CURRENT BIOGRAPHY

CURRENT BIOGRAPHY

WHO'S NEWS AND WHY

1944

EDITOR

Anna Rothe

ASSISTANT EDITOR

Helen Demarest

THE H. W. WILSON COMPANY

NEW YORK, N. Y.

Preface

In this, the fifth volume of the CURRENT BIOGRAPHY Yearbook, the "why" of "who's news" may be traced in events often identified with politics, war, and government. And yet not all figures move in public affairs, against a background of a world at war. Almost equally impressive in number, if not in the size of newspaper headlines in which their names appear, are personages in the worlds of literature, music, art, entertainment, education, and law. A quick survey of names in these and a number of other fields is provided by the "Classification by Profession" index at the back of this volume.

Like the volumes of the past four years, 1944 CURRENT BIOGRAPHY Yearbook is a one-alphabet cumulation of the biographical articles and obituary notices that appeared in the 1944 monthly numbers. However, before the articles were reprinted in the Yearbook, they were revised, when necessary, to include events that occurred in 1944 after the publication of those articles in the monthly numbers. While many biographies were thus rounded out as of December 31, 1944, that deadline of necessity left a few issues pending at the year's close. If a biographee died in 1944, the article includes facts up to the date of death.

The assembling of material for these biographies entails much research. Files of clippings are drawn upon when a name is selected for inclusion in CURRENT BIOGRAPHY. Indexes to magazine articles and books guide writers to a mass of information which is culled for biographical and background facts. Various "Who's Whos," encyclopedias, and other reference works contribute data. Information is also obtained from government offices and a variety of commercial and educational organizations. Whenever it is possible to get in touch with the biographees, they are asked to confirm or correct facts, but it should be pointed out these sketches are not authorized biographies. The biographees, too, may send their photographs, although a number of the prints are procured from duly credited photographers. The Press Association, Inc., 30 Rockefeller Plaza, New York, is the source of those photographs not supplied by biographees or photographers.

The following members of CURRENT BIOGRAPHY's staff have shared with the editors in the preparation of this Yearbook: Marian Prince, Ethel Ashworth, Vineta Blumoff, Frances Jennings, Ruth Lechlitner, Frances Rosenberg, Dana Rush, Charlotte Sills, and Frances Wallace, who wrote or revised sketches; Eileen Conlon and Sophie Starr, who assisted in the revision. Special acknowledgment is due Maxine Block, whose editorship ended with the June 1944 issue, after four and one-half years of valuable service.

A. R.

Contents

Explanations

Authorities for biographees' full names, with few exceptions, are the bibliographical publications of The Wilson Company. When a biographee prefers a certain name form, that is indicated in the heading of the article; for example, "McGeachy, Mary (Agnes) Craig" means that Miss McGeachy does not use the name of Agnes. When a professional name is used in the heading, for example, "Drake, Alfred," the real name, which in his case is Alfred Capurro, appears in the article itself.

The heading of each article includes the pronunciation of the name if it is difficult, date of birth (if obtainable), and occupation. The article is supplemented by a list of references to sources of information, in two alphabets: (1) newspapers and periodicals, (2) books. Space limitation requires that these bibliographies be kept short, but an effort is made to include the most useful references.

References to newspapers and periodicals are listed in abbreviated form; for example, "Sat Eve Post 217:14-15 S 30 '44 por" means *Saturday Evening Post,* volume 217, pages 14-15, for September 30, 1944, with portrait. (See the section "Periodicals and Newspapers Consulted" for full titles.) The books given as references are limited to those of a biographical nature, including such reference works as *Who's Who in America, Living Musicians,* etc. (See the section "Biographical References Consulted" for complete list.) Each obituary notice includes full dates when that information is available, and the reference is to the New York *Times.* When a name in the body of an article is followed by '40, '41, '42, '43, '44, the reference is to the 1940, 1941, 1942, 1943, or 1944 CURRENT BIOGRAPHY Yearbook, in which a biography of that person appears.

As indicated in the table of contents, this volume contains four name indexes, the purposes of which are self-evident. The all-inclusive index—the cumulated index to the biographies and obituary notices in the five CURRENT BIOGRAPHY Yearbooks published thus far—includes some four thousand names.

Key to Pronunciation
(By permission of Thorndike Century Senior Dictionary)

a	hat	u	cup	œ	as in French *peu.* Pronounce ā with the lips rounded as for ō.
ā	age	ů	full		
ã	care	ü	rule		
ä	far	ū	use		
e	let	zh	measure	N	as in French *bon.* The N is not pronounced, but shows that the vowel before it is nasal.
ē	equal				
ėr	term	ə	represents:		
		a	in about		
i	pin	e	in taken		
ī	ice	i	in pencil		
		o	in lemon		
o	hot	u	in circus	H	as in German *ach.* Pronounce k without closing the breath passage.
ō	open				
ô	order	FOREIGN SOUNDS			
oi	oil	Y as in French *du.* Pronounce ē with the lips rounded as for English ü in **rule**		′ = main accent.	
ou	house				
th	thin				
TH	then, smooth			″ = secondary accent.	

KEY TO ABBREVIATIONS

AAA — Agricultural Adjustment Administration
A.C.L.U. — American Civil Liberties Union
A.E.F. — American Expeditionary Force
A.F. of L. — American Federation of Labor
Ag — August
A.M.A. — American Medical Association
AMG — Allied Military Government
Ap — April
A.P. — Associated Press
ASCAP — American Society of Composers, Authors and Publishers
AYC — American Youth Congress
b. — business address
B.A. — Bachelor of Arts
BBC — British Broadcasting Corporation
B.D. — Bachelor of Divinity
B.E.F. — British Expeditionary Force
B.L. — Bachelor of Letters
B.S. — Bachelor of Science
C.B. — Companion of the Bath
C.B.E. — Commander of (the Order of) the British Empire
CBS — Columbia Broadcasting System
CIO — Congress of Industrial Organizations
C.M.G. — Companion of (the Order of) St. Michael and St. George
comp — compiler
cond — condensed
CWA — Civil Works Administration
D — December
D.A.R. — Daughters of the American Revolution
D.C.L. — Doctor of Civil Law
D.D. — Doctor of Divinity
D.Eng. — Doctor of Engineering
D.Litt. — Doctor of Literature
D.Mus. — Doctor of Music
Dr. — Doctor
D.Sc. — Doctor of Science
D.S.C. — Distinguished Service Cross
D.S.M. — Distinguished Service Medal
D.S.O. — Distinguished Service Order
ed — edited, edition, editor
EDB — Economic Defense Board
F — February
FBI — Federal Bureau of Investigation
FCC — Federal Communications Commission
FERA — Federal Emergency Relief Administration
F.F.I. — French Forces of the Interior
FHA — Federal Housing Administration
FSA — Farm Security Administration

G.B.E. — Knight or Dame Grand Cross Order of the British Empire
G.C.B. — Knight Grand Cross of the Bath
G.C.V.O. — Knight Grand Cross of Royal Victorian Order
GHQ — General Headquarters
GSO — General Staff Officer
h. — home address
H.M. — His Majesty
ICC — Interstate Commerce Commission
il — illustrated
I.L.G.W.U. — International Ladies' Garment Workers' Union
I.L.O. — International Labor Office
INS — International News Service
I.W.W. — Industrial Workers of the World
J — Journal
Ja — January
J.C.B. — Juris Canonici Bachelor
J.D. — Doctor of Jurisprudence
Je — June
Jl — July
K.C. — King's Council
K.C.B. — Knight Commander of the Bath
L.H.D. — Doctor of Humanities
Litt.D. — Doctor of Letters
LL.B. — Bachelor of Laws
LL.D. — Doctor of Laws
LL.M. — Master of Laws
M.A. — Master of Arts
mag — magazine
M.B.A. — Master of Business Administration
M.C. — Military Cross
M.C.E. — Master of Civil Engineering
M.D. — Doctor of Medicine
MGM — Metro-Goldwyn-Mayer
Mgr. — Monsignor, Monseigneur
M.Litt. — Master of Literature
M.P. — Member of Parliament
Mr — March
M.Sc. — Master of Science
My — May
N — November
NAM — National Association of Manufacturers
N.A.N.A. — North American Newspaper Alliance
NBC — National Broadcasting Company
nd — no date
NLRB — National Labor Relations Board
N.M.U. — National Maritime Union
no — number
NRPB — National Resources Planning Board
ns — new series
NYA — National Youth Administration
O — October
OCD — Office of Civilian Defense
ODT — Office of Defense Transportation
OPA — Office of Price Administration

OPM — Office of Production Management
OWI — Office of War Information
p — page
pam — pamphlet
P.E.N. — Poets, Playwrights, Editors, Essayists and Novelists (International Association)
Ph.B. — Bachelor of Philosophy
Ph.D. — Doctor of Philosophy
pl — plate, -s
por — portrait, -s
pseud — pseudonym
PWA — Public Works Administration
R — Review
R.A.F. — Royal Air Force
RCA — Radio Corporation of America
RFC — Reconstruction Finance Corporation
RKO — Radio Keith Orpheum
S — September
SEC — Security Exchange Commission
ser — series
SHAEF — Supreme Headquarters, Allied Expeditionary Force
S.J.D. — Doctor Juridical Science
SPAB — Supply Priorities and Allocation Board
S.T.B. — Bachelor of Sacred Theology
S.T.D. — Doctor of Sacred Theology
sup — supplement
S.W.O.C. — Steel Workers' Organizing Committee
tab — tabulation
TNEC — Temporary National Economic Committee
tr — translated, translation, translator
TVA — Tennessee Valley Authority
U.A.W.A. — United Auto Workers of America
U.M.W.A. — United Mine Workers of America
UNRRA — United Nations Relief and Rehabilitation Administration
U.P. — United Press
USO — United Service Organizations
U.S.S.R. — Union of Socialist Soviet Republics
v — volume
w — weekly
W.C.T.U. — Woman's Christian Temperance Union
W.L.A. — Women's Land Army
WLB — War Labor Board
WPA — Work Projects Administration
WPB — War Production Board
YM(W)CA — Young Men's (Women's) Christian Association
YM(W)HA — Young Men's (Women's) Hebrew Association

CURRENT BIOGRAPHY

1944

ACLAND, SIR RICHARD (THOMAS DYKE) (ak'land) Nov. 26, 1906- Member of the British Parliament; head of British Common Wealth Party

Address: b. House of Parliament, London; h. 10 Gerald Rd., London

The head of the radical British Common Wealth Party, which has been contesting elections in England in spite of the electoral truce between the Conservative and Labor Parties, is Sir Richard Acland, a "gaunt, bespectacled [ex-]millionaire and fifteenth baronet of his line." "Those reactionary ancestors of mine" is how he refers to his forebears, for in 1644 the Aclands were rewarded with their title when they fought for Charles I against Oliver Cromwell, and during the American Revolution one member of the family was a red-coat colonel who served under General Burgoyne in the New York campaign.

The present head of the family, Sir Richard Thomas Dyke Acland, the son of Sir Francis Acland, was born November 26, 1906. He was apparently a rebel from the very beginning. He was at Rugby when the British Government sent the notorious Black and Tans to Ireland, and was sentenced to ostracism for a week for criticizing this action. Nor could he decide to settle down peaceably to the law after studying at Oxford and qualifying as a barrister. Dissatisfied after practicing in London for a while, he took an architectural course —which at least enabled him to build yachts for his own use. He did follow tradition when he stood for Parliament in 1929—for a century Aclands had sat in Commons—but he broke the tradition when he lost this first electoral battle, and it was not until 1935, when he was elected to represent the Barnstaple Division of Devon, that he was able to join his father in Parliament. In 1937 the elder Acland died, and Sir Richard became the ninth successive head of his family to hold a Parliament seat. At the same time he inherited $80,000 as well as the vast estates that had been in his family for 400 years.

A member of the Liberal Party at this time, Acland supported the idea of an anti-fascist Popular Front of Liberals, Laborites, Independent Laborites, and Communists. In Commons he fought against the Government's policy of appeasing the fascists, arguing instead for collective security. When war came he joined the British Army as a private—but, according to one account, in drill squad the men kept complaining, "Everyone's in line except Dick." Whether this is true or not, he finally decided that he could be of more use

British Official Photo

SIR RICHARD ACLAND

to his country in Parliament than in uniform, asked for his discharge, and was released.

Not until after the outbreak of the Second World War had Acland become a Socialist. In 1940 he showed himself a very ardent convert, however, launching the Forward March Movement under the slogan, "Liberty, Equality, and Material Well-Being." In December of that year the Forward Marchers' aims were summed up: "We are fighting, not to restore the old order, but to establish a real democracy, economic as well as political. . . . There must be common ownership of great resources . . . because without this we cannot move forward to a new way of life based on service, not self —a way of life as different from the way of 1939 as free capitalism was from the feudal system that preceded it. . . . It is essential that you should, at the very minimum, take over the banks, the railways, the mines, the key industries, the engineering industry—and do it now." Both the Forward Marchers and J. B. Priestley's 1941 Committee, another pressure group with liberal aims, kept prodding the Government with demands for a definition of Britain's war and peace aims and for a more positive social consciousness. Acland's group was also responsible for an amendment to the declaration presented at the Malvern Conference of the Anglican Church. This amendment, overwhelmingly adopted, stated that

ACLAND, SIR RICHARD—*Continued*

the time had come for Christians to proclaim the need of seeking some form of society in which the stumbling block of private ownership of the great resources of the community would be removed.

In July 1942 the Forward Marchers merged with Priestley's 1941 Committee to become the Common Wealth Party—no longer a mere pressure group, but a political party determined to run its own candidates in by-elections against the Government coalition. (There has been no general election in England since 1935.) Priestley and Vernon Bartlett (an Independent Progressive M.P.) were original leaders along with Acland and Tom Wintringham. Their principles crystallized in a "Nine-Point Program," in the summer of 1942 they helped to elect an Independent to Parliament. In September of that year Acland announced his intention of placing a resolution on the order paper of the House proposing that immediate steps be taken for the re-election of at least one-third of the present Parliament. Soon afterwards Priestley resigned from Common Wealth, followed by Bartlett, but Acland and Tom Wintringham continued the work of setting up local Common Wealth organizations.

Common Wealth's manifesto was issued in July 1943: "An age is ending. A whole way of life is breaking down and is reaching its end. If the evidence before your own eyes does not convince you that this is true, no words of ours are likely to persuade you. The future struggles to be born." Major demands were: public ownership of land, factories, utilities, banks, and insurance companies (present owners to get "reasonable" compensation); self-government for the British colonies; immediate freedom for India; an international council to regulate post-War trade, shipping, and aviation; a general election in the United Kingdom; complete support for the Beveridge '43 Plan. In Acland's own words, "We want to amalgamate the Russian economic system with our own democratic political system."

In the first six months of 1943 there were twelve contested by-elections, in which the Government candidates polled 111,842 votes, other candidates 90,864 votes—54,412 of these opposition votes being for Common Wealth. In April 1943 the first candidate running under the Common Wealth label was elected to Parliament, and from a normally Conservative constituency. It was little wonder that those parties which continued to observe the Parliamentary truce, holding to the theory that partisan politics at this time would prove detrimental to the war effort, denounced Acland's "opportunism" with increasing intensity. Common Wealth was rapidly becoming a "convenient repository for votes of protest against everything about the Government that is not universally approved"—and in 1944 a labor politician, standing as an independent Socialist with Common Wealth backing and paid electioneers, won another seat for the new party.

According to Acland, the difference between Communism and Common Wealth is that Russia has an economic democracy, but not a political democracy. He believes that one must

be able to raise one's voice if one disagrees with the Government; that the people of England as a whole must own their own resources, too. He himself has given 16,000 acres of his inherited estates, worth about $1,000,000, to his country—the largest individual gift of land to the nation in the history of Britain's National Trust. This gift, he says, has left him without income other than the $2,400 a year earned as an M.P. ("I shall be a workingman, nothing else.") While Common Wealth has been attacked by the Communists, at the Unity Conference called by the British *Daily Worker* in March 1944 "the main division that appeared between Common Wealth and Communist delegates was that the former concentrated almost exclusively on the electoral and post-War issues, while the Communists wanted to put the first emphasis on united policy about coal, production, and other immediate issues of the War itself." Common Wealth's most caustic critic is probably H. G. Wells, who in *42 to 44* (1944) wrote:

"[This] versatile adventurer would apparently stop at nothing in his thirst for political leadership. Now, in the autumn of 1942, he reappears, happily leading a jumble of discontented people who find the existing administration of British affairs unendurable. The jumble is called 'Common Wealth.'. . . His intelligence is very limited and unstable. He is as imitative as a monkey, any claptrap that seems to be popular goes into his bag and any 'religious' cant, and his ambition for 'leadership' is uncontrollable."

Bartlett, Acland's former associate, expresses a different point of view in an article entitled "The Old Britain Is Gone Forever" in the New York *Times Magazine* of October 15, 1944. Although critical of Acland (calling his style of oratory "less suited to the House of Commons than to that strange corner of Hyde Park where enthusiasts for any cause under the sun stand on little ladders and harangue the crowd"), Bartlett nevertheless feels that the members of the House of Commons take Common Wealth less seriously than they should, for it has won the support of "many serious-minded, responsible lawyers or doctors or bank managers who in the old days were stanch supporters of the existing order." Bartlett thinks that at the close of the War, when the All-Party Government breaks up and elections are held again, Common Wealth may disappear and the "middle-class intellectuals" will vote along regular party lines, but he feels that the swing will continue to be toward radicalism. His explanation of this growth of liberalism in Great Britain is that the "common suffering, common sacrifice, and common effort (of the War) have given Britain a sense of social service such as her people have never known before."

Acland lives behind the British Museum, in a "shabby five-story Bloomsbury house," where the Common Wealth organization "boils and bubbles." He was married in 1936 to Anne Stella Alford, and has three children. Black-haired, thin-faced, with large spectacles perched on a jutting nose, Acland is described as bearing some resemblance to a reflective crane. He often rides his bicycle about London.

References
N Y Herald Tribune VII p9+ Ap 23
'44 por
Newsweek 21:46+ Ap 19 '43
Time 42:33-4 Jl 19 '43 por
Who's Who 1944

ADE, GEORGE (ād) Feb. 9, 1886—May 16, 1944 American who won fame with *Fables in Slang*, an adaptation of Aesop's literary form; began as newspaper reporter, rose to success as playwright, author, and wit; one of his plays, *The College Widow* (1904), later became a stage musical and a motion picture.

Obituary
N Y Times p19 My 17 '44 por

ADLER, LARRY Feb. 10, 1914- Musician
Address: b. 113 W. 57th St., New York City; h. 22 E. 67th St., New York City

One out of every thirteen persons in the United States plays the harmonica, according to statisticians; but one person in the world has raised the harmonica to the level of a virtuoso's concert instrument. Larry Adler, playing an instrument which the Musicians Union lists only as a toy, has given command performances for such high-ranking admirers as President Roosevelt '42, the two most recent English Georges and their Queens, Kings Haakon '40 of Norway, Gustav of Sweden '42, and Alfonso of Spain, the Windsors '44, and the Kents. "Adler is probably also the only soloist appearing in concert with symphony orchestras who . . . could not read a note of music and insisted cheerily on the public's knowing it."

Larry was born Lawrence Cecil Adler in Baltimore, Maryland, February 10, 1914, the son of Louis Adler and Sadie (Hack) Adler. He could carry a tune very early and loved to sing: according to a *New Yorker* article, "When he was two, he wandered away from home one day and was found by his father, two hours later, standing on a table in a downtown poolroom and singing a song called "I've Got Those Profiteering Blues" while the enchanted patrons stuffed money into his rompers pockets." At five, Larry was taken to a Rachmaninoff concert and developed a great admiration for that artist. The Adlers were not a highly musical family, but their orthodox Judaism gave Larry a chance for training in religious music. When he was ten Larry became the youngest cantor in Baltimore; and it is said that he was so zealously pious, "chiding his playmates for every lapse from orthodoxy, such as carrying money in their pockets on a Saturday, that soon nobody his age would speak to him. His unpopularity in public school made him unhappy, and he solved that problem by producing enough symptoms of a breakdown to convince the school doctor and his parents and to get himself sent to the Peabody School of Music."

Larry Adler was enrolled at the Peabody School to learn the piano, but was eventually dismissed for being "incorrigible, untalented, and entirely lacking in ear." Nevertheless, un-

LARRY ADLER

til 1941 he learned all his music by ear from phonograph records, never having learned to read music; and he can still play a long musical selection correctly after only two hearings. Larry, who had liked very little about the music school, had learned to love the piano. Since there was none in the home, eleven-year-old Larry, without bothering to consult his parents, selected a Mason & Hamlin piano and coolly ordered it. The proprietor, startled and amused by the boy's brashness and extreme youth, suggested that what Larry really wanted was a harmonica, and made him a present of one. But the boy exercised his powers of persuasion, and the expensive piano was sent to the Adler home on approval. Larry did some more fast talking, and actually persuaded his parents to keep the piano and pay for it on the installment plan over a period of years. From then on, the boy sold magazines on street corners so that he could buy concert tickets and phonograph records, from which he learned the music he played by ear on the piano and the harmonica.

In 1927 young Adler entered a harmonica contest conducted by the Baltimore *Sun*. All the other contestants played the few tunes to which a harmonica repertoire was then confined, on the order of "Turkey in the Straw" and "St. Louis Blues." But Adler, who knew many classical selections as well as popular music of the Jolson '40 type, astonished and gratified the judges by playing a Beethoven minuet. He was promptly awarded the silver cup.

Fourteen months later, Larry ran away to New York, taking his harmonica and his life's savings—$7. In a few days he had to wire home for more. His parents countered with an ultimatum: he could have the money, enough to keep him going for a reasonable period in New York. But if he did not succeed in finding work, then he would return to Baltimore, take up the life his parents had planned for him, and eventually justify their hopes by becoming a doctor or a lawyer. Although Larry

ADLER, LARRY—*Continued*

had to live in a cheap furnished room for months, eating little but cornflakes and milk (this for fear of violating the Jewish dietary laws), he stayed in New York, playing his harmonica under the windows and outside the stage doors of musical celebrities. In Kyle Crichton's words, "He interviewed three theatre managers and eight booking agents in one afternoon and was only saved from violence by his age." Finally he got into Rudy Vallee's dressing room and played Vallee into hiring him for the Heigh-Ho Club. Larry's engagement there was brief, but Vallee did help him to get a job playing the harmonica for "Mickey Mouse" cartoons.

Paul Ash, then the orchestra leader at the New York Paramount Theatre, heard Larry and placed him in a vaudeville unit. In the show Larry was presented as a ragged urchin, playing for pennies. Showmen were so pleased with the effect that afterwards they decked him out in torn knickers every time he went on the stage. The late Florenz Ziegfeld engaged Adler to appear in *Smiles*, after which Lew Leslie hired him for a revue called *Clowns in Clover* (1928)—and in both shows Adler was assigned the urchin routine. He breathed a sigh of relief when a producer promised not to make him an urchin if he would accept a part in *Flying Colors* (1933). The producer was as good as his word: Adler appeared as a bootblack.

A brief engagement in Hollywood where he appeared in the Paramount picture *Many Happy Returns* preceded a booking at the New York Palace Theatre in 1934. Adler, finally permitted to dress as he pleased, threw out the ragged garb and appeared in a well-cut dinner jacket. An English producer, C. B. Cochran [40], who happened to be in the audience, was as impressed with Adler's playing as he was with the novelty of seeing a man wear a dinner jacket to play the harmonica. He immediately engaged Adler at $350 a week to play in a London revue called *Streamline*.

The extent of Adler's London success may be measured in several ways. Shortly after his arrival there was a 2,000-per cent increase in harmonica sales throughout the British Empire; fan clubs, with a total membership numbering about 300,000, sprouted all over England; in 1937 an entire English revue, *Tune Inn*, was built around him; and he received more night-club offers than he could fill. He was paid $2,500 for a single evening when he played at a Monte Carlo party given for King Gustav of Sweden. He has since played for whatever royalty is left in the world and has performed piano duets with the late Duke of Kent.

Important English musicians were as enthusiastic about Adler as was the general public. Cyril Scott, the composer, wrote music especially for Adler and honored him by acting as his accompanist at a London recital. William Walton [40], another distinguished English composer, said, "The only two young musical geniuses in the world are Yehudi Menuhin [41] and Larry Adler."

Adler married an English mannequin named Eileen Walser in 1938. The following year he returned to New York after touring South

Africa and Australia. He found himself unknown to his countrymen and for a while had no engagements. Then a few radio and theatre engagements trickled in, the best of which was a $150-a-week offer from Eddy Duchin. It was through the efforts of Adler's friend, Leonard Lyons of the New York *Post*, that he landed a job at a New York night club, Féfé's Monte Carlo, which, in turn, led to $750-a-week offers from New York's Capitol and Loew's State Theatres. But Adler really "arrived" in the United States when he began to play classical music. His appearance as harmonica soloist with the Chicago Women's Symphony gained him national recognition. "Since I started with the symphonies," he states, "I've worked constantly, without a week off, and am more or less in the position of picking my engagements." In addition to his concert, radio, and theatre work, Adler has appeared in five motion pictures: *Many Happy Returns* (1934); *The Singing Marine* (1937); *St. Martin's Lane* (1938); *Sidewalks of London* (1940); and *The Big Broadcast of 1937*, which was billed in England as "Larry Adler and Jack Benny [41] in. . . ." *Broadcast* and *The Singing Marine* were made during a flying trip from England for that purpose. Adler dashed back to London as soon as he had fulfilled those contracts.

He has been collaborating with his good friend Paul Draper [44], the dancer, with whom he has appeared at the New York Savoy-Plaza and in a joint recital at Carnegie Hall. In January 1943 Adler and Draper returned from an unpublicized tour of United States Army camps and in August 1943 arrived in Cairo, Egypt with Jack Benny, Wini Shaw, and Anna Lee for a tour of the Middle East. While in Africa Adler wrote semi-weekly newsletters which were published in the Chicago *Sun*. His tours of American camps were distinguished by his insistence that enlisted men be seated first, and his refusal to allow discrimination against Negro troops in the seating at his performances. During the winter of 1943-1944 Adler and Draper were together again, on a tour that included Cleveland, Philadelphia, Cincinnati, and Pittsburgh.

During the summer of 1944 Adler accompanied Carole Landis, the film star, Martha Tilton, the singer, and Jack Benny (whom Adler considers one of the finest men he knows) on a USO overseas tour to the South Pacific. The troupe received a rousing reception from the servicemen, according to the Melbourne short-wave radio station. In November Adler gave two concerts with the San Francisco and Houston Symphony orchestras for the Sixth War Loan Drive. The next month Adler and Paul Draper appeared for the third time in a one-week joint engagement at the New York City Center Theatre. Adler was also featured in a motion picture, *Music for Millions* (1944), with Jimmy Durante and Margaret O'Brien.

Listeners have long marveled at Larry Adler's ability to draw from a harmonica "a tone reminiscent of many instruments, which tone is as varied as those that emerge from a symphony orchestra. The effects he obtains," adds the Chicago *Herald-American,* "are inconceivable—musical sounds to astonish and entrance layman or musician." To achieve a trumpet effect, he stands three feet back of the microphone, opens his hands on the harmonica, and blows a sharp, brassy tone; for a "wah-wah," muted-trumpet sound, he stands closer to the microphone, opening and closing his hands slowly; a violin tone is achieved by fluttering the hands fast and playing into the microphone from a distance of ten or twelve inches; a cello tone comes from blowing softly through the first three holes of the harmonica, about six inches away; and an oboe effect can be induced by vibrating the tongue rapidly.

Perhaps the most amazing thing about Adler is that until a few years ago he was unable to read a single note of music; yet (according to the San Francisco *Examiner*) "Adler, by a sort of genius, has raised the mouth-organ to the status of a concert instrument. His skill is incredible—the dash of his rhythm, the suppleness of his phrasing, and the richness of his tone color are masterly." Adler says today, however, that if he had his life to live over he would not leave school as he did at fourteen but would go on to college and study music. He feels one should really know the essentials of music to interpret it properly.

Adler learned all of his repertoire from phonograph records; his acute musical hearing enables him to play by ear whatever he listens to, whether it be classical or popular music. He was proud of his musical ignorance until the unhappy summer of 1940 "when Jean Berger, a French composer, wrote a harmonica concerto for him, and Adler realized darkly that no recording of the work existed. He had to learn to read the notes, and he has since studied all of his more important new numbers from a score, remarking that he never knew what he was missing."

When in New York the Adlers and their two children live in a terrace apartment, generally crowded with visitors, more than a thousand phonograph records, and Paul Draper. Adler's two hundred harmonicas used to be part of the household, but for the duration they are kept in a safe deposit vault from which one is withdrawn every few weeks, as needed. He used to wear one out every two or three performances; but now that his favorite German make is unobtainable, he has stopped "leaning on the high notes so hard," and makes his harmonicas last several times as long. With care and repairs, he hopes to be able to keep playing for the duration with his present stock. He has one pet extravagance—his wife. "When I pay a lot of money for anything," he says, "it usually turns out to be for her. After all, I have never bought a mink coat to wear myself."

References

Life 11:130-3 O 20 '41 il pors
Look 7:82 Ap 20 '43 por
N Y Post Mag p5 F 20 '43 por
New Yorker 18:19-24+ Jl 18 '42 por
Newsweek 18:63-4 D 1 '41 por
Time 37:50+ My 26 '41

AGAR, HERBERT (SEBASTIAN) (ā'-gär) Sept. 29, 1897- Diplomat; author; economist

Address: b. American Embassy, London; h. 2 Beekman Pl., New York City

G. Maillard Kesslere

HERBERT AGAR

"There is nothing worth fighting for except an idea, for it alone can last, can provide a basis for the developing future. Touch the American tradition anywhere, in any speech or document or song or ritual, and the same 'explosive idea' emerges, the one force that Hitler fears, the idea of *all men*." These words from Herbert Agar's *A Time for Greatness* (1942) form the basis of his democratic beliefs. Prominent among America's outstanding authors and journalists who advocate a liberal and progressive domestic and foreign policy, Herbert Agar, in his capacity as special assistant to Ambassador John G. Winant [41] in England, now occupies the responsible position of civilian adviser to "Army Talks," a forum program in the European Theatre of Operations designed to promote free discussion of "controversial national and international issues." An early disciple of intervention in the Second World War when many American intellectuals were inclined toward an isolationist viewpoint; one of the organizers and first president of Freedom House, Inc., founded in 1941 to promote international cooperation toward a just and lasting peace; for several years editor of the Louisville *Courier-Journal*, a paper noted for its liberal editorial stand; author of several books that "reflect brilliantly the feeling of liberal Americans"—Agar brings to his most recent appointment a strong conviction that soldiers "fight better when they know what they are fighting for."

Herbert Sebastian Agar was born in New Rochelle, New York, September 29, 1897, the son of John Giraud and Agnes Louise (Macdonough) Agar. Although Northern-born, Agar came of a family which had been "prominent in Louisiana for generations," a factor which doubtless led his interest in youth toward the literary and economic trends of the South. He received his preparatory education at the Newman School, Lakewood, New Jersey; then entered Columbia University. With

AGAR, HERBERT—*Continued*

the entrance of America into the First World War, however, he enlisted as a seaman in the United States Naval Reserve. Seriously injured while working at an ammunition depot, he was given a physical disability discharge. But in 1918 he returned to the Navy as chief quartermaster, and he was still in service when the Armistice was signed. After the War he returned to Columbia University, where in 1919 he took his B.A., with Phi Beta Kappa honors. He continued his education at Princeton University, receiving his M.A. in 1920 and his Ph.D in 1922. (Among the honorary degrees that have subsequently been awarded to him are Litt.D. from Southwestern University, Memphis, Tennessee, 1936, and LL.D. from Boston University, 1941.)

For some time Agar taught at the Hun Preparatory School at Princeton, New Jersey, but soon gave up teaching to devote his entire time to writing. He began his career as a journalist with the Louisville *Courier-Journal* and *Times,* for which papers he became London correspondent in 1929. The next five years Agar spent in England. There he was also literary editor of the *English Review,* and began contributing regularly to political weeklies in Great Britain and the United States. During part of this time he served as an attaché of the American Embassy in London.

In 1918 Agar had been married to Adeline Scott, from whom he was divorced in 1933. Their two children are William Scott and Agnes. He was then married to the Southern-born poet and novelist, Eleanor Carroll Chilton (author of *The Burning Fountain* [1929], *Follow the Furies* [1935], etc.), with whom he had collaborated on plays and collections of essays and poems.

Agar's first book, *Milton and Plato* (1928), was a scholarly essay published in the "Princeton Studies in English" series. In that year also appeared a volume of poems, *Fire and Sleet and Candlelight* (which he had written with Eleanor Carroll Chilton and Willis Fisher), verses "of high seriousness, a rather self-conscious dignity, and a great deal of monotony, both in cadence and epithet." Agar and Miss Chilton were also co-authors of a number of plays, one of which was produced in London by Basil Dean. Another Agar-Chilton collaboration, a collection of essays on poets and the influence of poetry in life, *Garment of Praise,* was published in 1929. This volume was described by Gorham B. Munson as "well informed by scholarship, agreeably written, and genuinely thoughtful." A reviewer for the *Nation,* however, felt that the authors "woefully misunderstood poets like Chaucer, Pope, and T. S. Eliot, who do not fit into their picture." The *Saturday Review of Literature,* with regard to Agar's contribution, found "his remarks, when they are vague, often dubious and sometimes dull." *Bread and Circuses,* another collection of essays, appeared in 1930.

It was not until he turned from literature to political studies that Herbert Agar won attention as a writer. His survey of American presidents from Washington to Harding, *The*

People's Choice, won the 1933 Pulitzer Prize in American history. The book gave evidence that Agar was dubious concerning a system of government that could produce so large a number of weak or incapable leaders. Agar's friends in the South gave him full support, Allen Tate commenting: "It is chiefly his firm sense of the real forces that have made modern America that gives the book its great interest and value." Henry S. Commager, however, was outspoken in his criticism of Agar's thesis: "He has, by begging every question, defying logic, scouting historical accuracy, and indulging in reckless generalization, made out the worst possible case for his theory, and his book calls irresistibly to mind that ancient adage about a little knowledge being a dangerous thing." John Chamberlain [40] (who became an ardent supporter of Agar's later books) wrote, "He is a T. S. Eliot of political literature. Mr. Agar certainly does not write as a democrat." The critic of the *New Republic* considered the book "a fine example of historical criticism . . . a lucid and interesting survey."

On his return to the United States, Agar had continued his work on the staff of the Louisville *Courier-Journal,* and in 1935 he published a second historical study, *Land of the Free.* In this he surveyed America's past economic history, analyzed its present condition, and offered a program for its rehabilitation. Critical reaction in general was divided. While one critic judged Agar "less convincing as a prescriber than as a diagnostician," another praised him for establishing the urgency of the question.

It was at this time that Agar became associated with the group of Southern writers—literary figures, economists, historians—known as the "Southern Agrarians." In 1936 a symposium by twenty-one of these "new regionalists" called *Who Owns America?* was edited by Agar and Allen Tate. According to Agar, "Our common ground is a belief that monopoly capitalism is evil and self-destructive, and that it is possible, while preserving private ownership, to build a true democracy in which men would be better off morally and physically." The regionalists sought to preserve the "American dream" by freeing small business from big business; they took an anti-Marxist stand and decried the system of mass production. Kenneth Burke's comments in the *New Republic* were representative of liberal reaction to the book: "In noting that big business is developed by the growth of corporations, the Agrarians would lump fascism and communism together as merely the extension of the corporate idea. Hence, they would draw upon our resistance to big business as a way of exhorting us against all collectives." Agar had further stated his beliefs at this time in an essay, "The Task for Conservatism," written for the *American Review*: "The present system is doomed, and if nothing is done to interfere with blind determinism the name of that doom is communism. But the task of the conservative is to find out how to interfere with blind determinism. And an important part of that task is to persuade those who are temperamentally his allies that man is not condemned to push forward if he happens to hate what lies ahead of him, that it is not true that the one thing man can never do is the thing he did yesterday. If this be admitted—and with it the possibility of choice, and hence of morality, in politics—there is the basis for conservatism."

By 1938, however, some critics thought that Agar was undergoing a change in his literary, social, and political affiliations and viewpoints. "Once a conservative who believed that democracy was a dismal failure," he became a supporter of Rooseveltian social measures. He began a syndicated newspaper column, "Time and Tide," which had "a resolutely New Deal aura," and his next book, *The Pursuit of Happiness* (1938), was a re-examination of the democratic ideal in a survey of the Democratic Party from Jeffersonian days. Said *Time*: "With the publication of *The Pursuit of Happiness* it was plain that author Agar had swung all the way around the circuit from Right to Left. Jefferson, called lacking in character in *The People's Choice,* emerges as his great hero. Bryan, damned as ignorant before, is pictured as an heir to Jefferson's ideals. And author Agar, in his best book to date, is more eloquent and convincing in defining democracy than he ever was in attacking it."

In January 1940 Herbert Agar became acting editor of the Louisville *Courier-Journal*, succeeding to the position once held by the famous "Marse" Henry Watterson, founder and for many years editor of the paper. At once Agar's "trenchant, forceful editorials advocating more militant action on the part of the United States" attracted considerable attention, particularly at a time when much of the Midwest and Southwest was isolationist in sympathy. Warmly disposed toward Great Britain because of his years of residence there, Agar saw the impact of war on the British people when he spent several weeks in London during the height of the blitz on that city. He returned to this country to impress upon Americans, in editorials and through lectures, the necessity of supporting England and other democracies. "What is happening," he said, "is a counter-revolution against our society," which can only be beaten back "by people who are willing to meet it on a military front." He defined our world as one of free peoples "who are trying to save themselves from this revolution. In the joining of the free peoples, our world will win."

With Helen Hill, Agar wrote *Beyond German Victory* (1940), which is concerned with America's position in a Hitler '42-dominated world. The book was termed "a compressed yet completely thorough statement of everything the advocates of an aggressive, dynamic foreign policy for America have on their hearts and minds." That year he was also a contributor to a symposium, *The City of Man: a Declaration on World Democracy* (1940).

In June 1940 Agar was one of the organizers of the Committee of Thirty, composed of authors and other professional people and formed to "urge immediate recognition of the fact that a state of war exists between this country and Germany. Commented the New York *Sun*: "This time no one can say it's Wall Street that is fanning up the war talk....

Herbert S. Agar, Pulitzer Prize winner, heading the committee list, is typical of workers in the cultural vineyard who have opposed war in all moods and tenses, some of whom have been stanch isolationists, but now ask for a showdown on what they consider the rescue of civilization. Not to try to confound Mr. Agar, but to cite the changing drift of straws in the wind, it is recalled that on November 2, 1935 he urged die-hard isolation before the New York Foreign Policy Association. 'If we ever learn how to run a single county in Indiana,' said Mr. Agar on that occasion, 'that will be time enough for us to begin curing the old misery along the Rhine.'"

But Agar, convinced by 1940 that "the frontier of our national interest is now on the Somme," continued crusading for a quick entry of America into the War. Early in 1941 he took a leading part in defending the Lend Lease Bill. With regard to what American papers should print he said, "I think the press can justify freedom of the press only when newspapers themselves have the courage to accept direct responsibility for their own interpretations and comment." Speaking at a conference of organized labor (May 1941), he called on the United States "to engage immediately in a double-barreled war against the dictatorships abroad and 'indecent' living and working conditions here."

In December 1941 Agar became one of the founders of Freedom House, Inc., an organization "established as a clearinghouse for all groups in the United States of America participating in the struggle for a free world." Through press and radio and pamphlets, Freedom House members worked to bring the issues of the conflict before the American public. It arranged several broadcasts, including the program *Our Secret Weapon,* with Rex Stout as the lie detector, as well as the *Giants of Freedom* series, with Carl Van Doren, the late Stephen Vincent Benét and Wendell Willkie '40, and others. As his own contribution, Agar wrote a series of articles, "What We Are Fighting For," which appeared in New York's *PM*. In his article for August 5, 1942 he deplored the prevalent fear that "Russia will dominate the world." If our economic system can supply enough to eat and do so without destroying freedom, we need not fear communism, he said. "So far nobody has found a way of curing the great flaw in communism: that the state which controls all property, and thus all jobs, inevitably becomes a tyrant state. If the state is the universal master, the citizens become slaves. If the Russians can find a way out of this dilemma, we need no longer fear communism. If they can't find a way out of this dilemma, we shall never be attracted to communism. Instead, we shall insist on improving the system we have, to make it serve our purpose."

Having made a brief trip to England during August 1941, Agar returned more convinced than ever that we should immediately enter the War—at least "before the supply of gallant foreigners runs out." He insisted also that we must not make promises in this War, as in the last, which we cannot carry out. After the last War "we did nothing to improve the lot of the Negro. We broke our

AGAR, HERBERT—*Continued*

promises." Speaking also before a Senate committee on the Poll Tax Bill, he said: "The result of a poll tax is to keep the poor from voting, or to keep the Negroes from voting, or both. If you keep the poor from voting, you make a joke of Jefferson. If you keep the Negroes from voting, you make a joke of Lincoln. If you do both these things, you make a joke of the American idea."

Above all, Agar believes, the American people need to be guided by a "great ideal," and he expresses that belief in his book *A Time for Greatness*. In this he said that the "long disease" which has afflicted our culture is "the loss of a fixed central faith." Agar's ideas of moral freedom are in part derived from his early studies of Milton and Plato. To help make our American concept of equality come true, Agar supports the kind of government planning advocated by Thurman Arnold [40] and Leon Henderson [40], since it is based on "the historic American tradition." But what we need most, he says, is a "change of mind and heart" rather than a change of system.

Widely read and discussed, the book won universal acclaim. Joseph Henry Jackson of the San Francisco *Chronicle* called it "the most valuable examination of America and Americans, their war and democracy, yet published." Lewis Gannett [41] said, "One of the shakingest and wakingest books I've read in some time." Of its style, Gerald Johnson wrote: "Anyone who is fascinated by the rapier thrust as well as by the crash of the battle-ax will find both here. Anyone, in short, who is looking for engrossing intellectual entertainment can hardly do better than turn to Mr. Agar's book." *A Time for Greatness* is to be translated into Norwegian, Dutch, and French.

In September 1942 Agar was made a lieutenant commander in the Navy. Early in 1943 he was "loaned" to the State Department to become special assistant to the United States Ambassador to the Court of St. James, John G. Winant. In England Agar has made several broadcasts and has written articles for British journals. In the London *Observer* he praised the "high-mindedness" of Henry Wallace's [40] recent speeches. "If we regard the suggestions of better people as an eccentricity sufficient to unfit a man for public life, we had better accustom ourselves to the thought that the future will be as disorderly and as sanguinary as the past. . . . Whatever justice and peace we enjoy in our public lives will be a by-product of our private lives."

In October 1943 Agar was appointed by Brigadier General Frederick Osborn [41], chief of the Special Service Division, as civilian adviser to "Army Talks," his duty being to train junior officers as discussion-group leaders. It was reported that "Army officers in touch with Agar's activity in arranging political discussion groups among our troops in Britain agree he is doing splendid work." One hour a week is earmarked for compulsory participation in these talks by all United States soldiers in Europe, "excepting the Air Force, where participation is optional with the unit commander." The selection of Agar to train

group leaders "is regarded as strong indication that the program will not fall into the hands of reactionary officers who want to plant their own prejudice in Army soil."

Agar is described by a New York *Herald Tribune* reporter as a popular speaker at his London discussion groups, his favorite topic being Anglo-American relations; and *Time* states also that "Herbert Agar . . . shows up cool and well groomed at luncheons and unveilings whenever his boss, United States Ambassador Winant, is otherwise engaged."

Herbert Agar is tall—well over six feet—an impressive figure, with a great deal of personal charm. He has a wide and scholarly brow and the sensitive, yet determined mouth characteristic of the fervor of a man who, as *Time* notes, has "some of the moral reach of the Old Testament prophets." Agar is a "self-styled creative conservative"; that is, "a man who insists on adapting our habits to our principles, on saving what is immortal." Men generally called conservatives, however, would probably consider Agar a radical. He combines, in fact, the qualities of both—along with those of the poet and mystic. He is an adherent of domestic, social, and economic reform based on the original principles of America's founding fathers, and of ideas of world reform in the shape of a genuinely democratic foreign policy that will give the people of Europe "something firm, definite, and final to believe in."

References

N Y Sun p24 Je 11 '40
N Y Times p17 F 4 '43
PM p9 O 17 '43 por
Time 40:100 N 9 '42 por
Kunitz, S. J. and Haycraft, H. eds.
    Twentieth Century Authors 1942
Who's Who in America 1944-45

ALBRIGHT, IVAN LE LORRAINE
Feb. 20, 1897- Artist

Address: b. and h. Albright Studio, Warrenville, Ill.

When Metro-Goldwyn-Mayer needed a progressively more hideous series of portraits for Oscar Wilde's *The Picture of Dorian Gray*, their choice fell upon Ivan Le Lorraine Albright, the painter of horrors. As one commentator remarked, MGM's only problem would then be to find an actor who could look like one of Albright's portraits. It would, however, be considerably more remarkable to find an actor who would be willing to look like an Albright painting, for that artist specializes in the repulsive. Obsessed by ugliness, by decay, by corruption, he paints these qualities with such lavishness of detail that one prize-winning study of a mortuary door took him ten years. Albright's work has been called "a world of midnight" (the title of one of his canvases), but the general tone of his work might more specifically be described as 3 a.m. under the harsh electric glare of the police court—if not the morgue. Those who wonder how anyone can make a living painting in such a fashion may find the explanation in Albright's comfortable private income, the result of his father's successful dealings in real estate. When he does sell a picture, however, his price is fabulous.

Ivan was one of twins born February 20, 1897 in Chicago, to Adam Emory and Clara Amelia (Wilson) Albright. The elder Albright, a painter of sweetly innocent childhood idyls which live up to his surname, expressed his artistic tastes in the middle names of his sons. Ivan was given Le Lorraine, after Claude Lorraine, "the wanderer through tranquil groves"; his brother became Malvin Marr, for Carl Marr, president of the Munich Academy of Arts; and another son was called Lisle Murillo, after the painter of sweet-faced Madonnas and winsome Spanish urchins. The twins were ideal models for their father, and so, "by the hour, Ivan posed with his twin brother in ragged breeches, dabbling his toes in silvery brooks or fishing with string and bent pin. Barefoot boy with cheek of umber. This gave him a disrespect for art and a passion for drawing."

Reacting from sweetness and light, the Albright twins abjured art for architecture. After a year's study at Northwestern University and another at the University of Illinois, Albright found himself in France as a private in the A.E.F. As *Time* tells the story, "During World War I Painter Albright sneaked into military hospitals in France, made methodical, painstakingly realistic sketches of wounds. The medical corps, struck with the accuracy of his anatomical paintings, requested a complete set for its permanent files," with the result that Albright served as official medical draftsman in the base hospital No. 11 at Nantes from 1918 to 1919. He also studied at the École des Beaux Arts in the same city.

Returning to the United States, Albright took up his studies at the Art Institute of Chicago, where he was a special scholarship student four times in four years. In 1923 he attended the Pennsylvania Academy of Fine Arts in Philadelphia, and in 1924, the National Academy of Design in New York. According to Daniel Catton Rich, director of the Chicago Art Institute, "Ivan learned more from advanced students than from men like Hawthorne and Seyffert. An exception was Henry McCarter. He 'upset' Ivan, and Ivan 'upset' him by laying a still-life arrangement on the floor and painting it from a chandelier angle. It took him forty-two days to conquer the technical problems involved."

Ivan Albright then settled down at Warrenville, a small town not far from Chicago, where all three of the painting Albrights (Malvin gave up architecture for art) have streets named after them, memorializing Adam Albright's success with real estate. They all live and work together, happily sharing a storeroom which was once a Methodist church. Adam continues to paint sunny pictures of rural American youth, while Ivan in his white studio (Malvin's is pink) cheerfully turns out his gruesome shockers and less startling lithographs. Malvin, a sculptor, paints under the name of Zsissly, in order to place himself at the end of catalog listings. The number of important prizes won by the three in art competitions comes to some two dozen.

IVAN LE LORRAINE ALBRIGHT

"For the first ten years," according to Daniel Catton Rich, Albright's chief admirer and interpreter, "there issued . . . [from his brush] a procession of obsessed figures. He chose rugged models from the neighborhood, a linesman or a blacksmith. Posed in harsh, unfeeling light which falls devouringly on leather, hair, or skin, these figures are somber in browns, dead tans, and faded blues." They won Albright honorable mention in the Chicago Art Institute's competition of 1926. Two years later, when his style had become less "external" and more "terrifying in its realism" (*Woman* is made up of "dead purple and black surfaces picked out in chalky whites"), Albright showed his works at the Carnegie International Exhibition in Pittsburgh and won the John C. Shaffer prize of $500. "In the scabrous faces and wrinkled, puffy hands" of his figures "may be read the whole backwash of pioneer optimism."

Abandoning short titles for "literary" long ones—a field in which he rivals Salvador Dali '40 and Joán Miró '40—Albright next produced *Into the World There Came A Soul Called Ida*, which *Time* describes conservatively as a "portrait of a massive, flabby, semi-nude varicose-veined prostitute primping herself," done in unhealthy green and purple tones, with bilious yellow shadows and convincingly repellent skin texture. *Ida* "caused a storm of protest when it was exhibited," but won Albright another honorable mention from the Chicago Art Institute in 1930. Admitting that the painting is horrifying in its ugliness, Director Rich insists that "nevertheless, it gives off a kind of disenchanted loveliness." Rich also holds that *And God Created Man in His Own Image* (1930) (called by *Time* "a terrifyingly seamed and ugly figure . . . whose every gray hair looks as if it could be plucked from its purple body") is "rendered with a fastidious delight in . . . tints and textures."

Even though repelled by the "detailed enormity" of Albright's canvases, critics had

ALBRIGHT, IVAN LE LORRAINE—
Continued

to admit his power, as well as his mastery of the craft of painting. In 1930 Albright won the Chicago Society of Artists Silver Medal, and in 1931, the Gold Medal. Meanwhile he continued his experiments. "In a still life, *Wherefore Now Arises the Illusion of the Third Dimension* (1931), he bent and wrenched space to suit his feeling. Apples in a dish are designed from varying perspectives; a glass of wine is seen from still another angle."

The following year Albright began a decade of work on his masterpiece, *That Which I Should Have Done I Did Not Do* (1931-1941). This eight-foot painting of a decrepit mortuary door with distorted funeral wreath "shows one touch of life—a woman's gnarled, bejeweled hand," holding a lace handkerchief, which rests on the intricately carved molding. Great and careful were the preparations," it is said. "An actual door was found and set up on a sill made from a discarded tombstone." For two years Albright lay prone to paint the bottom of the ceiling-height canvas, then finally made standing room by cutting a hole in the floor. "Diagrams were made of the flowers, some to be painted one foot above the ordinary line of vision, others from three feet below. The door itself was 'shot' from contrasting angles." A model with legs that Albright considered "wonderful" was hired to pose for the hand. After a year of spending all her Sundays in that pose she couldn't stand any more of it; so Albright took a plaster cast of her hand and wired it into position. He was delighted to find that the plaster cast was "more spectral" than its original. "Season after season the charcoal preparation was filled in, every mar, scratch, or blemish recorded. The full and empty spaces were welded together with new lines of force. After a decade it was finished, Albright's masterpiece."

In spite of the artist's dedication to this work, he found time during those ten years to win the Audubon Post Prize (1934), time to act as president (1933-1934) and vice president (1935-1936) of the Chicago Society of Artists and as chairman of the fund-raising Artists' Balls in 1934, 1935, and 1936. Albright won the Springfield (Massachusetts) Art League's first prize for painting in 1937 and for lithography in 1941, as well as the Philadelphia Water Color Club Prize of $200 (1940) and the Bower prize of $300 (1941).

Although Albright has received many honors, Earle Ludgin of Chicago has been the only collector to purchase any of his paintings. "Because his portraits looked as though their subjects had been removed from newly-opened graves," commented *Time*, "nobody gave him commissions. . . . Many a museum has bought his paintings, but no other collector. One reason is the fabulous prices Ivan Albright asks for them: as much as $30,000 for his biggest works. Independent Artist Albright, already well off on the proceeds of the Albright family real-estate business in Warrenville, really doesn't care very much whether people buy his paintings or not. He raised his price exactly forty-one per cent when

President Roosevelt '42 devalued the dollar, still sells his work on the gold standard."

That Which I Should Have Done I Did Not Do won a $500 prize at the Art Institute of Chicago and the Temple Gold Medal from Pittsburgh's Carnegie. In 1942 it was submitted in the open competition of Artists for Victory at the Metropolitan Museum of Art in New York. Out of some 600 paintings, selected from 11,000 original entries, *That Which* won the First Medal. Albright, who sets a high value on his own works, did not submit it for the purchase prize of $3,500 because he considers it worth much more. In the same year his works won the Fellowship Prize of the Philadelphia Academy of Fine Arts and the first prizes (for water color) of the Springfield Art League and of the Wustum Museum in Racine, Wisconsin. In 1943 he received the first prize for the best oil painting from the Butler Art Institute, Youngstown, Ohio; and in March 1944 the artist won the Altman Prize of $500 for a "milder" picture, *The Linesman*, described by Carlyle Burrows as "honest in treatment," and possessed of "a streak of originality"; and in October he exhibited a typical Albright, entitled *The Showcase Doll That Was Never Painted.*

A shy, meek, nervous little man "with eyes reddened from staring at visions," Albright "looks almost as old as his paintings, even though he is only forty-seven." However morbid his outlook as a painter, Albright is a cheerful person and, in his own field, something of a "joiner." His memberships include the Arts Congress (New York), the Arts Club of Chicago, the Chicago Society of Artists, the Association of Chicago Painters and Sculptors, the Art Institute of Chicago Alumni Association, the Laguna Beach (California) Art Association, the Springfield (Massachusetts) Art League, and the Philadelphia Water Color Club. He is a Fellow of the Pennsylvania Academy of Fine Arts, and a member of the Artists' Housing Commission for Chicago. For recreation he writes poetry.

The inseparable Albright twins were in 1944 installed in the studio on the Metro-Goldwyn-Mayer lot in which the late John Barrymore used to do his etchings. They have refurnished it "with a *décor* that's absolutely Wilde"—including two $2,000 Aubusson rugs —to help in their *Dorian Gray* pictures by giving them "the feel of the period." No figures have been released on the payment to be made, but it is said that Albright will get $75,000 merely for the use of the paintings, which he will continue to own. Asked when the pictures will be finished, the Albrights told interviewers, "Not before 1957." MGM, recalling a production schedule which required shooting to begin on January 15, 1944, hoped that these all-important properties would be ready considerably sooner.

For an interpretation of Albright's meaning we must turn to Rich: "This failure to understand the themes of his painting is a fault of our time. Through undue emphasis on form we have become such materialists that we are in danger of ignoring all meanings which reside in a work of art. . . . It is flesh . . . that Albright analyzes—a rabid, delicate autopsy on skin and tissue. . . . What is his purpose?

Does this vision spring from a cosmic bitterness, a personal cynicism, or an uncontrollable aggression against his fellow-men? I believe not. Rather it is the result of strong moral indignation, concealed (perhaps even from himself) under the guise of disgust. These maps of faces on which every sorrow or depravity is charted are named *Into the World There Came a Soul Called Ida* and *God Created Man in His Own Image*. The 'soul' of Ida is overwhelmed with the opacity of flesh; the 'image of God' is forever caught in a lava flow of matter. In an intense desire to portray a drama of corruption the painter spent ten years of his art in creating this cast of characters, and ten years more in designing a coffin in which they shall inevitably lie. Ivan Albright is like a page from Jeremiah."

References

Mag Art 36:48-51 F '43 il pors
Newsweek 22:82+ N 29 '43 il por
Time 38:81 N 24 '41 il por; 40:46-7 Jl
6 '42 il self por
Who's Who in America 1944-45
Who's Who in American Art 1940-41

ALONSO, JOSE IGNACIO RIVERO Y
See Rivero (y Alonso), J. I.

ALVAREZ QUINTERO, JOAQUIN
(äl'vä-räth kēn-tä'rō hwä-kēn') Jan. 1873—June 14, 1944 Leading Spanish dramatist; in collaboration with his brother Serafín, wrote some 200 dramas and sketches for the theatre; works tranlsatcd into English and seven other languages.

Obituary

N Y Times p19 Je 15 '44 por

ANDERSON, FREDERICK L(EWIS)
Oct. 4, 1905- United States Army Air Force officer
Address: b. c/o United States War Department, Washington, D.C.

Deputy commander for operations of the United States Strategic Air Forces in Europe since January 1944 is Major General Frederick L. Anderson, who was a 2nd lieutenant only ten years earlier. Before assignment to this post, he wielded, as commanding general of the 8th Air Force Bomber Command, "the greatest fire power ever directed constantly against an enemy nation by a single American." In cooperation with the R.A.F. his planes deliver the smashing blows which are crippling German war industries and weakening the enemy's resistance.

Frederick Lewis Anderson, Jr., was born October 4, 1905 in Kingston, New York. The eldest of six children, he was brought up on his father's farm near Stamford. Later the Andersons moved back to Kingston, where the boy entered high school in the fall of 1918, a month short of his thirteenth birthday. Upon graduation he hoped to enter the Military Academy at nearby West Point; but before taking the state's competitive examinations for entrance he had to spend two years in postgraduate study of mathematics and kindred subjects. During those years he tried without

U. S. Air Forces
MAJ. GEN. FREDERICK L. ANDERSON

much success to sell automobiles in his father's agency, and also chauffeured the local doctor. Entering West Point in 1924, young Anderson got on the football team but seldom on the field; he did, however, win the nickname of "Wild Indian"—short for "the wild Indian of the lacrosse field."

While at West Point, Cadet Lieutenant Anderson had his first airplane ride, and decided on a career in the Air Corps. Cadets were not able at that time to graduate into the air branch; therefore, on completing his West Point course in 1928, the aspiring airman acccptcd a commission as 2nd lieutenant of cavalry—and immediately requested flight training. At the same time he fulfilled a long-standing ambition to marry Betty Travis, the brunet daughter of one of his mother's friends.

Anderson's air training was begun the next fall at the Air Corps Primary Flying School in Brooks Field, Texas. After completing the primary course in June 1929, the Lieutenant went on to the Air Corps Advanced Flying School at Kelly Field, also in Texas. He won his wings in September, almost simultaneously with the birth of his daughter, Mary Winn. After graduation Anderson was assigned to the 99th Observation Squadron at Mitchel Field, Long Island. (He now holds the ratings of senior pilot and combat observer.)

On November 1, 1929 the flying cavalryman was finally transferred to the Air Corps and sent to the Philippine Islands. There he served in various post and unit staff capacities with the 4th Composite Group at Nichols Field, Riza. "Gosh," the General recalls now, "we were 2nd lieutenants for six years." If a 2nd lieutenant had, like Anderson, no private income, it was not easy for him to support a wife and child on a salary which had been cut fifteen per cent by an economy-minded Congress. But through it all Fred Anderson was true to an idea: "sanely and firmly," he came to the conclusion that "bombardment aviation would be the deciding factor in the next war," and

ANDERSON, FREDERICK L.—*Cont.*

in 1931 he transferred to the bombardment branch.

From that time on, in MacKinlay Kantor's words, "Fred Anderson forgot the burnished gilt bars that seemed to have taken root on his shoulders. He walked, slept, talked, ate, drank, and dreamed bombardment aviation in general and high-altitude precision bombing in particular." In those depression days, however, "there was very little to do with in the way of airplanes or equipment. Ammunition and bombs were a prize to be expended meagerly. Most of the bombing had to be done on paper, and that's a punk way to learn how to bomb."

On May 16, 1934 Anderson exchanged his gold bars for the silver of a 1st lieutenant. Mrs. Anderson, as a general's wife in practically servantless Washington, has said that she would gladly return to the 1st lieutenancy days in the Philippines where she had four servants; but at the time the family was delighted to get away from the tropics, where the young officer had suffered a siege of dengue fever and his wife and child were in delicate health. In October 1934 Anderson took his family back to the United States, where he was assigned to the 91st Observation Squadron at Crissy Field, California, shortly before the birth of a son, Travis Scott Anderson. Less than a month later Anderson became a hero.

Lieutenant Anderson was piloting an army plane over San Francisco when a fire broke out inside it. After ordering his mechanic to jump the young officer did not follow suit; rather than save himself and allow the abandoned plane to crash into the crowded street below, he "returned to the cockpit, despite the fact that it was almost completely enveloped in flames, piloted the burning plane away from the city and then jumped from the plane with his parachute into San Francisco Bay. The parachute submerged and he was in grave danger of drowning until he was rescued by one of the crew of the U.S.S. *Oklahoma*." This is quoted from the citation accompanying Anderson's Distinguished Flying Cross—which does not mention that doctors worked over him four hours before he was revived.

The next day Anderson was back at work—"Nobody told me I'd better stay home"—with a cough that persisted and was finally diagnosed as pulmonary tuberculosis. Before he could be invalided out of the Army the quick-thinking Lieutenant wangled a transfer to Colorado, where a three-month stay cured him. "The doctors tapped and peered and took pictures and couldn't believe that this miracle had occurred. Able to do staff work, possibly, but not fit for active flying—Fred Anderson grinned and went off to hunt up a nice fast-climbing airplane. He spent 300 hours flying on oxygen in the substratosphere during the next few months, and after that the medicos ran for cover and let him alone. The rest of his story is the story of high-altitude precision bombing in World War II."

In November 1935, after a temporary promotion and seven months on the Hamilton Field staff at San Rafael, California, Captain Anderson joined the Bombardment Squadron there. In September 1936 he was transferred to the famous 7th Bombardment Group as

flight commander and operations officer; and in June 1938 his temporary rank of captain was made permanent. Here Anderson collaborated with such fliers as Generals Clarence L. Tinker [42], Kenneth N. Walker, and George E. Stratemeyer to develop "the bombardment tactics now being used successfully throughout the world." (Tinker and Walker have since been killed in action.)

The thirty-three-year-old Captain was given command of the 21st Air Base Squadron at Lowry Field near Denver, in September 1938. At the beginning of 1940 he enrolled for a three-month course in the Air Corps Tactical School at Maxwell Field, Alabama, returning to Lowry Field after his April graduation as commanding officer, 2nd School Squadron. In July 1940 Anderson was selected as the first director of bombardier instruction at the Air Corps Tactical School, Lowry Field. This was the foundation for the tremendous bombardier training program put into effect since then. The young Director developed many of the bombardment tactics now used by United States forces, acquiring in the process "an exceptional reputation" and a promotion in January 1941 to the temporary rank of major. In May of that year, the Bombardier Instruction School well established, Major Anderson was sent to the Office of Chief of Air Corps in Washington as assistant to the chief of the Training Section, Training and Operations Division.

Ordered to England to observe bombardment methods and countermethods during the Battle of Britain, Anderson was flying over the equator above Brazil on his return trip when he heard the news of Pearl Harbor. Soon after his arrival in Washington he was made deputy director of bombardment at Army Air Forces headquarters with a promotion to lieutenant colonel (temporary). Upon reorganization of the Air Forces in March 1942 Colonel Anderson was selected as acting director of bombardment. "With foresight, aggressiveness, initiative, and superior qualities of leadership [according to the citation with his Legion of Merit decoration], he developed and crystallized many new ideas in relation to operation, tactics, and technique of bombardment aircraft."

Toward the beginning of 1943 Anderson was sent to North Africa as General Henry H. Arnold's [42] personal representative on bombardment matters. A few months afterward he was made a brigadier general (temporary) and placed in command of the 4th Bombardment Wing of Flying Fortresses: he led his bombers from their bases in the United Kingdom on a number of missions, winning the Air Medal and the Silver Star for gallantry. ("I find it much harder to stay on the ground," he says, "than to fly with my planes to their assigned objective.") Then on July 15, 1943 he succeeded Brigadier General Newton Longfellow as chief of the entire United States 8th Air Force Bomber Command. In this capacity General Anderson worked with the R.A.F.'s Air Chief Marshal Sir Charles Portal [41] and United States General Ira C. Eaker [42], his commanding general, on the April Plan for the bombing of Germany. (Named for the month it was put into effect, it is also called the Portal Plan, the Eaker Plan, and the

Strategic Bomber Plan.) This strategic blueprint, as described by Charles J. V. Murphy of *Fortune*, had as its objective "to reduce German resistance to a point where a Channel invasion could be launched with certain success."

"The airmen worked up their plan [in pursuance of a Casablanca directive] in collaboration with American and British economic analysts. The latter, from data accumulated by British Intelligence, singled out a number of 'economic structures,' the destruction of which would decisively weaken Germany's ability to wage war." "The British were to continue their massive strokes at night, aiming not at individual plants but rather at the enfolding social cortex—the integrated community services without which industry cannot function." "The American bomber force was to collaborate in a [daylight bombing] role suited to its precision methods," worked out by General Anderson. "This was to make sure that any important holes left by the R.A.F. would be taken care of."

But—still quoting Murphy—"the 8th Bomber Command was then well below the strength promised all through 1942. Only a token force of heavy bombers was in Britain. Many of our airmen were embarrassed and even humiliated by the questions they sensed in British minds"—this although "British and American airmen collaborated at every stage of the April Plan. After the targets had been selected a committee of four American and two British officers worked out the tactical methods for their destruction," which were then approved by Portal and by the Combined Chiefs of Staff in Washington. But for some reason "during the summer and fall [of 1943] the American deficit in heavy bombers and crews under the plan was such that only the highest-priority targets could be hit." "General Anderson's men maintained their tempo at a cost in sweat and blood that might have done credit to a country with its back to the wall."

"The 8th Bomber Force on its strongest raids was able to muster only a fraction of the force the British send on their 'heavy' raids. Yet with these weak numbers the Americans did extremely well. Their steady pounding of the submarine repair yards at Lorient, St. Nazaire, La Pallice, Brest, Bordeaux, and Trondheim, and the submarine building yards at Wilhelmshaven, Kiel, Hamburg, Vegesack, and Flensburg has been an important factor, perhaps the most important, in curbing the U-boat menace. And their bombing of the great synthetic-rubber plants at Hüls, on the edge of the Ruhr, and of the big Messerschmitt plant at Regensburg were supremely competent jobs. But all through the summer the scope of American operations was limited by the low intake of replacement aircraft and crews from across the Atlantic. As one American airman phrased the problem, 'After a certain point it meant risking our seed corn, and we had to save that.'"

One of the new techniques used by Anderson during this period was a "shuttle-bombing" route from England to Africa, hitting targets on the way over and on the way back. Other developments included a technique of "bombing through solid cloud," which gave "satisfactory" results. In September 1943 the

General sent his Flying Fortresses out on twilight raids (rather than their usual daylight attacks), another innovation. The following month an attack by his planes on the German ball- and roller-bearing works at Schweinfurt was described by General Arnold as "an engagement between large armies—a major campaign. In a period of a few hours we invaded German-held Europe to a depth of 500 miles, sacked and crippled one of her most vital enterprises"; and at the beginning of December 1943 Anderson was raised to the temporary rank of major general. At the age of thirty-nine one of the youngest major generals in the United States Army, Anderson was still only a captain in permanent rank.

That the shortage of men and planes reported by Murphy had been alleviated was indicated by a statement made by British Air Vice-Marshal H. W. L. Saunders in January 1944. He stated that the R.A.F. had watched "with amazement" the growth of the American Air Forces in England into a "magnificent" war machine. "Many people thought daily bombing would prove too costly," said the Air Marshal, "but the 8th has given the lie to them." In January 1944, when that force was inactivated, its head was made deputy commander in charge of operations of the United States Strategic Air Forces in Western Europe, under Lieutenant General Carl Spaatz [42]. And in February 1944, on the twenty-sixth anniversary of the Red Army the Soviets awarded Major General Frederick Lewis Anderson the Order of Suvorov (the highest Russian decoration) 3rd class.

The flying General is "built like a halfback" and "combines physical stamina with a kind of coltish ingrown shyness." His hair is brown, his eyebrows "ginger-colored," and his green eyes squint so that "half the time you can scarcely see his eyes when you are talking with him." Fred Anderson's wife and children are now living in Washington, but they all hope to retire after the War to a Western ranch with their three-legged setter. The General misses them "frightfully. They are his great love in life—they and the thousands of keen-eyed youngsters whom daily he manages in their task of skilled annihilation." "I think," comments an interviewer, "that when the crew of a Flying Fortress is lost in action, Fred Anderson feels as if he had lost ten of his kid brothers; and it's hard on you to lose a lot of kid brothers almost every day."

References

Am Mag 137:124 Ap '44 por
N Y Herald Tribune p23 Je 17 '43 por
N Y Sun p21 D 6 '43
N Y Times p5 Jl 16 '43 por
Sat Eve Post 216:16-17+ Ja 22 '44 pors
Who's Who in America 1944-45

ANTOINE, JOSEPHINE (an'twän) Oct. 27, 1908- Singer
Address: b. c/o Austin Wilder, 745 Fifth Ave., New York City; h. 45 Prospect Pl., New York City

The only American-trained singer at the Metropolitan Opera House who has never sung a subordinate role is Josephine Antoine. Ever since 1936, when she stepped directly from the

Bruno of Hollywood

JOSEPHINE ANTOINE

studios of the Juilliard School of Music in New York to the stage of the Metropolitan, Miss Antoine has had the distinction of singing only leading roles.

Josephine Louise Antoine was born in Colorado on October 27, 1908. Orphaned when she was only a few months old, she was chosen for adoption soon afterwards by Arthur H. and Bertha O. Antoine of Denver. Their chosen daughter has never attempted to trace her heredity. "I have never had any desire to trace the background of my antecedents," says Miss Antoine. "I owe everything to my foster parents, who gave me all they had from the time I was six months old. That is enough for me."

After five years Mr. Antoine's position as manager in a chain of grocery stores made it necessary for the family to move to Boulder, Colorado, where little Josephine was at first tutored at home. When she entered the one-room local school at the age of eight, it is told, she was so well drilled that she could answer eighth-grade questions, with the result that she was promoted through three grades in the first year. Yet, while Josephine was evidently fond of school, her real interest and delight was music. "Ever since I can remember," she says, "all I wanted to do was to sing and play the piano." On her eighth birthday part of this wish was fulfilled by the arrival of a piano and the neighborhood music teacher; and when Josephine entered high school, she had her first lesson in singing.

Her vocal training continued under Alexander Grant when she arrived at college age. She then became a student at the University of Colorado, where she majored in English. It was her intention to teach English and thus support herself while preparing for her career as a singer. Meanwhile, she says, "every penny went to buy recordings, or was laid aside for tickets on those rare occasions when some such famous diva as Amelita Galli-Curci visited

Denver." In 1928 the ambitious soprano entered a national competition for young American singers sponsored by the Atwater Kent Company; but, in her naïveté she prepared only one aria, "Caro Nome" from Rigoletto, and therefore had nothing to sing in the final audition. Undaunted, Miss Antoine re-entered the contest the following year, which was also the year of her graduation from college. After winning the regional trials, she went to New York City for the finals, taking third place—with the same aria from Rigoletto.

With her third prize—$1,500 plus one year's tuition at any American conservatory of her choice—the young coloratura soprano went off to Philadelphia to study at the Curtis Institute of Music under the great Marcella Sembrich, who had been one of the contest judges. After five months at the Institute, Miss Antoine was admitted to the graduate division of the Juilliard School of Music in New York, again under Mme. Sembrich. For the five years during which Miss Antoine studied in New York City, she supported herself by singing in churches. Albert Stoessel, the late director of the New York Oratorio Society, gave Miss Antoine her first professional opportunity by engaging her as one of the soloists in The Messiah, for a Carnegie Hall performance of Handel's oratorio. After this, she sang the role of Susanna under the direction of Fritz Reiner [41] in a Philadelphia Opera Company presentation of The Marriage of Figaro; she also appeared in the Cimarosa opera, The Secret Marriage, given at the Library of Congress during the Coolidge Festival. Mme. Sembrich, who avoided travel during the last years of her life, broke her own rule by traveling to Washington to hear her pupil's performance. In addition, Miss Antoine took part in the Juilliard production of Maria Malibran, an American opera by Robert Russell Bennett [42], and sang Zerbinetta in Richard Strauss's [44] Ariadne on Naxos.

The late Artur Bodansky, after attending one of the Juilliard productions in which Miss Antoine appeared, offered her an audition with the Metropolitan Opera. "I didn't think I'd make the Metropolitan," she recalls; "I thought they didn't need a new soprano." So it was that Miss Antoine went, in January 1935, for what she expected to be a routine audition—without high hopes and without the consequent nervousness of anxiety. Again, her choice was the "Caro Nome," followed by a Lucia aria and one from Mignon. And when the months went by with no word from the Metropolitan, it was only what the singer had expected. She dismissed the matter from her mind—and then, in June 1935, the opera company informed her that a contract awaited her signature.

Miss Antoine's debut at the Metropolitan was made on January 4, 1936 as Philine in a broadcast performance of Mignon, the first time that anyone had ever made an operatic and radio debut simultaneously. The new soprano was warmly received by the press and public, the reviewer of the New York Times writing that she sang "with such charm and animation that she scored an immediate hit with the large audience. . . . Blessed with an unusually attractive stage presence, Miss Antoine made a picturesque and engaging Philine. . . . Vocally, she handled the pyrotechnics of her numbers with ease and agility. She avoided forcing and her tones were pure and clear; the scale was even in quality."

Of her radio career, Miss Antoine reports that she has "done everything, from automobiles to soap and cheese." She has sung in the Chase and Sanborn *Opera in English* programs and with the various Sunday evening symphonic hours, such as those sponsored by the Ford and Packard motor car companies. She has appeared—in a somewhat lighter vein—on a radio series with the violinist Rubinoff and with Bing Crosby '41 on the *Kraft Music Hall* program. During 1943 and 1944 Miss Antoine has commuted to Chicago for her broadcasts on the coast-to-coast *Contented Hour*, a weekly Monday night program over the National Broadcasting Company's network.

Miss Antoine's subsequent singing engagements have taken her on tours from Canada to Puerto Rico. In the course of her travels she has sung all the usual coloratura roles with the Chicago Civic Opera, the San Francisco Opera Company, and with the Cincinnati Opera Company. Her extensive operatic repertoire includes the roles of Rosina in the *Barber of Seville*, Gilda in *Rigoletto*, Lucia in *Lucia di Lammermoor*, the Queen in *Le Coq d'Or*, Zerlina in *Don Giovanni*, and the Queen of the Night in *The Magic Flute*. Other operas in which she has appeared include *Die Fledermaus*, *The Bartered Bride*, *Martha*, and *The Tales of Hoffmann*. In recognition of her accomplishments, the Colorado-born singer has been awarded the first degree of Master of Fine Arts in Music ever conferred by the University of Colorado.

Nothing about Josephine Antoine suggests the prima donna—at least the popular idea of the prima donna—until she sings. Stage diction and cosmopolitan atmosphere have not affected her manner, which is friendly, direct, and natural. Those qualities and her blond hair, blue eyes, and medium stature give her "an infectious personality which matches an appearance of youth, charm, and spring-like freshness." That she does not claim the prerogatives of a diva is illustrated by an incident that occurred at a May Festival in Cleveland, where Miss Antoine was to have been the soprano soloist at a performance of Mahler's intricate Eighth Symphony. She tells of it herself: "When I arrived at Cleveland, after weeks of preparation, I found that Hilda Burke and I had been assigned the same role in error, but we were calmly informed that I was mistaken. I therefore took the other role and read it at sight. Luckily, I'd been taught the orchestral harmony, because that's a pretty difficult symphony. Anyway, I knew the soprano cues!" Not only did Miss Antoine sing the part at sight, but she gave what was considered an extraordinary performance.

In spite of her full schedule, Miss Antoine manages to give performances for service men and women, as well as benefits for bond and war fund drives. (In 1943 she was chosen Queen of the Illinois State Militia Ball.) Part of her spare time is spent in knitting, and another of her interests is antiques, particularly early American milk glass. Her favorite recreation is driving—"before and after the War," she has qualified the statement.

References

American Women 1939-40
Ewen, D. ed. Living Musicians 1940
Thompson, O. ed. International Cyclopedia of Music and Musicians 1943

ARMSTRONG, LOUIS July 4, 1900- Musician

Address: b. c/o Joe Glaser, Inc., 745 Fifth Ave., New York City

Louis Armstrong is "the irreplaceable hero of the very musicians who have received more votes than Louis himself in the swing magazine polls." And jazz critics are in complete accord. This Negro's "career set the pattern for the development of American jazz," wrote Leonard G. Feather in the New York *Times*. It is Virgil Thomson's '40 opinion that Armstrong's "style of improvisation would seem to have combined the highest reaches of instrumental virtuosity with the most tensely disciplined melodic structure and the most spontaneous emotional expression, all of which in one man you must admit to be pretty rare." Hugh Panassié believes Armstrong to be not only "the greatest of all jazz musicians," but "one of the most extraordinary creative geniuses that all music has ever known."

Not unlike jazz itself, Daniel Louis Armstrong was born in a back-of-town part of New Orleans at the turn of the century—on July 4, 1900. His mother, Mary-Ann, was a former house servant; his father, Willie Armstrong, was a turpentine worker. The marriage was not a very happy one, and when Louis was five his parents separated. The boy and his sister Beatrice then went to live with their mother and great-grandmother right in the city, around Liberty and Perdido Streets. The Perdido Street gang stayed around the streets most of the night, and were "always shooting dice and fighting," but there were things that Louis preferred to fighting. On warm nights he and some of the other boys in the gang would go down to the Mississippi and sit on the docks and sing together before going in for a swim; and soon they had formed a quartet in which he sang tenor. The quartet strolled the streets of the Storyville section of New Orleans, singing new jazz songs and passing the hat for pennies until chased away late every night. Louis' only instrument was a four-string guitar made of a cigar-box, copper wire, and a piece of flat wood for the neck, but every chance he got he would steal into the Dago Tony Tonk, where his hero Bunk Jones played the cornet. Bunk began teaching him to play by ear; and of everything he learned he liked the blues the best. He and Bunk felt things the same way, and he absorbed a good deal of Bunk's style— particularly Bunk's intense vibrato, and his way of hesitating, always behind the beat. Louis was only about eleven at the time.

It wasn't until later that the boy learned something about reading music. New Year's Eve 1913 was one which he celebrated by shooting off an old "38," and for that he was arrested and sent to the Waifs' Home for a year's discipline. It so happened that the Home was in charge of a man named Captain

LOUIS ARMSTRONG

Joseph Jones who did not believe in treating his charges as if they were criminals, and soon Louis began learning how to blow the bugle. When he had mastered the bugle he was given a cornet, and by the end of the year he was the leader of the Home's brass band, which was well known in New Orleans. When Louis was released from the Home he knew exactly what he wanted to do.

At fourteen, though, Louis was still too young to get a job in a band—and so for the next three years he sold newspapers and worked in a dairy. Whenever he could he picked up a job playing in one of the "gin mills" for a dollar a night, and he frequently visited the cabaret at which King Oliver played. He ran errands for Oliver's wife and finally began taking trumpet lessons from Oliver, who was the local idol in 1917 for his "powerful and original" trumpet work. Soon young Armstrong was able to take his teacher's place in occasional engagements, and when in 1917 Oliver left for Chicago Armstrong took Oliver's place in Kid Ory's band. The same year Armstrong married his childhood sweetheart, Daisy Parker.

The marriage was not too happy, and after a short time the Armstrongs were divorced. In November 1919 he signed up with Fate Marable's orchestra, which was playing on the Mississippi excursion boat *Dixie Belle*. When in 1920 and 1921 the *Dixie Belle* departed for its annual 2,000-mile summer cruise Armstrong went with it, and it was on these cruises that he learned what he didn't already know about reading music—from a melophone player, Dave Jones. After the second cruise he got a job at the Orchard Cabaret in New Orleans (at a salary of $21 a week), and then he played at Tom Anderson's cabaret, The Real Thing. He was already composing tunes, one of which, "I Wish I Could Shimmy Like My Sister Kate," he sold to Piron for $50.

At this time Chicago was rapidly becoming the jazz center of the United States, and King Oliver's and other Negro bands were having a

tremendous effect on white musicians there. In July 1922 the King sent for Armstrong, inviting him to join his orchestra as second cornettist. Armstrong didn't remain with the King long, but while he was with Oliver's band he made his first recordings, and it was also while with the band that he met his second wife, Lillian Hardin, whom he married in February 1924. A talented pianist and composer herself, she realized that Oliver's cornet style was having an unfortunate influence on Armstrong's own style, and engineered things so that he could join Ollie Powers at Dreamland as first trumpet. Then, in October 1924, Fletcher Henderson invited him to join his jazz band at the Roseland Ballroom in New York, and Armstrong thus went to that city for the first time. There nearly a year, he made little impression on Broadway, but before he returned to Chicago he had made a memorable series of recordings—among them the blues discs in which he accompanies Bessie Smith.

Armstrong returned to the unheard-of salary of $75 a week—his canny wife had been at work. On November 24, 1925 an advertisement appeared in the Chicago *Defender* announcing that Lil Hardin's Dreamland Syncopaters would feature the "World's Greatest Jazz Cornettist," Louis Armstrong. "At last," writes William Russell, "Louis was in his element and was playing the kind of music he knew and loved. The public loved it too. . . . It had to be loud and hot for the hip-liquor toter of the mid-twenties."

A month later Armstrong joined Erskine Tate's little symphony orchestra at the Vendome Theatre, and there he played solos, interspersed with his own brand of comedy and singing, before an appreciative audience. While still at the Vendome he left the Dreamland for the Sunset Cabaret, where he organized his own band and saw his name go up in lights for the first time. Soon, too, he was making Okeh recordings with a little group called Louis Armstrong's Hot Five (later, the Hot Seven). By this time Armstrong had abandoned the cornet for the trumpet, and his fame as a trumpeter spread. White musicians thronged to the Sunset, some of them offering "fabulous sums to learn Armstrong's tricks." Others studied *Fifty Hot Choruses of Armstrong*. Writes one critic: "Louis' phrasing and style were the admitted inspiration for almost every other prominent jazz trumpet player and vocalist. . . . Many of the jazz stars on instruments other than the trumpet have been influenced by Armstrong. Composers of so-called 'riff' tunes today are still borrowing, sometimes unconsciously, phrases invented in some of Armstrong's recorded improvisations a decade or two ago. . . . His spontaneous inventions laid the foundation for the 'swing' of 1941."

In early 1928 Armstrong resigned from the Vendome, but by April he found himself at Chicago's Savoy Ballroom, and there his salary was eventually raised to $200 a week. Panassié describes him during this period: "He would improvise on the same theme for a full half hour, taking twenty choruses in a row. Often he would be quite motionless as he played or sang —his eyes closed, like a man carried out of the world; tears would roll down his cheeks. His imagination seemed inexhaustible: for each new chorus he had new ideas more beautiful than those he had produced for the preceding chorus.

As he went along, his improvisation grew hotter, his style became more and more simple—until at the end there was nothing but the endless repetition of one fragment of melody—or even a single note insistently sounded and executed with cataclysmic intonations."

When the Savoy could no longer pay the musicians, most of them got together, put the band in Armstrong's name, and made their way to New York in four little automobiles. This was in the spring of 1929 and, though they had set out with only $20 apiece, they had good luck. They stopped at all the big towns they passed and were welcomed everywhere; when they reached New York they landed in one of the city's top spots, Connie's Inn. Soon Armstrong was also doubling with Leroy Smith in a revue produced by Connie on Broadway—and he and "Ain't Misbehavin'" became the rage. The *Hot Chocolates* revue ran through the winter and into the spring of 1930, and then Armstrong went on a triumphal summer tour as Lew Russell's featured trumpeter. In Hollywood the band was put in Armstrong's name and booked at Sebastian's Cotton Club, where it remained for almost a year, broadcasting every night and making many records. It was not until 1931 that he returned to Chicago and began to get a band of his own together again. (Armstrong has rarely led his own bands, in any case, and they have seldom been of great importance: they are always entirely subservient to him as a personality.)

Armstrong did not remain in Chicago long. After another road tour which included New Orleans and three or four months back in Hollywood he decided that it was time to see Europe. His recording of "You Rascal, You" had been a great hit in England, and when he arrived in London musicians and critics gave him a reception at the Ambassador that he will never forget. He proceeded to break the all-time record for a band at London's Palladium Theatre, playing with a group of swing musicians hastily rushed over from Paris, and then toured England and Scotland for four months with a ten-piece band of white musicians. He returned to New York on the day Roosevelt '42 was elected President for the first time. The next summer he again sailed for Europe, touring England during the summer and fall and during the winter of 1933-1934 making a continental tour which included Denmark, Sweden, Norway, and Holland. Back in London, he gave a performance before the present King, George VI '42, and the Duke of Windsor '44, then he went to Paris to "laze around" for three or four months. He ended up by giving two concerts in Paris and by touring Belgium, France, and Italy. After that came another United States tour; finally, in October 1935, he opened at Connie's Inn on Broadway with Luis Russell's band behind him. In October 1942, after his second divorce, he was married to his third wife, whom he had met at New York's Cotton Club.

Since 1923 Armstrong has put at least a thousand numbers on wax, and many of these records sell for $20 or more as collectors' items today. Among his best-known recordings are "Shine", "Chinatown", "Tiger Rag", "I Can't Give You Anything But Love", "Treasure Island"—and, of course, "Ain't Misbehavin'" and "You Rascal, You." He has also composed twenty-odd tunes, of which his favorites are "If We Never Meet Again" and "Struttin' With Some Barbecue." In 1944 a song he had written fifteen years before, "Go South, Young Man," was revived in the filmusical *Atlantic City*, in which he and his orchestra appeared in a "Harlem on Parade" sequence.

Oddly enough, Armstrong is better known in the United States "as a showman-comedian, a movie and stage star" than as "a great trumpet player and inspired singer." Even in the pictures which he has made—*Every Day's a Holiday* (1938), *Going Places* (1938), *Cabin in the Sky* (1943), and *Jam Session* (1944)—he has been regarded (in *Time*'s opinion) less as an artist than as a "picturesque, Sambo-style entertainer." This is certainly not because his creative powers have declined in recent years. Such a statement, according to Parnassié, "could only be made because of a total misunderstanding of this great trumpet player's evolution." The period from 1927 to 1931 was one of "highly imaginative improvisations in which he gave free rein to the almost frightening fluency of his technique. He employed vast and grandiose phrases, and used the most audacious and unforeseen melody lines. Here one feels that his invention is indeed limitless, that nothing can stop it." "Exhibitions of virtuosity" characterized the next four years, but since 1935 he has been given to stating his theme simply, "modifying it here and there with touches that give the most uninteresting phrases a beauty which transfigures them." Today, "in one or two notes, he concentrates all that he said earlier in a long phrase"; his present style has a "detached and sublime quality."

"Satchmo'" "has hardened his lip and jaw muscles and developed his abdominal air pressure to the point where he can strike and hold a high C for a greater length of time than any living swing trumpeter," and frequently "he plays up to high F and G, three and four tones, respectively, above C." "In every register," however, "Louis' tonal quality is unique; it surpasses in power that of all other jazz trumpet players; it is full and majestic, both fierce and polished, but at the same time it is heart-breaking and soothing." And he "surpasses all other singers in the same measure as he surpasses all other trumpeters. . . . His throaty, veiled voice touches one by its beautiful tone and by that same intense vibrato which he uses on the trumpet. . . . He is never hampered by the lyrics in improvising on the melody. . . . His singing swings as much as his trumpet." He is always experimenting. Richard M. Jones probably summed it all up when he said: "As long as those pearly teeth hold out, Louis'll still be playing something new, and all the others will be running after him trying to catch up."

References

Look 7:64-6 Mr 23 '43 il pors
N Y Times IX p6 O 26 '41
Armstrong, L. Swing That Music 1936
Hobson, W. American Jazz Music 1939
Parnassié, H. Hot Jazz 1936; Real Jazz 1942
Ramsey, F. and Smith, C. E. eds. Jazzmen 1939

ARMSTRONG, MARGARET (NEILSON) Sept. 24, 1867—July 18, 1944 American author who achieved distinction as an artist before publication of her two biographies, *Fanny Kemble* (1938) and *Trelawny* (1940); co-author of the *Field Book of Western Wild Flowers* (1915), still a standard reference work.

Obituary

N Y Times p19 Jl 19 '44

AUSTIN, WARREN R(OBINSON) Nov. 12, 1877- United States Senator from Vermont

Address: b. Senate Office Bldg., Washington, D. C.; h. 43 William St., Burlington, Vt.

The assistant Republican floor leader in Congress, Warren R. Austin from Vermont, is "one of those men who in any legislature, although they are strong party leaders, are capable of rising above partisanship when national crises arise." Although a bitter opponent of the New Deal, not only has Senator Austin consistently supported President Roosevelt's [42] foreign policy, but in some respects, according to Arthur Krock [43], he was many months and many realities ahead of the nation's President. He was at least two years ahead of many of his colleagues when in February 1941 (during discussion in the Senate of the Lease-Lend Bill) he said: "While Congress is writing a policy of full Anglo-American cooperation, members of Congress and other public leaders should express their views on what are our aims, and ask Britain what are her peace aims." In the same speech (which was called "historic" because he "was the first to voice such sentiments on the Senate floor") he expressed his own views when he said: "Furthermore, ought we not to ask Britain now to join us in an endeavor to establish something new . . . in the world hereafter, a new and different sanction of peace? This is not a mere dream. I believe we are in one of those great movements of civilization in which it advances to a higher step after it has slid backward."

Born in Highgate, Vermont, November 12, 1877, Warren Robinson Austin is the son of Chauncey Goodrich and Anne Mathilda (Robinson) Austin, whose ancestors fought in the American Revolutionary War. He was educated in the public schools and at the Brigham Academy in Bakersfield, Vermont, from which he was graduated in 1895. In 1899 he received the degree of Bachelor of Philosophy from the University of Vermont. He entered his father's law office in St. Albans, Vermont and in 1902 was admitted to the Vermont Bar. Many years of judiciary experience followed. In 1906 he was admitted to the Circuit Court of the Second Circuit of the United States; in 1914 to the Supreme Court of the United States; in 1917 to the United States Court for China; in 1919 to the District Court of the United States for the Eastern District of New York; and in 1931 to the Circuit Court of Appeals of the Second Circuit. His political career began at the age of twenty-seven when he became state's attorney for Franklin County; at thirty-two he was elected Mayor of St.

Albans, Vermont. During this time Austin also served as a United States Commissioner.

As the representative of the American International Corporation and the Seims-Carey Railway and Canal Company, Austin went to China in 1916 to negotiate two loans to the Chinese Republic, one of approximately $100,000,000 for the benefit of national railways, and one of $30,000,000 for national conservation and the dredging of the Grand Canal. On his return to the United States in 1917 he began his law practice in Burlington, Vermont, and during the boundary line dispute between New Hampshire and Vermont he served as special counsel for his state. Although Austin's clients included some of the most important business concerns in the New England states, his most sensational victory in the courts was won when he secured for his client in the Woodhouse *vs.* Woodhouse alienation case the largest damages ($465,000) ever secured in such a case. In addition to his legal practice he lectured at the University of Vermont from 1925 to 1928 on medical jurisprudence, and from 1917 to 1931 he was attorney for Vermont's State Medical Society. In 1923 he was elected president of the Vermont Bar Association.

Warren Austin came into prominence in national politics when he was chosen to second the nomination of Herbert Hoover [43] for President during the 1928 Republican convention. In 1931, when a Vermont seat in the Senate became vacant, Roy L. Patrick, a prominent Vermonter and New England industrialist, asked Austin if he would like to fill the unexpired term of Senator L. Greene. Austin hesitated—he had had no legislative experience and had held no public office outside his state. But Patrick and his many other Republican friends and admirers persuaded him to run, and he was elected to the Senate in March of that same year. Because of his extensive experience in judiciary circles he was made a member of the Senate's Judiciary Committee and also a member of the Military Affairs and the District of Columbia Committees. (In February 1944 when he was made a member of the important Senate Foreign Relations Committee, filling a post made vacant by the death of Senator Van Nuys, Austin resigned from the Judiciary Committee.) He was to be re-elected to the Senate in 1934 and again in 1940.

Austin's maiden speech (January 1932), against the Harrison amendment to the (Democratic) tariff bill which proposed taking from the President the power to change tariff rates, was well received by his colleagues. Like most freshman Senators, however, he played an inconspicuous role in the Senate for many months.

In 1934 he took the offensive against the Administration's action in canceling without warning the air-mail contracts, and he directed the inquiry of the Senate Air-Mail Committee into the activities of transport operators without contracts before and after the cancellation. In 1935 he was one of the leaders in the fight against the Tennessee Valley Authority; in 1936 he backed Alfred Landon [44] for the Presidency. In the summer of the latter year he sailed for Palestine to study conditions there under the British mandate, and upon his return asserted that the United States should insist that Great Britain perform her neglected duty there.

In 1937 Austin fought President Roosevelt's Supreme Court proposal, opposed the extension of the Reciprocal Trade Agreements Act, opposed the confirmation of Senator Black '41 for appointment to the Supreme Court, blocked the bill against WPA dismissals, and came out flatly against Senator Joseph C. O'Mahoney's TNEC (the committee for the investigation of such matters as industrial monopoly, unemployment, life insurance, and corporation methods—sometimes called "technology"), declaring that "it points the way to a collectivistic system akin to Nazi national socialism." He also considered the abolishing of tax exempt securities "a step in the direction of socialism." Late in 1937 he was sent to Puerto Rico to study that country's judicial system, and after his return in January 1938 he assailed the Government Reorganization Bill and the "pump-priming" bill, and offered an anti-political amendment to the Relief-Recovery Bill; the amendment was defeated. In 1938 and in 1939 as well as later, however, he supported defense measures which many of his Republican colleagues "made party issues." In March 1939 he defended American plane sales to France; after the outbreak of war in September he favored the cash-carry plan.

During the 1940 National Republican Convention, Austin, now senior Senator from Vermont, was a delegate at large and an ardent Wendell Willkie '40 supporter. According to the *Christian Science Monitor* (January 1941), "it would have lifted one of the heaviest loads from the shoulders of Wendell L. Willkie in the election" if Austin's colleagues had followed him. "It seemed sometimes as though Mr. Willkie didn't have the support of his own party in Congress."

In explanation of his stand on the international situation, Austin has said: "The foreign policy Mr. Roosevelt offers is not his policy, it is not mine or any other person's; it is the traditional American policy of aiding and upholding democracy." In this policy Austin had gone further than Roosevelt himself as early as 1937, when he favored independent sanctions against Japan by the United States if the League of Nations failed to apply them. And because of his views a bloc of Republican Senators who had held isolationist views before Pearl Harbor banded together in December 1942 (shortly before the winter session of Congress) in an effort to prevent Austin from serving as assistant minority leader. Austin had been chosen for the post by Senator Charles L. McNary '40, minority leader. The "incipient revolt" collapsed when McNary said flatly that Austin would continue to act as leader during his absence.

Austin again won against the isolationists of his party at the 1943 Mackinac Island conference. He was among the twoscore Governors, Senators, Representatives, and national committeemen invited to sit with Chairman Harrison E. Spangler's '43 Post-War Advisory Council to formulate a foreign and domestic policy. "As ranking member of the Senate Foreign Relations Committee, Arthur H. Vandenberg '40," stated *Newsweek*, "had come to

WARREN R. AUSTIN

Mackinac confident he had the Council in his pocket. . . . He favored his own Senate resolution to limit American participation in any post-War world organizations to steps which would not impair the nation's sovereignty. This was promptly scrapped by the bloc of New England and Northwestern Governors, along with the outstanding internationalist, Senator Austin. Austin even threatened to write a minority report. The revolt brought a compromise."

The foreign policy plank adopted by the Council was praised by the New York *Times* —especially the clause, "responsible participation by the United States in post-War cooperative organization among sovereign nations to prevent military aggression and to obtain permanent peace with organized justice in a free world." *PM*'s criticism of the plank was to the effect that the plank had "fifty-seven varieties of foreign policy, from the ultra isolationism of Clare Hoffman to the ultra internationalism of Warren Austin," and, if anything, "was vaguer than the 1920 platform, for at least that seemed to pledge the Republican Party to an association of nations." However, there has been nothing vague in Austin's statements on post-War peace plans. Both in the Senate and in public addresses he has urged his countrymen to adopt a definite peace policy which would commit the United States to membership in a world federation of nations with the power to enforce peace. He backed the Fulbright '43 and Connally '41 resolutions in the fall of 1943. And later, after the announcement of the Moscow joint three-nation declaration, he joined the Senators who supported Senator Claude Pepper's '41 amendment to the Connally resolution. The amendment asked for a revision of the resolution "to adopt the identical words adopted at the Moscow Conference," which would commit the Senate more specifically to "an international authority" to control the peace.

(Continued next page)

AUSTIN, WARREN R.—*Continued*

Austin's increasing activity in world peace groups during 1944 has caused him to be called the Republican Party's "most stalwart collaborationist." He was a member of the special bipartisan Senate group who consulted with Secretary Hull and the State Department on a post-War peace organization; a member of the five-man subcommittee to make the study of international communications authorized by the Senate; and he was drafted by the Republican Party to write the international plank in its campaign platform. *Time* Magazine was of the opinion that this plank closely followed the Mackinac Declaration of 1943. Much criticism followed its announcement, chief of which came from Senator Joseph Ball [43], Governor Edge of New Jersey, and the late Wendell Willkie. Willkie compared what he called its vagueness to the 1920 Republican foreign policy plank which enabled Warren G. Harding to technically escape any obligation to carry on a League of Nations, although the platform had pledged the party to an "association of nations." In the October issue of *World Affairs*, the American Peace Society bulletin, Austin declared that both the Republican and Democratic platform planks had been written to conform to the American plan offered at Dumbarton Oaks, after full information as to that plan had been given to the platform committees.

As early as 1940 Austin had interested himself in the manpower producing situation in the war effort, realizing that the Government must get quick deliveries of battleships, guns, and other equipment. "To get action, business needs efficient labor and an opportunity to get work out of labor," said Austin. At this time he proposed as a resolution a "five-man Industrial Council to manage rearmament," and in September 1942 he introduced an amendment to the Selective Service Act which would lower the military draft age to eighteen and make all men from eighteen to twenty-five deferred from military service liable to a manpower draft. The culmination of his efforts to draft the "home front" in the war effort came in February 1943 when he and Representative James W. Wadsworth [43] "dropped identical bills into the legislative hoppers of both Houses of Congress." These have become known as the Austin-Wadsworth Bill, a national war service measure authorizing the drafting of men from eighteen to sixty-five and of women from eighteen to fifty for war work. The bill provides that the President may direct the War Manpower Commission through the Selective Service Act system to provide workers for industries faced with labor shortages.

When the Senate Military Affairs Committee (of which Austin is a high ranking minority member) opened hearings on the measure "the military clashed with civilian ideas. Secretary of War Stimson [40] endorsed the bill, but War Manpower Commission Paul McNutt [40] opposed it on the ground that voluntary methods had not yet been plumbed. In this McNutt was seconded by Bernard M. Baruch [41], who termed the bill 'slavery' because it forced individuals to work for employers operating for profit." William

Green [42], president of the A. F. of L., also opposed the bill on the ground that it "imposes involuntary servitude in violation of the Thirteenth Amendment of the Federal Constitution and in violation of our basic and most cherished concepts of freedom." "Mr. Green's case," wrote Walter L. Lippmann [40], "is that men may be drafted to fight and that they also may be drafted to work, provided they are inducted into the Army. This means he thinks it right to compel certain American men to serve. But the rest, because they happen to be older, or cannot pass the Army's physical tests, or have dependents, or are women and not men, may not be compelled to do what they can. . . . The more we can obliterate the privilege which separates those who are compelled to serve from those who are not compelled, the nearer we shall be to the realities of democratic liberty. . . ."

In a *Look* Magazine article, Austin said that his method of solving the manpower problem "clearly is within the scope of the Constitution which recognizes the necessity of investing the Government with unusual powers during times of war. The soldier on the field of battle, risking his life, is not questioning the authority of his Government to draft him." On another occasion Austin said that he believed "a labor draft bill would prevent wartime strikes, such as those in the 1943 coal dispute, by ending competitive bidding for workers by employers." "This competitive bidding," pointed out Austin, "spurs the inflationary spiral and produces the higher prices which demand higher wages."

On January 11, 1944 the President in his wartime message to Congress recommended passage of a national service law, on the condition that bills covering four other points—stabilization renewal, subsidies, taxes, and continuance of the current renegotiation law—be passed. Austin quickly introduced a revision of his own bill (enabling draft boards to compel strikers to return to their jobs) to achieve purposes which he said were similar to those outlined by the President in his message. The Austin-Wadsworth Bill became the controversy of the month. Secretary of War Stimson made a far stronger appeal for its passage than the President had. The Secretary of the Navy, the Maritime Commission, the American Legion, and the Citizens' Committee urged its acceptance. Leading the opposition were the A.F. of L. and the CIO, the Chamber of Commerce of the United States, various women's organizations, and the Truman Committee. The *Congressional Digest* pointed out that the line-up of the pros and the cons indicated that the bill was political dynamite. Although the President in his qualified endorsement of the bill had declared that it would help to prevent strikes, Under-Secretary of War Robert Patterson [41], who handles the industrial contacts of the War Department, stated before the Senate Military Affairs Committee (an A.P. feature had reported that a canvass of the eighteen members of this committee showed only one certain vote for the measure) on January 26, 1944 that "no law will stop all strikes." Some Senators and Representatives, said the *Digest*, thought that if the President had given unqualified endorsement and exercised strong pressure in Congress, the bill might have had a chance. When interviewed, Austin said that various groups had set up to block its passage.

However, by June the manpower situation evoked an administrative order setting up a national system of "priority referrals" for employment. It came through WMC head Paul McNutt [40]. An editorial in the New York Herald Tribune said: "It is ironical that Congress, having failed to consider a national service act . . . now finds that measures on which it avoided commitment are to be taken on Executive order alone." Furthermore, the machinery and definitive authority of national service, pointed out the editorial, are needed not only to deal with dislocations of labor, but will be needed to deal with full-scale demobilization later.

During his terms in Congress, Senator Austin has voted against the Administration on many important issues not involving foreign policy. He voted for repeal of the President's order limiting salaries to $25,000 a year; for the modified version of the Ruml [43] plan; for the Smith [41]-Connally "Anti-Strike" Bill and for overriding the President's veto of the same bill; for limiting the National Labor Relations Board; against the appropriation of money for the National Resources Planning Board; and for the dismissal of Watson, Dodd, and Lovett [43]. He also opposed the Anti-Poll Tax Bill on the grounds that it was unconstitutional, voting instead to report to the Senate Senator O'Mahoney's resolution to abolish poll taxes by means of an amendment to the Constitution. He voted for overriding the President's veto on the tax bill (1944).

On the other hand, Austin was one of the six Republican Senators who voted against Senator Robert Taft's [40] amendment to the bill authorizing the merger of the Western Union and the Postal Telegraph, a bill opposed by the labor unions. He opposed the Bankhead [43] Bill to defer farm labor from the draft, and supported O'Mahoney's proposed amendment to that bill; he opposed the McKellar Bill requiring confirmation of most Federal employees making more than $4,500 a year; he opposed the inclusion of farm-labor costs in parity; he voted to continue the loan powers of the Farm Security Administration; he supported the continuation of the Administration's reciprocal trade agreement program without change in its present form. He also supported the Green-Lucas Soldier Vote Bill. His proposal (in collaboration with Senator Styles Bridges) for more liberal provisions for servicemen's mustering-out pay than the original Senator Barkley bill provided was accepted by the Military Affairs Committee. Austin voted for the bill barring further food subsidies after June 30, 1944; against the amendment which stripped the TVA of its revolving fund and limited its expenditures to Congressional appropriations; for the Bankhead amendment on price control legislation which would have forced the OPA to readjust ceilings on the cotton textiles; against the Kilgore-Murray $35-a-week unemployment compensation bill, and for the George reconversion bill.

Austin has the "Ethan Allen quality of independence and solidity." Known as a hard worker, he attributes his vigor to the fact that like most Vermonters he "has downed many dishes of baked beans, particularly before the tender age of two and a-half." But he is not the traditional Vermonter of Calvin Coolidge austerity. His manner is warm and cordial, and there is nothing he enjoys more than a friendly talk over a cigar and a highball. His liking for cigars puts him in the class of the cigaret chain-smoker. A lifelong friend, Roy L. Patrick, says that one of the Senator's most trying days occurred on a fishing trip in Canada a few years ago. Austin ran short of his favorite brand of cigars when they were deep in the Canadian woods. The Senator lighted the last one early in the morning and held it in his mouth throughout the day—a day "over trails and in a canoe under a continuous downpour." The trials of the day culminated that evening at the club house when a fellow club member (a United States Army general) brought out a box of a favorite brand of cigars—but failed to offer one to Austin. Austin never forgave the general until he won a major military victory in the Second World War. The Senator's favorite brand of cigars for many years was "No Appeal." "Appropriately named," says Patrick, "they had no appeal to anyone but Warren, who continued to smoke them until the company stopped making them."

The Senator is tall, straight, and always well-tailored. "In appearance," says a friend, "he is the type a Hollywood director would cast for the role of a—senator." He is red-cheeked, firm-jawed, and has iron-gray hair and smiling blue eyes. He is a member of the Congregational Church. On June 26, 1901 he was married to Mildred Marie Lucas. The Austins have two sons: Warren Robinson, Jr., a commander in the United States Coast Guard, and Edward Lucas, a major in an American tank-destroyer battalion which distinguished itself in an Anzio beachhead battle in the spring of 1944. Senator and Mrs. Austin have six grandchildren.

Austin's hobby is the growing of apples. In an orchard in the rear of his substantial red brick house in Burlington he works (in overalls) during summer vacations "conserving the native strains of American apples—strains which the commercial sellers will not carry." They are the Golden Russet, Spitzenburg, Jewett Red, Northern Spy, Quebec Sweet, and others—all in all, some sixty varieties. His greatest disappointment came when a storm uprooted a tree on which he had performed an interesting experiment. He had grafted a crab apple on a White Astrachan and produced a new type, a small-sized "ladies' apple."

Austin is a member of the Kappa Sigma fraternity and in 1939 was elected Kappa Sigma's "man of the year." He has been a trustee of the University of Vermont since 1914. He was the first president of Rotary in Burlington. He is a Mason, a Past Exalted Ruler of the Elks, an Odd Fellow, a member of Ahepan, the Military Order of the Loyal Legion of the United States, the Sons of the American Revolution, the China Society of America, the American Bar Association, and

AUSTIN, WARREN R.—*Continued*

the Far Eastern American Bar Association. In 1944 Columbia University conferred on Austin an honorary degree of Doctor of Laws. His clubs are: Ethan Allen (Burlington), St. Bernard (Canada), Alibi and Alfalfa (Washington, D.C.), the Farm Bureau, the Future Farmer, and the Bennington Club.

References

C S Mon p1 Ja 2 '41
Look 7:19 F 23 '43

Who's Who in America 1944-45
Who's Who in the Nation's Capital 1938-39

AVERY, SEWELL (LEE) (ā'vẽr-i sū'el)
Nov. 4, 1874- Corporation official
Address: b. Montgomery Ward & Co., Chicago; h. 209 Lake Shore Dr., Chicago

Sewell Avery's defiance of the Roosevelt Administration in April 1944—which resulted in the seizure of a plant of Montgomery Ward & Company of which he is chairman—highlighted a remarkable career of industrial organization and directorship that has Avery, according to *Fortune* Magazine in 1936, "pretty firmly established as the most important United States tycoon to make his reputation out of the depression."

Avery's career did not start at the bottom rung of the industrial ladder. His father, Waldo A. Avery, was a wealthy Michigan lumber man (Sewell was born to him and his wife, the former Ellen Lee, in Saginaw on November 4, 1874); and when Sewell was graduated from the University of Michigan in 1894 with a law degree, he went immediately into one of his father's companies, the Western Plaster Works. The young man had studied law, but he had never given much thought to the idea of practicing it. The opening in the gypsum company seemed a more satisfactory alternative.

His first position was as manager, and his first action was to change the name of the concern to the Alabaster Company. *Fortune* reports that he lived in "a couple of rooms near the lake" at Alabaster, Michigan, with his wife, the former Hortense Lenore Wisner, whom he had married October 11, 1899. He had "the first bathtub in town and made a couple of hundred dollars a month. Industrious, persuasive, ambitious, he got along well." Then in 1901 thirty Western gypsum manufacturers combined to form the U.S.G. Company, later reincorporated as the United States Gypsum Company; and Sewell Avery was made a director and Buffalo sales manager. In 1905 he became sales manager for a large Eastern district.

That same year the clash of interests within the new corporation resulted in an explosion that catapulted the thirty-year-old director into the presidency. (He became chairman of the board in 1937.) The first years in this office were trying ones, for Avery was faced with the job of pulling a tottering business through the financial panic of 1907. But he was a shrewd organizer. He hired chemists and engineers to find new uses for gypsum; he took on competent men to assist him. Under

his management the company profited by the post-War building boom, coasted through the price wars of the late '20's, and emerged from the depression, by 1936, a $60,000,000 corporation and the largest plaster company in the United States. (In December 1943 the Government started an anti-trust suit against Avery for joining in a "conspiracy in restraint of trade and commerce in gypsum products.")

By the summer of 1931 Avery had "an excellent reputation with the bankers," according to *Business Week*; and he was approached by J. P. Morgan & Company to become a director of the United States Steel Corporation, a Morgan company. Eight months later he took over the chairmanship (later the presidency) of another Morgan enterprise, Montgomery Ward & Company, as a "business doctor" with a yearly salary of $100,000, plus an option to buy 100,000 shares of stock at $11 a share. (Avery himself has said that he took on the last job, not as a favor to Morgan's, but at the insistence of Ward's directors. He explains that he was not a Wall Street man and did not wish to be identified with the banking interests.) At the end of 1935 Avery had "a list of directorships that read like a cross section of United States industry": Armour & Company, Chicago *Daily News*, Chicago Great Western Railroad, Commonwealth Edison Company, Container Corporation of America, Nash Motors Company, Northern Trust Company, Pullman, Inc., and Peoples Gas, Light & Coke Company.

Montgomery Ward & Company is the industry to which Avery now seems to devote most of his time. The gypsum company has been organized to a point where it can run itself fairly well without him. At the time when he took over Ward's, however, the company was badly in need of assistance. It was faced with overexpansion, a $5,700,000 deficit, and the threat of a merger with Sears, Roebuck and Company, by far the largest mail order house in the United States at the time. Most of Ward's directors were outsiders, and continuous friction resulted. Then, gradually, Avery's genius for organization began to show profits for the company. He hired top merchandising men from other fields and instituted numerous reforms.

Under his direction business improved until, by 1939, Ward's was three-fourths as big as Sears's and had a record gross of $474,900,000. Before long, however, there was dissension within the ranks of management. By 1940 several key men, including the president, had resigned. *Time* Magazine ventured two reasons: (1) Avery's desire to raise the class of Ward's stock from "overalls and manure-proof shoes" to Oriental rugs, guns, etc.; (2) his "preference for running a one-man show, keeping all the controls himself, playing and discarding favorites." When Raymond H. Folger, the president, departed, Sewell Avery became Ward president in his place, also retaining his position as chairman of the board. (In 1943 he relinquished the presidency to Clement D. Ryan.)

Almost with the advent of the New Deal, Avery became one of its foes—although he has said: "I find in every principle of the New Deal an essence to which I subscribe." *Fortune* wrote in 1935 that Ward's was "one of the greatest beneficiaries of Government relief," as it affected the company's farmer customers (Avery cites it as the largest single factor in Ward's improvement); but "because he does not feel that the Administration program is sound for the long pull he remains opposed to it in spite of the dictates of his own immediate interest." His opposition has remained firm. In 1935 Ward's was deprived of the use of the NRA Blue Eagle "for failure to pay its share of the cost of administering the retail NRA code," which Avery had claimed was "illegal" and "unfair." Avery also said that the Government's easy credit schemes would not be an inducement to widespread construction—for building represents a wide cross-section of American industry and will not revive until business as a whole regains confidence. "New Deal wastefulness is blighting the sunrise of a great new era of industrial and commercial prosperity," he stated in 1936. In recent years under Avery's leadership Ward's "has been combatting union expansion with increasing vigor . . . and has been challenging the right of the Government to regulate its relations with labor," wrote Marcus Duffield in the New York *Herald Tribune*. "In five different proceedings before the NLRB the company has been found guilty of unfair labor practices."

The basis of the "Montgomery Ward case" is this challenging of the Government's right to regulate its labor relations, by contesting the authority of the War Labor Board as well as the President's powers under the War Labor Disputes Act (Smith '41-Connally '41 Act). Events had come to the boiling point in November 1942 when the WLB directed Ward's to sign a long contested contract with the CIO's United Mail Order, Warehouse and Retail Employees Union, which in February had won a National Labor Relations Board election in the Chicago plant. One of the clauses which the union was fighting to insert was a maintenance-of-membership provision with a fifteen-day escape clause. The provision was evolved by the WLB as a compromise between the open and the closed shops and has been advocated by it as a measure of union protection since labor's no-strike pledge, which provided for creation of the Board. Such a provision, according to the Board, does not describe a closed shop, under which only workers who are members of the union can be employed, but stipulates instead that at the time the contract is signed all workers who are members of the union have fifteen days in which to resign. If they retain their membership after that period they must remain in good standing with the union for the duration of the contract or lose their jobs. Non-union workers are not compelled to join the union.

Avery, for his part, felt that the maintenance-of-membership clause was a step toward the closed shop—a deprivation of the company's right to manage its business, and a worker's right to join or not join a union at will—and he contended that the Board's directive to the company was illegal. His answer to the WLB directive was, therefore, to state that he would act only at the direction of President Roosevelt '42. As reported in the New York *Times*, after the company had spent some $400,000 advertising its objections in newspapers and after it had received two orders from the President, on December 18 it signed the contract with the disputed provision included.

During the run of the contract (in June 1943) Congress passed the Smith-Connally Act. From this act the WLB has received much of its present statutory powers (albeit "advisory powers," as Avery claims, without force behind them) to act in labor disputes "which may lead to substantial interference with the war effort." The President is given no power to act unless a dispute is referred to him by the Board. Then, as Congress has authorized, he may seize a plant if circumstances so justify—which was to be the eventual outcome of the Ward controversy.

The immediate effect of this latter phase of the Ward affair has been to raise the legal question of the proper interpretation of certain aspects of the Smith-Connally Act, which, in turn, may broaden into a constitutional issue over the scope of the Executive's wartime powers. ("The President, as Commander in Chief of the Army and Navy, [in time of war] has a great constitutional reserve of power, and no business of any kind is immune from that power"—legal opinion of Attorney General Francis Biddle '41 in the Ward case.) The act provides in part that the President's power to take possession of a plant found impeding the war effort through labor disturbances "shall also apply . . . to any plant, mine, or facility equipped for the manufacture, production, or mining of any articles or materials which may be required for the war effort or which may be useful in connection therewith." The stand on which Avery has based his defiance of the seizure of the Chicago plant is that the act "defined and limited" the President's jurisdiction to "war industries," which he claims the plant is not.

The last phase of the dispute leading up to the seizure began with the expiration of the contract in December 1943. Ward's had questioned whether the union still held a majority, since there had been an unusually large employee turnover during the contract period. The WLB decided that the union should petition the NLRB for an election within thirty days and that the company in the interval should extend the contract (the status quo), its action being made conditional upon the union's. (Later, when the Board found that Ward's had canceled contract provisions and broken off relations with the union, it directed that the union need not press for an election.) The union proceeded to act upon the WLB's directive; but Ward's refused to recognize it, and filed an injunction suit. In April the dispute was unanimously referred to the President when the union called a strike.

The President's answer was to set a deadline for both Ward's compliance and a cessation of the strike and to order an immediate NLRB election. (The strikers returned to their jobs the next day.) Avery's reply was that to grant maintenance-of-membership before an election was to violate the "employees' fundamental liberty of free choice" and to permit the union to demand discharge of union members who had resigned since the

SEWELL AVERY

end of the contract. The next move—the deadline having passed—was the expected seizure of the Chicago plant by the President and his turning it over to the Department of Commerce. This action involved a bit of drama. Upon refusing to leave his office and turn over records to the Government, Avery was bodily removed from the building by two military police. (He had refused to leave with several deputy marshals. Later he declared that he had forced his ouster to dramatize "the march of dictatorship" in the United States.)

Repercussions from the seizure were violent and nationwide. Some of the opposition to the action was felt in the Presidential primaries then taking place. Most of the press and Congress rallied to Avery's side. And an overwhelming majority of Montgomery Ward stockholders re-elected him chairman shortly after the seizure. Among those who sided with the Government's action was Marshall Field's [41] Chicago *Sun,* which printed a series of articles entitled "Sewell Avery *vs.* the People." Avery subsequently filed a $1,000,000 libel suit against Field.

A legal battle ensued over the Government's suit for a permanent injunction to enjoin the company from interference with the Government's management of the plant, but the legality of the seizure was not settled. When the Government finally returned the plant to the company—shortly before announcement that the union had won a three to two victory among the employees—the court refused to hand down a decision, ruling that the surrender of the plant ended the injunction suit. The election did not settle issues either, because Ward's declared that the NLRB had gerrymandered the bargaining units to insure a union victory, and, further, it would not sign a contract containing a maintenance-of-membership clause or provisions for check-off of union dues and compulsory arbitration of grievances. Avery declared, too, that through the action of the court "the com-

pany had again been denied the right to a decision in the courts," which he charged the WLB had persistently dodged in claiming that it had no legal authority. He also claimed that the Government had deprived Ward's of recourse to the courts by settling the dispute by force instead of legal action.

The Congressional committees investigating the Montgomery Ward case were faced with hotly contested issues. Foremost was the interpretation of the Smith-Connally Act, which would affect Presidential and WLB powers. (It would also determine whether the President's seizure power was less broad than the WLB's dispute powers under the act.) Montgomery Ward's had declared that its mail order business was a civilian industry and that if the Government could seize it under the act then it could construe the act to warrant seizure of any business in the United States, however small. In his letter to Ward's demanding compliance, President Roosevelt said that the dispute was delaying delivery of goods essential for the economy in wartime; and that it was in danger of spreading to other industries that were essential to both the civilian and the war economies. The Government, in its arguments in court, pointed out that these included the plants in Ward's entire corporation, employing approximately 78,000 workers. One plant—seized in June by the Government because of a contract dispute—manufactures parts for military aircraft, four others are manufacturing farm equipment. Affidavits from Government agencies showed that Ward's had applied for preferences and priorities for materials and that it held Lend-Lease contracts.

The WLB contended that if the Board were held to lack authority in the Montgomery Ward case, employees of that company would be freed from obligations under their no-strike pledge. If they were free to strike, workers in other plants, including war plants, would feel that they should have the same right. "It would not be possible as a practical matter to have one part of industry free to indulge in strikes and lockouts and another part bound to submit their disputes to this Board and to forego strikes and lockouts. We cannot expect to confine strikes to non-war establishments and keep war plants strikeless."

"Ward's experience with the WLB over a period of two years has convinced Ward's that the Board is a means by which special privileges are granted to labor unions," said Avery in his message to the President. His reference was to the John L. Lewis [42]-mine owners dispute in 1943. And there are many other people who argue that the Government has used "one policy—an easy one—for recalcitrant unions and another—a harsh one—for industry." Much of the discussion was about the actual seizure. Senator Harry F. Byrd [42], for example, has blamed the Government for not having "led an invading army into the office of Lewis." "The disturbance," said Max Lerner [42] in *PM,* "was actually at the mines, and it was there that the President sent the troops."

At the end of May a Senate judiciary subcommittee issued a report indicting every agency involved in the Government's seizure of the Chicago plant, beginning with the

Conciliation Service's original certification of the dispute to the WLB. A dissenting opinion declared that the subcommittee had not made "the kind of investigation calculated to get the facts required for a full report," and had called no witnesses. In September the House's investigating committee issued a majority report, written by the Democratic members, declaring that in ordering seizure of the plant the President had only performed his duty. The minority report, written by the Republican members, called the action unconstitutional and a "pattern for complete dictatorship."

At the end of July a unanimous decision of the United States Circuit Court of Appeals of the District of Columbia held that directives of the WLB are not subject to court review. This decision reversed an earlier opinion of a lower court and, in effect, dismissed the several pending suits in which Montgomery Ward's sought injunctions to prevent enforcement of WLB orders affecting its subsidiaries in several cities. Later in August the company dropped one of these suits, and in October the Federal Court of the District of Columbia dismissed six others. Then the United States Supreme Court in effect upheld this decision when it dismissed a new Ward injunction suit against the WLB. None of these decisions, however, ended the Chicago dispute. An eight-to-one vote of the WLB directing the company to extend their contract with the union, pending negotiations, continued to be defied by Ward's.

By December strikes were again threatening in Ward plants. Workers in four Detroit stores did go out on strike (claimed by the union to be the first strike, since labor's "no-strike" pledge, to be authorized by the CIO International), and workers in other cities were threatening walk-outs. The issue was two unobeyed WLB orders on retroactive wage adjustments (later partly complied with) and maintenance-of-membership. Ward's replied that these orders were "illegal and uneconomic" and had been declared by the courts to be "unenforceable and merely advisory." Following a now familiar pattern, the dispute was then referred to the President, and on December 28 he ordered the War Department to seize eleven properties in seven cities where Ward's had not complied with WLB directives. Avery himself was allowed to remain in his office to direct the business of plants not affected by the President's order. The termination of the long battle rested with the courts.

Sewell Avery, despite his years, is still agile. He is "a tall, distinguished, well-preserved gentleman with gray hair, brown eyes, and a great deal of personal charm," writes *Fortune* Magazine. "His eyes are his most distinctive feature, they have a depth and a sparkle that take years from his appearance." He is polished and articulate, has "a tendency to make a point by means of an anecdote," and he goes in a little for "homely philosophy." In addition to his industrial connections, he is trustee of the University of Chicago and the Museum of Science and Industry; and he belongs to numerous clubs. He and Mrs. Avery have had four children, Arla, Nancy, Sewell Lee, and Lenore.

References

Business Week p24-5 Ja 13 '32 por
Fortune 11:69-80 Ja '35 il pors; 13:86-92+ F '36 il pors

PM p9 D 11 '42; p8 Ap 24 '44 por
Time 48:11-13 My 8 '44 il por
Who's Who in America 1944-45
Who's Who in Commerce and Industry [1944]

BACCALONI, SALVATORE (bäk-kä-lō'ni säl-vä-tō'rä) Apr. 14, 1900- Opera singer

Address: b. c/o Metropolitan Opera House, Broadway and 39th St., New York City

Since the 1940-1941 season one of the most applauded singers at the Metropolitan Opera House has been the basso buffo of Falstaffian proportions, Salvatore Baccaloni, whose vocal and histrionic artistry had already captivated lovers of the opera on three continents. Considered by critics as the Metropolitan's best acquisition since Kirsten Flagstad, Baccaloni has added new life to such previously neglected works as Donizetti's *The Elixir of Love* and *Don Pasquale*. His operatic repertoire includes 160 roles.

Salvatore Baccaloni was born in Rome on April 14, 1900, the son of Joaquin and Ferminia (Desideri) Baccaloni. At the age of six his musical training was begun—he was a boy soprano in the school for choristers attached to the Sistine Choir. There, with 250 other boys, he received his basic musical education, as well as training in other subjects. As soon as he could read notes well he was sent as paid soloist to participate in the musical services of the various churches in Rome. He was allowed to keep half his fee and the other half was retained by the church Fathers to pay for his schooling and expenses at the choristers' school.

Shortly after his twelfth birthday, when his voice began to mature, Baccaloni left the Sistine Choir. He then entered the Academy of Fine Arts in Rome to please his father, a building contractor, who had urged the boy to utilize his gift for drawing and designing by becoming an architect. Accordingly, Salvatore persevered at his studies, which were interrupted by a period of military duty during the First World War. In 1920 he was graduated with a degree in architecture. Throughout his student years he had participated in amateur theatricals for diversion. To give his irrepressible musical and histrionic talents an outlet, even after obtaining a position as a draftsman in an architect's office, Baccaloni continued his singing. At an informal musicale in the home of a prominent Roman hostess, the well known baritone Giuseppe Kaschmann, who had been a member of the original company which opened the New York Metropolitan Opera back in 1883, remarked to the young singer: "Why be an architect when you have such a beautiful voice?"

Baccaloni, encouraged by the memory of a musical grandfather, promptly responded to the suggestion by deserting his drawing board and settling down in Kaschmann's studio with a sheaf of operatic scores. Within two years the young singer had mastered such roles as Dulcamara in *The Elixir of Love* and as Bartolo in *The Barber of Seville*, in which he made his debut in the Adriano Theatre in Rome at the age of twenty-two. Soon after he appeared in Bellini's *Norma* at the Augusteo.

(Continued next page)

SALVATORE BACCALONI

About three years later, while Baccaloni was singing the role of the tragic father in Charpentier's *Louise* in Bologna, Toscanini '42, who instantly recognized the power of the basso's voice and the vitality of his dramatic interpretations, became instrumental in bringing him to La Scala in Milan. Baccaloni's wide repertoire had included both serious and comic roles, until Toscanini counseled him to specialize in buffo parts. In pointing out the advantages of making comic roles in opera a lifetime work, the conductor observed that the tradition of singers with fine voices in these parts had for some reason not been maintained, perhaps through attempts of such singers to excel histrionically. "Comic roles," Toscanini added, "are played by old men who have lost their voices. I would like to have a young man in full voice to play them. You have the attitudes and the aptitude for comedy." Baccaloni followed the conductor's advice, and after the death of Azzolini he became La Scala's official basso buffo.

During the years Baccaloni sang regularly at La Scala, before he was engaged by the Metropolitan Opera, he was also captivating audiences in England, on the Continent, and in the Americas. He was invited to Covent Garden and to the Glyndebourne Festival in England, and appeared on the stages of all the important opera houses elsewhere in Europe. In 1930 he sailed to the United States to sing with the Chicago Opera Company, and San Francisco audiences welcomed him in 1938. (He is still on the roster of the San Francisco Opera Association.) A season at the Teatro Colón in Buenos Aires followed in the summer of 1940.

Baccaloni first delighted New York audiences on December 21, 1940 with his antics on the Metropolitan's stage as the lovesick, foolish old bachelor Don Pasquale. The considerable success of the return of *Don Pasquale* to the active repertory of the company, as well as of *The Daughter of the Regiment*, in which

Baccaloni disported himself as walrus-mustached Sergeant Sulpice, was largely attributed to the presence of the new star. "Not in memory has the company possessed a basso buffo of the gifts and personality of Salvatore Baccaloni," wrote Oscar Thompson in *Musical America*. "Mr. Baccaloni loomed above all the others as an operatic personality. . . . Not only was he droll without being downright farcical, but there were times when he fairly outsang his associates."

Baccaloni continued to hold the spotlight on the Metropolitan stage in such other roles as the crotchety Bartolo of *The Barber of Seville,* the farcical Leporello in *Don Giovanni,* the quack doctor Dulcamara in *The Elixir of Love,* Varlaam in *Boris Godunoff.* "A un Dottore," an aria from the second act of the *Barber,* has been returned to the score after a long omission because of the lack of suitable bass voices in the Metropolitan. "Nowhere is he better cast than as Doctor Bartolo," commented the New York *Times* after Baccaloni's appearance in this opera in 1943. "The humor with which he clothes the role is not only real humor, the sort of thing Cervantes depicted in *Don Quixote,* but it is fine art. It is not only convincing, it is exquisite and at the same time full-blooded." The basso buffo's "grotesque comedy and booming voice" as the deceitful self-appointed heir of Buoso Donati in the title role of Puccini's *Gianni Schicchi,* a one-act farce which was presented in January 1944 after a lapse of five years, was generally acknowledged as superb. Virgil Thomson '40 declared in the New York *Herald Tribune* that Baccaloni's portrayal was "one of the most tensely controlled and original bits of low comedy character acting in current repertory. Mr. Baccaloni, being an actor of irreducible power, quite regularly overplays his small parts. But give him a role in the center of things and he puts on a show that is without its equal, in kind, on the contemporary operatic stage." Two other roles of Baccaloni's, as Benoit and Alcindoro in *La Bohème,* presented at the Metropolitan in December 1944, were considered among the "choicest comedy bits."

Although criticized for descending to broad humor and overacting on occasion, Baccaloni usually holds his work within bounds. In analyzing the problems of his art, he wrote for *Etude*: "Comedy parts are, on the whole, more difficult to envisage because the very nature of comedy characterization implies the exaggeration of typical and outstanding qualities. Where an element of exaggeration exists, there is a great temptation, in inexperienced hands, to emphasize it into grotesquerie." However, he continued, the performer "must always subordinate himself to serving and emphasizing the inherent humor as the composer expressed it."

Good-humored and rotund Salvatore Baccaloni carries his 320 pounds erectly. He attributes this avoirdupois to resigning himself to comedy roles (and therefore not being obliged to preserve a hero's physique) and to enjoying the excellent cooking of his Bulgarian wife, Elena (Svilarova) Baccaloni. The singer's instantaneous success in New York won him a motion-picture contract in 1941, and in between his engagements at the Metropolitan he has devoted his talents to operatic concert tours throughout the United States. About 1942 Baccaloni formed his own opera company and toured with it in productions of *The Barber of Seville* and *Don Pasquale.* When Baccaloni is not singing, he busies himself with painting, designing costumes, and devising scenic effects. One day, he believes, he will combine his knowledge of the theatre, the opera, and his first profession, architecture, for the glorification of stage designing.

References

Etude 60:297+ My '42 por
N Y Times IX p6 N 24 '40
Opera News 5:45 D 2 '40 pors; 6:5 D 29 '41 por
Time 37:34 Ja 6 '41 por

BACHE, JULES S(EMON) (bāch) Nov. 9, 1861—Mar. 24, 1944 Banker; patron of art and owner of one of the world's finest private art collections; valued at millions, it was given to the State of New York in 1937; the collection is to become the property of the Metropolitan Museum of Art.

Obituary

N Y Times p15 Mr 25 '44 por

BAEKELAND, LEO H(ENDRIK) (bāk' land) Nov. 14, 1863—Feb. 23, 1944 Chemist noted for creation of bakelite, which gave impetus to the modern plastic industry, and of Velox, a photographic paper; president of the Bakelite Corporation; recipient of many awards from the American Chemical Society, Columbia University, Chemical Foundation, etc.

Obituary

N Y Times p15 F 24 '44 por

BAGRAMIAN, IVAN C(HRISTOFOR-OVICH) (bă-gram'yan khris-tō-fôr'ō-vich) 1895- Soviet Army officer

With the advance in October 1944 of the Russian commanding generals, Ivan Chernyakhovsky[44] of the 3rd White Russian Army and Ivan C. Bagramian of the 1st Baltic Army, into East Prussia, the battle for that territory developed into one of the bloodiest in history. Although only about 2,500,000 of Germany's 90,000,000 people live there, the province, the first to be invaded, is "the source of the whole German imperial tradition, the cornerstone of Junkerism, stamping ground of the Teutonic Knights."

Little was known about General Ivan Christoforovich Bagramian until 1942, when he whipped a German force at Kolesk-Sukhinichi and his military reputation spread over the entire Soviet Union. The only non-Slav to command a Red Army front, he was born in 1895 in Gyandzha (now Kirovobad) in that section of Armenia which is now part of the U.S.S.R. At an early age he became an officer in the Russian Army, and when the Soviet power was established he unreservedly went over to the Red Army, joining the cavalry regiment of an Armenian division. In 1922 the regiment in which he was squadron commander was stationed in the Ararat Valley, and two years later he was appointed regimental commander

for his distinguished service. Several years after that the regiment was transferred to Vagarshapat. Here, under Bagramian's guidance, the Armenian horsemen studied and trained near the ancient walls of Ejmiadzin, successfully mastering military science and displaying such excellent horsemanship that at maneuvers in the Transcaucasian Military Area the Armenian cavalry regiment won first place and a superior rating by the High Command. The same regiment was to produce a number of prominent commanders who developed under Bagramian's guidance, giving the Red Army four generals and a number of colonels and majors who today fight in defense of the U.S.S.R.

In 1930 Bagramian entered the Frunze Military Academy at Moscow. After graduation he continued his military education in the General Staff Academy, was graduated with honors, and for three years served as an instructor at the Academy. When Hitler[42] invaded the Soviet Union in June 1941 Bagramian was a colonel, serving in the Ukraine. His troops were among the first to defend the western frontiers of the Soviet Union, and before the end of 1941 he was a lieutenant general. Then in 1943 he helped to crack the Bryansk Front. In *Time*'s words, "He became tough Marshal Semyon Timoshenko's[41] Assistant Chief of Staff, tasted the bitterness of defeat, learned precious lessons. What he had learned, Bagramian put to good use in the 1942-1943 winter offensive, born in Stalingrad's ruins. At the head of 'X Army' he fought last spring [1943] on the approaches to Kharkov, won the Order of Kutuzov, First Class [that April 9]. Still later, in the fields of yellowing grain near Kursk, he took part in the great and decisive summer battle, was promoted to colonel general, became one of the chosen few to wear the treasured Order of Suvorov, First Class. Six weeks ago [November 1943]—probably after he took over the 1st Baltic Army—he became a full general."

The immediate task before Bagramian at this time was to take the tremendously powerful fortress of Vitebsk in White Russia. The winter-trained Siberian regiments of the new 1st Baltic Army had fought at Moscow, Stalingrad, and the Don, and the Germans themselves put its strength at fourteen infantry, one artillery, and two cavalry divisions, with two complete tank corps. After a powerful initial break-through in the "iron wall" before Nevel, Bagramian's white-clad ski troops held their momentum, and before the end of December 1943, fighting in the swampy, lake-dotted terrain known as Vitebsk Ridge, they had gathered up countless villages and were reported within eight miles of the Vitebsk fortress. At that time they had all but choked off supply routes into the city by taking a series of strong points fifteen miles northwest of Vitebsk on the road to Polotsk.

But the task was far from easy. The German command had poured tanks, aircraft, armored trains into Vitebsk—and until the spring of 1944 little was reported from this sector. It was not until June 23 that the Russians resumed the strong drive against Vitebsk. "Driving through a thick belt of forests, waterways, ravines, and marshes from the Vitebsk-Nevel Railroad, General Bagramian's 1st Baltic Army charged through a fifty-mile-wide hole in the

BAGRAMIAN, IVAN C.—*Continued*

deeply echeloned German defenses and reached the Dvina River, establishing a twenty-two-mile front along its northern bank. (The Dvina formed the main German defense line from Vitebsk through Polotsk to Riga, capital of Latvia.) Striking from southeast of Vitebsk, Colonel General Chernyakhovsky's new 3rd White Russian Army hurled through a maze of nine rows of entrenchments and antitank traps and tore another fifty-mile breach in the German lines. The two armies encircled Vitebsk, battered five defending Nazi divisions, and then stormed and captured the city." The city fell to the Russians on June 27, 1944. German General Fritz Gollwitzer later admitted that he had been left out on a limb at Vitebsk. also admitting that he himself had miscalculated the amount of ammunition his columns would need to punch an exit from the trap in which Bagramian and Chernyakhovsky had neatly placed him.

The next month Bagramian thrust a long salient into Lithuania. At the tip of it he occupied Shavli, cut the railroad from Riga to Tilsit in East Prussia, and left only a one-track line through Memel as an escape route for some thirty German divisions on the Baltic fronts. He then blocked even this loophole by broadening his salient northward to the junction at Jelgava. By August the battle of East Prussia was rushing toward a climax. Chernyakhovsky and Bagramian, on Chernyakhovsky's right flank, steadily pushed closer to the ancient stronghold of the Junkers. On the Gulf of Riga, Bagramian had established himself firmly on the coast, and four Russian armies had begun the task of liquidating twenty German divisions in Estonia and Latvia, cut off by his drive to the Baltic Sea coast. In October came the break-through. In eight days Bagramian's 1st Baltic Army drove down from the north, cleared the Memel territory, and laid siege to Memel and Tilsit, while Chernyakhovsky directed the main assault from the east, bursting through the most powerful and skillfully constructed defenses the Germans had been able to erect in those many months. This was the first invasion of German territory by the Russians in thirty years—and within a week the armies of Bagramian and Chernyakhovsky had scooped up 900 communities, 400 of them within the border of East Prussia. Not the least of the captured territories was that on which is Hermann Göring's [41] estate in the Rominten Forest. "Cooked food and French champagne were found in the dining room and kitchen," reports said, "and some of Göring's belongings, packed for evacuation, had not been moved." Meanwhile, on the southern border, Zakharov's 2nd White Russian Army was bringing up tank formations for a thrust toward Allenstein and eventually Danzig. In many German minds the Russian threat seemed more direful than the Anglo-American drive in the west.

General Bagramian is described as having a head "shaved as smooth as a billiard ball" and a natty, black mustache.

References

N Y Sun p18 Jl 12 '44
Time 43:25 Ja 3 '44

BAKER, GEORGE May 22, 1915- Cartoonist

Address: b. c/o Yank Magazine, 205 E. 42nd St., New York City

One of the outstanding figures of the Second World War has not yet attained the dizzy rank of private first class, and never will. He has been mentioned by General George Marshall [40] as a morale-booster in an official document, he has had his name painted on Liberator bombers, he has had clubs named after him, he has had songs composed about him. All profiteth him naught. He is Sad Sack, the cartoon character who appears in the Army magazine *Yank* every week, and "Sad Sacks just don't get promoted." The man responsible for this monstrous piece of injustice is Staff Sergeant George Baker, who since June 1942 has been seeing to it that no beam of light enters the darkened life of his creation—"a life of one great round of K.P., guard duty, duty, duty details, guardhouse." *Yank* readers have long been indignant about this; in 1944, with the appearance of *The Sad Sack,* a collection of 110 of the downtrodden private's misadventures, civilians were given an opportunity to become wrought up, too. Sad Sack himself has never uttered a syllable since the beginning of his unhappy Army career.

George Baker was born in Lowell, Massachusetts, on May 22, 1915, the son of Harry and Mary (Portman) Baker. Two years later his parents moved to Rock Island, Illinois, and there he lived until 1923, when the family went to Chicago. After finishing grammar school there he attended Lane Technical High School and Roosevelt High School, where his extracurricular activities included cartooning for the high school annual and a good deal of baseball. He was graduated in the middle of the depression, and for a while did various jobs such as fitting the paper bags on newly pressed clothes in a cleaning and dyeing establishment and loading and driving trucks. Fortified with a month and a half of art training in night school, he then found a job in a commercial art house, but soon grew tired of drawing pots and pans for newspaper advertisements. By 1937 he was ready to go West to play baseball with the minor leagues, and he would have ended up with the Los Angeles Angels if Walter Disney [40] hadn't offered him a job in his Hollywood studios.

With Disney until 1941, Baker worked on practically all of Disney's well known epics, including *Pinocchio, Fantasia, Dumbo,* and *Bambi.* What he specialized in was "effects"— the animation of objects other than human— clouds, thunderstorms, dancing trees, tumbling waterfalls. When in June 1941 Baker was drafted into the Army he had been out on strike for about a month, along with most of Disney's other employees.

"Everybody kicks about the Army Classification System," Baker says. "They say it makes cooks out of mechanics and vice versa. But I must say it worked perfectly in my case. I left Disney's animation department to join the Army. Three weeks later I was at Fort Monmouth, New Jersey, doing animation work on Signal Corps training movies."

It was while going through his basic training at Fort Monmouth that Baker got the "idea of doing a comic strip which would reveal, through the misadventures of a 'deadpan' recruit, the then mysterious intricacies of Army life." He drew a few strips dealing with such matters as K.P. and Inspection (similar to those which now appear in *Yank*, but untitled), submitted them in a contest conducted by the Defense Recreation Committee, and won the first prize, a portable typewriter. *Life* Magazine printed some of the cartoons—and after *Yank* began to collect a staff, in May 1942, Baker's strip was selected as the weekly's first permanent feature. The following month *Yank* started publication, and Baker was transferred to the staff. From the beginning "The Sad Sack" ("a whittled-down version of an old and unprintable epithet for an inept rookie") has drawn more fan mail from men in the Army than any other *Yank* feature. This means something: the eleven weekly printings of *Yank* at various global points run to approximately 2,000,000 copies, and it is estimated that each copy has five readers.

The ways in which this droopy little private boosts morale are obvious; the reasons for his own droopiness are even more obvious. Other enlisted men have suffered from Army red tape and ill-fitting uniforms, have had rank "pulled" on them numerous times, have seen their heroic labors go unnoticed and their unintentional mistakes called to everyone's attention; others have spent too much of their Army life hauling garbage, peeling potatoes, digging ditches, and being raked over the coals by their superiors through no fault of their own. But when they compare their lot with that of the mutely philosophic Sack they can all congratulate themselves. The Sack is doomed from the beginning. When he spends all day building himself a shower it is inevitable that he will find the sign "For Officers Only" on it by the time he is ready to use it. When he tries on a German uniform which he has picked up as a battle souvenir he should know that he will be made a prisoner of war by the Yanks. Even at the rare times when everything seems to be going smoothly for him there is sure to be trouble just around the corner. ("Of course he has the power to think," Baker says indignantly. "Circumstances just work against him.") Sergeants and girls find him equally unattractive; his relatives neglect him shamefully; he has no friends in the orderly room; and his barracksmates eat his food, muss up his bed, steal his clothes, and give him bad advice. Even the fact that he is honest, hard-working, and almost tremulously well-meaning seems to work against him.

In search of authentic methods of persecuting Sad Sack, Baker has toured about twenty-five Army camps in the United States, "hopped into foxholes on many fronts, and been under fire often enough to get four ribbons and a combat star." The artist "caricatures himself now and then in the strip as the apple-polisher who snags a three-day pass while Sad Sack

Yank

GEORGE BAKER

wistfully looks on, or as the 2nd lieutenant who steals Sad Sack's girl." He often makes deliberate mistakes in the strip, too, to test his reader response and to see how carefully his strip is read. Once the *Yank* editors were flooded with mail from all over the world protesting that Baker had given Sad Sack two left feet. All complainers received a printed reply: "Since when do two left feet keep a man out of the Army?"

Baker, a bachelor, lives about a block and a half from his job on East 42nd Street when he is in New York. Unlike his character, he is a tall, slim, very un-droopy staff sergeant whose chief hobbies are tennis and baseball. He holds the copyright on the name and character of Sad Sack, but will turn down all commercial exploitation offers until he is out of the Army. (Promoters have sought to put the Sack into a motion picture, a radio serial, and a syndicated comic; and to use him as an appliquéd design for clothing, a souvenir statuette, and a doll.) This has not confined the Sack to the columns of *Yank,* however. Many of the cartoons have been reprinted in current magazines and Sunday newspaper supplements; the Sack has been portrayed over CBS's *Report to the Nation;* he is the chief character in the Army revue *Hi Yank,* which is to be given at Army posts in the United States and overseas; Simon and Schuster has presented him to the public in book form (by October 1944, 55,000 copies had been sold); and his outline has even been cut into one of the ancient temple pillars in Panama. After the War Baker plans to muster the Sad Sack out of the Army and into a syndicated comic strip—probably in "a checkered suit, a striped tie, and brown and white shoes." But civilian life will not prove any happier for Mr. Sack than Army life has been: "He will be engaged by a number of businesses and invariably will be fired through no fault of his

BAKER, GEORGE—*Continued*

own." Any plan for full post-War employment must reckon with him.

References

N Y Herald Tribune VII p12 O 1 '44 por
N Y Times Mag p10-11+ N 21 '43 il por; p 16-17+ Jl 9 '44 il
New Yorker 20:20 My 27 '44
Newsweek 22:81 N 8 '43 il por

BALLANTINE, STUART (bal'an-tīn) Sept. 22, 1897—May 7, 1944 Radio engineer; devised the "throat microphone" for aviators; held patents on many other inventions; published numerous scientific articles.

Obituary

N Y Times p19 My 8 '44

BARBER, SAMUEL Mar. 9, 1910- Composer

Address: b. c/o G. Schirmer, Inc., 3 E. 43rd St., New York City; h. Mt. Kisco, N.Y.

The list of music composed in tribute to the armed forces has been lengthened by the "Symphony Dedicated to the Army Air Forces," the Second Symphony of young Corporal Samuel Barber, whose symphonies and shorter compositions have been performed by every major orchestra in the United States as well as abroad. The young composer has the further distinction of "chalking off" five Carnegie Hall performances of his two symphonies in a single week when they were played in New York in the spring of 1944. When he was commissioned to write the full-length symphony for the A.A.F., Barber said: "I am very happy that America is beginning to use composers in the same way Russia is using Shostakovich [44]."

Samuel Barber was born March 9, 1910, the son of a West Chester (Pennsylvania) physician, Dr. Samuel LeRoy Barber, and Marguerite McLeod (Beatty) Barber. He showed signs of unusual musical talent at the age of seven when he wrote his first composition. At thirteen he was considered a prodigy and accepted as a student of the piano by Isabelle Vengerova at the Curtis Institute, in Philadelphia. There he studied conducting with Fritz Reiner [41], composition with Rosario Scalero, and singing with Emilio de Gogorza. Before his graduation in 1932 he had composed "Serenade for String Quartet" (1929), "Dover Beach" (1931), for baritone voice and string quartet, and a sonata for cello and piano (1932). In 1933 Barber won the Bearns prize from Columbia University for his "Overture to 'The School for Scandal'" (1932). In 1935 *Musical America* wrote of that composition: "The young man has written an appealing work . . . investing a broad melody with shimmering color and tender mood." Other honors that came to him were the Prix de Rome of the American Academy in Rome in 1935 and the Pulitzer Prize for Music in 1935 and 1936. Barber was the first composer to win this award twice.

By 1937 the twenty-seven-year-old Samuel Barber had achieved an international reputation. While studying in Rome on the Academy fellowship, he composed his "Symphony in One Movement," which was first performed in that city in 1936. It was well received at its American première early in 1937, when the Cleveland Symphony Orchestra presented it under the direction of Artur Rodzinski [40]. Following four more performances of the symphony before appreciative New York audiences, in the summer of 1937 Rodzinski again conducted the symphony at the Salzburg Festival. Later that summer Rodzinski introduced Barber's work in England.

Barber's "Adagio for Strings" (1936) and "Essay for Orchestra" (1937) were given their world première by the NBC Symphony Orchestra in November 1938, Arturo Toscanini [42] conducting. The young composer received special recognition when the "Adagio" became the only American work recorded by Toscanini as well as the only American composition to be presented by that conductor and his orchestra on their South American tour. There was some criticism of the conductor's choice, the critics considering Barber's work not representative of modern music but as belonging to the tradition of romanticism. Robert Horan's opinion of Barber's non-symphonic works appeared in *Modern Music*: "Its design and its articulateness reveal a profound elegance of style and a personal anti-mechanical melancholy." His orchestration was "simple and aristocratic." In an age of emphasis on brass instruments, he wrote largely for strings. Commenting on the "Adagio for Strings," Horan praised its "disarming simplicity, its sonority, and its climax on a consonant chord."

According to a count made by Horan and reported in *Modern Music* in March 1943, Barber's compositions to that date totaled twenty-nine: seven orchestral and four chamber music compositions, six choral works, eleven songs with piano accompaniment, and one composition for the piano. Among the works Barber has written since then are a revised version of his First Symphony ("Symphony in One Movement"), his Second Symphony ("Symphony Dedicated to the Army Air Forces"), the "Commando March for Band," (first performed by the Air Forces Band at Atlantic City), "Second Essay" (first performed by Bruno Walter [42] and the New York Philharmonic Orchestra in April 1942), "A Stopwatch and an Ordnance Map" (for men's voices and kettle drums), and "The Virgin Martyrs" (for women's voices). He has also written seventeen new songs. Commenting on the earlier group of songs, Horan said that he considers it "unfortunate that Barber's songs are not better known to serious musicians, for they reveal an intimate, sensuous quality not always found in the larger works." Barber's songs were, however, not without hearings in 1944. In the spring the American Music Festival brought the seventeen later songs to Washington, and during the summer Jennie Tourel, mezzo-soprano of the Metropolitan Opera Company, included them in her concerts in Brazil.

The New York première of Barber's revised version of his "Symphony in One Movement" by the Philharmonic Symphony Orchestra on March 8, 1944, under the baton of Bruno Walter, received much notice in the newspapers. Commenting on its performance immediately after Schumann's Fourth Symphony in D Minor, the New York *Times* critic said: "That Mr. Barber's revised symphony was able to hold its ground and not appear anticlimatic after the Schumann masterpiece spoke worlds in its favor. If it lacked the melodic invention, simplicity, and freshness of that opus, it nevertheless was so skilled in its craftsmanship, so knowingly orchestrated and filled with character that it scored heavily with its hearers." Louis Biancolli, writing in the New York *World-Telegram*, considered the revised version a distinct improvement over the earlier— "compacter style and maturer grasp of idiom reveal it as possibly Corporal Barber's sturdiest symphonic work to date. The one-movement plan seems more logical now, also more expressive." To Virgil Thomson [40] of the New York *Herald Tribune* the symphony was "a lonely piece, a Hamlet-like meditation about Mr. Barber's private problems, the chief of which seems to be laying the ghost of romanticism without resorting to violence."

Twenty-four hours after the performance of the First Symphony, the "Symphony Dedicated to the Army Air Forces" was heard for the first time in New York when Serge Koussevitsky [40] conducted the Boston Symphony Orchestra in the performance. (The world première had been made a week earlier in Boston.) Barber had begun this symphony after his induction into the Army in 1943, while he was stationed at the Fort Worth Army Airfield, in Texas. Following its performance, recordings of the work were broadcast by the Office of War Information throughout the world, and scores were sent to England and Russia.

Critics were inclined to agree that while the Second Symphony is more in the modern idiom, it is of less musical merit than Barber's earlier works. Virgil Thomson confessed to "some uncertainty as to what it was all about," felt a "lack of striking melody and contrapuntal life," and could find little to be said for the handling of the instrumentation. Olin Downes [43] of the New York *Times* pointed out the inconsistency between the composer's assertion that the work was not "program music" and the use of a special electric "tone-generator" constructed by the Bell Telephone Laboratory to simulate the sound of a radio beam. In *PM* Henry Simon wrote: "Mr. Barber's fine sense of proportion is still evident in the construction of each of the three movements, but his new-found muscular extroversion does not yet sound very convincing. Maybe it presages a wider development in one of our finest composers." This critic compared the new symphony with the composer's "Essay for Orchestra" and "Dover Beach," which, he said, "move their hearers by emotional understatement."

The performance of Barber's violin concerto in Albert Hall, London, in the 1944 season, by the Australian violinist Eda Kersey and the orchestra under the direction of Sir Henry Wood, was considered by one critic as "the most genial and completely satisfying" of the "novelties" heard thus far in that season. "The composer seemed concerned with the true and clear presentation of his thought but not obsessed by the necessity of seeking originality of form or manner, and modern without mak-

Alexander

CPL. SAMUEL BARBER

ing a parody of modernity. . . . It is the work of an American composer who has something to say and says it honestly and without egotism, and therefore produces some genuine and interesting music."

Barber's new concerto, entitled "Capricorn," was presented in October 1944 by the Saidenberg Little Symphony at Town Hall, New York. It consists of three movements for flute, oboe, trumpet, and strings, and to Oscar Thompson of the New York *Sun* "they [the movements] are modern in spirit, and sonorities tingle. . . . They are always moving, though they don't seem to get anywhere in particular." Another new Barber work, three compositions for piano, entitled *Excursions*, was performed for the first time in late 1944 by Vladimir Horowitz [43]. The violin concerto, played in October 1944 by Roman Totenberg, concertmaster of the New York City Symphony, in a concert under the direction of Leopold Stokowski, has gained in popularity since its initial performance two years before. Olin Downes of the New York *Times* was of the opinion that Barber "had not produced a work for violin solo with orchestral accompaniment. . . . The fabric of the music and the orchestral treatment are symphonic." Downes continued: "The composition is markedly 'romantic' in character, especially in the first two movements. The finale is a more nervous and dissonant affair, and more satirical in effect."

Among the admirers of Samuel Barber are Josef Hofmann and Jean Sibelius; the Finnish composer wrote enthusiastically to the young American after hearing his works. Barber's compositions are also popular in Russia, where his scores are in constant demand. On May 21, 1944 the Soviet State Symphony Orchestra played the "Overture to 'The School for Scandal'" in a concert of all-American music. Barber's first violin concerto was chosen for performance in February 1941 by Albert Spalding [44] and the Philadelphia Orchestra. An analysis made by ASCAP revealed that Barber's works were played more often than any

BARBER, SAMUEL—*Continued*

other compositions on symphonic programs during the season of 1941-1942.

The tall, handsome bachelor composer is stationed at a flying field near New York, from which he was able to come to that city to take his bows in the uniform of the Army Air Forces at the New York premières of his symphonies. Incidentally, he is turning over his royalties from all performances of the Second Symphony to the Army Air Forces Aid Society.

References

> Thompson, O. ed. International Cyclopedia of Music and Musicians 1939
> Who's Who in America 1944-45

BARBOUR, RALPH HENRY Nov. 13, 1870—Feb. 19, 1944 Author, known as "the dean of sport writers for boys"; his books have been favorites for three generations; *The Half-Back* (1899) was reprinted every year for more than thirty years; sometimes used the pseudonym of Richard Stillman Powell.

Obituary

> N Y Times p36 F 20 '44 por

BARBOUR, W. WARREN (bär′bēr) July 31, 1888—Nov. 22, 1943 United States Senator from New Jersey; successful in business life, he was appointed to the Senate in 1931 and was elected Senator on the Republican ticket in 1932; he was defeated in the 1936 election but re-elected to the Senate in 1940.

Obituary

> N Y Times p1+ N 23 '43 por (p25)

BARNES, CLIFFORD W(EBSTER) Oct. 8, 1864—Sept. 18, 1944 Clergyman and philanthropist; founder of the Chicago Sunday Evening Club; vice-president of the World Alliance for International Friendship from 1927 to 1935; director of the Red Cross in Greece during the First World War; honorary secretary and chairman of the International Committee on Moral Training since 1907.

Obituary

> N Y Times p21 S 19 '44 por

BARRERE, GEORGES (ba″rär′ zhôrzh) Oct. 31, 1876—June 14, 1944 French-American flutist, composer, and conductor; perfected the technique of flute-playing; was largely responsible for the instrument's use in solo work rather than for decorative purposes; in 1914 founded the Barrère Little Symphony; from 1905 to 1928 was first flutist in New York Symphony Orchestra; appointed to faculty of Juilliard Graduate School in 1930.

Obituary

> N Y Times p19 Je 15 '44 por

BARTON, WILLIAM H(ENRY), JR. July 7, 1893—July 7, 1944 Chairman and curator of Hayden Planetarium of the American Museum of Natural History since 1941; wrote several books on astronomy and lectured on

CBS's *Men Behind the Stars*; since the beginning of the War he devoted the Planetarium's educational facilities to the teaching of navigation.

Obituary

> N Y Times p11 Jl 8 '44 por

BATES, H(ERBERT) E(RNEST) May 16, 1905- Author

Address: h. The Granary, Little Chart, Kent, England

One of the select corps of British authors who went into the uniform to serve and to write is H. E. Bates, before the War "the most talented and articulate of the young short story writers in England." His *Fair Stood the Wind for France*, a war story of the bravery of an English bomber crew and of the courage of a French girl in occupied France, was one of the two June 1944 choices of the Book-of-the-Month Club. It was also the first book selected for adaptation in the NBC *Words at War* program.

The son of Albert Ernest and Lucy Elizabeth (Lucas) Bates, Herbert Ernest Bates was born May 16, 1905, in Rushden, Northampton, one of England's Midland counties. To him, as to many of the youngsters of his heritage, the red-letter days of his childhood and the friendly rolling English countryside are two inseparable impressions—there were buggy rides and hunts for birds' eggs, violets, and butterfly orchids.

The boy was sent to the Grammar School in Kettering, and at seventeen began his apprenticeship for Fleet Street as a junior reporter on a country newspaper. Before long, however, he left provincial journalism to take a position as a clerk in a leather warehouse. This job in itself held little interest or promise for him, but it did give him a certain amount of freedom to write. It was at this time that he is said to have entered into a series of theological controversies with local church dignitaries, an activity which evidently gave him a little prestige and a kind of self-confidence. His mother's father, a "salty old farmer," full of reminiscences and folklore, was about the only person whose sympathies young Bates won during this interlude.

Before Bates was twenty both Edward Garnett, the critic, and his son David Garnett, the author, had measurably encouraged him. Of Bates's earlier writings the younger Garnett had said that they showed sensibility rather than originality, but also that "there is no living English writer of whose future work I feel more confident." Edward Garnett wrote the preface to Bates's first book, *The Two Sisters* (1926), which was published when Bates was twenty-one years old.

In the course of the decade that followed Bates reviewed books for the *Spectator* and the *Morning Post,* and wrote articles on a variety of subjects for almost every newspaper in London. Also, by 1938 Bates had produced seven novels and about a dozen books, largely collections of short stories, which won for him a sizable reputation. He has become, in time, thoroughly anthologized, not only in England but in the United States, appearing more often than any other author in Edward J. O'Brien's annual *Best British Short Stories.* A few plays also came from his pen as well as a good number of essays on country life. His development as an author was summed up a few years ago: "After working out from under the influence of Joseph Conrad, whose indirect method of narrative he imitated without much success, he has grown constantly in clarity and vigor. Conrad's influence was followed by that of Stephen Crane, and English critics frequently comment on the 'American' tone of Bates's work. Without being in any sense 'proletarian' in approach, his stories are nearly all concerned with the working class, and particularly with agricultural laborers or with those in small towns whose real background is of the country."

The heroism of R.A.F. fliers became the substance of Bates's writings after he put on his flight lieutenant's uniform in 1941. Under the pseudonym of Flying Officer X, the stories in his *There's Something in the Air* (1943) impressed Meyer Berger [43] as "sheer beauty in writing. . . . The short pieces will give the reader a clearer conception of the combat flier's thinking, fighting, living, than anything that has come before." But Bates wrote these stories, another critic held, with "so much understatement, and his young fliers exchange such brief and almost shamefaced talk about their feats, that only the streamlined modern Anglo-Saxon mind could appreciate the tribute which he pays them."

With *Fair Stood the Wind for France,* the young squadron leader discarded his wartime pseudonym at the same time that the censor released this first story of the fate of the men who man the bombers and who are brought down behind the German lines. That Bates's novel required approval by the censor may not be surprising in view of Henry Seidel Canby's opinion that "the new 'values' as well as the new casualties, of living, loving, and fighting in these war years cannot be always, perhaps not often, represented by factual accounts by correspondents and others. Fiction, good fiction, has a job here. Here, then, is one of the best stories of escape that have come out of the War." Yet the novel "would disappoint a reader who wants a good spy story," Harry Hansen [42] wrote in the New York *World-Telegram.* "Bates has never been as successful a novelist as a writer of short stories, primarily because he enjoys exploring a mood, for which the short story form is suited. But he also writes with the sensitivity of a poet." Orville Prescott criticized Bates's new novel as lacking in direction and purpose—"It seems to drift along aimlessly." The New York *Herald Tribune* reviewer Lewis Gannett [41] found that the author "reveals here again that intense instinct for catching the emotion of a countryside, that sensitivity for the moment in a man's life, which has given his short stories distinction."

Sometime in 1944 Bates visited the countryside of his childhood and saw his grandfather's farm in a twenty-five-year perspective; but military expediency had made the greatest change in the landscape in only the last five of those years. Three huge runways had been torn across the cornland, and "bits of woodland, other hedgerows, other fields," have been shorn "to make room for more men and more

H. E. BATES

aircraft." Those men are Americans, and Bates believes their influence will be far-reaching and long-lasting, even if it be limited to the impressions of English children who are constantly teasing the soldiers with "Got any gum, chum?" American boys, Bates tells, "grow to be part of English homes, marry English girls, and, when they are wounded or die, are mourned by English families." If there are "finer, securer, deeper ties than this between two peoples," the author says, "I don't know where you will find them."

In 1931 H. E. Bates was married to Marjorie Helen Cox. They have two sons and two daughters, and they make their home in Little Chart, Kent. Fair-haired and smooth-shaven, the writer is described as having something of Puck in his expression. Taut and tired from the tension of four years of war—"an officer first and a novelist second"—his best refresher during leaves, he says, is to have supper with his children after a half-day of work in his flower garden. It would seem that he has brought together these favorite relaxations in a small book he wrote in 1941— *The Seasons and the Gardener,* a book for children.

References

Book-of-the-Month Club N p5-6 My '44 por

Kunitz, S. J. and Haycraft, H. eds. Twentieth Century Authors 1942

Who's Who 1944

BAUSCH, EDWARD (boush) 1854-July 30, 1944 Chairman of the Board of the Bausch & Lomb Optical Company; played a leading part in the development of the American manufacture of precision optical instruments, particularly the microscope.

Obituary

N Y Times p13 Jl 31 '44 por

BAUSCH, WILLIAM (boush) 1861—Oct. 19, 1944 Chairman of the board of the Bausch and Lomb Optical Company; was responsible for the founding of the American optical plant in 1915 when optical glass was no longer available from European sources because of the First World War.

Obituary

N Y Times p19 O 20 '44 por

BEATON, CECIL (WALTER HARDY) (bē't'n ses'l) Jan. 14, 1904- Photographer; artist; author

Address: h. 8 Pelham Pl., London; Ashcombe House, Tollard Royal, Salisbury, England

"England's No. 1 photographer of beautiful women," Cecil Beaton, who started his career by making portraits of his sisters, reached its zenith when he became official photographer to the British Royal Family. His special ability for enhancing the charms of his sitters by placing them in an elaborate *décor* produced a series of glamorous photographs of Queen Elizabeth in Buckingham Palace in 1939. This commission was climaxed by the portraits he took of the young Princess Elizabeth[1], Heiress Presumptive to Britain's throne, prior to her coming of age in the spring of 1944.

Cecil Walter Hardy Beaton was born in London, January 14, 1904, the son of Ernest Walter Hardy Beaton, a London timber importer, and Etty (Sisson) Beaton. Educated at Harrow and Cambridge, he came away from the latter institution at the age of nineteen with two hobbies—painting and photography—that developed into professions. A third talent emerged as a corollary to his pictorial gifts. An inveterate diarist, he began to supplement the captions of his photographs with explanatory text, and then to write articles and books, and, finally, official war records for the British Government.

While at Harrow, Beaton had learned to paint in a sketching class, and from this elementary instruction evolved his own technique. "Brilliant histrionic talents" and an interest in costume complemented his artistic qualities and also proved valuable in the field of photography. As a beginner in this medium he had had a "certain romantic tendency to persuade the friends he photographed into unexpected attitudes, suspending them upside down or imprisoning them in cleft tree trunks or encouraging them to peep round curtains or through gashes in a paper sheet." He also experimented with double and triple exposures, costume pictures, and panorama portraits. But as his proficiency increased he became less preoccupied with the "chi-chi" of lilies and roses and baroque accessories that formerly had figured so largely in his compositions. Admitting that experience teaches certain useful tricks, he concluded that "the art of the serious photographer lies in knowing how to simplify for the sake of emphasis."

After five years of artistic activity Beaton had produced a galaxy of portraits and sketches of beauties and celebrities. Armed with these, and very limited financial backing, he came to the United States in 1928 expecting to make a lot of money quickly and easily. This notion was soon dispelled, but when Elsie de Wolfe (now Lady Mendl) loaned him her galleries for an exhibition in January 1929, his work caught the attention of New York's "glitter set." The New York *Times* critic found his talent rather fragile, but frequently expressive of piquancy and humor. Several years later, Beaton, who in the meantime had been to Hollywood and to his portraits of English society beauties had added exotic studies of American film stars, had two successful shows at the Delphic Studios in New York in 1931. *Art News* praised "his distinct flair for unusual effects of composition and chiaroscuro."

"Extracting enormous enjoyment from the world as he found it," Cecil Beaton led a very gay social life. He was especially addicted to party-going and dressing up. At one time there was "a period when for eight or ten days at a stretch he did not ever confront the world in ordinary costume, but, having removed his fancy dress to go to bed, stepped straight into a new disguise as soon as he emerged from slumber." An avid traveler, he photographed costumes and architecture in Central Europe, ruins in Greece, worshipped El Greco in Spain, read Gertrude Stein in the desert, attended bullfights in Mexico, contemplated vanished glory in Haiti, lingered in southern France. On the way to Moscow in 1936 he was awakened in the middle of the night and sent back to Berlin because Intourist had not informed him that a transit-visa for Poland was necessary. But, once in Moscow, he managed the almost unprecedented feat of visiting the Kremlin—accompanied by a guide, two armed guards, and the British Ambassador. These frequent travels provided material for articles, drawings, and photographs which Beaton contributed to *Harper's Bazaar, Vanity Fair,* the *Weekly Sketch* (London), *Life* Magazine, and *Vogue.*

Beaton made his debut as a stage designer in 1936. While still a schoolboy he had become interested in the Russian ballet, which, he said, provided the greatest emotional experience he had yet known. "I shall never forget the excitement of my first visit to the ballet," he wrote, "a new world of such visual loveliness was opened that, for me whose visual sense had always predominated, these colours, costumes, and scenery became an obsession." From then on he "saved his three and sixpences impatiently" in order to "repeat these raptures." Visits to the ballet provided an inexhaustible field for the subjects of his water colors, which were also influenced by the rich palettes of such designers as Bakst, Picasso[43], and Rouault. In between seasons Beaton often went to a Charing Cross Road shop where Cyril Beaumont presided over a large collection of "balletiana." His frequent visits were prompted by a desire to talk about ballet, but Beaumont was there to sell books, so young Beaton would have to accumulate the price of one—seven shillings and sixpence—before he could indulge in a chat with the proprietor. Determined to get full value for his money, he would also manage to look at about fifteen pounds' worth of books before departing with his purchase. Thus he became familiar with the history of ballet, the legends of Nijinsky, the features of ballerinas. Diaghileff became his hero.

These years of worship at the shrine of ballet eventually bore fruit. The producer Charles B. Cochran, who did not feel anything incongruous in inviting a photographer to design for the stage, gave Beaton carte blanche to do the scenery and costumes for the ballet scenes in two of his productions. "The First Shoot," in the Cochran revue *Follow the Sun,* tried out in Manchester on December 23, 1935, and then brought to the Adelphi Theatre in London the next month, was "a satirical parody of a 1905-vintage musical comedy depicting the manners and modes of Edwardian society." The critic of the *Dancing Times* found that Beaton's "full-scale debut in the art of theatrical decoration promises well for British ballet. His use of mauve and pale green in his landscape back cloth is particularly effective, but chief praise must go to his pheasant costumes." Beaton himself "was able to enjoy the experience of watching spellbound the velvet curtains part, to reveal the enormous, living, three-dimensional picture, for which he was responsible." His designs for "Apparitions," a ballet interlude in the Cochran Revue which opened at the Sadlers-Wells Theatre in February 1936, were also a great success. The ballroom costumes were considered amongst the most beautiful ever seen at the Wells. Boris Kochno, former secretary to Diaghileff and the scenarist for the Borodin-Lichine-Kochno ballet, *Le Pavillon,* saw some of Beaton's sketches, and as a result the artist was asked to do the scenery and costumes for this production, which was put on by Colonel de Basil's Ballet Russe de Monte Carlo at Covent Garden, London, in August 1936. Received with favor, this ballet of a lovers' tryst in the summerhouse in a garden became part of the regular repertoire of the de Basil company.

Cecil Beaton's show at the Carroll Carstairs Gallery in New York in 1936 "scooped the art world with his fashionable sitters, H.R.H. the Duke of Windsor '44 and Mrs. Wallis Simpson [now the Duchess of Windsor '44] being the most distinguished." Among other social figures were the beautiful Lady Abdy, Mrs. Harrison Williams, Alice Astor von Hofmannsthal, Princess Natalie Paley, and Mrs. Rhinelander Stewart. The attendance averaged 5,000 a week, and the exhibition was considered the most popular art event since the van Gogh exhibition at New York's Museum of Modern Art in 1935. Mary Fanton Roberts, in *Arts and Decoration,* labeled the opening "the most sublime and comprehensive gathering, not only of sketches but of smart society ladies, ever seen in New York. [Many of] the titled originals of the drawings were there, except Mrs. Simpson, with their admirers: and Mr. Beaton was there, much admired and applauded, and making so many luncheon and cocktail engagements that I don't see how he'll ever be able to get out of New York. Some of the sketches were charming, and all had that curious quality of fantasy with chic drawing that has made Mr. Beaton his international reputation."

At the suggestion of an artist friend, Christian Bérard, Beaton, who in 1930 had published a collection of portraits, *The Book of Beauty,* went through the more than fifty scrapbooks that he had filled during his career and made a selection of sketches, articles, and

CECIL BEATON

photographs for *Cecil Beaton's Scrapbook,* which came out in the autumn of 1937. The critic of the *Saturday Review of Literature* found the volume "the last word in snob appeal." Commenting on the superb reproduction of the photographs, he added that the highly personal, gossip column style of the articles might be improved with the scissors. The drawings he found "uniformly charming and showing great flair for fashion and the theatre." *The Scrapbook* was followed in 1938 by *Cecil Beaton's New York,* the young English artist-photographer's impressions of the city. This book aroused the ire of critics by its misinformation. The author himself, in the preface, disarmingly admits that he fears it is full of "howlers." But Katherine Woods, in the New York *Times,* found the pictures "seriously good ... the drawings swift and clever ... and a bright facility of phrase here and there in the text."

In January 1938 Beaton, "the highest paid and most sprightly talent" of *Vogue* Magazine, was the protagonist in a drama that cost him his job. Some microscopic lettering in a small corner of a sketch he had made for the February first issue of *Vogue* was discovered by Columnist Walter Winchell '43, who promptly broadcast the news to the nation. A decorative border for an article on cafe society included some tiny newspapers, among them the *Daily Mirror,* which carried Winchell's column. Under a subheading labeled "Broadway Filth" Beaton had written slurring comments on Jewish members of the Hollywood film-producer set. According to the artist, the marginal lettering, only visible through a magnifying glass, was never meant to be read, and but for the publicity which brought the incident to the attention of a wide public, might never have been noticed. Condé Nast, publisher of *Vogue,* protested that the whole thing was a mystery to his editors and held back the remaining 130,000 copies of the 280,000 issue to have the offending sketch altered. "My periodicals," he said, "have been free of attacks on race and creed

BEATON, CECIL—*Continued*

and I am determined that they must remain
free from such attacks, whether committed wit-
tingly or unwittingly." Beaton, interviewed at
the Waldorf-Astoria, declared that some of
his best friends were Jews, and called the occurrence "an aberration" of his artistic temperament, an expression of irritation caused
by some bad films he had just seen, and said
that he was unaware of the significance of some
of the slang words he had employed. As a result of this episode, Beaton resigned as a contributing photographer and artist on the staff
of *Vogue* Magazine. (After an interval of
several years, however, his work began to
appear in the pages of *Vogue* once more.)

Back in England, Beaton indulged his fancy
in writing a work of fiction, with the amusing
title *My Royal Past*, "by Baroness von Bülop,
née Princess Theodora Louise Alexina Ludmilla
Shophie von Eckermann-Waldstein, as told
to Cecil Beaton," which was published in the
fall of 1939. A satiric commentary on royal
diarists and biographers of royal personages,
this parody gave Beaton an opportunity to exploit his knowledge of the Victorian era. He
"omitted no aspect of idiot fashion or fatuous
social duty, as the press and biographer have so
many times represented them." Many drawings
full of "wicked observation and humour" accompanied the photographs of royal ladies and
gentlemen in "billowing trains, capes, and
starred uniforms of impressive grandeur" that
formed a record of the past. The critic of the
London *Times* called the volume a "luxury
leg-pull" and observed that Beaton had "taken
infinite pains to carry out an elaborate joke
with a smartness and finish that denote months
of preparation and a nicety of choice that makes
this book a triumph."

With the advent of the Second World War,
Beaton was assigned to the British Ministry
of Information to collect material and to take
documentary photographs for special Government reports. This assignment produced several books, some official, some brought out by
private publishers. *Air of Glory*, issued in 1941
by H. M. Stationery Office, a collection of photographs of wartime England, was followed by
History Under Fire, fifty-two photographs of
air-raid damage suffered by London buildings
in 1940-1941, with a commentary by James
Pope-Hennessy, who states that Beaton, in taking the photographs, has "earned the gratitude
not merely of contemporaries anxious to assess
the damage to London history, but of posterity."
Time Exposure, brought out by Batsford in
1941, is a collection of photographs representative of Beaton's career in photography, taken
during the period between 1923 and 1940, with
commentary by Peter Quennell, who considers
that the special value of the book lies in the
fact that it is a "continuous though partial reflection of the age," that is, the between-war
period. But Stark Young, in the *New Republic*, thought the book showed "profundity
of talent combined with flippancy of intention
. . . some congenital shallowness considerably
mixed with charm and the snobbery of British
getting on."

Winged Squadrons (1942) is the story of
the R.A.F. In March of that year Beaton was

"loaned" to the Air Ministry for a period of
three months to take documentary photographs
in the Middle East. Preceded by a case of 300
flash bulbs, and 10,000 films, he set out for
Africa. In Cairo, Cecil Beaton, the onetime
"pride of Mayfair," became No. 55561 of the
British Forces and donned the uniform of the
R.A.F., with "Official Photographer" on the
shoulders instead of a rank. No apparel, Beaton concedes, is more becoming than a uniform. Looking into a mirror, he "felt it was
a pity [he] was not fifteen years younger."
From Cairo, he proceeded to Alexandria to
photograph the fleet, and then toured the "forward" area in the months just previous to the
Allied disaster of Tobruk and the retreat to
El Alamein.

After Beaton left Africa he flew to Iraq,
where he photographed the Shah and his
family and also young King Feisal II. Next
on his itinerary was Jerusalem, where he
photographed various dignitaries, among them
His Beatitude, the Patriarch of the Greek
Orthodox Church. "I had given instructions
to Majesties and Air Marshals," said Beaton,
"but not before this had I the opportunity to
say, 'Please lower the chin, Your Beatitude.'"
Preparing to return home after his sojourn
with the R.A.F., Beaton was instructed by the
Ministry of Information to fly to Lisbon to
photograph the entire Portuguese Cabinet.
Although he had never been to Portugal, Lisbon did not appear strange to him because he
was so familiar with the ornate rococo decorations of the eighteenth century. He resumed
the pleasures of sightseeing with relish,
but he felt "that something was missing. It
was. The War." Neutral ground, Beaton
thinks, has something inhuman about it.

When he returned to England, Beaton, who
had scribbled in his diary "on the boat out, in
trains, in cars, and during countless airplane
trips," enjoyed reading his notes so much that
he thought others might do the same. So *The
Near East* came out in 1943, with many
photographs taken while on his mission. Before setting out on a new assignment Beaton
prepared a volume for the "Britain in Pictures" series, entitled *British Photographers*, in
which he traced the development of British
photography from the early experiments of
Henry Fox Talbot, a contemporary of Daguerre, to the latest methods of the photographers of today.

His next book will be called "The Far East,"
and will contain experiences of his nine-month
1944 assignment to China and India. Interviewed when he paused briefly in New York
on the way back from the Burma Front, he
said that he has now visited most of the countries of the world, except Japan. After five
years of photographing war scenes, he longs
to take up his stage designing again, and predicts a renaissance in the field of interior decorating. He also looks forward to being at
home in Tollard Royal, a sleepy little village
near the cathedral town of Salisbury, in the
South Downs, where his eighteenth-century
dwelling, Ashcombe House, provides a retreat
in which to work. While Beaton was in the
East, Tollard Royal was bombed, but little

damage was done beyond bringing down the ceiling in his bedroom.

References

N Y Times p10 N 13 '38
N Y World-Telegram p15 Ag 29 '44
Time p35+ F 7 '39 por
Beaton, Cecil Scrapbook 1937; The Near East 1943
Who's Who 1944

BEATRICE, MARIE VICTORIA FEODORA, PRINCESS OF ENGLAND Apr. 14, 1857—Oct. 26, 1944 Youngest and last surviving daughter of Queen Victoria; the mother of the ex-Queen of Spain and great-aunt of King George VI '42; Governor of the Isle of Wight since the death of her husband, Prince Henry of Battenberg, in 1896.

Obituary

N Y Times p23 O 27 '44 por

BEATTY, BESSIE Jan. 27, 1886- Radio commentator; journalist; author

Address: b. c/o Station WOR, 1440 Broadway, New York City; h. 142 E. 19th St., New York City

Bessie Beatty uses in her daily WOR radio program the lessons learned from thirty-six years of reporting, editing, writing, and public relations against a background that covers half the world. Miss Beatty is described as the type of friendly, unpretentious person one would expect to see conducting a women's forum. To her conversation she brings the extensive knowledge of people and places acquired over her years in Russia, Turkey, China, England, Mexico, Alaska, and the United States. And her practice of informal ad-libbed broadcasting draws forth from her noted guest stars the spontaneous, natural discussion one expects to hear in a roomful of friendly, intelligent people.

Bessie Beatty's parents, Thomas Edward and Jane Mary (Boxwell) Beatty, left a leisurely life in Ireland in the '80's to come to the United States on a gentlemen's farming project. Although they were unaccustomed to hardship, they went to undeveloped northwest Iowa, where they built their house. In a few years, however, disturbed by the loss of their first child and by forebodings of future hardships, the Beattys decided to move on across the country. They finally settled in Los Angeles, where Bessie, the first of five other children, was born on January 27, 1886; and there Mr. Beatty became one of the incorporators and directors of the first electric street railway in the city.

Before she was twelve Bessie had decided that she would be a writer. She clung to this idea all through school and by 1904 she was working for the Los Angeles *Herald*, having been hired on the strength of a story she had submitted while still a student at Occidental College in Los Angeles. At the end of three years she was drama editor and chief editor of the women's page. One day she was sent to the Nevada gold-mining district to do a story for the *Herald*. She became so interested in her subject that she gave up her newspaper

Blackstone

BESSIE BEATTY

work and moved into a cabin near the mines with the intention of writing a book on the district. (The book was published in 1907 as a series of sketches: *Who's Who in Nevada*.)

During her stay in Nevada she had occasion to entertain several visiting San Francisco newspapermen who had come to the region to investigate labor trouble and she was persuaded by them to go back into the newspaper field. Accordingly, she went to San Francisco and obtained a trial assignment on Fremont Older's famous *Bulletin*. The job was to edit a supplement celebrating the visit of the United States fleet to San Francisco; Miss Beatty's own visit to the city lasted about ten years—from 1907 to 1917. Ishbel Ross, in her history of American news women, writes that Miss Beatty proved herself a fearless, intelligent reporter after Older's own heart, and that he fostered her interest in "radical thought and social reform." (Before her San Francisco days Miss Beatty and her mother had campaigned together for equal suffrage.) During her association with the *Bulletin* she covered the Progressive movement in Washington, graft in Pittsburgh, life in Alaska; she organized the Red Stocking campaign and Happyland, a camp which she directed for six years for the underprivileged children of San Francisco; she originated a behind-the-news page called "On the Margin"; and in 1912 she published her *Political Primer for the New Voter*.

In 1917 Miss Beatty became interested in developments in Russia. In her determination to visit that country, she persuaded Older to let her do a series called "Around the World in Wartime." (She was four days out at sea on the Pacific when the news came that the United States had declared war on Germany.) Miss Beatty's first assignment took her to Japan and China, where she made a study of the people in those countries. She finally arrived alone in Russia in June. For the next eight months she lived at the "war hotel" in Petrograd, in the center of the

BEATTY, BESSIE—*Continued*

Revolution. Not content to be merely curious, Miss Beatty submerged herself in the turmoil of those hectic, vital days, seeing every phase of the struggle at close range. She visited the trenches on the southwestern Front; she lived for nearly a week with the women's famous Battalion of Death. She was on the scene for the Bolshevist uprising in July, the Kornilov rebellion, and the November Bolshevist Revolution. She was one of the first non-combatants to enter the Winter Palace when the Bolsheviks set up their dictatorship, and she attended the only meeting of the Constituent Assembly. Her whole absorption in the Revolution led her to talk to all kinds of people, the leaders, the soldiers, the working people. She was seeing the "new Russia emerging" and "she believed in the experiment she was watching." For a long time after she returned home, she says, everything that happened in the United States seemed like an anticlimax.

Back in the United States she wrote and lectured extensively on Russia. It was a difficult task, for people were suspicious of the new experiment, even though she urged them to try to understand the meaning of the political and economic revolutions she had witnessed. In 1918 she published *The Red Heart of Russia*, in which she summed up her experiences and conclusions. "Time," she wrote then, "will give to the world war, the political revolution, and the social revolution their true values. . . . To have failed to see the hope in the Russian Revolution is to be a blind man looking at a sunrise."

"I believe that progress," Miss Beatty said recently, "is made through a series of disillusionments, each one on a higher level of achievement. Revolution," she continued, "is a costly way of making progress, but history has shown repeatedly that there are conditions under which it is inevitable. Moreover, revolution, I feel, was inherent in Russia's past. . . . I believed and said in 1917 that the new regime in Russia was there to stay for a very long time. I think, however, that theories are always modified in practice. I have never doubted the deep sincerity of the Russian people in their attempt to make a new society, and I feel that that sincerity has been demonstrated by the manner in which they have endured every phase of hardship in this War."

For a three-year interlude after her return to the United States—from August 1918 to April 1921—Miss Beatty edited *McCall's* Magazine. She was accustomed to more excitement, however, and toward the end of 1921 she left for Russia again on a visit of nine months, this time as correspondent for *Good Housekeeping* and Hearst's *International* Magazine. She interviewed Lenin, Trotzky, Chicherin, and Mikhail Kalinin [42], with whom she toured the famine area along the Volga. Her articles were "intentionally designed to be non-controversial, non-political, non-economic, but colorfully descriptive of life as lived by such as butchers, bakers, and candlestickmakers as had survived seven years of war, revolution, and famine." On her trip home Miss Beatty toured the Near East and

Turkey, being one of the first Americans to enter Constantinople by the Black Sea after the War. In Turkey she studied the position of women under the new regime, but she was chiefly interested in the general effects of the new Turkish experiment on what seemed always to have been her primary preoccupation—the John and Mary Smiths of this world.

After her arrival in the United States, Miss Beatty called a halt to her active journalism for a brief period in order to write short stories and articles for such magazines as *Century, Good Housekeeping, New Republic,* and *Ladies' Home Journal.* Then, tired perhaps of comparative inactivity, in 1924 she succumbed once more to the temptations of newspaper work. She accepted an assignment from *Century* Magazine and embarked for England to do a series of articles on Ramsay Macdonald and the new Labor Government. The new Premier reminded Miss Beatty of Wilson. "He has his virtues and his limitations," she wrote. "I think he is honest, shrewd, able, liberal-minded, sentimental, religious, and fundamentally unrevolutionary." After her Russian experience, Miss Beatty could see the underlying conservatism of Macdonald's "socialism" even before the formation of the National Government in 1931.

In the succeeding years she continued to write for leading magazines in addition to her other work. For six months in 1926—following her marriage to the distinguished actor, William Sauter, on August 15—she wrote for MGM, among her other duties being an assignment to work with David Selznick [41] on the first production he did for the studio. After her brief experience with scenario-writing, however, she recognized the pitfalls in Hollywood for a serious writer, and refused further invitations to remain in California. She retained her interest in drama-writing, though, and the next year the play *Salt-chunk Mary,* of which she was co-author with Jack Black, was produced in Los Angeles. In 1932 it was produced on Broadway as *Jamboree.* Miss Beatty's connection with the theatre was philanthropic also. In 1933 she joined with her husband and a few leading theatrical figures to carry out Sauter's idea for the Actors' Dinner Club, a place where unemployed actors could get a meal and be entertained without the feeling of being charity cases. For two years she also served as its president.

Miss Beatty branched out into a new field in 1933. With the advent of the NRA she was invited by the clothing industry to handle their educational program to instruct the public in the buying of labeled clothes. For two years, as director of the National Label Council, she handled public relations for ten code organizations. Her own public relations bureau grew out of the demise of the NRA. Miss Beatty limited her publicity work to social organizations, handling accounts for such groups as the Museum of Costume Art, Greenwich House, the Neighborhood Playhouse School of the Theatre, New York State Commission for the Blind, and the Spanish Child Welfare Association. She also directed publicity for the women's division of the New York State Democratic Committee during the 1932 and 1936 campaigns. And as American secretary of the International P.E.N. Club founded by John Galsworthy and Mrs. Dawson Scott, she organized and directed the World's Congress of Writers at the World's Fair.

In 1939, as in the First World War, Miss Beatty was on the ocean when war was declared, on this occasion having started for Stockholm as American representative to the P.E.N. congress which never met. The Polish ship on which she was traveling reached Newcastle, instead of Stockholm, so the resourceful Miss Beatty toured England for a month collecting material for articles on the political, social, and economic aspects of war there, which she later sold to the *Christian Science Monitor.* A few months after her return to the United States she made a trip to Mexico for the New York *Post.*

For several years Miss Beatty had been working on the idea of a radio program, but her first introduction to broadcasting came in 1940 when she was a guest of, and on one occasion substituted for, Mary Margaret McBride '41 on the latter's own program as Martha Deane. Later in the year, when Miss McBride took over a program on another network, she recommended Miss Beatty for her old spot. The new morning program started on September 23, 1940 on WOR. Miss Beatty's routine every day from 10:15 to 11:00 o'clock consists of a fifteen to twenty minute period of answering questions and of chatting about her own activities, current events, books, plays, letters she has received. She then devotes ten or twelve minutes to her sponsors—in December 1943 she had twelve, the limit for a forty-five minute program, and she also had a waiting list. In an informal way she discusses the products, relating anecdotes and explaining methods of using the products. For the rest of the program she interviews guest stars, whose range includes actors, writers, librarians, social workers, and Mrs. Roosevelt '40.

Asked whether her radio work did not seem comparatively "tame" after her active newspaper career, Miss Beatty is quick to deny it. "It's strange," she comments, "that I am content to settle down after so much traveling, but I am." Everything she learned as journalist, editor, and publicist is used at one time or another. Furthermore, as she explains, it is stimulating to maintain day after day an interesting program. "It is a mistaken idea," she declares, "to claim that the mentality of radio audiences is on a fourteen-year-old level. A program finds its own audience, and our audience challenges us to give the best we have." Miss Beatty's own program encompasses everything which should be of interest to intelligent listeners. Her radio guests are chosen on a news basis— which may be a social question, an aspect of the international situation, a literary or theatrical or artistic event. Her philosophy of broadcasting is to present the program as though she, her guests, and her listeners were in the same room, talking together spontaneously as friends do. Miss Beatty works from rough notes, which supply only such facts as names and dates that might escape her. "Adlibbing," she explains, "is the only way I can

talk. I couldn't possibly do it if the gamble and spontaneity were taken away." She talks to her guests for only ten or fifteen minutes before going on the air, during which time voices are tested and Miss Beatty determines whether there is anything the individual particularly wishes mentioned or avoided.

Miss Beatty is assisted in chummy fashion by her talkative announcer, Dick Willard, and by her husband "Bill." William Sauter came to his radio assignment from a theatrical career in England and the United States. The role for which he is best known in this country is Osborn in *Journey's End.* (He played in the original road company that went on tour during the New York engagement, and he later played in the Broadway revival.) Sauter and Miss Beatty became acquainted in August 1924. They had once attended the same party given by a mutual friend; but their real introduction came when they both crossed the Atlantic—Sauter returning from England and Miss Beatty from France—on the *S.S. Arabic,* which had nearly been wrecked in a hurricane. They were married two years later, August 26, 1926. Sauter started out on the radio program with one or two casual appearances, until listeners more or less drafted him into appearing daily. He is a quiet, humorous man, "who contributes a felicitous conjugal note" to the program. He is slender and handsome, with a long, thin face, white hair, and a white mustache. (Although never heard on the air, Miss Beatty's dogs, Biddy and Biddy's son Terry, and her secretaries, the "angels," are also familiar to audiences.)

There seems to be no doubt that Miss Beatty is successful in her new endeavor. In 1942 she received the highest Crossley '41 rating for her type of program. In the same year the Office of Facts and Figures and *Variety Magazine* made a survey of radio's participation in the war effort, citing Miss Beatty's program for its efforts to draw listeners' attention to ways that they could help long before the survey was even contemplated. In 1943 she received the annual radio award of the Women's International Exposition of Arts and Industries for a "women's program which has performed an outstanding service and made a contribution to women throughout the country." Unofficial response has been large, too. Voluble housewives from all economic strata have written innumerable letters. Men, too, are regular listeners—dentists, doctors, defense workers, who are home during the day. When Miss Beatty recommends restaurants, plays, books, products, when she makes suggestions for civilian participation in the war effort or requests donations for charitable purposes, the response is immediate and sometimes overwhelming.

Miss Beatty is small, wears her somewhat graying light brown hair piled on the top of her head, and dresses simply but modishly. There is a happy combination of simplicity and assurance in her manner. Her fourstoried, narrow Gramercy Park home is described as gracious and homey. Her hobbies are the theatre, gardening (in her summer retreat, Goose Gables, at West Tremont, Maine), cooking, economics, Russia, and, since the War, entertaining United Nations servicemen

BEATTY, BESSIE—*Continued*

at her home on Thursday afternoons—an idea of her husband's. Miss Beatty is a member of the board of the International P.E.N. and a member of the Museum of Costume Art.

References

N Y Herald Tribune p6 Ag 20 '43 il pors
N Y Post p3 Ja 22 '41 por; p12 S 15 '43
N Y World-Telegram p6 O 15 '40 por
PM p13 O 25 '40 por
Pub W 144:266-7 Jl 24 '43
Time 40:52-3 S 21 '42 por
American Women 1939-40
Ross, I. Ladies of the Press 1936
Who's Who in America 1944-45

BECK, JOZEF (bek yu'zef) Oct. 4, 1894— June 6, 1944 Polish Foreign Minister at the outbreak of the War, appointed in 1932; served in Pulsudski's Polish Legion in the First World War; military attaché at Paris (1922-23); negotiated and signed non-aggression pact with Nazi Germany in 1934; after the invasion in 1939 fled from Poland and spent remainder of his days in retirement in Romania; death reported by the Nazi-controlled Romanian radio.

Obituary

N Y Times p19 Je 7 '44 por

BEDAUX, CHARLES E(UGENE) (be-dō') 1887 (?)—Feb. 14, 1944 French-born efficiency engineer; chairman of the board of International Bedaux Company and officer and director of many other corporations; citizen of the United States since 1917; severely criticized by labor for an industrial work plan which was termed "the old speed-up"; Duke of Windsor was married at his home in France; took his own life pending an indictment for treason against the United States; was a close associate of numerous Nazi and Vichy French officials.

Obituary

N Y Times p1+ F 20 '44 por

BELMONT, MRS. AUGUST Dec. 13, 1879- Chairman of the National Council of the American Red Cross Home Nursing Division; philanthropist; volunteer social service worker

Address: b. c/o Metropolitan Opera Guild, 654 Madison Ave., New York City; h. 1115 Fifth Ave., New York City

Eleanor Robson Belmont has made a marked success in many different fields. As Eleanor Robson, she was a well known and popular actress, retiring at the height of her career, and the co-author of a successful play. As the wealthy and socially prominent Mrs. August Belmont, her devotion to public service has brought her five important awards for distinguished achievement, three honorary degrees, and more than a dozen assorted chairmanships and directorates.

Born of a famous theatrical line in Wigan, Lancashire, England, December 13, 1879, Eleanor Elise Robson was the daughter of Madge (Carr) Robson, best remembered, as Madge Carr Cooke, for her portrayal of the title role in *Mrs. Wiggs of the Cabbage Patch*, and the granddaughter of Evelyn Cameron, a star of the English stage. Her father, Charles Robson, died not long after his daughter's birth. When the girl was seven, her mother brought her to the United States and placed her in a convent school, St. Peter's Academy on Staten Island, New York, while she herself continued with her work, trouping with Daniel Frawley's stock company of San Francisco. Upon graduation from school in 1897 seventeen-year-old Eleanor joined her mother and stepfather, the well known English actor Augustus Cooke. The shy, pigtailed girl had no intention of going on the stage; she arrived from her cross-continental trip with her paintbox under one arm, ready to put the glories of California scenery on canvas.

Nevertheless, Miss Robson was soon casually playing bit parts. "Not because I wanted to act," Mrs. Belmont now explains, "or because anybody else thought I could act, but merely because my mother wanted to have me with her as much as possible. Curiously enough, shy as I was [and Mrs. Belmont, in spite of her outward poise, has never wholly rid herself of shyness], I hadn't the least nervousness about those first appearances in public. That came later, when I accepted acting as my real work and realized how much depended on what I did." Miss Robson played only "insignificant" parts until the troupe's arrival in Honolulu, when they suddenly found themselves without an ingenue and with thirteen different plays to present in as many performances. "The only potential ingenue in sight," Miss Robson knew none of those roles; but she played in all the performances during what she says were the two most hectic weeks of her rather full life. Although the young girl still did not look upon acting as her true career, she did so well that the manager retained her as the ingenue during the rest of the tour and re-engaged her for the following season.

After this came seasons of stock in Denver and Milwaukee, where Eleanor Robson came to the attention of the playwright Augustus Thomas. Her first marked success was as Bonita Canby in his *Arizona*, which she first played in Chicago at the turn of the century. Her New York debut was made in this role in September 1900, when she was twenty-one, and was followed the next month by Constance in Robert Browning's *In a Balcony*. The spring of 1901 found her as Flossie Williams in *Unleavened Bread*, and in the fall she played the part of Mlle. de la Vire in *A Gentleman of France* in Ottawa, Canada. Throughout the 1902-1903 season the new star, who had been signed to a five-year contract by George C. Tyler, the theatrical manager, toured in the title role of *Audrey*; and in 1903 she headed an all-star cast in *Romeo and Juliet*. (Having missed the trial run because of mumps, she joined the cast for the New York opening after only twelve days of rehearsal.) Her features firm and well defined in a day when no lady accented her beauty with lipstick or eyebrow pencil, her waist small even in the age of hour-glass corsets, Eleanor Robson was a reigning beauty.

In 1903 she scored "a really phenomenal success" in *Merely Mary Ann*, a short story Israel Zangwill had dramatized at her suggestion. (It was she who later coined an immortal phrase by advising Zangwill to name a certain drama *The Melting Pot* instead of *The Crucible.*) Critics were "unanimously enthusiastic"; and after a Broadway triumph Miss Robson repeated her success in London the following year, when it was reported, "Her triumph . . . has had no parallel." The rising young dramatist Bernard Shaw '44 called her a "Joan of Arc" and wrote to her, explaining, "I am not interested in women, but I am interested in artists, and that is why I am writing you." When Miss Robson returned to the United States for the American tour Shaw corresponded with her concerning a play he proposed to write for her. One of the greatest disappointments in Mrs. Belmont's life is that when the play was finished she was so tied up by contracts that she was unable to appear in it; so the honor of creating the role of *Major Barbara* went to another actress.

After *Merely Mary Ann*, Miss Robson played Kate Hardcastle in an all-star revival of *She Stoops To Conquer*, produced in New York in the spring of 1905. The following year she alternated Zangwill's *Nurse Marjorie*, written especially for her, with *The Girl Who Has Everything, Susan in Search of a Husband*, and *A Tenement Tragedy*, also written expressly for her by Clotilde Graves. *Nurse Marjorie* won Miss Robson "curtain calls at the end of every act, and a storm of applause at the final scene." The following year, as "one of Bret Harte's roughest and tenderest heroines," Salomy Jane, she "won a personal success to warm any young actress' heart. Everyone will get to see the new play," it was predicted, "for the way it gripped its first audience showed that it will not let go as long as the present season lasts." After a brief appearance in *Vera, the Medium*, Miss Robson took the role of Glad in *The Dawn of a Tomorrow*, which opened in New York January 25, 1909. (She had asked the author, Frances Hodgson Burnett, to dramatize the story as a vehicle for her.) In this, which was to be her last appearance as an actress, Eleanor Robson's strangely appropriate final line was, "I'm going to be took care of now."

In February 1910, when Eleanor Robson was thirty-one, her engagement to the widowed Major August Belmont was announced; and two weeks later they were married. Major Belmont, then fifty-seven, was the son of the well known banker of that name. Himself a founder of the Rapid Transit Subway Company, he was best known as the owner of the famous Belmont racing stables and as chairman of the Jockey Club. Retiring from the stage at the time of her marriage, Eleanor Robson Belmont returned with her husband from their wedding trip in time for the opening of the Belmont Park racetrack. Although not previously interested in racing, Mrs. Belmont became a partner in the Belmont stables; but this, and the social duties devolving upon

Bachrach

MRS. AUGUST BELMONT

a Belmont, were not enough to engage all the energies of the former star.

Two years after her marriage Mrs. Belmont helped to organize the Working Girls' Vacation Association (now nationally known as the American Woman's Association), and founded the Spugs—Society for the Prevention of Useless Giving. "There exists," she said, "a distressing amount of duplication in appeals to the public, duplication which definitely limits, by its waste of money and effort, our capacity to accomplish the best results. We need a central planning agency." In 1913 Mrs. Belmont established the Educational Dramatic League, which she headed for six years. That spring "the Belmonts stood Manhattan society on its head by importing Ruby Helder, the English girl tenor with a voice 'like Caruso's,' to sing at a musicale at the Belmont house on East 34th Street. . . . The party cost them $10,000."

As soon as the United States went to war in 1917 Mrs. Belmont joined the Red Cross. Theodore Roosevelt recommended her for overseas duty so that she might "put before our people, as only she can do, what the real needs of our troops are. She has," he wrote, "a man's understanding, a woman's sympathy, and a sense of honor and gift of expression such as are possessed by very, very few, either among men or women." As a Red Cross worker, Mrs. Belmont made several trips to Europe (at a time when German U-boats were an ever-present menace to shipping) to inspect United States Army camps; founded a children's unit of the Red Cross in New York; and spoke in behalf of the Liberty Loan. In 1918 she was made assistant to the Red Cross War Council, since then serving also on various committees; and since 1942 she has been chairman of the National Council for Home Nursing courses. ("Today," Mrs. Belmont reports, "we have these classes in every part of the country, extending even to Hawaii and Alaska. They are attended by women of all

BELMONT, MRS. AUGUST—*Continued*
sorts, from illiterates to college graduates.
They are a perfect example of democracy at
work.") In 1919 Mrs. Belmont was elected to
membership in the Central Committee, the Red
Cross's governing body, a post she filled for a
quarter of a century.

One night in 1923, too tired to sleep after
finishing a strenuous Red Cross fund campaign, Mrs. Belmont borrowed a mystery novel
from her hostess, Amy Lowell. The book
chanced to be Harriet Ford's *In the Next
Room*; and as Eleanor Robson's old instinct for
dramatic material asserted itself, she conceived
the idea of turning the novel into a play. Produced on Broadway in 1923, the play, on which
she collaborated as Eleanor Robson with Miss
Ford, was an immediate success, and was
presented in London the following year.

Widowed in 1924, Eleanor Robson Belmont
put her husband's famous stable of 113 thoroughbreds up for auction, where they brought
some $500,000. Seven years later, in the
depths of the depression, she was appointed
chairman of the Women's Division of the
Emergency Unemployment Relief Commission
for New York City. In that year she broke
a precedent of one hundred years' standing by
delivering a commencement address at New
York University—the first woman ever to do
so. (In addition to her honorary degree from
that institution, Mrs. Belmont has been similarly honored by the University of Rochester
and Moravian Seminary and College.) At this
time, also, she founded the Adopt-a-Family
Committee, of which she became the chairman,
to care for white-collar workers who were not
unemployable but needed temporary relief. In
the two years that followed, Mrs. Belmont
proved herself "a super-saleswoman," persuading people to make generous contributions to
relief funds. "Borrow on your capital if your
income is curtailed," she told her auditors, "but
you must help!" Mrs. Belmont is still a member of the Adopt-a-Family Board of directors.
For a number of years she was also chairman
of the Nurses' House Committee of the Association for Improving the Condition of the
Poor and directed its drives for funds.

Elected to the board of directors of the Metropolitan Opera Association in 1933, Mrs.
Belmont was its first woman member. "I was
always interested in music," she recalls. "I
think that you will find that most people who
practice one art are concerned with all. At
the time I became active in the Metropolitan
it was in a bad shape financially. I felt that
its closing would mean an irreparable loss."
For the first time the "Met" sent out an appeal for support to the public; broadcast over
the radio, this brought in contributions totaling
$300,000. In 1935 it became clear that some
permanent coordinating agency was needed to
take financial care of the great opera house,
and so Mrs. Belmont organized the Metropolitan Opera Guild. For seven years she was
chairman of its board of directors, until she
resigned this post to give more time to war
activities. The Guild now has a membership
of some twenty thousand groups and individuals in various countries, most of whom are
reached through the medium of the weekly
opera broadcasts. It publishes a weekly mag-

azine, "books and literature for study purposes,
conducts backstage tours, broadcasts a weekly
explanatory program for the main event, gives
lectures, holds contests [and] children's performances, and contributes money and other
equipment to the Metropolitan."

Appointed chairman of the Guild's War Activities Committee in the winter of 1943, Mrs.
Belmont supervised the program of purchasing and distributing opera tickets to service
personnel; collecting, repairing, and distributing musical instruments for the North Atlantic Area of the American Red Cross; and
purchasing and distributing radios and operatic
recordings through Armed Forces Master
Records, Inc. Many another person would
have found this work with the Guild a full-
time job; but at the same time that she became its chairman she assumed the presidency
of the Motion Picture Research Council, an
organization designed to raise the standards of
American films. (She is now board chairman.)
She also became a member of the National
Broadcasting Company's advisory board. In
May 1944 Mrs. Belmont, who had decided to
return to active participation in the direction
of the Opera Guild, was unanimously elected
to the presidency. (She is also a trustee of the
Kathryn Long scholarship and award fund.)

Through all these years Mrs. Belmont has
continued her activities in the Red Cross,
which recognized her conspicuous services in
1934 by awarding her a gold medal. Again in
1939 she was presented with a medal for outstanding civil service by the Hundred Year
Association, the only woman to be thus honored. In April of 1943, her twenty-fifth year
in the Red Cross, Mrs. Belmont resigned from
its Central Committee, explaining that "the
important elective posts on the . . . governing
board of the Red Cross should be rotated
among the active leaders developed in recent
years." She has, however, continued her active interest in the organization, and remains
an honorary member of the Central Committee. In October 1944 she was elected to the
board of directors of the New York chapter
for a three-year term.

In 1939 Mrs. Belmont was awarded the gold
medal of the National Institute of Social Sciences; and in November 1940 the American
Woman's Association (of which she was a
founder) voted her its annual award for
"eminent achievement," for her work "on
the stage, in the fields of opera, social work,
and philanthropy." Still another award, for
"distinguished public service by a private citizen," came to Mrs. Belmont in October 1943,
when she received one of the three annual
Roosevelt Medals for, she said, "being a busy-
body."

These rewards of service did not mean that
the service was at an end, however. Mrs.
Belmont's vitality is still poured into movements for social betterment, and most of her
time is devoted to war activities of various
sorts. "Her threescore years rest as lightly
on her brow," it was said in 1943, "as her pow-
dery pompadour. Intense to the point of fervor, she has a nervous habit of fluffing up her
silvery-white hair while conversing." Her dark
blue eyes snap as her soft voice, which once
enchanted theatre audiences, is lifted in behalf
of money-raising drives for the Red Cross or

her beloved Opera. Eleanor Robson Belmont "has helped raise more millions probably than any other woman in America."

References

Am Mag 97:34+ Je '24 por
Etude 60:365+ Je '42 por
N Y Times Mag p13 O 24 '43 por
N Y World-Telegram p10 N 30 '40 pors
Who's Who in America 1944-45
Who's Who in the Theatre 1939

BELMONT, ELEANOR (ELISE) ROB-SON *See* Belmont, Mrs. A.

BENNETT, RICHARD 1872—Oct. 22, 1944 Former stage matinee idol and later a prominent Hollywood screen character actor; father of the three well known film actresses, Constance, Barbara, and Joan Bennett.

Obituary

N Y Times p19 O 23 '44 por

BERLIN, ELLIN (MACKAY) 1904- Author

Address: b. c/o Doubleday, Doran & Co., Inc., 14 W. 49th St., New York City

One of the reviewers of *Land I Have Chosen* (1944), by Ellin Berlin, said that it was a remarkable first novel for several reasons: "(1) its plot, a rigorous, old-fashioned narrative with beginning, middle, and end; (2) its portrait of Anne Brooke, a well-meaning attractive girl who begins as a Long Island debutante, ends as a Nazi sympathizer. But the book's chief interest is that it is the work of Mrs. Irving Berlin." It is also unusual because, unlike many first novels, it is not autobiographical.

It is not surprising that Ellin Mackay Berlin should write an "authentic, mature, and caustic story" with a background of Park Avenue and Long Island's Southampton, for her writing career began as far back as 1925 with what has been called a criticism of her own background. An article she wrote then for the *New Yorker* became front page news and drew forth comment in the editorial page of the conservative New York *Times*. The editorial writer called it an "indictment of modern society" and considered it "not only witty and audacious but true." Receiving less attention, although more noteworthy from the literary point of view, were Mrs. Berlin's short stories which appeared frequently from 1933 to 1940 in both the *Saturday Evening Post* and the *Ladies' Home Journal*.

Ellin Mackay Berlin, whose own life story suggests much of the romance of fiction, was born in 1904 near Roslyn, Long Island, on the $6,000,000 estate which her grandfather had given to her father, Clarence Hungerford Mackay when he was married to Katherine Alexander Duer. Among the properties Mackay inherited from his father, John W. Mackay, an Irish immigrant who "struck pay dirt" in Nevada in 1872, was a network of transatlantic cables. Mackay became the president of the Postal Telegraph and Cable Company and of the International Telephone

Pach

ELLIN BERLIN

and Telegraph Company, and developed his inheritance to a fortune reported to be in the thirty millions. Described as "dapper, debonair, and lavishly educated," Mackay gained additional prominence as an art collector, music patron (the New York Philharmonic was his particular godchild), a breeder of fine horses, and a squash player. His marriage to the bluestocking Katherine Alexander Duer, descendant of Colonel William A. Duer and Lady Katherine Alexander, who had settled in New York in 1768, established the Mackays in what was known in that year of 1898 as society's "400." Ellin, the second child of the marriage, was named for her grandmother Ellin Travers. In addition to her prominence in New York society, the young Mrs. Mackay was noted for her beauty, her interest in woman suffrage, and for her much talked of novel, *The Stone of Destiny* (1903) which reached a second edition and was translated into German.

In the early 1900's magazines carried photographs of the tall, gracefully slender society matron with her two daughters, little dark-haired Katherine and six-year old blond Ellin, the little girls in dotted swiss dresses and high-topped shoes. There were also articles on woman suffrage and other subjects by Mrs. Mackay in *Harper's* and in the *North American Review*. But in 1913 Mrs. Mackay surprised her world by obtaining a Paris divorce—giving the custody of her two daughters and young son to their father.

Added to the influence her mother's writings may have had on young Ellin was the example of the successful career of her cousin, the late Alice Duer Miller, whose narrative poem is the basis for the highly successful 1944 motion picture, *The White Cliffs of Dover*. Several of Mrs. Miller's stories were dramatized while Ellin was a child. One, under the title of *Come Out of the Kitchen* (1916), had a long Broadway

BERLIN, ELLIN—*Continued*

run with Ruth Chatterton in the starring role.

After making her debut at a ball given at the Ritz-Carlton Hotel, Ellin Mackay went to Barnard College for special courses, in preparation for a writing career. Her debutante and post-debutante days were in the "dizzy" twenties, when what is now known as cafe society first came into existence. Ellin Mackay defended the new custom of going to cabarets in the *New Yorker* article which caused so much comment: "It is not because fashionable young ladies are 'picturesquely depraved' that they go to cabarets," she said. "They go to find privacy." The exclusive "400" of her mother's young days was a thing of the past. The legend of exclusiveness still persisted, said Miss Mackay, despite the fact that invitation lists were "as long and as entrancing as the telephone directory." The dance program had also disappeared and in its place was the "miscellaneously flaccid stag line," young men who were privileged, without even the formality of an introduction, to cut in interminably, dooming their partners to "trodden toes and senseless conversation. So they [the young ladies] prefer rubbing elbows in a cabaret with 'fat drummers' to dancing at exclusive parties with all sorts of people." It was reported that Miss Mackay viewed the publicity which greeted her article with somewhat mixed emotions. She had tentatively planned other excursions into print but the publicity gave her pause. Her second *New Yorker* article, "The Declining Function" (December 12, 1925), was also recorded on front and editorial pages of newspapers. In it she emphasized, as a commentator put it, a statement she had made in the first article, "a determination to seek her joys where she finds them." More portentous was her statement, "Modern girls are conscious of their identity and they marry whom they choose, satisfied to satisfy themselves." A few weeks later, on January 4, 1926, she was married to Irving Berlin [42], America's foremost song writer, whose rise from poverty to an income of $500,000 a year had been duly publicized. The newspapers devoted tall headlines and much column space to the event. The Berlins had been married by a city clerk, without the sanction of Mrs. Berlin's Church—the Mackays were Roman Catholics, and Irving Berlin was of the Orthodox Jewish faith. Clarence Mackay, it was said, withheld his blessing until five years later, after his second marriage, to Anna Case, the opera singer. Mrs. Berlin's mother, who had remarried, made no comment at the time.

It was reported that the Berlins had met in Jim Kelly's Greenwich Village night club a year or so before their marriage. After the City Hall ceremony Mrs. Berlin telephoned Harold Ross [43], the *New Yorker's* publisher, to say that she would not be able to finish her article, which would have been the third of her series on society. A few days later the Berlins sailed in the presidential suite of the *Leviathan* for a European honeymoon. One of Berlin's wedding gifts to his bride was the copyright of his song hit

"Always," which he had written in 1925. Added to the sentimental value of the song, which had played a large part in Berlin's courtship, was its commercial value. Besides the yearly royalties on sheet music and other sales which the song has continued to earn, it has twice brought Mrs. Berlin a tidy sum from motion picture companies. Samuel Goldwyn [44] paid $15,000 for the "nonexclusive" use of it in the biographical picture of Lou Gehrig, *Pride of the Yankees* (1942). It had been the real-life romance song of the baseball star and his wife. Less than two years later "Always" brought Mrs. Berlin $18,500 from Universal for its "nonexclusive use" in Deanna Durbin's [41] *Christmas Holiday* (1944).

While Mrs. Berlin put aside her writing for the first years of her marriage, she resumed it in 1933. Her first short story was published in the *Saturday Evening Post*, in which others followed: "Say Not the Struggle" in 1936, "Limelight" and "To Them That Have" in 1938. In the *Ladies' Home Journal* appeared "Only the Nicest Girls" in 1933, "The First Mrs. Brooke" in 1936, and "Five-year Diary" and "Change Partners" in 1939.

Mrs. Berlin's *Land I Have Chosen* was bought by Warner Brothers for the largest price yet paid for the motion-picture rights to a first novel—$150,000. There was a divergence of opinion about the literary merits of the novel. Lewis Gannett [42], New York *Herald Tribune* reviewer, found it a "sober, sincere, colorful novel. Its characters are remarkably lifelike and convincing." Gannett thought that "one considerable weakness in the book is that its earnest patriotism defeats itself because America is depicted rather as a place in which one is safe than as one in which any definite and positive ideology of faith is typified." Orville Prescott of the New York *Times* thought that *Land I Have Chosen* "packs a nasty satirical wallop" in Anne Brooke, presented by Mrs. Berlin as a fairly normal, typical member of her society. Prescott found, however, "Lisa's story and the whole German section" of the book "dull and commonplace, just an echo of scores of other accounts of Nazi cruelty and those who suffer from it."

Mr. and Mrs. Berlin have three children: Mary Ellin, who will enter Bryn Mawr College in 1944, Linda Louise, and Elizabeth Irving. (A son, Irving Berlin, Jr., died as an infant.) The Berlins have moved from their New York town house to a hotel apartment for the duration of the War. They have a fifty-two-acre summer place near Livingston Manor in the Catskills. "The Berlins," says John Chapman in a *Saturday Evening Post* article on Berlin, "have always lived well, as befits Berlin's earning capacity, but not extravagantly."

Reference

Time 44:92+ Jl 3 '44

BERNSTEIN, LEONARD (bĕrn'stēn)
Aug. 25, 1918- Conductor; composer; pianist
Address: b. Philharmonic Symphony Society, Carnegie Hall, 113 W. 57th St., New York City

The classic story of the understudy who wins fame and fortune overnight by stepping into the star's role at the last minute very seldom comes true, particularly in the music world. When Leonard Bernstein, the twenty-five-year-old assistant conductor of the Philharmonic Symphony Orchestra of New York, shot into public notice in November 1943 by substituting for the renowned Bruno Walter '42, commentators went back fifty-seven years to find a parallel in the debut of Arturo Toscanini '42. Bernstein's success was even more remarkable in view of the fact that he had not had the opportunity for a single rehearsal, and had led the orchestra only twice in his entire association with the Philharmonic —both times in unimportant rehearsals.

Young Bernstein created the musical sensation of the season; concertgoers and critics alike welcomed the revelation of this new talent in a season that promised few, if any, important debuts. Enthusiastic responses to Bernstein's feat ranged all the way from Artur Rodzinski's '40 pronouncement of "prodigious talent" to a note of appreciation from the Junior Beethoven Club of Memphis, Tennessee signed by its twelve-year-old Vice-President in Charge of Listening to Radio Programs.

Leonard Bernstein is one of the few notable conductors to be entirely "made in America." He was born in Lawrence, Massachusetts, August 25, 1918, the son of Samuel Joseph and Jennie (Resnick) Bernstein. (Both his parents had come from Russia.) Definitely not a child prodigy, he showed no particular interest in music until his tenth year, when a relative sent her old upright piano to the Bernsteins to keep for her. Leonard found it a challenge: "I touched it. It made pretty sounds. Right away I screamed, 'Ma, give me lessons.'" A month of lessons convinced Leonard that he was going to be a musician when he grew up, but this decision interfered with his ordinary activities no more than if he had decided to become a doctor or a lawyer. At the Boston Latin School, Leonard was a crack athlete; at his summer camp he was the high-jump champion. Later he enrolled at Harvard University. With the intention of becoming a pianist, he studied the piano with Heinrich Gebhard and composition with Walter Piston and Edward Burlinghame Hill.

Upon graduation from Harvard in 1939 Bernstein felt that the piano "was not exhaustive enough from the point of view of expression. Mitropoulos '41, Roy Harris '40, and Aaron Copland '40 suggested that I study conducting. I don't know why in one month everybody should have decided I had the ability to be a conductor, but I had a good memory for music and a sense of style. You know, a sense of distinction between Couperin and Strauss." To this end Bernstein spent two years in graduate study at the Curtis Institute of Music in Philadelphia, where he studied conducting under Fritz Reiner '41, piano with the exacting Mme. Isabella Wengerova, and orchestration with Randall Thompson. During the summers he worked under Serge Koussevitzky '40, conductor of the Boston Symphony Orchestra, at the Berkshire Music Center in Tanglewood, Massachusetts.

LEONARD BERNSTEIN

In September 1942, after a season spent in teaching, composing a "Sonata for Clarinet" (his first published work), and producing a number of operas for the Boston Institute of Modern Art, Bernstein was appointed assistant to Koussevitzky. The "Sonata for Clarinet" was described as "a modest, economically written work," composed "with zest and with a great deal of relish for the contrasts possible in this instrumental combination" of the clarinet and piano. Bernstein was said to be clearly influenced by the generation of American composers that includes Copland and William Schuman '42, to each of whom he has dedicated one of his Seven Anniversaries. A recording of the sonata, with David Oppenheim as clarinetist and with the composer at the piano, was released in January 1944.

The following season found Bernstein appearing in New York as a pianist and conductor. His direction of one of the Serenade Concerts at the Museum of Modern Art conspicuously overshadowed the efforts of the other performers. Virgil Thomson '40 reported of the event: "That everything was heard so exactly is due . . . to the superb and musicianly conducting of Leonard Bernstein. . . . This young man, who proved himself recently at a Town Hall Music Forum to be a pianist of no mean technique and temperament, proved himself Tuesday night to be a conductor with a sure hand and, what is rarer, a sure mind about the music of his own time. He read the works with warmth as well as authority."

Scheduled for induction into the Army late in the summer of 1943, Bernstein was rejected because of asthma (the result of an allergy to dust). On the following day Artur Rodzinski offered him the post of assistant conductor of the New York Philharmonic Symphony Orchestra, which he accepted. On Saturday, November 12, 1943, the mezzo-soprano Jennie Tourel presented Bernstein's cycle of "Five Kid Songs" in a recital at Town Hall. Reviews mentioned the "sophisticated

BERNSTEIN, LEONARD—*Continued*

wit" of the group, which had the general title of *I Hate Music*. The following morning Bernstein was informed that the great Bruno Walter, who was to be guest conductor for the Philharmonic's Sunday concert, was ill and that Bernstein would have to take his place. There was no possibility of assembling the orchestra for a rehearsal, and Bernstein had time only for an hour's consultation with Walter. Fortunately he had realized the previous night that Walter's condition might not permit him to conduct: "I had an idea that I might have to do the concert. So I drank coffee at midnight, studied until two o'clock—not all night the way the newspapers said—and so I couldn't sleep. When I knew I had to do it I was scared out of my wits. It took me an hour to collect myself, to find that inner strength without which one would sink—unquote."

Music critics, however, found "no trace of strain or nervousness" as Bernstein led the orchestra through "one of the season's toughest programs," as Louis Biancolli commented. "Of course assistant conductors are supposed to meet such emergencies in stride. Still, a program of Schumann's *Manfred* overture, Strauss's '44 *Don Quixote*, Wagner's *Die Meistersinger* prelude, and a snaggy new score like Miklos Rosza's *Variations* would put any understudy on the spot, however primed. Then, stepping into the shoes of a Bruno Walter is no cinch either." Bernstein's parents and twelve-year-old brother, who had chanced to come down from Massachusetts to spend the week end with him, looked on proudly from a box as the audience became increasingly enthusiastic and finally "wildly demonstrative." During the intermission Bernstein received a telegram from Koussevitzky which said simply, "Listening now. Wonderful." During the intermission, too, Rodzinski, who had driven in from Stockbridge, Massachusetts, arrived. He announced that Bernstein showed "prodigious talent. We wish to give him every opportunity in the future." Later when the audience had finally left after bringing Bernstein back four times, Rodzinski told reporters that he had made his own debut under exactly similar circumstances in 1926 by replacing Leopold Stokowski as conductor of *Don Quixote* on a few hours' notice. Critics were agreed that Bernstein as a conductor was "indubitably to be reckoned with." His "brilliant musicianship" was praised, as well as the "excellent and exciting qualities" of his performance and "the authenticity of his interpretations." This "excellent impression" was reinforced later in the season, when the Philharmonic's second guest conductor, Howard Barlow '40, also succumbed to influenza and was replaced by Bernstein, this time with one rehearsal. "The tone of the orchestra throughout the evening was marked by clarity in every choir, but particularly the strings; the rhythms were precise, supple, and never exaggerated; the reading of *Paris* by Delius—the severest test on the program—was sensitive and imaginative."

Leonard Bernstein's next appearances as conductor were made in Pittsburgh and Boston,

where he made "a personal triumph" by leading programs which included the first performances of his symphony *Jeremiah* (1942), aided by Jennie Tourel's "superb" rendition of the Hebrew "Lamentations" assigned to her. Critics were agreed that its three sections were uneven, but Paul Bowles stated flatly that it "outranks every other symphonic product by any American composer of what is called the younger generation (meaning people up to forty) . . . using with complete ease an idiom which one is accustomed to hearing only haltingly." Robert Bagar, however, "fails to understand the euphuistic hullabaloo raised by the Pittsburgh and Boston critics," and considers that for two movements the symphony "wanders about uncertainly, aimlessly, and loaded down with superfluities, to boot. . . . The second movement rips and rivets and rears about in all sorts of broken rhythms—a well-marked Charleston beat not excluded—and all of it means little and sounds like less." Other critics, agreeing that Bernstein is a master of orchestration, mentioned both "the diffuse character of the composition" and its "shining brilliance and vibrant juxtapositions of color." *Jeremiah* won the New York Music Critics Circle Award for 1944 in the classification of orchestral compositions.

About a month later another Bernstein composition was premiered: the score for Jerome Robbins' *Fancy Free*, which had been commissioned by the Ballet Theatre the preceding October, before Bernstein "got the breaks." The ballet was a brilliant success, and the score proved "spicy, rhythmically complex, and jazzy music, interesting in itself and wedded to the choregraphy as neatly as stretched skin on a drum fits the shell." Bernstein's conducting received perhaps the most unanimous approval since his debut. His beat, said Edwin Denby, "was steady and, better still, it was buoyant. . . . He can give the illusion of an increase in speed by increasing this buoyancy and adding a dynamic crescendo; so he doesn't have to quicken the tempo to pep up the show. . . . And you could see that the dancers, even when they came on tired, responded to Mr. Bernstein like hepcats to Harry James '43." The young conductor has been commissioned to write a sequel, entitled *'Bye 'Bye, Jackie*.

While Bernstein and Adolph Green of the Revuers quintet were in a hospital recovering from operations, they worked on a musical play, *On the Town*, which Green was writing with Jerome Robbins and another Revuer, Betty Comden, using the basic plot idea of Robbins' *Fancy Free*. *On the Town*, which had both the RKO and MGM picture companies as investors, was said to be the first musical play to which film rights were sold (for a reported total of $250,000) before stage production. Having finished the score ("a six-month period out of my life") the composer was carrying on the normal routine of a popular guest conductor. "I was guest conductor of the Boston Symphony for a week in November," he told an interviewer. "It requires everything in you to do the job right. And all through the week I was getting calls from New York: the show needed two more measures for this song or another verse for that." Koussevitzky saw the *On the Town* tryout, liked it, and gave Bernstein a three-hour lecture for wasting his time on it. Impenitent, the young composer was soon discussing plans for an operatic version of Maxwell Anderson's '42 *Winterset,* for a possible novel, for scoring some future movie— "all the things that are fun." At the same time he realized, "I'm primarily a conductor. It's not easy to grow as a conductor when you're diverting your energies in so many other directions." (Bernstein, who is under contract to the Music Publishers' Holding Corporation as a composer, has also written a cycle of six anti-Fascist songs, a string quartet, and a violin sonata.)

On the Town opened in New York during Christmas Week of 1944 and soon established itself among the town's hit shows; by December 29 the advance ticket sales had reached $200,000—$50,000 more than the cost of production. Reviews as a whole were favorable, although a certain difference of opinion made itself felt in regard to Bernstein's music, among other things. *Variety's* own Ibee and Elie disagreed, the former writing, "If there is 'class' in *Town,* it's not evident." The latter, mentioning the composer's "more or less instrumental manner of writing for the voice," called Bernstein's music "smart and, for ballet purposes, "socko,' but it is not exactly show music. There is little feeling of repose or warmth or lyric grace in the romantic numbers, and there is a tendency to dress them up in clever orchestral scoring rather than to support their mood. The amusing tunes, such as 'I Get Carried Away", 'I Can Cook,' or 'You Got Me,' are 'terrif', however, and the three numbers all but carry the show." In contrast, Lewis Nichols called the music "unpedantic," while L. A. Sloper describes the "brilliant score, far more interesting than the average of musical comedy. It has, too," he concedes, "the weakness of most musical comedy writing—its romantic melodies are rather sticky. 'Lonely Town' may be voted the most likely in its class to succeed. On the other hand, some of the comedic songs are captivating in their intervals and in the variety of their rhythms. Such are 'I Get Carried Away', 'Lucky To Be Me,' and especially 'You Got Me.'" The *Christian Science Monitor's* E. C. Sherburne declared, "The varieties of his [Bernstein's] rhythms, his satirical tonal embroideries, and the surprises offered by his vaulting rhythms leave the listener startled with the realization that he made it, like the man on the flying trapeze."

Although Bernstein's other forms of success have overshadowed his career as an instrumentalist, he speaks of himself as a "pianist-composer-conductor"—in that order. He is "mad about boogie-woogie," gave three boogie-woogie piano concerts at Fort Dix in 1942, and is said to have six jazz songs in the hands of his publishers. Although *Cue Magazine* has described him as "small, dark, and handsome," Bernstein is of average height (five feet eight inches tall) and weighs 145 pounds. He has wavy brown hair, which insists on dipping over his right eye, a "medium-dark" complexion, and looks, in his own words, "like a well-built dope fiend." His photographs are sufficiently "glamorous" to explain the innumerable telephone calls from feminine admirers after his debut.

Lennie, as he is known to the men backstage, refuses to wear the traditional cut-away, substituting a dark jacket for concerts, and he would like to abolish the "striped pants" in favor of a less pretentious costume. He has never owned a hat. A leader who "conducts from his head to his heels," he says his greatest problem is refraining from stamping and swaying to a Latin beat, and he never uses a baton because it "unnerves" him. During the 1944 Presidential campaign, Bernstein was one of the many artists in various fields who made speeches in favor of President Roosevelt '42.

Although Leonard Bernstein gives his hobbies as "writing poetry, reading, swimming, and horseback riding," and although he is said to be expert at the rumba and conga, he has little time for any recreation except the motion pictures. "He can still swim fast but smokes too much these days to swim far." He boasts that he will eat or drink anything— including the breakfast which he prepares for himself—and says that he followed his debut concert with "four scotches and the best steak he's had in years." As an adherent to the Jewish religion, Bernstein feels deeply the problem of "a whole people in a world of no security," which moved him to write *Jeremiah;* but he feels himself too fortunate to be unhappy about anything. However, some interviewers have succeeded in annoying him by stating that he reads "Dick Tracy," which he hasn't done since coming to New York. (He refuses to read the New York *Daily News.)* "I have no idea," he protests, "what's happened since the beginning of Mrs. Pruneface."

References

C S Mon p6 S 25 '43; p6 N 20 '43
Cue 12 :11 D 4 '43 por
N Y Herald Tribune p12 N 15 '43 por
N Y Post Mag p29 N 16 '43 il pors
N Y Times p34 S 9 '43; p1+ N 15 '43 por
N Y World-Telegram p15 N 15 '43
New Yorker 19 :20 N 27 '43
Newsweek 23 :82 A p 10 '44 por
PM p22 Mr 31 '43; p25 D 2 '43 por

BESTOR, ARTHUR E(UGENE) May 19, 1879—Feb. 3, 1944 President of the Chautauqua Institution, Chautauqua, New York since 1915; a leader in the field of adult education; chairman of the Near East Relief; a former member of the Advisory Committee on Emergency Education.

Obituary

N Y Times p15 F 5 '44 por

BJORNSSON, SVEINN (bjèrn'sun svätn) Feb. 27, 1881- President of Iceland

Address: Reykjavik, Iceland

Before 1941 most Americans thought of Iceland as a distant and barren Thule, the home of sagas, and the jumping-off place for Leif Ericson's daring voyage to the continent of North America one thousand years ago. With the dispatch of American armed forces to Iceland in 1941, however, the history of Iceland, its language, literature, customs, and institutions became subjects of considerable popular interest in the United States. "The world's oldest democracy," Iceland elected its first presi-

SVEINN BJORNSSON

dent on June 17, 1944. He is Sveinn Björnsson, noted lawyer and diplomat, who until his presidency had served as Regent of Iceland since 1941.

Iceland's parliamentary system is the oldest in the world. The Althing, Iceland's legislative assembly, has been in almost continuous existence since the year 930. After the discovery of Iceland in the middle of the ninth century, Norsemen, Scots, and Irishmen settled there and in 1263 acknowledged the sovereignty of the King of Norway, at the same time maintaining their independence. Late in the fourteenth century, Iceland was brought into a union of the Scandinavian countries, Norway, Sweden, and Denmark. The Althing nevertheless continued to hold its sessions, and they were not brought to a halt until 1800 when the Althing was dissolved by Danish royal decree. Forty-three years later it was re-established, and it has flourished ever since.

Iceland was recognized an independent state in 1918, but it continued to recognize the Danish King as its monarch. With the outbreak of the Second World War, Iceland found itself in a strategic position guarding the sea lanes from the United States to Britain. On May 10, 1940, one month after the Nazis invaded Denmark, British troops moved into Iceland. When the Germans occupied Denmark, all connections with Denmark and its King were cut off. The Althing then declared that the Cabinet should exercise the royal functions, that Iceland should appoint her own diplomatic and consular representatives, and that it should defend her territorial waters. On June 14, 1941 the Althing elected Sveinn Björnsson as Regent.

The union between Iceland and Denmark rested on a treaty which expired on December 31, 1943. For four days, beginning on May 20, 1944, a popular referendum was held in Iceland in which about 97 per cent of the population voted for the abrogation of the treaty with Denmark and the re-establishment of the re-

publican form of government in Iceland. Iceland formally declared herself a republic on June 17, 1944, in the presence of special representatives of President Roosevelt [42] and King George VI [42], receiving also congratulations from the heads of most of the United Nations as well as from King Christian X [43] of Denmark. The first act of the new Parliament was to elect Sveinn Björnsson to the office of President, an act that was greeted with popular acclaim.

Iceland's first President has spent most of his life in the service of his island country. He was born in Reykjavik, February 27, 1881, the son of Björn and Elísabet (Sveinsdóttir) Jónsson. After studying at the Menntaskólinn School in Reykjavik, he went to Denmark, where he prepared for a career in law at the University of Copenhagen. Receiving his degree in 1907, Björnsson has had a distinguished career as a lawyer. He soon became a member of the bar of the Superior Court of Iceland. In 1920 he was admitted to practice before the Supreme Court, where he won valuable experience in international law. This knowledge was to become helpful to him when he later entered the diplomatic service.

Björnsson's first political post was as member of the City Council for Reykjavik; he later became president of the Council, an office which he held from 1912 to 1920. In 1914 he was elected to the Althing, served until 1916, and was re-elected in 1920. Meanwhile he was participating in several important diplomatic missions. He was special envoy to the United States in 1914 where he obtained for his country medicines, grain, and other goods which could not be imported from Europe because of the German and British blockades. One year later Björnsson was special envoy to London where he arranged the first trade agreement Iceland had negotiated with Great Britain. His most important diplomatic post was as minister to Denmark, a position which he filled, except for a brief interruption, from 1920 to 1941.

A firm believer in cooperation among the nations of the world, he headed the Icelandic delegation to the Genoa Conference in 1922 and, again, to the Monetary and Economic Conference in London in 1933. In 1930 he attended the Hague Conference for the Codification of International Law. He has negotiated commercial treaties for Iceland with Great Britain, the United States, Norway, Germany, Spain, Italy, and Greece.

Shortly after the military agreement between Iceland and the United States had been ratified in July 1941, Björnsson sent a message to President Roosevelt in which he emphasized the close cultural ties between his nation and the United States: "We recall that the great nation of the United States has always held on high the flag of liberty and democracy, which we, the nations of Scandinavian origin, history, language, and culture, respect so greatly."

In August 1944, two months after he had become President of Iceland, Björnsson visited the United States. At that time, in speaking of the agreement between the two republics, he said: "In the agreement, the United States pledged that immediately upon termination of the present international emergency all such military and naval forces will be at once withdrawn, leaving the people of Iceland and their Government in full sovereign control of their own territory. I have never had any doubt on this point. We know that the agreement will be carried out to the letter. . . . Developments have now been such that our relations with the United States have expanded greatly, in commercial, cultural and other fields."

In November, back in Iceland, Björnsson gave an interview to twelve visiting American newspapermen in which he again spoke of the closer ties with the United States, particularly in the development of air traffic. As summarized by Carl Levin in the New York *Herald Tribune*, "Iceland will welcome an important role, because of her strategic position, in peacetime international aviation, and she is looking to the United States for aid in building up her state air line." In a *Christian Science Monitor* dispatch, "Icelanders See Independence Linked to Continuing U.S. Tie," Albert D. Hughes reported that authoritative opinion in Iceland indicated that American military "occupation" had been found unburdensome to Iceland, "that United States troops have conducted themselves with credit, and that Iceland's economy has benefited from the occupation."

Björnsson has had business as well as political interests. He was president of the board of directors of the Icelandic Steamship Company from 1914 to 1920. In 1918 he was made director of the Fire Insurance Company and president of the board of directors of the Sea Insurance Company. He held both offices until 1920. In addition he has been a member of the bar association and president, from 1924 to 1926, of the Icelandic Red Cross.

Since 1908 Björnsson has been married to Georgia Hoff-Hansen whom he had met when he was studying law in Copenhagen. She has taken an important part in the women's movements in Iceland. The names of their six children are Björn, Anna, Henrik, Sveinn, Olafur, and Elisabet. A man of simple tastes, Björnsson's hobbies are salmon angling and golf. He is described as "of middle height, bulky without being fat, and of a very distinguished appearance." Like so many Icelanders he writes a fine prose and delivers his speeches expertly, "with a fire and eloquence that make him an outstanding orator."

Reference

International Who's Who 1942

BLAIR, DAVID H. Jan. 13, 1868—Sept. 12, 1944 Ex-commissioner of Internal Revenue of the United States Government, position he held from 1921 to 1929; was responsible for a simplification of the method of auditing income tax payments.

Obituary

N Y Times p23 S 14 '44 por

BOARDMAN, MABEL (THORP) Honorary secretary of the American National Red Cross
Address: h. 1801 P St., Washington, D.C.

In 1900 the American National Red Cross, then nearly nineteen years old, was a small society of 300 members, and its one-room of-

MABEL BOARDMAN

fice was managed by one employee. Forty-four years later, its senior and junior membership has increased to 29,000,000, it is housed in a white marble building near Washington's Potomac Park, and its officers, committee members, incorporators, and directors of services and activities form a roster of imposing names. This expansion is acknowledged to be largely the work of Mabel Boardman, "the administrative genius" of the American Red Cross. While 1940 marked Miss Boardman's retirement from the directorship of the department known as Volunteer Special Services, her years of service were not over. She still continued to be the national secretary of the American Red Cross and a member of its central committee—geared for the swift emergency action of another World War—until her retirement on December 13, 1944, when she became honorary secretary and honorary member of the central committee.

Of "distinguished family antecedents," Mabel Thorp Boardman was born in Cleveland, Ohio, the daughter of William Jarvis and Florence (Sheffield) Boardman. Following her education in private schools in Cleveland, New York, and in Europe, she was introduced to Washington society in those Victorian days when a young unmarried lady's activities were definitely circumscribed. Her life was not destined to remain within narrow limits, however, for her energy and imagination had already marked her for public service. In 1900, when Congress granted the American Red Cross a federal charter, Miss Boardman's name was placed on the organization's board of incorporators without her knowledge. It soon became clear that the young society woman's name was not merely to adorn the managerial roll of the Red Cross. She immediately put to work her talent for organizing, her grasp of details, and her unflagging enthusiasm, qualities that were given even wider scope when the growing importance of the organization demanded a new charter and

BOARDMAN, MABEL—*Continued*

a reincorporation, by Act of Congress in 1905. This placing of the Red Cross under government supervision obligated it "to serve the armed forces in time of war; to give voluntary relief, and to act in accord with military and naval authorities as a medium of communication between the people of the United States and their Army and Navy, or between the national societies of other governments; and to carry on a system of national and international relief in time of peace and to apply it in mitigating the suffering caused by disasters, and to devise and carry on measures for preventing these."

In less than a dozen years Miss Boardman's work was recognized in America and in other countries: In 1909 she was decorated by the King of Sweden and the Italian Government; in 1911 she was awarded an honorary M.A. degree by Yale University; in 1912 she received a decoration from the Emperor of Japan. She was also to receive the honorary degree of LL.D. from Western Reserve University and from Smith College, and decorations from Belgium, Portugal, Serbia, and Chile. Her French decorations are the Medal of Merit, 1st Class, and the Légion d'Honneur. During her first years with the Red Cross Miss Boardman made trips abroad to study methods in other countries, and in 1915 appeared her book *Under the Red Cross Flag at Home and Abroad*. She was a delegate to the 8th, 9th, 15th, and 16th International Red Cross Conferences held at London, Washington, Tokyo, and London, respectively.

A number of Mabel Boardman's accomplishments have been described in magazines and newspapers. In 1913, after Miss Boardman obtained $800,000 through public subscription and an appropriation from Congress, the Red Cross built the first of its new buildings on a site as large as a city square; during the First World War, at Miss Boardman's insistence, the now familiar uniform was adopted, a step that added "immeasurably to the enthusiasm, discipline, and satisfaction of the thousands who joined the Red Cross"; she opposed the disbanding of the Red Cross legions after the War; in 1931 she stood firm against having the Red Cross exposed to the danger of political interference by objecting to the acceptance of $25,000,000 of federal money for drought relief; and over and above all, was the forming, under Miss Boardman's direction, of more than 3,000 local chapters and 6,000 branches, which are required to turn over only 50c of each membership's contribution to the national body.

It was as head of the Volunteer Special Services that Miss Boardman was for many years the director behind the scenes of the Red Cross ministrations. In the sober language of an annual report, it is the purpose of the Services to maintain in every chapter the regular Red Cross services to the community and to keep volunteers trained by year-round activity for prompt and efficient service in peacetime floods, fires, and tornadoes, and now in war. The Services include seven Corps, of which their names and functions are: the Staff Assistance Corps provides volunteer office workers for chapters and branches; the Can-

teen Corps is an organization of workers who are trained in mass feeding for emergencies; the Motor Corps is organized to furnish economical and efficient transportation whenever and wherever it is needed; the Home Service Corps is a group of aides (receptionists, clerical helpers, etc.) who assist the Home Service staff; the Volunteer Nurse's Aide Corps is prepared to assist the professional nurse in community and government hospitals or in clinics; the Hospital and Recreation Corps, which includes the Gray Ladies, provides friendly nonprofessional aid to ill or disabled servicemen and ex-servicemen; the Production Corps (with an enrollment of 2,580,000 volunteers) performs the service of sewing, knitting, and making surgical dressings, which is carried on as a permanent activity of the chapters throughout the country in peacetime. It is tremendously increased during wartime to meet local, national, and foreign relief needs. Upon Miss Boardman's retirement from the "generalship" of the 2,720,000 members of the Volunteer Special Services her work was described as "effective, unselfish, and an inspiration and encouragement to Red Cross workers."

When Admiral Cary T. Grayson died in 1938, Miss Boardman was urged to succeed to his position as national chairman of the Red Cross. She declined to accept the chairmanship, as she had many times before, giving as her reason: "If there ever arises any doubt about the conduct of the Red Cross or its finances, investigators might be inclined to go easy with a woman. A man would have to accept a merciless inquiry." (President Roosevelt then appointed Norman T. Davis [40] to the post; upon Davis' death in July 1944, Basil O'Connor [44] was appointed to the chairmanship.)

As national secretary and member of the central committee of the American Red Cross, Miss Boardman directed the major relief problems of the Second World War until her retirement in mid-December 1944. The War Fund drives were launched to meet the rapidly increasing war needs. (The 1943 public response reached $147,000,000.) The magnitude of the organization's work is revealed by a few items taken from a recent report: During the year ending June 30, 1943, $42,391,000 was expended for assistance to personnel of the armed forces, disabled veterans, and their families; 1,545,692 families of servicemen were helped; from January 1, 1941, to June 30, 1943, the value of relief supplies shipped to United Nations prisoners of war in Europe and the Far East amounted to more then $17,000,000. At the outbreak of the War Miss Boardman praised the cooperation between the American and Japanese Red Cross societies, such cooperation being the duties devolving upon national societies which had acceded to the International Red Cross Treaty of Geneva. In April 1944, however, Miss Boardman wrote in the *Prisoners of War Bulletin*, published by the Red Cross for the relatives of prisoners: "Events have shown that such efforts as the Japanese Red Cross has made have been submerged under the all-powerful influence of the Japanese military."

Miss Boardman's retirement from her active to honorary post was marked by a testimonial luncheon given by the board of incorporators of the American Red Cross in Washington on December 13, 1944. The many notables present witnessed the decoration of Miss Boardman by Chairman O'Connor with the first Distinguished Service Medal ever awarded by the Red Cross. To the citation, which paid tribute to her as "inspirer, leader, and practical idealist," and the letters of praise from President Roosevelt and former Chief Justice Charles Evans Hughes '41, Miss Boardman replied briefly and wittily. As one reporter described it, Miss Boardman, who is past her eightieth year, "underplayed her own important role in Red Cross activities during the years of war and catastrophe at home." These years will doubtless be fully described in her memoirs which she is writing.

Miss Boardman has been called the chief volunteer of the American Red Cross, for it is said she has never accepted a salary for her forty-five years of daily work and has drawn upon her own income for trips to Europe and elsewhere for study and conferences. One of her co-workers has said that "her mental processes are like the mixing of concrete. Her mind is fluid and unprejudiced in considering arguments. But when the facts are in and the chemistry of her logic had acted on them, her mind hardens. Once it set, nothing can change her." Miss Boardman herself is described as "straight as a ramrod, serene, and at ease, but with a touch of military alertness." She has long been "the most conspicuous figure at the national capital," for, in addition to her Red Cross activities, she served for one term on the Washington Board of Commissioners, the District of Columbia's governing body. Her strong tall figure, graying pompadour, and pearls worn in the tradition of the grand lady convey a startling resemblance to England's Dowager Queen Mary. A story told of that likeness dates from one of the visits of the former Prince of Wales. When he caught his first glimpse of Miss Boardman at a reception, he exclaimed "There's Mother!"

References

C S Mon p5 My 9 '40
N Y Sun p 21 Ap 18 '41
Read Digest 34:70-4 Ap '39
American Women 1939-40
Who's Who in America 1944-45

BOGUSLAWSKI, MOISSAYE (bō-gū-slof'skē mu-i-syä'i) Nov. 1, 1887—Aug. 30, 1944 Noted concert pianist and head of the Boguslawski College of Music in Chicago; performed as a soloist with the Metropolitan Opera Company orchestra, the Detroit and Minneapolis Symphony Orchestras; developed a method of musical therapeutics as a mind restorer for insanity; author of *Piano-Play,* a series of ten volumes for child music study; editor of *Moderne Edition,* a book of piano music.

Obituary

N Y Times p17 Ag 31 '44

BONNEY, (MABEL) THERESE (bən'nē tä-räz') Photographer; war correspondent
Address: h. 117 E. 30th St., New York City

"The creator of the world's most shocking book," according to one reviewer, is Thérèse Bonney, documentary photographer, journalist, and war correspondent, whose *Europe's Children* has been one of the sensations of the fall publishing season of 1943. "Certainly no other recent book carries [such] terrific impact. . . . None has been so sharply moving, so overwhelmingly heartbreaking. None has made the meaning of war, the Nazi attempt to conquer the world, so quickly clear, nor moved so many people to tears who were not moved by words or casualty lists. This is a picture book about war and oppression . . . in which the camera proves mightier than the pen."

THERESE BONNEY

Mabel Thérèse Bonney was born in Syracuse, New York, the daughter of Anthony Le Roy and Addie (Robie) Bonney. At the age of five she went to live in California, where she remained until she was graduated from the University of California. The next year she took her M.A. in Romance languages at Harvard, and then went to Columbia University to prepare for her Ph.D. But she finished her studies in Paris, one of ten Americans to take the degree of Docteur ès Lettres at the Sorbonne, where she passed the examination with the highest honors. Before going to Paris, Miss Bonney had collaborated with Jacques Copeau, founder and director of the Théâtre du Vieux Colombier, who had brought his group of actors to New York City. Scholastic honors awarded to Miss Bonney include the Horatio Stebbins Scholarship; the Belknap, Baudrillart, and De Billy Fellowships; and the Carl Schurz Memorial Foundation's Oberlaender grant in 1936 to study "Germany's contribution to the history of photography"— its role during the last hundred years as a means of disseminating information.

In the next twenty years Thérèse Bonney spent the greater part of her time abroad. Her

BONNEY, THERESE—*Continued*

original intention of becoming a professor had been replaced by the idea of developing cultural relations between France and the United States. She established the European branch of the American Red Cross's Correspondence Exchange between the children of Europe and the children of America—a project of the Junior Red Cross provided for by the National Children's Fund established in 1919 to continue the relief work for children begun in Europe during the First World War. Miss Bonney traveled all over Europe, lecturing in four languages, and helping to organize Junior Red Cross groups. This cultural exchange was very important, for the children of European countries learned about the American way of life, the handicrafts, sports, and school activities.

During this period, Miss Bonney, who had her headquarters in Paris, was a frequent contributor to newspapers and periodicals in England, France, and America. She founded the first American illustrated press service in Europe—the Bonney Service—serving the press of thirty-three countries with feature spreads and articles. Much of her life was spent with artists, writers, and musicians. She did not herself follow any of these professions, but wrote with taste and discrimination on various phases of the decorative arts and was noted as a collector of fine French furniture, old photographs, and modern painting.

In 1929 Robert M. McBride & Company published a series of guide books prepared by Thérèse Bonney in collaboration with her sister, Louise Bonney. The first of these books, *Buying Antique and Modern Furniture in Paris*, was written with a collector's loving appreciation of the old, but also contained an exposition of the modern tendency in French furniture and *décor* of the twenties. These two interests are not so incompatible as might be thought, for, as the authors remind us, the antique furniture of today was the modern furniture of yesterday. In one of their lighter moments, the Bonneys gave instructions for discovering a little shop "where you search, and find, perhaps, a quaint old oil portrait, for an additional ancestor." There followed *A Shopping Guide to Paris* and a *Guide to the Restaurants of Paris*. The information in these books is now somewhat dated, but a fourth book is good for all time. It is *French Cooking for American Kitchens*. "A glance at any menu shows that the French love trouble," admit the Bonneys, but their culinary instructions have simplified the "trouble" enough to make most of the recipes practical.

A series of exhibitions evidenced Thérèse Bonney's gifts as an organizer. In November 1932 her own magnificent collection of photographs, many of them priceless, appeared under the title of "The Gay Nineties" at the Georges Petit Gallery in Paris, where it was "one of the outstanding events of the Grande Semaine," and later in New York, and various cities in the Midwest. The exhibition, which showed a cross section of *la vie*, as lived by all classes, but notably by European royalty," was also a record of Victorian fashion—"the feather boa, the pancake hat, the wasp waist, the taffeta bathing suit." "Art?" wrote Ed-

ward Alden Jewell, in the New York *Times*. "Maybe not, in the accepted, the sometimes rather stuffy, sense of the term. But Life!" A selection of these photographs was afterwards made into a book, *Remember When?* (1933), "a pictorial chronicle of the turn of the century and of the days known as Edwardian." Charles Dana Gibson, in the foreword, wrote: "M. Thérèse Bonney is rendering a unique service in preserving for us in photographs the history which isn't in the history books, but which is, nevertheless, of great social import. . . . Miss Bonney, in addition to her undoubted service to the social historian, has produced a book of charm and delight."

The following year Miss Bonney showed her collection of daguerreotypes at Knoedler's in New York in an exhibition called "The Second Empire," which commemorated the centenary of Nicéphore Niepce, inventor of photography. Niepce was closely associated with Louis Jacques Daguerre, the man who perfected the photographic process and whose name has since become a household word. Miss Bonney's collection was very choice, some of the examples being considered the finest in existence.

With the assistance of various patriotic societies, Thérèse Bonney directed the Lafayette Centenary Exhibition held in May 1934, the hundredth anniversary of the death of Lafayette. Chosen as the American delegate to a similar exhibition held in the Musée de l'Orangerie in Paris in July, Miss Bonney shared with Anne Morgan the distinction of being selected by the National Museums of France to collect the American relics of Lafayette. It was in the Orangerie, surrounded by the souvenirs of the great Revolutionary hero, that Henri Verne, Commander of the Légion d'Honneur, bestowed upon Thérèse Bonney the cross of the Légion in recognition of her untiring efforts to promote friendly understanding between the United States and France.

In the spring of 1935 a group of French and American leaders in art and education established in the Maison Française at Rockefeller Center a gallery of French art to foster cultural relations between France and America. Thérèse Bonney, director of the gallery, expressed the hope that the venture would be "an outstanding contribution to the civic and artistic life of New York City." For the opening exhibition Miss Bonney arranged a collection of portraits of famous Frenchwomen ranging from Jeanne d'Arc, by the classicist Ingres, to the Comtesse de Noailles, French poetess, painted by the modernist Vuillard. This exhibition was followed by a tribute to the liner *Normandie* and the ancient province for which she was named. Called "Normandie: The Province, Its People, and the Ship," the display celebrated the maiden voyage of the giant liner and was primarily ethnographical in character. In November of that year Miss Bonney directed a Napoleonic exhibition of memorabilia lent by various French museums and private collectors.

Becoming more and more exasperated with the poor quality and lack of dramatic content in the work of the photographers whom she employed in her picture-news service, Miss Bonney decided to take some pictures herself. The first big job she tackled was a behind-the-scenes sequence at the Vatican in 1938. Years before, she had tried to surmount the red tape involved in such an undertaking and had had to relinquish the idea. But in time the difficulties had been resolved. This venture resulted in an extensive series of photographs first brought out as a ten-page display in *Life* Magazine, and later made into a book, *The Vatican* (1939), with an introduction by the Reverend John La Farge [42]. The captions and descriptive text were written by Miss Bonney. Her career as a photographer was now assured, and as one reporter said, "The world was her oyster."

In 1939 Thérèse Bonney scooped the Russo-Finnish War. When other journalists were hurrying to the Balkans, she had gone to Finland on a "hunch," intending to photograph the preparations for the Olympic games which were to be held in Finland, but shot instead the great Finnish maneuvers at Karelia, where she was the only foreigner present, other than military attachés, and the only journalist permitted to interview and photograph Field Marshal Mannerheim [40] and his staff. As a result of her premonition she was in Finland at the outbreak of the War. In a letter to Anne Morgan (in the New York *Herald Tribune*) she wrote: "It is hard, hard work—bristling with risks—lucky if you come out of it, but a magnificent chance to contribute your brains and talent to a great cause, the world's—really a privilege." She described how she had slept only five hours in four days—motored all night for three nights running and one whole day, hiding in the forest or rolling in the snow when Russian planes appeared overhead. At the end of this particular trip the Finns decided, unofficially, that Miss Bonney possessed the "famous Finnish quality of *sisu* (a combination of guts plus grit)." Officially, at the request of Marshal Mannerheim, she was decorated with the highest order of Finland, the White Rose, an honor seldom accorded to a woman. While in Finland Miss Bonney was asked to help untangle an international press dispute and to mediate a strike of 150 foreign correspondents.

Thérèse Bonney left Scandinavia in 1940 just before the Nazi invasion, and went to France where she worked with the American Red Cross and with Anne Morgan's unit of the American Friends of France. At the Franco-Belgian frontier she helped with the evacuation of refugees day and night under bombardment. Finally "the refugee situation became impossible" and she went to Paris. In June 1940 she took the official photograph of General Weygand [40], receiving *carte blanche* for the Front, with car, gasoline, and telephone privileges. She was the only foreign correspondent at the Battle of the Meuse and she made the most complete record of the Battle of France. Retreating with the 9th Army, she at last reached Bordeaux.

Back in the United States she arranged an exhibition of her photographs for the Library of Congress, entitled "To Whom the Wars Are Done," showing the impact of the War upon the common man. Archibald MacLeish [40], in a preface to the exhibition, wrote: "Miss Bonney's photographs are exhibited in this library of a democratic people not only because they are eloquent and moving photographs but because they speak for the anonymous human beings to whom the wars are done.

"In these quiet and unarguing photographs the people's cause—the one eternal cause which neither force of arms nor fraud of lies can conquer—finds its words."

This exhibit was shown at the Museum of Modern Art in New York under the title "War Comes to the People," and then toured the United States.

Several scholars considered that Miss Bonney's work constituted a definite contribution to the raw materials of scholarship. And the Carnegie Corporation of New York made her a grant to ensure her return to Europe to photograph the aftermath of war and its impact on the civilian population. The grant stipulated that copies of each of the photographs taken should be deposited in the Library of Congress for a permanent record to be used for research.

When Thérèse Bonney started for Europe in February 1941 she took with her a basic outfit designed by a well known men's tailoring firm. "A woman needs to wear pants in War," she said, and then explained that the ski suit she had worn the year before had sometimes aroused suspicion that she might be a parachutist. The photographic equipment she uses for her "Truth Raids," as she calls her photographic expeditions, is very simple—an automatic Rolleiflex, Super-XX film, a flashgun, a synchronizer, and an exposure meter. She does not like to be bothered with a lot of gadgets and says that in her work the camera is incidental.

On this trip she went from Portugal to Spain, where she found that Death was playing a return engagement. During the Civil War death had come from bombs and bullets, but later hunger and disease took their toll. The straits to which the proud Spaniards have been reduced can be inferred from Miss Bonney's description of the way famished people would slip by, as she sat on a café terrace, and steal a bit of food from her plate. "*Hambre, señorita, hambre*," they would whisper, in extenuation. A caption from one of her photographs—"How aged the young look and how hopeless the old!"—makes a poignant comment on the tragic condition of the population.

In May 1941 Miss Bonney received the Croix de Guerre, with star, from the French Minister of War, General Huntziger. In Unoccupied France just as the first American Red Cross shipload of flour and canned milk was received, she witnessed its distribution to the French people. She also visited the schools where the Quakers operated their school-lunch program. In one school the children had made a picture book with colored crayons, in which Miss Bonney was portrayed as the Statue of Liberty, with her flash-bulb for a torch.

Later that same summer Miss Bonney spent several days with Gertrude Stein in her little cottage at a village called Bilignin par Belley Ain, near Grenoble. She felt that finding this writer who had loved the French people

BONNEY, THERESE—*Continued*

enough to remain with them in the tragedy of defeat was an important part of the task she had set herself—"looking for the great French artists of the pre-War world, the masters of the École de Paris." This quest took her to a small town in the south of France where she found Raoul Dufy in a sanatorium, badly crippled with rheumatism. On his first day out of bed, Miss Bonney and the doctor took him to spend the day with Aristide Maillol '43 the sculptor. They carried their own food—salad oil, a tiny pat of butter, wine, and a steak that represented all the meat ration tickets of Miss Bonney and her secretary for fifteen days and the doctor's family for one day. "Maillol grilled the steak over the fire of grapevine faggots and made a *saupiquet* of boiled white beans, garlic, and parsley, an incredible dish which is a specialty of the Basque country." Miss Bonney tried to persuade Dufy to return to America with her, but he refused to leave his country. But she did succeed in bringing back to America the water colors of roses that Dufy had created in his special "rhymed calligraphy." These pictures make the bare white walls of the studio in her New York apartment flame with luscious color.

Miss Bonney had made a record of blitzed England in 1941. In 1942, on her way back to Finland as a "lone wolf" correspondent for *Collier's*, she returned to England where she was the guest of Lord and Lady Astor '40 at Cliveden. Also at Cliveden were the George Bernard Shaws. Miss Bonney found Shaw "an irresistible exponent of the Lost Art of Conversation," who frequently gave out "pithy philosophy" at the breakfast table. "Today, people know the XYZ of everything," she quoted him as saying, "but they don't know the ABC." An enthusiastic photographer, he turned the tables on her when she tried to take his picture, and he himself made a little series on Thérèse Bonney. But she never saw the results, for Shaw sent her a letter with the information that the negatives had been "slightly overexposed." The moral of a week spent with G.B.S., according to Miss Bonney, is: "Don't let the passing of years—or anything else—dull your sense of humor."

The pictures that Miss Bonney took in Finland to add to her progressive war panorama —she was the first American correspondent to go there after the outbreak of the Russo-German war—include not only the battlefields, but also the shattering effects of war on Finnish children, and the determined efforts at reconstruction. In an article in *Collier's* she reported that everywhere she went she heard the words, *ei ole*—"no more." Never a land of abundance, Finland had been exhausted by three years of war and invasion. People were living on a scanty diet of potatoes and fish, and the babies were clothed in paper. On this trip Miss Bonney completed the sequence of photographs that she had spent four years in taking—the photographs that make *Europe's Children* so arresting a document, exposing to the world "the souls of helpless children under the awful shadow of total war." In a review in *Popular Pho-*

tography Bruce Downes compared these pictures to Goya's famous series on "The Disasters of War," but Miss Bonney replaces the sardonic Spaniard's cruel wit with "terrible pity." "Her picture story moves like a living drama to a . . . climax of overpowering poignancy."

Enlarged photographs from *Europe's Children* were on exhibit during the month of October 1943 for the benefit of the Coordinating Council of French Relief Societies, Inc., and later were sent to schools all over the United States.

This "unforgettable book" that shows "what Fascism does to children" was brought out by Thérèse Bonney herself, after ten publishers had refused it. "I look upon this book as the payment of my debt to those countries that are prisoners," she said. In January 1944, when the private edition of 2,000 copies had been exhausted in a "record breaking sell-out," Duell, Sloan & Pearce, Inc., published a trade edition.

After many months of crowded activities in New York, the "intrepid" Miss Bonney, who has crossed the Atlantic 104 times, is engrossed in preparations for her next expedition. She plans to go to Africa to continue her photographic record of the War and its impact on civilization. In the spacious living room of her New York apartment, packing cases and photographic equipment jostled some elegant little chairs whose green satin upholstery reflected the prevailing color in the Léger '43-designed rug. Five portraits of Miss Bonney dominated the scene. The one by Dufy is classed with the finest modern portraiture. Hung near it is a graciously beautiful portrait of Thérèse Bonney by Lurçat, while on another wall three interpretations by Georges Rouault present a strong contrast.

The dark-haired, vivacious photographer discussed her intention of experimenting with motion-picture technique. "The tempo and approach are quite different from that used for stills," she said, but she thinks that the results will be rewarding. She also spoke of the book on France that she was preparing with Antoine de St. Exupéry '40, which was interrupted when "St. Ex" went back to the Front. Now she feels that she wants to wait until she can show also the reconstruction of France— the "country of her adoption." And so Thérèse Bonney, who feels that "the most powerful propaganda is truth," prepares again to catch the dramatic moment "in this most momentous moment of the world's history."

References

C S Mon p6 F 18 '41 il por; p8 Mr 2 '43
N Y Herald Tribune V p5 F 28 '43
N Y Post Mag p7 O 27 '43
N Y World-Telegram p10 O 5 '43 por
Popular Photography p38+ D '43
Vogue Jl 1 '43
Women of Achievement 1940

BONO, EMILIO (GIUSEPPE GASPARE GIOVANNI) DE (bō'no ā-mē'lyō dä) 1866—Jan. 11, 1944 Commander in chief

of the Italian troops in East Africa (1935); chief of police and commander Fascist Militia

(1922); governor of Tripolitania (1925); high commissioner for Italian colonies in East Africa (January-November 1935); Marshal of Italy and Minister of State; Senator; reportedly executed by German firing squad.

Obituary

N Y Times p5 Ja 12 '44

BONOMI, IVANOE (bō-nô'mē) 1873-
Premier of Italy

Address: Rome, Italy

On June 22, 1944 "a tall, bespectacled man with a salt and pepper goatee" who had been chairman of the formerly underground Committee of National Liberation in Rome took the oath of office as Premier of the new Italian Government. Politically an Independent of moderately liberal views, before the rise of Mussolini '42 he served in many Italian Governments—twice as Minister of Public Works, once as Minister of Finance, once as Minister of War—and from July 1921 to February 1922 he was Premier of his country. With Count Sforza '42 he negotiated the Treaty of Rapallo and received the Supreme Order of Saint Annunziata.

Ivanoe Bonomi was born in Mantua, Italy, in 1873, the son of working-class parents. He taught school, then put himself through a law course, and when he was elected to the Chamber of Deputies from Ostiglia it was as a Socialist. At the Congress of Imola in September 1902 the Italian Socialist Party split into two wings—the Reformist and the Revolutionary—and he became one of the leaders of the first-named faction. For some time he helped to edit the Party paper, *Avanti*, but during the First World War he was expelled from the Socialist Party for advocating entrance into the War on the side of the Allies, and his post was taken over by Mussolini. He continued in politics as a moderate, however, and held several Cabinet posts both during and after the War. In 1916 he became Minister of Labor under Boselli; in 1919, a Minister in the Orlando '44 Cabinet; and for a short time he was a member of the Nitti Cabinet in 1920. He then entered the Giolitti Cabinet as Minister of War, and for a time worked with Badoglio '40 on a temporary reorganization of the Army. The next year he became Minister of Finance.

This was the time of great industrial strikes and of acts of Fascist violence in reprisal against the workers. Giolitti legitimized the Fascist terror, in which the Italian police connived; and his Government finally fell. In midyear of 1921 Ivanoe Bonomi became Premier of Italy, with a broad coalition Cabinet which included the *Popolari* (the Catholic Popular Party). Actually the Cabinet was under the rule of Don Sturzo, secretary of the *Popolari*. It did not take strong measures against the Fascists, who continued to attack the workers although the number of strikes in 1921 was only about one-half the number of the year before; and on August 3, 1921 Bonomi managed to patch up a peace covenant between the Socialist and Fascist members of Parliament. Mussolini's supporters, however, refused to stay in line, and Mussolini himself finally agreed to bury the covenant. In February of 1922 the Government fell because of dissension among the Liberals and the *Popolari* and a grave economic difficulty among the banks. One historian of this period calls Bonomi "a well-intentioned but vacillating Reformist-Socialist." It was during the administration of his successor that Mussolini's march on Rome took place.

Before 1910 Bonomi had written two books —on local finance and socialism. In 1924 he brought out another book, *Dal socialismo al fascismo* ("From Socialism to Fascism"). In it he commented: "When, in November 1918, the victory announced to the Italians their just prize for the sacrifices and struggles suffered, the Socialist Party was like a somnambulist who suddenly wakes up in a place he did not ever expect to be." He was sharply critical of the Socialist Party and its tactics during the period in which Mussolini's Blackshirts rose to power. The same year (1924) he made his last political speech denouncing Fascism, then retired from public life. It was never necessary for him to leave Italy, however, and he did not, but lived there in poverty on a meager pension, helping other lawyers with their briefs. It was not until 1944 that he emerged from obscurity—but when the Nazis were driven out of Rome it was revealed that he had been acting as the chairman of the Rome's Committee of National Liberation, the organization of Rome's party leaders. Early in June, when liberation leaders of Rome refused to serve under Marshal Badoglio because of his past association with Fascism and Badoglio retired, leaders of the six resistance parties got together and unanimously chose Bonomi as the new head of the Government.

Bonomi, who also took over the Ministry of Foreign Affairs and of the Interior, on June 9 filled the rest of the offices in his Cabinet with men who had no Fascist past to live down, dividing the seats about equally between underground liberation leaders who had operated in Rome during the German occupation and the anti-Fascist leaders of southern Italy who had joined Badoglio's Cabinet two months before to give it a broader base. All six of Italy's liberation parties were represented— Communist, Liberal, Christian Democratic, Social Democratic, Actionist, Socialist. Benedetto Croce '44, Count Sforza, and Palmiro Togliatti, who had been in the Badoglio Government, continued in Bonomi's Cabinet without portfolio. Said Bonomi: "Our program is brief. For the moment we are not considering social reforms, except insofar as we shall set up a completely democratic government. The one program we have all agreed upon is to intensify Italy's military effort in the war against Fascism." He also said that the question of the monarchy had been put off until after the War: the King had "half-resigned," and Prince Umberto '43 had given the new Government an absolutely free hand. Neither the United States nor Britain, he added, had sought to influence any of the decisions. He paid tribute to Badoglio, but said that he was not inviting the Marshal to join the Cabinet "because I have no place in it for anybody who has been compromised by Fascism or connected with Fascism in any way."

Bonomi's Government then returned to Salerno, but it was some days before the Allied Governments gave it their approval. The Greeks, the Yugoslavs, and the Russians were

BONOMI, IVANOE—*Continued*

reportedly satisfied with Bonomi's Government, but it was rumored that Churchill '42 was angered by General Sir Harold R. L. G. Alexander '42 for not only accepting Bonomi but giving practically no support to Badoglio in the new Government. Before accepting Bonomi and his Cabinet, the British Prime Minister was said to be insisting that each member of the new Cabinet sign the armistice (which both Badoglio and the King had previously signed) and accept its terms *in toto*. In spite of such rumors, on June 19 the Allied Advisory Council recognized Bonomi's Government, and on June 22 the new Government became official—without Badoglio.

On July 15, 1944, Bonomi took his Cabinet back to Rome after its protracted exile in Salerno. *Time* Magazine described the Cabinet's first meeting as "an unhappy, feckless affair. . . . It administered under the cloud of defeat, under the weight of the Allies' unpublished armistice." A few days later, reported the New York *Times* correspondent, Bonomi asked that the armistice terms be published, making it clear that Italy expected a modification of the "very stern" terms according to the contribution of Italy in the struggle against Germany.

The armistice terms rigidly limited the scope of Italian self-rule. However, the AMG gradually increased the authority of the new Government, and on August 15 the administrative authority of Rome and two adjacent provinces (about one-third of Italy) was given to the Bonomi Government. Although this gave the Italians direct responsibility for local administration and the power to make their own appointments to various public posts, AMG remained as an advisory-supervisory body.

Bonomi's Government almost from the start was faced with difficulties. Croce's withdrawal was one of the first indications of political trouble among the six political parties represented in the Cabinet. "There have been suggestions," reported the *Christian Science Monitor*, "that Croce felt the Leftist character of the Bonomi Government was too pronounced and therefore not representative of the political attitude of the Italian masses." Rightist elements then began an active campaign against the Government. "Significantly," remarked the *Monitor*, this "campaign . . . began with the gradual political emergence of former Premier Vittorio Orlando, who for two months—presumably with the full support of the Vatican—has been laying the groundwork for a new monarchist party."

On August 14 it was reported that negotiations were far advanced to replace the Bonomi Government with a "national concentration" Cabinet headed by Orlando, with Badoglio for Foreign Minister, and that Bonomi would receive a "consolation prize" of the most difficult job in the Cabinet—the Ministry of National Reconstruction. (The chief flaw in the plan was the refusal of the Communists and Socialists to participate in the proposed Government.) *PM* offered an explanation for the movement: "The Republican and Democratic Parties are afraid the six-party, anti-Fascist coalition, which is the backbone of the Bonomi Cabinet, is monopolizing the political field; an important group of Britons wants

IVANOE BONOMI

to see Italian monarchy represented in the Cabinet." But the Orlando boom collapsed, and on September 13 Pietro Nenni, the Socialist leader, announced in *Avanti* that the Socialist Party was willing to take power, and that after Milan had been freed the time would come for a solution to Italy's problem in other than the six-party rule under Bonomi.

On September 26 Bonomi averted a governmental crisis when he announced he would stay in office only if all six major parties loyally supported him, and all the Ministers accepted the Premier's condition. The New York *Times'* opinion was that Bonomi was in a strong position because he knew that no one else wanted to assume the thankless task of running the Government until northern Italy was freed.

In his foreign policy Bonomi showed that it was his aim to establish close and friendly relations with both Yugoslavia and France. The first public declaration of foreign policy by any member of his Cabinet was made by Count Carlo Sforza on August 20. He proposed that the port of Fiume, long a bone of contention between Italy and Yugoslavia, be made one of the seats of a super-League of Nations; that Trieste be retained by Italy, and that the port be internationalized under a consortium in which the Yugoslavs would feel themselves as much masters as the Italians. He further declared: "Italy owes atonement to Greece. . . . If the population of the Dodecanese Islands wishes to be annexed to Greece, we shall welcome this." In speaking of the African colonies he said, "Even in the interests of Western powers the colonies should be left to Italy. It never pays to violate a nation's rights." In a speech on September 13 Marshal Tito '43 claimed for Yugoslavia the Istrian and Slovene coastal areas, which would include Trieste. In addition, Italy's hope of retaining its colonies was blasted when Churchill stated in Parliament in September that Italy's empire "has been lost—irretrievably lost." Although the statement evoked a sharp reaction in Italy, Bonomi made no statement. (His Government under Allied armistice terms has no power to decide long-term foreign policies.)

Diplomatic relations with Italy were resumed by the United States and Great Britain in October (the Soviets previously had extended recognition to Bonomi's Government). In a speech to his Cabinet regarding this, Bonomi pleaded that "this formal action be given a practical basis." He asked how the return of Italy to the community of nations was compatible with the regime of control established by the armistice. Italy, he said, had a voice in the concert of nations but "none in her own house." Edward R. Stettinius [40], then Acting Secretary of State, said that it was the policy of the United States to return to the Italian Government control over its internal affairs as soon as it was possible to do so. He declined to discuss the armistice terms on the grounds that they still had to be kept secret for military reasons; he pointed out that peace could finally be concluded with Italy only through action in Congress, and that the terms to be given to Italy would have to be discussed at the peace conference after the War. Diplomatic recognition, he said, had been made because of the loyal cooperation of the Italian people and armed forces during the year, and in recognition of the founding of a healthy Government in Rome.

A number of significant factors contributed to the recurring political crisis during Bonomi's regime and led to his resignation on November 26. A *Newsweek* correspondent reported that in his opinion the people of Rome were suffering far worse hardships under the Allies than under the Germans and Fascists. Their troubles, he explained, were not actually due to either the Bonomi Government nor to the AMG. The real culprits were the Germans, who had stolen the trucks needed to bring food into Rome and who had blown up the great hydroelectric plants. Yet, disillusioned and confused, the Italians were inclined to blame their new Government and the Allies. Another unsettling factor was that the Leftists were convinced that there would be no change in the British attitude toward Italy's political problems, that the conservative trend might well become even more pronounced.

But one of the immediate causes of the last crisis was an interview Prince Umberto gave to Herbert L. Matthews [43] of the New York *Times*. "While obviously pleading for a plebiscite—Italian Monarchists would prefer a plebiscite to the constituent assembly demanded by the anti-Fascist parties—the Crown Prince emphasized that, in his opinion, the Italian monarchy must move Left." The interview caused a storm of indignation among the leaders of the anti-Fascist coalition. Bonomi's Cabinet tried to avoid a crisis by issuing a statement that the constitutional issue would be decided through a vote of a constituent assembly, but the debate preceding that statement led to a split among the coalition parties.

Another reason contributing to the split in the Government was the conflict of demands. The Communists, Socialists, and (with reservations) the Action Party, which has been described as militantly democratic without being either Socialist or Communist, were demanding a republic, a drastic purge of Fascists, and a strong dose of Socialism; the three other parties were for retaining the monarchy, purging with caution, and effecting social reforms without revolution.

In accordance with Italian constitutional procedure, Bonomi in presenting his resignation to Umberto also presented the resignations of all members of his Cabinet. In Herbert L. Matthews' opinion, Bonomi by his resignation had forced the issue which subsequently returned the Crown Prince to his constitutional position of genuine head of the State, and which gave him the power to summon the next candidate for the premiership. (Bonomi's first Government was formed without Umberto being consulted.)

Among the names suggested for the premiership was Count Sforza's, who had already accepted the appointment as Ambassador-designate to Washington. The British, who had expressed their disapproval of him for Foreign Minister in the first Bonomi Cabinet, immediately vetoed him for the position, and later for that of Foreign Minister. Foreign Secretary Anthony Eden [40] before the House of Commons declared that Sforza had been disloyal both to the Badoglio and the Bonomi Governments. Although Bonomi defended Sforza, saying that his long and close friendship with the Count did not permit him to believe that he had been disloyal, Eden repeated his contention. Most observers thought that England's move had been designed to force selection of a second and a more conservative Bonomi Cabinet. On December 4 it was reported that the Italian crisis would end within a few days and that Bonomi would head a new Government backed by all parties of the Committee of National Liberation, except the Action Party (of which Sforza is a leader). But by December 5 the Italian crisis had developed into an international crisis. United States Secretary of State Stettinius (backed by the President) administered a "sharp rebuke" to Britain by declaring that the United States expected the Italians to form a Government "without influence from the outside." The rebuke was made with the conviction that Britain was violating the spirit of the agreements reached at Moscow (1943) by the United States, Britain, and the U.S.S.R.—non-interference with liberal movements in reconstructed governments. Moreover, in exercising his veto of Sforza, Eden had acted without notifying the United States through the Italian Advisory Commission or the Allied Armistice Control Commission, mechanisms set up for precisely such a situation. The Socialist Party, which had expressed its willingness to support a new Cabinet, now turned its wrath upon Bonomi. On December 9 Bonomi presented the list of proposed Ministers for a Government to be formed by four members of the former six-party coalition—the Action and Socialist Parties refused to join—to the Allied Commission, and on December 12 Bonomi was again sworn in and Togliatti became Vice-Premier. (Count Sforza's refusal of the United States ambassadorship was accepted by the new Cabinet on December 20, and a week later he was retired from his post as High Commissioner for the Epuration, in which he had been responsible for the purging of Fascists.)

(Continued next page)

BONOMI, IVANOE—*Continued*

"Notwithstanding numerous Communist assertions to the contrary," observed the *Christian Science Monitor*, "the second Bonomi Government appears to have become part of a new setup, where it plays second fiddle to the Lieutenant General of the Realm, Crown Prince Umberto, and has the full support of Prime Minister Churchill, the strongly pro-monarchic Italian Army and Navy, and the most conservative sections of the Italian bourgeoisie." The New York *Times* correspondent, however, believed that the two key parties in the new Government were the Communists and the Christian Democrats, the latter the outgrowth of the old Popular Party, which might be called "the Christian Left, as opposed to the Marxist Left."

References

N Y Herald Tribune II p3 Je 25 '44 por
N Y Post p10 Je 9 '44
N Y Times p1+ Je 9 '44
International Who's Who 1942

BOSE, SUBHAS CHANDRA (bōs shəb-häsh' chun'drə) 1897- Indian politician

The only Indian Nationalist leader of any prominence to be won over by the Axis, Subhas Chandra Bose, is in 1944 head of the Japanese-sponsored "provisional government of India" and the commander of an Indian "army of liberation" accompanying the Japanese forces in eastern India. He is called "the greatest and most sinister Axis figure of the war in Asia." Yet this is the same man whom the fervently anti-Axis Nehru [41] was calling "dear and trusted comrade" not very many years ago, and whose early career paralleled Nehru's in many respects. His seems to be the story of an ambitious man guided by an intense hatred of the British.

Subhas Chandra Bose was born in Cuttack, Bengal, in 1897, the son of Jankinath Bose, a lawyer of some means. Unlike Nehru, he is not a Brahman, but he is a high-caste Hindu, and he received an education in keeping with his caste and his father's position. He was only five when sent to the Protestant European School at Cuttack, where the favoritism shown to Anglo-Indians and the severity of his headmaster made him very unhappy. He was glad to leave seven years later to enter the Ravenshaw Collegiate School of Cuttack, even though he found himself under a handicap there: his ignorance of his native language, Bengali. (His studies had been chiefly in English before.) An excellent student, however, soon he was receiving the highest marks in Bengali, and he became a close and zealous student of the Sanskrit Scriptures. At sixteen he had a religious seizure and ran away from home, wandering for a year through the Himalayas and holy cities of India in search of spiritual revelation. His parents finally discovered his whereabouts only when he was stricken with typhoid fever and recognized by a friend who happened to be in the vicinity.

At this time Bose had little or no interest in politics; the famous bomb incident of 1908, the first of Indian terrorist activities, had impressed him only briefly. After his matriculation at Presidency College of Calcutta, however, he apparently became less mystically inclined. In 1916 a certain Mr. O., an English teacher at Presidency College, manhandled some of the boys; and the students replied with the first organized students' strike, in which Bose was one of the leaders. When Mr. O. persisted in his treatment of the boys he was thrashed by a group of them. Although nothing could be proved against Bose, he was nevertheless expelled. Going to the distinguished Bengal lawyer C. R. Das (later a leader in the Nationalist movement) for advice, Bose decided to continue his education abroad. He was sent to Scottish Church College in England and later to Fitzwilliam Hall, Cambridge, taking high honors at both. In 1920, having completed his studies, he tried for a berth in the Indian Civil Service and came out fourth on the list in the difficult examinations. At about this time, however, Gandhi [42] was beginning his first civil disobedience campaign in India. Making what seemed a courageous decision, Bose resigned from the Indian Civil Service in May 1921 and hurried back to his own country.

Eager to have his questions answered, Bose interviewed Gandhi on the day he arrived in India, July 16, 1921. It was not the Mahatma but C. R. Das who finally induced him to join the civil disobedience campaign, however—and in December 1921 young Bose went to jail for the first of a number of times for his Nationalist activities. Upon his release he became Das's right-hand man, for two years editing the Nationalist daily *Forward,* the Calcutta paper founded by Das and himself. His career was interrupted by his second arrest in October 1924, at which time he had already been elected chief executive officer of the Calcutta municipality. He held this post for three years, personally seeing to the efficiency of every department under him. In 1926 he was elected to the Bengal Legislative Council as well, and soon afterward arrested again and removed to a prison in Mandalay. This gave him the opportunity to learn Burmese, a language which was to be very useful to him later.

At this time Bose was known as a Socialist with extremist views as to Indian independence: two English-language newspapers in Calcutta described him as "the brains of the revolutionary conspiracy" and the "soul" of terroristic activities in Bengal. From prison he sued the newspapers for libel, and since nothing could be proved against him he was awarded damages several months later. By this time (1927) he had been elected president of the Bengal National Congress and, along with Nehru, one of the two general secretaries of the All-India National Congress, "the largest and most representative political body in India, made up of illiterates and intellectuals, trade unionists and industrialists, poor peasants and wealthy landlords, conservatives and radicals, Hindus and many Moslems—all bound together by their opposition to British rule." Right-wing leaders in the Congress, alarmed, turned to Gandhi the next year to secure the Congress' acceptance of their report shelving the earlier demand for complete independence in favor of dominion status. Nehru and Bose formed the Indian Independence League, and when the Congress met at the end of the year they offered a counterresolution insisting on the immediate aim of complete independence, but they were defeated.

That same year (1928) Bose had started the Bengal Students' Conference and had been elected city councillor in Calcutta. He proceeded to become active in the trade union movement, too, together with Nehru. When in 1929 his terms as member of the Bengal Legislative Council and as general secretary of the All-India National Congress expired, he was elected president of the All-India Trade Union Congress. (He also remained president of the Bengal National Congress and Calcutta city councillor.) In 1930 he added to his offices that of mayor of Calcutta, but the city had to be administered from the British prison cell in which he found himself again. Finally released, Bose was jailed again in January 1932 during the period of most severe British repression in India, when the Congress itself was outlawed. He had always been treated with less consideration than Nehru—the British still considered him a terrorist, "heart and brain" of the Bengal cult of bomb-throwers, who was using his Congress allegiance as a mere façade—and the rigors of prison life had given him tuberculosis by this time. Later in 1932 he was therefore released on account of his ill health. Vallabhbhai Patel, one of the most radical leaders of the Nationalist movement and the first president of the All-India Congress, persuaded him to come to "neutral" Vienna, where Patel himself was living in exile, also broken in health.

Almost equally attracted to Mussolini '42 and to Stalin '42, Bose had in 1932 begun to advocate *Samyavada* (equality), a single-party state with no room for the idle rich and with authoritarian discipline. He had publicly approved Gandhi's meeting with Mussolini after the abortive London Round Table Conference in 1931, only regretting that Gandhi had not remained in Rome longer to "cultivate more personal contacts," and so it was logical that Bose should accept an invitation from Mussolini to visit him in Rome. It was logical, too, that he should become more and more the advocate of force as the only way to win Indian independence. In the summer of 1933 he announced that "no self-respecting Asiatic would ever bow to the arrogance of the Nazi race theory," but within a very few months he himself was on friendly terms with certain prominent Nazis. He was quoted as having said privately: "Fascism is essentially militarism. It will inevitably lead to a new world war and will offer India a unique opportunity to emancipate herself from the British yoke." In the fall of 1933 both Patel and Bose claimed that the time had finally come for direct action, and from Vienna they launched a joint attack on Gandhi's policy of nonviolence. When not very long afterward Bose rushed home from Vienna to his dying father (too late, however, to see his father alive) he was submitted to irksome restrictions on his freedom of movement especially decreed by the Government of India for him.

SUBHAS CHANDRA BOSE

For a long time Bose and Nehru had shared the limelight more or less equally as the idols of radical Indian youth, but Bose's political influence was now somewhat dim besides that of Nehru—partly because he was not favored with Gandhi's confidence. Patel's death, however, gave Bose something of the prestige of Patel himself. In 1934 he served as president of the Bengal National Congress again; in 1937 as an alderman. Still known as a Leftist, in his writings (chief among them his autobiography, *The Indian Struggle, 1920-34,* published in England in 1935 but banned in India), he continued to observe the socialist line. But he made frequent trips to Germany to "study the situation" and received mysterious visitors from the Reich.

In 1937 the Congress Party obtained control in eight out of eleven provincial governments. A bitter battle in the Congress itself followed, Gandhi and other Right-wing leaders wanting the elected candidates actually to take office and the Left-wing group opposing this course. A compromise formulated by Gandhi was finally adopted and the Congress Ministries took office, but in February 1938 Bose was elected president of the Congress. He and other Left-wing members grew louder than ever in their denunciation of Gandhi's conservative and compromising policies, and when Bose ran for the presidency again in 1939 it was against a candidate nominated by Gandhi and the Right-wing majority on the Congress Working Committee. Demanding the immediate launching of a nationwide struggle against British rule, Bose was elected by a narrow margin—the first president of the Congress during the period of Gandhi's leadership to be elected without the Mahatma's approval. This deepened the rift between Right and Left, a rift that was only partially healed when a resolution was adopted reaffirming confidence in the leadership and policies of Gandhi and requiring the new president to nominate his Working Committee in accordance with Gandhi's wishes. Bose and Gandhi could not agree

BOSE, SUBHAS CHANDRA—*Continued*

on the composition of the new Working Committee, and in April 1939 Bose resigned his office.

Bose promptly organized his followers into the Forward Bloc, "the aims of which," according to Kate L. Mitchell, "were declared to be to ensure that the Congress Ministries were effectively subordinated to the provincial and All-India Congress Committees; to establish direct and close ties between the Congress and the working-class, peasant, and States Peoples' organizations; to raise a permanent Volunteer Corps; and to intensify the national struggle against the Federal Constitution. Bose and his followers also maintained that the country was fit for a nonviolent civil disobedience campaign, and was only waiting for a lead from Congress." According to Nehru, the Forward Bloc was intended to be almost a rival organization of the Congress and, though it "petered out after a while," it "added to the disruptive tendencies and the general deterioration. Under cover of fine phrases, adventurist and opportunist elements found platforms, and I could not help thinking of the rise of the Nazi Party in Germany. Their way had been to mobilize mass support for one program and then to utilize this for an entirely different purpose." Alfred Tyrnauer, in the *Saturday Evening Post*, says that Bose extended his dual organization (the Forward Bloc had its "storm troop" as well as its parliamentary aspects) all over the country and, in collaboration with German and Japanese agents, contacted the governments and political parties of neighboring states—Burma, Thailand, Malaya, Singapore, Indo-China, Iran, Afghanistan.

In September 1939 the British Viceroy declared India a co-belligerent, without the approval of the Indian people. The British Government in India was empowered to rule by decree. The Congress forsook provisional self-government in protest, and by March 1940 was demanding complete independence from Britain, but there was disagreement about using the weapon of civil disobedience in time of war. Bose and his Forward Bloc failed to approve of Gandhi's conciliatory attitude, and in July 1940—even before Gandhi had launched his program of individual civil disobedience—Bose was jailed on the charge of plotting to raze the famous Black Hole monument at Calcutta. In November, elected a member of the Indian Legislative Assembly, he requested his release long enough for the formal installation. The British Raj denied the appeal, and Bose went on a hunger strike. Afraid that he would die in jail, the British transferred him to his luxurious home on Elgin Road in the European section of Calcutta, under guard. There, according to *Time* Magazine, "he professedly abandoned his faith in European medical science, took up yoga exercises with such fervor that friends feared for his sanity." In January 1941 he disappeared—but there was nothing mystical about his destination: late that year he turned up in Germany.

In March 1942 the Axis opened up a "Bose barrage." The Japanese-controlled Bangkok radio ran off phonograph records of his voice, all inflammatory speeches beamed at India.

These were particularly effective when in August of that year even consistently anti-Axis Nationalist leaders were arrested by the British. By June 1943 the owner of the voice had reached Tokyo, his arrival timed to coincide with Japan's big political offensive—promises of "independence" for Burma and preparations for "independence" in the Philippines, the award of four Shan states to Thailand, and the attempt to "appease" Chungking. From Tokyo, Bose went to Singapore, and on the day that Sir Archibald Wavell [41] ascended the vice-regal throne in Delhi (October 1943) Bose proclaimed the establishment of his countergovernment. The powerful Singapore radio—formerly British—was turned over to him for recruiting and for the dissemination of Nationalist propaganda. He praised Gandhi, whom he had always criticized in the past, claiming that the Mahatma secretly sided with him. (Chiang Kai-shek [40], too, he said, was fundamentally sympathetic to the Japanese—he had simply bowed to British and American coercion.) In addition, Bose had very real Indian grievances to play upon. He charged the British with deliberately depriving the Indians of food in order to "teach them a lesson," and offered the Indian Government 100,000 tons of rice to be delivered as the Government saw fit, professing astonishment when his offer was ignored.

Since there are fewer than 200,000 radio receiving sets in all of India, the effectiveness of this propaganda could be overestimated. Bose, however, also declared that he had agents at work in India, claiming Calcutta, the capital of Bengal, as the center of his underground organization and boasting that he was responsible for all the sabotage, rioting, and assassinations being committed behind the British lines guarding India's eastern frontier. Furthermore, the Japanese held about 60,000 Indian prisoners of war, who were subjected to constant propaganda telling how a victorious Japan would liberate India and how they must compose the vanguard of the "army of liberation." Setting his goal at 300,000 men, Bose announced the formation of such an army and started a vigorous drive to recruit Indians in Japanese-dominated territory, including Burma and Thailand. "On to Delhi!" was to be their battle-cry, and Indians in British India were to prepare themselves for the great day of "liberation." "Don't worry about arms and ammunition," Bose broadcast. "They will come. Do all you can to form widespread secret organizations. Brace yourself for action and sacrifice." It is thought that Bose may have as many as 30,000 Indians in his army.

A bland, plump bachelor, myopic and clean-shaven, Subhas Chandra Bose has a face which has always reminded Krishnalal Shridharani [42] "of the face of the Buddha as conceived by Chinese artists." Writes Johannes Steel [41]: "He is a forceful speaker, and his writing, though not of as high a literary quality as Nehru's, is clear and unpretentious. Careless of the moral scruples that have guided the political actions of the more moderate Indian leaders, he is bold, reckless, imaginative to an unusual degree in a country whose resistance to foreign rule in the main has been passive. For this reason the young hot-heads of Bengal worship him much as he worshipped C. R. Das in his youth."

References

N Y Sun p15 O 28 '43
Nation 157 :323-5 S 18 '43
Newsweek 19 :34 Mr 16 '42 por
Sat Eve Post 216 :22+ Mr 11 '44 por
Time 31 :19-20 Mr 7 '38 (por cover) ;
    37 :34 F 10 '41 ; 43 :36 Ap 17 '44 por
Bose, S. C. Indian Struggle, 1920-1934
    1935
International Who's Who 1942
Mitchell, K. L. India Without Fable
    1942
Nehru, J. Toward Freedom 1941
Sen, S. Testament of India p69-87
    1939
Shridharani, K. My India, My America
    p461-5 1941
Steel, J. Men Behind the War p324-9
    1942

BOSWORTH, HOBART (VAN ZANDT)
(vän zändt) Aug. 11, 1867—Dec. 30, 1943.
Stage and screen actor; film pioneer; played
lead in first movie made in Los Angeles, *The
Sultan's Power* (1909) ; star of many screen
epics.

Obituary

N Y Times p15 D 31 '43

**BOWEN, CATHERINE (SHOBER)
DRINKER** Jan. 1, 1897- Author; lecturer
Address: b. c/o Little, Brown Co., Boston;
h. Mt. Pleasant Rd., Bryn Mawr, Pa.

When Catherine Drinker Bowen, author of
several well-received "fictionalized" biographies
of musicians, turned from that field to write
Yankee From Olympus (1944), a study of
Justice Oliver Wendell Holmes, critical reaction was sharply divided. Some reviewers
applauded her warm, intimate, "humanized"
presentation of the Justice and the members of
his family; others objected to her "invention"
of the personal thoughts and feelings of the
characters. Max Lerner [42] was sure that
Holmes himself would not have liked Catherine
Bowen's book, "which is blurred where he was
sharp and soft where he was unsentimental."
H. S. Commager wrote, however : "If Holmes
had had his choice, we may well believe that
it is rather by this portrait that he would prefer to be known." The concurring or dissenting opinion of the Justice himself is unfortunately not available to settle the argument;
but Catherine Bowen's biography of him indisputably won enough readers to place it on
the top of the non-fiction best-seller lists shortly
after publication. It was, too, the choice of
the Book-of-the-Month Club, the second book
of Mrs. Bowen's to be thus recognized. (The
first was *Beloved Friend*, in 1937.)

Catherine Shober Drinker was born on New
Year's Day, 1897, at Haverford, Pennsylvania,
the youngest of six children "in a house always alive with music." Her father was
Henry Sturgis Drinker, a lawyer and for many
years president of Lehigh University; her
mother, Aimee Ernesta (Beaux) Drinker, was
a musician who gave to her children the music
she knew and loved. "There has never been a

CATHERINE DRINKER BOWEN

professional musician in our family," Catherine
Bowen writes, "and we all live together in a
quiet, practical succession of days. But strike
'A' on the piano, blow it on the pitch pipe, and
to a man we move to the fiddle cases."

Her childhood was spent in Bethlehem,
Pennsylvania; later she went to boarding
school at St. Timothy's in Catonsville, Maryland. When she was eight Catherine Drinker
heard a woman play the violin, and promptly
announced she was going to learn to play as
well as that. "The household of Dr. Henry S.
Drinker was, and is, one in which if you
announce yourself as going to do something,
you are not only helped to do it, but jolly well
expected to." By the time she was twelve
Catherine was good enough to be allowed to
try a friend's priceless Amati. Her decision
not to go to college came when—like the older
Drinker children—she was to sit for her portrait. It was then that she overheard a cousin
remark : "Not a forehead to paint . . . a forehead that will go to Bryn Mawr and write a
book." At that Catherine Drinker rebelled.
"Never, never to Bryn Mawr! I swore it,
kneeling against the sofa. Never to any of
their stuffy colleges, to be a spinster with a
forehead and her skirt hanging wrong. I
would play the violin. I would work and work
until I could play like Kreisler [44], like *two*
Kreislers."

So at eighteen Catherine Drinker left school,
and the years between 1915 and 1917 found her
working at the Peabody Conservatory of Music
in Baltimore, where Jan Van Hulsteyn was
her first teacher. "She insists that she did not
learn easily; and she might well have allowed
her interest to slump in the face of her father's
comment : 'I want you to keep your balance,
child, and to remember that with us music is
an accomplishment, not a profession.'" She
ruefully recalls her first orchestra practice,
when Strube, the conductor, would shout at
her : "Put your fiddle in the oven and burn it,
Gottforsaken amateur !" The young musician,
however, finished her course, and creditably.
Then she went on to New York, where she

BOWEN, CATHERINE DRINKER—
Continued

received a teacher's certificate from the Institute of Musical Art. Edouard Dethier was her violin teacher; Percy Goetschius, well known to music students, was also her teacher and friend. It was he who roared at her when she told him she was leaving the Institute to get married: "So! You will come back to us! Counterpoint is more interesting than cradle-rocking!" It was also Goetschius who later, at the age of eighty-four, wrote to her: "The world can get along without counterpoint, but not without babies."

Having decided on cradle-rocking, Catherine Drinker was married in 1919 to Ezra Bowen. They had two children: Ezra, born in 1921, and Catherine Drinker, born in 1924. With the children and her husband, a professor, she spent the long summer vacations in Bermuda, in England, and in the Tyrol. Since her career as a professional violinist was over, she began to give music lessons to her own and the neighbors' children and to write articles about yachting and—most of all—about music. These began to appear in *Current History*, *Pictorial Review*, the *Woman's Home Companion*. Her first books were *The Story of the Oak Tree* and a history of Lehigh University, both published in 1924. Then in 1932 came a novel, *Rufus Starbuck's Wife*, a story of married life, "an illuminating study of a human relationship extraordinarily complicated by civilization."

But it was music that remained Mrs. Bowen's first love. In 1935 appeared *Friends and Fiddlers*, a book of essays on music and musicians. Later, in 1937, Barbara von Meck brought to her the letters exchanged between the Russian composer Tchaikowsky and his wealthy patroness, Nedejda von Meck, with whom he had corresponded for many years. Barbara von Meck, whose husband was the grandson of Nadejda, made literal translations of the letters, and these, together with her notes and recollections of the persons and places involved, became *Beloved Friend*, published in 1937. In this well-documented life Mrs. Bowen found her real stride as a writer. Most music critics highly praised the book: "It is written with the true delicacy of feeling for music that only a fine musician can have"; "a most valuable addition to the knowledge we possess of the celebrated Russian composer and to the large record of the peculiarities of men of genius." The book was a Book-of-the-Month Club choice and was translated into Swedish, French, and German.

Free Artist (1939) was the story of the Rubinsteins, Anton and Nicholas, who had been Tchaikowsky's teachers. To gather material for the biography, in 1937 Mrs. Bowen spent several months visiting museums and libraries in Russia, Germany, and France and talking with people who had known the musicians. The book was termed "worthy to rank with the best biographies of any year," and was found "in some respects perhaps even superior" to *Beloved Friend*.

Mrs. Bowen had wanted to write a study of Mendelssohn, but she couldn't get abroad to work on the life of the musician. "My subject," she says, "had to be an intellectual from the nineteenth century, and somehow Holmes

appealed to me." By this time Mrs. Bowen had been divorced and remarried; and the story is told that her husband, Dr. Thomas McKean Downs (now a captain in the United States Navy Medical Corps), "put his foot down" when she suggested that she might shelve the life of Holmes in favor of a book on Carey Thomas, female feminist and educator. It seems that Catherine Bowen does her writing in the bedroom, and has the habit of scattering her manuscript pages all over the place. "I don't mind," said her husband firmly, "going to bed under Justice Holmes, but I'll never do it under piles of Carey Thomas." For her book Catherine Bowen spent four years of research on the background, family, and career of Oliver Wendell Holmes, Jr., Justice of the United States Supreme Court, the *Yankee from Olympus*.

Catherine Bowen says herself that her avowed intention was "to bring Justice Holmes out of legal terms into human terms." She devotes very little space to the man after he became a justice—much more to his boyhood and early years. A considerable portion of her book is also given to his famous father, Dr. Oliver Wendell Holmes (who "holds the all-time record of being a problem-father"), and to his grandfather, the Reverend Abiel Holmes. The main interests of the book, however, are the father-son relationship and the women of the Holmes family. Mrs. Bowen, says Frances Woodward, found it easier to cross Poland without a visa than it was to dig the material about Justice Holmes out of Boston and Washington. "Because," the author says, "being neither a lawyer, a Bostonian, nor a man, so much preliminary time was spent . . . explaining why I wanted to write about Oliver Wendell Holmes."

Many reviewers praised the book as "a mellow and lively biography", "full of long perspectives." According to Orville Prescott: "Justice Holmes lives in these pages in all his genuine nobility of mind, in all his fierce integrity of spirit, in all his salty, tolerant, practical wisdom." Dissenting opinion came from those who resented a life of the Justice in "fictionalized" form. "Who is Mrs. Bowen," wrote Edmund Wilson, "that she should be able to supply us with the unspoken thoughts of Justice Holmes and his distinguished family? Mrs. Bowen's own mind is too blunt, too limited, and too prosaic for her to be able to deal with the Holmeses as she has had the ambition to do. . . . One can never be sure what has been reliably reported by someone in a position to know, and what has been invented by the author." Max Lerner (the author of *The Mind and Faith of Justice Holmes*) said that "the semi-fictional form becomes in itself a symbol of the effort, in the literature of recognition, to make things easy that will never be anything but hard." From this point of view Catherine Bowen herself has frankly said of her book: "I disapprove intensely of the kind of biography I write. But without the scenes I have to create, my biographies read like children's notebooks."

Yankee From Olympus was one of four books restricted from reprinting and distribution to the Army and Navy—a War-Department-sponsored project. This ban resulted from the Soldiers' Vote Act, which prohibits the distribution among the armed forces of books containing political arguments. The curb brought forth protests from the Council on Books in Wartime as well as from the author herself, who called the ban sinister, dangerous, and terrifying. In November 1944 Mrs. Bowen revealed that two passages in the book were responsible for the ban. As reported in the New York *Post*, "one told of a visit to Holmes by the President shortly after his inauguration in 1933, during which Holmes was reported to have advised the President, then facing the battle against depression, that in war there is one rule: Form your battalions and fight. The other was a statement to the effect that in 1932 it was feared President Hoover might appoint Calvin Coolidge to fill the post left vacant by the retirement of Holmes." Before this report, however, an amendment canceling previous restrictions on soldier reading cleared Mrs. Bowen's book along with others formerly banned. It thus was among the titles chosen for first distribution to the armed forces. And in December it was announced that the dramatization of *Yankee From Olympus*, for motion picture showing, had been completed.

"A rangy, forceful woman in her mid-forties," said a New York *Post* interviewer in 1944, "Catherine Bowen likes to dress in tweeds. Her angular features and severely worn brown hair give an effect of austerity which vanishes as soon as she begins to speak. She talks rapidly, frequently resorting to slang, and she has a colorful sense of humor." (She often speaks at clubs and schools.) She and her family live in a country house near Bryn Mawr; her daughter, Catherine Bowen, Jr., uses the "Junior" because so many people ask her if she wrote the Bowen biographies; her stepson, Thomas Downs, Jr., is in the Army. Known among her friends as "Mrs. Dr. Downs," she does not share the tastes of the other members of her family for mystery stories and cocktails—but all like music and play instruments. As for literature, "John Donne and Samuel Butler have always been important in my life. But there are a great many more recent books that I admire: John Hersey's [44] *A Bell for Adano* is one, Charles Beard's [41] *The Rise of American Civilization* is another, and so is De Voto's [43] *Year of Decision*." She adds that C. S. Lewis' [44] *The Screwtape Letters* is her current favorite. That, she declares, is "the most wonderful book in a generation."

She confesses to "dozens of extravagances." "I like clothes," she says. "I am buying a fur coat with some of my book club money. I like to buy violins and violas and music." She hates cooking, isn't much interested in food, loves motion pictures, and thinks Humphrey Bogart is "wonderful." She particularly enjoys sailing and likes all sea craft. She is said to take seriously the world's present ills and "would like to see a planned economy here at home without people being afraid of it. She would like a United Nations organization with an international police force to back it up." For herself, she has one very special wish: "I'd give anything to play quartets with Albert Einstein [41]"; and one hope for the future: "When I am seventy I shall begin to go furiously to concerts. . . . And if I have not learned, acquired that peace of soul, that receptivity which is true innocence, then I had

rather be dead and worthy of no more various symphony than the rain upon my tombstone."

References

Book-of-the-Month Club p4-5 Ap '44
N Y Post Mag p37 My 10 '44 pors
Wilson Lib Bul 14:408 Ja '40 por
American Women 1939-40
Bowen, C. D. Friends and Fiddlers 1935

BOWES-LYON, CLAUD GEORGE, 14TH EARL OF STRATHMORE and KINGHORNE *See* Strathmore and Kinghorne, C.G.B.-L.

BOYD, JAMES July 2, 1888—Feb. 25, 1944 Leading author of historical novels dealing with the Revolutionary and Civil War eras; won fame with his first book, *Drums* (1926), and with *Marching On* (1927).

Obituary

N Y Times p13 F 26 '44 por

BRACKEN, EDDIE Feb. 7, 1920- Stage and motion-picture actor

Address: b. c/o Paramount Pictures, Inc., 5451 Marathon St., Hollywood, Calif.; h. Westwood Village, Hollywood, Calif.

"With infallible instinct Preston Sturges' [41] casts unknown actors in parts where they give brilliant performances," commented *Life* Magazine after the appearance of Eddie Bracken in two Sturges films, *The Miracle of Morgan's Creek* (1944) and *Hail the Conquering Hero* (1944). This comedian with the homely, expressive face and hair in one "vast cowlick" gained rather sudden wide popularity with these pictures, but he had been receiving critical recognition for several years before and had been acting since his childhood in Astoria, Long Island.

Except for young Eddie, says *Photoplay* Magazine, the Astoria Brackens had never shown any talent for music or acting. For one thing, explains the actor himself, his parents were too poor to spend money on such things as a piano and music lessons, and too busy to have many recreations or to encourage their three sons to have them. Eddie's father, Joseph L. Bracken, was a stove appliance salesman, and his mother worked in a department store. His older brothers, John and Joseph, also had un-theatrical concerns, and grew up to be, respectively, an accountant and a lawyer. Despite these liabilities, the youngest Bracken boy, only a few years after his birth on February 7, 1920, displayed an intense desire to entertain others. His first public appearance was perhaps an unwilling one—at four he won a prize in a baby contest—but by the age of five he had chosen to sing a solo in a nursery school performance and had followed this up with appearances in a church choir. In another few years Eddie was touring what he calls the local Knights of Columbus circuit to sing "mother" songs at special K.C. entertainments.

After several years of shrewdly capitalizing on his talent for making elderly ladies weep, he was rewarded with a contract with the American Sound Studios' Kiddie Troupers, a

A. L. Whitey Schafer

EDDIE BRACKEN

New York version of Hal Roach's "Our Gang" group of children in Hollywood. At the end of his engagement with the Eastern "Gang," Eddie went to California to make three pictures for Roach. Since he was just entering the ungainly stage of adolescence when he returned to New York in 1929, his parents, by now inured to their son's foibles, sent him to the Professional Children's School in that city for a year.

For many years following this course at the school young Bracken suffered a series of disappointments. For two years, as "Edward Bracken," the boy understudied other children in Broadway plays or acted small roles in unsuccessful productions. At the end of 1932, disgusted with this meager fare, he left Astoria with $4.20 and hitchhiked to Hollywood. He roomed with Junior Durkin, a former Broadway friend who had already become established as a film star; but Eddie himself was unable to find any openings. Finally, two and a half months later, he wired home for the bus money back to Astoria.

Back in New York, Eddie's fortunes did not improve markedly. His first piece of bad luck was a "bit" part in a tedious comedy entitled The Lady Refuses, starring Lou Tellegen. It opened in March 1933 and ran only seven performances. Following this venture, an offer to play Huckleberry Finn in a movie version of Mark Twain's book evaporated. The next March Eddie had the better fortune to be signed for the part of the small messenger boy in H. S. Smith's The Drunkard, or the Fallen Saved. Billed as "Master Bracken," the fourteen-year-old played for over ten months in the Fifty-Fifth Street Group's production of this five-act melodrama, first produced by P. T. Barnum in 1843 as a "Moral Lecture."

When the run of The Drunkard ended, Bracken was auditioned for a supporting role in Little Ol' Boy, starring his friend Junior Durkin, but was rejected for the part. The producer was George Abbott '40, with whom Eddie was afterward to become a leading

player. For a time after this first contact with him, however, the young actor was destined to play small parts in the brief runs of such productions as Life's Too Short (September 1935), So Proudly We Hail (September 1936), and Iron Men (October 1936), the last a morbid story about a steel construction crew. In this play sixteen-year-old Bracken portrayed very convincingly, it is reported, the role of a thirty-seven-year-old plumber. As a result of his interpretation, Abbott called in "Edward V. Bracken" at the end of 1936 to play the adult part of the commandant in the new play he was casting. That was Brother Rat, the John Monks, Jr.-Fred F. Finklehoffe comedy about cadet life at Virginia Military Academy. When the producer discovered the identity of the supposedly middle-aged character actor, he gave Eddie Bracken the role of Grant Bottome, the youngest cadet, in the road company. In June 1937, five months after the Broadway opening, the juvenile returned to New York to play for a time the leading role of Billy Randolph when Frank Albertson left the cast. Today Bracken says that the Abbott training in hair-trigger pacing he received for Brother Rat and for later Abbott productions has been his greatest acting asset.

The next spring Bracken expected to be given the lead in another Abbott production—Clifford Goldsmith's What a Life, the comedy which was to be the forerunner of the playwright's radio and film series about Henry Aldrich, the Booth Tarkington-ish adolescent. The Aldrich role in this first presentation (which opened in April 1938) went to the better-known Ezra Stone, however, and Eddie Bracken was given a subordinate part. Later, when the play went on tour, he played Henry, and in the second picture of the film series (Life With Henry, Paramount, 1941), he played the part of Dizzy opposite Jackie Cooper's Henry.

Following a summer of stock in 1939 Eddie Bracken went back to New York to make his musical comedy debut as one of the four male principals in the Rodgers '40 and Hart '40 energetic collegiate show, Too Many Girls. It was produced by George Abbott and opened in October with Richard Kollmar, Desi Arnaz, Hal LeRoy, and Marcy Westcott in the cast. The critics found it to be a pert, pleasing, high-spirited production and, moreover, according to Burns Mantle, "agreeable, clean entertainment that missed being stuffy." (It ran for seven months.) Abbott had been credited in the past with discovering many youthful, talented performers who acted with a natural exuberance; and in his latest "debonair gambol" Bracken, too, now an Abbott alumnus, displayed a "fresh, unhackneyed style" and a "natural grace and stage wit." His interpretation was later brought effectively to the screen in 1940, when RKO-Radio made "a faithful reconstruction" of the comedy. (He was under contract to another studio by this time and was loaned to RKO for the picture.)

Bracken's efforts in the Broadway version of Too Many Girls were rewarded by bids for his services from six major Hollywood studios, among them Paramount Pictures, with which he finally signed a five-year contract. In his second picture for the company, Reaching for the Sun (1941), he was given star rating, although in this film as in most of his later ones he continued to play supporting roles. The type of pictures in which he appeared were the cheerful, noisy comedies and frivolous musicals common to Hollywood: *Caught in the Draft* (1941), with Bob Hope [41] and Dorothy Lamour, *Sweater Girl* (1942), with June Preisser, and *Young and Willing* (1943), with Susan Hayworth and William Holden. The classification also included several films in which he was pummeled into recognition by the hoyden Betty Hutton: *The Fleet's In* (1942), *Happy-Go-Lucky* (a 1943 picture in which his acting is said to have given a wryly comic twist to belabored material), and *Star-Spangled Rhythm* (1943). In September 1942 the *Motion Picture Herald's* poll of Canadian film exhibitors revealed Bracken as "the most promising star of tomorrow." The next year the *Herald's* 1943 "Fame Poll" showed Bracken again to be the "star of tomorrow" winner in the estimation of those questioned.

The comedian rapidly became known to movie-goers for reliable comic performances in a somewhat bewildered style of acting; and in 1943 Paramount decided to take a gamble on his and Miss Hutton's special box office appeal and give them comedy leads. The company coupled the team with Preston Sturges, as writer and director, to produce *The Miracle of Morgan's Creek* (1944). For the film Sturges tackled the delicate problem of "spoofing the sacred realm of maternity," and succeeded in making his story, to quote Bosley Crowther in the New York *Times*, "so innocently amusing, so full of candor, that no one could take offense." And as director, Sturges got from all his actors "performances that made him look like inspired comedians," added the *Times* reviewer. Most of the other critics, too, felt that in spite of his occasional use of ridicule Sturges had displayed a rare feeling for satire and nonsense and that his cast had caught the spirit of the "Sturges world."

Following the success of Bracken in *The Miracle of Morgan's Creek*—although the predicament of Betty Hutton was the focal point of its plot—Paramount decided to put him in another Sturges picture, this time as the protagonist. Upon the release of *Hail the Conquering Hero* in the summer of 1944, the trade paper *Variety* announced that the young actor had "bounced back from his humorously absent-minded performance in *Miracle* to still a stronger hold on the star ladder" with his portrayal of a synthetic Marine hero who is unwillingly swept up in a tide of hometown hero worship. It is proof, said *Variety,* that "a capable director can take an actor who is willing to listen and get a better-than-good performance out of him." To the enthusiastic critics the picture firmly established Bracken as an actor as well as a comedian, if, to a few, a somewhat stylized one in his customary rôle of "the long-suffering, plaintive type who muddles through difficult situations, never knowing quite how he escapes with a whole skin." "Within the past two years," wrote Paul Kennedy in September 1944, "young Mr. Bracken has emerged as one of Hollywood's most competent exponents of a highly commercial type of comedy. It's a type that combines broadness, bordering almost on slapstick, with delicate overtones of the pathos and frustration of confused youth."

A later film attempt at zany satire, with Bracken as the star comic, proved less successful. Called *Rainbow Island* (1944), the picture was a lavish Technicolor spectacle with a South Sea island setting, complete with Dorothy Lamour. The reviewers' opinions of Bracken's comedy varied with their respective senses of humor. "When he is on the screen," wrote one, "there is constant cause for amusement, if only to look at him." He offers "masterful scoops of burlesque." In comparing Bracken and the second comic in the picture unfavorably with the team of Crosby [41] and Hope [41], another reviewer commented that Bracken "virtually broke his neck attempting to be wryly funny," retaining only the "mannerisms from his recent hits."

Two newer Bracken pictures, *Bring On the Girls* and *Out of This World*, have not yet been released to the general public. It has been reported that Harold Lloyd is ready to sell the film rights of two of his early pictures, *The Freshman* and *Grandma's Boy*, to Preston Sturges as starring vehicles for Bracken. In addition to making films Bracken has also toured for the USO and other entertainment units and made several radio appearances. It is said that he often writes his own material for these engagements. On February 4, 1945 the comedian will start a sponsored program over NBC, to be called the *Eddie Bracken Show.*

"Modest and clean-cut like his motion picture roles," say interviewers, Eddie Bracken has managed to remain unspoiled despite his rapid rise to stardom. In September 1939 he was married to the former Connie Nickerson (whom he met in the road company of *What a Life*). They admit that during their first months in California they temporarily lost their perspective—renting a large house and "an ermine-lined swimming pool"—but they now live quietly with their two daughters and a Dalmatian named Dizzy in a small house outside of Hollywood. Bracken enjoys gardening, making his own recordings, listening to Gilbert and Sullivan operas, playing bridge and baseball. During his unsuccessful days in New York City he even played semi-professional baseball between plays with the Oneida Indians at Forest Hills, Long Island. He is still interested in the legitimate stage, and his Paramount contract allows him the time to return to Broadway each year to appear in a play if the occasion arises. His ultimate ambition, however, is to be a producer-director—like the two men he admires, Abbott and Sturges—for both the theatre and the screen.

"I don't consider myself a comedian," Bracken declared in a New York *Post* interview in 1943, "although the things I've been associated with so far have all been laugh-getters. Actually, I'm no gag man. I couldn't carry on like Bob Hope if my life depended on it. I do best as the serious guy—like Harold Lloyd used to portray, for instance, who is constantly involved in comic situations—and that's the kind of part I'm always striving for." In the fall of 1944 it was reported that Sturges, pleased with the reception of *The Miracle of Morgan's Creek* and *Hail the Conquering Hero*, was set-

BRACKEN, EDDIE—*Continued*

ting up a stock company for the films and wanted Eddie Bracken as his comedy star.

References

N Y Herald Tribune VII p22-3 N 19 '44 por
N Y Post p11 My 22 '43 por
N Y Times II p3 S 10 '44
N Y World-Telegram p16 My 22 '41 por
Photoplay 24:59+ Mr '44 por
International Motion Picture Almanac 1943-44

BRAND, MAX, pseud. *See* Faust, R.

BRENTANO, ARTHUR (bran-tä′nō) Apr. 20, 1858—Jan. 29, 1944 Since 1915 President of Brentano's, Inc., the world's largest retail bookselling business, which began ninety years ago as a newsstand.

Obituary

N Y Times p38 Ja 30 '44

BRINKLEY, NELL 1888(?)—Oct. 21, 1944 Artist, creator of a distinctive type of elaborately sketched boy and girl drawings formerly syndicated throughout the United States; was largely self-taught; pen-and-ink technique; which required much time to develop, caused her to be regarded as one of the hardest working artists in the syndicate organization.

Obituary

N Y Times p19 O 23 '44

BRISTOW, JOSEPH LITTLE (bris′tō) July 22, 1861—July 14, 1944 Republican Senator from Kansas (1909-1915); joint author of the Seventeenth Amendment, providing for the election of Senators by popular vote.

Obituary

N Y Times p13 Jl 15 '44 por

BROMFIELD, LOUIS (brom′fēld) Dec. 27, 1896- Author; farmer
Address: b. and h. Malabar Farm, Lucas, Ohio

A lifelong devotion to both farming and writing and the achievement of definite success in each have made Louis Bromfield a unique personality in the American scene. Public recognition first came to Bromfield as an "expatriate" author who lived abroad after the First World War, and whose novels in the '20's merited high acclaim, one winning a Pulitzer award. Then Bromfield came home: to a thousand-acre farm, Malabar, in Ohio's Mohican Valley. He still wrote (at the rate of about a book a year), but his fiction evolved gradually into "sleek, sensational," Hollywood-slanted best sellers. There are some who believe that Bromfield's growing interest in his farm, in the American political scene as it affects farmers, and in wartime farm production has almost completely superseded his interest in creative writing.

From the very beginning Bromfield's has been a divided allegiance. He was born of Boston-Maryland ancestry on a farm in Mansfield, Ohio, December 27, 1896, the son of Charles and Annette Maria (Coulter) Bromfield and the grandson of an Abolitionist who was one of the founders of the Underground Railroad. He took his first job on a local newspaper at sixteen. When he reached college age, however, he entered Cornell University in 1914 to study agriculture. Then, after only a year there, the urge to write took him to Columbia University's School of Journalism. He had hoped to spend a year at four different colleges but the First World War interrupted that plan. He left college, joined the French Army as an ambulance driver, and later became a liaison man between French and British forces. For two years he saw service on almost every sector of the Front and was awarded the star of the Légion d'Honneur and the Croix de Guerre. Columbia University also gave him an honorary B.A. degree because of his distinguished war service.

On his return to the United States, Bromfield first worked for the New York City News Association, then for the Associated Press. Subsequent positions included those of private tutor, foreign editor and critic for *Musical America*, theatre, music, and art critic for the *Bookman*, assistant to a theatrical producer, and advertising manager for G. P. Putnam's Sons, the publishers. Bromfield was also one of the original staff members of *Time* Magazine.

In 1923 Bromfield married Mary Appleton Wood. (Their three daughters are Anne Chalmers, Mary Hope, and Ellen Margaret.) Shortly after their marriage the Bromfields went abroad, where Bromfield subsequently settled down to a writing career at Senlis, a village thirty miles north of Paris.

Although Bromfield lived abroad, his first four novels consisted of four panels in the American scene. *The Green Bay Tree* (1924), with its background a huge American steel town, won an excellent critical reception. Then a year later came *Possession*, the story of a girl's escape from the narrow confines of an Ohio town into the world of music. Again Bromfield had produced a book "rich in character and in drama." *Early Autumn* (1926), called "both a dramatic novel and a stinging satire," a book with "a mellowness and power of perspective which American fiction too often lacks," won the Pulitzer award for that year; but *A Good Woman* (1927), about a domineering mother who ruins her son's life, was thought by most critics to be Bromfield's best work in the series on America. The young novelist showed the influence of Dickens, Thackeray, and Balzac. Writing of his own work at that time, Louis Bromfield said: "I was aware first of all of the whole spectacle rather than any individual character in the story." He was more interested in the characters of women than of men and—in distinct contrast to many of his fellow expatriate authors—was uninterested in style for its own sake. One critic has written: "Simplicity and clarity are what he aims at. . . . He greatly prefers the writer who has a good deal to say and says it clumsily, to the artist in words who has little to say."

The Strange Case of Miss Annie Spragg (1928) was a departure in subject from his previous work, a brilliant tour de force. Consisting of several stories grouped around the central figure of an eccentric old maid living in Italy, it was called "an exhilarating, intelligent, brilliant book," with an "evidence of the sense of life that all great storytellers must possess . . . a sense of glamour." A little too much glamour, according to some critics, entered Bromfield's next three books, of which *Twenty-Four Hours* was the best received. It was not until *The Farm* (1933) that he returned to the substance and manner of his early series. This was a long, semi-autobiographical family chronicle concerning four generations of a family living on a northern Ohio farm. Although the "intellectual" critics have found fault with it, others believe that it still stands as "one of the solidest and most genuinely important books the author has written." Bromfield himself usually rates it as his best.

An interlude of residence in India produced a new background for Bromfield's fiction. *The Rains Came* (1937) had just about everything: skilled social commentary in the characters of Indians, Europeans, and Americans trying to work for a "better India"; also disaster, earthquake, flood, and plague. The "cosmopolitan parasites," whom Bromfield knew so well, figured in *Night in Bombay* (1940). By this time Hollywood had found Bromfield; and by this time, too (it was just before the Second World War), Bromfield was no longer happy in the decadent European scene.

Accordingly, in 1939, he came home to Ohio. "After twenty-five years of witnessing revolutions, inflations, and the ruin of whole nations," Bromfield said, "I knew that the nearest thing to security that unstable man could still have was the land." He first acquired some 600 acres near Mansfield, Ohio, where he was born, of which 400 were eroded, "rundown" land which he hoped to reclaim—"another wound in our American economy to heal." Named Malabar (after the coast where he had written his Indian novels), Bromfield's farm is run on a cooperative basis: "Any profits left after the first 5 per cent which is paid on the capital the author-farmer has invested in the enterprise are divided pro rata among the employees living on the place. The dozen tenants and their families not only live on the farm, they live 'off' it. They get their share of the vegetables, meats, poultry, eggs, and dairy products raised before the remainder is marketed." Squire Bromfield's farm neighbors were, according to report, at first suspicious, but his "simple and direct manner broke down their prejudices. His loud-checked shirts still startle them, his New Deal politics still rub some of them the wrong way, his speech, which he fills out with many a French idiom, amuses others, but his knowledge of farm marketing, crop rotation, soil conservation, and other problems which concern their daily lives has won him the respect of all."

By 1942 Malabar had become something of a show place. In the thirty-room house, "sitting rooms are decorated in striking combinations of gray and yellow, red, green, and white.

LOUIS BROMFIELD

Telephones and typewriters are found in every bedroom, with one exception: the author does his sleeping in a room in which neither is permitted. Pool and ping-pong tables fill a much-used game room. . . . Malabar is both an international post office and rendezvous. European refugees whom the Bromfields knew during their pre-War residence in France have their mail sent to the Ohio farm, where it is readdressed to wherever the unfortunate évacués have found temporary haven." The author and his wife entertain on a large scale. "At our own house," says Bromfield, "at least eighteen people sit down at table for every meal, with usually four or five visitors. We eat well and what we eat is the best in quality, fresh from garden or dairy or hen house. . . . Thousands of people from nearby and far away have paid us visits. Everywhere on the farm there are children helping with the haying and filling the silos, fishing and swimming in the ponds, learning to know and respect the farm animals as a part of God's scheme of things, discovering the satisfaction of honest work. My two older daughters, when home from school, have their place and responsibility. . . . Out of a life fortunate in adventure, travel, friendships, and work, the five years given to the farm have been the most rewarding of all my existence."

The novels Bromfield has written since he acquired Malabar have seldom struck deeper than the popular fiction level—*Wild Is the River* (1941), *Until the Day Break* (1942), *Mrs. Parkington* (1943). The motion picture rights for the latter were sold for $60,000 on the basis of a one-paragraph synopsis even before the book was written, and Greer Garson '42 played the title role. *What Became of Anna Bolton* (1944) is the tale of a rich American woman living in Europe during the late '30's who, when the Germans entered Paris, took the side of the driven and oppressed. Of what he calls the "strange case of Louis Bromfield," Orville Prescott writes: "In a recent interview . . . Mr. Bromfield said he didn't care if

BROMFIELD, LOUIS—*Continued*

reviewers spoke more highly of his old novels, that no one except himself could know what he needed to write, that when a writer imitates himself he is through. Just the same, if Bromfield would imitate his own best work he would at least be setting himself a commendably high standard. . . . Bromfield sometimes seems to be imitating writers much inferior to himself."

The World We Live In, a collection of nine Bromfield short stories and novelettes, the first in five years, was published in the fall of 1944. One reviewer finds Bromfield still "an excellent story-teller," while another thought that "generally the stories seem to hover on the verge of deep significance." Bromfield himself is of the opinion that some of the stories reveal a new trend, "a simplification of idiom" and "a Jean Jacques Rousseau naturalism."

It was as a practicing farmer and a critic chiefly of the New Deal's food administration that Bromfield came prominently into the news during 1943 and early 1944. Although a Democrat and a supporter of Roosevelt '42 policies in general, he became convinced that Administration "muddling" with the farm problem was drastically cutting food production, "threatening the American people with hunger, destroying hope for winning the peace by feeding Europe's starving millions after the War, and bringing disaster to the Democratic Party." In various articles and speeches, Bromfield stingingly condemned the policies of the Secretary of Agriculture, the War Production Board, and the Office of Price Administration. There is not, he said, and never has been any "authentic, coordinated food production program." He decried the cut in farm machinery production; criticized the "erratic price-ceiling policy" and the drafting of necessary skilled farm workers. "If the New Deal had hired Nazi Propaganda Minister Goebbels '41 to think up a [United States] farm policy" he couldn't have done half as much damage to the war effort, according to the author-farmer. Bromfield went so far as to predict a food famine in the United States by February 1944: "If it were possible, I would rather not think about next February. . . . No matter how much we produce, it will not be enough."

February came, however, and—as *PM* reported anent the Bromfield prophecies—people were still eating. According to an opinion in *Time* Magazine, however: "Bromfield as the sensational prophet last summer was hewing at the right tree, while Marvin Jones '43, the optimist, had lost sight of the forest. To eat well, the United States was drawing heavily on its food reserves carried over from years of abundance and underconsumption." When Bromfield "set his clock ahead" to April 1944 as a food shortage month, he was again mocked as a prophet. In June Bromfield quipped, "We'd have had a famine if I hadn't written the article," (in which he first made the prediction).

Several observers felt that his protest against the Administration's food policy had a personal basis. "Bromfield actually still is a Democrat," a friend of his is reported to have said, "and there's nothing between him and the Administration which couldn't be repaired by a two-minute meeting with the President . . . those two minutes in which the President should say: 'I hereby appoint you Secretary of Agriculture.'"

In July 1944 Bromfield covered the Democratic National Convention as a reporter. He called the convention "one of the most shameful spectacles in the history of politics"; and bolted the Democratic Party (of which he had been a lifelong member) in September to take the stump for the Republican ticket. He joined the Independent Voters' Protest Committee against the PAC of the CIO; and in October he headed the formation of the Independent Artists and Writers for Dewey. Said Bromfield: "No man and no administration can continue for four terms without becoming tired, weary, divided. I am voting Republican for the first time in my life because I believe we need a fresh and vigorous administration." He predicted that at least one-fourth of the Democrats of Ohio would oppose the President, and three or four million Democrats throughout the nation would vote Republican in November. Mrs. Bromfield, it was reported, was still for Roosevelt.

Whether or not Bromfield has political aspirations, few Americans have been more active in the anti-Fascist cause. He is on the executive board of the Emergency Committee To Save the Jewish People of Europe; a sponsor of the American Committee for the Protection of the Foreign Born; a signer of an appeal through the Union for Democratic Action for a restatement by the Government of its demand for the "unconditional surrender of Fascism." He is convinced that fascism is not simply a disease confined to nations. "It cuts across all nations. We have plenty of fascist-minded people right here in the United States—the kind who think 'the Fascist-Nazis would put the poor people in their place and protect my property and investments.'" He believes in "the sum total of the common sense of the common people." He has faith in the average American. He has defended organized labor, but has criticized its leadership ("some labor leaders are using the crisis . . . to build up personal prestige for reasons of politics inside their own organizations"), and the Administration policy toward labor.

The *New Yorker* in November 1942 described a few days that were characteristic of Bromfield's activities. "Monday he was in Ohio on his farm. He worked an hour on a novel, dictated replies to fifty letters, squared up the farm accounts, took a nap between three and four (he always does this), worked on a magazine article about a TVA development he'd recently inspected, and had six guests for dinner, including an FBI man with whom, after coffee, he returned to his study." That night he took a sleeper to New York. The next day he was interviewed by a delegate of Fighting French, two Negro 2nd lieutenants, three Austrian refugees, a child who wanted to interview him for a school paper, and an English lady who wanted help in getting permission to return to England with her children. Some movie people also turned up. After lunch with two naval officers, a woman from *Time*, and another from the Fifth Avenue Association he worked on a short-wave broadcast, then went to the Astor Hotel to help with seating arrangements for the Century of the Common Man dinner. Until the dinner, at which he made an address, he chatted with Sidney Hillman '40, Muriel Draper, and Joe Curran; afterward 'did the town' with Dan Golenpaul of *Information, Please."*

As Ben Ray Redman has said, the first impression one receives of Louis Bromfield "is that of abounding and intense vitality; the second impression is of a man who is willing to expend that vitality lavishly." He is described as "tall, spare, broad-shouldered, with legs and arms that are loosely but powerfully articulated; quick to smile and given to vivacious gestures. Bromfield strolls through life as an eager borrower . . ." who repays his debts with more than legal interest. "He is never in a hurry to be off and away. . . . He is never in a hurry to abandon a conversation, for the dullest of conversations is still human dialogue. . . . He is never in a hurry to dismiss an idea."

He is said to do all his literary work in a few hours daily. His secret is "knowing what to say before sitting down" at his desk. Two hours in the morning, another late at night suffice for his steady and large literary production. He writes entirely in longhand: his secretary, Hawkins, "has typed every word of his employer's almost illegible manuscripts for the last twelve years." Two of Bromfield's daughters apparently have inherited their father's literary gifts. The eldest, Anne, writes poetry; the youngest, Ellen, "incredibly long novels about horses and dogs." Mary is the family musician. Bromfield devotes more and more time to farming and politics. He is a member of the Farm Security Administration's advisory board; he is an active vice-president of Friends of the Land, a national conservation organization. At the end of 1944 Bromfield said he was at work on a non-fiction book about his life as an agriculturist. (Harper's stated the book, "Pleasant Valley," was scheduled for publication in the spring of 1945.) Bromfield said it was not to be an autobiography, however, for he believes a man should postpone that until he reaches the age of sixty-five.

References

N Y Herald Tribune Books p6 Ag 23 '42 il pors
N Y Times Mag p14+ Ag 16 '42 il pors
New Yorker 18:12-13 N 7 '42
Wilson Bul 5:100 O '30 por
Kunitz, S. J. and Haycraft, H. eds. Twentieth Century Authors 1942
Who's Who in America 1944-45

BROWDER, EARL (RUSSELL) May 20, 1891- Head of the Communist Political Association of the United States; journalist

Address: b. 35 E. 12th St., New York City; h. 7 Highland Pl., Yonkers, N. Y.

Earl Russell Browder, the present head of the Communist Political Association of the United States (formerly the Communist Party), was born in Wichita, Kansas, May 20, 1891, one of ten brothers and sisters. He is of old American stock. His father, William Browder, was one of the eighteen children of a circuit-riding Methodist parson of Illinois,

EARL BROWDER

and had himself intended to become a minister until he turned Unitarian under the influence of Emerson. After teaching school in Illinois he had been married to a miner's daughter of Scotch extraction, the former Martha Hankins, and had headed for Kansas to claim a homestead in the prairies; when farming proved unsuccessful he moved to Wichita to teach school again. In 1902 he had a complete breakdown, and it became necessary for Earl and the oldest boy, Waldo, to support the family. Earl's formal education therefore ended with the third grade. Studying in his spare time, he held jobs as a cash boy in a department store at $1.50 a week, as a telegraph messenger, as an errand boy in a wholesale drug house at $3.50 a week, as an office boy, as a ledger clerk, as a bookkeeper. By the time he was twenty-one he was earning $16 a week as an accountant. "I was well handled personally almost everywhere I worked," he says.

The elder Browder had, over the space of a few years, traveled from Unitarianism to Populism to Socialism, and Earl grew up in the atmosphere of radical discussion. He was only fifteen when he followed his father into the Socialist Party and began peddling *An Appeal to Reason*. But even the Socialist Party was a little mild for him, and after his family moved from Wichita to Kansas City, Missouri, he joined a branch of the Syndicalist League of North America, led by William Z. Foster. For a time he worked as trustee for an office workers' union and as associate editor of the Syndicalist magazine, the *Toiler*; then, after taking a correspondence course in law, he became office manager of the Farmers' Cooperative Store in Olathe, Kansas. Of this period in Browder's life, from 1915 to 1917, a writer in the *American Magazine* says: "Earl was a gay chap then, with a twinkle in his blue eyes and a ready wit. He liked to sit outside his cottage door on summer evenings and play little ballads on the flute. Once in Kansas City he organized and directed a boys' band, just for the fun of it. He liked to talk about

BROWDER, EARL—*Continued*

poetry, too, and sometimes wrote very nice couplets."

Then came America's entry into the First World War. Earl Browder and his brother Bill formed the League for Democratic Control, which sought a court order to restrain Missouri's Governor and sheriff from putting the draft laws into operation. For this they received a double sentence under two separate indictments—a year in the Platte County jail on the charge of refusing to register for the draft, and two years in the Federal penitentiary at Leavenworth on the charge of conspiracy to block the draft. Earl Browder does not seem to have been badly treated in prison, having been allowed access to all the books on economics and sociology he wanted. In the Platte County Jail he wrote a treatise entitled "A System of Accounts for a Small Consumer's Cooperative." In Leavenworth, in addition to serving as a bookkeeper and playing the flute in the prison band, he read not only Marx and Engels but made the acquaintance of his boyhood idol, "Big Bill" Haywood, the American labor leader. His sentence commuted after sixteen months, he was released in November 1920, but was not to be fully pardoned until 1933.

By 1920 the struggle between the reformists and militants within the Socialist Party had crystallized and led to a split and the formation of the Communist Party, which was forced to function under ground because of the "Red scare" that followed the War. Browder immediately became active in the underground movement; above ground, he organized the Office Service Associates to take care of the books of small businessmen in Kansas City. When that firm failed he and some relatives and friends pooled their resources and established a cooperative colony on a tract of land near Independence, Missouri. It was a short-lived experiment. Browder himself finally left for New York City, and there, after another brief interlude of bookkeeping, he went to work for the Trade Union Educational League, an independent radical organization headed by William Foster, with whom Browder had remained on excellent terms. With the title of managing editor of the *Labor Herald*, he served as Foster's man Friday. It was the beginning of a long association, uninterrupted to this day.

Both Browder and Foster met with the Executive Council of the underground Communist Party, although Foster was not yet a member of the party; and in the summer of 1921 they attended the congress of the Profintern or Red International of Labor Unions at Moscow as delegates from the T.U.E.L. (The Profintern was an industrial organization formed in 1921 under the auspices of the Third International as a militant international committee for the reorganization of the trade union movement.) In Moscow it was decided that the T.U.E.L. would organize "cells" in A.F. of L. unions to agitate for amalgamation along industrial lines; and when the American delegation returned from the convention, Foster joined the Communist Party.

By this time the underground Communist Party in the United States had organized the Workers Party of America as a legal political organization with which to camouflage its activities. As T.U.E.L. leaders, Foster and Browder worked in the latter organization, which was not affiliated with the Third International, after their return to the United States. Both of them believed that the Workers Party should supersede the underground organization in effect; and in April 1923 this took place, when the underground party was dissolved and merged with the legalized party. This new group was named the Workers (Communist) Party, and later became the Communist Party.

A great struggle for power now ensued between Foster and C. E. Ruthenberg, general secretary of the organization and one of the original Communist Party founders. By 1924 Foster had become leader of the majority, and Ruthenberg, though still general secretary, was left with much less power. The following year Browder, still Foster's man Friday, acted as general secretary of the party during Ruthenberg's absence in Moscow; and in 1926, as a member of the Executive Committee of the Profintern, he was sent to Moscow to attend a trade union conference. The Profintern promptly assigned him to go to China with an international labor delegation from the conference to the Chinese workers which included Tom Mann, of the British Communist Party, and Jacques Doriot [40], of the French Communist Party.

Browder and his associates journeyed northward from Canton to Hankow. They told the Chinese people how well Chiang Kai-shek [40] and the Communists were working together to liberate China from imperialist domination, but by the time they reached Hankow, Chiang was massacring his former Communist allies, and the group was forced to disband. In Hankow the Pan-Pacific Trade Union Secretariat was nevertheless formed to carry on propaganda in the trade unions of the countries bordering on the Pacific; Browder was elected its secretary. During most of the year 1928 he edited the underground *Pan-Pacific Worker* in Hankow, returning to the United States only a few days before the stock market crash of October 1929.

Browder found the Foster-Lovestone dispute within the Communist Party running high. Jay Lovestone was an ultramoderate who believed in playing down the revolutionary factors in American society; apparently, too, the great majority within the party was with him rather than with Foster. Browder was actually hooted down at the sixth convention of the party when he took Foster's side. But Foster was favored by the Comintern for the office of general secretary, and finally the convention endorsed his candidacy. (Lovestone's reluctance to yield to the demands of the Executive Committee of the Communist International led to his expulsion in 1929. Only a few hundred Communists followed him out of the party, to form the Independent Labor League of America.) Actually Foster served as general secretary for only a short time. Because of Foster's poor health, in 1930 Browder took over the office of general secretary of the party, and Foster became its chairman. Since there were far more prominent American Communist leaders available for the office, anti-Communists have attributed Browder's selection directly to Stalin '42, who, they say, was sure that he would be a pliable tool.

Whatever the truth in the matter, the American Communist Party was to attain its greatest influence under Browder's leadership, during the period of the Popular Front against Fascism. Early in 1935, when Browder was present in Moscow, the Communist International, during its Seventh World Congress, adopted a "new line" of united front collaboration with other radical and "bourgeois" parties against Fascism, and the Communist revolutionary line was abandoned. Although it was not until later that the American Communist Party adopted the slogan, "Communism is Twentieth Century Americanism," Browder's 1936 speech in which he accepted the Communist nomination for the Presidency of the United States was free from even a passing reference to Marx, Lenin, or Stalin; and in the campaign which followed the emphasis was on defeating Alf Landon '44 rather than on getting votes for Browder himself. In the NRA the Communists had found dangerous symptoms of fascism, but they saw Roosevelt '42 in a different light after General Hugh Johnson '40 was dismissed as the President's adviser and head of NRA and after the birth of the Liberty League. (Said Browder: "We think there is taking place a social regrouping in the country in the course of which all the most reactionary forces are tending toward the Republican ticket. . . . Roosevelt represents the effort to maintain a middle course between reaction on one hand and a progressive policy on the other.") During the 1936 campaign the Communist leader traveled 26,000 miles, visiting twenty-six states. At Tampa, Florida, he was locked out of the hall where he was supposed to speak; in Terre Haute, Indiana, he was jailed as a vagrant and pelted with eggs; in Atlanta, Georgia, he was refused permission to leave his train to speak.

During most of the next three years the Communists were among the most enthusiastic supporters of Roosevelt and the New Deal. But it was not on support of the New Deal but on the issue of resistance to Fascism abroad that the Popular Front was chiefly built. In 1935 and 1936, in speeches and writings that gained an ever-widening audience among liberals as well as Communists, Browder campaigned for action of the United States, in concert with England, France, and the Soviet Union, to apply sanctions to Italy for the protection of Ethiopia. In 1936 he announced that "the pack led by Hitler, Mussolini '42, and the Japanese militarists are getting ready to tear down civilization itself," and declared that if peace were to be maintained the non-Fascist nations must adopt one united international policy. (Peace was particularly important, he felt, because the chances of America's staying out of any general war were very slight: "Our imperialist ambitions or a new 'savior' delusion will draw us in.") In 1937 the Communist leader supported Roosevelt's Chicago speech advocating a quarantine of the aggressor nations; during the Spanish war he particularly urged lifting the embargo on republican Spain and laying an embargo on all commercial and economic relations with Germany, Italy, and Japan, pointing out that this would mean no danger of

war, since the United States could not be invaded. Until the Munich pact strengthened Germany, Browder insisted that the "warmakers," with their limited economic resources, could be brought to a halt by the peaceful joint action of the United States, France, and Britain, with the Soviet Union, saying that if the democracies continued to leave Spain and China to their fate, "we will have no one to blame but ourselves when we have to take up the full military burden under more unfavorable conditions." "Do you really think it is possible to defeat the Rome-Berlin-Tokyo axis without the cooperation of the Soviet Union?" he also asked. Wrote Reinhold Niebuhr '41 in 1938: "If war should come upon us because of the failure of the democratic capitalist powers, the question is whether the workers should be encouraged to participate in it or not. Upon that question Mr. Browder is silent."

Then, on the heels of Munich, came the Nazi-Soviet nonaggression pact of August 1939. Although Browder had been audibly questioning Chamberlain's '40 sincerity in attempting to make a military agreement with the Russians, he was obviously stunned by the news. After twenty-four hours of silence he came out with the prediction that the pact would contain an "escape clause"; but when the terms were made public there was no such clause. The Nazi attack on Poland followed, and on September 1, 1939 France and Britain formally declared war on Germany.

The American Communists, after another period of bewilderment, answered Niebuhr's question by denouncing the conflict as a second imperialist war and calling for an immediate end to it. According to Browder, Great Britain and France were fighting a "phony" war, had deserted Poland, and were striving merely to switch the war against the Soviet Union. In his opinion, the British and French Governments were angry at the Nazi-Soviet nonaggression pact only because it had frustrated their designs to turn Germany eastward and then let the Soviet Union fight the Nazis alone. With the outbreak of the Russo-Finnish War he felt the Communist thesis proved, for Chamberlain and Daladier '40 displayed considerably more inclination to help the Finns than they had any of the victims of previous aggression by the Nazis, and in America indignation against the Russians crowded the western "sitzkrieg" almost completely off the front pages. Even before the Second World War the Communists had criticized Roosevelt for his "abandonment of the Spanish republic" and for "allowing his lieutenants to claim for him 'credit' for Munich," although they continued to support the President as late as September 11, 1939. Now Roosevelt's hostility toward Russia caused them to withdraw the last shreds of their support and to bring out all the adjectives previously reserved for his enemies. On the domestic front, this did not mean that Browder had deserted the New Deal: the implication he gave was that Roosevelt had deserted it, had become a tool of Wall Street.

During this period the U.S.S.R. and all Communists had become intensely unpopular in the United States, particularly in the journals of liberal opinion, whose contributors had begun in August 1939 to regret their every pre-

BROWDER, EARL—_Continued_

pact word on behalf of the U.S.S.R. There was, however, talk of persecution and danger to civil liberties when in 1940 a Federal district court sentenced Browder to four years imprisonment and a $2,000 fine, and a Federal circuit court upheld the conviction. In 1939, testifying before the Dies '40 Committee, Browder had revealed that before 1934 he had traveled through Europe on passports bearing false names. This had been long enough ago for the offense to be outlawed; but in 1934, applying for a new passport under his right name, he had written "none" after the words: "My last passport was obtained from—." Browder was charged with having _used_ this passport unlawfully when he displayed it to immigration authorities to prove his citizenship upon his return from abroad, and it was on this charge that he was convicted. Browder himself maintained that this did not constitute a _use_ of the passport, since an American citizen must be admitted to his own country whether he displays a passport or not. The _New Republic_ pointed out that "the case of a song writer immediately following Browder's and substantially similar to his was disposed of with a $500 fine."

Free on bail, Browder carried the fight to the Supreme Court while running for President of the United States as Communist nominee in 1940, but he was forbidden to leave the New York area. In New York he was ruled off the ballot as having failed to receive the necessary number of bona-fide signatures of petitioners, and he charged in turn that intimidation had been used to get signers to repudiate their signatures. He nevertheless carried on an energetic campaign, which was chiefly centered around the charge that two candidates had never been more alike than Wendell L. Willkie '40 and Franklin D. Roosevelt: both of them represented Wall Street, he claimed; both were more than anxious to lead the American people into war. Browder's own idea of a correct foreign policy became clear when in October 1940 he came out for a Washington-Moscow-Chungking axis.

In March 1941, while Communists were denouncing the Lend-Lease Bill as loudly as they had the Selective Service Act, Browder started his four-year term at the United States Penitentiary at Atlanta, his Supreme Court appeal having been denied. Two months later came Germany's attack on the Soviet Union and Churchill's '42 prompt promise of all possible aid to Russia. For the surprised Communists, who had been warning of a "second Munich," the "imperialist" phase of the War was ended. They immediately began demanding all-out aid for both Britain and the U.S.S.R. and a no-strike policy for American labor—and President Roosevelt quickly regained his popularity with them. Browder himself remained in jail until May 1942, when President Roosevelt commuted his sentence without restoring his citizenship, of which he had automatically been deprived through his conviction on a felony charge.

In July 1942, in his first public speech since his release, Browder termed his fourteen months in jail "an incidental by-product of the desperate efforts of world reaction, headed by Hitler, to prevent by all means the realization of the United States-Soviet alliance which I, as spokesman for my party, had long advocated as essential to the national interests of our own country and to the whole freedom-loving world." During the next months one of his chief campaigns was for centralized control of war production; the other was for a Second Front in the West, for the lack of which, he charged, Churchill was to blame. Communist suspicion that Churchill might still manage that "second Munich" was, indeed, not entirely allayed until the Teheran conference of December 1943.

Teheran, to the Communists, represented a new turning point in world affairs—a sincere agreement among the United States, Britain, and Russia to cooperate both during and after the War. When the Third International had been dissolved in the spring of 1943, Browder had announced that the move would not affect his party decisions, since the American Communists had officially withdrawn from the International in November 1940. But Teheran produced a different reaction. In January 1944 the National Committee of the Communist Party announced: "It is beyond question that the post-War reconstruction, like production for the War at present, will be carried out under the system of free enterprise. It is equally evident that the political issues of this time will be decided within the form of the two-party system traditional in this country." At the Madison Square Garden meeting which followed it was announced that even such an "elementary measure" as a nationalization of banks, railroads, coal, and steel would be eliminated from the Communist program; since the American people were not prepared for socialism, any attempts in that direction would divide the United States and help the anti-Teheran forces to come to power. In May 1944 the Communist Party itself was officially dissolved, to be known henceforth as the Communist Political Association. Those who had long been urging that the Communist Party dissolve in the interests of national unity were not uniformly pleased, however. To some liberals, the new program seemed to be a total abandonment of Marxism, designed to win friends for Russia by appeasing such groups as the National Association of Manufacturers; conservatives were more inclined to disbelieve Browder's words. By the time of the Presidential campaign the Communists were being accused by Republicans of having seized control of the CIO's Political Action Committee, which was working for the re-election of President Roosevelt. Browder himself, testifying before a House investigating committee, said that some Communists were active in PAC but that some also were active in A.F. of L. political committees, "the Kiwanis, the Elks, the Democrats, the Republicans, the ministerial associations, and so forth." However, as the Presidential campaign progressed, Republicans repeated the charge, as did the Socialist Frederick Woltman, writer for the New York _World-Telegram_, who set forth his charges at length.

Browder has been responsible for the largest number of pamphlets published by any American Communist, and for several books, among them _Communism in the United States_ (1935), _What Is Communism?_ (1936), _The People's Front_ (1938), _Fighting for Peace_ (1939), _The Second Imperialist War_ (1940), _The Way Out_ (1941), _Victory—and After_ (1942), _Teheran— Our Path in War and Peace_ (1944). He is a frequent contributor to the *New Masses* and the *Daily Worker*, for which he served as correspondent in Spain in 1938. In June 1944 he was appointed editor in chief of the *Daily Worker*, a post which he had held previously for a short time in 1931.

Browder was married in 1926 in Moscow to the former Raissa Irene Berkman, a member of the Russian bar who had worked in one of the Soviet bureaus, but Mrs. Browder did not follow her husband to the United States until 1933. (Browder's first wife had divorced him and secured custody of their son.) In 1940 "Ria" Browder, as she is called by her friends, was arrested, found guilty of having entered the country illegally, and ordered deported. In April 1944, however, she was able to dissipate the doubts of the Board of Immigration Appeals as to her testimony that she was not a Communist, and the deportation order was withdrawn. Early in September Mrs. Browder received a visa from the Consul General in Montreal, the granting of which was recommended by the State Department Board of Appeals on visa cases after several Government agencies had protested against her re-entry into the United States.

The Browders, who live in a five-room apartment in Yonkers, New York, have three sons. Felix was born in Moscow, Andrew, in London, and William, in the United States. Browder is described as being highly indulgent with the children. "No one should be politically conscious before the age of fourteen," he has been quoted as saying. In June 1944 the Daughters of the American Revolution and the American Legion were among the organizations which honored Felix Browder with awards for scholarship upon his graduation from Yonkers Senior High School: among other things, he had attained a top mark of 100 in American history during his three years there.

Browder's salary has been variously reported as $35 and $40 a week, and he receives in addition royalties of several hundred dollars a year from his books. He has never owned an automobile, a house, or a plot of ground, and he works an average of twelve hours a day in his dingy little office on Twelfth Street in New York City. Recreation, when he finds time for it, consists of an occasional game of pool, bowling, the movies, or a baseball game. Only one male of the Browder line is not a member of the Communist Political Association—Earl's older brother Waldo. His brother Bill is treasurer of the New York State Committee.

The *Literary Digest* once described Browder as "a slight, stooped man with graying hair" who "looks about as much like the cartoonist's conception of a Communist as that incarnation of Middle Westernism, William Allen White '40." He impressed a *Current History* writer in 1936 as "a sweet-natured, almost wistful person, looking more like a lyric poet than the leader of a revolutionary faction." The *New Yorker* was less kind: "His tie is usually askew and his vest a little rumpled. He rarely buttons his coat and he has a hard time keeping the cuffs of his shirt from wholly engulfing his hands. . . . Going at full tilt, with one of the powerful cigars that he fancies clenched in his teeth, he could be readily mistaken for a harassed small-town lawyer."

References

Am Mag 121:29+ F '36
Cur Hist 45:93-7 O '36
Lit Digest 122:10 O 31 '36
New Yorker 14:20-4 S 24 '38; 14:24-9 O 1 '38
Time 31:9-11 My 30 '38; 34:20 N 13 '39
Who's Who in America 1944-45

BROWN, GILMOR Theatrical producer and director

Address: b. 39 S. El Moline Ave., Pasadena, Calif.

In the autumn of 1916 a young man, short on cash but long on determination, arrived in Pasadena, California, to put on some plays with his own little company of professional actors. He remained to found the Pasadena Community Playhouse, the "leading community theatre in America" as well as the oldest theatrical organization in the West. Under Gilmor Brown's direction that organization, which celebrated its twenty-fifth anniversary in 1943, has to its credit an impressive list of "firsts." It has produced more plays than any other organization in the world—an amazing total of 1,348 plays, of which seventy-six were world premières and twenty-four American premières. Called "one of the most complete theatrical-producing organizations in the world" and valued at $660,000, the Playhouse was the first organization in the world to produce *all* the plays of Shakespeare; and the first organization in the United States and second in the world to produce the ten Chronicle Plays of Shakespeare in chronological order. (Strangely enough, the first production of the Chronicle Plays was given in Germany by a group of striking coal miners.)

Gilmor Brown was born into a theatrical family. The event occurred in what can scarcely be called a theatrical center—New Salem, North Dakota. His father, Orville A. Brown, was a stock company owner and actor of English descent who was born in Illinois and who became a pioneer barnstormer in the Far West, where "sheer theatrical bravado" was necessary to continue a "professional existence." His mother, an actress, was Emma Louisa (Gilmor) Brown, born in Georgia of Scottish ancestry. Young Gilmor was educated in the public schools of New Salem and early in life acquired familiarity with every phase of theatrical activity in his parents' stock company. Impatient with the lack of facilities for theatrical study in the pioneer West, the young boy soon made his way to Chicago. There he studied with a distinguished teacher, Mrs. Milward Adams, onetime pupil of Steele MacKaye and André Antoine, the founders of the French Théâtre-Libre. Later Gilmor was fortunate to find a place with the famous Ben Greet Players, then fresh from England and appearing successfully in New York. He toured the country with them, later appearing in stock and road companies in the West.

By 1916 he had trained a small stock company, called the Savoy Players, and had brought them to Pasadena, together with his father and mother, his brother Frank, and his sister-in-law, the well known actress Vir-

GILMOR BROWN   Eaton

ginia Lykins Brown. As soon as they arrived Brown hired a bicycle and pedaled about the streets distributing handbills and posters to advertise his traveling players. His was no ordinary repertoire, for it included plays by Shaw, Barrie, Shakespeare, Ibsen, and Pinero. Brown was wise enough, however, to lighten this intellectual fare with *Ten Nights in a Barroom* and *Uncle Tom's Cabin*.

"To add to the suspicions of those not already altogether comfortable at the thought of live actors in their midst, the show duly opened at the unsavory 'Old Savoy,' where brazen hussies had oft kicked their heels in that doubtful entertainment known as 'burlesque.'" The ambitious and optimistic players opened to a small house that first evening in October 1916—a house that subsequently became smaller and smaller. In spite of this, Brown felt that Pasadena was a wonderful place to develop a permanent theatre. The next season he joined with the local Drama League in calling a public meeting for the purpose of establishing a community playhouse. Three hundred people attended, and on November 20, 1917 they put on their first show in the Shakespeare Club, working with a small number of professionals and an ambitious group of amateurs. The public showed a general apathy to the four one-act plays presented, but, nothing daunted, the group rented the "Old Savoy" and rechristened it the Community Playhouse.

In numbers of cities throughout the country, ambitious "little theatres" were starting, but most of them died a-borning. Not so the Community Playhouse, for it had the dynamic spirit of Gilmor Brown behind it. Even with volunteer actors and technicians, the Playhouse had tough sledding. Except for the providential donation of $500 from a Pasadena attorney, the Playhouse might have closed. The next year the group was incorporated as the Community Playhouse Association, and when another gift of $2,000 arrived the group was ready to go ahead—just in time

for the influenza epidemic of 1918-1919 to frighten away all but the most loyal. Playgoers as well as actors wore gauze masks. The audience suffered the inconveniences of a leaking tin roof, while the stage, says Brown, was so shallow that it gave the effect of a Greek frieze, and the actors were forced to "cross from one side of the stage to the other by running through the alley at the back of the building."

Under these conditions the Community Playhouse continued for eight years to present new, daring, and experimental plays. "There never was enough room, enough money, or enough anything except enthusiasm and loyalty and devotion at the old Playhouse," recalls Brown, but "today, the Playhouse has its own beautiful theatre, given us by the citizens of our community." The Playhouse, opened on May 18, 1925, is a striking and unusually beautiful building with its tree-shaded patio, old stone courtyard, and stone-covered corridors, "a lovely reminder of California's heritage from the days of the dons and the mission padres."

Brown's financial worries were still by no means over. Then a miracle happened. In May 1930 a quiet old lady stopped by the box office and asked how she might help. Told of the heavy mortgage which was keeping the management from expanding, she listened and left. The next day a check for $180,000 arrived, the gift of Mrs. Fannie Morrison, and again in 1936 Mrs. Morrison donated $160,000 for the acquisition of property adjoining the Playhouse and for the erection of a six-story annex so that all the various departments might be housed under one roof.

In addition to the main Playhouse there is the Laboratory Theatre, a training ground for developing players for the main theatre, which in 1928 became the Pasadena Playhouse School of the Theatre. By 1939 the school had 206 graduates out of a total of 371, who "were more or less steadily active in 'Theatre,' whether on Broadway, in pictures, in radio, in the teaching of theatre, or in directing and technical work in university and community theatres." Brown also has his own theatre, the Playbox, built in 1929. "An intimate theatre in its best sense," the tiny theatre seats about fifty and offers a unique opportunity for experiment in the drama.

The main Playhouse's regular production season is from October 1 to August 15. Brown explains that its purpose is "to give expression to the unusual play, the play of such artistic stature or vitality of statement as to be assured a place in dramatic literature, but which, because of cost of production or lack of immediate power to arouse general interest, is not readily available for the professional theatre." At the Playhouse, Brown says, "we may venture to offer plays like Masefield's *Melloney Holtspur* or Romain Rolland's *The Wolves* with the assurance that if only comparatively few care for them we soon shall be doing others with a greater general appeal; we can stage James Elroy Flecker's *Hassan* or *The Armored Train* by Vsevolod Ivanov because we have resources other than financial at our command which make their presentation possible. It is, I feel, a source of justifiable pride to us that many of these beautiful plays have first been presented to American audiences from the Playhouse stage."

One of the Playhouse activities which has brought it fame throughout the world is the series of Midsummer Drama Festivals which began in 1935. The first subject chosen was the ten Chronicle Plays of Shakespeare. "Perhaps," says Brown, "nothing the Playhouse has done, not even our much discussed production of Eugene O'Neill's *Lazarus Laughed*, has aroused more general interest among theatrical people of all countries." The second festival was again Shakespeare—the Greco-Roman plays. Then, as a gesture of gratitude to the California State Legislature for the honor of naming the Playhouse the State Theatre of California, the third festival was called "The Story of the Great Southwest" and included such plays as Gerhart Hauptmann's *The White Saviour* and Ramon Romero's *Miracle of the Swallows*. "Just before the opening curtain on the first night of *Miracle of the Swallows*," Brown says, "the Padre from San Juan Capistrano stepped suddenly from the wings to bless the work of the Playhouse, and the cast gathered on the stage waiting the opening scene of their play."

The fourth festival was called "Seven from Shaw." Brown had met the playwright and lunched at his home one day, discussing "the American theatre in general and the Playhouse in particular." The next two festivals, in 1939 and 1940, were devoted to the works of Maxwell Anderson '42 and Sir James M. Barrie. Since the outbreak of the War, the Playhouse has tried to contribute what it could "of relief and courage through the stabilizing influence of laughter." The festivals have consisted of the plays of George S. Kaufman '44, Booth Tarkington, and comedies by other American playwrights.

Gilmor Brown not only directs or supervises all the Playhouse productions—he frequently acts in them as well. Probably three of his best-remembered roles are those of Tiberius in *Lazarus Laughed*, Vershinin in *The Armored Train*, and Falstaff in *The Merry Wives of Windsor*. He is well known as a lecturer on the drama at the California Institute of Technology, the University of Southern California, and many other universities throughout the country. He was state director of the Federal Theatre Project from 1936 to 1937 and president of the National Theatre Conference. Many honors have been awarded him: he was the first recipient of the Arthur Noble Award gold medal, presented to him by the City Planning Commission of Pasadena as "the most useful citizen." In 1932 France made him an Officier de l'Instruction Publique for "significant service to the world at large in the arts," and he was awarded a bronze medal by the Société des Amitiés Françaises in 1936.

Tall, with a high forehead, fair hair, rather dreamy blue eyes, Brown is an extremely busy man who nevertheless gives the impression that he has time for every caller. Unlike many theatrical people, he is not dramatic of gesture, nor affected in speech. He is a bachelor. His day, and most of the evening too, is crowded with interviewing actors, playwrights, technicians, conferring with his assistants, conducting auditions and rehearsals, attending meetings, reading plays and seeing them produced. The Playhouse, under his direction, has taken a large part in war work, producing plays at nearby camps and entertaining servicemen visiting the theatre. Brown takes vacations merely to see new plays. His sole relaxation outside the theatre is reading himself to sleep at night with detective stories. Some time ago someone asked: "When does Gilmor Brown get any time for his personal life?" A friend who knows him well answered: "He has no personal life. His life *is* the theatre!"

References

National Theatre Conference Bul 5:3-14 Ap '43
Theatre Arts 19:513-17 Jl '35; 26:462 Jl '42; 27:411-20 Jl '43
Green, H. L. Gilmor Brown; Portrait of a Man and an Idea 1933
Who's Who in America 1944-45

BROWNELL, HERBERT, JR. Feb. 20, 1904- Chairman of the Republican National Committee

Address: b. Republican National Committee, Roosevelt Hotel, New York City; h. 140 E 19th St., New York City

Herbert Brownell, Jr., close personal friend of Thomas Dewey '44 and the least well known of the triumvirate (the other members are J. Russel Sprague and Edwin M. Jaeckle) which made possible Dewey's nomination as the Republican Presidential candidate in 1944, succeeded Harrison E. Spangler '43 as chairman of the Republican National Committee. His election to the office was announced on June 30, 1944, two days after Dewey had received the nomination.

A young lawyer who has served five terms in the New York State Legislature, Brownell was expected to assume a position of great responsibility in the National Government if the man whom he boosted for nomination had won the election in November 1944. The National Committee chairman is a native of Peru, Nebraska, where he was born February 20, 1904, the son of Herbert and May (Miller) Brownell. At an early age Brownell was taken to Lincoln, where his father taught at the University of Nebraska. As soon as Herbert, Jr., had been prepared for college, he enrolled at the University of Nebraska where he was elected to Phi Beta Kappa, and from which he was graduated in 1924.

Young Brownell then came East to study at the Yale Law School from which he received his L.L. B., *cum laude*, in 1927. He then became a law clerk in the New York City law firm of Root, Clark, Buckner, Howland, and Ballantine with which he remained two years. In 1932 he became a member of the law firm of Lord, Day, and Lord. Brownell's entry in politics was made as an election district captain in the old 10th Manhattan Assembly District. Working in the same district was another election captain, Thomas Dewey, and the two young political workers became good friends.

In 1931 Dewey acted as Brownell's campaign manager when the latter sought election to the New York State Assembly from the 10th

George Karger

HERBERT BROWNELL, JR.

District of New York County. Since this district housed the headquarters of Tammany Hall, then New York's most powerful Democratic organization, Brownell and Dewey had a stiff fight ahead of them. Their slogan was "100 per cent anti-Tammany," and they made use of at least one startling innovation—phonograph records with music and a speech by Brownell, which were sent to every voter in the district. (On these records it was Dewey who introduced Brownell.) Their vigorous campaigning did not win Brownell the election that year, but in 1932 he ran again and was then elected.

In the Assembly, where Brownell served from 1933 to 1937, he sponsored much progressive legislation, including a bill to give the people of New York City the opportunity to vote on a modern city charter, another bill providing for the official canvass of New York City election returns, and still another providing for "auditing" grand juries to investigate the government of counties twice a year. In 1934, Brownell, who had long taken an active interest in national as well as local activities of the Republican Party, was made head of the National Republican Committee on State Affairs.

There was some opposition to Brownell's candidacy in 1935 as Assembly majority leader because he was from New York City (it was felt that the leader should represent another area of the state), but he was nevertheless returned to office and continued to wield considerable power in the Assembly. Although Democratic Governor Herbert H. Lehman '43 was to leave one of the largest surpluses in the history of the state, Brownell was a frequent critic of Lehman's budget methods, objecting strongly to the deficits which existed in 1934 and 1935.

In 1937 Brownell announced that he would not be a candidate for renomination to the Assembly. He had, in the meanwhile, become interested in plans for the New York World's Fair, and when a New York State World's

Fair Commission was formed, Brownell became vice-chairman of the group.

Since 1941 Brownell's political fortunes have followed those of his friend, Thomas Dewey. In that year Dewey was honorary campaign chairman for Edgar J. Nathan, Jr., a Republican, who ran for the office of President of New York City's Borough of Manhattan. At Dewey's invitation Brownell became Nathan's campaign manager, and Edgar Nathan won the election. With this success behind him, Brownell turned to the management of Dewey's campaign for Governor in 1942. (Dewey had been a candidate in 1938 but was defeated by Governor Lehman.) Dewey won over John J. Bennett, the Democratic candidate, by nearly 650,000 votes, and Brownell went to Albany with Dewey to become one of his "key men."

The death in 1943 of New York's Lieutenant Governor, Thomas W. Wallace, necessitated the election of a new man to that post. Again Brownell managed a campaign, this time for Joe R. Hanley, and again his man won. With this record of political success it came as no surprise to political commentators that Dewey should immediately choose Brownell to manage his most important campaign—for the Presidency of the United States. Harrison E. Spangler, the former chairman, had won little popularity in liberal circles because of his avowed isolationist sympathies. Although it was thought that Brownell's appointment did not necessarily mean a repudiation of isolationism in the Republican Party, one commentator said Brownell's naming pointed to "the intention of forty-two-year-old Mr. Dewey both to make his a 'young man's campaign' and to effect a thoroughgoing housecleaning in the top ranks of the Republican national organization." John W. Bricker '43, Dewey's running mate, expressed hearty approval of Brownell's appointment.

Brownell promptly set to work organizing the campaign. He retained Spangler as general counsel for the committee and set up headquarters in New York City at the Roosevelt (he was careful to specify "Theodore Roosevelt") Hotel. He remained in constant communication with Governor Dewey and frequently served as his spokesman. Among Brownell's earliest statements was a criticism of President Roosevelt's '42 use of the title of Commander in Chief as "a pretext to perpetuate himself in political office." Brownell also saw "a misuse of wartime censorship" in what was reportedly a conference between the President and Robert E. Hannegan '44, the Democratic chairman, a few days before the opening of the Democratic Convention. In another statement Brownell charged the Democrats with being controlled by city machine bosses and radical Left-wingers. (In answer, R. J. Thomas '42, president of the United Automobile Workers and treasurer of the CIO Political Action Committee, denied that the CIO was conspiring with Democratic bosses.) Brownell also pointed to disunity within the Democratic ranks as presaging a Republican victory.

One of Brownell's most delicate tasks was to reconcile Wendell Willkie '40 sympathizers with the rest of the Republican Party. Announcing that he was determined that all factions in the party should have representation on the National Committee, he named several close political associates of Willkie's to important executive posts on the committee, and statements made to the press indicated that he expected Dewey support from Willkie. However, at the time of his death (October 8, 1944) Willkie had not come forth with an endorsement of Dewey nor declared himself at all on the election.

Believing that the part played by organized trade unionists and liberals, represented by the CIO's Political Action Committee, was one of the most important issues of the campaign, Brownell emphasized this, agreeing with the charge that the "Communist-led CIO" was playing a heavy part in the Roosevelt campaign and might attain undue influence in the Government if Roosevelt were re-elected. Brownell contended that union members were revolting against the attempts of Earl Browder '44, Communist chief, and Sidney Hillman '40, head of the Political Action Committee, to swing organized labor to New Deal candidates. Writing in the New York *Herald Tribune* on October 8, 1944, Brownell delineated his belief in the party system, declaring that victory for the Republican Party would mean its return to existence as a bona fide political party, thus safeguarding the political system under which the United States had developed into the world's greatest democracy. In this article Brownell expressed his belief that the emergence of the Political Action Committee is perhaps the most significant and alarming of all the developments in the metamorphosis of what was once a real American party (that is, the Democratic Party) into a mass of political automatons.

Until the day of the election in which President Roosevelt '42 was chosen for a fourth term, Brownell evinced faith in a sweeping Republican victory. While the Democratic press pointed out Brownell's "complete lack of experience in national politics," the young Manhattan lawyer was heartily praised by Republican papers at the end of the campaign. Said the New York *Herald Tribune* editorially: "One of the best deeds that Governor Dewey performed for the Republican Party in the recent campaign was his choice of Herbert Brownell, Jr., as chairman of the National Committee. This forty-year-old leader brought just about everything to the difficult job that he assumed. . . . He has brought youth, vigor, and a progressive outlook to an organization bogged down in caution and hesitation. We know that other careers have claims on him. But for the coming four years his continuing service as chairman seems to us the most important factor in the recovery of the party."

At the close of what the *New Republic* called the "bitterest election campaign in generations," Governor Dewey asked Brownell to stay on as chairman of the Republican National Committee. After Brownell's return in December from a month's vacation in Arizona, his part-time continuance as chairman was announced, although several Republican leaders in the Senate had earlier seen the chairmanship as a full-time job. Brownell immediately stated that he had called a meeting of the Republican National Committee for January 22, 1945, to be held in Indianapolis, for the purpose of authorizing "a vigorous, progressive, all-year-round program of party activity." Brownell had already expressed himself in favor of a definite party policy to take the place of mere criticism of the Roosevelt Administration. He has also advocated the strengthening of the committee's staff in preparation for the 1948 national election as well as the 1946 Congressional election.

In June 1944 Brownell celebrated the tenth anniversary of his marriage to the former Doris McCarter. Present at the celebration were their four children—Joan, Ann, Tom, and Jim. A youthful-looking man who is growing bald, friendly, soft-spoken Brownell says that his one relaxation is playing with his children.

References

N Y Times p1+ Jl 1 '44 por
Who's Who in New York 1938

BRYAN, GEORGE SANDS Sept. 6, 1879 —Dec. 22, 1943 Author, editor, and compiler; biographer of Thomas A. Edison and Sam Houston; former executive of *New Standard Encyclopedia*.

Obituary

N Y Times p19 D 23 '43

BURKE, CHARLES H. 1862—Apr. 7, 1944 Former United States Commissioner of Indian Affairs (1921-29) and one-time Congressman from South Dakota; member of the House of Representatives from 1899 to 1907 and from 1909 to 1915.

Obituary

N Y Times p13 Ap 8 '44 por

BUSCH, CARL (búsh) Mar. 29, 1862— Dec. 19, 1943 Internationally known composer and conductor; won Edwin Franko Goldman '42 Prize in 1920 for "the best composition for band by an American composer"; among his best-known choral works were *The Four Winds, May, Pan's Flute,* and *Sir Galahad*; conducted the Kansas City Symphony Orchestra for many years; was chiefly responsible for the development of the Kansas City Philharmonic Orchestra.

Obituary

N Y Times p23 D 20 '43 por

BUTLER, RICHARD AUSTEN Dec. 9, 1902- British Government official
Address: b. Board of Education, London; h. Stanstead Hall, Halstead, Essex, England

A highly significant development in Great Britain during these war years is the revolutionary recasting in 1944 of an educational system that had seen almost no change for the past seventy years. Considered by forward-looking Britons as important as the social recommendations of the Beveridge '43 plan, the drastic education reform "has for its objective the creation of a progressive system of education from nursery to college," in which "children would be treated as young citizens undergoing training for at least twelve of their most formative years." The program was published in July 1943 in the form of a White Paper by the alert young president of the British Board of Education, Richard Austen Butler, who has been called

British Official Photo

RICHARD AUSTEN BUTLER

"the outstanding Tory Socialist" in the House of Commons.

Richard Austen Butler was born in Attock Serai, India, on December 9, 1902, the eldest son of Sir Montagu S. D. Butler. While still a schoolboy he decided to make politics his career. From his public school, Marlborough, he went on to Pembroke College, Cambridge, where he soon became a leader in the university debates. He was president of the Union when Stanley Baldwin came to speak on the motion that "Oratory is the harlot of the arts." The Union was packed with students; when the votes were counted it was found that they were divided evenly. This meant that Butler, as chairman, had to cast the deciding vote. Without hesitation "he rose with a twinkle in his eye and blandly voted against his future political chief." At another time Butler led a Union debating team which argued against Columbia University's fastest talkers; the result was a draw.

After taking first class honors in modern languages and history Butler became a Fellow of Corpus Christi College (1925-29). In 1926 he was married to Sydney Courtauld, and he is now the father of three sons. Travel and parliamentary duties (he was elected M.P. from Saffron Walden in 1929) took up the next few years. In 1932 Butler was made Under-Secretary of State for India. His chief was Lord Halifax '40, who could speak only in the House of Lords. This meant that Butler had to carry in Commons the entire responsibility for the Foreign Office. However, he piloted the India Bill successfully through the House of Commons, and was personally responsible for the drafting of a good deal of it. He was Under-Secretary of State for Foreign Affairs from 1938 to 1941.

His own qualifications, plus a distinguished family background, led to Butler's appointment, in 1941, as the president of the British Board of Education. His father, Sir Montagu Butler, is Master of Pembroke College, Cambridge. Other scholars and teachers in the Butler family line included two headmasters of Harrow, and one of Haileybury, a professor at University College, London, and a master of Trinity College, Cambridge. On his mother's side Butler is the nephew of the late Sir George Adam Smith, principal of Aberdeen University.

Changed conditions brought about by the Second World War faced the new president of the Board of Education. One of these was the necessity of fostering education among Europeans who are exiled from their own countries. At a meeting in February 1942 of the ministers of education of the United Nations, Butler said: "Allied children attend our elementary and secondary schools with our children. We have established here a French lycée, several Belgian schools, a Belgian technical training institute, and a Czech army school, among other institutions. We hope to establish a special school for the children brought here from successful raids on Norwegian fjords." It was his belief, he said, that a common educational ideal would be the most important prelude to genuine European comity. In February 1944 it was reported that he was pressing a plan to facilitate post-War student exchanges, in talks with the representatives of Allied governments. The plan called for the elimination of matriculation examinations for students of countries which would participate in the proposed agreements.

The evacuation of children in England provided another unusual problem. The state school system had to handle this matter of evacuation, which meant "a drastic upheaval of educational methods and the doubling up of children from the city with country children in rural schools, with the consequent shortening of hours of instruction and lowering of standards." In other cases the evacuated city children returned to find that their former schools had been taken over as rest hostels or first-aid centers—or had been actually destroyed in bombing raids. Further, since England is a country which does not favor women teachers for boys beyond the age of eleven, the fact that 20,000 male teachers had joined the armed services created a serious shortage of teachers throughout England.

On the bright side of the ledger, however, the War has resulted "in greater powers being given to school authorities, and greater influence is wielded by those authorities over children." British traditionalists, it is said, dislike the fact that the trend of education is now away from private control. However, "the Board of Education professes to have little fear that exclusive public schools like Eton and Harrow will be harmful to the nation. It is pointed out that the predominance today of public school graduates with their old school ties, in the Cabinet as elsewhere in the life of this country, is due to the poor standard of schools generally thirty or forty years ago when the present leaders of Britain were youngsters."

By July 1943 the president of the Board of Education had in hand, to present to the House of Commons, a drastic and provocative new blueprint for recasting Britain's educational system. Like the Beveridge report, it was conceived on a grand scale with post-War Britain in mind. Called "the first truly fresh approach to the subject since 1870," Butler's plan contained reforms that would have significance "far beyond the walls of the schoolhouse, for they would strengthen the social fabric of the nation as a whole."

The new system encompasses raising the school-leaving age to sixteen (it is now fourteen) and the institution of a further "youth service" which envisages compulsory part-time education and physical education up to the age of eighteen, quite apart from the present voluntary system. Further, Britain's schools of the future must provide all children with supplementary food and medicine, and in cases of need, with shoes and clothing as well. There is to be a great increase in the number of nursery schools, not only in large cities but in country districts. In the next age grouping, five to eleven, more emphasis is to be placed on preparation for secondary school training. These secondary schools will offer not only work toward administrative and professional careers, but also courses in engineering, commerce, farming, and kindred subjects. The Butler plan envisages children required to remain in a secondary school until sixteen, or else put in part-time day attendance at a "young people's college" until eighteen. This would require the hiring of at least 60,000 more teachers.

Said Butler in his speech before the House of Commons: "From the point of view of the country's manufacturing industry, agriculture, and commerce, training afforded by a system of part-time education in conjunction with employment is long overdue. . . . More and more in the future it will be necessary to rely on the capacity, adaptability, and quality of our industrial and commercial personnel. Had fuller attention been given earlier to the all-important question of training young workers, some difficulties experienced by the services and industries during the present War would have been markedly less acute." He said further that, in response to a "very general wish," daily worship service and religious instruction had been recommended—with, of course, parents and teachers reserving the right to "withdraw if they choose."

In March 1944 Butler's liberal Education Bill was before the half-empty benches of the House of Commons. A Tory member rose to propose an amendment granting equal pay to women teachers. Gently Butler objected that equal pay had nothing to do with the Education Bill, and should be considered at some other time. All at once, in Time's words, "all the country's discontent with Winston Churchill's management of home affairs whistled over." In the ensuing debate Butler insisted that a vote for equal pay would be a vote against "the interests of this great reform," a vote "against the Government." When members asked why the House could not vote on teachers' pay without involving the question of confidence in the Government he retorted: "Childish. . . . I am here to give a lead. . . . I must put myself and the Government in the hands of the House. . . ." The resulting vote was 117 to 116 in favor of the amendment; Churchill's coalition Government had suffered parliamentary defeat for the first time.

The day after his defeat Churchill went to the House to demand a general vote of confidence, refusing to leave the amendment on the books. The next day a packed House gave him an overwhelming vote of confidence, yet "few even among his most ardent supporters could fail to see that he had lost ground as the nation's leader. The issue was not considered by many members to be an honest one."

That same afternoon Butler was greeted with prolonged applause. According to the New York Times, "He spoke about equal pay in the same terms as heretofore and then explained to a sympathetic audience the religious and political complexities of the Education Bill. He concluded by apologizing for having caused so great a commotion. This was pure good manners on his part, for every member appreciated the fact that undercurrents created the disturbance and not Mr. Butler's bill."

Final passage of the measure, which had taken Butler three years of hard work to frame and to pilot on a complex course through Parliament, came on August 3, 1944. A bewigged clerk in the House of Lords observed an ancient custom by speaking four words in Norman-French, "Le roy le veult" ("The King wills it"). Thus the Education Bill became an act, a major landmark in British history and a major triumph for its sponsor.

"Observers in both British and American educational systems recognize," reported the Christian Science Monitor, "that the British problem is complicated because there is so much of the old and traditional to scrub out in Britain." It is not claimed, however, that every inequality is ironed out with one stroke. "But for England, which in the past has certainly had big inequalities in education, this new Education Act ranks as revolutionary." It will be expensive—200 million pounds yearly when it is fully operative, compared with 120 million today. Teaching staffs will have to be increased 50 per cent. New schools will have to be built. All of which, under present wartime and the immediate post-War circumstances, does not promise rapid progress toward the goal. Nevertheless, there is nationwide confidence that British children are "well on their way to a new deal in fitting them to be better, happier citizens."

Richard Austen Butler (known to all his friends in the Commons smoking room as "Rab") is a man not only persuasive and convincing, but one who "usually gets his own way in the end—or at least finds a middle way along which all parties can travel to a common objective." That objective he has repeatedly stressed: "I want to see equal opportunities for every boy and girl in this country. Plans for the shaping of a new world are in hand. Education is one of the vital factors in a democratic way of life. If democracy is to work, we must have a well-informed and highly intelligent community. And we must have leaders—men of vision and ability. In the past a great number of our leaders have come from the public schools and universities. In the future it must be made possible for the child of the very poorest parents in our midst

BUTLER, RICHARD AUSTIN—*Continued*

to have the chance of a public school and university education."

References

N Y Sun p6 Ap 1 '44
N Y Times p4 F 12 '42; IV p9 Ja 31
'43 por; p7 Jl 18 '43; p8 Mr 31 '43;
IV p7 S 5 '43 por; p1+ Mr 31 '44
Time 43:35-6 Ap 10 '44
Who's Who 1944

CADOGAN, SIR ALEXANDER (GEORGE MONTAGU) (ka-dug'an) Nov. 25, 1884- British diplomat; Permanent Under-Secretary of State for Foreign Affairs

Address: b. The Foreign Office, London; h. 18 Sloane Gardens, London

Heading the British delegation to the exploratory four-power Dumbarton Oaks conference on peace and post-War security in August 1944 was the Honorable Sir Alexander Cadogan, Permanent Under-Secretary of State for Foreign Affairs. He is a frequent delegate to international conferences, having been present at Cairo and Quebec in 1943 and at Quebec in September 1944. An able diplomat, he holds one of the highest offices in the famous British civil service. Although the permanent department staffs, being nonpolitical public servants, carry out whatever policies are set forth by the various Parliamentary Ministers and Secretaries, the Permanent Under-Secretaries use their long experience in the field as advisers to the Secretaries, who are responsible to the Cabinet.

The Honorable Alexander George Montagu Cadogan was born November 25, 1884, the seventh and youngest child of George Henry, the fifth Earl of Cadogan, and Beatrix Jane, daughter of the second Earl of Craven. The Cadogans' lineage is traced to one Cadwgan ap Elystan of the fourth royal tribe of Wales; the surname took its present form about 1600.

SIR ALEXANDER CADOGAN

Before his son's birth the Earl had been Member of Parliament from Bath, Under-Secretary for War, and Under-Secretary for Colonies. During Alexander Cadogan's childhood the Earl was successively Lord Privy Seal, Lord Lieutenant of Ireland, and First Mayor of Chelsea, a metropolitan borough of London.

"Ouida . . . could not have imagined a background more completely in the tradition of Victorian diplomacy than Cadogan's." His education was typical of the training given those well-born younger sons who very largely make up the British foreign service and the higher civil service generally. At twenty-three, after attending Eton and Balliol College, Oxford, Cadogan entered the public service as a diplomatic attaché. In January 1909 he left England for Constantinople to take up his duties there; on arrival, he found a counter-revolution against the 1908 revolution of Young Turks in full swing. The newly arrived attaché at once set about learning Turkish, succeeding so well that in 1910 he was granted a special allowance for his knowledge of the language. In May of that year he received his first promotion, to third secretary of the Embassy.

After three and one-half years in Turkey, Cadogan was recalled to London, where he spent nine months at the Foreign Office. In August of that year (1912) he was married to Lady Theodosia Louisa Augusta Acheson, daughter of the fourth Earl of Gosford, whose family has large holdings in the British-American Tobacco Company. Then Cadogan was assigned to Vienna, where he arrived in the spring of 1913, a few months before another crisis culminated, on August 12, 1914, in Britain's declaration of war on Austria-Hungary. Two days later Cadogan left for London, where he returned to the Foreign Office as a junior clerk. In 1919 he was raised to first secretary and sent to Paris. As Secretary General of the United Kingdom delegation to the League of Nations, he was largely responsible for the British draft of the proposed convention on disarmament, and attended many conferences bearing on the problems of collective security.

After seven more years, in May 1926 Cadogan received the honor of Companion of St. Michael and St. George, and in 1928 he was promoted to counsellor in the Foreign Office. After the invasion of Manchuria by the Japanese in 1931 his chief concern in this post lay in the hope of establishing the means of security in the Western Hemisphere. In March 1932 Cadogan was created a Companion of the Bath, and two years later a Knight Commander of the Order of St. Michael and St. George. Then, in January 1934, he was sent to Peiping as Envoy Extraordinary and Minister Plenipotentiary to China, and when the British Legation was raised to the status of an embassy in May 1935, Sir Alexander became Ambassador.

Recalled to Whitehall in 1936 by Foreign Minister Anthony Eden [40], Cadogan was made Deputy Under-Secretary of State for Foreign Affairs, serving under Lord Vansittart [41], then Sir Robert Vansittart, the Permanent Under-Secretary. In January of 1938 when Lord Vansittart was "kicked upstairs" to the new post of Chief Diplomatic Adviser to the Foreign Office, Sir Alexander Cadogan succeeded him as Permanent Under-Secretary.

In this capacity Sir Alexander is in control not only of the Foreign Office's staff of experts, but of the British Intelligence and the Office's secret funds. As Permanent Under-Secretary, Sir Alexander is above any party control; he cannot be removed from office by the elected Government except for misconduct. While Foreign Secretaries may come and go with every Parliamentary shift, the Permanent Under-Secretaries remain in office.

In keeping with his position, in the 1939 New Year's Honors Sir Alexander was created a Knight Grand Cross of St. Michael and St. George, and two years later a Knight Commander of the Bath. Although his position does not ordinarily bring him into the public eye, Sir Alexander has been taking a vital part in most of the important conferences. In 1939 he accompanied Prime Minister Neville Chamberlain to Rome to confer with Mussolini '42; from the outbreak of war he has met with the Supreme War Council. In January 1942 he was present at the Stalin '42-Eden conference in Moscow, and later attended the Russian leader's discussions with Winston Churchill '42, whom he also accompanied to the Teheran conference of Allied war leaders in December 1943 and to other international discussions. And it was he who, with American Under-Secretary of State Sumner Welles '40, drafted the Atlantic Charter in the summer of 1941.

In 1944, in pursuance of the American-British-Russian-Chinese Moscow Declaration of October 30, 1943, the United States invited the three other powers to a preliminary discussion at Dumbarton Oaks, near Washington, to draft a proposal for a world organization to preserve the peace. This proposal was then to be submitted to all the United Nations. Sir Alexander was chosen to head the British delegation (the other chairmen were: for the United States, Under-Secretary of State Edward R. Stettinius, Jr. '40; Soviet Union, Ambassador Andrei A. Gromyko '43; China, Ambassador to England Dr. V. K. Wellington Koo '41.) At the one meeting open to the press Sir Alexander expressed a general view similar to that taken by the other speakers, Secretary of State Cordell Hull '40 and Gromyko (the Chinese delegation was not to arrive until the Soviet representatives had left, because of Russia's neutrality toward Japan). Cadogan's speech was considered by some commentators the most realistic of the three because he pointed out that "it is obvious that unless the Great Powers are united in aim and ready to assume and fulfill loyally their obligations, no machine for maintaining peace, however perfectly constructed, will in practice work." In his report to Commons, the Prime Minister declared, "His Majesty's Government could have had no more able official representative than Sir Alexander Cadogan."

The wiry, sloping-shouldered, mustached Under-Secretary is termed "a model diplomat." "Reticent, cool, meticulous, carefully colorless in manner and speech," he is also "thorough, neat, and precise . . . with a notable penchant for clarity and brevity" and "a passion for anonymity equal to that of all six Presidential assistants. He has "an engaging smile with which he can toss in an apt classic quotation and close a delicate subject." He and Lady Theodosia have one son, Alec Ambrose Patrick George, and three daughters, Patricia, Cynthia, and Gillian Moyra. Their father's own version of "doodling" is to draw quick sketches of visitors at the Foreign Office.

References

N Y Sun p16 Ap 10 '44
Newsweek 24:46 Ag 28 '44 por
Burke's Peerage 1936
International Who's Who 1942
Who's Who 1944

CANDEE, ROBERT C(HAPIN) (kan-dē) June 4, 1892- United States Army officer

Address: b. Army Air Forces, Washington, D.C.; h. 1507 W. Seventh Ave., Spokane, Wash.

Teaching what he learned as head of the American 8th Air Support Command "somewhere in England" is Brigadier General Robert Chapin Candee, who joined the Air Corps in 1922 after five years as a cavalry officer. He was born June 4, 1892, to Fred J. and Carrie N. (Hill) Candee in Hinsdale, Illinois, and attended the public schools there. Candee was graduated from Cornell University in 1915; and, after some graduate study, was commissioned a 2nd lieutenant in the United States Cavalry on November 30, 1916.

Candee saw duty with the cavalry on the Mexican border, and was then assigned as an instructor at Fort Bliss, Texas, where he remained until 1920. In that year he was ordered to the Philippines. While on duty there the young cavalryman enrolled in the air observer course at Clark Field and served three months with the 3rd Observation Squadron, becoming a qualified observer. He acted as aide to Governor General Leonard Wood until 1922, when he returned to the United States to enter primary flying school. In 1923, having been graduated from the Advanced Flying School at Kelly Field (Texas) and having served three months as air observer with the 3rd Observation Squadron, Candee completed a course in bombardment aviation which qualified him as a bombardment pilot. (He now holds the aeronautical ratings of command pilot and combat observer.) He then served as director and senior instructor of bombardment training at the Advanced Flying School and as a school executive until 1926, when he left to attend the Air Corps Tactical School at Langley Field (Virginia).

After a year of study at the Air Corps Tactical School and another at the Command and General Staff School (Fort Leavenworth, Kansas), Candee returned as instructor at the Tactical School, where he spent some four years. In 1928 he was married to Katharine Chickering. (They have one daughter, Katharine.) From July of 1932 to July of 1934 he was stationed in Panama as Air Officer and Executive of the 19th Wing, and was then assigned to the Office of the Chief of Air Corps in Washington, D.C. Two more years

BRIG. GEN. ROBERT C. CANDEE

of instruction followed: at the Army War College, 1935-1936, at the Navy War College, 1936-1937, and two years of service as executive of the 18th Wing in Hawaii. In September 1939 Candee returned to duty in the Office of the Chief of Air Corps, Washington, D.C.

Command of the 4th Air Support Command at Hamilton Field (California) was given to Candee in July 1941. He held this position until January 1942, when he was sent to Brazil on official business, returning to the United States in March. He was made commander of the 8th Air Support Command of the 8th Air Force; in June he received the promotion to brigadier general (temporary) in the Army of the United States; and in July he "proceeded to the European theatre of operations" and established his headquarters in England. General Candee describes his work there as "organizing and training the 8th Air Support Command somewhere in England for the coming invasion of Nazi-held Europe. The command furnished several units for the North African invasion and since July 16, 1943 has been actively engaged in attacks on German airdromes and installations in northern France, Belgium, and Holland."

On May 16, 1943 a correspondent reported, "General Candee's establishment is quite modest just now. He has some troop carriers (converted from airliners), some cargo gliders capable of carrying two pilots and either fifteen fully equipped troops or one jeep, and some Spitfires and some Piper Cubs for reconnaissance." By September of that year the 8th Air Support Command had been built up to the point where it was described officially as utilizing "reconnaissance planes, fighters, fighter-bombers, light and medium bombers, troop carrier planes, and gliders. Its targets, which include armored forces, bridges, supply depots, massed troops, etc., are close to the front, as contrasted with the more distant objectives of the long-range heavy bombers of a bomber command. The mission of a

support command is essentially offensive." Support Command planes will be responsible for carrying invading paratroops, dropping supplies to ground forces, and transporting air-borne infantrymen by glider. Aerial photographs are taken and dropped by parachute for ground troops to use as guides in their advance through enemy territory.

The key words in the Support Command setup are "cooperation" and "integration." Described originally as "established to coordinate activities of American bomber and fighter forces in support of American invasion troops," the Support Command is designed to work with and for the ground troops in closest harmony. "This," according to Drew Middleton, "necessitates a large but delicately adjusted system of signals. It seems best to have a single unit dealing with both reports from the air and requests for air support from advanced airfields and from the vanguard of the ground forces." Middleton further states that "The R.A.F.'s Tactical Air Force is anchored in the Fighter Command, which means that when operations start it can be called on freely for fighter support for its light and medium bombers. The same is true, to a large measure, in the American Air Support Command. However, it is likely that before the operations open on the Continent both the American and British T.A.F. will be merged into a single force, which will have the greatest leeway in calling for fighters, whether they bear the cockade of the R.A.F. or the star of the U.S.A.A.F."

A demonstration of Support Command operation was described thus: "A 'veep'—a jeep equipped with a two-way radio set—was drawn up. . . . 'I want you to imagine,' he [General Candee] said, 'that the veep is up with the forward elements of an American ground force, attacking a dangerous salient. Now watch what happens.' The veep was calling for air support. In a few minutes Spitfires zoomed over the tree tops, clearing a path for medium bombers sent to blast an enemy strong point barring the Americans' advance. In the early stages of the invasion radio messages will be sent by veeps flown over the sea in gliders. Air-borne troops will travel in 'sky trains'. . . . As a troop carrier, the sky train carries twenty-eight men; as an ambulance, eighteen stretchers in three tiers. . . . As Support Command's field headquarters calls for reconnaissance planes, fighters and bombers are handled in a control tent by high-ranking officers of both air and ground forces working together."

Since his arrival in England, General Candee has had little leisure for recreation; but in less hurried times he makes a hobby of photography, plays tennis and squash, and likes to watch football games and tennis matches. He is a member of the Scottish Rite and Shrine. The General makes a point of keeping his two precious loose-leaf notebooks up to date—they are filled with "graphic statistical presentation of facts" and he can find in them anything at all he wants to know about his command, instantly. He carefully maintains his skill as a pilot by keeping up his flying time, and has had his C-47 fitted up as a "flying headquarters, befitting a command that is in its nature mobile." By this means he frequently visited and inspected several stations in one day. According to *Time* Magazine, Brigadier General Candee "reads Ruskin before breakfast, is an expert grammarian, is often called 'poker face.' Officers jump when he speaks, learn well when he teaches his ground-air coordination specialty." By May 1944 Candee was back in Washington at the Army and Navy Staff College.

References

Time 40:68 Ag 10 '42 por

Directory of Living Alumni Cornell University 1938

CANEGATA, LEONARD LIONEL CORNELIUS See Lee, C.

CANIFF, MILTON A(RTHUR) (kan'if)
Feb. 28, 1907- Cartoonist
Address: b. Daily News Bldg., 220 E. 42 St., New York City; h. New City, Rockland County, N. Y.

When in 1930 the late Billy Ireland, cartoonist for the Columbus *Dispatch*, said to a young man who was wavering between art and the theatre for his future career, "Stick to your inkpots, kid, actors don't eat regularly," he little knew that he was influencing the lives of some twenty million people. Had Caniff not taken his advice, today those people would be opening their newspapers and not finding "Terry and the Pirates"—and what is sadder, they would not even be expecting to find it. In its ten years of life the comic strip "Terry and the Pirates," replete with mysterious Oriental intrigue, involving handsome, dashing heroes, beautiful menaced heroines, subtle, ingenious villains, and assorted remarkable characters, has become one of the most popular "comic" strips in the United States. (Actually, the term is a misnomer, as "Terry" is not a series of cartoons, but an adventure story told through the medium of the picture strip.) It is also running as a five-times-a-week serial on the Blue Network stations; but the radio show is not a presentation of the adventure strip. Instead, it uses the characters and setting Caniff has made popular in an original story. The artist asks only that the script writer, Al Barker, "do right by his characters"—and so far, he has had no complaints. Barker, who was selected for the *Terry* series after writing "more kid shows than anyone else in radio," describes the serial as "a kid show with sophistication for the adults—but plenty of *zing* for the kids." The description would serve as well for Caniff's original adventure strip.

Many of Caniff's fans are confident that if he was not born and bred in China, he must at least have spent a good many years there. He has not, however, so much as passed through China. Milton Arthur Caniff was born in Hillsboro, Ohio, on February 28, 1907, the only child of Scottish and Irish parents: John W. Caniff, a printer, and the former Elizabeth Burton. Young Caniff attended the public schools of Hillsboro, except during the winter, when the family migrated to Redlands, California. He received his high school education at Stivers High School in Dayton, Ohio,

Self-portrait

MILTON A. CANIFF

and, upon graduation, entered Ohio State University, where he participated in dramatics and served as art editor of the campus magazine, in addition to outside work on newspapers. In the words of the *New Yorker*, Milton Caniff "established himself as a big man both on and off the campus by belonging to Sigma Chi fraternity [which was in 1937 to present him with a 'Significant Sig' medal—the youngest of its members to be so honored] and [to] an impressive list of other social, dramatic, and honorary societies; by serving as art editor of his senior-year yearbook and of the college humor magazine; and by working afternoons at $17 a week as a retoucher in the art department of the Columbus *Dispatch*."

Caniff had been working in the art department of various papers since 1920. From 1920 until 1925 he was with the Dayton (Ohio) *Journal*. During the summer of 1925 he worked on the Miami (Florida) *Daily News*, and the following fall he started work on the Columbus (Ohio) *Dispatch*. During these early years he disliked drawing women; today his comic strips prove how successfully one can overcome one's youthful prejudices. Meanwhile Caniff was also dabbling in the theatre—he played a few bit parts for Hollywood films and worked in amateur theatrical and stock companies. When he received his B.A. from the University in the summer of 1930 he could not decide which of the two professions to choose. At the time he was working on the Columbus *Dispatch*, and Ireland gave him the advice which should by now be historic to properly appreciative "Terry" fans.

In 1932 the Associated Press offered the young artist a job, and he left Columbus to go to New York. For two years he drew the strips "Dickie Dare" and "The Gay Thirties" for A.P. Then in 1934 he was summoned by the Chicago *Tribune*-New York *Daily News* Syndicate. Captain Joseph M. Patterson [42], publisher of the *News*, had a specific idea for

CANIFF, MILTON A.—*Continued*

a comic strip in mind. He wanted a strip "based on a blood-and-thunder formula, carrying a juvenile angle, and packed with plenty of comedy, sex, and suspense. The locale, he insisted, must be the Orient—last outpost for adventure." Caniff knew nothing whatever about China, but he did extensive research, and discovered that in that country piracy was a standard occupation, handed down from father to son and, failing a son, from father to daughter. Recognizing the dramatic values inherent in this theme, Caniff created a beautiful villainess and called her the Dragon Lady. As dramatic foils, he went back to the types he had employed in "Dickie Dare"—a blond American boy (whom he called Terry Lee), traveling with his handsome and resourceful tutor (called, in this case, Pat Ryan). The two heroes and the search for a secret mine which Caniff used as the device to bring them to China were typical adventure story material. But as the story progressed, as Pat and Terry came into contact with the genuinely original character of the Dragon Lady, the secret mine was forgotten, and the strip took on credibility and relative depth of characterization. These qualities, plus Caniff's excellent draftsmanship, explain the great success of "Terry and the Pirates." In turn, they are perhaps traceable to Caniff's desire to achieve authenticity. His studio is a museum of Far Eastern lore. He has collected a large library of books on all subjects relating to the Orient, and twelve filing cases full of pictures, clippings, and documents, ranging from Chinese poetry to Chinese recipes and telegraph blanks. In addition, he has a collection of all sorts of objects he might have occasion to draw in the strip, including opium pipes and many weapons, modern and ancient. Perhaps the most important collection for his work is the group of accurate sketches he has made showing Chinese junks, soldiers, and anything not already in his files. Much of Caniff's authentic material he owes to a number of advisers in the Orient who are in a position to answer from first-hand observation any questions he may have; and he also subscribes to thirty publications. Probably this unusual knowledge of Far Eastern affairs enables Caniff to make his remarkably accurate prophecies of events there.

"Terry and the Pirates" showed both the full-scale Japanese invasion of China and the Japanese attack on the United States well in advance of their actual occurrence. "Long before German-Japanese collaboration in the Far East was a known fact, stiff, monocled German officers appeared as confederates of 'the invader.'" Several of Caniff's fiction weapons have turned out to be sober military fact; of one torpedo raft he portrayed, the Navy Department wrote Caniff an official letter asking him to let them know before putting such ideas in the funny paper.

In the ten years since Terry landed on the China coast, he has grown from a boy in knee-pants to a fighter pilot, serving under the wisecracking super-ace, Flip Corkin, a faithful portrait of Caniff's even more incredible college friend, Philip Cochran. His characterization is accurate in every detail, except that

"Cochran's real-life promotions have come so fast that his alter ego hasn't been able to keep pace," and Corkin was still being addressed as Major long after his model had become Colonel Cochran. Apart from this, the only fictional detail in Caniff's portrait is that Flip is pleasantly involved with a freckle-faced Army nurse, although, as Cochran says, "Taffy Tucker is still just an imaginary gal. Personally, I prefer hat-check chicks and showgirls."

Another character taken directly from life is Dude Hennick, actually Dude Higgs of the Chinese Government airline, Caniff's college friend and chief adviser on things Oriental. A comic strip tradition was broken when Caniff permitted the death of Hennick's sweetheart, heiress Raven Sherman. When she was buried, "the [comic strip] syndicate was flooded with telegrams, flowers, condolence cards, and more than 1,500 letters," on the order of: "Who do you think you are—God? You can't kill Raven and get away with it." Raven was only one of the charming women with whom Caniff has always liberally embellished "Terry and the Pirates"—all short-nosed, with full, small mouths, arched brows, generous curves, and incredibly tiny waists. Probably the most important of these, and the most original character, was the Dragon Lady, a seductive and resourceful half-caste pirate captain with definitely Occidental make-up—even to a lovely permanent wave coiffure. When the Japanese invasion became official, she followed the example of China's actual river pirates by leading her pirate crew as guerrillas organized against the enemy. Normandie Drake, Pat's demure heart-throb, has also made occasional appearances, as has Terry Lee's wide-eyed Southern junior miss, April Kane. Of the forty-five important characters who have appeared in "Terry," some, in the *New Yorker*'s words, are "calm, well-adjusted types, but many are bundles of emotional quirks. One character is troubled by an anxiety neurosis, another with nymphomania, and still another with transvestitism." But the greatest uproar was created by slinky, slangy Burma, the Jean Harlow-ish chorus girl with a heart of gold.

There was almost a revolution when, because of his syndicate's fear of infringement, Caniff had to eliminate Burma from the comic strip he contributes (free of charge) to over 1,000 service newspapers. Originally it was a special version of "Terry," slanted toward army tastes; but newspapers which had paid for exclusive rights to the feature complained, and so Caniff substituted another strip, "Male Call," with a completely different set of characters. This meant that Burma had to go—leaving a note saying that the soldiers could see her in the funny papers. "The transition," *Life* commented, "was easy for Caniff but very hard on the Army. . . . Caniff was flooded with complaints. Soldiers sent angry letters, sad letters, and some letters that sounded lovesick. On further acquaintance with Lace [Burma's wide-eyed brunet chorus friend and successor], however, the soldiers are beginning to feel reconciled to losing Burma."

Unlike Pat Ryan, now a naval officer, whom the tall, dark, blue-eyed Caniff resembles, the artist was rejected by the services for a childhood leg injury. He has, however, also served the Army by illustrating its *Pocket Guide to China*, which includes instructions on how to tell the difference between the Chinese and the Japanese. This official handbook is distributed to all United States soldiers in the Orient.

Radio producers, ever on the alert for material with demonstrated audience appeal, decided to cash in on "Terry's" huge following. On September 25, 1938, the first performance of *Terry and the Pirates* was broadcast. The serial was based on the strip, but used its own situations, and was presented three times a week. It went off the air on March 22, 1939, and was revived on January 1, 1942. As now presented, the program is broadcast five days a week over all the stations of the Blue Network. Caniff, although not concerning himself with any of the actual details of production, keeps the script-writer informed of any pending important changes in *Terry*, such as the introduction of new characters.

Today Caniff's income from Terry is written in five figures. He lives with his wife, a Great Dane, and a wire-haired fox terrier forty miles up the Hudson from New York City, in a "big white house," wrote Howard Whitman, "built by Henry Varnum Poor'[42], the artist, in what might be called a motif of modernistic Bohemianism. Though streamlined in design, it is made of cinderblock covered with waterproof paint with the same kind of surface both inside and out. The living room flooring is raw, untreated tulip wood, and the fireplace is flanked by bare firebrick. The idea was to keep everything in its natural state. Caniff covered over a beautiful mahogany radio-phonograph with raw wood to keep it from clashing. The house has no rugs or draperies, providing a stern, unfettered simplicity in which the art spirit undoubtedly feels at home."

Caniff works from noon to 6:00 a.m. with two assistant cartoonists, but is always behind schedule. "Male Call" is done in his so-called spare time. Although Caniff writes with his right hand, he draws with his left. He works plots out in his head as he goes along. At times he has enmeshed his characters so deeply in the problems he devised that, in his words, "I almost went nuts trying to get them out." He is helped in "fathoming the feminine angle" by his wife, the former Esther Parsons, to whom he was married in 1930. She is not one of the "Terry" readers. Assistance is also furnished by his secretary, and by the girl who poses for most of his feminine characters. The use of models is a distinctive feature of Caniff's comic strip technique.

Recognized as an excellent draftsman, Caniff has found time for painting. An exhibition of his sketches and adventure strip drawings, held at the Julien Levy Galleries in December 1940, was hailed as showing "a genuine creative talent in the field of modern Americana," and some of his work has hung in the Metropolitan Museum of Art. Its creator has been characterized by *Mademoiselle* as "sweet and kinda plump."

During the 1944 political campaign Caniff was an active member of the Rockland County artists' and writers' committee, led by actress Helen Hayes'[42] and playwright Maxwell Anderson'[42], which worked to unseat Republican Hamilton Fish'[41] from his long-held place in Congress. When the committee was threatened with a libel suit the late Wendell Willkie'[40] volunteered his legal services for the defense. The charge was subsequently dropped, and Augustus W. Bennet, a Republican endorsed by the Democrats, was elected to represent the district.

References

Life 10:34+ Ja 6 '41 il pors
New Yorker 19:25 Ja 8 '44
Newsweek 16:48 D 16 '40
Who's Who in America 1944-45
Who's Who in American Art 1940-41

CANNON, JAMES, JR., BISHOP Nov. 13, 1864—Sept. 6, 1944 For many years was an outstanding Prohibitionist, reformer, and religious leader in the Methodist Church in the South; Bishop of the Methodist Episcopal Church, South, from 1918 to 1938; chairman of the executive committee of the World League Against Alcoholism since 1919; chairman of the committee of Southern Anti-Smith Democrats in 1928.

Obituary

N Y Times p23 S 7 '44 por

CARNARVON, COUNTESS OF *See* Losch, T.

CARREL, ALEXIS (kar'el ä-lek'sis) June 28, 1873—Nov. 5, 1944 Noted French biologist and surgeon; co-developer with Charles A. Lindbergh'[41] of the "artificial heart"; received the Nobel Prize in 1912; after the fall of France was appointed director of the Foundation for the Study of Human Relations created by the Vichy regime; denied charges that he collaborated with the Germans; was author of *Man the Unknown* (1935), which stirred up considerable comment "because of his championship of the intellectually elite as the rulers in his scientific Utopia"; see sketch 1940 Yearbook.

Obituary

N Y Times p19 N 6 '44 por

CARRINGTON, ELAINE STERNE Author; radio writer

Address: b. c/o National Broadcasting Company, 30 Rockefeller Plaza, New York City; h. Bridgehampton, Long Island, N. Y.

The author of two of radio's most popular daytime serials, *Pepper Young's Family* and *When a Girl Marries,* is Elaine Sterne Carrington, a prolific writer who produces not only her 20,000 words a week for radio, but three-act plays for Broadway, many short stories for magazines, patriotic scripts, and (as a hobby) popular songs. Mrs. Carrington was already a successful story writer when she began her work for radio in 1932; since then, under the sponsorship of Procter &

ELAINE STERNE CARRINGTON

Gamble, "she has turned out the astonishing total of four million words for a single client, or the equivalent of some fifty average novels. Her entire output for radio almost doubles this amount of wordage." She has also brought up a son and daughter, who have furnished her with much of the material for her radio series—"the everyday happenings of a family like my own, a husband and wife, struggling to bring up two youngsters the very best way they can."

Tall, buxom, gray-haired Elaine Sterne Carrington was born and educated in New York City. She actually began writing "before she could write," when she told innumerable stories to an adoring grandmother. She spent summers during her childhood on her father's farm at Great Barrington, Massachusetts. At the supper table she would tell long, romantic tales. "When guests were coming, Elaine always made up a slew of tales the night before." At the age of twelve she had completed a masterpiece, "For Love's Sake." "It began this way," says Mrs. Carrington: "'Lady Helias Tivioli of Tivioli Chateau, heir to all the vast estates east of France. . .' and I signed the story 'Listrade Hall.'"

During her teens—having given up an earlier ambition to become a musical comedy star—Elaine Sterne bombarded editors with her stories. American magazine offices were flooded with manuscripts signed "Elaine Sterne, G. A." Many an editor puzzled over that "G. A." before he clipped on a rejection slip. "I never told a soul," Mrs. Carrington says. "It meant Great Author." The Great Author had turned out a novel, a musical comedy, and countless stories before, at the age of eighteen, she actually sold a story, "King of the Christmas Feast," to *St. Nicholas* Magazine.

A year later success came fast. The New York *Evening Sun* in cooperation with Vitagraph sponsored a scenario-writing contest. Despite her mother's objections to the title,

Sins of the Mothers, Elaine Sterne entered her script, and won the first prize of $1,000. That same year she won another scenario prize offered by the New York *Morning Telegraph*, and a short story contest sponsored by *Collier's* Magazine.

The next few years found Elaine Sterne busy writing picture scripts (although she never left New York for Hollywood) and short stories for the *Saturday Evening Post*, *Good Housekeeping, Redbook, Woman's Home Companion, Pictorial Review,* etc. She also tried her hand at a play, written for presentation at the Lambs Club under the name of John Ray. This was subsequently lengthened and produced as a motion picture under the title *Alibi* (1929).

The early '30's saw the rise of radio; and one day in 1932, when she was caught in a heavy downpour of rain, Elaine Carrington entered the NBC offices on upper Fifth Avenue. She had never written for radio, but she had with her the manuscripts of some one-act plays. She left the plays with Katherine Seymour of NBC's Continuity Department, who read them and suggested that Mrs. Carrington write a serial. "Write about what you know best," said Miss Seymour. What Mrs. Carrington knew most about, at this time, was the business of being a wife with two growing children. She had married George D. Carrington, an attorney, whom she had known ever since they both went to the same New York private school. The two children were Patricia and Robert Bruce. So she decided to write a script whose central characters were fashioned after her own experiences as a wife and mother. It was originally called *Red Adams*. "Into it she put all the heartaches and struggle of making ends meet, of giving the children the new dress or the new tuxedo they needed for a party; the effort on the part of both parents to understand and sympathize with the new point of view, and not spoil their children; in fact, all the pangs of adolescence from both the children's and parents' points of view."

This serial went on the air as *Red Davis*, immediately obtained a sponsor, and featured Burgess Meredith [40] in the leading role. After two years the show was bought by a new sponsor and renamed *Pepper Young's Family*. The serial (for which Mrs. Carrington currently gets a reported $2,500 weekly) was so successful that in 1939 she undertook another one, *When a Girl Marries*. Likewise based on a pattern of conflicts and events, big and little, in everyday home life, this too soon became a radio "best seller." In January 1944 it jumped to first place in the Hooper poll of listeners with a rating of 9.0, having climbed from a 5.8 rating in January 1940.

Variety, in a survey of "soap operas," calls *Pepper Young's Family* "above average both in quality and popularity. Only the most biased critics could quarrel with *Pepper*. Its story stresses everyday family situations, with little or no melodrama and nothing lurid or emotionally upsetting. If anything, the action is too mild for maximum dramatic effect. The pace is relatively slow and the dialogue is inclined to be a trifle innocuous." *Pepper Young's Family* has long enjoyed a top-place radio popularity rating. Listeners, who write many letters to Mrs. Carrington, include not only women, but men and children. The children, particularly, send in suggestions and observations, says Mrs. Carrington; and often her own youngsters inquire how such-and-such a situation is going to come out, or ask her to make the story go a certain way. Mrs. Carrington says she always answers her fan mail, because it keeps her in close contact with her audience; and also because, as a girl, she wrote many letters to actresses and authors, "but never once received a reply."

In writing a serial, the radio author faces certain problems in keeping his characters in step with the times. When America was swinging into preparedness for war, nineteen-year-old Pepper Young, then in college, decided to enlist. Mrs. Carrington found herself in a predicament. If Pepper enlisted he'd be off to camp, and she'd be out of pocket the $2,500 a week her sponsors were paying her for the serial. She had to keep Pepper on the air and still meet the demands of patriotism. Hearing of the CAA flying projects, which trained boys without requiring enlistment, she set up a CAA unit in Pepper's home town, Elmwood, and Pepper was saved for his country—and for radio.

"Daytime radio needn't hang its head in the presence of books, magazine fiction, or other so-called 'literature.' The much-criticized serials have a definite and legitimate place in modern American life. They can and sometimes do teach valuable lessons in human conduct. And if they aren't a hifalutin' form of art, they frequently contain profound wisdom expressed in universal terms." This is Elaine Carrington's belief about the kind of work she does in the radio field. She gets her "material" by watching and listening to her own children, their friends, and her neighbors. Her advice to young women who "want to write" is: "Just push the salt shaker and sugar bowl aside, clear elbow room on the table, and go to it. Let them write about the world they live in—if mother wants to talk about the grocery bill, tell them to listen and take notes. Some day they'll use those notes."

Mrs. Carrington now does her own writing in bed, dictating her scripts, since she "can write better and faster while she's lying comfortably stretched out smoking a cigaret and completely relaxed." After her secretary types the first draft she makes extensive revisions in pencil and the script is retyped. She always works in the morning, refusing to let herself get out of bed until the day's quota is finished. She always is at least three weeks ahead on her programs, which gives her ample leeway and avoids the feeling of pressure. It also gives the agency, directors, and actors plenty of time to familiarize themselves with the script, discuss problems, and make any other preparations. She submits monthly synopses and a yearly story outline to the agency, but "never sticks to it": Pepper Young characters have become so real they "often get out of hand," and twist the plot new ways. "Sometimes," she says, "the characters surprise me with what they do."

Witty, energetic, devoted to her family, Elaine Sterne Carrington lives and writes in her Bridgehampton, Long Island home which she calls "Shepherd Hill." "That's because there's no shepherd and no hill," she explains. The house is set on a grassy knoll that slopes down to a salt water lake. "There's a wharf and boats for fishing and sailing, a Victory garden, a horse called Kissie Missie, a raccoon named General 'Ike' Eisenhower [42] because his attacks are ceaseless," and several dogs and cats. Mrs. Carrington's secretary, Elsie Frank, lives here with the family. On week ends Major George D. Carrington, of the Judge Advocate General's Department, pays them visits. He is the only person permitted to blue-pencil the scripts before they reach the producing agency. Near the lake Mrs. Carrington has a one-room workshop, finished in natural wood. Just above her double studio lounge hangs a map of Stanwood, the fictitious town in *When a Girl Marries,* to which the author refers constantly as she works on her script dialogues.

In her spare time Mrs. Carrington helps the gardener with the Shepherd Hill Victory garden, or composes songs for her own amusement. One, called *Here's What You Are,* was heard on a *Hobby Lobby* program. She also writes patriotic scripts for the Treasury Department, for which she has received a citation for distinguished service. On September 29, 1944 another Carrington serial, titled *Rosemary,* went on the air, replacing the time-honored *Vic and Sade* program.

Mrs. Carrington's chief interests are, however, her children. Patricia, a student at Smith College, is already an author. When she was fifteen she was "the youngest writer to have a play accepted for the radio." It was a one-act drama, *Prepare to Die* (produced over NBC in May 1940), hinging on "an episode of Finland's tragedy during the Russian invasion." Like her mother, Patricia does her best work "in a confusion of noises, when her own and her brother's young friends are raising a ruckus." She got her practice writing plays for young friends who gave performances of them in the attic of the Carrington home in Brooklyn Heights. With her brother Bobby, now a student at Deerfield Academy, she wrote and edited a magazine for children, *The Jolly Roger.* With the children to carry on, the Carrington family looks forward to a thriving writing future. Elaine Carrington herself has just one remaining ambition: to live up to that "G. A."

References

N Y Post p13 Ja 25 '40 por
Newsweek 18:79 O 20 '41 por
PM p13 Ja 7 '41 por
Variety 138:38 My 8 '40; 151:34 Je 16 '43.

CARTER, JOHN RIDGELY Nov. 28, 1865 —June 3, 1944 Banker and diplomat; senior partner of Morgan et C¹ᵉ, Paris; Councilor of American Embassy in London (1905-09); Minister to the Balkans (1909-11); Acting Ambassador to Turkey (1910-11); a humanitarian, contributed much of his time and money to the care of blinded war veterans in France after the First World War.

Obituary

N Y Times p4 Je 4 '44 por

**CASTELNAU, EDOUARD DE CURI-
ERES DE** (kəs″tel″nō′ ã″dwar′ dė ky″ryãr′
dė) 1851—(?) 1944 General of the Armies
and oldest officer of France; chief of staff to
General Joffre; had share in early defense of
Verdun (1916); member of the Chamber of
Deputies (1919-24); report of death came
from a Swiss source.

Obituary

N Y Times p18 Mr 20 '44 por

CASTILLO, RAMON S. (käs-tē′yō rä-
môn′) Nov. 20, 1873—Oct. 12, 1944 President of Argentina from June 27, 1942 to June
5, 1943, when ousted from office by a military coup for his conservative views; had
actually ruled country as Vice-President since
July 1940; advocated neutrality for Argentina
in Second World War; see sketch 1941 Yearbook.

Obituary

N Y Times p19 O 13 '44 por

CATTELL, J(AMES) McKEEN (kə-tel′)
May 25, 1860—Jan. 20, 1944 Noted psychologist, educator, author; was recognized as the
"dean of American science"; editor and publisher of scientific journals and founder of
Science Press; his researches included the
measurement of behavior, studies of individual
and group differences, association of ideas, etc.

Obituary

N Y Times p17 Ja 21 '44 por

**CATTO, THOMAS SIVEWRIGHT CAT-
TO, 1ST BARON** (cat′tō sīv′rīt) Mar. 15,
1879- Governor of the Bank of England

Address: b. c/o Bank of England, London;
h. 7 Great Winchester St., London

The appointment of Thomas Sivewright
Catto, well known British businessman and
financier, to the Governorship of the Bank of
England in April 1944 created international
interest both because of the importance of the
position and because of the contrast between
Lord Catto and his predecessor, Montagu
Norman [40]. Catto is a self-made Scotsman
whose life story reads like a Horatio Alger
tale; Montagu Norman, seventy-three years
old at the time of his retirement, is an eccentric aristocrat with an Eton and Cambridge
background who, for a quarter of a century,
had dominated every move of the world's
greatest banking institution and whose name,
as Raymond Daniell [44] of the New York
Times stated, had become "synonymous with
the Bank of England."

Thomas Sivewright Catto, born March 15,
1879, is the son of William Catto and Isabella
(Yule) Catto of Peterhead, Aberdeenshire.
He attended school at the local academy at
Peterhead, where he won a scholarship to
Rutherford College at the busy shipbuilding
center of Newcastle-on-Tyne, not far from
the Scottish border in England. At Newcastle
the sixteen-year-old Scotsman began his business career by entering a shipping office.
Catto, even now only three inches over five
feet, could not then reach the wall telephones.

but settled this problem in what *Time* Magazine calls "true Alger-boy fashion" by piling
books upon the floor and standing on them.
Also, having discovered the combination of the
safe where the precious typewriters were kept
at night, he practiced nightly on the machines
until he became a proficient typist.

When he was nineteen Catto answered a
newspaper advertisement in which a firm of
merchants were asking for a man to go to
its office in the Caucasus in southern Russia—
and got the job. He quickly rose to be assistant general manager of the firm's business
throughout the whole of the Near and Middle
East, and when only twenty-nine he became
vice-president of a large company of ship
owners, MacAndrews and Forbes, Ltd., and
managed their business in America for eleven
years, until 1919.

His Russian experience led to appointment as
British Admiralty representative on the Russian commission to America during the First
World War. Later he transferred to the
British Food Mission, and in 1918-1919 served
as chairman of the British and Allied food
missions in the United States and Canada.
From there he went to India to become the
active head, as deputy chairman and managing director, of the trading firm of Andrew
Yule and Company of Calcutta, in 1928 becoming the chairman. He has also been
director of the London firm of Yule, Catto and
Company, Ltd., since 1919. In 1930 he became
a managing director of the banking house
of Morgan, Grenfell and Company. He further established a position for himself in
British banking circles by becoming director
of the Royal Bank of Scotland, the Royal
Exchange Assurance Corporation, the Mercantile Bank of India, the Union Castle Steamship Company, and in 1940 he was elected a
director of the Bank of England. The following June, Lord Catto resigned all these
directorships when he accepted the specially
created, unpaid post of financial adviser to the
British Treasury.

Before going to the Treasury he was for a
short time Director General of Equipment at
the Ministry of Supply and a member of the
Supply Council. In 1922-1923 he was a member of the Indian Government Retrenchment
Commission and at home in Britain his services were sought on the Coal Sales Commission. He was made a peer in 1936, becoming
1st Baron Catto of Cairncatto.

In the Treasury, Catto worked with John
Maynard Keynes [41], another wartime Treasury
adviser. The two men had adjoining offices
in the old Board of Trade building which
Treasury personnel nicknamed "Doggo" and
"Catto." Actually, according to *Time,* the two
men were fast friends and worked together
in perfect accord as Lord Catto's practical
experience supplemented the "unparalleled intellectual equipment" of the tall, gaunt Lord
Keynes. The selection of Lord Catto, instead
of Keynes, to be Governor of the Bank of
England suggested, the New York *Herald
Tribune* pointed out, that the directors were
thinking more about the "Bank's role in promoting British export trade after the War
than about its role in furthering a policy of
full employment at home. Had the latter
policy been foremost, it is considered that the

logical choice would have been Lord Keynes, the economist, who is identified with that policy in the public mind and who had been mentioned as Montagu Norman's possible successor."

Lord Catto has no easy task in following in the footsteps of the almost legendary Norman, particularly at a time when, as *Time* has pointed out, even "tougher responsibilities" may emerge from the present War than those with which Norman had to contend after the First World War. However, though he may not provide as much colorful newspaper copy as did the former Governor, Lord Catto's world-wide reputation as a shrewd and practical banker and economist and his work as joint adviser with John Maynard Keynes to the Treasury in Whitehall are the basis of a general feeling of confidence in him. As he himself has pointed out, his name in Gaelic means "fight," and in his family crest is the motto "Touch Not Gloveless."

The Bank of England, a large, imposing building in the center of London (often spoken of as the "Old Lady of Threadneedle Street"), is two hundred and fifty years old. It was founded in 1694 when a group of businessmen advanced £1,200,000 to King William III for a war loan. In return they received 8 per cent interest, an allowance of £4,000 for "expenses," and the right to conduct a profitable banking business. Since its foundation, no governor had served for more than five years until Montagu Norman took office in 1920.

"Few institutions have cast a more pervasive influence on history than the Old Lady of Threadneedle Street," says one commentator. The Bank is a private body which, although not controlled by the British Government, is banker to the Government. It is the center for the issue of bank notes, it handles the daily operations of the Government, manages its stocks and bonds, issues new loans, and advises the Government on problems in which public policy is related to business and finance. Under its leadership the pound sterling became, in the nineteenth century, a universal currency. The First World War shattered this system, brought about the collapse of the gold standard, left England burdened with debt.

The end of the Second World War will find England again in a serious financial condition. As *Time* indicates, she will be burdened by debt, faced with the loss of revenues from overseas investment and shipping, and faced, too, with the problems of a Europe in reconstruction. Her paramount need will be for a world-wide currency and financial system. Lord Catto himself, says *Time,* is the first to acknowledge that Britain cannot exist unless some system of trading and credit can be re-established at the War's end. The foremost question will be: What kind of a system? That he feels sure that some successful plan will be worked out is proven by a statement he made recently: "I am frequently asked whether Britain can regain its old financial and industrial leadership. I am full of quiet confidence."

Lord Catto, described as a "cheery, sturdy, gray-haired, twinkling-eyed little Scotchman," lives in a one-hundred-year-old house in Surrey. He was married in 1910 to Gladys Gordon,

THOMAS SIVEWRIGHT CATTO

daughter of Stephen Gordon of Elgin. There are four children, three of whom have records of service in the War. His eldest daughter is deputy head of the Young Women's Christian Association in Cairo; another daughter is in the Women's Auxiliary Air Force; while Catto's son Stephen is in the Royal Air Force. Another daughter is married to an R.A.F. squadron leader in India.

Lord Catto does not play golf, which is usually expected of a Scotsman, but he loves the country and finds his greatest relaxation in donning an old tweed suit and walking with his two spaniels over his forty-acre estate, which is about twenty-four miles south of London. He is a member of several London clubs as well as of the Bengal Club in Calcutta. Catto is the shortest Governor in the history of the Bank of England and, according to the New York *Herald Tribune*, probably the wealthiest, since he controls English and Indian concerns handling enormous business.

References

Illus London News 204:454 Ap 22 '44 por
N Y Herald Tribune p8 Ap 7 '44; p10 Ap 19 '44; VII p6-7 O 1 '44 il por
N Y Times p8 Ap 7 '44 por
Newsweek 23:54 Ap 17 '44
Time 43:79-82 Ap 17 '44 por
Who's Who 1944

CHAMINADE, CECILE (LOUISE STE-PHANIE)

(sha"mē"nad' sā-sēl' lwēz stä"fa"nē') 1861—1944 (?) French composer and pianist; one of the few women to achieve distinction in musical composition; her works include more than 500 songs, and piano and orchestral works; recipient of the ribbon of the Légion d'Honneur; death reported by Paris radio.

Obituary

N Y Times p23 Ap 19 '44 por

CHATEL, YVES (-CHARLES) (shä″tel′ ēv) 1885 (?)—Oct. 13, 1944 Former Vichy-appointed Governor General of Algeria until January 1943 when replaced by Marcel Peyrouton [43] after it became known he was not trusted by General Dwight Eisenhower [42]; had succeeded General Maxime Weygand [40] in November 1941; entered French Civil Service in 1909; became an administrator in 1911.

Obituary

N Y Times p13 O 14 '44

CHEN, EUGENE (chun) 1878—May 20, 1944 British-born Chinese publisher and politician; was four times Foreign Minister in various Chinese Governments, including the Left-Wing Hankow Government which fell in 1927, and twice a refugee when out of favor with the Nationalist Government; editor of the Peking and the Shanghai *Gazettes*; death reported by Domei, Japanese news agency.

Obituary

N Y Times p44 My 21 '44

CHERNYAKHOVSKY, IVAN D(ANILO-VICH) (chär″nyä-kof′ski) 1908(?)- Soviet Army officer

On June 24, 1944, inside the Kremlin walls, 224 cannon boomed forth twenty salvos three times to celebrate the Russian victories in Karelia and in the central sector of the Eastern Front. The Central Front victories, north and south of Vitebsk, of Generals Ivan Chernyakhovsky and Ivan Bagramian [44], who are directing operations in White Russia, merited twenty salvos each. And so Chernyakhovsky, the brilliant young Army officer who helped defend Voronezh in 1942, who was made a Hero of the Soviet Union for crossing the Dnieper in October 1943, whose singing soldiers led the way into liberated Kiev in November, and who in the spring of 1944 was leading an army belonging to the Third Ukrainian Front of Marshal Zhukov [42], started along the historic pathway trodden by Empress Elizabeth's troops on their way to Berlin in 1760.

As is the case with almost all Russian Army officers, it is difficult to find the details of Ivan Danilovich Chernyakovsky's life. He was born, it is said, in the west Ukraine, the son of a railway worker in Uman. In *Time* Magazine for July 3, 1944, his age was given as thirty-two; but the same magazine two weeks later spoke of him as thirty-six—as did *PM* for June 28—and other newspaper dispatches for about the same time gave his age as thirty-six or thirty-seven. However, any of these figures, viewed in the light of his accomplishments and his position as commander of the Third White Russian Army, an army large enough to have forty-nine generals or other senior officers singled out in Marshal Stalin's [42] order of the day addressed to Chernyakhovsky, lend special significance to news dispatches describing the young tank expert as a brilliant general.

When Russia chose the Central Front for the opening phase of the 1944 summer campaign, heading along the historic pathway between the Dnieper and the Dvina Rivers, the Red Army started on the shortest route to Berlin. To clear the way for a drive westward along the highway to Minsk, Warsaw, and eventually Berlin, the Russians began to clean up the three German strongholds of Vitebsk, Orsha, and Mogilev. Vitebsk was probably the most strongly fortified Russian city held by the Germans. Chernyakhovsky and Bagramian, veterans of three years of fighting, launched thrusts south and north of the city, by-passed it from fifteen to twenty-five miles, then closed the gap behind it, thus cutting off five German divisions. One day after the encirclement and only a brief four days after the beginning of the summer campaign, Stalin announced that Vitebsk was in Russian hands: Hitler's [42] chain of fortresses guarding the shortest route to Berlin was dented. Chernyakhovsky was promptly made a full general—the youngest full general in the Red Army, according to the New York *Times*. He had risen rapidly: he was a major general in November 1943, was promoted to colonel general in March, and was given his own army late in June.

Elements of the Third White Russian Army now branched off in the direction of Orsha, forty miles south of Vitebsk, and broke through its defenses, north of the Dnieper, to a depth of nine miles along a twelve-mile front. The credit for the fall of Orsha, site of one of the largest Luftwaffe bases in the east, went to Chernyakhovsky, who then turned westward toward Minsk. Along the Berezina River, scene of Napoleon's defeat in 1812, the forces of Chernyakhovsky's Third White Russian Army, Zakharov's Second, and the northern wing of Rokossovsky's [44] First joined. Chernyakhovsky's forces, taking Borisov, crossed the Berezina River on a sixty-eight-mile front north and southeast of the city. Stalin announced the fall of this important stronghold of the German defenses covering approaches to Minsk in an order of the day that called on the 224 Moscow guns to fire the salvos in a victory salute. Indicating the strength of the forces under Chernyakhovsky, Stalin paid tribute to thirteen infantry generals. Moscow dispatches said that the German High Command had failed to throw any reserves into the battle against the Third White Russian Army, which in nine days had covered more than one-third of the 360 miles from northwest of Orsha to East Prussia.

On July 3 the combined forces of Chernyakhovsky and Rokossovsky outflanked and then captured Minsk by storm. (Minsk is the ancient White Russian capital and last major enemy bastion in pre-War Russia on the road to Warsaw.) Chernyakhovsky's troops cut the railway on the northwest, and Rokossovsky hit from the southwest—and 324 Moscow guns fired twenty-four salvos to salute that victory. Chernyakhovsky's hard-riding cavalry pressed on ten miles into Poland toward Vilna, for twenty years a point of dispute between Poland and Lithuania. Advance troops were about 170 miles from German East Prussia. Other elements cleared the Orsha-Minsk Railroad. Molodechno, important rail center, fell to Chernyakhovsky on July 6, and again Moscow celebrated by twelve salvos of 124 guns.

By July 9 street fighting raged in Vilna as Soviet troops plunged to within ninety-five miles of the border of East Prussia. By the tenth the Third White Russian Army had surrounded Vilna. Chernyakhovsky's army severed Vilna's communications with the Latvian city of Dvinsk by cutting the Leningrad-Warsaw rail trunk line and thus depriving the German Baltic divisions of their main escape route through Poland. The capture of Lida collapsed all German defenses along the Vilna-Luninets rail line and put the young General's forces sixty-two miles northeast of Grodno, Nazi bulwark protecting the southern approaches to East Prussia and major bastion along the German main defense line in the east. On July 13 Chernyakhovsky's infantry troops still battled Germans in the streets of Vilna, while his tanks and cavalry by-passed the city and slashed into Lithuania. When Vilna finally fell to the Red Army after five days of house-to-house fighting, the capture was celebrated in Moscow with the salute of twenty-four salvos from 324 guns—a salute fired before in the Second World War only for the capture of Kiev, Petrozavodsk, and Minsk, all capitals of Soviet republics. With this citation by Stalin, Chernyakhovsky became the recipient of more orders of the day from Stalin than any other general in Soviet history.

In the days that followed Chernyakhovsky's forces pressed a growing offensive against the Niemen River, reached the river on a seventy-five-mile front, forced several crossings, established bridgeheads on the west bank, and attacked Grodno. On July 16 Moscow announced the capture of Grodno, greatest prize before East Prussia, by a combined thrust of the forces of Chernyakhovsky and Zakharov. A flanking move northwest of the city sent some units to the smaller town of Gozha. On this front Chernyakhovsky's Third White Russian Army was only forty miles from East Prussia proper, only two miles from the Suwalki Triangle, which Germany annexed to East Prussia in 1939. His capture of Kaunas, last Nazi defense bastion before East Prussia, was announced by Stalin on August 2, and spearheads of the army advanced thirty-six miles west of the city to within artillery range of the pre-War East Prussian border. Now Chernyakhovsky held within his grasp the honor of seeing his divisions the first to march upon the soil of Germany.

By August 5 the grimly fighting Russian troops, moving against fanatic German resistance, had inched to within eight miles of East Prussia. Fresh Nazi troops were rushed up, and the Russians were being forced to blast the Germans from villages one by one in fierce hand-to-hand fighting. By the sixteenth they were two miles from the border; by the eighteenth they had reached the border of the East Prussian frontier along the Sesupe River in western Lithuania. Great armored battles raged. Russian soldiers, for the first time since General Gavel K. Rennenkampf led his Czarist armies into East Prussia thirty years ago, seemed about to march onto the sacred soil of the Reich. Here the enemy was girded for a last-ditch fight. In ten days, the Germans dug 1,800 miles of trenches, and Russian patrols reported the mushrooming of machine-gun nests and tank ditches. Every able-bodied man and woman between fifteen and sixty-five was called out to work on the defenses. Chernyakhovsky's armies weathered one fierce counterattack after another, then waited for the convulsions to die out. Inside

GEN. IVAN DANILOVICH
CHERNYAKHOVSKY

the border Germans burned farm buildings—the first scorching of their own earth in the War.

As the world waited for the Red armies to enter East Prussia, Germany threw into the battle armored units brought from Italy and heavy catapult appliances (possibly rocket platforms). Chernyakhovsky had 150,000 men (by German count) massed on the province's eastern border. After an artillery barrage of 3,000 shells in twenty minutes, Chernyakhovsky's infantry closed in along the Kaunas-Königsberg Railroad. Soviet troops smashed their way into hurriedly prepared enemy trenches. General Zakharov's army group also closed in over the swampy ground from the south. Moscow radio announced on August 22 that East Prussia had been invaded by the Red Army, but this report was premature.

For two months the Russian Army waited at the northern border of East Prussia, reorganizing and collecting supplies while the world waited for news of the expected invasion. The situation was a dramatic one: three years and four months before the Germans had invaded Russia, and thirty years before, during the First World War, the Germans under Field Marshal Paul von Hindenburg had accomplished their defeat of the Russians in this same locale. Neither country had forgotten these events. The Russians were stronger in 1944 than in the 1914 campaign, but the Germans, according to Time Magazine, had "the most powerful and skillfully constructed defenses they had been able to erect in months." Then, too, the Prussians were defending their sacred soil and Germany's "bowels of iron and heart of steel," and their fighting was therefore more desperate.

Finally, in late October, when the weather had turned cold and the first winter snows had come, Chernyakhovsky smashed into East Prussia, leading his army of 500,000 men on an eighty-seven-mile front and capturing more than 400 towns and villages. Spearheads were

CHERNYAKHOVSKY, IVAN D.—*Cont.*
thrust as deep as nineteen miles into Nazi territory. This invasion, fulfilling predictions made for the General, was the deepest penetration of German soil yet made by any Allied force, and newspapers again hailed Chernyakhovsky as a brilliant tank expert. By the end of October his armored divisions were heading toward Königsberg, the capital of East Prussia, and Gumbinnen, where Germans and Russians had fought in the First World War. Around Gumbinnen the Russians found even stronger defenses than they had previously encountered. According to *PM*, by the middle of November Chernyakhovsky's artillery, tanks, and planes had blasted their way forward for twenty-six miles before they were checked.

General Chernyakhovsky is described as chunky and barrel-chested, iron-muscled, and iron-willed. His photographs show him to be a handsome man. The New York *Sun* characterizes him as an extraordinary organizer, one who makes decisions in combat with split-second speed.

References

N Y Times p4 Je 27 '44
Time 44:25 Jl 10 '44 por

CHODOROV, EDWARD (chä'dä-räv)
Apr. 17, 1904- Playwright; scenarist
Address: b. c/o Richard Maney, 1430 Broadway, New York City; h. 277 Park Ave., New York City

Into the middle of a Broadway season composed principally of musicals and plays concerned with murder, sex, and life with father, came (in February 1944) a new play, *Decision*, bluntly concerned with the dangers facing democracy on the home front now in 1944 and when the War is over. The author of this frank appeal to Americans is Edward Chodorov of Broadway and Hollywood, one of the two theatre-minded sons of Harry and Lena (Simmons) Chodorov.

Edward, the elder son, who turned out to be "less successful in the theatre than Jerome, but more adventurous," was born in New York City (Manhattan), April 17, 1904. He thinks that love of the theatre first came into the Chodorov veins when his Russian great-grandfather ran a little theatre in connection with his inn at Kiev; his father apparently inherited this interest, for he was an actor with Jacob Adler's company.

Stage-struck from childhood—as was his brother—Edward persuaded his parents to let him travel across the city to the Erasmus High School in Brooklyn, where such celebrities as Jane Cowl, Edward Everett Horton, and Barbara Stanwyck had been students. Following his graduation he went on to Brown University, although he soon left to find a job in the theatre.

For a while Chodorov spent many hours in New York automats discussing the drama with another young hopeful, Moss Hart[40]. When Hart finally procured a position as secretary to an executive of a theatrical booking agency he was able to get the inexperienced Chodorov a job as stage manager for the production of Anne Nichols' *Abie's Irish Rose*. (This was about 1922.) The work

young Chodorov did apparently proved to be satisfactory despite his inexperience, for he was next (1928) sent to South Africa as stage manager of *Is Zat So*, with Luther Adler and Harry Green in the cast.

Upon his return to the United States Chodorov found the country in the midst of the depression and work in the theatre scarce. He got a job with Columbia Pictures instead, and for a short time he did publicity work for that company. The outcome of the experience he received there was the farce-comedy *Wonder Boy,* which he wrote with a co-worker, Arthur Barton. Produced in 1931 by Jed Harris, the play was the hectic account of a futile attempt of a motion-picture company to make a star out of a young student. Full of "noisy confusion," as one critic wrote, its satire on Hollywood business methods was lost in the melee. In any case it lacked the swift satire of Moss Hart's and George S. Kaufman's[41] *Once in a Lifetime*, a play with a similar theme to which it was inevitably compared. Some reviewers, however, felt that in places *Wonder Boy* was impish, malicious, and very funny. Although the production ran for only forty-four performances, both Chodorov and the male lead, Gregory Ratoff[43], received offers from Hollywood.

Chodorov, still intent on his career in the theatre, was not tempted by Hollywood at first, but he soon capitulated to the lucrative offers. For a few years he stayed in the film capital writing and adapting scripts for both Warner Brothers and First National; then he returned to Broadway. Among those pictures on which he worked were *The Mayor of Hell* (1933), an original screen play which starred James Cagney[42]; *Captured* (1933), a picture based on a short story by Sir Philip Gibbs and starring Leslie Howard and Paul Lukas[42]; *Madame Du Barry* (1933), an opulent spectacle with Dolores del Rio; and *The World Changes* (1933), a picture with Paul Muni[44] based on a story by Sheridan Gibney. Chodorov said, after a later visit to Hollywood, that many of the things concerning his Hollywood career of which he was proudest were those that in a sense never happened. For example, he sold to Warner Brothers the idea of making a screen biography of Louis Pasteur, but left the studio after a disagreement and before he had written the script. At another time he talked himself out of adapting Sinclair Lewis' *Dodsworth* for the screen by persuading Samuel Goldwyn[44] that the motion picture should be made directly from the play.

Shortly after his return to New York, Chodorov's second play opened on Broadway—in April 1935. *Kind Lady*, based on a short story, *The Silver Mask*, by Hugh Walpole, is still called "one of the best melodramas of the modern theatre" and since 1935 has been produced in innumerable little theatres all over the United States, with a return engagement on Broadway in 1940. The script had gone the rounds of all the prominent producers in New York before two summer-theatre managers, Henry Potter and George Haight, read it and decided to handle it. A psychological thriller, it needed skillful acting to be effective. It received it, too, from Grace George, who made the role of gentle Mary Herries indubitably hers, and from Henry Daniell, who played the part of Henry Abbott in the first New York presentation. The plot concerns the subtle invasion by a gang of crooks of the home of a wealthy and lonely old spinster. Out of pity Mary Herries takes the charming vagrant, Henry, and his ill wife and child into her home—supposedly only until the doctor comes—and then finds herself a prisoner in her own house, kept there by the sinister Henry and his odious associates. As they slowly rob her of her possessions they torture her suavely, without a hint of overt violence, but with a world of meaning underneath their matter-of-fact, almost innocent, words. To quote Brooks Atkinson [42]: Chodorov has told the story with "mischievous detachment." With considerable skill, and with no words wasted, "the mood alters from ordinary friendliness to ominous villainy before you realize it. . . . The callousness of the characters develops slyly. Scene by scene the pressure of these vultures against the helpless lady becomes so agonizing that the theatre-goers are more relieved than she when at length she contrives her deliverance." (Chodorov had written two endings for the play and was advised for the sake of the audience to use the cheerful one.) "Mr. Chodorov," continued Atkinson, "is a man of few words and impeccable literary taste. What makes *Kind Lady* exciting is the austerity he uses to cover a torture tale." Similarly, the other reviewers praised this "artful, strangely compelling horror play"—with "gaps in it large enough to drive a horse and wagon through"—yet withal "an exceedingly skillful", "nervewracking tour de force."

His ability firmly established by the success of *Kind Lady,* Chodorov returned again to Hollywood. In 1935 he wrote the screen version of his play for Metro-Goldwyn-Mayer; and during the next eight or nine years, with time out for two more plays, he continued as adapter, writer, and producer for MGM and other picture companies, including Columbia and Paramount. Some of those films with which he was connected in one capacity or another were *Snowed Under* (1936), *Yellow Jack* (1938) with Robert Montgomery, *Woman Against Woman* (1938) with Herbert Marshall, *The Man From Dakota* (1940) with Wallace Beery, and Moss Hart's *Lady in the Dark* (1944) with Ginger Rogers [41]. Chodorov has said that he feels characterization should be made secondary in film writing, and the process reversed in play writing. A film story should be told, he says, in a series of dramatic highlights, each of the scenes advancing the action. There is no time in the progression for brilliant dialogue or clever characterization.

Chodorov's first vacation from Hollywood since 1935 had been used to write *Cue for Passion,* in collaboration with H. S. Kraft. This play opened in New York on December 19, 1940 under the aegis of Richard Aldrich and Richard Myers and closed twelve performances later. Chodorov and Kraft had written about an unlikable woman author and her obnoxious husband in the form of a social satire which, in the second and third acts, turned into a murder mystery. The *Theatre Arts Monthly* criticized the play for having

EDWARD CHODOROV

too much theme, plot, and character; and also objected to the abrupt change from the social satire of the first act to the later emphasis on sleuthing. The *New Yorker* commented that the play contained "badtempered" writing about two well known people, although in general it was felt that some of the characterizations had been cleverly done.

The next play of Chodorov's to appear on Broadway was *Those Endearing Young Charms,* which opened in June 1943 (for a short run) under the banner of Max Gordon [42]. Chodorov was writing of love in wartime, a subject close to many people in 1943, but the drama received a mixed reception despite its timeliness and the excellence of the cast of four players. The principal objection was to the playwright's resolution of his plot. For his purpose he had drawn the character of a spoiled man of the world, an aviator, who is apparently taking advantage of the love of a sweet young girl. Only at the end of the play is it revealed that the man is really a misunderstood person who actually wants to marry his sweetheart. Louis Kronenberger objected to this switch, saying that Chodorov had "shamelessly" used contradictory formulas, the "poignant-realistic" and the "pretty-romantic," in working out his story. Much of the writing was considered excellent, however, and was aided by the charm of Virginia Gilmore in the role of the young girl. The story was undoubtedly the kind which Hollywood could use, moreover, and both Warner Brothers and Samuel Goldwyn bid for it. According to *Variety*, it was finally sold to Goldwyn, who sold it to RKO in 1944.

Toward the end of 1943, the opening of *Those Endearing Young Charms* and his work on the screen adaptation of *Lady in the Dark* behind him, Chodorov settled down to finish a new play, to be called *Decision.* To offer to theatre audiences this thoughtful and daring play on fascism in America he had given up numerous attractive film offers for uncertain box office receipts from Broadway.

CHODOROV, EDWARD—*Continued*

In suspecting that most producers were wrong in thinking that wartime audiences want only escapist entertainment—or plays about war far from the United States—Chodorov and his young producer, Edward Choate, were taking a big financial risk. Since the opening of *Decision* at the Belasco Theatre on February 2, 1944, however, audiences have proved that Chodorov and Choate were right in their suspicions. When warned by friends not to use the theme, the playwright had answered: "Every other medium of intellectual dissemination has gone at the problem; and it is about time the theatre did." To present this problem of native fascism, Chodorov has written with earnest passion the story of a young soldier, wounded at the Sicilian battle front, who returns home to discover that freedom has to be fought for on the home front, too. He finds his father, a high school principal, in the midst of a struggle to reveal the insidious forces in high places which had instigated a race riot in his home town; and only when the father is framed and murdered does the boy come to his decision to carry on the battle in the dead man's stead.

Not only audiences but critics, too, were enthusiastic about Chodorov's play, which he himself had also directed. The propaganda aspect of the theme was inevitably discussed, as were certain technical faults, such as a slight luridness in the presentation of this theme and a rather unsatisfactory working out of the solution. However, as Howard Barnes wrote, echoing the rest of the press: "It has remarkable bite and vigor for all its . . . faults . . . it pulls very few punches in the telling." And, as if in answer to all criticisms which might be directed at the play, Louis Kronenberger added: "Whether in terms of higher criticism *Decision* is a good or bad play can wait. What is more to the point right now is that it is an immensely timely play and a very telling one, on as serious a theme as confronts this country today. Mr. Chodorov has tackled his theme with no mincing of words . . . he has given it a vigor to match its seriousness. It is good theatre. . . . Certainly the tone of *Decision* is didactic, as the plot is lurid. But there are moments in history when the drama, like every other instrument of communication, must raise a cry and sound a warning; and there are times when life itself catches up with the most melodramatic plots." In emphatic terms the *New Amsterdam News* announced that the play was "the most sincere thought-provoking drama on racial unity ever to grace the American stage." The case of the Negro "is stated emphatically and honestly, in a moving and courageous production.... If this play is propaganda, so is the New Testament."

Burns Mantle [44] included *Decision* in his selection of best plays of the 1943-1944 season. The play had only a moderately successful run, however, leaving Broadway after 158 performances. The screen rights to it were bought in July 1944 by Samuel Bronston, an independent producer for production by United Artists. In November, when the OWI issued a warning which indicated that export permit might be withheld because of the play's impli-

cation of fascism in America, Bronston planned to submit a new screen treatment. In December Chodorov was reported as having almost finished a new play for staging on Broadway by RKO. The play, *Common Ground*, is about the capture by the Nazis of a USO unit in Italy.

Chodorov has not limited his activities to the theatre. He has recently spoken on numerous vital subjects, including the problems of the playwright in wartime. *Time* Magazine has described Chodorov as a stocky, swart man who is quiet and untemperamental, yet at times stubborn and cantankerous. A New York *Post* reporter says that he has dark blue, lively eyes and curly brown hair, that he claims to have outgrown every sport except swimming, and reads everything except fiction. He loves the theatre and feels sorry for anybody who doesn't work in it, wondering "how they manage to get along and have any fun." The playwright is married and has two children. His wife, the former Marjorie Roth, was chairman in April 1944 of the women's division of the Joint Anti-Fascist Refugee Committee.

References

N Y Herald Tribune IV p2 Ja 30 '44
N Y Post Mag p25 Ap 25 '44
Time 43:62 F 14 '44

International Motion Picture Almanac 1943-44

CHRISTIE, JOHN WALTER 1866(?)—Jan. 11, 1943 Noted inventor, creator of the standard turret track for battleships, of gun mounts, carriages, and army tanks; contributed much to the development of the four-wheel drive for motor vehicles; his design for an automobile platform to sustain the 75-millimeter artillery both on land and water resulted in the world's first amphibian tank.

Obituary

N Y Times p23 Ja 12 '44 por

CIANO, GALEAZZO, CONTE (chä'nō gä'la-ät'tsō) Mar. 18, 1903—Jan. 11, 1944 Italian statesman; Minister of Foreign Affairs (1936-43); member of the Fascist Supreme Council; named Ambassador to Holy See (February 1943); married to Edda, daughter of Benito Mussolini [42]; reportedly executed by German firing squad; see sketch 1940 Yearbook.

Obituary

N Y Times p5 Ja 12 '44

CLAPPER, RAYMOND May 30, 1892—Feb.(?), 1944 Newspaper correspondent; commentator for Scripps-Howard Newspapers since January 1936; noted for his intense respect for the individual citizen and the sanity of the American mass mind; had built up an audience of over 10,000,000 readers; report of his death in an air collision over the Marshall Islands released by the Navy Department, February 3, 1944; see sketch 1940 Yearbook.

Obituary

N Y Times p3 F 4 '44 por

CLAYTON, WILLIAM L(OCKHART)

1880- United States Government official; cotton factor

Address: b. Department of State, Washington, D.C.; h. Houston, Tex.

When President Roosevelt '42 reorganized the State Department in December 1944, former Surplus War Property Administrator Will Clayton was named Assistant Secretary of State for Foreign Economic Affairs—an appointment which gratified conservative elements in this country, among whom he holds "an enviable reputation" for ability. Some liberals, however, took a dimmer view of the nomination, being less pleased with Clayton's record as Assistant Secretary of Commerce, his accomplishments as a tremendously successful cotton broker, and his administration of the five and one-half billion dollars' worth of Government property for which he was responsible in November 1944.

William Lockhart Clayton, who up to this time has been chiefly known as the world's No. 1 cotton factor, the head of the firm of Anderson, Clayton & Company, was born in 1880 on a cotton farm near Tupelo, Mississippi, the son of a railroad contractor. When young Will was six his family moved to the small town of Jackson, Tennessee, and there he attended local schools up to the eighth grade. By the time he was fourteen he was through with his formal education—and he was also the fastest stenographer in town. At fifteen he was working as a court reporter for trials at the local courthouse, spending days recording the horrors of homicide and the intricacies of railroad law. On the side he handled correspondence for the guests in the local hotel, among whom was William Jennings Bryan, who once made him retype a speech because the margins were too narrow. Jerome Hill, a cotton factor from St. Louis visiting there, recognized the boy's ability and eventually took him back to St. Louis with him as his secretary. Not long after that, Hill went to work for a large cotton firm in New York City and again took young Clayton along. The enterprising lad became secretary to Lamar Fleming, the father of the man who is now his own partner.

The temptations of the big city apparently held little appeal for the ambitious boy from Tennessee. He never smoked, drank, or swore, habits which he has not developed to this day; he worked nights; he sent his money to his mother; and he learned another language by living in a modest French boarding house in Manhattan. From 1896 to 1904 he was in New York learning about the cotton business, with an intermission when, at the age of seventeen, he went back to Tennessee to recuperate from pneumonia. For a while he resumed his work as a court reporter and even considered becoming a lawyer, but then his company asked him to return to New York, and he went. He had gained something from his stay in Tennessee, however: he had met Susan Vaughan, whom he married in 1902. (The Claytons now have four daughters.)

In 1904 Clayton realized that the firm he worked for was about to fail, and so he moved to Oklahoma to organize a new cotton firm, Anderson, Clayton & Company, with his

WILLIAM L. CLAYTON

brother-in-law, Frank E. Anderson, and his brother-in-law's brother, M. D. Anderson. In 1905 Clayton's brother Benjamin was taken in, too. (Frank E. Anderson died in 1924 and Benjamin Clayton retired in 1929, but M. D. Anderson remains a partner in the firm, which still has the same name.) Anderson, Clayton & Company grew with tremendous speed, taking over gins, branches, and business from the defunct firm for which Clayton had formerly worked. In 1916 it moved to Houston, Texas. It was one of the first to set up European offices and sell direct to mills in England, Russia, or Italy. The First World War gave this business a big impetus: during the latter years of the War the firm first handled more than 1,000,000 bales of cotton in one year. At this time, according to Delos Lovelace, Clayton served on Bernard M. Baruch's '41 famed War Industries Board, Cotton Division. By the middle 1920's Clayton's was the biggest cotton firm ever heard of, buying and selling about fourteen per cent of the entire American cotton crop.

Today Anderson, Clayton & Company, with business principally in cotton compressing, warehousing, and factoring, is the "biggest spot cotton house in the country, owning the world's largest compressing plant. From Mr. Clayton's huge warehouses more than half the Texas crop has gone out each year in chartered ships to hundreds of ports all over the world." According to a 1936 issue of *Time* Magazine, "It is a poor year in which Anderson, Clayton & Company does not handle 2,000,000 bales of United States cotton. It is a poor year in which the firm does not do twice as much business as its nearest private competitor, George H. McFadden & Brother. It has $40,000,000 capital and its credit is good for at least $150,000,000. The list of its branches and affiliates stemming from its headquarters in Houston's sixteen-story Cotton Exchange Building is a complete lesson in world cotton geography." Before the Second World War these branches or affiliates were

CLAYTON, WILLIAM L.—*Continued*

found not only all over North and South America, but in Bombay, Shanghai, Osaka, Alexandria, Le Havre, Milan, Liverpool; and the firm's representatives traveled from Sweden to Spain, from Poland to Portugal. Anderson, Clayton & Company, continued *Time,* "operates traveling gins in sparsely settled areas of Mexico, compresses to reduce the size of ordinary gin bales for overseas shipment, warehouses with a capacity of 2,000,000 bales, a barge line on the Ouachita, Mississippi, and Warrior Rivers to carry cotton to tidewater. It runs a school to teach the fine art of cotton grading, finances cotton growing in ordinary sections, has even distributed hogs to improve the lot of the cotton grower."

On the New York Cotton Exchange the company's operations are so tremendous that it has a separate member firm, Anderson, Clayton & Fleming. These operations are solely confined to "hedging," or insurance against price changes, in which the cotton merchant sells futures contracts short. Such a procedure is only without risk if he can deliver his real cotton against his contract for future cotton, however—and for a long time the Port of New York, to which the merchant could not possibly get his cotton in time, was the only acceptable port of delivery. In the 1920's, *Time* says, Clayton therefore "squeezed" other cotton men so hard that they forced the modification of this Cotton Exchange rule, and had certain cities in the South also designated as "delivery points." This was exactly what he had set out to do, and he promptly stopped "squeezing"—but he had already made enemies, and enemies who had the ear of Ellison D. ("Cotton Ed") Smith, senior Senator from South Carolina. Since that time there have been several cotton investigations—in 1928, 1929, 1930, and 1936—"all," according to *Time,* "apparently with the prime purpose of pinning something on Will Clayton," who, among other things, was accused of strangling the Exchange by "running it singlehanded from his Houston office." At all of these investigations, from which his enemies have received little satisfaction, Clayton has appeared and testified willingly.

But he has had things to say on many other occasions, too. Before the day of the Hoover [43] Farm Board, which attempted to peg falling cotton prices, his favorite hate was the tariff. Like Secretary of State Hull [40], he is a free trader who opposes "meddling" with the economic machine in any way. When the Farm Board came along he warned that not even the United States Government could buck "the law of supply and demand" in a world-wide product, but his warning went unheeded, and soon the Farm Board found itself the owner of millions of bales of cotton, with prices still down. In the seven seasons before 1935 Clayton's firm sold more than a billion dollars' worth of cotton, however, making at least half of its $13,000,000 reported profit as the result of the Government cotton policy, by Clayton's own admission.

After the Hoover Farm Board came the New Deal. Seeing that it would be disastrous to attempt to peg the price of cotton by Government buying unless production itself were restricted, the AAA guaranteed farmers a certain price if they would cut their acreage. At a public meeting held by the Department of Agriculture in Washington in June 1933 Clayton's was one of the two voices raised against the proposal to destroy a portion of the growing cotton crop as a means of raising the price: he said it would hand over American export cotton markets to foreign producers of cotton. Again he was ignored. In 1936 the Supreme Court held the AAA restriction law unconstitutional, but the Soil Conservation Act continued to keep cotton acreage low, and in the meanwhile foreign production, encouraged by the American cotton policy, had nearly doubled. Clayton himself had turned to South America, "where he taught the Brazilians to grow more cotton and gin it better." His firm also expanded its operations in Argentina and Paraguay, Clayton explaining in his testimony before the Senate Committee on Agriculture in February and March 1936 that this expansion was necessary to enable his firm to do business from Germany, since Exchange conditions hampered it from carrying on the trade from the United States.

There were other tangles with the New Deal, too. Hearings of the Senate Civil Liberties Committee in California disclosed that through a subsidiary firm Clayton was a supporter of Associated Farmers, and that the firm of Anderson, Clayton & Company was in part responsible for the importation of "tractored out" farmers to Arizona during the First World War and the years following in connection with the development of long-staple cotton. "The Clayton interests," according to *PM,* "contributed to an agricultural labor service in Arizona which functioned in an office adjoining the United States Employment Office and was found to have used the Government frank in circulating handbills promising farmers and farm workers prosperity in the Arizona cotton fields."

Clayton was found in the ranks of the Liberty League, to which he contributed $7,500, from 1933 to 1935. (He is politically a Democrat, but not, he says, "a New Deal Democrat.") During the 1936 Presidential campaign *Time* reports that his New Deal wife, inspired by his support of the Liberty League, decided to match what he had given the League by making out a check to James A. Farley [44]. Later in that campaign Republican Candidate Alf M. Landon [44] attacked Hull's reciprocal trade agreements, and Clayton himself came out with a strong statement for Roosevelt and Hull. In the summer of 1936, in a special cotton supplement in the New York *Journal of Commerce,* Clayton "gave the New Deal a hand for the first time in many a season." "The most significant development in cotton in the season just drawing to a close," he wrote, "is the fact that the Government is rapidly on the way out of the market. . . . Not having been slow to criticize Government entrance into the cotton market, it is a pleasure now to commend the wisdom of decision and the skill of execution in liquidation of Government cotton holdings." That the liquidation of Government cotton holdings did not solve everything became apparent, however, in the fall of 1937. American farmers had learned to grow more cotton on fewer acres, and with the great increase in foreign production it became obvious that the world was going to have the largest cotton crop in history. Prices skidded; the South, Congress, and the President grew concerned; a special session of Congress was called.

None of this was good for the export cotton market—and then came the Second World War. On June 27, 1940, in a speech before the Cotton Research Congress, William Clayton announced: "World trade, in any normal sense, lies prostrate . . . the future is so menacing that we must act as if we were already at war." By August of that year he had become even more forthright. "Our national defense ought to be 100 per cent," he said, "or we ought to leave it alone. . . . Every American citizen must be ready to make sacrifices." At the same time he warned that if the War continued cotton exports would show even more drastic decreases.

The War continued—and Clayton was soon called to public service. Says Delos Lovelace, "Mr. Clayton severed all his links with his vast business interests, except for relatively small investment holdings, when he went to Washington." The *United States News* for November 22, 1940 reported that he had "recently captured two key positions," as a raw materials adviser to Nelson Rockefeller's [41] Latin-American Division of the Defense Commission and as deputy administrator, under Jesse Jones [40], in the Federal Loan Agency, in charge of the purchase of critical and strategic materials. In the latter post he was to assist the directors of the Export-Import Bank in making loans to South America.

In January 1941, when the National Cotton Council held its third annual convention at Augusta, Georgia, Clayton spoke on the subject of democracy and cotton. He revealed that he still was quarreling with the New Deal's attempt "to peg the world price" of cotton, thus stimulating foreign production and killing for good any remaining foreign market for United States cotton. His was a straight plea for old-fashioned free trade, to which "the menacing power of Hitler" [42] was the chief obstacle.

More important Government posts were ahead for Clayton. In the spring of 1941 it was rumored that he would head a projected "Department of Economic Warfare," and that he might yet head the Inter-American Bank which was expected to play a big role in the economic development of Latin America. In May of that year he actually was named president of the new Airlines Credit Corporation, which was being organized to take over— by one means or another—the network of South American air services which had been operated by Axis interests. Finally, in July 1942, President Roosevelt nominated Clayton to be Assistant Secretary of Commerce, selected on the recommendation of Secretary of Commerce Jesse Jones, with whom he had worked in the Federal Loan Agency. *Time* described him at this time as "seldom heard of, never quoted, almost never seen outside his office. But through his big, able hands pass all the multi-zeroed dealings of Defense Supplies Corp., which trades vital loans for

Latin American raw materials, and other jobs." Labor and organizations like the National Farmers Union were not particularly friendly to the appointment. When the fight had occurred that year over a thirty-cent minimum wage and minimum sanitary and shelter conditions for cotton pickers the Clayton interests had joined the big growers in resisting the program established by the Farm Security Administration in the agreement with Mexico on the importation of Mexican farm workers. Clayton was pictured in terms of "big money" and "outside control" of the products and prices of agriculture.

In May 1943 the Assistant Secretary of Commerce was a United States delegate to the United Nations Conference on Food and Agriculture at Hot Springs, Virginia. The next month, during the feud between Henry A. Wallace's [40] Board of Economic Warfare and Jesse Jones's Reconstruction Finance Corporation, he testified on behalf of the RFC before the Byrd [42] Committee, stating that all the RFC now did was to foot the bills for purchases of strategic materials made by the BEW, and that BEW views on development programs prevailed when the two agencies differed. (One of the matters on which they differed was the inclusion of labor protective clauses in the procurement contracts for essential war materials negotiated by the BEW with firms in Latin America and elsewhere. On July 5 Clayton signed a letter to the BEW saying that he and Jones agreed to such a clause in the Bolivian tin contract "only on condition there is no intention to try to revolutionize the social and working conditions in these Latin-American countries . . . and that we will not be expected to provide any elaborate policing organization to check upon the contractors to make sure that they are living up to the clauses") The Vice-President's charges that actually the RFC and Jones had obstructed the war effort through their policies resulted in the abolishment of his own BEW post on July 15, 1943.

Appointed Surplus War Property Administrator in Justice James Byrnes's [41] Office of War Mobilization in February 1944, Clayton told a House of Representatives committee that the greatest problem in disposing of the surpluses was pressure from labor and industrial groups to prevent the sale of such goods in competition with new products. (Such a viewpoint was expressed by one Representative.) Clayton, whose administration came under the jurisdiction of four different House committees, succeeded in getting the four chairmen to question him at a joint hearing, saving three of the usual duplications which waste so much official time in Washington.

In May the Administrator stated that "the Government's interest in getting its money out of surplus property is certainly secondary to that of promoting and maintaining a sound domestic economy," but in a few months he was under fire for his apparent "business as usual" attitude. (That June, incidentally, Clayton was placed in an embarrassing position by the "rebellion" of Texas Democrats who threatened not to vote for the party's Presidential nominee unless certain unacceptable Southern demands—such as a platform declaration for "white supremacy"—were met; leaders of the

CLAYTON, WILLIAM L.—*Continued*

revolt included Lamar Fleming and another high official of Anderson, Clayton & Company. The Administrator himself repudiated all connection with the plan and offered to resign to save the Administration from embarrassment.)

In early July Clayton issued an order transferring his assistant, Colonel J. M. O'Byrne, to the Defense Supplies Corporation of the RFC, there to take charge of the disposal of some 14,000,000 acres of land no longer needed by the Army for military installations, which were similarly transferred. About 3,500,000 acres were said to be good farm land, suitable for high agricultural production. Officials of the Department of Agriculture and the Farm Security Administration immediately demanded to know why the RFC had been chosen, while the conservative Washington *Post* said that "Clayton might as reasonably allocate the disposal of surplus factories to the Office of Indian Affairs or the disposal of surplus ships to the Bureau of Entomology and Plant Quarantine. What does the RFC know about farming?" James G. Patton, president of the National Farmers Union, also expressed anxiety that this form of disposal would tend toward inflation of land prices, being dominated by the National Association of Real Estate Boards. Clayton therefore announced a policy of selling agricultural land in family-sized farms to buyers who would themselves buy and use the property, giving as additional objectives: to sell promptly at current values without undue disruption of the market (unlike the New Dealers, who saw in surplus disposal an instrument for reducing the power of monopolies and lowering prices); to give former owners first chance; to avoid sales to speculators; and to have land appraised by "experienced and disinterested men," usually drawn from the local community.

Nevertheless, the controversy continued, with Senator John H. Bankhead [43] of Alabama attempting by law to order the disposal of surplus farm land through the Department of Agriculture, Assistant Attorney General Norman Littell speaking for the Public Lands Division of the Department of Justice, and the War Food Administration entering the picture. James G. Patton charged that a Clayton regulation "returns to the system of exclusive franchises issued to real estate dealers that was so flagrantly abused in 1939-1941 as to result in a complete reorganization of Army real estate machinery and methods at the direct instance of General Brehon B. Somervell [42], head of the Army Service Forces. . . . The probabilities of scandalous profits and inflationary selling are very great if this course is pursued." As a result, on August 22 and 23 both houses of Congress passed bills providing for the disposal of the war surpluses and limiting sharply the Administrator's powers, the Senate bill going so far as to replace him by an eight-man board.

The compromise bill which finally went to the President was signed on October 4 with "considerable reluctance," as Roosevelt considered that "there is danger that the confused methods of disposition and the elaborate restrictions imposed by the bill will in many instances delay rather than expedite reconversion and re-employment." Clayton himself called the bill "unacceptable" and the three-man board

setup "unworkable," and therefore tendered his resignation, effective when a majority of the new board had taken office. However, he offered to remain unofficially for a reasonable period to be of assistance. On October 19 the Texan made a speech challenging the statement of the Republican Presidential nominee, Thomas E. Dewey [44], that he would continue the Hull program of reciprocal trade treaties; and at a committee hearing on the 27th, he advocated the reduction of tariff as well as the sale of surplus ships to other nations.

In early December 1944 President Roosevelt sent to the Senate for confirmation the appointment of Edward R. Stettinius, Jr. [40], as Secretary of State, replacing Cordell Hull, with Joseph C. Grew [41] as Under-Secretary. In a general reorganization of the Cabinet department, Clayton was one of three new Assistant Secretaries (the others were Librarian of Congress Archibald MacLeish [40] and Nelson Rockefeller, the young Coordinator of Inter-American Affairs). No one questioned Clayton's ability to handle the foreign economic affairs assigned to him; conservative opinion and business were pleased with his selection: even the Communist *Daily Worker* favored it on the grounds of unity, and warned its readers against an anti-big-business viewpoint. But there was highly vocal opposition, nonetheless: from cotton state Senators; from *PM* and the Philadelphia *Record*; from labor groups and others who did not necessarily have anything against the man himself but who looked askance on a State Department made up of too many persons of wealth and vested interests.

With other of the State Department nominees, Clayton was questioned as to his beliefs, and his record was scrutinized by the Senate Foreign Relations Committee. He was ready for the line of questioning and submitted a prepared statement: "It has been suggested by some persons that I am a believer in cartels. Nothing could be farther from the truth. . . . A cartel smells the same to me by whatever name it may be called or for whatever commercial purpose it may be organized." The New York *Times* reported further on the hearing: "Of alleged sales by his firm to Japan after the 'moral embargo' was imposed, Mr. Clayton asserted that such sales may have been made but not to his knowledge. To Southern Senators who appeared hostile to his views on cotton, Mr. Clayton declared that he favored shifting cotton farmers from submarginal lands to the growing of other commodities to advance the 'mechanization' of cotton and to prevent great surpluses in a declining cotton export market." The hearing lasted two and one-half hours. In the subsequent roll call of Senators, Clayton's nomination was confirmed by a vote of 52 to 19.

PM, which devoted a series of long articles and editorials to "exposing" Clayton, conceded that he is "a most unusual type of business-man . . . widely read . . . has thought deeply . . . not given in the least to the clichés which pass for ideas among average businessmen . . . an intellectual . . . as articulate and intelligent a spokesman for capitalist conservatism as Henry Wallace is of capitalist liberalism." The paper credited him also with "literacy, persuasiveness, and personal charm," but opposed him on the grounds that his economic thinking was unsuited to twentieth century problems.

The handsome, dark-browed cotton factor is described as tall (six feet three), lean, urbane, magnetic, with thick gray hair parted in the middle, humorous blue eyes, a modest manner, and a calm good humor which seldom leaves him. In Houston the Claytons live in a two-story brick house; they also have a summer home on Lookout Mountain, Chattanooga, Tennessee. There are few close friends, and Houston's golf links and clubs never saw much of Clayton; but even before his present responsibilities in Washington there was little enough time for his hobbies—horseback riding, bridge, mystery stories. Clayton is a member of the Committee on International Economic Policy, made up of prominent representatives of American banking, education, and business.

References

Am Mag 125:18-19+ Ap '38 il por
N Y Sun p28 N 22 '40
PM p4 F 23 '44 por
Time 27:80+ Ap 20 '36; 28:57-8+ Ag 17 '36 por; 37:62 F 10 '41
U S News 9:33 N 22 '40 por
Who's Who in America 1944-45

William B. Feakins, Inc.

UPTON CLOSE

CLOSE, UPTON Feb. 27, 1894- Radio commentator; writer; lecturer

Address: b. Rm. 207, 6777 Hollywood Blvd., Hollywood, Calif.; h. 3052 Lake Hollywood Dr., Los Angeles, Calif.

For many years a popular lecturer on Asia and the peoples of the Pacific Basin, Upton Close is the author of several books and of more than a thousand magazine and newspaper articles. Between travels in the Far East and Europe he has also substituted for radio commentator Lowell Thomas '40, has "voiced" Fox Movietone news films, taken part in educational conferences, written textbooks, and served as a college professor at the University of Washington. Today he is heard over the MBS network as a commentator on world affairs.

The son of Joseph Hall, a Yankee who had mined with Joaquin Miller, and of Lina (Ganty) Hall, a Frenchwoman educated in Sweden who had become a leader in music and art on the Pacific Coast, Upton Close was born Josef Washington Hall. The place was an Indian reservation on the Columbia River, at Kelso, Washington; the date was February 27, 1894. After studying at Washington Missionary College young Hall went on to George Washington University, where he took his B.A. degree in 1915. That same year he was married to Nettie Lipkaman.

It was in 1916 that Hall first set foot in the Far East. In Shantung during the Japanese invasion, from 1916 to 1919 he served as investigating officer for the United States Government, and during that time acquired his present nom de plume. ("Upton Close" was a code identity phrase which came from his habit of being "up close" to the fighting line.) From 1917 to 1922 he also worked as a newspaper correspondent in China, Japan, and Siberia; he also served as adviser to Chinese student revolutionaries and as foreign affairs chief in the regime of General Wu Pei-fu until typhoid fever sent him home an invalid. He returned to the West Coast to lecture on Oriental life and literature at the University of Wash-

ington until 1926, and in that period, in 1924, made his first broadcast with Lowell Thomas, establishing himself and Thomas as radio's first lecturers. While at the University of Washington he also wrote his first two books, *In the Land of the Laughing Buddha* (1925) and *Outline History of China* (with Dr. H. H. Gowen, 1926).

In 1926 Close became director of the annual American Cultural Expeditions to the Orient—expeditions of students, teachers, and professional people which he was to lead for nine years. From 1927 to 1931 he traveled in India, Russia, Syria; from 1932 to 1935, in the Orient and Europe. All in all, he has had a career of amazing adventure. Twice reported dead, he came back each time "bringing the corpse himself," in the words of a telegram he once sent to his wife. He has been through Chinese famines and floods; has been picked up in the streets of Hong Kong, unconscious from dengue fever; has been arrested and held in a Chinese military prison; has raced the tide of the Mediterranean in a motorcar; has ridden, tramped, wheelbarrowed, mule littered, and flown from one end to the other of the world's largest and most picturesque continent, Asia. It was his findings at the earthquake of Kansu, made famous under the title of "Where the Mountains Walked," that brought about his admittance to the Explorers Club in New York.

Close has managed to combine a great deal of writing with this life of adventure and travel. In 1927 came *The Revolt of Asia,* telling about a journey from Tokyo to Cairo and noting the cultural tone and political temper of each country passed through. Its chief thesis was that the hold of the United States on the East should be moral, not legal; and the New York *Times* critic judged the book "able, lucid, and constructive." *Moonlady,* a novel, appeared the same year; although it was a melodrama with a conventional triangular plot, the Chinese setting and Close's unquestioned knowledge of the country made it fascinating reading to most reviewers. *Eminent Asians* (1929)

CLOSE, UPTON—*Continued*

made Close's name known to more readers than any of his earlier books. The New York *Herald Tribune* critic wrote that Close's sketches of Sun Yat-sen, Yagamata, and Ito, Mustapha Kemal, Joseph Stalin '[42], and Mahatma Gandhi '[42] had "more adventure than Zane Grey could invent"; and the New York *Times* commended the book for "its style, its sincerity, and its historical completeness." *Challenge* (1934), which attempted to give a picture of modern Japan, was both criticized for its "glib certainties" and praised as an "excellent and painstaking work." Later revised and partially rewritten, it was republished in 1942 as *Behind the Face of Japan*. Many reviewers found the revised book informal and generally useful for reference work, although the *Saturday Review of Literature* countered that "with a few major deletions and a few fresh personality sketches the volume could have been a useful handbook." "Its chief merit is . . . that it makes the Japanese comprehensible and human," wrote the *Christian Science Monitor*.

But it is through his lectures, radio broadcasts, and articles—for such publications as the New York *Times*, New York *Journal-American* (since the fall of 1944 he has contributed frequently), *Saturday Evening Post*, *American Mercury*, *Reader's Digest*, *Cosmopolitan*—that Close has gained the largest public. Off and on since 1934 he has appeared on news programs over the National Broadcasting Company; from April 1941 to September 1942 he broadcast a Sunday afternoon sustaining program for the network as its authority on Far Eastern questions; and he also broadcast at intervals on the Miles Laboratory's *News of the World*, its nightly news roundup. Then, starting in September 1942, he began a Sunday afternoon commentary for the Sheaffer Pen Company over NBC, and also that fall started broadcasting on Sundays over the Mutual Broadcasting Company for the Lumberman's Mutual Casualty Company, which is headed by James S. Kemper '[41].

In November 1944 Close revealed that his contract with NBC would be ended as of December 10. (The Sheaffer Pen Company had not hired the commentator directly, but had arranged for his services through the broadcasting company.) Although Close told a reporter that "certain radical and communistic elements" or Government sources had forced the network's decision, Niles Trammell '[40], NBC president, declared that these charges were "completely false." "This decision on our part," Trammell said, "to replace one commentator with another [Max Hill, former Tokyo correspondent for the Associated Press] does not involve in the slightest degree the principle of free speech which we have always upheld. . . . In connection with all commercial commentators on NBC facilities, it is a standing policy of the company . . . that the selection of such commentators rests with NBC, inasmuch as the balanced presentation of news and comment is an obligation and responsibility of the broadcast station or network." Close had stated that he was considered "objectionable" because of discussion on "The Dangers of Communism" during his commentary. He announced that he would place the case before the Senate and House committees on interstate commerce, declaring that it raised the question of "Who, after all, is the censor of radio?"

The commentator has been charged in liberal columns, among them *PM*'s, with taking an isolationist, antilabor stand in his articles and broadcasts. (The United Automobile Workers of the CIO has stated that Close has an anti-union bias.) In August 1940, in an article in *Living Age*, he wrote that "we cannot crush European totalitarianism any more than Jefferson's America could abolish kings." In July 1944, marshaling arguments for its "isolationist" charges, *PM* stated that in March 1941 Close had told audiences: "I see less reason for having a war with Japan who is frayed out, eaten out at the heart, who has the blind staggers. . . . And if there is one thing that Japan hopes to do it is to avoid a clash with the American fleet." In September 1941 Close wrote that "we have established an American imperium in the Pacific. (Or will establish it in the process of knocking out anyone who has the temerity to challenge us there, which seems unlikely.)"

When the Japanese attack on Pearl Harbor came Close concluded that America's chief danger lay in the Pacific, not Europe, with the war in the Pacific being fought primarily for supremacy of the New Asia. Any hope of "brotherly love" between England, Russia, China, and the United States is unrealistic, he also claims, asserting that the Roosevelt '[42] Administration has been tricked by its allies, particularly Russia.

Although he usually broadcasts from Hollywood, when Close goes on one of his lecture trips across the continent his broadcasts are made from wherever he happens to be. He has frequently appeared before the New York Town Hall of the Air; his engagements vary from the National Industrial Conference Board and Pennsylvania Bankers Association to Leagues of Women Voters and Knife and Fork Clubs all over the country. Rotary conventions have voted him and Will Durant their "top" speakers.

Close is a member of the Peking, Town Hall, National Arts, and Explorers Clubs, and he was recently elected a member of the Society of American Historians. (In 1945 a new book, "The Ladder of History", a textbook history of the world for American high schools written with Merle Burke, is to appear.) He was married for the fourth time in 1942, to the former Julia Robinson, who makes a practice of accompanying him on his strenuous lecture tours. His four sons by his first wife, Louis Lipkaman, Clarence Victor, Josef Washington 3rd, and Marvell, are in 1944 all in the armed services, and he was recently presented with a fifth son, named Spencer Quintus Ultimus.

Reference

Who's Who in America 1944-45 .

COBB, IRVIN S(HREWSBURY) June 23, 1876—Mar. 10, 1944 Author, journalist, war correspondent, playwright, screen actor, and famous after-dinner speaker; prolific writer of short stories, essays, and novels; became famous through his Judge Priest stories; noted for his irony and humor.

Obituary

N Y Times p14 Mr 11 '44 por

COBURN, CHARLES June 19, 1877- Stage
and motion-picture actor
Address: b. c/o Columbia Pictures, 1438 Gower
St., Hollywood, Calif.

One of the awards made by the Academy of
Motion Picture Arts and Sciences which has
won heartiest public approval was that given to
Charles Coburn for the best supporting role
of 1943. This award was made in recognition
of his work in *The More the Merrier*.

Now celebrating his fiftieth year in show
business, Coburn, despite many previous tempting offers, did not enter the films until 1937.
His long and varied career as actor and manager in the theatre (his stage roles fill an entire column in *Who's Who in the Theatre*)
proved of no mean value in the film world.
"Charles Coburn steals the picture" is a comment often seen in the press reviews of the
picture in which he has appeared. His most
popular roles have been those in which he has
been placed in farcical situations; as a master
comedian he manages to impart an "elegance"
to slapstick.

Born on June 19, 1877 in Savannah, Georgia,
Charles Douville Coburn is the son of Moses
Douville and Emma Louise (Sprigman) Coburn. While employed as a program boy in a
Savannah theatre young Coburn decided upon
the stage as a career after he was given a
"bit" part in a visiting company of *The Mi-
kado*. "But no one would give me a chance to
act," he recalls. Many companies arrived at
the Savannah theatre during the two years he
was employed there, first as program boy and
later as house manager, with their casts complete and left without adding him to their
troupes. At nineteen he left Savannah for
New York, where he made the rounds of the
Broadway producers with no better luck. To
support himself he worked in the package delivery department of a store, was usher in a
theatre, and also rode in a six-day bicycle race.
He was on the point of returning home when
Fate handed him a job as an advance man for
a theatrical company. It was a Chicago stock
company's production of *Quo Vadis* that
brought Coburn his first professional engagement as an actor. Roles in numerous road companies touring the Middle West followed before he made his first New York appearance in
Up York State (1901) in the Fourteenth
Street Theatre. By 1904 Coburn was playing
the lead in a road company of *The Christian*.

The following year he organized the Coburn
Shakespearean Players. In the company was
Ivah Wills, with whom he fell in love while
playing Orlando to her Rosalind. After their
marriage in 1906 Ivah Coburn joined her husband in his managerial enterprises. More interested in the art of the theatre than its commercial advantages, the Coburns chose plays
for their artistic merit rather than their popular appeal. However, their repertory group had
its lighter moments, too. A baseball nine was
formed by the actors, and in between performances of *Hamlet* and *Lysistrata* they played
college teams and semi-pro teams in the towns
they visited.

"Mr. and Mrs. Coburn," as they were billed,
presented plays on Broadway, too. Their revival of *Yellow Jacket* (1916) was proclaimed
to be "the most imaginative and significant

CHARLES COBURN

production ever given of the famous Chinese play." It was done in the Chinese tradition, without formal stage sets. The props
that were used were handled by a character
called the Property Man, who sat in full
view of the audience as he worked a thunder
sheet for a storm effect or moved a ladder
to represent a mountain. Coburn, playing
the part of The Chorus, interpreted the action
from the background as the leading characters
performed at the front of the stage. After
a successful run on Broadway, the play was
added to the Coburns' repertoire, and was
presented to New York audiences in 1921 and
1928 and on the road during the season of
1933-1934.

Mr. and Mrs. Coburn's "biggest box-office"
play was *The Better 'Ole*, Captain Bruce
Bairnsfather's dramatization of his famous
cartoon character, Old Bill, a cockney soldier
of the First World War. Presented in New
York's Greenwich Village Theatre in 1918
with Coburn in the role of Old Bill, its popularity brought the play to an uptown theatre
shortly after its opening, where it continued
to play until 1920. Another successful role
of Coburn's stage career was that of Colonel
Ibbetson in the 1931 New York production of
Peter Ibbetson.

Coburn's love for the theatre prompted him
to carry on a campaign to have colleges and
universities supplement dramatic coaches with
professional actors in their drama courses. In
1941 he sent out brochures on the subject to
all the leading schools and made a series of
speeches along the Atlantic seaboard. Coburn
says, "After all, law is taught by jurists, medicine by experienced doctors. . . . Acting
should no less be taught by professionals who
know what every department of the theatre
is about. . . . The colleges are teaching acting
on the theory that the students can learn from
each other. That is not so. They can learn
only as much as their fellow performers
know." He pointed out also that the need

COBURN, CHARLES—*Continued*

for more professional training centers for stage aspirants had become alarmingly acute since the demise of the stock company in which most of the theatrical stars of other days had served their apprenticeship. Coburn tested his theory in Union College (Schenectady) in the summer of 1935, when with his wife and the College president, Dixon Ryan Fox, he founded the Mohawk Drama Festival. During the eight-week summer course Mr. and Mrs. Coburn were members of the faculty, and under their direction the class produced *Lysistrata, Rip Van Winkle, The Merry Wives of Windsor,* and *The Master of the Revels.* After the death of his wife in 1936, Coburn continued to guide the Drama Festival at Union College, returning each year from Hollywood to do so until the War drove it off the campus. In recognition of his work he was given the honorary Degree of Master of Letters by the College.

Regarding his own art, Coburn says that he tries to avoid being "typed." In his stage career his roles have ranged from Hamlet to the sentimental cockney of *The Better 'Ole.* In his film work he has free-lanced so that he might choose his parts. In 1943 he signed a long-term contract with Columbia Pictures, but he limited the contract to four films in two years so that he would be free to make pictures at other studios. Among the twenty or more films in which he has appeared, some of the outstanding ones are *Idiot's Delight* (1939) with Norma Shearer and Clark Gable, *The Devil and Miss Jones* (1941) with Jean Arthur and Robert Cummings, *Kings Row* (1941) with Ann Sheridan, *In This Our Life* (1942) with Bette Davis [41] and Olivia de Havilland [44], *George Washington Slept Here* (1942) with Jack Benny [41] and Ann Sheridan, *Princess O'Rourke* (1943) with Olivia de Havilland and Robert Cummings, *The Constant Nymph* (1943) with Joan Fontaine [44] and Charles Boyer [43], *Heaven Can Wait* (1943) with Gene Tierney and Don Ameche, *Knickerbocker Holiday* (1944) with Nelson Eddy [43] and Constance Dowling, *Wilson* (1944) with an all-star cast, *Impatient Years* (1944) with Jean Arthur, and *Together Again* (1944), in which Charles Boyer and Irene Dunne shared stellar honors with Coburn. Pictures awaiting release are *Rhapsody in Blue, Czarina,* with Tallulah Bankhead [41], and *Colonel Effingham's Raid.* In Ruth Gordon's [43] *Over 21,* which begins production in January 1945, Coburn will play the part of the newspaper publisher.

In *The More the Merrier* (1943), the picture which won him an "Oscar," Coburn played the part of Mr. Dingle, a "well-to-do retired millionaire" who, after persuading a young office worker (Jean Arthur) in crowded Washington to rent him a room in her apartment, decides she is lonesome and, unknown to her, rents a couch in his room to a young aviation expert (Joel McCrea). After many farcical complications a happy ending is reached. The New York *Herald Tribune* reviewer said that the director-producer could not have picked more expert players, but that Coburn "beats both the stars on more than one occasion in whipping up amusement by his crafty imper-

sonation of an elderly cupid." Coburn's increasing box-office value has prompted Columbia to offer him a more lucrative contract as well as star billing. In *My Kingdom for a Cook* (1943) Coburn played a star role, a George Bernard Shaw [44] character who "barges belligerently and humorously" through the story. "You might dismiss it," wrote the New York *World-Telegram,* "as a flimsy little farce, but you can't do that to a picture where Mr. Coburn is permitted to cut loose as he does in this one." Of himself, the veteran actor has said: "Most actors seem to start out playing slapstick and work up to roles so dignified you have to put a 'Mr.' before the fellow's name on the marquee. I started out with a slight bit of dignity, worked into Shakespeare, and now they call me Charlie and I get flapjacks in my face. But I wouldn't have it any other way." At any rate, one writer points out, Coburn receives as much as pin-up girls and wavy-haired leading men—something like $7,500 every Saturday.

There were various reports that Coburn planned to return to the stage in the winter of 1944, but he announced that his motion-picture contracts would not permit him to return to Broadway until October 1945, when he plans to produce *The Master of the Revels,* a play by Don Marquis about Henry VIII. Coburn had appeared in the play in 1935 with Mrs. Coburn in a tryout production by the Mohawk Drama Festival group.

A Hollywood columnist reports that if you ask the Hollywood girls who their favorite glamour boy is the answer will come in a chorus, "Charles Coburn." Despite his sixty-eight years, Coburn presents a dashing appearance, "with a monocle in one eye and a twinkle in the other and a trip-lightly in his step." Off the screen he wears bright yellow sport shirts and many chains—one on his wrist, one on his monocle, and a very long one on a cigar cutter. There is not a baseball, hockey, football, or tennis match (he bets mildly) at which Coburn is not the "loudest and most persistent yeller in the place." He dances the rumba and a version of the samba. He is what Hollywood calls "a solid sender." With Lucas, his houseboy, at war, Coburn lives quite alone in a Sunset Boulevard apartment.

References

N Y Post p11 Jl 24 '43 por
N Y Sun p24 Jl 28 '43
Who's Who in America 1944-45
Who's Who in the Theatre 1939

COFFIN, HENRY SLOANE, REV. Jan. 5, 1877- Clergyman; author; educator

Address: b. Union Theological Seminary, 120th St. and Broadway, New York City; h. 80 Claremont Ave., New York City

Perhaps the most important spiritual leader of 2,051,869 American Presbyterians is the Reverend Dr. Henry Sloane Coffin, past moderator of the General Assembly of the Presbyterian Church in the United States of America—"a brilliant preacher, an able theologian, and a voluminous author." His election as moderator climaxed forty years of service in the New York Presbytery, seventeen of them as president of the interdenominational Union Theological Seminary, from which position he is to retire in June 1945. Dr. Coffin is an eloquent liberal and a leader in the movement for church unity. In the words of the *Christian Century*, "He has elevated the importance of the moderatorship of the General Assembly in the eyes of Protestants on two continents by a ministry of reconciliation which has had few parallels in recent times. His words carry not only the resonant authority of ecumenical Christianity but also that rare overtone of irenic experience."

Henry Sloane Coffin was born January 5, 1877, in New York City. The son of Edmund and Euphemia (Sloane) Coffin, he came of a family of wealthy and philanthropic merchants. As might be expected, he attended Yale University, where he was elected to Phi Beta Kappa, Delta Kappa Epsilon, Skull and Bones, and Chi Alpha, receiving his B.A. degree in 1897. During the next two years he pursued graduate studies at New College, Edinburgh (Scotland), and at the University of Marburg (Germany). Returning to the United States, in 1900 Coffin received his M.A. degree from Yale. After studying at the Union Theological Seminary, that same year he received his degree of Bachelor of Divinity and was ordained a Presbyterian minister.

The Reverend Mr. Coffin first entered upon his pastoral duties at the Bedford Park Church in New York, where he remained from 1900 to 1905. Toward the end of this period he joined the faculty of Union Theological Seminary as associate professor of practical theology, a position he held until 1926.

In 1906 Henry Sloane Coffin received a D.D. from New York University, and on September 6 of that year he was married to Dorothy Prentice Eells. As pastor of the Madison Avenue Presbyterian Church, a post which he had entered the year before, Dr. Coffin was zealously putting his ideas on "practical theology" into effect. At that time the Madison Avenue Church included a chapel where services were held for the poor families of the East Side who could not afford to rent pews (often a considerable expense in those days, as one familiar with Clarence Day's *Life With Father* will remember). This chapel was supported by the pewholders of the church proper. Dr. Coffin proceeded to close the chapel, to bring the two very different congregations together as one, and to abolish all pew rentals—a daring innovation, but successful, for Dr. Coffin remained with the Madison Avenue Church until his resignation in 1926. During the early years of his ministry there he made a practice of taking a portable reed organ to nearby tenement houses in order to hold a morning service for street railway workers coming home from the night shift at 2 a.m.

Dr. Coffin's first book, *The Creed of Jesus*, was published in 1907. It was followed in 1910 by *Hymns of the Kingdom*, of which he was co-editor; in 1911 by *Social Aspects of the Cross*; in 1912 by *The Christian and the Church* and, in collaboration, *Some Social Aspects of the Gospel*; in 1914 by *University Sermons*; and in 1915, the year in which Dr. Coffin received a D.D. from Yale, by *The Ten*

REV. HENRY SLOANE COFFIN

Commandments and *Some Christian Convictions*. The Lyman Beecher lectures, given at Yale by Dr. Coffin, who has long been a popular guest preacher at leading universities, were published as *In a Day of Social Rebuilding* (1918). *A More Christian Industrial Order* followed in 1920; *What Is There in Religion?* in 1922, the year in which Dr. Coffin was awarded a D.D. by Harvard University; *Portraits of Jesus Christ* and *What To Preach* (the Warrack Lectures) in 1926.

After twenty-two years on the faculty of Union Theological Seminary, Dr. Coffin was elevated to its presidency in 1926. Upon his inauguration he announced his intention to "turn out men of adventurous spirit, unfettered by tradition." The Seminary had a history of liberalism dating back to 1892, when the General Assembly of the Presbyterian Church had suspended Professor Charles Augustus Briggs from the ministry because of his unorthodox interpretation of the Old Testament. Rather than separate Professor Briggs from the faculty, the Seminary separated itself from the Presbyterian fold, becoming interdenominational. Dr. Coffin has carried on and enriched this liberal tradition, "administering a ticklish job," it is said, "with absolute fairmindedness." A wide range of opinion has been represented at the Seminary, not only by students but by faculty members. "They have the liberty," Dr. Coffin points out, "of joining any organization they wish. One hopes that men in responsible positions will behave with Christian discretion."

Dr. Coffin has been a consistent opponent of racial discrimination and insists that the issue must not be met "timidly," but with the determination "to bring together the men and women [of the various groups] . . . so that they may understand one another and the partition wall of class feeling may fall away." Through his efforts Union became in 1942 the first major United States seminary to elect a Negro to membership on its Governing Board.

COFFIN, HENRY SLOANE, REV.—*Cont.*

During the years of his presidency Dr. Coffin has continued his activities as author and as guest preacher at local churches and at schools in the United States, England, and Scotland. In 1927 he was awarded an LL.D. by Amherst College; in 1928 a D.D. by Union College; and in 1931 a Litt.D. by the College of the Ozarks. In 1931 appeared his *The Meaning of the Cross*, in 1933 *What Men Are Asking*, and in 1934 *God's Turn*. In 1934, too, he received an LL.D. from St. Andrews' University at Dundee (Scotland). He was further honored with a D.D. from the Episcopal Seminary in 1935; an S.T.D. from the Jewish Theological Seminary and a Litt.D. from Western Reserve University in 1937; a Litt.D. from Hamilton College and a D.Théol. from the Faculté Libre de Théologie Protestante de Paris in 1938.

Two years later six lectures Dr. Coffin had delivered at New York and Emory Universities on the subject of changing religious beliefs and problems in America during the preceding fifty years were published under the title *Religion Yesterday and Today*. The New York *Times* called them "admirably lucid and comprehensive," the *Christian Century*, "stimulating and provocative"; but Dr. John Haynes Holmes[41] considered the book "a tired piece of work . . . [which] looks backward rather than forward, seeks recovery of old ideas rather than discovery of new, and even conveys a sense of satisfaction that the best religious thought of two generations gone by is tumbling today to ruins. One might accuse this book of cynicism, were it not for that ringing conviction of the Christian faith which has always been Dr. Coffin's most attractive and potent characteristic."

An admirer of the Russian people although not of Communism, Dr. Coffin gives his services as vice-president of Russian War Relief, Inc. In addition he is director of the Church Extension Committee of the Presbytery of New York, a member of the Board of Home Missions of the Presbyterian Church, a fellow of the corporation of Yale University, and a trustee of Atlanta University (Georgia) and of Robert College, Constantinople (Turkey). Dr. Coffin belongs to the Yale and University Clubs. As president of the Union Settlement Association of New York City he takes much interest in its work for unfortunate children.

On May 28, 1943 Dr. Coffin was elected moderator of the 155th General Assembly of the Presbyterian Church in the United States of America. In taking the chair Dr. Coffin "immediately declared that his major objective during the year he was to be in office would be to advance the cause of reunion between the Northern and the Southern branches of Presbyterianism." This cleavage, caused originally by "the tensions leading to the Civil War," resulted in the separate existence of the Presbyterian Church in the United States (the Northern branch is the Presbyterian Church in the United States *of America*), with a 1943 membership of 553,797. Dr. Coffin was also desirous of union with the Episcopal Church, which had been under consideration for six years "with unflagging

leisureliness" by a Joint Committee on Approaches to Unity, although opposed by New York's Bishop William T. Manning[40]. In September 1943, when the question came up before the Episcopal House of Bishops, they adopted an inconclusive and delaying resolution. "Later," adds *Time* Magazine, "scholarly, urbane Presbyterian Moderator Henry Sloane Coffin addressed the Episcopal Convention. Said he dryly, 'Our Church is committed to the principle of visible church unity, and never has sought to be merely a sect of the Holy Catholic Church.'" The *Christian Century* called his speech at this time "one of the most impressive in recent church history."

In Dr. Coffin's eyes the big issues before the Christian church are "the achievement of fellowship among nations, fellowship in the distribution of spiritual and economic goods, fellowship among races." Before these issues, he declares, "how irrelevant seem the questions of church government or forms of worship or the minor elaborations of doctrine which have divided their members into many communions! . . . To those who know at first hand how hampering, how wasteful, how ineffective for the real job our inherited divisions prove, how meaningless and repellent they appear to outsiders and to that large mass of indifferent nominal Christians whom the Church must recapture, it seems imperative [to achieve church unity]. Here and there leaders are trying to end the divisions of past centuries. . . . Otherwise traditionalism and inertia will block every effort."

At the election of a new moderator on May 25, 1944, Dr. Coffin's address as retiring moderator warned against a return to "hideous pagan isolation" and declared that "the Church must lay impatient hands on stubborn remnants of anti-Christian isolationism. . . . No plan of international cooperation to maintain order and secure peace has the slightest chance of success," he said, "which does not get all peoples employed with a prospect of an equitable share in the goods which God makes available to our world. . . . Obsolete economic structures must be torn down and carted off."

References

N Y Herald Tribune p19 My 28 '43 por
Time 41:50-1 Je 7 '43 por
Who's Who in America 1944-45

COLLIER, WILLIAM, SR. Nov. 1, 1866—Jan. 13, 1944 Stage and screen favorite for more than sixty years, writer, and director; appeared with George M. Cohan and with Weber and Fields; played in numerous shows in London, Australia, and the United States; wrote *Nothing but the Truth, Take My Advice, Caught in the Rain,* and many other hits.

Obituary

N Y Times p19 Ja 14 '44

COLVIN, MRS. D(AVID) LEIGH June 12, 1883- President of the National Woman's Christian Temperance Union

Address: b. c/o National Woman's Christian Temperance Union, 1730 Chicago Ave., Evanston, Ill.; h. 605 W. 184th St., New York City

For about a decade prohibition has been waiting for the pendulum of public opinion to swing
back in its direction, according to Mrs. D.
Leigh Colvin, who in November 1944 became
the seventh president of the National Woman's
Christian Temperance Union. Predicting a
great wave of drunkenness at the end of the
War, she sees as inevitable the return of prohibition.

Mrs. Colvin was born Mamie White, in
Westview, Ohio, on June 12, 1883, the daughter
of a Congregationalist minister, the Reverend
Levi White, and Belle (Hudelson) White. She
was graduated from the Manual Training High
School in Indianapolis, and from Wheaton College, Illinois, in 1905 with a B.A. degree. In
1906-1907 and again in 1909-1910 she did graduate work at Columbia University in economics,
sociology, and political science.

Mrs. Colvin's parents were ardent Prohibitionists, and she herself had entered the movement at an early age by joining the youth organization of the W.C.T.U. At Wheaton she
competed in contests of the Intercollegiate Prohibition Association, called the most extensive
system of oratorical contests in the United
States, and won successively the college, state,
and interstate contests and second place one
year in the national competition. While still
an undergraduate she was elected national vice-
president of the association, of which her future
husband was then president. The year after
her graduation from Wheaton, on September
19, 1906, she and David Leigh Colvin were
married. Colvin, too, has continued since their
marriage to be active in the movement, in 1916
running for United States Senator from New
York, in 1917 for Mayor of New York City,
and for Vice-President (1920) and President
(1936) of the United States—all on the ticket
of the Prohibition Party.

Mrs. Colvin was a member of the United
States delegation to the 1910 world W.C.T.U.
convention in Glasgow, after which she and
her husband spent four months in European
travel. Back in the United States, she helped
to organize in 1913 the Fort Washington
branch of the W.C.T.U. in New York City.
The following year she became corresponding
secretary of the county W.C.T.U., and in 1916
she became county president, a post which she
held until 1921. From then until 1926 she was
state vice-president, and in 1926 she became
state president. She served in this capacity,
and from 1933 as national vice-president as
well, until her present incumbency. Like her
husband, Mrs. Colvin has also run for public
office on the Prohibition ticket: as New York
candidate for Congress and as Lieutenant Governor, both in 1918, and as member of the
New York State Assembly in 1923. When
asked once if she thought women had done
much to reform politics, her answer was a
blunt "No!" They still have as much right as
men to vote, however, she added, whatever the
result.

It is the confirmed belief of the W.C.T.U.
leader that total abstinence is the only way
to fight alcohol. The term "moderate drinking," she says, is a snare: "Alcohol is no
respecter of moderate drinkers. Nobody knows
which moderate drinker will become an alcoholic—they must have all been moderate drinkers at first." Prohibition will come, she be-

MRS. D. LEIGH COLVIN

lieves, when the American people realize that
"stop-gaps," as she calls them, will never eradicate the root of the evil.

The liquor interests, Mrs. Colvin states, are
now conducting a campaign for moderate drinking, placing emphasis on medical and psychiatric care. These people are today "afraid
that prohibition will cut off their business," she
says, "and they are trying to solve the problem
of drunkenness by curing the alcoholics, and
allowing the business to continue. The result
of this," she says, "is an increase in the
number of alcoholics." "The W.C.T.U. is not
concerned primarily with these cures, though
of course we sympathize, but what we want to
do is to legislate the liquor industry out of business." Mrs. Colvin herself attended the Yale
University School of Alcohol Studies during
the summer of 1944, and her attendance is regarded as indicative of her realistic attitude
toward the alcohol problem. Some members of
the W.C.T.U. have not been in sympathy with
the Yale school, which is engaged in socio-
logic, legal, and statistical research relating to
the problem.

Mrs. Colvin has answered the challenge of
crime in connection with prohibition with the
spirit of the founders of the movement. "Wet
publicity!" she exclaimed. "There was bootlegging and drinking, of course, and there was
crime." But drink, and not prohibition, she
pointed out, was still the offender. The prohibition law was poorly enforced, she maintains. "Today, with the American people
accustomed to rationing, and the OPA experienced in handling black markets, prohibition
would be a success."

Speaking after her election to the W.C.T.U.
presidency, Mrs. Colvin stated that the "wets"
were preventing local option elections on prohibition. "They use as their strongest argument the one that we must not vote on prohibition while our soldiers are overseas," she said.
"We have a hard job ahead, but we major in
hard jobs. It took a great deal of agitation,
prayer, and hard work to bring about the

COLVIN, MRS. D. LEIGH—*Continued*

prohibition of liquor traffic, and I have faith that it will again be outlawed." The W.C.T.U. is asking people to abstain from the use of alcohol in their celebration of the coming day of victory at the end of the War. "Two states," the president says, "have already passed laws forbidding the sale of liquor on that day." But she is of the opinion that many people will of their own accord plan a solemn celebration.

In connection with her activities in the prohibition movement, Mrs. Colvin has lectured in almost all of the forty-eight states. She appeared before the New York Republican State Convention in 1930 during a hearing on the subject of repeal; and before the repeal of the Eighteenth Amendment she spoke at the Institute of Public Relations of the University of Virginia and at a course at Ohio Wesleyan. From 1926 to 1943 she was editor in chief of the *Woman's Temperance Work* (now the New York *Temperance Work*), official organ of the New York W.C.T.U., and she has also contributed to numerous temperance periodicals.

While the temperance cause and the W.C.T.U. are Mrs. Colvin's main interests, she has had a part in other movements. She is vice-president of the National Council of Women, founded by Frances E. Willard and Susan B. Anthony and composed of representatives of leading women's societies; she is vice-president of the Women's National Radio Committee, a group of women interested in promoting higher ethical standards for radio programs; and she is a member of the D.A.R. and the League of Women Voters. In addition she is active within the Methodist Church and has been a delegate to its General and Jurisdictional Conferences.

The W.C.T.U. president has won silver, gold, grand gold, diamond, and grand diamond medals in national oratorical contests; was made a member of Wheaton's Scholastic Honor Society in 1932; and in 1937 was awarded the honorary degree of Doctor of the Art of Oratory from Staley College of the Spoken Word in Brookline, Massachusetts. Unlike some of the early members of the prohibition movement, gray-haired Mrs. Colvin is no hatchet-swinging reformer. Plump and comfortable-looking, she disarms opponents with her gentle good humor. She is described as an effective speaker who presents her facts logically and without emotionalism. "One of the most competent women who ever carved out a woman's career in America," wrote one newspaperman after hearing her speak.

Shortly after their marriage Mr. and Mrs. Colvin bought five thousand acres of land in North Dakota and spent three summers there living in a sod house. Their permanent home has been New York City. Mrs. Colvin's new post may force a change of residence, however, to be nearer the W.C.T.U. headquarters in Evanston, Illinois, the old home of the second president, Frances Willard. Since Mr. Colvin is currently devoting himself to lecturing, Mrs. Colvin feels that Evanston or Chicago might serve just as well for their home. The Colvins have one daughter, Virginia Leigh.

References

N Y Herald Tribune p18 S 25 '44 por
N Y Sun p22 S 29 '44
PM Mag p5 O 22 '44 por
Union Signal 70:4-5+ N 4 '44
Who's Who in America 1944-45

COLVIN, MAMIE WHITE *See* Colvin, Mrs. D. L.

CONDON, EDDIE Nov. 16, 1905- Musician

Address: b. c/o Blue Network Co., Inc., 30 Rockefeller Plaza, New York City; h. 130 W. 12th St., New York City

Guitarist Eddie Condon is a musician who has been called "the moving force behind some of the greatest jazz records ever made" and "a catalyst of jazz, who never takes a chorus himself." Since 1942 he has been directing "hot jazz" concerts at Manhattan's Town Hall and the conservative old Carnegie Hall. His music has inspired Virgil Thomson [40] and other serious music critics to write comments like: "the most absorbing musical experience that I have been through as a consumer in some years." If hot jazz now rubs elbows with Beethoven and Brahms, it is in large part due to musicians like Condon.

It took thirty-six years for Condon and his guitar to reach Town Hall, however. Albert Edwin Condon was born November 16, 1905 in Goodland, Indiana, the son of John Henry and Margaret (McGraw) Condon. He was two years old when his family moved to Momence, Illinois—because, he says, "the state went dry and I couldn't take that." After eight years of what Eddie calls his "moments in Momence" the family moved to Chicago Heights, close to Chicago, and it was while in grade school there that Eddie graduated from the ukelele to the banjo. While taking in the first year of Bloom Township High School, he worked at non-union jobs like playing for Odd Fellows' dances: "I used to sleep through classes because I was up all night playing hot banjo with the cats." By the time he was fifteen he was a finished banjoist and guitarist, and he held a card in the musicians' union. He therefore decided against more formal education, and joined Homer Peavey's Jazz Bandits, playing one-night engagements throughout Wisconsin, Minnesota, and Iowa. Some months later he was to find himself playing with the already famous Bix Beiderbecke when he signed up with another band which was being assembled to play in Syracuse, New York. For some time Condon, Beiderbecke, and a couple of other musicians lived together in Syracuse, a few blocks away from their job at the Alhambra; on Sunday nights they would drive north to play at a pavilion at Oswego on Lake Ontario. The association did much to shape Condon's attitude toward music: his dislike of big bands and of jazz arrangements, his respect for improvisation. "I'm a free soul," says Condon. "Guys like me want to play hot jazz, the stuff you make up as you go along."

When Condon parted from Bix it was to return to Chicago, the Jazz Bandits, and more one-night dates—he was afraid of New York. After the Jazz Bandits he worked, he says, at about ninety-five places in Chicago. By 1925, at the age of nineteen, he was guitarist and

leader of the McKenzie-Condon Chicagoans,
who included such musicians as Gene Krupa
(then seventeen), Joe Sullivan, Bud Freeman,
Frank Teschmaker, Jimmy MacPartland, and
James Lannigan (now with the Chicago Symphony). The Chicago Rhythm Kings made
what have been called "marvelous records of
pure improvisations," some "among the very
finest things in all hot music." Ever since that
time Condon has been identified as a "Chicago-
style" musician, but he himself ridicules the
expression. There are two kinds of music,
good and bad, he says—and "if you're in Fairbanks, Alaska, and you can play the piano
good, you can play the piano."

In 1928 Condon went to New York and
found a job for his Chicago Rhythm Kings at
the Chateau Madrid. But the "Chicago style"
was still too rough for New York, which at
that time liked its jazz on the anemic side, and
the band was fired after a short time. They
then spent a week at the Palace, the Manhattan home of vaudeville, but they were not liked
there either. Discouraged, all of them except
Eddie returned to Chicago, and eventually Condon and Red McKenzie "struck up a little outfit that could be set up on a domino," the
Mound City Blue Blowers, which consisted of
McKenzie on a comb, Frank Billings on a
leather suitcase, Jack Bland on the guitar, and
Condon himself on the banjo. They played
mostly at fashionable cocktail parties, where
they were very popular, for all the guests
wanted to play the suitcase. For nine months
the Blowers were engaged at the Bath Club,
and they worked at the Stork Club three different times. One winter they even went to
Miami and commuted to dates at Palm Beach.
At another time Condon played the piano in
a five-piece band on a liner going to Buenos
Aires and back. "For 14,000 miles we played
in the key of F," he says—and when he was
welcomed back to New York he was introduced as "Eddie Condon, just back from Buenos
Aires, who can really make the piano talk.
And it says, 'Please let me alone.'"

In 1936 New York's Onyx Club, where the
swing craze of the '30's had just started, hired
McKenzie and Condon, but the musicians were
out on the street after the advent of the popular "The Music Goes Round and Round,"
which was not their type of song. Condon,
with Bunny Berigan, Joe Bushkin, and three
other men, promptly set up at the Famous
Door—and Benny Goodman '42 came on the
scene. For a while it seemed as though small
bands would become a thing of the past. In
1937, however, Nick's hired Bobby Hackett,
Pee Wee Russell '44, George Brunis, and Condon, and hot jazz found a home in Greenwich
Village. It kept that home, and soon Milt Gab-
ler began issuing his first Commodore records
with Condon's band, seeking to recapture the
spirit of Chicago jazz of the mid-'20's. Condon
also played the guitar with Artie Shaw's '41 orchestra in 1938, and the following year he organized the Summa Cum Laude Orchestra,
which Bud Breeman took to Chicago's Sherman
Hotel in 1940 and 1941.

On January 14, 1942 the advertising executive,
Ernest Anderson, promoted a Carnegie Hall
concert for the late Fats Waller '42. It was
such a success that Anderson decided to put
jazz into Town Hall, leaving the choosing of
musicians and the program entirely up to Con-

EDDIE CONDON

don, who was also to serve as guitarist and
unceremonious master of ceremonies and to do
whatever directing was needed. Although the
first of the concerts was not notably successful,
by 1944 crowds were overflowing into 43rd
Street outside of Town Hall, waiting to get in.
"It was wonderful," said Condon. "I could
look out over the house and not see those mal-
lard and deer that used to fly around in the
empty seats." In May 1944 the Blue Network
started broadcasting a program of hot jazz
directed by Condon, which originated from
Town Hall from 3:30 to 4:00 p.m. on Saturday afternoons; and the Columbia Broadcasting System selected his Town Hall Jazzopators
for the first television program to present a
jazz group. The following October Condon's
Jazz Concerts moved to Carnegie Hall. In
reviewing the first performance there *PM's*
writer said the vastness and austerity of the
larger auditorium discouraged audience participation. A New York *Times* critic, however,
said of a later concert in the same auditorium:
"There is no denying that the impromptu nature
of his [Condon's] group's performance makes
for an unusual musical experience and proves
that jazz has a real place in the music of our
time. The improvisations by groups of varying size are a unique thing and one to wonder
at." Condon himself regards these improvisations as pure jazz: "We can't honestly dictate
arrangements for these men to play. We believe they can create something better than anyone could write for them. And by this uninhibited improvisation you can be sure you know
just exactly where the talent lies."

For each concert Condon lines up from fifteen to twenty musicians, both Negro and
white. Most of them are from Nick's, "where
hot jazz still holds out against 'boogie-woogie.'"
Pee Wee Russell and Condon himself are ever-
present regulars, but anybody is apt to be asked
to drop around and sit in on a session. The
concerts are always informal and intimate.
Condon keeps the audience generally amused
with his patter, takes swipes at Guy Lombardo,
and recognizes friends in the gathering. He

CONDON, EDDIE—*Continued*

"introduces performers casually, he holds conferences on the stage with some of his associates while others are breaking out into solo splashes, and he tells the performers who is to take a chorus while the numbers are in progress, meanwhile setting tempi decisively." He himself never solos; however, in Charles Smith's words, "his guitar (or banjo) is so important a part of every rhythm section in which he plays that it would take very untrained ears to miss his contribution." In musician's polls in 1942 and 1943 he was awarded cups as the best guitarist. Condon says of himself: "I have been playing the guitar for fifteen years. For fifteen years people have been asking me why I don't play solos. I've spent fifteen years working up the answer, and it's now practically in final form."

Condon has written a number of musical compositions, some in collaboration with Louis Armstrong[44], Fats Waller, Johnny De Vries, and others. On November 16, 1942 he was married to Phyllis Smith Reay, a copywriter at the D'Arcy Advertising Company, of which Ernest Anderson is an executive. The couple have one daughter, Maggie McGraw Condon. In appearance, according to one writer, Eddie "looks like a college boy from the stage. Close up he shows his years and the fact that he dates back to the golden-horned days of the Mound City Blue Blowers." He is just under five feet eight inches tall, weighs 131 pounds, and is given to bow ties and striped shirts. His hair, according to George Frazier, is of that nondescript color that "makes you pause trying to decide whether it's reddish blond or sandy or light blond." As for his voice, it is "crisp and quick, but not quite quick enough for his mind." His chief hobby, recreation, and sport is conversation. "Night in, night out, he probably talks more than anyone you've ever met." According to *Newsweek*, "Condon has had an enormous influence on 'Le Jazz Intellectuel' for two reasons: his wizardry on his instrument, and the fact that he is articulate about his art. There are jazz pundits in every bar and record shop, but there are few fine players who are any good at talking about what they believe in. Condon, however, will talk to anybody about anything."

Condon is nevertheless not entirely sympathetic with "Le Jazz Intellectuel." Of Hugues Panassié, author of *Le Jazz Hot,* he asks: "How can he come to America and tell us about our native music? I wouldn't go to France and tell him how to jump on a grape." (In *Le Jazz Hot* Panassié writes of Condon: "Eddie Condon never plays one-string solos; he concentrates on supplying a powerful rhythmic foundation. From this point of view he is incomparable. Few musicians have so much to give to a hot orchestra as Eddie, with his metronomically regular rhythm which induces superb swing. Usually Eddie simply marks the four beats, but occasionally he plays eight chords to the measure, thus giving the effect of a sort of 'roll,' which gives the performance great tension.") Condon is also considerably irritated by the "semi-pro jazz critics" who call a clarinet a licorice-stick or a trombone a bicycle pump. "Stuff like that sets you back ten years when you're trying to sell people jazz."

References

Boston Herald Ap 2 '42 por
Down Beat p14-15 Jl 1 '43 il por
N Y World-Telegram p8 Jl 1 '44
New Yorker 18:13 Ap 11 '42
Newsweek 23:62 Ja 24 '44 por
Scholastic 44:40+ My 1 '44 por

CONINGHAM, SIR ARTHUR 1895-

Royal Air Force officer

Address: c/o British Air Ministry, London

Why did the Germans never launch an all-out counterattack in western France after the Allied invasion of June 6, 1944? This is a question frequently posed by military men and civilians alike. The main reason, suggests *Time* Magazine, may have been "the greatest tactical air operation in history." Directing this operation was Air Marshal Sir Arthur Coningham, K.C.B., chief of the 2nd Tactical Air Force, who had studied the German system of air and ground coordination and, with a few alterations, had turned it into one of the most decisive factors in the Allied offensive.

Although he was born in Brisbane, Australia, in 1895, Sir Arthur Coningham regards New Zealand, where he was reared, as his home. He received his advanced education at Wellington College and Victoria College. On the very first day of the First World War the nineteen-year-old youth enlisted in the infantry, shortly afterward transferring to the cavalry, with which he served a brief time in Egypt. There he contracted dysentery and typhoid fever, lost seventy-two pounds, and was sent home to New Zealand to recuperate. Six months later he was on his way to England to join the Royal Flying Corps. In France he won the Military Cross and the Distinguished Service Order within the space of a month. Wounded, he did home service for a while, then returned as a squadron leader to France, where he promptly bagged another medal.

After the War he remained with the Royal Air Force as a flight lieutenant and was sent to Iraq as a squadron leader. (The R.A.F. had been formed in April 1918 by an amalgamation of the Royal Naval Air Service and the Royal Flying Corps.) In 1924, following his service in Iraq, Coningham was assigned to staff and special duties in Egypt and the Middle East. In 1925 he led three De Havilland planes on a 5,600-mile contest flight from Cairo to Nigeria, winning the Air Force Cross. The flight blazed a trail for a trans-African route, which was to be used in the Second World War for the ferrying of supply aircraft to the Middle East, India, and Russia. After this exploit he served for a time as an instructor in England at the R.A.F. College and Central Flying School, and then was sent back to the Middle East at Khartoum in the Anglo-Egyptian Sudan. His next assignment was at the coastal area headquarters staff; and in 1937, as a group captain, he became the senior staff officer. He then took command of Calshot Station, leaving it just prior to the start of the Second World War to serve as an air commodore of a bomber group in England. In July 1941, as air vice-marshal, he was sent to the Middle East once more, this time to act as the air officer in command in the Western Desert (Egypt).

Coningham was now a seasoned airman. His technical skill, however, did not account entirely for his success, explains Lemuel F. Parton of the New York *Sun*. It was a success of personality as well. Coningham has a "prodigious memory and likes persons rather than people." He had a nickname for every officer in his Libyan bomber group, and the effect of this happy trait was a heightened sense of individuality among the men, a quality which plays a strong role in the efficiency and morale of the air force. At the same time, under Coningham's leadership, his Desert Air Force acquired such a high *esprit de corps* that when one of its American units was about to be transferred to another air force General Dwight Eisenhower '42 received a petition from the American pilots requesting that they be allowed to stay with the D.A.F.

In 1941 no British airman had a clear idea of what could be accomplished with a tactical air force, the cooperation of air and ground units. Coningham set about finding out. His first move was to size up the enemy. With a few brilliant exceptions most Germans were "poor stuff . . . incredible hoots," he decided, and called their celebrated Stuka dive bomber an "overrated crate." But about their courage and the success of their particular method of fighting he had few doubts. "The Germans have been brought up to be nasty to people," he said. "We've been brought up to be gentlemen, and that's a handicap to us in fighting this War. We've got to learn to give up being gentlemen for the duration."

One of the combat plans which the Marshal devised was that of ordering forth unusually powerful fighter escorts to protect small bomber formations, which so vitiated the enemy fighter strength that progressively smaller escorts were then possible and the number of bomber missions could be increased.

From his observation of the Luftwaffe and from his own fighting experience, Coningham pieced together his theory of air support. He saw that Erwin Rommel's '42 Luftwaffe always worked closely with tanks and artillery, and that his own tie-up with the ground commanders was too casual. He therefore became an exponent of the doctrine of concerted use of air power and land power, each equal in its own right, but mutually interdependent. In putting his plan into action he was greatly assisted by General Bernard Montgomery '42. Montgomery, in fact, was the first to voice the new doctrine: "We have one plan, one idea in mind. There is no army on one hand and an air force on the other. We work as a unit." Both men agreed, too, that the effectiveness of the air force should not be dissipated by tie-ups with each separate ground unit, but should be made to function in theatre-wide blows that struck at the enemy's most vulnerable spots. "The Germans know war from *A* to *Y*," declared Coningham. "They don't know *Z*."

At El Alamein, after a preliminary strategic pummeling of Rommel's transport columns, bases, and shipping, Coningham in an all-out air offensive at the end of 1942 delivered the knockout blow to the Luftwaffe. When two

AIR MARSHAL SIR ARTHUR CONINGHAM

weeks later Montgomery's infantry appeared on the scene, the joint work of the two men began to show effects. Coningham's bombers pulverized enemy rear lines, and his fighters strafed the front. The enemy's back was broken. The Germans still hadn't learned the last letter of the alphabet by the spring of 1943, moreover, and by that time it was too late. Rommel surrendered within forty-eight hours. Coningham today considers the Tunisian campaign his best job before the Normandy invasion.

In the meantime, in April 1943, in a reshuffling of the Allied air forces, Coningham was put in command of three separate United States and R.A.F. tactical air forces, which were called the 1st Tactical Air Force of the Northwest African Air Forces (under Lieutenant General Carl Spaatz '42). He was proud of the close cooperation between his British and American fliers. He once illustrated his point with this story: An American general had come into his caravan with a can of pineapple juice. "I put a little spot of gin in it," he said. "That's the sort of cooperation that exists." In Sicily Sir Arthur declared: "The German Air Force has been knocked out as far as we are concerned." The main objective of his T.A.F. was then to lend support to the Allied ground forces. The Marshal had a great admiration for the American air forces. Of the American fliers who bombed Rome with such deadly precision, he said: "Those chaps are marvelous—quite marvelous."

In January 1944 the Marshal was sent back to England to command the 2nd Tactical Air Force which was preparing for the invasion of Europe. A few months later Sir Archibald Sinclair '40, Secretary of State for Air, told the House of Commons that Coningham's 2nd, combined with the United States 9th Air Force under Major General Lewis H. Brereton '43 would be "powerful enough to cripple enemy defenses and drive the Luftwaffe from the skies" when the invasion started. (A delicate situation might have arisen out of the

CONINGHAM, SIR ARTHUR—*Continued*
fact that the American's force was larger than the Britisher's if the latter had not had a talent for collaboration.)

Weeks before D-Day (June 6) reconnaissance crews scouted the coastline between Cherbourg and Le Harve, ferreting out hidden gun positions, filming landmarks, and charting underwater obstacles which stood exposed at low tide. The enemy's radio location positions were discovered through the aid of Intelligence and wiped out so neatly that the enemy remained unaware of the impending invasion almost up to H-Hour. Ten days before D-Day Allied tactical bombers cut off the Germans' lines of communication, putting 75 per cent of their bridges out of service and throwing awry Nazi plans for troop and supply movements. In France Coningham's air forces also did an excellent job of "isolation" (cutting the Germans' communication lines around the battlefield perimeter so that they could not supply or reinforce units in the combat areas). The Germans had counted on some sixty bridges across the Seine and the Loire to bring up reinforcements when needed, but the Allied air forces put an end to that plan. On the day of invasion, when only 20 per cent of the expected all-out strength of the Luftwaffe appeared in the skies, Coningham switched a large part of his defensive umbrella to offensive operations.

While in Africa Coningham lived in a trailer with a red carpet and blue doors and curtains. After the Afrika Korps was driven from Tunisia he lived for a time in a luxurious Tunisian villa. He now carries on his work in more severe surroundings in London with his aide and two staff officers. A habitually early riser, he holds his conferences at 8:00 a.m. sharp. There, too, he keeps in close touch with aircraft on the manufacturing end. Jet-propelled fighters will be the next type of combat plane with which the Allies will have to reckon, he says. They will make the present fighters "as obsolete as the monoplane made the biplane."

In 1932 Sir Arthur was married to the widow of Sir H. G. Frank; he had competed with her in boat races for years. They have one daughter. Coningham is sometimes referred to as "Mary," which is a corruption of "Maori," a New Zealand aborigine. The nickname bothers red-blooded Coningham not in the least, but a newspaper reference to him as the scholarly type brought forth an outburst: "I'm *not* a scholar," he roared. "I'm an athlete." Were it not that his almost black hair is turning to silver gray after three years of war, he might be classified as "tall, dark, and handsome." "But he has never lost an atom of his bouncing confidence, overflowing energy, infectious good humor," says *Time* Magazine. He is over six feet tall and built accordingly. A non-smoker, he enjoys a drink now and then, and is an urbane and convivial individual. Winston Churchill [42] once said that Coningham was no mere technician but a redoubtable warrior. And the R.A.F. crews swear by him as the greatest commander that ever "pranged a Jerry."

References

N Y Sun p19 N 25 '41
N Y Times p4 Ag 16 '43; p6 Ja 26 '44

Newsweek 23:24 F 7 '44 por
Time 44:27-9 Ag 14 '44
Who's Who 1944

COOPER, KENT Mar. 22, 1880- Executive director and general manager of the Associated Press
Address: b. The Associated Press, 50 Rockefeller Plaza, New York City

"This War had to be because the nations of the European continent had no unbiased information whatever about their neighbors and no unbiased information about their own governments," said Kent Cooper, executive director and general manager of the Associated Press (the world's largest news association), in 1941. It is this belief that has prompted Cooper to crusade for inclusion of international agreements guaranteeing world-wide freedom of the press in the peace treaties at the end of the Second World War. With this end in view he has called upon members of the American press to ask for news representatives at the peace conferences. "Around those tables will be, as always, politicians and soldiers in the role of statesmen," says Cooper. "This, in spite of the fact that it is doubtful whether any politician or soldier can have any better understanding than a newspaperman of one basic cause of war, and that is perverted presentation of international news."

Kent Cooper was born March 22, 1880 in Columbus, Indiana; he is the son of George William and Sina (Green) Cooper. Indiana in the '80's was a Republican state in which the Democrats had a fighting chance: his father, a lawyer and a Democrat, was elected Mayor of Columbus in 1877, city attorney in 1879, and Representative to the United States Congress for three terms (1889-95). Election campaigns in that era and area were battles royal in which the whole population, regardless of age, participated with much gusto. To aid his father's election to Congress, twelve-year-old Kent organized his friends into the Cooper Club. One of the inducements to joining was the club uniform of white duck pants and a tin helmet. The young politicians paraded and campaigned in the towns of the Congressional district, accompanied by their own band, also organized by young Cooper. In between his father's political campaigns the boy earned pocket money by running a newspaper route. Today he boasts that even at that age he knew the value of speeding the news to the public: he arranged to leave school twenty minutes early so that his papers might be delivered promptly.

His family background also brought to him a love of music. (Cooper is the composer of a number of published songs.) When he was ten his father gave him a $5 violin (now being used by Cooper's grandson), which he learned to play by ear and upon which at family concerts he accompanied the piano-playing of his sisters. By the time Cooper was sixteen he had progressed to a place in the orchestra of Crump's Opera House, Columbus' only theatre, and to the composership of a song, "My Village Girl," which, while never published, was sung locally. Cooper once told an *Etude* reporter that no thrill had ever equaled the one he experienced when he heard the neighbors whistling his first composition. (He gets just as much pleasure today from putting a nickel in a juke box and hearing one of his own songs.)

The difference between $12 a week as a reporter and $1 a night as a musician in the theatre orchestra made him decide to desert music for journalistic work. The duties of his first job—working after school on the staff of the Columbus *Republican*—were to cover the railroad station for news of departures and arrivals. After graduation from high school he attended Indiana University, but at the end of the second year the death of his father (in 1899) forced him to seek a job.

In 1899 nineteen-year-old Cooper started as a reporter for the Indianapolis *Press,* shortly afterward becoming associated with the Scripps-McRae Press Association, which was later consolidated into the United Press Association. It was during this period that he met Roy W. Howard '40, who was to build the United Press into a formidable rival of the Associated Press.

After resigning from Scripps-McRae, Cooper showed his organizing ability in the press service he set up himself to supply small-town Indiana newspapers, using the telephone instead of the customary telegraph to transmit his news. When Scripps-McRae later bought his idea, Cooper returned to their employ as their Indianapolis bureau manager, making a specialty of supplying news to small newspapers at a low cost. In 1910 Cooper went to New York to try to convince telephone company officials of the practicability of his idea of setting up telephone circuits to service isolated newspapers. The American Telephone and Telegraph Company's general manager, impressed with the young Hoosier's knowledge of the intricate problem, gave him an introduction to Melville E. Stone, general manager of the Associated Press. The famous journalist, too, was impressed with Cooper's answers to questions that had puzzled experts, and hired him at once as a traveling inspector at $65 weekly, although he remained skeptical as to the possible accuracy of messages transmitted over a telephone circuit. Cooper's response was that he would tender his resignation if he could not prove his scheme more efficient than the telegraph.

Cooper did not need to resign—the new system was an immediate success. Two years later he established the traffic department and as its chief visited every A.P. bureau in the United States. The knowledge he acquired through his tours led to another drastic change in the A.P. system. By realigning routes on its leased wires and effecting other economies, Cooper converted in one year a threatened $50,000 deficit into a saving of $100,000. This assured Kent Cooper's future with the press service. In 1920 he was promoted to assistant general manager, in 1925 he was made general manager, and in 1943 he was elected executive director.

The Associated Press is a cooperative organization of newspaper owners that was established in 1848 after the advent of the telegraph made possible the speedy exchange of news. To produce the report of a single day (approximately 1,000,000 words), 65,000 men and women are engaged. It supports bureaus in virtually every capital and principal city in the world and has access to the news reports of affiliated foreign news

KENT COOPER

agencies in many countries. The great bulk of the news it gathers itself, a little comes from the outside through exchange arrangements, and considerable regional news is drawn from the 1,300 or more dailies that make up its membership

After sorting, careful checking, rewriting, and editing, the Association parcels this news supply among the members, of whom fully 800 are wholly dependent upon it for outside news. The A.P. spends $12,000,000 a year. Its assets are the office and news equipment and an emergency fund of $2,000,000. It declares no dividend. The annual budget is figured out and met by lumping the general charges, such as wire rental fees, foreign service, etc., and dividing them state by state, each newspaper within the state paying its share of the cost according to the percentage of population it serves in a ten-mile radius. Admission to the Association is controlled by a vote of the members, and until April 1942 a vote of 80 per cent was necessary to override a veto of a membership application. In the words of the *Nation,* an organization which claimed to be "merely a cooperative service club" had become "a powerful protective society for established newspapers." The really decisive factor in entering the A.P. was "the competitive position of the applicant in relation to existing members," concluded the *Nation.*

In April 1942 the bylaws were changed to permit the overriding of a veto by a simple majority vote instead of by a four-fifths vote at a general meeting, plus payment of a percentage of assessments previously collected from existing members in the same city and field, the fields being morning, evening, or Sunday.

Despite the revision, however, the Federal Government in the late summer of 1942 served suit on the A.P. for allegedly "harboring a monopoly." The decision handed down on October 6, 1943, was considered extraordinary by some commentators. While two of the three judges concluded that the present bylaws unlawfully restrict admission of mem-

COOPER, KENT—*Continued*

bers and stated that their enforcement should be enjoined, *Time* Magazine reported that "in a broader sense the Court ruled *for* the A.P. For the Court held that the A.P. not only may but must have the right to pass on the character of its membership. The Court took from the A.P. its possibilities of monopolistic profit. But the Court took from the A.P. none of its responsibility for maintaining the highest standards of integrity in news." "The Court found," said a *Saturday Evening Post* editorial, "that the A.P. was not a monopoly; and although it disapproved the method by which applicants for A.P. membership could be turned down, it went out of its way to indicate that it was possible for the A.P. to adopt substitutes which will restrict its admission. . . . The case went to the Supreme Court on issues too vague for comprehension." On the other hand, the *New Republic* announced that the decision declaring the A.P. guilty of violating the anti-trust laws was "a victory for a free press. . . . The ruling of the Court now makes it impossible for A.P. members to block the admission of a new member on the grounds of the applicant's status as a possible competitor."

On October 23, 1944 the A.P. filed with the Superior Court a protest which stated that the decision would result in "transferring the press from the field of enterprise to the status of a regulated public utility," and that the "case involves no question of monopoly, of domination, of power over others, or inadequacy of competition." The protest also contended that the court had acted in direct conflict with the public policy embodied in the First Amendment to the Constitution, which guarantees freedom of the press. In its own brief the Justice Department said that this protest was "without substance," and at the same time recommended to the Supreme Court that the A.P. be required to adopt an explicit bylaw which would admit new members without regard to local competitive situations. The Chicago *Sun*, which is seeking membership in the A.P. or access to its facilities, also filed a suit with the Supreme Court, suggesting that new bylaws be drawn so as to declare that membership shall not be denied to applicants except for cause—in the case of applicants not conducting bona fide newspapers or being unable to meet their financial obligations as members.

The Supreme Court took the case under advisement on December 6 after hearing the arguments on appeals from the summary judgment (decision based on affidavits and depositions) by a Federal District Court of New York. (A decision was expected early in 1945.) Later in December the A.P. asked outright dismissal of the Government's suit, contending that "the equalitarian [equal sharing] philosophy espoused by the Government has time and again been rejected by this court. . . . The burden of proof is on the Government to establish that the adoption of such a principle would not . . . destroy initiative, decrease competition, impair the efficiency of all new agencies and their capacity to perform their functions . . . and, as applied to the press, whether it would not destroy the right of first and exclusive publication—which is a fundamental characteristic of property of the mind."

During Cooper's association with the A.P. he has gradually erected a "modern structure on the solid-rock foundations laid by its founders, who were noted for their ultra-conservatism." One of these changes was that of "humanizing" the news. The A.P. had been content with its reputation for accuracy, but Cooper told his thousands of reporters and editors scattered over the globe that instead of dull, tedious recitals he wanted stories written entertainingly as well as factually, and that he also wanted stories of the humorous and unusual. He installed the Association's first feature service, which embraced a variety of subjects—from Hollywood to Broadway columns, to women's page activities, comic strips, and crossword puzzles.

Humanizing the news was only one phase of Cooper's rebuilding of the A.P. structure, however. In a profession where speed is a vital factor, Cooper was quick to perceive the advantage of new mechanical inventions relating to news coverage. Over the protests of some of the less imaginative board members he replaced the old-time Morse sending keys with high-speed telegraph printing machines. He was the first to perceive the practicability of sending photographs directly into newspaper offices by leased wires, side by side with the news. This mechanism is called Wirephoto and enables the sending of an ordinary sized photograph from a point as distant as San Francisco or New York in about eight minutes. His first proof of the value of this last service came with the A.P.'s scoop of pictures made at the scene of the Will Rogers-Wiley Post airplane crash in Alaska in 1935—after every other news service had turned down Wirephoto. In recent years Cooper has developed A.P. services to newspapers and radio stations in many countries outside of the United States.

Cooper has also been concerned about the individuals who work for him. It was this concern for them that led him in 1918 to foster A.P.'s pension plan years before the Federal Government's Social Security law was passed. Realizing that the swift pace of newspaper work caused men to slow up early in their careers, he introduced shorter hours and sickness and death benefits.

Although Kent Cooper has made newspaper history through his many innovations in the A.P. system, the general public knew little of him until the publication of his book *Barriers Down* in 1942. (It was dramatized in November 1944 by NBC.) In it he tells of his long battle to free the Associated Press, and through it the entire world press, from domination by foreign news services—the British Reuter's, the French Havas, and the German Wolff. These services had confined the A.P., by an old contract, originally to the United States, later to the Western Hemisphere. The A.P. was barred from selling news directly abroad, and it could not take news from individual papers anywhere outside the borders of the United States.

This meant at the start a complete censorship by the Big Three of foreign news received in America, although early in the century the A.P. began building up its own staff and direct sources abroad. But what was equally important was a complete misrepresentation of the United States in the news abroad. "What is more," said Oswald Garrison

Villard '40 in his review of the book, "the news was utilized for nationalistic propaganda and imperialistic purposes. Reuter's stood in with the British Government and played its game in Asia, Africa—all the continents. In France, Havas was the creature of the French Government." Cooper's feeling, in the words of Villard's review, is that "if Reuter's domination of the world had been ended, if the news sources had been freed from government control and from monopoly management by proper regulations in the Treaty of Versailles, the present global war could have been avoided."

He began his fight for unhampered reporting when he was a young and obscure newspaperman. In Paris during the framing of the Versailles Treaty he urged Colonel House, Woodrow Wilson's adviser, to advocate the inclusion of free press terms in the Treaty. House assured him that the matter would be adjusted, but the "adjustment" was the continuance of the cartel of European news agencies, with Reuter's and Havas confining Wolff's activities to Germany. This scheme, declared Cooper in a *Life* article for November 13, 1944, "was supposed to ensure so complete a news blockade around Germany that London and Paris could dictate to Germany—and to practically all of Europe—what foreign news would be received and what domestic would go out. . . . The post-War cartel worked so well that when Belgium tried to break away not even the personal intercession of King Albert was enough to release Reuter's and Havas' domination." Reuter's strangle hold on international news was broken in 1934 through the combined efforts of the A.P. and the U.P. "This unity," says Cooper, "won a victory over the cartel—not because of any change of heart on the part of the cartel members but because they feared the growing power of the American news agencies. During the present War the ownership of Reuter's passed voluntarily into the hands of England's truly free press, its newspapers."

Oswald Garrison Villard, formerly a director of the A.P., saw the beginning of Cooper's crusade, and declares that he would gladly testify to the truth of the story in *Barriers Down* and to the selflessness of the fight, its worth, its necessity, and its world-wide importance. Joseph L. Jones, vice-president and general foreign manager of the U.P., on the other hand, has declared that the U.P. foreign correspondents broke the foreign news monopoly by demanding and fighting for free access to foreign sources of news. "During the First World War," Jones asserted, "South American newspapers wanted an American news service to free them from the European monopoly. United Press was the only one not bound by agreements with that monopoly. It went into South America in 1916—years ahead of any other American service." (The Associated Press entered South America in 1919.) However that may be, it is generally agreed that Cooper, more than any other man, deserves credit for breaking Reuter's hold on the news. That organization is now owned by the associated newspapers of Britain in a setup similar to the A.P. Havas was taken over by the Germans upon the fall of France in 1940; but in September 1944 Léon Rollin, director of the Agence Française de la Presse born in the days of the battle for Paris, informed Cooper that the new agency expected to become an independent national news agency

modeled on the A.P.'s organization of cooperative gathering and dissemination of the news. The old Havas facilities have been taken over by the news agency.

Largely because of Cooper's efforts the Republican and Democratic Parties at the 1944 National Conventions adopted resolutions in favor of world-wide freedom of information. Secretary of State Edward R. Stettinius '40 has stated that he will support United Nations action on international press freedom. Both houses of Congress have unanimously endorsed the idea, and Senator Tom Connally '41 of the Foreign Relations Committee has prepared a resolution for nondiscriminatory communication tolls. "Obviously," says *Newsweek*, "this was aimed at preferential British Empire rates. (For example, the rates from the United States to some Empire points are eleven times the rates to the same points from Canada.)" Cooper has pointed out that it is "as easy to stop news at its sources by putting prohibitive prices on wordage as by outright censorship." In the opinion of *Newsweek*, the problem of communication tolls promises to be one of the most troublesome confronting American and British diplomacy. The A.P. executive believes that if the British Parliament were to follow the example of Congress, it would not only give the British press encouragement, but it would help enormously to promote news freedom everywhere in the world." Cooper warns in his *Life* article: "A heavy duty rests upon the Allied peoples. If they are not convinced that the adoption of free-news principles is their responsibility, then once again the next war is their war." He has proposed that newspaper correspondents be given diplomatic immunity in foreign countries without being attached to any diplomatic corps.

In December 1944 the American Society of Newspaper Editors issued a declaration on world freedom of the press which, *Newsweek* wrote, "embodies the idea championed by Kent Cooper . . . and Hugh Baillie, president of the United Press." A committee was appointed to tour Allied capitals to promote sponsorship of the program.

Cooper's press freedom campaign about the same time provoked an attack by the British *Economist*, which wrote that "in his [Cooper's] ode to liberty there is no suggestion that when all barriers are down the huge financial resources of the American agencies might enable them to dominate the world. . . . Democracy does not necessarily mean making the whole world safe for the A.P." To this Cooper replied: "Surely the *Economist* does not want the activities of all news agencies except the British confined to their own countries. . . . If there is commercial advantage to an American news association in making its news service available in other countries, there is, under the plan I advocate, the same opportunity for the British or any other news agency to make its news service available in other countries." A week later the general manager of Reuter's, Christopher Chancellor, commented on the repercussions of the *Economist* article, stating that he was satisfied that there was no dispute between the British and American press or between the British and American Governments on the issue of a free international press. "Reuter's will work hand in hand with the Associated Press in forwarding the principles

COOPER, KENT—*Continued*

in which both agencies believe." (It was later reported that a Soviet publication had published an open letter to Cooper stating, in effect, that Russians did not expect to impose their type of freedom on the rest of the world, nor to accept foreign ideas in Russia.)

Cooper's office in the A.P. building is furnished like a club lounge—and it has no desk. "People leave things," Cooper says, "if you have a desk to drop them on. Now everybody who comes in with a file gets an answer and carries the file out again. You get things done that way." The efficient A.P. executive, who has been described by fellow journalists as "tough-minded and keen," presents quite a different personality when he talks about music. He once told an *Etude* reporter that when he is composing he likes to sit in an easy chair in his home and "look at a fine old tree outside in the garden and listen to what it has to say." His first published song, "Dixie Girl," was broadcast over NBC in 1941. *Newsweek* called it "pleasant but a dated composition [it had been written in 1923], not overly melodic." A second work appeared in 1943 when, at the request of Henry Weber, the conductor, he developed all his unpublished songs into an operetta—*About the Girl*—for which he also wrote the book. A more serious effort was a piece, "America Needs You," which he composed for the Girl Scouts in the same year. Still another work, a symphonetta entitled "The Magic of the Violin," was presented in part by Paul Lavalle's Stradivari Orchestra over NBC in July 1944, and in October over the same station, Lavalle conducted Cooper's overture based on the life of Lola Montez.

The journalist-composer is tall and robust. He has keen brown eyes and graying brown hair, and he looks much younger than his years. In 1905 he was married to Daisy McBride, who died in 1920. By this marriage he had one daughter, Jane. His marriage to Marian Rothwell ended in divorce in 1940; and in 1942 he was married to Sarah A. Gibbs, formerly his secretary. In 1944 he was re-elected for a four-year term to the Pulitzer advisory board for journalism awards. He has received the honorary degree of LL.D. from Drake and Indiana Universities. Golf is Cooper's favorite sport, and he has often played with Bobby Jones on the champion's home course in Atlanta.

References

Etude 61:295+ My '43
Forbes 47:14+ Mr 1 '41 por
Fortune 15:89-91+ F '37
Newsweek 5:15 Ap 20 '35; 20:102-4 D 14 '42 por
Who's Who in America 1944-45

COT, PIERRE (kō pyär) 1895- French politician

"During my public life I committed mistakes," writes Pierre Cot, much-criticized French Minister of Air during Léon Blum's [40] Popular Front regime. "But I have never voluntarily been absent from a battle against fascism. In French politics I fought, in turn, against the Royalists, the Croix de Feu, the Cagoulards [the "hooded men"], the conservatives and the reactionaries of every stamp."

In *Triumph of Treason* (1944) Cot continues this battle, marshaling evidence to prove that France fell in June 1940 not because of the lack of courage among the soldiers and common people or because of lack of military equipment, but because of the weakness and treachery of the upper bourgeoisie and the officer class. Louis Dolivet calls this book "the most brilliant political exposé of the tragedy of the Third Republic. . . . Brilliantly written, dramatically presented, and clinging rigidly to the truth, it fills a gap that has long existed." Sterling North [43] finds the book "so circumstantial, well-documented, and closely reasoned that Cot's enemies will be hard pressed for an answer." Yet Eleanor Kittredge asks, in the New York *Times Book Review*: "Does logical correctness, in judging the mistakes of the past, endow one, necessarily, with the wisdom and the mercy to build a humanist future?"

Pierre Cot was born in 1895 in the southeastern part of France, in the province of Savoie. Both his father and his grandfather, members of the petite bourgeoisie of Savoie, held various elective posts in that province, and both of them opposed the royalists and reactionaries. During the Dreyfus affair the elder Cot fought against clericalism, but after his death in 1900, when Pierre was five years old, his "very pious" wife gave Pierre a Catholic education. When the First World War broke out in 1914 the nineteen-year-old youth volunteered for military service, and emerged in 1918 a Chevalier of the Légion d'Honneur, holding the Croix de Guerre with five citations.

After the War young Cot finished his studies, in 1919 receiving his Doctor of Laws degree from the University of Grenoble and in 1921 his Doctor of Political and Economic Sciences from the University of Paris. In 1922, having completed certain researches at the Thiers Foundation, he was accepted at the Concours d'Agrégation des Facultés de Droit et des Sciences Politiques, which gave him the right to teach in a French university. That same year he became a professor at the University of Rennes (Brittany), teaching public law and international public law. His *Manières juridiques des travaux publiques* was published the next year. After serving for a brief period as attorney at the Court of Appeals in Paris, Cot attracted the attention of Poincaré, and Poincaré asked Cot to work with him as a member of the Judicial Committee in the Foreign Affairs Department. Some years later the young specialist in public law had the opportunity to take part in studies that dealt with administrative reforms undertaken by the Ministry of the Interior.

Cot's real political career, however, developed from 1928 to 1940, "the period when the conservative bourgeoisie were being corrupted by Fascist theories." A member of the Left Wing of the not very radical Radical-Socialist Party, in 1928 he was elected a member of the Chamber of Deputies, and he held the post without interruption until June 1940, re-elected regularly by strong majorities in Savoie. (During the same period he served as mayor of his little mountain village.) "What attracted me to Parliament," he says, "was foreign rather than domestic politics. . . . The War had developed in me, as in many men of my generation, a profound horror of nationalism and militarism; we put our faith in the development of international institutions and the League of Nations. I had taken part in the activities of the Institute of International Law at The Hague and of the School of International Relations at Geneva." From 1928 to 1932 a member of the Commission of Foreign Affairs, in 1929 he was also named by Aristide Briand a member of the French delegation to the League of Nations, a post in which he remained for four years. Believing that the peace of the world was "in large measure dependent on the reconciliation of French and German democratic forces," until the rise of Hitler '42 Cot demanded in vain the fair application of the League of Nations pact, including the article relating to reconsideration of treaties. He visited Berlin after the Reichstag assembled in October 1930, and wrote afterwards: "We must help Germany to recover her equilibrium. We must act quickly. . . . The fate of Europe will be decided in Berlin this winter."

Cot participated in the Disarmament Conferences as a member of the French delegation, too, supporting Maxim Litvinov '41 in most of Litvinov's proposals for disarmament and earning the enmity of the French General Staff by his own. Before the Disarmament Conference which opened in February 1932 he wrote that three scandals must be ended: (1) the armaments race; (2) the inequalities between conquered and victorious nations; (3) the private manufacture of, and traffic in, arms and munitions of war. A few months later, by this time Under-Secretary of State for Foreign Affairs in the Paul-Boncour Cabinet, Cot suggested that the French delegation support the project submitted by the American delegation for the suppression of "offensive arms." In the spring of 1933 (he had succeeded Paul Painlevé as Minister of Aviation in February of that year) he was the only member of the French Government present at Geneva, and, hoping to force Hitler to unmask his batteries, he proposed that France and Germany agree to have short-term armies organized on the model of the Swiss militia. This idea brought even louder protests from the French nationalist press than from the Nazis.

And in many other ways Cot was making enemies. Painlevé had decided to expose irregularities in the financial administration of Aéropostale, the aerial navigation company connecting South America and France. Cot, as his successor, went ahead with this, bringing into court many people holding "high places in the triple hierarchy of money, society, and politics." A law he had helped to draft several years before as a member of the Aeronautic Commission also gave him the power to organize a national company uniting all French air lines under state control. This, the Compagnie Air-France, "saved the state several tens of millions annually" by its establishment, "and became the statement of a primary formula of 'nationalization.'"

It was as Minister of Aviation that Cot watched the uprising of February 6, 1934, when, after the Stavisky scandal, a mob largely led by Fascist organizations tried to

PIERRE COT

invade the Chamber of Deputies, and, according to Cot, to form a provisional government and overthrow the republican regime. Cot approved the Government's action in dispersing the mob by force and recommended that Premier Daladier '40 and the Minister of the Interior proclaim a state of siege. His advice was not followed, however, and the next day the Daladier Cabinet resigned, while the Fascists shouted their hatred of Cot as well as of Daladier. The next Cabinet, formed by Gaston Doumergue, included such men as Laval '40, Flandin '41, and Pétain '40, and was a preview of the Pétain Government of 1940.

Cot participated in the democratic opposition to this Cabinet and later to the Flandin and Laval Cabinets. It was during this period (1934-36) that the Popular Front was conceived. Cot, one of the first democrats to recommend the union of all anti-Fascist elements, including Communists, took an active part in its organization. In 1935 a hall in which he was speaking was invaded by Fascists, who wounded several people and threw an acid grenade at him. It hit him in the ear, and he has been slightly deaf ever since.

Cot pleads guilty to many of the "crimes" he was charged with, among them the sponsorship of a Franco-Soviet pact and collective security. As one of Herriot's co-workers he had arrived in Moscow in August 1933, accompanied by a mission of military and technical experts, to study "the bases of a rapprochement between Soviet and French aviation." At the end of the trip the Soviet Government had asked him to transmit confidentially to the French Government a proposal for the negotiation of a security pact. When in 1935 a committee was formed in France for the defense of the Ethiopian people and the application of sanctions to Fascist Italy, Cot was chosen its president. That same year his Le droit national socialiste was published. Not much later the International Peace Campaign, which became the world's most active movement in favor of collective security, came into

COT, PIERRE—*Continued*

being. Cot was elected co-president of the international organization with Lord Robert Cecil.

The Popular Front Government, with Léon Blum at its head, was organized in June 1936 after the overwhelming victory of the Left in the May elections of that year. On June 4, 1936 Cot became Minister of Aviation again, and it is for what he did in this post that he is best known abroad. For one thing, he opposed the policy of "nonintervention" in Spain adopted by Blum on August 8, and in 1937 actually sent the Spanish Loyalists about 130 planes as well as putting at their disposal some French training centers and schools and letting Loyalist aircraft be refueled at French airports. Pointing out that if he had not shipped planes to Spain the French Air Force would not have gained a single plane it could have used by 1940, he says he is only sorry that he did not send more. It is doubtful whether the Fascists hated him most for this, for his part in the proceedings against the Cagoulards in 1937, or for his role in the nationalization of the war industries. The nationalization of the war industries was a part of the Popular Front program which most of the political parties and veterans' organizations supported at this time, however, and one which was accomplished by a law which the Chamber and Senate voted almost unanimously. "By nationalizing the aircraft factories," Cot says, "I simply executed the mandate given me by Parliament, the legal interpreter of the will of the people."

According to Cot, "the essential cause of the failure of the Popular Front was its lack of daring." "What the Government needed was to imitate Robespierre, not Roosevelt '42. It needed to declare 'the Republic in danger,' to override the vote of the Senate, and to govern strictly on the basis of the Popular Front majority which the country had just elected—in short, to proclaim 'the dictatorship of the majority.'"

"The Popular Front experiment . . . proved above all the impossibility of establishing a democratic government simultaneously with a regime founded on capitalistic monopolies; the two cannot co-exist," Cot wrote in 1942.

In June 1937 the Senate overthrew the first Blum Cabinet, and a new Popular Front Cabinet was formed under the leadership of Camille Chautemps. Although it was far more conservative than the first, Cot remained as Minister of Aviation. In January 1938, when the Cabinet was reshuffled to exclude the Socialists entirely, Cot became Minister of Commerce and Industry. Then in March of that year Blum returned to power for a brief period with a purified Popular Front Cabinet that included neither Bonnet nor Chautemps, but Cot lost his post, too. The next month Blum's Government was overthrown by the Senate for the second time and Daladier set up a "concentration Cabinet" which remained in power until February 1940. The Socialists took no part in it, and Cot also refused to enter it, disapproving of its foreign and economic policy.

The Daladier Government, with Bonnet as Foreign Minister, so totally rejected the foreign policy of its Popular Front predecessors that, says Cot, "when Stalin '42 signed his famous pact with von Ribbentrop '41, French politics and diplomacy had left him no alternative." (Everything had been in readiness for an aviation pact signed by France, Czechoslovakia, and the U.S.S.R. when Cot had left the Air Ministry.) Not many months before Munich the former Air Minister wrote: "The key to [the democratic countries'] defense, strategically speaking, is Czechoslovakia." In two speeches by Hitler immediately before and after the Munich betrayal, Cot, one of the outstanding opponents of the Munich pact, was threatened personally. At about the same time the French reactionaries launched a campaign against him as "the warmonger and the man who sold out France to Russia," and his murder was demanded by Charles Maurras, leader of l'Action Française, and by the Cagoulards.

After the French declaration of war in September 1939 Cot says that a vast offensive against the working class was launched, disguised as an anti-Communist campaign; the Government's economic and social policy became more and more reactionary, so that the Fascists had their own way in the country at large and in the Army. During the fighting, moreover, he believes that 1,000,000 of France's best soldiers were purposely left behind in the Maginot Line, that enormous quantities of airplanes and tanks were purposely never thrown into the fray, and that General Weygand '40 took over for the sole purpose of selling France to the enemy, for there were sufficient men and matériel to carry on resistance from North Africa even after the fall of Paris. At the end of June 1940 Cot himself fled from Bordeaux to London. In August 1940 he landed in Montreal, hoping to join the faculty of some American university as a lecturer on international law; early the next month he was indicted for treason by the French Supreme Court of Justice at Riom along with Guy la Chambre, his successor in the Ministry of Aviation. La Chambre returned to France for the "trial," but Cot refused to recognize the legitimacy of the Vichy Government, which had already deprived him of his French citizenship.

As the author of *L'armée de l'air française* (1939), Cot is amply prepared to answer Vichy's charges that he was responsible for France's lack of planes in June 1940. In the first place, he says, the French Air Force could use in June 1940 only planes built in 1938 and 1939, when he was no longer Air Minister. In the second place, in 1940 France had all the planes the General Staff had considered necessary for her defense, although few of them appeared on the scene of battle. The aerial division and parachute units created in 1936 and 1937 by the Popular Front had been abolished in 1938 and 1939 at the express request of the General Staff, while Cot's proposals for the creation of an "attacking air force, with light multiplace airplanes, to be used in land warfare," the development of antiaircraft artillery, and the doubling of the number of planes in the air force had all been rejected in 1936 and 1937 by the Permanent Committee of National Defense, on which sat Daladier, General Gamelin '40—and Pétain.

Early in 1941 Cot was appointed to the faculty of Yale University to give a graduate sem-

inar in government. In addition to teaching
and working on his book he remained active
in the cause of France: as a member of the
executive committee of France Forever, as a
member of the international editorial board of
Free World Magazine, and as the author of
articles on French politics in such publications
as *Foreign Affairs*, the *American Journal of
Sociology*, and the *Nation*. In the fall of 1943
he left the United States for Algiers, and late
in November of that year the French Consultative Assembly there seated him after a lively
discussion of his policies as Air Minister. In
March 1944 Cot was sent to the Soviet Union
on a special mission to study rehabilitation.
Four months later, still in Moscow, he said:
"As always the people here are in sympathy
with any attempt to understand the individual,
especially if it is to rehabilitate him." Concerning industry he added that in ten or twenty
years Soviet production might equal that of
the United States. In the summer of 1944 his
Triumph of Treason was published in the original French for distribution in liberated France
and the French colonies.

"Small, scholarly, and dynamic", "even-
tempered, always willing to be interviewed,"
Pierre Cot has long been the delight of foreign newspapermen. His wife is an American citizen, the former Louise Phelps of
Boston ("Nena," her friends call her), who
grew up in Venezuela, where her father was
an ornithologist. Since the fall of France
she has been living in New York with the
three children—Françoise, Jean-Pierre, and
Catherine, the first of them by her former
marriage. Of her husband Mme. Cot says:
"He has never been interested in money. He
doesn't care for possessions. He is a plain
man from the mountains of Savoie," with the
keen blue eyes of all mountaineers. "He
would rather climb mountains than eat.
There is always a mountain in his life. No
matter where we go, his first question is,
'Have you a mountain in this town?'" One
misty day in New Hampshire, when Mount
Washington was proudly pointed out to him
for the first time, Cot announced: "I think
the foothills are lovely. I hope it is clear
tomorrow so I can see the mountains."

References

N Y Herald Tribune p3 Ag 27 '40
N Y Post Mag p18 Mr 28 '44 pors
N Y World-Telegram p36 Ap 19 '44
PM p5 Ag 26 '40; p13 Ag 27 '40 por
Cot, P. Triumph of Treason 1944
International Who's Who 1942

CRAIG, MALIN (may-lin) Aug. 5, 1876-
United States Army officer

Address: b. c/o Adjutant General, War Department, Washington, D. C.; h. 2126 Connecticut Ave., Washington, D. C.

With the traditional background of West
Point, Malin Craig, the son of an Army officer, began a military career that brought him
not only action, promotions, and decorations,
but the highest post the Army has to offer—
that of chief of staff from October 1935 to
August 1939, when he retired from active duty.
Then in 1941, at the age of sixty-seven, after

U. S. Army Signal Corps

GEN. MALIN CRAIG

having commanded every type of military unit
from cavalry troop to field army, he became
the head of the War Department's Personnel
Board.

Born in St. Joseph, Missouri, August 5,
1875, Malin Craig was the son of a cavalryman. After a boyhood spent mostly on the
Western Plains, he was appointed to the
United States Military Academy at West Point
from Pennsylvania in 1894. Though his scholastic record there was not called brilliant, he
made football history by kicking a field goal
while running with the ball and cornered by
opponents.

After serving with the 4th Infantry for a
short time following graduation, Craig joined
the 6th Cavalry, serving with this regiment
in Cuba during the Spanish-American War
and participating in the Santiago campaign.
In June 1900 he went to China with the Relief Expedition during the Boxer Rebellion,
and from there was sent to the Philippine Islands, where he "bushwhacked" through the
jungles under Major General J. Franklin Bell
until 1903. Upon his return to the United
States he attended the Infantry-Cavalry School
at Fort Leavenworth, Kansas, completing the
course as an honor graduate in 1904 and receiving a promotion to captain. He then attended the Army Staff College at Fort Leavenworth.

In 1906 his ability to "take charge of things
and keep them straight" won him the gratitude
of the entire Chinese population of San Francisco, where he stowed away and sorted out
"a squalling horde of Chinese babies" after the
earthquake.

After a second duty in the Philippine Islands Captain Craig returned to the United
States in September 1909 and enrolled for a
course at the Army War College in Washington, D. C. Upon completing the course he
remained at the college as an instructor until
March 1911. Following that he served at
Fort Sam Houston, Texas; at the Presidio of

CRAIG, MALIN—*Continued*

San Francisco; at Fort Yellowstone, Wyoming; and at the Presidio of Monterey, California. In September 1916 he was ordered to Fort Leavenworth as an instructor in the General Service School, where he remained until he was transferred to Washington, D. C. in January 1917. He served there in the office of the adjutant general and later in the office of the chief of staff, and received the rank of major in May 1917.

Following a short period in Camp Greene, North Carolina, where he served as division chief of staff, Major Craig sailed for France in September 1917. There he had ample opportunity to exercise his abilities as chief of staff of the 41st Division, then of the 1st Corps, and later of the 3rd Army. He participated in the Aisne and Champagne-Marne defensives and the Aisne-Marne, Saint-Mihiel, and Meuses-Argonne offensives, receiving the Distinguished Service Medal for his service in the latter campaigns, in which "his personal influence, aggressiveness, and untiring efforts were repeatedly displayed." He also received these foreign decorations: Commander of the Légion d'Honneur, France; Croix de Guerre, with two Palms, France; Companion of the Bath, England; Commander of the Order of the Crown, Belgium; Commander of the Order of the Liberator (Knight), Venezuela.

After the Armistice Craig remained in Europe until August 1919 as chief of staff of the Army of Occupation and later of the American forces in Germany which "wound up the watch on the Rhine." During the War he had received temporary promotions to lieutenant colonel, colonel, and brigadier general. Upon his return to the United States, Craig reverted to his permanent rank of major, Regular Army, but was promoted to colonel on July 1, 1920 and then to brigadier general two days later. He was director of the Army War College in Washington for a year; then commander at Camp Harry J. Jones, Arizona until August 1921, after which he spent two years as commandant of the Cavalry School at Fort Riley, Kansas. Craig's third tour of duty in the Far East took him again to the Philippine Islands, where he commanded the coast defenses of Manila and Subic Bays, with headquarters at Fort Mills, until the summer of 1924. At that time he was promoted to major general, chief of cavalry, and for the next few years he served as chief of cavalry at Washington, D.C.; as assistant chief of staff in charge of the Operations and Training Division of the War Department General Staff; and as commander of the 4th Corps Area with headquarters at Atlanta, Georgia. In the Panama Canal Zone he commanded the Panama Canal Division and later the Panama Canal Department. In October 1930 General Craig returned to the United States to be put in command of the 9th Corps Area, Presidio of San Francisco, simultaneously commanding the 4th Army, until January 1935. During that time "he handled with minimum red tape more CCC men than there were soldiers in the United States Army (116,000)." For the next few months he was commandant of the Army War College, Washington, D. C.

The big event of Craig's life came as a surprise. One afternoon in October 1935 when he returned home from a game of golf, his wife excitedly told him that President Roosevelt had just appointed him chief of staff of the United States Army (to succeed General McArthur '41). He put on his uniform and hurried to the War Department to report for duty. The President's selection did not surprise others at that time, but the sudden decision conveyed by a telegram sent in such informal fashion was attributed to the general world-wide war scare.

General Craig (promoted to the rank of full general at this time) took over in a purposeful way—"the Army knew it had a leader who would carry on with minimum nonsense and get things done." He fought successfully with Congress for appropriations to modernize the Army and its equipment; he revised mobilization plans, and encouraged a "new, critical approach by military men to military affairs." Back in the days when the Army neither desired nor expected war abroad, the office of the chief of staff nevertheless had complete plans on hand for immediate mobilization at any time for war anywhere, whether abroad or at home.

When General Craig became chief of staff many people suffered from the illusion that the Army could mobilize and equip from 2,000,000 to 10,000,000 men in practically no time at all. Under General Craig this "astronomical assumption" was shown to be quite false, but he put into effect plans whereby it would be possible to train and equip a million men should it be necessary. At the time he was criticized severely for spending so much money on the Army in peacetime, to which the reply was that the United States had had a war approximately every twenty-five years—with Indians, British, Mexicans, Spaniards, Germans—as well as the Civil War. It was the Army's job to be ready should an emergency arise. It was General Craig, too, who insisted that the United States Army have at least some antiaircraft equipment, tanks, antitank guns, modern artillery, bombs, etc. His desire was that every rifleman should be trained as a machine gunner, able to use his initiative in emergencies. He wanted experimentation in chemical warfare, improved artillery, and a variety of miscellaneous equipment then lacking.

After forty-one years in the Army, General Craig retired in August 1939. But he had not yet reached the end of his career. In September 1941, when the United States entry into the War seemed imminent, he was recalled to active duty and assigned to the Army Group in Washington, where he heads the War Department's Personnel Board, which passes upon promotions and civilians recommended for commissions.

The General's career has left little time for a personal life. Mrs. Craig, whom he married in 1901, has, like any Army wife, followed her husband to many camps and endured many separations. They have one son, Malin, Jr. Craig's brother, Major General Louis A. Craig, is commander of the United States 9th Infantry Division in Europe

General Craig has been described as "husky, muscular, square-jawed," and is known in the Army as "a soldier's soldier." He appears stern, but has always been called "a disciplinarian without 'barking.'" He has maintained his early reputation as an athlete and now "shoots golf in the low 80's and rides frequently, as becomes a crack cavalry man." His language when necessary can be most picturesque, and he has a liking for practical jokes. But he is best known as a stern, capable, hard-working and hard-hitting soldier, who conscientiously follows his own favorite maxim: "Don't be apostles of the obvious."

References

N Y Times Mag p15 My 2 '43 por
Who's Who in America 1944-45
Who's Who in the Nation's Capital 1938-39

CRAVEN, THOMAS Jan. 6, 1889- Author; art critic; lecturer
Address: h. 16 Nassau Dr., Great Neck, Long Island, N.Y.

Best known of all the American popularizers of art is Thomas Craven, a critic-journalist-lecturer whose special distinction is that he does know how to paint. His "irreverent, iconoclastic, positive" opinions have made him unpopular in the art world, and his allegedly arrogant and superficial style irritates some reviewers tremendously; but he remains one of the best liked, best paid writers and lecturers on the subject.

The son of Richard Price and Virginia (Bates) Craven, Thomas Craven was born in Salina, Kansas, January 6, 1889. At twelve he entered the Salina High School, where Glenn Martin '43 was one of his schoolmates, and upon graduation he matriculated at Kansas Wesleyan University. After receiving his B.A. degree in 1908, when he was nineteen, Craven went to work as a reporter in Denver, and then as night clerk for the Santa Fe Railroad at Las Vegas, Nevada. After this young Craven went to Paris to study art; and there he says, he "embarked seriously into the business of transforming myself into a Frenchman." As *Newsweek* put it, he "conscientiously set about becoming a Bohemian."

Craven returned to the United States with his love for art undimmed, but without plans for becoming a professional painter. He continued to paint for his own pleasure, and to write poetry, which seemed to be his true métier. He lived, of course, in Greenwich Village, the Montparnasse of New York, where he roomed with Thomas Benton '40. Benton is one of Craven's particular heroes, so it is likely that this period in the critic's life laid the foundations for his later concern with American regional art. At the time, however, Craven was still under the art-for-art's-sake influence of the Bohemians. Every so often, "in order to live," the poet-painter was forced to emerge from the Village into the world of materialism and take a job, wherever there was one, teaching Latin and Greek in "schools located anywhere from the West Coast to Puerto Rico." Before the

THOMAS CRAVEN

First World War broke out Craven was teaching at the University of San Juan, Puerto Rico. He became a seaman second class on a neutral ship, sailing before the mast in the West Indies, and "watching for spies, smugglers, and saboteurs."

After the War, Craven took up writing in a more professional way. He contributed book reviews and art criticism to various magazines, and wrote a novel, *Paint,* which was actually published in 1924 but has since been forgotten by everyone, including the author. Most of these earlier writings were concerned with the French moderns: Craven had yet to become "the prophet of a native American art" and the leading decrier of "the School of Paris and any manifestation of its influence on American painters." By 1927 strongly under the influence of H. L. Mencken Lewis Gannett '41 describes Craven as having "an acute case of Babbitt-baiting Menckenitis from which he has never completely recovered"—the budding critic published in *The American Mercury* an article which laid the foundation for his later reputation: "Have Painters Minds?" His answer was a ringing "No!"

In this forthright treatise he asserts that "writers on art are the toughest nuts in the literary basket. They seem to be incapable of lucidity and common sense; as a rule they know little of the actual problems of painting, and the best they can do is to deceive a public that knows less." Portrait-painting he dismisses as "artistically worthless," still life as pointless, studies of the nude as "either erotic trash or academic convention," and murals as "an extinct art." But his sharpest words are reserved for the modern painter, who is "dull and dumb and conceited," an "anti-social coward": "Of all the workers in the arts he is the least alive—no man of brains and education could waste his life in . . . the feebleness, stupidity, and ignorance of the painter. He is inarticulate and proud of it; in any society he is a nonentity."

(Continued next page)

CRAVEN, THOMAS—*Continued*

Somewhat more restrained was Craven's *Men of Art* (1931), an "intensely interesting and vital study of painting in the Western world." Described as "a combination of social history, biography, description, and criticism," it shows "significant movements and outstanding artists, choosing boldly those painters who seem to him typical of certain tendencies in the growth of civilization." Craven himself describes his book as "a tribute to the power and the glory of artists whose work is impregnated with human meanings and interwoven with the fabric of the social structure, as opposed to the futile practitioners of art for art's sake." Many of the reviews were very favorable; none were wholly condemnatory; and all agreed on such adjectives as "forthright", "vigorous", "dogmatic," and "stimulating."

This was followed, three years later, by a sequel, *Modern Art; the Men, the Movements, the Meaning* (1934). This presents, mainly through sketches of the artists, "a view of modern art which is at once brilliantly stated and consistently maintained." In the words of the *Yale Review*, "Craven is frankly a journalist: he writes about art as he might about politics or, better, gangsters. There is positive virtue in his refusal to consider painting as anything extraordinary or esoteric."

The year 1939 saw the publication of two compilations which Craven edited: *A Treasury of American Prints* and *A Treasury of Art Masterpieces*, both of which attracted considerable attention. Four years later came another compilation, *Cartoon Cavalcade*, in which the editor was assisted by Florence and Sydney Weiss, and another history, *The Story of Painting; From Cave Pictures to Modern Art.* "Iconoclasts and modern artists of distinction may well take furious issue with the author's bland 'God's-in-His-Heaven-and-the-disagreement-of-mere-mortals-troubles-me-not-at-all' tone of text," comments the *Library Journal.* "Nevertheless, the 101 pages may prove invaluable as introductory reading for young people or oldsters who need a quick brushing up."

In pursuance of his belief that "only art dealing with the human drama of the day . . . has any meaning to contemporary man," Craven is a propagandist for regional United States painting, especially "the Midwest group led by the late Grant Wood,'[40]" for folk art as represented by the cartoonists and comic-strip artists, and, above all, for Walt Disney'[40]. Readers of *Cartoon Cavalcade* might question the compiler's choice of drawings—particularly a sequence of "Terry and the Pirates" which shows only two of Milton Caniff's '[44] widely-known characters and none of his gorgeous girls—but few would doubt that the book was a labor of love. And, whatever the tone of Craven's comments, "the text in such a book as this is merely a publisher's convention." Craven again emphasized the function of art in the portrayal of human drama in his foreword to *Our Flying Navy*, the work of seven artists who depict the life of the aviator from pre-flight school days to combat.

This human-interest approach to art is one of the reasons for Craven's success as a lecturer. His discussion is not technical; he does not burden his audiences with praise of beauties invisible to them, in pursuance of concepts to which they are strangers; and thus he avoids the usual pitfall of art critics. Anyone who gives the public good reasons for liking what they already like and for disliking what they already dislike is sure of a certain amount of popularity. To this foundation, add Craven's energy, enthusiasm, and positiveness, plus an effective platform manner—and the result is one of the most popular lecturers on the circuit. The very dogmatism to which his critics object—"the approved Ruskinian style of 'Now be good little children and I will explain art to you'"—is probably a help to Craven, for people who come to be told about art come to be *told,* not asked. There are few things in that line more annoying than an indecisive lecturer; and positiveness, when backed by a knowledge of the subject, is a refreshing quality on the platform. Craven himself, when criticized, replied simply: "You make art as interesting as I do and you get rid of me."

Of medium height and blond, Craven is described as looking "the Middle Westerner he is, with his shrewd, lined face, long nose, and straight, lank hair." Since 1923 he has been married to an English writer, Aileen St. John-Brenon; they have one son, Richard Craven, born in 1928. Craven, who calls himself an independent Democrat, went back to fiction in the winter of 1943, and began work on a novel dealing with life in the Southwest.

References

N Y Herald Tribune p19 D 3 '43
Newsweek 22:82+ D 20 '43
Kunitz, S. J. and Haycraft, H. eds. Twentieth Century Authors 1942
Who's Who in America 1944-45

CREEL, GEORGE (EDWARD) (krēl)
Dec. 1, 1876- Journalist; author
Address: h. 2761 Divisadero, San Francisco

Propaganda has long been recognized as a tremendous force in modern warfare, yet the scientific study of it is a recent development. This study originated during the First World War when every major belligerent power established offices of wartime propaganda. One of the most important of these offices was the Committee on Public Information, organized when the United States entered the War in 1917 and headed by George Creel. In 1944 Creel remains vitally interested in the channels of war information. His most recent book, *War Criminals and Punishment* (1944), is a consideration of the problem "What shall be done with the war criminals of the Axis powers?"

George Creel was born in Lafayette County, Missouri, December 1, 1876, the son of Henry Clay and Virginia (Fackler) Creel. His father had been an officer in the Confederate Army and had moved to the West from Virginia after the Civil War. Creel received his education in the public schools of Kansas City and, after one year of high school where he gained early experience as a journalist by writing for the school paper, he left school to wander around the United States for several years. Creel worked as a professional newspaperman on the Kansas City *World* but he soon departed to try his luck in the East. He arrived in New York City on a cattle train in 1898. After some months of struggle, during which he shoveled snow and did other odd jobs, Creel was hired by the New York *Journal*. It was while working on the *Journal* in 1900 that Creel and a friend, Arthur Grisson, decided to return to Kansas City to found "a semi-literary weekly," the Kansas City *Independent*. Creel himself conducted a column of verse, jokes, and anecdotes in the weekly. In 1903 Creel became full owner, editor, and publisher of the *Independent*, which was advertised under the slogan "A Clean, Clever Paper for Intelligent People." After taking over, the young editor plunged immediately into a reform fight and in 1904 helped to elect Joseph Wingate Folk, the lawyer-politician-reformer, to the governorship of Missouri. After that, Creel says, his "crowd virtually reorganized the state."

The *Independent* was more than a literary publication, for Creel was interested also in social and economic issues. His political sympathies at that time were closest to those of the Socialist Party, but he was soon to become an ardent spokesman for the "New Freedom" program of the Democratic Party under Woodrow Wilson. In 1908 Creel decided to move to Colorado and offered the *Independent* for sale. But "when it looked like a wait," the owner gave it to two women and left to be editorial writer for the Denver *Post*. Before the year was out he had "quarreled spectacularly" with Tammen and Bonfils, the owners of the *Post*, and after a year of work on magazines in New York, he went back to Denver in 1911 as editor of the *Rocky Mountain News*, a post he retained until 1913. In these years he made the acquaintance of Judge Ben B. Lindsey, a friendship which "committed him more definitely than ever before to the liberal side of important social issues"; along with the judge and others Creel "filled the statute books with progressive legislation."

Creel had published his first book, a volume of verse called *Quatrains of Christ*, in 1908. The book won the praise of the poet Edwin Markham, and several years later Markham, Lindsey, and Creel collaborated on a study of the problems of child labor, *Children in Bondage* (1914). In politics Creel continued to pursue a liberal course as one of the young muckrakers, advocating large-scale social and political reforms. When Woodrow Wilson was elected to the Presidency in 1912, Creel's editorials in the *Rocky Mountain News* were enthusiastic in his support.

In addition to his newspaper work, Creel contributed many articles on the "New Freedom" to national magazines. In 1916 when Wilson was a candidate for re-election, Creel, at that time opposed to American intervention in the World War, published *Wilson and the Issues*, in which he urged that the President be re-elected and that his reform programs be continued. Wilson showed his gratitude for this support by inviting Creel to Washington "as a member of his [Wilson's] official family." Creel was unable to accept the invi-

GEORGE CREEL

tation, but, he writes: "When we entered the War on April 6, 1917, and the newspapers carried the news that some rigid form of censorship would be adopted, I wrote a letter of protest to the President in which I explained to him that the need was for expression not repression, and urged a campaign that would carry our war aims and peace terms not only to the United States, but to every neutral country, and also to England, France, and Italy."

Eight days after the declaration of war, on April 14, 1917, President Wilson created by Executive order the Committee on Public Information (CPI), whose members were the Secretaries of State, War, and Navy, and George Creel, civilian chairman. His appointment alarmed conservatives, many of whom still regarded him as "a radical writer." The New York *Times* declared editorially: "Whatever may have been the rights or the wrongs of his controversies, his career had been one of turbulence and mud-spattering; he had denounced and been denounced. His name stood for acrimonious contention." Throughout his service on the Committee of Public Information, Creel was severely criticized by his political enemies but staunchly defended by others who praised the efficiency, economy, and the democratic methods with which he organized and ran the Committee. With a staff of writers and the assistance of thousands of Americans who volunteered to serve as "Four-Minute Men," Creel and his Committee attempted to carry out the principle of voluntary censorship, at the same time boosting home morale and winning support for the war effort.

Under the jurisdiction of the CPI came "everything relating to public opinion, both at home and abroad." The foreign work of this organization was unique. Not only were the friendship and cooperation of the neutral nations sought, but, writes Creel, "The war-weary peoples of England, France, and Italy

CREEL, GEORGE—*Continued*

had to be bucked up by daily reports on our progress." To accomplish this, agencies were opened in every neutral and friendly belligerent nation. Both at home and abroad the Committee distributed news releases, pamphlets, material for speeches by the "Four-Minute Men," and advertising in motion pictures and posters. Bureaus were established for the various nationalities within the United States. "Each of these had a director who was responsible for keeping his particular racial group informed concerning the war activities of the United States and for keeping them loyal to America." Although the Committee was accused of wastefulness, its expenses were actually small. It has been estimated that the total cost to the taxpayer for the two years of the organization's existence was under $5,000,000.

Not the least of Creel's difficulties was the curbing of the wave of anti-German hysteria which swept through the United States. The Committee used no atrocity stories, and when criticized for not preaching hatred of the Germans, Creel replied: "It is true that this Committee has never preached any doctrine of hate, for it is not our duty to deal in emotional appeals but to give the people the facts from which conclusions may be drawn." James Mock and Cedric Larson comment in their book *Words That Won the War* (1939): "The CPI hoped that it could direct the nation's emotional energy into channels of constructive patriotism, not hysteria, but it was not always successful. Though only too well aware of how hysteria begins and grows, the Committee was forced to deal constantly with the material of panic, fear, and intolerance."

The CPI succeeded in directing American public opinion into the desired channels largely because it did not attempt to force new ideas upon the public, but rather "to codify and standardize ideas already widely current and to bring the powerful force of the emotions behind them." Creel's energy and enthusiasm were in large part held responsible for the success of this endeavor. During the War and the years which immediately followed Creel and the CPI were severely criticized by Congress. In June 1918 Congress cut in half the appropriation which Creel had requested for his Committee, and the CPI was asked to justify its existence before a Congressional committee. There were numerous political attacks made upon Creel. He later wrote: "It is these joined causes—the indecencies of partisanship, the noise and unintelligibility of a large portion of the press, the lack of trustworthy information, the dreary routine of mud-slinging that passes for political discussion—that have killed public opinion, or rather deafened it, confused it, bored it, disgusted it."

When the War ended and the Committee's work ceased, Creel went back to writing. He contributed articles on a variety of subjects to many of the national magazines and is in 1944 a staff writer for *Collier's*. His books include several works on the War—*How We Advertised America* (1920), an account of the CPI's activities, and *The War, the World and Wilson* (1920). He has also written biographies of Thomas Paine and Sam Houston,

a study of Irish history—*Ireland's Fight for Freedom* (1919), and a book on Mexico, *The People Next Door* (1926). His *War Criminals and Punishment*, published in the spring of 1944, condemns the theory that Hitler [42] does not represent the German people and calls it "the ultimate in falsehood and gullibility." Creel presents the case against the German war criminals, citing numerous atrocity incidents and their long tradition of militarism. Although, to quote Harry Hansen [42], "Mr. Creel is against the school that advocates total extermination of the Germans, he is also against letting the German people escape." Reviewers of the book, although some criticize the author's thesis, agree that it is a forthright and scholarly work.

A radio dramatization of *War Criminals and Punishment* entitled *Words at War* was presented over the NBC network on July 4, 1944. This program became the basis of a weekly *Words at War* script which, like the book, sought to arouse Americans to demand unconditional surrender of all war criminals "lest Hitler and his pals make suckers of us all." By October it had been chosen Script of the Month four times by the Writers' War Board. The original adaptation of Creel's book was also one of the winners in this series.

Creel has served in public life in several capacities. In 1933 he was appointed chairman of the San Francisco Regional Labor Board, and two years later he was made chairman of the National Advisory Committee of the Works Progress Administration. In 1934 he ran for the Democratic gubernatorial nomination against Upton Sinclair. Creel carried the state but "lost Los Angeles by a huge majority." In 1939 President Roosevelt [42] appointed him commissioner to the San Francisco International Exposition. Creel was an enthusiastic supporter of the New Deal in its early period, but with the outbreak of the Second World War his enthusiasm cooled somewhat. He was critical of the propaganda efforts of the Administration's wartime agencies, the OWI in particular, describing them as "blundering" and extravagant, and commenting: "A full twenty organizations now spend more than $130,000,000 a year to do the work that I did with $2,500,000 a year."

By 1944 Creel was described in liberal quarters as "no flaming liberal. . . . He belongs to that wing of the Democratic Party which in recent years has been anti-New Deal and anti-FDR." Creel himself says: "I have been a radical liberal all my life, but am now a 'reactionary,' because I refuse to admit that the Russian system is better than our own." A staunch admirer of Secretary of State Hull [40], Creel was one of the foremost defenders of the policies of the American State Department in early 1944 when that office was criticized for refusing to recognize General de Gaulle [40] for supporting the Badoglio [40] Government in Italy and for "coddling" General Franco [42]. In a *Collier's* article in March 1944 Creel described the critics of the State Department as Communist sympathizers, "ideologists," and "emotionalists."

In 1912 Creel was married to the actress Blanche Bates; the couple had two children, Frances Virginia and George Bates Creel. Miss Bates died in 1941, and in 1943 Creel was married to Alice May Rosseter. Although strong-jawed, rugged-looking Creel is best remembered for his work in the First World War, he is still regarded as the innovator of a propaganda system "destined to influence social thinking and action for years to come."

References

Newsweek 17:60 My 19 '41 por
Mock, J. R. and Larson, C. Words That Won the War 1939
Who's Who in America 1944-45

CRERAR, H(ENRY) D(UNCAN) G(RAHAM) (krē'rär) Apr. 26, 1888- Canadian Army officer

Address: b. c/o Department of National Defence (Army), Ottawa, Canada

Canadians have fought in many wars and won many proud victories but—until the fifth year of the Second World War—always under the Union Jack. It was in July 1944 that they first marched into battle under the flag of Canada, led by a Canadian general. That honor fell to Lieutenant General H. D. G. Crerar, C.B., D.S.O., of Ottawa, whose 1st Canadian Army is a part of the 21st Army Group led by Field Marshal Sir Bernard L. Montgomery '42. Four months later Crerar was made a full general.

Henry Duncan Graham Crerar was born in Hamilton, Ontario, on April 28, 1888. The son of Peter Duncan and Marion Elizabeth (Stinson) Crerar, he came of a nonmilitary family of middle-class Scotch-Canadians. Young Harry Crerar attended the local schools, studied at Upper Canada College in Toronto, and then entered the Royal Military College at Kingston, also in Ontario. Upon graduation in 1910 he was commissioned a lieutenant in the 4th Battery, Field Artillery. Lieutenant Crerar decided, however, that he could not get along on the pay of a junior officer, and therefore gave up active service for a job with the Ontario Hydro Electric Power Commission and a commission in the Non-Permanent Active Militia. When the Canadian Expeditionary Force was organized in 1914 Crerar joined it as a lieutenant and soon became a captain in the 3rd Brigade of the Canadian Field Artillery. The year 1916 found the twenty-eight-year-old officer a major, commanding the 11th Battalion, Field Artillery; at this time he was married in London to Verschoyle Cronyn, a handsome girl from Toronto.

Major Crerar continued to rise, was mentioned in Army dispatches, was awarded the Distinguished Service Order in the King's Birthday List of 1917, when he was brigade major of the 5th Canadian Divisional Artillery. That November he was appointed to be the Canadian Corps' staff officer for artillery, succeeding the present Chief of the Imperial General Staff, Sir Alan Brooke '41. After eleven months in this position Crerar was promoted to lieutenant colonel and made the counter-battery staff officer, succeeding another lieutenant colonel, the present Lieutenant General Andrew McNaughton '42, whom he was later to succeed as head of the 1st Canadian Army.

The Hydro Electric Power Commission had been holding Crerar's old job open for him, but on his return to Canada the thirty-one-year-old officer decided to remain in the Army

Canadian Army Photo

GEN. H. D. G. CRERAR

as a Permanent Force officer. In April 1920 he was appointed to the Canadian General Staff at Ottawa as an artillery expert with the permanent rank of major. Sent to England to attend the Staff College at Camberley and later the Imperial Defence College, he had a tour of duty at the Imperial War Office in 1925. As a General Staff officer on the Operations Staff, Crerar worked for a time directly under the future Field Marshal Sir Archibald Wavell '41, Viceroy of India. On his return to Canada in 1927 he was placed in command of B Battery, Royal Horse Artillery, and was soon afterward appointed professor of tactics at the Royal Military College in Kingston.

In 1929 Crerar began a six-year tour of duty as General Staff officer in charge of Operations at National Defence Headquarters, during which he designed the present structure of the Army and drew up plans for its organization in time of war. He accompanied the Dominion delegation to the 1932 Disarmament Conference in Geneva as its military adviser, returning with renewed determination to strengthen the Army, and served in a similar capacity at the London Imperial Conference five years later. At this time he was director of Military Operations and Intelligence at National Defence Headquarters.

At the outbreak of the Second World War in 1939 General Crerar was commandant of the Royal Military College. Within a month after Canada's declaration of war, he was sent overseas as senior combatant officer to establish headquarters and make plans for the training and landing in Britain of 100,000 Canadians. Returning to Canada in July 1940, he was immediately named Vice-Chief of Staff, and two weeks later was made Chief of the General Staff with the rank of major general. His first official action was to put the entire staff, including himself, on a seven-day work week. After three weeks of sixteen-hour days without a break, Crerar ordered all men to take one day of rest each week, to

CRERAR, H. D. G.—*Continued*

work no more than three nights a week under any circumstances, and to take one long week-end each month for "the maintenance of good health and mental well-being." On November 22, 1941 he was promoted to lieutenant general, but chose to revert to the rank of major general in order to leave his desk for overseas service. His wish was granted: exactly one month later Crerar was made the general officer commanding the 2nd Canadian Division. "I have given of my best," he told an interviewer, "in advising the Government in the establishment in Canada of a sound system of military training and an ordered, balanced, and speedy development of the armed forces. . . . I feel, therefore, that I can now accept the honor of an overseas command with the knowledge that my departure coincides with the completion of a definite phase of the Army expansion."

All Canadian troops overseas were volunteers, and at least one-fifth were from "those very French regions whose influence had prevented the Ottawa Government from sending conscripts overseas." Canadians comprised almost one-third of the R.A.F.'s fighting strength. But, in spite of the efforts of Canadian General McNaughton to combine the Canadian units into one Canadian army, they were scattered under various British commands. When McNaughton's headquarters were first set up in Britain in the spring of 1942, General Crerar was commanding the 1st Canadian Corps. This was sent to Sicily and Italy, where Crerar's troops distinguished themselves at Catania and Ortona. Among the General's officers there was his son Peter, who had enlisted in the ranks early in the War and won his commission in February 1942. (The Crerars also have a married daughter, Peggy.) From Italy Crerar was recalled to Britain in March 1944 to take command of the 1st (in every sense) Canadian Army, succeeding General McNaughton and the temporary commander, Lieutenant General Kenneth Stuart '44. From then until D-Day the Canadian General devoted himself to training his men for their part in the invasion of France, to such effect that in 1943 he was made a Companion of the Bath.

Civilians are inclined to think that a Canadian army is made up of Canadians, a British army of Britons, a United States army of Americans, and so forth. This is not wholly true. Canadian troops were withdrawn from the British 2nd Army to form the 1st Canadian Army, but it also included the famous 51st Scottish Highland Division, at least one British division (which makes up for the Canadian division attached to the British 8th Army), as well as Polish, Belgian, and Netherlands units; also some American and Czech units. In an interview on April 24, 1944 General Crerar announced that the 1st Canadian Army was prepared and eager to tackle the great task that lay ahead. "I am convinced," he said, "that it will maintain the high reputation gained by the Canadian Corps of 1915-1918 and already confirmed in this War. The Canadian Army also has a debt to settle—Dieppe [the August 19, 1942 raid in which nearly two-thirds of 5,000 Canadians involved

were lost]. And when the final story is told the price Canada paid at Dieppe will be repaid over and over again to the Allied armies of invasion in the not distant future."

"The not distant future," as the world was soon to know, began on June 6, 1944. On that long-awaited invasion day 10,000 of Crerar's men were landed from Canadian ships, protected by Canadian planes, and waded ashore at Bernières-sur-Mer, between Caen and the Orne River, under the Canadian national flag. Then they began the long, bloody fight to reach Falaise. In the words of *Time* Magazine, "at the beginning the Canadians had tough fighting and little glory. They and the British had the pick of [Field Marshal Erwin] Rommel's '42 armor, guns, and troops in front of them. Even after the capture of Caen they were held down and unmercifully pounded by German 88's [88mm. heavy guns]. Grimly they held on, giving United States Lieutenant General Omar Bradley '43 time to take Cherbourg [which fell on June 26]. Grimly, after the surprise United States break-through at Saint-Lô [forty miles west of Caen, on July 17], they pushed through and held the north arm of the Falaise-Argentan pincer." Their costly victories were won in a sector where, according to General Dwight D. Eisenhower '42, the supreme Allied commander, "every piece of dust represented diamonds, and every foot of ground was worth ten miles elsewhere."

Two days after the initial landings Crerar's men found the bodies of nineteen Canadian prisoners of war who had been shot by the Germans. At the General's request a board of inquiry composed of British, Canadian, and American senior officers investigated the charge and concluded that the soldiers had been willfully murdered. On August 2 General Crerar revealed to his men "the brief story of an abhorrent act," and warned that "the universal and natural determination of Canadian soldiers to avenge the death of our comrades must not under any circumstances take the form of retaliation in kind. The commission of atrocities will be left as a bestial prerogative of Hitler's '42 Germans. Instead, Canadian anger must be converted into a steel-hard determination to destroy the enemy in battle, to hit him harder, to advance faster, and above all never to stop fighting, and fighting hard, while life remains."

And fight hard they did, against a constant series of bitter German counterattacks. During the first month of "hedgerow" war the Canadians protected the vital Allied communications area around Caen, which they took from the Germans on July 9, and then fought toward the south, attacking the hinge of the German line. General Crerar, who had arrived in France on June 18, jeeped from one command post to another, "pausing to read reports with the avidity of a hungry wolf, to give orders in his quiet, precise, unbending manner." Nearly every day he inspected the battle lines from the air, once narrowly escaping being shot down, and once being forced to make a crash landing—from which, however, he emerged unhurt. At his camouflaged forest headquarters Crerar directed a staff of young officers trained in British and Canadian staff colleges; his emphasis on youth is said to have developed a "young, keen-fighting army in which innovations are not unusual." Several of these new methods were introduced at

Cintheaux August 7-8, the anniversary of the First World War battle of Amiens.

This assault, which was launched just at the moment when Marshal Rommel had committed many of his tanks to a counterattack against the advancing American forces, was described by correspondents as "unique in its use of new air-land tactics and novel devices." Preceded at 11:00 p.m. by an "awesome" attack by 1,000 R.A.F. bombers, it was "the first time heavy bombers had been employed in direct, close support of ground forces by night." The bombers, guided by giant flares and by special devices from the ground forces, left a path about 3,000 yards wide along the road for the tanks to advance. First came special "flail" tanks, later identified by reporters as Scorpions, equipped with rolling chains on prongs in front to beat the ground and explode mine fields without injury. Behind them, along "highways marked off on either side by streams of brilliant colored tracer shells, armored troop carriers smashed inside the enemy lines, unloading their cargoes of tough fighting men deep inside the German lines to rip and disorganize the foe. Engineers had been busy for days preparing the trucks [which one of Crerar's generals, Lieutenant General Guy G. Simonds [43], had improvised by stripping American self-propelled M-7 guns down to the chassis and adding truck bodies of two layers of steel separated by sand], and they came as a complete surprise to the Germans. . . . The enemy could not have known about them until his machine-gun and artillery shells began bouncing harmlessly off the plated monsters. Another surprise was the method of guiding them by tracers." Behind this spearhead marched the rest of the infantry with flame-throwers and machine guns, accompanied by self-propelled guns.

As this battle, said to be the heaviest since the landings, raged on into the daylight, British and American fighters, fighter-bombers, and rocket-firing planes patrolled the field, directed to specific targets by ground officers "like taxis called up by a starter." At noon there was an hour-long bombardment by American 8th Air Force planes. (Fortunately, a large supply of surgical cotton wool had been flown in and issued to the troops to stuff in their ears, just before the battle.) "It was like going into the gates of hell to get into that village," said a Canadian brigadier. "The hinge of the German line is loosening, and some screws are out," said the Army spokesman, "but the hinge is not yet off the door entirely."

The hinge was being pried farther and farther off the door as 1st Army infantrymen fought their way through the rolling plains and undulating wheat fields south of Caen to Falaise. In a night march on August 14, described as an Odyssey of endurance, they dominated the last main road over which German Marshal Guenther von Kluge's 7th Army was retreating from the encircled Argentan-Falaise sector. Here the Germans fought "inch by inch." The mine fields in the area were the thickest seen up to that point. But Falaise did fall on August 17, and thousands of Germans from several divisions were taken prisoner in the coordinated Canadian, British, Polish, and American drives which tightened a deadly noose around the trapped enemy. On August 27 the Manitoba Dragoons

(18th Armored Car Regiment) reached the Seine (which had been crossed by General George S. Patton's [43] United States 3rd Army a week before) in a drive which joined with British units to force the Germans into a pocket south of Le Havre and Rouen and northwest of Paris. The Falaise pocket, according to the official announcement, had been eliminated, yielding 50,000 prisoners.

Many of Crerar's officers, who had gone on the ill-fated Dieppe raid two years earlier, must have felt a special thrill as the Canadians returned in triumph behind their skirling bagpipers on September 1, 1944—a date which saw the Allies "advancing at a pace never equaled in military history and with scarcely a skirmish." While the British 2nd Army took Arras, the American 1st Army raced on toward Belgium at a speed which cut down to less than one-third the Germans' record for the distance from Paris to Brussels in the First World War, the American 3rd Army liberated Verdun, the French and Belgians mopped up by the way, and Crerar's men cleaned up the coastal areas on the extreme left (east) flank of the drive. A count of the 1st Canadian Army's prisoners showed 25,776 captured between August 8 and August 31.

But Crerar's Canadians, Poles, Britons, and Hollanders were still faced with a grim struggle for each advance. As *PM*'s Ernest Crown reported on September 8, "along the northwest coast of France fanatical Nazi troops were still fighting their damnedest to hold the ports—Brest, Le Havre, Calais, Boulogne." All these were then under siege of the Canadian 1st Army. An estimated 20,000 to 50,000 Germans were pinned against the Channel coast and the North Sea, 5,000 of them in Le Havre, and the German High Command was determined to hold the ports at all cost and thus hamper the Allies by forcing them to transport their material hundreds of miles farther. (Prefabricated artificial ports had, however, been towed across the Channel and were actually in use by the Allies.)

Against the German defensive system of pillboxes, barbed wire, and land mines, the Canadians employed flail tanks and the new flame-throwing "crocodile" tanks. On September 8 they took Nieuport and entered Ostend, while Crerar's Polish units broke through the Germans' rear-guard positions west of Ghent, Belgium, and captured whole companies at once. At this time the Germans flooded the Dunkerque area in which Nieuport lies, making movement difficult. Meanwhile Crerar's British soldiers besieged Le Havre, capturing it with 11,000 prisoners on September 13. Ten days later, on September 23, while the public eye was focused on the invasion of Germany and the plight of General Robert E. Urquhart's [44] air-borne troops in Holland, General Crerar's men finally wrested complete control of Boulogne from the Germans, freeing that port for Allied use and seizing 7,500 prisoners. In the next two days the 1st Army's Polish troops drove into the Netherlands, north of Ghent, taking an additional 1,700 prisoners. General Crerar was then reported to have before him a list reading: "Le Havre, done; Boulogne, nearly done; Calais and Dunkerque, about to be done; Scheldt going on now."

(Continued next page)

CRERAR, H. D. G.—*Continued*

On September 26 the 1st Army opened its attack on Calais, only twenty miles from England through the Straits of Dover and "one of the most formidable fortresses of Europe," from which German naval guns had "punished the southeast coast of England with dreadful monotony" for the preceding four years. Three days later the Canadian infantry, with close support from bombers, worked their way into the historic citadel, wearing lifebelts to help them swim the flooded fields. On the 29th a twenty-four-hour truce was arranged, during which 20,000 civilians were evacuated, leaving 4,000 Germans from an original garrison of 7,000; on the 30th all resistance collapsed. This brought the total bag of prisoners in the French coastal area up to 132,800, the equivalent of thirteen German divisions. The size of the captured garrisons ranged from a few hundred men at robot bomb launching sites to 30,000 at Cherbourg and 40,000 at Brest. The Canadian 1st Army's total "catch" through October 3 was 62,636. (They were joined in the freeing of Calais by an invited group of the King's Royal Rifle Corps, a battalion of which had fought in the desperate rear-guard action covering the 1940 retreat from Dunkerque.)

With the capture that same day of the last remaining German guns at Cap Gris Nez in the Pas-de-Calais area, the English coastal towns of "Hellfire Corner," Dover, Deal, and Folkestone, were considered liberated from the four-year siege of shelling and bombing which had caused two-thirds of their population to be evacuated and most of the remainder to take to caves during the final month. The grateful inhabitants sent messages of thanks to General Crerar and to the Canadian people through Prime Minister Mackenzie King [40] and Marshal Montgomery. Meanwhile other units of the Canadian Army smashed through Antwerp to the Dutch border, putting that city for the first time beyond the range of German guns. Still other units of Crerar's command pressed their siege of Dunkerque. On October 6, 1944 a sixty-four-hour truce to evacuate 20,000 civilians came to an end, and the battle was resumed, 100 miles behind the other four Anglo-American armies' lines; meanwhile Canadians battled grimly for the Scheldt estuary and for Breskens, guarding the entrance to the valuable port of Antwerp. Four days later the Canadian Army's bag of prisoners to date was announced as 72,392. At this time, the commanding general was in Britain, suffering from a three-week illness; on October 23, the Ottawa Government announced Crerar's impending return to his post.

In nearly a month of "hellish" struggle the Canadians won for themselves the enemy's epithet of "Allies' SS" (Elite Guard). They fought their way through South Beveland Isthmus; then eastward under point-blank fire along the narrow causeway to besiege the one unflooded fifth of Walcheren Island. Here German gun posts still held out and dominated the approaches to the Antwerp harbor. In late October Allied soldiers landed on three sides of the island, some of the British landing craft moving in through holes in the dikes. Because of the flooding, big guns and tanks could not well be moved into position, and the Canadian infantrymen had to scramble along the tops of the dikes, in full view of enemy machine gunners. Nevertheless they won the struggle for the city of Flushing (Vlissingen), and opened up the Allies' new supply route as far as enemy interference was concerned. On November 20 Crerar was made a full general; and on the 30th, after a few weeks' rest, his hard-fighting 1st Army moved into Germany on the extreme left flank of the seven-army Allied front. This placed them opposite Cleve, the northern end of the Siegfried Line, in the Nijmegen-Arnhem salient, which the Germans had also flooded by opening the Waal dikes. At this time the Canadian 1st Army and Lieutenant General Miles C. Dempsey's [44] British 2nd Army, at its flank, were the only ones of the seven not entirely committed, and therefore had somewhat the character of reserves.

Little has been written about the publicity-hating Canadian leader. When he assumed command of the 1st Army he was almost unknown even to the Canadian public. As undramatic in appearance as in personality, Crerar has a closely-cropped mustache, "impersonal" gray-blue eyes, and graying hair which is retreating in good order. Possessed of "the line soldier's devotion to drills, ceremonials, and discipline," he nevertheless has created a young organization which innovates new tactics and equipment. Described as formerly "so reticent that he had no cronies and few close acquaintances," Crerar gets along famously with his brilliant but difficult superior, General Montgomery, and has renewed his old friendship with Sir Alan Brooke. A believer in austerity, he "takes every opportunity to deny himself luxuries, especially food and drink"; but he has a file of salty stories to which his officers regularly contribute. (When he went overseas in 1942, however, he left the file in Ottawa.) Henry Duncan Graham Crerar is described officially as "a born strategist and a thoroughgoing administrator," and unofficially as having "a department store mind on a Napoleonic scale."

References

N Y Sun p18 Ag 10 '44
Newsweek 24:30 Ag 21 '44 por
Time 43:20 Ja 3 '44; 44:31 S 18 '44
Who's Who 1944

CROCE, BENEDETTO (krō′cha bā′nā-dat′tō) Feb. 25, 1866- Philosopher; Italian Senator

As a philosopher Benedetto Croce, who in 1943 emerged as one of Italy's political leaders, has been called "the most influential literary personality in Italy since the death of Carducci." In scholarly circles he is more widely known outside his own country than any Italian thinker since Galileo: his principal works have been translated into English, French, and German, and some of them into Russian and Japanese as well. Whether all of this aging philosopher's disciples understand him is something else again. His idealistic interpretation of the universe and of human life, according to one critic, puts him in "the company of those who make the world interesting" rather than in "the company of those who satisfy the mind's desire for intelligibility." According to another, his system of thought is "as clear as a starless night." On the other hand, H. L. Matthews[43], in *Fruits of Fascism*, describes Croce as "one of the greatest and clearest minds of our age."

Benedetto Croce was born February 25, 1866 in the village of Pescasseroli, near the Sangro River in the province of Aquila, the son of a well-to-do landowner whose main concern was the administration of his estate. His grandfather was a high magistrate under the Bourbons; one uncle was a professor of philosophy at the University of Naples; another uncle, Silvio Spaventa, was a member of the Italian Parliament and a leader of the Right. As for his mother, she was a highly cultured woman who encouraged her son's passion for books. When young Benedetto was only nine he was sent to a Catholic boarding school patronized by the aristocrats of the Bourbon party, and there he not only ran away with all the prizes but also gradually developed a "contempt for the cant of Liberalism and a hatred of pompous phrases and all rhetorical ostentation." Eventually he was to react to this intensive religious education by becoming an atheist, but "his acquaintance with scholastic philosophy left an indelible mark on his style of presentation, which is notable for distinctions so subtle that they exhaust both the subject matter and the reader, and for a tendency to slip into casuistry when the author is hard pressed." (Croce also remains one of the very few modern writers who are either ignorant of or indifferent to science and who ridicule it as a method of grappling with reality.)

In 1882, while he was still at the lyceum, Croce's first sketches, a group of rather satirical critical essays, were published in a literary journal. The next year his father, mother, and sisters were all killed in an earthquake from which he himself escaped only after having been buried for several hours, and, seriously injured, he went to live with his uncle Silvio in Rome. The next years were years of slow recovery from which he was to emerge a stoic towards pain and sorrow; they were also "the darkest and most bitter years of his life." He registered in jurisprudence at the University of Rome but seldom bothered to attend classes and "never sat for the examination," spending his days instead in the Casanatese library and, during his second year, attending Antonio Labriola's lectures on ethics, which deeply impressed him. Croce's *Juvenilia 1883-1887* nevertheless reveal the young philosopher as "a dilettante only superficially interested in ideas."

In 1886 young Croce returned to Naples, where, with the money inherited from his father, he bought the house in which Giovanni Battista Vico (an Italian philosopher who lived in the latter part of the seventeenth century and most of the first half of the eighteenth, and whom Croce calls "the philosopher most closely akin to myself") had lived. His independent income also enabled him to spend his time in antiquarian research for more than six years, traveling in Germany, Spain, France, and England. This period gave him material for such works as *I Teatri di Napoli* (1891) and *La Rivoluzione Napoletana del 1799* (4th ed. 1926); "and in the publication, at his own expense, of *Library*

of Neapolitan Literature and a magazine dealing with topographical and historical questions." His research in Germany also gave him a knowledge of the positivist historical method and certain mental characteristics which later inspired Will Durant to call him "a Germanized Italian."

In March 1893, after having read Vico's *New Science* in which art and history are connected philosophically, Croce read his first philosophical manifesto, *History Subsumed Under the General Concept of Art*, before the Accademia Pontaniana at Naples. His general theory, that art was "an activity aiming at the production of the beautiful," won much critical praise. He followed this by an essay upon methods of literary criticism, which also caused some stir. But he had not yet found himself. In April 1895 Labriola sent him the first of his essays on the materialistic conception of history. "I read it and reread it," says Croce; "and again I felt my whole mind burst into flame. . . . I broke off— I might almost say, gave up—my researches upon Spain in Italian life and threw myself, with inexpressible fervor, into the study of economy, of which till then I knew nothing." During the next five years the essays contained in *Materialismo Storico ed Economia Marxistica* (1900), translated as *Historical Materialism and the Economics of Karl Marx* in 1914, were written. Croce himself had flirted with socialism for a time, but now he concluded not only that Marxism was a bad philosophy of history, but that all philosophies of history were necessarily bad. He also maintained "that the capitalist society studied by Marx is not any society that ever has existed or does exist." Croce insists that his critique of society was largely influential in provoking the crisis in Italian socialism leading to syndicalism on the one hand, Italian revisionism on the other.

At the age of thirty-three there came another intellectual crisis. "I read almost nothing, walked for hours and hours, spent half my days and all my nights lying on a couch, searching assiduously within myself, and putting down on paper notes and ideas, each a criticism of the other." At length the young philosopher established his philosophical bearings "with an awakened and sure understanding of almost all the principal problems with which classical philosophers have toiled, an understanding which cannot be acquired by merely reading their books, but only by repeating within oneself, under the stimulus of life, their mental drama." The immediate result was, presumably, the *Estetica Come Scienza dell' Esperessione et Linguistica Generale*, the first volume of his *Filosofia Come Scienza dello Spirito* (*Aesthetic as Science of Expression and General Linguistic*, the first volume of *Philosophy of Mind*), published in Italy in 1902 and translated into English in 1909. Of this volume Croce, never famous for his modesty, says that it "inspired everything of importance that was produced [in Italy] in the field of philosophy and historical study, criticism of poetry, music, and the fine arts, linguistic studies, legal and economic science, the history of thought and civilization, and religious and educational controversies." In textbooks Croce's theory of art is

BENEDETTO CROCE

called "the Expressionist theory," and it is notable in that it makes no distinction between matter and form: the aesthetic intuition, when fully realized in the soul of an artist, is complete also in its expression, says Croce, and all that remains is to communicate it to the external world.

In January 1903 the first number of *La Critica*, a "review of literature, history, and philosophy," appeared under the joint editorship of Croce and of Professor Giovanni Gentile of the University of Palermo, who was later to become the chief philosopher of Fascism. Gentile was in charge of the philosophy section, Croce of the literary. In 1905 the second volume of *Filosofia Come Scienza dello Spirito, Logica Come Scienza del Concetto Puro* (translated as *Logic as the Science of the Pure Concept* in 1917), appeared; in this Croce maintained that there could be no reality external to the human mind nor knowledge separable from its object. That same year he discovered Hegel. "When I plunged into the reading of Hegel, I seemed to be plunging into myself," he said later; and in 1906 there appeared *Saggio Sullo Hegel* (translated as *What Is Living and What Is Dead in the Philosophy of Hegel* in 1915). In this book Croce followed Hegel in his basic idealism and in his view of reality as a spiritual life whose driving force is the conflict of opposites, but he rejected Hegel's "panlogism" and his concept of "the Absolute." (Croce absolutely rejects Transcendentalism, and does not search for reality beyond experience. In his *Aesthetic* he included a polemic against religion—chiefly Catholicism —which he maintains cannot even be conceived of as a pure form of mind to be ranked with art and philosophy.)

In 1906 Croce was persuaded by Laterza, a Bari publisher, to issue a series of "Classics of Modern Philosophy," edited with Gentile, and a series edited by himself devoted to the southern Italian writers of the Risorgimento and the early years of unity. He also edited a series of translations into the Italian of the classical authors of modern philosophy and himself translated Hegel's *Encyclopedia* for the series. In 1908 the third volume of his *Filosofia Come Scienza dello Spirito* was published, *Filosofia della Pratica—Economica ed Etica* (translated as *Philosophy of the Practical: Economic and Ethic* in 1913). This idealistic treatise assumed that volition and action, pleasure and the good were all indivisible. If the will was not realized in deed, it meant that the will was imperfect. Evil was always negative, meaning only that which is not willed. On this basis, the Machiavellian theory of power and the state was upheld, the Holy Inquisition apologized for as representing an unavoidable and philosophically legitimate use of violence in politics, right identified with might and justice with success and the *fait accompli*. At the same time Croce published a translation of Sorel's *Reflections on Violence* and accompanied the book with a flattering preface which Mussolini [42] was later to laud for its "clarity, sincerity, and probity in research." According to Mussolini, "Both [Croce and Sorel] are opposed to superficial positivism as well as metaphysical cloudiness; both teach men that life is struggle, sacrifice, conquest, a continuous surpassing of one's self."

In 1910 Croce was elected a Senator from Sonnino, becoming the youngest of Italian Senators, who retain their seats for life. The next year *La Filosofia di Giambattista Vico* (translated as *Philosophy of Giambattista Vico* in 1913) was published. Between 1912 and 1913 portions of Croce's *Teoria e Storia della Storiografia* were printed in the proceedings of Italian academies and reviews. (It appeared in book form in 1917 and was translated as *Theory and History of Historiography* in 1921. It was the fourth volume of his *Filosofia Come Scienza dello Spirito*.) In this volume he proclaimed the identity of philosophy and history and announced, moreover, that all history is contemporary history, since "past and future are purely psychological subdivisions within the present." ("In every new situation," Croce has written, "the individual begins his life all over again.")

According to G. A. Borgese, after his short-lived socialism Croce "had gone over, practically, to a resolute conservatism which even enabled him, during the municipal elections of 1914 at Naples, to head the coalition of the conservative parties . . . against the Leftist bloc." That same year marked two events: his marriage to Adèle Rossi of Turin, a history student much younger than he, and the outbreak of the First World War. Croce "sided with the Italian Germanophiles and urged Italian neutrality," denouncing war as a suicidal mania, and he remained aloof even after Italy threw in her lot with the Allies. "At the end of the War he joined the Italian Nationalists. He minimized Wilsonianism, Neo-Mazzinianism, and the League of Nations as sorry remnants of a Masonic and eighteenth century mentality which he had always hated. . . . He stressed national differences. . . . He scorned again and again the idea of 'state as justice.'" From June

1920 to July 1921 he served as Minister of Public Instruction, in the same Cabinet in which Count Sforza [42] was Minister for Foreign Affairs. With the fall of the Giolitti Government in 1921, however, he retired from office.

In his first speech in Parliament, on June 21, 1921, Mussolini said: "There is a philosopher on the Ministers' bench [Croce], and he certainly taught me that the neo-spiritualist philosophers, with their continuous wavering between metaphysics and lyrics, are very pernicious for small brains." G. A. Borgese argues that Mussolini borrowed many of his ideas from Croce's writings; Richard V. Burks writes that Croce's system of thought, in its origins, was "part of the rising tide of Neo-Romanticism, which latterly found political expression in Fascism." Croce had always emphasized the importance of action, the autonomy of politics, and the relativity of values. He had recognized the necessity of a ruling class, had criticized "individualistic democracy" and the "Masonic mentality." According to his ex-colleague Gentile, speaking in March 1925, "The whole philosophical education of Croce and his constant and most profound inspiration of thought make him a Fascist without a black shirt. . . . He, like many other fathers, does not want to recognize his sons."

Croce himself argues that "with the foundation of La Critica he had fought the irrational and morbid elements in the new Romanticism, denouncing Futurism in art, the new cult of nationalism in politics, and in philosophy actual idealism, Gentile's creation, now the official philosophy of the Fascist state." But it is also true that in its early years he saw the Fascist regime as a reform movement, potentially capable of injecting new life, vigor, and firmness into a weak government, and lent his vast prestige to Mussolini. It was not until late 1924, two years after the March on Rome and shortly after the murder of Matteotti, that he broke with Il Duce. At that time a group of deputies and senators withdrew from the Chamber and the Senate, seeking to defeat a still half-legal Fascism through their absence and passivity after the battle had already been lost —and thus forcing the Fascists into a frankly dictatorial government.

Croce, protected by his economic independence and tremendous popularity, then tried to rally an intellectual opposition to Fascism. A manifesto, "seemingly philosophical but intrinsically political, endorsed by a few score of signatures, found its way through the haze of dawning tyranny," and in 1925 Croce wrote hopefully: "It is . . . certain . . . that our Socialists and our authoritarians will gradually return to Liberalism, in proportion as they gain experience, and as thoughtfulness and a sense of responsibility resume sway over their policies." But the year 1929 marked the last open stand of the Liberals against Mussolini. In that year Croce not only was shouted down when he tried to speak in the Senate against coming to terms with the Vatican, but a law permitting only Fascists in the Chamber was passed. Virtually silenced now, having lost his chair at the University because of his refusal to take the oath of allegiance to the regime, he nevertheless continued to work at his villa in Sor-

rento amidst his library of 60,000 books (one of the finest private libraries in the world). The Fascists expelled him from one academy and society after another and used him as a major target of attacks; few of his associates stood by him; his books were not kept in Italian public libraries, and the circulation of his review La Critica was forbidden in all Italian schools; but Mussolini still did not dare brave international opinion by harming him. Besides, in his writings Croce had ceased to mention the word "Fascism" except indirectly, appeasing anti-Fascist youth who asked his advice by telling them: "Work for culture. He who works for culture works against Fascism."

The most important works of Croce's later years—Storia d'Italia dal 1871 al 1915 (3rd ed. 1928); Storia d'Europa nel Secolo Decimonono (3rd ed. 1932); La Storia Come Pensiero e Come Azione (2nd ed. 1938)—"are not only scarcely veiled attacks on Fascism; they are also attempts to reconcile Neo-Romantic and liberal-positivistic conceptions of history." The first of these books, translated as History of Italy, 1871-1915 in 1929, attempted to disprove the Fascist view of pre-War Italian history as an era of decline. The second, translated as History of Europe in the Nineteenth Century in 1933, was an attempt to reach an understanding of the underlying ideas and faiths, particularly the hope of "liberty," which motivated men's lives and made history during the period between the fall of Napoleon and the end of the First World War. It provoked a frenzy of argument throughout Italy and was put on the Catholic Index of Prohibited Books. The third, translated in 1941 as History as the Story of Liberty, advanced the thesis that "liberty is the eternal creature of history and itself the subject of every history, so that its development is forever incomplete"; liberty is present in every age either as an acquired fact or as an aspiration, and "when periods of barbarism and violence are approaching, it is only for the vile and the foolish that the ideal becomes unfreedom and slavery." In the words of one writer, "Croce's philosophy reconciles, or rather is a process of perpetually reconciling materialism and idealism"—an attempt to reconcile irreconcilables, according to G. A. Borgese, which sprang from "the dogmatic continuity of his personality which did not allow him to admit that once in his life he had been theoretically or practically wrong."

Croce's conception of "Liberty" was also developed in numerous articles which appeared in foreign publications throughout the years. To this conception socialism and communism were as antipathetic as Fascism; indeed, since Croce did not mention Fascism by name, one might almost have thought they were more so. "Under the name of socialism, communism had already been introduced into the political life and institutions of Europe before the War," he wrote in 1932. "Now it has reappeared, cruel and disruptive, a sterile thing that kills thought, religion, and art." In a later article he wrote: ". . . the fundamental and sole necessary condition for a liberal party is the rebirth of oppression or tyranny, whether lay or ecclesiastical, whatever its particular forms may be (demagogy, dictatorship, Bolshevism, and so forth)—

CROCE, BENEDETTO—*Continued*

the thesis which substantially provokes its anti-thesis." Moreover, his conception of liberalism was not one which placed much faith in the will of the majority. "Sound political sense," he wrote in 1937, "has never regarded the masses as the directing force of society, but has always delegated this directive function to a class which was not economic in its basis of selection, but political; one capable of governing. . . . Liberalism should be at one and the same time the friend and the foe of democracy . . . its friend, because the governing class is fluid . . . the foe of democracy when the latter tends to substitute mere numbers or quantity for quality, because by so doing democracy is preparing the way for demagoguery and, quite unintentionally, for dictatorship and tyranny and its own destruction."

With the fall of Mussolini in 1943, it was inevitable that Croce should use his voice again. Writing in *Giornale d'Italia* in August of that year, he stressed that what Italy needed most was the establishment beyond doubt of the practice of freedom, the principles and method of political debate, as a necessary preliminary condition of free political life. "Spain," he wrote, "aiming at liberty, tried to deal at the same time with a variety of disparate problems, from the struggle against the clergy to the agrarian reforms. On this her people were divided by a civil war and her soil was covered with blood. . . . No mingling or confusing of liberty's problems with the other particular problems must be tolerated. . . . One must not delude one's self that by holding forth the bait of particular economic reforms and advantages one can strengthen liberty."

Croce was at Sorrento in the German rear while the battle of Salerno was still raging violently, and the Germans reported that he had been arrested along with other anti-Fascist Italians, but in September a British force landed and succeeded in getting him away to safety. With Count Sforza's [42] return to Italy the names of the two men became linked in newspaper dispatches as the Liberals and leaders of the Committee of National Liberation who were best known abroad.

After long separation, these two found their ideas exactly the same on the political situation. Both favored a regency under Badoglio [40] with the six-year-old Prince of Naples as King; both insisted upon the abdication of Victor Emmanuel [43]; and, in spite of Badoglio's refusal to ask the King to abdicate and his dissolution of the volunteer army to fight beside the Allies which Sforza and Croce had championed, both continued for some time to "sympathize with Marshal Badoglio and place great hopes in him." Undoubtedly, however, it is Sforza who enjoys more popular support. At a public meeting at Naples late in November in Croce's honor there was protest when the aging philosopher referred to the Anglo-American war effort without mentioning Russia, and there was a tumultuous anti-monarchical demonstration. Even though he now opposes both Victor Emmanuel and his son, Croce has long been

a monarchist, and if he favors a regency it is because he sees it as the one way to save the monarchy in Italy. The Communists have declared themselves ready to support a government headed by Sforza but have said that they would oppose one formed by Croce.

In April 1944 Senator Croce was brought into the Badoglio Cabinet, with other representatives of the anti-Fascist movements, to "give it a broader base." After the liberation of Rome in early June the leaders of the six resistance parties forced Badoglio's resignation by refusing to serve under him because of his association with Fascism. With the unanimous election of Ivanoe Bonomi [44] as head of the Government, Croce, Sforza, and Communist Palmiro ("Ercole"—"Hercules") Togliatti [44] were retained as Ministers of State without portfolio; but in July the aged philosopher announced that he would resign his post when the Government moved to Rome on the 15th, giving as his reason the difficulty for him of constant trips there from his Sorrento home. The *Voce Republicana* declared, however, that this resignation was due in part to disagreement with the other Ministers over "such things as their refusal to take the oath of loyalty to the throne," swearing instead "on their honor . . . in the supreme interest of the nation." Croce's prestige as a thinker was enhanced by this retirement, according to Anne O'Hare McCormick [40]. Speaking not as president of the Liberal Party but simply as an Italian on the anniversary of Italy's declaration of war against Germany, the Senator asked in September for an end to Italy's co-belligerency. Stating that "this War is intrinsically a civil war and Italy has won its battle against Fascism," he asked that Italy be recognized as a full ally, and that the terms of the armistice, which "bind and impede the Italian Government in every movement," be revised, particularly in view of the milder terms imposed on Rumania and Finland. "In the face of so many of the provisions and nominations made by Allied authorities," he added, "I have often wished they would seek for and listen to an Italian lawyer who might enlighten them and prevent further errors."

In July 1944 Vincent Sheean's [41] translation of four Croce essays was published in New York as *Germany and Europe*; the introduction revealed that "the British Navy made a dash across Capri just to rescue Croce from the Germans." Describing himself as "an Italian Germanophile who cannot discover within himself in this respect anything for which he should repent," Croce says that the Nazi evil "was historically born, and will historically die; therefore it does not possess the character of a fantastic fact in physics, or rather in metaphysics, conferred upon it by the concept of race." Somewhat optimistically, he feels that "the shame which it [the German nation] cannot help but feel over the evil for which it has made itself the instrument will be converted into a force of good—as with those great saints who were once great sinners." Others, however, did not discount the numbers of those great sinners who failed to become saints of any degree. Reviewers called *Germany and Europe* a profoundly civilized book, and joined with the author in hoping that, though "perpetual peace is perpetual Utopia," we may hope, as Croce says, to "clear away from the mind every residuum and tear out every smallest root or filament of 'war as ideal.'" To Dorothy Thompson[40], the book is "a pleasure, like drinking from a clean pool after ditch water, or moving from a babelous market place into a quiet study where reason still reigns."

In October 1944 Benedetto Croce announced that the year's end would see the last of his famous magazine *La Critica*. "My new studies, such as a series of essays on Goethe's works that will integrate a volume I wrote previously on the same subject, will appear in a new review," he said, "which I will publish at irregular intervals, called *I Quaderna della Critica* ['Notebook of Critical Thought']. In this new magazine I intend to collect, besides my studies, those of old and new contributors who follow the same line of thought."

Croce is described as stout, short, blondish, bespectacled, with greenish gray eyes. He has four daughters, of whom *Life* reports that Alda, Sylvia, and Lydia are history students. He himself is a member of the Prussian Academy, the American Academy of Arts and Letters, and the British Academy. In 1920 he received a gold medal from Columbia University, and he was later honored with university degrees from Oxford, Freiburg in Baden, and Marburg. In 1934 he stood as the strongest candidate for the Nobel Prize, which for political reasons was awarded to Luigi Pirandello instead.

References

Life 15:126-9 N 22 '43 il pors
N Y Times p4 O 16 '43; p1+ O 31 '43
Borgese, G. A. Goliath: The March of Fascism 1937
Drake, W. A. Contemporary European Writers p43-51 1928
Durant, W. Story of Philosophy 1927
Kunitz, S. J. and Haycraft, H. eds. Twentieth Century Authors 1942
Matthews, H. L. Fruits of Fascism 1943
Riccio, P. M. Italian Authors of Today 1938
Schmitt, B. Some Historians of Modern Europe 1942
Who's Who 1944

CULLEN, THOMAS H. Mar. 29, 1868—Feb. 29, 1944 Democratic Congressman from Brooklyn since 1919; dean of the New York delegation in the House of Representatives since 1930; sat in the state Senate from 1896 to 1918; author of many tariff measures.

Obituary

N Y Times p18 Mr 2 '44 por

DAFOE, JOHN WESLEY 1866—Jan. 9, 1944 Canadian editor, author, and journalist; editor of the Winnipeg *Free Press*; adviser to Prime Minister of Canada during the Versailles Conference; Chancellor of Manitoba University in 1934; member of Royal Commission on Dominion Provincial Relations from 1937 to 1940; author of many publications, his last book was *Canada Fights* (1941).

Obituary

N Y Times Ja 10 '44

DAMROSCH, WALTER (JOHANNES) (dam'rosh) Jan. 30, 1862- Conductor; composer; pianist; music commentator
Address: h. 168 E. 71st St., New York City

Walter Damrosch, the dean of American music, "has achieved an eminence which no other conductor in all recorded history has even remotely approached"; yet many people who love and honor him have only a vague idea of the reasons for his fame. The composers for whom he battled have become classics; the innovations he made have become standard practice; the localities to which he introduced good music now have their own orchestras—and conductors who in some cases outshine him.

Walter Johannes Damrosch was born in Breslau, Silesia (Prussia), January 30, 1862, and brought up in an atmosphere permeated with music. His father was Dr. Leopold Damrosch, a well known violinist and conductor; his mother, Helene (von Heimburg) Damrosch, was an operatic soprano who created the role of Ortrude in *Lohengrin*; and his aunt Marie von Heimburg, who lived with them, was also an accomplished singer. In the year of Walter's birth Dr. Damrosch founded the Breslau Orchestral Society to support the Breslau Philharmonic Orchestra of which he was conductor. Such famous musicians as Liszt, Wagner, von Bülow, Clara Schumann, and Anton Rubinstein, as well as Haenselt, Carl Taussig, and Joseph Joachim, came to Breslau to take part in Dr. Damrosch's concerts and, usually, to stay at his modest home. Franz Liszt and Richard Wagner had stood as godfathers to Walter's elder brothers.

Dr. Damrosch was a stern and reserved father, in the German way; yet, in spite of his heavy responsibilities and financial difficulties, he found time to read fairy tales to his children. (At eight Walter's favorite reading was a metrical translation of Homer.) The boy had his whippings, in and out of school; he was sent supperless to bed or "confined to quarters" for such misdeeds as refusing to eat spinach, which he still detests; but Walter loved and revered his father and "used to enjoy trotting by his side" because "so many people would take off their hats to him deferentially as he passed."

In 1871 Dr. Leopold Damrosch was invited to come to New York as conductor of the German male choral society, the Männesängverein Arion. He had not only had great financial difficulty in Breslau, often giving up his own salary so that an orchestra member might be paid, but had become increasingly annoyed by the arrogance of the Prussian bureaucracy during and after the Austro-Prussian War. Dr. Damrosch accepted the invitation from America, hoping to popularize the radical, modern music of Liszt and Wagner in an atmosphere of greater freedom. The following year, when Walter was nine and his brother Frank twelve, Dr. Damrosch sent for his family. The boys did not know a word of English, and so were put in the beginning class at school, although they had both attended the Gymnasium (high school) in Germany and had both studied Latin. They were, however, quickly promoted through the grades as they learned more and more English.

WALTER DAMROSCH

Walter, who had begun early to study the piano, continued with Jean Vogt and then with Pruckner, von Inten, Max Pinner, and Boeckelman. The latter teacher unintentionally put an end to his pupil's chances for a pianistic career by having him exercise with a device intended to strengthen the fingers, which injured the third finger of Walter's right hand. For a time it seemed as though young Damrosch might become an artist, for he had "some talent for painting," and he studied drawing at Cooper Union. He was very skillful at construction, too, making doll's houses for his sisters and "quite a little flect of boats" which won a number of races in the Central Park pond. Probably his greatest achievement in that field, however, was as a puppet show impresario, presenting Wagnerian music-dramas. Thus, at the age of fourteen, he gave the first American production of *Das Rheingold.* By that time he was also singing as an alto in the Oratorio Society of New York, which his father had helped found in 1873, at the suggestion of Anton Rubinstein, performing new works by Liszt, Brahms, and Berlioz, as well as classic oratorios. Another novelty was their choral presentation of excerpts from Wagner operas, such as the first act finale of *Parsifal* and the third act of *Die Meistersinger.* At the presentation of Berlioz' *La Damnation de Faust* Walter played in "the last stand of the second violins," for Dr. Damrosch wanted him, as a future conductor, to be able to follow the leader's beat.

In 1878 Walter Damrosch was invited to act as accompanist for August Wilhelmj, the violinist, on a Southern concert tour. (Wilhelmj knew him to be experienced at accompanying his father, and needed a substitute for the regular accompanist, who had suddenly been taken ill.) Damrosch, then sixteen years old, received $100 a week and his train fare. Two years later Dr. Damrosch decided to hold a huge music festival, including the Berlioz *Requiem* among the

works to be performed; and, as there was no piano score of this work, eighteen-year-old Walter was entrusted with the task of making one from the original orchestral score. He therefore spent that summer in Amherst, Massachusetts, arranging the *Requiem,* practising the piano, and studying both French and Latin with Dr. Sauveur. On Walter's return, Dr. Damrosch turned over to him the training of two sections of the festival chorus (totaling 500 voices). At the same time young Damrosch played the piano accompaniment for all his father's rehearsals; and, at the festival, he played the organ accompaniments for the 1,500 performers. The festival was a huge success, drawing an audience of 10,000 to each performance. As a result of the festival the Newark Harmonic Society, which he had rehearsed, elected Walter Damrosch their permanent conductor in 1881. For four years he produced their choral works with orchestral accompaniment, holding weekly rehearsals and giving three or four such concerts a winter.

In the spring of 1882 Damrosch went to Germany to take the cure for his throat at Ems; but first he visited Weimar and called upon his father's old friend, Franz Liszt. Afterwards the youth attended the first performances of *Parsifal* at Bayreuth, where he "met scores of artists by whom I was cordially received because I was my father's son." Richard Wagner gave him a manuscript copy of the first act finale for presentation by his father, "a remarkable act of friendship."

That was the year when New York's Metropolitan Opera House was built. After one unsuccessful season of Italian opera at "the new yellow brewery on Broadway," the directors selected Dr. Leopold Damrosch to manage and conduct a season of German opera in 1884-1885. The season was a great success, but the strain of running an entire opera company and two musical societies proved too great for Dr. Damrosch. In February 1885 he contracted pneumonia. His twenty-year-old son had to step into the breach and conduct the final week's performances of *Walküre* and *Tannhäuser.* "They had been so splendidly rehearsed by my father and had been performed several times," says Damrosch. "I have, therefore, never claimed much credit for what many kind friends at the time considered an extraordinary feat." On Dr. Damrosch's death, young Walter, overcome by a tremendous sense of loss, was left "numb and overwhelmed by the terrible responsibilities which began to press in upon me." But he "had no opportunity for indulging in quiet grief." Not only did he succeed his father as director of the Oratorio and Symphony Societies, but "the contracts for the tour had to be met. My father's estate was technically liable, though he left literally no money. There was no one to assume the responsibility of taking the company on tour except me, and I accordingly set forth." On the very first trip the worst blizzard of the year struck their train and made them a day late in arriving. The tour was such a success, however, that the season was extended, and Damrosch produced two operas new to America although standard in Germany: Boïeldieu's *La Dame Blanche* and

Gluck's *Orpheus*. Meanwhile, the Metropolitan directors appointed Damrosch as assistant director and second conductor, "granting me a salary which was large enough to enable me to support my mother and my father's family decently." In 1885 he justified their confidence by obtaining the services of the famous artists Lilli Lehmann, Emil Fischer, Max Alvary, and Anton Seidl. As second conductor, however, Damrosch had no chance to lead the Wagnerian operas.

During the first years of Damrosch's career "unqualified and incessant damnation was heaped upon him as an incompetent and mediocrity." His conducting of the Symphony Society was "treated with routine consideration by the newspapers, while every star imported from Europe became the subject of speculation and analysis and even rhapsody occupying many columns." Yet "his rise was unbroken," his importance increased, and even his unfriendliest critics admitted the force and charm of his personality. "When he was young he was very handsome, with luxuriant blond hair rushing torrentially back from a bold brow, and a pair of radiant eyes." A photograph of the young Damrosch shows that the straight lines of his eyebrows, the strong square bone structure, and especially the uncompromising set of his jaw gave him an air of stern intensity which must have been most engaging in one so young. Then, when he flashed the famous Damrosch smile, no wonder that "many maidens regarded him wistfully." This gracious and tactful musician always had the knack of making friends, and "an unequalled ability to collect money and sympathy for a cause."

In the spring of 1887 Damrosch sailed for Europe to spend the summer studying with Hans von Bülow. On the trip across he made the acquaintance of the Andrew Carnegies, then on their wedding trip, who invited him to visit them at their Scottish castle when his studies were completed. This he did—after learning von Bülow's analysis of the Beethoven symphonies, and after politely refusing an invitation from the Prince of Hesse to join his household as court musician. At the Carnegies' were James G. Blaine, the former Congressman, Secretary of State, and candidate for President, with his wife and two daughters. "Music had entered but little into the lives of the Blaine family," wrote Damrosch, "and I was really delighted that for the first time in my life I was compelled to establish relations from a purely human standpoint and without the assistance of any of the 'romantic glamour' of my profession." Damrosch and the Blaines were both invited for a coaching trip through England and Scotland the following summer (broken by a concert Damrosch conducted in London, which included one of his father's concertos). The handsome young musician "laid siege to Margaret Blaine's affections." On October 1889 their engagement was announced, and on May 17, 1890 they were married.

In that year Damrosch gave his first series of public lecture recitals on Wagner; in that year, too, Damrosch got his "first real opportunity," when Anton Seidl's illness gave him a chance to conduct Cornelius' opera, *The Barber of Bagdad*. Beginning in 1891, however, the Metropolitan Opera House devoted itself entirely to operas of the French-Italian school, so that there was no possibility of his conducting Wagner, except for an occasional *Lohengrin* in Italian. In 1894, therefore, when Damrosch was asked to arrange a charity entertainment, he produced the *Götterdämmerung* at Carnegie Hall. This was followed by *Walküre,* both operas meeting with such remarkable success that, having failed to induce the Metropolitan to include Wagnerian operas in its repertoire, Damrosch decided to found his own German opera company. To finance this venture he sold his West 55th Street house and was instrumental in founding a Wagner Society to help in the sale of subscription seats. (The Metropolitan management assisted the young conductor in his debut as an impresario by letting him have the use of the Opera House for four weeks, in effect rent free.) Damrosch went to Germany for his singers and scenery, bringing back some of the best in each category. In 1895 the Damrosch Opera Company's thirteen-week season netted him $53,000; but the following year, with a longer season and an improved cast, he lost $43,000 of it. During the course of this tour Damrosch took Wagnerian operas to many places which had never heard any of them. It was at this time that his own *The Scarlet Letter* was presented, an opera which he considers "well written and orchestrated," but so Wagnerian that he agrees with Anton Seidl, who called it the New England Nibelungen Trilogy.

The Metropolitan directors now entered on a reciprocal arrangement with the young impresario whereby they interchanged certain performers. This enabled Damrosch to balance his repertoire by including some French and Italian operas. Besides this, the Philadelphia Academy of Music guaranteed him a regular season. In 1898 the great Nellie Melba joined the company, which then became a partnership, the Damrosch-Ellis Opera Company. (Charles Ellis was then Melba's manager.) After a successful season under the partnership Damrosch sold his half-interest to Ellis and withdrew permanently from the management phase of opera. In 1900, however, he returned to the Metropolitan to conduct the Wagnerian operas there, directing such famous singers as the de Reszkes, Schumann-Heink, Nordica, and Milka Ternina.

During all these years Damrosch continued active with the Symphony and Oratorio Societies. In 1891 he invited Tschaikowsky to appear with the New York Symphony, and also conducted the orchestra for Paderewski's first five concerts in America. The following year was the 150th anniversary of the first performance of Handel's *Messiah*, and Damrosch celebrated the occasion with a Handel festival, presenting a number of choral works. During the same year (1892) he gave the American première of Saint-Saëns' *Samson and Delilah,* again in concert form. Among the "novelties" introduced by the Oratorio Society under Damrosch were Berlioz' *Te Deum,* Liszt's *Christus,* and Eduard Grell's *Missa Solemnis.* In 1896 the Society gave the first American presentation of *Parsifal* with the

DAMROSCH, WALTER—*Continued*

assistance of soloists from the Metropolitan; two years later they presented Damrosch's *Manila Te Deum,* celebrating Dewey's victory at Manila. This last event was under the baton of Frank Damrosch at his introduction as conductor of the Oratorio Society to succeed his busy brother.

In the spring of 1902 the New York Philharmonic Society, Dr. Leopold Damrosch's old rival, invited his son to become its permanent conductor. The Philharmonic Society, a cooperative venture, rejected Damrosch's proposals for reorganization through the raising of a symphony fund administered by trustees, but his own New York Symphony Society was later reorganized in this manner and put on a permanent basis. Thus in 1903 Damrosch realized his dream of an orchestra devoted exclusively to symphonic music and assembling for daily rehearsals.

Keeping the New York Symphony together had from the first been Damrosch's main problem; in order to keep the orchestra occupied he had instituted long spring tours and resident summer engagements at expositions and in parks. Thus in spite of the hazards of travel and discomforts of work under crude conditions he brought great soloists and great symphonic music to people in the South and West who were unacquainted with them. The enthusiasm and interest thus aroused resulted eventually in the formation of many local orchestras, so that gradually the tours had come to be less necessary and important. The Damrosch Opera Company had for a time provided employment for the orchestra; but it had interfered with their concert schedule.

Now that Damrosch was able to carry out his "artistic plans" he gave a Beethoven cycle (1909), climaxed by a double performance of the Ninth Symphony and followed by a Brahms festival. In 1914 Harry Harkness Flagler, the president of the Orchestra Fund and a large contributor to it, decided to assume the entire financial responsibility for the orchestra himself. This princely gesture made possible the performance of more than one hundred symphony concerts a year, as well as several tours to Canada and the Middle West. Among these concerts were a series for young people and another for children, both with explanatory remarks. Among Damrosch's innovations was the Sunday symphonic concert, a daring move at the time, but now so effectively popularized that Sunday is the most crowded day of the musical week. Even before the reorganization, says Damrosch, "the foreign artists who came to America, such as Sarasate, Ysaye, d'Albert, Joseffy, Paderewski, Kubelik, and many others, always chose my orchestra to accompany them."

In the words of W. J. Henderson, "Mr. Damrosch . . . exhibited a catholicity of taste which went far toward establishing him as a pioneer. . . . No composer of worth and no school was permitted to escape his consideration." He introduced the Third and Fourth Symphonies of Brahms. "He was active in spreading the gospel of Tschaikowsky and induced the composer to come to this country." "He found abundant material in France at a time when its music was generally neg-

lected by our conductors." "Probably no other conductor produced more American novelties than Damrosch. The Modernists were also benefited by his study." (He prefaced the performance of one such work by telling the audience that he didn't understand it either.) "There can be no question that Damrosch's personal popularity obtained careful attention for works which might otherwise have been slighted."

Damrosch's *Cyrano de Bergérac,* an "American" opera, was presented by the Metropolitan company in 1913. Two years later Margaret Anglin commissioned the conductor to write incidental music for her productions of Euripides' *Iphigenia in Aulis* and *Medea* and Sophocles' *Electra.* This music "revealed Damrosch the composer at his best."

When the First World War began Damrosch faced and successfully solved the problem of keeping peace in an orchestra composed of thirteen warring nationalities. He was a naturalized citizen, and when the United States entered the War his sympathies were wholly on the side of America. Damrosch, then in his fifties, sailed to France. He was recommended by Theodore Roosevelt, who wrote: "I have known him thirty years; I vouch for him as if he were my brother." As president of the Society of American Friends of Musicians in France, his intention was to form an orchestra of French musicians with which to entertain the American soldiers. This proved impossible; but Damrosch was able to conduct several benefit concerts for the Red Cross. Invited by General Pershing to confer with him on the possible improvement of Army bands, he persuaded the General to give up the practice of using bandsmen as stretcher-bearers "except in cases of extreme military urgency." After examining the 200 bandmasters he organized a school for bandmasters and bandsmen, taught by the best French instructors.

After the War, Damrosch received invitations from the governments of France, Belgium, and Italy, from King George of England, and later from Cuba, to visit them with the New York Symphony. As representative American soloists he chose Albert Spalding '44 and John Powell, a composer-pianist. The tour, financed by Harry Harkness Flagler, was a great success. Damrosch was decorated by the French Légion d'Honneur and received the gold medal of the Banda Communale of Rome and the silver medal of the Worshipfull Company of Musicians of London. (He has since been made Chevalier of the Crown of Belgium, Officer of the Crown of Italy, and Officer of the Légion d'Honneur, and has also received honorary doctorates from Columbia, Princeton, Brown, New York, and New York State Universities.) Europe had been sending musical artists to America for years; Damrosch thus initiated traffic in the other direction. The conductor was very proud of his wife's activities in the movement for woman suffrage during this period.

Damrosch's autobiography, *My Musical Life,* was published in 1923, but in spite of the sixty-one years behind him the author had many years of achievement still in the future. In 1925 he again "pioneered," as he loved to do, by conducting the first symphony concert ever broadcast. Damrosch continued his activities with the New York Symphony until "in the middle of the 1926-1927 season, he surprised almost everybody by announcing his resignation from the conductorship of the symphony, giving as his reason 'a desire to lessen somewhat his public activities.'" Then he became musical counselor for NBC, but continued with the children's concerts, also serving as guest conductor of the New York Symphony and, for one season, of the new Philharmonic-Symphony (which had resulted from a "merger" of the two orchestras). In April 1929 at the age of sixty-five, Damrosch ended his association with that orchestra—though not with conducting.

Much of Damrosch's life had been spent in bringing music to the greatest possible number of people. Now he visualized an audience of millions in radio, as compared to the thousands in even the largest concert hall; and he remembered his brother Frank's statement that true musical culture would never flourish in America until musical education was begun with children in the schools. In years Walter Damrosch was an old man in 1929; but he launched himself on a new career with zest. After preliminary experiments he instituted the NBC Music Appreciation Course.

This course met with tremendous success. His fan mail amounted to some 40,000 letters a year, and soon it was estimated that six million school children (as well as three million adults) were listening to him conduct and explain good music. In New York City alone 200 schools listened to the first series in 1929; the entire school systems of several cities were equipped with radios for that purpose; and in rural schools without radios the pupils gathered about a radio-equipped car to hear "Papa Damrosch." Heads of schools in Mexico, the Bahamas, Bermuda, Cuba, and even Suchow, China, wrote for the teacher's manual of his course. Martin Goodale might snort at "the unctuous voice which rolls out cheerful sugar-coated music pills and . . . penetrates into millions of defenseless homes," but those homes—and schools—welcomed it warmly. His final series was heard on a hookup which included Latin America. In 1942 the NBC *Music Appreciation Hour* became a war casualty. The network asked Damrosch to cut down his program from an hour to thirty minutes because of the great demand for radio time; and the eighty-year-old musician, feeling that he could not do justice to his subject in so short a time, preferred to withdraw his course entirely.

Damrosch had not confined himself to teaching during those years. In 1935 he composed an "Abraham Lincoln Song," and in 1936 "Death and General Putnam." The Metropolitan produced his opera *The Man Without a Country* in 1937; and in 1939 Damrosch appeared in the motion picture *The Star Maker*. The venerable conductor then turned down a commission to write the musical score for *Gone With the Wind*, saying that his heart would not be in it, and returned to New York, where in 1941 he revised and directed the production of his old opera *Cyrano*. This inspired him to take up his piano practice again

—to such good effect that on March 28, 1941 he made his debut as a concert pianist. A "child prodigy," as he termed himself, of seventy-eight, Damrosch played in ensemble "with a beginner's zest and a veteran's zeal," drawing reviews highly complimentary to "the veteran who had given such an inspiring example of the interpreter's art." Toward the end of 1942 Damrosch the composer presented another opera, *The Opera Cloak*, which was produced by the New Opera Company that same year.

Among his other compositions are *The Dove of Peace* (an opera), *The Virgin Mary to the Child Jesus, The Canterbury Pilgrims* (a cantata), and a group of songs: "Danny Deever," "Mandalay," "To Sleep," "Was Ever Maid of Spain." In 1943 he composed the ballad "Dunkirk," for baritone, male chorus, and orchestra. John T. Howard has summed up critical opinion of Damrosch as a composer: "That branch of his work has been a diversion of his youth and his latter years; and no one begrudges him the enjoyment it has afforded, so long as he does not ask us to remember him by it instead of by his truly great achievements."

There are four daughters in the Damrosch family: Alice, Gretchen (Margaret), Anita, and Polly (Leopoldine), who was married to the late playwright Sidney Howard. Damrosch still builds models expertly and is considered a good cook. He is a famous host in a charming home decorated with pictures of Handel, Haydn, Gluck, Bach, Liszt, Beethoven, Schumann—and a bust of Wagner. He cherishes two precious possessions: the manuscript of a Beethoven trio which was given to him by Clara Schumann, having been left to Schumann by Mendelssohn; and the yellowed program of Dr. Leopold Damrosch's first concert in Steinway Hall, sent to his son by a stranger who had kept it for fifty years.

Perhaps the best definition of this venerable pioneer's standing in American music has been given by a distinguished critic, the late W. J. Henderson: "What impresses this writer most in making a retrospective view of the intensely interesting career of Walter Damrosch is the outstanding fact that he has acquired fame without gaining celebrity in any one department of his art." As David Ewen put it in *Man With the Baton*: "He has been, one must confess, a far greater personality than an artist. Even his most devoted admirer would hesitate to call him a great conductor, or even a very good one. Competent he was, and a fine musician as well; and we have yet to see a program maker who could repeatedly fashion concerts that possessed for so long a time such variety, freshness, and perpetual interest. . . . Even greater importance rests with Damrosch because of his valiant battle for the modern composers [such daring radicals as Wagner, Stravinsky '40, Tschaikowsky, Gershwin, Sibelius, Delius, Ravel, Elgar, Honegger '41] at a time when he stood virtually alone on the battlefield."

References
Am Mag 109:54+ My '30
Am Mercury 34:352-59 Mr '35
Century 115:23-9 N '27
Mus Q 18:1-8 Ja '32
(Continued next page)

DAMROSCH, WALTER—*Continued*

Damrosch, W. My Musical Life 1923
Ewen, D. Dictators of the Baton 1943
Ewen, D. The Man With the Baton 1936
Thompson, O. ed. International Cyclopedia of Music and Musicians 1943
Who's Who in America 1944-45

DANIELL, (FRANCIS) RAYMOND
(dan'yel) Oct. 22, 1901- Journalist; author
Address: b. c/o New York Times, 229 W. 43rd St., New York City; Hotel Savoy, London

"There are no glamour boys among the American correspondents resident in London," Raymond Daniell tells us in *Civilians Must Fight* (1941); but the hard-working newspapermen there took as many risks and stood in as much danger during the Battle for Britain as the more colorful correspondents assigned to the front lines. Daniell, "on furlough" from his work as chief of the London bureau of the New York *Times*, came home in 1941 to find "an interminable debate; a babble of paradoxes and contradictions from the interventionists; a chorus of half-truths and defeatism from the isolationists." Before Pearl Harbor his calm, dispassionate book pointed out to Americans that their only choice lay between fighting Nazism and accepting the terms of "a Hitler '42 astride three-quarters of the world." One month after Daniell's warning the United States was forced to recognize the truth of his analysis; two months later he was sailing back to England through submarine-infested seas.

Francis Raymond Daniell was born in New Haven, Connecticut, October 22, 1901, the son of Francis Guild and Maude Louise (Mazeine) Daniell. In spite of his nearness to Yale University, the youth attended Rutgers University in New Jersey. Without waiting to be graduated, he left in 1923 to join the reporting staff, first of the New Brunswick *Home News*, and then of the New York *Herald*. Somewhere in his experience Daniell also managed two weeks on the Newark *Ledger*. On June 13, 1924 Daniell was married to Blanche Elizabeth Naylor; they have two children, a daughter, Elizabeth Lake, and a son, Curtis Guild. (The Daniells were divorced in Reno seventeen years later.)

When the New York *Herald* merged with the New York *Tribune*, Daniell moved to the Associated Press. Later he took a job with the New York *Evening Post*, and in 1928 he joined the staff of the New York *Times*, with which he has remained. In his article, "Land of the Free," included in *We Saw It Happen* (1938), Daniell describes his years as a reporter, telling how "fashions in news, which move in cycles . . . began to change, and the emphasis shifted gradually from individuals and personalities to philosophies and movements. In the predepression era the big stories of the day were the 'bunion derbies,' the transatlantic flights, the prison riots, the dance marathons, and the murder trials and divorce suits. I have sat through some of the most sensational murder trials. . . . I have lived to report bits of local current history that have convinced me that there is more to municipal reform than the mere ousting of a figurehead for a corrupt machine. I have seen laid bare the corrupt alliance between politics and the underworld and have heard enough to satisfy me that racketeering flourished in our big cities because businessmen condoned and encouraged it.

"With the coming of the depression, my assignments ran more and more to politics and to matters of national concern. My unaccustomed typewriter began to tap out a song of social significance, and I began to obtain a firsthand impression of this 'land of the free,' an impression that clashed with the picture school and college had left with me." During the years that followed Daniell reported the "period of political-economic lunacy," and then "the period of economic realism." "I attended the inquest and the funeral for a dozen men who had been shot in the back by Chicago policemen firing into a parade of striking steelworkers. Later . . . at Monroe, Michigan, I was mildly gassed while watching the local vigilantes break a picket line around a plant of Republic Steel.

"The steel strike served as a reminder to me that violence, intolerance, and disrespect for minorities were not the exclusive weapon of the economic royalists. . . . I have heard violence defended in the name of Americanism. I have heard the New Deal attacked as fascism and again as communism. I have encountered bigotry and intolerance on the Left as well as on the Right. . . . It was in the South that I first realized that the unbelievable book-burning orgies of the Nazis could, save for the grace of God, be duplicated here, and realized that the Mussolini '42 castor-oil treatment was unknown here chiefly because our folkways dictated tar-and-feathers and flogging." This was borne in forcibly on Daniell when he covered the Scottsboro case and, later, when he investigated the plight of sharecroppers in Arkansas and miners in Kentucky, whom he found living in "conditions more squalid than would be tolerated in any city slum." Unable to obtain adequate education, undernourished, disfranchised by the poll tax, these "freeborn Americans living the lives of serfs" are held down by "night riders and vigilantes, terrorizing white and black alike."

Daniell's experiences and observations convinced him that "the mental attitude on which fascism feeds exists here just as it does in Germany and Italy, while the seeds of Marxism fall on barren soil. Often I wonder why it has not happened here. Americans like other peoples have been baffled by the increasing complexities of life, and like others have shown increasingly a predilection for ducking responsibilities and letting self-appointed leaders do their thinking for them. . . . To me, proud of a New England heritage, this resignation, acceptance of the inevitable, shirking of responsibility, and flouting of the rights of minorities are the most alarming phenomena of these unhappy times."

In September 1939, when Great Britain and France declared war against Germany, Daniell, who was a member of the *Times* editorial board, sailed for England to take charge of its London office. Suffering from pneumonia, he left on fourteen hours' notice to replace a man who might leave before he arrived, taking over a dangerous and exacting job at a foreign capital which might be in ruins when he got there. But "it was the biggest story in the world, and what newspaperman would say no?"

Still, says Daniell, "never having experienced it, I couldn't imagine the hellish nuisance of the blackout, the stupidity of wartime censors, the mental strain of bombardment—in anticipation and in reality—the dull routine of managing a large office and trying to be a reporter as well, the loneliness of being separated by an ocean from family and friends, with no means of communication except by letters, which sometimes took two months to reach their destination. Nor could I anticipate what rationing really meant. For months in that first winter of war I never saw the sunlight. Six hours difference in time between New York and London and the uncertainty of events . . . kept us in the office until 3 or 4 a.m. We slept until midafternoon, had breakfast, drew our blackout curtains, and then set out through the fog and darkness for another day of work. There were a dozen restaurants in London where I ate dinner without having the faintest idea how they looked from the outside, until summer came with its longer hours of daylight."

Sharing these discomforts with Daniell and the other male correspondents was Tania Long, of the New York *Herald Tribune*, who soon won the prize of the New York Newspaper Women's Club for the best reporting of the year. Daniell describes her in *Civilians Must Fight*, telling how she provided the correspondents "with as much competition as any man in London" at the same time that she looked after them with motherly care. After the Daniells' divorce, in November 1941 she and Daniell were married. Tania Long then came to work for the New York *Times* Magazine, in which capacity she accompanies her husband on his travels.

It was in the early spring of 1941 that Daniell arrived in the United States; at the beginning of November, *Civilians Must Fight* was published and favorably reviewed. The *Times* critic called the narrative "brief, swift, and simple. It avoids the melodramatic and the spectacular like the plague. It has few literary graces, but possesses the rare virtue of conciseness. . . . Mr. Daniell is the reverse of tedious." The month after Daniell's warning was published the United States entered the War; and when Daniell returned to England (in February 1942) he no longer represented a neutral but an Allied press. This, however, was only a change of labels, for, as he had written, "It is impossible to be neutral in thought when a city one has grown to love is being smashed to bits wantonly, when one's friends are being killed and injured every day, when one's own home has been wrecked. . . . Neutrality of thought was a luxury to which war correspondents in the First World War could afford to treat themselves. We, their successors, cannot. . . . Journalistic objectivity is quite another matter. Unneutral as most of us are, we manage to preserve that." Of the London correspondents, he said,

RAYMOND DANIELL

"They don't fall often or easily for propaganda. . . . [They] are Americans first and always."

On May 6, 1942, at its annual meeting in London, the Association of American Correspondents elected Daniell to a one-year term as its president. In September of the following year he returned to the United States, where his European experience provided a background for editorials. In March 1944 he was back at his London post replenishing this firsthand knowledge by channel-hopping between London and Paris and occasional trips to the front. He found liberated Paris "the same chic, gay city it has always been . . . but underneath . . . clashes and cleavages, grievances and suspicions" and a revolutionary air that carried a threat of mob rule. Radical Socialism might be the outcome, but Daniell deemed it more likely that "French realism, the national aptitude for compromise, and, above all, the influence of the individualistic peasant" would lead to "a kind of paternalistic democracy, emphasizing freedom of speech and social security." Daniell's long cable and wireless dispatches, originating in London, Paris, the Netherlands, the Lorraine front, or in Germany itself, continued to report on 1944 events military, political, and social. "On the spot," he described the robot bombs over England, the big events as well as the small incidents of the Allied advances, the grim German attack in December; and he discussed the political and social complexities of the Polish question and other inter-Allied problems.

Raymond Daniell is five feet six inches tall and has brown hair and eyes. He is an Episcopalian, a member of Delta Kappa Epsilon and the English Speaking Union, as well as the American Correspondents and Press Clubs in London.

References

N Y Herald Tribune p23 N 11 '41
N Y Times p21 N 7 '41 por; p28 O 8 '43
(Continued next page)

DANIELL, RAYMOND—*Continued*

Baldwin, H. W. and Stone, S. eds. We Saw It Happen 1938
Daniell, F. R. Civilians Must Fight 1941
Who's Who in America 1944-45

DANIELS, JOSEPHUS May 18, 1862- Newspaper publisher; author; former Secretary of the Navy and Ambassador to Mexico
Address: b. The News and Observer, Raleigh, N. C.

"A man is as old as his arteries and his interests. If he permits his economic, religious, or social arteries to harden, or loses interest in whatever concerns mankind ... he will need only six feet of earth." So speaks Josephus Daniels, Secretary of the Navy during the Wilson Administration, Ambassador to Mexico from 1933 to 1941, lifelong Democrat, Methodist, and Prohibitionist, and, at eighty-two, still editor and publisher of the Raleigh *News and Observer*. Daniels is also author of three volumes of reminiscences, *Tar Heel Editor* (1939), *Editor in Politics* (1941), and *The Wilson Era* (1944). The 1944 volume, described as a "valuable eye-witness account of a tremendous period," brings the memoirs up to the outbreak of the First World War. A fourth volume, which Daniels plans to write to complete the series, will be an account of the war years.

Josephus Daniels was born May 18, 1862 in the town of Washington, North Carolina—a town at that time under siege, sometimes in Confederate hands, sometimes in possession of the Federals. His father, Josephus Daniels, was a shipbuilder for the Confederacy in the Wilmington (North Carolina) Navy Yard, where he put ships in condition to run the blockade. When a cannoneer "made an orphan of Josephus Daniels before he was three years old," Mrs. Daniels, the former Mary Cleves, was left to rear her three sons alone. She supported them at first by keeping a small millinery and dressmaking establishment, later moving to Wilson, North Carolina, to become the town's postmistress. Her sons helped, too. Young Josephus worked as a cotton-picker, did odd jobs, and clerked in a drugstore while attending the Wilson Collegiate Institute.

Before he was twelve he had worked in a printing office. After that he was never to stay very far away from the smell of printer's ink. In his school debating society he frequently wrote on current topics, and when he was sixteen he and his brother Charles began to publish an amateur paper, the *Cornucopia*. Later young Josephus became one of the editors of *Our Free Blade*, and by the time he was eighteen, he was local editor of the weekly Wilson *Advance*, the paper for Wilson, Nash, and Greene Counties. He proved himself a businessman as well as journalist when he bought out his partners in the paper for $2,000 (his mother mortgaged their home to guarantee the payment) and put it on a paying basis. Though Daniels himself was not yet old enough to vote, his paper crusaded for such measures as a low tariff, and in 1881 its editor made his first speech—in favor of state-wide prohibition. Since then his papers have gen-

erally lived up to the policy of refusing to accept liquor advertisements.

Wilson was a town which, according to Daniels, contained but one white Republican, and Daniels himself was a stanch party Democrat. When in 1882 he and his brother Charles established in Kinston a second fighting paper, the *Free Press,* they took an active part in the election campaign, and their mother was later ousted as postmistress because of their political militancy. By 1884 Josephus Daniels was not only president of the North Carolina Press Association but also president of the Cleveland and Hendricks Club in Wilson. (Even before this he had hailed Grover Cleveland in the *Advance* as "the Democratic Moses who would lead his party into the Promised Land.") Cleveland's Presidential victory was the occasion for a celebration such as Wilson had never seen before.

Planning to practice law while editing his newspapers, in May 1885 Daniels entered the University Law School at Chapel Hill. In the meanwhile he had acquired the Raleigh *State Chronicle* and the *Farmer and Mechanic,* which he merged and named the *State Chronicle.* (The newspaper was published weekly.) He was admitted to the bar in October 1885, but he never practiced law, for the following year he decided to become a candidate for the office of Printer-to-the-State. In 1887 he was elected to that office, which bore a salary almost as large as the Governor's and which gave the Democratic Party imprimatur to its incumbent's newspaper. He was to be re-elected in 1889, 1891, and 1893, every time by an increased majority. On May 2, 1888 he was married to Addie Worth Bagley, the daughter of Major W. H. Bagley. They had four sons: Josephus, Worth Bagley, Jonathan Worth, and Frank A., 3rd. (In the fall of 1944 a new ship was named the S.S. *Addie Daniels* in honor of Mrs. Daniels, who died in 1943. Two granddaughters of the Daniels' officiated at the launching in Savannah.

The political influence of the *State Chronicle* continued to grow, particularly after it became a daily. Daniels had been strongly influenced by reading George Eliot's *Felix Holt, the Radical.* This, he says, turned his thought to "the labor problems, to labor's reaction, and to the championship of social justice, reasonable hours of work, collective bargaining, security legislation, the necessity for the organization of workers, and opposition to child labor, sweatshops, and treating men as 'hands.'" In the *State Chronicle* he therefore campaigned for aid to education, for the creation of a Railroad Commission in North Carolina, for free silver; he attacked the "Tobacco Trust", criticized the housing of mill workers, and advocated a child labor law and the reduction of working hours in the textile mills. "White supremacy," on the other hand, was to him as much a principle to be fought for as social justice. In 1892, when he sold the daily *State Chronicle* because it had been losing money and started the weekly *North Carolinian*, his new newspaper's campaign for "white supremacy" played a large part in the Democratic success in North Carolina, in the campaign that elected Cleveland to the Presidency of the United States.

Then the *North Carolinian* began losing money, too. Daniels wrote to the Secretary of the Interior saying that he would be happy to get a position in the Department of the Interior. In answer he received a telegram telling him to come to Washington for Cleveland's inauguration. On March 4, 1893 he arrived in Washington, and the morning after the inauguration was given temporary work in the Department at a salary of $1,600 a year. He was soon made chief of the Appointment Division, with a salary of $2,000, and eventually he became chief clerk, with a salary of $2,750, serving until 1895. He, his wife, baby, and Negro nurse lived on $100 a month, the rest being sent to Raleigh to keep the *North Carolinian* going. Says Daniels: "My youthful enthusiasm for Cleveland made me happy to serve even in a subordinate position in the administration of the man whose victory in 1884 had been to me the promise of a united America and of better government." It was only later that disillusionment came.

In the summer of 1894, while still serving as chief clerk in the Department of the Interior, Daniels bought the Raleigh *News and Observer,* consolidating the *State Chronicle* and *North Carolinian* with it. This was to become the only daily paper in the world having more subscribers than the population of the city in which it is published and so successful that before Daniels was sixty he was to refuse an offer of a million dollars from William Randolph Hearst. The years from 1893 to 1913 saw the rise of William Jennings Bryan, the beginnings of American imperialism, the emergence of Theodore Roosevelt, the administration of William Howard Taft, the split in the Republican Party, and the return of the Democrats to national power after sixteen years. In all of these events Daniels had his part to play—and not only as a newspaper publisher.

He was only thirty-four when he became a member of the Democratic National Committee from North Carolina. He was one of the first adherents of William Jennings Bryan, and during Bryan's campaign for the Presidency in 1896 he served as his publicity director, also accompanying the Democratic candidate on his swing through New England. (Even today Daniels believes that Bryan was cheated out of that election.) The *News and Observer* could always be relied upon to carry what was at that time the chief Democratic message to the South. In Daniels' own words, "Whenever there was any gross crime on the part of the Negroes, the *News and Observer* printed it in a lurid way, sometimes too lurid, in keeping with the spirit of the times." Daniels himself helped to establish Jim Crow railway cars, and his paper constantly demanded that the letter and spirit of the Jim Crow laws be carried out: "The people of North Carolina prefer to ride as they vote, as they go to church, and as they send their children to school," it said.

This era was also a period of personal journalism, and Daniels "practiced it to the nth degree." His newspaper opposed American imperialism in the Philippine Islands, battled with the Southern railroads entrenched in North Carolina politics, championed votes for women, defended strikers, campaigned against trusts.

Some called Daniels' paper the "Nuisance and Disturber," and a railroad once poured

JOSEPHUS DANIELS

$250,000 into another newspaper in an attempt to put him out of business, but no one ever accused the *News and Observer* of being dull. (Says Daniels: "Dullness is the only crime for which an editor ought to be hung.") And, though much of North Carolina is supposed to have disliked the *News and Observer's* editor, "he couldn't be scared and he couldn't be bought." In 1904, when arraigned for contempt of court, he refused to pay a $2,000 fine, saying he would go to jail rather than pay it. (He was released after three and a half days in jail.) And Daniels was not an inaccessible editor. In 1907, when a new building was to be erected for the *News and Observer* and a quiet sanctum in the rear was being planned for its editor, Daniels said: "The plan is all wrong. Put my office in the front, with the door wide open, so that anybody can see me at any time. No man can edit a paper in a town like Raleigh or a folksy state like North Carolina unless he is in close touch with all sorts of people, the more the better. And put this sign on my door: 'Office hours between 9 a.m. and 12:00 o'clock midnight. Can be seen at all other hours by calling Telephone 90.' "

The editor of the *News and Observer* was an enthusiastic advocate of Woodrow Wilson's nomination for the Presidency in 1912, and was a member of the Democratic Executive Committee which conducted the successful campaign for Wilson that year. He was rewarded with the Cabinet post of Secretary of the Navy, a post in which he served from March 5, 1913 to March 6, 1921. Thinking of himself as "managing editor of the Navy" rather than as a Cabinet official, Daniels stirred up controversy in Washington by some of his actions. Liberals criticized him in April 1914, when the Navy bombarded the Naval Academy at Vera Cruz and American troops landed in Mexico to oust the revolutionary Government of General Victoriano Huerta. Officers criticized him for taking

DANIELS, JOSEPHUS—*Continued*

away their shipboard beer and wine. Criticism came from other sources because of his attempts to make the Navy a "democracy," which, it was claimed, resulted in lack of discipline, lack of fighting spirit and fighting efficiency. It was also said that he showed much less interest in making the Navy a fighting force than in going after collusive bidders for armor plate, establishing vocational schools on shipboard for enlisted men, and increasing the number of chaplains in the Navy.

On Daniels' side it must be said that he has denied ordering the attack at Vera Cruz; certainly his hatred of war was strong, for he was the last member of Wilson's Cabinet to vote for the declaration of war in 1917. It is also true that "when it was called upon to meet the supreme test of war, the Navy was found ready—sound to the core, highly efficient prepared for action." Daniels himself went aloft in a rickety naval plane in order to encourage naval aviation. New records in construction were made; within six weeks after the United States entered the War there were American war vessels alongside those of Great Britain in Europe. Daniels was "rediscovered as one of the ablest heads the Navy ever had."

In 1919 Daniels' war addresses, entitled *The Navy and the Nation,* were published, and in 1922, after he had returned to Raleigh, his *Our Navy at War* appeared. These books were followed by his *Life of Woodrow Wilson* (1924), a "frank eulogy by a sincere and profoundly sympathetic admirer who . . . makes no claim to the perspective of the impartial historian."

Still active in national Democratic politics in 1924, the editor of the *News and Observer* helped to hold North Carolina's vote to McAdoo, but was spokesman for the committee that withdrew McAdoo from the balloting toward the end of a desolating month in New York. In 1928 Daniels opposed the nomination of Alfred E. Smith [44] for the Presidency, then afterward supported him because Smith could not change the "dry" laws, saying, "anyway, Hoover's [43] backers are wetter." In 1932, after refusing to run for the governorship of North Carolina, he made a speaking tour for Franklin Roosevelt [42], to whom he had given his national political start years before by making him his Assistant Secretary of the Navy. After Roosevelt's election he declined the post of head of a new transportation agency, but accepted the post of Ambassador to Mexico.

Immediately protests began, for the Mexicans remembered 1914. When Josephus Daniels arrived in Mexico City on April 15, 1933 the American Embassy was stoned. On April 24 he formally presented his credentials, however, and Mexican press comment on his speech was favorable. He and his wife then set out to improve Mexican relations by really putting a Good Neighbor policy into practice—and before long it was American conservatives who were attacking Daniels. He commended the new Mexican plan for universal popular education, thus acquiring Catholic disapproval. With the Franco [42] revolt in Spain, he realized from the first the deplorable effects the collapse of the Spanish republic would have on the Spanish-speaking countries of the Western Hemisphere, and, like the Mexican Government, he considered the loss of the Loyalist cause an American disaster. In February 1939 a Mexican newspaper reported that he had suppressed a strong note to Mexico on the land seizures; the following year, in a speech to American consuls in Mexico, he urged that American diplomatic officials and nationals refrain from interference in other countries' affairs. By October 1941, when Roosevelt announced Daniels' resignation because of his wife's ill health, there was universal regret among Mexicans.

Daniels resumed his old post as editor of the *News and Observer,* for his son Jonathan [42] had vacated it to join the Office of Civilian Defense, and the citizens of Raleigh found him as much the crusading journalist as ever. In July 1942 he was suggesting that all Army and Navy cadets at West Point and Annapolis be chosen by competitive examinations from Army and Navy ranks. In July 1943 he was writing strong editorials on the Navy's contract giving Standard Oil 36 per cent of the Navy's biggest reserve—the Elk Hills deal. In May 1944 he was calling for the setting up of one department of national defense—the consolidation of the Army and Navy: "The great god tradition still rules too strongly in Army and Navy strategy."

The third volume of Daniels' memoirs, *The Wilson Era,* which was published in November 1944, was thought by some reviewers to have a wider appeal than the first two volumes, which were described as "amazingly candid and untrammeled." The New York *Times* critic wrote: "Mr. Daniels is no Macaulay. . . . He is an editor and a storyteller who happened, to his great surprise, to become civilian chief of the Navy when the future of the United States was in terrible danger. . . . No biographer of Woodrow Wilson will fail to study Mr. Daniels' memoirs. Nor will those who write, in the years ahead, about Franklin D. Roosevelt, The World War of 1914 to 1918, or naval history." Gerald W. Johnson, writing in the New York *Herald Tribune,* points out that the Josephus Daniels of *The Wilson Era* looks like a much bigger man than the country editor who fought Tarheel politicians and privilege grabbers, but that he is still the same Josephus Daniels with the same courage and astuteness that marked those earlier years.

This is the *News and Observer*'s publisher, as one writer describes him: "Tall, heavy, a bit sloppy in appearance, his face is quite wrinkled. He usually wears a large black hat with flat top and flat brim. . . . And he is as friendly and affable as he looks. Has a reputation for a phenomenal memory for faces and names." Franklin Roosevelt still calls Daniels "the Chief," as he did back in 1917, and Daniels' own signatures in 1894 and 1944 can hardly be told apart. "I believe the Bible from cover to cover," says octogenarian Daniels, "except where it says a man's life is three-score years and ten. That, sirs, is a lie."

References

    Am Mercury 29:297-306 Jl '33
    Cur Hist 38:343-4 Je '33
    Lit Digest 115:8 Mr 25 '33
    Nation 153:476-7 N 15 '41 por

Newsweek 18:21 N 10 '41; 21:92-3 My 24 '43

Outlook 154:656 Ap 23 '30

Public 21:791-4, 822-5 Je 22-29 '18

Time 38:22 N 10 '41

Daniels, J. Tar Heel Editor 1939; Editor in Politics 1941; Wilson Era 1944

Who's Who in America 1944-45

DASHWOOD, MRS. EDMEE ELIZABETH MONICA (DE LA PASTURE)
See Delafield, E.M.

DAUSER, SUE S(OPHIA) (dô'sẻr) Sept. 20, 1888- Superintendent of the Navy Nurse Corps

Address: b. Bureau of Medicine and Surgery, Navy Dept., Washington, D.C.; h. 1900 F St., N. W., Washington, D. C.

Viewers-with-alarm have long inveighed against the assignment of women to overseas duty with the armed forces. And yet, while the Women's Reserves of the Navy and the Marine Corps were limited by Congressional decree to the continental United States, the most Victorian of conservatives took it for granted that the women nurses of the Navy—as well as the Army—serve wherever they are needed. Superintending the Navy Nurse Corps, which is serving afloat and ashore all over the world, is Captain Sue S. Dauser, a veteran whose rank is equivalent to the colonelcy of Florence A. Blanchfield [43], superintendent of the Army Nurse Corps, although the latter commands five times as many nurses.

The daughter of Francis X. and Mary Anna (Steuckle) Dauser, Sue Sophia Dauser was born in Anaheim, California, September 20, 1888. Graduated from the Fullerton High School in 1907, she attended Leland Stanford University for two years, after which she entered the California Hospital School of Nursing at Los Angeles. On her graduation in June 1914 Miss Dauser became surgical supervisor at the hospital, remaining in that position three years. In September 1917, five months after the entrance of the United States into the First World War, the twenty-nine-year-old nurse joined the Naval Reserve. One month later she entered Navy service, in which she has remained ever since.

After a one-month course of instruction at the Naval Hospital in San Diego, California, Miss Dauser was appointed a chief nurse, United States Naval Reserve, and placed in charge of the nursing activities of Base Hospital No. 3, which was organized in Los Angeles and in December 1917 mobilized in Philadelphia for shipment overseas. Eight months later, on July 10, 1918, her appointment as reserve nurse was terminated in order that she might be appointed nurse in the Regular Navy; the following day Miss Dauser was given this appointment and then immediately promoted to chief nurse, United States Navy. This was one month before the arrival of Base Hospital No. 3 in Edinburgh, Scotland, where it replaced a British naval hospital unit. (A base hospital is a semi-permanent unit, a fully equipped hospital which must nevertheless be capable both of sending mobile units wherever needed and of packing up and moving, as a unit, if troop movements make it necessary.)

For the three months remaining of the First World War, Miss Dauser was stationed at the base hospital in Scotland. After the Armistice, while awaiting transportation back to the United States, she was ordered to France for temporary duty in Brest. On her return, she was sent to the Naval Hospital at Brooklyn, New York, as chief nurse, and shortly afterward to the one at San Diego, California. Next she had a tour of sea duty in the hospital ship U.S.S. *Relief* on its cruise with the Pacific Fleet to Australia, New Zealand, and Samoa.

Although Navy nurses are not required to serve at sea except on hospital ships or when actually being transported to some point overseas, Miss Dauser was on duty in the *Argonne* in transport service from the East to the West Coast. When President Harding made the Alaskan cruise on the *Henderson* in 1923, she was aboard and nursed the President in his last illness.

From 1926 to 1928 Miss Dauser had "tropical duty" in Guam and the Philippines, after which she was made principal chief nurse in the San Diego hospital and, in 1931, transferred to Puget Sound, Washington, in the same capacity. Her next two assignments were at Mare Island, California (1934) and at the United States Naval Dispensary at Long Beach, California. There she was in charge of nursing activities from 1935 to 1939.

In 1939 Sue S. Dauser was made superintendent of the Navy Nurse Corps, responsible directly to the Surgeon General, Ross T. McIntire, personal physician to President Roosevelt [42]. As before, she had an officer's privileges but a special status. (Nurses had since 1908 been legally considered members of the Naval Service, though neither officers nor enlisted personnel.) As superintendent, her first duty was to organize the Naval Reserve Nurse Corps provided for by the Naval Reserve Act of 1938. Although reserve appointments were given to a steadily rising number of graduate nurses, the Nurse Corps numbered only 700—one-tenth the size of the Army Nurse Corps—when the United States entered the War. Working aboard her flagship, the hospital ship *Relief*, which moved with the Fleet on all its maneuvers, Miss Dauser was faced with the problem of building her corps up to the thousands required by a fighting navy. The Army offered nurses relative rank (officer's title and uniform, although not officer's commission, retirement privileges, dependents' allowances, or pay), while the Navy offered only vague "officer's privileges"—with the result that the Navy Nurse Corps was at a disadvantage in building up its reserves. This disparity was remedied in July 1942 by an Act of Congress, which provided that the Superintendent of the Nurse Corps receive the relative rank of lieutenant commander (senior rank, equivalent to an Army major). The injustice of less pay for the same rank ($90 for a nurse ensign, as compared with $150 base pay for a male ensign—and even that an improvement over the former $70 monthly for a nurse entering the service) was not remedied until the end of December 1942. And it was in February 1944 that Congress finally granted military commissions to members of the Navy Nurse Corps. This made official, though temporary, the relative rank of captain which had been granted to the Nurse Superintendent by

Bachrach

CAPT. SUE S. DAUSER

law the preceding December. Captain Dauser thus became the first American woman entitled to wear four gold stripes on the sleeve of her navy blue uniform. (Six months after the close of the War she will revert to the permanent relative rank of lieutenant commander.)

Throughout the fanfare attending the entrance of women into the armed forces and the publicizing of their commanders—Colonel Oveta Culp Hobby '42 of the Wacs, Captain Mildred H. McAfee '42 of the Waves, Major Ruth Cheney Streeter '43 of the Marines, and Captain Dorothy C. Stratton '43 of the Spars—Captain Dauser, who outranks them all, continued in her quiet and unpublicized way to command her 8,000 nurse officers. (They, in turn, are largely responsible for training and instructing the Navy's highly regarded enlisted hospital corpsmen.) Captain Dauser is described as soft-spoken and as having a firm pleasant face, brown eyes behind rimless glasses, and dark brown hair now turning gray. She is of the Catholic faith.

DAVENPORT, CHARLES B(ENEDICT) June 1, 1866—Feb. 18, 1944 Internationally known geneticist; author and editor of many scientific books and journals; noted for his research in animal, plant, and human heredity; was for thirty years director of the Carnegie Institution's Station for Experimental Evolution.

Obituary

N Y Times p13 F 19 '44 por

DAVENPORT, MARCIA June 9, 1903-
Author; music critic
Address: h. 1 East End Ave., New York City

Marcia Davenport has the sort of background which spells "glamour" to the public. Her mother, Alma Gluck, was known as one of the great lyric sopranos of the world; her stepfather is the celebrated violinist, Efrem

Zimbalist; her husband, Russell W. Davenport '44, is a leader of liberal thought; and she herself is a best-selling author whose writings have appeared in leading magazines since 1928.

Two years after her birth (New York, 1903), her mother was "discovered" and began to work hard at operatic training. "My life," says Marcia Davenport, "was not what most people consider a normal life for a child; that is, my mother had no room in her world for a child. I was fitted into my mother's existence along with the other exigencies. If I wanted companionship I had to come up to adult standards. Although my mother was very strict with me in the European fashion—which means that every detail of my conduct was known to her and sharply criticized—she gave me an absolute freedom in the range of my reading. . . . I did want to write books, and I knew it even then. I had a very lonely childhood except for books. I read fairy stories, and the people in them were my first companions."

When Marcia was four, Mme. Gluck's teacher, the late Maestro Arturo Buzzi-Peccia, returned to Europe. In order to continue her lessons, Mme. Gluck took Marcia and went along. "I marvel," Mrs. Davenport says now, "at the self-discipline, the strong character of a young and beautiful woman who was working terribly hard at music and yet would let herself be encumbered by a small child and all the annoyances that go with it." In Switzerland, Gatti-Casazza, then Director of the Metropolitan Opera House, happened to visit Buzzi-Peccia and hear Mme. Gluck. He immediately signed her to sing with the Metropolitan Opera Company.

From that time until the beginning of her schooling, little Marcia spent many hours sitting in the corners of opera houses while her mother rehearsed. In addition to being exposed to this musical "education" Marcia had to practice at the piano, "not because I had the least talent for it—we both knew that I hadn't any—but because she [my mother] believed, as I do, that work is most necessary for any human being; and also because she believed, as I do, that to permit a child to grow up illiterate in music is as bad as to permit general illiteracy. I think that it is just as necessary for anyone to know the way around in musical sources as to have read the classics of literature . . . and that it is no less desirable to be able to look at a sheet of music and to know what's on it and what the writer intended than it is to be able to look at a newspaper and understand what the print says."

Marcia was educated in the United States, attending the Friends School in Philadelphia and the Shipley School at Bryn Mawr. After two years at Wellesley College she returned to Europe, and finally was awarded the Bachelor's Degree by the University of Grenoble, France. Officially it was for "studies in French history and literature," but Mrs. Davenport says that what she did to earn it is "a permanent mystery." In April 1923, when she was not quite twenty, Marcia Gluck married Frank D. Clarke; and in March 1924, she became the mother of Patricia Delmas Clarke.

A year later, as a divorceé, Miss Gluck began her career as a writer of advertising copy.

From 1928 to 1931 she was a member of the editorial staff of the *New Yorker*; and on May 13, 1929 she was married to Russell W. Davenport, who became managing editor of *Fortune* shortly thereafter. Her first book, *Mozart*, was published in 1932. The *Saturday Review of Literature* says of it: "Marcia Davenport concludes the foreword of her life of Mozart with the statement that she has written 'neither a romance nor a textbook.' In this she is right. Hers is a carefully 'documented' account of one of the most extraordinary and most persistently misrepresented personalities of genius; she has accomplished her difficult and delicate task without the usual obligatory array of footnotes, and without allowing her keen and sympathetic treatment to get out of hand." *Mozart* has been translated into French, German, Spanish, and Portuguese.

Mrs. Davenport's second child, Cornelia Whipple Davenport, was born in April 1934. That year, after working in five different departments of the *New Yorker*, Marcia Davenport was chosen music critic of *Stage* Magazine, which position she occupied until 1939. Her second book, *Of Lena Geyer*, appeared in 1936 (when Mrs. Davenport was commentator on the Metropolitan Opera broadcasts), and resembled her first book in that it, too, was the biography of a musician, although a fictional one. Her story is told in the form of the facts and reminiscences collected by a great singer's biographer after her death. "Mrs. Davenport is not a literary stylist," said the *Manchester Guardian*, "She constantly misuses such words as 'fabulous' and 'phenomenal,' but she knows a great deal about music; her book is vital, her detail admirable, and in Lena Geyer she has created a character that can never be forgotten." John Erskine thought that "Mrs. Davenport is somewhat hard on singers, if she means that Lena's character is typical"; but the *Saturday Review of Literature* declared, "The memory of Lena Geyer as a great artist and a warmly lovable human being is not obscured by the history of her decline."

Mrs. Davenport spent five years on *The Valley of Decision*. Living in Pittsburgh for two years, she inspected the family records of Pittsburgh friends, interviewed steel mill managers and union heads, and collected upwards of 100,000 words of notes and charts on the steel industry. *The Valley of Decision* is a family saga, tracing the Scott Iron Works from the panic of 1873 to Pearl Harbor. In the words of *Time*, "Author Davenport has packed her book with descriptions of the unfeminine workings of Bessemers, open hearth furnaces, skip-hoists, cast-houses. The men who pump lifeblood through the heart of Pittsburgh come alive in her pages—Irish steelworkers of the 1870's, Slovaks and 'Hunkies' pouring in from the mills of Europe. Novelist Davenport's description of this hard, world-transforming valley of steel and furnaces is the most memorable part of her impressive work."

Reviews were generally favorable, although the *Catholic World* complained that "one would need the patience of Job to read the 788 pages of Marcia Davenport's interminable novel." That critic also condemned the por-

MARCIA DAVENPORT

trayal of wickedness and improprieties "to keep one's interest from flagging." Other reviews called *The Valley of Decision* "a rich and well-knit story . . . as enjoyable as it is distinguished," with "energy, boldness, and copiousness . . . a seeing eye, an understanding heart, and a surgeon's touch . . . a truly monumental work which never for one instant loses its quality of stirring human interest." The book appeared on five standard best-seller lists; and at the end of 1943, more than a year after its publication, it was still a best seller. MGM purchased it as a vehicle for Greer Garson [42], who was presumably to take the role of Mary Rafferty, an Irish "'tween-maid" who comes to work for the Scotts at fifteen and remains for seventy years. Mrs. Davenport is under contract to Paramount, also, to write an original story, tentatively called *Sophie Cooper*, which deals with the "public and private ambitions of an American woman, to be played by Claudette Colbert.

Although Mrs. Davenport "hates paid lecturing" and dislikes touring, she has made many lecture appearances for the United Czechoslovak Relief, of which she is a director, and the Russian War Relief, of which she is a member of the Executive Committee, women's division. A Democrat, in the fall of 1944 Mrs. Davenport campaigned for President Roosevelt [42], believing like her husband that Thomas E. Dewey's [44] election would mean "the loss of the peace." She works at her writing ten hours a day, confining her recreation to week-ends; her workplace is the book-lined living room of the East River apartment where she lives with her husband, Russell W. Davenport, and her two daughters. The girls are being brought up, like Mrs. Davenport herself, according to the standards of work and discipline which she inherited from her mother.

A zealot for hard work, Mrs. Davenport pursues the exacting avocation of needlepoint, the strenuous sport of sailing ("I must live

DAVENPORT, MARCIA—*Continued*

near a large body of water," she says, "or I can't function"), and the demanding recreation of listening to music. "Music to me is work. . . . When I listen to music it's with severe concentration. . . . I follow the score. I know just what each instrument is doing. I listen for the special developments that I know are to come. . . . It's a severe mental exercise."

Although the Davenports bought a large Vermont farm in 1932, they now live in the city. Mrs. Davenport says, "I hate the country and I don't like farms. I must live in the city or I can't work." The only way her husband could induce her to live for a brief time in the country was to give her a pet which could not be kept in a New York apartment. Mrs. Davenport is so nearsighted that, when she first saw this animal she thought her husband was bringing her a Great Dane pup; and so fond of cats that she was delighted to find it was a lion cub!

References

N Y Post p4 F 13 '43 il pors
N Y Times Book R p2+ F 28 '43 por
Who's Who in America 1944-45

DAVENPORT, RUSSELL W(HEELER)
July 12, 1899- Author; publicist
Address: h. 1 East End Ave., New York City

A poet and journalist with a background of industrialism, Russell W. Davenport never thought "free enterprise" meant opposition to other forms of freedom. An editor of the powerful Henry Luce '41 publications at thirty-eight, he turned his energies to politics at forty-two, becoming one of the late Wendell Willkie's '40 closest friends and advisers. In four years Davenport made himself notable as an eloquent and impassioned foe of isolationism, race discrimination, and injustice in all its forms; with Willkie's passing, leadership of the internationalist Republicans in the eastern United States gravitated to him.

Russell Wheeler Davenport was born in South Bethlehem, Pennsylvania, July 12, 1899, a descendant of New Haven Colony ministers. His father, Russell W. Davenport, Sr., was vice-president of Bethlehem Steel; his mother, the former Cornelia Whipple Farnum, had shocked her conservative Philadelphia circle by combining schoolteaching with her debutante activities. When young Russell was twelve he suffered from a siege of pneumonia which left his hearing permanently impaired. (Today he wears a hearing device which he does not use when conversation ceases to interest him.) For Russell's health, his family had to move to the less conservative atmosphere of California, where he attended the Thacher School at Ojai. Here he acquired the nickname of "Mitch"—perhaps from "Mitchy-Mitch," the pestiferous little brother in Tarkington's *Penrod*—by which he is still known. The background for his future internationalism was laid, perhaps, by his early schooling in Europe and by the summers the Davenports spent abroad; the inculcation of a love of freedom in him Davenport attributes to his mother.

Davenport was graduated from the Thacher School, just after the United States declared

war. "Most of my friends enlisted," he has been quoted as saying, "but they landed in camps peeling potatoes. None of that for me. I took my family on an automobile trip to New York, and when we arrived I joined the American Field Service. Then I went to Paris and enlisted in the American Army there." Davenport had wanted to be one of those dashing aviators who gave the only touch of glamour to a muddy and unglamorous war, but his defective hearing barred him from the air. He therefore "tried some lip reading," and was accepted as an ambulance driver, attaining the exalted rank of private, 1st class. Davenport enjoys the rare distinction of having been decorated with the Croix de Guerre twice. "They gave them out like watches," he explains, "figured they would give twenty here, twenty there. Just happened to hit me twice, that's all." The reason for the first award was that Davenport drove an ambulance to a battery under withering fire; the second Croix was given him for rescuing the mayor of a small town under terrific artillery bombardment, and driving him between the lines to safety. Beyond this, Davenport says, "Nothing happened to me. Oh, yes, I got a touch of malaria and I was gassed and my helmet was dented a few times. But I was fine."

Upon his discharge from the service, Davenport entered Yale University. At that time, according to his younger brother John (himself one of the editors of *Fortune*), "all his bad habits began." Chief among them is a preference for working at night, when there are fewer interruptions; this dates back to his freshman year, when he would begin all his assigned work at two in the morning and would work through until time for his nine o'clock class. With his hearing instrument off Davenport could work on, oblivious of the chatter and clatter of the all-night lunch stand in which he liked to study. Probably his huge consumption of coffee dates from that time; now he ordinarily drinks ten cups of coffee a day.

At Yale, too, young Davenport wrote poetry; became intercollegiate fencing champion ("because all the contests were held at night"); headed the Liberal Club, a group of "curious thinkers"; and was managing editor of the Yale *Literary Magazine*. He developed an interest in physics and metaphysics, but complains that "I can't ask people about the red shift of the nebulae. Damn few would know what I meant, whereas most people know their birth date." He now talks about astrology rather than astronomy. Davenport was graduated in 1923 with honors in philosophy and ethics, and then, so the story goes, was advised by his professors that he was too poetical to be a philosopher, and too philosophical to be a poet!

The next few years were spent trying to find a career for which he was neither too poetical nor too philosophical. Davenport did have one long poem published (*California Spring*), but gave up poetry when, after years of work on a group of lyrics, he accidentally left them in a taxi. For a while, when he was still writing poetry, he rented a cottage in an artists' colony in Colorado and "painted pictures of anything. Boy, they were terrible." He spent some months on the research staff of a new magazine called *Time*, and a few more as a reporter for the Spokane (Washington) *Review*. Then came an interlude in Paris, where he wrote several stories and a novel. The book, published in 1929 as *Through Traffic* (in England, as *Abominable Branch*) was the first—and, as it turned out, the last—of a planned series with businessmen as heroes. A reviewer called it "a practice flight by one who may live—such are the rewards of industry—to spin much finer. tales for your delight. Mr. Davenport's faults at present appear to be merely those inherent in youth and inexperience." In 1929, too, Davenport was married to Alma Gluck's daughter Marcia, an eminently successful author and music critic who writes as Marcia Davenport [44], and who was then on the editorial staff of the *New Yorker*.

Soon after his marriage Davenport joined the staff of *Fortune* Magazine. In 1937 he was made managing editor, a position he held until in 1940 he resigned to become Wendell L. Willkie's personal adviser and chief of his research staff for the Presidential campaign. Davenport first met Willkie at a *Fortune* Round Table Conference on unemployment, and was "taken by storm." *Fortune's* sister publication, *Life*, commented: "Russell ('Mitch') Davenport is a charter Willkieite as the result of conversational affinity. Their first meeting provoked an intellectual reaction something akin to the action of sodium on water. Ideas and theories fizzed and sputtered all over the room. . . . No politician, Mr. Davenport is Willkie's chief braintruster, the adviser on whom the candidate principally relies for guidance in speech-writing, selection of issues and formulation of campaign policy. . . . Davenport's diversified knowledge and trained editorial mind are of inestimable value on Willkie's current campaign trip. And Davenport is far more than a political adviser. He is also one of Wendell Willkie's closest personal friends." Actually it had been Davenport who had started the Willkie boom: the *Fortune* editor had seen an article by Willkie entitled "We, the People" and had had it published in the April 1940 *Fortune,* accompanied by an editorial on the merits of the author. Reprinted in pamphlet form by the thousand, this was the beginning of the Willkie-for-President campaign. Davenport worked tirelessly, "twenty-four hours a day, seven days a week," first for Willkie's nomination, then for his election. Financing himself, he worked in a little office with six assistants, beginning usually at midnight and exhausting them with his driving energy. (This strenuous vitality seems to be a family characteristic. At seventy-eight his mother still managed her leather goods shop in Philadelphia, still came into New York once a week or oftener to deal with wholesalers.)

In 1941 Davenport returned to *Fortune* as chairman of the board of editors. When Colonel Charles A. Lindbergh [41] made his first speech for the America First Committee, Davenport immediately came forth with a rebuttal, pointing out that "the force that drives him [Hitler [42]] on is a great revolution . . . an attack against freedom, against the free way of life. . . . Therefore Hitler's attack is an attack against America. Free

RUSSELL W. DAVENPORT

and democratic America is his ultimate objective. We cannot escape that terrible fact." Four months later Davenport joined the Office of Civilian Defense, under Mayor La Guardia [40], as head of a research bureau.

As early as February 1941 Davenport warned that "The democratic world that we have hitherto known is collapsing. Even if it succeeds in defeating the dictators, it cannot survive. The internal struggles of the last ten years have weakened it. The supreme effort of the War will shatter it. And what shall we put in its place?" The solution he offered was a world "based upon those values which democracy has discovered and proved to be good; a civilization of liberty and trade, and science applied to the needs of man. . . . There must be one common purpose among the nations who join in the open market— to raise the standard of living. Not just their own, but the standards of all the others. Since our standard is highest, we must take the leadership."

In 1942 Davenport was transferred to the tremendously successful weekly picture magazine, *Life*, as chief editorial writer. In the same year he was named president of "Citizens for Victory," which, he said, "liquidated the Committee to Defend America," and incorporated the Council for Democracy. He described it as "an experiment to determine whether people in a democracy can take care of themselves in wartime and take the responsibility for their own morale." (In August 1944 this was incorporated into Americans United for World Organization.)

In February 1944 Davenport left *Life* for "health reasons" and to do independent writing. That June he declared that the Roosevelt Administration, particularly the State Department, had "failed to give the American people the kind of leadership they are entitled to expect in a world crisis," and also demanded to be "convinced that the Republican Party is engaged in a crusade to interpret the American idea as a world idea." "I feel confident

DAVENPORT, RUSSELL W.—*Continued*
that I speak for millions of Republicans and
independents," he stated, "when I say that, if
my party fails me on this, the fundamental
issue of our time, I will not support that party."
That August, after the Republican National
Convention had nominated Governor Thomas
E. Dewey '44 for President, Davenport denounced both platforms as inadequate, citing
particularly the Democrats' failure to "give
meaning to the indispensable principle of racial
equality," and the Republicans' "dereliction in
domestic and foreign policy." Hailing the
newly organized Liberal Party, which was
formed originally of the Right Wing of Sidney Hillman's '40 American Labor Party, he declared, "I have the conviction that labor and
liberalism will be synonymous in the post-War
world." From that time on Davenport threw
himself into the work of convincing the public that there was "only one issue in this campaign—the issue of peace." He wrote what he
believed America ought to stand for, first in
prose, then in lectures, then in a sixty-two-page
poem, *My Country*.

This testament, which begins,

America is not a land of ease.
  We have not paused from action to beget
Heroic simile and song and frieze;
  We have no empire of the mind as yet,

states Davenport's main theme:

Yes, there are things to fear
(But let us fear the ones that there are
To fear, let us fear only in freedom's
  name) . . .
. . . .
It is not ours: we cannot bound its scope!
. . . .
But ever outward, over all the earth,
Where deserts wait the skulls, or eagles
  climb,
We must put forth the products of our
  birth;
Our faith, our laws, the meaning of our
  will;
. . . .
Put forth, not as in conquest, but to spread
Assurance of a world community,

and ends with the declaration,

Freedom is not to limit, but to share;
And freedom here is freedom everywhere.

Reviewers praised the skill with which the
poet handled his verse forms, particularly the
difficult *terzarima*; Irwin Edman called *My
Country,* "as a whole . . . an undeniable poetic
experience of a high order, though there are
parts of it that by purely literary standards
must be called less than good." Most agreed
that its strength and meaning lay in its power
to "make the pulses beat like drums and the
eyes grow misty," as the New York *Times*
reviewer put it. Said playwright Robert Sherwood '40, "There are no words in my vocabulary adequate for describing how deeply moved
and impressed I was by *My Country.* It is a
great job and, I think, a historic one." Of
My Country Virginia Kirkus '41 wrote: "Laud-
able sentiments all in a paean to American
progress which may find an audience—not
poetry lovers."

The first printed copy of *My Country*
reached its author on the very night of Willkie's death, and as Davenport read it he began
to realize he had unconsciously made Willkie
"the hero of the book," that is, had put Willkie's thoughts into poetic form. Although dis-
claiming any intention of speaking for his
friend, Davenport took up some of his burden
of leadership, becoming head of the Independent Republican Committee for Roosevelt, Eastern Division. Although he was "profoundly
dissatisfied with many aspects of the Roosevelt
Administration," and opposed to the theory of
a fourth term, he announced his support of the
President on the foreign policy issue, recommending that New Yorkers cast their votes on
the Liberal Party line, and called that party
"genuinely independent . . . controlled neither
by city bosses nor by bureaucrats."

A *PM* reporter, interviewing Davenport ten
days after his feverish campaigning had ended
with Roosevelt's re-election, found that "Davenport looks as though he knows where he's
going and indeed is on his way this very instant, each time he outlines each possible path.
. . . All of Davenport's paths are broad paths,
they all lead to magnificent destinations, and
none can be traversed in less than eight years."
Meanwhile he was considering developments
in his non-ivory New York tower, an office
filled with "hundreds and hundreds of books,
files and files of newspapers, a grand piano, a
specially built phonograph with volumes of
symphonies . . . a Cézanne print and a Michelangelo print on the walls . . . cigaret ashes on
the Persian carpet . . . a fireplace and unrelated easy chairs . . . and always that elevator
to get you the hell out in one minute flat."

Davenport loves the country, and himself
helped build the "very big house and things"
on the large Vermont farm he bought in 1932.
But the Davenports live in New York with
two daughters, Cornelia Whipple and Patricia
Delmas Clarke, because Mrs. Davenport hates
the country and dislikes farms. The two
share a passion for sailing their yawl, he as
navigator and she as the rest of the crew.
Davenport's other hobby is flying (although
he was not allowed to pilot a warplane), and
he has retained his skill at fencing.

Sylvia Porter '41 says of Davenport, "When
he smiles—and he smiles frequently—his
pale-green eyes sparkle and there is a suggestion of dimples in his smooth-shaven face.
There's something completely disarming about
this man with the mussed tan-brown hair, big
ears, and expensive suits that are rarely
pressed and never fit. [*Life* printed a full-
page picture of Davenport once, with a large
hole in one sole conspicuously in the foreground.] His conversation is a peculiar mixture of slang, when talking about himself or
other people, and of perfectly phrased sentences, when discussing liberty, democracy, or
freedom of enterprise. He'll quote the Bible
or a line out of Herbert Spencer at the drop
of a hat." Tall and solidly built, Davenport
has thick eyebrows which often develop a
satanic upward twist.

As Davenport puts it, "I have a helluva
stomach from overwork and too much coffee"
—not to mention afternoon tea and evening
highballs. He therefore carries a small
bottle of medicine wherever he goes and keeps

a large one in his office. He used to drink this like water during his conversations with Willkie. An Episcopalian, he was described by a former classmate as "intensely religious . . . but he hated being forced to go to chapel." Davenport belongs to Psi Upsilon and is a member of the University, Century, and Players Clubs, all of New York. He is, of course, a Republican, and a fervent believer in liberty, democracy, and "freedom of enterprise"—"those big ideas that make everything else seem unimportant." Albright College in Reading, Pennsylvania, awarded him an LL.D.

References

Life 7:79 S 30 '40 il por
N Y Herald Tribune X p7 Ag 18 '40 il pors
N Y Post Mag p25 O 30 '44 por
PM p14 N 17 '44 por
Who's Who in America 1944-45

DAVIS, NORMAN H(EZEKIAH) Aug. 9, 1878—July 2, 1944 Chairman of the American Red Cross since 1938, financier, and diplomat; was foreign emissary under Presidents Wilson, Coolidge, and Hoover '43, finally receiving the title of Ambassador at Large under President Roosevelt '42; known for his efforts in the cause of disarmament after the First World War; was strong advocate of the League of Nations; see sketch 1940 Yearbook.

Obituary

N Y Times p11 Jl 3 '44 por

DAVIS, ROBERT C(OURTNEY) Oct. 12, 1876—Sept. 2, 1944 Executive director of the New York Chapter of the American Red Cross since 1932; at death was a major general in the United States Army, retired; participated in four major conflicts during thirty years in Regular Army; won many decorations both from his own and allied governments; was an administrator of exceptional ability.

Obituary

N Y Times p27 S 3 '44 por

DE BONO, EMILIO (GIUSEPPE GASPARE GIOVANNI) *See* Bono, E. G. G. G. de

DE CASTELNAU, EDOUARD DE CURIERES *See* Castelnau, E. de C. de

DE HAUTECLOCQUE, JACQUES LECLERC *See* Leclerc, J.-P.

DE HAVILLAND, OLIVIA *See* Fontaine, J. and de Havilland, O.

DEJONG, DAVID C(ORNEL) (de-yong' cor'nel) June 9, 1905- Author

Address: b. c/o Harper and Brothers, 49 E. 33rd St., New York City; h. 119 Benefit St., Providence, R.I.; 845 Oakhill St., Grand Rapids, Mich.

Born in Holland, brought to the United States at the age of thirteen, and "Americanized" the hard way, David C. DeJong has won genuine distinction as a novelist by writing about his life both in the Netherlands and in the United States. Some of his experiences are to be found in his early novels; and the full story of his family and early boyhood has

been told in the autobiographical *With a Dutch Accent* (1944). According to critical opinion, that book deserves "an honorable position alongside the biographies or thinly disguised autobiographical fiction of such adopted sons of America as Rölvaag, Lewisohn, Adamic '40, and McFee."

David Cornel DeJong was born in Blija, Friesland, the Netherlands, on June 9, 1905. His parents, Raymond R. and Jantje deJong, were strict Calvinists: his Calvinistic upbringing, first in Holland and later in Grand Rapids, Michigan, was the dominant influence of his early years. Shortly after David was three his father, a carpenter, moved with his family to Wierum to take over the grandfather's building business. In this town, "hugging an elbow of the dike," David would have to learn to skate and to wear wooden shoes, "or the people would be offended." "I was reputed to have been a brilliant and unusual child," he writes. "Every so often I'm still reminded that if I hadn't become so willful, or so flighty, or so American, I might today be an ardent Dutch divine, an incomparable exegete, a great saver of souls in Borneo."

Although he was obviously not destined for "the cloth," young David's imagination led him to people the family's fuel room with Lost and Condemned Souls and to play biblical games in which God's wrath was always about to materialize. The special Christian school where the students learned they were "covenant children of the elect" didn't please David; and the headmaster considered him a "prideful boy" who would surely come to no good. His early schooling was often interrupted because of his ill health. "Physically I'd become quite a problem." He was allergic to many foods; he could not take part in games, so took to reading instead. "In spite of being absent a good deal, I regularly won all the prizes offered, especially if they were for arithmetic or geography." Having finished the six forms of school at eleven, David was then considered "of age" and, further schooling being financially beyond the family, it was decided to make him a member of "Ebenezer," the church's young men's society. He had to go to long solemn meetings where the young Calvinists tackled problems of predestination and divine grace and smoked long black cigars.

Then, when David was twelve, things suddenly looked better. His parents, who had long talked about going to America, definitely decided to migrate: they even mentioned the city where they'd live: Grand Rapids, in the state of Michigan. David's "new life," which began aboard ship, made a tremendous impression on him. Then some harrowing experiences on Ellis Island were compensated for in part by the exciting train ride across America to Grand Rapids. There the family moved into one of "a row of ugly little houses" in a neighborhood "entirely of Hollanders, all of the same faith" as they were. The house "had no toilet, nor even a water tap. . . . Mother sat down and wept." Even worse was the hostility of the "Christian" neighbors: the American-born Dutch boys, especially, made life miserable for the newcomers, singsonging their ceaseless

Dutchman, Dutchman, belly fulla straw,
Can't say nothin' but ja ja ja.

DAVID C. DEJONG

Soon, however, David got a job: a magnificent one that paid 50c a day for digging up dandelions in a small park. He was becoming an American.

But, because of his mother's long illness, he had to take care of a sickly baby and keep house for his active young brothers. His mother grew worse; and it was only the coming of a gaunt, homely "practical" nurse that gave the boy his first contact with true kindliness. She took the family under her wing—she even told David to go out and play. But he was fourteen, and had never learned how to play. "For the time being I just stood crying in the street, and didn't know what else to do. This, then, was love. This, then, was Christ's teaching put into practice. . . . No wonder they had crucified Him, and now twisted His Commandments their own way. This love was almost too much to receive, let alone to give."

David found himself more and more against the ultra-pious Reformed Dutch atmosphere of his neighborhood that opposed his longing to enter the real American world of baseball, sodas, moving pictures. At fifteen he was graduated from eighth grade; and, he says, "all summer afterward I worked as hard as I possibly could, hoping I might earn enough to be sent to high school in September." He worked in a drugstore; then, after a course at business school, got a job in a bank for a time, at $40 a month. "For the first time in my life, I was ashamed that I had to explain that I had been born in the Netherlands. . . . I had become an American, I told myself. . . . I realized only one thing concretely, unmistakably: I didn't want to be walking anywhere else."

After high school DeJong entered Calvin College in Grand Rapids and, following interludes of study at the University of Chicago and University of Wisconsin, he received his B.A. in 1929. At the Christian Reformed college he "managed to be on the disciplinary

committee's probation list for all of his college career except the first two months and last three days." As a senior he began writing, first poetry, then short stories. In 1930 he taught high school in Edmore, Michigan, to earn enough to continue his education; and in 1932 he went on a fellowship to Duke University at Durham, North Carolina, where he got his M.A. degree. His poems and short stories were then beginning to appear in *Poetry, Scribner's,* the *Virginia Quarterly Review,* etc. He entered Brown University to work toward a Ph.D. in 1933. In 1934, however, when his first novel was published, he decided to devote his time wholly to writing and translating. Accordingly, he moved to Providence, Rhode Island, in which vicinity he has since lived. Over the period of years from 1930 to 1943 he has written some forty short stories, in addition to articles and poetry.

Belly Fulla Straw, the chronicle of a Dutch immigrant family, was called "an extremely well-written novel . . . a rich and complete work with sound descriptions and penetration into the depths of character." It was followed in 1938 by *Old Haven,* which won the Houghton Mifflin annual fellowship for fiction for that year. Of it Howard Mumford Jones wrote: "Slow moving, rich in texture, built as solidly as the Dutch town wherein most of the action takes place, *Old Haven* is an extraordinary novel which makes most current fiction in comparison thin and pale. . . . It is without any qualification the ablest prize novel published this year." The book was not only successfully received in America, but was translated into six foreign languages.

In 1939 DeJong returned to Holland for a visit after several months' medical treatment for a paralysis of the vocal cords. The trip was the first time he had seen his native land since boyhood. Before that he had translated two books from the Dutch—Leonard Roggeveen's *Old Man Daantje's Beard* (1935) and C. Spoelstra's *Express to the East* 1937). His next novel, *Light Sons and Dark,* appeared in 1940. This, the story of an American family living on a nearly worthless Middle Western farm, was described as "a novel of hard realism and spiritual intensity", "strangely moving and cleansing." *Day of the Trumpet* (1941) returned to Holland for its setting—the story of a family in a small Dutch city during the opening war years, 1939 and 1940. "Without reservations," wrote Pierre van Paassen [42] of it, "*Day of the Trumpet* is an exceptionally mature work. . . . It was a dangerous undertaking on which DeJong embarked, for few writers have succeeded in steering clear of the melodramatic when their subject is dramatic. It also required poise and confidence to tackle events so close to the present and stretching so far into an uncertain future. But above all it took a sensitive and seasoned artist to write simply of people in the midst of impending catastrophe and to see them as they really are."

It was not until 1942 that DeJong's first book of poems, *Across the Board,* appeared—and met with a considerably less favorable reception than his fiction. One reviewer found the poems "hardly more than a collection of labored words and phrases arbitrarily divided into stanzas, with titles that bear no ascertainable relation to the pieces they purport to describe." Said Ruth Lechlitner in the New York *Herald Tribune Books*: "The general composition sometimes becomes diffuse and remote, lacking sharp focus or dynamic impact," but "more nearly than any other contemporary, Mr. DeJong approaches Wallace Stevens in his ability to take off from earthy fact into heights where humanity, foregoing its small concerns and petty memories, may walk in a fifth dimension of poetry in which imagination becomes pure reality."

A novel of DeJong's also appeared in 1942. It was *Benefit Street* (the locale of his home in Providence), which tells a story of fourteen tenants in a Providence boardinghouse and ends with the hurricane of September 1938. Milton Hindus called it "exciting enough to make you regret that you can't grab the first train out to Providence."

When *With a Dutch Accent*, his autobiography, appeared in 1944, it won high critical notice. Clara G. Stillman wrote: "The tempo of this book is slow at times, but this slowness seems to express its essence. . . . One has the sense of participating in a fundamental life pattern: in the slow, persistent rise of sap, in plant-like reaching for crevices, in compensatory branching toward light."

The picture on the jacket of De Jong's *With a Dutch Accent* is reproduced from one of his own water colors. Richard A. Cordell, the critic, has written that DeJong is also "a poet and painter as well as a writer," who not only describes the Dutch scene but "paints it and invests it with authentic beauty, not with the picturesque, inconsequential trappings of Dutch life that serve as tourist bait."

This author-poet-artist is tall, blond, blue-eyed; among his recreations are skating and swimming, and he likes cats, horses, and horse racing. He is unmarried and currently divides his time between working in his vegetable garden and on a new novel, as yet untitled.

References

New York Herald Tribune Books p4 F 20 '44 por
Sat R Lit 27:24 F 19 '44
DeJong, D. C. With a Dutch Accent 1944
Kunitz, S. J. and Haycraft, H. eds. Twentieth Century Authors 1942
Who's Who in America 1944-45

DELAFIELD, E(DMEE) M(ONICA) 1890—Dec. 2, 1943 In private life Mrs. Edmée Elizabeth Monica de la Pasture Dashwood; author; playwright; best known for her "gently satirical" novels portraying middle class English life; most famous work was *Diary of a Provincial Lady* (1931).

Obituary

N Y Times p23 D 3 '43 por

DELONCLE, EUGENE (dœ-loɴ'cle ü-zhañ') (?)—Jan. (?) 1944 Founder of the extreme Rightist French political organization, the Cagoulards ("hooded men"), under the Republic; became an ardent collaborationist when the Germans took control of Paris; reported dead by Vichy radio January 9, 1944.

Obituary

N Y Times p42 Ja 9 '44

DE LUCE, DANIEL (de lüce) June 8, 1911- Foreign correspondent
Address: b. c/o The Associated Press, 50 Rockefeller Plaza, New York City

A hackneyed pun in the Associated Press foreign news department is "De Luce is on da loose again." Daniel De Luce has traveled more than 100,000 miles. He has seen the Second World War from its beginning in Poland, and has followed it through Greece, Burma, North Africa, Sicily, and Italy. He has written vivid stories on Polish refugees, Greek artillerymen, Indian rioters, and the American G.I. When in May 1944 it was announced that he had won the Pulitzer Prize for his reporting of international affairs it was for no particular piece of reporting—but no one doubted that his exploit in October 1943, when he became the first American correspondent to return to Yugoslavia in two and a half years, had something to do with it.

Born in Yuma, Arizona, June 8, 1911, Daniel De Luce first joined the Associated Press in San Francisco eighteen years later, after being graduated from Los Angeles High School. When he attended the University of California in Los Angeles he continued to work a forty-eight-hour-week in A.P.'s Los Angeles bureau. This did not, however, prevent him from being graduated from the University in 1934 with Phi Beta Kappa honors. He had always wanted to be a foreign correspondent, and it didn't take him long to get abroad, after a period working for the Los Angeles *Examiner* as well as the Associated Press. In September 1939 he left his station in Budapest to cover the closing portions of the Polish campaign. From Lwów, where he found himself in a hotel with his wife, he wrote one of the War's first air-raid eyewitness dispatches. "As I write . . . two German bombers are raining heavy bombs. . . . The table under my hand is shaking like something alive. If [the hotel] holds together until I can get this off to Romania then I will believe in miracles." "One De Luce," commented H. L. Mencken upon reading this dispatch, "is worth all the gaudy journalistic wizards who sit in the safe hotels of unbombed capitals and tell us, not what has happened, but what they think."

And De Luce continued to tell the world "what happened." He saw the Italian adventure in Albania. He was with the Greeks during the fighting against the Italians, often writing dispatches from advanced Greek bases not a hundred yards from hidden Italian machine gun nests. When the Germans defeated the Greeks he escaped with his wife to Turkey in a fishing boat, and when the British and Russians occupied Iran he was there, too. He was with the British when they retreated from Burma in the spring of 1942, and he escaped in ten days by hiding in dry river beds and dodging Japanese strafers before getting a 2,000-mile jeep ride to Calcutta. By

DANIEL DE LUCE

this time he had sent grim stories about Allied inadequacies back to America. "Boys with matchless courage are being slaughtered because they are in inadequate numbers, ill-trained, poorly equipped. . . . The last tired companies of what were proud battalions . . . are in a galling retreat." What he wrote about India (in an article for *Collier's* in December 1942) was only a little more cheerful, for there was a species of civil war going on in Calcutta by the time he reached it. "This affair in Calcutta might be likened to New York, if the Japs were waiting up in Canada, and native rebels on the island of Manhattan had seized and isolated Greenwich Village and the Bowery, and Montana-born cops were ordered to clean them up."

After a rest in the United States to recover from malaria and dysentery, De Luce was assigned to North Africa. Early in 1943 he covered the American combat forces fighting their way into Tunisia, and later he covered the invasion of Sicily with the Americans. The invasion of Italy itself found him with the British 8th Army—and on September 15, 1943 British and American war correspondents with that Army made the first contact with the American 5th Army in Italy. De Luce arrived at 5th Army headquarters almost simultaneously with General Sir Harold R. L. G. Alexander '42, commander in chief of the Allied ground forces under Eisenhower '42, who was making his first visit to the battle scene. Said Alexander, "It was quite a trip." "Not half so tough as getting out of Burma with you, sir," De Luce replied. "The General, his face as dusty as mine, smiled at the recollection. 'You chaps get around extraordinarily well,' he commented."

One day the next month there was a flash from the A.P. Bureau chief at Algiers to the Manhattan headquarters of the Associated Press: DE LUCE MADE TRIP INTO BALKANS WHICH ARRANGED ITALY. WILL WRITE SERIES

STORIES. DE LUCE DESERVES HIGHEST CREDIT. Then came the first dispatch, with its sensational dateline, "A Partisan Brigade Headquarters in Yugoslavia."

If De Luce had become the first American correspondent to return to Yugoslavia in two and a half years and to get an eyewitness account of the Partisans, it was not because the trip had been made easy for him. He crossed the Adriatic from Italy to Yugoslavia in a small fishing boat with a wheezy engine, risking capture and death. As *Time* Magazine describes it, the little vessel dropped the young reporter on the rocky Dalmatian coast shortly before dawn and he climbed soundlessly into the wet woods, feeling his way to the appointed rendezvous with the Partisans. He was then passed swiftly from hand to hand, always upward, away from the sea, into the Dinaric Alps. The Partisans made full notes of all they told De Luce during his four-day trip, which included an afternoon with a Partisan brigade commander, going over maps, plans, and requirements. These notes were then forwarded to Tito '43 at his Bosnian headquarters.

The American reporter then wrote five articles on the Partisans, four of which were published (the censors "slightly mutilated" two of the published articles, halted the fifth entirely). De Luce's conclusions were: "Tito has welded his guerrillas into a tightly disciplined and hotly idealistic force that visibly shows more enthusiastic determination than any outfit I have seen since I met Major General Vasilly Novikoff's Caucasus army during the British-Russian occupation of Iran." "Communists and non-Communists are united by a common aim—resistance to Germany and the restoration of Yugoslavian freedom. Today I saw black-robed Catholic priests raise clenched right fists in greeting Partisan officers." "I've found not one scrap of evidence of Partisan terror." In January 1944 the Free Yugoslav radio, the organ of the Partisans, broadcast De Luce's series of dispatches, praising him for the accuracy and integrity of his reporting. After his trip, however, the Allied military authorities in Italy imposed restrictions on journeys to Yugoslavia. De Luce himself was the subject of an official investigation and report, but it could not be proved that he had violated any regulation. Efforts made to obtain permission for him to return as a correspondent attached to the Partisans proved futile, although Tito made two specific requests and offered to furnish transportation for him. On March 28, 1944 De Luce telegraphed his New York office that he had obtained "the only travel order issued a correspondent by Tito, but using it would make me liable to military arrest and disaccreditation by the Mediterranean command."

As a member of the A.P. staff in Italy on the Anzio beachhead, the tall (six feet three), blond, blue-eyed reporter was typing a story there when informed he had won the Pulitzer Prize in May 1944. "It's swell," he said. "Any newspaperman would be proud to receive this reward, and I am glad I was lucky enough to be in a place to get this break before the Allies shut the door on reporters going to Yugoslavia." Not many days later, on May 25, he was also "lucky enough" to be present when the two Allied fronts in Italy were united for the first time.

References

N Y Times p16 My 2 '44 por
Time 42:58 O 18 '43 por

DE MENTHON, FRANCOIS *See* Menthon, F. de

DEMPSEY, MILES CHRISTOPHER
Dec. 15, 1896- British Army officer
Address: b. c/o War Office, London

Lieutenant General Miles Christopher ("Lucky") Dempsey, C.B., D.S.O., M.C., is the young commander of the British Second Army which at the beginning of September 1944 sliced through the heart of Belgium and into Holland in less than forty-eight hours. Dempsey is said to be as able a tactician as General Montgomery '42, who commands the Twenty-first Army Group of which his Second Army is a part, and he is "a soldier who can describe foreign terrain so vividly from a map that it becomes almost a pictorial reality for his listeners." His Army's dash through Amiens, Arras, and Vimy Ridge "will produce some day a thousand sentimental essays. In two days these 1944 Britishers raced over battlefields that held and bled their fathers for more than two years during World War I."

Born on December 15, 1896, this youthful British general is the son of A. F. Dempsey of Hoylake, Cheshire, England. In 1915, after being graduated from the Shrewsbury School and Sandhurst Royal Military College, he was commissioned a second lieutenant in the Royal Berkshire Regiment. During the First World War he served in France, Belgium, and Iraq; he was wounded, mentioned in dispatches, and awarded the Military Cross.

Between wars Dempsey passed through the Staff College, commanded a company at the Royal Military College, Sandhurst, and served as staff captain at the War Office, brigade major in the Aldershot Command, and general staff officer, grade 2, with the Union Defence Force in South Africa. At intervals he returned to his regiment. But, although he had showed promise as a future commander of high quality while still at the Staff College, peacetime promotion was slow. In 1921 he was made a captain; in 1932 he became a major in the Fifth Infantry Brigade, Aldershot; and at the beginning of the Second World War he was a lieutenant colonel.

It was in the Second World War that he was given a chance to show what he could do, and he soon became one of the rapidly promoted officers in the British Army. In November 1939 he was made an acting brigadier and assumed the command of an infantry brigade of Royal Berkshires. During the "phony" war period he organized a pack of hunting hounds to provide an additional form of recreation for his men; and "when the real test came, in the spring of 1940, Dempsey's men distinguished themselves again and again, finally taking part in the rear-guard action at Dunkerque which saved the major portion of the British Army." He was awarded the Distinguished Service Order, and after Dunkerque was appointed to the General Staff to assist in the creation of a new army.

In June 1941 Dempsey was chosen to form a new armored division, which he commanded with the rank of acting major general. By December 1942 he was acting lieutenant general in command of the 13th Corps, a part of Montgomery's 8th Army, which was then chasing the Germans through Libya. Dempsey continued to command the 13th Corps as it fought from the Mareth Line through Enfidaville and Sicily and up the toe of Italy, taking part in the campaigns in Sicily and Italy until January 1944, and being made a Companion of the Bath for his gallant services there. By this time he was known as the 8th Army's expert in combined operations, for he had made at least nine different landings. In one, at Termoli, on the Adriatic coast of Italy, the surprise was so complete that General Heidrich, the German paratroop commander, had to flee in pajamas.

Montgomery had kept an eye on this young tactician, and when he returned to England for an important job in the coming invasion of France he brought Dempsey with him. In January 1944 Dempsey was appointed commander of the British Second Army. The name of the Second Army's commander was not to be revealed until June 1944, shortly after the Allied invasion of France, but as early as the winter of 1943-1944 America's General Bradley '43 was promising Dempsey a dinner in Paris on his (Bradley's) birthday (August 11).

Bradley was not far off. The Allied invasion of France came in June 1944. Until the Canadian First and the American Third Armies arrived in France and the Twelfth Army Group was formed, Bradley's American First Army was a part of the Twenty-First Army under Montgomery. In the middle of July 1944, attacking along the eastern section of the Allied battle lines in Normandy, Dempsey's Second Army drew to its Caen front the major share of the German forces, thus making it possible for Bradley, striking in the western section, to break through in five days. By the end of July the Second Army had joined the Allied offensive, too; and so rapid was the Allied advance from that point on that the two generals were almost able to keep their Paris engagement.

The speed of Dempsey's drive through Belgium was even more unprecedented. "This is a complete disaster for the Huns," the British General was quoted on September 4. "It will be reckoned as one of the greatest victories of history." His Second Army raced through northern Belgium, liberated Brussels, took Antwerp, then, having swept through crumbling German defenses in northeastern Belgium, penetrated southern Holland in a flanking drive aimed at the weaker north end of the Siegfried Line.

On September 20 Dempsey's patrols reached the south bank of the Neder Rijn, the northernmost branch of the Rhine River; but he was unable to reinforce adequately General R. E. Urquhart's '44 8,000 Red Devils of the British 1st Airborne Division, who were "marooned amidst a tornado" of German tank and

LT. GEN. MILES CHRISTOPHER
DEMPSEY

artillery fire at their Arnhem bridgehead. On the 25th, after nine unexpected days of heroic resistance, the 2,200 survivors were evacuated across the river. Not in vain, as Prime Minister Winston Churchill '42 declared, was the pride of those who survived and the epitaph of those who fell: Dempsey estimates that their stand saved his forces at least 25,000 casualties. To his army had fallen the task of fighting Germany's very best troops, the SS or Elite Guard, to clear them from the Rhine delta, above the northern tip of the Westwall.

On December 3, after what correspondents called a lull of weeks on the eastern Holland front, Dempsey's army crossed the Maas (or Meuse) against concentrated artillery fire and proceeded to drive the Germans from the west bank of that river. By December 15 all but one of the Allied armies at the front (the First French Army under General Jean de Lattre de Tassigny) had put some troops into Germany. Then, on the 16th, German Field Marshal Karl Rudolf Gerd von Runstedt sent his armored divisions westward in a drive from the Siegfried Line into eastern Belgium and Luxembourg, driving back the Allied line to form a "bulge." SHAEF censorship clamped down on the war news. As December wore on, it was clear that the Germans were being pushed back and their bulge reduced; but Second Army news was conspicuous by its absence. After General H. D. G. Crerar's '44 First Canadian Army, Dempsey's was the northernmost of the seven armies on the Allied line; in terms of their offensive, it was toward the extreme left flank.

A bachelor, Lieutenant General Dempsey looks in 1944 five years younger than his forty-seven years. "His slim, six-foot figure is always neatly dressed and his field boots are always polished to mirror brightness." He is modest to the point of shyness, but speaks vigorously and incisively when addressing his men or talking with his fellow officers on military topics. A great regard for detail is typical of him. His field maps are always carefully indexed and annotated, the annotations all in his tidy script.

References

N Y Sun p6 Jl 8 '44
Newsweek 24:25 Jl 10 '44 por

DES PORTES, FAY ALLEN (dā-pôrt') June 16, 1890—Sept. (?) 1944 Diplomat; resigned from the South Carolina State Senate in 1928 to become Minister to Bolivia (1933-36); was Minister to Guatemala (1936-43); appointed Ambassador to Costa Rica in March 1943, which post he held at time of death.

Obituary

N Y Times p19 S 18 '44 por

DEUTSCH, JULIUS (doich) Feb. 2, 1884- Austrian Socialist leader
Address: h. 243 Riverside Dr., New York City

Among prominent Austrian political refugees in the United States is General Julius Deutsch, onetime Secretary of War of the Austrian Republic, former general secretary of the Austrian Social Democratic Party, and commander in chief of the Republican Schutzbund which fought against the Fascist troops in the Dollfuss *coup d'état* of February 1934. In 1944 he is a member of the International Honorary Board of the Free World Association and a script editor in the Office of War Information.

Julius Deutsch was born February 2, 1884 in Lackenbach, Austria. He attended the universities of Vienna, Berlin, Zurich, and Paris, studying jurisprudence, economics, and philosophy. At the University of Zurich he received a first prize in recognition of his first book, *Die Kinderarbeit und ihre Bekämpfung* ("Child Labor and the Fight Against It"), and at the same University obtained the degree of Doctor in Political Science. Among other historical and economic studies were *Geschichte der österreichischen Gewerkschaftsbewegung* ("History of the Austrian Trade Union Movement"), in 1929 to be republished in a corrected and expanded two-volume edition; *Das moderne Proletariat,* a socio-psychological study written in collaboration with Professor Dr. Rudolf Broda; *Die Lohn und Arbeitsverhältnisse in den österreichischen Siemens-Schuckert-Werken* ("Wage and Working Conditions in the Austrian Siemens-Schuckert Plants"), a series of studies on collective bargaining. In 1914 he wrote a study about the migrations of European workers for the Carnegie Peace Foundation, but as a result of the outbreak of War the Foundation was not able to publish the study.

During the First World War, Deutsch served in the Austro-Hungarian Army as an artillery officer and was several times decorated for bravery. During the last months of the War he was commissioned by the Government to join the economic staff of the Imperial Secretary of War in order to supervise war production. After the breakup of the Austrian Monarchy the new Republican Government of Austria appointed him Under-Secretary of War. One of his principal tasks was to liquidate the Imperial Austro-Hungarian Army and to organize the new Republican forces, which were intended to be democratic in both composition and direction. The rights and duties enjoyed by civilians were to be enjoyed by enlisted men as well; such matters as clothing, conditions within the barracks, and discipline were placed under the direction of Soldiers' Councils elected by soldiers from their own companies. After the 1919 elections he became a Member of Parliament and was appointed Secretary of War in the Government in which the Social Democrats, the largest party in Parliament, held most of the important posts.

Deutsch remained chief of the Republican forces until his resignation from the Government at the end of 1920, when the Social Democrats retired permanently into opposition. (Although in Vienna they were in almost complete control, they were never to gain a majority in Parliament.) Parliament then elected Deutsch Parliamentary commissioner for the armed forces, and in this post he worked until 1933. General secretary of the Social Democratic Party, during this period he also did all he could to strengthen the Republican Defense Corps (Republikanischer Schutzbund), founded by the Socialists for the defense of the Republic, for he saw that the Austrian Republican Army was being turned into a reactionary instrument and that the Government was increasing the illegal armament of the Fascist Heimwehr and similar organizations as well as offering them the protection of police, Army, and courts of justice. From 1925 to 1934 he served as chairman of the International Commission for the Fight Against Fascism.

Clashes between Austrian Socialists and Fascists grew more and more frequent. In July 1927 a Socialist demonstration in Vienna protesting against the release of the assassinators of several Socialists developed into an open battle between workers and police, and finished in the shooting of many workers by the police. Although the Schutzbund had secret arms depots, the pacific character of the Social Democratic leaders is shown by the fact that they did not open them up at this time to arm the workers, but instead called a general strike which was broken within three days. The result was that they were criticized from the Left as having done "lackey service" to "capitalist reaction," attacked from the Right as having attempted what amounted to a Bolshevik revolution.

It was March 1933 when Dollfuss made himself dictator of Austria and created the authoritarian Austrian State; one of his first actions was to dissolve the Republican Schutzbund of which Deutsch was commander in chief, on the grounds that it was planning violence against the Government. Shortly afterward the small Communist Party of Austria was suppressed. Deutsch and Otto Bauer nevertheless offered Dollfuss their support if he would restore some semblance of parliamentary government, and when he refused they kept on hoping for some sort of compromise. In January 1934 they offered their cooperation again on condition of a popular referendum on the proposed new constitution, free elections to the new "corporations," and recognition of the rights of organization and collective bargaining. Dollfuss' response came: raids on all Socialist headquarters and the announcement of a discovery of a "Bolshevist-Marxist plot" during the first week of February, followed by the arrest of sundry leaders of the Schutzbund.

Finally, on February 12, the Heimwehr attempted to search the headquarters of the Linz Socialist Party for arms, were denied admittance, and stormed and took the building after heavy fighting. The Social Democratic leaders reluctantly decided on a general strike for 5:00 p.m., but the electrical workers struck at once for an undisclosed reason, stopping the presses which were to print the strike notices. The arrest of most of the Socialist leaders followed, and as Heimwehr forces, supported by police and troops, moved against the Socialists, these almost leaderless workers barricaded themselves in their municipal dwelling houses and for three days of siege defended them with arms from the few secret depots they succeeded in locating. They made no attempt to seize public buildings, telegraph and telephone offices, broadcasting centers, posts to command arterial roads and railway stations—and these were seized by the Heimwehr with the cooperation of the police and the Army. At the end Social Democracy in Austria was drowned in blood, with hundreds of Socialists dead, imprisoned, or executed, and the party, the Socialist unions, and all affiliated societies and clubs officially dissolved. In May 1934 the Social Democrats were illegally excluded from Parliament. Austria was no longer even nominally a republic.

All during the fighting the Government radio had told the workers that Bauer and Deutsch had "fled to Prague before a shot was fired with trunks full of money stolen from the party." Actually they had gone under ground in the days before the fighting, snatching what sleep they could in movie theatres while the Government was arresting most of the other key men, and carrying on conferences and staff discussions in public swimming-baths and Turkish baths. They had both taken part in the fighting until the end, when they fled into Czechoslovakia at Bratislava along with two-score other refugees. In the fighting Deutsch had been wounded just below the eye by a ricocheting bullet and had reached safety alone, feeling his way through the woods and across the fields. When challenged by the Heimwehr just before the frontier he acted like a drunken peasant.

At Brünn in Czechoslovakia the headquarters of the old party leaders were now established under Bauer and Deutsch. Here the daily newspaper of the Social Democrat Party, the *Arbeiterzeitung*, reappeared as a weekly and was smuggled into Austria to the number of 75,000 copies a week. In Austria itself illegal trades unions were formed, and the Schutzbund reconstituted itself as an independent body embracing both Socialist and Communist members. At a conference in Brünn the Socialists also decided to drop the word "democratic" and to call themselves the Austrian Revolutionary Socialists. Later the old name of the party, Social Democracy, was readopted.

(Continued next page)

JULIUS DEUTSCH

In 1936, following an invitation from the Spanish Republican Government, Deutsch offered his services as a general of the Loyalists in Spain. He became chief of the Coastal Defense and a member of the General Staff of the High Command, and until 1938 did intensive work training the recruits of the Spanish Republican Army. With the victory of Franco's '42 forces he escaped to France, and during 1939 and 1940 edited a military and scientific revue in Paris, *Krieg und Frieden* ("War and Peace"). Following the fall of France he escaped once more, and since January 1941 has been living in the United States, since 1942 employed as a script editor at the Office of War Information.

He has written several articles on Central European problems for publications like the *Nation* and the *Free World*, and he has taken part in many public discussions on the future of Austria. It is his view that a republic is the only possible form of government for Austria, but that "Austria is unable to exist alone. By sheer economic necessity," he says, "she is forced to unite with a larger territory, and here she faces the alternative: union [with Germany] or participation in a Danubian federation." Chances of the former being slight, the only answer is a federation of Danube states in the frame of a general European federation—composed of states that are all equally democratic, with a republican form of government. Austria would never join a federation of Central European states which might form a *cordon sanitaire* against the U.S.S.R., he also declares. In his pamphlet entitled *Austria in the Framework of a World Organization* (1944), published by the Free World Association, Deutsch sees a government of workers and farmers in post-War Austria, the neutrality of which would be established by an international act of law; he also proposes that Vienna be made the seat of an international organization of states.

DEVOE, RALPH G(ODWIN) June 15, 1883- United States Army Medical Corps officer
Address: b. and h. Halloran General Hospital, Staten Island, N. Y.

"History is full of the great accomplishments of individuals who are afflicted with handicaps. . . . It can happen that those of you whose handicaps now appear most grievous will be the ones called upon to leadership in the perilous and difficult years ahead. Some of you may think a republic soon forgets. This will be true of those who cease to exert themselves and sulk in their tents. . . . The physical handicap is nothing as compared with the mental attitude." These are excerpts from a letter Brigadier General Ralph G. DeVoe, commanding officer of Halloran General Hospital, Staten Island, New York, sent to the patients. Halloran is the first piece of the United States seen by the men who have been wounded in action while fighting abroad during the Second World War. Its place in the Army's scheme of healing and rehabilitation for that reason is strategic—a happy reception may influence the men's future attitude as citizens. DeVoe was selected because his background—his specialization in neuropsychiatry and his First World War experience as commanding officer of a base hospital in France—offered admirable qualifications for the post.

Ralph Godwin DeVoe, born in Indiana, Pennsylvania, on June 15, 1883, is of old American stock on both sides of his family. His father, Dr. Arthur DeVoe, is descended from a Huguenot family who settled in New York in 1643, the succeeding generations being of English, Irish, and Scotch stock. His mother was Sarah Alice Coleman, a descendant of General Archibald Campbell of the Revolutionary Army. Ralph DeVoe is the third of his family to choose medicine as a career. His grandfather practiced medicine in New York; his father practiced in Indiana, Pennsylvania, and (after the death of his wife when Ralph was only three years old) in Seattle, Washington, to which he had moved with his son. (The fourth generation in medicine is the General's son, Arthur Gerard DeVoe, who, until he entered the United States Army Medical Corps, was a leading eye specialist on the staff of the Columbia Presbyterian Medical Center in New York City.)

In Seattle DeVoe attended the public schools and was graduated from the Seattle High School in 1901. During the Spanish-American War a military camp situated near Seattle had aroused the young high school student's interest in army life. After high school he made application for a West Point appointment. His failure to receive the appointment that year made him decide to study medicine. Two years of pre-medical work at the University of Washington followed (1902-04). After graduation from the University of Pennsylvania Medical School, which gave him his M. D. degree in 1908, he interned at the City Emergency Hospital in Seattle, Washington.

Army life had lost none of its appeal, however. Passing with high honors his entrance examination for the Army Medical School in Washington, D. C., he was commissioned 1st lieutenant in the Medical Reserve Corps on September 1, 1909. After his graduation from the school on May 20, 1910 he was commissioned 1st lieutenant in the Army Medical Corps, serving at the Fort Worden Coast Defenses in Puget Sound until October 1911. He was then stationed in the Philippine Islands, where he served until October 1914, by which time he had received his captaincy. After his stay in the Philippines he served at Fort MacDowell, California, from October 1914 to September 1917.

A month after the United States entered the First World War, DeVoe was advanced to the rank of major. The following September he was made the commanding officer of Base Hospital 34. Under his able guidance the hospital unit (originally organized at the Episcopal Hospital in Philadelphia) went through its preliminary training at Allentown, Pennsylvania (Camp Crane), its "weather-beaten career at Camp Mills, Long Island, its ocean voyage, and its final settlement and work at Nantes, France. There not only did DeVoe direct the work of the hospital but he carried on the duties of a medical liaison officer to the Headquarters of the French 11th Army Corps Region, a position in which he did much to accentuate the cordial relations between the French and American Departments in that region."

Base Hospital 34, the central hospital of which had originally been a French seminary, went into actual operation on April 1, 1918. During the nine months that followed 9,100 patients were admitted. The hospital, under DeVoe's direction, made a record in countless ways. Statistics show successful operations by the hundreds—and a death rate of only 1 3/10 per cent. The wounded and sick alike were cared for. At one time during the heaviest fighting only thirteen medical cases were recorded among the hundreds of wounded admitted. A history of the hospital pays this tribute to it: "Other hospitals have records as deserving, but let it be realized that 34's accomplishments were of the highest order." DeVoe was promoted to the rank of lieutenant colonel on January 18, 1918, and to colonel on May 5, 1919. On January 16, 1919 Base Hospital 34, after thirteen months of service, ceasing to be a part of the American Expeditionary Forces, returned home. DeVoe remained in France as the commanding officer of the Hospital Center of Nantes. In recognition of his valuable work the French Government in 1918 awarded him the decoration of Chevalier of the Legion of Honor.

The General relates this amusing incident of his experience at Nantes: One of the soldiers admitted to the hospital was treated for a minor wound received in his left shoulder. After the wound had been healed the soldier, according to regular procedure, was signed up with another outfit and sent forth again. A month later he was returned to Base Hospital 34—the second bullet had entered in precisely the same spot as the first and did no more damage than to remove the scar of the first. Upon discharging the soldier for the second time, the surgeon advised him that the next time he heard a bullet coming his way he would do well to step two inches to the left.

Merin-Baliban

BRIG. GEN. RALPH G. DEVOE

After the War DeVoe, honorably discharged as colonel, was returned to the grade of major in February 1920. In August 1919 he had been appointed assistant to the post surgeon at Fort Slocum, New York. In September 1921 he became assistant professor in military science and tactics at New York University, a post he held until June 1924, and to which he returned in 1930 to remain for four more years. During the last part of 1924 he was at the Command and General Staff School at Fort Leavenworth, Kansas, and was then assigned as the commanding officer of the 1st Medical Regiment at the Carlisle Barracks, Pennsylvania, where he remained until 1927. His next assignment was as assistant to the 2nd Corps Area surgeon and division surgeon for the 1st Division at Governors Island, New York. In 1929 he was made acting surgeon of the latter post, where he remained until 1930. On May 20, 1930 DeVoe was promoted to lieutenant colonel. In 1934, after his second assignment with New York University, he was made the division surgeon of the 1st Cavalry Division at Fort Bliss, Texas, serving until 1939. On May 20, 1936 he was promoted to the rank of colonel; and four years later, after serving as the post surgeon at Fort Monroe, Virginia, through 1939-1940, he was assigned as the corps surgeon of the 2nd Army at Wilmington, Delaware (1940-41). Just prior to his assignment as the commanding officer of Halloran General Hospital, in October 1942, he had been the post surgeon at Fort Dix, New Jersey (1941-42). On May 28, 1944 he was promoted to the rank of brigadier general.

The Architectural Record gives DeVoe and his staff credit for the comprehensiveness and humanity that governed the conception of building the Halloran General Hospital. "Not only is Halloran a great medical plant equipped with every facility for medical, psychological, and surgical healing, but it is equipped to serve other social needs, whether of religion, education, sociability, or entertainment." The hospital originally had been planned as a home

DEVOE, RALPH G.—*Continued*
for mentally defective children, and the architects had only three weeks in which to prepare their plans for its conversion into a hospital. Throughout the rush, however, DeVoe never let it be forgotten that this was a hospital for "those who deserve the best." An atmosphere of cheerfulness was one of his aims. The Metropolitan Museum of Art was consulted about the decoration, and through the good will of the Museum's director, Henry Taylor, there were loaned to the hospital pieces of sculpture, paintings, and art objects of an aggregate value running into six figures.

Named after the late distinguished Army medical officer, Colonel Paul Stacy Halloran, the hospital was opened on October 19, 1942. It is located on a 383-acre plot of open and wooded terrain on Staten Island in New York harbor. It consists of many brick buildings of Georgian architecture—virtually a town with its own power plant, shops, gasoline depots for maintenance, chapel, library, crafts shop, outdoor theatre, motion-picture auditoriums, dance floor, bowling alleys, and playing fields. The heart of the institution, however, is the "PX" or post exchange, where the men talk while chain-drinking "cokes," have meals with visitors, and buy tobacco and magazines or gifts for friends. Quarters are provided not only for patients but for the staff, including nurses and Wacs. One-third of Halloran's patients are litter patients and they can be cleared for entry at the rate of 2,500 a day. The present bed-capacity is 3,000, with 3,500 expansion beds which may be made available in the event of an emergency or disaster. One emergency, not included in the "expected" was that of September 14, 1944, when a hurricane swept the Atlantic coast. One unit of an Army hospital in Atlantic City was incapacitated by the storm, and Halloran took in its patients on one day's notice. So perfectly organized is the staff under DeVoe that a day later there was no evidence that Halloran had answered an emergency call of such magnitude.

"The prime factor in the successful treatment of wounds with penicillin," says DeVoe, "is careful and thorough surgical procedures—without these the miracle drug often fails. In the First World War it was early realized that ordinary methods of surgery would not meet the then new conditions of war—trench fighting and the effects of modern artillery. The wounded soldier was eminently a dirty person, highly contaminated by his surroundings. It was soon realized that damaged tissues and foreign bodies in the tissues, such as shell fragments, bits of shattered bone, shoe leather, part of a belt buckle, manure (often not revealed by X-ray), caused infection. A method, revolutionary to surgery before the First World War, was introduced by Dr. Alexis Carrel [40], and a new antiseptic was originated by Dr. Thomas D. Dakin. The combination of these was known as the Carrel-Dakin method. The probing and cutting away of damaged tissue is still a necessary procedure in the treatment of wounds."

There are a number of new terms for the soldier who was described as "shell-shocked" in the First World War. These are "battle fatigue", "battle exhaustion", "hunger psychosis"—all of which the soldier sums up aptly under the term "bomb nuts." "Battle fatigue," DeVoe says,

"responds readily to a few days of good food, rest, and diversion." Some of the more serious cases are given the "shock treatment," an intravenous injection of metrazol which throws the patient into convulsions. An old-school medico compared the therapy to that of "throwing a patient into fits and then curing the fits." DeVoe has also emphasized the importance of music therapy: "It will stand high if not at the top of reconditioning agencies in wartime hospitals."

In 1908 DeVoe was married to Frances Reba Gerard. They have one son, the Army doctor, and two grandchildren, both boys. In 1944 the General was selected as the most outstanding alumnus for the year by the University of Pennsylvania. His favorite recreations are golf and horseback riding. He has never entirely outgrown his early interest in military science and says he cannot speak too highly of the men who planned the European invasion—"a truly magnificent achievement."

General DeVoe is five feet eleven, weighs 190 pounds, has a ruddy complexion, and brown eyes; his bearing is more that of the medical man than of the military. He has an easy, informal manner. Members of his staff speak enthusiastically of his sympathetic understanding and simplicity. Another of his attributes is his sense of humor. Once when told that he did not look his years by at least twenty, he said, "Youth is a matter of physiology rather than chronology," and illustrated his point with a story about Justice Holmes, who, at ninety-five, sighed when he saw a pretty girl passing and said, "Oh, to be ninety again!"

References

Arch Rec 95:71-8 Ja '44
Pitts, E. M. ed. Base Hospital 34 in the World War 1922

DEWART, WILLIAM T(HOMPSON) (dū'ert) Jan. 29, 1875—Jan. 27, 1944 President and principal owner of the New York *Sun*; a leader for many years in the newspaper publishing field.

Obituary

N Y Times p1 Ja 28 '44

DEWEY, JOHN Oct. 20, 1859- Philosopher; educator; author
Address: h. 1 W. 89th St., New York City

The philosopher who has removed the aura of remoteness from philosophy, who puts his theories into practice by active participation in American life, is "typically American" John Dewey, foremost spokesman of democracy and science. Variously labeled as instrumentalism, experimentalism, pragmatism, and humanistic naturalism, Dewey's philosophy, in his own words, is a system of thought that is "based on *experience* [instead of tradition or dogma] as the ultimate authority in knowledge and conduct."

Ranked with Paine, Jefferson, Emerson, and William James in his moral idealism, Dewey has been influencing contemporary thought since 1887. He has enunciated his ideas through a prodigious number of controversial books, articles, and lectures, not only on philosophy in its metaphysical aspects, but in the related realms of the moral, social, and political questions of modern society. ("Philosophy should be a method of understanding and rectifying specific social ills," believes Dewey, unlike those who treat it as an interpretation of life or as a consolation for existing and perhaps irremediable evils; and he has complete faith in the scientific method of inquiry and in the power of human intelligence to create a better society.) It is in the field of education that Dewey's philosophy has been most widely and most directly applied. Often misinterpreted, due to some extent to a complex, sometimes obscure style, Dewey has steadfastly weathered mordant criticism, as well as responded quietly to enthusiastic allegiance. In answer to his critics, Dewey has written: "It is less important that we all believe alike than that we all alike inquire freely and put at the disposal of one another such glimpses as we may attain of the truth for which we are in search."

The year 1859 saw several events which have deeply influenced the cultural history of the western world—the publication of Karl Marx's *Critique of Political Economy,* John Stuart Mill's essay "On Liberty," and Charles Darwin's *Origin of Species,* the births in Europe of Havelock Ellis and Henri Bergson, and in Burlington, Vermont on October 20, of John Dewey. However, John Dewey's early life was "painfully average, or, if you will, divinely average," as Max Eastman puts it. His father, Archibald Sprague Dewey, who kept a general store in that New England community, was famous in a small way as a humorist; a sign outside his establishment advertised: "Ham and Cigars—Smoked and Unsmoked." Lucina A. (Rich) Dewey, young Dewey's mother, boasted of a grandfather who served in Congress. The boy had to earn his spending money delivering papers after school for $1.00 a week, and at fourteen he found his first real job—$6.00 weekly—"tallying" in a lumber yard. Neither in grammar school nor in high school did the future philosopher distinguish himself.

Entering the University of Vermont (which was located in Burlington) at the early age of fifteen, Dewey still evinced no special talent, until in his senior year he led his class and won the highest marks on record in philosophy. This transformation in Dewey's scholastic record was occasioned by his accidental perusal of a physiology textbook written by Thomas Henry Huxley, the foremost supporter in England of Darwin's theory of evolution. Awakened to the excitement of the effort to understand the world, and beginning to doubt his early moralistic beliefs, Dewey delved into philosophy for an answer to the conflict between revealed dogma and the findings of science. This was the beginning of Dewey's lifelong task of reconciling these two poles.

As a temporary solution to earning a livelihood, upon receiving his B.A. in 1879, Dewey taught briefly at an Oil City (Pennsylvania) high school run by a female cousin, a period followed by a year's rural teaching in Charlotte, Vermont. Dewey continued his philosophical reading during this time, submitting his first original piece of writing, "The Meta-

physical Assumptions of Materialism," to W. T. Harris, publisher of the *Journal of Speculative Philosophy* in St. Louis. Encouraged by the acceptance of this and other articles by America's first major philosophical periodical, Dewey determined to become a "lay" philosopher.

Borrowing $500 from an aunt, Dewey entered the newly founded research university, Johns Hopkins, in the fall of 1882. Here he fell under the influence of George Sylvester Morris, who introduced him to the writings of Hegel and to those of the neo-Hegelian British school. "The immediate appeal of Hegel to Dewey," explains Sidney Hook, "lay in Hegel's opposition to dualisms of all sorts, in his historical approach to all cultural life, his mastery of concrete material, and his extraordinary acute perception of the continuities between matter and life, life and mind, mind and society," concepts which Dewey valued even after he had abandoned the idealism and artificial terminology of the German philosopher some ten years later.

With his Ph.D. (1884) Dewey proceeded to the University of Michigan, where, until 1888 he taught philosophy, first as instructor, then as assistant professor. The year 1887 saw the publication of Dewey's first book, *Psychology,* a textbook which placed him among those who pioneered to break psychology loose from philosophy, thereby giving it the status of a natural science.

In 1888 Dewey went on to the University of Minnesota, but returned to Michigan the next year to succeed his friend, Professor Morris, as head of the department of philosophy. Six years later President William R. Harper invited Dewey to come to the newly founded University of Chicago to head the combined departments of philosophy, psychology, and education. There Dewey laid the groundwork of his educational thought. He had already written, in 1889, with J. A. McLellan, *Applied Psychology: an Introduction to the Principles and Practice of Education.* With the encouragement of Mrs. Dewey, in 1896 Dewey established the now historic Experimental or Laboratory School, "the most important experimental venture in the whole history of American education," Sidney Hook declares. (Katherine Mayhew and Anna Edwards have written a detailed account of its operation in *The Dewey School,* published in 1936.) Supported by a group who, originally concerned with the education of their own children, had revolted against formalized traditional methods, the institution flourished for seven years. Chicago University's president did not share the enthusiasm of the founders, however, and in 1904 Dewey resigned. Dewey then accepted the Columbia University post at Teacher's College and in the department of philosophy which he held until 1930, when he retired. He is now professor emeritus.

The theories which Dewey tested and developed in his Experimental School appeared in print in his *School and Society* (1899), an educational classic which has been translated into dozens of languages and which "more than any other single writing hastened the pedagogic revolution." Later expanded and clarified in *How We Think* (1910; revised edi-

JOHN DEWEY

tion, 1929), and in *Democracy and Education* (1916), the characteristic features of Dewey's method have been to give the child the utmost freedom of initiative and curiosity, to make his experience in dealing with the world about him the basis of his learning rather than passive absorption of subject matter from textbooks, and to encourage him to work easily and happily with other members of a group. "The school is primarily a social institution," Dewey emphasizes repeatedly, and "education is a process of living ['the constant reconstruction of experience'] and not a preparation for future living"; the keynote of modern education is its continuity with life. "Education is the fundamental method of social progress and reform," and "the problem of problems in our education is to discover how to mature and make effective the scientific habit of mind."

It is generally acknowledged that Dewey is, more than anyone else, responsible for shaping education to the ways of modern life. Many of his doctrines have become commonplaces. Not only have many elementary schools throughout the United States adopted or modified the so-called activity program of progressive education, but Dewey's principles have come to the fore also in high schools and in colleges. In 1919 the Progressive Education Association (of which he became honorary president in 1934) was formed to further the steady growth of the modern method. In the years following the close of the First World War Dewey became the unofficial intellectual ambassador of the United States to the world. He visited China in 1919 and 1931, Japan (where he declined for democratic reasons the decoration of the Order of the Rising Sun), Turkey (whose schools, in 1924, the new revolutionary government delegated him to reorganize), Mexico in 1926, Russia in 1928, and South Africa. Dewey's praise for the educational accomplishments of the Lenin and Trotsky regime placed him to the left of liberals in America.

Dewey has been disparaged as an exponent of soft pedagogy, the "child-centered school" becoming a term of opprobrium in some quarters. These critics err, sympathizers maintain, in treating Deweyism and "progressivism" (the term used in describing the diverse and sometimes inconsistent methods of those who run the modern schools in his name) as synonymous. What Dewey advocates is learning through purposeful activities; his concept of freedom does not mean the absence of control and direction. In *Experience and Education* (1938) Dewey makes it clear that progressive education is not to be regarded as an exclusive antithesis with respect to conventional education. (*Education Today,* a resumé of his philosophy, followed in 1940.) "Despite its own grave shortcomings in interpretation and practice, progressive education has revealed the inadequacy of the formal stereotypes of traditional education," writes Hook. Other Dewey partisans include William H. Kilpatrick, Harold Rugg [41], Boyd H. Bode, and George S. Counts [41].

Dewey has consistently battled the arbitrary separation of vocational studies from academic education. In a strong attack upon that theory and upon the educational system sponsored by Dr. Robert Hutchins [40], president of the University of Chicago, Dewey stated in 1944: "At the very time when an important, perhaps the important, problem in education is to fill education having an occupational direction with a genuinely liberal content, we have a movement . . . to cut vocational training off from any contact with what is liberating by relegating it to special schools devoted to inculcation of technical skills." Certain educators, Dewey continued, are waging "a definite campaign to make the scientific attitude the scapegoat for present evils."

This philosophy of education is the most significant phase of Dewey's philosophy of instrumentalism, which he first formulated in *Studies in Logical Theory* (1903), later revised and amplified in *Essays in Experimental Logic* (1916). All thinking, he believes, is instrumental, an operation directed toward a definite end, and the truth of an idea lies in its practical effect. Pure thought cannot exist. William James, whose *Principles of Psychology* had marked one of the turning points in Dewey's philosophical development, spoke of the book as "the foundation of the philosophy of pragmatism" and welcomed the younger man as a peer. (James himself is regarded as the founder of that school of philosophy.)

Creative Intelligence (1917) is a statement of the pragmatic purpose behind Dewey's attempt to free philosophy from its attachment to remote, traditional problems. "What serious-minded men not engaged in the professional business of philosophy most want to know is what modifications and abandonments of intellectual inheritance are required by the newer industrial, political, and scientific movements," wrote Dewey. *Reconstruction in Philosophy* (1920) is a sketch of the development of European philosophy and a recapitulation of his own. In *Human Nature and Conduct* (1922), again expressing a view in marked contrast to general interpretation, Dewey advanced the idea that in habit—that is, in existing institutions and customs—and not in instinct or intelligence lay the why and wherefore of human actions. (Human nature *is* changeable, Dewey insists. He deplores the use of the belief that it is not, as a means of opposing economic or political change; under no illusions, he admits that the new project is, of course, contrary to some traits of human nature as they exist at the time.) H. M. Kallen commented on this analysis of human nature: "Highly abstract and concentratedly subtle though the book is compelled to be, it has a quality of vitality and abundance, an eloquence and emotional immediacy joined with epigrammatic sharpness unprecedented in Mr. Dewey's work, and rare among philosophers anywhere."

With the publication of *Experience and Nature* (1925) Dewey brought to light the basic metaphysical principles upon which his educational and social theories rest. Almost simultaneously with the celebration of his seventieth birthday appeared a volume, *The Quest for Certainty: a Study of the Relation of Knowledge and Action* (1929), which was hailed at that time as his crowning work, confirming, as Irwin Edman wrote, "the impression long current that he has initiated, more truly even than Kant, a Copernican revolution in philosophy." Philosophy, in Dewey's belief, must take cognizance of a changing world and must apply the experimental methods of science to its judgments concerning the values which control conduct, especially in its social phases. *Philosophy and Civilization,* a collection of essays reprinted from technical periodicals and other sources, appeared in 1931.

The publication of *Art as Experience* (1934) "marked, in a minor way," observes Hook, "a turning point in the reception of his philosophy." Although primarily an analysis of the esthetic experience, it served to clarify all of Dewey's leading ideas, constituting "the most persuasive introduction to his thought he has so far written for non-philosophers." Dewey here demonstrates what has often been denied, that art is "a mode of interaction of the live creature with his environment," his central thesis being what he terms the "continuity of esthetic with ordinary experience." Art is the freest and most universal means of communication between individuals and nations, and it also establishes the continuity of culture. A work of art is the ideal example of the fusion of means and ends; thus, "art itself is the best proof of the existence of a realized and therefore realizable union of the material and ideal"—art is what all life should be.

In accordance with his philosophy of experience, Dewey rejects the supernatural element in religion, and it is here that many of his supporters come to a parting of the ways with him. There is a difference between having a religion and being religious, Dewey thinks. To have a religion is to be committed to a set of doctrines which cannot always be scientifically proven; "to be religious," as Hook explains it, "is to have an unqualified allegiance to an imaginative ideal, based on the heart's deepest desire, which directs our fundamental choices, and does not yield before the tyranny of force and chance." Religious faith, says Dewey in *A Common Faith* (1934), is "the unification of the self through allegiance to inclusive ideal ends which imagination presents to us and to which the human will responds as worthy of controlling our desires and choices." The use of the concept of God is, in this sense, not a person or divine power or an embodied ideal, but simply another name for "the unity of all ideal ends arousing us to desire and action," the merging of the ideal with the actual through the use of the imagination.

Logic: The Theory of Inquiry (1938) was greeted as the consummate achievement of a great career. Again Dewey projected a new and challenging view; namely, that logical analysis is not restricted to formal proofs and procedures, but is synonymous with scientific methodology. Dewey's official definition, characteristic of the style his readers bemoan, is: "Inquiry is the controlled and directed transformation of an indeterminate situation into one that is so determinate in its constituent distinctions and relations as to convert the elements of the original situation into a unified whole." There is no other source of logic than inquiry itself, Dewey maintains. As an alternative to this dynamic, ever-changing conception, Mortimer Adler '40, for example, insists that the processes of inquiry resulting in security and wisdom can only be founded upon permanent and *a priori* known forms of thinking.

As is appropriate in one who believes that philosophy is a tendency to action, Dewey has played a significant part in the nation's political life, devoting many years to fostering and aiding progressive causes. A member of innumerable liberal and educational organizations, Dewey figured prominently in the Teachers Union in New York until it fell under political domination, whereupon, together with the original founders of the Union, he organized the Teachers Guild; he helped organize the American Civil Liberties Union as well as the American Association of University Professors. He protested strongly against the judgment in the Sacco-Vanzetti case. Skeptical of the success of the League of Nations, Dewey supported the activities of S. O. Levinson's tiny Committee for the Outlawry of War, which led to the Kellogg-Briand Treaty in 1929. (In 1915 Dewey's *German Philosophy and Politics*, favoring the War against Germany, had won the bitter derision of some of his disciples who saw it as war propaganda.)

Following the election of Hoover, Dewey created a stir by his proposal of a third party, whose policies would "deal mainly with the economic facts which the present major parties conspicuously ignore." He was among the founders of the League for Independent Political Action formed in 1929 to act as a clearing house for liberal sentiment throughout the country and to "carry on the work of research and education in order to build up that body of positive and constructive policies which alone give unity and endurance to a progressive party movement." Dewey has several times supported Norman Thomas, the Socialists' policies coming sufficiently near to representing the aims of the League. Dewey's action in the People's Lobby in Washington

DEWEY, JOHN—*Continued*

also helped to awaken a national sense of responsibility in relation to economic problems.

In 1937, at the age of seventy-eight, Dewey journeyed to Mexico to act as chairman of a commission of American scholars, educators, and labor leaders, which investigated the charges made against Leon Trotsky in the famous Moscow trials. Although disagreeing with the Russian's ideology, Dewey championed his innocence in an 800-page report: "The lesson for all American radicals and sympathizers with the U.S.S.R. is that they must go back and reconsider the whole question of means of bringing about social changes and of truly democratic methods of approach to progress." Dewey repeated his thesis that a bad means (such as government terror) can not justify a good end in his devastating criticism of the motion picture *Mission to Moscow* (1943), one of Hollywood's most controversial films. For its distortion of fact and history, he condemned it as "the first instance in our country of totalitarian propaganda for mass consumption." Dewey entered his eighty-first year as the leader and organizer of the American Committee for Cultural Freedom. In 1941, in company with eight others, he edited an angry volume, *The Bertrand Russell Case*, denouncing the "fundamental clerics, machine politicians, and professional patriots" who had succeeded in ousting the English mathematician and philosopher from the staff of the College of the City of New York for his writings on the subject of sexual ethics.

Dewey has expressed his social and political philosophy of liberalism, for the most part, in *The Public and Its Problems* (1927); *Characters and Events* (1929), which contains about 100 short articles, many of them from the *New Republic*—on whose staff he served many years as contributing editor—illustrating the application of his doctrine that progress can be achieved through an experimental social reconstruction; *Liberalism and Social Action* (1935); *Freedom and Culture* (1939). In furtherance of democracy, Dewey wishes to apply the scientific method to the study of human behavior as it is exemplified in the political field. The individual has been submerged in our predominantly capitalist economy, he argues. "Organized social planning, put into effect for the creation of an order in which industry is socially directed in behalf of institutions that provide the material basis for cultural liberation and growth of individuals, is now the sole method by which liberalism can realize its professed aims." Liberalism must today accept a form of collectivism: "Regimentation of material and mechanical forces is the only way by which the mass of individuals can be released from regimentation and consequent suppression of their cultural possibilities." However, "individuals are the finally decisive factors of the nature and movement of associated life."

The moral basis of Dewey's philosophy is his firm belief in democracy. Deploring the attempt to identify democracy with economic individualism as the essence of free action, or merely with a special political form, he defines democracy as a *personal* way of life, both individual and social, controlled by a working faith in the possibilities of human nature, in the capacity of human beings for intelligent judgment and action, and in the power of pooled and friendly cooperation. Democracy should not be thought of as simply institutional and external; it is a moral ideal, and so far as it becomes a fact it is a moral fact. Faith in democracy is one with faith in experience and education. (Essentially a moralist, Dewey, with James Hayden Tufts, has discussed many of the ethical problems of economic life in *Ethics*, first published in 1908 and later revised in 1932 and 1938.)

Although many of Dewey's contemporaries are convinced that the problems of social welfare in our time have never been so squarely faced, opposition to Dewey "has run the gamut all the way from the charge that he is an arch-radical," wrote Sidney Hook in 1935, "to empty denunciation of him as an apologist for finance capitalism [to George Santayana '" Dewey is "the devoted spokesman of the spirit of enterprise . . . of modern industry"]. The more technical criticism that his philosophy is too utilitarian, that it makes a fetish of action, and loses sight of ends in a narrow absorption in practical means, although not so fantastic, is no more better grounded." Dewey's style, too, which has "its own sturdy robustness, precise effect, and compelling honesty" is often impeached for its complex, closely-knit structure and its "treacherous terminology"—the use of familiar words such as logic, experience, intelligence, and nature with new, sometimes ambiguous, meanings which lead to constant misunderstanding.

More specifically, Morris R. Cohen attacks Dewey's attempt to reconstruct philosophy by denying the absolute character of things and events, thus transforming philosophy from a system into a critical, experimental method and abandoning all interest in the mystery of the universe at large. Harry Slochower believes, on the other hand, that Dewey's "repeated emphasis on relating philosophy to civilization has been a solitary antidote to that ghostly metaphysics which shuns the compulsions of time." To build a philosophy of life on science which is ever-changing, is perilous, many point out, and it is doubtful whether the scientific method can properly evaluate the entire range of human experience. To these critics, Dewey replies that the scientific method is not merely a technical method but an attitude of mind; that the particular technique of the physical sciences is not to be literally copied. In answer to those to whom "Dewey seems to deny all that is high and fine in life and all that is noble and enduring in philosophy," C. E. Ayres writes: "But that is just the point: he denies nothing. That is, he is not denying life, he is only denying the adequacy of any abstraction however fine to represent the whole of life." Thus, there is no absolute good in Dewey's ethical criterion except growth: "Not perfection as a final goal, but the ever-enduring process of perfecting, maturing, refining, is the aim in living."

To those who contend that Dewey is not a philosopher by virtue of the polemic character of his writings, his rejoinder is: "Better it is for philosophy to err in active participation in the living struggles and issues of its own age and times, than to maintain an immune monastic impeccability. To try to escape from the snares and pitfalls of time by recourse to traditional problems and interests —rather than that, let the dead bury their own dead."

Dewey's "bland way of going around with nothing on his mind but thoughts" was tempered by his wife's love of action; "she put 'guts and stuffing' into what had been with him mere intellectual conclusions," writes Max Eastman. Dewey met his wife when she was Alice Chipman, a student in one of his classes at the University of Michigan. Descended from a family of radicals and freethinkers, she was a resolute woman, with a crusading spirit and a strong interest in the life of ideas, and in July 1886 Dewey had married her. When they came to New York in the early 1900's they lived in a fourth-floor apartment on the noisy corner of Broadway and 56th Street. The father of six children (two died in childhood and he adopted another), he learned to concentrate amid domestic bustle. Since his wife's death in 1927 and his retirement from his Columbia professorship, Dewey has made his home at various times in Long Island (where he raised chickens and sold eggs), in Nova Scotia during the summers, or in Key West in winter.

At eighty-five, despite little attention to physical exercise, Dewey is still possessed of a remarkable physical vitality. It is said that forty years ago Dewey resembled portraits of Robert Louis Stevenson, "having the same flat hair, dark mustache, and luminous eyes." With none of the usual tricks of an effective speaker, in his slow, Vermont drawl, he lectured numerous students to sleep. But this was "a man actually *thinking* in the presence of a class," declared Irwin Edman, who felt that Dewey's greatest gift as a teacher was that of "initiating inquiry rather than disseminating a doctrine." Dewey spends most of his time thinking, but his favorite hobby is solving acrostic puzzles. He is said to type his manuscripts himself and to carry on a large correspondence in longhand, sometimes writing as many as eighteen letters in a morning.

In August 1944 Dewey was one of the contributors to the forum conducted by *American Scholar* on the subject "The function of the liberal arts college in a democratic society." In the fall of 1944 Dewey told reporters that he hoped to write another serious book soon but that at the time he was writing only articles for philosophical journals. *The Public Schools and Spiritual Values*, the seventh yearbook of the John Dewey Society, was published in October.

Although John Dewey has been honored with many awards and degrees, two volumes of essays in praise of him, and a bronze bust executed by Jacob Epstein, he is neglectful of his fame, and did not even attend the banquet given to celebrate his eightieth birthday though many of the world's most distinguished personages were present. In his relationship with people Dewey has been termed unassum-

ing, direct, and sincere. But "despite his gentleness there is a deep vein of Vermont marble in his character," writes Sidney Hook. "None have been so shocked as those who have mistaken this gentleness for softness. In controversy he does not give ground easily and hesitates not at all in getting rough with opponents whose good faith he has reason to challenge whether they are ambassadors or newspaper columnists."

Writing in *Fortune* Magazine for August 1944, Dewey answered charges of his responsibility for "undisciplined schools" by calling the Neo-Scholastics of the Hutchins school "historical illiterates." In the fall his beliefs were again under attack on several fronts. The director of the new Teachers' School in Buenos Aires called the Dewey influence on education pernicious; and Presidents Nicholas Murray Butler '40 of Columbia University, Robert M. Hutchins of the University of Chicago, and Robert G. Sproul of the University of California criticized progressive education. Dewey, taking up his long-standing disagreement with Hutchins, said at this time that Hutchins' conception of liberal education for a small elite group and vocational education for the masses seemed to him a completely reactionary and anti-democratic idea. To Butler, whose contention it was that progressive education is the "rabbit" type of learning (in which a child nibbles at his studies on a hit-or-miss basis), Dewey replied that progressive education stands for the most solid, enduring discipline that comes from growth and power in self-discipline. "The conduct of the boys on the battlefield shows what a democratic discipline developed from within is capable of accomplishing," he said.

But though John Dewey continued to attack and be attacked in the world of philosophy and education, on his eighty-fifth birthday on October 20, 1944 he was called by *Time* Magazine the "sage, grand old man of United States philosophy," and the New York *Times* wrote of him editorially as the "philosopher and beloved teacher of two generations . . . a steadfast figure in a troubled world."

References

Atlan 168:671-685 D '41

Durant, W. Story of Philosophy 1933
Hook, S. John Dewey: an Intellectual Portrait 1939
Kunitz, S. J. and Haycraft, H. eds. Twentieth Century Authors 1942
Leaders in Education 1941
Schilpp, P. A. ed. Philosophy of John Dewey 1939

Who's Who in America 1944-45
Who's Who in Philosophy 1942

DEWEY, THOMAS E(DMUND) Mar. 24, 1902- Governor of New York State; 1944 Presidential candidate of the Republican Party
Address: Executive Mansion, Albany, N. Y.

NOTE: This revised and enlarged article on Thomas E. Dewey supersedes the biography which appeared in the 1940 Yearbook, when he was District Attorney of New York County.

When in June 1944 the Republican Party chose Thomas E. Dewey as their candidate for

Greystone Studios

THOMAS E. DEWEY

the highest office in the United States, they picked one of the youngest men ever proposed for the Presidency. Yet, so prominent had the Governor of New York become in the thirteen years since his entrance into public life, that his almost unanimous choice to oppose President Franklin D. Roosevelt [42] was a foregone conclusion.

Thomas Edmund Dewey was born in Owosso, Michigan, March 24, 1902, the son of George Martin and Annie (Thomas) Dewey. His father, who died in 1927, was for many years Republican county chairman, postmaster of Owosso, and publisher of the Owosso *Times*. Admiral George Dewey, the hero of Manila Bay, was his grandfather's third cousin. Young Tom Dewey was a Boy Scout, sang in a choir, organized a magazine agency, won a bicycle for his services to the *Saturday Evening Post*, soon had ten other boys working under him, and occasionally won debating contests. In 1923 Dewey acquired a B.A. from the University of Michigan, and in the two years that followed he finished Columbia University's law course, which ordinarily required three years to complete. Back in Michigan he had taken singing lessons and had won contests in singing at the University of Michigan; in New York he continued with his voice lessons and sang in church and synagogue choirs to help pay his expenses.

In 1925 the new LL.B. entered practice in the firm of Larkin, Rathbone & Perry, where he stayed one year before associating himself with McNamara & Seymour. By 1931, when Dewey left McNamara & Seymour for a position as chief assistant to George Z. Medalie, newly appointed United States Attorney for the Southern District of New York, he was earning $8,000 a year in private practice. Dewey's assistantship ended in 1933 when Medalie resigned two days after the beginning of the trial of racketeer Waxey Gordon. For five weeks Dewey then served as United States Attorney. He resumed private practice for the next eighteen months, until, in July 1935, the

New York Grand Jury asked Governor Lehman [43] to appoint an investigator to root out racketeering and vice in New York. After four other prospects had refused the job, Dewey was offered the office of Special Prosecutor at Medalie's suggestion.

Following the much publicized prosecution and conviction of leaders of commercialized vice in 1936, Dewey conducted the more prosaic investigations of rackets in the poultry, trucking, restaurant, and baking businesses. In 1937 New York's anti-Tammany faction, headed by Fiorello La Guardia [40], nominated Dewey to run on its ticket as candidate for District Attorney. In December 1937 Dewey was elected by a margin of more than 100,000 votes. The New York *World-Telegram* announced: "Hoodlums Start Out As Dewey Starts In."

During Dewey's term as District Attorney the crimes and consequent convictions of such figures as Richard Whitney, Jimmy Hines, Fritz Kuhn, and Louis (Lepke) Buchalter were brought to the attention of newspaper readers throughout the country. Dewey's creation of the Volunteer Defenders, a panel of the best available legal talent to handle a certain number of cases every year without fee, did not make the headlines. During the end of his first year in office, the young District Attorney ran against Lehman for the governorship of New York, losing the election by only 65,000 votes. After his defeat he added to his record of convictions by the successful prosecution of such public menaces as Judge Manton, subway employees responsible for the theft of a fortune in nickels, ambulance-chasing lawyers, and landlords of fire-trap tenements.

In the fall of 1939 a petition was circulated among leading Republicans to "cooperate in the movement to elect Thomas E. Dewey President in 1940." The Gallup Polls revealed 60 per cent of the population in favor of his candidacy. Dewey's opponents charged that he was too young and inexperienced for the Presidential office; he was accused of "bullying hostile witnesses and coddling favorable ones, demanding exorbitant bail, wire-tapping, condoning the use of perjured testimony"; and he was said to have been "groomed by the moneyed crowd." Dewey was described as pompous, conceited, and unpopular; and Samuel Grafton [40] said of his social philosophy: "If a young man is as cold as this at thirty-seven, he will reach absolute zero by fifty." His supporters, in turn, pointed out that some of the experienced people then in office had not "polished off the nation's rough spots" too satisfactorily, that Dewey was "the only one of the leading candidates of proved executive ability," and that he had shown by his acts that he would not tolerate financial crookedness and that he had sympathy with the poor. (In his book *Dewey, an American of This Century*, published by Whittlesey House in September 1944, Stanley Walker [44] defends Dewey against these charges. He points out, for example, that Dewey supported the passage of a State bill which requires that a court order be issued before a wire can be tapped.)

Although the Republican nomination finally went to Wendell Willkie [40], Dewey and Robert A. Taft [40] ran a fairly close race at the Philadelphia convention. Afterward, the District Attorney campaigned for Willkie, condemning the New Deal on the grounds of inefficient re-armament, "open war on American business," defeatism, bureaucracy, extravagance, and corruption. ("It is Franklin Roosevelt who today is edging the country toward participation in the European war," stated Dewey in a nation-wide radio address in June 1940, to "cover the utter bankruptcy of his domestic policies . . . to hide the futility of his foreign policy.") Another of his points of attack was that the Administration had betrayed the nation by its diplomatic recognition of Soviet Russia's "godless regime."

Dewey's collected speeches were published in the book *The Case Against the New Deal*, which appeared shortly before the 1940 election. Although the Springfield *Republican* thought it "not as informing or effective for reading as several other books directed against the New Deal," the New York *Herald Tribune*'s reviewer considered that "his remarks have that surprising pertinence whose retention is the hallmark of statesmanship." At about the same time Rupert Hughes, the novelist, who had once written a "debunking" biography of George Washington, brought out *Attorney for the People; the Story of Thomas E. Dewey*, "less a personal portrait than an account of Mr. Dewey's career as a public prosecutor and a record of the underworld crime which he has uncovered and brought to conviction." Of the book, the *Christian Science Monitor* reviewer said: "Although Mr. Hughes has written an entirely uncritical biography, it is a useful one." I. F. Stone, of the *Nation*, was of the opinion that the author seemed "to have confused him [Dewey] with George Washington."

On April 30, 1941 Walter Hoving, president of the newly formed United Service Organizations for National Defense, asked Dewey to head 150,000 volunteer workers in the USO's drive for funds to equip clubhouses for the nation's growing Army. Accepting this post, Dewey called the appeal "a major challenge to the American people. If the Government should be compelled to provide these funds," he asserted, "the result would be Government control of the religious activity and private lives of the youth of America. To this all Americans are unalterably opposed." To determine the servicemen's actual recreational needs and desires, Dewey devoted six weeks to three inspection tours, traveling 41,000 miles to visit Army and Navy bases and near-by communities in all sections of the country. The goal of the drive was $10,500,000, but the first ten days brought in $10,765,000, and the final result was a total of $16,000,000. Later, in February 1942, when Dewey was back in private practice, he laid aside his lucrative civil cases for a time to accept the Navy Relief Society's fund-raising chairmanship for the Third Naval District.

"For the past eleven years," *Newsweek* commented in August 1941, "Thomas E. Dewey . . . has played the role of a St. George slaying the dragon of municipal graft and corruption. . . . Last week the handsome, black-haired racket-buster filled New York City's Fusion ranks with gloom and Tammany Hall with rejoicing when he announced flatly 'I shall not run for District Attorney' in November 1941 on the slate headed by Mayor

Fiorello H. La Guardia." He was, however, active in behalf of the Fusion candidates. Dewey's administrative assistant, Frank S. Hogan, was nominated by the Democrats and endorsed by the Republicans to succeed him. The very high level of efficiency (measured by the proportion of convictions secured to cases tried) which had been set by the retiring District Attorney has since been raised by his successor to 97.7 per cent, a fact to which Dewey's supporters point as evidence of the thorough streamlining he had given the District Attorney's office and of his success in recognizing and developing the abilities of his assistants.

Dewey himself announced his return to private practice. He was, however, regarded as a possibility for the Republican Presidential nomination, and a Gallup Poll taken in September 1941 showed him in third place in popularity among the Republican voters. In 1942, when the question of nominating a successor for Governor Lehman arose, the former District Attorney was the choice of the Old Guard Republicans, led by Herbert Hoover '43 and Alf M. Landon '44. Although *Time* Magazine described Dewey as having "no appeal to the interventionist majority of New York, no appeal to labor and liberal groups," being "personally disliked by many of the hardheaded local [Republican] bosses who are perforce supporting him," and having "weathervane views on all important matters," he was nominated without opposition. "He began his campaign at the upstate county fairs," it was reported, "mingling with the crowds, signing autographs, winning friends quietly." Standing on a platform said to have been written to meet Willkie's views, he "pledged full support of the War, proposed a liberal five-point labor program, dissected the state Democratic machines, and charged that 'the most reactionary element' in New York had taken over the Democratic Party."

Against Dewey there was only a "thoroughly disintegrated and demoralized" opposition—the Democrats, after twenty years of gubernatorial control, had been weakened by a struggle between President Roosevelt (who favored the nomination of Senator Mead) and State Chairman James A. Farley '44, and the American Labor Party had split off and named its own candidate. The final result was a Republican victory with 2,116,000 votes for Dewey, 1,505,-000 for the Democrats' Attorney General Bennett, and 400,000 for the A.L.P.'s Dean Alfange. Thomas Dewey was thus put into "the second biggest job in the country," as the New York governorship is generally considered. In spite of his announced intention to serve out his full four-year term, the nation's eyes would be on Dewey as a possible future President. His acceptance speech was regarded as setting a high tone: "We are not here tonight to celebrate a party victory. We are all of us interested in only one victory—total, uncompromising, crushing victory over our nation's enemies. . . . In all things needed for the winning of this War we are united in unswerving loyalty to our Commander in Chief." And his inaugural speech in January 1943 impressed the New York *Times* as "a model of what a wartime inaugural ought to be."

The advisers and cabinet members with whom the new Governor surrounded himself came

DEWEY, THOMAS E.—*Continued*

mostly from his racket-busting days. They included his secretary, Paul Lockwood; his research assistant, John Burton, whose appointment as Director of the State Budget was one of Dewey's first executive acts; his executive assistant, James C. Hagerty, former *Times* writer and "probably the most talented press secretary any Presidential candidate could acquire," in the opinion of one reporter. The State Superintendent of Banks was Elliott Bell, Dewey's financial adviser. To all his cabinet officers the Governor gave a free hand. Other advisers included Hickman Powell, a magazine writer and the Republican National Committee's researcher on farm problems; George Z. Medalie, who had started Dewey off in public life in 1931; Roger Williams Straus, the philanthropic president of the American Smelting and Refining Company, Dewey's expert on race relations and minorities; Harold Keller, who became public relations man for the Division of Commerce; and Lieutenant General Hugh A. Drum, whom Dewey appointed to head the State Guard on his retirement from the Army. The political angle was handled by "the three musketeers of the Dewey draft," Herbert Brownell '44 (Republican National Chairman), J. Russel Sprague (National Committeeman from New York), and State Chairman Edwin F. Jaeckle, whose law firm's former association with the Nazi-minded German-American Bund provided a talking point for the opposition. During the campaign Bennett charged that Jaeckle had used defamatory anti-Catholic and anti-Jewish propaganda for Dewey. *Fortune* asserts that this caused Dewey some embarrassment during the gubernatorial campaign, and that immediately upon his election the new Governor "purged Jaeckle from his councils." In 1944, however, they were reported on good terms, and Jaeckle's political machine was in motion for the nomination and then the election of Dewey to the Presidency. (After the election he resigned his post.) In the matter of general policy, particularly with regard to international affairs, Dewey's adviser was John Foster Dulles '44 of the Commission for a Just and Durable Peace of the Federal Council of Churches, whom *Life* Magazine described as "the world's highest-paid lawyer."

"On the whole," to quote Richard H. Rovere after the inauguration, "his [Dewey's] appointments seem good enough, no better or worse than those made by Smith '44, Roosevelt, or Lehman. All important jobs but two have gone to Republicans." Others considered Dewey's appointments a source of strength, pointing in particular to that of Justice Francis E. Rivers, a former State Assemblyman from the Harlem District who had been one of Dewey's most able assistant district attorneys, to the New York City Court, the highest judicial office ever held by a Negro in the state. (This appointment was later confirmed at the polls.) Another important appointment was that of former United States Solicitor General Thomas Thacher, who had worked tirelessly for the improvement of relations with Russia, to the highest state tribunal, the Court of Appeals. "Judge Thacher," said *Fortune*, "is Dewey's most impressive character witness." Evidently, said one commentator, the Governor considered quality of appointments more important than quantity: "He took two months to name a

Tax Commissioner ($365,000,000 in revenues to collect), five months to name a Mental Hygiene Commissioner (98,500 patients to care for), and nine months to find an Insurance Superintendent ($35,000,000,000 in assets to supervise)."

Financially the new administration was in a fortunate position. New York State, kept solvent under Governor Lehman, was accumulating a surplus by reason of its wartime rise in revenue, notably stock transfer levies, automobile licenses, and the state's share of the take from race-track betting; state expenditures for relief were no longer necessary, and construction was impossible. At Lehman's resignation, two months before the end of his term, the surplus was some forty million dollars. Even with the shortening of that fiscal year by Dewey, who moved the beginning of the next year from July 1 to April 1, the favorable balance was $70,000,000. (This change in the fiscal year was made to allow convenient quarterly payments of the income tax.) Under Dewey's administration this surplus continued to rise, enabling him to allow certain new ✓ "humanizing" deductions on the income tax, such as those for medical expenses and life insurance premiums. "These," it was pointed out by a commentator, "are distinct improvements, but they are all revisions of proposals that Governor Lehman was forced to veto in the lean years before the boom. Nothing new has been added." One minor but appreciated change was the introduction of a simplified income tax blank which, it was claimed, an average taxpayer could fill out in five or ten minutes. At the end of two years in office Governor Dewey announced an expected Treasury surplus of $140,000,000 (in April 1944 he gave the figure as $163,000,000) from the "hurricane of war" and proposed that it be "locked up in a separate fund to meet postWar reconstruction demands and offset possible falling revenues when war production had ceased." Such a bill was immediately introduced by an Assemblyman and promptly passed as Chapter I of the Laws of 1944.

This first bill seemed to set the precedent for other bills which Dewey favored. Through weekly dinners and frequent discussions with the Republican majority leaders of the state legislature, he exercised an effective control— many called it autocratic—over that body's deliberations. "No Republican bill is ever submitted," wrote Rovere in the May 1944 *Harper's*, "before it has gone to the Governor's office for approval and, as often as not, drastic revision. This is true even of bills that have no bearing on state policy and of those routine proposals that are submitted simply to cadge a little publicity for their sponsors." The New York *Times'* Warren Moscow reported at the end of the 1943-1944 legislative session that the measures Dewey favored were passed and virtually every bill he opposed failed of passage. In his second annual report on the state government administration, broadcast April 14, 1944, the Governor stated that tremendous progress had been made "on the task of cleaning out, from the departments and agencies of the state, the accumulated cobwebs of twenty years," and summarized the administration's accomplishments, mentioning: the drawing up of plans for public works by the Post War Planning Commission, including new housing projects, additions to overcrowded state hospitals, and a great arterial highway system; the Division of Commerce's help to businessmen planning reconversion for peace; the passage of eighteen bills proposed by Dewey to correct "long-standing evils" of corruption and inefficiency in the administration of workmen's compensation. "One of the most important things we did this winter," reported the Governor, "was to create . . . a state school of labor and industry at Cornell University. This school, blazing a great trail, will offer advanced studies in this rapidly expanding field, will prepare young men and women for useful careers of leadership in the solution of labor's perplexing problems." The Department of Mental Hygiene had been given "a thorough housecleaning," and Dewey had been able to have the law changed so that he could appoint a layman, not a psychiatrist, to its head, a change attacked by the psychiatrists' professional society. Inasmuch as the mental hospitals required fully a third of New York State's four-million-dollar budget, his shifting of the emphasis from care to cure was considered of great significance. Dewey also reported a number of measures designed to provide education, vocational training, and aid for the returned veteran, and he announced, "New York State today leads the nation in employment regardless of race, creed, or color."

"Your state administration," the Governor told his fellow New Yorkers, "also took the lead in proposing a simple, workable formula for soldier voting. Under the new state law . . . every member of the armed services desiring to vote has simply to send in his name and his home and service address. He will then receive in the mail a ballot and self-addressed envelope. . . . It will not deprive the soldier of his constitutional right to vote for every office to be filled. It will give every man and woman in the armed services, by the simple act of signing his name once, a valid vote for every candidate from President down to the local officers in his home town." This view drew the fire of a number of commentators, who claimed the law was neither simple nor workable, and it was attacked by some newspapers and by organizations ranging from the CIO to the National Lawyers' Guild and the Sweethearts of Servicemen. These critics saw in Dewey's stand an effort to cut down the votes of soldiers.

Governor Dewey based his position upon Article I, Section II of the state constitution. ". . . in time of war no elector in the actual military service of the State or of the United States, in the Army or Navy thereof, shall be deprived of his or her vote by reason of his or her absence from such election district." His opinion was that even optional use of a Federal ballot was in violation of the state constitution, as it (the Federal ballot) was limited to the main Federal offices and therefore constituted a denial of the citizen's right to vote for all offices elective by the people. This interpretation of that right was attacked by a number of lawyers, among them Morris Ernst [40] and by the National Lawyers Guild as a group.

In July Governor Dewey, by that time the Republican nominee for President (John W. Bricker [43], Governor of Ohio, had been nominated for Vice-President), having refused

to call a special session of the legislature to amend the criticized provisions, issued a statement charging that an unidentified "group with unlimited financial resources has been playing partisan politics with the right of New York's servicemen to vote" through "a campaign of deceit." Calling the state ballot "a model of simplicity," he reiterated that the Federal ballot "would be void and worthless under the constitution of this state. . . . In 1917 the same problem was before the people and the state of New York then insisted upon a full ballot for its soldiers as required by the constitution." Ernst challenged this statement in his summary of Chapter 815, Laws 1917, "which by no means covered each and every office for which the soldier would have been entitled to vote at home."

At the end of July Mayor La Guardia proclaimed a "War Ballot Week-End" for New York City, during which many organizations, including unions, churches, and business concerns, aided the city departments in distributing application forms for ballots to friends and relatives of servicemen as well as to the servicemen themselves. The demand for the forms was heavy at this time. Late in August a rising return of applications from absent servicemen was reported by the New York State Ballot Commission. This increase was attributed to Army and Navy distribution of the forms to members of the armed forces earlier in August. Stanley Walker asserted that both Dewey and anti-Dewey forces made a concerted drive to obtain as large a soldier vote as possible.

At the Governors' Conference held in Columbus, Georgia, in June 1943 "Tom Dewey delivered the week's most telling criticism of Roosevelt and its most cogent plea for states' rights. He urged the G.O.P. to take the lead in international planning. From the start he occupied the conference's leading role." Dewey, who reaffirmed his statement that he would not be a candidate for the Presidency, convinced some skeptics by making a sensible but politically dangerous proposal to avert a threatened milk shortage: he asked farmers in the Midwestern corn belt to cut down their hog population so that their feed could be used for the East's milch cows. Judging by the Gallup Poll results, this suggestion cost the New York Governor only 1 per cent of popular favor, leaving him the Presidential choice of 37 per cent of Republicans.

Dewey again stole the show at the Republican Post-War Advisory Council's meeting at Mackinac Island in September 1943. In a press conference he told a hundred reporters: "We have had a *de facto* military alliance with Great Britain practically ever since the War of 1812. In the two principal cases since, when war was made on Britain, we went to her defense. . . . I should think that [a post-War alliance with Great Britain] would be very likely and would be in our interest. . . . It would be hoped that in the working out of the peace Russia and China might be included." Then, according to *Time*, "newsmen, out of old antipathies from the days when young Tom Dewey was known as 'The Boy Scout,' asked needling questions, kept getting keen, straightforward answers. At the end of the conference Tom Dewey had won most of

DEWEY, THOMAS E.—*Continued*

them over, 100 per cent." Observers were puzzled at this forthright declaration by the habitually cautious and noncommittal Governor, who had been generally considered an isolationist. Three days later Gallup Poll results were published showing that 61 per cent of the electorate favored "a permanent military alliance with Great Britain."

This dependence on the trend of the times is a charge frequently raised against Dewey. Richard Rovere was speaking for many observers when he stated that "after twelve years in public life, with his sights on the Presidency . . . Dewey has yet to make anything resembling a full and coherent statement of his views on world affairs." The New York *Times* alone has devoted some half-dozen editorials to urging Dewey to declare himself. In 1938, when Dewey was a candidate for the governorship, the New Deal had been supported two years earlier by the greatest majority in history; Dewey let himself be called "a New Deal Republican," even going so far, it is said, as to forbid the other candidates on the state Republican ticket to discuss Roosevelt or his policies "under any provocation." "Since that time," in Rovere's words, "he has become increasingly outspoken in his opposition to Roosevelt, more and more so as each year has revealed new areas of public disenchantment. He is now a confirmed enemy of the Administration, but he has yet to give the country an adequate picture of what he proposes to do about the social and economic system. One gets the impression that he is an orthodox Republican who would like to reverse as many of Roosevelt's policies as is politically and economically feasible. But he himself has never said even that much," contenting himself with such vague but pleasant phrases as, "establish sound and consistent national policies."

In October the Governor launched an attack on the allegedly corrupt O'Connell Democratic machine which controlled Albany politically. This investigation, one of Dewey's few specific campaign objectives, was somewhat embarrassed by a threatened counterinvestigation of the perennially Republican state legislature, whose committee expense accounts were said to be ripe for an exposé.

The following November Governor Dewey faced what many regarded as his first real test of strength, when the death in office of his Lieutenant Governor forced him, under much pressure, to call a special election. Although Dewey was in excellent health and apparently not a candidate for higher office, he was regarded as anxious that a Republican be elected, so that the state would be kept in the hands of the faithful should he, the Governor, suddenly cease to govern. After the election, which Dewey's candidate, Senate majority leader Joe R. Hanley, won by 341,372 votes, the Governor proposed a bill ensuring that the Lieutenant Governor be elected along with the Governor on an indivisible ticket. In December Dewey was not in national headlines except for a statement approving the United States inter-American policy.

During the following months Governor Dewey came under the fire of educators and city officials for cutting the state aid to the schools. (This has long been a sore point with the city of New York—a Democratic stronghold in an otherwise Republican state—which holds that it would be well able to finance its own school system unaided if the state would cease to restrict its great metropolis' tax powers.) This was corrected by a supplementary budget issued later. The city representatives were also indignant over his plan to give more funds to the largely Republican communities upstate.

In late February 1944 Dewey's name was entered in the Republican primary election in Wisconsin, in which Wendell Willkie '40 was the chief contender. Although the nomination was withdrawn at Dewey's request, the Wisconsin Republicans put his name back on the slate by electing fifteen delegates pledged to vote for him at the coming National Convention, as compared with four for Commander Harold Stassen '40, three for General Douglas MacArthur '41, two unpledged sympathizers, and none for Willkie, who thereupon withdrew his candidacy. By May, *Time* reported that Chicago bookmakers were offering four to one that Dewey would win the nomination. "The wonder was that Tom Dewey had accomplished all this without any of the normal political dickering. His backers had not even set up headquarters. Dewey himself had not stirred from his New York home, except to vacation, since the Mackinac Conference last September [1943]. No campaign fund has been raised. No reporter could find a state boss anywhere . . . who had yet been promised a job, a favor, or even a pat on the back."

But Dewey still had to acquaint the public with his views. In 1942 the Governor had declared that business must learn to "bear in mind the national well-being" and to "work with the Government and like it." He predicted the cancellation of debts after the War and declared that "we shall have to lease, lend, and give away—and I favor mostly giving away—both to our allies and defeated enemies, food, medical aid, material, and equipment to rehabilitate their destitute peoples and to rebuild their well-torn lands." During about two years Governor Dewey did not commit himself on most of the issues agitating the country. But in the spring of 1944 he delivered a carefully worded speech which declared him in sympathy with the foreign policy of Secretary of State Cordell Hull '40—and voiced suspicion that the President was "privately" following a different course. Urging a "durable cohesion" of the United States and Britain, "together, I hope, with Russia and China," he pointed out that the U.S.S.R. was governed by "hardheaded, realistic leaders," and he hoped that the United States approach would be "equally realistic" and include "adequate force" to back the peace terms.

Thomas E. Dewey was absent when the Republican National Convention opened in June 1944, but his headquarters, staffed by a large complement of pretty, camera-wise girls (that they were professional models was denied by his supporters), was clicking with "machinelike efficiency" when he was nominated—1,056 to 1. He then flew from Albany to accept the nomination, announcing, "I have made no pledges, promises, or commitments, expressed or implied, to any man or woman. . . . The military conduct of the War is outside this campaign. . . . I stand firmly with the overwhelming majority of my fellow citizens in that great wide area of agreement . . . that America will participate with other sovereign nations in a cooperative effort to prevent future wars."

The Republican platform on which Dewey was officially running included: "We shall terminate rationing, price-fixing, and all other emergency powers. . . . We condemn the freezing of wage rates . . . and the binding of men to their jobs. . . . As soon as the War ends the present rate of taxation . . . should be reduced as far as is consistent with the payment of normal expenditures of government. . . . We will establish and maintain a fair protective tariff . . . [but] join with others in leadership in every cooperative effort to remove unnecessary and destructive barriers to trade." The platform also favored the "immediate feeding of starving children of our allies and friends in the Nazi-dominated countries," a constitutional amendment limiting the Presidency to two terms, and another establishing equal rights for men and women without pay discrimination. Another plank, which Walter White, president of the National Association for the Advancement of Colored People, termed "a splinter," pledged "an immediate Congressional inquiry to ascertain the extent to which mistreatment, segregation, and discrimination against Negroes who are in our armed forces are impairing morale and efficiency", "the adoption of corrective legislation," and "the establishment by Federal legislation of a permanent Fair Employment Practices Commission [such as the Administration had put into effect]." The Republicans also came out for a constitutional amendment against the poll tax and for early legislation against lynching.

One of the planks stated that "any treaty or [international] agreement" should be entered into only with a two-thirds vote of the Senate; tariffs "should be modified only by reciprocal bilateral trade agreements approved by Congress." Barely eight hours after the promulgation of the Republican platform, Governor Dewey announced that he favored Secretary Hull's program of multilateral trade agreements entered into by Executive action without the consent of Congress, and asserted that "that has always been a Republican policy." As the New York *Times* pointed out, however, Hull had encountered "violent Republican opposition" to his reciprocal trade treaty program. The candidate also emphasized his complete agreement with the Republican plank promising freedom from "civilian interference with the military and naval commands." Dewey thereby exposed himself to such comments as Helen Gahagan Douglas' [44], "The Republican nominee runs for the office of Commander in Chief on the solemn pledge that if elected he will not fulfill that duty."

In August 1944 the Republican nominee, aroused by the proposed Russian, British, and American plans for an organization to preserve world peace, warned against "cynical power politics"—subjecting "the nations of the world, great and small, permanently to the coercive power of the four nations [United States, Great Britain, Russia, and China] holding this [Dumbarton Oaks] conference." To this Secretary Hull responded with an invitation to Governor Dewey to confer with him. The

Governor accepted, but sent his adviser and presumptive choice for Secretary of State, John Foster Dulles, as his representative—a move which quelled many fears that the Republican attitude would revert to isolationism, as Dulles had spent years working for "a durable peace."

Dewey's cross-country campaign tour began September 7. The candidate made few platform appearances, concentrating on private discussions with local group leaders and on press conferences. His speeches were considered to be aimed at the radio audiences rather than at the listeners in auditoriums. The basic theme of his campaign was that the next President would serve the greater part of his term in peacetime, and that the conduct of the War was therefore not a campaign issue. This approach cost him the support of Walter Lippmann [40], who felt that a long and hard war lay before the country and it therefore should take precedence over all other issues.

Throughout the campaign Dewey pounded hard at the domestic policies of the New Deal, declaring that the country had been in the grip of the "Roosevelt Depression" until the outbreak of war, and charging "it was the New Deal that kept this country in a continuous state of depression for seven straight years." As his domestic policy, the Governor declared that he would keep all the reforms, the "good things the New Deal had done in its youth," but would administer them more fairly and efficiently and would put an end to extravagance, unnecessary bureaucracy, and the "endless public bickering" of an administration "grown tired, old, and quarrelsome in office." Dewey also charged that the Administration was afraid to discharge the soldiers promptly after the War because it feared unemployment, stating that there would be jobs under his administration and that post-War occupation of Germany and Japan could be left to volunteers. He promised to reduce most taxes, to extend social security and the pension system, and to bring the country to a golden mean between collectivism and unregulated private enterprise.

At the New York *Herald Tribune* Forum in October, Dewey took up the question of foreign policy, attacking the "personal diplomacy" which had, he charged, complicated relations with Italy, France, Poland, and Rumania, and had refreshed the German will to fight by the "Treasury's ill-conceived proposals." He later suggested that internationalizing the Ruhr industrial section of Germany would be desirable. On the foreign policy issue, however, he lost the support of the Chicago *Tribune* on the one hand, and of the New York *Times* on the other; and of such Republicans as Russell Davenport [44] and Senator Joseph Ball [43] of Minnesota. Dewey drew upon himself the severe rebuke of President Roosevelt when he stated that clashes between the President and the Congress would endanger "not only reconversion, but the peace of the world as well," whereas, "with a Congress and a President who will cooperate with each other, we need not fear the peace." Roosevelt pointed out that in Dewey's charge lay the "implication that the Republicans in Congress would cooperate [only] with a Republican President in establishing a world organization for peace." Possibly Dewey's sharpest charge was that "Mr. Roosevelt has put his party on the auction block," where

DEWEY, THOMAS E.—*Continued*

it was knocked down to "the Political Action Committee of Sidney Hillman'[40] and the Communists of Earl Browder.'[44]."

According to a survey of Press Research, Inc., Dewey had the backing of even more of the nation's press than had opposed Roosevelt in previous elections. Nevertheless, on November 7 he polled only 45.9 per cent of the popular vote to Roosevelt's 53.4 per cent, losing by 3,596,227 votes. (Dewey won 99 of the 531 electoral votes.) Unprecedentedly, his Republican National Campaign Committee ended the season with a surplus of $350,000, which, it was announced, would be used for a year-round campaign.

After his return from Georgia, where the Governor went to rest after the election, he told reporters that his and Dulles' "deep interest in the building of a lasting peace in the world" and joint efforts to that end would continue; and on December 8 Dulles went to Washington to confer with Secretary of State Edward R. Stettinius'[40], at the latter's invitation, the first of a series of such planned conferences. Later Dewey met in New York with Republican leaders of Congress, in the attempt to work out with them "a positive program for legislative action." His proposal was, however, "gently but firmly turned aside," by Senators Robert Taft'[40], Arthur Vandenberg'[40], and Wallace White, and Representatives Joseph A. Martin'[40] and Charles A. Halleck. The New York Governor also devoted some time to the preparation of his annual message to the State Assembly, in which it was announced that he would recommend an $800,000,000 highway construction program to be accomplished over a period of years, including state financing· of throughways through cities; also that an additional $35,000,000 of housing funds be allocated to New York City; and that the limit of state subsidies for repayment of public housing loans be raised by $1,250,00 annually. (This last would require a public referendum, and would also benefit New York City mainly.) There were also indications that the Governor was considering an upward revision of the educational budget.

According to Stanley Walker, supporters of Dewey contend that none of the principal objections to Dewey contain much substance. The objections, as summarized by Walker in his book *Dewey, an American of This Century*, are: Dewey lacks a thorough understanding of national and international affairs; he has changed his mind on such issues as the Lend-Lease and the participation of the United States in world affairs; he has not had the valuable experience of conferring with international leaders; he has the "mental cast" of the "prosecutor," not the judiciousness and open-mindedness of the administrator; he has "come along" too fast and needs "seasoning." To these criticisms Dewey's defenders answer that he has a clear perception of national and international affairs and can count on the co-operation of the best minds of the country; he has only changed his mind in the light of new evidence; he has an intimate acquaintance or long friendship with leaders in world affairs; he has demonstrated administrative ability; he is at the height of his physical and mental vigor. A number of commentators have re-

garded Dewey's probable choice of a Cabinet (were he elected President) as one of the strong points in his favor, for he is credited with an ability to pick good men who work together harmoniously.

In spite of the many jokes ·about Tom Dewey's size, he is actually of average height—just over five feet eight—and is considered handsome. His distinctive black mustache and heavy eyebrows make him a caricaturist's delight, as does his habit of rotating his piercing brown eyes. He has a fine baritone voice and enjoys singing duets with his wife, the former Frances Eileen Hutt of Oklahoma, who once sang the mezzo-soprano lead (as Eileen Hoyt) in George White's *Scandals.* (They met at their singing teacher's studio and were married in 1928.) The Deweys and their sons, Thomas Edmund and John Martin, spend their summers on their 486-acre Dapplemere Farm at Pawling, New York, which Dewey bought in 1937. An Episcopalian and a Mason, Dewey smokes a pack of cigarettes a day, sips water constantly, drinks alcohol sparingly, plays poker frugally, and appears cool and calm no matter how torrid the weather.

References

Am Mercury 50 :135-47 Je '40
Collier's 105 :14-15+ Je 8 '40 il por;
   113 :12+ Je 24 '44 por
Cur Hist 51 :35-9+ Ja '40 por
Harper 188 :481-90 My '44
Ladies' H J 41 :145 N '44 il pors
Life 8 :19-21 Mr 4 '40 il pors; 8 :28-9
   Ap 15 '40 il pors; 8 :84-6+ Ap 22 '40
   il pors; 17 :69-73 Jl 24 '44 il pors
Nation 150 :282 F 24 '40; 150 :356-60 Mr
   16 '40; 150 :551 Ap 27 '40
New Yorker 16 :24-8+ My 25 '40 il
Newsweek 24 :38-43 Jl 10 '44 por
Read Digest 45 :95-8 Ag '44
Sat Eve Post 216 :9-11+ Ja 22 '44;
   216 :26-7+ Ja 29 '44 il pors; 217 :9-
   10+ Ag 12 '44
Survey G 29 :286+ My '40
Time 35 :15-17 F 26 '40 pors; 35 :18-19
   Ap 15 '40; 42 :15-18 N 1 '43
Hughes, R. Attorney for the People 1940
Powell, H. Ninety Times Guilty 1939
Walker, S. Dewey: an American of This
   Century, 1944
Who's Who in America 1944-45
Who's Who in Law 1937

DICKERSON, ROY E(RNEST) Aug. 8, 1878—Feb. 24, 1944

Technical section chief of the Petroleum Division, Foreign Economics Administration; chief foreign geologist with Atlantic Refining Company before Government appointment.

Obituary

N Y Times p17 F 25 '44

DILL, SIR JOHN G(REER) 1881—Nov. 4, 1944

Outstanding British soldier and strategist; field marshal and head of the British Joint Staff Mission in the United States, where he died; as chief of the British General Staff from May to December 1940, he rebuilt the battered British Army into a formidable force

after Dunkerque defeat; see sketch 1941 Yearbook.

Obituary

N Y Times p54 N 5 '44 por

DINEHART, ALAN (din'härt) Oct. 3,
1890-July 17, 1944   Actor, producer, and
writer; featured Broadway actor, a few of
the plays in which he appeared were *The
Gipsy Trail* (1918), *Lawful Larceny* (1922),
Treat 'Em Rough (1925); co-author, director,
and co-producer of many plays: *Human Cargo*
(1936), *Step Lively Jeeves* (1937), *Rebecca of
Sunnybrook Farm* (1938) were three of his
numerous movie vehicles.

Obituary

N Y Times p19 Jl 18 '44 por

DITTER, J. WILLIAM Sept. 5, 1888—Nov.
21, 1943   United States Representative from
Pennsylvania; chairman of the Republican
National Congressional Committee; member
of the House of Representatives since 1932.

Obituary

N Y Times p1+ N 22 '43

**DOUGLAS, HELEN (MARY) GAHA-
GAN** (gā'hāgən) Nov. 25, 1900- United
States Representative from California; ac-
tress and singer

Address: b. House of Representatives Office
Bldg., Washington, D. C.; h. 7141 Senalda Rd.,
Los Angeles

When Helen Gahagan Douglas, successful
nominee for Congress from California's 14th
Congressional District, was scheduled to make
a fifteen-minute address to her party's national
convention in July 1944, she was referred to
by the press and public as the Democratic
counterpart of Republican Representative
Clare Boothe Luce '42 of Connecticut. Despite the
objections of both candidates, the comparison
was inevitable, for "both are svelte, beautiful,
and slick as all-get-out"; both have famous
husbands and a background of achievement
and theatrical glamour; each was one of the
first women to make such an address.   Mrs.
Melvyn Douglas may have had some advantage
in the second category, however, for her handsome spouse was at the time serving as an
Army captain in the China-Burma-India area.

Helen Mary Gahagan was born November
25, 1900 in Boonton, New Jersey, the daughter
of Walter Hamer Gahagan, a civil and contracting engineer who had, it is said, filled in
most of Long Island.   Her mother was Lillian
Rose (Mussen) Gahagan.   A descendant of
pioneers, little Helen was brought up in " a conservative, religious atmosphere," Republican and
Episcopalian, where the five children were
strictly disciplined.   A Brooklynite, Helen attended the Berkeley Institute for Girls (where
Elizabeth Grimball encouraged her interest in
the drama), and went on to Miss Capon's
School at Northampton, Massachusetts.   In
spite of Walter Gahagan's opposition, his
daughter was inevitably drawn to the stage. In
1922, when she had completed two years at
Barnard College of Columbia University, she

HELEN GAHAGAN DOUGLAS

and Alis de Sala wrote a play, *Shadows on the
Moon.* Her performance in this so impressed
Henry Wagstaff Gribble that he offered her
the lead in the three-performance professional
try-out of his *Shoot.* After this Miss Gahagan
was immediately offered a small professional
part—Sybil Herrington in the Henry Hull-
Leighton Osmun *Manhattan,* which Alexander
Woollcott '41 called "an artificial and desperately epigrammatic comedy which rings about
as true as a lead quarter."

Her beauty and talent made such an impression that after only two weeks in this
part the tall, vivid Helen Gahagan was selected
by William A. Brady for the leading feminine role of Anne Baldwin in Owen Davis'
Dreams for Sale.   This was in September
1922; by December the new ingenue was playing Paula in Ferenc Molnár's *Fashions for
Men* and giving an "admirable" performance.
In September 1923 Miss Gahagan starred as
Jean Trowbridge in Jules Goodman's *Chains;*
the following spring, in the title role of *Leah
Kleschna,* she undertook a part played twenty
years earlier by the famous Minnie Maddern
Fiske, whose supporting company included
George Arliss.   (Miss Gahagan's supporting
cast included a new actress known as Claudette Colbert.)   Three more plays, *Beyond,
The Sapphire Ring,* and *The Enchanted Cottage,* followed, respectively, in January, April,
and August 1925; and in November the young
actress appeared as Laura Simmons in John
van Druten's '44 *Young Woodley.*   This play,
banned in London on the grounds that it disparaged the British public schools, ran for 260
performances on Broadway.   The performance
of Glenn Hunter in the title role, however,
overshadowed that of his co-star.   In addition
to her rocket-like rise to full stardom, Miss
Gahagan became a reigning beauty: Heywood
Broun listed her as one of the twelve most
beautiful women in America, and one wit declared simply, "Helen Gahagan is the ten most
beautiful women in the world."

(Continued next page)

DOUGLAS, HELEN GAHAGAN—*Cont.*

While playing in *Young Woodley*, Miss Gahagan was introduced to Mme. Sofie Cehanovska, who had been head singing mistress at the Imperial Conservatory in St. Petersburg, and began some "very spasmodic studying" of voice with her. In spite of her success on the legitimate stage, Miss Gahagan had always remembered her mother's dream that she would be an opera star; and after appearing in two more plays, as Rose Trelawney in Pinero's *Trelawney of the Wells* and the Comtesse Zicka in Sardou's *Diplomacy*, the actress decided to give up her six-year-old stage career and devote herself completely to studying for the opera. Of the last performance she gave before going abroad to study, Stark Young wrote: "Mr. William Faversham and Miss Helen Gahagan alone are dressed with any air of this elegant [Sardou] *monde*. Mr. Ben-Ami and Miss Gahagan alone seem capable of any convincing emotion where Sardou's crafty palette requires it."

Miss Gahagan had made her first audition for the Victor Recording Company while playing in *Trelawney of the Wells*, after which she had promised the play's young publicity manager, "When I'm an opera star you'll be my press agent!" After finishing her tour in *Diplomacy*, she and Mme. Cehanovska left for Italy to work at fulfilling the prophecy. They stayed at Rimini, where Miss Gahagan worked hard at her singing. "In fact," she reported, "I did nothing but talk, sleep, and eat opera. Memorizing was very easy for me, because of my theatrical training. But it was hard work, just the same, for Madame and for me." When the American had learned the title role of *La Tosca* in Italian, she was invited through a member of the Metropolitan Opera to sing it at Morovska-Ostrava in Czechoslovakia. This, Miss Gahagan's opera debut, was the first time that she had ever sung with an orchestra. Without benefit of any rehearsal with the other actors (this is possible in operatic productions because every aspect of the performance is controlled by a rigid, unvarying "tradition"), the guest star had to depend entirely on her music for guidance, as the rest of the cast was singing in Czech, of which she understood not a word. "I sang as though I were a perfect wooden machine," she recalls, "oblivious to everything except my voice"—and she completely forgot about her acting. Then, although she had been invited to return two days later, she spent those two days crying. By the second performance everything was under control; altogether, the three performances she gave were successful.

"That's rather an achievement for a guest artist, you know, filling the house three times with the same opera—even though it doesn't sound modest for me to say so," she adds. The European newspaper critics praised her beauty, lauded her voice, but added that she had yet to learn to act. After this Miss Gahagan sang in many other places, including Salzburg, Augsburg, Belgrade, Graz, Berchtesgaden (known to Americans mainly as the later "palace" of Adolf Hitler '42), and Vienna. Again she sang Italian operas in the original language while the others sang in German, but this was fairly easy for her because she does understand German. At the time she tried not to walk through streets where she would see herself on the

advertising placards hung on lampposts—they made her nervous. But she loved the German and Austrian audiences. "They're so enthusiastic and friendly," she told one of her old acquaintances. "Crowds would wait at the stage door to cheer and they would make me feel like a mighty important person. That was fun, all right."

When "the bewitching Helen Gahagan" returned to the stage in September 1930, it was to play the opera singer in Belasco's last production, *Tonight or Never*. In the part of the temperamental and beautiful but love-starved prima donna, the soprano "made an unbelievable character no more unbelievable than she should be," sang several arias competently, and played what reviewers described as one of the most ardent love scenes on record with a member of the supporting cast, one Melvyn Douglas '42. This chore was probably made pleasanter because Miss Gahagan allegedly fell in love with her good-looking leading man ten minutes after their first meeting. They were married eight months later, in April 1931. (This was Douglas' second marriage. By his first, he had a son, Gregory, to whom Miss Gahagan is devoted.)

After the tour of *Tonight or Never* Miss Gahagan returned to New York from California to take part in a benefit performance of *Aïda* given on June 24, 1932, with Carmela Ponselle of the Metropolitan troupe as Amneris. Her voice was "resonant and clear" and she was recalled many times by the audience of 5,000. Within the month Miss Gahagan turned from grand opera to musical comedy, appearing in *The Cat and the Fiddle* in San Francisco. Later that year she had an experience which made her sharply aware of social problems.

"In 1932 I went out to Arizona by car with my husband," Mrs. Douglas recalls, "and we ran head-on into the migrants of those days. This was a migration which came from the cities, made up sometimes of young boys and young girls who had left their families—who could not face going home night after night to their jobless, unhappy homes. There were also fathers of families in the migration who simply had broken under the strain of not having a job and could not bear to stay home—thousands of them, living in box cars and in caves dug out of the sides of the hills. I saw this. I was shocked, and I really came of age at that time. I watched the New Deal cope with these problems and I became convinced it was the most enlightened administration that we'd had. At the same time, I realized that the Republicans had allowed this situation to come to pass." Although this experience changed Mrs. Douglas' political outlook, she did not go into politics at that time. For one thing, there was the trip around the world on which she and her husband were starting; for another, there was the birth, in October 1933, of Gahagan ("Peter") Douglas, who narrowly missed being born under the Japanese flag of the ship on which his parents were traveling.

In April 1934 New York again had a chance to see Helen Gahagan—in Dan Totheroh's *Moor Born*, the story of the Brontë sisters, staged by Mr. Douglas. In her favorite role she "demonstrated her very high artistry by a perceptive and understanding creation of Emily Brontë." Opinions about the play differed sharply and were perhaps weighted on the side of disapproval, but Miss Gahagan's performance was generally considered to be the best in the cast. The play was short-lived, however; and in August the star began a tour in the title role of Maxwell Anderson's '42 *Mary of Scotland*. The following December found Miss Gahagan co-producer and co-star with her husband of the Totheroth-George O'Neil *Mother Lode*. Completing the family effect, the supporting cast included her sister, Lillian Gahagan. Although the Douglases were considered "sound players and good in their parts" as "characters of bitter social portent" in early San Francisco, *Mother Lode* remained a "sentimental rhapsody." Another none-too-successful vehicle was the film version of H. Rider Haggard's *She* (1935), although Miss Gahagan was "properly impressive" in the title role of She-Who-Must-Be-Obeyed.

During the 1935-1936 season the actress-singer appeared in San Francisco and Los Angeles in *The Cat and the Fiddle* and *The Merry Widow*. October 1936 found her in New York with the Theatre Guild's unsuccessful *And Stars Remain*. In the spring of 1937 Miss Gahagan began a concert tour which she continued in the fall, and accepted an invitation to sing at the annual Salzburg Festival of Music. Then she continued her concert tour through Europe. Nazism made itself felt everywhere; Robert Armstrong, writing in *Collier's* in September 1944, says one official delicately suggested that Helen do a bit of spying for the Nazis in her native land! These facts, and the other observations she made during the tour, convinced the star that Nazism was an evil to be fought relentlessly. On returning to the United States she cabled at once to cancel her Vienna opera contract for the following year. Then she joined "every anti-Nazi organization she could find." She also threw herself into relief work in her own country, beginning with the Farm Security Administration on migratory workers' problems. In 1939 Mrs. Douglas was on the National Advisory Committee for WPA and the State Advisory Committee for NYA. (Mary Helen, the Douglases' second child, was born in 1938.) "When the Okies came," Mrs. Douglas told reporters in 1940, "I was interested in getting legislation to help them, and I wanted to get the larger picture. . . . That's how I got started [in politics], meeting people and talking—and I'm just as surprised as you are that I'm a [Democratic National] Committeewoman today." With her husband, the first actor ever elected a delegate to the Democratic convention, Mrs. Douglas was active in campaigning for the election of President Roosevelt '42 and Governor Olson of California; on occasion, the Douglases have visited the President in Washington and stayed at the White House. In 1941 Mrs. Douglas also found time to open a theatre in Del Monte, California, with a performance of Somerset Maugham's *The Constant Wife*.

But, much as she loved acting and singing, the star gave up the most lucrative years of her professional career. "I got into politics step by step," she recalls. "I always meant to stop. Offers kept coming from the theatre and pictures, and I couldn't accept—there was always something more pressing." Appointed in 1941 vice-chairman of the Democratic State Committee, an unsalaried post in which she was responsible for the expenses of the women's division, Mrs. Douglas was re-elected the following year. "I've helped pick candidates—progressive ones," she told a *PM* reporter in 1944, "and I've helped bring support to those progressives. I've had my fingers in the patronage pot, and I've seen to it that able people got the jobs. I've learned politics at the grass-roots level." In so doing, Mrs. Douglas, like her husband, made herself target of constant attacks from Hearst papers, and from the floor of Congress.

In 1942, after Melvyn Douglas joined the Army as a private (after having completed a year of unsalaried work in Washington, organizing the Arts Division program of the OCD), his statuesque wife began doing all the housework and cooking formerly delegated to two maids, as well as caring for the children and keeping up her relief and political activities. (Their hilltop house is a relatively modest one-story building, in which they "tried desperately to avoid elegance," the only really luxurious note being a swimming pool used by all the children of the neighborhood.) When the Democratic Congressman from California's 14th District, Thomas F. Ford, refused to run for renomination because he was disgusted with "being a member of the majority party and seeing the minority run the House with the aid of Southern reactionaries," Helen Douglas filed nomination papers with the California Secretary of State for his office. This district includes many low-income families (a California Representative need not live in the district which he represents) whom Mrs. Douglas acquainted with her views by going to the apartment houses and calling meetings in the lobbies to which the housewives came without stopping to take off their aprons.

"I am interested in politics," she told reporters, "because of deep convictions that government is just what you make it. If you are not interested, and do nothing about it, you have no right to complain about what your government does. Personally, I just feel very deeply about the situation we're in, and I hope I can help if I get elected to Congress. If we weren't in this situation I'd probably be singing or acting in one of the plays they've asked me to be in in New York." With her two-to-one victory over seven male opponents in the Democratic primaries, Mrs. Douglas' election was considered certain, as the polyglot 14th is predominantly Democratic. In her campaign she had the support of various labor groups, including the CIO and I.L.G.W.U. Disregarding all personal aspects, she campaigned on these issues: equal rights for members of all races and creeds, limited food subsidies, full respect for the rights of organized labor, full opportunity for honestly conducted private enterprise, protection of small business and small farmers, and adequate taxes based on ability to pay. And she won.

As a delegate to the National Convention in July 1944 Mrs. Douglas was forthright and businesslike. "Helen has really been in the smoke-filled rooms," as one political leader remarked, "and that's the first time that's happened with any woman." She was, inevitably, regarded as "the Democrats' answer to Clare Boothe Luce," the "glamour girl of the Re-

DOUGLAS, HELEN GAHAGAN—*Cont.*

publican convention," but Mrs. Douglas refused to be drawn into a duel with the playwright, for whom she professes great respect. "I'm not a fencer," she explains, "I'm not a wit. I don't say things smarter than other people. I'm not going to spar. It is nonsense, with people dying the world over, for anyone to carp." At press conferences she kept to the main issues, in spite of the typical insistence of certain male reporters in asking about her clothes and her measurements when she was talking about foreign policy and Henry A. Wallace[40], whom she had just nominated in a California caucus.

What the reporters did find out and faithfully record was that Mrs. Douglas is five feet seven inches tall and wears a size sixteen dress. Blue-eyed and brown-haired (her hair looks black or auburn depending on the lights), she walks with a long, athletic stride, dresses simply, never wears nail polish, and speaks in a strong, clear voice with no sign of affectation. She never kisses babies—except her own—and seems to have convinced the convention reporters that she is "terribly in earnest about her humanitarian and liberal beliefs. . . . She says she's in politics to stay as long as she is useful—and somehow you believe her." She has given up her tennis and horseback riding for the duration; in her free time she reads economics, history, social philosophy, and detective stories, and employs a political secretary and outside researchers. "On a quick guess," wrote one interviewer, "there probably aren't twenty members now in the House who are better posted on politics, economics, and foreign affairs than Miss Gahagan." In private life her best friends are said to be Orson Welles[41] and his wife Rita Hayworth. Mrs. Douglas' constituents greet her with "Hi, Helen!" In December 1944 she was voted the best-dressed woman in politics, replacing Mrs. Luce on the Fashion Academy's list of awards.

References

Collier's 114:40 S 23 '44 por
NY Post p30 Jl 19 '44 pors
PM p14 O 1 '44 il por

International Motion Picture Almanac 1937-38
Who's Who in America 1944-45
Who's Who in the Theatre 1939

DOW, WILLARD H(ENRY) Jan. 4, 1897- Chemist; industrialist

Address: b. Dow Chemical Co., Midland, Mich.; h. 923 W. Park Dr., Midland, Mich.

For his "dynamic and successful leadership in the American chemical industry," for his "daring enterprise in the direction of the extraction of bromine and of magnesium from sea water," and in the production of synthetic rubber and plastics "that have attracted worldwide attention," Willard H. Dow was awarded the 1943 Charles Frederick Chandler Medal, which Columbia University confers annually for notable achievements in the field of chemistry.

As president, general manager, and chairman of the board of directors of the Dow Chemical Company, Willard H. Dow controls "one of the greatest factors in American production of magnesium and synthetic rubber. Its [Dow's] list of products is a polysyllabic headache. . . . Its plants are scattered over the country . . . to Texas, North Carolina, and the upper peninsula of Michigan. . . . Dow provides many of the ingredients going into highly advertised products of other companies." Dow was "the first company [in the world] to extract magnesium from sea water, the first to break the German domination of synthetic aniline and indigo dyes, the first to increase oil well production by administering acid, and the first to make commercial production of styrene, which is needed for the Buna process of making synthetic rubber." The Dow policy has always been the finding of new and improved methods of production, rather than the development of new products.

Willard Henry Dow was born January 4, 1897, the son of Herbert Henry and Grace Anna (Ball) Dow, in Midland, Michigan. There his father had founded the Dow Chemical Company, which was incorporated that same year. Young Willard Dow attended the Midland schools and the University of Michigan, where in 1919 he received the degree of B.S. Then he joined his father's staff as a chemical engineer, having made a practice of working at the Dow factory during his summer vacations. Three years later he became a director and four years after that he was made assistant general manager. Upon Herbert Dow's death in 1930 his son succeeded him as president and general manager; and in 1941 Willard H. Dow was also elected chairman of the board of directors of the company. He has two honorary doctorates: a D.Sc. awarded by the Michigan College of Mining and Technology in 1939, and a D.Eng. from the University of Michigan in 1941. (Like his father, he is referred to as Dr. Dow.)

In 1941 the Dow Chemical Company received the yearly award of the magazine, *Chemical and Metallurgical Engineering*, for "pioneering work in the recovery of metallic magnesium from sea water." Colonel Alfred H. White, chairman of the Award Committee, said that one hundred per cent of the company's output of magnesium alloy, lighter and more durable than aluminum, was being used for defense purposes (this was said four days before Pearl Harbor); and that each day the company's process recovered 300,000,000 gallons of ocean water from which it produced the alloy.

The Dow Chemical Company dominates the life of Midland, a town of about 12,000 inhabitants, of whom 6,000 are employed by Dow. It has "some residential areas unmatched probably in the country for imaginative architecture [most of it the work of Dow's younger brother, architect Alden Dow] . . . one of the highest birth rates and one of the highest percentages of college graduates in the nation . . . and so many women's clubs that . . . the average housewife belongs to five of them." This is due mainly to the presence of the Dow research laboratories, staffed by "Ph.D.'s in the physical sciences" who "marry girls of virulently high I.Q." "Dow puts up between sixty-five and seventy cents for research against every dollar paid to stockholders—one of the highest ratios in the industry," says *Fortune*. "Research goes on in fifteen independent laboratories, answerable only to Dr. Dow. It is research primarily characterized by the development of new processes—not the discovery of new chemicals, but the engineering of known and new reactions into new or improved commercial production. Dow is probably the world's leading electro-chemical engineer in the chemistry of brine, and its research accumulation made it ready for protean development." And development has been great: "in other, peaceful times the extent of that empire might be expressed merely by noting that Dow's sales are running currently at a rate in excess of a phenomenal $100,000,000 [yearly]. . . . Dow's net after taxes on a twenty-five per cent increase in sales will barely top . . . $9,000,000."

Herbert H. Dow laid the foundations of the company but as *Fortune* states, Willard Dow "brought the organizing ability to expand them." Under his guidance the Dow Chemical Company turns out more than 500 products, of which forty per cent are chemicals used by industry; twenty-five per cent are magnesium products; ten per cent are pharmaceuticals; and the remaining twenty-five per cent include plastics such as Styran, Saran, phenolite, and Thiokol, as well as all the Dowicides. All this is built on a base of brine, vast deposits of which underlie the site selected for the plant's location. Thus it is the Dow specialty to "make something" of sea water. It is estimated that the Dow brine wells will last another 500,000 years. Water from the ocean is also being used for magnesium extraction. This makes the process more complicated, for ocean water is far less concentrated than Michigan brine, left from long-vanished seas.

Probably the greatest field for the Dow Company's future expansion is magnesium, which it extracts in pure form from the brine. The company now handles some 500,000,000 gallons of brine a day. Almost 1,000 pounds of magnesium are used in the average airplane, and Dow produces more than ninety-five per cent of all American magnesium. In addition, new Dowicides (fumigants, germicides, etc.) have been successfully developed; and the synthesizing of plastics offers interesting possibilities for improvement. At this time Dow is working on synthetic rubber, including Thiokol, which is used for retreading tires. "The advantages are that the process is simple, the plant easy to erect, the materials quickly accessible, and Thiokol can retread and retread a tire as long as the carcass stands up." The Baruch[41] report recommended increasing its production as a stopgap retread for civilian tires.

In March 1944 the Department of Justice brought an antitrust indictment against the Dow Company, charging it with a pre-War agreement with Germany's I. G. Farben, an agreement then believed to have brought about the United States magnesium shortage. Testifying before the Truman[42] Investigating Committee of the Senate at his own request, Dow assailed the Department of Justice as "authors and spreaders of a smear campaign" and denied the charges. A week later a report prepared by the Truman Committee cleared the company and praised it for turning out 61 per cent of all magnesium produced in the United States in 1943.

WILLARD H. DOW

In accepting the 1944 Gold Medal Award of the American Institute of Chemists, Dow issued a warning against controlled economy. "We are being told that . . . we must ease out of controls and that chaos would follow their sudden ending. By the very nature of our present controls we cannot ease out of them. We can only ease into permanent control. . . . Whatever may be the seeming dangers of throwing off our controls, they are as nothing in contrast to the dangers of being merely a tended herd." A few months later in an open letter to WPB Chief Donald M. Nelson[41], he asserted that it was "the plain duty of the War Production Board to remove at once all controls from the magnesium industry." As far as the needs of war were concerned, there was no longer any reason to keep the magnesium industry under any form of allocation control, he concluded. The Government's answer came in an action on October 4, 1944 lifting all controls on the use of magnesium. Conversion to peacetime industry became an immediate issue. One-third lighter than aluminum, magnesium has unlimited potentialities and will be used everywhere from the kitchen and nursery to automobile factories—any place where a lessening of weight is an advantage. About one-third of the present production capacity will be subject to conversion. The value of civilian products after from one to two post-War years is seen at about $75,000,000.

Dow's activities are not confined to the Dow Chemical Company itself, but are carried on in part by a string of subsidiaries, including "Dowell, Inc., to service oil wells; Io-Dow Chemical Company, to extract iodine from California oil well brines; Ethyl-Dow Chemical Company, to extract bromine for anti-knock fluid from sea water off North Carolina; Cliffs Dow Chemical Company, to

DOW, WILLARD H.—*Continued*

secure wood-product chemical supplies. And in 1938 Dow, in lieu of building a new West Coast plant, merged Great Western Electro-Chemical Company, for which it paid close to $10,000,000, into its corporate structure. Great Western makes a complementary line of products." Willard Dow is president of Midland Ammonia and of Ethyl-Dow.

Dow was married to Martha L. Pratt of Midland on September 3, 1921. They have two children, Helen Adeline and Herbert Henry Dow II. Described as "able, youngish-looking, with gray hair and a bright, gossipy humor," Dow is five feet eight inches tall, blue-eyed, and weighs 160 pounds. Presbyterian by creed, and a Republican, he is also a thirty-second degree Mason (Shriner) and a member of the American Chemical Society, the American Institute of Chemical Engineers, the Newcomen Society, the Torch Club, Theta Delta Chi, and Alpha Chi Sigma. His New York club is the Chemists, and he is also a member of the Detroit Club and of the Midland Country Club. He has been a member of Deutsche Chemische Gesellschaft, and is now on the advisory board of the Chicago Chemical Procurement District of the Chemical Warfare Service, United States Army.

References

Fortune 26:111+ D '42
Sat Eve Post 215:20+ My 1, '43 il por
Who's Who in America 1944-45
Who's Who in Commerce and Industry 1944

DRAKE, ALFRED   Oct. 7, 1914-   Singer; actor

Address: b. c/o Theatre Guild, 23 W. 53rd St., New York City

The choice of the young actor-baritone, Alfred Drake, for the male lead in the Theatre Guild's *Oklahoma!* was not a hasty one. Richard Rodgers '40, the composer, and the Guild had remembered him from their own shows and others in which the rapidly rising newcomer had acted and in which he had received consistently good reviews, despite the mediocre quality of some of the plays. Thus, after only a few years of appearing in several failures and a few minor successes, Drake had the good fortune to be chosen for a musical play which subsequently turned out to be a fabulously successful enterprise for him as well as for the producers.

The male lead in "one of the most captivating shows of the [1943-44] season" was born Alfred Capurro, October 1, 1914, in New York City, the son of John M. and Elena Teresa (Maggiolo) Capurro. Although Alfred began his professional career in 1935 while still a junior in the teacher-training course at Brooklyn College, he started his singing appearances much earlier—as a child in the choir of Brooklyn's Our Lady of Good Council Church. "Our choirmaster," says Drake, "was a Scotsman, and we sang many original and unorthodox masses by Beethoven, Schubert, and Brahms. It was very exciting; and I learned a lot there." Later he continued with his music at college in the glee club and in other extracurricular groups. Having this

interest and practice in singing, plus the encouragement of his musical mother and brother, it was natural that Drake should begin to think casually about singing as a possible career. Then one spring day in 1935 he happened to pass by the Adelphi Theatre in New York City, where auditions were in progress for R. H. Burnside's proposed season of Gilbert and Sullivan. It was a chance not to be missed: Drake went in to audition and, to his surprise, was hired as understudy and chorus boy. When the nine weeks' engagement ended he and his older brother Arthur finished up the summer singing with an itinerant opera company on the Steel Pier in Atlantic City. "We were damn good," says Alfred now, "but nobody listened."

At the end of the summer he went back to Brooklyn College to complete his course in education, although by then he had found that he was no longer interested in the teaching profession. Immediately after his graduation in 1936, therefore, he accepted the opportunity to return for another season with the opera company in Atlantic City. When he went back to New York in the fall he was able, with his brief experience, to secure another job as chorus boy and understudy in the elaborate musical spectacle *White Horse Inn*, which was opening at the Center Theatre that October. During Christmas week one of the stars, William Gaxton, became ill, and Drake was rushed into his part with scarcely any preparation. He says, in fact, that he had not even learned Gaxton's third-act lines and so was forced to memorize them during the intermissions. The novice played the role for only eight performances, but the time was long enough for him to be remembered in theatre circles.

As a result of the brief starring appearance (he continued as chorus boy for twenty-odd more weeks) Drake was given a part in Dwight Deere Wiman's jolly Rodgers and Hart '40 musical *Babes in Arms*, when it opened the following April. The new show had a long run—about forty-four weeks—and, although Drake was only one of the dozen or more gifted but unstarred young people in the cast, the engagement helped to establish him as a competent and dependable performer. "*Babes in Arms*," wrote the *Theatre Arts Monthly*, "is acted and sung and danced entirely, or almost entirely, by a group of players in or under their teens, who are so well skilled in their crafts that they very nearly override the fear lest—with vaudeville gone—we may soon have no comic actors for the revues that are Broadway's chief contribution to theatre form and bright entertainment. . . . The young actors in *Babes in Arms* . . . have a fresh and fluent skill, a theatre presence, and a developed power of projection that are distinctly disarming, not to say impressive." Following this engagement Drake became identified for a time with a number of other similar revues with young sprightly casts, although the other productions were not so consistently high in quality.

The next spring (1938) he was given a supporting role in the nostalgic Continental operetta *The Two Bouquets*, produced by Marc

Connelly. The reviewers who saw this escapist costume piece were very complimentary to Drake, mentioning his "especially charming voice" and light comedy touch. Drake's own comment was that he had lost a lot of weight hurrying in and out of his costumes during the few weeks of the run. His next play, which had had a tryout at the Suffern County (New York) Theatre during the summer of that same year, was brought to New York City in February 1939. It was a Nancy Hamilton revue, *One for the Money*; and in it Drake had an opportunity to burlesque Orson Welles '41, at which he was quite successful. As Robert Benchley '41 remarked: "Alfred Drake *is* Orson Welles." The opulent production, many of the sharply satirical Hamilton sketches, and the acting were all favorably reviewed, but according to most of the critics the revue on the whole was not the best of its kind. It was, wrote Burns Mantle, "a Right-wing revue . . . aimed directly at, and staged for, New York's cafe society set." The public, he reported, was slow to respond, but gradually the cleverness of the lyrics caught on, and the show ran until June, when it went on to Chicago for six weeks.

At the end of September of the same year Drake appeared in still another musical, *The Straw Hat Revue*. Two of the other young hopefuls in the cast were Danny Kaye '41 and Imogene Coca. There was little critical mention of individual performances; and the general comment on the production was that it contained everything from the "excellent to the execrable," and did not quite click. (It closed the first of December.) A bright note for Drake came from *Commonweal*, though, which noted that he had given "admirable assistance."

The following February (1940) another Nancy Hamilton revue, *Two for the Show*, was brought to Broadway with a cast that included Eve Arden, Betty Hutton, Richard Haydn, Brenda Forbes, and Drake. The show was a sequel in form to *One for the Money* of the previous season. The sketches were in the "*New Yorker* style," sophisticated, witty, and "sometimes a little brutal"—a popular enough blend for New York audiences—but the revue was not popular with the press. (It ran about sixteen weeks.) That same year, when Drake's brother Arthur tried out for the Metropolitan Opera Company through its radio auditions, Alfred "went along for the ride," as he expresses it. His older brother succeeded in winning a contract at the Metropolitan, where he is known as Arthur Kent, and Alfred himself got as far as the semifinals. (In recent years he has been studying singing with Clytie Hine Mundy, formerly connected with Covent Garden Opera in London.)

Since his graduation from college in 1936 Drake had thus been fortunate in being able to secure many roles, but, to his disappointment, they had all been singing ones. His baritone had received appreciative critical comment; yet his ambition, unlike his brother's, was to act. He finally got his opportunity the summer of 1940, when he played the male lead (Norman) in Francis Swann's comedy *Out of the Frying Pan* during its tryout run in Connecticut. The producers were some-

ALFRED DRAKE

what skeptical about his doing the part in the Broadway production, but at the insistence of the author he was in the play when it opened in New York in February 1941. *Out of the Frying Pan* proved to be a rather "foolish little item" about "adolescent trifles"—six stage-struck boys and girls attempting to get themselves established—but Drake received his customary good notices.

His next chance at a straight role was as the lead opposite Helen Craig in the short-lived production of *As You Like It* the following October. "The youngsters gathered on the stage," wrote the *Theatre Arts Monthly*, "treated their reverent playwright casually, but always with spirit and assurance. . . . Alfred Drake made a personable Orlando." His Orlando, said another critic, was "realistic, rather than romantic, but he is forthright and likable." At the close of this play Drake was scheduled to go into *The Admiral Takes a Wife*, a satire on the United States Navy in the Pacific, but the attack on Pearl Harbor in December stopped the show before it opened. After that brief excursion into satire he was given the male ingenue part in a Theatre Guild production, *Yesterday's Magic*, by Emlyn Williams '41. The play, the dirge of a dipsomaniac Shakespearean actor struggling to reform, opened in April 1942 with Paul Muni '44 as the protagonist. Criticisms of the script were gloomy: "hackneyed and hammy", "torturous", "lugubrious," and "sentimental." Even the star did not receive good notices. The New York *Times* reviewer wrote of Drake, though, that the young man, "who has never had a good part before, is playing . . . with force and clarity"; and the New York *Herald Tribune* critic remarked that Drake "does everything possible" with his "equivocal role" as the lover of the drunkard's crippled daughter. (This daughter was played by Jessica Tandy, who also was well received.)

The end of Drake's mediocre roles came with his engagement for the part of Curly in *Oklahoma!* (1943-44), the Theatre Guild's

DRAKE, ALFRED—*Continued*

musical adaptation of Lynn Riggs's serious play of the early Oklahoma Indian country, *Green Grow the Lilacs*. The cast for the Guild interpretation had been carefully chosen as to type. In addition, each person selected had to be a fine singer—although none of them, as it turned out, had had wide experience in the art of musical comedy. Composer Richard Rodgers, determined that the words of the songs should get over clearly to the audience, had held singing lessons for the cast every few days for four or five hours. The result of this intensive training was that many reviewers noted particularly that the group sang with the thought "that the audience might also like to hear Mr. Hammerstein's '44 poetry." The cumulative result of *Oklahoma!* was: "a beautifully coordinated and integrated and astonishingly different production from the rowdy musicals familiar to Broadway." Drake himself was given the happy chance to introduce and become identified with such attractive Rodgers' melodies as "The Surrey With the Fringe on Top", "Oh, What a Beautiful Mornin'", "People Will Say We're in Love," songs which soon became musical favorites of the public.

Recommendations of Drake for the role of Curly had come from Rodgers, who had remembered him from *Babes in Arms*, and from the Theatre Guild, which had engaged him for its *Yesterday's Magic*. All the criticisms of Drake's singing and his interpretation of his cowboy part seemed to justify the selection. *Variety*'s 1942-1943 poll of the New York drama critics, for example, credited him with giving the best male performance in a Broadway musical. He was "well chosen," wrote Stark Young for his fellow reviewers. He had "plenty of voice . . . without the banging and whacking methods of most musical comedy singing." Also, Young wrote, he had none of the "stale, ham lyricism that would spoil that amiable impression of sly, gay simplicity." He was "fresh and engaging", "pleasantly unaffected and direct . . . his acting more than adequate to the modest demands made upon it," added others. And Alfred Drake, as the *New Yorker* critic said, "is what every writer of musical plays will want in his shows."

The theatre, radio, and motion pictures soon signified that Drake was precisely what they wanted. In the fall of 1943 he signed a contract with Columbia Pictures, to begin in June 1944. The Theatre Guild made arrangements with him both to direct and act for it for three years in six months' intervals between his film work. (Drake declared in a Bessie Beatty '44 radio interview that his ambition was to have a repertory company of his own.) In addition to stage and screen commitments he had the job of the singing "emcee" on the sponsored weekly CBS *Broadway Matinee* during the fall and spring of 1943-1944. "His baritone and brilliance," declared *Cue* Magazine, were "the heart blood of this variety show."

Drake's feeling about leaving a successful play while it was still running was that by June 1944 *Oklahoma!* would be better off without him. "I think after an actor has been in a part for a certain length of time he's exhausted every possibility for improvement. . . . After that I believe it [one's performance] gets to be completely mechanical. For the good of the show an actor should then step out and let a newcomer in. In many cases a new actor will give the part a fresh slant and cause a general lift in the performance of the entire company."

Since Drake's Columbia contract did not call for an immediate picture, the actor was able, in December 1944, to open in the Theatre Guild's *Sing Out, Sweet Land*, with Burl Ives and Alma Kaye. In the role of Barnaby Goodchild, Drake played, according to Lawrence Langner '44 of the Guild, "a kind of immortal American song-and-dance man, who wanders from one century to the next, from Puritan times, through the Revolution, through the American frontiers . . . into industry, on up into modern times. This fellow becomes a kind of symbol of the national character, changing, developing as the country changes, develops, reflecting all this in his songs." While many critics found the book weak and a good idea unfortunately burlesqued in spots, they felt again that Drake proved himself a refreshing singer and an engaging actor, even though, in the words of some of the reviewers, he was occasionally required to be too "cute."

Besides singing and acting Drake has done some writing and composing. With Edward Eager he is co-author of an operetta, *The Burglar's Opera*, which was performed by the Columbia Workshop Theatre of Columbia University one week during the summer of 1942. Russell Lewis saw one of the performances at Columbia and as a result asked Drake and Eager to make an adaptation of Offenbach's *La Belle Hélène* as a possible vehicle for Grace Moore '44. The French composer, Darius Milhaud '41, has done the arrangements. Eager and Drake also made a "very free musical-comedy adaptation" of Goldoni's play *The Liar*; and Drake by himself is the composer and lyricist of *The People's War*. His hobbies are tennis and reading. He belongs to no political party, but says that he has a general inclination toward "liberal socialism."

Drake was married September 29, 1940 to the singer Alma Rowena Tollefsen, whom he met during his engagement with the Gilbert and Sullivan company in 1935. Following a divorce, he was married again, on March 10, 1944, to E. Harvey Brown, formerly of the *Oklahoma!* cast. He has wavy brown hair, light gray eyes, a "slow, easy smile," and a friendly voice. As a *Cue* reporter has put it, Drake has an "engaging air . . . also, more energy, erudition, and entertainment value" than the reporter had seen in a long time.

References

Cue 12:10 N 27 '43 por
N Y Herald Tribune IV p1+ F 13 '44
   por
N Y Journal-American p8 N 13 '43

DRAPER, PAUL Oct. 25, 1909- Dancer
Address: b. c/o Metropolitan Musical Bureau, 113 W. 57th St., New York City

"Almost inevitably, whenever a writer attempts to describe the dancing of Paul Draper, he immediately becomes involved in a series of seeming contradictions. This state of affairs originates in the free use which Draper makes of various dancing techniques; for while his dancing is, strictly speaking, based on both the methods of tap and ballet, in actual performance it resembles neither. What emerges, instead, is Draper's highly individualized fusion of the two types of dancing which is sometimes set to the music of Bach and Handel in a manner that would probably cause those old masters to wink slyly but happily at one another. "It is hard to write about him without firing a barrage of superlatives," stated a recent press notice. "No other dancer has ever succeeded so amazingly in combining classical forms with modern technique."

Dubbed "Dancing Hamlet" by his author-mother, the former Muriel Sanders, Paul Draper belongs to a socially prominent family of various talents. He is the great-grandson of Charles A. Dana, who founded the New York *Sun*, and the nephew of Ruth Draper, the inimitable monologuist. His father, also named Paul Draper, was a concert singer of some repute who was studying voice in Florence, Italy, at the time of his son's birth on October 25, 1909.

When Paul was two years old his family moved from Florence to London, where Muriel Draper took a large house in which she entertained enthusiastically, expensively, and "apparently ceaselessly." The Draper drawing room often bristled with the witticisms of Gertrude Stein, Henry James, Pablo Casals, Norman Douglas, Mabel Dodge, and Artur Rubinstein, among others. What Draper terms the constant "showing off" of his mother's guests had an unexpected effect on him; he developed a bad case of "inferiority complex," with an accompanying stutter. (After he became a top-notch celebrity himself, however, his stutter disappeared.)

Four years of living in London depleted the family's finances, and the Drapers returned to the United States. When Mr. and Mrs. Draper separated a year later, young Paul was sent to his maternal grandparents in Haverhill, Massachusetts. Later he was shunted over to an uncle in Pawling, New York. Finally, at the age of nine, he was taken to New York by his mother and sent to the progressive Lincoln School of Teachers College, from which he was expelled after two years. He had stopped a Christmas production of Good King Wenceslaus when he produced a large toy elephant in the midst of the scene in which he was appearing.

His first expulsion from school seems to have established a precedent, inasmuch as thereafter his stay in any one school was limited to two years. Following the Lincoln School, his mother enrolled him at a school in Morristown, New Jersey. Two years later, true to schedule, Paul was expelled, although he had won a number of scholastic prizes. In the hope that his allergy to school might be im-

PAUL DRAPER

proved by a change of scene, Paul's mother shipped him down to Virginia with instructions to cool his heels for a while. He remained in the South until he was sixteen, when, in an ostensibly chastened state of mind, he went off to the Loomis Institute in Windsor, Connecticut. This time he anticipated his superiors by leaving before they had a chance to expel him; besides, he argued, it was spring, he was seventeen, and exams were too near for comfort.

He went to New York City, borrowed some money, bought a used car, and set out for the literary colony at Woodstock, New York. There his funds ran low and he took a job digging ditches. One day he was discovered at his new occupation by his horrified Aunt Ruth. Recovering her composure, the famous monologuist extemporized a private monologue for her nephew's benefit which convinced him of the wisdom of taking an engineering course at the Polytechnic Institute of Brooklyn. Obediently he persevered at his studies for an entire year, during which he lived in Greenwich Village and worked nights at a drug store fountain.

When that phase of his life ended, Draper thought of entering the field of *belles lettres*. However, a rejection slip from *Commonweal* Magazine persuaded him to try journalism instead, and for a short time he worked on the old New York *World* as assistant music critic to Samuel Chotzinoff [40]. After that he solicited advertisements for what he calls a "phony" musical magazine. Draper stopped casting about for his real vocation in 1930, the year marked by the passing of the Charleston in favor of the Lindy Hop. The widespread mania for the new dance precipitated a drastic shortage of dancing teachers. Draper, who had a natural flair for dancing, applied persistently at an Arthur Murray [43] school until he was accepted as an instructor. The job ended abruptly, however, says Irving Drutman in the *Saturday Evening Post*, when Murray discovered he was giving "private lessons away from the school and pocketing the money."

(Continued next page)

DRAPER, PAUL—*Continued*

That winter (1930) Draper ran into a Broadway dancing school conducted by someone named Tommy Nip. Draper took half-a-dozen lessons in tap dancing, which left him with a hazy, theoretical notion of the basic step, the time-step. He then left the establishment of Mr. Nip, and has never taken another tap lesson.

Undaunted by the elementary state of his dancing, Draper sailed for London shortly after, fortified with many letters of introduction. These obtained for him numerous invitations to dinner but no jobs. After a long period of unemployment a friend of his found him a job as a dancer at the Plaza Theatre where an "eccentric" dancer was wanted. Draper's clumsiness was probably mistaken for his style. He was given an ill-fitting evening suit, white cotton gloves, and a burlesque make-up. "It was amazing how bad I was," he states. "Anyway, we assumed I was so bad I couldn't get worse. I finally worked and worked, and practiced myself right into the *Sensations of 1932*, where I did a double with a partner called Nina Ford." Draper was given a "flash routine" in which he danced on a marble pedestal. For twenty weeks they toured England—Draper, Miss Ford, and the pedestal. At the end of the engagement Draper and the pedestal crossed to France, where for some time he earned scant pay by dancing in various cafes.

Feeling discouraged, he then accepted an offer from his family to return home. The only stipulation they made was that he promise to give up dancing and enter his uncle's brokerage business. Paul agreed, with tongue in cheek. As expected, he no sooner was off the boat than he was up on the pedestal again, dancing at Cobina Wright's Sutton Club. Luck was suddenly with him, and the engagement was followed by others at the Roxy and Paramount Theatres, the Radio City Music Hall, and the Casino de Paris, which earned him between $150 and $200 a week. In 1935, still on the pedestal, he appeared in the musical production, *Thumbs Up*.

Then one fatal afternoon, while filling a Los Angeles engagement, Draper smashed the pedestal, with malice aforethought. It had annoyed him to such an extent that he wonders why he hadn't wrecked it sooner. That same season he nearly wrecked Warner Brothers by making a super-flop of a film for them called *Colleen* (1936). Draper objectively reports the outcome: "Warner Brothers looked me in the eye and told me confidently that I ought to take up pottery, or some other useful work, and leave show business to get along the best it could without me."

Indifferent to his Hollywood failure, Draper continued to dance and to listen to good music. He had also begun to study at the School of American Ballet, just in order to keep himself limber. Then, suddenly, an idea that was to constitute the turning point of his life occurred to him. He became aware of the possibilities that could be realized if his three interests—tap dancing, ballet, and music—were combined.

He spent three years of hard work developing his idea. After that he was able to name his own price. What he evolved was an eclectic manner of tap dancing based on the forms of the classic ballet. His dances, all of which are composed by himself, are set to modern blues and jazz tunes as well as to the music of Bach, Scarlatti, Beethoven, and Brahms. John Martin, the dance critic of the New York *Times*, has stated: "Draper is unique among tap dancers in that he considers his work as an art. He does not think up a series of tricks and merely join them together by means of time steps; he composes in terms of rhythms. . . . His footwork is exquisite, precise. . . . Draper is unquestionably an artist and a delightful one."

Jacques Porel, the French critic, compares Draper's dancing to that of Massine [40] and Lifar, whom he thinks Draper has now surpassed. "Natural in his movement," writes Porel, "genuine down to his smallest gesture, everything about him carries the stamp of authenticity—of truth. . . . He has enough originality and talent to become the greatest of living dancers." Of his style, Porel says: "He has succeeding in combining Russian choreography with the purely American form. . . . From the floor to the waist he is an American, but he uses this rhythm of the feet as an accompaniment, a sort of base to his true choreography. The upper part of his body has gone abroad, it has expatriated itself—he seems to dance on two continents. . . . He has created a new style which is at once startling and reassuring. He can beat out the rhythm of Handel with his obedient feet, dance to Debussy with a sure and unfaltering grace, and perform with equal certainty to any American folk tune. He is as close to the admirable Negro dancers of Harlem, to a dancer such as Bill Robinson [41], for example, as to that incredible Russian who left us one evening in his final leap through the open window. He dances the past, the present, and the future."

A part of Draper's dancing equipment is a section of floor which he carries from place to place. It acts as the sounding board for his taps, and on it depend the qualities and degrees of the shading. It is composed of metal against plywood, and it is so sensitive that a worn spot in any section of it will affect the sound of the tapping.

Draper became the idol of fashionable audiences in New York and London. For several seasons he has appeared as the featured dancer at smart supper clubs and in duo-recitals with the harmonica player, Larry Adler [44], several times holding forth with Adler at the New York City Center in a typical program ranging from Handel to Gershwin. These Center programs have proved highly successful. One of the features of them, and of other duo-concerts, has been an "ad-lib" duet in which the artists improvise to a medley of tunes called out by the audience.

In early 1944 the dancer gave a duo-recital with Duke Ellington [41], presenting a dance routine improvised especially for one of Duke Ellington's latest compositions. In 1941 he had made a successful tour of South America, and the following year he was one of the headliners in the musical revue *Priorities of 1942*. In 1944 Draper twice toured South America. "From my own experience at least," wrote Stark Young of one performance, "I should say he [Draper] is one of the major achievements to come out of our American theatre. . . . I have seen few things [there] more luminous, expert, and right."

This red-haired, poker-faced, slim dancer, who earns in the comfortable vicinity of $75,000 a year, has received as much as $5,000 for a single evening's performance at a private party. But if his dancing has brought Draper many advantages, it also has imposed severe restrictions on his time. A stage performance leaves him physically exhausted. He rarely can go anywhere because his work takes up most of his time, and by the time he is ready to call it a day everyone else he knows is usually asleep. Sundays excepted, he rises at about two in the afternoon, practices from four until seven, and is at work either at a theatre or night club from nine until midnight or later. If he had more time, he states, he wouldn't waste it on parties or entertainment—he would go off somewhere and learn to play a musical instrument.

It was in Rio de Janeiro in June 1941 that Draper suddenly decided to marry Heidi Vosseler, a ballerina of the Metropolitan Opera Company and of the American Ballet. He made a dash for the telephone, put through a long distance call to New York, and proposed to Miss Vosseler, whom he had known for five years. "Grab the next boat for Rio and let's get married here," he told the astonished ballerina. Miss Vosseler accepted, and they were married July 1. They now have a daughter, born September 16, 1943.

References

N Y Herald Tribune p2 Ap 19 '42
Sat Eve Post 215:16-17+ D 12 '42 il
    pors
Draper, M. Music at Midnight 1929

DREW, CHARLES R(ICHARD) 1904-
Professor of surgery
Address: b. Howard University College of Medicine, Washington, D. C.; h. 3324 Sherman Ave., N. W., Washington, D. C.

In March 1943 the National Association for the Advancement of Colored People announced that the twenty-ninth Spingarn Medal, "for the highest and noblest achievement by an American Negro during the preceding year or years," had been awarded to Dr. Charles R. Drew. Now chief of surgery at Freedmen's Hospital in Washington, D. C., as well as professor of surgery at Howard University's College of Medicine, Dr. Drew was given the medal because of his outstanding work with blood plasma. It was he who set up and ran the blood plasma bank in the Presbyterian Hospital in New York City which served as one of the models for the widespread system of blood banks now in operation for the American Red Cross. Ironically enough, at the time he set up the bank his own blood would have been rejected by the Red Cross if he had offered it. Even today it would be segregated.

Born in Washington, D. C., on June 3, 1904, Charles Richard Drew is the son of Richard Thomas and Nora Rosella (Burrell) Drew. After receiving his secondary schooling at Dunbar High School he was graduated from Amherst College in 1926 with a B.A. degree and the Howard Hill Mossman trophy for

DR. CHARLES R. DREW

having brought most honor to the school over a four-year period. Captain of the Amherst College track team, he won the National Junior A.A.U. championship in high hurdles during his last year in college. From Amherst he went to McGill University's Medical School at Montreal, Canada. There he not only won first prize in physiological anatomy and obtained two fellowships in medicine (Rosenwald and Williams), but he again distinguished himself in athletics: he was the all-time top scorer in a Canadian intercollegiate track competition. He became a member of Alpha Omega Alpha fraternity. In 1933 he received his M.D. and Master of Surgery from McGill, being graduated with top honors. By then he had served as extern-intern at Montreal's Royal Victoria Hospital and had held a general rotating internship at the Montreal General Hospital from 1933 to 1934. He now served for a year as a resident in medicine at the latter hospital as well as a diplomat of the National Board of Medical Examiners, and then in 1935 returned to the United States to become an instructor in pathology at the College of Medicine at Howard University. By the next year he had been promoted to assistant in surgery at Howard, and was also serving as a resident in surgery at Freedmen's Hospital. In 1938 he received a Rockefeller fellowship.

Some years of postgraduate work at Columbia University's College of Physicians and Surgeons followed—and in 1940 Dr. Drew obtained his Doctor of Medical Science degree from that university. Early in the War when it was decided by the Blood Transfusion Association to investigate the possibility of aiding the Allies by shipping plasma to Europe, a committee was selected to draw up plans for such a project. It consisted of Dr. E. H. L. Corwin, Dr. John Scudder, and Dr. Drew. (Dr. Drew had already done brilliant research in blood plasma with Dr. Scudder at the Presbyterian-Columbia Medical Center in New York.) When France fell, the plan was about

DREW, CHARLES R.—*Continued*

to go into effect as a means of aiding the French. Then, on October 1, 1940, in answer to the urgent call for help from Great Britain during the terrible blitz period, Dr. Drew was appointed full-time medical director of the plasma project for Great Britain, with the job of solving the many technical problems which had risen in this first great experiment in gross production of human plasma. He was unanimously chosen to direct the project by a distinguished group of blood experts, who described him as "the best qualified of anyone we know to act in this important development."

As a final report at the end of this project, which functioned at Presbyterian Hospital in New York, a complete summary of the organizational, technical, and medical problem that arose in the work was written. When published, this report served as a guide for the later developments in the United States for the United States Army and also for its Allies. In a review of Drew's pioneer work, the Blood Transfusion Betterment Association stated: "Since Drew, who is a recognized authority on the subject of blood preservation and blood substitutes, and, at the same time, an excellent organizer, has been in charge, our major troubles have vanished."

When this project ended in 1941 and the American Red Cross decided to set up blood donor stations to collect blood plasma for the American armed forces, Dr. Drew was appointed the first director of the new project and set up the first collection unit. When the project had been successfully running for three months he resigned to take the chair of surgery at Howard University.

Red Cross officials freely admit that their blood segregation policy represents an appeasement to prejudice, and that there is no scientific basis whatsoever for it. In connection with this policy, Dr. Drew said in 1942: "I feel that the recent ruling of the United States Army and Navy regarding the refusal of colored blood donors is an indefensible one from any point of view. As you know, there is no scientific basis for the separation of the bloods of different races except on the basis of the individual blood types or groups."

Drew has contributed over a dozen articles to medical publications, largely on the subject of blood. His wife is the former Minnie Lenore Robbins, and his three daughters are Bebe Roberta, Charlene Rosella, and Rhea Sylvia.

References

NAACP Bulletin 3:1+ Ap '44 por
N Y Times p23 Mr 31 '44
PM p11 Mr 30 '44
American Medical Directory 1942

DUDLEY, BIDE Sept. 8, 1877—Jan. 4, 1944 Drama critic, playwright, radio commentator, and theatrical columnist for more than thirty years; real name Walter Bronson Dudley; created the Theatre Club of the Air; was drama critic of radio station WOR; plays include *Come Along All* (1928), *Oh, Henry* (1928), and *Borrowed Love* (1929); father of actress Doris Dudley.

Obituary

N Y Times p17 Ja 5 '44

DUDLEY, WALTER BRONSON *See* Dudley, B.

DULLES, JOHN FOSTER (dul'les) Feb. 25, 1888- Lawyer; Chairman of the Commission on a Just and Durable Peace, Federal Council of Churches of Christ in America.

Address: b. 48 Wall St., New York City; h. 72 E. 91st St., New York City

Although for many years well known in the field of corporate law (he is the senior partner of Sullivan and Cromwell, perhaps the richest and most powerful law firm in downtown New York), John Foster Dulles is a man about whom the American public had first heard during the 1944 Presidential campaign. Since 1941, however, he has been chairman of the influential organization called the Commission on a Just and Durable Peace of the Federal Council of Churches of Christ in America. But the lawyer is best known as one of the "strong" men behind Governor Thomas E. Dewey '44: he is Dewey's "closest adviser on foreign policy," and—according to Richard H. Rovere—if Dewey had been elected President in 1944, his probable Secretary of State.

While Dulles has directed some of the largest corporations in the United States, his dominant interest is, and always has been, international relations. He grew up, as a matter of fact, in an atmosphere of statesmanship as the grandson of John W. Foster, American diplomat and Secretary of State during the Harrison Administration; and as the nephew of Mrs. Robert Lansing, whose husband was Secretary of State during the Wilson Administration. Born in Washington, D. C., February 25, 1888, John Foster Dulles is the son of Allen M. Dulles (a professor at Auburn Theological Seminary) and Edith Foster Dulles. After attending high school in Watertown, New York, he decided on law as a career and entered Princeton University. His interest in international affairs began while he was still an undergraduate at Princeton: at the age of nineteen he became secretary to a delegation at the 1907 Hague Peace Conference. Having received his B.A. degree at Princeton in 1908 (he was valedictorian of his class), he went to Paris for a year to study international law at the Sorbonne; then he returned to take his LL.B. in 1911 at George Washington University, in Washington, D. C. An LL.D. was awarded to him in 1939 by Tufts College, in Massachusetts. Early in 1911 Dulles began his law practice in association with the firm of Sullivan and Cromwell. He became a partner of the firm in 1920, and in 1944 is senior partner. In June 1912 he was married to Janet Pomeroy Avery. They have three children: John Watson Foster, Lillias Pomeroy (Mrs. Robert Y. Hinshaw), and Charles Avery.

Just before the United States entered the First World War, Dulles was designated by President Wilson as special agent to Panama to aid in bringing about the alignment of Panama and other Central American states to facilitate the successful defense of the Panama Canal. During the War he was commissioned as captain, later as major, in the United States Army and attached to the General Staff. In 1918 he became assistant to the chairman of the War Trade Board, in which capacity he took an active part in negotiating trade agreements with neutral Continental states designed to tighten the blockade of Germany and to give the United States more ships. After the War he was the principal American counsel on the Paris Peace Conference committees on reparations and financial matters and helped to draft the treaty clauses dealing with these subjects. He was also a member in 1919 of the Supreme Economic Council. Following the signing of the Treaty by Germany, Dulles became the first American member of the Reparations Commission as then constituted in provisional form.

Upon his return from Paris, Dulles resumed his association with Sullivan and Cromwell, becoming one of the leading international lawyers. He directed the legal aspects of many international financial affairs, including the financing of most of the countries of Europe and South America, as well as China and Japan. In 1927 he was engaged in Poland as legal adviser in connection with the Polish Plan of Monetary Stabilization. Writing in the '20's on various aspects of the peace of Europe, he praised the Dawes Report experts, saying: "They have produced a scientifically worked out plan, with checks and balances to insure equitable adjustments to meet future developments which cannot be accurately foreseen." In an article written in 1929 he stated that intervention by an international police force was "not a peculiarly obnoxious form of interference," but in many cases preferable to a policy of nonrecognition of a country's government with its resultant economic pressures. "Only if public opinion is founded on a recognition of practical considerations . . . can it serve as an effective and very proper curb upon governments during the time when international law is still in an undeveloped stage."

Following the collapse of the various foreign exchanges in 1932, Dulles represented the American bondholders at the three successive international debt conferences called by Dr. Hjalmar Schacht '44 in Berlin. He was chief counsel in the realization, for credits, of Kreuger & Toll assets after the collapse of that company. In 1938 he was in the Far East studying the political and economic situation there.

War, Peace and Change (1939) contained Dulles' philosophical analysis of the causes of war. In this book he stated that the reason war has so long been tolerated as a method of settling international disputes is that no procedures are available whereby changes in international relations can be made effective in order to meet changing conditions. Any procedure for settling international disputes, he wrote, implies the application of two principles, one ethical and the other political. "We cannot remove force and leave a vacuum. We must first know the nature and significance of that which we would remove." The *Saturday Review of Literature* considered Dulles' book a notable addition to the literature of "rare, careful analysis of the most vital and baffling issue

Jay Te Winburn

JOHN FOSTER DULLES

confronting humanity today. . . . His is not a particularly novel doctrine, nor does it promise quick results. It is by no means adequate in meeting some of the questions raised by current, conflicting ideologies and economic interests." G. A. Warp of the *Christian Century* saw the virtue of the book lying "in its endeavor to reach a solution of the problem of war by examining its origins and causes and in its urgent plea that the lessons of past wars be learned and applied today." The same critic believes, however, that readers "will charge that, in the present crisis, he [Dulles] is aiding those who would make force the sole arbiter of our destinies."

During 1940 and 1941 Dulles wrote several articles on the problems resulting from the various peace plans formulated since 1918. In "The Aftermath of the World War," he pointed out that the Treaty of Versailles contained liberal and forward-looking provisions in its projects for the League of Nations, the Permanent Court of International Justice, and progressive disarmament, but that it failed because of the "failure of nations to comprehend and to put to use the political mechanisms provided for the promotion of a healthy world order. . . . The League of Nations, dominated by France and her Continental allies, gradually became an alliance of the satisfied powers to maintain their status unimpaired. The emphasis was placed upon resistance to change. . . . One by one the governments of the dissatisfied peoples—Italian, German, and Japanese—departed from the League which to them assumed the character of a strait jacket." Dulles reviewed the procession of the Reparation Commission, Dawes plan, Disarmament Conference, and the World Economic Conference of 1933, the effectiveness of which was destroyed by the "excessive claims of nationalism. . . . The collapse of the Conference [of 1933] constituted the final demonstration that the nations of the world were operating on a basis of *sauve qui peut.* . . . International

DULLES, JOHN FOSTER—*Continued*

anarchy assumed its extreme form and general war was inevitable."

In 1941 a commission of twenty-two men was formed by the Federal Council of Churches with the help of seven other interdenominational agencies to "study the bases of a just and durable peace." Dulles, himself the son of a Presbyterian minister, and veteran of almost every peace parley since the 1907 Hague Conference, was made the chairman. "No churchgoer himself, he never thought to blame the failure of all the peace conferences he attended on lack of Christianity until he set out to draft a practical set of principles on which a peace conference might succeed. To his surprise, he found them an echo of Christianity, so back to the church he went." According to Dulles, " 'Practical' men of the world tell me that all this talk of the Gospels has no place in the world today, but it is only by bringing that Christian point of view to bear on world affairs that something really practical and constructive can be done to make peace last." It is reported that all of the commission members were "agreed that the United States must accept its responsibility in world affairs, not scuttle out of them as it did after Versailles." In May 1941 the commission put forward a proposal "that Congress immediately establish a governmental unit to study economic relations with other nations, and that no law dealing with foreign trade, immigration, or money exchange be enacted without first obtaining from this agency a full report on the effect this contemplated action would have on other nations. Said Dulles in the symposium, *A Righteous Faith for a Just and Durable Peace* (1942): "Our purpose is that the American people be filled with a righteous faith and a sense of mission in the world."

Two years after the organization of the Commission on a Just and Durable Peace it put forth its six broad "political propositions," or "pillars," representing the minimum practical application of the principles to world problems of the future. At a meeting of financial, labor, religious, and educational leaders in New York City on March 18, 1943, Chairman Dulles outlined the six "pillars of peace" as follows: (1) World political cooperation on the pattern of the United Nations; (2) control of economic and financial acts which may disturb international peace; (3) establishment of an organization to adapt the treaty to changing conditions; (4) autonomy for subject peoples; (5) international control of armaments; (6) religious and intellectual liberty. In his *How to Think About War and Peace* (1944), Mortimer Adler [40] made this criticism of the six-pillar plan: While it includes the notion of world government, the plan regards such a project "a remote objective to be approached through stages of progressively mitigated nationalism."

In July 1943 church leaders of fourteen nations met to discuss post-War reconstruction problems at an international round table in Princeton, New Jersey. The British Council of Churches group, including the Archbishops of Canterbury [42] and York, lent its support to the six-pillar program; endorsements came also from Sumner Welles [40], Senator Joseph H. Ball [43] of Minnesota, and Governor Thomas E. Dewey. Late in October 1943 some 5,000

Protestants met at the Cathedral of St. John the Divine in New York to inaugurate the Christian Mission of World Order. In a speech at this meeting Dulles said: "If we would be a nation of creative faith, we must be individuals of creative faith." In a subsequent address (before a group of ministers at the Collegiate Reformed Church), Dulles warned that the "rebuilt nations" would lean toward the Soviet Union if the United States did not revive a "creative spirit." Russia's influence, he said, "may spread because countries could derive inspirational material from her actions. . . . To date there has been no statement by President Roosevelt as to either war or peace objectives. First, he has no clear convictions on the matter. Second, he is being politically cautious . . . and last, it is impossible to know what Russia wants."

At a meeting in February 1944 of the Alliance of Reformed Churches, Dulles said that while "the Moscow Conference and the Senate resolution endorsing the Moscow Declaration envisaged a general world organization and approved the principle of control of armaments, no steps had as yet been taken toward setting up an organization to promote world economic and social changes essential to preserve peace and democratic progress." In April 1944 a Protestant appeal, issued through Dulles, was signed by 1,200 laymen and clergymen: it urged that "practical steps be taken immediately to form the nucleus of a general world organization as envisaged in the Moscow Declaration and the Connolly resolution adopted by the Senate."

It is in connection with the Republican Presidential candidacy of Governor Thomas E. Dewey that the name of John Foster Dulles appeared most frequently during 1944. In 1943 Dewey appointed his old friend and adviser as one of the new members of the New York State Banking Board; in March 1944 he was named as a delegate to the Republican National Convention from the 18th Congressional District. According to *Look*, "In Dewey, Dulles sees a dynamic vehicle for his own convictions that the world's problems will be solved not by generalized, wishful pacts but by a well analyzed, step-by-step progression from a primitive society to a civilized one. Today Dewey's views reflect ten years of conversation with Dulles."

During the summer and fall of 1944, the name of Dulles appeared with increasing frequency in newspaper headlines. His conference with Wendell Willkie in August resulted in a short joint statement which, Wyona Dashwood of the *Christian Science Monitor* said, "specifically eschewed interest for any presidential candidate." The statement: "We have conferred extensively about the various international problems bearing on world organization to assure lasting peace. There was a full exchange of views not animated by partisan consideration nor having to do with any candidacy, but by the desire of both of us that the United States should play a constructive and responsible part in assuring world order." Again representing Dewey in August, Dulles conferred with Secretary Hull [40] in response to the latter's invitation to discuss "in a nonpartisan spirit" the problem of post-War security, a move hailed in editorial columns as "genuine statesmanship." While it was stated that there was an agreement of views on many aspects of a world organization for peace, R. H. Shackford, United Press correspondent, reported: "Mr. Hull lost his attempt to get the Republican Presidential nominee to agree that the subject of future peace be 'kept entirely out of politics.' Mr. Dulles explained that Governor Dewey 'didn't feel that he could accept without his own interpretation the Secretary's phrase 'entirely out of politics.'"

In a press conference held in August at the Executive Mansion in Albany Dulles set forth his reasoning on foreign policy: that the occupation of Germany and Japan be assigned individually to the four big powers, with some parts of the task reassigned to smaller nations: that the task of world organization for peace belongs to all nations, large and small—the organization may fail if it is dominated completely by the four big powers; that the occupation must not be assigned to the world organization, which, if dominated by the big powers, might fail. Speaking later at church conferences in New York and Pittsburgh (the latter the meeting of the Federal Council of Churches of Christ in America), Dulles said that while he subscribed to the Dumbarton Oaks proposals, he feared the stability of world peace would be jeopardized by too much reliance on force. In December Dulles was in Washington again, for a talk with the new Secretary of State Stettinius [40], the first after the election that defeated his candidate. Of this meeting Stettinius said: "We have had a friendly exchange of views and general conversations regarding the Dumbarton Oaks proposals."

During the Presidential campaign the lawyer was the target of attack of those who would oppose him as a Secretary of State in the event that Dewey were sent to the White House. There were those who objected strongly to the injection of partisanship into the discussion of the post-War world. In the opinion of Life, "a Dulles enemy might read into his measured phrases on economics a fondness for a status quo that included the German cartel system." Dulles' attackers have also seen reason for criticism in some of his firm's clients, such as banking and industrial organizations of dictator countries.

Dr. Nicholas Murray Butler [40] announced the election of Dulles in May 1944 as a trustee of the Carnegie Endowment for International Peace. Dulles is also vice-president of the Bar Association of New York City and chairman of its committee on international law; trustee of the Rockefeller Foundation; director of the Bank of New York, the International Nickel Company, and the American Bank Note Company.

The *United States News* gives this picture of Dulles: "Mr. Dulles is restrained and quiet, a man of unruffled calm. . . .He wears habitually a solemn, almost lugubrious expression, which infrequently is broken by a broad grin." He is described as a tall man with gray hair and dark blue eyes. In the words of *Life,* Dulles is "an intellectual who likes material hobbies. . . .There is Dulles the political philosopher . . . there is a man who has a great deal of fun, a combination of the countryman and *bon vivant,* a man who is ornithologist and yachtsman, chef and tree surgeon, fisherman

and woodchopper, gregarious family man and lonely woods recluse." He indulges his various urges in his country home on Long Island Sound and in a rustic retreat near Lake Ontario. The books to which he turns oftenest, he says, are the Bible, Shakespeare's sonnets and plays, Beveridge's *Life of John Marshall,* and General Foster's *Diplomatic Memoirs.*

References

Life 17:84 Ag 21 '44 il pors
N Y Post p19 Ap 10 '44
N Y Sun p21 Mr 24 '43
N Y Times p36 My 15 '44 por
Newsweek 23:32 My 1 '44 por
Time 37:74 Ap 7 '41
International Who's Who 1942
Who's Who 1944
Who's Who in America 1944-45

DUNNINGER, JOSEPH Apr. 28, 1896- Mind reader; magician

Address: b. c/o National Concert and Artists Corp., 711 Fifth Ave., New York City

"Whether Joseph Dunninger, an accomplished magician who has sliced a cooperative lady into eight rejoinable pieces and therefore looks down upon ordinary, bisecting magicians, will ultimately be remembered as a sleight-of-hand expert, a mind reader, or a determined foe of spiritualistic mediums," writes the *New Yorker,* "is something that not even a Dunninger can state with precision." "I may turn out to be the world's greatest chemist," Dunninger once speculated. On another occasion he declared: "Fundamentally, I am the last of the great name magicians." A few days before he was heard to say: "I am not a magician, though I have been looked upon as the world's highest authority on magic. Fundamentally I am a mentalist, a demonstrator of telepathic communication." Billing himself as "The Man With the Miracle Mind" and "The Master Mind of Mental Mystery," Dunninger has artfully explained that his feats "could be done by a child of three—with thirty years of practice."

Joseph Dunninger was born in New York City, April 28, 1896, into a "strictly non-telepathic" family. His father was a textile manufacturer from Bavaria, and his two elder brothers were later to enter conventional professions, one in music, the other in painting. Dunninger discovered his unusual ability when as a boy in school he "thought-read" most of the answers in his classes, his correct "guessing," however, bringing on accusations of dishonesty. But with some fifty out of sixty minds concentrating on the correct answers, "How could I miss?" demands Dunninger. The boy began to startle his parents by casually announcing who was calling when the telephone rang or who was waiting at the door when the bell sounded, and by describing events that had happened at home while he was away.

Always fascinated by the mysterious and inspired by a glimpse of Harry Kellar, the leading magician of that time, Dunninger early began to practice sleight of hand and the performance of illusions. Following a number of exhibitions in which he appeared as "The Child Wonder Magician," he soon became so skillful that he worked evenings at the Eden Musée on

JOSEPH DUNNINGER

New York's West 23rd Street—for a period of sixty-five weeks, the longest run ever enjoyed by any performer at that establishment. In his daytime hours Dunninger worked at Wanamaker's department store to please his mother, who favored a business career for him.

After his success at the Musée Dunninger overcame maternal opposition and set out on a tour of the vaudeville circuits. At twenty he was a stage headliner. In his most extravagant phase his act was heralded as "Dunninger, the Master Mind of Mystery and His Company of Temple Dancers from the Far East . . . Producing a Beautiful Girl from Thin Air . . . The Flight of the Night Rider . . . Is It Dunninger or Is It Not? . . . The Balloon that Floats Out Over the Audience and Vanishes . . . And Many Other Baffling Features." Occasionally Dunninger caused an elephant to disappear. Some of the equipment he used then had been willed to him by his close friend Harry Houdini.

Between tours and after stage appearances Dunninger often performed at private parties and club banquets. At one such entertainment he "unveiled" for the first time his mind-reading act. Soon after he gave up his magic routine to turn "mentalist." Thereafter he faced his public "with nothing but a pencil, a writing board, and his peculiarly sensitive cerebral cells." Claiming "neither supernatural nor supernormal powers," unlike others of his trade, he worked minus assistants, props, or fanfare. In time commanding fabulous fees, Dunninger was able to number among his private clients such celebrities as the Prince of Wales before he became the Duke of Windsor '44, Cardinal Pacelli, who became Pope Pius XII '41, Steinmetz, Edison, Thomas E. Dewey '44, and Mrs. Franklin D. Roosevelt '40—all of whom were impressed. He has also mystified six United States Presidents. The first Chief Executive to invite him to the White House was Theodore Roosevelt, who, Dunninger found, was thinking of a poker hand. Harding had a streetcar line on his mind; Taft, a point of law; and Hoover, his mother. Dunninger has forgotten exactly what Coolidge was thinking about. President Roosevelt '42 has had him to Washington twice; the first time the President was wondering: "Will Huey Long or Ham Fish '41 be the next President of the United States?" On the next occasion he simply thought of 1600 Pennsylvania Avenue, the address of the White House.

Always skeptical of so-called "supernatural manifestations," since 1920 Dunninger has carried on an unrelenting attack against faked phenomena. In the thirties Dunninger accepted the chairmanship of the Universal Council for Psychic Research, becoming well known to the newspaper-reading public for his exposés. In 1933 he vainly offered $10,000 to a medium who could correctly reproduce the words of a code message Sir Arthur Conan Doyle had sent him before his death; in 1936 he tendered an identical sum for a bona fide haunted house. Ready to give another $10,000 to any dealer in the occult who can produce a psychic manifestation Dunninger himself can neither duplicate by trickery nor explain by natural or scientific means, the mind reader has attended over 1,000 séances; he is chairman, too, of the *Scientific American* Committee on Psychic Research (which was formed in March 1941). To date there have been no takers for any of the prize money. Dunninger has easily reproduced sham ghosts (these are often merely images applied with luminous paint on black velveteen), table levitation, automatic writing, rappings, and spirit voices; "ectoplasm" he has identified as cheesecloth, muslin, or as a bubbly mixture of peroxide and toothpaste. "Where a medium can ring a bell at a seance," Dunninger boasts, "I can get a ton of coal."

But Dunninger's own extraordinary exploits —in the field of mental telepathy—still bemuse layman and scientist alike. When the Master Mentalist made his radio debut on the Blue Network on September 12, 1943, he became subject to "the doubts and scrutiny of millions." (Some listeners may have remembered him as the NBC "thought-caster" of 1929; that is, those who had written to the network that they had received his silent communications.) Although *Variety* commented that the program was "apparently baffling and fascinating to the in-person audience, but difficult to visualize and somewhat so-whatish to those on the kilocycle end of the proceedings," it evoked wide popular enthusiasm. Many special bookings followed in the wake of his broadcasts, and in January 1944 Dunninger acquired a sponsor, the Sherwin-Williams Company. (The program continued on the air until December 27, 1944.)

After a warming-up period in which Dunninger entertained the studio audience with a few conjuring tricks, he distributed slips of paper to the spectators, on which they were requested to write various questions, names, or numbers; he then instructed them to seal these in the envelopes he had provided and to place them in their pockets or under their feet. During the proceedings (in which the mentalist, equipped with a writing board with high screening sides, shared the stage with several judges, some of them guest stars), Dunninger had revealed to his audience such facts as dates and names known only to themselves, private telephone numbers, and newspaper headlines as yet unprinted. (He rejected all questions involving prognostication, stressing that he is not a fortuneteller.) The half hour concluded with a "brainbuster" and a "projection" sent out to unseen listeners.

Two months after the initial radio demonstration, Waldemar Kaempffert [43], science editor of the New York *Times*, criticized the act, concluding: "It is significant that always more than one person is involved, and that always the one in the studio knows what Dunninger is to 'mind-read' and has to write it down. If there were no writing Dunninger would probably be stumped." "How he does it we don't know, admits Kaempffert, but adds, "No psychologist would accept the evidence of the broadcasts." Dunninger devoted a large part of his subsequent program to vindicating himself; he climaxed his rebuttal by "snatching" three words (chosen from the *Congressional Record*) from the mind of Representative William A. Rowan, 590 miles away. There is as yet no evidence to suggest that Dunninger gets his effects through collusion; Dunninger has a collection of voluntary testimonials "to prove they are as honest as they are unbelievable."

Nettled by skeptical discussions of his methods, Dunninger offers $10,000 to "anyone who can point out any paid employees, stooges, or confederates who could possibly assist him in his telepathic readings." He complains that "the greatest hindrance to public acceptance of my telepathic powers is that I was once a professional magician." When he misses one or two letters in the spelling of a foreign name or several digits in a number, he explains that he is not infallible: "I do not claim to be 100 per cent accurate; I am right only about 90 per cent of the time." Neither can he read the mind of everyone at any time, he admits; his mind goes into a special receptive state before a demonstration: "It's just as though I were putting a record on." "If I could read anybody's mind at any time, do you think I'd be working for a livelihood?"

"In his rare introspective moments," writes Lincoln Barnett in *Life* Magazine, "he describes his reception of thought impressions as an inner visual process. He discerns, he says, letters, words, numerals, as though inscribed by an unseen hand within the chamber of his mind." In analyzing his *modus operandi* Dunninger has said: "I definitely perform feats of genuine telepathic communication and thought reading. I have, however, a knowledge of magic and I believe that from the standpoint of showmanship I have the right to the professional license granted any entertainer to make his efforts more impressive. If I succeed in entertaining by mystification, regardless of how my results are obtained, I have succeeded in my endeavor." The ingredients of his technique include 60 per cent mind reading, 10 per cent psychology, 10 per cent hypnosis, 15 per cent self-hypnosis, and 5 per cent magic. "All of which adds up to 100 per cent entertainment."

In the recently published *What's On Your Mind* (1944) Dunninger covers the subject of telepathy (which he defines as "all forms of mental communication") for the general reader. After reviewing outstanding examples of telepathy, including accounts of his own prowess, and theories on its physical causes, he offers a series of twenty-four tests of telepathic ability which "may become the basis of a new parlor game," as *Bookweek* predicts. Dunninger believes that telepathy is a normal function though a latent one, and that one in ten persons is naturally telepathic.

Although it was generally thought that Dunninger was a bachelor, evidence of a sixteen-year-old common-law marriage came to light in 1944 when Chrystal Spencer Dunninger sued to be declared his legal wife. In October a Supreme Court ruling simultaneously declared her legally married and granted her a legal separation.

Dunninger is "a tall solid man with hypnotic eyes, a voice of cello-like resonance, and a tendency to say 'madim' and 'teleephone,'" writes Lincoln Barnett. A master of showmanship, Dunninger has a disarmingly convincing manner. "He is the only man I know," a friend is said to have observed, "who can mispronounce a word and make it sound authoritative." The "master mentalist" has a collection of antiques, Chinese *objets d'art,* first edition books, and autographs; he owns a collection of Buddhas, which, he says, exceeds 3,000. As a student of hypnotism, Dunninger is today assisting in three New York hospitals with the hypnotic treatment of patients. Adroit in the use of publicity, Dunninger has demonstrated and handed over to the United States Navy a device for camouflaging a warship to the point of invisibility; he refuses to explain his invention publicly on the grounds that it is both a military and a magical secret.

References

Life 16 :100-2+ Mr 13 '44 il pors
New Yorker 17 :26-30+ N 29 '41
Read Digest 44 :83-7 Ja '44 por
Dunninger, J. What's On Your Mind 1944

D'USSEAU, ARNAUD *See* Gow, J. E. and d'Usseau, A.

DWYFOR, DAVID LLOYD GEORGE, 1ST EARL OF *See* Lloyd George of Dwyfor, D., 1st Earl

DYER-BENNET, RICHARD Oct. 6, 1913- Ballad singer

Address: b. c/o Ted Zittel, 15 E. 40th St., New York City; h. 15 Charles St., New York City

The art of minstrelsy is as old as recorded history. It has won popular acclaim from the days when Homer recited his verses to the accompaniment of a stringed instrument, through the Middle Ages when troubadours enlivened the courts of feudal lords, to 1944 when Richard Dyer-Bennet, "the twentieth century minstrel," entertains in night clubs and concert halls. Dyer-Bennet makes no concessions to modernity and sings his ballads as simply and genuinely as they were sung centuries ago. His successful recitals at New York's Town Hall and Carnegie Hall have convinced music-lovers that folk songs have a definite place on the formal concert program.

The son of a British father and an American mother, Richard Stewart and Miriam

RICHARD DYER-BENNET

(Wolcott) Dyer-Bennet, Richard Dyer-Bennet
was born in England, October 6, 1913. "Probably the only United States radio entertainer
listed in *Burke's Peerage*," he chose to become
an American citizen on his twenty-first birthday. Although he studied voice at the University of California, the idea of making a career
of ballad-singing had not yet occurred to
Dyer-Bennet. His major interest as a boy had
been sports, particularly tennis and soccer, and
he had considered becoming a professional
soccer player. Quite by chance the noted voice
teacher, Gertrude Wheeler Becker, heard him
sing at a Christmas party. She was impressed
not so much with his voice as with his talent
for folk singing. It was not long before Dyer-
Bennet was studying with her and planning a
trip to Sweden to learn minstrelsy under the
noted Swedish minstrel, Sven Scholander. After a year of training in the United States,
during which he concentrated especially on the
development of "crystal clear enunciation,"
Dyer-Bennet bought passage to Europe on
a freighter. Equipped with a bicycle and a
lute, he set out to master the difficult and
unique art he had chosen.

Sven Scholander told Dyer-Bennet that minstrelsy could not be taught. He agreed, however, to sing a few old songs for the young
would-be minstrel. Dyer-Bennet immediately
realized that it was the greatest musical experience of his life. Although he had only a
few visits with Scholander (who died a year
later), and was taught only "that he should
sing to all of the people who would listen and
should learn various kinds of songs and try to
present them so that it would seem that the
songs were fresh," Dyer-Bennet knew that his
trip had not been in vain. He went to Wales,
"where good singing is traditional," and sang
for the miners. Dyer-Bennet did not charge
admission for these recitals, for he was gaining from them the practical experience of the
professional minstrel. With a repertoire consisting of a hundred German, Swedish, and
French songs Scholander had given to him,

the young singer returned to the United States.
He tried without success to get concert bookings. The public, he was told, would not be
interested in hearing the simple old songs of
their ancestors sung on the modern concert
stage. But Richard Dyer-Bennet was not discouraged. He determined to study American
and British balladry as he had already studied
the songs of other countries. The folk ballads of the South and the cowboy songs of
the West offered a wealth of material. In
addition, Dyer-Bennet composed his own ballads. (He now has a one-hundred-song repertoire of his own compositions, many of them
on the War and other subjects of current interest. Some of these have received a radio
hearing on the *March of Time* program.)

Dyer-Bennet entered the professional music
world via the night clubs. Visitors to New
York's Greenwich Village often claim credit
for his "discovery," for it was at the Village
Vanguard that he had his first really successful engagement, enchanting listeners with his
high tenor voice, his simple delivery, and his
varied repertoire. "It is the claim of long-
standing Vanguard votaries," wrote John T.
McManus in *PM*, "that Dick Dyer-Bennet has
never failed, in the two years he has been
singing at the Vanguard, to come up at least
once an evening with a tune none of them had
ever heard before." He would ask his audience to request songs, and rarely did he fail
to have the song ready.

The songs Dyer-Bennet sings range from old
folk ballads like "Lord Randal" and "Barbara
Allen" to American cowboy ballads. He believes that his listeners are primarily interested in the story he is telling and only second-
arily in the tune. For that reason Dyer-Bennet
has developed an "impeccable diction" and a
clear high tenor voice, and he delivers his
songs with a minimum of flourish. He conveys the mood of earnestness not "by facial
gymnastics nor with gesture or contortion, but
in his voice and his own conviction that he
has an interesting story to tell that the listener
will want to hear." Since ancient times it
has been the technique of the minstrel never to
intrude upon the story he is telling in music.
Dyer-Bennet's adherence to this princple has
won him great praise. Louis Biancolli said
in a review of one of the recitals: "Wrapped
around a Scottish border ballad or American
Revolutionary song, with the guitar twanging
in faintly, he seemed to grow into the music.
You forgot all about Richard Dyer-Bennet in
the illusion of a dim yesterday coming back
through the magic of remembered music."

From the Village Vanguard, Dyer-Bennet
moved uptown to the Ruban Bleu. His success there and at the Vanguard led to an
invitation from the OWI to broadcast his
own compositions overseas—"his robust tales
of Rommel '42 the Fox, the *Hood* and the
Bismarck, people's resistance in Norway, the
stirring 'Who Enters Russia by the Sword.'"
and others. Dyer-Bennet is hopeful that the
current interest in soldier songs will lead to a
general revival in ballad singing. "Ballad
singing," he says, "when it is really art must
be the telling of a human experience as though
it were . . . your own." Thus he has been
able to popularize Elizabethan songs with as

much ease as if they had been newly created in Tin Pan Alley.

On March 4, 1944 Richard Dyer-Bennet gave his first recital to a capacity audience at Town Hall in New York. In the informal, intimate style which was so successful in his two years of night-club work, Dyer-Bennet proved equally effective on the concert stage. He accompanied himself on the guitar—"never too much of it, usually just a few mild brush-strokes." One reviewer commented on Dyer-Bennet's excellent musicianship, but was even more enthusiastic about his "own real love for the folk songs of many centuries. He isn't just a collector of rare and known items of folk balladry. In his scheme each song is treated like something alive, long thought dead, but merely waiting for the art of fanning it back into life."

A slightly less enthusiastic judgment of his work appeared in the New York *Herald Tribune,* whose reviewer wrote: "The voice is soft, high and husky, without the unpleasant signs of partial cultivation which might easily be present in such a case. When he sings a song straight through simply and without too many art effects he is eminently enjoyable. He has, however, a tendency to exaggerate the mood of some of his numbers, particularly the ballads, by slowing down when he comes to a soft passage and singing loud when he comes to a fast section."

So successful was this first recital that another was given on April 4, and by November his audience had grown so large that he made his first appearance in the huge Carnegie Hall before a "capacity crowd." Besides his concert and radio work, he makes recordings and appears at benefits for the various war relief agencies. He no longer accompanies himself on the lute but prefers the Spanish guitar "because the latter is more flexible and he can develop technically as he couldn't with the lute."

References

C S Mon p6 Mr 1 '44 por
Look 8:66 F 9 '44 por
N Y Post Mag p34 F 25 '44 pors
N Y Times II p5 F 27 '44 por
Newsweek 23:94 Mr 13 '44 por
PM p21 Mr 2 '44 por
Time 38:60 O 13 '41 por

EASTMAN, JOSEPH B(ARTLETT) June 26, 1882—Mar. 15, 1944 Director of the Office of Defense Transportation and member of the Interstate Commerce Commission; a public official for thirty-one years and a leading authority on transportation; known as one of the hardest working as well as one of the ablest United States Federal administrators; see sketch 1942 Yearbook.

Obituary

N Y Times p19 Mr 16 '44 por

EBOUE, FELIX ADOLPHE (ā"bu"ā' fā"lĕks' a"dôlf') 1884—May 17, 1944 Governor General of French Equatorial Africa since 1939; first Negro ever to hold this rank; early supporter of General Charles de Gaulle '40 and the Free French; Secretary-General of Marti-

nique (1932-34); Governor of the French Sudan (1934-36) and of Guadeloupe (1936-38); death reported by Radio France in Algiers.

Obituary

N Y Times p19 My 18 '44

ELIZABETH, PRINCESS OF GREAT BRITAIN Apr. 21, 1926- Heiress Presumptive to the British Throne

In the past four centuries six queens have occupied the throne of Great Britain; of these the most illustrious were the Tudor Elizabeth and the nineteenth century Victoria, great-great-grandmother of the prospective second Queen Bess, eighteen-year-old Princess Elizabeth. The first member of a British royal family with any purely British blood since the end of the Stuart dynasty in 1714 (to name only a few of her ancestors, she can claim descent from Alfred the Great, William the Conqueror, Robert Bruce, Mary Stuart, Charlemagne, the Emperor Barbarossa, and Saint Louis of France), Princess Elizabeth stands first in succession to the Crown. Never before has there been such a plentiful supply of heirs, according to Henry Benson, there being 124 direct descendants of Queen Victoria now alive, without going back to the descendants of Victoria's uncles, the Dukes of Cumberland and Cambridge. This line of succession extends into most of the royal families of Europe, Crown Prince Olav of Norway being fourteenth in order.

Nearly two decades ago at daybreak on the morning of April 21, 1926 the bells of St. Paul's Cathedral rang out and forty-one gun salutes were fired in Hyde Park and the Tower of London to signalize the birth of a daughter to Prince Albert Frederick Arthur George '42, the Duke of York, and his Scottish wife, the former Lady Elizabeth Angela Marguerite Bowes-Lyon, third and youngest daughter of the fourteenth Earl of Strathmore and Kinghorne, an officer attached to the royal household. Sir William Joynson-Hicks, the Home Secretary, was in the house at the time, so, in keeping with historic custom, the Cabinet Minister was able to attest to the birth of the infant and telegraphed the fact to the Lord Mayor of London and the governors of all the Dominions and Colonies. Shortly afterward, careful not to splash the baptismal robe—made of laces worn by Good Queen Bess—with water from the Jordan, the Archbishop of Canterbury baptized the child Elizabeth (for the Virgin Queen) Alexandra (for Edward VII's widow, who had died the previous year) Mary (for the present Queen Mother). Then third in succession to the throne, the new Princess was acclaimed as a possible Queen Elizabeth II. The possibility grew as the Prince of Wales, her favorite uncle, continued to avoid marriage, to "live his own life," and to repeat his assertion that "York would make a much better king than I."

Elizabeth soon became the most publicized child in Great Britain, the "Empire's Favorite Little Girl," and the Duke of York was able to start a scrapbook of journalistic extravagances which he called "Things That Never

Cecil Beaton

PRINCESS ELIZABETH OF GREAT BRITAIN

Happened to Us." Multitudes of little girls were named after her, as were every imaginable kind of object from chocolates and china to hospital wards, and the narrow strip of Antarctica discovered by Sir Douglas Mawson during a New Zealand-Antarctic expedition is called Princess Elizabeth Land. Her photograph was soon seen in every home all over the Empire, and a doll with her golden hair, blue eyes, tilted nose, and wide mouth appeared in countless nurseries, as did a toy replica of the exquisite miniature cottage (called Y Bwythynn Bach to Gwellt—"The Little House With the Straw Roof") which the Principality of Wales gave Elizabeth for her sixth birthday. Elizabeth also set the pace in styles for little girls in Great Britain: when she first appeared in yellow tweed, weavers and dyers worked overtime to supply the demand. Her face soon adorned the Newfoundland stamp.

To keep this "fourth lady in the land"—or Lilybet, as she had called herself at eighteen months—from being spoiled by millions of admirers in the British Empire, the Duchess of York and Queen Mary instituted a strict surveillance over her deportment, education, and upbringing in general. Like any ordinary child she used to throw tantrums on the nursery floor, but usually minded her P's and Q's in public. On the principle that her royal birth was as much a responsibility as a privilege, her "precocious assumption of royal airs" was soon skillfully arrested. Elizabeth's autocratic tendencies were further subdued by the arrival in August 1930 of her baby sister, Margaret Rose, an irrepressible brown-eyed tomboy. (Elizabeth's thoughtfulness toward her sister has always been one of her attractive characteristics.) To accustom them to appearing in public (following the example of Queen Mary and Queen Alexandra with their children) the Duchess took her daughters with her on every possible occasion—although never permitting either of them to accept public or semi-public engagements.

Although the boys of the Royal Family have usually attended military and naval schools along with non-royal cadets, the Queen Mother and the Cabinet Ministers decided that Elizabeth's education should be private. Since infancy Elizabeth has been in the care of Nurse Clara Knight, the "nannie" of her mother's childhood. Despite the many official claims on her, the Duchess found time to give her daughter all her first lessons in the three R's. There was also tutoring from a French governess, Madame de Bellaigne. Then in October 1933 Miss Marion Crawford, Scottish, and a graduate of Edinburgh University, arrived as resident governess to preside over the lessons which began every morning except Sunday at 9:30 in the green-walled nursery at 145 Piccadilly and continued until 1:00 p.m. with a brief recess at 11:00. Grammar, composition, Latin, French, German, Scriptures, geography, arithmetic (which the Princess still struggles with), history, and constitutional law fill her course of study. Frequently she stands while studying in order to drill herself for long public appearances. Naturally musical, in 1930 she took her first piano lesson from Miss Mabel Lander, a pupil of Théodor Léschetizky (who had trained such famous pianists as Gabrilówitsch and Paderewski), and she later played duets with her sister. She has also been instructed by experts in dancing and in painting and sketching, and has become an apt pupil in these arts.

In spite of the many lessons a princess must master, Elizabeth has always had time for relaxation in hobbies and games, most of which give her the open air life which her mother sets great store by. At the age of four Elizabeth started her training as a horsewoman, when "Grandpapa England" (her name for King George V) presented her with a Shetland pony. In addition to their ponies, Elizabeth and Margaret Rose have as pets two Welsh Corgis, two collies, two fawns, and fifteen blue budgereegahs housed in the aviary at Royal Lodge. Elizabeth early became a successful gardener. She learned to skate, and to swim at the fashionable Bath Club in Dover Street.

This was a happy upbringing for a royal princess. Until Victoria became Queen—twenty-seven days after she had reached the age of eighteen—she had never been allowed to walk down a flight of steps unaccompanied lest an accident befall the Heiress Presumptive; the stern word "duty" was ever in her ears. The Tudor Princess, too, had never been permitted to be childlike or to lose sight of the fate that awaited her. The modern Princess, on the other hand, did not grow up amid the restraint and ostentation of an imposing palace, but in a house with a number in a street, with nothing to distinguish it from adjoining houses. When Margaret Rose was two the family acquired a country house of their own, Royal Lodge in Windsor Great Park, where they have been able to enjoy undisturbed privacy and a normal family life. Elizabeth's Welsh cottage stands in the garden. After a summer holiday at Glamis Castle, the ancestral home of the Duchess, the family used to travel north to share King George V's holiday at Balmoral, Scotland, and then on to their own small highland house, Birkhall. Christmas they spent at Sandringham Hall in Norfolk, and before George VI's accession they also visited Windsor Castle frequently.

The private life of the Yorks came to an end when they moved into Buckingham Palace after the abdication of Edward VIII (who later became the Duke of Windsor '44) on December 11, 1936. Thus Elizabeth's first important ordeal came on Wednesday, May 12, 1937, when, seated beside Queen Mary, the slender, dignified little girl of eleven was the first female heir presumptive in history to see her parents crowned—in a long and tiring ceremony at Westminster Abbey. Elizabeth continued all her usual pursuits, but during history lessons she heard hints of the possibilities of her future. Then, while poring over a genealogical tree one morning, she was told that some day she might be Queen of England. Her immediate response was: "If ever I am Queen, the first thing I shall do will be to make a law forbidding people to ride or drive on Sunday. Horses *must* have a holiday!"

Since the beginning of the War, Elizabeth and her sister have lived, for the most part, at Royal Lodge. Thirteen-and-one-half years old when Britain declared war on Germany on September 3, 1939, she has matured rapidly in the years of strain and crisis that have followed. In the comparative seclusion of their country home, where the King and Queen spend their brief week ends, the Princesses continue to study their lessons and to work at their many hobbies, to follow the progress of the War in the newspapers and on the radio, and to spend a considerable number of hours working for the various war services. When the War began Elizabeth's first company of Girl Guides (the English equivalent of Girl Scouts), composed mainly of children living in the Royal Mews at Buckingham Palace, was disbanded, but another was formed in the country among evacuated children. (As an important part of her training, Elizabeth was subject to ordinary rules of discipline of the Guides: she drilled, camped out, and passed her tests in first aid and various crafts, along with other girls of her age.) Recently she was promoted to membership in the Sea Rangers, who have developed a system of war training known as the Home Emergency Service, which includes first aid, home nursing, child welfare, and various other branches of civilian defense. Princess Elizabeth has incidentally acquired a good knowledge of electricity.

The first important task that Elizabeth performed as a member of the Royal Family was the delivery of a three-minute broadcast message over the BBC to the children of the Empire on October 13, 1940. In a clear, precise voice very like her mother's, she addressed herself to the many children then being evacuated either to the British countryside or to new homes in the Empire and in the United States.

Elizabeth's sixteenth birthday was marked by her official debut in public life. A rather severe-looking young person in a blue "utility" suit, she reviewed the 500 Grenadier Guards (the regiment of which she had been made a colonel two months before) as they marched past her to the strains of the famous "Grenadiers' March" on the Great Quadrangle outside Windsor Castle. That same week, wear-

ing her Girl Guide uniform, she registered under the Ministry of Labor's national service program along with 200,000 other Britons of her age group; to the national registration office she became Briton No. SWGC 55-1.

Prior to Elizabeth's attaining her majority the question of her future title was mooted in official circles. Despite the plea of leading Welshmen, including former Prime Minister David Lloyd George, that she be invested with the title of Princess of Wales, the King decided not to violate the tradition whereby no British king has conferred that peerage on his daughter. The fact that, as heir, she is only "presumptive" and not "apparent" debars her from receiving the Principality of Wales and the accompanying Dukedom of Cornwall, it has been pointed out. (The Princess' right to the throne would be annulled by the birth of a son—an Heir Apparent—to the King.)

In March 1944 it was announced that with the approval of the Cabinet the King had ordered that the Princess' training for her royal duties, either as Princess or Queen—an important form of national service—exempt her from the uniformed or industrial services. (One source reported that she had wished to join the Wrens.) Although many felt that she should be sent to a university—there being an advantage in having her associate with girls of her own age and learn for herself that "the best of us have equals"—this suggestion was rejected "both on account of the jealousy the selection would have caused and because the difficulty of finding a suitable course of study for a potential future queen and suitable companions proved insuperable." Then, too, a report of close friendship with a politically active family might throw doubt on the detachment of the Royal Family.

The groundwork of her education has already been completed. She has learned to speak French and German well, Italian and Spanish acceptably. In her studies in French literature she has read some of the writings of Molière, Corneille, Daudet, Montaigne, Ronsard, La Fontaine, La Bruyère, and she has memorized many of *Les cent meilleurs poèmes français*. Among the classics of her own tongue she has read *The Canterbury Tales*, most of Shakespeare, Coleridge, Keats, Browning, and Tennyson, some of the works of Scott, Dickens, Jane Austen, Anthony Trollope, and Robert Louis Stevenson; of the lighter authors she enjoys John Buchan, P. G. Wodehouse, and Conan Doyle. During the next year her studies in history and constitutional law will be redoubled. With C. H. K. Marten, vice-provost of Eton, she is now embarking on a course based on David S. Muzzey's *United States of America,* George M. Trevelyan's *History of England,* and Herbert A. Fisher's *History of Europe.* Trevelyan and Fisher have been regarded as "radical" historians who consider democracy to be Britain's foremost achievement—a view the Princess must accept and uphold. On the practical side, Elizabeth has more and more often been an interested listener at informal discussions of statecraft by the King and his Ministers, and she spends many hours talking with her father.

(Continued next page)

ELIZABETH, PRINCESS OF GREAT BRITAIN—*Continued*

Legally, Princess Elizabeth will reach her majority at twenty-one, but her eighteenth birthday marked the day on which she could ascend the throne without a Regency upon the death of the King. The day did not occasion any elaborate court function or fanfare. In accordance with her new status, the Duke of Gloucester, King George's younger brother, handed over to his niece those responsibilities he had held had he needed to be Regent. Elizabeth, by the revision of the Regency Act of 1937 (which George VI had requested of Parliament in the fall of 1943) is now serving as a member of the Council of State which deputizes for her father when he is out of the country. In July, while King George was in Italy, she exercised for the first time her new responsibilities as Councilor of State by signing a series of new Acts of Parliament. (As the act originally stood she would have been unable to serve as Councilor of State until the age of twenty-one.) She must await the end of the War for the separate establishment traditionally acquired by the heir to the Crown at this time; this household will include a comptroller, equerries, ladies in waiting, and a private secretary. Her full title is Her Royal Highness, Princess Elizabeth Alexandra Mary, Heiress Presumptive to the Throne; Colonel, Grenadier Guards; President, Royal College of Music; President, National Society for the Prevention of Cruelty to Children; President, Queen Elizabeth Hospital for Children; President, Children's League of the Princess Elizabeth of York Hospital for Children. It has been pointed out that her royal titles are by courtesy only, that inasmuch as she has been granted no peerage, orders of knighthood, decorations or rank of any kind, she is still a commoner.

Elizabeth will not in the immediate future appear more frequently in public, although these appearances are gradually increasing. In November 1943 she assisted her parents in entertaining the two Princes of Saudi Arabia, the Emirs Feisal and Khalid. She accompanied the King and Queen on a recent two-day visit to South Wales and was called upon to fill twelve engagements in as many hours, visiting factories and civilian defense posts, receiving civic delegations, and hearing herself cheered as "Ein Tywysoges"—"Our Princess." There will be other tours to all parts of Great Britain designed to give her a view of her probable subjects at work. As President of the Royal College of Music (an honorary title, though later she may follow the precedent of Edward VII, its founder, by presiding at the meetings), in late 1943 she presented the Tagore Gold Medal to Leonard Salzedo in London. And, interested in the American GI's in England, in the fall of 1944 she visited an 8th Air Force bomber base where she christened a Flying Fortress. In November she officiated alone, without either of her parents beside her, when she christened the greatest battleship ever built in the British Isles.

The high estate for which Princess Elizabeth is being prepared is by no means a sinecure or an ornamental office. In her future sovereignty over 500,000,000 subjects, in the words of Rebecca West, she must be "always and unalterably perfectly good, perfectly sensible, and perfectly sane." A constitutional monarch must always master State papers, must be equipped to make decisions of consequence, must grapple with political crises.

All rumors of a coming betrothal have been labeled as "ridiculous" by the department that handles press relations for the Royal Family. Court gossip has linked Elizabeth's name with two genealogically acceptable young commoners. They are Hugh Denis Charles Fitzroy, Earl of Euston, and Charles John Robert Manners, Duke of Rutland—both are twenty-five, Etonians, Cambridge men, and junior officers in the Grenadier Guards. Although discussion is officially frowned upon, it is reported likely "that her future consort will be selected from among Britain's peers, of whom five or six have the right age and background." Though Elizabeth may be restricted or even directed in her choice, it is significant that in a measure she will be permitted to follow the dictates of her own heart. In a domestic policy that began with Queen Victoria, marriage based upon personal choice—with domestic happiness instead of alliance with a foreign country in view—became a habit with the Royal Family. When the Duke of York married a commoner it had been more than two centuries since a prince in direct succession to the throne had married a subject other than a princess—George V having decided that his sons might marry whom they wished from the ranks of dukes, marquesses, or earls.

The future Queen Elizabeth II is a "pretty but not yet handsome" girl, slim and erect (at latest report she was five feet six and one-half inches tall), with light brown hair that is naturally wavy, gray-blue eyes, a slightly long nose, a determined jaw, an ingratiating smile, and a complexion that has an "almost unroyal color." She bears a striking resemblance to the Queen Mother at the same age.

Elizabeth has grown into a very human, poised, and unaffected—yet contemplative—young lady who can drive a motor car or a speedboat, jitterbug, swim expertly, and act rather creditably (both Princesses have starred in several Christmas pantomimes). Nevertheless, she still leads the most secluded life of any girl in Britain: she has never had a date, been in a bus or taxi, shopped alone, or been allowed to attend parties in other people's houses. But like every other Briton, she gets only forty-eight clothing ration coupons, and is "making the old clothes do." As a rule she does not dress gaily, favoring plain suits, especially tweeds in pastel shades, low-heeled shoes, and sober hats.

References

Atlantic Monthly 172:83-5 D '43
Lit Digest 123:11-12 Ja 2 '37 por
N Y Times Mag VI p14-15+ Je 20 '43
    pors; VI p11+ Ap 16 '44 por
Newsweek 23:44+ Ap 17 '44 pors
Asquith, C. M. E. C. The King's
    Daughters 1938

ENGEL, CARL July 21, 1883—May 6, 1944
French-born musician, composer, and publisher; president since 1934 of G. Schirmer, Inc., music publishers; editor of the *Music Quarterly* since 1929; chief of the music division of the Library of Congress from 1922 to 1934, then honorary consultant; held numerous posts and was honorary member of many societies.

Obituary

N Y Times p45 My 7 '44 por

EVERGOOD, PHILIP (HOWARD FRANCIS DIXON) Oct. 26, 1901- Painter and etcher

Address: h. 37-13 65th St., Woodside, Long Island, N. Y.; Barnstable, Mass.

"My only aim is to paint a good picture—a work of art—and, on this level plane, to say what I want about life." This is the credo of Philip Evergood, whose *Wheels for Victory* took in 1944 the second prize of $2,000 in the Pepsi-Cola Competition for American Artists, held under the auspices of Artists for Victory, Inc. The canvases submitted came from almost every state in the Union and contained everything in the way of subject matter from *genre* to self-portraits. But, curiously enough, Evergood's was the only industrial-war subject among the twelve winners. His painting, which shows a locomotive and an Army tank on a bridge with a group of war-workers and a Negro military guard, has, according to *Art News*, "the powerful and uncompromising quality of his best work." The top prize-winning paintings become the property of the Pepsi-Cola Company, forming the nucleus of a collection of American art which will later be given to the nation. One hundred and fifty canvases selected from the contest, including the prize winners, were shown in an exhibition, "Portrait of America," at New York's Metropolitan Museum of Art in October 1944, and then toured the country.

Philip Howard Francis Dixon Evergood was born in New York City on October 26, 1901, the son of Miles Evergood, an Australian artist, and Flora Jane (Perry) Evergood. At the age of ten he was sent to his mother's family in England to be educated, studying at Eton, and at Trinity Hall, Cambridge. Ostensibly reading law at the latter institution, Evergood was secretly making sketches on the side, and in 1921 he left Cambridge to be an apprentice in the studio of Harvard Thomas, the sculptor. Thomas showed some of Evergood's drawings to Henry Tonks, principal of the Slade School of Art in London, and Tonks, delighted with the humorous quality of the work, admitted young Evergood to his classes at once, in advance of a long waiting list. It was at the Slade that Philip Evergood learned the sound draftsmanship that underlies all of his painting. In 1923 he returned to America with the firm intention of devoting himself to his lifelong ambition of becoming a painter. A year at the Art Student's League in New York under George Luks and von Schlegel was followed by a few months at the Académie Julien in Paris, a sojourn at the British Academy in Rome, and short periods of study in Antwerp, Madrid, and other European art cen-

Alfredo Valente

PHILIP EVERGOOD

ters. His first exhibited work was shown at London's National Academy in 1924.

Back in New York, Evergood, who had "fled from the chance to live securely, prosperously and dully . . . in order to live more agreeably though precariously as an artist," held his first one-man show at the Dudensing Gallery in 1927. The exhibition comprised over fifty paintings and etchings, chiefly biblical in theme. In several succeeding exhibitions at the Montross Gallery, Evergood showed himself as an "artist of romantic inclination." The New York *Herald Tribune* found the spirited handling of his biblical subjects suggestive of Delacroix, and that hints from Picasso '43 were apparent in a painting titled *Hagar and Ishmael*; and the critic of the New York *Evening Post* noted the artist's increased power of spatial design and solidity of form. Later Evergood retreated somewhat from his preoccupation with the Bible and began to paint *genre* subjects. But according to Elizabeth McCausland, in *Parnassus*, his "emergence as a painter of the world about him" dated from New York's Museum of Modern Art's "Murals by American Painters and Photographers" exhibition in 1932, in which Evergood showed three mural panels. Although he still adhered to allegory and literary titles, these panels indicated his flair for design and his increasing interest in realistic subject matter. About this time critics noted a keying-up of his palette, "a brave new surge of color that at times fairly knocks one down."

In 1935 Evergood's *Evening Reading* received the M. V. Kohnstamm prize for the most commendable painting in the Chicago Art Institute's 46th Annual Exhibition of American Painting and Sculpture, an exhibition which caused a great stir among critics and patrons alike, many finding the canvases obscene, comic, or just plain dull. But defenders were not lacking to proclaim the show a "fresh and vital comment on present-day life." The jury, amazed at the reaction to their choice, contended that there had been "a deep shifting of values in the artist's world and the exhibition rightfully reflected this change." Selections had been due

EVERGOOD, PHILIP—*Continued*

not to the individual taste of the jurors, but to the character of the overwhelming majority of works submitted. Evergood's painting, which Eleanor Jewett of the Chicago *Tribune* called "a frightful clash of colors," and which Robert B. Harshe, director of the Institute, compared to van Gogh, shows a Bohemian interior in which a young man and a girl lolling on a couch are "reading Tolstoi and some radical manifestos."

Another controversy over Evergood's work occurred when a storm of resentment greeted the showing of his *Art on the Beach* in an exhibition at the National Gallery in Melbourne, Australia, in the autumn of 1937. This canvas, which portrays a sketch class on the beach at Provincetown painting a young woman in sailor pants while two sailors look on, is a chaos of "bustle, confusion, conflict of elements, characters, textures, shapes, and colors." A caricature held by one of the sketchers gives Evergood the opportunity for one of his sly bits of humor. Bitter arguments between the opposing museum factions— some 2,000 in number—led to blows between academicians and modernists, and guards had to be called to end the fighting. But admirers took up the cudgels for Evergood, and Sir John Longstaff, noted Australian artist, helped to raise a fund to purchase the disputed painting for the National Gallery's permanent collection.

One of the first artists to be employed by the Government, Evergood executed a huge canvas, *Government Report on North River,* for the Public Works Art Project, and then turned his energies to a mural for the Federal Art Project—*The Story of Richmond Hill,* for the Richmond Hill Branch of the Queens Borough Public Library, in Long Island. Finished in 1937 after two years' work, the mural presents the history, occupations, and diversions of the community. Although critics found the work a "sort of gay extravaganza, full of originality, and in its rollicking fashion very vigorous," some Richmond Hillers objected to it because it did not "realistically portray the rural beauty of the neighborhood as it was in 1870 when Albon Platt Man, wealthy lawyer, conceived the idea of building a garden community within reach of the great city." Others registered dissatisfaction with the portraits of the founders, color of the church, and even drawing and perspective. But the fundamental cause of protest was of a more delicate nature. The proprieties of these distinguished citizens had been outraged by "gross corporal references. . . ." "Even the horses were thought to be of an uncouth breed." Jerome Klein wrote in the New York *Post* that the ideas of these objectors had evidently changed little since the days of Frederick Marryat's visit to the country a century ago, when he observed that "well-bred American girls never used the coarse word 'leg'—it seems that even the tables and chairs stood on limbs." Klein was unable to blush when he saw the mural, which was defended by the National Society of Mural Painters, the American Artists Congress, and the Artists Union. However, when Evergood had made some alterations, the opposition party, after months of protest, was forced to give

way and the long controversy ended in the acceptance of the mural by the Queens Borough Library Board.

Evergood's next mural, *Cotton from Field to Mill,* was executed under Government auspices for the United States Post Office at Jackson, Georgia. A third mural, the result of a grant from the Carnegie Foundation, is *The Bridge to Life,* painted while Evergood was Carnegie Resident Artist at Kalamazoo College, Michigan, for about ten months in 1940-1941. During this time he also taught at the College, and painted various easel pictures, one of which, *The Little Accomplices,* placed by admirers among Evergood's most important smaller canvases, was bought in 1942 by the Kalamazoo Institute of Arts for its permanent collection. Another canvas from this period is the "brilliantly atmospheric *Kalamazoo in Winter,* with its daring contrast between fore- and background," which later won a $500 purchase prize at the "Artists for Victory" exhibition at the Metropolitan Museum in 1943.

It was inevitable that Philip Evergood, who believes "that the role of the artist in society has always been and always will be to express the life of his day," should identify himself with the American Contemporary Art Gallery, where for the past half-dozen years he has been holding one-man shows, for that gallery has been exhibiting the works of social comment painters since 1932. In his early exhibitions there Edward Alden Jewell of the New York *Times* noted that "elements of caricature are found in most of the pictures in the current display (1939), yet even now that he has to some extent transferred his interest from 'fantastic painting based on symbolism' to 'social consciousness' an incorruptible good humor remains a prime ingredient." Pictures exhibited during this period include *An American Tragedy* (1940), a much disputed painting of steel strikers clashing with the law, which Elizabeth McCausland, critic of the Springfield *Union and Republican,* found a "dynamic composition painted with great understanding of the kinesthetic realities of movement; but which Jewell of the New York *Times* considered "cheap and unconvincing as social comment, with little to recommend it aside from its excellent design and painting quality." *My Forebears Were Pioneers*—hung in the Contemporary Art Exhibition of the New York World's Fair (1939) and later shown at the Museum of Modern Art's "Romantic Painting in America" exhibition and at the A.C.A.—a painting in which "Evergood is completely and slyly and subtly and sardonically himself," according to Jewell, has a subject taken from the New England hurricane of 1938, which Evergood witnessed. The fantastic element in this canvas is heightened by a "brilliantly bizarre palette of acrid purples, greens, and yellows." The artist reached a high point in his development with *Lily and the Sparrows,* shown at the Whitney Annual in 1940 and at the A.C.A. the same year. According to Miss McCausland, this painting displays "a worship of life which in other societies was bestowed on religious symbols, in our time on humanity."

Illness and personal tragedy interrupted Evergood's work for almost a year. When he exhibited again, in October 1942, his work had taken on a touch of mysticism, reflected in the mysterious mood of *Turmoil*, which shows a questioning woman standing hesitatingly on a steep stairway and looking out with wondering eyes. Carlyle Burrows of the New York *Herald Tribune* thought highly of this painting, as did other critics. *Juju as a Wave* he considered "most distinctive"; but Emily Genauer of the New York *World-Telegram* found it "gauche and tasteless," although she described Evergood as "one of the country's most gifted, if uneven, painters."

Reaction to the War provided most of the subjects for the artist's next exhibition at the A.C.A. Gallery, in the spring of 1944. The paintings, which both repelled and attracted by the violence of their scenes, showed the profound horror that war had added to Evergood's constant sense of social injustice. Considered outstanding was *Don't Cry, Mother*, recently purchased by the Museum of Modern Art, in which distortion, elongation, and exaggerated perspective are predominant. Two other works which aroused especial interest were *Lone Survivor,* a fantastic representation of a "ravaged wood in which fragments of brightly dressed bodies hang from smoky trees, the lone survivor being a bedraggled old white horse"; and *Veteran of Stalingrad,* which symbolizes the heroic resistance of the Russian people in the War.

Although Evergood has functioned primarily as a creative artist, he has filled various posts in the art world. From 1933 to 1935 he was art director of the Gallery of American Indian Art, Inc.; in 1937-1938 he was managing supervisor of New York's Easel Division of the Federal Art Project; and in 1940-1941, Carnegie Resident Artist at Kalamazoo College, Kalamazoo, Michigan. An active member of the Artists' League of America and a former president of the old Artists' Union, Evergood is very articulate about his beliefs. His writings have appeared in various art magazines.

Called "a painter's painter," Philip Evergood has a "wide following among collectors, an enthusiastic personal following among younger artists." His is an art "based on the fusion of real experience with symbols extracted from contemporary life and history. It is an art, too, in which the present builds on the past, using particularly the complex plastic language of modern painting from the Renaissance up to now." His "beautiful paint quality and the clear blues, reds, and yellows he uses come from long hours of intensive experimentation with oil and duco and glazes and colors." According to Jack Tworkov it is part of Evergood's "positive attitude to draw with great devotion the minutiae of finger nails and wrinkles, eyelids and nostrils. He distorts freely, but avoids boneless generalization. The names most frequently on his lips are El Greco, Brueghel, Angelo, and Raphael."

Since painting is Evergood's hobby as well as his profession, his output is large. He has exhibited continuously since 1927, having put on ten one-man shows, and also displayed his work in major exhibitions in America and abroad. He is represented in the permanent collections of the Metropolitan Museum of Art, the Museum of Modern Art, and the Whitney Museum, in New York; the Brook-

lyn Museum; the Boston Museum of the Fine Arts; the Kalamazoo Institute of Arts, Michigan; the Arizona University Museum; the Widener Library, Harvard; the Carnegie Institute, Pittsburgh; the Albright Art Gallery, Buffalo; the National Gallery, Melbourne, Australia; the Geelong Gallery of Art, Victoria, Australia; and the Library of Congress. Many of his paintings are also owned by private collectors.

Evergood, who was married to the former Julia Vincent Cross, artist and dancer, on August 15, 1931, spends his winters in Woodside, Long Island, and his summers in Barnstable, Massachusetts. As might be expected of so socially minded a painter, he belongs to the American Labor Party. Said to resemble the English actor Charles Laughton, Philip Evergood has a sense of humor that is "delicious and very individual." Although his work is robust in the extreme, he himself retains the aristocratic aura of his Cambridge University education.

In the summer of 1944 the artist was busy at his Cape Cod home completing twelve paintings depicting American-Russian friendship since the birth of the American republic. The scenes, which have been reproduced in color for the 1945 calendar of Russian War Relief, Inc., were on exhibition at the A.C.A. Gallery in November. Some critics felt that these canvases did not rank with Evergood's best work, but they praised the vivid and exciting color and the skillful use of symbolism. Other activities of the summer included a talk, "Fundamentals, Functions, Frameworks of Art," delivered to the students of the Smith College summer session; and preparation for his next one-man show, which Herman Baron reports will be held at the A.C.A. Gallery in the spring of 1945.

References

Art Digest 14:20 Ap 1 '40
Coronet 2:174 My '37
Newsweek 23:93-4 Mr 27 '44 por
Parnassus 11:19-21 Mr '39
Who's Who in America 1944-45

FAIRFAX, BEATRICE 1878(?)- Columnist; reporter; author

Address: b. c/o King Features Syndicate, 235 E. 45th St., New York City; h. 1753 P St., N.W., Washington, D. C.

> *Just write to Beatrice Fairfax*
> *Whenever you are in doubt;*
> *Just write to Beatrice Fairfax*
> *And she will help you out.*

"Who is Beatrice Fairfax? Does anyone really know?" asks Ishbel Ross rhetorically in *Ladies of the Press.* "The dark suspicion that a pipe-smoking, cursing male takes the love confessions of harassed youth and wisecracks at their expense has provided many a newspaper joke." After the publication of Miss Fairfax's autobiographical *Ladies Now and Then* (1944), the reading public knows that Beatrice Fairfax is not only a woman but a mother, that she takes her correspondents very seriously indeed, and that apart from her column she is an author of many stories under her real name of Marie Manning. For years she

Harris & Ewing

BEATRICE FAIRFAX

was listed in *Who's Who in America* as Marie Manning—with a cross-reference to Mrs. Herman Edward Gasch. Today, however, "probably a handful of people know who Marie Manning is, but the name Beatrice Fairfax is as familiar as the national anthem."

Marie Manning was born in Washington, D. C., in the late '70's, the daughter of M. Charles and Elizabeth (Barrett) Manning. She was privately educated in Washington, New York, and London. After her mother's death, which occurred during Marie's childhood, the girl spent most of her time at a finshing school, taking "such oddments as were considered meet for a young gentlewoman to know." Here she was taught to play Rubinstein's "Melody in F," given her, she explains, because her hands were large enough to play it as it is written, without resorting to arpeggios. In her mid-teens, Marie, who grew to be four inches taller than the average man of the day, was so thin that her father feared she would "go into a decline" and sent her to a Western ranch to build up her strength. "I went on studying at the ladies' seminary even after my father's death," says Miss Fairfax, "because my guardian, Justice Martin F. Morris, didn't quite know what to do with a girl who was almost six feet tall, had no interest in clothes, and wouldn't go to 'pink teas,' as coming-out parties were apt to be called at the time." Something the Judge didn't know was that his lanky charge, who "adored the printed word and reverenced anybody connected with it," had become "a marked character, bereft of all privileges" at the school when it was discovered that she had been smuggling in sensational newspapers which she read during the period set aside for meditation.

Asked to fill in for an absent schoolmate at dinner, the twenty-year-old Miss Manning found that her partner was Arthur Brisbane, then editor of the New York *World*. On his invitation—after a ten-day siege of her guardian to get his consent—she came to New York to get a job on the *World*. Beginning

at "space rates," Miss Manning soon found reason to be glad of her private income, for her earnings often came to only five or six dollars a week. After a lucky chance got her an interview with ex-President Cleveland which had been refused all the paper's best reporters, this newest of cubs was put on the regular staff at the then very good salary of $30 a week. Shortly afterwards, however, Miss Manning joined the exodus of *World* employees to William Randolph Hearst's *Evening Journal*. The *Journal* staff was very well paid, and, as Miss Fairfax recalls, "full speed ahead was the order of the day, whether it was a murder story that the police had given up as practically insoluble, battering for cheaper freight rates for farmers, demanding postal savings banks, then regarded as a dangerous novelty, or sending tenement-house children for daily trips to the seashore."

Miss Manning and two other girls, incarcerated in a little office called the "Hen Coop," where erring male reporters were sent to expiate their misdeeds, wrote all the women's page articles, turned out book reviews and features, produced thrillers for the Sunday edition, and added "the 'woman's angle,' whatever that is," to murder trials. "It was an amiable little Victorian world that we young women viewed from the Hen Coop," writes Miss Fairfax, "with its treacly sweet interviews given by ladies bent on impressing the public with their domestic urges. . . . The really brazen thing for a woman to do was to work for suffrage"—as Miss Manning did— "or to try getting some of the more unjust old English common laws controlling women repealed."

Shortly after the close of the Spanish-American War, the *Journal's* editor brought three letters to the Hen Coop. Each of these writers asked for advice on a tragic personal problem, and as the letters hardly seemed to belong in the "People's Forum," Brisbane wanted them answered on the women's page. Miss Manning suggested a separate department, a public confessional, to specialize in just such letters, and later thought of the name Beatrice Fairfax (Beatrice for Dante's *Beata Beatrix*, and Fairfax after the Virginia county where the Manning family owned "a run-down place of sorts"). Her suggestion was adopted, and on July 20, 1898, she abandoned the cooking, etiquette, and "'very naïve beauty hints'" she had been writing, and became Beatrice Fairfax. As such she became nationally known with astonishing speed.

By the sophisticated, Beatrice Fairfax was considered as a supplier of "saccharine answers to the sentimental missives that blossomed in Hearst's column, 'Letters from the Lovelorn.' This column, which was an outgrowth of Annie Laurie's sob stuff, was even more popular," wrote Oliver Carlson and Ernest Sutherland Bates in their book on Hearst, "since it allowed moronic readers to be actors as well as audience."

But at that time, it is pointed out, there were practically no social agencies—"no well-organized Legal Aid, no Community Chest, no adult education or vocational training to bridge educational gaps and enable people to get better jobs. . . . Laws relating to women in many of the states were monstrously unjust." The air was heavy with conventional propriety, and there were "no generally accepted common-sense solutions to certain eternally familiar problems, as the deserted wife, abandoned children, or the girl who had loved well and unwisely. To a multitude of correspondents, the Beatrice Fairfax column represented the only medium through which they could discuss their perplexities and get an impartial answer from an unknown and unprejudiced person." And although Miss Fairfax had at first to dash off a few notes to herself, the column soon caught on. "Before long," she recalls, "I began to dread the sight of the office boys straining under mail sacks brought over from the post office." Soon porters had to be hired to carry the Fairfax mail, which came in such quantities—as high as 1,400 letters a day—that "Uncle Sam had washed his hands of us and declined to deliver more mail by carrier." "Circulation zoomed like an ascending airplane. . . . Editors all over the country, amazed at the pulling power of the 'lovelorn'"—a word Miss Fairfax detests—"founded heart clinics," and, as Jane Cobb was later to write, the lonely heart became lonely by courtesy only. "Reticent people, who ordinarily would not have confided in anyone, enjoyed seeing their own experiences mirrored in the columns.... That old, never-quenched curiosity about the secret springs of other peoples' lives got us hundreds of thousands of readers."

Not all the letters were tragic, nor were they all from adolescents. Correspondents asked advice on all sorts of subjects and often sent photographs. The favorite question, and still much asked, though now oftener by young men than by girls, was "What can I do to be more popular?" Still other frequent inquiries were, "Should the young man get down on his knees while proposing? Should he get the consent of the girl's parents first? . . . What should they do about a chaperon when they went out on a bicycle built for two? . . . Divorce problems, which make up the bulk of the Beatrice Fairfax letters now, were rarely mentioned in those days. Nor did the question of a girl keeping her job after marriage ever arise. All her yearnings were toward the ladylike."

As Beatrice Fairfax, Marie Manning took an entirely different tack from the sentimental vaporings of the period and avoided the "heavy sobbing" which characterized the column later, when written by others. Common sense was her motto and her method: "Dry your eyes, roll up your sleeves, and *dig for a practical solution*." Not that she was unsympathetic; on the contrary, she and her assistants were constantly trying to collect money from the *Journal* staff for particularly needy cases. But her philosophy was: "In any case, pick up the pieces and keep on going." When a question of law was involved—and "innumerable people know nothing of their legal rights"—Miss Fairfax got the answer from her old guardian, Judge Morris. Yet, even while carrying the Beatrice Fairfax burden, Marie Manning continued under her original name to go on reportorial assignments, interviewing William Jennings Bryan and other celebrities. Short stories from her pen appeared mainly in *Harper's Magazine* every few months; and she wrote several full-length books. *Lord Allingham, Bankrupt* came out in 1902, and *Judith of the Plains,* from which, Miss Fairfax says, David Belasco lifted the plot without credit for his *Girl of the Golden West,* was published in 1903. Three years later came *Truce, The Prophetess of the Land of No-Smoke,* and, in collaboration, *Under the Sunset.*

On June 12, 1905 Marie Manning retired from newspaper work to marry her old friend Herman Edward Gasch, one of the few men taller than she. "Of all queer sources of romance," says Miss Fairfax, "ours lay in the discovery that each was an addict of Boswell's *Life of Johnson.* H.E.G. had a first edition of *Journal of a Tour to the Hebrides* which I coveted mightily. Why not acquire the book honorably: marry the man and have it around the house? . . . And so we were married and went to the Hebrides on our honeymoon. . . . It may be a strange recipe for avoiding Reno, but we never agree on any subject, political, religious, ethical, or the better way of making coffee. Our arguments, which I beg you to believe are always conducted in a minor key, have cleared the domestic atmosphere, which otherwise might have grown stodgy."

For nearly a quarter-century (with a brief reunion during the First World War), "Beatrice Fairfax" was separated from Miss Manning and "fluttered from one pair of hands to another," remaining longest under the care of Lilian Lauferty. The new Mrs. Gasch devoted this time to her husband and sons, Oliver H. Gasch (during the Second World War a major in the Army of the United States) and Manning Gasch. Besides her domestic life in Washington and Virginia, where she grew delphiniums nearly as tall as herself, she worked for the cause of justice for women. "Unbelievable today," she writes, "was the apologetic spirit with which taxpaying women asked for a trifling betterment of laws concerning women and children. Children at that time were working eight and ten hours a day in cotton mills and the gentlemen on [Capitol] Hill were quoting Scripture to prove that the system was all that it should be." Mrs. Gasch, a witty and adroit speaker, led delegations of lobbyists, marched in parades, and "as an inconspicuous private . . . helped to fight the good fight for women." ("I've always felt a certain amount of shame," she says, "that I lacked the moral courage to go to jail with these women [who had been picketing the White House with banners demanding the vote], who were arrested on the grounds of obstructing traffic, a manifestly absurd charge.") Nor did Miss Manning completely lose track of her work; for every once in a while Arthur Brisbane called on her to cover a big story for the paper. Two of her short stories were published in 1910, and one each in 1920 and 1921, while her *Crete, the Beginning* came out in 1924.

Like many others, during the wild financial days of 1929 Marie Manning Gasch went "absolutely broke in an effort to get rich quick." "I've been through the stock market and lost every cent I had, put a mortgage on my house, borrowed ten thousand dollars from my husband, have one son just graduating from Princeton who wants to study law, another

FAIRFAX, BEATRICE—*Continued*

boy about to enter college.... Might I have a job, the sooner the better?" she asked Arthur Brisbane. So Mrs. Gasch again became Beatrice Fairfax, King Features' queen of the lovelorn, whose column is distributed by the Hearst syndicate to 200 newspapers throughout the country. (Each subscribing paper may edit the column to suit its own needs, and local "ghosts handle the local letters in certain parts of the country, so that there is good ground for the suspicion that Beatrice Fairfax is often in masquerade," as Ishbel Ross puts it.)

All the ancient problems were still going strong, of course, but the difference in the times was reflected in the Fairfax letters. For one thing, they were fewer. "Girls were more sophisticated. They seemed to have taken the bit in their teeth, a good many of them, and shown more initiative in solving their own problems." There were more letters from men, more from mature people than from the young, and many more about broken homes, "the forays of the love pirate, the ennui of the restless wife, and the problem of the children of divorced parents. In the nineties, when a girl got married practically all correspondence with Beatrice Fairfax ended. Now marriage is only the beginning of the widespread traffic with the love oracle. The effects of the Second World War on human lives, from its beginning, were reflected in the column; when the United States entered the War, these inquiries became much more frequent and varied. When the Office of Dependency Benefits was inaugurated, Miss Fairfax was "swamped with letters asking every conceivable sort of question about draft, enlistments, and so on. Also such questions as 'Why don't I receive my maintenance check? . . . Why don't they send me my husband's service number, for which I wrote? . . . How can I get in touch with my husband, who hasn't written me, and can he be forced to contribute some of his pay to me and the children?'" "The thousand and one questions most commonly asked by service men, their wives, and their sweethearts" were gathered into a book and published, with Miss Fairfax's answers, as *Personal Reply* (1943).

In addition to her duties as mother confessor and adviser-in-chief, Miss Fairfax covers the "woman's angle" on Washington for the International News Service, including Eleanor Roosevelt's [40] famous press conferences for ladies only. In May 1944 her *Ladies Now and Then,* a "chatty, casual, and occasionally serious" résumé of her life, was published. Hardly personal enough to be termed an autobiography, it was called by the *Library Journal* "superficial but very readable." Rose Feld thought it "a pleasant surprise to know that Beatrice Fairfax is a real person . . . and that she has a fine sense of humor, a warm heart, and a straight-thinking mind."

Even among a generation of women two inches taller than hers, Beatrice Fairfax is an impressive figure; five feet eleven inches tall, she weighs 170 pounds. Her graying brown hair, casually swept into an old-fashioned bun high on the back of her head, combined with her lack of cosmetics, make her look more like a homebody grandmother than a nationally known columnist and reporter. In keeping

with the first impression, Miss Fairfax says of her husband and herself: "We adore our children, we love all animals, we love to plant things in the garden—productive of more arguments—but we're not addicted to change. We've had the same house, the same children, the same servants or relatives and friends of these excellent people, all these years." Miss Fairfax is a member of the Arts and Woman's City Clubs, and a charter member of the Women's National Press Club and Newspaper Women's Club. Her New York club is the National Arts.

Remembering her part in the long and not yet finished campaign for women's rights, Miss Fairfax says, "I have a faint glow of reflected pride whenever I read of some woman's accomplishment, whether in the arts, letters, law, or medicine." In her own field, the best of the advice columns, in her opinion, is that of Dorothy Dix [40], her chief competitor. "Often," says Miss Fairfax, "I've envied her philosophy and wit in handling a knotty problem."

References

> Fairfax, B. Ladies Now and Then 1944
> Ross, I. Ladies of the Press 1936
> Who's Who in America 1936-37 (See Manning, Marie)
> Who's Who in the Nation's Capital, 1938-39 (See Manning, Marie)

FARLEY, JAMES A(LOYSIUS) May 30, 1888- Politician; businessman

Address: h. 1040 Fifth Ave., New York City; Haverstraw, N.Y.

James Aloysius Farley was born in Grassy Point, Rockland County, New York, May 30, 1888, of Irish antecedents. His father was James Farley, a brick manufacturer and one of the few Democrats in the county; his mother was the former Ellen Goldrick. "I was born a Democrat and I expect to die a Democrat," Farley himself has been quoted as saying. At any rate, his political talents showed themselves early. At the advanced age of eight young Jim Farley was carrying a torch in a "Bryan-for-President" parade; by the time he had reached high school years he was known as "that friendly-as-a-pup Farley kid"—he was addressing nearly everyone in town by his first name.

When Farley was not quite ten his father was killed by a horse, and Mrs. Farley was left with a half-interest in a little schooner that carried bricks thirty miles down the Hudson to New York, a small insurance policy—and five sons. Jim ran errands and sold newspapers until his mother bought a small grocery and saloon with her last $1,500. He then helped her in both ends of the business, and during the summers worked from 3.30 to 11 a.m. as a machine boy in Morrissey's brickyard for less than a dollar a day. Besides going to school he played a good deal of baseball. Nicknamed "Stretch" because he was the best first baseman the town had ever seen, he played on high school and semi-professional teams which won most of the local pennants. At the same time he managed to be a waltzing champion and a model young man who attended church regularly—he made and kept a confirmation vow to abstain from alcohol and tobacco.

When Farley was graduated from near-by Stony Point High School in 1905 he went to New York City to study bookkeeping at the Packard Commercial School, then took a position as bookkeeper in the Merlin, Keilholtz Paper Company in the same city, at a salary of $8 a week. But his natural affability and his talent for remembering "what kind of a tree it was that little Johnny fell out of and which arm he broke" wouldn't let him remain a bookkeeper long. His next position was with the Universal Gypsum Company, for which he worked fifteen years as bookkeeper, company correspondent, and finally as salesman.

In the summer of 1912 he entered politics when he announced his candidacy for the town clerkship of Stony Point. While selling on the road in southern New York six days a week he sent postal cards to everyone he knew in Stony Point (meaning nearly everyone); and, though the Democrats had not held the post since the swing away from Cleveland in 1894, he won the election hands down. He then wrote "thank-you" notes to every voter in Stony Point, to those who had voted for him as well as those who hadn't—and he made himself as useful and agreeable as possible in his non-paying office. He refused the small fees to which the law entitled him for various services; he delivered marriage licenses personally; he sold hunting licenses from door to door on the Sunday before the hunting season opened. It was little wonder that he was re-elected three times to the town clerkship by rising majorities, nor that he was soon associating with the real leaders of the Democratic Party in New York State. One of the first to urge Al Smith '44 to run for the governorship of the state, in the fall of 1918 he had the pleasure of adding his delegate's vote in the nomination of Smith for that office and of seeing him elected. The Governor later appointed him one of the wardens in the ancient office of port warden for New York at a salary of $5,000 a year. Farley describes the post (of inspecting cargoes on incoming boats for possible shifting or damage by water) as a sinecure: "I performed the duties of port warden for about a year, during which time it was evident to me that there was no real necessity for the place." In 1919 a Republican legislature abolished the office.

Farley then returned happily enough to his other labors: by this time he was chairman of the Rockland County Democratic Committee, and he was to serve as supervisor of Rockland County from 1920 to 1923. In April 1920 he was married to his childhood sweetheart, Elizabeth Finnegan, who, incidentally, has never been too interested in politics. In 1922 her husband engineered the renomination of Al Smith for Governor of New York over William Randolph Hearst, and was himself elected to the New York State Assembly. The following year he was defeated for re-election although nineteen bills he introduced to abolish the abuses of the "fee system" were enacted by the assembly. However, within a year Al Smith appointed him a member of the New York State Boxing Commission, a non-salaried position. Farley himself has said: "It wasn't very long until my idea about the new post's being a pleasant diversion was rudely shattered." Soon he was being severely criticized for a ruling on fouls and for allowing fights between

JAMES A. FARLEY

boxers of mixed weights. He also came under fire for his liberal distribution of free fight tickets among personal and political friends. Such gifts, critics pointed out, did not impede his ascent in politics. During this time Farley was still sales manager of the Universal Gypsum Company; a few years later, however, he organized his own business of supplying lime and cement to contractors, which, after several mergers, became the General Building Supply Corporation. He remained its president until 1933.

All along Farley was increasingly active in politics. He remained chairman of the Rockland County Democratic Committee until 1929, and in 1928 became secretary of the New York State Democratic Committee as well, helping to manage Franklin Delano Roosevelt's '42 first campaign for Governor of New York. (He had first met Roosevelt in 1920 at a crowded reception in Manhattan, but their real acquaintanceship had begun at the Democratic National Convention of 1924, and Farley had been one of Roosevelt's chief admirers for some time.) In 1930, when Farley became chairman of the State Democratic Committee, Roosevelt was re-elected Governor by the unprecedented plurality of 725,001. The day after the election Farley commented: "We have elected . . . the man who will be the next President of the United States," and he immediately set about to make his prophesy come true. Concentrating on the personal contact, in 1931 he made a whirlwind tour of eighteen states, renewing old acquaintanceships, winning new friends, and persuading everyone he met that "there is magic in the name of Roosevelt." Roosevelt's pre-nomination campaign was actually launched at the 1931 Elks' convention in Seattle. From that time until the convention Farley worked in conjunction with the late Louis McHenry Howe as organizer and "field man" for Roosevelt, his particular methods of contacting party workers being the personal letter, the long-distance telephone call, the handshake.

(Continued next page)

FARLEY, JAMES A.—*Continued*

At the 1932 convention, when Farley was the Roosevelt floor leader, Roosevelt had a heavy majority from the first. The voting seemed hopelessly deadlocked, however, until Farley made a deal that swung the Texas and California delegations, pledged to John Nance Garner, to his candidate. Garner received the nomination for Vice-President as a result; Farley took over the chairmanship of the Democratic National Committee, which badly needed the streamlining that he gave it. He added to his reputation not only as a master politician but as a political prophet when he announced before the November 1932 elections that the Democrats would win by a plurality of 7,500,-000 votes. He was off the mark by only 300,000.

Appointed Postmaster General by President Roosevelt, Farley continued to hold his posts as New York State Democratic chairman and National Democratic chairman. He soon became the chief target of Republican criticism, although he could never have been classed as a rabid New Dealer: he was, purely and simply, a Democrat. His yardstick for job-hunters in Washington was "party loyalty," and those who had been for Roosevelt before the 1932 convention found themselves particularly solid in his good graces. What is more, he delayed in awarding patronage until he saw how Congressmen voted on the essential part of the Roosevelt legislative program. Opponents of the New Deal therefore attacked him as a "spoilsman," though there were others to point out that Farley had not invented the patronage system, and, according to *Look,* all he introduced into it was "a more efficient card-index system." Both the Administration and Farley were criticized when, following the cancellation of the air-mail contracts with commercial lines and the subsequent flying of air mail by the Army, ten Army fliers were killed. He was, too, the target of criticism for presenting specimen sheets of stamps to Democratic bigwigs, a criticism that came also from some of Roosevelt's friends. In the face of such attacks, however, Farley remained cheerful and silent.

In August 1936 Postmaster General Farley took a leave of absence without pay in order to manage Roosevelt's second Presidential campaign—and he maintained his reputation as a prophet when, five days before the election, he forecast that Roosevelt would carry every state except Maine and Vermont. Early in 1938, when his memoirs, *Behind the Ballots,* appeared, he and the President were apparently still on excellent terms. Already, however, he was beginning to become annoyed by Tommy Corcoran [40], "something of a program writer for the New Deal"—and other irritations came thick and fast. The Supreme Court reorganization bill was something on which he had nothing whatsoever to say. The party purge that followed was a bad political mistake, in his opinion: wasn't a Democrat a Democrat? Roosevelt consulted him less and less in his dealings with Congress, and, according to some sources, discouraged him from becoming a candidate for Governor of New York State. Whatever Farley's feelings may have been, by the latter part of the year one writer was already reporting that Farley and Garner had signed a secret pact under which they would attempt to control the 1940 convention and keep either Roosevelt, or anyone picked by him, from getting the nomination.

Farley's visits to the White House became less frequent, and although there was no open break with the President, it was bruited about that Farley was opposed to a third term. It was also said that Farley himself had Presidential—or, at least, Vice-Presidential—aspirations. Then, in March 1940, Ernest K. Lindley [43] reported in his column that Roosevelt had told an unnamed Democrat that he 'would not run for a third term unless Germany overran England; that Hull [40] was his candidate; and that Farley was inacceptable as the Vice-Presidential nominee because some might think the Democrats "were using Cordell Hull as a stalking horse for the Pope." Shortly afterward Roosevelt himself stated that the column had been made up out of whole cloth, but it was too late: the next day Farley announced that his own name would be presented to the Democratic National Convention in Chicago—"and that's that." Talk of a Hull-Farley ticket revived; there were signs of overtures from Vice-President Garner's friends for an alliance with Farley; and Farley himself made a "speech-making, hand-shaking, post-office dedicating" tour of the country.

Even before the 1940 Democratic National Convention it became obvious that the President, who had remained publicly non-committal on the issue, would permit himself to be drafted for a third term. In 1937 Farley had said of Roosevelt: "While the breath in my body lingers, I will try to assist him in all he does"; but now he apparently felt himself betrayed. According to Charlie Michelson [40], he had misunderstood Roosevelt's reluctance to run again as a pledge that he would not be a candidate. In any case, Farley permitted his own name to go before the convention as a Presidential candidate (it was put up by Carter Glass [41]), and gained a total of 72 and a fraction votes on the roll call. Roosevelt having won renomination by 946 and a fraction votes, Farley moved that the nomination be made by acclamation, but shortly after the convention he resigned both as chairman of the Democratic National Committee and as Postmaster General. This was ostensibly in order to become new board chairman of the Coca-Cola Export Company, but the move was interpreted by some as a dignified protest against the "third termites." Farley's one-time critics, who had begun to see his good qualities as soon as he had lined up with the Roosevelt-must-go clique, immediately sympathized with him as one who had put principle and country above party, and who had been mistreated by Roosevelt. Farley himself, never sympathetic with party bolters (he had criticized his former friend Al Smith for teaming up with the Liberty League in 1932), announced that he was supporting the Democratic ticket, but conducted "only a perfunctory" campaign for Roosevelt in 1940.

His record as chairman of the State Democratic Committee from that time on was not one of undiminished success. In 1941 he backed William O'Dwyer, the Democratic nominee, in an unsuccessful bid for the mayoralty of New York. In 1942 he was successful in getting the Democratic nomination for Governor of New York for his candidate, John J. Bennett, against the opposition of Roosevelt, who was supporting James Mead '44; but the voters replied by electing the Republican candidate, Thomas E. Dewey '44. During 1943 Farley made many business trips in which he found time to talk with anti-Roosevelt Democrats all over the country, but particularly in the South. A "Byrd '42-for-President" campaign seemed to be shaping up there. Then, in the fall of 1943, the Republicans installed Joe R. Hanley as Lieutenant Governor of New York over the Democratic candidate, Lieutenant General William N. Haskell (retired). Farley saw Hanley's election as a sign that "the people are tired of being kicked around," and pointed to a "definite trend against the National Administration"; but New Dealers charged that he had not made "even the most elementary Democratic campaign efforts on behalf of Haskell." By April 1944 the O'Connell Democratic machine in Albany was attempting to oust him as chairman of the State Democratic Committee, but the move was not supported in Washington, and he was re-elected unanimously.

Farley resigned his chairmanship in June 1944, stating that business interests required his whole attention. This came as a surprise to those who had expected him to wait until after the Democratic National Convention. Although he could not have made his opposition to a fourth term for Roosevelt more evident, Democrats of all shades of opinion, 1,500 in number, attended a testimonial dinner in his honor the next month. No one assumed that he would entirely disappear from politics— and he did not. Later in July he was at the Democratic convention, telling reporters that he was not candidate for either nomination. His own half-votes, however, went to Alben Barkley '41 for Vice-President and to Harry F. Byrd for President; and Farley himself received two half-votes for the Presidential nomination from two of his intimate friends in the New York delegation. Although he announced after Roosevelt's nomination that he would support the Democratic ticket as usual, Mrs. Farley was by this time frankly avowing her support of Dewey.

Farley continued to be active in both national and international affairs. In September, along with John Foster Dulles '44, Alfred E. Smith, Sumner Wells '40, and other distinguished citizens, he signed an appeal for a clean Presidential campaign—a public request to all candidates to discourage the injection of religious and racial animosities into the campaign: "Such conduct is un-American . . . divides our people and betrays one of the cherished ideals for which we struggle." In October he acted as chairman of the celebration held in New York City in honor of the thirty-third birthday of the Chinese Republic. At that time he paid tribute to the late Wendell Willkie '40 for the service Willkie had rendered in strengthening the bond between the United States and China. A month later Farley spoke before the convention of the Alabama State Chamber of Commerce, stressing the need for more industry in the South to balance the agricultural production. And in December 1944, speaking at the twenty-sixth annual Guadalupe Day of the Mexico Pilgrims organization, Farley admonished Americans to drop the tendency "to talk down" to their Latin-American neighbors, but rather "to cement the ties between nations with true friendship."

Many things have been said for and against Farley, but there are some points on which both friend and foe agree. One is his phenomenal memory—a memory for names, faces, and personal details that has helped to win friends and influence people in a large way. Another is his dependability: "his pledge, once promised, is always kept . . . favor for favor, deed for deed." A third is his honesty. He made an annual $15,000 as Postmaster General, but was in debt when he left the office because he insisted that his General Building Supply Corporation, in which he still had a business interest, should not solicit orders where his influence would count and should reject all public business offered. If he had not received $65,000 for his memoirs when they were serialized in the American Magazine he would have been even more badly off. And a fourth quality is his affability. "I like people," Farley himself says, and boasts that he has 100,000 friends. He usually manages to stay on good terms personally with even his greatest political enemies, and he has always been universally popular with the press because he will quip or talk as seriously with a Daily Worker or New York Herald Tribune reporter as with representatives of more friendly newspapers.

Farley "has the look of what people living in the rural areas of the Boston diocese call a 'city Irishman.' Big, strapping [he is over six feet two], his bald head possessing an incredible shine, he has been marked by the metropolis in his manner, his bearing, his speech." According to the American Mercury in 1937, "He looks like a musical comedy butter-and-egg-man ripening for apoplexy, yet he bows the backs of five stenographers a day with his dictation orgies, sees sometimes as many as 200 visitors, and walks the occasional short corridor distances he has to negotiate between fast elevators, trains, and automobiles at a pace roughly equivalent to that of a championship football team charging into the Rose Bowl." "A lifelong non-smoking teetotaler," he consumes large quantities of milk, ice cream, chewing gum, and peppermint drops. He is also a model family man, although his wife and three children (Elizabeth, Ann, James A.) have always complained that they don't see enough of him; and he is a born "joiner"—a big man in the Elks, Redmen, Eagles, and Knights of Columbus. In all these things he is typically American, and his love for baseball is typically American, too. It has been frequently rumored that he is interested in buying a share in the New York Yankees, and he has on occasion been boomed for Judge Kenesaw M. Landis' '44 job as baseball commissioner.

References
  Am Mag 118:18-19+ N '34
  Am Mercury 27:13-19 S '32 por; 42:257-74 N '37
  Collier's 90:9+ S 17 '32 il pors
  Harper 170:385-94 Mr '35
  Look 4:20-3 My 7 '40 il pors
  N Y Herald Tribune II p2 My 5 '40 pors
  (Continued next page)

FARLEY, JAMES A.—*Continued*
New Repub 102:333-6 Mr 11 '40; 108:
440-1 Ap 5 '43
Sat Eve Post 208 :5-6+ Je 27 '36 il pors
Farley, J. Behind the Ballots 1938
Who's Who in America 1944-45

FAUST, FREDERICK (foust) May 29,
1892—May 12(?), 1944 Author under five
pseudonyms but best known as Max Brand;
known as "King of the Pulps" because of a
prodigious output of Western and action
thrillers; author of the Dr. Kildare series for
both books and films; at time of death was
war correspondent attached to Fifth Army in
Italy.

Obituary

N Y Times p3 My 17 '44

FERGUSON, ELSIE Aug. 19, 1885- Actress
Address: b. c/o Central Hanover Bank and
Trust Co., 70 Broadway, New York City;
h. 530 Park Ave., New York City; East Lyme,
Conn.

One of the events of the 1943-1944 theatrical season was the return of Elsie Ferguson,
stage and screen star, to the theatre after an
absence of fourteen years. Famed for her
beauty as well as the distinction of her acting,
Miss Ferguson held a stellar position in the
theatre for thirty years. In almost any town
that had a beauty shop in 1917 and thereabouts,
hopeful housewives would be pleading: "Please
try to make me look like Elsie Ferguson."
The nearest most of her imitators came to
looking like the star (whose pulchritude was
aptly described by a 1914 journalist as "the
shadow of beauty rather than beauty itself")
was the painted beauty spot that the star had
made the rage. When Miss Ferguson opened
in Rose Franken's[41] *Outrageous Fortune* (November 1943) critics jubilantly reported that
despite her fifty-odd years she still possessed
"the presence, the voice, the charm, and the
piquant profile" which made her so memorable
in what she now calls her "first career."

Born in New York August 19, 1885 (some
sources erroneously give 1883), Elsie Ferguson is the daughter of Hiram Benson and
Amelia Ferguson. In 1902 she began her career
as a chorus girl in a road show of *The Belle of
New York*. Her mother, a very good amateur
actress, who boasted of a German ancestor with
a royal decoration for oratory, did not object
to her daughter's choice of profession; her
father, a lawyer (with Scotch-Irish ancestors),
was also agreeable, although he had planned a
normal school education for Elsie. The sight
of a glittering electric sign—"Olga Nethersole
in *Sappho*"—had inspired the girl to become an
actress. "Some day," Miss Ferguson vowed
as she stood before it, "my name is going to
be in front of a theatre—and in lights."

Before the end of 1902, elevated to the position of show girl in *Liberty Belles*, on her
return to New York she won the title of the
"prettiest show girl on Broadway." Pictures
of her with her blond hair piled high in a
pompadour, her figure corseted to hourglass
lines, and a Trilby heart dangling stylishly from

a black ribbon around her throat illustrated the
dramatic sections of *Harper's Weekly, Cosmopolitan*, and other periodicals and newspapers.

In December 1904, while a member of the
New York musical *The Second Fiddle*, Elsie
Ferguson was married to Fred Hoey, shotgun
expert, "man about town, and Knight of
Bohemia," the son of a former president of
the Adams Express Company. Before Charles
Frohman gave her her first part in a straight
play—a one-line role—Miss Ferguson had also
appeared in the chorus lines of *Babes in Toy-
land* and *Mlle. Modiste*, and in the role of a
saleslady in *Julie Bon-Bon*.

Her next boost came when William A.
Brady gave her an important supporting role
in *The Bondman* (1907) ; back in 1903, on her
first European trip, she had caught his attention while appearing in London in a "bit"
part in *The Earl of Pawtucket*. When the
play toured the country, Miss Ferguson,
whose variegated talents made her "the most
original and piquant of serio-comediennes,"
dominated the theatrical pages of the newspapers.

Following a role in *Pierre of the Plains*
(1909), Miss Ferguson achieved stardom in
Channing Pollock's comedy, *Such a Little
Queen* (1909). The press was enthusiastic
in its praise, Adolph Klauber of the New
York *Times* noting "a loveliness akin to
Maude Adams" in her acting.

Miss Ferguson's next three vehicles (all in
1911) were failures, however—*Ambition, A
Matter of Money*, and *Dolly Madison*. The
last, rewritten as *The First Lady of the Land,*
though only a minor success, proved to be
another personal triumph for the star. The
year 1911 also saw the end of her marriage to
Fred Hoey, who, when queried about the
divorce, responded with, "She's a fine woman
—I'm sorry."

A milestone in Miss Ferguson's career was
her interpretation of Inez de Pierrefond in *The
Strange Woman* (1913). When the company
played in Washington, the President and Mrs.
Wilson invited Miss Ferguson to the White
House. But it was in *Outcast* (1914), "a very
honest, sincere and sober study of the mutual
responsibilities of a man and his mistress,"
that Miss Ferguson found the most successful
role of her "first career." Critics commented
that "a more expert and eloquent piece of acting, a more moving impersonation, it would be
hard to discover upon the contemporary stage."

In the year following *Outcast* Miss Ferguson seemed to be living up to the statement
she made to an interviewer at the time: "I
want to be an unguessed riddle, I hope the
public won't solve me and paste a label on me,
for quite a while yet." As Margaret Schiller
in *The Prime Minister* (January 1916) she
played a heavy dramatic role; as Portia to
Sir Herbert Tree's Shylock (May 1916) she
played Shakespeare for the first time ; and
during December 1916 she scored another distinct personal success as a comedienne in the
title role of *Shirley Kaye*. Al Woods, Broadway's most successful producer at the time,
said, "There can be no doubt as to Elsie Ferguson's supremacy on the stage." He pointed
out that she had wondrous beauty, ability, and
versatility. That year also saw her taking her

second step in matrimony. Her marriage to Thomas Benedict Clarke, a vice-president of the Harriman National Bank, was a social event of June 1916. (For years the marriage was considered a success by all their friends, but in 1923 it ended in a Paris divorce.)

"You have to step lively in this profession after once getting under way," observed Elsie Ferguson when she made the momentous decision to join the Famous Players-Lasky Corporation as a screen star in 1917. Her first picture, *Barbary Sheep* (1917), was followed by *The Rise of Jennie Cushing* (1917); *Rose of the World* (1918); *Song of Songs* (1918); *The Lie* (1918); *A Doll's House* (1918); and *The Danger Mark* (1918). In 1920, after three years of work in the films, she was welcomed back to the Broadway stage in *Sacred and Profane Love*. *Varying Shore* (1921) by Zoë Akins, which followed, although listed among Miss Ferguson's most successful vehicles, closed after only thirty-one performances.

Two more years in the films followed—her most outstanding picture being *Peter Ibbetson*, with Wallace Reid in the title role. In January 1923 she was again back in the theatre, opening in *The Wheel of Life*, in whose cast was the well known English actor, Frederick Worlock. In the spring of 1924 Miss Ferguson and Worlock were married. They appeared together again in Alfred Savoir's *The Grand Duchess and the Waiter* (1925).

The House of Women (1927), a dramatization of Louis Bromfield's [44] *The Green Bay Tree*, presented Miss Ferguson as Lilly Shane, the daughter with the "scarlet-lady complex." Benjamin De Casseres was of the opinion that the star could not do scarlet types, although he found her "pretty, charming, and inviting." In *Scarlet Pages* she appeared as a lawyer defending her illegitimate daughter in a murder trial. At the end of its run (1929) Miss Ferguson announced her retirement from the stage. Late in 1930 she sailed for Europe, where she secured a divorce from Frederick Worlock. During the next three years she traveled through Switzerland, France, Germany, and England—staying in Cannes during the summer, in Biarritz during the winter.

Broadway was not to see Miss Ferguson again until she emerged from her retirement in Rose Franken's *Outrageous Fortune*, which closed in January 1944 after a run of eight weeks. According to many of the metropolitan critics, the play was "confused and complex" because it dealt with two major social problems and was complicated by several minor ones, none of which was solved satisfactorily. Of Miss Ferguson's performance, critics wrote: "*Outrageous Fortune* gave Miss Ferguson ample opportunity to demonstrate that those fourteen years [of absence from the stage] were the theatre's loss"; "she gave a glowing performance of a woman wise in human relationships that attained to a deep-reaching effect"; "she brings with her the charm and winning manner of old." After the closing of *Outrageous Fortune*, it was reported that Miss Ferguson would play the leading role of the novelist in Rex Ingram's film production of the stage comedy *Escape to Autumn*.

ELSIE FERGUSON

In London in March 1934 Elsie Ferguson had been married to Victor Augustus Egan, a wealthy Irish sportsman of fifty-nine. Shortly after their marriage the Egans came to the United States, and they are now living on a farm in East Lyme, Connecticut, near the Boston Post Road. In an interview with Lucius Beebe [40] in 1943 Miss Ferguson said, "You have no idea how happy I have been these last few years among my country possessions. I have more than a hundred acres of land, a wonderful cow (very content, too) named Elsie, because she was given to me on my birthday, and I sell milk and eggs commercially. Of course, I have no idea how I am going to come out financially—no head for money, you know—but I have a sneaking suspicion I may come out about even."

Another commercial venture of the actress was the result of a gift from an admirer, a quaint old lady who had called backstage to pay homage while Miss Ferguson was on tour in 1911. As a token of her admiration she had presented the star with an English recipe for fruit cake that had been brought to Virginia in 1700 and was a treasured family heirloom. Miss Ferguson liked the cake made from the recipe so much that in 1922 she founded the Elsie Ferguson Fruit Cake Company.

According to Lucius Beebe, Miss Ferguson "has the assurance and humor that make her good company." In her own words, her philosophy is: "To strive for physical beauty only is to seek to be an object rather than a person. A woman who thinks of nothing but dressing up and decorating herself becomes a decoration, and a decoration is easily replaced by another decoration."

References

N Y Herald Tribune IV p1 O 31 '43
N Y Sun p22 O 29 '43
N Y Times II p1 O 31 '43
Who's Who in the Theatre 1939

FERGUSON, JAMES EDWARD Aug. 31, 1871—Sept. 21, 1944 Former Governor of Texas, impeached on twenty-one financial counts and removed from office in 1917; was barred by a 1924 ruling of the Texas Supreme Court from holding a state office, but continued to wield power through his wife, Mrs. Miriam A. Ferguson, who was elected Governor in 1924 and again in 1932.

Obituary

N Y Times p19 S 22 '44 por

FERRER, JOSE (fär-rär' hō-sā') Jan. 8, 1912- Actor

HAGEN, UTA (hä'gen ü'tä) June 12, 1919- Actress

Address: h. Ossining, N.Y.

"The most mispronounced couple on the American stage," José Ferrer and Uta Hagen have the additional distinction of being one of the few teams of co-starring spouses—the first to achieve stardom together. Iago and Desdemona of the longest-running *Othello* in history, the Ferrers have appeared together in a dozen other productions, ranging from farce to tragedy.

Born in Santurce, Puerto Rico, January 8, 1912, José Vicente Ferrer Otero y Cintron was brought to the United States at the age of six. (He had been there once before, at seven months, for an operation on his palate.) His Spanish-born parents, Rafael and María (Cintron) Ferrer, were naturalized United States citizens, and his father, an attorney, had given up the personal administration of his island real estate holdings so that his children might be brought up in the land of their citizenship. José attended public and private schools; and he studied music, showing such skill at the piano that for some time it was thought he would become a concert pianist. After graduation from school the boy passed the entrance examinations for Princeton. The university authorities, however, thought fourteen a bit too young for even "an awful brightie" like José to enter college; so he was sent to a Swiss boarding school for a year of preparation.

At Princeton, where young Ferrer spent five years studying architecture, he organized a band called "José Ferrer and His Pied Pipers," which played for college functions of various sorts. By its leader's third year the outfit had grown into a fourteen-piece unit which played for most of the big proms—mainly, Ferrer says, because during the depression the classes couldn't afford "name" bands. The Pied Pipers were good enough, however, to be booked for summer cruises to Bermuda and the West Indies and to tour Europe one season. The young Puerto Rican musician realized, however, that the stage was his true love when he acted with the Princeton Triangle Club, of which James Stewart [41] and Joshua Logan were the leading lights. The determining factor was a Triangle play of 1932, *It's the Valet*, with Ferrer as the valet. He spent the summer of 1934, it is said, "aboard the good ship *Periwinkle* in Long Island Sound, declaiming such ripe old melodramas as *The Ocean of Life, or Every*

Inch a Sailor and *The Bitter Reckoning, or Lady Haldane's Secret.*"

Nevertheless the future star endured a year of postgraduate work in Romance languages at Columbia University before realizing that teaching was not his true vocation. That summer (1935) he went to Suffern (New York) and got a job as assistant stage manager and occasional walk-on in Joshua Logan's stock company, including one with Helen Hayes [42] in Bernard Shaw's [44] *Caesar and Cleopatra.*

That fall he managed to do a similar job for *A Slight Case of Murder*. In addition to his backstage duties Ferrer played the Second Policeman, his role consisting of the deathless line, "What's going on here?" His efforts were rewarded with a part twice that length in the road company of *Boy Meets Girl* starting out in January 1936. The fall of that year he played the lead in a comedy, *Spring Dance*. In this Ferrer "neatly characterized" a brash youth, delivering such lines as this description of a woman's college: "The place where they teach the young boas how to constrict."

Next, "the youthful triumvirate of Frankie Albertson, Eddie Albert, and José Ferrer, playing the parts of cadets of Virginia Military Institute, helped to make *Brother Rat* (1936) one of the refreshing farce comedies of the season." This sprightly long-run play was followed by an unremarkable performance in an undistinguished drama, *How To Get Tough About It* (1938) and by the short-lived *Missouri Legend* (1938)—which remains, however, one of Ferrer's favorite plays. In the secondary role of a mournfully devoted mountaineer-poet the young actor had "an opportunity of which he took full advantage. . . . Billy Gashade, in his hands, is more than a figure from Currier and Ives"; he gave the play some necessary "robustness."

The spring season of 1939 saw José Ferrer "acquitting himself well" in the only important white role in *Mamba's Daughters* (which introduced Ethel Waters [41] as a dramatic actress). The summer before he played in stock, appearing at Ridgefield (Connecticut) opposite Uta Hagen in *Arms and the Man* and *Mr. Pim Passes By*. One scene in another play, *The Latitude of Love*, called for her to knock him unconscious—and she did.

The daughter of Dr. Oskar Frank Leonard Hagen, the well-known art historian, and Thyra A. (Leisner) Hagen, Uta Thyra Hagen was born in Göttingen, Germany, June 12, 1919. Her father, lecturer on fine art at the University of Göttingen, had been rejected for military service in the First World War—his mother was Welsh, his father American. He was a promising pupil of Humperdinck and was encouraged to devote free time to musicological research. It was largely he who "made Göttingen the center of a new Handel cult." For five consecutive years after the War Dr. Hagen "organized and directed the Göttingen Handel Festivals, in addition to editing and revising the opera scores which had not been heard for 200 years." His wife sang in many of these summer concerts. Little Uta spent her first six years in the confusion and depression of post-War Germany; but in 1924 her father came to the

United States for a semester as a Carl Schurz Foundation professor and founded the department of art history at the University of Wisconsin, where he remained as head of the department.

Uta's schooling was international, for every two or three years the family would go back to Europe so that Dr. Hagen could continue with his research. (It is far easier nowadays to persuade Uta Hagen to talk about her father than to discuss his daughter.)

Uta was always interested in the theatre; when she decided to become an actress her family sent her to England to attend the Royal Academy of Dramatic Art. Back in the United States, she wrote to Eva Le Gallienne '42 for an audition, which was arranged, and which won the aspiring ingenue the role of Ophelia in the Civic Repertory Theatre's production of *Hamlet*. Despite her success in this part, the following winter found Miss Hagen "practically starving to death and holding tightly to her last dime." This dime she used to phone for an audition for Nina in the Theatre Guild's 1938 production of *The Sea Gull*. Critics remarked that "the role of Nina, the bewildered child who thinks all artists belong to the great in spirit, the little 'sea gull' hunted to death by a bored hunter, is a heavy assignment for a player as new to the Broadway boards as Uta Hagen, and her performance must win her great credit." One reviewer went so far as to credit her with "outright theft of the show" from its stars, Alfred Lunt '41 and Lynn Fontanne '41. Then came summer stock at Ridgefield, and *The Latitude of Love*.

There is a story to the effect that Miss Hagen was married to José Ferrer one week after their first meeting; but the actual courtship involved considerably more time. In the words of Nathaniel Benchley, "Mr. Ferrer—and quite understandably—was one of the most ambitious of modern suitors." After *Latitude of Love* the two went into different plays, and "Mr. Ferrer's route while conducting the courtship looked something like Hannibal's on the way to Rome. He was living in New York, and each day included a visit to Miss Hagen wherever she was playing, his own rehearsal in another place, his show that night still somewhere else, and the return to New York and Miss Hagen. It involved, all in all, five hours in an automobile every day over a period of months, but the net result was worth the gas and time expended [José Ferrer and Uta Hagen were married the following December]. Few of your modern suitors would pay fifty cents to cross the George Washington Bridge unless they were sure the affair was in the bag."

A little less than a year after their marriage the Ferrers played together in Maxwell Anderson's '42 *Key Largo*, in which they both gave "admirable" performances, in spite of the difficulties of blank verse drama. "Together" is perhaps a misleading word, as they never met on-stage: José Ferrer was seen only in the prologue, lasting some twenty minutes, while Uta Hagen had the feminine lead opposite Paul Muni '44. This gave Ferrer the chance, usually denied working actors, to watch his fellow-professionals in action. On his re-

Alfredo Valente

JOSE FERRER and UTA HAGEN

turn he would report to his wife, who was "always glad to talk English again, after an hour or more of blank verse." A writer who came to interview Miss Hagen and met her husband and their two dogs described the couple as "just a little more famous and probably a lot nicer than most people you could name at random, and any interviewer who sat down with a list of prepared questions to ask them would feel more like a dope than they would."

In the summer of 1940 Ferrer was engaged to direct stock productions at the Westchester Playhouse in Mount Kisco, New York. When Walter Slezak got the idea of reviving the old farce *Charley's Aunt*, by Brandon Thomas, director Ferrer persuaded him to play in *Topaze* instead, and then proceeded to put on a startlingly successful version of *Charley's Aunt*, with José Ferrer as Lord Fancourt Babberley. The backers decided to bring the play to Broadway, with Ferrer retaining the lead and Joshua Logan directing, in October 1940. The birth of a daughter, Leticia, proved a fortunate omen for the play's success. That success did not surprise Ferrer: "With two of the best low comedy minds of the century working on it—mine and Logan's, I mean—how could it be anything else?" he mused. Reviewers generally agreed that the laughs were due mainly to bright ideas grafted onto the hoary script, as Ferrer "screamed about the stage, swinging from trees, getting out and then into his clothes again, and successfully eluding the clutches of two deluded gentlemen who thought him a fair dish."

While Ferrer made a star's name for himself as a comedian, Miss Hagen "got the smallest Ferrer into an organized way of living," put up hundreds of jars of the produce of their Ossining farm, and planned to return to the stage. "We have so much fun when we act in the same play," she told an interviewer later. "It's much nicer than having just one of us in a play with the other trailing along

FERRER, JOSE and HAGEN, UTA—*Cont.*

behind." In 1941 the producer-director José Ferrer began rehearsals on *The Admiral Takes a Wife*, starring Uta Hagen. This farce, satirizing the United States Pacific Fleet, began its out-of-town tour in Princeton, and was just about ready for Broadway when the Pearl Harbor attack cut short its existence.

The summer of 1942 they turned from low comedy to classic tragedy, appearing as Iago and Desdemona in a Cambridge (Massachusetts) production of *Othello*, with Paul Robeson [41] in the title role. At this time it was said that "Robeson's towering personality unbalanced the play by dwarfing Iago." "A great Iago can usually steal the show. As a pretty good Iago, José Ferrer . . . could not, against Robeson, even hold his own." The production was, however, a great success; but Robeson's concert commitments would not allow him to start a Broadway run until later.

That fall Miss Hagen and Ferrer were co-featured in *Vickie*, a comedy of which Ferrer was co-director. It proved to be a mistake all around. As though playing in it were not enough of a catastrophe, Miss Hagen slipped one night while making an exit and sprained her ankle. Reversing the usual attitude of the-show-must-go-on, her husband dashed offstage after her, leaving another member of the cast apparently talking to himself on-stage. Later, when Ferrer had been restored to the doctor's brandy, he announced to the audience, "My wife has met with a major disaster!" On her re-entrance she was greeted with cheers which started afresh each time she spoke a line.

When, in the spring of 1943 friend Danny Kaye [41] left *Let's Face It*, Iago Ferrer took over Kaye's part, proving "lively and likable" in his first musical comedy role. "He acts," reported Louis Kronenberger [44], "as though he were having the time of his life, which means that at best he has enormous gusto—though at his not-so-good he is unduly frolicsome. . . . There's no use pretending he has any voice, but he manages to slide through his songs (including the patter of 'Let's Not Talk About Love') without mishap." Ferrer had now scored successes with furious slapstick, impassioned tragedy, light comedy, scheming villainy, and musical comedy, but his record was not free of disappointments. "When I'm lousy in a part," he says, "I know it. Like I was in something called *In Clover*." The Ferrers had another sort of disappointment on the West Coast: "We loathed and despised Hollywood. No self-respecting person will stay there. I hated every minute of it, and hope never to see it again. The only thing I liked was the scenery, and I suppose that was because now and then it reminded me of Puerto Rico."

In the meantime on the radio the young Puerto Rican was playing the part of a young Mexican in an NBC daytime serial, *Woman of America*. His part varied "in length, in scope, and sometimes—serials being what they are—in character," reaching an all-time low when it was confined to an off-microphone ejaculation of "Alto!" addressed to a team-of-horses sound effect. Ferrer also acted as master of ceremonies on *Saludos Amigos*, a Latin-American musical program presented by the Coordinator of Inter-American Affairs every Sunday evening, until December 6, 1943 when he resigned. (He was replaced by Arnold Moss.)

In the winter of 1943 José Ferrer and Uta Hagen returned to their original roles in Margaret Webster's [40] New York presentation of *Othello*. The play scored a tremendous hit, both Ferrers being raised to co-stardom with Paul Robeson, at his request, after the 158th performance. This was the first Shakespearean play to run more than 157 performances, the record held jointly by Jane Cowl's *Romeo and Juliet* and Orson Welles's [41] *Julius Caesar*. In June 1944 the production won the award for "the most outstanding dramatic offering of the season" presented annually by the *Sign*, the Catholic magazine.

Miss Hagen's success, if not as spectacular as her husband's, was as certain. Burton Rascoe, reviewer of the New York *World-Telegram*, was profoundly impressed: In spite of the magnificence of Robeson's portrayal, he wrote, "the highest acting honors, as I see it, must go to José Ferrer as Iago and to Uta Hagen as Desdemona. It has immemorially been a commonplace that Iago steals the show; but Mr. Ferrer's interpretation goes far beyond the prodigal opportunities of the part. It is a character creation of the first magnitude, played in a manner I daresay you never saw it played before. . . . That Mr. Ferrer's interpretation has profound validity is to be found in Iago's key speech, his last: 'Demand me nothing; what you know, you know: From this time forth I'll never speak a word.' . . . Miss Hagen, who is very beautiful, is Desdemona as she is described in the play—'the sweetest innocent that e'er did lift an eye.' Trusting naïveté, plaintive bewilderment, suppliant misery—these moods Miss Hagen sustains in a glorious and heart-gripping performance."

Other reviewers, if not quite so highly impressed, found Miss Hagen's Desdemona "properly sweet and submissive and troubled, which is about all one can ask of a role that is dramatically pretty thankless"; but Nathaniel Benchley wrote flatly that her performance "will be held up as an example for future Desdemonas to try to equal. In this I don't envy the future Desdemonas, first because it is a very tough part to do sympathetically and well, and second because Miss Hagen leaves no room for improvement. This latter point is no surprise to those who have seen Miss Hagen before." Louis Kronenberger of *Time* and *PM*, who had thought Ferrer's Iago underplayed in the Cambridge production, found his presentation further developed; while still not agreeing with the actor's interpretation, Kronenberger conceded that Ferrer "conveys the workings of Iago's mind, the dexterity of his method, with uncommon intelligence; he works on Othello pretty convincingly; and his reading of Shakespearian verse is very skillful and flexible. He is an animated Iago without being a crude or melodramatic one."

"One rather sordid aspect of Miss Hagen's job," it was reported, "is that she is continually receiving letters from people who object to seeing a white woman play opposite a Negro." These letters read "like the mouthings of that old advocate of culture and learning, Dr. Joseph Goebbels '41. They make quite a colorful collection." The only other cloud for her in New York was the problem of most working women with children: a maid. "I've had eleven so far," she said at one point, "and in between shows and maids I did my own housework and played with the baby—and left pounds by the wayside. I'm only 115 pounds now, and that isn't much for someone who stands five feet seven," without heels. (The Ferrers' schedule during the New York run—they went on tour in September—was a demanding one as they are doing the uncut *Othello*. They had to move into town, for commuting was out of the question with such hours.) To Ferrer, however, playing an un-cut Iago eight times a week and appearing as master of ceremonies on Gladys Swarthout's '44 *Family Hour* on Sundays may not have been as strenuous as it seemed after his training in *Charley's Aunt*: then it was not unusual for him to lose five pounds at each performance.

In what is laughingly called their spare time the Ferrers play piano duets (José, who used to be an exponent of *le jazz hot*, now limits himself to Mozart, Haydn, and Bach), collect prints, and keep up with Letty, who can recognize pictures of "mommy and Joe" in the most unlikely costumes and poses. Ferrer is also a knuckle-cracker, a caricaturist, and an ardent baseball player on theatre teams. In June 1944 he was elected to a five-year term as one of the ten councilors of the governing board of Actors Equity.

Heredity being what it is, Leticia should grow up to be tall. Her father is five feet eleven inches, "but maybe I don't look it," he says. "I always stand crooked, never straight. I have short legs and a big head." Miss Hagen, model-tall and model-slim, is usually described as beautiful. Ferrer's dark coloring contrasts with his wife's fair skin, blue eyes, and brown hair. She calls it brown, although "others have called it everything from blond to red." An impartial observer found it brown, but with a sort of orange overtone that matches her Desdemona greasepaint.

References

N Y Herald Tribune VI p2 F 4 '40; VI p5 Mr 9 '41; IV p1 Ja 16 '44
N Y Post p10 O 25 '40 pors
N Y Sun p28 Mr 12 '43 self por; p11 O 9 '43 por
N Y Times X p7 D 8 '40
N Y World-Telegram p6 Mr 4 '44 por
New Yorker 16:15 N 2 '40

FERRERO, GINA L(OMBROSO) (fä-rä´rō jē´na) 1872—Mar. 29, 1944 Italian author and sociologist; called Italy's leading woman intellectual; an authority on feminine psychology; held Doctor's degrees in philosophy and medicine; wife of Guglielmo Ferrero, the late Italian historian.

Obituary

N Y Times p13 Ap 1 '44 por

FIRESTONE, HARVEY S(AMUEL), JR. Apr. 20, 1898- Industrialist
Address: b. Firestone Tire & Rubber Co., Akron, Ohio; h. 50 Twin Oaks Rd., Akron, Ohio

HARVEY S. FIRESTONE, JR.

It has been said that Harvey S. Firestone, Jr., president of the Firestone Tire and Rubber Company, is responsible more than any other man for the winning of America's fight for rubber freedom, a victory that was the aim of his father, the founder of the Firestone hierarchy. The younger Firestone has accomplished this by his development of the Firestone plantations in Liberia, West Africa, which in 1944 are one of the few remaining sources of raw rubber for the United States and her allies, as well as by his production of synthetic rubber.

When Harvey Samuel Firestone, Jr., was born on April 20, 1898 in Chicago, his father was the owner of a small carriage rubber tire business which he and one assistant were able to handle alone. The house in which Harvey was born was a modest one, and his mother—the former Idabelle Smith, the daughter of the inventor George T. Smith—ran the home on a small allowance. The Firestone side of the family was of colonial stock: its first member came with his family from the province of Alsace in 1752 and settled in Franklin County, Pennsylvania. One of his descendants migrated to Columbiana County, Ohio, where he in time became the richest man in that section. In his will he divided his land among his sons, with the provision that his wife should live in the house and choose which son was to maintain it. Her choice was Benjamin, grandfather of Harvey, Jr., and the man who, in his capacity as farmer and horse trader, taught Harvey's father, the future founder of the Firestone Tire and Rubber Company, the elements of shrewd salesmanship. The old home—"much larger than . . . any of his descendants have been able to use"—is situated some sixty miles from the present Firestone business in Akron and is often used for the annual picnic of Firestone office employees.

One of the memorable experiences in young Harvey's boyhood was his acquaintance with Thomas Edison. For many years Harvey accompanied his father and the famous inventor

FIRESTONE, HARVEY S., JR.—*Continued*

on camping trips with other friends. "Mr. Edison, it seemed to me," says Firestone now, "knew all about everything—he could talk on any subject with a knowledge which was amazing. It is impossible to express in words the inspiration this experience gave me." In 1916 Harvey was graduated from Asheville School in North Carolina, and the following year he entered Princeton University, from which he received a B.A. degree in 1920. (His schooling had been interrupted by the First World War, in which he served in naval aviation.) Then, by September, he was ready to enter the family company.

When Harvey was a year old his father had sold the Chicago business at a profit of $45,000, and a year later, in 1900, had founded the Firestone Tire and Rubber Company in Akron. At first the company did not make its own tires; but in 1903 an old foundry was bought and equipped with secondhand machinery, and there the manufacture of solid tires was begun. For the first ten years the family was forced to live very modestly so that it could buy up every possible share of stock. In addition, the change in tires at that time from solids to pneumatics added to their financial problems, for it necessitated the use of new equipment and methods. Young Harvey, incidentally, had his first automobile ride in a Maxwell car which his father had bought for use in experimenting with the pneumatics.

Their first customer was Henry Ford '44, whose order in 1905 for 2,000 sets of the tires established the Firestone Company in the new enterprise. By 1906 sales had reached the million-dollar mark, and when Harvey S. Firestone, Sr., died in 1938 at the age of sixty-nine, the company he had started with ten employees had 40,000 men on its payroll, thirty-two subsidiaries, and huge plantations in Liberia.

When Firestone entered his father's company at twenty-three he was put in charge of the steel products division. Under his direction this branch increased tremendously—and during the Second World War it has supplied numerous types of war matériel, including Bofors 40-mm. antiaircraft gun mounts and carriages, and machine-gun clips. Another phase of Firestone's activity through the years has been his direction of the expansion of the company into the foreign field: by 1940 foreign sales accounted for 23½ per cent of the company's consolidated net profit. Firestone also helped to establish the company's supply and service stores in the United States, which now form an important adjunct of the business. In 1944 the Firestone Company is supplying many rubber products which figure in the conduct of the War: barrage balloons, life belts, rubber boats, gas masks, and pontoon bridges. In both 1942 and 1943 the Akron plant was awarded the Army-Navy "E."

War contracts have increased the company's income from $187,000,000 in 1940 to $651,000,-000 in 1944. In 1940, in nineteen plants scattered throughout the United States, Firestone employed 26,000 workers; in 1944 that number had increased to 72,500. In an attempt to avoid another unemployment crisis at the end of the War, since the workers have been employed mainly on war materials, Firestone has created the Firestone Postwar Planning Division, a full-time organization geared for action. "The whole object of planning," it is said, "was to figure out how to make new and better products more economically and thus develop new markets, with an accompanying rise in employment and real income." As a result of a study of the post-War market, Firestone is branching into new fields. In addition to manufacturing tires, the company will make a complete line of aircraft products, tires, tubes, wheels, spark plugs, storage batteries; flying accessories and apparel for pilots, such as gloves, sun glasses, cameras, field glasses, and radio sets; and the company is already working in the autogiro and helicopter field.

But despite the importance of these activities to the company, Firestone's work in Liberia may have more lasting value. Since the early '20's Harvey S. Firestone, Sr., had been conducting a one-man crusade to have America grow its own rubber. During the First World War, American manufacturers had paid high prices for Dutch and British rubber, because, between them, Britain and Holland had controlled about 98 per cent of the raw material. In addition, in 1922 Great Britain had imposed a Rubber Restriction Act which shot up the price to an abnormally high level. "To give substance to his own protests against the British control," says Firestone, "my father sent me [in 1924] on a world-wide search to determine where Americans should best grow their own rubber." The twenty-six-year-old junior industrialist and his party of experts visited the Philippines, Sarawak, Java, Ceylon, Malaya, Sumatra, Singapore, and Mexico—where they experimented with planting—before the little country of Liberia in West Africa was selected for the project. In 1926 the Firestone Plantations Company was started, and young Firestone was put in full charge. (He became president in 1932.)

From Liberia's area of about 45,000 square miles, Firestone leased 1,500 square miles, or 1,000,000 acres. It has been said by some writers that the financial arrangements for the transaction "virtually mortgaged Liberia to the Firestone Company." It was implemented by a forty-year loan (of $5,000,000 at 7 per cent interest) from an American finance company, apparently established and financed by Firestone for that sole purpose, wrote Raymond Buell in 1928. The loan was a lien on the Liberian customs, which had to be applied first to the cost of collecting those customs and then to the payment of the service of the loan. The remainder was to go to the Liberian Government. Altogether interest and sinking-fund charges, plus salaries, were estimated to equal about two-fifths of the total expenditures of the Government in 1925.

Because of the Firestone Company's large holdings in the small republic, it has come in for a share of the criticism directed against Liberia's "ruling clique." When the enterprise was started the population of the country included some 12,000 descendants of former American slaves, who had set themselves up as a ruling aristocracy, and some million and a half native blacks. Slave-trading had been prevalent until exposed by a commission of the League of Nations, and had afterward continued covertly. According to a former Firestone employee, Arthur Hayman, Liberia's ruling clique permitted the company to come to Liberia "simply because the Government was penniless after years of graft and extravagance" and in need of the money the enterprise would bring and the employment it would provide.

An article of the Firestone agreement provided that the Liberian Government would assist the company in securing an adequate labor supply. To this end the Government established a labor bureau through which Firestone paid 1c per day to the Government and to the chiefs for each man recruited. Says Hayman in his book *Lighting Up Liberia:* "When the Firestone Company first came to Liberia it wanted to pay its native laborers the high wages, for Africa, of $1 a day. But the rulers insisted upon maintaining a coolie wage . . . for men with money in their pockets would eventually have demanded the ballot and schools for their children . . . would have eventually turned out the rotting little Cabinet and legislature in a political revolution that would have shaken the structures of foreign imperialism and domestic tyranny in huge, enslaved Africa."

To supplement the rubber supply from the Liberian plantation, Firestone has done considerable experimenting with synthetic materials, beginning as early as 1933 to make tires by a synthetic process. After Pearl Harbor the United States Government asked the four largest rubber companies in the country to build plants with funds provided by the Defense Plant Corporation and to operate them under Government contract. In April 1942 Firestone claimed that his company had become the first to produce synthetic rubber in one of these plants. He also reported that the Firestone facilities for reclaiming used rubber were the largest in the world. In the spring of 1944, speaking for the rubber industry as a whole, he said: "In two years of war we have licked, for good and all, one of the greatest problems car owners of America have constantly faced for years. . . . This year America will have an annual productive capacity in its own synthetic rubber plants nearly 25 per cent greater than our average annual consumption of rubber in the past three pre-War years." A post-War synthetic rubber industry, he had already declared, would need no tariff protection. He is optimistic about the outlook for both synthetic and natural rubber during the first peace years, holding that both types will be required to meet the huge pent-up demand. However, he loses no opportunity to repeat his faith in synthetic rubber as a "$700,000,000 insurance policy against high prices for natural rubber. It may be recalled," he said to a New York *Times* reporter, "that, during the six years following the Stevenson Restriction Act, consumers here paid $1,250,000,000 more for rubber than if the prices had held at the 14c level which prevailed when the restriction became effective."

In May 1944 one of the nation's largest integrated high-octane gasoline and synthetic rubber plants—operated by Cities Service Company and the Firestone Company—was opened in Louisiana. It was a joint project of the two companies and the United States Government and represented an investment of about $100,000,000, only about 25 per cent of which came from the Government. According to Firestone, the plant will produce enough to fill one-tenth of the nation's normal rubber demands.

Since December 1928 the company has had its own musical radio program, *The Voice of Firestone.* The opening and closing themes, "In My Garden" and "If I Could Tell You," respectively, were composed by Firestone's mother. He himself frequently addresses the public on the program. A series of his weekly talks from September 1931 to September 1932 has been published under the title *The Romance and Drama of the Rubber Industry* (1932).

Slender, dark-haired Harvey S. Firestone, Jr., has been president of the Firestone Tire and Rubber Company since 1941. (He was made vice-president in 1929.) He makes many business trips, and in Akron averages ten to eleven hours a day of work at the plant. In addition to the Akron plant and the Liberian plantations, moreover, his business connections are numerous. He is director or president-director of Firestone subsidiaries in England, Switzerland, and Central America and South America; in the United States he is director or president-director of eight companies, five of them bearing the Firestone name and manufacturing rubber and metal products. In addition he is president-director of the United States-Liberia Radio Corporation and of the Bank of Monrovia, Inc.

Outside of his business, he is active in various Episcopalian organizations; he is a trustee of Princeton University and a director of the Booker T. Washington Agricultural and Industrial Institute in Liberia and the National Association of Manufacturers. He is also a member of many clubs, a member of the International Committee of the YMCA, the chairman for the rubber industry of the National Citizens Committee of Navy Relief Society, and general chairman for the USO organizations in Ohio.

Despite Firestone's position in the rubber world, his private life has been little publicized, for he moves quietly in his own small social circle. For relaxation he plays tennis; and at one time he and his four younger brothers formed a creditable polo team. (There were five boys in the Firestone family and one girl. The men all hold high executive positions in the rubber company.) Music is a hobby he shares with his wife, Elizabeth Parke Firestone, whom he married in 1921. The couple have four children: Elizabeth Chambers, Martha Parke, Anne Idabelle, and Harvey Samuel 3d. Elizabeth, Firestone's daughter, has inherited the musical ability of her grandmother, Idabelle Firestone. Young Elizabeth has some forty compositions to her credit. Two of her lighter compositions have been featured by name bands and on radio programs.

References

Newsweek 18:44 N 17 '41 por
Sat Eve Post 216:12-13+ Mr 4 '44 il pors

(Continued next page)

FIRESTONE, HARVEY S., JR.—*Cont.*

Firestone, H. S. and Crowther, S. Men and Rubber 1926
Firestone, H. S., Jr. The Romance and Drama of the Rubber Industry 1932
Hayman, A. I. and Preece, H. Lighting Up Liberia 1943
Who's Who in America 1944-45

FLEMING, SIR ALEXANDER 1882(?)-
Scientist
Address: 20 Danvers St., London

FLOREY, SIR HOWARD W(ALTER)
Sept. 24, 1894- Scientist
Address: Lincoln College, Oxford, England

The discoverers of penicillin (pen-i-sil'-in), "the most valuable disease-fighting chemical in existence," are Professors Alexander Fleming of the University of London and Howard Florey of Oxford University. Few scientific discoveries have been received with so much acclaim as the mild drug secreted by a mold similar to the ordinary fungus growth on cheese and stale bread. Scientists usually disapprove of such terms as "miracle-worker" and "wonder-drug," but penicillin's power to cure infection where all other drugs fail and to work rapidly without harmful effect has caused even its original discoverer, Dr. Fleming, to admit: "People have called it a miracle. For once in my life as a scientist I agree. It is a miracle, and it will save lives by thousands."

No single individual is responsible for the discovery and development of the drug. First noticed by Dr. Fleming in 1928, it was for a time overshadowed by the great interest in sulfa drugs. Not until 1939, eleven years after Dr. Fleming's initial discovery, did a group of British and American scientists, financed by a Rockefeller grant and headed by Dr. Florey, begin intensive work at Oxford on Penicillin Chrysogenum notatum, the technical name of the mold. Since that time penicillin has made tremendous forward strides in actual clinical practice. With the outbreak of the Second World War the penicillin supply in the United States became the ward of the Federal Government, so that its very limited quantities might be properly allocated.

Alexander Fleming was born some sixty years ago at Lochfield near Darvel in Scotland, the son of Hugh Fleming. He attended Kilmarnock Academy, "where he took almost all the available prizes and scholarships," and from there went to St. Mary's Hospital Medical School in Paddington, England. Again Fleming won academic distinction, receiving, in addition to the senior entrance scholarship, numerous class prizes. A student at London University, he took honors in physiology, pharmacology, medicine, pathology, forensic medicine, and hygiene. In 1906 he received his Licentiate of the Royal College of Physicians and his membership in the Royal College of Surgeons and won the University's bacterial professorship.

During the next few years Dr. Fleming devoted almost all his attention to research work. He assisted the famous Sir Almroth Wright, the originator of the system of vaccinotherapy (therapeutic inoculation for bacterial infection). When Britain entered the First World War, Fleming served as a captain in the Royal Army Medical Corps. He saw action in France, where he specialized in the study of wounds.

At the conclusion of hostilities Fleming returned to his laboratory work. Interested in hospital conditions in England, he has worked under the Emergency Medical Scheme supervising a London district. Most of Dr. Fleming's time, however, has been spent at London University, where he is professor of bacteriology, and at St. Mary's Hospital in Paddington, where he first began his study of antiseptics nearly thirty years ago. A holder of a Royal Society Fellowship, Dr. Fleming is also well known for his discovery of lysozyme in 1929. Lysozyme is another antiseptic substance found both in the whites of eggs and in human tears.

Dr. Fleming is married to Sara McElroy, and they have one son who is studying medicine. Described as "studious, soft-spoken, rather careworn looking, blue-eyed, and gray-haired," Fleming finds recreation in swimming, shooting, and painting. He has won some distinction as an artist, particularly because of the extraordinary materials he uses for his painting. For paints he uses, in the manner of water colors, certain germ cultures which "when grown in an incubator produce vivid colors." His works, colorful and impressionistic, have been shown by the London Exhibition of the Medical Arts Society.

Howard Walter Florey, the co-discoverer of penicillin, was born in Australia, September 24, 1898, the son of Joseph Florey. He received his education at St. Peter's Collegiate School and Adelaide University. From there

SIR ALEXANDER FLEMING

he proceeded to Magdalen College, Oxford, winning academic honors. In 1921 Florey was a Rhodes Scholar for South Australia. He entered Cambridge in 1924 as a John Lucas Walker Student. In the following year Florey came to the United States as a Rockefeller Traveling Fellow. The year 1926 saw two academic honors awarded him—he was appointed Freedom Research Fellow at London Hospital and Fellow of Gonville and Cauis College at Cambridge. In that year, too, he was married to Mary Ethel Reed. They have two children.

Dr. Florey remained at Cambridge as Huddersfield Lecturer in special pathology for several years. In 1931 he went to the University of Sheffield as Joseph Hunter professor of pathology. Here he remained until 1935, when he became professor of pathology at Oxford University. Author of numerous articles on physiology and pathology, Dr. Florey has been working with American scientists and American drug companies to increase the supplies of penicillin. He brought his request for penicillin to the Committee on Medical Research of the Office of Scientific Research and Development, the National Research Council, and the United States Department of Agriculture. In the latter's offices in Peoria, Illinois, new methods were found to increase production of the mold, and new molds were developed which produced greater quantities of penicillin. Meanwhile three large American pharmaceutical companies, Merck and Company, E. R. Squibb and Sons, and Charles A. Pfizer and Company, among others, have set to work producing the drug.

The story of penicillin's discovery is a dramatic one, "a triumph of accident and shrewd observation." Dr. Fleming came upon it by accident in 1928 while doing some research on influenza. (A recent derivative of penicillin, patulin, may be a remedy for common colds.) He had left exposed in the open air some culture plates of staphylococcus colonies. In a short time ordinary spots of mold developed on the plates. This was not in itself a noteworthy development, but instead of throwing the culture away Dr. Fleming studied it under the microscope. Around the mold there had formed a ring perfectly free from bacteria. He realized then that the mold contained some substance that killed bacteria. As he has said: "Nothing is more certain than that, when I saw the bacteria fading away, I had no suspicion that I had got a clue to the most powerful therapeutic substance yet used to defeat bacterial infections in the human body. But the appearance of that culture plate was such that I thought it should not be neglected."

Dr. Fleming then began a series of experiments with molds. He succeeded in making a pure culture of the mold. He discovered that it thrived best in meat broth, but also in bread and cheese. Dr. Fleming's great difficulty, however, was in isolating the drug itself. He spent years of research on this problem, and although its therapeutic effects had not as yet been demonstrated, Dr. Fleming was encouraged

SIR HOWARD W. FLOREY

by the fact that this antiseptic did not damage blood corpuscles. He published the results of his experiments with the hope that someone would continue the work and discover a way to purify the drug. Dr. Charles Thom, the micrologist of the United States Department of Agriculture, identified the mold as a species of the Penicillin Chrysogenum notatum series.

In 1939 Dr. Florey and his Oxford associates took up Dr. Fleming's work. Their task was to extract the essential compound from the liquid in which penicillin grows. This was no easy assignment, since the properties of the drug were unknown. Although there are several ways of producing the drug, the most effective method is to grow mold cultures in a sugar solution, keeping them in incubators. The mold develops on the surface of the solution, and eventually "shining golden droplets of natural penicillin are excreted from the mold." These are extracted from the mold by evaporation and produce a yellowish-brown powder. On the average, 160 quarts of mold culture yield about one hundred standard doses of penicillin (about ten grains). The cost of producing a pound of penicillin is about $18,000, but the average dose is so small that it can be administered for only $2.

In 1940 a report on penicillin was issued to the medical world. The drug had already advanced beyond the experimental stages and was used on human beings to treat a variety of infections. The results were astounding. Not only did the patients recover in most cases, but their recoveries were almost invariably more rapid and less difficult than had ever before been known. It was not invariably successful, however—this due primarily to the limited quantities of the drug. So mild that it can be applied directly to a wound, penicillin is generally administered by injection into the veins or muscles. Since poisonous reactions occur only when huge quantities of the drug are used by an individual, relatively

FLEMING, SIR ALEXANDER and **FLOREY, SIR HOWARD W.**—*Continued*

large doses can be administered effectively and innocuously.

The amazing healing qualities of the drug soon brought it to the attention of the American and British public. It was hailed as a cure for osteomyelitis (bone infection), septicemia (blood poisoning), meningitis, pneumonia, gas gangrene, cellulitis, carbuncles, gonorrhea, and numerous other infections. It is being used in the treatment of cancer. It proved of tremendous value in curing wounds sustained by soldiers in the British 8th Army in North Africa, and was also used extensively on Normandy beaches, helping to keep casualty lists low. Dr. Florey has used penicillin in surgery with marked success. Like most of his fellow-scientists, however, he warns that "penicillin is as yet available only in the smallest quantities," the greater part of which has been diverted for wartime use. "All the penicillin in the United States at any one time," *Time* Magazine estimates, "has never been more than about enough to treat thirty cases."

The great demand for the drug in the United States has forced the Federal Government to step in to assure proper distribution of the penicillin supply. As plans were being made to speed production, Dr. Chester S. Keefer, chairman of the National Research Council's committee on chemical therapy, was placed in charge of the rationing of the drug. The Army gets fifty per cent of the penicillin supply, and Surgeon General Norman T. Kirk [44] reports: "The Army is working night and day to the end that not a single American soldier will have to die from an infected wound that might have been healed by penicillin." In March 1944 it was suggested, however, that "commercial rivalry is causing this holding back by various firms of unrestricted interchange of developments in techniques." The situation is so serious, *PM* reported, that the Chemicals Branch of the WPB called a conference of representatives from nineteen United States firms and two Canadian firms engaged in the production of penicillin. Despite these difficulties, it has been announced by a Department of Agriculture official that there may soon be available sufficient quantities of penicillin to treat 7,000 patients daily. Two thousand hospitals in the United States have already been designated as depots for the distribution of the drug. And in November 1944 the largest penicillin factory in the world was established in England. The main cause for production difficulty is the unusually long period of fermentation required before the drug is ready for use. Since much time is required to produce this "magic-worker," an electronic system of drying penicillin, which will accelerate its production, has been perfected by Radio Corporation of America.

In an effort to counteract the serious scarcity of the drug scientists have been seeking a method of making penicillin synthetically. A new penicillin B, supposedly even more effective than the original penicillin, has been isolated, and it works on the principle of destroying the bacteria by supply-

ing them with too much oxygen. Unfortunately this drug is even rarer than the original penicillin. In February 1944 it was announced that "common yeast is in some cases more potent than penicillin," and scientists are continuing to seek for other sources for the common drug.

Scientists, including Fleming and Florey themselves, are quick to warn against overenthusiasm. Penicillin, doctors point out, has amazing effectiveness. "But the danger is that people may think of it as a panacea. It isn't. It's only another medical tool." The War Department points out that although it has demonstrated "high efficiency" in fighting certain types of bacteria, it is "almost wholly ineffective" against other types. Perhaps its greatest contribution in the treatment of the wounded is that it affords quick relief from pain "and quick restoration of a normal appetite, even in seriously wounded men." Thus physical rehabilitation is expedited, and the necessary surgery can be employed with less danger.

In June 1944 the discoverer and co-discoverer of penicillin were knighted. Earlier, in December 1943 Doctors Fleming and Florey received the Award of Distinction from the American Pharmaceutical Manufacturers Association. In his speech of acceptance Dr. Fleming highlighted some of the important consequences of his and Dr. Florey's work: "The extraordinary merit of penicillin has trained the searchlight on a new field. The intensive research into the metabolic products of the lower fungi will inevitably lead to some most interesting results. What now remains is the synthesis of penicillin, and this has much wider significance than just an increase in production. The chemists will fasten on the molecule and modify it, as they have done with the sulfanilamide molecule in the last five years, so that derivatives of penicillin will appear more powerful, or with wider applications, and diseases now untouched will be conquered."

References

Liberty 20:36 Jl 24 '43
N Y Times p13 D 14 '43
N Y Times Mag VI p8 Ja 2 '44 por
N Y World-Telegram p29 O 6 '43 por
Who's Who 1944

FLOREY, SIR HOWARD W(ALTER)
See Fleming, A. and Florey, H. W.

FLOYD, WILLIAM Aug. 2, 1871—Nov. 26, 1943 Journalist; editor and publisher of the *Arbitrator*, "a humanist monthly"; a noted pacifist; author of *Social Progress* (1925).

Obituary

N Y Times p13 N 27 '43

FONTAINE, JOAN Oct. 22, 1917- Motion-picture actress

Address: b. c/o David O. Selznick Productions, Culver City, Calif.; h. Beverly Hills, Calif.; Indio, Calif.

DE HAVILLAND, OLIVIA July 1, 1916-
Motion-picture actress

Address: b. c/o Warner Brothers, Burbank,
Calif.; h. Cold Water Canyon, Beverly Hills,
Calif.

Joan Fontaine's life offers an irresistible
temptation to refer to her as the Cinderella
sister of Olivia de Havilland—Cinderella at
least in the sense that life up until a certain
point seemed to give Olivia all the good
breaks and all the bad ones to Joan. Whether
the influence which changed this order of
things was a new philosophy, or her marriage
to the successful actor Brian Aherne, or the
astute management of David O. Selznick [41],
ace star-maker of the films, is not easily decided—since they all entered her life in the
year she stepped from the obscurity of small
roles in "B" pictures to stardom in top-drawer
"A" pictures.

Olivia de Havilland and Joan Fontaine are
the daughters of Walter and Lillian (Ruse)
de Havilland. On their father's side they
are the descendants of Sir Peter de Havilland,
supporter of Cromwell against Charles I of
England; and other family notables are Lord
and Lady Nolesworth, patrons of Gilbert and
Sullivan. Their father, after graduation from
Cambridge, left England in 1893 to head a
firm of patent attorneys in Tokyo. Their
mother, a "nice English girl from Berkshire,"
met de Havilland while visiting her brother,
a teacher in the Imperial University of Tokyo.
In 1914 when de Havilland returned to England to enlist in the British Army he renewed
his acquaintance with Lillian Ruse, who at
the time was a student at Sir Beerbohm
Tree's Dramatic Academy. When he was rejected for service in the First World War
de Havilland asked Miss Ruse to return with
him to Japan as his wife. She was undecided,
so he suggested they toss a coin. "If it's a
head you go with me—" The coin came down
tails, but the omen was ignored. Olivia was
born July 1, 1916, and, because of the War,
her parents prayerfully named her after the
olive branch, signifying peace. Joan, born
October 22, 1917, was christened Joan de
Beauvoir. The success of the marriage was
doubtful from the start and, when both her
children proved to be sickly, Mrs. de Havilland on the advice of a physician bundled up
her babies and sailed for America, where she
made a home in Saratoga, a small town on
the Monterey peninsula near Del Monte, California.

Olivia was three and Joan two when their
parents separated. Following a tonsil operation, Olivia contracted pneumonia but upon
recovering grew into a plump, bouncing, and
pretty child. Joan, however, after having
miraculously survived a united attack of
measles and streptococcic infection, developed
anemia and sank steadily into invalidism, unable to ride or swim or play field hockey like
her glowingly healthy sister. "Livvy [the
family name for Olivia] can, Joan can't" was
a taunt which haunted her childhood. Frequently she was seen reading poetry in a
graveyard near her home. "This melancholy
pursuit seemed suitable," it was said, "since
she was a wasted looking creature and to all
appearances had one foot planted in the area."

JOAN FONTAINE

In 1925, leaving her children in the care of
a nurse, Mrs. de Havilland returned to Japan
for the purpose of arranging a divorce from
her husband. During her absence Joan and
Livvy became very friendly with George M.
Fontaine, a department store owner of
French-Canadian origin. On their mother's
return the girls introduced her to their new
friend—and marriage followed. About the
same time their father was married to a
Japanese girl. (When he was sixty-nine
years old, shortly after the outbreak of the
Second World War, de Havilland came to
California with his Japanese wife. Anti-
British feeling having forced him out of business in Japan, upon his arrival he stated, "I'm
here because I am forced by lack of money
to leave Japan." He is now living in Denver,
Colorado, with his wife, whom the Immigration Authorities had ordered out of the West
Coast war zone along with other Japanese
residents.)

Joan and Olivia were carefully brought up.
At an early age Mrs. Fontaine began giving
them lessons in diction and voice control.
Taffy-haired, timid Joan did not lag behind
dark-haired, vivacious Olivia in her studies.
Given intelligence tests when she was three
years old, Joan scored 160 (150 is supposed
to be the mark of a genius). On occasion the
sisters gave sketches from Shakespeare and
recited "coy duologues," which Miss Fontaine
now describes as "simply awful." The girls
were sent to the Saratoga elementary school
and to the high school in nearby Los Gatos.
When Joan was fifteen she went to Tokyo
to live with her father and his Japanese wife.
During her two-year stay in Japan her dismal
adolescence came to an end and she developed
into a wraith-like beauty.

By the time Joan returned to California,
Olivia had captured a film contract after a
brief stage appearance. Joan then made her
bow on the stage in Henry Duffy's West
Coast production of *Call It A Day* (1935),

OLIVIA DE HAVILLAND

an English domestic comedy by Dodie Smith which had been produced in New York by the Theatre Guild. "The quality of the work of Joan Fontaine as the girl next door was delightful," wrote a Los Angeles drama critic; but when Warner Brothers bought the picture rights the role she had played was given to her sister.

Joan had adopted her stepfather's name for her stage debut because she was determined to make her way independently of the famous Olivia; but in order to learn the technique of acting before the camera, she took a small part in a Joan Crawford picture, *No More Ladies* (1935), changing her name to Joan Burfield in order to conceal her identity. After she had made a dozen quickies under the names of Joan Burfield and Joan St. John, Jesse Lasky signed her to a contract which was later taken over by RKO. In 1937 under the name of Joan Fontaine she played small parts in *The Man Who Found Himself, Quality Street, You Can't Beat Love, Music for Madame,* and *A Damsel in Distress,* the last well-named as far as Miss Fontaine was concerned. Cast opposite Fred Astaire in a Ginger Rogers '41 singing and dancing role when she could neither sing nor dance, Miss Fontaine was described as "the weak spot in the picture . . . a wooden woman." After that RKO farmed her out for *The Duke of West Point* (1938) and *Man of Conquest* (1939). *Gunga Din* (1939), a Douglas Fairbanks' picture, finished her contract with RKO, and her option was not renewed. The week this happened she discovered that her secret negotiations to play Scarlett O'Hara in *Gone With The Wind* had failed—but that the role of Melanie, the second lead in the much publicized picture, had been won by Miss de Havilland.

Again she heard the childhood taunt, "Livvy can, Joan can't." Her latest romance was beginning to lose its glamour, too. Faced with failures, twenty-two-year-old Joan thought one night that the only way out was suicide. Then the intelligence which had won her the high I.Q. rating asserted itself. She decided against the Lily Maid of Astolat role for a plate of rum and bananas. Since she was all alone in the cottage she shared with her sister she went to the kitchen to prepare the dish (she prides herself on being a very good cook). With the food warming her inwardly, she tumbled into bed to read a new book—*Rebecca.* She became completely fascinated as she identified herself with the character of the second Mrs. de Winter. (After her success in the role she told her husband, "When I was a little girl unable to hold my own with those who should have been my friends, I knew the same quality of unhappiness the second Mrs. de Winter knew. I was fearful and timid. And I lived in constant horror of criticism.") At a dinner party the night following her discovery of *Rebecca* she found herself seated next to David O. Selznick. She told him of the book—and his response, "I bought it today. Will you test for it?" has become historic in motion-picture circles.

But that was only the beginning. She tested for six months—scores of other young actresses were trying out for the role, too, and Selznick does not decide quickly on the casts of his pictures. (Testing for *Gone With the Wind* went on for more than a year.) However, Miss Fontaine's tests won her a small but effective part in *The Women* (1939), and her work in that picture brought her the coveted *Rebecca* role. Another major event of her life happened during her waiting period for the role. She had attended a garden party at Brian Aherne's house. It was a big party, complete with a fortune teller, who told Miss Fontaine that she was going to be married to her host. Although she was engaged to another man and had met Aherne for the first time that day, she could not resist telling the actor of the prophecy. Later his secretary reported that the day after he had met Miss Fontaine, Aherne interrupted his dictation three times to murmur, "She's beautiful, very beautiful." After a month's courtship they were married in August 1939. The wedding in St. John's Chapel in Del Monte was a society event of the film colony.

The day after Miss Fontaine's return from their honeymoon she began work on *Rebecca.* The picture won the Academy Award of 1940, and the star was acclaimed a superb actress. "Joan," Miss de Havilland said, "wouldn't have been as wonderfully good as she was in *Rebecca* if she hadn't been married. With Brian and her home foremost in her life, she was able to be objective about her work. She didn't get too intense. We try too hard in our family. We get too anxious about things."

Selznick placed her under a long-term contract at a salary unofficially said to be $1,200 a week. In a January 1944 article, *Look* Magazine stated that Selznick, who has Ingrid Bergman '40 and a number of other stars under similar contracts, had hit upon a method of keeping his stars busy, as well as maintaining their box-office stature: he rented them to other studios. Deals involving the Misses Bergman and Fontaine have netted the producer close to $1,000,000. For Miss Fontaine's contributions to *The Constant Nymph* (1943), *Jane Eyre* (1944), and *Frenchman's Creek* (1944), the actress received $100,000 of the $385,000 these studios paid Selznick. Her second picture under the Selznick contract, *Suspicion* (1941), won her the 1941 Academy Award for the finest performance of the year. The occasion was made more dramatic because Olivia de Havilland had been among the nominees for her work in *Hold Back the Dawn* (1941). Although the rivalry of the two sisters for the much prized "Oscar" sounded like a Hollywood publicity story, it was nevertheless legitimate. Earlier in the year the New York Film Reviewers, in making their annual choice of the best actress of the year, had cast five ballots before getting the two-thirds majority necessary for a decision. During four of the ballots (and New York critics are not concerned with Hollywood publicity) Miss de Havilland had vied with Miss Fontaine for the honor. Moreover, it was the first time in the history of the two organizations that they had selected the same actress for the award. The Ugly Duckling or Cinderella elements made it a good story, and press tales of sisterly rivalry grew, not all of them sympathetic to Miss Fontaine. (The press, as an institution, seldom allows Miss Fontaine a bonus. In 1943 she was selected by the Hollywood Women's Press Club as the least cooperative actress of the year. Reporters invariably misinterpret her painful shyness and distrust of inquiring persons.)

Having become a star of major magnitude, Miss Fontaine turned down role after role until she came to *The Constant Nymph*. She had not wanted to act in Eric Knight's [42] *This Above All*, but Selznick said that either she must do that for him or he wouldn't permit her to do *The Constant Nymph*—and so she has appeared in both. Her interpretation of Tessa, the delicate teen-age girl of *The Constant Nymph*, has greatly added to her prestige as an actress. "A superb achievement," commented the New York *Times*, and although she did not win the Academy Award of 1943, her acting in the role placed her among the five nominees for the honor.

Jane Eyre (1944) proved to be another triumph for Miss Fontaine: "a superb actress," wrote the New York *Sun* reviewer, "who has the good fortune of always appearing in worthwhile pictures." New York critics were divided in their opinion of the star's interpretation of the bold and dashing Lady Dana St. Columb in Daphne du Maurier's [40] *Frenchman's Creek* (1944). Kate Cameron of the New York *Daily News* thought the star had made an error in choosing that role in order to get away from the casting that had made her a long-suffering screen heroine. "If Miss Fontaine's performance had been good, which it is not. . . ." *PM*'s critic found himself "unconvinced by most of the star's moods," but Eileen Creelman informed her New York *Sun* readers that Miss Fontaine plays "to the hilt," making the heroine a "warm and dashing figure."

In July 1944 Selznick, after Miss Fontaine had been under suspension for several months because of her refusal to play in *Double Fur-*

lough, accepted from Hal Wallis a contract for the star's appearance in *The Affairs of Susan,* a comedy about a thrice-divorced actress. In speaking of her preference for comedy to the psychological dramas in which she had achieved stardom, Miss Fontaine said, "That seems to be the kind of picture people want now, something light and happy and perhaps escapist." However, her schedule includes another psychological drama, Mildred Cram's *Forever.*

In May 1944 Miss Fontaine filed suit for divorce (granted June 1944) against Aherne. She blamed the marriage's failure on constant separation and said they had been separated so much that they might as well make it legal. One of the causes of this is Aherne's presence in Phoenix, Arizona. Before the War, Aherne and Miss Fontaine, along with some other film people, bought a tract of land and built an airfield for the training of civilian pilots. Now, during the War, the Government has leased this project, turning it into Thunderbird and Falcon Fields, where British, Chinese, and American pilots are trained. The venture has proved to be very profitable for the Ahernes but demands a great deal of his time at the fields.

They are both enthusiastic amateur pilots and before the War did most of their traveling in Aherne's private plane. As a contribution to the war effort they had converted their 160-acre place at Indio, California, into a stock and vegetable farm. During week ends spent upon the farm Miss Fontaine wore dungarees, her hair braided and caught under a bandana. Life in their Beverly Hills white Georgian house was very British. Tea was at four, with much shining silver, and they dressed for dinner every night. The announcement of their separation came as a surprise as it had been reported that they were very congenial—laughing at the same jokes, liking the same people, and some of their friends saw a growing resemblance to one another in manner and expression. Aherne has not changed his English citizenship but Miss Fontaine became an American citizen in 1943. Her favorite pet is a French poodle named Nicholas, who is the first to greet any visitor who rings the doorbell, and his nights are spent at the foot of his mistress' bed.

The shyness and unsureness of Miss Fontaine's early career are gone. When asked how she had gained confidence she said, "Perhaps I had learned my trade and knew it." She takes her work seriously. "I try to live each character I play; this calls for, for me at least, much concentration." She is five feet four inches tall, weighs 108 pounds, has blond hair and hazel eyes. Her favorite sitting position is with her feet tucked under her on the seat of the chair.

Someone has said that no matter what opportunity was presented to Olivia de Havilland she was prepared for it. It was not that she has been exceptionally studious or ambitious—things just came to Olivia. In her school days she was the kind of student who achieved high marks without being a bookworm, and who led in all extra-curricular activities: she was on the school paper, on the debating team, in the dramatic club; she

FONTAINE, JOAN and DE HAVIL-LAND, OLIVIA—Continued

edited the senior year book, wrote school plays, and she won her emblem at hockey and a cup for public speaking. After graduation from high school (1934) she won a scholarship from Mills College (Oakland, California), where she planned to major in English and Speech Arts in preparation for her chosen career as a teacher in those subjects.

Although she had appeared in many productions of the Saratoga Community Players, she never had seriously considered the stage as a career. The summer, however, in which she was all set to become a teacher, California had been made Shakespeare-conscious by Warner Brothers fanfare of publicity over their forthcoming production of *A Midsummer Night's Dream* to be directed by Max Reinhardt. The Saratoga Players put on an outdoor production of the play with Miss de Havilland cast as Puck. One of Reinhardt's talent scouts heard of her brilliant performance through a friend of a friend of a friend of hers—and Miss de Havilland, not quite knowing how it happened, found herself engaged as second understudy to Hermia (Mickey Rooney '42 was cast as Puck). The Hollywood Bowl presentation was to open September 17, and she arranged with Mills College to enter the school late. Six days before the opening she was told that she was to play Hermia, as the No. 1 and No. 2 Hermias had dropped out of the cast. The morning after the opening her telephone began ringing—agents wanting to represent her for screen work. Miss de Havilland refused: her four-week engagement as an actress was to be only an interlude to her career as a teacher. However, before the end of the tour Reinhardt had persuaded her to accept a contract from Warners and to play in the film version of *A Midsummer Night's Dream* (1935).

Dream, as the picture was known to the trade, was a critics' picture. Reinhardt and the cast were praised by film reviewers, but the picture itself failed to make a hit with the public. From Shakespeare Miss de Havilland stepped into Joe E. Brown's picture, *Alibi Ike* (1935), about a stupid baseball player. *The Irish in Us* (1935), with James Cagney, followed, but her big opportunity came when Mervyn Le Roy chose her to play Angela in *Anthony Adverse* (1936), a million dollar version of the best-selling novel by Hervey Allen. Critical approval of her work as Angela placed nineteen-year-old Olivia de Havilland among the important players of the motion-picture world.

Her success, however, did not spoil her. A writer assigned at the time to do a story on the new star for the *American* Magazine decided to ask some of her fellow workers what they thought of her. Mervyn Le Roy, her director in *Anthony Adverse*, said: "If there ever was a born actress, it is Olivia de Havilland. Her diction is superb. She can deliver a line with any inflection the director wants, as accurately as if it were played on a piano—and she has the greatest of arts—the ability to act as if she weren't acting at all." James Cagney, with whom she had

worked in two pictures, announced to one and all, "That girl can play any part ever written." Around the lot men and women from electricians to executives acclaimed her virtues—she was unsophisticatedly charming, forthright, trusting, democratic, modest, a small-town girl unspoiled by success. Even hard-boiled Los Angeles newspaper men, who pride themselves on knowing film actors, and who never go wrong in telling a "real one from a phony," went out of their way to sing her praises. The cameramen reported that she had a perfect photogenic face. The make-up men found no study in facial reconstruction necessary. "Hell's bells," said the writer finally. "Nobody could be as perfect as that. She must be human; there must be some weak spot in her character." There was—the next day when he lunched with her in the studio cafeteria he discovered it took her fifteen minutes to make up her mind to order a salad and a glass of milk. Miss de Havilland herself admits to being stubborn and quick-tempered.

Of the thirty or more pictures she has made during the nine years she has been in the films, the outstanding ones are the following: *The Great Garrick* (1937), *Adventures of Robin Hood* (1938), *Private Lives of Elizabeth and Essex* (1939), *Gone With the Wind* (1939), *Santa Fe Trail* (1940), *Strawberry Blonde* (1941), *Hold Back the Dawn* (1941), *In This Our Life* (1942), *Princess O'Rourke* (1943); and to be released in the fall of 1944 is a story of the Brontë sisters called *Devotion*. The picture *Hold Back the Dawn,* for her work in which Miss de Havilland ran a close second to her sister Joan for the Academy Award, was a Paramount picture based on Ketti Frings's novel of the same name. The story is of a European bounder (played by Charles Boyer '43) who snags and marries an American school-teacher (Miss de Havilland) in a Mexican border town, merely to gain admittance to the United States. (In the end the girl's honesty and charm win his love.) "The story is told in a manner so artful and honest that the producers and actors have fetched forth an amazingly poignant picture," commented the New York *Times*. "Miss de Havilland's interpretation of the role has authority and power." In the opinion of Howard Barnes, New York *Herald Tribune* reviewer, her work was the picture's chief support. When the award was given to Miss Fontaine for her role in *Suspicion*, Miss de Havilland clapped loudest of all and exclaimed, "We've won." Later she said, "If *Suspicion* had been delayed just a little it wouldn't have got under the wire for this year's award. I've been runner-up so often it isn't funny any more. If it happens again I'm likely to break something."

Although Miss de Havilland was not among the nominees for the 1943 award, *Princess O'Rourke*, in which she played the title role, was thought to be one of her best parts; and the author of the story won an "Oscar" for the best original screenplay. However, the only thing Miss de Havilland has succeeded in breaking so far is her contract with Warner Brothers, a move which may have been prompted by her failure to capture an "Oscar." As a contract player, she, unlike Miss Fontaine, had no choice in her pictures. In September 1943 the actress brought suit for declaratory relief from her contract, claiming her seven-year pact with Warners had ended. The studio replied that her contract had six months more to run as the result of five suspensions when Miss de Havilland had refused to play roles assigned to her. (In 1942 she had refused to play in *George Washington Slept Here* and in 1943 she had been suspended because of allegedly failing to report to Columbia under a loan-out deal.) On March 14, 1944 the Superior Court in Los Angeles ruled that a studio may not discipline a player by suspension for an indefinite period, adding the time to the end of the contract. The decision, which eliminated several months of suspension for Miss de Havilland, criticized the practice as "virtual peonage for employees, or even life bondage."

Unfortunately for the actress, the Superior Court's decision was appealed by Warners, and her subsequent petition for an injunction to restrain Warners from interfering with her contracting with other studios was denied in September. In December she won an appeal decision from a higher court, the District Court of Appeals, which upheld the ruling of the Superior Court. The producers and players of the film industry have been following the legal steps in the case closely, knowing that its outcome will establish a fundamental principle in relations between studio and "talent." The new decision strengthens the player's bargaining power and decreases the potency of the studio's threat of suspension.

As a result of the litigation Miss de Havilland had not made a picture in over a year. Unable to accept film work, the star appeared frequently in radio dramas. Among these were *This Above All, The Laughter,* and *Suspicion.* In the first and last dramas she played roles which sister Joan had played in the motion-picture versions. Miss de Havilland also took an active part in the 1944 Presidential election, and as a supporter of Roosevelt '42 she helped to found several political clubs. She has been on several personal appearance tours to camps for the USO. During her trip through the Southwest Pacific area the actress contracted pneumonia and was forced to remain in a hospital at Suva in the Fiji Islands for three weeks. Upon her return in December she was signed by Paramount to co-star in *The Well Groomed Bride* with Ray Milland and Dennis O'Keefe—her salary was reported to be $125,000 for the picture. The legal heads of the studio were reported believing that the decision of last court of appeals was clear-cut and that Warners would have no redress.

Despite reported stories of jealousy between the two stars, there is evidence that they are warm friends. On Miss de Havilland's table there is a framed picture of her sister in her wedding dress, and her favorite costume jewelry is a set of Mexican silver clips and earrings given to her by Miss Fontaine after a Mexican holiday. Miss de Havilland still lives in the cottage she shared with her sister before her marriage. It is situated on Cold Water Canyon, a long and lonely road between California hillsides in Beverly Hills. Her mother, who chaperoned her daughters when they first came to the film capital, now has her own apartment—and her own film career. She is making her debut as Jane Wyman's mother in *The Lost Weekend.* Miss de Havilland lives a bachelor-girl existence with one Negro maid to look after her wants. There is only one bedroom in the house, which is a one-story affair. "When I'm acting in pictures," she says, "I do most of my entertaining in my bedroom because I am so exhausted. I take a hot bath and go right to bed at the end of the day. So my dinner and friends are usually there, too. I eat off a tray and they eat off a bridge table in the corner." The garden, the most attractive part of the house, is located in a tiny V-shaped canyon between two hills. It has a small swimming pool and a doll-like duplicate of the big house for a playhouse. Inside the playhouse are a bar, a fireplace, and many books.

Olivia de Havilland is five feet four inches tall, weighs 107 pounds, and has reddish brown hair and brown eyes. The camera portrays her features as much smaller than they are, which causes her eyes to seem larger than they really are. She has been described as a "cellophane Hedy Lamarr—with candles lit inside, glowing, vibrant, alive."

References

    Am Mag 124:34 S '37 por
    Collier's 99:24+ F '37 por
    Liberty 20:33+ Ag 14 '43 por
    Life 12:88-94 My 4 '42 pors
    N Y Post Mag p9 F 6 '43 pors
    Photoplay 54:19+ Jl '40 por; 24:40+
      Mr '44 por
    Photoplay Movie Mirror 21:72+ Jl '42
      por

    International Motion Picture Almanac 1943-44

FORBES, KATHRYN Mar. 20, 1909- Author

Address: h. 910 Chula Vista, Burlingame, Calif.

On October 19, 1944 a simple, rambling *Life With Father*-ish folk drama—"vaguely defined as a play"—had its first performance before a reportedly delighted Broadway audience. Based on five short stories by Kathryn Forbes, *I Remember Mama* was called a "stage vignette of distinction and power," and even before its opening was slated by some Broadwayites for a long run.

Kathryn Forbes's short stories, published as *Mama's Bank Account,* were based on reminiscences of her own childhood in San Francisco, where she was born March 20, 1909. She is the daughter of Leon Ellis Anderson and Della (Jesser) Anderson, whose own mother was a Norwegian immigrant. (From her paternal grandmother she took her pen name of Forbes.) Kathryn Anderson was educated in the San Francisco schools, and graduated from the Mountain View High School in 1925. The following year, on October 31, she was married to Robert Edward McLean. They now have two sons, Robert Moore and Richard Edward.

Mama's Bank Account is the first book Miss Forbes has written, but not the only writing

Anita Fowler

KATHRYN FORBES

she has done. She sold her first short story in 1938, and since then others have appeared in the *American, Saturday Evening Post, Redbook, Collier's, Ladies' Home Journal*, and *Capper's Farmer*; she has done publicity work for clubs and parent-teacher associations; and she has written scripts for radio, this last work during 1938. *Mama* started out quite casually as a short piece for the Canadian paper, Toronto *Star Weekly*. The *Reader's Digest* picked it up shortly after and brought it to the attention of American readers in February 1941, two months later reprinting a second installment. The reader response to these two brief stories was enthusiastic and instantaneous, thousands of people writing in to demand more about Mama. In answer to these, therefore, the author set about to put down on paper more of her childhood recollections, and in the spring of 1943 Harcourt, Brace and Company published eight of the nostalgic episodes about Katrin's Norwegian-American immigrant family growing up in California around the early 1900's.

Each chapter in the 204-page volume related an incident in the life of one member of the family, but the "loving, understanding" mother presiding over it was reckoned the real heroine. "If there are any who may excusably be called 100 per cent American," wrote *Book Week*, "they are people like this Norwegian family who brought with them from the old country traits of courage, honesty, and straight thinking which we like to think make up the American character." "Once in a very blue moon indeed," said the Springfield *Republican*, "a book by a virtually unknown author appears without fanfare or even much more than hope on the publisher's part which is so completely endearing that it must be shared by all who read it." Although in the summing up it was recognized as frankly sentimental, *Mama's Bank Account* received a warm reception from most of the other reviewers, too. There was

brisk humor in these charming sketches, they said, and gentle irony, "a fine tribute to Mama." The War Department has ordered 50,000 G.I. copies of the book for servicemen overseas; it has been made into a Talking Book for the blind, and has been translated into Swedish.

In June 1944 it was announced that Richard Rodgers '40 and Oscar Hammerstein 2d '44, composer and lyricist, respectively, of the musical play *Oklahoma!*, had acquired the rights to the book in "one of those unusual deals with filmdom." According to the New York *Times*, RKO Radio Pictures had originally owned the rights to it and was ready to film the story, having obtained the services of Miss Forbes for conferences on the adaptation. A two-way deal was then arranged by which RKO would turn the rights over to Rodgers and Hammerstein (and ten limited partners), paying $2,500 weekly during the run of the play until a ceiling of $150,000 was reached, thus obtaining the film rights.

A cast headed by Mady Christians as Mama opened October 19 in John van Druten's '44 dramatization of the book. ("I claim," writes Miss Forbes, "the unique distinction of being one author who was very happy with the adaptation, interpretation, and presentation of her literary chee-ild.") New York's critical reception was substantially the same as that given the novel. "To Miss Forbes," wrote Howard Barnes of the New York *Herald Tribune*, "must go the chief credit for a gladsome show. Her Mama with her pretended bank account, Uncle Chris, three aunts, and a flock of kids are real and exciting." There were some static moments, critics commented, and overlong parts that could have been cut, but on the whole they considered it a beguiling, leisurely story about real people, presented in an episodic, unconventionally informal manner.

"There is nothing strikingly dramatic or especially gripping," said Wilella Waldorf of the New York *Post*. "Nobody will swoon with anguish. Nobody will actually roll in the aisles laughing. But Mr. van Druten has seen to it that it has quality and a certain quiet distinction that comes from Mama herself and her way of living and bringing up a family." "For this story," *PM* in effect continued, ". . . adds to homely warmth just enough humor and color to take the kinks out of reality without altogether removing the kernel. It prettifies family life, that is, without arrantly falsifying it; and at its best it is really touching or really funny."

"What had your family thought of the book?" a New York *Post* interviewer asked fair-haired, blue-eyed Miss Forbes after the opening of the play. "Well," replied the author, "one of my aunts said, 'It's a very nice book, Kathryn, but I don't see what all the shouting's about. Anyone in the family could have written it.'"

Miss Forbes is continuing to write, and at present is working on a novel and some short stories. But she is a sportswoman also, by conversion. Since her husband and sons are such ardent sportsmen, she says, she has had to learn how to hunt ducks, stalk trout, and land striped bass—and to cook the bag.

FORD, HENRY July 30, 1863- Automobile manufacturer

Address: Dearborn, Mich.

On his eighty-first birthday in July 1944, Henry Ford visualized a "great day" ahead, "if we apply what we have learned and mix it with plenty of hard work." Since the death of his only son Edsel in May 1943, this employer of 160,000 workers has again assumed the direction of his vast industrial empire with assets valued at a billion dollars. The symbol of the most characteristic aspect of American civilization—mass production—Ford is able to count yearly profits by the millions; the vertical structure of his and his family's holdings embraces, in addition to factories, a railroad, ships, steel mills, foundries, iron and coal mines, timberland, and rubber and soy bean plantations; and the peace- and wartime output of his factories and assembly plants on five continents has made his name a universal household word. While Ford's mastery of manufacturing, financing, and marketing is acknowledged, his stand on labor relations and military preparedness, and his excursions into peacemaking, politics, publishing, and social service have probably evoked more condemnation and ridicule than admiration.

Henry Ford was born on a farm near Dearborn, Michigan, on July 30, 1863. His father, William Ford, was a prosperous farmer who was married to Mary Litigot, of Dutch descent, in 1862. The boy went to a one-room school in Greenfield, where he studied the famous McGuffey readers, and he had his regular farm chores to do. But these tasks held little interest for him. "There was too much hard hand labor on our own and all other farms of the time," he writes in his *My Life and Work* (1922). "Even when very young I suspected that much might somehow be done in a better way. That is what took me into mechanics—although my mother always said that I was born a mechanic. . . . My father was not entirely in sympathy with my bent toward mechanics. He thought I ought to be a farmer."

The two biggest events of his boyhood, Ford relates, happened in his twelfth year: he received a watch and he saw a horseless vehicle for the first time—a road engine used for driving threshing machines. Already using crude tools to tinker with fragments of machinery, young Ford was able to put together a watch when he was thirteen, and a few years later had built a working model of the road engine. At seventeen he was ready to leave school and the farm, walking the nine miles to Detroit to take his first job, with the Michigan Car Works, where he made repairs for $1.10 a day. He stayed there only six days, going next to a foundry and machine shop where he received $2.50 a week. This meager wage was supplemented by the extra money he earned at night by cleaning and repairing watches. It was at this time that a fellow worker lent him an English magazine, *World of Science*, which contained a description of the recently invented Otto internal combustion engine. The article excited Ford's interest in engines, and he left the machine shop to work for a lower salary at the Dry Dock Engine Company. Within two more years his appren-

HENRY FORD

ticeship was ended—he had mastered the machinist's trade.

Ford's ambition in those days was to develop a plan for making watches so cheaply that they could be sold for $1 each. He gave up this idea, however, when, at his father's urging, he went home to help with the work on the farm. But all of his time was not devoted to agriculture. He attended a business college for three months in the winter of 1884-85, experimented with machinery in his well-equipped workshop, and courted Clara Bryant, the daughter of a neighboring farmer. On April 11, 1888 the couple were married. In 1943, on the occasion of their fifty-fifth wedding anniversary, Ford spoke of Mrs. Ford's steadfast encouragement of his efforts: "My wife believed in me so much that when many were doubting my early experiments I called her 'The Believer.'"

In the home which he had built for his wife on a forty-acre wooded tract his father had given to him, Henry Ford drew up the first diagram of a gasoline engine. Before this he had become convinced that the silent gas engine, not the steam engine, was to be the driving power of the future, and he had already had an opportunity to repair an Otto engine. He soon realized that he could not build his engine on a farm, but needed the superior mechanical equipment to be found in a city like Detroit. Thus, in 1891 the young couple moved to Detroit, where Ford found a machinist's job—a twelve-hour day paying $45 a month. In a small brick shed behind the Bagley Avenue home Ford continued work on the gasoline engine in his spare time. It was finished in a week and tested in December 1893 for the first time in the Ford kitchen where, clamped to the sink, its spark plug was connected to the overhead electric light socket and its oil cup was tended by Mrs. Ford. This engine, which has been exhibited many times, is described by William A. Simonds, Ford's biographer: "A length of one-inch gas pipe was reamed out to serve as a cylinder, and in it rested a homemade piston fitted with rings. This was at-

FORD, HENRY—*Continued*

tached by a rod to the crankshaft, and had a five-inch stroke. A hand-wheel off an old lathe served as the flywheel. A gear arrangement operated a cam, opening the exhaust valve and timing the spark much as is done in cars today. A piece of fiber with a wire through the center did for a 'spark plug.' It made contact with another wire at the end of the piston, and when this was broken a spark leaped across, exploding the gasoline."

The engine ran. Ford's ambition now was to make it drive a four-wheel carriage. That idea was not original with him, however. There had been several motor vehicles, European ones notably, which operated with some degree of success, but there was no commercial manufacture of any motorcar. Finally, in 1896 Ford actually drove his first automobile out of his backyard shop after breaking a hole in the shop's wall to permit the passage of the vehicle. Its two-cylinder, four horsepower motor shook the light frame mounted on four bicycle wheels. A bicycle saddle provided a seat on the three-gallon gas tank. A few weeks later, a buggy seat having been added, Ford drove the nine miles to the old home in Dearborn with Mrs. Ford and their young son Edsel. The boy had been born three years before and was named for a childhood friend of Ford's.

At this time Ford was working as chief engineer for the Detroit Edison Company. He was receiving $1,800 a year, a high salary in the late '90's, and when he sold that first car for $200 he was able to set about designing and building his second car. Meanwhile he had attracted the attention of several businessmen, who in 1898 offered Ford $10,000, enough to pay for building ten cars. In August 1899 he therefore left the Edison Company to become the chief engineer of the newly organized Detroit Automobile Company. But the connection was to be short-lived. Before long Ford and his backers parted company, and the re-organized firm eventually became the Cadillac Motor Car Company. With another group of backers Ford became chief engineer of the Henry Ford Company in 1901, which was capitalized for $60,000; but again disagreement arose between Ford and the other stockholders, and the company was dissolved in 1902. These disputes are ascribed to Ford's refusal to be hurried in his experiments and to his contention that success must come from manufacturing a car that could be sold at a low price. (Another point of difference with later stockholders was to be his insistence on "ploughing back" profits into the business.)

Ford went back to his experimenting in another little shop of his own, working on a four-cylinder motor. Intent on getting speed—a mile a minute—he and others then began building racing cars which drew tremendous publicity because of their exploits on the track. Ford built two models, the "Arrow" and "999"; he describes the sensation of driving them: "Going over Niagara Falls would have been but a pastime after a ride in one of them." Although the eighty horsepower engines gave the cars a tendency to leave the road, Barney Oldfield easily won the race with the "999" at the Grosse Pointe track in October 1902.

Meanwhile the "horseless carriage" had become an automobile, and a number of cars were appearing. The Oldsmobile and other companies were selling a total of 9,000 cars a year. Two months after the racing car had won the memorable race, Ford was able to find new investors, among them Alexander Malcolmson and James Couzens. With eight other stockholders, the Ford Motor Company was founded in June 1903, only $28,000 of its $100,000 capitalization being in cash.

The new company was soon at work producing the Fordmobile, to sell for $850. This was the Model A, constructed for practical, everyday purposes. Utility, not comfort or beauty, was Ford's aim. From his autobiography: "The business went along almost as by magic. The cars gained a reputation for standing up. They were tough, they were simple, and they were well made." A touring car, the Model B, was put on the market for $2,000, and an improved and cheaper Model C appeared in 1905. By 1906 a new plant had been built and generous dividends were declared. Ford controlled the company with 585 shares of stock.

In 1908, after putting out five other models, Ford began work on a new car, of which he later said: "It contained all that I was then able to put into a motorcar, plus the material which for the first time I was able to obtain." This was the Model T, Ford's best-known car, a noisy, uncomfortable, unattractive, but efficient automobile. With half a million of its kind on the roads within five years, it became the subject of jokes and cartoons which Ford recognized as good advertising. Strictly utilitarian, the car was painted black. Ford commented: "Any customer can have a car painted any color that he wants, so long as it is black." With the launching of the Model T the capital stock of the Ford Motor Company was increased to $2,000,000. In 1909 the one-year-old car won a cross-country race, covering the distance between New York and Seattle in twenty-two days and fifty-five minutes. By 1911 there were over 4,000 Ford employees producing 34,528 cars in the newly built Highland Park plant. Increased demand called for greatly increased speed in production, which was achieved after Ford began to experiment with the moving assembly belt in April 1913. He describes this process as "the reduction of the necessity for thought on the part of the worker, and the reduction of the movement to a minimum. He does as nearly as possible only one thing with only one movement. . . . He must have every second necessary but not a single unnecessary second." The speed with which conveyor belts could travel was studied and applied to the motor and the chassis, as well as to the making of parts, which had formerly been supplied by other manufacturers. The result was more cars per day driving off the assembly line under their own power. Critics of Ford have pointed to another result—an increased labor turnover attributed to the demoralizing effect of speed and monotony.

When the Ford Company made the sensational announcement in January 1914 that all its workers would receive a minimum wage of $5.00 for an eight-hour day, Ford became the most famous man in the country. Hailed by some as a humanitarian, he was also criticized for what it was suspected were good business motives. Eventually, with better wages workers could be expected to consume more goods, including cars. One immediate result of the new wage announcement was the appearance at the Ford Company's gates of hundreds of men clamoring for work; they were dispersed when a fire hose was turned upon them.

Ford's feelings about war were well known when, in 1915, a group of pacifists approached him with a plan to end the War. He believed that the First World War had been begun by international financiers and was deeply interested in cooperating in some action to end the conflict. When he could get no definite aid from President Wilson, Ford chartered an ocean liner to carry himself and the pacifists to Europe, there to "get the boys out of the trenches by Christmas." Although many prominent civic and social leaders endorsed the mission, when the day (December 4, 1915) came for the "Peace Ship" to sail, there were few people on board who could be expected to direct the mission successfully. Ford himself left the party at Christiania, returning to the United States within a month. His own comment was: "We learn more from our failures than from our successes." He continued, however, to speak strongly against preparedness for war until February 1917, when diplomatic relations were severed between the United States and Germany. Soon in Washington to discuss preparedness, he said, "If the War is to be won, it will be won by the nation that knows best how to use machinery and tools." "Once we were in the War," he wrote later, "every facility of the Ford industries was put at the disposal of the Government. We had, up to the time of the declaration of war, absolutely refused to take war orders from the foreign belligerents." From April 1917 until November 1918, the Ford Company manufactured army trucks, Liberty motors, aero cylinders, caissons, listening devices, steel helmets, and Eagle boats.

On December 31, 1918, Ford resigned from the company presidency in favor of his son. Early in 1919 Ford bought up all stock not owned by his family, the new company with a capitalization of $100,000,000 thus becoming a family property. (In 1943, 55 per cent of the stock was Ford's.) In January of 1919 he increased the minimum wage of workers to $6 a day. The same year saw the building of the River Rouge plant and the trial of the libel suit brought by Ford against the Chicago Tribune, which had called him an anarchist. (The Tribune had committed the name-calling in 1916, when Ford had opposed the expedition into Mexico in pursuit of Villa.) The amount sought was a million dollars; the verdict, in Ford's favor, awarded him six cents. But 1919 is also remembered for another event: Ford became the publisher of the Dearborn Independent, a weekly periodical edited first by E. G. Pipp, later by William J. Cameron. The purpose of the publication was announced on "Mr. Ford's Own Page": "This paper exists to spread ideas, the best that can be found. It aims to furnish food for thought. It desires to stir ambition and encourage independent thinking."

The Dearborn Independent began to publish a series of attacks on Jews, collectively and individually, on May 22, 1920. According to these articles, which were entitled The Inter-

national Jew, the Jews were planning to dominate the world. The Independent also reprinted parts of the notorious forgery, The Protocols of the Wise Men of Zion, a document used to foment pogroms in Czarist Russia and later used by the Nazis to justify Hitler's [42] anti-Semitism. The attack aroused both Jews and Christians. The protests and denunciations by eminent persons and important organizations were given wide publicity, and the Independent was barred from some libraries and newsstands. The articles continued to appear until 1927, however, and were given greater circulation when collected and reprinted in pamphlet form. In 1926 Ford was faced by two libel suits, the outcome of accusations made in The International Jew. Before either could be settled in court, however, Ford released an apology through Arthur Brisbane in which he stated he had not had time to keep informed on the contents of the Independent and that the articles justified the indignation of the Jews. He also asked for forgiveness and assured the Jews of his friendship.

There were to be repercussions later in Germany, where reprints of the pamphlet, the publication of which Ford had forbidden, fanned anti-Semitic feeling. Also, as late as 1942, Ford's legal representative requested the Ku Klux Klan to cease making use of the articles Ford had retracted. In August 1944, when Ford decried the philosophies that create hatreds and war ("There can be no peace where hatred exists"), The Friends of Democracy commended him on his attitude toward world peace the while they urged him to disassociate himself from those who used his name and prestige to further racial hatred and religious bigotry. No little criticism was also directed at Ford when, on his seventy-fifth birthday, in 1938, he received the Nazi decoration of the Grand Cross of the German Eagle. (In this connection Simonds points out that other foreign countries had similarly recognized Ford's achievement as the manufacturer of the low-priced automobile.) There now appears to be an acceptance of the idea that Ford had been imposed upon by those who managed the Independent, this despite Ford's own earlier criticism of Jews in the fields of finance and entertainment.

On two occasions the figure of Ford loomed upon the political horizon. In 1918 he accepted the Democratic nomination for United States Senator from Michigan. "There was nothing that Mr. Ford wanted less than political office," writes Simonds. "When the Republicans first approached him on the same matter he turned a deaf ear. It was the appeal of President Wilson that led him to set aside his own desires." Ford was defeated, however, by the Republican candidate Truman H. Newberry. Four years later, a "Ford-for-President" movement was attributed to the furor caused by his negotiations with the Federal Government for the purchase of the Muscle Shoals dam and electric plant. Leaders of both political parties recognized, however, that Ford could not carry an election, the boom ceased suddenly in the fall of 1923, and Congress turned down his Muscle Shoals offer.

In the sixteen years between 1908 and 1924, Ford had manufactured ten million Model T cars. In 1920 he weathered a "buyers' strike" and a serious financial crisis by closing the

FORD, HENRY—*Continued*

plant for two weeks, shipping out all cars to protesting dealers, collecting accounts receivable, disposing of Liberty bonds. He reduced prices almost annually until, in 1926, the touring car sold for $298 and the roadster for $260. He had also had the bodies painted green, brown, or blue. Yet sales began to drop. In 1924 competitors with an eye to good looks as well as practicality began to manufacture cars; and their prices were low enough to tempt buyers away from Ford. But Ford said on his sixty-fourth birthday: "The biggest job of my life is ahead of me." Bowing to necessity, Ford remodeled his "T" into a smooth, refined new Model A in 1928. According to one commentator, "Lizzie had become Elizabeth." Model A, however, was to lose its popularity four years later, when the V-8 appeared.

In reference to his relation with labor, Ford, ever the stanch individualist, said, "There is nothing that a union membership could do for our people." Workers complained about the speed and tension under which they had to work, about lay-offs and demotions. Ford's stand was: "We make no attempt to coddle the people who work with us. It is absolutely a give-and-take relationship." Another cause for complaint was the company sociological department's investigations of the private lives of the employees. Smoking, drinking, political activity were among the reasons for dismissals. Ford has also expressed his opinion on social work: "I have no patience with professional charity." Work should be a duty and pleasure; there would be no need for charity if everyone worked; and "in a sufficiently subdivided industry there are places which can be filled by the maimed, the halt, and the blind." (Later, in 1942, Ford expressed his stand on public housing when he opposed a Federal building project as "unnecessary" and "wasteful.")

The depression struck hard at the automobile capital, with wage cuts and layoffs. There was much unemployment in Detroit, and in March 1932 a group of workers, members of the Detroit Unemployed Councils and the Automobile Workers Union staged a "Ford hunger march." They had planned to send in a committee to petition Ford for jobs and improved working conditions, but as they neared the Rouge plant's gates they were met by police with tear gas and machine-gun fire. Four marchers were fatally wounded. The bitter struggle between the anti-union company and the workers, who were trying to organize, was to continue. There was more violence in 1937, when the workers' charges were set forth in the NLRB complaint.

In the Presidential election of 1932 Ford had opposed the election of Franklin Roosevelt [42], and he refused to sign the automobile codes of the NRA, which stipulated that employees had a right to organize. Said Ford: "Organization best serves evil purposes. Independence best serves good purposes." At last the National Labor Relations Board summoned the Ford Company to a hearing, charging "malicious and brutal assault" on United Automobile Workers' leaders; "using threats and coercion on its employees; circulating propaganda; and discharging employees for union activities, all for the purpose of interfering with the rights of employees to organize." Both Ford and his son refused to appear. The NLRB ordered the company "to cease and desist" from anti-union activity. The order was obeyed, but the plants remained unorganized. In April 1941 the workers went out on strike, and the NLRB ordered an election at the Ford plants. When the votes were counted 70 per cent were found to have been cast for the UAW-CIO as the bargaining agency for the plant. Accordingly, a contract was signed in June. Although both the company and the union officials have striven to keep production going at top speed during the War, there have been a number of short-lived unauthorized strikes at various plants. The result has been a somewhat lowered production on war orders, but it is agreed that production has generally been kept well up to schedule since 1943.

True to his pacifist convictions, Ford opposed the United States entry into the Second World War. Nevertheless, he agreed to build airplane motors for defense although he refused to build airplane engines for the British Government. In May 1940 he stated: "If it became necessary the Ford Motor Company could, with the counsel of men like Lindbergh [41] and Rickenbacker [40], under our own supervision and without meddling by Government agencies, swing into the production of a thousand airplanes of standard design a day." With the attack on Pearl Harbor, Ford went "all-out" in support of the war effort. The tremendous Willow Run plant was built and operated by the Ford Company to produce B-24 Liberator bombers. In addition, Ford's factories have turned out tanks, airplane engines, armored cars, jeeps, gliders, and engines for robot bombs.

In the midst of the heaviest production for war, Ford assumed the post he had relinquished nearly twenty-five years before. The sudden death of Edsel Ford in 1943 "shook the entire Ford empire, which had expected Edsel to assume command when advancing years should moderate Henry Ford's determination to be active until the day he died." Ford immediately took over his son's duties, and heir apparent to the Ford empire now is Henry Ford 2d, Edsel's son, who is executive vice-president of the company.

Ford's post-War plans include a $150,000,000 reconversion and expansion program; there will be new plants and depots. A new low-cost car is to be offered to the American public; it will be a "face-lifted" version of 1942 models. (Its price may be $800, f.o.b. Detroit.) The company, it is also reported, is ready to buy the Willow Run plant from the Government and to convert it into the world's largest farm machinery factory. (Ford peace production planning does not include continued manufacture of airplanes.) Looking toward the end of the War, Ford has spoken frequently in 1944 on the subject of world peace and post-War conditions: There must be a world organization formed to preserve peace; peace will only be an armistice unless greeds are eliminated, disunity in religion overcome, and national boundaries leveled. There should be the earliest possible removal of Government controls over material, production, and distribution. "A doctrine of continued control . . . means control over individual initiative.

. . . My thoughts today are with the young men who are coming home from war with a blank wall of inopportunity facing them."

One of Ford's closest friends was Thomas Edison, to whom the automobile manufacturer has built a veritable shrine. He moved to Dearborn the laboratory in which the inventor had worked, and opened it as a museum to the public. In addition, Ford has acquired and displayed a magnificent collection of Americana. He built Greenfield Village, a reproduction of the town in which Mrs. Ford was born. Into the Village, where he has established a model school, he has brought the original log cabin in which McGuffey, author of the famous readers, was born. There, too, are preserved the courthouse in which Lincoln first practiced law, the home of Stephen Foster's parents, other buildings of historical interest, as well as mementos of Ford's youth. Other projects for which Ford is responsible are the Ford Hospital, where Ford was a patient for one week in 1932 in his only serious illness, the Trade and Apprentice Schools, the Willow Run Aircraft Apprentice School, and the Rehabilitation Center for the Second World War veterans at Dearborn. (At its convention in September 1944 the American Legion awarded Ford its Distinguished Service Medal for his contributions to the rehabilitation of veterans of both wars.) Early in the War the Navy found facilities at the Rouge plant for its Training School for Aviation Mechanics.

Ford's interest in occupational training stems from his "tinkering" days in the farm workshop. Of the Ford schools, the Trade School is the oldest and best known. There boys between the ages of twelve and eighteen receive the fundamentals of a high school education and are taught a trade while they earn money in the process. In twenty-six years (by 1942) the school's enrollment had increased from six to 2,800, and there is a list of 12,000 applicants. (In December 1944 the NLRB reported that a majority of the eligible voters at the Trade School had elected to be represented by the Ford Industrial Education Association in collective bargaining. This action followed a decision that the students were actually employees of the Ford Company.) The Apprentice School was established to give employees a technical training.

In his eighty-first year Henry Ford's spare frame and lean face continue to appear in news picture as he meets General Henry H. Arnold '⁴², the head of the nation's air forces, or operates a reaper which he used seventy years ago; and the highlights of his life are pictured in the wartime advertisements of the company. Reporters take down his words on world peace and wages. Of the latter he spoke in September 1944, when he stated he wanted to raise wages as soon as possible, Government permitting: "As long as I live I want to pay the highest wages in the automobile business. If the men in our plants will give a full day's work for a full day's pay, there is no reason why we can't always do it. Everyman should make enough money to own a home, a piece of land, and a car."

Others of Ford's opinions are dateless, for they reveal few changes in his philosophy. He has long favored decentralization of industry,

life in the country, hard work, utilitarian education, the abstemious life, simple pleasures; among the things of which he has disapproved are tobacco, liquor, the employment of married women, idle people, idle money; and he has doubted that lawyers or bankers know much about business. Of himself Henry Ford has said, "I refuse to recognize that there are impossibilities."

References

Fortune 29:138-45+ Je '44 il pors
Woman's H C 70:22-3+ Jl '43 por
Bradford, G. The Quick and the Dead p113-48 1931
Ford, H. and Crowther, S. My Life and Work 1922; Edison as I Know Him 1930; Moving Forward 1930
Leonard, J. N. The Tragedy of Henry Ford 1932
Marquis, S. S. Henry Ford; an Interpretation 1923
Merz, C. And Then Came Ford 1929
Simonds, W. A. Henry Ford 1943

FOWLER, GENE Mar. 8, 1890- Journalist; author; scenarist

Address: h. 472 N. Barrington Ave., Los Angeles; Lotus Club, New York City

Although Gene Fowler ended his newspaper career in 1928, has since then written four novels, five biographies (three of them best sellers), one narrative poem, and one or two plays, and has had a hand in more than twenty-five Hollywood scripts, anecdotes in the best *Front Page* tradition are still being told about him by his former newspaper cronies. His career as a reporter on the "city hall beat" has put its stamp on his writing, too. His biographies and novels have been adversely criticized by some reviewers for their "gutter terms," although a greater number of critics have considered his two-fisted language suited to the subjects, who often were more infamous than famous and who were chosen by Fowler only because their careers illuminated some phase of American life. However, there has been no divergence of critical opinion on the importance of Fowler's contribution to Americana. And for his biography of his friend, John Barrymore, *Good Night, Sweet Prince* (1944), Fowler has won unanimous praise. Written with affection and "profound understanding," it is considered "one of the best biographies ever written of an actor."

Fowler describes himself as an American peasant, his birthplace as the "west bank of Miller's Mill Ditch" in Denver, Colorado. Born on March 8, 1890, he is the son of Charles Francis and Dora Grace Devlan. On the divorce of his parents and the marriage of his mother to Frank Fowler he was adopted by his stepfather. The reunion of father and son, as described by Fowler, has his touch of salty humor. Fowler was already grown when a strange, bearded man appeared at his door. He took one look at the beard and shouted: "So that's where you've been hiding all these years!"

Upon the death of his mother when he was thirteen, Fowler went to live with his grandmother. "Pride of the Rockies" is a nick-

GENE FOWLER

name he carried through his newspaper days because as a youngster his underwear, made from flour sacks, usually had the brand name "Pride of the Rockies" splashed boldly across the seat. From those days, too, dates his vegetarianism: When he was ten years old he had left school and gone to work for a taxidermist, the result being that he has never eaten meat since then. Later a more agreeable job as a printer's devil made him determined to become a newspaperman. Studying in his spare hours, he worked his way through one year at the University of Colorado and then secured a job as a reporter on a Denver paper. He served on several other newspapers before coming to New York City under the sponsorship of Damon Runyon '42 to work for a Hearst paper.

In 1918, while employed on the New York *American*, Fowler got himself in the bad graces of the city editor, but the drama editor liked the young "Pride of the Rockies," chiefly because he chewed tobacco while writing poems. "It shows you just don't give a damn," the drama editor said. It was the sympathetic drama editor who sent Gene Fowler to interview John Barrymore, then playing in Tolstoi's *Redemption*. *Newsweek* calls that interview a "classic." (It is the introductory episode to Fowler's biography of Barrymore.) Barrymore was not in the mood to be interviewed but, recognizing a fellow Bacchus-lover, he invited Fowler to join him in a visit to a friend after the matinee. The friend, a musty little man called the Baron who lived in a ramshackle boarding house, was making gin in his bathtub and cooking chili in his bedroom. Both were being prepared for Barrymore—but a pet pug dog ate the chili, and the two guests spent the time between the matinee and evening performances in doctoring the animal, whose canine stomach had rebelled against the highly spiced dish. Conversation revealed two bonds these characters, ("gay and gaudy, but with tears in their laughter") had in common—love

of animals and memories of an adored grandmother.

In 1924 Fowler became sports editor of the New York *Daily Mirror*; in 1925 he was transferred to the New York *American* as managing editor. He was with Hearst's King Features Syndicate when William Randolph Hearst (who had his own way of taking down the top man) wired from his California castle suggesting that the editor needed a rest and should make a trip to some far place. Fowler wired back: "Am taking off for Egypt. Is that far enough?" "Some of his exploits in the fields of journalism and movie-making," says *Newsweek*, "have assumed legendary proportions. Appointed editor of the New York *Morning Telegraph* (1928), he lured reporters away from rivals by salary increases of $200 a week, supplementing them with such stars as Ring Lardner, Ben Hecht '42, Charles MacArthur, David Belasco, and Maria Jeritza. Then his publisher discovered that his payroll resembled the Government's—and Mr. Fowler ceased being editor. In Hollywood, producers annoyed him by calling him up at all hours to get him to work on scripts. So he moved to an apartment whose door thereafter announced it as the residence of 'Horace Witherspoon, famous Polish impersonator.' He also informed the boss that he had settled in Santa Barbara and was commuting by plane to Hollywood. Thereafter he received no more midnight calls."

At odd moments in his career Fowler has acted as press agent for Queen Marie of Rumania and as manager for assorted prize fighters and wrestlers. When he first began writing books, Fowler says he had to write "fast" because the "sheriff was always at the door." In 1916 he had been married to Agnes Hubbard. (One story places the scene of his marriage in a natural amphitheatre near Denver, with a prize fight promoter and gambler as best men.) The Fowlers have three children, all married, and two grandchildren. Gene, Jr., now in the armed forces, but formerly a member of the Twentieth Century-Fox editing department, collaborated with his father on *Half a Deck Harrigan*, a story bought by Twentieth Century-Fox in August 1942. Will, the second son, is playing a screen role in Warner Brothers' production of the Broadway play, *Janie*. Daughter Jane, "with ambitions for boxing," according to her father, "is now retired."

By writing fast, Fowler produced two books in his first year of free-lance work. *Trumpet in the Dust* (1930) dealt with newspapers and their makers. The New York *Herald Tribune* called its leading character, Gordon, "a masterpiece"; the New York *Times* found Gordon always credible but most of the other characters shadowy and unreal creations. *The Great Mouthpiece* (1931), the life story of William J. Fallon, a New York City lawyer, "mouthpiece" for the underworld of crime, followed. Despite the fact that he had given his imagination plenty of range, in the opinion of the *American Mercury* the author was always "plausible, and his dialogue often pungent and amusing." The Springfield *Republican*, moreover, stated that Fowler had not only resurrected the incidents of Fallon's life, but the spirit in which it had been lived and the background which had given it color.

Shoe the Wild Mare (1931) followed. Ben Hecht's review stated that it was an exuberant story, neither realistic nor fantastic; the *Saturday Review of Literature* considered Fowler's writing "crude, sometimes to the verge of unbearable vulgarity," but admitted the subject suitably "illuminated" by such treatment. In 1932, with the assistance of Ben Hecht, Fowler turned playwright. *The Great Magoo,* pronounced by George Jean Nathan "college boy wash-room stuff," failed despite "an excellent production and several amusing lines." In 1933 came *Timber Line,* the life story of Bonfils and Tammen, respectively a bartender and a speculator, who "teamed together to run the Denver *Post.* They achieved fame and fortune by methods considered slightly unethical even in the days of the wild West. Stanley Walker '44, author and newspaperman, acclaimed it "gorgeous stuff"; *Forum* Magazine felt that "the squeamish will have reason to shudder at this slice of Americana, but nevertheless it is a rip-roaring, highly entertaining book." *Father Goose* (1934), a biography of Mack Sennett, founder of the slapstick movie comedies, was called by the *Saturday Review of Literature* "a valuable document of Americana, written in vigorous American language that should delight Mencken of Baltimore." The first "shooting script" of a film to be published, *The Mighty Barnum* (1934), was the combined work of Bess Meredyth and Gene Fowler. The stage directions were "crisply and robustly entertaining;" the story was a hilarious dramatization of the showman's life and era.

Salute to Yesterday (1937), a nostalgic tale of Fowler's Denver days, although splashing over with sentiment, gave a colorful picture of an age which has faded from American life. *Illusion in Java* (1939), a romantic tale, "compared favorably to the Hollywood version of Pearl Buck's *Good Earth.*" *The Jervis Bay Goes Down* (1941) was an epic poem of an Australian freighter's heroic fight with a powerful German warship. The freighter finally goes down with all guns blazing, but not before most of the ships in the convoy have escaped. Fowler called his ballad "a sprig of laurel laid upon the crypt of the dead." Composed for a broadcast program for Greek Relief, the subsequent demand for it caused it to be published.

One might question whether it would be possible to write an objective biography of a person with whom friendship had been long and deep. It is a question Fowler asks in the last pages of *Good Night, Sweet Prince:* "Could I . . . write of him [Barrymore] objectively? And should I write of him at all, or so soon after his own robust gaiety had gone out of the world?" His first self-query is answered affirmatively by the book itself, says Patricia Collinge in the New York *Times.* "For, apart from the momentum of the fine and simple writing, it is responsible, meticulous regard for truth that makes the biography a four-dimensional image of the man." The *New Yorker* thought "the fuzzy, raffish style" of the book "had its special appropriateness to the subject . . . a literary equivalent

for the atmosphere in which the events take place." *Time* Magazine commented: "No facets of Barrymore's character were left unexposed by Fowler. . . . Gaudy, gossipy, with a sob-sister lining to its Rabelaisian hide. . . . From it the Great Profile emerges both more tarnished and more dazzling, more fantastic and more real." The book proved to be a runaway best seller. In the first three weeks after its publication 105,000 copies were sold, and it remained on the best-seller list throughout 1944.

After an automobile accident some years ago, when Fowler thought he was going to die, he made a quick estimate of what he should have done that he hadn't done in his life. "I decided," says Fowler, "that the great waste had been the time that I put in writing things that I didn't want to write. The time gained was that time that I'd spent in writing to suit myself—and I like to write books." Writing books—unless they turn out to be best sellers —is an expensive whim for any writer in Hollywood pay. Fowler says that his novel *Illusion in Java* "cost me eighteen months of work, $25,000 in travel expenses, and contracts for $90,000 worth of movie work that I turned down. It brought me in the equivalent of two weeks' salary—$4,000." Nevertheless, he refused film contracts after the publication of *Good Night, Sweet Prince* in order to begin another book—an autobiography. It is not to be based upon *Solo in Tom-Toms,* Fowler's short autobiography published in a limited edition by Covici at the beginning of his career as a novelist, despite the many publicity releases to that effect. Concerning *Special Extra,* which also has been repeatedly named as a Fowler story, he says: "Not only have I not sold it, I haven't written it. And if I did write it, I wouldn't call it *Special Extra.*"

Fowler has been employed as a script writer for the films more or less regularly since the early '30's. *Union Depot* (1932), *The Mighty Barnum* (1934), *Call of the Wild* (1935), *Jesse James* (1939), and the *Earl of Chicago* (1940) are a few of the titles for which he has been responsible. Concerning his motion-picture work, Fowler says, "They appreciate industry out here. A lot of writers who came to Hollywood don't realize that and hold up pictures that should be made fast. Of course," he went on to explain, "work doesn't come quite so easy here because it is siesta country, and then there are all the Christmas tree ornaments of life here that are likely to fool you—the big houses, long week ends in the mountains or on the desert or in boats. When you get to believing you have to have these ornaments they become too important and it hurts your work."

Fowler is six feet, lithe, and gray-haired. He never exercises, and friends call him a "food burner" because he can stow away great quantities of food. He wears $25 suits but, strictly speaking, he no longer merits the nickname "Pride of the Rockies."

References

N Y Post Mag p37 Ja 28 '44
N Y Times Book R p2 S 15 '40
Newsweek 10:34 O 18 '37; 23:68 Ja 10 '44
Wilson Lib Bul 12:230 D '37
(Continued next page)

FOWLER, GENE—*Continued*

Fowler, G. Good Night, Sweet Prince p3-14 1944
International Motion Picture Almanac 1943-44
Kunitz, S. J. and Haycraft, H. eds. Twentieth Century Authors 1942
Who's Who in America 1944-45

FULMER, HAMPTON PITTS June 23, 1875—Oct. 19, 1944 Democratic Representative to the United States Congress from South Carolina, in his twelfth consecutive term; was chairman of the Agriculture Committee; author of the Agricultural Adjustment Act and the cotton-grading act; deeply interested in farm legislation.

Obituary

N Y Times p19 O 20 '44 por

GAHAGAN, HELEN (MARY) *See* Douglas, H. M. G.

GARDNER, ERLE STANLEY July 17, 1889- Author

Address: b. c/o Columbia Broadcasting Co., 485 Madison Ave., New York City; h. Rancho Del Paisano, Temecula, Calif.

One of the "kings of the 'time-killers' among American writers today" is Erle Stanley Gardner. A background as successful lawyer, sales executive, world traveler, and "pulp" magazine writer has aided Gardner in shaping his fast-moving detective stories. "With no pretensions to literary style, but with a sound understanding of action fiction, the Gardner yarns are a sure two-hour cure for anybody's boredom." And in 1943 they became a welcome addition to the housewife's afternoon radio schedule.

Erle Stanley Gardner has always led an exciting, unconventional existence. He was born in Malden, Massachusetts, July 17, 1889, but when he was very young his parents, Charles Walter and Grace Adelma (Waugh) Gardner, left Massachusetts to travel west toward the mining country. "Because his father knew about gold dredges, the boy grew up in a lot of odd places, mostly ramshackle little towns all the way from the Klondike [where he did some prospecting himself] to the latter-day mining camps of northern California." After a rather haphazard education that included a brief interlude in college, he decided that he wanted to become a professional boxer. The "chunky", "aggressive" young man did train a bit, and even had a few matches, before he realized that the ring did not have much to offer. He had received an unexpected talking-to from a district attorney because of an unlicensed fight, and the lecture had given Gardner the idea that the law might offer greater possibilities as a career.

His method of preparation for a legal career was as unconventional as the rest of his life was to be. Instead of attending law school, he worked in law offices during the day and studied his books at night. Finding that he was particularly interested in courtroom psychology, he moved about from one office to another in an attempt to work under outstanding attorneys with unique courtroom techniques. By 1911 his method had proved successful enough for him to be admitted to the California bar, after which he hung out his shingle in the little town of Oxnard.

Business came slowly during the next five years. For one thing, according to the literary critic Joseph Henry Jackson, the young lawyer had few social graces. In addition, he faced the competition of several graduates from the big Eastern law schools. "Much of his early practice was with the local Chinese who came to him with a tough case and stuck by them afterward because he kept them out of jail." Although some of the respectable citizens of Oxnard thought that many of these clients were better off in prison, Gardner stood by his Chinese friends. Much of what he learned from them he now employs in his detective stories. Then in 1916 one of his law cases brought him and a partner in contact with a sales agency, the Consolidated Sales Company. When the case was finished Gardner was offered a managerial position with the company, which he accepted, thinking the job might be an interesting sideline. In 1918 he was made president of the agency, but three years later he felt he had had enough of selling and left to return to law practice. With three others he set up the Sheridan, Orr, Drapeau, and Gardner law offices in Ventura, California, and practiced there for many years as a trial lawyer.

He found the practice of law fascinating, he says, and he was successful—usually as champion of the underdog—too successful, in fact, after his discovery of the equally fascinating profession of writing. His practice became "a continuing strain as well as a confining profession. If I had been in a larger field," he writes, " I could have specialized or raised my fees to such a point as to keep my practice within reasonable limits, but being in a smaller community I had to take things as they came." By degrees, therefore, he found he was relegating his law practice more and more into the background.

Joseph Henry Jackson feels that Gardner is essentially an experimenter. It is that habit of mind which has led him into most of the ventures of his career, and which led him into this next job. Jackson says Gardner doesn't quite know why he got the idea of becoming a writer, "nor can he explain how it first occurred to him or what made him think he could succeed at writing." But at the beginning of the 1920's he wrote and sold his first piece of work, and he has been writing steadily ever since. Before long the new author had discovered that the writing game paid. At the end of the first year, though devoting only spare hours to it, he had made almost $1,000. For the next five years, therefore, he experimented at writing everything imaginable: "Westerns, detective stories, confession yarns, motor-tour articles, pieces about hunting and fishing, disquisitions on archery [a hobby]." In his fifth year he made $6,627 at his spare-time venture. His next two steps were to cut down on his hours at the law office and to buy an electric typewriter. From then on his output was amazing, almost a million words a year. In 1931 alone he earned $20,525, and without writing a book: practically all the money had been earned by his contributions to pulp magazines. Editors, writes Jackson, "liked Gardner himself . . . because he was reliable, never went prima-donna on them, met his deadlines, kept up the quality of his output."

About this time Gardner went to China on a visit, having learned Chinese in odd moments. Shortly after his return, in the middle of 1932, the editorial offices of William Morrow, Inc., received the first signs of still another Gardner experiment. Morrow's had just decided to halt the production of detective fiction for a time when two manuscripts were submitted. The titles were curious, *The Case of the Velvet Claws* and *The Case of the Sulky Girl*, and they did the trick for Gardner. Both were published the next year (1933) and were the start of an institution: "Perry Mason, the shrewdest lawyer-detective in mystery history."

The years from 1933 to 1938, says *Newsweek*, were Gardner's "quantitative if not qualitative literary peak. He wrote 1,100,000 words a year . . . or the equivalent of a novel every five or six days [this included magazine stories as well as books]. . . . At the same time he kept up a brisk law practice." His Perry Mason had indeed caught on with the public. Year after year the stories poured out, all with arresting titles that seemed to appeal to readers: *Case of the Curious Bride* (1934), *Case of the Counterfeit Eye* (1935), *Case of the Lame Canary* (1937), *Case of the Careless Kitten* (1942), *Case of the Black-eyed Blonde* (1944). *Liberty* Magazine, *Cosmopolitan,* and the *Saturday Evening Post* began to serialize Perry Mason, and Hollywood made several movies about him, with Warren Williams as the sophisticated lawyer-detective. In recent years Gardner has also capitalized on two other fiction characters in his books, Terry Clane and Douglas Selby. These two, however, do not detect under the same "scrambled anapests" that the favored Perry docs. For one of the series Gardner uses such titles as *The D.A. Calls It Murder* (1937) and *The D.A. Goes to Trial* (1940); for the other he uses such unadorned ones as *Murder up My Sleeve* (1937). Altogether these three series number almost forty volumes, and they have been translated into all the major languages. In 1943 the Mason series sold over four and one-half million copies in all editions. (Some of Gardner's other mystery novels are published under pseudonyms.) His publishers have returned all his original manuscripts to him because of their possible future value.

In the fall of 1943 Gardner added another new job to his crowded schedule. Following the sensational murder of the wealthy Sir Harry Oakes in the Bahamas, Gardner was assigned by Hearst's New York *Journal-American* to report daily on the subsequent trial of Oakes's son-in-law, Alfred de Marigny. The articles were written as if they were by Perry Mason in the throes of detecting on a case. Gardner, however, employed very little supposition in his reports. In the middle of his work on the trial Gardner started another new job, that of preparing radio scripts for his detective. The Columbia Broadcasting Company started broadcasting these sponsored

ERLE STANLEY GARDNER

programs in October 1943. *Newsweek* Magazine estimates that these broadcasts bring Gardner about $50,000 a year. At present he keeps his book production down to four or five volumes a year.

He has abandoned his electrical typewriter for a group of human secretaries and for dictaphone apparatus. When he gets too far ahead of the secretaries—he usually works with two—a supply of words can always be stored away on cylinders.

Critics of Gardner's books, pro and con, continually use such expressions as "well-sustained tension", "fast and furious action", "rapid-fire dialogue", "brisk humor," and "surprising situations." Gardner himself admits that he is interested only in fiction that moves swiftly. His style follows a familiar pattern, and many of the tricks have become standbys, although the repertoire of clever, legal quirks used by his lawyer-detective are "seemingly inexhaustible," as one reviewer has exclaimed. "Mason," wrote Kay Irvin, "is a past master of courtroom strategy . . . cutting legal corners [in a particular book] more perilously than ever. . . . He skates with all his aplomb and vivacity along the edges of, to say the least, contempt of court." "He pits his legal wits," said Will Cuppy once, "against a battery of Grade-B brains." "Erle Stanley Gardner's books," continued Cuppy at another time, "may be a bit short on Old World Culture, but they're long on entertainment qualities for the deep-dyed fan." Perry Mason, it is true, gets into some critics' hair, according to one of them: the "slick", "familiar formula" annoys them. For most critics, however, Gardner's books have retained their "customary snappiness," regardless of the numerous times this formula has been repeated.

The author has in his possession correspondence from a prosecuting attorney in Phoenix, Arizona, which is a revealing sidelight on Gardner, the author, as a lawyer. The Arizona attorney, faced with a seemingly insurmountable legal technicality in prosecuting a

GARDNER, ERLE STANLEY—*Cont.*

man for murder, had decided to dismiss the case. Then the evening before the trial he found in a Gardner story that Perry Mason had met and circumvented the same legal difficulty. The Arizona man was able to apply the Mason technique in court the next day and to secure what had seemed to be an impossible conviction.

Despite warnings that he would wear himself out, Gardner remains "as inexhaustible as his famous character." "All I ask of life," he says, "is that it keep moving." He is a devotee of the out of doors and spends a great deal of his income so that he may live in the open in the manner that suits him. He is solidly built, about five feet eight inches tall, weighs 170 pounds, and "walks with the same light step he learned in his days in the ring. His grip is powerful and nervous; when he shakes hands he does it as though he meant it. . . . He has never learned to like alcohol much, and smokes only casually, like a man trying something new."

To keep in contact with people and ideas and yet maintain his amazing writing schedule, Gardner—before gasoline rationing—used to travel around the United States and Mexico with several trailers, following the sun. Clerks, secretaries, drivers, families, his and theirs, accompanied him. (Gardner was married April 9, 1912 to Natalie Talbert of Mississippi, and the couple have one child, Natalie Grace, now Mrs. Alan R. McKittrick.) Gardner has a 400-acre ranch near Temecula, California, 100 miles from Los Angeles. It is surrounded by an Indian reservation and a 96,000-acre cattle ranch. His own ranch has eight buildings: a social hall, his own quarters, a building for each member of his staff and for any possible guests. Once inside his own cabin, a person is never disturbed on the Gardner ranch. When he feels the need of company he adjourns to the social hall. When the owner of the ranch feels "stale" he asks to help his neighbor with the cattle. "As a cowpuncher," says Perry Mason's creator, "I'm the best mystery writer in the valley."

References

Newsweek 22:94-5 O 25 '43 por
Sat Eve Post 214:4 My 30 '42 por
Sat R Lit 18:10-12 Jl 16 '38 pors
White, Leslie T. Me, Detective p31-5 (1936)
Who's Who in America 1944-45

GASCH, MARIE MANNING. *See* Fairfax, B.

GAYLORD, ROBERT (MARCH) Oct. 11, 1888- Manufacturer

Address: b. Ingersoll Milling Machine Co., 2400 Douglas St., Rockford, Ill.; h. Spring Creek Rd., Rockford, Ill.

The 1944 president of the National Association of Manufacturers—whose present policy is to sell the public on free enterprise—was Robert Gaylord, president of the Ingersoll Milling Machine Company of Rockford, Illinois, a stanch believer in small business and free competition.

Robert March Gaylord was born October 11, 1888, in Minneapolis, Minnesota, the son of Edson Starr and Louise (March) Gaylord. Instead of following his father into the law profession, young Gaylord took a bench job with the Minneapolis Steel and Machinery Company, a tractor firm, immediately after his graduation in 1911 from the University of Minnesota. The next year he left there to work for the Emerson Brantingham Company in Rockford, Illinois, remaining with this company for two years. He made still another change in 1914, taking over the vice-presidency of the Gray Tractor Company in Minneapolis. The following year he had the good fortune to marry into the machine tool business, as he expresses it himself, through his marriage on October 30 to Mildred Ingersoll of the Ingersoll Milling Machine Company family in Rockford. In 1917 he left the Gray Tractor Company to assume the position of vice-president of the twenty-five-year-old Ingersoll firm, and in 1928 he became president, an office which he has held ever since.

The man to take over the leadership of the NAM, a post vacated by big-businessman Frederick C. Crawford'43, is professedly a small businessman, but one, adds *Time* Magazine, who has had "a hatful of big-business affiliations." The Ingersoll Milling Machine Company specializes in heavy machine tools, ranging from five to 250 tons in weight. In peacetime only a small firm, after the beginning of the War it doubled the number of its workers until, by December 1943, it was employing more than 900 men. In October 1941 the company received the Navy "E" in recognition of its "contribution in the design and manufacture of special machine tools for machining armor plate at speeds theretofore considered impossible."

Newsweek Magazine describes Gaylord's labor policies as liberal, citing his twenty-year record of no slow-downs or work stoppages and a labor absenteeism of less than two per cent for all causes since the start of the War. Since 1919 the company has had a profit-sharing plan for employees, plus an apprentice-training program. Neither the CIO nor the A.F. of L. however, has ever organized the Ingersoll plant, which has no written labor contract. The employees have an open-shop, independent union, the Industrial Employees Association. Under it, the company declares, any employee with a suggestion of a complaint can be assured of an answer within twenty-four hours. A war policy of the company is to meet eight times a year with the men to "tell what the business outlook is, where the machines are going, whether our stuff is doing a good job or not." The president sees no difference between management problems and labor problems. "Our [combined] job is to get the machines out the back door. . . . Given the best possible tools and the best possible working conditions, the workers will do the best possible job."

Gaylord's 1944 program for the NAM, as defined at his first press conference, was "anything to win the War"; his post-War plan is a simple slogan: "Save money and work." In addition Gaylord feels that top management should taken an active interest in the rehabilitation and training of disabled war veterans to prepare them for future employment.

From time to time during 1944 Gaylord spoke for NAM on national issues. In August he told the House Campaign Fund Investigation Committee that NAM is not a political organization, that its members are Republicans, Democrats, and New Dealers, and that "it would be improper to use common funds for partisan political purposes." With Eric Johnston '43, in October he urged the War Labor Board to maintain wage and price stabilization until the end of the War, advising the Board to consult farmers, families of servicemen, and the white collar workers before coming to any decision on a change in the "Little Steel" wage formula. On another occasion Gaylord answered critics who had been charging American industry with making exorbitant profits out of the War by pointing out that the rate of profit had declined from 3.1 per cent in 1939 to 2.8 per cent in 1943.

Earlier in the year, in April, Gaylord had declined to serve on a nine-man committee named by Donald M. Nelson '41, chairman of the War Production Board. This advisory committee on major reconversion policy had been selected from a cross section of the country in order to provide the WPB with varied opinions, but the president of the NAM claimed that such groups were unable to agree on anything but relatively unimportant subjects. Two months later he condemned the report of the Securities Exchange Commission in which it was stated that industry had sufficient working capital to convert to peacetime operation without financial aid. He insisted that business will need new capital if the country is to have the kind of post-War world it wants.

At the International Business Conference held in November at Rye, New York, Gaylord set forth the principles of foreign trade that are recognized by American manufacturers: "If we are to export goods, we must receive payment . . . in raw materials and in manufactured goods of other nations . . . if we are to export capital, we must be prepared to do so on a low-term basis and with the knowledge that it can be returned to us only in the shape of goods and services rendered by those who borrow." At NAM's annual meeting in December Gaylord expressed his organization's opposition to cartels, both private and governmental, and decried the British and French trend toward the acceptance of "collectivist principles." Upon his retirement from the presidency of NAM (Ira Mosher was elected as his successor) Gaylord assumed the association's board chairmanship.

In addition to the presidency of his own company and of the NAM, Gaylord's big-business affiliations have been, and are, numerous. From 1940 through 1943 he was a director of the NAM; since 1943 he has been a member of the governing board of the NAM-sponsored National Industrial Information Committee (to educate the public in behalf of the preservation of the American private enterprise system); and during 1943 he was chairman of the NAM Industrial Equipment Division. He was president of the National Machine Tool Builders Association in 1932. He has been a member of the executive committee of the Machinery and Allied Prod-

ROBERT GAYLORD

ucts Institute since 1934; vice-president of the same institute since 1937; a director and an officer of the Illinois Manufacturers' Association since 1938—president of the Association in 1941, and chairman in 1942 and 1943. (The Association is the largest state manufacturers' group in the United States.) Besides these duties, in December 1941 Gaylord served as an industry member of the President's Committee on Labor and Industry.

Gaylord is described as being a blue-eyed, ruddy-faced man, with sandy hair well flecked with gray. Tall, lean, and athletic, he is a hunting enthusiast, owning half-a-dozen hunting dogs and a camp in Minnesota. His reading tastes run toward the history of early America, of the Northwest, and of Indian tribes and lore. Mrs. Gaylord is active in civic affairs, most of them charitable and educational. The couple have four children: Robert March, a lieutenant, junior grade, in the Navy, who has seen active service in the South Pacific; Clayton Russell, a captain in the Army Air Forces; Edson Ingersoll, a private in the Army Artillery; and Helen Ingersoll, a student in the secondary schools of Rockford.

References

N Y Herald Tribune p20 D 11 '43 por
N Y Sun p18 Ap 17 '44
Newsweek 22:60+ D 20 '43
Time 42:83-4 D 20 '43 por
Who's Who in Commerce and Industry 1944

GEORGE, DAVID LLOYD, 1ST EARL OF DWYFOR *See* Lloyd George of Dwyfor, D., 1st Earl

GIBBS, WILLIAM FRANCIS Aug. 24, 1886- Naval architect; marine engineer
Address: b. 1 Broadway, New York City; h. 170 E. 79h St., New York City

WILLIAM FRANCIS GIBBS

The top executive of the chief United States firm of naval architects and marine engineers, the former WPB Controller of Shipbuilding, the designer of the Liberty ship, and the man responsible for three-fourths of the vessels built in the United States—these are all contained in one person, William Francis Gibbs, who never took a degree either in architecture or in engineering, but has been called "the greatest influence on naval design since John Ericsson," who designed the famous *Monitor*.

Ever since his birth in Philadelphia, on August 24, 1886, the son of William Warren and Frances Ayres (Johnson) Gibbs, he has been known to family and friends as Francis, without any abbreviation. Only *Time* Magazine has had the temerity to call him Willie. A delicate child, Francis was allowed to stay home from school much of the time, and therefore "loafed around the house twelve or fourteen hours a day, playing with blueprints, mathematical calculations, and treatises on shipbuilding." Graduated, eventually, from the Delancey School in Philadelphia, he wanted to study engineering; but his father, a financier whose fortune at one time reached fifteen million dollars and who was "a director of more corporations than any other man in America," disliked engineers. Francis therefore majored in economics at Harvard University, which he entered at twenty. After three years he left, because of "trouble with Latin," and entered Columbia University, where he studied law, acquiring both his LL.B. and his M.A. by 1913. In his free time Gibbs studied sea history and designed improvements for British battleships, the plans of which he found in certain technical publications. He continued this avocation during the year he was connected with a law firm specializing in real estate cases. Gibbs won the first case he tried, but was so disillusioned with the law that he left the firm soon after and never practiced law again.

To prepare himself for a career in naval architecture, the Philadelphian went into retirement for a year of "special research." Soon he was joined by his brother, Frederick H.

Gibbs, who was to handle the business aspects. The Gibbs fortune had been wiped out by the "rich man's panic" of 1907, and the brothers proceeded on the proverbial shoestring while Francis designed his first ship: a thousand-foot, thirty-knot vessel designed to cut down the time of the transatlantic run by ten hours. The brothers submitted the plans to authorities for criticism; designed proposed harbor developments for the projected line; and presented Frederick Gibbs's exhaustive economic studies in immigration to show its probable revenue. Then they laid the project before Ralph Peters, president of the Long Island Railroad, who was known to be interested in transatlantic ships. He in turn conferred with J. P. Morgan, who had the Gibbs brothers placed on the payroll of the International Mercantile Marine Company while they did further work on the project. The First World War ended work on this line, but Francis Gibbs was given other work, made a reputation, and was appointed chief designer; on the entrance of the United States into the War, he became naval architect to the Shipping Control Commission. He attended the Paris Peace Conference as special assistant to the chairman of the Shipping Control Board, after which he returned to New York and a position as chief of construction of the International Mercantile Marine Company.

In 1922, at the request of the United States Government, Frederick and William Francis Gibbs took on the job of reconditioning the *Leviathan*, organizing Gibbs Brothers, Inc. for that purpose. During the summer of 1923 the firm, with William Francis as its president, drew up the necessary plans, prepared the specifications, and supervised the work of reconditioning. Their success with this undertaking brought contracts for reconditioning other vessels, and then for building new ones. In the course of Gibbs Brothers' rise to prominence among naval architects and marine engineers, "Sir Francis" found good use for his knowledge of the intricacies of contract law.

Believing that orthodox shipbuilders were far from making their vessels "as unsinkable as humanly possible," Gibbs increased the number of compartments in the ship's hold, with watertight doors between. Then, if the vessel sprang a leak, the hold would not be flooded—the leaking compartment would be shut off, and the ship kept afloat. In 1927 he put his ideas to a practical test in the construction of the S.S. *Malolo*, commissioned by the Matson Line, which was to be the highest-powered merchant vessel ever built in the United States. Gibbs designed a hold composed of many compartments with sliding bulkhead doors controlled from the pilothouse. There was, however, one unfortunate aspect of this plan—the lack of any practical way for the designer to test the soundness of his theories. By a convenient coincidence, the *Malolo* was rammed during her trial run by a Norwegian freighter which tore a gash in her hull. Gibbs dashed into the pilothouse and pushed the proper button. The bulkhead door slid shut; the *Malolo* remained triumphantly afloat; and the multiple-compartment principle became standard practice in shipbuilding. "Wounded" ships have since been kept from sinking even when more than one compartment has sprung a leak and become filled with water.

During these years naval building was halted, so there was little opportunity in the field of warship design. While other countries with government-sponsored shipbuilding programs took over the world's trade, ship construction in the United States was perhaps at its lowest ebb. Almost the only keels laid were for yachts and luxury liners; so in 1929 Gibbs went into partnership with a well known yacht designer, Daniel Hargate Cox, and became vice-president of the new firm, Gibbs & Cox. In the same year the firm designed and supervised construction of the world's largest pleasure ship, the *Savarona*. Commissioned by Mrs. Richard M. Cadwalader, this yacht was equipped with such appointments as a public-address system, gold-plated doorknobs, and bathrooms inlaid with mother-of-pearl. Slightly less splendorous were the luxury liners *Santa Rosa, Santa Paula, Santa Elena,* and *Santa Lucia,* which Gibbs built for the Grace Lines in 1931. But it was not until two years later, when the United States Government began to build up its depleted Navy, that the designer really came into his own.

On behalf of three shipyards (United Dry Docks, the Federal Shipbuilding and Dry Dock Company, and the Bath Iron Works), Gibbs drew up plans for the Navy's proposed class of destroyers which featured "high-pressure, high-temperature [steam] propulsion." This was a highly advanced system which he had worked out in conjunction with five manufacturers. The plans were accepted, and Gibbs continued to undertake new destroyer designs each year (his plans were executed by the Bath Iron Works and the Federal Shipbuilding and Dry Docks Company). In the years 1937 to 1939 Gibbs also designed and supervised the construction of the S.S. *America,* the largest mail and passenger liner built in the United States, and of *Firefighter,* a fireboat commissioned by the City of New York, which introduced some revolutionary improvements. In 1936, foreseeing the inevitable war, Gibbs began enlarging his staff to cope with wartime demands, but continued to handle all shop and employee problems himself.

In 1939, the year in which Gibbs & Cox designed a class of light cruisers, William Francis Gibbs was investigated by the Dies [40] Committee. Testimony showed that he had once designed a battleship for the Russian Government, only to have his plans rejected. According to *Time*'s report, the U.S.S.R. had ordered from Gibbs "the finest battleship in the world, something about 35,000 tons." So Gibbs proceeded to design the finest battleship in the world—something about 85,000 tons, which dwarfed every battleship that had ever been built. This yielding to impulse cost Gibbs & Cox the order. (A "mystery man" because of the little information there is about him, Gibbs has also been investigated by seven other agencies, including the FBI, all of which took up half his time for one year but gave him clean bills of health.)

But Gibbs was keeping himself occupied, nonetheless. In 1940, when the United States Maritime Commission asked him to design a cargo vessel for mass production, Gibbs & Cox was supervising construction of a similar vessel for the British—"a little ugly duckling of 10,000 deadweight tons." Her parts were modified and standardized for mass production all over the country, using "simple reciprocating engines, fittings, gears, and pumps, all interchangeable." The result was the Liberty ship.

The real problem then arose: how to get the tradition-bound, custom-building ship construction industry into mass production. Gibbs not only simplified the various parts, but devised easier and more efficient ways of assembling them. Once Henry Kaiser [42] and the California Shipbuilding Corporation went into mass production under Gibbs's direction, shipbuilders were inspired to carry his time- and labor-saving ideas even further. Instead of building a vessel entirely on the ways, they learned to break construction down into operations which could be carried on in different places at the same time. This and other improved methods cut down production time from four years to four days. The same principles were applied to the far more complex construction of naval vessels, and produced comparable results. By September 1942 ship production had increased approximately 700 per cent over the pre-War rate.

Gibbs was not personally responsible for this entire "technological revolution"; but even from a purely quantitative viewpoint his share in it is impressive. Gibbs & Cox was responsible for some seventy per cent of all United States shipbuilding. In addition to the Liberty ship, the firm designed "merchant ships, destroyers, tankers, cruisers, and landing barges. It designs the means of building them swiftly and efficiently. It lays down their specifications and in many cases orders the materials" and supervises construction. "Every day," *Time* reported, "Gibbs & Cox turns out 8,000 to 10,000 blueprints, twenty-six acres of blueprints a month. . . . Not a day goes by that the company does not contract for at least $1,000,000 worth of materials."

In December 1942 WPB Vice-Chairman Charles E. Wilson [41] brought Gibbs in as controller of shipbuilding. His task was "to coordinate the programs of the Army, the Navy, and the Maritime Commission" and to make sure that shipbuilding was carried on with maximum efficiency. Gibbs, whose acid directness had already made him many enemies, predicted: "I'll be one of the most hated men around here in about three weeks. . . . But there'll be action." There was.

The new Shipbuilding Controller had accepted his appointment reluctantly, but he "hurled himself into battle" wholeheartedly—and "ran head-on into the Maritime Commission," which, under Rear Admiral Howard L. Vickery [43], had its own shipbuilding program "with an eye on a post-War merchant marine." The President's "don't fight in public" order dropped over the incident "like a black cloth over a parrot cage." "Betrayed only by muffled sounds," it was "quietly settled beneath the cloth." It is known, however, that Vickery held out for conversion to the larger and faster Victory ship, which would be a useful vessel after the War, while Gibbs's plan was to spur the production of Liberties. The first round was apparently won by Gibbs, with his appointment as chairman of the

GIBBS, WILLIAM FRANCIS—*Cont.*

American-British-Canadian Combined Committee on Standardization of Ship Design. (The establishment of this committee, incidentally, was not announced until August 1943, although it had been formed some months before. At the time it was said to have materially increased output.)

Whatever opposition he may have encountered, Gibbs succeeded "magnificently" in standardizing and simplifying ship design. Merchant ship types were reduced from six to three; geared turbines, from twenty-seven to eight; turbogenerators (which provide the power and light for all naval vessels), from seventy-seven to seventeen. These changes very greatly increased the interchangeability of parts, and thus made possible mass production on a much greater scale. In September 1943, having accomplished what he came to do, Gibbs handed in his resignation and went back to his waterfront office in New York City, "reputation intact."

In early 1944 reports of Liberty ships cracking open reached Congress, resulting in an investigation by the Truman [42] Committee. Hearings were held in Washington, Seattle, and New York, at which all operators of Liberty ships as well as many others concerned were shipping were questioned. Testimony showed that sixty-five or 3.21 per cent of the 2,000 Liberty ships in service had developed cracks. This was considered not to be an alarming figure in view of the speed of their construction and the tremendous strain they underwent in keeping up with convoys, carrying deck cargo for which they had not been designed, and meeting heavy weather with insufficient or incorrect ballasting. The basic design was not called into question, but faults were found with the construction of the damaged vessels. In March, Edgar F. Kaiser, general manager of the Oregon Shipbuilding Corporation, testified before the War Investigating Committee that changes in design had virtually eliminated the difficulties which caused "cracking" of some of the first Liberty ships.

At the end of the hearings it was decided that a program of converting Liberty ships to troop and hospital ships should be abandoned, as they were not designed for such use, and that the construction program should be devoted to faster vessels. (Meanwhile, Admiral Vickery's Maritime Commission canceled contracts for Liberty ships, replacing them with orders for ships about half their size.) It was emphasized, however, that (in the words of J. Lyell Wilson of the American Bureau of Shipping) "Liberty ships have been our salvation in carrying war materials."

The firm of Gibbs & Cox was under investigation by the House Naval Affairs Committee in May on the charge of collecting excessive profits on war contracts, but was cleared almost immediately. Criticism turned into commendation, the New York *Times* reported, when Chairman Carl Vinson and Rear Admiral E. L. Cochrane, chief of the Bureau of Ships, said that the firm's contribution to the shipbuilding program had been a definite factor in the record production.

In the fall of 1944 shipbuilders, steamship operators, and Government maritime officials discussed the question of the disposition of the Liberty ships when the war emergency should be over. Some of the proposals were to charter them to Allied nations, to lay them up as an emergency fleet, or to scrap them altogether. However, Vice-Admiral Emory S. Land [41], chairman of the Maritime Commission, defended the Libertys, claiming they would be 20 per cent more valuable as a peacetime unit.

Their designer, described variously as "dour", "acidulous", "bony", "long and stringy," is said to be "a profound skeptic" and to "look more like an undertaker than a real one. But his friends recognize this as a mannerism which they suspect is partly affectation. It includes wearing shiny, patched clothes, and shocking dinner parties with his sardonic comments." Although since 1927 Gibbs has been married to the socially prominent Vera (Cravath) Larkin, past president of the Metropolitan Opera Guild, he "avoids society, but pops into it every once in a while, throws himself into a chair like an old rug, and often turns out to be the lion of the party."

Gibbs, a Presbyterian, is a member of the Department of Commerce Safety of Life at Sea Commission, as well as of the Society of Naval Architects and Marine Engineers, the Institution of Naval Architects, the Institution of Aeronautical Sciences, and the New York Bar. His clubs are the Broad Street and the Piping Rock. The architect has been honored by the award of a doctorate in engineering from the Stevens Institute of Technology (1938), and by one of the American Design Awards given in recognition of his Liberty ship design. He avoids publicity and says that a man exposed to it "gets to thinking he is so goddam bright that it just paralyzes him."

References

Sat Eve Post 217:9-11+ Ja 20 '45 il pors; 217:20+ Ja 27 '45 il por; 217-20 F 3 '45 por

Time 40:20-2 S 28 '42; 42:21 S 20 '43

Who's Who in America 1944-45

GIEGENGACK, A(UGUSTUS) E(DWARD) (gē´gen-gak) Apr. 19, 1890- Public Printer of the United States

Address: b. United States Government Printing Office, N. Capitol and H Sts., Washington, D.C.; h. 3016 Tilden St., N.W., Washington, D.C.

When A. E. Giegengack was made Public Printer of the United States in 1934 he was almost as pleased with his new title as with the job. After years of patiently hearing himself referred to as everything from Mr. Backingoop to Hickenlooper, he welcomed with relief the right to be addressed simply as Mr. Public Printer. But the Public Printer is a happy man mainly because he has realized a life ambition. For fifteen years he had worked toward attaining to his present position.

Augustus Edward Giegengack was born in New York City's borough of Manhattan on April 19, 1890. His father was a German cafe owner; his mother was Irish and a printer's daughter who had worked in a printing office herself. When Augustus was two the family

moved to Brooklyn, where he later attended
St. Francis College, a parochial grade school.
At thirteen he took a business course in stenography and commercial law, then at fifteen
decided to pay his own way in the world. His
first job was an $8-a-week one with the
American News Company. But there was
more money in printing, advised his mother, so
he became an apprentice in the composing
room of the New York *Commercial,* a financial daily. In the next few years he made
several more moves: a linotype operator at
eighteen, a printer, successively, on the *World,*
the *Hudson County Observer* in Hoboken, and
with the McCall Company during his early
twenties, he became foreman of a Brooklyn
printing plant at the age of twenty-five.

Young Giegengack was now quite a man-
about-Brooklyn, according to the *New Yorker,*
"a connoisseur of girls, beer, and anecdotes,
especially the last." The First World War
gave him a fine opportunity to increase this
story repertoire. His career as a soldier got
off to a dramatic start with cases of measles,
scarlet fever, mumps, and diphtheria, all contracted in a row. He was all over the measles
by the time the boat docked at Liverpool,
but he was nonetheless taken on a stretcher
to a hospital, where he was placed by mistake
in a scarlet fever ward. In the ward were
also (by mistake, no doubt) a mumps case and
a diphtheria case. After he had recovered from
all the diseases he was finally released and
sent to an infantry replacement center in
France. Then, securing a job on the Army
newspaper *Stars and Stripes,* he was transferred to Paris as its production manager.

The *Stars and Stripes* staff then included
such fledgling celebrities as Alexander Woollcott '41, Grantland Rice '41, and Franklin P.
Adams '41. The production manager, a church-
going Catholic, was made much of by some
well-born French girls whose church he attended. This made possible his entry into chateau society, and his colleagues were both
awed and envious as he described the "elegant
soirees" that he attended. He was now a sergeant, with 200 soldier printers under him, and
a pillar on which the whole *Stars and Stripes*
staff could lean in moments of stress. "Nothing neglected, nothing slack, in the department
Giegengack" were the closing lines of a poetic
tribute paid to him in an anniversary edition
of the paper.

When the War was over Giegengack went
home to Brooklyn, and, as a commercial printer,
fared well during the next fifteen years. He
was, successively, foreman of the composing
room of the DeVinne Press, half-owner of the
Burkhardt Linotype Company, and partner in
the firm of Whittaker-Giegengack-Trapp, which
printed technical publications for McGraw-Hill
and also did work for Funk and Wagnalls. In
1920 he was married to Margaret A. Morrison,
a young Brooklyn schoolteacher. (They have
one daughter, Margaret Mary.)

By this time a leading figure in his profession, Giegengack served two years as president
of the Typographers Association of New York
and of the International Association of Printing House Craftsmen. Referred to by a friend
as "the type who succeeds instinctively in political organizations," he was to live up to this
"typing" during the 1932 elections. Public

A. E. GIEGENGACK

Printers were appointed by the President, and
a change in administration, Giegengack figured, would probably carry with it a change of
Printers. Banking on this chance, Giegengack
began to angle for the job by becoming active
in the Democratic Club of Rockville Center,
where he had purchased a home shortly after
his marriage. His next move was to organize
an "A. E. Giegengack for Public Printer" movement which solicited endorsements from numerous printing groups. In this way he secured
about 200 recommendations, which he had
bound in a gilt-edged volume and sent to Postmaster Farley '44, who in turn brought it to the
attention of President Roosevelt '42. Finally, on
July 2, 1934, Giegengack secured the desired
appointment.

When Giegengack took over his new post
as thirteenth Public Printer of the United
States he found the buildings of the Government Printing Office in bad condition. He immediately incorporated a series of photographs
of the most deteriorated parts into a booklet
which was distributed among Congressmen.
Impressed, the Congressmen voted a generous
appropriation which provided for the renovation
of two buildings and for the erection of two
new buildings where two others had been torn
down.

Giegengack found more than physical decay,
however, when he took control of the Printing
Office. It had such an unreliable system of
cost accounting that it would sometimes over-
charge on one job to make up for a job for
which it had charged too little. Ignorant of
Federal accounting procedure himself, Giegengack went to the Comptroller General of the
United States, who recommended Russell H.
Herrell, one of his chief investigators of Federal agencies. Herrell became administrative
assistant to the Public Printer and director of
personnel. He set up a cost accounting system by which it was possible to estimate more
accurately in advance the cost of a piece of
work. In addition, Giegengack always checks
funds available in the Federal appropriation for
a particular job before making a contract—his

GIEGENGACK, A. E.—*Continued*

policy is, no money, no contract. Profit is made on those Government publications sold to the public through the Division of Public Documents.

Extending this program of efficient management, Giegengack has integrated the systems of production and distribution to the public, speeding up both. He has further increased output at the home plant by introducing three working shifts and a seven-day week. (In dealing with his 8,000 employees, Giegengack has taken a firm stand on the subject of raises. Federal printing salaries are about equal to the average wage standard of private companies, and for this reason he feels that to raise the wages of Government printers would be unfair to private printers.)

"Giegengack has always been a magisterial Public Printer," says the *New Yorker*. Lack of cooperation from Federal agencies was a source of annoyance to him. Observing that untidy manuscripts turned in by the agencies were adding to the labor and expense of the composing room, he wrote in his 1938 annual report: "It is urged that each Federal agency designate a competent copy preparer, thoroughly familiar with Government Printing Office routine and its *Style Manual* and good usage in the English language, to contact in a cooperative manner the officials in his department who handle the editing of copy before it is sent to the Government Printing Office for publication."

Not only has the Printing Office become more efficient, but under the Giegengack regime Government printing has acquired a more attractive appearance. The *Congressional Record*, the only publication of which the Government Printing Office is editor as well as printer, now has the American eagle on its frontispiece and runs three instead of two columns to a page. This not only makes for greater readability, but the resultant conservation of space has cut down costs by 16.97 per cent. Type faces are more attractive. "We're not so 'corny-looking' as in the old days," said a Printing Office layout man. Among other innovations introduced by the Public Printer is chemically treated writing paper for the use of enemy prisoners of war. All invisible writing fluids, when brought in contact with the paper, turn bright green or red.

In 1934, when Giegengack became Public Printer, the plant was consuming about 28,000 tons of paper a year. By 1943 it used nearly 250,000 tons. This increase over a period of nine years is the result of material issued by the dozens of Government agencies that originated during the '30's, the "OPA instructions and questionnaires, Selective Service forms, and the gigantic and varied orders of the War and Navy Departments."

The Second World War alone has swollen the volume of "business" of the Printing Office to $65,000,000 a year. A statistician estimated that the 73,000,000,000 ration stamps it produced during a two-year period would be enough to spin a seventeen-inch web fourteen times around the earth. Foreseeing America's entry into the War, in 1940 Giegengack began making plans for handling the anticipated overflow of work. By means of questionnaires sent to thousands of commercial printers and engravers, he has obtained precise information as to their personnel, specialties, and equipment. With the aid of a classified index of these shops, he has thus been able to farm out over half his production, sending out members of his own staff to supervise and direct the work.

A story told about the Public Printer points him up as both shrewd and imaginative: Preparedness for the threatening paper shortage and a sudden cancellation of a Government order had left Giegengack's warehouse during the early part of the War with more than its quota of paper. The rumor that the Government was hoarding was picked up by *Life* Magazine, which immediately sent a reporter and a photographer to investigate. Greeting the *Life* representatives in person, Giegengack took them to the warehouse, bemoaning the fact that it now held only five freight cars, "though we have room for sixteen." Further investigation produced no evidence of the reported hoarding, and the disgruntled reporters left, unaware that they had missed a scoop. There was a basis for the rumor, but Giegengack had been tipped off and had shipped a dozen or more freight cars to Baltimore. He used up this extra paper two weeks later, and his conscience in the matter has thus always been clear.

The Public Printer keeps several scrapbooks about himself which he has had indexed. A section of an index presents a patchwork quilt picture of his personality: "Affable and bald. . . . Doing most astonishing work with all sorts of handicaps. . . . Dwarfs others in room. . . . Not only eminent executive but great, jolly mixer. . . . With coat off means business." He mentions as his hobbies baseball, football, and the theatre. Geoffrey T. Hellman of the *New Yorker* augments this list with "poker, scotch-and-sodas, long telephone conversations, and making the most of a gift for profanity." "He has the superficially gentle manner of a man who does not care to be imposed upon," adds Hellman. Giegengack and his family have a home in Washington, and in the summer go to their place in the Catskills.

Giegengack's position is an appointive one, revocable at will by the President. He has some objection to this and does not see why his office should not be permanent and nonpolitical as it is with his counterpart, the English Controller of His Majesty's Stationery Office and King's Printer of Acts of Parliament. He feels no particular apprehension about losing his appointive post, however. He has met war demands so effectively that it is thought unlikely that he will be forced to resign even with a change in administration. Whatever eventuates, he still has offers of twice his present salary awaiting him in private printing concerns.

References

New Yorker 19:24-8+ Je 12 '43 por; 19:28-30+ Je 19 '43; 19:24-8+ Je 26 '43

Who's Who in America 1944-45

GIFFORD, SANFORD R(OBINSON) Jan. 8, 1892—Feb. 25, 1944 Internationally known eye specialist and author; several hundred contributions to the field of ophthalmology were made by his research; two widely used texts are his *Hand-book of Ocular Therapeutics* (1932) and *Textbook of Ophthalmology* (1938).

Obituary

N Y Times p13 F 26 '44

GILES, BARNEY MCKINNEY (jīls) Sept. 13, 1892- United States Army Air Forces officer

Address: b. c/o War Department, Washington, D. C.

"In Washington last week," wrote *Newsweek* in May 1944, "a rangy, soft-spoken man with gray-sprinkled hair kept combat maps of Europe constantly before him, watching closely the greatest air offensive of all time." That man was Lieutenant General Barney McKinney Giles, Deputy Commander of the Army Air Forces and Chief of Air Staff of the United States Army Air Forces. For him the invasion of Western Europe began many months before the actual landings. "General Giles could take pride in his part in preparing the Air Forces for their D-Day," continued *Newsweek*. "For, under the sponsorship of General Arnold'[42], he was the leading exponent of long-range fighters as cover for invading bombers."

Still rated a command pilot, and technical and aircraft observer, no doubt Giles would have liked to fly an invading bomber himself. Born in Mineola, Texas, September 13, 1892, the son of Richard Portlock and Louisa (Reed) Giles, he and his twin brother Ben were dreaming of flying while still doing chores on their father's farm in Mineola, where neighbors remember them as "the out-workingest hands and the best danged bird hunters in Texas." They attended East Texas College and the University of Texas, planning to be lawyers, and then the First World War gave them an opportunity to fulfill their original dream. Before the United States entered the War the twins avidly read tales of Royal Flying Corps fliers dropping bricks, gasoline, and bottles on Germany and fighting air duels with shotguns. Finally the boys could stand it no longer. They pooled their resources, and Ben was the one chosen to go to Canada to find out about joining the Royal Flying Corps. Having barely crossed the border when the United States entered the War, he rushed back—and the adventurous brothers promptly betook themselves to an Army recruiting station. Ever since that time they have been waging "a cheerful feud for promotion." In 1944 Barney Giles is Chief of Air Staff; his brother, Major General Benjamin F. Giles, is commanding general of the United States Army Forces in the Middle East.

Barney Giles was appointed a flying cadet in the Army in September 1917, and until October he attended the School of Military Aeronautics at the University of Texas in Austin. After graduation he was transferred to Mitchel Field, New York, for observation training, and in December 1917 he went to Ellington Field in his home state for advanced flying training. Finally, on April 9, 1918, he received his commission as 2nd lieutenant in the Aviation Section of the Signal Reserve

U. S. Army Air Forces

LT. GEN. BARNEY MCKINNEY GILES

and was sent to Langley Field, Virginia, as an instructor in the School for Aerial Observers. During July 1918 he attended the Advanced Observation School at Taliaferro Field, Texas, then returned to Langley Field. It was September 1918 before he got to France, where he attended the aviation school at St. Maxient and the Aviation Instruction Center at Issoudun. In December of that same year, after the Armistice, he was assigned to duty with the 168th Observation Squadron, which was stationed successively at Toul until March 1919 and at Trampe, France, and Coblenz, Germany, until June 1919. Giles was then sent to Brest, as an inspector at that post. Upon his return to the United States in September 1919 he was assigned to Mitchell Field, New York. In October he went to Morrison, Virginia, as engineer officer at the Aviation Supply Depot; in April 1920 he was honorably discharged.

But this was by no means the end of Giles's Army career. He enlisted in the Regular Army, and on July 1, 1920, only a few months after his discharge, he was commissioned a 2nd lieutenant of Air Service and on the same date was promoted to 1st lieutenant. He was assigned to the Aviation Repair Depot in Dallas, Texas, until July 1921, when he went to the San Antonio, Texas, Air Intermediate Depot. He remained at that assignment until July 1924, and was then transferred to Kelly Field, Texas, for duty with the 68th Service Squadron.

In November 1924 Giles was assigned to the 43rd School Squadron at Kelly Field, and in July 1925 he went to Fairfield, Ohio, as assistant chief of the Maintenance Branch at Wright Field. In January 1926 he became chief of the Matériel Branch there; in May 1927 chief of the Maintenance Engineering Branch; and in May 1928 he was transferred to March Field, California. He served there as assistant engineering officer of the Air Corps Primary Flying School and instructor in that

GILES, BARNEY MCKINNEY—*Cont.*

school until September 1930, when he was transferred to the Rockwell Air Depot at Coronado, California, as chief engineer officer. On January 1, 1932 he was promoted to the rank of captain.

It was August 1934 when Captain Giles entered the Air Corps Tactical School at Maxwell Field, Alabama. Graduated in June 1935 and promoted that same month to the temporary rank of major, he was assigned to command the 20th Bombardment Squadron at Langley Field, Virginia. That year he became one of the first officers to fly a four-motored airplane—one of the original B-17 Flying Fortresses. In February 1936 he was participating in an aerial flight from Concord, New Hampshire, to East Brewster, Massachusetts, and return. Notified that seven Civilian Conservation Corps youths were stranded on an ice floe in Cape Cod Bay, he took off in an airplane during the hours of darkness, under dangerous flying conditions. He not only successfully found the men, but dropped a message to them and reported their location, thereby being chiefly responsible for saving their lives. For this act he was awarded the Distinguished Flying Cross.

In July 1936 Giles became operations officer of the 2nd Bombardment Group at Langley Field, serving until August 1937. He then attended the Command and General Staff School at Fort Leavenworth, Kansas, until June 1938, when he was assigned to the Office, Chief of Air Corps in Washington, D. C., as chief of the Inspection Division. On August 15, 1939 he was promoted to the permanent rank of major; on December 30, 1940, to the temporary rank of lieutenant colonel. During the days of the Battle of Britain he served for a short time as a combat observer there, and his study of air fighting in England convinced him that bomber losses could be cut sharply by fighter protection. Extra tanks, he thought, would allow the fighters to carry the fuel-loads necessary for long-range flights and still be useful as fighters. Experiments in this line apparently proved successful, but, according to *Newsweek*, many high officers were hard to convince.

Then came Pearl Harbor. In December 1941 Giles was ordered to the West Coast to organize the 4th Air Service Area Command and to take command of this unit at Hamilton Field, California. (On December 18, 1941 he was promoted to the permanent rank of lieutenant colonel, and on January 5, 1942 to the temporary rank of colonel.) In February 1942, promoted to the temporary rank of brigadier general, he became commanding general of the 4th Bomber Command at Hamilton Field, and the following September, as a temporary major general, he was designated commanding general of the Fourth Air Force at the Presidio of San Francisco. During all this time he had continued to advance his idea as to the importance of fighter protection for bombers.

In March 1943 Army Air Forces headquarters was reorganized to transform it into an over-all policy-making body. (The high command would continue to tell the field commanders "what to do," but not "how to

do it.") Giles was appointed one of the six assistant chiefs of the Air Staff under General Arnold, in charge of operations, commitments, and requirements. In this post he determined tactics and technique of aerial warfare and requirements for trained personnel and for aircraft, equipment, and supplies and had full control of War Organization and Movement. Miss Jacqueline Cochran [40], director of Women Pilots in the Air Forces, was one of his special assistants in the department.

Three months later, on July 27, 1943, Giles was appointed Chief of Air Staff, succeeding Major General George E. Stratemeyer. He was still faced by opposition to his theory, but by the fall of that year P-38's and P-51's were beginning to go into long-range action, and soon these long-range fighter escorts were beginning to cut bomber losses tremendously. (Today the flight radius of such planes is more than 600 miles.) On April 28, 1944 President Roosevelt [42] sent the name of Barney McKinney Giles to the Senate for promotion to the rank of lieutenant general.

After the Allied landings in Normandy on June 6, 1944 Giles expressed his surprise at the lack of immediate air opposition. "We had superiority in the air," he said, "but if the Luftwaffe had chosen to fight, we perhaps could not have claimed complete command." He expressed the opinion that the Luftwaffe could no longer hope to strike any decisive blows. Furthermore, "we still are building up our air strength in the United Kingdom. The Germans will find no let-down in the skies over France."

Two months later Giles went on a six-week tour of combat theatres in the European area. Upon his return in September he disclosed at a press conference the cost in men and planes since D-Day. From June 6 to September 11 the A.A.F. casualties totaled 10,284 killed or missing, and the loss of American aircraft, all types, numbered 2,870. After the defeat of Germany, the General remarked, the Air Forces plan to concentrate on three major types of fighter planes, two types of medium bombers, and four types of heavy bombers.

Giles was married to Hollyce Thomas Rice of Abilene, Texas, on April 18, 1922, and he and Mrs. Giles live in quarters in Fort Myer. The hard-working General arrives at his Washington office at 7:30 a.m. seven mornings a week and works until 8:30 p.m. every day except Sunday, when he tries to go home at 3:00. He likes bridge, poker, Scotch, is a par golfer and a "dead-eye bird hunter"; but there is little time for such things these days. Nor is there much time for social life, although he is a member of the Bolling Field Officers Club in Washington and the Columbia Country Club in Chevy Chase, Maryland. Every once in a while, however, he does manage to satisfy some of his desire for action. In 1942, as commander of the 4th Air Force, he flew up to Kiska and dropped some bombs on the Japanese himself. In early 1944 he toured the Mediterranean fronts and saw the fighting at Cassino both from the air and from the ground. And, according to *Newsweek*, in April 1944 he "hopped into the pilot's seat of the brand-new air giant *Constellation* and took off from Washington Airport with twelve officers as passengers. High over the Virginia hills, he purposely cut out two of the great ship's four motors. The officers behind him swallowed dryly and breathed easier only after the two dead engines had chimed in again. 'I just wanted to see what would happen,' General Giles told them."

References

N Y Times p9 Jl 28 '43
Newsweek 23:42 My 8 '44 por
Time 43:70 My 29 '44 por
Who's Who in Aviation 1942-43

GIRAUDOUX, JEAN (zhē-rō-dū zhän) 1882—Jan. 31, 1944 French novelist and playwright; his works include *Pathetic Simon* (1918), *Adorable Clio* (1920), *Siegfried and the Limousine* (1922); served as Secretary of Information 1939-1940.

Obituary

N Y Times p19 F 1 '44 por

GIRDLER, TOM M(ERCER) May 19, 1877- Industrialist

Address: b. Republic Steel Corp., Republic Bldg., Cleveland, Ohio; h. Greystone Farm, Mentor, Ohio

"Tom Mercer Girdler, steel man and airplane manufacturer, is a man of two reputations," says John Chamberlain in a review of Girdler's autobiographical *Boot Straps* (1943), in the writing of which the industrialist had the collaboration of Boyden Sparkes. Union men in the Chicago, Mahoning Valley, and Pittsburgh regions, Chamberlain states, still bitterly attack Tom Girdler. "Yet Tom Girdler, the man who refused to follow the lead of United States Steel in 'getting along' with the steel union, has been one of the production heroes of the War. In the year of Pearl Harbor one-half of all the steel in American-made airplanes was poured from the furnaces of Mr. Girdler's Republic Steel Corporation. Republic's light alloy electric furnace steel was for a long time practically the basis for our air power. But Tom Girdler has also been wartime boss of the Consolidated and Vultee Airplane Companies, which have done their own spectacular wartime jobs." As a matter of fact, in January 1944 Consolidated Vultee led the nation in the production of military aircraft, receiving a telegram of congratulation from the Aircraft Production Board because of its top position in the industry. Girdler has himself suggested that his contributions to the War may mean the difference between victory and defeat for the United Nations.

Tom M. Girdler prides himself on his American heritage. Although his mother, Elizabeth Mercer, was of English descent, and the Girdlers were "originally Gauls," there were both Mercers and Girdlers in Massachusetts before 1700. Before Tom Mercer Girdler ("not Thomas, Tom") arrived in the world his family had moved farther west—to Clark County, Indiana. There he was born, the third of five children, on May 19, 1877. At the time his father, Lewis, was superintendent of an Indiana cement mill, only one of many owned

TOM M. GIRDLER

by his sister and her husband. Tom grew up on a farm which raised the fodder needed for the horses and mules used in the mill operations. The boys did chores and worked in the mills during their vacations, but never knew real hardships.

When Tom was fourteen his family moved to the nearby town of Jeffersonville, Indiana, and he attended the Manual Training High School in Louisville, Kentucky—just across the river. There he received a thorough mechanical training which, combined with an unusual aptitude for technical work, made him a great asset to his father. While he was still in his teens he devised an engine to do what had formerly been the work of six mules, and but a short time later he built a locomotive from an old vertical-boiler twin engine. It was natural, then, that when his wealthy aunt sent him to Lehigh University in 1897 he chose to become a mechanical engineer.

At Lehigh young Girdler was an outstanding student who mastered everything except German without difficulty and who was vice-president of his class by his sophomore year. (He also sang in the choir and glee club and was an editor of the semi-weekly *The Brown and White* and a member of Beta Theta Pi fraternity.) When in March 1901 he took his degree in mechanical engineering, second in his class, a fraternity brother had already arranged a position for him with the Buffalo Forge Company at $12.50 a week. He spent two months at the home plant of the company, and then was sent to England to assist in the London branch. After almost a year abroad he began to grow homesick, however, and when in March 1902 he received an offer from the Oliver Iron & Steel Company in Pittsburgh, owned by the uncle of another college friend, he accepted. That was Girdler's first contact with the steel business, and the start of his real career. "Girdler, the mechanical engineer, now began his lifelong fight against conservative steelmaking processes."

(Continued next page)

GIRDLER, TOM M.—*Continued*

After three years with Oliver, two of them spent as superintendent of the nut factory, Girdler left Pittsburgh for a better position with the Colorado Fuel & Iron Company in Pueblo, Colorado. There he did a startling thing: walked into the general manager's office and asked for a job less rewarding financially and more taxing physically than his own—a job in the rail rolling mill. The work was hazardous, the hours nerve-wracking, and Girdler went from 148 pounds to a mere 125. But he has never regretted the time he spent in the mill, for he learned much about the making of steel.

From Colorado, Girdler went to the South in June 1907 to work as superintendent of the rolling mills of the Atlanta (now Atlantic) Steel Company. By the fall of 1908 he was general superintendent of the plant. "I ran that steel plant. I was its captain. I knew every part of it, every peculiarity of its machines, every virtue, every fault." As for the men—"I knew them all and knew their problems." But he was unhappy, isolated from the big steel centers, and he was eager to test himself on large problems. In 1914 he was hired by Pittsburgh's Jones & Laughlin Steel Corporation and put to work in their Woodlawn—now Aliquippa, Pennsylvania—plant. Within a year or two he became assistant general superintendent, the highest ranking official of the company living in Woodlawn, with the responsibility of running the steel town around the plant.

According to Girdler, Aliquippa was a model town, with recreational facilities, a good school system, "clean" living, and an absolute lack of friction. When the people wanted a new project of any sort they had only to ask him for it. "I was sort of a political boss," Girdler explains. "Certainly I had considerable power in politics without responsibility to 'the people.' . . . There was in Aliquippa, if you please, a benevolent dictatorship." According to *Fortune* Magazine, however, Girdler's labor policies at Aliquippa were such that the town "was known to steel men as 'the perfect company town' and to radicals as 'the Siberia of the industry.'"

In 1929 Girdler left Jones & Laughlin to join Cyrus Eaton in forming Republic Steel in Cleveland, Ohio. Girdler himself says that he resigned; Jones & Laughlin people say that he was let out of the company for dealing with Eaton. In either case, it would seem that Jones & Laughlin had reason to regret his departure, for by 1932 the company's earnings had slid from $29.04 a share (highest in the industry) to a loss of $20.86 a share (the greatest). And at first it looked as if Girdler might have reason to regret his departure, too. Republic was not too solid a corporation to begin with. Some of its companies were decided liabilities, others too new to be of any aid. At the time Girdler stepped in, the stock market was on the verge of its crash. Banks were not easily induced to extend credit, especially to an outfit which could offer very little in the way of collateral. Payrolls became "unending nightmares." It was only through Girdler's ceaseless efforts and unusual skill at management—he is "a formidable financial man as well as a crack operator"—that the business was kept alive. At first every year showed a heavy loss. Then in 1935 there was black ink in the books for the first time, and, though "the great force that seemed bent on our destruction thereafter was the Government of the United States," there has never been a deficit since. Republic has taken its place as one of the "big three" in the industry along with United States Steel and Bethlehem, and Girdler, having later dropped Eaton, not only became supreme boss of Republic but in his capacity as manager "drastically altered an enormous amount of property he does not own—revamping plants, bringing Corrigan, McKinney Steel Company, Truscon Steel Company, and Gulf States Steel Company under Republic's roof."

But once again he earned the enmity of labor by his tactics. In a *Fortune* article written in 1935 it was said that "he fired veteran foremen and mill hands so ruthlessly that his name is still cursed in the shabbier districts of Youngstown. . . . 'Before I spend the rest of my life dealing with William Green '42,' he told fellow steel men last year [1934], 'I'm going to raise apples and potatoes. . . . We are not going to deal with the Amalgamated or any other professional union, even if we have to shut down.'" In *Organized Labor and Production*, Philip Murray '41 and Morris L. Cooke said that the Republic Steel Corporation employed spies, discredited and attacked union leaders, incited violence, and "coerced employees into signing petitions opposing outside or independent unions."

Girdler devotes 144 out of the 470 pages of his autobiography to defending his company's role in the Little Steel strike of 1937. By that time the United States Steel Corporation and others had conferred with the Steel Workers Organizing Committee of the CIO and signed contracts. Although the CIO also claimed a majority of Republic's employees, Girdler refused to follow suit, insisting that the closed shop and the "checkoff" were not in his employees' interests. Girdler has stated that he did not oppose collective bargaining, but that the "employee representation plan"—more commonly known as the "company union"—was the form of unionism which the majority of his employees preferred.

One of the most violent struggles between Republic Steel and the union took place near the company's South Chicago plant on Memorial Day in 1937. The encounter between strikers and sympathizers on the one side (there were about 1,500 in the crowd, including women and children) and the police and company men on the other, in which tear gas, crude weapons, and firearms figured, resulted in ten deaths and many injured among the demonstrators as well as injured among the police.

According to Girdler, the crowd had obvious intentions of storming the plant, in which were hundreds of non-strikers. He said there were few Republic workers in the crowd, that women and children were used as "props," and that the affair was staged by Communists; he also stated that the police first ordered the demonstrators to disperse, using tear gas and guns only after they had been attacked. On the other hand, in disagreement with Girdler were many groups and individuals who protested the police action. The *New Republic*, which called the event a massacre, pointed to the Paramount newsreel taken on the scene as evidence of police aggression—uniformed men hurling tear gas into the crowd, shooting at fleeing demonstrators and striking some who had fallen. (The film itself was "shelved" for fear of the reaction of theatre audiences.) While subsequent investigations—Robert La Follette's [44] Civil Liberties Committee hearing, at which Girdler was questioned, was one—brought out different reports of the riot and the events that preceded it, Girdler maintained the whole story had not been told.

After four years, in which eight more men were killed near steel plants, at the end of 1941 the corporation, the NLRB, and the CIO (the Steel Workers Organizing Committee) signed a stipulation settling all charges of Wagner Act violation. Then, in August of 1942, when a count of union cards held by employees showed the majority wanted CIO representation, the union and Republic Steel Corporation signed a contract. Nearly 42,000 workers were brought under the agreement at the various plants of the corporation (of these several hundred were reinstated in jobs) and tens of thousands of dollars were paid in back wages. In Girdler's words, written in 1943: "Ever since we have done our conscientious best to make the relationship work to the mutual advantage of our employees and the company. In consequence, union officials with whom our people deal have stated publicly that relations with Republic Steel Corporation are favorable. But this does not mean that my opinions have changed."

In 1937 Girdler joined the board of the Cord Corporation, now known as the Vultee Aircraft Division of the Aviation Manufacturing Corporation. Under his management there were great advances in airplane designing and manufacturing, and Vultee grew. In 1941 Girdler tried to arrange a merger with Consolidated Aircraft Corporation, but was unsuccessful. Finally at the end of 1941 Vultee bought Consolidated, producers of long-range flying boats and four-engine bombers. (The merger was concluded in March 1943.) Girdler arrived in San Diego, California in January 1942 to take charge of Consolidated. He was changing careers at the age of sixty-five.

The veteran steel man is now chairman of the board and chief executive officer of both Consolidated and Vultee, while still retaining the chairmanship and policy direction of Republic. His is one of the top production assignments of the War: with interests extending from coast to coast, his companies' assets at the end of 1941 stood at nearly $600,000,000. Besides, through Aviation Corporation, he has a potent influence on New York Shipbuilding, on the new Liquid-Cooled Engine Division, on the American Propeller Corporation, on American Central Manufacturing Corporation, and other vital enterprises. He refuses any compensation beyond what he had been getting from Republic Steel, however, and Republic still continues to pay his salary of $275,000 a year.

And that Girdler has given value for that $275,000 a year is denied by no one. His plants have turned out some of the most effective planes to date—the PBY flying boat and the B-24 Liberator bomber. In 1942 Consolidated Vultee delivered around 53,000,000 pounds of planes, including spares. In 1943 this figure was multiplied almost two and one-half times—and Girdler accounts for this by "a steady increase of operation efficiency." At the Army Ordnance Association's annual dinner in New York City on January 19, 1944 Girdler, chairman of the Army Ordnance Association's Endowment Committee, received the Rice Gold Medal for distinguished ordnance service. In March 1944 *Time* Magazine announced that "for the year 1943 (excluding Vultee profits before the two companies merged last March), Board Chairman Girdler reported profits of $19,268,000, compared to $7,004,000 for both companies for the entire year 1942"—all this, Girdler pointed out, despite reductions of $171,000,000 in the price of planes as well as the relegating of $80,000,000 out of profits into a special renegotiation reserve.

In March Girdler addressed the St. Louis Chamber of Commerce, at which time he predicted that at the end of the War there would be an immediate need for 12,000,000 new automobiles in the United States and for years after production would have to be maintained at about 6,500,000 units annually. He also called for a three-point program to assure resumption of peacetime production without undue dislocation of basic economic groups; removal of all unnecessary Governmental restrictions when peace is restored; adoption of sound measures for contract cancellation and disposal of surplus war stocks; and the enactment of sound tax legislation.

In June Girdler warned against attempts to hold over wartime restrictions on industry to meet the conversion crisis. Speaking before the Cleveland Chamber of Commerce, he declared that there is real danger these restrictions will be required later to meet other crises, and "on and on into perpetuity." Referring to the post-War outlook for labor relations, he remarked that the growth of labor organizations in itself is not disturbing. "Collective bargaining is necessary in modern industry . . . but collective bargaining by government edict at the point of a bayonet ceases to be collective bargaining. It ceases to be democracy." Later in the year Girdler protested to William H. Davis [44], WLB chairman, over the wage award in the steel case: "In April 1941 steel prices were frozen at the 1939 level. Since that time the industry has absorbed two general wage increases without any price increase." A third increase, Girdler asserted, would endanger Republic's financial position.

Girdler cannot forget, however, how he has been attacked and criticized by labor and liberals. "I know I have been vilified not because I was Tom Girdler," he says, "but because I was a symbol of management, conspicuous because I dared to resist something I still believe should be resisted for the sake of my country." When government, labor, or any other force interferes with the rights of

GIRDLER, TOM M.—*Continued*

management he believes that it should be resisted, because it is management that is responsible for the great industries on which modern society is dependent. "Today," he says, "as a manager my right to work is seriously hampered . . . a terribly *disorganizing* influence is at work at the base of all industry in America. The boss is no longer boss." Girdler looks back nostalgically to his father's day, when a company had so few employees that a manager could know all his men and all their problems. "The whole relationship between my father and the mill men was marked by dignity, even though he was pretty much a tyrant. . . . He had labor troubles, of course; not unlike the problems of today except that father didn't have unions to contend with nor did the men. . . . There was something feudal in the relationship, something perhaps not to be defended on the Fourth of July. Nevertheless, I was brought up by a father who believed that the troubles of the men who worked for him were his troubles."

Says Benjamin Appel in the *Saturday Review of Literature*: "*Boot Straps* . . . is one of the most important works of this season, not so much as a literary job, although it is good interesting reading, but as a challenging blueprint, a candid document to be read and thought about as that other blueprint and document *Mein Kampf* was read and thought about. I am not saying that Girdler is a Fascist. I am saying that he is not a democrat." W. M. Houghton, the New York *Herald Tribune* critic wrote: "While Mr. Girdler is richly deserving of his day in court in the matter of this conflict (the steel strike) the best part of the book is that which is more intimately autobiographical."

In his sixties, the author of this "challenging blueprint" is as energetic and forceful as ever. According to a New York *Sun* interviewer, he "looks and acts like Bobby Clark of the stage and screen and he'd be even more like him if he wore dark glasses and flipped an acrobatic cigar. He has quick and jumpy movements, he is generally affable, but has top-sergeant toughness when he needs it." He is five feet eight inches tall, weighs 180 pounds, and is, he told one interviewer, "bald as hell." ("If I cuss a lot, it's possibly because I come from a long line of seagoing ancestors," he says.) He loves the outdoors, is fond of horses and dogs, and his newest passion is flying.

Early in his career Girdler was married to Mary Elizabeth Hayes, a girl from his home town. They had four children. Since her death in 1917 Girdler has been married three times. He is a member of clubs in New York City, Pittsburgh, and Sewickley, Pennsylvania.

References

C S Mon p13 O 30 '43
Fortune 12:76-84 D '35 por; 17:73 Mr '38 por; 26:88-93+ S '42 il pors
N Y Sun p1+ Ja 20 '42 por
Nation 144:668-9; 670-1 Je 12 '37
Newsweek 12:11 Ag 22 '38 por
R of Rs 95:30-1 Je '37 il pors
Sat R Lit 26:48+ D 4 '43

Girdler, T. M. Boot Straps 1943
Who's Who in America 1944-45

GISH, DOROTHY Mar. 11, 1898- Actress
GISH, LILLIAN Oct. 14, 1896- Actress

The names of Lillian and Dorothy Gish will always be associated with the "golden silent days of the motion pictures" although they began their careers on the stage, returned to the stage after the passing of the silent films, and are now appearing in Hollywood productions. In their early film careers they appeared separately or together in such history-making motion pictures as *The Birth of a Nation* (1915), *Hearts of the World* (1918), *Way Down East* (1920), *Orphans of the Storm* (1922), and *Romola* (1924).

Although a competent actress Dorothy never received the plaudits given to Lillian, who known in those days as the "First Lady of the Screen." Lillian's talent and beauty not only placed her among "the true immortals of the screen," but caused the literati to become lyrical. The caustic-tongued critic George Jean Nathan wrote: "The smile of the Gish girl is a bit of happiness trembling on a bed of death; the tears of the Gish girl . . . are the tears that Johann Strauss wrote in the rosemary of his waltzes. . . . Her particular genius lies in making the definite, charmingly indefinite." Joseph Hergesheimer compared her beauty to the "fragrant April moon of men's hopes," her eyes to "butterflies fluttering softly to their object." Albert Bigelow Paine in his book-length biography, *Life and Lillian Gish* (1932), said that Miss Gish had "never played a part as lovely as herself . . . as her own spirit." The great of her own profession extolled her histrionic ability and native intelligence: John Barrymore, after seeing her a second time in the film, *Way Down East,* described Miss Gish's performance "the most superlatively exquisite and poignantly enchaining thing" he had ever seen. The judgment of David Wark Griffith, under whose direction she rose to her cinema heights, was: "She is not only the best actress in her profession, but she has the best mind of any woman I have ever met."

Lillian Diana and Dorothy Gish are the daughters of James Lee and Mary Robinson (McConnell) Gish, both of whom came from old American stock. Mr. Gish, a traveling salesman from Pennsylvania, met his future wife in her native Urbana, Ohio. "Pretty May McConnell," as she was called, came from a family who boasted of an Ohio State Senator, President Zachary Taylor, and a poetess. Lillian was born October 14, 1896 in Springfield, Ohio, where her father was employed by a wholesale grocery house. The neighbors whispered that fame and fortune awaited the new baby—she had been born with a caul. Alfred Bigelow Paine gives Dorothy's birthplace as Dayton, Ohio, to which James Gish had moved his family after he had established a small confectionery there. A year and a half younger than Lillian, Dorothy was born March 11, 1898.

"The world was not kind to James Gish," is Paine's explanation of Gish's failure to provide for his family. After failing twice in the confectionery business, Gish moved his wife and two small daughters to New York City, finally deserting them. Before this, in order to help meet expenses, they had rented out two rooms of their West 39th Street apartment and Mrs. Gish had taken a part-time job. One day the furniture, which had been bought on the installment plan, was removed from the home, for Gish had failed to make the payments. Things looked rather desperate until one of the roomers, an actress, came in from a round of theatrical offices and announced that she could get a good part in an *East Lynne* road company if she were allowed to take Dorothy along to play the part of Little Willie. The inducements were a weekly salary of $15 for Dorothy, to be paid in advance, and a part for Lillian in another road company. Mrs. Gish, at first shocked by the idea of her little six- and four-year-old girls going away with strangers, finally consented.

Lillian made her stage debut in Risingsun, Ohio, in a barn which had been converted into a theatre; the play and time—*Convict Stripes,* 1902. Recalling her opening night some years later, Lillian Gish said, "The audience gave me a marvelous ovation," due, however, to her failure to follow stage instructions. The big scene of the play was the hero's rescue of Lillian from a stone quarry one second before a dynamite explosion. Lillian had been told to stay behind the wings while the hero in a daring leap with the aid of a rope picked up her dummy. Although she had also been told that there would be a loud noise in the scene, Lillian was unprepared for the explosion—she ran screaming to the footlights. The Risingsun audience was loud in its approval.

Lillian then played in other road melodramas, which were so popular in pre-motion picture days. There was one brief but memorable New York engagement, when she appeared in a bit part with Sarah Bernhardt. In order to be with her children, Mrs. Gish, too, went on the stage. "When a play required one child," says Lillian Gish, "I traveled alone, and mother and Dorothy would go with another company. Usually I was put in care of some older woman in the company, who looked out for me, and saw that I studied as time permitted. We seldom stayed over night in any town, and I can remember that on numerous occasions I slept on a folded coat on the telegraph desk in railroad stations. I was grown before I saw a Pullman car. . . . So we traveled through the East, the South, and sometimes as far West as Denver. One year was like another, except for those good years when we could all be together."

It was while Dorothy, Lillian, and Mrs. Gish were on tour in *The Little Red Schoolhouse,* by Hal Reid, the father of Wallace Reid, of the silent films, that they met Mary Pickford. The company had reached Toronto and needed another child. A little girl with lovely golden curls, who had acted with the local stock company, was sent for. In response to the summons, Mrs. Smith and Gladys Mary Smith arrived. The Smiths, who later took the name of Pickford, joined the company, and when the play closed in New York the two families lived together there through the summer. "It

LILLIAN GISH

was a wonderful thing," said Lillian Gish, "for Dorothy and me to have three other children [Miss Pickford's sister Lottie and brother Jack were with them] to associate with." (The friendship between the stars has continued through the years. Lillian, when acting in Hollywood films in 1943, was a guest at Pickfair.) During that summer in New York Mrs. Gish, who had learned candy-making from her husband, opened a pop-corn and candy stand in the Fort George amusement park near the north tip of Manhattan. The three stars-to-be thought it fun to help Mrs. Gish by wrapping and selling the sweet wares, and there were other things to enjoy—among them, ice-cream cones, which they called "mashed potatoes," and rides on the merry-go-round.

While the years on the stage had carried the family through an emergency, Mrs. Gish still looked forward to establishing a home for her children. That opportunity came when a brother in St. Louis died, leaving a widow. With her sister-in-law, Mrs. Gish opened a confectionery in East St. Louis, where the children went to school (Lillian to the Ursuline Academy) and helped in the store when business was brisk. But Mrs. Gish's hopes for a home there were not yet to be realized. A motion-picture theatre adjoining her candy shop was destroyed by fire—and the shop with it.

In the two years which followed, the girls lived with their Aunt Emily in Massillon, Ohio, where they went to school, while their mother worked in Springfield, about a hundred miles distant. It was during this time that a letter from their father's brother in Shawnee, Oklahoma, told that James Gish was gravely ill. Fourteen-year-old Lillian made the journey alone to Oklahoma, where she remained a year, attending school and working after school in a doctor's office. Upon her return to her Ohio relatives another year of school followed before James Gish's death and other circumstances made Mrs. Gish decide to take her daughters back to New York—and the stage.

(Continued next page)

A. L. Whitey Schafer

DOROTHY GISH

Ten years earlier, in 1903, William J. Dean had directed Dorothy in the part of Little Willie in *East Lynne*. In the meantime, Dean had become David Belasco's assistant, and it was through him that Lillian was engaged for the part of Morganie the fairy in Belasco's forthcoming production of *The Good Little Devil* (1913), the play in which Mary Pickford and Ernest Truex were starred. The name of Mary Pickford was not familiar to Lillian and Dorothy, for they had not learned that their childhood playmate, Gladys Smith, had changed her name to Pickford. Later, upon learning her identity and that she was working at the Biograph motion-picture studio in East 14th Street, Dorothy and Lillian visited her there. It was Miss Pickford who introduced the Misses Gish to David Wark Griffith, who even then was considered the master director of the new art. Their first work before the camera was as extras—spectators in a theatre audience. Quickly they graduated from extra-parts to roles—*The Unseen Enemy* (1912) was the motion picture in which Lillian and Dorothy made their screen debuts. As Griffith could not tell them apart, he had Lillian wear a blue ribbon in her hair, and Dorothy a red one. Then, when he wanted to direct them he called for red or blue to come into the scene or to exit, to laugh or to cry. They got in three days and an extra night on their first picture—$18 each. That was riches!

In the fall, as was his custom, Griffith took his company to California for the winter months, but Lillian remained in New York to rehearse for her stage role in the Belasco production. *The Good Little Devil,* after an out-of-town tryout, opened in New York, but again a mishap in "stage business" not only spoiled her scene but also caused a physical injury which so impaired her health that the doctor advised her to go to a milder climate. Griffith, in California, offered her and Dorothy places in his company at the princely salaries of $50 a week. The hard days were over.

California sunshine, fresh air, and exercise (all films were made out of doors in pre-Klieg light days) brought quick recovery to Lillian. In their first year with Griffith, both Dorothy and Lillian worked in many pictures. At that time no picture exceeded one reel in length, and as many as three pictures were made in a week. While the films had little artistic merit, they taught the sisters much about acting before the camera and made their faces and names known to the public.

The first important picture in which Lillian Gish appeared was *The Mothering Heart,* noteworthy because it was two reels long and cost $1,800. The comment of one critic was significant: "Her lack of so-called acting is the secret of her success." There were many other pictures before Lillian Gish and the lowly "movies" were recognized by the metropolitan press reviewers as an artist and an art, respectively. This recognition came with Griffith's *The Birth of a Nation,* the first motion picture to command $2 for orchestra seats and play a long run on Broadway. The artistic success of that motion picture is film history. The acclaim won by Miss Gish as Elsie Stoneman came as a surprise to both her and Griffith. At the time of the casting, Lilliam Gish was not the star of Griffith's players. The star was Blanche Sweet, who, it is reported, might have played opposite Henry Walthall (she as the Northern girl Elsie, he as the Southern Little Colonel) had she not been taller than the actor. Griffith's comment on the honors critics heaped upon Miss Gish was: "I merely thought she could play it. . . . I did not realize she would make anything special of it though, of course, by that time, I knew she would do it her own way."

In *Hearts of the World* (1918), "a First World War picture, made in France at the suggestion of Lloyd George and others, Griffith cast Lillian as a Belgian girl, captured and cruelly treated by the Germans, and Dorothy as the Little Disturber, a strolling singer, who "with a lute under her arm, romped through the war scenes with a jaunty swagger." Bobby Harron was the hero-lover of the story, but in real life it has been reported that he loved Dorothy until his death (he accidently shot himself). During the making of the picture the Misses Gish often played scenes close to the front lines of the battlefields. Lillian afterwards attributed her mother's death to the shock of air raids and similar hazards they all had experienced while making the picture.

Under the Griffith banner, Lillian Gish's distinguished work in the silent films continued to add to her prestige. The pinnacle of her successful roles, in the opinion of many critics, was that of the twelve-year-old child in *Broken Blossoms* (1919), the screen adaptation of Thomas Burke's "The Chink and the Child," the short story published in his collection, *Limehouse Nights.* The press was unanimous in its praise. "What impressed us all," said one reviewer, "was that all of her reactions were those of a child. Her wild terror in the closet scene, the finest example of emotional hysteria in the history of the screen, was the terror of a child." Morris Gest, the late producer, who saw it at a private showing, "went quite mad" over it. "Greatest picture the world has ever seen—charge what you please for it," he told Griffith. Orchestra seats were priced as high as three dollars. In *The Orphans of the Storm* (1922) Lillian and Dorothy Gish acted in the last picture they made under Griffith's direction. Although Lillian's salary had increased from $50 to $1,000 a week, (Dorothy's salary was lower) Griffith could not afford as an independent producer to pay them salaries to which their world-wide celebrity entitled them.

Before the Misses Gish left Griffith's company, however, Lillian displayed her versatility by taking over the direction of Dorothy in a picture entitled *Remodeling Her Husband* (1920). It had become necessary for Griffith to go to Florida and Dorothy's contract called for one more picture. Lillian, who believed no picture had brought out Dorothy's sweetness and comic sense, undertook the work of directing. In Griffith's opinion the picture was the best Dorothy had ever made. It was also a financial success, having cost $58,000 and netting $160,000.

In 1922 Lillian Gish signed a contract with the Tiffany Company at a salary of $1,250 a week and an added fifteen per cent of the pictures' earnings above a certain amount. In speaking of her choice of *The White Sister* (1923) as her first picture, Lillian Gish said: "Ever since my winter at the Ursuline School in St. Louis, I had thought of the nuns as earnest women, hard-working and kindly. There had been a time when I fancied I might have a vocation for the veil. . . . I have regretted, sometimes, that I did not follow that early inclination." (Miss Gish is of the Episcopalian faith and she has never been married.) Ronald Colman '43 was chosen for the lead opposite the star, his first motion-picture engagement. *The White Sister* was made in Italy. Although it was well received, reviewers did not consider it so good as some of Miss Gish's earlier roles—"a good deal of her personality was lost in the standardized costume of a nun." In 1924 she returned to Italy to play the title role in *Romola*, George Eliot's novel of Renaissance Italy. Dorothy Gish played the part of Tessa with "her usual skill." Dorothy's description, "a beautiful picture but an awfully dull one," echoed the press comments. "We had been so entranced with photographing the architecture and tapestries that we completely forgot the story."

There had been rumors that Lillian Gish was unhappy in the Tiffany Company; in January 1925 Charles H. Duell, president of Tiffany, brought suit against Miss Gish to prevent her acting under direction other than his. The suit made front page headlines when James Rennie, Dorothy's husband, was arrested by Duell on the charge of threatening him if he continued his suit against Lillian. Later Rennie was cleared of the charge. In May the Court dismissed the case against Miss Gish, who signed with Metro-Goldwyn-Mayer shortly afterwards.

La Bohème (1926), her first picture under her new contract, was another triumph for the star. Among the films which followed, *The Scarlet Letter* (1926) was the most outstanding. "She is not Hawthorne's Hester Prynne,"

said the Evening *Sun* reviewer, "but she is yours and mine."

With the arrival of the sound track on motion-picture reels, Lillian Gish, after making *One Romantic Night* (1930), a "talkie" which failed to register her voice effectively, returned to the stage as Helena in Chekhov's *Uncle Vanya* (1930). Charles Darnton in the New York *Times* wrote: "She was so luminous that the others faded into the background. . . . Try as you may, you cannot get her out of your eye. Just what this rare thing is I hesitate to say. But a first-nighter did say it for me, 'She is sublime.' " Joseph Wood Krutch, critic for the *Nation,* who had always regarded the actress as an enigma, said that after her performance in *Uncle Vanya* he was no more sure than he was in the days when she was the particular star of the Great Griffith—whether she had "real talents or merely certain odd deficiencies which a skillful director can utilize after the fashion of the marionette master." Her *Camille* (1932) Stark Young of the *New Republic* found to be "lovely in a sort of private essence," but he added that it did not have the technical skill behind it to give it the variation and shading needed. On the other hand, her performance in the first act "had really a kind of truth, muted in its eloquence, which made the rest of the play seem silly and false. . . . In her last scene she was "only a dying child."

In Sean O'Casey's *Within the Gates* (1934), Miss Gish, who had hitherto been cast only in sympathetic roles, played the part of the Young Whore. This new facet to the Gish characterizations again sent the critics into most laudatory superlatives. It was indeed a new Lillian Gish—saucy, pert, and gay. In 1936 she played Ophelia in Guthrie McClintic's '43 production of *Hamlet* with John Gielgud; *The Star Wagon* (1937) gave her her longest Broadway run; in the Chicago company of *Life With Father* (1941) she made a record run of sixty-six weeks outlasting any other star or play in Chicago theatrical history. The Theatre Guild production of *Mr. Sycamore* (1942), an imaginative tree fable adapted to the stage by Ketti Frings, brought Miss Gish back to Broadway. Although the play did not live up to the possibilities of its theme, the critics praised the actress. Brooks Atkinson wrote: "She can penetrate a character with extraordinary insight. There is nothing spectacular about her acting. . . . But every moment is filled with the fine integrity of a human character."

Miss Gish's return to motion pictures in 1943 was made in two minor roles, the Norwegian patriot in *The Commandos Strike at Dawn* and the mother in *The Top Man.* On June 21, 1944 a Hollywood sheet reported the return of the Great Gish under the direction of the old master, David Wark Griffith. Miss Gish will play the ax-murderess role she created in the play, *Nine Pine Street,* the story of Lizzie Borden. It is to be one of the first films of the Preston Sturges '41 producing unit.

In October 1944 the star signed an optional five-year contract calling for two pictures a year with Paramount. Her first Paramount picture, *Miss Susie Slagle's,* the Augusta Tucker novel, went before the cameras in October with Miss Gish in the title role, reported

GISH, DOROTHY, and GISH, LILLIAN
—*Continued*

to be her most important film part since her return to Hollywood. Upon the completion of this picture Miss Gish will begin rehearsals in Arthur Hopkins' Broadway presentation of *The Magnificent Yankee*, the biography of Justice Oliver Wendell Holmes. Between stage and film engagements since 1939 the actress has been writing *Silver Glory*, her history of Hollywood. The 1943-1944 season saw her touring the country for the lecture platform.

Lillian Gish is a slender woman; she is five feet six inches tall, and weighs 112 pounds. She has small feet, narrow shoulders, and long limbs, and her eyes are blue, her hair blond. Her abstinence from cigarets and liquor, observed Joseph Hergesheimer, is "so exactly right for her quaint rigidity of bearing." In speaking of her reserved manner, Miss Gish once said herself, "When I go to a party—it stops being a party. On the other hand, Dorothy *is* the party." Lillian reads omnivorously. Her biographer Paine says she is without envy or malice. Miss Gish, who has been a pacifist since her days near the European battlefields, was a member of the America First Committee and in the 1944 Presidential election she was a member of the Hollywood Committee for Dewey '44.

The story of Dorothy's and Lillian's first public appearance might be considered prophetic of the pattern Dorothy's life was to take as the younger sister of a famous star. When Lillian was five she was invited to "speak a piece" at a church entertainment. Dorothy heard the piece rehearsed so many times that when the big night arrived, she interrupted the applause for Lillian by calling out from her first-row seat, "I know a piece, too." The three-year-old Dorothy was then invited to the stage where she repeated the piece—an anti-climax for Lillian. That was probably the only time Dorothy topped Lillian. Not only are the sisters unusually devoted but their different personalities preclude rivalry for the same roles. In contrast to Lillian's reserve and studiousness, Dorothy is lively and outspoken—"a bright flag flying in the breeze." In comparing their work, Griffith said that Dorothy was quicker to get the director's idea but was satisfied with less than the ideal in her work, while Lillian, following more slowly, was satisfied with nothing less than perfection.

Dorothy's first starring pictures were *The Mountain Rat* (1914), a Western in which she played the part of a dance-hall girl, and *The Mysterious Shot* (1914), in which she co-starred with Jack Pickford. Her favorite role is that of the Little Disturber in *Hearts of the World* (1918). After leaving Griffith, Dorothy signed with Paramount, the company for whom in 1944 she played Maud Skinner in *Our Hearts Were Young and Gay* and which is now negotiating with her for a three-picture-a-year contract. Her last film in America, during her silent picture career, was *Clothes Make the Pirate* (1925). In England she made *Nell Gwyn* (1926) and *Madame Pompadour* (1927) for Herbert Wilcox, and appeared in her first talking picture, *Wolves,* with Charles Laughton.

In 1928 she returned to the stage in *Young Love*, which after a Broadway run pleased London audiences. Her most successful roles on the stage have been Maria in *The Inspector General* (1930), Leo in *Getting Married* (1931), Ellen Smith in *By Your Leave* (1934), Emily Dickinson in *Brittle Heaven* (1934), and Mrs. Howard in *Missouri Legend* (1938). With Louis Calhern, Dorothy headed the road company of *Life With Father* at the same time that Lillian was heading the Chicago company of the play. *The Great Big Doorstep* (1942) gave Dorothy Gish favorable reviews but failed to win the public. Of Miss Gish, the New York *Times* said: "She is excellent, with both a wry humor and a tenderness." Since 1924 she had made frequent radio appearances—her latest work was in *Redemption* on NBC's sustaining hour, *Arthur Hopkins Presents*.

In 1920 Dorothy Gish was married to James Rennie, the actor who played opposite her in *Remodeling Her Husband*. (The Rennies are now divorced.) She is five feet four and one-half inches tall, weighs 114 pounds and has gray eyes and blond hair. Like her sister, she is fond of books. Marcel Proust is her favorite author. As a Roosevelt '42 supporter, Miss Gish was one of the delegates representing the Independent Voters Committee of Arts and Sciences who called upon the President at the White House during the 1944 Presidential campaign.

References

Ladies' H J 42:19+ S '25 por
N Y Times II p3 O 24 '43
International Motion Picture Almanac 1943-44
Paine, A. B. Life and Lillian Gish 1932
Who's Who in America 1944-45
Who's Who in the Theatre 1939

GOLDEN, JOHN   June 27, 1874-   Producer; playwright; composer.

Address: b. 246 W. 44th St., New York City; h. Bayside, Long Island, N.Y.

In his time he has been bricklayer, law student, chemist, actor, song writer, playwright, and producer, but never, from the time he was a boy giving "pin shows," has John Golden given up the pursuit of his main interest—the theatre. Described as voluble and volatile, with "plenty of buckle and bounce," Golden in his twenty-odd years as a producer has presented seventy-one plays, thirty-three of which have been Broadway hits. He has written hundreds of songs, librettos for twelve musical shows, and has authored and collaborated on a number of dramatic plays.

John Golden was born June 27, 1874, in New York City. He spent his youth in Wauseon, Ohio, where his father Joseph Golden was not only a businessman but also a clarinet player in the local band. His mother, Amelia (Tyreler) Golden, sang in the village choir. In an *American Magazine* article, Golden, in speaking of his mother, said: "She was beautiful, and she had the refinement that goes to make a lady. She was a wonderful singer and taught me to appreciate good music." The musical education of the man who was later to have to his credit several hundred published songs, including such hits as *Poor Butterfly* and *Goodbye, Girls, I'm Through,* consisted of "six lessons on the fiddle, at twenty-five cents a lesson."

When Golden came to New York to make his own way at fourteen, his ambitions were directed toward architecture, and they inspired him to work as office boy for a firm of builders and contractors. One of his employers told him that the real way to learn to be an architect was to begin by laying bricks, and so young Golden worked eight months as a bricklayer. He says, however: "All the time while I was talking of being an architect, I was thinking of the theatre"— thinking and writing rhymes which later were to earn him enough money to stake his first Broadway play. When a letter to a theatrical manager obtained for him a part as a "super" (an extra) in a Broadway play, Golden finally deserted architecture.

While a "super" he went on writing rhymes, occasionally selling one to a newspaper for three or four dollars. Soon he discovered that if he set the rhymes to music he could get ten dollars for them from someone who would sing the song on the stage. And so he became a song writer. In a dramatic club (a little company of amateurs playing in a loft in Fourteenth Street) Golden obtained experience in acting dramatic roles, and in directing and producing plays. But since earning a little as a "super" and not much more as a song writer made for very "rough sledding," Golden decided to study law, and enrolled in the New York University Law School. "Three days later one of the Psi Upsilon boys found that I could act," says Golden, "and suggested that I form a dramatic club among the students. We did; and the club is still in existence." But the dramatic club ended his legal career. A play produced by the club ran a week, earning for Golden (whose share was fifty per cent of the profits) several hundred dollars. The money meant only one thing to him—the opportunity to return to the theatrical world in quest of a job and this time in prosperous looking "raiment."

Returning to Broadway, he secured his first speaking part on the professional stage. For two or three years he played small parts, but there were "long, bare spots," and during one of these he found a job selling chewing gum. "The chewing gum experience," says Golden, "led to my meeting a man who had more effect on the course of my life than anyone else. . . . His name was Oakes, and he was president of the Oakes Manufacturing Company, which made chemicals." Golden was twenty-one years old when he accepted a position as salesman with Oakes. Two years after he joined the company he was made president and general manager.

Golden remained with the company thirteen years. "But during all of that time," he says, "I never let up on my work for the theatre. . . . I wrote seven plays, all of which were successfully produced." One of them, *The Candy Shop* (1909), was played by stock companies for twenty years, earning a yearly income in royalties for its author. When he entered the business world Golden promised

JOHN GOLDEN

Phyfe

himself that when he had obtained an assured income he would devote himself to the thing he wanted to do. He reached that position when he was thirty-four and, returning to the theatre world, he wrote plays, vaudeville sketches and songs. Four of the Hippodrome shows, including lyrics, were authored by Golden. They were *Hip Hip Hooray* (1915); *The Big Show* (1916); *Cheer Up* (1917); and *Everything* (1918). Golden's song hit, *Poor Butterfly,* was introduced in one of these Hippodrome shows. Another of his successful songs, *Goodbye, Girls, I'm Through,* was sung for the first time in Charles Dillingham's production of *Chin-Chin,* in which Montgomery and Stone were starred. The lyric, written by Golden in less than half an hour during a *Chin-Chin* rehearsal to fill in a stage wait caused by costume changing, earned thousands of dollars for him. A royalty check for $3,400 from the song was, in fact, the initial stake for his first venture as an independent Broadway producer. *Turn to the Right* (1916) was the play, and it in turn netted for Golden hundreds of thousands of dollars. The play, a comedy, was written by Winchell Smith from a story told to him and Golden by Jack Hazzard. Golden and Smith had been on their way to Nantucket to do a benefit show for a golf club. The trip promised to be long and tiresome, and when Hazzard asked to accompany them Golden told him, "You can go with us as far as you can entertain us. But just as soon as you cease to be amusing, you're dropped off." The plot of *Turn to the Right* earned Hazzard's fare to Nantucket.

Winchell Smith and Golden were successful in their theatrical productions for many years. Golden on one occasion said: "Winchell Smith knows more about the theatre than any other living man. . . . And I believe I know something about the theatre myself." *Three Wise Fools* (1918), *Lightnin'* (1918), and *The First Year* (1920) were the most

GOLDEN, JOHN—*Continued*

successful of the comedies presented by Golden with Winchell Smith employed either as director or play doctor (sometimes in both capacities). On one show, however, Golden's judgment proved to be better than Smith's. From the beginning Smith had "hated *Three Wise Fools*." After its opening the play gave every sign of failure until the theatre was filled with cut-rate tickets. "Once we got audiences coming," says Golden, "the play was a great success and ran at the Criterion Theatre into two seasons." Then Golden discovered a vaudeville sketch which he thought had the makings of a Broadway play. Winchell Smith came in as a collaborator with its author, Frank Bacon, a veteran actor who had played in the sketch through the hinterlands for a score or more years. The result of the collaboration was called *Lightnin'*. It proved to be Golden's most successful production, holding the record for the longest run on Broadway (1,291 performances) until *Abie's Irish Rose* topped it.

Frank Craven wrote and starred in *The First Year*, a little "homespun comedy" which established itself "as the best" of the season, "if not the best ever written by an American." The New York *Times* pronounced the play "the most enjoyable comedy of the year," while Burns Mantle placed it among the ten best plays of the 1920-1921 season. *Current Opinion* thought that it "owed its buoyancy not only to the authorship and acting of Frank Craven, but also to the craftsmanship of Winchell Smith as director and John Golden as producer."

At Golden's suggestion, Austin Strong, author of *Three Wise Fools*, developed from a one-act melodrama of the Parisian underworld a full-length play called *Seventh Heaven*. Although partnership in the production was offered to Winchell Smith and other theatre men, no one had sufficient faith in *Seventh Heaven* to join Golden financially in its production. However, in May 1922 when he presented the play with Helen Menken, the star and the producer received "vociferous applause from the metropolitan critics," and the play itself was called a "new melodrama." "The newness of the play," wrote *Current Opinion*, "lies in the subtle and skillful treatment of a theme formulated by one of the characters: 'It is what is inside you—the idea—that makes you what you are.'" Golden's faith in *Seventh Heaven* was justified when the play achieved a two-year run on Broadway. *The Wisdom Tooth* by Marc Connelly, produced by Golden with Smith's cooperation again, received a favorable press and was listed by Burns Mantle as one of the ten best plays of the 1925-1926 season. Opening in February 1926, it ran for the season, through June of that year.

Another association of long standing which has proved to be a profitable one for Golden is that with Rachel Crothers. His production of Miss Crothers' *Let Us Be Gay* made the Burns Mantle list of best plays for the 1928-1929 season. Other plays by that distinguished playwright with the "John Golden presents" label are *As Husbands Go* (1931), *When Ladies Meet* (1932), and *Susan and God* (1937). The *Nation's* reviewer, Joseph

Wood Krutch, thought *When Ladies Meet* a "sentimental comedy." "However," added the reviewer, "it becomes my duty to report three things: first, that most of the critics liked it very much; second, that the general public seems to agree so thoroughly that the play promises to be the first large financial success of the dramatic season; third, that it is unusually well-performed." The *Theatre Arts Monthly* found *When Ladies Meet* "a warm and entertaining play peopled with well-drawn characters." (Walter Abel, Spring Byington, Selena Royle, and Frieda Inescort were in the cast.) But that same magazine's opinion of *Susan and God* was that it was not the "best of the good and gracious plays that Rachel Crothers and John Golden have added to the theatre's store, although, at the moment, aided by Gertrude Lawrence's [40] inspired playing, it seems to be." *Susan and God* nevertheless made the *Catholic World* reviewer feel like cheering and in his opinion offered the public a delightful evening. In 1939 Golden presented Gertrude Lawrence again in Samson Raphaelson's *Skylark*. *Time* Magazine called it a drawing-room comedy with "monogrammed wisecracks," and the *Nation* thought it "a sleazy affair" in which Miss Lawrence's performance was nothing more "than a mere bag of tricks." Despite this adverse criticism the play ran for 256 performances.

On February 12, 1941 Golden presented Rose Franken's *Claudia* to Broadway. The comedy played two long Broadway engagements, and with several companies touring the road, Golden reported the box office receipts on the play had exceeded $3,000,000. (The motion-picture rights, moreover, were sold to David O. Selznick [41] for $137,000.) *Three Is a Family*, a discreetly ribald and rib-tickling domestic farce by Phoebe and Henry Ephron came to Broadway under the Golden banner on May 5, 1943. Burton Rascoe of the New York *World-Telegram* wrote in his review that "the play is right out of the top drawer of the old reliable protector and champion of the sturdy, commonplace American home, John Golden." Although many of the metropolitan newspaper critics were not sure about its comedy value, it ran fourteen months, the seventh Golden play to achieve a year's run on Broadway. His production of the George Seaton comedy *But Not Goodbye* (1944) won favor on its road tryout but failed to capture the plaudits of New York critics. *Laughing Water*, the Phoebe and Henry Ephron comedy which opened on the road in November 1944, was considered too fragile for box office competition, and it was withdrawn for revision.

One of the few Broadway producers to accumulate a substantial fortune, Golden has done so by producing "clean" plays—never has he found it necessary to keep pace with the increasingly off-color plays presented by many producers. "Clean plays have been my crown and my cross," says Golden, "my punishment and my reward—my blessing and my curse. . . . They brought me the sneers of the sophisticates, the shy gibes and veiled innuendos of erudite critics. . . . I guess I've a sneaking idea that I wouldn't enjoy putting on a play that my mother could not sit through." Regarding the question of what type of play the public wants during war times, Golden, who has produced no plays about the War since Pearl Harbor, says: "People don't want the War in their theatrical entertainment. They want escape. Also, the best war plays are written after perspective comes, not during the heat of conflict."

"Although the Golden record bulks largest as a song writer of lyrics and of musical comedy librettos (he was writing songs for the late Marie Dressler as far back as her Koster and Bial days, and did the book for her first Broadway play, *Miss Print*) he has written a number of dramatic plays on his own and acted as a collaborator on others." Burns Mantle says: "John Golden has been fairly secretive about his activities as a playwright. He has worked on many scripts and with dozens of authors but has been entirely satisfied to permit the author to have the credit for whatever happened to the idea after it had been put into work at the Golden play factory. On one or two scripts, however, the authors themselves have insisted upon sharing the credit or dividing the blame. With Kenyon Nicholson, Golden wrote the comedy *Eva the Fifth,* which had a run of sixty-three performances in 1928. He wrote *After Tomorrow* with Hugh Stange, and this comedy ran seventy-seven times in 1931. It is not written in the record that the producer was the co-author of a comedy Dan Jarrett wrote called *Salt Water,* which Frank Craven played for eighty-three performances in 1929, but it so stands in the Golden files. He was also part author of *A Divine Drudge,* written with Vicki Baum and produced in 1933." Golden refers to the Vicki Baum play as his "favorite failure." His latest collaboration, *Another Heaven,* written with the late Bide Dudley, was given a tryout production in Toronto in August 1943. *Variety* reported that it lacked clarity and would need "plenty of revision," although there was drama, suspense, and a fine idea in the play. Nothing has been done with it, however, since the death of Dudley in January 1944.

Concerning his playwriting, Golden has said: "My job of producing plays for the American stage is not the hardest job in the world. It is only the second hardest. The hardest job is the one I have taken a shot at from time to time, and that is writing plays for the American stage. . . . In all the jobs of modern industry man is able to measure the value of what he is doing step by step as he does it. There are gauges and tests and statistical analyses to go by at every point. But in the theatre you're in the dark." As a producer he believes the author knows better than any director could possibly know just how a play should be staged and therefore he insists, whenever it is possible, that the author direct his own play. Elmer Rice '43, Rachel Crothers, Rose Franken '41, and the Ephrons have proved that Golden's idea is a good one, for they have directed their own plays and have been very successful at the job.

During the First World War Golden earned the rank of major in the United States Army by organizing a free-ticket service for men of the armed forces. In 1941, during the Second World War, he and Mrs. Julius Ochs Adler were named co-chairmen of the New York Defense Recreation Committee, whose object is to provide diversion for servicemen in the city. Golden was considered a happy choice for the project—"without a gun he succeeded in getting five million free theatre tickets from showmen for the boys and girls in the service." *The Army Play-by-Play* (five one-act prize winners in a contest sponsored by Golden) was presented by him and the Second Service Command at New York's 46th Street Theatre on the night of June 14, 1943, the entire proceeds going to the Soldiers and Sailors Club. "Appropriately enough (with one or two exceptions) everything he has touched has taken on a golden hue," commented S. J. Woolf, the artist-writer. A single performance of the contest playlets brought $130,000 into the box office. Another Golden project was the one-act play contest for noncommissioned personnel of the Third Naval District (including Waves and Spars). Five prizes were offered, and the winning plays were broadcast in September 1944 to vessels and naval stations throughout the world.

Another non-commercial enterprise to which Golden has contributed his time is the City Center of Music and Drama in New York City. Not only is he underwriter and incorporator of the municipal enterprise, but his production *Susan and God* opened the theatre in December 1943. Golden believes firmly in a "governmentally subsidized theatre; that is, a people's theatre, run by the people, for the people in the sense of its being operated at such low prices, as is possible when the grim necessity of making a profit is removed." In February 1944 the City Center was also the scene of another Golden enterprise: In an effort to help the theatre discover new talent and at the same time give aspiring young actors an opportunity for a hearing by the Broadway producers, Golden announced in 1943 a series of auditions open to anybody who registered. The response was overwhelming—exactly 1,007 responded and were duly auditioned. From that number thirty were picked for the finals—twenty of whom got jobs. One of them, Virginia Vass, played in the cast of *Three Is a Family.*

"No one on the street [Broadway of Times Square section] which is supposed to have no heart has more friends," says S. J. Woolf. "No one has been an easier touch than this business magnate who never grew up, and has been called a 'plutocratic Peter Pan.'" Proof of his popularity is the fact that he was elected in 1942 and re-elected in 1943 and 1944 Shepherd of the Lambs, exclusive club for men of the theatrical world. He also is an officer of the Stage Relief Fund and the Percy Williams Home for aged actors.

In June 1944, by his establishment of a $100,000 fund for the advancement of the legitimate theatre and the workers in it, Golden became the first active member in the field to contribute such a large sum. The fund is to be administered by the Foundation Advisory Committee of the Theatre and will be used for the various purposes outlined by Golden and his co-workers. The donor has explained that he hopes the money will supply the theatre

GOLDEN, JOHN—*Continued*

with new talent and also speed the establishment of a national civic theatre, "free to produce the finer things at low prices for the people." Approximately one-half of the fund will be used for cultural experiments, and the remainder for loans to needy actors, playwrights, and their associates. Projects already sponsored by the fund are a dramatic department at New York City College, and playwriting contests at Columbia and New York Universities and at City College in New York.

Golden's recreation is a game of gin rummy at the Lambs; his hobby is the theatre (he sees every play presented on Broadway); his greatest pride is an autographed picture from President Woodrow Wilson on which is written the commendation, "Well done" for Golden's work in recreation for the service men during the First World War. His office, pine-paneled, is atop a theatre in the Times Square district. He does not look the sixty-nine years with which *Who's Who in America* credits him. "Gray streaks his straight black hair, but his bushy eyebrows are still dark and cast heavy shadows over his flashing eyes. He is five feet ten and one-half inches tall and weighs 178 pounds.

In 1909 Golden was married to Margaret Hesterich, an actress before her marriage. The Goldens have no children of their own, but the gates of their twenty-one acre estate in Bayside, Long Island are never closed to those in the vicinity. A football and a baseball field were built by Golden for "his boys," many of whom have grown up since he moved to Bayside. Originally, it is said, his home had belonged to a former Shepherd of the Lambs and was the scene of that club's Annual Wash, a ritual observed by the members "to wash away the year's misdeeds." When Golden first saw the palatial house, spacious grounds, and private beach facing Little Neck Bay he was too poor to imagine anyone rich enough to live so grandly. On the death of its owner a few years later *Lightnin', Seventh Heaven*, and other Broadway successes had made it possible for John Golden to become lord of the manor.

References

Am Mag 93:18+ Mr '22 por
Cue 10:3 Ag 30 '41 por
N Y Post p31 Jl 6 '43 il pors
N Y Times Mag p16+ Jl 18 '43 por
PM p12 Ja 13 '42
Mantle, B. Contemporary American
 Playwrights 1938
Who's Who in America 1944-45
Who's Who in the Theatre 1939

GOLDTHWAITE, ANNE (gōld'thwāit) 1875 (?)—Jan. 29, 1944 American painter, etcher, and lithographer; acclaimed as one of the outstanding women artists in United States; her work is exhibited in the Congressional Library and in the art museums of Cleveland, Chicago, New York, and Baltimore.

Obituary

N Y Times p37 Ja 30 '44 por

GOLDWYN, SAMUEL Aug. 27, 1884(?)- Motion-picture producer

Address: b. Samuel Goldwyn, Inc., Ltd., 1210 Santa Monica Blvd., Hollywood, Calif.

Hollywood producer Samuel Goldwyn, a pioneer in the motion-picture field in the early days before the First World War, is recognized as one of the top men in the industry today. While others of early motion-picture fame have retired on their earnings and prestige, Samuel Goldwyn continues to turn out the best pictures he knows how to make, and each year the industry looks to him to set the pace.

The producer was born in Warsaw, Poland, of poor parents, who both died when the boy was still very young. When he was eleven he ran away to London, where he earned a meager living in blacksmith shops and glove factories. He lived with relatives at Manchester for a while, but when they tried to exercise authority over him, he crossed the Atlantic in the steerage and arrived in America, where he had no relatives to harass him. He was then thirteen.

Sam got a job at a machine in a glove factory in Gloversville, New York, an upstate factory town. After working at a glove machine for several years, Goldwyn was made a salesman, and is reported to have sold 15,000 pairs of gloves a year—something of a record. He was considered one of the greatest glove salesmen in the world by the time he was eighteen; he was able to dictate his own terms, and to travel to Europe for a month or two every year. (Goldwyn had already learned English in a year at evening school, and in 1902 he became a citizen of the United States.) He soon was made a partner in the glove company and, convinced that it would become prosperous, planned to stay in the business.

Shortly after his marriage to Blanche Lasky in 1910, however, he gave up a secure position to join forces with his brother-in-law, Jesse Lasky (a vaudeville producer), in a daring new venture—motion-picture production. There had already been in the United States some experiments with two- or three-reel films, but no long features had been presented to the American public until Adolph Zukor, in 1912, imported a four-reel French film starring Sarah Bernhardt.

The success of this picture convinced Zukor of the possibilities of feature-length pictures, and he set out to organize his own company, Famous Players in Famous Plays Company. Immediately the idea spread, and several other companies were formed. The most important of these was perhaps Lasky and Goldwyn's.

When with an estimated capital of $26,500 they formed the Jesse Lasky Feature Play Company, Cecil B. De Mille '42, a depressed young playwright who had been about to go to Mexico to seek glory and/or the grave in a local revolution, was made director at $100 a week. Their first picture, *The Squaw Man* (1913), starred Dustin Farnum. The first full-length film made in the United States, it was created in a studio which had started life as a stable. Farnum had no faith in the project and demanded $5,000 cash instead of the stock interest he was offered—

a stock interest which would have been worth
millions to him, for the picture was a tremendous hit and helped to revolutionize the
industry.

The only serious competitor of the Lasky
company was Adolph Zukor's Famous Players, with which a merger was effected in 1917.
Goldwyn, as a result of the deal, became
chairman of the board and director of the
new combine. The following year, however,
he sold out after a dispute with Zukor. Goldwyn's share of the sale amounted to $900,000.
"A billion-dollar pastime, movies had become
a fabulously rich giant in commerce," writes
Lewis Jacobs.

That same year, 1917, the new movie
magnate formed another company, the Goldwyn Pictures Corporation. The name was a
combination of Goldfish—the immigration authorities' translation of his Polish name—and
Selwyn, the name of his two partners, Arch
and Edgar, young Broadway producers.
Samuel Goldwyn became the president and
chief owner. (It was not until 1919 that
"Goldfish" had his name legally changed.)
The du Ponts and the Chase National Bank
also entered the field as backers of the corporation.

In 1919, after leaving Goldwyn Pictures,
he formed Eminent Authors Pictures, Inc.
He had to lay emphasis upon the writers,
because the firm he had just left had all the
big name stars under contract. Always an
enthusiastic pioneer, Goldwyn thought that he
could advertise the names of the writers in
big lights and the names of the stars in small
ones. For his new enterprise he imported
some of the best known writers to Hollywood
—Rex Beach, Rupert Hughes, Mary Roberts
Rinehart, Gertrude Atherton [40], and Maurice
Maeterlinck being only a few (although the
Hollywood writings of the Belgian playwright
were never made into a film). Goldwyn's venture established a custom. "Competition for
'name' writers became fierce . . . [and] Hollywood became the writer's Mecca."

Goldwyn, however, soon dissociated himself with Eminent Authors and, in 1925,
bought out another company to form Metro-
Goldwyn-Mayer. Shortly after the merger he
was defeated in a battle for control. He
promptly sold his interest for a large sum
and founded still another new company,
Samuel Goldwyn, Inc., Ltd., in which he
owned one hundred per cent of the stock.
Metro tried legally to prevent Goldwyn from
using his name in another picture company,
and Goldwyn finally agreed to label his pictures "Samuel Goldwyn Presents."

In 1926 Goldwyn allied himself with United
Artists for the distribution of his films and
in 1927 was elected an owner-member by its
members, Mary Pickford, Douglas Fairbanks,
Sr. [40], Charlie Chaplin [40], Alexander Korda,
and others. Ten years later he and Korda,
feeling that they were the only active partners, tried to buy the three-fifths they did not
own for a reported six million dollars. They
wanted primarily to limit the company's policy
of releasing the supposedly inferior pictures
of outside producers. When this failed Goldwyn filed suit against United Artists in 1939
for breach of contract. In February 1941 the
suit was settled with United Artists reputedly

SAMUEL GOLDWYN

buying in his stock for $300,000, a loss of
$300,000 for Goldwyn, since the stock was, he
claimed, worth $600,000. In May Goldwyn
signed an unprecedented contract for release
rights on his pictures with RKO.

The names of some of Goldwyn's discoveries
are among the greatest in the motion-picture
industry. They include Rudolph Valentino,
Bebe Daniels, Pola Negri, Anna Sten, Will
Rogers, Vilma Banky, and Ronald Colman [43].
Goldwyn is also credited with developing
Eddie Cantor [41] on the screen. Gary Cooper [41] was on Goldwyn pay rolls at $50 a week
when he was discovered by another producer
and signed up for $200 weekly. Several years
later Goldwyn got him back, a star, at $3,000
a week.

The films Goldwyn has made have also gone
down in the annals of the industry, ever since
his first film, *The Squaw Man*, in 1913. The
more modern ones—dating from his first
talkie, *Bulldog Drummond* in 1929—include:
All Quiet on the Western Front (1930);
Street Scene (1931); *Arrowsmith* (1931);
Dark Angel (1934); *Nana* (1934); *Stella
Dallas* (1937); *Dodsworth* (1937); *Dead End*
(1937); *Wuthering Heights* (1939); and *The
Westerner* (1940). Goldwyn produces only
from one to three pictures a year, since he
has always believed in quality rather than
quantity. He has campaigned heartily against
the double-feature bill, maintaining that the
policy is killing the industry by antagonizing
the picture-going public and by forcing producers to release inferior pictures to keep up
with the demand.

Goldwyn has always hired the "best," including Ben Hecht [42] and Charles MacArthur
as writers, the late Florenz Ziegfeld as the
producer of *Whoopee* (1930), and the President's [42] son, James Roosevelt, as his former
vice-president. Goldwyn reveres the writing
department above all the other branches of
the motion-picture industry. He pays fabulous sums to "Big Names," and if Shakespeare were alive, wags have said, Goldwyn

GOLDWYN, SAMUEL—*Continued*

would have him. Alva Johnston adds that some of the Bard's bad plays, such as *Cymbeline, Troilus and Cressida,* and *Pericles,* might have been tightened up into great drama if the playwright had had Goldwyn over him.

The producer, critics declare, has managed to develop taste and artistic conscience to the point where it is a compliment to nearly any motion picture to say that it looks like a Goldwyn production. Alva Johnston thought that Goldwyn was probably lucky in having had an education consisting of no more than one year at evening school, because "his power seems to consist in a simplicity and elemental directness of mind which does not always flourish under higher education." Goldwyn educated himself by "relentless inquisitiveness and by rare skill in searching other people's minds."

"Not long after World War I, producers got the idea that sensational pictures were 'good business,'" Goldwyn wrote in the New York *World-Telegram* in September 1944. "All this sensational stuff nearly wrecked the entire industry. . . .I'm serving warning that the underestimation of the audience mind will be just as nearly fatal. . . .I have always insisted that the screen's first function is to entertain. Entertainment, however, does not automatically exclude thought. The minds of an intelligent audience do not stop working even when they are most relaxed."

Since his alliance with RKO, Goldwyn has made *The Little Foxes* (1941) with Bette Davis [41]; *Ball of Fire* (1941) with Barbara Stanwyck and Gary Cooper; *Pride of the Yankees* (1942) with Cooper; *They Got Me Covered* (1943) with Bob Hope [41]; the much-discussed *The North Star* (1943), written by Lillian Hellman [41]; *Up in Arms* (1944) with Danny Kaye [41]; and *The Princess and the Pirate* (1944) with Hope.

The North Star, "a cinemilestone," to quote *Time* Magazine, was one of Goldwyn's most expensive and spectacular productions and had received an immense amount of advance publicity. For its lavish world première it opened simultaneously at two first-run Broadway houses, an unusual occurrence for a motion picture. The film was "the first major attempt by a major United States producer" to deal with the invasion of Russia; and the resulting controversy and excitement following the première were more intense than that over any picture in recent years.

Reviews varied from "rave" notices to bitter denunciations. *The North Star* was called "a simple, non-ideological and completely enthralling story"; "a lyric and savage picture"; and the first major American film to "present Russia's war with the Nazis in the way that Winston Churchill [42] saw it when the War began—not primarily as a struggle for Communism, but as a heroic defense by the Russian people of their homes." Yet most of the discussion was over a possible propaganda element in the picture. Accusations were based on the supposedly idyllic picturization of pre-War Russian life and on an atrocity incident in the film, the authenticity of which its critics claimed was

questionable. The most savage attacks came from the Hearst-controlled press. The first one and a half million copies of the New York Sunday *Mirror* following the opening contained a highly complimentary review. Printing of the paper was then halted, following a directive from the top to describe *The North Star* as pure Bolshevist propaganda, which could not be worse if it had been paid for by Stalin [42]. A new review was inserted in the paper, and the remainder of the copies carried a scathing denunciation of *The North Star.* Similar attacks were made in other Hearst papers; and an attack on the film was also made by George Sokolsky [41] in the New York *Sun.*

One of Goldwyn's most recent battles has been that against monopolies among motion-picture exhibitors, particularly those affecting the independent producer, who, he claims, has not been allowed sufficient percentage from the sale of tickets to cover rising wartime production costs. The independent producer, Goldwyn says, has made "significant and constructive forward steps" in the industry, as evidenced by such men as D. W. Griffith, Cecil B. DeMille, Walt Disney [40], Charles Chaplin, David O. Selznick [41], Darryl Zanuck [41]. Anything that obstructs them in turn affects "all producers, all distributors, and, in time, all exhibitors." Post-War world competition in the film market is another threat to the American producer, Goldwyn points out, and an additional financial worry. "The American motion picture is the voice and vision of the American way of life on the screens in our own and foreign lands. . . .For America to lose world film leadership would be a catastrophe to all American industry. . . . It is, therefore, to the selfish interest of the American exhibitor that he support the Hollywood output generously." Not only has Goldwyn voiced his opposition to monopoly control—he has supported his stand by action. He showed, for example, his 1944 film *Up in Arms* in a small independent theatre in Chicago (at a profit), later, in a converted dance hall in Reno.

As temperamental as any artist, Goldwyn goes into a kind of nervous state of concentration as pictures near completion or when he is working out a new idea. In 1936 he was ill and was forced to take a vacation. During this time he vowed to go easy when he went back to work, but the vow was quickly forgotten as his work mounted to its usual feverish pitch again. Goldwyn has had one book published, *Behind the Screen* (1923), memoirs written while he waited for one of his many settlements with companies he was leaving.

Goldwyn has won numerous film awards. In 1938 the now defunct *Stage* Magazine gave "to Samuel Goldwyn, producer extraordinary, who has yet to traffic deliberately with anything but the Class A product, who experiments consistently and cashes in regularly, a palm." As Alva Johnston wrote: "The routine is to ridicule Goldwyn for a while, and to denounce him for a while, and then to credit him with 'an instinctive love of beauty' and 'complete' or 'almost complete' artistic integrity."

Over the years a great deal has been written on the subject of the so-called "Goldwynisms" or malapropisms—such as "Include me out"—which have been attributed to the producer. These he and his publicity office deny, and Earl Wilson of the New York *Post* has reported that Howard Dietz, former Goldwyn publicity director, has not denied that he "'edited' some of Goldwyn's remarks to make them perfect Goldwynisms." According to Edward Hutchings, Jr., whose article on Goldwyn appeared in the April 8, 1944 issue of *Liberty,* the producer may once have encouraged his own press agents "to pin garbled-English anecdotes on him." Today, continues Hutchings, "speaking in a voice that still has more than a trace of accent, but getting all the right words in the right places, he denies it by the hour."

An "active, aggressive, determined" man, Goldwyn is tall and broad-shouldered, almost bald. He never carries money. "Sam," wrote Alva Johnston, "is too proud of his figure and his tailor to allow his lines to be distorted by currency in any form." After his divorce from Blanche Lasky (1915), Goldwyn married Frances Howard, a Broadway show girl, on April 23, 1925. They have one son, Samuel Goldwyn, Jr.

JAMES GOW and ARNAUD D'USSEAU

References

Liberty 21:30+ Ap 8 '44
New Yorker 1:13-14 Ap 25 '25
International Motion Picture Almanac 1941-42
Johnston, A. The Great Goldwyn 1937
Who's Who in America 1944-45
Who's Who in American Jewry 1938-39

GORDON, GODFREY JERVIS *See* Gordon, J.

GORDON, JAN Mar. 11, 1882—Feb. 2, 1944 British artist, author, lecturer, critic, folk musician, and traveler; known as the vagabond artist"; collaborated with his wife Cora in writing the "Vagabond" books; his paintings were on exhibit in various parts of the world.

Obituary

N Y Times p19 F 3 '44

GORDON, LEON May 25, 1889—Dec. 31, 1943 Russian-born illustrator and portrait painter; among his paintings were those of the late President Calvin Coolidge and Mrs. Coolidge, the late Will Rogers, Helen Keller '42 and Winston Churchill '42; famous for his group of America's eleven greatest women.

Obituary

N Y Times p13 Ja 1 '44

GOW, JAMES (ELLIS) Aug. 23, 1907-
Scenarist; playwright
Address: h. 161 W. 75th St., New York City

D'USSEAU, ARNAUD (dü'sō är-nō) Apr. 18, 1916- Scenarist; playwright
Address: h. 5 E. 54th St., New York City

During the 1942-1943 season Broadway saw so many war plays that were failures that the drama critics began saying, "Nazi plays are not so good." Then toward the tag end of the season (April 14, 1943) *Tomorrow the World* opened on Broadway, and the critics rejoiced—here at last was a Nazi play with a fresh angle, "containing a thoughtful and theatrically exciting study of one of the major problems of today—how to deal with the German people once the guns have ceased firing." The play was the work of two young men— James Gow and Arnaud d'Usseau. Their names were new to the Broadway theatre world, although they had authored a goodly number of Hollywood scripts, and Gow had collaborated on two plays which had been given tryouts in out-of-town productions.

Born in Creston, Iowa, August 23, 1907, James Ellis Gow is the son of James Ellis and Faith (James) Gow. He attended school from 1914 to 1920 in Greenfield, Iowa and from 1920 to 1924 in Vinton, Iowa. Two years in the University of Iowa followed (1924-26), but in 1926 he enrolled at the University of Colorado, where he obtained a B.A. degree in 1928. September of that year found him on the city staff of the old New York *World,* where he remained for one year. In 1929 he became a member of the *World's* dramatic department, remaining with that paper until it went out of existence.

From 1931 to 1943 Gow was employed as a writer for various studios in Hollywood. In collaboration with Edmund North he wrote the screen play for *One Night of Love* (1934), a Columbia picture in which Grace Moore '44 was starred. The story concerned an opera singer and contained several operatic arias. The picture was a success, and from then on Gow was considered an authority on pictures containing operatic music. Other pictures upon which Gow has worked include *I Dream Too Much* (1936) and *His Majesty, Bunker Bean* (1937) for RKO, and *Moonlight in Hawaii* (1941) for Universal Pictures.

In between picture assignments Gow has written for the theatre, though without much

GOW, JAMES, and D'USSEAU, ARNAUD
—Continued

success until *Tomorrow the World. The Drums, Professor,* a play written in collaboration with Edmund North, was announced for production by Guthrie McClintic [43] in 1932. When McClintic failed to produce the play Frank McCoy gave it a tryout (1935) in White Plains, New York. The reviews were far from favorable. A second collaboration with North, *Rhyme Without Reason,* was given a production by Arthur Beckhard, a New York producer who was trying out plays in San Francisco in the 1937-1938 season. Burns Mantle refers to the play as "a feather-weight affair, linking Hollywood and Broadway characters." It closed after one week.

Arnaud d'Usseau, the son of Leon and Ottola (Nesmith) d'Usseau, was born in Los Angeles, California, April 18, 1916. He was educated in the California schools, graduating from Beverly Hills High School. In 1932 he became a book clerk, and his first work as a writer was for the United Press in Arizona. He left the newspaper field when a Hollywood studio gave him a place in the scenic department as a set dresser during the making of a period picture. On his shoulders rested the responsibility for seeing that no Louis XVI chairs adorned the sets of a picture laid in Louis XIV's time. His reward for work well done was an assignment to write a treatment of a mystery story, a task for which he was apparently "eminently suited, since he had never read a mystery story." The thriller, *One Crowded Night* (1940), was successful, and from then on d'Usseau was a "mystery writer."

Gow, whose success with the screen adaptation of opera had also made him a victim of Hollywood's typing malady, met d'Usseau on the RKO lot. Collaboration on an original movie story, *Repent at Leisure* (1941), followed. It was a comedy, and its authors hoped to escape through it from the thrillers and operatic adaptations, but when it came to the question of who was to write the screen adaptation Gow and d'Usseau were told, "It's not your kind of picture." Gow then suggested collaboration on a play—and their first play, the saga of the effect of a possessive mother on a sensitive household, was called *How Like an Angel.*

In 1942 d'Usseau went over to the Twentieth Century-Fox lot, where he worked on the screen plays of *Who Is Hope Schuyler? The Man Who Wouldn't Die, Twelve Men in a Box,* and *Just Off Broadway.* In between their film jobs Gow and d'Usseau discussed ideas for a second play—a play which would have something to do with the world today. One unusually hot afternoon in July 1942 they met in Gow's apartment just outside of Hollywood. They began wondering what would happen if a Nazi-trained youngster were eventually brought into contact with democratic principles through coming to live with his uncle in the United States; the result was *Tomorrow the World.* Once the play was outlined, the climaxes established, and the curtains determined, they took turns sitting at the typewriter while the other paced the floor. The play was finished in November. (The first two acts as presented in New York remained essentially as written in the first draft, but the third act was rewritten three times, following the suggestions of the producer and Elliott Nugent [44], the director.)

Under contract to write a documentary film with Robert Riskin, chief of OWI's Overseas Motion Picture Bureau, the two came East, bringing the play with them. It was given to the agent who had been handling *How Like an Angel,* which had almost sold a couple of times but had not quite made the mark. After the first reading the play agent knew he had a winner; one month later Theron Bamberger bought it. The agent gave him a ten-day option in which to raise two-thirds of the capital. In ten days twenty-five investors (including Ralph Bellamy, who had been engaged to play the leading man, and Elliott Nugent, engaged as director) had put up $20,000. The production cost not much more than $17,000. Two months after the opening of the play the original investors received their investment back. *Variety* stated that no show in years with the exceptions of *Life With Father* and *Arsenic and Old Lace* "has kicked back the coin to its backers so quickly." From its opening week *Tomorrow the World* cleared approximately $5,000 weekly over its running expenses for the New York company alone, and in its tenth month on Broadway it was still drawing excellent grosses. A second company with Elissa Landi and Paul McGrath in the leading roles opened in September 1943 and in 1944 was playing in Chicago. The movie rights were sold to Lester Cowan, an independent producer, the contract calling for a "straight split" to the playwrights of 25 per cent of the gross profits.

Tomorrow the World, whose leading feminine role was played by Shirley Booth [42], was not acclaimed a literary masterpiece. Lewis Nichols of the New York *Times* wrote that there were flaws in it, but that "it gives an audience an evening that is sometimes moving, sometimes exciting and, in general, all on the credit side of the ledger." Howard Barnes in the New York *Herald Tribune* thought the authors had composed a show which is at times "vastly effective, at times rather luridly ridiculous." Much credit was given to Skippy Homeier, the child-actor who plays the Nazi-reared child, and to Joyce Van Patten, the other young player in the cast.

Although Gow and d'Usseau were drafted for the Army shortly after the production of *Tomorrow the World,* they were present during the rehearsals. "We actually had something to say about the production," they boasted to a reporter, recalling how little they had had to say about the motion-picture production of their screen scripts. "We shall always be grateful to Elliott Nugent. We learned more from him in six weeks about playwriting than we did in six years before." They also believe much credit is due to the cast for the success of the play—especially Ralph Bellamy for "the many small but subtle changes in dialogue. The modeling of the quarrel scene between Bellamy and Shirley Booth resulted from suggestions by the actress."

Tomorrow the World closed in June 1944, after a run of sixty-two weeks or 499 performances, a Broadway record for a play dealing with political or war problems. (The road company remained twenty-three weeks in Chicago.) A few months later the play was produced in Yiddish in a Brooklyn theatre, and in December the film version was released. Adapted by Ring Lardner, Jr., and Leopold Atlas, directed by Leslie Fenton, the picture was generally considered as having much merit as a story. Opinions varied as to some aspects of its treatment: in the opinion of some reviewers, the acting of Skippy Homeier was thought badly exaggerated before the camera, and situations "packed with dynamite" were "muffed."

The collaborators, who are now serving as privates in the Signal Corps Photographic Center, Long Island City, Long Island, agree on politics and religion. They are both "Win-the-War" Democrats and neither professes to any religious faith. In spare hours Gow likes to bowl or play a game of pool. His hobby is collecting phonograph records. Most of d'Usseau's leisure is spent in reading. Gow is five feet eight inches tall and weighs 145 pounds; his hair is light brown and his eyes a green-gray. On February 6, 1941 he was married to Olga Alexander. D'Usseau is five feet eleven inches tall and weighs 160 pounds; his hair and eyes are dark brown. On August 15, 1938 he was married to Susan Wells.

References

N Y Herald Tribune VI p3 Ag 1 '43
Film Daily Year Book 1943
International Motion Picture Almanac 1937-38

GRAHAM, MARTHA Dancer; teacher of the dance

Address: b. 66 Fifth Ave., New York City

In the days when Ruth St. Denis and Ted Shawn were weaning American dance tastes away from high-kicks, cartwheels, and other forms of acrobatic expression, one of their performances so affected a wide-eyed little girl as to determine the entire course of her life. The little girl was Martha Graham, who was later to be acknowledged as the greatest exponent of the modern dance. In the process of becoming an artist, Miss Graham discovered that there was no easy blueprint for her to follow: it was necessary, she found, that she evolve her own technique of dancing.

During the early days of her career Miss Graham wore her seriousness conspicuously on her sleeve; her dance works were, for the most part, abstractions expressed in severe, and often violent, angular movements. She had won an audience even then, but was regarded as "arty" in the manner of the so-called "morbid moderns." Long since artistically mature, Miss Graham has left these early abstractions behind her and has been composing dances of greater flexibility within a broader, less abstruse range of subject matter. Some of her more recent creations such as *Every Soul Is a Circus* and *Punch and the Judy* are instances of an approach that is witty, satiric, and at the same time full of warm understanding.

Martha Graham was born in Pittsburgh, Pennsylvania, and is, through her mother, a tenth direct descendant of Miles Standish. Her

Valenti

MARTHA GRAHAM

father, Dr. George Graham, was a specialist in nerve diseases. A legend is circulated to the effect that at the age of two Martha danced down the aisle during church services, but afterwards confined her dancing to the more private setting of the kitchen, with a nurse-maid for an audience. When she was eight years old her family moved to Santa Barbara, California, and a short time later, through a fortuitous circumstance, she determined to study dancing: a billboard poster of Ruth St. Denis, she explains, "finally awakened my dormant interest, and from that time on I made my family's life miserable until I was allowed to go to Los Angeles to study at the Denishawn School," conducted by Ruth St. Denis and Ted Shawn.

A brief stay at this establishment, however, precipitated a parental storm of objection which sent Martha back to complete her formal schooling. It seemed impossible at the time to modify her father's somewhat puritanical prejudice against dancing, and it was not until after his death, which occured when she was in her early teens, that she began to work seriously at her dancing.

Upon returning to the Denishawn School, Martha began her training under the direction of Ted Shawn. In her autobiography, *An Unfinished Life* (1939), Ruth St. Denis writes that as a student Martha was "exceedingly shy and quiet, with the same fascinating, homely face that she has today. Most of the time in my class she sat very still and listened. When she spoke it was only to ask an intelligent question." By contrast, this otherwise mousey girl danced like "a young tornado," and with "tremendous bursts of vitality." "If one saw Martha do a certain dance," states Miss St. Denis, "it was rendered innocuous and pale when any other girl attempted it."

Miss Graham made her first professional appearance in 1920 with Ted Shawn, with whom she made a six months' tour. Her

GRAHAM, MARTHA—*Continued*

first leading part was in Shawn's ballet *Xochitl*, based on an Aztec Indian legend. She remained four years with Shawn's company. In 1923 the peregrinations of the group having taken them to New York City, Miss Graham so impressed John Murray Anderson that he engaged the young dancer for the Greenwich Village Follies.

Two seasons as a solo dancer with the Follies convinced Miss Graham that she was working in an artistic vacuum. Her dances, which were Moorish and Oriental in character, were not original, but derived from her training. Accordingly, she went into retirement for two years and entered what she refers to as her "woolen period." "It was a natural reaction against the tinsel of Broadway," she explains. "I adopted simple, severe costumes, much to the disgust of my mother who couldn't understand why I didn't wear pretty costumes like the other dancers." During this interval she experimented with new types of choregraphy and with new methods of libretto-writing. "I was attempting something that I felt was a part of myself, and the going was hard. But I was sincere, and slowly my ideas began to take hold."

Upon a recommendation from Rouben Mamoulian, Miss Graham obtained a position as a dance instructor with the Eastman School of the Theatre (a division of the Eastman School of Music) in Rochester, New York, where she experimented with group dancing for the first time. In 1926 she gave her first independent recital in New York's Forty-eighth Street Theatre. Although it was unsponsored, the recitalist relatively unknown, and the press only "mildly cordial," the evening was a success because the box-office receipts covered the expenses. (According to *Time*, she had given the recital on $11.50 in cash and about $800 in credit.) Graham's dancing then was still a far cry from what it was to become; her program included exotic carry-overs from her Denishawn background; but, what was more significant, the program also contained three dances which bore imprints foreshadowing the characteristics of her later work. They were the *Danse Languide*, *Désir*, and the *Tanagar*. The following season she gave two more New York recitals and she has since appeared in that city every year. Two of her original early dances were choregraphic settings of Ernest Bloch's '41 *Baal Shem* and of Claude Debussy's *Nuages et Fêtes*." In 1930 Russian choreographer Léonide Massine '40 and conductor Leopold Stokowski '41 chose her for the leading female role in the United States première of Igor Stravinsky's '40 *Sacre du Printemps*.

One of the reasons why Miss Graham's dancing escapes formularization is that her restless curiosity is always ready to explore in unexpected directions. "Her sole purpose in her art is to awaken the 'awareness of life,'" said John Martin in the New York *Times*, "and for this end she has no formula and no set vocabulary of movements." Such a broad inclusive approach gives her the whole world to draw from and she can be counted on to vary her formula radically "about every third season."

In the early '30's she became interested in the Indian country of New Mexico, its landscape, its dark-skinned natives, and, above all, its religious rituals. All of this naturally had an effect upon her work. The following season she introduced two "primitive" dances to her audiences—*Primitive Canticles* and *Primitive Mysteries*; the next season she brought out *Incantation* and *Dolorosa*. In 1932 she was granted a Guggenheim Fellowship for a summer of study in Mexico, where she observed the native dances. This was the first time a dancer had received a Guggenheim award.

After the New Mexican period Miss Graham's dancing expressed anger at puritanism. Later she drew upon Emily Dickinson and the Brontës for inspiration. On another occasion she created dance patterns based on Georgia O'Keefe's flower paintings. The dancer's costuming has always been unorthodox. Sheet rubber has served her purposes on one occasion, and on another a dyed sponge was used effectively as a bit of decoration and is said to have influenced costume designers.

Besides fulfilling her ordinarily exhausting schedule every season, Miss Graham staged dances for the Katherine Cornell '41 production of Romeo and Juliet (1934); worked with Archibald MacLeish '40 on his verse drama of the financial crisis, *Panic*; and in the summer of 1935 she was one of a group of four who established the school of modern dance at the Bennington School of Arts of Bennington College in Vermont. The school soon became famous as a mecca for dance enthusiasts from all over the country. Miss Graham not only teaches there, but uses the school as an experimental workshop where she tries out new dance compositions and polishes up old ones in preparation for each oncoming season. She also "spends a good deal of her time teaching in a downtown Manhattan studio, counts many topnotchers among her pupils."

It was at the 1940 Festival at Bennington that Miss Graham presented her much discussed *Letter to the World* for the first time. The action of the dance is based on the legend of Emily Dickinson's life, and several characters are used to represent different aspects of the poet's personality. An innovation of the work was the introduction of spoken lines from Miss Dickinson's poems. When the dance appeared in its final form in New York, John Martin, who had written earlier that the dance was a "failure," stated that *Letter to the World* was "the finest work of Miss Graham's career and a bold venture into entirely new territory for the dance. On second seeing . . . the composition stands forth unmistakably as a work of pure genius." Of Graham's dancing Martin wrote: "Miss Graham's performance of the central role is a matchless accomplishment, and in the closing sections she touches the heights of tragic beauty."

After two season's absence from New York Miss Graham made a triumphant return in December 1943. "The house, scaled to a $3.30 top, was sold out the day the seats went on sale at the box office, and on the night of the performance people stood in line, many of them in the rain, waiting to be told that there was no more standing room to be had. When a second performance was announced for January 9 the management had to put on an extra secretary to handle the mail orders. The audience was as brilliant a one as has been seen hereabouts in years. Fully a quarter of it consisted of artists of achievement in various fields —actors, writers, painters, musicians, dancers. . . . Nor did she let them down."

At this time Miss Graham presented two new dances. One, *Deaths and Entrances*, created as an homage to stoic Emily Brontë, was described as "long, obscure, of intense interest and extraordinary richness of invention. But it is Miss Graham's own performance that is the extraordinary and fascinating focus in which one sees this irrational world as a real experience. The intensity with which she projects [emotions] . . . is a unique quality. Unique, too, is the extraordinary technique with which she makes every movement seem that of an actual person, not of a performer." Miss Graham's other new dance, a solo called *Salem Shore*, received similar though less high praise. It was, however, generally agreed that the works required a second viewing and a creative, responsive audience to be fully appreciated.

On May 7, 1944 Miss Graham, who had always performed one-night stands, departed from custom to present her most outstanding works during eight consecutive nights at the National Theatre in New York. Her repertoire ranged from the satirical *Punch and Judy* to the frenzied *Deaths and Entrances*. The audience was always responsive and even "choreographic illiterates . . . could sense the flashes of real beauty," said Louis Biancolli in the New York *World-Telegram*.

In *Time*'s words, "Martha Graham's dancing differs from the traditional ballet in much the same way as that of the late, great Isadora Duncan. It is less formal, less orthodox, less showy, more intensely expressive, with emphasis on current subject matter. Graham approaches her art with barefoot, Protestant simplicity, thinks of her choregraphy in terms of drama rather than pirouettes and *entre-chats*."

During the days when the public still looked at Martha Graham's revolutionary dance forms with suspicion, she received such epithets as "ugly, stark, neurotic, *précieuse*, angular, obscure, and intellectual." There may be some explanation at least for the first of these, according to John Martin, but there is not a trace of intellectuality in her dance. It "is based entirely in that subrational region of the mind where all subjective experiences dwell, and therein lies the basis of its uncanny truth."

Miss Graham warns aspiring neophytes of the hardships of a dance career and insists that they ought not to be encouraged to plan careers as dancers. "The modern dance," she states, "is something far more complicated than cavorting about in chiffon robes, expressing joy or despair or springtime." It is instead, she points out, a life requiring years of strenuous physical and mental training, as well as the courage with which to meet enormous hardships. "You either have to be a dancer or you don't," she declares. "The life is too hard to enter without a 'call.'"

After having achieved a record of brilliant successes, Miss Graham works at least six hours a day in her studio to keep her muscles in condition. Her work leaves the diminutive dancer without either the desire or the vitality to engage in active sports by way of diversion. "I just want to be amused in a restful way," she says. "I like the theatre and music, driving and reading, and for pets I have a couple of dachshunds. I live a very simple life, just like anyone else's. I disapprove of theatrical people who dramatize their lives offstage. It seems to me to mean they are not satisfied with their success on the stage." She is a "pert, slim, dark-haired woman" who "looks, offstage, more like a business executive than a ballerina."

References

N Y Post p15 Mr 17 '41 por
N Y Times VIII p2 Ag 11 '40 por; IX p2 Ja 26 '41; p16 Ag 11 '41; IX p8 Je 1 '41
Time 43:56+ Ja 10 '44 por

Armitage, M. ed. Martha Graham 1937
Morgan, B. Martha Graham 1941
St. Denis R. An Unfinished Life 1939

GRAU SAN MARTIN, RAMON (grou mär-tēn' rä-môn') Sept. 13, 1887- President of Cuba

Address: Presidential Palace, Havana, Cuba

The accession of Dr. Ramón Grau San Martín to the Cuban Presidency on October 10, 1944 was accomplished by the first completely free election in the history of the republic of Cuba. While Grau defeated the powerful Batista's protégé, lawyer Carlos Saladrigas, by a wide margin, it remained a subtle issue as to whose—Batista's or Grau's—was the moral victory. Grau was the popular choice, but his actual election was only made possible through the honest polls established by ex-President Batista. The picture of a onetime dictator dictating a free and honest election was so unique that it made Batista the main figure of the event. From his balcony he told his cheering people that true democracy was theirs at last and that if they ever needed him he would answer their cries. Grau, said *Time* Magazine, "undoubtedly heard and pondered" the outgoing dictator's promise. By the time the President-elect took the oath of office, however, he need have entertained little doubt as to his hold on the people's affections. "The greatest chorus of 'Vivas' was reserved for the new President, and celebrations lasted for three days. "The Cuban public," wrote *Newsweek*, "long disgruntled with the Batista regime, once again hoped for a new deal."

Ramón Grau San Martín was born in Pinar del Rio, Cuba, on September 13, 1887. His father was a prosperous tobacco merchant who wanted his business to become a family tradition, and the boy Ramón therefore took a commercial course in Havana. Although he saw the course through to its successful completion, his heart was really in medicine. He carried out his ambition to become a doctor in the face of family opposition, receiving his degree of Doctor of Medicine in 1908 from the University of Havana, at which he had earned part of his tuition as an assistant in the botany department. He rounded out his medical training by study in France, Italy, and Spain. Titles

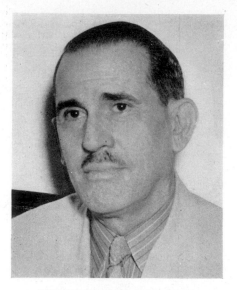

RAMON GRAU SAN MARTIN

of his published medical tracts take up almost a column in *Who's Who in Latin America*.

In 1921 Grau became titular professor of physiology at his own alma mater and acquired a large and devoted following among the students. Although his world was remote from politics, he did not have the usual academic detachment. In 1927 university students demonstrated against the Machado Government, and Grau, resigning from the University under protest, joined the students. In 1929, among other leaders, he was thrown into prison by the Machado faction, but the indomitable professor continued his classes in prison. When he was released after an amnesty for political prisoners was declared, he realized that the release was only temporary and left the country to conduct his revolutionary activities from Miami and New York.

After Machado was overthrown in 1933 and the moderation policy of Manuel de Cespedes incited the revolt of six sergeants, led by the Army stenographer, Fulgencio Batista[40], a junta took over the rule, and Grau became President. Though he was only one of the obscure presidents that came and went during the '30's his four-month tenure of office was worthy of notice. The "Cuba for the Cubans" slogan was coined during his term, and his progressive pro-labor policy established a Cuban precedent. Among the many reforms that he advanced two went through: an eight-hour working day and the Labor Nationalization law which established a 50 per cent quota for employment of foreign labor. Alien to moneyed interests, the liberal Grau acquired a "Red" label. The Right Wing of the ABC (the secret society formed to overthrow Machado), the island's industrialists, and numerous other reactionary groups opposed him. One of Grau's first acts was to denounce the Platt amendment, for which he was called "anti-American."

During his incumbency Grau promised his people the Cuban equivalent of "a chicken in every pot," and freedom from "Yankee imperialism," graft, and high taxes. He tried

earnestly to fulfill his promises, but the idealistic professor was no politician. He received at all hours every laborer or student with a problem or an idea. He was thus besieged by would-be advisers, and his office became a free-for-all forum. During the confusion workers struck in demand for higher wages, and a decline in business nearly emptied the Treasury. The new Government was afraid to declare a moratorium on debts for fear of jeopardizing recognition by the United States. To avert total anarchy, democratic ideals had to be abandoned for a temporary dictatorship.

In 1934, on Sumner Welles's[40] advice, the United States refused to extend recognition to the new Government on the grounds that it did not possess the complete support and approval of the people. Batista prepared to dismiss Grau, who, according to one commentator, did not need to be told to go. He had tired of the imbroglio and "slipped out of the side door of Cuba's unhappy palace on the afternoon of January 15, as rifle and machine-gun bullets were flattening against the barricaded building, and sped away to the semi-obscurity of private life." He was to return to the medical profession, building up a private practice of better than $50,000 a year.

The rifle and machine gun that played a tune to Grau's resignation were to continue in action for a few years. Batista, the "king-maker," made and unmade five Presidents, who came and went in quick succession. Carlos Hevía, succeeding Grau, remained in office from Monday, January 15, 1934 until 1:20 a.m. on Thursday, January 18, then "resigned under conditions of the utmost confusion." Carlos Mendieta, who became the next President, did better, remaining in office two years.

Calling it the "Cuban Terror," Grau San Martín criticized Mendieta's regime in an article that appeared in the *Nation*, April 3, 1935. "Cuba is at this moment in a state of veritable chaos," it began, and then went on to explain that that Administration had renewed all the worst features of the Machado Government, dissenting voices were silenced with violence, the only basic law that remained in force was a decree of prison or death without right of appeal to all those suspected of opposing the Government. The injustice of these bloody acts, Grau pointed out, was attested by the fact that they were directed against a public protest, essentially civic and peaceful, that had originated in a complaint against the neglect of the public schools. Only the War Department, he concluded, was "generously pampered by the Government."

Relations with the United States, however, improved during Mendieta's accession. President Roosevelt[42] recognized the Government and extended a $10,000,000 food credit to help feed the starving Cubans; a satisfactory sugar quota was fixed, allowing 1,944,000 short tons a year to be admitted to the United States. In May 1934 a new treaty was drafted and ratified, abrogating the Platt amendment passed in 1901. This amendment the Cubans had vigorously opposed because it restricted the freedom of their government in both domestic and international affairs. The United States had stipulated that the Platt amendment be added to the Cuban constitution before complete independence could be granted, and Cuba had had no choice but to accept. Although Americans regarded the amendment as only a paternal measure, the Cubans could not see this analogy. Nations, they felt, should learn by the trial-and-error method. Moreover, said Cosme de la Torriente y Peraza, Cuban Ambassador to the United States in the '20's, the amendment and its allowances for American intervention had been "exploited by unscrupulous politicians for selfish purposes."

Mendieta was succeeded by three puppet Presidents: José Barnet, who ruled for only a few months; Miguel Mariano Gómez, who was legally elected but whom Batista finally had impeached; and Laredo Bru, who remained President until 1940. During these years the anti-Batista forces had been strengthening themselves: in 1938 70 per cent of the electorate had boycotted the "king-maker" by staying home on election day. Although Batista had instituted certain social security measures, had built schools, hospitals, and orphan asylums, and had made attempts at Government control of the sugar industry, he was obviously not popular. In 1939 he therefore made a swift turn to the Left, ordering the Cuban Falange to dissolve itself, legalizing the Cuban Communist Party, and emerging a "progressive and democrat." Later that year he called for the election of a Constituent Assembly to draft a new constitution, and announced that he would become a candidate in the 1940 Presidential election under the new rules. The anti-Batista forces, led by Grau of the Auténticos (a center group), but also including members of the Cuban ABC, which had nearly overthrown Grau's liberal regime in 1933, won a majority of the delegates to the Assembly.

Outlining his views for the press as the opposition candidate for the Presidency, Grau declared that "Yankee imperialism" was now extinct and that close economic and political cooperation with the United States was indispensable to the prosperity and stability of Cuba. Its economic condition depended entirely on its sugar trade with the United States, he continued, and there was need for a permanent commercial treaty with that country. Significant was his reference to communism as one of the dangerous problems to be confronted. Envisioned as a radical by Cuba's nabobs because he was pro-labor, he also acquired the label of reactionary because he aligned his Cuban Revolutionary Party, the Auténticos, with the conservative Republican Party of the peasants to oppose the Batista Reds. "Communism," he said, "is foreign to Cuban ideals and temperament but carries a false allure in periods of economic stress like the present. At the same time certain outside influences are being felt in Cuba, and we must be on our guard against these." In his platform were also included plans for reduction of government expenditures and improved distribution of the national budget.

In July 1940, with the support of seven political parties ranging from the moderate Right to the Communist Party and the Socialist-Democratic coalition, Batista was elected President of Cuba. John Gunther[41] says that this election was fair and honest; Grau's supporters claim that their candidate actually had the votes. In any case, Batista's democratic aspirations were apparently sincere. Cuba's new constitution made voting compulsory, provided for social legislation, called for the division of

large estates to give land to the poor *colonos* (farmers). As President, Batista cooperated closely with the United States, and Cuba was one of the first Latin American countries to declare war on the Axis. In 1942, however, a parade of Grau's supporters is said to have dwarfed the official Fourth of July celebration in Havana.

In the elections Batista had won over Grau by a majority just short of a quarter of a million votes. Three years later few would take seriously his announced intention of quitting the Presidency, even though to discuss politics was no longer flirting with death. When Batista warned political parties that they had better prepare for the next election, everybody wondered what to expect. The electorate were finally convinced of his intentions when he thundered at his people that if a President were not elected by June 1, 1944, he would turn his office over to the president of the Senate.

Cuba's political conscience burst from its cocoon, and all the old parties revived in a fight for supremacy. The scattered parties finally integrated into two groups. The Coalitionist Party became the Government party, and the oppositionists (a disparate group of extreme Leftists and conservatives) lined up behind the Cuban Revolutionary Party or the Auténticos. Grau became the latter's candidate. The lawyer Carlos Saladrigas Zayas, former Prime Minister and protégé of Batista, was the Coalitionist candidate. There was little to favor the opposition, pointed out *Newsweek*. The country seemed satisfied with the incumbent Government, and everybody expected Batista's favorite to win in a walk.

But Batista had changed his views more completely than anyone would have suspected. He ordered a completely free election without the financial support even of American capitalists. This action had the unforeseen effect of giving Grau a strong advantage over Saladrigas, who had no "political sex appeal." In contrast to Saladrigas' costly campaign, Grau "stumped the country . . . in a soiled and wilted panama suit," arousing fervid response wherever he went. His sincerity and impassioned stand against corruption, his cheering talk of more schools, better roads, Pan-American solidarity, and "Cuba for the Cubans" struck a responsive chord among the peasants. Women knelt as before a saint, and there was even a myth prevalent that honest Grau would end taxes, rent, and electric and water bills. Saladrigas conceded defeat after only one-fourth of the votes had been counted. And, although the United States had rebuffed Grau eleven years before, President Roosevelt now waived all formalities to telephone his own congratulations.

The new form of ballot used in the elections permitted voters to vote for each office independently rather than on one slate for the first time in history. Thus Grau was successful independently of his own party, which lost to the coalition. When the new President took office October 10 the coalition held thirty of the fifty-four seats in the Senate and ninety of the Chamber's 127 seats. Political observers, according to the New York *Times*, believe that the coalition may be broken. Said the *Americas*, a review of Latin-American news: "The conditions affecting the Grau Government will be no less complex than the international situation.

(Continued next page)

GRAU SAN MARTIN, RAMON—*Cont.*

. . . His supporters, furthermore, range all the way from workers and peasants to Falangistas. . . . Which line of policy will Grau's Government choose? Blas Roca points out that the re-election of Roosevelt will strengthen the tendencies toward democracy in Cuba, as well as elsewhere, whereas his defeat would encourage the forces of reaction." Though not a doubt is cast on Grau's integrity and idealism, some observers are not so convinced of his administrative ability.

Grau promised that he would "never dictate laws of a personal nature." At a press conference he declared that dictatorships in the Western Hemisphere were only temporary and would disappear because they "do not represent the will of the people and their rule can only be imposed by force." The Spanish Falange, he said, had no influence in Cuba at present, and its activities had been practically abolished.

Briefly, Grau's stated policy is: collaboration in international relations; fair treatment of foreign capital; improved rural education; increased agricultural production; and the development of irrigation and communications. An immediate goal is to curb inflation and suppress the black market, which was the result, he said, of his predecessor's mismanagement of the war economy.

In his first message to the Cuban Congress Grau outlined a program for reforming the tax system, suppressing graft, setting up a currency system and bank of issue, and improving education, health, and sanitation. Early in November, following the killing of several of the police, Grau removed Batista henchmen from the Army and police and took personal command of keeping order in Cuba. All licenses to carry arms were canceled and the civilian population disarmed. Observers believe his next step in the Cuban "housecleaning" will be the reorganization of Government departments which will result in the discharge of employees whom Grau regards as drawing pay without working. In his effort to raise the price of Cuban sugar he is supporting the industry in its refusal to accept less than 3¼c a pound from the United States.

The President, who visited the United States for two weeks in September 1944, has been described as "so friendly that he once broke his right hand while shaking hands." He is tall, with gray hair and chestnut eyes deep-set in a grave face. "Elderly, soft-voiced, fine-mannered, non-lady killers," Grau and his Vice-President, Raul de Cardenas, "are a departure," says *Life* Magazine, "from Cuba's bully-boy tradition."

References

Inter-American 3:7 Je '44; 3:3-4 Jl '44
Life 16:81-4 Je 26 '44 pors
Lit Digest 117:14 Ja 27 '34
Pan Am Union Bul 77:490-2 S '44 por
Sat Eve Post 217:14-15+ S 30 '44 pors
Time 43:37-8 Je 12 '44
Moore, D. R. History of Latin America p624-5 1938
Who's Who in Latin America 1940

GRIFFIS, STANTON May 2, 1887- Investment banker; Red Cross commissioner

Address: b. 15 Broad St., New York City; h. Faraway Farm, New Canaan, Conn.

As an investment banker, business executive, and former Government official, Stanton Griffis, Red Cross commissioner in the Pacific area, has been a newsworthy figure ever since his graduation from Cornell University in 1910, when an address he made denouncing undergraduate activities as "side shows" won him an oratory prize and newspaper notices.

Stanton Griffis was born in Boston on May 2, 1887, one of the three children of Katherine Lyra (Stanton) Griffis and William Elliot Griffis, a Congregational minister and author, who was considered an authority on Japan. A few years after Stanton's birth the family moved to Ithaca, New York. There he went to Ithaca High School and to Cornell University, from which he was graduated in 1910 with a B.A. degree. At the University he had won many undergraduate honors, and in his senior year had been editor of the Cornell *Sun.* Two years after his graduation he was married to Dorothea Nixon, by whom he had two children, Theodora and Nixon. (Mrs. Griffis is now deceased.)

Immediately after leaving college, Griffis went out to Medford, Oregon, where he secured a job as manager of several large apple orchards. He is said to have nostalgic feelings now about the period he spent in the West; but, without the aura of accumulated years, the experiment seemed at the time too drab to the young man. In 1914, therefore, deciding that it would be more enjoyable to starve in lively New York City than to remain buried on a fruit farm in Oregon, he left for the East.

Although he had chosen an unpropitious moment to make his decision—with war starting in Europe and job opportunities in New York scarce—Griffis was able to find an opening with Hallgarten and Company, and later with Hemphill, White and Chamberlain, both investment firms. When the United States entered the War he was commissioned as a captain on the Army General Staff and sent to Washington. In 1919 he returned to Wall Street as a partner in the investment banking house of Hemphill, Noyes and Company, with which he has remained since that time, either as a general or special partner. Subsequently engaged in industrial underwritings and reorganizations of everything from paper bag companies to sewing machine firms, Griffis gradually accumulated a large fortune.

A paragraph from Ilka Chase's [42] autobiography, *Past Imperfect* (1942), tells something of Griffis' many interests and activities: "In his capacity of chairman of the executive committee of Paramount [Pictures], chairman of the board of Madison Square Garden, Wall Street tycoon, owner of Brentano's bookstore, and entertaining human being," she writes, "Mr. Griffis has at one time or another played host to most of the biggest names in finance, sport, and the arts."

One of these activities, Griffis' connection with Madison Square Garden, began in 1933, when, with Floyd B. Odlum [41], president of Atlas Corporation, he acquired control of the

Garden and set about to reorganize the corporation and put it on a paying basis. Two years later he took over the directorship of Paramount, which was just emerging from reorganization, and the following year he became chairman of the executive committee. Under his management the company has gone through a period of expansion and development and has paid off in excess of $50,000,000 in debt. In his executive capacity he has supported Paramount's backing of televised motion pictures, pointing out that sending these "canned" television-movies directly from the studios to the transmitters would be a cheaper procedure than wiring them to the stations. Furthermore, he has said, "televised movies must excel any performance acted directly for the television transmitter."

In 1942-1943 Griffis accepted a confidential Government commission. As part of his assignment he spent approximately six months visiting England, Sweden, Finland, Spain, and Portugal. (He was also engaged in business for Paramount.) After his return he took a leave from Paramount to become in the fall of 1943 the chief of the domestic OWI Motion Picture Bureau, succeeding Lowell Mellett '42, who had returned to the White House secretariat. In announcing Griffis' appointment, Palmer Hoyt '43, director of Domestic Operations for the OWI, pointed out that the already effective cooperation between the film industry and the Government made obvious the point that there was "no more need for the OWI to produce its own films than there was for it to publish its own newspapers." The duties of the new chief, he said, would be to supervise the relations between the Government and the film industry, coordinating all Government requests to the industry and channeling all the film industry's requests for information from the Government. In addition, Hoyt explained, Griffis would supervise all requests for motion-picture cooperation in war drives and in Governmental information programs. At the same time he would coordinate the film producing activities of other war agencies.

According to unofficial information from Hollywood, Griffis had hesitated about accepting the appointment—a popular one in the industry—until he was assured that he would be free of pressure from either Hollywood or Washington. He finally agreed to accept the position, the New York *Herald Tribune* stated, when Congress took such a slice out of the OWI domestic appropriations that only a small portion was left for the film bureau budget. "It's no secret," Griffis told a reporter, "that I am glad that OWI is out of domestic production." He believed that Hollywood companies were more ideally equipped to turn out short films with audience appeal, a quality usually lacking in the Government's documentary films. By early 1944, in fact, he was able to tell producers participating in the program that the "shorts" they had contributed had had a greater circulation than any commercial film in the history of the industry.

Griffis received a second governmental assignment in April 1944, when he was sent to England and Sweden for three months as a special representative of the Foreign Economics Administration. The American and British air

STANTON GRIFFIS

forces in England had been staging costly large-scale raids over the ball bearing centers in Schweinfurt, Germany, the effectiveness of which, it was held, was being weakened by exports to the Nazis of ball bearings from Sweden's huge SKF plant. General George C. Marshall '40, American Chief of Staff, had, in consequence, minced no words in demanding that action be taken to cut off this supply, and Griffis' appointment was a step toward this end. Sweden, for her part, had pleaded the excuse of "helpless neutral," and had maintained that American reports of the importance of SKF shipments were erroneous.

Together with Douglas Poteat of the Foreign Economic Administration and William Waring of the British Ministry of Supply, Griffis conducted negotiations with both the Swedish Government and with SKF officials. Reports were that he had been vested with the authority to spend a considerable sum of money, if necessary, to purchase all ball bearings produced by the company. It was also assumed that he would warn the Swedes of the threat of economic sanctions against the parent SKF concern and of the threat of economic action against its subsidiary in the United States if the exports to Germany were not curtailed.

On May 22 the omission of SKF from the State Department's blacklist of firms in neutral countries conducting business with the Axis gave an indication that Griffis' conferences were proceeding smoothly. The same day Prime Minister Per Albin Hansson '42 stated before his own party that Sweden had not succeeded in remaining neutral in all respects and that, while she must consider the actual situation and risks involved, there was also a limit to "concessions which can't be exceeded." Three weeks later, on June 13, the FEA announced that the negotiations had produced a temporary agreement with Sweden, whereby a "very substantial" reduction in ball bearing exports to Germany would be effected.

Details of the agreement remained a military secret, but I. F. Stone of *PM* questioned its efficacy. The term "substantial reduction" he

GRIFFIS, STANTON—Continued

pronounced as cryptic, and said further that this reduction, allegedly 50 per cent, represented only $8,000,000 worth of bearings—according to an admission he had procured from official FEA sources—the sum paid by the United States for the cut in Swedish exports to Germany. Since Griffis had been authorized to spend considerably more, reportedly $23,000,000, the actual purchase, Stone concluded, "would seem to leave the bulk of Swedish SKF's output still available to the Nazis." FEA officials, on the other hand, contended that the comparison in figures did not provide a fair picture of the concession won from the company. Though Griffis himself had told reporters upon his return from Sweden that the mission had been highly successful, a later remark attributed to him by the New York *Post* was that the Swedish industrialists were not interested in ideologies—"only in making money." On October 15 the Swedish Foreign Office announced that export of Swedish ball bearings to Germany had ceased. (In December it was revealed that Griffis' trip to Sweden had not been without hazard. He flew from England to Sweden strapped in the cargo bay of a Mosquito, arriving in Sweden numb and almost frozen. And in Stockholm he was soon warned that his life would be in danger if he persisted in his mission.)

Griffis' other connections and interests have encompassed a varied field. In 1930 he was appointed by Franklin Roosevelt '42 (in his capacity as Governor of New York) a trustee of Cornell University. He was reappointed by Herbert Lehman '43 in 1935 and 1940 for five-year terms. (In 1932 he was elected chairman of the finance committee.) In 1939 he was made a director of Famous Players Canadian Corporation, Ltd.; and he is director of the American Historical Society and a member of the Film Advisory Committee of the Museum of Modern Art in New York. In 1942 he devoted six months to working as chairman of the Special Events Committee of the Navy Relief Drive which raised over $10,000,000. And in another field, his friendship with Katharine Cornell '41 and Guthrie McClintic '43 led to his backing of a number of Broadway shows. In late September 1944 Griffis was appointed Red Cross commissioner for the Pacific island area, and in October he resigned from his post as chief of the OWI film bureau to go to his station in Honolulu. Since leaving the United States he was awarded an honorary LL.D. degree in absentia by Union College in Schenectady, New York.

According to Ilka Chase, "Massa," as she calls Griffis, lives simply for a rich man, although he has a few luxuries. He owns a yacht, on which he has entertained many celebrated persons, and he enjoys collecting books as well as art works, having amassed a valuable collection of the etchings of Anders Zorn, the Swedish artist. One of his recreations is tennis.

References

N Y Herald Tribune II p3 My 14 '44
  por
N Y Sun p16 Je 1 '44
N Y Times p43 S 26 '43
Who's Who in America 1944-45

GUBELMAN, MINEI IZRAILEVICH
See Yaroslavsky, E.

GUFFEY, JOSEPH F. Dec. 29, 1875-
United States Senator from Pennsylvania

Address: b. Senate Office Bldg., Washington, D. C.; h. 2929 Benton Pl., Washington, D. C.

Elected in 1934 as Pennsylvania's first Democratic Senator since 1875, Joseph F. Guffey thereupon became and remains President Roosevelt's '42 most faithful Senatorial wheel horse. At times when stanch friends of the New Deal occasionally wavered, Guffey could be counted on to support unreservedly all Roosevelt-advocated measures. Loudest booster and prognosticator of a third term, he was again loudest and most prophetic concerning term four for the President. In the course of ten years Senator Guffey has built up what has been called a modern, streamlined political machine—a "medieval machine" to which he has "harnessed the driving force of New Deal liberalism." As a result, it is said, "in the Democratic hierarchy, no other man except the President has wielded so much power." According to writers Joseph Alsop and Robert Kintner, whose article appeared in the *Saturday Evening Post*, Joseph F. Guffey is "the first of liberal bosses, liberal in platform and enjoying tremendous support from the Left wing."

The stocky, poker-faced, smartly tailored Senator from Pennsylvania was not always a politician of liberal persuasion. Prior to his Congressional career he had accumulated wealth through oil speculation and public utilities. Joseph Guffey was born in Westmoreland County, Pennsylvania, December 29, 1875, the son of John and Barbaretta (Hough) Guffey. There was a younger brother, Alexander (now deceased) and three sisters, Ida, Pauletta, and Emma, who have exerted considerable influence in Guffey's career (particularly Emma Guffey Miller, for some time his chief adviser on Pennsylvania state relief problems) and with whom, being unmarried, he makes his home. Guffey's ancestors, who were country squires, had moved in 1750 across the Alleghenies into Westmoreland County. By 1875, the year of Guffey's birth, his uncles had gone to Pittsburgh to speculate in oil. His father, however, stayed at home to farm in Westmoreland County, where the children went to the public schools. During the summers young Guffey found part-time jobs with the Greensburg, Pennsylvania, public utilities.

Joe Guffey received his preparatory education at the Princeton University Preparatory School and entered Princeton in 1890. There he joined the Democratic undergraduate club, and at one of its meetings he met Woodrow Wilson, then a professor at the University. Guffey at once conceived a great admiration for Wilson. From this admiration he has never swerved; he is still one of the country's most ardent supporters of Wilson's League of Nations plan. In a radio address on December 28, 1941 he said that the present world-wide conflict would have been avoided if the United States had accepted Wilson's peace plan.

The attractions of academic education, however, appealed less to Guffey than the attrac-

tions of business. He left Princeton after
two years and returned to Pittsburgh where,
at the age of twenty, he got a supervisory
job in the Pittsburgh Post Office. His salary
was $2,400 a year, and he had 300 employees
under him. On the side he worked for his
uncle in the political wards, and "solemnly
did some welfare work." He also made
friends. He soon attracted the attention of
Judge James Reed, a Republican and an old
friend of the Guffey family. It was through
Judge Reed, in 1899, that young Guffey got
his first job with a utilities company. He did
so well that within two years he had become
general manager of the whole Philadelphia
company. He was successful in a good many
maneuvers, such as persuading the West Virginia legislature to grant his company the
right of eminent domain. At this time Guffey
also promoted an Ohio coal company and
started dabbling in oil leases.

By the time he was thirty Joe Guffey was
on his way to becoming "a really rich man."
He entered politics actively in 1912 when he
became a delegate to the Democratic National
Convention, supporting Wilson. In 1916
Palmer and McCormick, state political bosses,
gave him the acting chairmanship of the Democratic State Committee. Guffey had not,
however, wholly forsaken business for politics: he had been busy building up the Guffey-
Gillespie Oil Company, of which in 1917 he
became president; he also had large interests
in the Atlantic Gulf Oil Company and the
Columbia Syndicate.

During the First World War, Joseph Guffey
was a member of the petroleum service division of the War Industries Board, as well
as director of sales for the Alien Property
Custodian Office. At the War's end Guffey's
business was booming: "he was rich and
great." His devotion to Wilson never wavered; when Wilson returned, broken and disillusioned, from the Paris Peace Conference,
"it was Guffey who put up the $15,000 for that
last cross-country speaking trip."

But in 1920 with the defeat of the Democratic Presidential candidate, Cox, and a fall
in the price of oil, Guffey's fortunes, political
and financial, suffered severe reverses. As
director of sales under the Alien Property
Custodian, Guffey received the interest of
$401,001.36 of the millions he deposited in
banks in the interval between sales and the
ultimate disposition of funds. As Alsop and
Kintner explain, "for some reason the Federal
Treasury was reluctant to accept the interest
on the Alien Property Custodian's funds. By
an ancient usage in certain cities and a few
states, the interest on public funds is the per-
quisite of the public official who deposits the
funds. Joe accepted this precedent." Francis
P. Garvan, who replaced A. Mitchell Palmer
as Alien Property Custodian with the coming
of the Harding Administration, "began to ask
questions" about the interest the banks had
turned over to Guffey. "Soon there was a
demand for immediate repayment." By dint
of scraping together everything he could realize on his own properties, and loans from his
sisters and friends, Guffey was able to pay the
Government the four hundred thousand dollars
in March 1921. "If there had been another

JOSEPH F. GUFFEY

Democratic President," he said, "they never
would have raided me. But that's all part of
the game."

In the words of the *Saturday Evening Post*
writers, "Guffey's ruin seemed to be complete"
when the Government charged him with illegal
tax avoidance involving more than a million
dollars. "But Joe is not the sort of man who
stays down long." With the help of his sisters
he organized the Thermatomic Carbon Company, which was soon bringing in good returns.
Then, in 1924, Guffey chose to endorse Alfred
E. Smith [44], thereby getting back much of his
state political power—a power unshaken by
Smith's failure to win the nomination. By
1926 Joseph Guffey was definitely on the way
up again, financially and politically. Smith,
his man, was strongly entrenched. Further,
Guffey had gotten in on the ground floor
with the flourishing East Texas Oil Company.
It was then that the Guffey family formed
the "Japi" (Joseph, Alexander, Pauletta, Ida)
Corporation, in which, if one Guffey dies, his
or her stock is turned over to the remaining
Guffeys.

Pennsylvania's Democratic organization in
1930 was "pretty anemic," but when Franklin
D. Roosevelt became the party candidate in
1932 Guffey at once "laid himself and his
followers at Roosevelt's feet." He was again
backing the right man. The Guffey machine
rolled smoothly along through the succeeding
years, its one object to bring out the New
Deal vote. "In transforming himself into a
Left-wing political boss, Guffey reversed his
previous history. The spectacle must have
affected the oligarchs of steel and aluminum,
coal and oil and banking in Pittsburgh much
as it would affect a general if he saw one of
his most familiar subordinates charging his
own battle lines." Previously an opponent of
organized labor, Guffey was now full of
praise for John L. Lewis [42] and the CIO.
As a modern machine boss, Joseph Guffey is
fond of stating his formula for success: "A
politician's business isn't to mold public opin-

GUFFEY, JOSEPH F.—*Continued*

ion. It's to find out what public opinion is and get ahead of it."

During the years of WPA Guffey was said to have made "refinements and improvements on the methods of earlier bosses: WPA's bountiful non-relief payroll took on his precinct committeemen." "The fellows who've done the work I believe is rewarding," said Guffey. "When a job comes vacant, I just try to think who deserves it. Ours isn't a machine; it's organization for service." The "organization for service" worked both ways: under the Guffey system, employees of the state government were "generally required to pay into the party treasury three per cent of salaries less than $1,800 and five per cent of salaries above $1,800." Guffey is also given credit for having instituted the "$100 dinner" in party finance. "It is better to raise funds from party workers," said Guffey, "than to sell yourself to big business."

Winning the Pennsylvania Negro vote was another Guffey accomplishment. By giving Robert L. Vann, owner of the Pittsburgh *Courier,* Pennsylvania's largest Negro paper, and several other Negro constituents first-class Federal jobs, and by proclaiming it a "criminal offense" for any Pennsylvania hotel-keeper or restaurant or theatre owner to refuse accommodations to Negroes, Guffey was able to establish "the first really effective Negro division a Democratic campaign ever had."

Guffey was a power in the United States Senate before he even ran for election. It was said that "Dave Reed and Jim Davis may not know it, but Joe Guffey is really both Senators from Pennsylvania." When in 1934 Guffey announced he would run for the Senate against David Reed he sent for George Earle (then in Austria) to run for Governor so that the machine would be left in capable hands. And, as the new Senator from Pennsylvania, Guffey continued to put himself and his mighty machine behind Roosevelt measures. In October 1935 he added to his influence by becoming chairman of the Senate Democratic Campaign Committee. In 1936 he predicted that Roosevelt, in the forthcoming election, would "carry every state he did in 1932, plus Connecticut and Pennsylvania."

Guffey's most important legislative act during his first Senatorial term was the Guffey-Vinson '43 Coal Bill of 1937, a formulated four-year plan to stabilize the bituminous coal industry. The United Mine Workers regarded this law of stabilization necessary because "through a system of federally prescribed minimum prices it protects the miners' wage-scale in times of lax demand for coal." (Signed by Roosevelt on April 27, 1937, in 1941 it was extended for two years, and in April 1943 it came up for consideration for further extension. Because opponents of the act felt that big wartime demands "had changed the situation," and that its operation now tended to "conflict with the law of supply and demand," on July 5, 1943 the Ways and Means Committee voted its disapproval of further extending the measure.)

Throughout 1937 and 1938 Senator Guffey was well to the fore among the defenders of liberal legislation. He backed Roosevelt's Supreme Court proposal; he made a broadcast praising both the A.F. of L. and the CIO and assailing strike-breaking; he strongly defended the Anti-Lynching Bill and the Government Reorganization Bill. By 1939 he was doing the job he liked best—getting his "machine" in good order for the forthcoming campaign year and ardently supporting a third term for Roosevelt. He stoutly affirmed that there was nothing in the Constitution that forbade any President from running for a third term, and as stoutly predicted that, should Roosevelt run, he would be re-elected by a substantial majority.

Up for re-election himself, the Senator won renomination in April 1940, after a bitter primary contest which he called "a clean-cut fight between the New Deal and those who would destroy it." Guffey's victory at the primaries was, for him, a heartening comeback, since Democratic state leaders had assigned him to the political doghouse after the 1938 primary, marked by "graft and corruption charges against members of the Earle administration." Guffey interpreted his victory as a victory for Roosevelt and a "test case" third term endorsement.

With Roosevelt re-elected, and Guffey assured six more years in the Senate, the latter offered an appropriation bill to end coal mine cave-ins, and continued to function as an impeccably liberal New Dealer. More than once it became Guffey's duty to sound off, in "advance" speeches, a forthcoming Presidential policy on which Roosevelt was not yet ready to commit himself. This was true particularly early in 1941, when the controversial question of protection of Britain-bound convoys by the American Navy came up. It was Senator Guffey who made the frank demand for outright convoying by the United States, at least in Atlantic waters. This was considered the first step in the President's intention to use American naval forces to escort aiding ships.

During 1942, when the assembling of men and materials for war was the paramount issue, Guffey worked quietly in support of administration business, appeared little in the news. It is considered one of the Senator's virtues, together with a very genuine personal modesty (he has the shortest biography, for instance, of anyone in the *Congressional Directory*) that he has never entertained illusions about himself as a statesman. He seems quite content to be a good machine boss and vote-getter, loyal to his party and its leader, happiest when he can promote both. Early March 1943 found him already paving the way for a fourth term for Roosevelt. In a speech before the Senate he declared that there was "no American tradition which says that a good President cannot serve four terms in the White House."

Putting himself emphatically on record for the Ball '43-Burton-Hill '43-Hatch '44 resolution before the Senate in March 1943, Guffey said: "I have always favored a world organization to keep the peace and I am for anything that will prevent another war. Because the League of Nations failed, this War will cost us 1,000,-000 men and $300,000,000,000 in world treasure before it is over." On March 27 he continued these sentiments in a radio broadcast. "As a practical politician I agree that it is not wise to discuss details of the peace before we know the exact post-War problems with which we will have to deal," he said. "But I do know that the time has come when we must make the great fundamental decisions which will clear up, once for all, in our minds as well as in that of our Allies, the question of whether we are to continue Wilson's and Roosevelt's wise and practical world policies or whether we are going . . . to return to normalcy, to phony isolation, to ignorance, greed and cowardice because we haven't the courage to stand up now and chart our own future course in dignity and in honor and truth." In October 1943 Guffey was to support Senators Ball, Burton, Hatch, Hill, Pepper '41, and others in demanding more specific commitments and provisions in the Connally '41 post-War peace resolution. He also actively backed a resolution calling for the establishment of a Presidential commission to plan immediate action for relieving the plight of Europe's persecuted Jews.

More than once in 1943 Guffey was charged by Republicans with "political corruption." When Russell H. Potter quit the New York District OPA, he said that "politicians are trying to make a patronage machine out of the OPA," accusing Guffey along with other Democratic bosses of dictating OPA appointments in his area. On June 12 "corruption" talk also flew thick and fast in the Senate when the compromise Anti-Strike Bill was up for a vote, and Guffey opposed inclusion of a House provision prohibiting political contributions by labor unions.

And Guffey was usually ready with counter-charges. When Republican leaders met at a "fund-raising" dinner in Pittsburgh, Guffey said it was to be a feast costing "$8,000 a plate," which would "outdo in many ways the biblical feast of Belshazzar at which they drank wine and praised the gods of gold and of silver, of brass, of iron, of wood and stone." Republican House Leader Joe Martin is said to have quipped: "I don't know any Republicans named Belshazzar." Guffey had a return quip with regard to the forthcoming meeting of the Republican post-War council in Michigan. Two Republicans—Vanderberg '40 of Michigan and Clare Luce '42 of Connecticut— had been found, he said, who agreed on a one-word platform, so he couldn't see why any meeting was necessary. The word was "globaloney." Later, Guffey and other Administration supporters blasted Nebraska's Republican Senator Hugh Butler, who returned from a South American trip to call the Good Neighbor policy a "six-billion-dollar boondoggle."

Domestic farm problems also occupied a share of Guffey's attention in 1943 and 1944. In August 1943 he called for the distribution of protein concentrate to Pennsylvania farmers as a means of depriving "monopolistic interests" of control over livestock feed. In January 1944 he accused Governor Dewey '44 and the "New York farm crowd" of making "a political football" of food problems. "They have cried about feed shortages, milk shortages, and reduced living standards of the people at the very time they have urged farmers to hoard feed and reduce production. . . . It is the rankest kind of partisan politics, absolutely inexcusable in wartime."

December 1943 found Senator Guffey agitating for Federal control on the Lucas-Green soldier vote issue. He accused certain Southern Democrats, under the leadership of Harry F. Byrd '42, of entering into an "unholy alliance" with Northern Republicans, under the leadership of Joseph N. Pew, Jr. '41, to defeat the bill. The Southern Democrats thereupon assailed the New Deal, and Senator Guffey in particular, demanding his resignation as chairman of the Democratic Senatorial Committee. It was not until January 29, 1944, that Guffey submitted his resignation, "to become effective as soon as a successor is chosen." Guffey charged that he had not resigned, but had been "removed" by Senate Leader Alben Barkley '41, at the demand of Southern democrats opposed to the Lucas-Green Bill. In February 1944, when Barkley himself resigned as Senate majority leader in protest against Roosevelt's veto of the Congressional tax bill, Guffey commented: "There they are, congratulating him on wrecking the Democratic Party."

A month later Guffey attacked the foes of the Federal Ballot plan for soldiers, declaring that they were afraid to let soldiers vote for fear they would vote for Roosevelt, and afraid that, "if the poll tax and registration are waived, the colored troops and poor whites may cast a vote." He also backed (April 4, 1944) an organization called "Parents and Wives of Fighting Americans" in a Virginia test of the constitutionality of the poll tax. The feud between Senator Guffey and the Southern Democrats continued when, on June 23, the former criticized Senator J. W. Bailey of North Carolina for having called Philip Murray '41 and Sidney Hillman '40, CIO leaders, "Communists." When Senator Taft attempted to secure War Department censorship of certain films and books (August 1944) Guffey called the act "bad and foolish. . . . The Taft amendment must be changed and I will do all in my power to have it changed." The Pennsylvania Senator's watch-dog alertness was demonstrated on September 22, 1944, when he caught an "error" in an insurance bill which would have forestalled the Justice Department from prosecuting 200 insurance firms indicted for price fixing and other monopoly practices.

In late January 1944 Guffey was worried, over the political situation in his own territory. With special elections Pennsylvania had replaced two United States House of Representative vacancies with two Republicans. This meant that "for the first time in thirteen years Democrats had less than a numerical majority" in the House of Representatives. The campaign for a fourth term, however, was officially launched and well under way, with Guffey ardently singing what the New York Sun called his theme song— You'd Be So Nice To Come Home To. It was Guffey who became chief backer for the renomination of Vice-President Wallace '40 at the Democratic National Convention, criticizing Chairman Hannegan '44 for influencing the nomination of Senator Truman '42. As a continuously faithful party man, however, the Senator from Pennsylvania campaigned vigorously for the Roosevelt-Truman ticket. He did not, however, approve of Roosevelt's six appointees to the State Department in December 1944. One of the bloc of four Senators who

GUFFEY, JOSEPH F.—*Continued*

worked for the defeat of the nominations, Guffey put searching questions to the appointees at the Senate committee hearing. In the vote subsequently taken, Archibald MacLeish's [40] appointment was near defeat in a tie vote of 10 to 10, when Guffey switched to MacLeish's support.

The "earthy canniness, the coolness of his calculation, the businesslike originality" of Senator Joseph Guffey has changed little since he came to Washington in 1934. "The quiet, expensive clothes, the chunky body and strutting gait, the broad, closed face, with the heavy eyebrows and the odd alternation of expression between perfect blankness and a knowing grin" are familiar to gallery visitors. "He is not, even in striped trousers, a tall Senator, and beside a long colleague he is squatty. . . . He likes to walk with hands clasped behind his back, although that is likely to sway his belt buckle way out in front."

References

N Y Sun p42 My 7 '43
Sat Eve Post 210:5-7+ Mr 26 '38 il pors; 210:16-17+ Ap 16 '38 il pors
Who's Who in America 1944-45

GUGGENHEIM, MRS. DANIEL (güg'en-hīm) Sept. 3, 1863—May 13, 1944 Widow of Daniel Guggenheim, leader in the copper industry; sponsor of the Goldman Concerts in New York City; president and a director of the Guggenheim Foundation; treasurer of the Women's National Republican Club 1921 to 1938; noted for her philanthropies, she gave her estate to the Institute of Aeronautical Sciences for a research center.

Obituary

N Y Times p45 My 14 '44 por

GUGGENHEIM, FLORENCE (SHLOSS) *See* Guggenheim, Mrs. D.

GUINNESS, WALTER EDWARD, 1ST BARON MOYNE *See* Moyne, W. E. G.

GUNN, SELSKAR MICHAEL May 25, 1883—Aug. 2, 1944 Public health authority; vice-president of Rockefeller Foundation since 1927; conducted campaigns against disease in Europe, China, and the United States; assisted former Governor Herbert H. Lehman [43] in his relief and rehabilitation work in Europe.

Obituary

N Y Times p19 Ag 3 '44 por

GWATHMEY, JAMES T(AYLOE) (gwăth'me) 1865—Feb. 11, 1944 One of America's leading authorities on anesthesia; his research on anesthetical techniques contributed largely to the present-day usages in operative surgery; his book *Anesthesia* (1914) is one of the most comprehensive and authoritative works in this field.

Obituary

N Y Times p13 F 12 '44 por

HACKETT, WALTER Nov. 10, 1876—Jan. 20, 1944 American playwright; co-author of *White Sister* (1909) and *It Pays to Advertise* (1914); majority of his successes were comedies; produced most of his plays in London, where he lived from 1915 to 1940.

Obituary

N Y Times p13 Ja 22 '44 por

HAGEN, UTA *See* Ferrer, J. and Hagen, U.

HALL, JOSEF WASHINGTON *See* Close, U.

HALSEY, MARGARET (FRANCES) Feb. 13, 1910- Author
Address: h. 244 E. 48th St., New York City

With the publication in 1938 of *With Malice Toward Some*, the English travel diary that is said to have made Anglophiles writhe, Margaret Halsey found herself being compared to such satirists as Dorothy Parker and H. L. Mencken. In her second book, *Some of My Best Friends Are Soldiers* (1944), the author has turned her barbs on the more serious subject of racial intolerance in her own country, the United States.

Margaret Frances Halsey was born February 13, 1910 in Yonkers, New York, and brought up in an outlying section of the city. Her father, Reinhold Henry Francis Halsey, was, until his retirement in the middle '30's, the deputy superintendent of New York City school buildings; her mother, Annie Shelton (Braithwaite) Halsey, had been a teacher at the time of her marriage. Gretchen, as the young Halsey girl was called until she was seven, was "sifted inconspicuously" through the Yonkers public schools after auspiciously starting her education at the age of four. This event was occasioned, relates Lee Wright, by the opening of a new school in the Halsey neighborhood which the borough was unable to fill and which apparently admitted very young children. Margaret proved to be a good student despite her few years, and in high school, while her classmates experimented with Cuban heels and face powder, the youthful Miss Halsey unconcernedly wore middy blouses and child's sandals.

In 1926, at sixteen, she entered Skidmore College in upstate New York. She had always been a voracious reader and at Skidmore she took many courses in the English department, although her actual major was secretarial science. "She was very thin," write her publishers now, "very earnest, and addicted to writing 'How true!' in book margins." She nevertheless became the college humorist, and wrote the "Skidmoronia" column for the student paper, patterning her witticisms after those of Franklin P. Adams [41] and Frank Sullivan.

After her graduation with a B.S. in 1930 Miss Halsey abandoned any literary aspirations that she might have had and took a stenographic job in a bank. The work seemed distressingly dull to her after only half a year, so she left, despite the fact that the depression had caused a shortage of jobs. Her next job—as dictaphone operator for a real estate company—"opened new vistas of ennui," and after a year and a half she resigned. Her third position was with Thomas L. Stix, the radio and literary agent, who gave her a secretarial job. The summer of that same year, 1933, she accompanied his wife and children to Martha's Vineyard. There Miss Halsey met Max Eastman, who offered her a position as his secretary to assist him with the manuscript of the book on which he was working, *Artists in Uniform* (published in 1934).

When Eastman's book was finished he secured a job for his young secretary in the publishing house of Simon and Schuster in New York, where Miss Halsey worked in the editorial department. At the end of a year, on June 29, 1935, in the midst of a case of German measles, she was married to Henry W. Simon, thirty-four-year-old Ph.D. and brother of publisher Richard L. Simon '41. Henry Simon was assistant professor of education at Teachers College, Columbia University; and in 1936 his wife took her M.A. degree in English there, with the intention of teaching.

Mrs. Simon was not to teach school, however. In May 1936 the couple sailed for England, where Mr. Simon was to be an exchange professor of English at the University College, Southwest, in Exeter, Devonshire. For six months, while her husband taught, Mrs. Simon struggled with English food, telephones, the "boneless quality" of the conversation, and kept a diary. This diary was undertaken at the suggestion of her former employer at Simon and Schuster's, to whom she had written letters telling of her disillusionment with certain aspects of England, notably its "gentry." When he saw some of her entries he at once commissioned her to turn the diary into a book. This Miss Halsey did, with some misgivings, having written nothing for publication since her graduation except one article for the *New Yorker*.

The book was published in the summer of 1938 under the title *With Malice Toward Some*, which had been changed from "The Travel Diary of a Professor's Wife." (It was illustrated by Peggy Bacon '40.) Full of sentences that were "innocent and conventional in their exteriors, but mined with adverbial phrases which detonated at just the right moment"—to quote Thomas Sugrue—the travel account provoked mixed emotions on both sides of the Atlantic. The majority of the American reviewers received it with much hilarity, calling it shrewdly analytical and full of charm and a deft, biting—if occasionally forced—wit. But regardless of, or because of, the individual opinion, interest in the book was keen, and by the end of 1940 the author's profits, according to the New York *World-Telegram*, had exceeded $100,000. In 1938 the Book-of-the-Month Club had made it its September choice; in February 1939 the American Booksellers Association had named it the most original book of the preceding season in its National Book Awards.

Summed up, Miss Halsey's likes, expressed with "an irresistible sense of humor" and the "most endearing figures of speech," included English cathedrals, scenery and the manners of the lower classes, or the "ungentry"; she was alarmed, on the other hand, by English food, treatment of servants, conversation at

MARGARET HALSEY

polite dinners, and the pervading dampness of the climate. Irwin Edman experimented with the book on some Devonshire friends and found, for example, that Miss Halsey's theory about English women's hats—that they are kept suspended from bedroom ceilings and dropped to the wearers' heads when needed—evoked smiles from his married host. Other portions of the volume caused considerable laughter, Edman also reported. The more professional critic of the London *Times* was not offended, either: "Accepted in the right spirit of give and take, her [Miss Halsey's] vivacious jesting should be thoroughly enjoyed, her criticisms not at all resented, and England as ready to welcome her again as she, apparently, to return to it." "Divested of wisecracks," wrote *Time* Magazine, "author Halsey's English impressions are surprisingly charitable—kinder than most English impressions of the United States" and "kinder even than the satire of the English when knocking their own gentry."

In January 1941, with the subject of "Aid-to-Britain" in the air, Miss Halsey was called upon to defend herself. "I was only writing women's page stuff," she commented, "but people attacked me as if I'd been doing editorials. They took with desperate seriousness something I had intended to be very casual. They thought I'd personally undertaken to destroy the British Empire, when all I attempted was hammock-reading." Denying that she was a "political animal," she asserted that she did, however, favor helping Britain win the War. "I wasn't uncomfortable in England," she added for a *World-Telegram* interviewer; "that is, not more than any American is; I was interested."

When asked in 1944 whether any special incident had roused her into writing her second book, "a kind of novel" on racial intolerance, after a six-year period of literary inactivity, Miss Halsey only replied that "racial discrimination is around all the time. It's just a

HALSEY, MARGARET—*Continued*

rather tawdry way of getting emotional satisfaction." *Some of My Best Friends Are Soldiers* is, according to Clifton Fadiman[41], "a queer duck among books—a story . . . that is deadly serious in intent, but consistently light-hearted and comical in tone." It is told in the form of letters from a Manhattan girl to her brother in the service. Opinion varied as to the effect of such a mixture, that is, the ultimate value of such a book. "She makes the lesson stick," was Fadiman's feeling, "perhaps more effectively than do all the propaganda, preachments, and solemn warnings. . . . Miss Halsey's style, of course, is the thing. She tosses out epigrams and glittery sentences literally by the hundreds, and has an unequaled knack for the humor of exaggeration. . . . If it has a fault, one might say that the author tries just a mite too hard. She might have hoarded about 20 per cent of her cleverness for her next novel."

Other reviewers, too, evidenced a feeling of encouragement on finding "a pen like Margaret Halsey's" "standing up for freedom," or on discerning "some good, hard common sense hidden in the fun," as Eleanor Roosevelt[40] wrote. A few, however, criticized what was termed "a thinly disguised sermon" running through a "brightly written book"—a book that was "a bit on the hollow side," in the opinion of Robert Molloy.

The book ran into censorship difficulties in October when, according to *Variety*, NBC refused to sanction a *March of Time* broadcast dramatizing it, including sections touching on intolerance. Later Frank Norris, director of the program, denied this version of the story, explaining that the script had been discarded because it had proven to be unsatisfactory dramatic material.

"I just have to work from my own experience," says Margaret Halsey, "and then make sweeping generalizations as most women do." Writing for her, she declares, is not easy. "I sweat blood," she explained to a New York *Post* interviewer. "I have a lot of self-doubt. 'I'm no good,' I say, rushing out of the room, and then people have to soothe me and persuade me that I'll get by. It took me a year and a half to write *Some of My Best Friends Are Soldiers*." Brown-haired, deep-voiced Miss Halsey is a slender five feet six inches. She says that sewing and travel are her hobbies; and she enjoys walking, swimming, and bowling. Her latest book was written at her parents' home in Connecticut while her second husband, Milton Reid Stern, was in the Army. (Following a divorce from Henry Simon, she was remarried in March 1944.) "My parents have never seen any author but me," she said with a grin to the *Post*'s Clip Boutell, "and they're impressed. They go around saying, 'Margaret's working. Watch!'"

References

Book-of-the-Month Club News np Ag 19 '38 por
N Y Post p22 S 28 '44
N Y World-Telegram p3 Ja 28 '41 por
Scholastic 33:4 O 1 '38
American Women 1939-40
Who's Who in America 1944-45

HAMILTON, CLIVE, pseud. *See* Lewis, C. S.

HAMMERSTEIN, OSCAR, 2d (ham'mĕr-stīn) July 12, 1895- Librettist; lyric writer
Address: b. c/o ASCAP 30 Rockefeller Plaza, New York City; h. 157 E. 61st St., New York City; Doylestown, Pa.

Representative of the third generation of "one of Broadway's most formidable dynasties" is Oscar Hammerstein 2d, who writes successful librettos and lyrics for successful musical plays. For more than twenty years he has contributed to such smash hits as *Show Boat* (1927), *Rose Marie* (1924), *Desert Song* (1926), and *Sunny* (1925), to name only a few. Captivating Broadway audiences in 1944 were *Oklahoma!* (March 1943) and *Carmen Jones* (December 1943), two hits for which Hammerstein supplied the books and lyrics.

Hammerstein's most outstanding accomplishments have been "musical plays," which he carefully distinguishes from the musical comedy and the operetta. He believes that the key to the difference between these forms is dialogue. "Musical comedy dialogue is like a cartoon of real speech—it's usually high-sounding and remote. A musical play has the same sort of production as these two, but its dialogue is close to natural speech." The colorful and "folksy" dialogue in *Oklahoma!* is a perfect illustration of this point.

Oscar Hammerstein 2d was born July 12, 1895 in New York City. His mother, the former Alice Nimmo, was of Scotch descent, while his father, William Hammerstein, the theatrical manager, was of German-Jewish extraction. His grandfather was the first and fabulous Oscar Hammerstein, who owned and operated the Manhattan Opera House. Despite this heritage Young Hammerstein was not reared in a theatrical environment, and, in fact, was never behind the footlights until his college years.

He began his schooling at the Hamilton Institute in New York and later went to Columbia University. Upon receiving his B.A. in 1916 he remained at Columbia for two years more, attending its law school. During that time the theatre as a profession never formed any part of his plans for the future. His only active connection with the stage was his extra-curricular participation in student performances.

It was because of his enjoyment of amateur productions that he joined the Columbia University Players Club. At the time of his entry into the Club its directors were casting for the annual show on the basis of a competition open to all students of the University. Hammerstein came off with a comedy part in an effort called *On Your Way*. Apparently he was an entertaining comedian, for the following year the Columbia Players gave him the leading comedy role in a show entitled *The Peace Pirates*. The amateur actor's first attempt at dramatic writing was made in connection with this production, to which he contributed a parodistic Shakespearean skit. During his last year at Columbia, Hammerstein wrote the book and lyrics for the

University show—an opus called *Home, James*
—and acted its principal comedy role.

Hammerstein was graduated from law
school and had actually worked in a law office (where a few of the clients were from
the theatre) for an entire year before he
became convinced that the theatre was his
real métier. Fortunately, his uncle Arthur
Hammerstein was a producer, and willing to
give Oscar a chance. To make sure that his
nephew would "write for the stage and not
for the library," Arthur Hammerstein determined that Oscar would spend a year learning
the various aspects of theatrical production
before he began his creative career, and
admonished him not to write a line during
this period of apprenticeship.

Young Hammerstein followed his uncle's
suggestions to the letter. He rolled up his
sleeves, went backstage, and moved scenery
and hauled props, among other things. In
time he was made the stage manager of an
Ed Wynn show, *Sometime* (1918), and later,
of *Tumble Inn*. He relates that while rehearsals went on he stood by with playbook
in hand "listening to the authors and actors,
and drinking in as much as I could at close
range." By 1919 Hammerstein was general
stage manager of his uncle's shows, supervising all of the road company performances.
By that time he was also well on his way
toward becoming a librettist and lyric writer;
hardly a year has passed since then without
the production of at least one Hammerstein
work.

Hammerstein's first play, a four-act drama,
was a box-office failure in its out-of-town tryouts. But his knowledge that every playwright has his share of "turkeys" counter-
balanced any discouragement he might have
felt, and his self confidence remained characteristically unruffled. In 1919 he wrote *The
Light* and the following year he turned out
the books for three productions, *Always You,
Jimmie,* and *Tickle Me.* These last two
works were written in collaboration with
Otto Harbach and Frank Mandel. Together
with Mandel he finished *Queen O'Hearts* in
1922, and alone he wrote the lyrics for *Daffy
Dill.*

The enormously popular *Wildflower* (1923)
was Hammerstein's first hit show and inaugurated a series of highly successful musical
plays whose lyrics were to survive as American classics. Two of these, *Rose Marie* and
Sunny, were produced in 1924; *The Song
of the Flame* opened a year later; and in
1926 the curtain rose on the romantic *Desert
Song.* Hammerstein's record of hits obviously indicated that his successes were not
merely the result of good luck; his books
were the products of the conscientious efforts
of a master craftsman. In 1927 he completed
the book for the predecessor (in popularity at
least) of *Oklahoma!* That work, which
threatened to run forever, was called *Show
Boat* and had a musical score by Jerome
Kern '42. The next season Hammerstein put
the finishing touches on *New Moon* and went
to work on two shows that opened in 1928,
Good Boy and *Rainbow.* Among his many later
works were *Sweet Adeline* (1929); *The Gang's
All Here* (1931); *Music in the Air* (1932);

OSCAR HAMMERSTEIN 2d

May Wine (1935); *Gentlemen Unafraid*
(1938); and, of course, *Oklahoma!* (1943) and
Carmen Jones (1943).

Both the book and lyrics of the extraodi-
narily popular *Oklahoma!* were written by
Hammerstein. His adaptation of Lynn Riggs'
play *Green Grow the Lilacs* (which Hammerstein says is the "wellspring of all that
is good in *Oklahoma!*") and the musical score
of Richard Rodgers '40 are undoubtedly two
of the decisive factors of the show's success.
One commentator has stated: "Plots are generally a nuisance in musical comedies, but the
narrative line in *Oklahoma!* is arresting and
even dramatic." Wrote Howard Barnes in
the *Herald Tribune*: "Hammerstein has collaborated with the composer triumphantly.
His lyrics are good as his adaptation of
the Riggs original. In more than one instance
they serve to illuminate the action in the true
sense of melodrama. "Poor Jud" is a masterpiece of musical comedy exposition. The other
words with music give the production its rich
American flavor in no uncertain terms." Some
of the "other words with music" from *Oklahoma!* are the melodious "Oh! What a Beautiful Mornin'," "People Will Say We're in
Love," and "The Surrey With the Fringe on
Top." In 1944 the Pulitzer Prize Committee
decided that there had been no production in
the season just past that was worthy of the
annual award for an original play by an American author. Instead, the committee made the
unusual decision to award a $500 prize to Ham-
merstein and Rodgers for their musical play.

In December 1943, about nine months after
the opening of *Oklahoma!,* a streamlined,
modernized version of Bizet's opera *Carmen,*
now surnamed *Jones,* was presented to New
York audiences with an all-Negro cast. The
adaptation from the original, which was made
by Hammerstein, has been described as
"definitely out of the top drawer." In Hammerstein's version of the opera, the main plot
and characters remain the same although the
time and place have been transposed from old-

HAMMERSTEIN, OSCAR, 2d—*Continued*
world Spain to the contemporary United States.
The heroine becomes a war worker in a
cigaret factory converted to making para-
chutes, soldier Don José becomes an M.P.
named Joe, and Escamillo, the bullfighter,
emerges as a prizefighter named Husky Miller.
"Mr. Hammerstein's lyrics," wrote Louis
Kronenberger[44] in *PM*, "are fresh and clean-
cut—at times humorous, at times poignant in
their simplicity. . . . It is a bit of a shock to
hear the Toreador Song banged out with 'Stand
up and fight until you hear the bell,' but the
song is none the worse for it." The *Times* reviewer agreed that "Mr. Hammerstein has done
a splendid job in translating the libretto and
lyrics into Negro dialect, with plenty of Har-
lemesque touches. He has succeeded admirably
too in making the gaiety and tragedy truly that
of the Negro race while preserving the essential
spirit of the original opera." Elsa Maxwell[43],
however, protested that Hammerstein had "substituted burlesque for satire and flashy tours
de force for sensitivity."

The team of Rodgers and Hammerstein became a producing unit in October 1944 when
their first production, a non-musical one, opened
on Broadway. The play was *I Remember
Mama*, John van Druten's[44] adaptation of the
Kathryn Forbes's[44] stories about a Norwegian-
American family of the early 1900's. The New
York *Post* critic commented that "even if they
lose their shirts [on the venture], they can
always run around the corner and buy a couple
of sweaters out of the profits of *Oklahoma!*";
but the reviews of pleased critics forecast a
profitable run for the play.

The librettist's present plans include writing
the screen play for the Twentieth Century-Fox
musical biography of his grandfather, Oscar
Hammerstein. The grandson will also be the
co-producer with director Otto Preminger.
Hammerstein's second project is the preparation
of the book and lyrics for the Theatre Guild's
adaptation of Ferenc Molnar's *Liliom*, for
which Richard Rodgers is doing the musical
score.

With a single exception, all of the songs for
which Hammerstein wrote the lyrics—such as
"Ol' Man River", "Make Believe", "Who", "Indian Love Call"—constituted parts of the complete scores of musical plays. The exception
was in the case of the nostalgic lyric "The
Last Time I Saw Paris," which swept the
country in 1940. "The words just came to me
about a week after Paris fell," he explains.
"The idea was based on my memories, and the
situation was presented to me without charge
by Herr Hitler[42]."

Hammerstein does not depend on moments
of inspiration, buoyed up by coffee and cigarets, to turn out these lyrics. He "is a methodical, consistently prolific fellow, punctual
to the day in delivering material," says *Life*.
He "generally turns out a complete libretto,
with song lyrics, in six to seven months. . . .
He spent three solid weeks on the brief lyric
of "When I Grow Too Old To Dream." Some
songs, however, come to him at one sitting.
"Oh! What a Beautiful Mornin'" was the work
of an hour and "The Last Time I Saw Paris"
was pure spontaneity. In fact, he says, "I
was so depressed by what was happening that
I couldn't keep my mind on the show I was

doing. I got it off my chest by writing that
lyric."

In 1943 Hammerstein joined the Music War
Committee which later merged with the American Theatre Wing. Its purpose, in addition to
recruiting blood donors and assisting in the war
effort generally, is to encourage the composition
of a rousing war song which will be the modern
counterpart of George M. Cohan's "Over
There." Hammerstein, who is now chairman,
says, "We are trying to sensitize the song
writer to the need of the right kind of war
songs, and we want to make his efforts in this
direction worth while by creating for him a
means of exploiting these songs once they are
written."

Since the War began, other responsibilities
have been added to Hammerstein's ordinarily
heavy routine. He has gone into partnership
with Dick Rodgers in a music publishing company called Williamson Music, Inc. (both are
sons of men named William). In 1944 the
librettist is vice-president and director of the
American Society of Composers, Authors and
Publishers, and, in addition to being a member of numerous boards and leagues, he is a
member of the famous theatre group, the
Lambs, and washes dishes once a week at New
York's Stage Door Canteen, where his wife
and daughter are hostesses. Hammerstein is
also one of the sponsors of the American Youth
Orchestra, under the direction of Dean Dixon[43], which is composed of young professional musicians and graduates of music schools.

Hammerstein is a little over six feet tall and
is described as "well-built, with a short, almost
G.I., haircut [and] a young and friendly face."
His wife, the former Dorothy Blanchard of
Melbourne, Australia, operates a successful interior decorating business in New York City.
The elder of the two Hammerstein sons, William, is in the Navy; the younger boy, Jimmy,
is certain that he is a composer. Hammerstein's daughter, Alice, the wife of Michael J.
Byrne, writes lyrics.

Hammerstein is a man of simple tastes and
habits. He rises every morning at 7:30 and is
generally in bed well before midnight. He prefers sarsaparilla and ice cream or beer to
liquor, and he has never smoked. For recreation he plays tennis and bridge. He does all
of his songwriting standing up because it saves
him the trouble of having to get up every time
he wants to pace the floor.

References

> N Y Post Mag p25 Je 28 '43 il pors
> Who's Who in America 1944-45
> Who's Who in the Theatre 1939

HAMMOND, GRAEME M. Feb. 1, 1858—
Oct. 30, 1944 Neurologist; sportsman; former
president of the American Neurological Association, the New York Athletic Club, and the
American Olympic Association; for many years
professor of neurology at the New York Post-
Graduate Hospital.

Obituary

> N Y Times p19 O 31 '44 por

HANNA, EDWARD JOSEPH July 21,
1860—July 10, 1944 Retired Catholic Archbishop of San Francisco and titular Arch-

bishop of Gortyna (Crete, Greece) since 1935; won national reputation as a fair arbitrator in labor disputes and as leader in the Americanization of immigrants.

Obituary

N Y Times p15 Jl 11 '44 por

HANNAGAN, STEVE Apr. 4, 1899- Publicity agent

Address: b. 247 Park Ave., New York City; h. 280 Park Ave., New York City; 5037 N. Bay Rd., Miami Beach, Fla.

The career of Steve Hannagan, publicity man extraordinary, exhibits the dash and color he senses in many of the subjects of his spectacular publicity campaigns. With all the "cocky verve of a motion-picture press agent and all the sustained energy of a Florida cyclone," this explosive, handsome Irishman from Indiana introduced the bathing beauty in the American press and publicized such stupendous undertakings as Miami Beach, Sun Valley, and the Indianapolis Speedway, in addition to large industrial organizations.

To Stephen Jerome Hannagan his amazing rise has been hard work. The son of poor parents, he was born to William J. and Johanna Gertrude (Enright) Hannagan on April 4, 1899, in Lafayette, Indiana. Like many other boys in his town, he attended the Jefferson High School, from which he was graduated in 1917; but, unlike many other Lafayette boys, at the age of fourteen he was already a newspaper reporter on the Lafayette *Morning Journal*, where he was later to become sports editor and then city editor. At seventeen he was writing signed articles for metropolitan dailies, and had achieved the "cheeky" feat of interviewing the great George Ade, who received him in the bathtub. After high school Steve enrolled at Purdue University, but stayed only two years. He says that it seemed illogical to him that a student should be making more money than his professors. At that time he was earning $28.50 a week as city editor of the Lafayette *Morning Journal*, plus $25 a week as correspondent for metropolitan newspapers. When he was offered a job as sports writer for the Indianapolis *Star*, at $30 a week, he accepted, although it was a step-down in salary. "His principal equipment consisted of a cap, a grin like a slashed cantaloupe, a nose for news, and a terrific amount of energy." He still has, says Stanley Jones in a magazine article, "the sustained energy of a turbine with direct pipe line to a gusher." Nevertheless, when his boss, Ralston Goss, outstanding sports editor of the Midwest, saw Hannagan for the first time, he looked the "skinny kid" over and said: "It's a darn good thing I hired you over the telephone." Goss was not displeased with his acquistion at the end of a year, but Hannagan decided to leave when he saw more opportunity in advertising, and in 1919 joined the Russel M. Seeds advertising agency, where products for which he wrote copy ranged from cough syrups to automobiles.

In that same year Hannagan's first big opportunity presented itself when he was engaged by Carl G. Fisher to publicize the Indianapolis Motor Speedway. The Speedway, the first 500-mile motor race track in the United States, had opened in 1911 before some 50,000 specta-

Bob Davis

STEVE HANNAGAN

tors. During the First World War the field was used for military purposes, and when racing was again resumed Fisher became dissatisfied with the publicity. "Hitherto concerned almost exclusively with motor parts and their workings, it lacked human interest. Not knowing a spark plug from a crankshaft, Hannagan did the only thing a good reporter could do—wrote about the men who drove the cars. . . . Hannagan's typewriter spilled their lives, their families, their superstitions, their 'color' into columns from coast to coast. Editors liked these faster paced stories. The Speedway got more publicity than it had ever had . . . and Hannagan became as much a part of the Indianapolis motor classic as the checkered finish flag." His office still does the Speedway publicity, although the Second World War has temporarily halted the racing.

In 1920 Hannagan met a group of influential publishers and writers, including Roy Howard, the late Ray Long, Jimmie Quirk, and Odd O. McIntyre. Howard sent him to Karl Bickel, then president of the United Press, and Hannagan, ever ready to forsake current opportunities for future gains, took a large slash in his salary and was given a job on the United Press for $50 a week. He covered every type of reporting from police stories to features and then went over to the N.E.A. Service as a feature writer and New York columnist. He also wrote for the United Features Syndicate.

By 1924 the energetic Hannagan, having made many contacts, was ready to open his own publicity office. Stanley Walker [*] says that during the brief time Hannagan worked as a newspaperman "he was hardly regarded as a promising journalist. Indeed, he [Hannagan] says, he was almost a total loss. He was wise when he took up the life of a press agent." The newspaper experience, however, was of much value to Hannagan in his press agent work. Having been a reporter he knew what papers would print, and he supplied them accordingly. Hannagan, at twenty-five, was now ready for

HANNAGAN, STEVE—*Continued*

the job which made his name synonymous with the most spectacular publicity.

Carl Fisher, who had hired Hannagan for the Speedway publicity, next turned to the promotion of Miami Beach, where he began to "build an incredible pleasure empire out of nothing. He pumped sand and soil from the floor of Biscayne Bay over the stumps of a mangrove thicket to make Miami Beach." Fisher needed Hannagan to tell the world about it and to make it a thriving vacation city. Hannagan was willing. Studying the man-made resort he found that Florida's waters were warmer in January than California's famed surf in August. Surf bathing naturally suggested pictures of beautiful girls in bathing suits in midwinter. Soon Hannagan became a "virtuoso in the technique of using pictures of shapely girls to get free newspaper space for his clients." The Miami Beach High School, filled with civic spirit, excused girl students occasionally to pose gratis for the series of stunt pictures which Hannagan dreamed up for the press and the newsreel photographers.

Steve Hannagan built bathing beauty publicity into an "art" and a big business in Miami Beach—a "hardheaded business despite its conscious absurdity." He organized the Miami Beach News Bureau, a publicity service staff of eleven experienced newspapermen, whose job it is to lure frost-bitten Northerners to the Florida resort. There Hannagan originated the "home-town paper, please note" idea of sending pictures and write-ups of vacationists to their home-town papers, an idea which stemmed from his own small-town beginnings. From the grateful Florida municipality Hannagan has received $25,000 a year for his services.

Hannagan has pleased newspaper editors by his policy, also unusual, of covering bad news in his territory, including a number of hurricanes, jewel robberies, and night club fracases. The high-powered press agent can't see much distinction between news that is created or news that just happens—"so long," he points out, "as the event *actually* occurs. We do lots of crazy things in our pursuit of contrasts for our publicity releases. In one season at Miami Beach we had an Austrian nobleman sliding down a manufactured snow slide bang into a swimming pool with a background of palm trees. At the same time, with snow packed deep around the hot springs pool out at a Western winter resort, we had a girl in a bathing suit diving off a springboard covered with snow! These things were true—they happened. Hence they are honest news."

Hannagan also managed successful publicity campaigns on heiresses and on such sports figures as Jack Dempsey and Gene Tunney '40; he is credited with the publicizing of Tunney as the prize fighter who read Shakespeare. But Hannagan usually shies away from "big name" personalities, especially those requiring character-renovating for the press. He accomplished such a feat, however, for the late Samuel Insull, an undertaking he has since regretted.

In 1933 Hannagan, having given up his own agency, became vice-president of Lord & Thomas in that advertising agency's Chicago office. In 1935 he left that firm to begin an agency in New York under his own name, on Park Avenue. He kept his Miami Beach office, however, and later expanded by opening a third office in Hollywood to take care of the volume of motion-picture work, newsreel contacts, and radio publicity for various clients. Gradually he dropped stunt publicity and became known for his more dignified, and incidentally more lucrative, industrial public relations for some of the most important corporations in the country. These included the Union Pacific Railroad, the Coca-Cola Company, the Electric Auto-Lite Company, Owens Illinois Glass Company, Winchester Arms, and Cities Service Company. In June 1944 Hannagan took over the publicity for the Jack Benny '41 radio show.

For the Union Pacific he began one of his most famous campaigns—that of publicizing Sun Valley, which he was also responsible for naming. In early 1936 he was sent out by the chairman of the board of the railroad, William Averill Harriman '41, to look into the prospect of making a winter resort—on some 3,300 acres of U.P. mountain-sheltered land—that would match the finest in Switzerland. Hannagan, a city-dweller with no instinctive love of nature, was not impressed with the inaccessible and lonely Idaho valley. "I couldn't see," he recalls, "why any living thing except a St. Bernard on a rescue expedition should ever want to go there." Then suddenly "the sun wheeled up over the Sawtooth Mountain, and soon I was perspiring at every step in the snow. Why a fellow could strip and take a sun bath!" With his accustomed cyclonic energy, Hannagan got busy. Newspapers, magazines, and newsreels soon contained stories and pictures of the hotels, ski slides, skating rinks, openair, glass-walled, hot-spring-fed swimming pools, and assorted night clubs. Even several motion pictures have used this "winter sports in a summer climate" resort for their locale.

A bit off the beaten track for Hannagan was the island of Puerto Rico, which he made attractive to vacationists by calling it "The Honolulu of the East." (Connections were severed when the island became a military operation in the Second World War.) But very much in his territory, according to Lucius Beebe '40, was New York's famous Stork Club which he helped to publicize and the policies of which he also helped to shape.

Steve Hannagan is a hard worker. He spends about sixteen hours a day in one of his three offices, or in a plane or train on his way to more work. He has no hobby except his business, which, he says, is diversion enough. Noted for his excellent memory and respected by his associates for his honesty, he works like a hard-driving city editor. Hannagan is not only a press agent: his clients pay close attention to his judgment in business matters. His friends number thousands—friends are the lifeblood of the publicity business. In Hollywood such motion-picture figures as Darryl Zanuck '41, Louis B. Mayer '43, Louella Parsons '40, Hedda Hopper '42, and Buddy de Sylva '43 call him constantly; in New York Walter Winchell '43, Danton Walker, and a score of other columnists and newspapermen keep in touch with him. The walls in Hannagan's New York office are covered from floor to ceiling with photographs of clients, friends, and celebrities in every field.

Genial, "stocky, moon-faced," with thick black hair flecked with gray, Steven Hannagan sprawls at his desk, a telephone at his ear most of the time. At work he wears horn-rimmed glasses. In 1931 he was married to Ruth Ellery; after a divorce he was married in 1939 to Suzanne Brewster, beautiful Hattie Carnegie '42 clothes model, from whom he was divorced in 1943. Although Hannagan has had much to do with resorts which feature skiing and swimming, he dislikes sports, except for the four weeks in which he retires to a physical culture farm to get himself into condition for another year of work. It is said he spends a considerable sum for his clothing, and has a passion for having everything possible mono-grammed or signed "Steve Hannagan."

References

Fortune 13:35-45+ Ja '36 il pors
Life 1:18-23 N 30 '36 por; 9:50+ O 7 '40 pors
Newsweek 7:46-7 Mr 14 '36
Walker, S. City Editor p138 1934
Who's Who in America 1944-45

HANNEGAN, ROBERT E(MMET) June 30, 1903- Chairman of National Democratic Committee; lawyer

Address: b. National Democratic Committee, Mayflower Hotel, Washington, D. C.

"I'm an old team man," says Robert E. Hannegan, chairman of the National Demo-cratic Committee in 1944. The third man to attempt to wear James Farley's shoes (the others were Edward J. Flynn '40 of New York and Postmaster General Frank C. Walker '40), he has more in common with Farley than either of his two predecessors. Like Farley, he is an Irish Catholic, a family man—and "a hand-shaker de luxe, a thorough believer in organized politics, devoted to the art of making friends by going out and hunting them up." Neither a New Dealer nor an anti-New Dealer, he sees it as his job to get along with Democrats of all political shades.

Born in St. Louis, Missouri, June 30, 1903, Robert Emmet Hannegan is the son a St. Louis police captain who rose to be chief of detec-tives. He attended public schools in St. Louis, and almost succeeded in taking a vacation from his first year at Yeatman High School through an effort to join the United States Marine Corps in 1917 by adding four years to his age. The attempted deception was unsuccessful, and when Bob Hannegan really turned eighteen in 1921 he signed up with St. Louis University rather than the Marines. A star athlete who won his letters in football, baseball, basketball, track, and swimming, he somehow found enough time for study, too, to take his law de-gree in 1925; and in 1924, the first year he could vote, he organized a Democratic club among his fellow students.

Young lawyers don't have an easy time dur-ing the first years of their practice, and after graduation Hannegan tided himself over this period by coaching football and swimming at his alma mater, also playing professional foot-ball and minor league baseball for a while. (Later he was to help organize "The Knights of the Cauliflower Ear," a group of leading business and professional men in St. Louis, dedicated to the proposition that St. Louis was a natural sports center.) As soon as he had begun to establish himself as a lawyer he was

ROBERT E. HANNEGAN

married to Irma Protzmann, whose best beau he had been ever since high school days. There are now four children, any one of whom could pose for a breakfast-food advertisement: Patri-cia, Robert, William, and Sally Ann, in order of appearance.

Although Hannegan never ran for any elec-tive office he was a good party Democrat and a born politician, and in 1933, at the beginning of Mayor Bernard F. Dickmann's first admin-istration, he was persuaded to take over as Democratic committeeman of St. Louis' Twen-ty-first Ward. Before the year was out he was chairman of the City Central Committee and co-boss, with the Mayor, of St. Louis' Demo-cratic machine. A party revolt deposed him in 1935, but the city of St. Louis promptly hired him as its legislative representative at the Gen-eral Assembly of Missouri, the Mayor "con-tinued him as the dispenser of patronage and favors," and in 1936, with the troublemakers eliminated, he returned to the chairmanship. That year the size of Dickmann's majority caused the Republicans to raise the cry of "ballot-box stuffing," and an investigation un-covered wholesale fraud which forced the Democratic Governor to remove the entire St. Louis election board. That Dickmann and Hannegan were not necessarily responsible for the fraud even their opponents had to admit, but the scandal did not help them later, when the Democrats accused the Republicans of simi-lar fraud.

What happened was this: In 1940 the Dick-mann-Hannegan combine nominated a St. Louis man for the governorship, instead of a "coun-try boy," as was customary. Their candidate lost the state by 3,613 votes, although Roose-velt '42 carried it by 88,000, and a Republican Governor (Forest Donnell) was elected for the first time in twelve years. At a St. Louis meeting called by Hannegan it was therefore decided to press for an "investigation" of the election by the Democratic-controlled legisla-ture, which responded by barring the Republi-can candidate from assuming office pending in-

HANNEGAN, ROBERT E.—*Continued*

vestigation. The Democratic Governor, left in office by this move, vetoed the legislature's resolution and called the whole thing a "shameless steal," but the legislature went ahead and Donnell appealed to the Missouri Supreme Court (also Democratic). After due deliberation it ordered Donnell inducted into office. The Democratic candidate then contested the vote, but the re-count revealed that his rival had been elected by 10,000 votes, not 3,613. By this time the newspapers were attacking Hannegan as the ringleader in the attempted "gubernatorial steal," along with Mayor Dickmann. Hannegan's friends still insist that neither he nor Dickmann approved of the legislature's tactics, but that the press and the people made them the scapegoats. Whatever the facts, when the Mayor ran for a third term in April 1941 he was overwhelmingly defeated, although Hannegan continued to serve as chairman of the City Central Committee until June 1942.

Later on the then Senator Harry Truman [43], who owed his narrow margin of victory in 1940 to the Dickmann-Hannegan machine, decided to show his gratitude. Early in 1942 the post of Collector of Internal Revenue of the Eastern District of Missouri fell vacant, and Senator Truman proposed Hannegan to Secretary of the Treasury Henry Morgenthau [40] for the post. In March the St. Louis press got wind of the fact that Hannegan was slated for the job, and furious opposition arose. Up to that time Hannegan himself had intended to turn down the job, but when the St. Louis *Post-Dispatch* protested that Truman's choice was "an affront to thousands" and the *Globe-Democrat* called him "the most discredited boss of a discredited political machine," he decided to fight. "I never quit under fire," he says. In the middle of the battle Truman announced: "Hannegan carried St. Louis three times for the President and for me. If he is not nominated, there will be no collector at St. Louis. I think I have enough friends in the Senate to see that no other person gets the job." In June 1942 President Roosevelt appointed Hannegan to the post, and to accept, Hannegan, under provisions of the Hatch [44] Act, was forced to resign from the City Central Committee post.

According to George Creel [44] in *Collier's*, Hannegan promptly disappointed his enemies by giving "the best administration in the history of the Office" of Collector of Internal Revenue. He was the first to arrive at the office every morning, the last to leave; the merit system was his bible insofar as appointments were concerned; he went to night school to study tax law; he tried to make taxpaying as painless as possible by eliminating long waiting lines and instructing his clerks in the rudiments of courtesy. When in October 1943 Secretary Morgenthau selected him as the country's outstanding collector and recommended his promotion to the Commissionership of Internal Revenue in Washington, D. C., a post which had just fallen vacant, Hannegan's old enemies remained very quiet.

Once in the Capital, Hannegan proceeded to make more friends than ever. When he arrived at the Internal Revenue Bureau he said that its arteries had hardened—that the business of collecting taxes was too cold and formal. He proceeded to make it less so, keeping himself so busy that his lunches consisted of hasty bites at his desk or in the cafeteria along with his office associates. He made a "habit of addressing all official mail by name instead of a mechanical 'Dear Sir,' of giving his staff pep talks and ordering politeness to taxpayers, and of signing nothing he hadn't read." He also made many exploratory trips into the field, visiting cities in order to phone the office of the local collector. Identifying himself as a taxpayer, he would request some tax information and record the replies. Those who answered discourteously received reprimands, but they never suspected the source of the complaints.

Postmaster General Frank Walker [40] had accepted the chairmanship of the National Democratic Committee in 1943 only on condition that he be relieved before the 1944 election campaigning hit its full stride, and when Senator Truman suggested Hannegan for this post the President called the Commissioner of Internal Revenue to the White House for a chat. Apparently he was pleased with what he found, for before the members of the National Committee met in January 1944 they had been advised that Hannegan was Roosevelt's choice—his resignation as Commissioner of Internal Revenue had been already sent to the White House, and Roosevelt's letter of acceptance was ready to be released. On January 22, in accepting the post, Hannegan described himself as a "plain, everyday, 100 per cent, straight organization Democrat," promised to keep away from party feuds, praised Farley, and announced he would seek that master politician's advice. He also said he was "frightened" in his new post. "This is the big league for me, as I'm used to the bush leagues out in the Ozarks."

He displayed few symptoms of fright in the months that followed, however. The "big, plushy" suite at the Mayflower Hotel which constituted Democratic National Committee headquarters had been described as "pretty sleepy" in recent years, inhabited by little more than Charlie Michelson [40] (for more than a decade publicity director of the National Democratic Committee) and a typewriter, and Hannegan discovered that since Farley's departure the party organization had practically fallen to pieces. There was neither an office for him in headquarters nor a mailing list of county chairmen; patronage was completely out of hand, for Cabinet members had almost entirely ignored the National Committee in making appointments; and, of course, there were a disturbing number of feuds in the party itself. Hannegan moved into headquarters. He planned a nationwide drive to aid war workers who were away from their homes in registering for the coming election; he planned "get-togethers" with precinct workers throughout the country, calling them the forgotten men of today; he announced that the 1944 campaign would find the National Committee working for the election or re-election of all Democratic nominees, without distinction between them. He took tours throughout the country from time to time, meeting party leaders in Minnesota, Texas, New England, the South. He did his best to mend party breaks. And by April he "had installed a new headquarters high command, traveled nearly 10,000 miles, and infused a new hopefulness in the outlook of the party's weary." By that time he had officially called the Democratic National Convention for July 19 in Chicago.

Quotations from Hannegan by this time had given an indication of the line the Democrats were planning to take in the election campaign. He credited the Administration with saving America from "the disaster of inflation," while the opposition had a record "of never offering constructive help, of never pointing to a better or more efficient way, of always and forever scolding and belittling." Although the National Committee had given an only slightly disguised endorsement to the Roosevelt candidacy six months in advance of the party's national convention, Hannegan announced that while he personally thought Roosevelt would be renominated—and "I am not averse to that"—his job was not to work on behalf of the nomination, but "to organize the party, so that whoever is the nominee he will be victorious in November."

He did ask, however, "What could hearten Hitler '42 or the Japanese war lords more than tidings that America has repudiated the Administration of Franklin Roosevelt?" Referring to the Republicans, who for twelve years have "been showering America with negations," he demanded: "Do they think the support of the American people can be bought by promising more gasoline when our bombers need it to blast Berlin and Tokyo? Do they believe that more sugar will gain somebody's vote when industrial alcohol is needed for munitions for ourselves and our allies? Do they feel that promises of higher prices to groups of producers will invite support when this Administration is battling valiantly and successfully to prevent inflation and to protect the value of the allotment of the fighting man's dependent?"

When Hannegan spoke at the annual $50-a-plate Jefferson Day dinner at the Hotel Commodore, May 8, 1944, he predicted that Roosevelt would be renominated in July and re-elected in November to a fourth term, for "our people have adjudged the life-and-death risks of total war too great to entrust the responsibility of waging it from here on to a novice or a lesser soldier of freedom."

At the twenty-ninth Democratic National Convention in July, Hannegan filled the dual role of national chairman and President Roosevelt's personal representative. Although in May Hannegan had predicted Roosevelt's renomination and re-election, the official answer to the question of whether the President would even accept nomination was not made public until a week before the convention. On July 12, in response to a letter from the National Democratic Committee chairman, which had stated that a majority of the delegates had been directed by their constituents to vote for the President's renomination, Roosevelt wrote that he would accept if "drafted."

In the months before this announcement political analysts were puzzled as to whom the Democrats could bring forth as a candidate should the Chief Executive not be a nominee again. The possibilities of Byrnes, Farley, Harry F. Byrd '42, Henry Wallace '40, Sam Rayburn '40, and Harry Truman were discussed. Party-wise Farley created a situation by resigning as New York State chairman; an anti-Roosevelt group of Democrats, named the American Democratic Committee, came out for John Bricker '43, later to be the Republican Vice-Presidential choice; and Democratic leaders in six Southern states met to formulate plans for their opposition to Roosevelt. Even the President's nomination by a vote of 1,086 to 90 did not bring about complete unity within the party.

Of almost equal concern at the convention was the selection of the Vice-Presidential candidate. For his part in the final choice, Hannegan has been criticized by Democrats (mainly supporters of the defeated Henry Wallace) and Republicans alike for "improperly using his position . . . to put over Truman on the convention." "In justice to him [Hannegan]," wrote Roscoe Drummond of the *Christian Science Monitor* at the time, ". . . it deserves to be put into the record that he did not take the lead in engineering the Truman strategy at his own initiative." Of those who took this stand, many felt that Hannegan was following Roosevelt's wishes in the matter of a running mate. The National Committee chairman, it is said, favored Truman for the post above Wallace, whom he considered as a political liability, despite, or because of, the backing of the CIO's Political Action Committee. (Hannegan and several other Democratic leaders are said to have made this feeling known to the President.) Two letters written by Roosevelt are believed to have been instrumental in swinging the nomination to Truman. The first, addressed to the permanent chairman of the convention, stated that if he (Roosevelt) were a delegate he would support Wallace, but that the choice lay with the convention. The second letter, solicited by Hannegan, who had asked the President's views on Truman and William O. Douglas '41, stated that either man would make a satisfactory running mate.

Re-elected chairman of the committee at the closing meeting, Hannegan in his speech "pitched the campaign to re-elect President Roosevelt on the keynote that mass voting was the secret to success in November." "People are not registered," he declared. "The Republican Party is not interested in doing anything about it. The more votes cast the better it is for us. We must wage a vigorous campaign of registration. The only way to do it is by a door-to-door campaign." Maintaining that Thomas E. Dewey '44 would not get more than Herbert Hoover '43 had in 1932 (Dewey got over 6,000,000 more) Hannegan set out to stimulate registration by a series of conferences with state and county Democratic leaders, this organizational work taking him across the continent. Of special concern to him was the vote of war workers, migratory workers, and Negroes.

There were a number of separate issues highlighted during the campaign on which Hannegan was especially vocal. One of these was the charge made by him that the Repub-

HANNEGAN, ROBERT E.—*Continued*

lican candidate, in his post as New York State Governor, was "resisting all proposals for simplification of New York's wartime ballot law." News of the existence of a Democratic campaign textbook, containing attacks on Farley, John J. Bennett, and Edward J. Flynn[40], made political headlines; later the offending volumes were destroyed, according to Hannegan, and apologies made. In a number of speeches Hannegan charged "the opposition" with avoiding fundamental issues, with making distortions, with promoting "a whispering campaign" about the President's health—this denied by Herbert Brownell[44], the Republican chairman. The CIO's PAC was the cause of much bitter controversy, and candidate Bricker charged that Roosevelt had instructed Hannegan to "Clear everything with Sidney [Hillman[40]]," chairman of the PAC. This Republican charge, that the Democratic Party was dominated by Hillman and a Communist element in the CIO group, was vehemently denied by Hannegan. Such criticisms of both opponent's supporters continued throughout the campaign: Among them were Hannegan's attacks on certain of Dewey's backers, and the Republican's criticism of the One Thousand Club, the members of which were supposed, according to Dewey himself, to receive special privileges for their campaign contributions of one thousand dollars. (This charge Hannegan denied for the White House, declaring it to be "wholly without substance.")

Finally, after a heavy turnout at the polls, at 11:49 on Election Night the Democratic Committee chairman was able to announce "the overwhelming victory" of President Roosevelt. While Hannegan was wrong in his prediction that his candidate would do better than he had in 1940 (Roosevelt's total was one and a half million less), Hannegan guessed wrong on only one electoral vote—Ohio's. The campaign, reports showed, had cost the Democrats $2,056,121.58; the Republicans $2,828,-651 in their unsuccessful race. For his work Hannegan had received a weekly salary of $384.61, but no Cabinet post, as rumors had first indicated. It was believed that he would continue as national chairman.

Robert Hannegan is a talkative, genial, aggressive, black-haired man with an Irish grin and "a youngish smooth face with impassive blue eyes." He is an inch over six feet tall and weighs 205 pounds. He "dresses carefully, with ties, socks, suit in color harmony. On the fourth finger of his left hand he wears a largish diamond ring." The onetime athlete now restricts his own athletic activities to golf, but he is found at a big prize fight or a football game more often than at the movies. He does little reading—he likes historical novels, but there hasn't been time for many of them lately.

In April 1944 Hannegan was elected vice-president of the Lawyers' Association of St. Louis. He is also a member of several athletic and country clubs and of the American and the Missouri Bar Associations.

References

Collier's 113:14+ Mr 25 '44 por
N Y Herald Tribune p23 Ja 23 '44 por;
  II p3 Ja 30 '44 por
N Y Post p4 Ja 29 '44 por; p21 Mr 1
  '44
N Y Post Mag p8 Ja 29 '44 pors
Newsweek 23:36+ Ja 31 '44 por; 23:27
  Ap 10 '44 por
Scholastic 44:8 F 14 '44 por
Time 43:14 Ja 24 '44 por; 39:16 Mr 23
  '42

HARRISON, JOAN (MARY) June 20, 1908(?)- Producer; scenarist

Address: b. Universal Studios, Universal City, Calif.; h. 874 Birchwood Dr., Los Angeles, Calif.

A producer, says Jesse Lasky, "must be a prophet and a general, a diplomat and a peacemaker, a miser and a spendthrift. He must have vision tempered by hindsight, daring governed by caution, the patience of a saint, and the iron of a Cromwell." One of the newest of these super-beings is Joan Harrison, scriptwriter and Alfred Hitchcock's[41] former "Girl Friday." With her first production, Universal's *Phantom Lady*, in early 1944, she became one of the few women producers in the history of Hollywood—others are Dorothy Davenport, Fanchon Royer, Lois Weber, Harriet Parsons, Mary Pickford—and one of those who, Leo Rosten[42] claims, have it within their power to "improve or ruin a picture at a hundred different points."

Joan Mary Harrison began life in Guildford, Surrey, England, the daughter of Walter and Maelia (Muir) Harrison. As the child of moderately well-to-do parents, she was given a good education in literature, philosophy, languages, and political economy in preparation for becoming an English lady. (On the side she read unladylike murder stories for her own amusement.) Following boarding school in Kent, she was sent to the Sorbonne for a year and then to St. Hugh's College at Oxford, where she received her B.A. degree. When she returned home to Surrey following her graduation she was hopeful of getting a newspaper job through her father, the publisher of two local papers. He and his wife, however, were more interested in seeing their daughter marry and settle down in respectable idleness than in helping her become "a tough journalist." In deference to their wishes, therefore, Miss Harrison pottered around home for several months; that is, until she found she could no longer stand the inactivity. She left Surrey and went up to London to try her own luck. For the next four or five years she worked at numerous jobs: as copy writer for the London Press Exchange, an advertising agency; as clerk in a dress shop, telling stout ladies they "looked darling in tweeds"; as a free-lancer for magazines, which gave her a meager livelihood; and as secretary for several writers.

Finally she had a stroke of good luck. She learned one morning that Alfred Hitchcock, the film director, was looking for a competent secretary. Miss Harrison's brief course in stenography had not made her exactly what Hitchcock was seeking, but she was determined to try for the opening. By the simple expedient of telling the man in charge of the outside office that her sister was expecting a baby and that she, Joan, was needed back at the hospital shortly, she got in to see the famous gentleman ahead of a large number of other applicants. The stories vary on how she got the job from Hitchcock, as well as the "entrée" to his office, but she was hired. That was in 1933, and Hitchcock was working on *The Man Who Knew Too Much.*

Miss Harrison proved very competent, but not as a secretary. In a short time she was graduated from stenographer to script-reader, and then to assistant at story conferences, starting with *The Thirty-nine Steps.* Hitchcock would not read scripts himself, so that part of her job had been to present the plots to him. After a time she began making improvements in those she outlined to him and by degrees she began making her own suggestions. In 1937 she had her first opportunity to collaborate on a screen adaptation when Hitchcock directed *The Girl Was Young;* and in 1939 she got her first screen credit for her collaboration on *Jamaica Inn.* In the nine years she worked for the English director she of course absorbed valuable knowledge on the making of motion pictures, particularly the type of psychological thriller on which Hitchcock specialized. When he came to the United States in April 1939 to work for David O. Selznick '41, Miss Harrison accompanied him as an important member of his staff. Until 1941 she continued to work with him in various capacities on such pictures as *Rebecca* (1940), the first American film on which she worked and for which she wrote her first full script; *Foreign Correspondent* (1940); *Suspicion* (1941); and *Saboteur* (1942)—all of them in the familiar Hitchcock vein.

By 1941, according to *Time* Magazine, "Secretary Harrison was (1) perhaps the most highly esteemed member of Hitchcock's permanent crew, (2) desperate." The explanation for her desperation was simple: "She had ideas and an ego, and she had been too close to a great man to do what she wanted with either." She left Hitchcock at the end of 1941, therefore, to concentrate on screen writing. During the next two years the results of her free-lancing were disappointing. The first film she started was for Paramount and was designed for Charles Boyer '43; but both his plans and those of the producer, Arthur Hornblow, were changed before the script ever reached the screen. (Miss Harrison was very fond of her story, but felt that Boyer was the only actor who could handle it the way she imagined it.) Another script-writing job was for MGM, for whom Miss Harrison did the adaptation of Marguerite Steen's '41 *The Sun Is My Undoing* (1941). That script, too, was shelved. Still another script, for Columbia Pictures, was so badly mangled in the transference to the screen that Miss Harrison complained that "what came out didn't even vaguely resemble what I had written. I was heartbroken."

Miss Harrison was about ready to abandon the idea of free-lance film-writing when she came across the mystery novel by William Irish entitled *The Phantom Lady,* which Universal Pictures was planning to film. She had

JOAN HARRISON

been given the rare opportunity to do the script—detective pictures usually being considered in the men's field—and while it was the kind of story she was most interested in doing, she was skeptical because of her recent experiences in the way a writer's work is treated. She finally agreed to do it, however; and when the time for the story conference came around she told the executives exactly how she wanted the picture done. Impressed by her firmness and her suggestions, the studio offered her the chance to act as associate producer for the production. It was an unusual offer to make to a woman, and Miss Harrison was not slow in accepting it.

Leo Rosten in his book *Hollywood* writes that the questions "What is a producer?" and "What does a producer do?" can be answered by another question, "Which producer?" "'Producer,'" he explains, "is a term which covers several meanings. There are producers who head small companies, executive-producers of large motion-picture corporations, producers who work on a salary, producers who get a percentage of the profits. There are producers who are employers, and producers who are employees." And the functions and jurisdiction of all of them vary from studio to studio. Rosten lists in seven categories the various types that he considers the most usual: the executive head of a studio, the executive in charge of the productions of his studio, the independent producer, the producer in charge of "A" pictures, the producer in charge of "B" pictures, the producer or associate producer, and the producer-director. As associate producer for Universal Miss Harrison worked under a budget and was concerned only with the actual production of the picture. She worked with her director "in planning the emphases and 'key' of a story, the handling of the cast." She was "in direct contact with

HARRISON, JOAN—*Continued*

all the technicians and departments entering into the making of the film."

According to *Time,* from the first Miss Harrison's working methods were rather unconventional: "they showed foresight and sharp common sense." Her first step was to hire an art director, John Goodman, then a screen-writer, B. C. Schoenfeld, a cameraman, "mood-wise" Elwood Bredell, and a director, Robert Siodmak, former director of German horror pictures. With each she worked very closely. Miss Harrison did all of her own casting, too, spending a reported $60,000 on Franchot Tone [40], her star, "on the theory that unusual casting brings a different flavor to your picture." Then, unlike other Hollywood producers, she worked for simplicity in her costuming and make-up in an effort to approach the naturalness that many other producers seem to scorn.

The total result of this maiden effort of Miss Harrison's received a mixed reception from the press when it opened in January 1944. (The story concerned a hunt for an elusive woman who could provide the alibi for a murder suspect—elusive because those who could assist in finding her have been bribed by the real murderer.) On the favorable side of the critical line-up were those who thought that *Phantom Lady* "lagged behind Hitchcock's best films, but had picked up enough from them to sprint laps ahead of most thrillers." A *PM* critic remarked that it was a "measured melodrama with some notable crests of melodramatic tension and endowed with more flesh and blood than Hitchcock ever permits in his graven characters." Those who considered the film often very exciting emphasized the clever use of lighting and photography to heighten the suspense and the effective use of silence in long sections of the sound track. As the New York *Herald Tribune* reviewer wrote in praise of the picture, these directorial tricks are still good suspense builders and, in the case of *Phantom Lady,* were at least less obvious than the usual whodunit routines. The best sequence in the film, in the opinion of several critics, was that of a jam session at which an attempt was made to loosen the tongue of one of the witnesses. In cagily handling the baser emotions, it was said, Miss Harrison produced a genuine "orgy, portrayed metaphorically, without a line of dialogue, suggestive or otherwise." On the negative side, however, were critics who found the film tedious. It was, according to the New York *Times* critic, "a perfect combination of the styles of the eminent Mr. Hitchcock and the old German psychological films . . . studiously constructed for weird and disturbing effects . . . severe and unrelenting, drenched in creeping morbidity and gloom," but on the whole a specious picture without a plausible, realistic plot.

At the conclusion of production on *Phantom Lady* at the end of 1943 Miss Harrison was reported to be planning to concentrate on mystery pictures "from the women's angle." "Women must have something to pull for," she explained, "whether it's a dog, a horse,

an old beggar, or even another woman."

The next thing for which Joan Harrison "pulled," as associate producer, was Benedict Bogeaus' production of *Dark Waters,* a melodrama of the Louisiana bayou country. Originally a *Saturday Evening Post* serial by Frank and Marian Cockrell, it had been adapted for United Artists by Miss Harrison and Miss Cockrell. For the inveterate "thriller" fan, the picture was, according to the New York *Times,* a "killer diller of a thriller," relying heavily on its dank and eerie locale and full of "a harsh, relentless menace."

Interviewers announce that Miss Harrison is blond, pretty, and shapely, an unusual combination for a Hollywood producer. Because of her attractive looks she is frequently asked why she does not get into camera range. She replies that she is definitely not an actress and that at present, as someone else put it, her job is "to make cops-and-robbers more exciting than Dorothy Lamour."

References

C S Mon p6 N 12 '43 por
Collier's 112:55+ Ag 14 '43 por
N Y Times 11 p3 Je 27 '43
N Y World-Telegram p15 S 28 '43 por
Time 43:93-4+ F 28 '44 il por
International Motion Picture Almanac 1942-43

HARSANYI, ZSOLT (hor'shä-nyi zhōlt) 1887—Dec.(?), 1943 Hungarian author and journalist; his fictional biography of Galileo, *The Star-Gazer* (1939), was the Book-of-the-Month Club selection in February 1940; his first book to be published in English was *Immortal Franz* (1937).

Obituary

N Y Times p17 F 28 '44 por

HARSCH, JOSEPH C(LOSE) (härsh) May 25, 1905- Radio commentator; journalist

Address: b. 1293 National Press Bldg., Washington, D. C.; h. 2800 O St., N. W., Washington, D. C.

After a distinguished career as foreign correspondent for the *Christian Science Monitor,* Joseph C. Harsch became in March 1943 the Washington commentator for the Columbia Broadcasting System. Like other correspondents in the early years of the Second World War, he had become known to the public through a book. His book, *Pattern of Conquest* (1941), was the result of observations made during his two years in Germany from 1939 to 1941. He had been on the scene when many of the critical events of the War occurred, but he had had little microphone experience—except for some broadcasts from Berlin for William Shirer [41] over CBS and some others from Australia and Denmark. (He still retains his connection with the *Monitor.*)

Like many other correspondents and commentators, Joseph Close Harsch is from the Middle West. He was born in Toledo, Ohio, on May 25, 1905, the son of Paul Arthur and Leila Katherine (Close) Harsch. After attending the Hackley School in Tarrytown,

JOSEPH C. HARSCH

New York, he entered Williams College, where he received his B.A. in 1927. (Williams College awarded him an honorary M.A. degree in 1943.) He then studied at Corpus Christi College of Cambridge University in England, where he was given a B.A. degree in 1929. It was in that year that he began his career as a newspaperman.

A member of the Christian Scientist Church, Harsch went directly to work for the *Christian Science Monitor* in Boston, and in 1931 the newspaper transferred him to its Washington bureau, where he remained until 1939. In this capacity he covered, in 1936, the last of the between-wars naval conferences in London. In 1939, when he was drafted by the State Department in Washington to serve for a year as an assistant director of the Inter-Governmental Committee on Political Refugees, of which Myron C. Taylor [40] was vice-chairman, he was granted a leave from the *Monitor*. After 1939 he became a foreign correspondent for his newspaper. He was first assigned to Rome for a brief time, and was then sent to Berlin to cover Germany in the early years of the War. He also reported from Czechoslovakia, Denmark, Belgium, Nazi-occupied France, and Vichy. He was on hand for Hitler's [42] great moment: his dictation of armistice terms to the French in the railway car at Compiègne. (In Denmark he made his actual microphone debut—from Copenhagen about a week after the German Army entered the city.)

On Harsch's return in 1941 from inside Germany, his *Pattern of Conquest* was published. Coming on the heels of William Shirer's best seller, *Berlin Diary* (1941), it offered the opportunity for some interesting conclusions and points of comparison. Readers found both books convincing because of their honest, thoughtful, undramatic objectivity. Reviewers described as "impressive" Harsch's description of the efficient and democratic organization of the German Army—an army well fed and well clothed at the expense of

civilians who were hungry and poorly clad. "And the nation which will defeat it," said Harsch, "must do the same." Reporting on the German home front a year after the Nazis went to war, he saw rationing and shortages, but he also saw that on the whole the Germans were faring well because of the immense amount of loot coming in from France and other conquered countries. In view of Allied air attacks over Germany in 1943, Harsch's predictions of the effect of the "pattern of conquest in reverse" were interesting. He said that if Nazi Germany disintegrates, history will trace that disintegration back to the night of August 26, 1940 when, for the first time, British airplanes dropped bombs on Berlin. "What will happen then, when the German people find themselves bombed with increasing accuracy and regularity?" he asked.

Harsch did not remain long in America following his return from Germany. A sixth sense for locating scenes of action or trouble spots prompted him to be on hand to record the Japanese attack on Pearl Harbor in December 1941. He then made a 4,125-mile trip by aircraft carrier and destroyer from Honolulu to New Zealand, with "more steam up than the Navy had in Washington." In February 1942 he could report: "The Battle of the Supply Line from America's factories to the Far Pacific battle front has been won. . . . During the long silent weeks since Pearl Harbor lines of communication vital to ultimate success have been nailed down hard with reinforcements and ceaseless naval patrols and hard jabs at enemy points of attack."

Harsch was in Java when the Japanese began their invasion of that island. Making his escape, the correspondent reached Australia just in time to greet the first contingent of disembarking American troops. And, "when General MacArthur's [41] arrival from embattled Bataan sent tremendous waves of enthusiasm surging through the Australian people, Harsch, as usual, was 'on the spot.'" Writing of events there he said: "Political Washington was largely responsible for setting up two separate commands in the Far Pacific, and it did this partly because of jealousy of MacArthur's great popularity and partly because the conservative opposition press launched a 'MacArthur-for-President' campaign—without any encouragement from the General himself."

While in Australia Harsch made several broadcasts, one for the Columbia Broadcasting System, others for the Canadian Broadcasting Company and the Australian airways. When the commentator returned to New York City, CBS's Paul White [40] persuaded Harsch to join the station's staff of news analysts. On his first broadcast on March 15, 1943 the correspondent called for "a peace which will make this war worth fighting." "Such arrangements," he said "are going to be made soon. Russia certainly isn't going to wait until the last gun has been fired before deciding whether to commit her future security either to a group organization or to her own isolated national strength. Stalin [42] is going to decide very soon whether his allies in war are worth working with after the War."

Around Washington, Harsch soon became recognized as an authority on foreign affairs, and his coverage of the political home front eventually became no less authoritative. On

HARSCH, JOSEPH C.—*Continued*

May 12, 1943 he gave the radio public a "split-second" report of the Churchill [42] arrival in Washington. Four minutes after the announcement that the Prime Minister was in the United States, Harsch came on the air for his analysis of "news behind the news." "He had written a full script on the Churchill visit," it is reported, "feeling sure that his judgment was right. It was a master stroke, for Columbia listeners heard that analysis and thus had full coverage of a stirring world event within barely ten minutes of the time it transpired."

Harsch's radio news comments and interpretations, made daily from 6:55 to 7:00 p.m. for the Columbia Broadcasting System, are careful, unspectacular, often shrewdly prophetic. The following comment, made in the summer of 1943, is characteristic of his manner and method: "The Balkans lie before us—still a long way off, but there at the end of the road. And the Balkans are also in the suggested path of Russian advance. Here is a potential giant pincers. It could close on everything the German armies hold today south of the Alps and the Carpathians, cutting Germany off from the food and oil of the Ukraine and the Balkans. This sounds almost like a dream, but it is the kind of dream which today's facts of war make into a bold, clear possibility."

During the winter of 1943 and the spring and summer of 1944 Harsch continued his weekly dispatches from Washington to the *Christian Science Monitor* in his column, "An Intimate Message From Washington." He also contributed to *Collier's* and the New York *Times Magazine*. His comments and interpretations covered various theatres of military action—the European land-fronts and the naval action in the Pacific—and occasionally internal political affairs in the United States. Early in 1944 he wrote a series of articles assessing conditions existing in Germany, finding that country "outclassed only by the sum total of Russian, British, American, and other Allied might."

In May 1944 came a series of pre-invasion articles; and of the historic event of June 6, Harsch said: "This is the day when the grand alliance of the United Nations has finally achieved its full stature . . . the day of all days that Adolf Hitler [42] never wrote into his calculations." Although he had nothing but admiration for the skill of Allied military strategy, Harsch—in both his writings and his radio comments—condemned from the start the feud between the United States State Department and General de Gaulle [40]. On June 14 he said, "The long confused record of American-French relations has moved to a resentful climax"; and on June 16 wrote: "The Russians and Poles have managed to produce some rather unsightly pages in the record of the United Nations, but nothing in their controversy has ever quite approached the vulgarity of the dispute between de Gaulle's French National Committee and the United States Government at the solemn moment of the invasion of France. . . . What happened to mar the invasion was the product of a long vicious downward spiral in human relations which no event or individual has proven capable of breaking." By July, however, Harsch noted more cheerfully that "progress is being made in putting the Allied political house into order. General de Gaulle is coming here . . . to see the President, and the British are recalling their Ambassador from Argentina. The two events have a closer connection than might appear on the surface." In a later article on the situation in Argentina (July 27, 1944) the commentator said he felt that "Nazism has fixed upon Argentina as the place where it will go underground when this War is over, not only as a refuge for its leaders but also as a warm nest within which the concepts of fascism are to be nurtured and a new attempt on the world spawned at some later day." In his significant comments on the German robot planes, Harsch revealed his understanding of Nazi character and psychology: "The prime German military problem is to meet and repel the invasion. The robot plane has shown up in its opening engagement not as an anti-invasion weapon, but as a weapon which is three years behind the War. The whole Nazi concept of war-making was based on the doctrine of conquest by terror. At this stage of the War, when terror has failed scores of times, when the technique of blackmail has been discredited by the staunchness of Britain, by the grim courage of Russia, by the industrial miracle of America—Nazi war-making relies for its salvation not on a real weapon of war but on a weapon of terror . . . an instrument built on the false foundation which underlies the whole German concept."

In September 1944 Harsch declared that the Allies had reached the point where they could do to Japan what had already been done to Germany. "The defeat of Germany," he wrote, "began with the tearing asunder of its economic foundation. . . . Once we have air and naval bases in the Philippines again, Japan will automatically lose access to the oil and rubber of the East Indies and the rice of Burma." He also posed the pertinent question of whether or not the Allied coalition could be applied as effectively to the concluding phases of war in the Pacific area as it already had been applied to the war in Europe. (Later he said that the Allied failure at Arnhem, the Netherlands, in September 1944, meant that victory over Germany could not be achieved that year.)

Harsch, writing in the *Christian Science Monitor* during October 1944, was concerned with the two major theatres of action, the European and the Pacific. He characterized as a stalemate Allied operations on the Western Front, but felt that "British and American forces were carrying the attack to the enemy all along the line without letup." He also observed the withdrawals of the Germans on several "useless fronts," but noted that in Italy "Kesselring's [42] campaign was coming to be regarded as the ablest of any German general." Following the daring and dramatic naval action in the Pacific, Harsch warned that General MacArthur's "landing in the Philippines marked not the beginning of the end, which is the liberation of these islands, but the beginning of a new venture of greater hazard and duration and difficulty than generally is appreciated." With a side glance at a future aspect of the war in Europe, Harsch in his radio report for October 25 touched on the situation in Spain: "Franco [42] is energetically trying to revive his own Falange Party . . . and is engaged in killing Spaniards who have just finished a fight for the liberation of France. Will de Gaulle deal with Franco or support those who have fought with him?"

Five feet six and one-half inches tall, blond, and smiling, Joe Harsch is popular around Washington, where he is a member of Chi Psi and the National Press Club. In December 1932 he was married to Anne Elizabeth Wood. The couple have two sons: Joseph William Wood and Jonathan Hannum.

References

Newsweek 18:64 S 8 '41 por
PM p7 S 18 '41 por
Who's Who in America 1944-45

HART, LORENZ May 2, 1895—Nov. 22, 1943 Song writer; for twenty years associated with Richard Rodgers '40; team wrote numerous successful musical comedies; see sketch 1940 Yearbook.

Obituary

N Y Times p25 N 23 '43

HASKIN, FREDERIC J. Dec. 13, 1872—Apr. 24, 1944 Author and columnist; his question-and-answer column established in 1916 appeared in more than 100 newspapers; author of *The American Government* (1911), *The Immigrant* (1913), *The Panama Canal* (1913), *Uncle Sam at Work* (1915), and *The American Government Today* (1935).

Obituary

N Y Times p23 Ap 25 '44

HASTIE, WILLIAM H(ENRY) (hăs'tē) Nov. 17, 1904- Educator; lawyer; judge *Address*: b. Howard University, Washington, D.C.; h. 1707 S St., N.W., Washington, D.C.

Enemy propagandists have been quick to seize on the inconsistency between the United States declaration for the rights of minorities —and the admitted discrimination practiced against the tenth of the American population who happen to be wholly or partly Negro. Among the many distinguished persons of both races who are leaders in the fight against such discrimination is William H. Hastie, one of the most prominent Negroes of the country. In January 1943 he resigned his position as civilian aide to the Secretary of War on Negro problems, charging that his recommendations had been disregarded in the carrying out of "reactionary policies and discriminatory practices" against Negroes in the Army, and particularly in the Army Air Forces.

William Henry Hastie came to this position with a distinguished record as jurist, educator, and leader of conservative Negro thought. Born in Knoxville, Tennessee, November 17, 1904, to William Henry and Roberta (Child) Hastie, he attended elementary schools there and in Washington, D. C. After his graduation from the Dunbar High School in Washington, Hastie entered Amherst College (Massachusetts), from which he received his bachelor's degree as top-ranking student of the class of 1925. He was elected to the Amherst chapter of Phi Beta Kappa, of which he is president. Hastie then joined the staff of the Bordentown (New Jersey) Manual Training School, where

he taught until 1927. In 1930 he received his LL.B. from Harvard University, where he was on the staff of the *Harvard Law Review*, and then joined the faculty of the Howard University School of Law, in Washington, D. C. He was admitted to the District of Columbia Bar in 1931, entering practice in association with the firm of Houston and Houston. A year later Harvard University awarded Hastie the degree of Doctor of Juridicial Science.

Dr. Hastie's service with the Government began in 1933, when he became Assistant Solicitor of the United States Department of the Interior. In 1937 he had the unprecedented honor of being appointed judge of the district court of the United States for the Virgin Islands—unprecedented because, although the Virgin Islands population is ninety per cent Negro, no colored person had ever before been appointed to a Federal judgeship.

At the end of his two-year term Hastie returned to Howard University as dean and professor of law. He took a leave of absence from the University in November 1940 so that he might accept the post of civilian aide to the Secretary of War. The understanding was that "all questions of policy and important proposals relating to Negroes should be referred to his office for comment or approval before final action." In this capacity he was active in the attempt to open all branches of the Army, and particularly the Air Force, to Negroes. During Dr. Hastie's incumbency the condition of Negroes in the Army was sufficiently improved for him to report, "In any view, the present status of the Negro officer is significantly better than his status during World War I. . . . Yet, in any view, the status of the Negro officer is far from what it should be and must be if the Army is to realize the tremendous potential value which the Negro officer represents both in himself and as an inspiration to the Negro soldier."

That statement is regarded as a conservative one when considered in relation to Hastie's revelations: "Many Negro soldiers could not even get information concerning officer candidate training from their immediate superiors" until the Secretary of War, acting presumably on the advice of Hastie, "gave explicit and unmistakable instructions to field commanders concerning the need for Negro officers," and "commanders were required to account for their failure to send Negro soldiers to these schools. . . . Proportionately [Negroes in the Medical Corps] represent a far smaller percentage of the available Negro professionals in these fields than the percentage of white physicians and dentists accepted for military duty. Moreover, service in general hospitals is still for white officers only. And, of the hundreds of station hospitals, only those at . . . [four camps and one overseas station] have Negro officers as members of the hospital staffs. Even as to these officers, the notion persists that Negro medical men can serve Negro patients only. . . . Generally, the Negro woman officer, like her brother officer, has been restricted, whatever her special qualifications may be, to service with or in command of Negro units. . . . As to them [nurses] also, restriction to the service of Negro patients is enforced by the device of establishing segregated wards for colored sol-

WILLIAM H. HASTIE

diers. Today the Army is unwilling to recruit additional Negro nurses, at a time when every effort is being made to recruit thousands of white nurses," and this recruitment is considerably behind its quota.

"The Army still is reluctant to assign to combat service those units which are officered entirely by Negroes. Only one such regiment is now known to be overseas and it is in an inactive theatre. Almost no use is made of Negro officers in administrative or other capacities where they must deal with white as well as colored troops. The promotion of the Negro officer and his use in the command of units higher than the platoon is still retarded by racial considerations. Although one Negro officer is a brigadier general and some ten Negroes command regiments or independent battalions or administrative units, such opportunities continue to be few and restricted. . . . While the promotion of a qualified white officer to the command of Negro troops or to any other assignment may proceed as a matter of routine, Negro officers are not similarly advanced until the War Department shall expressly indicate that a particular position is to be filled by a Negro. The result has been the freezing of many Negroes for long periods of time while white officers of no greater competency or experience are being advanced. This situation affects not only senior Reserve and National Guard officers, but also the best of the Officer Candidate School graduates." By the beginning of 1943 one white OCS graduate "had already risen to lieutenant colonel, several had become majors, and hundreds had been promoted to captaincies . . . but not a single Negro OCS graduate had been promoted beyond the grade of 1st lieutenant. . . . Failure of promotion is perhaps the most serious impediment to high morale and efficiency among Negro officers."

The Navy has long been criticized as a racially discriminating organization; with the emergence of the Army Air Force as an elite

corps, the problem of racial discrimination in it has become comparable. "In July 1941," when "instruction began in the first officer candidate schools, every arm and service except the Air Corps established an unsegregated school for the training of its officers. . . . Only the Air Corps, already more nearly independent than the public realized, was able to establish a segregated school for the training of Negro pilots." This center was established over Dr. Hastie's objections. "In December 1940," he said when explaining his resignation, "the Air Forces referred to me a plan for a segregated training center for Negro pursuit pilots at Tuskegee, Alabama. I expressed my entire disagreement with the plan, giving my reasons in detail. My views were disregarded. Since then the Air Command has never on its own initiative submitted any project to me for comment or recommendation." "'Aviation Squadrons (separate)' never would have come into existence except for the necessity of making some provision for Negro enlisted men in the Air Forces. Reluctant to use Negroes at all, the Air Command started off on the wrong foot by organizing some Negro labor units, while every effort was being made to recruit white volunteers with mechanical ability for skilled service."

Negro medical officers, Hastie charged, were getting only a small part of the special training in aviation medicine which was available to white doctors. In spite of the pressing need for weather officers, armorers, engineers, and service pilots, all Negro volunteers for these services were being rejected. Two applicants for service pilot who were actually accepted and ordered to report for training were sent home—as soon as it was discovered that they were Negroes.

"Even now," Dr. Hastie stated, "the Air Command views the use of the Negro as an 'experiment' designed to determine whether he can do this or that in the field of aviation. This attitude is the result of wholly unscientific notions that race somehow controls a man's capacity and aptitudes. The tragedy is that by not wanting the Negro in the first place and by doubting his capacity the Air Command has committed itself psychologically to courses of action which themselves become major obstacles to the success of Negroes in the Air Forces."

In January of 1943 Hastie learned of plans to establish a segregated officer candidate school for Negroes at Jefferson Barracks, Missouri. This climaxed the situation, and on January 18 he resigned from his position as civilian aide to the Secretary of War and returned to his work as dean and professor of law at Howard University. On July 19, 1943 he submitted a report to the National Lawyers Guild (of which he is vice-president), "reviewing a series of civilian and police assaults on Negro troops" in 1942, warning that in 1943 "both the seriousness of this form of lawlessness and the lack of any effective methods of control have become more apparent and increasingly grave in their implications," and criticizing the Federal and military authorities for not using their limited power "to restrain and punish such violence." (A number of his other papers have appeared, mainly in professional journals.) Finally, less than a year after Hastie's resignation, the Army High Command in March 1944 ordered that all Negro officers be trained with white candidates, and since then the experiment has been found successful. In April 1944 Hastie supported the National Committee to Abolish the Poll Tax in demanding Senatorial enactment of the bill which would outlaw the tax in Federal elections. In May 1944, after a Supreme Court decision had assured the Negro the vote in the South, the educator said that a "changed atmosphere" was evident throughout the Southern states as a result of the Court's decision. Most of the South, he said, is slowly grasping the fact that the Negroes' constitutional right to vote is at last being established.

Dr. Hastie is a member not only of Phi Beta Kappa and the National Lawyers Guild, but of the National and Washington Bar Associations and of Omega Phi Psi fraternity. He is a director of the National Association for the Advancement of Colored People, a Mason (English Constitution), and a member of the African Methodist Episcopal Church. On Christmas Day 1943 he was married to Beryl A. Lockhart.

In February 1943 the Honor Roll of Race Relations, a nationwide poll conducted by the trustees of the Schomburg Collection of Literature in the New York Public Library, named Dr. Hastie as one of the twelve Negroes who had most distinguished themselves during the year, "for his heroic efforts to achieve full integration of the Negro in the United States Army." In June 1943 he received the Spingarn medal, presented by the National Association for the Advancement of Colored People to the American Negro considered to have made "the most outstanding contribution to the advancement of the Negro status" in the preceding year, at the hands of Representative Will Rogers, Jr., before an audience of more than 23,000 in Detroit. The citation read, "As civilian aide to the Secretary of War, Hastie refused to temporize with racial bigotry, segregation or discrimination. Men of lesser character and of greater selfishness would have closed their eyes to prejudice in order to maintain themselves in a remunerative position. But Hastie refused to do this, resigning in protest against perpetuation of practices which more aptly would have characterized the racial ideology of a dictatorship than of a democracy."

References

Ann Am Acad 223:59 S '42

Who's Who in America 1944-45

HATCH, CARL A(TWOOD) Nov. 27, 1889- United States Senator from New Mexico; lawyer

Address: b. c/o Senate Office Bldg., Washington, D. C.; h. Clovis, N. M.

Author of the "clean politics" acts—the Hatch Acts—passed by the United States Congress in 1939 and 1940, to restrict campaign funds and proscribe pernicious political activities, is Democratic Senator Carl A. Hatch of New Mexico, acting chairman of the Senate Judiciary Committee.

Carl Atwood Hatch emerged from the West at the beginning of the '30's. He was born in Kirwin, Kansas, November 27, 1889, the son of pioneers, Harley Atwood and Esther Shannon (Ryan) Hatch. When he was still young he moved with his family to Eldorado, Oklahoma. At the age of sixteen he dropped his formal education to become a clerk in his father's hardware store, but the first step toward his political future was a job as printer's devil on the Eldorado *Courier*. Later, as reporter and half-owner of the small weekly, he covered the county courthouse, where the eloquence of the lawyers so impressed him that it cut short a potential newspaper career. Young Hatch took a law course at Cumberland University in Lebanon, Tennessee, and had his own practice by the time he was twenty-three. A year later, in September 1913, he was married to Ruth Caviness.

Before long Hatch was called to Clovis, New Mexico, to defend a nineteen-year-old youth who had run afoul of several statutes. There Hatch engaged a law firm with the euphonious name of Patton and Bratton to assist him, an association that foreshadowed his political career. When illness in the Hatch family later made it advisable to live in the drier climate of New Mexico, Clovis was selected for the new home because, Hatch said, it was the only place in which he knew anybody.

By that time Patton and Bratton were making progress, and they took Hatch along with them. Harry Patton became state attorney general in 1916 and made Hatch his assistant the next year. In 1923 Hatch succeeded Sam G. Bratton as district judge (of the 9th Judicial District), and succeeded himself in 1924.

The new district judge let no prairie grass grow under his feet. He held court in nearly every town in the state and made friends in the process. "As campaign manager for Senators, governors, and others, he became a local Jim Farley[44]," Alva Johnston wrote in the *Saturday Evening Post* in 1940 ". . . an extraordinary career for a 'newcomer'" to a state.

In 1929 Hatch resumed his private practice, leaving his old boss, Patton, to continue the relay as district judge in his place. The stick was passed on again four years later when Hatch, who had managed the campaign that had put Bratton in the United States Senate, was appointed to fill Bratton's unexpired term after the Senator resigned in 1933 to become a circuit judge. (Hatch was elected on his own the following year, and was re-elected in 1942.)

In the Senate Carl Hatch was an ardent New Dealer, but his attitude toward the Administration was not unlike that of a cautious parent toward a precocious child. He backed much of the Administration-favored legislation, until the bill to enlarge the Supreme Court was introduced in 1937. Hatch agreed that "new blood" was necessary in the Court, but felt also that if the proposed new appointments were made all at once the Executive would be in a position to control decisions on pending issues. He introduced an amendment that provided for five new Justices, with the stipulation that only one be appointed in any given year. Sharply scorned at first, this amendment was later sought for adoption as a face-saving compromise, but it was too late.

(Continued next page)

CARL A. HATCH

Senator Hatch's crusade for pure politics had originated in the early stages of his career in New Mexico when he became incensed over the patronage system. "Millions of Democrats have gone mad under similar circumstances," said Johnston, "but it has been a form of madness curable by election." Carl Hatch was an exception. His first attempt at reform legislation came in 1935, when, with the cooperation of Senator Harry F. Byrd [42], he introduced a bill to prohibit WPA contractors and others from making campaign contributions. But he dropped the issue when certain Congressmen assured him that this abuse was already covered by the Corrupt Practices Act of 1925 (defining crimes against the purity of elections). Later developments taught him to take "assurances" with a grain of salt, according to Alva Johnston (*Saturday Evening Post*, October 12, 1940), for even while those were being given the Democratic National Committee was obtaining contributions from persons and corporations holding Federal contracts. Contributions were made in proportion to the size of the contract and were in the guise of advertisements in the party's campaign book, which apparently had little value as an advertising medium; copies autographed by President Roosevelt [42] sold for $250 apiece.

In 1937 Hatch essayed a second reform bill, which forbade Federal employees to attend political conventions. Shelved for a year, it was later defeated by forces led by Senator Alben W. Barkley [41], who nonetheless was unwittingly responsible for its eventual passage. Coincidental with the battle of the payrolls during the 1938 gubernatorial race in Kentucky, investigation of the Sheppard Committee unearthed such political corruption that the Administration could no longer ignore WPA scandals. Taking advantage of the situation, Hatch reinforced his bill and brought it before the Senate in 1939, where it was passed by a vote of 242 to 133. It was not passed, however, contends Alva Johnston, in a spirit of penitence. Public sentiment was strongly on the side of Hatch. An attempt was made by the

House Judiciary Committee to dehorn the bill before it went before the House. The proposed amendment was defeated, however, and Vice-President John Garner "gaveled it [the bill] through to a chorus of 'Ayes' and nary a 'Nay.'" In essence, the measure forbids any Federal employee—in the words of Arnold J. Zurcher—"to use his position to influence political conduct; outlaws coercion of voters in national elections; prohibits solicitation of funds from employees on public relief projects; and forbids efforts to secure political support by the promise or denial of employment on any project made possible by national appropriations."

A year later the second Hatch bill was passed to extend that ruling to cover state employees whose salaries were paid in part from Federal funds. A filibuster against it in the Senate and an attempt to kill it in the House Judiciary Committee aroused such indignation that the bill was suddenly steamrollered through. (It was depicted as "too hot to handle" in a Rollin Kirby [44] cartoon which appeared in the New York *Post* in March 1940.) An additional amendment introduced by Senator John H. Bankhead [43] limited the annual expenditure of any political committee to $3,000,000 and cut down individual contributions to a national political committee to $5,000. Hatch is recorded as voting against this measure when it was first introduced, but in July 1940 he teamed up with Representative John Dempsey (also from New Mexico) to push it through.

In October 1942 the act was amended to assure teachers in schools and colleges the right to participate in political activities. (It had been Hatch's original intention to exempt teachers from the provisions of the act, but he had been defeated on a technicality.) In the summer of 1944 still another amendment was passed, this time by Senator Robert A. Taft [40]. It prevented electioneering through Government dissemination of political literature among the armed forces, and its application created a situation which newspapers throughout the country derided. In practice, the added provision led to the banning of literature that was not even indirectly propaganda. Protesting that the amendment had been misinterpreted, Taft proposed another amendment to ease the censorship.

Certain crippling amendments that have caused these Hatch Acts to be called, variously, the "Hatchet Acts", "Laws Horrible of Politics," and "Cannibal Bills," are laid to Senators who had hoped to estrange the bills' supporters. Hatch still feels, however, that his legislation saved the Democratic Party from scandals that would have wrecked it. Paradoxically, it was Hatch's early failures, plus persistence, that resulted in making him a headline figure. He "grew under punishment"; and his measures grew to significant proportions as attempts to thwart them revealed political skeletons in the closet.

Hatch himself has admitted that his reform measures are full of loopholes. Indignant at the huge 1940 campaign expenditures, he said in January 1941 that his law had been evaded through technicalities (loans and contributions to state committees which are exempt from the law). Legislation requiring the Federal Government to bear all campaign expenses in a Presidential year was preferable to the large campaign sums of today, he said. In July 1943 he considered proposing legislation to have the Treasury bear campaign expenses. In the meantime, Representative Emanuel Celler of the House Judiciary Committee, long-time opponent of the Hatch Acts, sought their repeal. They have been "flagrantly violated," he contended. (One judge had imposed a fine of 1c on an offender.) A year later the repeal of the acts as they affect Federal employees was demanded by the United Federal Workers of the Congress of Industrial Organizations, which earlier had filed suit in a lower court challenging their constitutionality. In August 1944, however, a three-man Federal court in Washington, D. C., upheld their constitutionality. Another attack made on the acts is that while they limit the campaign expenditures of a single political committee, they do not limit the number of committees which can be set up for each candidate. Since the 1944 campaign Hatch himself has advocated raising the $3,000,000 ceiling to discourage this practice.

Senator Hatch's crusade for clean politics has not been all on behalf of his own measures. In February 1943 he opposed the (Kenneth) McKellar bill (passed in June by the Senate with a vote of forty-two to twenty-nine) which proposed Presidential appointment and Senatorial approval of all executive officials of the Federal Government. The New York *Herald Tribune* regarded it as a clear invitation to logrolling. Hatch called it, in part, "completely destructive of the merit system . . . the greatest setback to civil service that has transpired in many years . . . as a matter of actual application . . . Senators would not advise and confirm, they would actually nominate and confirm."

In March 1943 Hatch joined forces with three other Senators (Republicans Joseph H. Ball [43] and Harold Burton, and Democrat Lister Hill [43]) to submit to the Senate a post-War peace resolution which they considered stronger than any that had up to then been introduced. Known as the Ball-Burton-Hatch-Hill resolution, or B2H2, as it was dubbed by Washington newspapermen, the bill proposed that the United States take the lead in forming a permanent United Nations organization with the power to rehabilitate and to protect with an international armed force the member nations. It was hailed by many as a good first step toward winning the peace, but it was attacked by others—mostly former isolationists—as controversial and therefore detrimental to national unity, tending to divert attention from the vital current task of winning the War. During the summer and fall a heated controversy over the bill ensued (while its sponsors stumped the country publicizing the measure). Finally, in October, the (Tom) Connally [41] resolution, drafted by a Foreign Relations subcommittee, was introduced in the Senate. (The House had already passed the [J. W.] Fulbright [43] resolution favoring the creation of international machinery to establish and maintain "a just and lasting peace.") Calling the Connally resolution too general and "rubber-worded," the internationalists in the Senate fought for revision. Voting was delayed until after the Moscow conference of the United States, Great Britain, and Russia, and

in November, by a vote of eighty-five to five, the Senate passed a compromise resolution (virtually reproducing the language used in Article 4 of the Moscow declaration), which recognized the necessity of a general international organization for the maintenance of international peace and security. In December, two of the B2H2 bipartisan group, Hatch and Ball, conferred with the President about the crises in Poland, Italy, Greece, and Belgium. Following the conference the two Senators issued a statement emphasizing the gravity of the international situation and the necessity for a "supreme effort" to overcome Allied disunity.

As acting chairman of the Senate Judiciary Committee—which has handled the statute extension resolutions postponing the courts-martial of General Walter C. Short and Admiral Husband E. Kimmel [42] for alleged culpability in the unpreparedness at Pearl Harbor in 1941—Hatch declared in November 1944: "I think in common with . . . every person in the United States I want to know the full facts concerning the disaster at Pearl Harbor. . . . But on the other hand . . . I do not want to start any investigation or do anything which might impede in any way the war effort which is so all-important at this time." (Hatch is also chairman of the Committee on Public Lands and Surveys.)

In New Mexico, Hatch is called "Smiling Carl"; and his smile is also well known in Washington, although it is said to be a little less ingenuous after eleven years in the Senate. His extreme affability and quiet, tactful nature have probably tempered his doses of reform medicine. He has never questioned a Senator's motives nor hurt his feelings, and his colleagues have reciprocated. As a debater, he is quietly competent and can puncture a "windbag" so deftly that the victim "will think Hatch has done him a favor." A rather slender five feet nine, the Senator weighs about 150 pounds. When the Senate is not in session he retires to his ranch and grain farm near Clovis, where he practices the terracing and soil conservation system recommended by the Department of Agriculture. There he also rides around on Senator, a five-gaited mare given to him by a friend. His son, Stewart Atwood, is beginning to follow the parental pattern—he was a newspaperman on the Houston *Chronicle* until his enlistment in the Army Air Corps in early 1942. At the end of 1944 he was a captain, stationed in France. The Hatchs' daughter, Marsha Naomi, is the wife of Glen Leet, a Rhode Island public welfare official, at the end of 1944 overseas with UNRRA. In his third term in Congress (the 1944 elections did not affect the Senator, whose term is not up until 1949), he still talks of returning to his law practice.

References

N Y Post p39 Mr 31 '43 pors
N Y Sun p30 Mr 13 '40; p28 Mr 17 '43
Sat Eve Post 213:31+ O 12 '40
Who's Who in America 1944-45

HAUCK, LOUISE PLATT (hôk) Aug. 15, 1883—Dec. 10, 1943 Author; published more than seventy historical and romantic novels; used noms de plume of Peter Ash,

HATCH, CARL A.—*Continued*

Louise Landon, Lane Archer, and Jean Randall.

Obituary
    N Y Times p15 D 11 '43

HAUTECLOCQUE, JACQUES LE-CLERC DE *See* Leclerc, J.-P.

HEIDEN, KONRAD (hí'den)   Aug. 7, 1901-   Author; journalist
Address: b. c/o Houghton Mifflin Co., 432 Fourth Ave., New York City

The last decade has brought forth a steadily increasing stock of literature on Adolf Hitler '42 and National Socialism—sensational revelations, scientific forecasts, and concrete proposals for their destruction. While Hitler does not as yet belong to history in the etymological sense of the word, without having the advantage of the necessary perspective of time, an internationally known authority on the Nazis, Konrad Heiden, has written soberly and objectively a definitive history of the move-

KONRAD HEIDEN

ment and its leader. Heiden brought a background of personal observation and experiences over a period of twenty-three years to the composition of his monumental opus, *Der Fuehrer; Hitler's Rise to Power* (1944). There is little doubt that he knows more about Hitler than any contemporary who is not a leading Nazi.

Born August 7, 1901, in Munich, Germany, the son of a labor union official, Konrad Heiden spent his youth in Frankfurt, then in 1920 returned to the city of his birth to study law and economics at the University. Here he encountered the subject of his lifelong work. "It is twenty-three years now since I first attended a National Socialist meeting," recalls Heiden in his preface to *Der Fuehrer*. "It is also twenty-three years since I saw, without

particular enjoyment, Herr Hitler at close range, and listened to the flood of nonsense— or so it then seemed to me—that he was spouting. It was only gradually that the effects of these speeches made me realize that behind all the nonsense there was unrivaled political cunning."

Elected president in 1922 of the Republican Student's Union, a small democratic group within the University, Heiden "tried, with all the earnestness of youth, and with complete lack of success, to annihilate Hitler by means of protest parades, mass meetings, and giant posters." Heiden thus claims the distinction of being perhaps the oldest anti-Nazi in the United States, "for there cannot be many in this country who came into conflict with Adolf Hitler and his handful of followers at so early a date." According to the Book-of-the-Month Club, Heiden may be credited with inventing the term "Nazi." Hitler's henchmen were originally known as the Nasos (the normal abbreviation of National Socialists); in the early 1920's Heiden derisively began to refer to them as the Nazis, a slang term for bumpkin or simpleton in the Bavarian villages. The nickname gained such currency that it was finally adopted officially by the party.

In 1923 Konrad Heiden joined the staff of the liberal *Frankfurter Zeitung*, drawing the special assignment of following up Nazi activities in Munich. In that year he observed the failure of the November *Putsch,* covered Hitler's trial for high treason, and saw him enter the Landsburg "prison," to emerge nine months later to give new life to his dispirited party. Heiden became known as "the man who kept Hitler waiting." It is said that on several occasions Hitler refused to start a meeting until the *Frankfurter Zeitung*'s correspondent had made his appearance.

After seven years with the *Frankfurter Zeitung*, Heiden went to Berlin to manage a newspaper syndicate formed to take up arms against Nazi propaganda. Trying to impress unconcerned democratic leaders with the virulence of Nazism, Heiden also wrote *A History of National Socialism*, which was suppressed and publicly burned. It is still a standard work outside Germany. (Published in the United States in 1935 by Alfred A. Knopf '43, *A History of National Socialism* is the joint translation of Heiden's two books, *Geschichte des Nationalsozialismus* [1932] and *Geburt des dritten Reiches* [1934].) Meanwhile, the rights had been sold to an English publishing house. "But when I got to London a year later," say Heiden, "I found that the book had not been translated and that my publishers had almost forgotten its existence." Baffled by this situation, he questioned his agent, only to learn that "the publishers were reluctant to issue a book about a dictator who tomorrow may be overthrown."

Outlawed by the Nazis because of the publication of *Geschichte des Nationalsozialismus*, Heiden was forced into hiding. In June 1933 he escaped to the Saar, then still under the jurisdiction of the League of Nations. Continuing his unremitting journalistic campaigning, he edited a paper opposing the return of the Saar to Nazi Germany. When in January

1935 the plebiscite went in favor of Germany, Heiden made his way to Paris, where he continued his writing in books and magazines.

The following year saw the publication of *Adolph Hitler: das Zeitalter der Verantwortungslosigkeit; eine Biographie* in German, French, and English. In the United States it was published under the title *Hitler; a Biography* (1936). Just as Heiden's first book had been considered the best study of National Socialism, so this new critically interpretive biography was greeted as the best book that had appeared to date on Hitler. John Gunther '41, whose criticism was representative, wrote that "the primary emphasis is on the internal forces of Hitler's character. It makes clear in terrifying detail what Europe may further expect from this man who combines the most rigid fixity of aim with apparently monstrous divagations. . . . Heiden's book is, to my mind, rigorously impartial, but impartiality in certain circumstances is tantamount to an indictment; and it would be difficult to read *Hitler* even cursorily without deriving from it emotions of awe, incredulity, and downright fright." In 1937 *Europäisches Schicksal* made its appearance in Amsterdam.

Heiden's next book was *The New Inquisition* (printed in Paris, 1939, as *Les Vêpres hitleriennes*), a brief, moving, yet restrained account of one of the most appalling chapters in modern history, the story of the Nazi pogrom of November 9, 1938 and the days immediately following. Writing from his Paris refuge, the author assures his readers that he "has drawn from and reproduced only such reports as he has conscientiously investigated in every respect, and for which he believes he can vouch." Hendrik Willem Van Loon says rightly in his introduction to *The New Inquisition* (1939): "Konrad Heiden has rendered us a signal service by writing this book which may well contain his own death sentence. . . . He has well deserved of the American people." The subsequent *One Man Against Europe* (England, 1939; New York, 1940) was only published in a limited edition.

In 1939 Heiden was placed in an internment camp by the French, freed through the intercession of Léon Blum '40, then again imprisoned when France was invaded. The prisoners having been evacuated as the Germans approached the camp, Heiden made the long adventurous trek south across France on foot. Reaching Lisbon, he sailed for America on October 4, 1940, in company with other German émigrés, including the novelists Franz Werfel '40 and Heinrich Mann, a brother of Thomas Mann '42.

For the last three years Heiden has made his home in New York, but has been in California gathering material at the Hoover library for *Der Fuehrer*. In 1941 the author-exile contributed the article "Europe Under the 'Master Race'" to a special supplement of the *Nation* (March 22) which made an attempt to prophesy the alternative results of either a Hitler peace or a Hitler defeat. Heiden pointed out that "the proposed New Order does not envisage a definite territorial reorganization of Europe any more than it does a new fixed legal code or a stable economy." Nor does it dream of "the establishment of a fixed and unshakable tyranny over the entire world" or "a thousand years 'peace' in which a minority exploits a tortured majority." Simply stated, "the New Order means a permanent state of war."

Heiden has also written the special introduction to the definitive new translation of *Mein Kampf* by Ralph Manheim, who rendered the journalist's own book into English. Heiden asserts that "for years *Mein Kampf* (it was first published in 1924) stood as proof of the blindness and complacency of the world," that Hitler again demonstrated "that there was no more effective method of concealment than the broadest publicity."

Finally published by Houghton Mifflin on January 28, 1944, *Der Fuehrer* was immediately acclaimed as a "must" book and became the February choice of the Book-of-the-Month Club. Actually a three-in-one volume of nearly 800 pages, *Der Fuehrer* is a comprehensive biography of the master of the Third Reich from birth to the climactic Blood Purge of 1934 ("an extraordinarily audacious and brilliant attempt to psychoanalyze him"); a sociological study of Germany since 1918 and the rise of National Socialism; and a penetrating examination of Germanic thought from Hegel to Hitler.

Throughout, Heiden is "remorselessly and ruthlessly objective." Only *Book Week* disputed his mastery of the facts, claiming that the author had accepted several historical forgeries in connection with Hitler's youth, but critics emphatically agreed that *Der Fuehrer* would be of permanent value chiefly as a source book. In part a retelling of the two earlier books (*A History of National Socialism* and *Hitler*), it contains much new information. Malcolm Cowley, writing in the *New Republic*, found it "sometimes confusing, not seldom repetitious, and . . . padded with familiar material until it is too long by almost a third"; other commentators found in it "passages of stormy eloquence" and felt that it "reads like a novel."

Dorothy Thompson '40, reviewing *Der Fuehrer* in the *Saturday Review of Literature*, said: "It is the most notable book to be written about National Socialism. . . . Not only a judgment of Der Führer, it is a judgment of our times." Miss Thompson particularly lauded the book for the way it emphasized the fact that fascism is a symptom of economic maladjustment that can occur in any country, rather than a distorted manifestation of the German character. Henry Seidel Canby '42, reporting on behalf of the Book-of-the-Month Club, commented that "the reader of this extraordinary story will follow, step by step, the beginnings and triumphs of a revolution as sinister as anything that has happened in history."

Heiden's thesis is the assertion that Hitler was not the author or guide of early Nazism. He informs us that "one scarcely need ask with what arts he conquered the masses, he did not conquer them; he portrayed and represented them." The junior officers, in their search for a proletarian following to boost them to power, "found their leader in the lowliest mass of their subordinates, and commanded him to follow." It is when Heiden denies that the German people as a whole, and most explicitly the German middle class, is responsible for Nazism that several leading

HEIDEN, KONRAD—*Continued*

critics take issue with him. He makes the National Socialist revolution a revolution of the "armed intellectuals" and the "armed bohemians." Lewis Gannett [41] points out that by the "armed intellectuals" Heiden means "a restless, principleless, white-collar man with a sense of superiority to the manual workman and a personal sense of defeat," and that "to call [National Socialism] a revolt of the intellectuals is dangerously misleading." In addition, Sterling North [43] comments that Heiden "makes the highly questionable statement that not Hegel but Friedrich Schiller, the humanist, was the dominant spiritual leader of Germany during the entire nineteenth century." On the other hand, George N. Shuster [41], writing for the New York *Times,* is in complete agreement with Heiden's statement.

Not pausing after the success of *Der Fuehrer,* early in 1944, Konrad Heiden is already indefatigably assembling material for "Hitler in Power," which Houghton Mifflin plans to publish.

Heiden has an "easy, unassuming manner, a nimble, shrewd, and comprehending mind." Apparently he does not believe in "art for art's sake." Introduced to Laura Z. Hobson (the author of *The Trespassers*) at a Dorothy Thompson party, he was told that Mrs. Hobson had also written a book. "Really?" remarked Heiden. "Against what?"

Reference

Book-of-the-Month Club N p4 Ja '44

HEIFETZ, JASCHA (hī′fets yä′sha) Feb. 2, 1901- Violinist

Address: b. c/o Columbia Concerts Corp., 113 W. 57th St., New York City; h. Redding, Conn; Harbor Island, Newport Beach, Calif.

As a rule the fame of a child prodigy is short-lived. By the time the infant phenomenon reaches adulthood, the once adoring public has forgotten him. Prominent among the exceptions who have achieved mature greatness after early precocity is the violinist Jascha Heifetz, whose name has long been synonymous with superlative musical interpretations. Heifetz began the study of the violin at the age of three; before he was halfway through his teens, he had aroused international comment; and his New York debut, made at the age of seventeen, immediately established him among the musical giants. "He plays the violin so well," wrote Deems Taylor [40] recently, "that he knows what a lesser artist will never know: how good violin playing might be. . . . He has only one rival, one violinist whom he is trying to beat: Jascha Heifetz."

Heifetz' immediate heritage was musical. His father, Ruvin Heifetz, held the first violinist's desk in the local orchestra at Vilna, Russia, where, on February 2, 1901, his only son, Jascha, was born. The father was highly pleased when he found that his child would cease crying whenever music was played. What he could not foresee, however, was that the normal life of the Heifetz household was to be

disrupted in a few years because of the boy's prodigious gifts.

Ruvin Heifetz guided the first musical steps of his son. He bought three-year-old Jascha a quarter-size violin upon which he instructed him in the rudiments of the instrument. Within a year, the boy's progress astonished even his parent, for he had not only mastered the five positions, but he played with the calm assurance of a veteran. The elder Heifetz sought the advice of Professor Elias Malkin as to whether his four-year-old son ought to receive formal training. Malkin suggested that he wait at least three more years, whereupon Ruvin Heifetz had Jascha play for him. Malkin was at once convinced that the child was extraordinary, and promptly accepted him as a student at the Royal School of Music in Vilna.

Jascha pursued his studies with the serious application of an adult. Before his fifth birthday he was one of the school's best students. Two years later he played as soloist in the Mendelssohn Concerto at Kovno; and by the time he was eight and a half he had completed the course at the Royal School of Music. He played the violin with an ease which appeared to come with spontaneous mastery, but which had been achieved by much strenuous work. In later years he remarked: "Don't imagine everything came to me out of a clear sky."

Fortunately for Jascha, Leopold Auer of the St. Petersburg Conservatory visited Vilna. During his stay Malkin approached him with reports of his exceptional student. Auer, to whom the very word "prodigy" was anathema, was at length persuaded to listen to Jascha. The boy's playing of the Mendelssohn Concerto and the twenty-fourth Caprice of Paganini caused Auer to forget that the performer was only nine years old. Overcome with joy, Auer embraced Jascha, promised him a magnificent future, and urged him to study with him at St. Petersburg.

As soon as Ruvin Heifetz had sold his possessions and resigned from his post he accompanied his son to St. Petersburg. There they called on Auer, who mistook the boy for just another child wonder. By the time they had identified themselves the period for enrollment at the Conservatory had elapsed. As a result it was arranged to have Jascha admitted to Auer's assistant. But another difficulty threatened to interfere with Jascha's stay in St. Petersburg. According to the law, Jews, with the exception of Conservatory students, were not permitted in the city of the Czar. The privilege granted to students, however, was not extended to their parents or relatives. The situation was saved by the quick resourcefulness of the Conservatory's director, who enrolled forty-year-old Ruvin Heifetz as a Conservatory pupil.

After six months of preliminary training Jascha entered Auer's class, where he outstripped his fellow students in very short order. He soon began to make public appearances in various Russian cities. When he played at the International Exposition in Odessa his safety was so endangered by the unrestrained enthusiasm of the audience that he required police protection all the way home. Similar scenes occurred in other cities.

Following his early concerts in Russia, young Heifetz embarked on his first European concert tour, which took him through Austria and Germany. In 1914 he was soloist with the Berlin Philharmonic under Artur Nikisch, who declared that never in his life had he heard such excellent violin playing. The German press pronounced him "a finished artist." A Berlin critic reported that "his technical supremacy is almost forgotten, it is so unobtrusively the vehicle of his conceptions; and such breadth, warmth, virility, and refinement do these conceptions display that one is at a loss to account for his mastery."

The occasion of Heifetz' New York debut was preceded by more than a flurry of interest. Musicians came from everywhere, eager to find out whether he would live up to advance notices. On October 27, 1917 a large and hypercritical audience, generously sprinkled with veteran virtuosos, had gathered to hear him. The atmosphere in Carnegie Hall was tense. Presently a slender, unsmiling young man in meticulous dress walked out upon the stage, tuned his instrument with care and deliberation, and began to play. Before he had finished his first selection storms of applause had broken out. On the following day the newspaper reviews compared Heifetz to Paganini and Kreisler. Pitts Sanborn concluded that "he is a modern miracle." Another critic wrote: "The newcomer plays with a tone so tragical, so intoxicatingly sweet, that only the molten gold of Fritz Kreisler can be conjured in comparison." One of the better-known musical anecdotes dates from the Heifetz debut. The story has it that Mischa Elman, then already a famous violinist, was sitting in the same box with Leopold Godowsky. As the recital proceeded and the ovation for Heifetz increased, Elman became visibly uneasy. Mopping the perspiration from under his collar he whispered to Godowsky: "It's hot in here, isn't it?" The latter replied dryly: "Not for pianists."

Subsequently Heifetz has given concerts in almost every country of the world, very often playing in the midst of national turmoil. He performed in Russia during the Revolution, in Ireland at the time of the Sinn Fein uprisings, in Japan during an earthquake, and in India while that country was seething with anti-British riots. An estimate made by the artist in 1940 indicated that he had spent 66,000 hours, or two-fifths of his waking career, at the violin, and had traveled the equivalent of more than two round trips to the moon.

Heifetz' stature as one of the great violinists of all time was not at all affected by a controversy which arose several years ago over his interpretations. He has always been regarded as a perfect technician. In some quarters, nevertheless, it was believed that his playing had become cold and aloof, and that his technical precision had been obtained at the cost of warmth and expressiveness. This criticism was answered with two explanations. Some advanced the theory that Heifetz was undergoing a transitional period in which he was "reacting away from the excessive emotionalism of his Russian temperament and training." But perhaps closer to reality was the suggestion of Deems Taylor, that Heifetz'

JASCHA HEIFETZ

severe facial expression produces an unfavorable effect on his audiences. Since audiences react to visual as well as to musical impressions, anyone watching him might easily confuse the sound of the playing with the appearance of the player." And Heifetz, Taylor reminded people, "is the least demonstrative of concert artists."

In 1934 the virtuoso returned to Russia for the first time in seventeen years. Devoted admirers came from remote Siberian outposts to hear him play. Some of these sold part of their clothing or furniture in order to get to the concert, and after each concert many followed him through the streets, shouting his praises. "That," states Heifetz, "was the greatest emotional experience of my life." It is a life that includes varied experiences. In 1926 he was made a Chevalier of the French Légion d'Honneur (in 1939 he was made an Officier); the preceding year he had donated a concert hall to Tel-Aviv, Palestine. In 1939 Heifetz appeared in *They Shall Have Music,* a motion picture produced by Samuel Goldwyn [44] for United Artists. Heifetz believes that motion pictures are a good educational medium for music and he would consider appearing in another film "if someone came along with a good story in which music were an integral part."

Among the violinist's transcriptions are two albums of twelve pieces by Scarlatti, which Heifetz has arranged for violin and piano from the composer's so-called sonatas for a keyboard instrument. "In all his work with these gems," writes *Musical America,* "Mr. Heifetz again displays the subtle understanding of characteristic style, the sense of proportion and the unimpeachable taste that have been hallmarks of all his previous arrangements and transcriptions."

Under the auspices of USO Camp Shows, in the summer of 1944 Heifetz made a tour of the Italian and North African theatres of war, giving forty-five concerts in eight weeks, some

HEIFETZ, JASCHA—*Continued*

of them at the front lines. In these concerts the violinist concentrated on the popular classics. At one performance, however, deciding to play a Bach prelude, he told his audience, "This number is like spinach—you may not like it but it's good for you." At the conclusion of the number the artist was overwhelmed to hear cries of "More spinach!" Wherever he went, in fact, he reports, he met intelligent, responsive listeners. At least 70 to 80 per cent of the soldiers, Heifetz believes, are interested in concerts of great music. Soldiers make the most challenging audience in the world, and they want the best that the artist has to give, he concluded.

Heifetz and his wife Florence Vidor, the former motion-picture actress, maintain two residences, a Connecticut farmhouse and a home at Newport Beach, California. The violinist, an air warden and airplane spotter in the Civilian Defense Corps, is fond of reading, gardening, and taking long walks with his children, Robert and Josepha. He also enjoys aquatic sports and dancing, plays a very good game of ping-pong, is addicted to cameras, and drinks moderately, usually Scotch and soda. Perhaps his favorite recreation is a busman's holiday—playing quartets with friends. He is the proud owner of two famous violins, one a 1731 Stradivarius. The other, which dates from 1742, is known as the "David Guarnerius" because it was formerly owned by Ferdinand David, a well known violinist of the last century.

The violinist's friends like to tell about the time that George Bernard Shaw [44] visited Heifetz backstage after a London recital. Shaw, it seems, scolded Heifetz for playing too perfectly. "Nothing may be perfect in this world," he said, "or the gods become jealous and destroy it. So would you mind playing one wrong note every night before you go to bed?"

References

Scholastic 36:23-4+ Mr 4 '40 il por
Ewen, D. ed. Living Musicians 1940
Kaufmann, H. L. and Hansl, E. E. Artists in Music for Today 1933
Taylor, D. Well Tempered Listener 1940
Thompson, O. ed. International Cyclopedia of Music and Musicians 1943
Who's Who in America 1944-45

HELBURN, THERESA *See* Langner, L. and Helburn, T.

HENRIOT, PHILIPPE (än"ryō' fē"lēp') ?—June 28, 1944 Vichy Minister of Propaganda killed by members of the underground movement; had been an extreme Right-wing Deputy from Bordeaux before the War; member of the notorious Croix de Feu; after the collapse of the Third Republic he became editor of the pro-German weekly *Gringoire* and a leading collaborationist radio commentator.

Obituary

N Y Times p1+ Je 29 '44 por

HERSEY, JOHN (RICHARD) June 17, 1914- War correspondent; author

Address: b. Time, Inc., 9 Rockefeller Plaza, New York City; h. 33 Sutton Pl., New York City

In his short span of years as a journalist—since 1939 as a war correspondent for Time, Inc.,—John Hersey has written his first three books, all inspired by the War. Two of these, *Into the Valley* (1943) and *A Bell for Adano* (1944), have been named by the Council of Books in Wartime as "imperative" wartime reading, and the latter volume has been dramatized in a Broadway production starring Fredric March [43].

Hersey's parents, Roscoe M. and Grace (Baird) Hersey, were American missionaries. In the early 1900's their work took them to the Orient, and their son, John Richard Hersey, was born in Tientsin, China, June 17, 1914. Speaking Chinese fluently before he knew a word of English, the boy had become a true cosmopolite at the age of three when his mother took him with her on a two-year trip around the world. His father had gone to France to serve with the YMCA, but Mrs. Hersey returned to the mission in Tientsin, where her son began his education at the Tientsin Grammar School, and later continued at the same city's American School. Unfortunately for Hersey, he lived in China while he was still too young to acquire any permanent memories, and despite the glamour which a childhood in the Orient implies, he feels that his was no more exciting than the average child's. Like most children, he merely tolerated school, always looking forward eagerly to summer vacations. To this day his strongest (and fondest) memories of China revolve about the months of each year which he and his parents spent at the seashore, devoting most of their time to donkey-riding.

When he was ten Hersey's parents returned to the United States, where he soon became thoroughly Americanized. Deciding early that he wanted to be a journalist, Hersey studied at Hotchkiss Preparatory School, then at Yale University, and after his graduation from Yale (1936) he went to Clare College, Cambridge, England, for postgraduate work. It was at Cambridge that he made up his mind that he would get a position on *Time*. "I was aware that I might have to wait a long while until there was an opening, but I didn't care. *Time* seemed to me the liveliest enterprise of its type, and I wanted, more than anything, to be connected with it." As things turned out, Hersey did not have a long wait. In the summer of 1937, after leaving Cambridge, he became private secretary to Sinclair Lewis; in the fall of the same year he began his career with *Time*.

In 1939 Hersey was sent to the Orient by *Time* to report on the Far Eastern situation. During the course of his assignment, he interviewed such internationally famed men as Chiang-Kai-shek [40], Matsuoka [41], and General Homma, who later conducted the campaign against MacArthur's [41] men on Bataan and then committed suicide after his failure to crush the Americans in later engagements. Not only did the journalist gather excellent material for a series of articles at the time, but he also gained a firsthand knowledge of the Japanese character, which later served him well when he wrote his books about the Second World War.

Even before the War, Hersey was considered an expert on Far Eastern matters, although in July 1940, in an article Ambassador Joseph Grew '41 published in *Life*, he himself took no position either for or against the "dynamic appeasement" of that country which Grew was still advocating.

When Hersey undertook to write *Men on Bataan* (1942), although he had not been on Bataan itself, he was "fortified with scads of already printed news dispatches, buttressed by hitherto unused by-products of *Time-Life's* vacuum cleaner system of detail gleanings and supplemented with original source material from friends of General MacArthur and from families of the fighting men." Believing that the story of the Bataan peninsula was inextricably linked with the life of Douglas MacArthur, in *Men on Bataan* Hersey avoided a sentimental glorification of either the battle or the man. The book contains concise vignettes of many of the participants—of General Pat Casey and his engineers, of the late Colin Kelly and Meyer Levin '40, of Father Duffy, and of many doctors and chaplains.

Sent to the Pacific area in July 1942 as correspondent for *Time*, in October Hersey arrived at Guadalcanal, where he "wangled permission to go along with the Marine company of Captain Charles Rigaud in an attack designed to pry the Japanese loose from the Matanikau River, which lies close to the now famous Henderson Field." While sharing the dangers of the men, who had by bad luck walked straight into a Japanese trap in the middle of the jungle, Hersey studied their reaction to danger, to their enemies, and to the War in general. Describing the skirmish in *Into the Valley*, he concludes that these men were more weary than frightened, that they were contemptuous of the character of the enemy but not of his fighting skill, and that, above all, they were fighting for home and for life as it used to be. Hersey had remained on Guadalcanal for two weeks, bunking with an Army aviator, swatting mosquitoes, dodging bombs, and helping to rescue wounded men under fire, as well as going into action with the Marines. Secretary of the Navy Knox '40 sent Hersey a letter of commendation for his conduct in aiding the removal of the wounded at Guadalcanal. Hersey has learned through actual experience that a foreign correspondent's part in this War is not one of smooth sailing and pleasant excitement. On four occasions, twice in the Pacific and twice in the Mediterranean, he survived airplane accidents, once suffering several broken ribs. One of the planes crashed in the water, capsized, and sank, and Hersey, freeing himself from the wreckage while it was still under water, reached the surface after what seemed hours, and immediately began to worry about the notes he had taken during the Guadalcanal expedition. "I thought about the notebooks right away," he says, "and felt in both my hip pockets. No books. Then something bumped my head, and there they were floating in the water within easy reach of

my hand. I never could figure out how they got there. By rights they should have sunk straight off."

In February 1943 John Chamberlain '40, New York *Times* book critic, heralded John Hersey's *Into the Valley* as evidence of "the birth of a new Hemingway, one whose single desire is to write 'truly,' basing every word on what the eyes have seen and the ears have heard." The following month Chamberlain's praise was echoed by the Council of Books in Wartime when it named Hersey's book an "'Imperative' . . . vital to the war effort and thought of the whole nation." That his book was so designated by the Council is a singular honor, for only one other, W. L. White's '43 *They Were Expendable,* had been selected previously. (The commendation was doubly impressive because Hersey was not quite twenty-nine years old at the time.)

From May to September 1943 Hersey was in an active zone again, this time the Mediterranean theatre. From Africa he accompanied the American invasion forces to Italy. "Although I would hardly call one type of warfare preferable to another," Hersey says, "now that I have had a chance to compare the two, I can see how much more horrible the War against the Japs is." Upon his return to the United States he began work on a novel—the story of a major of Italian antecedents who is doing his best to teach democracy to the peasants of an Italian village of which he is AMG officer in charge, until an irascible general, passing through, muddies the picture. Some pre-publication controversy was caused by the fact that the character of the general had apparently been created with an unfortunate episode in General Patton's '43 career in mind, and even before the publication of *A Bell for Adano* Virginia Kirkus '40 called it a prospective best seller. She also found it a sensitive and moving story, though perhaps not as important as all the furor about it would seem to imply.

After the publication of *A Bell for Adano* in early 1944, reviews revealed a division between outright praise of it and approval with reservations. "The whole thing," wrote Milton Hindus in the *Atlantic Monthly*, "adds up to a study in the crucible of experience of 'what America can and cannot do in Europe.' . . . Hersey is concerned with concrete observation rather than with theory, but if a credo does emerge from his book, it is one that is apt to be forgotten in the struggle of abstract slogans—that government, whatever its professions, can only be as good as the men who govern."

"The humanity, the rich humor, and the occasional pathos in *A Bell for Adano*," declared Edward Weeks, "are to be found in the lower ranks. . . . These people are as real to us as an Italian fruit stand, and to watch them react to the ruthless and destructive impersonality of the war machine is to realize what a long, tortuous road lies ahead of us in Europe." "The very speed of composition of Mr. Hersey's book," wrote Diana Trilling in the *Nation*, "gives it what interest it has, because, writing quickly, Mr. Hersey wrote out of a deep reservoir of folk-idealisms and popular assumptions. . . . There seems to me to be a great

JOHN HERSEY

deal of truth in Mr. Hersey's picture of an American." On the whole, the other reviewers felt that the correspondent had done a first-rate job reporting, but, on the artistic side, many felt that he had not produced a soundly constructed novel, and that his chief characters tended toward oversimplification.

The book by the end of 1944 had sold over 125,000 copies, a figure exclusive of the 200,000 copies distributed by the Literary Guild. French, Portuguese, Russian, and Swedish language rights have been sold, a Braille edition has been made, and Twentieth Century-Fox is making the book into a motion picture. In addition to calling the book "imperative" for wartime reading, the Council on Books in Wartime dramatized it on its radio program *Words at War.* The March of Time also made a short film of the novel (and is working on a short of Hersey's *Life* Magazine piece "Joe Is Home Now," a story on the rehabilitation of returning servicemen).

In December 1944 Paul Osborn's dramatization of the novel opened on Broadway. Produced by Leland Hayward, it starred Fredric March in the role of Major Joppolo, the American AMG officer who undertakes to govern the Sicilian village of Adano after its capture by the Allies. The play, reported Lewis Nichols of the New York *Times,* is a play of mood rather than of action, but Nichols, like those who agreed with him, felt that despite a certain episodic, straggling quality, *A Bell for Adano* was very effective. Others, more enthusiastic, declared the play beautiful and often eloquent. It had been announced that the production had been chosen by the Washington Committee for the Celebration of President Roosevelt's '42 Birthday to give a "command performance" in Washington. Such a performance is given annually to raise funds for the National Foundation for Infantile Paralysis, Inc. Later it was announced that the executive committee had decided that it would "be guilty of flaunting ODT regulations to bring to Washington for one performance such a substantial

number of people" (the cast included between twenty-five and thirty people). Hersey himself had not seen his play by the end of 1944. He had left for Moscow for Time, Inc., in August.

Hersey, who was married to Frances Ann Cannon on April 27, 1940, now has two sons, Martin Cannon and John Richard, Jr. When Hersey is at home he likes to relax by listening to music—in all forms, although he can "take swing or leave it"—as the occasion demands. There was a time when he used to "saw the violin." "But," he confesses rather sadly, "I gave it up because I am an ardent lover of good music."

References

N Y Herald Tribune p9 Je 1 '43
N Y Times p21 F 4 '43
N Y Times Book R p4 Je 7 '42; p9 Mr 28 '43

HERSHOLT, JEAN (hĕr'shōlt jēn) July 12, 1886- Actor

Address: b. c/o Columbia Broadcasting System, Hollywood, Calif.; h. Beverly Hills, Calif.

Danish-born Jean Hersholt is a veteran of more than thirty years in Hollywood films. From his early portrayals of villains and heroes, he turned to character roles, becoming universally known for his Dr. Dafoe, in the Dionne quintuplets film, and as another doctor, in the *Dr. Christian* screen and radio series. In 1944 he gave up his work before the camera for the duration of the War, in order to give more time to the war effort and to his duties as president of America Denmark Relief, Inc. He is continuing his acting, however, as Dr. Christian on a weekly CBS program.

Jean Hersholt was born July 12, 1886 in Copenhagen, Denmark. His parents, Henry and Claire (Petersen) Hersholt, were actors with the Danish Folk Theatre, but they discouraged him from going on the stage. He attended St. Knud College in Copenhagen. Although he studied to be an artist, from early youth Hersholt sought the career of an actor and in 1904, at eighteen, became an apprentice with the Dagmar Theatre in Copenhagen at $25 a month. His first part was that of Oswald in Ibsen's *Ghosts.* After obtaining his stage training at the Dagmar he toured in repertory throughout the Scandinavian countries. In 1906 he went into the movies, working for the Great Northern Film Company in the first motion picture produced in Denmark.

In 1912 the Scandinavian Steamship Line gave him free passage to America for entertaining passengers with his recitations. That first year he visited Montreal; and during his next visit the following year he toured various Danish clubs in the United States. On this trip he met a man named Hawkheimer who was associated with the Balboa Film Company. Hawkheimer gave Hersholt a letter to his brother on the West Coast with the airy prediction that the Dane would be at work before the week was out. Hersholt, who was going to San Francisco to direct and appear in a Danish stage production at the International Exposition, looked up Hawkheimer's brother on his arrival, found him to be a very pleasant man. "Your notices are fine," the second Hawkheimer told the actor. "Now I'll tell you wha you do—you act in the first two pictures for nothing and at the end of that time we'll be able to place your salary about where it should be." Hersholt declined and instead decided to look for an opening with a producing unit which had just been formed by the former actor Thomas H. Ince. Dressed in spats, cutaway, and derby hat (as any self-respecting European actor would be), and carrying a cane, Hersholt took a trolley to Santa Monica, transferred to Fisher's Wharf, then found he had two miles to walk to reach the company's studios. The road was dusty and the day hot. Ince was not there when he arrived. However, he was met by E. H. Allen. "Never mind the notices," said Allen, looking at him with fascination. "Are those your own clothes you got on?" "Yes," replied Hersholt, a bit surprised. "Do you have a tuxedo and a full dress suit?" "Yes," came the reply, this time more puzzled. "Well, you're hired," said Allen "Fifteen dollars a week." And so began Hersholt's American film career—under contract to Thomas Ince for 1914-1915.

The first picture in which Hersholt appeared was *Bullets and Brown Eyes*. To play the three parts he was assigned, he got up at 5:00 a.m. every day, took the streetcar to the end of the line, was met there by a team of oxen and taken to the set. (John Gilbert was in the picture, too, earning $12 a week.) When the picture was finished the Danish actor was given weekly assignments in half-a-dozen one-reel films in which he played the parts of villains, romantic leads, and old men. In April 1914 he was married to Via Andersen, whom he had met in Montreal, and they went to live in a $12-a-month house at Ocean Park. By the time Hersholt's pay had reached $25 a week, Universal took him on. For Universal he made eighty pictures the first year, mostly one-reelers. In those days the various companies at the studio played on one large outdoor platform, with bleacher seats above the stage for visitors who paid 25c for the privilege of applauding and hooting the actors. The stands held about 300 people, who were considered an excellent source of revenue by the company.

Sometime later Hersholt went with H. O. Davis at $60 a week, which in those days was "big money." Still later he went to Triangle for $75. (At this time Maurice Costello, highest paid of all actors, was getting $300 a week.) When Triangle failed in 1918, Hersholt went up to Portland to direct pictures for a company which planned to bring the screen industry to Oregon. The company soon failed, too, and he returned to Hollywood to direct Zane Grey Westerns for Ben Hampton. A still taken about this time on the set of *The Four Horsemen of the Apocalypse* (1921) shows a crowded drawing room scene in which one can detect that the black-bearded man standing behind Rudolph Valentino is Jean Hersholt.

Then he played the "heavy" with Mary Pickford in *Tess of the Storm Country* (1922). His success in the film made him one of the most sought-after "bad men" in Hollywood. It was followed by villain roles in such pictures as Erich von Stroheim's *Greed* (1924), *Stella Dallas* (1925), and Douglas Fairbanks' *Don Q* (1925). The first two he considers his best silent pictures. "It was a great experience," he says of working with von Stroheim in

JEAN HERSHOLT

Greed, the picture judged by many to be the best silent film ever made.

Stella Dallas brought him a starring contract at Universal, where he remained for four years. He made $2,500 a week and didn't like it, for he has always preferred character parts to stardom. Except for one ten-month period, he has been under contract steadily for more than thirty years, working successively for Universal, Metro-Goldwyn-Mayer, Twentieth Century-Fox, and RKO Radio.

It was his characterization as the kindly old professor in *The Student Prince* (1927) that freed him from villain roles. This, along with *The Old Soak* (1926), *Alias the Deacon* (1927), *Abie's Irish Rose* (1928), *Men in White* (1934), *The Country Doctor* (1936), *Sins of Man* (1936), and others, established him as one of the screen's best-loved personalities. He considers *Sins of Man* and *The Country Doctor* his best talking pictures.

When in 1935 Darryl Zanuck called him in to discuss the possibility of his portraying Dr. Allan Dafoe, the doctor who delivered the Dionne quintuplets, Jean Hersholt pointed out that it was useless to discuss his playing another part when shooting was to start on his new picture in two weeks. "If we let you do this picture," cried Zanuck, "you're practically made in movies. You can coast on this the rest of your life." This argument made little impression on Hersholt, who had been in movies since 1913 and had been working almost all that time, but the actor did know a good part when he saw it. Consequently he was on the train for Canada with the rest of the company the next morning. "For the first time in thirty-two years of acting," confessed Hersholt in 1939, "I had stage fright. I was to portray a man who not only was very much alive but who was to be right on hand as technical adviser on the picture."

Hersholt's playing of the fictionized counterpart of Dr. Dafoe put him before audiences in a new guise. The quintuplets' picture established him in the public mind as a country medico administering to sick souls and ailing

HERSHOLT, JEAN—Continued

bodies. It was his idea that the character would make a good radio series, and when the radio rights to the Dafoe impersonation proved unavailable "Dr. Christian" was born. The name was chosen mainly because of its meaning—the suggestion it conveyed—partly because it was Scandinavian and thus fitted his accent, partly because Hans Christian Andersen is Hersholt's favorite author

Practically without precedent in the radio industry, the *Dr. Christian* series was sold without an audition—sheerly on the basis of Hersholt's screen performance as Dafoe. It has been running successfully ever since 1937 and has an estimated weekly listening audience of twenty million. RKO has made several pictures based on the character. Listeners write to Dr. Christian for advice. Part of the success of the program since 1941 has undoubtedly been the result of Dr. Christian's keeping a finger on the public pulse through script contests. About 90 per cent of the scripts used on the program, a majority of which are by amateurs, come from almost 10,000 entries annually, with a $2,000 grand prize going to the winner. Hersholt reads the contest entries and helps the judges choose the fifty-two stories to be used each season. Though in 1943 he gave up commercial movies for the duration of the War, he continues his radio program. "I did not give up radio," he says, "because it isn't a difficult stint. The scripts are at my disposal. They entail a half hour's rehearsal a week, and a half hour's clocking time for the actual program. Besides, I enjoy being identified with Dr. Christian. The character is in my veins. It wouldn't be natural for me to drop him!"

In August 1944, in collaboration with the radio script writer Ruth Adams Knight[43], Hersholt made his radio character the hero of a novel—*Dr. Christian's Office*. Containing all the familiar radio characters, it was, in the opinion of the reviewers, a warm, sentimental story set against an authentic small-town background, and maintained, in the words of one critic, "a nice balance between reality and homily."

On September 1, 1944 Hersholt became a motion picture production executive. He is a partner of Sol Lesser and serves as chairman of the advisory board of Principal Pictures, Inc., the parent body of Lesser's various producing activities. He will continue his radio activities and his work in charitable and other fields.

The only film he has made since 1943 has been the subject of much controversy. That year he played, gratis, the part of the doctor in a health education film, *To the People of the United States*. This film was produced gratis by Walter Wanger, sponsored by the California Health Department and the United States Public Health Service, and approved by the War Activities Committee of the Office of War Information. Its purpose was to aid in the fight against syphilis. Arrangements were being made for national distribution through commercial motion picture houses throughout the nation when the Legion of Decency protested its commercial release on the grounds of its violation of the motion picture production code and its failure to stress the importance of moral standards in this question. Several revisions were recommended on the basis of the latter objection, and the film is to be shown to selected audiences only. Hersholt was "shocked and angered by the move for suppression of the film." "There is such a crying need for sex education," he declared, "it would be criminal negligence to overlook it. The Scandinavian countries were able to stamp out venereal disease almost completely by making blood tests and treatment compulsory. The time is coming when we shall have to do the same." His next short subject film will be on tuberculosis.

Hersholt is also prominent in Danish-American affairs. He now devotes nearly all of his time to America Denmark Relief, Inc., of which he is president. This association—the eighteenth group to be included in the National War Fund—is composed of about 600 churches, lodges, clubs, and other societies which are contributing large sums to aid Danish refugees in Sweden. America Denmark Relief maintains offices in New York, Chicago, and California, the latter having been supported by Hersholt for a year. The actor also makes frequent short-wave broadcasts to Denmark for the Office of War Information. Though his sister is still in Denmark, he believes she would wish him to continue this work of keeping up the courage of fellow Danes. Hersholt is proud of the fact that there are 5,000 Danish sailors in the service of the United Nations and that 800,000 tons of Danish shipping still sail the ocean.

Jean Hersholt has been an American citizen since 1918 and has an enviable record of public service. In Hollywood he is a civic figure. He is president of the Motion Picture Relief Fund, an organization which enables those of the film industry to take care of their own. He helped to establish the Fund and has been president since 1940. Under his guidance the motion picture industry built the Motion Picture Country House, a home for the aged and needy among its workers. Also, he is vice-president of the Academy of Motion Picture Arts and Sciences and of the American Federation of Radio Artists. For seven years he was president of the Screen Actors' Guild and is now a member of the board of directors of that organization. In March 1944 he was appointed to the Advisory Board of the Los Angeles War Council.

In 1943 Bowdoin College (Maine) awarded him an honorary Master of Arts degree. The year before he was honored with a degree of Doctor of Humanities at Rollins College in Florida. In 1939 the Academy of Motion Picture Arts and Sciences Award of Merit was given to him for services to the industry through charitable endeavors.

An ardent collector, the Danish actor owns one of the finest collections of Hans Christian Andersen rarities in existence, including original volumes, manuscripts, and letters, which he has described in an article for the June 1944 *American Scandinavian Review*. In 1944 Heritage Press published his translation of twenty-five of Andersen's fairy tales, and it is becoming a best seller in the field. For this volume he wrote a long introductory biography of Andersen which the *Christian Science Monitor* calls "a perfectly delightful introduction . . . about the poor cobbler's son whose own life was like a fairy tale." "Some things in this translation," commented the *Saturday Review of Literature,* "will shock certain people. Others will please them. The English that Mr. Hersholt uses is free, often colloquial. . . . Just the same there is a quality in his translation that will make it live. His approach is simple and direct, his wording fresh and vital. Obviously, the tales have lived with him since early childhood in the language in which they were written. They are a part of his proud Danish inheritance." "Jean Hersholt," says the *American Scandinavian Review,* "is probably the Dane in our time who in this country comes nearest to the universal popularity of his great compatriot Hans Christian Andersen."

A well known bibliophile, Hersholt has, in addition to his Andersen collection, a good Dickens group and many books by other favorites, e.g. Sinclair Lewis, Melville, Shakespeare, and Mark Twain. (In 1944 the Mark Twain Association of America elected Hersholt its president.) Books, however, are not his only hobby. He has a good collection of Currier and Ives prints, and enjoys painting, sketching, and photography. He is a member of several clubs, including the Elks and the Masons, and he belongs to The Players in New York and the Bohemian Club in San Francisco.

The Hersholts are among the oldest residents of Hollywood. In 1944 they celebrated their thirtieth wedding anniversary. Via Hersholt, a nonprofessional herself, attributes the success of their marriage especially to the fact that there is only one star in the family. They have one son, Allan, a film publicist, formerly married to Osa Massen, the Danish picture star.

Jean Hersholt is five feet eleven inches tall and weighs 190 pounds. He has black hair and wears a mustache. He is seldom seen without a pipe (he has a large collection of them), and is not averse to an occasional highball. The actor has been described as "a true cosmopolite, but one with honest sincerity, strong regard for simple things, and a marked sense of responsibility toward his fellow men." For over thirty years he has kept a diary. Some day a book, possibly his memoirs, will be based on it.

References

Collier's 97:17+ Ap 4 '36 por
N Y Post p15 My 27 '44 por
N Y World-Telegram p5 S 25 '43 por;
   p18 My 22 '44
Tune In 2:11-12 Ag '44 pors
Who's Who in America 1944-45

HICKEY, MARGARET A. Mar. 14, 1902-
Chairman of the Women's Advisory Committee, War Manpower Commission; personnel consultant

Address: b. Miss Hickey's Training School for Secretaries, 560 N. Skinker St., St. Louis, Mo.; h. 6808 Washington St., University City, Mo.

As chairman of the Women's Advisory Committee, Federal War Manpower Commission, Margaret A. Hickey heads the first wartime body of American women to influence major Government policy. The years leading up to her appointment in August 1942 were devoted mainly to career guidance for women.

MARGARET A. HICKEY

Born in Kansas City, Missouri, March 14, 1902, Margaret A. Hickey is the daughter of Charles Lawrence and Elizabeth (Wynne) Hickey. She received her secondary education at Mt. Marty High School, and became a personnel worker at the youthful age of sixteen. She left the personnel field six years later, in 1924, to study law at Kansas City University. To support herself in college she publicized the famous Chautauqua music series, thus providing a groundwork for public speaking. She received her LL. B. in 1928, subsequently became a member of the Missouri bar and the Women's Bar Association, and practiced law until 1933.

Returning to the personnel field she then founded in St. Louis Miss Hickey's Training School for Secretaries, a career school for women secretaries, administrative assistants, and business executives. Her school has provided government and industry with hundreds of women workers, and Miss Hickey herself has been directly responsible for recruiting women for the Wacs, Waves, Spars, Marines, and the American Red Cross. One of the first leaders in the vocational guidance movement in Missouri, Miss Hickey promoted business efficiency by bringing together employers, employees, and students in career conferences. She has championed the cause of women workers from coast to coast, lecturing on the importance of sound vocational preparedness. "New Career Frontiers for the Trained Woman (*Journal of the National Association of Deans of Women,* March 1941) and "Stepping Stones to Careers," a widely quoted article which appeared in the *Christian Science Monitor Magazine* on July 31, 1943, are among the numerous articles Miss Hickey has written in recent years. After the founding of her school for secretaries law entered her life again: On October 20, 1934 she was married to Joseph T. Strubinger, a lawyer.

The War Manpower Commission was aware that the problems affecting the employment of women in war industries were varied and numerous and required the special understand-

HICKEY, MARGARET A.—*Continued*

ing of competent, well-informed women. As chairman of the Commission, Paul V. Mc-Nutt[42] created the Women's Advisory Committee "to be concerned with the most effective use of women in the prosecution of the war effort" and appointed Miss Hickey its chairman. In that capacity she presides over fourteen women representing a geographical cross section of management, labor, and the general public. She appoints the subcommittees that work on specific problems and participates in the discussions of the Management-Labor Policy Committee; she is thus in a position to exchange the opinions and arguments of the two groups. Although not a member of the Management-Labor Policy Committee, she is frequently consulted by it: her argument for a forty-eight-hour week was instrumental in bringing about the passage of the bill for the longer work week.

Convening for the first time on October 1, 1942 the Women's Advisory Committee drew up recommendations, accepted as policy by the WMC, which called for: the removal of all barriers to the employment of women in any occupation from which they were or could be fitted; the admittance of women on a basis of equality with men to all forms of job training; and the determination of wage rates on the basis of the work performed, irrespective of sex. Subsequent recommendations incorporated into the policy provided safeguards for the physical and intellectual development of youths under eighteen years whose services might be required in the war effort; and called for child day-care centers for children of war workers.

The Women's Advisory Committee is urging the participation of the local groups of national women's organizations in action programs in all communities where more women are needed for war work. The cooperation of women's organizations is sought in the setting up of local over-all womanpower committees to work with the women's groups and the local WMC or United States Employment Offices. The responsibilities of the over-all community women's committee are: participation in educational programs regarding the recruitment, training, and employment of women; help in planning and executing educational campaigns to stimulate interest among women to accept training and employment opportunities; supplying of information about requirements of specific occupations; presenting the labor needs of local industries in which employers are hiring women.

Miss Hickey stresses always the importance of the family and has consistently urged the employment of older women on whom young children are not dependent. One of her subcommittees concerns itself solely with community facilities and services. A "community offensive," she points out, is an essential factor in lowering absenteeism in war industries. For such an offensive are recommended: day care for pre-school children, extended school hours for older children, supervised foster home care; more opportunities for the woman war worker to visit her bank, grocery store, and dentist; and the establishment of family restaurants and round-the-clock recreation. Work in

factories was not the only type of war work, she said: "Many have failed to see the direct relationship of simple humdrum jobs that must go on in every community if the war effort is to succeed." She cautioned women, too, against trying to make a career out of a war job. "This is not a time to satisfy career ambitions. . . . They [women] must work now to build the kind of a world in which a post-War job will be safe. . . . Any experience they gain now will always be valuable to them." (In the discussion that arose regarding a national work-or-fight measure, Miss Hickey came out in support of total mobilization of both men and women for war.)

Realizing that worry about post-War job security affected the workers' efficiency, as early as May 1943 Chairman Hickey appointed a subcommittee to make a special study of post-War problems. The most significant occupational development likely to result from the War, Miss Hickey predicted in "Stepping Stones to Careers," "bids fair to be the admission of women to those upper reaches of traditionally masculine employment." But on October 10, 1944 she warned against "danger signals on the horizons of post-War planning" as it applies to the employment of women. "It is well to remember," she cautioned, "that prejudices surrounding the employment of women have been shuffled around considerably during the War but have not been eliminated." A high level of production and broad scale of distribution "is the best way to prevent re-erection of pre-War barriers to women's employment."

In December 1943 the Committee put in its first bid for post-War consideration of women workers with a statement to Bernard M. Baruch[41], chairman of the Advisory Unit for War and Post-War Adjustment Policy in the Office of War Mobilization. The statement called for "a fair, honest, and accurate definition of 'full employment'" and "positive and specific planning for the appropriate placement of individual workers, regardless of sex." Servicemen would and should have their old jobs back after the War, the Committee acknowledged, but there would not be enough of these men to displace women who really needed work, for those women constitute a much larger group than is generally realized. Full employment is the goal of any democratic nation, the Committee asserted: "No society can boast of democratic ideals if it utilizes its womanpower in a crisis and neglects it in peace." Said Miss Hickey: "Some are discussing the demobilization of women as though the object were to deny them employment, regardless of their need to earn a living."

In March 1944, when cutbacks started affecting women in industry, a statement was released from the office of Chairman Hickey calling for certain policies to govern the immediate demobilization of women workers, voluntary resignation of women who wished eventually to return to civilian life, dismissals based on consideration of seniority on the job, and job counseling for those dismissed.

In July 1944 Miss Hickey's responsibilities increased still further when she was elected president of the National Federation of Business and Professional Women's Clubs. (In 1939 and 1941 she had been national education chairman and first vice-president.) In her acceptance speech she called women "the custodians of the great moral and spiritual heritage" in the United States. "The way to end wars," she added, "and to prevent their recurrence is to build and to keep on building the un-secret weapons of the spirit that will make this nation invincible in war and in peace."

Later in the year, in October, Miss Hickey, as president of the Federation, called a conference of the heads of eleven women's national organizations to discuss the procedure for securing equal pay legislation in the forty-three states which now lack such statutes. The decision was reached that similar conferences be called by the state federations to implement the drive. Both white collar and industrial groups will be asked to join the various women's organizations in uniting to press for immediate legislation.

Following up a White House conference in June, at which women's organizations discussed the procedure for recommending qualified women for Government positions dealing with problems of the post-War world, Miss Hickey in December issued a list of requisites for such nominees: outstanding competence in candidate's chosen field; quality of mind; recognized standing in community; maturity and stability of emotions; ability to express self orally and on paper; health, endurance; and availability. Miss Hickey feels that the correct placement of women in positions of influence is very important, inasmuch as "women make a valuable contribution, and for which, in many instances, their special skills and aptitudes are needed."

For a New Year's "contract" Miss Hickey asked the 80,000 members of the National Federation of Business and Professional Women's Clubs to keep this pledge in 1945: "To the men on the fields of battle, on the ocean, in the hospitals, and those who have their discharge papers, we, the women of the National Federation of Business and Professional Women's Clubs, pledge ourselves to help make the world of the future a better place in which to live . . . to bind the wounds, help the disabled back to usefulness, convert human power to peacetime pursuits, and destroy the tragic fraternity of want and war at home and abroad."

Referred to as a three-job woman, Miss Hickey spends three days a week in St. Louis, housekeeping for her husband and running her secretarial school. Then by plane or rail she dashes to her WMC post in Washington, where she also sits in on the meetings of the Management-Labor Policy Committee. Since 1938 she has been consultant for the Missouri Merit System Council for Unemployment Compensation, and since 1940 consultant for the State Social Security Commission. In addition, she has been vocational consultant for the American Youth Foundation at St. Louis since 1935, member of the board of representatives of the American Council for Guidance and Personnel Associations from 1939 to 1942, and since 1940 a member of the board of directors of the Washington University Y.M.C.A.

A tallish woman, five foot six, Miss Hickey dresses in soft blues and wine reds that show off to advantage her "large brown eyes, fresh skin, and softly bobbed hair." She once studied to be a concert pianist and collects music manuscripts as a hobby. She also has a liking for golf. When the exclusion of women from the Dumbarton Oaks conference in the fall of 1944 prompted ten women, distinguished in political and public life, to nominate fifty-six women they believed qualified to participate, the name of Margaret A. Hickey was included in the list.

References

C S Mon p6 Ap 27 '32
Ind Woman 23:233 Ag '44 por (cover)
N Y Sun p30 O 20 '43
N Y Times p18 O 11 '44

HILDEGARDE Feb. 1, 1906- Cafe and radio singer

Address: b. c/o Anna Sosenko, The Plaza, 5th Ave. and 59th St., New York City; h. The Plaza, 5th Ave. and 59th St., New York City

Darling, je vous aime beaucoup.
Je ne sais pas what to do.
Vous avez completely stolen my heart.

The sweet voice with the indefinable accent pauses, the music swells to a polite crescendo, and the master of ceremonies announces: "The incomparable Hildegarde!" The scene may be any smart supper club, or the song may be heard any place in the world where a radio receives or a phonograph spins. For Hildegarde, whom Irving Berlin '42 calls "the greatest artist and stylist of song in the profession today," is an international celebrity.

After receiving reams of publicity as a "mystery woman," the singer has gotten more by revealing herself as Hildegarde Loretta Sell, born in Wisconsin to a devout German Catholic family of humble background on February 1, 1906. When Hildegarde was twelve the Sells moved to Milwaukee, thus enabling press agents later to label her "The Dear That Made Milwaukee Famous." There she and her two sisters attended St. John's Cathedral High School, sang in the local choir, and played in the school orchestra. Hildegarde's instrument was the piano. Then as later, Hildegarde was "incurably romantic," and, like Frank Sinatra '43, she has found this helpful in "putting over" love songs.

During the next four years Hildegarde Sell developed into quite a proficient pianist. In her spare time she worked as a salesgirl in a local store, until at sixteen she got a job furnishing piano accompaniment for silent movies in the evenings, while studying music seriously at Marquette University during the day. Then Miss Sell joined a twelve-piece vaudeville orchestra, in which she was the only girl. She still has her union card.

When in 1928 a third-rate piano act called "Jerry and her Baby Grands" came to the theatre, Miss Sell asked for a job with them, and later joined the troupe, with which she toured for two seasons. After that the twenty-four-year-old pianist was on her own again. For a year she kept herself going by accompanying various performers, the most notable being Mickey Cochrane, the ballplayer, Ruth Etting, and the "Dancing DeMarrs," one of whom was later to become famous as

HILDEGARDE

Tony DeMarco. He remembers her as a plump blonde who carried a catechism, was self-conscious about her German accent, and disliked her first name.

While accompanying one Oklahoma Bob Albright, or a singer named Dora Early—nobody remembers exactly which—Hildegarde Sell stopped at a Camden (New Jersey) boardinghouse and struck up a friendship with her landlady's daughter, Anna Sosenko. When Miss Sosenko went to New York to seek her fortune as a songwriter, she asked Miss Sell to introduce her song "Time Was." The two became fast friends, and when the pianist was on the road she allowed Miss Sosenko to use her apartment, which rented for $12 a week, and also provided her with $7-a-week spending money while she looked for work. In return Miss Sosenko undertook to straighten out her friend's tangled financial affairs. Eventually the two reached a partnership, with Miss Sell performing, Miss Sosenko acting as her personal manager, and all income being entered in a joint bank account and divided equally between them. No written contract has ever been needed by Sell and Sosenko.

At first the money was hardly worth splitting. Hildegarde Sell slowly dwindled down to a song plugger in Irving Berlin's New York music office. Finally Jess Freeman of *Variety* and the comedian Joe Laurie, Jr., arranged to have Miss Sell audition for Gus Edwards, discoverer of many stars. After signing the Milwaukeean to a contract, Edwards shortened her name to Hildegarde, refreshed her accent, and put her in his revue *Stars on Parade*. Billed as "The Female Jack Pearl," after the creator of Baron Munchausen, she appeared as an immigrant girl singing "Two Hearts in Three-quarter Time." In spite of the length of *Stars on Parade*'s tour, which lasted more than a year, its closing found Hildegarde penniless in the bottom of the depression. "She was even worse off than before," comments J. Bryant

3rd, "because now she had no prospects. Vaudeville was dead and . . . most of New York's theatres were as dark as the future."

Hildegarde was singing at the Hotel Pierre for $100 a week (not much when expenses were deducted and the remainder divided) when, in January 1933, she auditioned for Martinus Poulsen, the director of London's "ultrasmart" Café de Paris, and was given a four weeks' contract for the following autumn. The American singer was not a complete failure at the Café de Paris, but she was not enough of a success to be re-engaged. One reason was that she was assigned to sing after a reigning star, Marion Harris, whose performance overshadowed hers. But this engagement, unimportant in itself, proved a turning point, for Sell and Sosenko began to study and apply tricks of technique to make a great night club personality. The first rule they learned from Marion Harris: "Never return to the room or remain after a performance. If your customers get to know you too well, they don't come back and pay money to see you." Hildegarde adopted this rule as her own. If important patrons wish to see her between shows, they must visit her in her dressing room. Deciding that Miss Harris' beautiful gowns made her glamorous, Miss Sosenko also invested a month's salary in creations for Hildegarde, and made a practice thereafter of dressing her with the greatest elegance they could afford.

After London Hildegarde and Miss Sosenko went to Paris, where they managed to scrape along for three years while the singer was learning cabaret technique. At this time Hildegarde was making as little as $40 a week for six performances a night—when she was working. But she was studying audience psychology: "There were little tricks she used to hold their interest, little ways she discovered of working on their hearts," says Miss Sosenko. Hildegarde acquired an international flavor by learning to sing in French, Russian, Italian, and Swedish, as well as English and German, and developed a precise diction which made every word clearly audible —and which reduced her accent to an unidentifiable exotic flavoring of her speech.

While Hildegarde was becoming a personality, her manager was making her into a personage. "I made her a sensation long before she was a sensation," says Miss Sosenko. "We're in a phony business, all glitter and glamour, and you have to play phony to get along." So Miss Sosenko created the "glitter and glamour" by spending as much money as the team could spare on American advertising of "the incomparable Hildegarde" and by deluging the press services with items from abroad about her. This method was so successful that it is now difficult to tell what in Hildegarde's European past is fact and what is fancy. The accepted story is that in 1934 the aged King Gustaf [42] of Sweden asked for her at the Club Casanova, which she had left; and, not wishing to offend his royal patron, the owner located Hildegarde and persuaded her to return—for an appropriate salary. Miss Sosenko saw to that, as well as to the resulting story in half the European press the next day. Kings are always news, and she could hardly have invented a better star for hitching purposes. Somehow no two accounts agreed as to the blond singer's nationality. A French newspaper referred to "the little Hollander," a Dutch paper to "the Viennese star," while an English paper had been unable to determine whether Hildegarde was "American with a French accent, or French with an American accent." This vagueness lent a glamorous mystery to the singer which considerably helped the sale of her phonograph records in America.

J. Bryant 3rd gives the chronology of Hildegarde's rise thus: "November 1934: A summons to sing at the Ritz Hotel, London, during the Duke of Kent's wedding festivities. January 1935: Part of a program televised from Paris—the first foreign star and the first representative of popular music to be thus honored. April 1935: The Ritz again, for King George V's Jubilee. Fall of 1935: Featured in an English movie, *Music Hath Charms*. February 1936: A tour of the English music halls. March 1936: Featured with Leslie Henson in an English revue, *Seeing the Stars*. July 1936: Back to New York; guest appearance on Rudy Vallee's program; sang at the Crystal Room in the Ritz. May 1937: Back to London Ritz for King George VI's '42 Coronation, at a salary of $8,500 for four weeks' work. September 1937: Back to New York; guest appearance on Ed Wynn's program, and had a sustaining program with NBC at $1,000 a week for two one-hour recitals."

The spaces were filled in with a long-term contract at the British Broadcasting Corporation; scores of recordings in London, Paris, and New York; and appearances at fashionable night clubs all over Europe and America—the Carlton, London; the Dolphin, Cannes; the Bœuf sur le Toit, Paris; the Diable Amoureux, Brussels; the Colony, Chicago; the Casino, Le Touquet; and private concerts for Albert Lebrun of France, Grand Duchess Kira of Russia, Elsie de Wolfe (Lady Mendl), and Prince Halim of Egypt.

When she returned to the United States, Hildegarde was invited to make guest appearances on several radio and television programs. Afterwards she was given a contract as a singing pianist with Raymond Paige's orchestra on *99 Men and a Girl* over CBS for the United States Rubber Company (reviewers said that the 99 Men made such a racket that the Girl was scarcely audible), and as a singer with Ripley's *Believe It or Not* (Nehi, Inc., for Royal Crown Cola, on CBS). *Radio Guide*'s poll of 750,000 listeners in June 1939 showed Hildegarde as fifth in popularity among women "sweet" singers, with 4.6 per cent of the vote.

After her guest broadcast she was engaged successively by the expensive Waldorf-Astoria and Ritz-Carlton Hotels in New York at $1000 a week—"and believe it or not," in Miss Sosenko's words "no one seemed to care whether Hildy sang or not. The Americans were harder to please than the Europeans." Once again Hildegarde buckled down to studying how to win applause and influence audiences. To catch the attention of New York's habitually indifferent cabaret patrons, she used dramatic lighting—a blackout pierced by special spotlights of flattering colors. Reportedly, Hildegarde is now

accompanied to any guest appearance by a truckload of lighting equipment. She learned to begin her program with an old favorite, like "Alouette," in which everyone can join, or "Chop-a-Nay-Cas," which calls for handclaps à la "Deep in the Heart of Texas." Later she organized a "Tinkle Club" of patrons who tinkled spoons in their glasses at the proper moments, and called men from ringside tables to dance with her during her act. She played up her acquaintance with many celebrities and luminaries of the "international set" by greeting publicly those audience members whom she knew. She carried audience participation to the point of kissing a strange soldier three times as a part of one act and commenting on a dowager's clothes.

This hard work paid off: booked into the lavish Versailles (New York) at less than half her previous salary, Hildegarde "wowed every last person in the night club." From then on it was one chic supper room after another in a rising crescendo of success, culminating in a six-year contract to sing at the Persian Room of the Plaza in New York. A Hildegarde cult developed, whose viewpoint is expressed by Harriet Van Horne of the New York *World-Telegram*: "When you see Hildegarde . . . tossing her blond topknot in those pink and golden lights, pinching young soldiers on the cheek, and kissing old soldiers on their bald spots, she is pure enchantment. You can't forget her playing the piano primly with her gloves on, telling her naughty jokes with the air of a youngster who has been eavesdropping—a chimera in rustling silks, who, you feel sure, goes back to the doll shop when the lights come up."

The dissenting opinion is delivered by *PM*'s Arnold Blom: "She is attractive, yes; but beautiful, no. She has a water-faucet charm, yes, but radiance, no. A natural for television? All she can offer is, (1) a so-so voice, with clear pronunciation its major recommendation; (2) an ability to play the piano with not extraordinary skill [*Life* quotes certain 'snide apostates' as maintaining that Hildegarde 'wears long gloves at the piano merely because she cannot play enough to keep herself warm']; (3) beautiful evening gowns, handkerchiefs, and gloves; and (4) a limited number of facial grimaces and contortions which, I shouldn't be surprised to learn, are carefully developed and rehearsed and used as occasion warrants. And still, from supper rooms, radio, and records, she earns about $150,000 a year. It just goes to show that, to coin a bromide, if there had been no Hildegarde, Anna Sosenko would have invented one." At a later date Blom amended this judgment: "I must admit," he said, "Hildegarde is quite a performer, at least as far as a visual audience is concerned."

In spite of the importance of visual appeal in Hildegarde's act, she is one of the leading recording personalities. Decca has released her albums of songs by Noel Coward '41 (1939), Rodgers '40 and Hart '40 (1939), Vernon Duke '41 (1940), Cole Porter '40 (1941), Moss Hart '40 and Kurt Weill '41 (1941), and again Rodgers and Hart (1942). In 1941 they also put out a *Hildegarde Souvenir Album* of her typical numbers, including her signature song "Darling, Je Vous Aime Beaucoup," which Anna Sosenko wrote with her help. She has

HILDEGARDE—*Continued*

made other records, including three Frank Loesser novelty numbers, her favorite "All the Things You Are" (1940), "I'll Be Seeing You" (1943), which she reintroduced, and "My Heart Sings" (1944), an unusual "staircase" melody.

After her unfortunate experiences in radio it was four years before Hildegarde again attempted the airwaves. In June 1943 Raleigh Cigarettes put her on the air as a summertime replacement for the Red Skelton show. In this dull program, *Beat the Band*, she acted as quiz mistress and sang only two songs an evening. But on June 13, 1944 Hildegarde moved from *Beat the Band* to a half-hour Tuesday night program on NBC, built around her talents, called the *Raleigh Room*. Produced by Anna Sosenko, it attempted to recreate the smart night club atmosphere of Hildegarde's usual surroundings, even going so far as to have the studio stage set with tables at which sit specially invited guests (on one program, Deems Taylor[40], Bert Lahr, and Georgie Price) and "volunteers drawn Hildy-nilly from the audience." The show became so popular that it was moved to another NBC studio, which, seating 1,200 people, is reputed to be the largest in the world. In the 1944 Hooper radio poll of listeners, Hildegarde's program won tenth place.

Hildegarde's working wardrobe includes some sixty evening gowns, designed by leading American couturiers, which cost from $175 to $400 apiece. A typical Hildegarde costume would be a sheath of some luxurious fabric, such as gold brocade (though it may be as simple as white crepe), with a low v-neck which flatters her round face as well as emphasizes the Hildegarde figure; long gloves ($20), specially designed to blend with her gowns, which add an air of sophisticated elegance, and in her hand one of seventy-five fragile imported lace handkerchiefs ($25 average, or up to $75) which she casually leaves on the piano while singing. Altogether, according to *Look* Magazine, Hildegarde spends more than $10,000 a year on her wardrobe— but, as *Life* revealed two years later, her evening slippers come from very inexpensive stores, and seldom cost more than $6 a pair.

A bubbling, exuberant performer, Hildegarde is said to be "as shy as Elsie Dinsmore" when only a few are present. She has been engaged three times, but never married. Five feet seven inches tall, counting her high heels, she has 128 pounds distributed in what *Variety* calls "an arresting chassis." Hildegarde has small pale blue eyes in a round, strong-jawed face, and blond hair swept into a flattering pompadour she calls her "fringe on top." She loves clothes, was delighted when Fashion Academy voted her one of the best-dressed women of 1940, but refuses to buy very expensive daytime garments. She collects foreign newspapers and water colors; her favorite recreation is bicycling. She still takes orders from Anna Sosenko, although, in Hildegarde's words, "we scrap and fight about new songs. . . . But after we finish the program is changed—the way she wants it."

"Withal, though," said one of her first American interviewers, "she's a swell girl and does her job superbly. She has kept utterly free

not only from scandal but from the affectations and idiocies that so often infest a stage celebrity." She is generous about playing benefits, attending war bond rallies, and reads books when she has time—which means twice a week, while she has her hair done. Her speech she defines as "occupied Milwaukee."

References

Collier's 106:21+ O 5 '40 por
Life 15:69-71+ N '43 pors
Look 5:32-5 F 25 '41 pors
N Y Herald Tribune p17 Mr 23 '40
N Y Post p3 D 22 '41 pors
Newsweek 19:56-7 Ja 19 '42 por; 23:82 Je 26 '44 por

Variety Radio Directory 1939-40

HINES, FRANK T(HOMAS) Apr. 11, 1879- United States Government official

Address: b. Veterans Administration, Washington, D.C.; h. 4900 Glenbrook Rd., Spring Valley, Va.

On February 21, 1944, some sixty hours after the Baruch[41]-Hancock demobilization recommendations had been made public, War Mobilization Director James F. Byrnes[41] named Brigadier General Frank T. Hines to the post of Retraining and Re-employment Director, a job in line with that of "work director" in Baruch's report. The office was later put under the new Office of War Mobilization and Reconversion created by Executive Order at the end of 1944. (Baruch himself had reportedly been offered the position and had refused it.) Hines, head of the Veterans Administration since 1930 and before that director of the Veterans Bureau, thus assumed the task of refitting possibly 10,000,000 men into America's post-War economy—the personnel side of reconversion.

Frank Thomas Hines was born in Salt Lake City, Utah, April 11, 1879, the son of Frank L. and Martha (Hollingsworth) Hines. He had just passed his nineteenth birthday when he enlisted in the Utah Light Artillery, and during the Spanish-American War he served as a sergeant and a 1st sergeant with Battery B before being commissioned a 2nd lieutenant on March 23, 1899. In August of that year he was honorably mustered out of the service, having served in twenty-two engagements in the Philippines and having been recommended for the Congressional Medal of Honor "for bravery in action against the Spaniards." On September 20, 1901 he was made a 2nd lieutenant in the Artillery Corps of the Regular Army. Three years later, by now an honor graduate of the United States Coast Artillery School, Fort Monroe, Virginia, he was advanced to the rank of 1st lieutenant, and on December 4, 1908 he became a captain in the Corps. He then proceeded to attend the advanced course at the Coast Artillery School until July 1911, and upon graduation was assigned to duty in the Office of the Quartermaster General, Washington, D.C., until June 1914.

The outbreak of war in Europe in the latter year found him in Athens, Greece, and there he was instructed to take charge of the embarkation of American citizens in the war zone en route home. Apparently he performed this duty with conspicuous success, for on August 5, 1917, after the United States had entered the First World War, he was not only promoted to the temporary rank of major but assigned as chief of staff of the Embarkation Service. On January 26, 1918 he was appointed chief of embarkation, controlling the entire embarkation of troops sent overseas. In February of the same year he was raised to the rank of lieutenant colonel in the National Army; in March, to colonel; in April, to brigadier general.

With the responsibility for the development of the organization which carried more than 2,082,000 soldiers to Europe in eighteen months and returned them home in eight months, Brigadier General Hines was a very busy man. With Secretary of War Baker he represented the United States at the Allied Maritime Transport Council in London in September 1919; and he was in England and in France early in 1919, representing the War Department in negotiations with the British, French, and Italian Governments on the relative costs of transportation and supplies. In April 1919 he was appointed chief of the Transportation Corps. On December 3, 1919 he was permanently appointed by President Wilson as a brigadier general in the Regular Army, and he held that grade until his resignation from the Army on August 31, 1920 to enter the shipping business. A week later he was appointed brigadier general in the Officers Reserve Corps. (On March 10, 1944, under the authority of Congress, the President appointed Hines a brigadier general in the Regular Army and immediately transferred him to the retired list.)

Hines did not remain in private life long, however. For a while he served as an officer of the Army and Navy Association, a membership organization in conjunction with retail stores which gave discounts to Association members; but when in 1923 President Harding chose him to direct the United States Veterans Bureau he accepted the appointment, and he was reappointed to this same post by both Coolidge and Hoover '43. In this post he practically controlled the rehabilitation of veterans of the First World War. He also had much to say about the controversial question of the so-called veterans' bonus which resulted in the Adjusted Compensation Act being passed over Coolidge's veto on May 19, 1924. This act provided for deferred payment of a "bonus" for veterans based on length of service in the United States and overseas, and after the depression Congress was besieged with demands for its immediate cash payment in full.

On July 8, 1930 the three veterans' agencies were consolidated by President Hoover, and Hines was appointed Administrator of Veterans Affairs, the head of a bureau with an annual budget of about $800,000,000. In this position he combatted the growing demands for immediate cash payment of the "bonus," attempting to show that the United States had already "dealt most generously with its veterans." In 1932, with the number of veterans seeking treatment for non-service disabilities rapidly increasing, he also told a joint Congressional committee named to study possible economies that restriction of relief to those

U. S. Army Signal Corps

FRANK T. HINES

who had actually suffered in the War would eventually save more than a billion dollars, and offered plans for the "prohibition of disability allowances to all veterans not permanently disabled to a degree of fifty per cent." He was not successful in all these economy efforts—in 1936 the "bonus" bill crossed the last hurdle—but he did conduct the Veterans Administration well within its Congressional appropriation, emerging with a surplus every year.

According to PM, "Friendly critics of General Hines say that his cautious business administration of veterans' affairs has made him slow to see the expansion in his operations required by this War. They point to the fact that [in January 1944] his agency was given first war priority for personnel. They further say that he has turned a deaf ear until recently to all who urged him to expand his hospital facilities." That Hines's "cautious business administration" pleased many others more than it pleased PM was, however, obvious from the fact that for three years a bill to let him return to the Army with the rank of major general and retire at that rank had not had favorable committee action in Congress. It evidently pleased James F. Byrnes particularly, for when on February 21, 1944 he named Hines Retraining and Re-employment Director it was before the post officially existed. President Roosevelt '42 rectified this three days later by issuing an executive order creating the position within the Office of War Mobilization. In November the Senate Finance Committee approved President Roosevelt's re-appointment of Hines as Retraining and Re-employment Administrator in the new Office of War Mobilization and Reconversion, a department created that fall to replace the OWM.

Hines is not only a close friend of War Mobilization Director Byrnes, who appointed him to this post, but also of Secretary of Commerce Jesse Jones '40, both conservative Democrats. He himself is a Republican, however:

HINES, FRANK T.—*Continued*

in 1932 he was listed by Robert Allen [41] and
Drew Pearson [41] in *More Merry-Go-Round*
as one of the leading figures in the late Senator Reed Smoot's private army of office-holders. Director Hines is an anti-New Dealer,
and people who have sat in interdepartmental
conferences with him as well as members of
veterans' organizations say he has often expressed fear that the moral fibre of the American people is in danger of being undermined
through work relief and security programs—
WPA, NYA, etc. (He has reportedly expressed the opinion that one hundred dollars
a month from a Government relief or Social
Security program would induce many citizens
to give up all effort to get private employment.)

Hines continues as administrator of Veterans Affairs, and in this position alone he
has a large job in front of him. He will be
cashier of any demobilization pay measure
Congress finally passes. He must continue to
administer a bureau which in January 1944
had upwards of 50,000 employees, a $1,000,-
000,000 appropriation, scores of hospital facilities for men and women with service-connected
disabilities, and more than 100,000 claims from
veterans of the Second World War awaiting
action.

The Servicemen's Readjustment Act of 1944
—popularly known as the G.I. Bill of Rights—
became law in June and will be put into effect
by the Veterans Administration under Hines.
Under the law, provisions are made for assisting discharged servicemen (excluding merchant
mariners) who have seen at least ninety days
of active service since September 16, 1940.
These provisions include unemployment benefits of $20 a week up to fifty-two weeks; job
placement and hospitalization facilities; educational aid up to $500 a year for at least a year,
plus $50 a month for subsistence and $25 for
dependents; a Government guaranty of 50 per
cent of a private or Federal loan for approved
purchase of home, farm, or small business, to
the limit of $2,000 on the guaranteed part and
at a maximum interest rate of 4 per cent. An
appropriation of $500,000,000 has been made
for additional veteran facilities, including new
hospital facilities.

To administer the law and to supply information to inquiring servicemen, stations are
being set up on a nationwide scale; centers are
being established in colleges and universities
throughout the country for vocational rehabilitation of returning veterans, and the FHA and
nearly 1,500 Federal savings and loan associations are among the agencies cooperating in
the benefit program. The Veterans Administration itself holds a status second only to the
War and Navy Departments in priorities of
personnel, equipment, supplies, and materials.
At the end of December Hines announced that
a medical panel was being named to advise on
the treatment of veterans suffering from rare
types of diseases encountered in distant battle
areas, as well as on the improvement of general
medical practices in the treatment of the men.

Statistics issued at the end of 1944 indicated
the extent to which returning servicemen were
availing themselves of the opportunities provided by the measure, as the various features

of it were slowly put into operation. Under
the educational provision over 12,000 men were
attending schools, including colleges, teacher-training and normal schools, trade schools,
junior colleges, and job-training schools in industrial plants. Up to December 31, Hines
announced, 36,778 applications for educational
assistance had been received and 33,256 had
been authorized.

The handling of the benefit provisions of the
G.I. Bill of Rights has proved to be a tremendous additional administrative task for the
already burdened Veterans Administration, and
critics have commented that certain features
of the VA have made it inadequate to handle
the new problem. It is the opinion of Sylvia
Porter [41], financial writer, that the bill itself
has been vaguely written and poorly publicized.
For one thing, she says, veterans are for the
most part unaware of the complexities of the
loan provisions and do not understand that their
own credentials must undergo a thorough
checking before a loan is granted. A great deal
of confusion exists on all sides, and only slow
progress is being made.

In a series of New York *Post* articles in December Marquis Childs [43] has summarized what,
in his own opinion, is the situation facing
Hines and his Administration. Red tape and
a top-heavy bureaucracy, he begins, "must be
slashed if the army of veterans out of this
War are to get the benefits Congress intended
them to have." It is Child's feeling that in
the matter of medical care "the inadequacy of
VA is perhaps most conspicuous," a fault
which he attributes to the favors which the
American Legion and other pressure groups
have demanded. Veterans' hospitals have had
no real control over their patients, he says; the
morale problem is of constant concern; there
is no legal control over insane veterans, and,
according to a substantiated report, there has
been maltreatment of insane veterans in one
hospital—which Hines blames largely on the
personnel problem resulting from the War. The
general level of the medical service is low,
Childs maintains. First-rate medical men have
not been attracted to the Service; veterans'
hospitals have had little or no contact with advanced ideas or new research; and the emphasis has not been on restoring men to usefulness.
"The old formula of permanent hospitalization,
plus pensions," is not in his opinion the solution to the problem of rehabilitation. The situation was complicated by the reported refusal
of the Veterans Administration to avail itself
of the services of trained Negroes, except to
staff four segregated hospitals in the South.
This practice was denied by the VA when exposed by *PM*; but at a Congressional committee hearing, it was admitted by George E. Ijans,
assistant veterans' administrator, under questioning by Representative Clare Boothe Luce [42].
At this time Ijans had just described the VA's
nurse shortage as "desperate."

"Dark, trim . . . middling tall," General
Hines is said to be quiet-spoken, "undemonstrative and reserved." The General was married to Nellie Vier on October 4, 1900 and had
two children (one is now deceased) and one
grandchild. Veterans' affairs are not his only
interests. In 1941 he was an active candidate
for the presidency of the New York Stock
Exchange, in whose operations he had been

interested for years, and he was backed for the post by some of the Exchange's most influential members. Outside business affairs take him to New York frequently, for he is a director and large stockholder in the Sperry Gyroscope Corporation. He is also a director of the Continental Trust Company in Washington, D. C.

Co-author of *Service of Coast Artillery*, Hines is a member of the Military Order of the World War, the American Legion Reserve Corps, the American Society of Mechanical Engineers, the Veterans of Foreign Wars, the United Spanish War Veterans. He also belongs to the less military Congressional Country Club and to Temple Noyes Lodge, No. 32. He has been awarded the Distinguished Service Medal by the Navy as well as the Army, and he has the privilege of wearing five foreign decorations.

The hard-working General usually reaches his desk by seven o'clock, and when he leaves around six it is often with a briefcase of unfinished work. Frequently he is found at his office on Sundays, too, although he tries not to let work interfere with his attendance at St. Thomas' Episcopal Church, where he is a vestryman. Whatever leisure time he has to devote to hobbies is given to philately. He also enjoys old-fashioned cowboy films, and he used to ride horseback every morning in order to keep fit.

References

N Y Post Mag p5 Mr 18 '44 pors
N Y Sun p12 Jl 27 '43
PM p6 F 27 '44 por
Who's Who in America 1944-45
Who's Who in Government 1932-33
Who's Who in the Nation's Capital 1938-39

HITCHCOCK, THOMAS Feb. 11, 1900— Apr. 19, 1944 Lieutenant colonel and commander of a P-51 Mustang fighter group in the 9th Air Support Command; a hero of the famous Lafayette Escadrille in the First World War; considered the greatest polo player of all time in the United States and one of the few ten-goal men recognized as such by the United States Polo Association; death occurred in a routine flight.

Obituary

N Y Times p1+ Ap 20 '44 por

HODZA, MILAN (hô'jä mi'län) 1878— June 27, 1944 Czechoslovak statesman; leader of Republican Agrarian Party; Prime Minister from 1935 to 1938; denounced by Nazi Germany for his negotiations for economic reconstruction in the Danube basin through reciprocal trade concessions; was a vice-president of first Czechoslovak State Council, formed in London on December 11, 1940, and acknowledged by the British Government.

Obituary

N Y Times p23 Je 29 '44

HOLM, CELESTE Actress
Address: h. Galeridge, Port Murray, N.J.

After a six-year period of acting in many dissimilar Broadway plays, the "amazingly versatile" actress Celeste Holm emerged in the musical play *Oklahoma!* (1943-44) as "a comedienne of important stature and capability." As long as she has an audience, she explains, she feels equally at home in straight and musical comedy roles, in a large theatre and an intimate cafe atmosphere.

Celeste Holm's introduction to the theatre came as a child at home both in New York, where she was born, and in Chicago, where she lived at one time. Her parents—Norwegian-born Theodor Holm, associated with the American branch of Lloyds of London, and Jean (Parke) Holm, the author and artist—were often hosts to literary and theatrical friends; and at an early age Celeste was taken to the New York plays. She was still a small child when an aunt taught her to sing and dance, and often the girl would entertain guests with her mimicry of current favorites in the theatre. Throughout her school years, too, Celeste never missed an opportunity to tread the boards. She participated in both backyard and schoolroom dramatics, culminating her amateur efforts with the portrayal of a mysterious Russian spy in a high school play. Her education was obtained from fourteen schools, including the Lycée Victor Durée in Paris and one in The Hague—two cities where exhibitions of her mother's paintings had taken the family. Training in dancing, singing, and acting was part of her educational background also; and at various times she has studied under such teachers as Adolph Bolm of the Ballet Theatre, Clytie Hine Mundy, formerly of the Covent Garden Opera, and Benno Schneider, whose teaching she claims is the most rewarding she has had.

There was never much doubt, of course, as to the profession Celeste would follow. When her academic education was completed she struck out on her own, haunting casting offices, at first only to receive the usual cool reception accorded novices. In a very short time, however, an offer to play ingenue leads with a summer stock company at Deer Lake, Pennsylvania, gave her the opening wedge. This was in the summer of 1936. After that jobs came fairly easily. The first real break was the chance in the winter of 1936-1937 to understudy for the part of Ophelia and play a small part in the road company of *Hamlet*. This engagement was followed in 1937 by a more prominent part in the road company of Clare Boothe's [42] sophisticated comedy *The Women*. As the homewrecker Crystal, Miss Holm toured the West in that siren's bubble bath.

But her primary concern was to appear on Broadway; so when a small part in *Gloriana* came along in the fall of 1938 she quickly accepted it. The play, a costume piece starring Blanche Yurka, dealt with the life and loves of England's Good Queen Bess. Although it had been well-received in European capitals under the title of *Elizabeth of England*, Broadway didn't care for it; and the produc-

Bruno of Hollywood

CELESTE HOLM

tion closed after a short run without Miss Holm's having received any critical mention.

The next fall, when the Theatre Guild started to cast William Saroyan's '40 *The Time of Your Life*, Miss Holm was auditioned for the role of the mysterious Mary L. She had been recommended by Lynn Fontanne '41, who had been impressed earlier in the year by her reading of Bianca for the Lunts' production of *The Taming of the Shrew*. (Miss Fontanne had not taken the girl at the time because she considered her too tall for the part.) On Miss Holm's first reading of middle-aged Mary she was rejected because of her youthful appearance. Convinced, however, that she was the one for the part, she then retired to a corner to make herself up more on the order of Crystal of *The Women*. Reappearing, she was given another chance to read, and she was subsequently hired.

The Saroyan comedy, which opened in October 1939, proved highly successful (it won the Pulitzer Prize); and Miss Holm's part was the one which, to date, she has most enjoyed. Although she was on the stage only briefly as the thirty-five-year-old Mary L., the part was important enough, and the young girl's playing of it good enough, for her to be singled out for praise. The *Theatre Arts Monthly*, for example, thought that Mary L. "was the most successful woman puppet which the playwright trots out for study. . . . Played by Celeste Holm . . . [it] has the poignant reality of a remembered dream." Other reviewers described Mary L. as an "excellent bit" and her portrayer as "the most appealing person of them all." Miss Holm appeared in the role during both its New York engagements: the first starting late in October 1939 and running through the first week in April, the second opening in September 1940 for a few weeks.

Before *The Time of Your Life* had ended its first New York run Miss Holm left the cast for the leading role of a Nazi sympathizer in *Another Sun*, the anti-Nazi play by Dorothy Thompson '40 and Fritz Kortner. It opened late in February 1940, and critics in general agreed that this was a poor play, despite the deep conviction and worthy motive which had inspired the authors. Again, however, the press had good words for Miss Holm—"one of the season's attractive leading ladies." Although her role was a "shallow" one, they found her playing of it "effective enough" and done with "considerable initiative."

With the early withdrawal of the production she continued to be described as "prettily engaging", "refreshing", and "an able actress" in a series of short-lived productions. One of these was *The Return of the Vagabond*, which George M. Cohan brought to Broadway in May 1940. It was a melodrama of the old school, written by Cohan in an attempt to recreate a vehicle in which he had been "a minor sensation" in 1920. As Miss Holm herself has remarked, it had a great many fine things in it, but the total effect was not quite successful. As Cohan's last leading lady, however, she says she learned much that was valuable, and she is "proud and happy to have been part of that theatrical tradition."

The next January found Miss Holm back on Broadway in *Eight O'Clock Tuesday*, a "confused and tiresome" mystery drama which rang down its final curtain soon after its première, although not before the appearance of critical comments on Miss Holm as "the most beautiful woman now playing in New York, as well as an unusually moving actress." In March she appeared in *My Fair Ladies*, a rather inane farce in which she played a stranded chorus girl masquerading as a titled English lady. This production received no better reception from New York than the previous effort, so, with the advent of June, Miss Holm joined the exodus to the summer theatres.

Since *The Time of Your Life* she had never had anything approaching a long run, although she had had no difficulty in getting leading parts and good notices. Then in January 1942 came the Theatre Guild's *Papa Is All*, a quaint comedy of the Pennsylvania Mennonites and a play for which Miss Holm had kind feelings. As the daughter in this good-humored study of manners and mores she again proved herself to be a versatile, delightful actress. This time the critics dealt as kindly with the playwright, Patterson Greene, as they did with the cast. In the face of this, the comparatively short life of the play was surprising. At the close of the production Miss Holm went into *All the Comforts of Home* (May 1942). It took only eight performances to establish the fact that a play in which Maude Adams had long ago triumphed held no particular interest for 1942 audiences.

In October of that same year Dwight Deere Wiman decided to produce John van Druten's '44 *The Damask Cheek*, in which Miss Holm was given the role of the actress, a slightly "tinseled piece of baggage." The New York *Times* described the van Druten work, laid in the New York of 1909, as a "pleasant excursion into polite comedy"; and, in commenting on the cast (which included Flora Robson), the critic said: "Celeste

Holm . . . plays the actress with grace and guile in the best performance she has given here in recent season"—a performance, according to Stark Young, that was "remarkably competent and witty."

Shortly before *The Damask Cheek* closed in January 1943 the Theatre Guild's musical version of Lynn Riggs's play of the Indian territory, *Green Grow the Lilacs*, was ready for casting. It was to be known as *Oklahoma!* Miss Holm, who had been studying singing with Clytie Mundy since 1940, felt ready for a musical, and she had wanted the part of the man-crazy Ado Annie ever since she had heard that the Guild was planning to do the show. In addition to its being a singing role, it was different in scope from any she had attempted before. For the audition she sang Schubert's "Who Is Sylvia." Richard Rodgers, composer of the score, asked her if she could "sing bad." "You know," he said, "you can't sing bad unless you're good." Whereupon Miss Holm, to quote her own words, "tried a song with a little comedy in it, sang bad, sort of rolled my eyes," and the part was hers.

Oklahoma! was an instantaneous hit, as was, among other things, Miss Holm's rendition of the plaintive, "rather naughty" ballad "I Cain't Say No." Following the opening in April 1943, all the papers carried enthusiastic reviews of "the young lady who simply tucks the show under her arm and lets the others touch it," to quote Burton Rascoe. And in similar tone the rest of the press reported on this "astonishing young woman . . . [with] too much talent to be quite believable." In a more analytical manner, Stark Young wrote: "The most interesting performance technically was that of Miss Celeste Holm as the love-lorn and impressionable Ado Annie Carnes. . . . [The only fault he could find with her was in her diction.] If you have seen her in other parts . . . you are impressed by this young actress' attempt to do something so sadly needed on our stage, which is to widen her range of characters, in the pursuit of which high creditable and intelligent vanity she includes a genuine study and use of make-up. Miss Holm is pretty enough in face and figure to compete with the rest of them, playing nothing but herself, and so it is all the more to her credit that she chooses otherwise."

New York's cafe society was quick to claim all this talent for their smart supper clubs. Several months after the opening of the musical play Miss Holm started an engagement (in between appearances on the St. James's stage) at La Vie Parisienne, where the overflow from the theatre was able to see her vivacious, witty, subtle brand of entertainment, the climax of which seemed to be "Eunice From Tunis", "a purified version of songs the soldiers sing." The following February she moved further uptown to the Persian Room of the Plaza Hotel, where she continued to entertain the after-theatre clientele with songs which are "especially tailored and fit her like a pair of lightly flirtatious opera gloves." "She has a mobile face with flexible eyebrows, an insouciance with which she can accomplish devastating satire or laughter at the flick of an artificial eyelash."

As a *PM* admirer commented: "She probably has the hugest vocabulary of contemporary female facial expressions of anybody in America." And she sings "with a consummate feminine charm that distinguishes her from every other singer of comedy songs."

On the other, non-comic, side she can also sing a light ballad with "freshness and sweetness." "When Celeste steps up to the microphone," added *PM*'s analysis of Miss Holm's night club performance, "you perceive . . . that she is a sensitive person. Not brash, not brassy, not blasé. A girl quite capable of being embarrassed; of having her feelings hurt. . . . And because of this, as she begins to sing you feel a sympathetic chill. . . . You are nervous for her. . . . And then it becomes apparent that Celeste is certainly not going to muff it. Her voice is sure. Her timing is exact. Her talent and her intelligence are in perfect control of the situation. She is funny and sweet, and the people stop scraping their chairs around . . . and the room is tense with their listening."

While Miss Holm was still playing in *Oklahoma!* producer John C. Wilson decided to build a musical around her. In October 1944 this show, *Bloomer Girl*, opened on Broadway with Miss Holm in the leading singing role. Joan McCracken from *Oklahoma!*, David Brooks, and Margaret Douglass were also in the cast. The play was laid in the Civil War years, the period when the intrepid Amelia Bloomer started a counter-civil war by suggesting that women wear bloomers and short skirts instead of hoops. After reading the script, in which she was to play the rebellious hoop-skirt-heiress niece of Amelia, Miss Holm had remarked, "Evelina is more me than anything I've done."

The play, on the whole, received good press notices, and even before its opening was a box-office success. Although the critics differed on the merits of the book, they found the production exceedingly attractive to the eye, and felt that the music by Harold Arlen and the choregraphy by Agnes de Mille had period charm. The reviewers were almost entirely agreed, too, on Celeste Holm's agreeable contribution to the proceedings, as in the past, although several felt that her voice was too light to carry a big musical. "Miss Holm makes an attractive and likable Evelina," wrote *PM*, "with a proper archness and dash." She is captivating," said *Variety*.

As might be gathered, Miss Holm is an exceedingly energetic young woman. In addition to stage and night club work, she has made several radio appearances, and with an entertainment unit she organized she has toured many Army camps. In July 1944 she signed a contract with Twentieth Century-Fox, effective in 1945. An "articulate and enthusiastic person, with an "intelligent, sensitive face," she has blue eyes, blond hair, is slender and about five feet five tall. In talking with her one is impressed by her honest, unaffected manner. A *PM* interviewer remarked once that Miss Holm "looks like the kind of girl you could take home and introduce to the folks without making Pop put his shoes on." In January 1940 she was married to Francis E. H. Davies, who, in March 1944, was in the armed forces. She

HOLM, CELESTE—*Continued.*

has one child, a son, by an earlier marriage. Her hobbies are sewing and cooking—and she claims she is a wonderful cook, "no kidding."

References

N Y Herald Tribune VI p1+ Jl 11 '43
PM p27 Ag 15 '43 por

HOLMES, (ELIAS) BURTON Jan. 8, 1870- Travel-lecturer

Address: h. 2 W. 67th St., New York City; Topside, Whitley Heights, Los Angeles, Calif.

In 1943 on the fiftieth anniversary of his first travel lecture, Burton Holmes told a reporter: "I suppose that the really remarkable thing about me is that I've been doing the same thing in the same way for fifty years and the public has stood for it." The public has stood for it so well that *Program*, the magazine of the lecture platform, reported in February 1944 that the seventy-three-year-old lecturer had that year not only sold out houses but had had to give extra lectures to accommodate his public. *Program's* explanation was: "America loves its Burton Holmes and says it with dollars." Not only does he have a record for continued drawing power in the entertainment world but he is also America's No. 1 traveler. He has been around the world six times, has spent some fifty-odd summers in foreign travel and at least fifty winters in traveling from one American city to another to fill his lecture engagements. These take him through seventeen states and the District of Columbia, not including the "spot dates" given in other states before and after his regular season. Despite this record, Holmes recently said, "I should be glad to have another three score years or more with this planet that I might know the good earth better than I do." The only accessible spots he has missed are Iraq, Iran, and Afghanistan.

Burton Elias Holmes, born January 8, 1870 in Chicago, is the son of Ira and Virginia (Burton) Holmes. He was named Elias for his paternal grandfather, a Congressman from New York, and Burton for his maternal grandfather, a Chicago pioneer. At the age of six he ran away—to school. A little private school had been opened in the neighborhood of his Michigan Avenue home, and young Burton without notifying anyone began his education. But at sixteen, after attending the Allen Academy and the Harvard School in Chicago, he walked out of school, never to return. His only diplomas or degrees, he says, have come from the Pullman Company and divers steamship and airway lines.

As a child Holmes traveled with his parents to Eastern summer resorts and, in the winter seasons, to Florida and California. He was only nine when he came for the first time under the spell of the oratory of John L. Stoddard, who for eighteen years had dominated the travel-lecture platform in the United States. After that he attended the Stoddard lectures regularly, not because he had any ambition at that time toward the lecture platform but because foreign lands fascinated him. In 1890, on his second European trip, he had the opportunity to make the acquaintance of

Stoddard when they were lodged under the same peasant roof in the little town of Oberammergau for the decennial presentation of the *Passion Play*. Later this acquaintanceship helped to establish Holmes on the lecture platform.

His first European trip had been made with his Grandmother Burton, who had traveled with her husband, before his death an importer of French wines and rare foods. His camera went with him. "And at that time," says Holmes, "to carry a camera was to be distinguished." (The day of the kodak had not yet arrived.) When he returned to Chicago after his second trip Holmes showed the lantern slides he had made from his "travel negatives" to his fellow members of the Chicago Camera Club. This was in 1890. "To take the edge off the silence, and keep the show moving," young Holmes wrote a brief account of his journey and read the script as the man at the stereoptican changed the slides. The lecture proved to be so successful that some member suggested that it might bring money in to the club's treasury if repeated with an admission price. "Through Europe With a Camera" brought in $350—and an idea to the young lecturer.

However, Holmes did not act upon the idea immediately. For the next two years he tried to sell real estate and when he proved a failure as a realtor he became a clerk with the Gayton A. Douglas photo-supply house in Chicago at $8 a week. When the job began to pall Holmes cajoled his family into staking him to a five-month visit to Japan. Upon boarding the train for the first stage of his journey Holmes found Stoddard in the same Pullman car—also bound for Japan. On the *Empress of Japan* their cabins were adjacent, and they were assigned to the same table in the ship's dining room. Their first impressions of Japan differed. The older man found Japan queer, comfortless, and almost repellent; to Holmes it was a fairyland, and, "despite the disillusions of later years, the charm has never been broken." On his return from this first Oriental trip he found the family finances suffering as a result of the 1893 depression, and to avoid returning to his clerkship, Holmes decided to try the lecture platform. He carefully prepared lectures on Japan with the first all-color set of slides. Two thousand announcements were sent out to his mother's visiting list as well as to selected addresses from the Blue Book. To his surprise people bought tickets in advance, and the balance-sheet for the short season (1893) showed a $700 profit. The job at the photo-supply house went to someone else.

His next three years were not profitable, but upon the retirement of Stoddard from the lecture platform Holmes decided to "make a play for his public." The capacious Central Music Hall in Chicago had for eighteen years been the Stoddard stronghold and Holmes, without money, boldly leased the hall for a course of five lectures. He had one advantage over Stoddard, the showing of a new invention, the motion pictures. The foreword of the advertising booklet prepared for the crucial season of 1897-1898 read as follows: "In addition to the lantern slides in color there will be presented *for the first time* in connection with a course of travel lectures, a series of pictures to which a modern miracle has added the illusion of life itself—the reproduction of recorded motion. Mr. Holmes has secured the most perfect instrument yet invented for the projection of Motion Pictures." At the lecture, shots of the Empire Express and galloping horses of a fire department followed lantern slides of cathedrals in Italy. Although motion picture exhibition was at that primitive stage when reel-changing meant an audience-wait of several minutes after a twenty-five-second showing of "recorded motion," the lecture public considered the "modern miracle" worth the waiting.

Having succeeded in Chicago, Holmes was tempted to fill the Stoddard dates in Eastern cities. Louis Francis Brown, Oscar Bennet Depue, and Holmes formed the Burton Holmes Lectures, Inc., starting with a capitalization of $50,000—and Brown set out for New York to interview Augustin Daly, whose theatre Stoddard had been packing year after year since 1879. It was on Stoddard's recommendation that the famous theatre owner booked Holmes for his theatre. Other "Big Time" dates followed. It took a number of years before Burton Holmes Lectures, Inc., made a profit, but "the worries of each winter were compensated by the travel joys of the succeeding summer." Eventually the box office began to report big business, and soon the Burton Holmes lecture season became a regular annual event in the leading cities of the United States.

The most popular of all the Holmes lectures, "The Panama Canal," was given in 1912 when the project was under construction. Other outstanding successes include "The Passion Play of Oberammergau", "The Glories and Frivolities of Paris", "Soviet Russia," and "The Magic of Mexico." Complete box office failures were the presentations of Siam, India, and other countries of the Far East. The highlights from the records show $2,500 for a matinee in Boston on Venice—the same subject in Pomona, California, yielded nothing because, as the house manager reported, "Nobody ain't came." Holmes says good management is as essential as a good lecture, and pays a warm tribute to Louis Francis Brown, who had secured his first "Big Time" date and who continued as his partner for twenty-eight years. Holmes makes 150 annual platform appearances, and before and after the closely booked regular season he fills "spot dates." During his fifty years as a lecturer he has missed only two lectures—in 1935 when dust got in his throat while he was flying over the Dust Bowl. At the end of 1944 he reported that he had closed his fifty-first season "with a record of overflowing houses nearly everywhere," adding, "not bad for a young seventy-five-year-old beginner."

The ambition to explore, to break new trails, has never appealed to Holmes. He says that he does not seek danger: "I'm a Cook's tourist, reporting how pleasant it is in such and such a place." His delivery has been described as "crisp." He makes his own pictures and builds his talk around what seems to him to be the most interesting of the countless events or scenes he has photographed.

BURTON HOLMES

Proof that his comments do read well was the success of the elaborately illustrated books in which his earlier lectures found permanent form—40,000 sets of fifteen volumes were sold. *Traveller's Russia* (1935) is the only book the lecturer has written that is not in travelogue style. He is responsible also for the editing and illustrations of a series of school readers for young people, and in the years from 1907 to 1912 he contributed a series of travel articles to the *Ladies' Home Journal*. Although he has not produced motion pictures regularly for the Hollywood companies, his Paramount releases from 1915 to 1921 had the longest run of any travel shorts in motion-picture history. Ten years later, in 1931, Metro-Goldwyn-Mayer commissioned him to do travel shorts in English, French, Italian, and Spanish. While in the film capital he also made a travelogue on Hollywood. Voluntarily appearing in his picture were Mary Pickford, Dolores del Rio, Jean Harlow, and other stars of the day.

The lecturer's only important radio broadcasts were made in 1933 when over a ten-week period he gave fifteen-minute talks for NBC about his daily experiences at the current Century of Progress Exposition in Chicago. He has made sundry guest appearances on other programs, and in May 1944 made his television debut on the Dumont Studio program *Thrills and Chills* with his film *Fantastic Bali*.

In 1914 Holmes was married to Margaret Oliver. They have a "palm-embowered home" called "Topside" in Whitley Heights, a suburb of Los Angeles. Their New York home is an apartment overlooking Central Park, in the same building in which they have lived for many years. Missing, however, is Holmes's elaborate Oriental studio, "Nirvana," in which was kept a forty-year accumulation of Japanese treasures. "Happily," says Holmes now, he disposed of these ten months before Pearl Harbor, although he still retains his large collection of foreign hats. A distinguished fig-

HOLMES, BURTON—*Continued*

ure, he has been photographed in the native costume of almost every land he has visited—on the lecture platform he appears in formal evening dress.

References

Program 10:22 N '43 por; 10:18 F '44
Who's Who in America 1944-45

HOLT, RACKHAM Mar. 5, 1899- Author

Address: b. c/o Doubleday, Doran & Co., 14 W. 49th St., New York City; h. Mt. Sinai, Long Island, N. Y.

Although Rackham Holt's writings have been published since 1933, it was not until ten years later that she came to the attention of the reading public. Mrs. Holt, known in private life as Margaret Van Vechten Saunders Holt, spent six of those ten years as a literary ghost—that is, she wrote books cred-

RACKHAM HOLT

ited to better-known persons with less literary ability. The last four years were devoted to *George Washington Carver,* a highly successful biography—the first of Mrs. Holt's books for which she received credit under the name of Rackham Holt. (The author was called "Rackham" by her friends because her fluffy red-gold hair and white skin made her look like an Arthur Rackham picture.)

The daughter of William L. and Ella M. (Plank) Saunders and the grandniece of Henry Wadsworth Longfellow, Margaret Van Vechten Saunders was born in Denver, Colorado, March 5, 1899. Her fondness for the old *St. Nicholas* Magazine led her, at the age of nine, to start writing herself. Throughout her school career, it is said, young Margaret edited school magazines; in addition she was one of the several high school students who edited the *Waste Basket*, which lasted exactly one year, at the end of which time its staff went off to either war or college. After graduation

from the Lake View High School in Chicago, to which city her parents had moved, the young editor went on to Columbia University in New York.

In 1919 Rackham Holt returned to Chicago and took a position in the public library there. Two years later she was reviewing books for the Chicago *Daily News*; the following year found her in Albany, assisting the editor of the New York State Library's *Book List*. Her next position was with the New York Public Library; in the same year (1923) she was married to Guy Holt, a publisher, who was a grandnephew of John Greenleaf Whittier. (Mr. Holt died in 1934, leaving Mrs. Holt with one daughter, Margaret Van Vechten Holt.)

Two years after her marriage Mrs. Holt joined the staff of G. P. Putnam's Sons, the well known publishers. She remained with the firm doing editorial work until 1933, when she decided to do "independent writing" exclusively. Her writing experience included not only daily racing sheets but work on other publications, including foreign trade bulletins, as well as feature stories on art, music, and books for newspapers in Chicago and Detroit. During a number of years Mrs. Holt traveled through Europe, the Orient, the West Indies, and the United States possessions, and ghosted, it is said, three best-selling biographies. She also wrote a number of magazine articles under her own name.

The great Negro scientist and artist George Washington Carver [40] aroused Mrs. Holt's admiration and her desire to write the first authentic story of his life. She therefore spent about three years collecting the material for his biography, which was finally published in 1943. Much of this time was spent with Dr. Carver at Tuskegee, where Mrs. Holt found that "as we talked together and as I read through his scrapbooks, each day brought stronger confirmation of his true greatness, his sweetness and humor, his wisdom and understanding."

It is hardly surprising, therefore, to find that "the author has engaged in no 'debunking.' Indeed, she approaches her subject with something of reverence and develops his life story with that loving tenderness which Dr. Carver was peculiarly able to evoke, particularly from white admirers." Another reviewer found the book "warm with intelligent understanding and unmarred by that fatuous indulgence which is only another kind of condescension. She sees quite clearly that certain aspects of Carver's personality were provincial or defensive, and shows us why. In one of the most attractive biographies of the season she puts an appropriately lyrical colloquial prose to good use in conveying the character of a gifted scientist, the most likable of ascetics. . . . If Mrs. Holt's book . . . has shortcomings, we may well blame its minor lacks on the difficulties of a pioneer work in a field that may have very broad implications." As a whole the reviews were very favorable. If the earlier portions of the book were considered "somewhat episodic, perhaps because of the antiquity and the fragmentary nature of the material, it soon swings into an epic stride. Not the least of Rackham Holt's virtues as a writer are her sense of the dramatic and her masterful manipulation of veiled irony. Here is a story that will cause you to chuckle, that will touch your heart, make your blood boil, and enlarge your soul."

Mrs. Holt is "deeply grateful for the privilege of knowing Dr. Carver through the daily communication we had over many months," and she is "deeply conscious of the honor of being the instrument through which his life has been recorded. If this book does anything to hold up a mirror and thereby help make others of his race better understood by white men who seldom look beyond the color of their skins to the living human being, our joint purpose will have been achieved, and George Washington Carver can rest in peace."

Half of Mrs. Holt's royalties have been assigned to the George Washington Carver Foundation at Tuskegee Institute and will be used toward scholarships for talented and needy young Negroes and toward laboratory facilities for those who carry on Dr. Carver's great work.

With the success of *George Washington Carver*, Rackham Holt qualified as a full-fledged celebrity and is included in the 1944 edition of *Who's Who in America*. The author, who gives her favorite spectator sports as "hockey, six-day bike races, and bullfights," says that her favorite recreation is "playing house—in the kitchen or garden" of her Long Island home. This old New England salt-box, built in 1665, is furnished throughout with a mélange of things the author has picked up all over the world, much in the manner, she believes, that its original sea-captain owner must have done. Her Ford touring car is "Madox" for short ("Ford Madox Ford")— but her dog is unimaginatively named Fido. There is always at least one dog chez Holt, and "anything else that comes along—cats, birds, fish, turtles, rabbits, snakes, mice."

Reference

Book-of-the-Month Club p27 Je '43

HOOVER, MRS. HERBERT 1875(?)— Jan. 7, 1944 Wife of the former President of the United States; one of Washington's most gracious hostesses; world traveler and relief worker; honorary chairman of the American Women's Division of the Commission for Relief in Belgium; honorary vice-president of the Girl Scouts.

Obituary

N Y Times p13 Ja 8 '44 por

HOOVER, LOU HENRY *See* Hoover, Mrs. H.

HOPKINS, ERNEST MARTIN Nov. 6, 1877- President of Dartmouth College

Address: b. Dartmouth College, Hanover, N. H.; h. Tuck Drive, Hanover, N. H.

The president of Dartmouth College, Ernest Martin Hopkins, long noteworthy for his activities in numerous government, educational, and industrial organizations, in August 1944 accepted the chairmanship of a new group, Americans United for World Organization,

formed for the purpose of promoting a better world order and a lasting peace.

Hopkins was born November 6, 1877 in Dunbarton, New Hampshire, the son of a country Baptist minister of colonial ancestry, Adoniram Judson Hopkins, and Mary Cheney (Martin) Hopkins. During the vacation periods of twelve school years the youth worked in a granite quarry, from which he gained a sturdiness of body still evident today. He later also earned money with which he partially paid for his schooling while at Worcester (Massachusetts) Academy by carrying the mail eight miles daily on foot. He taught grammar school for a year, too, before entering Dartmouth in the class of 1901.

Upon his graduation from college with a degree of Bachelor of Arts, he became secretary to William Jewett Tucker, the president of Dartmouth and an eminent American educator. In 1905 Hopkins became secretary of the College. He continued his studies and received the degree of Master of Arts in 1908. In 1910 he resigned the secretaryship and entered the business world, where he soon gained prominence as a pioneer expert in industrial personnel work. In the years from 1910 to 1916 he organized and developed the employment systems of Western Electric Company, Filene's in Boston, Curtis Publishing Company, and the New England Telephone Company. In 1916 he left this field to return to Dartmouth as its president.

Some 17,000 men have studied at Dartmouth in the years of "Hoppy's" presidency, and through the force of his personality and his administrative skill they have come to form one of the strongest supporting alumni bodies in the country. When he became president he was determined to make Dartmouth a college of "he-men." He developed the famed Outing Club, made Dartmouth a power in intercollegiate sports, introduced a new system of selection whereby freshmen were chosen not only for mental capacity but for all-round ability. A believer in developing responsibility in students, he introduced honors work, unlimited cuts, and a tutorial system. He was one of the first college presidents to denounce Prohibition. He let no one intimidate his liberal professors. When an irate alumnus offered $50,000 to Hopkins if he would discharge a professor who had denounced the 1921 Sacco-Vanzetti trial decision by Judge Webster Thayer (a Dartmouth man), he told the professor about the offer. The professor fumed, but Hopkins said, "Don't get excited. If you quit, I will too, and we'll split the $50,000."

With undergraduates of the '20's, whom he understood and liked, he was on intimate terms. Upper classmen had a standard prank they played on freshmen at the expense of their president: They would leave a note on some freshman's desk telling him to call "Hanover 65" (Hoppy's number) at 6:05 a.m. and to "ask for Ernie; he's in a jam." Hopkins got scores of such calls each year. But the undergraduates of the '30's baffled and saddened him. He considered them irresponsible, purposeless, prone to self-pity; and he assailed the New Deal for its effect on the imagination and aspirations of youth. He told one graduating class: "No real friend could wish that you should never face misfortune. It is not so that vigor of mind or strength of character is de-

Harris & Ewing

ERNEST MARTIN HOPKINS

veloped." By the end of the decade he was at loggerheads with the students and he angered them by exclaiming: "For some obscure reason . . . it has become a sign of intelligence to be pessimistic and . . . cynical—all of which seems to me to be contrary to the spirit of which the College should be representative." In the early '40's, however, he was relieved to note a change in undergraduate sentiment and evidences of student understanding of the crisis facing the country. A majority of the class of 1941 pressed for an immediate declaration of war on Germany. This attitude on the part of the students merited admiration, he believed, because they had arrived at it by their own intellectual striving. He said he recognized that the earlier views of the students had been based on a misrepresentation of facts with respect to the last war and that educators were partially to blame.

The alumni have reason to be proud of Hopkins for what he has done for Dartmouth. During his presidency the endowment has quadrupled, the physical plant has doubled, the percentage of annual expenditures for teaching purposes has climbed from 47 to nearly 64 per cent, and faculty and student bodies—until the start of the Second World War—had nearly doubled. The alumni are proud, too, of Hopkins' service to the nation in time of war. During the First World War he was appointed to the Army Quartermaster Department in charge of industrial relations; and the same year, 1918, he was assistant to Secretary of War Newton D. Baker in charge of industrial relations. He also represented the War Department on the War Labor Policies Board from July to September 1918. In the Second World War he was the executive director of the Minerals and Metals Group of the Priorities Division of the Office of Production Management from January 1941 until his resignation six months later.

In spite of his record as college president and his popularity with students, faculty, and alumni, Hopkins has had his critics. Some have said that in his concern for the "whole man"

he has neglected the scholastic side of Dartmouth and failed to bring world-renowned scholars to it; others have mistrusted his openmindedness and tolerance as revealed, for example, in his strong pronouncement in favor of the study of "isms" in institutions of higher learning so that each student could evaluate those "isms" for himself. He saw clearly as early as 1936 the challenge of Fascism the United States faced, and in June 1941 a New York *Times Magazine* article by Van Buren Thorne, Jr., quoted him as saying: "I do not believe that there are many people who would like to be pacifists better than I . . . but from Munich down to the present time it has seemed to me that the isolationists and noninterventionists were simply working toward saving the inevitable war for ourselves alone." He has seen many of his convictions substantiated by succeeding events. In answer to critics he has said: "The fundamental fact of the present situation seems clear: that liberty and freedom are available only to those capable and willing to protect them"; and again, "I think the whole theory of rights and privileges in a democracy has been overemphasized in our ideology of the past, as compared with our responsibilities and obligations, and I honestly don't think democracy can endure under the circumstances of the future excepting as we reverse those attributes."

Hopkins believes that "a people whose principle objective is security is a people whose idealism and moral stamina will inevitably be washed away in comfortable living." He opposes specialization in the liberal arts college in time of peace, for he believes that "the aim of the liberal college should be to be idealistic according to the root significance of the term" and that it is the responsibility of such institutions to develop in its students the "ability to think and provide or follow useful, thinking leadership." He asserts that "neither efficiency nor professional scholarship by itself alone makes for a sufficient goal in life to make a fight for survival worth while." As early as 1942, at the New York *Herald Tribune* Forum on current problems, he expressed a firm conviction that if people do not succeed in subordinating materialism and self-seeking to the common welfare of the peoples of the earth they will "contribute not only to the making of still another war but in the disappointment and disillusionment of those who return from waging this conflict [the Second World War]" there will be "the makings of what youth made of France after the last war."

Determined to do his share toward making the search for peace more concrete, Hopkins accepted in August 1944 the chairmanship of the board of directors of Americans United for World Organization, Inc., a nonpartisan group formed by the consolidation of a number of existing organizations. Represented in its officers and membership are many diverse shades of political opinion and of economic activity—labor, business, education, the bar, press, agriculture, and the arts. Local chapters throughout the United States will cooperate with the local units of collaborating educational organizations.

The three working principles of Americans United for World Organization, as stated by Ernest Hopkins, are: (1) to give every possible help to movements intelligently devised for world organization upon some basis of decency analogous to principles assumed to be essential among human beings in their dealings with one another; (2) to seek by every means at our command to insure the election of a Congress intelligent enough and purposeful enough to give expression to the popular will on these matters; (3) to make available to an eager public the knowledge by which they can identify and classify those individuals and agencies among us whose acquisitiveness for power, pride of position, or glorification of race lead them to positions and efforts which head straight to fascism and all of the hideous attributes of that cult.

In October 1944 Americans United arranged a meeting to which were invited representatives of eighty organizations, many of them not associated with the group. At a question-and-answer session the Dumbarton Oaks security proposals were discussed. These proposals Hopkins hailed as "a progressive step on the long road to make wars impossible," and the organization, he said, will, when the time comes, support the best plan which the Government "will have been able to obtain in negotiations with other peace-loving nations."

Hopkins is the possessor of more than a dozen honorary degrees—from Amherst, Rutgers, Brown, the University of New Hampshire, Yale, Harvard, William and Mary, and McGill University in Canada, to name a few. His activities in the field of education have been numerous. As early as 1922 he was invited to take the presidency of the University of Chicago. In 1925 he was lecturer at the Jayne Foundation in Philadelphia, and in 1932 he was appointed by the President as special investigator for the War Department of the Puerto Rican educational system. He has also been at various times a trustee of several educational institutions, including Worcester Academy, Phillips Academy at Andover, and the Brookings Institution. He has been, as well, a member of the Rockefeller Foundation and the General Education Board, succeeding John D. Rockefeller, Jr. '41, as chairman of the latter in 1939. He has kept his hand in business, too, and in 1944 is director of a number of organizations, among them the Boston and Maine Railroad, the Continental Can Company, the Encyclopaedia Britannica Films, Inc., and the Arctic Institute of North America.

In February 1911 Hopkins was married to Celia Stone, and the couple have one daughter, Dorothy Ann, now Mrs. John R. Potter. Hopkins enjoys golf, fishing, and boating, and likes watching a good game of football. He is a member of several clubs in Boston, New York, and Washington.

References

N Y Herald Tribune II p6 Je 8 '41
N Y Times Mag p13+ Je 15 '41 il
  pors
Time 37:59-60 Je 23 '41 por
Who's Who in America 1944-45

HOPPENOT, HENRI ETIENNE (ŏp'nō än-rē' ā-tyen') Oct. 26, 1891- French diplomat

Address: c/o Delegation of the French Committee of National Liberation, 1420 16th St., N.W., Washington, D. C.

From September 1943 until formal diplomatic relations between France and the United States were resumed in October 1944, Henri Etienne Hoppenot handled his country's affairs in Washington, D.C., as representative of the French Committee of National Liberation. In December Henri Bonnet, France's first Ambassador to the United States since her liberation, took Hoppenot's place in Washington.

Henri Etienne Hoppenot was born October 26, 1891 and entered the French diplomatic service twenty-six years later. He had acquired degrees in literature and in law and his diploma from L'Ecole des Sciences Politiques before being attached to the French Embassy at Berne in 1917, during the First World War. After that he held diplomatic posts of increasing importance. The year 1919 found him second secretary at Teheran; the year 1924, secretary, second class, to the Embassy at Rio de Janiero; the next year, first secretary at Berlin, where he spent a couple of years. In 1933 he went to Peiping, a move which led to his attending the abortive Brussels Conference on the Far East in 1937. Since 1936 he has also been an Officier of the Légion d'Honneur.

The years immediately before the outbreak of the Second World War found this career diplomat sub-director of Asiatic affairs in the French Foreign Ministry. It is said that in this post he was in close association with Paul Baudouin, general manager of the Banque d'Indo-Chine, who sent a telegram of congratulations to Hitler '42 after Munich. After the French collapse in June 1940 he was sent to Portugal as Vichy Ambassador by Baudouin, who was Vichy Foreign Minister at the time. Later Hoppenot was appointed Vichy Minister to Uruguay, arriving at Montevideo in November 1940.

Upon his arrival in Uruguay, he immediately antagonized the Free French there by his eulogies of Pétain '40. *PM* says that he disclaimed in the press the extent of German requisitions in Occupied France. In June of that same year he attempted to persuade the Uruguayan Government to bar de Gaullists from using radio stations, and later he tried to force the Government to apply sanctions against a publication which criticized *Le Maréchal*. In September 1942 he did everything within his power to prevent the minister of a foreign country from speaking before the microphone of a de Gaullist radio station. The next month he tried to get the Uruguayan University authorities not to recognize the validity of diplomas given out by the Lycée Français of Montevideo. He was, in other words, the loyal servant of the Government headed by Pétain and by Pierre Laval '40 up to October 25, 1942, just a few days before American troops landed in North Africa, when he resigned as Ambassador. According to de Gaullists, however, even in his letter of resignation he showed few symptoms of a change of heart. They say that on his own admission "he approved of capitulation, col-

HENRI ETIENNE HOPPENOT

laboration with the oppressor, of sending soldiers against the Russian Army, of actions by General Dentz, which opened the airports of Syria to the Germans, etc. In internal matters Hoppenot approved of all dictatorial measures taken by Pétain and Laval not only in occupied territory, but in unoccupied France —that part of France which Pétain had 'saved.' Hoppenot, therefore, approved persecutions against Republicans, anti-Semitic measures, denationalization of patriots, execution of patriots, etc." The former Vichy diplomat was nevertheless appointed to the French Military Mission to the United States headed by Giraud [42] on March 5, 1943.

And there were more important posts to come. In June 1943 there were civil demonstrations and disturbances in Martinique and Guadaloupe followed by a military revolt which forced Vichy's Admiral Robert [43] to ask a "change of authority to avoid bloodshed." In July, Hoppenot was appointed by the French Committee of National Liberation to talk with Admiral Robert and to negotiate the return of the French Antilles "into the union of the French Empire." He arrived at Martinique on Bastille Day, and Robert, after handing the French Antilles over to him, departed with his associates for Puerto Rico. Hoppenot immediately announced that the French warships, tankers, and merchant ships immobilized at Port au Prince since the fall of France would be sent to the United States for reconditioning preparatory to joining the Allied war effort. As French Delegate-Extraordinary to the French Antilles, he then restored the Republican Government, abrogated the laws of administration of Robert, and began the work of re-establishing economic life on Martinique and Guadaloupe.

Hoppenot was not destined to stay in Martinique long, however. On September 28, 1943, in spite of protests from the Montevideo chapter of France Forever, the French

Committee of National Liberation appointed him to represent the Committee in Washington. Returning from Martinique in October 1943, in one of his first interviews with the press he hinted that an Allied invasion of France might not be necessary to bring about a German collapse within the next six months, suggesting that Russian successes alone would bring the Red armies so close to Berlin that Hitler would resign and Germany would begin to ask "to discuss the terms of the 'unconditional surrender'" (with the Allies, of course).

These ideas were not agreeable to all Frenchmen, and neither was the purge of the high de Gaullist officials attached to the French Delegation in Washington which Hoppenot immediately began to carry out— reportedly at the request of René Massigli, a strong conservative who, it was said, had been forced on the Committee of National Liberation as Foreign Affairs Minister by the British. Fighting French delegations in South America continued to demand Hoppenot's removal, and on Armistice Day 1943 many refused to attend a rally in New York under the auspices of France Forever because he was speaking at it. That same month, however, in the midst of the purge of de Gaullists, Hoppenot made a speech in New York City before the Comité Républicain Français which was full of lavish praise of de Gaulle. General Giraud's resignation from the French Committee of National Liberation and the purge of the ex-Vichyites being carried on in Algiers may or may not have had something to do with it. In any case, it has been pointed out that while ex-Vichyites languished in North African prisons, Henri Hoppenot continued to represent the French Committee of National Liberation in Washington.

By the end of 1944, however, the picture had changed, for in October formal diplomatic relations between the United States and France had been resumed, Washington and eleven other Governments having accorded official recognition of the French de facto Government of de Gaulle as the French Provisional Government. In Hoppenot's place de Gaulle appointed Henri Bonnet as France's first Ambassador to the States since her liberation and Hoppenot himself returned to Paris when Bonnet took up his duties at the Embassy in December. The new Ambassador, it was said, is a champion of strong international ties, a former member of the League of Nations Secretariat, and the author of a number of books dealing with post-War plans for a world organization. Prior to his Embassy post he had been the Commissioner of Information in the French Committee. "Today," he has said, "the question of whether one is a Giraudist or a de Gaullist is not important. We have been appointed as a unit for France and we will serve as such."

On his departure for Paris in December, Henri Hoppenot said to the American press: "I leave full of love for your country and hope for the cooperation between your country and my country, which is certainly one of the bases for peace and freedom."

Hoppenot has been described by *Newsweek* as "a tall, dark, handsome man with an erect,

diplomatic bearing and a ready and gracious
smile."

References

N Y Sun p13 Jl 22 '43
PM p17 N 7 '43 por; p6 N 11 '43; p6 N
25 '43

HORDER, THOMAS J(EEVES), 1st BARON Jan. 7, 1871- British physician

Address: b. 141 Harley St., London

Physician in Ordinary to King George VI [43],
Baron Thomas J. Horder has been described
as the *enfant terrible* of medicine in England.
He has won this epithet as the result of his
strong, forward-looking social and medical
views, as expressed in his writings and practice. Prior to the Second World War Horder
had earned an international reputation in his
profession; and during the 1940 blitz Londoners in underground shelters came to know
well the friendly, small, stocky man who, as
chairman of the Shelter Hygiene Committee,
visited the shelters during London's worst
raids and instituted improvements to provide
greater comfort and safety.

Born January 7, 1871, in the little country
town of Shaftesbury in Dorset, Thomas
Jeeves Horder is the son of Albert Horder,
a draper. His family moved to Swindon when
he was a year old, and he spent his childhood
there. His early education was private until,
on reaching college age, he entered the University of London, where his career as a student was brilliant. In 1893 he obtained his
B.Sc. in physiology, with first class honors;
and in 1898 an M.B. with honors and gold
medals in medicine, midwifery, and forensic
medicine. A year later he took his M.D. To
supplement his readings in biology he studied
with the University Correspondence College,
which had on its staff a young biologist named
H. G. Wells, who graded Horder's papers.

For his further training Horder went on to
Saint Bartholomew's Hospital—familiarly
known in the profession as "Bart's"—with
which Horder has since been associated. He
began his career as a demonstrator of biology
there in 1895, subsequently holding every possible important post, including senior consulting physician, and becoming a governor of
the hospital in 1936.

After qualifying as a physician, Horder
started practice in Harley Street, London's
center of medical and surgical specialists.
Shortly afterward, in 1902, he was married
to Geraldine Rose Doggett, of Newnham
Manor, Hertfordshire. He is the father of a
son and two daughters.

During the First World War Horder served,
with the rank of captain, in the Royal Army
Medical Corps. He was knighted in 1918,
and in 1923 became Physician in Ordinary to
the Prince of Wales (now Duke of Windsor),
at the same time becoming the Baronet of
Shaston.

Horder soon earned a high reputation as a
diagnostician. Contributing his knowledge and
experience to the British literature of medicine, he wrote *Clinical Pathology in Practice*
(1910), *Cerebro-Spinal Fever* (1915), *Medical
Notes* (1921), and *Essentials of Medical Diagnosis* (1929), which is regarded as the

Barratt's

BARON THOMAS J. HORDER

authoritative work in that field. Shunning
mechanization and standardization of methods,
Horder has repeatedly declared that the most
essential factor in the diagnosis and treatment
of disease is the personal contact of doctor
and patient. The humanist attitude is the
one which enables the doctor to do his best
work, he continues. "The doctor must needs
be a priest as well as physician."

In a collection of lectures entitled *Health
and a Day* (1937), Horder set forth his conception of the function of the Ministry of
Health. Although regarded by many critics
as a visionary, he holds that, in the long view,
the ideal Ministry of Health would also be a
Ministry of Happiness. "My creed . . .
transcends politics," he declares. To achieve
the public happiness, he pleads for enough of
the right food, easy access to the fresh air,
shelter at a rent that leaves something to buy
food, leisure for play, the amenities of life,
"the giving of each human being a chance
before he is born, and, after death, the decent
disposal of his body in the best interests of
his fellow men."

A stanch advocate of cremation, Horder
is chairman of the council of the Cremation
Society, and regards "the integral burial of
corpses as inimical to hygiene." Also a champion of eugenics, he has written: "Any sane
nation must have birth control as one of the
planks in its platform." His other medical
interests include radiology, cancer research,
orthopedics, and the treatment of rheumatism.

Horder opposed the legalization of euthanasia (the practice of painlessly putting to death
persons suffering from incurable and painful
diseases) when the Voluntary Euthanasia Bill
was discussed in the House of Lords in December 1936. He asserted that the question of
euthanasia did not belong primarily to the medical profession. If the doctor cannot cure his
patients of their diseases, "then his duty is to
prolong life as far as may be, and to relieve
pain, both bodily and mental." The bill provided for the administration of euthanasia by

HORDER, THOMAS J.—*Continued*
a third party appointed by the Government
after the patient had voluntarily applied in
writing. Horder suggested that the criteria
which justify the decision to end life would
be very difficult to determine for every patient. The incurability of a disease can never
be more than a guess, the means of lessening
pain can certainly be expected to increase in the
future, and the judgment of a sick man is
too often confused and indeterminate.

Besides his work at "Bart's," Horder has
been consulting physician to many other fa-
mous British hospitals: the Royal Orthopedic,
the Royal Northern, and the hospitals of Bury
St. Edmunds, Swindon, Leatherhead, Becken-
ham, and Finchley. He became a member of
the advisory scientific committee of the British
Empire Cancer Campaign, president of the
Eugenics Society, of the Industrial Health
Education Society, and of the London Child
Guidance Society. He is also chairman of the
Noise Abatement League. Raised to the peer-
age in the New Year honors of 1933, he became
Baron Horder of Ashford in the county of
Southampton.

In October 1939 Horder was appointed honorary consulting physician to the Ministry of
Pensions, and eleven months later was selected
by Malcolm MacDonald, Minister of Health,
and Sir John Anderson[41], then Minister of
Home Security, as chairman of the Committee
on the Use of Public Air-Raid Shelters. He
toured the country examining shelters, and
was subsequently responsible for their improvement as well as for the provision of rest
centers for Civil Defence workers. Horder
voluntarily undertook to remain in London
during the severest air raids. A writer in the
London *News Chronicle* described him as the
"Blitz Doctor," who "shouldered his way into
dark underground doorways, through crowded
entrances, along alleyways, past bunks, into
Medical Aid Posts, into latrines, into every
dark corner. He noted a woman's pallor,
moved a child's head to a more comfortable
position without waking it, argued a medical
point with a health officer, measured the width
of a gangway, advised women against the
danger of cluttering up the place with their
belongings, pointed out to a nurse that the
key to the doctor's cupboard should be in the
doctor's pocket, not in hers." In March of
1944, protesting against the British Government's rejection of appeals for additional relief supplies for Nazi-occupied Europe, Horder
asserted that long undernourishment of those
populations would result in diseases from which
they would not recover for generations.

Although Lord Horder had passed seventy
at the time, he was as active as much younger
physicians during the Battle of Britain. When
he retires to his Hampshire home he finds
recreation in gardening. It is said that he is
as natural and friendly as a well brought up
child. "People are drawn to him by his extraordinary vitality. He looks a young man.
Health and good humor radiate from him.
His brown eyes sparkle behind his glasses;
his skin has a ruddy glow. Hs is 100 per

cent alive . . . a great doctor, a great gentleman, a great humanitarian."

Reference
Who's Who 1944

HORNE, LENA June 30, 1917 (?)- Sing-
er; motion-picture actress
Address: b. c/o Goldie & Gumm, 545 Fifth
Ave., New York City

The Negro blues singer Lena Horne "has
Hollywood agog," wrote columnist Elsa Maxwell[43] in 1943. "She has put poise into se-
duction, dignity into daring; she has given
glamour manners. Hollywood has never before seen such a combination."

The young Lena Horne spent many years
boarding with friends and relatives in cities
from Brooklyn, New York, where she was
born, to Atlanta and Miami. Her parents,
Edwin F. and Edna Horne, had been divorced
when she was three; and Mrs. Horne, an actress with the old Lafayette Stock Company
in Harlem, found she was not able to work and
at the same time take proper care of her only
child. It wasn't a very pleasant existence for
Lena, and by the time she was sixteen she decided to leave school—Girls' High School in
Brooklyn—to get a job. Through her mother's
connections she was able to land a place in
the chorus line at the famous Cotton Club in
Harlem—in the show "which gave the world
Ethel Waters[41] in 'Stormy Weather.'" For
the next two years Lena danced in the revues
at the club (and in addition in those that were
booked into theatres), sang occasional solos
in the early morning hours, and, for a brief
time in addition in October 1934, appeared in
a short-lived Broadway play on voodooism,
Dance With Your Gods.

The experience gained as a vocalist in those
two hectic years was very limited; but she had
picked up enough of the technique of phrasing
and of facing an audience to attract the attention of Flourney Miller, the actor, who recommended her to band leader Noble Sissle.
Sissle liked Miss Horne's voice, too; and in
February 1936 he started her on a road tour
with his band. One-night stands were a rigorous ordeal for the young girl, but they were
excellent training in showmanship. Sissle
coached her in delivery, and, as Miss Horne
expresses it, "those tank towns did wonders
for me. I learned how to 'sell' a song." While
in Pittsburgh during one engagement with
the band Miss Horne was introduced to Louis
J. Jones, a printer, and shortly afterwards, in
January 1937, they were married. (There are
two children, Gail, born December 1938, and
Edwin—Teddy—born February 1940.) When
Miss Horne finally left Sissle she had acquired a great deal of experience, some small
fame as a singer—enough to take a role offered her by Lew Leslie as a principal in the
February 1939 edition of his perennial *Black-
birds* revue. Despite former long-run successes, however, the edition with Miss Horne
closed after nine performances, and the young
singer went back to domesticity.

Her next professional engagement came almost two years later. By that time Lena
Horne Jones was disconsolate. Her marriage
was not working out satisfactorily (she was

finally divorced in June 1944), and no distraction in the guise of a singing job seemed available. Then one day in December 1940 she was hauled out of a New York movie theatre by an excited friend who had heard that Charlie Barnet was looking for a woman vocalist for his band. Miss Horne applied that afternoon and was hired on the spot for the evening show. While Barnet had used several Negro musicians in his band before, he did a rarer thing in the popular music field, according to *Billboard*, when he employed a Negro singer—and it showed great respect for her talent. In the months that she remained with the band she did radio work and made recordings with it as well as accompanying it on tours. "They were awfully nice to me," she says now. "They always tried to take me along wherever they went; but on Southern dates they left me behind—with pay—so there wouldn't be any embarrassment. One time upstate [New York] the whole gang got up and walked out of a restaurant because they wouldn't serve me."

While Miss Horne was with Barnet, John Henry Hammond, the swing expert and talent scout, heard about her singing and recommended her to Barney Josephson, owner of Cafe Society Downtown in New York City. The club had not been doing well since the opening of a more expensive uptown branch, at which Josephson's better-known entertainers were appearing. "The heart of what had made Cafe Society a mecca for hep-cats and Villagers," explains *PM,* had been "cut out and shipped uptown"; but after March 1941, when Miss Horne opened at the cafe, downtown business began to pick up again. The management, moreover, made no secret of the fact that its new blues singer was responsible for the noticeable change. Three weeks after her debut, for example, Josephson sponsored a concert for her at Carnegie Hall on the assumption that anyone good enough for him was good enough for Carnegie Hall, a theory which in the past had been extremely successful. As Helena Horne—an aristocratic touch—Lena Horne remained seven months at the night club. During that time she also appeared as featured vocalist on NBC's *Strictly From Dixie* program with "Hot Lips" Levine and on WOR's *Cats 'n' Jammers* show.

As "a solid, classy night club entertainer," with radio assignments behind her and a voice permanently recorded in two RCA-Victor record albums, Miss Horne next received an invitation to open in Hollywood's Little Troc cabaret in February 1942 and at the Mocambo in July. "She came on without an introduction," wrote a New York *Times* reporter of her Hollywood opening, "and started to sing without even announcing her number. . . . She just sang 'The Man I Love,' and 'Stormy Weather,' and a few other daisies. . . . And the crowd got chestnut happy. They whistled for more, like 'Embraceable You' and 'My Bill' and 'Can't Help Lovin' That Man.' . . . People who never went to night clubs pushed their way into the place four or five nights a week to hear Lena Horne sing straight versions of a lot of numbers they'd been hearing for years. To night-club owners who were used to their celebrated cus-

LENA HORNE

tomers eating right through their floor shows, Lena Horne was revolutionizing the business."

Before the end of the engagement Metro-Goldwyn-Mayer, on the recommendation of composer Roger Edens, had signed her up. Her first assignment was a small bit in *Panama Hattie* (1942) with Red Skelton and Ann Sothern, but her immediate popularity in the otherwise dull picture brought her the role of Georgia Brown in MGM's film version of the all-Negro musical, *Cabin in the Sky* (1943). (She now has a seven-year contract with Metro and star billing.) Miss Horne returned to New York in October 1942 to make personal appearances at the Capitol Theatre and followed up this engagement with one at the Savoy-Plaza Hotel's exclusive Cafe Lounge. As its first Negro entertainer, Miss Horne attracted capacity audiences every night during her stay, providing, according to *Time* Magazine, a record business for the night spot. "Unlike most Negro chanteuses," wrote *Time,* she "eschews the barrel-house manner . . . conducts herself with seductive reserve."

Upon Miss Horne's return to Hollywood in 1943 she made several more pictures for Metro: the all-Negro musical *Stormy Weather* (1943), *I Dood It* (1943), *Thousands Cheer* (1943), *Swing Fever* (1944), *Broadway Rhythm* (1944), *Two Girls and a Sailor* (1944), and a few others as yet unreleased. Although her roles in the pictures helped to "repeal the screen's unwritten law that Negroes appear on celluloid only in housemaids' uniforms"—to quote *PM*—the films themselves on the whole were little more than lavish or else merely humdrum. And in at least one she and the other Negro performers were "apparently regarded less as artists (despite their very high potential of artistry) than as picturesque, Sambo-style entertainers." This *Time* Magazine comment on *Stormy Weather* was, in fact, echoed by other reviewers in regard to more than one of the films. As one paper remarked, a Hollywood producers' pledge in

HORNE, LENA—*Continued*

1941 to play fair and square with the Negro had brought few outward results. "All we ask" of the motion-picture industry, Lena Horne says, "is that the Negro be portrayed as a normal person, as a voter at the polls, as a civil service worker, or an elected official. Perhaps I am being naïve when I voice such a desire. Perhaps these things will never be straightened out on the screen itself, but will have to wait until these problems are solved in real life."

Miss Horne herself has been received enthusiastically, with considerable mention of her "luscious", "dusky glamour." Her husky contralto voice, on the other hand, has been the subject of controversy. "Lena has a voice, a most clear, distinct, and articulate voice," said Elsa Maxwell. "Opinion about it may differ, but it is there. . . . As an artist she has one great fault: the fault of the cultured introvert. She hasn't the ability to project herself beyond herself. She lacks the great, warm human quality which takes in all feeling—the quality which makes a great artist like Ethel Waters." Miss Horne herself says she relies more on her personality than on her vocal cords, declaring that she is still learning how to sing. She has, however, "great technical proficiency," a *Collier's* writer commented, and is "an artist at projecting songs." "She makes up in styling and insinuating rhythms what her voice lacks in volume." "She picks her songs for the words," says Robert Rice, and tries to "confine her repertory to numbers that have stood the test of a little time at least. . . . Blues are her specialty, and if she's feeling good she's likely to sing torches all evening."

At the end of 1944 she was one of fifteen women, both Negro and white, who were nominated by the National Council of Negro Women as the most outstanding women of the year. Recognition by the Council is given in an effort to focus attention on the contributions to interracial cooperation being made by American women. These women were chosen, said the president of the organization, which represents 800,000 women, because their services had not been sufficiently recognized in other national polls and rosters of prominent people.

As has been said in many ways, Miss Horne is extraordinarily pretty, with a tall, lithe figure. "Being a brownskin woman," as she says, she generally wears white or vivid colors, which set off her golden-hued complexion. Much of her time today, she says, outside of her picture work, is taken up by the Hollywood Victory Committee and the USO camp shows as well as by work for various Negro causes. She is somewhat at a loss to explain her professional success. She is impressed, of course, "but she is by no means overcome." "She hasn't chased renown; she has fallen into it. She is possessed of no overwhelming compulsion to be famous; she is simply trying to make a living at a relatively pleasant and lucrative occupation."

References

Collier's 111:12 Je 26 '43 por
N Y Post p42 D 1 '42 por; p12 Jl 26 '43
Newsweek 21:65 Ja 4 '43 por

PM p19 D 15 '42 por
PM Mag p21 Ja 10 '43 pors (por cover)
Time 41:62 Ja 4 '43 por
Downs, K. E. Meet the Negro 1943

HORWOOD, SIR WILLIAM T(HOMAS) F(RANCIS) Nov. 1868—Nov. 16, 1943 Head of Scotland Yard from 1920 to 1928; brigadier general in First World War; instituted many reforms at Scotland Yard.

Obituary

N Y Times p19 N 19 '43 por

HUDSON, MANLEY O(TTMER) May 19, 1886- Professor of law; Judge of the World Court

Address: b. Harvard Law School, Cambridge, Mass.

The eighteenth century philosopher, Immanuel Kant, made the observation that nations lived in a state of anarchy toward each other and that so long as they refused to abide by international laws—as individuals are forced to obey national laws—devastating wars would continue. Manley O. Hudson, judge of the Permanent Court of International Justice (known in the United States as the World Court), member of the Permanent Court of Arbitration (the Hague Court), and Bemis Professor of International Law in the Harvard Law School, has worked tirelessly for more than a quarter of a century toward an effective administration of international law. After the United States entered the Second World War, Hudson declared that the "winning of the peace" depended greatly upon an extension and a strengthening of international law. With this end in view, Hudson became the guiding genius of 200 Americans and Canadians—judges, lawyers, university professors, and officials of national and international experience—who, under the sponsorship of the Carnegie Endowment for International Peace, began preparing a plan which would aid the peace makers. After two years of exhaustive research and labor the result of their work was announced in April 1944 under the title *The Future of International Law.* Critics consider the plan "the first comprehensive effort to implement the Four Nations' Moscow Declaration and the United States Senate's Connally [44] resolution, which advocate the speedy establishment of some form of international organization designed to guarantee peace."

Manley Ottmer Hudson, born May 19, 1886 in St. Peters, Missouri, is the son of David O. and Emma (Bibb) Hudson. He attended William Jewell College in Liberty, Missouri, where he obtained his B.A. degree in 1906 and an M.A. degree the next year. In 1910 Hudson received the degree of LL.B. from Harvard University and in the same year was given a professorship in law at the University of Missouri, which he held until 1919. In 1917 he received the degree of S.J.D. from Harvard and in 1928 the degree of LL.D. from William Jewell College. His degrees from other colleges include an LL.D. from the University of Missouri (1931), a D.C.L. from the University of Delaware (1934), and a Doctorate in Political Science from Peter Pazmány University in Budapest (1935).

Early in his career Hudson became interested in the world peace movement. He was acting as secretary to the Missouri Peace Society (1912-19) when Colonel E. H. House, Woodrow Wilson's adviser, succeeded in obtaining his appointment to the International Law Division of the American Commission to Negotiate Peace. During the Paris Peace Conference he acted as a special assistant in the Department of State (1918-19). On his return from Paris, Hudson was given a professorship in law at Harvard University, and in 1923 he was appointed Bemis Professor of International Law by the University.

His first official post with the League of Nations was as a member of the legal section of the League's Secretariat (1919-21), and ever since he has been "up and about all kinds of peace endeavors at Geneva, The Hague, as well as campaigning on the home front for American participation in the League and in the World Court." In 1935, 1938, 1943 he published a review of World Court activities under the title *World Court Reports,* and his handbook of the Court, entitled *The World Court* (1928), has gone through many editions and is considered one of the most valuable contributions to the literature on the subject. In 1924 he was made editor of the *American Journal of International Law.*

On May 5, 1933 President Roosevelt '42 rewarded Hudson's work in international activities by appointing him to membership in the Permanent Court of Arbitration. (He was reappointed in 1939.) This Court had come into existence in 1899 as a result of the Hague Convention. It is not quite what its name implies, however—it is neither permanent nor a court. A panel of men, appointed by the member-countries (each country is allowed four members), deals with arbitral cases between nations. From the panel, states are free to create tribunals to handle the cases which they are willing to refer to arbitration.

More than fifty nations have lent their support to the maintenance of the World Court. (The United States has never supported it in any way, although three Presidents and three Secretaries of State have suggested that such support be given. This failure was the subject of many articles by Hudson during the late '20's and early '30's when American support was under discussion.) The fifteen judges of the Court are elected by two electoral bodies, consisting of the Council and the Assembly of the League of Nations, plus the representatives of states which are parties to the Court Protocol but not members of the League of Nations. The term of the judges is nine years, and they receive salaries large enough to enable them to devote their entire time to the settlement of the cases. In October 1936 Hudson was elected to the World Court to succeed onetime United States Secretary of State Frank Billings Kellogg, who resigned before his nine-year term ended. Hudson's election to the bench was considered a happy one because of his knowledge of international law and the fact that he was not "political." (Incidentally, he was the fourth American, including Chief

MANLEY O. HUDSON

Justice Charles Evans Hughes '41, to be elected a judge of the Court.)

In speaking of the value of the Court, Hudson stated in an article published in the *Annals of the American Academy of Political and Social Science* (July 1942) that the "Court has settled more than fifty disputes between nations, and it has settled them in such a way as to remove festering centers of discord. Second, the Court by its advisory opinions has aided the smooth working of international organizations, such as the International Labor Organization, of which the United States is a member. Third, the Court has undoubtedly exercised a great influence on the settlement of disputes which were never referred to it—indeed, never referred to any court at all. In that respect it is like a national court; people often settle out of court in preference to going into court, but they would not do so if the court did not exist. Fourth, the Court has greatly facilitated the building of the law of pacific settlement. Fifth, the Court has greatly aided in the development of our substantive international law, and its judgments and opinions are constantly cited throughout the world."

As a consistent internationalist, Hudson has written many articles on America's role in the League of Nations. In a 1929 article which appeared in the *American Political Science Review,* he pointed out that despite the fact that the United States did not ratify the Covenant of the League and did not accept the place provided for her in the Assembly and the Council of the League, the Government of the United States, a few years after the League's establishment, had felt the necessity for such an organization. For instance, the year 1925 saw the American Government represented (as states members of the League were represented) at two important conferences in Geneva—the Conference on Opium and the Arms Traffic Conference. (This policy of regular representation, in conferences on matters of international humanitarian concern, had been

HUDSON, MANLEY O.—*Continued*

continued since 1925.) While pointing out that
it was not his present purpose to offer any
argument for changing our decision to stay out
of the League, he nevertheless saw "distinct
danger" in our position: "We do not have a
part in shaping the agenda, and our representatives arrive at a League conference to find a
chairman already chosen by the Council of the
League and preparations advanced to a great
extent by League committees over which our
Government has no control. And yet," he emphasized, "we must take part in the conferences
for the simple reason that our own interests
demand our representation when certain subjects of international importance are under consideration. . . . We simply cannot afford to
sit out when fifty other governments are sitting in."

The refusal of the United States Government to support the World Court was also
looked upon by Hudson as a moral failure in
our international duties. During his campaign
for American support of the Court he pointed
out that for more than a century and a quarter
the United States Government had been the
world's most conspicuous advocate of the pacific
settlement of international disputes. Furthermore, at both the 1899 and 1907 Hague Peace
Conferences, the United States had spoken in
favor of the largest possible extension of international arbitration.

Of particular interest was the relation between the Court and the League. Of this relationship Hudson said, "The Covenant is one
instrument, the Court Protocol of the adjoined
statute is another. The United States will not
become a party to the former by adhering to
the latter." His reply to the criticism that
"parties to one are also parties to the other"
was that if that were the case (which he did
not admit) "it will cease to be so when the
United States becomes a party to one without
becoming a party to the other. We shall cut
the cord." The chief opponent to the Court
and the League, Senator Borah, was answered
by Hudson in his book, *Progress in International Organization* (1932), published for the
University of Idaho upon the occasion of the
inauguration of the William Borah Foundation for the Outlawry of War. The *Harvard
Law Review* stated that Hudson's book had
rendered a great service in the cause of international understanding in making clear to the
students of Idaho the difference between "proclaiming pious platitudes and establishing and
cooperating in the machinery for preserving
international peace." The New York *Times*
reviewer expressed the hope that "Senator
Borah will read a chapter in it every night."

An outstanding work among Hudson's numerous books on international law agencies and
problems is his treatise on the World Court,
The Permanent Court of International Justice
(1925). Clyde Eagleton, reviewing the work
in the *Annals of the American Academy of
Political and Social Science,* pronounced it
"an invaluable study, whether to the student of
judicial organization and practice or to the
student of international organization."

The Carnegie Endowment for International
Peace and the Brookings Institution, together,
in 1944 published Hudson's *International Tri-*

bunals, Past and Present. (The two institutions
had given him grants-in-aid, which had enabled
him to devote time to its preparation over an
extended period.) The volume sketches the evolution of international tribunals since the Amer-
ican-British treaty of 1794; surveys the general
problems of these courts, and past solutions
adopted; and in conclusion it discusses future
problems and suggests future action which
might be taken on official proposals of later
years. Hudson, said Dexter Perkins in the
Saturday Review of Literature, "does not believe that courts can solve the major political
problems between nations"; thus he does not
exaggerate the role of international tribunals.
Both the Permanent Court of Arbitration and
the World Court, Hudson feels, should be continued, the latter with minimum change to
adapt it to new conditions. His conclusions on
planning the peace with law form "a practi-
cable, readable, handy guide for approaching the
problem," commented the New York *Times.*

Regarding *The Future of International Law,*
Dr. William E. Masterson, one of the 200 who
worked under Hudson's "masterly direction"
in preparing the post-War plan for peace, said
in a *Christian Science Monitor* Magazine article of April 22, 1944 that in many respects
the plan bears resemblance to the Covenant of
the League of Nations. However, it purports
to "eliminate the weakness of that Covenant
and to supply the omissions that proved eventually to be its undoing." The League of Nations is not an institution of government because its members accept no binding obligations towards it. "It is government by persuasion, but government by persuasion is persuasion and not government," said one critic
of the League. To overcome this weakness,
the new document called for the organization
of a "Community of States with a general de-
liberative organ, known as the General Assembly, in which all states should be represented, and a general executive organ, an Executive Council, in which states, playing a leading role in international affairs, should have
representation. Both the Assembly and the
Council are given power to deal with any
matter of concern to the Community of States."
Furthermore, the Council is given power to
take such action as it may deem necessary
should any state fail to carry out its obligations under international law, and "it may, with
the concurrence of the Assembly, adopt general provisions for preventing and suppressing
force by states, and to this end it may organize and employ military force."

Another weakness of the League lay in the
fact that the World Court did not have obligatory jurisdiction over all legal disputes. The
new plan provides this power for the Court,
and the Council is allowed to take action to
give effect to the Court's judgments. Further,
the Proposals (the document is made up of six
"Postulates," ten "Principles," and twenty-three
"Proposals") "make provisions for the revision of treaties and for the readjustment of
any situation which may endanger the good
understanding between states." One of the
criticisms of the World Court was based on
the absence of any "pacific means of modifying international law without the consent of
all states concerned." This omission was

righted through a provision giving the Assembly power to modify general rules of international law and to enact new ones, which opened the way for a modernization of the system of international law. The last two provisions were intended to placate the "have-not" nations, which had said that adherence to the League of Nations meant a continuation of an unfair distribution of colonies, of unfair boundary lines, and of the dependence of subject-nations, and that a power-state through high tariffs and other means might isolate a nation less fortunate in natural resources. Dr. Masterson believed that statesmen and politicians should find it a "constructive chart that would help to guide them past the perils that will be encountered on the way to peace."

As a follow-up of *The Future of International Law,* a shorter statement entitled *Design for a Charter of the General International Organization* was drawn up under the chairmanship of Hudson and reached publication through the Carnegie Endowment for International Peace in August 1944. The proposed organization differs from the League of Nations in that all existing States are to be members, with no provision for expulsion or withdrawal. All are to be bound by the principles of the charter, which, as the organic expression of international law, would become part of their own substantive law.

Hudson has stated that the most far-reaching feature of the organization is its universality. Eventually all nations would be bound by the law and all have the right to participate in its agencies. It is axiomatic, Hudson declared, that no one power could control the world and that the last 125 years of history have made it equally clear that no limited group of States could ensure permanent peace—because great powers did not always stay great or united. It is not enough to hold out universality as a goal—it must be adopted as a fundamental concept and as such it must shape the form and the purpose of the organization. Conversely, he said, if certain nations were excluded they would be spurred to form a rival and hostile organization. Among those who signed the *Design* were Raymond B. Fosdick, Clark M. Eichelberger, and James T. Shotwell[44]. Hudson in late 1944 was engaged in calling conferences for the purpose of preparing a statement on the Dumbarton Oaks conference.

Judge Hudson has not always written on weighty international subjects. In 1923 he contributed to a symposium, *These United States.* Writing on Missouri under the title, "Doesn't Want To Be Shown," he said: "The music-hall slogan, 'You've got to show me,' does not fit Missourians. You don't have to show a Missourian. He knows already." Hudson's reputation as a brilliant conversationalist springs from his gift for words, a "sweet reasonableness" in argument and an earthy sense of humor. The round-faced, silver-haired Judge works hard, but with Mrs. Hudson (he was married in 1930 to Janet Norton Aldrich) and their two sons he does find time to attend the motion pictures in Harvard Square, symphony concerts, and the plays of the Harvard Dramatic Club.

References

C S Mon Mag p2 Ap 22 '44
Who's Who in America 1944-45
Who's Who in Law 1937

HULL, JOHN ADLEY Aug. 7, 1874—Apr. 17, 1944 Army officer and lawyer; former Judge Advocate General of the United States Army (1924-28); legal adviser to Governor General of the Philippines (1930-32); in charge of insular litigation in the Circuit Court of Appeals (1932-36).

Obituary

N Y Times p21 Ap 18 '44 por

HUME, EDGAR ERSKINE Dec. 26, 1889- United States Army officer

Address: b. c/o War Department, Washington, D. C.; h. Frankfort, Ky.

In 1915 a young American doctor, Edgar Erskine Hume, came to Italy for postgraduate training and then found himself organizing earthquake relief. In 1918, an officer in the United States Army Medical Corps, he returned to serve with the Italian Army in France. Twenty-six years later Hume—"the most prolific writer in the armed forces," an internist and neurologist with dozens of honors and decorations—was back in Italy as the highest-ranking officer in the Allied Military Government of that liberated country.

Born in Frankfort, Kentucky, on December 26, 1889, Edgar Erskine Hume is the son of Dr. Enoch Edgar and Mary (South) Hume. At eighteen he was graduated from Centre College, Kentucky, where he was a member of both leading honor societies, Phi Beta Kappa and Sigma Xi. He remained there to work for his Master's degree, which he received the following year (1909). (Fourteen years later his old college also awarded him an honorary LL.D.) Enrolled in the medical course at Johns Hopkins University in Baltimore, young Hume received his M.D. in 1913, and after a year on the staff he left for study abroad. In 1914 he received a second doctorate from the University of Munich, and in 1915 a third from the University of Rome. He was present in Italy when in January 1915 an earthquake ruined sixty Italian towns, killed upwards of 30,000 persons and injured many thousands of others, as well as causing great property damage and starting disastrous fires. Young Dr. Hume became medical director of the American Relief Expedition which brought aid from the United States to the stricken areas—for as soon as the news of the disaster came out the American Red Cross had begun to receive many liberal contributions for the sufferers.

At the beginning of the European War in 1914 Hume was appointed a 1st lieutenant in the United States Army Medical Reserve Corps and detailed to the Army Medical School at Washington as a student. On January 14, 1917, while still attending classes, he was commissioned a 1st lieutenant in the Regular Army Medical Corps. At his graduation the following March Lieutenant Hume received the Hoff Medal for the highest standing in his class, and was then sent to Fort Leavenworth, Kansas, as parole officer and surgeon at the Disciplinary Barracks. From November to July

BRIG. GEN. EDGAR ERSKINE HUME

1918 he was on duty with the Division of Sanitation in the Surgeon General's Office in Washington, at which time he made a record for speed of promotion—to captain on March 28, to major the same day, and to lieutenant colonel (temporary) five days later.

Early in June 1918 Hume sailed for Europe, where he served as commanding officer of Base Hospital No. 102, first with the Italian Army and then with the British Expeditionary Force. According to a citation, Hume was considered to have "rendered professional services of a highly conspicuous character" when "in direct charge of an American base hospital which was later expanded by the addition of Italian hospitals into a composite hospital center in the Italian war zone." He was present at the battles of the Meuse-Argonne, St. Mihiel, and Vittorio-Veneto, and was wounded at the Piave River on November 2, 1918, winning the Purple Heart and the Silver Star for gallantry in aiding the wounded in the presence of the enemy. (A month after Hume went overseas he was married to Mary Swigert Hendrick, now deceased, daughter of Colonel John Buford Hendrick of his home town. Their one son, Edgar Erskine Hume, Jr., was born in 1924.)

After the close of the War, in 1919 Hume was chief medical officer in starving, disease-ridden Serbia (later a part of Yugoslavia). In this capacity and subsequently as American Red Cross Commissioner to Serbia, he fought and conquered an epidemic of typhus fever which had killed 80 per cent of the Serbian doctors. "With untiring energy, unremitting devotion to duty, and with rare administrative and professional skill, he organized and operated an American Sanitary Service, reorganizing hospitals, dispensaries, and dressing stations for soldiers and civilians alike" until June 1920, and winning for himself the Distinguished Service Medal with the citation quoted here. A grateful Serbia decorated Hume with four medals, including the Order of the White Eagle in the degree of commander, and the Order of St. Sava, of which he is a grand officer. Al-

together the American officer received eleven foreign decorations during the year 1919, five of them from Italy, including the Croce di Guerra and the Order of St. Maurice and St. Lazarus in the degree of officer.

After two months as assistant to the surgeon in the Post Hospital at Antwerp, Belgium, Hume returned to the United States, where in November 1920 he was assigned to duty as assistant to the commanding officer of the Corps Area Laboratory, 1st Corps Area, at Fort Banks, Massachusetts. In this capacity and later as commanding officer Hume remained in Massachusetts until June 1922, studying for his certificate in public health (1921) at Harvard University and the Massachusetts Institute of Technology, and for his doctorate of tropical medicine at Harvard (1922).

The Major's next assignment was to the congenial post of assistant librarian of the Army Medical Library, which is said to be the largest collection of medical literature that the world has ever seen. Here he edited the current volumes of its Index Catalogue, which is regarded by authorities as the greatest catalog ever compiled in any field. It indexes "every worthwhile article in every [medical book and] journal in every country in every language," and is the standard work of medical bibliography throughout the world. While in this post Hume was asked by the Association of Military Surgeons of the United States, which he had joined in 1920, to assume the temporary editorship of its journal on the sudden death of its elected secretary-editor. Hume then edited one volume of the *Military Surgeon* (for 1924—the year in which he received a diploma in public health from Johns Hopkins University) and parts of two others. He was then appointed assistant editor. This post he held for ten years, resigning in obedience to an act of Congress which forbids any active officer to be directly concerned with any publication containing advertisements of firms doing business with the Government. Then and in subsequent years Hume contributed many papers to this and other professional journals and to the publications of the Society of the Cincinnati, of which he is vice-president general.

In 1925 Hume was sent to Paris as the Army's delegate to the International Congress of Military Medicine; and in the spring of the following year he went to Fort Benning, Georgia, for a four-year period as medical inspector and epidemiologist. (In that year he was elected national president of Delta Omega fraternity, of which he was a founder.) At Benning he took the Infantry School's advanced course, which he completed in 1928. Leaving Georgia in October 1930, Hume went to Boston as instructor of the Massachusetts National Guard. In that year he was awarded honorary doctorates by the Universities of León (Nicaragua) and Kentucky; in the following five years he was to receive six more doctorates and twenty decorations from foreign countries. From May 15 to June 30, 1931 Hume was in Europe as secretary of the United States Delegation to the International Congress of Military Medicine at The Hague —the third of eight biennial congresses at which he represented the United States. After this he returned to Boston, where he remained until Septembr 1932.

Hume was then sent to the Army Medical Library, this time as librarian, a post he filled for four years. While there he wrote an essay for the *Military Surgeon*, which won the Wellcome Prize for 1933. In October 1936 the Major was assigned to study at the Medical Field Service School at Carlisle Barracks, Pennsylvania. After completing the course he was made director of the school's department of administration, and in January 1937 he was promoted to lieutenant colonel. That year, in which he studied in Germany on an Oberlaender Fellowship, saw the publication of his *Lafayette in Kentucky*, and the next year (1938) brought into print Hume's 495-page edition of *The Papers of the Society of the Cincinnati, 1783-1824*. In 1940 his *Medical Work of the Knights Hospitallers of St. John of Jerusalem* (of which Hume is a Knight) was called by *Commonweal* a fascinating account of a great achievement. The *American Historical Review*'s critic thought it "a labor of love," which could not be considered a thoroughly objective piece of critical scholarship, and which contained many panegyrical passages. The following year two scholarly volumes edited by Hume were published: the 472-page *General Washington's Correspondence Concerning the Society of the Cincinnati*, and *The Golden Jubilee of the Association of Military Surgeons of the United States*—an "exceptionally meritorious service in the field of military medicine" for which the author was rewarded with the first Founder's Medal ever presented.

Appointed Public Relations Officer of Carlisle Barracks in May 1941, Hume was promoted to colonel (temporary) the following month. In 1942 he published two monographs on historical aspects of the Army Medical Department. In January 1943 Colonel Hume was placed in command of the Winter Army General Hospital in Topeka, Kansas. That year his *Victories of Army Medicine* was hailed by the *Weekly Book Review* as "a distinguished service to the Army and to American medicine." The *New Yorker* found it "somewhat episodic and pious, but evidently comprehensive," while the *American Journal of Public Health* considered that "once again Colonel Hume has put the medical profession of the country in his debt. . . . It is a 'must' book for all medical libraries and contains information which all educated people generally should have." Also from Hume's pen is "War and Medicine," a lecture given at the New York Academy of Medicine and printed in *The March of Medicine* (1943). In this forty-seven-page historical review he calls war "the most terrible of all diseases," but points out that modern war is actually less brutal than ancient fighting. "The greater efficiency of modern weapons means that more men are injured, but not that the indivdual is more seriously hurt. . . . The suffering to be borne by the individual is nothing like so great as that caused by such ancient weapons as the spear, boiling oil, and battle-ax . . . infected wounds, as were wounds by other sharp instruments of battle." The science of preventive medicine is a recent development, as is the present efficient care of the sick and wounded. "The mighty war in which we are now engaged," said Hume, "is the first in which the unseen enemy [disease] has been less deadly than the visible enemy, and the difference is due not to the added lethal powers of modern weapons but to the advances of medical science."

Presumably Colonel Hume left the Winter General Hospital to attend the School of Military Government at Charlottesville, Virginia, for the following July he was in Sicily as chief health officer for the Allied Military Government of Occupied Territory attached to the United States 7th Army (Lieutenant General George S. Patton, Jr.,[43] commanding). In the opening stage of the invasion of Sicily, it was reported, "the doctors, lawyers, and public officials who formed the bulk of "Amgot's" personnel had to accept the common hardships of the soldier. They ate and slept on the ground. . . . Amgot officials have behaved with remarkable coolness at the front, often going into towns which were still under the fire of enemy guns." The civil affairs administration was at first badly understaffed. "Its officials were hamstrung by a low priority in Army transportation. Often they were compelled to hitchhike from one liberated town to another." Old Army officers, at first disdainful of "this interference from mere [former] civilians," became first respectful and then cordial as the joint American-British-Canadian military government proved its value in taking civil problems off the Army's hands and thus making military progress easier.

The first important test of the Allied Military Government's efficiency came with the capture of Palermo. Led by Lieutenant Colonel Charles Poletti[43], former Lieutenant Governor of New York State, the AMG enabled that wrecked city to resume functioning, thus freeing the 7th Army for purely military affairs. (It was about this time that the term Amgot was shortened to AMG.) The first day of real AMG control of central Italy from the seat of government at Salerno came in September 1943; the following month found Colonel Hume attached to the 5th Army (Lieutenant General Mark W. Clark[42] commanding) as military governor of the Naples district.

Not only did AMG have to cope in Naples with the wreckage of a city which had been a battlefield, but a report edited by Hume showed that the retreating German Army had destroyed or fouled all available food, and had destroyed the flour mills, the water supply, the sewage disposal system, the electric system, all transportation and communications—even to the tunnels through the hills. The doors of the prison had been thrown open, leaving criminals at large; the famous old University of Naples had been burned. The hospitals had been stripped of medical instruments, dressings, and medicines, leaving the Neapolitan doctors and nurses almost powerless to care for the innumerable victims. Naples, in short, was in a state of chaos. The stage was set for some devastating epidemic such as wars have brought in their train since antiquity; and in December 1943 Hume announced that the appearance of epidemic typhus had caused Naples to be placed off limits for the Army as a preventive measure. But this epidemic was successfully combatted, and Hume was awarded an honorary doctorate by the University in recognition of his public service.

(Continued next page)

HUME, EDGAR ERSKINE—*Continued*

Although AMG in Naples worked "a miracle" of recovery, it was sharply criticized from a political standpoint. The Allied press, as well as such Italian liberals as Count Carlo Sforza '42 and the historian Gaetano Salvemini '43 attacked it for being allegedly too lenient with Fascists and too strict with anti-Fascists. Local officials of the Fascist state were retained in office unless their personal records were known to be bad, while, on the other hand, anti-Fascist and anti-monarchist groups were not permitted to hold rallies demanding the abdication of King Victor Emmanuel III '43 and the end of the House of Savoy. AMG's official attitude was that a clean sweep of Fascists was impossible without disrupting the whole machinery of a state in which for twenty years every officeholder was required to be a member of the Fascist Party, while a directive from the Commander in Chief stated that no political activity of any kind was to be allowed. In January 1944 this restriction was lifted, and political meetings were permitted (subject only to military necessity). After Hume—promoted to brigadier general (temporary) in January 1944—moved on and was replaced as military governor of the Naples district by Poletti, the latter adopted much firmer measures toward all former Fascists, and removed from office the mayor, "utterly unacceptable to the anti-Fascists," whom the General had appointed.

When the 5th Army entered Rome on June 4 Hume and his staff were along to get to work on "the greatest collective problems ever to confront Allied civil administrators in the history of two World Wars." Unlike Naples, Rome proper (normally a city of about 1,300,000 population) was almost free of malicious damage; indeed, the American soldiers could hardly believe they had "taken a military objective they'd be able to enjoy." The water supply, however, was an even greater problem than in Naples; overcrowding was serious; the German Army had taken as much food as it could; there were land mines yet to be found, and the Nazis had again released thousands of convicts from Roman prisons. In addition, there were the special diplomatic problems created by the presence within the city of the neutral and hallowed Vatican State (in which, incidentally, the German, Hungarian, and Rumanian Ministers had taken refuge). Moreover, the AMG considered it necessary to round up Mussolini's '42 puppet police, the Polizia Africana Italiana, and the secret police, the Metropolitani. A force of 3,000 of the non-political, non-Fascist Carabinieri—professional soldiers detached for permanent police duty—had been assembled in Naples by AMG and specially trained for the policing of Rome. They were brought into the city in AMG trucks, thus becoming the only Italian troops to enter Rome with the liberators.

To succeed the interim mayor, General Roberto Bencivenga, who had been appointed by Premier Badoglio '40, General Hume appointed Prince Filippo Andrea Doria-Pamphili, who is married to an English nurse, and whose family's 17th century villa was one of the few Roman buildings defaced by the Germans.

This appointment and those to the City Council were made on the nomination of the new anti-Fascist Prime Minister Ivanoe Bonomi '44 and the six anti-Fascist parties. As before, once the reorganization of the city was well under way, General Hume moved on with the 5th Army on June 15, leaving Rome under the interim government of Colonel Norman Fiske until the arrival of Colonel Poletti, who had made an enviable record by his government of Naples.

Entering Florence three months later, Hume was confronted by a similar situation in "the most Fascist city in Italy." By late December a correspondent reported that "AMG has done a remarkable job in the past four months. This city is functioning in almost every respect. Its sewage system has been repaired, its water, light, gas, and telephone services have been restored, and its universities, schools, hospitals, and clinics have been opened. Four bridges have been built over the Arno River. The courts are working on a normal schedule. . . . So, if one shuts one's eyes to the dreadful mutilation caused in the heart of the city along the Arno [River] when the Germans blew up the bridges, Florence seems almost normal. It is only when one looks closely at the passers-by and talks to people that one realizes that they are hungry and can think of nothing else but food." Residents of the zone north of Naples, in which Florence lies, were given a ration of only 200 grams of bread, less than half a pound per day; AMG soup kitchens, which fed 30,000 persons every day, could not alleviate the real shortage. To make matters more difficult, President Roosevelt '42 had promised an increase which the authorities were unable to provide. Adding to Hume's problems was the question of the 4,500 Florentine Partisans or patriots, whom he had been ordered to disarm, to clothe and feed and organize the volunteers into labor battalions or soldiers for the regular Italian Army. Here there were two difficulties: the physical shortage of clothes and blankets for the bleak Italian winter, and the psychological—the patient but firm refusal of the patriots to give up the precious arms, with which they had fought the Germans, and of women guerrillas to give up the units in which they had battled. Civilian refugees from the countryside, on the other hand, were said to have "fared remarkably well in three centers that are models of their kind. Officers have come from France and Belgium to study the organization of these centers."

In addition to his three United States decorations, the scholarly head of AMG with the 5th Army has eight medals from other American nations and twenty-four from European countries. Besides his other honors, he is an honorary professor at the Military Institute of Warsaw and an honorary colonel in the Royal Serbian Army (no longer existent). A member of the Massachusetts Institute of Technology's advisory committee on public health, Hume was formerly a lecturer on medical history at Georgetown University. He has done translations and interpreting into and from both German and Italian, as well as writing some 250 original books and papers. The General's ninety-line entry in *Who's Who in America* lists among his memberships nine clubs, five fraternities, seventeen medical and other learned societies, and a number of miscellaneous organizations. An associate editor of the *Annals of Medical History,* Hume has contributed articles to the *Encyclopedia Britannica,* the *Encyclopedia Americana,* the *Dictionary of American Biography,* and Frederick Tice's *Practice of Medicine.*

Reference

Who's Who in America 1944-45

HURLEY, PATRICK J(AY) Jan. 8, 1883-
United States Ambassador to China; Army officer; lawyer

Address: b. c/o Department of State, Washington, D. C.; h. 301 Hillside Ave., Santa Fe, N. M.

On November 30, 1944 Major General Patrick J. Hurley became United States Ambassador to China, following the resignation of Clarence E. Gauss '41. General Hurley, stanch Republican, Hoover's '43 Secretary of War and spokesman of the Hoover Administration, strong critic of Franklin Delano Roosevelt in 1932 and later, thus became Roosevelt's Ambassador, in what has been called one of the hardest jobs in the world.

Patrick Jay Hurley—self-made millionaire, lawyer, banker, oil operator and businessman, veteran of two wars, Secretary of War under a Republican President, Minister to New Zealand under a Democratic President, most traveled man the Second World War has produced —has had a career typical of the American tradition. He was born on January 8, 1883, of Irish immigrant parents. Pierce Hurley had been married to Mary Kelly in Texas and moved to Lehigh, Oklahoma, then in Indian Territory, where Patrick was born. The family grubbed a living from the soil, and the boy's early years were years of hardship and poverty, largely because his father had, in falling from a horse, suffered injuries that made him an invalid.

On his mother's death, when he was only eleven, Pat went to work for 75c (some accounts say 25c) a day tending a trapdoor in a shaft at the Atoka Coal and Mining Company. Soon after he was promoted to the job of driving the mules that pulled coal cars out of the mine. The coal miners in the old Indian Territory were a rough lot, living poorly in company shacks, getting drunk on payday, and letting their children run wild. Physical strength alone counted in this environment. Pat knew the pangs of hunger often and ran around "without enough clothes to flag a handcar." He stood the bullying of the larger boys as long as they picked only on him, but went on a rampage once when one started teasing his sister. The manner in which he laid his adversary low and later turned the tables on another antagonist established his reputation, and the camp bullies decided to steer clear of the spindling youngster with the flashing temper and flashing fists.

When he was fourteen young Pat's education began, though it is a little obscure as to when he first learned to read. The first academic experience was brief, however, for the coal mine was shut down by a strike and Pat's pay and education stopped simultaneously. He then drifted into the Cherokee Nation country,

MAJ. GEN. PATRICK J. HURLEY

and later found a job on a ranch in Texas as a cowpuncher. He did not linger long on that ranch, for the Spanish-American War broke out. Burning with admiration for Teddy Roosevelt, Hurley set out to volunteer in the Rough Riders, but was turned down because of his youth. Going on to Muskogee, he next worked for another cattleman.

Some time after this, Baptist Indian University, now Bacone College, was established at Muskogee. Young Hurley met one of the students and through him was introduced to Dr. John Hart Scott, president of the institution. Dr. Scott inquired in friendly fashion whether the young man planned to get an education, and Hurley, warmed by the kindliness of the older man, replied, "I'm afraid I can't. I have my father and sisters to look after." Dr. Scott was impressed by the young man and decided something ought to be done for him. Encouraged by Dr. Scott and some friends, the young cowboy entered the University. By driving the delivery wagon for a Muskogee grocer, tending the school stables, and doing other part-time work, he was able to earn enough to pay his expenses. The academic standard of the college at that time is indicated by the fact that in his second year, when there was a shortage of teachers, Hurley became an instructor in American history and before his graduation was a professor in the same subject.

This was also the period of Hurley's first military experience. A home guard company, the Indian Territorial Volunteer Cavalry, was organized, and Hurley was one of the first volunteers. He quickly became a sergeant, then a captain in the Cavalry, which fought the Indians in the Crazy Snake Rebellion. In 1905 he received a B.A. degree from Indian University, at which he had been a leader among the students. He played the French horn in the orchestra, was first baseman on the baseball team, captained the football squad, was a member of the university choir, held the office of editor in chief of the student publication, and

HURLEY, PATRICK J.—*Continued*

was recognized as the leading debater of the institution.

After working for a while in the Indian Office at Muskogee, Hurley went to Washington to study law at National University and later at George Washington University. During this time he lived with Father Ketchum, a friend from the mining country, and earned enough to live on by dusting a law office and doing odd jobs. (Despite his ancestry and association with Ketchum and the fact that two of his sisters are nuns, Hurley is not a Catholic. He has said that if his mother had lived he probably would have been of that faith.) A short year after his arrival in Washington, in 1908 he received a degree of Bachelor of Laws from National University and returned to Oklahoma. He was admitted to the bar and opened a law office in Tulsa. From the start he was a successful lawyer. One of his first fees was a large block of prairie that became city blocks before long. With the opportunities the new state offered, Hurley's investments soon put him on the way to accumulating a fortune.

In 1910, at the age of twenty-seven, he was elected president of the Tulsa Bar Association. At this time he ran for State Senator on the Republican ticket in the dominantly Democratic state, and was defeated. Never since has he tried for an office, though he had the chance to run on the Republican ticket for the office of Governor of Oklahoma in later years. He continued his law practice, however, and in 1912 he was admitted to the bar of the Supreme Court of the United States. At this time he assisted Secretary of Commerce Wheeler in drafting the constitution of the United States Chamber of Commerce. An old friend, Victor Locke, was appointed Chief of the Choctaw Nation, and on Locke's recommendation Hurley was appointed attorney for the Choctaws. From 1912 until 1917 Hurley held that position at a salary of $5,000 a year and expenses, handling thirty-five million dollars in claims. Though his reappointment was refused by the Department of the Interior when President Wilson took office, Republican Hurley's retention was ordered by Wilson. During most of these years Hurley lived in Washington, since most of the cases came before the United States Supreme Court. It was this appointment that gave him legal prestige and the financial foundation on which to build his fortune. During this time, too, he was a member of the Oklahoma National Guard and in 1916 went to the Mexican border as a captain with his company on the expedition against Pancho Villa.

Upon enlisting in the Army in 1917 Hurley was assigned to duty in the Judge Advocate General's Office in Washington. Opportunity for promotion came at the same time as a chance to go overseas. He joined the first detachment of artillery to go to France and participated in a number of major battles, including the Aisne-Marne, Meuse-Argonne, and St. Mihiel offensives. During the War he reached the grades of major and lieutenant colonel and was cited for gallantry in action near Louppy, where he voluntarily made a reconnaissance under heavy enemy fire. After the Armistice he was made judge advocate of the 6th Army Corps and negotiated the agreement between the Grand Duchy of Luxemburg and the A.E.F. For his services he was awarded the Distinguished Service Medal.

Upon his return to the United States, Hurley hastened to bring to a conclusion his courtship of Ruth Wilson, daughter of Rear Admiral and Mrs. Henry B. Wilson. There are many stories of this courtship, but they all agree in that the third time Hurley met Miss Wilson he escorted her home and promptly proposed. Their wedding took place on December 5, 1919. (The Hurleys now have four children—three daughters and a son.)

With his bride, young Hurley returned to Tulsa—and his private law practice. He reopened his law office and built up a successful practice. His ventures in banking and the oil business were equally successful. As receiver for the Gilliland Oil Company he managed the company's affairs so well that he was able to sell it to Standard Oil for a profit of over three million dollars. He invested heavily in real estate and oil and grew rich. Soon he was one of the most important figures in Oklahoma, prominently mentioned as a candidate for the United States Senate but so busy with his private affairs he could not consider running. Once during these years, however, he was requested to assume authority, when there was a race riot in Tulsa. He organized a company of Rough Riders and Spanish-American and World War veterans and made it clear that "orders were orders." Within two hours customary tranquillity once more prevailed.

For many years Hurley steered clear of personal political activity, although he remained a stanch Republican. As early as 1925 he told newspapermen he knew that Herbert Hoover would be the next President. When John S. McGuire made a bitter attack on Hoover (then Secretary of Commerce) Hurley became so angered that he joined the forces actively backing Hoover. The pre-convention campaign was in full swing, and it was regarded as certain that the Oklahoma delegates would be for Curtis. Hurley spent a full Sunday writing a reply to McGuire, championing the Hoover cause in a state where it appeared hopeless. He then started a barnstorming political campaign about the state in his own airplane. An eloquent speaker, capable of making impromptu speeches, Hurley delivered forceful addresses to all who would listen. He paid all his own expenses and financed the entire Hoover battle in Oklahoma. The Old Guard organization that was backing Curtis was not pleased, and Hurley was denied a place on the state delegation to the Kansas City convention. Hurley went nevertheless and, when the showdown came, half the Oklahoma delegates supported Hoover. The Hoover campaign managers recognized Hurley's potential usefulness as a political diplomat and took him into the inner strategic councils. He was picked to persuade Curtis to accept the Vice Presidential nomination. During the election campaign he continued his activities, promising Oklahoma would go for Hoover by 175,000—it did, with 1,000 extra.

After the election Hoover offered Hurley a choice of three sub-Cabinet posts, including the post of Assistant Secretary of War. The Oklahoman accepted. On the death of Secretary Good, nine months later, Hurley was promoted to Secretary of War. He was sworn in on March 15, 1929, the first Oklahoman to sit in a Presidential Cabinet. At the time of the appointment, Hoover referred to Hurley as one of the "new patriots" (men who had made sacrifices to take low salaried positions in the Government). Secretary Hurley's special interest was the development of the air corps and the peacetime activities of the service. It was his firm belief that preparedness made for peace. Hurley proved an asset of no small value to the Hoover Administration. He grew in the confidence of the President as time passed and became the "eyes and ears" as well as the chief defender of the Administration. He traveled widely in pursuance of his duties and in every town he visited he got in a good word for Hoover. His Irish temper and fierce loyalty made him the fighting man of the Cabinet. *Time* Magazine has called him the "Ickes of his day," because he "took on Democrats by the carload."

In the summer of 1931 Hoover sent him to the Philippines to report on the movement for independence. He spent the time from September 1 to 26 in traveling the entire length of the Islands to question representative groups of all factions, and he reported the Islands were then not ready for independence. He was also assigned the disagreeable task of giving the order to oust the bonus marchers. Looking back over his Cabinet years, Hurley has said that the thing he is proudest of is his sponsorship of General Douglas MacArthur [41] for Chief of Staff. He promoted MacArthur over the heads of older men to make him the youngest officer to hold the post. He is proud, too, of his chairmanship of the War Policies Commission, set up to plan for mobilization.

By 1932 Hurley was being mentioned as a possible Vice-Presidential candidate. To all inquiries he replied adroitly without closing any doors on the future; he continued his defense of President Hoover as champion of the cause of individualism and author of the only constructive reconstruction program for fighting the depression.

When the New Deal swept the Republicans out of office, Hurley remained in Washington and built up a lucrative practice as a corporation lawyer. He represented Associated Gas and Electric Company during its long investigation by the Senate. In 1935 he sparred with the Senate Lobby Investigating Committee, insisting he had not lobbied but was paid merely for services in arranging for the company representatives to be heard by the committee considering the Public Utilities Bill, and remarked caustically: "My influence with this Congress wouldn't be worth anybody's nickel, and I don't fool my clients."

In 1936 he stumped Oklahoma for Hoover as he had in 1932. After the election, with the New Deal even more firmly entrenched in Washington, he returned to his law practice. In 1940 he arranged the settlement between the Mexican Government and the five companies whose oil Mexico had expropriated.

The Mexican Government gave him its highest official decoration, the Order of the Aztec Eagle; from the oil companies he got a fee in six figures. About this time, a group of industrialists and editors were reported to be grooming Hurley as a dark horse for the Presidential nomination should there be a deadlock between Taft and Dewey. They were said to have had a small campaign setup and literature reciting Hurley's record, ready to mail to national committeemen. His war record, public and private business record, and friendship with labor factions were regarded as good material. The movement died some months before the convention, at which Willkie [40] was nominated.

By September 12, 1941, at the launching of a new oil tanker built for Sinclair Refining Company, named in his honor and christened by his daughter, Hurley was declaring for repeal of the Neutrality Act, which he called a "cowardly surrender of freedom of the seas." He added: "We are a democracy and a democracy must survive on its integrity. If we are going into this war, we should not back into it."

Early in January 1942 Roosevelt called fifty-nine-year-old Hurley in and offered him a war task: to break the blockade of Bataan from the outside, get some food and ammunition to MacArthur's beleaguered soldiers. When Hurley's new temporary rank of brigadier general was approved by the Senate, he was already on his way to Australia with $1,000,000 in gold coin to buy ships to run the gantlet to Bataan. On three occasions Hurley ran the Japanese blockade of the Philippines and as a souvenir brought back three wounds. When his old friend, General Douglas MacArthur, flew out of Bataan to Australia, Hurley was there to greet him. Stimson called his blockade-running efforts very successful. An avowed "lifelong fighter for credit lines," Hurley said he got for once more than he deserved, since United States Army and Navy chiefs in Australia had given him "vital counsel and support."

On January 29, 1942 the White House announced General Hurley's appointment as first United States Minister to New Zealand. His army rank was unusual for an American diplomat, and many regarded his appointment as a move for closer coordination of American effort with that of other nations in the Pacific war against Japan. Hurley was reported popular in New Zealand. For four months he rallied New Zealanders, promising arms and ammunition to stem the Japs and praising the New Zealand war effort. He made it a rule never to speak more than four minutes. When asked to give some good advice, he replied: "Socrates was a Greek philosopher. He went about giving people a lot of good advice and they poisoned him." On July 17 Hurley's nomination for promotion to permanent grade of colonel went to the Senate.

Hurley appeared in Washington in September 1942 for an extended conference with the President. A few days later he disappeared, this time headed for Russia. Soon Stalin [42] and Hurley were described as hitting it off well. Hurley was impressed by Stalin the man of action; Stalin admired the representa-

HURLEY, PATRICK J.—*Continued*

tive of American capitalism with a career from coal miner to Cabinet member. Hurley asked point blank for permission to visit the Eastern Front, and got it. He is said to be the first foreigner to do so. In a bomber with two other American officers, General Hurley was flown over the Front where Russians were completing one of the most complicated encircling operations in military history. Later, the party toured the Front in a jeep, lived at field headquarters, had the best of Russian hospitality and co-operation. At the Don Front, General Hurley was asked to give the American war cry. Though the United States Army has no official war cry, General Hurley was too good a showman to disappoint his audience—he gave the high, piercing Choctaw battle cry, the original American war cry. For bringing home some of the specific reasons why the Russian Army is such a successful fighting force and for "organizing a blockade running service into the beleaguered Philippines" he was awarded the Oak Leaf Cluster to his Distinguished Service Medal in February 1943.

Upon his return from Russia in January 1943, Hurley formally resigned as Minister to New Zealand, and the President immediately named him as his "personal representative in the Near and Middle East." The key to the Near East is Iran, and Hurley concentrated his attention there. He found Iranians unhappy because of the virtual occupation of the country by the British and the Russians and fearful for their independence. He made three recommendations to remedy the situation: (1) that Iran be permitted to declare war on the Axis and as a belligerent attain parity with the other United Nations; (2) that the American Legation at Teheran be raised to an Embassy; (3) that the principles of the Atlantic Charter be extended to the Indian Ocean to insure post-War independence and territorial integrity of Iran.

President Roosevelt then sent Hurley to China to pave the way for the Cairo meeting with Chiang Kai-shek. En route he had a conference in New Delhi and saw General Claire Chennault [42]. In China he discovered the Generalissimo was very much interested in the fate of Iran since her problems were similar to those of China in many ways. The Cairo conference was his next stop. Here he convinced Roosevelt of the significance of applying the Atlantic Charter to Iran. He next proceeded to Teheran with the temporary rank of Ambassador to establish liaison with the Russians and assist in arranging for the President and the American delegation. Working with British, Russians, and Iranians, Hurley framed the Declaration of the Three Nations Regarding Iran for the Churchill, Stalin, Roosevelt signatures. He considers this the greatest success of his diplomatic career. The President immediately sent Hurley's nomination to temporary rank of major general to the Senate for confirmation. In June of 1943 Hurley's mission flights to the South Pacific, the Middle East, the Orient and Russia won for him the Distinguished Flying Cross.

In January of 1944 Hurley was again en route by plane on a Presidential mission—this time to Afghanistan. The present King of Afghanistan is determined to modernize the country and wants the help of the United States in doing so, believing there will be no interference in national politics. The General's trip was consequently for the purpose of discussing the country's problems and ambitions. In February he was reported to be handling the negotiations for the right of way for the proposed Saudi Arabian pipe line to establish an American military oil reserve on the Mediterranean, an assignment to which he brought his experience in the oil industry and his familiarity with the political and economic picture in Iran.

In August Roosevelt announced that Donald Nelson [41] and General Hurley would leave soon for China as his personal representatives to Chiang Kai-shek. Nelson was to handle the discussion of the economic problems, Hurley the military and military supply problems. En route to China the Presidential emissaries stopped in Moscow to confer with Russian leaders. On September 6 they arrived in Chungking, accompanied by General Stilwell [42], commander in chief of the United States forces in China, Burma, and India, and Chief of Staff to Chiang. (Stilwell had joined the group in India.) The nature of Hurley's mission was to work out arrangements for strengthening the command, training and equipping the interior forces, and forming a coalition government which would delegate top command to American officers.

His mission in China was soon to extend beyond the purely military. In a short time, in October, the worsening economic, political, and military situation in the country became the subject of much excited discussion in the press when Stilwell was unexpectedly relieved of his command by President Roosevelt. Simultaneously came the resignation of Ambassador Clarence E. Gauss—said by Roosevelt to be unrelated to the Stilwell recall—and a month later the Senate unanimously confirmed the President's nomination of Hurley as the new Ambassador to China.

According to President Roosevelt the recall of Stilwell was the culmination of differences between Chiang and the American general, "just a case of personalities." From correspondents who had served in China came somewhat more involved interpretations of the situation. These suggested that the two men had differed on many vital issues affecting the prosecution of the war, including the problems of supplies, military strategy, and the relationship of the Kuomintang and the Chinese Communists. When Stilwell was returned to Washington, his command, the China-Burma-India theatre, was divided into two areas: Major General Albert C. Wedemeyer was put in command of the United States Army Forces in the China area, including French Indo-China; and Lieutenant General Daniel I. Sultan was placed in command of the India-Burma theatre. Wedemeyer also replaced Stilwell as chief of staff to Chiang.

Ranking Chinese officials are said to have welcomed Hurley's appointment as Ambassador. His relations with the Generalissimo he himself has declared to be "direct and cordial." There has been no animosity of any kind between Chinese and American authorities over Stilwell's recall, the Ambassador said shortly after assuming his post. "General Chiang Kai-shek, the United States armed forces, China, and the American Embassy today are united as one and we have one common objective—the defeat of Japan."

A first impression of General Hurley is that he was born to affluence; close observation, however, sets him apart as a man who has known hard labor, for his well-built, slight but muscular frame reflects a physical strength that comes from vigorous effort. He is more than six feet in height, erect in bearing, square-shouldered. He has a close-cropped mustache, gray hair, square jaw, and blue eyes. He is handsome, suave and well-groomed, with the bearing of a successful career man. An impressive public speaker of charm and ability, Hurley has also been described as a man who "struts sitting down." His properties include eight large buildings in Oklahoma, Kansas, and Washington, an estate near Leesburg, Virginia, a house in Santa Fe and another near Washington.

References

Am Mercury 24:257-66 Jl '32; 58:610-16 My '44
N Y Post Mag p31 Mr 29 '43 por
N Y Sun p17 Je 15 '43; p14 S 26 '44
Nation's Business 32:23-4+ My '44 por
Outlook and Independent 159:365-7+ N 18 '41 il por
World's Work 59:58-60+ S '30 por
Who's Who in America 1944-45

HUTCHISON, MILLER REESE Aug. 6, 1876—Feb. 16, 1944 Inventor of many electrical and mechanical appliances, among them the Acousticon, the dictograph and the Klaxon horn; in 1913 he became chief engineer of the Edison Laboratory; formed the Hutchison Company in 1917; recipient of many awards and honorary titles; author of a number of authoritative works on electricity.

Obituary

N Y Times p17 F 18 '44

JACK, WILLIAM S(AUNDERS) Nov. 24, 1888- Industrialist

Address: b. Jack & Heintz, Inc., Solon Rd., Bedford, Ohio

"The most talked about war plant in the country" is Jack & Heintz (Jahco), Inc., producers of airplane starters, automatic pilots, flight instruments and accessories, generators, and landing gear retraction motors. First organized by William Jack and Ralph Heintz in Palo Alto, California, in February 1940, the company was later moved to Cleveland, where it was reorganized under the laws of Ohio in November 1940. Its tremendous production of war material has made it one of the most unique industrial phenomena of the Second World War.

Early in 1944 Jahco was in the headlines almost daily as its dynamic president, Bill Jack, fought a major battle against the United States Government over the question of renegotiation of war contracts. This was not the first nor the most sensational industrial dispute in which Jack's company had been involved. In 1942 the Naval Affairs Committee of the House of Representatives charged that "though the company itself reported profits of only about eleven per cent on its fifty-eight million dollars' worth of contracts with the Government, the Committee's investigation revealed that the profits had really approached one hundred per cent if certain charges and expenses were disallowed as a legitimate part of the company's costs." The "charges and expenses" referred to by the Committee were the high salaries and large bonuses paid by the company. One secretary, for example, had received over $39,000 in 1941, while every eligible employee (Jack prefers to call them "associates") had received a large cash bonus, free insurance, free lunches and work shoes, a wrist watch, and free vacations in company-leased cottages in Florida. The company maintains these charges are legitimate: A part of its established policy, they are generally accepted practices of American business and are not contrary to law. As to profits, the company has said: "Through the ingenuity of its organization, Jack & Heintz developed a better product at less cost, hence was able to earn a bigger profit. The Naval Affairs Committee found no evidence of fraud or scandal."

Bill Jack, who devised this program which many industrialists call revolutionary, is "a self-made man," until a few years ago a factory worker himself. Born in poverty, he is close to his workers because he was one of them for years. The son of a Canadian mother, the former Matilda Van Wyck, and a Scotch father, James Hood Jack, William S. Jack was born in Cleveland, Ohio, November 24, 1888. At the age of six he was selling newspapers on Cleveland streets and delivering laundry for his mother. who took in washing. When he was twelve, he left school to take a job as a magician's assistant. So many odd jobs followed that Jack cannot remember them all today. He won considerable success as an amateur boxer and baseball player. It was his talent for baseball, indeed, that was responsible for his decision to become a machinist. One day a machinist who had an amateur ball team of his own saw Jack play. He wanted the young man for his team, so he offered to teach him the die-sinking trade in exchange for his services as a baseball player. Bill Jack agreed and began work at the Hussey Drop Forge Company. He learned his trade by practicing it. At eighteen he was a journeyman machinist and a few years later business agent of the machinists' union in Cleveland. He was an aggressive union man, "building the membership from about a hundred to more than three thousand five hundred before he resigned."

When Bill Jack went into business for himself he remained loyal to the International Association of Machinists, and he has a contract with them at the present time. He is, he says, unwilling to sign with the CIO, because "to begin with, the organization [Jack and Heintz] started and still is 100 per cent I.A.M."

In 1917 Jack established the Accurate Machine Company on $2,500. In a short time he had more orders than he was able to fill. By borrowing, by increasing the incentive of his

Jack & Heintz Inc.

WILLIAM S. JACK

workers with high pay and bonuses, and by selling out at a large profit, Jack was able to build up and sell several large manufacturing enterprises. His most important business venture before the present War was the Pump Engineering Company, which Jack headed with the aid of his son William Russell Jack. This $2,000,000 corporation, employing some 265 men in 1939, had been started in an old garage six years before with a staff of four men and $500 capital.

In 1939 Jack went to California to establish an aircraft research department with Ralph M. Heintz, who was to head the experimental research. The plans for this enterprise fell through, but Jack and Heintz agreed to continue their association. Heintz had been experimenting on an improved airplane starter. Jack took his blueprints to Washington and persuaded the Government to give them an experimental contract. With an original investment of $100,000, Jack and Heintz, Inc., was organized in November 1940. At the end of the first year "business was booming to such an extent that William S. Jack and Ralph M. Heintz were able to plough back $254,000 out of company profits." The company meanwhile had moved back to Cleveland, after refusing to sign a closed shop agreement with the California unions.

The original $100,000 plus the $254,000 profit are the sole investments which Jack and Heintz have made in the business, aside from intangibles such as good credit. When, therefore, their profits soared to more than $8,000,000 in 1942, the United States War Department accused the company of "war profiteering." The major investment ($3,439,000 in equipment and $11,670,000 in cash) had been made by the Government, and so the War Department placed a renegotiation assessment against Jack and Heintz in order to get back some of its original investment and to prevent any company from making exorbitant profits out of the War.

Bill Jack did not accept the War Department's order quietly, however. Claiming that he needed his excess profits in order to build up a post-War reserve, Jack launched an expensive fight against the Government. He denied that his profits had been high and pointed out that most of the money had gone to employees of the company in the form of bonuses and other benefits. The officers and stockholders of Jack and Heintz, he has also said, are pledged not to take any profits in dividends on any war contract work.

Backed up wholeheartedly by his "associates," who are made to feel that they are a part of the business rather than employees, Jack threatened to take his renegotiation case to the courts. If he did that it would provide a test case on the question of whether a corporation that has come into existence because of the War and has made its profits through wartime contracts should "be allowed to build up an earnings reserve so that it can shift to large-scale peace production and compete with long-established concerns." Jack bought full-page advertisements in metropolitan papers in which he reprinted a telegram which the Jack and Heintz plants sent to every Congressman in Washington. His argument was that "free enterprise must be protected" and that "we are against the socialization of industry in any form." The profit reserve which Jack sought to establish would, he said, be used to "afford employment to our associates and our returning servicemen." In January 1944 Jack announced that, due to uncertainty about this reserve, he had been forced to withdraw his pledge to guarantee jobs to returning War veterans.

Determined to continue the "fight against the Government's war contract renegotiation program," Jack and Heintz carried their case to Congressmen by inviting all members of the House and Senate to a dinner which they gave in Washington on February 29. Seventy-odd Congressmen attended the dinner, heard speeches by Jack and other members of the company, and saw motion pictures showing employees "at work and at play."

In a recent address before the Advertising Club of New York Jack warned that industry would be "crippled" after the War "if it was not allowed to earmark for post-War conversion money that is being made currently." But in spite of his bitter fight against the Government, Jack is not popular with his fellow-industrialists, who admit very frankly that they cannot compete with him. While the manpower shortage is acute in Cleveland, Jack and Heintz has a waiting list of thousands who are eager to get on their payroll. Absenteeism is no problem for them. So completely do the workers have the company's interests at heart that the time clocks in the plants are used for keeping cost records. They are not used to time workers in or out when they begin or leave at the regular hours, for tardy and idle men are reproved by their fellow workers. The day begins with the playing of the National anthem over the public address system, and ends with the playing of "A Perfect Day" and "Pack Up Your Troubles."

The work week at Jack and Heintz averages eighty hours. Jack works as many hours as the other men and women in the plant, fraternizes with them, and has a loudspeaker system over which he frequently broadcasts "pep talks" to them. Thanks to vitamin pills, plenty of medical attention, steam-baths, foot treatments, diathermy, etc., the employees have achieved an enviable production record. Jack admits that he has instituted these improvements in working conditions as an incentive to increased output: "We are generous to our employees—as I term them, associates—from the floor sweeper to the top, because we believe that this is the only way for an all-out war production, to get it done quickly and get it ahead of schedule so that we can clean up the job that we have ahead of us." It has been pointed out, however, that actual hourly rates among the regular employees are not high. When calculated on an eighty-hour-week basis (with time and one-half for all work over forty hours) total salaries naturally seem very large.

There are just three owners of Jack and Heintz—Bill Jack, his son, and Ralph Heintz. They all work in the company; the employees call them by their first names. Jack himself is an indefatigable worker. He usually averages about five hours of sleep a night and has a couch in the plant so that he may spend all his time near his work. John Kouwenhoven writes in *Harper's*: "There is a tense quietness in his speech and in his motions, as if a restless and explosive energy were being automatically restrained by excessive weariness, and at moments his eyes fade as if he were starved for sleep." Short and stocky, Jack has little time for recreation but on rare occasions enjoys the movies or a sports game. He has been married since 1907 to his childhood sweetheart, the former Goldie White. In addition to their son, William Russell, they have a daughter named Betty. (Another son, Clarence, is deceased.) Simple in his own tastes (he generally wears work clothes like the men in the plants), Jack has refused an offer of $10,000,000 for a controlling interest in the company, saying: "I've got enough money already. It's worth a lot more to me to see those boys out there happy, like they are. I'd go all the way for any of them, and they know it." That the men do know it is reflected in the Jahco Victory Song which the employees sing at every gathering—

Bill and Ralph, you've stood by us,
We're all in back of you.
Anything you care to ask
We're waiting here to do.

References

Business Week p72-4 Mr 7 '43; p108
    My 22 '43
Harper 186:556-64 My '43
Liberty 21:12+ F 26 '44 por
Life 14:74-81 Mr 22 '43
N Y Post Mag p7 D 18 '43
New Repub 109:567-70 O 25 '43
Newsweek 29:48+ Ap 6 '42
Time 39:17 Ap 6 '42; 40:91-2 D 14 '42

JACKSON, CHARLES (REGINALD)
Apr. 6, 1903- Author
Address: h. Orford, N. H.

The story of five days in the life of a chronic alcoholic—the subject which Charles Jackson treated with great sensitivity in his first novel, *The Lost Weekend*—received excited discussion when it appeared early in 1944. Don Birnam, the alcoholic, is not one of the romantic drinkers of Hemingway or Scott Fitzgerald, but a "still" drinker whose five-day "binge" would be dreary reading in the extreme if it were not for the intimate and terrifying details given in its telling. These are so intimate that many of the literary critics have said the character is drawn too sharply not to be autobiographical, a fact which Jackson strongly denies. The reader is never conscious of any effort at drama, romance, or moral-pointing, yet Jackson has created "a suspense and a creepy psychological atmosphere that makes the reader follow the book to the end." As for its message, although Jackson indicates no reform of Birnam's character, John Chamberlain [40], the New York *Times* critic, calls it "the most moral book in a decade," a book which temperance lecturers ought to distribute to their audiences because it is the "best bet since Billy Sunday reformed and hit the sawdust trail." *The Lost Weekend* has proved to be a catapult to fame and fortune for Jackson. Acclaimed a masterpiece by some of the reviewers, it has reached the best-seller list, and Jackson was given a Hollywood contract by Metro-Goldwyn-Mayer.

Charles Reginald Jackson, born April 6, 1903 in Summit, New Jersey, is the son of Frederick and Sarah (Williams) Jackson. He grew up in Newark, New York, where his family had moved when he was quite young. From his childhood he has been an omnivorous reader, and when he was sixteen, he says, "I expected to make a real contribution to American letters, but at forty I know better. All I want is to be able to write, truly and well, stories that will hold the reader's interest and possibly tell him something about other people and maybe even about himself." One year at Syracuse University ended his formal education. Some years later, while ill with tuberculosis from 1927 to 1933, he had the opportunity for self-study. Four of those years were spent at Davos, Switzerland, the scene of Thomas Mann's [42] *Magic Mountain*.

Charles Jackson is one of those happy individuals who learn as they live; despite his lack of academic training he has won the description of "erudite" from his interviewers. His favorite authors are Thomas Mann, Walt Whitman, Tolstoy, and Shakespeare. "Shakespeare," he says, "is the author I'm always reading." While Jackson denies that *The Lost Weekend* is autobiographical, he admits that like many young men who grew up under prohibition he leaned on alcohol at times. "As sprawling and vague as my career was at that time, I wanted to be a writer—and one day I looked up and realized it was interfering. So I quit. No tapering off. I just stopped." (He has not had a drink in eight years.) Before he earned a living from his writing, Jack-

CHARLES JACKSON

son had been a bookseller, a feeder in a jig-saw factory in Boston, and a newspaperman.

Max Wylie '40, the Columbia Broadcasting System director and writer, in 1936 gave Jackson a trial at radio writing. He was a staff writer under Wylie for two years, and when he resigned in 1939 to free-lance Wylie made the following notation on Jackson's record card: "A talented person—has extraordinary ability for recognizing talent in other people. Highly esteemed for his work and well liked by his fellow workers." As a free lance Jackson contributed seven productions to the *Columbia Workshop* radio program, which gives him the distinction of having had more of his plays produced on that radio program than any other author. The first of these was an original story, *A Letter From Home* (1939). *The Devil and Daniel Webster, Outward Bound,* and *The Giant's Share* were his radio adaptations. In 1941 the Workshop presented Jackson's original radio play *Dress Rehearsal*, a story of the events and happenings immediately preceding the raising of the curtain on a stage play. The leading part was played by Joan Tetzel, a radio actress, who has been heard in several of CBS's serial dramas. In February 1944 Jackson wrote the radio adaptation of *Jane Eyre* for CBS, which was broadcast that month and again in April.

The Lost Weekend was written in a little over a year in the time left over from two jobs—teaching radio writing at New York University and, for a time, writing a five-times-a-week daytime radio serial. Although he does not consider that the writing of "popular stuff" is compromising to a serious writer, Jackson called the serial his "double life." The serial, *Sweet River*, heard over WJZ at 10 a.m. from Mondays through Fridays, took only three days a week to write, Jackson said—most of it is dictated to a public stenographer.

The Lost Weekend was published by Farrar & Rinehart in January 1944. Although there was a divergence of opinion among the reviewers on the reader-interest of the book,

all were agreed that Jackson had handled his subject brilliantly. Edmund Wilson of the *New Yorker* pronounced it a "tour de force of some merit. . . . The book, in fact," said Wilson, "has so much that is good that it ought to have been three times as good and a really satisfactory piece of fiction. As a whole, it is rather formless, and the writing, though fluent and smooth, is full of repetitions and tautologies." Chamberlain says that if "the story behind the story of Don Birnam's five liquor-soaked days never comes quite clear, that is probably quite in keeping with reality. For chronic alcoholics drink to forget, not to remember." Said A. C. Spectorsky: "There has never, to my knowledge, been a book like this. Its frankness is sometimes shocking but never aimed to shock. The aim, and it is unerring, is always for accuracy and . . . truth." As for its accuracy from a psychiatrist's point of view, Dr. Herbert L. Nossen, the noted psychiatric specialist, labeled the book, "expert and wonderful—the work of a courageous man." Jackson describes his work as a sketch, "variations on a theme, a five-day look into the mind of an abnormal, suffering human"—"a portrait of a neurotic personality, whose sensations probably were experienced by many persons who didn't happen to have taken up alcohol as a release." Despite the fact that the book contains so much accurate psychiatric information, Jackson says he does not know the subject academically, that the small knowledge he has of psychiatry has been picked up from personal observation or is largely intuitive.

Jackson was asked whether Don Birnam could "lick" alcohol and, if so, by what means. (In the book, friends, relatives, and a psychiatrist had failed to help Birnam.) "Don Birnam," said Jackson, "must help himself; no help from anyone will cure him. I have suggested throughout the book that he has character left. He has it within himself to work it out—that remorse is what he's going to build from—but at the end of the book he still isn't ready."

On March 4, 1938 Jackson was married to Rhoda Booth, an editorial writer on the magazine *Fortune*, whose home before she came to New York was Barre, Vermont. They have two daughters, Sarah Blann and Kate Winthrop. Jackson is a Beethoven fan, and in his collection of several hundred records he has every work of the composer ever recorded. He finds relaxation in painting in oils, which he says he does for fun, and he hopes no one will describe him as a painter with serious ambitions. The Jacksons are New Dealers, ardent admirers of Roosevelt '42, though Jackson's and his wife's families are Republicans. Mrs. Jackson is the business manager of the family. She feels very happy over the success *The Lost Weekend* has brought to her husband but she is highly amused when friends take every detail in the book literally. Jackson announced shortly after the publication of this first novel that he was working on his next book, which is about the regeneration of an alcoholic, a subject which he says he has found more fascinating than that of *The Lost Weekend*.

Jackson, who is described as smallish, balding, and soft-mannered, might be seen in his adaptation of *The Lost Weekend* for Paramount, for it has been reported that he will appear as an extra in one shot.

Reference

N Y World-Telegram p11 Mr 10 '44 por

JANEWAY, ELIZABETH (HALL) Oct. 7, 1913- Author

Address: b. c/o Doubleday Doran & Co., Inc., 14 W. 49th St., New York City; h. 444 E. 52nd St., New York City

"Brooklyn crashes through again!" said the New York *Post* when Elizabeth Janeway brought forth her successful first novel, *The Walsh Girls* (1943). Like Betty Smith [43], author of *A Tree Grows in Brooklyn* (1943), Mrs. Janeway is a native of the Dodgers' borough. The daughter of Charles H. and Jeannette F. Hall, she was born on Pineapple Street, October 7, 1913. After attending the Brooklyn schools Miss Hall was enrolled at Barnard College of Columbia University, and she began her writing career, it is reported, by taking the short story course "over and over in order that she might be forced to turn out a certain number of words a term." This method, however unorthodox, seems to have been successful, for Miss Hall won *Story* Magazine's Intercollegiate Short Story Contest for 1935. When the Hall family "went broke" during the depression Elizabeth left college to write advertisements for a department store's bargain basement. After a year of turning out masterpieces of persuasion which she summarizes as "Get these divine $3.98 dresses with a touch of Paris about them," she was able to return to Barnard and finish her course, graduating in June 1935.

Soon after her graduation Elizabeth Hall met Eliot Janeway, one of the editors of *Life* and *Fortune*; three months later they were married. At this time Mrs. Janeway began the short story which was eventually to develop into *The Walsh Girls*. She tore it up in disgust after two unsatisfactory versions had been produced, but Mr. Janeway "nagged" her into starting all over again. The third and final version was completed just in time for the birth of her second son, William Hall. (The Janeways already had one son, Michael Charles.)

Published in the fall of 1943, *The Walsh Girls* (a psychological study of two New England sisters) attracted critical attention to Mrs. Janeway as a writer of talent and great promise. "Since this novel is not in the least autobiographical," wrote John Chamberlain [40], "it is an augury of a long career." He compared Mrs. Janeway to Jane Austen, with the difference that the former is aware of "the larger theme of world tragedy" of her own time as well as the psychological interplay among her characters: "Figuratively speaking, she knows all about Napoleon." Although the Springfield *Republican*'s reviewer found that Mrs. Janeway's characters "made her [the reviewer] a little ashamed of women," and that the book was on a "dark, unhappy level," the *New Yorker* called *The Walsh Girls* "lucid and subtle," and the New York *Herald Tribune Books* considered it "Middletown in fiction, and that is no small achievement."

ELIZABETH JANEWAY

William DuBois, in the New York *Times*, remarked that "perhaps its tremulous stream-of-consciousness method, its awareness of things sensed but not seen in the amorphous half-world of the imagination, will frighten masculine readers away. . . . But no man who wishes to make even a fumble at understanding the other sex can afford to miss this novel." Several reviewers felt that the characters "are too much like those one has spent a lot of time avoiding in real life, neither 'bad' enough nor 'good' enough to arouse a sympathetic response"; but all agreed that "it introduces to us a new and brilliant young writer. Certainly it affirms that much may be expected from her succeeding work."

In reply to some of her critics, Mrs. Janeway said she would not rewrite *The Walsh Girls* for "love, money, fame, or even the critics." "By the time I got through writing the book the girls were bossing me around. They knew what they were going to do and did it, no matter how I felt about it." As to her writing in the future: "First, I'm going to write about much more decisive people. I'm not scared of them any more. Second, I want to write much more directly and tensely. . . . And I'm going to break my back to be a good technician. Who do I mean are good technicians? Well, I've just been rereading *Madame Bovary* and *A Farewell to Arms*. My God, I want to be that good. Delusions of grandeur, no doubt." Mrs. Janeway was reported to be in Connecticut in August 1944 at work on a "political" novel of New York. After throwing away an earlier attempt, she had 25,000 words written and hoped they would not, like the first book, have to be thrice rewritten. At a book meeting held under the auspices of the New York *Times* in February 1944, Mrs. Janeway expressed the belief that authors write novels, and other people read them, because "in a novel you can write about anything. . . . The novelist's characters are the extract, the essence of humanity as the author sees it."

(Continued next page)

JANEWAY, ELIZABETH—*Continued*

The author spends much time on trips around the country with her husband as he sounds out public opinion and gathers material for his articles. One of her greatest thrills came in California, when she launched the Liberty ship *George Sterling*. In addition, she has given many lectures and has appeared on *Information Please*. The Janeways have a duplex apartment overlooking the East River, where they live with their sons and, as always, a cat. The present incumbent, a Persian named General Krivitsky, is also known as "Fuzz Buzz." Mrs. Janeway likes to have "something big to work on in the way of reading—say six volumes"—and the Janeway apartment is lined with books. "I'm the happiest girl in the world," says Mrs. Janeway: "Two boy babies, a grand husband, a book."

Described as "an attractive young woman . . . with an upswept hair-do and a profile to match," Mrs. Janeway is five feet three inches tall and has dark brown hair and hazel eyes. She is fond of exotic food, particularly Swedish and Japanese specialties, although her interest extends only to the eating and not to the cooking. An accomplished knitter, Mrs. Janeway regrets her inability to sew or to tie a bow tie. This last is a particularly poignant regret, for Mr. Janeway cannot tie a bow tie either, and he is thus obliged to call on a neighbor for help whenever he puts on formal evening dress.

References

N Y Post Mag p33 N 4 '43 pors
N Y Times p17 O 19 '43 por
N Y Times Book R p1+ O 17 '43
Sat R Lit 26:18 N 6 '43

JANSON, PAUL EMILE 1872(?)—June(?) 1944 Belgian statesman; a leading member of the Liberal Party and prominent in Governmental affairs since 1914; Premier of Belgium in 1937-1938; something of an isolationist in foreign policy and a reformer in internal affairs; Minister of Justice at time of German invasion in 1940; arrested in 1943, he died in prison in Weimar, Germany.

Obituary

N Y Times p 17 Jl 5 '44 por

JASTROW, JOSEPH (jəs'trō) Jan. 30, 1863 —Jan. 8, 1944 Psychologist; professor at University of Wisconsin (1888-1927); author of many books on psychology; president of the American Psychological Association in 1900.

Obituary

N Y Times p4 Ja 9 '44

JOHNSON, DOUGLAS WILSON Nov. 30, 1878—Feb. 24, 1944 International authority on geology and physiography; division chief of boundary geography, American Peace Commission in Paris, 1918-1919; assistant on the New Jersey Geological Survey in 1911; geographical adviser of the United States State Department, 1919-1920; consulting physiographer to the Canadian Government in the Labrador boundary dispute in 1926; author of numerous works in his field.

Obituary

N Y Times p17 F 25 '44 por

JOHNSON, PAUL B(URNEY) Mar. 23, 1880—Dec. 26, 1943 Governor of Mississippi since 1939; former United States Representative (Democrat) to Congress from the 6th Mississippi District (1919-23).

Obituary

N Y Times p19 D 27 '43 por

JOHNSON, PHILIP G(USTAV) Nov. 5, 1894—Sept. 14, 1944 Aircraft official and engineer; president since 1939 of the Boeing Aircraft Company, builders of Army Flying fortresses, including the B-29's; an authority on aviation; was president of Varney Air Lines, Inc., from 1931 to 1933, the United Air Lines, Inc., during the same period, and vice-president of Trans-Canada Air Lines in 1937.

Obituary

N Y Times p19 S 15 '44 por

JONES, JENNIFER Mar. 2, 1919- Motion-picture actress

Address: b. c/o Twentieth Century-Fox Film Corp., Box 900, Beverly Hills, Calif.

The best performance by a motion-picture actress in 1943, by vote of 10,000 members of the Academy of Motion Picture Arts and Sciences, was given by a young mother playing her first important film role. Jennifer Jones, a tent-show girl from Oklahoma, won the Academy Award in competition with such experienced stars as Jean Arthur, Greer Garson [42], Joan Fontaine [44], and Ingrid Bergman [40].

The young actress who so successfully played the little saint in *The Song of Bernadette* (1943) started life as Phylis Isley in Tulsa, Oklahoma, March 2, 1919. Her parents, Phil R. and Flora Mae (Suber) Isley, were the owners, managers, and stars of the Isley Stock Company, a tent show which toured the rural districts of the Middle West. For ten cents admission—reserved seats twenty cents—the Isleys presented such tear-jerking dramas as *The Old Homestead*. Shows like theirs gave rise to the expression "Tomorrow night, *East Lynne!*" In their case it was not a joke, but an announcement of their next performance. However strenuous tent-show life may have been, the Isleys were financially comfortable. Their daughter was sent to the Edgemere Public School in Oklahoma City, where she was of course the leading actress in all class plays; summers were spent trouping with the show, in which her acting career began when she reached ten. The future star also sold candy, took tickets, and made herself generally useful.

After her graduation from elementary school the young actress was enrolled at Monte Cassino Junior College, a Benedictine Sisters school in Tulsa. There she continued to take the dramatic honors in student productions and to spend her summers touring in stock. In addition Miss Isley—not yet Miss Jones—appeared on Tulsa radio programs during the school year. Nevertheless, she felt that she was losing time from her career as an actress. (Tent-show performers are not considered actors by the "legitimate" professionals.) According to several interviewers she wrote to Katharine Cornell '41, her current idol, for advice on the burning question: Should a young beginner get started as soon as possible in a good New York dramatic school, or should she go to college? To everyone's surprise, Miss Cornell answered promptly, advising "a cultural background."

After a summer in stock with the Mansfield Players, Phylis Isley entered Northwestern University, majoring in dramatics. She continued to take leads in summer stock; her favorite role was Moonyean in *Smilin' Through*. Phil Isley was reluctant to have his daughter study for the stage; if the girl wanted to act, he felt, why didn't she go to Hollywood and make money at it? He'd give her a letter of introduction—for the elder Isleys were by then motion-picture exhibitors with a chain of theatres in Texas. But the future Jennifer Jones finally persuaded her parents to send her to the American Academy of Dramatic Arts in New York after one year at the University. This was at the beginning of 1938.

Among Miss Isley's classmates were Diana Barrymore and Robert Walker—the latter a lanky youth from Salt Lake City who had been the best actor at the San Diego Army and Navy Academy. He and Phylis became friends. When the two were cast as Robert Browning and Elizabeth Barrett in the Academy version of *The Barretts of Wimpole Street* "they played love scenes together from 2 to 4 p.m. and soon discovered they weren't play-acting." As Walker had no money, "they did their courting on Fifth Avenue busses, on the Staten Island ferry [a half-hour ride for a nickel], and on long walks." Another summer of stock, and then Miss Isley went back to the Academy while Walker looked for work so that they could be married. After a few weeks his young fiancée left school to join him in his search. The best the two could find were parts with Paul Gilmore's Cherry Lane troupe in Greenwich Village—fifty cents apiece per performance. Then came an offer from a Tulsa radio station: Would Miss Isley return to Oklahoma to take the feminine lead in a thirteen-week program, at $25 a week? Miss Isley would and did—and she knew just the man to play opposite her. Thirteen weeks later, on January 2, 1939, the anniversary of their meeting, she and Robert Walker were married.

On the suggestion of a prematurely enthusiastic talent scout the couple took a wedding trip to Hollywood, with great non-success. Young Mrs. Walker managed to get bit parts in two very unimportant Republic productions, *New Frontier* (1939) and *Dick Tracy's G-Men* (serial); young Mr. Walker achieved a two-line role in Warner Brothers' *Winter Carnival* (1939). The final blow was the failure of their test for Paramount, in which Phyllis was required to play her husband's mother. After that they sold their sky-blue automobile (a gift from the Isleys) for tickets back to New York.

Things were very difficult for the young couple, especially after the birth of Robert, Jr., in 1940. Phylis Walker sewed and cleaned and cooked—not very well at first—in a cold-water flat near the Elevated. After a while she got work modeling hats through the Powers agency. (A number of her pictures appeared in *Harper's Bazaar*, which is, for a fashion model, the equivalent of an accolade.) But she soon had to give up modeling. Less than a year after Bobby came Michael, and that made four Walkers to feed. Fortunately, Robert Walker got a chance to break into radio; and from there he went on to establish himself as an obscure but steady radio actor. By 1941 Walker was playing regularly in *Myrt and Marge*, and the family "had moved from two dingy rooms on the fringe of Hell's Kitchen to six sunlit rooms in Garden City, Long Island."

After seeing Rose Franken's '40 *Claudia* Mrs. Walker presented herself at David O. Selznick's '41 New York office to try out for the title role in his screen version. "They let me read the part," she says, "and I was very, very bad." Realizing this, the aspiring Claudia burst into tears. According to Selznick's official story, he happened to come in at that time, was impressed with the histrionic ability displayed, and had his secretary make an appointment with "this Miss Phylis Walker" for the following day. According to the lady herself, she thought the appointment just a device to stop her tears, and was at home shampooing her hair on the following day when the phone rang: Mr. Selznick was waiting to see her. Phylis hailed a cab and raced in from Long Island, frantically drying her hair all the way. The trip cost her $10 in cabfare but it won her a contract.

Selznick, who had already added Dorothy McGuire '41 to his crew of actresses under contract, had no intention of letting the Claudia role go to anyone else; but he saw Phylis Walker as a possibility for Nora in the movie version of *The Keys of the Kingdom* (which had been published in 1941). Two weeks after this interview the producer signed her to a long-term contract, and soon summoned his new discovery to Santa Barbara, California, to play in William Saroyan's '40 *Hello, Out There*. The play was given as curtain-raiser to a Shaw '44 production; but "to the surprise of everyone except Saroyan, the one-acter grabbed off all the good notices." After this Selznick sent Mrs. Walker back to New York to study under Sanford Meisner of the Group Theatre.

In February 1942 Selznick introduced Jennifer Jones, née Phylis Isley, to "a press that warmed up to her right off the bat." As one of its members wrote: "It wasn't just that she was so pretty, nor just the young excitement of an about-to-be-star. It was also that crisp, ups-a-daisy name, Jennifer Jones. When someone asked how she came by it, 'My mother must have been reading an old English novel,' said Jennifer with an *entre nous* grin. 'But I suppose they'll change it once I get to Hollywood.'" Reporters ferreted

JENNIFER JONES

out, however, the fact that "Mr. Selznick's earnest aides have spent the last several months thinking up that unbeatable name." The official story now is that Selznick bestowed the name on his discovery because he had always wanted a daughter named Jennifer.

Somehow *The Keys of the Kingdom*, which was to have been "Selznick's *Gone With the Wind* of 1942," turned out to be simply gone with the wind. After this introduction to the world Jennifer Jones spent almost a year in New York, learning how to talk, to walk, to act—and waiting for a wire from Hollywood. Finally, in December 1942 Twentieth Century-Fox announced that their search for an unknown to play the difficult and important role of Ste. Bernadette Soubirous in the film version of Franz Werfel's '40 *The Song of Bernadette* (published in 1942) was at an end. The role was to go to Jennifer Jones. Saroyan, by then in the Army, is said to have written to her: "After you become a big star because of Bernadette, you may want to play the lead again in a Saroyan play. Let me know when that is, and I will write a play for you. If I can find time between drills."

Just ten days after Miss Jones horrified the Selznick publicity organization by arriving with two energetic youngsters, her husband obtained a screen test from Metro-Goldwyn-Mayer, which led to his being cast as Sailor Purckett in *Bataan*. A pleasant sort of lightning struck twice in the Walker family. While Mrs. Walker worked on the exacting role of Bernadette (its 329 pages were called "enough to floor Helen Hayes" '42), Robert Walker drew critical praise for *Bataan* (1943) and was given the third lead in *Madame Curie* (1943), starring Greer Garson '42 and Walter Pidgeon '42. This was followed by the title role in *See Here, Private Hargrove* (1944). The Walkers' combined incomes came to $600 a week.

Inasmuch as Bernadette is a fifteen-year-old saint, the Selznick and Fox publicity offices

tried to protect their star from association in the minds of her future audiences with anything so earthly as being a wife and mother. This plan was slightly hampered, as in the case of Ingrid Bergman, by Mrs. Walker's pride in her family. When her husband also made a name for himself the clause in Jennifer Jones's contract forbidding her to be photographed with her husband and children quietly died. The tall young blond with the engaging grin, his dark, vivid wife, and their two handsome towheads formed too perfect a family group to be hidden from photographers; the couple's unprecedented double rocket-rise was far too newsworthy to be ignored. So the publicity was switched, and the model-couple, ideal family angle was played up for all it was worth. Then it backfired: the Walker household broke up. In spite of pressure from Selznick, Twentieth Century, and MGM, Jennifer Jones confirmed reports of "a friendly separation" in November 1943. (The day after her receipt of the Academy Award, while studio officials tore their hair and millions of sentimentalists sighed in disappointment, Miss Jones announced her intention of proceeding with a divorce action.) Meanwhile the ingenue, having finished work on *The Song of Bernadette*, went into *Since You Went Away*, in which she played the romantic lead opposite Robert Walker.

When *Bernadette* was released the critics approved Selznick's choice for the role. *Variety* called Jennifer Jones's portrayal of the title role "an inspirationally sensitive and arresting performance that sets her solid as a screen personality. Wistful, naïve, and at times angelic, Miss Jones takes command early." Other reviewers agreed that the film's success was due largely to "the simplicity and beauty of Miss Jones in the role. Her large, sad eyes and soft face, her wistful mouth and luminous smile are a thoroughly appealing exterior for the innocence which shines from within. And her manner, both dignified and humble, modest yet self-confident, is a wonderful contrast to the shadings of lay and clerical personalities which confront her on all sides." On Jennifer Jones's twenty-fifth birthday the Academy of Motion Picture Arts and Sciences presented her with the "Oscar" for the best performance of the year. (Altogether, *The Song of Bernadette* won five Academy awards for excellence.) Even before that, Twentieth Century-Fox, which had bought from Selznick a six-year option on her services in one picture a year, announced that Jennifer Jones would in the future receive star billing.

In the middle of 1944 Miss Jones appeared in the Selznick production *Since You Went Away*, a story of life on the home front in 1943. In the role of a girl who had felt the impact of the War, she was "surpassingly sweet as a well-bred American daughter in the first bloom of womanhood and love," in the opinion of Bosley Crowther of the New York *Times*. Selznick chose the role especially for Miss Jones, apprehensive lest her audience come to visualize her as "a sort of Bernadette in real life, an eminently worthy character, but lacking in variety."

Selznick's new star is tall—five feet seven —and has a long stride, a boyish figure, and a young, non-glamour-girl face. She has the brunet complexion that goes with her dark brown eyes and her dark hair which she wears in a mop of curls. The star prefers simple, tailored clothes, mainly suits and slacks, no hats, and low heels—low for Hollywood, at least. An expert swimmer and a good tennis player, she sleeps nine or ten hours each night, drinks a quart of milk a day, and never smokes. "The Jones girl" walks three miles a day, even in the rain, and does faithful calisthenics to stay slim, but she never bothers with a diet. She is devoting much of her spare time to the war effort, launching Red Cross Nurses Aid Drives; participating in bond drives; and visiting with wounded servicemen in hospitals.

References

Collier's 111:78+ Ap 24 '43 por
Ladies' H J 61:85 Ja '44 por
Liberty 20:16+ S 25 '43 pors
N Y Herald Tribune VII p20 N 21 '43 pors
N Y Post Mag p9 Jl 24 '43 pors
Newsweek 23:75-6 F 7 '44 il pors
Photoplay 24:38+ Mr '44 pors

JORDANA (Y SOUZA), FRANCISCO GOMEZ (hor-dä'na ē sō'zä frän-thēs'kō) 1876—Aug. 3, 1944 Former Spanish Foreign Minister; Army officer

Bulletin: Francisco Gómez Jordana died August 3, 1944.

From March 1944 issue:

When American oil shipments to Spain in the month of February 1944 were suspended by the American State Department, Secretary of State Hull '40 suggesting that perhaps Spain's "neutrality" in the Second World War was not all that it should be, most people who bear no love for Franco '42 breathed a sigh of relief and hoped the State Department was finally getting tough toward El Caudillo. At the same time there were some who could not help wondering about the fact that Jordana's son, Rafael Gómez, and Juan March's lawyer, Thomas Caballero Peire, had arrived in the United States just the month before with sixty-day visitors' permits. There were rumors that some sections of the State Department envisioned Jordana either as a possible successor for Franco or as a bridge for a monarchial restoration during a period of transition. In any case, Spanish Republicans doubted that the visit boded any good for the restoration of democratic government in Spain.

Looking into the past of Count General Francisco Gómez Jordana y Souza, it is difficult to understand why he has been pictured as more friendly to the democracies than either former Foreign Minister Ramón Serrano Suñer '40 or than Franco himself. Born in Spain in 1876 and educated at the Military Academy and Staff College, he fought in the war against Cuba as a very young man, and the year 1903 found him already on the Spanish General Staff, with the rank of captain. After having served as an instructor at the

FRANCISCO GOMEZ JORDANA

Escuela Superior de Guerra and having fought in Spain's costly war with Morocco he was promoted to the rank of colonel; by 1920 he was a brigadier general. During the dictatorship of Primo de Rivera, which lasted until January 1930, Jordana was in charge of Moroccan affairs. French cooperation was sought in finishing off Abd-el-Krim, and in 1925 Jordana served as both president of the Franco-Spanish Conference and as general of a division. From 1928 to 1930, after having taken part in the negotiations on Moroccan affairs in Paris, he acted as High Commissioner for Morocco (which had at last been "pacified"), with the rank of lieutenant general.

After the birth of the Spanish Republic in April 1931 Jordana was retired to relative obscurity. For many years, however, he had been a henchman of Juan March, who during the First World War built up Spain's greatest fortune as a tobacco smuggler and oil provider for Germany. During the days before Franco's coup of July 1936 March scurried around among Spain's aristocracy getting support for the coming revolt, and it was reportedly he, more than any other Spaniard, who brought the Nazis to Spain. March, who leased his Canary Islands lands to the Nazis for submarine bases in 1938, also acted as Franco's chief banker during the revolt; and it was natural that Jordana should rise to prominence in the Nationalist Government, proclaimed by Franco in the autumn of 1936. In 1936 Jordana served as president of Franco's High Court of Military Justice; from 1937 to 1938 as president of the Technical Council; from 1938 to 1939 as vice-president and Minister of Foreign Affairs. He was still Franco's Foreign Minister when the United States recognized Franco's Government in 1939, but the next year became president of the Council of State, surrendering the post of Foreign Minister to the Falange's Ramón Serrano Suñer.

(Continued next page)

JORDANA, FRANCISCO GOMEZ—*Cont.*

In September 1942 there were many who hailed Jordana's return to the post of Foreign Minister and Serrano Suñer's dismissal from Franco's Cabinet as an indication that Franco was becoming less friendly toward the Axis powers, for Jordana was reportedly no friend of the Falange. There were few proofs of Spain's increasing "neutrality" in the Second World War, however. Spain continued to serve as a base for espionage, sabotage, and pro-Axis propaganda through the Falange in the Western Hemisphere. Oil, nitrates, food, and other war supplies continued to be brought to Spain on "neutral" Spanish boats and transshipped to the Reichswehr. From submarine and air bases in Spanish Morocco, the Spanish Canaries and Balearics, and the Spanish mainland itself the Nazis continued to take their toll of United Nations ships. The Spanish Blue Division continued to fight against Russia. In November 1942, moreover, when Franco dissolved the national council of the Falange, he set up a new council that included Serrano Suñer.

As for Jordana himself, in December 1942, at a luncheon held in his honor by Portugal's Salazar[11], he announced the creation of an Iberian bloc strong enough to maintain the "neutrality" of Spain and Portugal and to influence international politics. On April 16, 1943, in a speech at Barcelona, he made it clear in what direction he wished to influence international politics. At that time he made an appeal for Great Britain and the United States on the one hand and the Axis powers on the other to shake hands and unite against Bolshevism, offering the "good offices" of Spain "to achieve the restoration of world peace" immediately. Jordana, who had seen Archbishop Spellman[40] during that dignitary's mission to Spain earlier in the year, continued: "The Holy See, which labors with such love for the welfare of humanity, and those nations the War has spared, will be able without doubt to facilitate the advent of peace and collaboration in the preparation of treaties that will organize the world from the point of view of equity and dispassion. . . ." These samples of Spain's "neutrality" and Jordana's friendliness toward the democracies were, however, overshadowed by the Foreign Minister's frankness in the fall of 1943. At that time he sent a message to José P. Laurel, President of the new Japanese puppet government in the Philippines, congratulating him in the name of Franco and the Spanish Government, and adding: "I can assure you that the relationship between the Philippines and Spain will always be on the plane of perfect comprehension and mutual understanding." (It was explained later that this message was simply the result of a spontaneous overflow of good will toward the Filipinos, and had no political significance whatsoever.)

Yet none of these acts discouraged the advocates of friendly relations with Franco's Spain, which still harbored a million and a half imprisoned Spanish Republicans. In December 1943 Jordana gave a sympathetic Scripps-Howard correspondent, Henry J. Taylor, his first interview in his office in the ancient palace of Santa Cruz. Stated Taylor,

in a subsequent account of the interview: "He [Jordana] is regarded in Washington, London, and here in Madrid as a forthright representative of Spain, and one who is her country's best hope for the improvement of her relations abroad. . . . What General Jordana most wants from the rest of the world is a clear understanding and belief in Spain's united determination for continued neutrality and independence." Jordana told Taylor: "It would be a grave error to shut out from the readjustment of the world those countries which have remained outside the conflict. . . . Their counsel and participation in shaping the new world is indispensable if the world hopes to arrive at a durable peace. . . . Only a complete distortion of the truth can explain how there are those in the United States, for example, who seem to believe that Spanish public opinion is divorced from the Government and does not support its policies and actions. We hear that even the loyalty of the Army is questioned from afar."

In January 1944 the New York *Times'* Harold Denny did Taylor one better. Jordana, according to Denny, was a "gentleman of statesmanlike qualities . . . a moderate in politics" who disliked the Falange, "which has steadily lost ground until now it is only tolerated by the regime it once aspired to dominate." (Actually the Falange had just had its state subsidy tripled, while the Falange militia had been bodily incorporated into the Spanish Army—according to Allan Chase, "to increase, not weaken, the Falange grip on the Army.") At the same time Denny "revealed" that the Nazis were rushing agents to Spain to save a situation which had "gone badly against her" there. These Germans, he said, were responsible for "present and forthcoming anti-Allied outbreaks by Falangist hoodlums in Spain." (Not long before bombs had been included in a shipment of oranges to Great Britain!) Germany's "original hope . . . that Spain would come in on the side of the Axis" had now been frustrated, he said, describing the Spanish Blue Division, still fighting against the Russians though now incorporated into the Nazi Army, as merely a clever means of ridding Spain of criminals "and otherwise undesirable elements."

Spanish Republicans in exile admitted, too, that things were happening in Spain, but they saw no reason for the Nazis to be angry at Franco unless his power was slipping. And that was undeniably true. Months before Juan March himself had told a friend in London that Franco was finished in Spain and that the only way to save Fascism there (and March's own vast holdings) would therefore be through a restoration of the monarchy. Thomas Caballero Peire, Juan March's lawyer, in whose firm Jordana's son is a partner, had reportedly been holding secret meetings with Colonel Juan Beigbeder of the Spanish Army since his arrival in the United States with young Jordana late in December 1943. According to Allan Chase, author of *Falange*, what was being planned for Spain was a fake anti-Nazi *Putsch* which would take place before the German armies in Europe could be destroyed by the combined forces of the United States, Great Britain, and the U.S.S.R., and Jordana was the key man "who, in the name of anti-Fascist revolution, is cut out to strengthen the power of Fascism." Chase continued: "He is neither more or less a Monarchist than Franco himself, but since the Nazis plan to restore Don Juan de Bourbon to the Spanish throne with Jordana as Prime Minister, the count's Monarchist sympathies are being played up." Publicity had already been given to a letter written by Don Juan de Bourbon to Jordana in April 1943 in which the claimant to the Spanish throne announced that he would not accept a monarchial restoration under the Franco regime and called for the "urgent installation of a new national regime which, like that of the traditional and Catholic monarchy, would find itself free from compromising positions and injurious ties and capable of carrying out the concept of strict neutrality."

Hull's angry statement of January 29, 1944, suspending oil shipments to Spain because of Franco's assistance to the Nazis, was replied to by a propaganda campaign seeking to convince the Spanish people that the United States was seeking to destroy Spanish "neutrality." (Actually the State Department had demanded that Franco stop shipping wolfram to the Nazis, withdraw Spanish soldiers from the Soviet Front, and release Italian ships held in Spanish ports.) Shortly afterward Great Britain clamped a rigid blockade on the Bay of Biscay for the announced purpose of stopping Spanish shipments of war materials to Germany via France; and on February 21 the American Foreign Economic Administration decided to continue the oil embargo against Spain during March and prepared a list of other economic sanctions in case the oil embargo failed to force Franco to stop aiding Hitler. (When Spain finally agreed to limit wolfram shipments to Germany to 280 tons for the remainder of 1944, a large share of the credit for the outcome of the negotiations belonged to Jordana, according to the Earl of Selbourne, Britain's Minister of Economic Warfare.)

Attorney General Francis Biddle [41], in the strongest speech yet made by any American government official, identified the Falangist movement as the Spanish counterpart of Nazism and Fascism, and mentioned Franco by name in placing the responsibility for Falangist activities in the Americas. But even these symptoms of increasing Allied pressure on the Spanish dictator did not satisfy everyone. On February 24 Representative John M. Coffee of Washington called for positive action on Spain—an immediate break with Franco and assistance to the Spanish people to help them throw the Germans out of Spain. Increasing Republican activities within Spain itself, he said, was causing the Nazis to consider getting rid of Franco and bringing back the Spanish monarchy, which would form a fake anti-Nazi government with Gil Robles as Premier and men like Jordana as ministers.

This Spaniard who may or may not play a leading role in his country in the future is blue-eyed, blond, "small-framed, quiet-mannered." He has the habit of showing up for work with his staff at 9 a.m., though the Spanish Ministry of Foreign Affairs does not open officially until 4 p.m. and closes at 10 p.m. A soldier as well as a politician, he is the author of *Studies on Military Art*.

References

N Y Times Ag 4 '44 por
N Y World Telegram p2 D 17 '43 por
PM p5 Ja 2 '44; p9 Ja 19 '44
International Who's Who 1942

JULIANA, CROWN PRINCESS OF THE NETHERLANDS Apr. 30, 1909-

Juliana of the Netherlands, Princess of Orange-Nassau and heir to the Dutch throne, is descended from ancient families, long illustrious in the history of their country. The Principality of Orange can be traced to the eighth century; and the origin of the Nassau family—whose prince, William the Silent, founded the Dutch Republic in 1579—goes back to the ninth. The Crown Princess Juliana, if she succeeds her mother Queen Wilhelmina [40], will be the twelfth of her house to rule her people, although actually, according to the custom in other countries, she is the first of a new dynasty, that of Mecklenburg-Schwerin, her father's family. The Dutch, however, most of them loyal supporters of the royal house, have traditionally identified their own fortunes with its fortunes and have consequently given her the Orange-Nassau title. So tenacious are they indeed of that lineage, and so wary of all that is non-Dutch, that in 1922 a constitutional amendment was passed limiting the succession to lineal descendants of Wilhelmina or, those failing, to descendants from the last deceased monarch not further removed than the third degree.

The birth of Juliana was received by the stolid Dutch with more than the usual rejoicing. The Orange-Nassau line had almost become extinct with the Crown Princess' maternal grandfather, William III, and almost again with his daughter Wilhelmina; and the Dutch people were fearful for the future of their country should the family die out. William's wife and sons had died in his old age, and, at the age of sixty-two, he had married the twenty-year-old Princess Emma of Waldeck-Pyrmont, a small German state. Wilhelmina was their only child. Her own marriage in 1901 to Henry Wladimir Albert Ernst, Duke of Mecklenburg-Schwerin and lieutenant in the Prussian Guards, had been joyously acclaimed, but eight years passed before their only child was born.

A fifty-one-gun salute on April 30, 1909 announced the arrival of the long-awaited heir. Two trumpeters rode through The Hague proclaiming the event, business houses closed, and people danced in the streets. Three weeks later the baby received her first military salute from the palace sentry; and on June 5, in the Willemskerk, she was baptized: Juliana Louise Emma Marie Wilhelmina, Princess of Orange-Nassau, Duchess of Meckenburg—Juliana for the mother of William the Silent, Louise for his fourth wife, Louise de Coligny.

The upbringing and education of the Princess were under the direction of her mother. The Queen herself had had a lonely girlhood under the supervision of the autocratic Queen Emma, and was determined that her own daughter should lead a more normal existence. A Socialist disturbance in 1918 had made Wilhelmina realize also that Holland might one

Karsh

CROWN PRINCESS JULIANA
OF THE NETHERLANDS

day become a republic again, so the young Juliana was taught to be a good citizen as well as a good queen. She studied in a palace classroom during her early years in the company of several girls of her own age. The lessons were those given to the average Dutch child; and the teacher was hired from the Jan Ligthart School, noted for its experiments in modern education. Much of the Princess' playtime, too, was like that of other children. When she was ten she joined a choral group composed of children from all economic strata, and on one occasion—to the dismay of some conventional people—sang in a public recital. Like all Dutch children she learned to ice skate, and when she fell she was made to pick herself up. Many summers were spent in travel with her parents; but when Juliana was in Holland she spent her summers at the beach or at girls' camps, where she proved to be a lively tomboy. From childhood she showed her dislike of form and ceremony. At her confirmation, for instance, at her own request she sat with other confirmands in preference to being confirmed alone. Like any normal child she was friendly, intelligent, generally obedient and willing, sometimes unruly and stubborn.

Juliana's youth was not altogether free and easy, however. In addition to her ordinary schooling, she was given severe training in other subjects. She began her religious studies early, she was tutored thoroughly in the Dutch arts of housework and sewing, and she received a rigid education for her future queenship. In many respects, too, although the Princess was brought up more liberally than was her mother, she was sheltered by the severely moral, Calvinist-educated Wilhelmina. "My mother takes me to church, my father to the movies," Juliana once said. She seldom appeared in public, moreover, without one of her parents, and when in 1933 the shy twenty-four-year-old girl made her first trip abroad alone,

this degree of emancipation received comment in the American press.

The Princess' secondary education was compressed into a three-year period, during which time emphasis was laid on modern languages—of foreign tongues she speaks German, Spanish, French, and English—history, and the arts. In 1927 at the age of eighteen Juliana was ready for the University of Leyden, founded in 1574 by her ancestor, William the Silent. The Princess was enrolled as Julia van Bueren, and every attempt was made to allow her to lead as normal a life as possible. With three friends she lived in a small furnished villa at Katwjk, a sea resort and fishermen's village on the outskirts of Leyden. Two ladies in waiting acted as chaperones, and Julia's chamberlain lived next door and sat in all of her classrooms—one of the few signs of the presence of royalty.

In classes Juliana rose with the other students when the professor entered and remained in the room until he had gone. She joined a debating society and the student club that was the center of university activities. In addition, she showed a keen interest in dramatics, writing several light plays which were performed by the students. She had specialized in economics, constitutional law, and Dutch literature, and in December 1929 she concluded her courses, receiving an honorary doctor's degree in literature and law, for which she had taken the required examinations. She has frequently referred to her university days as the happiest of her life; and for several years after leaving Leyden as a student she returned for class reunions. Lionel John Beresford Power, in his book *The Royal Ladies of The Netherlands,* comments that Juliana displayed a notable determination to follow up a point and probe any question, an unwillingness to take anything for granted, and a quick appreciation of a problem.

Juliana's eighteenth birthday was celebrated with the spendor befitting a royal princess; and with this coming of age and her entrance into Dutch society she began to assume some of her duties as heir to the throne. (The country has been a constitutional monarchy since 1814, with a parliament and government responsible to the throne.) She was given a small staff in the palace in the Kneuterdijk and granted a yearly income of over $100,000. She was also made a member of the Council of State, a fourteen-man body appointed by the Queen to which were referred certain legislative and executive matters. From 1931 to 1936 she acted as chairman of the National Crisis Committee that investigated relief and rehabilitation measures following the world depression; and upon the death of her father in 1934 she took over his duties as president of the Netherlands Red Cross.

Of utmost concern to the supporters of the House of Orange, upon Juliana's reaching her majority, was the problem of finding a suitable consort for her. More than a dozen times after 1927 rumors of her engagement were circulated, but Juliana herself showed no apparent interest in rushing into marriage. Potentially one of the most wealthy princesses in Europe (at her mother's death she would inherit a private fortune of $5,000,000 yearly), she had also attractive personal traits. She was credited with more than average intelligence and wit—not the least of the objects of her humor being her own plumpness. She was described as unpretentious, she mingled freely with the people, and took a keen interest in empire affairs. She was fond of sports, was a fine skater and tennis player, and with her mother she often visited the popular Continental winter resorts.

The position of Prince Consort of the Netherlands, however, had a few drawbacks. Foremost perhaps, as the *New Outlook* pointed out in 1935, was the minor and thankless job facing him in a small country, particularly one which had known feminine rule for such a long time. Another consideration was that no man would be acceptable to the Dutch who could conceivably become the ruler of another country or even be strong enough to influence the Dutch Queen. There was an obstacle, too, in the way of choosing someone from among Juliana's future subjects. There were in Holland no peers of the realm, as in England, with such titles and position that would make them eligible as Consort.

It was with mixed emotions, therefore, that the Dutch greeted the announcement, on September 8, 1936, of Juliana's engagement to the bespectacled Bernhard Leopold Frederic Everhard Jules Curt Charles Godfrey Pierre zu Lippe-Biesterfeld. The Prince, born June 29, 1911, was of an ancient German family, whose titles dated from the twelfth century. In 1909 Bernhard's uncle, the reigning prince of the minute principality of Lippe (abolished by the Weimar Republic), had made Armgard, Bernhard's mother, the Countess Biesterfeld, and in 1916 had further conferred upon her and her descendants the title of Lippe-Biesterfeld.

The cosmopolitan but impoverished Bernhard, a minor salaried employee of the colossal German dye trust, I. G. Farbenindustrie Aktiengesellschaft, had received a good education in Munich, Lausanne, and Berlin, having specialized in the legal aspects of international commerce. A good tennis player and skater, he had met the twenty-six-year-old Princess at the 1935 Olympics in Germany, and had, reportedly, proposed to her in Switzerland.

The choice of the German had been in some respects a surprise to the Dutch, but it seemed to be generally popular except with the Socialists, who, according to *Time* Magazine, disapproved of the selection of an "ex-Storm Trooper." It was pointed out, however, that "Benno's" apprenticeship to the dye trust had been served primarily in Paris and that his sympathies did not lie with the Nazis. And, as if in further assurance, Wilhelmina and her daughter broadcast to the world that the alliance would be a marriage for love, while the future bridegroom spoke of his "Hollandish" feelings.

Bernhard relinquished his German affiliations after the engagement was announced and became a naturalized Dutch citizen. He was given honorary naval and military ranks, including a captaincy in the Royal Dutch Huzzars. Upon his marriage he was to become His Royal Highness, Prince of the Netherlands—a title Wilhelmina's consort never held—and was to receive a Civil List from the Dutch Treasury of over $100,000 yearly—an improvement on the humiliating provision that had given Prince Hendrik an allowance out of his wife's private income. Bernhard, moreover, was to be made a member of the Council of State.

The political highlights of the few days before the wedding were of international interest. Attempts by the Germans before the ceremony to advertise it as an alliance of the Netherlands and Nazi Germany were received with dignified denials by the Dutch Government. To the indignation of Hitler '42 and his press, Bernhard refused to insist on the playing of the "Horst Wessel" song and "Deutschland über Alles" at his wedding and on having the streets lined with swastikas. For a time the piqued Germans withheld the passports of three princesses scheduled to be bridesmaids; and at the last moment—although Hitler sent tardy congratulations to the couple —all but one of the Nazi press correspondents were withdrawn from The Hague over a tiff concerning a fourth scheduled member of the wedding party.

One hundred and seven correspondents, however, from other parts of the world—plus the largest crowd in the capital's history—gathered on January 7, 1937, to watch the simple Calvinist ceremonies which united Juliana and Bernhard. A civil ceremony (followed by the customary "Dutch uncle" lecture) preceded the church services at the ancient Groote Kerk. Then, following a wedding breakfast at the Noordeinde, the royal couple slipped away, ostensibly to Innsbruck. But while an Innsbruck hotel manager made lavish preparations for the honeymoon, a Countess and Count von Sternburg—accompanied by twenty-one pieces of luggage and six pairs of skiis—arrived at the stylish Polish winter resort hotel in Krynica, Poland, managed by Jan Kiepura '43. And while even the staid New York *Times* announced in headlines that Juliana and the Prince had "mysteriously" disappeared, a terse royal telegram turned up at Innsbruck reporting that Their Royal Highnesses had made other plans.

Their Royal Highnesses went to live in the Soestdijk palace, a wedding present from the Queen—it had been modernized by the Dutch people as their contribution. The couple became active in relief and child welfare work; they were hosts to regular gatherings of young people, at which professionals debated economic and social questions and hosts and guests alike entered into the discussions. Both the press and the people remarked on the change in the appearance and actions of the Princess: she had bobbed her hair, for one thing, was slimmer, and dressed smartly. There was occurring, it appeared, a revival of the blithe spirit of Juliana's father that had prevailed despite the stiffness of the Dutch court. There was even a slight crisis over certain phases of the transformation. The Prince, it seemed, had a few modern ideas not always acceptable to Wilhelmina and many of her subjects; and the appearance, for example, of the royal couple drinking cocktails in public, and on the Sabbath, caused much criticism.

After the birth of the couple's first child, however, the feeling toward Bernhard softened and he became more popular with the Queen and the people. The child, a girl, was born on January 31, 1938 and was named Beatrix Wil-

JULIANA, CROWN PRINCESS OF THE NETHERLANDS—*Continued*

helmina Armgard, Beatrix being an unroyal, un-Dutch name meaning "happiness." A year later, on August 5, 1939, Irene Emma Elisabeth was born, and again an unroyal, un-Dutch name —meaning "peace"—was chosen.

With the invasion of Holland by the Nazis in 1940 all attempts at normal living came abruptly to an end for Juliana and Bernhard. The day before their country surrendered they escaped to England with their two children on a British destroyer. The following month—"to safeguard the future dynasty"—the Princess and her daughters left for Canada on a Dutch warship to be the guests of the Earl of Athlone, Governor General of Canada, and his wife, the Princess Alice. Bernhard, on the other hand, returned to France, where he fought with the Dutch and the British until the end of Allied resistance on the Continent. He then went back to England to act as aide-de-camp to Queen Wilhelmina (he was made honorary R.A.F. wing commander). In September 1944, when the Allied forces were again on the Continent, Bernard was made commander of the Netherlands interior forces under General Eisenhower [42].

"Never speak to me of the word pity," said the Princess on her arrival in North America. "Pity is for the weak, and our terrible fate has made us stronger than ever before." Thus, as "a private citizen," as she preferred to be called, Juliana set about to live even more simply and unostantatiously in Canada than she had at home, making no demands for the sympathy of her hosts. She moved into a ten-room rented house in Rockcliffe Park, a suburb of Ottawa, taking with her only two servants and a small personal staff. She dressed plainly, often did her own shopping, and helped with the care of the children. "Trix" and Irene were sent to the near-by Elmwood Nursery School and taught to speak English. Princess Juliana then made only two requests: that they be treated as the other children, and that they be relieved from hearing and reading stories involving fairy princesses. An interviewer from *Knickerbocker Weekly* visited them in 1943, later writing of the reticence of Juliana about her private life, which, he reported, was much like any middle-class Dutch family.

Wilhelmina only visited her daughter and grandchildren twice after their arrival in Canada. In the summer of 1942 she made her first trip—a two-and-one-half-month official visit—to North America, visiting Ottawa, Boston, Albany, New York, and Washington. During a part of her stay she and her family vacationed in the Berkshires. The following summer the Queen again flew to Canada, this time for a private visit with Juliana.

Bernhard visited Canada occasionally, too, usually after connection with Government missions for the Queen. One of his visits was for the birth of his third child, Margriet Francisca, on January 17, 1943. The baby was named after the marguerite, the May daisy which symbolizes the month Holland entered the War. The legal problem of the birth of royalty on foreign soil was adjusted through the granting of temporary extraterritorial rights to the hospital room where the Dutch Princess was born.

In December 1940 Juliana made her first trip to the United States as guest of President [42] and Mrs. Roosevelt [40]. After that she made numerous other journeys to the States to visit Dutch centers or to review Dutch activities, and she made frequent speeches. In 1941 she was present to receive honorary degrees from Hope College in Holland, Michigan, the seventy-five-year-old institution of Holland's Reformed Church in America, and from Mt. Holyoke College and Princeton University. In 1943 the Princess made the first visit for the Orange family to the Netherlands territories in the West Indies, and in 1944 she went there again. During the summer of 1944 she vacationed with her daughters on Cape Cod in Massachusetts. In September, with Allied successes on the Continent and the approaching liberation of her own country, she flew back to England to join her mother once more.

"Queen Wilhelmina never had a better envoy to represent the Netherlands in Canada and the United States than her daughter," a correspondent once said. The five-foot-eight-inch-tall Princess with her golden brown hair and bright blue eyes, impresses those whom she meets with her unassuming friendliness and intelligence. She is still shy and, when accompanied by the Prince at interviews, defers to him. The one favor she had asked of her hosts was that they give her children their smiles and her family their "strengthening love."

References

C S Mon p9 S 13 '40 por
Collier's 111:16+ Ja 23 '43 por
Knickerbocker W p 4-7 Ag 2 '43 il
Ladies' H J 37:183-4 Ap 20 il por
Lit Digest 122:13-14 S 19 '36 por; 123:
   11-12 Ja 16 '37 por
N Y World-Telegram p23 Je 4 '43 il por
New Outlook 165:55-6 F '35
Time 29:22-4 Ja '37 il por; 35:37 Je 24
   '40

International Who's Who 1942
Power, L. J. B. Royal Ladies of the
   Netherlands 1939

KAY-SCOTT, C(YRIL)   *See* Wellman, F. C.

KELLOGG, JOHN HARVEY   Feb. 26, 1852—Dec. 14, 1943   Surgeon, inventor, founder of the Battle Creek Sanitarium and the W. K. Kellogg Cereal Company; discoverer of therapeutic value of electric light and sinusoidal current; inventor of the electric light bath and improved apparatus and instruments for medical and surgical purposes.

Obituary

N Y Times p28 D 16 '43 por

KENNEDY, JOHN B(RIGHT)   Jan. 16, 1894-   Radio commentator; journalist

Address: b. c/o James S. Appell, 400 Madison Ave., New York City

One of the best-known voices in radio belongs to John B. Kennedy, the news analyst and commentator. Kennedy became one of radio's early star newscasters after a career as newspaperman, foreign correspondent, magazine writer, and editor. In January 1944 he left WNEW and through 1944 was heard regularly over the Blue Network of the National Broadcasting Company. A newsreel commentator on Hearst's *News of the Day* for about seven years, Kennedy's face is also familiar to motion-picture audiences. Of his persuasive reportorial manner an enthusiastic press agent has said that if Kennedy were to declare "the moon is made of green cheese," a listener might pause for just a moment and consider the possibility that Kennedy was right.

John Bright Kennedy probably inherited his way with words from his Irish father, John J. Kennedy, who with his French wife, Georgianna B. (Delara) Kennedy, was living in Quebec, Canada at the time of their son's birth there on January 16, 1894. Kennedy received most of his education in the United States, although he also attended schools in Canada and England. He was in such haste to begin writing that he left St. Louis University in 1913 to become a newspaper reporter in that city.

As soon as he had gained a toehold in the newspaper business Kennedy began to move up. He went from city room to city room, from Chicago to Canada to New York, always stepping into a better position. By the time the United States entered the First World War, Kennedy had been sent to Europe as a foreign correspondent.

He remained abroad after the Armistice had been signed in order to do relief work as a director of the Knights of Columbus. In that capacity he became associated with Herbert Hoover '43, who was serving in Europe as the Food Administrator for the United States. (Kennedy has been decorated by the Governments of France and Belgium for his relief work for victims of the First World War.) Kennedy's connection with the Knights of Columbus led him in 1921 to found a weekly magazine called *Columbia*; this periodical, of which Kennedy was the first editor, became the national publication of the Knights of Columbus. That same year his first magazine article, a brief piece dealing with the history of the Knights of Columbus, was published in *Current History* Magazine. (He was already co-author of a book, *The K. of C. in Peace and War,* published in 1920.)

Kennedy's entrance into the magazine field led him away from newspaper work, for in 1924, when he went back to his original occupation of writing, he joined the staff of *Collier's Weekly*. There he resumed the upward climb which had been interrupted by the War and by his duties in connection with the work of European rehabilitation. He was promoted to the post of managing editor of *Collier's* and later became associate editor of the magazine. His output during his stay with *Collier's* established something of a record: he produced nearly two hundred feature articles and short stories for that magazine, as well as numerous items for other publications such as the *Mentor* and the *American Mercury*.

The now familiar voice of Kennedy was heard over the radio for the first time in 1934 when he left his editorial post, temporarily he thought, in order to direct a radio pro-

JOHN B. KENNEDY

gram sponsored by *Collier's*. As a master of ceremonies on the air show he attracted many steady listeners who made their approval known with letters of praise. Although Kennedy had never considered giving up writing he had not foreseen the widespread popularity which the new medium of communication has given him— the audience he could reach through the radio dwarfed the largest magazine circulation. He hesitated, weighing the pros and cons of writing and broadcasting, before deciding that "the microphone was mightier than the pen."

Following his broadcasts for *Collier's* Kennedy became known as an ace announcer and a news commentator of great persuasion and conviction. His voice has been described as "biting, curt, incisive," and his manner of speech as "direct, hardbiting, and sincere." His admirers claim that if he chose to do so Kennedy could make a commonplace, trite statement sound like a newly discovered and highly original fact. For several seasons Kennedy's comments were a regular intermission feature of the General Motors radio concerts and of the *Magic Key*. He was graduated from the position of announcer for the NBC network programs to that of news commentator and political analyst for the same network, and later, for the Columbia Broadcasting System.

From April 1941 to January 7, 1944 Kennedy conducted his programs of news commentaries over the independent radio station WNEW. He has been with the Blue Network since midsummer of 1943. According to Chester La Roche, station executive, Kennedy is regarded as one of the Blue's most experienced and popular commentators. Sometimes well-timed predictions are fulfilled by the unfolding of events. In one instance in 1942 Kennedy announced to his listeners that Italy would be bombed into revolt against the Fascist regime, adding that because of the "cruel necessity of the devilish conflict Hitler '42 brewed," Italy would have to bear the first brunt of attack by the Allies. The

KENNEDY, JOHN B.—*Continued*

Italians, he said, would be reluctant to fight either the British or the Americans, and would use any pretext to avoid an armed clash.

Kennedy's work requires him to travel almost constantly; he probably has covered more territory than anyone else with the possible exception of Eleanor Roosevelt'[40] and those persons engaged in the transportation business. One week, for example, his broadcast may originate near the Golden Gate at San Francisco, and a few days later he may be found with a microphone on top of the Statue of Liberty in New York harbor. Kennedy himself rarely knows where his work will take him next. Very often he doesn't decide where he will go until the last minute; when he does decide, it sometimes is so late that he has to travel by plane to arrive on time.

Kennedy has been married to the former Blanche Gayhart of Toronto, Canada, since 1916. They have two daughters, Constance and Josephine.

A one-sport athlete, Kennedy plays a good game of golf. He can swim only, it is reported, with the help of a rope. He is more proficient in less strenuous forms of relaxation, however, such as drinking beer, talking to old Broadwayites, and smoking a pipe both in and out of bed. He never pays the slightest attention to his mail, and as often as he is allowed he will be found preparing his broadcasts in the Kennedy kitchen.

References

American Catholic Who's Who 1942-43
Variety Radio Directory 1938-39

KIESLER, FREDERICK J(OHN) (kēs' lẽr) Sept. 22, 1892- Architect; designer; teacher

Address: b. Juilliard School of Music, 120 Claremont Ave., New York City; h. 56 Seventh Ave., New York City

"My eyes have never bulged farther from their sockets than at this show," wrote Henry McBride of the New York *Sun*, reviewing the opening of the Guggenheim Art of This Century Gallery in October 1942. He was not referring to the futuristic art objects on display—those much-disputed works had been passed over. His exclamation was called forth by the startlingly original construction of the gallery itself. "Going through the rooms," wrote Emily Genauer, "is a mystifying and delightful experience. You feel like a child with a new toy that does all sorts of unpredictable things. . . . Frederick J. Kiesler, modern architect and designer, who is also director of the laboratory of Columbia University's School of Architecture, did . . . a job to make exhibition history. There are four separate divisions in this gallery, one . . . with [frameless] paintings fastened from triangular suspension columns . . . and with one wall a long undulating surface of marine blue canvas; a second . . . utilizing convex wood walls from which protrude . . . sawed-off baseball bats which can be adjusted so visitors may examine pictures from all angles; a third, in which pictures are shown automati-

cally, controlled by an invisible light beam; and a fourth room, which is really a painting library with special mobile stands and bins so that the visitor may devise a little exhibition all for himself." All this, in the designer's words, was to enable "the artist's work to stand forth as a vital entity in a spatial world, and art stand forth as a vital link in the structure of a new myth."

Frederick John Kiesler, who designed this startling gallery, was born in Vienna, September 22, 1892, the son of Julius and Rosemarie (Meister) Kiesler. He received his M.A. degree from the Technische Hochschule, Vienna, and from the Akademie der Bildenden Künste (Academy of Plastic Arts), also in Vienna, where he won "various first prizes."

Kiesler began his career as an architect by working with Adolf Loos on the first slum clearance and rehousing projects in Vienna. He made the first of his many innovations, the use of motion pictures rather than painted canvas as backdrops for the Berlin production of *R.U.R.*, in 1922. With the presentation of *The Emperor Jones*, Kiesler introduced the "space stage," with "continuous motion of scenery coordinated with acting, speech, and lighting." This "space stage" was again demonstrated in a full-size model in Vienna, where Kiesler was director and architect of the International Theatre and Music Festival, held in 1924. For the festival he devised the "Leger and Träger" (coined words, for which there is no exact translation) exhibition method, based on the suspension principle, which he applied to house construction in the model planned community at the Paris World's Fair. Kiesler was also named director of the theatre and film sections of the Austrian exhibit.

Kiesler came to the United States in 1926 at the invitation of the Theatre Guild, the Provincetown Playhouse, and the *Little Review* to create the exhibition of international theatre technique for the opening of Steinway Hall in New York. That same year he was commissioned to design the famous Museum of Modern Art.

Kiesler next entered into the prize competition for a community center and theatre at Woodstock, New York. His was the winning solution to the problem posed by a small group of permanent residents, augmented in summer by a large colony of experimental artists. By the use of movable partitions, runways, wheeled cycloramas, and arena stages, Kiesler devised a playhouse flexible enough to be suitable for any performance, from circus to grand opera, and for any size group, from convention to club meeting. In addition, the community center included club headquarters, exhibition halls, an open terrace restaurant, an emergency hotel, a gas station, parking space for 250 cars, and a housewife's dream of storage space!

Motion pictures, Kiesler felt, required an essentially different type of building from the standard theatre, but "we have never solved this problem—we have only increased the size and decoration of theatre buildings and used them for motion pictures." Planning the Film Guild Cinema auditorium in 1928 gave him a chance to put his ideas on the subject into practice. He eliminated the curtains, platform, and proscenium, replacing them by a device he called the "screen-o-scope." In 1928, too, he wrote *Contemporary Art Applied to the Store and Its Display*, which was published in 1930.

During the next six years, Kiesler built display windows for Saks Fifth Avenue; remodeled a bookstore; constructed the exhibition of the Association of American Designers; served as consulting architect for the National Public Housing Conference; created new lines of lighting equipment; and built a full-size model of his "space house" in New York City. He accepted a position on the faculty of the Juilliard School of Music as director of scenic design, creating, in 1934, settings and costumes for the school's production of Erskine's *Helen Retires* and Strauss's *Ariadne on Naxos*.

The 1935 City of Buffalo award for the best store design of the year went to Kiesler; but he spent most of the year designing opera productions for the Metropolitan Opera as well as for the Juilliard School. "Mr. Kiesler," said Samuel Chotzinoff '40 in *Town and Country*, "has the very rare ability to produce imaginative settings out of simple and inexpensive materials. The bills he runs up . . . are ideal for a depression era, yet his stage rooms and gardens offer no suggestion of parsimony. The figures for those productions of the Juilliard School that Mr. Kiesler created would make the stingiest board of directors happy. *Ariadne on Naxos* cost $1,500; *Helen Retires*, $500; and *Maria Malibran*, the princely sum of $4,000. . . . *In the Pasha's Garden*, which Mr. Kiesler mounted for the Metropolitan, set Gatti-Casazza back $1,500, probably the smallest sum that was ever expended on a good or bad opera at that lavish institution." Its sets included "a moon built to telescopic photographic design."

In 1937, after a year in which he devoted himself to interior designs and furniture construction, Kiesler wrote a series of articles, "The Architect in Search of Design Correlation," for the *Architectural Record*. "What we call forms," he wrote, "are only the visible trading posts of integrating and disintegrating forces mutating at a low rate of speed." "We must keep in mind that science in all its branches is based upon man's deficiency." "The one way to resolve this age-old contradiction [between beauty and utility] is to find one criterion which will do for all. This criterion, in my opinion, can only be health."

At this time Kiesler joined the School of Architecture of Columbia University as director of its laboratory for design correlation, which is "the coordination of paint, sculpture, industrial furnishing, and building structure into a heterogeneous unity called architecture."

Serving as member of the faculty and director of scenic design at the Juilliard School of Music, Kiesler created sets and costumes for operas by Mozart, Offenbach, and many others. An exhibition of his work for the school, "Ten Years of Opera Design," held in 1941 by the New York Public Library, drew this typical comment: "As remarkable as the fresh, imaginative quality of the work is the fact that it was all done by architects—by Kiesler himself and by selected students from the Columbia School of Architecture. Typical of the unconventional and highly successful solutions developed is the setting for *The Magic Flute*, in which a continuous roll of eleven

FREDERICK J. KIESLER

paintings, set in a baroque frame, meets the problem of simplifying a great variety of required backgrounds. . . . The setting for *Abduction from the Seraglio* . . . provided a single set for an opera normally considered to require three. . . . *Ariadne on Naxos* has a two-story set, with changes provided mainly by curtains. The stage design for *Helen Retires* harks back to Constructivist experiments, depends largely on lighting for its effect."

Kiesler has been quoted to the effect that "not only do architects make first-rate stage designers, but that stage design makes better architects. Reason is that in a few weeks the architect must meet and solve a myriad of problems involving both people and esthetic considerations. He must create a setting that permits every action of the singers to be properly carried out, take care of all mechanical requirement of lighting and scene-shifting, and produce a suitable atmosphere." The people involved include the actors and singers, director, business manager, stage-hands, property manager, and audience.

During this period Kiesler designed a display exhibition for the Museum of Modern Art; built a new exhibition hall for the School of Architecture of Columbia University; served as a member of the Advisory Board for the Advancement of Science and Art at Cooper Union; and published an article, "On Correalism and Biotechnique." "Design," he wrote, "is in my definition not the circumscription of a solid but a deliberate polarization of natural forces toward a specific human purpose." He advocated "continuous construction" aiming at "reduction of joints, making for higher resistance, higher rigidity, easier maintenance, lower costs." The year after this article appeared Kiesler's ideas were adopted by unanimous resolution of the Ann Arbor Conference on Design. In 1942 Kiesler announced the "first completion of extensive research work on sight, vision, and imagery, including design for a three-dimen-

KIESLER, FREDERICK J.—*Continued*
sional model for the demonstration of these
investigations" which had been carried on
since 1937.

Perhaps Kiesler's most spectacular achievement is the Art of this Century Gallery,
plans for which were completed in April
1942. This consists actually of four galleries,
one designed for Cubist and abstract paintings
and sculpture, two for Surrealist objects,
and one for changing exhibitions. All installations, including walls, are movable and
demountable, and all construction was designed to minimize expense, labor, and maintenance costs. Kiesler's aim was to coordinate architecture with painting and sculpture,
and all three with the spectator, by means
of his spatial-exhibition method. This "consists in not using walls for hanging pictures
or for placing pedestals . . . but of an arrangement . . . throughout the space available
using . . . various methods of cantilever and
suspension construction. One of the main
features of such spatial exhibition is the
necessity of eliminating all frames.

"Improvements in lighting have been attempted especially in one of the permanent
galleries where the indirect lighting can be
controlled for each painting individually. In
all galleries, however, the color, intensity, and
diffusion of light have been correlated in a
new manner . . . by planning the reflection
coefficients of all the surfaces of the room
in color as well as in volume and their combined effect upon the paintings." The daylight gallery gives the spectator a chance to
readjust or rearrange the paintings as he
chooses. "The fourth gallery is devoted to
an automatic method of showing pictures . . .
conceived to add more display space within
a small area." Art critics reviewing the exhibition devoted few words to the objects
exhibited, and almost complete columns to
Kiesler's presentation of them. Henry Mc-
Bride, writing in the New York *Sun,* summed
up opinion: "Frederick J. Kiesler . . . called
in . . . to install these amazing pictures and
carvings, has made such a startling job of it
that these still questionable works of art,
that have been disputed at every turn . . .
almost escape the question marks that are
usually hurled at them, and seem to tie
themselves naturally enough to the 'age of
demolition.' 'We, the inheritors of chaos,'
says Mr. Kiesler, 'must be the architects of
a new unity,' and the mere fact that the
pictures escape criticism suggests that something of his goal has been achieved."

In addition to his duties as a faculty
member of the Juilliard School of Music
and of the Columbia University School of
Architecture, Kiesler is now writing a book
on "biotechnique," doing illustrations for
Ovid, and planning several museum exhibits.
He would have all zoos except the "natural
area" type abolished, for his sympathies are
with the captive animals whose feet become
sore from the concrete floors of their cages.

Kiesler is a short man (five feet two inches
tall), weighing 145 pounds. His hair is
brown, his eyes are a "very dark brown," although his complexion is light. He is a naturalized citizen of the United States, and by

creed a Protestant. In 1920 he was married
to Stefi Fritsch; they have no children.

Kiesler joined the Dutch architects' organization, De Stijl, in 1923, and his favorite
recreations are typography, shooting, and
chess. It is not a usual combination; but he
has an even less usual characteristic—the ability to look at an ordinary object, such as a
bookcase, and design another which makes the
first one substandard.

References

Arch Rec 81:6-15 F '37 por
Who's Who in American Art 1940-41

KIMBALL, JAMES HENRY   Feb. 13,
1862—Dec. 21, 1943 Meteorologist, head of
the United States Weather Bureau in New
York; "unanimously regarded as one of the
world's outstanding meteorologists," he charted
historic flights such as those of Lindbergh '41,
Byrd '42, Chamberlin, and Williams and Yan-
cey; his *Storm Log of the North Atlantic*
has been a classic for many years.

Obituary

N Y Times p23 D 22 '43 por

KIMBROUGH, EMILY   (kim'brō)   Oct.
23, 1899-   Author; editor
Address: h. Avon Rd., Haverford, Pa.

Emily Kimbrough, writes her friend and
literary collaborator, Cornelia Otis Skinner '42,
"is that rare creature: a woman who is brilliantly witty and at the same time amazingly
kind. She loves people and has the priceless
gift of bringing out unsuspected qualities of
humor and gaiety in the most drab individual.
. . . To know Emily Kimbrough is to en-
hance one's days with gaiety, charm, and
occasional terror. . . . To quote her own
words, she 'attracts incident as serge attracts
lint.' The fact that she once set forth to visit
me in my modest New York apartment and
arrived by mistake . . . at the mansion of
Mr. J. P. Morgan, gives one a rough idea of
what to expect. She goes through life attended by adventure and a convoy of guardian
angels, for no matter how awkward the situation into which she hurtles, she invariably
emerges intact and triumphant."

Although Miss Kimbrough has been distinguished in the editorial and literary fields
since the middle nineteen-twenties, she did not
attain national celebrity until the publication
of the best-selling *Our Hearts Were Young
and Gay* (1942), which was written by Miss
Kimbrough in collaboration with Miss Skinner. Emily Kimbrough was born in Muncie,
Indiana, October 23, 1899, the daughter of
Hal Curry and Charlotte Emily (Wiles) Kimbrough. For her preparatory education she
attended girls' schools in Chicago, then went
to Bryn Mawr College, from which she received her B.A. degree in 1921. In 1923 she
did graduate work at the Sorbonne.

Sometime during the early 'twenties Miss
Kimbrough and her friend, Cornelia Otis
Skinner, saved the cost of a minimum passage
on a liner of the cabin class and undertook
to spend a summer's vacation in England and
France. Miss Skinner, who is the narrator

of their record of this perilous voyage (*Our Hearts Were Young and Gay*), refuses to give the exact date of the trip because, she informs the reader, they were both nineteen at the time and the date would therefore reveal their present ages. However, since Miss Kimbrough gives her birth year as 1899, she, at least, must have been a year or two older than nineteen.

The two of them enjoyed their summer's vacation even though "Emily had an inborn faculty for attracting disasters minor and major." Before they even arrived at the ocean they were shipwrecked—on the St. Lawrence River—and Emily hit a drowning man with a chair, which she had thrown to him instead of a life-preserver. As they were approaching England, Cornelia developed measles and had to be smuggled past the quarantine officials, thickly disguised in foundation cream and a white veil. "Their most side-splitting escapade," writes Beatrice Sherman, "was a bout of deck tennis. Both signed up for a tournament, were aghast when it turned out to be a game they'd never played, and nearly died of panic when Emily had to play in the first round partnered by the Australian champion against two businesslike Britishers. Emily went through with it, in high heels and a shirtwaist whose tail kept breezing out, and distinguished herself by beaning the titled umpire."

After these spectacular adventures (and a time at the Sorbonne without Cornelia) Miss Kimbrough returned to the United States, and in 1923 started her career as an advertising copy writer. In that same year, in Chicago, she became editor of the Marshall Field store's magazine *Fashions of the Hour*, and held that position until 1926, when she left to become fashion editor of the *Ladies' Home Journal*. In 1927 Miss Kimbrough became the managing editor of the *Journal*. In this year she married John Wrench, from whom she was divorced several years later. Her twin daughters, Margaret Achsah and Alis Emily, were born in 1929, and she gave up editorial work in order to devote more time to her family. Until 1942 she was a free-lance writer, her articles appearing in such magazines as *Country Life, House and Garden, Good Housekeeping*, etc. She also did promotional and publicity work for organizations in and around Philadelphia, where she had taken up residence on the Main Line, and she busied herself with civic affairs and war work.

"Although our trip abroad occurred in the early twenties," writes Miss Skinner, "it is still fresh in our memories and whenever we have both found ourselves at any gathering of kindred spirits, I have called upon Emily to relate this or that incident which took place on our delirious voyage. Last summer [1941] we hit upon the idea of writing it up. Emily, who has the memory of an elephant, was able to recall every detail of those giddy months, and she writes with the same humor with which she talks."

The record of their youthful adventures, *Our Hearts Were Young and Gay*, was published in 1942 with illustrations by Constantin Alajálov '42, and was an immediate success. "It is," wrote Beatrice Sherman in the New

York *Times*, "a fine, funny, effervescent tale. . . . *Our Hearts Were Young and Gay* ranks decidedly in the upper bracket of recent reminiscence books." That the book is a "joyous chronicle from beginning to end" was the general opinion of all the reviewers.

In 1943 both Miss Kimbrough and Miss Skinner were invited to Hollywood, on an expense account plus reportedly immense salaries, to write what, Burton Rascoe says, "turned out to be about . . . two recognizable words of the scenario of . . . *Our Hearts Were Young and Gay* for the movies." In December 1944, after it was announced that a film sequel to *Our Hearts Were Young and Gay* would go into production in January, Miss Skinner and Miss Kimbrough instituted action to restrain Paramount from using their names in the proposed film (entitled *Our Hearts Were Growing Up*). The authors held "it was never our understanding or intention to permit the defendant to use our names as the names of characters in a story or picture made entirely of fictional material and in no way connected with us or our lives."

Toward the end of 1943 *We Followed Our Hearts to Hollywood* (1943), written by Miss Kimbrough alone, appeared. Rascoe commented that the book is "not much more than a bread-and-butter open letter to all the people who entertained her and Cornelia Otis Skinner . . . when they went out to the cinema capital." The New York *Sun*'s critic called it "an entertaining book, made no less so by the Helen Hokinson illustrations, but it is far from being another *Hearts*. . . . Things which are naturally funny when they happen to those with young and gay hearts seem a little absurd when they involve those older and supposedly wiser." According to the New York *Times* reviewer, too, there are "some nervous moments of normality" in it.

The precise nature of Miss Kimbrough's humor has been a matter of interest to some of her literary critics. Although certain episodes in her book seem very close to broad farce, her tone, according to Rosemary Carr Benét, writing in the *Saturday Review of Literature*, is usually "a note of light, amusing reporting." Her attitude "is half the wide-eyed interest and surprise of a young person and half the sophisticated view of an experienced grown-up." It is this attitude, continues Mrs. Benét, which makes Miss Kimbrough's book "the record of a warm, outgiving personality with a talent for making friends and a zest for life." Sterling North '43 disagrees with Mrs. Benét: In her book about Hollywood, Emily Kimbrough shows herself "something of a snob and a lion hunter," he believes.

In November 1944 Miss Kimbrough's latest book, *How Dear to My Heart*, an account of life in Muncie, Indiana, at the turn of the century, was published. Critic Harry Hansen '42 of the *World-Telegram* finds "something of Booth Tarkington's landscape here. . . . Emily Kimbrough has made her story lively without making fun of anybody. . . . She has described pretty truthfully all the events that seem momentous to a little girl, in just the right manner." According to the New York *Sun*'s critic, "its interest is somewhat uneven,

EMILY KIMBROUGH

and it lacks the sparkle of *Our Hearts Were Young and Gay*. . . . It contains too many touches that have appeared in other books of reminiscence." And Nona Balakian wrote about the book in the New York *Times*: "Not to be classed with the other two 'heart' books, *How Dear to My Heart* is full of that wide-eyed exuberance which, unhappily most of us have put away with childish things. Unless you compare her to past masters of childhood lore, you will welcome Miss Kimbrough at her youngest if not her gayest."

At present Miss Kimbrough is lecturing on Hollywood and is working upon a book for children. "She finds time," writes Miss Skinner, "to raise, in addition to her twins, miniature poodles who prance out of the ring adorned with blue ribbons at dog shows. To give only two examples of the variety of her interests, she sings Bach with a choral society and works avidly over new dishes with a group of gastronomic epicures." Miss Kimbrough says of herself: "I have an uneasy feeling that there are certain things in my life about which I am inclined to be boastful; at least I like to bring them into the conversation. I made quite a large collection of butterflies when I was a child; I acted in the Greek plays with Margaret Anglin; I got the lowest mark in mathematics of anyone ever admitted to Bryn Mawr; I have twins; and Marian Anderson '40 is a friend of mine."

References

Ladies' Home J 60:17-18+ N '43
N Y Times Book R p5 N 22 '42
Sat R Lit 26:30 D 11 '43 por

Kimbrough, E. We Followed Our Hearts to Hollywood 1943
Skinner, C. O. and Kimbrough, E. Our Hearts Were Young and Gay 1942

KINGDON, FRANK Feb. 27, 1894- Educator; clergyman; commentator; author
Address: b. 120 E. 16th St., New York City; h. 58 Edgewood Ave., West Orange, N. J.

That Man in the White House (1944), Frank Kingdon's "succinct and unequivocal statement of the reasons why, in terms of both domestic and international issues, the writer considered it necessary to elect Franklin D. Roosevelt '42 for a fourth term as President," has been hailed by proponents of the fourth term as one of the most significant works of campaign literature produced in 1944. The author began his career as a minister, rose to the presidency of a university, and became, in the days before Pearl Harbor, an outspoken publicist for United States intervention in the Second World War and the champion of oppressed European minorities. In 1944 he is one of the foremost liberal political commentators on the air and has two radio programs—a Sunday morning spot over WOR Mutual and a program of daily news comment over station WMCA.

Although English-born, Frank Kingdon has held United States citizenship since 1918 and has identified himself completely with the American social and political scene. The youngest of thirteen children, he was born in London, February 27, 1894, the son of devoutly religious Wesleyan parents, John and Matilda (Caunt) Kingdon. Young Kingdon spent his boyhood in the heart of London. It was in the midst of crowded city life that he learned his first lessons in democracy, for the occasional sight of royalty driving through that part of town proved disillusioning to him. He ceased to be a royalist, Kingdon writes in his autobiography, *Jacob's Ladder* (1943), while witnessing Edward VII's funeral procession. As the long queue of European royalty rode past he realized that they were ordinary men, no different from the men who stood around him. Thus, Kingdon comments, "I count King Edward's funeral day as the definitive turning point in my political road. Solemnly I became a democratic man. An old loyalty became ashes, and from them a new spark passionately took flame, its fire burning more and more intensely with the unfolding years."

When Kingdon was eleven years old he won a scholarship to the University College School in London. Handicapped somewhat by a cockney accent which he soon lost, he made a good showing in his studies and in sports. Upon graduation he went to work as a clerk in a London office. London at the turn of the century was an exciting city, and young Kingdon was thrilled by his occasional visits to Fabian Society meetings where Bernard Shaw '44 and G. K. Chesterton debated, and to the theatre where he saw Sarah Bernhardt.

From childhood Kingdon had been deeply religious, and he had resolved, while still very young, to make the ministry his career. He has written: "As my childhood rounded through my eleventh toward my twelfth birthday, the strongest influences of my growing years gathered themselves together in my consciousness to produce in me a powerful religious experience." Teaching Sunday school and speaking for the Salvation Army won Kingdon valuable experience. His first ser-

mon from the pulpit was preached informally
at only a few minutes notice. When the regular preacher failed to appear for his sermon,
Kingdon was obliged to run all the way to
church in order to be there on time. At a loss
for a text, he chose an eight-stanza hymn
for the congregation to sing. Since it is the
English custom to sing every stanza of a
hymn, Kingdon had time to leaf through the
Bible for a text while the congregation was
singing.

His fervent admiration for democracy and
the fact that two of his best friends had
settled in the United States finally convinced
Kingdon that he should follow them. In 1912
he immigrated to Portland, Maine, where at
the age of eighteen he was ordained a minister
of the Methodist Church. Kingdon's first
parish was the rugged farm country of North
Palermo and China, Maine. The young minister spent most of his time traveling back and
forth through his parish, which was twenty-
five miles long and ten miles wide. It proved
a fruitful experience for Kingdon, rooting
him strongly in the American tradition. He
has written: "No better introduction to the
United States could any stranger have had.
Here was the community in its simplest form.
. . . To know it therefore was to know America from the beginning."

After one year in this area Kingdon was sent
to Harmony, Maine, where, he says, his chief
adventure was meeting and marrying Gertrude Littlefield. The marriage took place
February 27, 1915. By this time Kingdon had
adapted himself well to his new country. In
1914 he had campaigned vigorously for the
Bull Moose candidates in the Congressional
elections and had taken out his first papers
for American citizenship. Busy with family
life, church activities, and social work, Kingdon nevertheless looked forward to the time
when he might continue his formal education.
In 1916 he was appointed to the pastorate in
Hull, Massachusetts, and it was thus possible
for him to attend Boston University.

Kingdon became an American citizen in 1918.
Two years later he received his B.A. and his
Phi Beta Kappa key from Boston University
and was awarded a Jacob Sleeper Fellowship
at Harvard, where from 1920 to 1921 he studied philosophy and religion. In 1921 Kingdon moved to Michigan to accept the pastorate
of the Central Methodist Church in Lansing.
He remained there until 1928, taking additional
graduate work in social psychology at Michigan State College. He received the D.D.
degree from Albion College in 1927.

From Michigan, Frank Kingdon moved to
East Orange, New Jersey, to become the pastor
of Calvary Church. He played an active part
in New Jersey affairs and was soon "a prom-
inent figure in the cultural life of that state."
In 1934 he was offered the presidency of Dana
College in New Jersey and resigned from the
Calvary Church to accept this post. Two years
later Dana College merged with four other
Newark colleges to form the University of
Newark, with Frank Kingdon as its first presi-
dent. In addition to his university work, he
served as president of the Newark Welfare
Federation, campaign chairman of the Newark
Community Chest, and an active worker for

FRANK KINGDON

the National Conference of Christians and
Jews.

When the Second World War broke out
Kingdon took a leave of absence from his
university post to study movements in the
United States "designed to break down the
nation's democratic ideals." This work proved
so absorbing that in 1940 Kingdon resigned as
president of the University in order to devote
all his time to it. He served as educational
director of the Citizenship Educational Service,
a group "engaged in coordinating democratic
education among social welfare, civic, and labor
organizations." When the Committee To Defend America by Aiding the Allies was formed,
Kingdon became chairman of the New York
division. He also acted as chairman of the
Emergency Rescue Committee and as a member of the executive committee of the Committee for Refugee Education and of the
United States Committee for the Care of
European Children. Kingdon's lectures and
magazine articles soon won him nationwide
fame. He favored United States intervention in the War, arguing, "I do with all my
heart believe that democracy is not going
to be preserved by the world if it merely adopts
a defensive attitude behind barricades."

Kingdon has written that the War, which
he calls a "people's war," will mark a reorganization of Western institutions, particularly the institutions of laissez faire capitalism
and national sovereignty. The following elements will be included in the new world order:
"modification of laissez faire capitalism in the
interests of economic justice; the establishment
of recognized international law; and the repudiation of war." Although a bitter foe
of Nazism, Kingdon does not agree with Dr.
Richard M. Brickner's [43] theory that Germany
is psychologically "incurable," nor with the
program of Lord Vansittart [41]. He says: "To
dismember Germany is to deny history. She
is what she is, and what she is she will be."
Kingdon's plans for a post-War world would

KINGDON, FRANK—*Continued*

include action to feed and rehabilitate Europe, the establishment of an international congress and court, and an international army.

Kingdon started his regular radio broadcasts early in 1943. He proved himself an outspoken liberal, urging unity among the Allied powers, condemning the Smith '41-Connally '41 Act and other proposed anti-labor measures, deploring race and religious prejudice, the poll tax, and any attempt made to stifle free speech and criticism on the air. His advocacy of a fourth term for President Roosevelt did not come as a surprise to those who had followed his broadcasts and his magazine articles. In 1942 he had written of the President: "He is the greatest interpreter of democracy in our contemporary world. But no man can feel about democracy as he does without caring about human beings, and the weakness stemming from this is that he does not like to hurt people even when efficiency demands it. As an administrator, he suffers from the weakness inherent in the great strength of his character."

That Man in the White House was written in answer to a letter Kingdon had received from one of his sons who was serving overseas in the armed forces. In this letter his son had asked, "What is going to happen in 1944?" The book contains the father's answer. In a message appended to the book Rex Stout points out that the leaders of the United Nations would be suspicious of any newly elected Republican President at the peace table. "They will know, and he will know, that he is there because our isolationists, our chauvinists, our reactionaries, our labor baiters, our anti-Semites, our home-grown fascists helped to put him there." Frank Kingdon's thesis was not that Roosevelt was the indispensable man, but simply that at the time there was no man better equipped to take his place.

Comment on *That Man in the White House* was determined largely by the politics of each reviewer. Harry Hansen '42, while admitting that the author had "good arguments," disagreed with his thesis. Charles Hurd wrote in the New York *Times:* "The slim volume is written with the scholarly simplicity one expects of Dr. Kingdon; it contains considerable interesting material of a highly selective sort. But it has no purpose different from that of the handouts issued by the Democratic National Committee." Johannes Steel '41 called it "the most sensational and revealing book of the year for the people of America—and the world," while Upton Sinclair wrote enthusiastically: "It tells the American people exactly what they need to know in this greatest crisis in our history."

During the campaign Kingdon was an active member of the National Citizens Political Action Committee for the Reelection of President Roosevelt, an organization which included authors, writers, educators, businessmen, farm leaders, men and women in public affairs. He was also chairman of the New Jersey League of Independent Voters. In September a supplement to his book *That Man in the White House* entitled *The Inside Story of the Coming Election* was published. It discussed the party platforms and the events of the conventions, and brought up to date his analyses of

Dewey '44 and Roosevelt. In November it was announced that Kingdon was finishing another book, tentatively entitled "It's Time for a Change," which will deal with political, social, and economic aspects of the American scene. In December Kingdon participated in a debate on the Allied policy on liberated Europe (on the radio program *America's Town Meeting of the Air*), in which he held that the armed forces of the United Nations should not be used to force unwanted governments upon liberated peoples; and later that month Kingdon was chairman of a mass demonstration held in New York to demand severance of United States diplomatic relations with Franco Spain.

Kingdon's earlier published works are on religious themes—*Religious Implications of Modern Science* (1926), *Humane Religion* (1930), *When Half-Gods Go* (1933). He is also the author of a biography of John Cotton Dana, published in 1940; *1776, and Today* (1941), a series of addresses; and his autobiography, *Jacob's Ladder—the Days of My Youth*, appeared in 1943.

Kingdon has received numerous honors and awards, among them the Pi Lambda Phi gold medal for 1939 as "the outstanding interpreter of humanitarianism and brotherhood for the year," and an honorary LL.D. from Ohio Northern University in 1931.

The WMCA network closes its daily broadcasts with a prayer for the armed forces written by Kingdon. He has five children, four of whom are active in the war effort: John Gilmore is a ship designer, Frank Oliver is with the Army antiaircraft in New Guinea, David Charlton is with an air force ground crew in Hawaii, Barrie Knight is grinding crystals for precision instruments, and Gertrude Matilda's husband, Frank Behrle, is a bomber pilot in England.

References

N Y Herald Tribune p14 Ap 4 '40 por
N Y Post Mag p29 Ag 15 '44 pors
N Y Sun p28 Je 19 '40
PM Mag p3 My 21 '44 por
Kingdon, F. Jacob's Ladder 1943
Who's Who in America 1944-45
Who's Who in the Clergy 1935-36

KINKAID, THOMAS C(ASSIN) (kas' sin) Apr. 3, 1888- United States Navy officer

Address: b. c/o Navy Department, Washington, D. C.; h. 4915 Wynnefield Ave., Philadelphia

Gold braid runs in the family of Vice-Admiral Thomas C. Kinkaid, who "has shown himself to be one of the great naval leaders of our day," in General Douglas MacArthur's '41 words, by "turning a crisis into a glittering success" in the Second Battle of the Philippine Sea. In this battle, on October 22-27, 1944, the Japanese Imperial Navy was repaid with 200 per cent interest for the losses inflicted at Pearl Harbor.

Born in Hanover, New Hampshire, on April 3, 1888, Thomas Cassin Kinkaid is the son of Rear Admiral Thomas Wright Kinkaid and the former Virginia Lee Cassin, and was "brought up in the service." According to *Newsweek*, "as a 'Navy junior'—the title which children of naval officers proudly bestow upon themselves—his course was charted for him fathom by fathom." After graduating from Western High School in Washington, D. C., young "Kink" Kinkaid was appointed to Annapolis by President Theodore Roosevelt in 1904, when Kinkaid was sixteen. At the Naval Academy he played football, rowed on the Navy crew, and made the reputation of "a lively lad, equally fond of friendly tussling and eating." The Academy yearbook, the *Lucky Bag*, described him as a "black-eyed, rosy-cheeked, noisy Irishman . . . in every way a man of the first order." Graduated from Annapolis in 1908, Kinkaid was ordered to the battleship *Nebraska* for the two years as passed midshipman with the Fleet, then required before commissioning. In June 1910 he got the right to wear an ensign's single gold stripe on his sleeve, and one year later the twenty-three-year-old officer was married to Helen Sherbourne Ross of Philadelphia, where the Kinkaids now have their home.

As a commissioned officer Kinkaid was given what *Newsweek* calls "a series of choice assignments." Transferred to the battleship *Minnesota* in November 1911, he was detached in September 1913 for postgraduate instruction in ordnance, which was, "until recent years, the best path to an admiral's stars." This course, which included tours of duty at the Navy Yard in Washington, D. C., and the Naval Proving Ground at Indian Head, Maryland, as well as at various private industrial plants, was interrupted by nine months of sea duty in Mexican waters aboard the U.S.S. *Machias*. Resuming his studies in January 1915, the tall young Ensign completed the course in May 1916 and was promoted to lieutenant (junior grade) and assigned to the battleship *Pennsylvania*. "He was hot stuff then in gunnery," an old shipmate recalls; "Kinkaid used to come up on the quarterdeck after the day's work was done and do back dives off the top of the companion ladder, twenty-four feet into the water." That observer thought Kinkaid was "the finest young officer he had ever seen—and he still thinks so."

Kinkaid, who "played good enough golf, tennis, and bridge, was an amiable conversationalist, and drank reasonably," was ordered to duty with the British Admiralty, a quasi-diplomatic assignment, in December 1917, when he was a lieutenant. He never saw combat during the First World War. In April 1918 he went back to sea as gunnery officer of the battleship *Arizona*, which operated with the British Fleet for a time, and then escorted the transport *George Washington*, which carried President Wilson to France. In early 1919 the *Arizona* operated in Cuba and the West Indies, then cruised to France, Turkey, and Asia Minor; on her return to the United States in June, Kinkaid was detached with orders to the Navy Department's Bureau of Ordnance in Washington, D. C., for a three-year tour of shore duty.

At thirty-four Thomas Kinkaid was promoted to senior rank, lieutenant commander, and returned to the Near East as assistant chief of staff to Rear Admiral Mark L. Bristol, who commanded the naval detachment in Turkish waters. Two years later Kinkaid was given his first command, the U.S.S. *Isherwood*; and in July 1925 he went back to his specialty, ordnance, at the Naval Gun Factory in the Wash-

Official U. S. Navy Photo
VICE-ADM. THOMAS C. KINKAID

ington, D. C., Navy Yard. A year later Kinkaid was promoted to commander, and in November 1927 he was made fleet gunnery officer and aide to the commander in chief of the United States Fleet, Admiral H. A. Wiley.

Then Commander Kinkaid, who had completed the Naval War College's correspondence course in strategy and tactics, was ordered to the Naval War College at Newport to take the senior course (the Navy's top schooling for captains and commanders), which he finished in May 1930. Next the forty-year-old Commander was made secretary of the General Board, a commission of experienced high-rankers, usually retired, to advise on the preparation of the Fleet and the defense of the coast in case of war. While in this post Kinkaid served, in the fall of 1930, as naval adviser to the American members of the Preparatory Commission for the Disarmament Conference at Geneva; and in late 1932, having ended his tour with the General Board a year earlier, he went to Geneva as technical adviser with the United States delegation to the abortive General Disarmament Conference, to which Commander R. Kelly Turner[44] was aviation adviser.

At the beginning of 1933 Kinkaid was made executive officer of the battleship *Colorado*, in which he remained until October 1934, completing nearly sixteen years afloat. His next assignment in Washington was to the Officers' Detail Section of the Navy Department's Bureau of Navigation. Promoted to captain in January 1937, the officer was given his second sea command, the cruiser *Indianapolis*, six months later. In November 1938 he was back on shore duty. "Known throughout the Navy as a man with a rare talent for dealing with others," Kinkaid was handed the job of United States naval attaché and naval attaché for air in Rome during the period when Mussolini[42] was preparing to violate the Anglo-Italian treaty of April 1938. In April 1939, the month after Kinkaid was assigned additional duty in the same line at Belgrade, capital of Yugoslavia, Italy invaded Albania. The American

KINKAID, THOMAS C.—*Continued*

officer's poise and diplomatic ability were further tested when, on June 10, Mussolini announced war against "the plutocratic and reactionary democracies," and provoked from Kinkaid's Commander in Chief, President Roosevelt '42, the comment, "The hand that held the dagger has struck it into the back of its neighbor."

Captain and Mrs. Kinkaid returned to the United States in March 1941, and in June, after making his report, the fifty-three-year-old Captain was off to sea in command of another vessel. Flag rank came to him a month before Pearl Harbor, with his promotion to rear admiral (temporary), which was made permanent in April 1942.

Twenty minutes after the news of the Pearl Harbor disaster reached Washington, Admiral Kinkaid in mufti boarded a train for the West Coast, where he was to take command of a Pacific Fleet cruiser force. "Almost certainly," says Frank L. Kluckhohn, "he was the calmest man on that train." Seven days after Pearl Harbor he was "in there slugging; in almost every major engagement of a naval nature in the Pacific . . . he fought at the head of important elements or commands," and "once had under his command the only [United States aircraft] carrier capable of action in the Pacific." Kinkaid is entitled to the Presidential unit citation awarded every man aboard his flagship, the carrier *Enterprise*, for the fine record she made as "an ahead bulwark in the defense of the American Nation" (as the late Navy Secretary Frank Knox '40 described her). The *Enterprise*—and Kinkaid—took a notable part in the Gilbert and Marshall Islands raid on February 1, 1942, raided Wake Island on the 24th and Marcus Island ten days later. And on May 4-8, as a task force commander under Admiral Chester W. Nimitz '42, Kinkaid won the Distinguished Service Medal for his "aggressive leadership and determined action" in the battle of the Coral Sea, off the Solomon Islands, northeast of Australia, in which the American losses were less than one-tenth those suffered by the Japanese.

Less than a month later the "Big E," as the *Enterprise* was called, took an important part in the battle of Midway (June 4-6, 1942), which many consider the turning point of the Pacific war. Kinkaid's force not only damaged the Nipponese carriers but shot down three or four planes for each American plane lost. On August 7-8 Kinkaid led the *Enterprise* forces in "those wildly scrambled battles," as one correspondent described them, which made possible the occupation of Guadalcanal. Within sixteen days came the battle of Stewart Island (east and slightly north of Guadalcanal), during which Big E was attacked by a powerful force of Nipponese aircraft. The Admiral's "skillful leadership and extraordinary resourcefulness" throughout the battle and the campaign not only repelled the attack but destroyed the attackers with what the Navy termed minimum damage to his own ships. For this feat he was awarded a Gold Star in lieu of a second D.S.M. on January 22, 1943. The *Enterprise*, with Kinkaid aboard, further distinguished herself at the battle of Santa Cruz on October 26, and the Solomon Islands battle November 14-15; her Presidential citation states that the ship and her air group, "exclu-

sive of her far-flung destruction of hostile shore installations throughout the battle area, did sink or damage on her own a total of thirty-five Japanese vessels and shoot down a total of 185 Japanese aircraft."

With the South Pacific area relatively calm, Admiral Kinkaid was chosen to head the combined sea, land, and air operations to drive the Japanese from the Aleutian Islands off Alaska in the Bering Sea. In January 1943 he reported for duty as commander of the naval forces in the North Pacific, and set about building up Army-Navy cooperation, establishing a joint staff mess to replace the former separate ones. Working with Lieutenant General John L. De Witt '42, he proceeded to conduct "a determined and successful offensive drive," beginning immediately with bombing raids and later with bombardment by the big guns of warships, the first such naval raid since August 1942. On January 12, as the Navy announced in May, American forces commanded by Brigadier General Lloyd E. Jones and led by Navy Seabees and Army scouts, occupied Amchitka, one of the Rat Islands in the western Aleutians; by February 16 an air base for raids on Kiska, seventy-three miles northnorthwest, was completed. In spite of "terrific obstacles of North Pacific weather," the American and Canadian forces under Kinkaid kept up a constant bombardment of the Japanese bases; there was also occasional sea fighting.

On May 14, 1943 forces under Kinkaid's command invaded Attu Island, westernmost of the Aleutians, under the immediate direction of Rear Admiral Francis W. Rockwell. The Japanese under Colonel Yasuyo Yamazaki put up "incredibly bitter" resistance for two weeks and four days, culminating in a suicidal attack on the night of May 29, in which they were annihilated, except for snipers, by Major General Eugene M. Landrum's troops. Seventeen hundred and ninety-one Japanese were killed, and only eleven captured (others avoided capture by suicide); total United States casualties, including wounded and missing, came to 1,535. None of Admiral Kinkaid's warships were sunk or damaged. During and after the Aleutian fighting the Japanese Kiska garrison, estimated at from 8,000 to 10,000 men, was quietly being evacuated in submarines which slipped in and out under the fog-shrouded, turbulent Aleutian waters. Until the end of July, however, the Nipponese continued to build a road on the island where, on August 12, grimfaced Canadian and American soldiers found no enemy to oppose their advance.

At the conclusion of the Aleutians campaign Vice-Admiral Kinkaid (who had been promoted to that rank on June 9) was recalled to Washington, for which he left on October 12, 1943. Awarded a second Gold Star to his D.S.M., the Admiral stopped in Philadelphia to see Mrs. Kinkaid for the second time since the War started, then set off for Australia to take command of the Southwest Pacific naval forces cooperating with General Douglas MacArthur. MacArthur is considered by many Navy men "the most difficult of Army generals," according to *Newsweek*, but Kinkaid, himself a thoroughly un-dashing type of officer, got along smoothly with his photogenic superior. Following the example of General Dwight D. Eisenhower '42 working with the British in North Africa, Kinkaid forbade his men to criticize the other branch of the service, the first step in "a steady toning up of morale and unity of the forces."

As commander of the 7th Fleet, which "struggled along with a handful of destroyers and a heterogeneous cruiser task force including two Australian cruisers and a motley array of amphibious landing-support craft," Kinkaid was in charge of the naval aspects of the Southwest Pacific operations. In addition to air-sea work against the Japanese, this included landing fighting men and equipment on the islands General MacArthur occupied, providing sea and air support for the troops, and, on occasion, providing naval bombardment as an aid to the mopping-up process. On February 29, 1944 Kinkaid accompanied MacArthur on an inspection tour of Los Negros, one of the Admiralty Islands (at the northern entrance to the Bismarck Sea, adjacent to New Britain, New Guinea, and New Ireland), barely eight hours after the first landing, and "he supervised the General's first long jump up the New Guinea coast—500 miles to Hollandia," Netherlands New Guinea, in April. When the Americans landed on Biak Island in the Schoutens May 27, correspondents declared, "This was a daring thrust strategically as well as tactically. . . . Vice-Admiral Kinkaid's hard-worked amphibious fleet was the key to the whole operation. Its ability to move again so soon after the Hollandia and Wake landings was in itself remarkable. But the manner in which men and supplies were put ashore, despite reefs that made it impossible to land near the air strips, assured the success of the movement. The destroyer skippers were fearless in risking ships and ignoring the accurate shore batteries when the battle developed. Even when hit, the destroyer fire didn't slacken, and most of the shore batteries finally were silenced. . . . There is every indication that the enemy expected us to land closer to the Biak airdromes than we did, and were ready for us [there]."

Admiral Kinkaid was working months ahead on plans for the invasion of the Philippines. "Planning for the landing," reports Frank L. Kluckhohn, included the devising of a method of refueling at sea for hundreds of ships without slowing up the operation. "Under General MacArthur he was charged with command of the entire landing force until it was ashore," and was responsible for "any shift of plans that might be called for in the operation, which was subject to change both by weather and by enemy action."

In early September the Japanese radio predicted that MacArthur's forces, together with Kinkaid's 7th Naval Fleet, would attempt to move northward from New Guinea into Mindanao. But when the return to the Philippines promised by MacArthur was begun, it was the island of Leyte, 300 miles northeast of Mindanao and 425 miles southeast of Manila on Luzon, which American warships put under a devastating naval and air bombardment on October 17, toward the end of the typhoon season. Among the "battlewagons" hurling salvos from 14- and 16-inch guns into Leyte beach were the *West Virginia* and *California*, sunk by the Japanese at Pearl Harbor three years earlier. Enemy positions were bombarded, also, by cruisers of the Australian Squadron. Days before, a 600-ship convoy, stretched out over 900 miles of blue Pacific,

had started moving toward the central Philippines under Kinkaid's command. While the convoy was plowing along in the sweltering tropic heat the Japanese radio announcements made it clear, Kluckhohn reports, that "Admiral [William F.] Halsey '42, having a battle to the north, obviously might not be in a position to supply certain aid which was promised. Without hesitation Admiral Kinkaid decided not to delay the convoy or the landings," and showed no strain as he looked over reports and chatted with correspondents. And on October 18 units of the United States 6th Army stormed ashore under the personal command of General MacArthur, guarded by Kinkaid's 7th Fleet, the Australian Squadron, and supporting elements of Halsey's 3rd Fleet, and in the air by the Navy carrier planes, the Army Far Eastern Air Force, and the R.A.A.F. Capitalizing on the costly lesson of Tarawa (the Gilbert Island atoll invaded November 21, 1943 under Admiral Raymond A. Spruance '44), Navy minesweepers had cleared the surrounding waters in which the other warships were to operate.

On the 23rd and 24th Halsey's reconnaissance planes and Kinkaid's submarines brought word of three Japanese fleets converging against the invasion forces from different directions. The 7th Fleet itself was "virtually immobilized and on the defensive because its job was to guard the invasion vessels," and Kinkaid therefore used a smoke screen to protect the transports. The main Japanese carrier force was engaged by Halsey's 3rd Fleet on October 24 and effectively broken up. Admiral Kinkaid, although outnumbered in ships, made the bold decision to split his fleet and attack both the remaining Japanese forces at once. He sent his escort carriers ("baby flattops") northward to Samar Island under Rear Admiral Thomas L. Sprague to hold off the enemy from Leyte Gulf, which they did (aided by some of Halsey's planes) in an action Kinkaid termed unbelievable, until reinforced several hours later by battleships, cruisers, and fast carriers from the 3rd Fleet. This detachment of ships and planes sank two heavy enemy cruisers, damaged all four enemy battleships; the enemy then made off through San Bernardino Strait at high speed. Presumably he was impelled by the other fleets' fate. Meanwhile Kinkaid's PT (patrol torpedo) boats, destroyers, and battleships, under Rear Admiral Jesse Barret Oldendorf, sped southward and officially "wiped out" the Japanese detachment of sixteen warships in the Surigao Straits, in a night action October 24-25. During the battle Kinkaid retained his calm, to the extent of reading a detective story in the lulls; and at the battle's end he called in the news correspondents and asked, "Please don't say I made any dramatic statements. You know I am incapable of that."

But no statement from the Admiral was needed to add drama to his achievement: winning under great handicaps what his superior MacArthur called "one of history's very few 100 per cent naval victories." Said Kinkaid, "It brings the War that much closer to an end. I want to see this War over with as fast as possible so we can go home. I've had only seven weeks in the United States in the past three years."

After the amphibious landing at Ormoc Harbor on Leyte, General MacArthur sent

KINKAID, THOMAS C.—Continued

congratulations to Kinkaid's fleet, General Krueger's 6th Army, and General Kenney's air force on the success of the Ormoc operation: "It was executed with that cool courage, absolute determination, and indomitable will for victory which has so characterized our forces in all campaigns." Later, on December 26, when a Japanese task force slipped through the China Sea unchallenged by surface units and shelled the Mindoro beachhead, correspondent Frank Kelley explained that Halsey's force, "powerful as it is," has to retire periodically for refueling, repairs, and overhauling. "Could Kinkaid's 7th Fleet have remained on the spot?" he asked, and answered, "That fleet, less powerful than the formal title of 'fleet' indicates, has plenty of work to do in areas other than Mindoro. Moreover, to remain there it would require an air cover which is virtually impossible from air bases on Mindoro. These bases are just being built and are primarily offensive rather than defensive. . . . That [attack] is one of the hazards of war, and a risk any fighting American would assume in exchange for the strategic gain of putting air bases on Mindoro." Kinkaid and other commanders, meanwhile, were putting the final touches on "history's greatest overseas invasion," which Kinkaid was soon to command on the long journey to invade Luzon.

One would hardly suspect that the dignified, soft-spoken, publicity-shy Admiral has had to learn to control a temper. "It's only by years of schooling myself that I've learned to maintain a calm exterior," he told Frank L. Kluckhohn. Nor would one guess that, as *Look* reported, a full-rigged sailing ship is tattooed on Thomas Cassin Kinkaid's chest. The Admiral is tall and has some gray hair left; his eyes are black, as are his heavy jutting eyebrows. A member of Kinkaid's staff described him as "strict and conscientious without being overbearing . . . not afraid to delegate power, but he has a great eye for detail himself and knows what is going on all the time. For relaxation he reads detective stories omnivorously, likes the movies, likes to talk shop, and enjoys a sedate type of dinner party because he likes people. He'll swear at times, but doesn't make it a practice. When he shows his temper he is controlled, purposeful, more freezing than burning," and he is generous in his commendation of his colleagues. His post-War plan is simple: "After the War is over I want to spend my time fishing anywhere for any type of fish."

References

N Y Sun p14 N 7 '44
N Y Times p3 O 22 '44
N Y Times Mag p9+ N 5 '44 por
Newsweek 24:29+ N 6 '44 por
Register of Commissioned and Warrant Officers of the United States Navy and Marine Corps 1943
Who's Who in America 1944-45

KIRBY, ROLLIN Sept. 4, 1875- Cartoonist; author

Address: b. c/o New Yorker Magazine, 25 W. 43rd St., New York City

"New York Between Two Wars," the exhibition of Rollin Kirby's work which opened at the Museum of the City of New York in October 1944, covers the period between 1918 and 1940 in a way that no written history can. Kirby, three times Pulitzer Prize winner and one of America's most distinguished political cartoonists, has been making his bold comments on American life for more than three decades, and he is crusader as well as commentator. Writes the New York *Times*: "The broad sweep of the observer gathers in the return of the old A.E.F. from France, the ugly and ironic reign of prohibition, the bootleggers' rise to wealth and fame, and the wave of crime which afflicted the country in the wake of a noble experiment. It does not miss the stir that brought us woman's suffrage and incidentally bobbed hair and flaming youth, or the fabulous time when skyscrapers and stocks went up together; nor yet the crash of the stock market on the heels of prosperity gone mad and the lean and hungry days that followed. And it carries on right down to the period of doubt and uncertainty which preceded Pearl Harbor." Kirby has, in his time, turned his pictorial criticism against Harding, Coolidge, Hoover [43], Mayor Frank Hague, Wall Street, Tammany, Prohibitionists, imperialists, fascists, and the Ku Klux Klan. He has crusaded for civil liberties, woman suffrage, the New Deal— and in the 1944 campaign he was one of Roosevelt's [42] most fervent supporters.

Born in Galva, Illinois, on September 4, 1875, Rollin Kirby is the son of George Washington and Elizabeth (Maddox) Kirby. His childhood home was Hastings, Nebraska. He was nineteen when he came to New York City to enter the Art Students' League, and in those days he had every intention of becoming a painter. After studying under J. Carroll Beckwith and H. Siddons Mowbray at the New York school, he went to Paris, like most of the aspiring young artists of his time. There, at the Académie Rossi, he studied under the aging Whistler. He was enrolled also at the Académie Délecluse, Académie Julien, and the Beaux Arts; was influenced by the French impressionists; and learned to admire Charles Keene in *Punch*. Kenneth Stewart [43] adds that his social consciousness was awakened by the second Dreyfus trial.

Returning to New York in 1900, Kirby continued to paint. His paintings were exhibited at the National Academy, but even this did not bring sales. An order for a "large, light dining room picture" finally caused him to put his brushes away forever and turn to illustrating for magazines (*Collier's, McClure's, Life, American Magazine, Harper's*). In 1903 he was married to Estelle Carter, an actress.

Kirby found his first job as a newspaper cartoonist through his friend Franklin P. Adams [41], who at the time was with the New York *Mail*. This was in 1911, and after a few months a disagreement with the *Mail's* editor sent Kirby to the New York *Sun*. The year 1913 found him with the New York *World* as its pictorial reporter. A social cartoon, "The Trials of the Rich," was the beginning of a series later called "Sights of the Town," which finally evolved into Denys Wortman's "Metropolitan Movies." By that time Kirby had become the *World's* political cartoonist, and in the years that followed he was to play a large part in molding public opinion. "The idea," he says, "is 75 per cent of a cartoon. Given a good idea one can get by with mediocre drawing, but good drawing never makes a good cartoon if the idea is weak. So anyone who approaches cartooning primarily through his interest in art comes in at the wrong door, which is not to discount the importance of the artist's command of graphic language. One should wait for the maturity and the wisdom which qualify an editorial writer of a great newspaper to analyze and comment upon world affairs before thinking of becoming a cartoonist. For a cartoon is really an editorial. It must be judged by what it says rather than the way in which it says it, and what art there is in cartooning is the art of driving the message home."

It was Kirby who invented the paunchy figure frequently used by cartoonists of Democratic newspapers to represent the G.O.P., and it was he who created the long-nosed figure widely familiar as the symbol of prohibition. In an article he wrote for *Vanity Fair* in 1933 Kirby described the evolution of this figure— "tall, sour, weedy—something to express the canting hypocrisy we felt about the movement." While the symbol brought forth protests because of its quasi-ecclesiastical overtones, public opinion changed and other newspapers used the figure until it became the standardized symbol of prohibition.

In 1921 Kirby won the Pulitzer $500 prize for his cartoon "On the Road to Moscow"; in 1924 he won the award for the second time, with "News From the Outside World"; in 1928 "Tammany" made him a three-time Pulitzer winner. Today Kirby can scarcely remember these cartoons, but he does know that they were "terrible." He doesn't think of himself as an artist; he says editorial cartooning is a great art only "when it is practiced by a great artist like Forain or Daumier." And although he has been credited with playing a part in Hoover's defeat of 1932 by twisting the Republicans' 1928 slogan into "Two Chickens in Every Garage," he is not entirely certain that either political cartoons or editorials have the effect on public opinion that they once did.

Kirby was with the *World* until 1931, when the famous newspaper was merged with the New York *Telegram* of the Scripps-Howard chain. Said Kirby at the time: "The *Telegram* is about the only paper I could work for after the *World*. During my eighteen years on the *World* I was never once called off an issue or ordered to go light."

However, after the death in 1938 of Robert Paine Scripps, the editorial director, the *World-Telegram* grew more conservative, opposing many portions of the New Deal, and Kirby's old position of four-column prominence on the editorial page was not maintained. In March 1939 he resigned from the *World-Telegram*, voicing a "reluctance to support a point of view which seemed many times to be unfair. When the contract expired on April 1 Kirby said he would retire, but by July he had joined the New York *Post* under a two-year contract. "George Backer's [Backer was president and editor] idea of liberalism and my own are the same," he said at the time. "We both go back to the somewhat shopworn definition that human rights are more important than

ROLLIN KIRBY

property rights. That is the backbone of liberalism. This paper is going to represent a vehicle for the things in which I really believe. When I am through here I'm through for good." His first cartoon for the *Post*, published on July 10, 1939, attacked the Republican-controlled New York Legislature as imperiling state efficiency by its budget cuts. With the *Post* he was given a fairly free hand in his choice and treatment of subjects.

What he was not given was the salary that he had been receiving (according to the 1939 Treasury list, he had been given an annual $23,310 while with the *World-Telegram*). When his contract with the *Post* expired he got a renewal offer at a salary no larger, he said, than the first pay check he drew back in 1911 when F.P.A. got him his first cartoonist's job on the *Mail*. "I'm sure they didn't expect me to accept," he said—and he didn't. Since August 1942 he has been doing cartoons for *Look* Magazine, and editorials as well.

As an artist Kirby is noted, as one writer said, for "his facile and expressive line, his characteristic understatement, his beautifully handled composition, and the utter lack of anything commonplace or banal in his treatment even the dullest subjects." According to the *American Artist*, "in draftsmanship and dramatic power Kirby is a master. His figure drawing is unimpeachable. His line is articulate. His cartoons strike home with a terrific impact and they give instantaneous exposition of an idea." Today he declares that he would rather paint than do anything else, but he does not care to be a dabbler, and his brushes are packed away.

In the medium of words he is far from being a dabbler, however, for he has written and published verse, book reviews, articles, and a couple of short plays (as well as editorials) in such magazines as the old *Life*, the *Nation*, the *New Yorker*, *Vanity Fair*. He is also the author of the section on the cartoon in the United States in the fourteenth edition of the *Encyclo-*

KIRBY, ROLLIN—*Continued*

paedia Britannica. Nor has he hesitated to participate in politics. The winner of the Annie E. Gray Award of 1935, in September 1941 he was one of the signers of a telegram to President Roosevelt asking him to urge upon Congress the immediate declaration of war on Nazi Germany; in 1944 he was a prominent member of the National Independent Committee for Roosevelt.

Kirby is described by Kenneth Stewart as "lanky and limber, tanned from tennis and fishing, polished from his shoes to his iron-gray hair. Casual in manner, he is nevertheless smooth and dignified, with a bit of the professor and a bit of the clubman in his appearance. His quizzical expression, which can quickly become grave or fiery and jovial, marks him as the constant commentator on life." He makes his home in Westport, Connecticut. He has one daughter, Janet, now Mrs. Delos Chappell.

References

> Am Artist 4 :5-7 Je '40 ils
> Cur Hist 50 :31+ Ag '39 il por
> N Y Times VI p22 O 1 '44 il por
> Newsweek 14 :40 Jl 17 '39
> Time 40 :34 Jl 20 '42 por
> Who's Who in America 1944-45

KIRK, ALAN GOODRICH　Oct. 30, 1888-
United States naval officer

Address: b. c/o Navy Department, Washington, D.C.

June 6, 1944! Allied troops under General Sir Bernard Law Montgomery '42 began the assault on German Europe. Rear Admiral Alan Goodrich Kirk was one of the two naval commanders who landed them on the shores of France. Four months later, in October, he was made commander of the United States Naval Forces in France.

Alan Goodrich Kirk was born in Philadelphia, Pennsylvania, October 30, 1888, the son of William Thomson and Harriet (Goodrich) Kirk. Visits to the ships commanded by his uncle, Rear Admiral C. F. Goodrich, convinced young Alan that he, too, wanted to wear gold braid; so his father, a Democrat in Republican Pennsylvania, sought and found a New Jersey Congressman who would appoint his son to Annapolis. At the Naval Academy, for reasons unknown, young Kirk was dubbed "Hoboken Bill." There, too, he established a lasting friendship with another midshipman, Lewis H. Brereton '43, now in command of the Allied Air-borne Army. Graduated from the Academy in 1909, Kirk was "well on the topside of his class scholastically." After two years as passed midshipman with the Atlantic Fleet he was commissioned an ensign in 1911.

During the Chinese Revolution led by Sun Yat-sen against the Manchu imperium, Ensign Kirk was in Canton as gunnery officer in the gunboat *Wilmington.* Later he was transferred to the U. S. S. *Saratoga* which, as flagship of the Asiatic Fleet, was the fleet commander's floating headquarters. It was the gunnery officer's duty to fire the welcoming salutes for distinguished visitors; one of these salutes Kirk fired at such close range that he

blew the visiting notable's high silk hat off his head into the water. Promoted—nevertheless—to lieutenant (junior grade) in June 1914, Kirk was recalled to the United States to serve in the battleship *Utah* of the Atlantic Fleet. Two years later he was sent to the Naval Proving Ground at Dahlgren, Virginia for shore duty as testing and experimental officer. Throughout the First World War Kirk was stationed at the proving ground, where he tested the first 16-inch naval guns, the 14-inch railway guns later used in France, anti-submarine depth charges, and similar deadly weapons. Commissioned a lieutenant commander (temporary) in February 1918, Alan Kirk was married to Lydia Selden Chapin the following September.

In 1919 the future admiral was gunnery officer on the battleship *Connecticut* bringing troops home from France. In May 1920 he was transferred from the battleship *Arizona,* on which he was assistant gunnery officer, to the Presidential yacht *Mayflower* as executive officer and navigator with additional duty as aide to the White House. President Wilson, whose health was failing, used the yacht very little during the remaining months of his term, but his successor, President Harding, spent nearly a third of his leisure cruising aboard the *Mayflower.* Meanwhile, writes George Sessions Perry, "the executive officer of the yacht was busily applying himself to learning the mores of the great and near great, and seeing the astonishing effect that a casual word at precisely the right time can have in swaying the minds of the powerful."

At the end of 1922 Kirk, whose temporary rank had been made permanent in June 1921, began a two-year tour of shore duty centralizing material records at the Bureau of Ordnance. This was followed by a similar period as gunnery officer in the battleship *Maryland,* during which the Atlantic Fleet made a goodwill cruise to Australia and New Zealand. From September 1926 to July 1928 Commander Kirk was fleet gunnery officer on the staff of the Scouting Fleet commander, and was then sent to the Naval War College at Newport, Rhode Island. Here Kirk, who had already taken its correspondence course in strategy and tactics, was a student in the senior course (open only to captains and commanders). On its completion a year later he remained at Newport in the Operations Division of the College staff.

In 1931 Kirk returned to the sea in command of the destroyer *Schenck* of the Scouting Force, and the following year was executive officer of the battleship *West Virginia,* flagship of a battleship division of the Battle Force. He received letters of commendation from the Secretary of the Navy for his work in making his ship winner of the 1932-1933 Battle Efficiency Pennant and the gunnery, engineering, and communications trophies. This was followed by three years, June 1933-June 1936, as assistant director of the Ship Movements Division in the Office of the Chief of Naval Operations, and then a year at sea in command of the cruiser *Milwaukee.* In February 1937 Commander Kirk joined the staff of Admiral C. C. Bloch, commander of the Battle Force, as operations officer. A year later, after

promotion to the rank of captain, Alan Kirk
was detached from duty with the Battle Force
to continue on the staff of Admiral Bloch, who
had been made commander in chief of the
United States Fleet.

On June 7, 1939 the Captain arrived in
London as United States naval attaché and
naval attaché for air at the American Embassy.
He had the task of collecting American refugees from the European war and shipping them
back to the United States as quickly and safely
as possible. Hardly had these arrangements
been made when Britain declared war against
Germany. That day, September 3, the S.S.
Athenia was sunk and Kirk's investigation
established the fact that the ship had been torpedoed. Later, when the British seized American ships carrying contraband to neutral countries, "it was Kirk who adjudicated this business and saw that the American shippers
received a fair return for their confiscated
cargoes. Later still he did the British a good
turn on one of those many occasions when
Herr Goebbels'[41] orally sank the *Ark Royal*.
Kirk issued a statement that he had just visited
her and attended church services on her quarterdeck."

Captain Kirk, who was described by the
London press as "discreet, personable, and
leanly academic," was assigned a diplomatic
task of an E. Phillips Oppenheim character.
There was, according to George Sessions
Perry, "much vital secret material, such as
technical information about magnetic mines,
that . . . the American Navy felt it had to
have, and Kirk was delegated to get it—a mission requiring the most delicate blend of aggressiveness and discretion. That Kirk had
these qualities and succeeded in his mission
is denied by no one. The British liked him
as much for his firmness of character as for
his *politesse* and good taste."

At the end of 1940 Kirk returned to Washington to report to the President. After temporary duty in the Office of the Chief of Naval
Operations he became, in March 1941, director
of the Office of Naval Intelligence. Here, says
Perry, the Captain "beat the FBI to the
startling fact that the Italians were about to
scuttle their ships in Baltimore. He also
caught the Jap naval attaché red-handed acting
as an unqualified spy. But since at that time
the State Department was appeasing the Japs,
they would not let the Department of Justice
give the Jap official the business." In October 1941 Kirk was sent to sea in command
of a division of ships, and the following month
he was promoted to rear admiral. After the
Japanese attack on Pearl Harbor some newspapers, trying to fix responsibility for the
American forces' lack of preparedness, blamed
Kirk for inefficient Intelligence work. "And
at this point [Ambassador] Joe Kennedy'[40]
stepped in and called to mind a copy of a report which Kirk had circulated just before
leaving Intelligence. The report stated flatly
that due to our Fleet's poor antiaircraft equipment and lack of information about magnetic mines, and so on, the Japs could jump
it and lick the pants off it. That hard-headed
Joe Kennedy should have come to Kirk's defense was not surprising. He knew Kirk well,
and also knew that the American Navy could

not allow such capable men to be fed to the
wolves."

In March 1942 Admiral Kirk returned to
London as United States naval attaché as
well as chief of staff and senior aide to Admiral Harold Raynsford Stark'[40], commander
of the United States Fleet in European waters. Here, as before, the American got on
famously with "the rulers of the King's
navee," entertained Prince Bertil of Sweden
and King Peter II'[43] of Yugoslavia, and "at
times when Kirk felt like politics, he tootled
out to Cliveden and spent an evening with
Lady Astor's'[40] kaleidoscopic gang." At the
beginning of 1943 the Admiral was relieved
of his Embassy post, and in February he was
placed in command of the Atlantic Fleet's
Amphibious Force.

In June 1943 it was announced for the first
time that a "Unified Invasion Force," made
up of specially selected Army and Navy officers and men, was being "welded in preparation for assaults on enemy territory." Admiral Kirk, placed in command of the Atlantic Fleet's Amphibious Force, had arrived in
Norfolk to undertake "the endless complexities of his new job. To catalogue these complexities would require volumes. . . . Three
services, Army—both ground and air, Navy,
and Coast Guard, go to make up an amphibious force. Much of the equipment was not
battle-tried. . . . There was the necessity of
using naval gunfire not merely to fire pellmell
at the enemy beaches, but also to act as field
artillery for a highly mobile, unseen land
force. Far more than would ordinarily have
been the case, the outcome of the battle depended on the foresight and imagination of
the commander of such an operation. Again
Admiral Kirk delivered the goods"—a striking
force "ready to carry out with speed, precision, and perfect coordination the most difficult of military assignments—a landing on a
fortified hostile shore."

After "postgraduate training," Kirk's 500-
ship task force—of which he had assumed
command in October 1943—set out toward
Gibraltar in preparation for the Allies' invasion of Sicily. Two days out of port the
Admiral ordered Lieutenant John Mason
Brown'[42] of his staff to make a series of
"play-by-play" broadcasts over the flagship's
loudspeaker system for that 90 per cent of the
men on a modern battleship who cannot see
what is going on. (These broadcasts have
since been published in book form as *To All
Hands* [1943] with an introduction by Kirk.)
"Before a person can act independently without throwing out of gear a carefully drawn
plan he must have some idea of what it is
all about," said the Admiral. "This reliance
upon the individual is nowhere greater than in
amphibious warfare." His only recreation on
the trip over was said to have been Lieutenant
Brown's fifteen-minute broadcasts.

After a most unsatisfactory invasion rehearsal on a North African beach the task
force proceeded to demonstrate that old theatrical maxim, "A bad dress rehearsal means
a good first night." Admiral Kirk's ships,
part of the American unit commanded by Vice-
Admiral Henry K. Hewitt'[43] at sea and Lieutenant General George S. Patton, Jr.,'[43] on
land, dropped anchor at Scoglitti at the hinge

Official U. S. Navy Photo

REAR ADM. ALAN GOODRICH KIRK

of the invasion area before daylight on July 10, 1943 and set the 45th (Thunderbird) Army Division ashore in landing craft. The unloading of supplies, which General Patton had bet Kirk would take eight days, was accomplished in three days under incessant bombing without loss of a single vessel. Ninety casualties—a "microscopic fraction of one per cent"—were suffered by Kirk's men in the operation, which included the laying down of a barrage that not only blasted enemy strong points but stopped a heavy tank attack by the crack Hermann Goering '41 Division. The Admiral, himself a gunnery expert, told Captain Timothy F. Wellings and his men, "You shot better than anybody can. You were damn lucky, Gentlemen." This was Kirk's word on the entire invasion landing—an achievement for which he was awarded the Legion of Merit by Under-Secretary (later Secretary) of the Navy James C. Forrestal '42 in August 1943, and made a Companion of the Bath in February 1944. (The Admiral already had the Mexican Service medal, the Victory medal, the American Defense Service medal with Fleet Clasp, and the European-African-Middle Eastern Area campaign medal.)

Later in 1943 Admiral Kirk returned to England "on temporary duty for a series of conferences." On February 20, 1944 the Navy Department announced that Kirk had been named to command the United States task force operating directly under Admiral Stark and under the supreme naval command of British Admiral Sir Bertram Home Ramsay '44. Earlier, when asked by Admiral the Lord Louis Mountbatten '42 how he felt about taking an amphibious force against western Europe or Germany, Kirk is quoted as replying, "Louis, if they'll give me my own air [planes], the sooner the better."

What it was like for Kirk's men on D-Day has been published in a second compilation of Lieutenant Brown's intraship broadcasts, *Many a Watchful Night* (1944); Brown was

even sent ashore as the ship's "walking delegate" on June 8, to accompany General Omar N. Bradley '43 on his first inspection of the beachhead and report to the ship's company. On July 21 the Admiral told correspondents that ninety per cent of the targets the United States Navy had been asked to bombard had been hit effectively. (Kirk's flagship when he was commander of the western beachhead naval support was, incidentally, the *Augusta*, on which President Roosevelt '42 and Prime Minister Churchill '42 had drawn up the Atlantic Charter.) "Failure is not even contemplated when we launch an amphibious operation," said Admiral Kirk at a Navy Department press conference in Washington, where he was recalled for "temporary duty" in early summer. In the Normandy invasion, he recalled, there was no confusion among the hundreds of ships in his command (which included 125,000 sailors carrying the Army men), and no accidental shooting down of friendly planes; when his ship moved in to bombard shore installations they came so close that they could often fire by visual aim, while destroyer captains nearly grounded their ships in order to land their passengers as near as possible to the beach.

In October 1944 Admiral Harold R. Stark announced that Kirk had been named commander of the United States Naval Forces in France. At a press conference Kirk stated that "American amphibious technique is becoming virtually invincible." He particularly praised the ability of the United Nations to protect and use all of their sea power. Although a man of the sea, Kirk is frank enough to state that the success of the invasion of France must be credited to the infantry. Asked if he hopes "to get a crack at the Japanese," Admiral Kirk replied: "Every naval officer hopes for that."

The Admiral—described as "a handsome Philadelphian with a trace of Southern accent" who looks ten years younger than his age—is jaunty, freckled, and possessed of "dancing" blue eyes. His personality combines a fiery temper with "an almost Rooseveltian immunity to worry." Since the beginning of the War he has been separated from his family: his only son, Roger, his married daughter Marian young Deborah, a Wave, and Mrs. Kirk, who works in the office of the chief cable censor. An avid reader who "loves poetry next to naval gunnery" and has written learned treatises on ballistics, Kirk frequently reads a book a night and claims such unnautical friends as Harold Laski '41 and Justice Felix Frankfurter '41. He "smokes cigarettes on something approaching the chain scale, collects old silver at odd moments—which are odd in his case—and will go out of his way to pick up a rare naval print. He also "collects admirers, simply by being Alan Kirk, the brilliant, gracious fighter and statesman."

References

N Y Sun p15 Ag 9 '43; p20 My 19 '44; p7 Je 6 '44

Sat Eve Post 216:19+ O 30 '43 por

Register of Commissioned and Warrant Officers of the United-States Navy 1943

Who's Who in America 1944-45

KIRK, NORMAN T(HOMAS) Jan. 3, 1888- Surgeon General of the United States Army

Address: b. Office of the Surgeon General, War Department, Washington, D.C.; h. 1 Main Dr., Army Medical Center, Washington, D.C.

The tremendous responsibility for the health of every member of the Army of the United States, exposed to hazards of war and disease all over the globe, is borne by Major General Norman T. Kirk, Surgeon General of the United States Army. He returned from an inspection tour of the battlefronts in June 1943, to assume command of approximately 90,000 medical officers and 450,000 enlisted corpsmen. "When the War started," says Kirk, "we had 1,200 regular medical officers"—of whom he was one.— Thus far, according to the General, "the death rate from infections, diseases, and wounds is the lowest of any army at any time,—so low as to be almost unbelievable in the light of the medical experience of the First World War."

Norman Thomas Kirk was born in Rising Sun, Maryland, January 3, 1888, the son of Thomas and Anna May (Brown) Kirk. He attended the Tome School at Port Deposit, Maryland, and the University of Maryland, from which he was graduated in 1910 with the degree of M.D. He then spent a year as resident physician at the University Hospital in Baltimore. In 1912 Kirk was commissioned a 1st lieutenant in the United States Army Medical Corps. He has graduated from the Army Medical School the following year, and later completed the course given by the Graduate Field Service School. On September 27, 1917 Kirk was married to Anne Duryea. They have two daughters, Ann and Jane.

Kirk's advance through the various grades, from 1st lieutenant to colonel, was steady. From 1914 to 1924 he was chief of the amputation and orthopedic section of the Walter Reed General Hospital at Washington. His first paper to be published in a professional journal came out in October 1924, with the title, "End Results of 158 Consecutive Autogenous Bone Grafts for Non-Union in Long Bones: (A) in Simple Fractures; (B) in Astrophic Bone Following War Wounds and Chronic Suppurative Osteitis (Osteomyelitis)."

From 1924 to 1928 Kirk was chief of the orthopedic section of the Station Hospital in Fort Sam Houston, Texas. The next two years he spent as acting chief of the Sternberg General Hospital in Manila. He returned to the Walter Reed Hospital in 1930 and remained four years, after which he resumed his duties in the Philippines. In 1936 Kirk was made chief of surgical service at Letterman General Hospital in San Francisco, then commanding officer of Percy Jones General Hospital at Battle Creek, Michigan. During this period a number of Kirk's writings were published, including a book, *Amputations; Operative Technique* (1924); chapters on amputations in two medical encyclopedias, and on prosthesis and tetanus in two textbooks of surgery; and eleven articles in professional journals.

MAJ. GEN. NORMAN T. KIRK

Kirk, who had been promoted to the permanent rank of colonel in 1939, was given the wartime (temporary) promotion to brigadier general. This rank he held until June 1943, when the Senate confirmed his appointment as Surgeon General of the United States Army with the permanent rank of major general to succeed Dr. James C. Magee '43.

One of the problems confronting Surgeon General Kirk is that of bringing enough doctors and dentists into the Army to maintain the high medical standard set by his predecessor. (Recruitment of Army nurses is handled by the American Red Cross.) Since March 18, 1943 the Army has reduced the ratio of doctors to troops from the traditional 8.5 per 1,000, established by regulations at the time of the Spanish-American War, to a ratio of 6.6 in combat and 4.6 in non-combat areas. This reduced to 53,000 the number of civilian doctors (about 46,000 had been commissioned by August 15, 1943) who would have to be brought into the service. However, the commissioning of doctors fell behind its monthly quota. On July 9, 1943 Kirk reported that 7,000 more physicians and 600 more dentists were needed before the end of 1943 to ensure "even minimal care" of the wounded. Two thousand more nurses a month were needed, as well as occupational and physiotherapists.

The percentage of neuropsychiatric cases is too high, according to Kirk, constituting about forty per cent of the medical cases in the Army hospitals under his supervision. "The idea gets around," he said, "that the Army is making the boys crazy. The truth is the Army is finding it out. Some were simply born that way, and some were just spoiled. They were allowed to do too much as they pleased. They are the first to crack under strain. We are running into the same problem that General Pershing ran into in the last War, in that we have too many men physically fit to fight, but not mentally fit."

(Continued next page)

KIRK, NORMAN T.—*Continued*

Perhaps the most difficult problem facing Kirk is the procurement of surgical instruments, ninety per cent of which used to be imported. Now, when these essential hospital tools must all be made in the United States under wartime conditions, there is sometimes a six months' lag between order and delivery. Yet, in spite of these unsatisfactory conditions, the Medical Corps' record has been bright. Litter-bearers and ambulance drivers, as well as higher ranking personnel, "worked in some instances until they dropped from exhaustion." Lieutenant General Mark W. Clark '42, commanding the 5th Army, wrote to Kirk "the highest commendation for the wonderfully fine work performed by the medical units of this Army." General Dwight D. Eisenhower '42 told Kirk, "One of the most outstanding services of the whole A.E.F. in the Tunisian campaign was that rendered by the medical department." But the best proof of all is the record. "At no time in this War," says General Kirk, "has the venereal rate for troops in this country been as high as the *lowest* monthly rate for the last War." The death rate among battle casualties at evacuation hospitals during the Tunisian campaign averaged two and one-half to three and one-half per cent, as compared with fifteen to eighteen per cent in the First World War. Kirk reported also that the death rate from abdominal wounds and the incidence of infection for all wounds had been cut on the same scale. As major medical reasons he lists: first, the use of blood plasma (of which he urges the public to contribute 90,000 pints a week); next, improved medical and surgical techniques; and then the various sulfa compounds. "Drugs," he points out, "will never replace surgery in military medicine." But the main reason is non-medical—the use of airplanes to evacuate the wounded to base hospitals.

The statistics issued by Kirk, after approximately three years of war, on the health of the troops and the restoration to duty of wounded men is heartening. Kirk declared that 97 out of every 100 men hurt in battle are saved. This is credited in the first instance to the highly mobile surgical teams operating close to the front lines. It is axiomatic that the sooner a wounded soldier can receive surgical care the better are his chances of recovery. Soldiers on the battlefronts are receiving medical aid ten minutes after being injured, and X rays are being taken three miles behind the lines. The death rate caused by disease has been reduced to less than 6 per 10,000 men, a rate below that among civilians, and fifty per cent less than the level of the First World War. Of the 250,000 soldiers wounded in the three years of war, over 100,000 have returned to duty. This has been made possible by the Army's highly successful rehabilitation program which emphasizes the reconditioning of the mind as well as of the body. The crux of this learning program is summed up in Kirk's pamphlet, *It's Fun To Learn*: "The fun you will get out of learning something new will take your mind off your own troubles and give your body a chance to mend. . . . Pick a subject you will enjoy learning and that will help you."

At the end of the rehabilitation program those men discharged from the Army because of various disabilities "are not to be coddled but treated like normal human beings," emphasizes Kirk. The Surgeon General asserts that relatives and friends must continue to nurture the self-confidence which the Army has instilled in the disabled person. General Kirk has been appointed technical supervisor of the National Rehabilitation Committee, an organization sponsored by every major industry in the United States to help the new civilian readjust himself to a normal life.

The one dark spot in the medical picture is that "malaria, the most widespread disease to which American troops overseas are exposed, has increased during 1943 despite the relentless battle being waged against it." There is no prophylaxis against malaria, Kirk explains, and, because the best cure is prevention, a shipment of fine mosquito screening or netting is more essential than a shipment of tanks or planes. In the latter part of 1944 it was reported that the education program in malaria control for all ranks in the Army had been executed with very satisfying results. In November Kirk was able to tell the Association of Military Surgeons of the United States that the incidence of malaria had been reduced to one-fourth of what it was early in the War and that the death rate was only one-twentieth of what it was in the First World War.

"Tough little Surgeon General Norman T. Kirk," as *Time* calls him, stresses the "home folks'" influence on the soldiers and looks with favor on mothers reminding their sons by letter to watch their health. He warns the public to expect the return of wounded, maimed, and disfigured fighters, and reminds us that Army medicine can heal physical wounds but that family and friends must help in the readjustment of the injured. "Don't be callous . . . and don't be oversympathetic and overhelpful. Treat him as a normal human being." General Kirk is also thinking of the doctors who will be returning to civilian life after the War. In an article in the New York *Times Magazine* of November 26, 1944 ("School of Battle for Doctors") he discussed the lessons doctors are learning at the front that will prove invaluable to them in their civilian practice.

As Surgeon General, Kirk is an ex officio member of the following organizations: the Board of Commissioners of the United States Soldiers Home, the Association of Military Surgeons, the Board of Visitors of Saint Elizabeth's Hospital, the Central Committee of the American Red Cross, and many others, as well as being director of the Columbia Hospital for Women.

Hearty, wiry-haired General Kirk says that his favorite recreations are fishing and hunting, but he can have little time for sport. In addition to his heavy duties as Surgeon General, he is a Fellow and Governor of the American College of Surgeons, also a Fellow of the American College of Physicians; and a member of multitudinous organizations, including the American Surgical Association, American Medical Association, American Orthopaedic Association, American Association for the Surgery of Trauma, and American Academy of Orthopedic Surgeons.

References

N Y Times p6 My 4 '43
Time 42:94-6 Ji 26 '43 por
Directory of Medical Specialists Certified by American Boards 1942
Who's Who Among Physicians and Surgeons 1938

KNOX, (WILLIAM) FRANK(LIN) Jan. 1, 1874—Apr. 28, 1944 Secretary of the Navy from 1940 until his death; newspaper publisher, a soldier in two wars, and a leader of the Republican Party—its Vice-Presidential candidate in 1936; in his four years of office Knox directed the unprecedented development of the United States fleet from an inadequate, undermanned organization to the mightiest navy afloat; see sketch 1940 Yearbook.

Obituary

N Y Times p1+ Ap 29 '44 por

KOCH, FREDERICK H(ENRY) Sept. 12, 1877—Aug. 16, 1944 Author; head of the University of North Carolina Department of Dramatic Art; veteran of American folk playwriting; regarded as a pioneer in the development of creating drama out of native tradition and present-day life; founded numerous dramatic groups; editor of many play collections, among them *American Folk Plays* (1939); *Carolina Folk Plays* (1941).

Obituary

N Y Times p13 Ag 18 '44 por

KOENIG, JOSEPH-PIERRE (kē″nĕg′ zhō″zef′ pyār) 1898- French Army officer; Military Governor of Paris

Former commander in chief of the French Forces of the Interior, which contributed to Allied successes against the Nazis, is Lieutenant General Joseph-Pierre Koenig, who officially became Military Governor of Paris after its final liberation. His army, under the authority of General Dwight Eisenhower [42], included not only Maquis fighters (guerillas—*gens du maquis*, literally "bushrangers") operating under the direction of former French Army officers, but hundreds of thousands of others. By the end of August 1944, with the Allies only a few miles from Germany, the F.F.I. controlled 60,000 square miles of French territory.

Koenig himself is one of the younger French generals, thoroughly trained in modern warfare, and never afflicted with the "Maginot mentality." The hero of Bir Hacheim was born in 1898 in Alsace (hence his German name). He did not attend Saint-Cyr or the French Military Academy, but rose from the ranks of the French Army. A volunteer in the First World War, he later served with the Chasseurs Alpins as well as with the French Foreign Legion, fighting against the Riffs in Africa "until his hawklike face acquired a permanent deep sunburn." He rose slowly in the Army after suggesting a plan to reorganize and improve the cavalry, and by the time of the outbreak of the Second World War was a captain. With the Foreign Legion he fought above the Arctic Circle, in Norway, helping to capture Narvik. By this time a commander, he returned to France with the Legion to defend his country against the German invasion through the Low Countries. "His back to the Atlantic, he led a last-ditch defense in Normandy, then escaped in a Breton fisherman's boat to England—and de Gaulle [40]."

Made a colonel by de Gaulle and sent to Free French Africa, Koenig became chief of staff of the first French division, under the orders of General Legentilhomme. In this capacity he took Damas, and was rewarded by promotion to the rank of brigadier general. Libya was next. At the desert oasis of Bir Hacheim, in May and June 1942, he and his little force held off General Erwin Rommel's [42] tanks and dive bombers for sixteen days. "Two square miles of sandy, windswept ridge, Bir Hacheim was the southern anchor of the line defending Eastern Libya." With his men Koenig "scattered the armored cars which attacked them. When he was surrounded for three days he decided that the best way of breaking the blockade was to break through. Refusing to surrender, he burned the Germans' vehicles, destroyed their tanks, and brought back captives. With his men he attacked the German positions and set free 800 prisoners of the Indian Brigade. With his men he received twice the personal greetings of General Ritchie." He had rejected seven Axis demands for surrender by the time the Allied High Command demanded his withdrawal—and when the order came he "led three-fourths of the original French garrison through German mine fields to safety." The ultimatum which Rommel sent to Koenig on June 3, 1942 has been framed and now hangs above de Gaulle's desk in Algiers.

From that time on de Gaulle wished to put Koenig in an important position of command, but for a long time was frustrated by General Giraud [42]. Finally, in July 1943, with the unification of all the French fighting forces under de Gaulle and Giraud, Koenig was named assistant chief of staff for the Army. Unquestionably and outspokenly a de Gaullist, in December 1943 he was ordered confined to quarters for fifteen days when he expressed, in colorful, terse language, his criticism of proposals for cooperation with Giraud. (According to one report, he had flung his Cross of Lorraine on the table for added effect.) The matter was later settled amicably, however, and in April 1944 de Gaulle appointed Koenig military delegate, or liaison man, to represent the French Committee of National Liberation in the "northern theatre" of operations. His job would be "to supervise all military liaison with the Allied High Command and direct the part to be played by Frenchmen inside France in conformity with the plans of the Allied commander in chief."

In London, Koenig found it tough going. The British and American Governments, while refusing to recognize the Committee as the Provisional Government of France (recognition was accorded it in November) also re-

LT. GEN. JOSEPH-PIERRE KOENIG

frained from sending any specific directive to Eisenhower on the extent of recognition of the Committee as the civil authority in liberated France. It was therefore impossible for Eisenhower to negotiate a formal agreement with the Committee like those made with the exiled Governments of Norway, the Netherlands, and Belgium; and after the British forbade the exchange of messages in their own code between French representatives in London and the French Committee in Algiers it was also impossible for Koenig to contact de Gaulle. Whatever arrangements Koenig made with Eisenhower were therefore made on his own authority, particularly after the French Committee ordered the conversations suspended on May 6. They nevertheless worked out a plan whereby Committee appointees would be entrusted with the civil administration in France, having a free hand as long as it did not interfere with military operations; and French officers in London received liaison training on this basis.

Matters came to a head on D-Day. After flying to London, de Gaulle, according to Allied sources, canceled the "agreement" that had been made between the Supreme Headquarters civil affairs branch and Koenig and permitted only a token force of twenty French officers, out of the hundreds who were ready to go, to accompany the Anglo-American invasion troops. (To the Allied criticism of de Gaulle the French replied that no such agreement had been canceled because none had been signed.) Then, on June 14, de Gaulle, accompanied by Koenig, left England in a French destroyer and toured the beachhead areas freed by the Anglo-American forces in eight days of fighting. He installed his own group of officers in civil affairs positions, declaring that the French Committee would act on its own. But on June 22 it was revealed that an informal arrangement had finally been made whereby French representatives would serve as liaison officers and as governors of the liberated sections of

France under the control of Supreme Headquarters.

In the meanwhile the French underground forces had helped the Allies immeasurably. "On D-Day, armed with whatever came to hand, often with pitiable equipment and precarious supplies, the resistance army launched a vigorous offensive over almost the entire territory, carrying out in disciplined fashion the orders received from the Allied command. Their skillful work behind the German lines often had results which costly bombing sorties could not have obtained. In bitter clashes with the Wehrmacht they always inflicted losses on the enemy." On June 25 Koenig's appointment as commander in chief of the French Forces of the Interior and as a member of General Eisenhower's staff meant an elevation of the status of these underground forces, and also underlined the satisfactory relationship that now existed between Supreme Headquarters and the French. During the months before the invasion French resistance organizations had been calling in vain for more arms, and now more arms were promised.

Demonstrations of the thoroughness and precision of the French underground's operations continued. The flow of vital German military materials, equipment, and troops into the battle zone was more and more seriously hampered by patriot sabotage of rail and road lines, supply dumps, food stores, waterways; most of the telephone wires out of Paris were kept cut; life became increasingly more precarious for collaborationists everywhere. Koenig, having established contacts with underground centers all over France, saw to it that arms and munitions were distributed to them. He also sent experienced Army officers to the Maquis forces in a number of sectors, aiming to combine them into a single striking force whose action would be coordinated with that of the underground movement. The successes of the Maquis, now regrouped and reorganized, soon became the subject of announcements in German military communiques. Although the guerrillas had succeeded in establishing themselves most firmly in the mountainous regions, they also held some cities; and Hitler was forced to divert more and more of his battle strength to repressive measures. Reprisals were fierce, the Germans having rejected Eisenhower's pronouncement that the guerrillas formed an integral part of the Allied Expeditionary Force.

On August 12 the F.F.I. in eighteen French departments, including two near Paris, were ordered by Koenig to "attack immediately all elements directed toward the front. Not a German soldier or truck should be allowed to reinforce the enemy fighting against our allies." Four days later Koenig revealed that an armored detachment, operating in Brittany and composed entirely of patriots under his command, had for the first time directly participated in the battle of France. (During July alone the Maquis had received a total of 1,000 tons of arms and ammunition dropped from Allied aircraft.) On August 17 resistance forces throughout France, apparently inspired by the Allied invasion of southern France, had already captured at least nine towns and were fighting inside six others. Their zone of operations widened swiftly each day. It was announced officially on August 22 that the French Forces of the Interior had wrested fourteen departments, totaling 50,000 square miles in southern and central France, from German domination. In Paris itself the Germans reported violent battles between their troops and guerrillas. At the same time de Gaulle appointed Koenig Military Governor of the capital.

On August 23 General Koenig issued, prematurely, as it turned out, a statement of the complete liberation of Paris. It appeared later that the Germans, hard-pressed by the F.F.I. and unarmed civilian fighters, had asked for an armistice and then repudiated it after regrouping their forces or receiving reinforcements. The deliverance of Paris became a fact when the French 2nd Armored Division, led by General Jacques-Philippe Leclerc '44, and General Omar Bradley's '43 Americans entered the city on August 25, going into action alongside the F.F.I., steadily crushed remaining German resistance. The German commander ordered his troops to cease fire immediately. (Opposition continued in the outskirts of the city.)

On August 25, too, the French signed civil administration agreements with the United States and Great Britain that provided for a large measure of French authority in liberated regions outside military areas of operation and dealt with technical problems—captured war material and property, currency, the distribution of civilian relief supplies, and publicity. The "arrangements" with the United States, the terms of which were agreed to between French and American representatives in Washington, were placed in effect through an exchange of letters between General Koenig and General Eisenhower as United States Commanding General. The commander of the American forces which helped to free Paris officially delivered the city to Koenig, previously named Military Governor of Paris by de Gaulle, at noon on August 28.

In the latter part of September the Commissariat of War issued a decree incorporating the F.F.I. into the French Army, though retaining them as distinct F.F.I. units. Koenig declared that the F.F.I. war record has justified their inclusion into the French land, sea, and air forces. The Ministry of War also ruled that F.F.I. enlisted personnel and noncommissioned officers must be given the same consideration as Regular Army men in pay, promotions, and decorations.

Joseph-Pierre Koenig has been awarded the Legion of Merit by Eisenhower for outstanding leadership. He is, according to a French colleague, a man with "long features, a broken nose, chestnut-colored hair, a fine mouth with a short mustache, a direct and malicious glance, giving an impression of calm energy, of controlled activity, of an irony profoundly human. He is a man whom I have never seen in a hurry, for he never is late for an appointment. I have never seen him nervous, for he is never surprised; he is never surprised because he has seen all and proven all. I have never seen him disturbed, for there is no sacrifice that he has not experienced, that he has not accepted. Because he is never disturbed his men have confidence in him and because they have confidence in him he has a smile for them all. . . . When things went badly he would smile, declaring, 'You're going to see some pretty sport, old fellow!' "

References

N Y Herald Tribune II p3 Jl 2 '44 por
N Y Sun p18 My 11 '44
Newsweek 23:56 Ap 24 '44

KOSLOWSKI, LEON (kos-lof'ski le'ôn) 1892(?)—May 11, 1944   Premier of Poland during the Pilsudski regime; held previous positions in the Agriculture and Finance Ministries; was a professor of archeology at the University of Lwów.

Obituary

N Y Times p9 My 19 '44 por

KOSSAK (-SZCZUCKA), ZOFIA (kôs'säk shchūts'kä zô'fyä) 1890-   Polish author
Address: b. c/o A. N. Roy Publishers, 25 W. 45th St., New York City

The April 1944 choice of the Book-of-the-Month Club and the May 1944 choice of the Catholic Book Club was a novel by Zofia Kossak, a Polish woman writer who may not even know that Americans are reading her book—for she is believed to be still living in liberated Warsaw. *Blessed Are the Meek* (1944), her first book to be translated into English, is about St. Francis of Assisi and the Crusades of the thirteenth century. According to Henry Seidel Canby '42, it is "a remarkable achievement and as interesting as it is remarkable." Miss Kossak, according to Canby, "has the art of the tapestry designer who knows that his tapestry will be hung as a background against which the moving figures of men and women take on significance. . . . Her tapestry stretches from Italy to Asia to Egypt to Jerusalem." Sterling North '43 agrees. Calling Miss Kossak "one of the finest historical novelists Poland has ever produced," he nevertheless points out that her forte is "pageantry rather than character delineation." On the other hand, Harry Hansen '42 finds *Blessed Are the Meek* "both too mild and too unreal" as a picture of the times; and Franz Weiskopf calls it "but a pale descendant of that other Polish novel which can be considered the ancestor of the whole species: Sienkiewicz' *Quo Vadis?*"

Born in 1890, Zofia Kossak's own experiences can have been scarcely less tragic than those of the Crusaders of whom she writes, for she belongs to that generation of Poles who have lived through three wars. She spent her girlhood on a landed estate in Volhynia, in the eastern marches of Poland. Her father, Tadeusz Kossak, who had been an officer in the Austrian Army and later a major in the Polish cavalry, had finally left the military service, and went to live on an estate at Skowrotki. Here Zofia Kossak spent her youth and lived through the terrible years of 1917-1919, which she was to picture in her first book, *Pożoga* (The Blaze) (1923), a documentary account of her own and her neigh-

ZOFIA KOSSAK

bors' and relations' experiences in Volhynia during this period.

The Kossak family is well known in Poland because it has contributed so many outstanding talents to Polish culture. Juljusz Kossak, Zofia's grandfather, was one of Poland's greatest painters, and her uncle, Wojciech Kossak, was also well known in that field. Marja Pawlikowska, her cousin, was a prolific poet. Magdalena Samozwaniec, the daughter of Wojciech Kossak, is popular as a somewhat capricious but very talented writer. Zofia herself studied painting in Switzerland and must have been somewhat undecided for a time as to the direction in which her talents lay, but she has always been attracted to the historical novel.

Writes Edwin Seaver: "Poland has long had a great tradition in the field of the historical novel, of which Sienkiewicz and Żeromski are, perhaps, the most notable exponents. It was in this tradition that Mme. Kossak wrote her subsequent articles and novels. While these cannot be said to reach the dynamic, dramatic power of Sienkiewicz or the compelling lyricism of Żeromski, they, nevertheless, form a unique contribution to the Polish historical novel. For in her works Mme. Kossak has explored a sector which previous novelists either neglected or treated with minor consideration. This is the field of religious experience and emotion. Invariably the author reveals a profound grasp of the spiritual climate of the times of which she writes and the dialectical process involving religious ideologies and historical events." *Beatus Scelus* (Happy Misdeed) (1924), *Złota Wolność* (Golden Freedom) (1928), and *Bitva pod Lignicą* (Battle at Lignica) (1930) were among the first of such historical novels. But her talent shines out most brilliantly, according to her Polish publishers, in the cycle of her novels based on the Crusades of the thirteenth century. In 1935 four volumes of *Krzyżowcy* (The Crusaders) were published, after which came *Król Trędowaty* (King Trędowaty) and *Bez Oręża* (Without Arms), the last being the

best in "the rich array of Zofia Kossak's literary output."

Bez Oręża was published in Poland before the Second World War, and Zofia Kossak was a leading candidate for the Nobel Prize when War came. Her Polish publishers in Warsaw were bombed and pillaged out of existence; their entire stock of 2,000,000 books was stolen by the Nazi invaders. Her second husband, Zygmunt Szatkowski (she was married first to Stefan Szczucki), who had been a colonel in the Polish Army, was thrown into a Nazi concentration camp; of her two sons, also in the Polish Army, nothing is known. But something was saved. Marian and Hanna Kister, who own Roy Publishers, had brought American books to Poland before the War; now they managed to escape to the United States, where they published *Blessed Are the Meek* in 1944. When the novel was chosen by the Book-of-the-Month Club they were so happy that they had the news conveyed by short-wave radio to Poland. Miss Kossak's other novels are now in process of translation, and they will follow *Blessed Are the Meek* into print. One was expected to appear in the spring of 1945.

Reference

Book-of-the-Month Club N p4 Mr '44 por

KREISLER, FRITZ (krīs'lĕr frits) Feb. 2, 1875- Violinist; composer

Address: b. c/o Charles J. Foley, 230 Boylston St., Boston; h. 2 Sutton Pl., New York City

"It is one of the unhappy paradoxes of music criticism," says Deems Taylor [40], "that the very persons . . . to whom the professional listener looks forward with the greatest pleasure are those about whom it is most difficult to write." Thus he begins a discussion of Fritz Kreisler, "a virtuoso whose artistry is so nearly flawless that it is like a pane of clear glass through which one looks upon beauty. . . . One comes away from a Kreisler recital as one who returns from a visit to a beloved and trusted friend, saying simply, 'He is still there.'"

Fritz Kreisler was born in Vienna February 2, 1875, the son of an eminent physician who was also known as an amateur ichthyologist. His first memory is of chamber music being played by his father and friends. At four the boy fashioned a crude violin out of an old cigar box; and he knew how to read music before he knew how to read words. Dr. Kreisler, who always regretted that he had not become a concert violinist, had to force his reluctant son to practice; although extraordinarily talented, Fritz was simply not interested in the grind of practicing—nor has he become any fonder of it since. The boy's concert debut was made when he was seven, and led to his acceptance at the Vienna Conservatory, although his age was exactly half the minimum age at which pupils were accepted. There may have been some inexactness in reporting the boy's age, but it was his violin playing which gained him admittance. After three years of study under Hellmesberger and Auer, Fritz was awarded the gold medal for first prize in violin. (Realizing that he was surpassed in violin-playing by his ten-year-old son, the good Dr. Kreisler gave up that instrument for the cello, which he taught Fritz's younger brother Hugo to play. When Hugo was nine, however, he was such a proficient cellist that his father was forced to change again, this time to the viola.) At ten Fritz was sent to the Paris Conservatory to study violin under Massart and theory under Delibes. Here, after two years, he astounded his teachers by winning the Premier Grand Prix from a field of contestants averaging ten years older than he. That same day Fritz's playmates elected him chief of their "robber gang"—which meant a great deal more to him than any musical or academic honor.

In 1888, when the thirteen-year-old Fritz first came to America on a joint concert tour with the pianist Moritz Rosenthal, he "played charmingly enough to receive a few kind notices from the critics," but most of their attention was devoted to the pyrotechnics of his co-star. On his return to Austria, Fritz was refused the post of second violinist with the Vienna Philharmonic Orchestra. Convinced that the concert stage was not for his son, Dr. Kreisler enrolled Fritz in the Vienna Gymnasium to prepare him for a medical career. At seventeen, having successfully completed his preparation for the University, young Kreisler decided that painting was his goal, and left for Paris to study under Julien, from whom he received "glowing praises." He continued his art studies in Rome, living largely, it is said, on oranges and water in order to save money. At twenty Kreisler had to return to Austria for required peacetime military service. After intensive study he passed with high honors the examination which qualified him as a captain in a Uhlan regiment of skirmishers and scouts.

In spite of Kreisler's success in the Army, he abandoned this career avenue as he had medicine and art. With some reluctance he picked up his old violin, only to find his former suppleness of fingers gone. Eight weeks of retirement, devoted entirely to practicing—and then Fritz Kreisler emerged, in his own words, "as great a fiddler then as I have been ever since." His second debut was made in Berlin in 1899; but it was not until his American tour from 1901 to 1903 that "his supreme position among the violinists of his day" was recognized. The Austrian violinist's cheerful and friendly platform manner endeared him to audiences whom he amazed by what Deems Taylor calls "the warmth and vitality of his playing, the technical mastery so complete that it is taken for granted, his mastery of style and phrasing, and above all, his magnificent grasp of form, a musical vision of such breadth that he sees every bar . . . in its relation to all that has gone before and is to come after." In 1904 the London Philharmonic Society put its stamp of approval on Kreisler with the award of the Beethoven Gold Medal.

While en route to the United States, Kreisler met "a beautiful redheaded American girl," Harriet Lies of New York, with whom he fell in love almost immediately. Although Mr. Lies, a prominent tobacco merchant, was somewhat dubious about having his daughter espouse a "mere fiddler", the couple had two

FRITZ KREISLER

wedding ceremonies—one in a New York City church in 1902, and another performed by the Austrian Ambassador in London the following year. Kreisler is quick to admit how much his wife's "fine brain", "uncanny intuition," and executive ability have meant to him— "baffled," as he says he is, by "the ordinary things of life." From her he has absorbed his feeling that whatever he earns is merely a fund entrusted to his care for proper disbursement. "I am constantly endeavoring," he says, "to reduce my needs to a minimum. . . . In all these years of my so-called public success, we have not built a home for ourselves. Between it and us would stand all the homeless of the world." (Elsa Maxwell '43 reports, however, that Mrs. Kreisler wears an emerald "larger than the Hope Diamond.")

At the outbreak of war in 1914 Reserve Captain Kreisler returned in haste from Switzerland to rejoin his old company in Galicia. There were times during the campaign when the great violinist and his men were "more than three days at a time without any food whatsoever"; and many a time, he says, they had to "lick the dew from the grass for want of water." A Russian cavalry attack at Lemberg (Lwów) ended his Army career with a lance wound that put him in a hospital for a long stay. Exempted from further service, Captain Kreisler sought to serve his country in the one way open to him: by raising money and sympathy for the Austrian cause. To this end, he wrote *Four Weeks in the Trenches*, published in 1915; sold his precious Stradivarius (he now owns a famous Guarnerius del Gesù of 1737); and, with "a cheap $300 violin," set out for a concert tour in the neutral United States. "The months [sic] he had spent in the trenches had deepened Kreisler's feelings," wrote Konrad Bercovoci. "He actually did plead the Austrian cause on his violin"; and he earned great sums of money, of which all but his minimum living costs went for the support of "a veritable League of Nations of orphans," 1,500

KREISLER, FRITZ—*Continued*

starving artists, and his hard-pressed family. When the United States ranged itself with the Allies, Kreisler was denounced as a menace by the Civil War Veterans, the Daughters of 1812, and the D.A.R. Although "audiences in the East were large and cordial," small towns repeatedly canceled his bookings. "Generously and graciously," the violinist renounced all his concert engagements and retired to Maine for the duration of the War— but he continued, characteristically, to play free engagements for charity. Under these conditions he appeared for the first time as a member of an ensemble, giving some "wonderfully fine" performances.

On his return to the concert platform in October 1919, Kreisler was greeted with a stirring demonstration of affection when the entire Carnegie Hall audience rose spontaneously to its feet to greet him, remaining standing for more than five minutes. In David Ewen's words, "It has remained on its feet ever since." At the time, however, Kreisler's appearances were marked by American Legion riots; in Ithaca he continued playing in total darkness after invading Legionnaires had cut the electric light cable. One minister declared, "He stands for the principles of Prussianism and *kultur.*" The violinist himself spoke gently of the "well-intentioned zeal which is entirely natural after these long years of rampant hatred," and even accepted a request from the Legion to contribute his services for a benefit performance—which never was given after all. When the fog of wartime frenzies had died away, Fritz Kreisler stood in an even firmer position than before.

From 1919 to 1924 Kreisler remained in the United States; and in the years that followed, although his world tours made him internationally famous, and although he was presented with a house in Berlin, he always returned to the land that had first acclaimed him. It seemed impossible that anything scandalous could touch this artist; and yet in 1935 the music world was startled by the discovery of the now well known Kreisler hoax. "In current musical history," the *Musician* editorialized "no event has commanded wider public attention than Fritz Kreisler's confession that he is the sole author of a large group of popular compositions for the violin which for thirty years had been published and performed the world over as arrangements from such classic masters as Vivaldi, Pugnani, Martini, Porpora, Couperin, Francoeur, and others. The effect of this startling disclosure among musicians generally, and among violinists particularly, has been a composite of amusement, perplexity, resentment, and applause." When those compositions were first presented—with the explanation that Kreisler had happened on them in a monastery and bought them from the monks—the device was "a temporary expedient" to gain a wider circulation for the works of the little-known composer. Not many persons considered it likely that he intended, so to speak, a successful musical forgery; probably he expected to be soon unmasked, thus rousing even greater interest

in his works because they had been ranked with the old masters. But the fraud was all too successful, even though each published copy bore the warning, ". . . so freely treated that they constitute, in fact, original works."

Ten years after these "transcriptions" were first presented Kreisler brought out another group of arrangements, allegedly of Joseph Lanner, comprising the "Liebeslied" ("Love Song"), "Liebesfreud" ("Joy of Love"), and "Schön Rosmarin" ("Beautiful Rosemary"). When a Viennese critic rebuked Kreisler for his "impudence" in playing his own "Caprice viennois" in a group with "these gems of Lanner," the violinist indignantly revealed that the gems in question were also his own. This was commonly known among musicians; "one would therefore expect that Kreisler's other 'transcriptions' would have been subjected to a more rigorous scrutiny." Finally, the critic Olin Downes [43], applying to Kreisler for information about the Pugnani "Praeludium and Allegro," was told that it was original, as were all the rest—except the first eight measures of the Couperin "Chanson Louis XIII." Many musicians were indignant at the deception—Ernest Newman wrote a long and bitter attack—but the final effect was to add to Kreisler's reputation because of the perfection with which he mimicked the classics. "Wholly aside from ethical considerations, one cannot escape the conclusion that violin literature has been pricelessly richened by this music, which has brought unmeasured happiness to thousands of listeners."

Not all of Fritz Kreisler's compositions were first issued under another name. His Viennese background is clearly shown in his lilting operettas *Apple Blossoms* (London, 1920) and *Sissy* (Vienna, 1933). His music was used in the Columbia film *The King Steps Out* (1936), in which Grace Moore [44] sang such Kreisler melodies as "Stars in My Eyes" to Franchot Tone [40]. Among the dozens of other Kreisler compositions, "The Old Refrain" and "Tambourin chinois" are perhaps the most popular.

"Aside from his musical importance," Kreisler "long since has earned his right to a place among the world's intellectuals." "Nature," he says, "requires a balance. I am interested in *everything.* The artist should live in his age. . . . Those who are interested only in their art are not great artists." Kreisler's own particular "balance" is old books: "I was more flattered," he says, "when the bookseller's paper commended me for my knowledge of books than I have been by many a critical eulogy of my playing," and he "actually peruses the medieval books he buys." His knowledge of languages is great—he speaks eight fluently. After a street accident in April 1941 in which his skull was fractured, the sixty-six-year-old violinist suffered a temporary amnesia in which he spoke only in Latin and Greek. Mrs. Kreisler knew her husband was on the road to recovery when he started talking in "English, French, German, everything."

During the six weeks he was in the hospital "many thousands of friends and acquaintances" sent letters and telegrams, a hundred persons offered blood for a transfusion—though none was needed—and as for the flowers, "It's a sin! It's a positive sin!" said Mrs. Kreisler, who feels that "it was really this love that pulled him through." On the violinist's return to the concert stage in November 1942 he received a tremendous ovation, which he proceeded to justify by "the old brilliance and élan", "the same supreme authority as interpreter", the "unsullied tone," and "habitual wealth of exquisitely modulated sound." At this time the sixty-seven-year-old composer premiered his "Viennese Fantasia," which "won immediate favor."

In May 1943 Fritz Kreisler became a citizen of the United States. He gave his previous citizenship as French, explaining that when his native Austria was annexed by Germany, France had gladly smoothed the way for his naturalization. (Mrs. Kreisler had retained her American citizenship.) Early the next year it was announced that the venerable artist would break a twenty-year precedent by playing five radio concerts for the Bell Telephone program, beginning July 17, 1944 with Mendelssohn's Concerto in E Minor and two other compositions. Wartime travel restrictions had cut down on his concertizing, he explained, thus giving him a chance to study radio technique; and many persons otherwise unable to hear him had written asking him to accept some radio offer. The fee was not announced, but was known to be more than $5,000 for each half-hour broadcast. Another "first" occurred for the violinist that same summer when he gave his first Lewisohn Stadium (New York) concert on June 19.

After many seasons Kreisler was represented once more on Broadway, when in November 1944 the operetta *Rhapsody* opened, only to close two weeks later. The musical score had been based on Kreisler melodies in arrangements by Russell Bennett [42]. But the lavish production, "devoid of drama and direction," and dealing with intrigue in the court of Maria Theresa, did not suit the composer's music. "Where Kreisler's contributions called for gaiety, sparkle, and charm," wrote Lewis Nichols of the New York *Times,* "*Rhapsody* on the whole clumped along in hob-nailed heavy boots."

Great as is Kreisler's artistry, much of his popularity is due to the "Kreisler charm": his charity, his wit, the warmth and simplicity of his platform manner, and the fine yet widely appealing quality of his programs. (One classic remark of his is widely quoted and as widely attributed. A supercilious Chicago heiress, engaging him to perform at a party for a $3,000 fee, explained that he was not expected to mingle with the guests. "In that case, Madame," the violinist immediately answered, "the fee will be $2,000.") "What has aroused most adulation among music audiences has been Kreisler's profound cultural background, which is quite unique among musicians," embracing as it does mathematics, art, medicine, engineering, languages, philosophy, philology, an expert knowledge of chess, and "as great a skill with the piano as the violin." Perhaps the most endearing thing about this scholar and musician is that his wife can complain that she is forced to drive

him to the irreducible minimum of practice with: "You're lazy. You're good for nothing. You'll never amount to anything."

References

Am Mag 11:66-7+ F '31 pors
Musician 40:3 F '35
New Yorker 4:29-32 N 24 '28
Ewen, D. Composers of Today 1936; Living Musicians 1940; Men and Women Who Make Music p3-20 1939
Kaufmann, H. L. and Hansl, E. B. Artists in Music of Today 1933
Stidger, W. L. The Human Side of Greatness p68-77 1940
Taylor, D. Of Men and Music p190-3 1937
Thompson, O. ed. International Cyclopedia of Music and Musicians 1943

KRONENBERGER, LOUIS (JR.) Jan. 9, 1904- Dramatic critic; author

Address: b. c/o PM, 164 Duane St., New York City; h. 16 W. 77th St., New York City

There is a common belief that critics and editors are simply disappointed authors. Whatever the merits of this contention, in the case of Louis Kronenberger the theory falls to pieces. A daily drama reviewer for a New York newspaper, he has to his credit a novel, a historical work, a number of translations, several anthologies, many magazine articles, introductions to others' books, and contributions to literary symposiums of one sort or another.

Like many New Yorkers, *PM's* drama critic comes from the Middle West. The son of Louis and Mabel (Newwitter) Kronenberger, Louis, Jr., was born in Cincinnati, Ohio, December 9, 1904. There he attended the Hughes High School and, for three years, the University of Cincinnati. He began to write at thirteen. Until the budding author reached seventeen, "there was," in Kronenberger's own words, "hardly a day when I did not write half-a-dozen poems or get half-a-dozen back from various magazines. At times, indeed, I was as much involved with postage as with poetry. It was generally understood in suburban Cincinnati that I would become a poet by trade, and I received no little encouragement from the neighbors. I was not, mind you, a showy kind of poet—I did not wear the hair long or give readings."

When Kronenberger began his professional career, however, it was in the more prosaic role of an editor for the publishers, Boni and Liveright. Entering their employ in 1926, he remained with them for seven years; in 1929 they published his novel, *The Grand Manner.* In 1933, he joined the editorial staff of Alfred A. Knopf [43]; and while there, he edited an *Anthology of Light Verse* (1935) for the publishers of the Modern Library series. Leaving Knopf in 1935, Kronenberger edited *An Eighteenth Century Miscellany,* brought out by G. P. Putnam's Sons in 1936. The same year saw his translation of the *Maxims* of La Rochefoucauld, and his acceptance of an editorial position with *Fortune* Magazine; then, in 1938 Kronenberger became drama critic for the sister publication *Time.*

(Continued next page)

LOUIS KRONENBERGER

Leaving this last position in 1940, the thirty-six-year-old writer joined the newly formed *PM* as play reviewer and occasional columnist ("One Thing or Another"). He later resumed his writing for *Time*. In January 1940 he was married to Emmy L. Plaut. (They now have one son, John.) Kronenberger's next work was published by Knopf in 1942. Entitled *Kings and Desperate Men: Life in Eighteenth-Century England*, it was said to have "the virtues of Louis Kronenberger's best short pieces—vigor, discrimination, and social awareness, plus far greater breadth." According to Clifton Fadiman [41], Kronenberger "would rather be right than startling. Yet there is a constant shimmer and independence about his view of the great wits and politicians and writers of the period. He never astonishes, but he rarely echoes." Robert van Gelder in the New York *Times* remarked firmly that the book "was brilliantly written out of confidence and pleasure, with nothing in it that bored the author and nothing that bored me. . . . The emphasis in the book always is on men and women—the soldiers, the writers, the politicians, the fops and artists and rakes, on the best things they said, the most characteristic things they did, on what they intended and what they achieved. The pace never lets down, nor does the style, which is animated, colorful, and never strained."

As a reviewer of plays, Kronenberger does not hesitate to tear apart an unsatisfactory production. *Variety* listed him as the second in "toughness" among New York drama critics during the 1942-1943 season, as having "panned thirty-seven shows of the fifty-two he reviewed. Of these verdicts, forty-four were justified by the box-office results," giving him an average of 84.6 per cent accuracy and tying him for fourth place among the reviewers in correctness of judgment. In June 1944 he moved up to second place on the list with an 89.2 per cent accuracy; at the end of 1944 Kronenberger was first—.917 per cent

right—with the *Times* and *Mirror* reviewers trailing in second.

The critic, feeling "wholesale recognition can make a mere ragbag of achievement—can dishonor the first-rate by blowing the third-rate up to the same proportions," complains elsewhere of the indiscriminate use of "catsup poured on criticism . . . using the biggest words on what are not the biggest plays." He himself does not hesitate to condemn plays of which he disapproves, describing them in such phrases as "a pill-coated piece of sugar", "three triangle plots have seldom borne so great a resemblance to a triple bromide", "one of those comedies that would be positively brightened up by a little tragedy." Of Gertrude Lawrence's [40] performance in *Susan and God* at the City Center, he remarked, "Miss Lawrence does seem at times like a rather desperate performer in a game of charades; there are even moments when she appears to be playing both Susan and God at the same time."

Reviews of this sort provoked the theatrical producers, Lee and J. J. Shubert, to such an extent that they sought to cut short his "unfair, unjust, and cruel" remarks by discouraging his attendance at their theatres through withholding the complimentary tickets usually sent to reviewers. (This reprisal was occasioned by the tone of Kronenberger's remarks in *PM;* his *Time* reviews were not involved.) Other critics who had been similarly banned were Walter Winchell [43] and the late Alexander Woollcott [41].

Kronenberger summed up the 1943-1944 theatrical season in an article in which he called the season as a whole "dispiritingly dull. It was blanketed with the trite ideas, the facile words, the stock gags, the tired tunes, the glib showmanship of a Broadway as careless as it was competitive." He explained that he recognized the difficulties of producing in wartime, but warned that, "bad art, quite as much as bad money, tends to drive out good." Kronenberger deplored the lack of imagination, intensity, style, and insight in the modern theatre. The fault, according to him, lies in the fact that "the theatre today lacks real standards and as a result lacks real discipline." To help combat this situation, Kronenberger has voiced much enthusiasm for the establishment of a repertory theatre devoted to the production of established plays, "so as to constitute a gradual education in good drama instead of an occasional flirtation with a good play."

References

America's Young Men 1938-39
Who's Who in America 1944-45
Who's Who in American Jewry 1938-39

KRUG, J(ULIUS) A(LBERT) (krūg) Nov. 23, 1907- Chairman of the War Production Board

Address: b. War Production Board, Washington, D. C.; h. 100 Norris Rd., Norris, Tenn.

On August 24, 1944 the long-smoldering personality-and-policy feud between the War Production Board's chairman, Donald Nelson [41], and its executive vice-chairman, Charles E. Wilson [43], finally exploded, with Wilson spectacularly resigning, and Nelson sent by the President on a mission to China. Into the scene stepped a new acting chairman, thirty-six-year-old J. A. ("Cap") Krug, called out of the Navy, where he had been serving as a lieutenant commander. (He became chief after Nelson's resignation September 30.) Behind Krug lay an impressive record: as power manager for the Tennessee Valley Authority and later for the Office of Production Management, and as vice-chairman of WPB before he was drafted into service. Before him lay one of Washington's toughest jobs: the complex problem of shifting the country from war production to reconversion of industry for civilian needs.

Known to his associates simply as "Cap," Julius Albert Krug was born in Madison, Wisconsin, the son of Julius John and Emma (Korfmacher) Krug. It is said that the family doctor, who on November 23, 1907 looked over the big, robust baby boy, exclaimed: "Julius is no name for him! You ought to call him Captain Kidd!" And, though Julius was the traditional family name, the nickname—quickly abbreviated to "Cap"—stuck with the boy. Krug's grandparents were among those Germans who didn't like Bismarck's Germany and came to settle in America. His father, now a Wisconsin state fire warden, was a patrolman when his son was born, later became a detective, then sheriff. There were five sons and two daughters in the Krug family; the father, on the slim salaries his jobs paid, worked hard to send all the children through the University of Wisconsin at Madison. "Never once did I hear him—or my mother—complain," Krug affectionately recalls. "It was just pure unselfishness and sacrifice—and it made a profound impression on me."

Young Cap entered the State University at eighteen, where he worked at various jobs to help pay his way. He did not win any academic honors, but played football during his freshman year. At nineteen, in March of his sophomore year (1926), he was married to Margaret Catherine Dean, his neighborhood sweetheart. "I started assuming responsibilities quite early in life," he says. After that, while continuing his education, he went to work at almost anything that came to hand. He was, in turn, a laborer on a scaffolding gang that repaired the county courthouse, helper in a cabinetmaker's shop, engine-wiper in the roundhouse of the Milwaukee Railroad, iceman, driver of a moving-van, and filling station operator. He received his B.A. in 1929, his M.A., for which he had majored in utilities management and economics, a year later.

Fortunately, Krug says, he was able to get a position at once as business research analyst with the Wisconsin Telephone Company. After about two years charting business curves for this company, he became chief of the depreciation section of the Wisconsin Public Utilities Commission. There for about three years he handled technical work on public utility rates and evaluations, and became a good friend of David Lilienthal [44], then one of the commissioners, later chairman of the Tennessee Valley Authority. It was in 1935 that Krug first went to Washington—as public utilities expert with the Federal Communications Commission. He conducted the first government investigation into the affairs of the Long Lines Department

J. A. KRUG

of the American Telephone and Telegraph Company, as a result of which long distance tolls were substantially reduced. It was a job which, his friends say, "almost lost him to the New Dealers." Krug came to feel that the Federal Communications Commission was more interested in social reform than in doing a good job. He went back to Wisconsin in 1937, resolving never to become connected with the Federal Government again.

When, in that year, Governor Albert B. Chandler [43] of Kentucky decided that a reorganization of the Kentucky Public Service Commission was in order, he selected J. A. Krug for the job. Krug, whose investigations resulted in many public utility rate reductions, is said to be rather proud of his work there. After the disastrous Ohio River flood of 1937 it was his job to make recommendations for utilities to follow in their new installations on the Kentucky side of the river. It was said that no private engineer ever disagreed with his recommendations.

About this time the Tennessee Valley Authority, of which Lilienthal had then become a member, began angling for Krug. In 1938 he became their chief power engineer. "I dropped into a hornet's nest," said Krug—meaning the case in which the private power companies were making a last stand against the T.V.A. It was Krug who directed the purchasing of the private power firms in that area, his largest deal being the $80,000,000 transaction with the Tennessee Electric Company, controlled by Commonwealth and Southern, of which Wendell Willkie [40] was president. Krug and Willkie personally negotiated the transaction; after the deal Krug said: "I think we got the best of the bargain." The young power engineer came to believe thoroughly in the T.V.A; but he believed also that complete government ownership of all utilities would bring politics into action. In his words, "It is best for the nation not to give either public ownership or private ownership too much rope." T.V.A.'s construction

KRUG, J. A.—*Continued*

program proceeded rapidly under Krug's direction: a large steam plant, built in eastern Tennessee, was called "the fastest construction job in American history until that time." During his work with the T.V.A., however, friends of Krug remember best his long and patient defense of T.V.A. before a joint Congressional committee. "For seven solid days the massive, blue-eyed man sat at a desk in the middle of the horseshoe rostrum in a Senate committee room. His explanations were unhurried and unruffled, and in the end he effectively silenced his critics."

This work with the T.V.A. was a considerable achievement for a young man of thirty. In 1941 William L. Batt '[12] of the Office of Production Management wanted a defense power consultant, a man who would be "acceptable to men who were for and men who were against public ownership," but "not a tightrope artist." Krug got the job, and by July 1941 was head of the OPM power branch. When Krug took over it was said that Secretary Harold Ickes '[41], who wanted to be the nation's "energy" director, could forget his ambitions to be Power Coordinator as well as Petroleum Coordinator. Krug immediately promised the pooling of power resources through the country to provide maximum defense efficiency. At that time he warned that priorities might be ordered to assure power for defense production, and he forecast the dim-out of bright lights in New York and other cities. He fought for daylight saving in wartime, and constantly had to talk state legislatures out of going back to normal times. He said plans had been made to provide electric power needed for the expanding aluminum and magnesium production, and praised the cooperation of private, public, and Federal power interests which had made possible this achievement. "The job must be done," he said. "It will be done. Old controversies must be pushed in the background. 'Business as usual' is out." Krug apparently gained the cooperation of the public utilities with which the Administration had previously warred. He did not completely avert power shortages, but "he kept the huge new aluminum plants and all other war industries turning." As chief of OPM's power branch, Krug won a reputation for "administrative ability, a tactful firmness, and straight shooting."

Following OPM's reorganization into the War Production Board, in August 1942 Cap Krug was named Deputy Director-General for Priorities Control. For several months he ran WPB's raw-materials allocation plan. Then, on February 13, 1943, when Donald Nelson created the Office of War Utilities, Krug was chosen as its director, becoming at that time (according to the *Nation's Business*) "the greatest single personage in the public utilities field today." On March 3, after the ousting of Ferdinand Eberstadt '[42], Krug was named vice-chairman in charge of materials distribution, and chairman of the powerful WPB requirements committee. He was the man to whom the fourteen "claimant agencies" —Army, Navy, Civilian Supply, etc.—looked when they needed more materials. He had to see that a steady flow of raw materials got

into the right industries at the right times. In addition, as director of the Office of War Utilities, Krug had charge of all the country's electric power; of all natural and manufactured gas used in generating power in homes, industry, and business; of all water power; and of communications. From him came dim-out orders, orders that controlled the temperatures in buildings; rules on water supply, directives controlling long-distance phone calls. Other powers of WPB's No. 3 man were: collecting and analyzing requirements for food, petroleum products for uses under WPB jurisdiction, and requests for allocations of these items; and serving as the principle link between the WPB and Lend-Lease, the Board of Economic Warfare, the Office of Defense Transportation, the Solid Fuels Coordinator, and the Agriculture Department. Late in December 1943 Krug was named chairman and American member of a public utilities committee formed to recommend action concerning the re-establishment of electric, gas, and water services in liberated areas of Europe.

Krug's two jobs as WPB program chief and head of OWU kept him very busy for six days and three evenings a week. The rest of the time he reserved for necessary relaxation. But they were tough, burdensome jobs, and big Cap Krug was showing it. According to one interviewer: "Office work and lack of exercise have softened him up a bit, weighted him down a bit, inclined him to sag a bit at unguarded moments. His face is full and ruddy; his blue eyes are somewhat bloodshot and circled by strain and late hours at his desk; his lips are startlingly red, tight-skinned as grapes; his brown hair is parted precisely in the middle and sleeked sharply back; his jaw is fleshy, and his neck is short and thick." Keeping long hours at his desk, Krug said he found getting a haircut one of the most vexatious problems that Washington offers: "No wonder they call us the long-haired boys!"

Early in 1944 Krug became the *cause célèbre* in a bitter battle by the WPB to save many of its key men from the draft. Donald Nelson said flatly that nobody could touch "big, hardheaded" Cap Krug, thirty-six, and the father of two children, for "native intelligence, knowledge, ability, and dependability." Krug himself had not asked for a deferment, and when he heard that WPB had, he insisted that the request be withdrawn. Accordingly, when Krug's Clinton (Tennessee) draft board put him in 1-A, he quit his jobs in order to accept a commission as a lieutenant commander in the Navy. He went into training as a damage control officer and was assigned to a ship. But when the ship's sailing was delayed, the Navy seized the chance to send him abroad to make a survey of the post-War utilities requirements of France and Italy. When told that his ship would sail on September 15, 1944, he flew back home to finish his utilities survey report.

On August 24, 1944 Krug was lunching at Washington's Metropolitan Club when a page tapped him on the shoulder and told him he was wanted on the phone. It was the White House calling. Said Krug: "When I heard that Wilson had quit, Nelson was going to China, and the Big Boss wanted me to take over—well, it came like something right out of the clear blue sky." He didn't want to leave the Navy—it had been doing him a lot of good physically as well as mentally. As his wife told reporters: "I'm sorry to see him go back to WPB; he's looked ten years younger since he's been in the Navy!"

The selection of Lieutenant Commander Krug as acting head of the WPB was interpreted as a White House endorsement of Donald Nelson's reconversion policies. Krug was definitely not Wilson's choice; New Dealers claimed that he had quit WPB to join the Navy largely because of disagreements with Wilson. It was also rumored that Krug had actually been selected for the post even before Wilson's resignation. The appointment of Krug not only pleased liberals, but was understood to be entirely satisfactory to the Army and Navy. And Nelson's resignation on September 30 ended arguments as to whether or not Krug's job was temporary. Through him, it was said, the Nelson viewpoint would certainly "continue to prevail in WPB policy on current production problems and the more difficult reconversion problems." The Krug appointment was seen, also, to take command of WPB away from big businessmen. "Although not a zealous New Dealer type," one commentator wrote, "Mr. Krug has been sympathetic with New Deal aims, and his appointment will give a New Deal complexion to management of WPB. He can be expected to protect small business and labor in reconversion." There was some opposition to Krug. Republican Representative Charles A. Halleck of Indiana said that "he is the choice of the New Deal backstairs cabal who have succeeded in getting rid of many efficient men."

Young Krug, in his new post, found three major tasks confronting him: to cure his organization of the "schizophrenia" that led to the final Wilson-Nelson blowup; to find a way of stepping up production in the lagging programs that brought the military organizations down on WPB's neck; to take hold of the much discussed plans for reconversion, systematize them and supplement them with comprehensive programs for full reconversion when the military situation permits.

The first task called for immediate action: if Krug failed here, it was likely that subsequent reconversion planning would be taken out of WPB's hands entirely. Krug's first public statement, made before the Senate committee of which Senator James Mead '44 (following Truman's resignation) was chairman, was definite and tough: he said he had given orders that Nelson and Wilson men must work together on both war and peace plans, or heads would fall. As a result of this firm stand, the strife-torn agency seemed to change into a "smooth-working organization where bickering was at a minimum." Having stated what would happen to feuders and "snipers," Krug further told the committee that the WPB program would be a double-feature: first, the delivery of war materials; second, reconversion. Production must not let up. In a Labor Day order Krug said: "We have not yet reached the point where we can afford to relax in any of the key programs which are still behind schedule. . . . Our production must continue to increase if we are to meet the requirements of our armed services." He appealed to top WPB aides to stay on the job

and "hammer away"; and marked for "junking" the slow machinery for cutbacks that had been set up by Nelson.

In the problem of reconversion, Krug came out definitely for small business. "We feel that the small businessman is the key to conversion." Small business, he explained, could get back to civilian production promptly while big business was retooling. He promised prompt local action on applications for manufacturing the articles which had already been authorized by Nelson. Then, on September 5, 1944, Krug announced a formal WPB program resulting from findings that "there would be a reduction of about 40 per cent of war production within three months after the defeat of Germany, which would free over 4,000,000 workers." WPB had decided: (1) to remove almost all controls over materials immediately upon the defeat of Germany, except those necessary to beat Japan; (2) that the WPB and other agencies would do all in their powers to assist and encourage industry in resuming civilian production and maintaining employment; (3) that the board would maintain its organization and powers so as not to relinquish authority until it was certain that the war production program was adequate for victory over Japan. In effect, industry was told it could convert itself "to whatever it wants to make" upon the defeat of Germany. There would be an over-all cutback of about 40 per cent in munitions production after Germany's fall; the civilian economy, as a result, would be returned to a level of production about equal to that reached in 1939.

On September 30 (the day Krug became permanent chairman) a special task committee of the WPB released a draft recommending a revocation of 350 out of the Board's 500 restrictive orders following the defeat of Germany, plus a simplification of the remaining 150. These controls, according to the plan, would apply to materials in which shortages were expected to continue. Recognizing that the cutbacks would be uneven in their impact, this draft also recommended retention of some allocation and scheduling controls and of "its contingent authority to minimize the consequences of acute shortages when they developed."

One of Krug's first statements as chairman was that the Government "could not grant now the request of automobile manufacturers for priority on machine tools," since record-breaking munitions production schedules for the rest of the year stood in the way. In recognition, however, of the acute reconversion problems which will beset the aircraft industry when Germany surrenders, Krug suggested the establishment within the WPB of an aircraft division to deal exclusively with reconversion. Also, the production of 495,000 new shotguns and rifles for essential civilian uses was authorized. When there was complaint that a "feasible production" of refrigerators and washing machines was being held up, Krug replied that their manufacture was delayed by a shortage of labor in areas where appliance plants are located. In a letter to Krug, President Roosevelt stressed the need for the inclusion in reconversion plans of a greater manufacture of farm machinery for the production of huge amounts of food for home and foreign con-

KRUG, J. A.—*Continued*

sumption. To this Krug replied: "Of course, we are going to do everything possible to give the farmers all the farm machinery they want."

Recognizing the importance of rebuilding Russia's destroyed Dnieprostroy power plant, Krug authorized the manufacture of nine hydroelectric turbine generators for installation. And organized labor and the OPA, among others, were relieved when Krug vetoed a deal between his subordinates and the National Housing Administration which, by lifting many restrictions, would have "wrecked" the program for housing war workers.

Late in October 1944 the WPB chairman decried the lag in war production. Such a lag continued, he said, could "delay European victory for months." An encouraging note, however, was the report that so far in the War 240,000 aircraft had been built and that changes in production methods were bringing up to schedule the output of B-29's. About a month later, in early December, when the Army chiefs gave notice that more ammunition was imperative, Krug said the production of small-arms ammunition and mortar shells would be greatly increased. This called for 62,200 more workers and the reopening of shut-down plants.

This stepup in war production was dwarfed, however, by the order to halt reconversion in 126 cities in the supreme effort to meet the needs caused by the Allied reverses in the December German offensive, when losses were high in trucks, tires, artillery, ammunition, and other essential supplies. Production of passenger car tires was slashed for early 1945; all tire rationing certificates issued before March 1944 were voided; and all production of civilian goods was frozen until further notice. With the prospect facing America of a war continued "indefinitely," orders were given for the building of new factories at a cost of two hundred million dollars. Before this Krug had told a Senate committee that while it was too late for a national service law, specific authority was required to enforce manpower regulations—that legislation "with teeth in it" would keep workers in war plants. He also recommended the payment of bonuses to workers who stayed on their jobs as long as they were needed. Studies made by the WPB, he said, had convinced him that a measure was necessary to "halt the costly turnover of war workers."

Looking toward civilian needs, Krug in early December announced the allocation of cotton yarn for the production of children's undergarments and sleeping garments. Later he also stated that a program would be put into effect whereby a more equitable distribution among smaller merchants of low-cost clothing for men, women, and children would be made.

Krug took the attitude that there would not be serious post-War unemployment. "There will be some shocks, to be sure; we shouldn't kid ourselves about that. But I believe we'll be amazed how quickly industry will swing back into civilian production.... If some fellows seem about to be crushed, we'll give them help. Of course, we can't wet-nurse every one of the 200,000-odd enterprises expected to spring up after civilian production is resumed." Krug had his critics; but the majority opinion applauded (as one editorial writer put it) a "better than a fair demonstration of a young man getting a job done. . . . He's trampling all over the tenets of bureaucracy ... and he's talking out loud. There hasn't been such talk from inside the New Deal since Mr. Roosevelt's campaign speeches back in 1932." Rumors were circulated that Krug was being groomed for the over-all post of demobilization direction: the job would call for a "young, tough, rugged, and competent" man—a description which would seem to fit J. A. Krug.

But the No. 1 man of the WPB, whose six feet three inches and 235 pounds make him literally one of the biggest men in Washington, hasn't much time to consider additional jobs. The very few free evenings he has are spent with Mrs. Krug and their two children, Marilyn Ann and James Allan. He likes golf, but has no time to play. He likes to read, but hasn't read a single book "clear through" since he came to Washington. He usually takes time for a cocktail before dinner and a highball afterward. He is a big eater who "likes nothing better than a nice thick steak, preferably grilled with his own hands over an open charcoal fire." A conservative dresser, he usually wears brown suits and white shirts, and "doesn't want any women around" when he goes shopping. He took up aviation some years ago as a hobby and has several hours of flying time to his credit. He likes and respects the legal type of mind: many of his closer friends are lawyers. But he doesn't like personal publicity, and hopes to "keep personalities out" of the WPB as long as he is connected with it. Some day he hopes to go back to his home in Norris, Tennessee, "where the hill country slopes up to the Cumberlands and you can see the Smokies on a clear day."

References

Business Week p7 Ag 1 '42; p7 S 2 '44
N Y Herald Tribune II p3 S 3 '44 por
N Y Post Mag p7 My 22 '43 por; p5 S 3 '44 pors
N Y Sun p19 Ap 28 '43
N Y Times IV p2 Jl 27 '41; IV p2 S 3 '44
PM p19 Ag 27 '44 por
Time 40:21 Ag 10 '42; 43:21 Mr 20 '44

Who's Who in America 1944-45

KURENKO, MARIA (kū-ren′kō) Singer
Address: b. c/o Austin Wilder Concert Management, 745 Fifth Ave., New York City

The soprano chosen to headline the Carnegie Hall program commemorating, in the fall of 1943, the fiftieth anniversary of the death of Peter Ilich Tschaikowsky was Russian-born Maria Kurenko, star of the opera, concert stage, and radio. Considered by Serge Koussevitzky [40] the best living interpreter of Tschaikowsky's songs, Mme. Kurenko "sang at her best, which is one of the first 'bests' in the world in her field," the New York *Times'* critic wrote.

The youngest of five children of Michael and Countess Paraskeva Kurenko, Maria was born in Moscow to a family whose love of music amounted almost to a mania. Everyone either played an instrument or sang, including little Maria, who at the age of three began to add her vocal bit to the accompaniment of a guitar. As far back as she can remember, she wanted to become a singer, and in the child's world of fantasy she was already a famous diva. Even her dolls were transformed in her imagination to famous opera stars who unanimously acknowledged her as their peer.

Maria's father was an able pianist, but it was from her mother that she received her early musical training: lessons in piano, voice, and solfeggio. This was later supplemented with instruction from competent, if not brilliant, local teachers. When it was time for Maria to attend school, she entered the Moscow Conservatory, from which she was graduated with high honors, winning a gold medal for general excellence.

At the time of her enrollment at the Conservatory she also entered the University of Moscow. Although the Conservatory offered a sufficiently rigorous course of study, she did not want to risk becoming overspecialized. Girls had only shortly before been permitted to study at the University on an equal basis with men; in a great wave of what might be termed intellectual feminism, many Russian young women responded to the attractions of university life. Of the four Kurenko sisters, one became a physician, a second studied philology, and Maria, not to be outdone, worked for a degree in jurisprudence.

At the Conservatory she distinguished herself in her studies, which were directed by the well known Umberto Mazetti of Bologna. In 1915 she was graduated from both the University and the Conservatory. She was awarded a gold medal by the Conservatory, being the third woman to receive that honor in the fifty years of that institution's existence. Mme. Kurenko "sang her way" through school from the time of her tenth year. Throughout her childhood she sang as soloist in the choir of one of the large Moscow churches. Later, she was one of the highest paid soloists in the choir of Moscow University.

Mme. Kurenko made her debut in 1916 at the Opera House of the city of Kharkov. She created such a furor that she was called to Moscow and engaged by the Moscow Folk Opera. Overnight, practically, Kurenko the lawyer became Kurenko, a famous prima donna. Her first role was that of Antonida in Glinka's *Life for the Tsar.* So successful was her performance that she was assigned a number of other important roles. Two years later Mme. Kurenko became a member of the Moscow Grand Opera, where, in addition to Russian operas, she sang the leading soprano roles in *La Traviata, Manon Lescaut, Rigoletto,* and the *Barber of Seville.* During the Russian Revolution Mme. Kurenko continued to sing at the Opera. However, with the devaluation of the currency, she often received payment in food.

After the Revolution Maria Kurenko found it difficult to adjust herself to the widespread political "curiosity" and to what she considered the infringements on her personal freedom. She explains, too, that she wanted to see more of the world. As soon as the Russian Govern-

MARIA KURENKO

ment permitted her to leave for a concert tour, therefore, she departed from her native land. Her subsequent travels in Finland, Poland, and the Baltic countries brought her many rewarding professional appearances. In 1924 she made her home in Riga, remaining there for two years.

It was at one of her Paris recitals in 1926 that Jack Adams of the Wolfson Concert Bureau heard her sing and immediately urged her to sign a contract for a concert tour of the United States. The following year Mme. Kurenko made her American debut in *Lakmé* with the Los Angeles Opera Company. She was acclaimed by both the audience and the press; other appearances in opera and recital won for her many devoted followers in the country. Consequently, Mme. Kurenko returned to sing in the United States every season until she finally returned to make it her home.

In addition to recitals and appearances with leading opera companies, Mme. Kurenko has sung as soloist with major symphony orchestras conducted, among others, by Toscanini '42, Koussevitzky, Fritz Reiner '40, Molinari, and Gabrilowitsch. In 1930 she made a transcontinental American tour with the composer Gretchaninoff, singing many of his works, some of which have been dedicated to her. In 1936 she sang the role of Marfa in a New York performance of Rimsky-Korsakoff's rarely presented opera, *The Tsar's Bride.* In 1940, Victor selected her to record an album of Tschaikowsky songs in honor of the centenary of that composer's birth.

Mme. Kurenko is her own severest critic and constantly works to improve her depth and finish. Judging by the reviews of her recent recitals, her efforts are well rewarded. Noel Straus of the New York *Times* thought that Mme. Kurenko's voice "showed a remarkable gain in volume and in richness of texture. It was under superb control and capable of a new

KURENKO, MARIA—*Continued*

wealth of color effects." Jerome D. Bohm in the New York *Herald Tribune* commented: "Mme. Kurenko's voice has grown warmer, fuller, and darker since last I heard it and has lost none of its flexibility or range. The result is that her interpretations have gained immeasurably in conviction. Everything she undertook . . . was crowned with success." Virgil Thomson[40] is of the opinion, however, that Mme. Kurenko's understanding of music is incurably Slavic. Her Italian work lacks "the frankness and the bravura that are fundamental to Italian music"; her French songs, while clearly rendered, lack "simplicity and poetry," declares Thomson.

Mme. Kurenko's musical activities, however, have not been confined to recital work and opera. She has long been a favorite of radio listeners, having begun her radio career in 1927 with appearances on the Atwater-Kent "Celebrity" series. Since that time she has sung over many major networks, on programs sponsored by General Motors, Standard Oil, and Carnation Milk. From July 1943 to the following January the soprano sang on the Sunday night *Columbia Concerts* series, a CBS program featuring the Columbia Concert Orchestra under Howard Barlow[40]. In May 1944 she began her second appearance on the series, with Bernard Herrmann and Nicolai Berezowsky the alternate conductors. She has also been a frequent guest on CBS's *Invitation to Music* series and the *Gateway to Music* program of the American School of the Air. In May 1944 Mme. Kurenko sang in Washington, D. C., at the Chamber Music Guild concert, after which a reception was held in her honor at the Soviet Embassy.

Barclay Hudson of the New York *World-Telegram* has said of her radio voice: "Mme. Kurenko is reproduced with an extraordinary fidelity, which is a gratifying thing, particularly since the microphone has occasionally been known to wreak its little havoc on the best voices."

In 1936 Mme. Kurenko became a naturalized citizen. She mentions with special pride the two occasions when she was invited to sing at the White House. To her this represents as important a distinction as having world famous composers write music for her. (Among the composers who have dedicated songs to her are Glazunoff, Medtner, Gretchaninoff, and Berezowsky.)

While she has a stately stage presence, Mme. Kurenko is only five feet three inches tall. Whenever she smiles—and she smiles often—her brown eyes flash with humor and vitality. Her auburn hair is usually worn in a soft pompadour. She is married to Fedor Gontzoff; their son Vadim, who is now in the United States Army, is a Columbia University graduate and a former motion-picture actor, known in Hollywood as Victor Kendall. Like most opera stars, Mme. Kurenko is an accomplished linguist.

References

Ewen, D. ed. Living Musicians 1940
Who's Who in America 1944-45

LA FOLLETTE, ROBERT M(ARION, JR.) (lä fol'let) Feb. 6, 1895- United States Senator from Wisconsin

Address: b. Senate Office Bldg., Washington, D. C.; h. Maple Bluff Farm, Madison, Wis.

The Progressive Senator from Wisconsin, Robert Marion La Follette, Jr., son of "Fighting Bob" La Follette, has been identified with such major domestic issues as unemployment, labor relations, and taxation. A descendant of frontiersmen who had been in the vanguard of successive east-to-west migrations, he was born February 6, 1895, in Madison, Wisconsin. The political "insurgent" beliefs of the frontier motivated Wisconsin's elder statesman, whose doctrines comprised the "Wisconsin idea" which Young Bob, together with his brother Philip, absorbed in boyhood. The La Follette creed, that "the will of the people shall be the law of the land," fought for in terms both dramatic and realistic, made a lasting impression on him. His mother, Belle Case La Follette, was "a brilliant woman, to whose advice both her husband and her sons were much indebted."

When Young Bob was six his father had become Governor of Wisconsin, crusading to free the state from the control of railroad and lumber corporations. His earliest memories were "of the Governor's Mansion and the dramatic figure of his father, who made it frequently the center of national attention. . . . His earliest education was less in the Madison schools than in the absorbing political discussions between his father, his calm, even-tempered mother, and the other leaders of the Progressive movement who met in frequent council at the Governor's Mansion."

When his father went to Washington as Senator in 1906 the boy's education was transferred to national political issues: he spent much of his time listening to his father's brilliant participation in Senate debates. He was seventeen when his father made an almost successful bid for the Presidential nomination of 1912. Thereafter he watched the inauguration of Woodrow Wilson's "new freedom" and saw many of his father's liberal proposals adopted by a Democratic Administration which left him, at the same time, in relative isolation.

It is said, however, that Young Bob never wanted to go into politics: his main interests were banking and journalism, and he entered the University of Wisconsin for formal education in those subjects. At the University he was "a sufficient but not brilliant student." He had attended public grade school in Madison and had friends among the townspeople as well as among the students at the University. He was elected president of his class in his freshman year. But at the end of his second year at Madison he became critically ill with pneumonia and resulting complications, from which he did not recover for many months. Throughout this time his father (nationally denounced following his vote against the declaration of war) sat at his son's bedside.

On his recovery, Young Bob did not return to the University but became instead his father's secretary. In 1920 he had become sufficiently mature politically to accompany Gilbert Roe, his father's agent, to the national

Farmer-Labor convention. Then, during the Harding Administration, he helped his father plan the exposés of the oil scandals. For a time he was clerk to the Senate Committee on Manufactures. By 1924, when the elder La Follette undertook an independent campaign for the Presidency, Young Bob became his spokesman and participated in the management of his campaign.

Then, in 1925, Robert La Follette, Sr., died; it was imperative that a La Follette carry on the "Wisconsin idea" by filling his seat in the Senate. Young Bob's mother declined to be Senator in her husband's place; his brother Philip, who intended to make politics his career, was then too young for the Senate. It was up to Young Bob to be the candidate, and in the election which followed he won by a large majority.

"The youngest Senator since Henry Clay" took his seat in a Senate dominated by conservatives, and determined to carry on the insurgent role of his father. Some observers whispered that he would be only "a pale shadow" of Fighting Bob. Said one: "Robert M. La Follette, succeeding to his cyclonic father—ideal of the rough and shaggy Northwest where men are men—wears pearl-colored spats." But the Republicans were wary. They told him that if he cared to "moderate" his position he could have his choice of the better committee assignments. His reply was that he would continue to be the "same kind of Republican" his father had been. As a result the committees to which he was assigned were relatively unimportant. Young Bob didn't mind. He quietly bided his time, preparing himself by reading extensively in political biography and political science.

He did indicate his interests when he introduced a resolution for a Senate investigation of the Ward Food Products Corporation; demanded a Congressional investigation of conditions in the New Jersey textile mills that had led to the Passaic strike; assailed the inaction of the Coolidge Administration on farm relief; offered a resolution to bar from the Senate any candidate spending more than $25,000 in a primary or general election; and attacked the further tax reduction proposed by the Treasury under the late Andrew Mellon. In the field of foreign policy, he spoke strongly against the World Court. He has, however, supported various kinds of international cooperation, including the International Labor Office.

In 1927 La Follette became a more active insurgent. The question of a third term for Coolidge came up. La Follette promptly offered a resolution condemning the third term as a "flouting of American tradition" and praising Coolidge for adhering to this tradition by his "I do not choose to run" declaration. The Coolidge supporters were thus put on the spot and the resolution passed. La Follette also led in denouncing the Administration policy in Mexico and Nicaragua. On the labor front, he petitioned Governor Fuller of Massachusetts on behalf of Sacco and Vanzetti; later he made a final appeal on their behalf to President Coolidge.

During the 1928 session La Follette "began to develop into legislative form two of the issues which have been peculiarly his." The

ROBERT M. LA FOLLETTE

first was his conception of a national tax system based upon the principle of ability to pay according to income. The young Senator's second major concern was his attempt (April 1928) to draw an indifferent Senate's attention to a serious study of national unemployment.

The economic Jeremiah was not without honor, however, in his home state. Still cherishing the hope that the Republican Party might be made a progressive vehicle, in 1928 he went to the national convention as chairman of the Wisconsin delegation. There he presented a minority report which urged farm relief, public ownership of utilities, higher income taxes, aid to the St. Lawrence waterway, prohibition of injunctions in labor disputes, the curbing of stock market inflation. The delegates listened and applauded, but Hoover [43] got the votes. La Follette later attacked the Republican platform as reactionary and gave his attention to his own campaign in Wisconsin, running on a Progressive platform. In November 1928 he was re-elected by a large majority to a full six-year term.

That winter when La Follette returned to Washington he found his stride. One of his "most far-reaching exploits" was the abolition of secret sessions for consideration of executive appointments, and "the Supreme Court was brought under the control of public opinion for the first time in the nation's history." Furthermore, La Follette headed the coalition Progressives and Democrats who fought the conservative Smoot-Hawley Tariff Bill to a standstill.

Early in 1930 the conservative Republicans tried unsuccessfully to bar La Follette from a place on the Senate Finance Committee, to which he was assigned on January 12. He continued his attacks upon the inadequacies of Federal relief measures, and by the winter of that year Young Bob was accepted "not merely as the son of his father, but as a colleague" by such Senate leaders as George

LA FOLLETTE, ROBERT M.—*Continued*
W. Norris, Robert F. Wagner [41], Smith Brookhart, and William E. Borah [40]. Norris frequently referred to him as his successor in the Progressive movement. This position had been won "not by oratorical brilliance, but by sheer industry in committee and on the floor, his mastery of the subjects under discussion, and his fairness in debate." The three major policies upon which he was henceforth to concentrate his attention were those of unemployment, labor relations, and taxation.

The economic collapse of 1929-1930 substantiated La Follette's warnings of two years before. In 1930 he compiled nationwide statistics on the unemployed and declared before the Senate that the Federal Government had a responsibility which it could not evade. The La Follette-Costigan Bill for unemployment relief was defeated in February 1932; in July the Wagner substitute bill providing for loans rather than grants was accepted. It was, however, La Follette's drive "that compelled Hoover to admit by inference that he had been blocking relief," and that made the Tories of the Old Guard come to fear Young Bob "as much as they ever did his father." Continuing his fight for relief appropriations, La Follette caused consternation in Hoover circles by introducing a bill calling for a five-and-a-half-billion-dollar public works program.

It was the new President, Franklin D. Roosevelt [42], who saw eye to eye with La Follette on necessary relief measures. Early in 1933 the New Deal put into law many of his previous ideas on the subject. In 1934 La Follette introduced a bill to continue the PWA program; in 1935 he offered an amendment to the Work Relief Bill to increase appropriations to $9,880,000,000; in 1936 he was not only a sponsor of the Social Security Bill, but introduced a bill to put all government employees under civil service. But La Follette wanted more than New Deal "expediency" would grant: a government-owned central bank; public ownership of railroads; public development and operation of electric power; government ownership of munition plants.

Dedicated to the cause of labor from the beginning of his career, La Follette in 1936 became chairman of a Senate subcommittee to investigate abuses of civil liberties and denials of the right of labor to bargain collectively. This La Follette, or "Civil Liberties," Committee, of which Senator Elbert D. Thomas [42] of Utah was also a member, set a new and distinctive record. The Committee, after thorough investigation of five big detective agencies, revealed that, through an elaborate system of espionage, industry had for years been keeping tab on organizing activities among employees; and that such agencies had supplied spies, equipment, and men for breaking strikes. The Committee then turned its attention to the labor trouble in Harlan County, Kentucky, laying bare the "social and economic oligarchy" there. It also put into the record the personnel and methods of nationwide vigilante organizations. Possibly La Follette's most striking work in labor investigation was, however, his "painstaking case history" of the

Chicago Memorial Day incident, in which police clubbed and shot workers at Girdler's [44] Republic steel plant. "Observers have described the development of evidence in this investigation as excelling all previous committee investigations." The La Follette Committee on the whole, it is said, "has furnished the data upon which national and state labor legislation has been based . . . and facts which have guided administrative practice in labor relations."

In the field of taxation, La Follette has had "the most completely developed legislative program of his career." Throughout the Coolidge and Hoover regimes he hammered away at the need for levying taxes upon those who can pay, and in terms of their ability to pay. With the advent of the New Deal he was successful in securing the adoption of some of the main features of his tax program which has always been premised on the principle of taxation in accordance with ability to pay.

By 1938 Senator La Follette occupied a strategic place in party politics: with his brother Philip (then Governor of Wisconsin) he led the Progressive movement in the upper Mississippi valley, and he was often spoken of as the logical Presidential candidate for a national farmer-labor party. He was, moreover, strongly entrenched with the New Deal, although since opposing the World Court, La Follette had strongly opposed both war plans and "foreign entanglements" for enforcing the peace. He declined, in 1933, an invitation to be a delegate to the World Monetary and Economic Conference. By 1937 he was proposing a Constitutional amendment to provide for a national referendum on war except in case of attack by armed forces, actual or immediately threatened, upon the United States or its territorial possessions, or by any non-American nation against any country in the Western Hemisphere. In 1938 he assailed the arms expansion program before the Committee to Keep America out of War; in 1939 he fought the arms embargo repeal.

Up for Senatorial re-election in 1940, La Follette found himself in difficulties. While his isolationist stand was viewed with favor by many Wisconsin voters, he had come out in favor of a third term for Roosevelt, and the farmers had "turned sour" on the New Deal. With his third term endorsement he was also forced by the opposition to recall his anti-third term resolution in the days of Coolidge. But in many eyes the most damaging thing against La Follette was, ironically enough, the fact that in 1938 he had, along with some sixty other Congressmen, signed a joint message wishing success to the Loyalist Government in Spain. While many of these signers later repudiated their action, La Follette stood by his; and in 1940 the Republicans made good use of that fact among Catholic voters. The New Deal, however, threw its support behind the Wisconsin Progressive, and he won his hard fight for re-election.

He continued his vigorous opposition to the Administration's foreign policy, but remained ardently pro-labor. It was not easy going. His bill to outlaw oppressive labor practices passed the Senate on May 27, 1940, by a vote of 47 to 20, but was not reported from the House Committee on Labor and therefore failed to become law. In March 1941 the Senate Civil Liberties Committee, of which La Follette was chairman, issued reports covering the threatened strikes in the Little Steel group, saying that the nation, in view of its current defense effort, could not permit the Little Steel companies to take the same attitude they did in 1937 and oppose collective bargaining "with the same inevitable consequences of interrupted production." On March 2, 1942 he and Senator Thomas, also of the Senate Civil Liberties Committee, made a report on employer associations in California, which were found to be "waging war against industrial and agricultural labor alike," and "cloaking such policies in the name of national defense." In late 1942 La Follette and Thomas introduced in the Senate five bills designed to extend to farm workers many of the rights given urban workers by New Deal legislation: social security guarantees, unemployment insurance, agricultural wage boards, and a Labor Recruiting Act. In 1943 La Follette voted against limiting the National Labor Relations Board, against the Smith '41-Connally '41 Anti-Strike Bill and for upholding the President's veto of it. In 1944 he opposed the proposal to force unions and cooperatives to file annual income tax returns.

La Follette voted with the Administration on such national domestic issues as the dismissal of Watson, Dodd, and Lovett '43 and appropriations for the National Youth Administration and the National Resources Planning Board. But on much legislation involving farmers he found himself in opposition to Roosevelt, perhaps because Wisconsin farmers were against many aspects of the New Deal's anti-inflation program. In October 1942 the Senator from Wisconsin challenged Roosevelt's right to fix farm prices by executive order. In 1943 he voted to continue the loan powers of the Farm Security Administration, for an appropriation for soil conservation and crop insurance, and for Federal funds for a price rollback; but he also voted for the deferment of farm labor and for the inclusion of farm-labor costs in parity, and early in 1944 he voted approval of the Bankhead '46 Bill to forbid most existing food subsidy programs after June 30. He was appointed by a group of dairy state Senators to lead their fight against proposed elimination of the ten per cent tax on oleomargarine.

On taxation, his position was similarly anomalous. In 1943 he denounced the Ruml '43 tax plan, saying its passage would "force increases in tax rates later this year on middle and lower income groups"; yet he opposed the President's order imposing a $25,000 limit on salaries. In January 1944 he was one of four members of the Senate Finance Committee to warn that proposed amendments to the war contracts renegotiation law would breed "a new crop of war millionaires," and he effectively blocked certain amendments to the new tax bill to aid the war profiteers, as the Commerce Department reported record-breaking peaks in corporation profits in 1943. Furthermore, as one of the committee which drafted the new tax bill, he proclaimed himself "not satisfied" with it. He would have

made proposals on the Senate floor to better it if Senate Leader Alben W. Barkley '41 had given him any encouragement. Yet in February 1944, when Barkley made his dramatic speech of resignation in protest against the President's speech vetoing the bill, La Follette was one of the first to rise in tribute to Barkley, and he himself voted to override the President's veto.

The Senator has supported the Government-sponsored St. Lawrence River development. In December 1944 he accused its opponents of conducting an "underground campaign" to scuttle it, declaring that private utilities are now opposing the project, although they had approved of private development of the waterway. Railroad interests, he said, had joined in fighting the project because of Eastern financial control.

A front page story in the August 18, 1943 issue of the *Progressive,* a weekly paper published by the La Follettes, was headed "The New Deal Is Dead," and stated that "the progressive forces of America have lost faith in Franklin D. Roosevelt," that Roosevelt himself has been guilty of double dealing, "in each instance of which he tried to conceal the knife." (He has offered a resolution in the Senate [passed 56 to 26] stating that a departure from the precedent of limiting a President's term to eight years would be unwise and unpatriotic.)

Following America's entry into the War, La Follette was active, too, in legislation on behalf of the armed forces. In 1941 he blocked passage of a bill to prohibit the sale of alcoholic liquors near Army and Navy establishments; in June 1942 he led a successful fight for a $50 minimum base pay for Army privates and apprentice seamen. He also opposed a "dry rider" on the pending Teen-age Draft Bill. Following House and Senate debate on mustering-out pay for veterans, La Follette (with Senators Harley M. Kilgore '43, Harry S. Truman '42, and Ralph O. Brewster) introduced a bill which would "continue discharged veterans on the service payrolls until their compensation rights and other benefits have been determined by the Veterans Administration." La Follette backed the Green-Lucas Soldier Vote Bill; and on February 5, 1944 he authored an amendment which would "impose a penalty of $10,000 or five years in jail for anyone who polls any member of the armed forces on his political sentiments."

The Senator held his place on the Senate Foreign Relations Committee, continuing as one of its high-ranking members. He opposed the extension of the Reciprocal Trade Agreements Act when the amendment providing for Congressional revision of these agreements was defeated. He was one of the few Senators who refused to support the revised Connally resolution in November 1943, stating: "I think a great mistake is being made by the committee [Foreign Relations] in its present efforts to commit the United States to a future course in world relationships when the committee and the people of the United States are still in the dark as to the peace table demands and the post-War policies of the other United Nations, including Great Britain, China, and Russia."

(Continued next page)

LA FOLLETTE, ROBERT M.—*Continued*

La Follette in 1944 continued his opposition to the Administration's foreign policy. In May he said that there were signs that the Government was "repeating the tragic mistake which frustrated the fulfillment of the hopes and aspirations of people everywhere in World War I." He was against holding the Dumbarton Oaks Conference in August, declaring that the proposed security organization was being established too soon, with "almost frenzied haste." It is time, he said in October, for "America to break away from the imperial designs of Mr. Churchill and the Soviet drive for power of Mr. Stalin," and to "show Europe that. . .democracy is the great alternative for both." "The people of the United States," he continued, "understand. . .that the cause of peace will be enhanced through international cooperation." But he attacked the Administration's "practice of total secrecy," and charged that settlements were made under British or Russian direction. The Wisconsin Progressive Party under La Follette argues that the United States should not take part in any international organization until the terms of the peace settlements are known, and moreover, the acceptance by the other powers of America's conception of a just peace should be a condition of her entrance into the proposed league.

At the end of 1944 this Progressive Party, which once held the Governorship, all State offices, and control of both legislative houses, was suffering from the defeat of 1938 when Governor La Follette was defeated by the Republican candidate; and in the November 1944 elections the party lost heavily again to the Republicans, polling only six per cent of the vote. Although Bob La Follette declared a determination to carry on with Progressive principles, other leaders in the party advocated a return to the Republican Party from which the Progressives had broken away ten years before. In the Presidential election La Follette himself endorsed no candidates.

In December 1944 La Follette and Senators Joseph Guffey [44], Claude Pepper [41], and James Murray led the fight against confirmation of the President's State Department appointees. As a member of the Senate Foreign Relations Committee, he opposed closed hearings on the appointments and submitted considerable material in an attempt to defeat William L. Clayton's [44] nomination. When the final votes were taken, which confirmed the appointments, La Follette was the only one of the quartet to vote "Nay" on all the men.

That same month La Follette was appointed to a twelve-man committee which will study the "modernization" of Congressional procedures. Views of newspapermen, specialists in political science, authorities on business management, and members of Congress will be sought by this House-Senate joint committee. La Follette has already expressed his desire to see the abolition of twenty of the thirty-three standing Senate committees, and the limitation of each Senator to membership on only one major committee.

Senator Robert M. La Follette, Jr., is "slight of stature, though tending toward rotundity, round-faced and full-lipped. His hair is deep black and curly at the edges, and he keeps it slicked down." While "he never strikes the heroic poses which made his father such a picturesque figure," he has his father's "quick, nervous stride, the same habit of swift gesture in brushing back his hair or snapping out a pocket handkerchief while in the midst of debate." He is said to be "extremely cautious in all his contacts. He prefers to underestimate rather than overestimate a proposition. He shuns suggestions for stunts calculated to win favorable publicity." He is intensely serious and possesses much poise.

La Follette has few hobbies, but on vacation likes to fish; he plays what he calls a "rotten" game of golf; he dances occasionally, but is no "social light" and doesn't want to be. In 1930 he married his secretary, Rachel Wilson Young, whose experiences in the office, says Elmer Davis [40], "doubtless made her a pretty good La Follette by temperament before she married into the family." Their first child died shortly after birth. There are two children living, Joseph Oden and Bronson Cutting. Shortly after their marriage the La Follettes purchased an abandoned farm in near-by Virginia but they have never lived there, residing in the District of Columbia when in Washington. Senator La Follette considers as his home the farmhouse which belonged to his mother and father and which he has now purchased from the other heirs. Thus, his permanent home address is Maple Bluff Farm, Madison, Wisconsin.

References

Collier's 89:10-11+ Ap 23 '32 por
Cur Hist 42:475-80 Ag '35
Harper 178:267-77 F '39
Nation 132:235-7 Mr 4 '31
Salter, J. T. ed. The American Politician 1938
Tucker, R. T. and Barkley, F. R. Sons of the Wild Jackass 1932
Who's Who in America 1944-45

LANDES, BERTHA K(NIGHT) Oct. 19, 1868—Nov. 29, 1943 Former Mayor of Seattle; first woman to be elected mayor of a metropolitan city in the United States.

Obituary

NY Times p27 N 30 '43 por

LANDIS, KENESAW MOUNTAIN Nov. 20,1866—Nov. 25, 1944 Former baseball commissioner

Bulletin: Kenesaw Mountain Landis died November 25, 1944.

From May 1944 issue:

Judge Kenesaw Mountain Landis, baseball's seventy-eight-year-old Commissioner, is the only successful dictator in United States history. There is no recourse from his decisions; answerable to no one, he can impose any fine or punishment he wishes for failure to obey any rule he sets for the industry which employs him.

Born in Milville, Ohio, November 20, 1866, Kenesaw Mountain Landis is the son of Dr.

Abraham H. and Mary (Kumler) Landis. Although his parents' sixth child, Kenesaw was the first of his family born after the Civil War, and was therefore distinguished by the name of the battle (Kenesaw Mountain) in which his father was wounded while performing a battlefield amputation. The boy was seven when his family moved to the little town of Logansport, Indiana, where young Kenesaw delivered newspapers before school, did odd jobs after school, and worked on near-by farms during vacations. In the middle of his first high school term the youth decided that algebra was not for him and left school for work behind a grocery counter—without bothering to notify his parents of the change. It was six months before Dr. Landis found out about his son's action; he was not particularly pleased.

Young Landis never did finish high school From the grocery he advanced to reporting for the Logansport *Journal.* In addition to his regular work, he played on amateur and semi-professional baseball teams, receiving, it is said, many invitations to turn professional. These he always declined, saying he played "merely for sport and the love of the game," of which he remained an ardent spectator While covering trials for the *Journal,* Kenesaw was impressed by the court stenographer's facility with shorthand, and decided to aim for the same dizzy eminence. So well did he succeed in teaching himself shorthand from an old textbook that in 1883 he was appointed official stenographer of the local circuit court.

Again the youth's ambition was aroused, and he determined to study law. He managed somehow to save enough to attend the Union College School of Law in Chicago, from which he was graduated in 1891, at the age of twenty-five. Very soon after his admittance to the bar the young Democrat was appointed secretary to the Secretary of State, Walter Q. Gresham, who had been the colonel of Dr. Landis' regiment. In this capacity the brash Ohioan succeeded in antagonizing his dignified and rather formal colleagues—a faculty which he retained during his later career. President Cleveland, then in his second term, is said to have suggested Landis' removal; but Gresham defended his protégé. Rather than lose a Secretary over a secretary, the President softened his attitude toward Landis, even permitting him to attend Cabinet meetings in Gresham's absence (a duty normally carried out by the Under-Secretary of State). Eventually, in fact, Cleveland offered the young man the ministry to Venezuela; but he declined this offer, returning to Chicago to reopen his law practice. In July 1895 Kenesaw Mountain Landis was married to Winifred Reed. They have two children: Reed Gresham, a major in the First World War, and Susanne (Mrs. Richard W. Phillips).

Landis, who had originally been a Democrat, switched his allegiance to the Republican Party, later aligning himself with the Bull Moose Progressives. He continued his legal practice until 1905, when President Theodore Roosevelt appointed him Judge of the United States District Court of Northern Illinois, on the endorsement of the local Republican organization. Two years later, while still one of the youngest judges on the bench, Kenesaw Mountain Landis became a national figure on the basis of one judicial decision.

The Standard Oil Company of Indiana was accused by the Government of accepting freight rebates from the Chicago & Alton Railroad. When the case came up before Judge Landis he demanded the appearance, as witnesses, of various notables, including John D. Rockefeller, Sr., and then levied the largest fine in history—$29,240,000. (Later that same day the Judge spent hours over a case involving "a few pennies" of interest owed to a loan shark; finally he paid the interest from his own private pocket and dismissed the "bloodsucker," threatening to eject him personally.) The thirty-million-dollar fine naturally made all the front pages; the New York *World* called it "a great event in American political and financial history." Strangers would stop Judge Landis on the street to compliment him on the decision, and from it grew a tremendous reputation as a fearless and incorruptible oracle. It was even suggested that the Judge run for President, but this he indignantly declined: "To think that I would accept political preferment as a reward for what I have done on the bench," he said, "is to impeach my integrity as a judge and my honor as a man."

The almost legendary character of Landis' reputation as a judge was not dimmed by the fact that in July 1908 the Circuit Court of Appeals for the Northern District of Illinois, "in a decision that took Landis severely to task, revoked the $29,240,000 penalty and ordered a new trial for the Standard Oil Company"—which eventually paid no fine at all. Nor did "the Jedge" lose luster from the "startling frequency" of his reversals, which led him to refer to the higher court as "The Department of Chemistry and Microscopy." "It did not matter," reports Henry Pringle, "that his decisions were so often reversed; somehow the reversals were seldom given prominence in the newspapers. Few residents of the city that sprawls by Lake Michigan listened to grumbling by a few members of the bar that Landis was not learned in the law, that he wasted time in court, often treated them with scant respect, and invariably played to the gallery. He grew gradually to be an object of local civic pride. . . . Visitors to the city were taken to see him in action on the bench, and they rarely missed a performance long to be remembered. . . . Men stopped to listen when his drawling, back-country voice broke in to question a witness, when he assumed the role—as fancy moved him—of prosecutor or defense counsel or technical expert. Sometimes he would lunge far out, shaking a gaunt finger and twisting his face into a fearful contortion. It was thus that he interrogated some evasive unfortunate whom he suspected of perjury and reduced the man to a nervous wreck." The late Heywood Broun wrote of Landis: "His career typifies the heights to which dramatic talent may carry a man in America if only he has the foresight not to go on the stage"—

KENESAW MOUNTAIN LANDIS

but this, it must be remembered, was a minority opinion.

The majority opinion was definitely favorable. It is well expressed by William Fleming French, in an article called "The Most Interesting Man in America." "When T. R. left us," writes French, "the red-blooded youth, especially the soldiers, needed a hero to worship, a man of understanding, an intense patriot, someone absolutely fearless and square. There was one man to fill that need —as square and honest a man and as relentless a fighter as the Old Lion himself. The papers of the country blazed that name in bold type—Judge Kenesaw Mountain Landis. A fearless champion is what they wanted"— and found. The explanation for the great divergence of opinion with regard to Landis is given by Pringle: "Kenesaw Mountain Landis has lived by emotion rather than by reason in almost everything he has done. . . . Emotion—a factor not recognized in law and therefore a leading cause of his frequent reversals by the higher courts—sat with him on the bench in Chicago." Of Landis' honesty there has been no question; nor has anyone suggested that his emotions were not always on the side of the angels. Courage, patriotism, and human interest make a simple, direct appeal to the public. When the Judge reached into his own pocket to pay the rent for some unfortunate or gave a young first offender a suspended sentence, or when the newspapers reported that "Judge Landis has received infernal machines and bombs in the mail," the public felt a great personal affection as well as admiration for him.

Chicagoans got into the habit of coming to see the Judge in his chambers to have him settle their private quarrels; and it is certain that by such arbitration Landis prevented much expensive litigation. (One of the charges later brought against him was that of "using his office as district judge of the United States to settle disputes which might come into his court, as provided by the laws of the United States.") In general, the Judge was a successful arbitrator; but in at least one case he provoked economists and arbiters to remark that "Judge Landis has done more through his decision to discredit arbitration than all who favor it have done for it since the beginning of the labor movement." This was the dispute over wage scales in the building trades, placed before Landis by contractors and unions in September 1921.

Called in to rule on wages, Landis insisted on fixing working rules for some thirty construction unions, although he had no building trades experience and was occupied with his duties as judge and umpire during the three months before his decision. Not only was his ruling unsatisfactory and creative of much ill-will, but it was widely attacked as violating four generally accepted principles of arbitration. The charges were summed up as follows: (1) Entering upon arbitration proceedings even though some parties to the dispute had not submitted their cases to him and would not be bound in any way by his decision. (2) Going outside the boundaries of the dispute—settling problems which he had not been asked to settle. (3) Reduction of wages below those offered by the employers. (4) Establishment of one wage as both maximum and minimum. The award was repudiated by the workers, who agreed never to arbitrate their grievances again, and in January 1922 twenty-eight of the building trades unions signed a petition asking Judge Landis to resign. In the opinion of a well known arbiter, it would take twenty years to overcome the setback which the Landis award had given to arbitration of labor disputes.

In the seventeen years preceding this fiasco, Landis had tried some other notable cases. In 1916, when the Independent Federal League brought suit against the two big baseball leagues on charges of violating the Sherman Antitrust Act, the Judge dismissed the case. "Court's expert knowledge of baseball," he said, "obtained by more than thirty years' observation," indicated that such a suit would be, "if not destructive, at least vitally injurious to the game." Nevertheless, although the case was settled out of court, "the Judge spent many hours looking into baseball history, the national agreement, and other documents giving information concerning baseball. The knowledge acquired during this period made him a legal authority on the game's affairs," and brought him to the attention of the baseball world.

During the years before the First World War "Landis' hair grew snow-white and his reputation for wisdom increased accordingly. The Standard Oil fine was still remembered, but . . . the press associations mentioned him less and less. With the entrance of the United States into the World War in 1917 he again flashed into national prominence, however." According to Pringle, "Few men have been as zealous in the suppression of minorities, and his charges to juries were dangerously close to patriotic addresses." Even had the Judge been less fervent in his patriotism, "it is doubtful if he could have been impartial in trying men charged with sedition and conspiracy against the Government," for his only son, Major Reed Gresham Landis, was flying with the American forces in France, and Landis lived in constant dread of a telegram announcing the flier's death. As late as 1922 an admirer wrote that during the War, Landis had sat in judgment on "assassins, traitors, anarchists, and desperadoes of the most virulent character—men who for years had defied the laws of many countries. And back of these men were thousands of others, members of murdering secret societies. . . . Letters, threats, warnings, appeals, insults— they all poured in. If Judge Landis were wise, he would be indisposed, he would never try these men. Desperate men vowed he would never live to see them behind bars. Bombs came through the mails, the building that housed his court was dynamited, but the trial went on. The story of that trial is patriotic history—the people proved their case and Judge Landis exacted heavy penalty."

By 1927, when wartime fervor had subsided, Pringle could remind his readers that most of the I.W.W. defendants and all of the Socialists tried by Landis were later freed by the higher courts, Landis "being held specifically to have been prejudiced against the accused Socialists." Nevertheless, "the people of Chicago approved heartily of his conduct, and by Armistice Day he had become a sort of Windy City Solomon."

In 1920 the American sports world was rocked by the "White Sox Scandal"—the disclosure that the 1919 baseball World Series had been a fraud, some ten leading players having been bribed by "the gambling interests." As baseball is the leading sport of the United States, its professional aspect comes under the heading of big business and front-page news. "The outcry was agonized and long. Editorial writers took cognizance of the gravity of the situation. Sporting writers throughout the country demanded that something be done. Eventually even the baseball magnates were disturbed, since it seemed as though the gate receipts might fall off." Casting about for a one-man commission in whom the public would have faith, they recalled the name of United States District Judge Kenesaw Mountain Landis. A committee of eleven club-owners called on him to offer the job of arbiter with autocratic powers, at a salary of $50,000 a year. As the committee entered his courtroom, the Judge warned them sharply to be quiet; forty-five minutes later he agreed to take the position, specifying that his Federal salary of $7,500 be subtracted from the $50,000. Both Landis and the owners preferred that he retain his seat on the judicial bench, realizing the prestige it would afford his baseball decisions. In accepting the chairmanship of baseball, the Judge announced, "The only thing in anybody's mind now is to make and keep baseball what the millions of fans throughout the United States want it to be."

Unfortunately the two years during which Landis served both as judge and as baseball czar proved that there was something else in the minds of Congress, the press, and the American Bar Association—and that was the alleged impropriety of a Federal judge "neglecting his official duties for gainful occupation not connected therewith." In March 1921, aroused by Landis' parole of "a youthful

Ottawa bank teller trying to eke out his salary of $90 a month by embezzling $96,500," by the Judge's remark that low-paying employers were responsible for such crimes, by his building trades decision, and by his "appetite for cheap notoriety," two Congressmen sought his impeachment. (To similar talk, Landis had once remarked, "Don't it beat the devil what some Senators will do to pass the time?") Among the counts in the arraignment were those of lobbying before state legislatures "to procure the passage of state laws to prevent gambling in baseball, instead of discharging his duties as district judge of the United States"; and lending the sanction of his Federal judicial office to "a [baseball] trust which was declared illegal", "which tends to nullify the effect of the judgment of the Supreme Court of the District of Columbia and the baseball gambling indictments pending in the criminal courts." Landis remarked for publication, "Pish-tush. [Senator] Dial and [Representative] Welty demonstrate that I have a positive genius in the selection of my enemies." His off-the-record remarks were said to be somewhat more specific.

In March 1922 Judge Landis solved the problem by retiring from the bench. On his last day in court the newspapermen detailed to cover the courthouse came in a body to present "the Jedge" with a testimonial certificate. "What can I say to you fellows?" cried the recipient. "These people come in and say I'm a great man. But I know you fellows made me. You printed stuff about me and that's the reason I've got a fifty-thousand-dollar job. I don't kid myself." Since then, as head of baseball, the Commissioner has been first-rate sports page material, and no season has been complete without newspaper shots of him throwing out the first ball, yelling for a home run, eating a hot dog, or brooding over the pitcher's strategy. The baseball czar eventually abandoned the old-fashioned high collar and string tie which increased his resemblance to Andrew Jackson and to which he clung during the first years of his reign. Despite this, and although his snowy locks grew somewhat less flowing, he remained a picturesque and newsworthy figure.

In contrast to his spotlighted days on the bench, Landis' decisions are now largely made behind locked doors; but the importance attached to them is shown by the successive renewals of his seven-year contract, with all its autocratic provisions, and with an increase in salary to $65,000 per year. *Look* comments, "For twenty-three years he has been less approachable than United States Presidents, has been answerable only to himself. In his contract there appears the clause: 'The major and minor leagues severally agree to be bound by the decisions of the Commissioner rendered in accordance with this agreement and severally waive such rights of recourse to the courts as otherwise might have existed in their favor.' The only time this power was challenged [by Phil Ball, owner of the St. Louis Browns, in 1931] the case was thrown out of court." Should any of Landis' activities be questioned or any of his ukases greeted with less than complete respect, he need only threaten to tear up his contract. On business stationery headed BASEBALL he writes five-

LANDIS, KENESAW MOUNTAIN—
Continued

or ten-word letters—sometimes a simple "yes" or "no"—settling any question, from the ethics of hitting umpires with soda-bottles to the problem of keeping organized baseball from wartime extinction. These notes are almost as short, one hears, as the old gentleman's temper.

Since Pearl Harbor Judge Landis has guided the destinies of baseball through three wartime seasons, each year banning spring training in the South because of transportation priorities. Although many had predicted that the big leagues would have to "fold" for the duration of the War, Landis continued firm in his faith that the game could be continued with over-age and 4-F players. "Unless some sort of a rule is passed making it impossible to put nine men on the field, baseball is not dead," he asserted.

In July 1944 it was rumored that Judge Kenesaw Mountain Landis' contract might not be renewed because baseball leaders threatened rebellion, that the Judge might retire before the expiration of his term in January 1946, and that a three-man authority might be named to supplant his dictatorship. Sports writers and club owners began speculating on a possible successor; the names of James J. Walker, James A. Farley '44, Fred M. Vinson '43, General Douglas MacArthur '41, Harry S. McDevitt, Common Pleas Judge of Philadelphia, were discussed. In October 1944 ill health prevented Landis, for the first time in twenty-three years, from attending the opening of the World Series. The committees of the American and National Leagues, meeting jointly in Chicago on November 17, 1944 to "give consideration to the major league agreement which perpetuates the office of baseball commissioner," scotched all unconfirmed reports by giving Landis a vote of confidence and recommending that he be re-elected commissioner for another seven-year term.

Famous for his profanity and invective, the old Commissioner uses them upon baseball owners and players as readily as he does upon uncooperative golf balls and recalcitrant fish. Only one player, it is said, has ever dared an answer. In the early years of the czar's reign he fined a New York Giant catcher, Earl Smith, $100, and then gave him the alternative of apologizing to an umpire he had affronted. Looking at the Judge's famous white mane, Smith retorted, "You need that hundred dollars—buy yourself a hat and a haircut!"

As a rule, however, the Judge is feared, respected, and admired. He maintains this atmosphere by his unapproachability, never giving interviews or press conferences, and by the mystery and drama with which he surrounds all his actions. No one, for instance, knows the background of his secretary-treasurer, Leslie O'Connor. Like all dictators, Landis maintains "an elaborate espionage system" (to quote *Look*), which checks on enforcement of his rules, particularly his absolute prohibition of gambling in any form.

References

Harper 154:615-22 Ap '27
Illustrated World 37:34-5+ Mr '22 por
Lit Digest 67:46 D 4 '20 por
Look 7:84+ Ap 20 '43 pors
N Y World-Telegram p1+ N 25 '44 por
Who's Who in America 1944-45

LANDON, ALF(RED MOSSMAN) Sept. 9, 1887- Ex-Governor; oil operator
Address: h. Topeka, Kans.

In December 1943 Alf Landon, 1936 G.O.P. Presidential nominee, reappeared in the news and in the editorial columns of the country's newspapers. On a visit to Washington he had told a gathering of Republican junior Senators that endorsement by the Republican Party of the Moscow Pact before obtaining "much more precise and definite information" on it would be "disastrous to the country," and that adoption of similar declarations on foreign policy by the two major political parties "would accelerate the danger of a drift toward one party in our country." A few days later Herbert Hoover '43 came to the rescue with a statement that Kansas' ex-Governor had simply intended to recommend that the Republicans refrain from advance commitments on specific peace proposals until positive of what these are. But the damage had already been done. The Republican New York *Herald Tribune* editorialized: "In our judgment, Mr. Landon, in his new-found role of prophet and President-maker, is helping no one, least of all the Republican Party. . . . The party has a number of strong men with resolute convictions. They took charge boldly and effectively and placed the party on record for courage and the right at Mackinac. Every word that Mr. Landon now utters tends to undermine what they accomplished."

Alfred Mossman Landon was born September 9, 1887 in his maternal grandfather's Methodist parsonage in West Middlesex, Pennsylvania, the son of John Manuel, an oil prospector and promoter, and Anne (Mossman) Landon. Alfred was seventeen when the oil fields in southeastern Kansas were opened, and John Landon moved his family to Independence, Ohio. In Marietta, Ohio he attended Marietta Academy, making average grades, playing football until he broke his shoulder, and reading Sir Walter Scott and G. A. Henty. Going on to the University of Kansas in 1904, he joined Phi Gamma Delta fraternity, and "fraternity records show that he got the ice cream course eliminated from the house menu, tried and failed to have only one orchestra instead of two hired for the spring lawn party, outlawed gambling in the chapter house, opposed motions to install a stein rack and to discontinue 'Dr. Wilbur's Bible Lessons.'" He was, however, a member of Theta Nu Epsilon, a campus drinking society, and a "good dancer and a good dresser" who helped to introduce the tuxedo to the campus. He was also so expert at campus politics that he became known as "The Fox."

Young Landon received his LL.B. from the University in 1908. Law did not attract him, though, and after leaving the University he accepted a position as a bookkeeper in an Independence (Kansas) bank at a salary variously reported as $75 and as $90 a month. He invested part of his wages in oil-drilling ventures, and at the end of three years his savings account contained some $3,000. He managed to borrow some more, and in 1912 he and three other men formed A. M. Landon & Company, each of them putting $10,000 into the business. Landon was made president of the company—formed to develop strip oil wells—at a salary of $150 a month and traveling expenses. That same year he accompanied his father, a delegate, to the Bull Moose convention in Chicago, where he became acquainted with William Allen White '40 and with ex-Senator Allen of Kansas. He asked Allen's permission to organize his county for Theodore Roosevelt—and that year the Bull Moose party carried the county. Later the party was to become the progressive faction in the Republican Party in Kansas, and it was with that faction that Landon remained identified.

In January 1915 Landon was married to Margaret Fleming, by whom he had a daughter, Margaret Anne. As Mrs. Landon died when Margaret was only a year old, when the United States entered the First World War, Landon left his daughter with her grandparents and secured a commission as 1st lieutenant in the Chemical Warfare Division. The Armistice was signed while he was still in training, and he returned to Kansas to resume his oil operations, drilling for wells and selling whatever oil he found to the nearest pipeline company. (The year 1918, when oil sold as high as $3 a barrel, was the year of greatest prosperity for the Landon Company.) By 1929 he had reportedly accumulated something like $1,000,000.

But in the meanwhile there were other ventures in politics. When Allen became Governor of Kansas in 1922 he invited Landon to become his secretary. Although Landon spent only a few weeks in that position, he displayed his political acumen when he told the Governor one night after a speech: "You know, you aren't doing this thing right." "Didn't you like the speech?" asked Allen. "Oh, the speech was all right, but you should have stayed afterward and visited with those folks in the hall." From that time on Landon was the acknowledged leader of the Kansas "progressives," and in 1928 he was elected chairman of the Republican State Central Committee. Landon not only managed the successful campaign of Clyde Reed for Governor that year, but saw to it that his state gave Herbert Hoover more votes in proportion to its population than any other.

In 1931 Landon himself entered the primary election for Governor. (The year before he had married Theo Cobb, a talented musician and a charming hostess, the daughter of a Topeka bank president. The romance was allegedly engineered by daughter Peggy.) "Dressed in a soft shirt, no tie, high-laced oil boots, accompanied by his twelve-year-old daughter, he made a cracker-barrel campaign, walking into crossroad stores, holding out his hand in his friendly fashion and saying, 'I'm Alf Landon.' Kansas people liked him because he discussed their problems but never mentioned politics or asked for votes. He ran away from the field in the primary, and

ALF LANDON

in the 1932 Democratic landslide managed to be the only Republican Governor elected west of the Mississippi," though by a majority of only 6,000, and with only a nominal majority in his legislature. He was to be re-elected in the Democratic landslide of November 1934 by a much larger majority, 60,000, this time becoming the only Republican Governor elected in the entire United States.

Landon's two terms as Governor, beginning January 9, 1933, were the subject of considerable controversy during the 1936 Presidential campaign. As Governor, he supported some phases of the Agricultural Adjustment Act, although he opposed destruction of foodstuffs and processing taxes. He also supported the Federal Oil Control Bill, and on March 27, 1933, at an oil conference called by Harold L. Ickes '41, he declared that he wanted to "enlist for the duration of the war in this campaign of President Roosevelt's '42 to get America on its feet." "Even the raw hand of a dictator is better than paralysis," he said at this time. By December 1933 he was warning against some phases of the New Deal in references to the "constant fight for the people to hold their liberties," but his second inaugural address of January 14, 1935, might almost have been made by Roosevelt himself. "Our problems have been intensified by the great industrial plutocracy we have built since our last great depression of 1893," he said. "America bids fair to join the procession of nations of the world in their march toward a new social and economic philosophy. Some say this will lead to socialism, some communism, others fascism. For myself I am convinced that the ultimate goal will be a modified form of individual rights and ownership of property out of which will come a wider spread of prosperity and opportunity for a fuller, richer life." In another speech Landon announced: "Every right-thinking person sincerely desires to see the need for relief to the unemployed speedily pass away. Until

LANDON, ALF—*Continued*

that time comes it is reasonable—and nothing less than just—that the Government exert all its powers to prevent suffering among the less fortunate."

It was such words that led many to classify Landon as a "progressive" in 1936—and some of his acts support this conception. He kept the door of his office in the Capitol in Topeka wide open. He slashed his own pay from $5,000 to $3,750 a year. He pushed the prosecution in a bond scandal during his first term as Governor. In early 1933 a cash-basis law proposed by him was passed which allegedly had a good deal to do with the fact that his budgets were balanced. According to Raymond Gram Swing [40], he "imposed the budget system and the pay-as-you-go principle on all Kansas counties, municipalities, and school districts," and he "made 8,000 local boards face the financial realities of local government." He was responsible for a graduated income tax, the abolition of the poll tax, a farm-mortgage moratorium act, and a fifty per cent reduction in the motor-car license tags. He had the courage to bombard the Townsend Plan when it was at its peak and to oppose the teachers' oath. And, according to Swing, "in each of his two messages to the legislature he . . . urged legislation to benefit labor."

Landon's opponents, however, were to use the same record to prove other points. According to Harry L. Hopkins [41], Landon balanced his state budget only because Kansas did not put up "one thin dime" for work relief; according to other critics, Landon's books "would look sick" when Federal relief and AAA funds stopped flowing into the state. Landon was also accused of budget-balancing at the expense of state employees, whose salaries (already low) were slashed considerably. Furthermore, his enemies said, labor legislation passed under Landon was negligible. The Governor permitted prison labor to be used on a public works project and employed non-union labor in renovating the Executive Mansion. In June 1935 he ordered troops to the scene of a strike in the lead and zinc mines of southeastern Kansas, following a visit by a delegation of company lawyers, and the operators set up a company union under the cover of the militia's guns. Landon's own oil properties, which yielded him an income of $20,000 to $30,000 a year, were non-union, and, although not always friendly to Standard Oil, he stood with the big oil companies in most matters of policy. (He opposed all parts of the NRA, for example, except the oil code, which jacked up oil prices.) In the 1934 utility battle in Independence, he was also charged with covert support of the Kansas Gas and Electric Company's attempt to keep the city from using its own power facilities to supply its street-lighting system.

The only Republican Governor elected in 1934 was, however, due for some attention as a Presidential possibility, and the Kansas *Star* nursed his candidacy along. In the fall of 1935, when Landon attended the American Legion convention at St. Louis, a whole section of the convention pledged itself to the Landon-for-President movement. Then Landon again balanced his budget, and finally William Randolph Hearst grew interested and sent Damon Runyon [42] to Topeka to write an article for the *Cosmopolitan,* "Horse and Buggy Governor." (Said Runyon: "Here is a family man, a clean man, and withal a wholly sane man, who has bobbed up between suns, you might say, to capture the public imagination by his record of executive achievement.") After national comment had started Hearst himself visited Landon in Topeka, then told the readers of his twenty-six newspapers: "I think Landon is marvelous!" Landon set up pre-convention offices in Topeka, Kansas City, and New York and made "middle-of-the-road speeches" while John D. Hamilton, his campaign manager, solicited funds in Wall Street. By mid-February 1936 there was a continuous stream of Republican leaders flowing into Topeka, and the nomination was taken for granted. One fortunate factor was that Landon had been too inconspicuous in Republican politics before 1936 to have made any real enemies.

After much advance publicity the Republican National Convention took place in the summer of 1936. The state emblem of Kansas has on it the insignia of a sunflower, so sunflowers sprouted gaily in the buttonholes of Republican delegates; Landon was fond of *Oh, Susanna,* so the leader of the hotel orchestra where his staff was quartered was called on to play the piece no less than 800 times. And it was a Landon landslide: his nomination was almost unanimous on the first ballot. Colonel Frank Knox [40] was nominated as his running mate.

"Life, Liberty, and Landon!" was the slogan under which the Republicans presented their candidate to voters. He was pictured as Frugal Alf (in 1934 he had officially shortened his first name to Alf), "the poor man's Coolidge," who explained his well known budget-balancing feats by saying: "Don't spend what you haven't got!" He was also pictured as a character out of Edgar A. Guest's [41] *Just Folks,* "sound, sensible, friendly, simple." Everything about his personality was played up: his Midwest twang, his trick of borrowing cigarets from prospective voters, his love of home, family, and squash pie, his nickel bets on baseball games, and his habit of wearing his clothes until they wore out. The fact that he was inclined to say "he don't" and to mispronounce words was also not concealed. Raymond Gram Swing, who had interviewed him in pre-convention days, had given sanction to the picture. "On the personal side Landon is the friendliest man I ever met in public life," he wrote. He continued: "Like every typical Kansan he is an honest believer in self-government and civil liberties. . . . He has given cooperation to the New Deal, in so far as a governor was called upon to cooperate with it. He favors social insurance. He understands the force and usefulness of social taxation. He has the warmest recognition of the need for Federal relief. After talking with Rex Tugwell [41] early this year, he came back to praise him publicly for his intelligence. . . . He is not much, if at all,

less progressive in philosophy than Franklin
Delano Roosevelt; and if he only could, he
would improve the quality of government,
which in the last analysis means to scrap the
spoils system."

But Swing's picture of Landon as a sort
of Republican New Dealer was regarded by
some as not borne out in the campaign: In
his speech accepting the nomination, Landon
denounced the Administration for its "program of scarcity," although he had previously
maintained that "increased production has led
to poverty"; he deprecated "appeals to . . .
class feeling," although not long before he
had strongly attacked "industrial plutocracy" and "racketeers like Insull, Morgan, and
Van Sweringen." In addition, his insistence
that workers be protected against interference
from employers, fellow employees, "or any
other person" impressed labor leaders as a
declaration against union organizers.

In his campaign Landon, an active and tireless speaker, made four national tours radi-
ating in all directions from Topeka and gave
as many as twenty-eight short talks from the
rear platform of his campaign train. During
his first three tours his anti-New Deal statements were relatively moderate. He spoke of
"careless thinking, unworkable laws, and incompetent Administration . . . fumbling with
recovery." He spoke of broken promises, political corruption in the Democrats' handling
of relief, and Presidential tangles with the
Constitution. He announced that "national
economic planning violates the basic ideals
of the American system." But for a long time
he favored large parts of the New Deal and
only wanted to rid it of excessive cost and
restraint on business.

It was as the campaign went on that he
made more direct hits at the New Deal. In
Baltimore he announced: "It is the essence
of the New Deal that the Constitution must go
in order to give men in Washington the power
to make America over, to destroy the American way of life, and establish a foreign way
in its place." In Detroit he made friends with
Henry Ford '44, making a speech praising him
for having fought the NRA. In Albuquerque
he warned: "Franklin Delano Roosevelt proposes to destroy the right to elect your own
representatives, to talk politics on street corners, to march in political parades, to attend
the church of your faith, to be tried by jury,
and to own property." In the meanwhile John
D. Hamilton had been calling Roosevelt a
wrecker and a revolutionist whose administration was dominated by Communists.

Yet as the campaign went on it became
evident that it was Roosevelt who had the
audience appeal." (Landon's voice, for example, was monotonous, his delivery jerky
and halting.) In the end even the conservative
New York Times came out for Roosevelt on
the grounds that Landon had little to offer but
a second-hand New Deal, that the traditional
isolationism of the Republicans would injure
the United States, and that, "commanding the
confidence of the distressed masses, Roosevelt will provide insurance against radicalism
of the sort which the United States had most
to fear." Although the Literary Digest straw

vote on October 17, 1936 had given Landon
1,004,086 votes to Roosevelt's 728,088, the election that followed was a Democratic landslide. Landon received thirty-seven per cent
of the popular vote but only eight electoral
votes, or one and one-half per cent of the
electoral total—the "worst single defeat ever
suffered by an Also Ran." Maine and Vermont were the only states he carried.

Although the party's nominal head, after
the election the defeated candidate retired to
private life, spending most of his time at home
in Kansas attending to his oil business. In October 1937 he addressed a "nationwide mass
meeting" over the radio, and at this time he
listed as noteworthy New Deal failures relief,
taxes, the Social Security Act, the Wagner '41
Labor Relations Act, and Hugo Black's '41 appointment to the Supreme Court, and he called
on Congress to defend the Neutrality Act and
revise Roosevelt's international policy. In
December of that same year, however, he
wired Roosevelt: "I congratulate you on your
firm 'No' to the proposed legislation that
would take away the power of Congress to
declare war." Earlier that month he had
announced: "I have not had any idea of becoming a candidate [for the Presidency in
1940]. I will not accept the nomination in
the remote contingency that the Republican
convention may offer it." In 1938 Roosevelt
appointed his defeated rival a delegate to the
Pan-American Conference at Lima, Peru.

With the outbreak of the Second World
War, Landon's statements on foreign policy
became frequent. In September 1939 he supported modification of the Neutrality Act; in
May 1940 he pledged support to Roosevelt "in
his announced efforts to strengthen the nation against attack." He was promptly invited to lunch at the White House, but, suspecting that he might be offered a Cabinet position, he discussed things with Senator Robert
A. Taft '40 and came out flatly both against
a third term and against "coalition." The
luncheon took place, but its results were singularly negative: immediately afterward Landon
dictated another blast against the third term,
and the next month he denounced Roosevelt's
speech promising aid to the Allies "as a course
taken . . . on his own responsibility that is
in the direction of a war for which the nation
is utterly unprepared and to which a vast majority of people are opposed." Early in December 1940 Landon advocated subsidies to
Great Britain, but in January 1941 he announced: "Those who really mean all aid to
England short of war should specifically say:
'No convoying. No American ships in war
zones.'" The next month, testifying before
the Senate Foreign Relations Committee, he
opposed the Lease-Lend Bill. He stated that
he was merely for hemisphere defense, saying: "Let us arm ourselves so terrifically that
we can lick any nation or combination of
nations that are foolish enough to attack us
here."

In June 1941 the former candidate said
that "for the period of the unlimited emergency, we have not in form but in reality seen
the end of the Republic." He gave his support to the extension of the draft afterward,

LANDON, ALF—*Continued*

since "under the provocative words and bellicose policies and acts of the President and his
Cabinet we have gone too far not to be armed
to the teeth." But he remained as suspicious
as ever of Roosevelt's ideology. In October
1941 he was willing to help Russia (he had
opposed aiding her in July), but he held
that the President should not paint the U.S.S.R.
as anything but "a bloody, tyrannical, unfriendly, brutal, and godless duplicate of the
Nazis." "Under the smoke screen of national
defense a little group of New Dealers . . .
are attempting to establish a collective state
in America," he also said, contrasting the
picture to the "robust, vigorous, healthy Christian republic."

With Pearl Harbor, Landon supported the
American declaration of war, but whereas in
pre-Pearl Harbor days he had demanded that
we ask England what we would be fighting for
if we entered the War officially, he now
stated (March 1942): "To me it is a sheer
waste of precious time and energy to discuss
what we are aiming at, other than swift defeat of those who have attacked American
soil." He announced that President Roosevelt must refrain from planning war strategy;
that there must be no "new and untried changes
in our social and economic system"; and that
"frills and non-essentials" such as the National
Youth Administration must be cut out. "As
I have many times said, among the inevitable
results of war have been and always will be the
loss of social gains and a reduced standard
of living for all." In October 1942 he had
pointed out that his advice had not been
taken—that the New Deal had treated the War
"as a glorified WPA project"; in May 1943
he had found the "basic fault in our foreign
policy . . . the hallelujah approach." (The
month before, after a conference at the White
House, he had said that the President's plans
as they applied to the underprivileged peoples
of the world had "considerable merit.") The
food situation was the result of politics and
gross inefficiency on the part of the planners
in Washington. "Give the farmers the tools
for production and let them alone," was his
advice.

At the beginning of December 1943 Landon
came to Washington for a brief stay. "In
contrast to Willkie's '40 visit a few weeks ago,
Landon might have been traveling incognito,"
wrote *Time* Magazine. His speech to the
Republican "Freshman" Club on Capitol Hill,
which caused so much controversy, was chiefly
devoted to questioning the merits of the Moscow Pact. "It [the Moscow Pact] can be
blown up as a great achievement only because
everything in relation to the arrangement is so
completely indefinite," he said at that time.
"I can find no evidence that the Russians have
yielded one inch in regard to their well known
territorial aspirations or political ambitions
in Europe, the consistency of which with the
Atlantic Charter is obscure." (Later he was
to question the Teheran agreement for virtually the same reasons.) Regarding domestic
policies, Landon described Roosevelt as "the
life-term candidate." Willkie, to whom Landon's hostility had long been evident, now
commented: "If Governor Landon's recent

speeches represent the thinking of the Republican Party, then certainly someone other than
myself should lead the party in 1944." Landon
showed that he thoroughly agreed with Willkie in this, at least, when, after a talk with
New York's Governor Thomas Dewey '44 on
December 7, he told reporters that he regarded Dewey as "the outstanding possibility" for the Republican Presidential nomination in 1944.

Landon in 1944 again headed the Kansas
delegates-at-large to the Republican National
Convention. Previously he had come out for
a plank in the party platform pledging the
"removal of domestic and foreign trade barriers." The New York *Times* commended his
"courageous appeal to his fellow Republicans
to revise their traditional attitude on the tariff."
In one of his many speeches Landon had declared, "No territorial redistribution of the
world can equalize opportunities for all nations. But we can make the difference less irritating and burdensome by facilitating international trade. That not only means lower
tariffs—but also it means that as soon as possible all governments abandon artificial control
of currencies and exchange, quota restrictions
and 'imperial preference.' " In explanation of
this departure from party policy, Landon said
that a protective tariff system was justified
when the industrial system of the United States
was in its "infancy," but that today it has become a "colossus hungry for world markets."
As a member of the Platform and Foreign
Trade Committees at the national convention
at Chicago in June 1944, Landon continued his
attack on high tariffs. The tariff plank created
more controversy than any other one in the
proposed platform. Landon was made chairman of the subcommittee (the majority of the
members were high-tariff advocates) handling
the issue. Ralph Robey '41 of *Newsweek* described Landon's struggle with his co-workers
as a "real fight." But in the end, said Robey
the subcommittee adopted Landon's plank and
it was later approved by the Resolutions Committee. The *Newsweek* writer, while remarking
that the wording of the plank "could scarcely
have been worse from the point of view of
clarity," and that it gave the impression that
the Republican Party had "pledged itself to
move in two diametrically opposite direction
simultaneously," also said that inconsistency
arose from the fact that no one today can be
sure what the foreign trade policy of other nations will be in the post-War period, and that
the policy of the United States must be designed to meet world conditions. Landon had
applauded Secretary of State Hull's announcement in April that bipartisan committees of
Congress should help plan American foreign
trade policy. The New York *Times*, in commenting on the Republican tariff plank, stated
that it would destroy Hull's "multilateral trade
agreement plan" and put in its place bilateral
trade agreements "requiring specific Congressional approval of every change that is ever
made in any tariff item."

Among the campaign charges against Roosevelt made by the 1936 Republican Presidential
nominee were those that the President's foreign policy—"unconditional surrender"—was
"costing the lives of untold numbers of American soldiers"; that he had committed a "costly

blunder when he had sponsored Morgenthau's plan to reduce Germany to eighteenth century agriculture"; that he had blundered in his diplomacy toward China; and that the President himself was guilty of "isolationism" when he had remained aloof while allowing Churchill and Stalin to determine the framework for a post-War Europe. Landon urged a union of Democrats and Republicans to oust Roosevelt and "clean house" in Washington.

The 1936 Republican Presidential nominee is about five feet eight inches tall, "lamb-faced," with reddish-brown eyes gleaming through his rimless spectacles. He smokes a pipe, takes an occasional highball, plays bridge and poker, likes movies, and his chief exercise is horseback riding. He is a Methodist, a Mason, an Odd Fellow, and an Elk.

References

Collier's 97:10-11+ F 8 '36 pors; 98: 7-9+ Ag 15 '36 pors
Harper 172:584-91 Ap '36
Lit Digest 120:30-1 O 12 '35 por
Nation 142:39-41 Ja 8 '36; 142:70-2 Ja 15 '36; 143:7-8 Jl 4 '36; 143:475-6 O 24 '36
New Repub 85:272-4 Ja 15 '36; 87:122 4 Je 10 '36
Newsweek 6:20-1 N 16 '35 por; 7:10-12 Je 13 '36 por (cover); 8:9-10 Ag 1 '36 il por; 10:10-11 N 1 '37
Sat Eve Post 209:5-7+ Jl 18 '36 il pors; 209:10-11+ O 24 '36 il pors
Time 26:14-15 O 14 '35 il por; 27:15-19 My 18 '36 il pors; 28:13-14 O 5 '36 il por; 28:8-9 N 2 '36 por
Palmer, F. This Man Landon 1936
Stone, I. They Also Ran 1943
Who's Who in America 1944-45

LANGNER, LAWRENCE (lang'nẽr) May 30, 1890- Lawyer; theatrical producer; playwright

Address: b. c/o Theatre Guild, 23 W. 53rd St., New York City; h. 14 W. 11th St., New York City

HELBURN, THERESA Theatrical producer and director; playwright

Address: b. c/o Theatre Guild, 23 W. 53rd St., New York City

The Theatre Guild, America's most successful art theatre, in its early days was a group project, headed by a board of directors of six or seven people. It is generally conceded, however, that the founding of the Guild in 1919 was due largely to Lawrence Langner's initiative and enthusiasm, that almost from the start Langner and Theresa Helburn have been the guiding geniuses upon whom the chief managerial responsibility has rested. Since 1939 its destinies have been solely in their hands. Very capable hands, the theatre world decided when in the season of 1943-1944 (the 25th anniversary of the Guild) they presented three distinguished productions—*Othello*, *Jacobowsky and the Colonel*, and *Oklahoma!* the winner of a special Pulitzer award.

LAWRENCE LANGNER

Lawrence Langner, son of Braham and Cecile Langner, was born in the Welsh town of Swansea. A bit from Langner's description of his birthplace says: "One of its features was a jailyard, built conveniently low so that the townspeople could witness the hangings without stretching their own necks." Lawrence was spared the jailyard scenes when his family moved to London, where he continued his grammar school education. After the death of his father, a jeweler, thirteen-year-old Lawrence took his first job, as junior clerk with J. Bannister Howard and William Courtney, manager for Ellen Terry, whose office in Bedford Street was the home of the Ben Greet Players. In that year (1903) for the first time he saw a professional rehearsal— Ellen Terry in *The Merchant of Venice*. Gordon Craig was in charge of the costumes. These illustrious names failed to impress Langner's mother, who took her son out of the world he had grown to love and apprenticed him to Wallace Cranston Fairweather, a chartered patent agent. After taking patent law at Burbeck College, and science at Polytechnic Institute, Langner passed the examination of the British Chartered Institute of Patent Agents (attorneys) in 1910, and decided a year later to try his luck in the United States. By 1913 he had established himself as patent attorney; his business later became the firm of Langner, Parry, Card & Langner, a firm he still heads, and which has a large international patent law practice, with offices in New York, Chicago, and Washington.

But the theatre was in his blood and he divided his leisure hours between the "Greenwich Villages" of Chicago and New York. In New York he became the drama secretary of the Liberal Club. At their meetings in the back room of a Village bookshop, Langner and some of the other members organized the Washington Square Players, a group who were to become highly popular with the intelligentsia because of their experimental attitude toward the theatre. The first program of the group,

THERESA HELBURN

in 1914, included *Licensed*, a one-act play by Langner. During the group's existence Langner contributed other one-act plays to the programs and in 1917 a full-length comedy, *The Family Exit*, which was well received by critics. He also had short plays produced by the Provincetown Players during this period. When the United States entered the First World War the group disbanded, and Langner, who in 1917 had become an American citizen, became a consultant to the Ordnance Department on munition patents; and after the Armistice he was a member of the Advisory Council of the American committee for the preparation of the patent sections of the Versailles Treaty.

On December 18, 1918 Langner rallied some of the old members of the Washington Square Players for the purpose of forming a new art theatre. They were Helen Westley, actress, Philip Moeller, director and author of *Helena's Husband* (1916), a play which had been acclaimed as keen satire when it had been presented by the Washington Square Players, Lee Simonson, artist, Maurice Wertheim, banker, and Rollo Peters, artist. The last recruit was Theresa Helburn, who had been reading plays for the group while she had been employed as drama critic with the *Nation* (1918-19). With the exception of Miss Westley and Moeller, none of the six had any professional standing in the theatre. The Theatre Guild was founded "without a play, without a theatre, and without a scrap of scenery." Its sole asset was an idea. The idea was simple: "The theatre itself is bigger than any of the workers in it and . . . it should be employed for the creation of the finest drama of the time, drama definitely and honestly reflecting the author's vision of life or sense of style and beauty." This idea was a protest against the commercially minded Broadway producers, who at that time more or less dominated the theatre—"imposing their own ideas of what the public wanted upon helpless theatre-goers. . . . Playwriting had become a formula. If playwrights were unwilling to

write the usual 'happy ending' drama, their chances of a hearing in the theatre were slight."

Langner gave the first $500 toward financing the Guild; later Maurice Wertheim contributed a like sum. Langner's plan was to give a preliminary spring season of two plays to demonstrate to prospective audiences what could be done and, on the strength of that, invite subscriptions for the coming season, thus acquiring the necessary working capital. Subscription audiences were common in Europe and in the States for opera and concerts, but subscriptions for a series of plays had never been successfully put into practice in the United States. In the first season (1919) the Guild had 135 subscription patrons, by 1925 the number had grown to 25,000 in New York City, and an equal number in the five other cities to which they had extended their plan; in 1944 the number was 85,000 in thirteen American cities.

The name "Theatre Guild" was suggested by the medieval trade guilds who were noted for their cooperative organization and pride in craftsmanship—a policy the group followed even in the matter of salaries. In the beginning each member of the board received a $25-a-week salary. Each successive year the members received equal amounts based on the income of the organization. At times salaries would run as high as $5,000 a year. Otto Kahn who had befriended numerous artists, solved the problem of acquiring a theatre by sub-letting to the Guild the Garrick Theatre at a rental far below the Broadway rate. Seeking a meaningful play which had been ignored by the commercial theatre, the Guild selected *Bonds of Interest* (1919) by Jacinto Benavente. It lingered only a few weeks, but drama critics were encouraging, despite the fact that costumes and scenery were far from elaborate. Miss Helburn has recalled the distressing accident that happened to the leading woman's dress on the opening night. The dress was made of oilcloth that had been painted gold "because we could not afford cloth of gold," said Miss Helburn. "The actress stood up to make an exit and her chair came up with her. When Dudley Digges, who was playing opposite her, gently plucked the chair away from the dress—it left a great white patch." Today the production cost of the Guild's yearly program of six plays is approximately $100,000.

The financial failure of the Theatre Guild's first venture left it with a total capital of $19.50. The continuation of the newly formed group depended upon the success of the next production. It was at this point that Lawrence Langner walked into a bookstore one day as it was closing and saw a familiar name on the cover of a play. The author was St John Ervine, with whom Langner had debated in his earlier London days at a club known as the West London Parliament. The play was *John Ferguson* and Langner knew at once he must read it. Although the clerk declared it was against the rules to make a sale after store hours, she relented when Langner persisted. It was *John Ferguson* (1919) which became the Guild's first hit. It established the Guild artistically and earned a reserve fund for future productions. (*John Ferguson*'s production cost was $894, and it played to a gross of $125,000 in twenty-five weeks, netting $40,000.)

In the twenty-five years which followed, the Theatre Guild has given over 150 plays. There have been brilliant seasons and dull seasons; the treasury balance has fluctuated from $200 to $400,000, while in 1941 it became so low that for the first time in its history it had to seek outside capital. From 1926 to 1928 the Guild produced fourteen successful plays one after the other, a record which no other theatrical unit has equaled, and which the Guild has approached only in reverse—by producing some years later thirteen failures in a row. The big box office attractions (when a play proved popular enough for a long run it was moved to a Broadway house so that the regular program for the subscription patrons could be continued) of the early '20's established the Guild so solidly that in its fourth season it was able to borrow three-quarters of a million dollars to build its own playhouse.

"Though the Guild's adolescence was graced with paternal pats from friendly critics who saw hopeful promise in an organization which had dedicated itself to experiment, stimulation, and progress, it was not to be ever thus." When the Guild had a succession of poor plays, the critics who had once held illusions began to find disappointment instead, and wrote "bitterly of commercialism and sterility." George Jean Nathan, its most caustic critic, suggested in 1943 that "for the good of all concerned, including especially the Guild, the Shuberts or someone should take over the Theatre Guild. Whatever the result," concluded the critic, "they could not do any worse than the Guild has lately been doing."

On the whole, however, the Theatre Guild has a record which is a credit to the American theatre. Its plays have won many Pulitzer Prizes. It is older than any other American art theatre and its productions through a quarter of a century have added more glory to the theatre than any other one theatrical unit. As an experimental theatre it was the first to present a truly expressionistic play, From Morn to Midnight (1920) by George Keiser; it was first to present a radical play, The Adding Machine (1923) by Elmer Rice '43. Among other experimental ventures, to name only a few, were Processional (1925) by John Howard Lawson, Goat Song (1926) by Franz Werfel '40, and Man and the Masses (1924) by Ernst Toller.

Langner is responsible for the wide variety of Guild plays. As a patent attorney he has made trips all over the world from which he has brought back a new enthusiasm for such Europeans as Pirandello, Molnar, Werfel '40; and gradually these names have appeared in Guild programs. Through Langner's friendship with Ervine, he met George Bernard Shaw '44 and urged him to let the Guild produce Heartbreak House (1919). After that the Guild produced many other Shaw plays, including his series of plays written during the First World War and titled Back to Methuselah (1921). In putting on Methuselah, the Guild knew the group would not have a popular appeal and that the cost of production would be a total loss. However, only $20,000 of the 0,000 production cost was lost. Shaw imme-

diately sent a cable congratulating the Guild on making $10,000 on his play. When Langner had first approached Shaw on doing Back to Methuselah, Shaw consented, but when asked for a contract, he said, "That's unnecessary, no other producer would be fool enough to produce it."

It was Langner, also, who established the Guild's connection with Eugene O'Neill and urged the directors to produce his Strange Interlude in 1928. Langner said: "This play contains more deep knowledge of the dark corners of the human mind than anything I have ever read. . . . If we fail to do this experiment, we have lost one of the greatest opportunities in our history." The play was experimental in more than one way. The curtain went up at 5:30, three hours earlier than the accustomed hour. In it O'Neill reverted to the old "aside" of the theatre as a means for the characters to express their thoughts. Brilliantly acted with Lynn Fontanne '41 in the leading role, the play, for which financial success was not certain, grossed more at the box office than any other Guild play, although Oklahoma! the 1944 hit, is expected to break that record.

Perhaps the most noteworthy thing about Langner is that he has not only carried on successfully as a patent lawyer and as an executive director of Guild affairs, but that he has also written some twenty plays. In the season of 1933-1934 he was co-author of three plays: one a Broadway hit, called The Pursuit of Happiness, which he wrote with Mrs. Langner (Armina Marshall); one a modest success, The School for Husbands, which he adapted with Arthur Guiterman from Molière's L'Ecole des Maris; and a third, which ran a season, Champagne Sec, a rewriting, with Robert Simon, of Die Fledermaus. Other plays on which the Langners collaborated include On to Fortune, in 1936, and, in 1939, their Suzanna and the Elders. In summing up Langner's theatrical career, Burns Mantle has said: "As a dramatist, particularly as a collaborating dramatist, the Langner future is fraught with promise. As a founder and director he has long since arrived."

In addition to his activities with the Guild and Washington Square Players, Langner is founder and owner of the Country Playhouse at Westport. Out of this grew the New York Repertory Theatre in which he hoped to establish a theatre for the revival of important plays of other periods. The venture opened in the season of 1931-1932 with Dion Boucicault's The Streets of New York, which had a run of eleven weeks; Henrik Ibsen's Pillars of Society closed after two performances; the third production, The Bride the Sun Shines On, by Will Cotton, had a forced run of fifty-five performances, and then Langner's repertory properties went to the storehouse. The Playhouse, however, has operated for over twelve years and was the first to produce tryouts for Broadway.

Two of his brain children have played an important role in the Second World War. One is the National Inventors' Council, of which he was one of the organizers; the other is the National Advisory Council to the Committee on Patents of the House of Representatives,

**LANGNER, LAWRENCE, and HEL-
BURN, THERESA**—*Continued*

of which he has been executive secretary
since 1939. Besides his American law connection Langner is a member of the London firm
of patent agents Stevens, Langner, Parry &
Rollinson. He has written many articles on
international patent and trade-mark law, and
with Herbert Langner is the author of the
volume *Outline of Foreign Trade Mark Practice* (1923).

In 1924 Langner was married to Armina
Marshall, graduate of California University,
Southern Section, who has played prominent
parts in many Broadway successes. Mrs.
Langner is active at the Westport playhouse
and is administrative assistant to Langner
and Miss Helburn. The Langners have a son
Philip. (Langner has a daughter Phyllis Adair
by his marriage to Estelle Roege [1916], which
ended in divorce.) Summers are spent in their
Westport country place, which boasts an
oval swimming pool built so that Langner,
who describes himself as a "lazy swimmer,"
can avoid corners. In their New York Greenwich Village town house the Langners hold
one of the most distinguished salons of the
theatrical world.

Theresa Helburn, co-administrator of the
Theatre Guild, who has had a hand in the
supervision of more Broadway plays than any
other woman in New York's theatrical history,
was born in the heart of its theatrical district—
two blocks from Broadway on 45th Street. In
1944 she admitted to fifty-seven years, but
added that she could beat any woman of forty,
other than a ranking champion, at tennis. Her
parents, Julius and Hannah (Peyser) Helburn,
moved to Boston when she was a child, and
there she attended the fashionable Winsor
School. At the age of six she had already
begun to take an interest in things theatrical
through her discovery of the printed drama.
"I even plowed through Plato's dialogues," she
recalls. "I thought since they were dialogues
they had to be dramatic." She was not permitted, however, to attend any theatrical performance until she was nine, and then only
four times a year at holiday matinees. Her
first four plays, *As You Like It, Much Ado
About Nothing, Merchant of Venice,* and
School for Scandal, made such a deep impression on her that she feels that it was this
early love of fine drama which later influenced
her to seek a career in the art theatre.

At Bryn Mawr, where she obtained her B.A.
in 1908, she was an enthusiastic exponent of
the drama. She organized, managed, acted, and
wrote plays for the drama group, although
Bryn Mawr at that time was not enthusiastic
about the theatre. Miss Helburn says that
Bryn Mawr's library did not include modern
plays. Her sophomore thesis, nevertheless,
was on the plays of Arthur Wing Pinero, for
which she had to go to the Philadelphia library.

After leaving Bryn Mawr Miss Helburn attended Professor Baker's famous English "47"
at Radcliffe, then moved to New York, where
she first met the group that was ultimately to
start the Washington Square Players and the
Theatre Guild. Their mutual interest in the
theatre gave rise to weekly meetings at which
a play was read aloud, and it was from these
meetings that the impulse to form a theatre
originally stemmed.

From 1909 to 1913 Miss Helburn was writing
and publishing short stories and verse, and
was active in the Poetry Society of America
during the poetic renaissance in which Frost,
Masters, Lindsay, Teasdale, Amy Lowell, and
the imagists came to the fore. The year of
1913 she spent in Paris studying at the Sorbonne and writing. Shortly after her return
to America the Washington Square Players
got started, and she was cast for an important
role in their first offering, a playlet by Lawrence Langner entitled *Licensed.* After two
weeks of rehearsal her family forced her to
resign from the cast. They had disapproved
of her being an actress in the first place, she
says, but when they discovered that Langner's
play was concerned with birth control, a subject not mentioned in polite society, they pre-
emptorily intervened. This ended her career
as an actress until, ironically enough, she appeared many years later in a summer tryout of
another play by Langner, *Suzanna and the
Elders,* which dealt with the subject of free
love and multiple marriage in the Oneida Community.

Though bodily removed from the immediate
sphere of the theatre Miss Helburn could no
be separated from it, and immediately she began working seriously at playwriting. She
wrote a one-act play, *Enter the Hero,* which
the Washington Square Players accepted for
production and which has since been published
included in several anthologies, and is still
played by little theatres throughout the country. She then did a dramatization of Andrew
Lang's *Prince Prigio,* which was produced
twenty years later as a musical comedy by th
Federal Theatre. Another of her plays was
slightly satirical comedy on war hysteria, *Crop
and Croppers,* which was produced by B. Ide
Payne in 1918.

It was in that season that she functioned a
drama critic for the *Nation* and became asso
ciated with the new Theatre Guild as pla
advisor. In 1920 she wrote *Denbigh,* which
was to be produced eight years later by th
Shuberts, starring Alice Brady. After the firs
draft of this script was finished, Miss He
burn volunteered to act for a few weeks a
executive for the young Guild, which was go
ing through a moment of chaos and crisis. Th
day she took over as executive of the Guil
the business manager (an actress) resigned
a pique, and Miss Helburn, a novice in th
business of the theatre, was left to carry o
alone. She says she feels that she learned mo
in a month than she could otherwise have a
quired in years. Tact, economy, and a ne
business manager helped her through this di
ficult period, and she remained as executive d
rector until 1933. Then, after a year in Holl
wood, Miss Helburn returned to New Yo
to become administrative director of the Gui
with Lawrence Langner.

From the moment she became executive d
rector she ceased her own playwriting exce
for a few months in the summer of 1920, wh
she collaborated on *Other Lives* with Edwa
Goodman, later produced by Mark Klaw b
not brought to New York. Miss Helburn h
however, devoted much of her managerial ene
gies to working with playwrights on the d
velopment of their scripts. In 1934 she o
ganized the Bureau of New Plays, sponsor

by the seven major motion picture companies, and held two nationwide play competitions for college students and graduates. After this, the Bureau organized a seminar for the most promising of these playwrights. The seminar ultimately was transferred to the New School for Social Research under Miss Helburn's chairmanship.

It was through Miss Helburn's insistence that Alfred Lunt '41 and Lynn Fontanne were cast as a starring team in *The Guardsman* (1924), over strong opposition on the part of the play's agent and owner. Thus began the most distinguished dual acting team in the American theatre. The Lunts have remained with the Guild for more than twenty years. Their association since the production of the riotous *Taming of the Shrew* (1935) has been as independent actor-managers with only nominal supervision by the Guild—the Guild having a business interest in their productions. The success of the Lunt-Fontanne starring team probably had the most direct influence on the Guild's change of policy regarding the star system. In the beginning they had believed that "the play was the thing," later they came to the conclusion that actor and play are equally important.

In 1935 Miss Helburn turned her hand to directing in Langner's summer theatre at Westport, doing three new plays. One of them, *Chrysalis*, was produced in New York by Martin Beck in association with Langner and Miss Helburn. After this, at the request of Maxwell Anderson, she undertook, for the Guild, the production of *Mary of Scotland* (1933), with Helen Hayes '42. The play was listed by Burns Mantle among his ten best plays of the season and won acclaim from the press. After this Miss Helburn felt the strain of directing was too much to undertake with her other duties.

Theresa Helburn credits an indulgent husband, John B. Opdycke, with a considerable portion of what she has been able to accomplish. Opdycke, however, is no mean celebrity himself. During the thirty-five years he has spent in New York City's high schools as a teacher, he has written some twenty-two books on prose style and advertising technique, the most popular of which is *Don't Say It*. The Opdyckes live in a New York City apartment and spend their week-ends in their country place in the Connecticut hills near Westport. The house is called Terrytop, "Terry" being his pet name for his wife. Miss Helburn is an inch over five feet, slender, hazel-eyed, and white-haired, and is described as "merry, ebullient, and tactful."

In an interview for the New York *Times*, H. I. Brock asked Lawrence Langner and Miss Helburn, "Can the theatre be at the same time experimental and profitable?" Their answer was, "Yes, if the theatre is willing to put its profits into experiment." The Guild has never declared a dividend—all its profits have gone into experiments, while the directors serve on a salary basis. As for the future of the theatre, both Miss Helburn and Langner are agreed that it depends on the playwrights: "If no new ones are developed, God help us! The directors will have nothing to do but think up strange, wonderful, and curious ways of representing old plays." All of which may have

prompted the Guild to celebrate its 25th anniversary by presenting fifteen scholarships to young actors and playwrights. The scholarships are to be named in honor of Alfred Lunt, Dudley Digges, Henry Travers, Edward G. Robinson, Ernest Cossart, Helen Westley, Margalo Gillmore, Lynn Fontanne, Helen Hayes, Katharine Hepburn '42, George Bernard Shaw, Eugene O'Neill, S. N. Behrman '43, Maxwell Anderson '42, and Philip Barry, all of whom have been prominently associated with the Guild.

Since the beginning of the Second World War the Helburn-Langner co-administration has had great financial success. The hits of the early '40's have added large profits to the treasury—*Without Love* (1942) with Katharine Hepburn; the fabulously successful musical play *Oklahoma!* (1943), which made stars of Celeste Holm '44 and Alfred Drake '44; the record-breaking Shakespearean play, *Othello* (1943) with Paul Robeson '41; and *Jacobowsky and the Colonel* (1943), Franz Werfel's story of the Jewish refugee. Less fortunate were *Innocent Voyage* (1943), one of Burns Mantle's "ten best" plays of 1943; *Embezzled Heaven*, the dramatization of Werfel's novel with Ethel Barrymore '41; and *Sing Out, Sweet Land* (December 1944), a salute to American folk music and dancing, with Drake and Burl Ives.

In keeping with the prosperity brought them by 1943-1944 hit plays, in August 1944 Lawrence Langner and Theresa Helburn have moved out of the offices atop the Guild Theatre into a four-story mansion on West Fifty-third Street, near the Museum of Modern Art. Marble halls, thick velvet carpets, and Gobelin tapestries are "impressive enough to quell the initiative of the itinerant actor looking for a part." The building is furnished with props taken from old Guild shows. "Such is the scope of plays involved that Miss Helburn is thinking about attaching little placards to each prop, identifying it with the production in which it was used. Asked if the number of performances would be noted, Miss Helburn decided that it would."

References

N Y Herald Tribune VI p5 Ap 27 '41 por
N Y Post Mag p29 Ap 18 '44 por
N Y Times II p6 Mr 24 '40 por; VIII p1+ N 15 '42
N Y Times Mag p20-1+ Ap 16 '44
Newsweek 23:78 My 1 '44
Kunitz, S. J. and Haycraft, H. eds. Twentieth Century Authors 1942
Simonson, L. Part of a Lifetime p32-40 1943
Who's Who in America 1944-45

LAW, RICHARD K(IDSTON) (lô) Feb. 27, 1901- British Government official
Address: b. c/o House of Commons, London; h. Dolloways, Buxted, Sussex, England

With the appointment in September 1943 of Richard K. Law, one of the most "up and coming" of Britain's young Conservatives, as Minister of State in the Foreign Office, commentators have noted a decided shift to the Right in British internal policy. Long a prom-

RICHARD K. LAW

inent figure in both England and the United States, Richard Law actively favors post-War cooperation among the United Nations and urges that Britain play a leading role in the politics of post-War Europe. He has been an outspoken champion of the British Empire and holds up the British Commonwealth of Nations as a model for whatever world organization is to follow the Second World War. Late in December 1944 Law and a small group of British shipping and supply experts were sent to the United States to discuss, with the State Department, economic policies in liberated European areas.

Richard Kidston Law is the son of Annie Pitcairn Robley and of the late Andrew Bonar Law, Chancellor of the Exchequer during the First World War and Prime Minister of Great Britain in the years 1922 and 1923. He was born in Helensburgh, England, February 27, 1901. He attended the Shrewsbury School and St. John's College, Oxford, and on the completion of his formal education began a "grand tour" which took him through Asia Minor, India, Canada, South America, and the United States.

In 1927 Law came to the United States and worked on the editorial staff of the New York *Morning Post.* A year later he went to the New York *Herald Tribune,* and after that to the Philadelphia *Public Ledger.* His experiences in American journalism apparently had little effect upon his literary style, for according to *Time* Magazine he "writes waltzing British prose." But they served to broaden considerably his international outlook and to prepare him for the political career which he entered upon his return to England. Law has been a member of Parliament since 1931, when he was elected to the House as a Conservative from Southwest Hull. As a junior M.P., Law was often a critic of the British Government. During the lean days of the early 1930's he joined forces with Labor groups to demand more social reform from the Government, citing the Roosevelt [42] Administration in the

United States as an example which England should follow.

Although a Conservative member of Commons, Law opposed Neville Chamberlain's National Government on many issues, most particularly on foreign policy. With the outbreak of the Second World War, however, and Winston Churchill's [42] assumption of the office of Prime Minister in 1940, Richard Law entered the Government as Financial Secretary in the War Office. In 1941 he was transferred to the Foreign Office to become Under-Secretary of State. This position Law held until September 24, 1943, when he was appointed Minister of State in the Foreign Office, Anthony Eden's [40] first assistant. On January 1, 1943 he was named to the Privy Council.

Law served as his Government's spokesman both in the House of Commons and on foreign missions. In the summer of 1942 he visited the United States and gave a report on the American soldier in Britain. At that time he added his praise for Russian resistance to the German invasion and said he was confident that the Red Army could withstand the Nazi attack. In the House of Commons a few months later Law gave the exact figures on the amount of aid being sent the Soviet Union by Britain and the United States. He answered critics who felt that the Anglo-American war effort had not been so great as that of their Soviet ally by pointing to the difficulties of shipment abroad and the need for material in other theatres of war. "The effort to get those supplies to Russia, which on the whole has been most successful," he said, "has not been done without cost and has demanded of our seamen the most terrific and indeed, heroic feats of endurance." Law added that the success of the then newly launched Allied invasion of North Africa was due primarily to the United States attempt "to maintain its representatives in North Africa and prepare the ground for the arrival of the Allied forces." In December 1943 Law stated in the House of Commons that the resistance of General Tito's [43] Partisan armies to the Nazis in Yugoslavia was "very much greater" than that of General Mikhailovitch's [42] Chetniks. Since Law has so often expressed his Government's views on foreign policy, this statement was interpreted as the first real indication that British support would be offered to the Partisan forces.

In spite of his favorable attitude toward Anglo-American cooperation, Law was at first extremely cautious in his statements on post-War plans, agreeing to submit "all proposed agreements to the Commons for ratification." By 1943, however, he was outspoken in his demand that Britain should take a leading role in post-War organization, saying in one address: "If Britain turns its back on Europe as we did before, if we try to shuffle out of our world responsibilities in a narrow, shortsighted way, then the ideal of international structure will have no life in it whatever." In April of the same year he headed the British delegation to the Anglo-American Conference on War Refugee Problems held in Bermuda.

The Refugee Conference, which had been eagerly awaited particularly by Jewish organ zations all over the world, proved to be a keen disappointment to those who had expected immediate aid for the victims of Hitler's '42 persecution. It had little authority in itself and could only make recommendations for further international action. The only solution to the refugee problem, Law emphasized, was a victorious conclusion of the War. Beyond that he expressed the hope that refugees "should not be betrayed by false or premature hopes of what may be possible into a belief that aid is coming to them, when, in fact, we are unable to give them immediate succor." The Conference itself, Law felt, could only make a beginning and little could actually be done. Numerous groups protested against the Conference's failure to take more definite action and charged that this was due largely to Great Britain's refusal to open Palestine to European refugees.

While Law was still at the Refugee Conference it was announced from London that he would head the United Kingdom's delegation to the United Nations Conference on Food and Agriculture held in Hot Springs, Virginia, in May 1943. United States delegates to this conference had urged that the meeting "confine itself to the long-term problems of post-War reconstruction," but the British group proposed "that the questions of immediate relief for Europe as it is liberated from Nazi control and the whole broad field of post-War economic policy are so closely interrelated with the reconstruction problem that they also must be considered here." Law took the position that "freedom from want" was not a problem involving merely agricultural reform and readjustment but rather the "general problem of poverty and economic maladjustment." In a radio address from Hot Springs he advocated an "expanding rather than a contracting world economy," and said that he looked forward to other United Nations conferences on economic and social problems. Meanwhile he favored the establishment of a new international office modeled on the International Labor Office which would "collect world-wide statistical information regarding all important agricultural products and dietetic requirements, study consumption and production problems . . . and offer advice and recommendations as to how these problems should be solved."

Law did not visit the United States again until September 1943. (His appointment as Minister of State was announced while he was there.) He had gone to Washington with a number of British economic experts to confer on monetary and "other problems directly connected with the war effort." One of these problems was the United Nations Relief and Rehabilitation Administration, and Law was named to represent Great Britain at that conference in November 1943.

On New Year's Day of 1944 Richard Law made a radio address to the United States from Great Britain in which he said that the lasting peace which is to come out of the War "is really going to depend on the extent to which you and I, the ordinary men and women of the world, can understand that we are the same kind of creatures working together toward a common goal." He warned against the distrust which powerful interests,

both in the United States and in Britain, were trying to spread and said that only "common understanding" can insure the peace in the face of this opposition.

The next month a speech Law made to the American Chamber of Commerce in London revealed that he was dubious about an Anglo-American post-War alliance. Such an alliance, he said, "might create dangers more critical than those it sought to avert." According to a report of the speech, he favors a political and economic security system calling for the participation of many nations. A British-American alliance, he believes, would evoke counteralliances which would create friction.

The seriousness of the need for increased Allied relief shipments to liberated countries (a problem complicated by the shipping shortage) was emphasized when, at the end of 1944, Law and a small group of British experts were sent to the United States for discussions with Secretary of State Edward R. Stettinius '40 and other officials of the Department and UNRRA. In commenting on these conversations on Allied economic policy, James B. Reston of the New York *Times* pointed out that the grave economic situation in Belgium, Italy, Greece, and other countries was recognized by Government officials as partially responsible for the mounting political tension in those areas, and might in time affect Allied military plans. The purpose of the conversations, it was explained, was to see whether the flow of relief supplies could be increased without interfering with the already burdened military supply schedule. It was a problem which, according to one reporter, had put a greater strain on Allied diplomacy than any political differences between England and America. At the end of the discussions it was decided that a revision of supply schedules was necessary. While the military shipping problem remained serious, however, relief shipping would be allocated on a month-to-month basis.

In addition to his diplomatic duties, Law has found time to write several articles, two of which were printed late in 1943 in the "World To Live In" series in the *Rotarian*. The tone of these articles is entirely consistent with a statement made by the young Minister of State a year before in the House of Commons. At that time he had said that while Britain was willing to give up her extraterritorial rights in China, she did not intend to surrender Hong Kong. Similarly, Law points out in these articles that although Britain will make no further claim to foreign territory, it is only logical that she play a vital part in the politics of the new world order. "Britain must exert all her influence," he writes, "to prevent Europe [from] becoming the scene of further aggression by a power which, by descending to the eastern shores of the Atlantic, might again threaten her security or use those shores as a base for depredations similar to those which German aircraft have committed in Britain since 1940." Law holds no brief for power-politics, but he argues that power is not evil in itself— "power is nothing to be ashamed of, but there is much to be ashamed of when those who

LAW, RICHARD K.—*Continued*

are in a position of power refuse to exercise
that power or to recognize its obligations."
The concept of the United Nations, Law continues, can be realized only if the large nations "are prepared to discharge the responsibilities of great powers."

Law is a friendly, bespectacled gentleman
whom *Time* describes as "big and bland."
While in America in 1929 he met and was
married to Mary Virginia Nellis of Rochester,
New York. They have two sons. When he
is not delving deep into the problems of
post-War world organization and the national
affairs of Great Britain, Law finds relaxation
in sailing and in taking long walks.

References

N Y Herald Tribune p3 My 15 '43
N Y Times p1 My 15 '43
Rotarian 63:14-16+ N '43; 63:13-14 D
  '43
Time 40:35 N 30 '42; 41:22 My 31 '43
  por; 42:42 O 4 '43
International Who's Who 1942
Who's Who 1944

LAYCOCK, R(OBERT) E(DWARD) Apr.
18, 1907- British Army officer

Address: b. c/o War Office, Whitehall, London; h. Bracknell, Berkshire, England

Heading the famed Commandos is the
youngest major general in the British Army,
Chief of Combined Operations R. E. Laycock.
A veteran at thirty-seven, "Lucky" Laycock
has lived up to his nickname. His luck—and
skill—have taken him through a series of
exploits climaxed by a forty-day trek across
the Libyan desert with Marshal Rommel's '42
men hot on his heels.

Robert Edward Laycock was born April 18,
1907, the son of Brigadier General Sir Joseph
F. Laycock, of the Nottinghamshire Horse
Artillery, and Katherine M. (Hare) Laycock.
After preparing at Eton he attended the Royal
Military College at Sandhurst, where in 1936
he "achieved the highly prized distinction of
becoming senior under-officer." Despite his
choice of an Army career young Laycock
loved the sea. During vacations he sailed
aboard tramp steamers, acquiring a working
knowledge of Scandinavian and East African
harbors, as well as those of France, Belgium,
Germany, Italy, and the Netherlands. In
addition to being registered with Finland as
an able-bodied seaman, the youth was "a
keen amateur yachtsman," and used to charter
Brixham trawlers and sail them around the
British and French coasts.

Gazetted to the famous regiment of Royal
Horse Guards (the Blues) as a 2nd lieutenant in January 1927, the young officer later
became regimental adjutant. An excellent
mathematician, Laycock was then posted as an
instructor at the School of Military Engineering, becoming a full lieutenant in 1930. The
good fortune which won his nickname did not
desert Lucky Laycock even during that horrible
moment in 1935 when the electric lighting
system broke down five minutes before his
wedding ceremony. Five minutes later the
lights were on, and Laycock's marriage to
pretty eighteen-year-old Angela Dudley Ward,

daughter of the Marquise de Casamaury, proceeded on schedule. (They now have two
daughters and a son.)

In 1938 Laycock received a specialist's appointment to the War Office with the rank of
captain. When war was declared in 1939
the thirty-two-year-old officer was assigned to
the staff of General Headquarters, British
Expeditionary Force in France, where he
served until the spring of 1940. Then he was
recalled to take the shortened wartime course
at the Staff College, Camberley. Now a fully
qualified staff officer, Captain Laycock had
already been posted to the General Headquarters, Middle East Command, when, in
July 1940, the first call went out for volunteers for special service. He immediately
volunteered and was accepted.

The special service turned out to be Commando—the very first since the original Boer
raiders. Promoted from captain to acting
lieutenant colonel, Laycock was given the task
of raising and training a "Commando" (i.e., a
Commando unit), and took a leading part in
developing the methods which have since become famous. Himself "a man who can turn
his hand to almost anything" from celestial
navigation to cutting hair, Laycock was
superbly fitted for training Commandos. "He
thought nothing," it is said, "of marching
thirty miles with his men or showing them
the right way to climb a precipitous cliff."
Although a perfectionist with regard to drill
and discipline, Colonel Laycock encouraged the
individual initiative and imagination Commandos must have for split-second decisions.

At the end of 1940 Laycock sailed with
three Commando units from the United Kingdom for the Middle East, where he raised
two more. As commander of this Special
Service Battalion, known as Layforce, the
thirty-three-year-old Colonel had under him
men from almost every regiment in the British
Army—all volunteers. The combat history of
Layforce began the night of April 19, 1941,
just before the fall of Greece, when the
Colonel led a raiding party against the important enemy base of Bardia on the northern
coast of Libya. This raid was particularly
successful from a strategic viewpoint, as it
forced the Germans to divert "the greater part
of an armored brigade" from Sollum, just
across the border in Egypt, and reduced
pressure on the British all along the line.

Then, while British troops were being evacuated from Greece to the island of Crete,
one of Laycock's Commando units was sent
to reinforce the Cyprus garrison, while the
remaining four were held in reserve. Ordered
to join the battle of Crete near its end, these
assault troops, trained for hit-and-run raiding,
found themselves fighting a rear-guard action
to cover the British retreat from Sphakia.
Under constant fire by day, the Commandos
attacked at night, and were among the last
to be evacuated. Laycock himself left on the
last convoy; other Commandos, for whom
there was not enough shipping space, set out
in "small craft which, when petrol gave out,
they took to North Africa by means of sails
made out of blankets." Many of Laycock's
men had to be left behind. When the
Colonel's four Commandos were re-formed at

Tobruk, only one-quarter of their original number was left. Nevertheless, before the disbanding of Layforce and the return of its commander to London, Laycock's Commandos executed another raid from the Tobruk base.

Probably the best adventure story of the Commando leader's exploits was a raid on Field Marshal Erwin Rommel's Sidi Raffa headquarters in November 1941, after Laycock's return to Egypt. The fifty raiders landed from submarines on the Libyan coast. While the Colonel remained at the beachhead rendezvous with three men and the reserve rations and ammunition, his force was led by twenty-four-year old Geoffrey Keyes, the youngest lieutenant colonel in the British Army, on a daring attack for which Keyes subsequently received a posthumous Victoria Cross. Only eight Commandos survived the raid. High German officers were killed and much damage was done, but Rommel, the object of the attack, was away—at a birthday party in Rome. Rough seas prevented the few survivors from returning to their submarines, so Colonel Laycock and the other Commandos were forced to scatter and hide from the aroused enemy. Only two of the fifty escaped.

The two survivors, the Colonel and his sergeant, set out alone across the desert to join the 8th Army. The trip took them forty-one days, during which the two footsore Commandos lived on berries and rainwater. (It rained almost continuously for a biblical forty days.) They had practically no food, except when they happened to meet a party of Arabs or to capture a goat. Fortunately Sergeant Terry was a former butcher and Colonel Laycock an accomplished cook. Whenever the wanderers stopped to rest the Colonel would take advantage of his superior rank to read to the sergeant from a book he had brought along—Kenneth Grahame's *The Wind in the Willows*. Haggard and bearded, the two soldiers were finally found by an advancing Indian brigade of the 8th Army on Christmas Day, 1941. Inappropriately for the season, Laycock discovered that, being listed as missing, he had been reduced to the substantive rank of major, according to British custom. Although Laycock's colonelcy was restored, his lost pay was not, with the result that the poor accommodations of his forty days in the desert cost him some $2,000.

Recalled to Britain and given the rank of brigadier general in command of all Special Service troops, the young veteran helped plan all the raids carried out under Admiral Lord Louis Mountbatten*'* , chief of Combined Operations. He was also responsible for training the Commando and United States Ranger troops which made the famous raids on Dieppe, Boulogne, St. Nazaire, and Vaagö. When the North African campaign was plotted Brigadier Laycock was among the planners of "the assault phase," and in the early summer of 1943 he went to North Africa to lead his men in the invasion of Sicily, landing with a Royal Marine Commando in the initial assault on the Pachino Peninsula and fighting through the subsequent campaign, which won him the Distinguished Service

British Official Photo

MAJ. GEN. R. E. LAYCOCK

Order. The young Brigadier again landed with his leading troops at Salerno in September 1943. All objectives were seized, but the Germans counterattacked fiercely, day and night, with tanks and artillery support. For eleven days and nights Laycock was constantly in the front lines, visiting the most exposed positions and taking personal command of his rapidly depleted troops. Losses were so heavy and the counterattack so intense that even the orderlies at Brigade headquarters had to fire rifles and Bren guns from rooftops. When the battle was won Laycock, recalled to England, threw a German officer's field coat over his battle-stained garments and stepped into a plane. When he stepped out again in England the Brigadier's appearance caused at least one newspaperman to think him a German prisoner of war.

On October 22, 1943, Lord Mountbatten having been transferred to the Southeast Asia area as Allied commander in chief, Laycock succeeded him as chief of Combined Operations. At thirty-six he became the youngest major general in the British Army, and, as one writer remarked, "Soldier, sailor, and scientist, he is the very model of a modern major general." In December 1943 General Laycock attended the Allied military conferences at Cairo, and in September 1944 the second Quebec parley. And in January 1944 this announcement appeared in the list of promotions in British newspapers: "Captain [Acting Major General] R. E. Laycock is promoted to major."

This amphibious cavalryman is tall, dark, and cheerful-looking, but "no glamour boy." An experienced cutter of his friend's hair, he wears his own cropped short. Laycock has "the lithe figure of an equestrian and the alertness of the good marksman." An expert on chemical warfare and a former member of the Royal Yacht Squadron, he likes to read poetry, Greek philosophy, and the whimsical tales of Kenneth Grahame. This witty, plain-

LAYCOCK, R. E.—*Continued*

spoken General, equally adept at making plans and carrying them out, looks on his Commandos as one family. He has founded a Commando Benevolent Fund; and Mrs. Laycock, a dashing sportswoman who runs a canteen at her husband's headquarters, writes to every wounded Commando man and to the families of those killed in action.

References

N Y Herald Tribune p3 O 23 '43; IV
p3 O 31 '43
N Y Sun p13 N 2 '43

LEACOCK, STEPHEN (BUTLER) (lē-kok) Dec. 31, 1869—Mar. 28, 1944 Canadian humorist and for many years Professor of Political Economy at McGill University, Montreal; author of books on various subjects— literary essays, history, political economy, and biography; best known for his humorous writings.

Obituary

N Y Times p21 Mr 29 '44 por

LEARY, JOHN JOSEPH, JR. Feb. 2, 1874—Jan. 4, 1944 Journalist and economist; veteran New York newspaper man; Pulitzer Prize winner in 1920; noted for stories contributing to a better understanding of labor's problems; recently public relation counsel for building trades of the A.F. of L.

Obituary

N Y Times p17 Ja 5 '44 por

LECLERC, JACQUES-PHILIPPE (lē-klär′ zhäk fē″lēp′) 1902- French Army officer

"The wheel has come full circle. The first step toward victory has been taken by the first French prisoner to return to the fight." These words, said in 1943 of the two-star general known as Jacques-Philippe Leclerc, applied even more aptly in August 1944 when, as commander of the French 2nd Armored Division, he accepted the surrender of the German Army commander in Paris, General Dietrich von Choltitz. (While Leclerc's true name, Jacques Leclerc de Hautecloque, was revealed in September, "Leclerc" still remains his *nom de guerre*.)

Like many Fighting Frenchmen, de Hautecloque took his pseudonym to protect his family from possible German reprisals. (His brother, a career diplomat, was in 1944 Ambassador to Canada.) Scion of an old and aristocratic French family, he was born near Amiens in the north of France in late 1902. He attended the St. Cyr military academy, graduating in 1924, and then served as a 2nd lieutenant in a garrison in the south of France. Leclerc served next in Morocco as a 1st lieutenant, and was promoted to captain in 1934. He taught for a time at St. Cyr and also wrote many articles on social movements for the *Revue Catholique*. At this time, it is said, he was a cavalryman.

Wounded in the Battle of France in June 1940, Major Leclerc was taken prisoner at the Ailette River. When, as he explains, a German officer looked him up and down and promised him a quick end to his country, the Frenchman

determined on escape—and managed to do so before his captors could turn him over to a prison camp. Believing him too weak to move, they had placed him in a chateau belonging to some of his old friends. The officer persuaded one of the servants to bring him a butler's clothes. In this disguise he was enabled to find shelter among some peasants, who hid him on their farm and attended to his wounds as best they could. At the risk of severe punishment if caught, they listened to the BBC broadcasts, and during one of them Leclerc heard the voice of General Charles de Gaulle [40], former "special collaborator" at the War Ministry under the Reynaud [40] Government, declaring: "France has lost a battle, but France has not lost the war!" The hope contained in this message made Leclerc decide to join the new leader of the French in England.

Before starting on the long and dangerous journey to London to join de Gaulle and the Committee of National Liberation, Leclerc made his way to his home in Burgundy, from which he realized he would be entirely cut off until the liberation of France. He found it overrun with enemy soldiers. In the best adventure story tradition, he retrieved Mme. Leclerc's bicycle from a German soldier who was riding it by brusquely demanding, "Don't you know that these bicycles are for officers only?" and ordering the man to go about his business. Then Leclerc himself mounted the bicycle and set off for the Channel, some 400 miles away.

Reaching London after surmounting incredible difficulties, Leclerc formally joined de Gaulle's forces, and then entered a hospital for medical care. Just eight days after his arrival he was again on his way—this time to French Equatorial Africa to organize the Cameroun's two and a half million people for the Free French. This done, Leclerc, then a colonel, was ordered about 700 miles to the north, to Fort Lamy, capital of the Lake Chad district, to command the Desert Army. This was composed of the Chad Sharpshooters (one of France's famous Senegalese Negro regiments), the Tibesti Meharistes (an Arab camel corps), a few British officers, and a group of young Frenchmen who had completed their training at a Free French camp in England after the collapse of the metropolitan French armies (the term used in contrast to "colonial"). Air support was provided by daring and experienced fliers of the Bretagne Squadron in obsolescent planes.

After several audacious raids on Italian outposts in the Sahara had been carried out by forces under Leclerc's command, he personally led an attack on Kufra in Libya, a strong Italian fort and communications base some 700 miles northeast of the nearest French frontier post. The Italian garrison in January 1941 had been put on its guard by an unsuccessful British attempt, but the next month a fairly small French force put the oasis under siege. Later, when Kufra fell on March 1, the fort was found to be too large for the soldiers to guard without assistance, so that even their chaplain was forced to take a turn as sentry.

By the spring of 1942 Leclerc had been made a brigadier general. That March, although 650 miles from their base and opposed by Italian forces always superior in strength, the French pushed as far as Temissa near the Gulf of Sirte, seizing enemy posts on the way by hide-and-seek tactics. On March 8 a Free French communique revealed that General Leclerc's forces, after crossing 940 miles of "difficult country—absolutely isolated, sandy, and rocky—and despite sandstorms and absence of water," were continuing operations against the Italians in the region known as the Fezzan, Leclerc being determined on outright conquest. (The Fezzan is a region of oases in southwest Libya.) The mere accumulation of supplies for this undertaking was considerable, since everything had to be brought up from Brazzaville (at least 2,500 miles away as the crow flies) in French Equatorial Africa, the Free French headquarters. Traveling was done by means of slow heavy paddle boats, which could only navigate the Congo in the high-water season. But by November 1942 Leclerc was able to open his campaign, taking advantage of the winter decrease in temperature to 140 degrees in the sun (100 degrees in the shade) and the increased firmness of the sand. His column—estimates placed its strength between 10,000 and 40,000—included some American technicians and mechanics.

The first communique, issued on Christmas Day, announced that his motorized and camel-borne force had entered the Fezzan and won its first engagement. This feat meant that the Leclerc column had crossed more than 500 miles of desert and gone over the Tibesti Mountains just to reach Libya. As for the advance from there to the Italian post—in the words of Jacques Lorraine, "to travel 1,600 miles across one of the most forbidding deserts in the world without supply columns, after scaling the heights of the Tibesti range which rise to 10,000 feet in the wilderness, would have been a great achievement in peacetime, even as a test of endurance. But to storm, on the way, enemy forts long strengthened and equipped with mobile armored forces was a feat of arms beyond the wildest imagining.

"Fighting French troops achieved this in thirty-nine days . . . crossing in turn deserts of rock (the hammada), then of stones (those which the Arabs call the serir), and the erg, wide wastes of burning sand. . . . Inside the tanks the temperature reached 160 degrees. . . . [At night], above the still warm earth, the cold created whirlwinds of icy air. . . . Before dawn water bottles were replenished sparingly from the waterskins, each man getting less than a pint a day. Twenty times as much is really needed to make up for the day's evaporation by the sun." At least once all operations were prevented by a sandstorm.

In spite of these conditions, Leclerc's Negro sharpshooters retained their keenness of eye and actually shot down an Italian bombing plane with automatic rifles and muskets. Umm el Raneb was captured on January 4, by a force led by Colonel Ingold; El-Gatrun fell to Captain Sarazac's camel corps on January 6; and on the 12th the Leclerc column under Colonel Ingold made a triumphal entry into Murzuk, the religious capital, and Sebha, the chief military base of the region. Two days later Leclerc's communique announced: "In less than three weeks Fighting French forces have conquered the whole Fezzan territory.

BRIG. GEN. JACQUES-PHILIPPE LECLERC

The balance sheet of the campaign already shows more than 700 prisoners, forty guns, eighteen light armored cars, and a large number of weapons and vehicles captured. Three new flags have just been added to the four which already hang in the Hall of Honor of the Chad Senegalese Sharpshooters Regiment." And, on January 25, 1943, Leclerc's column, led by one Captain Ferret, entered Tripoli at the same time as General Sir Harold Alexander's [42] British 8th Army, which had just put Field Marshal Erwin Rommel [42] and his Afrika Korps to flight.

Leclerc then made contact with General Henri Honoré Giraud [42] at Bizerte. Later Leclerc relinquished his command to General Edouard René Marie de Larminat. Under de Larminat's command, the column was incorporated as a unit into General Sir Bernard L. Montgomery's [42] British 8th Army, of which Leclerc became a staff officer. He worked in that capacity throughout the Tunisian campaign. At this time he was wearing a French brigadier general's two stars, which he had refused to put on his sleeve until he had "justified them to himself" by a second attack on the Italian posts in Libya.

In April 1943 Leclerc and his troops received an enthusiastic popular demonstration upon their entrance into Gabès with units of the 8th Army under the New Zealander, General Bernard Freyberg [40]. Leclerc's name was usually mentioned in correspondent's stories together with that of General de Gaulle. At this time a certain amount of dissension arose when a group from Giraud's 19th Army Corps, attached to the British 1st Army, transferred itself unceremoniously to the Leclerc column. The fabulous General was twice decorated: by de Gaulle, who made him a Companion of the Order of Liberation for "showing the enemy that they were not finished with the French Army," and by President Roosevelt [42], who made him a Commander of the Legion of Merit.

(Continued next page)

LECLERC, JACQUES-PHILIPPE—*Cont.*

Leclerc himself dropped out of the news for a time while his reorganized and reinforced division was receiving preliminary invasion training in North Africa and a "final sharpening" in Great Britain. He reappeared in dispatches in August 1944, when his 2nd Armored Division landed in Normandy. Frenchmen roared their acclaim of the legendary leader and his red-capped Frenchmen, Arabs, and Negroes, who manned American-made General Sherman tanks given historic French names and decorated with the tricolor and the Cross of Lorraine on the map of France. Four of the tanks were named Athos, Porthos, Aramis, and d'Artagnan—a fitting touch, as the New York *Times* observed, for General Leclerc is "a fighter in the best Alexandre Dumas tradition." Their first clash with the occupation forces, at LeMans, caused an American general to describe the division as "one of the finest fighting outfits ever put together under any flag." From LeMans the men fought their way north alongside of American troops against the German 7th Army, on August 12 entering Alençon, the first large French city to be liberated by the French themselves. Leclerc's progress across the country had been made "over a carpet of flowers and a row of uplifted bottles of the French people's beloved *vin rouge* and cognac." Correspondents had informed the world how "dusty bottles of the rarest vintage that had been kept in hiding for the great day were trotted out and in many cases picked up on the fly by broadly grinning [tank] crews."

Leclerc's division was finally ordered with other Allied units to Paris, where in August F.F.I. guerrillas had pressed the Germans to the point of requesting an armistice. The Leclerc division and a force led by de Gaulle stormed their way in twin drives through German mine fields, artillery barrages, and barricades to the capital. Other Allied forces, including Canadian troops and the United States 1st Army under Lieutenant General Omar N. Bradley[43], which had entered the city at the same time, tactfully bivouacked near the city gates while General Leclerc's French division advanced to the Hôtel de Ville (City Hall). Paris became delirious with joy, even though two days fighting was necessary before the German commander surrendered to Leclerc, General Joinville of the F.F.I., and the American corps commander in the baggage room of a Paris railroad station. On August 25 General de Gaulle made his triumphal entry into Paris.

General Leclerc, who in the fall of 1944 shared with General Joseph-Pierre Koenig[44] of the F.F.I. the post of de Gaulle's second-in-command, was attached with his division to the United States 7th Army, under General Patch[43], and "participated brilliantly" in the encirclement of the German 7th Army. In November they broke through the Strasbourg defenses, and by the 25th had captured nearly all of the Alsatian capital. But there was still an inconveniently large number of snipers left—enough to force Leclerc to move his headquarters three times. The third time, he took action, without consulting General Jacob Devers[42], the Army Group commander, or General Patch. He posted a proclamation on November 29 announcing that for every French soldier shot, five hostages would be executed. Those would be taken "if necessary" from among the German prisoners of war. Supreme Headquarters immediately issued a statement pointing out that any sort of reprisals against prisoners of war was forbidden by the Geneva Convention; while military authorities have the right to take civilian hostages, the question was an academic one, as Leclerc had been relieved of the Strasbourg assignment for unspecified "further operations."

Hassoldt Davis, who dedicates his *Half Past When* (1944) to Leclerc, reports that the General was known to his motley troops as Barraca, which is Arabian for the "Invincible," and to the Italians as Il Grandissimo Generale. "The captured native troops," says Davis, "invariably asked to be allowed to search for the bullets they had shot at him, that supposedly had fallen at his feet. . . . It is because of Leclerc's personal modesty that the achievements of his troops are almost unknown." Another American reports in the New York *Herald Tribune*, "I think it can be fairly said, and this is the opinion of many of the highest Allied officers, that he is one of the most brilliant military figures to emerge from the War. Certainly his effect on the Free French movement has been enormous. He possesses the two attributes so long associated with the French officer: daring and imagination. . . . Noted for his charm, he is popular with the British and Americans as well as the French. He is a combination of the courtly Lafayette and the reckless D'Artagnan."

The General is said to be highly regarded by his tough soldiers as well as by the French public. He has been described as "little" and "blond", "thin, almost frail," and as having a cutting voice. Photographs show him to have straight hair, an aquiline nose, and a heavy dark mustache; his face, although by no means boyish, looks years younger than his age. Correspondents interviewing Leclerc after the liberation of Paris found him nervous and easily irritated, unwilling to answer personal questions—for fear, presumably, of involving his family. (He is married and has six children.) He is a devout Catholic. The long, knotty cane Leclerc carries everywhere has become legendary. With it he has traced his habitual "doodles" in the sands of Africa, the turf of England, and, finally, in the soil of his native France.

References

Collier's 114:51 O 28 '44 por
Free France 6:170 S 1-15 '44 il (por p169)
N Y Herald Tribune VII p9 O 29 '44 por
N Y Sun p38 Mr 19 '43; p10 Ag 19 '44; p4 S 28 '44
N Y Times p3 Ap 7 '43; p4 Ag 15 '44 por
Time 44:40 S 4 '44

LECUONA, ERNESTO (lä-cü-ō'nə er-näs'tō) Composer; conductor; pianist

Address: b. c/o Cuban Embassy, Washington, D. C.

One of the few Latin American composers to win early fame outside his own country is Ernesto Lecuona, the Cuban composer who first introduced rumba and conga rhythms to North America. His songs, loved throughout all Latin America, "have become as indelible a part of their culture as the Spanish and Portuguese tongues." Even in the United States "Lecuona's tunes outsell those of many a top-flight Tin Pan Alleyite." Many of his works have had a double life: the lovely concert boleros "Malagueña" and "Andalucía" from his *Andalucía* suite, for instance, have had their day on the hit parade in Tin Pan Alley arrangements called "At the Crossroads" and "The Breeze and I." Six or seven of the composer's major works are purely "serious," but most of his 300 published compositions are sung, whistled, hummed, and danced to—such tunes as "Always in My Heart", "La Comparsa", "Se Sue", "Para Vigo Me Voy" ("Say Si Si"), and the ubiquitous Cuban "Siboney."

Ernesto Lecuona, born in Guanabacoa, Cuba, a few years before the turn of the century, was taught the piano very early by his sister Ernestina. Oddly enough, although the elder Lecuonas were "completely unmusical"—Ernesto's father was a Havana newspaperman—the younger generation was highly talented. Ernesto's sisters Ernestina and Elisa are pianists and composers, his brothers Luís and Teodoro are respectively a pianist and a violinist, and his niece Margarita composed the widely-known "Babalu" and "Tabu." Ernesto himself was a genuine child prodigy, making his pianistic debut at the age of five, and studying with the famous Spanish composer Joaquín Nin (father of the musician Joaquín Nin-Culmell and the writer Anaïs Nin '44). At fifteen young Lecuona was certified by the National Conservatory at Havana as a teacher of singing and piano.

While still attending classes Ernesto organized his own band and appeared in Havana's movie houses in long trousers which he had borrowed from a friend. But he did not confine his activities to playing and conducting for, "like all reputable composers, Lecuona started cutting teeth and composing at about the same time." His first published number, a two-step called "Cuba y América," written when he was eleven, is still played by Cuban military bands.

The young musician came to New York in 1917 to give a piano recital and to make his first recordings for Victor. Today, after a number of visits to the United States, he still speaks little English. Lecuona's formal concert tours did not begin until 1919, however, with a trip to Spain. The following year found him playing engagements in Colombia and Venezuela. In 1922, returning to New York for eight weeks at the Capitol Theatre, the young Cuban pianist took part in some of the first broadcasts of theatrical performances ever made. (The late "Roxy" Rothafel, manager of the Capitol, was experimenting with this new form of advertising.) After

ERNESTO LECUONA

this Lecuona went to Paris for further study with Maurice Ravel, perhaps the most famous exponent of the bolero rhythm. (A bolero is what North Americans dance when they think they are doing the rumba—unless the beat is slow, in which case the so-called rumba is actually a *son*. The authentic rumba is an exhibition dance, no more adaptable to the ballroom than a tap dance.)

"Malagueña," which has been favorably compared by admirers with Liszt and Chopin compositions, was introduced by Lecuona at the Roxy Theatre, New York, in 1927. It has since sold an average of 100,000 sheet music copies a year in the United States alone, a remarkable record; pianists use it as a sure-fire applause-getter to end the recital or precede the intermission. In the same year, 1927, the composer presented the score of *Maria La O,* one of the thirty productions for which he has written the music, usually with Gustave Galarraga as librettist. (The latest of his musicals is *Vincent Youmans' '44* often-retitled revue, which opened in Baltimore in January 1944. Others include *El Cafetal, Rosa la China,* and *Lola Cruz*—all notably successful.) In 1929 Lecuona toured France, the Riviera, and Spain; the following year he was musical director for Metro-Goldwyn-Mayer's production *Under Cuban Skies (Bajo el Cielo de Cuba)*, with Lupe Velez and Lawrence Tibbett. The Cuban musician's first visit to Buenos Aires was made in 1936, with Esther Borja as interpreter of his songs; he returned in 1938 and 1940 for radio engagements and conducted several concerts while there.

During these years Lecuona did not confine himself to playing as a solo artist. He organized the Orquesta de la Habana, which played several hundred concerts in Havana, and he has conducted a number of concerts with symphony orchestra and chorus, as well as leading the Lecuona Cuban Boys, a dance band with which he toured all of Europe, South and Central America, and North Africa. The

LECUONA, ERNESTO—*Continued*

pianist-conductor-composer has also toured and recorded with the Havana Casino Orchestra and the Orquesta Lecuona. Meanwhile his more than three hundred compositions published in "various countries and in several languages" have won popularity for themselves, and "fabulous eminence" for their composer in Latin America.

On March 24, 1943, Lecuona was appointed honorary cultural attaché at the Cuban Embassy in the United States. At the time he was in that country to conduct the première of his new "serious" work, *Black Rhapsody (Rapsodia Negra)*, and another new composition, *Aragón*. These were presented at a concert of Cuban music to celebrate Cuban Independence Day, at which twenty-one of the twenty-seven compositions were by Ernesto Lecuona and one by Ernestina. One critic found that "the new works, along the same lines as Lecuona's earlier output, proved like his conducting and pianism, clean-cut and brilliant, if all much in the light vein of the sort of thing favored in the cafes and night clubs of Cuban communities." Others considered that "*Black Rhapsody* turned out to be very Gershwinesque in conception—which is not too remarkable, because Lecuona is a great admirer of Gershwin's and George himself was crazy about Cuban rhythms. . . . *Black Rhapsody* may not have been 'great music,' but it certainly made great listening." To gain his effects in this work the composer used native Afro-Cuban instruments, including *una quijada*—the jawbone of an ass.

Ever since Ernestina Lecuona first taught her little brother to play the piano, she has been trying to get him to practice. "But he is strictly a man of moods," it is said, "and won't go near the instrument unless his muse is upon him. Like most Latins, he plays with a beautiful rhythm but a very heavy hand." Brewing Cuban coffee is taken much more seriously by Lecuona—one observer described his coffee-making as "a nerve-wracking Shubert production." Like most concert stars he really likes to play his instrument, however, and claims to like best of all being alone with his music. Nonetheless, the Cuban composer dutifully makes the rounds of night clubs, churches, and museums. When he gives parties he is likely either to go out for a walk at the height of the festivities, or to stop conversation by inquiring if anybody minds if he plays the piano. Fortunately, since this may well be the first performance of a new work, nobody ever does mind.

Although he spends very little time there Ernesto Lecuona makes his home on a *finca* (farm) in the tropical interior of Cuba, far away from tourists, where "the native Afro-Cuban music is kept away from the trashy influences of civilized tunesmiths"—but which can be reached from Havana in less than an hour. He is described by Americans as "modest and quiet"—though his sketchy English may have something to do with that—fond of fine clothes, and possessed of "big, black expressive eyes which make him look alarmingly like [the comedian] Zero Mostel [43]." The resemblance means he is "a limp and slightly saddened sort of Charles Boyer [43] type." Lecuona

calls himself "a bachelor by nativity," that is, a born bachelor. However, when *Time*'s interviewer asked what he'd most like to take home from the United States, the Cuban's pensive answer was, "I'd like to collect American women—they are the most beautiful in the world."

References

Cue 12:11 O 9 '43
Inter-American 2:36 Je '43 por
New Yorker 19:20 O 16 '43
Newsweek 22:97 O 18 '43 por
Time 42:50 O 25 '43 por
Wier, A. E. ed. Macmillan Encyclopedia of Music and Musicians 1938

LEE, CANADA   May 3, 1907-   Actor

Address: h. 555 Edgecombe Ave., New York City

"All my life," said Canada Lee once, "I've been on the verge of being something. I'm almost becoming a concert violinist and I run away to the races. I'm almost a good jockey and I go overweight. I'm almost a champion prize fighter and my eyes go bad." Today, though, there is no "almost" about his success. Since his rise to fame overnight as Bigger Thomas in the stage version of Richard Wright's [40] *Native Son* in 1941, he has become, next to Paul Robeson [41], the best-known Negro actor on the American stage.

He was born Leonard Lionel Cornelius Canegata; Canegata was a Danish name taken by his West Indian forefathers. His grandfather had been an importer and shipowner in the West Indies, and his father had shipped to New York as a cabin boy and stayed there. Canada was born May 3, 1907 in Manhattan's San Juan Hill district and went to school at P.S. No. 5 in Harlem. James Cornelius and Lydia (Whaley) Canegata, unlike the parents of Bigger Thomas, were able to give their son many cultural advantages, and at seven he was studying the violin under Negro composer J. Rosamond Johnson and soon after playing Drdla's "Serenade" in a student concert at Aeolian Hall. But apparently he had inherited a spirit of adventure. At fourteen he grew bored with school and the violin and ran away to the races at Saratoga, chiefly in order to impress an eleven-year-old damsel who, in Lee's words, "didn't even care if I existed."

Lee was a jockey at Belmont, Aqueduct, and Jamaica and on the Canadian circuit, but he never had a "good hand" on a horse, he admits now. "I only came close to winning a couple of times." After three or four years of life as a jockey, then as an exerciser when he grew overweight, he returned home practically penniless, to find his damsel totally unimpressed. He didn't know what to do for a living either until he ran into a friend who had turned prize fighter, and remembered that he had successfully taken on the fighter years before. He therefore went into the basement of the nearby Methodist Church to put the boxing gloves on for the first time, and the trainer immediately took him in hand. Within a short time he had won ninety out of 100 amateur fights and had acquired the national amateur lightweight title; by 1926 he was able to turn

professional. During the next few years
he was to fight in more than 200 professional
bouts, losing only about twenty-five of them,
to move up from lightweight to leading contender for the welterweight championship, and
to acquire the name "Canada Lee" when the late
announcer Joe Humphries refused to wrestle
any longer with "Lee Canegata." Battling such
men as Jack Britton, Vince Dundee, Izzy
Grove, Bucky Lawless, and Jimmy Britt, Lee
had made and spent something under $100,000
before he had to quit the ring in 1933: a blow
had detached the retina of one eye, and he was
almost going blind.

The realization that he was through in the
ring was a sad one for Canada Lee, and he
has never lost his love for the fighting game.
"Boxing, that's like hot music," he says. "You
have to think. You feint to make the other
guy do what you want him to do. That's the
fun, not nailing him." Fighting gave him stage
presence, he believes, and neither his cauliflower
ears nor his broken nose handicap him in the
kind of roles he plays. "In the ring I learned
balance and fluidity of movement. There I
learned that when I made a false move I had
to correct it in a hurry."

In 1934 Lee was almost broke again: he had
returned to music, leading his own jazz band,
but no one compared him with Louis Armstrong '44. He began his acting career entirely
by accident. "I played the fiddle but I just
bulldozed," he says. "When it came to the
easy passages, I could play them, but not much
else. I was wondering what I was going to
do. I couldn't stand the idea of a routine job;
I just couldn't do it. I kept telling myself,
'You gotta work like other people work.' I'm
walking through the Harlem 'Y' one day and
saw Frank Wilson casting a play. I always
admired actors and stuff—romance, glamour,
you know—and I sat down about three rows
back of the others watching. Wilson finally
called the names of everybody and when he
got to me I was on the verge of saying, 'Oh,
I'm just a spectator.' But somebody else
shouted out, 'Canada Lee!' I thought, 'Oh,
what can I lose?'" The readings were for
the WPA production of Brother Mose, and
Canada Lee was given a part in the production.
From then on he was an actor. He played the
part of Blacksnake in the Theatre Union revival of Stevedore; he played Banquo in the
Federal Theatre's Negro Macbeth, making
friends with its producer, Orson Welles '41; he
played Jean Christophe in Haiti; he had a
minor role in Mamba's Daughters when it went
on tour. "I never studied acting once," Lee
says; "you don't have to study."

When Orson Welles got ready to cast Native
Son he knew exactly whom he wanted for the
part of Bigger Thomas, and early in 1941 John
Houseman asked Lee to read the part. "When
I read Richard Wright's novel," Lee said after
the play opened, "I never thought I'd be Bigger
Thomas. . . . It isn't difficult for me to play
Bigger Thomas. I've known guys like Bigger
Thomas all my life. I saw them at the race-
tracks. When I was there they were a haven
for ex-convicts, thieves, and all kinds of cutthroats. I saw some in school and I grew up
with some pretty tough guys. Some of them
are in jail now and some of them went to the

CANADA LEE

electric chair." But he doesn't believe he himself has much in common with Bigger, the
Chicago Negro whom racial animosities finally
drive to murder. "I knew guys who were
hungry to death, and I knew guys who said
being colored was a bar to everything they
hoped to be, but it wasn't so with me. I never
had a tough break."

Native Son, which had its Broadway opening
in the spring of 1941, was "by all odds the
strongest drama of the season," according to
Time Magazine; and Lee's portrait of Bigger
Thomas was hailed as "the most vital piece of
acting on the current stage." Wrote Richard
Watts, Jr., in the New York Herald Tribune:
"Without making any obvious appeal to sympathy, Mr. Lee makes Bigger an understandable and strangely touching human being as
he struggles snarlingly against a doom he cannot understand . . . a fine actor, giving one of
the season's best performances." The play was
revived at popular prices the following year,
and Brooks Atkinson '42 wrote of Lee's performance: "A superbly imaginative player.
When he is on the stage he inhabits it—knows
where all the doors lead, what the windows
look out at, knows where he can be seen or
not seen from other parts of the room; he is
aware of what is going on all through the
house where the play is set. . . . The quality
of life Mr. Lee imparts to a scene is overwhelming—partly physical, partly magnetic."

Lee himself had said of Native Son: "We're
making history in the theatre. The Negro has
never been given the scope that I'm given in
this play. Now things are going to happen.
Now they'll think of the Negro as an actor and
not as some butler-valet type, some ignorant
person. . . . This play will give writers an
opportunity to do things." But it seemed that
few writers were capable of producing a Native
Son. Lee appeared in William Saroyan's '40
Across the Board on Tomorrow Morning in
1942, but its run was short. He then accepted
a part in South Pacific, which told the story of
a cynical, individualistic Negro sailor who

LEE, CANADA—*Continued*

refuses to help in the war against the Japanese until he sees that no man can stand alone; the play opened in December 1943 and ran for only five performances. Not long afterward came the première of *Lifeboat* (1944), an Alfred Hitchcock '41 film in which Lee had played the part of a Negro steward. This was not only attacked from many quarters because of its exaltation of Nazi cunning, but Lee's role was criticized as giving the usual cliché picture of the Negro, although, according to the New York *Post*, the actor gave "a performance of dignity to a role of dubious significance."

More successful than any of these in making the American public aware of the Negro as a human being rather than as "some butler-valet type" was *New World A-Coming*, a radio series by Roi Ottley '43 which began in 1944 and was presented every Sunday afternoon at 3:02 over Manhattan's radio station WMCA. In this Lee served as narrator. This, the first radio series ever to be devoted to the Negro question in the United States, was called by the New York *Times* critic "a public invitation to decent thinking." "Mr. Lee, one of Broadway's better actors, is extremely effective as narrator precisely because he is not an actor giving a performance but an intelligent man saying, calmly and patiently, 'This is how it is. . . .'"

During the same year Lee appeared in many other radio shows which had much the same purpose. He was master of ceremonies for a program given over NBC during Negro News-paper Week, emphasizing Negro contributions to the war effort. He appeared on a new radio feature, *Tolerance Through Music*. He made one of the drama episodes on Mutual's *Green Valley, U.S.A.* "an effective plea for racial harmony." Nor did he confine himself to Negro roles: he was the narrator on a half-hour dramatic show over NBC entitled *Un-official Ambassadors*, for which he was chosen for his acting ability.

He was active politically during 1944 as well. In March he visited Washington with a delega-tion representing the entertainment industry, urging Congress to adopt the Federal ballot for soldiers. In June he appeared at a Negro Freedom rally at Madison Square Garden. In September he became a member of the National Citizens Political Action Committee, and in the 1944 elections he was active in the Independent Voters Committee of the Arts and Sciences for Roosevelt, also appearing in a cavalcade organized by the Nonpartisan Association for Franchise Education, Inc., urging people to register and vote.

On the stage, his next role after that in *South Pacific* was in *Anna Lucasta* (1944), whose players he had coached before the open-ing. The play had originally been presented in Harlem by the American Negro Theatre. When it was brought to Broadway Lee offered to lend his name to the production by taking a small role because he believed in the signifi-cance of the play—a study of the Negro as an individual rather than as a racial figure.

There had been some rumors that he would star in a production of *Emperor Jones* late in 1944, but instead he accepted the role of Caliban in Margaret Webster's '40 production of *The*

Tempest, with Zorina '41 and Arnold Moss. The play is to open in January. Lee's only previous appearance in a Shakespearean role had been at the Studio Theatre of the New School of Social Research in the spring of 1944, when he appeared as Othello in Act III, scene 3 of the play. Of his performance one critic had written that he "lacks the towering stature and the organ-like tones of Mr. Robe-son, and he has a good deal to learn about speaking blank verse, but there was a dignity, a sympathetic understanding of the dramatic aspects of the role, and a strong emotional quality in his characterization indicating that one of these days Mr. Lee might easily do a very good Othello."

Stocky, broad-shouldered, every inch an ex-boxer, Lee says he always has to have excite-ment. "I have to fight, get on a horse, see lots of people, even try to write songs. It's all there pushing out of me somehow and I don't know why, got to do something, got to be somebody." In addition to all his other activities, he is the father of a lively young son, Carl Vincent Canegata (Lee was mar-ried to Juanita Waller in December 1925); for a time he owned a Harlem restaurant, the Chicken Coop, which set out "the best Southern fried chicken and French fried sweet potatoes you ever ate"; and in 1941 he was training and financing Buddy Moore, a young Negro heavy-weight, working at this nearly every day. He lives in a penthouse apartment from which one sees the panorama of the Hudson River and New Jersey.

References

Cue 10:42 Mr 15 '41
N Y Herald Tribune VI p5 Mr 30 '41;
　IV p1 D 26 '43
N Y Post p3 Mr 31 '41 por
N Y Times IX p1 Mr 30 '41
N Y World Telegram p37 Ap 3 '41
PM p21 Mr 30 '41 por
Time 37:76-7 Ap 7 '41 por

LEE, JOHN CLIFFORD HODGES Aug. 1, 1887- United States Army officer
Address: b. c/o War Department, Washing-ton, D.C.

Leading "the combat echelon of American industry," the "Communications Zone," in the Allied invasion of Europe is the deputy com-mander of American forces, Lieutenant Gen-eral John Clifford Hodges Lee. "Administra-tion is the better part of warfare"—especially modern warfare—and General Lee, a former Army engineer and experienced administrator, is proceeding calmly with "a feat in supply and transportation that would be tremendous even were there no enemy to be overcome."

"Few laymen, even few soldiers, appreciate the immense task which was undertaken by Lieutenant General John C. H. Lee," reports correspondent Ned Russell. "With his chief of staff, Brigadier General Royal Lord, he had to procure, bring across the Atlantic, and send to [continental] Europe almost every item of supply which is being employed by American troops in the great assault today. It meant the mobilization of 700,000 different items of supply. An 'item' might be toothbrushes or . . . a giant locomotive built especially for certain European railroad tracks. . . . The position was as if the Services of Supply had been charged with the task of taking the population of a big American city, say Chicago or Boston, and feeding, housing, and even entertaining it. Also, of course, the population had to get the weapons for fighting. It had to be kept in the best possible health and it had to be made mobile. . . . The complexity of this job was almost beyond comprehension. . . . The awkwardness of the [existing English] geography had to be remedied. Many miles of new roads had to be made . . . and about 150 miles of new tracks laid down. A complete new system of exchanges and telephone lines had to be installed to give the military their own communications. . . . Besides arranging for the housing, feeding, sanitation, and equipment of the gigantic forces employed, General Lee and his thousands of logistics experts had to devise means of sustaining the flow of supplies" from America to Britain, to the fighting forces, and to the liberated areas.

The son born to Charles Fenlon Lee on August 1, 1887 in Junction City, Kansas, was named after his mother, John Clifford (Hodges) Lee—who had herself been given her father's name. His ambition to become a soldier was the result of visits to the cavalry post at near-by Fort Riley, where an uncle was stationed. A subsequent trip to West Point heightened his ardor for the military life. At eighteen young "Cliff" Lee entered West Point; and in 1909, when he was graduated with his B.S. and his commission as a 2d lieutenant, he entered the Corps of Engineers, the destination, it is said, of the Academy's most brilliant graduates. He served three months on river and harbor duty at Detroit before being ordered to the Panama Canal Zone, from which he returned in May 1910. After another three months at Rock Island, Illinois, and Pittsburgh, the young Lieutenant entered the Army's Engineer School at Washington Barracks, D.C.

From October 1911 to August 1912 Lee was on duty as a member of the 3rd Engineer Battalion at the National Guard Camp of Instruction in Fort Leavenworth, Kansas; and on February 27, 1912, after three years of service, he was promoted to a 1st lieutenancy. Chosen as secretary of the 1913 Presidential Inaugural Committee's military section, Lee was sent to the Office of the Chief of Staff in Washington, and then to Texas City, Texas. In September 1913 he left for duty in connection with the military survey of Guam; and in July 1914, toward the beginning of the First World War, he proceeded to the Philippines for the military survey of Luzon. There the Lieutenant was made senior topographical inspector and prepared the Philippine Department's *Manual for Topographers* (1915).

On his return to the United States, Lee served in district engineer work at Wheeling, West Virginia, and was made a captain on June 3, 1916. The twenty-eight-year-old Captain was then put in charge of constructing a dam on the Ohio River (all navigable rivers in the United States are under the care of the War Department), after which he returned to Wheeling. Chosen by Major General Leonard Wood to be his aide, Lee served with him at Governors Island, New York, and in Charleston, South Carolina, where the young officer

U. S. Army Signal Corps
LT. GEN. JOHN CLIFFORD HODGES LEE

was a member of the Camp Site Board for the Southeastern Department. Promotion to senior rank came in August 1917, when Lee was thirty. Raised to the temporary rank of major, he served as acting chief of staff for the 89th Division at Camp Funston, Kansas; and at the end of September he was married to Sarah Ann Row. (In 1939, after twenty-two years of married life, Mrs. Lee died, leaving one son, John Clifford Hodges Lee, Jr., like his father an officer in the United States Army.)

Appointed a lieutenant colonel (temporary) on February 4, 1918, Lee sailed for France two weeks later. There he was put through the Army General Staff College at Langres, graduating on May 30, and served as assistant chief of staff for Army Intelligence (G-2), 82nd Division. During this period Colonel Lee was attached to the British Expeditionary Force's 71st Division "in line opposite Albert," and then moved into reserve until July 18, after which he was promoted to full colonel (temporary). Assigned next to the Reynal Training Area as assistant chief of staff for Operations and Training (G-3), he remained there until the following October. During the battle of St. Mihiel, September 12-16, 1918, Lee served at Novient and Flirey. At Euvezin he helped in the "battle reorganization," serving at division headquarters there and at Commercy and Recicourt while "the 89th Division moved from sector to reserve in the rear of the Argonne offensive." The progress of the American forces can be easily followed through the names of places where Lee served successively: La Dhuy, Barricourt, Tailly, and Stenay, France; Dampicourt and St. Leger, Belgium; Mersch and Echternach, Luxembourg; and finally Kyllburgh, Germany.

"In the preparations for the drive in the St. Mihiel salient in September, and for the Argonne-Meuse offensive in October, he had charge of the detailed arrangements for and the subsequent execution of the operations of the 89th Division." Colonel Lee's "splendid

LEE, JOHN CLIFFORD HODGES—
Continued

staff coordination, marked tactical ability, and
sound judgment" were rewarded with the Distinguished Service Medal; and his "gallantry
in action . . . while leading a patrol which
penetrated into the enemy lines" won him the
Silver Star. France decorated the American
Colonel with the Croix de Guerre, with Palms,
and made him an Officier in the Légion d'Honneur.

In June 1919 Lee returned to the United
States to demobilize the 89th Division head-
quarters at Camp Upton and Camp Funston.
Then, after a few months in the Office of the
Chief of Engineers, the Colonel joined the
General Staff Corps of the 6th Corps Area.
In April 1921, with the permanent rank of
major to which he had reverted in March 1920,
Lee left for two more years' service in the
Philippine Islands, after which he went back
to the Office of the Chief of Engineers. Here
he remained from September 1923 to July
1926, at which time he was made district engineer in charge of navigation improvement
and flood control work on the Mississippi
River with headquarters at Vicksburg, Mississippi. During the next five years Major Lee
also worked on improvements (such as widening and deepening) of three smaller rivers,
the Red, Ouachita, and Yazoo, with their
tributaries.

This done, Lee entered the Army War College in Washington, which gives the highest
training in the United States Army. Completing his course June 30, 1932, he became an
instructor at the Army Industrial College, also
in Washington, receiving his lieutenant-colo-
nelcy in December 1933. The following year,
after five months in the Office of the District
Engineer, South Atlantic Division, and the
Civic Works Authority, Colonel Lee was sent
to Philadelphia as district engineer for the
North Atlantic Division. Four years later, in
April 1938, he assumed the duties of assistant and division engineer, North Pacific Division, with headquarters at Portland, Oregon;
and in June 1938 he was made a full colonel.
The following year, from May to August 1939,
he put in temporary duty with the Air Corps.

On October 1, 1940, at the age of fifty-three,
Colonel Lee was promoted to brigadier general (temporary) and ordered to Fort Mason,
California, to take command of the port of
embarkation. Thus he became one of the few
high-ranking officers of the wartime forces
who achieved general's rank before the outbreak of hostilities. (Among those who had
not, are Generals Mark W. Clark '42, George S.
Patton '43, Carl Spaatz '42, Ira C. Eaker '42, and
Lee's commander, Dwight D. Eisenhower '42.)
After a year in California the General was
assigned to the 2nd Infantry Division at Fort
Sam Houston, Texas, where he was in command from November 1941 to May 1942. In
February 1942 he was promoted to major general (temporary); on May 23, 1942 he arrived
in England to "stake out a claim" for the
American forces, and the following July it
was announced that General Lee would command the Services of Supply in the European
theatre of war.

Perhaps the first significant test of the supply
chief's efficiency was the North African campaign, which he stage-managed. Everything
was there when needed—even to traffic signs
written in English. In January 1944, when
General Eisenhower assumed command of
United States forces in the European theatre
in addition to his duties as supreme Allied
commander, he appointed John Clifford Hodges
Lee as his deputy. In this post, held in addition to his other duties, Lee was to "act in all
appropriate cases" for his commander. Inasmuch as General Eisenhower has been occupied
with planning the invasion, it was clear that
General Lee would be in effective charge of
the Americans; and in February 1944 he was
promoted to lieutenant general (temporary).

As head of the service forces, Lee "bossed
the A.E.F.'s housekeeping troops (except the
Air Forces) in all the endless work from
unloading ships to feeding the troops, building their camps, tending them when they are
sick, shipping their bodies home when they die"
—everything except actual fighting. Commented *Time* Magazine, "If an officer can be
judged from his peacetime career, square-
jawed, orderly General Lee is the man for the
job." By April 1943, when the rest of the
Army had discarded the ambiguous "S. O. S."
(Services of Supply) in favor of "A. S. F."
(Army Service Forces), the magazine reported
that "the cherubic, bald, bee-busy United
States supply chief in England refuses to
change his outfit's name . . . until officially and
specifically ordered to do so. He has not yet
received such an order. [In June 1944 his
command was redesignated as the Communications Zone, ETOUSA.] Military men regard
his organization as a model of efficiency in all
things great and small. As an example, S. O. S.
men in London last week pointed with pride to
an American-English glossary General Lee
had had printed for his men. Immediate reason: someone almost sent to the United States
for garbage cans when there were plenty in
England, disguised as 'dust bins.'" Among the
mysteries revealed in this glossary are: that
blowtorches and storage batteries are known,
respectively, as "brazing lamps" and "accumu-
lators"; that "paraffin" means kerosene in
England; and that thumbtacks, monkey
wrenches, and bobby pins suffer a sea change
to "drawing pins", "adjustable spanners," and
"hair grips" in crossing the ocean. This is
but one indication of the complexity of the
problems facing the supply service.

This prodigious job was made easier for
General Lee and his staff of experts—former
governors, railroad presidents, and managers
of grocery chains, now wearing the uniforms
of majors and colonels—by the full cooperation of the British. In the General's words,
"We have been given hundreds of buildings
as quarters for our troops, many scores of
airdromes, hospitals, depots, and headquarters
accommodations . . . the use of all ports, transportation facilities, and other services . . .
more than 100 well-equipped American Red
Cross leave centers . . . all these and more. . . .
Britons have moved out of their traditional
homes and villages to provide billets for our
troops. They have given up without protest
their fields and hedges, so dear to an Englishman's heart, so that our field forces might
have room to maneuver." This generosity he

repaid by doing what everyone called a superb job.

For months after Lee's arrival in England his engineers worked without letup to build bases, prepare the transportation, and work out plans for the handling of thousands of troops. Mere space was a greater problem than one might think. For every infantryman who wades ashore to invade the Continent, "about eight tons of supplies of various sorts must go with him, and fifty or sixty pounds more must get to him every day." It is in the British Isles that "the supplies were converging to be assembled, sorted, stored, and guarded until time came to rush them on. . . . These islands now hold the greatest arsenal in history," as Harold Denny pointed out, "and the puzzle is how, in the area of one good-sized American state, already crowded with their own war equipment, troops, and airdromes, they have found room for all the men and supplies we are importing. . . . The operation of this arsenal is a business so colossal it makes the biggest private enterprise look like a corner newsstand."

In spite of the heavy pressure of his duties, General Lee managed whenever he possibly could to attend morning service in an Episcopal church, in addition to the "regular and stated devotions" conducted by his own chaplain at field headquarters. A *Christian Science Monitor* reporter discovered, on one occasion, that he and the General were reading the same devotional quarterly; and among Lee's orders is one that "No member of the command who desires to attend Sunday services will be placed on duty that prevents such attendance."

One of the General's few setbacks occurred in March 1944, when he suggested that instead of an endless series of "FDR's" in *Stars and Stripes* headlines, some other term—he suggested CINC, short for Commander in Chief—might be more dignified. The soldier-editors of the overseas service paper, whose tradition of independence dates back to the First World War, blandly ignored the memorandum, which was subsequently withdrawn. More typical was the occasion when the General noticed that tires on a certain transport unit were soft—and whipped a pressure gauge out of his swagger stick to prove it.

The General who mounted the invasion is of medium height and sturdy build. His eyes still sparkle with mischief, reminiscent of his grammar school class which was so "ornery" that one principal, in a moment of acute distress, prophesied that the members would all land in the penitentiary. Lee spends about half of his time on tours of inspection that follow a minutely fixed timetable. He dislikes the words "substantially," "approximately," and "about," because in war approximations substituted for exact computations cost lives.

References

N Y Sun p18 Ap 4 '44
Sat Eve Post 217:9-11+ S 2 '44 il por
Time 40:56 Jl 27 '42; 44:21-2 S 25 '44 il

Who's Who in America 1944-45

LEESE, SIR OLIVER (WILLIAM HARGREAVES) Oct. 27, 1894- British Army officer

Address: h. The Lower Hall, Worfield, Bridgnorth, Shropshire, England

In November 1944 Lieutenant General Sir Oliver Leese, formerly head of the British 8th Army in Italy, was appointed commander of the newly organized 11th Army Group which will operate in southeast Asia under the direction of Admiral Lord Louis Mountbatten[42]. This appointment advances a distinguished military career which began when Leese was a young subaltern in the First World War. One of the youngest of the high-ranking British officers of the present time, he is considered an able commander with a reputation for great energy, fearlessness, and imperturbability.

Oliver William Hargreaves Leese was born in Shropshire, England, on October 27, 1894, the eldest son of William Hargreaves Leese, a solicitor and second holder of a baronetcy created in 1908. (Oliver succeeded to the baronetcy in 1937.) His mother was Violet Mary Sandeman, daughter of the late Albert George Sandeman. Young Leese received a conventional education at Ludgrove and Eton, and was commissioned in the Coldstream Guards before going to Flanders in 1914. Here, according to *Newsweek*, the young "blue blood" proved to his associates that he had grown up entirely unspoiled by displaying an engagingly informal manner and a complete disregard for rank or seniority. "Officers in the company mess, his sergeant, a sentry in the line, or the divisional general were all treated as though they had been in the same house with him at Eton." His infectious good spirits and his nonchalance in the fact of battle were the basis of many stories which have lasted through the years. According to these tales, Sir Oliver refused to treat war as any different from a field day in Windsor Park, yet "he was always where the danger was." He was wounded three times between 1914 and 1918; he received the Distinguished Service Order; and was twice mentioned in dispatches.

During the years following the First World War—or, as one writer expressed it, "between wars"—Sir Oliver's career was that of the British professional soldier. He had various staff positions and advanced rapidly. From 1920 to 1922 he was adjutant in the 3rd Battalion of the Coldstream Guards, and following this for three years he was adjutant at the Officers' Training Corps at Eton. He was staff officer at the College of Camberley for the year 1927-1928; and then brigade major with the 1st Guards Brigade; he was general staff officer, 2nd grade, in the War Office in 1935-1936; and then commanded the 1st Battalion of the Coldstream Guards for two years. From 1938 to 1940 he was general staff officer and chief instructor at the Staff College in Quetta, British Baluchistan (India). He also traveled throughout India and Africa studying the terrain. Returning to England after the start of the Second World War, he was appointed deputy chief of staff to Field Marshal Viscount Gort[40] with the British Expeditionary Force in France. Sir Oliver had command of troops at the time of the British evacuation

British Official Photo

LT. GEN. SIR OLIVER LEESE

from Dunkerque, and then commanded the
29th Independent Brigade Group stationed in
the Dover area, where he was charged with
the job of bearing the brunt of any German
invasion across the Dover Strait. It is said
that he was one of the last to leave Dunkerque,
crossing the Channel with Marshal Gort in
"something with a one-lung motor that just
lasted to the English shore."

Sir Oliver was a tank-warfare expert, and
during the months spent in England after
Dunkerque he trained a guards division when
it was converted from an infantry to an
armored division; this experience was to prove
excellent training for his work in 1942 when
he joined General Sir Bernard Montgomery '42
in the Middle East. Leese's appointment as
commander of the 30th Corps of the 8th Army
was an important one, for this corps was to
be the tank spearhead in the push across the
desert from El Alamein to Tunis. (The spearhead of the attack is the unit which makes the
principal attack and upon whose success victory
is usually dependent.) And the British attack
on the Axis forces in Egypt was considered
of great importance, for it represented an all-
out attack for the defenses of Cairo and Alexandria and for the elimination of Field Marshal
Erwin Rommel's '42 famous Afrika Korps from
North Africa.

The story of the "long seesaw African campaign" in which Leese participated as chief of
the 30th Corps is a chronicle of two armies
fighting doggedly in the "dusty glare of the
desert sun"—a chronicle of grim reality to
which there is added, ironically, an undercurrent of humor in the picture of Rommel, the
"Desert Fox," being chased across the coastal
highway. According to the *New Republic*, the
British Government's documentary film, *Desert
Victory*, gives an excellent and clear account
of this campaign, portraying vividly the start
of the British troops, barely holding a thirty-
mile front between the Qattara depression and
the sea, and ending thirteen weeks later and

1,300 miles further west through the gates of
Tripoli. This pursuit of Rommel, called the
"longest chase in history," began at El Alamein in October 1942, continued (with stops
at Tobruk, Bengazi, and El Agheila) until the
British entered Tripoli in January 1943, and
ended with the swift and sudden fall of Tunis
and Bizerte in May 1943. The New York
Times reported that the Allies had achieved a
"major and clean-cut victory . . . as the famous
Afrika Korps, shattered and wounded, tried
grimly to escape disaster." *Time* Magazine
described the campaign in these words: "The
Fox lost his tail. . . . Rommel let Montgomery
overtake him and, before he knew it, Montgomery had bitten off his brush." In a more
serious mood, *Time* also expressed the opinion
that "the defeat of the Afrika Korps was an
indispensable preliminary to the invasion of
southern Europe."

Sir Oliver was proud of the polyglot 8th
Army troops who fought with him in the
Middle East and Italy. As one Englishman
said, "It is in some measure the British Com-
monwealth in being, for it has the United
Kingdom as its core, and also divisions from
India, New Zealand, South Africa, and Canada.
That is how Leese likes to look at it—the
Commonwealth in being." Prime Minister
Winston Churchill '42 said of these hard-fighting
soldiers when he visited them in Tripoli, "I
have never seen troops march with the style of
this desert army. Talk about spit and polish!"
Later Polish troops joined the 8th Army, and
Leese permitted them to wear the Crusader's
patch, insignia of the 8th, on their shoulders
as special mark of their achievements in the
Italian campaign.

In July 1943, when Allied troops landed in
Sicily in a "vast amphibian sea-borne land
force synchronized with air and naval attacks,"
Leese again led the 30th Corps of the 8th
Army as it spearheaded this long-awaited invasion, called by President Franklin Roosevelt '42,
"the beginning of the end." The campaign in
Sicily lasted until August, when the Allied
troops entered Messina. In September the
Allies crossed the Strait of Messina and invaded
Italy—three years and three months after Dunkerque. Then in January 1944 Montgomery
was called to England to take over the command of the British ground forces under
General Dwight Eisenhower '42, and he recommended Sir Oliver as his successor to command
the 8th Army.

In March the furious aerial assault on
Cassino was begun; in May, four months after
they had waded ashore at Anzio and Nettuno,
General Mark Clark's '42 5th Army of Americans and Britons struck from the Anzio beachhead while the 8th Army struck smashing
blows at the Hitler Line. Brendan Bracken '41,
British Minister of Information, reported that
the intensity of the fighting was beyond all
description. The Germans were resisting stubbornly, but by the end of May the 5th Army
was within seventeen miles of Rome, and more
than 15,000 German prisoners had been taken.
Eighth Army troops were now at the eastern
end of the expanded line. As they pushed
north from Ceprano they were often delayed
by the necessity of building bridges over rivers
where the enemy had blown up the crossings;

earlier in the spring snowbanks in the mountains had delayed movement.

On June 4 Rome fell to Allied troops; three days later the 8th Army was twelve miles northeast of Rome and had captured the town of Monerotondo. As the summer wore on, the drive to the north of Italy continued along the west coast ten miles south of Grossito and in the center of Perugia; later there was a general advance along a 100-mile front across western Italy and thirty miles closer to Florence. In July, in an announcement from Headquarters, General Sir Harold Alexander '42 said: "The Allied armies in Italy have driven a battered enemy over 150 miles to the north of Rome within one month in a campaign that must rank with the most vigorous and carefully planned campaigns in modern blitz warfare." The 8th Army, described at this time as "welded into a fast-moving fighting machine," captured 10,000 prisoners, bringing the total bag to about 40,000, which meant that Field Marshal Albert Kesselring's '42 forces had been reduced, in prisoners alone, by four divisions. A BBC speaker said: "And so the old Desert Army has smashed on again, its men covered with dust that is white instead of the old golden yellow."

In August Leese's troops crossed the Arno River on the "debris-littered Ponte Vecchio" and entered the heart of Florence. On September 22 Greek troops of the 8th Army entered Rimini, the once beautiful resort and port city. An editorial in the New York Herald-Tribune described the event: "The Greek troops which fought their way into Rimini . . . took part in the closing of a year-old chapter of savage mountain warfare and the opening of a new chapter in the broad valley of the Po. Ever since the original landing on the tip of the Italian boot, on September 3, 1943, the ideal defensive terrain provided by endless ridges of the Apennines has held back the Allied advance. After a final month of bitter fighting, Lieutenant General Sir Oliver Leese's forces have emerged on the far side of those stubborn barriers." As the 8th Army poured onto the Lombardy plain the campaign for central Italy came to a close and the battle for northern Italy began.

During October and the early part of November the American 5th Army had been slowly making its way toward Bologna. The British 8th Army, to the east, worked painfully along the Bologna-Rimini highway, still thirty-nine miles southeast of Bologna. *Time* Magazine called the Italian battle front "the forgotten front," and described the difficulties—rain, mud, wind, high rivers, all but impassable roads and mountains—with which the Allied armies had to contend. Allied Commander in Chief General Sir Harold Alexander admitted that the autumn rains had bogged down the drive before the Po Valley was conquered and that the campaign had reached a stalemate. Hanson W. Baldwin '42, writing of the Italian campaign in the New York *Times*, said: "General Alexander and Lieutenant Generals Mark Clark and Oliver Leese have . . . done well with the tools given them. The primary problem in Italy has been a lack of means, particularly an insufficiency of ground strength and of landing craft and shipping."

Meanwhile, in the southeast Asia battle area a reorganization of commands was taking place following the recall of General Joseph Stilwell '42 to Washington. In November Sir Oliver was appointed commander of the newly organized 11th Army Group which was to operate under the direction of Admiral Lord Louis Mountbatten. (A group contains more than one army, but the only part identified at the time of Leese's appointment was the British 14th Army which was operating in Burma.) General Leese's appointment, observed the New York *Times,* was the strongest indication so far "of a build-up in Admiral Mountbatten's ground forces, whose southeast Asia command includes Ceylon, Burma, Thailand, Malay, and a part of Sumatra." Leese's own group contained a mixture of troops such as he had commanded in Italy, for the 11th Army Group contains the 14th Army, and American and Chinese forces, formerly directed by General Stilwell in northern Burma, are also a part of this army and therefore are under General Leese's over-all generalship. Leese succeeds General Sir George Giffard in the Burma post.

Sir Oliver is described as a "bull of a man, about six feet four inches tall" with a boyish zest for life and adventure and a tremendous capacity for work. Although his training was with the Coldstream Guards, he is informal, often casual in his dress, at times wearing a khaki shirt for dinner unadorned by badges of rank. He likes to be out and about visiting his troops and getting as far forward in the lines as possible. He has a gift for knowing the idiosyncrasies of his commanders and the characteristics of his diverse troops. When a problem confronts him he studies it deeply, but once he has made up his mind he does not change it easily. He dislikes paper work and will not have long documents presented to him.

Sir Oliver was married in 1933 to Margaret Alice, the only daughter of Cuthbert Leicester-Warren. He is fond of country sports, especially fishing. His clubs are the Turf and Guards'. He was made a Commander of the Order of the British Empire in 1940, a Companion of the Bath in 1942, and Knight Commander of the Bath in 1943.

References

N Y Herald Tribune p3 Ja 6 '44
N Y Times p6 Ja 6 '44
Newsweek 23:23-4 Ja 17 '44 por
Time 43:24 Ja 17 '44
Who's Who 1944

LEIGH-MALLORY, SIR TRAFFORD L(EIGH) (lē' mal'ō-ri) July 11, 1892—Nov. 14(?), 1944 British Air Chief Marshal

Bulletin: Air Chief Marshal Sir Trafford L. Leigh-Mallory was reported missing in November 1944 on flight to assume post as air commander in chief of the Southeast Asia Command.

From March 1944 issue:

When the Allied troops rushed ashore from their landing craft for the invasion of Fortress Europa, their fate depended largely on the air support they received. To provide this

British Official Photo

AIR CHIEF MARSHAL SIR TRAFFORD
L. LEIGH-MALLORY

1927 he was appointed commandant of the School of Army Cooperation, leaving this post in 1930 to become an instructor at the Staff College, Camberley. After a year there and three as deputy director of staff duties at the Air Ministry he was sent to the Imperial Defence College, and was then given command of No. 2 Flying Training School at Digby, Lincoln. From 1936 to 1937 Leigh-Mallory was senior air staff officer in Iraq, returning to England to assume command of the No. 12 Fighter Group at Hucknall. He was air officer commanding this group in 1939 when the German Luftwaffe began the Battle of Britain.

During this battle Leigh-Mallory directed the work of a wing which destroyed some 150 German aircraft in seven engagements. "On many occasions in 1940 he sat in the control room of his fighter station and directed as many as three wings of fighters at a time." In July of that year Leigh-Mallory, by then air vice-marshal, was awarded the Order of Companion of the Bath for this "distinguished service rendered in recent operations." Later he was transferred to No. 11 Fighter Group, again as air officer commanding. At the same time he was helping to organize and develop the Polish Air Force in England. In recognition of his work he was awarded the Polonia Restituta Medal in June 1942.

In August 1942 Air Marshal Leigh-Mallory came to international notice by providing the "air umbrella" for the raid on Dieppe. It was his responsibility to hold back the Luftwaffe and prevent it from bombing and strafing the attacking troops, and he carried it out with brilliant success. "Some of the fruits of that hair-raising raid were sour," according to one commentator, "but the Air Marshal's parasol was beyond criticism." Units of the American, Polish, and other Allied air forces, as well as squadrons from R.A.F. bomber, fighter, and Army cooperation commands, were under Leigh-Mallory's direction. Long before dawn the planes took off to "clear the air" above Dieppe and the Channel. Blenheims and Bostons laid smoke screens and attacked German strong points, knocking gun posts out of the battle, while Hurricanes and Spitfires brought down ninety-one enemy aircraft with another one hundred "probables." Only ninety-eight British planes were lost, from which thirty fighter pilots were saved. With characteristic British understatement, it was announced that "German aircraft were prevented from hindering the landing operations, the work undertaken ashore, and the re-embarkation by direction sent from the headquarters of a fighter group under Leigh-Mallory."

On November 28, 1942 Leigh-Mallory was appointed air officer commanding in chief, in charge of the entire Fighter Command. So intense was the work of this command during the winter months that "in recognition of the day and night raids, the fighter and reconnaissance sweeps, the train-busting and intruder expeditions, he was created a Knight Commander of the Bath in the 1943 New Year's Honors." By this time his planes had already destroyed some 5,000 enemy aircraft. Just one year later came the announcement that Sir Trafford had been appointed to head

support was the task of the Allied Tactical Air Force and the particular responsibility of British Air Chief Marshal Sir Trafford L. Leigh-Mallory, who is known as "a master of air-ground coordination."

Sir Trafford Leigh Leigh-Mallory was born July 11, 1892 at Mobberley, Cheshire, where his father and grandfather had both been rectors. His father was the Reverend Herbert Leigh Mallory, who changed his name by royal assent to Herbert Leigh Leigh-Mallory in 1914; Trafford's mother, the former Annie Beridge Jebb, was herself the daughter of a clergyman. Notwithstanding this clerical tradition, young Trafford intended to become a lawyer; and, after preparing at the Haileybury School, he read law at Magdalene College of Cambridge University. He received his LL.B. in 1914, just in time for him to enter the Army as a private of the 10th Battalion, Liverpool Territorial Regiment.

In August 1914 young Leigh-Mallory was commissioned a 2nd lieutenant in the 4th Battalion of Lancashire Fusiliers. Wounded in the battle of Ypres, he took time off in 1915 to marry Doris Jean Sawyer (their son was invalided home from the RAF in this War, while their daughter, Jacqueline, an officer in the WAAF, married an American air officer in May 1944). In July 1916 Leigh-Mallory left the Army to join the Royal Flying Corps, to which he was seconded as a flying officer. The young airman served in France with such distinction that he was mentioned in dispatches and awarded the Distinguished Service Order. In 1919, when the Royal Flying Corps had become the Royal Air Force, he gave up law permanently for a career in the air, and accepted a commission as squadron leader in the R.A.F.

Becoming interested in cooperation between the air and ground forces, Leigh-Mallory spent a number of years "studying and experimenting" with the combination. In the tactical air forces under General Eisenhower's[42] command; this appointment was followed by his promotion to the post of air chief marshal on December 31, 1943.

In February 1944 Britain's Secretary of State for Air, announced the passing of one of the great names of the War, the Fighter Command of the R.A.F., which had gained the first great Allied victory against the Germans in the Battle of Britain. This command was henceforth to work with the Army Cooperation Command in the British 2nd Tactical Air Force. With the United States 9th Air Force this organization constituted the Allied Expeditionary Air Forces in Western Europe, which eventually became the greatest assemblage of air power ever known, under the expert command of Air Chief Marshal Sir Trafford Leigh-Mallory. Sir Trafford was thus responsible for the coordinated air offensive that preceded and accompanied the successful invasion of Western Europe and the rapid sweep of the Allied armies through France and Belgium.

On D-Day, June 6, 1944, Leigh-Mallory's "air umbrella" was again beyond criticism, air support reaching an almost fantastic peak, with 16,000 tons of bombs being used during that day alone. The assault climaxed the end of a fifty-day period of aerial preparation during which enemy transportation was reported to have been disrupted along a deep coastal strip extending from Holland to the Bay of Biscay; and in the eighty-four hours preceding the invasion 15,000 tons of bombs were estimated to have been dropped upon Nazi rail lines, highways, fortifications, and other installations in the area. "The offensive fell into four main phases," explained Guy Rhoades, writing in *PM,* "the attack on yards and bases from which the Nazis launched their U-boats against Britain's lifeline; the attack on aircraft factories, munitions plants, and other industries supplying the Nazi war machine; the attack on enemy air bases in Germany and the occupied countries; the attack on enemy coastal fortifications and lines of communications." In recognition of his success, early in October Leigh-Mallory received the Soviet Order of Kutuzov, First Class, and on November 3 General Eisenhower awarded him the degree of Chief Commander of the American Legion of Merit.

After making this major contribution to initial Allied victories in the West, on October 15, 1944 Leigh-Mallory was named Allied air commander in chief in southeast Asia. Authority over air operations in Western Europe was taken over by General Eisenhower's deputy over-all commander, Air Chief Marshal Sir Arthur Tedder[43]. Leigh-Mallory's transfer to the staff of Admiral Mountbatten[42] in Asia emphasized the shift from the slow and difficult operations of the rainy monsoon season to the more rapid tempo of operations that were now expected in Burma, in the opinion of Hanson W. Baldwin[42] in the New York *Times.*

Sir Trafford is described as a "soft-voiced, quiet man who has a gift for resounding phrases and writes a neat, precise, tight hand, so characteristic that the initials 'L-M' which he signs to his memoranda and orders are superfluous." All the R.A.F. knows the Air Chief Marshal as "L-M." Although he and Lady Leigh-Mallory have lived in R.A.F. quarters at "one air station after another," he likes a "bright and homelike" atmosphere—"gay flowers in the living room and a cheery coal fire in the grate." As might be expected of an invasion chief, however, he spends little time at home. Even in normal times, Sir Trafford has few interests except his work.

While *Time* describes the air chief as "a calm, strapping, fifty-one-year-old six-footer," *Newsweek* sees him as "small, dark. . . . Has mind that can work like lightning in emergencies." Leigh-Mallory's photographs show him as dark and of medium height.

References

N Y Times VI p7 Ja 23 '44 por; p1+
    N 18 '44
Newsweek 23:22 Ja 10 '44
Time 43:26 Ja 10 '44
Who's Who 1944

LEMAY, CURTIS E(MERSON) Nov. 15, 1906- United States Army officer

Address: b. c/o War Department, Washington, D.C.; h. 1478 Orchard Pl., Lakewood, Ohio

Although the youngest major general in the United States Army, Curtis E. LeMay holds the most important pioneering job in air combat today, in the opinion of many analysts. Chief of the 20th Bomber Command in the China-Burma-India area, he commands the A.A.F.'s gigantic new Superfortresses, the B-29's.

An Ohioan, born in Cleveland on November 15, 1906, Curtis Emerson LeMay began his military career immediately after his graduation from Ohio State University with an engineering degree. He was appointed a 2nd lieutenant in June 1928, and for three months was stationed at Camp Knox, Kentucky, in the 62nd Field Artillery Brigade, Field Artillery Reserve. At the end of this time he decided to change over to the then young United States Air Corps. He enlisted in the Regular Army as a flying cadet and was sent to the Air Corps Primary Flying School at March Field, California. Following his graduation in June 1929 he entered the Air Corps Advanced Flying School at Kelly Field, Texas, and on October 12 was commissioned a 2nd lieutenant in the Air Reserve. Ordered into active service the next day, he served with the 27th Pursuit Squadron at Selfridge Field, Michigan, until January 1930, when he was made a 2nd lieutenant in the Air Corps of the Regular Army.

In September 1931 he was sent to Norton Field in his home town of Columbus as assistant engineer and operations officer. He remained there until the following March, when he returned to Selfridge Field. Except for two months spent at Langley Field, Virginia, where he received training in advanced aviation, he served with the 27th Pursuit Squadron at Selfridge until October 1934, when he joined the 18th Pursuit Group at Schofield Barracks, Hawaii. While in Hawaii he was advanced to 1st lieutenant (temporary) on March 12, 1935, this rank becoming permanent two months later.

(Continued next page)

LEMAY, CURTIS E.—_Continued_

In January 1937 he was assigned once more to Langley Field, in General Headquarters, Air Force, this time as operations and intelligence officer and navigator-bomber of a B-17, with the 49th Bombardment Squadron. (On March 1 the first of the new B-17 Flying Fortresses had been delivered to the 2nd Bombardment Group at Langley Field.) In May 1939 Lieutenant LeMay left the field to enter the Air Corps Tactical School at Maxwell Field, Alabama, graduating in August 1939. Rejoining the 49th Bombardment Squadron at this time, he served as a commander of a B-17 until February 1940, when he was transferred to the 41st Reconnaissance Squadron, also at Langley Field, as operations and intelligence officer. A month prior to this he had been advanced to the rank of captain.

Assigned to the 7th Bombardment Squadron, 34th Bombardment Group, in January 1941, he served with that unit, both at Langley Field and at Westover Field, Massachusetts, as squadron commander and later as group operations officer, until March 1942. Shortly before Pearl Harbor, LeMay had a chance to prove his ability when he was assigned to copilot a B-24 Liberator on an initial survey flight from Bolling Field in Washington, D.C., over the South Atlantic route to Africa and Asia Minor. It was a record-making 24,700-mile flight on which were members of the Harriman [41] mission. On this flight airports were surveyed for use by the Ferrying Command, bases of operation were selected, and recommendations were made for the establishment of new airports to serve as alternates on transoceanic flights. As a result of this flight LeMay received the Distinguished Flying Cross for displaying, said the citation, "outstanding initiative, resourcefulness, and a high degree of skill under the many trying conditions encountered on this hazardous mission of great responsibility." During the period with the 7th Bombardment Squadron he was also advanced in rank: to major (temporary) on March 21, 1941; to lieutenant colonel (temporary) on January 5, 1942; and to colonel (temporary) on March 1, 1942. In April 1942 he was given command of the 305th Bombardment Group (a heavy bombardment division) at Muroc, California, and in September was ordered to take the group to England on a mission with the 8th Air Force. (The 8th Air Force had been established that January as the daylight strategic bombing force of a combined British-based air offensive against Germany. In cooperation with the Italian-based 15th Air Force and the night-bombing Royal Air Force, its objective was the destruction of the German war machine.)

The commander was a sharp disciplinarian. After he received orders to toughen up his men for service in the European theatre he drilled them night and day on gunnery, navigation, and bombing. But the close supervision and insistence on efficiency was effective. In the twenty-five missions his group of Britain-based B-17 Flying Fortresses made against Germany from October 1942 until the middle of November 1943, only thirteen of the heavy bombers were lost. "Some of the best formations in which American bombers now fly against German targets," wrote one commenta-

tor in September 1944, "were worked out by the youthful, burly, critical LeMay," a leader in the development of daylight precision bombing. These heavy bombers at first had no fighter escort for their deep penetrations into enemy territory, and it was LeMay who helped to develop the trend toward close formations and concentration of fire power. One of the formations for which he is responsible is the defense flight formation, in which planes are staggered at different heights instead of in the less effective V-formation of three planes at the same altitude.

As the months advanced during the period LeMay was in England the newspaper headlines told a story of increasingly heavy 8th Air Force raids over the Continent. In December 1942 the U-boat pens at Lorient, France, were bombed. In January 1943 came the first United States bomber attack on Germany, in which fifty-three B-17's struck at Wilhelmshaven. Then on August 17, 1943 a group of 126 B-17's with a P-47 Thunderbolt escort hit at Regensburg, South Bavaria, in what was called the first notable example by the A.A.F. of shuttle bombing, with planes crossing Europe and landing in North African bases. On the return trip the Focke-Wulf plant at Bordeaux was attacked.

LeMay participated personally in this shuttle bombing by the Forts (as he had in several of the other raids), planning and leading the attack of his division. For this he received the Distinguished Service Cross for "extraordinary heroism" on a mission in which he had not been expected to participate "through obligations or reason of duty." While in the European theatre he also received the Air Medal (February 1943) for combat flights over Germany, and the Silver Star (March). And on September 28 his rank was advanced to brigadier general (temporary), the following March 2 to major general, also temporary.

Simple and to the point was LeMay's motto: "More bombs on the target." In October 1943, predicting that Germany's power to make war would be neutralized by the next spring, he declared: "Weather is not a factor which determines the frequency of our attacks. Replacement of airplanes is the primary factor, and if the flow to this theatre continues, as it will, German industry will be destroyed by spring."

In July 1944, after a brief period in the United States visiting air force commands and training centers, General LeMay was transferred to the China-Burma-India area, and in August made chief of the 20th Bomber Command, to succeed General Kenneth Wolfe. This Command was the first field organization of the 20th Air Force, the global air force created especially to direct the Army's new Superfortresses, the B-29's, in the air war against Japan. (In March the 21st Bomber Command was activated. It is now under General Haywood Hansell and operates from Saipan. The planes assigned to General LeMay's group were operating out of bases in China and India.) "If production and acquisition of bases can be advanced sufficiently before Japan is knocked out of the War," said Sidney Shallett in August, "the B-29's, in the opinion of their advocates here [Washington, D.C.], should prove a decisive factor in the final stages of the campaign against the Japanese homeland itself." LeMay's new job was not to be an easy one. "The B-29's," declared *Time* Magazine, "have more tricks to be solved than any Flying Fortress pilot ever dreamed of—such as remote-control guns, cabin supercharging, a set of high-powered engines that can suck tanks dry long before their time if controls are not set just right. Because they have a lot of new tricks, they call for a whole set of new tactics."

By the end of August the "mammoth, slim-nosed bombers"—about one and one-half times as large as the Flying Fortress and estimated to fly more than 300 miles per hour—had made approximately seven missions on five dates since their first appearance on June 15, 1944. Five of these missions were against Japan proper, one against enemy industrial targets in Manchuria and occupied China, and one against the oil refineries in Sumatra.

By September it seemed apparent that B-29 raids against Japan would be carried on with increasing ferocity. On the 8th an estimated force of 100 Superfortresses struck in daylight at strategic industrial targets in Anshan. It was the greatest force yet employed, and the second raid against this important area. General LeMay, it was reported, had presumably led the attack himself. A third attack against Anshan of more than 100 of the huge B-29's occurred at the end of the month. "Every plane that left the ground returned safely," said Brigadier General Lauris Norstadt, Chief of Staff of the 20th Air Force, after that raid. "This would be a remarkable record on a bombing mission by planes of any type," he added, "and it is all the more remarkable when applied to the B-29, which is still relatively experimental and is flying such vast distances." LeMay had evidently lost none of his toughness as a commander. And for this mission he received a congratulatory message from General Henry H. Arnold '42, commanding general of the Army Air Forces and direct commander of the 20th Air Force.

But in LeMay's own words, "the best show yet" was the October 14 successful Superfortress raid on Okayama, a vital Japanese repair base and supply depot on the island of Formosa. The tenth expedition of the Superfortresses, it marked the beginning of a new phase of B-29 operations, according to LeMay. Previous operations were largely preliminary while the crews learned to use the great new weapon with confidence. The first phase of combat testing is satisfactorily ended. From now on the real job begins, and greater damage with each sortie can be expected." In October he reported that the first nine raids of his B-29's set the record of not losing one single plane shot down by enemy fighters. Seven were lost to enemy action, but there was not a single authenticated case of a plane reported downed by Japanese interceptors.

In the remaining weeks of October and through November the number of B-29 raids increased. On November 11, on the sixteenth mission of LeMay's group (the seventh in twenty-seven days), the big planes struck for the second time at the Omura aircraft factory on Kyushu, the southernmost of Japan's home islands. Some of the planes, diverted by hurricane weather, hit docks and storage facilities at

MAJ. GEN. CURTIS E. LEMAY

Shanghai and Nanking in the first B-29 raid on these Japanese-held targets. One plane was reported lost. Ten days later eighty to one hundred B-29's made the 3,000-mile round trip to strike again at Kyushu (some of the planes also hitting Shanghai and Nanking). This time the Superfortresses encountered their first strong fighter opposition, according to a communique from 20th Air Force headquarters. Two planes were shot down and one was missing, the first planes to be lost to enemy fighter interception since June 15 when the 20th Bomber Command was inaugurated.

Then on November 24 the news was flashed to the United States that Tokyo had been hit for the second time in the War by American bombers. The daylight raid was the first attack on the enemy capital since the flight on April 18, 1942 of sixteen carrier-based medium bombers, led by the then Lieutenant Colonel James H. Doolittle '42. The November B-29 mission, it was revealed, had been conducted by the newly established 21st Bomber Command, operating from bases on Saipan in the Marianas under the command of General H. S. Hansell. "We have brought Japan within range of our Superfortresses from the east as well as from the west," declared General Millard F. Harmon '42, new deputy commander of the 20th Air Force. "No part of the homeland of Japan is now safe from land-based air attacks. We can hit where and when we choose." The 21st Bomber Command bases, closer to Japan than LeMay's bases in China and India, have a great logistics advantage over the old bases. Until the completion in late November of the main portion of a new oil line into Burma, the B-29's had been supplied with fuel by planes flown in from India.

After its twentieth mission against Japanese targets (including those in Singapore, Rangoon, Sumatra, Shanghai, and Japan itself) it was reported on December 14 by the 20th Bomber Command that in its six months of operations its Superforts had flown 55,000 miles, dropped a total of 4,500 tons of bombs,

LEMAY, CURTIS E.—*Continued*

knocked down 120 enemy fighters, probably destroyed 90 others, and damaged 170 more. Most of these attacks were made in daylight, in formation. Many points on the Japanese production line were being attacked regularly by both the 20th and 21st Bomber Commands. According to LeMay, the B-29 is "the best airplane we have ever built; we have had to make fewer modifications in the B-29 than in any other plane we have produced." The B-29 has become the deadliest aerial weapon in the United States Air Forces with the introduction of an "aircraft gunfire-control system."

If LeMay is hard with his men, he is harder with himself. Before the Wilhelmshaven flight he reassured his nervous men: "Now don't let the flak disturb you. Keep on the bombing run. You'll be able to see how it is because I'm going to be the first one in and I'll get it first." A stern rather than colorful hero, he is reported to have earned more respect than popularity. But his own respect for his job has made him an invaluable man in the war of the air. In April 1944 General LeMay received the Order of Patriotic Warfare, 1st Degree, from the Soviet Government; in December he received the Distinguished Service Medal for his previous work with his Flying Fortress unit in England.

LeMay looks his part. Five feet eight inches tall and weighing 180 pounds, he is a square-jawed man with a heavy shock of unruly black hair. He has a taste for cigars and poker. There are times when the General's stern front radiates a certain comfort among his men. "Pilots, navigators, and bombardiers are happier," says the New York *Sun,* "when they see his black head, wreathed with smoke from his eternal cigar, climb into the lead plane at the start of a tough mission."

References

N Y Herald Tribune p2 Mr 12 '44
N Y Sun p18 S 5 '44
N Y Times p52 D 12 '43; p5 My 14 '44;
　　p16 Ag 14 '44 por
Newsweek 24:33 Ag 28 '44
Time 42:72 Ag 21 '44 por

LENTAIGNE, WALTER D(AVID) A(LEXANDER) (len-tān') July 15, 1899-

British Army officer; leader of the Chindits
Address: b. c/o War Office, Whitehall, London; h. Camberley, Surrey, England

Behind the Japanese lines in Burma the Chindits, "a motley crew of intellectuals and cutthroats," British, Indian, Gurkha, and Burmese troops, led by Major General Walter D. A. Lentaigne, harass the Nipponese. First known to the public as "Wingate's Raiders" (they were so called for the fabulous General who organized and led them on an epic march through the jungle), this redoubtable group is commanded by one of its first members and assisted by the United States Army Air Forces. The name "Chindit" comes from the *Chinthey,* a mythical griffin, half-lion and half-eagle, whose statues guard Burmese temples against evil spirits. The lion-eagle combination symbolizes the cooperation between

ground and air forces. "To retreat like a Chinthey" is the Burmese phrase for a proud, courageous retreat second only to a victory.

The Chindit leader's connection with Burma began at his birth on July 15, 1899. Walter David Alexander Lentaigne— "Joe" for short —was the son of a Burma judge. Educated in England, he attended St. Anthony's in Eastbourne and Oratory in Birmingham. During the First World War young Lentaigne embarked for India on Christmas Day of 1917, and was commissioned a 2nd lieutenant in the British Army on his arrival. Although he has since passed the staff college at Camberley (England), thus qualifying as a staff officer, Lentaigne "is not nor ever has been an office soldier." Between wars he spent as much time as he could on the North-West Frontier of India, "that training ground for keen soldiers." In the course of his seventeen years of bloody campaigns against the mountain tribes of Waziristan—Waziri, Pathans, Afridi, and Mohmands—the young officer made a reputation as a "desperately keen soldier." By 1919 he was a full lieutenant, by 1924 a captain, and by 1936 a major—his present substantive rank.

In 1937, aroused by the new Indian constitution's proviso that the mountain tribes remain under military government, Ali Naggar, the Fakir of Ipi and self-styled "Savior of Islam," proclaimed an independent "Republic of the Frontier Tribes." Among the troops assigned to crush this revolt was Lentaigne, who led a brigade in a "remarkable night march over high mountains with mules and guns" in an attempt to capture the Fakir. The experience was excellent preparation for his later work with the Chindits. In the meantime, however, Major Lentaigne served in the less dramatic post of deputy assistant quartermaster general.

When the Japanese invaded Burma in 1941, Joe Lentaigne was in command of a battalion of the 4th Gurkha Rifles in India. "A magnificent commanding officer," he is said to have gained "an almost legendary reputation for bravery. His Gurkhas would have followed him literally anywhere." According to an official British report, when Lentaigne was ambushed and disarmed by four Japanese it was the work of a moment for him to seize the leader's sword, finish its owner, whirl on the others, kill one, and chase the two remaining enemy soldiers back into the jungle! Brigadier Lentaigne's exploits have a curious myth-like quality in that observers who agree on the general outline of an incident have a way of disagreeing on such details as whether it was four or eight men he killed in a given charge.

Lentaigne's "keen-eyed little Gurkhas" debarked in Burma in February 1942, just two days before the fall of Rangoon. Completely surrounded by the enemy, he should by all the rules have surrendered—but instead he simply turned his 700 men around and marched them back to India, picking up small British detachments on the way. When Lentaigne arrived he was "practically naked," having literally fought himself out of his clothes; but his troops numbered some 2,500, even after battle losses. In June 1942 the officer was decorated with the Distinguished Service Order for this achievement. (His younger brother, Captain C. N. Lentaigne, has also received the D.S.O.)

After a month's rest Lentaigne returned to the frontier with a brigade of the 17th Indian Division, "training for the jungle and killing Japs whenever opportunity occurred." His views on the proper tactics for jungle fighting agreeing exactly with those of General Orde Charles Wingate, Britain's learned, eccentric young military genius, Lentaigne applied for transfer to the new outfit Wingate was organizing in April 1942, and soon became the younger General's most trusted lieutenant. From then until Wingate's untimely death a year later, the story of Wingate's Raiders is the story of Joe Lentaigne.

The new command was made up of Gurkhas, Kachins, Shans, Burmese, and a regiment of second-line, city-bred English troops, all above "the optimum combat age," who had never been under fire. For "six sweltering months" Wingate hardened his men so intensively that actual operations behind the Japanese lines seemed "a piece of cake compared to the training," and illness was incredibly low for an area where malaria, dengue, filariasis, dysentery, typhoid, cholera, and leeches are all prevalent, and where practically every communicable disease has been reported. (Burma is also infested with poisonous snakes, and every Chindit was equipped with a razor blade to cut off the poisoned flesh in case of a bite.)

The Raider organization was, Wingate explained, "built around two weapons—the plane and the radio—which have never been fully exploited. Our supplies will be dropped from the air; we shall have no other line of communication. We shall maintain contact by radio with the R.A.F. and between the [eight] columns, which are self-contained mobile units prepared to operate at great distances from one another."

In February 1943 Lentaigne's chief led his Raiders across the Chindwin River and into North Burma to fight an entirely new kind of war against the Japanese. This army, "looking like a gang of hillbilly assassins, was in fact the last word in twentieth century techniques." The Raiders advanced "through dense jungles, over razor-back mountains, along paths not more than three feet wide flanked by sheer precipices, then down into valleys where the elephant grass grows taller than a man. Rotting skeletons marked the tracks over which the Allies had retreated the summer before." Keeping clear of beaten trails, the Raiders laboriously hacked their way through the jungle, taking elaborate precautions to cover up footprints and to lay false trails. All waking hours were spent fighting or marching. Contact between columns was maintained by radio, messenger dogs, carrier pigeons, and strange bird calls; equipment was carried by elephants, bullocks, and mules. Each column had an R.A.F. flying officer marching with it to select the site for dropping supplies and to notify the Assam base, by coded radio message, of the exact time and place for the next delivery. All told, 500,000 pounds of supplies were dropped to Wingate's men—including propaganda leaflets and such personal service items as monocles, kilts, false teeth, boxes of snuff, a recently published life of

MAJ. GEN. WALTER D. A. LENTAIGNE

Bernard Shaw'", an unsigned will, and 400 pounds of fine chocolate.

For three months the Chindits ranged over a 300-mile front, wrecking enemy airfields and hangars, exploding ammunition dumps, blowing up bridges, cutting rail lines, destroying remote outposts, skirmishing endlessly with enemy patrols, keeping an area of 10,000 square miles in a state of confusion and panic—and disappearing before the startled Nipponese could regain their balance. A whole Japanese division, ten times the number of Chindits, was sent to search for this army of ghosts; but, though scouts of the opposing forces often ran into each other in the steaming jungle, the Japanese never caught up with the Raiders in force. When the Chindits had penetrated 300 miles into Burma, within 120 miles of the Burma Road, they were ordered to return to India before the monsoon season broke. On the way back they were stopped at the Irrawaddy River by heavy enemy fire. After this, although the Chindits managed to slip away from the Japanese, they were closely hunted. To increase their speed, they were forced to get rid of their heavy equipment, which they smashed and buried. Without radio communication all air-borne supplies were cut off. First they ate their bullocks and mules, then "rice, snakes, vultures, banana palms, jungle roots, and boiled grass soup." Wingate drove his men to the very limit of their endurance—and brought them back to India. (The Japanese in Burma were busy on repair work all that summer and fall.)

High adventure though this mission was, "it was much more than pure adventure," as Charles J. Rolo pointed out in an article (later expanded into a book, Wingate's Raiders [1944]), "for the expedition accomplished important strategic aims. It relieved pressure on the Chinese and on the heroic little force of Burmese tribesmen still holding out in the north. It gathered information which enabled the R.A.F. to make devastating raids on Japa-

LENTAIGNE, WALTER D. A.—*Continued*

nese concentration points . . . probably staved
off an invasion of India . . . beat the Japanese soldier at his own game, and showed him
he was no longer master of the jungle."

Brigadier Lentaigne was in command of a
Raider Brigade in March 1944, when the outfit
again came into the news: they landed from
transport planes and seized a field behind the
Japanese lines on which they built an air strip,
thus turning it into a landing field for their
planes. "The keynote of the whole operation
is Anglo-American cooperation," a correspondent wrote at that time. "The air-borne force
. . . depends for its supplies on American aircraft flown by American pilots [the American
Air Commandos under Colonel Philip Cochran,
the original of Milton Caniff's '44 "Flip Corkin"]. It lives on American rations. Casualties
are evacuated by air, and replacements of arms
and equipment are flown in. Even food for
mules must be delivered by plane."

On March 24 General Wingate was killed
in an airplane crash. As soon as this report
was officially confirmed, Lord Mountbatten '42,
the supreme commander of the Southeast Asia
area, recalled Lentaigne from the Burma jungle
to headquarters and promoted him from brigadier to major general, placing him in command of "the orphaned Raiders." Under his
command these orphans proceeded to "cut the
Burma railway between Myitkyina and Katha
and control the Irrawaddy River in two places,
cutting off the Japs who opposed General Stilwell's advance down the Mogaung Valley from
their bases." The following months found
the Chindits using their old tricks in the battle
for Myitkyina in north Burma.

On June 24, 1944 the British Chindits seized
the strategic trail junction of Sawngching,
twelve miles west of the beleaguered railway
town, Mogaung. The possession of that base
closed the last southern escape route for the
Japanese garrison trapped at Mogaung, which
fell to Lieutenant General Joseph W. Stilwell's
forces two days later. This victory enabled
the Allies to increase their pressure on Myitkyina, which was finally taken on August 4.
During July Lentaigne's Chindits had continued
to inflict numerous casualties on the Japanese
and to seize ammunition and equipment in their
attacks on isolated units. In August they
pushed farther south along the Myitkyina-
Mandalay rail line. By the middle of October,
when British troops had captured the important
northwestern Burma base of Tiddim, which
had been held by the enemy for almost a year,
"the final and decisive chapter to the Japanese
invasion of India" had been reached, Hanson
W. Baldwin '42 wrote in the New York *Times*.
It was reported in November 1944 that Major
General Walter Lentaigne "is in England for
consultations."

The chief Raider is an impressive figure:
six feet four inches tall and lean; he has blue
eyes and sandy hair and mustache. Mrs. Lentaigne keeps the home fires burning for him in
Camberley, Surrey, England, with their two
daughters, Susan and Jane. Their son Victor,
despite his father's prominence in the land
forces, is at the Royal Naval College.

**LEOPOLD III, KING OF THE BEL-
GIANS** Nov. 3, 1901-

Twice within a generation the little country
of Belgium, a snug, prosperous, and highly
industrialized kingdom, with a rich jungle empire in the Congo, has been invaded by German
armies. Back in 1839 (nine years after Belgium
had won her independence from the Netherlands), Britain, France, Austria, Russia, and
Prussia had first guaranteed the integrity of
Belgium in a pact which declared that "Belgium shall form an independent and perpetually
neutral state." This agreement was in force
when the Kaiser sent his armies through Belgium in 1914 to attack France. Twenty-six
years later, in 1940, Germany again violated
Belgium's neutrality, which had been guaranteed by the Locarno Pact. (A short-lived
defense agreement with France and England
had been terminated by Belgium in 1937 to re-
establish her neutrality.) Sweeping around the
end of the Maginot Line, the Nazi armies overran the small kingdom and made a prisoner of
its ruler, Leopold III. Despite the calumnia-
tions heaped on Leopold immediately following
his capitulation to the Wehrmacht, the monarchy
in Belgium still holds much prestige and is
regarded as the stabilizing factor in Belgian
politics.

The father of Leopold III was Albert I,
who was married to Princess Elizabeth of
Bavaria. Leopold, their first son, was born
November 3, 1901. Upon Albert's succession
to the throne in 1909 the eight-year-old boy
became Crown Prince, and at fourteen he was
already a veteran of the First World War: in
1915 he had demanded to be allowed to enlist
as a private in the Belgian ranks, and he then
went into the front line with the famous 12th
Regiment and dug defense trenches under the
fire of German guns. After six months' service he was sent over to England, to Eton College, much against his will. "It was awfully
difficult to go back to book learning," he said.
But the Crown Prince was a good student.
After Eton he was tutored for four years
under King Albert's direction, with the emphasis laid on economics. His education was
rounded out by travel. In 1919 Leopold accompanied his royal parents on their tour of the
United States, astonishing newspapermen with
his expert poker playing. (Leopold always refused to tell who had taught him the game; a
suspect, however, was General Pershing.) Then
the Prince visited Brazil and Egypt with
Albert. A few years later, after visiting
Africa and the East, he prepared a series of
comparative reports on colonial administration
in the Belgian Congo, British India, the Netherlands Indies, the Philippines, and French Indo-
China; these earned him ranking as his father's
colonial adviser. Leopold drew the attention
of the Senate, of which he was an active
member, to the conditions and prices under
which quinine, the vital drug in the tropics,
was available; his recommendations led to the
State's supplying the drug free to needy natives.

At the age of thirty-two Leopold was called
to the throne after his father, one of the best-
loved personages of the First World War
years, was tragically killed, on February 17,
1934, by a fall while climbing a mountain peak
near Namur. On the day following the funeral,

February 23, Leopold was proclaimed King when he took the simple oath: "I swear to observe the constitution and the laws of the Belgian people and to maintain the national independence and integrity of territory." A year and a half later, in August 1935, Leopold's life was again overshadowed by tragedy when his Swedish-born Queen Astrid, whom he had married in 1926, was killed in a motor accident in Switzerland.

The Europe that confronted the fourth King of the Belgians was suffering from the effects of the civil war in Austria and from the threat of a Hitlerite Germany ready to force the Austro-German union. It was expected that Leopold would continue Albert's policy of colonial development and of constructing eastern fortifications to overlap those of France and form a bulwark against attack from Germany; and that he would pursue his course under the influence of the conservative diplomats, financiers, and economists who had directed Belgian affairs of state. Among these Belgian leaders were Georges Theunis, the economist who had negotiated the United States war debt settlement at Washington, and Paul van Zeeland, an expert in central banking.

Leopold III also had to cope with the internal strain of a national autonomy movement. More than half of Belgium's population, which inhabits Flanders, in northern Belgium, is Flemish—a people racially, culturally, and linguistically related to the Germans. The people in the industrial south, on the other hand, speak French, or its Walloon patois. These linguistic differences were first exploited for political purposes during the First World War when the Germans promised Flanders cultural autonomy. In his first speech as King, Leopold had pledged his efforts to the preservation of a united Belgium, yet a Flemish autonomy movement was flourishing with the aid and encouragement of Nazi Germany. Many Flemings were supporting Léon Degrelle, young would-be Belgian "Führer" and leader of the Rexist organization.

When the Germans seized the Rhineland in March 1936 in violation of the 1925 Locarno Pact, Belgium, under Leopold III's leadership, adopted a policy of neutrality. At first Belgium, along with Britain and France, hastily planned allied military action in the event of a German attack; but as fear of the Reich subsided Belgium felt that such an alliance would only antagonize her powerful neighbor. Accordingly the King negotiated in person with the British Government and in April 1937 received assurances that Great Britain and France as well would release Belgium from the obligations of the Locarno Pact and the Anglo-Franco-Belgian agreement of March 19, 1936 by which Belgium had promised to help defend Britain and France against attack, while the other two Governments had promised to come to the immediate aid of Belgium if she were attacked. Leopold was to maintain an army capable of holding off a German attack, and Belgium was to serve as a "listening post" for enemy bombers flying over her land. This venture of the King into statecraft was fully approved afterward by Belgium's Parliament, press, and public. Six months later Germany pledged that she too would protect Belgian

territory from all aggression. Belgium consistently refused to jeopardize her neutrality by permitting the British and French armies to prepare against the inevitable aggression by actual movements on Belgian soil.

Leopold was not regarded as merely an idealistic optimist in his firm policy of non-aggression and self-defense. He was convinced that Europe's piling up of armaments could only lead to a major war. The alternative to war, he believed, was "for statesmen to learn something about economics and apply what they learned toward easing the world's stresses and strains instead of holding endless conferences in terms of politics and prestige." In July 1937 Leopold made public an appeal for action in this direction, of which the conservative London *Morning Post* declared: "The very least that countries to which the appeal was directed can do is to give the proposal their urgent and sympathetic consideration." Leopold had stated: "Give humanity, especially the Far Eastern countries, not words, but proofs that the Western countries have, above their more immediate problems of material nature, a spiritual force emanating from the spirit of brotherhood. . . . If we are really to avoid war and bring back humanity to more peaceful sentiments, we must have the courage to face economic questions in their broadest aspect and find a solution for such great problems threatening peace as these: (1) distribution of raw materials; (2) apportionment of the elements of monetary exchange; (3) distribution of employment; (4) establishment of an equilibrium between agricultural and industrial nations."

In 1939 King Leopold joined King Haakon '40 of Norway, King Christian '43 of Denmark, King Gustav '42 of Sweden, Queen Wilhelmina '40 of Holland, and an informal international group of peace-lovers—who called themselves, after Jules Romains' book, Men of Good Will—in an attempt to secure peace by mediation (this has been described by Romains in *Seven Mysteries of Europe*). They hoped for a peace conference, to be called by one of the five sovereigns of northern Europe. Four of them were to write to the fifth, Leopold, urging him to save the peace of Europe. Leopold was then to appeal to Chamberlain, Daladier '40, Mussolini '42, and Hitler '42. The plan failed, however.

But despite her efforts to remain neutral in a Europe at war, Belgium was to become a victim of German aggression for a second time. At 4:00 o'clock on the morning of May 10, 1940, without warning, Hitler's forces swarmed into the Netherlands, Luxembourg, and Belgium. At 8:00 a.m. that fateful day Bulow-Schwante, the German Ambassador to Belgium, handed an ultimatum to Foreign Minister Paul-Henry Spaak after the Nazi armies had been fighting for several hours. Leopold took command of the Army as his father had done in 1914. By May 18 the Germans had occupied Brussels, Louvain, Malines, and Antwerp. On May 24 Premier Hubert Pierlot and other Cabinet members unsuccessfully urged Leopold to leave the country with them in order to strengthen an absentee Government. The Cabinet left next morning by plane for London and later went to Paris. As early as the week before the last

LEOPOLD III, KING OF THE BELGIANS

day of Belgian resistance Leopold had warned the Allies of the grim possibility of surrender unless sufficient aid were sent to him. His Army of more than 500,000—one Belgian out of every sixteen—fought gallantly until overwhelming German superiority in armored divisions and air power made further resistance useless. On May 28 Leopold ordered his troops to lay down their arms in unconditional surrender. The Nazis confined the King to his palace at Laeken, on the outskirts of Brussels.

The news of the end of the battle for Belgium was received with consternation, bewilderment, and denunciations in Great Britain and France. Parisians shouted "Treason!" and "Pro-German!" The British press called Leopold "King Quisling" and "King of the Fifth Column." The Fascist sympathies attributed to him were ascribed to his Flemish court and his Italian brother-in-law, Crown Prince Umberto '43. Paul Renaud laid the rout of the French Army to Leopold's defalcation. Meeting somewhere in France, the Belgian Cabinet, supported by the Belgian Parliament, decided to continue the struggle by the side of the Allies, and decreed that Leopold could no longer rule, although it was constitutionally unable to deprive him of his crown. On June 6 Great Britain recognized the Belgian Government-in-Exile as the only legal government of Belgium, and on October 22 the Belgian Cabinet established its seat in London.

A few months after Leopold's surrender a process of vindication got under way. As early as July 1940 Premier Pierlot advocated national unity around the King. In September 1941 the Belgian Government-in-Exile published an official account of the events, completely exonerating "a very gallant soldier" from charges of treason and defeatism. John Cudahy, United States Ambassador to Belgium at the time of the invasion, who visited the imprisoned King, and other diplomats testified to the fact that Leopold had no alternative but surrender and that both Britain and France knew this step was not far off.

Meanwhile, Belgium occupied a relatively favorable position among the conquered nations of Europe. Although its territory on the Continent was being administered by Nazis and a few Belgian quislings, Belgium continued to play the part of an active belligerent under the direction of the Government-in-Exile. Well-armed troops, refugees, and recruits from the Congo, as well as the resources of her colonies, made an important contribution to the United Nations war effort. King Leopold steadfastly refused to collaborate with his captors; he spurned all invitations to cooperate with the Nazis and an "all-Belgian" Ministry composed of pro-German Rexists and Flemish Nationalists. Significantly, the influence of the Rexist leader, Degrelle, declined steadily.

Within twenty-four hours after the Allies landed in Normandy in June 1944 Leopold was sent to Germany with his second wife, the commoner, Mary Lilian Baels, to whom he had been married in September 1941. Within a month the royal Belgian children were also deported to Germany—Princess Josephine Charlotte, Prince Baudouin, and Prince Albert, Astrid's children; and Philip, the child of his second marriage. (In mid-November 1944, it is reported, he was interned in the closely guarded Hotel Dreesen in Bad Godesberg, the scene of the Chamberlain-Hitler meeting in September 1938.) On September 2 the liberation of Belgium began when the American 1st Army crossed the French-Belgian border. The next day General Dwight Eisenhower '42 ordered Belgium's underground resistance army, which had been organized almost immediately after the arrival of the invaders, to fight in the open with the Allies in sweeping the Germans out of the Low Countries. On September 4 British troops entered Brussels, the fourth of Europe's capitals to be freed of the Nazis.

After four years in exile, on September 8 the Belgian Government returned to take over from the Allied military authorities the administration of civil affairs. Twelve days later the Belgian Parliament met for the first time since the decisive days of May 1940. It elected the younger brother of the King, Prince Charles, Count of Flanders, to serve as Regent pending Leopold's return from his German captivity. Within the week Pierlot was again named Premier and he announced the formation of a new and expanded Cabinet, whose most pressing problems are the deflation of prices, currency circulation, and the securing of an adequate food supply. At the end of December it was announced that arrangements had been made with the Belgian Government and Allied military authorities for the distribution of private relief to Belgium. The need of clothing is said to be acute, and the rise of tuberculosis among the children of working classes is alarming.

The Premier, Hubert Pierlot, belongs to the Conservative Catholic Party, which thus becomes the dominant political group; the Fascist Rexists and extreme Flemish Nationalists are in flight or hiding, while the Communists have two members in the Cabinet. The new Government has laid plans for a general election, but this cannot take place for nearly a year, inasmuch as 600,000 Belgian prisoners in Germany and 200,000 workers who were deported by the Germans must first be returned. In early November 1944 it was reported that posters were appearing in Brussels and in other Belgian cities demanding the resignation of the Pierlot Government and the establishment of Allied military control over civilian affairs. It was said, however, that the Supreme Headquarters of the Allied Expeditionary Force mission in Belgium, had no thought of assuming the direction of the country.

It is not certain, commentators believe, that Leopold will be accepted as King of the Belgians once he is released from his internment. In the four years that followed defeat many Belgians came to approve and respect his determination to share the captivity of his people. But there is opposition to him, which springs primarily from his marriage to a Flemish commoner, daughter of a former Cabinet Minister. Many members of the Socialist Party, which is the second strongest in both houses of Parliament, favor a republic. Meanwhile, it has been rumored that the Germans have offered to exchange Leopold for Rudolf Hess [41], who flew to England in 1941. (Queen Mother Elizabeth remains in Belgium.)

The King is a tall, grave, blue-eyed man, with graying hair that once was blond. He has the handsome figure, well-set shoulders, and ruddy skin of the athlete, and in happier days enjoyed skiing, mountain climbing, and golf.

References

Life 9:74-83 N 25 '40 il pors
Time 30:22-4 N 22 '37; 35:25-8 My 20 '40 por

Forbes, R. These Men I Knew p201-6 1940
International Who's Who 1942
Statesman's Yearbook 1943

LEWIS, C(LIVE) S(TAPLES) Nov. 29, 1898- Author

Address: b. Magdalen College, Oxford, England

Few contemporary writers of major importance have worked in the difficult genre of the satiric fantasy, but early in 1942 Clive Staples Lewis, a shy, sensitively poetic, scholarly Fellow of Magdalen College, Oxford, made literary news with the publication of a timely religio-psychological discourse, *The Screwtape Letters*. On reading these letters from the Devil to a young disciple, Leonard Bacon [41] saw in Mr. Lewis "a spectacular and satisfactory nova in the bleak sky of satire." *Out of the Silent Planet* (1938, England), Lewis' next book to be published in the United States, was a tale of life on the planet Mars that followed the astral-romance pattern of H. G. Wells, with Swiftian overtones and special moral trimmings. *The Problem of Pain*, which followed later in 1943, was, however, straight exposition of the Christian position toward suffering—and George N. Shuster [41] suggested that "perhaps Mr. Lewis succeeds better with straight argument than he does with parable." In 1944 *The Christian Saviour* and *Perelandra*, the latter a parable set in the

C. S. LEWIS

planet Venus, were published in the United States.

Clive Staples Lewis was born in Belfast, Ireland, November 29, 1898, the son of A. J. Lewis (a solicitor of that city) and Flora Augusta (Hamilton) Lewis. Following a year at Malvern College, he was privately educated by W. T. Kirkpatrick, the former Headmaster of Lurgan College. In 1918 he became a scholar at University College, Oxford. During the First World War he served as a 2nd lieutenant in the Somerset Light Infantry. In 1924 he became a lecturer at University College; a year later, Fellow and Tutor of Magdalen College, Oxford, where since that time he has been a special lecturer on English literature and has done considerable research in Anglo-Saxon and medieval literature.

Under the pseudonym of Clive Hamilton, Lewis published his first book, *Dymer*, in 1926. In 1933 appeared *Pilgrim's Regress*, "an allegorical apology for Christianity, reason, and Romanticism." *Allegory of Love* (1936) brought to its author considerable critical and scholarly attention, and was awarded the Hawthornden Prize for that year. Its theme is "the slow evolution of the passion of romantic love, and the slow evolution of the literary expression of that passion through the Middle Ages." Most reviewers found the book "learned, witty, and sensible." Writing in the New York *Herald Tribune*, Albert Guerard, Jr., said, "The purely historical study of the growth and decline of allegory and courtly love is a careful piece of scholarship, and the first and second chapters are excellent essays in comparative literature. With the third chapter, however, it is evident that the author has become more interested in individual poets than in historical tendencies."

Among other scholarly studies by Lewis to attract favorable notice, in both Great Britain and America, was his *Preface to*

LEWIS, C. S.—*Continued*

Paradise Lost (published in the United States early in 1943). Lewis stated in his introduction that his purpose was "to remove those obstacles to the enjoyment of *Paradise Lost* which have recently been accumulating." According to a review in the New York *Times,* "His emphasis on tradition leads Mr. Lewis to a preliminary consideration of epic poetry in general, which is both fresh and sound. But his most valiant service is to protect us against the many students of Milton who have not been able to see the woods for the trees."

The Screwtape Letters (1942) received almost unqualified praise from both British and American critics. An elderly Devil named Screwtape writes a series of letters of instruction to his ambitious young nephew, Wormwood, on the best way of winning to eternal perdition the soul of a certain "patient" living in the world today. Wormwood, helped along by war conditions, is inclined to go all out for "spectacular wickedness." But his wiser uncle keeps reminding him that the safest road to hell is "the gradual one." The real thing that matters, he admonishes, is "the extent to which you separate the man from the Enemy (God)." Unfortunately for Wormwood, his victim escapes him when "snatched into salvation by a bomb" during an air raid on London. Said the *Manchester Guardian*: "In a book of any length satire easily topples over into farce and any levity in the treatment of such a subject would be fatal. Mr. Lewis never fails. The book is sparkling yet truly reverent, in fact a perfect joy, and should become a classic." According to C. E. M. Joad, "Mr. Lewis possesses the rare gift of being able to make righteousness readable." Leonard Bacon found the book "the most exciting piece of Christian apologetics that has turned up in a long time."

The fantasy *Out of the Silent Planet* (1943) has been likewise termed "a genuinely significant criticism of the great forces which sway Western thinking today." Mr. Lewis' projection of what life may be like on the planet Malacandra (Mars) is "ethical and philosophical rather than scientific." Reviewers have agreed that the novel is, as *Time* puts it, "sub-Wellsian fantasy, tinted with irony and as pitted with morality as *Pilgrim's Progress.*" Others have called it "a story of strange fascination, not to be resisted even by an impatient and skeptical reader." "The descriptions of Malacandra have considerable beauty, and the picture of its pacific organization, contrasted with the behavior of our planet, makes effective criticism." Christopher Morley says of Lewis: "To me he is to this year's reading what Major Grey used to be on the pantry shelf when chutney was still available."

In *Out of the Silent Planet* Dr. Ransom, a Cambridge philologist, is kidnapped and taken in a space ship to Malacandra by two scientists: the fascist-minded physicist, Weston, and the gold-hunting materialist, Devine. When they land on the planet, Ransom escapes his companions and explores Malacandra on his own. He finds the atmosphere very cold and light, the rivers and lakes deep blue and warm, the vegetation fantastically thin and tall.

The inhabitants, too, are thin and stilt-like. These are creatures of three kinds, whose speech the philologist gradually learns: the *hrossa,* gentle and seal-like, who excel in singing and poetry; the *séroni,* tall and feathered, who do the thinking; and the *pfifltriggi,* smaller froglike creatures who are excellent mechanics and builders. There are also the *eldila,* ghostlike "higher" beings whom the Martians can see, but Ransom cannot. They all live peaceably and harmoniously under their god, Oyarsa, who in turn rules by grace of the supreme being of the universe, Maleldil. Ransom learns from Oyarsa that Thulcandra (the Earth) is called "the silent planet" because the Oyarsa of the Earth long ago became wicked, and Earth was shut off from all intercourse with other planets in space. There is mutual like and trust between Ransom and the inhabitants of Malacandra; but the latter are intelligent enough to realize that such *hnau* as Weston and Devine are "bent" (evil) specimens. They are given a ninety-day supply of oxygen and ordered back to Earth; Ransom decides to return with them, his task in the future to be to do all he can to counteract the bad intentions of men like Weston and Devine, and to convert humans "from the conception of Space to the conception of Heaven," —which would indeed be "a *hmān*-size job."

In *The Problem of Pain* (1943) Lewis insists that the universe may not be evil because the Ruler of it believes in Discipline. According to George N. Shuster, the book "not only makes uncommon good sense, but it is great writing." *In Perelandra* (Perelandra is Venus) we are wafted to that planet with Ransom, in the latest of Lewis' astral tours. Venus is depicted resplendent with beauty and overflowing with goodness and sweetness, devoid of pain, death, and diabolism. Dr. Weston, in the form of the devil, arrives on Perelandra obsessed with the idea of reproducing our form of life on all the planets. He tries through the means of bribery and temptation to ingratiate himself with the new Eve. Ransom, realizing that this would result in a repetition of the fall of man "entailing all the sacrifice and chaotic cruelty of earthward history," wages a victorious battle with Weston. The book's allegorical quality is found in its numerous subtle analogies to the present struggles on our own planet. In the opinion of Lewis Gannett of the New York *Herald Tribune,* "it is limited in range and intensity, yet, it is still an attractive novel of ideas." The New York *Sun* critic finds "Lewis a very intelligent and earnest fabulist. . . . But the book as a whole is heavy."

Very little is known of Lewis aside from his writings. He is said to be practically a recluse in his personal life, and so shy that he has been known to lock himself in his study whenever a woman was reported on the way to visit the College. One form of relaxation he enjoys is discussing poetry, theology, and nonsense over tea and beer. During the War he has broadcast over BBC and given talks on religion at R.A.F. airfields.

Reference

Who's Who 1944

LEWIS, LAWRENCE June 22, 1879—Dec. 9, 1943 United States Representative (Democrat) from Colorado to Congress since 1933; on House Rules Committee.

Obituary

N Y Times p29 D 10 '43 por

LICHTENBERG, BERNARD (lik'ten-bĕrg) Aug. 11, 1892—Oct. 3, 1944 Leading publicist; president and founder of the Institute of Public Relations; vice-chairman and a director of the Better Business Bureau of New York; vice-president and director of the Alexander Hamilton Institute from 1909 to 1935; awarded gold medal by Advertising Club of New York for "valuable contributions to advertising education"; author of many publications on policies and principles of advertising.

Obituary

N Y Times p19 O 4 '44 por

LILIENTHAL, DAVID E(LI) (lil'yen-thäl) July 8, 1899- Chairman of Tennessee Valley Authority

Address: b. New Sprankle Bldg., Knoxville, Tenn.; h. 81 Pine Rd., Norris, Tenn.

"I believe men may learn to work in harmony with the forces of nature, neither despoiling what God has given nor helpless to put them to use," writes David E. Lilienthal, chairman of the Tennessee Valley Authority. ". . . I believe that through the practice of democracy the world of technology holds out the greatest opportunity in all history for the development of the individual, according to his own talents, aspirations, and willingness to carry the responsibilities of a free man. We have a choice: to use science either for evil or for good. I believe men can make themselves free. These convictions have been fortified as I have seen them take on substance and become part of the life of this valley and of its people."

Born in Morton, Illinois, July 8, 1899, the son of Leo and Minna (Rosenak) Lilienthal, David Eli Lilienthal learned to become a fighter early in life—when a professional known as the Tacoma Tiger took him in hand. "He damn near killed me in the process, but he taught me something about coming up off the floor and taking more—which has come in handy." At DePauw University in Greencastle, Indiana, where he took his B.A. in 1920, he came away with a Phi Beta Kappa key—and a reputation as a light heavyweight boxer. It was at DePauw, too, that he met his future wife, Helen Marian Lamb; and when he went on to Harvard Law School she took postgraduate work at nearby Radcliffe College. On September 4, 1923, after Lilienthal had taken his LL.B. from Harvard, the young couple were married. That same year Lilienthal was admitted to the Illinois bar.

From 1923 to 1926 the young lawyer was associated in the practice of law with Donald R. Richberg in Chicago, and he participated in important cases involving the rights of labor. At the same time he contributed numerous articles to such publications as the *Nation* and the *New Outlook* as well as to legal journals—and when he wrote, in 1925, that "our government, and every government, is and must be a government of *men* and not of laws," he was expressing a thought which he is still paraphrasing today. Practicing law alone after 1926, in his own right he became special counsel for the city of Chicago in the famous telephone-rate controversy which ultimately resulted in the United States Supreme Court's ordering a refund of $20,000,000 overcharge to telephone subscribers. From 1926 to 1931 he also edited the *Public Utilities and Carriers Service* for Chicago's Commerce Clearing House. Most of the customers of this legal service were members of the power trust or their attorneys, and the service gave them up-to-date digests of legislative and court decisions affecting their operations.

Lilienthal's knowledge of the utilities led Governor Philip La Follette to ask him to become a member of the Wisconsin Public Service Commission in 1931. In this capacity Lilienthal reorganized the Commission and revised the public utilities statutes of Wisconsin in such a way that they became the model for half a dozen other states. His work came to the attention of President Roosevelt '42, and in 1933, after the Tennessee Valley Authority project sponsored by Senator Norris had been authorized by Congress, Lilienthal was chosen one of the TVA's three co-directors. (Lilienthal attributes the success of the TVA to its sponsor, former Senator George W. Norris: "Without him there would be no TVA; his statesmanship and integrity are deeply engraved upon every chapter of TVA's legislative history.")

When TVA first came to Tennessee Valley there were 14,000,000 acres sending their top-soil into the waters of the Tennessee, causing floods, and filling up the reservoirs of power dams. The three main objectives of the new project, which involved the harnessing of the giant river by a system of twenty-one dams, were the development of hydro-electric power, flood control, and the development of navigation on the river. This meant the clearing of 175,000 acres of land and the building or relocation of 1,200 miles of highway and 140 miles of railroad. And all these operations directly affected some 1,350,000 people living on 225,000 farms—originally under the most depressed rural conditions.

Naturally there was controversy both as to the TVA's objectives and methods, and not all of the battles were against the utilities: some of them took place within the administration of the TVA itself. The other co-directors were chairman Dr. Arthur Morgan, who had come from the presidency of Antioch College, and Dr. H. A. Morgan. By 1934 Arthur Morgan and Lilienthal were at swords' points; and in May 1936 Morgan opposed Lilienthal's reappointment. Lilienthal was reappointed nevertheless, and he and H. A. Morgan voted together against the chairman on almost every issue. Arthur Morgan is said to have wanted to make the people of the Valley follow certain methods and procedures for their own good, while Lilienthal and H. A. Morgan believed that the voluntary cooperation of local people should be enlisted instead. When early in 1938 Arthur Morgan began to make

DAVID E. LILIENTHAL

public charges of "corruption" against his fellow directors he was discharged by President Roosevelt for "contumacy" and H. A. Morgan was made chairman of the board. The investigation which followed brought unfavorable publicity for TVA, but it was generally agreed that Lilienthal and H. A. Morgan came out on top. They are, moreover, still working together. In September 1941, upon the request of H. A. Morgan, Lilienthal was designated as chairman of the board of directors of the TVA, and Morgan became vice-chairman.

The people of the Tennessee Valley have not only benefited through the TVA—they have done much of the planning and have participated in most of TVA's decisions. Individual farmers were persuaded to let their farms be used as "demonstration farms" by accepting the counsel of TVA's agricultural experts; and the results encouraged others to adopt some or all of the changes on their own farms. Inspired by TVA, farmers also organized their own electric cooperatives, sometimes against the opposition of private agencies. Leaders of organized labor were encouraged to participate in the affairs of the TVA, which from the beginning bargained collectively with the international labor unions whose craftsmen it employs. Businessmen, too, were drawn into the task of unified development. TVA technicians were made available to industry for counsel, and the methods TVA developed aided in the creation of new private enterprises, especially small business ventures. All of this, to Lilienthal, is democracy in action.

And in ten years the results have been obvious. Writes Lilienthal: "The average citizen will measure the change . . . in the records of new private industries established in the Valley, of failing enterprises revived, more money in people's hands, less tax delinquencies, increased bank deposits, a greater volume of buying at the stores—trends clearly established before the War. The citizen may read of the decade's change in records of new public library service or state parks established

where none had been before, more hospitals, county health units almost doubled, less tuberculosis and malaria and other 'low-income diseases.' He may read of the number of miles of lines built to bring power to the farms of the area and the rapid increase in the amount of electricity used by the people—unprecedented in this country. He may reflect on the better quality of food produced and the increased yield per acre on the land, or analyze the ton-miles of traffic increase on the river." TVA's yardstick rates have forced lower electric rates on private utility companies and the great increase in use of electricity has greatly increased the prosperity of the very companies whose early enmity to TVA "went beyond the multiplicity of suits in the courts, in propaganda, in elections, and, as some suggest, even in puissant friendship and enmity to newspapers." Furthermore, of TVA's overall cost of $750,000,000, sixty-five per cent will be paid off in thirty years from electric power revenue alone.

A great deal of the success of TVA's administrators in gaining the support and cooperation of farmer, townsman, labor leader, and businessman alike is due to their "grass roots" administration. Lilienthal believes in the wisdom of people when they are given half a chance to be wise, and he has "no confidence in progress that comes from plans concocted by supermen and imposed upon the rest of the community for its own good." He believes that technicians of various kinds must live together and work together among the people whom they serve, thus learning to understand what the people want rather than what the experts want, and also learning to induce the action of laymen by explaining "why" as well as "what." The administration of government, in other words, must be decentralized. This does not mean, however, that he is "attracted by that appealing combination of big business and little government." He believes that a "federal government must have large grants of power progressively to deal with problems that are national in their consequences and remedy, problems too broad to be handled by local political units. . . . Future responsibility will have to be assumed by the central government to deal with national issues which centralized business inevitably creates." In a few words, along with decentralized administration must go centralized authority.

Much of TVA's success, too, lies in its nonpolitical administration. TVA has full control over its personnel, hiring on a merit system of its own, and since it gives no civil service protection to employees, each man must continue to make good in order to hold his job. All political activities except voting are absolutely forbidden for TVA employees, who can't even take part in municipal politics. "TVA if politically managed could become a curse to this Valley," says Lilienthal.

Senator McKellar of Tennessee apparently differs on this last point. In the winter of 1941-1942, with TVA's power program rapidly expanding to meet defense needs, Lilienthal decided to build Douglas Dam to get another 100,000 kilowatts of power for aluminum expansion in a hurry. The land that was to be flooded was 12,000 acres owned mostly by influential canning interests, McKellar's friends, and the Senator blocked the dam for two months before giving in. His surrender was only temporary. In May 1942 he tried to "attach a dog collar for TVA" to an appropriation bill that would abolish TVA's revolving fund and make it turn to Congress for every penny, although Lilienthal announced that the effect would be to take TVA out of the War. In March 1944 the Senator added to the TVA portion of the Independent Offices Appropriation Bill sixteen "ripper" amendments that would bring the Government's corporation "under his own thumb."

While this controversy was going on, Lilienthal's book, *TVA—Democracy on the March* (1944) appeared. Selected as the April book of the Scientific Book Club, it was a work which New Dealers like Henry A. Wallace '40 and anti-New Dealers like Louis Bromfield found equally "exciting" and inspiring, and which Arthur H. Compton '40 described as "characterized by direct and lucent prose, clear and logical thinking, and a high faith, founded on proved fact, that such projects as TVA are workable and advantageous, regionally, nationally, and internationally." Such unanimity of opinion about the TVA and its administration did McKellar very little good: although the Senate passed his amendments, the New York *Times*, like most of the press, denounced them as making it difficult or impossible for the TVA to carry on its business. As for the provision requiring Senatorial confirmation of all appointments to executive agencies carrying salaries of $4,500 or more, this was "one of the biggest patronage grabs in history."

In October 1944 Lilienthal proposed "an American development program" to extend from now until 1975. First on the program would be restoration and preservation of soil fertility, which Lilienthal maintained would simultaneously mean jobs and opportunities in factories making chemicals, machinery, tractors, barns, and rural school material. A second consideration would be control of America's rivers so that they will "work for and not against the people." Just a month later President Roosevelt advocated the revival of a plan for the development of seven of the country's major watersheds along TVA lines. Although the President did not name the proposed new regional authorities, he mentioned in a news conference the Missouri, Arkansas, Columbia, Cumberland, Mississippi, and St. Lawrence Rivers.

Jonathan Daniels '42 has described the TVA's chairman as "a big man, a stout man in the root sense of the word, a pleasant, round-faced man, spectacled. He grins, wide and shrewd, and there is none of the wide-eyed staring of the Utopian in his eyes. He can laugh as well as talk. A Middle Western man in Tennessee, he can be serious without violating Tennessee's traditional Rule No. 5: 'Don't take yourself too damned seriously!'" Lilienthal is a good speaker who understands modern publicity and its value; a thoroughgoing realist, he is not very sensitive to personal criticism. He likes to refer to himself as an amateur athlete (he still boxes, plays badminton, and rides an elderly five-gaited horse), an amateur author (he is puzzled by the popularity of his book—it was serialized in digest form in *PM*, and its publisher announced that it would be translated into nearly twenty languages), and an amateur administrator. Although his salary is $10,000 a year, he is particularly insistent on the last-mentioned designation. One of the very few agency heads named in the early days of the New Deal who is still in the same post, he says that he always keeps his suitcase packed. "I'm not keen about a career in public service. It gives some people a desire for security that weakens their ability to stand up to things."

Lilienthal lives with his family (there are two children, Nancy Alice, now studying at Radcliffe, and David Eli, Jr.) in a pleasant house in Norris, Tennessee, a town of 300 houses, twenty miles out of Knoxville in rugged mountainous country. His reading tastes run to biography—he has read practically everything ever written about Jefferson, Hamilton, Clay, and Lincoln. He is also a movie-lover who "cries at any mention of home or mother" and who is "addicted to the sort of indecorous laughter that makes the neighbors say 'You were at the movies last night—I heard you!'" He is a member of the American Bar Association, Delta Upsilon, Delta Sigma Rho, and Sigma Delta Chi, and he was admitted to the Tennessee bar in 1934.

References

Harper 177:352-61 S '38
N Y Post Mag p5 My 6 '44 por
Nation 143:385-6 O 3 '36
New Repub 96:34-7 Ag 17 '38; 96:95-8 Ag 31 '38
Newsweek 11:11 Mr 28 '38; 11:10-11 Je 6 '38 por
Sat R Lit 17:6-8 Ap 23 '38 il por
Daniels, J. A Southerner Discovers the South p46-97 1938
Lilienthal, D. E. TVA—Democracy on the March 1944
Who's Who in America 1944-45

LINCOLN, JOSEPH C(ROSBY) Feb. 13, 1870—Mar. 10, 1944 American author, humorist, and poet; his short stories, sketches, and verse were as popular as his numerous novels; all of his works dealt with Cape Cod folk, their ways, thoughts, and surroundings; *Galusha, the Magnificent* (1921), *Silas Bradford's Boy* (1928), and *Blowing Clear* (1930) were some of his best-liked novels.

Obituary

N Y Times p13 Mr 11 '44 por

LINTON, FRANK B(ENTON) A(SHLEY) Feb. 26, 1871—Nov. 13, 1943 Artist; his painting, *The Last Touch*, was awarded the Médaille de Bronze of the Paris Salons in 1927 and was bought by the French Government for inclusion in the Louvre.

Obituary

N Y Times p23 N 16 '43

LITTLE, CLARENCE C(OOK) Oct. 6, 1888- Biologist

Address: b. Roscoe B. Jackson Memorial Laboratory, Bar Harbor, Me.; h. Bar Harbor, Me.

An account of Clarence C. Little's fight against cancer is, literally, a story of mice and men. When he gave up his career as a college president in 1929 to head the American Society for the Control of Cancer (since October 1944, American Cancer Society) and to direct cancer research at the new Roscoe B. Jackson Memorial Laboratory at Bar Harbor, Maine, Little took with him the progeny of the special strains of mice he had begun to breed while still an undergraduate at Harvard University. It is the descendants of these mice, carefully housed, labeled, and studied at the Bar Harbor laboratory, which have played such an important part in the scientist's work in genetics as applied to cancer research. The many experiments made with cancerous and noncancerous strains of mice in this laboratory (and in others which have been supplied with Little's specially bred mice) have led to certain important findings with regard to the nature and cause of cancer in human beings, and the hope of new cures for this scourge that, next to heart disorders, is the greatest cause of death by disease in the United States.

Clarence Cook Little was born in Brookline, Massachusetts, October 6, 1888, the son of James Lovell and Mary Robbins (Revere) Little. It is said that "Pete" Little became a geneticist at a very early age: when he was three someone gave him a pair of pigeons, and by the time he was seven he had bred a pair which won a first prize in a show. About this time the young geneticist took up the care and breeding of mice. After his graduation from the Noble and Greenough School in Boston in 1906, he entered Harvard University to study biology. He inbred his first pair of mice while he was a junior at Harvard. In 1910 he received his B.A. degree with Phi Beta Kappa honors; in 1912 his M.S. at the Harvard Graduate School of Applied Science; and the degree of Doctor of Science in 1914. For two years, 1910-1912, he had served as secretary to the Corporation of Harvard University; while working for his science degree he was research assistant in genetics. He continued his specialized studies in genetics with mice while he was research fellow in cancer at Harvard (1913-17). During 1916 he also served as assistant dean and acting University marshal. In 1917-1918 he was an associate in comparative pathology at the Harvard Medical School.

At the Plattsburg (New York) officers' training camp in 1917, Little became a captain in Aviation Section, Reserve Corps; then a major in the Adjutant-General's Department in August 1918. He was given an honorable discharge in December 1918. (During the Second World War he served as vice-chairman of Civilian Defense for Maine in 1941.) Little returned to his laboratory at Harvard for two years of research there, and in 1921 became assistant director of the Station for Experimental Evolution at the Carnegie Institution in Washington.

When, at the age of thirty-four, Little left his laboratory research to accept the presidency of the University of Maine, he took the descendants of his inbred mice with him and established them in a laboratory next to his office. In 1925 he took them along to Ann Arbor when he became president of the University of Michigan. At Michigan, according to *Time* Magazine, "after their initial enthusiasm for the youngest university president of his time, the University regents heckled him for his liberal views on education and student behavior, and for his refusal to let Michigan politicians dispose of University money." The *Michigan Alumnus* commented on his "high idealism in university education," but Little felt he must resign because the regents were "not fully appreciative of certain policies of significance" in the development of his plans for the University. His ideas on college education were published in his book *The Awakening College* (1930). In it he discussed the changes going on in American colleges, and the signs that educators were awakening to the fact that modern youth demanded independence and should be upheld in its demand. Although "scathing and bitter" in some of its indictments, the book was termed "full of wholesome and constructive criticism of things academic," and "a significant and stimulating book which progressive thinkers will appreciate as a truthful picture of the college situation."

The year 1929 was a significant one in Little's life. That year the American Society for the Control of Cancer appointed him its managing director at a salary of $9,000 a year; and in the fall the Roscoe B. Jackson Memorial Laboratory opened its doors, with the biologist as its $3,000-a-year director. While still at Michigan he had interested Roscoe B. Jackson, then president of the Hudson Motor Company, in the idea of a laboratory for cancer research. Little had definitely decided by that time against the scholastic world in favor of mice, "whose behavior seemed to him more rational, and in the present state of affairs perhaps even more important, since through mice he hoped to get a better understanding of men." Soon after the construction of the laboratory Little had wanted began, Jackson died. But his family and several of his friends completed the building as a memorial, and in 1929 Little resigned as president of the University of Michigan to accept its management.

That same year the new director obtained a divorce from his wife, the former Katherine D. Andrews, daughter of a Boston architect, to whom he had been married in 1911. In 1930 Little was remarried, to Beatrice W Johnson, who had been an enthusiastic laboratory assistant of his while he was at the University of Maine, and who had later come to Michigan to be a supervisor of women students. Mrs. Little, it is said, still take an active interest in the mice at the Bar Harbor laboratory, besides managing the Littl home near the water front and the two chil dren, Richard Warren and Laura Revere (Little also has three children by his firs wife, Edward Revere, Louise, and Robert Andrews.)

Along with his major interest in genetics during the '20's Little was also much interested in eugenics. He was secretary general and chairman of the Executive Committee of the Second International Congress of Eugenics meeting in New York in 1921, and has been a member of the Eugenics Committee of the United States since 1922. He has also been a director of the American Birth Control League since 1925. He was on the Executive Committee of the First World Population Conference at Geneva in 1927, and president of the Race Betterment Congress in 1928 and 1929. He was also president of the International Neo-Malthusian League in 1925, and a member of the American Euthanasia Society from 1938 to 1943. As a long-time champion of birth control, Little has been outspoken in condemnation of what he terms religious bigotry against the movement. In an article in the *Scientific American* for June 1933, for example, he deplored the inadequacy of certain conservative religious groups to meet modern conditions.

The early '30's were lean years for the new Jackson Memorial Laboratory. There was no endowment, and public support during the depression was reduced to a minimum. But research in the severely plain brick building went on, even though the staff worked only half time, and spent the other half in fishing, gardening, and canning to provide food. The Rockefeller Foundation was so much impressed, however, by the progress made in research that in 1937 it granted $40,000 to enlarge the laboratory. By 1941 the laboratory was receiving some $50,000 a year from donations and from the sale of its specially bred mice to other laboratories.

In the fight against cancer, however, Little knew that laboratory work alone was not enough. To combat a disease that was exacting an annual toll of from 150,000 to 160,000 lives in the United States the public itself must be educated concerning it. In March 1937 Little, as head of the American Society for the Control of Cancer, directed the organization of the Women's Field Army of one-half million to carry on the educational campaign in thirty-nine states. Since women are the victims of certain forms of cancer, the Women's Field Army set out to teach women the value of regular physical examination, and of consulting a doctor immediately when certain symptoms are noticed. "There is no longer need to fight cancer alone," said Little. "The menace of a common enemy and the inspiration of fighting it together may have a sorely needed and deeply significant religious and moral force." He called cancer everyone's fight because "it is no respecter of any age, sex, or social group."

In an article in *Hygeia* for April 1940, Little discussed the three fields in which progress against the disease is being made: research, treatment, education. In research, he described the genetic method, with the use of mice, of which the Bar Harbor laboratory is the largest center; and the increased use of the cyclotron, or atom smasher, at the University of California. Diagnosis of cancer, he stated, "requires the services of a trained pathologist, and the choice of proper treatment often needs the group judgment of specialists. The education of the medical profession has been largely

CLARENCE C. LITTLE

accomplished through the American College of Surgeons, the American Society for the Control of Cancer, and the American Medical Association." Little pointed out the menace of quackery always in the background. "In no other sector of medicine has this black art been developed to such a high degree of plausible treachery." Quacks prey on ignorant persons who want to avoid surgical treatment or costly irradiation. The only three methods of treatment so far approved by the medical profession are, according to Little, surgery, X rays, and radium, or a combination of them.

To inform people further about the disease Little published, in 1939, his *Civilization Against Cancer*. The book discussed cancer in its early stages, its various forms, its possibilities of cure, and the present state of cancer research. Although one critic lamented the author's seeming inability to "say exactly what he means," another found it "the best popular interpretation of its kind that has come to this reviewer's notice," which "should be distributed all over the land as an educational document of the highest importance."

Because of the great importance of mice used genetically in cancer research, it has been said that "when the problem of cancer is finally solved we'll owe a gold statue to the mouse." At the Jackson Laboratory the rooms have racks "lined with thousands of wire-topped wooden boxes . . . in each of which is a family of mice, a pile of shavings for a nest, a water bottle, and a rack for food. No human city has a tenth as much sanitation, policing, social security, and accurate vital statistics as Mousetown." Here the family histories of nearly one million mice have been recorded. Mice have been chosen for experimentation because they differ little, biologically, from men; because mouse cancer can scarcely be distinguished from human cancer; and because mice multiply so fast that several generations may be studied in a short time: one month of mouse life equals two years of human life. By 1941 several years' observation of mice had resulted

LITTLE, CLARENCE C.—*Continued*

in some definitely established trends. It was learned that susceptibility to breast cancer, for instance, was not purely hereditary, but that cancer was transmitted, even to a healthy strain, through a cancerous mouse mother's milk. This would indicate that, by bottle feeding babies of families in which breast cancer has occurred, breast cancer in humans might be wiped out in a few generations.

Another big accomplishment of the laboratory is confirmation of the theory that cancer is not one disease, but many. It is "not a unity, and many factors must be considered in attempting to blot it out—heredity, sex hormones, diet, sunlight, vitamins, and others." The only bond between all types of cancer is that all apparently result from a breakdown in the adult body of the powerful forces that limit growth—they are cells that "grow wild," and grow almost without limit. Hence, besides charting "mutations in heredity," Little's staff has worked to correlate genetic principles with other aspects of cancer development. Glands have been transplanted from one mouse to another to test the influence of hormone secretions. Mice have even been sutured together, Siamese-twin fashion, to discover whether cancer can be transferred by circulation. The most recent development to come out of research laboratories is "an understanding of the relationship between the glandular system and the growth of cancer," particularly the endocrine glands, which control the growth and development of the body. "Any disturbance of the endocrine glands results in an upheaval of normal growth."

In an article in *Look*, May 30, 1944, Little wrote of the new work of prevention clinics for the study and cure of cancer in human beings. Evidence has been accumulated, for instance, that "proper hormone balance may be an extremely important factor in delaying or even in preventing the onset of cancer of certain organs." To demonstrate the necessity of early diagnosis (in its early stages, cancer is curable) four "preventatorium" clinics have been operating in recent years—two in New York, one in Chicago, one in Philadelphia—all staffed by and maintained exclusively for women. Of 1,757 apparently normal and healthy women examined in the clinics at Memorial Hospital and New York Infirmary for Women and Children, almost one-third were found to have malignant or benign tumors. Little also mentions the importance of physical checkups which is demonstrated in the work of Dr. Harold Harvey, who has conducted a simple type of stomach examination on volunteers with no particular symptoms. By his method Harvey has detected many early and operable cases of cancer. "Clearly, the major reason for needless deaths from cancer is delay—caused for the most part by ignorance or by fear of consulting a doctor. . . . Only 'late' cases become incurable. . . . This means that people must learn to recognize—and report at once—signs and symptoms that may spell cancer."

At conferences of scientists in September 1944 at Bar Harbor, called to discuss the effects of heredity and environment on cancer, Little presented his annual report: "Enough evidence has been gathered," he said, "to prove conclusively that Mendel's law of inheritance, by itself, is not enough to explain the influence which parents can and do exert upon the development of their offspring." The forty attending scientists decided that "cancer research in widely separated fields would make more rapid progress if it were planned and organized," and adopted a fourteen-point charter to govern cancer study. One of the points provides for the establishment of an agency national in scope; another recommends that the United States Bureau of Census and various state departments of health be asked to cooperate in gathering data about persons known to have cancer or who have died from the disease.

It was announced in October 1944 that the newly named American Cancer Society (until 1944, the American Society for the Control of Cancer) had merged with the National Foundation for the Care of Advanced Cancer Patients. The thirty-one-year-old society, with Little still as director, will now devote part of its funds to providing care for incurable cancer patients of moderate means. This will supplement its present activities of supporting research and education in the prevention and cure of cancer.

Many times Little has called for more funds to carry on the important work of cancer research. He has said that much greater progress in the control of cancer could be made if the public would give the same support to the fight against cancer that it gives to other diseases with a much lower mortality rate. He has pointed out that the "total public and private budget for the drive against cancer is somewhere around a million dollars a year—approximately what the President's Birthday Balls alone raise for the work of infantile paralysis." Yet, even in an epidemic year, poliomyelitis kills or maims less than a hundredth the toll of cancer.

Clarence C. Little is a "big, dynamic individual with tremendous enthusiasms and a magnificent Harvard accent." His avocation and hobby is the breeding of dogs: Little's father had abandoned architecture, which he liked, to go into business, which he disliked, and the breeding of Scottish terriers, spaniels, and dachshunds was compensation. The son followed his father's avocation: he breeds Scotties and dachshunds in his own Newcastle Kennels at Bar Harbor, and is said to be a qualified judge of other breeds.

References

Collier's 107:21+ F 8 '41
Liberty 21:26-7+ Jl 29 '44 por
Life 8:36 Je 17 '40 por
Time 29:49+ Mr 22 '37 por
American Men of Science 1938
Who's Who in America 1944-45

LLOYD, JAMES T(IGHLMAN) Aug. 28, 1857—Apr. 3, 1944 Representative in United States Congress from the first Missouri district, 1897 to 1917; chairman of the Democratic Congressional Committee, 1908 to 1912.

Obituary

N Y Times p19 Ap 5 '44

LLOYD GEORGE OF DWYFOR, DAVID LLOYD GEORGE, 1ST EARL

Jan. 17, 1863- Member of the British Parliament

Address: h. Bron-y-de, Churt, Surrey; Ty Newydd, Llanystumdwy, Caernarvonshire, Wales

David Lloyd George in December 1944 announced his retirement as Member of Parliament, after having served a record non-stop fifty-four years in the British House of Commons. Britain's First World War Prime Minister, now 1st Earl of Dwyfor, had heard Disraeli and Gladstone speak. For seventeen of those years he had served continuously in a British Cabinet; for six years of War and Armistice he had dominated the history of his time. He had heard himself damned by every political party in England, including his own, and had heard himself compared to Gladstone and Pitt. British history holds few more fascinating figures than this "Welsh Wizard," who during his long career has been accused of almost everything except cowardice. According to Winston Churchill '42, "no British politician in my day has possessed half his competence as a mover of men and affairs."

David Lloyd George was born January 17, 1863 in a mean street in Manchester, England. He is the son of Welsh parents, William and Elizabeth (Lloyd) George. His father was an unsuccessful schoolmaster who turned to farming in South Wales, where he died when his son was not quite two years old. His death left Mrs. George practically penniless, and David never forgot how he and his sister piled stones in front of the gateway of their house to prevent the removal of his mother's furniture at a compulsory sale. After selling everything to pay the family's debts, Mrs. George went north to the village of Llanystumdwy in Caernarvonshire, to live with her bachelor brother, Richard Lloyd, a cobbler and pastor of the Campbellite Baptists. It was this remarkable man who educated David for the law, investing his life's savings of £200 in the boy's education and learning French and Latin himself in order to tutor his nephew in those subjects. By the time he was sixteen David Lloyd George had passed his law preliminary and was ready to be articled to a firm of solicitors in Portmadoc; at twenty-one he qualified as a solicitor himself. He gradually built up one of the largest practices in North Wales, his local reputation made by a successful fight, carried to the High Court, in defense of the right of a Nonconformist to burial in the churchyard of a Church of England parish. In 1888 he was married to Margaret Owen of Mynyddednyfed.

Belonging to a strict Nonconformist sect with definite leanings toward Calvinism, Lloyd George was an orator in the pulpit as well as in law courts. He also plunged into politics, writing articles for the North Wales *Express,* joining debating societies, becoming secretary of the South Caernarvonshire Anti-Tithe League which struggled against the payment of taxes for the Church of England, and stumping the countryside on behalf of land reform and temperance. (He is still a teetotaler.) An impassioned advocate of Welsh Home Rule, in 1888 he founded a paper called the *Trumpet of Freedom* and was adopted as a Liberal candidate for Caernarvon Borough. The following year he was chosen as Alderman for Caernarvonshire; and in 1890 he was elected to the British House of Commons from Caernarvon. "My friends, my countrymen, the day of the cottage-bred man has at last dawned!" he exulted during that first electoral campaign—and it is true that Lloyd George was one of the first men without a public school background to be elected to Commons. By this time his brother had assumed entire charge of his law office in order to support the young politician through the initial, unremunerative stages of his Parliamentary career.

Lloyd George entered the House of Commons during octogenarian Gladstone's crusade for Irish Home Rule, an influence on his fight for Welsh Home Rule. His speeches were full of eloquent references to mountain valleys and the glamour of sunrise upon the Welsh hills; they made the Welsh ecstatic, and they could reduce even a London audience to tears. Only gradually did he cease to be a Welsh Nationalist and develop into an English radical. By 1896, in a debate on the Agricultural Rates Bill, Lloyd George was speaking of all landlords as his avowed enemies. In 1899 his pacifist speeches in opposition to the Boer War brought him into really national prominence: he became the most hated of all pro-Boers, and during the South African crisis was mobbed more than once. The Conservatives' Education Bill of 1920, designed to strengthen the position of the Church of England, caused him to organize the principality of Wales into what amounted to a rebellion against enforcement of the act. Then the Tariff Reform movement was launched, and he became one of the most effective upholders of Free Trade in all Commons, one of the few men on the Liberal side who could gainsay Joseph Chamberlain.

With the return of the Liberals to power in 1905 the "little Welsh attorney" was appointed president of the Board of Trade. Responsible for the passage of the Port of London Act and the reorganization of an antiquated department, he proved himself the "businessman of the Cabinet," and upon Campbell-Bannerman's death in 1908 and the elevation of Asquith to the Premiership, he became Chancellor of the Exchequer. The appointment was well received even in the City of London, which knew him as the man who in 1907 had averted a threatened railway strike through his persuasive eloquence.

But Conservative approval did not last long. In 1908 Lloyd George made a tour of Germany to study the German system of national insurance, and after his return he and Winston Churchill became allies in advocating the use of the budget for raising money to "wage implacable warfare on poverty and squalidness." When the House of Lords vetoed the momentous Budget of 1909 and the Liberals called a general election to decide the issue, Lloyd George (noted for his good nature in private life) surpassed all his colleagues in the vehemence of his attacks on that aristocratic body. He declaimed against the "idle rich"; he denounced landlords as "blackmailers"; he called certain noblemen "Mr. Balfour's poodles"; he

DAVID LLOYD GEORGE, EARL LLOYD
GEORGE OF DWYFOR

defended his "People's Budget" in caustic speeches which came to be known as "Limehouse" (the locale where many of them were given). (His speeches of this period have been collected in a book called *Better Times.*) The election victory of 1910 was his, and another general election resulted in victory for his bill depriving the House of Lords of the right to veto. To the Tories he was "the perfect example of the cad in politics," and they liked him no better for his National Health Insurance Bill of 1911 and his National Unemployment Insurance Bill.

Karl Radek called Lloyd George the champion of the "peasants" against the landowners rather than of the working class as such, but during these years Lloyd George's reputation as a radical seemed secure. Only a few found any great significance in the fact that he made no bold stand for woman suffrage (to which Asquith was opposed); fewer still wondered to what his passion for "getting the parties together and settling the case out of court," as evinced in his settlement of the 1911 railway strike, might lead in the end. His famous Agadir speech of 1911, in which the great advocate of disarmament hinted that Germany had gone far enough in Morocco and practically threatened war, shocked those who thought of him as a pacifist, but even they were soon reassured. As late as January 1914 the Chancellor of the Exchequer spoke of the necessity of disarmament and stated that the prospects of peace were better than they had ever been, and in the summer of the same year, when Sir Edward Grey wanted to warn Germany that any attack on France would lead to England's intervention, Lloyd George refused to support him.

Then war broke out; and with the invasion of Belgium Lloyd George voted to declare war on imperialist Germany. His support of the War was so wholehearted from that moment on that all of his desire for social reform was put aside. During the next few years the Nonconformist was to postpone the carrying out of Welsh disestablishment; the radical was to become the foremost foe of the militant suffragettes; the advocate of land reform was to suspend the Land Tax; the Free Trader was to bring in Protection. Lloyd George was to become the bogeyman of Labor, the idol of the Right.

Emil Ludwig accounts for this turn to the Right by saying that Lloyd George "had so often pursued the policy of expediency rather than principle that he became too pliant." As War Finance Minister, he sought expert advice and acted on it, averting a serious financial crash and again winning the confidence of the City of London. Then in May 1915 the Liberal Government was broken up because of the Dardanelles crisis and the munitions shortage, and Lloyd George became Minister of Munitions in the Liberal-Conservative coalition administration of Asquith and Bonar Law. In this post it is generally agreed that he mobilized the industries of the country more quickly and effectively than anyone else could have done, even if in the process he "made hay of the legislative safeguards that in the course of tedious years had been put around the interests of England's laboring classes." In the fall of 1915 he became a vehement advocate of compulsory military service, although Liberal sentiment was against conscription, and he managed to swing the Cabinet to his point of view. ("I have seen him turn a Cabinet around in less than ten minutes," Winston Churchill has said of Lloyd George, "and yet when the process was complete no one could remember any particular argument to which to attribute their change of view.")

In June 1916 Lloyd George succeeded the unfortunate Lord Kitchener as Secretary of State for War; he continued to excel in pushing on the production of munitions, and he successfully organized the military railways in France. So far as war strategy was concerned, however, he was always at odds with Asquith. Not only did he find the machinery for directing the War cumbersome and slow, but he thought it folly to seek a military decision on the Western Front, where the enemy was strongest, and he bitterly resented allowing Serbia and then Rumania to go under. The resignation of Asquith, although perhaps inevitable, was hastened in part by the "political wire-pulling and personal intrigue of his former protégé, assisted by Conservative leaders." Most of the Liberals in the Coalition Cabinet, indignant at Lloyd George's "disloyalty," resigned with Asquith, and in December 1916 Lloyd George became Prime Minister. He immediately created "a small coalition War Directory of five or six members in which he was supreme, while the chief Ministers outside this Directory formed a quasi-Cabinet for Home Affairs. He did not hesitate to seek able men outside Parliament as Departmental Ministers, for whom seats were found in the Commons. His most significant innovation was the Imperial War Cabinet—sessions of the War Directory to which were invited the Prime Ministers of the Dominions and representatives of India." At the height of his power, a power based on the Defence of the Realm Act, Lloyd George was often called the "Prime Minister of Europe."

Lloyd George's actual contribution to the eventual Allied victory is a subject of considerable dispute. He has been called "the man who won the War" and "the man who almost lost the War." Even his enemies admit that his faith in victory, his dynamic energy, and his ability to keep the confidence of the public were invaluable to the Allied cause, and that his speeches sustained the spirits of the country at its darkest moments. His friends say also that he "had in him the makings of a greater soldier than anyone engaged on either side"; according to Churchill, "his intuition fitted the crisis better than the logical reasoning of more rigid minds." Others accuse him of interfering with generals and admirals to no good purpose, pointing out that the final victory was brought about by methods he had opposed. All that is indisputable is that at the most critical stage of the War he "spoke with two voices," in one breath talking of a "knockout blow" against Germany and in another seeming to commit himself to a peace without victory."

What is also indisputable is the esteem in which he was held in 1918. The "coupon election" of December 14, 1918 which followed the Armistice (and which Lloyd George has been criticized for calling so soon) was primarily a vote of confidence in the Prime Minister, and his candidates received 80 per cent of the whole vote of the British electorate. The chief battle cries of this khaki election concerned "making Germany pay the whole cost of the War" and "hanging the Kaiser"—slogans which Lloyd George permitted his supporters to use, although they were somewhat modified in his own speeches. The Prime Minister excluded from his candidates all Liberals of Cabinet rank who had not supported him, and all but destroyed the "Asquithians" at the polls. As a result he found himself in a strange position; the majority returned to Commons consisted of 358 Conservatives and only 136 Coalition Liberals.

By this election Lloyd George was already committed to a policy of vengeance against Germany when he went to the Paris Peace Conference in 1919 as the principal British delegate, even though he sincerely supported the idea of a League of Nations and had no personal desire to crush Germany. When at one time it was rumored that he was showing signs of moderation, a telegram from 370 of his new supporters in Parliament brought him home to protest that his purpose was as ruthless as ever. And, according to J. M. Keynes '41, even Lloyd George's talents for conciliation were the undoing of the Treaty of Versailles. It was his role to "explain the President to Clemenceau and Clemenceau to the President and seduce everybody all around"; and since the "Welsh Wizard" exercised more sway over Wilson than over Clemenceau, the Frenchman had things more or less his own way. When later Lloyd George tried to undo what he had helped to do he succeeded only in antagonizing the French and his own supporters back home. Even after the signing of the Treaty, Britain's Prime Minister continued to try to obtain revision of Allied demands on Germany, but, fearful of the collapse of the Entente, he was forced to give way whenever France countered with threats of an independent policy toward Germany.

Back in England, Lloyd George referred to the continuance of the Coalition of which he was a "prisoner" as the one salvation from the "Bolshevism" of the Labor Party, while continuing to be "a master orator for the rights of the common man." He broke the 1919 railroad strike in ten days, appointed the Sankey Commission to investigate the coal crisis, then rejected its recommendation that the mines be nationalized. In 1920 he developed a sort of "New Deal" of his own. Free public education was to be enormously extended, the poor rehoused, a national maximum working week of forty-eight hours and a national minimum wage instituted; there were to be industrial councils on which both workers and employers would be represented; the great estates were to be broken up and their idle land put to use. When, however, these proposals were met by an "Anti-Waste" campaign on the part of the Conservatives, the Prime Minister reconsidered and began to effect such widespread economies that a halt was again called to social reform.

So far as foreign affairs were concerned he was thought of as even more inconsistent. After having made a bid for peace with the Russian people he surrendered to Churchill, who advocated intervention on behalf of the Whites; then took advantage of the victory of the Soviets to call off intervention and conclude a commercial treaty with the U.S.S.R. He abandoned the Armenians to the Turks, but encouraged the Greeks to persist in their hopeless attack upon the rising Turkish power in Asia Minor. During 1920 and the first half of 1921 he permitted the use of Black and Tans and Auxiliaries in Ireland, then antagonized the Tories by arranging a series of negotiations with De Valera '40 and leading Irishmen which resulted in the Treaty of December 6, 1921. This was one of the chief causes of the downfall of his Coalition Government in October 1922, along with the Chanak crisis in the Greco-Turkish War. The Conservatives left the Coalition, Lloyd George resigned, and in the 1922 election Stanley Baldwin gained a majority. The same election gave the Liberals only fifty-five members, and those were divided among themselves.

Lloyd George's association with what Churchill calls the "orthodox or professional Imperialist forces of the Right" was now finished forever, but it had left the Liberal Party almost a corpse. Denounced by the Tories, England's war leader was attacked even more by the Asquith Liberals and the Socialists. For a time he was almost a nonentity in Commons. But his political career was by no means over: his own courage and charm were no mean allies. In 1923 his followers and the Asquith Liberals came together on the issue of free trade, and in 1925, when Asquith was elevated to the peerage as Earl of Oxford and Asquith, Lloyd George became the Liberal leader in Commons.

This alliance with his old enemies was not to last long, but once more Lloyd George

LLOYD GEORGE OF DWYFOR, DAVID LLOYD GEORGE, 1ST EARL
—Continued

came out the victor. In his not altogether successful attempts to make new friends among Labor and the Socialists he intervened again and again in the coal dispute as a critic of the Government; he backed the miners' appeal for funds in the United States; he assailed British imperialism in China and pleaded the cause of the Cantonese Nationalists; and during the general strike in the spring of 1926 he advocated negotiations with the strike leaders to end the conflict. Read out of the Liberal Party for his independence, he refused to accept his expulsion. He had the sympathy of most of the Liberal press, his oratory retained its old magic so far as the rank and file were concerned, and he had the trump card up his sleeve. Funds at the disposal of the Liberal Party organization had dwindled to little or nothing, while under his personal control was a huge political fund, the income of which he offered to put at the disposal of the Liberal organization; and in January 1927 the Liberal Administrative Committee accepted the offer, repaying him by calling for the resignation of the members of the party's organizational committee who were hostile to him.

But the Liberal Party could not be revived by funds alone, and four years later came Lloyd George's permanent break with the Liberals. In 1931 he refused to support Ramsay MacDonald's election program, at a time when his fellow Liberals were united in MacDonald's support and when MacDonald was being denounced as a traitor by the more militant members of his own Labor Party. Lloyd George, who could have been in MacDonald's new National Cabinet, took his place on the opposition benches along with his son Gwilym, his daughter Megan, and Gwilym's brother-in-law. Some wondered if he would join the Labor Party, but he remained an Independent Liberal, and in January 1935 staged a reentrance into politics with a program for dealing with the depression. (It was submitted to the Government and rejected by Baldwin.) In the general election which followed Lloyd George proceeded to work for a combination of the Labor and Liberal Parties against the Conservatives, forming the Council of Action of Peace and Reconstruction. After the Tory victory this organization of a couple of dozen members was chiefly used to harry the Government in general and Prime Minister Neville Chamberlain in particular.

In his opposition to the appeasement policy which characterized the Chamberlain Government during the '30's, Lloyd George was an earlier and more consistent foe of Fascism than Churchill himself, if his speeches carried somewhat less weight. In 1935 he hinted that Japan had gone far enough in China, decried the effectiveness of sanctions against Italy, and opposed the Hoare[40]-Laval[40] proposals. In 1937 he attacked the "nonintervention" agreement on Spain, calling Foreign Minister Anthony Eden[40] a "first-class chauffeur," and warned Great Britain against a deal with Germany. When in 1938 Eden himself resigned in protest against further appeasement Lloyd George issued a nationwide call for his reinstatement, again assailing the British-Italian pact and the British policy in Spain. In the fall of the same year he denounced Chamberlain's entire foreign policy, which had culminated in the Munich betrayal of Czechoslovakia. In 1939 he called for the speedy conclusion of a military agreement with the U.S.S.R.—otherwise Britain, dangerously unprepared, would have no means of implementing her promises to Poland, he said. Blaming Chamberlain for the Nazi-Soviet nonaggression pact of August 1939, when the Second World War broke out he also criticized Polish unpreparedness, called Poland's the worst feudal system in Europe, and welcomed Stalin's[42] march into that country. Lloyd George finally, in May 1940, attacked the Prime Minister for what he called his bungling in Norway and called upon him to resign. Immediately afterward he began rallying support for the Churchill Government.

This veteran fighter has often found himself among Churchill's critics, too. In April 1941 he warned that a food crisis for England was near, and claimed that land produce could be doubled if acres were conscripted. In May of the same year he called for the inclusion of "no" men in Churchill's Cabinet and warned that it would be a long time before United States aid could really become a factor in the War. In January 1943 he was quoted as saying: "I sometimes wonder what we're doing. Here we are in the fourth year of the War and we've hardly tackled our main enemy, Germany." In February 1943 he voted against the Government on its treatment of the Beveridge[43] report, along with a number of Laborites and a few other Liberals.

Twenty-five years after the Paris Peace Conference, Lloyd George in November 1944 emphatically stated his belief that "things would have gone differently" after the last war if America had not abandoned the League of Nations. "The surest way of preventing a third war, he said at one of his rare interviews, would be "by America's acting differently this time," for her commitments to a future world organization would perhaps be the great stabilizer. Germany should be completely disarmed after the War, he counseled, believing that "good Germans would welcome disarmament, involuntary or otherwise."

After fifty-four years of service as an M.P., the "father" of the House of Commons in December 28, 1944, announced that, on the advice of his physician, he would retire from Parliament when his term expired. In a statement to his constituents he said that his decision had been made with great regret, as he had hoped to continue as their representative "to the end." The year before, his successor as Prime Minister in the Second World War had declared, "The prime parent of all national insurance schemes is, of course, Lloyd George. I was his lieutenant in those distant days [between 1908 and the First World War]." In King George's[42] New Year's honors list, made public three days after Lloyd George's announcement, the veteran statesman received an earldom. He became Earl Lloyd George of Dwyfor, taking his name from the mountain stream near his farm in Wales. The earldom was made possible by his retirement, for he could not receive a title and hold a seat in Commons at the same time. As an earl he was allowed to sit in the House of Lords.

The first Mrs. Lloyd George died in January 1941, and in October 1943 the onetime Prime Minister was married to the former Frances Louise Stevenson, who had been his secretary for thirty years. By the first marriage there are two daughters and two sons (one was killed in the First World War). Gwilym Lloyd George has been a Member of Parliament since 1922, Minister of Fuel and Power since 1942; daughter Megan has served in Parliament since 1929.

Short, thickset, with a ruddy complexion, a mane of white hair, and keen, twinkling eyes, this energetic octogenarian is still noted for his eloquence, his caustic wit, his personal magnetism, his intuitive understanding of people, his ability to put on a good show. Of him Churchill said once, "At his best he could almost talk a bird out of a tree," while J. M. Keynes speaks about his "unerring, almost medium-like sensibility to everyone and everything around him." These are not always considered particularly British characteristics, so it is little wonder that he has frequently been called un-English. It has almost as frequently been pointed out that his erudition is neither accurate nor extensive, that he makes frequent errors of fact in his speeches, and that he apparently confines himself to newspapers so far as his reading is concerned. As a historian, however, he remains infinitely more readable than many of his more scholarly contemporaries, even though his *War Memoirs* (six volumes, 1933-36) and his *The Truth About the Peace Treaty* (two volumes, 1938) reveal little that is not "devastatingly on his side." He has been called the "world's greatest living journalist."

References

Cur Hist 42:25-30 Ap '35
For Affairs 9:457-68 Ap '31
Harper 143:423-8 S '21
Liv Age 340:283-5 My '31
New Repub 82:91-3 Mr 6 '35
R of Rs 68:512-16 N '23
Time 33:24 My 1 '39

Bigham, C. The Prime Ministers of Britain 1721-1921 p340-4 1924
Churchill, W. L. S. Amid These Storms p51-61 1932
Davies, W. W. Lloyd George 1863-1914 1939
Keynes, J. M. Essays in Biography p31-41 1933
Lloyd George, D. War Memoirs 1933-1936; The Truth About the Peace Treaty 1938
Ludwig, E. Nine Etched From Life p207-50 1934
Radek, K. Portraits and Pamphlets p69-81 1935
Who's Who 1944

LOCKE, ALAIN (LE ROY) (lok) Sept. 13, 1886- Author; educator
Address: b. Howard University, Washington, D. C; h. 1326 R St., N.W., Washington, D. C.

As an educator and author, Alain Le Roy Locke has been for many years an outstanding

James L. Allen

ALAIN LOCKE

interpreter of the cultural contributions and achievements of the Negro, an analyst of the problems of his race and of race relations in both national and international aspects. He has written several books on the Negro in American art, is well known for his work as contributing editor to the *Survey Graphic*, and in 1918 became head of the philosophy department at Howard University, Washington, D. C.

Alain Le Roy Locke, the son of Pliny I. and Mary (Hawkins) Locke, was born in Philadelphia, Pennsylvania, September 13, 1886. From the Philadelphia Central High School he entered Harvard, where he took his B.A. in 1908 with Phi Beta Kappa honors. Study abroad followed: he was a Rhodes Scholar from Pennsylvania to Oxford (1907-10); then a graduate student in philosophy at the University of Berlin. Locke returned to the United States in 1912 to become assistant professor of philosophy and education at Howard University. In 1918 he took his Ph.D. at Harvard, and thereupon returned to Howard University to head the department of philosophy. For one year (1927-28) he was exchange professor to Fisk University. In 1943 he was Inter-American Exchange Professor to Haiti.

While he was a graduate student Locke began his writings on racial problems: his first work, *Race Contacts and Inter-racial Relations*, appeared in 1916; his doctoral thesis, *The Problem of Classification in Theory of Value,* in 1918. But it was in 1925, with the appearance of *The New Negro,* that Locke gained nationwide attention, becoming one of the recognized critical authorities on Negro cultural achievement. In his title essay Locke said: "The fiction is that the life of the races is separate, and increasingly so. The fact is that they touch too closely at the unfavorable and too lightly at the favorable levels." Of his work in this volume Sterling Brown has written: "The best statement of

LOCKE, ALAIN—*Continued*

the aims of the New Negro movement is to be found in his several essays in *The New Negro*. In spite of certain hopes that were to fail and certain emphases later abandoned, this volume performed valuable services. It focused attention upon creditable works of Negro artists, it placed creative writing among Negroes in a position of self-respect, it gave something of a unifying bond to struggling Negro artists, whose loneliness is even greater than the proverbial loneliness of the artist in America."

As editor of the Harlem number of the *Survey Graphic* in March 1925, Locke brought before the American public the social problems and also the cultural awakening of Negroes in America. His special number of that magazine for November 1942, on "Color: Unfinished Business of Democracy," provides an interesting contrast study to the 1925 Harlem number.

In 1927 Locke was co-editor with Montgomery Gregory of an anthology of *Plays of Negro Life*. A comprehensive social study, *The Negro in America*, appeared in 1933. This was followed by *The Negro and His Music* (1936) and *Negro Art· Past and Present* (1937).

In 1941 appeared his highly praised *The Negro in Art,* a record of the Negro artist and of the Negro theme in art. The book's opening section was devoted to illustrations of the work of Negroes, largely American, from the days of the slave apprentices to the modern days of the Federal Arts projects. The second section showed the Negro as the artist's subject. A concluding section portrayed the ancestral arts as they appeared in Africa and as their influence reappears in modern painting and sculpture. According to a review of the book in *Theatre Arts:* "His guiding hand, his excellent taste, his keen distinction, his broad human sympathy and appreciation are on every page."

When Peoples Meet: a Study in Race and Culture Contacts, co-edited wth Bernhard J. Stern, was published in 1942. This symposium on what happens when dominant and minority groups meet in various countries of the world included analyses by such authors as Ruth Benedict '41, Franz Boas '40, Margaret Mead '40. Said one critic of the book: "If between the covers of any other volume as much richness is to be found on the subject of majority and minority population elements, dominant and submerged peoples, as in this book, I am sure I don't know what it can be." Another study of Locke's was *Le Rôle du Nègre dans la Culture Américaine* (1943), written while he was in Haiti.

Alain Locke is a member of the American Negro Academy and of the National Order of Honor and Merit (Haiti), and an Honorary Fellow of the Sociedad de Estudios Afro-Cubanos. He is also a member of the International Institute of African Languages and Culture; a Corresponding Member of the Académie des Sciences Coloniales (Paris); and a Founding Member of the Conference on Science, Philosophy, and Religion. Besides his editorial work for the *Survey Graphic,*

he has for some years been secretary-editor of the Associates in Negro Folk Education. He was one of the twelve Negroes named in the 1942 Honor Roll of Race Relations, an annual nationwide poll which selected those who most distinguished themselves during the year.

References

Mag Art 34:370-4 Ag '41
Who's Who in America 1944-45

LOSCH, TILLY Nov. 15, 1907- Dancer; artist

Address: h. Hotel Ambassador, New York City

In 1944 Tilly Losch, internationally famous dancer and actress, made her debut as a painter with a successful exhibit at a New York art gallery. "An exotic figure, a well-known dancer, a bona fide countess [Miss Losch is the Countess of Carnarvon], and one of the most glamorous of personalities," Miss Losch proved that she was not confined to one field of expression in the arts. Art critics agreed that she had revealed "the magic touch of the real artist."

Ottilie Ethel Losch (she shortened her first name to Tilly when she went on the stage) was born in Vienna, November 15, 1907, the daughter of Otto Emil and Eugenie (Dreucker) Losch. Her first appearance as a dancer was at the State Opera House in Vienna in 1912. The little girl grew up in the Vienna Opera Ballet. By the time she was twenty she was one of its most popular dancers and the recipient of an invitation from Max Reinhardt to dance the role of the First Fairy in his Salzburg production of *A Midsummer Night's Dream.*

Miss Losch's decision to leave the Vienna Ballet was not an easy one to make. The Vienna Opera and Ballet were subsidized by the State. When a dancer was engaged, although she received a very small salary, she was assured security for life with a pension when she retired. Reinhardt's original invitation to Miss Losch had been for the summer and, since the opera was closed during the summer season, she felt free to accept it. Leaving the opera permamently was another matter, however, and, but for the intervention of riots in Vienna, Miss Losch might never have left. On the last day that she might sign her contract for the following season Miss Losch started out for the Opera House—only to discover that she could not reach it because of an uprising of the Viennese workers. She tried to get there by darting from doorway to doorway, but the rioting made it impossible for her to cross the square in front of the Opera House. Miss Losch therefore left for Salzburg without signing the contract.

During that summer Reinhardt invited her to come to the United States with his company. Visiting America had long been the young dancer's dream, but, still loyal to the Vienna Ballet, she returned to ask for a year's leave of absence. The leave was refused, although she was invited to renew her contract. Miss Losch then took a deep breath and made perhaps the most important decision of her life—to leave the Vienna Ballet and come to the United States in 1928 with Reinhardt's company.

At Reinhardt's suggestion Miss Losch did choreography as well as dancing. Since she had never done choreography before, she was somewhat overwhelmed when he suggested that she arrange the dances for *A Midsummer Night's Dream.* "You can do it," Reinhardt told her, and she proceeded not only to do it, but to arrange all the dances for Reinhardt's productions of *Everyman* and *Danton's Death.* "You must have somebody who believes in you," Miss Losch says, and she admits that she has been fortunate in receiving the necessary encouragement in her dancing, her acting, and her painting. It was Reinhardt who told her she could act and gave her the role of the Nun in his London revival of *The Miracle* (1932).

In the meanwhile another of Miss Losch's dreams was realized. While dancing at Salzburg in the summer of 1927 she met the famous London impressario, Charles B. Cochran. Cochran had managed some of the greatest stars in the theatre, and when he signed her to appear in London, Miss Losch knew her career was in good hands. She made her London debut in 1928 in the Noel Coward '41 play, *This Year of Grace.* In the following year she appeared in London in *Wake Up and Dream* and came to the United States with that production.

In the early 1930's Miss Losch gave several dance recitals in the United States with Harald Kreutzberg. She was also kept busy producing the ballet for *The Gang's All Here* (1931) and dancing with Fred and Adele Astaire in *The Bandwagon* (1931). She made numerous trips between England and the United States to dance and act for Reinhardt and to appear in the United States with her own ballet company. She has danced with the Russian Ballet under the direction of George Balanchine '42 and with the Ballet Theatre, too. "I have worked all my life," she comments, "but I never considered it work because I loved it."

Hollywood producers were much impressed with Miss Losch's exotic beauty and her acting ability. After she had made two brief but very successful appearances on the American screen as the dancing girl in *The Garden of Allah* (1936) and as Lotus in *The Good Earth* (1937), Louis B. Mayer '43 gave her a one-year contract and proclaimed enthusiastically that she would be a great star. Miss Losch waited patiently for a year, but nothing happened. She admits that she was not happy in Hollywood. "It was an isolated life," she says, "with too many artists all striving for fame." Most of its residents, she continues, were playing "the great American game of promise." That "game" is one of Miss Losch's pet aversions. "If people would stop making promises they cannot fulfill, there would be less bad blood everywhere among individuals and among nations."

Tilly Losch began painting accidentally in 1938. Although she had often dabbled with water colors, and had long felt the urge for expression in a medium other than the dance, she did not begin painting in earnest until, as with her dancing and her acting, someone said, "You can do it." The someone

TILLY LOSCH

this time was John Churchill, Winston Churchill's '42 nephew, who painted her portrait and who, when he learned of her secret desire to paint, urged her to go ahead and paint fearlessly. Her first work was a self-portrait in oils—and she has worked in oils ever since. "To my amazement," she relates, "a sort of mystic greeny-blue face appeared and gradually took shape. I've been painting ever since. . . . I shall go on painting, for I love it as much as dancing." Miss Losch received further encouragement from the noted British artist and designer Cecil Beaton '44, who advised her never, in painting, to consider herself nor the obstacles that might stand in her way. "If you are going to paint, paint," he told her.

The first one-man exhibit of her paintings, held at the Bignou Gallery in New York City in the spring of 1944, revealed an artist of unusual grace and skill. Although slightly reminiscent of the French primitive school, her paintings are actually in no "school" of art. Miss Losch says: "I want to find my own way of painting, even if it isn't the right way; I don't want to be a poor reproduction of somebody else." Art critics found that Miss Losch had captured on canvas something of the rhythm and grace of the dance. She blends romanticism and mysticism into what has been called "a curious and evocative order of magic; a gift of divination." Some of her paintings have autobiographical significance; many are on dancing themes. (She never uses models, Miss Losch says.) Her *Saga in Five Movements* portrays the life of woman in five allegorical stages, while *Out of My Life* reveals a series of events moving from the dancing of little children on the street to a female figure stretched out upon a cross.

Miss Losch confesses that as the date for her art exhibit approached she suffered from the worst case of stage fright she had ever experienced. But the success of the exhibit and the fact that one of her paintings, *Creek,* was bought by the noted art collector Alfred Barnes for exhibition at the Barnes Founda-

LOSCH, TILLY—*Continued*

tion ("an accolade professionally") restored her confidence. The exhibit was moved to Philadelphia, where again it was well received, and in the summer of 1944 Miss Losch took it to California.

For the present Miss Losch plans only to continue painting. (She practices her dancing every day but has given it up except for a few appearances with the Ballet Theatre in New York and dance recitals for War reliefs.) In 1939 she became an English Countess when she married the Earl of Carnarvon, now a major in the British Army. (Her first marriage, to Edward James, ended in divorce in 1934.) Strikingly beautiful, Miss Losch wears her red hair in a long bob. While her painting is taking up most of her time she also works hard at knitting and needlework, and she would like to learn how to cook. She has a deep love for the United States, which she compares to a magnificent machine of numerous different little parts which somehow fit together and run smoothly and beautifully. In 1943 she tried to express her love for America in a letter to President Roosevelt[42], but "at the last minute she became shy and did not send it."

> *References*
> N Y Herald Tribune p38 Ap 23 '44 por
> N Y Post Mag p41 My 3 '44 pors
> N Y Times Mag p25 Ap 30 '44 il
> Time 43:37 My 15 '44 por
> Who's Who in the Theatre 1939

LUHRING, OSCAR RAYMOND (lūr'ing) Feb. 11, 1879—Aug. 18, 1944 Member of the District Court of the United States for the District of Columbia, for the past fourteen years; a Republican member of Congress from 1913 to 1923 (Indiana); and a prosecuting attorney and member of the Indiana State Legislature before going to Washington.

> *Obituary*
> N Y Times p11 Ag 19 '44 por

LUTYENS, SIR EDWIN L(ANDSEER) (lut'yenz) Mar. 29, 1869—Jan. 1, 1944 Foremost architect in Great Britain; president of Royal Academy since 1938; presided over plans for the rebuilding of London after the War; one of the principal architects for the Imperial War Graves Commission during First World War; his works included the British Embassy in Washington, D.C., the Government House, New Delhi, India, the British School of Art, Rome, and the British Art Exhibition Building, Rome; see sketch 1942 Yearbook.

> *Obituary*
> N Y Times p38 Ja 2 '44 por

LUTZ, FRANK E(UGENE) (lūts) Sept. 15, 1879—Nov. 27, 1943 Entomologist; curator of the Department of Insects and Spiders at American Museum of Natural History; member of the Museum's staff since 1909; noted educator and research worker.

> *Obituary*
> N Y Times p69 N 28 '43

LYONS, EUGENE July 1, 1898- Editor; author; journalist

Address: b. Pageant, 1476 Broadway, New York City; h. 62 E. 91st St., New York City

Although his progress from the Lower East Side of New York to the editorial chair of the *American Mercury*—then in 1944 to a new publication, *Pageant*—was not, perhaps, quite so spectacular as that of a Horatio Alger hero, Eugene Lyons is the protagonist of what he himself calls an "up-from-the-gutter" type of story. He does not, however, according to his autobiography, take too great a pleasure in his achievement. Those who "romanticize the glories of a hard, poverty-ridden youth" as a prelude to great success, he says, "overlook the more vital fact that when he does achieve wealth he generally carries the scars of the unequal struggle on his mind and spirit forever. He can rarely attain the mellow quality of the full, cultured existence of those whose rise was more orderly, less desperate."

Eugene Lyons was born in Uzlian, Russia on July 1, 1898, the son of Nathan H. and Minnie (Privin) Lyons. When he was nine years old his family emigrated to the United States. "As a child," he writes in *Assignment to Utopia*, "down in a stinking steerage hole . . . in one of the foul ships which, at that time, dumped cargoes of bewildered immigrants on the American shores, I treasured a vision of the fairyland called America. I shut my eyes and saw it clearly—the glittering streets, the happy faces, the new shiny land stocked with beauty. That lovely vision broke sickeningly on the garbage cans of the Corlears Hook section of New York. The specters of 'slack' seasons, of strikes for a living wage, of illness that cut off all earnings for a large family—the sight of my father's cadaverous face after a long day at the machine . . . these were less horrible when viewed as aspects of the perpetual class hostilities and as prelude to an ineffable triumph."

Consequently, before he was thirteen Eugene found himself enrolled in a "Socialist Sunday School" on East Broadway, run by the Workman's Circle. There he met a little girl of seven named Yetta (Billy) Siegel, whom he was to marry ten years later. From the Socialist Sunday School he graduated naturally into the "Yipsels," the Young People's Socialist League, where he "debated weighty questions and took courses in Marx and Spencer and distributed leaflets for Socialist candidates without the slightest hope of their election."

Fortunately for the boy, his parents had decided that he was to be a lawyer, and he was therefore to be sent to high school and college, thus escaping the fate of his older brother who "since the age of thirteen, had been among the sweated legions bending over sewing machines." His father and mother, however, could barely afford to provide Eugene with food, clothing, and shelter, and it was up to him to acquire money for carfare and incidental expenses himself. This he obtained by working after school hours at the Educational Alliance. Later for two or three years he earned $3 a week as "assistant professor" in one of the speed-up preparatory schools for adults. "My function was chiefly the correction of examination papers on subjects about which I knew precisely nothing. One night I would remain up, hurriedly digesting *As You Like It* in preparation for a set of test papers; another night it might be *Hamlet* or *Silas Marner*."

Lyons was graduated from De Witt Clinton High School in 1916. When the Russian Revolution began in March 1917 he was a freshman at City College in New York. For him and his friends the Revolution was "the rapturous harbinger of that Great Change in the glow of which we had warmed our spirits." Despite the fact that after this the First World War itself seemed anticlimactic, Lyons served as a private in the Student Army Training Corps, and in 1918 he studied at Columbia University. In 1919 his unit was demobilized. "On the very day when I removed my Army uniform," he says, "I wrote my first publicity story on the Workers Defense Union. . . . Day after day I composed these stories, destined for the New York *Call* and other radical publications, recounting the sufferings of IWW's and other political prisoners, the depredations of the Department of Justice on a rampage, the havoc being wrought by the American Legion. It was a time of raids on radicals, 'Treat 'em rough!' hooliganism, and mass deportations. Tales of horror poured in upon our Workers Defense Union." On May Day of 1919 the riots against the radicals were most spectacular. The "patriotic marauders" even climbed up the fire-escapes of the Rand School, where the offices of the Workers Defense Union were maintained. Lyons and his colleagues were all ready to fight to the end, but the rioters missed their room.

For the next two years Lyons worked as a reporter on various newspapers, including the Erie (Pennsylvania) *Dispatch*, and *Financial America* in Wall Street. He also wrote copy for some months in the publicity department of a motion-picture company and succeeded in "getting several high-pitched effusions into arty little magazines." His work in the radical movement was, however, most important to him. In 1920 there were reports of an impending Communist revolution in Italy, and there Lyons journeyed with credentials from the Federated Press, "a struggling labor news agency," and the *Liberator*. The revolution failed to mature, but Lyons had work to do in Italy. He had been commissioned by the Workers Defense Union to arouse all Italy to the significance of an obscure case in Boston concerning a fish-monger named Bartolomeo Vanzetti and a shoemaker named Nicola Sacco. "The Italian labor movement," Lyons discovered, "had other things to worry about." Finally he was deported from Italy and deposited in France.

Landing in Paris without a penny, Lyons obtained a job on the Paris *Herald* despite his lack of knowledge of the French language. "I . . . rewrote items out of the French paper largely by intuition during the month I survived on the job," Lyons explains. "The in-

tuition played me false on occasion and Americans on the Continent, I fear, were given some strange versions of French current events." By the end of the month Lyons received a check from America which would just pay his fare home, and accordingly he returned to New York.

Unfortunately the ship needed some repairs which kept the passengers waiting in Le Havre for some days. Lyons had no money for food, and was almost starving by the time the ship finally was ready. When they docked at the pier in New York he had to borrow a nickel from a fellow passenger in order to get him to his parents' home in Brooklyn. At the end of his first week in the States he was on his way to Boston where Sacco and Vanzetti had already been condemned to death. With him was his fiancée, Billy, whom he married a few weeks later on September 6, 1921. They spent fourteen months in a small, inexpensive apartment in Back Bay. For furniture a friend of theirs provided them with some that the late Supreme Court Justice Brandeis had stored in a Brookline cellar to which she held the key. A year later Lyons met Justice Brandeis, confessed the "theft," and found that their friend had "not overestimated his generosity."

The Lyonses returned to New York just before the birth of their daughter, Eugenie Rose, in November 1922. In New York Lyons found that "what had been a many-sided radical movement had disintegrated into so many sects. . . . Unhesitatingly I cast my lot with the Communists." The next five years he devoted largely to pro-Soviet activities. From 1922 until 1923 he edited the first popular American magazine about Russia, the *Soviet Russia Pictorial*; and for four years thereafter, until the day he sailed for the U.S.S.R., Lyons worked as assistant director for the official Soviet news agency, Tass. He says, nevertheless: "I did not join the Communist Party and consequently was never on the inside of its involved and embittered political life. Such close-ups of the internal party machinery as I had by reason of my everyday work strengthened my obstinacy in resisting solicitations to join up. In any organization which rests on absolute discipline, there is no intermediate role between leadership and blind obedience. I had not the slightest taste for one and a definite distaste for the other."

Since Russia followed the details of the Sacco-Vanzetti case more anxiously than did any other nation, Lyons again became involved in it. In 1927, shortly after the execution of the two men, Lyons' book, *The Life and Death of Sacco and Vanzetti*, was published. "Leafing through *The Life and Death of Sacco and Vanzetti* ten years later, Lyons himself wrote, "I am astonished to find passages so eloquent in their passionate restraint that they seem to have been written by another person. At points in the terse narrative I find a poetic vein that transcends my own normal literary powers. It was the alchemy of feeling too deep for tears precipitating a style of their own. . . . The book was translated into German, Italian, Russian, and Yiddish, and widely read in those

Portrait by Leon Gordon

EUGENE LYONS

languages. Two Russian editions, published while I was in Moscow, sold some 130,000 copies. Only the original English version never reached more than a few thousand readers. In 1933, the Nazis paid the book the compliment of immolation on their funeral pyre to German culture. It burned in as fine a literary company as was ever assembled outside a library."

Tass had exchanged facilities with the United Press, and when, in 1926, the post of the U.P. Moscow correspondent fell vacant, Lyons was suggested as a possible candidate. That time he was not chosen, but the following year the post again fell vacant, and Lyons was selected to fill it. He reached Russia in February 1928. He writes: "If anyone ever went to the Soviet realm with a deep and earnest determination to understand the Revolution, to slough off petty detail, and dig down to the hard, enduring core of a great event in human history, it was the newly-appointed United Press correspondent. My problem, I felt, would be to tone down the rhapsody to the humdrum level of American journalism. I was not deserting the direct service of the cause for the fleshpots of capitalism. (The United Press, as a matter of fact, was paying me only a few dollars more than Tass.) I was accepting, rather, a post of immense strategic importance in the further service of that cause, and doing so with the wholehearted agreement and understanding of my chiefs in Tass and, therefore, presumably of the Soviet Foreign Office."

Lyons and his family spent the next six years in Russia. His first impressions were favorable. "Ardently if illogically," he says, "I gave the Revolution credit for everything cultural that it had inherited from the czarist era." Once in Russia his natural move was, he writes, toward the Communist foreign colony, which included a number of former friends. He had expected confidently that his "Moscow friends and political guidance would come from that direction." As a rep-

resentative of the capitalist press, he found that, in crossing the Soviet frontier, he and his family had, in his own words, "been turned mysteriously into untouchables. How were we to surmise that in visiting old friends we were exposing them to capitalist contagions and, what is more to the point, endangering the most valuable asset in their political climbing—their spotless orthodoxy?"

During all of the years that he spent in Russia, Lyons' family lived with him there. His daughter was for a while educated in Berlin instead of in Russia, at the advice of a Russian official who expressed surprise that Lyons should want the child given a Russian education when he could send her out of the country. When the Nazis came into power she was sent to one of Moscow's model schools, where Stalin's [42] children were her schoolmates.

As a correspondent, Lyons scored two major scoops—in 1930 he got the first interview that Stalin gave after his rise to power; later he interviewed the Shah of Persia. During the course of his career in Russia, Lyons' understanding with the authorities kept fluctuating; occasionally he was in good repute with the Soviet powers, more often, despite his political sympathies, he was not. Finally he dispatched a story about a Soviet-Japanese border incident; this story, Lyons says, was based on Soviet sources but was denied by the Soviet Government, which insisted that Lyons be recalled from Russia. On January 30, 1934 Lyons left Moscow, and before his return to the United States he spent several months touring Europe on an assignment for *Cosmopolitan* Magazine.

In 1935, the year in which Lyons went to work for the publicity firm of Ames and Norr in the United States, his first book about Russia, *Moscow Carrousel,* was published. "The book is easy reading," wrote the *Saturday Review of Literature*'s critic, "but nonetheless it is probably the confusing truth about Russia, because what Mr. Lyons writes is not prejudiced either for or against the proletarian dictatorship." Other critics found the book possibly "too slick" and "journalistic," but otherwise commendable, and F. L. Schuman called the writer "a well-balanced, sympathetic, critical, and eminently human interpreter of the social scene in the U.S.S.R."

"The man who burns his Soviet bridges behind him . . . by telling what he considers the truth . . . is foregoing . . . the field of literary opportunism where so many other commentators on Russia luxuriate," Lyons had written in *Moscow Carrousel*; later he dismissed the book with contempt. When he wrote it he could not yet bear to disillusion people about the Soviet Union, he says—and he had to pass through more than one moral crisis before the publication of "To Tell or Not To Tell" in *Harper's* in June 1935, when his career as an anti-Soviet writer was firmly launched. In 1937 his autobiography, *Assignment in Utopia,* appeared. This book, which told of Lyons' disillusionment with the Communist ideals, aroused great agitation in the radical press, but on the whole the book was well received. "This book," wrote the reviewer for the New York *Times,* "is a book that any supporter of any dictatorial system will find hard to answer—

and it is a book that has no kin with the products of former radicals who turn reactionary because of the proffered fleshpots of Egypt."

In 1939 Lyons accepted the editorship of the *American Mercury*, the magazine founded by H. L. Mencken. (The following year he added to his editorial duties those of radio commentator on the New York radio station WMCA.) Many political articles by Lyons, most of them still dealing with the Soviet Union, have been published in the *Mercury* and other magazines since that time. Fascism and Nazism were merely the offspring of the Russian "phantasmagoria of cruelty and death," he wrote in October 1939, following the Nazi-Soviet non-aggression pact—and both parent and progeny must be "exposed, analyzed, and disowned." Before the War he had opposed the Soviet type of "collective security" but after the War started he was among the first to support all aid to France and Britain and a selective service act for the United States. In 1940 Lyons' biography of the Russian leader, *Stalin, Czar of All the Russias,* appeared. On one side the New York *Times'* critic considered it a "carefully planned and brilliantly written, comprehensive, and well-rounded story of Stalin's amazing career," and the London *Times'* critic was essentially in accord. Joseph Barnes of the New York *Herald Tribune* called it "sustained diatribe" and "political pamphleteering," written "not with a rapier but a bludgeon." Its picture of Stalin, as Lyons pointed out in this book, was in marked contrast to that in Lyons' published interview with Stalin which had taken place ten years before.

Early in 1941 Lyons wrote that the Russo-Finnish War was "unquestionably" a "segment of the prearranged Russo-German encirclement of Scandinavia," while if Russia's economic aid to the Reich had been disappointing, it was due merely to the "sad economic picture inside Russia." "Russo-German collaboration is as reliable as any of the alliances extant, if only because it rests on genuine mutual self-interest," he continued, basing his statement on the belief that Russia was the area where the "foundation of popular loyalties" was the weakest in the world, and that "the Russian military machine is too weak to venture a test of major warfare." In August 1941 the editor of the *American Mercury* wrote: "We are witnessing the violent and ignominious end of . . . Stalin." The Russian leader, he claimed, was faced by a Germany which now had the "support" of a Europe which "hates Stalin even more than it fears Hitler," and was fighting a war on "two fronts": "against the German invader and against his own people." As for Britain and America, they "wish only to prolong his [Stalin's] agony, knowing too well that he will capitulate and betray them at the first good opportunity." In November of that same year Lyons announced that he supported lend-lease aid for Russia only because "a decisive Russian victory is not even a remote possibility."

The year after America entered the War, Lyons' study of American Communism was published: *The Red Decade; the Stalinist Penetration of America,* a study of the activi-

ties of Communists and fellow travelers in the United States during the decade from 1930 to 1940. Favorably reviewed by such writers as Max Eastman, W. H. Chamberlin, and Benjamin de Casseres, this book was criticized for inaccuracy and exaggeration by such others as the New York *Times'* Ralph Thompson and the *Herald Tribune's* Lewis Gannett [43]. Legal action in regard to the book was taken when Corliss Lamont instituted a libel suit against the publishers, Bobbs-Merrill. Settlement was made in March 1942 when the company agreed to change several statements in the text if there should be a new edition (which by the end of 1944 there had not been).

In 1943 Lyons wrote that the Administration and many Americans were uncritical in their attitude toward Russia. "Rarely in history, indeed, has a nation made its eagerness for friendship and understanding more manifest. There have been no corresponding gestures of friendship at the Russian end," he wrote in May 1943, calling attention to, among other things, the fact that Russia was not fighting Japan. *Mission to Moscow* and Wendell Willkie's [40] *One World* he called examples of "Stalin-Worship."

In the fall of 1943 Lyons and the *American Mercury* were attacked several times by the newsletter *In Fact* for alleged Fascist leanings. The *American Mercury*, in turn, in a national campaign through the radio, the press, and the mails as well as its own columns, called the newsletter a Communist organ. (*In Fact* is published by George Seldes [41].)

In the 1944 Presidential campaign Lyons, writing for Scripps-Howard, counseled voters to recognize that "the Communist influence in the Goverment, in labor, and in American life generally" was an important issue in the campaign. It was not, he wrote, "a red herring dragged into the fight by the Republicans." He pointed to the effects of "totalitarian conspiracies" in European countries, and warned against self-delusion about such influences in the United States, stating that Communist efforts to re-elect Roosevelt in 1944, capture the American Labor Party in New York, control the CIO's PAC, and infiltrate into the Administration were evidences of Communist strength in America.

Lyons' association with the *American Mercury* came to an end in June 1944, when he left to edit a new pocket-sized monthly called *Pageant*. This magazine, which first appeared on the newsstands in November, contains humor, fiction, and articles on public affairs. Most of the material in *Pageant* originates with the magazine, that is, the magazine does not rely on reprinted material; and color photography is a specialty. There is no advertising on its pages. Lyons has declared that the magazine has no particular cause to promote; it will serve, among other things, as a medium for debate on current topics. At the end of December it was announced in the press that Lyons would also be a member of the board of editors of the *New Leader*, which will change from newspaper to magazine format. Among others on the board are Max Eastman, John Dewey [44], Sidney Hook, Harry Gideonse [40], William Henry Chamberlin.

(Continued next page)

LYONS, EUGENE—*Continued*

The journalist and editor, who wrties on the current scene as well as on Russia, is known as a lecturer and as editor of *Six Soviet Plays*, an anthology (1943), and of *We Cover the World* (1937), a symposium of foreign correspondents to which he contributed "Persian Interlude." He is a founder and past president of the Overseas Press Club. Lyons is of medium height, stocky, and dark. He lives with his wife and daughter in New York City.

References

Sat R Lit 16:40 O 9 '37 por (p10)
Va Q R 14:150-3 [Ja] '38
Wilson Lib Bul 16:346 Ja '42 por

Lyons, E. Assignment in Utopia 1939
Who's Who in America 1944-45
Who's Who in American Jewry 1938-39

MACCALLUM, WILLIAM GEORGE

Apr. 18, 1874—Feb. 3, 1944 Professor of pathology of the Johns Hopkins Medical School from 1917 until 1943; widely known in the scientific world for his research in this field and in endocrinology; his *Textbook of Pathology* (1916) became a standard book on the subject in all leading medical schools.

Obituary

N Y Times p15 F 4 '44

MCGEACHY, CRAIG *See* McGeachy, M. A. C.

MCGEACHY, MARY (AGNES) CRAIG

(mə-gay'hee) Nov. 7, 1904- Social administrator; diplomat

Address: b. c/o Welfare Division, United Nations Relief and Rehabilitation Administration, Washington, D.C.; h. 2709 O St., N.W., Washington, D.C.

Responsibility for the Welfare Division of the United Nations Relief and Rehabilitation Administration rests with an attractive young woman, Mary Craig McGeachy, who has never had any formal training or professional experience in social work. The first woman to receive an appointment as a full-fledged British diplomat to a major power, the blond Canadian is, after a ten-year apprenticeship to the League of Nations, an international authority on the problems of living standards.

Mary Agnes Craig McGeachy was born in Sarnia, Ontario, Canada, November 7, 1904. Her parents are the Reverend Donald and Anna Jeanette McGeachy; they had come to Canada from the Hebrides, islands off the coast of Scotland. In her homes at Ails Craig and Sarnia (just across the St. Clair from Port Huron, Michigan) she developed a social consciousness early, becoming "interested in politics and economics as soon as she knew the meaning of the words." Young Mary Craig McGeachy ("the 'Agnes' is silent") majored in history and philosophy at the University of Toronto, then went abroad to continue her studies at the Sorbonne in Paris. From June 1928 to May 1929 she represented the British-American Student Relief Fund at universities

in France, Austria, Hungary, Czechoslovakia, and Germany.

From the Graduate School of Higher International Studies at the University of Geneva to the Permanent Secretariat of the League of Nations was but a step for the twenty-six-year-old Canadian. In July 1930 she joined the League's section on public health, social welfare, and economic studies. During the next ten years she served as liaison officer for the League with the British Dominions, in addition to her technical duties with the Advisory Committee on Nutrition. Miss McGeachy acquired an expert's knowledge of raw materials, food supply, health, relief—all the factors affecting the standard of living; and her work in the Information Section, of which she rose to be acting director, was primarily that of publicizing the League's findings on commercial access to raw materials. "If that study of raw materials had been made two years earlier," she once told an interviewer, "it might have prevented the War."

While at Geneva, Miss McGeachy was active as liaison officer to the international women's organizations which had their headquarters there. She made many trips to North America to represent the Secretary General of the League before women's conventions as well as groups interested in international relations. Eventually she was drawn into the League's committee to study the status of women throughout the world. It is said that "ushers at the League of Nations Building, if they saw a lone woman wandering around looking as if she needed a friend, would tell her that Miss McGeachy was expecting her."

In August 1940 the young executive joined the Press and Parliamentary Section of the Ministry of Economic Warfare in London, where she also helped organize various women's defense units. After six months in that much-bombed capital—her own Georgian house was destroyed by the raiders—Miss McGeachy was transferred to Washington as public relations officer for the British Embassy on questions relating to economic warfare. Her special mission was to explain the British food blockade to indignant Americans, and she handled it with tact and skill. With Lord Halifax [40] and his wife, the Countess, she toured the Middle West, and "proved invaluable as a well-informed and graceful member of their public relations staff. A certain Canadian breeziness, which she has never lost, helps her in her relations with Americans and does much to offset conceptions of British diplomatic austerity." Since coming to the United States, Miss McGeachy has crossed the Atlantic each year "to carry news of what women are thinking and doing on both sides" and to keep herself up to date on the subject. In July 1942 she "took over questions of post-War relief preparation," as she phrases it.

On the first of October 1942 Britain's Foreign Secretary Anthony Eden [40] announced to Parliament the appointment of Miss Mary Agnes Craig McGeachy as first secretary of the British Embassy in the United States, on the recommendation of the Ambassador and the Minister of Economic Warfare. This appointment attracted a great deal of attention, as only one woman had ever held a comparable post in the British diplomatic corps—and that was the distinguished archeologist Gertrude Bell, in Iraq. Miss McGeachy herself remarked that there were half-a-dozen first secretaries in the Embassy, so why make such a fuss over her? She did tell interviewers, however, that "the appointment was given her as a way of honoring British women for the part they have been playing in the War" (i.e., as a response to pressure from women voters, who have long campaigned for Britain to follow the lead of other countries in admitting qualified women to the diplomatic corps).

The new First Secretary's duties were much the same as before, and included "keeping abreast of import and export statistics"—which means "to know from week to week what goes on in Europe, to see the whole picture and to analyze it. For example, Germany broadcasts that she has upped her civilian bread and meat rations: Miss McGeachy is able to deduce, as she does in a recent article, that this means a cut in cattle fodder and not, as might be assumed, an increase in grain and meat stocks from new sources." The public relations aspect of her job included "contact and diplomatic work involved in pursuing the Ministry of Economic Warfare's program in the Western Hemisphere," and also, as she was the highest-ranking woman at the Embassy, being "a contact person for all sorts of women's groups." In this capacity the young diplomat has traveled widely, addressed many groups, and written a number of articles. In addition to economic warfare, she showed herself particularly interested in labor relations and in post-War rehabilitation of stricken areas.

Although Miss McGeachy "has never attended a school of social work nor done a day's work as a professional social case worker," she was a logical nominee to head the United Nations Relief and Rehabilitation Administration's welfare division. Lord Halifax recommended her for the post; and on January 30, 1944 Herbert H. Lehman [43], director general of UNRRA, announced that she had resigned as first secretary of the Embassy to accept that position. The conservative New York *Herald Tribune* noted editorially its "hearty approval" of Miss McGeachy's appointment to head the important welfare division, "because of the experience and knowledge that competent young woman brings to this most pressing problem."

That competent young woman will be responsible for "the planning, supervision, and organization of essential relief for distressed persons, including specially dependent groups such as the aged, children, and nursing and pregnant women in liberated areas. She will also assist in redeveloping the national and community welfare organizations of those areas." Official intelligence and underground reports from the occupied countries indicate that "the framework of social agencies still exists," contrary to the Nazis' statements— Miss McGeachy explains that "the Germans would have you believe that chaos exists, but I go on the assumption they must be wrong— as they are about so many things." Her aim, therefore, is to strengthen these agencies and

British Official Photo
MARY CRAIG MCGEACHY

work through them to solve the problems of food, housing, and health, rather than setting up an entirely new organization. As for herself, "I'll probably stay here plotting the job, letting other people do the glamorous parts," she predicted lightly when questioned. The new division chief's choice of assistants was itself a delicate and important decision, as "she may pick experts from the entire world for her staff." The UNRRA took the occasion of Miss McGeachy's appointment to announce that its professional personnel was "to be selected without regard to sex."

The young executive who will administer this great work is not only capable but attractive. A woman interviewer described her as "disarming," and a man wrote that she is "remarkably pretty." Her eyes are piquantly slanted under strong, arched brows, and her firm-jawed face has an expression of quiet humor. Her skin is fair, as befits the copper-blond hair into which she often pins a ribbon bow. A good cook and a good hostess who loves to give small parties, Miss McGeachy gives an impression of "simplicity and self-assurance, very direct, very relaxed, and completely serene." Although a quiet person, when she has something to say to a co-worker or to a mass meeting she says it "easily and volubly in a soft Scots voice." Her clothes are simple but feminine, and photographs always show her with every hair in place.

Miss McGeachy's particular prides are a brace of fine springer spaniels and an unusual collection of ancient Greek sculpture—both "in storage" for the duration. In spite of the fact that she and her two sisters (one a doctor, the other a nurse) are all professional workers, and in spite of the brilliance of her own career, she dislikes above all others the term "career woman."

On December 21, 1944, in an old London church, Mary Agnes Craig McGeachy was married to Vienna-born Erwin Schuller, who was on leave from the National Council of Social

MCGEACHY, MARY CRAIG—*Continued*
Services (London) to the UNRRA Bureau of
Supply. Formerly associated with Lever
Brothers and Lazard Frères, Schuller was then
helping to develop a special training program
for UNRRA personnel.

References

> Ind Woman 21:321 N '42 por
> N Y Herald Tribune p9 Ja 20 '41 por;
>   p7 Ja 31 '44
> N Y Sun p22 F 4 '44
> N Y Times p14 Ja 31 '44 por
> N Y Times Mag p16 Ap 11 '43 por

MCGILLICUDY, CORNELIUS *See*
Mack, C.

MCGROARTY, JOHN STEVEN (ma-
grō'ĕr-ti) Aug. 20, 1862—Aug. 7, 1944 Ex-
Congressman, playwright, and lawyer; elected
poet laureate of California by state legislation
in 1933; Congressman from California (Democrat) in 1934, he served two terms; championed the Townsend Old Age Plan; *The Mission Play* (1911), which ran for twenty years,
and *California, Its History and Romance*
(1911) are two of his better known works.

Obituary

> N Y Times p17 Ag 8 '44 por

MACHADO, BERNARDINO (LUIZ)
(ma-sha'THŪ bĕr-nĕr-dē'nŪ lū-ēsh') 1851—
Apr. 29, 1944 Portuguese statesman; President of Portugal from 1915 to 1917 and again
in 1925; Minister of Foreign Affairs in provisional government in 1910; Prime Minister
in 1914; envoy to the United States before
the turn of the century.

Obituary

> N Y Times p46 Ap 30 '44 por

MCINTYRE, MARVIN H(UNTER) Nov.
27, 1878—Dec. 13, 1943 Secretary to President Roosevelt since he entered the White
House in 1933; as assistant secretary, had
charge of Presidential appointments for his
first six years as a member of the secretariat;
advanced to rank of secretary upon death of
Louis McHenry Howe.

Obituary

> N Y Times p27 D 14 '43 por

MACK, CONNIE Dec. 22, 1862- Baseball
club manager
Address: b. c/o Philadelphia American League
Baseball Club, Philadelphia

No other club manager in baseball history
has won so many championships or ended so
many seasons at the bottom of the list as Connie Mack, eighty-two-year old president, treasurer, and co-owner of the Philadelphia Athletics. Even though his team is a standing
joke among baseball enthusiasts, Mack himself is regarded with affectionate awe as "Mr.
Baseball," the sport's most beloved figure.

Connie Mack—or, as he was called by his
parents, Cornelius McGillicuddy—was born in
East Brookfield, Massachusetts, in 1862.
(After celebrating seventy-five of his birth-
days on December 23, Mack discovered that
his actual birth date was the 22nd, but decided
it was too late to change.) At nine the tall,
thin "Slats" McGillicuddy began to work in
a cotton mill during the summers, carrying
stock, running errands, and operating the elevator. When the boy was in his teens his
father, Michael McGillicuddy, died, and as
Mack recalls, left "the business of feeding
a sizeable and hollow-legged Irish family
squarely on my hatrack shoulders."

Entering a shoe factory at sixteen, young
McGillicuddy worked himself up to the job
of foreman at twenty. He also played semi-
professional baseball as catcher for the East
Brookfield team of the Central Massachusetts
League earning his "share of whatever was
dropped in the hat." In 1884, when the youth
was twenty-one, he was offered the then
princely sum of $90 a month by the Meriden
baseball club (Connecticut State League).
Much as he loved the game, a young man
had to think twice before giving up a good
job to cast his lot with a sport considered—
not without reason—as "beneath the notice of
decent society." Cornelius McGillicuddy
thought twice—and then joined the Meriden
club, where his name was shortened to "Connie Mack" to fit on the scorecards.

No statistics are available to show Mack's
earliest performances on the diamond; but
baseball managers were not paying $90 a
month lightly in those days. "I would have
played with them for half that if they had
only known it," he says. "And I was afraid
to let the other boys on the club know what
a plutocrat I was." After one year at Meriden, Mack joined the Hartford team of the
same league, later playing for Newark, New
Jersey. The Newark records have been preserved and show that Connie Mack ran up a
batting average of .500 and a fielding average
of .917. After a second year with Hartford,
batting .248 and fielding .953, he was sold,
with four other players, to the Washington
National League Club. The price for all
five was $3,500—"a big amount for talent in
those days."

Mack's batting average in the major leagues
was never the same after a certain change in
the rules. He "got along pretty well" when
the "throwers" were required to pitch the
batters the kind of balls they ordered; but
when they stopped giving him the high balls
he wanted, then he "couldn't hit for sour
apples"—and neither could a lot of top batters.
During the four seasons Mack played with
Washington he batted .361, .220, .186, and
.292—with the dead ball; as catcher he was
fielding .932, .904, .916, and .903. He caught
barehanded, according to the custom, picking
up the underhanded pitch on the first bounce
from forty-five feet away. "In the '80's the
rule for major league batters was seven balls
and three strikes, except for one year, 1887,
when it was four strikes." Those were the
days when players provided their own equipment, attended to their own injuries, played if
they could stand up, and might with impunity
knock down an umpire by way of expressing
disagreement. Three or four thousand spec-

tators constituted a great crowd. Throwing a curve ball was known to be impossible: eminent physicists declared it contrary to the laws of nature.

In the fall of 1888 the National League, alarmed by players' rising salaries, enacted the Brush Classification Rule, which allowed players an annual minimum of $1,500 and a maximum of $2,500. When 1889 proved an especially profitable baseball season, the Brotherhood of Professional Players determined that its members should have a greater share of the gate receipts; and in 1890, having found financial backers, they formed the Players' League of eight clubs. Connie Mack was catcher-infielder for the Buffalo club, batting .268 and fielding .939.

The Players' League was a financial wreck at the end of one season; and, after a general shake-up, Mack joined the new twelve-club National League's Pittsburgh team. He caught for them six seasons in addition to the managerial duties he assumed in 1894, batting .210, .257, .325, .257, .362, and .210, and fielding .941, .949, .885, .938, .916, and .933. Now that he had a chance to put his ideas on baseball management into practice he took the unprecedented step of forbidding his men to drink during the season. As was customary, however, "the bad blood and heat of the game carried right on through and far into the night. The fans sometimes horned into these brawls, and pop bottles flew like confetti."

From Pittsburgh, Mack went to the Western League's Milwaukee club as manager in 1897. Here for the last time he played on the team as catcher-first baseman, batting .254 and fielding .962. In the twelve years of his major league playing career Mack played in a total of 736 games, came to bat 2,827 times, and scored 421 runs from 705 hits for a total of 860 bases. He made 3,311 put-outs and was credited with 910 assists, as compared with 342 errors. Mack's all-time batting and fielding averages stand at .249 and .925; he never made a home run.

At the turn of the century, when the National League cut down its membership from twelve clubs to the original eight, the way was clear for the newly formed American League to establish teams in the four deprived cities. This encouraged the new group to expand, establishing four Eastern clubs in competition with the National. As Connie Mack modestly put it, "The Philadelphia franchise fell to me, and I betook myself to that city to interest local capital." This he found in Benjamin F. Shibe, a manufacturer of baseball equipment, who became the club president. All Mack needed then was a baseball park and a team to play in it. Having disposed of these problems and discovered the fabulous Rube Waddell, Mack made of the Athletics "a team that had something to say about who won what and why"—to the extent of winning the 1902 championship. After that season the National League agreed to recognize its new rival, and a National Commission was set up to arbitrate disputes between clubs. (This body was replaced by a single commissioner, Judge Kenesaw Mountain Landis '44, after the "White Sox scandal" of 1920.)

With his gift of practical psychology Connie Mack turned a jeering phrase into a useful slogan by adopting "White Elephants" as his team's nickname and insigne. Second in 1903, the club won the American League championship in 1905 and again in 1910, the year when the "dead" ball was replaced by the "lively" baseball. In the latter year the Philadelphia team also won the World Series from the National League champions, giving them the world championship. This accomplished, Mack began to reorganize his Series-winning team. "I had started in 1901," he explains, "with a veteran outfit which was right at its peak or maybe coming down a little bit on the sunset side, and I saw the need of young blood." This policy naturally displeased the fans, who could see no reason for selling their favorites "down the river." Meanwhile the Athletics' new ball grounds, Shibe Park, was being built to an unprecedented size. In 1907 and at the end of the 1909 season, during which thousands were turned away from the "over-ambitious" ball park, the Athletics finished second in the League, losing to Detroit by a game and a half. Mack was slowly grooming his "gang of kids" for a championship.

"The timeless flavor of his policy," remarks John Lardner, "is a rebuke to impatient churls . . . who can hardly wait till next year. Philadelphia is willing to wait fifteen or twenty years for Mr. Mack." Mack's success with this long-range approach in a league whose clubs average one new manager every 2.9 years can be attributed in part to his own baseball "know-how," part to the peculiar temperament of the Philadelphia fan, who becomes bored with persistent winners, and part to the share of the Philadelphia Athletics owned by Connie Mack.

The Athletics finished the 1910 season fifteen games ahead of the League and went on to win the World Series from the Chicago Cubs. This feat they repeated in 1911, with the famed "$100,000 infield" of Baker, Barry, Collins, and McInnis, any one of whom would bring more than that amount today. The team's World Series opponents in 1911 were the New York Giants. "We won in 1910 and 1911," Connie Mack muses, "and in 1912 we were at our best—but we lost." That season the backers of the newly formed New York Highlanders offered him a "pretty fabulous" salary to be their manager; but the Shibes appealed to his loyalty, and he stayed with the Athletics. (The Highlanders did all right without him, however, especially after their name was changed to the Yankees.) Next the Athletics "took another pennant and went into their annual act with the Giants," emerging as the 1913 world champions.

This team broke up, too, due to the efforts of the rival Federal League; although the Athletics won the pennant the next year, they lost all four World Series games to the Boston Braves. After two leading players had jumped to the Federal League, Mack salvaged the rest by selling them to other American League teams. (The Federal League, in spite of its strong financial backing, was dissolved in 1915.) Mack "took a beating from the public who didn't know the inside reasons for

CONNIE MACK

the breakup." As he dryly commented, "The fact that the local fans had been staying away from Shibe Park in droves and yawning with boredom when they read of another Athletic victory didn't soften the storm of abuse that was showered upon my head." Then came the First World War. "I pulled my purse in and nickeled along through the first of seven lean years, establishing a new all-time record for remaining in the baseball cellar. Then, when the War was over . . . I was a couple of years behind the procession when I finally got under way again." In 1926, 1927, and 1928 the Athletics were contenders once more, however, and in 1929 they were again World Series winners. In that Series Mack pulled "the biggest surprise in the history of baseball" when he started with pitcher Howard Ehmke, who was known to be ripe for retirement. Ehmke thereupon confounded all observers by striking out thirteen Cubs, setting a record which still stands. His manager was awarded the 1929 Bok Prize—$10,000, a gold medal, and a citation—for service to Philadelphia. This was the first time the award had been made to anyone but some eminent intellectual; yet, as the New York *Herald Tribune* remarked, "Connie Mack has given the Bok Prize publicity it never had before."

Mack's team won the 1930 World Series and again took the American League pennant in 1931. But the attendance dropped off in 1930, becoming still worse the following years— although Mack had "the highest-priced ball club in the history of the game." Once again he was forced to break up a great team because it was too good for Philadelphia. This happened, too, in 1935, when he sold four of his star players to Boston. Since that time the Philadelphia Athletics have seldom been long out of last place in the baseball listings, piling up "a record of defeat never equaled by any other team in major league baseball." But Connie Mack, as always, has taken his time about building up "one of those fine teams that

Philadelphia expects him to supply once in every generation or so."

"Life Begins at Seventy-three" was the appropriate title for the first article of a series Mack wrote about his experiences for the *Saturday Evening Post* in 1936. In these he said: "I never let my personal liking or dislike for a player influence me in my treatment of him . . . but the moment I make up my mind that forbearance and toleration will not work with that player I am through with him once and for all." "It has hurt me worse to break up my great teams than it has the fans." "I am rather proud to say that I began the business of conducting [pre-game conference] meetings. . . . There was only one unfortunate aftermath. The boys all began to ask me questions I couldn't answer."

It is said that "Some managers never think about the players when they leave the club. Still others take good care to see that a star doesn't go to a serious contender. Not Connie. He thinks of the players." Eddie Collins, who starred under Mack, spent several years as his assistant, and then became manager of the Boston team, thinks "You would have to comb the world to find a man possessed of such ability to make human beings extend themselves." A poll of sportswriters in May 1944 gave him first place as the manager most liked by players as well as writers.

Even when the Athletics' poor showing had become a tradition Philadelphians would say, "Let's go watch Connie this afternoon." On January 11, 1937 Mack was elected president and treasurer of the Club; and when the National Baseball Museum was opened at Cooperstown, New York, in July 1938, Connie Mack was one of the fifteen "Builders of Baseball" immortalized in its Hall of Fame. In 1940 he increased his share of the Athletics to fifty per cent. The following year the Pennsylvania Government set each May 17 as a state Connie Mack Day; George M. Cohan, from his home town, wrote a song entitled "Connie Mack Is the Grand Old Name"; and 15,000 baseball fans assembled to honor the seventy-eight-year-old veteran, against his wishes, by changing the name of Shibe Park to Connie Mack Stadium.

More honors came to Mack in August 1944, on the fiftieth anniversary of his entrance into major league management. A giant baseball supported on ten-foot bats was set up before the Philadelphia city hall, bearing the town's congratulations. Gifts poured in. More than twenty-nine thousand enthusiasts braved the ninety-six degree heat and the serious transit strike to jam Shibe Park for the ceremonies, at which Ted Husing '42 was master of ceremonies, Abbott '41 and Costello '41 entertained, a band played, a congratulatory telegram from President Roosevelt '42 was read. As a climax, specially invited members of Mack's "dream team" of living stars appeared in their old uniforms: Babe Ruth '44, Bill Dickey, George Sisler, Eddie Collins, Honus Wagner, Lefty Grove, Walter Johnson, Tris Speaker, and Frank (Home Run) Baker. (The other two members, Mickey Cochrane and Ty Cobb, were occupied, respectively, with Navy duty and poison ivy.) Grove and Collins had played for Philadelphia; the others represented six different clubs. Far from thinking of retirement, the star of the occasion was making plans for rebuilding his ball park, at a cost of $1,000,000, and was working on deals to acquire several new farm clubs, first establishing a "working agreement" with the Toronto Maple Leafs. (This means that the major team contributes to the minor's expenses, getting first choice of their best players in return.)

"It's such a little time I've been around," says Connie Mack. And he intends to continue telling his boys what to do until they have to tell him—even though, as he says, "I'm old. I've never been strong physically. I've got to save myself during the day." Every afternoon for a number of years he has stopped work to take a thirty-minute nap; and not until a game starts does he appear in the dugout, dressed in his characteristic blue suit. If it's a hot day there will be a handkerchief wrapped around his long neck under the high stiff collar. After the game Mack goes straight to his Germantown home, never willingly leaving it during the evening. "But of course Mrs. Mack likes the theatre," he adds, "and so in season we always go." Mrs. Mack is the former Katherine Hallahan, whom Mack married in 1910. Three sons by a previous marriage are associated with him in the Athletics: Roy Mack as vice-president and secretary, Earle Mack as assistant manager and coach, and Connie Mack, Jr., in the business office. Connie Mack, 3rd, is batboy.

"Despite his years in a business where tobacco is more often chewed than smoked," comments *Newsweek*, "Mack has remained the prim, stiff-collared Germantown gentleman. The frantic wavings of his scorecard as he transmits his famous wigwag signals to the field are punctuated only by such exclamations as 'Gracious!' and 'Goodness me!' But . . . Mr. Mack can be just as tough as the rarin'est tearin'est manager in the business." Devoutly religious, "the Old Man" has acted throughout his career on the assumption that "it is possible to be aggressive without resorting to rowdy tactics." A Philadelphia institution, he would rather people didn't pay so much attention to him when he enters some public place: a slight hush falls, and everyone straightens up. And well they may, for Connie Mack's six feet one and 150 pounds are carried with an erectness that would do credit to a cadet a quarter of his age. "He was never in a hurry," says John Lardner, "and time, like Philadelphia, will just have to wait for Connie Mack."

References

Am Mag 109:42-3+ Je '30 il pors
Newsweek 20:78-9 D 28 '42 pors
Sat Eve Post 208:5-7+ F 22 '36 il pors; 208:16-17+ Ap 4 '36 il; 211:20-1+ O 1 '38 pors
Time 31:34-6 Ja 3 '38 il pors
Kern, J. D. and Griggs, I. eds. This America p501-9 1942
Spink, J. G. T. ed. Baseball Register 1943
Who's Who in America 1944-45

MCKITTRICK, THOMAS H(ARRINGTON) Mar. 14, 1889- President of International Bank of Settlements

Address: b. Centralbahnstrasse 7, Basle, Switzerland; h. Milton, Mass.

"A neutral in office hours" is Thomas H. McKittrick, American president of the German-controlled Bank of International Settlements which has offices in Basle, Switzerland. The other executives of the bank are a German, a Vichyite, an Italian, and a Dutchman, and since the outbreak of war in 1939 "these men have been sitting side by side each morning, with discussions limited strictly to financial problems." There is a tacit agreement that politics and war will never be discussed while they carry on the bank's activities.

The B.I.S. was conceived in 1929, ostensibly to handle German reparation payments, its directors made up of the leading central bankers of the world. Protocols signed by the leading European powers in 1930 and 1936 (and intended to give sanctuary to the funds of the B.I.S. wherever deposited and to protect the assets of neutrals in countries at war) make its activities "immune from any disabilities and from any restrictive measures such as censorship, requisition, seizure, or confiscation, in time of peace or war." For years, however, most of the funds deposited at the B.I.S. have been loaned to the Germans, who have also absorbed most of their fellow stockholders' interests through seizure of the central banks in the occupied countries, and in 1944 the overwhelming majority of the bank's shares as well as its executive officers and directors are controlled by the Axis. Commentators hint that in using the facilities of the B.I.S. big business in Germany hopes to survive after the War and "even continue to dominate European economy."

Thomas Harrington McKittrick was born March 14, 1889 in St. Louis, Missouri, the son of Thomas Harrington and Hildegarde (Sterling) McKittrick. After studying at the St. Louis Manual Training School for two years, he attended the Hackley School in Tarrytown, New York, from 1905 to 1907, and then went on to Harvard. He received his B.A. from that university in 1911.

At Harvard young McKittrick had edited the *Crimson*, but this was his last venture in journalism. He returned to St. Louis to enter his father's wholesale firm, the Hargadine, McKittrick Dry Goods Company, and he remained in the dry goods business for the next three years. For a year (1914-15) he was with the St. Louis Union Trust Company while taking postgraduate work at St. Louis University. In 1916 he went East to join the National City Bank of New York, and that same year he was sent to Genoa, Italy, by the bank. His banking career was interrupted by America's entrance into the First World War. In 1918 he served as a 2nd lieutenant in the American Expeditionary Force, and the next year he was promoted to the rank of 1st lieutenant and cited for meritorious services.

When McKittrick returned to the United States in 1919 it was to join Lee Higginson & Company in New York City. This firm is closely associated with Higginson & Company

THOMAS H. MCKITTRICK

in London, and in 1922 he was sent to England to join the latter firm. From 1924 to 1929 he was a partner in the London house. In 1930 he also became a member of the executive committee and honorary treasurer of the American Relief Society and a director of the American Chamber of Commerce in London. The next year he became a member of the German Credits Arbitration Committee, whose vice-chairman he was to be in 1933. It was not until June 1939 that he was elected to the presidency of the Bank of International Settlements, the first American to hold this post since 1935. (Before that date the B.I.S. had had two American presidents.)

The B.I.S. had been more or less a brain child of Dr. Hjalmar Schacht '44, who was a member of its board of directors until 1938 and who is still its "leading brain," according to Heinz Pol in *PM*. Organized in Paris in June 1929, when the Young Committee had decided that a world bank was needed to receive German reparations payments without dislocating the currencies of the receiving nations, the bank was established at Basle the next year, with an authorized initial capital of $100,000,000 and with $25,000,000 paid in. (Actually all the B.I.S. keeps is books—all sums of money were to be shifted and transferred.) Each of the great central banks of England, France, Germany, Italy, and Belgium had their representatives on the board of directors, and Japan and the United States participated through commercial banks. Fifty-six per cent of the bank's shares were owned by these large central and commercial banks, and the remaining 44 per cent were distributed among the central banks of eleven smaller nations. According to one commentator, this meant that "the self-interest of the bank—except conceivably in the case of a war with Russia, where banking is not thought much of—would inevitably be on the side of peace." (This statement, however, meant one thing in January 1930—another in 1944.)

Five months after the birth of the B.I.S. the Wall Street market crashed, and it was not much later, on June 15, 1931, that Germany's reparations payments ended. It was believed, however, that the B.I.S. would be useful in expediting capital transfers, stabilizing currencies, and rushing short-term funds to danger points; and its directors continued to meet. In any case, according to Leon Fraser, a former president of the B.I.S., the functions not connected with reparations, though ostensibly secondary, had actually been the predominant motives for the establishment of the B.I.S. The institution, he said, had been envisaged primarily as an instrument for opening up new fields of world trade by means of fresh extensions of credit.

Actually the functions of the bank grew more and more limited, its character less and less genuinely international. Of the 200,000 shares outstanding in B.I.S., 20,000 had originally been sold in the United States through a consortium of the First National Bank of New York, First National of Chicago, and J. P. Morgan & Company. When Britain and the United States went off the gold standard Americans sold all but 3,000 of their shares to European individuals and organizations. The continuation of the world depression, with the contraction of foreign trade and international investment, also prevented the bank from developing very far as an international clearinghouse for the transfer of credit. Soon a great part of the bank's assets were largely invested in Hitler's '42 Germany and in Axis satellite countries. Basle became mainly a place where leading financiers of the world discussed their common fiscal worries every spring.

And even before the War the majority on the B.I.S. directorate were friendly to Germany. Some time prior to Munich the Czech Government removed part of its banking funds from Prague and deposited gold bullion amounting to some $30,000,000 with the B.I.S. The Czech gold had then been handed over to the Bank of England (whose governor, Montagu Norman '40, was also a member of the B.I.S. directorate) for safekeeping. In March 1939, however, the Nazis occupied Prague. An order was presented to B.I.S. to transfer the gold to the German account; the order was honored, and Norman was instructed to pay the gold to the Reichsbank. He obeyed. It was shortly after this, while anti-Nazis were criticizing Norman and saying that the B.I.S. should be dissolved, that McKittrick accepted the presidency of the bank. He did not actually take over the post until January 1, 1940, however; before that date he visited London, Berlin, Paris, and Rome, talking to the governors of the various banks of issue. As he put it later, all told him to cut down the business of the bank and to follow a policy of strict neutrality.

With the coming of the Second World War the Nazis, if they had wished to do so, could have compelled the B.I.S. to close its doors at any moment—for by that time B.I.S. funds loaned to Germany were in excess of the capital of the bank. The Nazi Government, however, continued to transfer in dollars, at the appointed dates, the interest accruing on its debt. This enabled the bank to remunerate its shareholders with a dividend of 6 per cent every year until 1944, when the dividend was only 4 per cent—due, no doubt, to Allied bombings. Four times—in the springs of 1940, 1941, 1942, and 1943—McKittrick walked into the empty room of the bank's five-story building in Basle and went by himself through the motions of presenting and accepting the annual report and declaring the annual dividend, authorized to do so by the proxies of the bank's absent directors. In May 1940 the Nazi invasion of France resulted in B.I.S. headquarters being set up temporarily in Chateau-d'Oex, a little mountain resort near Lake Geneva, for Basle was uncomfortably close to the gunfire. Free from any kind of traveling restrictions, the president continued to visit Berlin, Rome, London, and other capitals. (In the spring of 1943, when he returned to Europe after a vacation in the United States, he used an Italian diplomatic visa.) After Pearl Harbor he kept his post at the request of German and Italian members of the B.I.S. "I realize it is my duty to perform a neutral task in wartime," he told a New York *Herald Tribune* interviewer. "It is an extremely difficult and trying thing to do, but I do the best I can. . . . The policy of the bank can only be to remain entirely outside all matters of politics."

But as the War went on, criticism of British and American participation in the bank increased. Wrote *Time* Magazine in 1943: "Periodically the B.I.S. is accused in the House of Commons, the United States Congress, and elsewhere of being: (1) a clearinghouse of international espionage; (2) a shelter of international finance; (3) an instrument of possible appeasement. On such occasions high United States or British officials come to the bank's defense and explain that its business, under McKittrick, is so conducted that none of its operations could possibly confer an advantage on any belligerent nation at the expense of another. These operations consist chiefly of: (1) collecting interest; (2) semiautomatic renewal of maturing investments (no new ones are made); (3) extending limited credits to central banks; (4) handling payments under the international postal agreement and pre-War treaties: (5) acting as banker for the International Red Cross organizations operating from Switzerland."

Yet the criticism went on. According to Heinz Pol in *PM*, among the funds of the bank is a long-term deposit of 76,000,000 gold francs belonging to high German officials who want an emergency fund in a place whose safety is beyond doubt. Pol says, too, that German and Vichy French directors of the B.I.S. participated in a scheme to get money belonging to certain Franco-German cartels out of Europe and into Algiers, where it was exchanged for American dollars. Dr. Harry White '44, monetary adviser to Secretary of the Treasury Henry A. Morgenthau '40, has charged that Germany is anxious to keep the B.I.S. alive "because she hopes to use it as an instrumentality for getting back into financial power." And the New York *Post* claimed, in February 1944, that through the B.I.S. the German World Economic Society, an organization of Germany's biggest industrialists and

financiers, was keeping in touch with a powerful group in England which before the War had been identified with appeasement. The Society had prepared the "Schacht Plan," offering the United States and Great Britain joint ownership with the present owners of German industry in return for a guarantee that Germany's financial leaders would choose the political leaders of post-War Germany and that the new German regime would be permitted an armed police force to keep "order."

Finally, on May 10, 1944, twelve days before the fourteenth annual "meeting" of B.I.S. directors at Basle, Representative John M. Coffee introduced a resolution into the United States Congress saying that such a meeting was an affront to the patriotic people of America, Britain, and the Soviet Union and constituted trading with the enemy. The New York *Herald Tribune* apparently agreed, in an editorial saying that the Germans were still on the B.I.S. board "prepared to do what they can to see to it that Germany escapes the financial consequences of the Second World War, now nearing its climax, as she did of the first. . . . Funds from the bank may be made to play a part in the Reich's next defalcation. That gigantic fraud will follow gigantic pillage and slaughter is taken for granted."

The Coffee resolution asked the United States State Department (which said it had granted no passports to any American bankers to go to Basle) to forbid McKittrick's participation at the session; but on May 22 McKittrick was present for the fifth time. (This time Ernst Weber, Swiss chairman of the board of directors, declared the dividend, however, while McKittrick, along with the German assistant general manager merely watched the votes being counted.) After the meeting the American president announced: "It naturally needs a considerable amount of tact on behalf of every one of us, but up to now we've been getting along nicely and expect to do so in the future. . . . The bank's annual meeting has dwindled during the past five years. We keep the machine ticking, however, because when the armistice comes the formerly hostile powers will need an efficient instrument such as the B.I.S."

But criticism of the B.I.S. had barely subsided when it arose again as the result of a resolution introduced by the Norwegian delegation at the World Monetary Conference held at Bretton Woods, New Hampshire, in July. The Norwegians requested the immediate post-War liquidation of the B.I.S. and the establishment of a United Nations commission to investigate the bank's transactions during the War. According to *PM*, the reasons behind the resolution are the danger that the bank will be an avenue of financial escape for the Axis, and the obstacle the bank presents to better world financial order which the United Nations are striving to bring about at the monetary meeting. However, the associate financial editor Edward H. Collins of the New York *Herald Tribune* held a different view. Collins maintained that the proposal was completely extraneous to the business of the conference and that whether the B.I.S. would be preferable to some new institution for purposes of currency stabilization was not particularly im-

MCKITTRICK, THOMAS H.—*Continued*
portant to the discussion at Bretton Woods.
The matter of the B.I.S. was not discussed at
the conference.

A white-haired man, self-effacing and mild,
Thomas McKittrick avoids the limelight as
much as he can. He speaks four languages—
and needs them, for most of his permanent
staff of 100 in Basle are German, French,
Italian, and other nationals. He relaxes by
writing papers on the life and habits of sea
birds, and is a member of the British Ornithologists' Union and an associate member of the
American Ornithologists' Union. His clubs
are the Harvard (New York City) and the
American (London). McKittrick was married on November 9, 1921 to Marjorie Benson,
and there are four children: Marjorie Sterling,
Elizabeth Benson, Mary, and Frances Anne.

References

Fortune 20:108 Ag '39 por
N Y Herald Tribune p10 D 7 '42
N Y Times p8 My 19 '43
Newsweek 15:63 Je 10 '40; 20:56 O 26
    '42
PM p6 My 11 '44
Time 41:87 Je 7 '43 por
Who's Who in America 1944-45

MCMANAMY, FRANK (mak-man'ə-mē)
Sept. 3, 1870—Oct. 3, 1944 Former chairman
of the Interstate Commerce Commission from
1930 to 1938; had been a member of the Commission for twenty-seven years, entering its
service in 1911 as assistant chief inspector of
locomotives.

Obituary

N Y Times p23 O 5 '44 por

**MCMURTRIE, DOUGLAS C(RAW-
FORD)** (mak-mėr'trē) July 20, 1888—Sept.
29, 1944 Designer of typography

Bulletin: Douglas C. McMurtrie died on
September 29, 1944.

From July 1944 issue:

Douglas C. McMurtrie is an important authority in the field of graphic arts. Combining
a practical knowledge of printing with a large
store of scholarly learning, he has made numerous valuable contributions to the study of
typography, bookmaking, and bibliography.

The son of William and Helen (Douglass)
McMurtrie, Douglas Crawford McMurtrie was
born in Belmar, New Jersey, July 20, 1888.
After attending the Hamilton Institute and
the Horace Mann School in New York City
and gaining valuable experience in journalism
by founding and editing a class magazine, he
went to Pennsylvania to study at the Hill
School. Douglas' father was a chemical engineer and planned a career in the sciences for
his son. The boy was sent to the Massachusetts Institute of Technology to study electrical engineering, but he soon discovered that
he was far more interested in journalism. Besides editing school publications, young Mc-
Murtrie served as Institute correspondent for
three of the Boston daily papers.

McMurtrie's first job was as statistician for
the Pittsburgh Typhoid Fever Commission.
The printing business proved so attractive to
him, however, that within a short time he returned to New York to do free-lance work as
a designer and producer of printing. Not
long afterward McMurtrie established his own
business. When a boyhood friend, Edward
Goodman, became a theatrical producer, Mc-
Murtrie designed and printed the weekly program for his productions. One of these programs came to the attention of Ingalls Kimball, the co-designer of the famous Cheltenham type and president of the Cheltenham
Advertising Agency. He was so impressed
with McMurtrie's work that he hired him as
general manager of the Cheltenham Press
and typographical adviser to the Cheltenham
Advertising Agency.

In 1917 McMurtrie became director of the
Columbia University Printing Office. Two
years later he left to become president of the
Arbor Press. McMurtrie had long had the
idea that the perfect location for a printing
press would be in the country, "yet close
enough to a large city to have easy contact
with customers and materials." The perfect
location turned out to be Greenwich, Connecticut, where he designed and built a model
printing plant. The printing work was of exceptional quality, all the more praised since
it was done in "a period when facilities for
the production of fine printing were relatively
scarce." But the expense of turning out such
printing was tremendous. In 1921 McMurtrie
sold out to the Condé Nast Publications. He
remained with that organization as general
manager of the Condé Nast Press until 1923;
then, for two more years he remained in New
York to engage in the production of fine printing. In 1925 he moved to Chicago to become
director of typography for the Cuneo Press.

One year later McMurtrie was offered the
post of director of typography of the Ludlow
Typograph Company, in Chicago. He accepted the position and has held it ever since.
In the meanwhile he continued ever-zealous in
improving American typography. He designed publications for the Metropolitan Museum of Art, for the Macmillan Company, and
for other organizations. Much of his work
has been included among the "Fifty Books of
the Year," a selection made by the American
Institute of Graphic Arts on the basis of the
physical excellence of the books—typographic
design, binding, paper, etc. McMurtrie has
published articles urging that printing innovations be adopted, and for one year he edited
the journal *Ars Typographica*.

Many forward strides in the field of typography were being made in Europe, and Mc-
Murtrie favored closer study of these methods. His own study resulted in the writing
of the book *Modern Typography and Layout*
(1929). In addition to helping to form the
Continental Typefounders Association which
brought many European type faces to the
United States, he imported certain types himself—Astrée, original Didot, Le Mercure, Nar-
ciss, and Cochin—and designed two type faces
which he had cut in matrices: "McMurtrie
Title" and "Vanity Fair Capitals." In 1944
he is chairman of the educational commission

of the International Association of Printing House Craftsmen, Inc.

It is for his bibliographical activities that McMurtrie is perhaps best known. Early in his career he became interested in the history of printing in the United States. Since the only book he could find on the subject had been published in 1810, he decided to write an up-to-date work. It was no small task, for there was little information on early American printing. His research began, therefore, with an investigation of local printing history, and, with the assistance of Albert H. Allen he began publishing histories of printing with bibliographies of local imprints for the separate states of the United States. The final result of this research will be a four-volume *History of Printing in the United States,* of which Volume II (the first to be published) appeared in 1936 and received excellent reviews. (This research was interrupted in 1936, when McMurtrie became the head of a WPA project.) By the end of 1942 McMurtrie's writings and compilations included 327 separate titles on the history of printing, many of them pamphlets and magazine articles. In the opinion of Lawrence C. Wroth, with Evans' *American Bibliography* and Brigham's *American Newspapers* as a foundation, McMurtrie has so fully recorded the history of the press in the United States in his twenty-three years of research "that little remains for the . . . historians to do except interpret its implications."

In the course of his bibliographical research McMurtrie discovered thousands of American imprints in libraries all over the country which he did not have time to record. In 1936 McMurtrie was offered the aid of WPA workers, and a WPA project known as the American Imprints Inventory was established with McMurtrie as its national editor. The project did elaborate research, issued forty-two publications, and when the WPA was discontinued the work was continued by the Bibliographical Society of America, which is financed by a grant from the Rockefeller Foundation.

Much of McMurtrie's work has been of great interest to scholars in fields other than the graphic arts. His publication of English translations of documents relating to the biography of Johann Gutenberg (*The Gutenberg Documents,* 1940) was well received as a contribution to the studies of fifteenth century history and law. In 1927 McMurtrie published *The Golden Book,* a history of the printed book. After going through four editions, *The Golden Book* went out of print, and in 1938 he published a revised and re-written work, *The Book.* A handsome volume, beautifully illustrated and printed, *The Book* traces the history of bookmaking from the first records of man's writing, through medieval manuscripts and early presses, down to the most modern printing devices. *The Book* was praised both for its erudition and popular appeal. McMurtrie, in collaboration with Don Farran, has also written the story of Johann Gutenberg, for children, under the title *Wings for Words* (1940). The other titles in the field of printing which he has either written or edited make a long list in *Who's Who in America.*

George Nelidoff

DOUGLAS C. McMURTRIE

Since 1912 McMurtrie's avocational interest has been the care and education of crippled children and the rehabilitation of all cripples. He soon discovered that there was little literature on the subject, and so he began to collect a library of his own. As editor of the *American Journal of Care for Cripples* from 1912 to 1919 McMurtrie was able to assemble and publish some much needed information. In 1915 he became president of the Federation of Associations for Cripples. When the First World War broke out he gave special attention to "the then new science of re-educating war cripples," and became director of the Red Cross Institute for Crippled and Disabled Men. The work of this group included the training of cripples for jobs, an employment service for them, research, and the establishment of an artificial limb shop on modern manufacturing principles. McMurtrie has described this work in his *The Disabled Soldier* (1919) and *Vocational Re-education of Disabled Soldiers and Sailors* (1918). In recent years McMurtrie has had a new interest—the underground press of Europe, a subject "so fascinating that he could not escape it." He has published several articles and has written a book on the subject, which will be published soon.

McMurtrie is described as a large man weighing over 275 pounds, "with graying hair verging toward white." Friendly and jovial, he finds recreation in dancing. Since February 20, 1915 he has been married to the former Adele Koehler. The couple have three children, Havelock Heydon, Helen Josephine, and Baskerville.

References

C S Mon p7 Mr 23 '40 por
N Y Herald Tribune Books p28 O 29 '44
Who's Who in America 1944-45

MCNAIR, LESLEY J(AMES) (mak-nār')
May 25, 1883—July (?) 1944 Lieutenant General, one of the "big four" of the United States
Army, who as commanding general of the
Army Ground Forces, directed the greatest
military training and conditioning job in history; killed by an American bomb while observing action of our front-line troops; credited by the War Department for saving untold
thousands of American lives through his insistence on realistic "battle conditioning"; see
sketch 1942 Yearbook.

Obituary

N Y Times p1+ Jl 28 '44 por

MCNARNEY, JOSEPH T(AGGART)
Aug. 28, 1893- United States Army officer
Address: b. c/o War Department, Washington, D. C.; h. 3133 Connecticut Ave., N. W.,
Washington, D. C.

In October 1944 announcement was made
of the appointment of Lieutenant General
Joseph T. McNarney as Deputy Supreme Allied Commander in the Mediterranean. Before
this, as General Marshall's [40] "right arm," McNarney served as Deputy Chief of Staff. He
was born in Emporium, Pennsylvania, August
28, 1893, the son of James Pollard McNarney
(a lawyer and "a tough prosecutor") and of
the former Helen Taggart ("an indomitable
temperance worker"). At the United States
Military Academy at West Point, from which
he was graduated in 1915, General Omar
Bradley [43] was one of his classmates. On
June 12, 1915 he was commissioned a 2nd
lieutenant of infantry.

After service with the 21st Infantry at
Vancouver, Washington, young McNarney
was transferred to Yuma, Arizona, where he
served from April to July 1916. Promoted
to the rank of 1st lieutenant, he then became
a student instructor at the Signal Corps Aviation School at San Diego, California. It was
there that he met his future wife, Helen
Bamberger, a San Diego schoolteacher, to
whom he was married in June 1917. By that
time McNarney had completed his flying
training, had received the rating of junior
military aviator, the permanent rank of captain, and the temporary rank of major, and,
after teaching at the school as an instructor
in meteorology and radio telegraphy until May
1917, had been assigned to duty with the 1st
Aero Squadron at Columbus, New Mexico.

In August 1917 McNarney was ordered to
France. From September 1917 to January 1918
he was on duty with the 1st Aero Squadron
at Etampes, Avord, and Amanty, also serving as assistant director of the 1st Corps Aeronautical School. By July 1918 he had seen
duty with Headquarters Air Service, General
Headquarters; service as director of the 2nd
Corps Aeronautical School; duty with Headquarters, Zone of Advance; service as flight
commander with the 1st Aero Squadron, Toul
Sector; and service on the staff of the 4th
Corps Observation Group. During the Chateau-Thierry offensive he was commanding officer of the Observation Group of the 1st
Corps and chief of air service of the 3rd Corps,
also serving on the staff of the chief of air
service of the 1st Army. During the St. Mihiel

offensive he commanded the Observation Group
of the 4th Corps; during the Meuse-Argonne
offensive, from August to October 1918, he
commanded the Observation Group of the 5th
Corps. Until February 1919 he was the air
service commander of the 6th Corps, after
which he commanded the Army Observation
Group of the 2nd Army until April of the
same year. On May 22, 1919 he was promoted
to the temporary rank of lieutenant colonel.
By this time he was on duty at General Headquarters in Paris, assisting in writing a manual
on observation.

McNarney remained in Paris until June, and
shortly after his return to the United States
was assigned to command Godman Field, Fort
Knox, Kentucky, until October 1919. He was
then placed in command of the flying school
at Gerstner Field, Lake Charles, Louisiana.
On February 21, 1920 he reverted to his permanent rank of captain, but on July 1, 1920
he was promoted to the permanent rank of
major, and on that same date was transferred
to the Air Service. In November 1920 he was
assigned to Langley Field, Virginia, and there
he was stationed for the next five years as
instructor at the Field Officers' School, the designation of which was later changed to the Air
Corps Tactical School. During the school
year 1920-1921 he was a student as well as an
instructor, and in June 1921 he received his
graduation certificate. In the fall of 1925 he
was assigned as a student at the Command and
General Staff School, Fort Leavenworth, Kansas, from which he was graduated in June
of the following year as an honor graduate.

Following a tour of duty of three years as
a member of the War Department General
Staff in the Air Section, Military Intelligence
Division, Washington, D.C., McNarney became a student at the Army War College,
Washington, D. C. In August 1930, after his
graduation, he was assigned as the commandant of the Primary Flying School at March
Field, Riverside, California. When this school
was transferred to Randolph Field, Texas, he
remained at March Field, California, on duty
as the commanding officer of the 7th Bombardment Group. At various times he also served
as executive officer and as the commanding officer of the 1st Bombardment Wing.

His next assignment was as instructor at
the Army War College, Washington, D. C., in
August 1933; he remained there until March
1935, when he was promoted to the temporary
rank of lieutenant colonel and transferred to
Langley Field, Virginia, to serve as assistant chief of staff, G-4, General Headquarters,
Air Force. He remained in this post until July
1938, being promoted to the permanent rank
of lieutenant colonel in June 1936, and was
then assigned to Hamilton Field, California.
There he remained until March 1939, when he
went to Washington, D. C., for duty in the
War Plans Division of the War Department
General Staff. After two months of this he
was appointed a member of the Joint Army and
Navy Planning Committee.

Then came the Second World War—and
in May 1940, promoted to the temporary rank
of colonel, McNarney was appointed a member of the Permanent Joint Defense Board
for Canada and the United States. On April

7, 1941 he received the temporary rank of brigadier general, and from May to December of that year he served as a member of the Special Observers Group in London, England. From December 1941 to January 1942 he was a member of the Roberts Commission that investigated the attack on Pearl Harbor. Then, promoted to the temporary rank of major general, he became chairman of the Reorganization Committee of the War Department. When in March 1942 the War Department put its streamlined reorganization into effect, giving added importance to the Air Forces and creating a more youthful General Staff (reduced to one-fifth its former size), McNarney was designated Deputy Chief of Staff of the United States Army, replacing two older officers. According to *Time* Magazine, his rise to the post was "in some ways symbolic of the Air Forces' new prestige in the Army. McNarney has a job of the first importance which might have gone to a groundsman. As General Marshall's trusted deputy, he alone is empowered to act in the name of the Chief on many matters which otherwise would sponge up General Marshall's crowded hours." Two months after this appointment McNarney was promoted to the temporary rank of lieutenant general, the rank which he still holds.

Considered a man who speaks only when he knows his facts, since his appointment McNarney has often served as spokesman for the War Department before the public and Congress. In November 1942 he criticized armchair strategists, saying that if the American public insisted upon passing judgment on the war effort without knowledge of the facts, it would pay dearly for its impatience. At the same time he insisted that the induction of eighteen- and nineteen-year-olds was a military necessity. The following month, in a *Labor for Victory* program broadcast over the NBC network, he predicted that the months just ahead would see the Allied forces extend offensive fronts into Europe and Asia.

In January 1943 the Senate Military Affairs Committee questioned the Deputy Chief of Staff about the present and proposed sizes of the Army, and he gave them good reasons for the Army's demand for 8,240,000 men, including officers, by the end of that year. In June the Army's budget of seven and a half billions, the largest appropriation bill in the history of any country, passed the House. No changes were made or even suggested in it after McNarney had told Congress that those decisive dollars would be "translated into decisive strategic and tactical plans." That same month, before a subcommittee of the Senate Committee on Appropriations, he disclosed the Army's intention of bringing the War home to Japan "in a most violent and destructive way."

In September 1943 McNarney appeared before the Senate Military Affairs Committee to announce that the General Staff believed that 7,700,000 men was the minimum force for the task ahead. This figure represented a reduction of 540,000 men in the original estimates of Army needs—a reduction due to the increase in shipments of equipment and the consequent reduction in shipping space.

U. S. Army Signal Corps

LT. GEN. JOSEPH T. MCNARNEY

That same month he told a conference of industrial, labor, and newspaper leaders that the German military leaders had given up hope of winning the War and were directing all their efforts to staving off defeat. Though the actual collapse of either Germany or Japan was remote, the stage was all set for decisive action by the Allies, he said.

In April 1944 it was McNarney who presented the details of a plan approved by the War Department for the post-War integration of the Army and Navy into a single department of the armed forces, before the special House committee on post-War military planning. He advocated a single "secretary of the armed forces"—under him three undersecretaries (one for the Army, one for the Navy, and a third for Air) and a common supply service. The chief of staff to the commander in chief would direct the military planning of the new department, heading a group that would include the military commanders of the Army, Navy, and Air Forces; planning would be done from the top down rather than from the bottom up, thus eliminating delays, overlapping, and needless expense. McNarney urged that the shift be made not later than six months after the end of the War, but that the details be left to the process of evolution. In May 1944 Senator Hill [43] of Alabama, Democratic whip, introduced a bill patterned on his suggestions. Opposition reared its head chiefly in the Navy: naval officials were reportedly concerned about the possible loss of control of their air arm.

During all these months McNarney's promotion to the rank of permanent major general had been held up, at first because he had appeared on the same list with General Patton [42], later because of Congressional debate over an order he himself had sent to command areas. In June, however, his nomination to the rank of permanent major general was finally approved. That same month a House appropriations committee recommended a fifty-billion-

MCNARNEY, JOSEPH T.—*Continued*

dollar fund to finance fighting troops during the fiscal year starting July 1, calling attention to McNarney's testimony that the approaching period would be one of heavy fighting, involving great numbers of American troops. Later the Deputy Chief of Staff's testimony before the Senate Appropriations Committee considering the House-approved measure was made public, and his prediction revealed that the United States would have an overseas fighting force of 5,000,000 by the end of the year, and that the movement would likely continue at a high rate during 1945.

The opportunity to see service on a fighting front finally came to McNarney in October 1944, when he was appointed Deputy Supreme Allied Commander in the Mediterranean, to succeed Lieutenant General Jacob L. Devers.[42] He will also serve as commanding general of the United States Mediterranean theatre of operations. Before his departure for overseas the General was awarded the Distinguished Service Medal for his work in directing the War Department Reorganization Committee, and the Legion of Merit for his service as chief of staff of the Special Army Observers' Group in London from May to December, 1941.

Lean and of medium height, with dark hair that is rapidly disappearing, McNarney has been called "dour, taciturn, officially ruthless." According to the New York *Times Magazine*, he is known as "one of the most ruthlessly honest executives in uniform. . . . Scotch-Irish conscience wouldn't let him give his best friend a break." Still rated as a command pilot, combat observer, and technical observer, he always takes the controls on flying trips, and he has frequently contributed articles on aviation and related subjects to military journals. He is a member of the Order of Daedalians; his clubs include the Army and Navy and the Army, Navy, and Marine Country Clubs in Washington, D. C.

References

N Y Sun p16 Jl 3 '43
N Y Times Mag p45 N 21 '43 por
Who's Who in Aviation 1942-43

MCNARY, CHARLES L(INZA) (mak-när'i) June 12, 1874—Feb. 25, 1944 Republican floor leader of the Senate, and a Senator from Oregon for twenty-six consecutive years—appointed in 1917; noted as a friend of the farmer; fought for farm aid legislation; see sketch 1940 Yearbook.

Obituary

N Y Times p1+ F 26 '44 por

MCPHERSON, AIMEE SEMPLE (mak-fér'sun) Oct. 9, 1890—Sept. 27, 1944 Evangelist; spent thirty-four years in spectacular evangelism, frequently punctuated by sensational episodes in her personal life; enabled to found and build the Angelus Temple in Los Angeles with contributions of her disciples.

Obituary

N Y Times p19 S 28 '44 por

MACRAE, JOHN Aug. 25, 1866—Feb. 18, 1944 President since 1923 of E. P. Dutton & Company, publishers; considered book publishing a public responsibility; fought the advent of book clubs.

Obituary

N Y Times p35 F 20 '44 por

MAGLIONE, LUIGI, CARDINAL (mäl-yō'nä) 1877—Aug. 22, 1944 Papal Secretary of State since 1939; titular Archbishop of Casarea in Palestine and Papal Nuncio to Switzerland in 1920; from 1926 to 1936, Papal Nuncio to France; elevated to the Cardinalate in 1935; called back to Rome to head the important Congregation of the Council in 1936, which position he held until appointed Secretary of State.

Obituary

N Y Times p19 Ag 23 '44 por

MAILLOL, ARISTIDE (JOSEPH BONAVENTURE) (ma"yôl' a"rēs"tēd') Dec. 8, 1861—Oct. (?) 1944 French sculptor, considered by some the greatest since Auguste Rodin; carved monuments to Blanqui and Cézanne and a number of large graceful statues executed in the Greek tradition of the fifth century B.C.; see sketch 1942 Yearbook.

Obituary

N Y Times p10 O 6 '44

MALINOVSKY, RODION Y(AKOVLEVICH) (mä-le-nôf'-ske rō-dión ya-ku-vlye-vich) 1899(?)- Soviet Army officer

Address: Commissariat for Defense, Moscow

In perhaps the most dramatic home-coming of the Second World War, Marshal (then General) Rodion Y. Malinovsky recaptured his native city of Odessa on April 10, 1944, driving the enemy into the Black Sea. The triumph was symbolical to all Russians. It had been the mother city of the anti-Czarist revolution and the first major Soviet city to fall to the Nazi invaders. Moscow gave Malinovsky's 3rd Ukrainian Army its biggest salute—twenty-four salvos of red, white, and green flares, and the thunder of 324 massed artillery guns.

Like most of the commanders of the Soviet Army, Rodion Yakovlevich Malinovsky is young. He was born some forty-five years ago in Odessa. Before he was eighteen he was a corporal in the Imperial Russian Army, fighting in the First World War. He was sent to France with his division in 1915, making the slow journey via Siberia, Singapore, the Indian Ocean, and the Mediterranean Sea. In the trenches of France at Amiens and Saint-Mihiel he fought side by side with French, British, and American troops, and he comments today: "I shall never forget the British. Shaving in the darkest days, pipes perpetually between their teeth, they never moved faster than a walk whether in advance or retreat." Of the Americans Malinovsky says: "In spirit the Russians and the Americans got along together better than any two nationalities—especially when it came to having a drink or smashing glasses in a cafe."

While still in France Malinovsky heard rumors of a revolution in Russia. The men in his brigade refused to fight, much to the chagrin of the Allied forces around them, and demanded to return to Russia to take part in the uprising. Malinovsky managed to get to Siberia, where he joined a Red rifle division and became an officer. When the Revolution ended Malinovsky remained in the Army. He studied at Soviet military schools and prepared for a career of leadership in the Red Army.

When the Second World War broke out Malinovsky was a major general. He took part in the action against German General von Kleist '43 near Dnepropetrovsk in 1941 and was awarded the Order of Lenin for his work there. In 1942 he was present at Stalingrad when General von Manstein '42 tried to come to the aid of the German divisions of General von Paulus trapped in the city. Along with Generals Rokossovsky '44, Konev '43, and Tolbukhin (known as "the Four Horsemen of the German Apocalypse"), Malinovsky turned the German counteroffensive into a rout. His troops captured Kotelnikovo and, by this capture, says Walter Kerr, they "ended any hope Hitler '42 may have had of rescuing his trapped 6th Army at Stalingrad."

On January 29, 1943 Malinovsky received one of the highest honors his country offers, the Order of Suvorov, 1st Degree. In less than one month's time he proved that the honor had not been undeserved by leading his troops to recapture Rostov, "the gateway to the Caucasus." Rostov was the key to the entire Donets River bend region, a tremendously valuable industrial area. Almost simultaneous with the fall of Rostov came the announcement of the capture of Voroshilovgrad, "biggest industrial city in the Donets Basin" and a strong point in the German defense line.

Malinovsky was promoted from colonel general to the rank of full army general in April 1943. Meanwhile his armies were pressing the siege on German-held Kharkov, Russia's fourth largest city. Kharkov did not fall until the summer of 1943, but Malinovsky recognized the fact that the city was doomed long before the Nazis surrendered. Early in 1943 he had said, "The German Army will never be able to conduct an offensive on the same scale as it did last summer. But on one sector at a time, with a more limited objective, it will be able to launch strong offensive operations." Shortly before the fall of Rostov he reported a "faltering quality of German generalship and indecision in the Nazi High Command."

One of the most bitterly contested campaigns in the fall of 1943 took place around Zaporozhye, an important industrial city in the Dnieper region. Although his armies had begun their offensive here early in September, capturing the city of Stalino and freeing the Donets River Basin, Malinovsky realized that "the complicated nature of the German defensive system made it clear the enemy was prepared to fight a major battle to hold the city." Only sheer strength and persistence made it possible for the Russians to break down the German defenses at Zaporozhye. General Malinovsky's plan for storming Zaporozhye,"

MARSHAL RODION Y. MALINOVSKY

writes Ralph Parker in the New York Times, "consisted of punching two gaps at points nearest the city, to split the defenders into three isolated parts." His victory there was hailed as "a decisive blow at the entire German line from the Crimea northwestward to White Russia."

From Zaporozhye, Malinovsky's troops advanced on Melitopol. Around this city some of the bloodiest fighting of the War took place. The Germans had fortified the city strongly with trenches and anti-tank systems, and in many places the Russians were forced "to cut their way in with the bayonet." The Red armies were held back temporarily as Hitler issued a "stand-or-die" order to the Nazis in Melitopol. But the city fell to the Russians on October 23, and the drive in the Dnieper region continued. Three days later Malinovsky's men crossed the Dnieper River and effected a union with the armies of General Konev, thus virtually freeing the Dnieper bend area. The industrial centers of Dnepropetrovsk and Dneprodzerzhinsk both fell to the Red Army. Krivoi Rog, the last important city of the vital Ukrainian region, was under assault. Here once more the Germans put up a strong defense, and the siege was long and bitter. Meanwhile Malinovsky was leading an army southwest of Dnepropetrovsk in the direction of Nikopol while another army under the leadership of General Tolbukhin also advanced on that city.

Early in 1944 it was estimated that more than five German divisions had been trapped in the region between Krivoi Rog and Nikopol. As General Vatutin's '44 troops raced into pre-1939 Poland, Malinovsky and his armies tightened their hold on some 90,000 Germans trapped in this area. "After months of stalemate in the Dnieper bend, General Malinovsky's troops leaped forward in four-day gains ranging from twenty-eight to thirty-seven miles. Stalin's '42 citations disclosed that every Red Army service was employed, in-

MALINOVSKY, RODION Y.—*Continued*

fantry, tanks, artillery, and planes, in the break-through northeast of Krivoi Rog and Nikopol." And Nikopol, the city which had supplied the Nazis with sixty per cent of their vitally needed manganese, was captured by the Red Army on February 8, after days of desperate street fighting between the Nazis and Malinovsky's men. In spite of freak weather —snows, rains, and flood—the 3rd Ukrainian Army continued to strike at the very center of German forces at Krivoi Rog. On February 22 Malinovsky's men captured that city.

"Malinovsky took Odessa on April 10 with a typical Red Army maneuver," wrote *PM*'s Ken Clark. "Cavalry and mobile forces, in a swift flanking movement, clamped a siege arc about the city and when the circle was complete, heavy forces made a frontal attack." They were aided by an army of 10,000 Odessans who had lived underground for two years in the sewers and catacombs. With the Ukraine back in Russian hands, Hitler's satellite states were now within reach.

The Red Army on the south Russian front held its fire through the summer months; then, when Rumania broke with the Axis in August 1944, it "struck in thunder." Storming through the Galati Gap into Rumania, Malinovsky's 2nd Ukrainian Army marched down the Carpathian flank to Iasi, which fell after twenty-four hours hand-to-hand fighting. After taking Focsani to the south it captured the Ploesti oil fields which supplied more than one-third of Hitler's war machine. Thirty-three German generals were among the prisoners. A few days later Malinovsky's men entered Bucharest, the capital of Rumania and the first enemy capital taken by the Red Army.

About a week later (September 12) Malinovsky, on behalf of the United Nations, signed an armistice with Rumania, and was simultaneously promoted to marshal. By mid-October his 2nd Ukrainian Army was in Hungary and had crossed the Tisza River in the drive on Budapest. During the next six weeks a stream of dispatches from that front recorded the combined advance of Malinovsky's and Marshal Fedor I. Tolbukhin's armies upon the Hungarian capital. While part of the forces had completed the encirclement of the city by the end of December other moves brought the 2nd Ukrainian Army across the Slovak border to within approximately one hundred miles of Vienna.

Malinovsky, who is of "medium height, stocky and with thick black hair," is regarded by Soviet Army authorities as "a subtle and original tactician, second only to Rokossovsky as a daring and two-fisted commander." He is married and the father of two children. Walter Kerr reports an interview with him which Malinovsky opened by commenting: "It's not bad weather. It's good for war."

References

Time 41:24 F 8 '43; 42:26 S 13 '43
Kerr, W. The Russian Army 1943

MANNING, MARIE *See* **FAIRFAX, B.**

MANSON, JOHN T(HOMAS) Aug. 30, 1861—Feb. 21, 1944 Industrialist, banker, and church leader; former director of the Equitable Life Assurance Society; president of the American Bible Society; a former vice-moderator of the Presbyterian Church in the United States.

Obituary

N Y Times p23 F 22 '44

MANTLE, (ROBERT) BURNS Dec. 23, 1873- Dramatic critic and theatre annalist

Address: b. 220 E. 42nd St., New York City; h. 44 Seasongood Rd., Forest Hills Gardens, Long Island, N. Y.

The yearbooks of the American drama edited by Burns Mantle (*Best Plays of 1919-1920*, *Best Plays of 1920-1921*, etc.) have been unanimously acclaimed for their accuracy and for their invaluable usefulness in any library which keeps a record of the theatre in the United States. In the reference field Mantle's name is as prominently associated with the theatre as Webster's is with dictionaries or Bartlett's with quotations. Mantle, critic emeritus of the New York *Daily News* and dean of New York drama critics before his retirement in 1943 after forty-five years of devotion to the theatre, has achieved an enviable reputation for integrity in his work.

Born in Watertown, New York, on December 23, 1873, Robert Burns Mantle is the son of Robert Burns and Susan (Lawrence) Mantle. When he was still very young, his family moved to Denver, where he attended elementary school. After that a great-aunt who had been an essayist tutored him in high-school subjects. He began his newspaper career in California as a printer's devil, and by 1892 had become an expert linotype operator. Today Mantle's sensitive fingers are still so "fussy about the touch and speed of his typewriter that he keeps his machine padlocked when he is not using it."

When Mantle was a child he appeared once on the stage—as the interlocutor in a children's minstrel show—and as a youth he became an avid theatre-goer, spending as much as he could spare from his linotypist's salary on theatre tickets. This enthusiasm opened the way to his career as a critic. Although he was preparing to enter Stanford University, on his way to the Chicago World's Fair in 1892 he stopped off in Denver, where he ended up as a substitute linotypist with the Denver *Post*. While he was there an amusing incident occurred which may have given him a suggestion for his future profession. One evening the acting dramatic critic for the paper, scholarly Frederick W. White from New York, handed in a review he had scribbled a short time before his deadline. When linotypist Mantle was unable to decipher the writing, he wrote a short review of his own, having seen the performance that afternoon at the Tabor Grand Opera House. White, when he heard the story, was amused and pleased, Mantle reports.

Shortly after this Mantle became a reporter on the Denver *Times*, and in the course of six years became its drama editor after an unsuccessful try as columnist of theatrical news. He held the new post for two years, in 1900 going over to the Denver *Republican,* and the next year moving on to Chicago where he worked first as drama critic on the *Inter-Ocean* (1901-07) and later on the Chicago *Tribune* (1907-08). In 1908 he became the *Tribune's* Sunday editor. In speaking of his Sunday editorship, Mantle has said that he was no worse than any other Sunday editor, but that after he had printed the Hope diamond story three times he decided it was time to make a change.

It was as a salesman for the young Chicago *Tribune* syndicate that Mantle first came to New York, on September 25, 1911, the opening date of George M. Cohan's *The Little Millionaire.* He approached T. E. Niles, managing editor of the *Evening Mail* (now defunct), hoping to sell him some syndicate features. "We don't need any features," Niles is reported to have snapped, "we need a drama critic." Mantle's reputation as a critic, his "bright, newsy, and comprehensive style, extensively quoted from Chicago to the Rocky Mountains," had preceded him to New York. He agreed to stay with the *Mail* long enough to review the Cohan play. He remained, however, until 1922, when he moved to the *Daily News.* During this time Mantle had become one of the foremost drama critics in New York. Besides reviewing for the *Mail* he contributed a monthly article to the *Green Book* during 1918-1919, a weekly New York letter to the Chicago *Herald,* and articles to the New York *Dramatic Mirror, Munsey's, Collier's,* and other magazines. During this period Mantle also worked spasmodically for the movies. Among other assignments, was the one to title pictures for Constance and Norma Talmadge.

In 1913 Mantle was crusading against certain self-appointed critics of the drama. In an article for *Munsey's* he rejoiced in the passing of a first-night audience known as the "Death Watch," a group made up of a "sprinkling of 'the 400,' but the greater part the smart crowd of the 'Tenderloin Zone.'" It had its Diamond Jim Bradys, its Jerome Siegels, its idle actors and their friends." Their "velvet knocks," circulated by word of mouth, had ruined the chances of many deserving productions. Some of the plays cited by Mantle which had survived the Death Watch only because their producers had carried them at a loss until the ill effects had been counteracted were the now-famous musical *Floradora* and *Peter Pan.* Although Belasco, William A. Brady, and George M. Cohan had made efforts to break the influence of the Death Watch, its demise came about unassisted during the busy 1912-1913 season when almost nightly openings changed theatre-going for the Death Watch from a social event to a task. "With the first-night fad a dead issue socially," Mantle said, "resident New Yorkers acquired the habit of waiting for first night verdicts from the professional reviewers instead of creating them."

With the passing of the Death Watch, Mantle turned his pen against so-called "professional" reviewers who would sacrifice unbiased criticism for the sake of a witticism or a *bon mot.* In a 1914 New York *Dra-*

BURNS MANTLE

matic Mirror article, he said: "There are, according to my opinion, perhaps a dozen drama critics in America . . . men of the standing of George Pierce Baker or Brander Matthews— but there are six or seven thousand professional play-goers (an erudite specialist employed by a newspaper to keep its readers informed as to what is going on in the theatre). Misunderstandings frequently arise because the six or seven thousand have been called critics for so long that they have come to believe the classification true." "A critic," defined Mantle, "should be a good reporter and he should be sensible of his responsibility." Mantle always regarded himself as a reporter or professional play-goer rather than as a critic, with the result that his reviews were kindlier than most. If he disagreed violently with another critic about a play he seldom acknowledged it. But in 1938, when the irate playwright Jack Kirkland punched critic Richard Watts, Mantle wrote: "I can understand the urge. I get pretty peeved with those drama critics myself on occasion."

As critic for the New York *Daily News* he instituted a star system to simplify for readers his rating of the entertainment or artistic value of a production. Four stars at the head of his review signified "excellent," the top rating. In 1943, when the *News* made him critic emeritus. To John Chapman, his successor, Mantle wrote in his farewell letter: "Broadway is your oyster. Open it. Season it with a dash of salt and a lot of pep—but go easy with the tabasco." During his forty-five years as a play reviewer Mantle had seen on an average 200 plays a year. He conscientiously covered not only the Broadway plays but was present at the little theatre groups' productions. He has said that the percentage of good plays remains the same as earlier in his career: twenty successes to eighty failures. Among the plays he has listed as "the best" of his long career of theatre-going are *Déclassée,* Sacha Guitry's *Deburau, A Bill of Divorcement, Anna*

MANTLE, BURNS—*Continued*

Christie, Dover Road, and Galsworthy's *Loyalties*. The most amusing mishap in the theatre that he has ever witnessed occurred in a Western theatre where the attraction was Lincoln J. Carter's *Tornado*. Carter was famous for his sensational scenic effects. A "colossal" one in the *Tornado* was when the heroine, mounted on a mechanical horse, was supposed to escape from the villain by jumping her horse across a chasm. On this particular night the horse bounded into the air, got half way across the chasm, then stuck, its mechanical legs working furiously backward and forward as it pawed the air, and the audience roared, "Get an automobile!"

Mantle's career as a theatre annalist began in 1919 when the first of his yearbooks was published. Titled *The Best Plays of [19-] and Year Book of the Drama in America*, each volume contains introductory chapters covering the theatrical season in New York City, Chicago, San Francisco, and Southern California; an abridged version of each of the plays he has selected as the season's ten best; data on each New York production of the year, including author, producer, cast, number of performances, opening and closing dates, theatre in which played, and a brief synopsis. From the beginning drama critics and book reviewers have been unanimous in their praise. "A much needed piece of work and well done," wrote Rosamond Gilder in the *Theatre Arts Monthly*; a "treasurable annual anthology," said the *Saturday Review of Literature*. Concerning the introductory chapters, John Mason Brown[42] has said they are "shrewdly drawn, unsparing miniatures which preserve the features and spirit of the theatrical seasons for posterity." In praise of the abbreviated "best plays," Brander Matthews has written: "The extracts are prepared with surprising deftness and dexterity, the editor's [Mantle's] passages leading up adroitly to long stretches of dialogue."

As America's recognized annual play-picker, Mantle has seldom caused many disputes over his selections, although in some years he has included plays that have been adversely criticized by a majority of the reviewers. The 1932-1933 yearbook included Elmer Rice's[43] *We, the People*, which had been condemned as poor drama on its opening. The 1940-1941 list named Robert Sherwood's[40] *There Shall Be No Night* as the "most stirring event of the season" over William Saroyan's Pulitzer Prize winner, *The Time of Your Life*. In 1944, when the Drama Critics' Circle (composed of seventeen members, nine representing the metropolitan daily press, the others representing weeklies, monthlies, and trade papers) made no award for the 1943-1944 season, Mantle criticized their failure to select a "best play," also "telling off the Pulitzer Prize committee for acting similarly." Asked Mantle: "What right has either of these critical groups to belittle the American theatre by announcing loudly that for twelve months there has not been a play produced in the world's capital that is worthy of anybody's vote as a prize winner? Is that helping the theatre? Or the drama? . . . . Let them persist in this attitude of snooty superiority to the theatre's contribu-

tions to art and the chronicles of the time. Let them keep it up and do real injury to the theatre."

Wilella Waldorf, the New York *Post* critic, came to the defense of the Critics' Circle, saying that she and other "no-awarders" were not lacking interest in the theatre but did not believe in giving a prize to a play unless it was "sufficiently fine to bear the label 'prize play.'" Mantle admitted that the 1943-1944 season had been a poor one, but his yearbook contained his customary selection of the season's "ten best." Three of the plays he chose had been unsuccessful—*Outrageous Fortune, The Innocent Voyage*, and *Storm Operation*—but, as one critic commented, despite their financial failure, on the printed page they seemed worthy of a place in any list of good drama.

In collaboration with Garrison P. Sherwood, Mantle has added two volumes (edited on a similar plan) to his yearbooks. The additions, *Best Plays of 1899-1909* (1944) and *Best Plays of 1909-1919* (1933, reissued 1943), were written to fill the gap between the published and the planned records of Professor George C. D. Odell.[44] Odell's published records cover the theatre from its beginning in the American colonies to 1888 and have been published in thirteen volumes under the title *Annals of the New York Stage*. (The period from 1888 to 1899 is in preparation.)

In more informal style Mantle has given in three volumes a fairly complete picture of the foremost American playwrights since 1919, and the great playwrights of the world from Aeschylus to Eugene O'Neill. The first of these, *American Playwrights of Today* (1929), was in the opinion of the *Theatre Arts Monthly* too casual in quality: the criticism discounted the value of the material offered and laid the book "open to the charge of inaccuracy." Brooks Atkinson[42] of the New York *Times*, however, found it "a genial volume, invaluable to those associated with the theatre." *A Treasury of the Theatre* (1935), co-edited with John Gassner, is an omnibus of the great plays from the time of the early Greek dramatists to Eugene O'Neill. Atkinson called it "the best buy that has yet been issued in the way of an anthology." *Contemporary American Playwrights* (1938) contains biographical data on some 300 American dramatists. "Much of the information is not to be found conveniently elsewhere," pointed out the *Nation*, "and the volume is indispensable for the reference shelf of everyone connected with the theatre."

A list of the activities of the critic emeritus offers proof that his retirement from the *Daily News* was not the result of old age but that he is, as fellow journalists have reported, as young and vigorous as any of them. He is a member of the Writers' War Board committee on scripts for soldier and sailor shows; he is assistant secretary of *The Players*, a member of its house committee and chairman of its library committee. On October 1, 1944 he began a series of Sunday drama commentaries over WNEW. Included as an innovation was a "court of appeal for actors and playwrights" who feel they have been unjustly criticized by the press. In late 1944 he is preparing a history of *Best Plays*, with an index covering all volumes.

On August 20, 1903 Mantle was married to
Lydia Sears; they have one daughter, Margaret Burns, who in 1942 became Mrs. Edward Gerard. Mrs. Mantle, as popular as
her husband with first-night critics, told reporters on his retirement that for the first time
in forty years of theatre-going she would have
a husband who would take her home after a
play instead of rushing off to write a review.
Mantle's study on the third floor of his Forest
Hills house has no pictures of "drama queens,
and he has never drunk champagne from a
star's slipper. His after-work beaker is orange
juice or milk, although he takes an occasional
cocktail. His clothes are the kind that would
look appropriate on Wall Street" (his tailored
shirts are monogramed). He has a pink, unlined face, is five feet six and weighs 146
pounds. His religion is eclectic, his politics
liberal, and his recreations are theatre-going
and a "'umblin' game of golf." John Chapman, who has known Mantle since his Denver
Post days, says that Mantle's standards of
truth and decency in the theatre are high and
unwavering. "He fights for them," Chapman
adds, "but subtly: he just won't cuss and call
names."

References

> Time 42:62 Ag 23 '43
> Kunitz, S. J. and Haycraft, H. eds.
> Twentieth Century Authors 1942
> Who's Who in America 1944-45
> Who's Who in the Theatre 1939

MAPES, VICTOR March 10, 1870—Sept.
27, 1943. Playwright, producer, and drama
critic; wrote many successful comedy hits,
several in collaboration with Winchell Smith
and William Collier, and one novel, *The
Gilded Way* (1910).

Obituary

> N Y Times p69 D 12 '43

**MARIA THERESA, ARCHDUCHESS
OF AUSTRIA** Aug. 24, 1855—Feb. (?),
1944 Grandmother of Prince Franz Joseph of
Liechtenstein; stepmother of Archduke Francis Ferdinand, whose assassination in 1914 at
Sarajevo led to the outbreak of the First
World War.

Obituary

> N Y Times p17 F 16 '44

MARQUIS, ALBERT NELSON (mär'-
wis) Jan. 10, 1854(?)—Dec. 21, 1943 Publisher and editor; founder of the A. N. Marquis Company, especially noted for its biographical publication, *Who's Who in America*,
issued biennially since 1899.

Obituary

> N Y Times p23 D 22 '43 por

MARTIN, MARY Dec. 1, 1914- Stage and
motion-picture actress

Address: b. c/o Jean Dalrymple, 122 E. 42nd
St., New York City

In 1938 a young unknown Texan named
Mary Martin sang "My Heart Belongs to

Daddy" in one scene of the Broadway show,
Leave It To Me. That single song brought
her motion-picture stardom; five years later she
returned to New York in the title role of
One Touch of Venus, the musical comedy that
became a hit of the 1943-1944 season.

Merry and roguish Mary Martin, born December 1, 1914, is a native of Weatherford,
Texas, where her father practiced law and
her mother gave violin lessons. Mary studied
at the Ward-Belmont School in Nashville,
Tennessee until the family finances felt the
effects of the market crash of 1929. She
then enrolled at the University of Texas and
began taking voice lessons there. At the end
of her freshman year, however, she left
academic life to marry a Weatherford lawyer
named Ben Hageman. Later she realized that
this important step had been taken too hastily
and too early in life. Shortly after the
birth of their son, Larry, the Hagemans were
divorced.

Mary Martin's first professional venture
was the conducting, together with Mildred
Woods, of a dancing school in her home
town. The school, she explains, was begun
"more as a joke than anything else. The joke
turned out to be on me when I found myself
with a booming little business on my hands
and only two feet with which to cover all the
ground." Extra instructors had to be hired,
and two additional schools were opened in
neighboring towns.

The unexpected flourishing of her dancing
school enterprise persuaded Mary to brush
up on her own dance routines by taking a
summer course at the Hollywood studios of
Fanchon and Marco. "All summer I toiled
away without creating a ripple, and when I
returned home in the fall the waters of Hollywood closed over my head with not even a
bubble."

Upon her return to Weatherford she undertook voice study quite seriously with a
teacher whose encouragement was to constitute the turning point of her life. Things
ran along smoothly that year but without any
promise whatever of a brilliant future. Then
one night the building which housed her
Weatherford school burned to the ground.
Excitedly, Mary ran to Mildred Woods, exclaiming, "It's a sign. Let's go to Hollywood."

If Hollywood was aware of the signs and
portents involved in Mary Martin's arrival
there, it concealed the fact very effectively; so
effectively, in fact, that it thoroughly coldshouldered the young aspirant, despite the
combined operations of Martin and Woods to
gain attention. Miss Woods acted as agent
and "front man" for the future star—pulling
strings, planning wardrobes on their small
means, and arranging auditions. Their perseverance finally was rewarded, for after
many attempts they obtained a screen test for
Mary at one of the studios. The first test,
however, was a failure. So were all of the
other tests she made elsewhere, until at length
she became known as "Audition Mary."

Refusing to accept defeat, Mary and Mildred moved into cheaper quarters, determined
to wait for their luck to change. Small engagements came along, such as occasional
radio and night club jobs, none of them of
any consequence. Just as discouragement be-

MARY MARTIN

gan to catch up with Mary, she encountered her former voice teacher from Nashville, Tennessee. He was unimpressed by her recital of bad fortune; rather than offering sympathy, he suggested that she devote the next six months exclusively to serious vocal study.

Several months of singing lessons may have improved her voice but it nearly wrecked her already precarious finances. Mildred Woods decided that Mary ought to sing at one of the "Opportunity Nights" sponsored by Hollywood's Trocadero in the hope of obtaining a two-week engagement there. At that time the collective resources of the two girls could not produce an evening gown that would meet Hollywood standards for the occasion. Of necessity, Mary daringly appeared before her lavishly bejewelled audience in a collegiate sweater and skirt—very simple and smart.

When her turn to sing came, Mary puzzled her listeners by beginning to sing "Il Bacio," an inappropriate selection, to say the least, under the circumstances. But just as her restive listeners were about to show their disapproval she swung into a "solid," fast blues beat. "Suddenly," she states, "the place was alive and shouting. They wouldn't let me go, the very ones on whose doors I had been beating for months and months."

One of patrons at the Trocadero that evening was the producer Lawrence Schwab, who signed Mary for a New York show. Soon after her arrival in that city, accompanied of course by Miss Woods, she learned that the production had been canceled. Schwab, however, managed to find her a small part in the musical comedy Leave It to Me (1938). Although the show starred such veterans as Sophie Tucker and Victor Moore, Mary Martin stole the spotlight with her "scorching" rendition of "My Heart Belongs to Daddy," a song which she made famous—and which did the same service for her.

Shortly afterward, in 1939, she made her night club debut in New York's swank Rain-

bow Room, which, according to the newspapers, she took "by storm." One account stated, "She's a cute little package of dynamite, and she left the usually dignified and restrained Rainbow Room patrons cheering and yelling for more of her songs."

New York, Miss Martin felt, was her oyster; besides, after her stay in Hollywood, it offered more fun and gaiety than she had had in a long time. It was therefore understandable that she should ignore Hollywood offers as they came in. But at length her silent partner, Miss Woods, and a talent scout for Paramount Pictures persuaded her to sign a movie contract. Following her first part in The Great Victor Herbert (1939), Miss Martin was cast in a series of rickety vehicles: Rhythm on the River and Love Thy Neighbor in 1940; New York Town, Birth of the Blues, and Kiss the Boys Goodbye in 1941. (The latter was described as a highly diluted version of Clare Boothe's [42] stage play.) In 1943 she appeared in Star Spangled Rhythm, in Happy-Go-Lucky, which was pronounced "a straggling exhibit," but in which, nevertheless, Miss Martin made good use of "her superb sense of vocal timing"; and in True to Life, described by Time as "likable, sometimes genuinely laughable."

Miss Martin has little love for Hollywood, of which her impression is, "No time to think. It's shoot. Boom. If you don't get it right the first time do it again." She tried to break her contract on the grounds that choice roles were being withheld from her. The studio compromised by giving her a leave of absence in which to do One Touch of Venus. When her present contract does expire—in less than a year—Miss Martin intends to give up the motion pictures altogether in favor of the theatre.

She is happier on the stage, and her success there explains her preference. Almost five years after her New York debut, she returned to the stage as the lady Venus herself in One Touch of Venus. Its story is by S. J. Perelman and Ogden Nash [41], with music by Kurt Weill [43] and choreography by Agnes de Mille [43]. She was hailed as "one of the brightest stars to descend on the musical comedy stage in many a long year." Wrote Howard Barnes in the New York Herald Tribune: "It is the great good fortune of the show that it has Mary Martin in the leading role. . . . Miss Martin has the touch. When she comes to life after three thousand years of petrification she acts with all the astonishment and guile that one would expect from the top glamour gal of the Hellenic golden age." (The play is scheduled for motion picture production by Mary Pickford in 1945. It is expected that Miss Martin will play Venus.)

More than a year later her outstanding success in One Touch of Venus saw Miss Martin unspoiled by stardom. Her stage goddess, she confesses, was kept alive by a good many people, ranging all the way from her dressing room maid to her co-star, John Boles. She considered 1944 in New York City the most exciting of her life. She was chosen the year's best musical comedy actress (the Donaldson award, highly valued because it is a selection by other show people) and she was voted the best-dressed woman in the theatrical profession by the Fashion Academy. During the year she frequently made radio appearances and contributed her services to war bond rallies.

This twentieth-century Venus is five feet four and a half inches tall, weighs 112 pounds, has reddish brown hair and brown eyes set wide apart, and she is "full of life and humor." She is not "beautiful," though, according to Hollywood standards. Her chin, she was informed, is too small and her neck too long. Wearied by ineffective attempts to disguise these points, she eventually reversed matters by accentuating them. When it was time for the dress designer Mainbocher '42 to costume her Venus, he too followed this plan of dramatizing her physical "defects"—to such effect, that Miss Martin was often photographed for fashion magazines during the run of the play.

Since May 1940 Miss Martin has been the wife of Richard Halliday, formerly a literary agent, but now her manager. They have a daughter named Mary Heller Halliday. Miss Martin is proud of her honorary membership in the Texas Rangers. Appropriately enough, she likes horseback riding, and can't resist a shooting gallery.

As a star, Miss Martin remains grateful to the people who helped her along the way. "You could tell the short, short story of my life by the people I'm grateful to," the actress maintains. She includes in this group her parents, producer Cheryl Crawford, her first voice teacher, her friend Mildred Woods, and Cole Porter '40, who wrote "My Heart Belongs to Daddy."

References

Am Mag 135:44 Ap '43 por
Cue 12:19 N 13 '43; 13:8-9 Ag 19 '44 il por
Liberty 17:51 F 24 '40
Life 15:98-9+ D 27 '43 il pors
N Y Herald Tribune IV p1+Ag 20 '44 pors
Newsweek 22:86+ O 18 '43
PM Mag p15 N 28 '43 por

MARTINU, BOHUSLAV (mär′tin-ū bō′hū-släf) Composer

Address: h. 24 W. 58th St., New York City

While Bohuslav Martinů was still more or less "the property of musical scholars and specialists" so far as the United States was concerned, the European critics, André Coeuroy and Nikolai Lopatnikoff were calling him "one of the most happily endowed musicians not only of Czechoslovakia, but of all contemporary Europe," and "the most promising musician of the younger generation." Today American critics echo these earlier, European admirers. In 1944 many say that Martinů is undoubtedly the "Composer of the Year" and one increasingly appreciated by the general concert public. He has written well over 100 works, including operas, choral works, ballets, compositions for orchestra, concertos for solo instruments and orchestra, and more than thirty chamber pieces; and although most of his early compositions have been lost, since 1941 his American works have received their premières as fast as he has composed them. Of his work *Time* Magazine

BOHUSLAV MARTINU

writes: "Though he inherits the great Czech tradition of Friedrich Smetana and Antonin Dvořák Martinů does not work in their sun-lit, melodically fecund vein. The emotional tone of his music is measured, but it has genuine dignity, drama, and decided individuality."

According to Martinů's biographer, Miloš Šafránek, one of the keys to the singularly detached quality of Bohuslav Martinů's work and personality is the curious circumstance that he was born and brought up in the tower of a country church. He was born in the same region as Smetana, in the small town of Polička in eastern Bohemia, December 8, 1890. He is the son of Ferdinand and Karolina (Klimes) Martinů. His father was a shoemaker and keeper of the local church tower, in which young Martinů spent practically his entire childhood, "devoted to music, looking down from above, and at a distance, upon life in the town and in the beautiful countryside." Only six when he began violin study, by the time he was eight he was appearing in concerts, and when he was sixteen his skill on the violin prompted some wealthy citizens to send him to the Prague Conservatory of Music. At twenty-three he completed his studies in the violin department of the Conservatory and became a member of the Czech Philharmonic Orchestra in Prague.

Martinů was to remain a member of the orchestra from 1913 to 1923, though he had no desire to be merely a virtuoso. When he was ten he wrote his first musical composition, a piece for a string quintet. As a composer, he is almost entirely self-taught: he began Josef Suk's course in composition at the Prague Conservatory but never finished it. According to Šafránek, during those years in Prague Martinů's works were significant chiefly for what they seemed to foreshadow. With the exception of the "Czech Rhapsody" (1919), "a spontaneous outpouring of the sentiments of a liberated nation and of the enthusiasm of its masses . . . composed to celebrate the liberation of the

MARTINU, BOHUSLAV—*Continued*

Czechoslovak nation," his compositions showed the influence of Debussy and impressionism even more than that of Dvořák. At a time when his contemporaries were emphasizing the metaphysical and literary qualities of music he was concentrating on "sound in and for itself." Among the works of this period are a full-evening ballet, *Istar* (1921), based on Oriental themes, and a series of impressionistic compositions, such as "Vanishing Midnight" (1922), a symphonic poem for orchestra, and songs to exotic texts.

In the autumn of 1923 the composer went to Paris, intending to stay only a few months: he was to remain for seventeen years. The first years were difficult. He "composed very little, did not give his works to the public, and destroyed many of them . . . he clung to impressionism and homophonic style, having no confidence in the current polyphony." For only a few moderns—chiefly Stravinsky '40 and Honegger '41—did he conceive any enthusiasm. Albert Roussel, who from the first was more an adviser than a teacher, encouraged him and assured him that he was on the right track; but it was not until the rhythmically incisive "Half-Time," composed in 1925 and first performed in Prague that year, that his work began to interest the general public. The "Second String Quartet" (1926) showed a conscious development of the elements used in "Half-Time"; and in two later compositions for large orchestra—"La Bagarre" (1927), "Rhapsody" (1928)—the composer "exploited the rhythmic and dynamic elements that were a feature of modern music in the '20's." Then in 1930 came *Trios*, five short pieces for violin, cello, and piano in which "a new, direct, and reckless polyphony suddenly appeared," marking "a turning point in Martinů's work towards new forms of musical lyricism and rhythm." For some time after this Martinů abandoned the large orchestra almost completely in order to devote himself to chamber music. In the compositions that followed he cast off external influences (specifically the French influence) and achieved a style distinctly his own. Among the results were "Serenade" (1930), "Partita" for string orchestra (1931), "String Quartet With Orchestra" (1931), and "String Sextet" (1931), the manuscript of which is in the Library of Congress and which won the Elizabeth Sprague Coolidge '41 Prize in 1932. It was not until 1934, with "Inventions" for grand orchestra, that the composer returned "to his old preoccupation with sonorities as well as to characteristically Czech music."

During those years in Paris the Czech composer had also composed many operatic works: operas, short works for radio, ballets, music for motion pictures. Returning to Prague every year, he had slowly built up a group of young collaborators there who in his absence were able to present his work according to his intentions. Among the best known of these works is *Špaliček* (1931), a great ballet with singing, based on folk songs, folk dances, and folk customs. According to Šafránek, the most perfect of Martinů's operas are two later works: *The Miracle of Our Lady* (1933) and the fantastic *Juliette* (or *The Key to Dreams*)

(1936-37). These are by no means ordinary operas. Martinů sees opera as "a spectacle, transformed by music . . . not a fragment of real life but a theatrical performance." His operatic principles are said to be exactly the opposite of Wagner's: believing that by putting stress on the words and their meaning "opera loses its freedom of action, its power, and even its *raison d'être*," he "maintains a primary interest in the unity of the musical conception, never sacrificing it to considerations of action or characterization." *Juliette* is, in essence, a great symphonic poem.

"Martinů's tendency towards absolute music becomes clearly evident in his 'Concerto Grosso,' composed in 1938," in which "he sought to create something between chamber and symphonic music." This was an ill-fated work. The composer's plans to have it published in Vienna in 1938 were frustrated by the Austrian *Anschluss*; the Paris première scheduled for the same year was canceled because the score and orchestral material could not be obtained in time from Vienna; and the Munich crisis prevented it from being performed in Prague. At the time of Munich, Martinů was visiting in Switzerland, but he listened daily to the news bulletins on his radio while working on his "Double Concerto," "the most perfect and most forceful of his works." When, on February 5, 1940, Paul Sacher performed the "Double Concerto" in Geneva, the critics as well as the public felt the tragedy of Martinů's homeland expressed in its melodies."

Upon his return from Geneva to Paris, Martinů collaborated with the Czechoslovak National Committee in France, in 1940 writing "Field Mass" for the Czechoslovak Army volunteers and "Military March" for the Czechoslovak Army Band there. In the winter of 1939-1940 he also composed one of his best chamber music works, his "First Sonata" for violoncello and piano, the manuscript of which is still somewhere in France. This work was performed in May 1940; the première of "Concerto Grosso" was planned for the same month, but the imminent downfall of France made its performance impossible. In June the Czech composer, who was on the Nazi blacklist, was forced to flee Paris, leaving his manuscripts behind.

Martinů now settled in Aix-en-Provence, traveling to Marseilles almost every day in the attempt to procure an American visa. His "Sinfonietta Giocosa" for piano and chamber orchestra was composed between October 14 and November 12, 1940—mostly in the uncomfortable trolley car which ran between Aix-en-Provence and Marseilles—and was written on the last sheets of music paper obtainable in Marseilles. Actually the hitherto unperformed "Concerto Grosso," which he had believed forever lost, preceded the composer and his new work to the United States. George Szell had rescued a copy of the manuscript from Prague and had brought it via Australia to New York, where it received its première in January 1941 by the Boston Symphony Orchestra under Serge Koussevitzky '40, who had first introduced Martinů's work to the American public in 1927. Of "Concerto Grosso" the New York *Times* Noel Straus wrote: "Not only expertly contrived in its orchestration, but also replete with interesting musical ideas."

On March 31, 1941 Martinů himself arrived in New York, and he was soon at work again. His first work to be composed on American soil was a mazurka, for piano, written for the Paderewski memorial program. This was followed, in the summer of 1941, by "Concerto da Camera" in F minor, written as an expression of gratitude to friends in Switzerland and sent off to Basle, where it was performed in January 1942. Martinů's "Second Sonata" for violoncello and piano was composed in Jamaica, Long Island, in November and December 1941, and was followed by an extraordinarily productive period. His "Variations on a Theme of Rossini" for violoncello, his "Madrigal Sonata" for flute, violin, and piano, a collection of six little songs on folk texts entitled the *New Špalíček*, and his "First Piano Quartet" were all written in 1942, as was his famous First Symphony.

The latter work, commissioned by the Koussevitzky Music Foundation, was completed in less than four months, about half of it being composed while Martinů was teaching as one of the faculty at Koussevitzky's summer Berkshire Music Center at Stockbridge, Massachusetts. In the program notes for this symphony the composer says: "Each composer and each creator of our epoch feels himself, to a certain extent, obliged to espouse sentiments of grandeur and tragedy. . . . The tendency, the desire to be greater than one is, can lead directly to an emphasis which, to say the least, is not essentially musical. . . . Sheer orchestral power does not necessarily imply either grandeur or elevation." His own symphony, in contrast, is based on an "extremely simple theme that appears in all four movements and isn't much more in its unadorned form than one note followed by the next above it," but is worked out with stunning orchestral virtuosity and variety in the opinion of Henry Simon, *PM* critic.

The première of the First Symphony in November 1942 inspired Virgil Thomson[40] to write: "The Martinů symphony is a beaut. It is wholly lovely and doesn't sound like anything else. . . . The shining sounds of it sing as well as shine; the instrumental complication is a part of the musical conception, not an icing laid over it. Personal indeed is the delicate but vigorous rhythmic animation, the singing (rather than dynamic) syncopation that permeates the work. Personal and individual, too, is the whole orchestral sound of it, the acoustical superstructure that shimmers constantly."

During the two weeks between October 28 and November 9, 1943 eleven performances of Martinů's works were given in New York, Philadelphia, and Cleveland alone. And seldom had a living composer been more overwhelmed by premières. The Cleveland Orchestra under Erich Leinsdorf[40] conducted the première of Martinů's Second Symphony, commissioned by Clevelanders of Czechoslovak origin and dedicated to them; the New York Philharmonic under Artur Rodzinski[40] conducted the première of the symphonic poem "Memorial to Lidice," commissioned by the League of Composers; the Philadelphia Symphony under Eugene Ormandy[41] conducted the première of a third new Martinů composition, "Concerto for Two Pianos and Orchestra," composed on commission from pianists Pierre Luboschutz and Genia Nemenoff. Later, in December, came the première of the "Third Violin Concerto," commissioned by Mischa Elman. Martinů missed the New York première of "Memorial to Lidice" through attending the Cleveland première of his Second Symphony; he got to Philadelphia for the initial performance of the two-piano concerto, but was attending the first New York performance of the Second Symphony while his "Violin Concerto" was being introduced in Boston, and had to listen to the latter by means of portable radio at Carnegie Hall.

Critical comment on nearly all of these new compositions was less unanimously laudatory than that on the First Symphony had been. Though Olin Downes[43] found the Second Symphony "simple and frank and sunny," Virgil Thomson thought that it was less fresh than Martinů's First, its melodic material being "a little too plain and sensible for the ornate figurations in which it is embedded." The two-piano concerto was described by Henry Simon as "salty harmonically, piquant rhythmically, and full of clever color effects," but as leaving "the impression of a skillful workman turning out a neat but uninspired job." As for the "Violin Concerto," it was praised by Olin Downes as "a perfect fit" for Mischa Elman, but dismissed as a "hastily conceived and dispatched opus" by Paul Bowles. Only "Memorial to Lidice" was universally greeted as a minor masterpiece. Olin Downes found it "untheatrical but noble, masterfully developed from short germinal motives suggestive of ancient hymns and folk chants . . . the latest token of Martinů's complete sincerity, his constantly growing mastery of his material, his selflessness in his art."

Martinů is surprised at how easy it is for him to compose. "I just work and work," he says, "and then I write fast." By September 1944 he had completed his Third Symphony, which the Boston Symphony Orchestra was to introduce during the coming season. This, unlike his other recent works, had not been commissioned, but was intended as a gift to the Boston orchestra. Martinů is particularly grateful to Koussevitzky, who first introduced his music in the United States and who has encouraged him since his arrival there.

On March 21, 1932 the composer was married to Charlotte Quennehen. He is a soft-spoken, serious-minded, shy man, who composes daily for three or four hours in the forenoon, studies physics and biology for relaxation, and likes to go for solitary walks late at night. He often composes without a piano. According to Šafránek, "for Martinů, form—organic unity, the complete realization of an idea, the perfect conformity of content and expression—is the main problem." Šafránek also says that the composer will never write "American" music, although America is "freeing the composer of certain constrictive traditions of the Old World." "He is, so to speak, emerging

MARTINU, BOHUSLAV—*Continued*
from a closed room and beginning to breathe
the open air."

References

Mus Q 29 :329-54 Jl '43 por
Newsweek 23 :72 Ja 17 '44 ; 24 :106-7
S 11 '44 por
Time 42 :70 N 8 '43 por
Ewen, D. ed. Composers of Today 1934
International Who's Who 1942
Šafránek, M. Bohuslav Martinů : The
Man and His Music 1944
Thompson, O. ed. International Cyclo-
pedia of Music and Musicians 1943

MASARYK, JAN (GARRIGUE) (ma′sa-
rik yan ga-rēg′) 1886- Foreign Minister and
Deputy Prime Minister of Czechoslovakia
Address: h. 58 Westminster Gardens, Mar-
sham St., London

Jan Masaryk is the Foreign Minister of the
Czechoslovak Government-in-Exile and one of
the most popular figures in the 1944 international scene. A progressive in politics and an
ardent champion of democracy, he has not
been content to live in the reflected glory of
his distinguished father, the first President of
the Czechoslovak Republic, Thomas Masaryk.
Instead he has made a career of his own as a
diplomat and writer on international affairs.
In the spring of 1944, as victorious armies of
the Soviet Union pushed on to within a few
miles of the Czech eastern frontier, the Czech
Government in London issued an order to its
people to join in "an armed uprising" against
their Nazi rulers, and Jan Masaryk prepared
to return to his native land.

The son of Thomas Masaryk and an American mother, Charlotte Garrigue, Jan Garrigue
Masaryk was born in Prague September 14,
1886. Since his father had spent many years
in the United States teaching and later lecturing for the cause of Czechoslovak independence, Jan Masaryk had an American as well
as a European background. A graduate of
Prague University, he has studied at Boston
University and worked in the United States
as an ironworker and as a pianist in a motion-
picture theatre. It was while working in an
iron foundry, Masaryk says, that he learned
the fundamentals of diplomacy. "There were
Slovaks, Swedes, Poles, Norwegians—absolutely everyone. I bought a blackboard and
four times a week taught them to read and
write. That was the strongest influence of
my Europeanism."

As a boy Jan Masaryk reacted against the
serious scholarly atmosphere of his home by
developing his sense of humor to the utmost.
He determined to be a black sheep in his otherwise model family, but succeeded only to a
limited degree when at twenty he left home
and came to the United States with only $80
in cash. It was not long, however, before
young Masaryk became involved in European
politics himself. The outbreak of the First
World War found the Czech people, under the
leadership of the elder Masaryk, engaged in
a movement for national independence. In 1914
what is now Czechoslovakia was a part of
Austria-Hungary. Thomas Masaryk was quick

to realize that as long as the Czechs remained
under the rule of the Hapsburgs they would be
the puppets of their traditional enemy, Germany. He wrote in *The Making of a State*
(1927) : "Once the proud rulers of the Holy
Roman Empire, the Hapsburgs had sunk to the
level of being a mere vanguard of the eastward march of pan-Germanism."

Austria's declaration of war against Serbia
in 1914 and the consequent general mobilization
forced the Czechs and Slovaks to take up arms
for Austria although their sympathies were
clearly with the Serbians, the Russians, and the
French. S. Harrison Thomson writes: "The
Czech soldiers who were called to the colors
made their sentiments known immediately.
Some few refused to obey the order, and the
great majority sang Slav songs interspersed
with anti-German cries as their trains pulled
out of the Prague stations. The civilian popu-
lace was openly and vociferously of the same
mind."

Jan Masaryk had been in Austria at the
time of the outbreak of war and was therefore
forced to serve, against his will, in the Austro-Hungarian infantry. That his sympathies
were not with the Central Powers was made
clear when his "political unreliability" nearly
won him a death sentence from the Austrian
Government. Meanwhile Thomas Masaryk
continued his struggle for Czech independence.
He left his country on December 17, 1914 "to
go abroad in order to establish connection with
influential individuals in the Entente capitals
and set up an organization able to maintain
the necessary communications between Prague
and the outside world." Four years later
Thomas Masaryk returned to his native land
as President of the Czechoslovak Republic.

As soon as the War ended Jan Masaryk
joined his father in Prague to aid in the establishment of an independent Czechoslovakia.
He served his diplomatic apprenticeship in the
Ministry of Foreign Affairs. In 1919 he was
sent to the United States to serve as chargé
d'affaires in Washington. Two years later he
joined the Czechoslovak Legation in London,
acting as private secretary to Dr. Eduard
Beneš[42]. After serving in Prague with the
Czechoslovak Ministry of Foreign Affairs,
Masaryk was appointed Minister to Great Britain in 1925.

In London and in the United States, which
he visited frequently during those years, Jan
Masaryk was the most popular of Continental
statesmen. His ready wit, his energy and
enthusiasm, his talent for telling "unprintable
stories" and playing the piano (*Time* calls him
"the best pianist among contemporary foreign
ministers"), combined with keen political
acumen and a genuine faith in democracy—
all served to make him a key figure in international affairs. Like his father and his
father's successor to the Presidency of Czechoslovakia, Eduard Beneš, Masaryk felt that his
country had a definite role to play in Europe.
He realized that the Soviet Union was a
powerful force that had to be recognized as
a world power, that the pan-Slavism movement would not serve Czechoslovakia's best
interests, and that his country should be considered part of democratic Europe.

The deeply rooted Czech fear of German
domination was proved entirely justified when

Adolf Hitler [42] demanded that the so-called Sudeten land be given to Nazi Germany. The German propaganda line concentrated upon Czechoslovakia's friendly relations with the Soviet Union and its menace to German security. By May 1938, after Austria's *Anschluss* with Germany, there were German armies on the northern Czech borders. The small nation was determined to resist aggression, however, and issued a general mobilization call. Hence its betrayal at Munich in September 1938, when France and England recommended that it bow to Germany's demands, proved the source of bitter humiliation to the Czech people. Masaryk promptly resigned from his office as envoy to the Court of St. James. Although he recognized the fact that his country had been the victim of a policy of deceit and appeasement, Masaryk himself held little bitterness against the British or the French. Even in a speech made just after his resignation he reaffirmed his friendship for England: "I want nothing better for the world than that all countries should have the same qualities as these islands of England."

With characteristic blitzkrieg tactics Czechoslovakia was soon swept by German armies. Beneš was forced to resign, and all liberal and Left-wing elements were dissolved. In March 1939 German troops marched into Czech territory, and Hitler entered Prague, committing the final ignominy by spending a night in the ancient castle which had been the home of Thomas Masaryk for seventeen years.

It was not until after the fall of France that the democracies recognized a Czechoslovak Government-in-Exile. In July 1940 such a provisional government was recognized with Beneš as its President and Masaryk as its Foreign Minister and later as its deputy Prime Minister. One year later Great Britain, the United States, and the Soviet Union granted the Government full *de jure* recognition. Masaryk and Beneš were free to go ahead with their plans for a post-War European program. Their aims, briefly described, included: "A disarmed, decentralized German confederation; similar regional federations in the Balkans, in western Europe, in Scandinavia; all these regional federations ultimately to form a Federation of Europe; inclusion of Russia in a cooperative European settlement."

Masaryk has spent the years since the outbreak of the Second World War shuttling back and forth between Great Britain and the United States lecturing and writing. In London he conducts a short-wave broadcast to Czechoslovakia. Although his listeners know that there is a death penalty for listening to these talks, he has a large audience and is in some measure responsible for the strength and unity of the Czech underground. Early in the War Masaryk did not urge armed resistance against the Germans, knowing that such action had no chance of success. Instead he advised workers to slow down and be inefficient. As time passed, however, the underground became more and more active, and when, in April 1944, Russian armies stood on the borders of Czechoslovakia, Beneš and Masaryk ordered their people to join these

JAN MASARYK

"armies of liberation" in offering armed resistance to the Nazis.

The Czech Foreign Minister has always been a stern realist in his discussion of Europe's future. Confident of ultimate Allied victory, he nevertheless warned: "There is no fence to sit upon. Tanks do not stop for fences. Impatient people tell me daily that neither Great Britain nor America is doing enough. There is something to be said for that complaint, but I say they are doing a terrific lot and they are going to do more and they are going to be quick about it and we all must do more, much more and then still more."

The destruction of the little town of Lidice, Masaryk pointed out, was typical of what was happening not only in Czechoslovakia, but in Yugoslavia, Poland, and every other country occupied by the Nazis. He has written: "The War cannot be said to have ended until the last Reich official and the last Reich soldier are kicked out of Czechoslovakia dead or alive, but preferably dead." He urged that German cities be bombed and that the Reich be invaded, saying the German people must "be taught the meaning of war by firsthand experience."

Masaryk has written and lectured extensively on post-War planning. Holding that the security of small nations must be guaranteed, he has opposed spheres of influence and the balance of power argument. In an article printed in the New York *Times Magazine*, Masaryk cautioned that in an attempt to avoid any tinge of isolationism many post-War planners have gone too far to the other extreme in planning too elaborately for the rehabilitation of Europe. That is a job, he feels, for the occupied countries themselves: "Domination is hateful even when the dominating power is paternal, solicitous, and beneficent. Europe is not a kindergarten, and as a wise British statesman once put it, self-government is better than good government."

(Continued next page)

MASARYK, JAN—*Continued*

Masaryk is sure that the new world holds great promise, if it is carefully planned and intelligently governed. A political liberal though a member of no political party, he argues: "Let us face the fact that we can never go back to either 1918 or 1939 or even to 1942. It is in our hands to make this new world ring free. The people in Europe and Asia expect that from us and we dare not disappoint them."

The Czech Government-in-Exile has always been on friendly terms with the Soviet Union. Both Masaryk and Beneš have looked to that country as "the greatest Continental power." Masaryk points out that the U.S.S.R. is responsible for stopping German aggression in Europe and says: "We intend to live our own life in our own way and we know that Russia will respect our way of living." In order to avoid offending the Soviet Union Masaryk and Beneš refrained from taking a stand in the diplomatic difficulties between Poland and the U.S.S.R.

In November 1943 Masaryk announced that President Beneš would visit Moscow. One month later the Soviet-Czechoslovak mutual assistance pact was signed. Commentators at first feared that this pact symbolized Czechoslovakia's withdrawal from the politics of Western Europe to those of Eastern Europe. Masaryk insisted, however, that Czechoslovak sovereignty had not been jeopardized and that this move would simply strengthen his country's position in Western Europe: "Soviet Russia not only is a European power but she will be the most powerful European power when the War is over. In negotiating the treaty we have just signed, we did not sell out to Russia. We know that without Russia's friendship none of her small neighbors can revert to independent national life." (In May 1944 a Soviet-Czech Liberation Pact was signed. Under its terms the liberated areas of Czechoslovakia would be placed under the supreme authority of the Soviet (Allied) military commander. Czechoslovak civil administrators take the control as the fighting ends.)

An article Masaryk wrote for the *Nation* in December 1944, discussing a future Czecho-Polish confederation against aggression, received criticism from the Soviet publication *War and the Working Class.* The small countries, alone or together, have not been able to withstand German imperialism, the magazine stated. "Salvation was only brought to the Czech and Polish people by the Red Army."

Jan Masaryk was his country's delegate to the United Nations Relief and Rehabilitation Administration. In a public address made to that group he urged that Poland, Yugoslavia, and Greece be given food priorities over his own country. "Czechoslovakia, when the War is over, will have had six years of purgatory. Poland, Yugoslavia, and Greece started later, but got a greater and more devastating dose. The food situation, though bad in any country, is not as bad as in the three countries I mention. Therefore they should get priority." The Foreign Minister, as deputy Prime Minister, headed the Czechoslovak delegation to the conference of the International Labor Office held in Philadelphia in the spring of 1944.

Sharp debates were held on the war guilt of the German people. Said Masaryk: "Czechs have been neighbors of Germans for a thousand years and there is nothing anybody can teach us about their certain bellicose and goose-stepping German qualities." They must be taught, he said, "that aggression does not and never will pay."

The Czechoslovak Government in November presented identical notes to the United States, British, Russian, and French Governments. The notes contained the Czech Government's plans for handling the 3,000,000 Germans living in Sudeten land before the War. These plans, it is said, propose to allow between 800,000 to 1,000,000 Germans, those with good records, to remain in Czechoslovakia. The rest will be deported. The Germans remaining will cease to exist as a separate unit, with special language and privileges.

In 1944 Masaryk is recognized as a worthy successor to his father's great name and "a chip off a colossal old block." Partly bald, six feet two inches tall, he looks like "a successful American businessman, an elegant European *bon vivant*, a world-famous orchestra leader, a magnetic political boss," *Time* says. Masaryk's wit is the subject of many anecdotes. One story, according to a New York *Post* columnist, has it that he quite upset immigration officials on one of his visits to the United States. In filling out a certain form Masaryk hesitated a bit over the word "Race," then wrote down "Human." In explanation he said that he was a Czechoslovakian by nationality, but, he insisted, "I belong to the human race." Nonplused, the officials let it stand. In 1924 he was married to Frances Crane Leatherbee. The marriage ended in divorce in 1931.

References

Scholastic p9 D 13 '43
Time p28+ Mr 27 '44 (por cov)
International Who's Who 1942
Who's Who 1944

MAVERICK, MAURY (mav′rik mô′rē) Oct. 23, 1895- United States Government official; lawyer

Address: b. Smaller War Plants Corp., Washington, D. C.; h. 1829 Jefferson Pl., N.W., Washington, D. C.; San Antonio, Tex.

A "maverick," according to standard dictionary definition, is "a calf not marked with its owner's brand," hence a stray of any kind. The word is derived from the name Sam Maverick, a Texas cattle owner of the nineteenth century, onetime mayor of San Antonio and a signer of the Texas declaration of independence who had refused to brand his cattle. Sam Maverick's grandson, Maury Maverick, former Congressman and also onetime mayor of San Antonio, named in January 1944 to head the Smaller War Plants Corporation of the War Production Board, is carrying on the tradition of political independence which his grandfather established. His career has been a stormy series of political "ups and downs," and he is one of the few figures in the American scene who has survived his own political funeral.

Maury Maverick's ancestry includes not only the doughty cattleman Sam Maverick, but also the famous pioneer-explorer Meriwether Lewis (of Lewis and Clark), the Maury family of Virginia, and Judge Lynch, from whose name is derived the word "lynch." (Maverick, incidentally, was one of the few Southern Congressmen who favored the passage of an anti-lynch law.) Born in San Antonio, Texas, October 23, 1895, he is the son of Albert and Jane Lewis (Maury) Maverick. Although his family was a distinguished one, his parents were not wealthy, and Maury's education was irregular. He received some early schooling from his mother, whom he describes as "the best cultured and best educated woman I know," but spent most of his time in the saddle working at odd ranch jobs. After a year at the Virginia Military Institute, from 1912 to 1913, Maverick entered the University of Texas, where he remained until 1916. He was then admitted to the Texas bar. (In 1917 he studied at St. Mary's University.) He began law practice in San Antonio, but when the United States entered the First World War he promptly enlisted and was commissioned a 1st lieutenant. He saw active duty overseas both in the battle of Saint-Mihiel (where he brought in twenty-six German prisoners singlehandedly) and in the Argonne. Maverick was severely wounded during the Argonne battle and received a citation for "gallantry in action," the Silver Star, and the Purple Heart.

Maverick's war experiences left him with a sober determination to enter politics and fight for what he believed in—"peace, preservation of personal and Constitutional liberties." His friends and enemies agree that Maverick never "pussyfoots" or equivocates. When asked once why he was so outspoken he answered, "Having died twice in France, it isn't worthwhile to avoid one political death by being a demagogue."

Back in San Antonio, Maverick took an active interest in civic affairs. He fought the Ku Klux Klan, fought the local political machine, was elected president of the San Antonio Bar Association, and organized a Citizens' League in that city. During the boom years of the '20's Maverick went into the lumber business and made a small fortune building cheap houses, which he says "were a disgrace to American civilization." In 1929 Maverick was elected state and county tax collector for Bexar County, Texas, a job that paid him more than $12,000 a year. But when the depression came Maverick was deeply moved by the poverty which he saw all about him. He "went exploring into the hobo jungles . . . and subsequently founded a cooperative camp in San Antonio for the relief of starving transients."

The depression convinced him that capitalism "needed serious readjustments," but Maverick did not favor any radical step that would effect a readjustment. He became an ardent New Dealer and, in spite of the numerous political enemies he had made, was elected to Congress in 1935 as a Representative from the 20th Texas District. He got there, according to the late Sherwood Anderson, "by buying the Mexican vote"; that is, Mexicans had previously been classified as

MAURY MAVERICK

Negroes "in the census and other records, Federal and state," thus unable to vote in most Texas primaries. Maverick forced their classification as white men and thus won the Mexican vote. He went to Congress as a Southern New Dealer and soon became one of the most colorful figures in Washington.

A group of liberal insurgents in the House led by the Texas Representative were called "mavericks," and they were known for their wholehearted support of all New Deal measures. Maverick fought for anti-trust legislation, favored President Roosevelt's '12 plan to enlarge the Supreme Court, led the House in the fight for TVA and slum clearance, and, as an upholder of civil liberties, opposed the Tydings-McCormick Bill which was aimed against communism and would "punish efforts to incite members of the Army and Navy to disobedience." Maverick's reputation as a liberal was well established. Although he was at this time a pacifist and bitterly opposed to the building of a powerful offensive army and navy (he proposed a bill to make required reading in the Reserve Officers' Training Corps such books as Remarque's *All Quiet on the Western Front* [1930] and Dos Passos' '40 *Three Soldiers* [1921]), he was nevertheless an avowed enemy of fascism—"As much as he hates war," Hamilton Basso wrote in 1937, "he hates fascism even more." By 1938 Maverick was advocating the training of 100,000 pilots and the building of 50,000 planes for a defensive United States Air Force.

Meanwhile Maverick was writing numerous articles concerning the administration of local governments, and of schools, hospitals, prisons, and business. Then, in 1937, he published his autobiography, *A Maverick American*. The book was well received and praised for its humor and absence of "pomposity and ponderosity." Duncan Aikman, writing in the *Saturday Review of Literature*, said, "The whalebone of pedantry, the bloat of oratorical gasses, the poison meat taints of political self-righteousness

MAVERICK, MAURY—*Continued*

simply are not in him." In 1939 Maverick published *In Blood and Ink*, comments on the origins of the Constitution of the United States and the significance of the document today. The reviewers were again enthusiastic, and the New York *Times* critic wrote: "Mr. Maverick's liberalism speaks with simplicity and vigorous warmth as well as seriousness and with a vigorous and sometimes dramatic turn of phrase."

Maverick announced his endorsement of a third term for President Roosevelt in 1939. But he declared himself unalterably opposed to Vice-President John Nance Garner of Texas, thus launching his own war against the old-guard conservative political machine in his home state. A year before Maverick had been defeated for Congress in the Democratic primaries, but in 1939 he announced his candidacy for mayor of San Antonio, running on a Fusion ticket. In May of that year, just one hundred years after his grandfather had been elected to that office, Maury Maverick became mayor of San Antonio. The late Heywood Broun hailed his election as a signal victory for the New Deal. Supported by the CIO, by the Mexican and Negro vote, and by numerous other groups who sought reform in city politics, Maverick began work on an elaborate program of slum clearance, public health, and general civic improvement.

Only two weeks after he took office, however, Maverick ran into serious difficulties. He was attacked editorially because he had not reduced municipal expenses, because he was using "collectivist" methods, and he was called "the No. 1 Communist of Texas." A dramatic climax was reached when Maverick refused to revoke a permit issued before he became mayor to a Communist group, permitting them to hold a meeting in the San Antonio Municipal Auditorium. The speaker at this meeting was to be a Mexican girl named Emma Tenayucca, known as "La Pasionara," and Maverick said that he could not bar her from the right of free speech anymore than he could bar a Republican or an Elk. Realizing that there would be trouble, Maverick ordered a police guard for the Auditorium on the night of the meeting. There was a riot, several people were injured, and Maverick was burned in effigy by a group of rioters.

Late in 1939 Maverick's political opponents had the Mayor arrested on a charge of paying the poll tax of another person. Maverick had received $1,000 from David Dubinsky [42], head of the International Ladies' Garment Workers' Union, for his mayoralty campaign. In return Maverick gave $250 to the San Antonio local of the I.L.G.W.U. "The prosecution claimed that this $250 was to be used for the illegal payment of poll taxes, but Maverick successfully maintained that the money had been intended only to help the union carry on a publicity campaign to encourage their members to pay their own poll taxes."

Actually Maverick's opponents had little hope of having him convicted on the charge. They went to court, according to Charles Curtis Munz, "so that the testimony, true and false together, could be spread on the public record." Munz thinks that his foes erred because by making Maverick something of a political martyr they increased his political strength. This did not prove to be exactly the case, however. Maverick was acquitted and finished out his term of office, but when he was renominated for mayor he lost a closely contested race by 1,000 votes. It was nevertheless agreed by political commentators that Maverick had survived his "political funeral."

Maverick's liberalism has classed him with the group of progressive Southern legislators who have opposed the poll tax as a hindrance upon the economic advance of the entire South. He testified before a House subcommittee: "I want the South to be run by Southerners, and the poll tax keeps that from happening. The poll tax makes the South a sort of piecemeal, part-time, fractional, divided democracy." Typical of these young Southern liberals, Maverick wants to dismiss all the romantic myths about the Old South and to promote its development as an independent, self-supporting economic unit. He writes: "The past, present, and future of the South are not alone important for the South itself, but its conditions bear an exact relation to conditions in the rest of the United States."

In 1940 Maverick was cited for his race-relations work by the Schomburg Collection of the New York Public Library and the Negro Life and History Study Association. In the same year he took an active part in Aid-to-Britain work, warning that if England fell the United States would be attacked. And in the summer of 1941, fully six months before the Japanese attack at Pearl Harbor, Maverick urged United States action against Japan. In the fall of that year he was named OPA assistant to study price administration in the United States territories and possessions.

From the OPA Maverick was transferred to the War Production Board, where he headed the Governmental Division from 1941 to 1944. This division embraces priorities of all civil branches of the Government (there being 170,000 state and local governments), war training programs, schools, colleges, hospitals, and prison industries.

In January 1944 WPB Chairman Donald M. Nelson [41], calling Maverick "an able, vigorous administrator," announced his appointment as vice-chairman of the WPB in charge of the Smaller War Plants Corporation. Maverick's new job was described as a "graveyard assignment," since most of his predecessors had been forced to resign after a short period in office. His job was "to get small business a fair share of renewed civilian output and of materials for reconversion." And, as I. F. Stone wrote: "It's going to be more difficult than ever as expanded big business, with cutbacks in their war contracts, hungrily eye the limited materials being made available for a limited resumption of civilian production." One of Maverick's first steps in his job was to adopt a new loan policy for the SWPC. Under the new system "the amount that banks are permitted to carry under a deferred participation was raised to $250,000 from the previous limit of $100,000, where the bank takes a direct participation in the loan of ten per cent or more." Maverick predicted that the new policy would be of tremendous advantage for small business, which he defined as "any business that can't hire a lobbyist in Washington."

According to one Washington column, written in January 1944, under Maverick there has been none of the "yoppy-yi-yaying and boisterous confusion" in the SWPC that some people had been led to expect by "re-reading fading clippings on earlier phases of the Maverick career." Nor had there been any "sudden characteristic political influx of Maverick protégés into SWPC personnel." Maverick "launched a series of weekly to-staff meetings that already have straightened out any number of wrinkles in the central organization"— and in one week SWPC "helped place approximately 350 contracts and 330 sub-contracts with a total value of $31,000,000 among small businessmen all over the country." Maverick had had a number of years of business experience (lumber) before entering politics, with the Hillyer-Deutsch-Jarratt Company, and from 1921 to 1930 with the Kelley-Maverick Company. Even in his SWPC office he had a small factory with 9,000 workers—a hive of honeybees which Agriculture Secretary Claude Wickard '40 had given him.

The SWPC chairman has expressed his views in reports to Congress, in articles for various publications, and in many speeches. He was insistent that small plants (those having fewer than 500 employees) which did not have war production contracts and could not get any, be allowed to convert to civilian production immediately. In May 1944 the War Production Board came around to this viewpoint and freed war plants with fewer than 100 workers from restrictions, thus allowing them to make essential civilian goods when manpower and surplus materials were available. In the critical manpower shortage areas, this applied only to plants with a payroll of fifty. This move was, however, blocked by the Army.

Over and over Maverick has pointed out the "unfair advantages" accruing to big business as such. These include ready and inexpensive credit, technological research facilities, access to management advice, and availability of raw materials. "He [little businessman] even suffers from inadequate representation with his Government"—so Maverick made himself "the little businessman's lobbyist in Washington." "The Government is an umpire," he stated, "but let's get this umpire business straight. It shouldn't let a team of supermen that has a patent pool on its side, plus cartel agreements, take on a team of sand-lot boys. A no-hit game in that case would be unfair. The Government should step in where such inequalities exist, and give the small businessman a chance to compete. Then, if he can't hit the ball, let him be called out." His solution: "treat the small businessman as well as you do the farmer. Any farmer can get management advice from Uncle Sam [through the Department of Agriculture]. He can get laboratory help too. And the farmed is nothing but a businessman who lives out in the country. Give the little man in town at least as much encouragement."

Specifically, Maverick advocates: (1) the enforcement of antitrust and anticartel laws; (2) "giving the little man first right at reconversion"; (3) selling all Government surplus property in small lots and with wide publicity so that the small buyer can get a share; (4) "multiple rental" of large Government-owned plants no longer needed for war production (Secretary Ickes '40 estimated that one-third of the country's factories were in 1944 owned by the nation), to permit several smaller businesses to use the facilities which otherwise only huge concerns could afford. In the field of finance, Maverick says, "Let the Smaller War Plants Corporation set up a bank insurance plan similar to the one used by the Federal Housing Authority." And about taxation: "Increase well beyond $10,000 the excess-profit exemption provided in the Revenue Act of 1943. Make it $50,000 at least. It could, if necessary, be restricted to corporations with excess-profits net income—before exemption—of not over $50,000." Other Maverick recommendations are for "carry-overs and carry-backs" of operating losses, and liberal depreciation allowances on new plants and equipment. Not only should Government-owned patents be available and well publicized, but "the Government should make it possible through cooperative laboratory systems for small producers to secure aid in developing new processes and new products. This can be done with existing private laboratories, the land-grant colleges, universities, and numerous Government laboratories which have a wealth of help that is not being used fully. In none of these, I claim, is the little man being given an advantage. He now has handicaps, and I propose taking them off."

While working for this end, Maverick won editorial praise from coast to coast by denouncing what he termed "gobbledygook"—the use of the long, involved, pompous, polysyllabic terminology or officialdom. "Anyone using the word 'activate' or 'implement' will be shot," he warned his underlings. The SWPC head found time also to write articles demanding free guide service for visitors to the National Capital; to make inspection trips to England; to advocate a post-War chain of superhighways costing some ten billion dollars; and to get from Congress appropriations of many millions of dollars—and an increase in his own salary from $8,000 to $10,000. He had previously been receiving less than some of his own aides. In later 1944 emphasis in the SWPC began to be placed on the returning veteran, using its "virtually unlimited credit facilities, tools, and materials . . . and a fund of technical information embracing both the experience of America's leading corporations and the pool of patents sequestered from owners in enemy countries." The SWPC already had made arrangements with the Alien Property Custodian by which they brought to the attention of small business the 45,000 alien patents "on a nonexclusive basis for fifteen dollars each. By careful abstracting of the patents," Maverick reported, "we are making it much simpler for the small manufacturer to find those he can use. These patents must be kept for the American people, and little, and big, business."

Maury Maverick is fair-complexioned and just under average in height. Interested from both the institutional and humanitarian viewpoints in "prisons, jails, houses of detention, hospitals, and schools," he is a member of six public-minded associations (also the Sons of the American Revolution, the American

MAVERICK, MAURY—*Continued*

Legion, the V.F.W., the National Press Club, and Army and Navy Club). He has founded a pan-American center and restored an old Spanish village, called the "Villita." Maverick calls himself "a student of Latin-American relations," and is a collector of Americana and a numismatist. Reflecting the Texas influence, he is proud also of his collection of saddles; and he is a designer of silver and gold pillboxes.

Maverick is described as "big-boned and full-cheeked, with a curving waistline that is beginning to crease over his belt." He has been called "a remarkably able and engaging speaker." In 1920 he was married to Terrell Louise Dobbs, and they now have two children, Terrelita Fontaine, and Maury, Jr., a Marine Corps officer. Bluff and brusque in manner, Maverick has not had a smooth career, and he says that he does not expect any smoother sailing in the future: "I figure on trouble with my undertaker, who will probably try to bury me in a dress suit."

References

Am Mag 130:22-3+ S '40 pors
Forum and Century 95:354-8 Je '36 por
Nation 149:673-4 D 16 '39 por
New Repub 90:315-17 Ap 21 '37 por;
102:398-400 Mr 25 '40; 152:557-8
My 10 '41 por
Sat R Lit 16:3-4+ Je 26 '37 pors
Maverick, M. A Maverick American 1937
Who's Who in America 1944-45

MAY, CHARLES H(ENRY) Aug. 7, 1861
—Dec. 7, 1943 Ophthalmologist; for nearly sixty years a specialist in diseases of the eye; author of *Manual of the Diseases of the Eye* (1900), which reached its seventeenth edition in 1941, and was translated into ten foreign languages.

Obituary

N Y Times p27 D 9 '43 por

MEAD, JAMES M(ICHAEL) Dec. 27, 1885- United States Senator from New York
Address: b. Senate Office Bldg., Washington, D.C.; h. 79 Ideal St., Buffalo, N.Y.

James M. Mead, junior Senator from New York, was born December 27, 1885, the son of Thomas and Jane (Kelly) Mead, in a clapboard shack along the Lackawanna Railroad tracks at Mount Morris, Livingston County, New York. His father was a section boss on the Lackawanna Railroad and very poor: the shack itself was provided by the railroad. Jim Mead's brothers and uncles were railroad workers, too: one brother was a fireman, two were trainmen; three uncles were trainmen, three were switchmen. His own future was therefore cut out for him. After attending grammar school in Buffalo, where his family moved when he was five, he went to work at the age of twelve as water boy for the Lackawanna, earning $1.15 a day. Six months later he was promoted to a job taking care of switch lamps; a year later he became a maintenance-of-way man. Once when the men went out on strike for better working conditions and higher pay the boy joined his seniors, but his father promptly ordered him back to work.

In 1904 and 1905, while employed on the Lackawanna Railroad in charge of switch and signal lights, Mead attended the Caton School of Engineering and later the Buffalo Institute of Technology, taking an engineering course. In 1910 the Democrats captured the lower House of Congress and when the party came to power in 1911, Mead, a good Democrat himself, was appointed a member of the Capitol Police Force. It was a job which he held for only six or eight months. He was on duty from midnight until 8:00 a.m., utilizing much of the time during the day studying law and listening to Congressional harangues. When he left Washington he told his fellow guards that he himself would be in Congress in ten years. Actually he was two years off: it took him eight.

Returning to Buffalo to take an active part in the local political campaign, Mead soon became an election inspector, committeeman from his district, and in 1913 a candidate for supervisor. Throughout the next year he served on the Erie County Board of Supervisors, representing the 11th Ward. At the same time he was employed as a yard switchman on the Erie Railroad, and in the fall of 1914 he was elected president of his union local, serving until January 1915. Today he holds one of the two lifetime silver membership cards issued by the Switchmen's Union of North America. In the fall of 1914 Mead was also elected to the New York Assembly (state legislature), where he served four successive terms. At the time much social and labor legislation was being framed. Mead acted as spokesman for all railroad-labor legislation, leading a successful fight to prevent repeal of the state's "full crew" law and also helping to put through the Eight-Hour Day Act. On August 25, 1915 he was married to Alice M. Dillon, a schoolteacher.

In November 1918, running for Congress at the request of organized labor and other progressives, Mead was elected in spite of the fact that most of the United States went Republican that year, also in spite of the fact that the 42nd District was itself normally Republican. For twenty years, through Harding, Coolidge, and Hoover '43 landslides, he was to keep his seat—his vote going up at each election. In 1918 his majority was only 1,000; in 1936 it approximated 25,000.

In Congress, Mead—as a member of the House Post Office and Post Roads Committee, of which he became chairman after the Democrats were returned to power in 1931—championed legislation for shorter hours and increased pay for postal service employees. The author of the Mead Air Mail Act and of the Forty-Four-Hour Week law (later, the Forty-Hour Week law) for postal workers, he has been honored by the members of the Buffalo Letter Carriers' Union, who have named their local the "James M. Mead Branch." The young Congressman was also one of the outstanding supporters of the amendments widening the scope of the Locomotive Inspection Act, and he played a prominent part in helping defeat the anti-strike provisions of the Cummins-Esch law. With La Guardia '40 he fought Hoover's plan for a general sales tax, helped defeat anti-labor bills, supported all bills for workmen's compensation, for mothers' and widows' pensions, and for a shorter work-day, and stood by labor during the long fight over the Howell-Barkley Railroad Bill. Throughout the depression he battled for Federal relief for the unemployed, for a public works program, against wage reductions. When Roosevelt '42 became President, Mead became known as one of the most loyal supporters of the New Deal, always reporting for votes on crucial measures. When he ran for re-election in 1936 his defeat was urged by Father Coughlin '40.

On December 2, 1938 Mead resigned from the House of Representatives, a month after having been elected to the Senate to fill the vacancy caused by the death of Royal S. Copeland, a Republican. (Mead's vote-getting talents are underscored by the fact that the 42nd New York District, which had been sending him to Congress for so many years, fell back into Republican hands.) In the Senate, to which he was re-elected for a six-year term in 1940, running against Bruce Barton, he continued to be known as an ardent supporter of the New Deal. As a member of the Labor and Appropriations Committees, he consistently defended the National Labor Relations Board and fought against cuts in relief appropriations and restrictive labor legislation. As a member of the Temporary National Economic Committee and, later, of the Murray Committee, he defended the interests of small business, urging more and more sub-contracting on war jobs and the relaxation of existing loan restrictions of the Federal Reserve System. In the international sphere he supported President Roosevelt's foreign policy at all times, backing revision of the Neutrality Act, the Lend-Lease Bill, the Selective Service Act. In October 1941, entering the controversy over Administration efforts to get greater Catholic support for American aid to Russia, he read to the Senate "concrete, documentary evidence that Hitler '42 and the Nazi police are destroying the Catholic Church in Germany."

Early in 1942 Mead was designated by the Civil Service Committee of the Senate to pilot through the Senate what was popularly known as the "Pensions for Congress" measure. This measure, which Mead said was almost universally misunderstood, would have granted annuities to members of Congress who, like all other Government officials and employees, paid 5 per cent of their salaries into a retirement fund, and it had as its aim nothing more than the broadening of the present retirement system. It specifically excluded from its benefits those "already subject to another retirement act," and Mead himself was covered by the retirement act of New York State—but the Senator came in for much criticism during the press campaign which forced Congress to repeal the measure.

Much worse things were said about Mead, however, when in July 1942 President Roosevelt backed him for the Democratic nomination for Governor of New York after James A. Farley, state Democratic chairman, already had secured commitments from fifty-one out of sixty-two county delegations for his own man, Attorney General John J. Bennett, Jr.

JAMES M. MEAD

The American Labor Party, which had often held the balance of power in New York state, insisted it would not support Bennett for Governor if he were nominated, and the President said that he did not believe that the Democrats could win with Bennett. But the real stake in this battle between Farley and Roosevelt, it was believed, was control of the ninety-four New York delegates to the 1944 Democratic convention.

Within an hour after Mead announced his own candidacy Jim Farley cited nine occasions on which Mead had said he didn't want to be Governor. Claiming that Mead was "scared" of the job and would make a "terrible" governor, Farley announced that the "draft-Mead move" was a "piece of political fakery" and that Mead's record was one of "inconsistency . . . vacillation . . . plain and unadulterated deceit." (In 1940 Farley had said he was remaining as New York state chairman only in order to see Mead renominated and re-elected.) Westbrook Pegler '40 took Mead to task for being "what the unioneers call a labor stiff, meaning a union politician," and blamed him for not having cleaned up all the racketeering in the American labor movement (in this connection, Mead himself states he was never a salaried union official, that he always served without compensation); others attacked him for enjoying the support of the Left wing as well as the Right wing of the American Labor Party. (Mead finally disavowed the former.) In the meanwhile Mead was busy making speeches. At a CIO second-front rally he announced boldly: "We should declare a war against poverty, against ignorance, against persecution, against prejudice, against inequality, against exploitation. We can win *that* war just as we are going to win *this* war."

But the really important issue was: Who controlled the delegates to the Democratic state convention? And the answer came in August 1942, when Bennett was nominated by a vote of 623 to 393. Mead joined Bennett in a series of campaign appearances after Roose-

MEAD, JAMES M.—*Continued*

velt declared Bennett "the best fitted" of the three candidates for Governor, but both Left and Right wings of the American Labor Party continued to refuse support to Bennett. In November 1942 Thomas E. Dewey '44, the Republican candidate, was elected Governor of New York.

The junior Senator from New York continued to be a "loyal Administration wheel horse." In 1943 he led the fight in the Senate to prevent the dismissal of Watson, Dodd, and Lovett '43. His only major votes against the Administration were in opposition to an appropriation for crop insurance and in opposition to the proposed $25,000 limit on salaries, and at every opportunity he denounced "labor baiters whose object is to slip the knave card to organized labor for absenteeism, slow-downs, and wage profiteering in war production."

As a member of the five-man subcommittee of the Truman '42 Committee studying the manpower problem, in June 1943 Mead, together with four other Senators, was given the opportunity to visit the war fronts of the world in an Army bomber. The five returned late in September. They had questioned such leaders as Churchill '42, Eisenhower '42, Chiang Kai-shek '40, and MacArthur '41; had talked to the men fighting this global war in England, Africa, the Middle East, China, and the Far East, and had reached a number of conclusions. Mead and the fellow member of his subcommittee, Ralph O. Brewster (Republican), had been specifically assigned to investigate the provision of airport agreements with foreign nations, and in the Senate they advanced the thesis that the United States should acquire permanent possession of those air bases which it had built in other countries. Mead also told the Senate that the United States should formulate a foreign oil policy as a guarantee of adequate future supplies, since, he claimed, the Western Hemisphere was supplying a disproportionate share of the War's petroleum needs. But that his chief impressions of America's fighting forces and leadership were more than favorable was made evident in May 1944, when he became the first Senator to report in book form on his trip. According to Harry Hansen, his book, *Tell the Folks Back Home* (1944), is "not a stuffy, formal report such as Senators are supposed to enjoy, nor a barrage of oratory and grandiloquence. It is a readable, informal, chatty story of a trip to the camps at the Front." Under a provision of the Soldiers Vote Act it was found at first to be unsuitable for distribution to servicemen; later this provision was amended. Proceeds from the book are being turned over by Mead to the Red Cross and other war service agencies.

In 1944 Senator Mead has fought particularly hard against overriding Roosevelt's veto of the tax bill, against stripping the Tennessee Valley Authority of its revolving fund, cutting appropriations for the Federal Communications Commission's radio intelligence work, restricting the use of the Federal ballot by servicemen in the 1944 election, and dissolving the Fair Employment Practices Committee. As floor manager for the Marcantonio bill which would have prohibited eight

Southern states from charging a tax as a voting requirement, he battled unsuccessfully for cloture to allow a vote on the poll tax.

In November Mead opposed the policy of the State Department in regarding the St. Lawrence seaway project as an Executive agreement with Canada instead of a treaty. "It would set a dangerous precedent for future treaties with other countries," he declared. However, he called for hearings on the project in the next session of Congress, asserting that he endorsed the hydroelectric power plan, but was uncertain as to the wisdom of opening the St. Lawrence to large vessels until reciprocal privileges had been assured. As a member of the Senate Small Business Committee the Senator in December advocated the enactment of a bill empowering the OPA to establish rent ceilings on business properties where it considered these ceilings essential.

Upon the resignation of Harry S. Truman as chairman of the Senate's War Investigating Committee in August, Senator Mead was elected its chairman. After December hearings on manpower shortages, Mead declared that legislation is not the solution to current critical shortages of war materials. He believes a labor draft unlikely, that the Army, Navy, Maritime Commission, WPB and WMC "can and will work the thing out." His committee, charging that over-buying of some materials by the armed services had contributed to shortages of others, made an additional report to the Senate on its study of war needs and shortages. It contained a six-point program for "improving supply and . . . reducing to the minimum" problems of surplus disposal.

Many of Mead's most telling speeches are made outside the Senate. According to *Time* Magazine, "he never misses a chance to talk at a Democratic fish fry or a labor meeting." In May 1944 he addressed the Polish-American Congress at the opening of its convention in Buffalo, and, after hearing heated attacks on the Soviet Union from other speakers, he affirmed the need for unity among Americans and the United Nations and warned the Congress that "complicated questions should be resolved after the termination of hostilities."

Mead campaigned vigorously for the President's re-election in 1944. He urged the defeat of "isolationists" in Congress; he assailed Dewey's labor policy, stating that there was no danger of wartime labor restrictions remaining permanent; and he charged Governor Dewey and Herbert Hoover '43 with initiating an undercover campaign "to drive the late Wendell Willkie '40 out of the Republican Party."

A political forecast for Mead was made by James A. Haggerty of the New York *Times* in December 1944: Should Governor Thomas Dewey seek re-election to Albany in 1946, Haggerty wrote, it is expected he will be opposed by Mead, who will offer stronger opposition than Bennett did in 1942. The Senator, it is certain, will have the backing of the Labor Party, the political arm of the Political Action Committee in New York State.

Six feet two, the Senator has wavy dark hair that is now graying and a habitual wide smile. He doesn't smoke, he drinks only occasionally, and athletics is still one of his chief interests. He was instrumental in getting a gymnasium for Congressmen; as a student of boxing, he never misses a heavyweight title fight; and he is an enthusiastic fisherman. But it is baseball that is his true love. A veteran of sandlot baseball teams and railroad workers' scratch teams who once tried for a place on a Class-A minor league team, he is vice-president and part owner of the Buffalo Baseball Club. He had a leading role in persuading the powers-that-be that baseball has a definite place in the war program, and he has tried to get all-star baseball teams to visit the fighting fronts. He himself is top man on the Democratic ball team which meets the Republican team every year in an annual charity tilt in Washington, and at Angola, New York, where he has a farm, he is the mainstay of the softball team when not engaged in raising grapes, berries, and a few chickens. Senator and Mrs. Mead have one son, James M. Mead, Jr., who entered the service as a private and in 1944 is a 2nd lieutenant. Member of a bomber crew, he was wounded in action in the European theatre of war. (A younger brother, George, now a lieutenant in the Navy, was State Department Commander of the American Legion.)

Mead's election day ritual includes a reunion with friends of sandlot and schoolhouse days in Hankie Dean's Tavern in East Buffalo, where he eats clams, chowder, and goulash while waiting for the returns. Whether he will ever again carry out this ritual is another story. In the spring of 1944 there was a rumor that he would be Democratic candidate for Governor in 1946—another that he was hankering to give up his Senatorial toga and to become Mayor of Buffalo and president of the Buffalo Baseball Club.

References

N Y Post p4 Ap 26 '44
Newsweek 20:31 Ag 3 '42
PM Mag p14-15 Ag 2 '42 pors
Time 40:18 Ag 3 '42 por
Who's Who in America 1944-45

MENTHON, FRANCOIS DE 1900(?)- (mäṅ″tôn′ frän″swä′ dé) French Government official; lawyer; educator

Address: Office of the Commissioner of Justice, French Provisional Government, Paris

The chief problem of François de Menthon, who was appointed Commissioner of Justice in the French Provisional Government in August 1944, is the carrying out of the purge of traitors and collaborationists in France. Before the liberation of Paris he was Commissioner of Justice in the Committee of National Liberation. In this post he was in charge of studies made by its short-lived Purge Commission.

Born in 1900, de Menthon can speak of a past which, according to *La Lettre de la France au Combat*, "duplicates that of countless Frenchmen: a studious and hard-working childhood and youth, a profession carefully prepared and achieved step by step; marriage, children, a quiet, happy home life." The year 1938 found him in the chair of law and political economy at Lyons University. (He had already served as professor of political economy at Nancy, where he also was municipal attorney.) In 1938, "with France again threatened from the North and the freedom of peoples and na-

tions everywhere endangered, François de Menthon—like Frenchmen everywhere—found himself confronted with the question: 'Can the Republic forfeit her pledges, retreat before the ever-growing German menace?' Munich was the answer. To François de Menthon, as to countless other Frenchmen, Munich was the 'first indelible stain.'"

Although, as the father of six children, he had not been called up for service, when France declared war on Germany in September 1939 de Menthon volunteered for active service. At the front he lived through the "long months of strange and troubling inactivity" that characterized the "Sitzkrieg," the "phoney War." In the disastrous month of May 1940 he noted: "We are fighting without planes, without tanks, without anti-tank guns. How was such a lack of preparation possible?" He hoped in vain that "the Republic would galvanize Army and people to a supreme effort."

June 1940 found him wounded and a prisoner, sick with rage at having been "betrayed before, during, and after the combat." He heard Petain's [40] voice "quavering words of senile consolation." Then he heard another voice: de Gaulle's [40]. Hope was born again. "The fight goes on. France carries on. Nothing is irretrievably lost."

Four months later François de Menthon escaped from prison to Unoccupied France—only to find a government "that speaks of reconstruction, honor, tradition . . . and accepts defeat as final, while the War goes on elsewhere. A government that makes defeat the cornerstone of the regime, a regime inspired by the enemy and contrary to all French traditions—and whose supporters seem blind and insensible to their shameful destiny." He had returned to the chair of law and political economy at Lyons University, but he determined to "fight Hitler [42] and Mussolini [42] and their French disciples who would impose on our land a totalitarian regime. . . . Fight for Strasbourg and Metz, for our Empire—and more than that: fight for the soul of France that can only be stifled in a Nazified Europe."

Dismissed from the Lyons faculty by Vichy in August 1942, this quiet professor became a major thorn in the side of the Germans. He was the founder of an underground movement in southern France called Liberté, which later merged with the strongly de Gaullist Combat, of which he was made co-director. (Combat, made up chiefly of anti-Nazi intellectuals, and Libération, whose leadership is mainly trade unionist, have been called the two leading underground movements in France.) De Menthon directed the "study committee" to which all the resistance movements sent delegates, and also directed the clandestine sheet published by Combat, which is reportedly read by 750,000 French men and women. The "study committee" under his guidance "sought to work out general political principles for the resistance movement—which naturally takes in the Communists—and to determine a minimum program for France after liberation." De Menthon's own ideas of that minimum program are hinted at in the first number of *Les Cahiers politiques*, another clandestine publication that aimed at defining the "general trend of the future political, economic, and

FRANCOIS DE MENTHON

social regime" from the point of view of French resistance. In an article (then anonymous) entitled "Why I Am a Republican," he wrote:

"The Republic, for us, is a constant, ordered collaboration of all citizens in the march of public affairs and the direction of collective interests. . . . It demands a common soul, a complete faith in the destiny of our land and the respect of certain fundamental values. . . . There must be mutual confidence among individuals and classes . . . and the convergence of all efforts toward a common end: human progress in its deepest sense, transcending purely material gains. . . . Prepared in struggle, sacrifice, and captivity, founded in the blood of the martyrs of resistance, our Republic will be no field for sordid intrigue or personal ambition; it will usher in a great period of humanity."

In August 1943 de Menthon escaped from France by fleeing to England, although the Nazis had placed a prize of a million francs (about $20,000) on his head. On September 6, 1943 it was announced that he had been appointed Commissioner of Justice by the French Committee of National Liberation. This appointment, with the approval of the entire Committee, forged the strongest link that had yet been established with the mother country. The Committee was about to name its Purge Commission—the body that would seek to purge the French Empire of all collaborationists, Vichyites, underminers of the French Republican Constitution, and men of uncertain loyalties—and it was the function of the Commissioner of Justice to put the Purge Commission into operation. In his first interview in London, de Menthon said that French organizations demanded stern action against collaborationists. "It is not a question of vengeance but of patriotism. We have suffered too much not to demand sanctions and a purge of the handful of Frenchmen

who have led us into such misery. There must be a purge of civilian and military cadres." At the same time he revealed that since April resistance inside France had been coordinated by a Council of Resistance representing eight underground movements.

One of de Menthon's first actions was a detailed legal analysis of the Crémieux decree of 1870 giving French citizenship to Algerian-born Jews, which had been revoked by General Giraud '42 in March 1943. On October 21, 1943, following his analysis and his statement that the French resistance movement had regretted and resented the Crémieux abrogation, the decree was declared again in full force by the French Committee of National Liberation. De Menthon also made many speeches over Radio France, and on November 14, 1943, in one of his broadcasts to France, was able to announce that the French Committee had "at last taken on the characteristics of a real government." (General Giraud had recently resigned.) At the same time he invited the Communists to take part in it so that it might be truly representative of French resistance in which they played such an important role.

These moves were generally popular with the Provisional Consultative Assembly set up at Algiers, but many members of the Assembly did not feel that the purge of the long list of men whom they considered traitors to France was going on fast enough. Since it was de Menthon's department which was in charge of studies by the Purge Commission, by this time headed by Charles Laurent, it was to the Commissioner of Justice that complaints were addressed. Finally, in January 1944, the impatience of the Assembly, which week by week was gaining power at the expense of the French Committee of National Liberation, reached a climax. Some of the disgruntled members of the French underground resistance group announced that if punishment was further delayed they would deal with the traitors themselves or go back to France again to continue their battle against the Nazis. That the delay in the punishment of former collaborationists was entirely de Menthon's fault seemed dubious, however. De Gaulle himself blamed the Allies for "painful, dolorous negotiations." The British had reportedly been putting on strong pressure on behalf of Pierre-Etienne Flandin '41; the United States on behalf of both Pierre Boisson '43 and Marcel Peyrouton '43.

At the beginning of March, de Menthon announced from Algiers that the Purge Commission had examined 1,473 cases and 491 were pending. The Commissariat of Colonies had punished seventy-six officials, among them eleven governors; while the Commissariat of Justice had penalized ninety-three collaborationists. Although the work of the Purge Commission had been finished the month before, a purge of the North African press would be continued, he said, by members of the Committee of National Liberation.

When the French Provisional Government headed by de Gaulle was formed at the end of August, following the liberation of Paris, de Menthon continued in his post as Commissioner of Justice (Commissioner is a rank equivalent to Minister). By early September the Provisional Government had already ordered the arrest of many prominent collaborationists, as well as a French branch of the Gestapo which had been unearthed. Orders were issued by the new Commissioner to stop these arrests from being made by any authority other than his own department or the prefecture of police.

On September 15 de Menthon announced that the arrest of Marshal Pétain and all members of the Vichy Cabinet had been ordered. Action against these functionaries was part of a campaign to restore republican laws, he said, although some Vichy degrees would remain in force. "Government action since June 16, 1940 has no legal basis," he explained, "but we cannot cancel everything and even must maintain some decrees, otherwise it would mean disorder in the national administration." The new Government, he added, did not intend "to hold responsible any auxiliary officials who had taken no initiative and limited themselves to carrying out orders."

Indications from different parts of liberated France were that the purge was soon under way, special courts having been instituted in every department to try the cases. (Later a High Court of Justice to try high Vichy officials was established.) A *Christian Science Monitor* writer at the end of September expressed concern over some signs of the existence of popular justice, as revealed in the executions of minor collaborationists. "If political criminals are summarily punished. . ." the article commented, "republican legality and the authority of the new de Gaulle Government will be seriously compromised." However, de Menthon and de Gaulle himself had made it clear that they were opposed to the rule of "terror" in France, stating that collaborationists would be punished according to republican penal law.

As the purge progressed, a sharp division of opinion was apparent. In December when a Lyon court pronounced the death penalty on a collaborator the judges were denounced with cries of "Assassins!" This was not a unique view among Frenchmen, according to the New York *Times*, but one that had not been given much notice in the press. At the same time, in Paris de Menthon was assailed by members of the Consultative Assembly for not speeding up the purge throughout the country. As *Newsweek* wrote, "Echoing the revolutionary cry of 1792 they [the members] asked for heads and, amid ringing cheers, named the heads that they wanted to roll." A public opinion poll held at the end of the year found that 70 per cent of the people did not approve of the methods in which the purge was being carried out. Of these, the majority objected to the slowness of action against the collaborators; others felt that outstanding collaborationists were going unpunished; while still others protested against arbitrary arrests and excessive punishment.

At the end of the year de Menthon expressed the hope that the purge would end by February. Figures issued by the Ministry of Justice in December revealed that some 300 death sentences had already been imposed, although all of these collaborations had not been executed and commutations had been granted in some instances. While admitting to imperfections in the system, de Menthon emphasized that the

Government had not failed to make provision for the administration of justice. The Government, he reiterated before the Council of State in December, "has as its principal task the restoration of republican legality."

De Menthon is described as "slightly built, mild tempered." He is devoted to General de Gaulle, who, he once announced over Radio France, "for us is not only the symbol of liberty but who will be tomorrow, who is already, the leader of national liberation, the general, even the President, Charles de Gaulle."

References

La Lettre de la France au Combat 3:
8-9+ S '43
N Y Times p11 S 7 '43
Newsweek 22:64 S 20 '43

MERRILL, FRANK (DOW) Dec. 4, 1903-
United States Army officer
Address: b. c/o War Department, Washington,
D. C.

The opening of the Allied invasion of Europe in June of 1944 overshadowed the bitter two-year campaign against the Japanese in Burma; yet "no other American force anywhere had marched as far, fought as continuously, or has had to display such endurance as Major General Frank Merrill's swift-moving, hard-hitting Marauders," who have since been disbanded as a unit.

Frank Dow Merrill, known as "the Army's outstanding authority on the Japanese military system and mind," was born in Hopkinton, Massachusetts, December 4, 1903, and was brought up in Amesbury. (His wife and two sons now live in New Hampshire.) Unable to secure an appointment to West Point from a Congressman, Merrill enlisted in the Regular Army on June 14, 1922, when he was nineteen. Shipped to Panama with Company A of the 11th Engineers, he rose in three years from private to staff sergeant. On five different occasions Merrill took the competitive examinations for entrance to West Point, and each time he was rejected for a physical deficiency: he wears eyeglasses to correct astigmatism. The young soldier's sixth attempt to enter the Point was successful, however; and in June 1929 he was graduated from the Military Academy and commissioned a 2nd lieutenant of cavalry.

The following October, Lieutenant Merrill reported for duty with the 3rd Cavalry at Fort Ethan Allen, Vermont. After a year there he was transferred to the 2nd Armored Car Squadron (Cavalry) at Fort Eustis, Virginia; and then in May 1931 he was assigned to study special weapons at the Ordnance School of Watertown Arsenal, Watertown, Massachusetts, from which he was graduated a year later. The following month the Lieutenant obtained the degree of B.S. in Military Engineering from the Massachusetts Institute of Technology, after which he joined the 13th Cavalry at Fort Riley, Kansas.

Ordered to Brownbranch, Missouri, in August 1933, the thirty-year-old officer spent four months on Civilian Conservation Corps duty, rejoining the 13th Cavalry as a regimental motor officer at the beginning of 1934.

MAJ. GEN. FRANK MERRILL

While at Fort Riley, Merrill was detailed to the Cavalry School, which he was attending in November 1934 when his promotion to 1st lieutenant came through. After his graduation in June 1935 he remained at the Cavalry School as an instructor. Three years later Merrill was sent to the United States Embassy in Tokyo to study Japanese. As assistant military attaché he was attached to the Japanese Army on maneuvers and cultivated the friendship of the young Japanese officers, including many who are now high in the enemy's forces. In addition to Japanese, Merrill learned Chinese dialects, which are very useful in his present relations with Chinese troops.

Presumably Lieutenant Merrill made a highly favorable impression on his superiors, for the forty months of his stay in Japan brought him two promotions: to captain in June 1939 and to major (temporary) in October 1941. The following November the new Major was assigned to duty in Manila as General Douglas MacArthur's [41] intelligence officer. When the Japanese struck at Pearl Harbor, Merrill was in Rangoon on a flying mission for MacArthur; he remained there to become Lieutenant General Joseph W. Stilwell's [42] "right hand" in the China-Burma-India theatre of operations.

When Stilwell's forces "got run out of Burma" by the Japanese in the spring of 1942 Merrill marched into India with him and his "polyglot party of weary, hungry, sick American, British, and Chinese Army officers, enlisted men, Burmese women nurses [under the direction of Dr. Gordon Seagrave [43]], Naga, Chin, and Shan tribesmen, and a devil's brew of Indian and Malayan mechanics, railwaymen, cooks, refugees, cipher clerks, and mixed breeds of Southern Asia." On May 25 Merrill was promoted to lieutenant colonel, and in July he was awarded the Order of the Purple Heart for his "singularly meritorious acts of essential service in Burma between March 15, 1942 and May 1, 1942." (This deco-

ration, originally for wounds received in action, when revived in 1932 was also awarded for meritorious acts. As of September 1942 it is no longer awarded for the latter reason.) "By his most efficient and tactful handling of the duties of liaison officer with the British forces and between him and the Chinese forces," the citation read, "which frequently exposed him to heavy bombings in a country infested with Fifth Columnists, and by his accurate and careful observations, Lieutenant Colonel Merrill provided invaluable and dependable information upon which action was based." From then on Merrill helped his chief to discover the cause of the Allied failure in Burma and make plans to return and retake Burma from the Japanese. At the beginning of 1943 he was promoted to colonel (temporary).

In October 1943 volunteers were assembled in answer to President Roosevelt's [42] call for "a dangerous and hazardous mission." As Time Magazine reported, "From the jungle training bases of Trinidad and the Canal Zone, from Guadalcanal and New Georgia came many veteran Regular Army men itching for action. . . . Others were young, unmarried zealots who usually make fine soldiers." Frank Merrill set about welding these men into a long-range penetration group on the model of General Wingate's famous British Chindits (now under Major General W. D. A. Lentaigne [44]), who had made a daring raid into Burma the preceding spring. The "foresight, superior judgment, energy, and devotion to duty" Merrill displayed in planning future operations from January to November 1943 won him the Legion of Merit decoration and his promotion, at the age of thirty-nine, to brigadier general (temporary).

After intensive training in the latest techniques of jungle warfare, "Merrill's Marauders" became the first American infantrymen to fight on the Asiatic mainland. From Ledo in the northwest Indian province of Assam, they set out in February 1944 on a hundred-mile circling march to the rear of the Japanese concentrations at Maingkwan. Handicapped by constant rains and by having to train their own pack animals—a shipment of 600 mules had been sunk—the Marauders averaged twenty miles a day over the Naga Hills and through the sweltering, disease-ridden jungle, taking all precautions against ambush. "Iron rations" were dropped from 10th Air Force planes based in India. Arrived at their destination, a point ten miles behind the enemy lines, Merrill's men proceeded to cut the Japanese supply line through the Hukawng Valley. This roadblock technique, first applied by the Nipponese against Stilwell, was turned against its originators with such effect that part of a veteran Japanese division was trapped between Merrill's Americans and Stilwell's Chinese. "This isn't battle," correspondent Frank Hewlett reported, "it's wholesale slaughter." At least 2,000 Japanese were killed—650 by Merrill's Marauders—and as many more wounded, while the Americans had the amazingly low number of seven dead and thirty-seven wounded.

General Merrill, who had been given his orders for the campaign in a five-minute talk with Stilwell, was on his own after that. At times he directed the supporting fighter planes in their attacks on enemy columns and communications; at others the pilots hit "targets of opportunity." "Militarily," as General Stilwell commented, "elements of two Chinese divisions, a unit of tanks operated by Chinese and commanded by an American, and American combat troops worked smoothly together in the happy job of exterminating the common enemy."

Next Merrill led the main group of his Marauders on a "nearly incredible" outflanking left-end march of seventy miles in three days, most of the way over steep timbered mountains, and set up a roadblock barring the enemy's retreat from Shaduzup, forty miles to the south, which the Marauder unit proceeded to capture. Pursued into the hills by a Japanese column trying an encirclement of its own, one of Merrill's battalions fought a bitter two-week battle at Npum Ga, aided by "artillery dropped from planes in action so close that the American gunners ignored their gunsights and simply fired in the direction of the enemy." Finally other Marauder units came to the rescue; the surrounded raiders suddenly shifted from the defensive to the offensive and "virtually annihilated" their attackers. During these operations the General became ill, and on April 11, 1944 he was flown to an American hospital in India by "a plane which landed virtually under the noses of the Japanese." (In spite of a heart ailment, Merrill refused to be evacuated then or in May when he was again hospitalized. "Taking cognizance of his great popularity with his men," Stilwell permitted him to return to his command in June, but he was back in the hospital in July, with malaria.)

After a few days of reorganization and integration with Chinese troops, Merrill's Marauders set off for their biggest job, the assault on Myitkyina. They "marched 112 miles, mostly over a narrow mountain trail, winning two victories over the Japanese en route. They fought through heavy pre-monsoon rains, at times slogging through ankle-deep mud. They crossed mountains which tribesmen had told them were impassable. . . . In one sector they went from 1,000 feet to 6,000 feet almost straight up. It took them nearly two days to make one mile in altitude. At times they crawled on hands and knees, and many of their sure-footed pack animals plunged over precipices [carrying precious equipment] . . . . They fought at times for thirty-six hours without food or water." Merrill's troops did, however, have close air support from Brigadier General John Egan's Tactical Air Force and a complete air umbrella in the latter part of the campaign.

Arrived at the outskirts of Myitkyina, the largest city in northern Burma, the Marauders put into operation a strategy which Merrill had helped General Stilwell to plan. In "a brilliantly conceived and intrepidly executed attack" reminiscent of Robert E. Lee's Chancellorsville plan, columns of Marauders and Chinese troops slid through Japanese lines, emerged north, south, and west of Myitkyina, seized the enemy airfield and made it ready for the landing of planes which brought reinforcements and equipment—an air-borne army that immediately began the assault on the city itself, already under attack by Stilwell's Chinese and menaced by General Lentaigne's Chindits. With hardly a pause, the Marauders were "smashing" the Japanese garrison—units of two divisions and auxiliaries commanded by Lieutenant General Renya Mataguchi, the captor of Singapore, with whom the American Generals had that old score to settle. They fought "street by street and house by house," handicapped by the heavy pre-monsoon rains. This, the largest air-borne troop movement up to that time (the German invasion of Crete in May 1941 was the only comparable operation), was hailed by commentators as a demonstration that "when the enemy air power is comparatively low . . . it is not safe [for him] to have any flat piece of ground big enough for an airplane to land on without a guard if there is a military objective near it."

General Merrill directed the attack from a *basha* made of bamboo and parachute rayon in a valley camp which "comes as near to being like the movies as reality can get without becoming ridiculous." Such is the confusion of jungle fighting that a commander may often find, as Merrill once reported to Stilwell, "I would have to be either a liar or a magician to tell you where the troops are today."

In early August 1944 the War Department released the information that the famous Marauders had suffered "an almost complete breakdown in morale," bringing out Senator Robert Rice Reynolds' [40] demand for an investigation. As Merrill himself told the story in Washington, the Marauders had been in combat one hundred days, carrying out three campaigns involving 750 miles of marching, five major battles, and thirty-two minor engagements, culminating at Myitkyina. At this time the hospitalization rate was high, and included the General. When the Japanese at Myitkyina were bringing up reinforcements, Stilwell scraped the bottom of the manpower barrel and issued an order to return to the front all convalescents fit for full field duty. By error, it was transmitted as calling for men fit to walk. Merrill and the hospital authorities questioned the order, but by the time it had been checked with Stilwell some plane-loads of convalescents had already been sent forward. ("Uncle Joe" Stilwell is said to have wept when he heard this.) "A lot of my men got very indignant," says Merrill. "I was goddam indignant myself, but . . . I am positive that if we had asked for volunteers every one of them would have gone back." In ten days, the General declared, the "storm in a teapot" was over, and the Marauders were to be reorganized as a numbered regiment, instead of remaining "orphaned" as an experimental organization—thus allowing for a regular promotion system.

General Stilwell emphasized that Merrill was in no way to blame for the occurrence, and transferred him to "less arduous but equally important duty" as head of the Allied headquarters liaison group for the CBI theatre. "General Merrill," he stated, "is a very high-class officer, and my full confidence in him should be obvious from the duty he is now performing." (Brigadier General Theodore F.

MERRILL, FRANK—*Continued*

Wessels was given command of the Marauders.) In September 1944 President Roosevelt's [42] nomination of Merrill for promotion to major general (temporary) was confirmed by the Senate, and in December he was appointed deputy United States commander in the Burma-India theatre, under Lieutenant General Daniel I. Sultan.

Ordinarily, General Merrill, a tall, well-built soldier whose sandy hair was already graying at forty, smokes a pipe endlessly and jokes with his associates in a cool New England voice; when the situation is discouraging, his staff know the danger signals which warn them to "keep out of the 'Old Man's' way." "He has always outworked and overworked his aides." Said to have much quiet charm, the General is particularly popular with the Chinese, who reportedly hold him in an esteem second only to Major General Claire L. Chennault [42] of the 14th Air Force. One correspondent who found him "brushing up on his Japanese" remembered that Merrill "knows personally most of the Japanese commanders against whom he is fighting, including the Japanese general he is outsmarting at the moment." The writer was reminded, too, of the late Stephen Vincent Benét's words in *The Devil and Daniel Webster*: "If two New Hampshiremen can't lick the devil, we might as well give the country back to the Indians."

References

C S Mon II p2 Mr 8 '44 por
N Y Sun p16 Mr 14 '44
N Y World-Telegram p1 Mr 6 '44
Newsweek 23:19 Mr 20 '44
Scholastic 44:9 Mr 27 '44 por

MICHAEL V, KING OF RUMANIA Oct. 25, 1921-

Address: Royal Palace, Bucharest

Probably the only king in history to precede and succeed his father is youthful King Michael V of Rumania. In both instances he fell heir to the tottering throne of a kingdom wracked by internal dissension and court intrigue and menaced by enemies at all its boundaries. Formed through the union of the Principalities of Wallachia and Moldavia in 1859, Rumania won her independence from the Turks in 1877. As a reward for joining the Allies during the First World War, Rumania won wide territories which had previously belonged to her neighbors, Austria, Hungary, Bulgaria, and Russia, and over which she instituted a strong policy of repression of minorities. The Rumanians soon realized that the spoils of war were more of a handicap than a blessing. The country's contested geographical position, the ingrained loyalty of most of her citizens to the Allied cause, and her great natural wealth—she is especially rich in oil and grain—placed that small country in the Second World War in an extremely critical position in the Balkan peninsula. Falling under the sway of the Nazis in 1940, Rumania in August 1944 deserted the Axis camp to become a cobelligerent with the United Nations.

On July 20, 1927 a shy, quiet boy born not quite six years before (on October 25, 1921), Prince Michael (Mihai) of Rumania, suc-

ceeded to the crown of his grandfather, the late King Ferdinand I. The heir apparent, Michael's father, former Crown Prince Carol [40], who first caught the attention of the world as a playboy prince, had renounced his right to the throne for the sake of a love affair, of which the Royal Family disapproved. Married in 1921 to Princess Helen of Greece, Michael's mother, Carol maintained a liaison with the half-Jewish Magda Lupescu [40] to the point where it became a public scandal, precipitating an open break with the court. In December 1925 Carol disclaimed his hereditary rights, an action almost immediately confirmed by a parliamentary law which declared his son heir to the throne and which consigned Carol to ten years' banishment. Little interested in ruling a kingdom, six-year-old Michael is said to have cried plaintively to his mother at the close of the coronation ceremonies: "Let's go home, mama, I'm hungry."

During Michael's minority the country was to be administered by a regency council. This was composed of the child's uncle, Prince Nicholas, the Patriarch Miron Cristea, and Supreme Court Justice G. V. Buzdugan. The latter two were appointees of Premier Ion Bratianu, the "invisible dictator" of Rumania and the head of the so-called Liberal Party, which represented banking, commercial, and industrial interests. Bratianu was the astute statesman whose father had brought the weak Hohenzollern Prince Ferdinand into power in Rumania, and, it is claimed, adroitly made use of Carol's estrangement from his father to build up the regency to counteract any possible attempt by Carol to return. Despite his son's accession Carol retained the title of King, indicating that his exile had been forced rather than voluntary. Carol thus became the center of discontented forces in his native land. These included certain factions in the Army as well as the United National Peasant Party, representative of the mass of Rumanian peasants, led by Juliu Maniu, who raised the question of the legality of the regency. Intensifying the political instability of the boy-king's reign was the reputed desire of his grandmother, the late Dowager Queen Marie, to become sole regent. Meanwhile many political leaders were inclined to agree that a prince who could forswear his inheritance and desert his wife and son was hardly the type of person who, as king, could bolster an insecure dynasty.

Three years later, nonetheless, the small boy installed in Cotroceni Palace in Bucharest was displaced by his father, who dramatically returned from exile to become King Carol II. The downfall of the Liberal Party, Carol's avowed enemy, had been hastened by the death of Ion Bratianu in November 1927 and by the real though not apparent success of the giant National Peasant Congress held at Alba Julia in May 1928. Then, in November of that year, Juliu Maniu succeeded Vintila Bratianu as Prime Minister, with promises of honest government that would favor the workers. Thus the dictatorship of the brothers Bratianu, who had at least nominally guarded the throne for Michael, finally ceased in a bloodless revolution which overthrew a half-century of comparatively uninterrupted rule by aristocratic and capitalistic interests.

On the evening of June 6, 1930 former Prince Carol of Rumania landed on the flying field of Bucharest and within forty-eight hours was proclaimed King and head of the House of Hohenzollern-Sigmaringen, by virtue of an act of Parliament. What seemed to be a spontaneous *coup d'état* was soon revealed to be a premeditated measure of the Rumanian Government, headed by Premier Juliu Maniu and Prince Nicholas, who had taken advantage of the struggles of reactionary factions to effect their purpose. The first political result of the accession, however, was the upsetting of Maniu's Peasant Government.

Now relieved of his royal responsibilities and demoted to Crown Prince, Michael shed the burden of kingship with a light heart and, with his new title of Grand Voevod of Alba Julia, returned to his play and to his studies. Since infancy the boy with "the precociously grave smile" had been in the constant charge of an English nurse, Miss St. John, and had received his early education at the hands of Rumanian tutors. His mother, Princess Helen, who came from a family of disciplinarians, gave Michael a strict upbringing, yet allowed him some childhood pleasures. It is recorded that the American Minister to Rumania, when paying a state call at the palace, more than once got down on his knees to play with the young King's expensive set of blocks or to have explained to him the newest royal locomotive. By the time he was twelve Michael had already mastered three foreign languages—English, French, and Greek.

On his return to Bucharest King Carol sent Helen into exile and himself assumed a stern control over his son's education. Two Hungarian writers for *World* Magazine report that Michael, deprived at this point of the companionship of his domineering mother, to whom he was deeply devoted, formed a strong dislike for his father and Magda Lupescu. A natural outlet for the emotions of the politically immature Crown Prince, *World* continues, was to join the Fascist Iron Guard, the chief aim of which was the removal of Carol and Lupescu. (This Iron Guard movement was an outgrowth of the League of the Archangel Gabriel, founded in 1924 by the anti-Semitic zealot, Corneliu Zelea Codrianu. Supplied with Nazi funds, it first became politically dangerous in 1934.) Until his disillusionment with the Nazis, Michael therefore remained with the Guards.

For his part, Carol supplied his son with companions of both sexes and from all classes of people, and Michael was made to spend long hours of study under exacting teachers who taught him military science, government, history, mathematics, and philosophy. In 1940 the Crown Prince was certified to have passed his examinations, taken orally in the presence of his father. He also completed his military training and for a time worked as a mechanic in the Ford automobile plant in Bucharest. His father, perforce, was almost his constant companion, and Michael was frequently at his side during the conduct of official business. On his eighteenth birthday Michael was made a Senator, a member of the Rumanian Academy, and a lieutenant in the Army.

MICHAEL V, KING OF RUMANIA

During his ten-year tenancy of the Rumanian throne the new King, too impulsive and temperamental ever to be a wise ruler, was unable to avert the disintegration threatening his land. Many of Rumania's grievances were laid at the door of Mme. Lupescu, whom Carol had falsely pledged to leave behind when he returned. Ministerial Cabinets followed one another rapidly, two Premiers (Duca in 1934 and Calinescu in 1939) were assassinated, and Carol himself escaped assassination several times. In 1938 he virtually proclaimed a royal dictatorship, forming a one-party state and making the ministers personally responsible to the Crown. He has also been accused of graft. The Iron Guard, too, contributed to the discontent and disorder in Rumania. At Carol's sporadic attempts at repression, the Iron Guards redoubled their campaign against Rumania's 1,000,000 Jews—in which Carol collaborated by signing anti-Semitic decrees—and played a large part in changing the Government's traditional pro-French policy. Nazi Germany had not been slow to cast covetous eyes on Rumanian oil and grain, and in March 1939 Carol signed a trade treaty with her. In early 1940 the fight of German, French, and British interests over Rumanian oil fast approached a climax.

In the crucial year of 1940 Rumania was forced to yield some of her territorial gains of the First World War. In June she lost about 19,300 square miles of land and an estimated population of 3,500,000 when Russia occupied Bessarabia and Northern Bukovina. (Bessarabia had belonged to Russia from 1812 to 1918, when Rumania had taken advantage of the Bolshevik Revolution by seizing and annexing the territory. In Bessarabia the Moldavians formed the largest part of the population; in Northern Bukovina—which from 1774 to 1918 had been part of the Austro-Hungarian Empire—the Ukrainians were predominant. The former territory was therefore incorporated by the U.S.S.R. with the Moldavian autonomous republic; the latter with the Ukrainian Soviet Socialist Republic.) In

MICHAEL V, KING OF RUMANIA—
Continued

the wake of the Russian invasion a Nazi regime was established in Rumania. Only two months later the Vienna Award dictated by the Foreign Ministers of Germany and Italy, Ribbentrop [41] and Ciano '[40], handed over to Hungary a large area in Transylvania. In an effort to appease German demands, Carol appointed to head his Government General Ion Antonescu '[40], who with German support established the Fascist Iron Guard as the only recognized party in the state. With the Iron Guard in full revolt, on September 6, 1940, Antonescu forced Carol to abdicate. Two days later Antonescu's collaborationist Government ceded the Southern Dobruja to Bulgaria. Seeking to keep Rumania neutral, Carol had first relied on a British-French territorial guaranty, then had helplessly watched Rumania diminish to a virtual military protectorate of Germany, which, with Italy, guaranteed the new borders against aggression.

For the second time Carol's son, a somber tall youth of eighteen who preferred to tinker with motorboats, automobiles, and radio sets, ascended the throne—of a smaller Rumania. Helen was recalled from her ten-year exile, and as Queen Mother she lived with Michael in the palace at Sinaia in the country. Deprived of all his constitutional rights by Antonescu, who, with the title of Conductor, wielded all legislative and executive authority, Michael was more a prisoner than a king. He seldom appeared in public, and under compulsion he delivered prepared speeches. In 1942, from his refuge in Mexico City, Carol announced that he would release Michael from his bondage as soon as he could organize his Free Rumania movement.

In October 1940, a month after Michael's accession, German troops poured into Rumania, occupying the capital and vital oil fields in an operation that exemplified the perfection of the Nazi technique of attaining an objective by military and political threats, but without actual armed action. Completing their subservience to the Nazis, the Antonescu Government welcomed the invaders. It was pointed out that Rumania had been rendered defenseless in a military sense largely because of the Vienna Award, while at the same time the abdication created an internal crisis; this coincided, too, with a crisis between Bucharest and London, the Germans having long charged the British with attempts to destroy the oil wells, which were largely controlled by British, French, Dutch, and American capital. In November Rumania, together with Finland and Hungary, signed the Anti-Comintern Pact in Berlin. In the months that followed, the country sank into civil war and anarchy, even factions of the Iron Guard revolting against German rule as they watched the results of the occupation.

In June 1941 Rumanian troops marched out with the Wehrmacht in its attack on Russia, and later Rumania declared war against Great Britain and the United States. With the help of the Germans, Rumania retook Bessarabia and Northern Bukovina, and conquered other Russian territories; in October 1941 a decree was issued incorporating Odessa and an area beyond the Dneister into Rumania. But despite this regaining of her lost territory, Rumania was merely "a gasoline station and a granary" for Hitler. Although the official policy of the Rumanian Government had followed the line of least resistance in bowing to Axis demands, since the summer of 1940 the popular tendencies were moving ever more strongly toward a more independent economic and political relationship with Germany.

By early 1943, although there were comparatively few conspicuous signs of discontent and sabotage in Rumania, reports made it clear that a vigorous anti-German feeling was growing among the population, which protested the mounting casualties on the fighting fronts and the increased Nazi demands for oil and food. Rumanians felt also that Hungary was profiting from the War at the expense of Rumania. It was rumored that several armistice overtures to the Allies had been made, and by May observers saw Rumania ready to drop out of the War at the earliest opportunity. It was further reported that Socialist, Communist, and Liberal forces in the embattled country were banding together against the Antonescu regime under the leadership of Maniu, who favored friendly relations with the Allies. At this time, too, King Michael, in an open clash with Antonescu, revealed that his antagonism to the pro-Axis policy was no longer a secret. Tightening their grip on Rumania, the Germans became increasingly suspicious of the King and his mother, who were now in constant touch with Maniu. In an attempt to ease the Balkan satellites away from Hitler, in December 1943 United States Secretary of State Cordell Hull '[40] warned Rumania and the other nations that they would share the "consequences of the terrible defeat that United Nations arms were so surely bringing to Nazi Germany." Then, as the Russians advanced speedily toward the Rumanian borders in March 1944, Antonescu, almost defenseless with most of his forces locked up in the Crimea, sent peace emissaries to Turkey to bargain with the Allies.

In April, giving the lie to German propaganda and reaffirming Russia's adherence to the principles of the Atlantic Charter, Russian Commissar V. M. Molotov '[40] authoritatively pledged that in the invasion of Rumania the Soviet Government did not "pursue the aim of acquiring any part of Rumanian territory [beyond Bessarabia, which she regarded as her own] or altering the existing social system in Rumania"; the U.S.S.R.'s only objective, he said, was "to pursue the enemy until his final rout and capitulation." Accordingly, as the Red Army occupied the country, it instituted a strict policy of nonintervention in local affairs in the areas taken from the Axis. In May 1944 the Mediterranean Allied Air Forces completely destroyed the Astra Romana oil refineries at Ploesti. In July peace negotiations broke down again; and at the time no likelihood was seen of their resumption.

On the night of August 23, 1944 twenty-two-year-old King Michael, taking matters into his own hands apparently for the first time, broke Rumania's ties with the Axis and switched to the Allied camp as a cobelligerent in a sudden *coup d'état*. (In an anonymous *PM* article written by a Rumanian student of Balkan affairs it was stated, however, that the coup was a political maneuver executed by Michael's pro-Nazi mother to save the throne and to retain for future use "her position as go-between for the conservative Nazis [in their dealings with] other world powers." Michael, the article also said, is still under the domination of the Queen Mother.) The determining factor in the King's decision was said to be the swift August offensive of the Soviets on Rumanian soil. It was later announced that Antonescu had been imprisoned on the order of the King, backed by a few loyal military leaders, when the Marshal refused to conclude an armistice with the Allies or resign his office. Other arrests of the entire pro-German Cabinet followed. Then, in a proclamation over the Bucharest radio, King Michael ordered his armies to cease hostilities against the forces of the Allies, declaring that he had accepted their terms of unconditional surrender in the name of the nation. He called upon his subjects to take up the fight alongside Russian troops against the common enemy, Germany. (War was declared August 25.) The new regime also denounced the Vienna Award of 1940, making it clear that Rumania was at war with Hungary and sought Allied help in the recovery of Transylvania. Michael named General Constantin Sanatescu, the master of his military household, as Chief of Government and Marshal of Rumania. Other new Cabinet members included Peasant Party leader Juliu Maniu and Dino Bratianu, head of the Liberal Party, as well as representatives of the Communist and Socialist Democrat Parties.

Rumania was thus the first Axis satellite in the Balkans to desert Germany. Her action was viewed as a major triumph for the Allies, in both a political and military sense. The armistice terms signed with the United Nations on September 13 provided, in part, that Rumania throw its military strength against Germany under Allied (Soviet) command; disband all Fascist organizations; restore everything taken from the Allies, including the return of Bukovina and Bessarabia to Russia; pay to Russia $300,000,000 occupation damages in goods within six years; and accept direction by an Allied Control Commission until a final peace was signed. In return it was also provided that the Rumanian surrender of Transylvania to Germany under the Vienna Award would be voided; that she would retain civil administration in noncombat zones; and that Soviet troops would assist Rumania against Germany and Hungary. Russia had continued her sweeping operations through the Balkan peninsula, entrapping numerous fleeing German divisions; and in Rumania itself, in the period between August 20 and 31 (on which day the Russians entered Bucharest), her army killed or captured 418,600 enemy troops.

Reports eminating from Rumania after the armistice soon showed that Rumania's problems were not solved by her change of allegiance in the War. A New York *Times* correspondent wrote in October that the leaders of the four major parties represented in the Cabinet—the National Peasant and the Liberal Parties on the one hand, and the Social Democratic and the Communist on the other—seemed unable to reach a compromise on the formation of the Government. The Generals who made up the Cabinet, reported to be almost entirely pro-Fascist or reactionary, had no knowledge of civil administration. The Government departments were functioning badly, and the country was disorganized. In November Russia sent a stiff note to the Government accusing it of not living up to the terms of the armistice— not all German-Hungarian citizens had been interned, German-Hungarian business interests had not been put under Government control, and Allied nationals held in the country were not being aided. As a result of the note, the Cabinet resigned and Premier Sanatescu took over the post of War Minister. A second crisis soon developed, however, and in early December a new Government was installed, with Sanatescu out and General Nicolai Radescu the new Premier. A week later King Michael signed a decree abolishing Jewish restrictions and paving the way for the return of full citizenship rights to Rumanian Jews.

References

C S Mon p4 S 9 '40 pors
N Y Herald Tribune p4 S 7 '40
PM p8-10 S 13 '44 il pors
World 2:76 O '44
International Who's Who 1942
Statesman's Yearbook 1943

MICHAEL, MOINA 1870 (?)—May 10, 1944 Known as the "Poppy Lady"; originated Poppy Day in 1918, an idea which has raised millions for war veterans; it was sponsored in August 1920 by the American Legion and adopted in 1921 by the British Legion.

Obituary

N Y Times p19 My 11 '44 por

MIDGLEY, THOMAS, JR. (mij'lē) May 18, 1889—Nov. 2, 1944 Noted American chemist; invented ethyl gasoline and was one of the first to do research with synthetic rubber; recipient of many awards, among them the Longstreth Medal of Franklin Institute in 1925, and the Willard Gibbs Medal in 1942.

Obituary

N Y Times p21 N 3 '44 por

MIKOLAJCZYK, STANISLAW (me-ko-li'chek stä-nē'släf) July 18, 1901- Former Premier of Polish Government-in-Exile

Address: Polish Government-in-Exile, London

Stanislaw Mikolajczyk, ex-Premier of the Polish Government-in-Exile, was born July 18, 1901 in the German province of Westphalia, where his father, a migrant Polish laborer, had gone to work in a coal mine. He was still a boy when his family returned to their native province of Poznan, then under German rule, where his father had established a homestead in Borzecice. He attended elementary school there and, resuming his studies some years later, was graduated from an agricultural college and the Dalki folk college.

By his sixteenth year young Mikolajczyk had already started to work in a sugar-beet refinery and had become an active participant in Polish patriotic youth organizations which were preparing an insurrection against German rule. At eighteen he enlisted in the Polish Army, then fighting against the Germans to enforce the decision of the Versailles

STANISLAW MIKOLAJCZYK

Peace Conference that gave Poznan province to Poland. In 1920 he fought as a private in the war against Soviet Russia when Pilsudski, Poland's post-War leader, attacked Russia with the avowed aim of including the Ukraine in a new Polish-Lithuanian Empire. Mikolajczyk was mustered out after he was wounded. He then returned to the fifty-acre farm which his father had bought. Some years later he was to move to his own farm.

Since early youth Mikolajczyk had been very active as a community organizer, and in many educational and cooperative organizations as well as in the Right Wing of the Peasant Party. Elected to the local village council, he subsequently became county supervisor and a member of the provincial legislature, and from 1930 to 1935 he represented the Peasant Party in the Sejm, or Polish Parliament. In 1935, after serving as regional secretary of the Peasant Party for Poznan province, he became vice-chairman of the party's executive committee.

In January 1934 Pilsudski had introduced an authoritarian constitution in Poland, and Foreign Minister Beck had signed a pact of non-aggression with Nazi Germany. A few months later Pilsudski died, and a species of fascism came to Poland. The dream of empire was revived, with hopes of help from a Nazified Germany. The authoritarian constitution of April 1935 was frankly based on the principle of "solidarity of the élite." Persecution of minority groups grew. The Communist Party and allied organizations were outlawed. Vincent Witos, chairman of the Peasant Party, was exiled, and Mikolajczyk became one of the party's deputy leaders. The party, although strongly nationalistic, had a pro-French orientation and took a firm stand in favor of democratic and civil rights. In April 1937 it called a ten-day strike to prevent supplies from reaching the cities when Beck's Government remained deaf to its demands for a democratic constitution, free elections, and the return of Witos. That same year, according to

the official Polish news agency, Mikolajczyk was called upon to accept the presidency of the Peasant Party. Dr. Tewik Rustu Aras, Turkish Foreign Minister for thirteen years, has said, however, that "the largest majority of Poles never heard of Mikolajczyk," and it does seem to be true that the names of Peasant leaders like Witos, Thugutt, and Rataj are better known in Poland itself.

When the War began in 1939, Mikolajczyk fought as a private that September in the defense of Warsaw against the invading German troops. With the surviving members of his unit he then escaped to Hungary, where he was interned. Ultimately he and many of his comrades escaped to France by way of Yugoslavia and Italy. There the late General Wladyslaw Sikorski [40] had formed a new Polish Army, 100,000 strong. There, too, the Polish National Council, headed by Ignace Jan Paderewski, had been formed to replace the Polish Parliament for the duration of the War. Mikolajczyk was named Paderewski's deputy vice-chairman after serving for a brief time on the National Council, and upon the death of the statesman-pianist he succeeded him as president of the Council, which had moved to London after French resistance collapsed. Sikorski, after fighting at Narvik and in Flanders, had succeeded in getting the bulk of his forces to England, too; and in 1941 Mikolajczyk was appointed deputy Prime Minister and Minister of the Interior in Sikorski's Cabinet.

As Minister of the Interior in the Polish Government-in-Exile, Mikolajczyk's chief duties were to maintain contacts with the official Polish underground and to act as its popular representative in all government affairs. It was he who coordinated all communications between the various government departments and officials and their "opposite numbers" in occupied Poland. His office handled all underground finances and the continuing vital statistics of the nation at war, including a comprehensive census. Representatives of the United Nations knew him as the custodian of the most extensive blacklist of Nazi criminals in all of occupied Europe. He was the man whom Burnet Hershey described as the Polish "J. Edgar Hoover [40], Prosecuting Attorney, Sheriff—and, one hopes—Lord High Executioner" all rolled into one. "From his office on the fourth floor of Stratton House, Piccadilly," Hershey wrote, "he holds the reins of the strangest bureaucracy in the world, controlling a vast army of conspirators and plotters, all working under the very nose of the enemy. . . . He [Mikolajczyk] has virtually prepared the decrees for the execution of Hitler [42] and Himmler [41], and only a sense of respect for orderly justice restrains him from signing the documents before the court convenes."

In the meanwhile Premier Sikorski, who advocated a policy of friendship with Poland's traditional enemy, Russia, had apparently won out over the strong anti-Soviet forces in his own Government. On July 30, 1941 Sikorski and the Soviet Ambassador in London, Ivan Maisky [41], signed an agreement that formally ended the state of war existing between Poland and the U.S.S.R. and joined them in a military alliance. Polish prisoners taken by the Red

Army when it invaded eastern Poland in September 1939 were freed by the Russians to fight again. A new Polish Army was to be recruited, trained, and equipped in the U.S.S.R., it being understood that the Poles would be ready for battle alongside the Red Army by October 1941. The commander in chief, General Wladyslaw Anders, kept insisting that his army was not ready to fight, however, and when early in 1942 the Polish Government-in-Exile decided to evacuate its troops from Russia to Iran the Russians raised no objections.

This experience did not further good Polish-Soviet relations. And the fact that the border dispute had not been settled was another source of constant friction. By virtue of the treaty of July 1941 the Russo-German pact of September 28, 1939 partitioning Poland had been annulled, but no new arrangement was put in its stead and the question of post-War boundaries remained open. Before signing the treaty Sikorski had suggested that the Soviet Government should recognize Poland's pre-War frontiers, but had met with a flat refusal.

In this dispute, Poland's claims were chiefly historical. Poland in medieval times was one of the largest empires in Europe, stretching from the Baltic in the north to the Black Sea in the south and taking in Lithuania, part of what later became Latvia, the Ukraine, and northwest or White Russia. Russia and Poland were traditional enemies: in 1610, for example, Polish troops seized Moscow; in 1764 and 1794 Russian armies occupied Warsaw. In the early 1800's the kingdom of Poland was partitioned between Russia, Prussia, and Austria, and in 1815 the Russian Czar set up a "Congress Kingdom" limited to ethnical Poland, refusing to include the non-Polish provinces which had belonged to Poland before. The Treaty of Versailles fixed Poland's western boundary but left the problem of her eastern frontiers open. An Allied commission headed by Britain's Foreign Secretary, Lord Curzon, nevertheless attempted to delineate the ethnical boundary between Russia and Poland, and the famous "Curzon Line" was drawn in December 1919. This put Poland's eastern frontier almost exactly where the Soviet-German pact of September 1939 later drew the demarcation line, both leaving the western Ukraine and western White Russia within the U.S.S.R., although in 1939 the Russians also occupied the regions of Bialystok and Lwów.

The Curzon Line was merely a general plan, details of which were to be elaborated later by the Governments of the new Poland and the U.S.S.R., for both countries were then torn by civil strife. But the Poles would have none of it. Still dreaming of the "Greater Poland" of the past, Marshal Pilsudski sought to expand the Polish boundaries as far eastward as possible, and made demands for a wide stretch of land mainly inhabited by White Russians. War broke out over these claims, and in 1919 Polish forces overran eastern Galicia; Vilna, just awarded to Lithuania by the Allies, was seized; and in April 1920 Pilsudski attacked Russia in an attempt to seize the Ukraine. The Russians succeeded in driving the Poles out of the Ukraine, and Soviet troops even reached the gates of Warsaw, but France's General Weygand [40] hurled them back almost to the Curzon Line, and under the Treaty of Riga, concluded in 1921, Poland retained extensive Ukrainian and White Russian territories. At the time the United States denounced the treaty, for one of Wilson's Fourteen Points had stipulated: "An independent Polish State should be erected which should include the territories inhabited by indisputably Polish populations." It is estimated that the Ukrainian population of pre-War Poland was 6,257,000, and, according to the New York *Times,* "there were not more than 2,500,000 Poles of a population of 11,000,000 in the provinces east of the Curzon Line when the last reliable census was taken in 1931."

In eastern Poland, moreover, "huge latifundia, covering thousands of acres, were in the hands of a few wealthy noblemen, while the masses of the rural population lived in misery." Discontent led to sporadic outbreaks of violence, and in the Polish "pacification" of the Ukraine in 1930 dozens of villages were burnt down by Polish policemen and thousands of peasants and workers were subjected to brutal treatment. In the autumn of 1934 Poland declared that it would no longer accept control by the League of Nations over the fulfillment of its obligation to minorities within its borders, as defined in minority treaties it had accepted in 1919, "thus," according to a *Foreign Policy Report,* "freeing its hands for measures of repression against Ukrainians, Jews, and other minority groups."

It is true, however, that the Soviet-German agreement of September 1939 gave to Russia territory which included 5,274,000 Polish-speaking inhabitants as well as 7,413,000 non-Poles. And although presumably the U.S.S.R. would be willing to restore to Poland the regions of Bialystok and Lwów, both west of the Curzon Line, where at least one-fifth of the Polish-speaking inhabitants of the entire eastern area lived, the dispossessed landowners, bankers, and industrialists among the Polish émigrés have a very tangible interest in preserving Poland's 1939 frontier. In December 1942 the Polish National Council in London passed a resolution formally laying claim to nearly all territories acquired under the Treaty of Riga, as well as to German territories on the west. Sikorski, yielding to pressure, himself issued a formal statement in February 1943 asserting Poland's claim to the lost provinces. On March 30 he also announced that if Polish "rights" were not respected at the conclusion of the War, Poles would be united to the last man to "resist any claims which aim at the sovereignty of our country, from whatever quarter they might be raised." The Soviet press, never known for its tact, responded in kind. The Union of Polish Patriots in the U.S.S.R. had already been formed under the leadership of the pro-Soviet Polish novelist Wanda Wasilewska [41], and a new Polish fighting force had been formed, made up of Polish officers and soldiers who had preferred not to leave Russia along with Anders.

On April 25, 1943 came the first open rupture between members of the United Nations. The Nazis had charged that 10,000 Polish

MIKOLAJCZYK, STANISLAW—Cont.

officer prisoners had been murdered by the Russians in 1940 near Smolensk (territory under German control for almost two years). The Poles promptly asked the International Red Cross to investigate, and the Russians, saying that any investigation on Nazi-held territory would be a farce and charging the Germans with responsibility for whatever murders had been committed, "suspended" relations with the Polish Government-in-Exile and accused the Poles of "contact and accord" with the enemy. Three days later Wanda Wasilewska disputed the right of the Sikorski Government to speak in the name of the Polish people, and although the Russians refrained from giving official status to her Union of Polish Patriots, this organization in Moscow was eventually to develop into a virtual counter-government.

Only a few weeks after this crisis in Polish-Soviet affairs Sikorski was killed in a plane crash on his way back from the Middle East, where the Polish armed forces were stationed—and hopes of a Polish-Soviet reconciliation grew dimmer than ever. On July 14 Mikolajczyk was named Premier of a new Government which included two other members of the Peasant Party, three Socialists, two National Liberals, two National Democrats, and three non-party men. The new Government hardly represented a determined break with the past, however. The official policy of the London leadership of even the Polish labor movement, the Polish Peasant Party, and the Polish Socialist Party was to uphold the integrity of the Polish frontiers of 1939. As for one Rightist in the Cabinet—Foreign Minister Romer—was the man who, as Polish Ambassador in Tokyo, had preached the doctrine that Poland should have a special alliance with Japan so that in the coming war against Bolshevism the U.S.S.R. could be attacked on two fronts. President Wladyslaw Raczkiewicz, formerly a loyal Pilsudski man, held almost equally vehement anti-Soviet views, and he named as commander in chief of the Polish Army the anti-Semitic General Kazimierz Sosnkowski, who had previously resigned from the Government because he had opposed Sikorski's pact with Russia. According to Time Magazine, "Since its army in Britain and the Near East is Poland's greatest military and political force until Polish soil is reconquered, Sosnkowski's political influence will presumably exceed that of the Premier."

Comments made by Mikolajczyk himself on July 16, 1943 showed, according to the New York Times' David Anderson, "an unmistakable thread of militant nationalism." Mikolajczyk said his Government "fully subscribed" to the idea of a federation of central European nations outlined by Sikorski in 1940. "What he chose not to recall today was the collapse of the plan when the Russians indicated their distaste for it."

The Polish-Russian border quarrel grew more serious as the Nazis retreated in the Ukraine and the Red armies neared the pre-1939 Polish border. As early as December 1943 the U.S.S.R. had charged that Sosnkowski had instigated systematic murders of Poles in eastern Poland who gave allegiance to Moscow; and on January 3, 1944 Premier Mikolajczyk announced in a Reuters interview: "I can say unhesitatingly that provided complications arising from demands to certain Polish territories could be removed we would gladly, in execution of a common strategic plan, cooperate with the Russians when they reach Poland." This was seen by some as a threat that the Polish underground would be ordered to refuse to cooperate with the Red Army unless the demands of the Polish Government-in-Exile were met. It was generally believed, however, that Mikolajczyk himself had thrown his weight in the direction of "moderation" toward Russia. A government statement of January 5 frankly demanding the restoration of Russo-Polish relations as the price of underground cooperation with the Red Army was reportedly toned down by him, although the modified statement, released as the Russians advanced across the pre-1939 frontier of Poland on January 6, was also regarded as sowing distrust of Russia.

The crisis came on January 11, when the Moscow radio announced that Russia was prepared to guarantee a "strong and independent" Poland—presumably including slices of Germany—provided the Polish Government-in-Exile agreed to accept the Curzon Line as the basis of discussions. (Poland was also invited to become signatory to the Russian-Czech treaty of alliance, mutual assistance, and post-War collaboration.) The Polish Government-in-Exile replied on January 14 that it was willing to submit "all outstanding questions" to the judgment of a four-power conference including Britain and the United States, but this was not enough for Moscow, which promptly denounced the Polish Government-in-Exile as having rejected the Curzon Line. Russia also indicated that anti-Soviet elements would have to be removed from the Polish Cabinet before she would consider resuming relations with the Polish Government.

Mikolajczyk and Foreign Minister Romer prepared to go to the United States in February 1944, apparently in hopes of winning State Department support; but the trip was postponed by Washington. In the meanwhile the British attempted to break the deadlock, but failed. At the end of February 1944 the attitude of the Polish Government-in-Exile was still that it could not accept the Curzon Line as a final settlement without a mandate from the Polish people, although it would be willing to accept a temporary border nearer to Soviet demands; and that it was not willing to change its personnel in order to please Moscow. (It did, however, order its underground organization to cooperate with the Red Army.) Actually, according to the authoritarian Polish constitution of 1935, under which the Polish Government operates, the uniform and indivisible state power rests in the President's hands. He has the legal right to declare war, to decide about peace, to make agreements with foreign countries, and to ratify such agreements—none of these actions requiring more than the signature of the Prime Minister. The President and Premier Mikolajczyk alone are thus constitutionally entitled to make an agreement with the U.S.S.R. in regard to the border dispute or any other question; but the constitution itself is denounced by many Poles as illegal.

For more than a year, beginning in April 1943, when the Soviet Union severed diplomatic relations with Poland, to the middle of 1944, Great Britain and the United States sought by various means at their disposal to heal the breach between the Soviet Union and Poland, but to no avail. In June 1944 Premier Mikolajczyk journeyed to Washington for a conference with President Roosevelt [42], which resulted in an understanding that the President would approach Moscow anew. In August Mikolajczyk, aware of the implications in the Soviet recognition of the rival Lublin National Committee of Liberation as the de facto government, was received in Moscow, but within a few days the meeting was "temporarily suspended." Each of the rival factions announced that the other's authority was "self-assumed and illegal." No agreement was reached on the fundamental issues of boundary lines and of the form of constitutional government for liberated Poland. It was reported that although Mikolajczyk was willing to reshuffle his Cabinet to include members of the Liberation Committee, he was offered no more than a chance to join the National Committee of Liberation, which was anxious to have him.

By September the Russo-Polish situation had reached the boiling point. The Polish patriots of Warsaw, responding to instructions from the Moscow radio, rose to fight alongside the Russians who were reported on the outskirts of the Polish capital. After sixty-three days of bitter fighting, in which eighty-five per cent of the city was destroyed and 200,000 were killed and wounded, General Bor, the leader of the patriots, surrendered his armies to the Germans. Before capitulation, Bor appealed to Britain and the United States for aid after hearing that the Russians could not force the Vistula River and would not permit the use of Russian air bases as loading stations for American fliers assigned to drop food and ammunition to the Polish patriots. It was rumored in some quarters that the Russians had deliberately allowed the Germans to liquidate Warsaw's patriots. Said the Moscow radio: "A libel on the Soviet High Command. . . . The London Polish circles responsible for the Warsaw uprising made no attempt to coordinate the revolt with the Soviet High Command. The responsibility thus lies with the Polish émigré circles in London." Colonel General Michael Rola-Zymierski, chief of Polish forces established in Moscow, branded the Warsaw uprising as an "irresponsible undertaking" and asserted "it was launched purely for political reasons to strengthen the position of Mikolajczyk."

In a renewed attempt to create some agreement between Stalin and the Poles in London, Prime Minister Churchill and Foreign Secretary Eden [40] flew to Moscow in October. Twenty-four hours after their arrival in the Russian capital, an invitation was extended to Mikolajczyk to join the meeting. This conference brought them no nearer to a solution. It was announced that Stalin was absolutely firm on the Curzon Line, offering, however, an extension of Poland's western boundary into Germany along the Oder and Neisse Rivers. In the early part of November the Polish Gov-

ernment-in-Exile proclaimed that it could not accept the Curzon Line as its eastern boundary without a more detailed and comprehensive plan which would solve other disputed points. The rift between the Lublin Committee in Lublin and the Polish Government-in-Exile had been steadily growing with the insistence of the Soviet-sponsored National Committee that the constitution of 1921 be substituted for the constitution of 1935 for liberated Poland. (The latter constitution is the one under which the Polish Government-in-Exile is functioning.) The Lublin Committee has also charged the London Poles with organized terrorist opposition to their agrarian reforms, although both groups call such reforms necessary.

Mikolajczyk's position was an extraordinarily difficult one. When he went to Russia, according to Raymond Daniell [44], he "found W. Averell Harriman [41], the American Ambassador, a silent neutral observer while Premier Stalin sat as judge and jury and Mr. Churchill had the role of public prosecutor. . . . He made inquiries through diplomatic channels in Washington about the American Government's attitude toward the agreement between London and Moscow which, it had become all too painfully apparent to him, meant that Poland would come out of the War without half the territory with which she had entered it. . . . He received assurance that the United States would prefer to see the final settlement of all frontier problems deferred to the conclusion of hostilities but that, if Poland felt that it was to her interest to resolve hers now, the United States would be glad to serve as an intermediary to support Poland's claim to Lwów and the oil centers." Mikolajczyk's Government felt that acceptance of this offer would imply a surrender of all the other territories in question, and the upshot was that the Premier and Cabinet resigned. His first successor was unable to form a Cabinet; and Mikolajczyk and his Peasant Party refused to join the Government finally formed by the Socialist Tomasz Arcisewski in late November.

Mikolajczyk's resignation was considered a calamity by the British and Russians; the former's attitude toward his successor was noticeably cooler. Inasmuch as the Peasants were the largest party in the last free Polish elections, it was felt that no Government in which they were not represented could succeed. The Lublin Committee's head, Edward Osubska-Morawski, invited him to come to Lublin and join them to work for the rebuilding of Poland on the basis of their program. Mikolajczyk was said to be a "catch" for the Lublin Poles because of his prestige, but he did not accept the invitation, and the situation remained confused.

Mikolajczyk is a stocky, smooth-shaven man who "dresses like Anthony Eden [40]." In November 1943 it was reported that his sixteen-year-old son, Marian, had escaped from the Nazi prison at Lublin and was hiding somewhere in Poland. Mikolajczyk's wife, Cecelia, had been seized by the Nazis in July 1942 together with her son and was at the time a hostage in the Oswiecim concentration camp.

References

For Policy Rep 19:122-39 Ag 15 '43
N Y World-Telegram p13 Jl 16 '43

(Continued next page)

MIKOLAJCZYK, STANISLAW—*Cont.*

Newsweek 22:31 Jl 26 '43 por
Sat Eve Post 215:16-17 Je 12 '43
Scholastic 43:9 Ja 24 '44 por

MILANOV, ZINKA (mē-lä'nov zēn'ka)
May 17, 1906- Singer

Address: b. c/o Columbia Concerts, Inc., 113 W. 57th St., New York City; h. 25 Central Park West, New York City

Unofficial ambassador from Yugoslavia to the world of opera is Zinka Milanov, the Metropolitan Opera Company's first Norma since Gina Cigna and Rosa Ponselle sang that role. A proud compatriot of the fighting Partisans, she has, however, lived in the United States since 1937. Before the War began, each performance of hers that was to be broadcast from the Metropolitan stage was announced in the newspapers of her native Zagreb so that everyone who could get near a short-wave radio set might listen to her voice.

The prima donna was born Zinka Kunc on May 17, 1906, in Zagreb, Yugoslavia, the Croatian birthplace of General Tito [43] (Josip Broz), of whom she therefore feels particularly proud. She was the daughter of a local banker, Rudolf Kunc, and Ljubica (Smiciklas) Kunc. Young Zinka's brother, a talented child pianist, composed twenty-five songs for her early recitals. Zinka herself started "real singing" at the age of four, performing at her friends' and neighbors' parties; at eight, then a mezzo-soprano, she sang the role of Carmen at a home performance. When the girl was twelve, however, the register of her voice changed to soprano. Two years later her voice was sufficiently matured for admittance to the Royal Music Academy in her native city. (She also studied at a girls' high school and college in Zagreb.)

Zinka Kunc's first appearance on the concert stage, made when she was fifteen, was attended by Milka Ternina, the Wagnerian soprano (then retired) who created the role of Kundry in the Metropolitan Opera production of *Parsifal* and was a member of the Academy's board of advisers. The famous singer was so much impressed by Zinka's performance that she offered to teach this promising young girl. Zinka accordingly studied for three years with Mme. Ternina, whom she describes as "a Brünnhilde who was not afraid of her horse," and who is "a great figure still" in the lives of her countrymen. (The singer has also studied in Italy and Germany with Professor Jacques Stueckhold.) After Zinka's graduation with the first prize, she continued her musical studies at the Royal Music Academy, also in Zagreb. She then passed the state examinations which qualified her to sing at the State Opera. Mme. Ternina coached her in her debut role of Leonora in *Il Trovatore* (sung, like other Italian operas, in German or in the native Yugoslav, but never in Italian). Her debut, made in October 1927, was followed by successful appearances with opera companies in Germany, Italy, and Czechoslovakia—during all of which the young soprano never sang a word of Italian, even in Italy. From 1928 to 1935 she also sang the leading roles in operas at the National Theatre. The famous conductor Bruno Walter [42] in-

vited her to be guest soloist with his orchestra in Hamburg and again in Vienna. Finally, for the 1937 Salzburg Festival, the great Arturo Toscanini [42] selected her as soprano soloist in Verdi's *Requiem*—the first of thirteen performances under his baton.

Mme. Milanov—for Zinka Kunc had married in July 1937 a handsome Zagreb actor-director, Predrag Milanov—was approached after the festival by Edward Johnson [43], manager of the Metropolitan Opera Company who was on his annual European talent-hunt. Johnson offered her one of the most unusual contracts in musical history: mindful of the Metropolitan's requirements in the way of sopranos, it bound her, within three months, to learn three complete roles in Italian and to lose at least twenty-five pounds. This was quite an order, but—with the aid of a physician and an Italian teacher—she arrived in New York three months later, twenty-five pounds lighter, with a doctor's certificate to testify that the diet had not impaired her singing ability, ready to make at once her American and Italian-language debuts. The vehicle for this double debut in December 1937 was, again, Leonora—after some seventy-five European performances of the Verdi opera, Mme. Milanov was going to sing it in the language of its composer.

In estimating her performance, music critics were unusually considerate of the new singer's language difficulty and of the tension attendant on a Metropolitan debut; both of these factors, wrote Olin Downes [43] of the New York *Times*, "may explain some of the discrepancies" and "conspicuous defects" of Mme. Milanov's singing, such as "the frequent unsteadiness and spreading of tones of the top register, intonation not always accurate, and shrillness in fortissimo passages." These faults were overshadowed some weeks later by a forceful interpretation of Aïda which caused the same reviewer to comment: "It will not be long before the news of her qualities spreads, for she presented a conception of the role which was at least thoroughly Italianized. Mme. Milanov phrased the music expertly and sang much of it with superior vocal quality." A more recent performance in the same role (given in February 1944) "brought the old thrill" to Downes's spine—"the kind of intoxication at such moments as was oftener the privilege of our forefathers in the great old days of grand opera singing than of ourselves in this present period which tends toward tenuity and refinement." "Mme. Milanov's magnificent voice," he remarked, "has seldom been used with such complete effect, variety of color, and emotional communication. And she has by nature and instinct the grand manner. She may not always be articulate in bodily plastic, or even in the quality of her song, but she has a presence and a glorious voice. She is a soprano for Aïda."

In the years since coming to America Mme. Milanov is said to have progressed as a singer. "Always the possessor of a remarkably beautiful voice," in the opinion of a New York *Herald Tribune* critic, "she was formerly most undependable as to pitch, to placement, and to power. She is still not a perfect vocalist, but her tremolo is subsiding, and her placement is more unified throughout her range than it was. She has developed a remarkably touching low register, and her powerful high notes are often of the utmost beauty. . . . With a voice of such transcendent beauty as hers and with the sort of conscientious discipline she is obviously submitting it to, she could become one of the great opera singers of our century; and I suspect she will."

In December 1943 the Metropolitan returned *Norma* to its repertoire, from which that opera had been absent for over six years. The extremely difficult title role—of which Lilli Lehmann, its creator, remarked that "singing the three Brünnhildes in one evening would be easier than one *Norma*"—was taken by Mme. Milanov, who had sung the role five times in the space of eleven days with the Buenos Aires opera two years earlier. It is her favorite of all her parts, perhaps because Norma has two children. The singer is so fond of children that "her official offspring" onstage "are so delighted by her attentions that their caresses have more than once impeded a performance." In this role she drew from Robert Bagar of the New York *World-Telegram* the comment: "Mme. Milanov can proudly claim one of the best voices at the Metropolitan. She has a good deal of breadth and power and sometimes she shows a surprising flexibility in the use of her voice. Not always is she the perfect musician, though she often does creditably in that department." Another reviewer noted "earnest effort and some very good vocalization on the part of Zinka Milanov, but there is too much that is labored and variable in her production, and too much that is wooden in her acting, conscientious though it is, to keep the opera alive." (Other roles which Mme. Milanov has sung at the Metropolitan are Donna Anna in *Don Giovanni*, Zantuzza in *Cavalleria Rusticana*, Leonora in *La Forza del Destino*, Amelia in *The Masked Ball*, and the title role in *La Gioconda*.)

At a Stadium performance of *Aïda* in New York in June 1944, Bagar found that Mme. Milanov "seems to have come into her own quite suddenly. There was a new-found thrust to her singing, besides increased elasticity and warmth. She was always on key . . . and to complement that her acting showed vast improvement, though she still favored a bit of bodily weaving in the over-heroic mold." Reviews of other critics in 1944 indicated that Mme. Milanov was continuing to develop, both musically and dramatically. However, there were also indications that she still lacked sufficient technique, especially in the bravura passages. "It is indeed unfortunate," wrote Jerome D. Bohm in December 1944, "that the possessor of such remarkable native gifts should not be able to learn to employ them more expertly."

In South America the singer is hailed with the "pelting flowers, bravos, and stamping feet" of a demonstrative public. The opera seasons in different parts of the Western Hemisphere interlock so neatly that many singers, including Mme. Milanov, sing during the season in Buenos Aires or Rio de Janeiro, as well as with the Metropolitan or another North American company. In 1940 the Yugoslavian

ZINKA MILANOV

soprano opened no less than three grand opera seasons—singing in *Andrea Chenier* in Buenos Aires, *Turandot* in Rio, and *Aïda* in Chicago. Her success at the Brazilian Teatro Colón was so great that she has sung there regularly ever since. After her Norma in 1942 the leading residents of Buenos Aires actually signed a petition asking her to sing in *La Forza del Destino*, which was soon revived at the Metropolitan. She has also sung several seasons at the Teatro Municipale in Rio de Janeiro. But, in spite of her affection for her Latin audiences, Mme. Milanov "works hard at her English" (and Italian) "and her diet and her milliner—not to speak of her tireless vocalises —in her desire to live up to the streamlined standards of a Metropolitan prima donna." Like most divas, she has given many successful concerts in Europe and America, and has made a number of recordings.

Mme. Milanov relaxes after a performance by cooking for a dozen people, specializing in pastry and in the substantial dishes of her native country. She and her husband, who gave up his separate and successful career to devote himself to managing her business affairs and coaching her in acting, live in a modern Central Park West duplex apartment. "I love my house," she says, "probably because I must be away from it so much rehearsing." "We Yugoslav women," she adds, "are very shy. We are not accustomed to society. We live quietly in our homes with our husbands and children. I would like to have time to have children."

The "sultry-eyed, chestnut-haired" soprano, who is described as "tall and classically built," is particularly fond of swimming. Called by the *Opera News* "half child, half woman—entirely prima donna," Mme. Milanov is said to have a ready smile and "the warm, glowing temperament of the South." Her only confessed superstition is that she must kiss her husband before going onstage. The singer, who has been decorated with the Order of St. Sava for her patriotic services, shows her

MILANOV, ZINKA—*Continued*

Yugoslav origin in an accent she calls "a little like Russian but not so soft," and in her flaming pride and belief in her people and particularly in the Partisans. (Her cousin, a painter, fights in their ranks.) "Tito is a great man. . . . Oh, I do not *hope*—I am *sure* my people are going to win. They are fighting so with heart and soul!"

References

Etude 58:729+ N '40
Newsweek 11:30 Ja 10 '38
Opera News p12-14 D 25 '39
Ewen, D. ed. Living Musicians 1940
Who Is Who in Music 1941
Who's Who in America 1944-45

MILLER, BENJAMIN MEEK (?)—Feb. 6, 1944 Ex-governor of Alabama from 1931 to 1935; elevated to the state's Supreme Court bench in 1921; served as circuit judge of the 4th Alabama Judicial District for sixteen years.

Obituary

N Y Times p15 F 7 '44

MITSCHER, MARC A(NDREW) Jan. 26, 1887- United States naval officer

Address: b. c/o Navy Department, Washington, D.C.

"The most powerful and destructive unit in the history of sea warfare," according to the official description, is Task Force 58, built up under Vice-Admiral Marc A. Mitscher, of the United States 3rd Fleet in the Pacific. While the "battleship admirals" try to lure the Imperial Japanese Navy out to fight, Mitscher's carrier planes bring the fight to the enemy, as well as help to provide the necessary air cover for amphibious operations. Such smashing victories as his force has achieved are the best answer to those Navy diehards who "have never quite forgiven the Wright brothers for inventing the airplane." (Mitscher's new assignment was a military secret as of the end of December 1944.)

Marc Andrew Mitscher was born January 26, 1887, the son of Oscar and Myrta (Spear) Mitscher. Although he was born in Hillsboro, Wisconsin, at the age of two he was taken to Oklahoma, where his father became an agent for the Osage Indian tribe; then to Washington, D. C., where he attended the grade and high schools. Unfortunately for young Washingtonians with dreams of a naval career, the District of Columbia has no representation in the Federal Government, and therefore all appointments to West Point or Annapolis for deserving youths are made by the President of the United States. Nineteen-year-old Marc Mitscher would have liked to get into the Military Academy, but the best that could be managed was to have him appointed to Annapolis from Oklahoma. At the Naval Academy, as *Time* Magazine reports, young Mitscher was "a hell-raiser" who soon became known as "Oklahoma Pete from the wild prairies," later shortened to Pete, and was "kicked out" for hazing underclassmen unduly —and reinstated four days later. Although only an average student, Pete Mitscher hoped to be

assigned to naval aviation, but was not able to realize this ambition for five years after he had completed the course.

Graduated as passed midshipman in 1910, Mitscher was assigned to duty in the battleship *Colorado*, and started on the climb upward through the grades. After the *Colorado* he served in another battleship, the *South Dakota*. Next came tours of duty in the gunboats *Vicksburg* and *Annapolis,* and then the twenty-six-year-old Ensign (commissioned in 1912) took time off, in January 1913, to marry Frances Smalley of Tacoma, Washington. The following August Mitscher joined the *San Diego* (then the U.S.S. *California*), in which he served on the West Coast during Pershing's expedition against the troops of Pancho Villa. (This campaign came to an end in 1916, after a battle between Villa's men and those of General Pershing.)

After duty in the destroyers *Whipple* and *Stewart*, Mitscher joined the newly formed naval air force, reporting for flight training at the Naval Air Station at Pensacola in October 1915. He was the thirty-second pilot to receive his wings from the now famous "Annapolis of the Air"; since then, his service is interwoven with the history of naval aviation. On April 30, 1917, the newly fledged flier, a lieutenant (junior grade) since 1915, reported to the U.S.S. *Huntington* to take part in experiments with the catapulting of planes, which has made possible the use of carrier-borne aircraft. These experiments were halted by the entrance of the United States into the First World War: the *Huntington*—and Mitscher— were soon occupied in convoying troopships. But in October 1917 the thirty-year-old airman reported at Montauk Point, Long Island; and the following February, he was given command of the Naval Air Station at Rockaway, Long Island. One month later, Mitscher was ordered to Miami to assume command of the naval air training station there.

During the First World War the little open-cockpit planes, which gave their pilots a distinctive, red-leathery complexion, were originally considered useful for scouting and observation; although dogfights became common (starting a wave of aviation battle fiction which supported a prosperous list of pulp magazines on First World War stories up to the outbreak of the Second), flying in itself was considered much more of an adventure in those days. Mitscher, by then a full lieutenant, started out in one of those old seaplanes, the NC-1, in May 1919, in company with two others, to make the first Navy transatlantic flight. After flying from Long Island to Newfoundland, they started from Trepassey for Lisbon; but the NC-1 was forced down in heavy fog off the Azores, and sank while being towed to port. (The NC-4 completed the flight to Lisbon, and then went on to Plymouth, England.) In spite of this mishap, Mitscher was decorated with the Navy Cross and the Portuguese Order of Tower and Sword, in the grade of Officer, for his "distinguished service in the line of his profession." (Today this 1,314-mile hop from Newfoundland to the Azores is one of the standard routes, and the islands are one of the crossroads of the world's airways.)

In September 1919 Mitscher joined the U.S.S. *Aroostook*, flagship of the admiral in command of the Pacific Fleet's air detachment. Fifteen months later, in December 1920, he was assigned the additional duty of commanding the detachment of air forces at the Fleet Air Base in San Diego, California, and in 1921 he was promoted to lieutenant commander. From June 1922 to November 1925 he was in command of the experimental station at Anacostia, D. C., where new airplanes and equipment are tested, and was then assigned to the airplane tender *Langley*. When the first American aircraft carrier, the *Saratoga*, was being fitted out by the American Brown Boveri Electric Corporation at Camden, New Jersey, in November 1926, Mitscher was assigned to the ship; and when she was commissioned a year later, he went along as head of her air department. On July 11, 1928 Lieutenant Commander Mitscher landed the first plane on her new flight deck.

Mitscher returned to the *Langley* in June 1929, this time as her executive officer, a post he held for one year. Next he had a three-year tour of shore duty in the Bureau of Aeronautics of the Navy Department at Washington. During this period, in October 1930, he was made a full commander, one of 491 in the peacetime Navy. (At that time the highest ranking naval officers were rear admirals, of which there were sixty-four.) In June 1933 the Commander returned to the sea as chief of staff to the admiral commanding the Base Force's aircraft, with headquarters on the airplane tender *Wright*. One year as executive officer of the *Saratoga*—still the largest, as well as the oldest, of the United States aircraft carriers—was followed by two at the Bureau of Aeronautics; and in May 1937 Mitscher returned to the *Wright* as her commanding officer. Raised to a captaincy in 1938, he commanded Patrol Wing 1 from November of that year to the following June, when he reported as assistant chief of the Bureau of Aeronautics.

According to one interviewer, the period in Mitscher's career of which he seems most proud is his tour as chief of staff to Rear Admiral Alfred W. Johnson in the mid-'thirties. "We made 'em fly—fly a long way," he recalls. "Always before, our planes, although capable of long flights, had hung around close to their bases. But Admiral Johnson and his staff made 'em fly." On January 10 and 11, 1934, Mitscher traveled in a six-plane flight from San Francisco to Pearl Harbor, covering 2,400 miles in less than twenty-five hours, thus setting a precedent. Then, a year later, he helped plan and fly a forty-eight-plane jaunt from San Diego to Panama. All forty-eight planes arrived safely at the end of the 3,000 miles. Mitscher says, incidentally, that he had only three "serious" crashes in his flying days, injuring his arm in one of them. Once he walked away from his plane after a flat spin, a feat ordinarily regarded as impossible.

In October 1941 Captain Mitscher commissioned the aircraft carrier *Hornet*, which he was to command for nearly two years. Three days before the Japanese attack on Pearl Harbor plunged the United States into war, the Captain was promoted to rear admiral. He was then fifty-four and had spent thirty-five years in the Navy and more than seventeen years at sea. His ship, the *Hornet*, was the "Shangri-La" from which American planes, under the command of Major General James

Doolittle [42], made their "impossible" bombing raid on Tokyo and four other Japanese cities on April 18, 1942. These Army fliers had received special training after boarding the ship at San Francisco; and Admiral Mitscher brought the *Hornet* within 800 miles of the military objectives for the planes' take-off.

Just two weeks after that sensational tour de force, the *Hornet* was involved in the Battle of Midway (June 4 to 6, 1942). Pete Mitscher was one of the commanders who, first under Admiral Frank J. Fletcher and then under Admiral Raymond Ames Spruance [44], helped to win an unmistakable victory over a much larger and stronger Japanese force. Thus he was in the two actions which probably did the most to raise American morale after the first defeats and prove that the Japanese were not invincible. The following month Admiral Mitscher was detached from the *Hornet* (which was subsequently sunk in the Battle of Santa Cruz, October 26, 1942) to take command of Patrol Wing 2.

On April 1, 1943 Mitscher took over as air commander on Guadalcanal in the Solomon Islands, where he was in charge of Army Air Corps units, Navy and Marine Corps aviation groups, and contingents of the Royal New Zealand Air Force. During the first four months Mitscher filled this post he achieved "distinctive success in coordinating these various forces into a powerful offensive weapon against the enemy Japanese. By the effective tactical employment of the forces under his command for maximum combat efficiency, he inflicted tremendous losses upon the enemy, destroying more than 500 Japanese aircraft and sinking more than twenty vessels." For this achievement he was decorated with the Distinguished Service Medal with the citation quoted above. Mitscher, who had learned to hate the Japanese, was putting into action his theory that "the only way to win this War is to kill so many they can't exist as a nation."

In January and February 1944, as commanding officer of a carrier force, part of Admiral Spruance's Central Pacific Force, Mitscher provided a superb air umbrella for the invasion troops which took the Marshall Islands. His attacks against the invasion objectives and against hostile bases within supporting distance were very largely responsible for the amphibious forces' success; as for the three-day pre-invasion bombardment laid down by his planes and the shore-based craft of Rear Admiral John H. Hoover, "correspondents ran out of adjectives attempting to describe" it. It literally leveled everything on some of the islands, and so disorganized the Japanese defense that the American task force's casualties were amazingly light—far lighter than those of the defenders. On February 16 and 17, while a task force under Rear Admiral R. Kelly Turner [44] invaded Eniwetok atoll in the Marshalls, Mitscher provided the air support for Admiral Spruance's "brilliant diversionary attack" on the Japanese base of Truk in the Caroline Islands, some 750 statute miles to the east. "All I knew about Truk," Mitscher recalls "was what I'd read in the *National Geographic*—and the writer was wrong about some things."

Five days later Admiral Mitscher led his task force of carriers, cruisers, destroyers, and battleships on an attack against the Japanese-held Tinian and Saipan Islands in the Marianas

VICE-ADM. MARC A. MITSCHER

group. While proceeding toward the objective as well as during the attack, the task force was detected and intercepted by enemy torpedo and bombing planes. Nevertheless the Admiral pressed home two attacks on the Saipan anchorage and naval repair base and the Tinian naval air base with a side blow at Guam, the U.S. island 125 miles to the south which the Japanese had captured early in the War. Although these islands, less than 1,400 miles south of Tokyo, were defended by fierce aerial and antiaircraft opposition, the American force succeeded in destroying a total of 135 planes, sinking several ships, and inflicting other damages on the enemy, while itself suffering the loss of only six planes. No ships were so much as touched in spite of the Japanese advantage in the ability to use land-based aircraft. As Admiral Mitscher said in a message of commendation to his men, "This attack was history-making for daring and tenacity of execution." "As a result of Admiral Mitscher's brilliant leadership and indomitable fighting spirit," to quote the citation which accompanied the Gold Star which indicates a second award of the D.S.M., "the Central Pacific Force obtained and maintained complete control of the air throughout this vital area." On March 21, 1944 Mitscher was promoted to vice-admiral, which was confirmed retroactively by the United States Senate on May 25, 1944.

Eight days later, on March 29, Vice-Admiral Mitscher, who had led an attack on Ponope and Kusaie in the Carolines on March 5, was again making headlines. Under the tactical command of Admiral Spruance, he led a three-day attack on three widely-separated islands 1,000 miles inside the Japanese Central Pacific defense perimeter. Mitscher's Task Force 58, described officially as the most powerful naval striking force ever assembled in the Pacific, was subdivided into several strong task groups. One attacked the Palau Islands, an air and sea base only 550 miles east of the Philippines, with carrier dive-bombers and torpedo planes.

One struck at bases on Yap Island and Ulithi Atoll, 100 miles apart in the western Carolines. Woleai, an atoll about halfway between Palau and Truk, was also heavily attacked by Mitscher's force. Theses operations, described in the longest communiqué ever issued by Admiral Nimitz [42], commander in chief of the Pacific Fleet, were "far more extensive than any previous carrier raids." The total Japanese killed in these encounters might, it was estimated, exceed the totals run up in any of the amphibious operations in the Pacific at that time, while American losses were held to the amazingly low figure of twenty-five planes and eighteen lives. There was no damage to the United States surface ships; not one piece of metal from an enemy gun fell on any of them.

Admiral Mitscher's Task Force 58, as announced the following June, had been formed six months earlier of the latest and swiftest carriers, battleships, cruisers, and destroyers in the United States Fleet, with the entire Pacific its beat. Its carriers could launch more than 1,000 planes from 1,250,000 square feet of runway; its ships could pound the enemy with more than 850 guns, ranging in size up to the largest coastal defense guns, and equal in their total power to seventy standard Army field artillery units. The force was equipped to take care of its own antiaircraft protection and supply problems—the latter by means of a vast "fleet train," protected by its own carriers, cruisers, and destroyers, capable of providing food, fuel, replacement aircraft and pilots wherever the task force might go. This, officially described as "the most mobile strategic air force yet seen in warfare," provided the air support for the American invasion of Hollandia and Tanahmera, Dutch New Guinea, and Aitape, Australian New Guinea, led by General Douglas MacArthur [41] on April 22, 1944. This, the first recapture of Netherlands territory since the beginning of the War, was completed six days later, and Mitscher's ships steamed off to take part in a much fiercer battle, the fight for Saipan and other Marianas Islands. (Two days later his superior officer, Admiral Spruance, was designated commander of the 5th United States Fleet.)

The Marianas campaign was opened by air attacks on June 10 and 11, presumably by units of Admiral Mitscher's task force. Bombardment of Saipan by the 5th Fleet's naval guns was begun June 12; and two days later, American marines of the 2nd and 4th Divisions and infantrymen of the 27th Army Division swarmed ashore to begin the actual invasion. At this time Mitscher's force pinned down the Japanese in the Bonin (Ogasawara) Islands, 800 miles to the north and only 783 miles from the heart of Japan, to prevent them from interfering with the Saipan action; and some four days later the task force rejoined Spruance's fleet. Although the American admirals were avowedly desperate for a battle with the Japanese Imperial Grand Battle Fleet, the Nipponese Navy resisted all provocation to come out and fight. "Like most naval actions today, this one was fought at a distance of hundreds of miles." It was Mitscher's carrier-based aircraft that brought the fight to the elusive enemy. On June 18 a smashing victory was achieved over the hundreds of Japanese planes which attacked the 5th Fleet—so great, in fact, that the Americans concluded the Nipponese must be sending out inferior pilots. Three hundred fifty-three enemy planes were lost, as compared with twenty-one American planes; before going down they managed to inflict superficial damage on only three ships. Admiral Mitscher's force pursued the Japanese remnants, attacked, and defeated them—402 planes and six ships to 122 planes lost, on June 19 in the Battle of the Eastern Philippines. This air-sea battle, which enabled the invasion forces to proceed without interference from the sea or air, drew from naval commander in chief Admiral Ernest J. King [42] a message of commendation for an achievement "unequaled in all seagoing aviation."

The carrier-based planes did not, of course, win the Battle of Saipan; that was won by sleepless foot soldiers in three and one-half weeks of bitter fighting against a fanatical enemy provided with all modern equipment, including twenty-seven tanks. Credit even for the air operations must be shared with Marine Corps fliers and, toward the end, with some Army Air Force planes. But Mitscher's men can rightly claim an important part in what was possibly the hardest campaign in American military history; they share responsibility for the surrender which, on July 10, gave the Americans a base within bomber range of Tokyo—one which the Nipponese had had a quarter-century to fortify. And they sustained the longest sea-air assault in naval history with attacks preceding and covering the invasions of Guam and Tinian.

A report by Navy Secretary James Forrestal [42] to the President on Admiral Halsey's (3rd Fleet) fast carrier force (58) has revealed that, "except for one period of fifteen days from September 23 to October 9, the fast carrier task force was not out of action for more than five consecutive days during its entire cruise—a cruise that lasted beyond this chronology for a total period of almost three months beyond the sortie date of August 28 . . . ranging over 1,800 miles from north to south." In the first two months of these operations, said the Secretary, the 3rd Fleet Task Force (which was transferred to the 5th Fleet in August) engaged in twenty-one combat actions and had to be refueled, resupplied, or refitted twenty-six times while at sea. Its planes flew 18,226 sorties, using up 6,000 tons of bombs, 331 torpedoes, 7,752 rockets, and enormous amounts of fuel and provisions; 325 planes were lost in combat and operational accidents (according to Hanson Baldwin [42], more than ten times as many Navy planes are lost operationally than by enemy action); and 297 of its pilots and aircrewmen were casualties. On August 10 Admiral Nimitz paid a surprise visit to Mitscher at an advanced Marshalls base to decorate him with a second Bronze Star to his D.S.M. (for work in the Marshalls and the raids on Truk and the Marianas). At this time Task Force 58 was "ranging over the seas, looking for trouble." From August to September Mitscher's planes made a series of strikes against the Bonins, Volcanoes, Palau, and Mindanao in the Philippines. The Palau campaign began in September; on September 21 the 3rd Fleet further taunted the Nipponese

admirals with a "superlatively successful attack which apparently caught the enemy completely by surprise" on the Manila area, causing them to put the Philippines under martial law. Keeping the enemy off balance, Mitscher next directed a "bold, brilliantly executed" strike against the Ryukyu archipelago from 200 miles off southern Japan to Formosa, encountering no air or sea opposition. This brought the score for Mitscher's planes up to more than 1,000 planes and 500 surface craft, with no damage to American surface ships, and with "light" plane losses. (At the same time, other 3rd Fleet forces were striking at Marcus Island, 1,500 miles farther east.) Japanese fire was heavy, but the real hazard was the weather: the carriers, including Mitscher's flagship, had to sail on the fringe of a typhoon to reach jump-off position. It looked for a time as though the Admiral had finally drummed up a real, old-fashioned sea fight, but the approaching Japanese task force scurried away after getting one quick look at the size of the American fleet.

Toward the end of the typhoon season General Douglas MacArthur's [41] invasion fleet started moving toward the Philippines, while American warships put Leyte, 425 miles southeast of Luzon, under a devastating naval and air bombardment. Meanwhile Mitscher's planes were carrying out a daring operation against Formosa that brought his ships within range of strong land-based enemy airpower. (Later they were joined by some of Major General Curtis E. LeMay's [44] Superfortresses from western China.) This "two-week series of feints and thrusts" by Mitscher's task force "kept the Japanese forces off balance while whittling down their aerial strength by some 900 planes. These successes indicated the feasibility of advancing the date for the invasion of the Philippines." Mitscher joined "MacArthur's Navy"— the 7th Fleet of Vice-Admiral Thomas C. Kinkaid [44]—in support of the landings on Leyte; his carriers were posted in the sea south of Luzon, between Samar and Mindoro. On Tuesday, September 24, they engaged the Japanese task force coming through the Sibuyan Sea, while under a very heavy air attack by hundreds of land-based enemy planes. (Two other Japanese fleets were routed by the 3rd and 7th Fleets.) Individual credit is not easy to assess, but Mitscher's men, planes, and ships further distinguished themselves in the great victory of the battle for Leyte, the second battle of the Philippine Seas.

A résumé of Task Force 58's operations from January 29 through October 27, 1944 (when it was part of Halsey's 3rd Fleet) shows 795 Japanese naval and merchant vessels sunk or damaged; 4,425 planes were destroyed, 2,569 in the air and 1,857 on the ground. Admiral Mitscher went to great lengths to protect his pilots and aircrewmen: during the great battle of June 19 he broke the strict blackout to have searchlights guide the planes back to their carriers, and detached some of the protecting destroyers to search for those which had gone down on the sea—this in addition to the normal air-sea rescue service. "We lost nearly one hundred planes that night," writes Elmont Waite, "but less than half that number of pilots and crewmen. That is one reason morale aboard Mitscher's carriers is no prob-

MITSCHER, MARC A.—*Continued*
lem. Another is his amazing knowledge of how
these youngsters will think and act and feel.
To him, of course, this is not amazing at all.
It's just that he used to be a young naval
aviator himself, and still is, in spirit at least."

Throughout his campaigns Admiral Mitscher
directed his ships and planes from his customary seat on the flag bridge of his flagship.
Here he sat, facing aft, his feet propped
against the base of a compass, his special green
canvas cap with a huge visor shading his eyes.
The Admiral is a small, raw-boned, wizened
man whose leathery face reveals the old-time
aviator, whose eyes are "icy," and whose hair
is, or was, tow colored. *Life*'s Noel Busch, who
reported the Saipan expedition from Mitscher's
flagship, says he is fast becoming a legend in
the Pacific theatre for "taciturnity, reticence,
and built-in gyroscopic resistance to the display of any emotions under any circumstances.
Mitscher comments are delivered in an almost
inaudible growl and often have a special pun-
gence. . . . Mitscher's feeling for the Japanese is whole-hearted, one-track loathing." Yet
this formidable figure, in private life, has no
heart for hunting—he likes to fish and to pitch
horseshoes. The Mitschers have no children,
and have not gotten around to selecting a permanent home; meanwhile Mrs. Mitscher is living in a California hotel.

References

> Newsweek 23:25 F 14 '44 por
> Sat Eve Post 217:20 D 2 '44 il pors
> Scholastic 44:9 My 1 '44
> Register of Commissioned and Warrant
> Officers of the Navy and Marine
> Corps July 1, 1943
> Who's Who in America 1944-45

MOFFATT, JAMES, REV. (mof'at) July
4, 1870—June 27, 1944 Theologian; author;
noted for translation of the Bible, which bears
his name; came to United States from Glasgow, Scotland in 1927 to assume post of professor of church history at Union Theological
Seminary in New York; a prolific writer, his
books include The *Historical New Testament*
(1901), *The Presbyterian Churches* (1928),
The Books of the Prophets (1939).

Obituary

> N Y Times p23 Je 28 '44

MOLLOY, DANIEL M(URRAH) (mol-
loi') Feb. 19, 1892—Jan. 29, 1944 Field
representative in Central America for the
international health division of the Rockefeller Foundation from 1914 until 1940; credited with the elimination of yellow fever;
made progress in conquering malaria and the
establishment of an efficient health department in Nicaragua.

Obituary

> N Y Times p37 Ja 30 '44

MONDRIAAN, PIET(ER CORNELIS)
(mon'drē-an pē'tėr) Mar. 7, 1872—Feb. 1,
1944 Dutch painter; renowned in the field of
non-objective painting; exerted influence in
Europe on architecture, design, painting, and
sculpture; his work is included in the collec-

tion of the Museum of Modern Art, the
Philadelphia Museum of Art, and the Wadsworth Athenaeum, Hartford, Connecticut.

Obituary

> N Y Times p21 F 2 '44 por

MOORE, GRACE Dec. 5, 1901- Singer
Address: b. c/o W. Colston Leigh, Inc., 521
Fifth Ave., New York City; h. Far Away
Meadows Farm, Sandy Hook, Conn.

Opera, radio, and screen star Grace Moore
has added a new attainment to her already
crowded list of achievements—in February
1944 her informal, chatty autobiography,
You're Only Human Once, was published.
Writing has long been one of Miss Moore's
hobbies, but her musical career has left her
little time for it. Although she is a recognized star of the Metropolitan Opera Company and one of the few native American
artists who have won international fame in
the field of music, her career is not a dazzling
and breath-taking success story, but rather
a record of long years of hard work and
study, discouragement, and ultimate triumph.

Grace Moore was born December 5, 1901, in
Slabtown, Cocke County, Tennessee, the
daughter of Richard L. and Tessie Jane
(Stokely) Moore. Her hometown is not
Slabtown, however, but Jellico, Tennessee,
where the family moved a few years after
her birth. Here she grew up, as she relates
it, "a skinny, long-legged, ugly girl" and something of a tomboy. She had her first taste
of music when she sang in the church choir,
but it was the church rather than the music
which attracted her, and her early ambition
was to be a missionary.

Miss Moore was sent to the Ward-Belmont
School in Nashville. One day the girls at
the school were taken to hear a recital by
Mary Garden, the famous opera singer. Later
Miss Garden permitted the group to visit her
backstage and, as a result of the concert and
the interview with the prima donna, Grace
Moore resolved to become an opera star. For
a time she wrote almost daily to Miss Garden,
confiding in the singer all her dreams and ambitions. In spite of the opposition of her
family she finally managed to persuade her
father to send her to the Wilson-Green
Academy of Music in Chevy Chase, Maryland, to study voice.

Grace Moore made her musical debut in
Washington in 1918, singing on a program
with the well known tenor Giovanni Martinelli. The young girl ambitiously selected
for her solo a difficult aria from *Aida*, "Ri-
torna Vincitor," and was considerably dwarfed
by Martinelli's singing. One critic wrote
the next day: "A lion and a mouse gave a
concert yesterday. The lion made way for
the mouse, who disclosed a pretty and charming voice with a future." Encouraged by this
left-handed compliment, Miss Moore set out
for New York to begin her career in earnest.

In true romantic fashion she soon found
herself in New York's Greenwich Village,
jobless and almost penniless. A job soon
came along, though it was not the kind the
would-be opera star had expected—a singing
engagement at the Black Cat, a Greenwich

Village night club. Her first New York voice teacher was recommended by a friend as "good and cheap," but who, unfortunately proved to be far from good for Miss Moore's voice. "Instead of permitting my voice to grow and become stronger naturally," relates the singer, "I was being forced into vocal fatigue." One day she discovered that her vocal cords had been injured and that she could no longer sing a note of music. On the advice of a noted voice teacher she retired to Canada, where for months she rested her voice and studied languages in preparation for operatic roles.

Recovering, she went into the musical show, —*Suite Sixteen*, in which Miss Moore sang, with appropriate hip-swinging, "First You Wiggle, Then You Waggle"; *Kitchy Koo* (1921); *Up in the Clouds* (1922); Irving Berlin's *Music Box Revue* of 1923. With the money she earned in musical comedy Grace Moore was able to pay for voice lessons and to save for her long-dreamed-of trip to Europe. New York audiences hailed her as "the new singing Elsie Ferguson '44."

She sailed for Europe to study in France. Months of intensive study and practice followed, but Miss Moore also found time to make friends, many of whom she describes in her autobiography—Noel Coward '41, Cole Porter '40, Elsa Maxwell '43, the late Alexander Woollcott '41, and Condé Nast. One of her closest friends was Mary Garden, whom she had admired years before.

Returning to New York, she sang in another of the *Music Box Revues* and had two auditions at the Metropolitan Opera House. Although one was favorable, she did not win a contract then. Nevertheless, the singer was not discouraged. She even made a bet with one of the judges that she would be singing at the Metropolitan within two years. Then Miss Moore sailed for Europe again, giving only about twelve hours' notice to the producers of the *Revue*.

Grace Moore won her bet. She returned to the United States to make her operatic debut as Mimi in *La Bohème* on February 7, 1928. Opera audiences received her enthusiastically. In 1928 young American singers were a rarity, and this American prima donna who combined talent with glamour was little short of a sensation. The critics, while not quite so enthusiastic as the general public, nevertheless conceded that "the voice is a soprano young and fresh but light and thin. It possesses a definite sweetness and purity."

For the next five seasons Miss Moore was one of the stars of the Metropolitan. Her repertoire included the roles of Mimi, Manon, Juliet, Marguerite, Madame Butterfly, Louise, and many others. She has sung with the American-German Opera Company in Paris and Nice, at Covent Garden in London, and at the Opéra Comique in Paris. Her favorite role is Louise, the heroine of Gustave Charpentier's opera *Louise*, a story of Parisian middle-class life. Charpentier first heard Miss Moore sing the role at the Opéra Comique and coached her in it, even acting as an adviser when the film version of the opera was made in 1938. "Miss Moore's Louise," writes Olin Downes '43, "is a thoughtful, sincere, and dramatically effective accomplishment . . . the

GRACE MOORE

conception, dramatically as well as in song, is excellently constructed and carried out in detail."

In 1930 Grace Moore accepted a Hollywood offer, went on a strict diet to satisfy Hollywood figure standards, and made her film debut in *A Lady's Morals*, a motion picture based on the life of the Swedish soprano Jenny Lind. As in the case of her Metropolitan auditions, Miss Moore's first two appearances in motion pictures were unsuccessful. Both *A Lady's Morals* and *New Moon* (1930), in which she was co-starred with Lawrence Tibbett, did poorly at the box office. "A trained voice, cool, thin, mechanically perfect but without much color, beautifully recorded," wrote Otis Ferguson of Grace Moore; and he continued, "When it comes to stage genius and stage presence there are scores of little girls in Hollywood who can run wide star, a plot somewhat similar to Miss Moore's starred in *One Night of Love* (1934) that she won world-wide fame as a film star. *One Night of Love* was the story of a rising young opera star, a plot somewhat similar to Miss Moore's own life story. It was the first film in which classical music was presented in a pleasant, almost informal manner fitting naturally into the plot. In it Miss Moore sang excerpts from *Carmen* and *Madame Butterfly* as well as the popular song "Chiribiribin" (a song always identified with Miss Moore, who sings it at nearly every recital) and the title song, "One Night of Love." Technically *One Night of Love* was far in advance of its time—the sound recording was clearer and more lifelike than in any earlier musical film.

Miss Moore was awarded a medal in 1935 by the American Society of Arts and Sciences for her work in *One Night of Love*. Frankly proud of her achievement (she says, "I am as susceptible to human vanity as anyone"), Miss Moore considers her performance "a contribution to the cinema." She says: "I made the motion-picture public opera conscious!

(Continued next page)

MOORE, GRACE—*Continued*

I am the girl who took the high hat off grand opera."

One Night of Love was followed by a series of pictures which, according to Miss Moore, were the same picture under four different names—*Love Me Forever* (1935), *The King Steps Out* (1936), *When You're in Love* (1937), and *I'll Take Romance* (1937). Although Miss Moore says enthusiastically, "Hollywood made my face, my voice, my name completely recognizable here, in Europe, throughout the world," she realized that the public was beginning to tire of the same formula.

Hollywood had not interfered seriously with Miss Moore's operatic career; it had, indeed, increased her opera audiences tremendously. In 1933 she returned to the New York stage for a short run in *The DuBarry*. Returning to opera, Miss Moore sang at Covent Garden in 1935 and received one of the greatest ovations ever accorded a singer there. It was a command performance for Queen Mary, and Miss Moore has sung for other European royalty, including King Haakon [40] of Norway, King Christian [12] of Denmark, and King Gustav [12] of Sweden. She has received decorations from Norway, Sweden, Denmark, Belgium, France, Cuba, Mexico, and other countries.

In recent years Miss Moore has added two more roles to her repertoire—Tosca and Fiora, the heroine of Montemezzi's opera, *The Love of Three Kings*. Miss Moore had met the composer Italo Montemezzi in 1923 and received special coaching from him before undertaking the role. On February 7, 1941 *The Love of Three Kings* was given at the Metropolitan Opera House with the composer conducting. It was well received, although Miss Moore's acting was criticized as stiff and overdramatic.

Miss Moore's Tosca, critics agree, had developed from an awkward and harsh interpretation to a minor musical triumph. She has always sung the role convincingly, but her acting has been a serious drawback. Robert Bagar writes: "Miss Moore is, no doubt, vitally attached to acting. She spends enormous energy on it. She happens, regrettably, not to be a natural actress. She overdoes things."

In February 1942 Virgil Thomson [40] devoted a column to what he called "The Grace Moore Case." Although he criticized the singer severely, he pointed out that with her Tosca "she has 'arrived' at a quite indisputable and authentic stardom." Thompson wrote: "Her faults were so abundant, her talents, musical and dramatic, so limited, that it has often been occasion for wonder that so much energy and hard work should be deployed on so seemingly hopeless an errand." But, he concluded: "Miss Moore gives a thoroughly worked out rendition of whatever she does. That working out, moreover, is done on no eclectic precept or personal basis. It is a sincere attempt to observe a great tradition. And somehow, by sheer good will, hard work, and intellectual modesty, Miss Moore manages to produce the best performance now available in that tradition."

In 1942 Miss Moore took over the management of her own career and proved that artists do not necessarily lack "good business heads." She has had her own radio program and has appeared as guest star on many radio shows. A "star-maker," she discovered the well known lyric soprano Dorothy Kirsten. In the spring of 1943 Miss Moore broke all precedents for opera stars by going into vaudeville and accepting an engagement at the Roxy Theatre in New York City for $10,000 a week. Four times a day she sang everything from "Minnie the Moocher" to the beautiful aria from *Tosca*, "Vissi d'Arti," and became what *PM* called "a frantic hit." When reporters asked her why she had made the appearance, she admitted that the salary was an important consideration, but added: "My greatest ambition is in reaching as many people as possible; and the movie houses offer the audience of the largest possible size. Not only that, these people listen with their hearts, and that, I say, is the most important thing about them." In August the following year her belief was substantiated at her first outdoor concert. Miss Moore made her debut at the Lewisohn Stadium in New York before an audience of 22,000. Although the critics agreed she was not in too good voice, she was enthusiastically received.

Since 1931 Grace Moore has been married to Valentin Parera, handsome Spanish actor who was formerly known as "the Spanish Ronald Colman [43]." She has had homes in France, California, and Connecticut, but is happiest in her two-hundred-year-old farmhouse in Sandy Hook, Connecticut, which she remodeled and furnished with the antiques she collects as a hobby. She was very proud to hear, after the restoration of France, that her villa there had been used as a relay station for patriots fleeing from the Gestapo, but regretted that no bombs had destroyed the kitchen, which is the worst she has ever seen. Blond and attractive, Miss Moore was chosen one of the best-dressed women in the world. Her autobiography, *You're Only Human Once,* is considered a frank and charming self-portrait. During the War Miss Moore has been singing at Army hospitals and canteens.

References

C S Mon p9 Ap 1 '41 pors
N Y Post p15 F 7 '41 por
Opera N 5:11 Mr 31 '41 por
PM Mag p8-9 Je 11 '44 pors
Ewen, D. ed. Living Musicians 1940
International Motion Picture Almanac 1943-44
Moore, G. You're Only Human Once 1944
Thompson, O. ed. International Cyclopedia of Music and Musicians 1943
Who's Who in America 1944-45

MORDKIN, MIKHAIL (môrt′kyin myi-ku-ēl′) 1881 (?)—July 15, 1944 Ballet master, former partner of Pavlova; organizer of the Mordkin Ballet; first male ballet dancer to gain popularity in the United States.

Obituary

N Y Times p31 Jl 16 '44

MORE, ADELYNE, pseud. *See* Ogden, C. K.

MORRIS, DAVE HENNEN Apr. 24, 1872—May 4, 1944 Lawyer and diplomat; Ambassador to Belgium and Minister to Luxembourg from 1933 to 1937; active in many fields, he held directorates in several business corporations and was a leader in educational organizations; an old friend of President Roosevelt's '42.

Obituary

N Y Times p19 My 5 '44 por

MOULTON, HAROLD G(LENN) Nov. 7, 1883- President of the Brookings Institution; economist

Address: b. The Brookings Institution, Washington, D. C.; h. 3700 Oliver St., Washington, D. C.

While many economic treatises gather dust on library shelves, the publications issued by the Brookings Institution in Washington, D. C., are being studied by economists, industrialists, and statesmen. The basic purpose of this Institution is to ferret out facts on weighty national and international economic and governmental problems and to publish them in the interests of public enlightenment and the development of sound national policies. President of this fact-finding, non-profit-making body is former University of Chicago economics professor, Harold G. Moulton, whose writings are known for their scientific accuracy and comprehensiveness. Moulton's most recent book, *The Control of Germany and Japan* (1944), written in collaboration with Louis Marlio, the French industrialist and economist who served on committees of the League of Nations, is regarded by Harry Scherman '43 of the Book-of-the-Month Club as "the most enlightening document on the peace, from the point of view of practicality, that has as yet been published." (The Book-of-the-Month Club distributed more than 600,000 complimentary copies of Moulton and Marlio's book to its members.)

Harold Glenn Moulton was born in LeRoy, Michigan, on November 7, 1883, the son of Belah G. and Mary C. (Smith) Moulton. After studying at Albion College in his home state for a period of two years, he studied at the University of Chicago, which in 1907 awarded him his first academic degree, Bachelor of Philosophy, and a Phi Beta Kappa key. The following year Moulton became an instructor at the Evanston Collegiate Institute in Evanston, Illinois. In 1910 he was appointed an instructor in political economy at the University of Chicago, subsequently attaining the rank of professor. In 1914 he earned his Ph.D. from that University, and several other universities have since honored him with degrees.

During his years on the Chicago faculty Moulton made several analytic studies in economics which were published by the Chicago University Press. Among these were *Principles of Money and Banking* (1916) and *The Financial Organization of Society* (1922), a textbook recommended for the experienced banker as well as for the student. Moulton's

arguments were considered cogent and convincing, his views moderate and fair-minded. (The latter volume was considerably amplified and republished in 1938 as *Financial Organization and the Economic System*.)

Resigning from the University in 1922, Moulton continued writing his treatises on economics as director of the Institute of Economics in Washington, D.C., a body which has devoted a considerable part of its energies to a nonpartisan investigation of the problem of reparations and the international economic reconstruction following the First World War. The resultant volumes included *Germany's Capacity To Pay* (1923), a survey written in collaboration with C. E. McGuire, which helped the reparations experts in Paris to formulate the Dawes Plan, and *The Reparation Plan* (1924), an analysis of the Dawes report. Shortly afterward Moulton co-authored *Russia's Debts and Russian Reconstruction* (1924), *The French Debt Problem* (1925), *World War Debt Settlements* (1926), then *Japan, an Economic and Financial Appraisal* (1931), and subsequently in 1932, *War Debts and World Prosperity,* a synthesis of all the previous publications on the subject.

In 1927 the Institute of Economics was merged with the Institute for Government Research and the Robert Brookings Graduate School of Economics and Government to form the Brookings Institution, "devoted to public service through research and training in the humanistic sciences." The late Robert Brookings, a former hardware salesman who amassed a fortune of several million dollars, had been instrumental in forming these three Washington institutions engaged in the study of social and economic questions. In addition to the endowment left by the founder, funds for research are contributed by such philanthropic trusts as the Rockefeller Foundation and the Carnegie Institute. A permanent staff of specialists co-operate in conducting the Institution's broader investigations, aided by graduate fellowship students, who receive training in research methods. Moulton has been president of the Brookings Institution since its founding and is thereby responsible for "formulating general policies and coordinating the activities of the various divisions of the Institution."

Often Federal or state officials request the Institution to conduct special investigations. In 1933 the National Transportation Committee, under the chairmanship of Calvin Coolidge, leaned heavily on the Institution's 900-page report, *The American Transportation Problem,* in forming its recommendations. State governments have asked Brookings economics experts to study their administrative setup and to suggest changes for economy and increased efficiency.

In 1932 the Brookings Institution initiated an exploratory study in an attempt to answer the question: Do the country's economic ills result from the maldistribution of wealth and income? The first volume of the series was *America's Capacity To Produce,* prepared by Edward G. Nourse and others of the staff. In 1934 appeared *America's Capacity To Consume,* the work of Moulton and Harold Leven, and in 1935 Moulton's *The Formation of Capital* and *Income and Economic Progress.* In gen-

Blackstone Studios

HAROLD G. MOULTON

eral, in these as elsewhere, Moulton argues the converse of the familiar thesis that higher wages and shorter hours are necessary to compensate for the displacement of workers by technological progress. On the basic premise that it is the social function of the capitalist system to bring the masses progressively higher living standards, he holds that the solution to economic recovery lies in the reduction of prices as production becomes more and more efficient (wage increases can reach only about 40 per cent of the population); increased production; and wider distribution of buying power. Brookings again gave the subject careful consideration in *The Recovery Problem in the United States* (1937), a volume which reviewed the causes of the depression and discussed New Deal measures used in combatting it. Moulton has many times challenged the efficacy of New Deal economic policies. Although the Institution has been attacked at various times, as when the late General Hugh S. Johnson, NRA administrator, charged that it represented the opinions of but one man, Harold G. Moulton, its scientific reputation is high and it is said to have much influence on Government policy.

Under Moulton's direction, in 1938 the Brookings Institution plowed deep into a study of the factors responsible for the prevailing stagnation in American capital markets, concluding, in *Capital Expansion, Employment, and Economic Stability* (1940), that, contrary to the views of many economists, the United States had by no means reached a stage of "economic maturity," and that there consequently is likelihood of further opportunity for private capital. Changes in Federal taxation to promote equity financing were recommended.

Among other outstanding Brookings publications was its president's *The New Philosophy of Public Debt* (1943), written in language which the layman could readily understand. Moulton contrasted the traditional view "that

a continuously unbalanced budget and rapidly rising public debt imperil the financial stability of the nation" with the new concept that "continuous deficit spending is essential to the economic prosperity of the nation" and that a balanced budget is outmoded. The more recent view, Moulton believes, is thoroughly unsound and invites inflation and a tottering economy.

In *The Control of Germany and Japan* (published in September 1944), the Brookings Institution discussed the controversial question of how to deal with the German and Japanese industrial machines at the close of this War. Its authors, Moulton and Louis Marlio, reject as inadequate proposals to dismember Germany territorially; to reduce her to an agricultural status (in view of the tremendous unemployment problem that would inevitably result); to place exclusive faith in general control of the importation of strategic raw materials. The fundamental objectives of the United Nations should be to institute preventative measures, they declare, not merely to check the resurgence of military power of the Axis. Thus Moulton and Marlio recommend for Germany the control of selected key industries—the control of the production of alloy steel, the prohibition of synthetic oil and aluminum ingot production—and the prohibition of all commercial as well as military aviation. The same basic principles are advocated in the treatment of Japan; she must be deprived of all her colonies and annexed areas since her war power depends upon their natural resources and industries.

These economic measures must be backed by a "requisite military force" at the disposal of an International Rearmament Detection and Prevention Board set up as the pivot of a combined system of detection of military preparations and their coercion, the authors conclude. In addition, the German-Japanese peace problem being separate from that of the cooperative handling of other international issues, an international organization should be established to develop a system of universal collective security. *The Control of Germany and Japan* was considered in many quarters a remarkably clear and realistic discussion of a controversial subject, the approach being scientific rather than emotional. "The layman could not easily find a simpler or more complete guide" to the problem, observed Arthur D. Gayer in the New York *Times*. I. F. Stone of *PM* sees the book as a "soft peace" plea and declares that the authors' objections to extensive economic controls is that "a general system of economic control would work strongly against private enterprise." (Stone considers it significant that Marlio was chairman of the International Aluminum Cartel—from 1926 to 1938, according to Moulton.)

Moulton is a stocky, white-haired man. Despite his 200 pounds he plays good games of squash and tennis. With the memory of a keen sports fan Moulton can recall at a moment's notice a staggering array of batting averages, football scores, and swimming records made years ago. He operates his own farm in Shenandoah Valley near Charlestown, West Virginia, but lives in Washington, D. C., with his wife, the former, Frances C. Rawlins (to whom he was married in 1912) and their two children, Barbara and John Rawlins.

Reference

Who's Who in America 1944-45

MOYNE, WALTER EDWARD GUINNESS, 1ST BARON 1880—Nov. 6, 1944 Irish-born British Resident Minister in the Middle East since January 1944; held numerous posts in the British Government, among them joint Parliamentary Secretary to the Ministry of Agriculture (1940-41), Secretary of State for the Colonies, and Leader of the House of Lords (1941-42); assassinated by two Palestine Jews, members of the Stern terrorist organization, denounced by Jews all over the world.

Obituary

N Y Times p1+ N 7 '44 por

MUNCH, EDVARD (mɔngk ed'värt) 1863—Jan. (?), 1944 Distinguished Norwegian painter; as a founder of the modern, expressionistic school of painting he exerted great influence throughout Europe; reported dead by Oslo radio January 25, 1944; see sketch 1940 Yearbook.

Obituary

N Y Times p19 Ja 25 '44

MUNI, PAUL (mü'ni) Sept. 22, 1895- Stage and screen actor
Address: b. c/o Columbia Pictures Corp., 1438 Gower St., Hollywood, Calif.; h. Encino, Calif.

Character actor supreme, Paul Muni has earned for himself the titles of the "man who is always somebody else" and the "man of many faces," and other similar epithets. In the last decade he has made his name synonymous with Zola, Pasteur, Juárez, and other real life heroes in his brilliant gallery of screen impersonations. He has never repeated a performance. By no means unattractive, he has not often been cast as a "handsome leading man spreading glamour all over the place." He exhibits none of the personal mannerisms that are the lucrative trademarks of many a Hollywood star, because he reverses the usual acting procedure of transforming the character into the actor. Avoiding the ballyhoo of the cinema capital, Muni is forever debunking the star system and intermittently threatens to retire in order to escape the "slavery of stardom," as he phrases it. He is of the ever-increasing roster who occasionally desert their mecca for a Broadway fling. He is as good an actor today as when he first became the talk of the town in the late '20's. Back in 1931, the late John Anderson wrote this succinct bit of tribute: "Muni knows how to make every moment in a performance count, and is willing to take his time in doing it. He leaves no blurred edges, nor any frayed outlines. They are sharp, clear, in full focus because he sees them himself, and commands the fluency and vitality to show what he is thinking about. There is power and richness of texture in his acting, and a sort of personal violence that is

PAUL MUNI

carefully used for touches that are compelling and unforgettable."

Born Muni Weisenfreund in the little town of Lemberg, in a part of Austria-Hungary that is now Poland, on September 22, 1895, Paul Muni was reared in the fascinating insecurity of the familiar theatrical trunk. His Thespian parents, Nathan Philip and Sally (Weisberg) Weisenfreund, were strolling players who sang, danced, and acted in the ghettos, trekking from one European capital to the other. This nomadic life brought the Weisenfreunds to London, where Muni attended his first school. The next year, 1902, found them thankfully viewing the Statue of Liberty for the first time. In New York Muni was enrolled at Public School No. 20 at Rivington and Forsythe Streets on the East Side, but his formal education was haphazard from then on, for the Weisenfreunds trouped through the Yiddish variety theatres in the States, with Muni and his two brothers in tow.

Shunning the financial hazards of their profession, Muni's parents had mapped out a musical career for their son. A good part of their combined weekly salaries went for violin lessons for the boy. But the stage-struck youth did not remain long behind the scenes. At thirteen or thereabouts young Muni masked his youth behind a heavy beard and make-up and filled in for a member of his parents' troupe who had fallen ill. The time was 1908, in Cleveland; the play was a sketch called *Two Corpses at Breakfast* in which Muni emerged as the ancient president of a lodge. He did so well that he soon became a regular member of the company—until 1913. From 1914 to 1917 he performed with a traveling troupe in the Middle Western states.

Weisenfreund Senior had been heartbroken at his son's ambition and had sorrowfully broken the precious violin across his knee. However, Paul managed to reconcile his father to his career, happily aided by the fact that he took the place of a $10-a-week actor

MUNI, PAUL—*Continued*

in his parents' company. He played every-thing from Ibsen and Strindberg to circuit burlesque—all in his native tongue, Yiddish.

Thus Muni learned to act in the most prac-tical school—acting itself. In his teens his roles were generally those of the "bearded variety"—from a Russian Cossack to a learned rabbi. Even in these early years he exhibited a flair for make-up. He loved to buy second-hand wigs and to wash and patch them up; he had fun molding his face with putty and donning whiskers. He once proudly perfected a make-up for Mephistopheles by pasting gold paper on his eyelids. To his delight, fire shot out of his eyes when the spotlight was turned on him. For eighteen years he played in Yiddish stock companies in and out of New York and Chicago.

There is a legend extant, according to Mor-ton Eustis in *Theatre Arts Monthly*, of "a wizened old man with long, straggly hair and a flowing beard who was wont to terrify the street urchins playing in the alley back of the old Yiddish Theatre in the Bowery by skat-ing past them with wild agility." The ini-tiated recognized him as the youthful Muni exercising between the acts while he waited for his cues. Another tale tells of a madman playing marbles who sent the whole East Side into a panic.

In 1918 Muni was spotted by Maurice Schwartz, who speedily signed him up at the munificent salary of $45 weekly as a member of the Yiddish Art Theatre. Under his tute-lage Muni toured the United States and Eng-land until 1926, playing the roles of Yivanov in Shalom Aleichem's *Hard To Be a Jew*; David Leizer in Andreev's *Anathema*; Osip in Gogol's *Inspector General*; the father in Gorky's *Middle Class People*; and the aristo-crat in Romain Rolland's *Wolves*. The Yid-dish theatre world paid homage to him as a brilliant and sensitive actor. On May 8, 1921 he had been married to a slim, dark-eyed girl, Bella Finkel, whose family were known as the Barrymores of the East Side.

On October 12, 1926 Muni moved to Broad-way when he appeared in his first English-speaking role at the Eltinge Theatre, as Morris Levine, the aged, orthodox Jewish father of *We, Americans*. He was an "instantaneous success," and the play ran for 118 perform-ances. He was only thirty-one, but some bemused critics expressed pity that "this old man should have spent a lifetime waiting a chance to appear on Broadway." John Golden recognized his talents and the following sea-son cast him as Benny Horowitz, the sturdy New York tough just out of prison, in the hit drama by Dana Burnet and George Ab-bott [40], *Four Walls* (1927). For once he played the part of a young man. Mrs. Muni was also in the cast.

Inevitably, it was not long before he at-tracted the Hollywood eyes of Winnie Shee-han, who lured him to Hollywood to do *The Valiant*, one of the first short talkies. In the film, released in 1929, Muni enacted the role of James Dyke, the youth who killed for hon-or's sake and then hid his identity on giving himself up in order to spare his family. When William Fox saw the first reel and a half he had qualms about Muni's performance because he thought the actor would not appeal to feminine audiences. However, Muni's sin-cerity in making the most of the rather melo-dramatic script made his first film something of a minor success. Six months later *Seven Faces* (1929) exhibited him at the height of his versatility as the simple, talkative janitor of a waxworks that came to life. Muni tackled the varying roles of Napoleon, Don Juan, Svengali, Franz Schubert, the Negro prize fighter Joe Gans, and a costermonger. The picture was a "flop" so Muni made his way back to New York.

Broadway welcomed his reappearance in October 1930 in *This One Man*, a thrilling psychological melodrama written by Sidney Robert Buchman. As the tough gangster Saul Holland, the idol of his weakling brother, Muni basked in the warm plaudits of the critics. Richard Dana Skinner wrote in the *Commonweal*: "Those who saw Paul Muni in *Four Walls* will remember the very great promise he then showed. He has not only amazing force and vitality, but a rich under-standing and an excellent technical equipment which enables him to put infinite variety not only into the use of his fine voice, but into gesture and action." Four months later, in February 1931, he again won applause as Steven Moorhead, the Middle Western hero of *Rock Me, Julie*, although the play closed after seven performances.

The following November Muni's star was in the ascendant. The play, which had a first run of 258 performances, was Elmer Rice's [43] *Counsellor-at-Law*, a heart-warming story of realistic humanity. Muni created the role of George Simon, the self-made, dynamic Jewish lawyer who is by turns full of exuberance, pretension, sentimentalism, shrewdness, un-selfishness, and human sympathy. The approval of Stark Young, writing in the *New Republic*, was typical: Muni's "performance exhibited above all things that gift not uncommon among Jewish actors, of passing with the greatest ease and persuasiveness from one emotion to another, and of rendering everything with the most disarming truth to reality. He showed also qualities of tenderness and sympathetic understanding that were very fine."

While Muni's name was adorning the Ply-mouth marquee, Strand Theatre patrons wit-nessed his first hit movie. With the aid of an ugly gash across his check, Muni was "snarl-ing and pillaging for Howard Hughes [41]" and United Artists in the role of Tony Camonte, a crack-brained, arrogant mobster. Rated as per-haps the best motion picture of its class, be-cause its gangster hero was drawn as a brutal thug who shows a yellow streak when the law gets him—a welcome change in screen treat-ment—*Scarface* (1932) had been banned by the Hays [43] office, but taken off the shelf sixteen months later when it had been revised and cut.

In the summer of 1932 Muni returned to the Coast to fulfill a picture commitment, while Otto Kruger substituted for him in *Counsellor-at-Law*. He resumed his role in the play in September, and during the winter the play was sent on tour with Muni again starring, returning to New York for a final two weeks' engagement, 378 Broadway performances *in toto*. Meanwhile, under the sponsorship of Warners, Muni appeared on the screen again as the hunted James Allen of *I Am a Fugitive from a Chain Gang* (1932), a grim and blasting depiction of life in Southern prison camps.

Broadway was not to see Muni in the flesh again for eight years. In 1933 First National put him into *The World Changes* in the role of the beef baron, Orin Nordholm, Jr., a captain of industry. "Beginning in pioneer days in 1865, the story traces the lines of four generations of the Nordholm family—from the soil in the Dakota territory to the meatpacking business in Chicago, to the crash of 1929 in Wall Street, and back to the land." Venturing into comedy in *Hi, Nellie!* (1934), Muni stepped into the shoes of Samuel N. Bradshaw, a wisecracking managing editor demoted to the "Heartthrobs" column under the pen name of Nellie Nelson.

Muni soon established a reputation for his painstaking methods in preparing for a role. For *Bordertown* (1935), in which, opposite Bette Davis '41, he brought to life Johnny Ramirez, a snarling (again), ambitious, and embittered Mexican youth, he wended his way down to the Mexican border town of Mexicali to get his local color at firsthand. Before rehearsing in *Black Fury* (1935) Muni perambulated through an Eastern mining district, where he acquired the dialect as well as a large fund of technical knowledge. In *Black Fury* Muni appeared as the Hunky Joe Radek, a robust, puzzled, illiterate miner full of consummate fury, who is thrust into the blind leadership of a labor war that is a setup for the strikebreaking agency behind it. Muni was far less enthusiastic about his next role, that of studious Dr. Lee Caldwell in the gangster opus, *Dr. Socrates* (1935), in which he singlehandedly rounded up a gang that had kidnapped his sweetheart. However, critics agreed that Muni performed with his customary effectiveness.

Just as Warner Brothers had pioneered with the controversial topic of *Black Fury*, so they laid claim to having originated the trend of screen biographies of great men. Muni's portrayal of the zealous French bacteriologist who braved the sneering, stodgy academicians won him the Academy Award in 1936. But with the release of *The Story of Louis Pasteur* (1935) Muni announced that he was quitting in order to be idle for a while.

Muni made his next deep impression on cinema audiences in MGM's epical production, *The Good Earth* (1937), which dramatized man's eternal courageous struggle with nature. As the simple Chinese peasant, Wang Lung, Muni nearly obliterated himself with nine separate make-ups during the span of the years, but several critics felt that Muni was never completely Chinese. In *The Woman I Love* (1937) which followed he gave an industrious performance as Lieutenant Claude Maury, a moody pilot of the last war, caught in a shopworn triangle with Miriam Hopkins and Louis Hayward.

Cheers accompanied Paul Muni's exit after the Hollywood première of *The Life of Émile Zola* (1937), his thirteenth and most successful picture. Warner Brothers billed him as "Mr. Paul Muni," with emphasis on the *Mister*. His brilliant portrayal of the fearless novelist and reformer who wrestled with hypocrisy and injustice in the cause of truth and freedom was again the result of conscientious preparation. He pored through Zola's most characteristic literary works, read accounts of his life and of the Dreyfus case, studied portraits, then experimented with make-ups, mastered the man's gestures and personal habits. As is his custom in perfecting a role, he recited his lines into a dictating machine at home and listened intently to his intonations and inflections.

After the success of *Zola* the Warners cast about for another biographical screen subject for their star. Colonel Gorgas, Victor Hugo, Anatole France, Haym Solomon, Lincoln, Beethoven, even Napoleon were projected. But Muni demurred. Afraid that both Pasteur and Zola were roles too similar to be repeated, he was through with biographies. Instead, he decided to take a long vacation, setting out on a world trip with his wife in November 1937, avoiding any war zones.

Juárez (1939) marked his return to the Hollywood fold. In a Prince Albert and a stovepipe hat, Muni *was* the man Benito Pablo Juárez, the stolid, idealistic Indian who overcame a foreign, European despotism and established a democracy in Mexico. Muni turned to modern romanticism and an English accent in the picturization of *We Are Not Alone* (1939), James Hilton's '42 sympathetic story of lovable, bewildered Dr. Newcombe, who befriends a homeless Viennese dancer.

Muni is one of the few stars who has the last word on his screen vehicles. He reads a script first to determine its general story value, then decides whether the character is an interesting human being. The majority of his films may be classified as sociological dramas, although he has expressed his indifference to crusading. "The reason, I suppose," he says, "is my insistence upon a role that is vital and lifelike. It so happens that characters like that are found in the more human, the earthier, and timelier stories."

During his Hollywood sojourn Muni hankered for another try at Broadway and read dozens of scripts before Maxwell Anderson's '42 *Key Largo* (1939) came his way. This was the tragedy of disillusioned King McCloud who deserts his American companions trapped by the Franco '42 forces because he cannot justify his dying, but lives to be tormented by a sense of guilt. Muni's distinguished miming, which won the Drama League award for the outstanding performance of the season of 1939 to 1940, contributed largely to the success of the play, "providing it with the depth, the richness, the dignity, and integrity it demands."

Muni commenced his free-lance work for the screen with *Hudson's Bay* (1941), another historical epic though not a particularly happy choice. He appeared as Pierre Radisson, unshaven French trapper and practical idealist, who was directly responsible for the formation of Canada's Hudson's Bay Company. On April 14, 1942 Muni was back on Broadway in Emlyn William's '41 hackneyed, sentimental *Yesterday's Magic*, playing the role of Maddoc Thomas, a broken-down, inebriated actor who tries to make a comeback as Lear. (Muni himself does not have this typical actor's

MUNI, PAUL—*Continued*

dream of playing Shakespeare.) The critical consensus was that Muni played too literally, without exhibiting the touch of humor that might have put the part over. *Time* commented that "actor Muni has the good sense not to overact in a part he lacked the good sense to turn down."

Muni once more returned to the coast after a two years' absence, this time to make *The Commandos Strike at Dawn* (1943) for Columbia, a picture praised for its realism in depicting Norwegian sabotage and rebellion against Nazi invasion, and directed by John Farrow of *Wake Island* fame. As the patriot Eric Toreson who leads the resistance against the oppressors, reviewers felt that Muni played with fine restraint and sincerity. In *Stage Door Canteen* (1943) he appeared fleetingly along with a host of other "name" players. In the winter of 1943 he was at Columbia working on *A Song To Remember*, as Joseph Elsner, instructor and mentor to Frederic Chopin. With Muni in the picture are Merle Oberon [41] as George Sand and Cornel Wilde as Chopin. The film was to be released in early 1945, along with *Counterattack*, in which Muni plays Kulkov, the Russian guerrilla. It is also reported that Twentieth Century-Fox is considering a screen biography of Victor Hugo. If it materializes, Paul Muni is slated for the role.

On November 24, 1942 John Golden revived *Counsellor-at-Law*, in which Muni had made his first smashing success eleven years before. Again Muni played "with his usual charm, authority, and artistry." The play did not end its run at the Royale Theatre until July 17, 1943. In March 1943 Muni acted as principal narrator of the dramatic mass memorial for the 2,000,000 Jews killed in Europe, *We Will Never Die*, at Madison Square Garden.

Muni is a handsome, dark-haired man, tallish and slender, "with unusually expressive [black] eyes and a quick merry smile." He is an inveterate worrier, dreamy, sensitive, impractical, unobtrusive, and unpublicized. Statistics are his weakness, be they true or false; he never doubts anyone who quotes figures. A good game of pinochle is his idea of a perfect nightly recreation. He still plays the violin, and he enjoys painting, too. Mrs. Muni has been an invaluable aid to him; she is the boss of the set in her own quiet way, and at the end of each "take" Muni looks to her for approbation or disapproval.

He does not like to analyze his art. "I have been in the business for years," he explains, "but can't for the life of me tell what acting is or how it is done. I know I have not tried to learn the 'art' of acting, whatever that may be. I try to grasp the mind of the character I'm playing. I think his thoughts, and unconsciously they motivate my hands, my voice, my face, my body. You cannot become a good actor, I believe, if you merely imitate a character, if you are thinking: 'Now I'll move a hand, now I'll shrug my shoulders, now I'll get my face closer to the camera. . . .'" He likes to think that the character he is portraying is not Paul Muni, but he adds that there is always something of himself in any part he plays, as well as something of the writer who created the part.

References

Am M 125:42-3+ F '38 pors
Am Theatre Mag 1:18-20 Mr '40 pors
N Y Herald Tribune VI p 1+ N 22 '42
Scholastic 31:39 S 18 '37 pors
Theatre Arts 24:194-205 Mr '40 pors
Time 30:34-5 Ag 16 '37 por (cover)
International Motion Picture Almanac 1941-42
Sobel, B. ed. Theatre Handbook 1940
Who's Who 1944
Who's Who in America 1944-45
Who's Who in American Jewry 1938-39
Who's Who in the Theatre 1939

MUNK, KAJ (kĭ) 1898 (?)—Jan. 5, 1944 Danish clergyman; Denmark's foremost poet, playwright, and most outspoken anti-Nazi pamphleteer; arrested by Nazis in September 1943 and released two months later; kidnapped and shot to death, reportedly by Nazis.

Obituary

N Y Times p4 Ja 6 '44 por

MUNN, FRANK 1895- Radio singer

Address: b. c/o Hummert Radio Features Co., 247 Park Ave., New York City

Radio and Frank Munn, the singer, have been faithful to each other. Unlike most professional singers, Munn has devoted himself exclusively to radio; the only exception has been his recordings for Brunswick and other record houses. He has never sung in night clubs, concert halls, motion-picture houses, or theatres since he made his first radio appearance in December 1923 on the old Brunswick radio hour. Radio has rewarded him by giving him twenty-one years of commercial programs—something of a record, since top stars like Frank Sinatra [43], Bing Crosby [41], and Connee Boswell have served their time on radio sustaining programs while seeking a sponsor. Moreover, the Hummert Radio Features Company, producers of his present programs, the *American Album of Familiar Music* and *Waltz Time*, report that until 1944, when he took a two-week vacation, he never missed a concert on either of the programs in the thirteen years he has been with them as soloist.

Frank Munn was born in The Bronx, New York, in 1895, the son of George H. Munn, a policeman. He is of Irish-German stock. Both parents died when he was a baby, and he was brought up by his grandmother. There was very little money, and so as soon as he was old enough to work Frank found a job as a shuttle-boy in an embroidery factory for $3 a week. He had a natural love for music, and it is said that the rhythm of the factory machines "led him to hum and keep time with them." As the next step in his musical education he studied phonograph records of singers.

In his boyhood he belonged to a Bronx recreation club called the Church House, a place where neighborhood boys played basketball, gave little concerts, and enjoyed other social activities. He was soon asked to sing at one of the concerts. Since he could not read music, in order to learn a song he had to play a record over and over again until he had memorized the phrasing and air perfectly. The first song he mastered in this way was "Dear Old Pal o' Mine." He was a great success, and after that, Munn says, "Nothing could keep me quiet."

Declared physically unfit for service in the armed forces during the First World War, Munn went to work as a machinist, building turbine engines. At the urging of his friends, in his spare hours he began taking singing lessons—his first teacher was Dudley Buck. His reputation as a singer grew, and he frequently sang in churches and at amateur concerts. On one of these occasions Gustave (better known as Gus) Haenschen, National Broadcasting Company conductor, heard him sing. Haenschen, who at the time was organizing the recording division of Brunswick-Balke-Callender, offered Munn $300 to make a record of "Little Mother o' Mine" for Brunswick. In those days recording companies paid a flat sum to artists and no royalties. However, the $300 looked big to Munn, who until then had been paid not much more than the proverbial coffee and cake for his singing. The record proved to be a money-maker, and after that Munn became a regular contributor to the record house. One of his early successes in records was "As Time Goes By," which has been revived recently. The friendship and business association with Haenschen formed at that time has continued ever since.

In December 1923 Munn joined the *Brunswick Hour of Music* radio program organized and conducted by Haenschen. The conductor introduced Munn as "The Golden Voice of Radio," a title still used and one which is considered fitting because of the unusually rich and mellow tones of his tenor voice. His first song on the Brunswick program was the one in which he had made his debut in records, "Little Mother o' Mine." Since then his work has been confined almost exclusively to popular ballads, which he repeats again and again because of the public's demand. Among the songs he has sung more than a hundred times are "Forgotten", "The Rose of Tralee", "Rose of Picardy", "Somewhere a Voice Is Calling", "The Rosary," and "Auf Wiedersehen." There are two words he refuses to sing: one is "baby" and the other "pal." Munn says the nicest compliment ever paid him was when at Oley Speaks's request he sang Speaks's song "Sylvia." The composer was so delighted with Munn's enunciation and the perfection of his interpretation that he called a cab and dashed to the NBC studio to congratulate the singer in person.

Munn's connection with Frank Hummert of the Hummert Radio Features began in 1931 when Hummert engaged the singer as soloist on *American Album of Familiar Music,* a Sunday night program which can be heard over NBC's Red Network. In 1933 Hummert, in collaboration with his wife, Anne Hummert, originated and produced *Waltz Time,* a Friday night program also on NBC's

FRANK MUNN

Red Network, and Munn was engaged as featured soloist. In radio circles both programs come under the category, "moderately-priced familiar music program," a form of program which *Variety* gives credit to Hummert for originating. Because they are produced on a small budget, Munn's salary is a modest one when compared to other radio stars. Royalties from his records, however, are large. Through ASCAP's efforts artists today are paid a royalty of one-and-a-half to two cents on each record by the recording companies. Royalties on a popular number often net the artist $10,000 or more.

Despite the fact that Munn has had no publicity through personal appearances outside radio studios, he has been voted to sixth place in popularity polls conducted by *Radio Guide* and his program *Waltz Time* won second place in the *Radio Guide*'s 1939 poll among its readers. Munn is well liked by his fellow workers, who say that he has a keen sense of humor, and that his favorite bit of advice, "Take it easy," is the one which he applies to his own life. He likes to tinker with machinery (he has a talent for mechanics) and to cook goulash in his Garden City home, where he lives a bachelor's existence. He plays golf—his most prized possessions are his clubs. He likes to watch football, and has seen many games from the coach's bench with his friend and mutual fan, the ex-footballer John Francis (Chick) Meehan. Munn is very fond of grand opera, his favorite operas including *Norma, La Bohème, La Traviata, Tosca, Rigoletto,* and *Pagliacci.* He is a Mason and belongs to a Protestant church. He is five feet nine inches tall, is large framed, and weighs over the 200 pound mark. His hair and eyes are brown.

Reference

Variety Radio Directory 1940-41

NELLES, PERCY WALKER (nel'las)
Jan. 7, 1892- Chief of Canadian Naval Staff
Address: b. Navy Building, Elgin St., Ottawa,
Canada; h. Vine Lynne, 7 Rideau Gate, Ottawa, Canada

The senior man in the Canadian Navy, in
every sense, is Vice-Admiral Percy W. Nelles,
chief of the Canadian Naval Staff, appointed
Senior Canadian Flag Officer Overseas in
January 1944. Not only does he hold the
highest rank, but he was the first of all its
members to enlist; yet he was in 1938 the
youngest man in the entire British Navy to
hold the rank of rear admiral. Nelles' promotion to vice-admiral causes him to outrank
his famous father, Brigadier General Charles
Macklem Nelles.

Percy Walker Nelles was born in Brantford, Ontario, on January 7, 1892. His mother
was Ida Maud Mary (Walker) Nelles. He
was educated at Lakefield Preparatory School
and at Bishop's College School, Port Hope,
Ontario. In 1908, when the Canadian Navy
was first formed under Rear Admiral Kingsmill, Nelles was sixteen. He immediately
volunteered for training as a naval cadet and
was the second man to enlist in the new Navy.
(The first person to enlist transferred to the
Air Force during the First World War; later,
when he sought to re-enter the Navy, he was
unable to pass the medical examination.
Nelles is therefore the senior man in point
of service.) After his preliminary training,
Nelles was assigned to H.M.S. *Dreadnought*,
the first modern capital ship; next he saw
service on cruisers. Nelles has served in "all
kinds of ships—bar subs, which are a specialty
—and done all kinds of navy work." In 1914
he became a lieutenant in the Navy; and on
May 17, 1915 he was married to Helen Schuyler Allen. They now have two sons, Charles
Macklem and William Allen.

The Canadian Navy was "pitifully weak";
the public simply was not interested in building
up a strong Navy, and "Parliament never supplied the money to do a decent navy job." In
1911 Nelles, then a junior officer aboard the
Niobe, was present at a demonstration intended
to arouse public interest in building up the
Navy. A political picnic was held "down Yarmouth way" in Nova Scotia; orators harangued
the crowd on the need for a strong Navy; and
then, at the dramatic moment, the *Niobe*
steamed smartly into view off the coast—and
ran aground. Half the Canadian Navy was
stuck in the mud!

During the First World War Nelles served
as an officer aboard cruisers convoying Canadian
troops from Halifax to Clyde. In 1914 he was
decorated with the Star; toward the end of
the War he was recalled to Ottawa to serve as
aide to Admiral Kingsmill at Naval Service
Headquarters. Nelles also received the British
War and Victory medals, and in 1918 was
given intensive training at the Royal Navy
Staff College and the Imperial Defence College,
both in England. Eleven years later he became
the first Canadian-trained officer to take command of a British cruiser, H.M.S. *Dragon*.
Promotion to the rank of captain came in 1933;
and the following year Nelles succeeded the
retiring Commodore Hose as chief of the

Canadian naval staff, with the rank of commodore first class.

As commander of the Canadian Navy Nelles
was faced with a number of difficult problems.
The personnel and equipment at his command
were pathetically inadequate for the protection
of Canada's long, irregular coastline. "As
chief of the naval staff Nelles was responsible
for every aspect of training, every item of
equipment, every detail of operations." He was
faced particularly with the problem of creating
an organization which could serve as a "trained
nucleus capable, without conflict, confusion, or
waste, of an immediate expansion along a prearranged course." Nelles arranged for his men
to have the benefit of training on ships of the
Royal Navy so that they might come up to
the strict British standards; in winter he sent
Canadian destroyers to the iceless West Indian
waters. Fortunately, Nelles brought to his
command a "fanatic devotion to the Navy" and
a popularity among his men which brought
their fullest cooperation. Nelles' men said that,
before the present War started, he knew the
name of every Canadian vessel—including private merchant and pleasure craft, even to sailboats and launches—and had fitted each one
into its place for greatest effectiveness in case
of emergency. In 1938, when Nelles was promoted to rear admiral, he was the youngest
man ever to hold that rank in the British Navy.

In August 1939 the Royal Canadian Navy
had only fifteen ships, with 131 officers and
1,643 enlisted men in active service; but Admiral Nelles foresaw the tremendous expansion
of the coming war, and reorganized the staff
along the lines of the British Navy, similar to
those of any well-run army. Although the admiral remains as chief of the naval staff, each
of the other staff members has a definite sphere
of responsibility, for no one man could hope to
handle the training, equipment, and operational
activities of the present Canadian Navy. By
November 1941, when Nelles was promoted to
vice-admiral (the first Canadian ever to hold
that rank), his command had been built up to
a strength of some 400 ships and 27,000 personnel, and was continuing to expand.

In January 1944, when Nelles was appointed
Senior Canadian Flag Officer with general
supervision of affairs over the Canadian Navy
in European waters, the Navy had multiplied
"fortyfold," comprising "250 combat ships and
400 auxiliary craft with a total personnel of
80,000." It had been almost entirely responsible for the naval convoy work in the western
half of the North Atlantic, with the assistance
of R.C.A.F. patrols. British Navy Minister
Angus Macdonald, announcing Nelles' transfer
to London, explained that while it "did not
imply actual command in action of Canadian
units, as they would be intermingled with other
Allied navies," it did mean that "the Canadian
Navy will maintain an entity of its own and
not be merely an adjunct of the British Navy."
As the Canadian Navy is "largely made up of
destroyers, frigates, corvettes, and smaller craft,
[it] will be supplemented in a few months by
two medium cruisers of modern design from
the British Navy, and by two aircraft carriers
which will be manned by Canadian seamen and
officers, while the aircraft and air personnel
will be supplied by the Royal Navy." Admiral

Royal Canadian Navy Photo
VICE-ADM. PERCY WALKER NELLES

Nelles will be "working with the Admiralty, and might sit on a naval war council, if one is created." He was replaced as chief of staff in Canada by Rear Admiral G. C. Jones.

After the invasion of the Continent in June it was revealed that Nelles had gone to London with Lieutenant General Kenneth Stuart '44 and Air Marshal Lloyd S. Breadner to correlate invasion plans. When D-Day came "ships of the Royal Canadian Navy carried the men of the Canadian Army [led by Lieutenant General H. D. G. Crerar '44], landed the first assault waves and their reinforcements, and then commenced a sleepless period of day-and-night ferry service to the beachheads. Above, the men of the Royal Canadian Air Force held the skies." "It was news," wrote *Newsweek*, "that an all-Canadian team had been formed in England to strike its own blow; that from Canada's 11,500,000 citizens had been drawn ground, sea, and air forces in sufficient strength to earn a distinct place in the greatest assault in history." At least three Canadian flotillas of destroyers, frigates, corvettes, mine sweepers, and motor torpedo boats were engaged in the landing operations, the Navy disclosed afterward. Nelles, commented the New York *Times,* had done more than any other man to make the tiny fleet that Canada had at the start of the War into a great fighting force.

Admiral Nelles is described as "rather on the short side, thick-set but not overweight, with a chubby face surmounted by an unruly crest of graying hair. He wears tortoise-shell glasses, is clean-shaven." Nelles has the knack of maintaining discipline and efficiency while remaining on the best of terms with his subordinates. In spite of his masses of heavy gold braid, and his many service ribbons, "there is no 'side' or 'top-hat' about him, no clearings of the throat and shootings of the gold-encased cuffs. He is . . . an Ontario kind of · democrat who combines the free-and-easy style with a sense of humor and rather a predisposition to the wisecrack."

The Admiral, a member of the Church of England, has received the King George V Coronation and Jubilee medals. On January 1, 1943 he was decorated by the King with the Order of Companion of the Bath. When he has some time free from his duties in "the King's navee," Nelles takes his mind off his work by going swimming.

References

N Y Sun p21 Ap 25 '41 por
Who's Who 1944
Who's Who in Canada 1940-41

NEWCOMER, MABEL July 2, 1891-
Economist; educator
Address: b. c/o Vassar College, Poughkeepsie, N. Y.

Among the world monetary experts gathered at the United Nations Monetary and Financial Conference in July 1944 to discuss plans for an International Stabilization Fund and a World Bank for Reconstruction and Development was Mabel Newcomer, the only woman delegate selected by the United States Government. Miss Newcomer is head of the economics department of Vassar College and has previously served as an expert in economics to New York and California State authorities, as well as for the United States Treasury. Other members of the American delegation at the first major world financial conference since the ill-fated one at London in 1933 were Henry Morgenthau, Jr.'40, Secretary of the Treasury and president of the conclave; Harry D. White '44, chief author of the projects under discussion; Dean Acheson '41, Assistant Secretary of State; Marriner S. Eccles '41, chairman of the Federal Reserve Bank; Fred M. Vinson '43, Economic Stabilization Director. Congress was represented by Democrats Robert F. Wagner '41 and Brent Spence and by Republicans Jesse P. Wolcott and Charles W. Tobey.

Mabel Newcomer was born in Oregon, Illinois, on July 2, 1891, the daughter of Alphonso Gerald and Carrie Mabel (Jackson) Newcomer. There was an academic tradition in her family, for her father was the head of the English Department at Stanford University. It was there that Miss Newcomer took her bachelor's degree as a Phi Beta Kappa student in 1913 and her M.A. the following year. In 1917 she won her Ph.D. from Columbia University, after completing her thesis, *The Separation of State and Local Revenues in the United States.*

Miss Newcomer began her teaching career in 1917 as an instructor in economics at Barnard College. A year later she went to Vassar College in Poughkeepsie, New York, attaining the rank of professor in 1926. Since 1932 she has been the head of the combined departments of economics, sociology, and anthropology. She has taught also as visiting professor at Stanford University, the University of Chicago, and Columbia University.

But Miss Newcomer's energies have not been confined to the classroom. Her specialty is taxes, and she has served as an expert in this connection for the tax authorities of New York and California, and for the United States Treasury. Miss Newcomer's first practical experience in fiscal matters came with her appointment as special investigator for the New

Alman Co.

MABEL NEWCOMER

York State Joint Committee on Taxation and Retrenchment from 1921 to 1926. During this period she also worked on two studies, *The Chemical Industry in New York and Its Environs* (1924) and, as economist for the Educational Finance Inquiry (1922-23), *Financial Statistics of Public Education in the United States, 1910-20* (1924). In 1928 she again served as consulting economist, this time for the California Tax Commission. Miss Newcomer next became a special investigator for the New York State Commission on the Revision of the Tax Law from 1931 to 1932, the year in which she completed *The Use of State Revenues for the Support of Local Functions in New York* and also acted on Governor Franklin D. Roosevelt's '42 Commission on Rural Homes.

In 1934 Miss Newcomer received a grant-in-aid from the Social Science Research Council for a study which resulted in a 381-page volume, *Central and Local Finance in Germany and England* (1937). Then, following a special investigation for the New York State Commission on State Aid (1935-36), in 1937 she acted as tax consultant on two more committees, the Advisory Committee on Education and the New York State Joint Legislative Committee on Fiscal Policies. In that year, too, Miss Newcomer was the joint author of *Facing the Tax Problem*. Throughout all these activities, Miss Newcomer also contributed numerous articles to technical periodicals and wrote pamphlets such as *You Are a Taxpayer* (1939) and an addition to the Columbia University Series on Current Problems in American Life, *Taxation and Fiscal Policy* (1940).

As a member of the Committee on Intergovernmental Fiscal Relations, for the Treasury Department, which began its consultations in 1941, Miss Newcomer helped prepare a six-volume report, *Federal, State, and Local Fiscal Relations*, made public in March 1943. The two others on the committee were Luther Gulick,

director of the Institute of Public Administration, and Harold M. Groves, professor of economics at Wisconsin University. The three independent experts outlined a post-War fiscal program for the United States to fit the new world envisioned by the President's National Resources Planning Board. Designed primarily to simplify and coordinate overlapping taxes, the report contains sixty-nine recommendations, among which the more important are public investment in public health, regional development, housing, and nutrition in order "to underwrite the maintenance of a high level of economic opportunity and full use of resources and plant capacity in the United States," expanded Federal aid programs to include relief and public education, broader social security to include groups now uncovered, more Federal aid to poor states, Federal incorporation of companies doing interstate business, and the adoption of a more progressive tax system. Copies of the report were sent to President Roosevelt, to the Governors of the forty-eight states, and to members of the House Ways and Means and Senate Finance Committees. Although a Democrat herself, in 1943 Miss Newcomer served on Governor Thomas E. Dewey's '44 Committee on Taxation.

Miss Newcomer's next task for the United States Government was in the capacity of specialist in international finance and foreign exchange at the United Nations Monetary and Financial Conference which convened in Bretton Woods, New Hampshire, on July 1, 1944, having as its objectives the stabilizing of post-War exchange and the promoting of world trade. The sole woman negotiator in the American group, Miss Newcomer was appointed a member of both Commission No. 1, which considered the $8,000,000,000 International Stabilization Fund principally authored by Harry D. White, and of Commission No. 2, which debated the merits of a world bank for reconstruction where relief measures end. By July 22, the closing date of the conference, forty-four United and Associated Nations had submerged their differences and approved both proposals aiming at international cooperation. President Roosevelt predicted that this pact—although it is yet to be ratified by the home governments, as well as by the United States Congress—was one step toward the establishment of "a dynamic and soundly expanding" post-War world economy. At the second conference of women, held at the New York *Times* Hall in December of 1944, Miss Newcomer pointed out the significance of the Bretton Woods conference. "We are now where England used to be," she said; but now the tables are turned—"we are the great industrial nation. We want free trade. The English do not. . . . That was really the battle of Bretton Woods. We are trying to persuade England not to protect against us."

This student of intergovernmental fiscal problems lives on a two-acre place at Poughkeepsie, where she operates a large garden which, she says as an economist, makes her kitchen entirely self-sufficient. Although her favorite recreation is climbing mountains, Miss Newcomer was so occupied at the monetary conference that she did not attempt to scale the slopes of Mount Washington, which towered 5,000 feet above the conference setting.

References

N Y Times p20 Jl 5 '44 por
Who's Who in America 1944-45

NIN, ANAIS (nēn a-nä-ēss′) Author; printer

Address: h. 215 W. 13th St., New York City

Anaïs Nin is one "uncommercial" writer who has solved the problem of reaching her public without the help of a commercial publisher. Concluding that "no real writer should try to earn a living from writing because if his work is valuable to society, it is surely not for immediate, agreeable, and harmless consumption," she chose to "write sincerely" and print her own books, selling them to whomever she could interest. Although rejected by the commercial publishers, the manuscript of the *Winter of Artifice* had been favorably criticized by such leading independent critics as Rebecca West, who said: "I think the whole thing quite marvelous, particularly in its use of absolutely new material. You seem to me to have real and unmistakable genius." Henry Miller and William Carlos Williams published long articles on Miss Nin's writings, which won praise also from a number of others, including Kay Boyle '42, Carl Van Vechten, and Paul Rosenfeld.

Miss Nin, "a writer since the age of eleven," whose diary now includes more than sixty volumes, was born in Paris, the daughter of Joaquín and Rosa (Culmell) Nin. Her maternal grandfather was a Dane who had settled in Cuba. As a child she worshipped her father, who (in Paul Rosenfeld's words) was "an elegant, spoiled Spanish musician and composer whom some authorities set in an artistic category above Manuel De Falla." When his daughter was eleven he deserted his family, who thereupon sailed to New York. The abrupt transposition from one country to another was bewildering, and the brutality of a father she adored was a profound shock to the young girl.

"To help make the desolation of life endurable, she began to keep a journal." According to the novelist and essayist Henry Miller, a personal friend of Miss Nin's, "there is a very significant fact attached to the origin of this diary, and that is that it was begun in artistic fashion. By that I do not mean that it was done with the skill of an artist, with the conscious use of a technique; no, but it was begun as something to be read by someone else, as something to influence someone else. . . . Begun during the voyage to a foreign land, the diary is a silent communion with the father who has deserted her, a gift which she intends to send him from their new home, a gift of love which she hopes will reunite them. And so, in the very beginning of her diary the child behaves precisely like the artist who, through the medium of his expression, sets about to conquer the world which has denied him. . . . Thinking originally to woo and enchant the father by the testimony of her grief, thwarted in all

Deigh-Navin

ANAIS NIN

her attempts to recover him, she begins little by little to regard the separation as a punishment for her own inadequacy. . . . The diary becomes the confession of her inability to make herself worthy of this lost father who has become for her the very paragon of perfection."

At fifteen Miss Nin left school and obtained work as a fashion mannequin and artists' model. She supported her mother and brothers in this manner for two years until her marriage in 1920 to Ian Hugo, whose copperplate engravings now illustrate her books. Later she became "a dancer of Spanish dances" and gave one recital in Paris during the early '30's, after which she decided that dancing was too strenuous for her health and gave it up to study psychoanalysis. After a year of practice Miss Nin concluded that psychoanalysis was also too strenuous for her and therefore abandoned it. In the meantime she had written "an unprofessional study of D. H. Lawrence," an essay published in 1930. During 1931 she wrote *The House of Incest*, and in 1935, *Winter of Artifice*. A short story, "Birth," was listed in O'Brien's *Best Short Stories* for 1937. During all this time she "produced on the side, in the midst of an intensely active life, a monumental confession which [in the opinion of Henry Miller] when given to the world will take its place beside the revelations of St. Augustine, Petronius, Rousseau, Proust, and others. Of the twenty years recorded, half the time was spent in America, half in Europe. The diary is full of voyages; in fact, like life itself it might be regarded as nothing but a voyage . . . a mythological voyage towards the source and fountainhead of life."

"She writes in the dark but unfalteringly," Henry Miller has written elsewhere. "She clings to her European authors, her European habits of mind, in the most formative years of her life, when any other child would have succumbed to the strong rhythm of American life. She holds herself silently superior to the

NIN, ANAIS—*Continued*

whole American scene, a fact in itself which impresses me as quite magnificent. . . . For me it is a foregone conclusion that the Journal is a work of the highest standing, that it is indeed . . . a unique human contribution." (In 1944 Miss Nin announced her plan to "convert and transpose the diary of sixty-five volumes into a full, long novel of the thirty years between 1914 and 1944—between two wars." Among the themes will be the artistic life of Paris, the drama of psychoanalysis, the transition from romanticism to realism, the birth and death of surrealism, and woman in her relationship to the present-day world.)

In 1942 Miss Nin, then in New York, found that the manuscript of *Winter of Artifice* drew high praise from critics but no offers from publishers, who called it "uncommercial." But Miss Nin "did not accept this condemnation," for "a real writer does not need the publicity that is granted with equal fervor to a toothpaste. A real writer only wants his book read by those people who want to read it, and if there are one hundred of them it is enough to keep his work alive and sustain his productivity. But there are two obstacles to his finding these hundred persons: one, the publisher, who is interested only in large and immediate returns; the second, the writer himself, who needs to earn a living." Miss Nin thinks that anyone can follow her example who is willing to "write sincerely and to earn his living by some other means."

First Miss Nin arranged with the Gotham Book Mart to advance her $100 for copies of the book; then she raised a similar amount in subscriptions from "a few friends." With this she bought a second-hand foot-power printing press and some type, persuaded the paper supplier and the bookbinder to give her thirty days' credit, and set about learning from a friend how to print. After a month of working "eight and nine hours a day," Miss Nin was able to print two and then four pages a day. After two more months she had turned out 500 copies of *Winter of Artifice*, illustrated with six of her husband's engravings (which she printed directly from the copperplates, using "an old forgotten method invented by William Blake"). The total cost was $400, including $75 for the press and $100 for the type. With "no money to spend on advertising," Miss Nin printed her own announcements, circularized everyone she knew had been interested in her earlier writings, and visited the bookstores, persuading them to include *Winter of Artifice* in their catalogs. By these methods she succeeded in selling some 400 copies, more than enough to cover all expenses. The surplus went toward the paper for a 300-copy edition of her next book, *Under a Glass Bell* published in the spring of 1944.

"I have met," Miss Nin says, "with only one insuperable obstacle: the reviewers. They side with the commercial publishers. They will not review books by small presses unless these small presses . . . get themselves publicized." Nevertheless, *Winter of Artifice* was reviewed in the New York *Herald Tribune* book section and in the *Nation*. The former found it "a little overfull of . . . people saying mystic things about themselves, about others, about life. It

presents stories about stories and conclusions that come before the fact. Over all this there is a rather piquant icing of good language." The *Nation's* reviewer held, however, that "Anaïs Nin's writing will come to be regarded as one of the most admirable of purely lyrical efforts."

Both reviewers found reflections of Miss Nin's life in the two stories which make up this book—"Both 'Winter of Artifice' and 'The Voice' are rooted in psychoanalysis." According to Rosenfeld, "the first was incidental to her seductive parent's long-looked-for reappearance in her life. In the course of an effective portrait of him we see Joaquín Nin take her to stay in the south of France. . . . Shortly the disharmony which had always existed between their ways of living grows plain. She becomes aware that she has outgrown her need of him." The second story, "The Voice", "offers more personality contrasts than the first. This is the story of a psychoanalyst, or more accurately it is the story of his failure to be anything but a psychoanalyst."

"The *universal* quality which publishers pretend to recognize," says Miss Nin, "is impossible to define as they do. My book, which was not supposed to have this universal quality, was bought and read by all kinds of people. In the public library of my quarter it has been reserved, and people are waiting to read it. The girl who washes my hair bought it and commented on it with perception. The grown colored boy of the woman who cleans my apartment got his schoolmates to chip in twenty-five cents so as to own a copy. . . . I was not 'put over' or 'pushed over' or 'sold.' I was simply saved from the middleman and found my public alone."

Of *Under a Glass Bell,* Miss Nin says, "These stories represent the moment when many like myself had found only one answer to the suffering of the world: to dream, to tell fairy tales, to elaborate, and to follow the labyrinth of fantasy. . . . I am in the difficult position of presenting stories which are dreams and of having to say: 'But now, although I give you these, I am awake!'" The first edition was sold out, and the author-printer set about printing 1,000 more. Edmund Wilson, reviewing it in the *New Yorker,* said, "'The Mouse', 'Under a Glass Bell', 'Rag Time,' and 'Birth,' are really beautiful little pieces. . . . They are half short stories, half dreams, and they mix a sometimes exquisite poetry with a homely realistic observation. They take place in a special world, a world of feminine perception and fancy which is all the more curious and charming for being innocently international. . . . There are passages in her prose which may perhaps suffer a little from an hallucinatory vein of writing which the surrealists have overdone: a mere reeling-out of images, each of which is designed to be surprising but which, strung together, simply fatigue. In Miss Nin's case, however, the imagery does convey something and is always appropriate. . . . But perhaps the main thing to say is that Miss Nin is a very good artist, as perhaps none of the literary surrealists is. . . . The book, like her others, has been printed by Miss Nin herself and is distributed through the Gotham Book Mart. . . . It is well worth the trouble of sending for." (The author's next book was to be "This Hunger," scheduled for publication in the spring of 1945.)

Miss Nin, whose favorite recreations are music and dancing, is five and one-half feet tall —and slender. She has "brown-red hair, green eyes, pale mat skin." Her home is in a "sort of walk-up studio penthouse with roof-terrace" in Greenwich Village, where she faithfully keeps on with her diary.

References

N Y Herald Tribune Books p14 N 8 '42
Nation 155:276-7 S 26 '42

Laughlin, J. ed. New Directions p429-36 1942

NOBLE, EDWARD J(OHN) Aug. 8, 1882- Manufacturer; radio network owner

Address: b. 30 Rockefeller Plaza, New York City; h. Round Hill Rd., Greenwich, Conn.

A boyhood dream to make a mark in the advertising world was realized when Edward J. Noble, Life Saver candy millionaire, bought the Blue Network in July 1943. The purchase made history in the radio world because Noble was the first individual to own a national chain of radio stations. *Variety* estimates that the sponsored programs on the Blue Network will yield Noble more than two million dollars in annual profits. The purchase price was $8,000,000 in cash, with an outlay of an equal sum required for new equipment and offices six months after the War ends.

Born in Gouverneur, New York, August 8, 1882, Edward John Noble is the son of Harvey H. and Edna L. (Wood) Noble. Although the Nobles were far from well-to-do, young Noble managed to spend summer vacations in the nearby Thousand Islands with his chum, Roy Allen. They dreamed or rather planned to make fortunes for themselves and decided that this could be done in advertising, which was in their opinion a "coming business." While attending Syracuse University, Noble worked as a reporter on the Watertown *Daily Times* and as treasurer of the Gouverneur Athenian Society. Later he went to Yale University, where he obtained his B.A. degree in 1905. "Broke when he entered Yale, Noble organized and ran an eating club and marked himself as likely to succeed by accumulating a financial surplus by the time he left the University." As planned in his boyhood, he entered the advertising field as a space salesman for the card advertising specialists, Ward & Gow of New York City.

Becoming familiar with the profits made in advertised specialties, young Noble kept "his eyes open for one to promote by himself." In 1913 he discovered Life Savers, a hard mint candy manufactured as a sideline by Clarence A. Crane, maker of Mary Garden chocolates. Noble felt that they could be made to sell on a bigger scale and so urged Crane to advertise them. The manufacturer, not having that much faith in his product, offered to sell Noble his trademark and his stock of mints for $5,000. Noble presented the proposition to his friend J. Roy Allen: "a $50-a-day repeat business"—a product they could de-

velop by advertising. Allen liked the proposition and they started to raise the purchase money. Allen borrowed $1,500 from his mother; Noble put in his savings and agreed to keep his salaried job and put in cash each week. Allen was to devote all of his time to the enterprise.

Since the young men could raise only $3,900 and needed $1,000 for initial expenses, Crane accepted $2,900 for Life Savers. Loft space in New York City was rented; six girls at $5 a week were hired. But when Allen called on Crane's customers for "repeat" orders he discovered "their dream business was indeed a dream." Life Savers were a "flop." Noble, concluding the fault lay in the cardboard package, designed a new package, a light foil wrap which not only kept the mints fresh but was easy to open and yet kept the contents from spilling even after it had been opened. With the new package Allen started to look for outlets not supplied with the Crane product. He found that one outlet was the saloon. Life Savers thus became a competitor of the standard dish of cloves at the end of the bar. At the same time Noble designed a light cardboard shipping container so made that it could be set up as a miniature display case on the counter near the cash register, the first of the kind now seen in so many stores. Noble feels that the display container was a big contributor to the success of Life Savers. "Calling for no effort from the retailer, it simply sat on the counter and caught the nickels which cashiers were instructed to include in a customer's change when possible."

But sales were slow and cash ran low. It was necessary to keep the staff late on Saturday afternoons so that Noble might have time to cash his advertising job's pay check to pay them. It was only after hard months that repeat sales began to show volume. Sales of 940,000 tubes in 1914 increased to 6,725,000 in 1915. When the First World War interrupted Noble's business career (from 1917 to 1919 he served as a major in the Ordnance Department of the United States Army) Life Savers carried on during his absence, and in 1918 showed a net profit of $280,000. In 1920 a modern factory was erected in Port Chester, New York. A subsidiary company started in Australia with an investment of $30,000 was sold within a year for a $500,000 cash profit. By 1920 Life Savers had made a million dollars in profits.

When twenty per cent of the stock in Life Savers, Inc., was sold to the public in 1925 through the Wall Street firm of Hornblower & Weeks, J. Roy Allen retired from the company with a "cool profit of $3,300,000," and the twelve-year-old company now had a value of $11,550,000. According to *Fortune* Magazine, in the years from 1925 to 1938 Life Savers, Inc., continued to average a yearly net profit of $1,000.000 on a gross of only $4,000,000; and at the end of 1938 the estimated value of the business was $22,000,000.

In the years between 1925 and 1938 Noble kept himself looking "younger than his years" by turning his duties over to an executive who managed the details of Life Savers, which Noble described as "a happy, whimsical little business." His time was divided between

EDWARD J. NOBLE

Florida, where he fished from his eighty-foot *Monatoana*, and the Thousand Islands, where he owns the Thousand Islands Country Club. Near-by, Noble has a summer home on the Canadian mainland from which he flies his own plane (he has been a flier and an investor in aviation companies since 1928) on trips to New York and Port Chester.

When the President set up the Civil Aeronautics Authority to develop an "air transportation system properly adapted to the . . . need of . . . commerce," to control it much as the Interstate Commerce Commission controls land transportation, and to function entirely free from all government branches except the White House, commercial aviation was pleased. It was "even more pleased," said *Fortune* Magazine, "on appointment of its chairman, Edward J. Noble. The reason: aviation wanted no hangar theorist, no political kibitzer." While still serving as chairman of the Authority (August 1938 to May 1939), Noble was chosen by Secretary of Commerce Harry L. Hopkins '41 to be his No. 1 assistant; and when the office of Under-Secretary of Commerce was created (June 1939) Noble was appointed to the position. Though reported to have been on warm social terms with the President, when Noble resigned (August 1940) as Under-Secretary of Commerce he informed his White House friends that he was still a Republican—that he was, in fact, resigning to take an active part in the Willkie '40 Presidential campaign. In January 1941 Noble bought New York's WMCA radio station from Donald Flamm for the sum of $850,000.

Later Flamm brought suit in the New York courts to invalidate the sale, charging it had been made under pressure from the Federal Communications Commission and "greased from the White House down." His complaint prompted the President to order a special investigation. In February 1944 the special House committee investigating the FCC listened to Flamm, who testified that he had previously turned down offers of more than a million dollars but had been intimidated into selling WMCA for a mere $850,000 to Noble. At the end of the probe of FCC (December 16, 1944) "a hint from one member of the committee" indicated that the sale of the station would not be a subject of condemnation unless Representative Richard Wigglesworth, Republican committee member, who had made charges of "obstruction, intimidation, and sabotage" against the investigation by the Administration, turned in a one-man report. In his testimony before the committee Noble denied using coercion on Flamm. He said that "it was true he had bought the station for $850,000 and sold it for $1,125,000, but that he had substantially increased WMCA's earnings in the meantime." The report of the House committee is expected early in January 1945.

Noble's purchase of the Blue Network (July 30, 1943) created much discussion in radio circles because of the network's history. The National Broadcasting Company, a Radio Corporation of America subsidiary, owned the Blue and Red Networks (so-called because of colored pencils used by telephone company engineers in mapping the station hookups of the system) until the Federal Communications Commission issued its anti-monopoly regulations and ordered the NBC to dispose of one of the networks (May 1941). The Commission later amended the regulations so that disposition of the network could be indefinitely postponed to avoid a forced sale. However, NBC proceeded to separate the two chains immediately; network affiliates, wholly owned stations, and programs were shifted; and two separate staffs were set up (January 1942). After a year of independent operation, the Blue, for the first time in the sixteen years of its existence, began to show a profit. While under NBC management it had been "truly a stepchild," receiving none of the advertising plums and having to carry a load of highbrow and high-cost sustainers to uphold NBC's record of public service.

Noble bought the Blue Network from the Radio Corporation of America for $8,000,000, outbidding two other interested purchasers and a score of "window shoppers." The investment banking house of Dillon, Read & Company, representing Paramount Pictures Corporation, went as high as $7,000,000 but balked at $8,000,000 (with a virtually full cash payment) because Paramount felt it would cost an additional $7,000,000 to streamline the network for future needs. The second bidder was a "reported representative of Marshall Field '41."

Part of the excitement caused by Noble's purchase of the Blue Network was due to the fact that "for the first time in the meteoric rise of the industry a value had been set on radio broadcasting." *Business Week* pointed out that "virtually the only other standard of value for sale of a top-ranking station was established seven years ago when the Columbia Broadcasting Company bought KNX, Hollywood, for a price of $1,250,000." The three stations which the Blue owns and operates (WJZ, New York City, a full-time 50,000 watt station; San Francisco's KGO, a 7,500 watt station; and Chicago's WENR, which operates half-time, sharing its wave length with WLS, an independent station but affiliated with the

Blue) constitute the principal asset which Noble acquired, for the network represents only a collection of valuable, but nonetheless alterable, contracts with 195 stations.

On December 28, 1943 it was reported that Noble has sold more than a quarter of the Blue's common stock. The principal purchasers were Time, Inc., and Chester La Roche, each buying 12½ per cent at a price reported to be $1,000,000. Other purchasers for an unknown amount were Mark Woods, president of the Blue, and Edgar Kobak, vice-president of the network at the time, but who has since resigned. In September 1944 La Roche, onetime board chairman of Young and Rubicam [43], was appointed vice-chairman of the Blue, directly under Noble. After its purchase Time, Inc., announced that it would exercise no authority over the Blue's programs, but that it would supplement its news service with reports and cables from its own correspondents. Noble announced at the time that he intended retaining his present holdings for an indefinite period.

And there was little doubt that Noble had purchased "a humming business." The Blue's gross time sales in 1942 totaled $16,-152,088—a twenty-nine per cent increase over 1941. "Its net profits for the first six months of 1943 were somewhat over $1,000,000, while the whole year showed an increase of 60 per cent in gross sales over 1942. In December 1944 the Blue stated that its listening audience had increased to 23,558,000, a gain of 843,000; sponsored hours had increased from 2,887 to 5,178. Hooper reports for the last ten months of 1944 disclosed that the Blue was the only one of the three major networks whose daytime ratings were going up. The evening programs, while improving, were not so popular as those of the other networks—for example, an evening half-hour on the Blue cost almost four thousand dollars less than the same time on CBS. FCC has granted Noble the authority to change the name of the Blue to the American Broadcasting Company, Inc., which lends itself nicely to the signature ABC—an obvious advantage in any alphabetical listing of networks. Since a goodly sum has been spent on promoting the Blue name, the change will not be a sudden one, however. Eventually Noble must find new headquarters (the Blue is now with NBC in Radio City) and buy necessary and expensive equipment. Furthermore, the Blue has lost the right to participate in RCA-NBC experimental work in television and frequency modulation and will have to begin its own development program.

Time Magazine reports Noble considers "radio broadcasting a public service enterprise. I'd be perfectly happy with meager profits." He would like to make the Blue a "sort of New York *Times* of the industry." When the approval of Noble as the owner of a national network came up before the Federal Communications Commission, its chairman, James L. Fly [40], asked for a written statement from Noble on his policy in giving out time on his stations. Fly took the occasion also to issue a rebuke to the National Association of Broadcasters for the practice of donating but not selling broadcast time to labor organizations and cooperative groups, calling the practice "a backdoor handout." The *Christian Science Monitor* in commenting on Fly's statement said: "Were all the applicants for time on the air put on a strictly commercial basis, organizations with overflowing treasuries might succeed in shutting out altogether worthy causes and sections of opinion which have no huge publicity funds at their disposal." The approval of Noble as owner of the Blue was given by the FCC on October 12, 1943.

"Ed," as Noble is popularly called, is remarkably young-looking for his sixty-odd years. He is tall, athletic, and soft-spoken—a voluble and genial talker who displays fine teeth when he laughs, which is often and heartily. He has been described as "rich, happy, and dollar-wise." His eyes are widely set and framed with heavy eyebrows. He was married to Ethel Louise Tinkham on November 6, 1920. The Nobles have one daughter, June. (Their other daughter, Sally, died early in 1944.)

Other business interests of Edward Noble's are, among others, the Heart Island Operating Company, Heart Island Transportation Corporation. He is also chairman of the board of directors of Life Savers, Inc., a director of the Commercial National Bank and Trust Company, a member of the Industrial Advisory Commission of the Federal Reserve Bank, and a trustee and the founder of the Edward John Noble Foundation, a charitable organization. He is a member of Beta Theta Pi and is president of the board of trustees of St. Lawrence University. His clubs include Round Hill, Field, Beach, and Greenwich Riding in Connecticut; the Chevy Chase in Maryland; the Cloud and Yale in New York; and the Thousand Islands Club in Alexandria Bay, New York.

References

Business Week p78 Ag 7 '43
Fortune 17:87+ F '38; 18:132 S '38 por
Time 32:35 Jl 18 '38; 62:62 Ag 9 '43
Who's Who in America 1944-45

NOCK, ALBERT JAY   Author

Address: c/o Harper & Brothers, 49 E. 33rd St., New York City

Essayist Albert Jay Nock has spent so many decades successfully avoiding personal publicity that no one seems to know in exactly which of those decades he was born, but some few *Who's Who*-ish details could not avoid creeping into his *Memoirs of a Superfluous Man* (1943). One learns, for example, that he was not born in Paris in 1810—or presumably he was not, for that was when he would have chosen to be born. One learns, too, that his earliest years were spent in Brooklyn, City of Churches. But from then on names and dates are almost entirely missing—for this is "the autobiography of a mind in relation to the society in which it found itself."

Apparently it found itself very early. Nock doesn't remember how he learned his letters, but he does remember teaching himself to piece them together into words, and certainly

NOCK, ALBERT JAY—*Continued*

he knew how to read by the time he was three. It was soon afterward that Webster's dictionary became his bosom friend. His intellectual life was entirely self-directed up to the age of eight, when he began to study Latin and Greek with some slight assistance from his father; but he was by no means a bookish introvert. "I was a child of the great outdoors, active, strong, never ill." He had just turned ten when his father accepted a professional opportunity in a town on the upper shores of Lake Huron, which was forty-five miles from any railway and completely isolated during the bitter winters. The boy found its social and cultural climate no less congenial than Brooklyn's: it was a community that "might have served pretty well as a standing advertisement for Mr. Jefferson's notion that the virtues which he regarded as distinctively American thrive best in the absence of government." He went on with his studies in the same happy-go-lucky fashion as before until, just turning fourteen, he was sent off to a boarding school on the banks of the Illinois River—a school with poor, primitive material equipment, but with an unusual atmosphere of freedom and with masters of unusual calibre.

According to *Twentieth Century Authors*, Nock received his B.A. and Litt.D. from St. Stephen's College, New York, now a component part of Columbia University. Aside from certain Jesuit institutions, it was possibly the last in America to stick by "the grand old fortifying classical curriculum." Of students there were less than a hundred; and they were all made to understand that the burden of education was on them and no one else, least of all their instructors. Nock came out knowing nothing of the natural sciences this side of Aristotle, Theophrastus, and Pliny; nothing of any history since 1500 A. D.; and since his ignorance of other subjects was quite as complete, he had "no accumulated lumber of prepossession or formula to be cleared away."

Since that time he has watched the progress of the "educational revolution" in America with superior amusement. Today, he says, training is called education, on the theory that very few are really educable, but that practically anyone can be trained. To Nock universal education is no more desirable than universal literacy, which to his mind has merely resulted in bad literature driving out the good. In our "neolithic society" an educable person is a "superfluous man," in any case.

After leaving college Nock did graduate work for most of three years in different institutions, finally qualifying for an advanced degree more by accident than intention. Uninterested in devoting his life to making money, in his early thirties he perceived, he says, "that I could get on better outside my native land than in it, so I decided to put in as much as possible of my lifetime in some other part of the world." "Living in Brussels in the years before 1914 was to me curiously like living with one's best girl in the days of chivalry and romance."

Then came the First World War. The Spanish War, "our first full-blown adventure in overseas imperialism," had impressed him as a dastardly affair; his version of it is that "British imperialism did not want either French imperialism or the newer imperialism of Germany to get into a stronger position in the southwestern Pacific by taking the Philippines . . . so the architects of our foreign policy obligingly put themselves at England's convenience . . . and . . . committed the United States to follow the fortunes of British imperialism in perpetuity." Nock's first book, *How Diplomats Make War*, was written with Francis Neilson and published in 1916; in 1922 his *Myth of a Guilty Nation* appeared. The second book was a compilation and transcription of documentary material showing that the German Government's guilt in bringing about the War was very small—that England, Russia, and France had a far larger role. Nearly a quarter of the volume, according to Sidney B. Fay, was filled with material carefully handpicked by Junker propagandists from the mass of diplomatic papers in the Brussels archives.

In the decade following the War, Nock lived in New York for four years, engaged in getting out the *Freeman*, a publication modeled after the old *London Spectator*. What success it had surprised him considerably, for it was "quite generally acknowledged to be the best paper published in our language." It was, Nock says, a radical publication in the true sense of the word—that is, its writers stuck straight through to the root of whatever subject they discussed. An avowed Jeffersonian, Nock still cleaved optimistically to the theory of the infinite improvability of man. He was unalterably opposed to giving the State any more power than it already had, however, and so was as opposed as any man who refused to take part in the cynical business of politics could be to most of the projects for social and political reform espoused by liberals (the income tax, for example). The State seemed to him an anti-social institution, used by one group of "mass-men" or another to legalize their appropriation of the product of others' work without compensation. The effect of all revolutions was merely "to reapportion the use of the political means" for this form of exploitation. In 1923 this disciple of Henry George was nevertheless still dimly hopeful that a transition from "political" to "administrative" government would eventually come about; he even thought he saw the beginnings of such a transition in Russia.

In 1926 Nock's study of Thomas Jefferson, *Jefferson*, was published. Although criticized for certain inaccuracies, the book was described by reviewers as sparkling, charming, witty, and all the other adjectives inevitably called forth by Nock's inimitable prose style; and Claude G. Bowers[41] wrote: "Mr. Nock set out to give us a study of Jefferson that would illuminate both his personality and philosophy, and he has achieved a distinctive success." Collections of Nock's essays, already published in such magazines as *Harper's*, the *Atlantic Monthly*, and H. L. Mencken's *American Mercury*, followed: *On Doing the Right Thing and Other Essays* (1928) and *Book of Journeyman* (1930).

Dealing with everything from free speech (Nock is not for "liberty" but for "license," like the Russians in Lincoln Steffens' story) to the control of wealth by women, from the horrors of so-called American civilization to the benefits of hearing bad music, they both charmed and exasperated critics.

In 1929 appeared *Francis Rabelais*, written with Catherine Rose Wilson; critical comment ranged from the *New Republic*'s "authoritative and convincing" to the *Nation*'s opinion that the authors' scholarship was not always of the best and that they had approached their subject in a spirit that was "at best sublimated prudery." (Nock, who says he owes much to Rabelais, brought much more interest to helping edit the Urquhart-Motteux translation of Rabelais' works than to any of his own books, however.) Toward the end of the 1920's Nock had come to the United States for two winters to give two university courses, and the result was another book, the iconoclastic *Theory of Education in the United States* (1932). This little volume was followed by *Journal of Thèse Days: June 1932-December 1933* (1934), ranging from "characteristic condemnation of American civilization to curiosity over the absence of mosquitoes in Seville."

For some time during the 1930's, under the editorship of Paul Palmer, Nock conducted an intensely anti-New Deal column in the *American Mercury* called "The State of the Nation." Long before this he had discarded his optimistic view of human improvability entirely, inspired by the late Ralph Adams Cram's [42] essay on "Why We Do Not Behave Like Human Beings." (According to Cram, in the evolutionary process only occasional individuals have reached the level of *homo sapiens*, of the psychically-human being—all the rest are sub-human.) In his *Memoirs* Nock writes: "I could see how democracy might do very well in a society of saints and sages led by an Alfred or an Antonious Pius. Short of that, I was unable to see how it could come to anything but an ochlocracy of mass men led by a sagacious knave." Today the one-time "radical" is called a "reactionary." And yet it is true that few of his ideas have changed. Even in the 1920's—in the day of Harding, Coolidge, Hoover [43]—he saw in the United States a growth of what he calls "Statism," a "floundering progress toward collectivism." As early as 1927 he wrote, "Mr. Jefferson said that if a centralization of power were ever effected at Washington, the United States would have the most corrupt government on earth." In *Our Enemy the State* (1935) his views on the anti-social nature of the State (combining those of "Confucius, Karl Marx, and the National Association of Manufacturers," according to George Soule) are expressed in much the same terms as in the pages of the old *Freeman*; only the dim hopefulness about the future is gone. If "Communism, the New Deal, Fascism, Nazism, are merely so many trade-names for collectivist Statism," why, he might ask, should one think more of Roosevelt [42] than of Hitler [42]?

Of the Second World War, Nock says: "This War, like the last, has held no interest for me. I have had no curiosity about its progress, have read nothing of it, and all I have heard has been casual." He makes his views on it clear, however. "At any time after 1936 it was evident that a European war would not be unwelcome to the Administration at Washington; largely as a means of diverting public attention from its flock of uncouth economic chickens on their way home to roost, but chiefly as a means of strengthening its malign grasp upon the country's political and economic machinery. . . . The principality of Monaco, the Grand Duchy of Luxemburg, would have taken up arms against the United States on receipt of such a note as the State Department sent the Japanese Government on the eve of Pearl Harbor." Before the United States entered the War, Nock says he did not go in with any of the non-interventionist movements, "partly because I knew their efforts were futile, but mainly because I was not sure they were well-advised." In 1941 he did contribute several articles to the isolationist *Scribner's Commentator*, however. That same year two articles by him on "The Jewish Problem in America" were published in the *Atlantic Monthly*. His observation of anti-Semitism was that "the sudden flaring-up of anti-Jewish sentiment in this country . . . was coincident with the deepest depression in 1929, and it was clamped down only by the sheer accident of encountering a great wave of sympathy for the mistreated Jews of Europe."

Memoirs of a Superfluous Man was Nock's first book since 1939, when *Henry George; an Essay* appeared. His last collection of essays had been *Free Speech and Plain Language* (1937). Of the *Memoirs* Clifton Fadiman [41] wrote: "I have not since the days of the early Mencken read a more eloquently written blast against democracy or enjoyed more fully a display of crusted prejudice. Mr. Nock is a highly civilized man who does not like our civilization and will have no part of it. He is a rare bird, one of an almost extinct species, and, as he very properly puts it, a superfluous man. We are not apt to see his like again." "The *Memoirs* strikes me as one of the vainest, most cocksure, most self-satisfied books in years," wrote Orville Prescott of the New York *Times*. The New York *Herald Tribune*'s Isabel Paterson was more admiring. "An adequate review would require twice the space of the book itself. . . . Whether for instruction or for entertainment, this is a unique book, of instant timeliness and permanent value." Another opinion comes from H. I. Brock, who wrote in the *Times*: ". . . this book is packed with things that make it worth reading. The reward will be both entertainment and profit, coupled with admiration (sometimes reluctant) for a master craftsman and plenty of wholesome exasperation with a vagarious author."

By Nock's own description he has "blue eyes, blond complexion running to the rubicund, what one of my sinful friends calls the veritable boozehister's complexion, fit to ornament a retired admiral of the Royal Navy. A thin skin, scanty blond hair, small pudgy hands and feet, a villainous tendency

NOCK, ALBERT JAY—*Continued*

to gout, rheumatism, arthritis; these, I believe, make up the lot." Among his enthusiasms (nearly as numerous as his prejudices) are beer, wine, Chinese food, Portugal and its Government, Artemus Ward, Montague Glass, Finley Peter Dunne, and Angela Thirkell. Nock believes that the one invincible and implacable enemy of art is the writer's self-consciousness, his pre-occupation with the subjective. Among the few specific modern literary works of which he approves are *Les Thibaults* by Roger Martin du Gard, *Father Malachy's Miracle* by Bruce Marshall, *The Beloved Vagabond* by William J. Locke, and *H. M. Pulham, Esquire* by J. P. Marquand.'⁴².

References

Haycraft, H. and Kunitz, S. J. Twentieth Century Authors 1942
Nock, A. J. Memoirs of a Superfluous Man 1943

NORRIS, GEORGE W(ILLIAM) July 11, 1861—Sept. 3, 1944 Former Senator from Nebraska; one of the nation's foremost liberals and a veteran of forty years in Congress, from 1913 to 1943; father of the TVA and author of the Twentieth Amendment to the Constitution; champion of rights for the underprivileged and a tireless advocate of governmental reform; honorary chairman of the National Citizens Political Action Committee at time of death.

Obituary

N Y Times p1+ S 3 '44 por

NORTON, MARY T(ERESA HOPKINS) Mar. 7, 1875- United States Representative from New Jersey

Address: b. House of Representatives Office Bldg., Washington, D. C.; h. 2600 Boulevard, Jersey City, N. J.; The Kennedy-Warren, Washington, D. C.

The dean of women Representatives in the United States Congress and breaker of precedent is Mary T. Norton, chairman of the House of Representatives Labor Committee, who has represented Jersey City continuously since the ratification of the woman suffrage amendment in 1920. A follower of the tough political boss, Frank Hague, she has also been able to give consistent support in Congress to liberal and pro-labor measures. Although an able and successful politician, she still believes that woman's place is in the home.

Representative Norton was originally Mary Teresa Hopkins, one of the five children of Thomas Hopkins, a well-to-do road builder, and Marie (Shea) Hopkins. Born in Jersey City on March 7, 1875, she attended the public schools there, and had just finished high school when her mother died. Young Mary Hopkins spent the next five years managing the household. Then she took a secretarial course at the Packard Business College in New York, and worked as a stenographer and secretary until her marriage, in April 1909, when she was thirty-four, to Robert Francis Norton. After the death of her only child, Robert Francis, Jr., Mrs. Norton turned her energies

to welfare work for others' children. The newly formed Queen's Daughters Day Nursery, organized by a Catholic welfare group, elected her secretary in 1913, and in 1916 she became president of the Day Nurseries Association of Jersey City, which cared for the children of working women.

In addition to this, Mrs. Norton was engaged in other charitable activities of the Queen's Daughters; when municipal aid was needed, it was she who went to City Hall to arrange it. Often she solicited funds from Mayor Frank Hague, called "the nation's most powerful and disreputable political boss." On one such occasion, in June 1920, when only one more state's vote was needed to ratify the Nineteenth Amendment, Hague asked Mrs. Norton to become the representative of Hudson County (Jersey City and Bayonne) women on the State Democratic Committee; and on August 30, two days after Tennessee had cast the ratifying vote for woman suffrage, he told her, "It is your duty to organize the women of Jersey City." In spite of her unfamiliarity with politics, Mrs. Norton did so well that she was elected vice-chairman of the state committee in 1921, a post she held for twelve years. In 1923 she became the first woman member of the Board of Chosen Freeholders of Hudson County, the elective county legislature. A hard party worker, Mrs. Norton gained more political experience as a delegate-at-large to the 1924 Democratic National Convention; President Wilson's secretary said of her, "Mary Norton has more common sense than most men I know."

With the Hague machine behind her, the new Congresswoman was sent to the Sixty-ninth Congress (1925) to represent the 12th New Jersey District as the first Democratic woman to be elected to Congress and the first woman Representative of any Eastern state. As such, Representative Norton had to cope with the conservative attitude of male Congressmen who were often gallant to "the gentlewoman from New Jersey" but were seldom fair. (Women, like independents were seldom placed on the most important committees.) Once, when a fellow Congressman agreed to "yield to the *lady*," she retorted, "I'm no lady, I'm a member of Congress, and I'll proceed on that basis." As a freshman Representative, Mrs. Norton was placed on the Veterans Committee (later on the District of Columbia, Memorials, and Labor Committees). She introduced one unsuccessful amendment to increase the personal income tax exemption, and was the first person to introduce a bill for the repeal of the Eighteenth Amendment to the Constitution, which was finally repealed by the Twenty-first Amendment.

At the end of her two-year term Mrs. Norton was re-elected to Congress. Her "amendment teas" during the primary campaign were widely publicized, and she remained a vigorous worker to organize women politically; and she continued to be a staunch defender of Hague, Jimmy Walker, the late Al Smith '⁴⁴, and the Democrats in general. In 1928 she was a delegate to the national convention which nominated Smith, one of her particular heroes, for the Presidency. The following year she opposed the Hawley-Smoot tariff, urging women to unite to defeat a bill which she felt would "increase the cost of everything they wear. . . . Lipsticks, perfumes, and the like once were luxuries," she pointed out. "Today they are necessities." The following year St. Elizabeth's, the oldest women's college in New Jersey, conferred upon Mrs. Norton its first honorary degree of Doctor of Laws in recognition of her "constructive humanitarian work in welfare and politics." (In 1937 she was similarly honored by Rider College.) At the 1932 Democratic Convention Mrs. Norton worked for the renomination of Smith, but loyally supported the chosen candidate, Franklin Delano Roosevelt '42.

When the Gillett bill (to remove birth control information from the purview of the obscenity laws under certain circumstances) was considered by a Congressional committee, Mrs. Norton was one of the prominent Catholics who opposed the measure. Testifying against it, she stated that "the fine womanhood of America . . . consider . . . the pressure of a baby face against their own the highest form of earthly happiness. . . . Does anyone believe that any kind of information would help the feeble-minded? . . . Nothing abnormal and contrary to the laws of nature will tend to safeguard the health of any woman."

In 1932, during Representative Norton's fourth term of office, she was the ranking member in point of seniority on the Seventy-second Congress' Committee on the District of Columbia, and was therefore appointed its chairman. The first woman ever to head a Congressional committee, Mrs. Norton was the "Mayor of Washington," whose group of twenty-one Congressmen shared with fifteen Senators the difficult and thankless task of legislating for the 900,000 voteless Washingtonians "in all cases whatsoever." One of Chairman Norton's first acts was to conclude a street railways merger on which negotiations had been pending for thirty-two years. Often some 250 bills a week passed through her hands, dealing with every item of administration from street names to street cleaning—budgets, schools, hospitals, police and fire departments, maintenance, waterworks. Because of the pressure of her work, Mrs. Norton resigned in 1935 from the chairmanship of the New Jersey Democratic Committee (it carries responsibility for the state's entire Federal patronage) to which she had been elected in 1932 as the first woman state chairman of either party, and resumed the vice-chairmanship. During her terms as "Mayor" in the Seventy-second and Seventy-third Congresses the Representative "wrung" $1,500,000 from the PWA for a hospital for the Capital's tubercular patients, cleared some of Washington's disgraceful slums, and legalized boxing and liquor selling.

The death of Representative William P. Connery in 1937 left the House Labor Committee chairmanship vacant. Mrs. Norton resigned her District of Columbia chairmanship to succeed him, explaining, "I represent a labor district in New Jersey [since 1933 the 13th] and I feel the people of that district have more claim on me than do the people of the District [of Columbia]." In this capacity "Aunt Mary" (a term Washington correspondents picked up from Marion McDonagh, Mrs. Norton's niece, committee clerk, and secretary-

MARY T. NORTON

companion since Mr. Norton's death in 1935) had to steer President Roosevelt's '42 pending Wages and Hours Bill through the House against vigorous opposition from conservatives, Republicans, Southerners, and the "sweatshop lobby." Passing this bill she considers the Congress' greatest forward step. In May 1940 Mrs. Norton and Majority Leader John W. McCormack '43 successfully defended the act from a series of proposed revisions by tacking their own amendments onto each amendment offered until the final revision was unacceptable to the House as a whole. "Twelve miserable dollars and sixty cents [the minimum set by the act for a forty-two-hour week] is a pittance for any family to live on," she cried. "That is really our fight—whether Congress wants to go on record as believing that less than $12.60 is sufficient for the ordinary American worker. I do not believe so. I think that when members get their monthly checks for $833 they cannot look at that check and face their conscience if they refuse to vote for American workers who are getting only $12.60 a week."

It was Mrs. Norton's task to defend the progressive New Deal labor legislation from the attacks of the Republican-Southern Democratic coalition which sought to undo it. In March 1941 she stated, "I am unalterably opposed to [anti] strike legislation but I have sense enough to know that, unless labor unions get together and declare a truce for the duration of the War in jurisdictional disputes, and employers and employees compromise their differences, it will be impossible for all the true friends of labor—and there are many of us— to prevent this legislation or even to preserve the legislation we have worked so hard to enact." That November Mrs. Norton introduced a bill calling for Congressional reconstitution of the President's National Defense Mediation Board, composed of representatives of labor, industry, and the public, with the power to order sixty-day "cooling-off" periods.

(Continued next page)

NORTON, MARY T.—*Continued*

If agreement could not be reached by the Board in a given dispute, the issue was to be settled, by a novel provision, on the vote of the members representing the public. The plant seizure provision of the Smith '41-Connally '41 bill was included as a penalty for using "other methods" than recourse to the Board for settling disputes, while failure to obey the Board's "cease and desist" order would empower the Attorney General to get an injunction. This would set aside the Norris-La Guardia '40 Anti-Injunction Act. The Labor Committee bill was one of several passed over in favor of the Smith-Connally Anti-Strike Act.

Liberals who find Representative Norton's attitude a contrast to that of labor-baiting Boss Hague are forced to believe that, as she says, he has never once attempted to dictate her vote. This, it has been remarked, "was very clever on his part, as the immaculate Mrs. Norton is as ardent a 'regular' as the ward politicians that Jersey City used to send [to Congress], and much more conscientious and personable." Moreover, she has gone on record as thinking Hague a great and noble leader, and asserted in September 1943, "He has never asked any of us to do anything our conscience would not approve our doing." In 1944 Mrs. Norton continued to vote along the regular Democratic lines, that is, with the Administration, although she was against expenditures for rural electrification and did not vote on extension of the Reciprocal Trade Treaties Act.

Writing in *Collier's*, Amy Porter describes the Labor Committee as "ineffectual," and states that Mrs. Norton actually "has as little to say on labor as Mme. Perkins '40," the Cabinet officer whose functions as Secretary of Labor have increasingly been taken over by other agencies, such as the War Labor Board and War Manpower Commission. While this description may be exaggerated, there is no doubt that certain other committees, particularly those on Naval Affairs and Military Affairs, have been passing on bills dealing with labor problems. On March 17, 1943, when the former approved the Johnson bill which dealt exclusively and drastically with labor, Mrs. Norton sent a letter of protest to Representative Carl Vinson '42, Naval Affairs chairman. "Mr. Vinson's committee is infringing on labor legislation," she told reporters. "There is no doubt of it and, I believe, no excuse for it." That June, when asked her views on women's place in post-War affairs, Mrs. Norton pointed out that much important legislation had been "stolen" from the Labor Committee, and stated her belief that this was done because the committee is headed by a woman.

"Those who really know our social system," she declared, "know that women have never had very much opportunity. . . . Women are going to be pushed in a corner, and very soon at that." After the War, when, she feels, they will be forced to vacate jobs they have been handling capably, she believes women's position will be "heartbreaking." (In June 1944 the New Jersey Congresswoman offered a bill providing that wage determination under the War Labor Disputes Act, the Fair Labor Standards Act, and other statutes "shall apply to workers without regard to sex.") On other occasions Mrs. Norton has said that the reason women are not given offices commensurate with their abilities is that they fail to apply pressure as a group. "We won't see a dozen women in Congress in our day," Mrs. Norton predicts, "because women won't vote for women." She stands with other women Congressmen, however, in stressing that each represents her own district, and more would be lost than gained by the formation of a "woman's bloc" like that in the British Parliament.

At the Democratic National Convention in July 1940 Mrs. Norton helped set another precedent: the Resolutions and Platform Subcommittee was the first major convention committee on which women were equally represented with men. And at the 1944 convention, where this practice was followed on all the major committees, Mrs. Norton was co-chairman with Majority Leader McCormack of Platform and Resolutions. Reporter Mary Braggiotti described her as "working tooth and nail in her usual forthright manner," while others mentioned the "lusty comebacks for which she is noted." The following month Mrs. Norton resigned from the New Jersey Democratic chairmanship, to which she had been re-elected in 1943, to devote herself to "the critical vital problems currently before Congress."

One of the most pressing of the problems before the Labor Committee was the establishment of a permanent Fair Employment Practice Committee. The FEPC, originally a volunteer President's committee, had been set up in May 1943 in pursuance of an Executive order of June 1941. The opposition it aroused was on much the same order as that aroused by the Wages and Hours Bill, except that fewer Republicans were opposed, and a few discriminatory labor unions were. Overcoming the parliamentary maneuvers of the "White Supremacy" group of Southern Democrats, the FEPC had been given legislative status on a wartime basis in June 1944; it forbade racial and religious discrimination in employment by any Federal agency, any war plant, any contractor working for the Government, and any labor union in such an industry. At their conventions, both Republican and Democratic Parties had listed a permanent FEPC in their platforms. The bill reported out by the Norton Committee was a composite of three submitted by Representatives Michael Scanlon, William L. Dawson, and Robert La Follette '44. It failed of passage by the outgoing "Lame-duck" Congress; but Mrs. Norton announced that she would resubmit it to the Seventy-ninth Congress in 1945. (Re-elected in November to her eleventh consecutive term, the Representative had been assured at the polls of the company in the House of three Democrats of her own sex, Helen Gahagan Douglas '44 of California, Emily Taft Douglas of Illinois, and Chase Going Woodhouse of Connecticut.)

Another bill which she introduced in December 1944, calling for pensions for Congressmen, required considerable moral courage on her part, for a similar bill had been greeted with national ridicule ("Bundles for Congress") not long before. As Mrs. Norton pointed out, however, the bill would simply extend the Federal employee's retirement system to cover elective and executive offices. She could have added that the lack of a pension is often mentioned by students of government as a weakness of the present system, and that it may often result in long-time Congressmen, such as the late Senator George Norris, dying in near-poverty after they have left Congress.

Dark-haired and dark-eyed, the matronly Representative from Hudson County is described as genial and unassuming. "Cool, witty, and competent," in debate or discussion, she "knows when to yield a point and when to fight back. And she knows how to fight back effectively when she judges it wise to take off the gloves." Since the marriages of her two nieces, who have successively served as her secretary-companions, Mrs. Norton lives alone with one servant. Long known as one who lives for her work, Mrs. Norton has been deprived by war conditions of her only recreations, motoring and theatre-going. A member of the New Jersey Housing League, the Friends of Lafayette, and Zonta, she has retained her interest in welfare work, and is a constant reader of newspapers, detective stories, and history, with emphasis on labor and church affairs. Mrs. Norton is said to have "no social life outside her home. She can't be dragged to the big formal affairs everyone is supposed to attend." Duff Gilfond wrote in the *American Mercury*, back in 1929, "To snooty Washington society she is a business school graduate, Tammany, and Catholic, and hence unacceptable. But then, so was Al Smith, and Mrs. Norton is proud to be in any category with him."

References

Am Mercury 18:159 O '29
Collier's 112:22 Ag '43 por
Ladies' H J 50:117 My '33
Lit Digest 119:24 Mr 30 '35 por
N Y Post Mag p5 N 28 '42 por
Newsweek 19:17-18 Je 26 '37 por
Scholastic 30:10 My 15 '37 por
Time 31:14-15 My 16 '38 por
U S News p37 My 10 '40 por

American Catholic Who's Who 1942-43
American Women 1939-40
Who's Who in America 1944-45
Who's Who in the Nation's Capital 1938-39

NUGENT, ELLIOTT (nū'jent) Sept. 20, 1900- Actor; director; playwright
Address: h. 3 E. 84th St., New York City

One of the most versatile figures in the modern theatre is Elliott Nugent. Not only does he hold a high average of excellence as an actor, playwright, director, and producer both in Hollywood and on Broadway, but he manages to keep active in all of these departments of the show business. The year 1943 saw him directing the stage hit *Tomorrow, the World* and the successful film *Up in Arms,* which introduced Danny Kaye to the cinema audiences, and winning top honors for his acting in Broadway's leading drama, *The Voice of the Turtle.* That also won for him the New York drama critics' vote for the best actor's performance of the 1943-1944 season.

Vandamm

ELLIOTT NUGENT

The holder of this all-star record came by his talents naturally. He is the son of John Charles Nugent, the playwright, director, and actor, and Grace Mary Fertig, the actress. At the time of his birth, September 20, 1900 in Dover, Ohio, his parents were headliners on the Keith-Orpheum vaudeville circuit. Young Elliott accompanied them on their tours, and at the age of four made his debut as a monologuist in the Los Angeles Orpheum Theatre when another act failed to show up at the last moment. A yellowed and tattered clipping of a notice from the Los Angeles *Times* of 1904 gives proof that Master Nugent possessed the same charm and presence which have been attributed to his work in *The Voice of the Turtle.* The 1904 reviewer described him as frank, unabashed, and poised, without conscious mannerisms. These qualities and his precocious talent won him five encores. In 1943 Lewis Nichols, the New York *Times* critic, said: "Mr. Nugent's system of acting is simply to be Elliott Nugent. He is calm, casual . . . he wanders around the stage as though it were his home and he is comfortable in it."

For several years following this auspicious beginning, Elliott was booked regularly on all the programs in which his parents appeared. When he reached his teens he left the stage to attend high school in Dover, Ohio, the native heath of the Nugents. Four years at Ohio State University followed. After school, in preparation for a career in the legitimate theatre, he joined the famous Stuart Walker stock company in Cincinnati, Ohio. And, according to Burns Mantle[44], it was by this stock group that Nugent had his first play produced. It was *Charlie,* a collaboration with Clifford Goldsmith, who was to become the author of the radio serial *The Aldrich Family.* The play failed, however, to find a Broadway producer.

Nugent's first New York role was that of Tom Sterrett, the juvenile in *Dulcy* (1921),

NUGENT, ELLIOTT—*Continued*

the play which established Lynn Fontanne [41] as a star. A more important member of the company in young Nugent's opinion, however, was the pretty blond ingenue, Norma Lee. The ingenue and juvenile fell in love, and when they were sure *Dulcy* was in for at least a six-month run, Nugent says, they decided that that was "enough security financially for anybody to be married on." Married one morning, they turned up for the evening performance; and for many years following Norma Nugent continued to appear with her husband on the stage and screen. Their three daughters were born during this period. Annabelle Lee, the eldest, was born in New York when Mrs. Nugent was playing with her husband in *The Poor Nut* (1925), Barbara Ruth was born in Chicago during the run of *Hoosiers Abroad* (1927), and Nancy Elliott was born in Hollywood in 1933. (Nugent's three daughters are "beginning young" in the theatre business: in December 1944 they were among the forty-one investors in the new Howard Lindsay [42]-Russel Crouse [41] production, *The Hasty Heart,* John Patrick's drama of convalescent G.I.'s in the Far East.)

The first successful play of Nugent's playwriting career was *Kempy* (1922), written in collaboration with his father. It not only won favor on Broadway but it also provided parts for the acting Nugents—father Nugent, known as "J. C.," sister Ruth Nugent, Elliott, and, in the latter part of its run, Elliott's wife and Ruth's husband, Alan Bunce. Elliott played the leading role of Kempy, a plumber's helper who was forced into a spite marriage with a lady novelist. *The Dumb-Bell* (1923), *The Rising Sun* (1924), *The Poor Nut* (1925), *Human Nature* (1925), *The Trouper* (1926), and other plays were jointly conceived, jointly directed, and usually jointly played, by father and son—but none attained the popularity of *Kempy.* During this period in Nugent's career he appeared also in plays in whose authorship he had no share. Included in these were *The Wild Westcotts* (1923) and *Hoosiers Abroad.*

Hollywood, ever on the alert for seasoned theatrical talent, signed Nugent in 1929 to a three-way contract, calling for his services as an actor, writer, and director. His first film appearance was made in *College Life* (the picturization of *Dulcy*). The adaptation of his play *Kempy* under the title *The Wise Girls* (1930) followed, with Nugent and his wife in their Broadway roles. In the ten years that followed, Nugent, with the exception of a week's run on Broadway, remained in Hollywood employed either as a director, writer, or actor—and in some instances in all three capacities at the same time—on twenty-odd motion pictures. He also managed to collaborate on three plays between films. *Fast Service* (1931), written and acted by Elliott and "J. C.," was presented on Broadway by Edgar Selwyn, after a tryout in San Francisco, with the Nugents in the cast. (The play closed after a week's run.) *The World's My Onion* (1935), also from Nugent *père* and *fils,* had a tryout at the Pasadena Playhouse but did not reach the East. *The Fight's On*

(1937), the result of Nugent's collaboration with Ernest V. Heyn, screen magazine editor, and Hagar Wilde, was produced in London.

Nugent's return to Broadway came about through his collaboration on the play *The Male Animal* (1940), with James Thurber [40], the famous humorist-cartoonist. Thurber and Nugent had been fellow graduates in the 1920 class of Ohio State University. It was during their joint editorship of the college paper, *The Lantern*, that they had first planned to collaborate on a play. "It took us twenty years to get around to it," Nugent says, "but once started we did the job in three months." After a Hollywood tryout, Herman Shumlin [41] presented *The Male Animal* on Broadway with Nugent playing the leading role. The play won immediate favor with New York audiences and critics, and later was sold for $150,000 to Warner Brothers, who filmed it in 1942 with Henry Fonda and Olivia de Havilland [44] in the leading roles. On Broadway it ran for 187 performances, and it was listed among Burns Mantle's ten best plays of the 1939-1940 season. The plot concerns the marital misunderstandings of a young professor who believes that his wife has fallen for the charms of a former sweetheart, an ex-football player and successful businessman. The professor's efforts to be reasonable about this situation, together with the complications arising from the fact that he had planned to read Vanzetti's last letter as part of his course in English literature, provide enough hilarious situations to make a gay play. Regarding Nugent's work as an actor, Rosamond Gilder said in the *Theatre Arts Monthly*: "Nugent's rueful countenance and neat understatement are the perfect embodiment of the character. Again and again he strikes the note so exactly that it reverberates in the listener's ear with implications wider than the immediate issue."

Nugent's success as an actor and author in *The Male Animal* began what has been described as "The Nugent Marathon." While the play was in preparation for its New York production Nugent returned to Hollywood to direct *The Cat and the Canary* (1939), after which he dashed to New York for further polishing of the Thurber collaboration. That completed, he returned to Hollywood again for the Bob Hope [41] picture *Nothing But the Truth* (released in 1941), finishing in time to come to New York for rehearsals of *The Male Animal.* At the end of that play's run Nugent went back to Hollywood for another directorial chore, after which he became a producer with Robert Montgomery and Jesse Duncan of a play called *All in Favor* (1942). "But they weren't," he recalls. (The play closed in its first week on Broadway.) *The Crystal Ball* (1943), his next Hollywood directorial assignment, also failed to win critical approval, despite a talented cast which included Paulette Goddard, Ray Milland, and Gladys George. Then Broadway recalled Nugent to play opposite Katharine Hepburn [42] in *Without Love* (1942). Although the play ran a season on Broadway, the press was divided in its opinion of the play's merit, and Nugent as an actor came in for his share of the adverse criticism. Brooks Atkinson [42] of the New York Times found that while Nugent's acting was done in an "agreeably humorous style it was not particularly well suited to the character."

During his appearance in *Without Love,* Nugent continued his "marathon" by directing *Tomorrow, the World.* In this play Nancy, his youngest daughter, made her bow on the stage—the third generation of the Nugent family to follow the profession of acting. Ten-year-old Nancy played opposite Skippy Homeier, who portrayed the Nazi boy villain of the play, until his two-coast father took his family to Hollywood in order to direct *Up in Arms.* This picture won critical praise with Nugent "coming in on the glory side" for pacing the comedy with "infectious zest" and making a "top film star of Danny Kaye in his first film role."

With this triumph in picture direction added to his record, Nugent consented to play opposite Margaret Sullavan[44] in John van Druten's[44] three-character play, *The Voice of the Turtle.* His "wonderfully natural" interpretation of the sergeant in this play won unanimous acclaim, placing him among the top stellar names of the theatre. But Nugent did not rest upon his laurels. In February 1944 he was commuting between New York and Philadelphia for the tryout of the Frank Craven-Billie Burke vehicle, *Mrs. January and Mr. Ex,* which he had undertaken to direct. It was generally conceded by Broadway reviewers, however, that not even "the expert direction of Nugent" could make credible the inconsistencies of the play's plot. In between directorial and acting jobs Nugent squeezed a number of radio appearances, the direction of a USO overseas presentation of *The Male Animal,* became a member of the newly formed play-producing firm of Nugent, (Robert) Montgomery & Duncan, and wrote a play, as yet untitled. The play is scheduled for production in 1945 by John Golden[44], in association with Nugent and Montgomery.

Concerning his active life (he has had only four days vacation in six years) Nugent says, "Work is a drug, and the human system acquires a greater tolerance for it as time goes on. By the time I'm eighty I expect I shall be acting, writing plays, producing, directing, lighting, and designing sets for them, all at the same time. I'm really just beginning to get versatile." Nugent has not overlooked the business end of the theatre, either. He was part owner of *Tomorrow, the World, The Voice of the Turtle* (both 1943-1944's biggest money-makers), and *Mrs. January and Mr. Ex.* In 1944 Nugent, Russel Crouse, Howard Stix Cullman, and Howard Lindsay bought New York's Hudson Theatre for $300,000.

Nugent is six feet, slender, gray-eyed, and blond. His personality in private life has "some of the flavor of small-town-America—the leaves raked after school, the granite-topped soda fountain, the 5:45 local." His collaborator, James Thurber, says: "He is the best-rounded guy I know. He only gets mad on second Sundays in October every fourth year." Although *The Voice of the Turtle* closed in June for two months so that its stars could have a vacation, its popularity has made Broadwayites predict a record run for it. During the summer of 1944 Nugent coached his

daughters in their stock company appearances on the straw hat circuits. When in New York the Nugents live in a penthouse apartment in the East Eighties. Their California home is in Bel Air.

References

N Y Herald Tribune VI p5 Ja 18 '42; IV p2 D 19 '43
N Y Sun p20 F 24 '44
N Y Times IX pl Ag 4 '40
N Y World-Telegram p14 Ap 30 '40 por
International Motion Picture Almanac 1943-44
Who's Who in America 1944-45
Who's Who in the Theatre 1939

O'CONNELL, WILLIAM (HENRY), CARDINAL Dec. 8, 1859—Apr. 22, 1944 Cardinal Archbishop of Boston; New England's first and only prince of the Church of Rome; named assistant at the Pontifical Throne in 1905 and later the same year, papal Envoy to Japan; succeeded to the See of Boston on death of Archbishop Williams in 1907; elevated to the cardinalate in 1911; recipient of many honorary awards; see sketch 1941 Yearbook.

Obituary

N Y Times p1+ Ap 23 '44 por

O'CONNOR, BASIL Jan. 8, 1892- National Chairman of the American Red Cross; lawyer; president of the National Foundation for Infantile Paralysis

Address: b. 120 Broadway, New York City; h. 1220 Park Ave., New York City

The new chairman of the central committee of the American Red Cross is Basil O'Connor, prominent New York lawyer who has been identified for many years with humanitarian and educational projects. When on July 13, 1944 President Roosevelt[42] announced the appointment of his friend and former law partner to serve the remainder of the unfinished term (to December 11, 1944) of the late Norman H. Davis[40], he said: "Mr. O'Connor is admirably qualified for this position because of his firsthand knowledge of almost every part of the United States and because of his association with the medical and nursing problems through the years he has served as president of the National Foundation for Infantile Paralysis. All this is in addition to his excellent executive ability." O'Connor's temporary status ended five months later, on December 13, when he was reappointed chairman of the American Red Cross and elected a member of its board of incorporators.

Basil O'Connor was born in Taunton, Massachusetts, January 8, 1892. His parents were Daniel Basil and Elizabeth Ann (O'Gorman) O'Connor. "My mother," O'Connor has said, "had a passion for education and she made it seem important to me." He therefore fulfilled his boyhood resolve to become a lawyer by going first to Dartmouth College, where he earned his expenses by playing the violin in the town's orchestra. After earning his B.A. degree from that college in 1912, he went to Harvard Law School, from which he obtained his LL.B. degree in 1915. St. John's University (Brook-

BASIL O'CONNOR

lyn, New York) and Blackburn College (Carlinville, Illinois) conferred the honorary degree of LL.D. upon him, both in 1941.

O'Connor was admitted to the Massachusetts bar in 1915, and to the New York bar the following year, when he became connected with the law firm of Cravath & Henderson in New York City. After a year he returned to his native state to join the firm of Streeter & Holmes in Boston. By 1919 he was back in New York, where he practiced alone for five years.

It was in 1925 that O'Connor became the partner of Franklin D. Roosevelt in the firm of Roosevelt & O'Connor, which was not dissolved until 1933, when the senior partner entered the White House. Then, after another year, O'Connor formed the firm of O'Connor & Farber. In the course of their years of association, O'Connor has addressed Roosevelt, successively, as "Franklin", "Governor," and "Mr. President," while the President still calls his friend "Doc," which is not derived from any medical interest of O'Connor's but from an early admiration for Dartmouth's coach, Dr. John F. O'Connor. The friendship of the former law partners continued: in 1941 Raymond Clapper [40] listed O'Connor as a member of "F.D.R.'s Unofficial Cabinet," which was described as "kindred spirits, articulate men with hairtrigger minds who spark the President's thinking." In two of Roosevelt's chief philanthropic interests O'Connor has served long and faithfully: as chairman of the executive committee, treasurer, and trustee of the Georgia Warm Springs Foundation, in which he has been active the past twenty years, and as president and trustee of the National Foundation for Infantile Paralysis since its formation in 1938. (He is also president and trustee of the Franklin Delano Roosevelt Library, Inc., which is housed in its own building on the President's Hyde Park estate.)

As was reported in detail in the bulletin issued by the National Foundation for Infantile Paralysis, O'Connor has frequently visited various parts of the United States to speak on the progress in the fight against poliomyelitis and on the problems still to be solved. One of the most important phases of the Foundation's work is its support of Elizabeth Kenny [42] and her method of treating infantile paralysis, more than $500,000 having been spent in four years in testing and evaluating the method and in training doctors, nurses, and therapists in its technique; the Foundation expended $107,000 for the study of the Kenny method of after-treatment at the University of Minnesota. O'Connor regarded a controversy with the Kenny Institute in Minneapolis in 1943 as not involving the Foundation, which is continuing to sponsor Miss Kenny herself. O'Connor's interest in infantile paralysis sprang from his old friendship with the President, an interest which, he says, has become the crusade of his life.

The day after O'Connor's appointment to the national chairmanship of the American Red Cross, under authority of legislation passed in 1905 giving the President that power, the New York *Herald Tribune* pointed out that the President's choice was hardly a disinterested one. While the editorial credited O'Connor with a deep concern for humanitarian achievement, it maintained he had but a "limited equipment for direction of activities reaching out to all corners of the globe," and questioned his qualifications to head the Red Cross "in wartime and what may be the still more difficult post-War period." Recalling that it had earlier urged a "fresh and vigorous new leadership" of the Red Cross, the newspaper held that O'Connor's record gave no evidence of his "wish or ability to combat the traditionalism which . . . tends to become the guiding force in an enterprise such as the Red Cross. For that battle a complete and rugged independence of every political influence is essential." The New York *Times* also commented that "an old friendship must have played some part in President Roosevelt's choice of his former law partner," but declared that the association was "mostly cemented by good works in a field which eminently qualifies O'Connor for his new position. The records of O'Connor's mature life reveal many interests, but he is chiefly known for his unselfish devotion to public causes . . . to which he has given generously his money, his time, and his enthusiasm."

At a press conference he held a few days after his appointment, O'Connor spoke of his admiration for the Red Cross and of the humility with which he approached his new responsibilities. "Despite the magnitude of its contacts and services," he stated, "the Red Cross is respected as a personal and spiritual element in our national life. In so far as I can help, it shall remain that way." He mentioned his special interest in the blood bank, touching upon his own recovery from an illness after receiving thirteen blood transfusions. He announced he would forego, as had his predecessor, the annual salary of $12,000 provided for the national chairman: "For twenty years I have gladly given over a third of my time to charitable work. . . . I have never expected or received any compensation for that work. It therefore goes, almost without saying, that I shall accept no salary as chairman of the American Red Cross." Except for his presidency of the National Foundation for Infantile Paralysis, O'Connor will give up all his other activities, including his legal practice in New York, in order to devote himself to his new task. He promptly began making plans for an overseas trip to visit Red Cross establishments. Never before connected with any phase of the Red Cross, he says his present role is that of a student "with plenty of homework to do."

In emphasizing that health and medical problems touched virtually every aspect of Red Cross activities, O'Connor appointed a special medical and health committee composed of eleven men, prominent in their respective fields, to survey current Red Cross medical and health operations and to recommend plans for the post-War period. In October he went abroad to study, at firsthand, conditions in the field. Returning twenty-eight days later after inspecting installations in the Paris area and having an interview with Pope Pius XII [41], he reported that "the great need can be summed up in one word: transportation. There is considerable malnutrition in all these countries, and it will be a bad winter. The chief need is for food and clothing. If we can obtain transportation, the most important need, I would say, would be clothing. If there is no transportation the need will then be for food and fuel." O'Connor also predicted that the end of the "shooting war" would mean greater burdens than ever for the Red Cross, involving new tasks and sharper morale problems to be faced by American Red Cross field workers. "It will be far more difficult to keep up good morale when the shooting stops," he asserted. "In the restlessness and anxiety to get home, the need for diversion and entertainment will increase."

In December 1944 O'Connor sent messages to all Red Cross chapter chairmen, requesting their assistance in enlisting military nurses. The Red Cross, recruiting agency for the Army and Navy Nurse Corps, appealed for ten thousand Army nurses urgently needed overseas. Stressing the urgency of the situation, O'Connor said that the nurses "must be drawn at the risk of inconveniencing civilians and curtailing all except the most essential nursing care."

In his capacity as president of the National Foundation for Infantile Paralysis, he has also been active in the affairs of that organization. In December 1944 he reported on the work of the Foundation during the infantile paralysis epidemic of the summer of 1944, the second largest epidemic in the history of the country. O'Connor announced that almost one million dollars was spent in providing care for stricken patients. Stating that the nation was better prepared for fighting the disease than ever before, he said that the organization's work in the future "would see a further expansion in the fields of physical therapy as a possible cure."

A partial list of the organizations to which the new head of the American Red Cross has given his time indicates the scope of his interests: He is a trustee, officer, or member of the American Museum of Health, Finlay Institute of the Americas (organized to foster research and scientific development in the Caribbean area), Human Engineering Laboratory, La Rabida Sanitarium, National Conference of Christians and Jews, Tuskegee Institute. In addition, he is active in five bar associations as well as in the Committee on Character and Fitness (of the Supreme Court, Appellate Division, 1st Judicial Department), the Joint Conference on Legal Education, and Friends of Harvard Law School Library. Two business enterprises engage some of his attention—he is director of the American Reserve Insurance Company and of the West Indies Sugar Corporation. A clubman, too, O'Connor belongs to a number, among them the Dartmouth, Harvard, University, Bankers', Catholic, Manhattan, and New York Yacht.

An eighteen-hour day of work leaves O'Connor little time for the recreations he used to enjoy—bicycling, softball, playing the violin. His reading includes a vast number of legal books and papers, biographies, and histories, with an occasional novel for diversion. A special hobby is collecting Dartmouth literary items and first editions. With Mrs. O'Connor (the former Elvira Miller, whom he married in 1918), he spends year-round week-ends at their country place at Westhampton Beach, Long Island. Their two children are Bettyann (Mrs. Sidney Culver) and Sheelagh.

O'Connor summed up his busy life in a recent interview: "Scarcely any man has had such an opportunity to live two lives at once. . . . I take no vacations and don't need any." And the realistic manner in which he is said to approach any problem is epitomized in the challenging words that hang on his office wall—WHAT ARE THE FACTS?

References

N Y Post Mag p33 Ag 2 '44 pors
N Y Times p1+ Jl 14 '44
Who's Who in America 1944-45

ODELL, GEORGE C(LINTON) D(ENSMORE) Mar. 19, 1866- Historian of the theatre; educator
Address: h. Hotel Seymour, 50 W. 45th St., New York City

The *Annals of the New York Stage* (1927-1942), described as the "greatest piece of individual scholarship that the United States has known," is the work of George C. D. Odell, Brander Matthews professor emeritus of dramatic literature in residence, Columbia University. The prodigious scope of the fourteen volume work, which embraces all professional performances of the New York entertainment world—operas, concerts, lectures, carnivals, circuses, and the theatre—from about 1732 to 1888 (with the end of the nineteenth century as the author's goal), has been unanimously acclaimed by reviewers. "Merely contemplating the labor that Odell has put into the *Annals*," said John Mason Brown [42], former drama critic, "is enough to break the spirit of lesser men." The fourteen volumes contain almost 9,000 pages—volume thirteen alone, though it covers only three years (1885-88), includes 27,552 references to plays and artists.

George Clinton Densmore Odell's devotion to the theatre began in his boyhood, although his early environment was in no way connected with the theatre. Born in Newburgh, New York, on March 19, 1866, he is the son of Benjamin Barker Odell, a businessman who served six terms as Mayor of Newburgh. His elder

ODELL, GEORGE C. D.—*Continued*

brother, Benjamin Barker Odell, Jr., merchant and president of the Newburgh Electric Light Company, after serving in several public offices was elected Governor of New York State in 1900, and re-elected in 1902. On both sides of his house he is of old American stock: his mother, the former Ophelia Bookstaver, is a descendant of an old New York family; the first member on the Odell side to come to America settled in the western part of Connecticut in 1637, having emigrated from Bedfordshire, England. At the age of ten Odell began spending his allowance on pictures of actresses. These early pictures were the beginning of what is now an important theatre collection. The many illustrations in the *Annals*, except where credit is expressly given, are from Odell's private collection. "In fact," says the historian, "one of the objects of the work is to justify—in my own eyes, at least— my lifelong habit of accumulating mementos of the stage."

After graduation from Siglar Preparatory School in 1885 young Odell chose Columbia for his university so that he might attend the theatre in New York. In looking back Odell says that he feels his undergraduate years, 1885 to 1889, were the golden years of great actors, "the years of supremacy of Augustin Daly's stock company." Daly's stock company at that time included the famous Mrs. G. H. Gilbert, John Drew, Ada Rehan, Otis Skinner, and Edith Kingdon, who was to become the first Mrs. George Gould. An unforgettable Daly production which Odell recalls was that of *The Taming of the Shrew*, with Ada Rehan as Katharine, John Drew as Petruchio, Otis Skinner as Lucentio, and Mrs. Gilbert as Curtis. "Of course," says Odell, "the acting was the chief allurement. Ada Rehan reached the peak of her fame in the role of Katharine. I believe I may say her stormy entrance as the shrew, with her flame-red hair and her rich dress of superb mahogany colored damask, was the most magnificent stage entry I have ever seen. And her change from shrew to loving wife was an exquisite bit of acting, placing Miss Rehan among the great artists of dramatic history." Another major event in stage history which the young college student attended was the first American opera performance of *Tristan und Isolde*, with Lilli Lehmann as the star.

Odell obtained his B.A. degree from Columbia in 1889, his M.A. in 1890, and in 1893 a doctorate of philosophy. His first published work, *Simile and Metaphor in the English and Scottish Ballads* (1893), was followed by his editions of *Julius Cæsar* and *Henry V* which he prepared for students. In 1895 he became connected with the department of English at Columbia University. His first important work in theatre history was published in 1920. What the *Annals of the New York Stage* has done for American theatre history, this earlier work, *Shakespeare From Betterton to Irving* (in two volumes), has done for the theatres of London. A review in the New York *Times* said: "Professor Odell has undertaken to do for all Shakespeare's plays . . . what has hitherto been attempted for two of the tragedies only. . . . He has organized his two volumes in eight

chronological divisions: the age of Betterton (1660-1710); the age of Cibber (1710-42); the age of Garrick (1742-76); the age of Kemble (1776-1817); the leaderless age (1817-37); the age of Macready (1837-43); the age of Phelps and Charles Kean (1843-79); and the age of Irving (1879-1902). Not only does he give us what is to a certain extent a history of the theatres of London, he also supplies us what is almost (not quite) a history of the evolution of the art of scene painting." "It is no dry-as-dust chronicle," commented Brander Matthews, "it is a readable book, abounding in apt anecdote, in illuminating quotation, and in genial comment." Matthews pointed out also that although Odell had to "correct many blunders and misstatements of many predecessors, he spared us the acrimony of controversy."

In 1924 Odell succeeded Brander Matthews as professor of dramatic literature at Columbia University, a post he held until his retirement in 1939, when the University made him Brander Matthews professor emeritus of dramatic literature. In 1927 the first two volumes of the *Annals of the New York Stage* were published. These covered the American amusement world from its beginnings in about 1732 to 1821. Each of these and each succeeding volume (covering the remaining years to 1891) runs over 600 pages in length. Although there have been other chronicles of the American theatre, Odell's history is considered to be the most authoritative and comprehensive of all. "The material," says Odell, "has been collected solely from contemporary newspapers, pamphlets, diaries, letters, autobiographies, playbills, account books, etc. From such original sources I have tried to depict the city in successive eras, with all its prejudices and all its predilections, social, artistic, and dramatic."

Despite the fact that Odell has acknowledged that he spent almost a lifetime in garnering the material, and that since 1920 has been actively engaged in writing and editing the published and forthcoming volumes, reviewers have marveled over the wealth of detailed information contained in the histories. Still more amazing is Odell's statement that he has never employed any assistants on the work. All research and proofreading have been and are done by the author. "I prefer my mistakes and not those I pay other people to make," he said once in an interview; then added with warranted pride, "In the thirteen volumes published I have found twelve mistakes." He never trusts to memory for a date or the spelling of a name, and he must see personally all sources of information. He once took a trip to Philadelphia to read six lines of a newspaper. The guiding source of his research in the years after 1830 has been the New York *Herald*. Page-proofing of each published volume took nine months in a schedule of a ten-hour day and a seven-day work week. The index to each volume was a four-month job. "There have been hardships all along the line," says Odell, "but, despite the fact I have never earned any royalties from the *Annals*, I have been happy in the work." "Wedded to his art" applies literally to Odell inasmuch as he has never married. In reviewing the earlier volumes Brander Matthews said: "[They] picture life as it was lived on Manhattan Island before the Revolution and for nearly a half of a century after our Independence. They set before us the manners and customs of these distant days; and they do this by combining a lively narrative with the serious facts of history."

Odell is the fourth scholar in 150 years to receive the gold medal "for achievement in history" from the New York Historical Society. The presentation of the award in October 1942 took place before 400 persons in the Society's auditorium in New York City. Joseph Wood Krutch, author, drama critic, and professor of English at Columbia University, declared that "no theatrical work anywhere in the world in all history compares with the *Annals* in charm, completeness, and accuracy." Others who gave praise in the same vein were Walter Hampden, actor, the late William Lyon Phelps [43], author and critic, Arthur Quinn, and Burns Mantle [44], the twentieth century's theatre annalist. The Society also prepared an exhibition in honor of Odell's work. Pictures of Joseph Jefferson, Edwin Booth, a dress worn by Geraldine Farrar, a costume worn by Enrico Caruso, and playbills, programs, and theatre tickets, supplemented the photographs and personal objects of those now vanished giants of the entertainment world.

Odell is six feet three inches tall, slender, and straight. He is silver-haired and has deep-set blue eyes. His manner is gentle and genial. He lives simply in a small hotel near Times Square. Although he has said, "Happy is the man whose avocation merges finally into an absorbing vocation," and makes no complaint because his valuable history has not paid him a cent in royalties, he is concerned over the loss the Columbia University Press has taken in the publication of the work. In the fourteenth volume, covering the years from 1888 to 1891 and published in December 1944, the author succeeds even "more vividly in bringing to life the people of the theatre's past, as his research has now entered upon a period within his own memory. He witnessed, with the passing of Edwin Booth, Lawrence Barrett, and Mary Anderson, the end of the grand style in the acting of tragedy, and saw the light of old comedy portrayal quenched with the deaths of Lester Wallack and John Gilbert. He was on hand for the beginning of a new era in 1891, when Pinero and Henry Arthur Jones became leading exemplars of the 'well-made' play, and Shakespeare and Sheridan began their steady decline in the minds of managers and audiences. At the same time music advanced in a decade of great orchestras and a matchless aggregation of great artists—the famous De Reszke group—at the Metropolitan Opera House. A rich era in operettas and extravaganzas also opened in the years covered by this unique reference work." Material has been accumulated and some writing done on the remaining nine years of the nineteenth century in theatre history, but Odell says these years, because of the ever increasing attractions in New York City, will require more volumes than the same number of years in the earlier period.

References

N Y Herald Tribune p7 O 24 '42
N Y Times IV p2 O 25 '42 por
Who's Who in America 1944-45

OGDEN, C(HARLES) K(AY) 1889- Author; educator; language psychologist

Address: c/o Orthological Institute, 45 Gordon Sq., London

When Prime Minister Winston Churchill [42], speaking at Harvard University on September 6, 1943, called to his audience's attention the advantages of using Basic English as an international language, a public which is becoming increasingly internationally minded looked with new interest toward this movement and toward its founder, C. K. Ogden.

While I. A. Richards, now at Harvard, is Basic's leading publicist, its inventor is Charles Kay Ogden, educator and language psychologist. Ogden has been working on the idea of an international auxiliary language since the early 1920's, and Basic made its first general appearance in 1930. Within a few years his system won world-wide support. Basic has been taught in the schools of thirty countries representing every continent. Several literary classics, including Plato's *Meno*, *Robinson Crusoe*, Lamb's *Tales from Shakespeare*, and the *Bible*, have been translated into Basic, as well as such full-length standard works as Raymond McGrath's *Twentieth Century House* (one hundred thousand words). It won more praise when Winston Churchill said: "I like to think of British and Americans moving about freely over each other's wide estates with hardly a sense of being foreigners to one another. But I do not see why we should not try to spread our common language even more widely through the globe and, without seeking selfish advantage over any, possess ourselves of this invaluable amenity and birthright." This was promptly hailed as giving Mr. Ogden's invention "the biggest boost any international language had ever received." When the Prime Minister further announced that he had asked his Cabinet to study and give him a report on Basic, and that President Roosevelt [42] also recognized its merits, Basic English became one of the most discussed factors in post-War planning.

Charles Kay Ogden, born in 1889, has spent the greater part of his life at Cambridge University in England. He first went to Cambridge in 1908 as a scholar of Magdalene College. Before he was twenty he had begun work on problems of international communication, and this proved to be his all-consuming interest. Commencing with Greek thought, Ogden began an exhaustive study of the influence of language on thought. He became an accomplished linguist, and, convinced that "language is the basic instrument by which social relationships are managed," he gave equal attention to social psychology.

In 1910 Cambridge University awarded him First Class Honors, Classical Tripos, and he remained at the University, founding the famous *Cambridge Magazine* two years later. This periodical, an organ of international opinion, had the largest circulation of any English weekly from 1916 to 1919.

Meanwhile Ogden continued his investigations on methods of language teaching. He traveled widely on the Continent and in India, and in 1914 published his first work on education, *The Problem of the Continuation School*, a book hailed by Professor Elie

Portrait by James Wood

C. K. OGDEN

Halévy as "chiefly responsible for the Education Act of 1918." In line with his interest in education and society, Ogden in the same year translated the work of the German educator Georg Kerschensteiner, *The Schools and the Nation*. His dominant interest, however, was still the relation of language and thought, and it was Ogden's study of contemporary German language and philosophy which led to his translation of Hans Driesch's *History and Theory of Vitalism* (1914), a work which has since influenced the course of much modern psychology.

Still concerned with the power of language, Ogden began research in the field of modern economic theory. He became interested in industrial relations and trade disputes, and when, in 1915, the British Association Committee on Industrial Fatigue appointed him an honorary research investigator, he prepared a valuable and unusual report in which special attention was given to terminology and general clarification of terms.

During the First World War Ogden was busy making linguistic studies and correlating them with his "experience of the influence of word-magic in wartime." He continued to edit the *Cambridge Magazine* but devoted most of his time to a special study of the problem of color notation. The results of this study were not widely publicized, but its implications foreshadowed the establishment of Basic English; for in his color study Ogden was seeking to create an international scientific language for color "by analogy with the notation of sound."

Less scholarly but more widely read were two books published in 1917 under his pseudonym of Adelyne More—*Fecundity versus Civilization* (for which Arnold Bennett wrote a preface) and *Militarism versus Feminism*. These books, the first-mentioned in particular, were strongly sympathetic to the rising feminist movement and named over-population as the cause of war and the chief obstacle to the emancipation of women.

Meanwhile, by this time Ogden's studies in the field of the influence of language had convinced him that "the citizen of today is the victim of new forms of word magic so universal and so subtle that he is unable ever to escape their influence." No subject was too large or too small for his linguistic investigations. In the field of aesthetics Ogden's research led him to collaborate with I. A. Richards and James Wood on *The Foundations of Aesthetics* (1922), wherein the importance of art in the daily life of society was stressed.

Richards and Ogden had known each other since their student days in Magdalene College in Cambridge. In the early 1920's the two men, both deeply interested in the study of the symbolism of words, decided to set forth general principles for the understanding of their functions in a book called *The Meaning of Meaning*. Considered one of the most important books of the decade, *The Meaning of Meaning* was a tantalizing study of language abstractions, "a concrete approach to theoretical confusions about language." Their book was of unquestionable value because it pointed to the extent and to the numerous difficulties of the problems of language. One reviewer called *The Meaning of Meaning* "formless and unequal," but the majority opinion was expressed by another reviewer who wrote, "Messrs. Ogden and Richards are no mere sophists, no clever hair-splitters. It is doubtful if the essential limitations of speech have ever been more vividly yet sympathetically realized than in their radical study of symbolism."

The Ogden and Richard approach discarded "mystical relations between the knower and the known" and treating knowledge "as a causal affair open to ordinary scientific investigation," they insisted that there was no direct and immediate relation between the object perceived (the "referent") and the symbol, the word or phrase by which the object is verbalized. The relationship, instead, was complicated by a third factor, namely the psychological process of "reference" or thought by which we interpret the object before we verbalize it. The word we use, therefore, is no more than a gesture; it means nothing concrete in itself. Hence the authors caution against the misuse of abstractions, pointing out that in a discussion it is wise "to start with things to which one can point . . . then ascend the abstraction ladder gingerly, pausing for frequent checks." They set up five canons for good language and conclude that "only such a set of canons will enable the philosopher to discuss more important matters than his own or his colleagues' peculiarities of expression."

It has been said that the approach of *The Meaning of Meaning* to its problem was "orthological" rather than "psychological." Knowing the limited field of semantics, and disliking such terms as "significs," Ogden decided in 1927 to adopt the unexploited title "orthology," or the art of using words correctly, for the normative science of signs and symbols on which general linguistics must be based. He therefore called the research organization which he had gradually been building up the Ortholog-ical Institute.

The idea for Basic English "derived from Ogden's earlier interest (1909-12) in the analytic principles of Wilkins and Horne Tooke, and from concrete investigations of certain tendencies of American English (1925)." Also, failing "to find satisfaction in Aristotelian logic or its modern mathematical developments, Ogden had been specially influenced (1912-13) by the speculations of C. S. Peirce on 'semeiotic.' Between 1919 and 1923 collaboration on *The Meaning of Meaning* removed a number of bogus philosophical difficulties connected with emotive terms, and the way was open for a new approach to traditional grammar. The idea of Basic English first took definite shape in the years 1925-27, when the significance of Ogden's classification of 'operators' and 'directives' was realized. This discovery led to a more careful examination (at the suggestion of the late F. G. Crookshank) of the neglected contributions to linguistics undertaken by Jeremy Bentham in 1815 in the interests of legal reform. The final requirements of a minimum vocabulary were worked out between 1927 and 1930, with the help of a group of collaborators, amongst them Miss L. W. Lockhart (now Mrs. A. H. Hannay)."

Gradually Ogden evolved a theory of word elimination as a means of simplifying a language so that it might be used internationally. He felt that "there might be some limited set of words in terms of which the meanings of all other words might be stated," and managed to get rid of 4,000 English verbs "by combining ten fundamental operations of physics with twenty directions of geometry." Ogden then began to work on nouns. "If you have the words 'dog' and 'young,' you do not need the word 'puppy.'" In this manner Ogden was finally able to break the English language down to a system of 850 words (600 nouns, 150 adjectives, and 100 "operators," comprising the eighteen elementary verbs and the eighty-two other words which help to "operate" and complete the system). These can be printed on a single side of a sheet of note-paper, and are governed by seven simple grammatical rules—"the smallest number necessary for the clear statement of ideas." (Ogden's *Basic English and Grammatical Reform* is perhaps "his most important exposition of the theoretical background of Basic.")

Basic proved to be surprisingly flexible in spite of the limitations of its vocabulary. One critic has written, "To read a translation into Basic done by one who has made himself at home in this medium is to note not only an exceptional fluency and spontaneity but also a peculiar sharpness probably resulting from the fact that so many ideas are expressed by analysis or definition." Although word order in Basic is standardized, it is at all times a normal English.

Through the 1920's Ogden was busy formulating his system of Basic. Meanwhile, he had numerous other interests. In 1922 he assumed the editorship of *Psyche*, the international psychological journal which specialized in the publication of research "in connection with linguistic psychology and international language problems." A year later he took over financial control of the journal, and

in the same year organized the International Library of Psychology, Philosophy, and Scientific Method. Within the next decade this organization published nearly one hundred volumes under Ogden's editorship. He also set going the famous "Today and Tomorrow" series which published one hundred volumes on educational subjects between 1923 and 1929, and he has planned and been the sole editor of the "History of Civilization" series since its start.

In 1924 Ogden translated two important Continental works—from the German of the idealistic-positivist Hans Vaihinger he translated *The Philosophy of As-If* and from Jules Romains' French, *Eyeless Sight*. Vaihinger's work interested Ogden because of its relevance to the theory of linguistic fictions (the same interest led to his translation in the next year of Henri Piéron's *Thought and the Brain*). These and other translations, including Paulhan's *The Laws of Feeling*, gave him further material for his theory of color notation and for linguistic analysis.

The Meaning of Psychology was published in 1925. This popularly written introduction to the subject was well received by reviewers. Ellsworth Faris commented, "There exists no comparable volume where the untechnical reader can so quickly and so adequately learn what psychology is all about." Ogden later adapted this book for British publication in 1928 under the title *The A B C of Psychology*. Gradually Ogden's ideas on linguistic psychology were winning a wider audience. The "Psyche Miniature" series which he planned and edited began to issue Basic English works, and when, in 1925, he visited America as science adviser for the *Forum*, his reputation as an authority on language was well established.

Other translations and original works followed. Ogden's translation of August Forel's two-volume lifework, *The Social Life of the Ants* (1926), was hailed as an important contribution to the study of animal communication. He organized and edited two more educational series, "Science for You" and the "Library of Educational Psychology," and wrote the article on Aesthetics for the thirteenth edition of the *Encyclopedia Britannica*. By 1927 his Basic English system and the entire orthological program were formulated.

The Orthological Institute which Ogden heads has its headquarters in Cambridge, England. From 1928 to 1930 it made a survey of the problem of invention in the modern world, "developing a variety of inventions and apparatus for the recording and reproduction of language in connection with Basic English." In addition to its linguistic functions, the Institute further worked on proposals for the reform of patent laws. The proposals, published in *Psyche*, "formed a basis for the patents discussion at the British Association meeting in 1931."

The year 1932 marked the publication of one of Ogden's most important books, *Bentham's Theory of Fictions*. The early nineteenth century British philosopher, Jeremy Bentham, had been one of the first to insist that language should be a system of communication. He had written, "Fictions owe their existence entirely to language," and for this

OGDEN, C. K.—*Continued*

Ogden credits him "with the spark that inspired *The Meaning of Meaning.*"

Basic English was meanwhile winning its inventor national fame. Basic books were printed in Czech, Danish, Latvian, Swedish, Russian, Chinese, and Japanese. A Basic institute was founded in China, and in the U.S.S.R. Basic English was taught by Madame Ivy Litvinov. In 1930 Ogden was named a fellow of Magdalene College, Cambridge, and in 1932 he was invited to address the Royal Institute of International Relations on the subject of Basic English. In the same year he delivered the Bentham Centenary Lecture at University College, London. (This lecture was enlarged and later published as *Jeremy Bentham, 1832-2032* [1932]. In 1931 Ogden's *Bentham's Theory of Legislation* was published and presumably brought about the invitation to deliver the lecture.) Ogden published *The System of Basic English* in 1934. In this book he presented the thesis that "The so-called national barriers of today are, for the most part, ultimately language barriers. The absence of a common medium of communication is the chief obstacle to international understanding and consequently the chief underlying cause of war."

Generally from the start two aspects of the Basic question have been recognized. The first was its value as a method of teaching English to foreigners (Basic can be mastered in one month, while it is estimated that it takes four years of study to acquire a good working knowledge of English). The other aspect was the value of Basic English as an international language. Although Basic was already well established in some thirty different countries by 1935, the outbreak of the Second World War brought up more fundamental issues of international communication.

Meanwhile, on March 9, 1944, an important part of Ogden's Basic program was officially accepted by the British Government. Distinguishing between Basic as a method for the teaching of ordinary English, and as an auxiliary international language, the Government formulated plans for developing it for the latter use. The British Council, it was decided, would include among its activities the teaching of Basic wherever there was a demand for it; diplomatic and commercial representatives abroad would be asked to encourage its spread; more works would be translated into Basic, and more instruction manuals circulated; Colonial Governments would be invited to experiment with handbooks on agriculture, hygiene, etc., for their people; the BBC would be asked to cooperate; and the Foreign Office would be given primary responsibility for its development, with a special committee to act as a contact between the various Governmental departments concerned in the program.

Basic was already in common use in international communication and trade, and since February 1941, when it was established, the Harvard Commission on English Language Studies has been studying certain accepted educational applications of Basic as related to the special needs of American education. I. A. Richards has been working with this Commission to establish a Basic English center at Harvard.

References

N Y Times p20 S 10 '43
N Y Times Mag p12 S 19 '43
New Repub 78:328-31 My 2 '34
Newsweek 22:82 S 20 '43
Time 23:74-5 Mr 12 '34 por; 42:44 Ag 16 '43

O'HARA, MARY July 10, 1885- Author; composer

Address: b. c/o J. B. Lippincott Co., 227-231 S. 6th St., Philadelphia; h. Remount Ranch, Granite Canyon, Wyo.

Two remarkable stories about a boy and his horse, written with a sensitive understanding of both animal and human nature, are the work of Mary O'Hara. *My Friend Flicka* (1941), a best seller, was followed by a sequel, *Thunderhead* (1943). They have won special praise as books enjoyed by adults as well as older boys and girls, a category in which, as Lewis Gannett[41] has remarked, "some of the best-loved books in the English tongue hold their immortality." Their author, who has lived for several years on a Western ranch and is the mother of two grown children, received her literary training as a child by listening to the sermons of her father, an Episcopal clergyman. Besides writing stories, she has composed music and has adapted several scripts for motion pictures.

Mary O'Hara is the pen name of Mary O'Hara Alsop Sture-Vasa. She was born at Cape May Point, New Jersey, July 10, 1885, the daughter of the Rev. Reese Fell Alsop and Mary Lee (Spring) Alsop. She comes of an old American family, naming Jonathan Edwards and William Penn among her forebears; on her father's side the family were Philadelphia Quakers. A great-grandfather, Gardiner Spring, was pastor of the Brick Church, New York; Spring Street, New York, was named after him. Mary was named for Mary O'Hara Denny of Pittsburgh, who married the son of Gardiner Spring, and has used that name as a pseudonym in all her writings.

Mary Alsop grew up in Brooklyn Heights, where her father filled the pulpit of an Episcopal church. Though city-bred, the girl always loved horses. It is said that when she was a child, someone promised her a colt. She never got it, "but the longing for it and the hope of it were the secret joys of her life for many years." At the age of eight she began to write, she says—"fine and careful penmanship crowded into copybooks, the titles all rather sad and alliterative, like 'Lonely Laurie.'" She wrote both her own and her brother's compositions during their school days, and also began early to compose music. Educated at Ingleside, a finishing school in New Milford, Connecticut, and a Packer Institute, Brooklyn, she did not attend a university, but spent two years in Europe studying music and languages.

Miss O'Hara's first marriage, to Kent Karr Parrot, took her to California, where she began writing for the motion pictures. "A chance meeting on the golf course with an Eastern playwright whose success had taken him to Hollywood led to her employment in the studios, first as the playwright's assistant in choosing material." She soon became a special reader, then an assistant to the general supervisor, collaborating closely with the staff of continuity writers. One day the late Rex Ingram, at that time the best known director in Hollywood, sent for her, told her that her continuities were the best he had seen, and asked her to become his staff writer. It was for Ingram that Miss O'Hara wrote the adaptations and continuities of numerous films, including *Toilers of the Sea* (1923); *Black Oxen* (1924); *Turn to the Right* (1927); and *The Prisoner of Zenda* (1937). Miss O'Hara remained until "she decided that Hollywood success was not the kind she wanted," and in 1930 moved to a ranch in Wyoming, where she ran a dairy single-handed.

A ten-year-old boy and his wild colt, Flicka, which he loves more than anything else in the world, are the chief characters of Miss O'Hara's first full-length book, *My Friend Flicka*. On a Wyoming ranch his father, an ex-Army officer, was raising blooded horses; and the horse young Ken McLaughlin chose for his very own was a beautiful, half "loco," and almost untamable young filly. The dramatic tension in the story rises from the conflict between the boy and his father, and an understanding mother "who knows the heart of a small boy." Some reviewers felt that the story had definite touches of sentimentality and melodrama; but all agreed upon its grace and simplicity. "*My Friend Flicka* has the quality of *The Yearling*, but it is tougher and wilder; the great winds of Wyoming, rather than the soft breezes of Florida, sweep through it. It has the intensity of Lincoln Steffens' memorable little tale of his own Christmas pony, and has the strength of John Steinbeck's [40] stories of Joady and his red pony. It also has an undercurrent of boy-and-parent relationship running with bitter honesty through all its pages." The book was produced as a motion picture by Twentieth Century-Fox, with Roddy McDowall starring as young Ken.

Three months before the publication of Flicka's successor, *Thunderhead*, in October 1943, advance sales stood at 50,000. In this story Ken has reached the age of fourteen, and Thunderhead is Flicka's first foal, a swift, strong stallion—but a throw-back to his wild outlaw ancestors. Wrote Orville Prescott in the New York *Times*: "It is that rare achievement, a sequel to a great and richly deserved success that in no way disappoints or falls short of its distinguished predecessor. . . . In Miss O'Hara, I believe, we have one of the most important and most enduring novelists now writing in America. When other topical and fiercely contemporary books are long since forgotten, timeless tales like hers will always find a new public awaiting them as fast as new generations who like children and like horses grow up enough to read them. No writer that I can recall has ever written about animals of any kind the way Miss O'Hara does about horses, with such love and understanding, such blazing skill in individualizing them with striking personalities and yet such absence of anthropo-

Maurine

MARY O'HARA

morphical romanticizing." (Three months after its publication, *Thunderhead* was purchased by Twentieth Century-Fox.)

In 1922 Miss O'Hara was married to Helge Sture-Vasa. Her two children by her former marriage are Mary O'Hara Parrot and Kent Karre Parrot, Jr., now a captain with the United States Army Air Corps.

Mary O'Hara is a slender person with dark hair and dark eyes and strong regular features. Concurrently with her career as a writer she has won success in musical composition. A number of her works have been published by Schirmer of New York and Presser of Philadelphia. A Christmas carol of hers was sung in 1942 by the famous choir of the Paulist Fathers in New York. She says that she loves to compose music more than anything else; however, "I'll go on writing till the end of my days. I have been writing too long to stop." In late 1943 Miss O'Hara was in Hollywood conferring on the projected motion picture *Thunderhead, Son of Flicka*, which was to be independent of the book *Thunderhead*, not just a film version of the novel. The picture will be released early in 1945.

References

N Y Herald Tribune p15 Ag 21 '41 por
N Y Times p17 Ag 27 '41 por; p21 O 6 '43 por
New Repub 105:380 S 22 '41
Pub W 140:463 Ag 16 '41
Who's Who in America 1944-45

O'LEARY, JAMES A. Apr. 23, 1889—Mar. 16, 1944 New York Democratic Representative in Congress since 1935; author of numerous measures aiding the merchant marine; served as chairman of the House Committee on Expenditures in Executive Departments.

Obituary

N Y Times p17 Mr 17 '44 por

ORLANDO, VITTORIO EMANUELE

(or-län'do vĕt-tô'ryō ä'mä-nwä'la) Mar.
19(?), 1860- Lawyer; statesman

Address: h. Via Andrea Cesalpino 4, Rome,
Italy

In the dramatic coup of July 1943 during
which Benito Mussolini '⁴² and many of his
followers were overthrown and Pietro Badoglio '⁴⁰ assumed the premiership of Italy, an
old man, almost unknown to the younger generation of Italian Fascists, made a radio address appealing to the people of Sicily (then
besieged by Allied forces) for unity and
loyalty to the motherland. The speaker was
Vittorio Orlando, who had figured so prominently in Italy's government during the First
World War and had been one of the "Big
Four" (Woodrow Wilson, Georges Clemenceau,
and David Lloyd George '⁴⁴ being the other
three) at the Paris Peace Conference of 1919.
For the past twenty years he has lived in
obscurity; but with the Allied invasion of
Sicily in the summer of 1943 and the subsequent ousting of Mussolini, Orlando presented
himself as "a heroic symbol" to the Italian
people. In his radio address of August 18,
1943 he did little more than to reiterate what
Marshal Badoglio had already said and to repeat that "the salvation and the fate of Sicily
are closely linked to the salvation and the
fate of the rest of Italy." It was suggested,
however, that Orlando's words carried much
weight, since he represented to Italy its past
glory as a victor nation when he guided that
country, as he writes in his memoirs, "from
the abyss of defeat to the height of glory."
The Germans apparently felt that Orlando's
presence in Italy was a menace to themselves,
and in December 1943, as Allied armies pressed
their drive on Rome, he was arrested by the
Nazi authority in Italy. From the day of
Mussolini's fall, however, he has been "Rome's
elder statesman."

The son of Camillo and Carmela (Barab-
bino) Orlando, Vittorio Emanuele Orlando
was born in Palermo in March 1860. He
was evidently a precocious child, and as he
grew older he proved to be an apt student,
producing a mythological study, *Prometeo*, at
the age of nineteen. Abandoning myths for
the law, he took his degree in constitutional
law and when twenty-one wrote his thesis on
electoral reform (*Della Riforma Eletorale*,
1883). Orlando began his teaching career as
professor of law at the University of Palermo
in 1882. In 1885 he taught at the University
of Modena and in the following year at Messina. Meanwhile he was working on several
books on administrative and constitutional
law.

Vittorio Orlando entered political life in
1897 when he was elected to the Chamber of
Deputies as a representative of Partinico,
Sicily. Almost at once he impressed listeners
with his eloquent speech and his complete
mastery of the law. Decidedly a liberal, his
legalistic education marked him as a statesman
rather than a politician, and it was his analytic mind, his "precision of thought and clearness of expression," which accounted for his
rise in the government.

As Minister of Education in the Giolitti-
Tittoni Cabinet from 1903 to 1905 and as

Minister of Justice in the Giolitti Cabinet
from 1907 to 1909, Orlando was a witness to
the diplomatic maneuverings of his country
as it strove desperately to maintain the status
quo in Europe and at the same time to enlarge
its own territorial holdings. After the First
World War broke out Orlando served in the
Cabinet of Prime Minister Salandra who
favored Italian intervention in the War on
the side of the Allies. Although Italy was
committed to the Central Powers by an alliance, the territorial and economic advantages
offered her by the Allies in the Treaty of
London proved tempting. For a while she
maintained hesitant neutrality, reflecting the
views of Minister Giolitti, but many, including Orlando himself, though Giolittian at
heart, favored Italian intervention. The pressure at last proved effective, and Italy declared
war on Austria in May 1915.

The Salandra Cabinet resigned in June 1916,
but Orlando remained in office as Minister of
the Interior under Boselli. Then in October
1917, "on the same day that the Italian Front
was broken at Caporetto, and Italy . . . was
experiencing the greatest danger in its history,"
Boselli resigned and Orlando became Prime
Minister of Italy.

Few leaders have been so successful in restoring morale to a defeated people as was Orlando
in 1917 and 1918. Within a month after their
victory at Caporetto the Austrians were routed
and began to sue for peace. The Italians were
jubilant, for they had long regarded Austria
as the greatest menace to their national well-
being. With this menace out of the War they
looked forward to the general armistice when
they might proclaim their territorial demands.

Orlando went to Paris as president of the
Italian peace delegation to take part in the most
memorable meeting of nations since the Congress of Vienna. Each of the representatives
at the Paris Conference had his own claims
to press, but Orlando's were perhaps the most
definite and the most frankly demanding.
Robert Lansing, United States Secretary of
State under President Wilson, commented in
his recollections of the Conference: "My impression is that Signor Orlando came to Paris
with the definite purpose of obtaining, so far
as the Adriatic was concerned, the territorial
concessions laid down in the Pact of London."

The least influential of the "Big Four," handicapped by his inability to speak English and by
friction among the members of his own delegation, Orlando nevertheless made a favorable
impression upon his associates in Paris. Lloyd
George described him as "a learned, cultured,
and eminent lawyer possessing considerable
oratorical gifts," and commented on "his integrity and genuine patriotism" and his "liberal
and democratic" views. Robert Lansing was
equally kind in his description—"Signor Orlando
possessed physical and mental characteristics
which have left pleasant memories."

Like so many other delegates who were
"bound by considerations of home politics to
fight for certain terms of settlement which they
had given their people reason to expect,"
Orlando was committed to a policy which necessarily conflicted with the Fourteen Points.
While he praised the Points as high in ideals,
he stressed the "defenselessness of the Italian

coast in the Adriatic," and added, "Italy wants no more and no less than this: the completion of her national unity and the security of her frontiers on land and sea."

The inevitable break between the Italians and the other negotiators at the Conference came over the issue of the small city of Fiume, under Hungarian control before 1914 and incorporated, in 1919, in the new Kingdom of Yugoslavia. Italian nationalist groups at home had long been agitating for control of this city. To reconcile and satisfy these groups Orlando demanded that Fiume be given to Italy. Italian sentiment was so strong on the Fiume question that when President Wilson published his manifesto urging Italy "to subscribe wholeheartedly to the new order of things, of which the League of Nations was the embodiment," and to abandon its claim on the city, the Italian delegation indignantly left Paris and returned to Rome. Orlando defended this move with the statement that, "To oppose . . . the Italian Government and people would be to admit that this great free nation could submit to the yoke of a will other than its own, and I shall be forced to protest vigorously against such supposition, unjustly offensive to my country."

Back in Rome Orlando found nationalist sentiment so intense that all possibility of accepting a compromise settlement (which he personally might have wished to accept) was eliminated. He was given a vote of confidence and hailed as the champion of a united Italy. Still determined not to break completely with the Allies, however, he returned to Paris a few weeks later to resume his place at the peace table. According to most commentators, the Italian delegation had acted impulsively and had done their cause great harm by leaving the Conference. "They were coming back empty-handed, and if they had ever expected that their return would be bought by concessions, their move had been a distinct failure, which left them, if anything, in a weakened position."

Like Clemenceau and Wilson, Orlando was soon repudiated by his own people. The difficulties of post-War readjustment had upset Italy's economy. There was conflict within his Cabinet, and the Chamber of Deputies voted against him. Finally, on June 19, 1919, Orlando resigned as Prime Minister.

Orlando's political career was not yet finished, however. In December 1919 he was elected president of the Chamber of Deputies. (After "a stormy leadership" he resigned and was sent to Brazil as King Victor Emmanuel's [43] envoy.) When the Black Shirts marched on Rome in 1922 Orlando took some interest in Fascist politics, supported Mussolini, and was re-elected to the Chamber in 1924. But when the Socialist leader Matteotti was murdered and prominent Fascist Party leaders were implicated in the crime, Orlando withdrew his support and became an opponent of Fascism, refusing to take the Fascist Party oath. In 1925 he declared his hostility to Mussolini by running for office as an anti-Fascist. He was defeated, and after being the victim of an attack by a mob in the streets of Palermo, Sicily, he retired from political life and went to the University of

VITTORIO EMANUELE ORLANDO

Rome to teach international law. But he was forced to give this up, too, in 1931.

Orlando emerged in October 1935 to proclaim his devotion to the Fascist cause, but his offer of service was ignored. Characterized by *Time* Magazine as "an off-and-on" friend of Fascism, Orlando defended Fascism on the grounds that it was vindicating the wrongs of the Treaty of Versailles (to which he had been the sole opponent at the Paris Conference). Of his own retirement he wrote, "A profound oblivion has descended on my name. It is useless to search for the causes; I can only say that I have accepted this oblivion as the rational necessity of a historical situation imposed by destiny."

In April 1944 *Time* reported that eighty-four-year-old Vittorio Orlando was one of 300 hostages shot by the Gestapo in retaliation for a bomb thrown by anti-Nazis. That June, however, the New York *Times* Herbert L. Matthews [43] reported him "still very much alive and very much of a force in Italian politics. Nor is it by any means excluded that he will not again be an important figure in the peace negotiations to follow the Second World War." Orlando, who had been given charge of the Roman Parliament's Palazzo di Monte Citorio and archives, was called by Matthews "Rome's elder statesman, consulted first by the King, and then, during the German occupation, by National Liberation leaders. Recently, when the Government was formed here, he was consulted by all politicians, and above all by Crown Prince Humbert [43]. His home on the Via Cesalpino is a mecca. . . . It is a place to get advice and counsel and words of moderation in the midst of an atmosphere that is naturally extremist. . . . Signor Orlando speaks noble words of nineteenth century liberalism in a country that has forgotten what liberalism means."

The former Premier opposes the punishment of Fascists as such. "The Allies are wrong in thinking that Fascism was strong in Italy and that it must be eradicated," he says. "There is

ORLANDO, VITTORIO EMANUELE—
Continued

nothing to eradicate, and proof came on July 25 when the Fascist regime was blown away like dust. What followed was German activity." The liberal attitude, he feels, is that everyone is entitled to his political opinions, and that goes for Fascists as well as anybody else. He is also opposed to the strong anti-monarchist movement, headed by Count Carlo Sforza '42 and Professor Adolfo Omodeo; the monarchy, in his view, is "one of the few remaining cohesive factors in Italy," while a coalition government with "its varied theories and programs represents a luxury that Italy cannot afford." Similarly, though a Sicilian, he opposes the movement for Sicilian independence, which he claims would mean only subservience to England. "For the next fifty years," he declares, "Italy is to be faced with the problem of survival. I can't even think any longer about the subtleties of party politics. They have no reality in the face of the overwhelming fact that Italy is going to be dominated and prostrate and in danger of internal strife for two generations. That is the only basis upon which practical politicians can think today."

Orlando, who came to America with his wife in 1934 to visit a married daughter, impressed reporters at that time with his youthful appearance and his "razor-keen" mind. He refused to discuss politics or his own career, although he has been known to say, "The truth is that when I am confronted with a problem, I cannot do less than consider with fairness all its aspects, even those which are against me: and this seems weakness. Indeed in politics it is weakness"

References

N Y Sun p13 Ag 23 '43
N Y Times p4 Ag 19 '43
Albrecht, C. R. Italy at the Paris Peace
     Conference 1938
Chi è? 1936
International Who's Who 1942
Lansing, R. The Big Four and Others
     of the Peace Conference 1921
Lloyd George, D. Memoirs of the
     Peace Conference 1939

ORLEMANSKI, STANISLAUS, REV.
(or"le-män'ski) Dec. 9, 1889- Catholic priest
Address: h. Rectory, Our Lady of the Holy Rosary Church, Springfield, Mass.

Stanislaus Orlemanski, the obscure priest who in the spring of 1944 became the center of an international controversy by attempting a "Moscow mission" on his own, was born December 9, 1889. He was the son of Polish immigrants who had come to America twenty-one years before and had finally settled in Erie, Pennsylvania, where he was born. (His father, incidentally, had been awarded the Carnegie Hero Medal, the inscription on one side of it reading: "Greater love had no man than this, that a man lay down his life for his friends.") Both Stanislaus and his three brothers were destined for the priesthood, and he studied at the Orchard Lake Seminary in Michigan and at St. Francis Seminary in Wisconsin before being ordained in 1915.

Two years later, in *PM*'s words, "a group of Polish residents in Springfield, Massachusetts, for whom he had been conducting masses in a Syrian church every Sunday, asked him to leave a neighboring town and help them build a church of their own. Catholic authorities gave their permission, and in 1917, with Father Orlemanski as the pastor, fewer than 100 families raised enough money to build a hall which served both as church and community center—a building which has been converted into a parochial grammar school, standing next to the new church."

PM continued: "Ten years ago came the split in the parish which, apparently, no Springfield Pole has forgotten. According to both parishioners and those who left the church, the disagreement came when Father Orlemanski announced that the room which was used for masses and church services would be made into a recreation hall, and the former recreation room would be used as the church proper. Protests were raised by some who thought the change would be sacrilege, and who objected to having their church dues used for the conversion without their approval. Father Orlemanski persisted in the plan, however, and slightly less than half his congregation, which had grown considerably, left to form the Polish National Catholic Church of Springfield. This church is not a Roman Catholic church, but affiliated with the Polish National Catholic Church of America, organized about sixty years ago. It does not recognize the Pope as its spiritual head."

Father Orlemanski's parish gained new members, however: in 1944 it has more than 3,000 members, Irish as well as Polish, while the Polish National Catholic Church has about 1,100. In 1939, together with the workmen in his congregation, Father Orlemanski helped to design a new church and, donning an old cassock, went to work on it "side by side with his parishioners, plastering the walls, sawing wood, and laying bricks." In fourteen months the red brick, Doric-columned structure was finished, and in July 1940 it was dedicated. "On a little grassy hill, banked at the front and sides with shrubs and flowers," the Church of Our Lady of the Holy Rosary seats nearly 1,000 worshippers and is considered one of the East's most beautiful Catholic edifices. Today Father Orlemanski still tends the church furnace and mows the lawn.

Father Orlemanski's loyal parishioners tell how he has encouraged them to save money—to invest it in real estate and in war bonds. They tell how he got the money together to establish the little Polish National Home in Springfield, a combined fraternal order and social hall whose 150 members "gather for weddings and banquets and bridal showers, stop in for a beer of an evening, hold dances and meetings." The financial soundness of the home, which includes a substantial bank fund and $15,000 in war bonds, they attribute to Father Orlemanski's guidance.

But Father Orlemanski's activities have not been confined to his own parish. About 800 of his parishioners are reportedly members of the Kosciuszko League "for a free Poland," which he organized in Detroit in November 1943 and of which he is honorary president. Father Orlemanski has said that when the

Russians "organized the First Polish Division they named it the Kosciuszko Division. Kosciuszko being an American patriot, I thought it proper for me as an American citizen of Polish descent to support the move. Kosciuszko is our American hero, and bringing Kosciuszko to Poland means American democracy." He therefore "traveled through Canada in support of the League, visiting all big cities from Montreal to Winnipeg." Furthermore, he announced in a speech at Town Hall that he would "organize a branch in every town, village, and city of America and Canada. The Kosciuszko Division in Russia will help destroy Hitlerism in Europe, and the Kosciuszko League will help to completely destroy the pro-Nazi Polish publications, the pro-Nazi Polish leaders in our organizations, and also the pro-Nazi Polish leaders among our clergy here in America."

In "My Outlook," an article written in Polish and published in *Nasz Swiat*, a national Polish-American magazine, he proposed a military alliance between Poland and Russia and supported the Russian claims to the Ukraine and White Russia, saying that eastern Prussia would be much more beneficial to Poland. "After the conclusion of this War," he announced, "Poland must have a new progressive government, a new program, and a new policy towards her neighbors. . . . If the lot of the Polish workers and peasants is not improved to meet the standards of the workers and peasants of other powerful states . . . sooner or later such a Poland must disappear."

It was late in 1943 when Orlemanski made up his mind to go to Russia and "see what was on the other side of the fence." "I didn't want to work in the blind," he explained later. Sometime in January 1944 he wrote to Secretary of State Cordell Hull [40] asking him for a passport to go to the Soviet Union. When he received no answer he wrote again and asked for permission to investigate for himself and to study the Polish question there. The answer was that such a visit would be acceptable to the American Government, but that the Soviet Government might not approve. Father Orlemanski therefore wrote to the Russian consulate in New York, and finally an invitation came from Stalin [42] himself. In April 1944, after receiving permission from the United States War Department, Father Orlemanski went to Great Falls, Montana, where there was a Russian transport returning to Russia from America. His trip from Great Falls to Russia cost no one a penny, he says: "Those planes either carry cargo or go empty, and I was the cargo." He was also the first American Roman Catholic priest to visit Russia since 1934.

Father Orlemanski spent twelve days in Moscow and other points in Russia. His reception was beyond anything he had anticipated. Not only did he visit and address the Polish Army and visit a Soviet home for Polish children, but he was granted two interviews—each more than two hours long—with Stalin himself. The priest had told the Russian consulate before he left that if he didn't get to see Stalin personally he "would take the first plane back," but he had expected nothing like this. He found Stalin "very

REV. STANISLAUS ORLEMANSKI

democratic, very open," he said later. "I told Stalin that the most important problem to solve is the religious problem. He said, 'How would you go about this? What would you do?' I told him I wanted to ask two questions." These and their answers were:

Q. "Do you think that cooperation with the Holy Father, Pope Pius XII [41], in the matter of struggle against coercion and persecution of the Catholic Church is possible?"

A. "I think it is possible."

Q. "Do you think it admissible for the Soviet Government to pursue a policy of persecution and coercion with regard to the Catholic Church?"

A. "As an advocate of freedom of conscience and that of worship I consider such a policy to be inadmissible and precluded."

When Father Orlemanski emerged from the second conference it was as emissary bearing secret proposals direct from Stalin to the Pope, which he planned to transmit to the Pope through the apostolic delegate in Washington. Stalin had given to the priest his written promise that he would do all in his power to cooperate with the Church so that there would be no persecutions anywhere. He had also entrusted him with proposals of "tremendous significance" dealing with the Polish political question, the nature of which was not divulged even later, although Father Orlemanski assured everyone that "Stalin wants a free, independent, and democratic Poland."

Back home there were repercussions from all this. Professor Oscar Lange of the University of Chicago, who held views similar to the priest's on Polish-Soviet relations, was visiting Russia at the same time, and supporters of the Polish Government-in-Exile were angered at the Roosevelt [42] Administration for having granted the two passports. The act was called a "breach of good faith" which "indicated the stamp of approval of our Government on communistic activities in this country." Equally disapproving were many

ORLEMANSKI, STANISLAUS, REV.—
Continued

Catholic officials. The Right Reverend Michael J. Ready, National Catholic Welfare Conference Secretary, denounced the journey as "a political burlesque . . . the phoniest propaganda that the usually clever idea men in Russia have palmed off on the United States."

On his return trip Father Orlemanski took a Russian plane, stopping first at Fairbanks, Alaska, where he found he was running short of money and borrowed $200 from a Catholic Army chaplain. He arrived at Springfield on May 13. Only four hours after his arrival his suspension was ordered by Bishop Thomas M. O'Leary, head of the Springfield Diocese of the Roman Catholic Church, who possesses as Bishop the powers of order and jurisdiction in his diocese in due submission to the primacy of the Pope. (Father Orlemanski, whose vows of the priesthood involve obedience to his superiors, had as yet made no explanations to him.) The priest was charged, among other things, with having acted "contrary to the general doctrine of the Catholic Church as enunciated by Popes Leo XIII, Pius XI, and Pius XII" in "treating with Communists." His activities in the Kosciuszko League and his absence from his diocese without permission also entered into the picture, it was stated.

Much agitated, Father Orlemanski told reporters, after receiving the suspension orders: "What this is all about, I don't know. If it is about my trip to Moscow, I am willing to be crucified for my Church, because I went to Moscow for my Church. . . . I have done nothing immoral, nothing transgressing God's law. I feel I am defending my Church. Why should I receive a letter?" He added that he did not want a "communistic system installed in Poland, but an American system." "I openly told this to the Polish Army, too," he went on. "I belong to no party, no clique. I am working for the good of the Polish people and my country. I am an independent man, not tied up to anybody." He announced that he was appealing his case to the apostolic delegate at Washington, claiming that such an appeal would nullify Bishop O'Leary's suspension and give him the right to continue with whatever church functions he desired to carry on. The Reverend George A. Shea, chancellor of Father Orlemanski's diocese, disputed this interpretation, however, saying that Father Orlemanski was forbidden to perform divine office, to preach or make public appearances, to teach or lecture, and was also required to leave the parish and retire to a monastery of his own choosing until "further notice."

And Father Orlemanski, who had not actually appealed his case at this time, went into complete seclusion. He did not say Mass the next day, as he had said he might; nor did he appear in his parish. On May 15 his doctor announced that he was confined to bed in his rectory, threatened with a "complete physical and nervous breakdown," and that complete quiet and rest had been ordered. He did not lack for sympathy. His parish remained loyal, and radio commentator Johannes Steel [41] apparently spoke for many when he said that the punishment of Reverend Orlemanski by Bishop Thomas H. O'Leary was "in sharp contrast to the failure of the hierarchy in the past to discipline such pro-Fascist agitators as Father Coughlin [40] and Father Curran." Such Catholic organs as the British *Catholic Herald*, however, saw the Orlemanski controversy as playing into the hands of "the people who in recent years have sought to create a distinction within the Catholic Church."

On May 16, 1944 Father Orlemanski was reinstated to good standing in the Church after having made full apology to his Bishop and having promised to adhere in the future "to the rule and the mind of the Catholic Church." Father Orlemanski, like other priests, has always been required to get his Bishop's approval in order to make extended trips outside his parish (such as he had been doing in furtherance of the program of the Kosciuszko League), and to obtain the Bishop's imprimatur on any of his writings which might touch on faith and morals. Even writings on current or future Polish problems might involve faith and morals, it was now indicated, however.

An echo of Orlemanski's mission was heard in July, when there were several unconfirmed rumors that he would visit the Vatican to report to Pope Pius on the Russian trip.

Father Orlemanski is described as "a tall, powerfully built man, with piercing eyes behind rimless spectacles. He talks with emphatic gestures and, in frequent moments of excitement, with the trace of an accent."

References

N Y Herald Tribune p1+ Ap 29 '44;
   p1+ Ap 30 '44; p1+ My 14 '44
N Y Times p4 Ap 28 '44; p1+ My 7
   '44; p1+ My 13 '44; p1+ My 14 '44
PM p9 My 9 '44 por; p2 My 16 '44
Time 43:23 My 8 '44 por

OSMEÑA, SERGIO (ōs-mā′nyä ser′hyō)
Sept. 9, 1878- President of the Philippine Commonwealth

Sergio Osmeña, second President of the Commonwealth of the Philippines, took his oath of office on August 1, 1944, a few hours after his dynamic chief, Manuel L. Quezon [41], had died. In comparing the new President with his predecessor, *Time* Magazine says that the Filipinos thought of Osmeña as "a gray bird flying beside a brightly plumaged jungle cock." But underneath the pale plumage his countrymen see a brilliant mind and a steadfast purpose. Lacking Quezon's power to project his assets before the public eye, Osmeña had nonetheless maintained a quiet, steady popularity throughout the decades that the two men fought side by side for freedom. In 1941 he was re-elected to the Vice-Presidency by an even higher margin than the 7-to-1 vote polled by his chief.

Born September 9, 1878, in Cebu, a central island in the Philippines, Sergio Osmeña is a mestizo of humble parentage. (A mestizo is of native and Chinese blood.) San Carlos Seminary in Cebu and San Juan de Letran in Manila gave him his secondary education and prepared him for Santo Tomás University, where after two years his studies were interrupted in 1896 by the rising revolt against Spain.

At Santo Tomás a chance meeting occurred that subsequent events were to magnify into an historic significance. Osmeña, a law student on a scholarship, met Manuel Quezon, another scholarship student majoring in law. An immediate friendship was formed, the first effects of which were felt by their class, which was regarded by one professor as "the most distinct and rebellious" at the time. It is likely that Quezon provided most of the éclat, for Osmeña has always been the quiet complement to the vigorous personality, willing to remain as runner-up.

Too young to bear arms at the beginning of the Philippines' revolutionary period, Osmeña took up the cudgels as a newspaper writer and subsequently as publisher. When peace finally came to the Philippines he emerged as a young journalist with embryonic plans for a campaign for liberty. But Osmeña's ambition to be a lawyer still dominated and after further study he was admitted to the bar in 1903. A brief but successful record as a lawyer provided the springboard for his leap into public office; in 1906 he was elected provincial governor of Cebu. Paralleling his friend's progress in law, Quezon was simultaneously elected governor of Manila.

Osmeña was only twenty-eight years old at the time and had little political experience, but his administrative ability and political finesse based on genuine understanding and liking for the people made him a "natural" for public office. Upon his inception he was immediately faced with an urgent problem. Years of insurrection had destroyed all semblance of public order. He realized that cooperation between municipal enforcement officers and the people as a whole was the first step toward establishing a coordinated community. To his fairness and firmness is attributed the success with which he brought order out of chaos, "a [peaceful] situation that has not existed before within the memory of living people," according to the report of the Philippine Commission. An incident of his administration is regarded as illustrative of his honesty. By promising the leader of a notorious armed band that he would not be arrested, Osmeña was able to talk to the bandit. While the capture would have heaped glory on Osmeña, the young Governor not only allowed the man to go free but even carried integrity to the point of admitting that surrender would not guarantee a pardon.

Striving for complete independence for the Philippines has been the driving force of Osmeña's career. In 1902 he joined forces to petition Governor General Taft for permission to form a political party advocating independence. United States civil authorities, then opposed to the move, turned down the petition. In 1906, at the first Convention of Provincial Governors in Manila, Osmeña was one of a small nucleus who openly urged eventual independence. Although he belonged to this minority he was elected President of the Convention. When the ban on pro-independence parties was lifted prior to the first Philippine Assembly in 1907, Osmeña aided in forming the Nacionalista Party, which elected an overwhelming majority of its members to the new body. By a unanimous vote Osmeña became speaker of the Assembly and Quezon became leader of the majority. Realizing that he could do more for Philippine independence in Washington, Quezon went there in 1909 as Resident Commissioner, thus obtaining a voice (but not a vote) in Congress.

The Philippine Assembly patterned its procedure on the parliamentary rules of the Fifty-ninth Congress of the United States, in some respects even anticipating reforms in the rules of the American Congress. Osmeña remained its speaker through the nine years of its existence, steering the young legislative body past two pitfalls: it could have traveled along with the American officials, shouldering lightly the burden of state, or it could have adopted obstructionist tactics, opposing the sovereign power at every turn. The wisdom and ability of Speaker Osmeña are regarded as having been largely responsible for guiding the Assembly past these hazards and making it a responsible and effective legislative body. Meanwhile, Quezon remained in Washington, where he succeeded in 1916 in obtaining the enactment of the Jones law, which specifically stated the intention of the United States to give the Philippine Islands eventual independence. It thus gave the Islands a greater measure of self-government and provided for the election of a Senate composed of Filipinos. Osmeña, who chose to remain with the lower house (renamed the House of Representatives), was speaker of that body until 1922.

Of Osmeña at this period, J. R. Hayden writes in his *The Philippines; a Study of National Development*: "Astute, patient, tenacious, skilled in the delicate art of composing differences, and arranging compromises between his colleagues, this young assemblyman showed positive genius in parliamentary leadership. . . . By sheer industry he made himself the master of every problem to be dealt with. . . . His charm and tact made his suggestions easy to accept."

Wielding a strong influence in the Government—in power and prestige he was actually second only to the Governor General, who was appointed by the President of the United States—Speaker Osmeña was able to speed the ascendancy of Filipino self-government. Contributing factors were his position as leader of the dominant political party plus his own persuasive personality. Americans who held the post of Governor General evidenced their respect by consulting him not only about necessary legislation but also about the administration of the executive departments. In 1918 Governor General Francis B. Harrison formalized the arrangement by creating a Council of State, the Governor General acting as Chairman and Osmeña as Vice-Chairman. The Council actually functioned as a cabinet.

In 1922 a disagreement over the leadership question between Osmeña and Quezon drove a wedge between their close harmony. Osmeña maintained that a national leadership was essential for promoting Filipino self-government while Quezon advocated collective leadership. Their friendship survived, but the wedge succeeded in splitting the Nacionalista Party. In the 1922 elections Osmeña, instead of running for re-election to the House, presented his candidacy for the Senate and was elected Senator from Cebu, which position he held until his election to the Vice-Presidency of the Philippine Commonwealth in 1935. But a common objective fortified by a long-established

Blackstone Studios

SERGIO OSMENA

friendship kept the rift from remaining permanent. Osmeña supported Quezon in the legislature and before the elections of 1925 the two factions reunited to form the Partido Nacionalista Consolidado, with Quezon as leader.

It now became Osmeña's turn to journey to the United States to crusade for Philippine independence. In 1924 he was a member of the Third Philippine Mission to the United States; in 1925 he was special envoy of the Philippine Legislature to the United States; in succeeding years he was chairman of several other legislative missions; and in 1931 he was head of the Ninth Independence Mission, which culminated in passage by the American Congress of the Hare-Hawes-Cutting Act, forerunner of the Philippine Independence Act.

The Hare-Hawes-Cutting Act incited another party split, this time of more lasting consequence. Senate President Quezon and many other leaders objected strongly to certain provisions of the bill. Osmeña, after protracted wrangling with American Congressional leaders, felt that it was the best that could be secured under the circumstances. The act was contingent, however, upon the approval of the Philippine Legislature, and Quezon set about to defeat it. The "Pros" and "Antis" emerged as separate parties, and on October 17, 1933, Quezon and his Antis won: the Philippine Legislature rejected the act.

Although the two parties retained their separate identities, Osmeña and Quezon soon renewed their political cooperation. In 1934, when the latter secured passage by the American Congress of the Tydings-McDuffie Act, a modified version of the defeated act, Osmeña gave it his wholehearted support. This act provided for the complete independence of the Philippine Islands, for the adoption of a constitution, and a form of government. Ten years after the date of the inauguration of the Commonwealth Government, July 4, 1946, the Philippines are to have complete independence.

The Philippine Constitution drafted, the country prepared to elect its first President and Vice-President under the Commonwealth Government. Complete independence was now in sight and the attainment of this end could only be entrusted to "the greatest Filipinos of their generation." Instead of engaging in a political battle royal, Osmeña and Quezon buried temporary differences and ran for Vice-President and President, respectively, on a coalition ticket. Two years after the 1935 elections they merged their parties, and in 1941 were re-elected on a single party ticket—the Partido Nacionalista.

In 1938, on Osmeña's sixtieth birthday, Quezon in a public address gave a shrewd analysis of both his own and his colleague's characters: "He is by nature an evolutionist, and I have been all my life a revolutionist. . . . That and that alone was the cause of our misunderstandings. . . . I always wanted to move in a hurry—never satisfied. I always wanted to go without looking back, while he, ever measuring the distance, always looked ahead, but without forgetting what was behind. It was only for this reason that we clashed . . . but since there were never fundamentally serious differences in our aims and purposes, it has always been possible for us to join hands again."

Osmeña's responsibilities as Vice-President were by no means dwarfed by those of his chief. He filled the important position of Secretary of Public Instruction and was a member of the President's Cabinet. His became the difficult role of representing the President during his extended absences from the country and long periods of illness later. "The importance of the Vice-Presidency has been greatly enhanced," J. R. Hayden writes, "by the fact that the first person to fill the office has been the Honorable Sergio Osmeña. Preferring entrance into a coalition with the majority party to risking the national unity by fighting the Quezon-led Antis to a finish in the first Presidential elections, Mr. Osmeña brought to the support of the new Commonwealth Government his own power, prestige, and abilities as well as those of his followers, among whom were included a majority of the first-rate political leaders of the day."

In 1940, just before Quezon's six-year term had expired, a constitutional amendment changed the Presidential term to four years with right to re-election for one term. Quezon having been re-elected in 1941, it naturally followed that he would remain in office until November 15, 1943. But that day found the country occupied by the Japanese, and President Quezon, though half a world away with the Government-in-Exile at Washington, still stood as a symbol of freedom to his conquered people. It was Vice-President Osmeña himself who wrote a letter to the American Congress asking that "the ailing but still fighting President" be continued in office for the duration thereby setting "an example of loyalty and unity by giving up his constitutional right to succeed President Quezon." Thus the Philippine Constitution was temporarily suspended and Quezon was to be retained in office for the duration of the War.

On the zigzagging perilous route of the Government-in-Exile from Manila to Washington Osmeña was almost lost when his plane was grounded in the Australian desert. Following his arrival in the United States he shouldered "much more than the ordinary burden of a Vice-President" while Quezon lay helplessly ill at Saranac Lake. He represented him at meetings of the Pacific War Council and made most of the public speeches. On September 15, 1943, he was appointed chairman of the Post-War Planning Board of the Philippine Government and on July 14, 1944, chairman of the Filipino representatives of the Filipino Rehabilitation Commission, which was created by an act of the Congress of the United States to plan for the relief, rehabilitation, and reconstruction of the Philippines, and for future trade relations between the United States and the Philippines. On August 1, 1944, when his chief died, Osmeña succeeded to the Presidency. When Philippine independence is proclaimed, he will be able to run for election as President of an independent Philippines which will succeed the Commonwealth Government.

President Osmeña organized his new Government on the basis of a pledge of full post-War cooperation with the United States. He named a war Cabinet and appointed Colonel Carlos P. Romulo [43], former aide to General Douglas MacArthur [41], to the post of Philippine Resident Commissioner to the United States, in addition to his office of Secretary of Information and Public Relations. Ray Cronin, in the *Christian Science Monitor,* suggests that Quezon's passing may bring "a decided decrease in the strength of the all-powerful Quezon Nacionalista Party—abandonment of Mr. Quezon's theory of one-party government, the formation of new political factions and rebirth of old parties that went to pieces on the rocks of Quezon rule, free-for-all political fight for control of the Government as an independent republic."

Osmeña's Presidency-in-Exile lasted less than three months. In the latter part of October 1944 he returned home when he accompanied General Douglas MacArthur and the American invasion troops. After rallying the Filipinos, urging unity and summoning them to rise up and fight the Japanese when the tide of battle reached their towns, Osmeña and his Government immediately began work on the many problems confronting them as the Islands were progressively liberated. (General Ruperto Kangelon, guerrilla leader, was chosen the acting Governor of Leyte.) The President's first step was to incorporate the guerrilla troops into the reorganized Filipino branch of the United States Army. (MacArthur has praised the magnificent work of the Filipinos under his command.) The next step was to rid the Islands of all the effects of the Japanese occupation: American patterns of education were re-instituted and a board was created to investigate Filipinos suspected of disloyalty; post offices were reopened, and "victory" currency based on the American dollar was issued; Leyte Provincial Hospital, with free dispensaries and a social service center, was also reopened. A joint resolution of the United States Congress, signed by President Roosevelt on June 30, 1944, had advanced the day of liberation, formerly July 4, 1946, to take effect "as soon as possible after constitutional processes and normal functions of government have been restored" in the Islands. The same resolution also provided for the maintenance of land and air bases by the United States, in addition to naval bases for the "mutual protection" of the Philippines and the United States. Osmeña, while completely in accord with all provisions of the resolution, has expressed the hope that Philippine independence will be granted August 13, 1945, which is the forty-seventh anniversary of the landing of American forces in Manila under Admiral George Dewey.

During the Japanese occupation, Osmeña said, the Filipino people "remained faithful to the cause all Allied nations are fighting for." When Carlos P. Romulo went to the United States at the end of the year he told of the smooth transition from military to civil government that was taking place on Leyte, unlike the situation in liberated Europe. He attributed this to "the Philippines satisfaction with past American policy, advance preparations by President Osmeña, and the eagerness of the Filipino people for restoration of their constitutional rights." Few Filipinos suspected of disloyalty were actually guilty, Romulo said. President Osmeña and his Government are faced, however, with many economic problems in the rehabilitation of his people. Civilian supplies and boats for inter-island transportation are scarce, and there is threat of inflation. From his temporary capital at Tacloban, on Leyte, Osmeña said in December that when the Tydings-McDuffie Act expires the Philippines hope that a trade treaty with the United States will establish close economic ties between the two republics.

In appearance as well as temperament Osmeña carries out his complement to Quezon. His tall build accentuates his air of composure and his features give an impression of oriental calm in contrast to the mobile Latin countenance of the late President. Frank L. Kluckhohn of the New York *Times* writes that Osmeña is said "never to make snap decisions or act on impulse, but always to go into all aspects of the problem he is called on to resolve." Kluckhohn says also that Osmeña has a keen sense of humor and can illustrate Philippine history with "pithy remarks" about the people involved. When he was in the States he displayed a keen liking for dancing.

In December it was reported that Mrs. Osmeña and three of their children were being held by the Japanese as hostages. Four of the Osmeñas' sons, all of whom were educated at American colleges, were in the Filipinos' guerrilla forces. (Two were reported killed, and one missing.) María, a daughter, who was official hostess for her father in Washington, is a lyric soprano, having studied in America and Europe. Married to James M. Charnley shortly before her father's return to the Islands, she is under contract to lecture in the United States on the Filipinos. The Osmeñas, like nearly all Filipinos, are Roman Catholic.

References

Ann Am Acad 228:25-9 Jl '43
Collier's 110:27+ Ag 1 '42
For Affairs 21:289-96 Ja '43

(Continued next page)

OSMENA, SERGIO—*Continued*

N Y Sun p19 Je 9 '41

Newsweek 18:22 N 24 '41

PM p9 Ag 2 '44 por

International Who's Who 1942

Who's Who in America 1944-45

OTERO, MIGUEL ANTONIO Oct. 17, 1859—Aug. 7, 1944 Governor of the Territory of New Mexico from 1897 to 1906; author and businessman; wrote *The Real Billy the Kid* (1936), *My Life on the Frontier, 1864-1882* (1935).

Obituary

N Y Times p17 Ag 8 '44 por

OWEN, RUTH BRYAN Oct. 2, 1885- Lecturer and author; former Minister to Denmark; former United States Representative from Florida

Address: b. c/o Harold R. Peat, Inc., 2 W. 45th St., New York City; h. 903 Park Ave., New York City

Among the twenty-five women most often mentioned as eligible for a seat at the peace conference at the end of the War is Ruth Bryan Owen (Mrs. Borge Rohde), who is considered qualified by her experience as a member of the United States Congress, as the first American woman to represent her country abroad, a world traveler and nationally known lecturer, an educator, a welfare executive, and as an ardent worker for peace.

Born in Jacksonville, Illinois, on October 2, 1885, Ruth Bryan grew up in an atmosphere of politics and publicity. She was the eldest daughter of William Jennings Bryan, perhaps the most famous American orator, and the former Mary Baird, a lady of "indomitable will and biting wit" who had gone to college in a day when higher education for women was not generally approved. When Ruth was five, her father was elected to Congress from Nebraska; she often sat beside him in the House. A leader of the Democratic Party from then until his death, Bryan was nominated for the Presidency at thirty-six. It was at this convention of 1897 that he made his famous "Cross of Gold" speech: "You shall not press down upon the brow of labor this crown of thorns [the gold standard], you shall not crucify mankind upon a cross of gold!" While her father stumped the country on a whirlwind campaign tour, twelve-year-old Ruth's poise was often tested. Once, it is said, she came to class at the local school to find on her desk a magazine open to a cruel caricature of William Jennings Bryan, which she inspected without any sign of emotion. Bryan was defeated for the Presidency by William McKinley, but was renominated by acclamation in 1900 on an anti-imperialism platform. At this time his daughter was attending the Monticello Seminary at Godfrey, Illinois. In 1901 she entered the University of Nebraska, where she was active in athletics and was elected to Delta Gamma and Chi Delta Phi.

Ruth Bryan's marriage at eighteen to the artist William Homer Leavitt ended her college career, but did not dim her interest in politics. When Bryan made his third try for the Presidency in 1908 his tall, vital young daughter accompanied him as his secretary. She did not, however, permit her father's rigid Presbyterian fundamentalism to stop her from terminating an unhappy marriage by divorce in 1909 (she herself is an Episcopalian); and in May 1910, after a winter of voice study in Germany, she was married to Major Reginald Altham Owen of the Royal (British) Engineers. The next few years Mrs. Owen spent in Jamaica, British West Indies, where her husband was stationed, devoting herself to the care of her four children: Ruth Leavitt (later Mrs. Robert Lehman), John Bryan Leavitt (now deceased), Reginald Bryan Owen, and Helen Rudd Owen (later Mrs. Walter W. Harris, Jr.). After three years in the West Indies the Owens went to London at the beginning of the First World War.

When Major Owen was called to the front his wife worked jointly with Lou Hoover, wife of Herbert Hoover'[43], as secretary-treasurer of the American Woman's War Relief Fund in London, which operated five workrooms for unemployed London women and a war hospital in Devonshire. In 1915 Mrs. Owen left for the Middle East to serve as a nurse with a voluntary aid group attached to the British Army during the three-year Egypt-Palestine campaign. Major Owen became ill during the War, and so at its conclusion the family settled in Florida, where the Bryans had moved after the "Great Commoner's" retirement from President Wilson's Cabinet in 1915.

Florida, already under the Bryan spell, took the "Peerless Leader's" daughter to its collective heart. Beginning in 1919, she lectured regularly in the Lyceum and Chautauqua series, touring the country on the topics "Opening Doors" and "Modern Arabian Knights." Pointing out that "public opinion is a force like snow," she urged "those who have in their hearts a wish for international arbitration" to "bury war forever under a great white avalanche of peace." It was not long before Mrs. Owen was chairman, director, or president of "every civic, church, or educational movement in the state," including the Daughters of the American Revolution, Consumers' League, the Parent-Teachers' Association, and the 2,000-member Woman's Club. On Sundays she superintended the local Bible school. When the University of Miami was founded in 1925 Mrs. Owen was vice-president of its board of regents, and also joined its faculty as a member of the public speaking department, putting her salary into scholarships for deserving students. The University's honorary public speaking fraternity is still called Rho Beta Omicron, from the initial letters of Ruth Bryan Owen. Mrs. Owen also became the Florida member of the National Council on Child Welfare, and she was elected president of the Community Council of Civic Clubs, which included the Lions, Exchange, Kiwanis, Rotary, the Chamber of Commerce, and "every other group interested in the development of a then very young city."

In 1926 Mrs. Owen announced her candidacy for Congress, but was defeated by a 770-vote margin. Her direction of the Community Council's relief work after the 1927 hurricane increased her stature, and in that year Rollins

College honored her with the presentation of an LL. D. for her public services. In 1928, only nine years after Florida had rejected the woman suffrage amendment to the Constitution (the Nineteenth), the gray-haired Mrs. Owen (widowed the preceding December) opened her second campaign for election to Congress. Her earlier defeat had shown her that "there was not the friendliest feeling toward any woman taking her place in political life." Therefore, she says, "in order to overcome that handicap I felt it was positively necessary to meet the voters personally and let them see and hear what I had to say. I first made friends with the editors, ninety of them, in my district. I went right into their offices and frankly told them I wanted to go to Congress, and briefly what I hoped to accomplish while in office. I have great faith in the power and integrity of the press. Of course I told the editors that my advertising matter [short daily comments headed RUTH BRYAN OWEN SAYS] would reach them in due time and that they would receive also a regular run of news of the campaign."

Then Mrs. Owen acquired one of the new Ford coupes—not yet available to the public —and set off to visit each community in her eighteen-county district at least once. "When I started out with the car," she recalls, "it attracted so much attention whenever I pulled into a town that I got a crowd automatically." During the campaign the energetic candidate made some 500 speeches, an average of four daily, and sometimes addressed seven meetings in one day, snatching restorative sleep whenever she had a few minutes free. In addition to her stump speaking she gave lectures to senior and junior high school assemblies on government and citizenship, as she believes that young people's civic education is being neglected. (Later she brought a boy and a girl—chosen for good state citizenship by vote of the school children—from each county in her district to Washington, at her own expense, to study the National Government in action. And still later she persuaded the Daughters of the American Revolution in convention assembled to take over and continue these "Patriotic Pilgrimages" on a national basis.) Mrs. Owen won the Democratic primary—tantamount to election in the "solid South" state of Florida—from a seventh-term Congressman. At the ceremonial of a general election in November 1928, she polled 67,130 votes, to her Republican opponent's 36,288, and was duly elected to represent the 4th Florida District in the Seventy-first Congress, the first woman sent to Congress from the Deep South. Her absence from the one rally in Florida for Alfred E. Smith [44], the Democratic Party's Presidential candidate, "put her in wrong with many of its leaders," reported Duff Gilfond, "but it also put her into Congress from a violently anti-Catholic state."

On Mrs. Owen's arrival in Congress she was "rushed like the most popular coed on a campus," and the Foreign Affairs Committee was enlarged to include her. "Handsome elderly boys from the Senate came over to the House floor to sit by her side, and when she swung over to the higher chamber to listen to a debate dozens of Senators would leave their seats to shake hands with her. In a very short time she captivated Washington completely, over-

RUTH BRYAN OWEN

shadowing even such celebrities as Gentlewomen McCormick [of Illinois] and Pratt [of Manhattan], who are far richer." The gentlewomen referred to by Miss Gilfond were the House's two other Ruths, both Republicans, who had entered in the same election. (Other women in Congress at that time were Representative Mary T. Norton [44] of New Jersey and four ladies who had replaced their husbands, including Edith Nourse Rogers [42] of Massachusetts.) In 1929 Representative Owen's seat was contested by her former opponent, William C. Lawson, who contended that she had forfeited her United States citizenship by her marriage to a British subject. A Representative whose seat is contested is allowed $2,000 in lawyers' fees to defend his election, but Mrs. Owen chose to save the Treasury that expense by pleading her own case. Both the majority and minority reports of the Elections Committee upheld her right, although on different grounds.

In 1930 Mrs. Owen surprised everybody by voting "Aye" on the Smoot-Hawley Protective Tariff Bill, which no one expected of William Jennings Bryan's daughter. In that year, also, she proposed that the Everglades, Florida's famous swampy jungle, be made a national park. She also introduced a bill creating a Department of Home and Child, with Cabinet rank, to be made up of eight agencies then divided among six Departments (Agriculture, Commerce, Labor, Justice, Interior, and Treasury) and two separate boards, each concerned with certain aspects of the problem. "When I wish to obtain helpful information for the wives and mothers of my district," she declared, "I have to play a game of hide-and-seek with a series of separate boards and bureaus." Mrs. Owen also pointed out the overlapping, lack of coordination, and unbalanced expenditures inevitable under such a system. Her bill failed of passage, but she still hopes some day to see the formation of such a department, probably under another name—Department of Welfare has been suggested.

(Continued next page)

OWEN, RUTH BRYAN—*Continued*

Re-elected to the Seventy-second Congress in 1930, Mrs. Owen was honored the following year by the award of an L.H.D. from Russell Sage College and another from Temple University. In that year her book *Elements of Public Speaking* was published. The New York *Times* reviewer found it "sensible, practical, direct, and to the point," possessed of "much colorful personal interest." In 1932 Mrs. Owen, who had asked for a state referendum on prohibition, was defeated for renomination by James Mark Wilcox, who offered to ignore that formality. As a "lame duck" (Congressman defeated for re-election) she voted for the repeal of the Eighteenth (prohibition) Amendment, not because her "dry" views had changed, but because her district had thus made its wishes known; and she supplied "the only good-natured comment by any lame duck" in the form of a rhymed last will and testament leaving all Congress' problems to the successors.

In April 1933 President Franklin D. Roosevelt [42] appointed Mrs. Owen Envoy Extraordinary and Minister Plenipotentiary to Denmark, where she and the children had taken a trailer trip in 1931. Denmark was reportedly "delighted to be the nation to greet our first Madam Minister," particularly when she arrived to assume her duties accompanied by "an enchanting crowd of young people" (three of her children and three of her grandchildren, offspring of her daughter Ruth), and spent her first evening taking them to the famous old Tivoli amusement park. The first woman Minister was, however, "received with skepticism, and this was a decided handicap to her at the start of her mission." According to the *New Outlook*, "her clever political handling of negotiations with the Danes soon convinced them, however, that she was well chosen on a basis of ability."

Alexandra Kollontay [43], who had begun her diplomatic career in 1923 as the Soviet Union's Minister to Norway, had set a precedent of treatment on exactly the same basis as any other envoy. Mrs. Owen, on the other hand, graciously exacted the deference due a lady. As the first woman ever to appear at the annual New Year's levee in 1934, she asked the pleasure of the Court as to bowing or curtsying, and then quietly stood first in line to make her curtsy to King Christian X [43], although from the viewpoint of seniority she should have come last of all the diplomats and Cabinet members. She decorated the Legation like an American home, using her own favorite pictures and antiques, and served typical American food to "all Copenhagen's most interesting people"—and typical Danish food to visiting Americans. The vivacious United States Minister "practically never spent an evening without entertaining or being entertained"; and in Greenland, the Danish possession which she visited in 1934, the Eskimos named her Inunguak—"Dear Real Human Being." (On her return to the United States on vacation Mrs. Owen purchased 150 Christmas gifts for her Eskimo friends.) There was a brief flurry when a Senator charged that the Coast Guard cutter *Champlain* which brought her home had thereby been kept from emergency duty at the scene of the *Morro Castle* disaster; the Coast

Guard denied that rescue work had been hampered.

Three years later, soon after Mrs. Owen's return to the United States in July 1936, she was married to Captain Borge Rohde of the Danish Royal Guards, a tall, broad-shouldered Gentleman-in-Waiting to King Christian. (In classic American fashion, the couple took a wedding trip to Niagara Falls.) It was Mrs. Owen's intention to keep the name by which she was internationally known, and to continue as Minister to Denmark. By Danish law, however, the wife of a Danish subject automatically has his nationality conferred on her, thus giving Mrs. Owen a dual citizenship; and in August 1936 she therefore resigned from the Foreign Service. After this she toured the United States in a trailer with her husband, campaigning for the re-election of President Roosevelt. When an accident in which she broke her leg ended her tour for a time, the ex-Minister said, "Well, I needed a rest anyway." However, when this required rest was over she resumed her speaking for Roosevelt with speeches in Tennessee.

Since her resignation, Mrs. Owen has written several books, among them *Leaves From a Greenland Diary*, published in 1935; and *Denmark Caravan* in 1936, semi-fiction based on her own trailer trip in 1931. "The author's genuine feeling for the country to which she went as Minister, and her fine understanding of the children she is introducing to Denmark," appealed to the *Atlantic Monthly* reviewer, who considered the book "an indispensable one for an adult as well as the child traveler to Denmark." The author's choice of illustrators is considered particularly good in this book, as in *The Castle in the Silver Wood and Other Danish Fairy Tales Retold* (1939), which the *Library Journal* called, "altogether a fine addition to our fairy tale collections, and, what is more important, a popular one which children will enjoy." Of *Picture Tales From Scandinavia*, which was published the same year, it was said, "a few well-known stories have not gained by retelling, but unfamiliar ones will be a welcome addition."

In 1938 Mrs. Owen presented a modern Greenland Eskimo collection to the American Museum of Natural History. She continued her lecture career, becoming, it is said, the best-known and best-paid platform speaker in the United States and a director of the American Platform Guild since its formation. Among her "set pieces" are "New Horizons for America", "Building the Peace", "There'll Always Be a Denmark," and "After the War—What?" According to the five lecture bureaus who book her, these addresses "bring new inspiration . . . bring clarity where there has been confusion, and show us paths ahead that will bring us to a sane and abiding peace." In 1939 Mrs. Owen became visiting professor of political science to give a group of lectures each year at Monticello College, her old school in Illinois, where a scholarship had been founded in her honor four years earlier.

After the United States entry into the Second World War, Borge Rohde (Borge is pronounced Bore'ga, Rohde rhymes with soda), who had become an American citizen, entered the Coast Artillery with the rank of major and went overseas. Meanwhile his wife continued her work for world peace organization, which had occupied her attention since the First World War. At the beginning of 1943 her *Look Forward, Warrior* appeared. The book presents "a plan, and specifically a constitution, for a United Nations of the World, based to a large extent on the principles and forms of the United States Government." The *Saturday Review of Literature* called "this very short volume . . . packed with more constructive suggestions than most blueprints of the post-War world . . . a valuable contribution to the idea of world peace." Lincoln Colcord found Mrs. Owen's plan, on the other hand, "argued with calm assurance and persuasive power," but "strangely unsubstantial," as overlooking the immense difficulties involved in relinquishing sovereignty, and incomplete in its analysis of the League of Nations' failure. "Less persuasive in her own plan than in her exhortations to find one," Mrs. Owen was said by the New York *Herald Tribune Books* to have provided "perhaps the most simply and directly written of all the peace plans so far."

A speaker of great charm and effectiveness, Ruth Bryan Owen Rohde is "strikingly handsome" and distinguished in appearance. Tall and classically proportioned, she is always smartly dressed. Her hair, which was gray at forty, is "cleverly cut to the shape of a most graceful head"; her eyebrows are still dark above her drooping-lidded gray-green eyes. Her contralto voice still carries a "State Department accent"; and she used to speak fondly of "my farmers", "my fishermen," and "my little Danes." Too busy, she says, to have any hobbies beside her work and her family, Mrs. Owen loves music and travel and "often smiles to think what a joiner she has been." One of four women appointed by the President to the board of directors of the Federal Reformatory for Women (known as "Uncle Sam's Finishing School" for its campus atmosphere) which is situated near her summer home in West Virginia, she is also a trustee of the Starr Commonwealth for Boys in Michigan. Mrs. Owen is honorary president of the Women's Council for Postwar Europe, vice-chairman of the World Education Council, an executive of the Women's Action Committee for Victory and Lasting Peace, and a member of the Public Affairs Committee and the Americans United for World Organization. "Everything I've done between the First and Second World Wars," she says, "has been working toward building a mechanism for collective security for the world."

References

Am Mercury 18 :152 O '29
New Outlook 163 :37 My '34
Newsweek 6 :22-3 S 28 '35 por
American Women 1939-40
Congressional Directory 1930
Who's Who in America 1944-45

OXNAM, G(ARFIELD) BROMLEY, BISHOP (oks'nam) Aug. 14, 1891- Bishop of New York Methodist Area; author and lecturer

Address: b. Methodist Bldg., 150 Fifth Ave., New York City; h. 1165 Fifth Ave., New York City

Methodist Bishop of the New York Area, G. Bromley Oxnam, is a liberal-minded churchman whose interest in labor dates from his early California days when his father was an industrialist who "employed many men and encouraged an awareness in his son that grew during student days." Today Bishop Oxnam is, according to *Time*, one of the few bishops in the United States who are aggressively outspoken friends of labor. He is also a crusader for a new post-War world order and a champion of all minority groups. In the thirty years since his graduation from the University of Southern California he has been pastor, college professor, lecturer, author, and editor. During all his years of activity and accomplishment he has succeeded in combining his belief that "men and not things are the goal of social living" with a practical interpretation of current world problems.

Garfield Bromley Oxnam was born in Sonora, California, on August 14, 1891. His parents were Thomas Henry and Mamie (Job) Oxnam. His father was a mining engineer and a member of the board of trustees of the University of Southern California. The relationship between father and son was a close one, according to the Bishop, and they traveled over the world together. Young Oxnam attended Los Angeles High School, and received his B.A. degree from the University of Southern California in 1913. His marriage to Ruth Fisher took place on August 19, 1914. In 1915 he received the degree of S.T.B. from Boston University and then did additional graduate work at Harvard University and Massachusetts Institute of Technology. He also traveled and studied in Japan, China, and India, and in England. He was ordained in the Methodist Church in 1916, and began his career as pastor of the Methodist Church in Poplar, California, where he remained about a year. In one of his books, *Facing the Future Unafraid* (1944), Bishop Oxnam describes his introduction to his first pastorate, giving the reader an insight into the Oxnam character. He had grown up in the city and trained for service in the industrial and polyglot East Side of Los Angeles; he had not thought of Christian service in the country and was disappointed when he learned of his appointment to an unknown town in the San Joaquin Valley. When he arrived in Poplar he set out to make calls on the people of his parish; he found the president of the Church trustees out harvesting beans. Oxnam asked for another pitchfork and talked to the man as they worked together in the field.

From 1917 to 1927 he was pastor of the Church of all Nations, head of the All Nations Foundation in Los Angeles, and executive secretary of the Los Angeles Missionary and Church Extension Society. During the years from 1919 to 1923 he served as professor at the University of Southern California, giving a course in social ethics. In 1927 and 1928 he was professor of practical theology at the Boston University School of Theology. In 1928 he went to DePauw University (Indiana) to become its president. There, according to *Time,* he was popular with students because he permitted dancing, but unpopular with the American Legion because he abolished the R.O.T.C. He remained at DePauw until 1936, when he was elected a Bishop of the Methodist

Methodist Information

BISHOP G. BROMLEY OXNAM

Church and assigned to the Omaha Area. That same year, *Time* reports, Mrs. Elizabeth Dilling, author of *The Red Network*, got out an anti-Oxnam pamphlet for distribution at Omaha's eight Methodist churches. Oxnam was said to be on Mrs. Dilling's blacklist because he had abolished compulsory military training at DePauw, had once been secretary to Sherwood Eddy, and active in the Methodist Federation of Social Service. *Time* also mentions a page on Oxnam in *The Red Network*, which he is said to have provoked by an admiration for Russia.

Following the three years as Bishop of the Omaha Area, Oxnam's church leadership took him to the East, where he was Bishop of the Boston Area from 1939 until the New York appointment in 1944. In Boston he presided over the Conferences of more than 1,000 churches in four New England states. In June 1944 Bishop Oxnam assumed jurisdiction of the New York Area, covering Conferences in parts of New York, New Jersey, Vermont, and Connecticut, and including approximately 1,438 churches.

Bishop Oxnam has written the following books: *The Mexican in Los Angeles* (1920), *Social Principles of Jesus* (1923), *Russian Impressions* (1927), *Youth and the New America* (1928), *The Ethical Ideals of Jesus in a Changing World* (1941). He edited *Effective Preaching* (1929), *Creative Preaching* (1930), *Contemporary Preaching* (1931), *Varieties of Present Day Preaching* (1932), and *Preaching and the Social Crisis* (1933). He has also contributed numerous articles on social, international, industrial, and religious subjects. Two books by Bishop Oxnam have been published in 1944: *Behold Thy Mother*, and *Facing the Future Unafraid*. *Preaching in a Revolutionary Age* will be published in the fall of 1944, and *Labor in Tomorrow's World* will be published in February 1945. *Behold Thy Mother* is described as a "brief meditation on motherhood, divine and human."

In an address entitled "Ethical Idealism in a Changing World," delivered while he was president of DePauw University and published in the *Journal of the National Education Association* for April 1935, Bishop Oxnam discusses the economic, international, and religious changes taking place in the world; from competitive struggle to cooperative enterprise in the economic field, from selfish nationalism with its warring imperialism to sensible internationalism with its world law and order in the international field, and from religion grounded in authority to religion grounded in reality. These changes, basic in nature, Bishop Oxnam explains, are wrought out peaceably in some lands, through conflict in others. Beneath all this struggle is a spiritual urge; man demands life abundant, but in ignorance he may lay hold on methods that do not possess power to satisfy his dreams. Intelligent leadership will find means calculated to bring the good life to all. It is imperative that we lay hold on ideals that have been proved valid. He suggests these ideals: (1) Men and not things are the goal of social living; that is, personality is to be recognized as the supreme value. All other things are to be regarded as instrumental, instruments to be used to enrich personality. Personality-making, not profit-making, must become the major objective. (2) The solidarity of the human family, that is, we are all one family. (3) The supremacy of the common good. The attainment of this ideal demands the maintenance of democracy; fascism and communism are political and economic systems that challenge democracy and crush out freedom. (4) Equal rights for all; the right to be well-born, the right to a home, the right to play, the right to an education, the right to work. (5) Cooperation, not selfish competition, is the law of progress. (6) Love and not force is the social bond. These six ideals seem to form the basis of Bishop Oxnam's social creed; they appear, in various forms, again and again in his addresses and writings.

In 1940 the Bishop wrote of the crucifixion of democracy and freedom by the weapons of totalitarian propaganda, pointing out that if we are to preserve freedom we must move in crusade to victory over those who would crucify mankind. In 1941 Oxnam delivered the Merrick lectures at Ohio Wesleyan University. The volume containing these lectures bears the title *By This Sign Conquer*. The theme of the lectures is again that of the contemporary crucifixion of mankind and the crusade which will save it. J. S. Cleavinger, writing in the *Library Journal*, describes the book as a "stimulating volume for clergymen and social leaders and helpful to thoughtful Christian laymen."

The Bishop has expressed himself in both an idealistic and a practical way on the subject of the Second World War. This book was written before the entrance of the United States into the War, but in the preface, written at the time of the publication of the volume in 1942, the author states: "I believed from the first that the issues involved in the European conflict would involve the United States and eventually carry the War to the Pacific. I was fearful lest the democratic peoples, mobilizing their military strength to resist and destroy totalitarian aggression, might see that as their major task, rather than as a necessary and tragic first step in the fundamental endeavor to build a world community upon foundations of economic justice and brotherhood." In March 1944 Oxnam, on a *March of Time* broadcast, said that the "obliteration bombing of German cities was a revolting necessity" which the best military judgment believes to be necessary to Germany's defeat. Oxnam spoke in reply to twenty-eight clergymen and other leaders who had called for the cessation of such bombings.

A request that V-E Day be made one of religious thanksgiving and not a wild celebration was put forth by Bishop Oxnam in October 1944 in a joint pastoral letter. This message said, in part, ". . . it seems fitting that the recognition of victory should be characterized by reverence, repentence, and the stern resolve that we will do our part to build a better world."

Oxnam, in addition to his episcopal duties, is serving as president (elected in November 1944) of the Federal Council of Churches of Christ in America and as a member of the Federal Council's Commission to Study the Bases of a Just and Durable Peace. He is secretary of the Council of Bishops, chairman of the Division of Foreign Missions of the Board of Missions, a member of the Methodist Commission on Chaplains and of the General Commission on Army and Navy Chaplains, and has been serving on the National War Labor Board as a special mediator in labor disputes.

For several years Bishop Oxnam has also been active in directing the Methodist Church in a crusade for United States participation in a world government. This work has been carried on by means of meetings and by letters, from people throughout the country, sent to Washington urging the Government to participate in an international organization. In January 1944 he was one of four Methodist bishops at a meeting of 2,000 people in Brooklyn, New York, at which he urged that force be used to maintain post-War peace. In February he was one of the delegates from the Federal Council of Churches of Christ in America to visit President Roosevelt '42 for a discussion of this same matter; and in September he was a speaker at a New York Forum on the subject "Building for a Better World." Bishop Oxnam also believes that the Christianization of "the last man in the last corner of the globe" is essential to post-War peace. Late in 1944 he spoke at an American-Russian Friendship Day rally at Madison Square Garden, and at a rally in the Garden demanding severance of United States diplomatic relations with Franco '42 Spain.

In an article written soon after his appointment as Bishop of the New York Area, *Time* Magazine describes Bishop Oxnam as "social-minded", "labor-loving," and "against injustice." The Methodist Church, with its membership of 8,000,000, is, according to *Time*, the biggest of all United States Protestant churches; it is also the "most active and vocal in advocating social and economic reform." Since 1907 the Methodist Federation for Social Service has worked against all forms of social injustice, and more and more Bishop Oxnam "has become the voice of the Federation." He also takes part, continues *Time*, in editing Methodism's *Social Creed* and has repeatedly cautioned Methodists against the dangers of developing an anti-labor attitude in the minds of soldiers and sailors since the future of all lies in the ability of management and labor to work together. Other statements of the Bishop's quoted by *Time* are: "Business tomorrow will not be as usual," and "anti-Semitism is not only a threat to Jewish liberty, but to Protestant liberty, and Catholic liberty, too." His statement that the anti-Semitic attacks were an expression of incipient fascism was called by *PM*, "one of the most courageous and forthright declarations [ever made] by a New England clergyman."

The Bishop's travels have taken him to most of the countries of Europe and Asia (he has visited Russia three times); and, according to one commentator, he has covered as much as 30,000 miles a year, mostly by plane, on his preaching and lecture tours. He was a member of the American delegation to Russia in 1926, a delegate to the World Conference of Faith and Order at Edinburgh and Oxford in 1937, and in 1940 he was Enoch Pond lecturer at Bangor Theological Seminary.

He is a trustee of Boston University, Wilbraham Academy, and a member of the American Geographical Society. He is also a member of the American Academy of Political and Social Sciences, the American Historical Association, and the National Economic League. Several colleges have recognized his work with honorary degrees: he holds the D.D. degree from the College of the Pacific; the LL.D. degree from Ohio Wesleyan University, Wabash College, Indiana, and the University of Southern California; the Litt.D. degree from Boston University and Northeastern University; the D.Sc. from Rose Polytechnic Institute, Indiana; and the L.H.D. from DePauw University.

Bishop Oxnam is described as a tall, heavy-set man with a friendly but businesslike manner. He is a dynamic speaker, talking in the pulpit with "machine-gun rapidity," pounding his palm with his clenched fist to stress his points. The Bishop and Mrs. Oxnam live in New York City in an apartment near the Metropolitan Museum of Art, where they enjoy going to pursue a long-standing interest in the study of paintings. The Bishop does some painting himself and owns a few originals by famous masters. He is also interested in autograph collecting, and enjoys watching football games. The Oxnams' daughter, Bette Ruth, is employed at a motion-picture company in Hollywood. Of their two sons, Robert is an infantry officer, and Philip is an Army chaplain. Known as the "Foxhole Chaplain," Philip at the end of 1944 was commended for accompanying an American Ranger unit on a dangerous reconnaissance trip into enemy territory on the Yugoslavian mainland. *Facing the Future Unafraid*, a book of the Bishop's published in 1944, is a tribute to these soldier sons.

References

Time 43:88-92 Je 26 '44 por

International Who's Who 1942

Oxnam, G. B. Facing the Future Unafraid p73-4 1944

Who's Who in America 1944-45

Who's Who in American Education 1941-42

Who's Who in the Clergy 1935-36

PAASIKIVI, JUHO KUSTI (pä-sē'kē-vē yū'hō) Nov. 27, 1870- Premier of Finland
Address: Helsinki, Finland

Since November 1944 the head of the Council of State of Suomen Tasavalta—a title better known abroad as Premier of the Finnish Republic—has been Juho Kusti Paasikivi, who has "fewer inhibitions about talking out in meeting than most Finnish leaders." He twice headed Finnish delegations which negotiated peace with the Russians: the first time at Dorpat in 1920, the second time at Moscow in 1940. He is, moreover, one of the few conservative Finns who admits quite frankly that he likes Stalin '⁴² and doesn't find Communism too disagreeable.

Juho Kusti Paasikivi was born in Tampere in western Finland, November 27, 1870, the son of Johan August Hellsten and Karolina Welhelmina (Selin) Hellsten. Since medieval times the Swedish minority in Finland, constituting some eleven per cent of the total population, had to a large extent controlled the economic life of the country; and it was to this minority that his father, a merchant, belonged. He himself was christened Johan Gustav Hellsten, but later he "Finnified" his name.

Young Paasikivi studied law in universities in Finland, in Stockholm and Uppsala, and in Leipzig; and for a year, in 1891, he studied languages at a Czarist Russian university. He received his LL.D. in 1901, that same year became secretary of the Union of Pellervo, and two years later was elected a member of its board of directors. Under Czarist Russia, which since 1809 had ruled Finland as a semi-autonomous grand duchy, he rose to public office: from 1907 to 1913 he was a member of Parliament; from 1908 to 1909 he was Minister of Finance. In private life he has been a director of the Salama Life Insurance Company since 1910 (he became vice-president of the same company in 1918); and he served as managing director of the Kansallis Osake Pankki (National Joint State Bank) from 1914 to 1934 and as a member and vice-president of the Helsingfors Exchange from 1916 to 1930.

With the March 1917 Revolution in Russia the Russian Provisional Government of Kerensky restored representative government in Finland, but refused to give that country complete independence. At the elections of 1916 the Finnish Socialists had obtained a small majority in the Diet, however, and in July 1917 the Diet formally declared the independence of Finland. Kerensky replied by dissolving the Diet, and when the October elections gave the Finnish bourgeoisie a small majority a Cabinet was formed which excluded the Socialists. By this time the Bolsheviks had come to power in Russia and the old Diet had declared Finland a republic within Russia. It was therefore the propertied classes who were clamoring loudest of all for complete Finnish independence, and on December 6, 1917 the new Diet proclaimed Finland an independent and sovereign republic. In the meanwhile, too, the Finnish conservatives had been forming a "White Guard," and the Socialists, who regarded the elections as unjust and the White Guard as a challenge,

had been organizing a "Red Guard" of laborers and Russian soldiers. Civil war broke out. In January 1918 the Finnish Socialist Workmen's Republic was proclaimed at Viborg, and the old Government fled to Vasa. The treaty between the "Red" Government and the Russian Bolsheviks which followed confirmed Finland's independence. The "White" Government, however, concluded a treaty a few days later which made Finland Germany's ally and vassal, and in the spring of 1918 German intervention brought victory to the previously defeated White Guard.

The period of the "White Terror" began, with thousands of "Reds" executed, many more imprisoned. In the June 1918 Diet the Socialists were excluded from the register, and the crown of Finland was offered to the brother-in-law of the German Emperor. Only the defeat of Germany by the Allies in November kept Finland from becoming a monarchy. In December 1918, however, the pro-German Pehr Svinhufvud was succeeded by the White Guards' Baron von Mannerheim '⁴⁰ as regent, and six months later Mannerheim himself was defeated when he ran for President. On June 17, 1919 the Finnish Diet established a republic, and on October 14, 1920 a peace treaty with the U.S.S.R. was signed at Dorpat. Paasikivi, who had served as Finnish Prime Minister for a brief period in 1918, headed the Finnish delegation which negotiated this peace. Through it Petsamo was ceded to Finland, which thus obtained an outlet on the Arctic Ocean.

From 1924 to 1928 Paasikivi served as vice-president of the Finnish section of the International Chamber of Commerce, of which he has been president since 1928. In 1927 he was president of the Finnish delegation to the International Conference at Geneva, and since 1934 he has been a member of the advisory board of the Kansallis Osake Pankki (of which he was formerly managing director). He was made Finland's envoy to Stockholm in 1936.

This was a period of great prosperity for Finland—a period of full employment, of boom times for industry, agriculture, and foreign trade, and of social reforms. The Fascist Lappo movement, so active in the early 1930's, had been forced underground; the parties of the Left had a majority in the Diet (this did not include the Communist Party, which had been outlawed in 1923). Yet, according to Joachim Joesten '⁴², during this same period the Finnish Army was imbued with the Prussian tradition and the Nazi spirit. The Finnish High Command was made up of generals trained in Germany; the German and Finnish armies "fraternized and conspired" continuously; Germans trained the Finnish Air Force; the Finnish Navy was frankly Nazi; and German engineers helped to build the Mannerheim Line, laying out and erecting a chain of forty large air bases along the Karelian border from which German and Finnish airmen were later to operate against Murmansk and Soviet Karelia, and sink American ships in the Arctic Ocean. Shortly before the Second World War it was estimated that from sixty to seventy per cent of all Finnish students belonged to irredentist organizations, agitating for a "Greater Finland."

It was against such a background that in September 1939, shortly after the signing of the Russo-German non-aggression pact, the Kremlin invited the Finnish Government to send a delegation to Moscow for the discussion of certain unspecified points. Eventually Helsinki accepted, and Paasikivi, who not only spoke fluent Russian but who was a friend of the Russian Minister to Stockholm, Alexandra Kollontay '43, was called from his Stockholm post to lead the Finnish delegation. The Russians reportedly resented the fact that Finland sent neither its Foreign Minister nor any other Cabinet members, but in any case it seems that Paasikivi got along well with Stalin personally.

The Russian demands were that the Finns lease the harbor of Hangö for thirty years and permit the establishment of a Red naval base there; that the Red naval forces be allowed to use the port of Lappvik near Hangö, too; that five small but strategic islands in the Gulf of Finland and a strip of land on the Karelian isthmus and another on the Rybachi peninsula in the Arctic be ceded to Russia (altogether, 2,761 square kilometers). In return an area of 5,529 square kilometers in eastern Karelia would be ceded by Russia to Finland. Neither power was to make any treaty with a third power that might be directed against the other, and both were to dismantle their fortifications in the Karelian isthmus. According to Paasikivi, "The Russians would speak now of a possible attack by England, now of an attack by Germany which might also come by Finland. [Leningrad's central parts actually lay within artillery range of the Mannerheim Line.] 'But you have an agreement of friendship with Germany,' I said. 'That is the case now, but in this world everything can change.'"

Whether or not Paasikivi could have come to an agreement with the Russians if his hands had not been tied by instructions from home is not known; as it was, no agreement was reached. Things worsened when Foreign Minister Väinö Tanner joined him at the head of the delegation. "In most of the talks, while Tanner and Viacheslav Molotov '40 did the hard-headed bargaining, Paasikivi swapped jokes with Stalin and used his chuckle to smooth things over when Tanner got a little heated." But by mid-November there was a complete deadlock, and the Finnish delegation went home. At a press interview immediately after his return from his third journey to Moscow, Paasikivi announced: "I regard Stalin as a comfortable man to get on with, a man with a sense of humor." Paasikivi says he then expected that negotiations would be taken up again, and he was surprised at the "frontier incident" that followed soon after the Finnish delegation's departure. A few hours after the "incident" came a Russian ultimatum to Finland demanding the withdrawal of Finnish troops on the Karelian isthmus twelve to fifteen miles to the rear. Helsinki refused; and at dawn on November 30, 1939 war broke out. The puppet "People's Government of the Finnish Democratic Republic" was set up by a handful of Finnish

JUHO KUSTI PAASIKIVI

Communists, and it signed a pact of peace and military assistance with Moscow. The Finnish Government did not, however.

During the Russo-Finnish War of 1939-1940 Paasikivi expressed the opinion more than once that Russia's reasons were primarily defensive, even if "pathologically" defensive. He continued to say that he liked Stalin the man. "He is now waging a bloody and, in my opinion, altogether unpardonable war on Finland. This, however, cannot alter the impression made on me during negotiations." When in March 1940 it became evident that the Finns would have to make peace, Paasikivi was the logical choice as chairman of the Finnish-Russian Peace Commission, and he signed the treaty whereby Finland ceded to Russia about one-tenth of her national territory, with a population of 450,000. For a brief time after that Paasikivi, a leading member of the Unionist Party, was Minister without Portfolio in the Finnish Cabinet.

But Paasikivi's counsel did not prevail in Helsinki, which moved more and more into the German orbit. On September 24, 1940 Finland concluded a "transit agreement" with the Nazis, amounting to permission for the Nazi troops to occupy Finland and turn it into a base of attack. During the winter of 1940-1941 and the following spring the peaceful Nazi penetration went on; and on June 27, 1941 President Risto Ryti '41 declared war on Russia, thus allying Finland with Germany and her "leader of genius, Reichschancellor Adolf Hitler '42." On November 25, 1941 Finland signed the anti-Comintern pact, having consistently rejected all suggestions of a separate peace, although she had long since recovered all the territory lost the year before. The Finns fought on the Don, bombed Russian villages, launched attacks on British and American merchantmen, and although even Paasikivi told a Danish reporter in August 1942 that Finland was fighting only to "ward off Russian attacks" and that the Finns saw "no chance of peace,"

PAASIKIVI, JUHO KUSTI—*Continued*

he continued to say: "Stalin did not want war with Finland. I went to Moscow nearly three years ago to negotiate with Stalin and Molotov about the Russian demands on Finland. I am still really on that journey. Both Stalin and Molotov explained that it was essential for Russia to protect her northwestern frontiers. I am absolutely convinced that neither of these men thought it would be necessary to go to war. Stalin undoubtedly believed that we would bow to his demands."

With the Nazi reversals in Russia rumors of a separate peace between Finland and Russia floated out of Stockholm from time to time. But the Finnish Government apparently hoped that if the War continued long enough the United States, which had not declared war on Finland, would help her to get better terms from Russia than she could get by herself. Relations between Finland and the United States grew less and less warm, however. On December 8, 1942, at the Japanese Legation at Helsinki, the Finnish Prime Minister and Foreign Minister expressed their hopes that Japan would soon sink the rest of the American Navy.

In August 1943 it was reported that fifty important Finns had called on President Ryti and asked him to shelve Prime Minister Edwin Linkomies and give the post to Paasikivi. Whether there was truth in the rumor or not, Paasikivi did not become Prime Minister until a year later. On January 31, 1944, however, Secretary of State Hull [40] sent an ultimatum to Finland saying that she must break off her alliance with Germany or suffer the consequences. This was probably the most effective thing that could have been done, short of an actual American declaration of war, to produce a genuine Finnish peace move; and the next month Paasikivi arrived at Stockholm. Although he said he was there so that his wife could consult a doctor and he could catch up on his reading, everyone was sure that he was actually there to negotiate with his friend Madame Kollontay. He was quite willing to discuss Communism with reporters, too. "I am sure that after Russia has won the War," he was quoted, "Communism will further strengthen its position, wherefore there can be no question that the country will then return to capitalism and other formulas scrapped by Communism. Only the collaboration of industrialism, capitalism, and liberalism has made people strive to hoard wealth." On February 23, 1944 he left Stockholm for Helsinki, still refusing to discuss the negotiations for getting his country out of the War.

The Soviet armistice terms, it was learned only a few days afterwards, included: (1) the rupture of relations with Germany and the internment of German troops and ships in Finland, a task in which the Soviet Union was prepared to render assistance if necessary; (2) re-establishment of the Soviet-Finnish agreement of 1940 and withdrawal of Finnish troops to the 1940 boundaries; (3) the immediate return of Allied and Soviet war prisoners and civilians in concentration camps or used for labor purposes (the Finnish Board of Forestry was using Polish slave labor recruited for her by Hitler, for example); (4) questions concerning demobilization, repara-

tions, and the Petsamo region to be left for negotiations in Moscow. In general, the terms were considered mild by the foreign press, and even the Swedish Government urged the Finns to accept, promising to help feed them if they would break with the Axis.

On March 26 Paasikivi flew to Moscow, returning to Stockholm on April 1, but Finland rejected the revised peace terms which he brought back and broke off conversations, according to a Russian announcement of April 22. To the Finnish assertion that the Soviet demands would deprive their country of its independence, the Russians replied that Finland was no longer independent in any case, and that Helsinki "wants to retain Finland as a vassal of Germany." Stockholm sources reported that Finnish Right-wing elements were still contending that Germany might not lose the War. It was also said that the Finns feared that any attempt to intern or drive out the German troops in Finland would turn their country into another Italy: the result would be civil war, with the Finnish Nazis and a considerable part of the Finnish Army siding with the Nazi troops. Finland's official objections were to the payment of reparations of $600,000,000 (which the Russians said represented about one-half the estimated damage inflicted on the U.S.S.R. by the Finns during the War), but the Russians believed this an evasive move inspired by Berlin, since neither Paasikivi nor his colleague had raised this objection during negotiations.

Finland's position in the international scene did not improve after negotiations with Russia were terminated. A stiff Allied note in May to the Government (and to Hungary, Rumania, and Bulgaria), warning her to "get out of the War" and "cease aiding Germany," was followed by the blacklisting of eighty-four Finnish firms by the United States Department of State. Then, on June 16, the day after Finland had made her semi-annual war debt payment, the American State Department asked the Finnish Minister to the States, Hjalmar Procopé [43], and three Legation counselors to leave the country because of activities "inimical to the interests of the United States." At the end of the month the Germans entered Helsinki to aid the Finns against the Russians, and three days later the United States broke off relations with the little country because of this alliance with the Nazis. "There is no choice for Finland but to fight for the present and the future," said the Premier. "Otherwise she would have to abandon herself to the tender mercies of the enemy."

In the months that followed, however, Finland swung back into the Allied camp. A new Russian offensive that had started in June after a thirty-one month lull had brought the Red Army extensive gains. Throughout June and July a delicate political situation prevailed in Finland as a result, and reports persisted that a shakeup in the Cabinet was imminent. Demands for peace were made by leading Finns, who insisted that Paasikivi be asked to form a new Government, and rumors of peace overtures appeared in the press several times. Paasikivi himself is said to have criticized the Linkomies Government openly for not accepting the Soviet peace conditions, declaring that it had only itself to blame for the predicament.

The situation began to crystallize on August 1 when President Risto Ryti resigned, the penalty, said the New York *Times* reporter, for his attempt to sell Finland to the Nazis behind the back of Parliament. Mannerheim was appointed President in his place by a special parliamentary decree legalizing the appointment without an election. This was followed three days later by the resignation of Premier Linkomies and the formation of a so-called "peace Cabinet," headed by Antti U. Hackzell, an intimate friend of Paasikivi's. A whole month elapsed, however, before announcement came from Helsinki on September 3 that a truce with Russia had been reached. Under its terms all German troops were to be cleared from the country by the 15th, while all those remaining were to be disarmed and turned over to the Allies as prisoners of war, and Finland was to publicly announce her break with Germany. The armistice terms were announced on the 19th: they repeated the provision regarding German troops; in addition the Finns were to pay a $300,000,000 reparation debt over a six-year period; the 1940 border was to be recognized, giving Russia Karelia and Petsamo; the headland near Helsinki was to be leased to Russia for fifty years as a military base; the merchant fleet, airdromes, and various military supplies were to be put at the disposal of the Allies; and Finland's military force was to be reduced to a peacetime footing.

In September, after the resignation of the Premier because of ill health, Urho Castren was named Premier. Although under the new Government political prisoners were released, Axis subjects were interned, and diplomatic relations with Japan were broken off, a large section of northern Finland remained occupied by German troops, in contradiction to the terms of the armistice. This provoked criticism from the Russians, who, at the end of the month, sent troops to assist the Finns in driving out the Nazis. Not until the end of December, however, was it possible to announce that all the Germans had finally retreated beyond the borders. Meanwhile, another Government crisis loomed. In November it was revealed that certain units of the Finnish White Guard Militia had refused to be disarmed in accordance with the armistice provision banning Fascist and pro-Nazi organizations, and an open break with the Government seemed unavoidable. Inharmonious elements within the Cabinet and the killing of two Russian officers in Helsinki heightened the political tension. Finally, on November 11, Castren resigned, and Paasikivi was made Premier. Included in the new Government for the first time was a Communist, Yrjoe Leino, who was made Assistant Minister of Labor. On assuming his post Paasikivi pledged his Government to "work in mutual understanding with the Soviet Union, and meticulously to fulfill the armistice terms." On December 11 it was announced that Finland's army had been completely demobilized in accordance with these terms.

Premier Juho Kusti Paasikivi is a ruddy-faced, square-headed man. He has an "Elihu Root cast of eye, hair clipped *en brosse*, and a paunch." In 1897 he was married to Anna Matilda Forsman, who died in 1931; he has been married to his second wife, the former Alli Valve Hilden, since 1934.

References

Life 8:10-11 Mr 4 '40 por
N Y Herald Tribune II p3 F 20 '44 por
N Y Sun p15 N 23 '43
Scholastic 44:8 F 28 '44 por
International Who's Who 1942
Who's Who in Central and East Europe 1935-36

PACCIARDI, RANDOLFO (pa-chär'dē ran-dol'fō) Jan. 1, 1899- General Secretary of the Italian Republican Party; journalist

Address: b. c/o L'Italia Libera, 100 Fifth Ave., New York City; h. 190 Waverly Pl., New York City

Not the least serious of the problems facing the Allied Governments is this: How shall the countries released from Fascist domination be governed? Shall the former Fascist leaders who surrender to the Allies be permitted to retain their power on grounds of military and political "expediency," or shall popular movements, led by anti-Fascists who are working in the European underground or are refugees in the United States and Great Britain, be allowed to join the Allies in battle today and in democratic government tomorrow? One of the leading champions for the rights of these popular movements is Randolfo Pacciardi, "Italy's foremost anti-Fascist military hero."

Since the beginnings of the Black Shirt movement in Italy, Pacciardi has been a militant foe of Fascism. He fought against it first openly in Italy and then in the underground and in Spain, where he commanded the Italian division of the International Brigade. Early in 1944, after having tried unsuccessfully to join the American Army, he was in the United States organizing a Free Italian movement and seeking permission from the State Department to return to Italy to fight the Germans. By summer he finally received the permission.

A veteran of the First World War, Randolfo Pacciardi was born in Grosetto, Italy, January 1, 1899, the son of Giovanni and Elvira (Guidoni) Pacciardi. He was a sensitive child but soon learned a lesson which was to prove of inestimable value to him later in life. "At about the age of twelve," he relates, "one of the bigger boys with whom I played and who had always teased me infuriated me to such a degree that I pounced upon him and gave him a beating. I feel that this was what finally woke me up. Suddenly, I was no longer afraid. I had found that faith in myself that is so necessary in every human being."

From childhood Pacciardi had been an ardent Italian nationalist. His boyhood heroes were Dante and Mazzini, and at fifteen he wrote an article, "Dante and Mazzini," which was published in a local newspaper. (Years later, in 1921, he wrote a book on Mazzini.) When the First World War broke out, Pacciardi volunteered for military service as soon as he was old enough. Decorated three times for bravery (he received both the British and the Italian Military Crosses), the young

RANDOLFO PACCIARDI

man became an officer of the Bersaglieri, the infantry corps of sharpshooters.

After the Armistice, Pacciardi returned to civilian life and prepared for a career in the law, taking his Doctor of Law degree at the University of Rome in 1921. He was soon engaged in another struggle, this time against the rising tide of Fascism within his own country. In 1923, the same year in which he was married to Luigina Civinini, he organized a Free Italy Movement in opposition to Mussolini's '42 Black Shirts. Of this he has said: "Mussolini had been trying to prove that he truly represented youth and its wishes. I organized 100,000 young people who were against Fascism. I dreamed of overthrowing Mussolini's regime." The Fascists already had the upper hand in Italy, but Pacciardi continued the struggle. In 1924 he served as defense counsel for an Italian newspaper which had accused the prominent commander of the Fascist Militzia, General Italo Balbo, of being responsible for the murder of a priest, Don Menzoni. Pacciardi won the case for the newspaper but in so doing sacrificed his own safety in Italy. He was wounded twice when Fascists tried to assassinate him in the streets.

In spite of these attempts upon his life, Pacciardi continued his work in Italy. In 1926 the Fascists passed a law which permitted arrest and deportation of all anti-Fascists to penal colonies without trial. Pacciardi was arrested and sentenced to five years imprisonment. He managed to escape, however, and fled into Switzerland, where he made contact with the Italian underground and began intensive propaganda work. So effective were his activities that *in absentia* Pacciardi was tried three times in Italy for his work abroad. He became almost a legendary figure to the people of Italy, and when in 1933 Picciardi uncovered a Fascist spy ring in Switzerland, Mussolini determined to get him out of that country. As Pacciardi himself tells the story: "Mussolini brought pressure on the Swiss

Government, threatening to bring two divisions to the Swiss frontier if I was not expelled." The Duce succeeded at last and Pacciardi went to France, where he continued his anti-Fascist propaganda activities until 1936.

When civil war broke out in Spain in 1936, and it became clear that the Fascist governments of Italy and Germany were to be open allies of the Rebels under General Franco '42, Pacciardi began to organize a legion of anti-Fascist Italians to fight in Spain on the side of the Loyalist Government. Within two years the membership of that legion grew from 500 to 5,000. "Its mere existence," Pacciardi later wrote, "was of greater value to the anti-Fascist movement in Italy than all our political work in the previous ten years." Pacciardi became the commander of the Garibaldi Brigade, part of the International Brigade—an army made up of Americans, British, French, and men of other nationalities who had joined together to combat the Axis in Spain. He participated in seventeen battles, and on five occasions received citations for bravery. Wounded during the battle of Madrid, he was sent to France to recuperate, but when the Fascist attack at Guadelajara was launched, Pacciardi hurried back to Spain to lead a counterattack which proved disastrous for the enemy. His use of loudspeakers to broadcast propaganda against Mussolini was held an important factor in the victory. "It was believed that the bewilderment of the Fascist soldiers in finding their own countrymen on the enemy side was a contributing cause to their defeat in that battle."

In 1938 Pacciardi visited the United States to mobilize Italians in this country for the fight in Spain. But the war ended before he could return with an army and Pacciardi went back to France to continue his anti-Fascist propaganda work. There he organized an Italian youth movement and edited a newspaper with a militantly anti-Fascist policy.

With the fall of France Pacciardi moved the headquarters for his anti-Fascist activities to the United States. Here he resumed his fight for a free Italian legion which would "organize Italians everywhere to fight against Fascism." In an article published in the *Nation* in October 1942 Pacciardi described the work which such an organization would do. He pointed out that until Italy actually faced military defeat, invasion of her own territory, there was no possibility of an open revolt there. But the psychological effects of the appearance of anti-Fascist Italians, fighting on the side of the Allied invaders, would be of tremendous value in inspiring the Italian people to overthrow their Fascist leaders.

At the International Congress of Italians of 1942, held in Montevideo, Uruguay, this free Italian Legion, designed "to be their equivalent of the Fighting French," was officially organized, with Pacciardi as its leader and Count Carlo Sforza '42 as one of its backers. The Legion was to have a military rather than an administrative function. According to Pacciardi: "Our position is not identical with that of those national groups which had constitutionally established governments until they became a prey to the Nazi conquerer.

Our National Committee will do everything in its power to help the Italian people win their liberation. But its functions cease at their frontier; Italy, when free, will choose its own government."

Since 1942 Pacciardi has been traveling through the United States trying to recruit volunteers for the Legion, writing newspaper and magazine articles, and editing the newspaper *Italia Libera*. He has published a book, *Il Battaglione Garibaldi* (1938), which is an account of anti-Fascist activity in the Spanish Civil War.

The Allied invasion of the Italian mainland, Mussolini's downfall, and the subsequent establishment and Allied recognition of the Government of King Victor Emmanuel [43] and Marshal Pietro Badoglio [40]—all led to an intensification of Pacciardi's efforts to return to his homeland and fight for democracy. He made no effort to conceal his disapproval of the new Italian Government, calling it anti-democratic and corrupt. He pointed out, in an article entitled "Traitors Cannot Lead," that King Victor Emmanuel had betrayed his country two decades ago by calling in Mussolini, by defending him, by declaring war in Abyssinia, by signing an alliance with Nazi Germany, and by aiding Franco's forces in Spain; finally, when things looked bad, he had betrayed Hitler [42]. Pacciardi continued, "We anti-Fascist Italians want to fight the Germans. If we are given no other choice than to fight the Nazis and Fascists under the flag of Savoy, it means that the democratic powers have deliberately renounced Italian anti-Fascists as their allies. Yet they are the only ones who can arouse the whole of Italy against the Germans." According to Gaetano Salvemini [43], if Pacciardi and his volunteers had been available in Sicily the day that Mussolini fell and had been sent immediately to Civitavecchia with intentions of marching on Rome, the Germans might have had no opportunity to occupy Italy. In May 1944 he resigned from the International Honorary Board of the Free World Association, along with Salvemini and G. A. Borgese, in protest against Carlo Sforza's and Alberto Tarchiani's joining of the Badoglio Cabinet.

After eighteen years of exile, Pacciardi returned to Italy in June 1944 on a mission which had the full approval of the United States. In an interview before his departure Pacciardi said he would place himself at the disposal of the Allied military command, adding: "We Italians hope that . . . not an inch of Italian national territory will be separated from our country. . . . Peace can only be maintained if European territorial problems are solved with justice."

Within a month the once famous organ of the Italian Republican Party, *Voce Republicana*, which had been suppressed during the Fascist regime, resumed publication. Its first, challenging editorial was written by Pacciardi. He made it clear that the Republican Party would be strongly left and at the same time have nationalistic tendencies. In a series of sharp criticisms of the Allies (also printed in the *Voce*) Pacciardi pointed out that the Italian Government had only incomplete control of the territory south of Salerno, and

that Sardinia and Corsica were under Allied high commissioners, a situation he held to be abnormal. His bitterest complaint was against the Allies' backing of a "monarchistic, Fascistic Italy," and their refusal of the Italian offer of military contributions to the Allied fighting forces.

Pacciardi says of himself: "I have my weaknesses and fears as every man does. I am rather nervous, but it reacts in such a way that in critical moments it turns into calmness. I am naturally pessimistic, too, but my pessimism watches over my idealism." Youthful-looking, serious, and firm in manner, he says of his plans for the future: "All I wish is to be allowed to go back to fight the Germans. I will go anywhere to do this. To Italy. To Yugoslavia. Anywhere. I would like to organize guerrillas, shock troops. Or I would be willing to serve under any military authorities of the United Nations. The only thing I do not want is to compromise with Fascism."

References

N Y Post Mag p33 N 22 '43 il pors
Nation 155:299-300 O 3 '42

PALMER, JOHN LESLIE 1885—Aug. 5, 1944 British author, dramatic critic, and editor; member of Permanent Secretariat of the League of Nations (1920-39); member of the British delegation to the peace conference in Paris in 1919; better known for his literary criticisms than as a diplomat; three of his works are *The Comedy of Manners* (1913), *Molière* (1930), *Ben Jonson* (1934).

Obituary

N Y Times p17 Ag 8 '44

PAPANDREOU, GEORGE (ANDREAS) (pä-pän-drä'ü än-drä"äs') Jan. 1888- Premier of Greece
Address: b. c/o Greek Government, Athens; h. Kastri-Kifissiar, Greece

When George Papandreou took office in Cairo in May 1944 as the new Premier of the Greek Government-in-Exile, he said: "I am coming as a crusader of our national union. . . . Our motto must be 'one country, one government, one army.'" These words were greeted with cheers by the people of the small Mediterranean country which has suffered so acutely from invasion and famine, political disunity and civil strife. Greece has since been liberated from German domination, and the Government has returned to Athens—and to a civil war.

The son of Andreas Papandreou, George Andreas Papandreou was born in Patras, Greece, in January 1888. He was graduated from Athens University with an LL.D. about 1911, and also studied at Berlin and Leipzig Universities. He practiced law in Athens, and in 1915 he began his political career as Prefect of Chios. He then joined, in Salonika, the provisional government of national defense formed by the late Venizelos, which brought Greece into the First World War on the side of the Allies after having forced the abdication of the pro-German King Constantine in 1917. From 1917 to 1920 Papandreou was Governor General of the Aegean Islands; then in 1923, dur-

GEORGE PAPANDREOU

ing the regime of General Plastiras, he was Minister of the Interior. He was elected a member of the Greek Parliament in 1923 from the constituency of Lesbos, which returned him until 1936. From 1929 to 1933 he was Minister of Education in the Government of Premier Venizelos. As Minister of Education he was responsible for many progressive educational and ecclesiastical reforms and for the building of 4,000 new schools.

In 1935 Papandreou seceded from the Left wing of the Liberal Party to which he belonged to form the Republican Socialist Party. During most of the years of the Metaxas '40 dictatorship from 1936 to 1940 he was an exile on Andros and Kythera islands, released after the outbreak of war between Italy and Greece in 1940. After the Nazi occupation of the country he used his influence among the Greek political parties and in the underground movement to encourage united action against the Axis. The Germans at last arrested him for what they considered an attitude inimical to their occupation, and he was held in the Averoff prison in Athens where he is said to have worked in his cell on the plans for a Greek constitution. He made his escape from prison ten days before going to Cairo to take part in the newly formed Government.

The types of Greek governments since the end of the First World War have been as variable as the personalities behind them; the New York *Herald Tribune* points out that Greece's political past contains "dynamite for the future." Except for the interest and friendship of Great Britain, there appears to be little in the story of King George II '43 to give him any assurance of a stable position on the throne should he return to it. Between 1917 and March 25, 1924, when the General Assembly proclaimed a republic in Greece and the nation's name was changed from "Kingdom of Greece" to "Hellenic State," George had been a banished Diadoch, an unpopular and exiled king. During part of his exile he lived in London (where he is always welcomed as the great-

grandson of Queen Victoria) and Greece continued as a republic with Eleutherios Venizelos as Premier and head of the Liberal Party until his defeat by Tsaldares in 1933. Later when George Kondylis, War Minister in the Tsaldares Cabinet, took over the Government, in October 1935 by means of an Army coup—proclaiming Greece a monarchy and himself the Regent—George was recalled to the throne. After both Kondylis and Venizelos died George arranged in August 1936 for the return of Metaxas, the Monarchist leader who had been Greek Chief of Staff under George's father, Constantine, and Metaxas appointed himself dictator. The dictatorship of Metaxas has been described as "a mixture of a National Socialist regime and the capitalist state of the eighteenth century." Neither the King nor dictator was popular but the people were powerless to do anything about the existing state of affairs as all democratic demonstrations were repressed by Metaxas.

On April 6, 1941 the Nazis invaded Greece. By this time Metaxas was dead and the late Alexander Korizis '41 was Premier. Accused of Fifth Column activity, Korizis committed suicide and on April 21 Emmanuel Tsouderos was appointed Premier. On April 22 George and the Government abandoned Athens for Crete and the Axis bombing of Greece began its devastating work. George again went to London, reaching there in September 1941. He had formed a new Cabinet in June, retaining Tsouderos as Premier, and this new Cabinet was then recognized as the Greek Government-in-Exile and transferred to Cairo in the fall of 1942. It was quite clear, however, that the Greek people did not want a return to a dictatorship—nor, for that matter, did they seem to want a king, since an effort had been made in February to depose George, and it was agreed that a national plebiscite would be held after the liberation of Greece to decide whether or not George would be accepted. George agreed to this plan and promised a truly representative government if he should come back. The following summer, when George again promised free elections, the *New Republic* wrote: "George's democratic gestures in Cairo are to be interpreted as the maneuvers of a man, unsure of himself, fishing for an invitation to come back home."

As the Nazi occupation of Greece continued, armed underground political groups which had formed began a feud that threatened to jeopardize the anti-Nazi fight. The most powerful of these groups, known as EAM from the initials of the Greek words for National Liberation Front, was a liberal coalition group corresponding roughly to the organization of Marshal Tito '43 in Yugoslavia. Its guerrilla cadres fought under the name of ELAS (Greek Popular Liberation Army). The ELAS cadres were estimated in 1944 at more than 40,000 regulars and 100,000 reserves, making it the largest guerrilla organization in Greece. EDES, the Greek National Democratic Army, the second largest guerrilla organization, had an estimated following of 10,000. Also a liberal group, but with what the New York *Times* called middle-of-the-road leanings, it operated under the leadership of Brigadier General Napoleon Zervas, who had sworn his allegiance to the King. In the fall of 1942 there were numerous clashes between EDES and ELAS; on August

6, 1943 six guerrilla leaders were smuggled out of Greece and they soon appeared in Cairo to demand that King George stay out of Greece (after its liberation) until the people could choose a post-War government. Although the Cabinet endorsed this demand, the King objected; the guerrilla envoys therefore returned to Greece, and civil war was resumed.

The Tsouderos Cabinet continued in power until April 1944, when King George, knowing that Greek affairs were not progressing satisfactorily, flew to Cairo, as *Time* Magazine said, "to steady the rocking boat of the Greek Government-in-Exile." He persuaded liberal Sophocles Venizelos, son of the former Greek Premier, to become temporary Premier. Wrote *Time*: "Popular Premier Venizelos knew what most Greeks in the Middle East urgently wanted—an end to the old Tsouderos Cabinet's dilatoriness, a broadened government capable of administering liberated Greece until elections could be held. His crushing task was to find the right Ministers for a 'Panhellenic' Government, men who would be acceptable to fighting Greeks in Greece, where the Leftist EAM dominates."

Papandreou, colleague of the Premier's late father, Eleutherios Venizelos, seemed the right person to form this Government. Reconstruction plans were begun immediately upon his arrival in Cairo, and the tense crisis which had been gripping Greek politics seemed to lessen. In May informal parleys were held at a small hotel at Beirut, Lebanon, all political parties and national resistance groups being represented at these meetings. Blueprints for a new Greek Cabinet were formed and the new Cabinet was sworn in. George Papandreou, Social Democrat, the third Greek Premier within a fortnight, assumed the twin portfolios of Premier and Minister of Foreign Affairs, as well as temporary War Minister. The feeling that the King had become too autocractic had been steadily growing; it was evident that a more democratic form of government was wanted. George himself sensed this and again declared his willingness to await the result of a post-War plebiscite before attempting a return to the throne. The representatives at Lebanon agreed on a *modus vivendi* which provided that until the War ended all questions regarding a permanent regime should be put aside, and that all guerrilla bands fighting the Germans should be reorganized into a new national army making common cause under the Government's orders.

The new Cabinet headed by Papandreou did not include representatives of the Leftist resistance group or of the Communist Party, although Papandreou had notified the heads of these groups that he was keeping four Cabinet posts open for them. In a joint letter they replied that they were *not* satisfied with the preliminary discussions. The situation therefore became complex: unless the Government included EAM it could not command support of the ELAS guerrilla bands inside Greece. By July 8 there had been no reconciliation and, moreover, inside the country there had been formed a new provisional government opposing the new national coalition Government in Cairo. In August EAM asked that Papandreou resign, with the apparent idea that with Papandreou removed from the Cabinet the Government's solidarity would be impaired and EAM would

have a better chance of achieving its ends. The demands of EAM were considered at an all-day Cabinet meeting, but were rejected unanimously. However, in a speech to the Ministers (and in a reply drafted to EAM) the Premier said that "in no case would the person of the Premier be allowed to form an obstacle to achievement of national unity." This Cabinet crisis was finally ended on August 18 with EAM's decision to join the Cabinet. The EAM-sponsored Political Committee of National Liberation, consisting of political units besides those in the Leftist EAM, and the Communist Party also decided to participate in the Government, and five members of EAM came out of their mountain hide-outs in Greece to be sworn in as members of Papandreou's Cabinet. During the summer die-hard Royalists in Cairo and die-hard Leftists in Greece continued to disagree; there were occasional mutinies among soldiers who were disgruntled by what they considered a Royalist Government; and Premier Papandreou, to use the words of *Time*, was "pitched and tossed in the blanket of Greek politics."

Then, in October 1944, after three years and six months of Axis domination—during which time, it has been estimated, 500,000 Greeks were executed or died from starvation and mistreatment—Greece was liberated. Athens was jubilant. However, with "all Peloponnesus under ELAS thumb" (to quote a New York *Times* headline), the city was the scene of victory parades that led to street battles and rioting. In November, Premier Papandreou, to avoid more civil strife, announced that the ELAS would police Greece until December 1, when the maintenance of order would be placed in the hands of a nonpartisan army under the War Ministry. It was also decided that all guerrilla groups would be dissolved a few weeks later. This order was issued after a conference between Papandreou and Lieutenant General Ronald Scobie, British commander in chief in Greece. The New York *Times* quoted the Premier as saying: "After the complete liberation of Greece our heroic resistance is ended. Thus it is natural that ELAS and EDES units be demobilized."

By November 4 British troops and Greek patriots had driven the Germans completely out of Greece, but, as *Life* points out, Greece is now in "very bad shape," with 80 per cent of the children tubercular and 30 per cent of the real wealth of Greece stolen or destroyed. Also, in *Time*'s words, "Greece is not free from the twin problems of inflation and the EAM." M. W. Fodor, writing from Athens for *PM*, presents a more cheerful note: "The revolution now occurring in Greece is probably the calmest, quietest political change that has marked the Balkans in recent years. . . . Although 'incidents' are unavoidable, the dignified emergence of a nation after nearly nine years of dictatorship . . . is impressive." That Premier Papandreou sees the possibility of the spread of revolution and communism in Greece was evident in his first speech on home soil in which he said: "Our aim is not only for national liberation but for complete integrity of our nation."

The New York *Times* felt that the country is faced by a more critical post-War situation than any of the other European nations. Will the demobilization of the guerrilla organiza-

PAPANDREOU, GEORGE—*Continued*

tions, other commentators asked, and the formation of a Regular Army be satisfying to a people whose patriotism led them into a fervor for Left-wing organizations? Will a plebiscite decide in favor of George II, or in favor of a republic? Do the Greeks want their country to be a "British sphere of influence," or, as *PM* expresses it, "will there be a democratic Greek Government or King George, riding in on a British imperial chariot?"

The situation exploded in early December. Accounts vary widely, but what happened was approximately this: The Papandreou Government issued an order to disarm and disband the ELAS Resistance Army, claiming that "it would be impossible to proceed with the task of establishing a nationally representative Government so long as armed ELAS groups controlled much of rural Greece"; later it charged that the ELAS was "conducting a brutal reign of terror throughout the countryside," and was planning a Left-wing revolutionary *coup d'état*. The National Liberation Front, on the other hand, claimed that its ELAS needed arms to protect itself from police brutality, and the country from a royalist coup by the Rightists; certain units of the Regular Army were, it claimed, reactionary and determined to wipe out the EAM, and the Army was not required to lay down its arms. According to Joseph G. Harrison of the *Christian Science Monitor*, political leader Themistokles Sophoulis declared that "one of the principal causes of the present strife was the refusal of Premier Papandreou to lay down power after the liberation of Greece from the Germans. Mr. Sophoulis said that it had been agreed when Mr. Papandreou went to Cairo to form the Greek Government that as soon as Greece was freed the Premier would resign and permit all parties to reach the political balance which most nearly met the country's needs." According to reports, however, Papandreou's resignation had been refused by the King.

On December 1 General Scobie broadcast to the Greek people to remind them that the British troops had come to Greece, "first to drive out the invader, secondly to bring relief, and thirdly to help restore prosperity," and he announced that he "stood firm behind the existing constitutional Government until the State could be re-established with legal armed force behind it and free elections could be held." On the 2nd six EAM representatives resigned from the Cabinet in protest against the disarmament order, and a mass protest demonstration was held the following day in Constitution Square. According to the official Greek and British version, bombs were thrown at policemen and some were forcibly disarmed; the EAM claim, supported by a report from *Life* photographer Dmitri Kessel, is that police fired on the demonstrators without provocation. At any rate, civil war broke out. A general strike was called by the National Liberation Front, which cut off all public utilities in Athens and stopped the unloading of UNRRA relief ships, leaving many Greeks without food. It was soon reported that the ELAS had taken Salonika and established a "proletarian dictatorship." While the

United States maintained a much criticized "hands off" policy, the British took an even more criticized part in supporting the Greek Government. General Scobie was commander in chief of Allied forces in Greece, including the ELAS and EDES (by the Caserta Agreement of September). Ordered to take over military command of Athens and to restore and maintain order by whatever measures were necessary, he thereupon prepared to fight "a full campaign" with troops, planes, tanks, and field artillery.

"For three or four days, or more," Prime Minister Churchill [42] reported to the British Parliament, "it was a struggle to prevent a hideous massacre in the center of Athens." The EAM already held and governed much of the countryside on its own terms. On December 12 Scobie conferred with the EAM emissary, Porphyrogennis, giving as his terms that the ELAS, being under his [Scobie's] command, should carry out his orders to evacuate Attica, and that EAM supporters in Athens and Piraeus should lay down their arms. But on the 13th ELAS forces shelled Athens with heavy guns, and also made "determined attacks" on Regular Greek and British troops. Scobie thereupon opened a tank assault on the ELAS concentrations. According to one description, ELAS had the men but not the arms to win the bloody civil war; while Scobie had the arms but only a small number of troops. On Christmas Day Churchill and his Foreign Secretary, Anthony Eden [40], arrived in Athens for conferences. The outcome was the naming of a regent, subject to the King's approval (Premier Papandreou had advocated a three-man regency). This regent was Archbishop Damaskinos, whose surname happened also to be Papandreou. By the end of the year, however, the situation had not been entirely resolved.

Papandreou is described by *Time* as a "tall, stoop-shouldered man with a mighty tongue and a little mustache," who utters "firm, authoritative commands," and sometimes speaks "bitterly" and "passionately." He was married in 1913 to Sofia Mineiko. After the termination of this union Papandreou was married again, to the former Kyveli Theodoridou, in 1938. He has two sons, George Papandreou, Jr., and Andreas G. Papandreou, the elder a former Harvard University instructor, who in 1944 is in the United States Navy. For many years Papandreou has had a home on Mytilene, the island home of the poet Sappho. He himself is the author of *The Future of Greece* (1913), and a number of his speeches have been published. He also organized the National Theatre of Greece.

References

C S Mon p2 Ap 29 '44
N Y Sun p18 My 1 '44
Time 44:28 My 8 '44
European Who's Who 1932

PARKER, LOUIS N(APOLEON) Oct. 21, 1852—Sept. 21, 1944 Dramatist, composer, and pageant-master; probably best known to American audiences as the author of *Disraeli*; has written alone or in collaboration more than 100 dramatic works, among them *The Vaga-*

bond King, The Monkey's Paw, Pomander Walk, The White Sister, and *Mr. Garrick*

Obituary

N Y Times p19 S 22 '44

PEIRCE, WALDO   Dec. 17, 1884-   Artist; author

Address: b. c/o Midtown Galleries, 605 Madison Ave., New York City

"The American Renoir," bearded and Bohemian Waldo Peirce, made news again in July 1944 when his *Maine Swimming Hole* took first prize of $2,500 in the nationwide Pepsi-Cola Competition for American Artists, held under the auspices of Artists for Victory, Inc. The painter has a legendary past in which he "is pictured individually and severally as a Gargantua, an Elizabethan husky, a Paul Bunyan, or a 'Man-Mountain' Dean." "Gusto is a word that always comes to mind in viewing Peirce's work for it is carried out *con brio* with immense verve." His prize-winning painting was shown with the group of 150 canvases, selected from 5,000 entries, in the "Portrait of America" exhibition at New York's Metropolitan Museum of Art in October; it has also been reproduced in the Pepsi-Cola Company's 1945 calendar.

Waldo Peirce was born on December 17, 1884, in Bangor, Maine, the son of Mellen Chamberlain and Anna (Hayford) Peirce. He received his preparatory education at Phillips Academy, Andover, Massachusetts, then entered Harvard in 1903. He took a prominent part in athletics, playing on the football team. He also "made" Professor Charles Copeland's classes in English, considered an indication of literary promise; some of his best friends thought he would be a poet. But Waldo and his brother Hayford—now an authority on Byzantine art—were both much more interested in making sketches and cartoons for the Harvard *Lampoon.* After graduation Waldo Peirce enrolled in the Art Students' League in New York City, later studying at the Académie Julien in Paris. His parents had no objection to his art career, and his mother often went abroad to stay with him. In 1912, while on a visit to Rome, he decided to break away from formal training and begin to paint for himself. His first picture was *Ruins, Roman Forum,* painted in oils on a wooden panel. But architecture, critics have remarked, is not Peirce's forte.

For the next twenty years Peirce lived abroad, a semi-expatriate who returned to the United States only on visits to his family. He took an apartment in Paris as headquarters, and then roamed about Europe in search of adventure. In 1912 he went to Spain, where he married his first wife, also an artist, and a follower of Zuloaga. The Peirces took a house in Segovia and painted in an old church that Zuloaga had turned into a studio. The work that Peirce did at this time is considered mediocre. With the coming of the First World War he left Spain for the United States, via England. But he returned to France in 1915 to drive a Model-T Ford for the American Ambulance Unit, in the Vosges and "up and down the shell-shattered roads to Verdun," and was awarded the Croix de Guerre for valor under fire. Somehow he

WALDO PEIRCE

found time to do "a whole galaxy of military portraits, honest and realistic, though hurriedly executed." And one day in December, he recalls, "3,000,000 beards, including those of marshals and generals and Peirce's, were shaved off," because gas masks wouldn't fit otherwise. When America entered the War, Peirce was appointed to the Intelligence Division of the United States Army and was stationed in Madrid, where he spent a good deal of time copying Goya, from whom, it is said, he learned to portray movement.

After the War Peirce lived off and on in Paris, where he still maintained his apartment in the Rue Lille. This apartment was occupied by so many unknown guests during the War that Peirce never knew whom he would find in his bed. "He remembers that the Tolstoi family made his flat their headquarters, drinking tea through the night and finally making off with many books." A year in the south of France, near Monet's garden in Giverny, stimulated his impressionistic ideas. Then, in 1920 following a divorce from his first wife, he was married again and went to French Africa, where he spent three years in Tunis, painting the Arab scene. Later he was "corrupted by the Matisse '43 stuff," an influence that surged up repeatedly in his work until the '30's. In 1927 he went back to Spain with Ernest Hemingway, and the liberating influence of Goya almost obliterated the tendency to loose composition and soft form that Matisse had engendered. This was the period of his Pamplona bull pictures, full of violent movement and rich color.

At the end of the '20's Peirce returned to America to "paint things closer to his own nature, broad, generous, devoid of complexities." After a second divorce, he was married, in 1930, to Alzira Boehm, a rising young artist whom he had met at an exhibition of Matisse. The Peirce twins were born a year later in Paris, and soon afterward the artist and his family settled in Maine, and Peirce started

PEIRCE, WALDO—*Continued*

off on that next period of his painting life that "has made his family an American institution." According to John O'Connor, Jr., of Pittsburgh's Carnegie Institute, Peirce is "the most natural of painters. There is nothing artificial, precious, or pretentious about his pictures." As he painted the American scene in his "free, vibrant, impromptu" style, the unconstructive influences of his European period fell away.

Peirce had exhibited constantly in Paris, where he had become a Sociétaire du Salon d'Automne with the very first picture he had submitted, a painting of Tunis. And in 1926 he had his first American exhibition, at the Wildenstein Gallery in New York. The New York *Times* critic noted the influence of Matisse, and commented on Peirce's color, which "sang a radiant song in orange and purple." The artist's next one-man show, at The Gallery, in New York in 1934, displayed the new depth and tenderness that critics found had come into his work. Contrasted with his earlier show, which had been preoccupied with his European experiences, the paintings in this exhibition were mostly "contented domestic documents," of which the most striking were *Summer,* a family idyl, and the portraits of the now famous twins, in *Concert Champêtre* and *Chamber Music,* "delightfully amusing and though solidly painted, with a touch of the whimsical about them." These "robust, vigorously constructed pieces reflect . . . his sensuous appreciation of the joy of living, and in their luscious chromatic color they suggest a Renoir more solid and less lyric than the great French painter." The artist's predilection for dramatic themes is evident in the *Fiesta of St. Fermin,* which echoes "the vivid animation of a Goya." *After the Show,* a circus subject, was marked with a new restraint, and a smoothness, subtlety, and spaciousness that attracted the attention of critics. Later this painting was bought by Juliana Force for the Whitney Museum of American Art in New York. Jerome Klein, writing in the New York *Post,* called a subsequent New York exhibition at the Midtown Galleries in 1936 the best one-man show of the season. That same year Peirce did a series of three panels of the Harvard Tercentenary celebration. His class (1907) bought one to present to the University. A second panel hangs in the Harvard Club in New York.

In September 1937 the Midtown Galleries arranged a retrospective exhibition of the previous six years of Peirce's work, which exemplified "all the major aspects of his talent." According to Melville Upton in the New York *Sun,* Peirce "is not concerned with social problems or probings into the subconscious. His seems a red-blooded, carefree art, pulsating with color and the joy of living." Edward Alden Jewell of the New York *Times* found the artist, like George Luks, "a gusty extrovert in paint." His sheer exuberance, Jewell wrote, constituted a problem that could not always be resolved successfully, tending to flout form and sometimes resulting in an excess of coarseness that could negative in some degree the essential effect toward which the artist aspired. But he also felt that there was "a great deal more quality in his paint than there had been a few years ago; and a great

deal more quality in his color and the color relationships." One of the outstanding oils shown was *Haircut by the Sea,* a painting that had been displayed in other general exhibitions, the Carnegie International in Pittsburgh, the Corcoran Gallery of Art in Washington, and the Art Institute of Chicago. Later this canvas was purchased by the Metropolitan Museum. The water colors in this show were "delightfully spontaneous and effective," with the personal accent usually found in Peirce's work. Included in this group were the Key West pictures, the aftermath of a visit to Ernest Hemingway—*Sloppy Joe's, Key West,* "with its swirling group of girls and white-clad sailors from the fleet, and the equally lively, though more decorous, *Rest Beach, Key West,* with its careless vigor and indifference to the literal that it is conceivable might pain the academically minded." This exhibition was sent, at the conclusion of its New York showing, on a tour of the country.

Peirce became interested in murals, and in 1939 executed designs, under Government auspices, for three post office buildings. The first, for the Westbrook (Maine) Post Office, was a logging scene showing lumberjacks at work stripping bark—an interesting choice of subject, for the Peirce family fortune was made in lumber. This was followed by two panels for the Troy (New York) Post Office, depicting Rip Van Winkle and the Legend of Sleepy Hollow. A third mural, painted for the post office at Peabody, Massachusetts, was called *The Bull Pen.*

A "healthy hedonism" characterized the artist's 1939 one-man show, in which Emily Genauer of the New York *World-Telegram* noticed "greater complexity of design, more reliance on texture and less on broad planes, and an earthiness which is less sensuous than Renoir, a thing compounded of fresh air, new hay, breeze-swept beaches, and noisy kids." She recalled that Matisse had once named Peirce as "one of America's truly great and indigenous painters." In the fall of 1939 Peirce was awarded the First Purchase Prize of $400 at the National Watercolor Exhibition of the Los Angeles County Fair Art Exhibit at Pomona, California, for *On Penobscot Bay.*

In the winter of 1941 Peirce was asked to make some sketches for the young American Ballet Theatre. The backstage scenes, and the sketches he made for *Billy the Kid,* are distinguished by their disregard of the Degas tradition, a tradition which had become an almost unavoidable precedent in any ballet subject. *Art News* found some of the ballerina pictures displaying Peirce's "unfortunate tendency to softness," lacking the nervous incisiveness so inherent in the subject. But in his scenes of movement the treatment is "marvelously fresh, with a sense of rapidity permeated with love of this life." The following spring the Midtown Galleries arranged the first Peirce all water-color show. These sketches of "rural comment, woodland interiors, and land-and-water compositions" were "all executed with zest and sparkle." *Art Digest* noted that "he maintains a uniform color scheme, and if he starts in a light key, as in *Jones Port,* he keeps it there, or if he goes in for dramatic darks, like in *Old Cemetery,* he manages to retain the effect with a brooding sky and shadowy trees, relieved only by the sunlight on dried grass and the white tombstones." Peirce used one of the tombstones in *Old Cemetery* for his signature— "Hic jacet W.P. 21 Nov. '42." A few weeks later, in May 1942, two one-man shows— Waldo Peirce, and Maurice de Vlaminck— were put on by the Wildenstein Gallery in New York in cooperation with the Hyperion Press, which had just published biographies of the two artists. According to the New York *Times* critic, it was interesting to pass from one large room to the other and compare the respective styles of these two men. "There is a very wide divergence here," he wrote, "yet both styles are vigorous and very personal."

The sensation of Peirce's 1944 spring show was his *Siesta in the Barn*, the nude figure of a young girl, whose rosy flesh makes a strong contrast to the barn's sober timbers, earth floor, and haymow. The artist does not specialize in nudes, but for years he has wanted to paint one in this unusual setting. Because of the old-fashioned prejudices of Maine society, however, the project had to be carried out in two different locales—the barn was sketched in Maine, but the nude study was made in Peirce's New York studio. Then the final painting was done from the two sketches. Other paintings attracting attention in this exhibition which employed the artist's "rare gifts of humor, fine observation, and the reflection of a rich and varied personality" were the *Fire at East Orrington*, a spectacular canvas crowded with figures, *Trio*, and *Apple Pickers*. Nineteen forty-four was a prize year for Peirce, for in addition to the award in the Pepsi-Cola Competition he also received an Honorable Mention, carrying with it $400, in Carnegie Institute's "Painting in the United States" exhibition, at Pittsburgh, for his *Black-Eyed Susans*, "a warmly painted picture of a bouquet set out of doors."

Peirce's most recent achievement is the illustration of *The Children's Hour*, a collection of verse brought out by the Hyperion Press in the fall of 1944. The artist, who has had an almost lifelong interest in poetry, feels that poems such as Blake's "Tiger," Shakespeare's incidental songs, the verses of Christina Rossetti, and other poets included in the book are not beyond the enjoyment of children. Give them Mother Goose, by all means, he says, but let them have the great poets also. May Lamberton Becker [41] of the New York *Herald Tribune* evidently shares this opinion, for she writes, "This is now my favorite collection of poetry for children, not altogether for the lively colored pictures dancing over its large pages, though these give unexpected sidelights on the poems . . . but because in all these lovely pages is not one poem that is not pure beauty." Peirce also illustrated two earlier books. *Squawky and Bawky,* a tale of twin penguins written by Lynne Lofting, the daughter of Hugh Lofting of *Dr. Dolittle* fame, was published in 1939. The penguins, named Squawky and Bawky by the Peirce twins, are pictured on ice floes near the North Pole, but Peirce, of course, drew them at the Battery in New York City. Five years later, in the spring of 1944, the artist made the illustrations for Mary Norton's hilarious story of some English children's adventures in witchcraft, *The Magic Bed-Knob*. Waldo Peirce's "lusciously colored pictures," notes the New York *Times,* "mirror the mood" of the book.

Under a contract to write his memoirs for Scribner's, Peirce several years ago accepted an advance of $500 on the project. For a time this advance worried him, for although he wrote and wrote, the end of the manuscript did not appear to be much nearer. Then he solved the problem by leaving the publisher $500 in his will, in case the memoirs should never be finished. He is a prolific writer of verse, long narrative poems or "ballades," as he calls them. These are bound by hand, with the text written in, and expressive water-color illustrations pasted on facing pages. One manuscript, written in French (Peirce speaks French and Spanish fluently), contains the exploits of a friend in Paris, "Redacteur Rehm." Another, "Unser Kent," is Rockwell Kent [42] as Waldo Peirce sees him; and a third, "Don Ernesto, Pamplona," written in Spanish, recounts the escapades of his friend, Ernest Hemingway, in Spain. The illustrations for this last one are very choice. One in particular shows "Don Ernesto" reclining on a slain bull, into whose blood he dips a quill in order to continue writing his manuscript—while in the background "the sun also rises."

Paintings by Peirce have been shown in all important national and international exhibitions in the United States, and also at the Wildenstein Gallery in London and the Museum of Modern Art in Paris. He is represented in the permanent collections of the Metropolitan Museum, the Whitney Museum, the Pennsylvania Academy of the Fine Arts, the Addison Gallery of American Art at Andover, Massachusetts, the Brooklyn Museum, the University of Arizona, and in private collections throughout the United States.

Waldo Peirce has three residences—a home in Bangor, Maine, one in Haverstraw, New York, and a studio-apartment in the Greenwich Village section of New York City. When not at work in his studio he roams the city, making sketches. He has also made many water colors at the New York Chapter of the American Red Cross, especially at the Blood Bank, where he himself is a frequent donor. He aspires to be a member of the "gallon" club, and has just one more pint to give before becoming eligible. In moments of relaxation Peirce reads detective stories, being partial to those of Georges Simenon. Tall, broad-shouldered, Peirce, a man of great physical strength, weighs 210 pounds and has thick blond hair now turning gray. He is mild and gracious in manner. His wife, dark-eyed, dark-haired Alzira Peirce, herself a serious artist, exhibits frequently her sturdy genre scenes of New York and Maine. The Peirce children, Chamberlain and Michael (the twins) and Anna Gabriella—Bill, Mike, and Anna Gabby, as they are familiarly known—also paint. Their father, whom they address as "Waldo," is very proud of their efforts.

References

Art N 40:27+ My 1 '41 por
Cue p6 S 4 '37
N Y Sun p14 My 15 '44
Varga, M. Waldo Peirce 1941
Who's Who in America 1944-45

PELLETIER, WILFRED (pel"le"-tyā' wil'fred) June 30, 1896- Conductor; pianist
Address: b. c/o Metropolitan Opera Association, 1425 Broadway, New York City; h. 400 Park Ave., New York City

When the Metropolitan Opera Association opened its sixtieth season on November 27, 1944, the honor of conducting the first night went to Wilfred Pelletier, who led a "workmanlike performance of *Faust*." This was also his twenty-seventh anniversary with the company and his first batoning of a first night.

One of a large and musical French-Canadian family, Pelletier was born in Montreal, Quebec, June 30, 1896, the son of Elzear and Zelire Pelletier, who named him Wilfrid (later Anglicized to Wilfred). The elder Pelletier conducted an amateur orchestra, and from his earliest youth Wilfrid was surrounded by rehearsals, at which various members of the family acted as leader. The boy learned from an older brother to play the drums and timpani; at seven he graduated to the piano. It is said that he was soon able to play all the instruments of the orchestra. While continuing his general education in the Montreal schools, Wilfrid was tutored by his father in harmony, composition, and piano. At nine he was playing regular engagements as a drummer with small amateur bands; at eleven he had a part-time job playing at a skating rink in the evenings. In 1910, when the little drummer was fourteen, he saw his first opera and chose that medium for his career.

In 1914 Pelletier won the Province of Quebec Prix d'Europe, a scholarship for study abroad. This enabled the youth to go to Paris to study piano under Isidor Philipp, harmony with Samuel Rousseau, composition with Charles Widor, and operatic tradition and repertoire with Camille Bellaigue. On his return two years later, the young Canadian was appointed assistant conductor and chorus master of the Montreal Opera Company, and in 1917 he was engaged by the Metropolitan Opera Association in the same capacity.

For the next five years Pelletier, one of a dozen assistants, worked under some of the greatest conductors of the day, including Artur Bodanzky, Gennaro Papi, Tullio Serafin, and Roberto Moranzoni. The conductor to whom an opera was assigned for production would explain his exact wishes to "Pelly," who would then work out the details of the performance with each singer. No opera star is too experienced to be thus coached, and Pelletier assisted such luminaries as Enrico Caruso, Lucrezia Bori, Margaret Matzenauer, Geraldine Farrar, and Antonio Scotti, with whose opera company Pelletier toured for a time after the First World War. In an *Etude* article written two decades later, the conductor stated that such a coach must have "a knowledge of orchestration and instrumentation . . . as thorough as that of any conductor, and he must be as fluent at the piano as any accompanist. Moreover, he must know the languages in which the standard works are sung; he must be able to detect and correct errors in tone production; he must be conversant with dramatic acting and stage deportment; and, most important of all, he must be familiar with the authentic traditions of the Italian, French, German, and similar 'schools' of opera. . . . The

coach must be able to arouse the same confidence in the singer that a good physician would."

While on the regular staff of the Metropolitan as assistant conductor, Pelletier began in 1921 to lead the Ravinia (Illinois) Opera Company during the summers and to conduct the San Francisco Opera Company in the autumns, which he continued to do for ten years. In 1922 the twenty-six-year-old musician was promoted to second-string conductor, one of six at the Metropolitan, and put in charge of the Sunday night concerts, at which new Metropolitan recruits were tested and veterans tried out new roles. Pelletier's first operatic assignment was *Carmen*; since then he has conducted German, Russian, Italian, and other French operas with "intelligence, force, and perception." In 1925 the Canadian conductor was married to Queena Mario, American soprano then singing at the Metropolitan. (His first wife had been Berthe Jeannotte, daughter of a Canadian physician of high professional and social standing. There are two sons of that union.)

For ten years Pelletier continued his Metropolitan-Ravinia-San Francisco routine, conducting the premières of several modern works, notably Louis Gruenberg's *The Emperor Jones*, Henri Rabaud's *Marouf*, and Rimsky-Korsakoff's *Le Coq d'Or* in California, and Deems Taylor's [40] *Peter Ibbetson*, (which he conducted at the Metropolitan in the 1934-1935 season) in Chicago. He also made records for RCA-Victor in the days when, in his words, "soloists, conductors, and engineers congratulated themselves when they completed one twelve-inch record in eight hours." Many of these early records, so painfully produced, were scratchy and indistinct. But Pelletier had faith in the new medium, and is now one of the top recording conductors. He has made records and albums with sopranos Grace Moore [44], Gladys Swarthout [44], and Lily Pons [44]; with baritones Lawrence Tibbett and Igor Gorin [42]; and with tenors Beniamino Gigli, Giovanni Martinelli, Richard Crooks, Jan Peerce, and James Melton; as well as some purely choral and orchestral works.

In 1932 Pelletier succeeded to the post of first conductor at the Metropolitan. Two years later he began his radio work as musical director-composer-conductor for *Roses and Drums*, a continued Civil War story over the NBC Blue Network, sponsored by the Union Central Life Insurance Company, which lasted through 1936. In 1934-1935, too, he appeared regularly on the Chase and Sanborn Coffee Hour over the NBC Red Network. "Radio work is much more difficult than any of the other musical fields," he found. "It requires everything that most other fields do—with the possible exception of good looks—and a great deal more besides. . . . As for the conductor or director, he must be a symphonic expert, an operatic expert, a popular waltz, march, and ballad expert, an instrument factory, a music library, and a past master of theory, harmony, counterpoint, and orchestration—all of these rolled into one and prepared to function at sixty miles an hour." Pelletier also points out that it is necessary, in radio work, to play popular music with "the same smoothness and sincerity that you put into Debussy." "Personally," he declares, "I do not consider popular music as 'bad.' It is not bad! It is simply different; and we of the radio must learn to respect it, provided it keeps in its own place."

Until 1936 Wilfred Pelletier made few appearances as conductor of complete operas at the Metropolitan, but when the *Metropolitan Opera Auditions* went on the air in 1935 over NBC Blue under the sponsorship of the Sherwin-Williams Paint Company, he was the conductor, personally coached each contestant for one or two weeks, and was one of a committee of judges. Auditioning young and not-so-young musical hopefuls was very largely his responsibility anyway, and he listened to some nine hundred each year—as many as forty-five singers in one day. The *Auditions of the Air* have been the gateway to "Met" contracts for nearly forty aspirants, including Eleanor Steber [43], Patrice Munsel, Mary Van Kirk, Leonard Warren, Martial Singher, Arthur Carron, and Mack Harrell. Others, such as Dorothy Sarnoff and Alfred Drake [44] (whose brother Arthur Kent was a contract winner) were eliminated from the competition but were "discovered" and starred by other producers. In 1944 the program was revised: as *The Metropolitan Opera Presents*, it featured one guest soloist from the opera company and only one singer competing for a contract.

Maestro Pelletier looks forward to opera casts made up entirely of Americans, so that operas can be sung in the language of the audience and be intelligible—as they are not when sung with strong and varying foreign accents. "Opera in this country will never be as popular as it is in Europe," he declares, "until the audience can understand what it's all about and can appreciate every point of dramatic action. As it is, the majority of those who attend the opera haven't the faintest idea of what it is all about. What they are really listening to, as far as they are concerned, is a concert in costume." The *Auditions of the Air*, he believes, do "immeasurable good" in finding qualified singers, but there should be a training system by which each large center would have a small opera company in conjunction with its symphony orchestra. The Metropolitan would be the "focal point" for the singers. "With many opera companies functioning," says Pelletier with, perhaps, one eye on the Metropolitan's regular deficits, "we might have dollar opera in English and make money."

During the summer of 1935, the Ravinia Opera Company having come to an end, Pelletier returned to his native Montreal and fulfilled a long-standing ambition by forming the Montreal Festival Orchestra. This he led in the first of that city's Bach-Beethoven concerts and later in symphonic concerts, as well as in a series of Saturday afternoon music presentations for children ("Matinées d'initiation symphonique") which he was to conduct for four years. The following year he was awarded a Mus.D. by the University of Montreal. That August the Pelletiers were divorced, and in May 1937 the forty-one-year-old conductor was married to the Metropolitan soprano Rose Bampton [40]. The couple have collaborated on more than twenty recordings, on some of which Pelletier is pianist rather than conductor. Among the most popular of these records are "Ah, malgré moi" from *Alceste* and "Vissi d' Arte" from *La Tosca*. In

De Bellis Studio

WILFRED PELLETIER

the summer of 1944 the conductor and his tall young wife also co-starred on the air in a program called *Vacation Serenade*.

Three years earlier, when the France-Film Company found its importation of foreign pictures cut off and therefore turned its resources to the field of music, it supported Pelletier in establishing a fall season of opera in Quebec. For this he used the Montreal Festival Orchestra, which he had founded seven years before. In 1942 the Canadian conductor fulfilled another desire when the Institute of Music and Dramatic Art of the Province of Quebec opened its doors. Pelletier had worked tirelessly for the establishment of just such a school, the first of its kind in North America, where talented young people could get a musical education at government expense; everyone was pleased but no one was surprised when the Provincial Secretary named him director. Pelletier then turned his attention to the next step: providing job opportunities for the graduates. This he hoped to do by establishing "small symphonic units" to tour the Canadian provinces, providing music for cities and towns which had no orchestras of their own. "We can do it and we will!" says Pelletier, who has made himself an international commuter in order to devote several days of alternate weeks to his Canadian students.

In addition to his regular conducting duties, Pelletier is a popular guest conductor, and has led many of the Saturday afternoon Metropolitan Opera broadcasts. He has directed symphonic broadcasts for the Ford [44], Packard, Simmons, and Firestone [44] radio hours, and has appeared with leading symphony orchestras throughout the United States, including those of Detroit, Chicago, San Francisco, and Cincinnati. When Paramount Pictures engaged Kirsten Flagstad for an operatic sequence in *The Big Broadcast of 1938*, Pelletier was chosen to direct it; the following spring he toured South Africa. In 1944 the Canadian conducted the *World of Song* program, featuring soloists from the Metropolitan Opera As-

PELLETIER, WILFRED—*Continued*

sociation. In April of that year he conducted three Metropolitan operas (*Aïda, Carmen,* and *Mignon*) in four days, a "most unusual" assignment, especially as his performance schedule there has never been heavy. During the whole of the 1943-1944 season he directed only three other operas, *Faust, The Barber of Seville,* and another *Aïda.* Pelletier has found time to play numberless benefits, and, since the War began, to entertain as pianist or conductor at most of the service hospitals and bases in the United States and Canada. Pelletier's two sons entered the United States service: Camille became a major in the tank corps, and Frank (François) was made a sergeant in the Signal Corps.

A "driving and propulsive" conductor, Pelletier is a short man (five feet four inches tall, weighing 150 pounds) and has blue-gray eyes and gray hair which used to be brown. His hobby—which he caught from Roland Young and passed on to Miss Bampton—is collecting penguins of all sorts except real ones ("there isn't enough room in my icebox"); he wears two little penguin figures on his watch chain, one a gift from Miss Bampton, the other from Lily Pons. He also has a collection of old musical instruments. The conductor is said to be indefatigable, capable of working around the clock with only a short nap; his agent says he is "tireless, painstaking, adaptable, and cosmopolitan," and has a "wonderful" sense of humor. It is perhaps typical of Pelletier that he has, not a Victory garden, but a seventy-seven-acre farm near Southbury, Connecticut, on which he and his wife raise fruit, vegetables, and chickens. The chickens are in the Maestro's department, and he is reported to have made some successful experiments in crossbreeding. When Pelletier and Miss Bampton both have to rush off to musical engagements the latter's parents, who live nearby, keep things going until the Pelletiers get back.

No mourner of past glories, Pelletier finds that musical teaching has improved, and standards of musicianship have risen in America during the past decade. "I have been at the Metropolitan for twenty-five years," he said in 1942, "and I have never seen the secondary parts taken so well as they are today. A generation ago such high standards of musicianship could not have been expected, even among foreign singers. . . . Even some of our greatest artists of the past, like Antonio Scotti and Angelo Bada, could not read music as these youngsters can." The *Opera News* describes the conductor as "a man who has grown young with the youth he loves."

References

N Y Times p10 O 24 '42

Ewen, D. ed. Living Musicians 1940
Thompson, O. ed. International Cyclopedia of Music and Musicians 1943
Variety Radio Directory 1940-41
Who Is Who in Music 1940
Who's Who in America 1944-45

PENNELL, JOSEPH STANLEY (pen'nel") July 4, 1908- Author

Address: b. c/o Charles Scribner's Sons, 597 Fifth Ave., New York City; h. 802½ N. Washington St., Junction City, Kan.

When Joseph Stanley Pennell's novel of the Civil War, *The History of Rome Hanks and Kindred Matters,* was published in July 1944, most reviewers named Pennell the successor to the late Thomas Wolfe. Apart from this concensus of critical opinion, reactions varied, ranging from "certain to be a landmark among novels of its type" to "an irritating, perplexing, overwritten, and inchoate book"; from "the best novel about the Civil War I have read, with the natural exception of *The Red Badge of Courage,*" to "nothing, either in writing or conception, but self-indulgence." Majority opinion decried the book's confused, torrential style and undisciplined construction, but praised it nonetheless as powerful, eloquent, intense, and superb. Orville Prescott in the New York *Times* predicted: "It is unlikely that any novel this year [1944] will cause such furious disagreements, such enthusiasm, and such rage."

The author of *The History of Rome Hanks* found the material and background for his novel in the history of his own family. He turned also to the pioneer and Civil War days of the town in which he was born and grew up, once host to "Wild Bill" Hickok, General Custer, and other historic figures: Junction City, Kansas (Fork City in the book). Joseph Stanley Pennell was born there July 4, 1908, the son of Joseph Judd and Edith (Stanley) Pennell. His father came across the plains from North Carolina at the age of sixteen; his mother "might be said to be the daughter of pioneers, as she did a lot of traveling in covered wagons and saw a lot of Indians." An array of great-great-grandfathers and great-uncles fought in the Civil War—some for the North, others for the South.

From St. Francis Xavier's School, Pennell entered the University of Kansas. After one year of study there he continued his university work at Pembroke College, Oxford, where he received his B.A. in 1929. He began his career as a newspaperman during vacations while a student, and on returning to his own country worked as a reporter on various newspapers, including the Denver *Post,* the Los Angeles *Examiner,* and the Los Angeles *Post-Record.* He was also for a time managing editor of the Huntington Park (California) *Signal.* Other jobs included radio work, and teaching at the John Burroughs School.

Pennell began his creative writing with verse, which for the most part was published in *Poetry* Magazine. He also wrote articles for the *North American Review,* and his short stories have appeared in *Harper's Bazaar, Mademoiselle,* and other magazines. *The History of Rome Hanks,* his first novel, was written at Junction City, and finished just before his induction into the Army. At the end of 1944 Pennell, who is unmarried, was serving as a lieutenant in an antiaircraft battery.

As "a curious and arresting blend of the American past and present," *The History of Rome Hanks* was begun, actually, as a record of the author's search for the answer to the questions: What am I? How did I get to be what I am? Specifically, it is an account of the American forebears of the young man in the story, Robert Lee Harrington, who closely resembles Pennell himself. Piqued by the bored remark of his girl friend, Christa Schell: "I'm sure your grandfather must have been a fine

old Southern gentleman," Lee Harrington decides to find out something about the lives and
experiences of persons in his ancestral background. Several different stories make up the
book. The first narrator is the Reverend
Thomas Wagnal, D. D., a surgeon in the 117th
"Ioway" Regiment; then there is the story of
Thomas Beckham, who married the daughter
of Rome Hanks; and the story of Lee's North
Carolina ancestors, as told by his great-uncle
Pinckney Harrington. Through these narra-
tives Lee learns about his great-grandfather,
Romulus Lycurgus Hanks, kind and gentle
and a fine soldier. He learns, too, about Clint
Belton, a coward and a thief, who became a
general and later Secretary of War; of the
bloody battle of Shiloh; of Pickett's charge at
Gettysburg; of life in the Andersonville prison; of the Reconstruction days in the South.
Though the book centers about the Civil War,
it is brought down to the modern scene when
it ends with Lee Harrington's birth.

Much of the effectiveness of the novel, as
several reviewers pointed out, was lost through
a lack of sound basic construction, experimentation with the stream-of-consciousness method, and through the use of the movie flashback
technique. They felt, too, that the book suffered from the mixed influences of Wolfe,
Faulkner, Joyce, Proust, Dos Passos '40, and
others. As Hamilton Basso put it: "Mr. Pennell, like Wolfe, commits just about every sin
known to literary man and, again like Wolfe,
thinks up a few on his own." George May-
berry, writing in the *New Republic*, said: "The
method of the book is pretentious and clumsy
. . . the style could stand several good night
sweats." In the *Nation*, "Mr. Pennell tells us
simple and obvious things," said Diana Trilling,
"so elaborately as to make us believe he is being profound. . . . It is certainly the case
that in Mr. Pennell's novel the assertion of
the glory that is America shows itself to be
basically only an assertion of the glory that is
the author himself."

Many things, however, were said on the
credit side. In the *Saturday Review of Literature* Harrison Smith wrote: "He has a gift
unrivaled among our younger writers for narrative description that at times almost over-
whelms the reader, and a remarkably varied
vocabulary. . . . A solid and memorable volume
in the fictional history of America." Virginia
Kirkus '41 called it "definitely a man's book—
few women will like it. But Pennell has succeeded in translating with modern idiom and
emotional value the men of the armies of the
War between the States. These men are as
alive as the men in Ernie Pyle's '41 columns."
Orville Prescott said: "The emotion, excitement, exhilaration, disgust, horror, and slaughter of battle have rarely been captured better
in print. The thousands of fragmentary episodes of which battles are made, the mutilation, death, self-sacrifice, brutality, cowardice,
and even humor are superbly conveyed. Out
of such fires as these did America grow and
take its shape."

The History of Rome Hanks commanded
immediate interest and wide popular appeal in
spite of the reservations of some reviewers.
"But the effect of their praise," commented
Time Magazine, "plus lavish advertisements,
was immediate. *Rome Hanks* sold out its first
edition overnight." New interest in and sales

John Engstead

LT. JOSEPH STANLEY PENNELL

stimulation to the novel came when, on August
8, 1944, after complaints were issued by New
England's Watch and Ward Society, several
booksellers in Boston and Cambridge banned it
as more improper than Lillian Smith's '44
Strange Fruit. An elderly lady bookseller had
found passages in *Rome Hanks* containing
"raw vulgarity." The Boston police petitioned
the municipal court for an obscenity complaint;
and a decision was left under advisement of
the court. In other sections of the country
the book continued to be in high popular demand and throughout 1944 held a place on the
nation's best-seller lists.

References

N Y Times p13 Jl 17 '44 por; p15 Ag
    8 '44
Newsweek 24:80-1 Jl 31 '44

PERON, JUAN (DOMINGO) (pe-ron'
hwän dō-mĕng'gō) 1896(?)- Vice-President
of Argentina

Address: Buenos Aires, Argentina

Since June 1943 Argentina has had four
Presidents and an unestimated number of "palace" revolutions. The man who has remained
the most powerful behind-the-scenes figure
throughout all these shifts in government is
young Colonel Juan Perón, considered "the
brains" behind the totalitarian movement in
Argentina. Almost unknown outside of his
own country before the summer of 1943,
by the middle of 1944 Perón held the triple
posts of Vice-President, Minister of War, and
Secretary of Labor and Social Welfare.

Juan Domingo Perón was born in southern
Argentina a little less than fifty years ago.
The son of a well-to-do rancher, he grew up on
his father's ranch and was educated at the
Army's Military Academy. At eighteen he
was a sub-lieutenant and two years later he
was raised to the rank of full lieutenant. Little
is known about Perón's early career except
that he was an excellent athlete and a good

COL. JUAN PERON

student of military affairs. He is the author
of several books on military strategy, and was,
according to his associates, "a good soldier,
a strict disciplinarian who was liked by his
subordinates." Although Perón has not been
able to put his military knowledge to the test
in actual warfare, he has applied it, with
marked success, to the internal political scene.

Leading "a crusade for spiritual renovation,"
Perón set out to reorganize the Argentine
Government on the basis of an extreme nationalism. He worked with a group of young
Army officers who soon became known as the
GOU or Grupo de Oficiales Unidos (Group
of United Officers). Their activities were
little publicized until June 4, 1943, when a
palace revolution brought about the ousting of
President Ramón Castillo '41 and the prodemo-
cratic members of his Cabinet. It was soon
recognized that the new President, Pedro
Ramirez '43 (Arturo Rawson had been President for a few days immediately following the
coup), was working in close cooperation with
Perón, whose office was then Chief of the Secretariat of the Ministry of War and President
of the National Labor Department.

Perón quickly won himself a reputation for
intelligence combined with ruthlessness in dealing with his political enemies. His power over
President Ramirez was said to be absolute.
It is reported that he told the President, "You
can't resign until we are ready to let you
quit." His friendship for the Axis powers
was disquieting to observers in the United
States. John W. White reported in the New
York Herald Tribune: "Perón is said to supply the brains for a group of pro-Nazi colonels who plotted to overthrow Castillo because
they did not consider him sufficiently pro-
German." Together with his group of associates known as "the Colonel's clique," Perón
established a governing system described as
not unfamiliar to those who had watched the
rise of Nazism in Germany. Foremost among
his plans was the control of Argentine labor.

He succeeded in dissolving the strongest union
in Argentina, the Confederación General de
Trabajo, with a membership of 250,000. "I
am disposed to end all labor difficulties in the
country," he said; "I will not allow any action
by elements of dissolution and agitation which
in the majority of cases are . . . aliens who
do not know how to respect my country."

In the early stages of his public career Perón
voiced a definite hostility against the United
States and Great Britain. He is reported to
have said, "Argentina is no longer going to
be kicked around by Washington and London,"
and "We are not anti-capitalists, but we will
not allow capital to dominate us." Several
times Perón has admitted his admiration for
German military efficiency, but, according to
Time Magazine, "Perón is a home-grown authoritarian, not a Nazi stooge. Perhaps he
would like to be a real dictator; at present he
is merely a brainy man who generally out-
maneuvers the other militarists."

Late in 1943 Perón indicated the extent to
which Argentina was becoming a corporate
state by announcing that the state would thereafter "bring workers and employers into a
joint cooperative organization." He said that
"future decisions will be based on a principle
higher than the principle of law, this being
'welfare of the country.'" As a result of this
totalitarian trend, diplomatic relations between
Argentina and the United States became increasingly cooler. Former United States Under-Secretary of State Sumner Welles '40 described Perón as "young, forceful, a fanatical
Fascist and bent upon becoming an Argentine
dictator."

The young Colonel's rise to power was not
interrupted by this or other criticism. In February 1944 President Ramirez was obliged to
retire because of illness ("more diplomatic than
medical," commentators agreed). Through
Perón's efforts his close friend General Edel-
miro Farrell, Vice-President under Ramirez,
was raised to the Presidency, with Perón himself as Minister of War. Although one month
earlier Argentina had broken off diplomatic
relations with Germany and Japan, the new
shift in government was seen as unfriendly
to the United Nations. It was felt that this
most recent coup had been motivated by
Perón's fear that Ramirez' regime might declare war on the Axis.

Coincidental with Perón's growing power
there has also arisen opposition to him. In
spite of his frequent attempts to stifle a
free press, Perón has not been able to silence
his opposition, perhaps because he has not
employed large scale "Gestapo methods."
Time reports that although the press is restricted, it still exists, and although labor
unions are under Government control, they
too still exist. A formidable democratic
underground is said to be flourishing in Argentina.

While the United States had broken off relations with Argentina in March, the American
Ambassador, Norman Armour, was not immediately recalled, for Perón was seen as
inclined to establish a more moderate regime.
What good intentions he might have had were
somewhat overshadowed by a "saber-rattling"
speech he made on June 10 at the University
of La Plata, a speech he claimed was misin-

terpreted but which did not please the United
States, the democratic Latin American countries, nor Great Britain. (Its main thesis was
that so far as Argentina was concerned there
was no essential difference between an Axis or
United Nations victory, and that a militaristic
Argentina was necessary for the gaining of
that country's totalitarian aims.) While Perón
later showed himself "expansive and amiable"
to the foreign press, within about two weeks
the United States and British Ambassadors
were recalled.

Meanwhile, however, a five-month struggle
between Perón and General Luis Perlinger,
the Minister of the Interior, for the control
of the Government was brought to a sudden
close by the "resignation" of Perlinger and
the appointment of Perón as Vice-President.
The withdrawal of Perlinger, an extreme
nationalist, who had been considered to have
been responsible for press censorship and
large-scale arrests of liberals, was looked upon
as a gesture of appeasement toward the
"Colossus of the North" and Great Britain.
Commentators believe Perón was able to effect
this coup without opposition by the strongly
Fascist-minded factions (in March he had
dissolved the GOU) because the recall of the
Ambassadors constituted a threat of economic
sanctions which Argentina could ill afford to
have applied against her tremendous export
trade. Other moderating measures followed:
some political prisoners were freed, workers'
wages were raised, cooperation between capital
and labor urged, a pro-Nazi newspaper was
suspended for criticizing the United States.
Also, press censorship was modified—correspondents might send uncensored dispatches
abroad although they would be held account-
able for their reports.

Late in August, Alberto Baldrich, the outspoken Nazi-minded Minister of Justice and
Education, was ousted, and not long after
Perón announced that the military phase of
the revolution was over, although he said he
could not name the date of transfer of power
to the people. Nevertheless, his plan to "prepare the nation for war" by "conscripting"
youth and women did not clarify the outlook,
nor did his commitments entirely satisfy
Washington (the United States had not yet
recognized his Government). By December
commentators were discussing Perón's ambitions to be Argentina's next President, ambitions that might not be acceptable to either
the liberal groups or to the extreme nationalist
groups who had frowned on his efforts to win
United States approval.

"Tall and handsome," Perón impresses reporters with his pleasant manners and friendly
sense of humor. A widower, Perón's has one
daughter. He is a hard worker who finds
relaxation in cooking, fishing, and hunting.

Reference

Time 43:38-40 Ap 24 '44 por

PERONI, CARLO 1889 (?)—Mar. 12, 1944
Italian-born operatic conductor; music director
of the San Carlo Opera Company for more
than twenty years; a scholarly musician, he

knew sixty operatic scores by memory; conductor of the Chicago Opera Company in 1941
and 1942; often guest conductor at numerous
musical events.

Obituary

N Y Times p15 Mr 13 '44 por

PETRY, LUCILE (pē'trē) Nurse-admin-
istrator; educator
Address: b. Nurse Education Division, United
States Public Health Service, Bethesda, Md.

As director of the United States Cadet
Nurse Corps, it is Lucile Petry's task to bring
girls into an accelerated training program to
relieve the wartime shortage of nurses. The
welfare of the civilian sick and even of the
wounded soldiers may, to a very large extent,
depend on the success of this small gray-clad
woman in persuading others to wear the cadet
uniform.

The daughter of a small-town school principal, Miss Petry was brought up to accept
responsibility. While still a young girl, it
is said, she spent her vacations working—in
a drygoods store, a broker's office, and a can-
nery. This habit of hard work proved valuable to the girl when she chose nursing as her
vocation, for a student nurse's probationary
period is traditionally wearing. Miss Petry's
professional history began in 1924, when she
was graduated with honors from the University of Delaware, and enrolled at the
famous Johns Hopkins School of Nursing in
Baltimore, Maryland, later specializing in
psychiatric nursing at the Henry Phipps Clinic
of Johns Hopkins Hospital. After winning
the white cap of a graduate nurse, she was
awarded a scholarship which enabled her to
study for her M.A. at Teachers College of
Columbia University. During these years
Miss Petry's so-called vacations were spent
in further study at various colleges and universities, such as Yale, which have well known
schools of nursing.

Four years after receiving her B.A., Miss
Petry returned to Johns Hopkins Hospital as
head nurse and supervisor. She left the hospital staff in 1929, taking a position as assistant director of the University of Minnesota
School of Nursing, where she spent ten years.
In ten summers, Miss Petry accumulated most
of the credits required for her doctorate; but
in 1941 her education was interrupted by an
appointment to the United States Public
Health Service as its first woman administrator. For two years Miss Petry served as
senior public health nursing consultant, retaining that position when, in May 1943, she was
appointed as the first dean of Cornell University-New York Hospital School of Nursing in
New York City.

Wartime always creates an especially heavy
demand for nurses; today the relatively long
training and high requirements for nursing
make such a demand harder to fill than ever
before. While the armed forces busily recruited nurses, civilian hospitals were seriously
inconvenienced by this loss of personnel.

(Continued next page)

LUCILE PETRY

Finally, feeling that the public health was threatened, Congress passed a bill creating the Student War Nurse Reserve on a subsidized basis. Dr. Thomas Parran [40], surgeon general of the United States Public Health Service, who was to administer the program, announced on June 16, 1943 the creation of the Cadet Nurse Corps as a major administrative division of the Service, with Miss Petry as director.

One month after Miss Petry's appointment as dean of the Cornell University-New York Hospital School of Nursing, she was given a year's leave of absence to take charge of the Cadet Nurse Corps. There being no Army schools for nurses, as there were in the First World War, some agency was necessary to direct and stimulate nurse training in the civilian hospitals, and to relieve the pressure on civilian health facilities. "The increased hospital enrollment and the assignment of cadet nurses to Army hospitals will," Miss Petry declared, "release graduate nurses immediately, although the full effect of the new act will not be felt until next July [1944]." The effect was seen that July, when it was revealed that 65,000 new student nurses had entered the corps, exceeding the quota by 500, and making Miss Petry chief of the largest group of women in wartime service.

The Cadet Corps Administrator charged with the training of "the first women ever to receive free professional educations" launched her recruiting campaign immediately. Telegrams were sent to the 1,294 nursing schools eligible to enter the program—"not," she emphasized, "as a dramatic gesture, but because new classes were forming and it was imperative that both students and schools be able to make their plans." She stressed the fact that "the oath the cadet nurse will take requires no more from her than her original motive to render service as a nurse. It is just a guarantee that she will work at the profession during the emergency." In ex-

change for all-expense scholarships, a monthly cash allowance ($15 to $30, according to grade), and smart gray street uniforms with scarlet epaulets, the student nurses bind themselves only to take a more concentrated course—thirty to thirty-four months instead of the usual thirty-six. (When state laws require a full three years' training, the student nurse continues as a senior cadet, "receiving important nursing assignments under supervision.") Of this, "their last six to twelve months will be cleared so they won't have to have instruction during that time." (Instruction time will thus be cut down from three to two years.) Miss Petry's division "will in no way endeavor to standardize schools of nursing. The student will continue to meet the admission, scholastic, and graduation requirements of the particular school in which she is enrolled" and which she herself chooses. "Cadets are to wear the uniforms of their own hospitals while on duty," and may choose between military and civilian nursing.

Miss Petry, the nurse-administrator of the cadets, is smaller than most of them. She is "short and slim, with a youthful appearance which belies her graying hair," worn short and curly, on which pert little hats with veils used to be poised. Now, however, Delos Lovelace writes, "the petite, erect, fresh-as-a-daisy Miss Petry is even prettier in uniform than in civilian dress."

References

N Y Sun p5 F 5 '44
N Y Times p21 My 5 '43; p18 Je 17 '43
N Y World-Telegram p17 Ag 17 '43

POIRET, PAUL (pwä″rä′) Apr. 20, 1879—Apr. 30, 1944 Famous French dress designer; had been couturier to most of European royalty; became established in Paris in 1903 but lost his business and wealth in 1929.

Obituary

N Y Times p19 My 3 '44 por

PONS, LILY (pōns) Apr. 12, 1904- Singer

Address: b. c/o Metropolitan Musical Bureau, Inc., 113 W. 57th St., New York City; h. 322 E. 57th St., New York City; Silvermine, Norwalk, Conn.

"Trapeze artist of the Metropolitan Opera" are the words *Opera News* has used to describe Lily Pons, the tiny coloratura soprano "who can trill on a sixteenth note and take a scale from middle C to the F sharp above high C." The seemingly effortless manner with which she meets difficult vocal requirements are, in reality, the result of strenuous training and a disciplined program of living. "I am afraid," she states, "too many people think that it is possible to accomplish something in art without study and hard work. They are looking for short cuts, and in art there are none."

Born near Cannes, France, April 12, 1904, Lily Pons was named Alice Joséphine by her Italian mother and French father, who were Maria (Naso) and Auguste Pons. During childhood, Lily and her two sisters were taken for a weekly treat to the village bakeshop where they each were allowed to choose either a *baba* or a strawberry tart. One of the first things Miss Pons did upon achieving her early success was to visit the same bakeshop and buy both a *baba* and a tart!

It was Miss Pons's first ambition to become a pianist. Having begun to study the piano at Cannes, she entered the Paris Conservatory for further study at the age of thirteen, and at fifteen she had won a prize for excellence. Her plans for a future as a concert pianist, however, were frustrated by an illness: doctor's orders forbade her to play the piano for two unhappy years. Shortly after the Armistice, she had sufficiently regained her health to play in Paris hospitals for convalescent soldiers. Once, at one of these recitals, a *poilu* asked her to sing. The applause with which her first song was received caused Miss Pons to "discover" her voice; and with true Gallic persuasiveness she convinced Max Dearly, the manager of the *Théâtre des Variétés*, that she was an experienced singer. As a result, she obtained a small part in one of his productions. Some of her colleagues were so impressed by her excellent performance that they predicted a rosy future for her in the *Comédie Française*.

Instead of working to fulfill their hopes, Miss Pons left the stage in 1923 and married August Mesritz, a wealthy, middle-aged Dutchman who was a retired lawyer and newspaper publisher. Her husband directed her interest from the theatre to singing, and convinced her that she had a voice worth cultivating. He arranged to have her study with Alberti di Gorostiaga, the noted vocal coach. For three years, accompanied by Mesritz, Miss Pons went to the Spaniard's studio for a daily one hour lesson. So diligent were Mr. and Mrs. Mesritz that they followed the teacher on his summer vacations in order not to miss any lessons. Señor di Gorostiaga, who is as familiar with the intricacies of *bel canto* as he is indifferent to the niceties of gender, has commented warmly: "Mademoiselle Pons, he is charming, a gentle lady, he is the most hard-working pupil of my life, he has the range of Patti."

In 1928 Miss Pons made her operatic debut in *Lakmé* at the opera house of Mulhouse, Alsace. She was not very successful, but she continued to sing in various French provinces until she by chance won the attention of the late Maria Gay and her husband, Giovanni Zenatello, who persuaded her to go to the United States for an audition at the Metropolitan. For four months after her arrival in America Miss Pons spent an hour a day working on one song she proposed to sing at her audition. She had reason to be fearful, for she had never before sung in a major opera house and she had only five roles in her repertoire. Other singers usually had twenty roles at their command.

When the important day arrived, Miss Pons appeared before Giulio Gatti-Casazza, Otto Kahn, and Tullio Serafin. After she had sung the aria from *Lucia* and the "Bell Song" from *Lakmé*, the triumvirate exchanged knowing glances and approving nods. On the follow-

LILY PONS

ing day Miss Pons was awarded a five-year contract beginning at $445 a week. She now earns $1,000 for each performance.

Without the usual publicity that heralds the presentation of a new coloratura, Miss Pons stepped upon the stage of the Metropolitan in 1931 for her debut as a "sensational" Lucia di Lammermoor. Critics employed rarely used superlatives. Olin Downes [43] praised her at length. "Her voice has range and freshness," he stated. "Certain passages were sung with marked tonal beauty and emotional color. . . . Miss Pons gave the impression of sincerity, intelligence, and the ability to work. She never did a cheap thing and when possible subjected technical display to musical expression."

Thereafter, the singer's fame spread swiftly and securely. She has sung practically all over the world. In Rio de Janeiro police reinforcements were required to restrain the public enthusiasm in her honor. Frantic admirers twice tore the doors from her car. The French made her a Chevalier in the Légion d'Honneur; the Belgians awarded her the Order of the Crown; Americans named two locomotives and a town in Maryland after her. Her audiences broke attendance records from California to New York. At one concert held in Chicago's Grant Park she drew approximately 300,000 listeners. At the Metropolitan, old, neglected operas have been revived to serve as vehicles for her extraordinary voice, among them *Lakmé, La Sonnambula, Linda di Chamounix, Le Coq d'Or* and *The Daughter of the Regiment*. In April 1943 she was presented with the yearly achievement award of the Essex County Symphony Society for her contributions "to opera and musical art in America during the past decade and for her unselfish contributions to the war effort." At the end of the year (and again in 1944) she won *Radio Daily*'s poll of radio edi-

PONS, LILY—*Continued*

tors throughout the country as the best female classical vocalist. In 1944 she was awarded honorary life membership in the Philadelphia Orchestra Pension Foundation.

Miss Pons has been the soloist over many coast-to-coast broadcasts and has appeared in three Hollywood pictures, *I Dream Too Much* (1935); *That Girl From Paris* (1936); and *Hitting a New High* (1937). Fortunately she has remained immune to the lure of easy success offered by the films; she dislikes making them because "the machine comes between the artist and the audience."

On the whole, critical opinion of Miss Pons is highly favorable. She is commended for both her musicianship and for the freshness and conviction her acting imparts to many otherwise wilted operatic roles. The scope of her characterizations extends from the flippant Rosina in *The Barber* to the tragic Lucia in Gaetano Donizetti's *Lucia di Lammermoor.* "Her voice is velvet," wrote one reviewer. "She produces it without much apparent effort, and she has the gift of looking pretty with her mouth wide open." These distinct qualities are regarded as compensatory for her occasional tendency to sing out of tune. One commentator's remarks upon a recent Pons recital sum up this attitude: "She accomplished much that was charming, especially after the customary uncertainties of pitch. . . were disposed of."

Miss Pons was divorced from her first husband in 1933. Five years later, after a transcontinental courtship, she married André Kostelanetz [42], the noted conductor, with whose orchestra she has been appearing for several years. The petite soprano, who became an American citizen in December 1940, measures five feet one, weighs 104 pounds, and wears a size two shoe. She wears her dark hair in a smooth pageboy bob. Despite her diminutive size she has astonishing vitality, which she attributes to her careful daily regimen. She exercises an hour and a half a day in half-hour periods, either by riding, walking, or playing tennis. Cinderella-like, she retires from the gayest gatherings before midnight, and she neither drinks nor smokes.

During the summer of 1944 Miss Pons and Kostelanetz, accompanied by a pianist and a flutist, made a thirteen-week tour of the Middle East, North Africa, and Italy for USO Camp Shows. During their tour they covered 25,000 miles, giving in all, 50 hour-and-a-half concerts to approximately 400,000 soldiers. Although when on concert tours in the States Miss Pons limits herself to two appearances a week, on her USO trip she made as many as twenty-eight within thirty days. The various orchestras which accompanied her singing throughout this tour were recruited by her husband from among the soldiers at each post which they visited. Her programs usually contained the "Bell Song", "The Blue Danube", "Estrellita", "Song of India," and Gounod's "Ave Maria."

The Kostelanetz' were both so pleased with the success of their tour, that they canceled all professional engagements for 1945, including Miss Pons's Metropolitan Opera performances, to start out in December 1944 on a thirteen-week tour of European and China-Burma-India theatres of war. They are planning to return to Europe after the end of the War to give concerts in the liberated countries, feeling that when the necessities of life have been supplied the people of these countries, they will respond to mental and spiritual rehabilitation too. In December 1944 Miss Pons and her husband received citations from the Iranian Institute's School of Asiatic Studies for their "valuable contribution to the cause of international cooperation between Iran and the United States.

When announcement of the liberation of Paris was flashed to the world in August 1944, Miss Pons participated in a celebration at Rockefeller Plaza in New York City when she sang "La Marseillaise" before an assembled crowd of 20,000 persons. Earlier that year in Italy, while on the USO tour, she had seen the Allied forces massing for the invasion which liberated southern France where she was born.

An incurable collector, Miss Pons loves to poke about in antique shops. She has accumulated quantities of authentic period pieces, South American colonial silver, and old American glass. These, together with cages of many brilliantly plumed Brazilian birds, adorn her smart New York duplex apartment and her Norman farmhouse near Silvermine, Connecticut. The latter residence, her thirteenth, is named La Gentilhommière; it was designed and decorated by Miss Pons. The farm yields innumerable chickens, and quantities of vegetables for wartime canning. The singer points out that thirteen is her lucky number: she was born on Friday the thirteenth; her auto license is marked LP-13; and she married Kostelanetz after his thirteenth proposal.

References

N Y Times VII p9+ Ja 5 '41 por; p5 D 7 '40 por
N Y World-Telegram p16 Je 30 '43 por
New Yorker 7:23+ Ja 16 '32
Time 36:30-1 D 30 '40 il (por cover)
Ewen, D. ed. Living Musicians 1936
Flanner, J. American in Paris p155-66 1940
Henderson, W. J. Art of Singing p409-17 1938
Kaufmann, Mrs. H. L. and Hansl, Mrs. E. E. Von B. Artists in Music of Today p79 1941
Thompson, O. ed. International Cyclopedia of Music and Musicians 1943
Who Is Who in Music 1941
Who's Who 1944
Who's Who in America 1944-45

POTTER, BEATRIX 1866(?)—Dec. 22, 1943 English author and artist of some of the best-known children's books ever published, *The Tale of Peter Rabbit, Benjamin Bunny, Mrs. Tittlemous, Jemima Puddle-Duck,* etc.; her charming watercolor illustrations are as famous as the stories.

POULTON, SIR EDWARD BAGNALL
(pōl'ton) Jan. 27, 1856—Nov. 21, 1943
Zoologist and entomologist; for forty years
(1893-1933) professor of zoology at Oxford
University; disciple of Charles Darwin.

Obituary

N Y Times p19 N 22 '43

PRIBICHEVICH, STOYAN (pri-bē'che-
vich stoi'ən) 1905(?)- Author; journalist
Address: b. c/o Time Magazine, 14 W. 49th
St., New York City

Returning to his native country for the first
time in twelve years, in May 1944 Stoyan Pribichevich became the first American newsman
to meet and talk with the fabulous Marshal
Tito '43 face to face. Shortly afterward Pribichevich earned another distinction by becoming the first Allied correspondent captured by
the Nazis to escape from them. Speaking both
Serbo-Croatian and German, he thus had a
unique opportunity to report on the mood and
temper of the Partisan fighters and of the Nazis
who are being bested by them in this "new
kind of war."

The son of Svetozar Pribichevich, a liberal
Serbian statesman, from his youth Stoyan Pribichevich has been familiar with the turbulent
politics of the Balkans. He was born in Zagreb,
now the capital of Croatia in Yugoslavia but
at the time a part of old Austria-Hungary. At
the close of the First World War his father
helped to create the Kingdom of Yugoslavia
and from 1919 to 1925 served in its government
as Minister of the Interior. Exiled shortly
afterward for opposing King Alexander's dictatorship, the elder Pribichevich went to Paris,
and there his son joined him in 1932. A doctor
of political science and a practicing lawyer in
Belgrade, young Stoyan had become involved
in Yugoslav university students' riots and in
printing pamphlets against Alexander's regime.
He had managed to cross the Yugoslav frontier
disguised as a peasant before the political police could seize him.

During his two years in Paris, young Pribichevich helped his father write a book on
democracy, and, he says, quarreled with the
painters of Montparnasse on art, played the
violin (he had once planned to become a concert violinist), and argued in smoke-clouded
cafes with his exiled countrymen about the
"perfect democratic society"—which, they
agreed, Yugoslavia was not. Then, he continues, "I thought I would visit a relative of
mine in New York. I signed under oath a long
printed paper in English declaring that I was
not a bomb thrower, lunatic, or venereal
patient, and landed in Manhattan."

America was strange to him—at least at
first. "I could not understand why the country
with the largest workers' population in the
world should have no labor party; why centralization should be advocated by liberals, and
States' rights defended by big corporations;
why Tom Mooney should be in jail for murder
and Al Capone for tax evasion; why aliens
should be regarded with contempt by the sons
of aliens; why religion should be separated
from the state, and Darwin's theory of evolution banned by one State in the name of the
Bible; why bishops should oppose child-labor
regulation; why gangsters and kidnappers

STOYAN PRIBICHEVICH

should grow up next door to the strange
prophets and utopians of the Share-the-Wealth,
Epic, Social Justice, and Old-Age-Pension
plans; why the dictatorships of Louisiana and
Jersey City should flourish under a democratic
federal Constitution.

"Only gradually did I begin to grasp the
deep significance of American inconsistencies
. . . to realize that they were mere symptoms
of growth, showing a slow trend of the nation
toward ever-increasing democracy. In this
country I experienced for the first time the
magnificent feeling of absolute personal freedom. . . . I decided to stay here—and went
back to France to change my legal clothes. I
obtained an immigration visa and, toward the
end of 1935, returned to America as an immigrant."

But it was difficult for Pribichevich to find
work in Manhattan, despite his four languages
and his legal training. At a party in New
York the young lawyer had met a manufacturer
from Cleveland, who had teasingly told him
that as a newcomer to America he should learn
about American life by spending a few months
as a worker in his shop. Penniless in New
York, Pribichevich finally decided to take the
offer, and wrote to ask if the invitation was
still open. It was—and one gray, foggy morning in the beginning of 1937 Pribichevich got
off the train in Cleveland, bound for Warner
and Swasey's machine tool plant. He was depressed—he knew no one in the city, he had
never done physical work before, and he was
without money for the return trip. Assigned
to the second shift as a mechanic's helper, he
did rough work on that first night. As he
described it later, "I swept the floor and picked
up waste and dirt with my bare hands. I carried heavy machine parts in my arms or on
my shoulders. I screwed big pipes together."
That night he "slept like a dead man."

But the men in the shop were helpful, and
Pribichevich made friends among them. In
a full year at the plant he learned much about
America, in both its democratic and undemo-
cratic aspects—and more about American work-

PRIBICHEVICH, STOYAN—*Continued*

ers. When he returned to New York his friend Louis Adamic[40] encouraged him to write about his experiences, and his first article, "In an American Factory," appeared in *Harper's* Magazine in September 1938.

By this time he was working on a book, too. In Cleveland he had given a series of lectures on Central Europe and the Balkans (and been called "Doc" by his fellow-workers in the shop the next day); and he felt that no adequate treatment of the subject had yet been published in English. *World Without End* (1939), his own informal history of the countries of Southeastern Europe, was praised by reviewers as just such a book. It was also a book which showed his belief in the ultimate triumph of democracy and freedom in those lands which had known so little of either.

In 1940 Pribichevich accepted another invitation—to join the staff of *Fortune* Magazine. (He is now an associate editor.) The next year he showed his political acumen by insisting that under no conditions would the Yugoslavs accept a pact with the Axis and permit the passage of German munitions for use against the Greeks and British. "This apparently naïve opinion," he says, "was based, not on any inside information, but merely on a knowledge of the character and temperament of the people." After Yugoslavia was overrun by the Nazis in the spring of 1941 he tried to get back to his own country as a correspondent for *Time* and *Fortune,* but until the fall of 1943 he could get no closer than London. In the spring of 1942 he spent two months in England, on the London staff of the Luce publications, studying the various governments in exile and the free movements there. The result was an article in *Fortune* in August 1942, "The Exiled Governments," in which he concluded: ". . . a distinguished exile sums up—no one knows the names of the new European forms of government, but everywhere the common man will win. . . . You have never seen the faces of the men of Europe who will sit at the conference tables the next time." (He made no mention of the Partisan movement in Yugoslavia as yet, however: Mikhailovitch[42] was still the man of the hour.) A later *Fortune* article was his account of the total of six weeks spent at sea. An opinion of it was: "Much has been written about the Battle of the Atlantic, but few men have succeeded as well as Mr. Pribichevich in conveying the daily realities of this ceaseless struggle for mastery of the Western Ocean."

Later in 1942 Pribichevich again returned to London, where he sent back a series of reports on the British at war to *Fortune* and at the same time kept in close touch with the Balkan underground. (He has one cousin who is now a lieutenant on Tito's general staff, another who is an official on the Partisan National Committee.) *Time* Magazine was probably the first non-Leftist publication in America to tell the real story of Mikhailovitch, in November 1942 publishing an account of the Partisan movement in Yugoslavia based on Pribichevich's information; and in June 1943

Fortune published his comprehensive article on the Mikhailovitch-Partisan struggle, "Fratricide in Yugoslavia." This last article was followed by "Allied Strategy in Yugoslavia" in September 1943.

Finally, in the early winter of 1943, after returning to the United States, Pribichevich was sent to Cairo as a correspondent accredited to the Mediterranean theatre. As soon as he reached Egypt he began practicing parachute jumping in order to be ready at a moment's notice to be dropped on his native land. He broke his left foot in one jump, but in less than a month the plaster cast was off, and in the spring of 1944 he was notified by the military authorities that he had been chosen by lot to represent the entire American press in Yugoslavia. Shortly before he received the news he had cabled *Time*: "If I am chosen I may not see you until the end of the European war."

In February 1944 Pribichevich wrote a long story on Marshal Tito for *Life* Magazine. Then, early in May, he was flown into Yugoslavia to join Tito's forces, along with a Reuters' correspondent and two photographers. Landed ten miles behind the fighting front one starry night, they were met by Randolph Churchill, the son of Winston Churchill[42], and driven to the Partisan leader's mountain stronghold. "As I write this dispatch," Pribichevich noted afterward, "sitting on the grass with my typewriter on my knees, I can gaze at the deep perpendicular cleft cut in the huge rock where I had dinner with Marshal Tito last night. . . . I remember an Allied official who had expressed doubts as to whether certain territories of Yugoslavia could be called 'liberated' in the strictest sense of the word. Well, I entered Partisan territory ten miles behind the fighting line, traveled twenty-five miles in an automobile, saw a Partisan train, and visited the last session of the Anti-Fascist Congress. . . . This is liberated enough for me."

On the morning of May 25 Pribichevich was captured by Nazi paratroopers. Lined up against a wall for execution, he managed to talk the Nazis out of killing him in that particular fashion, but was then forced by the Nazis to follow them through a thick hail of Partisan fire. Finally the German front line began reeling back under the Partisan advance, however, and Pribichevich, ordered to carry a wounded German, pretended to retreat while actually dropping behind to let the Partisans catch up with him. With the Reuters' correspondent still in the hands of the Germans, as long as Pribichevich remained in Yugoslavia he represented the combined American and British press. The next month found him in Italy to re-equip himself and write his stories, after which he was to rejoin Tito.

Now a United States citizen, Stoyan Pribichevich makes his bachelor home in Connecticut when not on foreign assignment. He is an enthusiastic amateur musician.

References

Harper 177:362-73 S '38
Time 43:15 My 29 '44 por; 43:15, 69-70+ Je 26 '44

PRIMUS, PEARL (prē'mus) Nov. 29, 1919- Dancer
Address: h. 536 Madison St., Brooklyn, N.Y.

"Pearl Primus," said a glib magazine commentator once, "can bounce in the air like a rubber ball, an achievement rarely found in young girls on their way to their Master's degree at Hunter College." Her talent for bouncing is, however, the least amazing quality possessed by this dancer, who came to her profession quite by accident. After less than four years of study she is described as not only one of the outstanding dancers of the Negro race, but as one of the most important dancers of any race.

This gifted young dancer was born November 29, 1919, in Trinidad, British West Indies, the daughter of Edward and Emily (Jackson) Primus. In the United States, where her parents had taken her when she was very young, she attended Hunter College High School and Hunter College with no thought of ever becoming a dancer. Her ambition was to be a doctor and it was with that in mind that she took her B.A. at Hunter in biology and premedical sciences. Even after graduation in 1940, when she found that as a Negro she could get no laboratory work in New York, she continued studying at night. During her first year of graduate work she took health education courses at New York University, changing to the psychology department at Hunter the following year. (These psychology courses have helped her a great deal as a dancer, she says, in her approach to her audiences.)

Although Miss Primus was busy in the evenings with her graduate work, she wanted to find a paying job during the daytime. In 1940, therefore, with no position open to her in the field for which she was qualified, she turned to the National Youth Administration for assistance. The office was also unable to find her the work she wanted, so she was put into an NYA dance group as an understudy. She had had no previous training of any kind along this line, but she was able, with her innate vitality and sense of motion, to translate the movements she was taught into rhythm. Her adaptability to the medium was so amazing and her progress so noticeable that around July 1941 friends dared the novice to try for one of the scholarships offered by the New Dance Group in New York City. She tried for, and won, the scholarship, becoming the first Negro to enroll at the school—but even then she gave no thought to making the dance her career.

At about the same time the dance group at the NYA was discontinued, and Miss Primus looked about for other work. For a time she was a photographer for the Administration, and following that she went from one unrelated job to another. During the summers she taught health education in Manhattan and Brooklyn and held dancing classes at a camp. During the winters she was employed, successively, as a worker in a tin factory, a welder-burner at the Todd Shipyard in Hoboken, a clerk at the National Maritime Union, and a switchboard operator for the United Office and Professional Workers of America (CIO). Then, at the beginning of

Gerda Peterich

PEARL PRIMUS

1942, she began for the first time to think seriously about her dancing. The previous December, six months after winning the scholarship, she had appeared in a recital as a member of the New Dance Group's Performing Company, and the event had made her think of the dance as more than an avocation. In the latter part of 1942, while continuing to hold a job during the day, she therefore began to study with representatives of all the various dance techniques. (Today reviewers notice that her own individual style has not been marked by any of these teachers.) In addition to working and studying she also continued to appear in dance recitals with the Performing Company.

Finally, on February 14, 1943, Miss Primus was ready to give her first professional concert as a recognized artist. Her debut took place at the New York City Young Men's Hebrew Association, which makes a practice of giving new dancers an opportunity to appear before a public. Through its Dance Theatre the Association offers its facilities to those experienced artists who do not happen to have the machinery to give their own performances. Miss Primus' debut took place on a program with four other accomplished dancers, but she "walked away with the lion's share of the honors." John Martin of the New York *Times* wrote at the time that "if ever a young dancer was entitled to a company of her own and the freedom to do what she chooses with it, she is it."

Even after this successful appearance at the Y.M.H.A. Miss Primus did not completely give up the idea of becoming a doctor. But in a short time she found herself faced with making a decision about her professional future. That spring (1943) Cafe Society Downtown offered her a position as an entertainer. She had been finding the dance a satisfactory means of expression—particularly the expression of her feelings about her race and about democracy—but as yet she was not sure of its social value as opposed to

PRIMUS, PEARL—*Continued*

that of the medical profession. For advice she turned to John Martin, the reviewer. His feeling was that in a final survey of history one would never be able to say conclusively whether it was one of the creative arts or medicine that had had the greater curative power. With this in mind, Miss Primus finally decided in favor of continuing with her dancing, and in April 1943 she started an engagement with the night club (Cafe Society). She remained there ten months, leaving in February 1944 in order to conserve her energy for study, recitals, canteen work, and teaching—since November 1942 she has been a member of the faculty of the New Dance Group.

Her successful first solo performance, given in April 1944 at the New York City Y.M.H.A., was followed by an engagement at Cafe Society Uptown. In October Miss Primus made her Broadway debut, when she opened a ten-day run at the Belasco Theatre. Her troupe consisted of four male dancers, a five-piece jazz band, two drummers, two singers, a narrator, and the ballad singer Josh White [44], who sang "Hard Time Blues." Miss Primus introduced two new numbers: "Slave Market," which portrays the old slave custom of singing spirituals as a secret code for the Underground Railroad, and "Rock Daniel," a lesson on jazz. An innovation was a running commentary by which a narrator integrated the various numbers to produce an over-all picture of the Negro. Two months later the young dancer made her first appearance in a motion picture theatre, the Roxy, in New York City. She presented an elaborate version of her "African Ceremonial" with an ensemble of fourteen dancers. It was John Martin's comment that "it looked as if it might be a bit difficult for Miss Primus to top her company as soloist, but when the time came she did so without the slightest effort."

In a discussion of Miss Primus' work critics invariably mention her exceptional technical capacity and compositional skill. The technique which she has developed is based on a strange type of movement which she admits she does not yet quite understand herself. But to her a firm groundwork in technique is essential to good dancing. Too many of the newer dancers show an uninhibited style, she claims, which reveals a distressing lack of muscular control and training. In spite of this, however, she would like to draw from these young dancers in building a group of her own, for as yet they are not set in their style and are full of new ideas.

To Miss Primus her dancing is an intensely serious medium of expression. She considers it not a form of amusement but a method of education, a means of communicating to others her deep emotional and intellectual feeling about democracy and about the Negro as a race and as a member of the society in which he lives. "She is an artist of the people," writes a Negro critic, "in the same sense that Paul Robeson [41] is a people's singer." Her medium is "an odd combination of intellectualized choreography and free emotional drive." "Throughout," wrote the *Daily Worker* of

one of her concerts, "there is movement which is gorgeously exciting, stimulating, and deeply meaningful because of the thematic choice."

Her method of presentation is to offer selections from her six groups of dances. The first, the primitive group, is based on the authentic steps of the African and West Indian Negro, which she has adapted to American taste and understanding. She tries to suggest the fundamental dignity of these dances because, as she explains "in expressing primitive emotions it is easy to cross over the borderline into the vulgar." Miss Primus feels strongly about this group of dances, for she remembers from her own school years how ashamed she and her Negro classmates were of the one-sided version of the African Negro —pictured as totally lacking in any dignity— that was presented to them by their teachers. In presenting this group she is accompanied by two African and Haitian drummers. Her second group extends from the primitive period through the period of slavery and includes dances based on folk songs, spirituals, revivals, and on Langston Hughes's [40] poem "The Negro Speaks of Rivers." Her third group of dances covers the jazz and blues period in America. Real jitterbugging is an art in New York's Harlem, Miss Primus says, and her version of the dance has been formalized in its transition to the concert stage. The fourth group is concerned with social unrest, and one of the dances is built around Louis Allen's powerful poem of a lynching, "Strange Fruit," which is spoken during the dance. In offering these social themes Miss Primus is emphasizing clearly her strong feeling that the "Negro problem," so-called, is in reality a problem of democracy. As she dances she is saying to her audiences that, as in other countries men and women fight against Hitler's suppression of minorities, so they must fight against Fascist ideas in the United States.

At first the repertoire consisted only of these four groups of dances, which deal primarily with the Negro. Then, as her perspective broadened, she added a fifth group. The dances in this group speak not simply of the struggle of her race for justice and security but of the struggle of all races against suppression; and as a Negro she is speaking for the whole world. She has become, wrote the *Daily Worker,* "a potent voice not only for Negro America, but for all America and a free world." Miss Primus has dedicated these dances to the Underground in every country; and in her presentation of them she employs a musical version of Langston Hughes's poem of the Underground, "Our Spring Will Come," to emphasize her message.

Her audiences, whether they be Negro or white, frequently prove to be "wildly enthusiastic," although Miss Primus says she senses a certain antagonism when she first steps on the stage before a Negro audience. They are very tense at first—a little suspicious of her, a little afraid of what she may say— but the tension soon leaves them as she begins to dance. And critical response to her dancing has been, for the most part, as appreciative as that of her different audiences. "No other Negro dancer has yet appeared with anything like her artistic range or her innate equipment," says John Martin. "Her gifts are racially rooted, but not bound by any means to mere topical treatment." She is "a broadly creative dancer", "with tremendous power, a fine dramatic sense, the gayest kind of comedy lilt, and a technique that bowls you over. She can jump over the Brooklyn Bridge [a feat Miss Primus thinks she should try someday], and when in her impassioned dance to the poem 'Strange Fruit' she throws herself down and rolls across the floor at forty miles an hour it makes your hair curl with excitement."

"What she intends her gestures to mean," notes Edwin Denby, "is always completely clear." And in addition to telling the story, her movement is powerful and thrilling. "The roots of her real quality," writes John Martin, "lie in her apparent awareness of her racial heritage at its richest and truest, but it would be manifestly unfair to classify her merely as an outstanding Negro dancer, for by any standard of comparison she is an outstanding dancer without regard for race."

Occasionally during 1944 a review would indicate that Miss Primus had displayed signs of self-consciousness in some of her dance patterns, her more serious numbers at times revealing too great care for form, at the expense of feeling. "But when she really let go, as she did in 'Rock Daniel' and in. . . 'Hard Time Blues,'" said *PM* after one of these performances, "her unique personality and skill moved the large and very sympathetic audience to explosive enthusiasm." "One wishes she would dance . . . more in her personal, playful way," wrote Edwin Denby after another performance, "where her invention is most brilliant and free, and her personality warm and charmingly dignified."

Miss Primus' own opinion regarding the Negro artist in America—as with a Negro in any field—is that he should be thought of as an American and not as one in a category apart from his fellow artists and citizens. Although she herself has had offers to appear in motion pictures, she realizes that the time is not ripe for such a venture. "Until my name carries more weight," she explains, "I do not think that I could have much influence on the manner in which the Negro character is handled by Hollywood. As nationally established artists like Paul Robeson, Lena Horne [44], and Hazel Scott [43] continue to criticize the conventional way in which the Negro is presented on the screen, much will be accomplished."

In talking with this young dancer one cannot help being impressed with her sincerity and the deep feeling she shows for her work. She is a friendly, articulate person, well able to make herself understood both as a Negro and as an artist, and she has great personal vitality and charm. In appearance she is small and slender, with a pretty, intelligent face. She enjoys reading the Greek classics and poetry, and in school her own poetry-writing was encouraged by her teachers. Since the beginning of the War, she has been keeping up a correspondence with servicemen who have seen her dance at their canteens, Army camps, and Cafe Society, and with others who have only seen her picture. In addition to USO performances, Miss Primus

in 1944 also contributed her services to a Negro Freedom Rally at Madison Square Garden, and to Roosevelt rallies during the Presidential campaign.

References
Mademoiselle p203 N '43
PM p15 Ap 4 '44 pors
Vogue p48 Ag 1, '43 por

PUCHEU, PIERRE (pY"shœ' pyãr) (?)—Mar. 20, 1944 French politician and industrialist; former Vichy Interior Minister (1941-42); found guilty of treason by a special French military tribunal and executed by firing squad.

Obituary
N Y Times p1+ Mr 21 '44

QUEZON, MANUEL L(UIS) (kā'sôn mä-nwel' lū-ēs') Aug. 19, 1878—Aug. 1, 1944 Exiled President of the Philippine Commonwealth; a loyal friend of the United States despite a long and stubborn fight for the independence of his native islands, climaxed by the passage of the Philippine Independence Act of 1934 and his own election as first President of the Philippines in September 1935; persuaded to flee from his country before Japanese conquest, he reached Washington, D.C. in May 1942; see sketch 1941 Yearbook.

Obituary
N Y Times p4 Ag 2 '44 por

QUILLER-COUCH, SIR ARTHUR THOMAS (kwil'ẽr-küch') Nov. 21, 1863—May 12, 1944 Anthologist, poet, critical essayist, and lecturer; authority on English literature, professor at Cambridge University and compiler of *The Oxford Book of English Verse* (1939); author of some fifty literary works.

Obituary
N Y Times p19 My 13 '44

QUINTERO, JOAQUIN ALVAREZ *See* Alvarez Quintero, J.

RAMM, FREDRIK (?)—Nov. 15, 1943 Norwegian editor; was New York *Times* correspondent on dirigible *Norge* when it crossed the North Pole in 1926; former editor in chief of *Morgenbladet* and member of the Oxford Group in Norway; released from a German concentration camp shortly before his death.

Obituary
N Y Times p25 N 17 '43

RAMSAY, SIR BERTRAM (HOME) Jan. 20, 1883- British naval officer
Address: b. c/o British Admiralty, London; h. Bughtrig, Coldstream, Berwickshire, England

"Ramsay got 'em off, and Ramsay'll get 'em on again!" This was a common British reaction to Churchill's [42] appointment of Ad-

VICE-ADM. SIR BERTRAM RAMSAY

miral Sir Bertram Ramsay in 1943 as Allied
naval commander in chief on General Eisenhower's [42] invasion staff. This admiral, who
organized and directed the evacuation of British troops from Dunkerque three years before,
did indeed bring them back—in "the greatest
armada of specially constructed landing craft
ever floated on any sea."

Like his colleague, Canadian Admiral Nelles [44], Bertram Home Ramsay is the son of a
brigadier general, the late W. A. Ramsay, whom
he now outranks. He was born January 20,
1883 at Hampton Court, London. Again like
Nelles, Ramsay entered the Royal Navy as
a midshipman. His first promotion, to sub-
lieutenant, came in 1902, and his second, to
lieutenant, in 1904, after an early amphibious
action in Somaliland. He was graduated from
the Staff College and by 1915 had risen to the
command of Monitor No. 25. During the
First World War he commanded the famous
Dover patrol in the flotilla leader H.M.S.
Broke, and was made a member of the Royal
Victorian Order in 1918.

In 1919 Ramsay accompanied Lord Jellicoe,
commander of the Grand Fleet during the
First World War, on a mission to India and
the Dominions. From that time on he advanced steadily, alternating commands at sea
with duty ashore. After the flagship H.M.S.
Benbow, he was promoted to captain in 1923
and placed in command of cruisers: H.M.S.
Weymouth (1924-25) and the *Danae* (1925-
27). Ramsay spent two years on the staff
of the Royal Navy War College. From
1929 to 1931, while in command of H.M.S.
Kent, he was chief of staff for the China
Station. Ramsay was married in 1929 to
Helen Margaret, daughter of Colonel Charles
T. Menzies, the former commander of the
Berwickshire militia; the Ramsays now have
two sons.

The Admiral was ordered back from the
China Station in 1931 to join the staff of the
Imperial Defence College. He remained
there until 1933, and then assumed command
of H.M.S. *Royal Sovereign.* In 1935 Ramsay
was appointed chief of staff for the Home
Fleet and naval aide-de-camp to King George
V. In 1936 he was made a Companion of the
Bath, and in 1938, after forty years of service in the Royal Navy, Admiral Ramsay retired to his picturesque home, Bughtrig. He
resigned in December (with the usual promotion on retirement) at the age of fifty-five,
because he felt his appointment that August
as chief of staff to Admiral Sir Roger Back-
house was beneath his rank. Sir Roger had
been so favorably impressed by his work,
however, that when he became First Sea Lord
he recalled Vice-Admiral Ramsay on a war
appointment during the Munich crisis.

Soon after the outbreak of the Second
World War in 1939, Ramsay returned to
active service as flag officer commanding at
the port of Dover. "This," according to one
commentator, "was a not-too-demanding post
for a 'retired gaffer' and somewhat of a familiar job for Admiral Ramsay," who, "though
fully occupied, disappeared from public notice."
Dover was made an independent command.
Then came June 1940 and the blitzkrieg
through France. Britain looked on in horrified amazement as "German panzers slashed
through the French lines to Abbeville. The
Germans began a steady squeeze that compressed the British and French into a pocket
by the channel at Dunkerque," from which
they could neither counterattack nor escape.
The United Kingdom braced itself to face the
return of shattered remnants of the British
Expeditionary Force—and Admiral Ramsay
quietly sent out questionnaires to every boat
owner on the English coast.

Finally the time came for the Admiral's
plans to be put into action. He and his assistants worked feverishly through four days
and nights to "keep the ferry working"—the
"ferry" which saved hundreds of thousands
of British (and some French and Belgian)
troops from death or capture. In the words
of *Time*, "Inside the blazing lines of warships
lay transports of every description, from big
merchantmen and passenger steamers to channel ferries, private yachts, fishing smacks, tug-
drawn coal barges. [Many were manned by
boys and old men, some by women. Many
were not built for open water.] Over these
craft wheeled swarms of German high bombers,
down at them plunged wedge after wedge of
dive-bombers. Day and night the sea air was
filled with screaming gulls and bats of death,
including two whole German air corps. . . .
When German bombs blew up the locks which
held water in the [harbor] basins at low tide,
Dunkerque's inner loading piers became a
muddy, smoldering shambles. Embarkation
had to be carried out by shallow-draft ships
at the mole or by whaleboats, dories, rafts,
and wreckage bobbing in the surf along the
flat shelf of seashore. A calm sea and bright
sunshine made the rescue ships perfect bomb
targets for two days, and dozens of them were
smashed, burned, sunk. Britain admitted the
loss of thirty warships. Then a blessed fog

rolled in for forty-eight hours, saving countless lives. . . .

"Crossing the water to Dover, Ramsgate, or Sheerness was a prolongation of the stupefying nightmare. For beside the German armadas aloft, German motorboats raced alongside firing torpedoes. Each successive boatload that came in safely seemed so precious and triumphant that British morale soared out of the jaws of death." Although Dunkerque was an unquestioned military defeat for the British, who lost twenty per cent of their expeditionary force and much valuable equipment and material, the retreat was so brilliant as to seem almost a victory. Psychologically, it was a victory. French Vice-Admiral Jean Marie Charles Abrial commanded the Dunkerque naval area, but the British knew that Admiral Ramsay was responsible for this great rescue. His services were recognized by the King, who conferred on him the rank of Knight Commander of the Bath, and by his colleagues in the service, who conferred on him the nickname of "Dynamo" (short for "Operation Dynamo," the code name for the Dunkerque evacuation).

Another great task fell to Sir Bertram in April 1942, when the Admiralty selected him as flag officer to organize the secret Anglo-American expedition to North Africa (which made the Algiers and Oran landings). Seven months later, while Admiral Cunningham[41] was in the United States, Ramsay was the expedition's naval commander in chief with the acting rank of admiral. In this position, and later as deputy naval commander, Sir Bertram's service drew mention in official dispatches and praise from General Eisenhower.

After the "cleaning up" of Tunisia, Eisenhower selected Sir Bertram to plan the naval details of the Sicilian campaign, which has been called "a triumph in sea-borne transport." Ramsay "used more than 3,000 troopships and landing craft to bridge the water gap between Tunisia and Sicily," and was in command of the British area during the operations. Afterwards Eisenhower praised the "precise timing and perfect technique displayed" with "an enthusiastic and grateful 'well done.'" Ramsay repeated this success with the invasion of Salerno, and was rewarded by King George[42] with the K. B. E.

On December 29, 1943 Sir Bertram was appointed Allied naval commander in chief on Eisenhower's invasion staff. (In April 1944 the Admiralty finally changed him from the retired to the active list, and promoted him to full admiral.) From that day until June 6, 1944, when the Allied armies, comprising the greatest amphibious force ever to assault a hostile shore, stormed the French coast, Sir Bertram and his staff labored with United States naval leaders in formulating the detailed plans for the invasion of the Continent. The Navy's over-all plan for the operations provided for organizing the force; moving it across; and sustaining it on the beachhead. This operation necessitated the use of 4,000 ships, 11,000 planes and hundreds of thousands of men, machines and guns. D-Day-plus-one found Sir Bertram, having persuaded Churchill[42] not to accompany him, cruising to and from the invasion beach, inspecting operations,

and conferring with the operational commanders. "Everything has gone according to plan," he reported. "We have won the first round and can see no signs that the enemy will be in a position to beat us in the second round. . . . We have put about 100 per cent of our troops over," despite "very naughty" weather; "we have got through the defended beach zone and we have now made it possible for Montgomery[42] to fight a land battle."

Three unpublicized months later, the Admiral announced that two and a half million men had been landed on the Continent, with one and a half million vehicles and four million tons of supplies, exclusive of the supplies that had been flown in. In November he revealed that the American Navy was then responsible for the Atlantic ports from Brest to Le Havre, while the British were responsible for Dieppe, Calais, Ostend, Boulogne, Zeebrugge, and Antwerp. He pointed out also that the landings at Walcheren Island were done by the Navy and marines without any air support, and that the naval commanders had the task of putting the liberated and captured ports into operation.

In the words of one writer, Sir Bertram "could wear any kind of regalia and still look like what he is—a British naval officer. He is short but erect, with a thin nose, graying hair rather thin on top, and eyes that squint habitually from long peering out from an open bridge." One correspondent describes him as "austere, studious-looking"; another as "shy, stern, daring"; and a third as "a tough, slit-mouthed, energetic officer who well deserves his nickname, 'Dynamo.'"

References

N Y Times p7 D 30 '43
N Y Times Mag p7 Ja 23 '44
N Y World-Telegram p21 Ja 5 '44
International Who's Who 1942
Who's Who 1944

RAND, JAMES HENRY, SR. May 29, 1859—Sept. 15, 1944 Industrialist; pioneer in the business machine industry and founder of the company now known as Remington-Rand, Inc.; developed the visible index for blind-card files and the visible-name ledger.

Obituary

N Y Times p41 S 17 '44 por

RANK, JOSEPH 1854(?)—Nov. 13, 1943 British industrialist and philanthropist; his flour mills were said to "produce enough bread for one-seventh of the population of the United Kingdom"; one of the wealthiest men in England.

Obituary

N Y Times p19 N 15 '43 por

RANKIN, JOHN E(LLIOTT) Mar. 29, 1882- United States Representative from Mississippi

Address: b. House of Representatives Office Bldg., Washington, D. C.; h. Tupelo, Miss.

John E. Rankin, the Congressman who has represented the 1st District of Mississippi since

JOHN E. RANKIN

he took his first seat in the 68th Congress in 1921, was re-elected for the twelfth time in July 1944. Known as a fighter for "White Supremacy" and consequently vehemently opposed to the repeal of the poll-tax, in 1944 he was co-sponsor of the "States' rights" Eastland-Rankin Soldier Vote Bill; and as chairman of the House War Veterans Committee, he had much to say about the shaping of the G.I. Bill of Rights.

John Elliott Rankin was born in Itawamba County, Mississippi, March 29, 1882, the son of Thomas Braxton and Venola Modeste (Rutledge) Rankin. ("My people were slaveholders, and their ex-slaves lived around us during my day," he says. "They had more respect for me than for any flannel-mouthed demagogue who ever came around to tell them they were our social equals.") After receiving his LL.B. from the University of Mississippi in 1910 he hung out his shingle in Tupelo, where he served as prosecuting attorney from 1911 to 1915. Aside from time that he spent in an officers' training camp during the First World War, his law career was uninterrupted until 1920, when he was elected for the first time to the United States House of Representatives from the 1st Mississippi District, which gave him 10,400 votes out of a population of 200,158. The year before, in October, he had been married to Annie Laurie Burrous. They have one daughter, Annie Laurie.

This belligerent Southern Democrat whom Time Magazine calls "No. 1 Jew-baiter of the House" is also vehemently anti-Negro, anti-Communist, anti-union. Yet his Congressional record was such in 1937 that Stanley High, in an article in the Saturday Evening Post on Congressmen to the left of the New Deal, could call him a "veteran liberal." High pointed out that after years of denunciation of high electric rates and the power trust Rankin was co-author, with Senator George Norris, of the Administration's bill to create the Tennessee Valley Authority. "He managed to get most of

northeastern Mississippi tied into the TVA," continued High, "and, in every county of his own district, he has organized electric-power associations and instituted a movement to bring cheap electricity into the rural areas." Rankin has adopted as his slogan, "Let's electrify every farm home in America."

The Congressman from Mississippi represents a primarily agricultural district, the constituents of which are not only traditionally suspicious of Wall Street and the "trusts" but who stand to benefit directly by the rural electrification program; and the town where Rankin himself lives is one of those now using TVA power. His views on monopolies, utilities, and public power, which in the past frequently lined him up with New Dealers and which led him to campaign for Senator Norris in 1936, are therefore understandable. But the New Deal has stood for many things which he opposes more than he opposes "trusts." Even before the Second World War he fought the Anti-Lynching Bill, attacked the National Labor Relations Board, supported revision of the Wage-Hour Bill. One of the earliest bills he sponsored was to prohibit the intermarriage of whites and Negroes or Mongolians in the District of Columbia.

Time says that Rankin is (among other things) "an almost perfect example" of "the Ashurstian definition of a Congressman—'A man who votes for all appropriations and against all taxes.'" The first part of that statement, at least, is very much exaggerated; but it is true that as chairman of the House Committee on Veterans' Legislation he received many millions of dollars from the Treasury. As early as 1924 he assailed the Presidential veto of the Soldiers' Bonus Bill, and during the early '30's he was again active on behalf of the bonus, also getting passed by the House a bill safeguarding the estates of insane veterans. In March 1940 he succeeded in obtaining from the Veterans' Legislation committee what Time called "the most galumptious pension bill yet framed. Its terms: to pension all widows, children, and dependent parents of World War veterans who have died from any cause whatever." More recently he sponsored and put through a bill calling for the issuance of a flag to "the nearest relatives of certain persons who die in service of the land or naval forces of the United States."

As for foreign policy, after the outbreak of the Second World War the Mississippi Congressman voted for the fortification of Guam, for the military airplanes appropriation, for conscription, Lend-Lease, draft extension, and the repeal of the ban on arming ships. (He opposed the Administration only on revision of the Neutrality Act, on the lifting of the arms embargo, and on redefinition of "belligerent zones.") But more than once he tried to convince the House that the time was ripe for a negotiated peace between Great Britain and Germany, and in June 1941 he told the House: "Mr. Speaker, Wall Street and a little group of our international Jewish brethren are still attempting to harass the President . . . and the Congress of the United States into plunging us into the European War, unprepared. . . . These international bankers are so afraid that this peace movement . . . might take root . . .

before they can get us into it that on yesterday they held a rally on Wall Street and made a plea to that effect." New York's Congressman Michael M. Edelstein immediately jumped to his feet to compare this talk of "international Jewish brethren" to that of Hitler '42—then left, and dropped dead from a heart attack. When John Roy Carlson '43, author of *Under Cover*, interviewed Rankin he was told: "There is only one way to win this fight and that is to expose the international Jewish bankers as the war mongers. Tell the people that it is the Jews who want war. Do that and you've got the battle won."

Comparable with Rankin's anti-Semitism is his attitude toward Negroes. He once protested against a measure to end discrimination against Negroes in public places in the District of Columbia on the grounds that it would encourage assaults on white women. He has called the anti-discrimination orders of the Fair Employment Practice Committee "revolutionary, illegal, and destructive." In May 1942 he contended: "Mr. Speaker, one of the most vicious movements that has yet been instituted by the crackpots, the Communists, and parlor pinks of this country is trying to browbeat the American Red Cross into taking the labels off the blood bank they are building up for our wounded boys in the service so that it will not show whether it is Negro blood or white blood. That seems to be one of the schemes of these fellow travelers to try to mongrelize this nation." "If you people keep stirring up trouble for us in the South, we are going to need our young men trained when the War is over in order to take care of the domestic situation," he said at another time. In June 1943 he asserted that the Detroit race riots had been caused by the Administration's effort to eliminate Negro discrimination in war industries, telling those who supported the Anti-Poll Tax Bill that "their chickens are coming home to roost"; the next month he blamed the riots on "communistic Jews and Negroes," his charge being inserted in the *Congressional Record* without objection from the floor. Ever consistent in his policy toward the Negro, Rankin stated that "his greatest fear had been realized in the decision of the Supreme Court" when the United States Supreme Court in 1944 upheld the right of the Negroes to vote in primary elections. Rankin continued: "The Congress of the United States is the last hope of constitutional government as we know it." Some time before, in March 1943 he maintained: "If the Department of Justice as now constituted is destined to degenerate into a Gestapo for the persecution of the white people throughout the South and for the persecution of white Gentiles throughout the country generally, and for the stirring up of race hatred and promoting race strife, I must say it is well on its way." The next month, speaking of the indictment of seditionists, he told his fellow Congressmen: "Read this indictment . . . and ask yourself if the white Gentiles of this country have no rights left that the Department of Justice is bound to respect."

On the legislative front, Rankin has nevertheless voted with the Administration on some issues in 1943. He supported it on the $25,000 limit on salaries after taxes, voted against the Ruml '43 tax collection plan (and also against the Carlson-Ruml Bill, Robertson-Forand Bill, and the conference tax report), voted for more money for soil conservation, against prohibiting incentive payments for certain crops, and against limiting policy makers on price regulations. In April 1943 he got the appropriation for the Rural Electrification Administration restored through an amendment. In September he supported the Fulbright '43 post-War collaboration resolution.

Many a Republican has given the Administration more support, however. In 1942 Rankin demanded repeal of the Wagner Act and the wage-hour law, which would "destroy individual liberty"; he voted for restrictive labor legislation, opposed time-and-a-half pay for overtime, voted against price control legislation and for the inflationary farm-parity amendment, fought the Geyer Anti-Poll Tax Bill, and attacked the War Labor Board's handling of the Montgomery Ward case as an attempt to "turn that great enterprise over to the labor agitators in the CIO without any legal or Constitutional authority."

In 1943 he voted for the Hobbs Anti-Racketeering Bill and for the Smith '41-Connally '41 Bill and for overriding the President's veto of it. He opposed incentive payments to farmers or the granting of funds for a price rollback, voted for reduced funds for OPA enforcement and for legislation outlawing the Administration's consumer food subsidy program in extending the life of the Commodity Credit Corporation. He voted to abolish the domestic branch of the Office of War Information, to create the Smith Committee, to continue the Dies '40 Committee, and to dismiss Watson, Dodd, and Lovett '43. He called the President's post-War program "the most fantastic conglomeration of bureaucratic nonsense that ever has been sent to the Congress. It would wreck this Republic, wipe out the Constitution, destroy our form of government, set up a totalitarian regime, eliminate private enterprise, regiment our people indefinitely, and pile upon their backs a burden of expenditures that no nation on earth could bear." He attacked the proposed War Security Act, providing the death penalty for sabotage and lengthy imprisonment for espionage, declaring that "under this bill you could indict Congress, the American Legion, and the Daughters of the American Revolution." He called the bill to outlaw the poll tax communistic. He opposed repealing the Chinese Exclusion Act on the grounds that such action would play directly "into the hands of the Japs," who, he said, are trying to break down our immigration laws so as to flood the country after the War.

In October 1943 the House Privileges and Elections Committee, of which Rankin is ranking majority member, began to consider legislation for a Federal ballot commission to supervise soldier votes. Said Rankin: "We are not going to take it lying down when Congress attempts to interfere with the election laws"—and he described the Green-Lucas Service Men's

RANKIN, JOHN E.—*Continued*

Absentee Voting Bill, which had been introduced in the Senate, as a "monstrous" measure.

The Federal Soldier Vote Bill sponsored by Representative Eugene Worley of Texas was defeated in the House by a teller vote in January. (Of the 233 votes cast against a roll-call vote, 52 were cast by Democrats, of whom Rankin was one.) When President Roosevelt challenged the House to "stand up and be counted," the roll-call vote (224 to 168) again rejected the Administration-supported Worley bill. In another roll-call vote of 328 to 69, the Congressmen then passed (on February 3) the "States' rights" Eastland-Rankin Bill "designed to leave the service balloting to the several states, but with recommendations for state and Federal cooperation to carry to the maximum the opportunity for those under arms, and those working with them overseas, to vote." Jubilant Rankin hailed the passage of his bill as "the greatest victory for 'States' rights' and constitutional government that has been won in this Capitol in fifty years."

At about this time, however, the Senate passed the Green-Lucas Bill, a Federal ballot bill, making it necessary to work out a compromise between the conflicting measures. After a two-week deadlock, the Senate-House conferees finally agreed on a plan by which the use of the Federal ballot could be "restricted to those who could not vote legally by state ballot and those who, having applied for a legalized state absentee ballot, had not received one by October 1, and that only on the condition that the governor of the home state of the voter had certified by August 1 that the Federal ballot would be acceptable for counting under the state law." Rankin's was the only dissenting vote in the conference. While the "revolt" against Rankin was described by Thomas L. Stokes, Scripps-Howard writer, as an example of the "liberalizing movement which is germinating in the South," the compromise bill was branded by liberals as an attempt to rob servicemen of their vote. The bill was finally enacted, President Roosevelt signing it in mid-March after the House and Senate had approved it. (The President called this provision for the soldier vote inadequate.)

In January 1944 identical bills (commonly known as the G.I. Bill of Rights) were introduced in both the Senate and House. "An omnibus measure," in the words of *PM*, "the bill covers a wide range of benefits for the war veterans—hospitalization; education; loans for the purchase of homes, businesses, or farms; employment guidance; and unemployment benefits." The Senate, after amending "slightly" some of the provisions, approved it; but in April it was not yet reported out of the House War Veterans Committee, of which Representative Rankin was chairman. Early in May it reached the House after undergoing amendments, the major alterations being the reduction of fifty per cent of the unemployment compensation for returned soldiers. (Rankin had denounced any unemployment benefits that "would make idleness more attractive than jobs.") On the other hand, the committee raised the ceiling on loans to veterans from $1,000 to $2,000; loans also were made easier—three months instead of six months of service making an ex-soldier eligible for a loan. The

main provisions of the educational opportunities for veterans were left unchanged except for their limitation to men who were under twenty-five when they entered the service. The House committee also added an amendment that will supply artificial limbs for those who need them and train the veterans in their use; and the committee removed the Senate's $500,000,000 limit for building veterans' hospitals. ("We may need more than that," said Rankin, "so we authorized such appropriations as may be necessary.") In June the bill was approved in a House vote of 379 to 0.

In July Rankin pressed for a tidewater channel from New Orleans to the Gulf of Mexico—"Such a channel is needed for both commerce and defense purposes"; in October he called for an investigation of the "Battle of the Statler," in which two naval officers and members of the Teamsters Union were involved; and in November he offered a bill to raise the vocational rehabilitation allowance for the disabled veterans.

White-haired Rankin has been described as small and wiry. According to a New York *Sun* writer, "Words of all sorts come easily to him . . . he has a low oratorical boiling point." (Some of his fiery speeches have been given ovations.) Vigorous and apparently tireless, he declared himself against the 1944 Easter holiday for the national legislators: "It is necessary in my opinion for Congress to stay on the job."

References

Collier's 110:15+ S 19 '42
Nation 155:438 O 31 '42
PM p3-4 D 6 '43 por
Sat Eve Post 209:10+ My 22 '37
Time 35:14 Ap 8 '40 por
Who's Who in America 1944-45

RAY, CHARLES   1891—Nov. 23, 1943

Star of silent films; won fame "for his portrayal of country bumpkin roles"; produced some of his own films.

Obituary

N Y Times p21 N 24 '43 por

REED, JAMES A.   Nov. 9, 1861—Sept. 8, 1944 Former Missouri Senator, served three terms in the United States Congress, from 1911 to 1929; bitter foe of the League of Nations, the Hoover [43] Administration in 1932, and the New Deal; fought the World Court as a creature of the League; in 1928 and 1932 a contender for the Democratic Presidential nomination.

Obituary

N Y Times p15 S 9 '44 por

RENAULT, LOUIS   (rē-nō' lwē)   1877 (?)—Oct. 24, 1944 Pioneer automobile manufacturer who developed, with his brother, the largest motorcar plant in France; was arrested on September 23, 1944 on the charge of aiding the Nazis during their occupation of France; death occurred before a trial could be held.

Obituary

N Y Times p21 O 25 '44 por

REVENTLOW, ERNST, GRAF ZU (re-vent'lō) Aug. 18, 1869—Nov. (?), 1943 German author and journalist; although frequently a critic of Hitler '42, he was an ardent anti-Semite and one of the founders of the Nazi neo-pagan movement.

Obituary

N Y Times p19 N 22 '43

RIVERO (Y ALONSO), JOSE IGNACIO (rē-vä'rō hō-sä' ĕg-nä'syō) Feb. 3, 1895—Apr. 1, 1944 Havana publisher; a strong "nationalist" and anti-Communist, he received medals from Hitler '42 and from King Victor Emmanuel '43 shortly before the Second World War; in 1941 received Cabot Prize in journalism at Columbia University while his paper, *El Diario*, was honored with a bronze plaque.

Obituary

N Y Times p40 Ap 2 '44 por

RIZA SHAH PAHLAVI (ri-zä' shä' pa'-la-vē) 1877-July 26, 1944 Shah of Iran from 1925 to 1941; in 1921 he assisted in the overthrow of the Persian Government; Prime Minister from 1923 to 1925; chosen Shah by National Assembly after deposition of Ahmed Shah in 1925; was responsible for the change in name from Persia to Iran; abdicated in 1941, succeeded by his son Mohammed Riza Pahlavi.

Obituary

N Y Times p17 Jl 27 '44 por

ROBERTS, SIR CHARLES G(EORGE) D(OUGLAS) Jan. 10, 1860—Nov. 26, 1943 Canadian poet and author; leading figure in the development of a Canadian national literature.

Obituary

N Y Times p13 N 27 '43

ROBINSON, WILLIAM HEATH May 31, 1872—Sept. 13, 1944 Noted English artist and cartoonist; contributed humorous drawings to many English and American periodicals; a few of his illustrated works are the *Arabian Nights, The Water Babies,* Hans Andersen's *Fairy Tales,* and Walter de la Mare's *Peacock Pie.*

Obituary

N Y Times p23 S 14 '44

ROHDE, RUTH BRYAN OWEN *See* Owen, R. B.

ROKOSSOVSKY, KONSTANTIN (ru-ku-sôf'ske) 1895(?)- Soviet Army officer
Address: b. c/o Commissariat for Defense, Moscow

Marshal Konstantin Rokossovsky, veteran of the battles of Moscow, Stalingrad, and Orel, is known as one of the most capable officers in the Red Army. A handsome, romantic figure, his rise in military ranks has been swift and steady. He has enjoyed one of the most unique personal triumphs of the War,

MARSHAL KONSTANTIN ROKOSSOVSKY

the victory at Stalingrad, and the subsequent capture of twenty-two divisions of Nazi soldiers with the biggest prize of all, their commander, Field Marshal Friedrich von Paulus. With Konev '43, Malinovsky '44, and Tolbukhin, he is known as one of "The Four Horsemen of the German Apocalypse."

Like nearly all of the Russian Army officers who have distinguished themselves in the present War, Rokossovsky is a product of the Revolution and the Frunze Military Academy, "nursery of Soviet generals." Although in recent months his name has figured prominently in communiqués from the front, Rokossovsky's biography is a riddle and a mystery. Reports on the date of his birth vary from a questionable 1893 to an even more doubtful 1905. The former date seems more reliable, since it is further reported that he fought in the First World War and held the rank of major in the Czarist armies. In 1917, it is claimed, he joined the Red Guards, took part in the civil wars which followed and in the 1920 Russo-Polish campaign. A more imaginative but probably less reliable account has it that he was an orphan boy wandering homeless about the streets during the years between 1914 and the establishment of the Soviet Government. War correspondents have referred to Rokossovsky as "Polish-born."

It is certain, in any event, that Rokossovsky attended the Frunze Military Academy. There he specialized in tank and air warfare, both of which he has used effectively in the field against the Germans. Walter Kerr in *The Russian Army* (1944) says that he has heard that at the time of the German invasion of the U.S.S.R., Rokossovsky, then a colonel, was either in retirement or confined to quarters as a result of the purge of Red Army generals in 1937 and 1938. According to the same sources, Marshal Shaposhnikov '42, then chief of staff of the Army, asked Stalin '42 to release him because he was needed at the front, and Stalin assented. Kerr cannot

ROKOSSOVSKY, KONSTANTIN—*Cont.*

vouch for the story's authenticity. At any rate, soon after the outbreak of hostilities Rokossovsky was promoted to major general "because of a heady, stubborn defense that stalled the first Nazi Blitz for a month back of Smolensk." The battle of Smolensk, which has been described as a Pyrrhic victory for the Germans and "one of the bloodiest episodes of the Russo-German War," was waged during the summer of 1941. The 8th Panzer Division and the 5th and 137th German Infantry Divisions suffered severe casualties. By the time the Russians were finally forced back they had gained valuable knowledge of German tactics, and Rokossovsky had "acquired a disdain for the German Army, even while he recognized its mechanical strength." Within a few months "he set going Russia's first counteroffensive."

Rokossovsky's experience at Smolensk contributed heavily to his planning for the defense of Moscow. "By studying German tactics," he said, "we changed our own method of attack and step by step inflicted increasing losses." He was confident that the German blitzkrieg was not invincible and stated in a radio speech, "I fought against the fathers. Now I'm fighting the sons. . . . I do honestly think the fathers were better soldiers. . . . Hitler '42 has ruined the German Army. It is an *ersatz* army. It is obsessed with the desire for gain. . . . The quality of any troops must atrophy under such conditions."

Rokossovsky was in command of one of the seven armies which were responsible for the defense of Moscow in the winter of 1941-1942, and for the Russian counteroffensive. The *Wehrmacht*, with overwhelmingly superior forces, had captured the important railway center of Orel to the south of Moscow, broken the Front at Medyn, and by November 25 Rokossovsky, driven back through Istra just thirty miles from the capital, was fighting a losing battle along the highway that runs northwest from Moscow. That night the telephone rang in his dugout. As he himself describes the conversation: " 'Stalin speaking. What's the situation?' I explained it to him in detail, trying not to forget even the small things. I explained our position on every point of my sector. Then I heard the quiet voice again. 'Hold even stronger. We'll help you. That's all.' " Headquarters then began throwing its strategic reserves into the battle up and down the Moscow Front; but Rokossovsky had some bad days before they could come to his aid. At one place several German tanks and a company or so of infantry got in behind him and were not destroyed until they reached a village only fifteen miles from Moscow.

By the end of November the seven armies and two cavalry corps were operating in four groups, guarding the four main approaches to Moscow, Rokossovsky's army constituting the bulk of the northwestern group assigned to defend the highways leading in from Leningrad and Volokolamsk. And on December 6 his 16th Army was able to start its counteroffensive. By that time others had straightened out the line, and Rokossovsky

began with everything he had because he knew that the Nazis had exhausted their reserves. The next afternoon the Germans were retreating on a wide front, after many stubborn counterattacks. Rokossovsky used the numerous partisans operating around Istra and Volokolamsk to good advantage, and the retreat grew disorderly. He then sent in a cavalry corps, and the Nazis fled in terror. Soon the four groups of armies in their westward march converged to such a point that Rokossovsky's could be pulled out of line and sent south to help the army that had swept all the way from Tula south of Moscow to Kaluga south of Mozhaisk; and from then on it operated with the southern group.

Using anti-tank rifles, hand grenades, "Molotov cocktails", and cavalry units against persistant German tank attacks, Rokossovsky's men had struck "the major blow in the Russian counterattack," putting nearly 200 enemy tanks and 29,000 enemy troops out of action; and Soviet newspapers hailed General Rokossovsky as "the victor of Moscow." In an interview he described his own tactics in the battle of Moscow as follows: "There [at the approaches to the city] the Germans tried to encircle and annihilate my forces. In the battle of Moscow, we used maneuver tactics very widely. While beating off frontal attacks, we strengthened our flanks, parried the German flanking movements, and, at the same time, struck many blows at the enemy's rear lines, with tank-borne troops also attacking their flanks." Rokossovsky went on to describe the bloody fighting and estimated that the Germans lost more than fifty per cent of their forces. He ended with a tribute to his men. "But the chief reason for the collapse of the German offensive is the supreme courage and unparalleled heroism of our men and their commanders. They fought like lions with their backs to Moscow."

For several months after the battle of Moscow little was heard of Rokossovsky, and it was assumed that he was recuperating from a wound received during battle. Early in 1943, however, he was commanding the six Soviet armies of the Don Front when they began their liquidation of the German 6th Army which was surrounded inside and just west of the city of Stalingrad. An ultimatum to surrender issued to the Germans had not been answered, and so the Russian "annihilation drive" was launched. While the Russians advanced from the west the Germans kept backing into Stalingrad (an exact reversal of their positions a few months before), and on January 27 General Chuikov's '43 62nd Army inside Stalingrad joined Rokossovsky's other armies in the final destruction of the surrounded groups. On January 29, raised to the rank of colonel general, Rokossovsky received the highest military honor offered by the Soviet Union, the order of Suvorov, First Degree.

On February 2, 1943 a special Moscow communiqué announced the end of the battle of Stalingrad, "perhaps the most costly military operation the world has ever known," and the capture of a total of twenty-four German generals and one field marshal. In a dramatic and history-making scene Generals Rokossovsky and Voronov reviewed their victorious troops and the seemingly endless lines of German prisoners. They interviewed Field Marshal von Paulus, surveyed the extent of Nazi losses, and Rokossovsky found occasion to repeat one of his favorite sayings, "The myth of German invincibility is built on sand."

Called to Moscow, Rokossovsky received Premier Stalin's personal congratulations. The strategy for the battle of Stalingrad had been drawn up by the Supreme Command, but, says Time Magazine, "the tactical execution was Rokossovsky's." In the weeks that followed the victory, Rokossovsky concentrated on "mopping-up" operations in the Don region. In April 1943 he was promoted to the rank of army general.

With the advent of summer a German offensive was expected. Before such a drive could be launched effectively, however, the Red Army had begun its own offensive, on July 15, on the fronts north and east of the "key German base" of Orel. Rokossovsky was one of the leaders in this summer offensive, along with Generals Vatutin [44] Sokolovsky, Konev, and Popov. The progress of Russian troops was steady and notably successful. By July 24 Joseph Stalin was able to proclaim "that the Nazi plans for a summer offensive must be considered as completely frustrated." Early in August Orel and Belgorod were captured, and a 120-gun salute was fired in Moscow for the victorious troops of General Rokossovsky and his fellow generals.

Rokossovsky was then placed in charge of the Sevsk drive. His troops penetrated the northern Ukraine, cut the Bryansk-Sumy Railroad and captured 200 towns within five days. In the face of his drive, the Germans began a "systematic evacuation" of the entire area. Sevsk fell, and Moscow had occasion to fire another 124-gun salvo in celebration. Wasting no time, Rokossovsky led his troops in a powerful drive toward Kiev. On September 10 it was announced that Bakhmach, a key railroad town on the road to Kiev, had fallen to Rokossovsky's forces, who were again honored with a cannon salvo in Moscow. They continued their advance southward, weaving, according to the New York Times, "a web of defeat along the Dnieper." By December they had penetrated deep into the strong German defense line virtually from one end of White Russia to the other, and were fighting in snowdrifts more than three feet deep in their drive on Zhlobin and Rogachev, rail hubs of the Gomel region. Rokossovsky's drive on Zhlobin was generally regarded as preparation for an expected winter offensive from Nevel to Riga.

Rokossovsky opened the year of 1944 with a drive on the White Russian front against Mozyr, a town of 12,000 about 125 miles northwest of Kiev. Described as "the Red Army's ablest fortifications-buster," he ripped an eighteen-mile gap in the defenses of the stronghold, during the first twenty-four hours of that battle, attacking from the north, northeast, east, and southeast. At this time it was revealed that Partisan guerrillas, who had been operating in the desolate 250-mile-long Pripet Marshes of pre-War Poland, had joined Rokossovsky's troops and were acting as guides and forerunners. On February 22, when the cold froze swamps and rivers and the clear skies allowed the Soviet Air Force to operate, he unleashed another offensive, aimed at the heavily fortified cities of Zhoblin and Bobruisk, key points of the German White Russian defense line. Within four days his men had taken Rogachev and "several other inhabited places," and by late June they had fought their way up to and then into Zhoblin. In Stalin's order of the day for June 26, fifty of Rokossovsky's subordinate generals were commended, and on the 29th their commander was made a marshal.

Rokossovsky and his fellow Army leaders now faced no natural barriers, but only the same open country of plains and marshes across which Hitler's [42] panzers had raced three years earlier. The first stop on the road to Berlin for his 1st White Russian Army was Bobruisk, where it encircled five German divisions and killed a reported 8,000 Germans in a day. This put his command only seventy-four miles northeast of Minsk, the local capital; the 1st Army's bag of prisoners for the last week in June was 35,680, according to the Moscow communiqué. On July 4, the eleventh day of "a whirlwind Soviet offensive that had driven the Nazis back 165 miles across White Russia and Poland and cost them more than 213,000 men killed or captured," Minsk fell to the combined forces of Rokossovsky and General Ivan D. Chernyakhovsky [44] of the 3rd White Russian Army. This victory, saluted in Moscow with twenty-four salvos from 324 guns, was regarded there as "one of the decisive battles of the War," for it drove the Germans into a disorderly retreat. Rokossovsky's army moved southward to replace Zukov's 1st Ukrainian Army before Kowel, which was soon captured.

Eleven days after taking Minsk, Rokossovsky forced the Yaselda and Pripet Rivers in a naval action, and sent his tanks and infantry in to capture the German supply base of Pinsk. His northern wing drove simultaneously toward Białystok and the Brest Litovsk railroad, joining General Zakharov in a pincers movement aimed at Białystok. While Rokossovsky's forces outflanked Brest Litovsk, Red airplanes dropped leaflets on the Germans before Warsaw which read simply, "Rokossovsky Kommt!" —Rokossovsky is coming! By late July it was reported that "Brest Litovsk and Białystok, bastions guarding the roads to Warsaw, now were of little use to the Germans because of the Russian drives around them," and Rokossovsky's troops of the 1st White Russian Front were attacking in a broad sweep toward Warsaw.

On July 23 tank, cavalry, and infantry detachments of the White Russian Front armies broke into Lublin, which fell on the 25th. (This city, which the Germans had made notorious as a slaughterhouse for Jewish captives, soon became the headquarters for the Moscow-approved Polish Committee of National Liberation.) At this time Moscow reported that Rokossovsky's army had "torn more than 9,000 square miles out of the Axis grip in German-occupied Poland, and beyond their immediate objective, Warsaw, lay the plains leading to Germany on the shortest road to Berlin—365 airline miles from Siedlce." For the month from late June to late July the 1st White Russian Army was credited with 182,236 Germans: more than 120,000 killed and 62,236 captured.

(Continued next page)

ROKOSSOVSKY, KONSTANTIN—*Cont.*

At this time commentators stated that "Rokossovsky and Konev and a half-dozen other generals are moving on the Germans with the greatest military force ever engaged in a single operation, at a pace never before attained except by small mobile columns. The force, with its reserves, is estimated by the United Press at 400 divisions (about 6,000,000 men). The speed of its spearheads, operating over a front of 1,000 miles—the front is continually broadening—is sometimes as much as forty miles in a single day. One of the greatest military miracles of all history is being performed in supplying front troops of possibly 3,000,000 men . . . . This huge front has been treated like a single battle, in which armies were moved like divisions and regiments like platoons. The observer also noted that the Russians are fighting with complete disregard of losses in order to attain their ends, which include the destruction of the power of the German Army."

Rokossovsky had little opposition on the road to Warsaw, and his troops were therefore able to move with great speed; but the approaches to the occupied capital itself were fiercely defended. Huge tank battles were reported there, with Moscow claiming that the Germans had lost 151 tanks on August 4 alone (and the Nazis claiming to have knocked out 192 Soviet tanks). On July 30, when Rokossovsky's patrols had penetrated into the east bank suburb of Praga, the Kosciusko Station in Moscow allegedly broadcast the message, "People of Warsaw, to arms! Let the entire population stand together and . . . attack the Germans." (Russian stations had made a series of such demands earlier.) On August 1 "General Bor" (Tadeusz Komorowski, chief of staff to Sosnkowski), who recognized the authority of the Polish Government-in-Exile in London, led the Warsaw population in an uprising against their German oppressors. But the Russian patrols were turned back, and Soviet artillery fire against Praga ceased on August 3, leaving General Bor to "defend a desperate situation" alone, while Rokossovsky regrouped his forces. On August 15, when it was evident that the Warsaw patriots were being "cut to ribbons," the Polish Government-in-Exile made the first of a series of protests against the lack of aid from Poland's allies. And on August 17 the Soviet newspaper *Izvestia* charged the Polish commander in chief, General Kazimierz Sosnkowski, with ordering the Warsawites into a hopeless fight in order to embarrass the Russians. Charges and countercharges flew from Pole to Russian; Churchill '42 spoke of the "heroic struggle" in Warsaw, "watched by the whole world."

On September 1 Sosnkowski charged in an order of the day that Warsaw had been abandoned by her allies. A few days later Mayor Fiorello H. La Guardia '40 of New York received a message from the Mayor of Warsaw which said, "The day we chose for the beginning of our uprising was the last that could have saved us from the Germans' putting into practice their destructive plans for the extermination and deportation of the inhabitants of our city. Why are we left alone. . . ? Why is there no air succor coming?" On September 11 La Guardia urged quick relief for Warsaw on his radio program; and on the next day

(whether or not there was a connection) Rokossovsky reopened his attack on Warsaw, after regrouping his forces. General Zakharov's army joined him on the banks of the Bug River, forming a straight twenty-one-mile front north of the city's eastern limits. And finally, after the Warsaw patriots had withstood the German siege for seven bitter weeks, Rokossovsky's patrols crossed the Vistula and established contact with General Bor's hard-pressed force, whose casualties were estimated at 200,-000. Although the Russians had taken Praga, they were still faced with the problem of capturing Warsaw itself, which is located on a 130-foot bluff across the 450-yard Vistula. (Among Rokossovsky's troops here was the Polish 1st Division of General Zygmunt Berling's command, under General Berzuik, which gave allegiance to the Lublin Committee.) On October 3, 1944, the London Poles announced the surrender of the patriots after sixty-three days of fighting; and on October 26 Rokossovsky opened a renewed drive, which continued as the year drew to a close.

The reasons for Rokossovsky's failure to aid the Warsaw fighters more effectively remained a mystery. "One may reason," wrote Edwin L. James, "that the Russians saw greater value in devoting themselves to their very brilliant politico-military campaign in the Balkans, or one may reason that the German line in Poland was too tough to crack." Each of these hypotheses presented certain difficulties to the observer.

Marshal Rokossovsky is six feet four inches tall, blue-eyed, and "huge and ebullient." He is married, and his wife heads one of the Women's Councils in Moscow, in charge of the welfare of the wives, mothers, and children of Red Army men. Well liked by the men he commands, Rokossovsky has a reputation for cheerfulness and calm. He has said, on several occasions when his armies faced defeat and destruction: "The German Army is a machine, and machines can be broken."

References

N Y Herald Tribune p8 D 15 '41
N Y Sun p13 My 6 '43
N Y Times p3 Ja 30 '43; p3 Je 18 '43
Time 41:24 F 8 '43; 42:24 Ag 23 '43
    (por cover); 42:26-7 S 13 '43 por
Kerr, W. The Russian Army 1944

ROMMEL, ERWIN (rŏm'əl er'vēn) 1891

—July 18(?), 1944 Field marshal and foremost Nazi soldier; reported dead after strafing of his car in France by an Allied plane; a ruthless, colorful master of tank warfare tactics; attained great prestige as commander of the Afrika Korps in 1942; often referred to as the "Desert Fox"; see sketch 1942 Yearbook.

Obituary

N Y Times p1+ O 16 '44 por

ROOSEVELT, THEODORE, JR. Sept.

13, 1887-July 12, 1944 United States Army officer, public official, explorer, author, publisher; eldest son of the twenty-sixth President of the United States, he served in both World Wars; was brigadier general at the time of his death from heart attack at the Normandy front; active in public life: elected New York State Assemblyman in 1919; Assistant Secretary of the Navy (1921-24); Governor of Puerto Rico (1929-32); Governor General of Philippine Islands (1932-33); author and co-author of seven books; since 1935 was officer of publishing house Doubleday, Doran & Company.

Obituary

N Y Times p1+ Jl 14 '44 por

ROSS, MALCOLM June 1, 1895- United States Government official; author

Address: b. Fair Employment Practice Committee, Washington, D.C.; h. Route 1, Vienna, Va.

Malcolm Ross, in 1944 head of the United States Fair Employment Practice Committee, was born in Newark, New Jersey, June 1, 1895, the son of William Lawrence and Gertrude Estelle (Ross) Ross. His ancestors had come to this "ugly industrial city" from Connecticut 200 years before. His was not an adventurous childhood—although he was to make up for it later. "I was trotted to Sunday school once a week for all my growing years. We had family prayers and sang hymns on Sunday night. My mother had the local Epworth League, and every Monday afternoon I was there with a Bible verse learned and ready to have a gold star stuck on my card." After three years in the local high school, young Malcolm was sent to a Hudson River private school "where my parents thought I would pick up a bit of polish." After a short time there an instructor friend warned him that he needed a couple more years of decent college preparation, and recommended him to Hotchkiss Preparatory School for a scholarship. From Hotchkiss he graduated into Yale in 1915.

In *Death of a Yale Man* (1939) Ross tells about his four years at that University, where the religion of the undergraduate was "success in extra-curriculum activities." Nearly two years spent as a first lieutenant in the Army Air Service (he left Yale to enter a training camp in April 1917 and did not return until the early winter of 1918-1919) did not materially change his outlook on life. Having received his B.A. in 1919, within a month of his return, he therefore accepted a job as messenger in the New York office of Lee Higginson & Company, the stock brokers. His allotted district included a block on lower Broadway and eastward to Little Italy and Chinatown as well as the Jewish Cemetery. He hated his work, not so much because he disapproved of Wall Street (he was as eager as anyone to become rich), but because "my hands got clammy and my tongue thick whenever I tackled a prospect." It was not long before he made a compact with a friend, a former Yale acquaintance who now worked for the same firm, to quit and go adventuring in the hinterlands with only the work of their hands to support them. Boredom and the itch for adventure were Ross's real motives for taking this rash step, rather than early symptoms of social consciousness. "Workers were remote beings, a race of underlings tra-

MALCOLM ROSS

ditionally dedicated to supporting the higher civilization—which was New York and ourselves."

Ross's first step was to take a flier in oil in the Texas oil fields. This turned out badly he has written; "thereafter I wandered the West with nothing in my hand but a naïve pleasure in hardboiled men and day-for-the-day living." An older Yale graduate got him a job on a pipe-line gang, and later Ross started a little grocery business, but on the whole, he says, his career in the oil fields was a dismal failure. "I turned my back on the opportunity to work my way up in my sponsor's oil company. I let oil madness lead me into absurd ventures. I panned this unpromising claim for nuggets of beauty when I should have been peddling my groceries. Yet one thing I learned. He who lives among working people has to make his own way."

From Texas he drifted to Arizona, having salvaged enough cash from the grocery business to buy a ticket for Bisbee, where his friend from New York was digging ore as a mucker in the Copper Queen Mine. Ross got a job in the same mine, first as a mucker to a mule skinner. There, working with the miners, talking to them, sharing their working conditions, he learned more. "I came to understand that my pals in Texas were an ornery lot. . . . The copper miners were of finer stuff." When the world price of copper fell, emptying Bisbee and all the other copper towns, he went willingly enough back to New York to work for a firm of efficiency engineers "who had persuaded the Government to let them put the United States Post Office on a bing-bing-bing basis." At first sent to tell the old-timer clerks in Detroit "where to get off," then assigned to take inventory in an elevator factory, he grew bored again. For some time he had had vague newspaper ambitions, and now he did something about them. As a Yale man, he needed barely to mention them before he found himself heading back

ROSS, MALCOLM—*Continued*

to Texas with an assured job as a cub reporter on the Dallas *News*.

On the Dallas *News* Ross was assigned to cover the criminal courts and to write a "daily poem." He spent a year doing this, then turned up in Kentucky, with the Louisville *Courier-Journal*. By the mid-twenties he found himself on the New York *Morning World*, but a couple of years before that newspaper stopped publication he left it to become a novelist. Incidentally, although Ross's grief over the passing of the *World* was as great as that of most of his colleagues, he later came to believe that it died of "little-heartedness." "What was happening to the people in fetid tenements was deserving of no inquiry, unless there was conspicuous violence."

Ross's first novel was *Deep Enough* (1927), the story of the experiences of an ex-bond salesman who drifts westward and, laboring with his hands for the first time, gets beneath the surface of life and finds among laborers and miners the only contacts free from pretense and artificiality. Of it the *World*'s reviewer wrote: "On the whole it is first-rate stuff." Ross was generally praised for his vivid writing and for his fresh and interesting material, but the book was not considered of great importance by most reviewers. Of *Deep Enough* Ross himself says: "I did a fairly good job in reproducing the Texas roustabouts and Arizona muckers of my *Wanderjahr*, but, because I had seen them with the romantic eyes of an uneducated Yale man, I completely neglected them as workers playing a part in an exciting industrial game. Their physical life I knew and shared. In my raw ignorance I skipped their problems."

A second novel, *Penny Dreadful* (1929), "tried to make fiction out of my hatred of what the tabloids have done to newspapers." *Penny Dreadful* was the story of a sob writer for the tabloids who attempts to ruin the lives of her ex-husband and the girl he loves, but whose vindictiveness acts as a boomerang. The New York *Evening Post* called it "fast-moving and pleasant," the *Saturday Review of Literature* "heavy-footed and dull," but neither publication thought it belonged to the ages. Ross explains that his publishers set in type the first draft, which he considered spoiled by a "dragged-in-at-the-heels" love story, on irretrievable galleys while he was abroad.

Where he was was in Italy, working on a third novel about Labrador. He had learned to know that country as a New York newspaper reporter sent to cover the arrival of the Army World Flight, but, he says, "my training in unreality inspired me to clutter up good material on the real people of Labrador with an inane fictional hero." *Hymn to the Sun* (1930) has as its plot the attempts of an artistic idler to win the wife of a medical missionary in Labrador. Critics agreed that the book was highly dramatic, and Stanley Walker [44] suggested that it "should form the basis of one of the grandest motion pictures ever made," but Ross asks: "Why did not we scribblers of the 1920's, supposed observers of life, have courage to look it in the eye?"

Hymn to the Sun was Ross's last novel. He returned from Italy in time for the stock-market crash of October 1929 and for a time was out of a job, but then became assistant editor of the *Sportsman Pilot*, a glossy magazine dedicated to the increase of amateur aviation. Later he found himself "editor, rewrite desk, make-up man, and part-time worrier about our finances, which were pretty sick." After working for a year and a half to keep the magazine alive, he finally heard that the aviation financiers downtown had decided not to support it any longer. The chief result of this job was a lifelong interest in aviation and a book, *Sailing the Skies* (1931), a history of the development of gliding machines and of gliding as a sport. The New York *Times* called this "no academic treatise on a subject of which the author writes with detached interest, but a contagiously hearty account of an activity in which he himself plainly enjoys taking part."

After Ross had edited a book on industrial research, *Profitable Practice in Industrial Research* (1932), for the National Research Council, the Quakers asked him to come to the coal fields to live and work with them in the mine towns scattered all over Kentucky, West Virginia, and Tennessee, to observe what was happening, and to write about it. What was happening in the years 1931 and 1932 was—to put it bluntly—starvation. Ross's "tempered descriptions" of what he saw in *Machine Age in the Hills* (1933) were "but misty reflections of the misery in the mine valleys that winter," where the Quakers had been ordered by President Hoover [43] to feed the miners' children. Although Ross's book, which included an account of terrorism in Harlan County by the mine operators, received almost unanimously good reviews, "few took any interest in my thesis, and . . . I let old habits drag me back to New York."

In early 1933 Ross was living in a borrowed basement apartment on New York's West Side. All his short stories having been rejected by the magazine editors, he decided to take a cabin in the Connecticut hills in order to write. He had slept in his cabin exactly one night when, returning to pick up some things in New York the next day, he found a telegram suggesting the possibility of a job in Washington. Immediately he went south, and upon reaching Washington he was attached to the Consumers Advisory Board, "a trained flea in General Johnson's [40] circus." During the period of the NRA he fought in vain for grade labeling. Then NRA was killed by the Supreme Court, and Ross was asked by Francis Biddle [41], at the time chairman of the National Labor Relations Board, to join his Labor Board staff. Since then Ross has been connected at some stage with practically all the important labor relations agencies of the Federal Government, in 1936 becoming Director of Information for the National Labor Relations Board. "When the big issue was discrimination on the job against men who belonged to labor unions, Ross was sweating away at the unhappy task of trying to get the newspapers to print the story of the NLRB." In *Death of a Yale Man* Ross tells the story of the Rand hearings, the Big Steel and Little Steel strikes, and other history-making labor dramas. He himself had become a charter member of the NRA Lodge of the American Federation of Government Employees (A.F. of L.).

The autobiographical *Death of a Yale Man* was published in 1939, its theme the author's development from a bond-selling Yale graduate to a position on the NLRB. The *Nation* called *Death of a Yale Man* "a book you wish every middle-class American might read"; the New York *Times* announced that it would "please those who believe that the Wagner '40 Act is perfect"; the *Saturday Review of Literature* described it as "the post-War equivalent of Lincoln Steffens' *Autobiography*," adding that "Ross surpasses Steffens in variety and scope of language and style."

In May 1943 Monsignor Francis J. Haas '43 was appointed head of the Fair Employment Practice Committee, set up by President Roosevelt '42 to combat discrimination because of race, creed, or color in industries which have been awarded Government contracts. In July, Ross was appointed executive director of the Committee, and three months later Monsignor Haas, who had been made bishop of Grand Rapids, took leave of the FEPC. He had declined to name his successor, but Ross had been named to that post on October 15, and he was promptly sworn into "Washington's No. 1 hot spot." Shortly afterward Comptroller General Lindsay Warren announced that Executive Order 9346 on contracting agencies (to incorporate a non-discrimination clause in each contract awarded by them) was not of a mandatory nature: was not an order but a "directive." This decision apparently struck a death blow to the power of the FEPC to enforce its non-discrimination orders. On October 30 Ross announced that the FEPC had asked Attorney General Francis Biddle to consider the scope and meaning of the Executive order. President Roosevelt himself promptly announced that his order had been mandatory.

There were many reasons why Roosevelt's firmness was important. In September FEPC hearings had been held on discrimination against Negroes in the railroad industry. Late in November the FEPC notified twenty railroads and seven railway unions that in thirty days they must cease all discriminatory practices—practices whose chief effect had been to prevent the promotion of Negroes to better jobs on the railroads. On December 13 sixteen Southern railroads termed the FEPC's orders empty of authority, and two weeks later the FEPC, having been openly defied by both employers and unions, certified the Committee's orders to the White House "for such action as the President may determine." The certification preceded the Presidential order directing the Government's seizure of the railroads. At the same time encouragement was given to the recalcitrant employers and unions by the Smith '41 Committee of the House, which launched a long-anticipated Congressional attempt to "get" the FEPC by ordering the seizure of the records on the railroad case. On January 3, 1944 President Roosevelt appointed a three-man committee to study the same case, and Ross welcomed this step.

This committee was headed by Judge Walter P. Stacy of North Carolina, who held a number of conferences, but little progress was reported, or for that matter, expected. Herbert Corey, in an article for *Nation's Business,* declared that it was the opposition of seven railroad brotherhoods to Negro workers which had caused the trouble, and not the employers' opposition. "Anyone who has a bowing acquaintance with practicality," stated the article, "knows that, if the brotherhoods refused to accept colored workers on even terms, the roads would be as powerless as so many sick cats." Nevertheless, in April Ross was able to announce that the Pennsylvania Railroad Company had agreed to employ qualified dining car stewards (a position until then held only by white men) without regard to race, color, creed, or national origin. At the same time this company told Ross that ten new skilled occupations in the mechanical departments were open to Negroes.

The FEPC's jurisdiction is more limited than is generally believed. Its jurisdiction is specifically limited to complaints against agencies of the Federal Government, complaints against employers (and the unions in their plants) having contracts with the Government, and complaints against employers (and the unions) regarded as essential to the war effort. The FEPC has held that steamship lines, railroads, telephone and telegraph companies, and local street railway systems in vital industrial areas are essential war industries. Should the committee's directives be defied, such violation can be referred to the proper contracting agency or to the President. The FEPC has stated that cases of non-compliance also can be brought to the attention of the WMC, which is interested in securing maximum employment of Negroes and other minorities in order to fill manpower requirements. WMC may use its referral powers to enforce an FEPC order by denying workers to an employer who refuses to accept Negro workers, or by denying further job referrals to workers who refuse to work with Negroes. In practice, these techniques are seldom used. Since it was established (1941) the committee has handled approximately 5,000 complaints of discrimination in employment, of which 3,000 were disposed of satisfactorily.

The FEPC prefers that no publicity be given its settlements, says *Business Week,* unless it is confronted with a crisis requiring dramatic action—that is why there have been only about a dozen public hearings. One of these was called in 1943 to settle the case of the Philadelphia Transportation Company. The FEPC had begun conferences with this company in August after complaints had been received that the line had refused to upgrade their Negro employees to operating jobs. The independent employee union, the company protested, was unwilling to work with Negroes as motormen. A public hearing was finally held and a directive issued calling for the upgrading. No steps were taken by the company, however, to put this order into effect. In the meantime, the independent union had lost to the CIO Transport Union the right to represent the employees. This CIO group notified the FEPC that it had no objection to the use of Negroes in operating jobs, and the company thereupon moved to upgrade eight

ROSS, MALCOLM—*Continued*

of its Negro workers. The result of this action was an unauthorized "wildcat" protest strike of 6,000 white Philadelphia Transportation Company employees, a strike which turned into a riot in which a number of people were injured. The strike was referred to the President, who ordered the Army to take over the transit system. The ending of the drawn-out affair was the arrest of the strike leaders, and the upgrading of the eight men—another victory for the FEPC.

A fight in Congress, led by a group of Southern Democrats, to "snuff out" the FEPC by cutting off its appropriations was defeated in June 1944. One of seventeen agencies asking for appropriations to continue their work under the War Agencies Bill, the FEPC had become the target of a four-day fight. At the end of 1944 the Scanlon-Dawson-La Follette [44] bill to provide for a permanent agency had failed of passage, but Representative Mary T. Norton [44], chairman of the House Labor Committee, announced that the bill would be re-submitted in early 1945. Other similar bills were expected to be introduced in the Seventy-ninth Congress; and the idea of a permanent FEPC has been sponsored by "hundreds" of various social groups, according to Representative Norton, as well as by many prominent persons. Ross, in pleading for passage of such a bill, has said, "I think there are specific and practical reasons, aside from the common decency of not condemning any group of citizens to menial labor, why minority group members should be given specialized assistance in these limited respects."

The crusading head of the FEPC is said to be about six feet three inches tall, "with Grecian profile, curls, and pointed ears." On April 18, 1936 he was married to Camille Miller, one of the "many beautiful girls who had come to Washington to work for the Government." They have two sons, Alexander Clinton and Malcolm, Jr. Ross was once called the most popular dinner guest in New York. His ability to play the guitar and to improvise songs does not detract from his popularity, and at least one of these improvised songs, *Tennessee Valley*, has become well known. At his friend Francis Biddle's suggestion Ross composed this song about his findings in the Tennessee Valley, where he had gone on an NLRB investigation, and Paul Robeson [41] first sang it in 1941. Ross was one of the six white persons chosen for the 1943 Honor Roll of Race Relations by the Schomburg Collection of Negro Literature of the New York Public Library. Every year the Schomburg Collection conducts a nationwide poll to determine the twelve Negro individuals, organizations, or institutions who have most distinguished themselves during the year and the six white individuals, organizations, or institutions over the same period who have done the most for the improvement of race relations, "in terms of real democracy."

When attacked by a reporter for the Patterson [42]-McCormick [42] press as a Communist sympathizer in January 1944, Ross replied: "I don't know where Mr. Edwards' present sympathies lie, but he is a master of under-statement if he described my present emotions toward the Russian drive against Germany as mere 'sympathies.' . . . But I suspect the truth to be that Mr. Edwards, and the newspaper he adorns, is not so much interested in harassing me as an individual as he is, and they are, interested in striking old familiar chords against the FEPC. . . . If such reporters, holding in trust the power of the printed word, wish to learn the roots of my belief in the American form of government, let me tell them that it stems from ancestors who for 300 years have fought this country's wars, tilled its soil, and built its structures, and that one of them, Captain James Lawrence, once said—in a similar perilous situation: 'Don't give up the ship!'"

References

N Y Sun p17 Jl 2 '41; p13 O 26 '43
Nation's Bus 32:36-40+ F '44 por
PM p17 O 17 '43
Ross, M. Death of a Yale Man 1939
Who's Who in America 1944-45

ROSTEN, NORMAN (rä'sten) Jan. 1, 1914- Poet; playwright

Address: b. c/o Farrar & Rinehart, 232 Madison Ave., New York City; h. 18 Schermerhorn St., Brooklyn, N.Y.

Outstanding among young American poets for the vigor of his themes and for his emotional "directness and sincerity," Norman Rosten has had two books of verse published and has written a considerable number of verse plays for radio and stage. Like Carl Sandburg [40] and the late Stephen Vincent Benét, Rosten believes in a poetry about the people and for the people. "What I am concerned with most in my poetry," he writes, "is the external world and its action, for the beliefs and heroisms of that world are, finally, the sources of poetry. I do not belong to that school which holds to the curious belief that poetry is written for poets and should be as difficult and obscure as possible. Poetry . . . should neither exhaust nor confuse, but invigorate and clarify."

As Isidor Schneider, in an estimate of Rosten's work, has pointed out, there have been two major movements in American poetry. "One was the attempt by poets in the Middle West, where the transforming and creative elements of American life were more active than in the East, to have poetry deal with common life and be an expression of the people. These poets of the Middle West, Carl Sandburg, Vachel Lindsay, Edgar Lee Masters, wrote almost the only poetry that a mass public in America read and unself-consciously enjoyed. The other movement came from the East, Amy Lowell and her immediate followers, or from American emigrés to Europe, T. S. Eliot, Ezra Pound [42], H. D. [Hilda Doolittle], who wanted poetry to be the perception of the exquisite individual transmitted to an elite. They succeeded in turning poetry into a sort of solitary vice, deepening the psychopathic taint that had fallen upon it." Rosten's influences derive from the first group. Those who believe in this tradition in American writing have admired his work; those who subscribe to the "intellectual," or individual and "elite" school, have as heartily condemned it.

"I did not begin to write until I was twenty-two [in 1936]," says Norman Rosten, "and am pleased I was not a prodigy." He was born in New York City, January 1, 1914, the son of Louis and Celia Rosten. The early years of his life were spent in the small up-state town of Hurleyville, where he thought of being a farmer, and in 1931, after high school, he went to Ithaca to the Agricultural College of Cornell University for six months. Apparently he had decided on a literary career by the time he entered Brooklyn College. He took his B.A. degree at Brooklyn in 1935, and his M.A. at New York University a year later. Between school years, to earn the money for his education, he worked as a garage mechanic.

On a playwrighting scholarship Rosten went to the University of Michigan School of the Drama in 1937. His poetic drama *This Proud Pilgrimage* was written there and produced in January 1938 at the University Theatre. Of it a critic said: "Mr. Norman Rosten's dramatic poem, based on the puzzling and tragic history of the Chicago Haymarket riot, is a skillful, sincere, and illuminating treatment of apparently uncompromising materials. Above all else it is successful stage drama, written by an author whose sense of the stage is always adequate, and often something more." The same play was later produced at the Heckscher Foundation, New York City, in June 1940, and won the National Theatre Conference Award in 1942. At Michigan, Rosten also won the Avery Hopwood Awards (1938) in both poetry and drama.

On returning to New York in 1939 Rosten worked for the New York Federal Theatre. He also began to write verse plays for radio. Two of these, *Death of a King* and *Samson Agonistes*, were given over NBC. For *Cavalcade of America* Rosten wrote a number of plays on American literary figures, including Edgar Allan Poe, O. Henry, and Emily Dickinson. Concerning the production of the latter Leonard Lyons wrote: "After the cast had rehearsed the program thoroughly the producers discovered that the eight Dickinson poems quoted in the show were copyrighted—and that the copyrights belonged to an octogenarian niece of Emily Dickinson. The venerable niece, now living in the South, refused to permit these poems to be broadcast. The frantic producers notified Rosten at his home in New Britain, Connecticut. 'Don't worry,' he assured them. 'I'm taking the train to New York and everything will be all right.' During that train ride of little more than an hour Rosten composed eight poems in the style of Emily Dickinson, which were used on that program without anyone suspecting."

Rosten's first book of poems, *Return Again, Traveler,* was the 1940 winner in the "Yale Series of Younger Poets." Speaking of "the lustiness and the mockery, the affirmation and the questioning" that formed the basis of Rosten's American theme, Stephen Vincent Benét, then editor of the Yale Series, wrote: "It seems to me that he has dealt with it boldly, freshly, and successfully. Here is a revaluation of certain American things by a young,

affirmative mind that can laugh and yet be deeply concerned. I don't agree with everything he says and I am continuously interested in what he has to say. For his verse can be enthusiastic or irate, but there is one thing it never is, and that is indifferent."

It was a hitch-hiking trip during the summer of 1937 to Salt Lake City and back that gave Rosten the original idea for *Return Again, Traveler,* as a foreword to which he wrote:

> *Wanderer,*
> *homeless one, anxious for answers. . . .*
> *Return again, traveler,*
> *into our history as we have lived it*
> *and find direction there.*

Of the book the New York *Herald Tribune Books* wrote: "If he has profited not a little from the trail blazers, at least he has found his way among the wide open spaces of the cities and the billboarded prairies to make discoveries of his own. . . . Mr. Rosten sets down what he sees in good, idiomatic American: tough, sentimental, oratorical, hyperbolical, as the mood or character demand. He follows the trail of Johnny Appleseed, builds the Union Pacific, celebrates John Brown, and remembers 'the good shoemaker and the peddler of fish'; he also tells us how Mike Carter died, of Ludwig Valna taking out citizenship papers, of Blondie Johnson in a 42nd Street burlesque." Said the *Christian Science Monitor:* "Mr. Rosten is a young poet who combines sincerity and emotional balance to a degree unusual in a person of his years. . . . It would be difficult to imagine a more timely book of poems. It is the kind of poetry that translates thought into action. It is poetry serving at the front lines in the battle for the survival of democracy."

A Guggenheim Fellowship in poetry was awarded Rosten for 1941-1942. In January 1941 his initial venture at a play for Broadway, *First Stop to Heaven,* was decidedly not a success. Writing of it in retrospect, however, the late drama critic, John Anderson, urged that the Sidney Howard Memorial Award for a promising young playwright be given to Norman Rosten. "I volunteer as a witness for a young author whose play disappeared so quickly under the critical barrage that he hardly had time to see it himself," wrote Mr. Anderson. "By looking back over the files of this department you may discover that I, along with all the others on January 6, 1941, panned a flimsy show at the Windsor Theatre called *First Stop to Heaven.* That was Mr. Rosten's Broadway baptism of fire. It was not a very good play, but I still insist that it was a much better play than anyone could guess from the tenth-rate production Margaret Hewes gave it. . . . I still have a deep suspicion that the aisle boys took Mr. Rosten to the woodshed for sins he didn't commit."

During 1942 Rosten continued his work for radio, writing several plays for the *Treasury Star Parade* series, and was represented by three in the radio play anthology *Treasury Star Parade* (1942). Probably the best known and most highly praised of Rosten's verse for radio was his *Ballad of Bataan,* called "one of the great poems of this War." It was first read by Alfred Lunt [41], later repeated twice

NORMAN ROSTEN

by Orson Welles '41, and has been recorded for use on over 800 radio stations and used in Army reception centers, USO groups, etc. Of it the author writes: "It is a poem for radio, which is not exactly pure poetry, but the boys sure like it!"

A number of sketches were also produced by Rosten for the *Lunch Hour Follies,* performed by theatrical groups in war-production factories during lunch hours and shift changes; and he did several scripts for the OWI short wave and domestic shows. During the winter of 1942 he wrote for Orson Welles's Pan-American program, *Hello, Americans,* one verse play on the conquest of the Andes and another on Mexico. "During one show of this series (which originated from California) we were short by six minutes, and I had to rush out six minutes of blank verse by teletype from New York." In April 1943 Rosten's was the final script for the Council for Democracy in the radio series *Day of Reckoning.* "I took care of Goebbels '41, Göring '41, and Himmler '41. But good," says Rosten. This script, *The Unholy Three,* was considered by Judy Dupuy of *PM* "the most effective of the Council for Democracy's *Day of Reckoning,* radio trials of the dictators. It meted out punishment without hysteria. It stated clearly 'our theme is not revenge but justice.' . . . The script, written partly in blank verse, partly in dialogue, 'studied the disease of fascism, searched out its guilt.'" Rosten's poem *Song for America* was set to music by Leo Sowerby and performed as a cantata over the NBC network in November 1942, with a repeat performance a year later.

The Fourth Decade and Other Poems, Rosten's second collection of verse, appeared in October 1943. The book opens with his radio poem *Bataan.* There follows a section of shorter poems on the American scene in the late '30's and on the War that began during the days of "peace in our time," concluding with our walk to the exits "into a

burning world" and the beginning of a new decade:

> As the seas are joined, and our suffering,
> so our veins flow toward a single future.
> We gather in the resurrection of belief,
> miracle of ashes and pain and the wound,
> out of which new cities take shape and rise.
>
> Believe, man and woman,
> for history is the bed you sleep upon.
> This is your death and your life:
> it is your own son about to be born.

Critical notices were largely favorable, the dissenters being among those who prefer the "intellectuals" in American verse. Leo Kennedy reported in *Book Week*: "These poems about Europe and America in the '30's and about Bataan and Sevastopol in the '40's have qualities of fire and ice. They are written in a cold rage and heroic shout. They celebrate the knavery and cowardice of the big men who necessarily started the War, and the courage and strength of the little men who as necessarily will finish it. This is poetry by an impatient, angry man addressing not a few other poets but all other people. Consequently it is nowhere difficult or obscure; it is not heavy with the writer's own personal word associations and private jokes and memories." William Poster, on the other hand, said in the *New Republic*: "Primarily Rosten tries to write for a wide, popular audience . . . and succeeds by writing for them in the language, spirit, and mood of a rhapsodic newspaper editorial, with Marxist implications and gleanings of the more threadbare devices from a type of poetry he deplores and disclaims." In the New York *Times Book Review* Robert Gorham Davis said: "Norman Rosten, except for line separation, writes not poetry but a very bare prose, rising occasionally to the excitement of names and exclamations. . . . It is not clear to me what he gives us—except for greater selectivity—that we do not get from newspaper accounts." William Rose Benét, however, in the *Saturday Review of Literature,* commented: "It is good to have a book like this, alive to great issues. . . . He writes with the full force of good prose, not always with the full force of poetry, but that does not so much matter. . . . He knows what price this age is paying that the spirit of man may go on. This is a good book, like an automatic, compact and hard." Joy Davidman, in the *New Masses,* wrote: "*The Fourth Decade* is a delight for its own sake. And it is equally valuable as a symptom of the healthy morale of the American people that such poetry should appear just now, that Norman Rosten should be able to reach millions over the radio with the *Ballad of Bataan* while defeatist poets must live by taking in one another's washing. . . . If *The Fourth Decade* is any indication, American poetry is even now coming back to the people for good and all." (During 1943 Rosten won the Lola Ridge Memorial Award contest.)

In March 1944 Rosten was at work "on a long narrative poem dealing with the construction of the Alcan Highway and the vision of roads connecting the hemispheres via Alaska." The young poet says he has had "no hobbies, unless you could call prodigious writing of postcards a hobby. I like museums, post offices, and subways—the latter being a place where I write a good deal of poetry (particularly the stretch between 59th and 125th on the Independent). So far I have resisted Hollywood offers in order to stick to poetry and playwriting. Sure is tough on the resistance cells! After the War I promise to write a good poetic drama. And that long poem. Lots of work for post-War. . . ."

In 1940 Rosten was married to Hedda Rowinski, "who is my unnamed collaborator in poetry and, as a psychologist, finds me very interesting."

References

Sat R Lit 26:22 D 4 '43
Scholastic 43:14 Ja 17 '44

RUSSELL, CHARLES ELLSWORTH
See Russell, P. W.

RUSSELL, PEE WEE Mar. 27, 1906-
Musician

Address: b. c/o Nick's, 170 W. 10th St., New York City; h. 49 W. 12th St., New York City

Nick's is a small night club in New York's Greenwich Village which ever since the '20's has been patronized by those who want to listen to "hot jazz"—jazz played the way the musicians feel like playing it, and never the same way twice. The faces in the band at Nick's are not always the same faces, but apparently Pee Wee Russell, who will also answer to the first names of Charles Ellsworth, "comes with the rent of the place"—he has been blowing his clarinet there for seven years.

The number of Pee Wee's admirers can hardly be measured by the size of the crowd at Nick's place, however: the small but fanatical "Pee Wee cult" has members all over the world, most of whom know their favorite clarinetist only through records, or through the jazz concerts broadcast from Town Hall. Many of those admirers are in England. In February 1944 there was a "Pee Wee Russell Edition" of the London magazine *Discography*; and during the Battle of England a group of R.A.F. fliers wrote to Russell to say that they always played his records "for courage" before going up. In the United States Pee Wee has received the *Down Beat* Award for the best clarinet player for four years running: in 1942 he won by thirty votes; in 1943 he had 1,632 more votes than his nearest competitor. One of his records, "I Ain't Gonna Give Nobody None of My Jellyroll," is in the collection of the Congressional Library as the best example of jazz clarinet. (Oklahoma seems to be about the only scene of a defeat: it was there, at the age of nine, that Russell lost a violin contest.)

Pee Wee Russell, called "Ellsworth" by no one except members of his immediate family, was born Charles Ellsworth Russell III or IV—he is not quite sure which—on March 27, 1906. The place was Webster Groves, Missouri, according to his birth certificate; his parents were Charles Ellsworth and Ella Mary (Ballard) Russell, both of Southern stock.

Myron Ehrenberg
PEE WEE RUSSELL

The family moved to Oklahoma when Pee Wee was very young, and there he had his first music lessons when seven years old, from a "lady teacher": the instrument was not the clarinet, but the violin. Mr. Russell had made a considerable fortune from oil wells, and Pee Wee's education, musical and otherwise, was not neglected. He was evidently a born musician, in spite of the fact that all the other men in his family had been physicians, and it was assumed that he would eventually become a doctor. After the violin came the piano, drums, and clarinet. Afterwards, by himself, Pee Wee was to take up every wind instrument imaginable; today he is interested in seventeenth century musical instruments, particularly the harpsichord.

Pee Wee was still playing the clarinet, however, when he attended Western Military School at Alton, Illinois, at the age of twelve. "In the school band he was fourth clarinet and that, in his own words, 'meant there were four clarinet players in school, and I was the fourth worst.'" For a couple of years he was a student at the University of Missouri, but spent more time playing with local bands than attending classes. Most of his jobs were on Saturday nights. "Sometimes," he explained to Charles E. Smith, "I'd go away on a Saturday and turn up in college on Tuesday afternoon in time for a Monday class at eight o'clock." During this time he was already developing an individual clarinet style. He listened to the Negro bands playing on the riverboats; in St. Louis he heard Charlie Creath, a cornet player "who created his own blues style, playing with a deep, rough tone." For a few months, too, he studied clarinet with Tony Sarley of the St. Louis Symphony Orchestra.

For one interviewer Pee Wee Russell has summed up his later varied career in a few sentences. He played in a tent show for a while, then went with Herbert Berger to Juarez, Mexico, and played in the Big Kid's

RUSSELL, PEE WEE—*Continued*

Palace. "James Cruze, the movie director, was there . . . that was in the early '20's, making the *Covered Wagon,* and he liked the band so much he took us back to Hollywood with him. Rudy Wiedoff was in that band then. We made pictures, I forget what, and then we went back to St. Louis. We were playing there when Red Nichols came through town and heard us. Then Red left town. I stayed on with Berger. Frankie Trambauer, he was my next boss [at the Arcadia Ballroom, in St. Louis]. Bix Beiderbecke was in that band. Frankie took over Gene Goldkette's band." Soon after that Pee Wee was fired. "But I wouldn't leave, so that was all right. I just wasn't paid. Then the band split up. Bix went to New York and I went to Chicago. A wire came from Red Nichols. 'Come to New York' . . . so I went. We made some records with Miff Mole. 'Ida' was one." In succession Pee Wee played the clarinet with Cass Hagan and the Five Pennies; with Paul Specht at New York's Capitol Theatre; with Louis Prima both at New York's Famous Door and in Hollywood's Famous Door. "Then I got a wire from Eddie Condon [44] and Red McKenzie to come to New York and play at Nick's. . . . I've been here ever since." Not that Nick's is the only place Russell's clarinet may be heard. With Eddie Condon, who leads informal programs of "hot rhythm," and such artists as Bobby Hackett, Ernie Caceres, Joe Marsala, and Bob Haggart, Russell played his clarinet at Town Hall and Carnegie Hall in the summer and fall of 1944. Once upon a time in those seven years (he can't remember dates), he wrote a book of clarinet solos for Leo Feist, the music publisher.

During all these years Pee Wee Russell has constantly turned down offers to play in large bands. Writes George Frazier: "He could be affluent, if he would but accept any one of the jobs offered him in big bands, but he doesn't like affluence that much. He plays what he feels and there are no confining arrangements to imprison his imagination. He is playing for the sheer joy of playing and not because a leader is paying him a fat salary. His life and his hard times and the stuff he dreams up on his clarinet are in the true jazz tradition. He is everything that Glenn Miller [42] and Tommy and Jimmy Dorsey [42] aren't. He is jazz, and the best too."

The almost legendary figures of early jazz, who belonged to the same tradition, were among Pee Wee's friends. Pee Wee was Bix Beiderbecke's closest friend, although he never mentions it: it took the New York *World-Telegram* to dig that fact up, in an article appropriately entitled "George Washington Slept Here." He and the late Frankie Teschmaker were "musical kids together": they learned from each other, copied one another's style. Even Benny Goodman [42] was influenced by Pee Wee. "Goodman, on his early records, seemed to vacillate between Tesch's phrasing and Pee Wee's growl." Sometimes today when Pee Wee listens to Goodman he murmurs, "Thief"—but he believes Goodman is the greatest clarinet player who ever lived. (Next, in his opinion, come Omer Simeon, Edmond Hall, and Johnny Dodds.)

Other jazz addicts have gone into literary rhapsodies, some of them incomprehensible to the uninitiated, over Pee Wee Russell's "moist, breathy, broken" clarinet solos. Writes Ann Chidester, in *No Longer Fugitive* (1943): "The music began slow, easy as the rising of a bird over a prairie land with spaces of sky to twirl in and to fall. It began like the timid prayer of a child, sank into fallow fields, drew forth the lovely water-crested sprouts, shot up, fell down, wept and bespoke a heart of darkness. It went on in a torrent like an ageless river, like a woman in red slippers tottering slightly. . . ." Virgil Thomson [40] is more restrained: "Mr. Russell's clarinet work is musical, imaginative, and brilliantly skillful. He has an unequaled repertory of 'dirty' sonorities; and he slides better than almost anybody. He is a great master in a great tradition."

Carlton Brown writes that Pee Wee "probably doesn't know the stream-of-consciousness method from the Gowanus Canal in theory, but in practice, he does with musical phrases just about exactly what Joyce did with words— he breaks them up, violently rearranged their structure and accustomed order, and puts them together into fascinating new patterns. Pee Wee Russell makes a clarinet sound like a unique and marvelous instrument that he invented for his own ruggedly individualistic purposes. He is by turns hilarious and tragic; he can express the heart of melancholy with overwhelming directness, or make surprising satirical comments composed of incredible dissonances and ornate embroideries." And Hugh Panassié, the French critic, writes in *Hot Jazz*: "Among all hot clarinetists, Pee Wee Russell is undoubtedly the one who uses the soberest melodic style: short phrases of uncomplicated, clear contour played in an even, measured tone. It is the sort of style which should be a model to all others. Another peculiarity of his is his 'dirty' tone, full of definite huskiness. Curiously enough, even though Pee Wee fills his playing with these effects, his tone keeps its finish and polish. . . . His intonations are very beautiful and vibrant, and his attack is exceptionally forceful."

George Frazier describes Pee Wee Russell as "tall and spindly, with patent-leather hair and a long, seamed face that reminds you of a clown's. He is scarcely what you would call an impressive-looking man. But that is before he takes his clarinet to his mouth and begins to play. Then he is one of the most eloquent men on the face of the earth. It is an aged clarinet that he plays and it is kept serviceable only through the judicious use of rubber bands, but in Pee Wee's hands it is an instrument of surpassing beauty." The "aged clarinet" held together by rubber bands is, however, a thing of legend. Actually Pee Wee's clarinet is one of the most expensive instruments made, and he takes as good care of it as if it were his child, sometimes taking his own overcoat off to wrap around it on a particularly cold day. There are a host of similar anecdotes about Pee Wee which may be just as apocryphal, since he never bothers to contradict them— after all, they make good publicity. As Charles E. Smith puts it, "Off the stand he looks like the sort of person about whom anecdotes are told, an attitude he inspires whether he wills it or not. One story told about him concerns the Chicago El, on which tokens were three for a quarter. Passing through the gate, Pee Wee paid a quarter each time, pocketing the two tokens change. Gradually they accumulated and he talked it over with an acquaintance. He explained how he got the tokens, and said, 'Now what do I do with them?'"

Pee Wee Russell was married to Mary S. Chaloff on March 11, 1943. She also comes from a musical family: her uncle, Eugene Plotnikoff, was conductor of the Imperial Opera at Moscow until the Russian Revolution; her brother, Herman Chaloff, is a composer. Russell gives some figures and facts about himself: He is one-half inch under six feet, weighs 140 pounds, and has black hair and dark eyes. His favorite hobby is "being with a gal named Mary." Of the numerous magazines and newspapers in which articles about him have appeared, Russell says, "Don't know dates, don't keep clippings, don't even read them." Out of the hundreds of records which Pee Wee has made with various bands he and his wife remember with special affection "Hello Lola", "Home Cooking", "The Eel", "Embraceable You" (on Commodore), and "Serenade to a Shylock" (with Jack Teagarden). "Serenade to a Shylock" and "I'm Through With Love" are among his own compositions; he made $8,000 out of the latter, and managed to spend it in less than a week. "Mammy o' Mine" is his worst record, he says—he never succeeded in getting off one note.

References

Band Leaders 1:12-13+ Jl '44
Cosmopolitan 113:42 N '42
Pic 15:29 Mr 28 '44 por

Ramsey, F. and Smith, C. E. eds. Jazzmen p174-5 1939

RUTH, BABE Feb. 6, 1895- Retired baseball star

Address: h. 173 Riverside Dr., New York City

When Japanese soldiers attempted to storm the United States Marine lines on Cape Gloucester, New Britain, in April 1944, they charged to their deaths with the battle cry, "To hell with Babe Ruth!" Strange as it sounded to other ears, it reflected the Babe's status as a national hero and as a symbol of the United States, undimmed by his retirement. Nine years earlier Matsutaro Shoriki, a Tokyo newspaper publisher, had been stabbed by a member of the secret Warlike Gods Society for sponsoring the successful barnstorming tour of Ruth's baseball team in Japan. Evidently the Nipponese patriots resented the arousing of Japanese admiration for the Babe and enthusiasm for the American game he played.

After the celebration of his fortieth birthday on February 6, 1934, Babe Ruth discovered that he was a year younger, having been born in Baltimore, Maryland, on February 6, 1895. His birth name was reportedly George Herman Ehrhardt. Just when and why the Babe's name became Ruth is not clear, but he has called himself George Herman Ruth throughout his career. "His true antecedents—that is, his father and mother —apparently will always remain misty and unexplored," says Paul Gallico. Ruth is often

referred to as an orphan, but this the Babe denies: "My folks lived in Baltimore and my father worked in the [waterfront] district where I was raised," he says. "We were very poor. And there were times when we never knew where the next meal was coming from. But I never minded. I was no worse off than the other kids with whom I played and fought." It was with considerable reluctance that the unruly George went to live at St. Mary's Industrial School, an institution staffed by the Brothers of a Catholic teaching order. One of the staff, Brother Gilbert, took a particular interest in the big, black-haired seven-year-old and helped him to adjust himself. "Once I had been introduced to school athletics," Ruth recalls, "I was satisfied and happy. Even as a kid I was big for my years, and because of my size I used to get most any job I liked on the team. . . . It was all the same to me. All I wanted was to play. I didn't care much where."

At eighteen Ruth was "as funny looking a kid as ever got a trouncing for cutting classes to go fishing"—and an outstanding ballplayer. Brother Gilbert wrote to Jack Dunn, manager of the minor league Baltimore Orioles baseball team, suggesting that Dunn come and see this promising youngster. After a half-hour observation of Ruth's pitching, Dunn offered to sign him to a contract, paying him $600 for a six-months season, and took out papers as his guardian. When the eager youth reported at the Oriole clubhouse in 1914, the team's coach took one look and exclaimed, "Well, here's Jack's newest babe now!" And "The Babe" Ruth became and remained, to all but a few intimates, for the rest of his highly-publicized career.

It might be expected that a young man making his professional debut would feel a certain nervousness, but not the Babe. His self-confidence was justified before the month was up, for, though Dunn had not started him in any regular games, Ruth pitched and won an exhibition game against Connie Mack's Philadelphia Athletics, then at the top of the National League. His salary as pitcher-outfielder with the Orioles (officially the Baltimore-Providence Club of the International League) was doubled; at the end of another month, it was increased to just three times the amount originally agreed on. During this season the young "southpaw" played in forty-six games, of which he pitched twenty-two winners, nine losing games, and four ties; he batted .231 and fielded .964; his pitching average was .709.

"With the Red Sox," Ruth says, "I really began to learn a little baseball . . . I didn't think much of becoming a slugger. I liked to hit . . . but it was pitching that took my time in Boston." After playing forty-two games during the 1915 season, of which he pitched thirty-two—eighteen won, six lost— Ruth entered one World Series game with the National League champions as a pinch-hitter for a string of zeros. During one game in Detroit, the Babe struck out three great batters—Bob Veach, Sam Crawford, and the immortal Ty Cobb—in succession, an achievement roughly comparable to an actor-playwright-director's winning a major award in each department simultaneously. "No home

BABE RUTH

home runs increased; and in 1919 he led the league with twenty-nine of them. This brought him to the attention of Colonel Ruppert, owner of the New York Yankees, who bought him in January 1920 for $125,000. When a player is sent to another team he generally gets a bonus and an increase in salary; Ruth's increase was a flat 100 per cent. It was with the Yankees that Babe Ruth began his "spectacular and scandal-spangled career" as a nationally and even internationally known personality.

"It would be an unpardonable bore," as John Terence McGovern said in *Diogenes Discovers Us,* "to write [in detail] of Babe's achievements as a baseball player. Every schoolboy and practically every adult in America knows his amazing personal history." The *Baseball Register* devotes twenty-three lines of fine print to just the baseball records he set—records most or all of which still stand. To mention a few, he led the American League in home runs from 1919 through 1924 (he was ill in 1925) and again from 1926 through 1931. He played in the most World Series (ten) and most often on the winning club (seven times). Pitchers were so unwilling to risk one of his deadly clouts that they passed him by 2,056 times, the world's record for bases on balls. In 1923 the American League voted Babe Ruth their most valuable player. From 1926 through 1931 and again in 1933 and 1934, he was picked for the League's all-star team. By any standard he was the greatest home run hitter in history, and—a typically Ruthian touch—he also holds the world's record for striking out 1,330 times.

By the time Babe Ruth joined the Yankees, he had already acquired an unusual hold over the public, such that a baseball crowd which had reacted fairly casually to home runs by other players would become, in the words of the great pitcher Walter Johnson, "so crazy with excitement that they were ready to tear up the stands" if Ruth drove out a home run [even] when the game was already won and there was nothing particularly at stake.... If the opposing pitcher tries to slip Babe free transportation to first [a base on balls] they take it as a personal insult.... The crowd has become so accustomed to seeing him knock out home runs that they expect it from him, and they don't give him credit for his remarkable hitting otherwise."

Part of the explanation for the Babe's unprecedented box-office draw was, of course, the incredible frequency of his home runs—fifty-four in 1920, fifty-nine the next year, and then it fluctuated about the forties, rising to sixty in 1927. But much, perhaps most, of his popularity was due to his emotional appeal to the fans. "He played ball," writes Paul Gallico in *Farewell to Sport,* "on the same enormous scale on which he lived his life, intensely, fervently, and with tremendous sincerity and passion. It was impossible to watch him at bat without experiencing an emotion. I have seen hundreds of ballplayers at the plate, and none of them managed to convey the message of impending doom to a pitcher that Babe Ruth did with the cock of his head, the position of his legs, and the little, gentle waving of his bat, feathered in

run in the world ever brought a greater kick than that!" says Ruth. His salary was going up, too. The Red Sox, who had started him in 1914 at $1,300, almost trebled that amount the following year, when his contract called for $3,500. (Even the most accurately reported salary figures do not necessarily give a complete picture of a player's baseball income, even apart from other sources. The players on a World Series team, for instance, share a percentage of the profits which usually figures out to a considerable sum. Exhibition games bring in more. Bonuses are used as a method of payment according to merit. The contractual amount, therefore, is to be regarded only as base pay.)

In 1914 Ruth's contract was sold to the world champion Boston Red Sox (American League) for a reported $2,900. Called on to play in only five games during the season, Ruth pitched four, winning two and losing one, batting .200 and fielding 1.000. That summer, when the pitcher was nineteen (but, not aware of his true birth date, he thought he was twenty) he married Helen Woodford, a sixteen-year-old waitress from Texas. They had two children who died in early infancy. As might be expected of an underprivileged boy suddenly come into money and public notice, Ruth led a wild and extravagant life, getting into various sorts of trouble. Being, as he puts it, "cursed with an iron constitution. . . I could commit those excesses . . . without apparent harm for a number of years."

From 1916, when Ruth pitched and won the longest game in World Series history (fourteen innings, against Brooklyn) to 1920, the Babe played for Boston as pitcher-outfielder and, in 1918, as first baseman. (In that year, too, he pitched and won two World Series games.) By then he was getting a salary of $7,000; the following year it was $10,000. Although Ruth's pitching average went down 135 points during this period, his

his two big paws. . . . The Babe is the only man I have ever known as spectacular in failure as he is in success. Just as when he connected the result was the most perfect thing of its kind, a ball whacked so high, wide, and handsome that no stadium in the entire country could contain it, so was his strikeout the absolute acme of frustration. He would swing himself twice around until his legs were braided. Often he would twist himself clear off his feet. . . . Every move that Ruth made brought some kind of answering sound from the crowd in the stands. . . . Ruth's throws to home plate from the outfield, or to a base, so accurate that the receiver never had to move a step from his position to receive them, always brought ripples of incredulous laughter, the 'I'm seeing it, but I don't believe it' kind. And of course his home runs brought forth pandemonium."

The name of Babe Ruth appeared so often in the sports columns that sportswriters thought up synonyms—"The Sultan of Swat", "The King of Clout," even "The Behemoth of Bust." They translated Babe into "Bambino," and then shortened it to "Bam" for headline purposes. And the Bambino provided them with a constant flow of colorful material on field and off. For one thing, there was his pay, a salary of $30,000 in 1921, $52,000 for each of the five following years, $70,000 from 1927 through 1929, and $80,000—more than that allotted the President of the United States —in 1930 and 1931. Nor do these figures include prize money and bonuses; among others, Ruth's arrangement with Ruppert specified that he was to receive $100 for each home run hit. Also, there were the crowds he attracted, which justified his huge income and, from an economic standpoint, would have justified a much higher one: When Ruth was absent from the line-up the Yankees' ball games drew only half their normal 15,000-20,000 weekday patrons and 60,000-70,000 on Saturdays and Sundays. The Yankee Stadium is still known as "The House that Ruth Built," and right field is still called "Ruthville." There were his innumerable free appearances for charitable organizations, especially the Knights of Columbus, to which he belongs. There were the Babe's other and profitable activities: the five motion-picture shorts and two features, one with Anna Q. Nilsson, in which he starred; the magazine and widely-syndicated newspaper articles under his name; the books, *Babe Ruth's Own Book of Baseball* (1928) and *How To Play Baseball* (1931), with "George Herman Ruth" on the title page.

Another source of income for the star— and one which sometimes got him into trouble with the baseball powers-that-be— was his barnstorming in exhibition games and vaudeville tours. Then there were radio broadcasts and endorsements of commercial products. Various sporting goods and a candy bar used his name—and paid generously for the privilege. These financial details were handled by Christy Walsh, a shrewd Irish sportswriter who managed Ruth's outside activities, syndicated his articles, and

split the profits with him fifty-fifty. (In 1924, with the help of "Mrs. Babe," Walsh accomplished the incredible feat of persuading the extravagant and always debt-ridden Ruth to deposit all the money thus earned in a trust fund to protect his future.) There was only one commercial exploitation of Ruth's fame from which he drew no profit: an enterprising producer clipped newsreel shots of the Babe in action and strung them together into two shorts, *Babe Ruth: How He Makes His Home-Runs* and *Over the Fence,* using scenes from photographs of practice sessions and early games. In 1920 Ruth sued Educational Films, Inc., for an injunction and damages; but the application was denied by the New York Supreme Court, Appellate Division, on the ground that "the public's interest in the plaintiff's current accomplishments . . . brought his past activities within the field of permissible news coverage."

"There are some men to whom has been given the faculty of living all their lives in newsprint. They have a natural attraction for headlines." As for George Herman Ruth, "the only walls he has ever known have been the parallel columns of the newspapers." Whatever he did seemed always to have somehow a dramatic touch. In the summer of 1920 a man died of excitement watching the Babe hit a ball into the bleachers. In 1921 the slugger was so unmanageable that the Yankees' manager, Miller Huggins, upheld by Commissioner Kenesaw Mountain Landis [4], suspended him from playing for a time. During the 1922 season George Herman Ruth got into about as much assorted trouble as a man could without being either imprisoned or excommunicated as a result. He committed "the gravest sin in baseball," leaving the field to chase a patron whose remarks he had resented; he drank too much, gambled far too heavily, fought with Judge Landis and everyone else in authority, and ran into various traffic charges and civil suits; he even played bad baseball. At the annual dinner of the Baseball Writers Association, New York State Senator Jimmy Walker (later the mayor of New York) made a personal but public plea to Babe Ruth to reform and make himself worthy of the "dirty-faced kids in the streets" who worshipped him—not to shirk his great responsibility to the youth of the nation. And "Ruth robbed it of all cheapness, of all sensationalism or everything that was vulgarly maudlin, by getting to his feet and with tears streaming down his big ugly face, promising the dirty-faced kids of the nation to behave, for their sake. And then he kept his promise. He was never in trouble again. . . . Nor did it make him the less a picturesque character, because he never went sissy or holy on the boys. He retained all of his appetites and gusto for living. He merely toned them down." Everyone read about the great reformation, and everyone loved Babe for it.

Returning from spring training in the South in 1925 Ruth, who ordinarily ate some ten daily meals punctuated with bicarbonate of soda, felt the need of a snack. By one report, it consisted of ten or twelve railroad station frankfurters, washed down with eight bottles of soda pop. The result was a case of acutest indigestion, one which caused the trip to be

RUTH, BABE—*Continued*

interrupted and the stricken man brought home to New York City and rushed to St. Vincent's Hospital. There "a baseball player lay close to death, and an entire nation held its breath, worried and fretted, and bought every edition of the newspapers to read the bulletins as though the life of a personal friend or a member of the family was at stake. . . . Even in England the penny papers watched at his bedside. That *is* fame." When Babe recovered, the country—one might almost say the world—breathed a great sigh of relief. And, although his playing season was shortened by his illness, Ruth had time to clout twenty-five home runs before it came to an end.

There are two stories about Ruth, both attested to by reliable witnesses, which neatly sum up the qualities that made him a beloved figure. One occurred in 1926, when a child named Johnny Sylvester lay seriously weakened after an operation. Learning that Babe Ruth was Johnny's particular idol, the doctor decided—perhaps with the help of some alert newspaperman—that a visit from his hero might give the child the will to live. So the Babe came and chatted, gave Johnny an autographed baseball and then, before he left for the stadium, promised to hit a home run that afternoon and dedicate it to Johnny. And he did.

Perhaps the most impressive single action of Ruth's career was seen in the 1932 World Series, the last in which he ever played. The Yankees were opposing the Chicago Cubs on the latter's home grounds. The Cubs were deliberately "riding" the Babe—insulting and reviling him—to make him lose his head; the Chicago fans were obviously hostile. When Ruth, who had already hit one home run, came to bat again and missed the first pitch, the crowd hooted him; when he missed the second, they laughed and booed as he calmly held up two fingers to indicate that those were only two strikes. And then, before the third strike, Ruth pointed dramatically to the center-field flagpole, showing that he would drive the next pitch out of the park at that point. And—incredibly—he did.

After the tragic death by fire of Babe Ruth's young wife, from whom he had been separated, he courted the widow, Claire Hodgson, who was a former Ziegfeld girl. They were married three months later, in April 1929. The ceremony was performed at a 6:30 a.m. nuptial mass, in order to avoid a crowd, but nonetheless some 150 strangers crowded around afterwards to congratulate the national hero, (and during the giving of the ring a photographer's flashbulb popped.) Next day the newly married Babe opened the Yankees' season with a home run. Ruth adopted his wife's daughter Julia, then thirteen, five years older than his own Dorothy. The second Mrs. Ruth proved to be an excellent manager who persuaded her husband to save, "kept him from going back to his old ways," and nursed him tenderly through his illnesses, real and exaggerated.

In 1932 baseball began to feel the depression. All salaries were cut down, and the outcome of Ruth's annual dispute with Colonel Ruppert was a salary no higher than the President's; the following year it was back to $52,000.

In 1934 it was $35,000. In this, his last year as an active player, the Babe hit only twenty-two home runs. Then, having rounded out twenty years in the American League, Ruth left the Yankees. He had always expressed an ambition to become a club manager after his playing days were over, and it was expected that such a position would be offered him. No such offer came, however. In April 1935, Ruth joined the Boston Braves (not of his old league, but of the National League) as vice-president, assistant manager, and part-time player with a reported salary of $30,000. After ninety-seven days with the Braves, for whom he hit six home runs, Ruth left the club because of a bad cold, a leg injury, and endless bickering. In 1936 he published a pamphlet of baseball advice. His coaching of the National League's Brooklyn Dodgers in 1938 was the Babe's last attempt at professional baseball. He "drew more attention from the fans than the Dodgers and their opponents combined," but a reported secret clause in his contract provided that Ruth was never to become manager of the Dodgers.

Writing in the January 1941 issue of *Friday* Ed Hughes explained baseball management's "blacklist" of Ruth as due to resentment because he had "almost automatically raised the pay of every ballplayer in the land." It is a fact that other players would use his salary as a yardstick—would say to their employers, "I'm not Babe Ruth, but I'm worth three-quarters (or one-half or one-third) what he is to the club, so I should get three-quarters or (one-half or one-third) of his salary." Ruth was, says Hughes, "a one-man union without realizing it. He forced the magnates to shell out players' wages commensurate with the gate receipts they helped to swell." Asked by Hughes for a statement in the matter, Ruth replied, "I don't want to say anything that makes me look like a bad sport. You know—on account of the kids."

And so the Babe is in a paradoxical position. He is still the idol of children who could never possibly have seen him play—some of whom were not born at the time—as well as of their elders, who remember the days when he was making his records. He is still sought after for charity performances. He is still certain of the loudest ovation anytime a crowd glimpses his huge six feet two bulk or catches sight of the distinctively pigeon-toed mincing trot of his oddly slim ankles—and that is true even of a non-baseball crowd. And yet, although his unlisted telephone number still has to be changed every few months because fans manage to find it out and call him up so often, there is, apparently, no place for Babe Ruth in the game he led. Since his retirement he has played himself in RKO's *Pride of the Yankees* (1942), a picturization of the life of Lou Gehrig '⁴⁰, his brilliant runner-up for batting honors. In 1943 he began broadcasting a fifteen-minute program over WEAF on Saturday mornings and continued it in 1944; audience reaction demonstrated that he is still the children's idol. He has taken up golf and bowling to keep down his weight; he has made innumerable appearances at bond rallies and has talked his deep bass voice hoarse entertaining service men. He can't go overseas on a USO tour—half a dozen doctors have forbidden it. His smoking has been reduced from twenty to only four cigars a day and his pipe. Stanley Frank wrote in the New York *Post* in April 1944: "The Big Guy was down and it was depressing to see him without the ebullience and bounce and lusty bawdiness that you always associated with him. . . . 'It's hell to grow old,' Babe Ruth said plaintively. And it's hell to watch him grow old."

On the subjects of age and bygone days Ruth did not appear too downhearted when he and Mrs. Ruth registered in the fall of 1944 (before voting for Governor Dewey '44—"Mr. Roosevelt '42 is a great man, but we've got to have a change"). He gave his age as "over twenty-one" and answered the question as to occupation with "retired." On the radio, too, he has delivered his comic lines "beautifully." In commenting on the old Ruth spirit, exhibited on a Blue Network broadcast with Milton Berle, *Variety* wrote: "The Bambino 'went along with the gags' like an old trouper and took care of his lines and biz as easily as he used to take care of those American League pitchers a few seasons back."

References

Lit Digest 83:58 O 4 '24 por; 90:46 Jl 31 '26 por
New Yorker 2:15 Jl 31 '26 por
Newsweek 4:17 Jl 14 '34 por
Cook, T. R. ed. Essays in Modern Thought p98-104 1935
Gallico, P. Farewell to Sport p30-43 1941
Johnston, C. H. L. Famous American Athletes of Today 1938
McGovern, J. T. Diogenes Discovers Us p73-88 1933
Ruth, G. H. Babe Ruth's Own Book of Baseball 1928
Spink, J. G. T. Baseball Register 1941

RUTH, GEORGE HERMAN *See* Ruth, B.

SACHS, BERNARD (säks) Jan. 2, 1858— Feb. 8, 1944 One of the world's outstanding neurologists; leader in field for more than fifty years; author of *Mental and Nervous Disorders of Children* and numerous monographs; president of a number of American medical societies.

Obituary

N Y Times p19 F 9 '44 por

SACHS, CURT June 29, 1881- Musicologist *Address*: h. 1781 Riverside Dr., New York City

Dr. Curt Sachs, one of the great living German musicologists, who has received refuge and veneration in America, defines his field as "the backbone of all musical knowledge. What philology and historical research do for literature, musicology performs for music." Its special subjects of research—the historical study of musical instruments, investigation of sources, gathering and organization of data—have been Dr. Sachs's life work, for which he has won international renown

CURT SACHS

Curt Sachs was born in Berlin on June 20, 1881, the son of Louis Edward and Anna (Frölich) Sachs. As a youth he attended the Königliches französisches Gymnasium in that city; later he enrolled at the University of Berlin, where he specialized in the history of art and studied music history with Oscar Fleischer. In 1904 he received his Ph.D. degree for his thesis on the sculpture of Verrocchio.

Thus Dr. Sachs's early interests were divided between art and music, and he had already entered the field of art criticism before he turned to research in music. He then devoted some years to the intensive study of the subject under Hermann Kretzschmar and Johannes Wolf. The first significant result of that study was the publication of his history of musical life at the Hohenzollern court.

While delving into hitherto unexplored fields of music, Dr. Sachs gradually became convinced that the musical instruments of the past would reveal as much about the quality of ancient music as notation could about the melody. He believed also that the history of music could be traced through a study of the musical instruments of bygone ages. Accordingly, his first contribution to that knowledge was his *Reallexikon der Musikinstrumente* (a dictionary of musical instruments), published in 1913. It was then considered the best authority in the field. Later he met Erich M. von Hornbostel, an eminent scholar in comparative musicology, with whom he collaborated in arranging a new classification of instruments based on the principles of sound production. The system evolved by them has since been used in the organization of collections of instruments.

Widespread recognition of Dr. Sachs's scholarship caused every important German institution of higher musical learning to seek his services. In 1919 the Berlin State Museum of Musical Instruments entrusted him with their precious collections. During the same year

SACHS, CURT—*Continued*

he was appointed professor of musicology at
the University of Berlin and the following year
he was made professor of music history at
the National Academy of Music. Several
years later the Academy for Church and School
Music offered him a professorship. Dr. Sachs,
who held the three professorships and the museum post simultaneously, still found time to do
private research, making public many important works on his findings. He also prepared
a series of phonograph records of ancient music, *Two Thousand Years of Music*, which was
completed in Berlin in 1930. In those years,
too, lecturing took him to many of the European countries as well as to the United States.

The full appreciation of Dr. Sachs's achievement is inevitably limited to a small and highly
specialized group of musical devotees; but, his
fame among such groups is international. Specialists throughout the world have acknowledged
his authority and sought his advice. In 1930
and again in 1932, for example, he was invited
by the Egyptian Government to inquire into
the problem of developing the traditional music
of the Orient in order that Egyptian music
might be revived and, at the same time, be
kept free of European influence.

In 1933 Dr. Sachs resigned his professorial
posts in Germany and left the country for
political reasons. He stayed in London for a
few days and then went to France. There
a grant from the Rockefeller Foundation enabled him to carry on his work in Paris, where
the musicologist became a member of the
staff at the Ethnographical Museum. In 1934
Dr. Sachs was chosen to prepare another series
of records, *Anthologie Sonore*. That was an
especially interesting undertaking: its purpose
was "to create a medium of teaching music
history and to present living illustrations to
the history of music without pedagogical intentions" by recreating and recording old music
exactly as it had been written. A total of
one hundred recordings of long-neglected music
was made, sixty of which have been released in
the United States. A French society awarded
him its Grand Prix five times for such recordings.

Before Dr. Sachs came to the United States
in 1937 he had already been appointed by the
Graduate School of New York University to
the post of visiting professor of musicology.
Upon his arrival he was also made music consultant to the New York Public Library and
he later was commissioned by the Metropolitan
Museum to take charge of the project to restore the treasured Crosby-Brown collection
of musical instruments. Just as he and his
assistants had begun to work on the Crosby-
Brown collection, however, the funds were exhausted and the project was discontinued.

Dr. Sachs is the author of many important
works on musical history. His *World History
of the Dance*, "comprehensive, thorough, and
exhaustively documented," was translated in
1937 and immediately won high praise from
English and American reviewers. But perhaps
his most valuable work is the *History of Musical Instruments*, published in 1940 after thirty
years of research and preparation. The book
is the only comprehensive survey of its kind.
It is further distinguished, reviewers agreed,
by a happy combination of scholarship and
readability which makes it enjoyable both to
the specialist and to the layman. This history was the first book Dr. Sachs had written
in English. A reviewer for the New York
Times commented: "It is vivid proof of what
this country has gained by opening its gates
to scholars like Dr. Sachs." Paul Rosenfeld
wrote in the *New Republic*: "Dr. Sachs is a
manner of unicorn among musicologists. A
sincere, enthusiastic scholar, he carries his
immense learning lightly: he is something of a
bel esprit."

Dr. Sachs followed this study with another
history, published in 1943. It is *The Rise of
Music in the Ancient World, East and West*.
In addition to offering "the first comprehensive
study in any language of oriental musical systems and their relation to the music of the
West," the book was hailed as a splendid summary of modern research in the field of music
history. George Herzog, reviewing the book
for the *Saturday Review of Literature*, wrote:
"Professor Sachs's book represents a heroic
and also daring accomplishment. It brings into
an organized scheme a great diversity of materials that are scattered, uneven, incomplete;
it offers ingenious solutions for old controversies."

In late 1944 Curt Sachs compiled, and the
Edward B. Marks Music Corporation published,
The Evolution of Piano Music, a survey of
keyboard music which extends from as early as
1350 to approximately 1770. In a foreword to
the collection, he insists that "the music in
this album is not stale and dusty 'ancient music.' . . . It is no more ancient than Rem-
brandt's paintings or Gothic cathedrals. . . . It
is written in the style of generations past, but
in a spirit that has not changed, and will never
change, the spirit of solid workmanship, pep
and genius."

America, Dr. Sachs believes, offers the intellectual freedom necessary to the creative
artist. But he feels, too, that American composers have too little appreciation of the country's musical tradition, which can only be given
permanence when it is representative of the
people from whom it springs. Jazz music,
for example, is built upon a true tradition because it is rooted in Negro culture.

A gracious old-world scholar, Curt Sachs is
a soft-spoken, modest man, with gray eyes
and a short beard. Musicians, students, and
laymen who come to him with questions are
kindly received. He finds relaxation in any
sort of puzzle—provided it is sufficiently complicated—or in his hobby of deciphering Sanskrit texts, Greek and Hebrew manuscripts,
or Egyptian hieroglyphics.

References

Musical Q 27:263-79 Jl '41
Baker's Biographical Dictionary of Mu-
    sicians 1940
Thompson, O. ed. International Cyclo-
    pedia of Music and Musicians 1943
Who's Who in America 1944-45

ST. GEORGE, THOMAS R(ICHARD)

Nov. 23, 1919- Author; cartoonist

Address: b. c/o Thomas Y. Crowell Co., 432 Fourth Ave., New York City; h. Simpson, Minn.

"Last January [1943]," explains the introduction to *c/o Postmaster*, "from somewhere in Australia there drifted into the offices of the San Francisco *Chronicle* a piece . . . describing the life of an American soldier in that curiously new Antipodean world. With the piece were some drawings . . . and accompanying the material was a letter, rather on the plaintive side, explaining that this was No. 14 in a series, that the idea was that the *Chronicle* just might like the stuff enough to print it, and that if so the signatory to this document would be pleased and proud." In conclusion, the hopeful writer, the then Corporal Thomas St. George, added that maybe the other pieces hadn't come through yet, but if the editor would just wait, they probably would. The editor needed no coaxing, as bit by bit other pieces did come through, each "complete with neat rectangles cut by the censor's scissors." Their publication in the newspaper began a sequence of events culminating in the book for which the publisher, as announced to the trade, issued "one of the largest and certainly one of the screwiest series of ads in the one hundred years" of the history of the company.

When Robert Crowell of the Thomas Y. Crowell Company discovered these illustrated articles in the "This World" section of the *Chronicle*, he obtained the author's address from Joseph Henry Jackson, the book reviewer of the paper, and wrote immediately to St. George. "The answer came back like a boomerang." "There is nothing," the delighted Corporal replied, "that would interest me more than authoring a small, illustrated book describing Army life abroad." Before this announcement could be answered, St. George sent a second letter from Australia. "I don't know why I didn't think of this before," he wrote, "but how long is a 'small' book?" When the matter was finally straightened out there followed an "astonishingly active communication," considering the mileage. The new author, moreover, was not only prompt; he was also cooperative. "You can edit all to hell," he offered. "Just leave my name on the title page and I'll be happy. . . . I've been too close to it for too long to feel very sure about the general tone, but I'm pretty sure it won't read like Mama's and little Isadore's trip to Cincinnati." The publisher didn't change a word, however. The result was a best seller, which became one of the two selections of the Book-of-the-Month Club for October 1943.

The soldier-author of this long-distance publishing event was born to John J. and Cecelia St. George in Simpson, Minnesota—a town of eighty inhabitants—on 10:00 a. m. of a Sunday, November 23, 1919. His parents were of Irish-English ancestry. The specific hour of his arrival seems to have left its mark on him, for he writes: "In the years that followed I continued to experience a considerable amount of difficulty in getting started on anything prior to 10:00 a.m.

SGT. THOMAS R. ST. GEORGE

"Otherwise," he continues, "I was a rather unremarkable child, with a tendency to play by myself, probably because I preferred my own way but, being underweight, couldn't insist on it. The only child, I survived the combined attentions of one mother, one father, three aunts, two uncles, one grandmother, and a succession of star boarders." Although given the abridgeable Christian names of Thomas Richard, during his youth St. George acquired the nickname Ozzie through, his parents have reluctantly explained, his fond attachment for a monkey named Oswald.

St. George went the usual number of years to grammar and high school in Simpson, recited "Paul Revere's Ride"— "practically intact"—at the age of nine, and gained the reputation for being, "generally, a good boy in school." Then, apparently in revulsion against this state of affairs, he began a peculiarly hectic period of his education. In the junior college in Rochester, Minnesota he tried, "in rapid succession, pre-aeronautics, pre-engineering, pre-law, and pre-business, failing miserably in all." "This," he notes, "led to the dean's remarking, on numerous occasions in the sanctity of his office, that I hadn't grown up, that I was 'horsing around.'" To this the student responded that it was probably the school's fault if he wasn't interested. In spite of the rebuffs, the two managed to struggle along for several years, until the literary Ozzie was expelled for "ghostwriting four themes, all alike, for four students, all alike, in the same rhetoric class." On more sober consideration, St. George has decided that it was "one hell of a poor gag. Happening as it did the afternoon before the spring prom, my departure under forced draft was quite a blow both to myself and my date."

Apparently the stigma of his expulsion was too much for the University of Minnesota, for, after a summer of manual labor for the Reid Murdoch Company, he was told by the University in the fall of 1940 that it could do without his kind. He "settled" for the

ST. GEORGE, THOMAS R.—*Continued*

Minneapolis Institute of Arts as a result and "spent a rather delightful year at the Institute, learning a great deal about life, though very little indeed about drawing." In February, deciding that he was "essentially a raconteur," he enrolled in a University extension course in short story writing. Enrolling was about as far as he got with that branch of his formal education. He went to one session, found he didn't like the course, and left; but that one class brought him in contact with a "Friend of an Editor." This chance meeting led to his selling a humorous article and four drawings to the Minneapolis *Star Journal* for $5. Thus encouraged, St. George gave up his art lessons shortly before the end of the term, and took a summer job again with the Reid Murdoch Company, collecting $300 from them for his efforts. The following fall he started anew in another course, at the University's School of Journalism. This time his status from the beginning was probationary. Whether this was due to the draft number he had acquired during the summer, or to other matters, St. George doesn't make clear. Between the time he entered and February 1942, he tells, "I pledged Phi Delta Theta, spent the three 'C's,' broke probation, took (and successfully completed) three psychology exams for 'brothers' at the quarter's end, then ran to the waiting arms of my local draft board." He was inducted into the Army on February 13.

That he had had a college education was never exactly determined at the time of his induction; that he had had "experience bussing dishes, sweeping floors, mowing lawns, pushing wheelbarrows, and raking gravel, nobody could or tried to deny; and the Army immediately put those of my talents to work." Approximately thirteen weeks later, shortly after 5:00 a.m. on a certain morning in the spring of 1942, at a camp at San Luis Obispo, St. George and fifty-six other average young men, "buttoned to the ears," stood at attention and listened to "a short lecture (prepared by the War Department and butchered by a 2nd lieutenant) to the effect that we were undoubtedly the finest type of Young Americans, leaving to defend our heritage." Under the mistaken impression that they were off to defend that heritage in Fort Leonard Wood, Missouri, they were "considerably happier than our lieutenant throughout the performance." Their basic training or "Glorified Boy Scout stage of soldiering," as St. George calls it, was over; but they were not on their way to Missouri.

Their destination was Australia. Out of this trip and the period from their arrival in Australia to their departure to New Guinea for active service, St. George has drawn a series of principally amusing, "somewhat irreverent" anecdotes, made more colorful by his wash drawings, with their "authentic, daffy, scrambled quality," to quote the *New Yorker*. Other sketches hold an undercurrent of seriousness that is "effective and moving," the best-remembered being the visit with the little Australian minister who listened quietly while St. George and a few other soldiers boasted of their hardships, and who,

they later learned, had been through the experience of the Japanese landing on Rabaul. "Some of the characters," writes the author-artist in his preface, "are not entirely fictitious, but their resemblance to any person, living or dead, is incidental and done without malice aforethought." The result is primarily a portrait of the author, but also, as Stanley Hyman says, "a portrait of the American Army, of the Yank of this War. St. George is far from the typical soldier . . . but he does exemplify most of the faults of the American Army (primarily in his total unconcern with the larger meanings of the War), as well as many of its virtues." "He has got on paper, in words and drawings, the authentic spirit of the American soldier in Australia." "It is not a bad-tempered book in any way," wrote Orville Prescott. "It is a cheerful, foolish, merry one, filled with laughter and zest for an experience that may be dull and trying much of the time, but which is often interesting, too, at least to St. George."

As some of the critics have remarked, there should be nothing particularly exciting about another soldier's book. St. George's differs from most, however, in that its location is outside the United States and in that the author is in the infantry rather than in the air corps, where the majority of the writers seem to have found themselves. In addition, the reviewers seem to agree with the New York *Times* critic that "it is one of the best and funniest soldier books yet written." St. George's arrival in the land of the Diggers (he tripped down the gangplank of the Matson liner and "literally fell onto the continent . . . a fraction of a second ahead of and directly beneath by barracks bag") is typical of the "delectable, screwball quality"—to quote his publishers—that pervades his book. The *New Yorker*, comparing its amusing, original way of writing with other soldier books, remarked that it is "evidently G.I. stuff rather than the sort of clever corn we've been getting." "The laughter is free," wrote William Soskin," the kind you cannot find in many armies or nations these days, and the book, in its artless, innocent fashion, suggests the species of a laughing, joking, kidding army of democracy fighting its way into other nations so that the peoples of the world may laugh with them."

Ozzie St. George in the fall of 1943 was in the southwest Pacific area. He had left the division headquarters of an infantry division in the Chemical Warfare Section to become a staff correspondent for the Army magazine *Yank* on the Down Under edition, for which he writes feature articles and editorials. And on the back cover of most of the issues appears one of his "inanely cockeyed" cartoons. He has written feature articles for *Yank Published Down Under* on the battles of Salamaura and Lae. His adventures, needless to say, are continuing outside the covers of *c/o Postmaster*. Since the publication of the book he has managed to fall out of a landing craft while doing a bit of journalism, to get himself drunk on jungle juice (a drink reported to be composed less of fruit juices than of alcohol), and to grab a ride on the first glider to New Guinea. According to Sergeant Dave Richardson, staff correspondent for *Yank* and a friend of St. George's, the soldier is the type of fellow who can sleep three days in a row and then get up and work steadily, although for how long Richardson doesn't say. In 1944 Sergeant St. George had a new locale for his adventures; his publishers reported in November that he had arrived in the Philippines from New Guinea. His new book, "Proceed Without Delay," was announced for publication in the spring of 1945.

St. George's mother has been made custodian of his Book-of-the-Month Club royalties for the duration. His only requests were, according to his parents, Mr. and Mrs. John St. George, who visited New York City during October, that he be sent a carton of cigarets, and that their house in Simpson be reshingled. The soldier-author admits that in spite of what he may have said "at various other times, usually reveille, this Army has been, all in all, the best thing that ever happened to me. Next week: *East Lynne.*"

References

Book-of-the-Month Club N p26-7 N '43
Pub W 144:404-5 Ag 7 '43 por

SALTER, ANDREW May 9, 1914- Psychologist

Address: b. 1000 Park Ave., New York City

What Is Hypnosis? (1944) is a small monograph presenting a completely new approach to hypnosis by the American whose development of autohypnosis gave a somewhat neglected branch of psychology a new impetus in 1941. H. G. Wells, much interested in Andrew Salter's work, writes of it: "I have read this with admiration and approval." Says Aldous Huxley: "Fundamentally sound, lucid, forceful. Unlike all too many scientific monographs, this little book can be read with real pleasure." Thomas Mann '42 finds the book "captivatingly written."

The son of Morris George and Frances (Saltzman) Salter, Andrew Salter was born May 9, 1914 in Waterbury, Connecticut, where his father and three uncles were employed as watchmakers. As a psychologist he emphasizes the importance of the early years: "Overlove your child rather than underlove it," he says to parents. He himself had extremely sympathetic and cooperative parents—"My early conditioning was lucky." And apparently he was something of a child prodigy. After he moved to New York City in the middle of his eighth year in grammar school his Connecticut teacher used to point to the seat he once occupied and hope audibly that the eighth grader who sat there would prove worthy of it.

As a boy Salter's special talents in school were cryptography and poetry (Robert Frost was impressed enough with his poetry to send him a Christmas card one year); and in 1932, after attending New York University for a year, he took a long vacation from formal education about which he remains poetically vague, except that it was filled with reading and youthful *Sturm und Drang*. By 1934 the *Sturm* had somewhat abated; in any case, he returned to the University with the prosaic intention of teaching psychology.

This notion didn't last long. The thought of the years of study before him if he was to teach psychology soon made him impatient. Besides, "I had no desire to spend the rest of my life studying the reactions of rats lost in labyrinths." Salter finally decided to dispense with his Doctor's degree and to do research on his own, and hypnosis seemed like a good field. Even before he was graduated from N.Y.U. in June 1937 he had made some slight dent in the literature of the subject. The fact that he could read five languages helped some, especially when he began to wonder if there weren't some relation between hypnosis and the self-induced phenomena produced by Indian Yogi. And then, what about habit formation? The bibliography began to encompass the entire field of psychology as his curiosity grew.

He was barely a year out of college when he began wondering if autohypnosis was not possible. Posthypnotic suggestions, given by hypnotist to patient, had such a temporary effect that hypnosis had almost been discarded as a tool in psychotherapy: a patient could not keep coming back to a hypnotist for the rest of his life. But what if the patient were taught to hypnotize himself and give himself posthypnotic suggestions while in the trance? It seemed like a simple and obvious idea; it just happened that no one else had apparently thought of it before. Unfortunately, Salter didn't seem to be equipped to do much about it. He hadn't even a Ph.D.; he had no research facilities.

He nevertheless set about to answer his own question. A few interested physicians tossed him an assortment of stutterers, insomniacs, and alcoholics that they couldn't seem to do much with, and these served as his guinea pigs. By the end of 1938 he had proved not only that the thing could be done, but had devised three techniques for doing it, and had begun asking himself a great many more questions. The next step was, in all logic, to publish a paper on his findings.

But it was far easier to write the paper than to get it published. Salter had had a private psychological practice since 1940, but what professional standing did a mere B.S. have? The professional journals were afraid to touch his article until he sent a copy to Professor Clark Leonard Hull of Yale's psychology department, who is probably the world's chief authority on hypnotism and allied phenomena and who is also an editor of the erudite *Journal of General Psychology*. Hull, impressed, turned the article over to the *Journal*, and it appeared in April 1941 under the title "Three Techniques of Autohypnosis."

The first of Salter's three techniques was the most obvious. Having determined that the potential subject could be hypnotized through the ordinary procedure, Salter would explain to him exactly what he was going to do. He would then hypnotize him and tell him while in the trance that he would be able to induce the same state in himself merely by settling himself somewhere comfortably and letting the thought flash through his mind that he would like to hypnotize himself. While in the resulting autohypnotic trance he could, of course, give himself whatever suggestions he

Benmosché

ANDREW SALTER

wished, and could "wake up" whenever he wanted to, feeling fine. Throughout the instructions Salter always emphasized the fact that it makes no difference whether the suggestions come from "within" or "without."

The second technique could also be used successfully on previously tested subjects. Such a subject would be told to memorize some typed autohypnotic material paralleling the "heterohypnotic" suggestions already found effective with him—and after instruction and practice he would usually find that he could put himself in an autohypnotic trance merely by repeating them silently to himself.

But it was the third method that was later to prove most rewarding to Salter in his search for an explanation of hypnosis. In this the trance state of hypnosis was assumed to be composed of discrete parts, and a subject on whom certain minor effects could be easily produced by waking suggestion (a catalepsy of the arm or leg, for example) would be taught to produce the deeper trance phenomena by autosuggestion, first separately, then all at once. Heterohypnotic aid would be necessary only in the final stages, and that usually very slight.

Naturally enough, it was the first and most spectacular technique that attracted most attention. Letters to Salter began pouring in from prospective patients. *Time, Life, Coronet,* and the New York *Times* ran articles; Elsa Maxwell '43 wrote about him in her column. The young psychologist began turning down lucrative offers outside the field of private practice—from lecture bureaus, from a radio entrepreneur who wanted him for a series of sponsored self-help programs, from a movie producer who wanted him to make a movie short demonstrating autohypnosis, and from an insurance company that wanted him to turn all three techniques on its lazy sales force.

In the meanwhile, after further experiments on subjects selected from employment agencies and on his own cooperative patients,

Salter was beginning to find the paper which had created such a sensation a bit on the primitive side. He was learning that the autohypnotic trance was not at all important in itself, for all of the phenomena of hypnosis could be produced with the subject in complete auto-control and in a waking state at all times. (Incidentally, the trance itself is much more closely related to the waking state than to real sleep.) In association with William Henry Gardiner, M.D., he trained three subjects to remain completely insensitive to pain and the sounds of guns in a waking state, for example—trained them to turn the anaesthesias on and off, by themselves, in any part of the body at will. Hypnosis, he concluded, involves nothing but a conditioning process—the same process involved in habit formation. "Other factors being equal, intelligence facilitates it, and the 'trance' is nothing but a pattern of specific conditionings," brought about through ringing a number of verbal "bells" to which the subject's past experiences have already trained him to respond somatically. Furthermore, "The complicated phenomena of posthypnotic suggestion reduce themselves to nothing but a series of conditioned speech and body muscle acts. In the creation of moods in a subject glandular conditionings may be involved, and previously established feelings are sympathetically vibrated. 'You are bored,' or 'you are happy, very happy.' In the poor and frequent use of hypnosis there is often a conditioned muscular inhibition. 'You will not bite your nails.' 'You will not tremble in front of an audience.'"

The implications of this theory, carrying Pavlov's conclusions one step farther, should be immediately obvious to the psychiatrist or psychoanalyst—and somewhat annoying. According to Salter, Freud had a fallacious concept of hypnosis when he stopped using it, although hypnosis *per se* is in no sense psychotherapy. ("Any fool can hypnotize.") If a neurosis is nothing more than the result of conditioning, as Salter believes it to be, once the unfortunate pattern of conditioning that produced it is revealed a neurotic can be shown how to do the real work of the cure—partly through his autohypnotic ability, but chiefly through the concepts which he absorbs in the process of acquiring it. Salter's theory is completely devoid of unnaturalistic complications. Personality is to him as unmysterious as putty.

No more than two people out of five, and probably no more than one person out of five, can go into the deepest hypnotic trances—hypnotic susceptibility, like intelligence or any other measurable characteristic, seems to be distributed along the probability curve. But Salter says that ninety-nine per cent of all people can at least be shown how to function on all cylinders, provided that the actual situation in which they find themselves is not impossible. Most often his patients are people who are, purely and simply, deeply unhappy. Then, of course, there are the women who want to keep to diets, the insomniacs, the shy and unself-confident, the incipient dipsomaniacs, the artists who can no longer express themselves or who have lost the "will to work." All of these can be helped—many of them in not more than six sessions, and for fees of $1,000 up. Few unsuspected talents have been uncovered, however, except a talent for acting: Salter has come to the conclusion that anyone can act, once self-consciousness and inhibitions are removed. A middle-aged traveling salesman who had been to the theatre only once or twice in his life was put in a trance and told he was Hamlet; "he was better than Barrymore or Maurice Evans '⁴⁰!'"

Asked what the larger implications of his psychological concepts are, Salter replies that they make it possible for the process of evolution to be carried on. "All the frontal lobes have done so far is to allow the human race to rationalize"; in this sense Hitler '⁴² was right in saying, "We think with our blood." If the tail has been wagging the dog, the time has come for the dog to understand the tail and the laws by which it works.

Five feet seven, dark, enthusiastic, and talkative, Salter gives the impression that the greater part of his revelations are yet to come. He declines to write a "popular" book on autohypnosis—a *You, Too, Can Be Hypnotized* or *Recondition Yourself!*—but he has an impressive number of other projects in mind. One important long-term project is already accomplished: on September 24, 1943 he was married to Rhoda Kazan, a former teacher of sociology at the University of Minnesota. Although Salter specialized in putting the savor back into the lives of his Park Avenue clientele, he confesses that some of it has gone out of his own: it has become so relatively simple for him to predict reactions that the unexpected hardly exists any more. But he could never pose for the portrait of a bored man. In recent years he has found his work a fascinating enough hobby for anyone, and he no longer even writes poetry—perhaps his one great interest aside from his experiments is in good music. Apparently, too, experiments on the genus *homo sapiens* are enough for him: he owns no dog or cat, and he is still unfascinated by rats in mazes. Above the door of his office, however, are two sculptured figures: a squirrel and an owl. He didn't choose his office because of them, but he now finds the symbolism quite appropriate for those who pass through its doors.

References

   Coronet 10:107-12 S '41
   Life 11:83-6+ N 10 '41 il pors
   N Y Post p12 Ag 6 '43
   Newsweek 23:78 F 28 '44
   Time 37:40 Je 2 '41; 43:90+ Mr 6 '44
     por
   Salter, A. What Is Hypnosis 1944

SALTER, SIR (JAMES) ARTHUR Mar. 15, 1881- Economist; statesman; author; teacher

Address: b. All Souls College, Oxford University, Oxford, England

Sir Arthur Salter, formerly one of the two heads of the Combined Shipping Adjustment Board in Washington, D. C., in 1944 senior deputy director general of the United Nations Relief and Rehabilitation Administration, is not only an economist and an authority on shipping, but an author, a teacher, and a states-

SIR ARTHUR SALTER

man. He has held so many official positions under the British Government that he has been called the "civil servant par excellence." It is in nautical affairs, however, that he remains true to his heritage, for it was his family that built the boats "in which Oxford's young gentlemen bump each other on the Thames."

James Arthur Salter is an Oxford man by birth as well as education. He was born in Oxford, March 15, 1881, the son of James E. Salter. Arthur Salter received both his preparatory and his higher education at Oxford. He attended Brasenose College, where his academic record was good but not outstanding. Upon leaving school in 1904 he secured a position in the transport department of the Admiralty. The rest of his career has consisted of moving from one civil service job to another. In 1913 he became assistant secretary of the British National Health Insurance Commission. During the First World War he won prominence as the organizer of world shipping—first as assistant director of Transports (1915), then as director of Ship Requisitioning (1917). The following year he was appointed secretary of the Allied Maritime Transport Council, and he rose to be chairman of the Allied Maritime Transport Executive. In 1919 he became a member of the Supreme Economic Council.

The end of the First World War and the consequent peace planning found Salter "the center of the best of the League's activities at Geneva" in the capacity of director of the Economic and Finance Section of the League of Nations, a position which he held from 1919 until 1920 and from 1922 until 1931. During those years he earned the title of "the worst-dressed man in Geneva." From 1920 until 1922 Salter was general secretary of the Reparation Commission. He had been made a Companion of the Bath in 1918, and in 1922 he was knighted for his achievements. (In 1944, on the New Year's honors list, he

SALTER, SIR ARTHUR—*Continued*

was raised to Knight Grand Cross of the Order of the British Empire.)

In 1930 Sir Arthur was sent on a mission to India, and in 1931 and 1933 he was sent to China. In 1932 he was appointed chairman of the Road-Rail Conference in England and was also made a member of the Economic Advisory Council, a position which he still retains.

Since 1934 Salter has been professor of political theory and institutions at Oxford University and since 1937, contrary to custom, he has been an Independent Member of Parliament for his home borough, Oxford. In the latter capacity he has been called "one of the most useful private members of the House of Commons." Meanwhile he has held other positions as well. From 1936 until 1939 he served as chairman of the Railway Staff of the National Tribunal, and from 1939 until 1941 he acted as parliamentary secretary to the Ministry of Shipping. In the spring of 1941 Salter visited Washington, D. C. as head of the British Shipping Mission and member of the British Supply Council in North America. There he told reporters that the War might depend on the United States shipyards and asked for another "miracle of 1918," when 4,000,000 gross tons of shipping were produced by the United States. In June he became joint parliamentary secretary to the Ministry of War Transports, another position he still retains.

In January 1942, soon after the United States entered the Second World War, an Anglo-American Combined Shipping Adjustment Board was set up to pool British and American shipping in wartime. Salter and Rear Admiral Land '41 became the heads of the combined board in Washington; Lord Leathers '41 and William A. Harriman '41 were appointed to the London board. Not many months later Roosevelt '42 and Churchill '42 were conferring with Salter, Land, and other shipping experts on shipping requirements for offensive strategy. Since that time Salter has frequently spoken on United Nations ship losses and building, on the U-boat warfare situation, on the importance of merchant shipbuilding, and on other aspects of shipping on which he is well qualified to give an opinion. When Herbert H. Lehman '43 appointed him senior director deputy general of the UNRRA he brought extremely useful experience to his new position, for UNRRA and the Anglo-American Combined Boards (Combined Food Board, Combined Raw Materials Board, and Combined Production and Resources Board, as well as Combined Shipping Adjustment Board) must work together a great deal. UNRRA, for example, must ask the Boards whenever it need supplies for relief. Salter planned to remain in Washington temporarily to help Lehman to develop UNRRA, although he resigned from the Combined Shipping Adjustment Board there.

In June 1944 Sir Arthur returned to London. To casual questioners he replied that he wanted to "sit in" on some sessions of Parliament. However, with Lehman unable to travel at the time, it was generally thought Sir Arthur went to take part in the secret conferences having to

do with UNRRA's post-invasion role in Europe, and that he went with full authority to make the necessary decisions. In September he attended the Montreal meeting of the UNRRA, at which was discussed the question of aid to occupied enemy territory.

Despite his numerous duties, Salter has found the time to write a number of books on economic questions. In 1921 he wrote *Allied Shipping Control: an Experiment in International Administration. Recovery: the Second Effort* did not appear until eleven years later. The following year, in 1933, two of his books were published: *The Framework of an Ordered Society* and *The United States of Europe. World Trade and Its Future* appeared in 1936. *Security, Can We Retrieve It,* his latest volume to date, was published in 1939. The book, a study of the British imperial security of the moment, was regarded by American critics as being, on the whole, rather confused. The opinions of English critics were somewhat more favorable. One wrote that Salter's "picture of the change wrought in England by the abolition of our insular position, his account of the economics and strategy of the dictatorships, and his summary of recent British policy and League history are lucid and valuable."

In addition to the honors he has received from Britain's Crown, Sir Arthur has been decorated with Belgian (1919), French (1920), Italian (1922), and Chinese (1937) orders. He holds a number of honorary degrees from the English universities of Oxford and Manchester, from the University of Vienna (Austria), from the universities of Harvard, Columbia, and California, and from McGill University in Montreal.

Salter has been described as "small in stature, strong and resolute in appearance, and decisive in speech." He is known, writes H. C. O'Neill, for his "ability to state a case with convincing clarity, calm judgment, and a flair for affairs." *Time* Magazine called Salter "a shrewd, wary, grim little man, a firm believer in the hunch school of statesmanship." Another source described him as "a busy and humorous sparrow in large round spectacles." Wherever the little Englishman —he is five feet four inches tall—goes, "the fur," according to *Time,* "will fly." Sir Arthur's arrival in Washington was likened to a medium tank making its way through underbrush.

Sir Arthur has been active in the Air-Raid Defence League. His favorite recreation is swimming. Previous to the year 1940 he was described as "one of the world's great bachelors," but this no longer holds true, for in that year he married the widowed Mrs. Arthur Bullard of Washington, D. C.

References

    Time 37 :18 Ap 14 '41

    Who's Who 1944

SALTONSTALL, LEVERETT (sôl't'n-stôl) Sept. 1, 1892- Governor of Massachusetts; United States Senator-elect from Massachusetts

Address: h. Chestnut Hill, Mass.

In November 1944, in his third term as Republican Governor of Massachusetts, Leverett

Saltonstall was elected to the United States Senate by what was "probably the most crushing plurality in Massachusetts politics." Known as "New England's favorite son," Saltonstall has won a popularity which, in the words of Marquis W. Childs [43] "blurs over party lines." Saltonstall will take his seat on January 3, 1945, in the 79th Congress, where he will fill the unexpired term of Henry Cabot Lodge, Jr., [43] which ends January 3, 1949.

The Bay State Governor can count eight former governors of Massachusetts among his forebears, and his is reputedly the wealthiest family in Massachusetts today: his mother is the daughter of Peter C. Brooks, a multi-millionaire. One Saltonstall was Lord Mayor of London in the days of Queen Elizabeth; another, Oliver Cromwell's Ambassador to Holland; another, Governor of the Massachusetts Bay Colony. Some of the Saltonstalls favored the Tory side in the Revolutionary War, although the Governor's direct ancestor did not, and four Brookses fought in the Revolution. The fact that he is a descendant of a certain Margery Sullivan from County Cork permits him to be a member of Boston's Charitable Irish Society.

Leverett Saltonstall was born in Chestnut Hill, a fashionable suburb of Boston, Massachusetts, September 1, 1892, the son of Richard Middlecott and Eleanor (Brooks) Saltonstall. He grew up in his parents' fifteen-room red brick house (complete with greenhouse, swimming pool, tennis court, gardener's cottage, and barn), riding ponies and playing in the fields with his neighbor, James Lowell, who is still his best friend. Young Leverett attended Boston's Noble and Greenough private day school until 1910, when he went on to Harvard.

The tenth Saltonstall in his direct line to go through Harvard, Saltonstall became a member of Hasty Pudding and the Porcellian Club, which is tops socially. He made good grades by sheer hard labor, and made his record in athletics in much the same way. Dropped from the ice hockey squad, the youth practiced skating daily until taken back, and in one game had the honor of ending the longest deadlock in Harvard's hockey history, scoring the winning goal when sent on the ice late in the game. By the end of his junior year he was a substitute on the varsity crew, too, and in his senior year he captained the Jayvee crew that won the Henley Grand Challenge in England. His father, grandfather, and great-grandfather had all been lawyers, and after receiving his B.A. in 1914 he went on to law school. There he made a "B" average and emerged with his LL.B. in 1917. By this time (June 27, 1916) he was already married to Alice Wesselhoeft, whom he had first met years before at dancing school.

Then came the First World War. Saltonstall served in France for six months as a 1st lieutenant, but participated in no actual combat. In 1919 admitted to the Massachusetts bar, he began his practice at Boston as attorney and trustee, also becoming a director in various financial institutions, as well as in the Boston & Albany Railroad. Then the Republican chieftain of the city of Newton suggested he run for the Board of Aldermen. He

was elected and served a two-year term (1920-22), also serving from 1921 to 1922 as assistant district attorney for Middlesex County. He has been in politics ever since. In 1923 Saltonstall was elected to the state legislature (known since 1629 as General Court). Regularly re-elected, he eventually gave up all his directorships except those in charitable institutions and abandoned the active practice of law.

According to the Massachusetts State Federation of Labor, in the legislature Saltonstall voted thirty-seven times "against" labor, only three times "for." When in 1929 he announced his candidacy for Speaker, a Boston Republican, speaking before the legislature, said: "He was not born, Mr. Speaker, in the ways that you and I were. He was born with a diamond-studded spoon in his mouth. He knows only one side of life—the coupon-clipping side." This speaker announced that the election of Saltonstall would be "a surrender to all that is hostile to the interests of the common people"—that it would make any future Republican victories in Massachusetts impossible. Saltonstall was nevertheless elected, and as Speaker he began to give some support to measures providing for old-age security, mothers' aid, a mandatory minimum wage, unemployment insurance, peaceful picketing, the outlawing of "yellow dog" contracts, and anti-injunction regulation. Furthermore, after the Republican rout in 1934 he warned his fellow Republicans that they should cooperate with President Roosevelt [42].

By this time he had shattered tradition by being re-elected in 1932 after having already served four years as Speaker—and by being re-elected again in 1934. Personally so popular that when his rulings were questioned Democrats usually joined with Republicans to uphold him, Saltonstall was in general a mild presiding officer. Once, however, when a measure he considered dangerous seemed likely to pass he banged his gavel, declared the House adjourned, and marched out with the gavel still in his hand so that no one else could take it up and carry on the session. At another time a bill came up to establish in every community of any size a place where speakers would not require a permit. It was going through with a majority of one when he stepped down from the rostrum—an unusual procedure—and voted against it. The vote was tied, and the bill failed to pass.

By 1936 Saltonstall "had joined nearly all the fraternal orders, had made innumerable addresses to all sorts of organizations, ranging from the Ancient and Honorable Artillery Company to the Young People's Society of Christian Endeavor. He had been careful not to stir up trouble or antipathy, discouraging legislative investigations and resolutions offering gratuitous advice to Congress. He had kept most of his public utterances on safe territory." When nominated for Lieutenant Governor that year he was defeated, but in 1938 he announced his candidacy for the governorship, and his old enemy of 1929 promptly hailed him as "the one white hope of the Republican Party," the man with "everything the public demands, everything Massachusetts likes to honor and trust." Saltonstall's was a "thorough and plugging" campaign for Governor that year: an agency sampled public

LEVERETT SALTONSTALL

opinion on certain campaign issues for him; he appeared three times in every important city and covered three sections of his state every week; and he shook more hands than any candidate in Massachusetts history. In his speeches he stressed his liberal outlook, and he defeated Boston's James Michael Curley (who was trying to make a comeback) by a large majority, becoming the first Republican Governor of Massachusetts since the depression.

As soon as he moved into the State House, Saltonstall ordered the elevator operators to discontinue the old custom of turning the elevator into a nonstop express when the Governor was aboard. "I like to ride with the people," he said. Assembling his staff for the Governor's office, he warned all his male assistants that they were to be at their desks at nine, freshly shaved, and cautioned them about drinking. His most spectacular feat during his first term was the settlement of a great truck drivers' strike which tied up the city of Boston not long after he took office. He conferred with conciliators, with the Mayor, the strike leaders, and the truck owners, who together worked out a compromise program. With the militia as an implied threat, he then got both sides to accept the program.

Saltonstall was easily re-elected in 1940, although in the Presidential race Roosevelt carried the state by 137,000 votes, and his re-election in 1942 made him Governor of Massachusetts for the longest stretch in ninety-odd years. Although known as a "plodding type," he has been a pioneer in many ways. Massachusetts' plan for home defense was the first state plan, and became the model for other states. Before Pearl Harbor, Saltonstall also began a planning board for a "post-defense" revision of Massachusetts' entire manufacturing economy (now called the Post-War Readjustment Committee). The committee, which advises consumers, businessmen, and labor leaders, has as its aim the restoration of Massachusetts' once-privileged industrial

position in the reconversion of the state's leading industries to peacetime production.

The Governor is by no means a "Roosevelt Republican," however. Like Ohio's Bricker '43, he is proud of his "economy" record. When he entered office there was a deficit and no sales tax. By the end of 1944 he will have cut the deficit of forty-one million by ninety-two per cent. He speaks frequently about the dangers of "bureaucracy," the necessity for the decentralization of government, "States' rights," and the safeguarding of "private enterprise," although he is not for discarding all of the New Deal. In 1942, when the cry went up for a Federal grant of 300 millions for the relief of unemployment in Detroit because of the reconversion of the automobile industry, he led the winning fight of the governors against it. Saltonstall has not escaped criticism from liberals, in spite of his internationalism and what even liberals consider a good record on such issues as civil liberties. In the fall of 1943 he was charged with leading a lobby of governors for the fire insurance lobby's bill to protect insurance companies from anti-trust prosecution. At about the same time there were many anti-Jewish incidents in Boston, although the Boston press kept quiet about them. The New York newspaper *PM* finally printed a documented story about them and demanded that Saltonstall take some action. Saltonstall, at first angered by the story, later said that he had had a "rude awakening." He then appointed a permanent seven-man, inter-faith advisory committee to deal with the problem and ordered the State Public Safety Commissioner to investigate the anti-Semitic outbreaks. The ultimate result was a new police commissioner.

A believer in international cooperation, he finds in the Moscow pact and the Cairo and Teheran parleys evidence that nations can get along together. On the domestic front, he believes that helping returning war veterans "to get back on their own feet" should be the first and foremost concern of the United States. He was also an advocate of the Federal soldier vote, and the law of his state permitted the maximum of servicemen to vote in 1944. Enjoying great prestige among his fellow governors, in June 1943 he was elected chairman of the Governors' Conference and in November of the same year president of the Council of State Governments. He also delivered the keynote address at the Michigan Republican Convention in Detroit in the spring of 1944.

Saltonstall stated his view on the issue of Federal-State relationships in a brief opening address he made as chairman of the thirty-sixth annual Governors' Conference in Hershey, Pennsylvania, in May 1944: "This question of which unit of government, Federal or State, can best meet the problem involved throws a spotlight on the whole fundamental question of what the average citizen expects of his government in relation to himself, his family, his home, and his job. We want freedom and opportunity. Yet we can't have the fullest freedom and opportunity if we turn to government to provide the initiative and the wherewithal for us in ever-increasing degree. . . . We want our country to be governed from the bottom up, and not from the top down. The government under which the states rose to greatness is government that begins at home." In a ceremony at Gettysburg the next day, Saltonstall representing the Old North, and Governor J. Melville Broughton of North Carolina representing the Old South, symbolized the unity of the two sections. In his address Saltonstall emphasized also the need for unity between government and business—"A country cannot go forward where government seeks to destroy opportunities in business and business seeks to weaken the reasonable authority of government." On labor relations, his words were: "We must insist upon the willingness and ability of the labor leaders to cooperate with the management of our industries. . . . We must insist that management cooperate with labor." Governor Saltonstall also demanded that the United States take its share of "neighborly responsibility" in the society of nations.

With liberal views such as these well known, it was not strange that Republican Saltonstall received strong support from Massachusetts Democrats in his race for the junior seat in the United States Senate. (He had indicated his candidacy in February 1944, when he had appointed Sinclair Weeks to fill the vacancy left by Senator Cabot Lodge, who went into service, and he had been nominated in July.) Because of his pro-Dewey [44] activities in the Presidential campaign, Saltonstall had the "tacit," if not formal, support of the PAC-CIO. Voters cut across party lines to give him a plurality of more than 400,000 over his Democratic opponent, Mayor John H. Corcoran of Cambridge; and he carried Democratic Boston by 66,046 votes, more than Mayor Maurice J. Tobin received in his successful race for the Governorship. As Arthur Krock described it, Saltonstall was "the first Republican to perform that political miracle since Calvin Coolidge achieved it in the three-man Presidential contest of 1924." One comment on the significance of Saltonstall's election to the Senate was that the Republicans, in seeking to become as united as possible on the issue of international security, had done well in the Massachusetts election. And Mark Sullivan wrote: "Such a proof of personal strength weighs in politics. Mr. Saltonstall, in the Senate during the coming four years, has a chance to impress himself on the country."

"Tall, long-faced, homely, Saltonstall is a typical old-family Bostonian (though he lives, technically, outside the city limits). He has a nasal twang, a Harvard accent, is reserved and easy-mannered, at home in anything from formal morning clothes to old flannels." According to *Time* Magazine, "Saltonstall's political charm is that he strikes people as an old shoe rather than an old tie. His engagingly homely face is his No. 1 political asset, with its drooping eyelids, lean cheeks, long nose, wide-spaced teeth, and the famed 'cowcatcher' chin. That reassuring face has been termed 'a well-worn American antique' and 'the most distinctive face in United States public life.' Deviousness would have a hard time finding a hiding place there. It is a face New Englanders trust." And his personal habits and tastes are equally reassuring to New Englanders. He drinks rarely, smokes almost never.

His Chestnut Hill house is "a fourteen-room frame affair" from which he commutes to Boston, and he frequently walks the mile from the Back Bay Station to the State House in the mornings. Even when driven around in his two-door 1941 Chevrolet he usually rides up front with his ununiformed chauffeur. Week ends he goes to his eighty-nine-acre farm at Dover, fifteen miles southwest of Boston. There he puts on old clothes, pitches hay, saws wood, beds down his horses; and in 1943 he sold 1,600 dozen eggs.

Governor and Mrs. Saltonstall have four children. Leverett, Jr., is a lieutenant in the Army Engineers; Emily is a Wave stationed in Washington; the two youngest children are William and Susan. Another son, Marine Sergeant Peter B. Saltonstall, was killed in action on Guam in August 1944. Called a "tweedy family" before three of them put on uniforms, they all used to ride with the Norfolk Hunt. Saltonstall himself prefers riding and farming to parties or even to reading. He is "also an accomplished sailor, but mediocre dancer and bridge player." His clubs are the Harvard, Exchange, Somerset, Norfolk Hunt, and Country clubs. In addition, he is secretary of his Harvard class of 1914 and president of the Harvard Board of Overseers, a trustee of the Massachusetts Eye and Ear Infirmary, manager of the Farm and Trade School, a member of the board of the directors of the Central Safety Deposit & Trust Company, and a member of such organizations as the Council Against Intolerance in America and the National Committee Against Nazi Persecution and Extermination of the Jews. He is a Unitarian, a Mason, and an Elk.

References

Nation 149:255 S 2 '39
Newsweek 21:88 Mr 22 '43
Scrib Mag 105:7-11+ My '39 por
Time 36:sup (8) N 11 '40 por; 43:19-22 Ap 10 '44 il pors
Who's Who in America 1944-45

SANDERS, JARED YOUNG Jan. 29, 1869—Mar. 23, 1944 Former Governor of Louisiana (1908-12); elected to United States Congress in 1917; served two terms as a Democratic Representative.

Obituary

N Y Times p19 Mr 24 '44

SANGER, MARGARET (HIGGINS) Sept. 14, 1883- Leader of birth control movement
Address: b. Margaret Sanger Research Bureau, 17 W. 16th St., New York City; h. Fishkill, N. Y.; Tucson, Ariz.

Margaret Sanger, the leader of the birth control movement in the United States, has fought long against a formidable array of opponents, including the United States Government itself. Her crusade has brought her persecution, a prison sentence, much mental anguish, and little rest, but she has seen what few pioneers see—"wide breaches in the walls at which she has battered" for so many years. Today "birth control" is in every com-

SANGER, MARGARET—*Continued*

prehensive dictionary and encyclopedia in the world.

Margaret Sanger's childhood in the industrial town of Corning, New York, says Beulah Amidon, "probably turned her thought to the problem of too many children born too rapidly into a home of uncertain income." Her tubercular Irish mother, Anne Purcell Higgins, died young, after bearing eleven children. But the heritage of the child's fun-loving, free-thinking Irish father had its influence, too. Michael Hennessy Higgins was "a philosopher, a rebel, and an artist" who made his living chiseling tombstone angels and saints out of stone. It was a precarious livelihood, and in time his persistent radicalism cut off much of his trade. He had always fought for woman suffrage; for "freedom of the mind from dogma and cant"; for free libraries and education and schoolbooks; for such things as the single tax and socialism. In the 1940's his family might have been called liberal; in the 1880's it was classed as little better than "heathen" by the neighbors.

Although the eleven little red-headed Higginses found some time to play-act in their barn or go hunting in the nearby woods, their youth—especially Margaret's—was mainly taken up with dreary household chores and the care of younger brothers and sisters. Even at the school at Claverack, New York, it was necessary for Margaret to work to supplement the money for expenses supplied by her parents and two elder sisters. The three years she spent at the coeducational Methodist institution were happy ones, however. She debated such subjects as woman suffrage and free silver, and during these years of development it was pointed out for the first time that the young girl—mature for her age—showed signs of leadership.

Immediately after leaving Claverack Margaret Higgins taught school for a brief period in New Jersey until she was called home to nurse her dying mother. After Anne Higgins' death an awakened interest in medicine and a latent desire to be of service to the world led Margaret to a nursing career. She studied at the White Plains Hospital in New York, a poorly equipped, small-town institution where the work was often unpaid drudgery. The latter part of the course—a relatively leisurely experience—was taken at the Manhattan Eye and Ear Hospital in New York City. Shortly after her graduation Miss Higgins was married in 1900 to William Sanger, an artist and architect.

The couple settled down in a New York City apartment, but before a year had passed young Mrs. Sanger discovered that the long hours with her tubercular mother and the subsequent months of overwork in the hospital had produced in her the incipient signs of tuberculosis. The next few years, spent near Saranac, New York, in the Adirondacks, were difficult ones for her. Finally, less than a year after the birth of her first child Stuart, in November 1905, she returned to her family in an attempt to regain her health in her own home. The move proved to be a wise one. For the following five or six years—although Margaret Sanger was never very strong—she and her family lived happily in a small town in New York State, where two other children,

Grant and Peggy, were born. At the end of this time, feeling a certain incompleteness in their small-town existence, the Sangers moved back to the city, where they plunged "into the rushing stream of New York life."

During the next few years William and Margaret Sanger took an active part in the vigorous intellectual revolution that was then sweeping the country. Their friends were radicals of all shades—John Reed, Mabel Dodge Luhan, Bill Haywood, Emma Goldman, Alexander Berkman, Jessie Ashley. Mrs. Sanger herself worked for the Socialist Party; lectured, and wrote health articles for the Socialist *Call*, which were later published in book form as *What Every Girl Should Know* (1916) and *What Every Mother Should Know* (1917).

The immediate motivating force that shaped Mrs. Sanger's lifework was not directly these Socialist activities, however, but her nursing, which she had taken up again. Her work was limited to maternity cases, principally from New York's teeming Lower East Side. Many of the patients were wives of small shopkeepers, truck drivers, pushcart vendors. Others were from a lower stratum of society in truly desperate circumstances. "These submerged, untouched classes were beyond the scope of organized charity or religion. No labor union, no church, not even the Salvation Army reached them." Among the women, pregnancy was "a chronic condition." The young nurse saw them, weary and old at thirty-five, resorting to self-induced abortions, which were frequently the cause of their deaths. The hopelessness of the distressed, poverty-stricken souls she attended became a recurrent nightmare to her. Finally in 1912, haunted by them and unable to stand her own inability to help and advise, Mrs. Sanger renounced nursing forever. "I came," she has written, "to a sudden realization that my work as a nurse and my activities in social service were entirely palliative and consequently futile and useless to relieve the misery I saw all about me." Determined to "seek out the root of the evil," she felt that the purely economic struggle to raise a man's wage was not sufficient.

Impeding her at every step were ignorance, prejudice, religious tenets, and the legal threat of the Comstock Act of 1873, which classified contraceptive information as obscene. Even progressive women, Socialists, and doctors offered her no assistance: fighters for women suffrage seemed more concerned with the vote than with Margaret Sanger's immediate problem, and doctors seemed to fear Comstock's law; in most cases, moreover, the doctors had no reliable information to offer. For nearly a year the ex-nurse read every available scrap of pertinent material, of which there was little to be had. Then, at the end of 1913, she went abroad to study conditions in Scotland and France.

Upon her return to the United States in 1914 the self-appointed pioneer started a defiant little magazine, the *Woman Rebel,* with the slogan: "No gods; no masters!" In the face of all kinds of opposition she wrote of the need for contraceptive control. Sympathy, charity, maternity centers, child labor laws—these were not enough. Contrary to the accusation that she wanted to lower the birth rate, she visualized families of rich and poor alike where children were wanted and given every advantage. She saw her program not solely one of health, but with economic and social aspects.

There were seven specific circumstances or principles, Mrs. Sanger emphasized, which governed birth control: (1) when either husband or wife had a transmissible disease; (2) when the wife suffered from a temporary affection of the lungs, heart, or kidneys, the cure of which might be retarded through pregnancy; (3) when parents, though normal, had subnormal children; (4) when husband or wife were adolescent; (5) when the income of the family was inadequate; (6) births should be spaced according to the mother's health; and (7) birth control should be practiced for at least a year after marriage so that the couple could become adjusted to their married life.

In 1914, with a small group of loyal friends Mrs. Sanger founded the National Birth Control League—thus launching in the United States the crusade for birth control under a name she chose herself. From the beginning the movement met almost insuperable obstacles, but at the same time interest in it spread even to Europe. Although the articles in the *Woman Rebel* kept strictly to the letter of the Comstock law in offering no contraceptive information, most of the issues were banned by the New York Post Office. Finally, in August 1914, the United States Government chose, as Margaret Sanger puts it, "to sever diplomatic relations" with her. She was indicted on nine counts and made liable to a prison term of forty-five years.

The impetus of this indictment paved the way for much of Mrs. Sanger's later actions. Refusing to plead guilty to test a law she felt was wrong—and being refused sufficient time to prepare an adequate defense—she left the United States on the eve of her trial. In the next year—from about October 1914 to September 1915—she visited England, Holland, France, and Spain in an attempt to study her subject from every angle and to prepare an historically sound case. The eventual outcome was a quashing of the indictment in February 1916 before the case came to trial. Interest in it had been greatly aroused, it appeared, and a letter signed by a long list of prominent English liberals had been sent to President Wilson requesting dismissal of the charges against Mrs. Sanger.

The victory was, however, only a moral one for the birth control proponent. The Comstock law had not been changed or clearly defined, and no tangible help had appeared for the women Mrs. Sanger was devoting her life to aid. (The National Birth Control League had been reorganized in her absence, and Mrs. Sanger no longer felt in harmony with it.) In Holland she had visited the birth control clinics —the first of their kind in the world—established by Dr. Aletta Jacobs, and the American woman now decided that the opening of similar clinics in the United States was the best procedure. In this way, she felt, could be given the necessary personal instruction that it was impossible to supply through printed information. As an additional step Mrs. Sanger continued to distribute a pamphlet she had begun to mail for the first time on the eve of her

Taylor-Sargent, N.Y.

MARGARET SANGER

departure for Europe. It was *Family Limitation*, compiled from information brought back from her first visit to France and complete with formulas and drawings. (She often tried to obtain legal judgment on this pamphlet but never succeeded.) During 1916 she also made a three-month lecture tour of the United States and was influential in starting in Pennsylvania the first state birth control league.

The clinic idea was still uppermost in Mrs. Sanger's mind, however, although no one volunteered to help her. Finally in 1916 she and a sister, Mrs. Ethel Byrne, a trained nurse, and another friend opened a clinic in the Brownsville section of Brooklyn, New York. The legislative approach, writes Mrs. Sanger, had "seemed a slow and tortuous method of making clinics legal; we stood a better and quicker chance by securing a favorable judicial interpretation through challenging the law directly." One section of the New York law stated that no one could give contraceptive information to anyone for any reason; another stated that physicians could give prescriptions for the cure or prevention of disease—interpreted as the cure or prevention of venereal diseases and applicable to male patients only.

The effect of the clinic was a favorable decision from the United States Court of Appeals. After nine days' service the office had been closed, ostensibly as a public nuisance, and both sisters had been given thirty-day prison terms for conducting the clinic. But their appeal had resulted in a decision—not given until January 1918—which at last allowed doctors to give contraceptive advice to women for the "cure and prevention of disease," the interpretation of "disease" being the broad one in *Webster's International Dictionary*.

During the prison term Mrs. Sanger reached the conclusion that the tempestuous period of agitation must end and that a new program of education, organization, and legislation must be initiated. "I based my program," she wrote, "on the existence in the country of a forceful sentiment which, if coordinated, could become

SANGER, MARGARET—*Continued*

powerful enough to change laws." But, she continued, "the public had to be educated before it could be organized and before the laws could be changed." One of the first steps in this educational stage was the founding of the *Birth Control Review* in February 1917 while its editor was still in prison.

Even this new approach was not easy. There were still the ever-present problems of raising money, of combatting opposition as well as the apathy of selfish or fair-weather friends. Many of these were afraid to approve a still controversial movement; others were daunted by the prospect of drudgery and unpleasant obstacles; while still others used the movement for personal aggrandizement. Physicians, moreover, were slow to take advantage of the 1918 court decision. Among the strongest opponents Mrs. Sanger found the anti-vice groups, the religious groups headed by the Catholic Church, and the orthodox Socialists who, she declared, opposed the birth control movement on the theory that to dull the edge of poverty was to make labor less dissatisfied with its lot, and thus less revolutionary. Discouraging, also, were the tentative forays Mrs. Sanger made into the legislative field in the early '20's, the bills proposed before New York, New Jersey, and Connecticut state legislatures being defeated.

But even with so many obstacles and such discouragement, the birth control movement and its followers increased. In the fall of 1921 the First National Birth Control Conference was held in New York and was attended by outstanding doctors, scientists, and lay supporters, including a representative of the movement from England. (An incident of this conference was the peremptory closing of the last session by police at the instance of Archbishop Patrick J. Hayes.) That same year the American Birth Control League was started by Mrs. Sanger "to build up public opinion so that women should demand instruction from doctors, to assemble the findings of scientists, to remove hampering Federal statutes, to send out field workers into those states where laws did not prevent clinics, to cooperate with similar bodies in studying population problems, food supplies, world peace." Several years later Dr. James F. Cooper made a successful tour of the United States for Mrs. Sanger in an effort to enlist the aid of the medical profession and to get laymen to apply pressure to the physicians. Mrs. Sanger herself had made an extensive tour, going in 1922 to Japan, Korea, and China, where her talks were instrumental in forwarding the movement.

Interest and support of the movement was obviously spreading, but Mrs. Sanger was beginning to find that the acceptance of the theory of birth control was ahead of the means of practicing it. A formula brought back from Germany by Mrs. Sanger after the First World War had proved too expensive, and the bootlegging of other supplies from abroad could not continue indefinitely. Consequently another method was devised by Dr. Stone and Dr. Cooper and its manufacture assumed by an American company, formed in 1923 for that purpose.

Another important step during these early years was the opening in January 1923 in New York City of Clinical Research, a bureau where a doctor—later Hannah M. Stone—prescribed contraceptives in cases where they were deemed advisable. In this office, case histories were kept which went toward forming a scientific basis for the birth control arguments. Later this office expanded into the Birth Control Clinical Research Bureau. In April 1929 it was raided by the New York City police. The confiscation of confidential records by the police, however, aroused the medical profession, for it was a case of violation of medical ethics. Morris L. Ernst [40] represented the clinic in this case. The charge was finally dismissed, Police Commissioner Grover A. Whalen [44] apologizing. Mrs. Sanger stated later that private sources of information indicated the raid was made at the suggestion of Catholic authorities.

Economists, sociologists, eugenists, biologists, and other scientists were now joining the crusade. The International Birth Control Conference, held in New York City in 1925, was attended by delegates from seventeen countries. Two years later Mrs. Sanger organized a World Population Conference, held in Geneva, at which the relationship between war and overpopulation was studied. In 1930 an International Contraceptive Conference (held in Zurich) was organized by her to correlate and unify the accomplishments of the various countries. In 1934 she organized the American Conference on Birth Control and National Recovery in Washington, D.C., and in 1936, the Conference on Contraceptive Practice and Clinical Research in New York.

By 1927 Mrs. Sanger found that the American Birth Control League was losing its old aggressive spirit and acting as though the movement was a year-in, year-out routine job. She, on the other hand, saw it as "something temporary, something to sweep through, to be done with and finished; it was merely an instrument for accomplishment. I wanted us to avail ourselves," she says, "of every psychological event, to push ahead until hospitals and public health agencies took over birth control as part of their regular program, which would end our function." Finding herself at odds with the League, therefore, she resigned in 1928 as president and continued instead to devote herself to the research clinic and to the legislative phase of the movement.

At first, in her fight to mitigate women's suffering, she had seen the progress of the battle as one of freedom of expression and had consciously violated the Comstock law. Later she realized that it was more imperative to change this law and others in order to establish research clinics, to enlist the support of the medical profession so that women could be helped by trained doctors. Simply repealing the objectionable laws, she saw, would mean permitting "anyone to give and send contraceptive devices and information through the mails, regardless of standards and quality."

In 1926 Mrs. Sanger had already begun to sound out Congressmen on birth control legislation, and in 1931, with friends, she founded the National Committee on Federal Legislation for Birth Control. During the early '30's this group fought to win Congressional support, only to have its measures defeated each year. Finally, a fortuitous event occurred which made further action on the part of the committee unnecessary. A shipment of contraceptives sent from Japan to Dr. Hannah Stone had been intercepted by the United States Customs authorities. The case was taken to court, and in 1936 lawyer Morris Ernst succeeded in winning a decision allowing doctors to import contraceptives, send them through the mails, and use them for the well-being of their patients. The Federal campaign was dissolved, but it had won many supporters.

Today the birth control movement has attained a respected position in the United States. Surveys show that, despite the fears of those who opposed it on moral grounds, the marriage curve has increased greatly over that of prostitution and abortion. Since 1936 it has been legal in forty-six states "for a physician to give pregnancy-spacing advice to his patient when her health requires it." In 1937 the conservative American Medical Association recognized the movement by recommending the teaching of birth control methods in medical schools. Other medical and social groups, as well as official church bodies representing many of the leading denominations in the country, have in one way or another sanctioned birth control under medical supervision. Surveys show that public support, too, is behind the movement. In August 1943 a *Fortune* Magazine poll revealed that 84.9 per cent of the women questioned approved, an opinion shared by 69 per cent of the Catholics questioned. Similar polls taken among both men and women of all religious denominations since 1930 have shown increasing approval. Although there is still widespread misunderstanding and fear among individuals, only the Roman Catholic Church remains, on religious grounds, the principal organized opponent. In 1931, however, the Pope sanctioned the practice of continence as a means of preventing conception, and since then ecclesiastical approbation has been given to the "safe period" or "rhythm" method.

In 1939 the old American Birth Control League merged with the Birth Control Clinical Research Bureau to form the Birth Control Federation of America with Mrs. Sanger as honorary chairman. In 1942 the new federation changed its name to the more positive Planned Parenthood Federation of America (with headquarters in New York City). The present activity of the Federation—an associate member of the National Health Council—is to continue to "inform the public, the medical and other professional groups on the health, sociological, and economic values in planned parenthood." It makes no effort to influence Federal or state legislation, but it seeks "to encourage Federal and state [and local] public health policies favorable to making contraceptive information available in accordance with existing laws." Seven states, as a result, now officially include child spacing as a part of their public health services; hundreds of public health and hospital clinics are cooperating; and the United States Public Health Service has a policy whereby a child-spacing program undertaken by a state's Department of Health will be given "the same consideration as would be given to any other proposal in connection with the health program of the state." Numerous state leagues and local committees are affiliated with the Federation, through which are promoted programs of education and clinic services. The Federation also works toward providing "adequate teaching in medical, nursing, social work, and theological schools" and toward providing technical information for practicing physicians and nurses. An increasing emphasis is placed on the problem of infertility as well as on conception control and on the proper care of the mother and her children.

Mrs. Sanger in 1935 founded the scientific *Journal of Contraception* (now *Human Fertility*) and she is the author of numerous books on birth control and sex education, including, *The Pivot of Civilization* (1922), *Woman and the New Race* (1923), *Happiness in Marriage* (1926), and two autobiographies, *My Fight for Birth Control* (1931) and *Margaret Sanger: an Autobiography* (1938). "Few will read her stirring autobiography," wrote Beulah Amidon of the latter book, "without a fresh sense of the mystery of what we call 'genius,' a new realization of the power of an idea." In 1931 Mrs. Sanger received the American Woman's Association award for "integrity, vision, and valor"; and in 1936 she won the Town Hall award of honor for the "most conspicuous contribution to the enlargement and enrichment of life."

Margaret Sanger now lives in Arizona and in New York. Her second husband, J. Noah H. Slee, to whom she was married in 1922, died in June 1943. (She and William Sanger had been amicably divorced, but she has retained the name by which she was best known.) Her two sons are both physicians. This crusader, "by far the most prominent leader of the movement throughout the world", "is a wistful, fragile little woman, with the courage of a wounded tiger," wrote Lowell Brentano in 1935. "Quiet, unassuming, retiring, she could and did battle like a Dempsey" for her idea of a better world. She has given all "her money, her health, and almost her life" to the movement. Heywood Broun once remarked that Margaret Sanger had no sense of humor. To which the leader of the birth control movement has replied: "I am the protagonist of women who have nothing to laugh at."

References

New Repub 97:152 D 7 '38
Sat R Lit 19:6 N 12 '38 por
World Tomorrow 12:296-6 Jl '29 por
American Women 1939-40
Sanger, M. My Fight for Birth Control 1931; Margaret Sanger: an Autobiography 1938
Who's Who in America 1944-45

SAN MARTIN, RAMON GRAU *See* Grau San Martín, R.

SANTAYANA, GEORGE (sän-tä-yä′nä) Dec. 16, 1863- Spanish-American philosopher; poet; critic; novelist

Address: b. c/o Charles Scribner's Sons, 597 Fifth Ave., New York City; c/o Brown, Shipley and Co., 123 Pall Mall, London

Somewhere in Rome there lives a philosopher in his eighties who has remained unperturbed throughout the bombing and

GEORGE SANTAYANA

upheavals in embattled Italy. It is the cosmopolite, George Santayana, who has achieved a reputation as one of the most eminent philosophers of modern times. Dubbed the "Mona Lisa of philosophy," in his eclectic system of "critical realism" he has reconciled materialism (naturalism) and idealism (otherworldliness or Platonism), classicism and romanticism, Catholicism and paganism. In his detachment he is compared to Emerson; in his comprehensiveness he is likened to Benedetto Croce '44. Not merely a moral philosopher and metaphysician, the versatile Santayana is poet, critic, essayist, novelist, humorist, and prose stylist in addition. There is some ambiguity as to precisely where his chief distinction lies; it has been suggested that his literary influence supersedes the philosophical. While antagonizing, bewildering, or delighting professional philosophers, in the best-selling *The Last Puritan* (1936) and the more recent *Persons and Places* (1944), he has also engaged the interest of the general reader and the student of literature.

The explanation for the elusive character of Santayana's personality and philosophy lies in part in his early Spanish and Catholic background. It was in Madrid that George Santayana was born, December 16, 1863, the son of Don Augustín Ruiz de Santayana and Doña Josefina Borrás (a native of Glasgow though wholly Spanish), and on the following New Year's Day he was christened Jorge Augustín Nicolás de Santayana (Jorge after his mother's first husband). Santayana's mother, an independent and passionless woman, was the daughter of a free-thinking Spanish republican who migrated to Virginia and eventually settled down as a Government official in the Philippines when Doña Josefina was nine. Her first marriage was to a young Boston merchant named Sturgis, to whom she had borne five children by the time of his death. On a visit to Madrid in 1862 she married Augustín Ruiz de Santayana, who had been a friend of the Sturgises in the Philippines. The

elder Santayana, a liberal in Catholic and conservative Spain, was a retired civil servant who in his youth had worked for a professional painter of the school of Goya and had translated the tragedies of Seneca into Spanish verse. Santayana thus found a reverence for art and literature and a stimulus to creative work in his own home.

Santayana lived in Spain the first nine years of his life, during which his parents were separated when his mother took her Sturgis children to America. Although Santayana speaks without the least hint of a Spanish accent, has never written a book in his native tongue, and until the composition of *Persons and Places* had seldom mentioned Spain in his writings, those few years made a profounder spiritual impression upon him than all his nearly forty years of life in America. When the boy was three the family moved from Madrid to the small town of Avila in Castile (and he was "nearly seventy when it ceased to be the center of my deepest legal and affectionate ties"). Although he learned his catechism and prayers as was inevitable in Spain, Santayana is not a devout believer in Catholicism. His attachment to that religion is "a matter of sympathy and traditional allegiance, not of philosophy," he has said. He early agreed with his parents in regarding "all religions as a work of human imagination."

In 1872, aged nine, Santayana was transported to Puritan Boston to rejoin the Sturgis family and to receive a Boston and Harvard education. This was the beginning of the fusion of the Spanish and American influences. Looking back from the vantage point of eighty years, he realizes that "there was a terrible moral disinheritance involved, an emotional and intellectual chill, a pettiness and practicality of outlook and ambition, which I should not have encountered amid the complex passions and intrigues of a Spanish environment." During his first winter in Boston, Santayana was sent to Miss Welchman's Kindergarten, where he "picked up English by ear before knowing how it was written."

After attending the Brimmer public grammar school (1873-74) he entered the historic Boston Latin School, the oldest of American public schools, for eight years of submission to a time-honored regime of mental discipline. It was here that his first literary effort, the witty *Lines on Leaving the Bedford Street Schoolhouse,* saw the light of print. While he was not a literary prodigy, his verses showed generally smooth metre, and in 1881 he became one of the original board of editors of the *Boston Latin Register.*

Almost at the age of nineteen, in 1882 Santayana registered at Harvard College, where he was to do his most distinguished work in philosophy and English composition. He has disparaged Harvard as a place where "much generous intellectual sincerity went with such spiritual penury and moral confusion as to offer nothing but a lottery ticket or a chance at the grabbag to the orphan mind." Though introspective and unlike the typical New England student, he was by no means a recluse nor of unsociable cast. "This 'Harvard indifference' was not due to intense study on my part or to misanthropy," avers Santayana. He played the leading lady in Institute theatricals of 1884; for three years contributed a steady output of drawings (marked by touches of philosophy) to the *Lampoon;* helped to found the *Harvard Monthly* (1885); belonged to the Art Club, the Chess Club, the Everett Athenaeum, Hasty Pudding, the Institute of 1770, the O.K. Society, Phi Beta Kappa, the Philosophical Club (president), and the Shakespeare Club.

Receiving his B.A. and a fellowship in June 1886, for the next two years Santayana enjoyed the comparative academic freedom of the University of Berlin. Paradoxically, it was in Germany, the country whose philosophy has always been most repellent to him, that he was first led to the study of Greek philosophy. In this he found a view of life to which he has given his staunchest allegiance. After his return to Harvard for an additional year of graduate study, in 1889 he was awarded the combined degrees of Master of Arts and Doctor of Philosophy. (Later, in 1912, he won a Litt.D. degree from the University of Wisconsin.)

In the fall of 1889, at the age of twenty-six, Santayana was inducted into the Harvard department of philosophy, joining the brilliant ranks of his former teachers, William James, Josiah Royce, and George H. Palmer. Although he enjoyed teaching, Santayana has admitted that he "always hated to be a professor." In his discussions with his father during his regular summer trips to Spain, after considering the Spanish Army and the diplomatic service, he had come to the conclusion that "the prospect of a quiet academic existence seemed the least of evils." He would have preferred, he adds, the life of a wandering student, like those of the Middle Ages.

A popular lecturer, Santayana soon won repute through his courses. Harvard alumni who attended his classes included such names as T. S. Eliot, Conrad Aiken, Walter Lippmann [40], Felix Frankfurter [41], and Robert Benchley [41], who admitted that Santayana's words baffled him, but that their music enthralled him. Continuing to live in solitude in Stoughton Hall, Santayana, a handsome, exotic young foreigner, was a familiar mystery on the campus. Outside of Harvard Yard he visited his mother and sister regularly at their home in Brookline. His favorite recreation was watching athletic games.

It was not long before Santayana's reputation extended beyond the classroom. His first poems, *Sonnets and Other Verses*, were published in 1894, when he was thirty-one. Receiving scant critical recognition until the turn of the century, these poems, "simply my philosophy in the making," are an expression of Santayana's abjuration of Catholicism in favor of naturalism, the most significant event of his life. A reprint of the volume, with additions, appeared in 1896; his other poetical ventures were *Lucifer: A Theological Tragedy* (1899) and *The Hermit of Carmel and Other Poems* (1901). Critical opinion was divided. While the verses were praised for their restraint and mastery of form, the judgment of the *Independent* (1902) was representative:

"His verse leaves us cold; aspiring to a classical severity, it often succeeds in being only austere." Santayana has himself declared that he is no poet. The ideal poet, he felt, "should live in the continual presence of all experience and respect it; he should at the same time understand nature, the ground of that experience; and he should also have a delicate sense for the ideal echoes of his own passions, and for all the colors of his possible happiness." It is this poet's task "to reconstitute the shattered picture of the world."

Santayana's first philosophical work, *The Sense of Beauty* (1896), was generally well received. Adjudged the finest book on aesthetics written by an American by his colleague Hugo Münsterberg, it is not only the first systematic philosophical treatise on aesthetics from the standpoint of psychological research, but also a philosophy of art. As one critic, George Howgate, has recently pointed out, Santayana felt that the moral justification of art lay not primarily in its representation of truth, but in its creation of beauty, the "objectification of pleasure."

The unorthodox views of *Interpretations of Poetry and Religion*, in which Santayana applied the theory of his first book to literary criticism, jolted the reading public of 1900. Santayana's underlying thesis is, in his own words, that "religion and poetry are identical in essence, and differ merely in the way in which they are attached to practical affairs. Poetry is called religion when it intervenes in life and religion, when it merely supervenes upon life, is seen to be nothing but poetry." While the religious press condemned the philosophy as pagan, the literary world was angered by Santayana's attack on the poetry of Whitman, Browning, Keats, and even Shakespeare on moral grounds. The philosopher charged that much of their work was the poetry of barbarism, that they did not fulfill the poet's proper function of remolding common experience, and that they were unconcerned with a religious ideal. William James wrote of the volume: "What a perfection of rottenness in a philosophy! I don't think I ever knew the anti-realistic view to be propounded with so impudently superior an air. . . . Although I absolutely reject the Platonism of it, I have literally squealed with delight at the imperturbable perfection with which the position is laid down page after page." The fascination of Santayana's style was early recognized by detractors and admirers alike.

By 1910 Santayana was no longer known as a young poet who had toyed with philosophy; with the publication in 1905 and 1906 of the five volumes of *The Life of Reason: or the Phases of Human Progress (Introduction and Reason in Common Sense, Reason in Society, Reason in Religion, Reason in Art, and Reason in Science)* and *Three Philosophical Poets: Lucretius, Dante, and Goethe* in 1910, he was established as a moral philosopher of note. The opposite poles of Santayana's early philosophy, as Howgate explains it, were Platonism, which "tended to justify a moral order based upon values rather than facts," and naturalism, which "with its mechanical explanation of the universe looked

SANTAYANA, GEORGE—*Continued*

upon values as ephemeral and dependent upon the facts which brought them into being." *The Life of Reason*, the phrase Santayana used as "the name for that part of experience which perceives and pursues ideals," is an inquiry into the facts of existence and the values of human life. In this, his most ambitious work, he gathered together all his opinions on morals, art, literature, and metaphysics, from a point of view which Howgate has summarized as "materialistic in regard to origins, pragmatic in regard to effects, and Platonic in regard to ultimate values." Critics noted also a subjective and hedonistic emphasis in his conception of the ultimate aim of life: "Happiness is the only sanction of life; where happiness fails existence remains a mad and lamentable experiment." The understanding was set up as the sole criterion of truth.

Its technical metaphysics precluding appeal for the general reader, for the most part the literary critics valued *The Life of Reason* more highly than did the professional philosophers, who were admittedly puzzled by Santayana's purpose and the distracting beauty of his style. It is significant that many of the philosopher's statements are not fundamentally original. As Lewis Mumford [40] wrote in the *Freeman* (1923): "His philosophy, in fact, is in good part an attempt to consolidate fragments of spiritual experience which more precipitous thinkers had conquered. . . . Is it not a tribute to the catholicity of Mr. Santayana's work to observe that it contained in its matrix the nuggets of other men's thoughts, sometimes indeed before those nuggets were brought to light." Santayana was to write later (in the introduction to *Scepticism and Animal Faith*), "My system is not mine, nor new."

Three Philosophical Poets, a more popular volume than its predecessor, is Santayana's most scholarly and comprehensive contribution to literary criticism. His unexpected defense of the romanticism of Shelley and Dickens is the most generally admired of his critical pieces.

In 1912, after twenty-two years of teaching, Santayana resigned from Harvard when he received a legacy. Turning his back on America, apparently with no intention of ever returning, he was drawn first to Spain. He spent two winters in Seville, his summers in Paris, then settled in Oxford, remaining in England for five years of leisurely meditation. His Harvard departure had been marked by the publication of a controversial volume, *Winds of Doctrine* (1913). Actively engaged in writing as always, at intervals from November 1914 to January 1916 he sent a series of topical articles across the ocean to the *New Republic*. At no other time has he paid so much attention to public affairs.

This English sojourn saw the inspiration for his next three volumes. *Egotism in German Philosophy* (1916) was a timely thrust at the fundamental moral principle in German idealism "which led to wilfulness in conduct and in time found an inevitable outlet in international war," as Howgate clarifies it. In spite of simplification of the facts and a definite personal bias, the book is especially valuable for its attack on moral absolutism everywhere, it was commented. *Character and Opinion in the United States* (1920), another book of generalizations, contains the well known essays on "Materialism and Idealism in American Life" and "The Genteel Tradition in American Philosophy."

Soliloquies in England and Later Soliloquies (1922), the most widely saluted book he had thus far written, established Santayana as an essayist of considerable distinction. It is in the brief essay called "Carnival" that some critics find the core of his whole philosophy of life: Life is perpetually changing, only the spirit is immutable; man must recognize his limitations in the face of nature, accept them courageously, and delight in the humor in the great carnival of life. "Everything in nature is lyrical in its ideal essence, tragic in its fate, and comic in its existence," Santayana concluded. Logan Pearsall Smith's anthology, *Little Essays Drawn from the Works of George Santayana* (1920), had already brought the philosopher's literary powers to the fore. Critics have repeatedly paid lavish tribute to Santayana's epigrammatic style, the abundance of metaphors, the rhythm of his sentences, the humor and ironical understatement. Irwin Edman has written: "Lovers of literature are enchanted by a prose as supple and picturesque, as musical and as just as exists in our time."

After the War Santayana moved to Paris for a short time, then in 1923 installed himself in an obscure hotel room in Rome. A voluntary exile from the world, he made few public appearances. In 1932 he delivered lectures at The Hague and in London as part of the tercentenary celebration of the birth of Locke and Spinoza. Out of his retirement he has formulated what some commentators pronounce to be one of the great philosophical systems of modern times.

Scepticism in Animal Faith (1923); *Dialogues in Limbo* (1925); *Platonism and the Spiritual Life* (1927); and the first two volumes of *The Realms of Being, The Realm of Essence* (1927) and *The Realm of Matter* (1930) marked the return of Santayana to the regions of metaphysics. *Scepticism in Animal Faith* is a general introduction to his system; *Platonism and the Spiritual Life* is a forerunner of the realm of spirit. The conception of "essence" is most difficult for layman and scholar alike to understand; Santayana means by essence not "the mental or the neural act of sensation, but rather the quality sensed," Howgate explains. Reviewers agreed that *The Realms of Being* made the philosopher the foremost champion of "critical realism" (which Sterling North [43] has defined as a composite of pragmatism, hedonism, materialism [or naturalism], and classicism).

During the composition of *The Realms of Being* over a period of fifteen years (the later volumes were *The Realm of Truth* [1938] and *The Realm of Spirit* [1940]), Santayana also wrote two series of essays in *The Genteel Tradition at Bay* (1931) and *Some Turns of Thought in Modern Philosophy* (1933), and the novel *The Last Puritan* (1936). *Obiter Scripta* (1936), also published in this period, is a miscellaneous collection of his papers and addresses on literary subjects during the preceding thirty years, co-edited by Justus Buchler and Benjamin Schwartz.

Six weeks after Santayana's seventy-second birthday, Scribner's issued the philosopher's first and only novel, *The Last Puritan*, a Book-of-the-Month Club selection, which immediately won a place on best-seller lists. The first of his works to achieve a wide popularity since *Soliloquies in England* (1922), *The Last Puritan* was begun in the 'nineties as a college story; the author calls it "a memoir in the form of a novel." Partly a discussion of United States manners and customs, it is an application of his philosophy of materialism to his American experiences. The hero of this epic is Oliver Alden, a straightforward young New Englander, who says of himself: "You don't see that I am struggling with a terrible problem, that I am trying to save my soul." He plays football, chooses his education, makes an attempt at courtship, fights in the War although he doesn't know what it is he is fighting for (ironically, he is killed by a motorcycle after the Armistice)—all from a sense of duty. Puritanism did not mean priggishness or asceticism to Oliver. "It is a popular error," says Santayana, "to suppose that Puritanism has anything to do with purity"; nor was it "mere timidity or fanaticism or calculated hardness: it was a deep and speculative thing: hatred of all shams, scorn of all mummeries, a bitter merciless pleasure in the hard facts."

The Last Puritan is "a book worth attacking, worth defending, worth digesting," Henry Seidel Canby [42] declared in the *Saturday Review of Literature*. Henry Hazlitt was of the opinion that "since Henry James there has been no American novel so rich in thought and analysis"; many reviews, on the other hand, noted that *The Last Puritan* was a novel in name only, "just a front for an argument." Admitting that it has no plot, characters, dialogue, or climax as the modern reader understands it, Canby observed that since the eighteenth century the novel has been the traditional vehicle for the unburdening of theories and philosophical observations. Ellen Glasgow remarked: "I should heartily recommend it to all those who prefer to think while they read, who relish a deep inward irony, who are interested more in the drama of ideas than in the play of conditioned reflexes."

At the beginning of the Second World War, Santayana was still living in Rome, in a nursing home conducted by the Blue Nuns, his Spanish citizenship preventing wartime embarrassment. Following the completion of *The Realms of Being* in 1940, he devoted his energies to the composition of his autobiography, *Persons and Places,* the first volume of which arrived at Scribner's printing plant by devious means through the cooperation of the State Department. Published on January 7, 1944, it was one of a dual selection of the Book-of-the-Month Club.

Accounting for the first thirty years of the author's life, *Persons and Places: The Background of My Life* is a reflective biography that interprets the fusion of the Spanish and American forces that made Santayana the man he is. Irwin Edman has predicted that these memoirs are more likely to become a classic than the more obscurely philosophical *Realms of Being,* and Edmund Wilson in the *New Yorker* compared it to Yeats's *Autobiographies* (1927) and *The Education of Henry Adams* (1927). In a representative comment, the *Times*'s Orville Prescott wrote: "This is a contemplative, intellectualized, discursive, mellow book, one that is sometimes dull and academic. . . . It is permeated with the fastidious, aristocratic, tolerant, and disillusioned wisdom of its author." Emphasizing Santayana's characteristic aloofness, Malcolm Cowley of the *New Republic* attested: "It seems as cold, bare, and drafty as a Venetian palace in winter. . . . It is as if, dwelling among ideas, he greeted the world of men with a limp handclasp and a somewhat chilly eye." Although the book contains no indication that it was written during the present War, several critics feel that it is a most timely one from the standpoint of our Latin-American relations, because it "link[s] the cultures of North and South America and interweave[s] them in the old romantic culture of Spain." (Santayana's only recognition of recent events, it is said, has been to write an additional chapter for the new edition of *Egotism in German Philosophy* [1940], in which he is openly critical of the Nazis. In *Persons and Places* Santayana says: "I love Tory England and honor conservative Spain, but not with any dogmatic or prescriptive passion. . . .")

The purely literary influence of Santayana has been wider perhaps than the philosophical. As early as 1920 Prof. Morris Cohen wrote: "Santayana has failed to draw fire because few people are interested in a frankly speculative and detached philosophy that departs radically from the accepted traditions and makes no appeal to the partisan zeal of either conservatives or reformers." Today critics still deplore the fact that he "sees and feels too many disparate things to make a slogan of any one point of view." Mortimer J. Adler [40] projects the claim that Santayana is not a philosopher at all, his views being "so precisely perverse and so delicately personal that they do not deserve the name of philosophy."

More sympathetic, George Howgate asserts: "In some ways the whole burden of Santayana's philosophy has been to make mankind more genuinely happy by a fuller realization of both its limitations and its possibilities. Certainly the most exacting moralist cannot call that an unworthy aim. And if Santayana's methods are not those of the humanitarian and the reformer, his desire to build happiness from within is in the great humanistic tradition and is all the more precious for its rare emphasis upon beauty and harmony and repose."

Santayana has chosen to live out his bachelorhood (it is rumored that in his Cambridge days there was some mysterious lady to whom he lost his heart) in Rome, chiefly "because Rome of all places on earth brings him closest to the two traditions of the ancient and Christian worlds." He carries on a wide correspondence, sees few visitors, has no friends who live permanently in Rome, does not make an effort to meet other philosophers or men of letters, even sometimes passes days with-

SANTAYANA, GEORGE—*Continued*

out speaking to anyone. His favorite exercise, and the best for a philosopher, he believes, is a solitary walk. "Santayana is nevertheless a jolly good-humored person," Howgate claims. "He is fond of young people and takes great pleasure in showing them the sights of Rome. . . . In conversation his mirth is constantly ruffled into those silvery ripples of laughter which no one who has ever heard them will ever forget. He loves a good story and tells one with gusto himself." He admires Lucretius, Spinoza, and Proust, reads Jacques Maritain[42], is interested in Spengler, Freud, Hindu philosophy.

Margaret Münsterberg, who saw him frequently when he and her father were both teaching at Harvard, has described his appearance: "His face was handsome, delicate, pale against the black hair and small mustache; it seemed the face of a dreamer rather than a scholarly thinker." His hair has thinned and grayed now; still in good health, he is slightly stout, wears sedate dark clothes, and might be mistaken for a prosperous English banker, were it not for his dark complexion, *Time* reports. That the philosopher still has gleaming eyes and an infectious grin is the report of Herbert Matthews, who saw him in June 1944, when Rome had been liberated. "Time had ceased to mean anything to this man, who is a philosopher in the old tradition, living apart from the world," wrote Matthews. Thus, while the correspondent interviewed the philosopher, the philosopher also interviewed the correspondent, questioning him particularly on Russia. On that occasion, too, Santayana said he felt neither approval of nor opposition to communism or fascism—he views conflict as an incident in an eternal scheme. "Doubtless there are good things in both, as well as bad," he said to another reporter. "I think it is right that there should be new movements, suitable to new generations and periods. They shock and disturb those who are attached to the old institutions, but they are not meant for them. It is true, of course, that although they are intended to be 'for the people,' they end up by being for those who are running the State." "I shall never leave here [the convent in Rome where he lives]," he said in 1944. "There has been so much killing and so much suffering in the world's history."

Another visitor to Santayana in 1944, an American soldier, James F. Brewster, wrote back to the United States that although the philosopher "has been living in rather severe conditions (no meat, no fuel all winter), he is apparently in good health, thin, but active, his mind quick and clear." Writing is almost automatic with him, Santayana said. He "has written two books, one his autobiography . . . the other a book on religion. This latter grew out of the fact that for quite a while he had nothing to read but the religious books of the convent. . . . He has now written all the books he ever planned to write, except a book on politics, which he began in 1900 and dropped, half finished, at the outbreak of the First World War, expecting new developments after the War. When the War was over the political situation was too complex for him, so he gave up the project altogether.

. . . His own favorite among his own books is *The Last Puritan*; he said it is the only one of his books he has reread, which he does because of the associations of passages with events in his life. . . . Most of the characters are composites of various people he has known, and he feels that this may make some readers feel that they are unreal, though they are very real to him." Santayana is the last of the descendants of one grandfather, Brewster also wrote in his letter, commenting, "this giving him some satisfaction, as if he had won a race." He has expressed surprise at the popularity of the first volume of his autobiography. (The second volume of the three-volume memoirs, on which he has been working in the convent, is scheduled for publication in the spring of 1945.)

Santayana explains that his detachment from things and persons is "affectionate, and simply what the ancients called philosophy." He insists that "my security in my own happiness is not indifference to that of others. . . . It is because I love life that I wish to keep it sweet . . . and all I wish for others . . . is that they should keep their lives sweet also, not after my fashion, but each man in his own way. . . ."

Answering another criticism, Santayana retorts: "Now I am sometimes blamed for not laboring more earnestly to bring down the good of which I prate into the lives of other men. . . . Alas, their propagandas! How they have filled this world with hatred, darkness, and blood! . . . I wish individuals, and races, and nations to be themselves, and to multiply the forms of perfection and happiness, as nature prompts them. . . . The good, as I conceive it, is happiness, happiness for each man after his own heart, and for each hour according to its inspiration. I should dread to transplant my happiness into other people; it might die in that soil. . . . Ah, I know why my critics murmur and are dissatisfied. I do not endeavor to deceive myself, not to deceive them, not to aid them in deceiving themselves. They will never prevail on me to do that. I am a disciple of Socrates."

References

N Y Times Mag p6+ D 17 '33 por
Time 27:75-9 F 3 '36 por (cover)
Fadiman, C. ed. I Believe 1941
Howgate, G. W. George Santayana 1938
Kunitz, S. J. and Haycraft, H. eds. Twentieth Century Authors 1942
Santayana, G. Persons and Places 1944
Who's Who 1944

SCHACHT, HJALMAR (HORACE GREELEY) (shäkt yäl'mär) Jan. 22, 1877- German financier; former public official

Address: Baden Allee 9, Berlin-Charlottenburg, Germany

Hjalmar Schacht has been labeled as "the Talleyrand of the German Revolution" because, like Talleyrand, he has successfully changed his political colors at least three times, always falling in with the party in power at the most favorable moment. Before the First World War he was associated with the Pan-German League; with the advent of the Weimar Republic he became a founder and one of the chairmen of the Democratic Party; and at least three years before Hitler '42 came to power he was giving the Nazi salute when the brownshirts paraded in Berlin. In Sigrid Schultz's '44 words, "No man has worked harder for the Nazis and for German world supremacy"—but at the same time he has managed to preserve a reputation in some British and American circles as a sort of anti-Nazi Nazi. Schacht himself has stated that all his apparent inconsistency has been the result of having to serve his country within his own sphere under the best available conditions. "I am not a politician. I am an economist, nothing but an economist," he has claimed; but others see him as one of the most ambitious and unscrupulous politicians of his time. Some of his enemies, who credit him with at least as much genius as his friends do, would not be too surprised to see him successfully "brush the swastikas from his lapel" as the Allies march into Germany and, "beaming with cordiality . . . begin the task of beating the Allies out of their victory." Rumors that he had been executed in connection with the Army revolt against Hitler in the summer of 1944 cheered them not at all, for rumors that Schacht was at odds with the Nazis have been carefully planted for years.

The fact that Hjalmar Horace Greeley Schacht lived in the United States as a boy and that he speaks fluent, colloquial English has been a great asset to him in his career. His mother, Constanze, Baroness von Eggers, was of Danish descent. His father, William Schacht, was a German merchant (and a great admirer of Horace Greeley) who emigrated to New York in 1864 but returned to Germany before Hjalmar was born on January 22, 1877 in Tingleff. Soon afterward the family again moved to the United States, and Hjalmar attended school in Brooklyn until he was twelve years old, when his family returned to Germany to remain there permanently. In Hamburg he was a pupil at the Johanneum Gymnasium, where he failed in sixth form arithmetic and was described on the school records an "an industrious boy, in no way outstanding, either at work or at play." When he left the Gymnasium for the University of Kiel, however, his teachers remarked that he "had talent; regards himself as destined to greatness."

Until he began his university studies at Kiel young Schacht had firmly intended to become a Protestant minister. At the University he turned to medicine, but finally enrolled in the Faculty of Philosophy, where he devoted himself to the economic branch. In 1899 he became one of the first men in Germany to acquire a Ph.D. with a thesis in economics—*British Mercantilism During the Sixteenth and Seventeenth Centuries*. For this he had made special studies in Paris, Brussels, and London, gaining great fluency in foreign languages.

Something of a prodigy, in 1901 Schacht became managing secretary of the Society of Commercial Treaties. In 1903 (the year in which he was married to Luise Sowa, the daughter of a police commissioner) the society's chairman transferred him to the statistical department of his bank, the Dresdner Bank, and there Schacht was given the work of compiling the statistics that made up the bank's

HJALMAR SCHACHT

weekly bulletin. He soon added to the statistics a bit of editorial comment, "couched in the same aggressive and provocative terms which characterize his later writings." This led to his appointment as the bank's assistant manager in 1908. He remained in that position until after the outbreak of the First World War, politically associated during this period with the Young Liberals, a party that was actually nationalist in character rather than liberal.

The German occupation of Belgium found Schacht in that country acting as financial administrator; next to the military governor the thirty-seven-year-old banker was the most powerful man in the occupied territory, having a free hand in Belgium's economic administration. With the endorsement of the military government, he issued several millions of counterfeited banknotes to "pay" for supplies bought from the Belgians, but Berlin authorities became suspicious when he never accounted for the bulk of this money. Also accused of having seen to it that his banking connections profited from his knowledge of Government secrets, Schacht finally resigned under fire and returned to Berlin. He spent the rest of the War as managing partner in the Nationalbank, a private bank, originally much less influential than the Dresdner, which under Schacht's guidance became, it is said, one of the most powerful and aggressive banking institutions in Germany. (In 1922 it was merged with the Darmstädter Bank.)

After the Armistice, Schacht climbed on the republican bandwagon when in 1919 he helped to found the Democratic Party, a Left-liberal, non-Socialist group. The disastrous German inflation that followed the War was no disaster for him financially, and it was a definite asset to him politically: in November 1923, when it seemed that no one could keep the mark from falling further, he was appointed Reich Currency Commissioner. With dictatorial powers at his disposal, he stopped the inflation within a week, whereupon Germans hailed him as "the man who saved the mark." The next year,

SCHACHT, HJALMAR—*Continued*

arguing that settlement of the reparations question was necessary if foreign capital was to be attracted into German industry and long-term investments, Schacht put his prestige behind the Dawes plan (envisaging a system of reparations payments to be made chiefly by goods). Germany accepted the plan—and, thanks to the Dawes agreements, the German Reichsbank was re-established as the powerful Central Bank of Germany. Schacht then threatened to resign as Currency Commissioner unless given the presidency of the Reichsbank. He received the appointment despite the unanimous opposition of the Reichsbank's board of directors, who had not forgotten his record in Belgium.

As president of the Reichsbank and as German delegate to the various reparations conferences of the '20's, Schacht played an important role in the Weimar Republic during its period of greatest material prosperity. Bankers everywhere began lending Germany money—money which built German roads and gave the country the finest industrial plants in Europe. "Under Schacht's guidance, Germany doled out four and a half billions in reparations, and got back five and a half billions in loans. On top of this gain, he persuaded foreign capital to invest two billions in German bond issues, industrial enterprises, and real property." But Germany's prosperity was built on a precarious basis. By 1928 foreign holdings amounted to one-quarter of the total national wealth; new loans only sufficed to pay the interest on the vast debt, and the supply of foreign capital had begun to thin. Schacht therefore refused to pay interest on the bonds foreigners had purchased, and began to announce that further reparations payments were beyond Germany's capacity. At the Paris conference of 1928, called to frame a new reparations plan, he not only demanded the return of Germany's colonies but took such a belligerent attitude toward reparations themselves that the conference nearly blew up; and all that summer and fall he directed a barrage of criticism against the Young plan (by which German reparation deliveries would be superseded entirely by money payments). With the stock-market crash of 1929 foreign loans to Germany stopped entirely, and the other powers also began to close their doors to foreign goods. German banks were failing, unemployment spreading. Schacht appeared at the second Hague reparations conference that year to attack the Bank of International Settlements and to threaten non-cooperation by the Reichsbank; and in January 1930 he resigned as president of the Reichsbank because the Young plan had passed the Reichstag.

By this time he was officially a man without a party. (In 1926 he had resigned from the Democratic Party because it had supported a movement for expropriating the property of the German princes, saying that as president of the Reichsbank he would lose the confidence of international finance if he associated himself with any such movement.) But now, from his large estate where he had retired in order to raise pigs, Schacht began giving out statements announcing that the German republican regime was doomed, and arguing that there must either be a united front against communism or complete socialization. Such a united front, it was soon obvious, could only be with the Nazis.

The Nazis received some 6,000,000 votes in the 1930 Reichstag elections, or about 18 per cent of the total. When in 1931 Dorothy Thompson[40] asked Schacht who would run German economics if the Nazis should come to power he replied, "I will!" Later that same year Schacht, who seemed to have maintained some reputation as a liberal abroad, made a lecture tour of the United States on Hitler's behalf; back in Germany, he is said to have persuaded Fritz Thyssen[40] to provide Hitler with $875,000 on the eve of the 1932 Presidential elections. When in 1933 Hitler became Chancellor of Germany, Schacht had helped immeasurably in establishing the new Government. Schacht then took over his old $120,000-a-year post as president of the Reichsbank, and on August 2, 1934, the day the aged President von Hindenburg died, he was also made Minister of Economics.

Generally regarded as the man who rescued the banks and trusts from their bankruptcy of 1932 through huge subsidies of the State, during the next years "Schacht's influence rested upon the backing of the Army and the dominant capitalist monopolies." At the same time his international business acquaintanceship was a tremendous asset to Hitler. It was Schacht who "fought and wheedled" until the Hoover[43] moratorium on reparations payments was extended to private loans, so that by 1934 foreign debt payments were suspended entirely. But he apparently had a genius for reassurance. In March 1933 he told a British economist and newspaper-owner: "Hitler is now doing as he wants, but just wait a month or two and he will have to do what I tell him to do and then we will have safety." The Englishman immediately flew back to London to write that no violent economic experiments need be feared from Hitler's Germany so long as Schacht remained in office. In December 1933 the British protested against Schacht's policies. Schacht promptly made it known through Montagu Norman[40], governor of the Bank of England, "that he was doing his best to keep the Nazis in check and to satisfy them with these comparatively small demands." And in October 1934 he wrote in *Foreign Affairs* that it was "unworthy of the American people to oppose the new *Weltanschauung* which has been built up in Germany today, the more so as this new conception of life rests upon the noblest human sentiments: fidelity to duty, national unity without differences of class, contempt for all privileges of birth, rank, and position, but recognition of all personal achievement."

It was Schacht who brought Germany's foreign trade under absolute government control. Under the slogan "Barter or Ersatz!" he centralized all exporting and developed a system of barter by which Germany was able to obtain war-essential minerals and oil in return for cheap toys and cameras, and to wreck the economies of the countries she intended to invade later. He invented the blocked mark and a whole series of currencies which could be spent only in Germany or for German goods and had no value elsewhere. And while he thus financed German rearmament, London and New York continued to regard him as the spokesman for a group of Nazi "moderates" who were attempting to obtain foreign trade and loans chiefly in order to prevent the Nazi "radicals" from taking advantage of Germany's economic situation to obtain control. Goering '41 (never a friend of Schacht's) described him as "unloved, unwanted—indispensable," and Hitler presented him with the golden party badge in order to make him, *ex post facto*, an "old member" of the Nazi gang.

Then, in October 1936, Goering's Four-Year Plan was inaugurated, and Goering got the role of "economic dictator and buffer between Schacht and the Nazi rank and file." Walter Funk '40, one of Schacht's former disciples, soon succeeded Schacht as Minister of Economics—and Schacht, from his Reichsbank post, began to snipe openly at the self-sufficiency plans of the Nazi extremists. On the other hand he emphasized that "he would never follow any other policy than that of the Führer"; in December 1938 he went to London in a futile attempt to persuade those interested in rescuing the Jews from Germany to pay a "ransom" in the form of increased purchases of German goods; and he remained at the service of the German Government as Reichsminister without portfolio even after Funk succeeded him as president of the Reichsbank in January 1939. Sent on a world tour to investigate Nazi interests, he made a long and mysterious visit to India, and in the summer of 1939 appeared in France and Britain to warn the chancelleries of the imminence of war and to whisper "in strictest confidence" details of Nazi military might. When Sumner Welles '40 visited Germany in March 1940 Schacht lunched with him, and *Time* Magazine pointed out: "If any scheme was abroad for a world bank to redistribute gold along the lines proposed by the State Department's Braintruster Adolf Berle '40, Dr. Schacht was the man to discuss it with."

By May of 1940 it was reported that Schacht had again retired to his estate in East Prussia; entrusted by Hitler with the task of perfecting the Nazi scheme for the economic reconstruction of Europe after the War, he was at work with a staff of secretaries and translators on a book setting forth his views. At the time the project was of some importance, but as the prospect of a post-War Nazi Europe became less and less likely Schacht was apparently entrusted by Hitler with another, less publicized mission: that of contacting British and American industrial-financial groups on the prospects of peace. According to some sources, by 1943 he had a "peace" plan readied for feelers abroad—a plan under which American and British industry and finance would be given joint ownership of German industry with the present owners, while German industrialists and financiers would get a free hand in choosing the political leaders of post-War Germany and the right to maintain an armed police force to keep order. True or not, it was in that year that Schacht moved one of his residences to Zurich, an hour's train ride from Basle, the home of the Bank of International Settlements. Although the fact that Schacht was permitted to travel proved his good relations with the Nazi regime at this time, there were the usual rumors that he was in Hitler's disfavor.

As the defeat of Germany draws nearer, there are many who wonder what has happened to Schacht. There are some who can see him as a prospective post-War leader for Germany. In December 1943 William Shirer '41 reported that a cabinet minister in the Belgian Government-in-Exile had told him: "If Dr. Schacht is in power in Berlin after this War, we can certainly do business with him." Countess Rosie Waldeck, in *Meet Mr. Blank* (1943), has many kind things to say about Schacht in the same role. And in early 1944 Max Immanuel wrote that while Hitler and the High Command would undoubtedly be given short shrift by the Allies, Schacht might be accepted by Britain and the United States as a post-War negotiator. According to Paul Winkler, Schacht "represents a much greater danger for the peace of the world than Hitler." And in late 1944 there were recurring rumors of Schacht's arrest by the Nazis and of his putting forth of peace feelers in behalf of the Nazis. These coincidences, commentators have warned, may be evidences of a plan to make him appear anti-Nazi and therefore more acceptable to the Allies.

In appearance Schacht has been described as "about six feet three inches tall, with Clark Gable ears and a G.I. haircut." His collar is regarded as his trademark—it is of gleaming white celluloid and about four inches high. He is said to be a man of considerable charm and somewhat obtrusive culture. He reads biography, history, political economy; he has written two books, *The Stabilization of the Mark* (1927) and *The End of Reparations* (1931), as well as some poetry, which he has had privately printed for his friends; he designs book covers and silver boxes, and collects paintings. By his first marriage he has a son and married daughter—Jens Hjalmar and Inge. Early in 1940 it was reported that he had divorced his first wife (who died in the spring of that year) and had married a well known German sculptress; but in March 1941 he reportedly was married to the former Mauzika Vogler, aged thirty-three.

References

Collier's 96:23+ D 7 '35
Contemp p107-10 Ag '41
Cur Hist 40:285-90 Je '34
19th Cent 127:464-70 Ap '40
Read Digest 44:59-62 My '44
International Who's Who 1942
Waldeck, R. Meet Mr. Blank 1943
Wer Ist's 1935

SCHEIBERLING, EDWARD N(ICHOLAS (shi'bér-ling) Dec. 2, 1888- 1944-1945 national commander of the American Legion; lawyer

Address: b. 91 State St., Albany, N. Y.; h. 117 Euclid Ave., Albany, N.Y.

The American Legion, in its annual national convention in September 1944, took a strong stand for the unconditional surrender and permanent disarmament of Germany and Japan, active American membership in an international police force to maintain peace, and universal military training after the War. At the final session of the convention Edward N. Scheiber-

EDWARD N. SCHEIBERLING

ling, Albany lawyer and former state office-holder, was chosen as the new national commander, to succeed Warren H. Atherton '43.

A native of Albany, New York, Edward Nicholas Scheiberling was born on December 2, 1888, the son of Martin and Mary (Schneider) Scheiberling. Following his graduation from Albany High School, he attended Union University, earning an LL.B. in 1912. Except for a few years, since that year Scheiberling has been engaged in the practice of law in the city of his birth. Now senior member of the firm of Scheiberling and Schneider, he had first served as legal examiner for New York State's Comptroller's Office. Then in 1916 the young lawyer enlisted in the infantry during the First World War. The following year he was commissioned a 2nd lieutenant in the 312th Infantry of the 78th (Lightning) Division and promoted to 1st lieutenant by December of the same year. He participated in the Meuse-Argonne offensive, and before the Armistice had been advanced to captain.

For several years following the War he was senior auditor in the State Income Tax Bureau. He then served as an Albany city judge from 1924 to 1929, when he entered private practice. Since 1920 Scheiberling had taken an active part in the American Legion. In 1935 Scheiberling became, for a year, the New York State commander of the American Legion; he was vice-president and director of the national convention in New York City in 1937. In the years 1939, 1940, and 1941 Scheiberling was a member of the national legislative committee; in 1943 he became its vice-chairman. As the culmination of his activities in the Legion, Scheiberling in September 1944 was unanimously elected national commander of the Legion's one and a half million members at the annual meeting in Chicago.

The convention at this time adopted a foreign relations resolution calling for a post-War international organization of "free and sovereign nations," with the power to maintain peace and prevent aggression. It demanded that Germany and Japan be permanently disarmed, and

warned that the United States must not be misled by propaganda into approving a "soft peace" and following an isolationist policy. This statement was indicative of the development in American public opinion since the Legion only endorsed international cooperation and Lend-Lease after bitter opposition at Milwaukee in September 1941. "We reaffirm our faith in the foreign policy of our Government," the new resolution asserted. "The consummation of the policies and principles declared at the Moscow, Cairo, and Teheran conferences should command the united support of all Americans." An indication of official reaction to the Legion's pronouncement on foreign policy was given by Senator Tom Connally's '41 praise of its stand, in an unexpected appearance before the convention.

A second resolution, on national defense, called upon Congress to enact legislation immediately that would require every young man in America to undergo a year's military training when the Selective Service Act ceases to operate, and, for a reasonable period after his training, to serve in a component of the National Guard or Naval Reserve, as provided for in the National Defense Act of 1920. It urged that Congress form a committee of educators, military experts, and other civilian experts to recommend a program. James Forrestal '42, Secretary of the Navy, told the convention that the Navy favored legislation for universal military service. Scheiberling pledged that the enactment of such a law would be made the Legion's major legislative objective in the coming year; he declared that the Legion had never taken a wrong position on any vital national defense issue and urged the nation to heed its future counsels on the winning of the peace.

A third resolution adopted by the Legion concerned post-War employment. The members "urge the extension and improvement of unemployment coverage and benefits; oppose its federalization; support experience ratings; continue to study methods of employment stabilization and insist that state funds be maintained to protect the worker adequately." Advocating minimum government control over labor and business, in his inaugural address Scheiberling said that the Legion would "help private industry absorb returning veterans in gainful employment." The Legion also emphasized in its program adequate care and protection for all veterans, war widows, and war orphans.

In Scheiberling's opinion, veterans of the Second World War will "dominate political trends in the nation for years—they will be very powerful for twenty-five years"; the logical result of this situation, he predicted, would be the election of one of these veterans as President of the United States in the not too distant future. (By December 1944 more than 300,000 Second World War veterans had joined the Legion.) He pointed out that he referred to veterans generally and not to Legionnaires in particular, because "the Legion takes no part in political campaigns; an elective officeholder or candidate cannot hold office in the Legion." He therefore opposed suggestions to move Legion headquarters to Washington, D.C., fearing that there it might come under the dominance of a political party. However, Scheiberling believes that the Legion must become more and more active politically so that legislation for the benefit of its members may be enacted. More active campaigning will assure the adoption of its recommendations, he promised in October 1944.

"We will have to take more vigorous action in Washington to put our program into effect. After the War is over and we try to keep the country out of war we will have to go into the districts and tell the people that 'we want this bill' or 'we want this man for Congress.' A majority of people now say that the Legion stand on important issues was right during the last twenty-five years. The Legion program after the last War was not put into effect because we were too quiet about it." Scheiberling also maintained that if the Legion program had been prosecuted more vigorously in the past "we might not have got into this War." He announced that the Legion had already taken steps to "present its case more adequately to the court of public opinion" by the creation of a public relations committee made up of men active in advertising and journalism.

In an address on Armistice Day at the Tomb of the Unknown Soldier, Scheiberling said that veterans should be given a place at the peace conference to assure a lasting peace. Stating that the last peace was lost on the "altar of political expediency and public indifference," he added: "This tragic blunder must not be repeated. Representatives of those who have fought in World War I and World War II should certainly sit at the peace table and exercise an active influence in formulating the terms of peace."

Speaking before the annual convention of the American Federation of Labor in November, Scheiberling was looking toward the post-War world when he warned that "any attempt upon the part of any segment of our people to maintain wartime advantages gained solely because of the absence of millions of men and women in the service will create one of the most tremendous employment problems we have ever faced." Earlier that year he had told state commanders and adjutants of the Legion that a nationwide survey made by the organization had revealed that thousands of widows and orphans of war veterans were "living on the verge of destitution in the midst of . . . war prosperity." He urged passage of legislation in Congress to provide a "bare minimum of subsistence" for them. A measure to provide for this, he pointed out was in the Senate Finance Committee of the Seventy-eighth Congress.

Legionnaire Scheiberling, a heavy-set man well over six feet, has given his time and energies to other organizations as well. From 1935 to 1941 he was chairman of the New York State World War Memorial Authority. In 1939 he assumed the chairmanship of the Community Chest Campaign; in 1941, the Albany USO campaign. He is director of the Albany County American Red Cross and a member of the National Council of the Boy Scouts of America. In 1939 Scheiberling was married to Ethel F. Fitzpatrick; a son, Edward N. Scheiberling, was born in 1941. Scheiberling's favorite recreation is fishing.

Reference

N Y Herald Tribune p20 S 21 '44 por

SCHICK, BELA (shik bā'la) July 16, 1877-
Pediatrician
Address: h. 17 E. 84th St., New York City

With the exception of smallpox, diphtheria is the one disease for which medical research has found the surest means of both prevention and cure. This was by no means a sudden achievement, for diphtheria first became a serious subject for investigation during the last half of the nineteenth century with the development of the science of bacteriology. Friedrich Löffler and Edwin Klebs discovered the diphtheria bacillus in 1883; seven years later Emil von Behring and Shibasaburo Kitazato of Japan demonstrated an effective curative agent in antitoxin; and in 1913 the leading pediatrician Béla Schick, a pioneer in the movement for universal immunization, perfected his test for determining susceptibility. While the steady decline (since about 1870) in diphtheria mortality is generally attributed to the use of deliberate prophylactic measures, it has been suggested that the underlying cause (inasmuch as the decrease in deaths began before public health procedures could have had major effect) is a change in the virulence of the diphtheria germ.

Béla Schick was born in Boglar, Hungary, July 16, 1877, the son of Jacob and Johanna (Pichler) Schick. He began his training at the second Staats Gymnasium at Graz, Austria, from which he was graduated in 1894, and six years later he received his medical degree from the Karl Franz University in the same city. Since that year, 1900, Schick has devoted his energies to his medical practice, to scientific research, and to teaching. From 1902 to 1923 he served as a staff member of the University of Vienna, in the successive capacities of intern, assistant in the pediatrics clinic, lecturer, and finally, beginning in 1918, of professor of pediatrics.

In 1905, in collaboration with Clemens von Pirquet, Schick had recorded in the monograph *Serumkrankheit* the results of a significant study, which "not only gave the first description of serum sickness but also established fundamental principles of allergy." With Theodore Escherich in 1912 he produced another notable monograph, *Scarlet Fever*, and in 1918, *Pirquetsche System der Ernahrung*.

The discovery for which Dr. Schick has won his chief distinction is the test for detecting susceptibility to diphtheria. After a series of investigations, Schick adapted to diphtheria a method which has been used in the diagnosis of other diseases. By injecting into the skin of the arm a very minute quantity of diluted diphtheria toxin, he was able to determine whether or not the subject possessed resistance to the disease. A swelling and reddening at the site of the injection indicates, he discovered, a positive reaction; if an amount of natural antitoxin sufficient to cause immunity is present in the blood no irritation occurs. At intervals after the inoculation of Schick positives, retests are made to check whether the reaction has been rendered negative. When the findings were published in 1913 this easily

BELA SCHICK

performed test created a stir in medical circles, but its practical value was not immediately evident.

Subsequent observations and large-scale experimentation proved the reliability of the test to be of a high order. Through the increasing campaigns conducted by public health and school authorities to overcome the apathy of the public, the utilization of the test to ascertain both the need for and the effect of immunization became widespread in the last two decades. Recently Schick could report that "in certain communities where practically universal immunization of children is carried out, the disease has been almost obliterated." It is preferable, physicians say, for every child to be immunized between the ages of nine months and one year, and Schick testing is advocated for all children entering school, even if previously immunized, in order to ascertain any possible need for further prophylactic treatment. The use of toxin-antitoxin (a mixture of toxin treated with antitoxin) has in general practice been supplanted by that of alum-precipitated toxoid for immunizing children; the other is still used for adults, since they sometimes suffer severe after-effects from the use of toxoid.

In 1923 Dr. Schick left Vienna to become pediatrician-in-chief at Mount Sinai Hospital in New York City. This post he held until his retirement in May 1943, when he was appointed consulting pediatrician at the hospital. In his long years of service as a child specialist Dr. Schick has also been director of the pediatrics division at Sea View Hospital in Staten Island, New York, consulting pediatrician at the Willard Parker Hospital, the Beth Israel Hospital, and the New York Infirmary for Women and Children, in addition to carrying out his teaching duties as clinical professor of diseases of children at Columbia University's College of Physicians and Surgeons since 1936.

Dr. Schick has also contributed to American and foreign periodicals important studies of infantile tuberculosis, of metabolism in infectious diseases, of the nutrition of newborn children, and of allergy. For more popular reading, with his colleague, William Rosenson, Schick wrote *Child Care Today* (1932), in which he urges parents to realize that "the foundation for sound physical and mental health should be laid in infancy and childhood."

Dr. Schick is a member of the New York Academy of Medicine, the American Pediatric Society, the American Academy of Pediatrics (of which he was a founder), the Society for Experimental Biology and Medicine, the American Association of Immunologists, the Deutsche Gesellschaft für Kinderheilkünde, and the Gesellschaft der Arzte in Vienna. He holds honorary membership in the Harvey Society, the Society of Pediatric Research, the Association for the Study of Allergy, and the Bronx Pediatric Society. In 1938, on the occasion of the twenty-fifth anniversary of the publication of his work on immunity in diphtheria, Dr. Schick was awarded the Medal of the New York Academy of Medicine—one of many honors he has won in his lifetime.

This indefatigable pediatrician finds his relaxation in music and travel. Occasionally taking a busman's holiday, he has toured the United States, Europe, and Mexico, at the same time attending international pediatric meetings in Stockholm, London, Rome, and Mexico City. Schick was married in 1925 to Catharine C. Fries.

References

American Men of Science 1938
Who's Who in America 1944-45
Who's Who in American Jewry 1938-39

SCHULLER, MARY CRAIG MCGEACHY *See* McGeachy, M. A. C.

SCHULTHESS, EDMUND (shəlt'hes et'-mənt) 1868—Apr. 22, 1944 Swiss statesman and lawyer; four times President of the Swiss Confederation; during First World War distinguished himself as food administrator; at all times a strong advocate of Swiss neutrality.

Obituary

N Y Times p41 Ap 23 '44

SCHULTZ, SIGRID (LILLIAN) (shŭlts) Journalist; author

Address: b. c/o Reynal and Hitchcock, 386 Fourth Ave., New York City; h. 32 Elm St., Westport, Conn.

"No other American correspondent in Berlin knew so much of what was going on behind the scenes in Germany as did Sigrid Schultz." So writes the noted correspondent William L. Shirer[41] in his review of Miss Schultz's 1944 book, *Germany Will Try It Again.* Sigrid Schultz, though American by birth, has spent the greater part of her life in Germany. She was a witness of Germany's reaction to defeat in the First World War. She watched the futile struggle to establish a republican form of government in the '20's, the rise of the Nazi Party, and the steady and deliberate preparation of all elements within Germany for the Second World War. Out of her wide experience Miss Schultz has written a book which, reviewers agree, is an important contribution to the great debate on the topic "What to do about Germany."

Sigrid Lillian Schultz was born in Chicago, the daughter of Herman and Hedwig (Jaskewitz) Schultz. Her parents are of Scandinavian descent, and her father was a well known portrait painter. His career took him to many of the capitals of Europe, where he painted royalty and important government figures. After some early schooling in the United States—in Ravenswood, Chicago— Sigrid Schultz went abroad with her parents in 1911 and continued her education at the Lycée Racine in Paris. In 1914 she received a Diplome de Certificat d'Études Supérieures from the Sorbonne in Paris. In the same year Miss Schultz went to Germany with her parents. There she witnessed the Kaiser's declaration of the First World War, a scene which she was later to compare with Hitler's announcement, on September 1, 1939, that Nazi troops had marched into Poland. The American citizenship of the Schultz family made them neutrals during the first three years of the struggle. They were, nevertheless, forced to suffer many wartime hardships, including a food shortage during which cooked crow was considered something of a delicacy.

Miss Schultz continued her studies at Berlin University, where she specialized in history and international law. When the United States entered the War in 1917 she and her family became enemy aliens and were obliged to report regularly to the German police. Her first job during these lean years was as secretary to the Mayor of Bagdad, who had come to Berlin to study law but did not know the German language. Miss Schultz acted as his interpreter and attended classes for him at the University, reporting to him in French on the lectures.

With the end of the War and the collapse of the German Empire, Miss Schultz began her career as foreign correspondent. Her first position was as assistant and secretary to Richard Henry Little of the Chicago *Tribune*. She had had no technical training for a career in journalism, but her knowledge of languages (she is fluent in German, French, Polish, and Dutch), combined with her training in international law and history, had given her the background for becoming "an authority on military strategy and armaments." For the rest, "she simply carried out the terse instructions contained in letter and cables from her paper's cable editor." Her first independent assignment was reporting the wedding of the ex-Kaiser in Doorn.

During the days of the establishment of the German Republic Miss Schultz risked her life more than once to cover an assignment. She has "dodged bullets in the Tiergarten, and in the '20's, at the time of the Kapp *Putsch*, she stepped over corpses in the lobby of the Hotel Adlon." In spite of all this there was considerable prejudice against women journalists, and Harry W. Flannery[43] writes in his *Assignment to Berlin* (1942): "Sigrid told me she had to plunge into the midst of a Communist riot before the *Tribune* thought her capable at all." Miss Schultz's newspaper reports now fill twelve huge volumes.

SIGRID SCHULTZ

It was not long, however, before the Chicago *Tribune* thought her capable enough to make her chief, in 1925, of their Berlin bureau. In this capacity she was official Berlin hostess for the Foreign Press Association. She met and entertained important international figures, knew "everybody from the Hohenzollerns and Nazis to the Communists," and with the rise of the Nazi Party one of her frequent guests was Field Marshal Hermann Goering[41], who tried to win the sympathy and favor of foreign correspondents by explaining that "the only way to treat a woman was to beat her and that the greatest thrill comes to a man when he kills another."

As early as 1931 Miss Schultz had her first interview with Hitler[42]. Other interviews with him followed, and during one of them the Führer told her that she could never understand the Nazi movement because "You think with your head and not with your heart." Miss Schultz's open dislike of Nazi methods and Nazi ideology made her position in Germany most precarious. The Propaganda Ministry attempted to have her expelled from Germany but failed. They wanted to get her out of Germany, William Shirer explains, "because of her independence and knowledge of things behind the scenes." Another attempt to oust her was made by Mrs. Elizabeth Dilling, who in 1944 was on trial in the United States for sedition. Mrs. Dilling requested the Munich Propaganda Office to deport Miss Schultz and another correspondent, Wallace Deuel[42], for writing articles which were not favorable to the Nazi cause.

Miss Schultz dates the beginning of the Second World War from November 11, 1918. She writes in *Germany Will Try It Again*: "The Allies wanted peace in 1918. The Ger-

SCHULTZ, SIGRID—*Continued*

man masses wanted peace in 1918. But the German General Staff merely wanted a breathing spell in which to rearm." Hitler's declaration of war in 1939 was merely the climax to these years of preparation.

In 1938, during the Munich Conference, Miss Schultz began broadcasting from Berlin. She continued these weekly broadcasts for the Mutual Broadcasting System until she left Germany. In August 1940, during a British air raid on the German capital, she was wounded in the leg by shrapnel. She made her way to the studio that night in spite of the raid and went through with her broadcast, only to discover afterwards that owing to technical difficulties her talk had never reached the United States.

Miss Schultz returned to the United States in February 1941. After recovering from a long siege of war typhus she began a series of lecture tours. She had no intention at first of writing a book on her experiences in Germany, but she resolved to do so when she realized that many Americans "do not have the faintest conception of what Nazism means and how wholeheartedly Germany stood behind Hitler when he was winning.... Wherever I went I was impressed by the number of well-meaning people who had been won to the German thesis that this War could have been avoided if 'we had been kinder to the Germans' after the last War. . . . Anyone who witnessed their joy in loot and their indifference to crimes perpetrated in their name cannot remain silent."

Germany Will Try It Again, published early in 1944, was Miss Schultz's "contribution to peace." She has written it as a warning against false sentimentalism towards Germany and the German people. Nazism, she argues, is not a disease restricted to the Germans. It has certain specific propaganda appeals to the democracies—appeals which Miss Schultz calls "Trojan horses." She lists and explains these—the "We want a leader" idea (one which frowns on free debate and criticism), the idea that "Nazism protects private enterprise" (offering special privileges to capitalist groups), the threat of "the menace of Soviet Russia," the stirring up of "racial friction," the calculating use of Christian teachings to win forgiveness for German faults, the fomenting of "distrust among the Allies," and, finally, the idea that "only German industries can rebuild Europe."

One of the most valuable sections of Miss Schultz's book is her analysis of the German woman. Under the heading "Women Nazis Are the Worst," Miss Schultz points out that they are more hysterical in their fervor for the Nazi ideology than their husbands and more dangerous, since they will continue to educate their children in the Nazi tradition. She warns that even now the German people are preparing "to win the peace even if the War were lost." She feels, moreover, that the German people themselves are responsible for their Government. "The friendly German . . . is the German of yesterday. It is the German of today with whom we have to deal, the arrogant, ruthless, intelligent schemer who either suavely hides his intentions or openly boasts of his brutality."

Although she has little faith in the possibility of a democratic, peace-loving Germany evolving from the War, Miss Schultz nevertheless believes that Germany must be allowed to work out her own destiny. The United Nations, she argues, must form an iron ring around Germany and must remain armed to the teeth as insurance against further aggression. But within that country the various conflicting groups must "fight it out among themselves." The duty of the United Nations is "to keep on guard—unremittingly—eternally. At the first sign of weakness on our part, they'll try it again."

Miss Schultz's book has received generally favorable notices. Harry Hansen [42] describes *Germany Will Try It Again* as "a crisp, violent denunciation of modern Germany." While criticizing it for bad organization and writing, Orville Prescott, writing in the New York *Times*, praised its effective propaganda, saying, "Until the peace has been won and Germany disarmed, in fact as well as in theory, it would be well if we had books like this once a month." And M. W. Fodor, reviewing the book in the *Saturday Review of Literature*, wrote: "This is the most revealing, very serious, and yet most readable book on post-1918 Germany. It is full of information and valuable material by means of which we can learn all of the machinations the Germans used after the last War—'tricks' which, according to Miss Schultz, they intend to employ once more after the hue and cry of the present battle has receded."

In the spring of 1944 Miss Schultz was busy lecturing and preparing for a new assignment on one of the battle fronts. Described as "buoyant and cheerful," she is slightly over five feet tall, weighs 120 pounds, and has blond hair ("very blond turning white," she writes). Spending what little spare time she has at her country home in Connecticut, she finds relaxation in experimenting with new dishes, growing herbs, and planning menus and entertainment for her friends. She is unmarried.

Although not pessimistic in her attitude toward the post-War world, Sigrid Schultz takes a sober and serious view of the future. She writes: "If the audiences keep asking for prescriptions on just how to handle our German enemy, I may get tempted to write some kind of blueprint of what we should do —though to date I have held that it is more important for us to know the facts of recent history, the technique of our enemy, and thus be able to act swiftly and with a definite unity of purpose when he lays down his arms. The War is not over and we won't know what our enemies are really up to until they have surrendered. In working out blueprints we shall have to take into consideration not only the nature and ambitions of our enemies, but we must also remember our own psychological make-up. We are very kindhearted, and that may prove dangerous for us."

References

C S Mon p10 Jl 28 '42 por
Ind Woman 20:8 Ja '41

American Women 1939-40
Schultz, S. Germany Will Try It Again
1944
Shirer, W. Berlin Diary 1941
Who's Who in America 1944-45

SCHULZ, LEO (shülts) 1865—Aug. 12, 1944
Noted cellist; soloist and first cellist with New
York Philharmonic Society for thirty-eight
years, retired in 1929; professor of music at
Yale; composer of many works for the violin-
cello; played with many great men, among
them Brahms, Wagner, Liszt, Tschaikowsky,
Dvorak, Grieg, Richard Strauss '44, and Walter
Damrosch '44.

Obituary

N Y Times p34 Ag 20 '44 por

SCOTT, C(YRIL) KAY- *See* Wellman,
F. C.

SEARS, WILLIAM JOSEPH, SR. Dec.
4, 1874—Mar. 30, 1944 Former United States
Democratic Representative in Congress from
Florida; served from 1915 to 1929 and from
1933 to 1937.

Obituary

N Y Times p21 Mr 31 '44 por

SEITZ, GEORGE B. Jan. 3, 1888—July 8,
1944 Veteran of the motion-picture industry;
directed for most of the major Hollywood
companies; made most of the *Andy Hardy*
series for MGM; wrote scenarios, produced,
acted in, and directed early serials, including
The Perils of Pauline, in which Pearl White
was starred.

Obituary

N Y Times p35 Jl 9 '44

SELL, HILDEGARDE LORETTA *See*
Hildegarde

SELWYN, EDGAR (sel'win) Oct. 20,
1875—Feb. 13, 1944 Producer, actor, and
director of stage and screen; joined Metro-
Goldwyn-Mayer in 1929 as a writer and director; director of Helen Hayes's '42 first motion picture.

Obituary

N Y Times p17 F 14 '44

SELZNICK, MYRON (selz'nik) Oct. 5,
1898—Mar. 23, 1944 Hollywood's leading actors' agent; represented more than 300 actors
and directors; a founder of Selznick International Pictures; responsible for the discovery of Vivien Leigh, who played Scarlett
O'Hara in *Gone With the Wind.*

Obituary

N Y Times p19 Mr 24 '44 por

SERGIO, LISA (sãr'-jē-o lē'zä) Mar. 17,
1905- Radio commentator

Address: b. c/o Radio Station WQXR, 730
Fifth Ave., New York City; h. Low Bridge,
160 Brookside Dr., Larchmont, N.Y.

"The radio station with a soul," WQXR,
extolled for its quality performances by lovers
of music and literature, added another feather
to its cap in 1939 by the discovery of one of
the most successful women commentators on
foreign affairs in America today. She is internationally famous Lisa Sergio, once known as
the "Golden Voice of Rome." Having begun
her career in Fascist Italy as Europe's first
woman radio commentator, she brings to her
news appraisals an unusual background of
personal acquaintance with Fascist aims,
methods, and party men.

Lisa Sergio was the first person ever to
refer to the "Rome-Berlin axis" in the English language. This occurred in November
1936 when she followed Mussolini '42 on the
air in an almost simultaneous English translation of one of his blustering speeches.
"There exists now between Berlin and Rome,"
she reported to the world, "an *axis* around
which the destinies of the other nations will
soon revolve, and around which they may
cooperate if they wish."

One of Fascism's most uncompromising
critics in the United States, she was born Elisa
Sergio in Florence, Italy, March 17, 1905.
Baron Agostino Sergio, her father, an Italian
nobleman who died in 1915, came of a Naples
family that had long supported the cause of
Italian independence; despite some Scotch
blood he traced his descent to the Roman
house of the Sergii, in whose honor an arch
had been erected at Pola on the Adriatic some
2,000 years ago. The other half of her ancestry is thoroughly American; there is a
treasured gold cup in the family presented by
Lafayette on his second visit to Virginia in
recognition of the hospitality accorded him
by one of her ancestors. In spite of this
heritage, her mother, the former Margaret
Fitzgerald, socially prominent in Baltimore,
Maryland, was eventually to become a supporter of Mussolini's regime.

While Miss Sergio as a child had so little
formal education that she does not possess
even the equivalent of a grade school certificate, through private tutoring, traveling about
Europe, and being simply wide awake and
receptive, she acquired a more comprehensive
liberal arts education than many holders of
B.A. degrees today can boast. At an early
age she had mastered English, French, and
Italian and found her way around in Spanish
and German. From the first her chief interest lay in antiquities and art. At fifteen
she was unaccountably intrigued by Bible
studies and the theatre; she translated a well
known French play into Italian and then had
the thrill of seeing it produced. She also took
courses at the University of Florence that
were of a cultural nature.

Rebelling against the traditional idleness of
the conservative young women of her social
milieu, in 1922 she managed to become the
associate editor of the *Italian Mail.* At the
time she was only seventeen, had had no

LISA SERGIO

journalistic experience, and had no specific qualification for her position other than her excellent knowledge of English. To this literary weekly published in Florence, the English-American colony in Italy, including Walter Savage Landor, D. H. Lawrence, Norman Douglas, and Wyckham Steed, contributed without charge. At first it avoided politics and was unhampered by governmental restrictions, but later Mussolini sought to use it as a propaganda sheet. Before her resignation in 1928 Miss Sergio had advanced to the editorship.

The ambitious Miss Sergio turned next to the field of archaeology, which had always fascinated her. She found a job as general secretary for the Association of Mediterranean Studies. This was an organization formed in 1929 to include the directors of the Foreign Academies in Rome and the most eminent foreign scholars resident in Italy in order to cooperate in the excavation of antiquities— under the approval and patronage of the Department of Fine Arts of the Italian Government. She also worked as assistant to Eugénie Sellers Strong, the famed woman archaeologist who was the first to recognize Roman portraiture as a field of study. At Ostia in 1930 the superintendent of excavations named several tombs after Miss Sergio. In 1934 she wrote an English guide to the city of Pompeii, still a standard handbook and issued also in French and in Italian by the Department of Fine Arts.

As Fascist regulations in archaeology increased, so did Lisa Sergio's contacts with the Foreign Office. Finding Florence too "stuffy," in 1930 she had moved to Rome. In 1933 when Italy inaugurated Europe's first short-wave broadcasts in foreign languages Miss Sergio was offered the job of news commentator. (Mussolini had heard of her reputation among social and intellectual leaders on the Continent for a quick mind and wide knowledge of languages.) At the urging of a long-

standing family friend, Count Marconi, who could not foresee that the telegraph he had invented simply for a means of communication was to become such a potent propaganda weapon, she accepted without misgivings. In addition, since American funds for the archaeological excavations had been cut off during the depression and the Association was petering out, it seemed a sensible thing to do, Miss Sergio now recalls.

Miss Sergio was soon given the assignment of news broadcaster in both French and English on Rome's short-wave radio station under the direction of Count Ciano '40, then head of the Press Bureau. The Italian statesman who was executed by a German firing squad in early 1944 ("He was a capable young man with not too lofty ideals," she declares) could be properly grateful to her when he rose to power. He had made use of her suggestion that he create a Ministry of Propaganda in order to avoid, among other things, the issuance of conflicting official bulletins from the Foreign Office and the Home Office; Miss Sergio was well acquainted with the straits of the foreign correspondents who often checked their stories through her.

So successful was the "Golden Voice of Rome" that she eventually helped to set up the short-wave radio programs in twenty-one different languages. In addition, she began teaching Italian to her listeners in England, supplementing her radio lessons with a weekly column printed in *World-Radio*, one of the publications of the British Broadcasting Corporation. In 1937 she authored an Italian-English grammar that was published in London.

It was not long, however, before Miss Sergio had realized that there was "something rotten in the state of Denmark." More and more she recognized the malignancy of the Fascist regime and the chicanery of its methods. In her teens she had seen the Italian youth bewitched by Mussolini: their social consciousness aroused by a war in which they were too young to fight, they were eager to spend their unused enthusiasm on a popular movement. Then she had believed that Fascism was a "good thing." One of her own dancing partners, Alessandro Pavolini, was later to become secretary general of the Fascist Party.

Miss Sergio, then, became increasingly critical of the Government dispatches she was handed to broadcast. Her conception of news integrity strained, she began to tamper with certain of the official bulletins she thought questionable or entirely fabricated—omitting an item or changing its import. Meanwhile her anti-Fascist friendships among newsmen and archaeologists and in other intellectual circles began to be noted by the authorities; expostulatory telephone conversations and other indiscreet actions added to the accumulation of evidence against her desirability as a citizen of Fascist Italy. She disregarded indulgent warnings, and her defiant conduct during the Ethiopian War hastened the inevitable climax.

It was on March 10, 1937 that after three and a half years of service the Boss of the Palazzo Venezia signed the order for her dismissal—due to "ill-health." For several weeks the ex-commentator remained in Rome, practically unmolested despite the continuance of her association with marked anti-Fascists. Then Marconi advised her to go to America before the opportunity went by, using his influence to procure her a passport. A warrant for her arrest was issued a few days after her sailing.

On her arrival in New York in July 1937 the Italian Consulate was particularly courteous toward her, eased the official red tape in the filing of her first citizenship papers. Then when she refused to aid its Fascist propaganda machine it campaigned violently against her. Nevertheless, she continued her tireless fight against Fascism both in the United States and abroad. (In Italy the Government threatened to seize her property, which she thereupon deeded to her mother.)

Her English and French short-wave broadcasts, as well as several appearances on WJZ's *The Magic Key,* had made Miss Sergio well known to American radio men. Within a fortnight of her arrival in this country David Sarnoff '40, president of the Radio Corporation of America, hired her to serve as guest commentator for the National Broadcasting Company. A week later she was on the air, acting as narrator for a special broadcast to commemorate the sudden death of Marconi. Then she announced such programs as the Metropolitan Opera broadcasts, the Berkshire Festival of Music, and the Music Guild. She also assisted NBC in setting up its short-wave radio division for Italian and French listeners. From December 1937 to August 1938 she appeared regularly for WJZ on *Let's Talk It Over,* a program in which Miss Sergio interviewed distinguished guest stars. From April to June 1938 she wrote and announced WEAF's *Tales of Great Rivers,* a series featuring the great music that expressed the spirit of such rivers as the Danube, the Volga, and the Mississippi. For a short time afterward she worked in the radio division of the Young and Rubicam '43 Advertising Agency.

It was in March 1939 that WQXR devotees heard the initial broadcast of *The Column of the Air,* which Lisa Sergio now conducts seven times weekly—Monday through Friday at 7:00 p.m. and Monday and Friday at 10:00 a.m. Practically alone in the company of full-time men analysts (there are Estelle Sternberger's *Washington Front* and Dorothy Thompson's '40 regular Sunday evening broadcast), Miss Sergio commands a wide radio audience which listens to her "with respect and admiration." Her fan mail includes praise from both housewives and Wall Street brokers. In 1943 she received the New Jersey Women's Press Club's Radio Award.

Miss Sergio's use of the right of free speech is always based upon sound reasoning and careful research. Her statements are well authenticated by her extensive sources of information. In April 1943, for example, *In Fact* reported that (with the exception of Bryce Oliver on WEVD) Miss Sergio was the sole commentator who disclosed the complete story of the protest that the Protestant Textbook Commission to Eliminate Anti-Semitic Statements in American Textbooks had sent to President Roosevelt '42 on the printing for the armed forces of a version of the Bible containing anti-labor and anti-Semitic subheads and footnotes. (The *World-Telegram* was the only New York newspaper which printed the account.)

Miss Sergio has devoted time on her program to a discussion of the action of the State Department in keeping Italian exiles from returning to their native land; and in March 1944 she was among the more than seventy prominent Americans of foreign birth who signed the Declaration of American Unity sponsored by the American Commission for Protection of the Foreign Born. She contrasts the attitude of the United States and Great Britain with Russia's "realistic view" in its constructive policy toward both Italy and France: "The democratization of the Badoglio '40 Cabinet in April 1944 was a victory for the quick-action and no-dilly-dally method of our ally in Moscow who demanded that the dissension between the Badoglio regime and the anti-Fascist groups end and an agreement be reached." In the case of de Gaulle '40 and the French Committee of National Liberation, the United States and Great Britain continued to withhold their recognition long after Moscow had already made its own decision. "Towards which of the three major powers do we suppose the French are going to gravitate in the future?" she asks. Miss Sergio deplores also the lack of cooperative action among the Allies; "if there were a council, as there should be," many mistakes would be avoided.

On the question of Italy's future, Miss Sergio maintains that with time the Government can attain a strong democratic basis and can even become a pillar of democracy in the Mediterranean. There are few die-hard monarchists left in the country, and the Italian people recognize that the prestige of the throne cannot be restored "merely by letting tall, dark-eyed, and weak-minded Umberto '43 push the little stubborn King off the velvet seat." There is in the new Italian Cabinet that was formed on April 21, 1944 (which contains representatives of all six parties in the opposition junta—Actionists, Communists, Labor Democrats, Liberals, Socialists, and Christian Democrats) an uncle of Miss Sergio's, Giulo Rodinó, a Christian Democrat who is serving as Minister of State without portfolio. The avowed purpose of this new Cabinet is to expel the Germans from Italy, to win the War, and to eliminate all traces of the Black Shirt regime.

Of all the social problems created by the War, Miss Sergio believes the rise in juvenile delinquency to be the most dangerous, the failure of communities to provide sufficient education and welfare services for their children in wartime creating potential Fascists as well as delinquents. "Neglected children, youths who are bored and have no place to go, unknowingly offer fertile soil for enemy propaganda to grow upon," she declares, remembering how Italian youth responded to Mussolini's beckoning at the close of the First World War.

In addition to her daily commentaries, Miss Sergio is a frequent speaker at high school assemblies and colleges, Masonic lodges, men's and women's clubs, forums, and other organizations, as well as Government and war relief groups in the war effort. Occasionally

SERGIO, LISA—*Continued*
she writes magazine and newspaper articles,
too, and at the request of several publishers
she has made tentative plans to write a
book. "I would like to have more time to
write," she says, although through the radio
and her lectures she is able to reach a very
wide audience. Her radio audience became even
larger when, in October 1944, she began a new
program *One Woman's Opinion,* which is heard
on Monday mornings.

With the area of liberated territory becoming
greater with each new advance of the Allied
armies, Miss Sergio has given more time to the
discussion of the political situations in those
countries. At the second Conference of Women
held in New York in December 1944, at which
the topic discussed was "No World War III—
A Challenge," she contended that there had
never been a people's peace in history, that the
political disorders in Europe today represented
the determination of the people "not to let the
making of the peace slip out of their hands."

This Italian-born commentator, who became
an American citizen in September 1944, is
slender, dark-haired, and vivacious, and has a
contralto voice whose exceptional beauty the
Italians were quick to recognize. Since her late
teens she has been known for her chic, her
practical habit of wearing only black, red, and
white, and her incessant smoking. In her home
at Larchmont, New York (which she owns
with her adopted mother, Ann Batchelder, associate editor of the *Ladies' Home Journal*),
she is a good hand at gardening, dressmaking,
painting, carpentry, and electric wiring. She
finds relaxation also in solving countless crossword puzzles and in re-reading the Bible,
Shakespeare, d'Annunzio, and Dante. She is of
the Roman Catholic faith.

Rarely has Miss Sergio felt that being a
woman has been a handicap in her field. The
War has increased the responsibilities of the
business of news analysis, "but I do not believe that, as a woman, I recognize them less
clearly nor accept them less honestly than my
male colleagues. Women, as a whole, make a
smaller fuss about accepting responsibilities,
of whatever nature, than men. That is probably why they get less credit for fulfilling them
and more criticism if they fail. That is why
they have to work harder to make a place
for themselves and to hold it."

More specifically, she points out the necessary qualifications of the news evaluator: "One
must have mental energy and some physical
stamina, too; a mind free from prejudice and
stocked with as many facts and realities as
it will hold. Whether it is a man or a woman
collecting material, analyzing it, writing it up,
making deductions, and presenting the picture
to the unseen audience, the most important
single factor is sincerity. On the strength of
that the audience, forgetting the sex, will con-
done the inaccuracies and errors when they
occur. Mental honesty is essential because the
microphone has a strange and impolite way of
sending over the air waves not only what the
commentators say, but also what they think
in the silent recesses of their minds."

References

N Y Herald Tribune VI p8 S 12 '43 por
N Y Post p5 S 23 '41 por; p12 N 22 '43
N Y World-Telegram p6 Ap 2 '41 por
Vogue p86 Ap 15 '43

SERGIUS, METROPOLITAN (sẽr'ji-us)
1866 (?)—May 15, 1944 Patriarch of Moscow and all Russia; acting head of the Russian Orthodox Church for more than a decade
when it was without a formal leader; elected
Patriarch in September 1943 when the Church
was officially restored in Russia.

Obituary

N Y Times p21 My 16 '44 por

SEWELL, JAMES LUTHER *See* Sewell,
L.

SEWELL, LUKE   Jan. 15, 1901- Baseball
club manager

Address: b. c/o St. Louis American League
Baseball Club, St. Louis, Mo.

"Baseball's poor relations, the underdog
Brownies, once more got there firstest with the
leastest." Thus said sports writers when the
St. Louis baseball club, under the management
of Luke Sewell, won the American League
pennant for 1944. With the St. Louis Cardinals, Sewell's team then proceeded to give
St. Louis its first home-town series, the sixth
intracity World Series in history. (Chicago
had had one, New York five.)

The Brown's "miraculous" manager, James
Luther Sewell (dubbed "Luke" by one of his
first teachers) had to choose between two family occupations, medicine and baseball. Born
to Susan (Hannon) Sewell in Titus, Alabama,
on January 15, 1901, he is the son of one
doctor, J. W. Sewell, and the brother of
another. Two brothers, Joseph and Thomas,
went into baseball, as did Luke's third cousin,
pitcher Truett (Rip) Sewell. Luke himself,
planning to become a doctor, took a science
course at the University of Alabama, but he
also caught for the University's team. After
his graduation in 1921, the twenty-year-old
Alabaman joined the Columbus American Association minor league team as a catcher. After
playing in seventeen games, during which he
batted .327, fielded .932, and made 52 putouts,
Sewell was put in the Cleveland Indians
(American League) club, where his brother
Joie Sewell was already an infielder. He was
to remain with Cleveland for twelve years.

In 41 games during 1922 Sewell made 108
putouts, batted .264 and fielded .963. The following year, for some reason, his averages
sank by 64 points and 130 points, respectively,
and in 10 games he made 5 putouts. In 1924,
however, the catcher played in 63 games, making 171 putouts, and in 1925 in 74, making 222;
his batting average rose to .291 and then went
down again to .232, while his fielding average
went from .959 to .971. Such figures do not,
of course, give a full picture of Sewell's value
to his team. As a catcher, he was the only
player on the field with a view of the entire
area, and thus the only one in a position to
grasp the whole strategic picture of the game

as it unfolded. For this reason a catcher's quickness and judgment are of extra importance to his team.

For four years, beginning in 1926, Sewell played some 125 games a season, making 437, 402, 430, and 433 putouts; his batting average, .238 in 1926, rose to .293 and .270, then fell to .236, while his fielding average went from .983 to .963, .972, and then .966. During this period Luke Sewell was married, in 1926, to Edna Ridge of Akron, Ohio, where the Sewells and their two daughters now have their home.

In 1930, playing in only 76 games, Sewell made 283 putouts and raised his batting score 21 points to .257 and his fielding to .974. The following year he made 384 putouts in 108 games, batted .275, fielded .980; in 1932 it was 306 putouts from 87 games, .253 and .978. During the usual pre-season dickering in January 1933, the depression-struck Cleveland Club traded Sewell to the Washington Senators (American League) for another catcher, Roy H. Spencer. The Senators kept their new acquisition busy during that pennant-winning season, putting him in 141 games, in which he made 516 putouts, batted .264 and fielded .990. Sewell caught five World Series games against the National League champions that year, during which he made 23 putouts, fielding 1.000 (no errors) and came to bat seventeen times for a .176 average. (Sewell pocketed a loser's share of the receipts, $3,019.86.) In 1934 an occupational hazard put Sewell out of the line-up for six weeks; he was "beaned"—struck on the left temple—by a pitch from "Bump" Hadley of the St. Louis Browns. He was, however, fortunate enough to escape with nothing worse than "a queer lump" on his forehead and bruised nerves which pain him in damp weather. Ironically enough, in January of the next year the Southern-born catcher was traded to the Browns in exchange for the same Irving D. Hadley. The St. Louis Club, in turn, sold his contract to the Chicago White Sox (American League) for an unannounced price.

If either the Indians' or Browns' powers-that-were acted on the assumption that Luke Sewell's value as a player was reduced by his "beaning," they were mistaken. In the course of 118 games during the 1935 season he made 399 putouts and only 6 errors, raising his batting average 8 points to .285, while his fielding went down 6 points to .988. The White Sox kept Sewell three more seasons, during which he batted .251, .269, and .213, and fielded .984, .985, and again .985. In 1938, his last season with Chicago, he played in only half as many games as usual, and that December the Brooklyn Dodgers (National League) claimed his services for the price of a waiver from the various American League clubs. (The teams of a league have first choice on any player dropped by any of their member clubs.) The following April, however, the Dodgers gave Sewell an unconditional release. A free agent again, the ballplayer immediately signed a contract with his old team, the Cleveland Indians, and became one of their coaches in June, after the season was under way. In addition to coaching he was called on to play in 16 games during the 1939 season, batting .150 and fielding .966.

LUKE SEWELL

On June 5, 1941, Don Barnes, owner of the St. Louis Browns, brought Luke Sewell in to replace Fred Haney in the unenviable position of manager—unenviable because the Browns were the only team in either league who had never won a championship. They had not even come out among the first four since 1929, when they were fourth. So many baseball men had tried unsuccessfully to salvage the Browns that the club was known as "the graveyard of managers." When Luke Sewell took over the job a month after the season had opened, the Browns were in seventh place in the eight-club league. He "pulled them into a tie for sixth." By methods still viewed as miraculous, Sewell pulled the club together into a team which ranked third in 1942. "It cannot be said that the Browns have vulgarly bought their way up in the world," commented *Newsweek*, "for the management has no money to spend on such foolish luxuries as good baseball players. Instead, the credit for the incredible devolves on one man, Luke Sewell, a lead-pipe cinch for the title of Manager of 1942. . . . Smart trading and a good break on the rookie crop have stood him in good stead. Pitcher Steve Sundra from the [Washington] Senators and catcher Frankie Hayes from [Connie Mack's '44 Philadelphia] Athletics have bolstered his crew. Shortstop Vernon Stephens, currently hitting around .300, has proved one of the freshman finds of the season. Outfielder Chet Laabs went on an extra-base hitting spree in midseason which did much to buck the Brownies up, and more lately outfielder Walter Judnich has been batting the ball around with abandon (and a bat). Nevertheless, Sewell ignores the legitimate amazement of the rest of the league at his team's performance and thinks things could be a lot better than they are. 'Give us a power hitter like Ted Williams or Joe DiMaggio '41,' he recently sighed to a group of bewildered baseball scribes, 'and I think we

SEWELL, LUKE—*Continued*

could have won the league [championship] pennant this year.'"

With the Browns' manager and both coaches former catchers—and not so former either, as Sewell himself returned to his old trade when necessary—the club was, Sewell declared, "too full of strategy." But for the first time in years it had something else: "We just don't figure on losing." At the end of the 1943 season the Browns were fifth in the American League, and Luke Sewell was signed for another two years as manager.

"No man ever did so much with so little," was the typical reaction to Sewell's 1944 team. His "odd assortment of talent" consisted mainly of "guys nobody ever heard of and nobody wanted." One of his pitchers, Jack Kramer, an ex-Seabee, wasn't even listed in the *Sporting News' Baseball Register*, "an omission which to major leaguers is like having your name left out of the phone book"; another, Sig Jakucki, also a war worker, had been pitching semi-professionally the previous year. Gene Moore, an infielder, had "seen more towns than Rand McNally" as a member of seventeen clubs and nine leagues before landing with the Browns, while one Al Hollingsworth had worked for fourteen clubs and "thought he was about ready for semi-pro ball" when he was tapped for Sewell's team. Perhaps the most striking example was Floyd Baker, whose batting average for the season was an almost unprecedentedly low .177. (After the Series the Browns bought Pete Gray, a one-armed outfielder from Memphis.) While the world wondered the Browns took the bit in their collective teeth in April 1944 and won their first nine games in a row. They "fell out for a few weeks in May, bounded back on June 1, and opened a margin that by mid-August made them look like a shoo-in. In September, however, they went into a tailspin that sent them skidding out of the lead and, when first the [New York] Yankees and then the even more formidable-looking [Detroit] Tigers passed them, it looked as though St. Louis' World Series mirage had vanished. Then, even after the Browns recovered their poise, their case still looked pretty hopeless as they entered a final four-game series with the still-in-the-running Yankees, while the Tigers, one game in front, had only to feast upon the tail-enders from Washington."

This was a dramatic moment, for the Browns were known to have been "feuding" with the Washington Senators all season. In Lowell Mellett's words, "The Browns, it seemed, not out of anger but with cool purpose, made it their custom to deride their Washington visitors [largely Cubans and Venezuelans replacing players then in the armed forces] on the score of their nationality and color." A certain amount of psychological warfare against the other team's morale is permissible, but "there are limits beyond which most players do not go. . . . The resentment on the part of the Washington team was such that the final game in St. Louis was marked by a fist fight on the field." This situation caused a complete break between Sewell and the Washington manager, Ossie Bluege, his onetime roommate. At the end of the American League pennant race, the Browns' victory depended on the team they had abused so unfairly on their own home grounds, for if the Detroit Tigers won their last two games against Washington the pennant—and the World Series money—would go to them rather than to St. Louis. No one would have blamed the last-place team for cheating their tormentors of a pennant by losing both games to the powerful Detroit team, especially as their own position could not be worsened. But they dug in and fought two winning games, which ended the season and gave Sewell's club the 1944 American League championship.

It may perhaps have been this experience which caused the post-season World Series against the National League St. Louis Cardinals to be conspicuously well-mannered. Or it may have been because Sewell and the Cardinals' manager, Billy Southworth [44], not only share the same St. Louis playing field, Sportsman's Park, but the same St. Louis apartment. (This worked out well because both teams were on the road alternately.) During the World Series, Sewell was already installed in their common apartment, so Southworth took up residence in a near-by hotel. The two managers rode home from the field together after the games, however. Whatever the reason, the greatest feature of the six-game Series was a sportsmanship which attracted comment, from Grantland Rice's [41] "Here was an example . . . that should be carried through from now on," to Tom O'Reilly's "Everybody seems too darned friendly. . . . Are these teams playing for money, or just to carry on a nice tradition?" Pepper Martin, a veteran Cardinal, complained, "We jest ain't havin' no fun!"

The Series was remarkable in other ways, most importantly perhaps, for the non-Series caliber of Sewell's personnel, and for the performance he drew from them. None of his players had ever been in a World Series before; pitcher Denny Galehouse, for one, a war plant worker, had never even seen one of the baseball classics. Granted that the 1944 Browns were a wartime freak, the Cardinals were widely regarded as the only team of pre-War quality. "On paper there was just no comparison between the two teams." The Series was conceded to the Cardinals by all the experts, but "those never-say-die Brownies made them work hard to attain it. The championship belongs to the Redbirds," to quote Arthur Daley, "but Luke Sewell deserves a brisk pat on the back for even getting his odd assortment of talent into the classic. No man ever did so much with so little."

The 1944 Series was notable also for its lack of one-sided fan partisanship; the St. Louisans, trained by three years of success to look with pride on the Cardinals, were also highly sympathetic to the Browns' role of a Cinderella, or an underdog fighting his way back up. More remarkably, no base runner even attempted a steal. No hit-and-run play was tried. The two sets of pitchers struck out ninety-two men, an all-time record.

Besides the Series glory, Sewell and his men received a share of the players' pool (the total Series receipts minus expenses and administration). As the losing team, the Browns divided twenty-eight per cent of the $309,590.91 player pool, each receiving about $2,840—the smallest loser's cut since 1931, when the Brooklyn Dodgers each got $2,419.60. And as a business organization the club paid "a handsome little dividend," for the first time in twenty-two years. The total attendance for 1944 at the Browns' home games was 510,000, while they drew 712,000 on the road; the disparity between these figures gave credence to rumors that the club president, Don Barnes, was planning to move the team's franchise to some more hospitable city, Brooklyn and Pittsburgh being most often mentioned. The Associated Press's year-end poll of sports editors voted the Browns first place as the "comeback" of the year, as the surprise of the year (and almost as the "flop" of the year). When the vote was taken Luke Sewell was already overseas with one of the five units of baseball men and sports writers playing the USO Camp Shows circuit; his unit's tour covered 35,000 miles in the China-Burma-India theatre of war.

From the first, Luke Sewell told reporters, "It's the men, not me." He has, he says, just one rule on his club: "Don't kid me or lie to me. I can only work with the truth." In spite of his years in Akron, the ex-catcher's speech reminds hearers of his Alabama birth. Just under five feet ten, dark (black hair and brown eyes), and good-looking, he has added five pounds to his playing weight of 175. He is fond of all sports, particularly golf and hunting; he likes to read, too. The Sewells' pretty daughter Suzanne (her younger sister's name is Lois) plans to carry on the family medical tradition, which her father thinks "a great idea. It's my only security for old age. If I'm sick, Suzy will be right there with the pills."

References

N Y World-Telegram p17 Ag 10 '44
Newsweek 22:74-5 Ag 2 '43 por
Baseball Register 1943

SEYMOUR, HARRIET AYER (se'môr) 1876(?)—July 30, 1944 A leading American advocate of the general use of music as a cure for illness; founded the Seymour School of Musical Re-education; seven years chairman of the hospital music committee of the New York State Charities Aid Association; founder and president of the National Foundation of Musical Therapy.

Obituary

N Y Times p13 Jl 31 '44

SHANG CHEN (shong chun) 1889- Chinese Army officer; head of military mission to the United States

Address: b. c/o Chinese Embassy, Washington, D.C.

Heading the second Chinese military mission to the United States in 1944 is General Shang Chen (sometimes written Shang Cheng), who has spent the past thirty-five years fighting to free China—first from the Manchus, then from the war lords, and now from the Japanese.

Born in Paoting, China, in 1889, Shang Chen grew up in Hopei, the province in northeastern China which is bounded by the Great Wall and has Peiping (Peking) as its capital. Orphaned at an early age, Shang was reared and educated by his grandmother, the customary head of a Chinese family. Many of his ancestors had been killed in opposing the Manchu invasion three centuries earlier, and their stories, particularly that of one Shang known as "the Heavenly Official" (Shang Tien Kuan), inspired the boy with a desire to avenge them and liberate his country. To prepare for this revolution, Shang Chen entered the Peiyang Military Academy in Tientsin during the Ching Dynasty. Graduated in 1909, he went to Japan to join Dr. Sun Yat-sen's expatriate revolutionary party, the Chung Kuo Tung Meng Hui. Among the veteran revolutionaries whose acquaintance he made there was Sung Chiao-jen—Charles Jones Soong (father of Mme. Sun '44, Mme. Chiang Kai-shek '40, Mme. H. H. Kung, and T. V. Soong '41, the Chinese Foreign Minister.)

Returning to China, Shang went, on Dr. Sun's instructions, to southern Manchuria, where he joined the Army and was placed in command of the 20th Division of the Fengtien forces of Shengking (then Liaoning) Province, later becoming a staff officer. While a military-school teacher and a junior officer he "devoted himself to the spreading of revolutionary ideas" and "engaged in secret revolutionary activities . . . and liaison work with different parties." Later he joined in an unsuccessful plot to revolt during autumn maneuvers at Luan-chow; after its failure Shang assumed another name and returned to Manchuria, where he again joined the Army. "In spite of many hardships and hazards," to quote the General's official biography, "he was not the least disheartened, and this contributed much towards laying down the foundation of the Chinese Revolution." In the fall of 1911 the twenty-two-year-old Shang, with Lan Tien-wei, was inspired by the Wuhan revolutionary troops to organize the Manchurian People's Army, of which Shang was commander in chief, while Lan was elected Governor of Manchuria.

Soon after the success of the Revolution and the establishment of the Chinese Republic, Dr. Sun resigned from the presidency of the provisional government. His successor, Yuan Shih-kai, an avowed monarchist who had been the Dowager Empress' viceroy, appointed Shang commander of a mixed brigade and later adviser to the Ministry of War. When Yuan, looking askance at the size of Shang's People's Army, ordered him to reduce his forces, the General left Chefoo in Shantung Province for the neighboring province of Shensi, taking his army with him. In 1913 an unsuccessful rebellion by Dr. Sun against the Yuan Government led to suppression and proscription of the Kuomintang. Shang was arrested on suspicion, but soon released.

In 1915, as commander of the Shensi Provincial Army's 1st Regiment, Shang was at the same time in command of the bandit-suppression forces in northern Shensi, which borders on Hopei. The following year he led his forces some 300 miles from Shensi to Shansi Province, where he became commander of the 4th Mixed Regiment, rising through command of the 1st Mixed Brigade and then the 1st Division to be field commander of the Shansi Army and defense commissioner of southern Shansi. When President Yuan's at-

GEN. SHANG CHEN

tempt to restore the Imperium in 1917 brought on another revolution, General Shang had the honor of leading his troops into Peiping as the first provincial army to reach the capital.

Appointed Tutung (military commissioner) of the Suiyuan Special District, Inner Mongolia, in 1926, Shang was named Governor of Suiyan Province the following year. At this time, when the young Chinese Republic embarked on the Northern Expedition to suppress the unruly war lords and bring the northern provinces into the republic, the Shansi forces were incorporated into Chiang Kai-shek's '40 Nationalist Revolutionary Army. Shang, placed in command of the 3rd Group Army's left wing, fought against the Fengtien forces and was soon promoted to field commander of the entire 3rd Group Army. Fighting their way eastward, General Shang's forces recaptured Peiping and Tientsin, and in 1928 the General entered his native Paoting in triumph.

The National Government then appointed Shang Governor of his native province (chairman of the Hopei Provincial Government) and concurrently acting garrison commander for Peiping and Tientsin. In 1929, when the Civil War ended, he became Governor of Shansi Province and also took on the duties of commander of the 32nd Army, member of the Peiping Branch Military Affairs Commission, and reserve member of the Central Supervisory Committee. "In these capacities," it is said, "he introduced drastic reforms in provincial administration" and endeared himself to the people by "advocating the elimination of corrupt practices and the removal of heavy taxes and unwholesome measures against the people. . . . He championed leniency and simplicity in government administration and helped to restore prosperity by reviving the energy of the people and by readjusting finances."

At the age of forty, Governor General Shang set out to learn English with United States Ambassador Nelson T. Johnson '40 as his teacher. Today, it is said, he feels at home wherever English is spoken. He got a chance

to practice this language at polo and boxing matches with English and Americans, having organized the first Chinese teams and won for himself the nickname of "General Polo."

In August 1931, when "bandit" uprisings created disturbances along the Peiping-Hankow Railway, Shang was ordered to lead his gendarmerie to Manchuria to quell the revolt and restore the communication system between northern and southern China. (The word "bandit" is used impartially for brigands and Communists, against whom Chiang's forces were waging an avowed war of annihilation.) Stationed after this in Shun-teh in southern Hopei, the General paid particular attention to the physical training of his troops and endeavored to improve their living conditions and habits. It was in September of 1931 that "the Mukden incident" opened Japan's undeclared war of aggression against China. Shang Chen fought, it is said, in "practically all of China's major battles in the War of Resistance, and when the Japanese were at the east end of the Great Wall in 1933 General Shang led the Chinese troops that stood off the foe."

The following year, when Generalissimo Chiang Kai-shek established the Lu-shan Officers' Training Center for the higher Army officers, he chose Shang Chen as assistant superintendent, reappointing him for three consecutive terms. After this Shang returned to the north, where he soon became acting chairman of the National Military Council's Peiping Branch. In June 1935, when the Japanese were conspiring to seize Peiping and Tientsin, the Nationalist Government appointed Shang Governor of Hopei Province, in which both cities are located, Mayor of Tientsin, and garrison commander of an area only one hundred miles across the Gulf of Pohai from the Japanese-held Port Arthur. He stood firm in all dealings with the Japanese, but was too late to stop the allegedly Nippon-sponsored movement of the Five Northern Provinces for autonomy and therefore led the members of his provincial government in tendering their resignations in a body in December 1935.

Four days later the General was appointed Governor of Honan Province, just south of Hopei in northeastern China. Stationed at Kaifeng, he devoted himself solely to preparing for the inevitable war with Japan. On the night of July 7, 1937 "the Marco Polo Bridge incident" opened the intensified Sino-Japanese War. General Shang led his forces northward to Shih-chia-chuang and met the Japanese in combat at different times in Hopei, Honan, Shansi, Hupeh, Hunan, and Kiangsi—all along the line of the Peiping-Hankow Railway. "And he was one of the leaders who brought victory out of Taierhchwang in 1938. That was the feat that convinced everybody that Japan had something to think about." In this battle the well equipped Nipponese force—including some thirty-five tanks—which claimed on April 5 to have captured Taierhchwang, was routed on April 8. More than 30,000 were killed, many prisoners taken, much booty seized, and the remainder pursued and besieged in Yihsien by the poorly equipped Chinese. (One month later the Chinese Government severed diplomatic relations with Japan.) Not long after, General Shang's command blasted the Yellow River dikes, unleashing great floods to halt the intensified Japanese advance on the Lung-hai Railway.

In May 1940 General Shang was transferred from his command, the 6th War Area, to the directorship of the National Military Council and of its Foreign Affairs Bureau. In this capacity Shang led a Chinese military mission to Malaya; and in September 1941 he was appointed head of a liaison staff to work with the United States military mission to China. His "extraordinary fidelity and essential service" in cooperation with American forces in China was recognized in July 1943, on the sixth anniversary of the War of Resistance: General Stilwell conferred on him the Legion of Merit (awarded to outstanding officers and enlisted men of the United States or of friendly nations) in the degree of Commander.

In December 1943 Chiang Kai-shek chose General Shang to accompany him as senior Chinese military officer at the Cairo conference of American, British, and Chinese leaders. At this time he became acquainted with many of the most important figures in the Allied commands, which acquaintance is useful to him as a liaison officer. Shang's work attracted the favorable attention of the British, and in March 1944 King George VI '42 conferred on him and four other Chinese generals the Order of the Bath. At the same time it was announced that the General would head a Chinese military mission to the United States —the only extra-ambassadorial representation of China since the first military mission, led by Lieutenant General S. F. Hsiung '42, left Washington "in a huff" a year before after many months of patient pleading. Observers expected General Shang and his six aides to take a much more active and important part in the work of the Combined Chiefs of Staff, pointing out that, unlike his predecessor, he was familiar with the language and knew the men with whom he would have to deal. It was considered as a good sign, too, that the United States Army sent a welcoming party of half-a-dozen officers, including a few major generals, to meet him.

On July 7, 1944, the seventh anniversary of China's war against Japanese aggression, General Shang spoke before an audience of three thousand at New York's City Hall Plaza. China's armies, he declared, had thus far engaged the enemy in 29,000 battles and inflicted 2,700,000 casualties. The year that lay ahead would be the hardest of all for China, he said, even though the morale of its armies and people was high. In an address the day before (July 6), Shang had stated it was important for the United States to send heavy arms to China in order to ward off Japan's attempt to set up munitions plants in China's interior, a move that would lengthen the War.

The bald, bespectacled, mustached General Shang is said to be one of Generalissimo Chiang's oldest and most trusted advisers. "China's number one sport fan," he is particularly fond of horseback riding and hunting. He speaks English rapidly but with a heavy accent. The courtesy name by which Shang Chen's friends call him is Chi-yu. Literally translated, that means "lifting the canopy of heaven."

References

N Y Herald Tribune II p3 My 28 '44 por

N Y Post p4 My 23 '44 por

N Y Sun p22 My 24 '44

China Handbook 1937-43

Who's Who in China 1936

SHAPIRO, KARL (JAY) Nov. 10, 1913- Poet

Address: b. c/o Evalyn Katz, 245 E. 55th St., New York City

Outstanding among young American poets now in service, Karl Shapiro, with the United States Army Medical Corps, has published three books of poems since he entered the Army in 1941, and has been the recipient of several major poetry awards. His work has been highly acclaimed by many critics; Malcolm Cowley has called him "perhaps the most interesting of our younger poets."

Born on November 10, 1913 in Baltimore, Maryland, Karl Jay Shapiro is the son of Joseph and Sarah (Omansky) Shapiro. At the age of nineteen he attended the University of Virginia for one year (1932-33), and a small collection of his poems appeared shortly after. Then following various positions—as clerk, salesman, and librarian, he again returned to his studies. He entered Johns Hopkins University in 1936, remaining there until 1939, and the following year he took a course in library training at the Enoch Pratt Free Library in Baltimore. He had begun writing while at the University of Virginia, and since 1934 his poems have appeared in *Poetry* Magazine, the *Nation*, the *New Yorker*, the *New Republic*, *Harper's*, and other magazines, as well as in various anthologies of contemporary verse.

Shapiro's work first attracted attention in 1941 when a group of his poems appeared under the title of *Noun* in *Five Young American Poets* (published by New Directions). In his foreword to these poems Shapiro wrote: "The reader will see that I write about myself, my house, my street, and my city, and not about America, the word that is the chief enemy of modern poetry." In her review of the poems Louise Bogan said: "I venture to predict that his work will become a sort of touchstone for his generation."

In March 1941 Shapiro was inducted into the Army, and a year later was on the Indian Ocean, bound for New Guinea. His first full-length book of poems, *Person, Place and Thing,* edited by his agent and fiancée, Evalyn Katz, appeared in 1942. The poems, displaying considerable variety in form and subject, consisted of both serious and satiric observations of persons and places in his own experience. As Malcolm Cowley wrote in his review of the book: "The poems tell much of his background—one on the University of Virginia, one on Johns Hopkins, 'the Oxford of all sickness.' He seems to be one of those young men who are not rich, not athletic, not socially proficient or popular with their classmates, and who therefore take refuge in that other world where they have a chance to excel, the world of their minds. Their one offensive weapon and their only armor is to be intelli-

KARL SHAPIRO

gent. By using their wits they can punish the Philistines—as Shapiro punished the University of Virginia; and by using their wits they can devise a literary style that is not easily open to attack, since it is self-deprecatory and written with a smile."

Most reviewers found *Person, Place and Thing* a highly original, brilliant volume. Delmore Schwartz in the *Nation* called it "a book which everyone interested in modern poetry ought to read." Writing in the *New Republic*, Selden Rodman emphasized the importance and significance of the actual war poems in the book. "They are few in number," he wrote, "and perhaps slight in intention. But they make me feel doubly confident that Shapiro is a true spokesman of our generation." Rice Estes found his short lyrics and ballads "uneven in quality, some being packed with intensity and highly polished in style, while a few suffer from confusion and harshness of tone." In the New York *Herald Tribune Books*, Ruth Lechlitner wrote: "He is expert with images that shock and sear, that send a chill down the spine or leave a brown and bitter taste on the tongue." The poems, however, "are more sharply impressive on first reading than on subsequent rereading and study. . . . His social criticism for the most part takes the form of contrasts between privilege and poverty. When Shapiro is not being viciously clever or satirically brilliant, when his observation is quiet, cool, exact, he gains an indisputable validity."

As the recipient of two of *Poetry's* annual awards—the Jeanette Sewell Davis Prize of 1941 and the Levinson Prize of 1942—and with his appearance in several anthologies, Shapiro's work became generally well known to readers of poetry. He published another volume, *The Place of Love*, in Australia in 1942.

In April 1944 Karl Shapiro was one of the three men in active war service to receive a Guggenheim award of $2,500 for creative work —one of the first grants from a $200,000 fellowship fund set aside by the Guggenheim

Foundation for men and women serving the nation in the Second World War, being distinct from the regular fellowship awards designed to advance research and creative work. In 1944 Shapiro was also the recipient of a special award of $1,000 from the American Academy of Arts and Letters.

V-Letter and Other Poems, Shapiro's third collection, appeared in the United States in August 1944. The entire book, with the exception of one poem, was written in the southwest Pacific area where the author had been on active duty. Many of the poems are about the War, or about the new lands and people the author had come to know. In his introduction to this book, however, Shapiro wrote: "I have tried to be on guard against becoming a 'war poet.' . . . We know very well that the most resounding slogans ring dead after a few years, and that it is not for poetry to keep pace with public speeches and the strategy of events. We learn that war is an affection of the human spirit, without any particular reference to 'values.' In the totality of striving and suffering we come to see the great configuration abstractedly, with oneself at the center reduced in size but not in meaning, like a V-letter."

As his other work had been, *V-Letter* was received with considerable interest by poetry readers and reviewers. In a discussion of the two sorts of war poets—"those who speak with a public voice and those who speak with a private one"—F. Cudworth Flint wrote of the book in the New York *Times Book Review*: "It is often supposed that individuality must be achieved by looking into one's own heart. Mr. Shapiro has begun more promisingly by noticing the outsides of things. He has the knack of catching up into his mind many kinds of phenomena. Crisply he puts down his notations side by side. Yet what results is no clutter but material growing into form—form that is the shape of an idea." For an example the reviewer quotes from Shapiro's poem on troops in a troop train:

> *We hang as from a cornucopia*
> *In total friendliness, with faces bunched*
> *To spray the streets with catcalls and*
> *   with leers.*
> *A bottle smashes on the moving ties*
> *And eyes fixed on a lady smiling pink*
> *Stretch like a rubber band.*

Other poems, drawn direct from the soldier-poet's personal observation (particularly in his job with the Medical Corps) are among his most recently published work. Close observation and sympathetic identification mark the following characteristic stanzas from "The Leg," a poem on a soldier who has suffered amputation:

> *One day beside some flowers near his*
> *   nose*
> *He will be thinking, When will I look*
> *   at it?*
> *And pain, still in the middle distance,*
> *   will reply,*
> *At what? and he will know it's gone,*
> *O where! and begin to tremble and cry.*
> *He will begin to cry as a child cries*
> *Whose puppy is mangled under a*
> *   screaming wheel.*

Later, as if deliberately, his fingers
Begin to explore the stump. He learns
*   a shape*
That is comfortable and tucked in like
*   a sock.*
This has a sense of humor, this can
*   despise*
The finest surgical limb, the dignity of
*   limping,*
The nonsense of wheel chairs. Now he
*   smiles to the wall:*
The amputation becomes an acquisition.

As Flint observes further, "In an age more
noted for the fecund originality of its comments than of its tunes, Mr. Shapiro has built
his poetry on comments. And so his single
voice becomes as well a lasting inflection in
the total voice of his time."

References

N Y Times p17 Ap 10 '44; p17 Jl 19 '44
Poetry 61:620-2 F '43; 63:299-305 Mr
   '44
Time 43:37 My 8 '44

SHAW, (GEORGE) BERNARD (bẽr'-
nẽrd) July 26, 1856-   Irish playwright;
critic; essayist; lecturer

Address: b. 4 Whitehall Court, London; h.
Ayot St., Lawrence, Hertfordshire, England

   "Around the names of great men there ac-
cretes a crust of legend and fable. Most have
to wait until they are dead; Shaw has achieved
a legendary fame while still alive."   The world-
renowned Irish playwright has "outlived his
age," but "as a figure, a personality, a hydra-
headed genius, he is more fascinating than the
finest of his works."   Almost all Shavian
critics agree with his latest biographer, Hesketh Pearson, that his greatness lies "not in
his beliefs, but in his humor, not in his preaching, but his personality."

   George Bernard Shaw was born in Dublin,
July 26, 1856, of a "shabby but genteel" family.
His father, George Carr Shaw, was a merchant, second cousin to a baronet, whose frequent "alcoholic antics" made the family socially shunned but whose superb gift for comedy was passed on to and became an armor
of wit and arrogance for his shy, sensitive
son.   The boy owed much, however, to his
capable, musically talented mother, the former
Lucinda Elizabeth Gurly: through her teaching and her professional musical associates he
memorized the works of the masters, particularly Mozart, one of the great influences of his
life. Sent to the Wesleyan Connexional in Dublin at ten, he soon found he hated school, especially languages and mathematics, but he loved
art. As for literature and writing, "I can remember no time when a page of print was not
intelligible to me. . . . I was saturated with
the Bible and Shakespeare by the time I was
ten."   He disliked games and longed to play
"wicked baritones in operas," or "to be another Michelangelo."

   Young Shaw, at fourteen, started his career
as a junior clerk, and made good. He so disliked the work, however, that in 1876 he left
Dublin (he did not return to Ireland until
1905), where his mother was then teaching
singing.   During those first lonely years in

GEORGE BERNARD SHAW

London, while he wrote five novels which no
publisher would accept, "my mother worked for
my living instead of preaching that it was my
duty to work for hers; therefore take off your
hat to her and blush."

   Having failed as a novelist, Shaw became
a critic: William Archer got him work reviewing books, and later art.   "He had the
four great virtues of a great journalist critic:
readability, irreverence, individuality, and courage."   As "Corno di Bassetto," a music critic
on Frank Harris' *Saturday Review,* Shaw
championed Wagner, then new and disliked.
Later, when he became drama critic, the plays
he saw "exasperated and irritated" him; they
were about romantic love, and for that tender
sentiment he had no use.   He attacked Shakespeare, partly to "draw attention to himself,"
mostly to obtain proper recognition of Ibsen,
whom he greatly admired.   A critical study,
The Quintessence of Ibsenism, appeared in
1891.

   At twenty-six, influenced by Henry George,
Shaw became a Socialist; he says also that the
reading of Marx was the turning point in his
career.   He was one of the original members
of the Fabian Society which was organized
in England in 1884.   Having recruited Sidney
Webb, his "natural complement," Shaw is credited with working out "the distinctively British
brand of socialism known as Fabianism."   He
soon became "in such demand as a principal
speaker that he was never at a loss for a
platform."   Shaw was "supreme in exposition,
a master of apt illustration and analogy, superb in repartee."   As a speaker he had everything, it was said, "but the power to touch the
emotions."   He was, however, a bourgeois intellectual, the "parlor" type of reformer: when
the police once attacked a Socialist meeting in
Trafalgar Square, Shaw was the first to run.
"When the shooting begins I shall always get
under the bed," he cheerfully admits.   One of
his outstanding contributions to the literature
of socialism has been *The Intelligent Woman's*

SHAW, BERNARD—*Continued*

Guide to Socialism and Capitalism (1928), which contains "everything that he had thought and felt on the subject for over forty years." Shaw has said that his sole contribution to socialist thought was to agree with the man in the street "that socialism means equal incomes for all." He served briefly as a London vestryman and borough councilor, his only experience in active politics. When urged later to run for political office he stoutly declined: "Better a leader of Fabianism than a chorus man in Parliament."

These political-social experiences, however, furnished him with the material for his first play, *Widowers' Houses* (produced in 1892), dealing with the evils of slum landlordism. The budding social dramatist "woke to find himself infamous." He was so violently attacked that he "felt convinced he was a born dramatist," and energetically went on writing his "pleasant" and "unpleasant" plays. His failures, his troubles with censorship, with actors, with critics are now integral parts of the Shavian legend. Success at last came with *Candida* (1897). "He was, and remains, the only playwright who has successfully dramatized the religious temperament . . . the source of all the emotion he was able to express on the stage."

His first financial success was achieved in America, with *The Devil's Disciple* (1900). It freed him from the drudgery of writing criticism; it also gave him the courage to marry a wealthy woman, long his friend and fellow Fabian. She was Charlotte Payne-Townshend, Irish, "born with a social conscience," and "plain, green-eyed, very ladylike," as Shaw said when he wrote Ellen Terry about her. She had become his secretary; and when he was seriously ill from overwork and a badly infected foot, she came to take care of him. Married in 1898, the Shaws became a devotedly happy though childless couple. And to Shaw, his wife remained his "best critic."

After his marriage Shaw, who liked to call himself "the incorrigible philanderer," continued his long, romantic correspondence with actress Ellen Terry, his "literary love," whom he had never met. In 1899 he wrote the role of Lady Cicely in *Captain Brassbound's Conversion* especially for her. By 1913 Shaw was at the apex of his career with the appearance of two of his best plays, *Androcles and the Lion* and *Pygmalion*, the latter starring Mrs. Patrick Campbell, another platonic love.

Some critics rate Shaw's historical plays higher than those with a contemporary "social" message. But it is the consensus of critical opinion that he will not be remembered as a dramatist of the highest rank. "All his plays form a cycle of mystical faith in which he proclaims that each one of us is a Man of Destiny, a servant of the Life Force, a temple of the Holy Ghost." His characters, as mouthpieces for social criticism, were "seldom objectively created, genuine personalities." Says Archibald Henderson, his official biographer: "He has almost succeeded in eliminating the red corpuscle from art"; his plays are "dramatic algebra," the characters of which have only "vegetable passions." Benjamin de Casseres says he "can never be great because his humor is not tragic": and Joseph Wood Krutch considers him valuable chiefly as a stimulant. Many Shavian devotees, however, agree with C. E. M. Joad: "The richness of the intellectual content, the play of ideas, the whizz-slap-bang of the dialogue, the regular discomfiture of the pompous and the powerful raised me to a level of mental exhilaration."

The critics have unanimously agreed that Bernard Shaw at his finest is to be found in the less well known Prefaces to his printed plays, a uniform collected edition of which appeared in 1930. Called "little masterpieces of essay writing" in "the best prose style since Swift," they are said to have cost him far more labor than his dramas and, as they more nearly expressed his own personal viewpoint on all subjects, Shaw himself thought them more important than his plays. For their witty, sharply ironic, cleanly effective commentary on whatever most vitally interested Shaw—marriage customs, medical practice, vivisection, censorship, creative evolution (his "religion") —they are, as John Mason Brown '42 has remarked, "among the glories of the language."

Since the beginning of the Second World War several of Shaw's plays have won new popularity through stage revivals and motion-picture adaptations. It was not until 1938 that he allowed *Pygmalion* to be filmed. An English producer, Gabriel Pascal '42, who had no money and no reputation, persuaded Shaw that only a man of his genius could write the film scripts of his plays. Rejuvenated in a new career, Shaw became a screen enthusiast. When his *Major Barbara* was filmed at Denham, England, in 1940, the white-bearded author had a wonderful time: he wrote and rewrote new scenes; he puttered around the sets "like a fussy gardener in his flower beds." Even when Luftwaffe bombs dropped all over the lot, the peppery old man refused to take shelter. A consummate actor himself, he thoroughly enjoyed being filmed for the picture's introductory speech. While the cameras turned "he was vivacious almost to the point of hamminess. When the cameras stopped and the lights dimmed Mr. Pascal leaned over and kissed G.B.S. gently, where his forelock used to be. Mr. Shaw slumped in his chair. The act was over. 'May I go home, now?' he pleaded." American film audiences in 1941 saw the photogenic old man reading his message to them: "I am sending you my old plays, just as you are sending us your old destroyers. . . . At any moment a bomb may crash through this roof and blow me to atoms. . . . If it does happen, it will not matter very much to me. As you see, I am in my eighty-fifth year. I have shot my bolt. I have done my work. But if my films are still being shown in America, my soul will go marching on, and that will satisfy me." *Major Barbara* was called "one of the most provocative films ever made. . . . Still ahead of the times upon the screen, which speaks very well for Shaw." *Caesar and Cleopatra* was being filmed by Gabriel Pascal in England in late 1944. *Geneva* (1939), his fiftieth play, the leading characters of which were based on the personalities of Hitler '42, Mussolini '42, and Stalin '42, was staged by Maurice Colbourne in New York in January 1940. A 1942 Broadway revival of *In*

Good King Charles's Golden Days (1939) was praised by Richard Watts as "Shaw at his mellowest and most charming."

A new book, *Everybody's Political What's What* (October 1944) was an effort "to track down some of the mistakes that have landed us in two wars in twenty-five years." Although Shaw said in his preface, "Written in my second childhood . . . it is just a child's guide to politics," most of the critics found it sound and brilliant. Bernard De Voto '⁴³ called it "the most exhilarating experience of the season . . . the most remarkable book ever written by a man in his eighties." And, regarding Shaw's pronouncements, Francis Hackett wrote: "How superb it is to have had such vivid humane convictions, to have searched into them, to have lived by them, and to carry them like a sword."

Long before Shaw had reached his height as a playwright he had been busy promoting the career that has survived and surpassed Shaw the writer: Shaw the Personality, the most fabulous, best-advertised Public Figure of his time. The red-bearded Fabian became the white-whiskered philosopher-patriarch; the gadfly-irritant of the status quo assumed the honored, entrusted role of Britain's Grand Old Boy. In his overly sensitive youth, G.B.S. had developed a formula upon which—as a Famous Man—he could capitalize: If you want to influence people, insult them first, win them afterward. Then you can say anything you like as long as people think you don't mean it. "Most mocking when most serious, most fantastic when most earnest," Shaw's word as a wit too often belied his intent: the "preacher by nature and Archbishop of the Universe by self-appointment" became his own worst enemy.

Shaw's act as a Public Figure was greatly bolstered by certain personal idiosyncrasies and convictions. He was a vegetarian, not as a faddist, but because he genuinely loved animals: the use of animal flesh as food was obnoxious to him, as was the wearing of furs by women. Because of a tender regard for all living things, he became one of the most rabid of anti-vivisectionists. He also violently attacked compulsory vaccination, for the reason that, though vaccinated in early youth, he got smallpox nevertheless. His dislike of doctors—particularly of modern surgical science—is well known. But that he has not always lived up to the letter of the law in his convictions has also been demonstrated: stricken with pernicious anemia at seventy, he owes his own survival to injections of liver extract, an animal product whose curative power was determined only after experiments with animals.

Always the "bourgeois Puritan" in revolt against social custom and convention, Shaw upheld socialism and feminism until they became generally accepted. Early in the '30's he decided to support Communism and stunned the old-time Fabians by saying: "We are Socialists. The Russian side is our side." When Stalin split with Trotsky, "Shaw took Stalin's view as a matter of course." And when he visited Russia he "was made as much of as if he had been Karl Marx in person." He liked almost everything about the Soviet Union, from its black bread and cabbage to its chief. When the Russo-German pact was signed in 1939 Shaw wrote one of his innumerable letters to the London *Times* pointing out that England should be grateful to Stalin for checking Germany—"a master stroke of foreign policy with six million Red soldiers at its back." It was predicted, however, of the unpredictable G.B.S. that when Russia got "respectable" Shaw would be ready, politically, to take up something else.

Although long past the age when an octogenarian is entitled to an armchair view of life, Shaw since the outbreak of the Second World War has been more vociferous than he was during the First World War, when he attacked and outraged Britons to the point of being called pro-German. In his role as "England's Bad Boy No. 1," he has made a good many caustic comments on Britain's war efforts. "I would welcome a German attack on London. They are knocking down a good many things we ought to have knocked down ourselves many years ago. I should hate to see them bomb Westminster Abbey, but I should be happy for them to bomb some of the monuments in it. The same applies to the House of Commons and its members." He denounced a radio ban on Leftist speakers. He called the detention of Gandhi '⁴² a "stupid blunder of the Right-wing diehards." He condemned the Atlantic Charter as not worth the paper it was written on; said that "we the British shall have to look to our step between the United States and the U.S.S.R. if we are to keep our eminence among the powers." On his eighty-eighth birthday in 1944 Shaw said that he did not believe Germany should be split up into small states, but "treated decently." He said that none of the Allies, except Russia, had shown sufficient talent in governing themselves to fit them to govern Germany. (As a birthday gift, he presented his home at Ayot St. Lawrence to the nation.) And in December, when he described the War as "a mere bubble in the froth of history," he scorned the thought that the punishment of Hitler would prevent future wars. As for women as keepers of the peace, Shaw declared: "Men are pugnacious and women are very pugnacious."

When the Irish are under fire Shaw becomes a good Irishman—his support of Eire's neutrality is characteristic: "Mr. de Valera '⁴⁰ should inform Mr. Churchill '⁴² privately that he cannot give him the naval bases without compromising Ireland's neutrality and perhaps losing his job and power for good, but that he cannot prevent him from taking them." But when Mrs. George Bernard Shaw died in September 1943 and set aside in her will some $400,000 to "teach the Irish the rudiments of social conduct and to abolish from their lives the social defects of shyness and inarticulate conversation," many an outraged Irishman read the fine Irish hand of her husband in the bequest. "They need it," Shaw said. "They get no training. They have no manners. They are ignorant." Further, "at the time my wife made that will I was seriously considering doing the same for the English."

The "highest paid playwright in the world" hotly complains that, because of taxation, the more he earns the poorer he gets. Nonetheless, "if taxes leave me anything," he hopes to leave his entire fortune to establishing a forty-two-letter alphabet and a system of simplified spelling. By eliminating one letter from every

SHAW, BERNARD—*Continued*

word possible, "we can save enough labor, machinery, and paper to pay for an offensive and maybe the whole War."

Photographed, painted, "sculptured," and caricatured innumerable times, any likeness of the white-whiskered, Mephistophelean-eyebrowed G.B.S. is universally recognized. Today "his snowy beard and his white hair make him look as antiseptic as his prose style and also give his head an appearance of patriarchal altitude." His nose is "big and blunt"; his ears (according to Shaw himself) "stick straight out like the doors of a triptych, and I was born with them full size, so that on windy days my nurse had to hold me by the waistband to prevent my being blown away." His eyes are "bluc and self-conscious," his pink complexion "the envy of Hollywood." According to Hesketh Pearson: "His clothes were perhaps symbolic of his soul. His collars were always soft, and he did not wear a shirt, believing it was wrong to swaddle one's middle with a double thickness of material. Instead, he wore some head-to-foot undergarment known only to its maker." Because he makes his suits last several years, "they acquire individuality and become characteristic of me. They take human shape with knees and elbows recognizably mine."

The thin, energetically erect oldster "always walks as though he had an appointment with himself and might be late for it." Until he was past eighty his favorite exercises were walking, swimming, bicycling, and motoring. He never played games, explaining that no one liked to play with him because he never cared whether he won or lost. "He had a Kiplingesque love of knowing how things were done; technicalities delighted him, and so did pianolas, gramophones, wireless, and calculators. . . . He experimented for hours with his cameras, and never tired of talking about photography."

At the age of seventy-five Shaw made a world tour, but his only visit to the United States was in 1933. "I have been particularly careful never to say a civil word to the United States," he said. "I have defined the 100 per cent American as 99 per cent idiot. And they just adore me." In December 1944 he emphatically denied he thought of coming to the United States for the première of the film of his play *Caesar and Cleopatra*. Refusing honors was another Shavian habit which brought much publicity. In 1925 he won the Nobel Prize for literature, which he called "a token of gratitude for a sense of world relief that I had published nothing that year." He turned the money over to the Anglo-Swedish Literary Alliance. He refused a knighthood and also the Order of Merit: "It has come simply to mean 'Old Man.'" He did join the P.E.N. Club, but said authors should not associate because "their minds inbreed and produce abortions." Another "hate" is his own first name, George; for some years he has signed his works with "Bernard Shaw."

It has been said that Shaw's scorn for emotion, his "lack of a common touch with humanity," is the saddest thing about him. Oscar Wilde remarked: "An excellent man: he has no enemies, and none of his friends like him."

Though he has made a legend of himself as a "tightwad," his admirers say this is only an act: he is "the most generous man of his generation." According to Brooks Atkinson [42]: "Although he is no fool with his purse, he is a generous man. His relations with people have always been kind and often magnanimous. . . . In fact, it was probably through socialism that he acquired humanity."

Shaw has "gone through life afflicted by a multiplicity of personalities." Always the realist, "it is my deliberate, cheerful, and entirely self-respecting intention to continue to the end of my life deceiving people, avoiding danger, making my bargain with publishers and managers on principles of supply and demand instead of abstract justice." As the basis of his philosophic conviction, Shaw thinks the man who believes there is a purpose in the universe is "the effective man and the happy man." Further, "we have no more right to consume happiness without producing it than we have to consume wealth without producing it." The Grand Old Boy of English Letters thus sums it up: "I am of the opinion that my life belongs to the whole community, and as long as I live it is my privilege to do for it whatsoever I can. . . . I rejoice in life for its own sake. It is a sort of splendid torch which I have got hold of for the moment, and I want to make it burn as brightly as possible before handing it on to future generations."

References

Am Mercury 58:233-8 F '44

N Y Herald Tribune p26 S 14 '43

N Y Times IX p1 Je 1 '41; VII p15 Je 1 '41 pors

N Y Times Mag p18 F 6 '44 por

Colbourne, M. The Real Bernard Shaw 1940

Harris, F. Bernard Shaw 1931

Henderson, A. George Bernard Shaw 1918

Kunitz, S. J. and Haycraft, H. eds. Twentieth Century Authors 1942

Pearson, H. G.B.S. Full-Length Portrait 1942

Who's Who 1944

SHERROD, ROBERT (LEE) (sher-rod)
Feb. 8, 1909- War correspondent

Address: b. c/o Time, Inc., Rockefeller Plaza, New York City; h. 4833 Rodman St., N. W., Washington, D. C.

When the fifth wave of marines waded neck-deep, amidst Japanese machine-gun fire, to the beach of Tarawa in 1943, Robert Sherrod, correspondent for *Time* Magazine, was with them. "I was never so scared in all my life as when our little boat headed for the beach through a barrage of Jap mortar shells and automatic weapons. The first two boats we met had already been disabled. I gritted my teeth and tried to smile at the scared marine next to me. . . . I don't know when it was that I realized I wasn't frightened any longer. Perhaps it was when I noticed the bullets were hitting six inches to the right or six inches to the left." Having witnessed the terrific slaughter of American boys under constant fire, Sherrod and a fellow correspondent dug a foxhole that night—and did not sleep.

"A war correspondent's life expectancy may not be long, but what there is of it is rarely dull," Robert Sherrod commented in *Tarawa: the Story of a Battle* (1944), his account of that four-day struggle, late in November 1943, for the Gilbert Island atoll. Called "perhaps the best firsthand description of action that has yet come out of the War", "one of the most vivid pieces of writing on record," and "as near as you can get, in an armchair, to being in the midst of battle," much of the book was actually written while the author, under fire, crouched behind the seawall and jotted down what he saw, heard, smelled, and felt.

The "quiet but fundamentally pugnacious" young reporter was the first of *Time*'s correspondents to be sent overseas to cover United States forces in the War. He was born in Thomas County, Georgia, February 8, 1909, the son of Joseph Arnold and Victoria Ellen (Evers) Sherrod. After attending the Thomasville High School in Georgia, he entered the University of Georgia, where he received his B.A. degree in 1929. Upon his graduation he immediately began his career as a newspaperman, reporting for the Atlanta *Constitution*. During the next four years his experiences in newspaper work were varied: he was advertising writer for the Davison-Paxon Company, Atlanta; reporter for the Florida *Palm Beach Daily News*, for the *Hampton Chronicle* of Westhampton Beach, Long Island, and for the New York *Herald Tribune* (1932-34). Sherrod began his work for *Time* Magazine in 1935 as its Washington correspondent. He became its associate editor in 1942, which position he still held in December 1944. (In 1936 he was married to Elizabeth Harvey Hudson; there are two sons, John Hudson and Robert Lee, Jr.)

Assigned as a war correspondent to the South Pacific in January 1942, Sherrod left with one of the first convoys for Australia in February of that year. He got his first taste of enemy bombings during six critical months when the Allies had only a scant handful of planes to meet the Zeroes. After sharing experiences with General MacArthur's [41] men in Australia and New Guinea, Sherrod flew to the Aleutians in time to cover the final period of the battle for Attu.

Of a correspondent's life in Attu he cabled (July 1943): "This was no taxicab war. The only way to get to the battle lines was to walk over mountains where a mile an hour was fair speed. Most of the fighting was done on mountain peaks a thousand feet or more straight up. Some reporters did not get to take their shoes off for days, and the icy Aleutian winds numbed an ungloved hand so quickly that taking notes outdoors was all but impossible. . . . There was no way to take a typewriter over the mountains, so to write a story we had to tramp all the way back to the beach, board a ship, then borrow a typewriter. After that we had to walk back an hour or more to G-2 headquarters for censoring. We all dressed in one to three sets of long wool underwear, field jacket, parka, sweaters, woolen cap beneath the helmet, two or more pairs of heavy wool socks, shoe pacs or leather boots, and raincoats. Yet we always seemed to be cold." He also reported that one field hospital on Attu, "with a staff of three surgeons,

Dimitri Kessel

ROBERT SHERROD

has treated 529 men wounded in battle landed a month ago. Only three casualties have died. Not one case of infection has turned up in the muddy little hospital area. Doctors credited this record to debridement (cutting of dead tissues) and sulfanilamide." Sherrod was one of the nine correspondents commended by the Army for their conduct during the twenty-day fight on Attu, and was the recipient of a Navy Department citation in May 1943. Following a brief time in New York, Sherrod left in September 1943 for the Central Pacific in time to go on the Wake Island raid.

Robert Sherrod was thus already a battle-seasoned correspondent when he boarded the outmoded old battleship (called by the crew the "U.S.S. Blisterbutt") which was to help shell Tarawa preparatory to the invasion of the atoll by Admiral Spruance's [44] troops. After the shelling, early in the morning of November 20, 1943, Sherrod and two other newsmen, Richard Johnston of the U.P. and William Hipple of the A.P., climbed down the ship's rope nets into one of the landing boats. It was found at the outset that the Higgins boats couldn't land on the atoll's shallow reef; they had to resort to the smaller and slower "amphtracks" (amphibious tractors), which meant wading the 700 yards to shore under vicious machine-gun fire. Sherrod made it, suffering most of all from the initial shock of seeing men die all around him. "All during that first day of Tarawa dozens of marines were being killed every five minutes. Anyone who ventured beyond the precarious beachhead we held behind the retaining wall was more likely to become a casualty than not. Jap snipers were hidden so carefully in the tops of coconut trees or under earth-mounded coconut logs that they could rarely be seen. Machine guns from slits in those fortifications covered the beach and the areas behind the beach, chattering incessantly as they raked the Americans." Sherrod crouched behind a broken-down bulldozer, dried out his note

SHERROD, ROBERT—Continued

paper, and was soon busy asking the names of the men beside him, reporting individual cases of remarkable heroism, such as that of Lieutenant William Deane Hawkins of El Paso, "the bravest man I have ever known."

That night ("quite certain it was to be my last") he and Hipple of the A.P. dug themselves a foxhole. "My knees shook. My whole body trembled like jelly. I peered into the darkness over the seawall, seeing nothing, hearing nothing except an occasional shot from a Jap sniper's rifle. . . . Why should I be afraid to die? My family will be well provided for with my own insurance and the insurance my company carries on its own war correspondents. It will be tough on my children, growing up without a father, but at least they will have a very capable mother and the satisfaction of knowing their father died in line of duty." On the second day the third-assault battalions held their footholds. And at night the two correspondents, in a new foxhole that already held the body of a dead Japanese, slept for the first time since landing.

Sherrod lived to write his story of an atoll of 5,000 American and Japanese dead—the casualty list of Americans at the close of his book includes 685 killed, 77 dead of wounds, and 2,100 wounded. By the end of November 1943 the correspondent was back in Honolulu, putting together his notes. There he read American newspapers and heard radio commentators groaning about the heavy casualties. This made him "pretty mad." The truth was, he felt, that "many Americans were not prepared psychologically to accept the cruel facts of war." Sherrod was even more incensed over conditions on the home front. "My trip back to the United States since the War began was a letdown. I had imagined that everybody, after two years, would realize the seriousness of the War and the necessity of working as hard as possible toward ending it. But I found a nation wallowing in unprecedented prosperity. There was a steel strike going on and a rail strike threatened. Men lobbying for special privileges swarmed around a Congress which appeared afraid to tax the people's new-found, inflationary wealth."

Tarawa was written mainly to impress people of the horrors of battle: "Our information services," wrote Sherrod, "have failed to impress people with the hard facts of war. . . . There is no easy way to win. There will be other and bigger Tarawas." The book was brought to American readers in less than four months from the first landing on Tarawa to the finished manuscript. Sherrod says that he made his last proof corrections only ten days before the first 5,000 copies were delivered.

Beyond the success of his book, Robert Sherrod is possibly proudest of his Marine Corps citation direct from Lieutenant Colonel Evans "Raider" Carlson '43. Praising the young correspondent's "courage, fortitude, and superb aplomb," Colonel Carlson said: "I came to know Mr. Sherrod when we shared the same transport en route to the target area and gained a respect for his ability to evaluate events. It did not occur to me that he would attempt to land before a reasonable beachhead had been secured. However, I met him on the beach during the critical first day and learned that he, in company with William Hipple of the Associated Press, had accompanied the assault waves of the center battalion ashore. Such devotion to factual reporting deserves special commendation."

During March 1944 Robert Sherrod spent a great deal of his available time lecturing and speaking on the radio. He was besieged with more speech-making requests than he could fill. But there was one address that he had to make. His maid had lost the folder containing the Sherrod family's ration books. It was found by a New York University medical student who gave it to the dean of the school, who, in turn, surrendered it to Mrs. Sherrod on condition that her husband make a speech.

In early June 1944, Sherrod was on his way to a new assignment in the Pacific area. During that month and in July he witnessed much of the action in the taking of Japanese-held Saipan Island. In the first week of August he cabled to *Time* the gruesome story of civilian mass suicides among the Japanese there. In August Sherrod returned from Saipan with 1,500 photographs taken by *Life* and *Time* cameramen. He expected to use a dozen of the best of these in his forthcoming book on the Saipan campaign.

References

> Time 41:17 Je 14 '43; 42-15 Jl 5 '43; 42:24-5 D 6 '43; 43:6 Ja 10 '44; 43:15 Mr 27 '44
>
> Sherrod, R. Tarawa: the Story of a Battle 1944

SHOTWELL, JAMES T(HOMSON) Aug. 6, 1874- Historian; author; chairman of the Commission to Study the Organization of Peace

Address: b. Commission to Study the Organization of Peace, 405 W. 117th St., New York City

One of the most indefatigable planners in the cause of world peace is the American scholar of history, James T. Shotwell. Since his participation in the Versailles conclave following the First World War, Shotwell has been intimately associated with the statesmen and leaders of public opinion in both Europe and America. Advocating international cooperation for collective security, in 1939 he organized the Commission to Study the Organization of Peace, which has become one of the leading agencies investigating the problems of the post-War world. Shotwell, professor emeritus of the history of international relations at Columbia University, is also director of the Division of Economics and History of the Carnegie Endowment for International Peace.

Of American-Quaker ancestry, James Thomson Shotwell was born in Canada, in Strathroy, Ontario, on August 6, 1874. His parents were John B. and Anne (Thomson) Shotwell. He received his Bachelor of Arts degree from Toronto University in 1898, and in 1900 was appointed as lecturer in history at Columbia University in New York. On earning his Ph.D. in 1903 he became an instructor, in 1908, a professor, teaching regularly for the next thirty-four years. In 1937 Shotwell was made Bryce Professor of the history of international relations, and on his retirement in 1942 continued his membership in the Columbia faculty as a special lecturer. Shotwell holds an LL.D. from Columbia and honorary degrees from nine other universities, including the University of Budapest and Johns Hopkins.

With the late James Harvey Robinson and other scholars, Shotwell played a large part in the movement to adapt the scientific method to historical criticism and to the teaching of history—"the recasting of traditional perspectives in the light of original source materials." In connection with this movement Shotwell planned an extensive library of studies and translations into English of original documents of European history, under the title *Records of Civilization: Sources and Studies.* Called into government service in 1917, Shotwell was able to edit only seven volumes; and the series was taken over by the history department of Columbia University. (The volumes were published between 1915 and 1921.) His first published work had been *The Religious Revolution of Today* (1913).

Shotwell's long career in the field of international affairs began soon after the United States entered the First World War. Granted a leave of absence from Columbia, in the spring of 1917 he assumed the chairmanship of the National Board for Historical Service, formed by a group of Americans during the War. In September Colonel House, the personal adviser of President Wilson, invited Shotwell to join in the deliberations of The Inquiry, a committee composed largely of university professors charged with studying the political, economic, legal, and historical phases of the problems which would have to be faced in the peace conference at the end of the War. At Versailles The Inquiry became a working part of the American delegation as a whole. Shotwell was made chief of the Division of History of the American Commission to Negotiate Peace and a member of the International Labor Legislation Commission, whose discussions resulted in the setting up of the International Labor Organization. (Shotwell's *Labor Provisions in the Peace Treaty* was published in 1919.) He was also the American member of the organizing committee of the International Labor Conference in 1919.

It was at this time that Shotwell first proposed that the Covenant of the envisaged League of Nations be changed so that the League would include, in addition to the regular members, an "Associate Membership for those nations which for one reason or another might not accept the full obligations of membership" (i.e., the principle of collective security as set forth in Articles Ten and Sixteen of the Covenant). The link between the two types of members was to be a system of conferences between them all to deal with "all the peacetime activities and interests of nations which do not have to do with the preservation of peace itself." Shotwell's experience in the making of the labor section of the Treaty, which had erected a world organization to

JAMES T. SHOTWELL

deal with questions affecting labor, suggested to him similar structures for international cooperation in the other major fields of national interests: "These bodies, each limited to its own task of labor, finance, communications, health, disarmament, etc., would, it seemed to me," Shotwell later wrote, "be more efficient than any single parliament of the world could ever be." He advocated United States entry into the League with an Associate Membership. In 1920 Shotwell co-authored *A History of the Peace Conference of Paris, Labor as an International Problem,* and *The League of Nations Starts.*

The preceding year, the American historian had become editor of the Carnegie Endowment for International Peace *Economic and Social History of the World War* series, and spent most of the following six years working in Europe on leave of absence from Columbia. The individual volumes were prepared under "a comprehensive system of editorial boards in each of the European countries." The survey covered sixteen of those countries and was described by its editor as "the first time that any historian had ever tried to measure the displacement caused by the war in the processes of civilization." Shotwell also completed his *Introduction to the History of History* (1922), which he had originally intended as an introduction to *Records of Civilization,* but which now emerged as an independent study of the origins and development of history in the ancient world. The *New Republic* commented: "Not only is Professor Shotwell's work one of high scholarship and interpretative profundity, but it is also admirably written, and the stylistic effort rarely demands a sacrifice of accuracy." Said the *American Historical Review:* "Professor Shotwell approaches the history of history with a contagious sense for the philosophic implications and the wide human interest of his theme. His book abounds in striking thoughts strikingly expressed. Without neglecting the needful bibliographical details he has thrown open, to all who can read a serious

SHOTWELL, JAMES T.—*Continued*
book, a subject ordinarily reserved as part of
the strict discipline of a profession." Other
opinions were similar, the *Scottish Historical
Review*'s critic going so far as to call it "an
entrancing book, which no student of history
can read without feeling his pulse beat faster."

In 1923 Professor Shotwell was in Brussels
as American president of the Fifth International Congress of Historical Sciences. In
1924 Shotwell became a trustee of the Carnegie Endowment and director of its Division
of Economics and History. In 1924 Shotwell
formed a committee to tackle the problems of
disarmament. This study group drew up its
proposals in the form of a Draft Treaty of
Disarmament and Security which provided for
a World Parliament on Disarmament to meet
once every three years. This seemed a bold
innovation to many, and the document also
opened new lines of political thinking—declaring an "aggressive war to be an international
crime" and defining an aggressor as "a state
which goes to war in violation of its given
pledge to take its case to court." The document was circulated as an official document
of the Assembly of the League and was discussed along with the Assembly's own Protocol of Geneva, which was rejected in favor
of the Locarno Treaties of 1925.

Taking a leading part in the movement in
the United States which led to the Kellogg-
Briand Peace Pact signed in Paris in 1928,
Shotwell was especially equipped to write his
*War as an Instrument of National Policy, and
Its Renunciation in the Pact of Paris* (1929),
a documentary record of the unofficial intrigue
and popular agitation which accompanied the
negotiations. In his analysis, which critics felt
was characterized by fairness and moderation,
Shotwell declared optimistically: "The renunciation of war . . . even if only as the instrument of national policy, establishes a new basis
for international law.... The instruments of
national justice are not yet perfected, and the
Pact of Paris leaves this problem unsolved,
but henceforth, with the arbitrament of war
no longer permitted and all disputes referred
to settlement by 'pacific means,' these means
will be developed through the practical experience of the coming years."

Shotwell continued to figure prominently in
international affairs as director of the Division of International Relations of the Social
Science Research Council from 1931 to 1933.
In 1932 he was made chairman of the National
Committee of the U.S.A. on International Intellectual Cooperation of the League of Nations,
a post he held until 1943. In 1935 Shotwell
was elected president of the League of Nations
Association, resigning in 1939 to undertake the
chairmanship of the newly formed Commission
to Study the Organization of Peace. The
Commission came into being on November 5,
1939, when Poland had just been overrun by
Nazi Panzer divisions.

The Commission to Study the Organization
of Peace, often known as the "Shotwell Commission" after its founder, has since become
one of the best-known and most effective
groups engaged in studying the blueprints for
a post-War society. Receiving financial assistance from the Carnegie Endowment for Inter-

national Peace, the Woodrow Wilson Foundation, and substantial individual contributions,
the Commission consists of a panel of 100 experts in various fields related to international
affairs, which meets about eight times yearly
in New York City. In addition, there are a
number of regional groups set up on similar
lines in other sections of the country. The
first annual report of the New York Commission, released in November 1940, called for a
world federation of states, presumably, as the
Herald Tribune explained, a super-League of
Nations in which the various national units
would have a status similar to that which American states now have in the American Federal
Union. The world faces two alternatives if it
wishes peace, the report stated: "empire
achieved by conquest, or some form of association." It also advocated outlawing aggressive armaments and creating in their place an
international police force.

The second report of the Commission surveyed such problems of the transitional period
following the War as famine, disease, social
security, and political control. The 13,000-word
study issued in February 1943 recommended
that the United Nations take steps to organize
as a "continuing conference" to draw up a program for a better world based upon the principles of the Atlantic Charter, with an international Bill of Human Rights, disarmament of
conquered nations, the substitution of the concept of "trusteeship" for that of imperialism,
and joint settlement of disputes without recourse to war. In May 1944 the Shotwell Commission urged the immediate establishment under the auspices of the United Nations of a
Human Rights Commission as a permanent international appeals body for the protection of
human rights.

In addition to his leadership of the confabu-
lations of the Commission to Study the Organization of Peace, since 1940 Shotwell has been
a member of the Advisory Committee of the
Department of Cultural Relations of the Department of State. In July 1943 Shotwell became chairman of the board of directors of the
newly established United Nations Association,
the purpose of which was to conduct a nationwide educational campaign for the entry of the
United States into a permanent world organization for collective security. He was a consultant of the State Department in 1942 and
1943 with reference to the preparation of post-
War plans which led eventually to the negotiations at Dumbarton Oaks, and was a member also of four other committees of the State
Department.

Throughout all these activities Shotwell continued his lecturing, editing, and writing. *The
Heritage of Freedom* (1934) was a historical
survey of the effect of the First World War
on the foreign policies of the United States
and Canada; in 1936 he began the editorship
of the series *Canadian-American Relations*. In
On the Rim of the Abyss (1936) Shotwell reviewed the history of the League of Nations
from its inception up to the Ethiopian crisis of
1936. While frankly exposing the weaknesses
and errors of the League, he revived his proposals for Associate Memberships in the
League and for periodic disarmament conferences. He concluded that the only way of
averting a second world war was "the readjustment of nations to a readjusted League.

Regionalism must be the keynote to security; but it must be bound to the whole world by the moral categories of the Pact of Paris." The *Saturday Review of Literature* declared: "His book is well written and despite his partisanship usually dispassionate." The following year saw the publication of *At the Paris Peace Conference*, a daily record of what Shotwell observed of the making of the treaties. Another useful volume for reference is his well-documented and readable *Turkey at the Straits* (1940), a history of the Straits from the dawn of history to the present time, written in collaboration with Frances Déak. In 1940, too, Shotwell edited *Governments of Continental Europe*.

In *What Germany Forgot* (1940) Shotwell exposed the Nazi claim that the peace terms of the Versailles Treaty wrecked post-War Germany, though he by no means regarded the 1919 settlement as an ideal arrangement. In a representative comment Rustem Vambery of the *Nation* wrote: "It is not easy to overrate the great value of Professor Shotwell's book. He proves with the dispassionate argumentation of the historian and the scholarly comprehension of a sociologist that the War itself, Germany's wartime economy, its continuation in the Hindenburg program of heavy expenditures, the devastating inflation, the 'false recovery,' based on the 'miracle' of the Rentenmark, the tariffs of the post-War period, and other economic fallacies, rather than the Treaty, produced that morass of despair from which eventually rose the miasma of Nazism. This is not only 'what Germany forgot,' but what insistent propaganda in this country kept Americans from perceiving."

The Great Decision, published in the summer of 1944, is Shotwell's summary of the conclusions of the Commission to Study the Organization of Peace. His basic premise is the self-evident fact that scientific militarism has rendered war "no longer a directable and controllable instrument of international policy." In place of the agency of war, international institutions (already partly in existence) based on national security, economic and social welfare, justice, and the safeguarding of human rights must be substituted. Shotwell favors a political body which would in large measure resemble the League of Nations, with the addition of an international air force to provide for rapid action against any aggressor. He argues that police action be delegated to an air force rather than to sea or land power, inasmuch as "its prodigious power of concentrated destruction . . . if used in time may make unnecessary the extreme diversion of national economies." A thoroughgoing reform of international law, again outlawing war as an instrument of national policy, is imperative, Shotwell maintains.

While the *Saturday Review of Literature* condemned Shotwell's propositions as "pallid," in a more typical appraisal H. B. Parkes of the New York *Herald Tribune* wrote: "But although this book cannot be recommended to readers in search of intellectual provocation or excitement, it is, nonetheless, a contribution to the education of American opinion. It summarizes carefully what has already been accomplished in the building of a world order; and its suggestions for the future are the more

persuasive because of the restraint, the tone of cautious optimism, and the avoidance of controversial issues with which they are presented." Points which impressed other reviewers included the introduction of the idea of "graded responsibility," by which "obligations incurred by membership in the United Nations would differ according to the situation of the country concerned and its relation to the particular question involved."

The agreements reached by the American-British-Chinese-Russian conferees at Dumbarton Oaks, Shotwell termed "stronger" than the League Covenant, because the later plan "attempts to place the military sanctions as well as the economic primarily in the hands of the Executive Council of the United Nations. It recognizes the need for extreme haste in preventive action at the time of crisis." In November 1944 Shotwell was one of six distinguished specialists in international law and affairs who signed an open letter stating that "there can be no doubt of the propriety of the President's use of his powers to carry out a commitment for participation in international policing such as that proposed at Dumbarton Oaks. Nor can there be doubt of his Constitutional right to utilize contingents of the armed forces for this purpose." He approved also of its provision for "the coordination of all that vast and growing field of the economic and humanitarian interplay of nations." He reiterated his aversion to "taking part in a world labor congress with representatives of the Soviet Union and the CIO," although urging confidence in the U.S.S.R. as a partner in peace. (Early in December, incidentally, the Commission to Study the Organization of Peace presented the results of a four-year study of colonial problems, with the recommendation that colonies taken from the enemy be placed under the trusteeship of the United Nations.)

Shotwell is a fair-haired, tallish man with a kindly face and "an over-all air as persuasive as it is assured." In recognition of his exhaustive efforts in the field of international relations, five countries have given him decorations. Besides being the author and editor of numerous works on contemporary history, in 1904-1905 Shotwell edited the eleventh edition of the *Encyclopaedia Britannica*, for which he was both assistant general editor and a contributor. He was married in 1901 to Margaret Harvey; they have two daughters, Margaret Grace and Helen Harvey.

References

N Y Times p18 Je 8 '42

Kunitz, S. J. and Haycraft, H. eds. Twentieth Century Authors 1942

Who's Who in America 1944-45

SIMMS, HILDA Apr. 15, 1920- Actress
Address: h. Webster Hotel, 40 W. 45th St., New York City

With the opening on Broadway in August 1944 of a new play, *Anna Lucasta*, American theatre history was being made. Unknown Hilda Simms came to the fore as an extremely promising young dramatic actress, and Broadway audiences saw, perhaps for the

George Karger

HILDA SIMMS

first time, a Negro cast perform a play about people, rather than about a race of people.

The young actress was born Hilda Moses in Minneapolis, April 15, 1920. Her mother, Lydia (Webber) Moses, was reared in a convent; her father, Emile Moses, was a musician who at one time had had his own orchestra. A few of Hilda's eight living brothers and sisters, of whom she is the eldest, are musicians, too, but although Hilda herself has a pleasant voice, she declares that she has no particular gift for music. During her youth the family was very poor, and she began early to help out by doing odd jobs on afternoons and week-ends while attending school. She won a scholarship to St. Margaret's Academy in Minneapolis (she was the first Negro to be admitted there), then following her graduation was enrolled at the General College of the University of Minnesota. The college had been organized by Dr. Malcolm MacLean and offered an accelerated two-year course for those students who could not afford to take the regular university course or who were in some way not qualified for it. During her first year at the General College Hilda Moses showed such promise that she was transferred to the College of Education to prepare for a teaching career.

In the meanwhile the teen-age girl had continued to work in her spare time to pay for her education. For a time she was employed as a maid in the Homewood Theatre in the city, and when she was eighteen she started modeling for portrait and sculpture classes at the Minneapolis Art Institute, being the first Negro girl to do so there. Her earliest professional interest had been in the field of social work, and from 1936 until she went East she also worked as girls' recreational assistant in the Phyllis Wheatley Settlement House, where she taught the first classes ever held in modern dancing for Negroes.

She had also begun to develop a keen interest in the theatre, although her first public "appearance," at the age of fifteen, was not on a theatre stage but as a Malayan girl in the Frank Buck '43 Bring 'Em Back Alive show then stopping in Minneapolis. Her real theatrical bow was made a little later when she appeared with the Edythe Bushe Players as Maimie in Clare Boothe's '42 Kiss the Boys Good-bye. Press notices called her performance the best in the play, and she was afterward asked to appear as Rheba with the Minneapolis Coach House players in their production of the New York success You Can't Take It With You. When she was at the University she acted with its Little Theatre group, too, in a few plays— as Marion in Noel Coward's '41 Cavalcade and as Irene in Eugene O'Neill's The Dreamy Kid.

At the end of a year and a half at the University, when the girl found she could no longer afford to remain in school, she left to take a job making salads in a Minneapolis restaurant. Shortly after, on August 15, 1941, she was married to William Simms, a graduate of Coe College, Iowa, whom she had met six years before. Then, only a week after her marriage, Malcolm MacLean, who had left Minnesota to take the presidency of Hampton Institute in Virginia, offered her a teaching fellowship, the first of its sort that the Institute had ever granted. While working for her B.S. there (her husband during this period was serving as director of public relations at Virginia State College), Miss Simms taught English, radio drama, and speech correction, and directed a USO group which she had organized. This group, called the First Nighters, was drawn from the townsfolk from near-by Newport News and toured Negro Army camps throughout the South. (Although its director is no longer actively connected with it, she still acts as its adviser.) During her year and a half at Hampton Miss Simms also acted in a number of plays presented by its drama group, including Kind Lady, The Divine Comedy, and Wuthering Heights, in which she played the lead.

After completing her course at Hampton in the spring of 1943 twenty-three-year-old Hilda Simms turned down several teaching offers to go north to New York City. Her first work in New York was as feature writer for the OWI of scripts being broadcast to the West Indies. After eight months she left to take the position of publicity assistant with Artkino Pictures, the agency which distributes Russian motion pictures in the United States; she later took complete charge of publicity and was also assistant to the vice-president of the company.

During her spare time Miss Simms did radio work. For several months she sang over WLIB on Joe Bostic's program The Negro Sings, also handling commercials for the station. In addition to making the WLIB broadcasts, she took small parts on programs heard over WNYC, WOR, and WEVD, appearing with the latter station on Clifford Burdette's series of sketches on the Negro. Since her Broadway debut she has made a few guest appearances on other stations, including one she made in Roi Ottley's '43 New World A-Coming.

Soon after her arrival in New York the actress joined the American Negro Theatre, the organization founded in Harlem in 1940 by Frederick O'Neal, a young actor from St. Louis, in collaboration with Abram Hill and six associates. This Harlem group is the nucleus of a series of community theatres which O'Neal, its guiding spirit, hopes to establish in cities throughout the United States with large Negro populations. No color barrier, however, is raised among those wishing to participate. (An example is Harry Wagstaff Gribble, director of *Anna Lucasta*.) As was the case with Miss Simms, the actors are very often young working people who are able to give only their leisure time to the group.

While she was actively associated with the A.N.T., Miss Simms says, she was not only actress but sound effects woman, property custodian, and publicity agent. Her first appearance with it as an actress was in the A.N.T. production of the Broadway comedy *Three Is a Family*, in which she played the Southern ingenue, Marion. Then came the turning point in her career, her first nineteen performances in the title role of Philip Yordan's *Anna Lucasta*, for which director Gribble had cast her without ever hearing her read the part.

Since the founding of the A.N.T. Broadway critics, screen representatives, and agents had been visiting the tiny, uncomfortable theatre in the basement of the 135th Street Public Library, and when *Anna Lucasta* opened there in June 1944 many of them were present. Yordan's play concerned the conflict between a scheming middle-class family and a wayward daughter trying to bring some happiness out of her sordid life. In the original draft the Lucastas had been Polish-Americans, but, as the playwright pointed out, there seemed to be no reason why they should not be Negroes, since their problems were unrelated to the color of their skins. (The few necessary changes were made by O'Neal and Hill.)

Like Hilda Simms, a number of the cast had had little or no professional experience, and the play itself, according to the visiting reviewers, had many weaknesses. Nevertheless, the critical reception the production received was almost unanimously excellent. The play, it was said, had a basic honesty that was sometimes curiously moving, however crude or clumsy portions of the writing were; and the cast, for the most part, acted it with great vitality and skill. For Miss Simms, the praise of her natural and sympathetic talent was high. Immediately, interest among the downtown commercial producers was aroused, and by the end of August the play had opened on Broadway under the banner of John Wildberg, producer of *One Touch of Venus*, *Porgy and Bess*, and other hits. In the cast were its star and five others of the original cast.

For prospective Broadway audiences *Anna* had received numerous revisions, including a happy ending. From the start of the run, however, many critics placed more emphasis on the fine acting, feeling that the script changes had made the characterizations less honest and some of the formerly lusty lines more farcical or calculated. Nonetheless, from a long-run point of view, the production was considered an important event in the American theatre. "It is not only top-notch theatre," wrote Burton Rascoe, ". . . but it is the first American play, designed for an all-Negro cast, to treat of Negro life without a certain amused condescension; the first play of Negro life to

recognize the fact that Negroes are individuals with pretty much the same problems, ways of living, speech, and points of view as the whites."

As for the new star of the production, the critics were unanimously enthusiastic. "The event of the evening," wrote the *Newsweek* reviewer after the opening, "is Hilda Simms's exciting portrayal." Similarly, other reviewers wrote of the "beauty and intelligence" she brought to her "vivid characterization" of the leading role. In October her work was further recognized when she was made the recipient of the Achievement Award as the outstanding actress of the year offered by the Salute to Young America Committee. Hollywood, too, has evidenced an interest, but studio offers to cast her in conventional singing and dancing roles do not appeal to the actress.

"I wish to be a great actress," Miss Simms says when asked her ambition, "and a writer," she will add. She is eager to be invited to study at the famous Moscow Art Theatre, perhaps on a scholarship, and at present she is studying the Russian language. Some day she hopes she will have a chance to play Shaw's [44] *Saint Joan*. Her strong interest in writing has been nurtured in several ways. She started writing in high school when she was editor of her school magazine, and since those days her interest has been fostered by her friend Malcolm MacLean. She has done a great deal of publicity work; at Hampton she wrote a play for Founders' Day; and in October 1944 she had an article published in the new magazine *Broadway*. In late 1944 she was working on a book about the people she knows—"something light with a little iron underneath the silk." In the political field she has been busy too, during the 1944 Presidential campaign working for the CIO's Political Action Committee. On the 1944 Race Relations Honor Roll of the Negro weekly the Chicago *Defender*, Miss Simms was named along with General Eisenhower [42], William Hastie [44], and eighteen other Americans. The actress has been described in many ways as lovely looking, and she has, in addition to her beauty, a vital, earnest quality, and, to quote *PM*, "a meat-and-potatoes healthiness" about her.

References

N Y Post p12 S 13 '44
N Y Post Mag p33 O 12 '44 pors
PM p20 S 1 '44 por

SINGER, ISRAEL J(OSHUA) Nov. 30, 1893—Feb. 10, 1944 Yiddish author and playwright; his works have been translated into many languages; two hit plays were *Yoshe Kalb* (1933) and *The Family Carnovsky* (1943).

Obituary

N Y Times p19 F 11 '44 por

SMART, DAVID A. Oct. 4, 1892- Publisher

Address: b. Esquire, Inc., 919 N. Michigan Ave., Chicago, Ill.; h. Golf, Ill.

Even constant readers of *Esquire*, that "unholy combination of erudition and sex," may not know that it is published by David A.

DAVID A. SMART

Smart of Chicago. They may not know either that Smart has been at one time or another the publisher of five other magazines, including three clothing-trade publications and *Coronet* and *Ken*. But even the most casual readers of *Esquire*, and some people who have never read it, are aware of its reputation and the controversy that has been stirred up over the denial by the United States Post Office Department in December 1943 of its second-class mailing privileges.

The man behind this controversial publication was born in Omaha, Nebraska, October 4, 1892, the son of Louis and Mary (Aronson) Smart. While still a small boy David was brought by his parents to Chicago, where he has lived ever since. He attended the Crane Technical High School for a short time; then, in 1911, he secured a position as an advertising salesman for the Chicago *Tribune*. He soon saw for himself the opportunities that lay in advertising and in 1914 established his own agency for the manufacture and sale of advertising and promotional material. The First World War interrupted his career, however, for when the United States declared war on Germany Smart was sent overseas with the A.E.F. in the Field Artillery.

A 2nd class private, he emerged slightly wounded from the War, and once more entered the advertising business. A few months later, however, he began speculating in the commodity markets. His luck, until the war boom broke, was phenomenal: in a short time he had made $750,000. When the crash eventually came he was able to clear out with $50,000. Following this adventure in speculating he went back for a second time to the safer field of advertising. In 1921, with his brother Alfred as his secretary-treasurer, he started the David A. Smart Publishing Company. Through the early '20's they "sold ideas to banks, haberdasheries, and furniture stores." The start of what was soon to be a successful enterprise for them came in 1927 with the inclusion of William

Hobart Weintraub in the partnership and the trio's entrance into the publishing business. Their first venture was with the *National Men's Wear Salesman*, a "mildly successful" trade magazine "modeled after *Printers' Ink*." A short time later they began publishing the *Gentleman's Quarterly*, "a smartly illustrated stylebook for men's shops to give away." For its editor they hired young Arnold Gingrich, who was to remain with them to edit *Esquire* in later years.

In 1930 one of the four conceived the idea of photographing the best dressed (and famous) gentlemen attending New York theatre openings and of rushing the results by telephoto to haberdashery subscribers. As these "red hot" releases appeared in store windows, style-conscious customers were supposed to dash in to purchase outfits similar to those in the photographs. When the first pictures were released in November 1930 the Fairchild Publishers, leaders in the textile apparel news field, protested loudly that the pictures were pre-opening ones taken of models in a studio. In retaliation Weintraub proposed that the Smarts establish themselves as Fairchild's competitors in the men's wear field. Their competitive offering, which appeared in December 1931, was, and still is, *Apparel Arts*, a trade magazine "so elaborately printed that it makes *Fortune* look like a pulp magazine." The price was $1.50. Colorful *Apparel Arts* was expensive to print, so only about 10,000 copies were printed—eight times a year. (It is now a monthly, selling for 50c a copy.) It proved to be popular almost at once—so popular, in fact, that haberdashers reported that customers were stealing copies from the clothing stores. Realizing from this experience the success they might have with a men's fashion magazine which could be sold on the newsstands, the partners began work on elaborate plans for a quarterly publication. This magazine was to be *Esquire: The Magazine for Men*, which first appeared October 15, 1933. "This magazine got its title through a fluke," according to the *Literary Digest*. "Every title imaginable had been copyrighted. When the firm's lawyer wrote that all proposed names were 'out,' he had addressed the letter to Arnold Gingrich, Esq. Seeing it, Smart shouted, 'Esquire! That's our title!'"

The publishing company had no vast resources, so part of the money to launch the publication had come from the partners' private funds. Prophets, moreover, were skeptical of the whole idea. Publishing costs would be too high, they said; and since the enterprise was starting in the middle of the depression, the thought that readers must pay 50c for a luxury item was fantastic. Furthermore, *Esquire* would have to sell two new ideas to prospective advertisers: that the men's clothing industry ought to advertise on a large scale, and that women are not the only people who read ads. In spite of the risks involved, however, work on *Esquire* proceeded. The plan for its distribution was to persuade 1,000 haberdasheries over the United States to buy one hundred copies each of this new magazine emphasizing men's fashions, which the stores in turn would sell to their customers.

The maiden issue was "relatively dignified." The cover was "staid," for *Esquire*'s cover trademark, the impudent, ribald Esky puppet, did not appear until the second issue. Furthermore, Nicholas Murray Butler [40] was represented in an "as told to" article. "*Esquire*," wrote its editors sedately for the debut, "is, as its name implies, a magazine for men. To analyze its name more closely, Esquire means, in the encyclopedia and dictionary sense, that class just below knighthood—the cream of that great middle class between the nobility and the peasantry. In a market sense, however, Esquire simply means Mister —the man of the middle class. Once it was the fashion to call him Babbitt, and to think of him as a wheelhorse, with no interests outside of business. That's very outmoded thinking, however. For today he represents the New Leisure Class. . . ." This idea of the New Leisure Class that had been brought into existence by the advent of the New Deal was the basis of a vague editorial policy for the first few issues. *Esquire* was supposed to supply that bewildered new class with the answer to the puzzling question: "What to do? What to eat, what to drink, what to wear, how to play, what to read—in short, a magazine dedicated to the improvement of a new leisure." Today, aside from aiming to present numerous big names in addition to the *Esquire* ladies, Esquire, Inc., disclaims any editorial policy. Smart says that the publication is "as useless as cigarets or liquor," which, he adds for the benefit of advertisers, people go right on buying anyway. The average reader of this luxury, the editors say, "is a very shaky bet to endow any universities, or to leave monuments behind him in the shape of any such good and lasting works. . . . Try as we may we have yet to find a subject which he considers sacred." Henry F. Pringle's comment in 1938 on the typical *Esquire* reader is that "he is a far cry from the devotee of the New Deal's New Leisure for whom, when it all began, the magazine was to be edited. He cares not a whit for better wages for the masses, better working conditions, or shorter hours. What he likes is the Old Leisure of 1929—and what he stands for is more mistresses and more champagne."

Esquire made money from the start. It was "an overnight hit," and with the second issue it became a monthly. According to *Time* Magazine, "publishers like it because it made the men's clothing industry 'ad' conscious; women like it for the effect it has on male dressing [moreover, advertisements are now being addressed to women readers]; advertising men like it because it is the United States male *Vogue*; and men like it because it is still the best smoking-room magazine in the land." Contrary to expectations of the prophets, the cost of publication was not prohibitive, and the advertising revenue was high. Editorial costs were low, for one thing. Smart could get his big names cheaply because in most cases there was no competition for the type of articles used. Smart was willing to publish "virtually anything" that well known authors offered, which most often meant things other publishers would turn down. (One famous article, "Latins Are Lousy Lovers," caused the magazine to be barred from Cuba.) Writers

were not forced to stick to formulas and could thus forget their inhibitions, as one explained: "Sometimes it's fun to let your hair down—slop over on the intellectual side, the bawdy, or what have you." The same was true of the cartoonists. Henry Pringle figured in 1938 that the editorial content cost Smart an average of $200 per article and that the cartoons ranged from $40 to $75 each.

Names of contributors to *Esquire*, as *Esquire* advertises, are eyecatchers. H. L. Mencken, Paul Gallico, Maurice Hindus, Ernest Hemingway, Stuart Cloete, Richard Aldington, John Dos Passos [40], Louis Paul (an *Esquire* "discovery"), the late William Lyon Phelps [43], Bennett Cerf [41], and Gilbert Seldes are only a few of the names which have appeared and reappeared in it. Pietro di Donato's *Christ in Concrete* first appeared as a short story in the magazine; a short story by Paul reprinted from the magazine won the O. Henry Memorial Award in 1934; and other authors' contributions have been included in the O'Brien collection of best short stories of the year. Artistic lures are Salvador Dali [40], George Hurrell, George Petty, and Alberto Varga. The resulting combination of "sex and erudition," as Henry Pringle remarks, "works out very well in the pages of *Esquire*." It is, he claims, "like Thomas Mann [42] [an article of whose was once used, through the courtesy of his agent], Hemingway, or Dos Passos reading from their works at a burlesque." "Subtlety or even variety are not of the essence of *Esquire*." There is a sameness about the cartoons and the written matter. There are also several regular departments appearing each month, concerned with books, the theatre, food, music, and clothes. And there is a great deal of advertising. (The circulation and advertising departments are the largest on the magazine's staff.)

Although *Esquire* editors have contended that it "is not a stag magazine devoted to smoking-car type of entertainment" (adding that "on the other hand . . . it is not edited . . . for the sense and sensibilities of the fourteen-year-old miss"), in September 1943 it was arraigned before a board of the United States Post Office Department to show cause why its second-class mailing privileges should not be revoked on the grounds of obscenity. During the subsequent hearings a lively "and sometimes amusing" discussion ensued as to whether the contents of the magazine were "obscene, lascivious, or even lewd," as the Post Office Department maintained. *Esquire* marshaled an imposing array of witnesses, including a neuropsychologist and the executive director of New England's Watch and Ward Society, "the watchdog of New England morals," to defend it. Despite their testimony, at the end of December Postmaster Frank C. Walker [40] overruled a two-to-one vote of his own judges in the magazine's favor to decide, "without ruling directly on the question of whether the magazine was obscene," that it failed to meet the statutory requirement of being "originated and published for the dissemination of information of a public character or devoted to literature, the sciences, arts, or some special industry" contributing to the public welfare and the public good. The revocation

SMART, DAVID A.—*Continued*

order, which, it was estimated, would cost Smart a half-million dollars a year, was to be effective February 28, 1944, unless the publisher was successful in obtaining an injunction.

The decision of Postmaster Walker, who had previously opposed a bill to bar anti-Semitic and fascist propaganda from the mails, stirred up a turmoil which even reached Congress. It was suggested by Senator Dennis Chavez that perhaps Congress should "make more specific the regulations under which publications can be thrown out of the mails." Smart himself was reported anxious to force the case into the Supreme Court "for a thorough clarification of the statute on second-class mailing rates," which was passed in 1879. Defenders of freedom of the press, too, saw in the Post Office ban the setting of an extremely dangerous precedent. The New York *Post* demanded the removal of Walker from his post because of his high-handed action. The American Civil Liberties Union was equally alarmed and indignant. And Dr. Daniel A. Poling '43, while making it clear that he did not endorse *Esquire*, declared that the ban was dangerous and outside the Bill of Rights. Another form of criticism came from the New York *Herald Tribune*, which remarked that "to bar *Esquire* for the reason given, while permitting floods of the most puerile and vapid stuff imaginable to fill our newsstands . . . is to indulge in an odd form of reasoning." Some *Esquire* supporters even seriously suggested that there might be a lowering of soldiers' morale if the Varga girl were removed from the mails. In June the American Newspaper Publishers Association filed a brief with the District of Columbia Federal Court, asking for a dismissal of the Postmaster's order of suspension of second-class mailing privilege. Following a ruling on July 15 by Justice T. Whitfield Davidson (of that court) which sustained Postmaster Walker's action, *Esquire*'s attorneys stated they would appeal.

Smart has also had business difficulties of quite another sort. In May 1941 a Chicago Federal Grand Jury indicted him, his brother Alfred, and ten others, including seven Wall Street brokers, for conspiracy to violate the Securities and Exchange Act of 1934 by artificially raising the price of stock in Esquire-Coronet, Inc. (now Esquire, Inc.) during a sales period. (During such a period the price must remain stable, according to the law.) A plea was entered of "accepting judgment without admitting guilt."

On the basis of this plea, in September 1941 the court fined Smart $10,000 and sentenced him to two years in prison. Eight other defendants were fined up to $10,000 each and given prison terms of from a year and a day to two years. All prison sentences were suspended on payment of the fines. A week before the verdict Esquire, Inc., announced a dividend of 30c a share. *Business Week* promptly pointed out that the Smarts, who still owned a majority of the stock, had to pay fines amounting to but 10c a share while receiving the dividends amounting to 30c.

Although Smart had decided by 1937 that the "publishing game . . . is a cinch," all of his publications have not hit the "jackpot" in quite the sense that *Apparel Arts* and *Esquire* did. In November 1936 Smart attempted to invade the territory of the *Reader's Digest* with his elaborate, pocket-sized *Coronet*. The magazine contains a wide assortment of art, fact, and fiction, but no advertising. Like *Esquire*, noted the *Literary Digest*, it "compensates in colorful, harum-scarum editing . . . and luck" for its "lack of caution and down-to-earth 'policies.'" Originally intended for non-*Esquire* minds, it used to carry a reproduction of an old masterpiece on its cover and several other reproductions inside. Recently this cover was changed—to a more conventional one—and the emphasis on classical art disappeared. In 1943 its circulation reportedly increased tremendously.

Two years after *Coronet*'s debut Smart tried competing in still another field: that of the news magazine—with pictures. The appearance of *Ken*, a bi-weekly, in April 1938 had been eagerly anticipated by liberals all over the country, for it had been heralded with much fanfare. In an article for the *Nation* that month, George Seldes '41 told "the inside story" of the magazine's birthpangs and early life. The idea for *Ken: The Insiders' World* originated with Smart, Gingrich, and Jay Cooke Allen '41 in the spring of 1937. They had seen the disillusionment of many Americans with the newspapers, and their magazine was to be for those who had lost faith in the integrity of the press. *Ken* was to be "one step left of center . . . antiwar and anti-fascist," and biased in favor of the awakening liberal-labor movement in America. Its staff was to be composed of left and liberal writers, headed by Cooke, with assistants such as John Spivak, Ernest Hemingway, and Paul de Kruif '42. Smart himself saw it as something like a cross between the *Nation* and *Life*—"liberal and lively, something for the millions, not highbrow . . . but popular [and] full of illustrations." A new corporation, Ken, Inc., was formed to keep the project separate from *Esquire* and its advertising.

But *Ken*'s career was brief and unprofitable. Almost at once it was in difficulties because of conflict between editorial policies and potential advertising, according to Seldes, and Smart was forced to make various changes in an effort to save the publication. *Ken*'s format was changed; it became a weekly; the price was reduced from 25c to 10c; and finally there came the demise of the publication, in August 1939, when the editors announced that they "had backed the wrong horse." Their deficit was $404,000.

Previous to his experiences with *Ken* and *Coronet*, Smart had ventured into the syndicate business, becoming interested two years after the advent of *Esquire* when he sold a fashion article to one hundred newspapers. An idea took shape which in July 1936 became Esquire Features, Inc. Among the types of material handled by the syndicate are humor and nature articles, cartoons, and women's and children's features. Still another Esquire, Inc., business deal was consummated when, in the summer of 1939, Smart bought for a reputed $11,000 the 80,000 circulation of *Scribner's Magazine*, which had suspended publication the preceding May.

In March 1944 Esquire published *Jazz Book*, edited by Paul Eduard Miller. The magazine also sold Petty and Varga calendars, booklets of reprints, and various items of the "pin-up" variety. Smart also sold the title "The Varga Girl" to movie producer Charles R. Rogers, and allowed "Varga Girls" to be used in the show *DuBarry Was a Lady*.

Esquire, Inc., in addition to handling its own publishing projects, is the American representative for the "artistic and literary" French quarterly *Verve*. The magazine, copies of which were translated into English for foreign readers, began its existence in December 1937, only to suspend publication in 1940. It was a sumptuous "collector's item" of articles, photographs, and careful reproductions of the works of famous artists; and it sold for $2.50 and $3.50 an issue. Some of *Verve*'s reproductions were said to be "among the best examples of craftsmanship in color plates that have yet appeared."

As president of Esquire, Inc., Smart works in a room which is said to resemble a Hollywood movie-set office. Smart himself is a "cinema-like" man, small, peppery, and alert, with wavy black hair and gray-green eyes. One interviewer described him as "fiercely erratic, 'lazy,'" yet a man who will work sixteen hours a day, often until three or four in the morning. "He dresses fastidiously, but not quite in the extreme manner of the *Esquire* fashion drawings." He is fond of fishing and, when enjoying the sport in his Florida retreat, thinks nothing of ripping apart at long distance a magazine make-up. In October 1942 Smart was married to the former Gaby Dure, fashion model and designer. Smart, through *Esquire*, contributed to the war effort in January 1944 when the magazine sponsored a jazz concert at the Metropolitan Opera House for the opening of the 4th War Loan Drive.

References

Lit Dig 123:20-1 F 6 '37 il
Scribner's 103:33-9+ Mr '38 il
Time 34:34 S 4 '39 por
Who's Who in America 1944-45

SMEDLEY, AGNES 1894- Author

Address: b. c/o Alfred A. Knopf, Inc., 501 Madison Ave., New York City

China has been described by John Chamberlain '40 as "a land of lurid contrasts, a land of 'squeeze' and bribery and war lords and political dictatorship on the one hand, and a faith and devoted courage and democratic feeling on the other." It is for this second China that American-born Agnes Smedley has expended the passionate sincerity and incisive vigor of her writing. Accused of partiality by an American military attaché, she retorted: "Of course, I am not impartial, and make no such pretense. Yet I do not lie, do not distort, do not misrepresent. I merely tell what I see with my own eyes and experi-

AGNES SMEDLEY

ence day by day." For twelve years Miss Smedley has lived among the Chinese—campaigning with the Red armies at the front (the only white woman to do so), traveling with guerrilla units, winning the friendship of peasants, mill laborers, students, Red Cross workers, Army generals.

Battle Hymn of China, published in September 1943, is in part autobiographical, an account of a Colorado girl whose sympathy with the underdog in Asia was first awakened by her contact with exiled Indian revolutionaries in New York and Berlin. Agnes Smedley was born in northern Missouri in 1894, the daughter of Charles H. and Sarah (Ralls) Smedley. Of her ancestry she writes: "One strain—my mother's—was of a hard-working, gentle, and devout folk. The other consisted of rebels, wanderers, tellers of tall tales, singers of songs. . . . The two family strains, meeting in me, made my spirit a battlefield across which a civil war raged endlessly." When she was a little girl the family moved to the Colorado mining country, "where Rockefeller's Colorado Fuel and Iron Company owned everything but the air." They lived a primitive, hardy life in the camps, "but I now understand that our intellectual poverty was far worse than our physical condition. . . . My father did unskilled labor and drank to forget his hopes, and my mother worked intermittently as a washerwoman and a keeper of boarders." Young Agnes became strong and self-reliant: "I fought boys with jimsom weeds and rocks, and nothing could make a little lady of me." None of the five Smedley children ever went to high school. Agnes acquired her education largely by her own reading. "I was in my early twenties before I learned who Shakespeare was, and in my forties before I read his plays."

When Miss Smedley was sixteen, her mother's death left her with the responsibility of taking care of the younger children and her older sister's baby. "Had I been

SMEDLEY, AGNES—*Continued*

more like my mother and less like my father, I would have accepted this burden as inevitable. But I resented my mother's suffering and refused to follow in her footsteps. . . . It seemed that men could go anywhere, do anything, discover new worlds, but that women could only trail behind or sit at home having babies. Such a fate I rejected. After making a few rudimentary arrangements for the care of my sister and baby nephew and leaving my small brothers to my father, I began a life of semi-vagabondage that was to last for years."

With the help of an aunt she learned stenography, but for some time took any job she could get—she was a waitress, tobacco-stripper, book agent. One year she spent as a special student in the Normal School at Tempe, Arizona. It was here that she met and married a young engineer. The marriage did not last long—"he soon divorced me"—but afterwards the couple became good friends. Comments Miss Smedley: "For women marriage is at best an economic investment; at its worst, a relic of human slavery. I have, however, heard of no society which has solved this problem."

In her early twenties Agnes Smedley left the Southwest for New York City. Here she worked during the day and in the evenings attended lectures at New York University, becoming greatly absorbed in the problems of India. In 1918, because of her work for the Indian revolutionary cause, she was "accused of aiding German espionage" (a German society had sent money to the Indian nationalists), arrested, and confined for some time in the Tombs, where she occupied her time by writing several short stories. Soon after the Armistice she was released. A year later she got a job as stewardess on a Polish-American freighter.

Once in Europe, she went directly to Berlin, where she met the young Indian revolutionary leader, Virendranath Chattopadhyaya. Although he was married to a Catholic who refused to divorce him, Miss Smedley was regarded as his wife during their association of some eight years. But "life with Viren had endless difficulties" that "drove me almost to the verge of insanity." With the rise of Hitler [42] he fled from Germany and sought refuge in Moscow. In Berlin, Miss Smedley had been teaching English to university students. She herself wanted to study for a Ph.D., but lacked the essential educational prerequisites.

In 1927 she wrote a semi-autobiographical novel, *Daughter of Earth,* "a desperate attempt to re-orient my life." Published in 1929, it described the life of Marie Rogers, who spent her childhood on a barren Wisconsin farm, "with a dissipated, half-Indian father, a weary drudge for a mother, and an ever-increasing brood of younger brothers and sisters." Of it one reviewer wrote: "It is impossible to regard this story as a novel. It is too bitterly, too passionately authentic. People cannot write with such intensity of things they have not intimately experienced."

Miss Smedley's career as a journalist began in 1928 when she became the correspondent of the Frankfurter *Zeitung* in China. The ap-

palling conditions of Chinese poverty and illiteracy immediately made a profound and indelible impression upon her. "Everywhere she went she witnessed the feudal contrasts of great families living on walled estates and the innumerable, omnipresent poor who begged on the outer side of the walls." The first account of these experiences appeared in 1933, in *Chinese Destinies.* While lauded as a book of "sheer and stark power", "accurate, absorbing, and of great political significance," some critics pointed out its Communist bias. Miss Smedley has explained, however, that she has never been a Communist. "For years I listened to Communists with sympathy, and in later years in China I gave them my active support. But I could never place my life and mind unquestionably at the disposal of their leaders."

While spending the year 1933 in the Soviet Union, Miss Smedley wrote her next book, *China's Red Army Marches* (1934). The story of the organization and growth of the Red Army—its struggles and campaigns between 1927 and 1931, its striking defense against the "merciless invasion by the Kuomintang armies" —was again eyewitness reporting, for Miss Smedley had traveled with that army and known its personnel. Said one reviewer: "It is a book which cannot be ignored. It is exciting, powerful in its sweep and challenging in its implications." Another wrote: "Though it is sometimes repetitious, is an important contribution to a subject about which very little has been known."

Of her third book, *China Fights Back* (1938), Lewis Gannett [41] said: "If you want the feeling of the war in China, not as it is fought on the spectacular fronts where the big guns thunder, but in the lonely mountains where small bands of men harrass the Japanese lines of communication, attacking, retreating, and preaching a gospel of a new China, you will find it in *China Fights Back.* This is the story of that 8th Route Army which . . . in the 'long march' around the fringes of China performed a modern military miracle." Either walking or riding horseback, or—with her back badly sprained —traveling in a stretcher, Miss Smedley lived the life of that army, saw the floods and famine of the land through which it passed. Those months were the happiest days of her life, she has said; "with that ragged army Agnes Smedley had found a democratic satisfaction which she had not felt in the backwoods of Missouri, in the coal fields of Colorado, or in the cosmopolitan city of Shanghai. . . . Of such stuff, in all ages, martyrs have been made. Martyrs can never have been comfortable people to have around the house. But they have made history and literature."

Battle Hymn of China, the November 1943 selection of the Book Find Club, is the full record of her years in China, from 1929 to 1941. Again she writes of the blood, sweat, and tears of the common man, in whose resurgence she sees China's only hope of salvation. Of her underlying attitude John Chamberlain has written: "In her passionate concern for the underdog everywhere, Miss Smedley is often guilty of thinking that middle-class origins and interests are *ipso facto* proof that one is a potential Fascist, or at least a hypocrite . . . that only a rarefied diabolism could have ever countenanced selling oil to Japan, and she would snort if you argued that Cordell Hull's [40] motive in permitting the sales was to delay the Japanese attack on Borneo and Sumatra." Miss Smedley makes it clear that she likes neither Chiang Kai-shek [40] nor the Kuomintang, which she fears as a "reactionary" clique. But because of its "forthrightness, its compassion, its significant love and understanding," the book won high praise from other reviewers, including Ralph Bates, Malcolm Cowley, Leo Kennedy, and Mark Gayn. And, as if in answer to Chamberlain, Colonel Evans F. Carlson [43] wrote: "Because of addiction to sugar-coated literature there will be many who will not like Agnes Smedley's *Battle Hymn of China*, for Miss Smedley does not pull her punches, nor does she insult the spade by attempting to disguise it as a heart. In common with our soldiers at the front she has lived in close proximity to suffering and death, and like them she sees life in terms of black or white, good or bad. It is odd, extremely odd, what a power for good the presence of death can be. In its presence man returns to fundamental honesty and to truth."

From 1938 to 1941 Miss Smedley worked as publicist and field worker for the Chinese Red Cross Medical Corps. Late in December 1941 she returned to the United States to recuperate from several attacks of malaria and other illnesses she had contracted in China's interior. In subsequent interviews she described, among other things, the "educational revolution" in China, in which schools traveling with the armies teach thousands of illiterate soldiers to read and write, and through impromptu lectures explain the history of China and why China is fighting. In a radio program, *Author Meets Critic* (November 1943), she emphasized the fact that the United States and Great Britain are largely responsible for the backward conditions in China today, because of their imperialistic foreign policies.

In the winter of 1944, Miss Smedley is working on a play about China; she also has in mind a "revolutionary novel" on the same theme. In her lectures and radio appearances she is busy carrying out her primary aim—to enlighten America on the plight of the Chinese. Writing a series of articles for *PM*, (October and November of 1944) Miss Smedley interpreted the current crisis in China. National unity, she said, could only be accomplished by lifting the four-year-old blockade (imposed by the powerful men surrounding Chiang Kai-shek) against the Chinese Communist 18th Group and the new 4th Armies.

Apart from her writing, farming is Miss Smedley's chief recreation. On a recent vacation in upstate New York, she worked on a farm, tending chickens and packing eggs. "She would rather see a good play than eat and, while food does not interest her, she loves coffee, and missed it terribly in China." Literature on the Far East, the work of Chaucer, and the notebooks of Da Vinci are her favorite reading. Jawaharlal Nehru [41] is her political and intellectual idol; she considers his autobiography, *Toward Freedom* (1941), one of the great books of our times.

References

N Y Herald Tribune p17 S 7 '43 por; p23 O 27 '43
N Y Post p40 S 8 '43 il pors
N Y Times p15 S 18 '43 por
Sat R Lit 26:22 S 18 '43
Kunitz, S. J. and Haycraft, H. eds. Twentieth Century Authors 1942
Smedley, A. Battle Hymn of China 1943

SMETONA, ANTANAS (smet'tô-nä' än-tä'näs) 1874(?)—Jan. 9, 1944 President-in-Exile of Lithuania; a former editor, he became a leader in the movement for Lithuanian independence from Russia before the First World War; head of National Party; First President of the Lithuanian State Council and of Lithuanian Republic (1920-21); re-elected in 1926; held office until Russian occupation in June 1940.

Obituary

N Y Times p1+ Ja 10 '44 por

SMITH, ALFRED E(MANUEL) Dec. 30, 1873—Oct. 5, 1944 Former Governor of New York State

Bulletin: Alfred E. Smith died on October 5, 1944

From September 1944 issue:

The story of Alfred E. Smith is that of "a plain man" who, as he writes in his autobiography, "received during his lifetime, to the fullest possible extent, the benefit of the free institutions of his country." It is also the story of a man who rose from New York's East Side to within reach of his country's highest office, only to be defeated by politically manipulated religious and social prejudices that seemingly belied the benefit of those free institutions. A Democratic Governor who had been called "the hope of liberalism in America," following that Presidential defeat, Smith retired to private life, became the affluent president of the Empire State Building corporation, and bolted his party to support Republican Presidential candidates.

Alfred Emanuel Smith was born at 174 South Street, New York City, on December 30, 1873, the son of Catholic parents, Alfred Emanuel and Catherine (Mulvehill) Smith. His mother was of sound Irish stock, intelligent and hard-working; his father, a fun-loving, good-natured truckman. When the father died the mother took a job as umbrella-maker, then ran a small candy-and-grocery store in order that her son and daughter might "grow up respectably." Thanks to her, Alfred was able "to sift out the East Side's pure gold and walk jauntily amid its vice and crime." The busy East River wharves, where clipper ships docked, provided activity and amusement. His gymnasium was the bowsprit and rigging of ships, his swimming pool was the river, and his pets were the gifts of sailors: "For a time I had a West Indian goat, four dogs, a parrot, and a monkey all living in peace and harmony in the garret of the South Street house." The building of the Brooklyn Bridge was probably the most absorb-

ALFRED E. SMITH

ing interest of his early years—"The bridge and I grew up together," Smith says.

Young Alfred (he was not called "Al" in those days) went to the neighborhood parochial school, sold newspapers after school, and waited at the counter in his mother's store in the evening until bedtime. Neighborhood life centered around St. James's Church, where he served as an altar boy. His earliest ambition was to be a fireman, and at fifteen he became a volunteer member of the neighborhood fire company. At that age he was in the eighth grade, not a very good student, and he therefore did not mind leaving school to take a job as an errand boy at $3 a week. In 1892 he got a better job—at the Fulton Fish Market, working for $12 a week from 4:00 in the morning till 4:00 in the afternoon. Al Smith's years in the fish market "loom as large in his public career as the cherry tree in Washington's, the log cabin in Lincoln's." At the market he picked up some of the similes he was later to use in speeches ("a man with an eye like a dead cod" is one example) and he liked to remark that he had only one degree: F.F.M. (Fulton Fish Market).

At about that time the young man became active in a group of amateur actors known as the St. James Players. The Players reproduced some of New York's current plays, in which, Smith says, he played a variety of roles, most often that of the villain. Menacing roles apparently did not detract from his popularity for his natural friendliness and gift for ready speech made him well regarded in the neighborhood. This easy manner with people, and the poise and the flair for acting that his little-theatre experiences developed, also made him a natural choice for political office. In the year 1895 he was appointed to his first public office—to the post of clerk in the office of the Commissioner of Jurors. Tom Foley, Tammany boss of the Dover Street district had already singled him

out and was to become his mentor during his early political career.

Smith was an active member of Tammany when, in 1900, he was married to Catherine (Katie) A. Dunn of The Bronx. While Mrs. Smith was self-effacing in Smith's political life, as a devoted wife and mother she was all-important to him in his rise to eminence. When Mrs. Smith died in May 1944 Archbishop Spellman [40] said a Requiem High Mass for her in St. Patrick's Cathedral, which was attended by 16,000 people. Journalists recalled her lifelong devotion to her husband, mentioning as particularly touching the games of cards the husband and wife played every night. Five children were born to the Smiths: Alfred E. Jr., Emily (Mrs. J. A. Warner), Catherine (Mrs. Francis Quillinan), Arthur, and Walter.

In 1903 Smith, with the help of Tom Foley, was nominated for the New York State Assembly. During his first sessions at the assembly he followed Foley's advice: "Don't speak until you have something to say. . . . Never promise anything that you are not perfectly sure you can deliver." Smith quietly observed proceedings and studied hard. It is said that he was the only member of the assembly ever to read the appropriations bills from beginning to end. "By 1907 I had so well established myself," Smith says, "that renominations came practically as a matter of course." A few years later, according to Henry F. Pringle, "he was a cocksure, hard-boiled, practical politician." In 1911 he became majority leader, and in 1913 speaker of the assembly. "He was wagged by Tammany," observed R. L. Duffus, "till he got to the point where he could and did wag Tammany." An indication of his interest in social legislation was seen in 1911 following the catastrophic Triangle Waist Company fire, in which 148 women lost their lives because of the non-enforcement of fire laws in factories. Robert Wagner [41] became chairman, and Smith vice-chairman, of the commission formed to investigate conditions in factories of the state; as a result of their efforts, New York wrote on its statute books what is generally held to be the most enlightened labor code in the country.

Smith served as a member of the State Constitutional Convention in 1913, his efforts being directed toward making the constitution "an instrument of social liberalism." In 1915 his election as sheriff of New York County was backed by the Citizens' Union and organized labor. That office, which paid fees of from $50,000 to $60,000 annually, was a boon to a man with a large family. In 1917 Smith became president of the Board of Aldermen of Greater New York, and by 1918, a commentator at the state convention said, it was clear that the Democrats had nobody to compare with Smith, "who stood on his record and his personality." After a close contest Smith won the election, and his forty-fifth birthday was celebrated by the Smith family in the Executive Mansion in Albany. He had only one ambition, he said then: "to make good for the state of New York." He described the people with whom he surrounded himself as being "of all political faiths as well as of no political faith." They were associates from Tammany Hall, social reformers, and intellectuals.

Notable among these people was Belle Moskowitz. Although her name is seldom mentioned in *Up to Now* (1929), Smith's autobiography, and not at all in *Up From the City Streets* (1927), the book on Smith written by her husband, Henry Moskowitz, and Norman Hapgood, it has been said by Henry F. Pringle that "the story of Smith cannot be told without telling the story of Belle Moskowitz." Having had considerable experience in social reform before becoming Smith's "councilor extraordinary," throughout all his terms as Governor she well earned the title of "the Colonel House of the Smith Administration." Her advice on countless matters he valued, it has been said, above that of all other persons, and she taught him that "loyalty to the state and to himself was a better thing than loyalty to Tammany." She was secretary of his Reconstruction Commission and during his campaign for President she was director of his publicity. After his defeat she became president of Publicity Associates, continuing to serve Smith in private life as she had during his public career. At her death in January 1933 the ex-Governor said: "She had the greatest brain of anybody I ever knew." In an observation on Smith's apparent reversal of his previous liberal social outlook after 1934, Dorothy Dunbar Bromley has remarked: "It is quite possible that if Mrs. Moskowitz were living today, his public utterances would reflect a sounder judgment."

During his first term as Governor, Smith's measures were impeded by a Republican majority. But the complete victory he won over William Randolph Hearst marked a high point in his political career. In 1917 the Republican state administration had placed regulatory control of the state milk supply in the hands of a board responsible only to the lawmakers. As Governor, Smith could do nothing but urge action against this milk trust, but Hearst's newspapers attacked Smith by saying he was in league with the milk trust and that he ignored "pleading mothers and starving children." Incensed, Smith challenged the publisher to a debate at Carnegie Hall in 1919, a challenge Hearst did not accept. Smith delivered such an effective speech that an organized committee urged that public opinion be directed against "the insidious and disintegrating opinions" of the journals owned by Hearst. From that time Smith never ceased to express his scorn of Hearst: in 1922 he balked Tammany by refusing to be considered as a running mate with Hearst on the Democratic ticket—and it was Hearst who withdrew. "It was Alfred E. Smith's greatest victory. . . . From this struggle he rose, figuratively speaking, to discard the brown derby. He was ready to go back to Albany with obligations to no one."

When Smith was defeated in his candidacy for Governor in 1920 by the favorite of big-business Republicans, Nathan L. Miller, he served two years as chairman of the United States Trucking Corporation. When he again ran against Miller in 1922 he won by an unprecedented majority of 385,932, considered the largest plurality ever given any candidate for governor in the history of the United States. It was during his successive years as Governor, from 1923 to 1928, that Smith accomplished his most important work. According to Hapgood and Moskowitz, he "demanded that the state be looked upon as an instrument for the service of the people and that economy be measured not by the amount of money spent, but by the amount obtained for the people in return." Said Smith: "My advocacy of the four great bond issues for state hospitals, public works improvements, grade crossing elimination, and public parks gave my enemies an opportunity to call me 'Smith the Spender.'" He succeeded in liberalizing the labor law and the Workman's Compensation Act; he fought hard for the forty-eight-hour bill for women and children, but strong opposition by the manufacturers' lobby caused its defeat. He vetoed bills seeking "loyalty tests" for teachers and the licensing of private schools, calling them "an unwarranted interference with freedom of opinion." He secured salary increases for teachers and increased appropriations for rural schools. A special session of the legislature which he called passed a housing relief law in 1926. It was a compromise, but he felt it was "a beginning of a lasting movement to wipe out . . . those old, dilapidated, dark, unsanitary, unsafe tenement houses unfit for human habitation."

Smith's governorship was noteworthy for other measures. One of his most important services was to take state highways out of the hands of politicians. He also established a Department of Public Works (1925); but his fight to keep the hands of the "power barons" off the state's water-power resources and to create a state agency was branded as socialistic, and it failed. Democratic job-seekers were angry when he went outside the party to make appointments (one was the selection of a Farmer-Labor man to the post of state architect). He won liberal admiration when he vetoed the Lusk bills, by which the Republican legislature had undertaken to deprive five Socialist Assemblymen from New York City of their seats. Smith's statement at that time was: "Although I am unalterably opposed to the fundamental principles of the Socialist Party, it is inconceivable that a minority party duly constituted and legally organized should be deprived of its right to expression. . . . Our faith in American democracy is confirmed not only by its results, but by its methods and organs of free expression."

One of Smith's hardest tasks as Governor was having to see death sentences carried out. He thought that the power of the Governor to pardon in capital cases should be taken away, and he favored less severe sentences and more psychiatric study of criminals. He felt, too, that the attitude of the state should not be one of seeking vengeance. Notable were his pardons in 1922 of Jim Larkin and in 1925 of Benjamin Gitlow who had been convicted under the criminal anarchy statute.

At the Democratic convention of 1924, Smith's name had been put up for nomination for President by Franklin D. Roosevelt, who was to become Governor of New York five years later. Roosevelt's words on that occasion were: "On our Governor for over twenty years the white light of publicity has pitilessly beaten, and revealed only spotless integrity. . . . He has won not only the undivided support of his own party but the public endorsement of great civic non-partisan bodies of the city and state." Smith's

SMITH, ALFRED E.—*Continued*

strength at that convention came from the big cities, but the Middle West, the Far West, and the South, the "dry" states, repudiated him. (He had become known as an aggressive champion of the "Wets" when he induced the New York Legislature to adopt a 2.75 beer bill as a test of the Volstead Act and sponsored a repeal of the state enforcement law.) But after Davis won the 1924 nomination Smith felt convinced that what really had prevented his nomination was his religion.

Smith won the nomination in 1928 only to be defeated in his race for the Presidency, according to some opinions, by the three P's: Prohibition, Prejudice, and Prosperity—and the greatest of these was the second. In 1927 discussion of his religion as a barrier to the office had already begun. The *Atlantic Monthly,* for example, published a long article by a Episcopalian lawyer, Charles C. Marshall, challenging Smith on the grounds that his religious faith and patriotism did not mix; Smith's reply, called the high point among all his public papers, ended with: "I recognize no power in the institutions of my Church to interfere with the operations of the Constitution of the United States or the enforcement of the law of the land. I believe in absolute freedom of conscience for all men and in equality of all churches, all sects, and all beliefs before the law as a matter of right and not as a matter of favor. . . . And I believe in the common brotherhood of man under the common fatherhood of God." Thereafter the charge of "Catholic" was not made openly during the campaign—Smith's enemies concentrated mainly on the Prohibition and Tammany issues.

Al Smith's East Side background and political beginnings were not in his favor, even though liberal supporters wrote enthusiastically of him—"an heroic figure, embodying in his person and spirit the deep aspirations of the people", "the first man of the new immigration who is completely available as a candidate for President." Although Smith was frequently compared to Abraham Lincoln and Andrew Jackson, villagers and farmers regarded him as a product of the "corrupt" city slums and as carrying the stigma of Tammany. Many women, it was said, refused to vote for him because his wife had once done all her own housework. Smith's diction also was against him: in spite of the best efforts of Mrs. Moskowitz and others to "refine" it, the accent and idioms of the East Side cropped out. Heywood Broun said that millions were induced to vote against him because he called the radio "raddio." Nonetheless, as the "Happy Warrior" Smith put up a good fight. He toured the country, making innumerable speeches from notes jotted on the backs of envelopes. The radio, too, made his personality and voice known.

Following his defeat by Herbert Hoover [43] in 1928 Smith retired to private life. Becoming president of the corporation controlling the Empire State Building, he received an annual salary of $50,000. Smith was on his way toward wealth. But like the men of wealth who became his associates (John Raskob, William Kenny, etc.), Smith was hard hit by the depression. The man who had been a Lower East Side boy now sat in the half-rented Empire State Building and watched the limelight swing to a man from the banks of the Hudson, from a family of impeccable background and social status. And, though that man had once been among the former Governor's best friends and supporters, it was only natural, many thought, that a "corroding bitterness" toward Franklin D. Roosevelt should grow in Smith's mind. It is said that many of his wealthy friends ("Smith is peculiarly a creature of friendships") fed that bitterness. Smith gave Roosevelt belated support in the 1932 campaign; but the change in his viewpoint could be seen in April 1932 when he said at a Jefferson Day dinner: "I will take off my coat and fight to the end any candidate who persists in any demagogic appeal to the masses of the working people of the country to destroy themselves by setting class against class and rich against the poor." He objected to the "soak-the-rich" policy, argued in favor of a general sales tax, complained about the taxes on his fifteen-room Fifth Avenue penthouse. He became one of the founders of the American Liberty League; and in 1933 he defended big business against the N.R.A. In the *New Outlook* (of which he was editor from 1932 to 1934) he extolled private initiative; and in November 1933 he wrote in that periodical: "After careful, and I may say almost prayerful, consideration of the arguments for and against the Child Labor Amendment, I wish to be recorded in the negative." At this time, too, he said, "the forgotten man is a myth."

Although Dorothy Bromley observed that a psychoanalyst might say Smith's change could be traced to "an unconscious desire to strike at Roosevelt," others felt that the real Smith was just emerging. Pringle in his book had pointed out that Smith was "not an outstanding liberal, but a conservative with a liberal mind." It was in 1936 that Smith turned completely against Roosevelt, saying in a speech that his fellow countrymen "would have to choose between Washington and Moscow; between the 'Star Spangled Banner' and the 'Internationale.' " He said the party had "walked away from the Democrats," and that therefore he himself was "taking a walk."

In 1940, announcing that he was an anti-third-term, Jeffersonian Democrat, Smith "took another walk" to support Wendell Willkie [40]. The next year Smith characterized a rumored regulation of life insurance companies by the Federal Government as a plan "imported directly from Russia." (Critics pointed out that Smith's connection with an insurance company might have been a reason for his feeling.) Smith also urged the medical profession to organize as a pressure group in order to combat the coming New Deal "socialist" program of public health insurance. In a radio address in May he approved a Presidential statement for the first time, Roosevelt's statement being "we will not participate in foreign wars and we will not send our armies, naval, or air forces to fight in foreign lands." After Pearl Harbor, Smith continued to defend Roosevelt's foreign policy (while still vigorously attacking domestic issues), and newspapers reported a reconciliation between the two men.

However, when Smith was invited to be a delegate to the 1944 Democratic National Convention he said: "No, I couldn't go. I feel, somehow, that I'd be as welcome as an electric razor at a barber's convention." While he did not make public whether or not he would vote for Roosevelt, he was one of a number of important public figures who signed an appeal for a "clean" campaign, a plea addressed to candidates and voters "to discourage the injection of religious and racial animosities into the current campaign."

In recent years Smith has devoted much time to the fund-raising campaigns of numerous organizations, among them the Catholic Charities, the USO, and the American Red Cross. He was appointed a member of the national advisory committee of the Johns Hopkins Institute of Law, and in 1944 he was chairman of the New York City Committee for Economic Development. In September 1944 his name was on the list of incorporators of the Health Insurance Plan of Greater New York, which will operate a comprehensive plan of medical and surgical care for all persons living or working in the city and earning not more than $5,000 annually. The former Governor has been honored by the leading universities of the country: He received the LL.D. degree from Columbia, Fordham, Harvard, University of the State of New York, Manhattan College, as well as from Dublin University; the Catholic University of America awarded him an honorary D.Litt; and the University of Notre Dame awarded him the Laetare Medal in 1929.

In his seventieth year Al Smith continued to use his eloquence to never-failing effect in War Loan drives. On that birthday he received a letter of blessing from the Pope, and a warm birthday greeting from President Roosevelt. When admirers proposed that he become the candidate for the United States Senate if his old friend Robert Wagner declined, Smith refused, saying it would be impossible for him to live on the salary of a Senator because of his financial responsibilities.

Alfred Smith is of medium height—"a stocky man, yet never pudgy." In 1928 William Allen White [40] described him: "He is smooth-shaven, oval-faced, mean-jawed, with a pugnacious set to his head, which wags with fine self-assertion." In 1943, his seventieth year, he was, "physically, the same Al Smith, ruddy and with one of his traditional cigars in the side of his mouth."

References

Broun, H. Collected Edition of Heywood Broun p270-3; p298-300; p347-9 1941
Hapgood, N. and Moskowitz, H. Up From the City Streets 1927
Lippmann, W. Men of Destiny p1-9 1927
Pringle, H. F. Alfred E. Smith 1927
Smith, A. E. Up to Now 1929
White, W. A. Masks in a Pageant p463-79 1928
Who's Who in America 1944-45

SMITH, (SIR) C(HARLES) AUBREY
July 21, 1863- Stage and motion-picture actor
Address: h. 2881 Coldwater Canyon, Beverly Hills, Calif.

Some of the most effective promotion of Anglo-American friendship has been done by British actors who, in the course of their daily work, have kept before the American public a sympathetic picture of the British. One of the most effective of these actors has been C. Aubrey Smith, whose "towering form and jutty eyebrows" are familiar to all movie-goers and remembered by old-time lovers of the theatre. His services to the Empire have been officially recognized by his creation as a Knight Bachelor; and audiences have been so thoroughly trained by his roles that when the Allies were suffering reverses in the Orient in the early part of the Second World War, "thousands of movie fans undoubtedly felt that the British Government would do well to put him in a field marshal's regalia and ship him off to India to get that tangle straightened out."

Charles Aubrey Smith was born in London on July 21, 1863, the son of Dr. Charles John Smith, a surgeon, and Sarah Ann (Clode) Smith, of Brighton. After preparing at Charterhouse, he attended Cambridge University, where he took up dramatics casually and cricket seriously. His unusual style of bowling—Americans would call it pitching—caused him, it is said, to be nicknamed "Round Corner." But it did not prevent him from making a great reputation as a cricket player. After his graduation from Cambridge in 1884, Smith became captain of the Sussex team, and later led English teams in Australia and South Africa. No matter where his travels have taken him since, the actor's admirers claim that in sixty years he has never missed his weekly game of cricket.

The future Sir Aubrey made his first appearance on the professional stage in 1892, when he was twenty-nine, as a member of A. B. Tapping's seaside stock company in Hastings. Here he played in *The Idler, Jim the Penman*, and *Not Such a Fool as He Looks*, and then went on tour in *Bootles' Baby* and *The Love Chase*. In 1894 he toured in the male lead of Pinero's *The Second Mrs. Tanqueray*, and in March 1895 Smith made his London debut as the Reverend Amos Winterfield in *The Notorious Mrs. Ebbsmith*. He toured with various companies for another year, reaching the United States with Sir John Hare. Perhaps the most noteworthy of these roles was that of the villainous Black Michael in *The Prisoner of Zenda*, which he played with Sir George Alexander's company in 1896. That August the thirty-three-year-old actor was married to Isabel Mary Wood. (He and Lady Smith have one daughter, Honor Beryl Clode, now Mrs. Robert Cobb.)

C. Aubrey Smith's first professional Shakespearian appearance was as another usurper, Duke Frederick, in a production of *As You Like It* which opened in London in December 1896. The following March he began a long series of military roles—for which his stern face, impressive figure, and military bearing made him a director's dream—by playing Lieutenant Colonel Arthur Eave in *The Princess and the Butterfly*. It was a series interrupted briefly, however, when, after an appearance at the beginning of 1898 as Cyril Charteris in

C. AUBREY SMITH

The Happy Life, Smith left the stage—but not the theatre—to become business manager of the St. James playhouse in London.

On Smith's return to his stage military career in 1900 he was demoted to major for *The Ambassador;* since then, he has played three stage colonels (in *Alice Sit-by-the-Fire* [1905]; *The Green Cord* [1922]; and *Posessions* [1925]), and a general (in *Paddy the Next Best Thing* [1929]), as well as enough movie senior officers to staff a medium-sized army. Not all the sixty-odd stage roles to his credit since the beginning of the twentieth century were military or menacing, however. They include one duke, two lords (Darlington in *Lady Windermere's Fan* [1904], and Emsworth in *The Best People* [1910]), one marquis, two "Honourables," two M.P.'s, and ten assorted knights and baronets. In 1903 he played opposite the legendary Mrs. Patrick Campbell in *The Second Mrs. Tanqueray* and later in *Warp and Woof.* One of Smith's best roles was that of Torpenhow, the war correspondent and friend of the hero of *The Light That Failed,* in which he toured the United States in 1903 and 1904. Three years later he returned to America and scored a great success in the title role of *The Morals of Marcus.* Smith again crossed the ocean in 1909 for an American tour, and in 1911 to support Billie Burke in *The Runaway.* In 1913 he resumed the part of Torpenhow for Forbes-Robertson's farewell revival of *The Light That Failed.*

Two roles later, in the fall of 1914, the English actor was again in New York to play in *Evidence.* That December he took the part of Noll Dibdin in *The Lie* and toured in it during 1915. This was made into a silent film in New York, and was followed by three others, including Daniel Frohman's *Builder of Bridges.* At that time an actor of the legitimate stage was reluctant to admit that he had worked in the "flickers," so data on C. Aubrey Smith's early film career are scanty.

When the tour on which Smith was engaged in 1916 ended, the fifty-three-year-old actor re-turned to England to be available if called for military service. Meanwhile he was engaged in the pacific activity of playing the title role in *Daddy Long-Legs,* for which his six feet four inches fitted him admirably. Some of the more notable of Smith's endless succession of parts were Professor Henry Higgins in Shaw's '44 *Pygmalion* (1920), Gray Meredith in *A Bill of Divorcement* (1921), and George Marden in A. A. Milne's *Mr. Pim Passes By* (1922). In 1923 the star was back in New York for *Mary, Mary, Quite Contrary;* and the following year he combined managing with acting at the Comedy in London. Three years later Smith took part in another memorable performance in New York, playing opposite Ethel Barrymore '41 in Somerset Maugham's *The Constant Wife.*

In February 1928 the veteran actor began his role as the gruff but sentimental Sir Basil Winterton in Edward Childs Carpenter's *The Bachelor Father.* Although some reviewers found the play, which dealt with the efforts of a former rake to "gather under one roof his varied brood," unworthy of its players' efforts, they praised "the sure skill and admirable propriety of taste and wit that he [C. Aubrey Smith] always brings to his comedy playing, and that is a lesson to our younger actors." *The Bachelor Father,* a great success, ran for a year in New York, was brought to London in 1929, and was made into a "talkie" in 1930. In addition to the title-roleist, the picture cast included Marion Davies and Doris Lloyd.

This was the beginning of a new career for its sixty-eight-year-old star, for C. Aubrey Smith soon became a familiar name to moviegoers. On the stage he had been leading man for England's and America's greatest actresses, but Hollywood found in him a character actor, one of those dependable veterans used constantly in supporting roles with featured billing. In 1933 "C. Aubrey Smith" appeared on cast listings in Paramount's *Luxury Liner* (starring George Brent, Frank Morgan, and Zita Johann), Fox's *Adorable* (Janet Gaynor), United Artists' *Secrets* (Mary Pickford-Leslie Howard), Metro-Goldwyn-Mayer's *The Barbarian* (Myrna Loy-Ramon Navarro) and *Bombshell* (Jean Harlow-Lee Tracy). In addition to these bright screen luminaries, he also supported two rising youngsters named Katharine Hepburn '42 and Douglas Fairbanks, Jr., '41 in RKO's *Morning Glory.*

Producers evidently agreed with studio press agents that the tall British actor was "a personality who epitomized the grace and charm of yesterday's school of manners," for they proceeded to cast him in a series of important costume pictures. From Claudette Colbert's *Cleopatra* (Paramount, 1934) through Garbo's *Queen Christina* (MGM, 1934) and Dietrich's *Scarlet Empress* (Paramount, 1934) to Ronald Colman's '43 regal *Prisoner of Zenda* (UA, 1937), few royal courts were complete without C. Aubrey Smith somewhere in the offing. *The Crusades* (Paramount, 1935) required his attention, as did *Lloyds of London* (20th Century-Fox, 1936), which introduced Tyrone Power as the male lead, *The House of Rothschild* (UA, 1934), *Clive of India* (UA, 1935), *Dr. Jekyll and Mr. Hyde* (MGM, 1942), and *Madame Curie* (MGM, 1943). And when in 1936 MGM produced *Romeo and Juliet*, with Leslie Howard and Norma Shearer in the title roles, Smith was garbed in "marvelous" robes for the part of Juliet's father, which he "endowed with his proper distinction."

In between Smith played a series of brisk Britishers with assorted titles, uniforms, and/or hearts of gold in such Anglophilia as Paramount's outstanding *Lives of a Bengal Lancer* (1935), UA's *Little Lord Fauntleroy* (1936), 20th Century-Fox's *Wee Willie Winkie* (1937) and *Four Men and a Prayer* (1938), Universal's *The Sun Never Sets* (1939), RKO's *Forever and a Day* (1943), and MGM's *The White Cliffs of Dover* (1944), as well as the British-made *Sixty Glorious Years* (Imperator-RKO, 1943) and *The Four Feathers* (London Film-UA, 1939). Although Smith's film career has been confined almost exclusively to "A" pictures—large-budget productions of the leading studios—not all his vehicles have been pretentious. In addition to aiding most of the reigning glamour boys and girls, he has supported the casual Bing Crosby '41 (in Universal's *East Side of Heaven*, 1939) and such youngsters as Gloria Jean, Fred—then Freddie—Bartholomew, Mickey Rooney '42, and Judy Garland '41, and has "lent his always welcome note of mellowness" to such light comedies as MGM's *Maisie Was a Lady* (1941) and Andrew Stone's *Sensations of 1945*. Once, for *The Adventures of Mark Twain* (WB, 1944), Smith had to recreate an incident he had witnessed thirty-seven years earlier: the presentation of an honorary degree to Samuel Clemens by the vice-chancellor of Oxford University.

In the winter of 1941-1942 C. Aubrey Smith returned to the stage with Grace George in the Isabel Leighton-Bertram Bloch *Spring Again*, "a vehicle which though mild was at least merry." During the run of this play Smith celebrated the fiftieth anniversary of his first professional performance. "People will think I must have to be wheeled on the stage in an invalid's chair," remarked the seventy-nine-year-old actor. "As a matter of fact I never felt better." Reviewers concluded that "winter has never caught up with Miss Grace George and Mr. C. Aubrey Smith who are now the center of a comedy which would be negligible were it not for the skill of these two prime favorites. It's a long time since the stage has been dignified by the presence of Mr. Smith who, eschewing the many titles that have been his on the screen, is now modestly appearing as the son of a very famous Civil War general whose reflection of glory is the son's whole career." *Spring Again* ran throughout the season, closing when Smith was recalled to Hollywood.

When, after Pearl Harbor, the United States Government asked the people to grow as much food as they could, Smith plowed up his beloved private bowling green and planted Golden Bantam corn. While a confirmed gardener, he also undertook to raise "two goats, twenty rabbits, a dozen chickens, one sow, and three piglets" at his home, The Round Corner, which perches above a canyon in Beverly Hills. In June 1944 King George VI '42 of Great Britain conferred knighthood upon the eighty-one-year-old actor, who had been created a Commander of the British Empire six years earlier. It

was then recalled that Smith had headed the appeal for a memorial to the late King George V and had worked so enthusiastically to establish the game of cricket in California that a cricket-pitch in Griffith Park in Los Angeles had been named for him.

The new Sir Aubrey, who supposed that he'd have to drop the "C." from his name, indignantly denied any intention of retiring from the screen. Nor did he plan to cut down on his three hours daily of reading or the painting, sculpturing, gardening, dancing, and cricket with which he fills the intervals between transferring his familiar blue-eyed twinkle and glare to film. He is said also to be an excellent musician and to have set Kipling's *Barrack Room Ballads* to music. Unlike most actors, he arises at six even when not working on a picture, using the time since the War began to write to some of the twenty servicemen overseas with whom he corresponds. In the evenings Sir Aubrey may perhaps be found at the Hollywood Canteen, telling some of the stories he has gathered in half a century of acting.

References

N Y Sun p6 Je 10 '44
International Motion Picture Almanac 1943-44
Who's Who 1944
Who's Who in the Theatre 1939

SMITH, LILLIAN (EUGENIA) 1897-
Author; editor; social worker
Address: b. c/o South Today, Clayton, Ga.; h. Clayton, Ga.

"Segregation, 'White Supremacy,' the Negroes' Place are not words to me, nor theories," writes Lillian Smith, author of the 1944 novel *Strange Fruit*, "but a way of life, a tragic way which I, and others like me, white and Negro, have lived since birth." "The relationship of the two races," she explains in *Common Ground* (Autumn 1943), "has become so intertwined with hate and love and fear and guilt and poverty and greed, with churches and lynchings, with attraction and repulsion that it has taken on the ambivalent qualities, the subtle conflicts of a terrible and terrifying illness." The author of this sensitive novel on Negro-white relations in the Deep South sees that her Southern white neighbors, by their pattern of living, have stunted their emotional growth and shut themselves off from the creative and human in life; the warped, distorted frame they have forced around the Negroes they have placed around themselves as well. The Negro's humiliation is matched, she explains, by the dull complacency of the white; fear is matched by arrogance; hate by the cruel cheapening of human worth; ignorance by willful hypocrisy and blindness to honest thinking; and the Negro's hurt is equaled by the aching conflict in the white man's soul between his conscience and the culture to which he has been bred since birth. "This deep inner conflict," says Miss Smith, "this wearing fear of bringing disaster to the innocent is the price we pay for being human in the Deep South." Comparatively few Southerners hate Negroes, she believes, but they act as they do out of great fear. "We do evil things, or countenance

LILLIAN SMITH

them through fear of what others will say, fear of being ostracized, fear of losing a job."

In a searching resumé of her background and that of her eight brothers and sisters, which she wrote for *Common Ground*, Miss Smith traces a pattern which is a familiar one to many Southerners. Jasper, Florida, where she was born in 1897, had a population about equally white and Negro. Her ancestors were among the earliest settlers in the state. Her father, who made money purely for the excitement of it, for several decades was a planter and owned and managed lumber mills and turpentine stills that employed hundreds of whites and Negroes. At one time he also owned water and electric utilities, an ice plant, and a large mercantile firm. He paid his employees "the prevailing low wages and worked them the prevailing long hours"; he built mill towns, churches, and commissaries where the usual high prices were charged. At the same time he was an influential and respected civic leader in church, educational, and town government organizations.

Lillian Smith was raised in a home where tolerance, courtesy, and democracy were emphasized. But, she continues, the mother "who taught me what I know of tenderness and love and compassion taught me also the bleak ritual of keeping the Negro in his place. The father who rebuked me for an air of superiority toward schoolmates from the mill settlement and rounded out his rebuke by gravely reminding me that 'all men are brothers' also taught me the steel-like, inhuman decorums I must demand of every colored male. . . . I do not remember how or when but I know that by the time I had learned that God is love, that Jesus is His Son, that all men are brothers with a common father, I also knew that I was better than a Negro, that all black folks have their place and must be kept in it, and that a terrifying disaster would befall the South if ever I treated a Negro as my social equal. I had learned that God so loved the

world that He gave His only begotten Son that we might have segregated churches in which it was my duty to worship every Sunday and on Wednesday at evening prayers. I learned that white Southern people are a hospitable, courteous, tactful, and warmhearted people who treat those of their own color with consideration and as carefully observe Jim-Crow customs, segregating from all the richness of life—'for their own good and welfare'—thirteen million people whose skin is colored a little differently from my own."

There were other things the small child learned, too: that one shook hands with old Negro friends; that "nigger" was an unpardonable word, as was "mister" in addressing a Negro; that one gave presents to this black man instead of love and esteem; and—one of the hardest things to comprehend—that it wasn't wrong to "cheapen with tears and sentimental talk of 'my old mammy' one of the profound and tender relationships" of her life. It was an upbringing that showed Lillian it was possible to be "a Southerner and Christian simultaneously; to be a gentlewoman and an arrogant and callous creature in the same moment; to believe in freedom, to glow when the word is used, and to practice slavery from morning to night." Gradually as she grew older, however, the sensitive girl discovered "somehow, somewhere", "in heart and imagination, what it means to be rejected by one's fellowmen."

One of the contributing factors to this discovery, she writes in *Common Ground*, developed within her own family while she was still very young. A small waif, apparently white, had been found taking refuge in a Negro home in Lillian's town. The child, a girl, was taken into the Smith household to share Lillian's room and clothes and affection until indignant whites could find a suitable place for her. Lillian became very fond of Julie; and then one bleak day it was discovered that Julie was black. The imposter was immediately hustled away, and the little white child was left behind to wonder. "You liked Julie," she pleaded with her mother; "you said she had nice manners. And she's the same little girl she was yesterday." But Mrs. Smith would only answer that Lillian was too young to understand. Lillian may indeed have been too young, but she was not too young to feel the pain of separation nor to begin to doubt for the first time her parents' words and the sincerity of their religion. Unconsciously, perhaps, she was identifying herself with Julie's shame and bewilderment. She was still too young to completely understand her emotions, but she "felt a profound reluctance ever again to accept something" simply because it was told her by her elders.

Another thing in which Lillian and her brothers and sisters were trained was the realization that each must have a profession of use to the world. Above an interest in books, music, and art was emphasized the need for planning "to do something" with their lives. In pursuit of a useful profession, therefore, Lillian went first to Piedmont College in Georgia; then, being particularly interested in the piano, she studied for four years at the Peabody Conservatory in Baltimore. At the end of that period she went for a year to Columbia

University. Then, about 1921, she went to Huchow, China, to teach music in a Methodist mission school. In China she saw again a pattern familiar to her: white people imposing their social code on an "inferior" race, this time the yellow one. It was one more example for her of how people could talk about love and Christianity without meaning what they said.

On her return to the United States at the time of her father's death in 1924, Lillian Smith started the fashionable Laurel Falls Girls' Camp at her parents' home in Clayton. With her close friend and associate, Paula Snelling, she has directed ever since this successful summer camp (which takes white girls from six to sixteen). The work has been another one of the contributing factors which have directed her interest into the field of race relations. In observing the effects the inherited pattern of race prejudice was having on the girls, she came to realize that the price the South has paid in blighted emotional growth is too high for another generation to pay. White and Negro alike, she declares firmly, must be allowed to grow up to full emotional maturity. "Self-esteem, human prestige, willingness to share are as important to personality growth as vitamins are to physical growth." Miss Smith does not hate the South, nor does she wish to hurt anyone by her writings. Her wish is that they will shake the South out of its complacency and blindness and cause it to change its "hating suicidal ways into creative cooperative ways of living."

The essence of what Miss Smith believes about her South and the trouble which it faces is found in her first novel, *Strange Fruit* (1944). (Originally this book was to have been called *Jordan Is So Chilly*.) Reception of the book has been excellent and has included favorable comment from educators, sociologists, and clergymen as well as from the nation's reviewers. (Sales at the end of the first month were over 35,000.) Southerners, too, despite the nature of the theme, have acclaimed Miss Smith's story of the tragic outcome of the love of a white man and a Negro girl in the Deep South. Thousands of Southerners—many of them women—have begged Miss Smith to continue her work in race relations. People in the North, the author says, do not know how conscientious many Southern women are. For a decade, she explains, churchwomen in the South have been trying to do away with segregation in their churches, showing far more courage than the ministers. Prominent Southern women, Miss Smith goes on to say, have worked against injustice to the Negro, although having been endoctrinated with the theory of States' rights, they have unfortunately not yet demanded Federal legislation to right the wrongs.

In the North reviews revealed that critics were deeply moved not only by Miss Smith's daring in overriding the Southern convention of silence but by the significance, tender understanding, and tremendous emotional impact of her book. "It is a passionate novel," wrote one critic, "about two decent people impossibly in love" in a small town where such a love is considered indecent. Told in outline, commented Florence Haxton Bullock, the story

would seem to be no different from one by Faulkner or Erskine Caldwell [40]. The difference is in Miss Smith's approach. In the foreground of her story she continually holds up the psychology of the Southern Negro who is taught by his parents the black's law of survival in the South: servility to his white overlord. She offers no solution to the sorrowful problem of "love-across-the-color-line," Miss Bullock continues, "but for that sense of inferiority that is beaten into the colored South regardless of individual talent or character she has no sympathy." With genuine compassion, wrote William Du Bois [40], she shows both Negroes and whites caught in an economic, ethnic, and emotional web that "only evolution can untangle or revolution break." Her characters she has made "deep and terrifyingly human." "It is a regional novel in the finest sense," adds Du Bois. "It offers a magnificently detailed picture of the small-town South, lashed by an urge for self-destruction as old as time. The author has suggested no cure for that urge: you will find no black messiahs here, no white devils. But the tragedy of the South is explicit in every line. It should be required reading in every deanery, every parsonage, and every legislature on both sides of the Mason-Dixon Line." There has never been a more truthful picture of the Southern Negro's desperate plight, said Richard Wright [40], Negro author of *Native Son* (1940).

As the publisher, Reynal & Hitchcock, had predicted, *Strange Fruit* has been "eagerly read and heatedly discussed." One of the most vehement of the debates has been in Massachusetts. At the end of March the Boston Board of Retail Book Merchants ordered the removal of the book from local bookstores following a protest of obscenity made by Boston Police Commissioner Thomas F. Sullivan. Reportedly it was not Sullivan's own complaint but that of a Boston resident, for whom he had complained to a clerk in a store that was a member of the Board. It was explained by Sullivan, *PM* reported, that the book was not formally "banned," but that there existed a "gentlemen's agreement" whereby any suggestion from him, the district attorney, or "somebody else" was usually complied with by the Board. A similar ban eventually extended throughout almost all of Massachusetts.

Individuals and organizations protested, of course. ("The immorality referred to in *Strange Fruit*," explained a Massachusetts minister, "is the result of an evil situation. A careful reading of the book might well stimulate changes [in the South] which would reduce the real causes.") And Miss Smith and her publishers announced that no effort would be made to tamper with the book to please official tastes. Finally in Cambridge, where the chief of police had formally banned the novel, an effort was made to test the legality of the ban. Bernard De Voto [43], the author, and Abraham Isenstadt, a bookseller, collaborated in the sale of the book to De Voto after the police had been advised in advance. (Isenstadt was defended by an attorney for the Massachusetts branch of the Civil Liberties Union.) In April the court

SMITH, LILLIAN—*Continued*

ruled the book "obscene, impure, and indecent," although the judge added that it contained a story "that might well be told." The case against De Voto was dismissed. Isenstadt was fined $200. When the fine was upheld by the Cambridge court, the bookseller's counsel stated that an appeal would be taken to the State Supreme Court.

The Massachusetts Library Association submitted a bill to the state legislature in an effort to correct the present Boston methods of prosecuting booksellers who displease the Watch and Ward Society. The proposed bill would "transfer obscene book complaints from the criminal to the civil courts, calling for court action against the book itself rather than against a bookseller." Booksellers in Detroit fared better than their Boston fellow tradesmen. The fact that the Detroit Public Library insisted on keeping *Strange Fruit* in circulation made it possible for booksellers there to maintain a firm stand against efforts to ban the book. In New York, the publishers of the book were notified by the Post Office Department that the book would be barred from the mails, only to be informed a few hours later that the book could be mailed, at the risk of prosecution, however.

Meanwhile, the sales of the book continued to mount through the remainder of 1944, as many as 15,000 copies being sold in one week. By the end of the year Miss Smith's work had reached its fifteenth printing, a total of approximately 475,000 copies. Meanwhile, too, Miss Smith, who was actively pro-Roosevelt in the Presidential campaign, was appearing at important radio and platform forums and writing for magazines and newspapers. She was also at work on a dramatization of her book for presentation on Broadway.

In 1936 Miss Smith and her friend Paula Snelling started a literary quarterly called *Pseudopodia* (the "extra" foot of an amoeba). The following year the magazine became the *North Georgia Review* and changed its emphasis from purely literary matters to social and political trends in the South. In 1942 the magazine again changed its name, this time to *South Today*. Today this magazine, according to *Common Ground*, is "one of the most forward-looking of Southern publications", "a dynamic and increasingly influential forum," says Alfred Deutsch, "for the frank discussion of regional, economic, social, and racial problems." By 1943 its circulation had increased to 5,000, from the 200 subscribers of 1936. To keep herself abreast of Southern thought, Miss Smith tours the South each year. (Her traveling has not been limited to the South, either. She has traveled widely in the United States and Canada and she spent one year in Brazil.) In addition to editing, Miss Smith lectures frequently. Recognized as an authority on children, she often speaks before parent-teachers' and women's groups in the South.

In 1943 she won a place on the 1942 Honor Roll of Race Relations, a nationwide poll conducted yearly by the Schomburg Collection of Negro Literature of the New York Public Library. "It determines the twelve Negroes (individuals, organizations, or institutions) who have most distinguished themselves during the year and the six white persons (also individuals, organizations, or institutions) who have done the most for the improvement of race relations." Miss Smith's citation said that, as editor of the *South Today,* she "has maintained a consistent liberalism in a land where it takes courage to be liberal." Miss Smith is on the board of directors of the Southern Conference for Human Welfare.

Lillian Smith, says Dorothy Dunbar Bromley, "does not look like a woman who leads a movement. Slight and soft-spoken, she has in her face the tranquillity of spirit which comes from listening to the pines on the mountain top," Old Screamer, "where she lives and has deep roots in the soil and the community. There is nothing of the righteous reformer about her, nothing of the exhibitionist who takes pleasure in shocking." She dresses smartly, has gray hair, "rich blue eyes, and an extremely sensitive face." She declares she is a good cook, particularly fond of Georgia coast dishes. Her extravagances—dictated by her mood of the moment—are clothes, records, and early American furniture. Her more serious interests are writing, books, music, modern dance, children, psychoanalysis, China, folk cultures, Southern people, and gardening. She also enjoys the theatre—she crams in all the plays she can during her yearly visit to New York City—and she is interested in the motion picture as an art form. Lillian Smith talks about human problems, says Albert Deutsch, "with quiet conviction and impressive clarity, exhibiting always a deep understanding of human beings and an abiding faith in their ultimate goodness." Two other books of hers may see early publication. They are a book of nonfiction and, possibly, "a leisurely chronicle," "The Harris Children," which she says she has been writing more or less all her life.

References

Common Ground 4:47-52 Autumn '43
N Y Herald Tribune p13 F 29 '44 por;
   IV p9 Mr 12 '44
N Y Post Mag p33 Mr 17 '44 por
PM Mag p11 Mr 5 '44 por; p10 Mr 13
   '44

SMITH, WALTER BEDELL (bē̄d'l) Oct. 5, 1895- United States Army officer

Address: b. c/o War Department, Washington, D.C.; h. 4314 36th St., Washington, D.C.

One of the most important and difficult posts in the Allied armies is filled by one of the least publicized generals: Lieutenant General Walter Bedell Smith, chief of staff of the Allied and American Expeditionary Forces for the invasion of northwestern Europe. Chiefs of staff do not usually make headlines; they make plans. Churchill[42] calls Bedell Smith "Bulldog"; *Time* calls him "perhaps the hardest-working officer in the United States Army"; and General Eisenhower[42] calls him "one of the great chiefs of staff of all time."

"The infinitude of detail" involved in planning military operations, according to Major George Fielding Eliot[40], "can hardly be grasped by the lay mind." These details are the responsibility of the chief of staff, among whose duties is that of keeping the commander informed of "the enemy situation and of the situation of the command as to location, strength, morale, training, equipment, supply, and general effectiveness." When the commander makes his decisions, on the basis of the information assembled and presented to him, it is up to the chief of staff to turn those decisions into action—to make all supplementary decisions, issue all necessary orders and instructions, assign and supervise the detail work, and coordinate the whole into a completed over-all plan, which is submitted to the commander for approval. In general the chief of staff directs and coordinates the work of the five staff departments—personnel, military intelligence, operations and training, supply, and the new Civil Affairs Section, G-5 —"in all their relations with the special staff, with the troops, and with each other." In addition, as the *Staff Officers' Field Manual* conservatively puts it, he "makes a continuous study of the situation with a view to being prepared for future contingencies."

Walter Bedell Smith, General Eisenhower's staff chief, was born in Indianapolis, Indiana, October 5, 1895, the son of William L. Smith of that city. Unlike most high-ranking officers, he never attended the Military Academy, nor did he rise through the non-commissioned ranks of the Regular Army. An infantry reserve officer in the First World War, after high school and work he won his commission at the Officers' Training Camp, Fort Benjamin Harrison, Indiana, which he attended from August 26 to November 27, 1917. On the completion of his three months' training the new 2nd Lieutenant was assigned to the 39th Infantry, 4th Division, at Camp Greene, North Carolina. On April 20, 1918 the division embarked for France, where Smith served four months.

As Bedell Smith was about to get on the ship, his German grandfather gave him a word of advice. The old man, who had fought in the Franco-Prussian War, was reportedly somewhat confused about the later conflict, for his words were "Just remember the French Army has never been able to withstand the onslaught of the Prussian cavalry." Without disabusing his grandfather, the young Lieutenant proceeded to fight with the French at Château-Thierry and in the third battle of the Marne. He was wounded by shrapnel and, with the entire "Ivy Division," received a unit citation for gallantry.

At the end of that time he returned to the United States for duty in Washington with the War Department's Bureau of Military Intelligence, and on September 30, 1918 he was promoted to 1st lieutenant. After a period in Washington, Smith went to Camp Sherman, Ohio, as intelligence officer and adjutant of the 379th Infantry. In February 1919 he was assigned to the 163rd Depot Brigade at Camp Dodge, Iowa, and in March to the 2nd Infantry.

The Hoosier Lieutenant must have made a brilliant record, for at the expiration of his temporary commission he was appointed a 1st lieutenant of infantry in the Regular Army (July 1, 1920). This was decidedly unusual, as reserve officers remaining in the Army after the War were ordinarily required

U. S. Army Signal Corps
LT. GEN. WALTER BEDELL SMITH

to accept demotions. Smith, however, remained with the 2nd Infantry until October 16, 1922, when he was assigned to the 6th Corps Area (headquarters at Chicago), later returning to Fort Sheridan, Illinois, as aide to General George Van Horn Moseley. The Lieutenant's next assignment was as adjutant of the 12th Infantry Brigade at Fort Sheridan. This post he held until April 25, 1925, when he was ordered to Washington as assistant to the chief coordinator, Bureau of the Budget. (In July 1917 Walter Bedell Smith had married the "tall, tweedy, charming" Mary Eleanor Cline, daughter of an Indianapolis real estate broker.) Promotions came very slowly in those days, particularly in the lower ranks of officers, and many first lieutenants had to wait a long time for advancement.

Four years later the Lieutenant was sent to the Philippine Islands to serve with the 45th Infantry at Fort William McKinley. While there, he was made a captain on September 24, 1929. Returning to the United States in March 1931, Captain Smith was assigned to study at the Infantry School, Fort Benning, Georgia. (Between wars, says *Life*, Smith "devoured war classics, studied and worked hard to make up for lack of West Point or college training.") Having completed the advanced course (June 1, 1932), he remained there as an instructor in weapons until August 1933. After two years of study at the Command and General Staff School (Fort Leavenworth, Kansas) the thirty-eight-year-old Captain returned to the Infantry School for another year of teaching. He then entered the Army War College in Washington, the most advanced training school in the United States Army, from which he was graduated June 23, 1937. He returned to the Infantry School faculty and at the beginning of 1939 was promoted to the rank of major.

In October of that year Major Smith was appointed to the War Department General Staff in Washington as assistant secretary.

SMITH, WALTER BEDELL—*Continued*
There, on April 18, 1941, he received the
temporary rank of lieutenant colonel, which
was made permanent seventeen days later.
Less than two months after that Smith was
promoted to colonel (temporary). He held
this rank at the beginning of September,
when appointed full secretary of the General
Staff, a position he occupied for five months.
On February 2, 1942 the Colonel became a
brigadier general (temporary); and eight
days later he was appointed United States
secretary of the Combined Chiefs of Staff,
with additional duty as secretary of the Joint
Board. In the former capacity he "had the
job of selling the United States plans to the
Combined Chiefs of Staff, principally to the
British. . . . Those who worked with General Smith during the spring of 1942 in Washington say he did a magnificent job of salesmanship as well as of organization. In spite
of his habit of speaking his mind in no uncertain terms, he displayed remarkable diplomatic skill" during those trying days of building up Allied cooperation, and was "one of
the best-known and best-liked Army figures in
Washington."

The following September the forty-seven-
year-old General was made chief of staff in
the European theatre of operations with
headquarters in England, while preparations
for the North African campaign were being
made. When General Eisenhower moved on
to the Mediterranean area, Smith followed
as his chief of staff. The official announcement was made November 20, 1942, and was
soon followed by Smith's promotion to major
general (temporary). In his work as chief
of staff Smith aroused the admiration of
other armies as well as of the United States
War Department. The famous French colonial cavalry known as the 2nd Spahis inducted
him as an honorary private first class. As
Time of May 31, 1943 described the scene:
"Hard-bitten French professionals, returned
to honor and glory in Tunisia, had seen no
finer staff officer than Major General Walter
B. Smith, Eisenhower's chief of staff. . . .
General de Goutel laid the colonial cavalry
regiment's scarlet *burnous* [an ankle-length
cape] on 'Beedle' Smith's shoulders and pinned the outfit's medal badge on his olive
drab blouse."

In July 1943 the General was awarded a
Distinguished Service Medal for his work as
first secretary of the United States Joint
Chiefs of Staff, with a citation praising his
"initiative, foresight, tact, and administrative
ability of a high degree, as well as superior
judgment." In lieu of a second D.S.M.,
Smith also received a bronze Oak Leaf
Cluster for the "great courage, tact, resolution, and sound judgment" he had displayed
as chief of staff of the Allied force headquarters.

General Smith's analysis of the Sicilian
campaign, in an August 15, 1943 interview,
was the first disclosure that the Allied invaders had been outnumbered by one-third
at the outset. "The measures taken to achieve
surprise," he pointed out, "must be utterly
fantastic in some instances, but the results
were worthwhile, for . . . even if strategic
surprise is impossible, there is always the

chance of achieving tactical surprise." To
do so requires the most complete information
and the most thoroughly worked-out plans
possible; certainly Smith himself was partly
responsible for the Allied success in this campaign. On September 3, 1943 he had the
pleasure of signing the Italian surrender
agreement, General Castellano representing
Italy—under an appropriate olive tree. The
Allied emissaries, Generals Smith and K. W.
D. Strong, had had to choose among the three
rival official Italian armistice commissions, sent
respectively by Premier Badoglio '40, the Ministry of Foreign Affairs, and the Italian Supreme Command.

When General Eisenhower was chosen by
the Combined Allied Chiefs of Staff as supreme commander of the northwestern Europe expeditionary forces, it was presumed
that he would retain Smith as his chief of
staff. On January 9 this was officially announced, and on the 23rd the General was
also named chief of staff of United States
forces in the European Theatre of Operations
(ETOUSA). (He was replaced in the Mediterranean area by Lieutenant General James
A. H. Gammell, former general officer of
the Eastern command of the United Kingdom.) This was just two days after Smith's
promotion to the temporary rank of lieutenant general. In permanent rank, however, he
was still a lieutenant colonel, for his promotion to brigadier general, asked by the President the preceding October, was among those
held up because of the appearance of General
Patton's '43 name on the executive calendar
of nominations for that day. If the promotion had failed to go through and Smith reverted to the rank of lieutenant colonel after
the War, he would have been able to draw
what satisfaction he could from styling himself
"Lieutenant Colonel Sir Walter Bedell
Smith"—in January 1944, King George VI '42
of England created him Knight Commander
of the Order of the Bath, the highest honor
awarded any of the thirty-one American soldiers decorated after the Allied landings in
North Africa. Tunisia made him a Grand
Officer of Nishan Iftikar, Morocco made him
a Grand Officer of Alouite, and the French
made him a Commander of the Légion d'Honneur.

When a definitive history of the invasion of
Europe can be written, to quote Charles Christian Wertenbaker, "it will be discovered that
General Smith was the man who saw it most
clearly, from its inception." Bedell Smith
(whose Wac secretary had a hard time preventing the British from hyphenating those
names and alphabetizing the General under *B*)
forgot his desire for a field command in the
absorption of working out the greatest military operation in history. "The problem was
so complex that only a trained military mind
could grasp it. Geography complicated the four
traditional essentials: mission, means, enemy,
terrain. New equipment had to be designed,
tested, produced, issued. Men had to be specially trained in amphibious operations. Air,
sea, and ground forces had to be coordinated
in a way never seen before in history. Weather,
tides, and the moon had to be just right. . . .
Meanwhile the enemy was also making preparations, which had to be anticipated or spied out,

then countered. This called for more training, more weapons." When Eisenhower wanted to know anything, it was up to Smith to give the answer. And when the troops were committed to the battle, the SHAEF staff was already working far ahead on plans for the next phase, as always.

Life gives this description of the General: He "looks like a bulldog, both in legs and face. . . . His eyes are brown, intelligent, hard. His manner is straightforward to the point of brusqueness; he never wastes a word. Yet there is no discourtesy about him. Although his job does not bring him into much contact with correspondents, he has a strong belief in the public's right to correct information and will take time and trouble to give it," though not personally desirous of publicity. The peacetime Walter Bedell Smith is "a gregarious, friendly individual with an immense personality," who loves dogs and horses and the Red Radiance roses he grows in his garden. The General is described as an excellent bridge and chess player and "a handy man to have around the house."

References

Life 10:94 Je 12 '44 pors
N Y Sun p14 F 21 '44
Who's Who in America 1944-45

SMYTH, DAME ETHEL MARY Apr. 23, 1858—May 8, 1944 British composer, author, journalist, suffragette; her *March of the Women* was the battle song of the suffragist movement; of her numerous compositions, the opera *Der Wald* and the Mass in D won wide recognition; author of many books, one of which, *As Time Went On* (1935), received high critical praise.

Obituary

N Y Times p19 My 10 '44 por

SOUTHWORTH, BILLY Mar. 9, 1893- Baseball club manager

Address: b. c/o St. Louis National League Baseball Club, St. Louis, Mo.; h. Sunbury, Ohio

William H. "Billy the Kid" Southworth, manager of the World Series-winning St. Louis Cardinals, first entered baseball against his father's wishes. One of seven children of Scotch, Irish, and English ancestry, he was born to Mr. and Mrs. Orlando Phelps Southworth on March 9, 1893, at Harvard, Nebraska. When Billy was nine, the Southworths moved to Columbus, Ohio, where he entered the Avondale School—and interscholastic baseball, as catcher, pitcher, or third baseman. The boy took his playing so seriously, in fact, that he ripped open the cellar floor to make a practice sliding pit. Orlando Southworth disapproved vigorously, as became a blacksmith, and continued to disapprove as his Billy moved on to catch for the West High School team. He greeted with no pleasure the prospect of his youngest son's becoming a professional ballplayer: "I don't want none of that baseball money around this house!" he roared. "Stop knocking those fool balls around!"

But young Southworth continued to knock those balls around, and at eighteen he reported

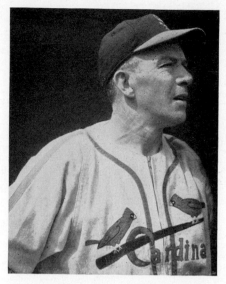

BILLY SOUTHWORTH

for a tryout by the Portsmouth Club of the Ohio State League. He was a catcher; but the only position open was right field, and there were five other candidates for that. Southworth got it, and remained an outfielder throughout his playing career. During the 1912 season he batted .278 (he bats left-handed, throws right) and fielded .947. After 77 games in 1913, during which he ran up averages of .306 and .927, the little outfielder was taken over by the Toledo Club, American Association; and after 37 games for them he was called to the major league Cleveland Indians (American League). The Indians' manager, Joe Birmingham, took a dislike to Southworth, refused to let him practice, and sent him into only one game, customary before firing a ballplayer. Southworth got a base on balls. Back he went to the American Association for two more years of seasoning. In 1915 Southworth's batting average had gone up to .336 when the Indians recalled him to play in 60 of their games. Then off he went to the Portland (Oregon) Pacific Coast League Club for his final 25 games of the season. He played all the next season with Portland, but the following year found him with the Birmingham Club of the Southern Association. (Somewhere around this time Southworth married a hometown girl, Lida Ruth Brale: they had a son, William, Jr., a major in the U.S.A.A.F. in the Second World War.)

In 1918 Billy Southworth started moving around some more. Starting with Birmingham, he was called to Pittsburgh by the National League Pirates. They put him into 64 games that first season, and he batted .341 and fielded .980. Next year he batted .280, fielded .968, and tied with Rogers Hornsby for leadership of the National League in making triples (three-base hits) with fourteen. In 1920 Southworth led all outfielders in fielding with .991; he was batting .284 that season. Before the 1921 season began, however, he was traded to the Boston Braves (National League), along with an infielder and another outfielder plus

SOUTHWORTH, BILLY—*Continued*
$15,000, for shortstop Walter (Rabbit) Maranville.

According to Burt Whitman, a Boston sportswriter, "Bill was one of the best. . . . We always bracketed him with Harry Hooper as the greatest of all Boston right fielders. When you needed a whale of a catch, Southworth would make it for you." In spite of a knee injury he batted .307, .322, and .319 during his stay in Boston, and fielded .975, .955, and .943. At the end of the 1923 season Southworth was again traded to John J. McGraw's New York Giants (National League) along with a pitcher, for a shortstop and two outfielders. (One of those outfielders was Casey Stengel, later manager of the Boston Braves.) This put the Ohioan on a pennant-winning team which won again that year after a bitter three-cornered fight with Brooklyn and Pittsburgh. During the season Southworth, a "brilliant, erratic, and unlucky player," batted .256 and fielded .935. He played in five of the seven 1924 World Series games against the Washington Senators, made no hits, but fielded perfectly (1.000). As a member of the losing team Southworth received $3,820.29 as his share of the receipts of $1,093,104.00.

Next year Billy Southworth's record was .292 and .964. In June 1926, when the season was a month old, McGraw gave up trying to turn Billy into a center fielder. He was traded again, this time with the St. Louis Cardinals for another outfielder, Clarence Mueller. This deal put Southworth on "a razzle-dazzle gang of guileful gaffers" whom Rogers Hornsby was shepherding to the first St. Louis National League pennant. Southworth's .320 batting and .970 fielding helped, and it was Billy the Kid himself whose home run against the Giants clinched the flag for Hornsby. And in the "dramatic rip-snorting" post-season World Series against Miller Huggins' New York Yankees which smashed all records for attendance and receipts, he played all seven games, hit a 407-foot home run, batted an average .345 and fielded 1.000. As a member of the winning team, Southworth received $5,584.51 for the Series.

In 1927 Southworth batted .301 and fielded .970 for St. Louis; but a recurrence of an ankle injury from his Cleveland days put him out of the line-up for a time. After that Branch Rickey, the Cardinals' vice-president and dictator of their chain of ball clubs, offered Southworth the management of their Rochester "farm" club (International League).

He accepted, and proceeded to win the 1928 International League pennant. The new manager was aided considerably by the fact that "the line-up was packed with Paul Derringers, Pepper Martins, and Tex Carletons on their way up to the big leagues, and with [other stars] . . . on their way down." Nor did Billy content himself with masterminding; in 1928 he played in 124 games, batting .361 and fielding .980. Meanwhile the Cardinals had won the league pennant, and had gone on to lose the World Series to the Yankees four games straight. Sam Breadon, the president, demoted the Cardinals' manager, Bill McKechnie, and sent for Southworth to replace him. When spring training began in 1929, Billy laid down the law to his old teammates. But players like the great Grover Cleveland Alex-

ander, Chick Hafey, Frankie Frisch (later to be manager of the Cardinals and of the Pittsburgh Pirates), Andy High, and Jimmy Wilson were antagonized by Southworth's methods. His attempts to discipline them won him the name of Billy the Heel, and in July Southworth was sent back to Rochester, where he won the next three pennants in succession.

In spite of his minor league victories, Southworth seemed to be embittered by his major league disappointments, for he lost interest and made enemies. In the middle of the 1932 season the Cardinals' "front office" transferred the player-manager from Rochester to the "bedraggled" Columbus Club (American Association) of their chain. Young Billy, Jr., welcomed the change—Pop would be home now; but Pop knew that he was being eased out. During that season Mrs. Southworth became fatally ill, and Billy, distracted by worry, lost his chance to straighten himself out. At the end of the season he was dropped entirely from the Cardinal chain.

The little ex-manager was given a job as third-string coach of the New York Giants by his old friend and ex-roommate, Bill Terry, in 1933. But this lasted no longer than a spring training trip to Galveston, Texas. Both he and Terry have repeatedly denied that Southworth gave his then boss the black eye he wore when Southworth made his abrupt departure. Anyhow, Billy went home to Columbus and his first non-baseball job.

It was far from easy to find work in those depression days, but the forty-one-year-old ball player was given a position selling cottonseed oil for a Columbus distributor. He became friendly with an attractive bookkeeper at the office, Mabel Stemen, and on January 7, 1934, they were married. Southworth became a teetotaler. For a year he worked at pulling himself together, and at teaching his tall young son, then a student at the University of Ohio, the baseball lore of his twenty years on the diamond. Then, in 1935, Branch Rickey offered Billy the management of the lowest Cardinal training camp—officially the Asheville (North Carolina) Club of the Piedmont League. And Southworth made a success of it. The technique he had used to teach young Billy worked on the Cardinals' rawest recruits. "He was the sort of guy," says Stanley Frank, "who went to the station early in the morning to meet a kid fresh out of the deep brush, then put him up at his home until the bewildered kid was at ease in his new surroundings." Southworth still regards the team he built up there as his greatest triumph. (That year, too, Mrs. Southworth bore him a daughter, Carole.)

In 1936 Southworth was promoted to management of the Memphis Chicks (Southern Association), and made "a fine record on the field and off. By 1937," says Charles Dexter, "he'd evolved into a successful baseball business man." He developed and sold a number of good players, and "the Chick's profits touched $100,000." As a reward, Southworth was promoted to the management of the Rochester Red Wings, which he had lost seven years earlier, in 1939—the year in which his son was voted the most valuable player in the Canadian-American League.

Meanwhile, Breadon had sold most of the Cardinals' baseball talent, including such stars as Joe (Ducky Wucky) Medwick, Curt Davis, and Mickey Owen, for $368,500. In June 1940 the remaining Cardinals were running last in the pennant race; so Breadon fired their manager, Ray Blades, and gave his job to Billy Southworth. The current quip was "Breadon's run out of new managers—he's starting all over again," and there was loud speculation about which of Southworth's predecessors would succeed him, and when. To everyone's amazement, Billy took the Cardinal remnants and whipped up a team which ran close on the heels of the star-studded Brooklyn Dodgers and ended the season in the first division, behind the Cincinnati Reds and the Brooklyn team.

The next year Southworth had a chance to train his team according to his own ideas. Emphasis was on the rookies, whose special problems were too often neglected under ordinary circumstances. The little manager had worked out a training chart system, "the most unusual split-second schedule anybody had ever heard of on a baseball field" to eliminate wasted time and motion and to insure adequate practice for each man. Billy not only made certain that the recruit got his full chance at the plate, but he installed an automatic pitching machine for anyone who wanted extra batting practice. He saw to it that the players got the benefit of the experience of veterans, such as catcher Gus Mancuso and pitcher Lon Warneke, and that the greenest rookie's stupid questions got serious and adequate answers. "Bill's the most considerate manager I ever worked for," Lon Warneke told a writer. "He never second-guesses you. And I never saw any manager in my life who could build up what you-all call morale like this guy does." For instance, he held sliding practice only at the end of a workout, just before the players changed their clothes. Southworth instituted a rule that no player would ever go to the front office without his permission, thus protecting his authority against the divisive influence of the players' former close relationship with Branch Rickey.

Apart from this, however, Billy formulated only those rules that had the players' approval, and sometimes liberalized their own decisions. He welcomed suggestions from anyone, and he put the team idea above all else, even turning down the services of a star, Bobo Newsom, in 1942, because the individualistic veteran "just wasn't our type," Bill said. "All we've got and all we want is a team that has youth and speed [Said Casey Stengel: If you can make a Redbird slide, you've won a moral victory] and no solo ambitions." But the Southworth system did bring out some new stars, among them Terry Moore and Enos (Country) Slaughter, "the best outfielders in the league"; a dazzling shortstop, Martin (Slats) Marion, called the league's most valuable 1944 player; the Cooper brothers: pitcher Morton, voted the most valuable player of 1942, and catcher Walker; Stan Musial and Jimmy Brown; and "the best crop of young pitchers anybody could remember." When the time came for cutting down his Redbirds to the allowed maximum of twenty-five, Southworth was over-burdened with riches. He had to sell Lon Warneke in order to keep Johnny Beazley: a return to the minors would, he felt, break the latter's morale. In 1941 the St. Louis team came out second

highest in the National League in spite of a debilitating series of injuries, and Southworth was named Manager of 1941 by the *Sporting News*. The winning Dodgers were "hot" again the next season—at one time they led the league by ten and a half games—but the Cardinals cooled them off in an exciting September double-header. Altogether Southworth's team won forty-three of their last fifty-two games, 106 league victories in all, and went on to defeat the supposedly unbeatable New York Yankees in the World Series, four games out of five. Each Cardinals' share in the $1,105,-249 receipts was $6,192.53. The baseball bible again named Southworth the Major League Manager of the Year.

The 1943 Cardinals, like every other team, had their quota of losses to the armed forces. Nevertheless, Southworth's Redbirds repeated their 1942 league victory, winning 105 games and losing 49. They lost the World Series to the Yankees exactly as the New York team had lost it to them in 1942: taking the first game and losing the next four. Southworth made the bad tactical error of barring reporters from his team's dressing room. But he collected his loser's share of $4,321.96, along with the other Cardinals, and also collected the annual award of the Sportsmanship Brotherhood.

Next year Southworth's Cardinals were generally considered "the only team of pre-War quality left in baseball." Although twenty-seven of them had gone into the service, Billy was able to fill their places with excellent substitutes, and also recalled the veteran Pepper Martin. His Cardinals, wrote Grantland Rice [41], "have the game's best catcher. . . . They have the game's best pitching staff. . . . They have the game's best infield . . . and the strongest outfield." They took the pennant easily, and went into the World Series with Billy's friend Luke Sewell's [44] Browns to give St. Louis its first all-city series. As expected, the Cardinals won the classic, but they met unexpectedly tough opposition from the Browns, and the Series went into six games. "The excellence of the Cardinals' defensive play," it was said, "was something the like of which never had been seen in World Series competition." The team handled 224 chances and made only one error. Southworth and his Cardinals each pocketed about $4,334, the smallest winners' cut since 1933. (As Sewell was already installed in the St. Louis apartment he shares with Southworth, the latter stayed at a near-by hotel.)

"Southworth is the perfect baseball manager," said Branch Rickey in 1944. "He's a gentleman, a shrewd baseball man, and an inspirational leader. . . . I think he's wonderful." Although there were rumors of team dissension after the 1944 Series, the consensus seems to be very definitely in Southworth's favor. Stanley Frank calls him "perhaps the easiest of all baseball managers to interview," and he tied for third place on a sportswriters' poll as "Manager Best Liked by Players," in May 1944. His tactful young wife is a help, too, She never talks baseball, but when something is worrying a Cardinal she quietly finds out what it is so that the problem can be solved.

Billy the Kid Southworth is of average height, five feet eight and a half, but most ball-players tower over him, so that he must stand on tiptoe to whisper instructions or congratu-

SOUTHWORTH, BILLY—*Continued*

lations to his men. This fact, plus his trim 170-pound build and his boyish grin, explains the blue-eyed, brown-haired manager's ambiguous nickname. Southworth loves to hunt, fish, bowl, attend football games, talk constantly of baseball. Although balding, the Redbird manager "still looks like a little boy down there at the third-base coaching line," says Roy Stockton; but baseball men are agreed that he coaches like an expert.

References

Collier's 112:21+ O 9 '43 por
Liberty 21:24-5+ O 7 '44 pors
Sat Eve Post 214:18+ Ag 9 '41 pors
Baseball Register 1943

SOUTHWORTH, WILLIAM H. *See* Southworth, B.

SPALDING, ALBERT Aug. 15, 1888-
Violinist
Address: b. 465 Park Ave., New York City; h. Great Barrington, Mass.

In *Rise To Follow* (November 1943) "America's own violinist," Albert Spalding, made his debut as an author. In urbane, graphic, and often witty prose, the musician relates, "not too exhaustively and not at all egotistically, the story of what seems to have been an exceptionally happy life." The autobiography does not follow the traditional pattern of success in that Spalding's difficulties have been comparatively few and slight. At a time when an American name was considered of little consequence on the concert stage Spalding won recognition as a virtuoso of the violin. Spalding has since played in nearly every civilized country on the globe.

Albert Spalding was born into a family of pioneer ancestry, on August 15, 1888, the son of J. W. and Marie (Boardman) Spalding. Spalding describes his parents as being opposites in tastes and temperament. His father, a partner in the well known sporting goods firm of A. G. Spalding & Brother, Inc., was a "sober and balanced" man; his mother, a talented musician, was "unpredictable and irrational." Of his early years he remembers most vividly the fascination that the Steinway grand piano in the drawing room held for him, and how he would stand behind his mother, "often on tiptoe, to watch the miraculous manipulation of the keys." Mrs. Spalding gave numerous evening parties in which the house was filled with musicians, many long-haired or bearded; these were always singers and pianists. And so, when Spalding was seven years old, for no reason that he can remember, he asked for a violin one Christmas while the family was wintering in Florence, Italy. (The Spaldings divided each year between Florence and New Jersey as a measure of "economy" after the 1893 panic.)

His parents were skeptical about having their son begin his musical training with the violin instead of the piano. But Santa Claus (in the person of indulgent Sally Guest, his mother's great-aunt) presented him with a "new, red, shining, half-sized fiddle with a

bow of sorts, to boot," for which she had paid the princely sum of twenty lire—in American money, about four dollars. The boy's joy in owning the precious instrument soon paled when he discovered that the mere possession of the instrument was somehow not sufficient to produce the music he had expected to play. Overcoming his initial dismay, young Albert fondly and energetically scraped at the open strings with the bow, producing weird, grating sounds that threatened to unhinge the nerves of the household. In self-defense, he explains, his family hastened to provide him with a teacher, one Ulpiano Chiti of Florence, who was as much renowned as a brilliant performer as he was feared as a highly impatient teacher. Chiti's reputed irritability, however, was mollified by his pride in his new student's natural aptitude for the violin. There were times later on, when Spalding used his talent to conceal his occasional laziness, that he felt the sharp sting of a swift rap on the knuckles. When the family spent their summers at Monmouth Beach, New Jersey, the young violinist's mother did not allow the season to become a vacation from violin practice. She engaged a South American teacher named Juan Buitrago, an excellent drill master, for the boy.

From time to time, while in Italy, Albert and his brother Boardman, who played the cello, were called upon to perform at local benefit concerts, much to the alarm of their father. Nevertheless, although the elder Spalding did not approve of a musical career for his sons, regarding such a profession as "of doubtful masculinity," he never discouraged them. The musical training of the Spalding brothers was supplemented by regular schooling at a Franco-Italian day school presided over by a certain Professor Domenjé. Occasionally, too, they attended concerts in Florence given by Pablo de Sarasate and Joseph Joachim, among others.

When Spalding was fourteen his teacher Chiti proposed that he go to Bologna to play for the examining board at the Conservatory in an attempt to obtain a diploma. A ruling of the Conservatory allowed outsiders to compete for the diploma if they complied with the rather formidable examination requirements. To the boy's amazement, he received the highest honors ever won by anyone of his age since the time of Mozart. The event made the front pages in the Italian newspapers, whereupon a procession of managers urged him to appear as a child prodigy. Spalding refused these offers and went on to Paris where, for another two years, he studied violin with Lefort of the National Conservatory, and counterpoint and composition with Antonio Scontrino.

On June 6, 1905 Spalding made his debut in Paris, at the Nouveau Théâtre, playing as the chief compositions the Concerto in B Minor by Saint-Saëns and the Bach *Chaconne*. The Paris *Figaro* hailed him for his "remarkable talent" and for playing described as "classically pure and noble in its simplicity." A short time after his debut Spalding was invited to appear on the same program with Adelina Patti, who had emerged from her retirement to make one last appearance. The concert was eagerly anticipated; Spalding, too, was particularly elated and eager to do his best. At the last moment, however, his accompanist did not appear. Patti came to the rescue by offering the distraught violinist the services of her accompanist.

Though his Paris recitals had gained Spalding a certain amount of prestige, they brought him no money. His father took a practical view of the situation, pointing out to his son that unless he became self-supporting in his chosen calling he would be regarded by people as a semi-dilettante. He argued that it was futile to give recitals at a loss in big cities if one could play for a fee—albeit a small one —in the provinces. Accordingly, Spalding embarked on a barnstorming tour of the French provinces with a Gallic soprano and her high-strung accompanist. From France, Spalding went on to London, which, he found, was "certainly not a citadel to be carried by assault." After having basked in the warm responsiveness of his Continental audiences, he felt his London listeners to be rather cool, despite the favorable reviews. By the time Spalding made his American debut he was a seasoned performer. His many European appearances had elicited the personal praise of such musical titans as Saint-Saëns, Joachim and Ysaye. Spalding played for the first time in this country on November 8, 1908, at Carnegie Hall as soloist with the New York Symphony Orchestra under the leadership of Walter Damrosch [44]. The violinist reports that never in his life, neither before nor since, has he been so nervous as on that occasion. The next morning's reviews confirmed the cause of his panic; the musical oracle of the country, Henry E. Krehbiel of the New York Tribune, pronounced his performance a cacophony of "rasping, raucous, snarling, unmusical sounds." Even though other critics praised Spalding's talent, Krehbiel's verdict carried the most weight. Walter Damrosch and others immediately rallied to Spalding's side, offering encouragement and insisting that he ignore the "vindictive" review.

Spalding had, however, arrived professionally by the time the First World War broke out. Upon the entry of this country into the conflict Spalding canceled more than $35,000 worth of signed engagements to enlist in the Army as a private in the aviation service; he was promoted to lieutenant and made adjutant to Major Fiorello La Guardia [40], then as now "a dynamo of energy," with the A.E.F. in Italy. Spalding the soldier soon acquired more titles than a rajah. "I was a judge advocate, a personnel officer, an adjutant, the assistant representative of the Joint Army and Navy Air Board, and a few other things." Specifically, he was being trained as observer to command bombing planes over the Italian Front. For his services with the A.E.F. the violinist was decorated by the Italian Government with the Cross of the Crown of Italy; France likewise honored him with the ribbon of the Chevalier of the Légion d'Honneur, although the Armistice came before his aerial training was completed. Lieutenant Spalding was, incidentally, one of the few soldiers who took along both a violin and a copy of Plato's Dialogues.

Shortly after the Armistice, Spalding resumed his place in the musical world as a dis-

ALBERT SPALDING

tinguished violinist on the American concert stage. Since then he has given from sixty to ninety concerts each season in this country alone, as well as some fifty concerts a year in Europe. He has performed as soloist with every leading American, and with practically every major European, orchestra. He has the distinction of being the only American violinist (and one of the five world famous violinists) who has played in Milan's La Scala Opera House. He is, besides, the only American who has ever been honored with an invitation to perform as soloist with the Paris Conservatory Orchestra. Only two other violinists, Fritz Kreisler [44] and Eugène Ysaye, are said to have shared this honor, a story Spalding has been denying for years: "Many other violinists have, to my knowledge, appeared as soloists with the Paris Conservatory Orchestra," he has said, "but fiction continues to overcome fact in spite of that."

Through his frequent radio appearances, too, Spalding has built up a large appreciative audience. During 1941 and 1942 he served regularly as master of ceremonies on the Columbia Network's Pause That Refreshes on the Air, the André Kostelanetz [42] program.

While critical opinion hardly concedes to Spalding the attributes of genius, it praises him for the unwavering excellence of his interpretations. Olin Downes [43], for one, calls attention to Spalding's "solicitude for scrupulous and expressive interpretation." A review by Howard Taubman epitomizes the critics' consensus: "Albert Spalding is a violinist who can be depended upon to play with excellent taste and with high sincerity of purpose. His performances . . . seldom, if ever, fall below this reliable level, and occasionally they soar higher. It is this consistency of standard that has secured Mr. Spalding's place in the nation's musical scheme of things. He may not achieve the interpretive heights of two or three of the greatest fiddlers, but he holds to his position steadily and honorably."

(Continued next page)

SPALDING, ALBERT—Continued

Spalding is also the composer of a large number of original works which include two violin concertos, four orchestral works, four quartets, and many compositions for the violin and piano.

"Above all else the violin is a singing instrument," says Spalding. "Beauty of tone—a tone distinct from that of any other musical mechanism is its province. While it is true that contrapuntal, rhythmic, and harmonic effects are extremely important in violin playing, the instrument is most advantageously utilized in lyric and melodic passages. Recognizing this fact, I choose for my radio recitals those works —whether from the so-called classics or semi-classics—which by their melodic and lyric beauty are most naturally violinistic."

Albert Spalding's autobiography, *Rise To Follow*, was greeted with generally favorable reviews. "Every concert artist should have a good story to tell about his career," commented Gilbert Chase, "because his job involves going places and meeting people—important people. . . . This book contains the proof that Spalding must be counted among the best of the musical storytellers." Some critics considered that "he presents the colorless details of his career so unsparingly that one is tempted to skim over them," while others found *Rise To Follow* "a very readable and entertaining book . . . written with honesty, discernment, gaiety, and charm." Wrote John Erskine, "Now he [Spalding] must give us volume two, with an account equally complete of his concerts in the Western Hemisphere, of his fine work as a teacher in the Juilliard School and in private, of his composing, of his radio performances, and of his miscellaneous activities on behalf of the usual profession." Even as the reviews were being written, arrangements were being completed for the author to join the Office of War Information's Psychological Warfare Branch in the spring, when he had canceled his concert and orchestral engagements. The violinist would serve, it was announced, as an assistant and counselor to the civilian head of the Branch.

Spalding is "tall, dark-haired, and dark-eyed," and has well-defined features. Louis Sherwin, interviewing him for the New York *Post*, wrote: "Spalding is not merely the virtuoso; he happens, like Toscanini[42], to be afflicted with intellect. A ratiocinating, perceptive man, he is for a musician fantastically articulate, knowing not merely his job but what it is all about."

On July 19, 1919 Spalding was married to Mary Vanderhof Pyle. During summer vacations at their estate in Great Barrington, Massachusetts, Spalding swims, plays golf and tennis. Occasionally he picks up rare pieces of English china or valuable first editions for his well-stocked library. Fast-moving mystery stories are his favorite reading.

References

Harper 184:356+ Mr '42; 184:501-8 Ap '42; 184:595-603 My '42; 185:55-62 Je '42
N Y Times p32 Ja 26 '41; p33 N 18 '41; p34 Je 20 '43
Newsweek 17:73 My 26 '41
Ewen, D. ed. Living Musicians 1940
Spalding, A. Rise to Follow 1943
Thompson, O. ed. International Cyclopedia of Music and Musicians 1943
Who Is Who in Music 1941
Who's Who in America 1944-45

SPRUANCE, RAYMOND AMES Jan. 3, 1886- United States naval officer

Address: b. c/o Navy Department, Washington, D. C.

"Nothing you can say about him would be praise enough" is Admiral Nimitz'[42] opinion of his chief of staff, Admiral Raymond Ames Spruance. As ranking United States naval officer at the Midway battle in the Second World War he won a brilliant victory with an outnumbered fleet; as commander of the Central Pacific area he planned and directed the successful invasions of the Gilbert and Marshall Islands which brought his ships closer to Tokyo than to the United States. As a four-star admiral, he took part in the Truk engagement aboard one of the fighting ships—an unprecedented action for an officer of his rank.

Raymond Ames Spruance was born in Baltimore, Maryland, July 3, 1886, the son of Alexander P. and Annie A. (Hiss) Spruance, and attended grade and high schools in East Orange, New Jersey, staying with three maiden aunts, and in Indianapolis, Indiana. He is remembered as neat, diligent, and gentle. His father wanted the boy to enter West Point, but Raymond had other ideas, and after preparing at the Stevens Preparatory School in Hoboken, New Jersey, he entered the Naval Academy in July 1903. The youth, who was then seventeen years old, was appointed from Indiana. He stood in the first section of his class scholastically—twenty-sixth, to be precise—at his graduation in September 1906. After service aboard the battleship *Iowa*, Spruance "made the world cruise" in the U.S.S. *Minnesota*. Commissioned an ensign in 1908, he had a tour of shore duty, taking a postgraduate course in electrical engineering at Schenectady, and was then ordered to the China station. After sea duty on the battleship *Connecticut* and the cruiser *Cincinnati*, the young officer was assigned to the *Bainbridge*, U. S. Destroyer No. 1, which he commanded until 1914. (On December 30 of that year Spruance was married to Margaret Vance Dean, the gay, handsome daughter of an Indianapolis businessman. They have a daughter, Margaret, and a son, Lieutenant Commander Edward Dean Spruance, a submarine captain, who was awarded the Silver Star for gallantry in action in the Pacific.)

In 1914 Spruance, who is described as "an expert on the myriad instruments, engines, and gun equipment that go into a modern battleship," was appointed assistant inspector of machinery at the Newport News Shipbuilding and Dry Dock Company in Virginia, which was then outfitting the U.S.S. *Pennsylvania*. When that battleship went to sea in June 1916 he went with her. In the Admiral's words, "I was shanghaied ashore in November of the next year to take over as electrical superintendent at the New York Navy Yard. I finally wangled two months at sea, in 1918, before the War was over. The following year they made me executive officer of the transport *Agamemnon*, bringing troops home from France. It was interesting work, but I wouldn't want to do it for a living." More to the officer's liking, perhaps, was the study of foreign methods of fire control, which "temporary additional duty" took him to London and Edinburgh in 1918.

After completing his service on the *Agamemnon*, Spruance was ordered to duty in connection with fitting out the destroyer *Aaron Ward*, and then to command of that ship. His next command was the U.S.S. *Perceval*, which sea duty ended in 1921. The next three years were spent with the Navy Department's Bureau of Engineering in Washington, D. C.; after the first, he was appointed a member of the Board on Doctrine of Aircraft in connection with fleet fire control.

Spruance's steady rise, according to *Newsweek,* "has borne the imprint of his personality —unobtrusive but undeviating. Early in his career he was catalogued as someone to watch; there was never any possibility that he would be passed over in the lists for promotion. His sea duty, a pretty good index of a man's professional standing in the Navy, compared favorably with that of old seadogs such as Admiral Ingersoll '42." A two-year tour of duty as assistant chief of staff to the commander of naval forces in Europe (1924-25) was followed by Spruance's return to the United States for a year of study at the Naval War College at Newport, Rhode Island. He took the senior course (open only to captains and commanders), completing it in 1927, after which he was assigned to two years of duty in the Office of Naval Intelligence.

The forty-three-year-old Commander's next sea service was on the battleship *Mississippi* (1929-31), followed by his return to the Naval War College as a staff member. Spruance's promotion to the rank of captain came on June 30, 1932; and in 1933 he was assigned to serve as chief of staff and aide to the commander of a destroyer scouting force. After another three-year tour of duty at the Naval War College the Captain was ordered to sea in the U.S.S. *Mississippi*, this time as its commander. This was in July 1938.

By 1939, when Spruance was fifty-three, he had spent eighteen years in sea service. In December of that year he was promoted to rear admiral and in February 1940 was placed in command of the 10th Naval District (the Caribbean Area), with headquarters at San Juan, Puerto Rico. The following year the new Admiral was assigned to command a division of cruisers in the Pacific under Admiral Nimitz; he was in this post on June 4, 1942, when the Japanese Navy attacked Midway Island in force. When Vice-Admiral F. J. Fletcher's flagship, the aircraft carrier *Yorktown*, was put out of action, Spruance "took over" and, in Nimitz' words, "did a remarkable job." The United States force was greatly outclassed both in size and number of ships; but Spruance and his officers used what strength they had so cleverly that after a four-day battle two Japanese fleets totaling eighty warships were routed, at least ten were sunk and as many more damaged,

Official U. S. Navy
ADM. RAYMOND AMES SPRUANCE

275 Japanese planes were lost, and 4,800 Japanese killed—with a total American loss of one destroyer, one aircraft carrier, and 307 men.

This victory had a great effect on the morale of a nation which had not fully recovered from the effects of Japan's first smashing attacks. Spruance received the Distinguished Service Medal for his exploit and, in May 1943, his promotion to vice-admiral. Admiral Nimitz was sufficiently impressed by the performance at Midway to make Spruance his chief of staff, a position in which he dropped out of the public eye, as his was a planning, rather than an operational job. Later, however, Nimitz named him commander of the disputed Central Pacific Area. Spruance thus became responsible for the planning and execution of the attack on the Gilbert Islands in November 1943 which brought him a Gold Star in lieu of a second D. S. M.

These islands, lying near the juncture of the international date line with the equator, were British colonies taken over by the Japanese soon after Pearl Harbor. Since then they had made Betio in Tarawa atoll "the hardest nut," in the words of Rear Admiral Harry W. Hill, "that any naval or military commander has ever been ordered to crack." Betio's defenses included heavy guns, tank traps, boat traps, barbed wire, machine-gun nests, remarkably solid blockhouses and pillboxes (some received and withstood direct hits during the bombardment)—the whole connected by a system of protected communications and concealed foxholes. "The principal points to be kept in mind about the Japanese defensive," commented Major George Fielding Eliot '40, "is its interlocking nature and the astonishing strength of its construction." But the islands, possessed of good landing strips and an adequate naval base, were considered worth the risk of high casualties. The battle, which began at dawn on November 21, 1943 and continued for

SPRUANCE, RAYMOND AMES—*Cont.*

seventy-six hours, resulted in American possession of the Gilberts, at a cost of 2,950 casualties. The figure was high—but it compared favorably with upwards of 4,500 Japanese killed, wounded, or captured. The attack was planned and directed by Admiral Spruance, with the assistance of Rear Admirals R. Kelly Turner '44 and Harry W. Hill, and three generals named Smith.

Just two months later United States forces launched an attack on Kwajalein atoll in the Marshall Islands. "The most powerful naval striking force in history" was supported by aircraft based at the Gilberts airfields. After three days of pulverizing bombardment by these and carrier-based aircraft, as well as by battleships and other seacraft, Marines swarmed ashore on Roi islet and captured it the same day. "The quick success of the offensive," according to commentators, "was attributed to the strategic daring by which Vice-Admiral R. A. Spruance's forces cut behind the eastern chain of the Marshalls. The Japanese had been battered for weeks by aerial bombardment and knew the invasion was imminent. But they expected it to come at the obvious and exposed outer fringe, and when we struck at the heart of the archipelago with a huge fleet which had approached undetected we enjoyed complete tactical surprise." Amphibious operations were again directed by Admiral Turner, and assault troops by Major General Holland M. Smith, U.S.M.C.; shore-based aircraft were under the command of Rear Admiral John H. Hoover, and carrier planes were directed by Rear Admiral Marc A. Mitscher '44.

Four days after the invasion was begun the immediate objectives—the Roi air base, the Namur supply depot, and the Kwajalein naval base—were all taken; by February 8 all organized resistance had ceased, and the Kwajalein atoll was under the United States flag. As Secretary of the Navy Frank Knox '40 put it, "The Japanese had been there twenty years. But we went in and took their possessions in a few days, without loss of a single ship." On February 10 President Roosevelt's '42 nomination of Spruance for promotion to full admiral was "approved unanimously by the Senate and the country"—but, because of a printing error on the executive calendar of nominations, he was officially "promoted" only to his former rank of vice-admiral.

Although Kwajalein atoll was in American hands, the rest of the Marshalls group remained to be dealt with. They comprise "some thirty islands and more than eight hundred reefs scattered over hundreds of square miles of ocean, the whole area powerfully fortified by the Japanese." On February 16 and 17 Admiral Spruance directed an attack on Truk, a great naval and air base called by some "the Japanese Pearl Harbor," at the same time that American forces under Admiral R. Kelly Turner '44 were striking Eniwetok atoll in the Marshalls, some 700 miles to the west. Spruance himself directed a task group of battleships, destroyers, and cruisers which "left the protection of the main body and went hunting the Japanese ships that fled the rain of aerial missiles." This was said to be the first time

that a four-star admiral participated in a sea action aboard one of the ships engaged. "Admiral Spruance commanded," a correspondent reported, "with deadly precision." Nineteen Japanese ships were sunk, seven more probably sunk, more than 200 of their planes destroyed, and their installations bombed and strafed, as compared to a loss of only seventeen American planes and not one ship.

Admiral Spruance's victories come about because, like every successful commander, he literally thinks of everything. "Probably the plans for the [relatively small] attack on Tarawa, as finally assembled and approved, occupied about 200 pages of legal-size typewriter paper." Admiral Nimitz said of the Kwajalein invasion, "Surprise was just one of the factors in our success. That success was due primarily to complete planning of the operation," involving a new method of disposing naval power, "used here for the first time. It is built mostly around [aircraft] carriers, and its composition enables us to combine our strength very quickly. It is distinctly an American development."

Presumably the Admiral was referring to Mitscher's Task Force 58, the "most powerful and destructive unit on the history of sea warfare," which went into action as a unit immediately after the Marshalls operations. Five days later Spruance sent the Mitscher force on a "history-making" attack against the Marianas islands of Tinian and Saipan in which the fierce defenders did not succeed in inflicting any damage on the American ships. On March 29 Spruance took tactical command of a three-pronged attack against the Palau Islands (550 miles east of the Philippines), and Yap Island and Ulithi atoll, in the western Carolines. In this three-day operation, the most extensive one ever undertaken by carriers, American losses were amazingly low—twenty-five planes, eighteen lives, and no ships, for "not one piece of metal from an enemy gun fell on any of them." On April 22 Task Force 58 supported the American invasion of Hollandia and Tanahmers in Dutch New Guinea and Aitape in Australian New Guinea led by General Douglas MacArthur '41. It was on the last day of this invasion, April 28, that Admiral Spruance's command was redesignated as the 5th Fleet. (In June it was announced that Admiral Halsey '42 had been given command of the 3rd Fleet, and later that year Task Force 58 was transferred to his fleet from Spruance's.)

Events in the Pacific in early June 1944 were, of course, overshadowed by the Allied invasion of Western Europe under General Dwight D. Eisenhower '42. Yet, as Navy Lieutenant Oliver Jensen points out, "in that operation a distance of less than 100 sea miles was involved, and the air umbrella under which Allied troops stormed the beaches was based on a near-by civilized shore. On the other hand, Spruance's anchorage was a bare, humid pinprick in the Pacific. From here he was jumping a long 1,200 miles, twice as far as the distance from London to Berlin, and carrying his extraordinary air force with him. Thus Task Force 58 . . . was making the offensive possible. To its carrier pilots was entrusted the primary task of wiping out enemy air power all up and down the 600-mile-long Mariana Islands chain. To its planes and heavy surface guns belonged the responsibility for protecting the new beach-head against all assaults of the Japanese Navy or Air Force."

The Saipan (Marianas) campaign began on June 10 with air attacks; Spruance's naval guns opened bombardment June 12; and two days later, while Mitscher led a diversionary attack on the Bonins 800 miles to the north, American marines and infantrymen swarmed ashore. (Certain British naval units also helped support the landings.) Four days or so later, when Mitscher rejoined Spruance and the rest of the 5th Fleet, the Admirals were hopeful of a classic battle with the Nipponese Imperial Grand Battle Fleet, but only the carrier planes were able to reach the Japanese ships. On June 18, however, hundreds of Japanese planes attacked the 5th Fleet, and were so overwhelmingly defeated (losses of 353 Japanese planes to twenty-one American aircraft) that the Americans were amazed. Before going down, the Nipponese managed to inflict superficial damage on only three ships. Mitscher pursued the enemy planes and carriers and attacked them the following day in the battle of the Eastern Philippines, running up a score of 402 planes and 6 ships with a loss of 122 planes from his own carriers. British Prime Minister Winston Churchill '42 wrote to Navy Secretary James Forrestal '43, "Admiral Spruance is again to be congratulated for another fine job. . . . My personal congratulations." Spruance's ships had accomplished this without the firing of one salvo, and had prevented the Japanese Fleet from bringing reinforcements to the Saipan garrison.

The fleet units protecting the Marianas invasion troops were also under Spruance's command. In a seven-week campaign, 55 enemy ships were sunk, 5 probably sunk, and 74 damaged, while 1,132 Japanese planes were knocked out of action. The American loss was 199 planes, 128 flight personnel, and damage to 4 warships. During those seven weeks the 5th Fleet burned up 630,000,000 gallons of fuel oil, which is enough to fill 105 fleet oilers, and more than the entire Pacific Fleet used in the entire year of 1943.

In August, at a press conference at newly captured Guam, Admiral Chester Nimitz '42 gave reporters to understand that his forces would work as two teams: the 3rd Fleet team under Halsey, which included the 3rd Amphibious Group and the 3rd Corps, under Rear Admiral Conolly and Major General Roy Geiger respectively; and the 5th Fleet team under Spruance, including Rear Admiral Harry Hill's 5th Amphibious Group and Marine Major General Harry Schmidt's 5th Amphibious Corps. These two teams were to alternate blows at the enemy, to keep him always off balance. The Guam invasion itself was begun by Halsey's team on July 21, preceded by seventeen days of heavy bombing and a week of increasingly intense shelling by his warships. Spruance himself dropped out of the news for a time. In October 1944, however, he was present in San Francisco at the conference of high-ranking Navy commanders, who were summarized as "Secretary Forrestal, who will provide the weapons; Admiral [Ernest J.] King '42, who makes the strategy; Vice-Admiral [Randall] Jacobs '42, who provides the men; Admiral Nimitz, who will give the orders; Vice-Ad-

miral [Aubrey Wray] Fitch, who plans the air support; and Admiral Spruance to execute, with Admiral Halsey, the tactics."

An acknowledged expert at planning naval operations, Spruance is described by his friend and superior Nimitz as "a fine man, a sterling character, and a great leader." Admiral William L. Calhoun, who has known Spruance forty-two years, calls him "a cold-blooded fighting fool. If he possesses one fault, it is that he believes too much in work and doesn't get enough play." When Spruance feels the need of recreation he turns to symphonic music, and when he wants exercise, to walking. He thinks nothing of walking eight or ten miles a day, and in the course of a two-hour interview "he stood or walked about all the time—not restlessly, but slowly and deliberately." That interviewer described him as "a man of medium build, with a rugged face, well weathered by years of sea duty," and his "coarse brown hair is flecked with gray. A pair of steel-blue eyes bore you like needles, and the set of his mouth and chin hint that he isn't to be fooled with." Others see him as "lean and thoughtful", "mild-mannered", "a poker-faced, taciturn fighter", "a quiet little man with drooping shoulders." The Admiral, who never smokes and drinks little (although said to be one of the best drink-mixers in the Pacific), does enjoy hot chocolate, which he prefers to make for himself each morning. He misses the companionship of his pet schnauzer particularly. Spruance lives on board his flagship, while his wife and daughter wait in "duration quarters" at Monrovia, California. Like all Navy families, the Spruances have lived in many places—but prefer Indianapolis.

The Admiral's medals include the Cuban Pacification Medal, the Victory Medal with Overseas Clasp, the American Defense Service Medal with Fleet Clasp, and the Asiatic-Pacific Area Campaign Medal. In addition to the Distinguished Service Medal, he was decorated in 1924 with the Gold Cross of Chevalier of the Greek Order of the Savior. Spruance is said to dislike all personal publicity—his entry in Who's Who in America is only three lines long, including his full name—and he has the reputation of freezing reporters who invade his privacy. But Frank Morris, who interviewed him for Collier's, found the Admiral "as formidable as an old shoe."

References

Collier's 113:17+ Ja 1 '44 por
N Y Herald Tribune p3 F 11 '44
N Y Sun p18 F 14 '44
Newsweek 23:25 F 11 '44
Scholastic 44:8 F 28 '44
Who's Who in America 1944-45

STAGG, (AMOS) ALONZO Aug. 16, 1862-
Football coach

Address: b. c/o College of the Pacific, Stockton, Calif; h. 127 W. Euclid Ave., Stockton, Calif.

Probably the only ex-divinity student ever to be elected America's "Football Man of the Year" (1943) is the famous old coach Alonzo Stagg. "Football's 'Old Man River' not only keeps rolling along—he keeps picking up new

ALONZO STAGG

him the honorary degree of Master of Physical Education in 1912.

At this time Stagg's erstwhile Bible professor, William Rainey Harper, was appointed president of the newly founded University of Chicago; and he offered young Stagg $1,500 a year to head the physical education department at the University. According to *Time* Magazine, Stagg was made speechless at the princely sum, a munificent salary for such a post in those days. Dr. Harper, mistaking Stagg's silence, raised the offer to $2,000 along with an assistant professorship. By the time Stagg found his voice to accept, he found himself in possession of a yearly stipend of $2,500 and a lifetime associate professorship (Amos Alonzo Stagg, M.A., is still listed in the catalog of the University of Chicago as Professor Emeritus of Physical Education). The professorship was unheard of in a day when coaches were not regarded as members of the faculty.

Stagg was thirty in 1892 when he came to the University of Chicago. It was then that romance entered his life, for he met Stella Robertson, a co-ed, his junior by thirteen years. They were married in the fall of 1894, and celebrated the fiftieth anniversary of their wedding in 1944. Mrs. Stagg, her husband says, has been "the best assistant coach a man ever had." (They have three children—Amos Alonzo, Ruth, and Paul.)

For forty-one years Stagg remained at Chicago, winning 268 games and losing 141. There he originated some of the basic forms of modern football—the tackling dummy, the end-around play, the tackle-back shift, and the hidden ball principle. The scene of his first triumphs was the small athletic field which he built largely with the help of voluntary student labor and money raised by the students and faculty. The famous Stagg Field, dedicated in 1914, has a total seating capacity of 57,000. While the University no longer plays football on a grand scale, Stagg Field still includes football fields, as well as lawn bowling rinks, an ice-skating and hockey rink, five tennis courts, golf greens, and a quarter-mile running-track. At Chicago Coach Stagg trained such "all-time greats" as Fritz Crisler, Walter Eckersall, and Hugo Bezdek. Alonzo Stagg, Jr., was on the team in 1922, but did not win his letter, for his father never sent him into a game, even as substitute.

From 1896 to 1911 Coach Stagg represented the University at the Inter-Collegiate Conference of Faculty Representatives. Since 1904 he has been a member of the Football Rules Committee (in 1932 Stagg was voted a life membership); and he was a member of the American committee for the Olympic Games at Athens in 1906, London in 1908, Stockholm in 1912, Antwerp in 1920, Paris in 1924 (also coaching the middle distance runners), Amsterdam in 1928, and Los Angeles in 1932. In 1911-1912 he was president of the Society of Directors of Physical Education in Colleges, and in the latter year was a Presidential elector for the Progressive Party. Since 1922 he has been athletic adviser of the Order of De-Molay, and chairman of the track and field records committee of the National Collegiate Athletic Association. He has two books to his credit as co-author: *Treatise on Football*,

honors along the way." Although he was retired in 1933 from his job as coach at the University of Chicago because he was "too old," in 1944 he is still "going strong," having made the football team of the College of the Pacific in Stockton, California, one of the "hardest-to-beat 'little' teams in the country."

Amos Alonzo Stagg was born August 16, 1862, in West Orange, New Jersey, to Amos Lindsley and Eunice (Pierson) Stagg. His father was a shoemaker, so poor that he also cut hay on neighboring farms in order to provide for the family. When the boy was old enough to handle a scythe, he worked in the hayfields with his father. While attending Orange High School he thus managed to save enough money to enable him to enter the fashionable Phillips Exeter Academy to make up the extra credits he needed in order to enter Yale University. The next year young Stagg entered Yale with a capital of $32. He allowed himself 20c a day for food, which brought about a collapse from malnutrition within three months. His classmates then got him a job as their student-waiter.

After receiving his B.A. degree from Yale, Stagg took one year of graduate work and one year at the Yale Divinity School. Both as undergraduate and divinity student he pitched Yale to five baseball championships. Gaining a reputation as one of the best pitchers in the United States, he was offered jobs by big-league teams which he refused. During his last year at Yale, Stagg was chosen an end on Walter Camp's first All-America football eleven in 1899. He is a member of Psi Upsilon and Skull and Bones.

While a student at the Yale Divinity School, Stagg discovered that he was not suited to be a preacher because of his lack of oratorical ability. He left Divinity School, therefore, and went to the International YMCA College at Springfield, Massachusetts, where he took up physical education. That college, from which he was graduated in 1891, gave with Williams (1893); and *Touchdown!* with Wesley W. Stout (1927).

At the age of seventy mandatory retirement was in order for Stagg. The year before the University of Chicago had offered to make him chairman of an Advisory Committee on Athletics and representative in the "Big Ten" Council. Stagg preferred the active life, however, and refused the offer. When he retired the next year he accepted the post of football coach at the relatively little known College of the Pacific, the oldest college in California.

Stagg's California Tigers did not pile up victories immediately (in ten years they won less than half the games). However, when the United States was preparing for the Second World War, the Army and Navy began to send trainees to various colleges and universities, and the College of the Pacific was able to get veteran football players for its team. In 1938, when the team was invited to play the University of Chicago team, the visitors won with a score of 32 to 0. In 1939 they lost only one game. In 1942 they lost six times, but the next year they were victorious over seven out of nine opponents, including the University of California at Los Angeles and the University of California, both on their home grounds.

By 1943 sports writers were beginning to say not only that the Tigers looked like the strongest team on the Pacific Coast, but that it was Stagg's best team since the year 1924, when Chicago ruled the Big Ten Conference. "The outstanding sports comeback of 1943," Stagg was named Football Man of the Year by the Football Writers' Association, and Coach of the Year by a New York *World-Telegram* poll of 128 coaches. Among earlier honors had been the dedication to him of the 1939 convention of the Coaches' Association in Los Angeles when Stagg had reached his fiftieth year of coaching and the establishment of the A. Alonzo Stagg award as the Association's highest honor. In 1944 he was also made an honorary life member. In March 1944, also, the Stockton Round Table planted a tree in honor of its Grand Old Man; they had elected him an Honorary Knight in October 1939, thus putting him in a class with Burbank, Edison, Charles Evans Hughes '41, Professor Robert A. Millikan, Wilfred Grenfell, Rear Admiral Richard E. Byrd '42, Baron Baden-Powell, Cordell Hull '40, and the four others similarly honored since 1922. The American Educational Association presented Stagg with an award in 1933, and two years later the Boy Scouts of America gave him the Silver Buffalo for "distinguished service to boyhood." Other awards in his collection are the New York City Touchdown Club award for 1940 and the Edward N. Tarbell medallion from Springfield College in 1941.

In 1913 an editorial in the *University of Chicago Magazine* paid this tribute to him: "The West is pretty unanimous in the opinion that as a football coach Mr. Stagg is the best ever known. But his value to Chicago as a moral force he is extraordinary. . . . Rough play, rough speech, a lack of sportsmanship he will not tolerate; and they are eliminated not by his exhortation but because they die in the shadow of his personality." From early days

at Chicago the undergraduates affectionately called him The Old Man.

Devout white-haired Stagg has never drunk, smoked, nor sworn; nor has he permitted his players to do so. Formerly he used to celebrate a football victory by eating a pint of ice cream; today, because of wartime shortages, he has had to substitute a dish of fresh figs. He weighs 158 pounds—only eight pounds more than his weight sixty years ago. Although he never got his degree in divinity, in 1922 Oberlin College awarded him an M.A., and in 1933 he received an honorary LL.D. from Wooster College. Perhaps his great success as a football coach is due, writers say, to the fact that he does not consider football as warfare on a small scale, or even as an activity to which academic studies should be subordinated. To Stagg football is simply a game.

References

Collier's 108:20 D 6 '41
Newsweek 22:98 O 25 '43 por
Read Digest 44:55-8 F '44
Time 42:55-7 O 25 '43
Who's Who in America 1944-45

STEAGALL, HENRY BASCOM (stē'gəl) May 19, 1873—Nov. 19, 1943 United States Representative from Alabama (1915-43); chairman of the House Banking and Currency Committee; member of the farm bloc and a leader in the fight against subsidies; co-sponsor of the Glass '41-Steagall Banking Reform Act (1933).

Obituary

N Y Times p25 N 23 '43

STEELE, FREDERIC DORR Aug. 6, 1873—July 5, 1944 American artist; achieved reputation for his illustrations for *The Return of Sherlock Holmes* and other Conan Doyle tales, as well as for the books of other well known American and British authors; contributed to leading American periodicals since 1897; the first living illustrator to have representation in the Cabinet of American Illustration of the Library of Congress.

Obituary

N Y Times p15 Jl 7 '44

STEFAN, PAUL (ste'fän) Nov. 25, 1879—Nov. 12, 1943 Austrian music critic; author and biographer; wrote biographies of Gustav Mahler, Arnold Schoenberg '42, Franz Schubert, Arturo Toscanini '42, and others; died in New York, a refugee from Nazi Germany.

Obituary

N Y Times p13 N 13 '43 por

STEIG, WILLIAM (stīg) Nov. 14, 1907- Artist; sculptor

Address: h. 133 W. 11th St., New York City

The creator of the "Small Fry" drawings in the *New Yorker* is a man whose sympathies hardly seem to lie with the world of adults. He himself says that little boys "are not as quickly socially-conditioned as little girls and

WILLIAM STEIG

not as artificial as adults. They furnish the best clues to the intrinsic nature of man." Born in New York City on November 14, 1907, the son of Joseph and Laura (Ebel) Steig, William Steig admits that he largely depends on memory for his "kid drawings," for he still vividly recalls life at his Alma Mater, P.S. 53 in the Bronx. He must have learned a thing or two about human nature since that time, however, for such specialists in it as Margaret Mead '40, Karen Horney '41, Karl Menninger, and A. A. Brill have praised his rather frightening collections of "psychographs," *About People* (1939), *The Lonely Ones* (1942), and *All Embarrassed* (1944).

William Steig received his art training at the National Academy of Design, New York City, which he attended from 1925 to 1929. (He had previously had two years at City College of New York, where he achieved fame as a water-polo player rather than as a scholar.) Even his years at the Academy, he confesses, were "purely to stall off a career," and he "got all his fun playing football in the backyard." Finally, in 1930, he set out to earn his living in the cartooning field, and since then his drawings have appeared in *Life, Judge,* the *New Yorker, Vanity Fair, Collier's,* and other magazines. His arrogant small boys and girls became particularly well known —so well known that in 1942 a manufacturer of children's clothes created a collection of Small Fry suits, dresses, overalls, shirts, and play clothes.

On January 2, 1936 Steig was married to Elizabeth Mead, and the young couple moved to a country house in Connecticut. There he and his brother, Henry Anton Steig, pruned fruit trees and stacked dead wood in a shed. One day William picked up a chunk of the wood and began whittling it. Thereafter all of his male carvings have been known in the family as Jason, all of his female carvings as Tessie. And these Jasons and Tessies were the beginnings of a new career—as a sculptor.

According to Steig, "one brought up in the city is bound to become entirely preoccupied with people; they are not only the protagonists, but also the setting. Country landscape is beautiful . . . but not related to people. Thus it seemed more logical to me to carve than to draw here. In the city one is impressed with what people *do*. In the country, where there is little activity, one becomes preoccupied with what people *are*." His sculptured figures, it seemed to him, not only expressed better than his drawings what people are, but were of such a character that they would not "seem out of place in the cabbage fumes of apartment houses." (Since they now sell for as much as $250 they have probably escaped a great many cabbage fumes, but it was still a good idea.)

Steig's first one-man show was of fourteen of these wood carvings—in 1939, at New York City's Downtown Gallery. Wrote one critic: "*Mal de Tête*, picturing a fat, chubby woman prone on a couch, is right out of one of his *New Yorker* drawings. Other works, like his *Matriarch*, have about them a primitive quality that is akin to African sculpture. . . . Steig in his carved figures aims at humor, whereas in his drawings his aim is at being funny." The *Magazine of Art* commented, however: "In his less than foot high wood sculptures . . . he doesn't cut as instinctively as he draws, nor as mean a figure, and he uses pat formulas which are never apparent in his ink drawings. Each head is a boring egg shape, each foot a club, and all noses flat, vertical vases. One surface is like another—barren, shaven, and the whole thing is pretty much a one-sided affair, lacking in formal distinction. It is humorous on the cute side, definitely conservative."

Apparently at about the same time Steig decided that it was possible to show "what people are" at least as well in pen and ink as in wood, for in 1939 *About People* appeared. A book of 105 symbolical drawings, it "illustrated decided neurotic symptoms like kleptomania and amnesia, more common everyday ones like nausea and lassitude, and the more interesting determined types of personality in our society: the *Pleasant chap but never a friend,* and the *One who would like to be left alone.* There was hardly a facet of modern-day behavior that Steig didn't touch; he analyzed even as seemingly inoffensive a manifestation as the catnap for its *sub rosa* quality." A. A. Brill wrote: "Mr. Steig has the rare faculty of sensing the essentials of human nature and the capacity of depicting them in a most poignant manner." Karl Menninger commented that Steig's drawings were "a new kind of art and a new kind of humor. They illustrated beautifully some of the principles of human behavior which Freud studied psychologically." And another psychoanalyst remarked that the drawings "combine incisive humorous comment with deep sympathetic understanding of the dilemma of man in the modern world."

This collection was followed by a second one, *The Lonely Ones* (1942), forty-six drawings of which one critic wrote: "Without the earlier shading in the drawings, with one small person to a page and no back or foreground, its subjects are much further off the beaten path into psychosis. . . . Though the attempt is still illustrative, he has here cut away much of his photographic excess, and relies more on the abstract quality of his line. . . . Steig has a genius for instinctively noting in line the quality of an upset mind or stomach. Most of all he is a kind of trusted spokesman for the masochist. . . ." According to the New York *Herald Tribune Books*, however, "Here with or without the grace of God, are all of us X-rayed, to catch, as not even the sincerest self-criticism can catch, those moods of egotism, vain dejection, and insane conceit that surge at times across everyone." Diana Trilling agreed, in the *New Republic*: "Mr. Steig's vision of mankind is awesome and awful; certainly to one reviewer this latest work of a humorist is anything but funny. But it isn't singular, except in degree. . . . You need only have ridden with your eyes open in a New York subway during rush hour to recognize many of Mr. Steig's obsessed types." *The Lonely Ones* was reprinted seven times in 1943, and on March 1944 *About People* was reissued.

In June 1944 *All Embarrassed*, a third collection of drawings, was published. Wrote Arthur Steig, the artist's brother, in the foreword: "The man of the fifth decade of the twentieth century is the Embarrassed Man. . . . The well of the embarrassment illustrated in this book is the interior chaos born in a world of façades. The artist illustrates it with the eye of a poet, satirist, and the eclectic (embarrassed) eye of a contemporary." According to Steig himself, "The title of every drawing in this book is EMBARRASSMENT. Other titles are to be regarded as subtitles."

"Most people have reached a stage of embarrassment," he told a *PM* reporter. "They're stymied. . . . They can't do anything about their suppressed anger at corruption and lack of freedom. Everybody wants a beautiful life. People want to live and love. They run into so much profanity, it gums them up. Money, profit, profanity—they're all bad for the soul. A person feels embarrassed when he doesn't respect what he's doing. He's all bottled up. . . . One of the most common feelings is rage—anger at the way things are being done, at the lack of grace, order, and honesty in the world. . . . Most people feel it and aren't aware of it." In *All Embarrassed*, he said, he tried to increase people's awareness.

Yet another Steig book appeared in November 1944—*Small Fry*, no less—a collection of more than a hundred drawings of the city-bred "half-pints." "What they prove to the parents and elders," wrote the New York *Times* reviewer, "is that eight-year-olds do not change from one generation to another, that the world of childhood is compounded of miniature terrors and glorious day-dreams, and that Mr. Steig—not to put to fine a point upon it—is wonderful."

By this time Steig had had other exhibitions of his work, both sculpture and drawings, in February 1940 at Smith College, in late 1942 at a New York gallery. Innovations in his sculpture by now were the use of such materials as brush-bristles and rope for hair and wire mesh for veiling. Wrote Emily Genauer in the New York *World-Telegram*, commenting on such characters as *Comic Corpse*, *Nos-*

talgia, *Lady With Veil*, *Settled Man*, *Sad and Lonely*, *Fool No. 1*, and *Proud Woman*: "It's amazing how Steig, with a simply modeled figure bedizened with a bit of rope, perhaps, or a few beads, or without any accouterments at all, can satirize a whole class."

This versatile artist is "a quiet young man with lazy, stone-blue eyes, a wide grin, and upstanding stiff brown hair." He is also a quick, sure workman, whose left hand sketches out drawings "with almost incredible speed." He has a son and daughter, who probably constitute his closest approximation to a hobby. (Once, asked if he regarded his woodwork as a hobby, he replied, with stern realism: "If it sells, it's not a hobby.") His children constitute something of a problem, too, in that Steig has always thought of other people as older than he is, identifying himself with the youngsters in his drawings. Since he has become a parent he doesn't know quite where he stands. "That's one problem I've still got to work out," he says.

References

    Am Artist 7:17-19 Mr '43 il por
    Mag Art 36:13-15 Ja '43 il
    PM Mag p4 Je 18 '44 por
    Time 33:43 Ap 3 '39 il
    Who's Who in America 1944-45

STEPHENS, WILLIAM D(ENNISON)
Dec. 26, 1859—Apr. 25, 1944 Former Governor of California (1917-22); Republican Representative in Congress (1910-17); in 1918 commuted Tom Mooney's sentence to life imprisonment.

Obituary

    N Y Times p19 Ap 26 '44 por

STIMSON, FREDERIC JESUP July 20, 1855—Nov. 19, 1943 Former United States Ambassador to Argentina and Brazil; author of books on legal, political, and Constitutional subjects and novels (under the nom de plume of J. S. of Dale); held state offices in Massachusetts.

Obituary

    N Y Times p57 N 21 '43 por

STRAIGHT, MICHAEL (WHITNEY)
Sept. 1, 1916- Economist; journalist; author
Address: b. c/o New Republic, 1721 Eye St., Washington, D.C.; h. Weyanoke, Va.

As the day of the final victory of the United Nations draws nearer, it is increasingly evident to many observers that military victory alone cannot ensure the durability of the peace to follow. It is only in our own day, Mortimer J. Adler [40] says in *How To Think About War and Peace* (1944), that a substantial number of men—a minority but an articulate one—have considered both the possibility and the probability of a lasting and world-wide peace. Adler finds contemporary thought on war and peace divided into two major camps, the pessimists and the optimists. The pessimists predict that future wars are inevitable, advocate the postponement of the next world war through the

Ankers

MICHAEL STRAIGHT

timeworn machinery of balance of power diplomacy, and insist that nations will never consent to forego their sovereignity as the fundamental condition of world federation. The optimists, on the other hand, hold that through the establishment of a federated world government, built on the principles of political justice and liberty for all and the complete abolition of national independence, it is quite probable that permanent peace can be achieved after the Second World War. Of all the representatives of the latter position, "none is as clear, as realistic, and yet as uncompromisingly idealistic" as economist Michael Straight in his *Make This the Last War* (1943), maintains Adler. This American's proposal for an interdependent world society has been outlined in detail in the recently published *Searchlight on Peace Plans* (1944) by Edith Wynner and Georgia Lloyd.

Not only an ardent crusader but a sound student of world affairs, Michael Whitney Straight was born in Southampton, New York, September 1, 1916, the son of Willard D. Straight (business associate of J. P. Morgan and diplomat who financed the *New Republic* during its first year of publication) and of Dorothy Payne (Whitney) Straight, the daughter of William C. Whitney. His parents bequeathed their liberal ideas to both Michael and his older brother, now Wing Commander Whitney Willard Straight of the R.A.F.

Straight began his school life at the progressive Lincoln School in New York City, and when he was ten he was sent to Dartington Hall, Totnes, England, to prepare for college. In 1932 he entered the London School of Economics for a year of study under Harold J. Laski [41], who exerted a profound influence upon him. From 1933 to 1937 Straight attended Trinity College, Cambridge, where, as a special student of John Maynard Keynes [41], the English economist, he took his M.A. in economics with "triple-first" honors. He was a Parliamentary candidate for Cambridge on the Labor Party ticket, and he was the first American to be elected president of the Cambridge Union (1936).

Straight returned to the United States to a position in the State Department as adviser on international economics in 1938. From May 1939 to September 1940 he worked with Benjamin Cohen [41] and Thomas G. Corcoran [40] in the National Power Policy Committee in the Department of the Interior. A year later Straight returned to the Department of State to join the staff of the European Division as an economist. In May 1941 he resigned to become Washington correspondent of the *New Republic,* and in June 1943 he was made an editor. (On September 10, 1939 he had been married to Belinda Crompton. They have one son, David Willard.)

In Washington Straight attracted attention as a 100 per cent New Dealer, an idealistic, self-confident, and energetic young man with a well-grounded education and practical experience in economics and government. He was active in organizing the Washington Chapter of the Fight for Freedom Committee and served for a time as its vice-chairman. He became a member of the Union for Democratic Action and of the advisory board of the Chinese Industrial Cooperatives. He also became president of the William C. Whitney Foundation, a philanthropic body, and a director of the East and West Association. As an editor of the *City Reporter* and *Free World* he has published articles on national and international problems, while in his contributions to the *New Republic* "he has been far more emphatic and belligerent than his editors, who are now getting a bit wide around the waist," Harry Hansen [42] wrote in 1943. Since February 1, 1943, Straight has been serving in the United States Army Air Forces.

While awaiting induction into the Army, Straight consolidated his views on the future of the post-War world into a volume "both substantial and exciting," *Make This the Last War: the Future of the United Nations,* 410 pages laden with facts, statistics, and argument. "The issue is no longer the old world or the new in victory; it is the new world or defeat," Straight contends. We can make this the last war if we recognize the conditions of world progress. These are: (1) the "affirmative society" or "the social service state," a society which guarantees to all of its citizens "the right to constructive work at fair wages; to good low-cost housing; to minimum standards of nutrition, clothing, and medical care; to full opportunities for training and adult education; to real social security—basic rights which the state must fulfill where private enterprise unaided cannot.; (2) national development as the means of liberation of the dependent, poverty-stricken peoples in Asia, Africa, and Latin America, instead of the resumption after the War of their exploitation by the imperialist countries; (3) a European federation to secure the rights of its interdependent peoples on the basis of an industrially developed economic system because "the union that is a vision for the rest of the world, for Europe is a matter of physical survival"; and (4) for the well-being of all peoples, a federated world organization engaged in the search for peace, economic security, social progress, and freedom.

"The future is within us," Straight stresses again and again. "We need have only one war aim—to recognize what we have already created." He points out that from the framework of the United Nations (created on January 1, 1942 by the pledge of twenty-six nations, two-thirds of the population of the world, to endure the trials of war together to the end), with its bill of rights embodied in the Atlantic Charter, its councils for the planning of military strategy, and its various forms of control with their own staffs of the distribution of supplies, a future federal government need only grow. The machinery of the United Nations proves that "there are no administrative barriers between us and a world government if the will to world unity exists." Secondly, Straight believes, through the extension of governmental powers in the democracies in this War (namely, the full mobilization of resources—both of materials and manpower, price and wage control, and the development of a new fiscal policy), the fundamental conditions of an affirmative, equalitarian society are coming to life. As a counterpoise to increased federal interference is the growth of community organizations, especially in the civil defense programs, evidence of increased participation in democracy. For all the weaknesses of government enterprise, its results are too impressive, Straight maintains, for any group in America to cut short.

Thirdly, Straight sees the opportunity to break down the inequities of imperialism as lying in the present physical destruction of the empires of the Allies in Southeast Asia, in the industrialization of undeveloped areas, and in the reawakening of democratic forces and the strivings for self-government in these countries. Finally, although Europe cannot, of course, be united under their leadership, the Nazis have forged the basis for a United Europe in their centralized control over industry, thereby demolishing the economic sovereignty of the defeated lands. Thus Straight concludes that federation for Europe now requires the destruction of her unlimited political and cultural sovereignty.

Straight is no vague idealist in Adler's opinion; he is aware of the economic and political difficulties of his case. Straight suggests a detailed program for the relief and rehabilitation of Europe in the transition period after the War through the machinery of the United Nations. He says, however, that it is not his purpose to indicate the precise way in which a political settlement will be reached, nor the manner in which each nation must bind itself to world authority. "This is your fight," Straight asserts, urging his readers to become members of the Free World Association—to fight by enlarging the roster of this international movement which aims at world federation.

Make This the Last War, one of the works on the future of the United Nations which "contains more fire, vigor, and indignation prompted by our lapses in politics, economics, and war-making than all the jeremiads pronounced on our time by authors from Agar '44 to Sorokin '42," according to Harry Hansen, raised considerable controversy. While the ranks of reaction could hardly sympathize with Straight's sweeping thrusts at imperialism and capitalism or his espousal of New Deal policies, the critical consensus rated the substance of his argument and his detailed analyses sound, stimulating, and deserving of the widest reading and careful study. Wrote Clifton Fadiman '41: "It will be read with care, I think, not by visionaries or utopians but by thousands of plain people." Some, finding his tone impatient and dogmatic, were repelled by his emotional approach. Allan Nevins commented in the New York *Herald Tribune*: "It throbs and crackles; it is full of electric currents of attraction and repulsion. It is a book to agree with enthusiastically on one page and quarrel with furiously on another. . . . Among its cardinal virtues is the author's soaring faith that the world can be remade."

Straight thinks of this War primarily as a world-wide economic revolution. He warns that our only assurance against another world war will be to bring our economic and social systems into harmony with each other. "If we want to keep the peace," he declares, "then our armed forces are within our own nations. They are happy citizens, mobilized in the great task of keeping the whole world at work in all-out production for a century to come. If we want to keep the peace, then our international police force is the civil service of the United Nations warring ceaselessly on malnutrition, overcrowding, disease, and all the conditions that set man against man."

Reference

Wilson Lib Bul 18:202 N '43

STRATHMORE and KINGHORNE, CLAUD GEORGE BOWES-LYON, 14TH EARL OF Mar. 14, 1855—Nov. 7, 1944 Father of present Queen Elizabeth of Great Britain; family is one of the oldest in Scottish nobility, claiming descent from King Robert II; family castle, Glamis, used by Shakespeare as setting for *Macbeth*.

Obituary

N Y Times p17 N 8 '44 por

STRAUS, NATHAN May 27, 1889- Housing expert; radio station owner
Address: b. 1657 Broadway, New York City; h. Valhalla, N.Y.

In his time Nathan Straus has been a newspaperman, a department-store executive, an editor and publisher, a state senator, and the administrator of the United States Housing Authority; but he finds his present state, that of owner of the New York City radio station WMCA, the happiest one of all. Owning a radio station is "the best way of reaching the greatest number of people in disseminating the truth," he believes. "A station ought to be a force of information and entertainment, and I want to make this

NATHAN STRAUS

peculiarly New York's station. We'll pick up anything of interest to the people of this great city, and give it to them free if necessary, even though we have to throw commercials off the air. A station ought to pay its way, but not be a kept station any more than a kept girl. We want to keep it in the black, and we're going to keep it in the black."

Straus is, in other words, something of a practical crusader—and he has been known as such for most of his life. The son of Nathan and Lina (Gutherz) Straus, he was born in the family mansion in Manhattan, May 27, 1889. After attending the Collegiate School in the same city he matriculated at Princeton University in 1906. The next year found him at Heidelberg, but he returned to Princeton in 1908 and the following year received a special diploma, *cum laude*.

Nathan Straus, Sr., was a partner in R. H. Macy & Company, the department store, but young Straus was less interested in business than in journalism (Arthur Brisbane was an old friend of the family's), and he promptly found a job with the old New York *Globe*. It was of short duration. In 1910 his father fell ill, and for a few years the son worked at Macy's. Then, in 1914, he bought the humorous weekly *Puck,* and until 1917 edited and published it. Possibly he would still be editing and publishing it if it had not been for the First World War. In 1917 he enlisted in the United States Navy, and after his honorable discharge he went back to the *Globe* as assistant editor. That was in 1919. The following year he ran for the New York Senate from his district—and was elected.

In the New York Senate for the next six years, Straus served as chairman of the Committee on Agriculture, as a member of committees on conservation, taxation, and retrenchment, and sponsored much liberal legislation. A Democrat, he worked with Franklin Delano Roosevelt [42], and when in 1928 Roosevelt ran for Governor of New York he almost made Straus his running mate for Lieutenant Gover-

nor. By this time Straus was back in private life, president of Nathan Straus-Duparquet, Inc., the largest hotel-restaurant equipment company in the United States. But he was by no means entirely concerned with business. In 1933 he sponsored a limited-dividend housing project, Hillside Homes, whose 118 modern buildings provided 1,415 apartments for lower-income families at an average monthly rental of $11 per room. In 1935 he was appointed by Mayor La Guardia [40] special housing commissioner for the City of New York to make a European housing survey.

In 1937 a $526,000,000 Federal housing program was hammered through a reluctant Congress by New York's Senator Robert Wagner [41]. Under the United States Housing Act the Federal Government became a financing agency through which funds were made available to qualified borrowers and grantees, all responsibility for initiating, constructing, financing, and operating the housing and slum clearance developments lying with the local authorities. The Housing Act could not function without subsidiary state, county, and city organizations. The President nominated Straus as administrator of the United States Housing Authority. Wagner supported Straus, but La Guardia accused his former special housing commissioner of "stargazing" and announced that "one can't move families into blueprints." In October 1937 Straus resigned the $24,000-a-year presidency of Nathan Straus-Duparquet, Inc., and the following month took over his new duties, calling it a job which "calls for action and very little talk."

It did call for all his powers of persuasion, however. For a while he had to roam the country, answering arguments against public housing and persuading the cities to set up housing authorities. In time local opposition was overcome and the cities obtained the necessary enabling laws, successfully defending them from constitutional attack, tearing down slums, giving tax exemption to the new projects, building and managing them. But the building-and-loan and real estate lobbies remained opposed to public housing, and they then concentrated all their force on Washington. By the end of 1941 nearly a billion dollars worth of public housing had been built, and the Truman [42] Committee had publicly commended Straus's work as Housing Administrator, but he had powerful enemies in Congress. A House Committee finally refused to appropriate any more money for his agency while he remained at the head of it, and in January 1942 he resigned, soon afterwards making public a letter in which he condemned the public housing foes who had brought about his resignation. The United States Housing Authority was reorganized as a branch of the National Housing Agency.

In *Seven Myths of Housing* (1944) Straus explodes those myths broadcast by the enemies of public housing. He shows that there are slums in every town, even in rural communities. He shows that the agitation for the Government to "buy up the slums" comes from slum owners who would like the Government to "bail them out"—that the practical way to clear the slums is to provide better houses for slum dwellers. He shows that the slum dweller does not "create the slums"; he shows that public housing neither injures private business nor threatens to bankrupt the country. In post-War years he would like to see 900,000 homes built every year for five years, one-third of them subsidized. Cities should buy land for future use, and six years hence all substandard housing should be outlawed. Although some critics disagreed with this post-War program for one reason or another, nearly all of them agreed that Straus's book was a valuable contribution to an understanding of housing. According to *Annals of the American Academy*, "The writing is simple, direct, and on the whole sweetly reasonable. Mr. Straus marshals facts in a way that should appeal to a businessman or civic leader seeking light."

In March 1944 Straus told the members of a women's organization: "With the real estate interests and slum owners completely in the saddle, we're going to lose the fight for good housing unless women do something about it. It's their natural field." He pointed out that slum clearance could be obtained only with a complete reorganization of the tax structure and with a drastic scaling down of valuations on slum property. "There is no hope for proper housing so long as real estate values are greater than human values."

At this time Straus was already owner of WMCA, acquired in September 1943 from Edward Noble.[43] Among new programs launched were *New World A-Coming*, based on the book by Roi Ottley[43], and dealing with the place of the Negro in American life, the paradox of his economic and social frustration in a democracy, and the hopes and problems that lie ahead; *Wake Up, America,* a forum in which "we get people to talk about everything from how to bring up children to what to do with the world of tomorrow"; and *Let's Listen to a Story*. (The last program Straus describes as unlike the type of children's program that "specializes in blood and murder. It's just an old-fashioned idea. Not goody-goody stuff, just telling stories to a different group of children every Sunday.")

In June 1944 the New York Newspaper Guild presented Straus with its Page One award for the "alert and constructive service" WMCA rendered through such programs as *New World A-Coming, We Hold These Truths, Labor Arbitration, Christmas Overseas,* and *Wake Up, America.* Straus did not receive praise from other quarters about a month later, however, when references to Communism and "bureaucratic Administration" were cut from a radio address being made by State Senator Frederick R. Coudert, Jr.[41] Straus defended the action of his station, maintaining that the deletions consisted of "aspersions on our allied and other material calculated to spread disunity at home." In September the president of WMCA announced that the station was prepared to broadcast the sessions of Congress, a proposal supported by Senator Claude Pepper[41] of Florida, who introduced a resolution that would provide the necessary authority. While permission was not granted, early in December the program *Halls of Congress* was begun, a program of verbatim dramatizations of debates and speeches selected from the *Congressional Record.* According to *Variety,* that program and

other public service programs account for WMCA's ending 1944 "with virtually no profit, despite a gross for the year of one and one-half million dollars." The station "in the past year, is said to have nixed [refused] some $300,000 in gross revenue from advertisers it didn't want. . . . The trade impression is that Straus's attitude is a healthy one for radio."

"I don't think there is any issue you ought not to talk about," Straus says. "I don't know what good thing but isn't made better by giving it publicity. I don't know what bad thing but isn't killed by bringing it out into the light." He has therefore taken issue with the National Association of Broadcasters, which does not permit its members to sell time for the discussion of controversial subjects. WMCA will sell time to labor unions and other organizations for the discussion of such subjects, provided another sponsor can be found for the other side. Both sides of the question must be presented on a similar basis, however; neither may be combined with entertainment features; and neither can promote racial or religious intolerance or encourage discrimination on account of color, race, or creed. Thus the radio station manager is virtually ruled out as a judge of what should or should not be heard over the radio, and the public is protected against "one-sided answers to two-sided questions." This policy is intended to supplement the practice of donating time for the discussion of controversial subjects, not to supplant it.

A quiet, friendly man who wears "glasses like Henry Morgenthau's[40]," Straus spends long hours in his large, blue-carpeted office on the floor above WMCA's studios. "Gosh, I've been working ten and sometimes fourteen hours a day," he says, "and so has Helen." (Helen is his wife, the former Helen E. Sachs, to whom he was married on April 29, 1915. She is in charge of all educational and children's programs.) The Strauses have four sons—Nathan, Barnard Sachs, Irving Lehman and Ronald Peter. All of the sons are in service, or they might be working for WMCA ten and fourteen hours a day, too.

References

New Repub 93:168 D 15 '37
Newsweek 10:13 N 1 '37 por
PM Mag p3 Ap 16 '44 por
Who's Who in America 1944-45
Who's Who in New York 1938

STRAUS, OSKAR Apr. 6, 1870- Composer

Address: b. c/o Hans Bartsch, 1674 Broadway, New York City; h. Hotel Meurice, 145 W. 58th St., New York City

"Wherever I go," laments Oskar Straus, "people ask me how I am related to Johann Strauss. They say, isn't it wonderful how I have inherited the gift! So I explain to them that I spell my name with one final 's,' that all my ancestors have spelled their name with one 's,' and that there isn't the remotest connection between the 'Strauses' and the 'Strausses.'" Nevertheless, people invariably associate Oskar Straus in some vague way with the Waltz King. The only connection

OSKAR STRAUS

between the two is an artistic one, for Oskar Straus singlehandedly carried on the tradition of the Viennese waltz as originated by Johann Strauss. He was also instrumental in establishing Vienna as the operetta center of the world.

Now that Straus is past seventy years of age, he can look back over a long and successful musical life. He was born in the legendary atmosphere of old Vienna, April 6, 1870, the son of Louis and Gabriele (Stern) Straus. The elder Straus was a merchant, but young Oskar aspired to become a second Beethoven. He prepared for this career by studying composition with Hermann Grädener and Adolph Prosniz in Vienna, and then went to Berlin for study with the famous Max Bruch, who has not spoken to him since he began writing operettas.

For five years, from 1895 to 1900, Straus was engaged as conductor in Brunn, Teplitz, Mainz, and Berlin theatres. At Berlin he was Kapellmeister for E. von Wolzogen's Uber-brettl, for which he wrote many compositions. This was "an artistic cabaret" designed to "raise the standards of the variety theatre and make it express modern thought and feeling." It lasted only one year, but while he was its conductor Straus wrote two of his best songs—"Der lustige Ehemann" and "Die Haselnuss."

Soon Straus began to feel the limitations of even the superior cabaret's form of entertainment. At the turn of the century he retired from the theatre so that he might devote his entire time to composition. Before he turned to the field that was to bring him international fame Straus tried his hand at various operatic forms. His first effort was a comic opera entitled *Der schwarze Mann* (1900), which was followed by an opera, *Columbine* (1904). Straus then demonstrated his talent for parody in his next works, *Die lustigen Nibelungen* (1904) and *Hugdietrich's Brautfahrt* (1906), which were musical travesties of Wagnerian operas.

Straus gained world-wide attention in 1907 with his first major success, *Ein Walzertraum* ("Waltz Dream"). The next year he assured his claim to fame with *Der tapfere Soldat* ("The Chocolate Soldier"). Its instantaneous popularity caused it to be played everywhere—in Berlin, Paris, London, and New York as well as in countless lesser known places. The English version of the operetta was performed on the London stage for several seasons and was produced all over the United States. The plot of *The Chocolate Soldier* was an adaptation by Rudolph Bernauer and Leopold Jacobson of George Bernard Shaw's [44] *Arms and the Man.* One reviewer remarked that the combination of a satiric story with equally effective musical satire had not been employed since the period of Gilbert and Sullivan. Straus's score established new standards for operetta music; with *The Chocolate Soldier* he freed the operetta from the vulgarities of musical hack-writing by proving that musical lyrics could be catchy without ever becoming commonplace. Straus also contributed to the operetta form by making use of new dance forms for music, such as the shimmy and fox-trot.

While *The Chocolate Soldier* was enjoying its early triumphs, Straus announced to the world that he intended to abandon operetta composition. Although he considered *The Chocolate Soldier* his best work, Strauss stated that it was to be the last work of its kind which he would write; in the future he would devote himself exclusively to the composition of serious works. Straus obviously did not put his intentions into practice, however, for he continued to turn out operettas. *Die kleine Freundin* ("The Little Friend," Vienna, 1911), soon opened in New York. In the opinion of the late Percy Hammond, its music was the best that Straus had ever written. The weaknesses of the libretto, which portrayed life in the Latin Quarter of Paris, were compensated for by the unusual excellence of the Straus score—which, incidentally, saved the show from failure.

Subsequent Straus operettas include *Rund um die Liebe* (1914), which was produced in New York in 1917 as *All Around Love*; *Die schöne Unbekannte* (Vienna, 1915), which was produced in New York as *My Lady's Glove* in 1917; *Mariette*, which was produced in London, Paris, Berlin, and Vienna in 1929 and 1930; *Drei Walzer*, which was given in Zurich in 1935, and in 1938 it was produced in New York as *Three Waltzes*.

Among the composer's "serious" works are an overture, *Der Traum ein Leben* (Grillparzer); a violin sonata in A minor; a serenade for string orchestra; "Russalka," for solo, chorus, and orchestra; a "Bilderbuch ohne Bilder," for piano (four hands); a "Suite in Tanzform," for violin, cello, and piano; "Alt Wiener Reigen," for string orchestra; and miscellaneous violin, cello, and piano compositions.

In 1930 Straus was awarded the Order of Merit by the Austrian Government in recognition of his musical achievement. During the same year he went to Hollywood to write music for motion pictures. Straus remained in Hollywood for some months during which time he contributed some songs to the Grace Moore [44] film *A Lady's Morals* (1930) and provided the musical score for *Daybreak* (1931), a film based upon a novel by Arthur Schnitzler. During subsequent visits to Hollywood Straus composed music for Bobby Breen and Maurice Chevalier films; perhaps the most sparkling scores Straus turned out while in Hollywood were those for Maurice Chevalier's *Smiling Lieutenant* (1931) and *One Hour With You* (1932).

The composer had left Berlin in 1927, when he went to Paris. He resided there for many years and became a French citizen the day that the Second World War was declared. Before he escaped to America, Straus instituted legal proceedings against Germany to obtain the royalties on his works; they were being sent to the Reich rather than to him. After the fall of France, Straus waited five months in Vichy for permission to go to the United States. In 1940 he arrived in America, where he will probably remain for the duration of the War. In 1942 he made a lengthy concert tour under independent auspices. The recent adaptation of his *Chocolate Soldier* and the sundry revivals of old Straus operettas brought in large box office receipts. Straus believes that American appreciation of music has increased immeasurably in the past twenty years. "You are producing great artists," he says, "great singers and great instrumentalists. And now you have begun to create a great American music." Straus is also highly optimistic in his attitude toward motion pictures which, he hopes, may one day rival grand opera as a musical vehicle; he thinks films are an excellent medium through which great music may be preserved.

The composer has been married twice. His first wife from whom he was to be divorced, was a celebrated Austrian violinist known as Irmen, for whom the composer wrote serious violin music. His second marriage in 1908 was to Clara Singer. The Strauses have three children, two sons and a daughter.

A recent interviewer described Straus as a "long, angular, and dignified" man who "peers pleasantly at the world through a pair of horn-rimmed glasses perched atop his great crag of a nose. What there is of his hair is white." Fat, black cigars are his trademark, and he smokes them constantly. Straus estimates that he has smoked well over 25,000 such cigars by this time. His fondness for cigars is matched only by his dislike of New York City and jazz. Both are too "noisy" to suit him. Once, after a particularly stormy Atlantic crossing, Straus declared that jazz had probably been invented by a seasick musician. Jerome Kern [42] and the late George Gershwin are the most tolerable American composers, believes Straus, because their music is the least "noisy."

In the summer of 1943, at the age of seventy-three, the composer began work on a new operetta, *Do-Si-Do*, which was announced as completed in December 1944. He had conducted the "preview" of the feature song, "Handsome Is as Handsome Does," over Mutual's *Treasure Hour of Song* in February 1944. Sung by Licia Albanese, soprano of the Metropolitan Opera Company, it was in the composer's typical lilting waltz style.

Johann Strauss is not the only person with whom Oskar Straus has been erroneously associated. The Hollywood movie mogul who once succeeded in inducing Straus to come to the cinema mecca thought he had hired Richard Strauss [44]. The matter was clarified when Oskar Straus after it became known that in some Hollywood circles Richard Strauss, the composer of "Death and Transfiguration," *Salome*, and other ponderous works, was thought to have written "The Beautiful Blue Danube."

References

N Y Herald Tribune p4 F 28 '40

Baker's Biographical Dictionary of Musicians 1940

Thompson, O. ed. International Cyclopedia of Music and Musicians 1943

Variety Radio Directory 1940-41

Who's Who in Central and East-Europe 1935-36

Who's Who in the Theatre 1939

STRAUS, PERCY SELDEN June 27, 1876 —Apr. 6, 1944 Chairman of the board of R. H. Macy & Company, Inc.; directorship of the New York Life Insurance Company and a trusteeship of the New York Public Library were just a few of his posts; he was one of a small group of men responsible for the New York World's Fair of 1939-1940; in 1929 he gave an unrestricted endowment of $1,000,000 to New York University.

Obituary

N Y Times p13 Ap 8 '44 por

STRAUSS, RICHARD (shtrous rik'ärt) June 11, 1864- Composer; conductor
Address: h. Villa Strauss, Zöppritzstrasse No. 46, Garmisch-Partenkirchen, Bavaria, Germany

"He *was* a genius." These words of Ernest Newman's are perhaps the music world's evaluation of the composer Richard Strauss. The "flaming genius", "anarch of art," and "supreme master of the orchestra" who revolutionized musical style has become, with the years, the possessor of "a mere talent." Yet he stands today, by virtue of past performance, as a great figure in the history of music.

The son of Franz S. Strauss, first hornist at the Munich Court Opera, and Josephine (Pschorr) Strauss, of the well known family of musically inclined brewers, Richard Strauss made his entrance into the world in an apartment two floors above a Munich restaurant on June 11, 1864—the year Richard Wagner came to conduct the Royal Orchestra. Franz Strauss was among those responsible for Wagner's eventual departure. Although he played the master's music "lusciously" (being the best hornist in Germany and a professor at the Royal Academy of Music), Strauss made no secret of his hatred for Wagner's music and his person. Little Richard's musical education was conducted along classical lines. Frau Strauss started her son off on the violin and piano at the age of four and then turned the precocious child over to August Tombo, harpist in the Royal Orchestra, and F. W. Meyer.

(Continued next page)

RICHARD STRAUSS

Little Richard Strauss wrote musical notes before he knew the letters of the alphabet, composing nearly a hundred pieces before he began numbering them. Opus 1, a "Festmarsch," was published when he was twelve, and some of his works were played while he was still in school. These early works show the influence of the classical masters he was taught to revere. "Strauss's astonishing later development has made us underestimate his youthful works," comments Guy Maier. "The early songs, instrumental solos, and chamber music are rewarding, possess astonishing vitality, and deserve frequent hearing."

At eighteen, when Strauss was graduated from the Gymnasium and entered the University of Munich, he heard his two-year-old Symphony in D Minor played in concert by the great Wagnerian conductor Hermann Levi. Meanwhile the youth had been converted from passionate anti-Wagnerism to equally passionate Wagnerism by Alexander Ritter. This conversion was also helped by Hans von Bülow, who recognized and encouraged Richard in spite of the misery he, as Wagner's apostle, had suffered at the hands of the elder Strauss. He gave Richard a chance to conduct his own "Serenade for Wind Instruments" (with great success, although the youth had never led an orchestra before). When in 1885 the Meiningen Ducal Orchestra needed a new *Hofmusikdirector* to assist von Bülow he chose Richard Strauss, although the latter was only twenty-one. The pay was small, but the honor was great, and so was the opportunity for study under the greatest conductor of his day.

According to von Bülow "Strauss's debut as a conductor as well as a pianist was simply stunning," and when von Bülow resigned his protégé remained as the sole conductor. After five months in this post the tall young musician became alarmed at rumors that the Duke of Meiningen intended to disband his famous orchestra and therefore accepted an invitation to join the Munich Opera as *Musikdirector*

and third conductor. As a conductor, Strauss was given little opportunity to show any initiative in his new post; but it did leave much of his time free for composing. Immediately upon signing the new contract Strauss left for a vacation trip through Italy, which he loved and celebrated in a symphonic fantasy, *Aus Italien* ("From Italy"), in a style new to him. In the composer's words, it was "the connecting link between the old and the new"—between the influence of Brahms and the influence of Liszt.

The first performance of this fantasy, conducted by the twenty-two-year-old composer, set the pattern for the reception of his future works: "general amazement and wrath," he reported, "because I too have now dared to go my own way, create my own form, and bother the heads of indolent persons. . . . No one has ever become a great artist who was not held by thousands to be crazy." Von Bülow himself did not approve of the "cacaphonic and programmatic" tendencies of his young friend; but, recognizing Strauss as one of the most important of contemporary composers, he welcomed the younger man's new tone poems, "Macbeth" (1887), the soon-popular "Don Juan" (1888), and the awesome "Death and Transfiguration" ("Tod und Verklärung," 1889). It was at this time, too, that Strauss wrote his most popular song, the "Serenade."

Again through von Bülow, the composer was appointed in 1889 to succeed Liszt as court conductor at Weimar, which had been built into a music center by his predecessor. Strauss followed Liszt's motto, "First Place to the Living," conducting programs which he called "madly modern" but which were "well attended and much applauded." In the concerts he featured the not-yet-appreciated works of Liszt, and at the opera house he devoted himself to Wagner. The young conductor prepared himself for this by repeated visits to Wagner's shrine of Bayreuth, where one summer he directed the chorus in *Parsifal* and made himself generally useful; and in 1894 he was invited to conduct the Bayreuth *Tannhäuser*. The widowed Cosima Wagner's comment was, "So young and so modern, yet how well you conduct *Tannhäuser!*"

To show his admiration for Wagner, Strauss, who ordinarily sat while conducting, stood whenever he led a Wagner composition. He gave lecture recitals at the piano to help others understand them; it is said that, once near death from illness, he had just resigned himself to leaving life when he reconsidered: "No! Before I die I should like to conduct *Tristan*." The first Strauss opera, *Guntram*, written mainly in 1892, is frankly Wagnerian in theme, treatment, and even names of characters. (After its resounding failure it was dropped and has never been revived except to complete a Strauss cycle. One reason for its failure was its unnatural and unnecessarily ascetic ending; another was said to be that "a public already beginning to tire of Wagner would not stomach imitation Wagner.") Freihild, the heroine, was sung by Pauline de Ahna, the niece of one of Strauss's neighbors, who also portrayed Elizabeth in *Tannhäuser*. In September 1894, after a four-month engagement, she and Richard Strauss were married. From that time on, the young Frau Strauss devoted her talents to popularizing her husband's songs by recitals at which he often accompanied her on the piano.

A month after his marriage Strauss returned to Munich to become the successor of Generalmusikdirector Levi. In spite of the *Guntram* failure, the composer was becoming an ever more important figure in music. During the 1894-1895 season he began to fulfill regular engagements with the Berlin Philharmonic Orchestra and subsequently toured all Europe with it. His songs and tone poems, which came to include "The Merry Pranks of Till Eulenspiegel" (1895), "Thus Spake Zarathustra" (1896), and "Don Quixote" (1897), grew in popularity. These longer works were violently attacked on the basis of their acknowledged difficulty, their allegedly crude realism (sheep bleating and wind-machines in "Don Quixote," for instance), and their "unmelodious construction." It was also considered pretty shocking to base a musical work on Friedrich Nietzsche's anarchistic *Also sprach Zarathustra*, and as for setting philosophic and scientific ideas to music—! The violent abuse Strauss's works drew furnished invaluable advertising; it made him notorious and also reminded people that the same words were hurled at "Richard I" (Wagner) as at "Richard II" (Strauss). "Consequently the concert halls were crowded whenever a new work by this bold, bad man was performed"; and in 1889 Strauss, as the most famous orchestral conductor of the time, was engaged by the Royal Opera in Berlin.

This position allowed him frequent leaves of absence for concert tours. There were many Strauss festivals all over Europe, a number of them lasting a week, and the composer was always invited. (Later "he could not begin to accept all the invitations that came to him.") "Paris was most hospitable to his operas, thoroughly un-French though they are; and London went through several Strauss crazes." It was only in Berlin itself that Germany's outstanding musician had any trouble in "asserting himself in the concert halls" and had to build up and train his own *Tonkünstlerorchester* (tone-art orchestra) to carry out his concert plans. With this he gave a series of Modern Concerts, presenting the works of talented but not yet recognized composers of many countries, and interpreting all of Liszt's symphonic poems in chronological order and "with such sympathetic insight that . . . even 'Hamlet,' which had previously been coldly received, was honored with stormy applause." As for Strauss's own works, "under his own direction his complicated and very difficult scores were not subject to misinterpretation."

These concerts were not given for profit—a wealthy friend made up the deficits—but were "by way of preaching progressive principles and helping composers who had not had their fair share of attention." Strauss himself has always had an "almost miraculous" knack for the profitable, being one of the few composers who could live well from his royalties, even without the income from his concert tours and conductorships—and he is also notoriously tight-fisted. Nevertheless, he has devoted "a vast amount of time and energy" to the aid of less well known musicians. He discovered

and popularized Engelbert Humperdinck; and in 1898 Strauss was one of the founders of the Genossenschaft Deutscher Tonsetzer, a sort of German ASCAP to secure composers royalties on the performances of their works. This was purely altruistic on his part— "Strauss had ways of his own of getting his dues"—yet he was forced to overcome much opposition from both sides and had to write scores of letters, public and private, in behalf of the new organization. In 1901 "Richard II" was also elected president of the Allgemeine Deutsche Musikverein for the advancement of modern music by means of annual festivals. (This post he retained for eight years.) In addition, he was for a time editor of a periodical, *Der Morgen*.

With all this activity, Strauss continued to compose. For the Kaiser, who did not like his other "noisy" music, Strauss wrote two military marches and was rewarded with the decoration of Kronenorden, 3rd class. In 1899 he began work on a second opera, *Feuersnot* ("Fire Famine"), the libretto being based on an old legend. Critics and the public found it highly objectionable, and concluded that "the climax calls for an attitude too medieval for modern audiences." Musically, however, *Feuersnot* represents a great advancement over *Guntram;* much freer from Wagnerism, it is "entirely the product of Strauss's own mind and ripest methods," alternating simple folk tunes with "the utmost complications of polyphonic structure."

When in 1903 Strauss brought forth an operatic version of *Salome* (in Hedwig Lachman's translation) it was generally assumed that he chose scandalous subjects because they suited his nature, although Oscar Wilde's play was tremendously popular in Germany. First performed in Dresden in 1905, *Salome* proved forbiddingly complex and difficult but became very popular. The "objectionable features" of its libretto caused it to be "edited" in London; and in the United States, as Deems Taylor [40] puts it, "the critics went up into the attic and dusted off adjectives that hadn't been in use since Ibsen was first produced in London. I remember that 'bestial', 'fetid', 'slimy,' and 'nauseous' were among the more complimentary terms that they applied to the score." Nowadays *Salome* is standard in the operatic repertoire; so is *Elektra*, first presented in 1909, in which "all the peculiarities of Strauss, especially his mania for needless dissonances and excessive polyphonic complexity, as well as his disregard for the possibilities of vocal achievement," were said to have reached "a climax which alarmed even his devoted followers and made them wonder, 'What next?'" This work was the first product of Strauss's long and fruitful collaboration with the distinguished poet Hugo von Hoffmannsthal. (Their correspondence has since been published, edited by Dr. Franz Strauss, the composer's son.) The *Elektra* libretto, a Freudian interpretation, proved offensive to many when first presented, but was a decided success.

The autobiographical quality of *Feuersnot*—containing, as it does, puns on the names of Wagner and Strauss (which means fight, bouquet, or ostrich)—pales beside the egoism of

STRAUSS, RICHARD—*Continued*

the tone poem "Ein Heldenleben" ("A Hero's Life"), written in 1898, and the "Sinfonia Domestica," written five years later. In "Heldenleben" Strauss strikes back at all his critics in sections known as "The Hero's Adversaries" and "The Hero's Battlefield"—the latter "full of unmitigated horror." Lest there be any doubt as to the protagonist's identity, "The Hero's Works" are recalled—twenty-three Strauss themes in all. The dissonances Strauss hurled at his critics have been blamed for the wave of modernists who make harshness and atonality "an end in themselves, applicable at all times, including situations in which Strauss himself would have used honeyed strains." In the "Domestic Symphony" 108 musicians spend forty-five minutes in reporting the doings of the Strauss household during one day and night, from a family quarrel to the baby splashing in his bath.

Having reached what then seemed the heights—or depths—of music in choice of theme and manner, Strauss managed yet another surprise: "This time," said he, "I will write a Mozart opera." Von Hoffmannsthal furnished him with a libretto of eighteenth-century Viennese intrigue in the romantic comedy vein, descending sometimes to farce; and Strauss began working on the music— including a number of anachronistic but charming waltzes—as soon as the draft of the first act reached him. (It is said that he was never entirely satisfied with the last act development.) This opera, produced as *Der Rosenkavalier* ("The Bearer of the Rose"), was strikingly different from any of his previous works. "With its fine period feeling and its attractive blend of artificiality and humanity, [this] must be one of the six best operatic libretti in the world," according to Eric Blom, "and although Strauss's setting is too heavy and highly wrought, his music has a glamour and pointed allusiveness and mastery. . . . Even its uncertainty of style is redeemed by its glowing beauty and sincerity of feeling." First presented in 1911, *Der Rosenkavalier* is the best known and most popular of Strauss's operas. The Metropolitan Opera Company has presented it some seventy times, and the role of the seventeen-year-old Octavian (scored for a mezzo-soprano who must disguise herself as a man disguised as a woman) is a particular favorite of Risë Stevens[41].

In 1926 the opera was made into a silent motion picture, von Hoffmannsthal adapting the book, and the composer adapting and adding three new pieces of music (to be played by an accompanying orchestra). Highly praised in Germany, it was less well received by the English critics, who thought that the film was disappointing, but that the music made up for it.

In a retrospective view of the Strauss operas published in February 1944, Herbert F. Peyser comments: "Today it is almost incredible that this or that page of *Der Rosenkavalier* should have been labeled 'Mozartian.' For in good truth Strauss was never more absolutely Strauss than in this opera which has taken a secure place as one of the great lyric comedies of musical literature, by the

side of Mozart's *Figaro*, Wagner's *Meistersinger,* and Verdi's *Falstaff*. No, the leopard had not changed his spots. It was the public which had caught up with Strauss. The worst charges that could be leveled at *Der Rosenkavalier* were that the opera was vulgar, overwritten, and in a measure commonplace, all of which was and still is true. But the musical idiom remained what Strauss's idiom had always been, and so it came to pass that the once dreaded *Salome*—not to speak of *Elektra* —grew intelligible and lost its awfulness when looked at from the vantage point of *Rosenkavalier*. . . . Long ago the dread of Strauss's dissonances gave place to the frank admission that his sugared, even middle-class sentimentalism ran the danger of palling. For a time the gall of his tone poems and operas appeared to outweigh the sugar. Then the phenomenon reversed itself."

With the success of *Der Rosenkavalier,* Richard Strauss stood at the very peak of the musical world. As a conductor he "continued fine"; but as a composer he repeatedly disappointed his expectant admirers. *Ariadne auf Naxos* (1912), a two-act opera intended as an interlude to Molière's *Le Bourgeois gentilhomme,* consists of two contrasted scenes played at once, one from the tragi comic Ariadne myth, the other a sprightly Italian *commedia dell' arte*. Von Hoffmannsthal and Count Harry von Kessler provided Strauss with the scenario for the ballet *Eine Joseph-Legende* (1914), which "does not belong to the best of the composer's output." "Eine Alpensinfonie," a long and complex work written in 100 days, came out in 1915 and showed "complete exhaustion" of inspiration. "There was scarcely anything in this work he had not said much better before."

The next Strauss opera, *Die Frau ohne Schatten* ("The Woman Without a Shadow"), proved to be a complicated, mystical allegory which "lured some fine music from the composer, but not a consistently great score," and amounted at times "almost to self-plagiarism." A second ballet, *Schlagobers* ("Whipped Cream"), produced in 1924, was as sweet, light and evanescent as its subject. It was rumored that the lavish production of this ballet was one reason for Strauss's resignation from the co-directorship of the Vienna Staatsoper "to devote all his time to composition." As might have been expected, the composer had aroused antagonism by his "excessive production of his own works."

Since 1917 Strauss had been working on and off at an operatic presentation of an incident of his early married life, *Intermezzo,* produced in 1925. Musically it "contained nothing new apart from the transparency of its texture and an endeavor to revert to a *bel canto* style of singing." The next libretto was furnished again by von Hoffmannsthal. *Die ägyptische Helena* ("The Egyptian Helen") was, like *Elektra,* "the psychological subtilization of a classical subject"—the return from Troy of the ever-glamorous Helen. But the poet "overdid it," producing such a mélange of magic and menace that audiences were left bewildered; nor, it was charged, did Strauss's music redeem the book. Nevertheless, as was customary with Strauss premières, *Helena* "proved the musical sensation of the [1928] season." At his death in 1929 Hugo von Hoffmannsthal left his friend and collaborator another operatic libretto, "a slight but charming and poetic story," *Arabella*. Produced in 1933, it "turned out to be the most refined thing the composer had ever written for the orchestra, exquisite in sound from beginning to end," but "very unlikely to last."

When Adolf Hitler's '42 National Socialists came into power in Germany, Richard Strauss was sixty-nine and the country's foremost composer. Like many Germans, he took the situation calmly and, failing to realize its full implications, accepted the chairmanship of the new Reichsmusikkammer (State Music Office). Nevertheless, Strauss made arrangements to be guest conductor at the 1934 Salzburg Music Festival, at a time when all Austria was in mourning for her Chancellor, Engelbert Dollfuss—murdered, it was considered, by the Nazis. And although this plan was canceled at the last moment, the Austrians went ahead with their plans to present a cycle of four Strauss operas.

Because of the composer's great eminence, the new regime graciously overlooked his former undesirable associations; and on Strauss's seventieth birthday he was presented with "warmly inscribed" photographs of Hitler and his chief lieutenant. Now that Strauss's "non-Aryan" librettist was so conveniently dead the Nazis expected no further indiscretions along that line. To their pained surprise, the new librettist proved to be the famous novelist Stefan Zweig, author of *The Case of Sergeant Grischa*—an Austrian and a Jew to boot. He provided Strauss with the book of *Die schweigsame Frau* ("The Silent Woman"), based on Jonson's *Epicoene*. Produced at Dresden in 1935, the opera was snubbed by the official critics and immediately dropped from the repertory; the librettist's name appeared nowhere on the program. When Strauss asked Zweig for two more librettos the novelist declined the honor, since his works could not even be produced. "Nonsense!" retorted Strauss by letter, pointing out that he as an old man would write more slowly than he used to; by the time he had finished the score "the gang now in power" would be out, and there would be no more trouble. This cheerful view was not appreciated by the Nazis, who were of course reading the mail; and a few months later Herr Doktor Strauss resigned from the Music Office because of the weight of his years.

Later that year the seventy-two-year-old composer announced his choice of a new, acceptable librettist, Dr. Joseph Gregor of the National Library at Vienna. Rehearsals were well under way and all arrangements had been made for the 1938 première of their historical German opera when the score was released to the public—and the Nazi militarists discovered that the "obstinate Bavarian Strauss and his guaranteed 'Aryan' librettist had concocted an impassioned plea against war!" Titled *Der Friedenstag* ("The Day of Peace"), its music was considered simpler and less daring than Strauss's earlier works. "But it contains spots (notably a central love scene) of noble and eloquent music." Little is known of the next Strauss-Gregor opera, announced for 1938 production, except its innocuous title, *Daphne*.

Richard Strauss was able to defy the dictator because of his unique position as "Naziland's No. 1 cultural exhibit." He can hardly, on his record, be *persona grata* to the touchy rulers of the Reich; yet his seventy-fifth birthday in 1939 was the first one of nationwide importance which Der Führer himself attended. The reason is his tremendous musical eminence: "A half-dozen lusty, brilliantly orchestrated tone poems" are played by the major symphony orchestras "almost as often as Beethoven's symphonies." *Der Rosenkavalier* is universally popular; *Salome* and *Elektra* are performed regularly. Strauss's high standing as a conductor is admitted even by his ill-wishers; and at least a dozen of the 150 difficult songs for which, by 1929, he had written the music are permanent additions to the list of German *Lieder* classics. The best known include "Morgen", "Cäcilie", "Allerseelen" ("All Soul's Day"), and "Traum durch die Dämmerung" ("Twilight Dream"). Strauss has also written chamber music and various choral and orchestral pieces. His favorite among his works is *Intermezzo*—"for personal reasons."

The fate of all innovators has come to Strauss—to be called old-fashioned. To this he grins, "My music is the most modern." Other famed—and exiled—German modernists, such as Paul Hindemith '41 and Arnold Schoenberg '42, the composer refuses to discuss. His favorite in music is Mozart, followed by Beethoven, and he admires the works of Johann (no relative) Strauss, the Waltz King. Jazz he dismisses as abominable. (His tastes in painting are equally conservative: he likes and owns El Grecos, Rubens', and Tintorettos.)

In spite of his views on Nazism, in 1940 Strauss composed and dedicated to the Axis partner Emperor Hirohito '42 a piece in honor of the 2,600th anniversary of the Imperial Japanese Dynasty. In the years that followed he was the subject of various rumors. In August 1944, when a number of his public appearances were canceled, it was reported that he was placed under house arrest "somewhere in Austria." According to the *Schweizer Illustrierte Zeitung* of Zurich, the octogenarian had refused to billet a dozen air-raid refugees at his villa near Hitler's Berchtesgaden retreat, claiming his need for peace and privacy. Threatened with cancellation of his planned national birthday celebrations, Strauss was unmoved. Instead, the Nazis merely refused him a passport to Zurich to conduct *Elektra*. *Time* wrote: "International music circles, remembering Strauss's huge international royalties in the past, knowing him for a highly practical artist, were inclined to discount the heroism in his stubbornness. On the other hand, it was quite conceivable that the eighty-year-old composer might have balked at riding the few remaining miles to music's Valhalla aboard the Nazi bandwagon."

Herr Doktor Strauss—he uses the title in the German way although it is honorary—"looks more like a conservative country squire than a world-renowned conductor and composer. Ruddy-complexioned, with clear pale blue childlike eyes, he carries his full six feet three with an easy natural dignity. Bent slightly with the weight of his many years,

STRAUSS, RICHARD—*Continued*

his tall figure is still spare and vigorous. There is no trace of pose or affectation about him." Even in his own idyllic Bavarian villa this eminent composer, who did not shrink from defying Hitler, has to wipe his feet on three different doormats before he dares enter Frau Strauss's spotless house.

References

Mentor 17 :24-6 F '29 il
Newsweek 3 :16 Je 16 '34 por; 13 :31-2 Je 12 '39 por
Time 32 :30-3 Jl 25 '38 (por cover)
Brockway, W. and Weinstock, H. Men of Music p520-36 1939
Ewen, D. ed. Book of Modern Composers p49-66 1942; Composers of Today 1936
Finck, H. T. Richard Strauss: the Man and His Works 1917
Huneker, J. Overtones p1-63 1904
Pannain, G. Modern Composers p17-34 1933
Rosenfeld, P. Musical Portraits p27-56 1920
Thompson, O. ed. International Cyclopedia of Music and Musicians 1943

STUART, KENNETH Sept. 9, 1891- Canadian Army officer; author

Address: h. 162 Metcalfe St., Ottawa, Canada

Lieutenant General Kenneth Stuart (inactive since November 1944), Canada's ex-chief of staff, is an author, editor, and teacher as well as a soldier; "he might, too, be called a prophet because a decade before the outbreak of the Second Great War he foresaw the course it would take, had determined correctly the use that was to be made of aircraft and mechanized armies, and had written of their importance." General Stuart's blueprint of the war to come had been drafted during the years (1929 to 1939) in which he edited, in his spare time, the *Canadian Defence Quarterly,* published by a "Committee of Officers at Ottawa." For the *Defence Quarterly* he wrote editorials, expert articles on the art of war, and reviews of books by such military masters as General Pershing, Major General J. F. C. Fuller, and Captain B. H. Liddell Hart[40]. To those who read General Stuart's predictions, the German "lightning war," it is said, "could have come as no surprise."

General Stuart's military career has followed much the same pattern as those of Generals McNaughton[42] and Crerar[44] the latter having been chief of the General Staff when Stuart was deputy and vice-chief. A Scot by descent, "but not of the dour, traditional type," Kenneth Stuart comes from a long line of fighting men. He was born at Three Rivers, Quebec, September 9, 1891, the son of the Reverend H. C. and Annie M. (Colston) Stuart. Although his father was a Church of England clergyman, his forefathers "for years back had been warriors." At an early age Kenneth Stuart decided that he would have a military career, too; and after attending Bishop's College School at Lennoxville, Quebec, he entered the Royal Military College, from which he was graduated in 1911. Commissioned in the Canadian

Canadian Army Photo

LT. GEN. KENNETH STUART

Engineers, he proceeded to the School of Military Engineering at Chatham, England. After serving briefly with the Army Staff College at Camberley, England, he returned to Canada.

On the outbreak of the First World War, young Stuart went overseas in command of the 1st Army Troop Company of the Royal Canadian Engineers. By 1917 he had won a promotion to lieutenant colonel and was commanding the 7th Field Company of the Royal Canadian Engineers at Vimy and Passchendale. The next year found them operating at Hangard Wood, where, under the personal supervision of the colonel, they advanced "under heavy shell-fire" to bridge a river. Again official dispatches mention Stuart "personally reconnoitering the route for artillery under heavy fire." For these demonstrations of courage and for "consistent good work and devotion to duty," Stuart was awarded a Distinguished Service Order and a Military Cross.

Back in Canada at the end of the War, Stuart held various staff appointments: senior engineer officer at Calgary (1919-20); district engineer officer at Quebec (1920-25); district engineer officer at Victoria (1928-29). He was also assistant director of Military Intelligence at Ottawa in 1929. From 1934 to 1937 he was a general staff officer at the Royal Military College, and for a year thereafter chief instructor on military subjects. Because he had disliked lectures and examinations when he was there as a student, Stuart as a staff member "did away with them as nearly as possible." He also revamped the College's basic course in civil engineering.

After serving as director of Military Operations and Intelligence at Ottawa, Stuart returned to the Royal Military College as commandant, 1939 to 1940. He served as deputy chief of the General Staff during the following year. As vice-chief of staff to Major General Crerar in 1941, he went overseas to learn the lessons of the present war. When Crerar took command of the 2nd Canadian Division, General Stuart succeeded him, becoming chief of staff in December 1941.

As chief of the General Staff, Stuart was specifically charged with the "coordination of the work undertaken by each of the four staff branches of the Department." (These four branches comprise the General Staff, which directs policy of mobilization and equipment as well as training, intelligence, and operations; that of the adjutant general, which deals with personnel; that of the quartermaster general, which deals with supplies; and that of the master general of ordnance, which deals with guns, rifles, tanks, shells, and equipment.) The chief of the General Staff must also oversee the system of National Defence. The Government of Canada decides the policy under which the Department of National Defence (like all government departments) is run. The General Staff branch translates that policy into terms of military action, coordinated always with the broad strategy of the United Nations.

One of the original members of the Canadian-American Joint Defence Board, General Stuart became the Army member of the Canadian Section in August 1940. In June 1942 the Canadian Minister of National Defence announced that General Stuart had taken over temporary command of the Pacific area "in order to deal with the organization plans arising out of the expansion of Army forces in that command." On June 21 the acting commander in chief of the West Coast Defences reported direct enemy action: Estevan Point on Vancouver Island was shelled by an enemy submarine, presumably Japanese. The attack —the first against Canadian soil in the history of Canada as a dominion—had as its objective the government wireless and telegraph station at Estevan Point. Although no damage was done, the shells having landed on the rocks well beyond the building, the incident brought severe protests from British Columbia members of Parliament "against what they regard as the insufficiency of defenses on the Pacific Coast."

By December 1943, however, Canadian waters had been made so safe that General Stuart, who had "organized the Canadian participation in the invasion of Kiska in the Aleutian Islands," was transferred to England to succeed General McNaughton in command of the 1st Canadian Army. Having formed an army under the Canadian flag from Dominion units scattered under various British commands, McNaughton retired. As his successor, Stuart commanded this army four months, and began the training for their part in the invasion, a training which General Crerar took over in March 1944, when he was recalled from Italy for the purpose. And in November 1944 the Department of National Defence announced that General Kenneth Stuart, C.B., D.S.O., M.C., was on leave pending retirement.

General Stuart is said to be a "down to earth sort of person, thoroughly democratic, and as popular with the men in the ranks as with officers." As one private summed it up after Stuart made a camp inspection: "He may be a brass hat but he's no stuffed shirt."

He is slim, tall, athletic, ruddy with "gray hair brushed straight back from the forehead; mustache close-clipped, neat; straight blue eyes, affable manner. . . . If you met him in civilian clothes, you would probably take him for a lawyer, certainly a professional man. Before retirement, he was described as working 'a full seven-day week: Stuart's "day begins at 8:45; often his lunch is brought to his desk; his afternoon work continues until 7 or 7:30; and he is back at his desk by 8:30 to carry on until midnight or later." He is said to be "high strung, quick in thought and movement. Long arms shoot out for desired papers, he begins to answer questions before you have finished asking them. True, this man could be stern and ruthless. There is a glint of steel in those eyes. But as you talk with him in his office at headquarters he is relaxed. His humor is not of the dry sort; it is spontaneous."

General Stuart was made a Companion of the Bath in the King's Honor List on January 1, 1943, receiving this award from the hands of King George VI '42 at a subsequent investiture. Since 1916 he has been married to Marguerite Dorothy Stuart; they have one daughter, Marguerite Coleridge, and one son, Victor Cuthbert Henry, a flight lieutenant in the Royal Canadian Air Force.

Reference

Who's Who in Canada 1940-41

STURE-VASA, MARY ALSOP *See* O'Hara, M.

SUES, (ILONA) RALF (sū'es i-lō'na rälf) Author

Address: c/o Little, Brown & Co., 34 Beacon St., Boston

The forthright woman who wrote the revealing book on China—*Shark's Fins and Millet* (1944)—is Ilona Ralf Sues, "Polish intellectual, journalist, and Left-wing idealist." Miss Sues was born in Lodz, Poland, the daughter of a businessman and sportsman and of a former concert violinist. Most of her life has been lived in the atmosphere of international activity, and her traveling has taken her all over the world. She went to school in both Poland and Silesia and in her teens lived for two years with an aunt and uncle in Montreal. During this Canadian visit she learned English by painstakingly reading Shaw '44, Wilde, Dickens, and Poe with a dictionary in her lap. (Her language repertoire also includes Polish, Russian, German, and French.) She also learned shorthand while in Canada and worked a while for her uncle as a secretary. On her return to Europe her jobs became a series of hops, skips, and jumps over the Continent. According to the New York *Post* she was interpreter for the American Relief Administration in Warsaw after the First World War, then private secretary of the American adviser to the Polish Minister of Railways and to Major T. Reade Ryan, whom she followed to Berlin when he became American delegate to the Reparations Commission there. For an interlude after that she "studied life" in Paris. Her next job was as interpreter for Colonel Edward B. Lowry, European representative for

Shelbourne Studios

RALF SUES

Will Hays [43] and the American film industry, as he traveled from capital to capital on the Continent conferring with the various ministers of education.

By 1929 Miss Sues had gravitated to Geneva, where the world's hope for lasting peace was located. She was not directly associated with the League of Nations, however, but with the Anti-Opium Information Bureau, "a very small private organization, whose aim it was to make the League and the individual governments live up to their international pledges." "We had to be on the alert constantly, watch every word, every move: the vested interests and the League's Secretariat were up to a new trick every day to sabotage inconvenient international agreements. As soon as we learned of a novel one we would tip off the press and the Victim Bloc [a group of non-manufacturing and nonproducing countries], raise hell in one of our blue press notes or communiques, or prepare a meticulously accurate paper for some ambitious delegate in search of a good non-political speech, and get him to 'spill the beans' on opium at the League's Assembly or the Council table."

In spite of the noble efforts of the Bureau, however, its work seems to have been in vain. By 1936 Miss Sues had become disgusted with the evasion, hypocrisy, and appeasement of the various governments and had decided there was no solution to the opium problem. The whole atmosphere of Geneva, she said, was vitiating, and nowhere in the international field, except in China, did it appear that anything constructive was going on. Attracted to the Chinese delegates, she had already begun to learn Chinese; and in the spring of 1936 she sold her couch, bought a Leica camera, and with her cat and her typewriter set out as a freelance journalist to study China's reconstruction.

It was Miss Sues's idea to see things for herself and to publish "Letters to Tom, Dick, and Harry" as she went along, although she improvidently made no effort to obtain either a publishing contract or a newspaper assignment. For financial support she made only an oral agreement with a London news-photo agency, an agreement which soon fell through, and she was obliged to fall back on secretarial work or teaching now and then. "But living in China is cheap," she reported, "and I am anything but ambitious."

The Chinese travelogue began unexpectedly in Hong Kong, where the inquisitive Miss Sues had disembarked from her Shanghai-bound vessel after hearing that Generalissimo Chiang Kai-shek [40] had just arrived in nearby Canton, had ousted the Kwangtung Autonomous Provincial Government, and was incorporating the province into the territory of the National Government. Simultaneously, it was learned, he was negotiating with the overlords of the neighboring Kwangsi Province to fall in line as well. Miss Sues, it seemed, had landed in China on a historical occasion, for the pacification of the Kwangsi Province would mean that all of China would be united except for the territory of the Red Army, which at that time, she says, Chiang still expected to conquer.

From her vantage point in Canton, Miss Sues watched the reconstruction of Kwangtung Province. In September 1936 the Chiangs' New Life Movement (inaugurated in 1934) officially came to the Cantonese. She looked on curiously as "spic and span eagle-eyed" policemen tried to see to it that the people acted in the manner that was now expected of "perfect citizens." Gambling, slovenliness, spitting and smoking in the streets—all forms of ill-breeding—were now forbidden by the Movement. Offenders were spoken to sharply, beaten, or even sent to prison. To Miss Sues there was "something disquieting" about this method of introducing a new era to China; to the Chinese the whole business was amusing, even though the spiritual Movement, with its code of ethics (courtesy, service, honesty, honor) and its emphasis on cleanliness and manners, seemed as little likely to solve China's pressing economic problems as to help her repel the invader.

It was while Miss Sues was in Shanghai (December 1936) that the Generalissimo was "kidnapped" in Sian by the Young Marshal, Chang Hsueh-liang. Without Sian, she writes, China's present United Anti-Japanese Front would not have been born. According to her version of the event, the Generalissimo was isolated from his people by "an iron ring of the most reactionary and pro-Japanese Cabinet China ever had." The leader of this group was the Minister of War, Ho Ying-chin [41], who sought to keep from Chiang the fact that the majority of the people wanted him to stop the civil war against the Communists and to prepare a resistance against Japan. The Young Marshal, Miss Sues explains, did not "capture" the Generalissimo, but detained him in Sian long enough to acquaint him with these facts. Ho Ying-chin, on the other hand, was so determined to prevent this that he dispatched an air force to Sian with the order to blast that city to pieces. Only a terrific snowstorm, she declares, saved the lives of Chiang, Mme. Chiang [40], and their friends. (Agnes

Smedley [44], who was in the city at the time, writes, on the contrary, that the weather was excellent.)

Miss Sues was in Tsingtao in July 1937 when Japan invaded China. In September she offered her services to the Chinese Government and was subsequently asked to come to Nanking, then the capital of the country. While being considered for a position in the Propaganda Ministry under Cheng Kung-po, she was casually asked by the Minister to draft a scheme showing how China's propaganda should be handled abroad. Miss Sues was familiar with the complicated maze involved in news gathering in China; accordingly, in her forthright way she outlined a practical plan of consolidation with a definite system for issuing news. (China's position in the outside world was often complicated by the lack of an efficient news system.) She sent a copy of her notes to W. H. Donald with the suggestion that the Chiangs might be interested and then proceeded to forget the whole matter.

It was in Shanghai that Miss Sues had been introduced to the legendary Donald. This fascinating, volcanic, brutally frank man, she wrote then, "was the only person in China who could tell anybody what he thought and get away with it." As unofficial "adviser" to the Chiangs he was the person anyone who wanted to know about China had to meet. No one could even see either of the Chiangs without Donald. Miss Sues credits the man with a large part of the reorientation of China's international policy in the middle '30's from one of "painfully introvert Chinese diplomacy" to "a keenly alert extrovert policy." And as she began to know him better she more and more felt that he was daily re-enacting Shaw's *Pygmalion* with Madame as Eliza. Without Donald, says Miss Sues, Madame seemed incapable of handling important situations.

Donald did not permit Miss Sues to forget about the memo which she had sent to him. In October she learned that Mme. Chiang—who was anxious to purge the Kuomintang—was pleased with it and wanted Miss Sues to act as her unofficial adviser on foreign publicity. At first Miss Sues worked in Donald's office, learning the ropes, writing daily articles for the foreign press on any subject she chose, and assisting Donald with Madame's voluminous correspondence. On one occasion she worked with Mme. Chiang herself to help out with a particular rush of mail. The second time she saw Madame was when they discussed the reorganization of the publicity bureau along the lines suggested by the memo. As the First Lady of China outlined rules and details, Miss Sues writes, she herself became "thrilled." "Here was Madame as she really was, pulsating, vibrating, dynamic—not the sentimental Good Samaritan, not the widely publicized pious Bible quoter, not the bluestocking reformer, but Mme. Chiang Kai-shek the Fighter. A courageous, temperamental little lady with no party to support her [the reactionary clique of the Kuomintang continually attempted to estrange her from the Generalissimo, who depended on her advice], with no foreign power to back her, all alone."

Miss Sues was so enthusiastic over Madame's attitude that she at once dramatically offered to present, in three short days, evidences of corruption in Cheng's bureaucratic organization. In the required time she did the investigating, drew up her radical conclusions, and presented them. The final decision was left to the Generalissimo. Before he could decide favorably, however, Madame's enemies in the Kuomintang got the upper hand, and the reorganization program was never effected as outlined. Madame had a breakdown as a result and declared she was through with publicity; and Miss Sues, who had innocently mentioned Madame's name in public—an unpardonable sin—parted from her. When Nanking was evacuated at the end of the year Miss Sues was sent on to Hankow as a member of the Central Publicity Bureau of the Propaganda Ministry. For a time she acted as English editor and foreign press censor. Finally, tired of the unproductive job and of the sabotage on the part of those members she had suggested firing, she made a few suggestions and gave them to her chief. A few days later she found herself inexplicably dismissed.

Miss Sues' portrait of Mme. Chiang is one for which a large portion of the Occidental world was unprepared. She saw Madame as a "sparkling political cocktail—radical by nature, Christian by education, capitalist by circumstances, pseudo-democrat by conviction, and temperamentally a dictator. Democracy to her is not the inalienable right of the people, but a candy which the Government may in time dole out as a reward for good behavior." Moreover, declares Miss Sues, she has never had any real understanding of the Chinese people. But "selfish, petty, and capricious" as she often is "inside her four walls," she has the "fighting spirit of a lioness, courage, tenacity, and ruse." On her shoulders she is carrying two supremely difficult tasks: that of intensifying the collaboration with America, and that of purging the Government of inefficiency and corruption.

Shortly after her adventures with the Chinese Government, Miss Sues became determined to visit the Communist territory of the Red Army. Throughout her trip her enthusiasm for what she was seeing and learning was tremendous. The spirit of the 8th Route Army, she writes, is completely democratic. Its system of training the soldiers, contrary to the traditional policy of the National Government, is based on the idea that "the average Chinese is intelligent, reliable, resourceful, and an individualist." As it marches across the country its administration establishes free schools and hospitals, cooperatives, and discussion groups, extends the franchise to all the people, and aids them in setting up their own governing units. "Notwithstanding all statements to the contrary," Miss Sues writes, "the Chinese people are ripe for democracy. Given a chance, they understand and practice it."

Back in Hankow, Miss Sues took over the French and English broadcasts of the Propaganda Section of the Military Affairs Commission of the National Defense Council, an organization outside of Kuomintang influence. Her job—her rank was colonel—was to pick

SUES, RALF—*Continued*

out and arrange the material to be used and then to broadcast it. This work lasted until the Government withdrew to Chungking, when Miss Sues, because of poor health, resigned and made ready to go home to Geneva.

A year after the Second World War began Miss Sues decided that she was homesick enough for China to "live on millet and a dollar a month and work for the Chinese Defence League." She left Geneva for America on her way East, but when she arrived in the United States at the beginning of 1941 she found that she would no longer be welcome in China. In February a radio interview with Johannes Steel [41] had broadcast to the world Miss Sues' opinions on the situation in the East. She had expressed her feeling that the Fascist-minded military clique was isolating Chiang from his people, advising him to make peace with Japan and fight the Communists again. Soon after the broadcast Miss Sues was warned by T. V. Soong's [41] No. 1 adviser in Washington that she would be shot on sight if she returned to China. Reaction, she knew then, had indeed grown strong in that country. W. H. Donald had disappeared, as he had promised to do when reaction got the upper hand, and without him Mme. Chiang seemed to lack support for the time being.

What China needs most of all now is national unity, declares Miss Sues. This implies "the reorganization of the Army, the placing of China's war economy on a war footing, the recognition of all political parties [to end the one-party authoritarian rule of the Kuomintang], and the people's participation in the Government." In the heart and hands of Chiang Kai-shek lies now the answer to China's dilemma.

Shark's Fins and Millet has been dedicated to the "Nameless Builders of a free, democratic China," the little men and women of China whom Miss Sues sees as its hope for the future. Her title is the key to the contents of her book: the two extremes of Chinese life. Shark's fins are the delicacy of the rich and powerful; millet, the food of the masses. Her story is lively and full of anecdotes and intimate portraits of the people she encountered during her three-year sojourn. In "rubbing all the glamour off the face of the ruling clique of our Far Eastern Ally," says Agnes Smedley, all kinds of people get hurt—some deservedly, some less so; even innocent bystanders are not safe. Some of these are men who are really victims of this ruling clique. Miss Smedley also finds many small inaccuracies. "However, Miss Sues has written," says Orville Prescott, "the most interesting book about China that I have read in years Her book is not objective, judicious, well-organized, or well-written. It is emotional, partisan, violent, personal, and even a little coy and girlish. But it sheds more light on contemporary China, presents information that has not been printed elsewhere . . . more than given in half a dozen of the usual variety of Chinese books added together."

The woman who "barged in everywhere in China" and "made Chinese fur fly" with her frank criticisms is "Ralf" to her friends. She is "small, vivacious, dark, quick-witted, and almost painfully honest," writes Sterling North [43]. Her dark brown boyish bob is slashed with a streak of white, says another interviewer. "Her level brown eyes look at you keenly through light-rimmed spectacles," and she speaks with "a definite but easy-to-understand Polish accent." Her reading interests incline toward biography and international affairs.

References

N Y Post Mag p23 F 16 '44 por

Sues, I. R. Shark's Fins and Millet 1944

SULLAVAN, MARGARET May 16, 1911-Actress

Address: b. c/o Leland Hayward, Inc., 444 Madison Ave., New York City; h. Brentwood, Calif.

Margaret Sullavan's "magnificent performance" in John van Druten's [44] three-character comedy, *The Voice of the Turtle* (1943), has established her as one of the top-ranking stars in the theatre—an achievement which fulfills an ambition she has never relinquished even though she has been a motion-picture star since 1933. The New York drama critics considered her acting in *The Voice of the Turtle* the best performance given by any actress in the 1943-1944 season.

Born May 16, 1911 in Norfolk, Virginia, Margaret Brooke Sullavan is the daughter of Cornelius H. and Garland (Council) Sullavan. (Dudley Digges, whose Dublin Abbey Players origin makes him an authority on things Irish, has assured Miss Sullavan that the *a* instead of the *i* in Sullavan is so authentically Irish that she could without other credentials be elected to a high office in the Ancient Order of Hiberians.) Miss Sullavan's ancestors were in America during Revolutionary days. The combination of Irish, American Revolutionary, and Tidewater Virginia stock is one writer's explanation for "the willful little star who has gone against Hollywood tradition but who nevertheless has gained her goal."

Her parents were "confirmed gentle people and sufficiently well off on the proceeds of Mr. Sullavan's brokerage business to maintain an inflexible Southern front before the world." But Margaret found the children of Norfolk's poor folk more exciting than the "nice" playmates of whom her mother approved. It was when the Sullavans discovered her habit of climbing down a lattice from her bedroom window to prowl about the countryside that they placed her in Miss Turnbull's Norfolk Tutoring School for Girls. Participation in school plays fixed her desire to be an actress, which had begun with recitations in the Sullavan back parlor at the age of six. Mr. and Mrs. Sullavan liked this idea even less than her visits on the wrong side of the railroad tracks, and she was removed from the local school to the Walter Herron Taylor School. St. George's private school and Chatham Episcopal Institute followed. None of these educational pilgrimages settled the family row over the stage or curbed her high spirits. Stories of school pranks are legion.

There is one that Howard Sharpe related in a *Liberty* Magazine article which concerns a midnight frog hunt and the school principal's surprise on finding a live frog in his desk the following morning, and another tells of her caricatures of her schoolmates in a school play. Sullins College in Bristol, Virginia, gave the finishing touches to Miss Sullavan's education.

With the ending of her school days, the question of the stage came up again. A compromise was arrived at—Margaret would study dancing. Three weeks of hopping about the dance studio of the Denishawn School in Boston convinced Miss Sullavan that her career was in the drama, and she transferred to the E. E. Clive Dramatic School in the same city. Her father had offered her an allowance, but she rejected it and earned her way by selling books in the Harvard Cooperative Store. Some sources credit Miss Sullavan with having formed the University Players Guild, a group composed of students from Harvard, Princeton, and Smith College, who produced plays at Falmouth, on Cape Cod. The Guild was a community venture, and the revenue was divided equally among the members of the company and just about paid their board and the running expenses. The summer of 1928 found Miss Sullavan enrolled with the Guild, playing leading roles opposite Henry Fonda, to whom she later was married. "Peggy and Hank," as they called each other, did not fall in love that first summer—conversations were said to have been in the Sullavan "argumentative vein" rather than the sentimental. At the end of the season Miss Sullavan called upon the New York producers—the best they could do for her was to give her the role of an offstage voice in *Karl and Anna,* a German play which proved to be a failure. She was considering joining the Jitney Players, who barnstormed towns missed by the Chautauqua Players, when her father persuaded her to return to Norfolk so that she might make a proper debut. Her season as a belle was terminated when she joined Fonda and other members of the University Players for another summer at Cape Cod. Now that she definitely had made her decision to seek a career in the theatre, Miss Sullavan was apparently happy. One writer reports that her disposition noticeably improved. At any rate it has been said that no more cooperative or friendly young actress than Margaret Sullavan ever worked in a Little Theatre barn.

There was not much time for romance—the group decided to build their own theatre, and in between rehearsals the players pitched in to help the carpenters and decorators rush through the finishing touches on the new theatre. In the night club, which the Guild ran as an adjunct of the theatre, Miss Sullavan, with true community spirit, carried trays of refreshments to patrons or acted as stooge to Fonda's mad magician act. At the end of the season she and Fonda obtained a marriage license but on sober second thought decided to postpone using it. That year, 1930, the New York producers gave Miss Sullavan the lead in the Southern company of Preston Sturgess' [41] hit play, *Strictly Dishonorable.* The role of Isabella Parry, a Southern girl,

MARGARET SULLAVAN

was considered ideally suited to the young actress, who, at the time, was described as "fiercely ambitious, and at the same time utterly soft, feminine, and bewitching." So successful was her interpretation of Isabella Parry that when she played the part in her home town her parents were reconciled to her career.

At the end of the run Miss Sullavan joined the University Players in Baltimore, where they had moved for a season of stock. Henry Fonda was among them. The couple were married on Christmas Day, 1930, in the hotel banquet hall. Bretaigne Windust '43, then a member of the group, played their favorite song during the ceremony—the theme number of the *Constant Nymph,* in which play they both had acted at Cape Cod. The marriage lasted less than a year.

In May 1931 Miss Sullavan made her bow on Broadway in the leading role of *A Modern Virgin,* a Lee Shubert production. The story of her interview with the well known showman is amusing and typical of the man who is famous for his quick decisions. Suffering from laryngitis when she was called for the part, Miss Sullavan told him in hoarse tones of her theatrical experience. Without asking for a reading or anything further, Shubert said, "You're hired." When she asked how he could judge her so quickly, he said, "You have a voice like Helen Morgan and Ethel Barrymore—they're stars." It is reported that even after her voice cleared Miss Sullavan played *A Modern Virgin* "down her gullet." The play lasted for only twenty-nine performances, but the critics were kind to the new leading actress—which may account for the present "throaty notes" in the star's voice. Despite the fact that during the following two years Miss Sullavan had the misfortune to appear in four failures, her prestige as an actress continued to grow. One reviewer predicted that "someday someone will find a real part for her—and then—!"

Taking no more chances on untried plays, Miss Sullavan took over in 1933 the Paula

SULLAVAN, MARGARET—*Continued*

Jordan role in *Dinner at Eight* (1932), an established hit play, when Marguerite Churchill left to fill a motion-picture contract. Frequently, during her two years on Broadway, Miss Sullavan had refused motion-picture contracts because of her devotion to the theatre. During the run of *Dinner at Eight,* nevertheless, Universal Pictures succeeded in getting her to sign a three-year contract by limiting the contract to two pictures a year with summers free for theatre work. To leave the stage before originating one successful role was irritating, however, and as a result she immediately "clashed with both studio and press." "Acting in the movies is just like ditch-digging," she informed one executive; and when she saw the "rushes" of her first picture, *Only Yesterday* (1933) (which turned out to be a four-star triumph for both Miss Sullavan and the picture), she offered the company $2,500 to release her. Universal refused. The summer of 1934 found Miss Sullavan exercising her privilege to return to the theatre when she appeared as Norma Besant in a summer theatre revival of *Coquette* at Mount Kisco, New York.

It was during the filming of her third picture, *The Good Fairy* (1935), that Miss Sullavan was married to William Wyler, the distinguished director, who was to win the Academy award for *Mrs. Miniver* in 1942. (Wyler, a cousin of Carl Laemmle, had been born in Alsace-Lorraine.) The story of their romance, as reported by Howard Sharpe, is that Wyler had been having difficulties with Miss Sullavan. Reaching the limit of his patience one day, Wyler pointed out to her before a group of listening workers that she had demoralized him, disrupted the company, and caused the picture, thus far, to require twelve weeks of shooting when the schedule called for a maximum of seven weeks. The quarrel ended in a dinner engagement, and a week later Wyler and Miss Sullavan were married in Yuma, Arizona, in 1934. (Miss Sullavan and Wyler were divorced two years later.)

From the beginning of her motion-picture career Miss Sullavan had not only been fortunate enough to appear in successful pictures but to earn high praise for her work. She continued her triumphant career in the pictures *So Red the Rose* (1935), *Next Time We Love* (1936), and *The Moon's Our Home* (1936), but upon the expiration of her contract with Universal Miss Sullavan left her stellar position in Hollywood to play an unstarred part in the Broadway play *Stage Door*. When the producer offered to place her name in electric lights over the marquee, Margaret Sullavan conscientiously refused, saying that she had not yet earned stardom in the theatre. Conscientiousness to that degree added to her reputation as an enigma. By those who have been allowed to interview her (she has refused to accede to the usual motion-picture buildup of personal appearances or to show up "for booming flashlights on a Hollywood opening night") she has been variously described as shy, as an electric personality who seems more alive than most people, as retiring, conscientious, willful, and unconventional.

Leland Hayward, one of the most important Hollywood agents, had had Miss Sullavan under contract for a number of years. During the Broadway run of *Stage Door* (1936) they were married at the Newport home of his parents. The successful run of the play was interrupted by "an act of God"—and Miss Sullavan returned to Los Angeles, where Brooke, their first daughter, was born in 1937. The Haywards live in a rambling house in Brentwood, California. A second daughter, Bridget, was born in 1939, and William Leland was born in 1941. In addition to his highly lucrative theatrical agency, Hayward is president of the Southwest Airways' new Thunderbird Field, which in 1941 was one of forty-eight "kindergartens" for Army airmen. The field is twelve miles from Phoenix, Arizona, and was financed by Hollywood and Broadway money. Brian Aherne and Gilbert Miller are among its stockholders. Hayward is also a TWA director. Friends have reported that "Margaret's happy married life has changed her completely. She is much calmer, softer, and is completely domesticated." Hayward and intimate friends often call her "Maggie."

Since her third marriage Miss Sullavan has made a number of pictures, the most important of which are: *Three Comrades* (1938), *The Mortal Storm* (1940), *Back Street* (1941), and *Cry Havoc* (1943). She returned to Broadway in December 1943 in *The Voice of the Turtle* as Sally, a whimsical and struggling young actress who falls in love with an Army sergeant on leave who had been "stood up by her girl friend." Howard Barnes, New York *Herald Tribune* critic, voiced the opinion of his fellow reviewers when he proclaimed her portrayal to be "impeccably right . . . little short of magnificent. . . . She reads her lines and plays her business so aptly that there is no questioning the fact that one is witnessing the finest actress of our day in the theatre."

In addition to the critical acclaim she received for her work in *The Voice of the Turtle,* the play promises to be financially profitable for Miss Sullavan. She invested $3,000 in its production; that makes her an important stockholder of a piece of property which Hal Wallis and others have been considering at the price of $3,000,000 for the basic copyright—including the future theatre box-office receipts, stock, radio, television, motion picture, and foreign rights. The film rights were finally sold to Warner Brothers for $500,000 (according to a newspaper account) plus a percentage of the profits, which, it is thought, will bring the figure to several millions. The "takings" of *The Voice of the Turtle* on Broadway alone in the forty-four weeks it played in 1944 (there was a summer hiatus of six weeks while the cast had a vacation) amounted to $968,000. (If the gross for the Chicago company is added, the total was $1,229,000.) On the advice of her physician, Miss Sullavan, then reported as underweight, left the cast in mid-December, a few days later leaving for California with her husband. Both are reported as pleased with their investment in *The Voice of the Turtle,* and Leland Hayward's good fortune has continued: he is the producer of *A Bell For Adano,* one of the highly successful plays on Broadway in the 1944-1945 season.

Miss Sullavan is five feet two and one-half inches tall, weighs 109 pounds, has gray eyes, naturally arched eyebrows, and a tawny shade of hair. In a recent *Theatre Arts Monthly* article John van Druten said in a description of her that she has the rarest and one of the most attractive things in a woman, hair-colored hair and skin-colored skin. "She has a simplicity, an almost embarrassing directness, and a friendliness that have nothing of the theatre-gush about them." Others who know her report that she likes to go barefoot and wear slacks, and cares little about dressing-up, but when she does she can be dazzling.

References

Liberty 20:18+ My 29 '43 por
Life 8:42 Je 17 '40 pors
N Y Post p11 Mr 14 '40
Theatre Arts Monthly 28:272 My '44
International Motion Picture Almanac 1943-44
Who's Who in the Theatre 1939

SULZBERGER C(YRUS) L(EO, 2d)
(sulz'bur"gẻr) Oct. 27, 1912- Foreign correspondent
Address: b. c/o New York Times, 229 W. 43rd St., New York City

Rated among the ablest of the New York *Times*'s large staff of foreign correspondents, C. L. Sulzberger became in December 1944 the chief overseas correspondent of that newspaper. Since 1940, when he joined the paper's London bureau, his front-page stories and his feature articles in the *Times*'s magazine section have carefully informed readers of the complex situation in the Near and Middle East and the Russian scene; in the spring of 1944 he was assigned to the American 5th Army in Italy. "Still young, and a nephew of New York *Times* publisher Arthur Hayes Sulzberger '43, he has bested both handicaps, has won the respect of *Times* men on his own merits."

Cyrus Leo Sulzberger 2d was born October 27, 1912, in New York City. His father was the late Leo Sulzberger, and his mother, now Mrs. Ely Jacques Kahn, was the former Beatrice Josephi. At the age of seventeen young Leo was graduated from the Horace Mann School for Boys, after which he went to Harvard. Four years later he received his B.S., *magna cum laude*. Other distinctions he won at college were the Phi Beta Kappa key and the Lloyd McKim Garrison prize for the best undergraduate poem (1934).

Asserting that he would not work for his family's New York *Times* until the paper sought his services, "Cy" Sulzberger left the East and began his career on the Pittsburgh *Press* as a general reporter and rewrite man. He is said to have spent most of his slim salary on books and modern art. In 1935 he went to Washington for the United Press, covering the Treasury, the Federal Reserve System, and Labor. "There he was distinguished as the worst-dressed Washington reporter, wearing a frayed trench coat in all weathers."

Sulzberger's interest in labor in those years (1935-1938) resulted in a book, *Sit Down With John L. Lewis* (1938). Edward Levinson's criticism in the *Nation* was representative: "Despite a style made annoying by repetition and staccato journalese, Sulzberger paints a rounded portrait of Lewis '42 that contains many hitherto unavailable details. . . . Sulzberger's comments on other CIO leaders are largely snap judgments, and he is far better at reporting than analysis. His labor history shows but a perfunctory attempt to understand the movement and its development, and there are errors on that score. However, for those who want to understand Lewis and the mainsprings of his behavior *Sit Down With John L. Lewis* will prove of great value."

Following a brief period of free-lancing in the United States, Sulzberger went abroad in 1938, where he became a foreign correspondent for the London *Evening Standard* with a roving commission in Europe. During the Albanian crisis he rejoined the United Press, sending his articles from Bulgaria and Greece. He also worked for the North American Newspaper Alliance and the British Broadcasting Corporation. Receiving the *Times* offer in 1940, he joined its London bureau and within another year had won the Overseas Press Club Award for the best reporting on the German-Russian front. Within four years he had traveled approximately 100,000 miles in thirty countries, visiting many of the fronts of the Second World War. "He wrote so many needling articles about Balkan and Axis politics that he was successively banned from Hungary, Rumania, Bulgaria, and Italy." In particular he aroused the ire of the late Italian propaganda chief, Virginio Gayda '40, who called him "a creeping tartantula, going from country to country, spreading poison."

In 1940 Italian leaders were incensed by Sulzberger's reports of Italian troop movements in Albania; early in 1941 he was on hand to dispatch eyewitness accounts of the fighting in Yugoslavia during the opening days of the hostilities. Traveling on a time schedule "a few hours ahead of the Germans," he joined the Yugoslav Army on the Albania frontier. While in Yugoslavia he interviewed the head of the German espionage system there, who assured him: "Ich bin nur Himmelspion. I am only a spy of the heavens. I look to see if there will be a good crops in this friendly country." Sulzberger and Ed Kennedy of the Associated Press shared several adventures. In Preshov they were both accused of espionage and marched off to jail. When a policeman got up and testified that Kennedy was a Hungarian who had been brought up with him in the border town of Kassa, they both laughed so much that even the Gestapo knew there must be a mistake, and released them. Back in Budapest, and about to leave for Rumania, they ran into the German DNB correspondent for Belgrade. "What on earth are you doing here?" they asked. "Oh," he said with obvious disappointment, "we heard about the arrest and disappearance of two American correspondents in Slovakia. I came to write the story."

Although arrested by Serbian gendarmes (at the time he was wearing a skiing costume and driving a heavily loaded automobile) Sulzberger was able to witness most of the action before proceeding to Greece via Turkey. His journey there terminated "with a five-hour

C. L. SULZBERGER

rowboat trip across the Aegean. . . . The wind came up fresh and strong, shoving clouds beneath the incredible stars in these seas and the oars dipped up phosphorescent pools. Only by threatening my two boatmen with a revolver was I able to induce them to proceed." But it was already "all over with" in Greece; he learned about the last hours of that country as a free kingdom from a refugee Cabinet minister seeking to escape.

Early in May 1941 Sulzberger was sending his dispatches to the *Times* from Ankara, Turkey. He reported that Russian troops were massing on the Iranian border, that Germany was reconcentrating her armies in Bulgaria and Rumania and threatening Turkish-British communications.

Romance, as well as adventure, came to young Cy Sulzberger during those years in the Near East. Before the Nazis had taken Greece he met Marina Ladas in Athens. (While Greece was fighting, Marina had refused to leave her country.) The story is told that she listened in to Sulzberger's short-wave broadcasts to the *Times* from Turkey—broadcasts during which Sulzberger spelled out the difficult words: "T for Tom, H for Harry," etc. She heard him say: "M for Marina." She managed to smuggle a message to him: "If you receive this, in your next broadcast say 'R for roses.'" Sure enough, from Ankara came Sulzberger's "M for Marina", "R for roses." She got another message through: "If you want me to leave here, say 'B for blossoms.'" After his next broadcast, when he all but shouted "B for blossoms," Marina made her way to Ankara. But their wedding had to wait: when she got to Turkey she found that the *Times* had rushed Sulzberger to the newest war front—Russia. On his return late in 1942 they were married in Beirut, Syria. (A daughter, Marina Beatrice, was born to the Sulzbergers in September 1944.)

Sulzberger reached Russia in July 1941. He was initially struck "by the famine in consumer goods when wandering about the stores of Leninkana, a bustling Armenian frontier town, and retained this impression throughout. . . . To a lesser degree this is true of Moscow." He was highly impressed by the Red Army; he commented also that the Soviets "have produced the only good war songs heard so far on the Allied side." After spending the better part of six months in the U.S.S.R., he concluded that the Soviet Union had its good points as well as its faults: "This correspondent hasn't been back home in almost four years, but it is his impression that we have spent far too much time recently in examing the latter."

After a brief interlude at home Sulzberger was sent by the *Times* back to Syria. From Beirut he reported that the Arab Terantine population feared a Zionist-dominated Palestine in the post-War era; he also condemned the harmful effect of the "lack of an official United States policy" in the Middle East. Toward the end of May Sulzberger was on his way to Russia again—via the Iranian "Burma Road." "Boar hunts in jeeps, cockfights between trained wild partridges, Afridi Commandos who don't speak English, and the best crap-shooting chaplain in the United States Army" were among the routine spectacles, according to his report, found along that "overland trail to Russia across backward, disease-ridden, famine-verging Iran, across which the United States Army's Persian Gulf Service Command is delivering the goods to the Soviet." It was a perilous, strange, drama-highlighted hitch-hiking trip that the young correspondent recorded in his diary.

Having arrived in Moscow, he dispatched a story to his paper on Stalin's [42] dissolution of the Comintern. Stalin's statement, said Sulzberger, "can be accepted by other nations as a pledge that under his direction the Soviet Union and the Communist Party will permit free political and religious development within foreign domains." He wrote further: "One of the most startling facts, to which some of the smugger elements of the world must awaken, is that after this War one of the greatest powers on the globe and almost certainly the greatest in Europe will be the Soviet Union. This would appear to be incontrovertible." He stated that he considered unlikely any post-War efforts to "communize" Europe on the part of Russia. "Many Russians with whom the writer has talked have frankly discussed the dangers of a communized Germany." The world, however, "is moving gradually toward the Left, and Moscow—now the center of that movement—knows its position and certainly has no intention of relinquishing it." He added that "isolationism" in the U.S.S.R. is dead, and that "Moscow is ready to place a trust in the West commensurate with that invested in her."

Returning to Cairo, Sulzberger cabled dispatches on the Near and Middle East situation. In an article (September 19, 1943) he stressed the troubled position in which the Balkans, Yugoslavia, Greece, etc. found themselves, caught between the ideologies of the Western powers and those of the East as dominated by Soviet Russia. "As the tides of war recede, leaving the hideous debris exposed on the lands released to freedom, the strange, formidable terrors of peace, which for so long have remained within the domain of theoretical cafe conversation, emerge in all their stark complexity. On their disposition and adjustment across the intervening space between ideals of West and East depends the fate of this generation and perhaps the next." On October 16 he wrote: "The greatest aid that England, America, and Russia could afford the Balkans at present would be to unify their resistance efforts and to prevent the situation from getting worse. The present Anglo-American policy is to back any group fighting the Germans with equal enthusiasm, but sometimes this results in the growth of mutual jealousies."

Possibly Sulzberger's most distinguished work as a foreign correspondent came with his carefully documented analysis of the two guerrilla movements in Yugoslavia: the Chetniks led by General Mikhailovitch '42, and the Partisan or People's Army led by Marshal Tito'43. On October 24, 1943 Sulzberger cabled his first detailed story of the origins, activities, and alignments of the two guerrilla forces. Initially, he said, the two leaders collaborated: "Their troops entered liberated villages bearing, respectively, pictures of King Peter '43 and Premier Joseph Stalin, and word circulated among the enthusiastic peasantry that 'our Peter is going to marry Stalin's daughter.'"

But "in 1941 and 1942 active outbreaks occurred between the rival guerrilla forces." Both leaders claimed they were being attacked by the other side. Mikhailovitch, strategically, maintained "only a small active force, preferring to await an Allied invasion," while Tito "has maintained a constant and growing pressure against the Axis with all the strength at his command." As a result, the British by the spring of 1943 were forced to recognize "the strength of the Partisans," and King Peter ordered Mikhailovitch to "cease fighting the Partisans except in self-defense."

In a further series of dispatches (called "epic" by Time Magazine) to the New York Times, December 21-28, 1943, Sulzberger described in full the rise, history, and special significance of Marshal Tito's Yugoslav Partisan Movement. The result of these dispatches was "widespread recognition in the world's press that the Partisans are doing the fighting in Yugoslavia." Wrote Sulzberger: "There are now more than 250,000 men and women organized into approximately twenty-six divisions fighting a savage war against some of Adolf Hitler's '42 best veteran units along Yugoslavia's frontiers." These Communist-led forces, as a result of their stubborn fight, "are receiving American material and military aid, and accompanying them are American and British missions that soon will be joined by one from Russia." Sulzberger described the heroism of these Partisans who, with almost no tanks or planes, few arms, and food that was mostly grass and raw meat, have battled Axis forces for three years. He told of leaders such as Olga Dedier, a major in the People's Army Medical Corps, whose arm was amputated: "When one of the few available ampules of heart stimulant was brought to her, still conscious, she refused it saying, 'Don't give it to me. Save it for those who will live.'" He described the terrible winter retreat under terrific German bombardment in 1942, on which Tito took 4,500 wounded "rather than risk their

capture"; and the strong counteroffensive by Tito the following June. Concluded Sulzberger: "This is the history of the desperate and incredible suffering of the popular movement against a background of misery so manifold that few can yet be aware of what large areas of Europe look like today. It is a tale that the world has not yet heard, because the limited radio facilities in this island of resistance can be devoted only to the most salient facts. It is an indication of the sort of developments that may well be anticipated in many Continental countries before this War ends."

After covering the Teheran meeting of the Allied leaders in December 1943, Sulzberger early in 1944 was assigned to follow the American 5th Army in the Italian campaign. He reported the various aspects of the battle for Cassino: the days of house-to-house fighting, the concentrated artillery barrages, the work of American dive-bombers and fighters, the bombing of the Cassino Abbey. In March 1944 Sulzberger flew in one of the Mitchells that dropped bombs on the Abbey during that 3,500-ton raid. He also described the arduous lot of the average doughboy in the "terrible process of troops bleeding their way forward" and the "lonely, tough, eye-straining job" of night-fighter squadrons. Although the Italian campaign seemed "disappointing and negative in its results," it was nevertheless a positive accomplishment, he said, because it forced the Germans to use crack anti-invasion troops in Italy, thus continuously draining their reserve pool of fighting men. Further, "Fritz, the German Landser . . . is after four and a half years of war not the cocky, boastful, spick and span, heavy-set, lusty fellow that his older brother was. He is not so comfortably equipped. He is not luxuriously fed. He is not so overwhelmingly impressed with his own prowess. He is quite definitely depressed when he hears an airplane." Fritz is, however, "still an intelligent, dogged soldier, good because he comes of a warrior race, and in his veins runs soldier's blood . . . good because Herr Feldwebel is there to see to it that he is good. Herr Feldwebel represents force and authority, and that is what Fritz respects. . . . Make no mistake about that."

Continuing his assignment in Italy, Sulzberger reported on a Polish corps in the British 8th Army. He had been on the scene in Russia when the first Polish units were organized and had followed their training in Iran during the summer of 1943. "The British 8th Army's Polish corps," Sulzberger writes, "represents the materialization of the dream that these men have had ever since their country was overrun in September 1939—of fighting once again to liberate it." Sulzberger has also covered the activities of Indian troops fighting in the 8th Army.

Back again in the Middle East, Sulzberger cabled his dispatches on the situation there from Cairo (April 1944) and Beirut (May 1944). He continued to follow the progress of Marshal Tito. British and Soviet policy were now supporting Tito, he said, while "American policy has not yet crystallized." An exchange of correspondence between Sulzberger and General Mikhailovich was subsequently published in the New York Times

SULZBERGER, C. L.—*Continued*
(August 6, 1944.) In answer to Sulzberger's
questions, Mikhailovich said that he did not
believe it possible to unite his forces with
those of Marshal Tito in view of his past unsuccessful efforts at such unity. However,
if a third Yugoslav general were found acceptable to both his forces and the Partisans,
he would be glad to place himself under the
command of that leader. In Rome, in December, Sulzberger revealed in one of his
last cables in 1944 the reasons behind the
eclipse of Mikhailovich. As reported in
Newsweek, "the chief one was the General's
policy of conserving the strength of his forces
and not striking against the Germans until
an Allied invasion of the Balkans occurred."
While this was agreeable to the British at
first, the invasion failed to materialize, and
the British "slowly shifted their support to
Tito's Partisans."

Sulzberger reported also various angles of
the increasingly critical situation in Greece
that began with mutiny aboard Greek warships in early April. Shortly after this,
George Papandreou '44 became the new Greek
Prime Minister, "favorably looked upon by
both the British and the American embassies."
For a while harmony between factions prevailed; on one thing they were agreed: "King
George and his regime would not be welcome." But Sulzberger's statement in July
1944 that the Greek civil war had been
"brought to an end" through British intervention, was not borne out in the light of
later events. He reported in August of that
year the new territorial claims by Greece
included control of the Dodecanese Islands
(a claim regarded as just by Italy and Turkey); Cyprus, now part of the British Empire; southern Albania; and a new Bulgarian
frontier. According to Greek spokesmen,
"Greece cannot play her part as a true, wholehearted friend of the great democracies of
the West who are also rulers of the sea if
she is not made really safe in the spirit of the
Atlantic Charter and of the Four Freedoms."

Writing from Ankara, Sulzberger surveyed
the situation in Turkey, whose price to enter
the War on the Allies' side could be "summarized in terms of material"—planes, tanks
and other weapons. However, the leaders of
a Fascist movement in that country were
brought to trial—a gesture by which Turkey
hoped to impress the Allies. It was not until
August 1944 that Turkey severed diplomatic
relations with Germany.

Concerning simultaneous developments in
Rumania during August, Sulzberger cabled
that King Michael '44 had arrested Marshal
Antonescu '40 and his pro-German Cabinet, thus
precipitating the about-face of the wealthiest
Balkan state. In this coup, said Sulzberger,
King Michael had wide popular backing.

"Tall, dark-haired" Cyrus Sulzberger is an
"omnivorous reader of history and philosophy,"
and he likes music and art. The story is told
that he once bought a painting by Dali for
$300. When, in 1938, he needed money in
Bulgaria, he wired the New York art dealer
with whom he had stored the painting to sell
it. Then, when he returned to America in
November 1944, he wanted to buy his painting

back—but found its price had increased tremendously in six years. However, its owner,
Thomas J. Watson, head of the International
Business Machine Corporation, generously re-
sold the Dali to Sulzberger for the exact
amount which the correspondent had received
for it in 1938. The fact that Sulzberger
is also an accomplished linguist adds much to
his qualifications as a foreign correspondent.
Like many other New York *Times* men covering the battle fronts, he does not stress the
"personalized" incident. A detached, carefully
studied, objective viewpoint characterizes his
work in general.

References

Life 13:78 Jl 20 '42
Time 41:90 Ap 12 '43
Who's Who in America 1944-45

SUN FO (sŭn fŭ) Oct. 1891- Chinese
Government official
Address: b. Legislative Yuan, Chinese Central
Government, Chungking, China

Sun Fo, president of the Legislative Yuan
of China, and author of *China Looks Forward*
(1944), is the only son of the late Dr. Sun
Yat-sen, the "Father of the Chinese Revolution." Born in Choy Heng Village in the
Chung-shan District of Kwangtung in October
1891, he was, like the Soongs, brought up in
the Christian faith and the Western tradition.
Until after his graduation from high school
he studied foreign languages and science in
Honolulu, and from 1908 to 1911 served as
associate editor of the *Liberty News*, a Chinese-
language newspaper there. Then, in October
1911, came the successful Chinese Revolution
against the Manchu Imperium. The Kuomintang (People's Party), which his father had
founded, turned the anti-Manchu tide into a
pro-republican movement, and in January 1912
Sun Yat-sen returned from England to take
the oath of office as President of the Provisional Government of the new republic. Young
Sun Fo spent a few months in his native land
at that time, but was sent to the United States
to finish his education that same year. Until
1916 he attended the University of California,
majoring in economics and political science for
his B.A. degree; in 1917 he received his M.A.
from Columbia University. It was only then
that he returned to China to live, arriving in
August 1917.

Some time before this Sun Yat-sen, who had
finally resigned the Presidency of China in the
interests of national unity and had accepted the
post of Director-General of Transport and
Trade under Yuan Shih-k'ai, had broken with
the reactionary Yuan and declared the southern
provinces of China independent of the northern.
His second revolution had been crushed, but by
1916 he was back in China, campaigning for
his constitutional government, and by 1917 he
was "Generalissimo" of a provisional military
government in Canton, the focus of all revolutionary activity. (In 1915 Dr. Sun had married Soong Chingling '44, sister of Chiang Kai-
shek's '40 future wife.) Sun Fo took part in
the organization of this government. During
1918-1919 he also served as secretary of the

Canton National Assembly, and during the winter of 1919-1920 he was associate editor of the Canton *Times*.

Sun Yat-sen soon found it impossible to cooperate with the military leaders in Canton. He and his followers fled, and from July to October in 1920 Sun Fo helped to organize and finance his father's campaign against the militarists. It was successful, and Sun Yat-sen returned to Canton in 1921 to be elected President of China. At the end of 1920 Sun Fo was appointed Provincial Government Director of the Canton Municipal Office and, concurrently, Director-General of the Kwangtung River Conservancy Board; in February 1921 he also became the first Mayor of Canton. He had already made a great reputation for himself as a municipal administrator when in June 1922 another revolt forced him to flee Canton again with his father.

The next year Sun Yat-sen made an agreement with the Russian Bolsheviks by which they were to supply him with military and political advisers, money, and munitions. As for the Chinese Communists, they were allowed to join the Kuomintang. As a result the leader of the revolt was soon defeated, and Sun Yat-sen was acknowledged chief executive of the province of Kwangtung. Sun Fo became Mayor of Canton again in December 1923, and during the next year, in addition to his administrative duties, he made several visits to Mukden and Shanghai as his father's representative to confer with the leaders of other parties on the political affairs of China. When Dr. Sun died on March 12, 1925 a section of the Kuomintang believed that his son should head the organization, but when the Nationalist Government was formed in Canton in July 1925 Sun Fo was simply a member of the Government Council. In May 1926 he began his third term as Mayor of Canton, serving concurrently as Commissioner of Reconstruction and acting chairman of the Kwangtung Provincial Government, and he was also elected a member of the Central Executive Committee and of the Political Council of the Kuomintang Party.

That same year Chiang Kai-shek, the leader of the Kuomintang's armies, had set out to unite all China by force of arms. By November 1926 Hankow had been taken, and the seat of the Nationalist Government was moved from Canton to Hankow in conformity with the decision of the Central Committee of the Kuomintang. Sun Fo became Minister of Communications in the Hankow Government, chairman of the War Economic Council, director of Military Aviation, and a member of the Committee of Military Affairs. This Government continued to cooperate with the Communists, but early the next year Chiang, supported by the Right Wing of the Kuomintang, set up another Government at Nanking as soon as that city fell to his forces. When Shanghai fell, too, he made a deal with the Shanghai bankers by which he promised to turn on his former Communist allies and break with Moscow in return for their support. The massacre of Communists and trade unionists followed in Nanking, Canton, and Shanghai, and the Hankow Government, which still retained the loyalty of twenty-one out of the thirty-three members of the Central Executive Committee of the Kuomintang, immediately repudiated Chiang. But Hankow was weak in military force and

SUN FO

strategically vulnerable, and within a few months after Chiang started his military campaign against that Wuhan city most of the Left Kuomintang members had deserted the Communists. Others, including Mme. Sun, fled to Moscow.

Sun Fo and the Left Kuomintang group still refused to support Nanking so long as the Generalissimo headed the Government, however, and in August 1927 Chiang resigned. The Nanking Government was definitely organized in October of the same year, and Sun Fo accepted the post of Minister of Finance. Then, in January 1928, Chiang returned to power. Sun Fo resigned his post in protest, but was given the post of Minister of Reconstruction shortly afterward and then departed for Europe and America, where he discussed with bankers and Government officials the possibility of enlisting foreign aid in the reconstruction schemes of the Chinese Government. He returned to find all of China proper theoretically under Nanking's control, and Chiang head of the Nationalist Government and commander in chief of the Army, Navy, and Air Force.

From October 1928 to May 1931 Sun Fo held the post of Minister of Railways in this Government, serving concurrently as vice-president of the Examination Yuan; in 1929 he organized and became president of the National Aviation Corporation, the first company to undertake commercial aviation in China. During this period he was apparently completely reconciled to Chiang and his policies, and the fact that he enjoyed the confidence and respect of foreign bankers was of great assistance to Chiang's Government. In December 1928, in a speech at the American University Club in Shanghai in which he asked for technical and financial assistance from America and Western Europe, Sun Fo announced: "It is the fundamental aim of the Kuomintang to prepare the nation for full democracy through the temporary exercise of national political power." In March 1929 he rejoiced that "the insidious influence of the Communist

SUN FO—*Continued*

Party, which deceptively plots to absorb his [Sun Yat-sen's] legacy, has been wiped out."

At the same time, however, there was a southern faction which remained jealous of Chiang, being particularly opposed to national (as versus provincial) disposition of revenues. In February 1929 the Central Political Council at Nanking refused to approve the proposal of the Wuhan division of the Council that the latter supervise the national revenues in the area under its control. The next month the Kwangsi army replied with a revolt against the Government at Hankow, and although the uprising was crushed within a week the Kwangsi leaders returned to their province to join with the other southern dissidents in the Political Council of the Southwest at Canton. In May 1931 Sun Fo went over to the Canton insurgents who aimed to oust Chiang Kai-shek, and soon accepted a high post in the new Kuomintang military government. A group of Chiang's military leaders "revealed" that the real reason for Sun Fo's flight had been because as Minister of Railways he had appropriated to his own use large sums of the public moneys, but they declared their willingness to accept him back if he would "cooperate" with them.

During the next months there were many attempts at reconciliation between Nanking and Canton, particularly after the Japanese invasion of Manchuria in September 1931, and Sun Fo was one of the principal negotiators. Chiang finally agreed to resign if the Canton Government would dissolve, and in the new Government approved by the plenary session of the Kuomintang late in December, Sun Fo held the post of president of the Executive Yuan. A month later, however, Chiang returned, and the Kuomintang created the post of Secretary-General for him. It was Sun Fo's turn to resign, and he did not rejoin the Nanking regime until June 1932, although officially he has been president of the Legislative Yuan since March 1932.

Though divided into committees, the Legislative Yuan is not a representative body, nor is it able to enact laws independently of the other agencies of the Government: chiefly it is a legislative drafting and research agency. Its president has a good deal of power, and when in 1933 a Constitutional Drafting Committee was formed Sun Fo headed it. The following year the Legislative Yuan undertook the drafting of a permanent constitution for China, and Sun Fo had much to say about the provisions of that constitution.

But Sun Fo has been equally influential in the sphere of foreign policy. Even in 1932 one of the principal reasons for his opposition to Chiang was his belief that China should unconditionally resume political relations with the Soviet Union as a preliminary step toward effective resistance against further Japanese aggression on Chinese territory, and that a united front should again be formed with the Chinese Communists. During all the years while Chiang was intent on attempting to liquidate the "Communist bandits," even though it meant appeasing Japan, Sun Fo was known as anti-Japanese. In 1934 he made a trip to Honolulu, where he met President Franklin D. Roosevelt [42] and, it is said, presented proposals concerning the continuance and observance of the Nine-Power Treaty and possibly a further appeal to the United States for financial and economic assistance against Japan. In February 1937, on the heels of the Sian incident, he was one of the signers of a joint proposal to the Kuomintang openly advising a return to the policies of cooperation with the Communists and of alliance with the Soviet Union, and shortly afterward the Central Executive Committee of the Kuomintang accepted the Communist offer of United Front collaboration. That same spring Sun Fo went to Moscow as China's confidential messenger, and on April 1 he returned with proposals that China and Russia conclude non-aggression and mutual assistance pacts. (Chiang procrastinated in accepting these proposals until the undeclared Sino-Japanese War actually broke out in July 1937. After that the Kremlin refused to make an alliance with China, although a nonaggression pact was signed on August 21, 1937.) When the following spring there was a serious schism in the Chinese Government over the issue of arming the Chinese masses, Sun Fo sided against the big bankers and landlords, who opposed guerrilla warfare; and that same year he revisited Russia and toured the European capitals, seeking aid for his country.

The son of the great Sun Yat-sen manages to be both internationally minded and pro-Chinese in his speeches. Since 1930 he has been tactfully showing how the abolition of extraterritoriality was essential to the international development of his country. In January 1942 he announced that if British and American concentration on the defeat of Germany gave Japan a free hand in the Far East, there was "grave doubt in Chungking as to the wisdom of China's continuing to fight." In March 1942 he urged Roosevelt and Churchill [42] to announce a Pacific Charter which would pledge the United Nations to recognize the independence of India, French Indo-China, Korea, and the Philippines. In January 1943 he attempted to refute some of the fallacious theories that seemed to be gaining currency abroad in regard to China—that a powerful China would be as dangerous to America as a powerful Japan, for example, and that Japan's military strength must therefore be restored after her defeat. In November 1943 he praised the United States repeal of the Chinese Exclusion Act. In January 1944 he announced that Germany would be knocked out between spring and summer of that year, and added that China believed that when that time came her ally, the Soviet Union, would turn her forces to the East and participate in the war against Japan.

Always known as a democrat who liked to dwell on the three Peoples' Principles expounded by his father—Nationalism, Democracy, Livelihood—and who put more emphasis on the second and third of those principles than most Kuomintang leaders, Sun Fo really emerged as a frank critic of the Kuomintang's reactionary tendencies in 1944. Then talk of the lack of democracy in Chiang Kai-shek's regime was at its height abroad, the Nationalist blockade of Communist troops provoking particular condemnation. In March 1944, broadcasting to the United States by short wave on Sun Yat-sen Day, Sun Fo announced that "the Kuomintang and the Communists must once and for all sink their little differences and find a permanent solution for the present difficulty. Such a solution will be found in the introduction of constitutional democratic government." In April 1944 he stated that "in these twenty years the machinery and practice of the Kuomintang have turned in a wrong direction, inconsistent with the Party Constitution drafted by Dr. Sun Yat-sen in 1923 and contrary to the spirit of democracy. . . . We have in the past assumed unwillingly the attitude and habit of a ruling caste. . . . The number of our party members is less than 1 per cent of the Chinese population. . . . The local election . . . is mostly a false one based on bogus recordings of votes. . . . There is not a single councilor of the hsien People's Political Council or a hsien administrator elected by the people." (A "hsien" is a subdivision of a province, and is sometimes translated as "county.") Moreover, he continued, public opinion in Great Britain and the United States held that "the suppression of opposition parties, the strict censorship of press and speech, and the limitation of meeting and assembly are imitations of Hitlerite Germany, Mussolinian Italy, and militarist Japan. . . . This suspicion is a great danger to the future of China." He finished by saying that if Sun Yat-sen's third principle was to be carried out China must, while democratizing her politics, "adopt a planned economy little different from that of the Soviet Union."

Even more sensational, in the eyes of foreign observers, was Sun Fo's speech in August 1944 to the training class of the Kuomintang, when he urged the Kuomintang to resume its original Leftist direction. "The democratic world is veering to the Left," he said, "and we shall have to keep in step with the world. . . . To oppose the Communists we opposed the Left and identified ourselves with the Right. This has been the great error committed by our party. . . . After the expulsion of the Communists, and in order to guard against 'outsiders,' we have even stifled democratic institutions. . . . To obtain foreign funds we must first win the confidence of foreign countries."

The *New Republic* called such speeches "models not only of democratic faith but of plain speaking," and commented: "It is obvious that a man with his honesty, instinct for democracy, and courage might easily play a great role in a China which was turning in a democratic direction." Nothing in Sun Fo's career or personality is regarded as an indication that he, as the "Crown Prince," would have any aversion to playing such a role. John Gunther[41] describes him as "an intelligent man, pleasant in appearance, rich, cultivated, ambitious." Vincent Sheean[41] wrote in 1927 that he looked like an American railway president and called him the "Babbitt" of the Hankow Government, but found him "competent, cool, hard-working, matter-of-fact—a very businesslike person" who quoted statistics when one asked him a question about the Revolution.

References

Asia 27:815 O '27 por
Far Eastern R 27:337-8+ Je '31
Gunther, J. Inside Asia 1939
Sun Fo China Looks Forward 1944
Who's Who in China 1936

SUN YAT-SEN, MME. (sŭn) 1890- Chinese political leader
Address: c/o Kuomintang Central Executive Committee, Chungking, China

Of the three world-famous Soong sisters, Mme. Chiang Kai-shek's[40] name is probably the best known outside her own country, and yet Vincent Sheean[41] once declared, after an interview with Mme. Sun Yat-sen: "No figure in China received the spontaneous respect of all men as did Soong Chingling." Ilona Ralf Sues[44], in her book *Shark's Fins and Millet* (1944), repeats a saying of the illiterate Chinese masses referring to the Soong sisters: "One loves money, one loves China, one loves glory." Although the saying is doubtless unfair to her two sisters, Mme. Sun Yat-sen's selfless love for her country is not questioned even by her enemies. Politically (though never personally) estranged from the rest of her family during the period when she believed Chiang Kai-shek[40] was betraying her late husband's principles, even today this shy, retiring woman, who by temperament was meant neither for politics nor leadership, does not hesitate to speak out for greater democracy in China than it has known under the rule of the Right wing of the Kuomintang. "Reaction and fascism in China are strong" began a message from her which reached the United States in February 1944.

Soong Chingling (her foreign name is Rosamonde) was born at Shanghai, Kiangsu, in 1890, the second daughter of the wealthy Mr. and Mrs. Charles Jones Soong of Shanghai. Soong had come to the United States, almost penniless, in 1880, and there had not only added the name Charles Jones to his family name of Soong but had become a Christian. Back in China, he had made a good business out of printing Bibles; investing the proceeds at the exorbitant Chinese interest rates, he had eventually become a merchant prince. He was a remarkable man in more than one way: he wanted his daughters to have as good an education as his sons. Ai-ling (who is now Mme. H. H. Kung), Chingling, and Mei-ling (the present Mme. Chiang Kai-shek) were all enrolled at the McTyeire School for Girls at Shanghai, the most important foreign-style school for Chinese girls in that city. Lessons continued during summer vacations, an Englishwoman tutoring the girls in English and Latin, a male instructor teaching them the classics.

For Chingling, the next step after McTyeire was Wesleyan College in Macon, Georgia, where Ai-ling, the eldest, was already studying. Chingling was eighteen and Mei-ling twelve when they followed their older sister to the United States. Chingling's schoolmates say that her sisters were more Americanized than she, and also less serious, studious, and dreamy. Chingling was also the least interested in such frivolous things as clothes—her sisters constantly criticized the way she dressed—and the most interested in moral and philosophical questions. She had no trouble with her studies, except with mathematics, which she had to figure out in Chinese first. And she was already concerned with her country's problems. A

MME. SUN YAT-SEN

theme written and published in 1911 was entitled "The Influence of Foreign Educated Students on China."

October 1911 saw the successful Chinese Revolution against the Manchu Government, a revolution with which Sun Yat-sen's personal influence had much to do. The organization of the Kuomintang (known as the People's party), which he had established, turned the anti-Manchu tide into a pro-republican movement, and in January 1912 he returned to China from England to take the oath of office as President of the Provisional Government of the new republic at the request of the National Convention in Nanking. Only a month later, however, he realized the impossibility of uniting the country under his own presidency and resigned in favor of Yuan Shih-k'ai, accepting the post of Director-General of Transport and Trade but continuing to wield his chief influence through the Kuomintang. When the news of the successful revolution reached Georgia, Chingling immediately set about to write a paper on it entitled "The Greatest Event of the Twentieth Century"; when the new Five-Barred Flag was sent to her she pulled down the Dragon Banner from her wall and stamped on it, crying: "Down with the Dragon! Up with the flag of the Republic!"

Graduated from Wesleyan in the spring of 1913 with a B.A. degree, Chingling returned to China not long afterward. From California she wrote to a teacher: "I shall soon be on my way home. I am taking a box of California fruit to Dr. Sun from his admirers here, and I am also the proud bearer of a private letter to him." When she arrived in Shanghai she found her politically-conscious family closely attached to Dr. Sun, Ai-ling acting as secretary to the great man. And for that very reason they did not remain long in Shanghai. Dr. Sun soon broke with Yuan Shih-k'ai and declared the Southern provinces of China independent of the North-

ern. His second revolution, however, was quickly crushed, and Dr. Sun fled to Japan along with his chief followers in the Kuomintang, among them the Soongs.

In Japan the Soongs lived first in Kobe, later in Tokyo and then Yokohama, where they settled down for almost two years. While there Ai-ling married H. H. Kung[43], recommending Chingling to Dr. Sun as his secretary; and it was not long afterward that Dr. Sun's new secretary announced her intention of marrying him. The "Father of the Chinese Revolution" was not only much older than she, but was already married, and Chingling's parents were horrified, particularly since both Chingling and Dr. Sun were Christians. Chingling, however, was as adamant as she has always shown herself once she makes up her mind, and in October 1915 she ran away and was married to Dr. Sun. Her family neither disinherited her nor broke with Dr. Sun politically; in putting the best possible face on the matter they were typically Chinese.

Now began an unsettled, turbulent life of work and struggle, in which the timid, delicate girl moved in a constant glare of publicity. She held no party office during her husband's life, but she acted as his secretary and assistant, accompanied him on his journeys and on the political platform, and was "stared at, mobbed by enthusiastic crowds, and photographed within an inch of her life." In 1916 it became possible for Dr. Sun (and the Soongs) to return to Shanghai. In January 1917 a monarchy was declared and then forsworn by Yuan, who died in June of that year. Dr. Sun began once more to campaign for his constitutional government, and when China declared war on Germany (August 14, 1917) he was in Canton leading the outcry against his country's participation in the conflict. Not long afterward he was appointed "Generalissimo" of a provisional military government, but the strength of his support had always been Kwantung province, and he soon found it impossible to cooperate with the military leaders in Canton. He therefore returned to Shanghai in disgust, not coming back to Canton until 1920, when the military regime there was driven out and he was elected "President of China." But it was far from the "free and united China" for which the Kuomintang agitated: the provinces were ruled and plundered by semi-feudal war lords who secured the aid of foreign capital in exchange for economic concessions, and who were continually fighting among themselves for loot and power. In 1922 a revolt caused the Suns to flee Canton again, with Mme. Sun disguised as an old countrywoman, carrying a basket of vegetables. The couple again found refuge in Shanghai until February 1923, when Dr. Sun called to his aid troops from Kwangsi and Yunnan and the leader of the 1922 revolt was defeated. Until his death he was acknowledged chief executive of the province, and although his effective sway did not extend far beyond Canton, his ideological influence remained dominant in the Kuomintang as long as he lived.

On March 12, 1925 Dr. Sun died in Peking of cancer of the liver. It was now both natural and politically advisable that his wife, "identified in the popular mind with his personal influence," should take office in the Political Council, the Central Executive Committee of the Kuomintang, and other party and government bodies. She had always been particularly interested in the feminist movement, in the education of women and the development of women's organizations within the Kuomintang, and the Women's Institute of Political Training in Hankow was her creation. But she was soon to show that to her the liberation of Chinese women was only a part of a much broader picture: the awakening of the entire Chinese people.

And she was soon to find herself in conflict with Chiang Kai-shek, commander in chief of the Kuomintang Army, which had won the day for the Nationalists when Dr. Sun's Canton Government stood close to defeat. Chiang's political influence increased with his military victories against the feudal war lords which the Kuomintang set out to conquer, in a final attempt to unify China. Dr. Sun had had an entente with the U.S.S.R. and the Chinese Communists, and Chiang himself used the Communists in his march north until all of southern China was united under the Kuomintang banner. But the peasants, under Communist influence, made louder and louder demands for the abolition of excessive taxes and the abolition of the gentry. Such demands seemed only natural to Mme. Sun, for her husband's three-cornered doctrine had called for the immediate awakening, emancipation, and enfranchisement of China's millions, the regeneration of the nation on a broad socio-democratic basis, and "death to the tyranny of militarism," and her husband had repeatedly secured raises in wages for the Canton workers. Chiang, however, grew alarmed. The Right wing of the Kuomintang had opposed collaboration with the Communists for some time, and only a series of offensives against the Canton Government by the still-powerful war lords had helped to maintain the united front at all after Dr. Sun's death.

In 1926 the Nationalist Government had been moved from Canton to Hankow, but early the next year Chiang, supported by the Right wing of the Kuomintang, set up another Government at Nanking. Following the fall of Shanghai to his forces he turned to the Shanghai bankers for aid. They promised to support him if he would turn on his former Communist allies and would break with Moscow, and the wholesale slaughter of Chinese Communists and trade unionists followed—in Nanking and Canton as well as Shanghai. The Left-wing Hankow Government repudiated Chiang Kai-shek, and through the dark days of April and May 1927 Mme. Sun remained in Hankow—against the wishes of her own family, and in spite of the fact that she was offered "refuge" on a Japanese destroyer on the theory that she was being "held prisoner" in Hankow by the Communists.

The fall of the Hankow Government was inevitable, however. After July 5, when the U.S.S.R. and the Kuomintang were formally divorced, the Russians in Hankow returned to Russia, and the most important Chinese who had remained loyal to the Left-wing program also sought refuge there. Mme.

Sun, too, fled to Moscow, but not before making public a farewell message (July 14, 1927): "Some members of the party executive are so defining the principles and policies of Dr. Sun Yat-sen that they seem to me to do violence to Dr. Sun's ideas and ideals. Feeling thus, I must disassociate myself from active participation in carrying out the new policies of the party. In the last analysis, all revolutions must be social revolutions, based upon fundamental changes in society; otherwise it is not a revolution, but merely a change in government." Claiming that Dr. Sun's third and most vital principle, "the livelihood of the people," was at stake, she announced: "We must not betray the people. We have built up in them a great hope. They have placed in us a great faith. . . . Today the lot of the Chinese peasant is even more wretched than in those days when Dr. Sun was driven by his great sense of human wrongs into a life of revolution."

Mme. Sun was living in Moscow in December 1927, when her sister Mei-ling, after a long courtship, was married to Chiang Kai-shek. Not long afterward Chingling went, in voluntary exile, to Berlin, where she lived in inexpensive pensions for some time. The Nationalists attempted to persuade her to return to China, but she refused to associate herself with the Chiang Kai-shek regime in any way; in consequence, all sorts of gossip was circulated about her. It was whispered that she was married to various persons in Russia and Germany (in China the remarriage of any widow is a great loss in dignity, and the remarriage of Dr. Sun's widow would be unthinkable); it was said frequently and aloud that she was completely dominated by Moscow. (Declared Mme. Sun: "When I make any statement they will not concede that I, a woman, can have an opinion. All my opinions have been influenced, it seems, and usually by Moscow.")

In the meanwhile she continued to make political pronouncements from time to time. In 1928 she was quoted: "There is no despair in my heart for the revolution. My disheartenment is only for the path into which some of those who had been leading the revolution have strayed." On August 1, 1929 she sent a telegram to the Anti-Imperialist League in Berlin on the occasion of international anti-war day. (This was during the tension between China and the U.S.S.R.) "While the oppressed nationalities today form a solid front against imperialist war and militarism," she wrote, "the reactionary Nanking Government is combining forces with the imperialists in brutal repressions against the Chinese masses. Never has the treacherous character of the counterrevolutionary Kuomintang leaders been so shamelessly exposed to the world as today. Having betrayed the Nationalist revolution, they have inevitably degenerated into imperialist tools and attempted to provoke war with Russia. But the Chinese masses, undaunted by repression and undeceived by lying propaganda, will fight only on the side of revolution. . . ."

At last, on May 6, 1929, Mme. Sun announced that she was proceeding to China to attend the removal of the remains of Dr. Sun

SUN YAT-SEN, MME.—*Continued*

to the Purple Mountain, where he had asked to be buried. "I emphatically adhere to my declaration made at Hankow," she also announced, however. In the spring of 1929, at the hand-picked Congress, she had been elected *in absentia* to the Central Executive Committee of the Kuomintang, but she refused to lend her prestige to that body. After all the ceremonies attendant upon the removal of her husband's remains she returned to her plainly furnished house in the Rue Molière in Shanghai, in the French Concession. It was possibly during this period that a member of the Nationalist Government called upon her and said, in effect, "If you were anyone but Mme. Sun we would cut your head off." She replied, smilingly: "If you were the revolutionists you pretend to be, you'd cut it off anyway."

During the next years Chiang Kai-shek was chiefly occupied in attempting to liquidate the "Communist bandits," even though it meant appeasing Japan, which invaded Manchuria in September 1931, in 1932 thrust at the Chapei and Shanghai area, and then began encroaching on North China and Inner Mongolia. As early as 1931 Mme. Sun had pleaded for national unification against the Japanese, speaking scornfully of all appeasers as sufferers from "fear-of-Japan-sickness"; and in January 1933 the provisional Chinese Soviet Government made its first comprehensive offer to all groups within China for united action against Japan. Mme. Sun urged the Nanking Government to reach an agreement with the Communists, and she was the inspiration of the contemporary Left-wing movement in the Kuomintang known as the National Salvation Group, many of whose members were arrested for "premature" anti-Japanese activity. The National Salvation Group supported the demands made on Chiang Kai-shek when he was "kidnapped" by the Young Marshal in December 1936 in an attempt to force him to an agreement for united action against Japan.

In July 1937 the undeclared Sino-Japanese War began; by August the Japanese were bombing Shanghai. When Shanghai fell that month Mme. Sun went in voluntary exile to Hong Kong as a guest of the British Government, refusing to take part in a non-democratic government. In Hong Kong she personally conducted the work of the China Defence League, which collected funds, foodstuffs, medical supplies, and clothing for the wounded and needy, and she sold her jewels and household possessions in order to carry on the work. The League had been founded after Mme. Sun had failed to obtain help from abroad for wounded Chinese soldiers. As chairman (her brother T. V. Soong [41] is president) she worked indefatigably, without even a secretary to assist her with correspondence and articles. She spent much of her time in Canton, too, until that city's fall. (During the last days of Canton as a part of Free China she was there almost all the time, leading protest parades and urging her followers to greater efforts of resistance. She wrote in disgust to the governor of Kwangtung, calling his attention to the number of able-bodied Cantonese who were pouring into Hong Kong instead of fighting against the invaders.) And as the Nanking Government drew closer to her friends (the National Anti-Japanese United Front was finally formed in 1937), Mme. Sun made more and more personal appearances, published more and more of her writings. After 1938 she again became a member of the Central Executive Committee of the Kuomintang.

In September of 1937 Mme. Sun had written in *Asia* Magazine: "When I consider the New Life Movement, I think it unfortunate that, well-meaning as the author doubtless meant it to be, he has not yet realized that the most fundamental need of the Chinese masses is economic development. . . . I propose to replace this pedantic movement by another—that is, a great campaign to improve peoples' livelihood through improvement of methods of production, especially in agriculture." Since the New Life Movement remains Mme. Chiang Kai-shek's own prized creation, it might be thought that the sisters are still at complete odds politically. Both of them, however, cooperated in the formation of the Chinese Industrial Cooperatives, which, according to Mme. Sun, "stand for human rehabilitation, economic progress, and democratic education"; and the year 1940 found all three of the sisters together. In February of 1940 Mme. Chiang Kai-shek went to Hong Kong to visit Mme. H. H. Kung, and Mme. Sun joined the household temporarily. They gossiped, cooked, joked, tried on each other's clothes; Chingling proposed Ai-ling as chairman of the Friends of the Wounded Association which she and Mei-ling formed during the visit; and all three appeared together in the Hong Kong Hotel and dined there—the first time they had been seen together in ten years. This was soon after the inauguration of the Japanese puppet Wang Ching-wei [40], and it did much to squelch rumors of a split in the family and consequently in the Government. In April the sisters flew to Chungking—the first time Chingling had visited any stamping ground of the National Government in many a year—and Chingling lived in the Kung house for a while, participating in the feverish round of Chungking social activity, addressing meetings, attending dedications, etc. She was no doubt glad to return to Hong Kong.

Articles published by Mme. Sun in 1941 show, however, that she was as concerned as ever with the "reactionary minority within the leadership" of the Kuomintang "which has forgotten the teachings of Sun Yat-sen." She warned that in this group were to be found "China's chief proponents of a Rome-Berlin-Axis orientation and of a speedy compromise with Japan." She criticized the lack of freedom of speech, press, and assembly in China. She announced that "lack of democracy in wartime Free China is the chief cause of the military clashes that occur between Chinese units [Kuomintang troops and the Communists], to the benefit of the enemy."

On December 8, 1941, the day after Pearl Harbor, Mme. H. H. Kung informed Mme. Sun that there was a plane for Chungking in which they could leave Hong Kong; there was no time to return home and pack her belongings, so she fled with a small grip, leaving behind some of her husband's mementos, many personal documents and letters. In Chungking since then she has lived "very modestly in a house belonging to the Chinese Foreign Office, given her because of the prolonged absence of her brother, T. V. Soong. The house is modestly furnished. It has a large basement which Madame has occasionally used as a dance hall for American enlisted men. She likes to entertain American officers and soldiers stationed in Chungking. She wants to give a good time to foreigners come from so far to fight in China. Americans who are attached to General Stilwell's '42 staff . . . adore Madame and love her parties."

But, much to the discomfort of some elements in the Kuomintang and of the Generalissimo himself, she has not confined herself to parties. In articles in *Asia* in 1942 she pointed out how the national revolutionary movement had made the liberation of women one of its basic demands and how the Kuomintang, captured by the Right wing, had abolished the women's department that had done so much to bring it victory. In a message reaching the United States in February 1944 she spoke angrily of "the diversion of part of our national army to the task of blockading and 'guarding' the guerrilla [Communist] areas." of the fact that "some still hold private profit above the national interest," of the "oppression of the peasantry," and of "the absence of a true labor movement" in China. She again claimed that "some Chinese reactionaries are preparing [civil war] to destroy a democratic sector in our struggle. That sector is the guerrilla bases in North Shensi and behind the enemy lines. . . . " On March 12, broadcasting to the meeting at the Metropolitan Opera House in New York City commemorating the nineteenth anniversary of Sun Yatsen's death, she asked that convocation of a "democratic national convention" in China be carried out as expeditiously as possible." She also asked for support for her demands from abroad by saying that her husband never would have regarded as "interference detrimental to our sovereignty the support given to our people's movement by our foreign friends."

When Vice-President of the United States Henry Wallace '40 visited China in 1944, he carried with him a copy of the China Defence League's three-year report, *In Guerrilla China* (1943) which Mme. Sun edited. Publication in China being impossible, she had sent the manuscript to the China Aid Council in New York, and Wallace's visit gave her her first chance to see the printed report. *In Guerrilla China* tells how the League, under Mme. Sun's chairmanship, was reconstituted after the flight from Hong Kong. "The International Peace Hospitals, which are the League's main responsibility, had for a long time been victims of the internal political blockade through which no supplies could be sent and money could be transmitted only with difficulty. The situation was aggravated by circumstances which affected all relief agencies equally. The internal purchasing power of the Chinese dollar underwent a terrific decline.

Prices rose to an average of from 50 to 200 times their pre-War level. Since the foreign exchange rate increased only four times, this meant that from ten to twenty times the previous amounts of foreign currency were needed in order to cover the same commitments. At the same time, the means at the disposal of the League for publicizing its needs and mobilizing support were drastically reduced. . . .

"The League took part in the joint effort of all relief organizations to secure an adjustment in the rate of exchange . . . a Government subsidy of 100 per cent on remitted funds for direct relief, and 50 per cent on those for indirect relief. In the face of constantly depreciating values—estimated at 15 per cent per month—the subsidy has been lamentably insufficient but it has served to compensate in a small way for the gross inequities of the previous situation. . . . In the winter and spring of 1942-43, in China's sixth year of war, her third year of strength-sapping internal friction, and her second year of being almost totally cut off on land and sea, all previous difficulties were aggravated by a famine of horrifying dimensions [which continued throughout 1943]. In Honan an estimated five million people perished, and in Kwangtung additional millions were affected." Except for one occasion, the blockade of the Northwest Region had prevented medical supplies from reaching the guerrillas, and the International Peace Hospitals, which serve a population of 52,000,000, had to rely on such medicines as could be produced locally. "Operations are done without anesthetics, while bamboo pincers, wooden retractors, and scalpels made from parts of Japanese planes shot down in battle have been fashioned by the doctors themselves to replace broken or missing instruments." These were augmented only by such supplies as the guerrillas might be able to capture on the battlefield.

In addition to the medical services, the League sponsored Bethune Medical College to train doctors, nurses, and pharmacists, and pays the expenses of the students; its drugs were produced at the "drug manufactory" of the 18th Group Army and other units. The famine was successfully combatted in the Honan area by the guerrilla Hopei-Shansi-Honan-Shantung Border Government. In the Shensi-Kansu-Ninghsia Border Region more than 100,000 refugees were received, cared for, resettled, and made full guerrilla citizens. The League also sponsors the industrial cooperatives, which since 1940 have suffered equally with the hospitals from the blockade, and provides medical and other care for mothers, children, and pregnant women— specifically, it supports twenty-six day nurseries, an elementary school, and a technical academy.

Few who have seen Mme. Sun disagree as to her possession of beauty. Ilona Ralf Sues becomes lyrical: "She was beautiful. . . . In Mme. Sun's presence one could breathe more freely, one felt the abundance of life and kindness and purpose. She was so small, so simple in her black dress, with that jet black hair brushed straight back and rolled into a knot in her nape. She was so exquisitely lovely; the fine oval of her face, the delicate

SUN YAT-SEN, MME.—*Continued*

complexion, the high forehead, those large, deep, pensive eyes, that sensitive mouth of a child who has eaten too much bitterness. And when she smiled, she had dimples in both cheeks. Yet any description of her must be painfully inadequate, because the great harmony of her personality, the warm light she radiates the whole atmosphere around her, cannot be expressed in words. It can only be felt." And Vincent Sheean wrote, back in 1927, that she was "a tiny, exquisite, almost doll-like creature, with a voice and manner which few who meet her can resist. In spite of her intelligence and courage, she was never made for a public career: she is very shy, she cannot make her voice heard more than four feet away, and she has none of the assertiveness and arrogance which politics demands of its participants." Sheean at the same time spoke of her "modesty and sense of humor," and a quality for which he knew "only the foolish word 'breeding.'"

References

Asia 27:852+ O '27 il por
Lit Digest 92:36-8 Mr 12 '27 por; 122: 15-16 Ag 29 '36 por
N Y Herald Tribune VI p7 Ag 15 '43
Nation 130:109-10 Ja 22 '30
Gunther, J. Inside Asia 1939
Hahn, E. The Soong Sisters 1940
Sues, I. R. Shark's Fins and Millet 1944
Who's Who in China 1936

SUN, CHINGLING (SOONG) *See* Sun Yat-sen, Mme.

SVINHUFVUD, PEHR EVIND (svēn'hüfüd pär ā'vind) 1861 (?)—Feb. (?), 1944 Finnish statesman; President of Finland from 1931 to 1937; played a leading part in his country's fight for independence; was banished to Siberia by the Czar; known as pro-German, anti-Russian; death officially announced in Helsinki according to a Nazi DNB broadcast.

Obituary

N Y Times p17 Mr 1 '44 por

SWARTHOUT GLADYS (swôr'THout) Dec. 25, 1904- Singer
Address: b. c/o National Concert & Artists Corp., 711 Fifth Ave., New York City; h. 25 East End Ave., New York City

Gladys Swarthout, "the prettiest Carmen on record" and one of the best-dressed women in America, was one of the first singers to prove that a Metropolitan Opera star need not be fat, frumpy, or foreign. She was born in Deepwater, Missouri (population 1,093), December 25, 1904, the daughter of Frank Leslie and Ruth (Wonser) Swarthout. Appropriately for a Christmas baby, Gladys was gifted not only with perfect health, but with absolute pitch, a retentive musical memory, and superb vocal equipment. Even when she was a child her singing brought compliments

to Mrs. Swarthout from neighbors who assumed that so full and mature a voice must belong to a grown woman. This inspired Gladys, whose family had never paid any particular attention to her singing, to even lustier vocal efforts. She sang so much and so loudly that her mother, afraid that Gladys would ruin her voice, arranged for singing lessons with Belle Vickers.

At the age of seven Gladys had decided to obtain the position of contralto soloist in a certain Kansas City (Missouri) church—"because I disliked the way the incumbent soloist held her music. . . . I remembered telling mother after one service on Sunday that I would one day be contralto soloist and show the woman how to hold her music." At thirteen, while still attending school, Gladys decided she was now ready to apply for this post. She took the precaution of dressing herself in adult fashion, pinning up her curls, thus adding some half-dozen years to her age. Whatever the choirmaster may have thought of the girl's appearance, after hearing her beautiful voice he engaged her as soloist, a post she held several years.

At Gladys' first public recital, given during her early teens, it happened that she missed a high note. With perfect poise she stopped, went back to the beginning of the aria, and sang it through, inspiring the audience to wild applause. Her performance so impressed a wealthy Kansas City family that they offered to finance her during the years of study which lay ahead. Although she did not have to work hard to develop her voice, the young singer needed to work on her interpretations and to achieve finesse.

After her graduation in 1920 from the Central High School of Kansas City, Miss Swarthout enrolled at the Bush Conservatory of Music in Chicago. She studied there for three years, meanwhile continuing with her church singing. Then she made a successful concert tour with her older sister, Roma, to help repay the cost of her training. These concerts aroused such a favorable response that Miss Swarthout's friends insisted that she try for the opera. But she did not know a single complete operatic role, and was further deterred from entering the operatic world by her mother's disapproval. However, in 1924 some friends arranged an audition with Herbert Johnson, manager of the renamed Chicago Civic Opera Company, which led to a contract for the following season. In a few weeks of intensive study during the summer preceding her debut, the ambitious mezzosoprano learned twenty-three complete roles.

Miss Swarthout's operatic debut was made in the part of an offstage shepherd in *Tosca;* her next role, again as a shepherd, allowed her to come onstage in *Tannhäuser;* and she continued to progress, singing in over half the Civic Opera's performances during the 1924-1925 season. Towards the end of the season, on March 22, 1925, Gladys Swarthout was married to Harry Richmond Kern. (He died six years later.)

During the summers from 1927 to 1929 Miss Swarthout gained more valuable operatic experience with Ravinia Opera Company near Chicago, after which she was engaged by the

Metropolitan Opera Company of New York. On November 15, 1929 she made her Metropolitan debut in the role of La Cieca, the blind old mother of *La Gioconda.* Two months later she received featured billing when she sang Niejata in the American première of Rimsky-Korsakov's *Sadko.* Upon the retirement of the contralto Marion Telva, Miss Swarthout took over many of her roles. Since then she has sung fifty-two characters, including most of the leading mezzo-soprano roles. She created the part of Cathos in the American première of Lattuada's *Le Preziose Ridicole,* and has "coped successfully with the difficult and high-lying music of Adalgisa in Bellini's *Norma.*" Operas in which she has appeared include *Faust, Lakmé, Peter Ibbetson, Romeo and Juliet, La Forza del Destino,* and *Boris Godunov.* But it is with the role of Carmen that she is particularly identified.

Miss Swarthout was welcomed as "a mezzo of great warmth, richness, and purity," and was praised for her "beauty, grace, and freshness"; but it was thought by many that she was "too much of a lady" for the best interpretation of her favorite role of Carmen. "It was a pleasant little baggage she portrayed," wrote Henry Simon, "marred by the inconsistency of an invincible gentility. Her angers were reminiscent of the frustrations of a student council president." Other reviewers described it as "a pleasant, small-scale Carmen, but of a routine rather than a distinctive savor." Robert Bagar, however, considered her "probably the most natural actress at the Metropolitan. She is very communicative, but never obvious. In her Carmen, for example, she attempts to achieve her acting aims in a manner that is in good keeping with such things as artistic restraint . . . and unforced realism. Miss Swarthout, for all her youth, is a veteran. She is a thoroughly dependable one, as the years have proved. And not the least valid of her attributes is the ability to be in the picture at all times and at the same time give a very good account of herself personally."

It was only a question of time before Hollywood called Miss Swarthout. With her voice, her beauty, her acting experience, and her following, she seemed a perfect choice for film stardom, especially with the wave of motion pictures with operatic backgrounds started by Grace Moore '44. But somehow she was the victim of the same poor story selection that Lily Pons '44 was; and although *Rose of the Rancho* (1936) went off well, the succeeding pictures—*Give Us This Night* (1936) in which she played opposite Jan Kiepura '43, *Champagne Waltz* (1937), and *Romance in the Dark* (1938)—were disappointments. Finally, for the last picture on her contract, she was cast in *Ambush* (1939)—a "rootin'-tootin'-shootin' mellerdrammer" in which she didn't sing a note! It was the only one she enjoyed making, for there were no arias to be cut out of the completed film.

In recent years Miss Swarthout has confined her operatic appearances to *Carmen.* In one of her performances, given at the Lewisohn Stadium on July 16, 1943, her interpretation had been developed to such an extent that, as Henry Simon put it, "it's practically a new role compared with the Carmen Miss Swarthout used to reveal at the Met several years

Alfredo Valente

GLADYS SWARTHOUT

ago. . . . She had acquired a tough, almost sluttish slouch. She smoldered, threw herself about the stage, and rose to real dramatic anger in the second and last acts. She sidled up to the officers in one mood, threw her cards to the wind in desperate determination in another, and acted the whole as a many-sided but always consistent peasant-gypsy. She was in excellent voice throughout the evening and the coloring she gave the music . . . matched her dramatic interpretation."

Lately Miss Swarthout has been devoting herself to radio and concert work. "An excellent concert singer," she has, according to Robert Lawrence, "everything in her favor but that combination of flame and profundity that makes for genius." He mentions her "natural good looks", "unspoiled presence on the platform," and the "cool, dusky beauty of her voice," and concludes that "Miss Swarthout is a genuine mezzo-soprano, the best among present-day American singers of this genre." Other reviewers agree that she is good to look at and to listen to; and in February 1944 a nationwide poll of radio editors gave her first place among concert singers.

In the opinion of Miss Swarthout and others, her best concert renditions are of the simple, well-loved English and American songs like "Home, Sweet Home" and "Long, Long Ago." She admits she cannot "put over" popular songs of the Tin Pan Alley sort, although Victor recorded a well-received album of her most requested ones in 1942. Unlike many in the world of classical music, she does not seek to explain this by calling popular songs intrinsically worthless: "The popular song," she says, "is as difficult as the most arduous aria. . . . Any good coach can teach you the opera and art-song tradition, and if you have the voice, the talent, and the elbow grease, you can learn it. With 'pops' it's different. A coach can't help you—or at least not me. I went to some of the best Broadway coaches, and they told me things I just couldn't do with the training I'd had. . . . Anyway, singing 'pops' is a matter of develop-

SWARTHOUT, GLADYS—_Continued_

ing your own individuality. If you sing a French art-song nearly as well as, say, Maggie Teyte, you're doing fine, but if you sing 'Smoke Gets in Your Eyes' like Dinah Shore '42, you're just an imitation of Dinah Shore and probably not so good. . . . For Verdi or Schubert you need to know tradition first of all; for 'pops' numbers you need individuality; but for 'Home, Sweet Home' you need only a heart."

Since her first radio performance for General Motors in 1930, the mezzo-soprano has appeared regularly on such programs as _The Magic Key_, the _Camel Caravan_, and the _Ford Symphony_. For three more years she was the star on the _Prudential Family Hour_, never missing one of its broadcasts except for her vacation—which was spent filling concert and guest radio engagements. During the concert slack season Miss Swarthout plans her programs for the coming season, building a working repertoire of forty songs. When with the _Family_ she often spent five nights a week on Pullmans, often made "hectic plane-train-car junkets to fill engagements in the West and get back to New York for Sunday broadcasts." Like many people whose work forces them to spend much time in travel, she loves to "do everything around the house—except cook and sew," while her husband is said to be an excellent amateur chef. She is a collector of fine china and figurines.

Since 1932 Miss Swarthout has been married to Frank M. Chapman, Jr., son of the famous ornithologist. They met in Florence, while Chapman, a baritone of distinction, was singing with the Italian National Opera Company, and later attended each other's American opera debuts. In 1931 they appeared on the same recital program; a year later they were married. Although Chapman has since appeared in operas throughout the country, has given many song recitals, and has also been featured on a number of radio programs, his main attention has been devoted to acting as Miss Swarthout's manager. He helped her plan the wardrobe which caused her to be twice voted one of the ten best-dressed women in America by a conference of designers. Having sold their California home to Greta Garbo, the Chapmans now have two homes: a New York apartment on the East River, and a 225-year-old farm near Redding Ridge, Connecticut where, it is said, Mr. Chapman found the graves of some of his ancestors. The couple are described as "earnest gourmets" and slightly less earnest athletes: Miss Swarthout often used to annoy her husband by stopping in the middle of a set of tennis. Frank Chapman is now serving as a captain in the Marine Corps.

Although Miss Swarthout works hard at her profession, she is careful to preserve her glowing health. She manages somehow to obtain her full quota of sleep, setting aside one night a week for "nerve repair." When in New York she exercises faithfully with a rowing machine on the balcony of her apartment; but she had to give up dancing because "the quick warming up and cooling off" gave her colds. For her devotion to duty, Miss Swarthout has been rewarded by a popularity which brings her a reported gross income of $200,000 (her net income is about fifteen per cent of that figure), by an honorary degree of Doctor of Music from the Bush Conservatory, and by election to Mu Pi Delta as the first woman member of that honorary music fraternity. Probably the greatest distinction conferred upon the Missouri-born mezzo-soprano was her selection to sing before the President, the Supreme Court, the entire assembled Congress, and the Diplomatic Corps on the occasion of the 150th anniversary of the Federal legislature. Miss Swarthout is a patriot who once remarked to an interviewer, "After all, we are first and last Americans—individualists. I want to be what I am as an American, sing our songs, standing on our soil. I'm a product of this country, and I'm proud to be."

In November 1943 a "career book" Miss Swarthout had written was published with the title _Come Soon, Tomorrow_. "Sometimes one suspects," commented the _Opera News_, "that Miss Swarthout was trying hard not to write her autobiography." That is to say that although names are carefully fictionized, sometimes it seems as though the writer were frantically signaling that Emmy Norton is Gladys Swarthout and no one else. There is a close parallel of background and life between the two. Even Emmy's personal description fits the author: "brown hair and eyes", "olive complexion", "an oval face"; Emmy has also heavy hair "simply parted in the center and brushed up and backward"—in the style which has become a Swarthout trademark. Emmy's desire to dress so as to appear taller reminds one that her five-feet-three creator has her clothes made by Valentina. (When she likes a dress design, she may have it made up in several different colors, and will then wear it for years. "When I stand in the bend of a grand piano dressed in one of these fine Rodier wools," she said of one such five-version creation, "no one is aware of a few moth holes!")

Notwithstanding the close personal parallel, "if Miss Swarthout had kept more closely to her own career" the _Opera News_ "would have liked her book better. Her own fascinating progress from an off-stage shepherd in _Tosca_ to the _Tannhäuser_ shepherd boy makes better reading than the jump made by Emmy Norton from concert appearances to Maddalena, Siebel, and Carmen. It is when she describes someone she has known well, like Maria Savage, who can be suspected in Mme. Mansard, that the narrative takes on its most intense interest."

The portrait of Emmy "throws new light on Gladys. She is hardworking, amiable, sentimental, conscientious, capable of warm affections, but never ignited by divine frenzy. The reader wonders if this is Miss Swarthout's picture of what she believes an American opera singer to be, or if she is unconsciously holding the mirror up to her own nature. Swarthout fans will surely find interest in solving this question for themselves."

References

C S Mon p10 Ap 13 '43
Cue 12:8 Ap 24 '43
N Y Post Mag p3 Ag 21 '43

Opera N 4:11 Ap 8 '40
PM p26 Jl 14 '43 por

Ewen, D. ed. Living Musicians 1940
Thompson, O. ed. International Cyclo-
    pedia of Music and Musicians 1943
Who's Who in America 1944-45

SWOPE, HERBERT BAYARD (swōp)
Jan. 5, 1882- Publicist; journalist
Address: b. 745 Fifth Ave., New York City;
h. Sands Point, Long Island, N. Y.

"The *World*'s greatest reporter—New York
World or the whole wide world"—was the
sweeping encomium by which a colleague once
referred to Herbert Bayard Swope, publicist
and former executive editor of the now defunct New York newspaper. If Swope had
overheard these words of praise he might conceivably have nodded in quiet agreement, for
a healthy ego is considered not the least among
the factors that have made him a legend. Possibly a more important factor is his dynamic
rise from obscurity.

The prelude to this dynamic career was
singularly unindicative—a very usual Middle
Western boyhood marked by a love of football. Herbert Bayard Swope was born in St.
Louis, Missouri, on January 5, 1882, to Isaac
and Ida S. Swope. After high school he decided to forego a college education for a year
in Europe. His trip was cut short, however,
when, after skinning his knee in a swimming
pool in the Black Forest, the wound developed
into a bad infection. He went back to St.
Louis, still at loose ends. It was no particular
urge to write that started him on his reporting career but a $100-prize offer from a local
department store for the best essay on why
it was the fastest growing business in town.
Eighteen-year-old Herbert won with the
judges' commendation that he was "a good
observer and writer." The fact that he was
later to become outstanding among reporters
really boils down to his continuing to be a
good observer. About his writing the late
Spencer Bull of the New York *Telegraph*
said: "In general style he is a master of tur-
gidity . . . but as a story-getter—irresistible,
unsurpassable."

Buoyed up by this evidence of a talent,
Swope sought and got a job on the St. Louis
Post Dispatch as a cub reporter. But, displeas-
ing his superiors by mixing in football with
routine work, he was soon suspended. His
next job, on the Chicago *Tribune*, was not
much more than a whistle stop on his way to
New York and fame. In New York he got
a job on the *Herald*, then for the next few
years shuttled back and forth between it and
the Morning *Telegraph*, doing some work for
Joseph Pulitzer's *World* in between.

Swope now began to be known as a man
about town. He discovered that to arrive late
focused attention on himself as an individual
and he was said to make a point of never being on time. In its early stages this habit got
him into trouble. When he began arriving
four hours late for work every day his boss,
Leo Redding, threatened to fire him. "But
Leo," argued young Swope, "when I come in
at 5:00 o'clock I'm still worth any two men

HERBERT BAYARD SWOPE

on your staff." Redding had to agree, and
Swope won the first round in his battle for
complete independence. (Bennett Cerf[41] says
in *Try and Stop Me* (1944) that Swope "is
never less than thirty minutes late for an appointment. He once was responsible for getting a popular actress to her own husband's
funeral an hour after the services had started.")

But his career did not really begin until
1909 when Sherman Morse, who had once
roomed with him, became city editor of the
New York *World* and asked Swope to join the
staff. H.B.S., as he was called on the paper,
now began to get into his stride. He kept his
finger on the pulse of the news by making
friends with politicians, gamblers, policemen,
elevator men, or any other individual who
crossed his reporter's path. "When you think
of news," he would tell people, "think of Herbert Bayard Swope."

But in 1912, the year of the famous Becker-
Rosenthal case, they needed no reminder.
Swope's releases on this case made him one
of the top-ranking newspapermen of the city.
A gambler, Herman Rosenthal, had "talked"
concerning police protection, and the *World*
was the first paper to print his affidavit. Then,
shortly before Rosenthal was to appear before
Charles Seymour Whitman, the District Attorney, he was shot and killed in front of the
Hotel Metropole. As a result of the investigation the police lieutenant, Charles Becker, went
to the electric chair along with four gunmen.
Whitman's handling of this case won him the
governorship, but considerable credit went
to H.B.S. On the scene of the murder himself only a few minutes after it occurred,
Swope got Whitman out of bed and to the
scene of the crime before any corrupt policeman might have time to cover up the evidence.
He was at the District Attorney's side thereafter, with suggestions and guidance, even
writing some of his statements. According to
Stanley Walker[44], Swope would snatch the
halting words out of Whitman's mouth, inject
cogent meaning into them, and then with a sly

SWOPE, HERBERT BAYARD—*Cont.*

"That was what you wanted to say, wasn't it?" give Whitman all the credit.

Writing on a "space rates" arrangement and winning frequently at the races, Swope began to make money; and in 1912 he was married to Margaret Pearl Honeyman Powell from Far Rockaway, New York. In 1914 he was still dazzling New York, this time from long distance. He was the *World's* foreign correspondent in Germany and sent exclusive dispatches of the sinking of the battleships *Crecy, Abou-Kir,* and *Hogue* by the German submarine, U-9. By his persuasive methods in searching out the news he was able to get around the German High Command and other Teutonic dignitaries. "He made James W. Gerard, American Ambassador to Germany, virtually a member of the *World's* staff," said Stanley Walker. When Swope's boat docked in New York no one knew whether to acclaim the foreign correspondent or the Ambassador. (Two years later there was no doubt, for, on a similar return trip Swope proved to be the major attraction for ship reporters.) Swope was now a recognized authority on war stories. In 1915 he was made city editor of the *World,* and in this post "exercised a proprietary interest in the news," said James Wyman Barrett, last city editor of the paper, in his *Joseph Pulitzer and His World* (1941). "Who is covering my Republican committee . . . subway accident . . . my murder trial?" Swope would ask. Coming in late one wintry day, he established his claims on nature: "Who's covering my snowstorm?" he demanded. And Swope regarded the telephone as his personal genie. Inclined to become confused in face-to-face conversation, his thoughts came out in clear, concise, and chronological order over the wires. He once roughly estimated the number of telephones in his various homes and offices as seventy-five.

Swope continued his reporting of the War, his investigations in 1916 during a second trip to Germany being serialized in the *World.* For this piece of work he received, in 1917, the Pulitzer Prize, the first reporter to receive that distinction. His articles were later published in book form under the title *Inside the German Empire* (1917). When the United States entered the First World War Swope was commissioned a lieutenant commander in the Navy, and then appointed to the War Industries Board as associate member and assistant to Bernard M. Baruch '41.

Chief correspondent of the four men the *World* sent to cover the Peace Conference at Versailles, Swope made the day of departure a memorable event in newspaper lore. The hour of sailing approaching—with no Swope in sight—his frenzied colleagues persuaded the captain to hold the ship for a half hour. Finally, when what seemed to be only a split second before the gangplank was to be removed, the "Paul Bunyan" of journalism hove in sight, perched atop his pile of baggage on an electric truck.

According to European diplomatic tradition, reporters were to be barred from the Conference. Swope was selected by the American journalists as chairman to lead the battle for American newspaper rights, and finally the European statesmen gave begrudging admission to a selected few. But Swope for some reason was not one of them. Completely undeterred he crashed the gates in top hat and cutaway as a diplomat, then cabled one scoop after another back to the *World.*

After each trip abroad Swope came home to a prize or new appointment. The plum that was waiting for him upon his return from Versailles in 1920 was the executive editorship of the *World,* a title created by Ralph Pulitzer expressly for Swope. Merging the executive editorship with the job of managing editor, Swope now reached his zenith as a newspaperman. Under his direction the *World* became a crusading paper, exposing the Ku Klux Klan, the peonage scandal in Georgia, and the radium poisonings in a watch factory. But this paper, famous for its "courageously liberal" tone, was beginning to fail. Various theories for its decline were advanced: Ralph and Herbert Pulitzer had not inherited enough of their father's talent for journalism; poor financial management; the fact that the paper "simply did not have the solid news coverage of its two conservative competitors, the *Times* and the *Herald Tribune.*" "Fine writing," said J. W. Barrett, "began to take the place of news." The "Op Ed," a special page opposite the editorial page that had been Swope's idea, had such by-lines as Heywood Broun, Franklin P. Adams '41, Alexander Woollcott '41, Laurence Stallings, Deems Taylor '40, William Bolitho, and Harry Hansen '42, but it was maintained at terrific cost. Old advertisers grew skeptical of the new elevated tone of the paper, and when the price went up from 2c to 3c, a move which Swope had opposed, there was a decided drop in circulation.

Finally, feeling that the *World* "no longer coincided with his personal ambition," said J. W. Barrett, Swope left it in 1929 just before the paper's sudden decline. "He it was," added Barrett, "who put the handwriting on the wall." The executive editor's resignation was a scoop in itself and was observed with innumerable farewell dinners and a special editor's edition of the paper in which every headline and story read simply: "Swope Quits."

During his newspaper years Swope, a gambler by instinct and an expert in games of chance, had become devoted to horseracing—it was said he edited the *World* from Belmont Park. In 1934, when betting became legal in New York State, the State Racing Commission was composed of the late Payne Whitney, John Sloan, the architect, and Swope as chairman. Though the chairmanship offered no salary, Swope tackled it with his typical crusading zest and made racing a respectable and popular sport, from which part of the profits went to the state. At the race track he introduced such innovations as the electric eye, the camera finish, the saliva test to detect drugging of horses, and the Australian barrier for starting races. He acquired a stable of his own and quite a reputation as a namer of thoroughbreds, among them Wrecker, Devastation, and Sidereal. Reappointed chairman in 1941, Swope was a familiar figure at the track, and is said to be a heavy stockholder in the Tropical racetrack.

The tenth report issued by Swope as chairman of the Racing Commission begins, "The New York thoroughbred racing season of 1944 was the most successful ever known to the sport—in any year, anywhere in the world."

For the six years of 1934 through 1939, before the adoption of the mutuels system of betting, total attendance was shown as 8,015,445; purse distribution was $10,454,620; and state revenue derived therefrom came to $3,026,745.41. As for the five years since the adoption of pari-mutuel betting, "the exact total of the public pools was $1,107,707,987; the whole attendance figure was 15,414,856; the purse distribution $19,273,030; and the state's net revenue, the immense figure of $70,830,486.37." This was to be Swope's last report in this capacity, as he tendered his resignation in December, to take effect at the end of January 1945. Three days after he did so, came War Mobilization Director James F. Byrnes' order to shut down all racing, to take effect January 3.

Swope is deeply nostalgic about his newspaper past. In fact, he has never been able to make a clean break, and keeps constantly in touch with editors and reporters, giving hints, advice, divulging "inside" information. In politics he has always been a Democrat. He turned "king-maker" with the late Alfred E. Smith '44, whom he had singled out as a potential statesman when Smith was sheriff of New York County. It was Swope who drew out Smith's opinion about the repeal of Prohibition and published it in the *World*. In 1924 Swope also succeeded in bringing to New York the Democratic National Convention, the first time one had been held in the city since 1868. In 1933 President Roosevelt '42 sent Swope along with Raymond Moley to the London Economic Conference. It was a failure, and for once Swope was not the returning hero. Neither he nor Moley divulged their version of the Conference at the time.

The ex-journalist's activities are still numerous. In 1942 he was named consultant to Secretary of War Stimson '40. He is a member of the executive committee of the Columbia Broadcasting System, and chairman of the Overseas News Agency and of the Turf Committee of America, which has raised over $3,000,000 for war relief. He is a director of the Beekman Street Hospital, the Humane Society, and the Child Welfare Society; member of the Committee on Control of Crime in New York, the Citizens Welfare Committee, the Committee to Defend America, and numerous other associations. Swope is also treasurer of Freedom House. He has honorary degrees from Hobart College and Colgate University, and is an honorary Phi Beta Kappa.

Past his sixtieth year, Swope takes little exercise but plays croquet with "skill and ferocity" and will let no one tell him it is not a man's game. Alexander Woollcott in one of his letters to Lilly Bonner describes Swope at the croquet court: "Burdened with Gerald Brooks as a croquet partner, he became so violent that Brooks agreed to do only what he was told and thereafter became a mute automaton, a condition which Swope enjoyed hugely. Brooks never moved his mallet or approached a ball without being told by Swope: 'Now Brooksy, you go through this wicket. That's fine. Now you shoot down to position. Perfect!' And so on. Finally before an enthralled audience, Swope said: 'Now you hit the ball up here in the road. That's right. Now you put your little foot on *your* ball and drive the other buckety-buckety off into the orchard. Perfect!' It was

only then, from the shrieks of onlookers, that Swope discovered it was his own ball which had been driven off."

Solidly built, Swope is just over six feet tall. His face has been called a "crimson bomb," and his hair is described as pinkish. He likes to smile and when he does it is with his whole face. From certain angles he is supposed to resemble Franklin Roosevelt, a fact that is said to please them both. He is famous for his gift of apt and ready speech, and has a voluminous store of assorted knowledge and an answer for every question, if "not always the right one," as Barrett once said.

Swope is fast becoming a patriarch in his Long Island home. Under its sprawling roof live three generations of his family, including in-laws and his own grownup children, Jane Marion and Herbert Bayard. His friends are those of long standing, as is his staff of Negro servants. Swope is at his best as a host, and his week-end parties are casual and pleasant. They are governed by only one law: the host's deeply rooted custom of making late appearances. Sometimes numbering thirty, his guests range from the Marx Brothers to William Randolph Hearst, Jr.

In summarizing Swope's career J. W. Barrett writes: "H.B.S.'s newspaper career was so outstanding, so dynamic, so brilliant, in some respects so disastrous, that even today . . . he is referred to in the press not so often as chairman of the New York State Racing Commission but as the former executive editor of the *World*. He is today's most distinguished ex-journalist."

References

Sat Eve Post 210:10-11+ Je 4 '38 il pors
Barrett, J. W. Joseph Pulitzer and His World p324-7; 344-6; 360-6 1941
Who's Who in America 1944-45

TARBELL, IDA M(INERVA) (tar-b-l) Nov. 5, 1875—Jan. 6, 1944 Dean of women authors in America; won recognition by her exposé of Standard Oil trust; associate editor of *McClure's Magazine* from 1894 to 1906; associate editor of *American Magazine* from 1906 to 1915; famous for her biographical studies of Abraham Lincoln.

Obituary

N Y Times p17 Ja 7 '44 por

TEMPLE, WILLIAM, ARCHBISHOP OF CANTERBURY Oct. 15, 1881—Oct. 26, 1944 Archbishop and Primate of All England since April 1942; was Archbishop of York, second highest dignitary in the Church of England, from 1929 until 1942; founder and first president of World Council of Churches; outstanding statesman, preacher, and writer; see sketch 1942 Yearbook.

Obituary

N Y Times p23 O 27 '44 por

TEMPSKI, ARMINE VON Apr. 1, 1899—Dec. 2, 1943 Author and lecturer; wrote many novels with Hawaiian background; most

TEMPSKI, ARMINE VON—*Continued*

successful book was autobiography, *Born in Paradise* (1940).

Obituary

N Y Times p23 D 3 '43

THOMAS, NORMAN (MATTOON) Nov. 20, 1884- The 1944 Presidential candidate of the Socialist Party of the United States

Address: h. 20 Gramercy Park, New York City

Norman Thomas, who has been the Socialist Party's unsuccessful Presidential candidate five times (the first in 1928), is regarded by his supporters as "a fearless inspired messiah," "the world's clearest, most civilized spokesman for the 'Brotherhood of Man to Come.'" In the crucial Presidential election year of 1932 Thomas received 884,781 votes, but since Franklin Delano Roosevelt [42] went into the White House the Socialist national vote has been dropping. In 1940 Thomas received 116,796 votes, and in the 1944 election, counting the "write-in" votes (which were disputed in several states) something over 100,000 ballots were cast for him. In December 1944 Thomas acknowledged, after his fifth defeat, that the "Socialist Party is finished as an electoral factor in the nation"—in the words of Robert S. Bird, the New York *Herald Tribune* writer. Thomas believes, however, that a new third party will emerge to elect a President. In this, the Socialist Party has an important, "even indispensable role as an educational factor." The new party will be social democrat, "with a small *s*," Thomas said, "and may not call itself a party at all. It may be a federation composed of a number of existing regional groups, and draw its electoral strength from the millions who vote Republican or Democrat, although factually they are neither." Thomas has said that the favorite sport of Americans during national election years is "choosing the lesser of two evils." The two major parties, which he has called "Tweedledum and Tweedledee," are, in his opinion, "like identical glass bottles with different labels and both empty."

Born in Marion, Ohio (Warren G. Harding's home town) on November 20, 1884, Norman Mattoon Thomas comes of a family of preachers of the rigid Calvinistic creed, from whom he undoubtedly inherited the gift of oratory. One grandfather was a missionary, the other preached the gospel until he was more than eighty, and his father was the Reverend Welling Evan Thomas. His mother was the former Emma Mattoon. The family was middle-class and of moderate means: he attended public schools in Marion, delivered Harding's newspaper, the *Daily Star,* from door to door, and when his father moved to a parish in Pennsylvania he was sent to Bucknell College. After a year at Bucknell a well-to-do relative gave him money enough to enable him to go to Princeton University to prepare for the ministry.

While studying at the Princeton Theological Seminary, Thomas, a shy, studious young man, took every available course in sociology; and on graduation day in 1905 he won a debate over Raymond B. Fosdick (now president of the Rockefeller Foundation) by arguing the thesis that "municipal governments should own their street railway systems." But socialism was apparently far from his thoughts at the time: as late as 1908 he was voting Republican, for Taft. And as yet he had no idea of becoming anything but a minister, even though after graduation he volunteered for work at the East Side Settlement in New York City at a salary of $500 a year. After two years in the New York slums he made a trip around the world, then took up work as assistant pastor at Christ Church, New York. It was there that he met Frances Violet Stewart, a social worker who had come to organize one of the first clinics in New York for the treatment of tuberculosis, and on September 1, 1910 they were married. The next year Thomas, who had been studying at Union Theological Seminary, was ordained a Presbyterian clergyman and for a few months he served as assistant to the Reverend Henry Van Dyke at New York's fashionable Brick Presbyterian Church on Fifth Avenue. That same year he was appointed pastor of the East Harlem Church and chairman of the American Parish, in the heart of Italian working-class Harlem, and he was to remain there for seven years.

While he was preaching in the East Harlem Church the United States entered the First World War. Thomas was a pacifist and he continued to preach against war; when the more belligerent church elders stopped financing his social service work at the American Parish he resigned his pastorate and joined the Socialist Party. He was not to leave the ministry formally until his mother's death in 1931, but from the beginning he could afford to give full time to the Socialist cause: his wife had inherited a comfortable trust fund from her grandfather. He therefore accepted the position of secretary of the anti-war Fellowship of Reconciliation, and in 1918 founded and became editor of the F.O.R. organ, the *New World* (renamed the *World Tomorrow* a few months later), of which Postmaster General Burleson, who had been barring pacifist and Socialist publications from the mails, declared: "Thomas is more insidious than Debs." With Roger N. Baldwin [40] he also helped to found the National Civil Liberties Bureau (now the American Civil Liberties Union), espousing the cause of conscientious objectors in particular. (He himself was exempt from the draft because of four children, but his own brother had been sentenced to Fort Leavenworth for defying conscription.)

After the War, in 1919 he helped to lead the Passaic, New Jersey, textile workers' strike. While he was making a speech to the workers the police entered the hall and cut off all the lights; Thomas lit a candle and read the constitution of the state. When ten Socialists were expelled from the New York State Assembly as a result of the Red scare which followed the War, Thomas was a "star" witness in the trial that followed. For a year following his resignation as editor of the *World Tomorrow* in 1921 he was an associate editor of the *Nation;* then he joined Harry W. Laidler in building up the League for Industrial Democracy out of the old Intercollegiate Socialist Society, and served as its director in

1922. By 1924, the year the Socialists supported La Follette for the Presidency, Thomas was running as Socialist nominee for Governor of New York. In 1925 he ran for Mayor of New York; in 1926, for state Senator; in 1927, for Alderman. In 1926 he also managed to be in Passaic (New Jersey) nearly every day, addressing the striking wool workers and protesting "unconstitutional police measures" to end the strike. He was finally arrested, but five months later a grand jury refused to indict him.

In 1928, "when Coolidge prosperity was up and socialism struck its hardest times," Thomas ran for President of the United States for the first time and succeeded in polling a quarter of a million votes. In 1929, while the Emergency Committee for Strikers' Relief (organized by the League for Industrial Democracy and directed by Thomas) was assisting in the textile strikes in Tennessee and the Carolinas, he ran for Mayor of New York for the second time. Three non-Socialist New York newspapers counseled their readers to vote for him, which 175,000 people did.

Then came the depression, and Thomas' following increased. Much of his program for relieving unemployment—public works, unemployment insurance as part of a general scheme of social insurance against old age and sickness, and the shortening of the work week—was later to be adopted by the New Deal. At the 1932 Socialist convention he was not only nominated for the Presidency by a vote of 252 to 1, but was instrumental in persuading the party to change its unsympathetic attitude toward the U.S.S.R., held since 1920. Even at this time he was no Marxist, however, and was firmly opposed to the idea of bringing about social change by force. On his insistence the Socialist convention that year voted down a resolution declaring for confiscation of property, but his views made enemies for him among the extreme Left-wingers in the Socialist Party as well as among the Old Guard. Thomas nevertheless received almost 900,000 votes in November 1932, after a campaign in which he charged that "Hoover's [43] record is a record of mistake piled on mistake," and that "the party which dares to take the name of Thomas Jefferson is in the South the party with the most outrageous racial discrimination, and in the North the party of the most flagrant corruption in our cities."

But subsequent events were to show that 1932 was apparently the peak of the Socialist Party's influence since the beginning of Thomas' leadership. In the years following, Roosevelt's [42] New Deal enlisted the support of many liberals and radicals who had formerly found a home in the Socialist Party. During the 1936 election campaign, when Thomas was again the Socialist Presidential candidate, his viewpoint was that it made little difference whether Roosevelt or Landon [44] were elected: "the drift in either case is toward war and fascism. . . . The issue this year is between socialism and capitalism." Cough drops, he pointed out, "may differ in color and taste, but they are all cough drops, and they will not cure tuberculosis." Election results, however, showed that the bulk of those who had voted the Socialist ticket in 1932 were willing to try the New Deal measures.

NORMAN THOMAS

Thomas' old followers were further split over his attitude toward "collective security" in the international sphere. In 1934 he had declared that America should join the World Court and the League of Nations and take the lead in disarmament, but at the same time he had announced that "we would have to take the most elaborate precautions against being drawn into wars to enforce peace. Especially we must not be trapped into giving any guarantee that we will support other nations in military or economic war against an 'aggressor' nation." That same year he had invited "unattached radicals," including those recently expelled from the Communist Party, to join the Socialist Party, and in early 1936 the Socialist Party itself had been "purged" of those favoring cooperation with the Communists. Under Thomas the Socialist Party therefore refused to support any front against Fascism, even though at the time of the Spanish civil war he opposed the sudden imposition, by the United States, of the embargo on arms to Spain. All sanctions and pressures against aggressor nations should be applied by unofficial groups, he believed; if applied by governments, war would become a likelihood, and "the minute war was declared, America would become a fascist state or a military despotism." In November 1938 the Socialist leader wrote, in Harper's Magazine: "A sound program of opposition to war will insist on clear-cut opposition to all imperialism and to the militarism of the big navy and mobilization bills. It will demand the recall of troops and ships from belligerent zones where no good that they can do is worth the risk they run. It will consent to no alliances, tacit or open, for war in the name of collective security. It will uphold the general policy of emphasis on peace trade, not war trade, which we have discussed. It will favor a popular referendum on the declaration of war."

Long before this Thomas had changed his views about the progressivism of the Russian

THOMAS, NORMAN—*Continued*

Government, maintaining that "Stalin'42 was a pioneer, ahead of Hitler'42, in purges, concentration camps, and all the techniques of modern regimentation"; and after the Nazi-Soviet non-aggression pact of August 1939 he also attacked Stalin for "giving Hitler the green light which cleared the way for his aggressive campaigns in Europe." While he approved the original Neutrality Act revision which permitted arms sales to Great Britain and admitted that he would prefer a British victory, he steadily insisted that the United States should maintain a position as neutral as Russia's in the Second World War. At the Socialist Party's national convention in 1940 he led the majority of the convention which opposed resolutions favoring aid to Great Britain and France as well as one demanding an embargo on goods to Japan. In July 1940 he denounced conscription before the Senate Military Affairs Committee; in January 1941 he testified before the House Foreign Affairs Committee against the Lend-Lease Bill; and throughout 1941 he was one of the chief speakers at peace rallies under the joint auspices of the America First Committee and the Keep America Out of War Congress. (At the time the *New Republic* pointed out that "although he stayed clear of the Popular Front several years ago Mr. Thomas has now united himself with a very different collection of elements, not on the Left but chiefly on the Right.")

Before Russia entered the War, Thomas' position was, in brief, that "the economics of war will practically doom democracy." When Hitler attacked Stalin he prophesied: "Of all the present rulers and regimes of the world, if eventually America loses herself in total war, the most likely victor is Stalin or his regime. . . . In my judgment there is not enough difference between the kind and quality of totalitarian rule under Stalin and the quality of state-ism under Hitler to justify the death of a generation of America's chosen youth." "Neither Japan nor Germany, nor both combined, can or will aggressively attack us in this hemisphere or even in the Philippines unless first they are convinced that, come what may, we intend and we are ready aggressively to attack them," he also said.

After Pearl Harbor the Socialist Party officially ceased its efforts to keep America out of war, but Thomas still did not "want to continue this War indefinitely only to the end that Stalin may become lord over most of Europe and Asia." He continued to declare that America, under Roosevelt, was on the road to dictatorship; he opposed the Department of Justice prosecutions, saying that "civil liberties in America are in a worse case than they were under Mr. Wilson"; and he forecast a third world war as a result of Roosevelt's policies abroad. In 1944 he deplored mass bombings of Axis cities and stated that "at Moscow, Cairo, and Teheran the America whose destiny should have been the vindication of democracy and of cooperation between peoples apparently underwrote the British and Russian empires." At the Socialist convention in June 1944 which nominated him as its Presidential candidate for the fifth time, he secured the adoption of a plank in his party's platform voicing a demand for "an immediate political peace offensive based on the offer of an armistice to the peoples of the Axis nations," and condemning Allied demands for Germany's unconditional surrender. (At the same convention Darlington Hoopes of Reading, Pennsylvania, was nominated for the Vice-Presidency. A former member of the Pennsylvania Legislature, he is credited with having won state ratification of the Federal Child Labor Amendment.)

Thomas' program for a sound and lasting peace would be based on three principles: (1) no vengeance against any people; (2) the abandonment of imperialism as a principle of world organization; (3) economic and political cooperation through regional federations and an over-all world federation, as opposed to a highly centralized world state. On the domestic scene, the Socialist Party proposes "social ownership and democratic management of the means of production and distribution." Thomas pointed out, however, that his party "does not stand blindly for government ownership. That depends," he said, "on who owns the government. We do not reject government of the workers by the bosses, for the profit of absentee owners, in favor of government of the workers by the bureaucrats for the glory and power of a military or totalitarian state. We are pointing the way in which people can save themselves."

During his 1944 Presidential campaign Thomas stated that in the field of post-War organization both major candidates had acclaimed the Dumbarton Oaks agreement, which he considered as meaning no more than "an association of major powers, with minor satellites, whose members hope to freeze the shape of the world indefinitely. It is an attempt to accomplish what has never been successful in world history; an attempt to make permanent the gains of a power alliance against the peoples of the world." "Dumbarton Oaks," he continued, "points the way to a post-War world that will insure new wars, either of the Big Three [Russia, Britain, and the United States] against revolutionary uprisings throughout all Europe and Asia, or among the victorious powers themselves." The National Committee of Thomas' party stated that in contrast to the foreign policy of both the Republican and Democratic parties the Socialists were not for a combination of imperialist powers "holding their own," but were for a combination of the peoples of the world, organized on a logical federal and economic basis, which would share the goods of the world equally, without regard to racial, geographical, and economic barriers. They believe the wealth of the world belongs to the people who produce it, and until such a distribution takes place, there will be no end of wars.

An open letter Thomas sent to Sidney Hillman, chairman of the Political Action Committee of the CIO, was described as "a slashing attack, delivered in the best Thomas style." Characterizing the activities of PAC in the election as "company unionism in politics," he declared that the CIO had deliberately scuttled an excellent opportunity for independent political action on the part of the workers and instead had joined the "Southern Bourbons" and the city bosses of the Democratic machine.

In the *Rotarian* of November 1943 Thomas declared: With all the mistakes and blunders the Government has made on the economic front in planning for war, it has practically abolished unemployment and enormously increased the national income. Men are going to insist after the War that if that kind of a job can be done for war, a better job can be done for peace by the right sort of social planning. . . . In the United States at the end of the War the Government will be the employer or the comptroller of practically all the manpower, the purchaser of at least 75 per cent of the national income, and the banker extraordinary for all enterprise."

Other articles by Thomas have appeared in such publications as the New York *Times*, the *American Mercury* ("Credo of an Old-fashioned Socialist" in April 1943), and in *Harper's*. (In May 1942 that magazine published an article by him in which he recommended legislative action by the states or by the Federal Government as a remedy for the "underlying lack of democracy in the labor union setup.") He often speaks on radio forums such as the *American Forum of the Air* and the *Commentators' Round Table*, and he remained a trustee of *America's Town Meeting* after the *Reader's Digest* took over its sponsorship, having pronounced himself satisfied that there would be no editorial interference or exercising of control over the program. Under the management of the Columbia Lecture Bureau, he also "earns more than pin money from lecturing at colleges and liberal clubs," and in 1932 Princeton, his own university, bestowed an honorary Litt.D. upon him.

The conservative press is not often very unkind to Thomas. As Matthew Josephson put it in 1932, "He has nearly always retained the respectful tolerance of his most conservative contemporaries. . . . There is something naïve in the big-hearted social worker who espouses the idea of reform. His type is perfectly familiar in our history: that of the 'Goo-Goos,' or Good Government Boys, whom Lincoln Steffens describes so well in his autobiography; and opponents have learned not to fear his type. By preference or by natural disposition Norman Thomas is less concerned with the reform of labor and its preparation for the conquest of power than he is with the moral need for socialism." The Socialist leader's tendency, according to Josephson, is "to make his appeal to a mildly rebellious section of the middle class from which he himself springs, and which he understands. For the laboring masses, whose language he speaks but haltingly, his appeal will be weaker."

Whether Josephson's estimate is true or not, Thomas has frequently been arrested or prevented from speaking—particularly in Mayor Hague's Jersey City bailiwick. The most famous episode was in 1938, when he was "deported" from the city by the police for attempting to address a Socialist meeting. A few weeks later he tried to deliver the same speech in Newark, but was again stopped.

Thomas is the author of numerous books and pamphlets, among them *The Conscientious Objector in America* (1923), later revised and reprinted under the title *Is Conscience a Crime?*

(1927); *America's Way Out—a Program for Democracy* (1930); *As I See It* (1932); *What's the Matter With New York?* (with Paul Blanchard, 1932); *Human Exploitation in the United States* (1934); *Socialism on the Defensive* (1938); *Keep America Out of War* (with Bertram D. Wolfe, 1939); *We Have a Future* (1941); and *What Is Our Destiny?* (1944).

As described by a Republican writer in 1932, he "looks like a cultivated aristocrat, with his high-domed head—not unlike that of John Galsworthy—his thin gray hair, his narrow nose and sensitive nostrils, his firm lips and thoughtful blue-gray eyes. He is tall and slender, slightly stooped in the shoulders, neat and conventional in attire, and dignified in his bearing. He belongs to the Woodrow Wilson type, depending more upon logic than upon emotions, and his manner is faintly academic. He would fit naturally into the atmosphere of an English house party with Balfour and Asquith. He is emphatically a gentleman. He has an ineradicable sense of humor with which he enlivens his arguments. About him there is something magnetic. And he has a charming smile. It should be understood that he is fully the peer of Mr. Hoover and Mr. Roosevelt in cultural antecedents . . . his hands are white and uncalloused. He is hardly aware from personal experience what it is to perform manual labor under economic compulsion. . . . He would behave in the White House like the well-born, well-bred aristocrat that he is."

According to another writer, he "still has the air of a prosperous preacher. Even in groups of two or three, he talks in ringing tones and strides back and forth, pulpit-style, as he expounds some favorite Socialist doctrine. . . . His personal habits are clerically ascetic. He seldom smokes or drinks." He and Mrs. Thomas, to whom he dictates most of his correspondence and speeches, live in a New York City apartment overlooking Gramercy Park and filled with "overstuffed chairs and pastoral paintings." They also own a country house in Cold Spring Harbor, Long Island, where Mrs. Thomas used to raise pure-blooded cocker spaniels. The Thomas' have five grown children.

References

Am Mag 130:44-5+ Jl '40 il pors
Commonweal 16:422-4 Ag 31 '32
Cur Hist 37:1-6 O '32; 45:71-5 O '36
Nation 134:365-7 Mr 30 '32
New Repub 71:332-6 Ag 10 '32
World Tomorrow 13:259-63 Je '30
Who's Who in America 1944-45

THOMASON, JOHN WILLIAM, JR. (tom'a-sun) Feb. 28, 1893—Mar. 12, 1944 Author; colonel in United States Marine Corps; veteran of the First World War; wrote biography, history, and fiction from his experiences and often sketched his own illustrations; *Fix Bayonets* (1926), *Red Pants* (1927), *Marines and Others* (1929) were some of his well known books.

Obituary

N Y Times p15 Mr 13 '44 por

THOMPSON, WILLIAM HALE (May 14, 1869—Mar. 19, 1944 Mayor of Chicago for three terms from 1915 to 1923 and 1927 to 1931; one of the most picturesque figures in Chicago's political history; known as "Big Bill" Thompson; during First World War was isolationist; in '20's launched short-lived America First Foundation and attempted to "purify" American history books.

Obituary

N Y Times p17 Mr 20 '44 por

TIETJENS, EUNICE (tē'jens) July 29, 1884—Sept. 6, 1944 Poet, lecturer, and author of books for young people; a former associate editor of *Poetry* Magazine; gained prominence for her poetical interpretations of Oriental life; her first book of poems, *Profiles From China,* was published in 1917; was followed by several other volumes on China and Japan.

Obituary

N Y Times p23 S 7 '44

TOBIN, RICHARD L(ARDNER) Aug. 9, 1910- Journalist

Address: b. c/o New York Herald Tribune, 230 W. 41st St., New York City; h. 4 Dartmouth St., Forest Hills, Long Island, N.Y.

Invasion Journal (1944), by Richard L. Tobin, is not, strictly speaking, a journal of the Allied invasion of Western Europe, for Tobin could spend comparatively little time at the Normandy beaches between April and August 1944, the period his journal covers. It is, however, in Bernard De Voto's [43] words, "a very serviceable instrument for conveying the feel of London in the period just before and just after D-Day . . . a different and useful kind of war book, frequently subjective and concerned principally with the marginal stories of invasion, the rumors that reach the press corps, the impact of military events on civilians and on the lower ranks at headquarters, the suspense and confusion and doubt and foreboding north of the Channel during the climactic hour." Sam Halper also finds it a warm book, for "Tobin knows what the War is all about and his anti-Fascism is stout and extends far back from the Front in France to the apartment house in Forest Hills where he lives."

Richard Lardner Tobin was born in Chicago on the day his mother (sister of the late Ring Lardner) had been to see a double-header between the White Sox and the Philadelphia Athletics at Comiskey Park. The date was August 9, 1910; the sports-loving parents were Richard Griswold and Ann (Lardner) Tobin. When old Charley Comiskey heard about the new arrival he sent the elder Tobin, who had been covering the White Sox for the Chicago *Inter-Ocean,* a baby carriage filled with a case of Scotch whisky.

It was some time after this that the family moved to Canada, and there the elder Tobin published a magazine, *Canada Monthly,* for a while. Later he became owner of his own newspaper in his wife's home town, Niles, Michigan; and it was in the enormous old Lardner house, in the aura of Ring Lardner's fame, that young Richard spent most of his early life. All in all, it was little wonder that he decided to become a newspaperman himself. From 1917 until he went to the University of Michigan in 1928 his father ran the Niles *Daily Star* and he was "vice-commissar" —when he was not playing football and breaking his nose five times in one season. For a while, too, he worked on the South Bend (Indiana) *News-Times* as a sports writer. By his senior year at Michigan he was managing editor of the Michigan *Daily.*

It was directly due to the president of the University of Michigan, however, that Tobin finally got a job on the New York *Herald Tribune.* "I was thrown out of Michigan for publishing editorials about campus graft or some such thing," he explains, "but the State Board of Regents made it an issue of free speech and overruled the president of the University, so I was reinstated with much flourish. *Time* Magazine picked it up and the resultant publicity caused Stanley Walker [44], city editor of the New York *Herald Tribune,* to hire me by letter. That was the very bottom of the depression and Walker said he could pay me $25 a week. It was $20 a week by the time I had been graduated in June [1932]. It was $18 a week six weeks after I got to New York because of a 10 per cent cut." At any rate he began working on the *Herald Tribune* the day after he left the University of Michigan, and he has been with that paper ever since. Those first years in Manhattan he shared an apartment with John Lardner, Jim Lardner (cousins), and Don Skene at 37 West 8th Street. "It was sailor's rest," he says. "Damon Runyon [42] would visit us with strange characters tagging along. We never locked the door and we never knew who'd be sleeping in the living room next day."

Life with the *Herald Tribune* was not dull, either. "I covered general assignments for several years, eventually drifting into crime news, which was pretty exciting stuff in the gangster era. I covered many a famous murder case at Police Headquarters and criminal courts; the beginning of Tom Dewey [44]; the La Guardia [40] overthrow of Tammany Hall; politics for a spell; then the Lindbergh [41] case from the hour that Bruno Richard Hauptmann was arrested until the minute he died. I witnessed his execution in the hot, dreadful little brick house inside the prison at Trenton, covering the story for the *Herald Tribune.* In 1937 I covered the Ohio-Mississippi floods from Pittsburgh to New Orleans, leaving the city desk temporarily.

"After the Hauptmann case had ended, the *Herald Tribune* put me on the city desk, as an assistant city editor. I was assistant day city editor for three years, 1935, 1936, and 1937. Then I was appointed assistant night city editor, where I stayed until the day after election in November 1942. The *Herald Tribune* then began to experiment with television and F.M. [nearly static-free frequency modulation] news broadcasting, and I was assigned to establish and maintain a broadcasting division of the *Herald Tribune.* For two years I broadcast four times a day, six days a week, over F.M. station WABF, and gave a nightly newscast over WOR at 11:15 p.m., meanwhile experimenting with telecasting of news. With the invasion imminent, and the radio television department pretty well established, the *Herald Tribune* sent me to London to coordinate the coverage of the invasion of northwest Europe, besides covering daily stories and broadcasting from London over WOR-Mutual."

In October 1937 Tobin had been married to the former Sylvia Cleveland of Cleveland, Ohio, and by this time there is a son, Mark. In April 1944, then, it was to Sylvia and Mark that he bade good-bye before boarding a ship bound for England. The entries in his journal dealing with life aboard the ship are more than graphic. Used to privacy and uncomfortable himself in a cabin that held six, he found it difficult to imagine how the troops—sleeping, eating, standing, waiting, and being seasick "within the same few square feet of dank smells"—managed to endure the passage. More discomforts awaited him in England; before long he had decided that the real reason the British couldn't be beaten in 1940 and 1941 was that even war could make little difference in their way of living: they had always been used to cold rooms, food that tasted like "waterlogged cardboard."

Most of the rest of *Invasion Journal* concerns the life of a newspaper correspondent in London in the days before and after D-Day. The nightmare of flying bombs; the attempted assassination of Hitler '42 and the excitement it created among newspaper correspondents; thoughts on de Gaulle '40, Irish neutrality, censorship, anti-Semitism, British class distinctions, and peanut butter—all find a place in his journal. Tobin made only a brief trip to France, of which he records talks with Germans prisoners, a Frenchwoman's defense of shaving the heads of women who had "comforted" the Germans, a visit to a field hospital. General Eisenhower '42 he calls "the least stuffy man in high place I've ever met, except Ambassador Winant '41, who thinks he's Lincoln, and overdoes it." Of the American soldier he says: "Yankee self-confidence is winning the War, and Yankee courage is measuring up to the actuality of having your foot or hand torn off by a mine." Scotch-Irish by ancestry, Episcopalian by faith, and democratic by conviction, Tobin has always been a firm believer in a stiff peace for Germany, and all that he has seen in London and in France has made him even less able to understand the advocates of a "soft peace."

While the *Library Journal*'s reviewer thought *Invasion Diary* "fairly interesting, but not too important," the Springfield *Republican*'s book critic came to the conclusion that "Mr. Tobin, with his training, could not be a poor reporter if he tried. . . . Mr. Tobin's account of his personal reaction to the dreadful robot bomb is one of the most vivid pieces to come out of that theatre." Wrote Brigadier General Donald Armstrong in the *Saturday Review of Literature*: "Excellent reading to supplement the exclusively military accounts of the invasion of France. . . . The G.I.'s in the crowded hold of a transport and in the British Isles, England and the English, London and the Londoners, are described by a capable and compassionate observer." Although General Armstrong found reason to remark on Tobin's impatience with Army "slowness" ("Will civil-

RICHARD L. TOBIN

ians ever appreciate the magnitude of the supply problem in modern war, and its effect on strategy?"), that reviewer, too, has praise for the author's discussion of the flying bombs: "After being close enough to these man-made meteorites to be knocked off his feet, Mr. Tobin writes feelingly and vividly of their development, present use, and future menace. . . . For this reason his book merits wide circulation among a people who forget readily the peril from a congenitally aggressor nation and from the self-propelled long-range projectiles that this nation [Germany] has developed and is reportedly ready to use."

At the conclusion of *Invasion Journal* Tobin was on his way back to the front, and since that time he has been covering the battle for Western Europe from Supreme Headquarters of the Allied Expeditionary Force. "When I get back from overseas, and the War has been won," he says, "we're going to buy an eighteenth century house on Nantucket. We've spent our vacations at sea—every single vacation for seven years. We've been to Haiti more times than we've been to Brooklyn. I was never a very happy man until I got married." Whether he will return to teaching he does not say; in 1940 he had begun to teach, one day a week, at the Pulitzer School of Journalism at Columbia University, and since then he has taught and lectured there as an assistant professor. Journalist Tobin's second book, written with Roscoe Ellard, his colleague in the reporting course, and tentatively titled "Reporters Tell the World," is scheduled for early publication. Aside from "telling the world," Tobin's hobbies are "tennis, swimming, football, Big League baseball, gardening, sea travel, reading, any kind of music, almost any play or movie."

References

N Y Herald Tribune p13 O 14 '40 por

Tobin, R. Invasion Journal 1944

TREANOR, TOM 1909 (?)—Aug. 19, 1944
War correspondent for the National Broad-
casting Company and the Los Angeles *Times;*
author of the best seller *One Damn Thing
After Another* (1944), which described his
war experiences in North Africa, Sicily, and
Italy; fatally injured in a jeep accident in
France.

Obituary

N Y Times p4 Ag 22 '44 por

TURNER, R(ICHMOND) KELLY May
27, 1885- United States naval officer
Address: b. c/o Navy Department, Washington, D. C.; h. Carmel, Calif.

The American Navy's leading expert on
amphibious warfare, according to *Time,* is a
vice-admiral who signs the pay roll R. Kelly
Turner. Personally thanked by Emperor
Hirohito '40 for bringing the ashes of the
Japanese ambassador, Hirosi Saito, back to

Official U.S. Navy Photo
VICE-ADM. R. KELLY TURNER

Japan in an American cruiser, he saw that
cruiser sunk by the Japanese less than three
years later, in 1942. Now he is "doing the
spadework for the advance to Japan" via "the
pinpoints of the Pacific."

Richmond Kelly Turner was born in Portland, Oregon, May 27, 1885, the son of Enoch
and Laura Frances (Kelly) Turner. He attended high school in Stockton, California,
entering the Naval Academy from that state
at twenty. There Turner was manager of the
baseball team and editor of the *Lucky Bag.*
He is said to have been a star hurdler.
On graduation he stood fifth in his class.
After duty at sea he was commissioned an
ensign on June 5, 1910, and was married to
Harriet Sterling the following August.
Turner has spent nearly half the succeeding
years afloat.

By 1913 the young officer had risen to
command of the U. S. S. *Stewart.* After this

tour of sea duty Turner was sent to the
Naval Ordnance School, from which he was
graduated in 1916. During the First World
War he served aboard a number of battleships, none of which, it is said, saw any action. At any rate, Turner's next command
was the U. S. S. *Mervine* (1924-25). In
spite of his forty-two years the air-minded
officer studied at the Naval Aviation School
at Pensacola, Florida, winning in 1927 the
wings which, like Admiral Halsey '42, he still
wears. The knowledge thus gained was put
to practical use at the head of an aircraft
squadron of the Asiatic Fleet, which, with
the command of the U. S. S. *Jason,* occupied
Turner's attention until July 29, 1929.

At this time the enterprising airman was
made chief of the Navy Bureau of Aeronautics' Planning Division. He attended the
abortive Geneva Conference on Disarmament
(December 1931-December 1932) as aviation
adviser to the American delegation, then was
ordered back to the United States to become
executive officer on the aircraft carrier *Saratoga.* Two years later Turner was appointed
chief of staff of the Aircraft Battle Force;
on July 1, 1935, at the age of fifty, he was
promoted to captain and assigned to the
Naval War College.

After five years of shore duty Captain
Turner returned to the sea in 1938 as skipper
of the cruiser *Astoria.* It was the *Astoria*
which brought Ambassador Saito's mortal remains back to Japan, as an indication of sympathy and respect on the part of the United
States. (On August 9, 1942 the *Astoria* was
sunk by the Japanese off Savo Island, just
north of Guadalcanal in the Solomons area.)
Turner had the opportunity, then and in his
days with the Asiatic Fleet, of coming to
know many of the high Japanese officers.
"He does not despise them," according to
Newsweek, "any more than he does a Japanese infantryman." He left the *Astoria* in
October 1940 to become director of the Navy
Department's War Plans Division, and then
assistant chief of staff to the fleet commander
in chief. His promotion to rear admiral
came in January 1941.

Ordered to the South Pacific in July 1942
to put his plans into effect, the fifty-seven-
year-old Admiral had no firsthand experience with island fighting. Neither had anyone else. This was a new kind of war, and
it was up to Kelly Turner to devise a new
technique to fit it. He "had to write the
rules as he went along"—and many of them
were learned the hard way. To quote the
citation for his Distinguished Service Medal
(awarded March 22, 1943 at an advanced
South Pacific base): "During the period of
August 7 to December 10 [1942] he was in
charge of task forces of occupation in the
Solomon Islands. The forces under his command have been repeatedly subject to enemy
submarine, surface, and air attack. The continued success of American arms has been in
a large degree due to his skillful organizing,
dynamic leadership, executive ability, and
personal fearlessness. He demonstrated professional skill of the highest order under the
most difficult of conditions." There were
some "disastrous naval losses for which
Turner must be held partly to blame," yet

his performance as a whole was so successful that he was also awarded the Navy Cross.

After the attack on Japanese-held Guadalcanal in the Solomons the middle-aged veteran "collapsed with malaria and dengue fever. Still gray with sickness, he set up headquarters on Guadalcanal preparatory to the New Georgia invasion. 'Terrible' Turner's bridge was a jungle clearing marked by a wooden sign: 'U. S. S. *Crocodile*—Flagship—Amphibious Forces South Pacific.' Under the scorching tropic sun," as reported in *Time*, "he taught the new amphibious doctrine, which he was learning himself, to the officers under his heterogeneous command: air officers, marine colonels, brigadier generals, destroyer captains, PT commanders, crusty transport skippers. Preached this old-line Navy man: 'The fellow we are working for is the fellow that walks on the ground. Whatever we are doing we are doing solely to get that boy onto the beach.' Cooperation was his passionate credo. More than any other man in the Pacific he was charged with combining all operations into one fast striking force."

Unlike most admirals, Turner had his flagship, the *McCawley*, shot out from under him during the Rendova attack, and was forced to shift with his staff to another destroyer. But the operation was highly successful nonetheless: all the soldiers were brought from their ships onto the beach without the loss of a single life. Responsibility for amphibious operations in the New Georgia campaign was shared by Turner with Rear Admiral Theodore S. Wilkinson; but, in Admiral Halsey's words, "There is plenty of glory for all."

After the successful completion of that campaign Turner was transferred to the Central Pacific area, under the command of Vice-Admiral Raymond Ames Spruance '⁴⁴. While Spruance had the strategic and naval command, and various generals directed the actual fighting, it was up to Kelly Turner to see that the men and equipment got off the ships and onto the beach. (This included the highly skilled and important art of combat loading—that is, loading the transports so that each item shall come off them in the order that makes for greatest efficiency.) In November 1943 United States forces attacked the Gilbert Islands (lying between Hawaii and New Guinea), which had been powerfully fortified by the Japanese in the twenty-three months since their seizure from the British. The assault was successful, both in gaining possession of the islands and in the favorable ratio of American to Japanese losses; but the number of American casualties, particularly in the battle for Betio Island in the Tarawa atoll, was the highest in the War up to that point (2,950). Many unexpected losses came about because landing craft were caught on boat traps built among the reefs.

By February 1944, with the Marshall Islands attack, it was clear that the commanders had learned how to deal with the strong and interlocking enemy defenses. These islands, mandates of the Nipponese Empire after the First World War, were considered by Japan a part of her homeland—and she had had a quarter-century to prepare their fortifications.

Under any circumstances it is axiomatic that the invaders lose more men than the defenders; yet the American task force's casualties were far fewer than the Japanese. Part of the explanation lay in surprise, part in superb coordination, but the chief factor was considered to be the tremendous, crushing power of the drive. It was preceded by three days of intense bombardment, which "correspondents ran out of adjectives attempting to describe," and which left nothing standing on one island except "the charred ribs of a hangar and one palm tree, from which the Yanks hung the Stars and Stripes." This first drive, with Turner in command of the southern task force as well as of the landings, captured all the immediate objectives on the important Kwajalein atoll. (However, some two dozen islands, scattered over three hundred miles of reef-studded Pacific waters, remained untaken in the Marshall group.) On February 10, 1944 Rear Admiral Richmond Kelly Turner's name was sent to the Senate, along with his commander's, for promotion to the rank of vice-admiral. He got it.

But the Admirals did not rest on their laurels. On February 16 and 17, 1944 Vice-Admiral Turner led an invasion of Eniwetok atoll, 379 statute miles north of Kwajalein, while Admiral Spruance directed a brilliant diversionary attack on the Japanese base at Truk in the Caroline Islands, some 750 miles farther east. Turner's amphibious forces were led by Rear Admiral Harry Hill, and his assault troops by Brigadier General Thomas E. Watson, U.S.M.C. Before the invasion there were "strong preliminary attacks" by carrier-based aircraft and heavy warships. According to a correspondent with the troops, "Engebi [Island in Eniwetok atoll] looked as if it had been run over by some giant lawn mower." During the operation, Admiral Spruance's command was redesignated the 5th Fleet.

Kelly Turner won a second-award Gold Star to his D.S.M. for the Marianas campaign early in June 1944, which opened with the invasion of Saipan. While the American public was watching the Normandy beaches, the Spruance-Turner-Mitscher '⁴⁴-Admiral Richard Conolly-Marine General Holland M. Smith team was carrying out an invasion from 120 times the distance across the English Channel, and taking their own supplies and air support with them. Turner put on the beach three veteran divisions, the 2nd and 4th Marines and the 27th Infantry, while Mitscher and Spruance prevented the Japanese from interfering by sea or air (in the battle of the Eastern Philippines, June 19). In August, while the fight for Guam was still going on, Admiral Turner had the satisfaction of announcing that he had established his headquarters on Saipan, 110 miles to the north. This put him 3,800 miles west of Pearl Harbor, in a strategic location equidistant (1,300 miles) from Japan and the Philippines. Soon Saipan was also a base for B-29 Superfortresses, and it was pointed out that the Marianas "will provide land bases of enough extent to stage large troop forces for the western drive to the Philippines and China, and an advanced naval base from which American task forces can intercept Japanese convoys to and from the home islands."

(Continued next page)

TURNER, R. KELLY—*Continued*

Turner's job, as described by *Newsweek*, was "to organize the transports, the supply ships, and the preliminary land force moves. This he does with what is considered a small staff, which always includes Army and Marine officers as well as Navy men. A great practicer of service cooperation, he composes his views with ground force commanders easily." That this composition is sometimes achieved rather less than easily is indicated by Major General Holland Smith, whose Army and Marine troops Turner put ashore: "We fought. We argued like hell. We were nasty to each other. But when we came up from the mat we were friends. I like that guy."

There is some evidence, however, that Admiral Turner is not universally loved. He is described as "hot-tempered", "impatient of failure", "abrasive as a file." A *Newsweek* comment: "To slack subordinates he is mercilessly harsh (some say he is unnecessarily arrogant); to superiors he will speak his mind sharply. He is usually right." "Men remember that the ships he ran were 'taut' rather than 'happy.'" This impression is aided by the Admiral's appearance, with his firmly set mouth—he claims "the longest Irish upper lip in the Navy"—and cold blue eyes under very heavy eyebrows, still startlingly black, although what there is of his hair is gray.

A candid shot of Turner at his desk without his cap and with his eyeglasses, however, catches an entirely different aspect of his personality. It shows the Kelly Turner who used to spend his leaves "with his wife and Lhasa terriers at their comfortable Carmel, California, home, playing golf, fishing, talking incessantly, growing roses, reading Conrad through gold-rimmed spectacles, and dreaming of the day when he would retire and take a round-the-world cruise aboard a freighter." The wandering life he has had as a Navy man is reflected in the list of organizations to which he belongs: in addition to the United States Naval Institute, they include the Army and Navy Country Club in Washington, D. C., the New York Yacht Club, the Monterey Peninsula Country Club in California, and the Manila Golf Club in the Philippines.

References

> N Y Herald Tribune p9 Mr 24 '43 por; 11 p3 F 6 '44 por
> N Y Sun p15 My 10 '43
> N Y Times p7 F 11 '44
> Newsweek 23:25 F 14 '44 por
> Time 43:19 F 7 '44
> Who's Who in America 1944-45

TYLER, ALICE S(ARAH) Apr. 27, 1859— Apr. 18, 1944 Dean emeritus of Western Reserve University's School of Library Science and an internationally known library organizer and authority on library law; former head of the State of Iowa Library Commission and the American Council of Library Workers; president of a number of library associations.

Obituary

> N Y Times p23 Ap 19 '44 por

ULLSTEIN, HERMANN 1875(?)—Nov. 23, 1943 German publisher; former partner in the Ullstein Company, one of the largest publishing houses in the world; his company taken over by the Nazis, he came to the United States in 1939.

Obituary

> N Y Times p21 N 24 '43

UNDERWOOD, BERT E(LIAS) 1862 (?) —Dec. 27, 1943 Photographer; founder and former president of the internationally known firm of Underwood & Underwood, photographers; one of the first to sense the possibilities of news photos.

Obituary

> N Y Times p17 D 29 '43 por

URQUHART, SIR ROBERT E(LLI-OTT) (ēr'kert) Nov. 28, 1901- British Army officer

Address: b. c/o War Office, London; h. Chudleigh, Devonshire, England

"The British near Arnhem fought like lions. . . . The best soldiers we have met since the invasion," said the enemy of Major General R. E. Urquhart's 1st Air-borne Division, the "Red Devil" division that fought behind the German lines in Holland during nine days and nights in September 1944, in a battle in which three-fourths of the men were lost. "There can be few episodes more glorious than the epic of Arnhem," Field Marshal Sir Bernard L. Montgomery[42] declared in a message to the division's commander.

This British general, Robert ("Roy") Elliott Urquhart, born November 28, 1901, is the son of Dr. Alexander Urquhart. The boy was graduated from Saint Paul's school in London, the public school which Field Marshal Montgomery attended. On December 24, 1920 he was commissioned a 2nd lieutenant in the Highland Light Infantry, the 140-year-old Scottish regiment. Two years later he was made a full lieutenant. He took a keen interest in sports and regularly as a junior officer won the hurdling and quarter-mile contests of the H.L.I. He was extremely popular with the men of the regiment—who called him "Walad," the Arabic for "bloke"—and today Lieutenant Colonel David Niven says he remembers Urquhart for his friendliness to newcomers. During the sixteen peacetime years following Urquhart's commission as 1st lieutenant, he advanced slowly, becoming a captain in March 1929, and a major in August 1938. From May 1933 to January 1936 he served as adjutant; from October 1938 to May 1939 as staff captain in India; and from May 1939 to October 1940 as deputy assistant quartermaster general.

After the outbreak of the Second World War he became, in December 1940, an acting lieutenant colonel, and the following March he was given a promotion to that temporary rank. In the summer of 1942 he accompanied General Montgomery to the Middle East with the famous 51st Highland Division (now part of the 1st Canadian Army). Colonel Urquhart fought with the division from El Alamein to Tunisia in the rout of the Afrika Korps from North Africa, and for his bravery was awarded the

D.S.O., with which the General invested him in a field ceremony in June 1943.

A few weeks before the Sicilian landings that followed in July, Urquhart was made a brigadier and then placed in command of the 231st Malta Brigade. The men of this unit, West Country troops, were then inexperienced in field warfare, although on Malta they had seen service under severe conditions. During the long siege of the island, on scanty rations and under heavy bombardment, they had serviced aircraft, repaired airfields, and unloaded cargoes. For the first few weeks after Urquhart assumed command of the brigade they were trained intensively by him in landing and assault exercises. Then, in the Allied invasion of southeastern Sicily on July 10 (under the command of General Dwight D. Eisenhower '42), the Malta Brigade was landed on the east of Cape Passero. Quickly attaining their objective, the men pushed ahead across the island. At Leonforte they distinguished themselves in their push through minefields over difficult country and against strong opposition. For his part in the fighting their commander received the D.S.O. Bar, gazetted September 23, 1944. The citation read: "His personal courage, leadership, and example under fire on the beaches, coupled with calm direction of operations, were a great inspiration to his brigade in their first battle." Urquhart received the decoration from General Montgomery in the field.

From Sicily Urquhart was sent in September to Italy, where his air-borne infantry troops were landed at the naval base of Taranto. He displayed courage there, too, and when seriously wounded near Pizzo refused medical aid until he could deploy his men. Upon his return to England Urquhart was made a major general and given command of the 1st British Airborne Division, which he trained during the winter of 1943-1944 on Salisbury Plain.

"If in years to come any man says to you, 'I fought with the Arnhem Air-borne Force,' take off your hat to him and buy him a drink, for his is the stuff of which Britain's greatness is made." Thus wrote correspondent Alan Wood from the Arnhem area on September 24, 1944. Seven days before, General Urquhart and 8,000 of his "Red Devils," members of the 1st Air-borne Division, had been landed near the town of Arnhem, which is situated on the north bank of the Neder Rijn in southeastern Holland. The Allies had considered the river a vital gateway to northern Germany, in fact, the last great water barrier guarding the plain eastward to Berlin, and were determined to establish bridgeheads there, as well as at the approaches at Grave and Nijmegen, and also to loosen and surround, as far as possible, the garrison of perhaps 120,000 German troops in western Holland. (Just above Nijmegen and Arnhem the Rhine divides into the Neder Rijn and the Waal. The former, the northern branch reaches the North Sea as the Lek or the Oude Rijn; the latter or southern branch, on which Nijmegen is situated, joins the Maas —the Meuse in France—on which Grave is situated.) In general, the assignment of each British air-borne force was to secure passage over the Neder Rijn and to throw out protection on the flanks for General Miles Dempsey's '44 advancing British 2nd Army below Nijmegen. (The British ground forces which reached Nijmegen were commanded by Lieu-

British Official Photo

MAJ. GEN. SIR ROBERT E. URQUHART

tenant General B. G. Horrocks.) American airborne units (the 101st and the 82nd) had been dropped near that city, and these units succeeded in making contact with the armored division and securing the bridge there.

When the British parachutists and glider troops were dropped west of Arnhem that Sunday in September (a smaller group also landed on Monday), one battalion made for the main road bridge in the city. Only 200 men managed to reach it, however, and they were able to hold out only until Wednesday night. By then there were not enough fit men left to withstand the withering German assaults, some made at point blank range, and the few survivors were forced to retreat. (It is thought that perhaps four escaped.) The rest of the men had meanwhile carved out a "perilous bridgehead" on the edge of the town, while the enemy incessantly sprayed the perimeter with everything from giant gunfire and flame-throwers to the Tiger tanks with which Urquhart later declared his men could not cope.

For nine days and nights these Red Devils hung on with their light weapons against insurmountable odds. By the fifth day they were on one-sixth normal rations; their only water was what they could catch in their raincoats. At the end the Germans were fighting within the paratroopers' own contracted lines outside the town. Then, using tanks, the enemy methodically blew up each street in Arnhem, house by house, until there were no more streets on which to fall back.

On September 25 the order came to retreat. According to Urquhart, his men could not have held out another twenty-four hours. "All will be ordered to break out rather than surrender," he radioed in a final message. "We have attempted our best and will continue to do our best as long as possible." The evacuation of the 2,000 "hollow-eyed, gaunt" survivors of the division was carried out at night through a forest in the pouring rain. An artillery division on the south bank of the Neder Rijn laid down a protective cover for

URQUHART, SIR ROBERT E.—*Cont.*

the troops as, Indian file in groups of ten to twenty, they filtered through the German ring around their hilltop camp. Their steps muffled by bits of torn blankets around their boots, the weary men followed a white parachute-tape trail laid earlier by "cheeky" patrols. "John Bull" was their password; "Operation Berlin" the code name for their escape plan.

British 2nd Army units had meanwhile crossed the river at Nijmegen and pushed along the ten-mile highway to Arnhem. A Polish parachute regiment had been dropped near Elst, south of the Neder Rijn, and when the two forces joined they fought through the pocket between the two arms of the river until they reached the branch before Arnhem where they were to evacuate the beleaguered Red Devils. The worst part of the march for the paratroopers, an eyewitness reported, was waiting by the river until one's turn came to be ferried to the south side by these rescuers. At dawn German gunfire made further crossings impossible, and the remaining survivors were left until the following night. The record of the invasion was 1,200 wounded—left behind with the Germans with some British doctors in attendance—and 4,800 killed or taken prisoner. It had been, to one survivor, "the kind of hell" he never dreamed could exist on earth.

The heavy loss of men, in the opinion of commentators, was due to the late arrival of air-borne fighter reinforcements as well as to the failure of sufficient air-borne supplies to reach the Red Devils, both because of bad weather and heavy flak; a stronger enemy force than was anticipated—a reason given by General Urquhart himself; and the inability of ground forces to break through to the division in sufficient strength. "It is possible," wrote William H. Stringer of the *Christian Science Monitor*, "[that] if ground forces [of the 2nd Army] had been a little faster during the first twenty-four hours, they might have reached Arnhem before the enemy ambush strengthened. Perhaps if troops assigned to cover the flanks had driven northward faster, the last bridge [at Arnhem] might have been crossed and held." But, Stringer went on to explain, the Germans were too well prepared for the Allies to repeat with complete success the brilliant move which carried them from the Seine to Brussels in August and early September. The Germans were prepared, moreover, with the best SS (Elite Guard) and Panzer troops available, wrote Ned Russell of the New York *Herald Tribune*. In addition, he continued, they interfered so successfully with flow of overland supplies during the attack that, although such an eventuality had been considered by the Allies in the original plans, the cutting of the supply routes had a serious effect on the pace of the whole thrust.

But, despite the fact that the Allies suffered a severe setback, General Montgomery has called the operation 80 to 85 per cent successful. Behind them the British paratroopers left 12,000 to 15,000 German Elite troops dead. And, it was pointed out, if the German forces had not been occupied by the Red Devils, the great bridge at Nijmegen, "one of the biggest prizes in Holland," might not have been captured. If the air-borne troops had not clung to the Arnhem bridge, the Germans might have had a direct road for rushing troops south-

ward to oppose the Allied thrust at Nijmegen. Although the German High Command announced that the British attempt had failed, it was soon reported that German troops were being thrown into the Arnhem area as Dempsey massed his 2nd Army forces south of the city in a great northern salient. By the end of September the Germans to balk pursuit had blown up the approaches to the Arnhem bridge that the Red Devils had fought so desperately to hold, and the British had increased to twenty miles their hold on the west bank of the Meuse River facing Germany. "Not in vain," said Winston Churchill [42] to the House of Commons, "may be the pride of those who survived and the epitaph of those who fell."

General Urquhart himself played no small part in the fierce battle. At one time he was reported captured, although actually he had been cut off from his division for thirty-six hours. He had been visiting one of his brigadiers when German troops opened fire on the area, marooning the brigade. Just before dark he was forced with two others to hide in the loft of a house until he could escape in the morning with a passing Red Devil unit.

The robust General, said to look like a mustached edition of Jack Dempsey, is over six feet tall. Until recently he smoked heavily, only giving up the habit to toughen himself for the rigors of the air-borne service. Since his return from Arnhem he appears outwardly unchanged, talking freely and undramatically of the experience, only becoming moved when recalling the fighting qualities of his paratroopers and the R.A.F. pilots. Upon his return to London, a friend commented, he turned up at his club wearing his maroon beret and swinging his walking stick as though he had just returned from a hike.

Urquhart was married in Lahore Cathedral, during his service in India, to Pamela Condon, the daughter of Colonel W. E. H. Condon. The Urquharts have two children, Elspeth and Judith. After Urquhart's return home from Arnhem on September 29 he was knighted as a Commander of the Bath.

VANDERBILT, WILLIAM K(ISSAM)
Oct. 26, 1878—Jan. 8, 1944 Sportsman; former president of the New York Central Railroad; founder of the Vanderbilt Cup races; great-grandson of Commodore Cornelius Vanderbilt.

Obituary

N Y Times p13 Ja 8 '44 por

VAN DRUTEN, JOHN (WILLIAM)
June 1, 1901- Playwright; novelist; scenarist
Address: b. c/o Monica McCall, 610 Fifth Ave., New York City; h. A.J.C. Ranch, Thermal, Calif.

Although most widely known as a dramatist, John van Druten has achieved an "enviable reputation as a novelist, and the magnates of Hollywood have paid substantial tribute to his prestige" in the years since the early '30's. His 1943-1944 Broadway plays were two of the season's finest and most financially successful. *The Voice of the Turtle* (1943), acclaimed the most brilliant comedy in many seasons, was placed in the honor list of best plays in both the Burns Mantle [44] and George

Jean Nathan yearbooks. *I Remember Mama* (1944), his first departure from drawing room comedy, is an American folk drama which "glows with human warmth."

Born in London on June 1, 1901, John William van Druten is the son of a Dutch father, Wilhelmus van Druten, and an English mother. After his marriage Wilhelmus van Druten became a partner in a Dutch banking firm in London. Lloyd Morris in a New York *Herald Tribune* article says that van Druten's boyhood home resembled that London household which he portrayed in his play *After All.* ("The play is the saga of a family who are socially sub-Forsythe," said the London *Saturday Review*. "They do not run to picture-buying . . . or smart houses in Westminster. They keep the solider suburbs going, pay their taxes, and provide a living for private and public schools.") In school van Druten was unpopular and lonely because he was poor at games and especially apt at his studies. Like many other children in similar circumstances, however, he discovered substitutes—books, writing, and a toy theatre—for his lack of companions.

Graduated at seventeen from the University College School in London, young van Druten proposed to make writing his career. His practical-minded father demurred: "The boy must have a profession until he could earn his living by writing." Van Druten chose the law. He was articled to a London firm of lawyers and for five years worked in their office, attending lectures and classes at the Law Society's School and writing conscientiously at night. In 1923 he was qualified with honors in the solicitors' examination and was admitted as a solicitor of the Supreme Court of Judicature. He also took the degree of LL.B. at London University. The practice of law, however, was not to his liking, which turned toward the academic side of his profession. He therefore applied for and obtained a post (which he held from 1923 to 1926) as special lecturer in English law and legal history at the University College of Wales in the town of Aberystwyth."

"I was always going to be a writer," says van Druten in an article published in the *Writer*. At seventeen he had decided that he was going to be a poet, but his poems kept on coming back from the magazines to which he sent them. He wanted someone to tell him whether he was "crazy still to believe in them or not." He found that person in Sir John Squire, editor of the London *Mercury*, who was both a poet and "a kind and gentle man," and who asked the young van Druten to call and bring his poems with him. "It was without a doubt the most momentous thing that had happened to me," says van Druten "I arrived at the office with a mouth and tongue that were completely dry, and a throat constricted almost to a non-speaking point with nervousness. . . . Inspired by the poets whom I most admired . . . I was at the age when gloom and pessimism greatly appealed to me." He had written poems in imitation of Shelley's *Stanzas Written in Dejection*, forgetting that Shelley had had some reason for dejection while he, a normal youth of eighteen with a healthy appetite, had none. Sir John

JOHN VAN DRUTEN

pointed this out to him after he had read his poems, saying, "No genuine work of art has been produced unless the artist was first genuinely moved by the subject matter himself." Slowly in the next few weeks van Druten found he was beginning to set up this advice as a standard for everything he tried to write. At the end of a year's effort one of his poems was printed in the London *Mercury*; his career as an author had begun. Van Druten says Sir John's advice made him "not only a better writer, but also a better person . . . my first lesson in the difficult art of sincerity, without which nothing of real and lasting value is ever produced."

His debut in the London *Mercury* was followed by a commission to write reviews of fiction and plays for an obscure English paper published in Switzerland. This connection enabled him to meet people in the theatrical and literary world; so during the five years he spent in studying law he succeeded also in developing the life he planned to follow later. In 1923 a three-act play entitled *The Return Half* was produced by the Ex-Students' Club of the Royal Academy of Dramatic Art. The play received encouraging reviews and in 1924 was produced by the Little Theatre, a non-commercial Baltimore group. In his earlier days he also made contributions to *Punch* (under his own name and under the pseudonym, John Harewood) some of which were parodies of plays then current in London.

It is the American theatre, however, which takes credit for the discovery of van Druten; and his next play, *Young Woodley*—written during his residence in Wales as a lecturer in the University—established him as a playwright in the professional theatre. The play had been bought by a New York producer, George Tyler, following its ban by a British censor on the grounds that it was disparaging to the English public school system. Stark Young in the *New Republic* called it a "delightful and gentle thing" with something "more permanent than most theatrical writ-

VAN DRUTEN, JOHN—*Continued*

ing." According to Burns Mantle, though, much of the reviewers' enthusiasm was centered on Glenn Hunter's interpretation of young Woodley. (Critics have always been inclined to give greater credit to the actors in a van Druten play than to the author. In *The Voice of the Turtle* it was nevertheless recognized that the very naturalness of his situations and the fluency and honesty of the dialogue made the performers the interpreters rather than merely personalities. Or, as Benjamin De Casseres put it: "Van Druten tells us the obvious. But he says, 'I'm, as you see, obviously obvious about the very obvious.'") *Young Woodley* ran for 260 performances on Broadway and was the "hardy perennial of one hundred stock companies, playing under every conceivable producer's management from Broadway to Sauk Center." After the success of the American production public clamor in England compelled the censor to reverse his decision. The play was given a private performance by the London Stage Society in 1927 and early in 1928 was presented at the Savoy Theatre, where it ran for the rest of the year.

During the time the play was under the ban, moreover, van Druten, eager to win recognition in his native country for the play which had brought him fame in the United States, turned to the medium of the novel. In this form *Young Woodley* (1928) was favorably received by the critics, Arnold Bennett declaring that "a good play becomes a better book."

In 1926, after the death of his mother, van Druten resigned from his post at the University and left Wales to make a lecture tour of the United States. (He remembers gratefully the three years he spent in Wales: they afforded him leisure time to read, think, and write—and through his direction of the University's dramatic society he gained experience in staging plays.) No account of his career in the theatre would be complete, van Druten himself also says, "without a tribute paid to the late Auriol Lee, who directed all my plays between 1928 and her death in 1941, and to Mr. Dwight Deere Wiman, who has produced a number of them."

Chance Acquaintance (1927), a light comedy described by van Druten as the story of "a respectable 'pick up,'" met with little success when it was produced in London. *Diversion* (1928), another study of adolescence, but with quite a different treatment from that given *Young Woodley*, was the first of his plays to be directed by Auriol Lee. (Jane Cowl directed the New York production.) The critic of the London *Saturday Review* found the power of this play so persuasive and some of its comedy scenes so penetrating that he preferred to approve the whole rather than grumble over parts less pleasing. In those early years of van Druten's writing career the subject of youth's disillusionment with love recurred frequently. The July 1927 issue of the American magazine *Poetry* had contained a short poem by the young writer entitled *Week-End Leave*. The poem told of a young soldier's disenchantment with love after "stolen leaves with Phyllis in her flat."

Van Druten's next play, a dramatization of Rebecca West's novel, *The Return of the Soldier* (1928), was followed by *After All* (a play about an English upper middle-class family). *After All* was first produced by the Three Hundred Club in London. In 1931 when it was presented in London's Criterion Theatre it was called by *Saturday Review* "an excellent little play" deserving success because of its qualities of "simplicity, truthfulness, gentle humor." It ran for eight months in London but closed after twenty performances when presented in New York in December 1931. The thirty-year-old British dramatist was, however, gathering "critical orchids and much gold from both sides of the Atlantic." His writing activities were no longer confined to the theatre and poetry. He had two novels to his credit (*Young Woodley* [1928] and *Woman on Her Way* [1931]) and he had been employed as a scenarist by both British and American motion-picture companies.

The second novel, *Woman on her Way* (1931), was considered by the New York *Times* as showing "dramatic sense, uncommon ability in the characterization of both men and women, and a convincing speech which never gives to the dialogue the effect of being a superimposed pattern." The London *Times Literary Supplement* found not one dull paragraph, but thought the author's excellent gift of characterization and narrative, as well as his really beautiful prose, were a "little wasted in a book that is so of the moment that it might be labeled 'the very latest.'" Van Druten was not to return to the novel as a medium for his creative work until 1937 when his *And Then You Wish* was published. This work the *Saturday Review of Literature* found a "pleasant, civilized book . . . filling beautifully the far too vacant void between the novel described as hammock reading and the novel with a purpose." The London *Times Literary Supplement,* however, thought that it had "neither wit nor imagination nor information."

During the year 1931 van Druten collaborated with Auriol Lee on *Sea Fever*, a play from the French, and with Benn W. Levy on *Hollywood Holiday*. The latter play met with a "pleasing response" when presented by the Pasadena Playhouse. *London Wall* (1931) ran all the same season in London. In it van Druten was concerned with the problem of marriage as an escape for underpaid English office girls. "A typical van Druten play—true and untheatrical, yet never dull," commented one critic. The playwright's biggest success of the year, however, was a four-character play, *There's Always Juliet*. Its London production was followed by an American production starting February 15, 1932. With Herbert Marshall, Edna Best, Dame May Whitty, and Cyril Raymond in the cast, the comedy ran for 108 performances in New York. The play had very little, if any, plot—"a duologue," wrote one critic, "on the subject of love, object matrimony." And, although the charm and naturalness of its dialogue and situations found high favor with the public, most of the credit for its success was given to its cast.

Somebody Knows, a London production (1932), was a psychological study of an unsolved murder case. "The play's failure to please the public," says van Druten, "was largely due to the fact that no one knew whether the hero was the murderer or not." The *Spectator*'s critic, though praising the "unassuming realism" of van Druten's dialogue, found "gaps in the psychological evidence which weakened the value of the play." In August of the same year *Behold, We Live* (a London production with Gertrude Lawrence '40 in the cast) also received unfavorable notices. Van Druten returned to comedy in *The Distaff Side*, which won favor with London audiences in 1933 and in 1934 was also popular with New York audiences. The play is concerned with the matriarchal side of an English family and displays woman in all her aspects: as a tyrannical old curmudgeon, a passionate birth-control advocate, a conventional and an unconventional lass, and a motherly fuss-budget. *Commonweal*'s critic observed: "It is a play, like the others of its author, which acted inexpertly, would vanish into thin air."

With the "cash register still jingling" in the box office of the *Distaff Side*, van Druten, after the London failure of his *Flowers of the Forest* (1934), came to New York for the play's production by Guthrie McClintic '43 and Auriol Lee. Joseph Wood Krutch, in reviewing *Flowers of the Forest* for the *Nation*, pointed out that van Druten, when nothing more is required "than a pleasant picture of pleasant domesticity," has a style of his own. "But he is not really at home anywhere except the drawing room; and even there he is lost if the drawing room atmosphere is disturbed by so much as a gentle draft from anywhere outside the walls which were built to inclose quiet affection and self-control." Despite the impeccable production and the presence of Katharine Cornell '41 and Burgess Meredith '40 in the cast, the play closed after a short run. *Most of the Game*, a 1935 New York production, also failed.

Ashley Dukes, reviewing the English theatre for *Theatre Arts Monthly*, thought that the subject of a 1937 production, *Gertie Maude*, was "better suited to the novel than to the stage." The story centers on a showgirl of England's "lower classes" who commits suicide when jilted by her aristocratic lover. *Leave Her to Heaven* (1940), another story of love, murder, and suicide, in the opinion of *Time* Magazine had "the effect of melodrama without the excitement, the violence of love without the poignancy." The play closed after fifteen performances in New York.

Old Acquaintance (1941), with Jane Cowl and Peggy Wood '42 in the New York production, enjoyed a successful run of 170 performances and had a command showing at Washington's National Theatre in aid of the President's Infantile Paralysis Fund, although *Time* Magazine considered the play less notable than the "team of Cowl and Wood." (It was made into a not-so-successful motion picture in 1943 with the team of Miriam Hopkins and Bette Davis '41.) New York saw two van Druten plays the following year. The first, *Solitaire*, fashioned from an Edwin Corle novel, proved to be "fragile fare for a full-length play" and despite its "considerable charm" failed to win the public. The second 1942 offering, *The Damask Cheek*, was written in collaboration with Lloyd Morris and,

in the opinion of Burton Rascoe of the New York *World-Telegram*, was a perfect comedy. Brooks Atkinson '42 of the New York *Times* said, however, that while the play was written with taste, it was "neither written or acted brilliantly enough to fill the theatre with the sort of gay brightness which makes comedies of manners irresistible." The story centered on an upper middle-class family of the brownstone era of New York City in 1909. After a three months' run the play closed in January 1943.

Since the filming of *Young Woodley* (for which he wrote the dialogue) by British International Pictures in 1930, van Druten has worked in most of the major Hollywood studios. He wrote the story and dialogue for Paramount's *Unfaithful* (1931); the story for *New Morals for Old* (1932), a Metro-Goldwyn-Mayer production; the story of *If I Were Free* (1933), an RKO production; and he collaborated on *I Love a Soldier* (1936). In 1937 he wrote the screen plays for *Night Must Fall* and *Parnell*, both Metro-Goldwyn-Mayer pictures; in 1939, for *Raffles*, a Samuel Goldwyn '43 picture; in 1940, for RKO's *Lucky Partners*. In 1941 his play *There's Always Juliet* was the basis for Paramount's *One Night in Lisbon*. In 1943 he had sole responsibility for the script of James Cagney's '42 *Johnny Come Lately*, and in the same year he collaborated on the screen story of his play *Old Acquaintance*. In 1944 he received, from Warner Brothers, $500,000 and a percentage of the profits for the film rights of *The Voice of the Turtle*; sold *The Damask Cheek* to Sam Goldwyn; and had a share in the film rights of *I Remember Mama*. He was one of three authors who adapted the stage play, *Angel Street*, into the exciting screen play entitled *Gaslight* (1944), which gave Ingrid Bergman '40 the 1943-1944 Academy award for the best star role of the year. "The only picture I have enjoyed writing," stated van Druten in 1944, "or taken any pride in was the screen adaptation of the play *Night Must Fall*, by Emlyn Williams '41."

Van Druten's *The Voice of the Turtle*, a three-character play, concerns a soldier on a week-end visit to New York and a young actress from Missouri who has just experienced an unhappy love affair. When circumstances force the soldier to spend the week-end in the girl's apartment "they hear the Song of Solomon" (from which the play draws its title). The comedy, "winningly gay in spirit," is achieved without wisecracks or farcical situations. Van Druten's "dialogue is never overstressed. On the contrary it is muted. His situations are almost always dramatically natural rather than contrived," wrote Howard Barnes in the New York *Herald Tribune*. In his review Lewis Nichols proclaimed the play to be "very little this side of classic"; Kronenberger of *PM* found the craftsmanship superlatively adroit; and Herrick Brown of the New York *Sun* called it "a sparkling bit of topflight theatre."

Since the death of Miss Lee the British-born playwright, who has contributed so richly to the American theatre that Lewis Nichols of the New York *Times* confessed that he was tempted to say that "the American theatre consists of John van Druten," has directed his own

VAN DRUTEN, JOHN—*Continued*

plays. His adherence to the qualities of sincerity and simplicity which he has followed in his writing ever since his first false start is evident in his direction of a play and has no small part in the artistic value. Among the honors accorded *The Voice* was its selection for the traditional command performance at the Capital's National Theatre in 1944, again in aid of President Roosevelt's [42] Infantile Paralysis Fund. Margaret Sullavan [44] and Elliott Nugent [44] originated the leading roles. Miss Sullavan's role has since been played by Betty Field in the New York company and by K. T. Stevens in the Chicago company, which was organized shortly after the New York company. The enormous success of the comedy, van Druten says, has been more of a surprise to him than anything that has happened in his theatrical career. Although when the idea came to him he immediately fell in love with it and felt compelled to write it, putting aside a serious play of which he had finished the first act, at no time did he foresee that the play would win such high favor. Furthermore, he cannot point out the elements or rather how he contrived to get the effects which have placed the play as a comedy, "in the proper sense of that misused word." *I Remember Mama*, adapted from Kathryn Forbes's [44] book of stories called *Mama's Bank Account*, also promises to enrich still further van Druten's own bank account. (He and his associates have been trying to make motion picture contracts which would spread the earnings of these superhits over a period of what may be leaner years, instead of having all the profits fall within the income of one year.) "Mama," played by Mady Christians, is the mother of a Norwegian-American family living at the foot of a San Francisco hill in the early 1900's. The play, which has no formal plot, is composed of little incidents that might have happened in any family. The lion's share of the praise bestowed upon the play went to van Druten. the director, not to van Druten, the adapter. "The play succeeds in being 'theatre,'" commented one critic, "partly because it never struggles to be; geared to a world in which drama seems out of place, you never ask for any."

John van Druten works "tirelessly and unflaggingly because he has a passion for writing." There is no substitute for careful writing, he believes. His own first drafts are cut and polished to a point where every sentence satisfies him. He keeps a notebook of ideas and plot material but generally forgets to use it or cannot remember where it is when he wants it. "His friends," says Lloyd Morris, "can readily observe the sources of his art as a novelist. They are apparent always in his conversation, which is rich in two kinds of humor: one very Dickensian and the other personal, whimsical, and often flavored with malicious wit. . . . Beneath the sophisticated and skeptical façade which van Druten presents to the world, there is always lurking a shy, reticent spirit, a little bewildered by its own fortune, and happy in a world which, astonishingly, has rewarded it for being what it is." His autobiography, *The Way to the Present* (1938), though not found so amusing as Noel Coward's [41] *Present Indicative*,

has been praised for the simplicity and clarity of its style.

Van Druten is of rather more than medium height, with wavy dark brown hair, remarkable large eyes which betray his sensibility, and "the friendliest of boyish smiles." "The low pitch of his voice and the inflection are unmistakably English. In our friendship," says Morris, "there are two insurmountable barriers. One is herring salad. The other is the collected works of Charles Dickens." Van Druten is devoted to both, but has long since given up Morris as a possible convert.

Now a permanent resident of the United States, of which he expects to become a citizen in 1944, John van Druten lives in Thermal, California, a small place in the desert—"I have a ranch of 120 acres, raising dates, corn, onions, and other produce." He spends about three months of each year in New York. His hobby, he says, is writing long letters.

References

N Y Herald Tribune Mag p8 S 20 '31 por; p17 Ja 16 '35 por
The Writer 55:244 Ag '42
International Motion Picture Almanac 1943-44
Kunitz, S. J. and Haycraft, H. eds. Twentieth Century Authors 1942
Sobel, B. ed. Theatre Handbook 1940
Who's Who in America 1944-45
Who's Who in the Theatre 1939

VAN LOON, HENDRIK WILLEM (van-lōn') Jan. 14, 1882—Mar. 11, 1944 Dutch-American historian; journalist and lecturer; author of six best sellers, the first of which was *The Story of Mankind* (1921); wrote on numerous subjects: art, ancient history, music, explorations, etc.; in 1924 Queen Wilhelmina conferred upon him the Order of Knight of the Netherlands Lion in recognition of his work in the cause of Dutch freedom.

Obituary

N Y Times p37 Mr 12 '44 por

VAN NUYS, FREDERICK (van-nīs') Apr. 16, 1874—Jan. 25, 1944 Member of the United States Senate (Democrat) since 1933; chairman of the Senate Committee on the Judiciary; opposed reorganization of the Supreme Court.

Obituary

N Y Times p19 Ja 25 '44 por

VATUTIN, NIKOLAI F(EDOROVICH) (vu-tü'tyin) 1900(?)- Soviet Army officer

Bulletin: General Nikolai F. Vatutin died on April 14, 1944.

From February 1944 issue:

The year 1944 was launched auspiciously on the Eastern Front by a series of uninterrupted Russian victories proving, even the most cautious observers agreed, that the invincibility of the Wehrmacht was now a thing of the past. Leading the 1st Ukrainian Army that was sweeping relentlessly against the Germans in pre-War Poland and threatening thousands of German troops in the Dnieper River bend is "driving" General Nikolai F. Vatutin, veteran of every major Soviet campaign of the Second World War. Largely because of efforts of his armies, the people of the Soviet Union and of all the United Nations celebrated in January 1944 their happiest New Year since the War began.

Like all of his fellow generals in the Red Army, Vatutin's fame rests entirely upon what he has done in the field. Of his personal life very little is known. He was born of peasant stock about 1900, served as a private in a tank division in the First World War, and with the outbreak of the Revolution, though still a very young man, he gained considerable prominence as the commander of a cavalry division. It is safe to assume that during the years following the Revolution Vatutin attended the most famous of schools for the training of Russian Army officers, the Frunze Military Academy.

When the Nazi invasion of the Soviet Union was launched in 1941 Vatutin commanded an army in the Ukraine under Marshal Semyon Timoshenko '41. There he experienced bitter defeat, fighting desperately to prevent that region rich in minerals, grain, and industrial power from falling to the German Blitzkrieg. Forced to retreat, Vatutin nevertheless aided Timoshenko in successful counterattacks, and even while Hitler '42 was proclaiming triumphantly that "the enemy is already broken and will never rise again," Soviet armies were slowly but surely regaining the initiative on every front. By late 1942 it became apparent that the Germans had met their equal in the Red Army: Moscow and Leningrad were still in Russian hands; Stalingrad was holding fast against a powerful German siege; and the Red armies were starting their own counteroffensives all along the Front.

Vatutin led his troops in the great southwest drive across the Don River bend, heading for Rostov, which is located at the mouth of the Don. The drive was important not only for the strategic advantage it would give the Russians but also as an example of the "flexibility of the Soviet military machine," for it was carried out successfully on a 1,200-mile front. By January 1943 the enemy was said to be "in complete rout" in the face of Colonel General Vatutin's onslaught. Threatened with encirclement, and suffering from the cold and the shortage of supplies, the German Army seemed to lose much of its fighting spirit; and Ralph Parker, the New York *Times* correspondent, wrote of this drive: "Small groups of hungry, cold Germans are reported to be wandering about the Don steppes behind the Russian lines seeking an opportunity to surrender." Gains were made on all sectors of the Front, but perhaps the most important were those made by General Vatutin's armies. In a period of two and one-half months they had advanced 289 miles from the upper Don River along the eighty mile Kharkov Front, 280 miles south in the Yama region, and had captured numerous positions of strategic importance. Vatutin's attacks were marked by extreme mobility and "abrupt changes of direction which have caught the enemy off balance repeatedly," and he used tanks, ski troops, airplane motored sleds, light and heavy artillery, and air power.

Vatutin's break-through on the Don was the start of the 1943 Soviet offensive. In recognition of his achievement the Soviet Government awarded him the Order of Suvorov, first degree, and in February 1943 he was promoted to the rank of army general. In that same month Vatutin led his armies across the Donets River to capture Izyum, a town of tremendous strategic value since it was on the railway line between Kharkov and Rostov. His armies took Kharkov, but supplies were held up because of a spring thaw, and he was forced to abandon the city. Vatutin continued to direct the struggle south of Voronezh, and by late summer 1943 Hitler's invasion line was crumbling in at least five different localities. Kharkov was finally recaptured in August. The generals responsible for this feat were Konev '43, Vatutin, and Malinovsky, and it was celebrated in Moscow by a twenty salvo salute fired from 224 guns.

Sumy, industrial and rail center to the northwest of Kharkov, fell next to Vatutin's armies, and at almost the same time the link between the German central and southern fronts, the Bryansk-Kiev Railway, was cut. Meanwhile Vatutin's 1st Ukrainian Army was inflicting "enormous losses of manpower" on the Germans, who were fleeing in disorder. On November 6, 1943, the eve of the twenty-sixth anniversary of the Russian Revolution, Generals Vatutin and Rokossovsky '44 and their troops received Stalin's '42 congratulations for the recapture of Kiev. Vatutin's armies began immediately to fan out in all directions around Kiev. Speed and surprise were the characteristics of these Russian drives; it was clear that the offensive in White Russia was headed for the old Polish border and that nothing could stop it. Vatutin's 1st Ukrainian Army raced westward while, in spite of snow and severe cold, his three other armies southwest, west, and northwest of Kiev advanced as much as ten miles a day. Thousands of German troops faced surrender or annihilation in the Dnieper bend region and in the Crimea.

By November 13 Zhitomir, the last major Ukrainian junction still in German hands, was being shelled by Vatutin's Ukrainian Army. Vatutin drove next on Korosten but suffered a temporary setback in the Zhitomir area when part of his army "ranged far ahead of the main body of his troops which, because of deteriorating weather, had been unable to join the vanguards."

The Germans made several serious attempts to stop Vatutin's onrush, withdrawing men and material from other fronts to hurl against him. They managed to push his forces back toward Kiev and the Dnieper line, but it was at terrific cost to themselves. The 1st Ukrainian Army stubbornly resisted the German "armored avalanche." Russian strategy, working on the thesis that "the only offensive action promising decisive success is one conducted simultaneously at several points on a broad front," soon proved the master. General Vatutin sent infantry, artillery, tanks, and dive bombers against Field Marshal von Manstein's '42 troops, and by the end of November German resistance was nearly broken. Vatu-

VATUTIN, NIKOLAI F.—*Continued*

tin's attack was concentrated in two spearheads: the northern one headed for the borders of old Poland, and the southern one threatening the south Ukraine and Romania.

General Vatutin's counteroffensive around Zhitomir threatened the Germans with almost as severe a disaster as they had met with less than a year before at Stalingrad. In their six-day offensive in the Korosten area, Vatutin's armies freed a total of 310 towns and inflicted heavy casualties upon the enemy. At the close of 1943 the Russians took Korosten and on December 30 swept into Zhitomir, pursuing "routed and demoralized German forces." The entire German Ukrainian Front seemed to collapse. Twenty-two German divisions (some 300,000 men) began their retreat into pre-1939 Poland with the Russians close at their heels.

As a result of this "greatest German military debacle since Stalingrad" the Red Army plunged ahead into pre-War Poland, and Vatutin's armies threatened to encircle fifty German divisions in the south Ukraine. By January 3 one spearhead was within eighty-five miles of Romania and, according to a Moscow dispatch, all branches of his army were "rolling with irresistible momentum." Ralph Parker wrote: "General Vatutin's massive power is so great that the enemy's stiffening resistance is unable to check it." The steady Russian advance was seen as a threat to Germany's own boundaries, and Radio Vichy reported in alarm that Vatutin's forces numbered over 1,000,000, and that the offensive was "probably the most gigantic ever mounted by the Russians."

On March 5, when Vatutin had led his 1st Army 200 miles in two months to Lutsk, Stalin announced that he had been relieved because of illness. He was replaced by Marshal Georgi Zhukov [42], the "brains of the Red Army," and retired for surgical treatment to Kiev, the city which he had liberated. The General is described as "massive, square-faced, pugnacious-looking"; his broad head is set so close to his shoulders that his troops call him "the man without a neck." The same men also know him as a hard driver, but one who shares the hardships of the field with them.

References

N Y Times IV p5 N 21 '43
Scholastic 43:9 D 6 '43
Time 41:24 F 8 '43; 42:26 S 13 '43

VERMILYE, WILLIAM MOORHEAD (ver-mil′yē) Apr. 6, 1880—Aug. 29, 1944 Executive and industrialist; substitute industry member of the regional War Labor Board; endowed the Vermilye medal, awarded biannually, for contributions to industrial management by the Franklin Institute of Pennsylvania.

Obituary

N Y Times p17 Ag 31 '44 por

VIAN, SIR PHILIP (LOUIS) (vī′ən) 1894- British naval officer

Address: b. c/o The Admiralty, Whitehall, London

The British naval commander in the invasion of western Europe was Rear Admiral Sir

Philip Vian, C.B., K.B.E., D.S.O.—better know as "Vian of the Cossack" and hero of several remarkable naval battles with German forces off Norway and Italian forces off Malta.

The son of Alsager Vian of Gilridge, Kent, Philip Louis Vian was born of French Huguenot ancestry in 1894. Preparing for a naval career, he attended the Royal Naval College in Dartmouth, becoming a midshipman in 1912. During the First World War Vian was a junior officer serving in destroyers. Promoted to a lieutenancy, he qualified in gunnery and was assigned to cruisers and battleships. Part of the time Lieutenant Vian was attached to the Australian Navy; he also had shore duty at the Admiralty. In 1929 the thirty-five-year-old Lieutenant was married to Marjorie Haig of Highfields Park, Sussex, the daughter of a colonel in the British Army; they have two daughters.

Promoted to captain in 1934, Vian was placed in command of a destroyer the following year. This was followed by a series of destroyer and small cruiser commands, and in 1937 the officer was in the cruiser *Arethusa* as flag captain and chief staff officer to the rear admiral commanding the 3rd Cruiser Squadron of the Mediterranean Fleet. At the beginning of the Second World War in 1939 he was given command of the destroyer *Cossack*: and the following February the Captain carried out an exploit which made "Vian of the Cossack" a familiar name. The *Cossack* was one of two destroyers and a cruiser ordered to intercept the German prison ship *Altmark* off the coast of Norway, then neutral. The *Altmark*, which had been a tender of the *Graf Spee* until the scuttling of that ship the preceding December, took refuge from her pursuers in Jösing Fiord, only 200 yards wide between its steep, rocky walls. To enter such a narrow inlet without a pilot familiar with the waters, is a risk not usually taken. But Vian did it. He took the *Cossack* right in after the *Altmark*, forced the prison ship aground, boarded her, and brought off the 299 British sailors imprisoned there. This feat was rewarded with the Distinguished Service Order.

Placed in command of a flotilla of destroyers a short time later, Captain Vian led them in the destruction of a whole German convoy near Narvik. Later he himself had the experience of having his ship, the *Afridi*, bombed and sunk under him while escorting a troopship convoy during the withdrawal from Namsos in Norway; but, in spite of an incessant air attack by the Luftwaffe, not one of the transports the *Afridi* was escorting was touched. In May 1941, back in the *Cossack,* Vian commanded a force of destroyers in the mass hunt of the German battleship *Bismarck;* torpedoes from his ships helped sink her. The captain, who had already added a bar to his D.S.O. (indicating that he had again qualified for that decoration) by "gallantry and resource against the enemy," was awarded another bar for the "masterly determination and skill" he showed in this action, and was soon promoted to rear admiral. The following September Vian's force fought another engagement in Norwegian waters against a German convoy, scattering the convoy and sinking four enemy ships without suffering any losses of its own.

A dramatic atmosphere was provided by the North Cape fog, out of which Vian's ships would suddenly appear, one by one, to blast the enemy at point-blank range.

In March 1942 Admiral Vian was escorting a convoy bound for the beleaguered British island of Malta when his light squadron of cruisers and destroyers sailed head-on into "an overwhelmingly powerful Italian fleet." None of the war correspondents aboard gave themselves "the remotest chance of getting back to Alexandria alive," the British fleet's destruction seeming so inevitable. The Italian fleet included one battleship, six cruisers, and a screen of destroyers, and was aided throughout by bombers and torpedo-bombing planes, while "there wasn't a single gun in the entire British squadron that could more than make a minor dent in the Italian battleship." But— with the aid of some remarkably bad Italian gunnery—Admiral Vian so confused the enemy with "darting attacks and withdrawals" made under cover of "an intricate smoke screen" that after five hours the vastly superior Italian force withdrew. Every British warship returned to harbor, and the Italian ships didn't even come near the convoy (although one transport was lost as the group approached Malta afterward). In the words of one of the ship captains, "Our admiral has fought one of the most brilliant actions against greatly superior forces ever successfully brought off," and Prime Minister Winston Churchill [42] offered all concerned "the compliments of the British nation." A few days later the Admiral was created a Knight Commander of the British Empire.

Sir Philip's convoy escorts for Malta-bound transports helped make it possible for that much bombed little island to hold out so long against the German attacks. Two of his convoys completely escaped any attack from the main enemy fleet which was lying in wait for them, while Vian's warships torpedoed one of the enemy battleships and sunk one of their cruisers. This accomplishment drew mention in the House of Commons in June 1942. Later Vian was listed by the First Lord of the Admiralty, A. V. Alexander [40], as one of the chief officers responsible for the surrender of the Italian fleet.

During the Allied invasion of Salerno in September 1943, Vian was one of the British naval task force commanders under Admiral Sir Bertram Ramsay [44] (the American naval force was under Vice-Admiral Henry K. Hewitt [43] and included Rear Admiral Alan G. Kirk [44]). At this time, according to Alexander P. DeSeversky [41], "ignoring the lessons of Kasserine Pass, when our forces had ventured beyond the shielding wings of airpower, we undertook a landing at the extreme range of our land-based aviation. We escaped disastrous defeat only through the ingenuity of airmen like Lieutenant General Carl Spaatz [42], Air Chief Marshal Sir Arthur William Tedder [43], and Rear Admiral Sir Philip Vian. They improvised an ingenious defense that made it possible to use carrier planes. By using land-based aviation to protect the carriers, they freed the carrier-based aviation to protect the landing forces." Vian's role in the landing operations won him the congratulations

British Official Photo

REAR ADM. SIR PHILIP VIAN

of Admiral Sir Andrew Browne Cunningham [41].

With the opening of the great Allied invasion of western Europe on June 6, 1944, Admiral Vian again came into the news. He and United States Admiral Kirk led the eastern and western naval task forces, respectively. About sixty per cent of the warships engaged were British, the rest being Canadian, Polish, and other Allies' vessels. All together the invasion fleet consisted of 4,000 ships and several thousand smaller craft. "Heaving to off the Normandy coast," in the words of Newsweek, "the ships laid down a blistering barrage on German positions. The shore-bombardment forces were formidable enough to throw in 2,000 tons of shells in the first twenty minutes. These were battleships— among them the British Ramillies, Rodney, Nelson, and Warspite, and the American Texas, Arkansas, and Nevada—15-inch gun monitors, cruisers, and hosts of destroyers and smaller craft including rocket boats. [Admiral Vian commanded his ships from the cruiser H.M.S. Scylla.] They sought opportunities to fight it out with shore batteries, and their big guns reached out far behind the battle lines to crumple German strong points. . . . The Rodney whipped scores of 16-inch shells miles inland, enabling British infantry to capture two positions. Cruisers moved in to perilous ranges while destroyers poked their noses as close as their drafts would allow. The Allied navies dominated the coastal waters completely." A loss of 10 per cent or more had been expected by the Supreme Command; but the Allied naval forces brought the invasion troops across the choppy English Channel in bad weather, landed them on the hostile shore of Normandy, and laid down a protective barrage which blasted the enemy out of various points, with what Admiral Ramsay, the supreme naval commander, called "in effect" 100 per cent success. On June 7, the King's official birthday,

VIAN, SIR PHILIP—*Continued*

Vian was made a Companion of the Order of the Bath.

A modest, taciturn fighter who dislikes publicity, Sir Philip Vian is considerate of those who serve under him, but "in the highest degree intolerant of incompetence." Tall and spare, he has penetrating blue eyes in a face that seems to be made up entirely of straight lines; his pictures show a C. Aubrey Smith profile.

Reference

Who's Who 1944

VIENOT, PIERRE (vyɔN″ō′ pyȧr) 1897 (?)—July 20, 1944 Head of the French Committee of National Liberation in London; a bitter opponent of Pierre Laval [40]; was Under-Secretary for Foreign Affairs in the Blum [40] regime (1936-37); considered an authority on German affairs.

Obituary

N Y Times p19 Jl 21 '44 por

VISHINSKY, ANDREI Y(ANUARIE-VICH) (vish-ɪn′ski un-dɪ ā′i yan-ü-är′ē-vich) Feb. 10, 1883- Soviet Government official

Address: c/o The Kremlin, Moscow

Vice-Commissar of Foreign Affairs of the U.S.S.R. and former delegate to the Allied Advisory Council, Andrei Vishinsky, noted lawyer and jurist, holds a key position in international affairs. Second only to Viacheslav Molotov [40] as the chief diplomatic representative of the Soviet Union, Vishinsky first won world-wide fame when he acted as state prosecutor in the famous Moscow trials of 1936 and 1938.

Andrei Yanuarievich Vishinsky was born of bourgeois parents in Odessa, February 10, 1883. He prepared for a career in the law by studying at the College of Law of Kiev University. At eighteen, while still a student at Kiev, he began to take part in the revolutionary activities of the Social Democratic Party. In 1905 he was made secretary of the Baku Soviet and, like so many of his contemporaries, spent long periods in Czarist prisons or in exile. When the Revolution broke out Vishinsky took part in the fighting and in the complicated organizational work which followed. He joined the Communist Party in 1920 and during the years of the post-Revolution famine he was a member of the Staff Commissariat for Food Supply, a job which is said to have given him important training for later diplomatic work. His next appointment was as state procurator of the U.S.S.R. in 1923. In this capacity he acted as a state prosecutor and "rapidly gained fame as an outstanding legal orator."

Vishinsky is today called "one of the fathers of the Soviet judicial system." His interest in the law covers all fields—general theory, political, civil, and criminal law—and he is the author of more than 100 books, including *The Organization of the Soviet State* (Moscow, 1937) and *Marx on the Problem of Law and State* (Moscow, 1938). "The first to give the correct definition of Socialist comprehension of law in literature," Vishinsky has given special consideration to Soviet criminal procedure. It is his belief that the courts have an educational as well as a corrective function, and the New York *Sun* describes him as "one of those just men 'by whom impartial laws are written.'" The extent of Vishinsky's impartiality has been a matter of some question to his political enemies, but in the Soviet Union he enjoys an unchallenged reputation as a lawyer and a teacher. "Technically," *Time* Magazine reported in 1937, "it is not Vishinsky, state public prosecutor, who interprets the constitution or the laws; but years of Soviet press, radio, and cinema propaganda have made his ominous features spell 'The Law' to millions of Russians."

Vishinsky began his teaching career in 1925 when he was appointed professor of jurisprudence at Moscow University, the oldest Russian university. He served as rector of the University and as a member of the Collegium of Education. In 1928 he was called upon to act as presiding judge at the Shakhty trial, at which fifty Russians and three Germans were charged with counter-revolution.

From that time forward Vishinsky was obliged to divide his time between academic work and actual courtroom duties. He had already gained considerable experience as Commissar for Justice and as deputy public prosecutor. During the 1930's his duties as public prosecutor assumed new importance, for it was Vishinsky who argued the state case against the prominent Russian officials accused of conspiring with Leon Trotsky to overthrow the Government of the U.S.S.R. In 1933 Vishinsky was prosecutor at the Metro-Vickers trial. The following year he led the investigation of the famous Kirov assassination, and from 1936 to 1938 he conducted the Government's case against the Trotskyist-Zinoviev "terrorist" factions. These highly controversial trials brought Vishinsky into considerable prominence outside his own country. The case, as he conducted it, always proved dramatic and exciting. The New York *Sun* reports: "Some of his former students gasped as they saw the once-mild-mannered professor turn tiger, run his hand over his red hair, shout until his pince-nez trembled on his nose, and hurl blazing epithets at the accused."

Honors meanwhile came thick and fast to Vishinsky. In 1935 he received the Order of the Red Banner of Labor "for his struggle against counterrevolution." Two years later he was elected to the Supreme Soviets. 1938 saw his appointment as vice-chairman of the Union Council of the People's Commissars of the U.S.S.R., and in 1939 he was elected a member of the Academy of Sciences of the U.S.S.R., the first representative of "the science of law" to be so honored.

With the outbreak of the Second World War, Vishinsky became Deputy People's Commissar for Foreign Affairs and was recruited to serve directly under Molotov, "Stalin's [42] head man in foreign affairs." As a neutral and a signer of a non-aggression pact with Germany, every diplomatic move made by the Soviet Union was closely watched by the rest of the world. Vishinsky's job was to act as Envoy Plenipotentiary representing his country on numerous diplomatic missions. In 1940 he was engaged in conversations with Sir Stafford Cripps '⁴⁰, presumably on "the possibility of an Anglo-Russian rapprochement, with special emphasis on a united front of Great Britain, the United States, and Russia against Japan."

In 1941, several months before the invasion of the Soviet Union, Vishinsky handed a strong statement to the Bulgarian Minister informing Bulgaria, which had accepted German occupation without resistance, that the German move threatened "extension of the War," and that the Soviet Union, "true to her policy of peace, cannot render any support to the Bulgarian Government in the application of its present policy." In April 1941, after Hungary had invaded Yugoslavia, Vishinsky had several conversations with the Hungarian Minister to Moscow, who had requested that the Soviet Union endorse the Hungarian move. Vishinsky, speaking for his Government, refused the request in no uncertain terms and sent this grim warning to the Hungarian Government: "It is not difficult to realize what would be the position of Hungary should she herself get into trouble and be torn to bits, since it is known that there are national minorities in Hungary too."

During the first two years of fighting between the Soviet and Nazi armies Vishinsky's work somewhat lessened in importance, but in May 1943 he was back in the news as his Government's spokesman on the delicate Polish question. Although efforts were being made to reconcile the Russian Government with the Polish Government-in-Exile, Vishinsky pressed the Russian charge that the Polish group "was under the influence of pro-Hitlerite elements." He pointed out that the Soviet had encouraged and financed the establishment of a Polish Army which was formed in Russia. "But," Vishinsky said, "the Polish Government kept postponing their dispatch to the front. The Polish commander never even raised the question of sending their army to the Soviet-German Front."

In September 1943 Vishinsky was appointed his Government's representative on the Allied Mediterranean Commission, a board "designed to meet the immediate task of settling the political issues arising from the military operations in Italy." The formation of such a commission had first been suggested by Premier Stalin, and it was held that the Commission would deal with political issues involving not only Italy but France, Yugoslavia, Greece, and Turkey as well.

The first meetings of the Commission were held in Algiers. In that city Vishinsky and the other members listened to speeches by members of the French Committee of National Liberation. Neither comment nor action on the French situation was expected from the representatives, and most of the time was spent in the organization of the Allied Advisory Council for Italy.

In December 1943 Vishinsky and the other council members visited Italy. The Russian delegate showed particular interest in the demolitions and atrocities committed by the German armies as they made their retreat.

In Naples he commented: "We can tell from studying the Germans' demolitions as they lose towns and cities whether they expect to be able to retake those places. When they simply run amuck, dynamiting and burning everything, we know they don't expect to come back. The fact that they are doing these things in Italy confirms that they are haunted by the knowledge they have lost the War. They are running wild now."

Early in 1944 Vishinsky and the Commission met with Italian political leaders Carlo Sforza '⁴² and Benedetto Croce '⁴⁴, who were demanding that King Victor Emmanuel '⁴³ abdicate in favor of his grandson, the six-year-old Prince of Naples. On his birthday, in 1944, Vishinsky, who had returned to Russia, was decorated with the Order of Lenin by Mikhail Kalinin '⁴², President of the U.S.S.R., as a tribute to his "distinguished services to the State." On March 12 it was announced that Alexander E. Bogomolov, Soviet representative with the French Committee of National Liberation, had replaced Vishinsky on the Allied Advisory Council for Italy. The following day the Soviet Union extended official recognition to the Badoglio '⁴⁰ Government, and on April 16 Vishinsky announced that his country favored "immediate formation of an Italian government representing all democratic elements of the country."

He had made an equally important announcement on March 21—Finland had rejected the Soviet Union's revised peace terms. The Swedish press deeply deplored the break, hoping, however, that there was something to the vague hints Vishinsky had made that the door was still open for Finland. "Time worked against Finland," commented *Svenska Dagbladet*; "the terms now published seem more severe than those reported on March 1. Consequently, nothing came of the rumored 'modifications' which the Swedish Foreign Office felt it could regard as 'authoritative.' "

In May the Vice-Commissar announced that an agreement had been reached between Czechoslovakia and the Soviet Union. The *Christian Science Monitor* observed that the terms clearly indicated the wide basis of cooperation existing between the Kremlin and the Czech Government-in-Exile. Describing Vishinsky as "dynamic and rapier-minded," the *Monitor* also gave him a share of credit for the cordial relations existing between his country and France, and later (November) pointed out that his visit to Bucharest had brought beneficial results. Moscow's "immense patience" with Rumanian internal affairs and the generous terms of the armistice with Bulgaria were, in the opinion of this newspaper, indications that the Russians did not want to rule the Balkan peninsula.

The most recent book which Vishinsky has edited is *The Criminal Responsibility of the Hitlerites*, written by Alexander Trainin, president of the Moscow Institute of Law. "Because of its authorship and sponsorship," to quote Maurice Hindus, "it must be accepted as the most complete and authoritative discussion of the subject that has yet appeared in Russia." In Hindus' summary, the thesis is that individual German soldiers are responsible each for his own crimes (acts in violation of international law or the German legal code): that the Nazi chiefs, "guilty of creating and

VISHINSKY, ANDREI Y.—*Continued*

realizing a policy that outrages international law and which promotes this system of organized state banditry," are subject to death by hanging; and that various other classifications are to be treated and stand trial as common criminals. This includes industrialists and financiers supplying the German Army or benefitting from its "thefts and murders," all receivers of stolen Russian goods looted by the Germans, and all employers of Russian slave laborers.

References

N Y Sun p20 Ap 7 '41; p13 S 24 '43
N Y Times p28 S 8 '40
Time 30:24 N 8 '37 por
International Who's Who 1942

VON TEMPSKI, ARMINE *See* Tempski, Armine von

VON ZELL, HARRY July 11, 1906- Radio announcer and actor

Address: b. c/o National Broadcasting Co., 30 Rockefeller Plaza, New York City

Harry von Zell, the veteran announcer-actor-master of ceremonies of the well-known laugh, has been broadcasting to American audiences since 1926. His success is said to be due to

HARRY VON ZELL

"dignity with a giggle." That giggle—which has been described as not quite a giggle nor even a chuckle, and which should be seen as well as heard to be appreciated—goes back to his high school days, when his nickname was "Giggles." Its value is its sincerity and its contagion. Von Zell himself did not count it an asset for his radio work until a certain day when he was speaking to a radio audience before the broadcast. "A bandsman made a funny crack and Harry's chuckle went into action. It caught on at once, made the audi-

ence join in, and was promptly added to his announcing repertoire." Its good humor runs through everything he says and gives the impression that he believes what he says, that he enjoys talking about his product, and that he is sharing a good time with his whole radio audience. "Whether Harry is reading prosaic blurbs or doubling as a member of the cast, he gives the impression of having the time of his life."

Harry von Zell was born on July 11, 1906, in Indianapolis. His father was a sports reporter for the Indianapolis *Star* and the boy's early memories are of covering the major sports events with his father and later relating the yarns to his envious pals; that is, when he wasn't fishing on Rush Creek. The von Zells started moving west while Harry was still in high school, so he finished his courses in Sioux City, Iowa. The family promptly moved farther west, to California, and Harry entered the University of California at Los Angeles, where he joined the musical and dramatic clubs. He also played football for a year, until he was injured on the field and was forced to quit. It took him some time to get over the injury, but that didn't cure him of his liking for athletics, for he became a lightweight boxer. He won three bouts, lost one decision, and fought a draw. That cured him.

When Harry was nineteen he thought it was time to settle down to something sensible, so he got himself a job as a bank messenger. He held this for a few months and then became a payroll clerk for a small railroad company.

But von Zell wasn't cut out to be a financier; he still had a hankering for the entertainment field. In free hours he therefore studied singing, although, as he says himself, he suspected that his was only an indifferent voice. One afternoon he went to see a radio program rehearsal. He was with some friends —the sort of friends who thought it funny to play a practical joke by announcing that von Zell was one of the performers. He had to sing. The joke, however, was on his friends, because this first experience on the air actually led to engagements on some of the smaller stations. Von Zell felt sure that he had found what he wanted in life and he thought he was well on his way to getting it. He wasn't the only one who had faith in his destiny. Minerva McGarvey ("Mickey" to him) met him about that time, and they were married on October 20, 1925. Then in 1926 KMIC (Inglewood, California) was looking for a singer-announcer and gave von Zell the job. KMIC was just a springboard, for when the officials of KMTR, then a CBS outlet, heard him, they hired him as sports announcer and singer-producer-writer. From there he went on to KGB in San Diego as program director.

Von Zell's first real break came in 1929, when Paul Whiteman started his first series on the air and chose the young man from among 250 contestants to handle the commercials. At the end of the series von Zell went back to New York with Whiteman as a staff announcer for CBS. That was in May of 1930. About this time von Zell decided that announcing alone did not furnish enough fun. He practiced comedy and volunteered for small parts with Fred Allen '41, Phil Baker, and Colonel Stoopnagle, and before long he was doing comedy bits and acting as stooge. Sometimes he played as many as six characters on a single broadcast. In another year or so his voice was familiar to coast-to-coast audiences.

A list of some of the programs on which von Zell has officiated sounds like a summary of all radio has to offer in the way of light entertainment. He has appeared with Will Rogers, Phil Baker, Fred Allen, Stoopnagle and Budd, Roy Atwell, Lou Holtz, "Whispering Jack" Smith, Ed Wynn, Eddy Duchin, Walter O'Keefe, Ben Bernie '41, and Ed Gardner '43, he has been on such shows as *Flying Red Horse Tavern, Vick's Open House, We the People, Hobby Lobby,* and *The Aldrich Family.* In addition he has broadcast for *The March of Time, Newspaper of the Air,* and the Richard E. Byrd '42 programs from the antarctic. His broadcasts take him back and forth between Hollywood and New York, and in 1943 he toured Army camps with Eddie Cantor '41, with whom he is still appearing on the *Time to Smile* show on NBC. In a nationwide poll of radio editors Harry von Zell has several times been voted the most popular announcer in the country. He was also a production executive in the radio department of the Young and Rubicam '43 advertising agency until he resigned in April 1944 to add the *Truth or Consequences* program to his radio work.

When the fiendishly ingenious radio director of *Truth or Consequences,* Ralph Edwards '43, was drafted by the Army in the spring the program's sponsors began a frantic search for a replacement. After spending six weeks and $6,500 on the search and testing scores of comedians, they signed up von Zell to take over the strenuous position vacated by Edwards. Then, after one von Zell broadcast, the Army rejected Edwards, throwing the situation into complete confusion, while for two weeks the two "emcees" shared the program. A financial settlement was finally worked out, but for a time everybody stayed on the alert lest the Army make other plans necessary.

Von Zell has been on a number of programs since receiving the biggest forfeit ever paid by *Truth or Consequences.* In October he was given a small part in the Fred Allen picture, *It's in the Bag.* Later the part was enlarged and predictions in the film capital are that the radio comedian will soon have a comfortable berth in the "flickers." In December von Zell replaced Bill Goodwin on the George Burns '40-Gracie Allen '40 radio show.

When in New York von Zell lives at Oyster Bay, Long Island, where, before the War, he managed to get in short cruises with his family on their powerboat. The craft is called *Mi-Har,* a combination of his and his wife's names. Their house has a family name, too— Kenhurst, after son Kenneth Harry.

Harry von Zell still suggests the athlete in his build and hobbies. He is five feet ten inches tall and weighs 175 pounds. He is an expert swimmer and a more than indifferently good tennis player. One of his clubs is The Lambs, where he enjoys telling about some of his unrehearsed bits on the air—for instance,

the time his tongue slipped and he called the ex-President, "Hoobert Herver." And another time was when he broke a cardinal rule of radio: He was sitting in the studio announcing "WABC, New York" every half hour between dance programs, when a friend came in to play blackjack with him. Von Zell didn't forget his semi-hourly announcements, but he did forget to switch off the microphone—for thirty minutes his progress in the game could be followed clear out to California.

Reference

Variety Radio Directory 1940-41

WAITE, HENRY MATSON 1869 (?)— Sept. 1, 1944 Engineer; deputy administrator of the Public Works Administration in 1933 and 1934; consultant on war projects in the United States Budget Bureau at time of death.

Obituary

N Y Times p11 S 2 '44 por

WAKASUGI, KENAME (wä-kä-sü'gē ke'-nä-mē) July 1883—Dec. 10, 1943 Former Japanese Minister to Washington; counselor under Ambassador Nomura '41 in 1941 pre-Pearl Harbor negotiations with the United States State Department; said to be a member of the "pro-American" faction of the Japanese diplomatic service.

Obituary

N Y Times p15 D 11 '43 por

WALKER, STANLEY Oct. 21, 1898- Journalist; author

Address: b. c/o New York Herald Tribune, 230 W. 41st St., New York City

The legendary former city editor of the New York *Herald Tribune,* Stanley Walker, came into the limelight again in 1944 with his biography of Thomas E. Dewey '44, making his reappearance after a series of ups and downs in the newspaper field that followed his resignation from the post in 1935.

A New Yorker now by preference, Stanley Walker was reared in Lampasas County in the center of Texas. The son of Walter and Cora (Stanley) Walker, he was born October 21, 1898 in the family's rambling one-story ranch house built by his maternal grandfather. Stanley's own father—a country schoolteacher as well as a stockman—saw to it that the boy's education was not restricted to the schoolhouse walls. Before he was ten, Walker says of himself, he had read or browsed through Ridpath's *History of the World* and Gibbon's *Decline and Fall of the Roman Empire* and he had memorized portions of Cicero's orations, the Hayne-Webster debate, and lectures of the atheist Colonel Bob Ingersoll. His grandfathers, one a Confederate veteran, the other a onetime Indian fighter, often told him horrendous stories of an earlier, lustier West, but the ranch people Stanley knew were for the most part sober, industrious individuals. It was impressed upon him at an early age that work, hard work, was the only honorable way to accumulate money, a dictum that for some years the boy never questioned. Then, when he was ten, he won a cash prize with an essay

STANLEY WALKER

outlining his unsuccessful attempts to raise corn, and the result convinced him that money actually need not be earned by manual labor.

When he was seventeen young Walker enrolled at the University of Texas, and worked on the Austin *American* as a cub reporter while there. After three years he left college for a job on the Dallas *Morning News*. For a brief time in 1919 he also served as secretary to the Mayor of the city. That year, however, he finally left both the *News* and Texas behind to try his luck in the East. The twenty-one-year-old reporter "hit New York City," writes *Newsweek* Magazine, "with $20 in his pocket, hope in his heart, and a head bulging with one year's reportorial experience. It took him all of half an hour," continues the magazine, "to land a job in the big city"—as reporter on the old morning *Herald*. In early 1920 the paper was bought by Frank Munsey, who owned the New York *Sun*, and young Walker went along with the combined staffs. "I was a pretty good reporter," Walker says of himself during those early years, "never brilliant, but accurate, fast, and reliable."

He was a reliable worker with an insatiable curiosity for the city he covered. In his spare time, says one commentator, he rambled into little known parts of town, talking to all kinds of people, "testing the shifting currents of conversation." By the time the *Herald* and the *Tribune* were merged in 1924 Walker already had a part-time desk job, and that year he became a re-write man for the new paper. Thereafter his rise was rapid. In 1926 he was made night city editor—a young man for such a position; and in 1928, at twenty-nine, he was named city editor of the big Republican daily.

In his foreword to Walker's *City Editor* (1934), Alexander Woollcott [41] declared: "If I am justified in my impression that he is the most notable city editor of his time, you need look no further than these pages for explanation. They are so obviously the work of one with an avid interest in the craftsmanship of his trade, one who further is insatiably fascinated by its material. . . . To Walker it is all

new and endlessly entertaining. Probably only a fellow from the hinterland would find it so in such full measure." Walker's regime, from 1928 through 1934—called by *Time* Magazine "seven sparkling years"—is still a popular topic of conversation, says *Newsweek*, in the favorite haunts of Tribunites. "It was an era in which the city staff—spurred by a mildly acid tongue, amused at times by zany antics, often astonished by an incredible intuitional flash—hit new peaks of performance." The "metooric" city editor became legendary in city rooms and to cub reporters all over the country. According to the *Literary Digest* in 1937, he was the most written about city editor in the United States.

Prohibition was in force during his years on the city desk, and in his off hours he roamed through the gaudy night clubs, dance halls, and speakeasies that mushroomed over the city, familiarizing himself with the curious people and manifestations that were becoming a part of American life during those early '30's. The products of his observations were numerous articles for the *American Mercury, Forum, Today, Vanity Fair, Harper's Magazine,* and two best sellers. The first book, *Night Club Era* (1933), received a generally enthusiastic reception from the press for what was called an amusing, accurate, and sometimes vivid account of contemporary New York.

The "cynical" *Mrs. Astor's Horse* (1935), Walker's third book, enlarged this kaleidoscopic view to cover his fifteen years as a New York newspaperman. Men and women like Daddy Browning, Earl Carroll, Sally Rand, Chic Sale, Queen Marie of Rumania, and similarly colorful individuals appeared in the chronicle. Some reviewers compared the prose style of the breezy, entertaining reminiscences to H. L. Mencken's. The *New Republic*'s M. R. Werner commented, on the other hand, that although Walker claimed he took no stock in the antics he described, his remarks lacked "the bite of satire and the exuberance of wit." Franklin P. Adams [41] wrote, however, that there was charm in the author's attitude of: "All this is silly, but I was part of most of it and I love it because it was all fascinating."

In 1934 Walker's *City Editor* was published —his comments and observations on journalism, sketches of famous reporters and editors, notes on ethics and good form, and discussions on the value of journalism schools, freedom of the press, and women in the newspaper field. This book, too, was well received and in some schools of journalism became required reading. Many reviewers found the style fresh and lively, and the points Walker made valuable because they were enforced by concrete examples—although it was noted by one critic that Walker had unfortunately slighted the major issues in the subject of freedom of the press.

In January 1935 Walker surprised many people by resigning from his $12,000-a-year post on the *Herald Tribune* to take over the managing editorship of Hearst's *Daily Mirror*, then the ten-year-old minor competitor of the New York *Daily News*. Walker's own feeling in the matter was said to have been that he saw the opening as a great opportunity to develop ideas that he had expressed in *City Editor*, such as making a tabloid-sized paper a more serious, better-edited contender in the news field. It is said that he planned to make the *Mirror* "authentic" and to see employed a "crisp, compact" style in "good, straight English." Less than nine months later he was shifted—according to the *Literary Digest* on a whim of the paper's publisher—to the now defunct New York *American*. Only a short time afterward Walker resigned, with the remark that he was "recovering from an attack of Hearst."

The next few years were said to be hectic, disappointing ones for Stanley Walker. In the fall of 1935 he went to the *New Yorker* as an associate editor, with the task of supervising the magazine's factual content. His stay there was brief, too, for he left the following fall, dissatisfied with the only semi-journalistic opportunities that the work offered. Early in 1937 Walker took over the editorship of the *New York Woman*. This magazine, started the previous September by J. Wilfred Megargre and W. E. Wheeler, former national advertising manager of the New York *Post,* had never been successful with the reading public, and Walker had been hired to stimulate circulation. There were evidences that he was troubled by the "woman's angle" he was to handle, although he offered a constructive policy on which to proceed. In spite of this, no one could "scare up enough money to turn the presses" for his first issue, and that March Walker was again out of a job.

For a few years he worked on the *Herald Tribune* again, first as assistant managing editor, then simply as an editorial writer. He continued to write articles for such magazines as the *American Mercury,* the *Saturday Evening Post,* and the *Woman's Home Companion.* Among these was the well known "The Decline of the Newspaper Souse," in which Walker declared: "The new generation of newspapermen, particularly in the larger cities, is an extra dull collection of serious-minded, supposedly socially conscious, immature moppets. They know Marx and Engels but they have trouble getting genuine feeling into what they write."

Then in April 1939 he was called to Philadelphia to take over the editorship of the Philadelphia *Evening Public Ledger,* with free reign in matters of policy and personnel, according to *Newsweek*. The paper announced Walker's coming in a full-page advertisement in the *Editor and Publisher,* but before nine months were out the new editor had resigned and gone back to New York. *Time* Magazine gives several reasons for this sudden move. The *Ledger* was another publication whose main problem had been one of circulation, and Walker had been called in to try to put it on its feet. He worked long and hard at the job, instituted new features and columns, increased the local news coverage. In spite of this the *Ledger* continued to lose money, and Colonel Guy T. Viskniskki, the efficiency expert, was called in to make a survey. Among the reforms he suggested, according to *Time,* was the removal of the new editor. *Time* also writes, however, that Walker himself, an inveterate New Yorker, was unhappy in Philadelphia (in an article for *Look* Magazine in April 1940 he "ripped Philadelphia apart with much fervor"). *Variety,* too, writes that Walker was in disagreement with Viskniskki over some of his proposals. In any case, his resignation from the *Ledger* was followed by a general upheaval of the staff, including the resigna-

tion of several additional members. George Kearney, the paper's president, was named to take Walker's place.

After leaving the *Ledger,* Walker continued to write, contributing articles and humorous verse to the *New Yorker* and book reviews to the *Saturday Review of Literature* and the New York *Herald Tribune,* of which he is still an associate editor. Then, in August 1944, his fourth book appeared, *Dewey, an American of This Century.* Its publication followed a week after his appointment as director of publicity for the Republican Presidential campaign in New York State. Although the biography is an unofficial one, the New York *Post* reports that Dewey, whom Walker has known since the former District Attorney's racket-busting days, was shown some of the chapters in advance of publication.

Walker's plan has been to give an account—called excellent, crisp, and fast-moving—of Dewey's beginnings, family, personality, and career in public office up to his nomination, supplemented by twenty-three of his major speeches. In addition, Walker answered the chief stock objections to the candidate, such as his height, mustache, lack of "color," as well as arguments on serious levels. These latter, he conceded, "at least have the merit of a certain surface plausibility." In refutation, he presents a figure "singularly devoid of the psychic disturbances of many rising statesmen", "innocent of self-hypnosis," unbossed, able, a steadfast, tireless worker. The book was felt generally to be unlike the "typical buttery campaign biography of a Presidential candidate," as *Newsweek* put it; in fact, a book in which Walker, for the most part, let the record speak for itself without his own interpretation. It was a "frankly friendly and respectful appraisal by a seasoned evaluator of phenomena" in New York, declared Wyona Dashwood of the *Christian Science Monitor.*

Particularly praiseworthy, wrote many reviewers, was the section on Dewey's conquest of organized crime in New York City. When it came to the section on his term as Governor of New York, in the words of Alan Nevins of the New York *Times,* Walker wrote "with less gusto and color. As an argument for the election of Dewey to the Presidency the book suffered from a hiatus in logic."

In the pages following the biographical chapters on his subject, Walker hit out at Dewey's opposition. After discussing the differences of what he called "sober, intelligent, and fairminded" persons, he shifted to "all that tatterdemalion crew whose members range from the merely foolish to the downright malicious." Brushing aside those who simply do not like Dewey for "vague reasons which they cannot precisely put into words," the author concentrated his fire on the more articulate leaders of the Dewey-haters—principally authors and newspapermen—in Manhattan's cafe society. Among them, he declared, being anti-Dewey is a fashionable pose, sometimes akin to hysteria. Because these "delightfully giddy people," some of them the "best-dressed and most acute thinkers" in the country, are "not only very talkative," according to Walker, but because "some of them, unless far gone in crapulence, can actually write" and fill much magazine and newspaper space, he declared that they have considerable influence, not to be overlooked.

(Continued next page)

WALKER, STANLEY—*Continued*

"It is quite true that many writers are against Dewey for President," wrote Harry Hansen [42] in response, but "Stanley Walker's book would have been stronger if he had discussed the reasons seriously. Writers, on the whole," he continued, "are not conservatives; they are in the vanguard of reform and fear the conservative influence of Dewey, in spite of what they call the conservative tendencies of the Roosevelt [42] Administration." (One of the theories advanced by Walker for this hatred is that these people do not like anyone, apparently even themselves, unless it is possibly Franklin D. Roosevelt.) There was a feeling among some critics on this score that Walker's argument was, in the words of Samuel Grafton [40], an "anti-intellectualism" campaign line.

On January 2, 1923, when Walker was a reporter on the *Herald Tribune*, he was married to Mary Louise Sandefer, who died in 1944. The couple had two children: Joan, born 1925, and James, born 1931. The small "wiry, mild-voiced" Texan enjoys boxing, shooting, walking, and ranching; and he also likes to cook.

References

Lit Dig 119:31 Ja 19 '35 por; 122:35 O 3 '36 por
New Yorker 17:78-84 D 13 '41; 19:79-85 O 23 '43
Newsweek 9:32+ Mr 13 '37; 13:34 My 1 '39 por
Time 35:46 Ja 15 '40 por
America's Young Men 1938-39
Who's Who in America 1944-45

WALLACE, DEWITT 1891(?)- Publisher

Address: b. Reader's Digest, Pleasantville, N. Y.; h. Mount Kisco, N. Y.

The greatest publishing success story in the world is undoubtedly that of the *Reader's Digest,* which in twenty-odd years has grown from a gleam in DeWitt Wallace's eye to a monthly with Spanish, British, Portuguese, Swedish, Arabic, and Chinese editions, and with an official circulation of "over 7,000,000" in the United States. ("Over 7,000,000" is said with a wink that means "well over"; in the spring of 1944 estimates of actual circulation varied between 9,000,000 and 10,000,-000, with 1,750,000 copies going to men in the armed forces, and an estimated four readers for every copy.) There is, in addition, a High School edition of 600,000 with a special insert for vocabulary and reading tests; 3,600 copies of the magazine every month are printed in Braille for the blind; and on request, key articles are reprinted in leaflet form—often for special distribution by such organizations as the National Association of Manufacturers and the Book-of-the-Month Club.

The publicity-shy publisher and editor of this national institution (well on its way toward becoming an international one) is DeWitt Wallace, born in St. Paul, Minnesota fifty-odd years ago, the son of Dr. James and Janet (Davis) Wallace. Dr. Wallace was then president of little Macalester College in St. Paul; later he wrote *The Great Betrayal,* denouncing those Senators who blocked Amer-

ican membership in the League of Nations, and he was to continue to deliver lectures with vigor when in his nineties. His son attended Macalester for two years, from 1907 to 1909, but at the end of his sophomore year transferred to the University of California. There he enrolled as a freshman again, and in 1911, after finishing his sophomore year for the second time, decided that he had had enough formal education. He promptly found a job with the book department of the Webb Publishing Company in St. Paul, publishers of farm magazines and high school textbooks, and after four years with that company spent a year trying to sell direct-mail advertising for Brown & Bigelow, the biggest calendar printers in the United States. While taking a Christmas vacation in Tacoma, Washington, he had met his future wife, Lila Bell Acheson, the daughter of a Presbyterian minister there, and at some time during this period he saw her again when she came to St. Paul as traveling secretary for the Presbyterian Church in charge of facilities for migrant workers.

With the First World War, Wallace enlisted with the 35th Division of the United States Army, becoming a sergeant. On the fifth day of the Verdun offensive he was hospitalized, with a hole through his neck, a piece of shrapnel in his lung. According to most stories, it was while he lay in the hospital that he shaped plans for the *Digest.* It had always seemed to him that magazine articles took too long to read, and he practiced cutting scores of them to a fraction of their original length while still retaining essential facts and making for smooth reading.

Nothing was done with the idea immediately, however. When he got home he reportedly outlined his plans to his father, who said that the venture would cost at least $10,000 and that its chances of success would be small. (He also pointed out that his son had been none too good at English at Macalester College.) Replied Wallace: "I have read hundreds of periodicals, and I'm convinced that the events of the world can be told far more simply and convincingly by economy of words. We're living in a fast-moving world, and people are impatient to get at the nub of all matters." He continued to nurse the idea while working with his brother Ben in the foreign publicity department of the Westinghouse Electrical & Manufacturing Company in Pittsburgh from 1920 to 1921, trimming more magazine articles during his spare time.

Then came the depression. Wallace, the last to be hired by Westinghouse, was the first to be fired, whereupon he went to New York with a sample copy of his collected condensations. He looked up Lila Bell Acheson there, interested her in the project, and she became co-founder, co-editor, and business partner in the *Digest.* He had already borrowed $300 from his brother and a similar sum from his father, and after writing promotion circulars for the scheme for three months he had collected $5,000. He and Miss Acheson established the Reader's Digest Association in October 1921, renting a basement storeroom for an office at No. 1 Minetta Lane, in Greenwich Village. After mailing out circulars asking for subscriptions to their new magazine they were married (October 15, 1921) and went on their honeymoon. When they got back they found the returns pretty good, and they went to work to produce the first issue. They couldn't afford to buy all the periodicals from which they wanted to digest material, so for a long time they spent many of their days in the New York Public Library, calling for one magazine after another.

At first Wallace estimated that he needed 5,000 readers to pay expenses, and the first issue of the *Digest*, which appeared in February 1922, had a printing of only 5,000 copies. Then, as now, it sold at 25c a copy, $3 a year, so profits were not tremendous. By 1923, however, there were 7,000 subscriptions on the books, and the borrowed money had been paid back, so with a small operating surplus the Wallaces moved to Pleasantville, in the heart of the rich, suburban Westchester County, New York. There they rented a garage and pony shed on the property of a friend. They had their living quarters above the shed, and the two buildings thus served as both home and headquarters for the next three years.

By 1925 circulation of the *Digest* was 20,000; there were two girl clerks working in the pony shed; there was money in the bank. The *Digest*'s editors therefore bought an adjoining property and built a Norman-style home, the ground-floor study in their house becoming the new office. Later the *Digest* "took over successively two floors of one Pleasantville bank building, three floors of another, the upper floor and basement of the post office, and other space." By this time the original conception of the magazine, which they had first seen as appealing chiefly to women, had changed somewhat: articles were chosen which would appeal equally to the intelligent high school student and to the college professor. "The specific criteria for any articles were three: (1) applicability (i. e., the reader should feel that the subject concerns himself); (2) lasting interest (it should be worth reading a year hence); (3) constructiveness. Nothing is taboo except defeatism. Preference is given to stories of good works." Apparently the editorial formula was correct, for the circulation nearly doubled every year—by 1929, when the *Digest* was first offered on the newsstands, it was 109,000.

And it was in 1929 that Wallace began offering checks to other magazines for reprint rights. In the beginning other publications had felt recompensed by the publicity of a credit line in the *Digest*, but now he could well afford to offer more than a credit line. Apparently, however, some publications felt that the rising circulation of the *Digest* threatened their own. *Scribner's* withdrew the right of reprint; the *Atlantic Monthly* and *Forum* threatened to do likewise, but were finally persuaded that the *Digest* helped them by stimulating mass reader interest in high quality reading. Then imitators began to appear. Wallace, in self-protection, proposed contracts with other magazines giving the *Digest* the exclusive right to reprint an article a month. Then he conceived the notion that a certain amount of original mate-

rial in the *Digest* would also make it less vulnerable to competition and withdrawn reprint rights, and in February 1933 the first by-line appeared among the magazine credits in the *Digest*'s table of contents. More and more free-lancers began to join the *Digest* staff, giving their full time to writing for it. At the same time, as the *Digest*'s income grew, Wallace voluntarily raised his payments both to writers and to the publications with which he had contracts. In 1936 *Fortune* guessed that the top price for a three-year contract was over $30,000, and added: "No secret is the fact that in the case of more than one struggling magazine the *Digest* payments have come to make the difference between red ink and black." This is a proposition denied by Wallace himself, and by most of the publications with which he has contracts.

All this time special departments of fillers, short pieces, and compilations of items dug up by *Digest* researchers had been increasing; a sixteen-page condensation of a significant non-fiction book had been added, one of the first selected having been Alexis Carrel's [40] *Man the Unknown*; the size of the magazine had grown from sixty-four pages to 128; the typography and editorial technique had been steadily improving. Reprint material was selected by a staff of reader-editors who tackled the same thirty or forty magazines every month, examining the articles and grading them. The articles were then reread and the grades often readjusted, and the surviving articles were ordered cut as possible reprints—most of them reduced to a quarter of their original length. In early 1935 Wallace began offering original articles free to magazines that wanted them, usually reprinting them in the *Digest* afterward with a magazine credit line. More original material thus appears in the *Digest* than the table of contents would indicate.

In 1936 the *Digest* management gave out the circulation figure of 750,000; since the magazine took no advertising there were no advantages in admitting the true circulation, which other sources put at 1,801,400 in October of that year. This was the largest ever achieved by a magazine without fiction or pictures—larger than any other magazine costing 25c a copy, except Hearst's *Good Housekeeping* (2,155,800). By 1938 the circulation was rumored to be about 3,000,000, and workmen were busy completing a big, red, brick building on an eighty-acre tract just outside Chappaqua, New York, to which the *Digest* "snippers and clippers" were to move from their Pleasantville offices. That same year the *Digest* entered the foreign field with a British edition, published in London, which soon had the largest circulation of all monthly magazines there. With the Second World War the circulation of the British edition was frozen because of the paper shortage, but in December 1940 Wallace entered South America with *Selecciones* (a Spanish-language edition). This sold, for the most part, at the equivalent of 10c, carried advertising, and by 1944 had the largest circulation of any publication in South America—about 900,000. The State Department, including Secretary of State Hull [40], expressed enthusiasm about

WALLACE, DEWITT—*Continued*

the project, and the Office of War Information not only helped to distribute the magazine in Spain but suggested a Swedish edition, which was started in 1943, along with an Arabic edition. *Seleções*, a Portuguese edition for Latin America, had been already born, in February 1942. Plans for Turkish and French editions were postponed until after the War.

In the meanwhile, however, the *Digest* had been making a number of enemies for itself among liberals and radicals through many of the articles which it published. For some time the magazine had been attacked as going out of its way to find articles with a reactionary point of view—in 1938, for example, it had been quick to reprint a pro-Franco [42] newspaper article by Ellery Sedgwick of the *Atlantic Monthly*—and as printing far more pieces with an anti-union, anti-New Deal slant than it could justify by claiming to represent a cross-section of American opinion. Most of the articles on labor concerned companies whose employees were "more content" without union representation, or they exposed "labor racketeers" in such a way as to leave all unions, good and bad, lumped together in the mind of the reader. Typical was a June 1943 piece headed "Remove Union Restrictions and Increase Shipyard Production by One-third," filled with stories of "feather-bedding" in which both characters and shipyards remained unidentified. Attacks on New Deal "bureaucracy", "global idealism," and "radicalism" were also frequent.

Nor did some *Digest* pieces on the War and on America's Allies please all of its readers. In November 1939 the *Digest* printed an article by Charles A. Lindbergh [41] in which the famous aviator spoke of guarding "our heritage from Mongol, Persian, and Moor" and holding back "the infiltration of inferior blood." In March 1940 the *Digest* told its readers "Why Russia Can't Fight." Isolationist articles by writers like Freda Utley appeared in the *Digest* as late as December 1941. A fourteen-page lead-off, written especially for the *Digest* by Max Eastman, appeared in July 1943. (The latter article, attacking Russia and what Eastman considered the Administration's overfriendly attitude toward that country, was reportedly used by the Nazis in their propaganda broadcasts.) In one issue, in August 1943, appeared "Boondoggling on a Global Basis" by Henry J. Taylor; "Too Much Wishful Thinking About China" by Hanson Baldwin; "America Is Being Made Over—And We Won't Like It" by Senator Joseph C. O'Mahoney; and Louis Bromfield's "We Aren't Going to Have Enough to Eat." All of these were original articles, not reprints.

Wallace's choice of editors and writers was also criticized by those who found the *Digest* "slyly reactionary." George Eggleston, former *Scribner's Commentator* editor, was hired briefly by the *Digest*. Lawrence Dennis [41], indicted in January 1944 on Federal charges of conspiracy to incite mutiny in the armed forces and overthrow the Government, was for a while paid by Paul

Palmer, a senior editor, "to help in a critical way, making suggestions." Another article, a piece by Heizer Wright, former New York *Daily News* copy editor under indictment as an alleged secret agent of Japan from 1931 to 1941, appeared in the *Digest* in 1943. (It, however, was a "perfectly innocuous piece" detailing the mechanism by which the War Department notifies relatives of the deaths of their nearest-of-kin, and was okayed by the War Department "several times.") It was also pointed out that José María Torres Peroña, one of the editors of *Selecciones*, had been a founder of one of the largest Falangist organizations in the country, and was a most ardent supporter of Franco.

But perhaps the biggest storm was provoked by Senator Hugh Butler's charges, in the December 1943 issue of the *Digest*, that the Administration had wasted the great part of an alleged $6,000,000,000 spent in furthering hemispheric solidarity. Butler based his charges on figures and information gathered during a hasty junket to South America, and Senator Guffey [44] promptly charged that the trip had been arranged by the *Reader's Digest*, a member of whose research staff had allegedly accompanied the Senator. (According to Wallace, the trip was entirely Butler's own idea, and he paid his own expenses.) Secretary of State Cordell Hull attacked Butler's "misrepresentations," and Senator Kenneth McKellar of Tennessee produced figures to show that Butler's were ninety-five per cent wrong because of duplications and exaggerated estimates—according to McKellar, $324,185,000 was the amount the Administration had really spent. Butler produced a statement by a firm of certified public accountants showing that his accounts had been correctly totaled, but Administration supporters pointed out that this proved nothing about the accuracy of his estimates. In the meantime Butler's article was also being attacked on the grounds that it gave arguments to Nazi sympathizers in South America, helping to undermine the Good Neighbor policy (which Butler and the *Digest* both claimed to support) and produce suspicion of the United States in Latin American minds.

At about the same time it was reported that "Administration circles have been flirting with the idea of an antitrust action aimed at the *Digest's* policy of sewing up reprint sources with exclusive contracts." By this time the contracts which all expired at different times, included such well known magazines as the *Nation, Liberty, American Mercury*, the *Atlantic Monthly, American Magazine, Collier's, Coronet, Esquire, Harper's, Life*, the *New Republic, Newsweek, Time*, and all the Curtis and Hearst publications, as well as a great number of more obscure periodicals.

In February 1944 the *New Yorker* refused to renew an agreement with the *Digest* permitting the reprinting of *New Yorker* articles because it held the *Digest* had ceased to be essentially a reprint magazine and was "beginning to generate a considerable fraction of the contents of American magazines." "This gives us the creeps, as does any centralization of Genius," the *New Yorker* editors explained in form letters sent out to their contributors. "The fact seems to be that some publications are already as good as subsidized by the *Digest*. Our feeling is that if the *Digest* wants to publish a magazine of original material it should do so in a direct manner . . . not operate through other publications to keep alive the reprint myth. . . . We were willing to be digested, but we are not willing to be first supplied, then digested. . . . " Said Wallace: "Six or eight magazines have at various times in the past ten years refused to permit quotation in the *Digest*. By far the most rapid growth of the *Digest* has occurred during this period. Spasmodic opposition from other magazines has had a highly salutory effect in keeping us on our toes editorially."

In March the *New Republic* said it would "no longer use material which originates in the *Digest* office and is intended for eventual reprint there," although, "if the *Digest* wants to expose its 9,000,000 readers to some of the good liberal doctrine from the pages of the *New Republic*, we shall be happy to have it do so—happy and surprised, in view of the way its policy has recently been shaped. . . . Unless it returns to its former principles, it will have to take its place openly as an extremely conservative magazine, prepared by its own staff of contributors, and on all fours with other conservative magazines like the Crowell, Curtis, and Hearst chains."

Wallace himself denies that he has "political views." "Feeling runs high in an election year," he says, "and a lot of people see an occasional article as though it were spread out on a billboard. I don't have any strong political bias that I am aware of. I think that there is a lot of hokum in politics and that the high feelings in an election year are rather amusing. I haven't decided whether or not to vote for F.D.R., but I have no strong feelings against him." He says, further, that the *Digest* is now looking for fresh articles showing good works in government, and that neither the *Digest* nor he himself opposes unions. ("William Hard, who writes many of our labor stories, is a most fair-minded man.") "The over-all emphasis, for twenty-one years," he continues, "has been a more or less conscious effort to find articles that tend to promote a Better America, with capital letters, with a fuller life for all and with a place for the United States of increasing influence and respect in world affairs." Even those who do not like the *Digest* admit that it pioneered in discussing syphilis openly, that it has printed articles on both sides of the controversy over birth control, and that it has published a number of consumer articles of the sort avoided by most magazines which accept advertising. And in the fall of 1944 the *Digest* expanded its interests into the fields of radio and motion picture. It assumed the sponsorship of *America's Town Meeting of the Air* in September, the same month in which it contracted with Metro-Goldwyn-Mayer for the production of a series of eight short features based on material appearing in its pages.

It is also generally admitted that Wallace is not only generous in financial arrangements with writers (the standard payment for *Digest* originals is $1,200, and top-flight writers get $1,500 and more; authors of articles reprinted by the *Digest* get $150 a page), but that the *Digest* plant is a very pleasant place in which to work. "There among the majestic hills of suburban Westchester County near Chappaqua, New York," is "a neat Georgian colonial structure of red brick, suggesting a small New England college. . . . Inside is peace and quiet, comfort and harmony." At intervals during the day there is Muzak; at 3:30, the end of the working day for *Digest* employees, the voices of a quartet come through the amplifiers, singing *Good Night, Ladies*. Before 8:30 each morning a company bus makes the rounds from Ossining, White Plains, Katonah, and Mount Kisco to pick up the employees, and the same bus takes them home each afternoon. For ordinary employees there are pension plans, health and surgical insurance, a month's vacation, and liberal bonuses. For top executives the rewards are even greater: in 1942 the *Digest*'s general manager was paid $84,500, while the managing editor received $48,500 in salary and a bonus of $35,425.54. Wallace himself owns fifty-two per cent of the *Digest* stock, his wife forty-eight per cent, so that his own 1942 salary of $99,500 does not represent the extent of his earnings. He has seldom been accused, however, of wanting to make money for its own sake, and he confesses that the first struggling years of the *Digest* were the best of his life.

Of Wallace, *Fortune* wrote in 1936: "He is tall, lean, slightly stooped, and he is dressed in the tweedy elegance of the English professor with the private income. He is forty-seven and looks five years younger, although his hair is a bit gray. Generally ill at ease with strangers, he is always shy, soft-voiced, and speaks haltingly." *Fortune*'s photographers were not permitted to take their cameras beyond the thresholds of the *Digest*'s office doorways, for Wallace has always disliked personal publicity.

Wallace did, however, allow Kenneth Stewart[43] of *PM* to interview him early in 1944. According to Stewart, Wallace's friends say that he is shy and complex, often giving the impression of being unsophisticated, even naïve. He is wide-eyed toward success and successful people, and surprised when "big shots" seek him out. He is "gracious, kind, and generous in personal relationships and scrupulously fair in financial dealings"; he has "a passion for wanting to make the wheels go around smoothly" and "an executive flair which belies his bewildered manner." Moreover, he calls himself a liberal. As for appearance, to Stewart the *Digest* publisher "seemed more the bashful country lad dressed up for a visit to the city" than the English professor described by *Fortune*. "He wore a pin-striped brown business suit, a tan-striped shirt and green silk figured tie. Tall and lithe, he still has a boyish look and manner despite a slight stoop and receding gray hair. Deep lines from mouth and nose begin to suggest his fifty-two years." To Stewart "he talked about his wife and early accomplishments with obvious affection and pride. Of his successes he spoke with amusement and some self-consciousness, about his staff with loyalty, and about his critics with the feeling of a man misunderstood."

(Continued next page)

WALLACE, DEWITT—*Continued*

Mr. and Mrs. Wallace live a few miles from their plant "in a stylized structure high on a ridge, between Mount Kisco and Chappaqua. With its circular peaked turret rising above the tree-tops and gleaming white against the sky, with its blue tile chimneys, it is on bright days a Maxfield Parrish painting—a fairyland scene befitting the fairy tale lives of its occupants." The Wallaces entertain very seldom, but they used to travel abroad almost every year, and in the days before gas rationing occasionally drove to Manhattan to a theatre or night club. Poker and erratic golf are two of Wallace's forms of recreation.

References

Fortune 14:121-4+ N '36 il tab por
New Repub 109:195 Ag 9 '43; 110:303-4
    Mr 6 '44
PM Mag p1+ Mr 5 '44 il por; p2-5
    Mr 12 '44 il por
Time 32:45 N 14 '38 por
Who's Who in America 1944-45

WALLER, FATS May 21, 1904—Dec. 15, 1943 Internationally known Negro jazz composer, pianist, and band leader; a few of his most popular songs were "I've Got a Feelin' I'm Fallin'," "Squeeze Me", "Ain't Misbehavin'," and "Honeysuckle Rose"; was singer, organist, pianist, and master of ceremonies for the Columbia Broadcasting System; appeared in the films *Hooray for Love* (1935), *King of Burlesque* (1935), and *Stormy Weather* (1943); see sketch 1942 Yearbook.

Obituary

N Y Times p23 D 16 '43 por

WALLER, THOMAS WRIGHT *See* Waller, F.

WARREN, EARL Mar. 19, 1891- Governor of California; lawyer
Address: b. Executive Mansion, Sacramento, Calif.; h. 1526 H St., Sacramento, Calif.

One of the liveliest "dark horse" Republican Presidential possibilities in 1944 was California's Governor Earl Warren. Within one month after being sent to the Executive Mansion by California's voters in 1942, he was presented by a writer in the Patterson '42-McCormick '42 papers as possible Presidential timber or at least "a cinch for Vice-President," and he was hailed by the Hearst newspapers as "A Great American." The Scripps-Howard press supported him, and he was favorably treated in feature stories in the *Saturday Evening Post, Life, Look,* and *Time* Magazines. Even New Dealer Carey McWilliams '43, writing in the *New Republic* in October 1943, was forced to warn Democrats: "The Warren boom should receive careful attention, for it is not an idle or merely sentimental favorite-son ballyhoo."

Earl Warren was born in Los Angeles, California, March 19, 1891, the son of Methias H. and Crystal (Hernland) Warren. Methias Warren was a master car builder who lost his job and home when the railroad workers organized and struck for better working conditions. In those days the railroad companies could and did fire striking workers. The family moved, therefore, to Bakersfield, California, where Methias Warren found another railroad position. Young Earl grew up in Bakersfield and still carries his membership card in the musicians' union which he joined when he played the clarinet in the local band.

Although the elder Warren was employed, the family was still far from prosperous, and Earl was forced to work his way through the University of California, from which he was graduated in 1912. During the summers he worked as a farm hand and freight hustler. He received his law degree in 1914 from the University and was admitted to the Bar on May 14. Until 1917 Warren was employed in a law office in San Francisco, apparently acquiring some stature in his profession, for he was vice-president of the Alameda County Bar Association from 1916 to 1918. (He has since served as vice-chairman of the Committee on Administration of Justice of the California Bar—from 1935 through 1938—and he has been a member of the Committee since 1933.) When the United States entered the First World War Warren was drafted in the infantry as a private, to emerge as a 1st lieutenant. He was "in the country all the time," he says, in Company 1 of the 363rd Infantry. In 1919, after he was discharged from the Army, he started on his active political career as a clerk on the judiciary committee of the California State Legislature, retaining, however, a captaincy in the United States Infantry Reserve Corps from 1919 to 1935.

Later in 1919 Warren moved to Oakland on his appointment to the position of deputy city attorney. He held that position until 1920, when he became deputy district attorney for Alameda County, in which Oakland is situated. When he took this job he intended to remain in public life, he says, for only two years, and then to return to private practice. He stayed until 1923, however, when he was promoted to the position of chief deputy district attorney. In 1925 he was elected district attorney "by talking to more people than any candidate ever had before." He held the position until 1938. (From 1931 to 1932 he was president of the District Attorneys' Association of California, and from 1932 through 1938 he served as its secretary.)

As district attorney of Alameda County from 1925 to January 1, 1939, Warren, according to the *Saturday Evening Post*, became a "new broom in a sensational cleanup campaign," clearing up race-track gamblers "practically singlehanded," waging war against racketeers, annoying the Ku Klux Klan, and sweeping the Mayor of Oakland and all but one member of the Oakland city council out of office. His political opponents charge that he also sent three prominent trade unionists to jail in 1936 on a "framed" charge that they had conspired to murder the chief engineer of a freighter who had been found stabbed to death.

In 1928 Warren had become alternate delegate to the Republican National Convention, and four years later he became a full delegate. From 1934 until 1936 he served as chairman of the Republican State Central Committee; subsequently he became Republican National

committeeman from California, a position which
he held until 1940. In 1938 he was elected
state attorney general on the Republican ticket,
although that year the Democrats won the
governorship for the first time in forty years,
the second time in the history of the state.

According to the New York *World-Telegram*, as attorney general of California Earl
Warren was extremely active in the prosecution of saboteurs, fifth columnists, and other
obstructors of the war effort, being one of
the first to suggest to Congress that the Japanese population of the West Coast formed a
menace to the aircraft plants; he proposed
that they be put under a modified form
of martial law. Nevertheless, the *World-
Telegram* continues, "voters of the state know
that . . . Warren is not one to go witch-hunt-
ing. For early in February [1942] . . . a move
was made to cleanse the civil service lists
[in California] of American job eligibles descended from Italian, German, and Japanese
nationals, and he was instrumental in blocking
the ruling." According to Carey McWilliams, however, Warren "was a very mediocre attorney general of California. Despite
his election pledges of an undying devotion to
civil liberties, he refused to lift a hand when
local law enforcement completely broke down
during the Westwood lumber strike." McWilliams adds that when the Democratic Governor
nominated Dr. Max Radin, distinguished authority on international law, to the Supreme
Court, the appointment had to be confirmed by
an advisory board of which Warren was a
member, and Warren succeeded in blocking the
appointment by the use of a letter in which
Radin had urged clemency for a group of social
workers found in contempt of a "Little Dies"
committee of the California legislature.

Running as a nonpartisan, he came extremely close to being nominated for state
Governor in 1942 on both Republican
and Democratic tickets. Having a candidate
running on the tickets of the two parties which,
at least elsewhere in the country, are bitter
rivals, is a practice not at all uncommon in
California. Warren won the Republican nomination and also gave Governor Culbert Olson
a hot battle for the Democratic nomination, but
lost the latter by 100,000 votes. After winning the Republican nomination, Warren, feeling "reasonably certain" of election, pledged
support to President Roosevelt [42] in furthering
the war effort. Continuing as a nonpartisan,
and allowing no other Republican candidate to
appear with him on a platform, he made
four major campaign pledges: tax reduction;
higher old-age pensions; reorganization of the
state guard; and a post-War planning program. "It is time to promise less and provide
more," he said. Although California had
2,300,000 enrolled Democrats and only 1,370,000
registered Republicans, Warren defeated Olson
by a majority of 342,000. Some 400,000 conservative Democrats voted for him, and when
Warren was asked how he had managed to
carry all fifty-eight counties, he exclaimed, "I
did it with Democrats!"

Governor Olson had been unable to carry
out most of his campaign pledges because the
California legislature had been unfriendly to
him, but under Warren the legislature had

EARL WARREN

passed 1,291 bills by May 9, 1943, when its
session ended. With "no labor problem, no unemployment problem, no tax problem" confronting him, Warren was able to keep his
promises to the letter. An almost disconcert-
ingly large surplus of state funds permitted
him to reduce taxes. He signed a pension
measure raising the old-age pension maximum
to $50 a month, the highest in the United
States, "obligingly approved by substantially
the same legislature that had bitterly fought
Olson's every attempt to obtain a more adequate old-age-pension system." The sum of
$43,000,000 was appropriated for post-War
planning and rehabilitation, and a commitment
to provide $1,500,000 for child-care centers
was also made. As reported in one magazine article, "Warren's first order to his
gubernatorial secretaries was, 'Leave the door
open,' and the story goes that it has been open
ever since, open to any citizen who wants to
crash in and offer suggestions about state government. Warren reserved his mornings for
informal discussions with members of the legislature, men with whom ex-Governor Olson
had been constantly at odds." McWilliams
says that Warren "has been very adroit and
successful in his relations with organized
groups and has shown far more political
finesse than his predecessor." Moreover, having run as an independent, he surprised everyone by behaving as one in his appointments.
"He went into both major parties for good men
and even beyond the parties into the non-political world of civil service."

In addition to carrying out his campaign
pledges, Warren overhauled California's
prison system, passed an anti-crime conspiracy statute which makes ringleaders as liable
as their tools, and established a new youth
commission authority which supervises all
criminals under twenty-five. One of his
greatest problems after taking office was the
notorious Los Angeles "zoot suit" riots, directed against Negro and Mexican youths.

(Continued next page)

WARREN, EARL—*Continued*

"Nothing could be more injurious to our cause and nothing could be more helpful to our enemies," said Warren, "than to have the spirit of riot and disorder take hold of us whether it is directed against individuals, groups, or against the conduct of affairs. . . . Our boys cannot successfully fight for tolerance if we cannot observe it here at home. We will do whatever is necessary in California to suppress riots and will strive to remove the conditions which bring them into being."

Yet in spite of Warren's record as Governor, in spite of the fact that Warren declared a "labor truce" and even consulted the CIO on appointments more than once, the labor press remained hostile to him, picturing him as the puppet of Hearst, of Harry Chandler, owner of the conservative Los Angeles *Times*, which supported him for President, and of Joseph Knowland of the Oakland *Tribune*. Wrote McWilliams: "Years ago Warren was singled out for future political favor by the most powerful industrial and political cliques in California. . . . They have carefully built Warren up as a political figure over a period of years; and have seen to it that his record, on most major social and economic issues, is an almost perfect blank. He is not the type of candidate to be embarrassed by statements made, or positions taken, earlier in his career. He has made few statements and, while invariably compliant toward these interests, has artfully avoided public commitments." Russell Davenport [44], writing in *Life* in 1943, declared that Warren, while being praised by the isolationist Hearst, failed to make a major pronouncement on foreign policy aside from stating that he looks forward to expanding world trade. (In December 1943 Warren announced that he also looks forward to some sort of organization for international cooperation, though not one "too rigid or too ambitious" or one involving a "scheme for international policing which would call for the sending of American boys to the ends of the earth.")

On the other hand, a 1944 *Life* feature article on Warren pointed out that "it can be proved with equal facility that he is a tool of the 'interests' or a friend of the masses. . . . He draws his support," continued the article, "from every element and class. Left-wingers may deplore his views; intellectuals may look down on what one of them called his 'middle-class mind,' but few people have ever come away from a talk with him without feeling that he will always do the best he can according to the highlights of his conscience."

On domestic issues California's Governor announced himself strongly opposed to centralization of power in the United States Government, anxious to protect States' rights, and equally anxious for the return of "private enterprise." "It is my view," he said, "that the nation cannot go along much longer with the expansion of Federal control over industry and the lives of individuals without departing completely from the original concept and purposes of our democracy." Furthermore, "We must return to the fundamentals; we must re-attach ourselves to the old moorings—the family, the home, religion, and free government. The more I think of this War, the more I am convinced that it all reduces itself to the dream of every good man and woman—the desire to have a home and a fireside—to have happy, healthy children, taught by a good mother the virtues of mankind as she might choose to interpret them from the Good Book."

In the summer of 1943, speaking before the Conference of Governors at Columbus, Ohio, Warren selected as his topic the problem of keeping the Japanese out of California. At the time he was opposed to any of them (including American citizens) ever returning to the state. However, when the Army, with the approval of the United States Supreme Court, issued an order (effective January 2, 1945) which lifted restrictions on the American-born Japanese and permitted them as much freedom in travel and residence as any other American citizen, Warren made "forthright appeals to Coast residents to pursue courses worthy of Americans."

According to the New York *Post*, "When the Republican Post-War Advisory Council had completed its September session at Mackinac Island, Michigan, one commentator wrote that 'Thomas E. Dewey' [44] cast the longest shadow,' but that 'California's Earl Warren did surprisingly well'; and 'if Dewey emerged the leading Presidential possibility, Warren emerged the liveliest dark horse.' Yet at that conference Warren declared he was not a candidate for any place on the ticket. . . . [In November 1943] he sent a message to the California Assembly, stating he was not a candidate for either President or Vice-President. Ignoring the message, the Assembly, after a two-day meeting, committed itself to the support of Warren as a 'favorite son' candidate for the 1944 Presidential nomination." Later that month Warren attended a meeting of the Interstate Committee on Post-War Reconstruction and Development at Chicago, where he announced that if he entered the Presidential primary it would be only because he was assured that California Republicans wanted him to head the convention delegation, and that this would leave the delegation free to back any candidate at the convention.

He was considered valuable to the ticket not only because of his "frank, engaging, and refreshing" personality, but because California was one of the states needed to carry the election for the Republicans, and Warren was the only man considered strong enough to win the state. Although from the beginning he had said that he was not a candidate, his supporters, believing that he, "like Tom Dewey, only needed urging," were surprised when on the eve of the balloting at the National Convention Warren "finally shut the door against the draft." There were various reasons given for his refusal to accept the honor. (His own had been that he could not conscientiously desert his stewardship of California during the critical period of the War.) *PM*, calling his refusal "a bitter blow to the Dewey camp," said that it indicated that Warren did not believe 1944 a Republican year and that, "by remaining off a losing ticket, he was saving himself for a top spot in 1948." *Time* pointed out that the governorship of California in the next four years would be not only one of the nation's most important jobs, but one of the most exciting: "Its war job, already enormous, will be vastly greater when the German war ends, and it becomes the funnel through which most of the United States war effort will be poured." Its post-War problems "seem likely to dwarf those of the other forty-seven states, for its main efforts have been in airplane-making and shipbuilding . . . the two which probably will be cut back the deepest when war ends."

After the Republican National Convention Arthur Krock '43 reported that it had been the opinion of the majority at the convention that Warren would have been a definite asset on the ticket, but that his reason for declining had been respected. Warren had stated that the reason his home commitments would not permit him to make the race was that his Lieutenant Governor was the Republican candidate for Senator, and in the event that both of them were elected, the people who had voted for them would be henceforth governed by a representative of the group they had cast out of office. After the refusal of Charles Evans Hughes '41 to make the keynote speech at the National Convention, Warren was selected for the honor. The New York *Herald Tribune*, describing him as a forceful speaker —his sentences "homely and forthright"—said that his "downright sincerity had captured the convention"; *PM* considered him "the best talent on the scene." He was one of three governors who in August opened the Republican Presidential speaking campaign over the Blue Network, but in October while making speeches in behalf of Dewey, the Californian was forced to retire from the campaign because of illness.

"Handsome, strapping" Governor Warren is said to make friends "as easily as rolling off a log." In 1925 he was married to Nina P. Meyers of Oakland. The couple have six children: James (in the United States Army), Virginia, Earl, Jr., Dorothy, Nina, and Robert. Warren is a great joiner: besides being a Republican, he is a Mason (Grand Master in California from 1935 to 1936), an Elk, and a member of more than a dozen organizations with large memberships. He is also a member of the National Association of Attorney Generals, and from 1932 through 1938 he was a research associate of the Bureau of Public Administration at the University of California. Warren, too, has always been very active in police work and law enforcement. He is chairman of the Advisory Board of the California Technical Institute for Police Training; he has been treasurer of the Interstate Commission on Crime since 1940; he was chairman of the Board of Managers of the State Bureau of Criminal Identification and Investigation from 1926 through 1938; and he has contributed articles on law enforcement to various periodicals. In 1934 he was awarded a medal by the United States Flag Association for outstanding work in the field of law enforcement; the Peace Officers Association of California has made him an active member in recognition of his services in behalf of law enforcement; and the International Association of Chiefs of Police has awarded him an honorary life membership for the same reason.

References

Life 15:106+ S 6 '43; 16:100 Ap 24 '44
N Y Herald Tribune II p4 D 19 '43 por
N Y Post p49 N 10 '43 pors
N Y World-Telegram p9 N 4 '42
New Repub 109:514+ O 18 '43 por
Sat Eve Post 216:22+ Ag 7 '43 il pors
Time 40:29 S 7 '42; 43:20 Ja 31 '44
Who's Who in America 1944-45

WASILEWSKA, WANDA (vä-shē-ef'skä vän'dä) 1905- Polish author; journalist; politician
Address: b. c/o Simon & Schuster, Inc., 1230 Sixth Ave., New York City

In the Russo-Polish controversy during the Second World War, Wanda Wasilewska, the author-journalist and Polish-born citizen of the U.S.S.R., has been one of the leaders of the Polish Communist faction. As one of those Poles backed by the Soviet Government, she headed the Union of Polish Patriots and later served as vice-chairman of the Polish Committee of National Liberation until its re-formation as the Lublin provisional government in December 1944.

This Wanda Wasilewska—author as well as international figure—was born in 1905 in the suburbs of Kraków, the daughter of revolutionary parents. Her father, Leon Wasilewski, was a member of the Polish Socialist Party and an official in the first Government formed after Poland's liberation in 1918. According to the Polish Government Information Center in New York, he was also one of the authors of the Treaty of Riga of 1921, which established the Polish-Soviet frontier. (Other information about Wanda Wasilewska's youth comes from a Russian book, *Wanda Wasilewska* (1941) by E. Usslevich, which has been made available by the American Russian Cultural Association of New York.)

Wanda's parents were concerned principally with their political activities and gave scant attention to their children. Her earliest playmates were children of the laborers of Kraków, among whom the Wasilewski family lived in the only large house in their section, and Wanda soon learned to hate those who exploited the poor. During the First World War, when her parents gave their entire time to the Polish nationalist movement, the child became even more conscious of the extreme suffering common then in the country, where she lived with her grandmother, and of the hatred of the peasants for their oppressors. Moreover, for the Russian war prisoners whom she met she felt keen sympathy. In 1918 when Poland became free Wanda encountered anti-Semitism for the first time. It is said that when the high school students were told to separate into groups of Jews and Gentiles, she became so indignant that she stood with the Jewish girls. In the university in Kraków where she specialized in philology, her contacts were with the workers, and in 1923 she participated in a revolutionary uprising which was crushed. Her first husband was a university student and a revolutionary who later died, and her second husband, Marion Bogatko, was a mason.

(Continued next page)

WANDA WASILEWSKA

After her graduation from the university in 1927 Wanda Wasilewska became a teacher in one of the high schools in the city, but she had to change her jobs frequently because of her political convictions. She became associated with the Left wing of the Polish Socialist Party and for a time was a member of its governing board. She also worked with a union of Polish teachers, organizing a teachers' strike during the '30's, and entered into contact with the illegalized Polish Communist Party. Since early childhood she had been writing poetry; later her interest changed to prose. She edited a Warsaw magazine for children, *Płomyk*, which was published by the Association of Polish Teachers, and wrote the book "A Room in the Garret" for young people. In 1937 she was removed from her editorial post because of her Communist sympathies. According to one source, in 1939 she became associated with another paper, *Nowe Widnokregi* ("New Horizons"), put out by the group of Polish radicals whom she headed.

Prior to the publication of *The Rainbow* (U.S.S.R., 1942)—the only one of her books to be translated into English and published in the United States—Wanda Wasilewska had written four proletarian novels. The first of these, the title of which has been translated as "The Image of the Day," was published in Poland in 1934 and immediately banned. Three others followed this one into print and have since been published in the Soviet Union in several languages. In these books—"Motherland" (Poland, 1935), "Earth in Bondage" (Poland, 1938), and a trilogy, "Flames in the Marshes" (Poland, 1939)—Wanda Wasilewska "raised the curtain which concealed the sufferings of the workers, peasants, and farmhands, the poverty and the exhausting labor of the working people, and the luxury, cruelty, and arbitrary rule of their exploiters." Of "Flames in the Marshes" she says: "It is the result of the strong protest which grew in me when I observed how the Ukrainian and Byelorussian

peasants perished of hunger, rose up, and fell again. I wanted to show people of good will in Poland that this was not Polish land, that in passing off a certain strange 'local' dialect as the native tongue of several million people, official statistics lied, for this was nothing other than the Ukrainian and Byelorussian languages."

Reports conflict as to whether or not Wanda Wasilewska visited the U.S.S.R. before 1939, but at the time her country was invaded she was in Poland. She immediately offered her services to the Russians, and soon afterward went to Russia herself, where she became a citizen. Since then her energies have been directed into several channels: she was chairman of the Union of Polish Patriots in the U.S.S.R., an editor of the Union's Polish-language newspaper *Wolna Polska* ("Free Poland"), and a correspondent with the Red Army; and she has also been general secretary of the Polish Communist Party and a deputy to the Supreme Soviet of the U.S.S.R.

After early 1943 Wanda Wasilewska's Union of Polish Patriots became a focal point in the Russo-Polish border dispute. The 1939 Russo-German pact partitioning Poland had been abrogated after the Nazi invasion of the U.S.S.R. in 1941, and Poland and Russia had signed an agreement ending the war between them, but the border question remained unsettled: the Polish Government-in-Exile was unwilling to give up the territory which Poland had gained after the First World War. In addition, a 1941 Polish promise of military aid to Russia had been withdrawn, intensifying the ill feeling on both sides. From Polish sources comes the declaration that the Russians had announced that they had neither food nor arms for the Polish Army. At the Russians' express demand, the Poles say, this army was then evacuated to the Middle East.

The Russian answer to this dilemma was to look about for other Polish collaborators. They were not hard to find. In early 1943 the Russian-sponsored Union of Polish Patriots in the U.S.S.R.—composed primarily of Polish Leftists already in Russia—came into being under the "spirited leadership" of Wanda Wasilewska. (Anti-Russian Poles have declared that the Patriots were Soviet citizens like their leader.) In March the Union began publication of *Wolna Polska*, with the chairman as one of the editors. She had previously become editor of *Nowe Widnokregi*, the publication of which had been resumed in May 1942, after a period of suspension following Germany's attack on Russia. In May, under the sponsorship of the Union, a Polish division in the Red Army was started. This Kościuszko division is, claims the New York *Sun*, "one of Wanda Wasilewska's most dramatic achievements to date. . . . She talked it into being, saw that its flag was Poland's traditional eagle on a white ground, and used a military truck as a rostrum to bid it goodbye and good hunting." In mid-October of 1943 she announced that another Polish division was then in training and that plans had been made for the formation of "an entire Polish army corps." She herself has been made an honorary colonel in the Red Army, said by one author to be the only instance of such an occurrence in the U.S.S.R.

"The makings of a Polish counter-government in Moscow were thus far progressed," explains Joachim Joesten [42] in *What Russia Wants,* "when the Soviet Government on April 25, 1943 formally severed relations with the Polish Government-in-Exile in London." The basis for this diplomatic move was the credence given by the Poles to the Nazi charge that 10,000 Polish officers had been murdered by the Russians in 1940 near Smolensk, territory under German control for almost two years. The Poles had proceeded to make the tactical mistake, said *Newsweek,* "of asking the [International] Red Cross to investigate the charges." Three days later Wanda Wasilewska in an article in *Izvestia* "flatly disputed the right of the Sikorski [40] Government to speak in the name of the Polish people," and denounced its silencing of "all truly democratic and progressively patriotic elements" within Poland and its compromising "dealings with enemy governments." The Polish state, she has said since, must be "recreated democratically by the people in Poland and not by emigrés."

British and American diplomats persuaded the Soviet Government for the time being not to give official status to the Union of Polish Patriots, but in the following months little was accomplished. By January 1944 Russia had made it clear that removal of anti-Soviet elements from the Polish Cabinet was necessary before restoration of Russo-Polish relations could be effected; and the Polish Government for its part had refused to accept the Russian-advocated "Curzon Line"—without a mandate from the Polish people—as the basis for border negotiations. Wanda Wasilewska has since taken the stand that the line is the only possible realistic approach to a solution. (The Curzon Line is the unofficial result of an attempt by an Allied commission in 1919 to limit Poland's long-disputed eastern boundaries to ethnical Poland. It left the western Ukraine and western White Russia, which had not belonged to Poland for more than a century, within the U.S.S.R.)

Another Russian step toward a solution of the trouble came in February 1944, when it was announced from Moscow that the Union of Polish Patriots had organized a National Council inside Poland, with Wanda Wasilewska as its head. (Polish sources have stated that the names of only two members were ever revealed, and Wanda Wasilewska's was not one of them.) The council included representatives "of the Polish Peasant Party, Polish Socialists, the Polish Workers Party, and other democratic national groupings," and it soon claimed to represent a majority within the occupied homeland. According to most unofficial interpretations in the other Allied countries, this move "was one of the sharpest warnings yet that a framework was being erected that could possibly become a Polish government recognized by Russia." An article in *Pravda* discussing the step asserted that the Polish Government-in-Exile "has completely cut itself off from the real Polish people. . . . The London Polish politicians are backed by no one in Poland except pro-Fascist agents who are helping the Germans." A protest was later reported to have reached the Government-in-Exile from the official Polish underground and the parliament, known as the Council of National Unity, to the effect that the new group was composed of Communists intent on forming a temporary government (in opposition to the Government in London) to make an alliance with Russia. It was "attempting to disintegrate the unity of the Poles" and "create a diversion in the Polish underground movement's struggles against the Germans," the Council was reported to have warned, denying, however, that the Communists had any real political force in Poland.

In May it was reported that representatives of this underground National Council, including Wanda Wasilewska, had met with Stalin for the purpose of informing him fully of the situation in Poland, of the activities of the council and the Polish People's Army.

As the Red Army drew closer to the Polish borders it became clear to the world that the Russians were abandoning the idea of dealing with the Polish Government in London. The day in late July 1944 that Chelm, the first large Polish town to fall to the Russians, was liberated from the Germans, the newly formed Polish Committee of National Liberation took over. Anti-Soviet Poles saw the move as merely another step nearer the end toward which the Russians had been moving all along, the destruction of Poland as a republic and its re-creation as the seventeenth republic of the Soviet Union. The members of this committee (appointed by the National Council) consisted mainly of Poles from within occupied Poland. Edward Boleslaw Osubka-Morawski was its chairman; and Wanda Wasilewska was one of its two deputy chairman.

The Moscow radio announced that the committee would perform all the civil functions that the exiled Polish Government had hoped to undertake in the territory liberated by the Red Army. The Polish Army in Russia and the underground in Poland, it was said, would be merged under the committee's single command. In addition, the Union of Polish Patriots and all Polish activities in Russia would be put under its jurisdiction, the Union acting as a sort of "cabinet." As the Soviet offensive progressed, the headquarters of the committee were transferred to Lublin, which gave the group its name. At the end of December this Moscow-backed Lublin Committee announced itself as the Provisional Government of Poland, but the name of Wanda Wasilewska had been dropped from the list of members. (The Premier was Osubka-Morawski.) Edgar Ansel Mowrer [41] said in November 1944 that Wanda Wasilewska supposedly had offended Stalin by protesting the awarding of the Order of Suvorov to a Polish general: General Suvorov had killed 32,000 Poles in 1794.

The politician has also been recognized as an author. Her stories have been dramatized by the little Polish Theatre in New York City; and four of her short stories have been included in Mark Van Doren's collection of stories on the Russian war, *The Night of the Summer Solstice* (1943). Her war novel, *The Rainbow,* was published in the U.S.S.R. in October 1942 (and published in the United States in 1944, with a foreword by Joseph E. Davies [42]). Its first edition of 400,000 copies was sold out in two days, and in 1943 the book

WASILEWSKA, WANDA—*Continued*
won the Stalin Prize of 100,000 rubles for the
most outstanding work in 1943 in the field of
belles-lettres. Wanda Wasilewska's third husband, the Ukrainian-born playwright-novelist-
politician, Alexander Korneichuk, also won a
Stalin Prize for his play *Front*, in which he
attacked "incompetent, irresolute, and old-
fashioned generals."

The awarding of this Stalin prize to a Pole
for her grim story of the effect of the War
on a Ukrainian village was not surprising,
especially in the U.S.S.R., "where politics and
literature have never been divorced," commented one American reviewer. There was
some feeling among critics that *The Rainbow*
was a naïve piece of propaganda—but "as a
hymn of Russian hate against Nazi *Schreck-
lichkeit*," said *Time* Magazine, "the book is
understandable." "In a sense," wrote the New
York *Times* critic, "it is an atrocity story,"
but "better than columns of newspaper stories"
it "explains why thousands of people jammed
Kharkov's public square to watch three Nazi
war criminals hanged a few weeks ago." "The
triumphant quality of Wanda Wasilewska's
story," wrote Lewis Gannett [41], "is that you
will remember the stoic courage of the peasants
more than the horror stories of the Germans."

There were differences of opinion about the
artistic merits of the book, too. Some critics
called it "skillful", "compact, well constructed,
and extraordinarily vivid"—"full of an inherent
poetry," said Franz Carl Weiskopf in the *Saturday Review of Literature*. Others felt—as
one critic remarked—that it was "quite inferior to the artistic standards set by Russian
writers," and in the opinion of *Time* it was
"possibly one of the worst novels ever written."
The book was made into a film in the U.S.S.R.,
which was released in the United States in
October 1944. The critics agreed in their appraisal of the picture. They regarded the
production itself, according to American standards, as "glaringly weak," but allowance was
made for the fact that the film had been made
under hazardous war conditions. However,
the characterization and the drama made it a
prize film in any tongue, in the opinion of one
reviewer. *PM* regarded it as "testimony
against the greatest barbarism of our time . . .
and a damning indictment of unspeakable Nazi
horror." In the spring the Polish author was
working on a book for children, a story of a
war orphan adopted by a worker's family.

Wanda Wasilewska is tall, square-shouldered,
a trifle heavy, "dark [she has jet-black hair],
full-lipped, quietly intense." She has a strong,
heavy voice, reports a U.P. interviewer, and
smokes incessantly. Her husband was formerly Vice-Commissar of Foreign Affairs in
Russia, and in 1944 became Foreign Minister of
the new Ukrainian republic, one of sixteen component republics of the Soviet Union which
in 1944 were granted autonomy. Some commentators attribute her political eclipse in
late 1944 to this unneutral tie. Her daughter, Eva, by an earlier marriage, is a nurse
with the Polish division in the Red Army
which Wanda Wasilewska helped to organize.

References

N Y Herald Tribune p15 Mr 17 '44 por
N Y Sun p22 Mr 3 '44

Cardwell, A. S. Poland and Russia
1944 p171-81
Joesten, J. What Russia Wants 1944

WEAVER, WALTER REED Feb. 23,
1885—Oct. 27, 1944 Major general, in United
States Army; head of the Technical Division
Training Command of the Army Air Forces
since March 1942; was responsible for the
almost impossible feat of training half a
million ground and air crew technicians in two
and a quarter years; since the First World
War had held high ranking positions at various air bases and training centers.

Obituary

N Y Times p 15 O 28 '44 por

WECTER, DIXON (wek'tĕr) Jan. 12, 1906-
Historian; educator

Address: b. c/o Huntington Library, San Marino, Calif.; h. 2055 Lombardy Rd., San Marino, Calif.

The complex problem of demobilization of
American soldiers following the World War
has become not only a political issue, but one
that greatly interests almost all American civilians. In his book *When Johnny Comes Marching Home* (1944), Dixon Wecter, social historian, has written accounts of "the road back"
after three previous wars—the Revolution, the
Civil War, and the First World War—and
from these has drawn the lessons of history
for today's immediate objective. Winner of the
"Life-in-America" prize of $2500, a Houghton
Mifflin award, *When Johnny Comes Marching
Home* has been called "a distinguished, timely
book on the most pressing of all peace problems," one which "should be read by veterans,
civilians, and present combatants, for it deals
with a subject close to the hearts of all three
groups."

Dixon Wecter was born in Houston, Texas,
January 12, 1906, the son of John Joseph and
Eugenia (Dixon) Wecter. His father, an employee of the Southern Pacific Railroad, died
when the boy was four, and afterward his
mother earned a living for her family by
teaching junior high school.

After receiving his B.A. at Baylor University (Waco, Texas) in 1925, Wecter went on
to Yale, where he took his M.A. the following year. He held a Sterling Junior Research
fellowship there in 1927-1928. (In 1936 he
also received his Ph.D. at Yale.) A Rhodes
scholarship took him to Merton College, Oxford, where he studied from 1928 to 1930.
There, interested also in athletics, he "pulled
an oar on the Thames," and played on a college tennis team. "But my doubles partner
was a strain on the nerves," Wecter recalls.
"He was a Hindu and had all the serenity of
the East. He stayed at the base line and
wouldn't join me in rallies. A Hindu can grow
explosive only over Mother India."

Wecter returned to the United States in 1933
to become an assistant professor at the University of Denver, where he remained a year.
The following year he accepted the position
of assistant professor at the University of
Colorado, which he held until 1936 when he
was made associate professor. One of the stu-

dents in his English classes was Elizabeth Farrar, to whom Wecter was married in December 1937. He taught at the University of Colorado until 1939, when he became a professor of English at the University of California at Los Angeles. There he has currently been instructing Army students and—since 1943—conducting some classes for Navy men at the California Institute of Technology. He asserts that "the boys are teaching me a good deal more than I am teaching them." Since 1943 he has also been research associate at the Henry E. Huntington Library at San Marino, California. Early in 1944 he gave a series of lectures at Princeton, Swarthmore, and the New School for Social Research in New York City.

The Saga of American Society, Dixon Wecter's first book, was published in 1937: it is said that his friend, the late Thomas Wolfe, the novelist, had encouraged him to write it. R. L. Duffus of the New York *Times* wrote of the book: "A volume . . . that will probably have to be on the shelves of any student who wishes to know the human history of America." The *Saturday Review of Literature* considered it "a serious piece of work, compiled and written by an author of erudition and literary skill . . . who records skillfully, wittily, and benignly a phase of American civilization which will never be seen again."

Edmund Burke and His Kinsmen, a University of Colorado publication, appeared in 1939. Wecter was becoming more and more interested in history, largely through the influence of the University of Colorado's president, George Norlin, who had been Roosevelt Professor of history in Germany at the time of Hitler's '42 rise. Wecter has also been greatly influenced by the social historian, Arthur M. Schlesinger. *The Hero in America* (1941), a study of the great personalities in American public life (presidents, generals, frontiersmen, etc.) helped define, according to R. L. Duffus, the nature of Americanism. Bernard De Voto '43 called it the best book of the year on American history: "Though he writes so brilliantly that he must be denied the highest rank as a historian, the Easy Chair summons the Pulitzer Prize committee in history to relax its *esprit de corps* and take account of his book." James Truslow Adams '41 cited *The Saga of American Society* and *The Hero in America* as "excellent examples of the newest school of historical writing which stresses synthesis and interpretation rather than the piling up of facts and which has emerged on the hither side of the debunking period into the realm of sane and balanced treatment of characters and events."

In preparation for his book on the soldier's return, Wecter delved into the whole range of American military history. In 1943 he edited, in collaboration with William Matthews, *Our Soldiers Speak: 1755-1918.* A great deal of the research for *When Johnny Comes Marching Home* was done during the year of Wecter's Guggenheim Fellowship, in 1942-1943. According to George F. Whicher: "He has consulted masses of War Department records and innumerable special studies, and he has also searched the diaries and letters of individual soldiers and conferred with many veterans of this war and the last in the effort to under-

DIXON WECTER

stand feelingly the motives and opinions of the men themselves." Published in September, 1944, at a time when events were shaping toward a swift end of the war in Europe, and the problem of demobilizing soldiers was being widely discussed, *When Johnny Comes Marching Home* was given "must" consideration in American book review columns, and in December was selected as the two thousandth American "ambassador" book to be sent to the English branch of Books Across the Sea.

Although no two wars are alike, the returning men from all America's wars, Wecter points out, faced many common problems. As one Continental soldier wrote: "I com down by the markett and sits down all alone allmost Descureged and begun to think over how I had ben in the army, what ill success I had met with there . . . and how that I could not get into any besness . . . you may well think how I felt." People looked with suspicion and resentment upon the returning Revolutionary Johnnies; it was not until 1818 that needy veterans began receiving pensions—$8 per month. After the Civil War the plight of returning Confederate veterans was pitiable; even in the North "veterans often discovered that an army record was something to conceal rather than to display." But when the Grand Army of the Republic became a major political force, pension claims poured in. New land in the West solved the problem for many Civil War soldiers. But the returning Doughboy of the First World War didn't want a homestead. His chief problem was one of morale rather than economics: he felt "let down," and "mocked by his countrymen as a sucker who had fought in vain." He was convinced, too, that statesmen had lost the peace. In a period of civilian cynicism, the newly formed American Legion plunged into a crusade for Americanism. To the jobless, labor became "the target for marked dislike of slackers, saboteurs, profiteers of labor, foreigners and no-damn-goods in general."

(Continued next page)

WECTER, DIXON—*Continued*

Apple-selling, and the results of the march of the Bonus Army on Washington, have not been forgotten.

In the final section of his book Wecter presents the return of G. I. Joe. "With an Iron Cross or Japanese helmet stowed in his kit, the tan of foreign suns on his face and the cheerful glint of survival in his eyes, he will come striding up the street, give and take his measure of handshakes and kisses, sit up talking far into the night—and the next morning, over the ham and eggs, leaf hastily past the international news, his brawny forearm coming to rest across the sports page and the comics. Those who expected very bad things of him, like those who anticipated very wise ones, will be puzzled. . . . Of his real self and the tensile strength of human nature, and about the gods that live in machines, he will know more than when he marched away. Getting back, he will feel with even greater certainty that his United States has been worth fighting for. . . . As he went forth, so he will return: friendly, generous, easy-going, brave, the citizen soldier of America." But these returning soldiers are "likely to be less patient with political bumblers and unemployment." In order to avoid the mistakes of the past, Wecter suggests that a dollar today will serve better than ten dollars in the future. "Let Uncle Sam help the veteran early and promptly, equip him by training to get as good or a better job than before, leave him with unemployment insurance, and then (unless a high degree of service-incurred disability remains) wipe the slate of obligation clean."

In a recent interview, Wecter suggested that veterans of the First World War could be the "ideal go-between in misunderstandings between today's G. I. Joe and the civilian population. They will be the best guides on readjustment and rehabilitation for the men who have come back." Wecter also (in a series of articles for the New York *World-Telegram*) wrote of what the home folks should do in helping the returning veteran make his readjustments. "Civilians as a whole—mothers, sisters, wives, neighbors, friends, employers—should learn as much as they can about the psychology of veterans, and act accordingly. The returnee can no more slip effortlessly into the old life than he can blot out the memory of a thousand things which the stay-at-homes have not shared with him. . . . When in doubt, let him alone." Further, "the soldier is prone to be a realist and should be treated like one." The author finds it encouraging to note that disabled veterans will be treated more wisely after this war.

In the spring of 1945 Dixon Wecter will go to the University of Sydney as the first incumbent of a chair of American history, the first one to be set up in Australia. Reported to be currently at work on the thirteenth volume in the *History of American Life* series, Wecter is also associate editor of the newly announced project, *The Literary History of the United States*.

Reference

N Y Times p15 Ja 4 '44; p7 S 18 '44

WELLMAN, FREDERICK CREIGHTON Jan. 3, 1871- Author; scientist; artist; explorer

Address: b. c/o Willis Kingsley Wing, 522 Fifth Ave., New York City

Successful careers in many professions—medicine, science, mining, business, teaching, writing, painting, farming—in Europe, Africa, South America, and the United States, make up the amazing life of Frederick Creighton Wellman, who writes—and has lived—under the pseudonym of Cyril Kay-Scott. In the introduction to his autobiography, *Life Is Too Short* (1943), his son, Paul I. Wellman (also an author), writes: "His personality has too many facets, there is too much that he has seen and done, his thinking is too varied, to permit of his ever being card-indexed, which presents some problems to his prefacist. The life of Dr. Wellman has consisted, in large measure, of an almost unbelievable series of contrasts. Extremes of poverty and obscurity have been balanced by heights of recognition and position; his adventures have taken place over four continents, and he has been equally at home among the most primitive savage tribes and in the world's most sophisticated capitals. One after another he has grappled with and mastered more than a dozen separate careers, and then tossed them aside, almost negligently." Dr. Wellman himself attributes these varied interests to the fact that there was "a cleavage in my impulses and tastes, so that I was at times attracted by great physical activity; then, for definite periods, I read, thought, studied, and wrote."

Frederick Creighton Wellman was born near Independence, Missouri, January 3, 1871, the son of Wheeler Montgomery and Nellie Jane (Blake) Wellman. By no means a precocious child, he learned to talk and read somewhat later than usual, and recalls his worried mother's plaint: "His father and I sometimes think he may not be all there." His father, more optimistic, said: "Let's see what the boy will do." The boy spent his summers on his father's farm, playing Robinson Crusoe, practicing to be a crack shot, and, from the time he was nine, dreaming about going to Africa. He loved poetry and wrote several poems at an early age, including "interminable plays in blank verse." With the money earned from working on farms and doing various jobs while attending college, he was able to put himself through Chicago Seminary, from which he received his B.A. degree. He then went to Kansas City Medical College for his M.D. After spending a year as an intern in the Kansas City Public Hospital he was married to Lydia Jeanette Isely, "the first girl I met who would consent to go to Central Africa with me."

When their son Paul was a year old Dr. Wellman was appointed as medical officer to the American Mission at Bihé, in Portuguese West Africa. Shocked by the barbarous treatment of the natives, Wellman did much to effect better treatment of them. While practicing as the only physician in the interior, he built up a hospital unit and clinic. During his nine years' stay in Africa Dr. Wellman contributed about seventy-five reports in five languages to the literature on tropical medicine, and wrote articles on big game hunting and native customs. Three other children were born to the Wellmans in Africa: Frederick, Manly, and Alice.

Leaving Africa, Wellman's next habitation was England, where he studied tropical medicine at the University of London and carried on extensive research with several authorities in the field. Having built up his reputation as an entomologist in Europe, he then went with his family to Washington, D. C., where he worked with the Smithsonian Institution and other collections. He also gave advice on African travel to Theodore Roosevelt, who was then planning a safari. In the meantime his marriage had become "impossible," his wife having given "full rein to an inherited puritanism." The couple were divorced, and for a number of years Wellman did not see his four children. "Another of my lives was over and done with."

Wellman found his next career in America —medical education in California. For the United States Public Health and Marine Hospital Service he undertook researches on the bubonic plague and then taught tropical medicine at Oakland Medical College. Research in the Canal Zone aroused his interest in South America and drew him toward further tropical adventure. Although married by this time to a wealthy Southern socialite, he soon met Elsie Dunn, who shared his intellectual and scientific interests. "She was probably more interested in getting away from her family than she was in me," but nonetheless she consented to go to South America with Wellman as his common-law wife. Assuming the names of Cyril Kay-Scott and Evelyn Scott (under which name Miss Dunn later became well known as a novelist), they sailed for Brazil.

As Cyril Kay-Scott, Wellman left his scientific reputation behind him. "I persisted in remaining Cyril Kay-Scott in spite of the severest hardships, which also affected those dependent upon me." In Brazil he got a job as bookkeeper in a small Singer Sewing Machine Company store in Rio de Janeiro. He made good at this, and soon became superintendent of the company branch there. Moving again, Wellman took his family—his wife, their son (Creighton), and his mother-in-law—to the interior of Brazil, where he became a sheep rancher. Just as the prospects of wealth were bright an infectious disease killed the entire flock.

For months thereafter Wellman labored with a hoe in the manioc fields to keep his family from starvation. Constantly reproached by his wife and mother-in-law, he decided to investigate a new mining project, some sixty miles away; he walked to the place, told the American manager he knew all about mining, and got a job. By constantly studying technical journals he did learn something about mining, "enough to be entrusted with projects that involved big sums of money." He eventually became manager of all the company's manganese operations in Brazil. Once again he had reached the top in a new career. Before leaving Brazil (during the First World War) he had an exciting adventure as a

FREDERICK CREIGHTON WELLMAN

Government agent. While uncovering needed evidence in a sabotage case, he was knifed by one of the enemy and almost lost his life.

When he returned to the United States after the War, Wellman (still Cyril Kay-Scott) thought he would now like to be a writer. He reviewed books, read manuscripts for publishers, and in 1921 wrote his first novel, Blind Mice. Built around the "mother-in-law situation," it was considered "powerfully realistic, but depressing." His life in Greenwich Village was the basis for his second novel, Sinbad (1923), in which he depicted the Village as "an unhealthy community, a turgid welter of emotions, unsatisfied restlessness, and banal cynicism." Siren was his third venture in fiction; he wrote also, in collaboration with Evelyn Scott, a children's book, In the Endless Sands. When the books didn't sell, he found a job in the research department of the Guaranty Trust Company.

Having been divorced from his wife—"she was breaking down everything in sight, including herself"—Wellman determined to try his hand at painting. He went to Paris to study art and to wander about Europe. Following an exhibition of his work, he "definitely arrived as a painter," and sold several pictures at good prices. He then met the great romance of his life—the brilliant and beautiful Mlle. Elise-Marie Edviges, with whom he lived happily until her sudden death in the Near East.

Upon his return to America the artist Kay-Scott founded a school of painting in Santa Fe, where he was married again, this time to a young writer, Phyllis Crawford '40. The marriage was short-lived, but the Art School was successful. At the request of the trustees of Denver University he turned his school over to the University as a summer school and accepted the posts of dean of the University's Art School and director of the Denver Art Museum, which he was asked to organize. It was in Wichita, Kansas, that he became reunited with the children of his first marriage·

WELLMAN, FREDERICK CREIGHTON—*Continued*

"I was very proud that every one of my children had achieved success in his or her chosen work." Paul had become a successful novelist, Frederick a well known botanist, Manly a short story writer, Alice a professional musician. Creighton, with a talent for drawing, had also published a novel, and became a broadcaster for NBC with the outbreak of the Second World War.

At the age of seventy-two, Wellman has written his autobiography, *Life Is Too Short* ("by C. Kay-Scott"). Of it a New York *Times* reviewer wrote: "Dr. Wellman is successful in delineating the surface pattern of a complex fascinating life, but not in revealing much of its motivation. His book has the quality of the memoirs that elderly men so often write as a record for their family and friends." Said Harry Hansen [42]: "Packed full of human adventure, this record of life in half-a-dozen climes and in three or four separate personalities offers so much in observation and entertainment that it should be food for weeks of reading. When you read *Life Is Too Short* you will agree that this book is, too." "I have known Cyril Kay-Scott," wrote Lewis Gannett, "and have known him well. . . . I know no more fantastic story than this, and few more lovable men than Cyril Kay-Scott. His book presents the fantasy, but the pride with which it is told obscures the rich charm of the man." Wellman's miscellaneous writings total about 150 monographs, articles, notes, and other contributions on a number of subjects, among them medicine, science, and art.

Wellman has been elected a fellow or member of more than a dozen scientific societies and academies in Europe and the United States, has held offices in four of them, and has represented the United States at International Entomological Congresses. His "outside" interests in earlier years were shooting, boxing, fencing, and playing tennis. He now takes pleasure in walking and swimming, and his hobbies are tropical botany and medieval literature. He is two inches under six feet tall and weighs 180 pounds. His complexion and hair are dark, his eyes blue.

This author-scientist-artist, listed twice in *Who's Who in America*—as the scientist, Dr. Frederick C. Wellman, and as the writer, Cyril Kay-Scott—has by no means closed the pages of his life. In early 1944 he is writing magazine articles and working on another book. As his son Paul Wellman says: "It would not surprise me to see him, at almost any day now, create yet another spectacular career."

References

N Y Times Book R p7 O 3 '43 por
Nation 117:120 Ag 1 '23
Pub W 144:333 Jl 31 '43
Sat R Lit 26:7-8 N 6 '43 por
Kay-Scott, C. Life Is Too Short 1943
Who's Who in America 1916-17

WERNTZ, CARL N. July 9, 1874—Oct. 27, 1944 Painter; teacher; illustrator; founder, director, and president of the Chicago Academy of Fine Arts; his covers and illustrations have appeared in *Redbook, Life, Century, Harper's Magazine, Asia,* New York *Times, Illustrated London News,* and *Australian Quarterly.*

Obituary

N Y Times p15 O 28 '44 por

WESLEY, CHARLES H(ARRIS) Dec. 2, 1891- Educator; author; historian
Address: b. Wilberforce University, Wilberforce, Ohio

"A consistent and continuous effort has been made during the history of the United States to present American Negroes as inferior beings and as a folk different from the normal American stock." The vicious myth of racial superiority and inferiority is fast being destroyed by scholars of all races, and some of the most valuable contributions to this work have been made by Charles H. Wesley, the noted Negro educator and author. Charles Wesley's career has been a study in devotion to a cause. His cause, he explains, is this: "History is an expanding concept embracing the ways in which *all* people have lived throughout the ages." History, he feels, must not, therefore, be subjective, reflecting only one people, one race, one religion. It must tell the whole story, honestly and objectively.

The son of Charles and Matilda (Harris) Wesley, Charles Harris Wesley was born in Louisville, Kentucky, December 2, 1891. He received his early education in the public schools of Louisville, graduating from the Central High School there in 1906. After a year at the Fisk Academy, Wesley entered Fisk University in Nashville, Tennessee, and took his B.A. in 1911. Thanks to his extraordinarily high academic record he was able to overcome the usual handicaps with which the Negro student is faced. Yale University awarded him a University scholarship in 1911 and again in 1912, and Wesley took his M.A. there in 1913, having specialized in history. He also attended Howard University Law School in 1915-1916.

For the next five years Wesley taught history and modern languages at Howard University, taking time in 1914 to study at the Guilde Internationale in Paris. His rise in the academic field was rapid. In 1918 he was made assistant professor of history at Howard, and a year later he became associate professor. In the meanwhile, on November 25, 1915, Wesley had been married to Louise Johnson. The couple have two daughters, Louise Johnson and Charlotte Harris.

Although he remained at Howard University during the First World War, Wesley devoted much of his time to social work in connection with the armed forces. In 1918 he served as secretary at the army YMCA at Camp Meade in Maryland, and in 1919 he was secretary of the National War Work Council, Colored Men's Department, of the YMCA. The War over, Wesley went back to full-time teaching. The Austin Teacher's Scholarship awarded him by Harvard University in 1920 enabled him to begin work toward his Ph.D. degree, which he received in 1925. In the same year (1920) he was made full professor and chairman of the History Department at Howard, a position which he held until 1942.

Wesley was not content with study and teaching but actively interested himself in social and educational reform as well. He has written numerous articles for scholarly journals on problems of Negro education. One subject of particular interest to him is the question of graduate education for Negroes. Interested in education on all levels, he feels, nevertheless, that "on the graduate level the difficulties beset a smaller number with greater force." Requirements for teaching positions have been raised (a year of graduate study is required for secondary school teaching in many states), but the Negro's opportunity to meet these requirements is extremely limited. Wesley argues that until adequate higher education is made available for all, Negro groups must form and support their own units for graduate and professional study. "From these," he writes, "will come the Negro scholars whose intellectual integrity and expanding brotherhood will cross the barriers of the segregated school and the segregated life to make a way of life serviceable to all people."

Another of Wesley's major concerns has been the problem of education for citizenship. He has made an intensive study of the Negro's struggle for the rights extended by citizenship in the United States. Advocating "a wider extension of suffrage, the abolition of poll taxes, the encouragement of participation in voting," Wesley has outlined a program for teaching citizenship in a democracy. He has warned, however, that "teaching citizenship . . . should not be permitted to degenerate into teaching politics," and he is hopeful that "the goals of good citizenship can be taught and practiced by educators so that democracy's program can be extended and the nation become increasingly democratic,"

In 1927 Wesley wrote *Negro Labor in the United States, 1850-1925,* a work that grew out of his doctoral dissertation at Harvard. This carefully documented "history of Negro labor from the period of slavery in the South to the great exodus to the industrial life of the Northern states, and the effect of that exodus upon the American labor problem and upon American economic and social life" was well received by scholars and reading public alike. The New York *Times* called it "a valuable contribution to the economic history of the country," and another reviewer described it as "admirable in clearness of statement and marshaling of pertinent facts."

Wesley's researches in the history of Negro labor have carried him from scholarly studies of the early slave trade to investigations of the Negro's position in modern trade unionism. In an article published in 1939 he pointed out that "organized labor throughout its history in the United States has not only failed to unite its forces but it has also permitted racial barriers to maintain additional divisions in its ranks." Strongly advocating increased cooperation between Negro and white workers for mutual advantage, the historian indicated that "it can well be envisioned that racial lines may be broken at first in labor organization. . . ."

For twenty years (1918 to 1938) Charles Wesley was pastor and presiding elder of the Ebenezer and Campbell African Methodist Episcopal Church in Washington, D.C. His interest in the church led Wesley to make a study of the Negro Methodist minister, Richard Allen, who organized the first church for Negroes in the United States. This study, *Richard Allen, Apostle of Freedom,* was published in 1935. Three years afterward one of Wesley's most important books appeared— *The Collapse of the Confederacy,* a study of "the disintegrating internal factors" that caused the Confederacy's downfall. In this book the author considers the resources of both sides in the struggle, "the lack of spirit of cooperation in politics and society" in the South, and the question of "whether the morale of the Confederacy was in any measure responsible for the outcome." Finally he reviews "the progress of the proposals to employ Negroes in the military service" and shows "their significant relations to the collapse." Wesley's thesis, briefly stated, is that the Confederacy did not collapse because of the superior forces which were pitted against it but because of a lack of "a will to fight in the South."

Reviewers of the book agreed that Charles Wesley's scholarship was sound and that his presentation was sincere and convincing. A. B. Miller, writing for the *Annals of the American Academy of Political and Social Science,* has commented, "In general Wesley has done his modest share toward shattering the illusion . . . that the Southern states presented a single, devoted front to their foe."

Wesley's other published works include a *History of Alpha Phi Alpha,* the Negro fraternity (1929, 1935, 1939, 1942), a *Manual of Research and Thesis Writing* (1941), and a collection of Howard University lectures which he edited under the title *The Negro in the Americas* (1940).

After serving as director of the summer school (1937), as dean of the Graduate School (1937 to 1942), and as dean of the College of Liberal Arts (1937 to 1938) of Howard University, Wesley resigned from the University in 1942 to become president of Wilberforce University in Wilberforce, Ohio. Still active in many social movements he is a member of the Executive Council of the Association for the Study of Negro Life and History, of which Mary M. Bethune '42 is the president and Carter G. Woodson '44 is the research director. Charles Wesley is firm in his belief that relations between the races can be improved. He has written: "The Negro in the United States must be viewed without blind prejudice, and his contributions to American life and history should be included with those of other peoples. When this is done, without doubt some Negroes will appear inferior to some whites and some whites will appear inferior to some Negroes. Any other position is contrary to the facts and their logical interpretation."

Wesley spent 1930-1931 in London as a Guggenheim Fellow. He has received several prizes for historical articles which have appeared in the *Journal of Negro History,* as well as a grant-in-aid in 1936 from the Social Science Research Council. He has received the honorary degree of LL.D. from Allen University (1932) and Virginia State College

WESLEY, CHARLES H.—*Continued*

(1943), and the degree of D.D. from Wilberforce University (1928). He is a Mason and an Odd Fellow. His favorite recreations are music, tennis, and golf. At the end of 1944 he was at work on a study of the Negro in United States politics and on a college textbook of Negro history.

References

Who's Who in America 1944-45
Who's Who in American Education 1942
Who's Who in Colored America 1941-44

WHALEN, GROVER A(LOYSIUS) June 2, 1886- Businessman; promoter

Address: b. 423 W. 55th St., New York City; h. 998 Fifth Ave., New York City

When the history of twentieth century New York City is written, the name of Grover Whalen will probably appear in it more frequently than that of anyone else; and in the listing of the various offices he has held

GROVER A. WHALEN

over the years will be mentioned Secretary to the Mayor, Police Commissioner, Commissioner of Plant and Structures, Chairman of the Board of Purchases, General Manager of John Wanamaker, New York City NRA administrator, President of the New York World's Fair, Chairman of the CDVO for New York City. As Elmer Davis'40 wrote in 1938, "London has the British Royal Family and New York has Grover Whalen."

One of four children (his two sisters are now nuns and his brother was killed in the First World War), Grover Aloysius Whalen was born on the Lower East Side of New York City on June 2, 1886, the son of Michael Henry and Esther (DeNee) Whalen. His father, who was in the general contracting and engineering business, had been brought from Ireland when he was two years old; his mother was of French-Canadian descent. Both of them were good Democrats, and their son was named

Grover because he was born the day Grover Cleveland was married to Frances Folsom in the White House.

Young Grover received most of his education at public schools, but for a time he attended Clason Point Military Academy. He then went on to Packard Commercial College in New York City and to New York Law School, which he was forced to leave at the age of twenty when his father died. Promptly taking a desk in the office of his father's contracting company, young Whalen ran the company until he was attracted by politics. This was in 1916, when he organized the Business Men's Civic League for the express purpose of "civic betterment." New York, in Elmer Davis' words, had been groaning for years under a reform administration, and in 1917 Whalen's organization endorsed John F. Hylan—the Hearst candidate—for Mayor. The United States had just entered the First World War, but Whalen was not drafted: in April 1913 he had been married to Anne Dolores Kelly (the daughter of a West India merchant and banker of Washington Square), and by the time the War began he was the father of a daughter, Mary. When in 1917 Hylan was elected Mayor, Whalen was therefore free to accept the position of Mayor's secretary and most trusted adviser—at $6,500 a year. (Whalen now has two other children: Grover, born in 1921, and Esther Anne, born in 1923.)

Before long the multiplicity of Whalen's municipal duties made him almost indistinguishable from the Mayor himself. In 1919 Whalen became Manhattan's Commissioner of Plant and Structures, chairman of the city's Board of Purchases, and member of the New York and New Jersey Bridge and Tunnel Commission; at the same time he served as secretary of the Mayor's Committee To Welcome the Homecoming Troops, a project conceived just after the Armistice by Rodman Wanamaker, a stanch Tammany supporter. When a department was established to test liquor under the old state enforcement act Whalen headed that also. Under Hylan, too, he campaigned for the abolition of trolley cars in Manhattan, set up New York's first system of municipal bus lines, streamlined the operation of municipal ferries, put traffic lights on Broadway, agitated for a triborough bridge, and originated the municipal radio station WNYC. It has been said that "Hylan finally got Whalen an executive job in Wanamaker's New York store to withdraw him from the public gaze." In any case, in 1924 Whalen became associated with the John Wanamaker department store, for which he was general manager off and on until 1934—building, according to *PM*, a reputation as a shrewd and capable executive.

But as general manager of a department store Whalen was by no means retired from public life. In 1925 he supported James Walker for Mayor after Walker had beaten Hylan in the primaries, and during Walker's administration he was again as prominent as any mayor. As New York's official greeter until the fall of 1929, Whalen, with "his faultless attire, his military bearing, his carefully groomed mustache," his white carnation—known libelously as a gardenia—met all the important guests. New York's distinguished visitors—among them the Prince of Wales (Duke of Windsor '44), Ruth Elder, Charles A. Lind-

bergh '41, Admiral Richard Byrd '42, Queen
Marie of Rumania—provided the occasion for
spectacular receptions. In these Whalen's well
known indifference to expense helped a great
deal (the Lindbergh welcome broke all records
for cost), but so did Whalen's sense of timing.
Since vast crowds simply would not turn out
for such celebrities as the Belgian Debt Re-
funding Commission or Spain's Duke of Alba,
Whalen always brought such visitors down
lower Broadway preceded by screeching sirens
between noon and 2:00 p.m., when that thor-
oughfare would be jammed with lunch crowds.
It was also Whalen who popularized the ticker
tape and telephone directory snowstorm so
frequently featured in newsreel pictures of in-
coming celebrities.

Whalen's own presence was, it is said,
enough to make any visitor feel important.
Someone has said that "a mere glimpse of him
is as restorative as an afternoon in the Metropolitan Museum of Art"; and Robert Rice
once commented in *PM* that Whalen's elegance,
sartorial and otherwise, "borders on the absurd,
yet somehow produces the opposite effect. . . .
Perhaps this is the key to his splendor," Rice
continued; "Grover Whalen accepts himself
and everything he does with the utmost
gravity." Whalen has been called a greater
showman than Barnum, and during his period
as greeter he acquired a host of other labels,
among them "Billion Dollar Barker", "Apostle
of the Grand Manner", "Doorman of the Western Hemisphere", "Gardenia Grover," and
"Gorgeous Greeter."

Late in 1928, when there was considerable
public outcry over the fact that the Arnold
Rothstein murder case remained unsolved, he
was appointed to succeed Joseph A. Warren
as New York's Police Commissioner (leaving
his executive job in the store temporarily).
While the new Commissioner was not able
to solve the Rothstein case, his first public acts did draw attention to his office.
He designed a new uniform for the department, ordered a special badge for himself with
four diamond studded stars, and bought a special barber chair for his exclusive use at headquarters. By New Year's Day he had also
demoted two veteran deputy commissioners,
abolished the homicide squad and "gumshoe"
squad, set up six strong-arm squads, and
rounded up several hundred "suspects"—most
of whom were immediately set free by indignant magistrates. He endorsed third-degree
methods, saying that "nowhere in the law books
is there anything about the rights of criminals." He declared war on speakeasies (he
himself neither smokes nor drinks), gambling
resorts, and other disorderly places, and conducted a number of raids on such places with
ax squads. He personally took over murder
investigations, rushed to the scenes of fires and
holdups, and denounced and threatened Communists with dire penalties.

That all of the publicity about Whalen was
not favorable was to be expected. Magistrate
David Hirshfield of Brooklyn referred to him
as "a snobbish, self-centered, would-be society
Police Commissioner in high hat, long-tail coat,
striped trousers, and light spats"; and Heywood Broun wrote in the *Nation*: "Mr. Whalen
leads all competitors in making the concepts of
melodrama come true in real life. . . . He

foams with ink and takes not a single step
until a roll of newsprint has been spread before
him like a red carpet." It has, however, been
pointed out that as Police Commissioner Whal-
en started an excellent Police Academy, organized a Crime Prevention Bureau and filled
it with experienced social workers to work
with underprivileged youths, and devised a
traffic system which still prevails in the Times
Square district at theatre time. When in May
1930 he went back to Wanamaker's the New
York *World* wrote that "no one else can hope
to equal his record in starting things that he
cannot finish"; but more than one commentator
has in retrospect called him New York's best
police commissioner.

Again at Wanamaker's, in 1932 Whalen was
made chairman of a local committee for New
York's celebration of the George Washington
Bicentennial, which spent a good deal of money
in anticipation of an improvement in business
conditions to meet the bills. While the Whalen
deficit was not met, it did not hurt the
Whalen reputation. The following year, drafted
by President Roosevelt '42 as New York City
administrator of the NRA, he organized the
greatest parade ever seen in New York—in
honor of the Blue Eagle. The same year he
settled by arbitration 130 strikes in New York
industries, mainly by the simple expedient of
locking the contesting parties in a conference
room until an agreement was reached. At the
time he was frequently mentioned as a possible
candidate for Mayor, but the Tammany Democratic organization was not popular, and in
1933 Fiorello H. La Guardia '40 won on a Fusion
ticket. Shortly afterward, with the death of
Rodman Wanamaker and the repeal of Prohibition, Whalen left the department store to
become chairman of the board of Schenley
Products Corporation and one of its three
executive and finance committeemen. Although
in 1937 he entered the Democratic primary for
Mayor with Roosevelt and Farley backing, he
withdrew from the race when Tammany put
up Jeremiah J. Mahoney against him.

Then, in 1939, Whalen came back into national view. Since 1936 he had headed the non-
profit corporation in charge of the New York
World's Fair, at a salary of $1 a year. In
1937 he left Schenley's to become president
of the Fair, with a reputed salary of $100,000
($25,000 of it for expenses). When some
European countries showed themselves not
eager to exhibit at the Fair he went to Moscow, signed up the U.S.S.R., and then dared
the rest of Europe to be put to shame by the
Russians. In three months he made a successful 30,000-mile tour of Europe, crossing and
recrossing forty-four frontiers. He also sold
innumerable bonds to big corporations and
"badgered them until they bought exhibition
space." With the well known Whalen enthusiasm and energy he worked day and night
and spurred his workers onward with the slogan, "Time Tears On!" The Fair opened on
schedule in the summer of 1939, Whalen having spent about $155,000,000 on it. The ex-
pensive project proved to be a financial failure
for investors, only paying off 39.2 cents on the
dollar, and in the spring of 1940 the bondholders eased Whalen out of control and went about
the details of keeping down the deficit. It was
Whalen, however, who was sent to Europe and
South America to induce forty-nine nations,

WHALEN, GROVER A.—*Continued*
including some belligerents, to maintain their
exhibits a second year. (For courtesies extended to their countries at the time of the
Fair, several European Governments conferred
decorations upon Whalen.)

In April 1941 super-promoter Whalen, who
had remained a director of the John Wanamaker store in Philadelphia, was snapped up
by Coty, Inc., cosmetic manufacturers, as chairman of their board. In the fall of the same
year he was appointed gasoline czar by Mayor
La Guardia; in the spring of 1942 he became
chairman of the Mayor's Committee for the
Mobilization of New York at War and staged
a mammoth "New York at War" parade; and
in the following fall he raised money for Russian War Relief as head of the "Thanks-to-
Russia" month. Next he became special civilian
adviser to the commanding general of the new
Alaska highway project, and he was about
to be commissioned an Army colonel and serve
as control officer in that area when in February 1943 he was released in order to accept
the job of Director of Civilian Defense for
New York City. In this position he has been
responsible for "the recruiting and placement
of all volunteers, for block organization, for
salvage, for youth services, for consumer education, for information concerning any and all
aspects of civilian defense." Soon after Whalen took over the office he made a successful
drive for 2,500 volunteers for the Aircraft
Warning Service, he effected much organizational streamlining, and he brought the CDVO
back into the Federal defense picture from
which it had been removed by Mayor La
Guardia. In recognition of his service to the
city, in June 1944 he was presented with the
CDVO gold ribbon award for 5,000 hours of
work.

For twenty years Whalen had been thinking
of a project that would make New York City
a world fashion center. Now he interested La
Guardia in his idea, and a committee was appointed to work on it. In January 1944 the
plans were revealed. Features of the center,
according to Whalen, were to include schools
of industrial art, studios of design, acres of
showrooms for all types of garments, a war
memorial auditorium seating 25,000, and a civic
opera house. Whalen was directed to prepare
a broad plan, including models and sketches
superimposed on aerial maps, to present before
the National Retail Drygoods Association in
June. The center, businessmen were assured,
would be self-liquidating, would be financed by
private enterprise, and would conflict in no way
with the manufacturing establishment of the
industry. The cost of the project was estimated to be between fifty and sixty million
dollars. By July the sober New York *Herald
Tribune* was calling it an "interesting and
promising" project; only realty interests remained to be won over.

At the end of Whalen's long working day
there has been little time for relaxation. In
addition to the dozen or more national and
municipal offices he has held, his executive
positions in seven business concerns, and his
directorship in many public service agencies,
he has been a member of several clubs and
of educational and philanthropic institutions.
However, he has what he calls an interest in

architecture, and in his spare time he has
equipped his New York City home with many
elaborate devices for both convenience and
pleasure. He also likes horseback riding, and
before the War enjoyed hunting at his country home at Roslyn, Long Island.

References

Esquire 11:53+ My '39 por
PM Mag p17-20 My 2 '43 pors
Who's Who in America 1944-45
Who's Who in Commerce and Industry
1940-41
Who's Who in New York 1938

WHEAT, WILLIAM HOWARD Feb.
19, 1879—Jan. 16, 1944 United States Representative (Republican) from Illinois since
1939; member of the Naval Affairs Committee.

Obituary

N Y Times Ja 17 '44 por

WHITE, HARRY D(EXTER) Oct. 29,
1892- United States Government official;
economist
Address: b. Department of the Treasury,
Washington, D. C.; h. 6810 Fairfax Rd., Bethesda, Md.

The United Nations Monetary and Financial
Conference, held in Bretton Woods, New
Hampshire, in July 1944, was the third in a
series of international parleys at which the
Allies, under the leadership of the United
States, have debated major post-War problems
before the day of final victory. The chief
author of the measures under discussion—which
aimed at the facilitation of currency stabilization, expanded world trade, high-level production, and maximum employment—was hard-
working Harry D. White, the United States
Treasury's Director of Monetary Research.

Preceded by the United Nations Conference
on Food and Agriculture at Hot Springs, Virginia, in June 1943 and the United Nations Relief and Rehabilitation Administration Council,
which had its initial meeting in November
1943, this third meeting was the first at which
permanent machinery for international cooperation was debated. (With the exception of
these three, other Allied conferences have dealt
with military or production problems.) President Roosevelt [42] has pointed out that this approach is in marked contrast to that in 1918
when President Wilson came to the peace
table with neatly packaged plans which had not
been previously discussed with the Allies. The
acceptance (subject to ratification by their respective governments) by the delegations of
forty-four Allied and Associated Nations of
the International Currency Stabilization Fund
and the International Bank for Reconstruction
and Development is seen by many observers as
a milestone on the path to international security and as the springboard for the envisioned
surrender of sovereign rights by nations and
the establishment of a world government. As
Secretary of the Treasury Morgenthau [40] observed, the aims of the broad economic program in which these proposals were included

were agreed upon in the Atlantic Charter and Article VII of the Lend-Lease Agreements.

Born in Boston, Massachusetts, October 29, 1892, Harry Dexter White did not decide upon an academic career until he had reached his late twenties. Early years in business were interrupted by the First World War, in which he served overseas as a lieutenant in the Infantry. On his return to the United States White directed an A.E.F. orphan asylum for two years. Then, resuming his education at Stanford University, he earned his B.A. in 1924, and a year later an M.A. In 1935 White received a Ph.D. from Harvard. Some six years earlier he had been an instructor in economics at that university, and then had gone on to Lawrence College in Appleton, Wisconsin, as a professor.

In June 1934 Professor Jacob Viner of the University of Chicago brought Dr. White to the Treasury Department to make a special study. White has since stayed there, having become Director of Monetary Research, a title created for him. In 1935 he was dispatched to England to study economic and monetary questions, the first of his official posts as Treasury spokesman there and in other countries. White took over the managing of the Treasury's $2,000,000,000 stabilization fund in 1941, and he has represented the Treasury at the committee meetings of the Economic Defense Board. He also sits on the board of trustees of the Export-Import Bank of Washington, and is a member of the Committee for Reciprocity Information.

Never one to seek headlines, the scholarly Treasury aide in 1943 became known to newspaper readers as the man behind Secretary Morgenthau's post-War monetary proposals. For nearly two years White had investigated conditions, discussed and revised details with other Government departments, and conferred with technical experts from foreign countries. His report was made public on April 6, 1943 after the London press had "scooped" the plan before the Secretary of the Treasury had presented it to Congressional committees. A British counterproposal, formulated by Lord Keynes '41, economist and adviser to the Exchequer, had been described in a London dispatch published on March 29.

Both plans, dealing primarily with currency and short-term credit, were considered by their authors as "preliminary drafts," of a tentative rather than an iron-clad, policy forming nature, and designed to serve as a groundwork for a formal conference of the United Nations; significantly, both agreed on the same general objectives of combatting currency fluctuation and promoting world commerce, but not on the means of their achievement. The White plan (an elaboration of the Tripartite Agreement between the United States, Great Britain, and France) called for an International Stabilization Fund of United and Associated Nations, with some $5,000,000,000 of capital (of which the United States might contribute as much as $2,000,000,000, the amount of the Treasury's present stabilization fund), with member nations making initial payments of one-half of the subscription in the form of gold, currency, and government securities. The international trade money would be a gold monetary unit called "unitas" (a name created by Morgenthau from United Nations and Associates),

HARRY D. WHITE

equal in value to $10 or 137 1/7 grains of gold; it would be merely a bookkeeping device in terms of which the fund would be kept.

The Keynes plan wished to name the new organization the International Clearing Union; it would have no actual assets (that is, no deposit of quotas), these being established by book entries with quotas based on the extent of the participating nation's trade volume in pre-War years. These would be valued in terms of "bancor" (coined by Keynes, it is a combination of the French words "banque" for bank and "or" for gold), a gold unit subject to revaluation as future conditions might require.

The two plans are "heroically international" in aim, but "characteristically national" in approach, observed one commentator. The chief difference revolved around the question of apportionment of control, according to officials, which under the White plan would be on the basis of capital participation—under the British plan, on that of a nation's pre-War world trade; the latter would thereby give Britain a greater voice than the United States. The role that gold should play was a second cause for discord: the unitas is redeemable in gold, the bancor, because its gold value is not fixed and inflexible, is not. "The purpose of the Clearing Union is to supplant gold as a governing factor, but not to dispense with it," asserted Keynes.

The text of the "preliminary draft" of the White plan was immediately sent to the Finance Ministers of thirty-seven United Nations for their consideration. The months that followed were filled with scores of discussions and even bitter controversy over the respective merits of the two plans, as well as a third, similar to the American, which Canada had later added. (The most extreme criticism has come from Dr. Benjamin M. Anderson of the University of California, who urged a return to the gold standard and international competition instead of cooperation.) Monetary experts of the United and Associated Nations for more than four months followed one another to

WHITE, HARRY D.—*Continued*

Washington, and toward the end of August 1943 White revised his plan, making more than a dozen major changes. The two most prominent ones were a larger gold requirement than in the original scheme and the relinquishing by the United States of its claimed right to veto alterations in exchange rates—it still retains the power in certain particulars. It again insisted on capital assets and deposits from all.

Discussions and revisions continued. On October 8, 1943 White disclosed another unofficial and tentative plan—a United Nations Bank for Reconstruction and Development to supplement the fund. On November 23 more details were released and a draft outline was sent to forty-three United and Associated Nations. The proposed institution was to have an aggregate capital of $10,000,000,000, of which the United States would provide one-third.

Substantial progress was reported between Keynes and White, and on April 21, 1943 Morgenthau announced as a basis for action a joint agreement, including an $8,000,000,000 stabilization fund, to which the United States would contribute at least $2,225,000,000, in gold and local currencies, agreed on by about thirty nations including the U.S.S.R. and all the exiled governments. Voting power and quotas were to be based on world trade, national incomes, and gold holdings and output (this status of gold was described as "a modified and managed gold standard"). The names unitas and bancor were dropped.

In May White attacked the resolution introduced to the House by Republican Representative Charles S. Dewey, an assistant secretary of the Treasury in the '20's, proposing a central reconstruction fund of $500,000,000 to make foreign reconstruction loans and otherwise contribute to post-War rehabilitation and currency stabilization, all strictly under American control. Regarded by some as a leading alternative proposal, it "does not begin to meet the problem" because it provides for little more than that which is at present authorized, said White.

On May 26 American diplomatic representatives delivered invitations from the President for the expected United Nations Monetary and Financial Conference to some forty countries and the French Committee of National Liberation, to begin July 1, 1944 at Bretton Woods. Roosevelt admonished the delegates that theirs was "the responsibility for demonstrating to the world that international post-War cooperation is possible," and that they were expected to adhere to the joint statement of principles of the international monetary fund announced in April. Alternate proposals were prepared by about seventy experts from fifteen nations who took part in an unpublicized two-week meeting in Atlantic City at the end of June.

When the conference, which set itself a three-week deadline, opened on schedule in the White Mountains, the personnel of the American delegation included, aside from technical experts, a Chicago banker and two Democrats and two Republicans who were members of the banking and currency committees of Congress. Secretary Morgenthau, chairman of the American group, was appointed conference president at the opening session, to preside over the delegates from forty-four nations (Denmark, a

forty-fifth, sent an observer). White, the American chief technical expert, went to the conference having won the first round, it being generally conceded that the "joint statement" more clearly resembled his original proposal than did the scheme of Keynes. Holding the first of scheduled daily press conferences on July 2, in which he summarized and analyzed the happenings in committee meetings—a procedure in great contrast to the air of secrecy at the United Nations Food Conference—White reported that already nearly 100 amendments or alternative provisions had been submitted by divers nations.

The conference was split into three task "commissions," the Stabilization Fund Committee, of which White was chairman, the World Bank Committee led by Keynes, and a third which considered all other proposals submitted. As the members came to grips with specific problems, the major controversial issues were seen to be the quotas required of each nation, the gold contribution, the composition of the executive directive, the nature of the first exchange rates to be set up, the procedure for changing rates to meet future changes in relative trade positions of member countries. A bipartisan appeal by twenty-five Western Senators for the inclusion of silver in the plans and thus establishing bimetallism met a chilly response from the American delegation and was dropped.

A final compromise agreement on all features, substantially the same as before the beginning of the deliberations, was reached (with some reservations) by the forty-four countries on July 15. The aggregate capital of the Fund was increased to $8,800,000,000, as compared to the original $8,000,000,000 and a subsequent proposal of $8,500,000,000. The Russian quota was raised $350,000,000, thereby increasing her prestige and voting power as well as her capacity to receive foreign exchange with which to finance post-War buying; the proposal of the Soviet Union to reduce gold payments of devastated countries was denied, however, as it was believed that this might make it impossible to get Congressional approval of the fund. Gold contributions will therefore be either 25 per cent of each country's quota or 10 per cent of official gold holdings, whichever is smaller. The pact will go into effect as soon as the governments of nations holding 65 per cent of the aggregate voting power, based largely on the size of their investment, notify the United States of their acceptance. (The United States holds 28 per cent of the voting strength, and Congress must approve the plan before the country can become a member.)

To recapitulate, quoting Sylvia F. Porter's [41] summary, "the forty-four nations agreed to establish an $8,800,000,000 currency stabilization fund to which every member would subscribe some gold and currency. The United States would put up $2,750,000,000, a little in gold, the most in dollars. England would be next with a $1,300,000,000 subscription in gold and pounds. Russia would be third with a $1,200,000,000 quota in gold and rubles. The Fund first would fix the rates of each member currency—the franc, peso, pound, ruble—in terms of gold or United States dollars. . . . Its objective would be to maintain those rates so we all can trade with each other in 'the certainty,' as Morgenthau remarked, 'that the money we receive on due date will have the value contracted for.'

"To make sure of this, the Fund wouldn't let any nation change its currency rate by more than 10 per cent unless the majority of the members agreed the move was essential. (In other words, the world would be tying up with gold again, but not in any rigid way. Gold would be the basis for currencies, but flexibility would be the basis at all times. It might be called a 'gold link' standard.) Then, to help out a member that was buying more goods than it was selling and thus owed, say, dollars to us, the Fund would sell that country the dollars it needed up to a specified amount and thus let the nation settle its debt to us. The Fund would check up on the country borrowing currencies to make certain it was using the money as it had promised. It would ration its own assets, if necessary. And it would be managed by a board of directors and an executive committee that would guard its activities constantly."

On July 21 the conferees unanimously voted to accept the plan for an $8,800,000,000 International Economic Bank of Reconstruction and Development in order to guarantee post-War international investments. (The U.S.S.R. had deadlocked the conference on quotas, demanding a lower capital subscription, as did several others, in reverse to her position on the Fund.) Described by a spokesman of the United States group as "a very conservative institution," the present draft provides for a one-to-one ratio of assets to guarantees; an earlier plan devised by White would have allowed it to guarantee a volume of loans one and one-half times the capital. The United States had to abandon her stand that bank subscriptions, which represent each nation's risks in guaranteeing international loans, be the same as quotas in the Fund, which represent that country's right to acquire foreign exchange with which to purchase materials in the world market. The United States increased its own subscription to $3,175,000,000, or $425,000,000 more than its original $2,750,-000,000 quota in the Fund. The American share of the risk will therefore be more than 36 per cent instead of one-third as promulgated on July 1.

The difference between the Bank and the Fund, which puzzled many people, is this (in the words of Miss Porter) : "The fund would help stabilize currencies by providing needy nations with the money necessary to settle their day-to-day transactions. The bank would help expand trade and create prosperity by providing nations with the money necessary for long-term construction and development. According to Harry White," she adds, "the Fund would raise our [United States] average annual trade after this war to seven billion dollars or possibly to ten billion dollars, a level higher than anything ever seen and comparing with our pre-War yearly average of three billion dollars."

Although the home governments had still to approve the "recommendations" of their delegates, there was a general feeling that the conference had been a success since contradicting philosophies and methods had been compromised. It is "one step in the broad program of international action necessary for the shaping of a free future," Morgenthau stated in a radio broadcast on July 22, marking the completion of the conference. "There is a curious notion," he added, "that the protection of national interest and the development of international cooperation are conflicting philosophies."

Most of the opposition for the two proposals came from United States bankers, "the only American group articulate about the conference," wrote *Time* Magazine on July 17, 1944, "perhaps partly out of fear of losing some of their power in foreign exchange and foreign investment business, partly out of dislike of all change and from misunderstanding of the Bretton Woods proposals." The bank, argues Morgenthau, "would indeed limit the control which certain private bankers have in the past exercised over international finance. It would by no means restrict the investment sphere in which bankers could engage. On the contrary, it would expand greatly this sphere by enlarging the volume of international investment and would act as an enormously effective stabilizer and guarantor of loans which they might make."

The direst note on this monetary plan was sounded by William B. Ziff in *The Gentlemen Talk of Peace* (1944). "It would last only so long as the member Powers did not feel that it was operating to their disadvantage, or were compelled to acquiesce by the threat of stark force. . . . The international governing body controlling the Bank soon would acquire powers of life and death over the commerce of at least the smaller States, giving the Bank a peculiarly decisive political position. The introduction of any of the control forms referred to would create a new series of mammoth superbureaucracies with all the vices inherent in such structures. These bureaucracies, or the bodies which controlled them, would be the real wielders of power and would themselves become the object of competition and seizure. The totalitarians with their planned production and socialized controls would make better adjustment to international economic regulation than would the free trade countries. They also would show infinitely more skill in evading those portions of the law which proved onerous or profitless. The introduction of an international regulatory apparatus accordingly would enable any powerful authoritarian country of dishonest bent to wreck the business of the free trade State by subtle methods not easily recognized early enough to be of value . . . and result in a true authoritarian world."

A group of British and United States financiers want the Nazi-dominated Bank of International Settlements at Basel kept alive, writes I. F. Stone in *PM*. These Anglo-American banking interests, states Stone, sponsor the establishment of a bilateral Anglo-American financial pact under Wall Street dictatorship; Leon Fraser, president of the First National Bank of New York, ex-president and ex-board chairman of the Bank of International Settlements (a group of American banks headed by First National are still members), was the key figure in working out this program. (During the conference the Norwegians had submitted a resolution urging the conference to recommend

WHITE, HARRY D.—*Continued*

the liquidation and investigation of the B.I.S., to which the Treasury has long been hostile. In November 1943 White had disparaged the existing B.I.S. as a possible medium for fulfilling the purposes of a world bank. "It has no significance in connection with this," White said. "It is German controlled. She [Germany] is being very nice and hopes to use it to get back into financial power. There's an American president [Thomas H. McKittrick[44]] doing business with the Germans.") Favoring direct American loans unsupervised by a cooperative international organization, Senator Robert A. Taft[40] has predicted Congressional disapproval of the two plans.

To fears expressed in conservative financial and economic circles that when dollars become scarce in the fund the American people will realize that the fund has thrown good American dollars "down a rathole" and has acquired worthless paper money in varied foreign currencies, White and his confreres answered that the United States must also adopt a commercial policy based on the principle that we must buy as well as sell abroad, and we must lower tariff barriers. "Few delegates," explains John H. Crider in the New York *Times*, "would claim that [the proposed institutions] represent anywhere near the complete economic arsenal of the United Nations to prevent disorder and recurrent depressions in the post-War era. The whole fabric of post-War economic apparatus, as envisioned by American technicians, would include international agreements on ocean shipping, air transport commodities, cartel policy, and, most important, commercial policy." The machinery of the plans is not enough. Both White and Keynes emphasize the interrelationship of the fund with the International Bank of Reconstruction and Development. One of the principal arguments for the latter, American sponsors believe, is that "if it accomplishes nothing more, it at least spreads responsibility for the financing of war reconstruction"—instead of again placing the whole burden on the United States. "The American taxpayer and the American businessman stand to gain, though the American banker may lose," by the adoption of these plans, forecasts I. F. Stone. *Newsweek* points out that "a basic defect of the new monetary agreement is its failure to recognize that internal financial stability of a country is the first requisite of international financial stability."

President Roosevelt had asked Secretary of State Cordell Hull[40], Secretary of War Stimson[41], and Secretary of the Treasury Morgenthau to work out a policy for the treatment of Germany after the War. Harry White drew up the so-called "Morgenthau plan," an idea of which was conveyed to the public in September 1944. Highly controversial in nature, it called for the prevention of German rearmament by changing that country from an industrial economy to an agrarian one; the other members of the policy committee apparently favored a less rigorous settlement, such as the restriction of certain kinds of industry (aviation and aluminum, for instance) that are particularly easily converted to war uses. The two main proposals soon became known as the "hard peace" and the "soft peace," respectively, although it was pointed

out that the so-called "soft peace" was hardly so in fact.

"There are many things wrong with the Morgenthau-White Treasury plan," wrote Max Lerner[42]. "It is always disheartening if you have to go against the grain of technological advance. It is always a negative solution if you have to turn the wheels of industry backward, diminish production rather than expand it, discourage rather than encourage the march of science. No one likes these features of the plan, and no one celebrates them—not even those who drew the plan up in the first instance. But . . . for the first time the whole subject of what to do with Germany has been brought down to the bedrock of reality. . . . The virtue of the Morgenthau-White plan is that it cuts through all these problems of selecting and deciding on what is to be controlled, the problems of policing, and the problems of who is to do the controlling and policing. It thus not only strips the Germans of their war potential. It also effectively removes Germany as the great bone of Allied contention. Where there is no German industrial machine, there can be no struggle for power over it between America and Britain and Russia. And despite the discreet efforts to hide it, the fact is that such a struggle for power does actually exist today."

Among other objections to the plan were: that an agricultural Germany could not support her present population; and that the loss of German industry would be a serious blow to world trade and to the Europe which she has devastated and ought to restore. To the population problem, the answer is given: Hitler and the Nazis have already liquidated millions of Germans and driven others to foreign homes; many more have died in combat, from disease and from the effects of bombings; the eleven million foreign workers brought to Germany by force will all go home; and Germany's population, in short, will have been drastically reduced from its pre-War level. German industry, it is suggested, could be dismantled and set up as replacement for men and machines stolen from her victims, thus answering the second objection. "Almost one-third of Germany's soil is still covered with forests," William B. Ziff points out in his book, "which are capable of yielding valuable products to a country operating on a semi-agrarian base. Less than half of the area which might be intensively worked is at present under the plow. The German earth is not extremely fertile but it is well able to produce all of the food and fodder crops necessary to keep the German people in health." Ziff does, indeed, go farther than White, and "makes the plan attributed to Mr. Henry Morgenthau seem, in comparison, the benevolence of some kindly old gentleman." As he points out, however, "on the whole, an amputated Reich would still remain a favored country, containing ample resources for a population content to live modestly as do those of Poland, Yugoslavia, France, or Spain."

Harry D. White is a solidly built man of medium height. He lives with his wife, Anne Terry White, a writer of children's books, and their two children in Bethesda, Maryland, on the northern outskirts of the Capital. On Sundays White plays volleyball and a good game of tennis—when he has not brought home a bulging brief case from the office.

References

Business Week p19 Ap 17 '43 por
N Y Herald Tribune II p3 Ap 11 '43
Who's Who in America 1944-45

WHITE, JOSH   Feb. 11, 1915-   Ballad singer

Address: b. c/o Cafe Society Downtown, 2 Sheridan Sq., New York City; h. 466 W. 151st St., New York City

The American, Josh White, called "the most famous folk singer of his race," has acquired a reputation for transmitting to his audience through his music what the Negro feels and thinks about himself and his place in the world picture. Like all true artists, wrote a critic, this particular one has a quality none can imitate.

Josh White was prepared for his profession in an unusual way. He was born in Greenville, South Carolina, February 11, 1915, and christened Joshua Daniel. This name was given to him, he explains, by his deeply religious parents—Dennis and Daisy Elizabeth (Humphrey) White—because they expected great things of him. (His father was a preacher.) The first inkling of his destiny came to him when, at the age of seven, he helped a blind man to cross a street in the Whites' home town. The boy, much awed by what he suspected was the Christian deed he had been born to do, rushed home to tell his mother. The blind man, it developed, had asked whether Joshua might lead him around every day after school, and, since the White family was desperately in need of money, the boy was allowed to assume the responsibility.

For the next ten years he followed a strange profession, traveling from city to city with a variety of blind musicians. His weekly stipend was only $4, although his charges often took in over $100 for a week of singing and playing. Joshua himself performed on the tambourine or the guitar (which he taught himself to play) and sang the spirituals he learned from the singers. After a time he became known as the "Singing Christian."

Although Joshua had never had a real music lesson, by the time he was eleven he had made his first recording (in Chicago). A number of years later—about 1933—he was asked to make recordings of spirituals for the Columbia Recording Corporation in New York. In the two-day contract period the teen-age Joshua made seventeen recordings, for which he received, reports *PM*, the sum of $100.

As the Singing Christian he became popular through these and other records, many of which were bought by churches for the salutary effect they had on their congregations. It is told that some of the churches, wanting all the singer's records, began receiving blues songs along with the spirituals. The non-pious ones were later distinguished by the label "Pinewood Tom." In addition to his recordings, White was also singing and playing his guitar with the Southernaires on their NBC program.

JOSH WHITE

One day in the late '30's Josh White fell and severely cut his hand on a milk bottle he had been carrying. For the next three years his right hand was paralyzed and could not be used to strum the guitar. During the period of his comparative prosperity—in 1935—the young ballad singer had met and married Carol Carr, a New Yorker; and he was now faced with the prospects of supporting a wife and a small daughter, Deborah, while his former means of earning an income was closed to him. (He now has three other children: Beverly, Joshua, Jr., and Caroline.) For a time White worked as an elevator operator, and then, at the end of 1939, he got a bit part in Sam Byrd's production of *John Henry*, starring Paul Robeson [41]. This musicalized version of Roark Bradford's tale of a Negro Paul Bunyan opened on Broadway on January 10, 1940, with Joshua White in the role of Blind Lemon, a character based on one of the blind men White had led around as a boy. Bradford had met the Singing Christian on his travels and had written this part for the singer into the show. "Joshua White played the guitar and sang excellently," wrote the *Theatre Arts Monthly*; but his opportunity was short-lived. The play, despite its handsome production and fine cast, was dull, and closed after only seven performances. In 1940 and 1941, however, White made two record albums. *Chain Gang* (for Columbia) and *Southern Exposure* (for Keynote)—albums which, reportedly, provoked Ku Klux Klan attacks on his family in Greenville.

Since 1940 White has appeared as a guest on a number of radio programs, including Norman Corwin's [40] *Dorie Got a Medal*; and in May 1944 he started broadcasting for WNEW, on a fifteen-minute sustaining program given every Sunday noon. Since August 1943 he has been appearing at Barney Josephson's famous Cafe Society Downtown, "the mecca for hepcats" in New York City. Seldom, wrote the New York *World-Telegram*

WHITE, JOSH—*Continued*

after the ballad singer's opening, is Josh White able to leave the floor without singing six or seven songs, such as, "Evil-hearted Man", "The Girl With the Delicate Air", "I Am Going To Move on the Outskirts of Town," or "Strange Fruit." "A terrific show-stopper," echoed the New York *Herald Tribune,* "he had to do about fifteen numbers at the supper show on the night of our visit. Even a broken string on his guitar didn't help him. He repaired the damage on the floor and went on with his work. Josh White is one of the great night club acts." From time to time, too, White has appeared with other important artists, notably Pearl Primus[44] and Libby Holman. Of the White-Holman concert, "Early American Blues and Other Songs" (November 1944), Malcolm Johnson of the New York *Sun* wrote: "We never dreamed we'd ever hear any white person sing these songs in the electrifying way this new, this more dynamic Libby Holman sings them."

Josh White claims, writes Dorothy Norman of the New York *Post,* that he has to sing his "fighting blues," with his guitar in his hand, in order to express what he really wants to say. "He cannot say what he wants through the spoken word alone," so, this writer continues, "you find him with his guitar, singing his incomparable ballads nightly, at Cafe Society Downtown—holding his audiences spellbound. For that is where he has the greatest freedom to sing what he wants to say." Although his repertoire consists of innumerable folk ballads learned from his blind employers, he is not satisfied with these forms alone. To them he adds his "social conscience" ballads, many of his own composition, that deal with Jim Crowism, poor housing, slums, and lynching. Negro spirituals such as, "Swing Low Sweet Chariot" and "Go Down Moses" he now objects to singing, because, *PM* writes, he feels that they represent "the Negroes' years of slavery and oppression." As a "sensitive and proud member of his race," he refused not long ago to accept lucrative motion-picture offers, too, because they were offers to play the conventional "Uncle Tom" parts usually accorded Negro entertainers. At the time of his refusal, in fact, he had already had such an experience in Hollywood, having made two full-length films which he now chooses to forget.

Josh White has sung by invitation three times at the White House, one of these times being his appearance at the 1940 Presidential inauguration. In addition he has given six concerts in the Library of Congress; he was sent under Government auspices on a good-will tour to Mexico in 1941; and he has been doing many benefit programs, plus twelve broadcasts a week over the BBC for the OWI. His recreation, in his brief free periods, is playing tennis.

References

N Y Post Mag p29 Je 21 '44 pors
PM p21 My 25 '44 por

WHITE, WILBERT WEBSTER, REV.
Jan. 16, 1863—Aug. 12, 1944 Presbyterian minister who in 1900 founded the Biblical Seminary (New York City), of which he was president until his retirement in 1939; author of many religious works, two of which are *Studies in Old Testament Characters* (1900) and *Thirty Studies in the Gospel by Matthew* (1903).

Obituary

N Y Times p35 Ag 13 '44 por

WHITE, WILLIAM ALLEN Feb. 10, 1868—Jan. 29, 1944 World-famous publisher and editor of the Emporia (Kansas) *Gazette;* novelist and biographer; considered a great influence on American journalism and politics; awarded the Pulitzer Prize for the best editorial ("To an Anxious Friend") written in 1922; "Mary White," an essay written about his daughter's death, is now regarded as a classic; see sketch 1940 Yearbook.

Obituary

N Y Times p38 Ja 30 '44 por

WILEY, WILLIAM FOUST 1874 (?)—Aug. 24, 1944 Publisher; one of America's leading newspaper executives; head of the Cincinnati *Enquirer* since 1936; chairman of the Committee on Federal Laws of the American Newspaper Publishers Association; fought vigorously much of the New Deal legislation; staunch battler for a free press.

Obituary

N Y Times p13 Ag 25 '44 por

WILLKIE, WENDELL L(EWIS) (wil' kē) Feb. 18, 1892—Oct. 8, 1944 Presidential nominee in 1940; leader of the internationalist wing of the Republican Party; wielded tremendous political influence although holding no office and controlling no political machine; assumed the vital task of rallying President Roosevelt's[42] opponents in support of the Administration's foreign policy for the sake of national unity in time of emergency; see sketch 1940 Yearbook.

Obituary

N Y Times p1+ O 8 '44 por

WILSON, DON(ALD HARLOW) Sept. 1, 1900- Radio announcer
Address: h. 13909 Magnolia Blvd., Van Nuys, Calif.

With the growing importance of radio advertising, it has become as necessary for sponsors to find the right announcer to read their commercials as it is to find the right talent to sponsor. Products are advertised with studied eloquence or with a wry prove-it-yourself manner; and men like Don Wilson are becoming as closely identified in the American public's mind with a particular product as the comedian or singer who may be the star of the show.

Donald Harlow Wilson was born in Lincoln, Nebraska, September 1, 1900. He considers himself a native of Colorado, however; his parents, Lincoln and C. Louise (Hatch) Wilson, moved to Denver when Don was only two years old. During his four years at the University of Colorado young Wilson contradicted the legend that academic studies and devotion to athletics do not mix, becoming one of the University's star football men.

Upon his graduation in 1923, Wilson started his business career as a salesman, soon deserting commerce to join a vocal trio. "I never expected anything to develop out of the idea," Wilson says. "At first, it merely seemed a way to have some fun, but before long I realized that I had been mistaken— also pleasantly surprised." The singers made a successful tour of the Mountain states, gradually working their way to California. An advertiser, who heard them in San Francisco, in 1927 put them on the air for a year over Station KFRC. On the expiration of their contract, Wilson and one of the other members of the trio headed for Los Angeles, where together they put on various radio programs for more than a year.

Abandoning singing as a profession, in the fall of 1929 Wilson joined the staff of KFI as an announcer, advancing shortly afterward to the post of chief announcer. He gained such wide popularity for his broadcasts of sports events that, in 1933, one of his admirers, John F. Royal, vice-president of the National Broadcasting Company, induced the announcer to come East to cover sports for NBC. At the same time Wilson was also connected with many of NBC's high-ranking programs, on which he extolled the merits of every imaginable sort of product. In 1934 Wilson, won the job of lauding "those six delicious flavors" on Jack Benny's '41 Sunday night broadcasts. In a short time Wilson became an integral part of the show, also taking part in the skits and acting as "straight man" as well.

Wilson has a ranch home in Van Nuys, California, where he lives with his wife, the former Countess Radunska of Poland, to whom he was married in December 1942. Wilson devotes most of his free time to his horses. With the exception of football, his favorite sport is golf. Still retaining his love for music, Wilson takes in as many concerts and operas as he can when he comes to New York with the Benny cast. "I suppose preferences in music are primarily dependent upon a person's mood at the moment," Wilson declares. "But I am nearly always in the mood for Debussy's 'Afternoon of a Faun,' the third act entrance to Lohengrin, and Tschaikowsky's Fourth." Although he worked with Harry James '43 on the trumpeter's last series of broadcasts and has the highest regard for James as a musician, Wilson says, "I'm afraid I just don't understand swing."

Wilson's size makes him the butt of many of Jack Benny's jokes. The announcer weighs 220 pounds and is six feet two inches tall. The comedian's continual quips, however, have created the impression that Wilson is really a lot more massive than he actually is. In fact, Benny boasts that he has "made Don the biggest man in radio." Whatever Benny's opinion is, it is true that Wilson is "tops" among announcers, having been voted the most popular by press and listeners every year since 1937. And when the word "popular" is mentioned, Don will even the score with Benny by saying with seeming serious-

Ray Lee Jackson

DON WILSON

ness that Fred Allen '41 is his favorite comedian. But the statement is always followed by the announcer's famous laugh.

References

Variety Radio Directory 1940-41
Who's Who in America 1944-45

WINDSOR, EDWARD, DUKE OF June 23, 1894- Governor of the Bahama Islands
WINDSOR, WALLIS (WARFIELD), DUCHESS OF June 19, 1896-

Address: Government House, Nassau, Bahama Islands

Back in 1936 the romance of King Edward VIII and the American divorcée, Wallis Warfield Simpson, was the biggest news story of the year, precipitating the "greatest constitutional crisis of all times." Even before the British King's dramatic abdication of his throne for "the woman I love," there were two schools of thought on the situation. Throughout the years since then pros and cons have continued to follow the career of Edward as the Duke of Windsor, particularly since his appointment, in 1940, to the governorship of the Bahama Islands. While anti-Edwardians felt that Windsor, the "selfish, shallow man" who let the Empire down, had been successfully shelved in an unimportant post, pro-Edwardians believed the Bahamian governorship of strategic importance during the war years, through which the "uncompromising, courageous, royal democrat" could well serve his country, and where his American-born duchess could also play a part in promoting friendly Anglo-American relations. While the character, ambitions, and destiny of the Duke of Windsor still remain something of an enigma, there is no doubt (so far as the American press is concerned) that the Windsors remain a happy, romantic couple whose least word and act are news.

Edward Albert Christian George Andrew Patrick David, the first Duke of Windsor, was born June 23, 1894 at White Lodge, Rich-

DUKE and DUCHESS OF WINDSOR

mond Park, England, the first child of King George V and Queen Mary, at that time Duke and Duchess of York. During the years from 1902 to 1907 the boy was prepared for the Navy and in the spring of 1907 he entered Osborne. Two years later he was sent to the Royal Naval College at Dartmouth, where "he was not to be favored in any way." Of his life as a cadet Edward has said: "I wasn't much of a shark at any of my studies, so I won no distinction in scholarship. I wasn't especially good at any of the sports, nor much gratified in any case when boys seemed to think it good form to let me win. I was not even hazed like other lads. . . . So I didn't get friendships." Although very shy, he actually "punched chaps in the nose" because they "royal-highnessed" him.

At the close of his Dartmouth training, in June 1911, he became a Knight of the Garter and, after his father's accession that same year, he was created Prince of Wales. (His other titles were of the ranks of baron, earl, and duke in peerages of the United Kingdom, England, and Scotland.) Shortly afterward the Prince served as a midshipman on the H.M.S. *Hindustan.* In October 1912 he entered Magdalen College, Oxford. His university career, however, ended with the outbreak of the First World War, when in August 1914 he was gazetted to the Grenadier Guards. As aide-de-camp to Sir John French, he served for eighteen months with the Expeditionary Force in Flanders and in France. In 1916 he was appointed to the staff of the officer commanding the Mediterranean Expeditionary Force. From 1917 to 1918 he served on the Italian Front; then he returned to France and was attached to the Canadian Corps. in which he was serving at the time of the Armistice. His assignments to safe positions are said to have irked him: "What difference does it make if I am killed? The King has three other sons!"

In February 1919 Edward returned to England to take up his public duties. For ten years the personable, golden-haired, pleasure-loving young Prince, who had "more than a touch of his grandfather in him," traveled throughout the British Empire and the rest of the world on official engagements. He became the "Empire's Salesman," the "best-known man in the world," the "arbiter of men's fashions, a fearless horseman, tireless dancer, idol of bachelors, dream of spinsters." These and similar descriptions appeared in the American press, particularly during his 1919 and 1923 visits to the United States. In 1927 he toured many of the great industrial centers in Great Britain, including the desolated mining districts. On these visits his comments drew much public attention to the miner's sufferings. At about this time, because of the many demands for his presence throughout England, on his insistence a plane was placed at his disposal which he learned to pilot himself.

By 1935 the Prince of Wales, while too outspoken in his comments and too indifferent to the traditions of royal dignity to please conservative British upper classes, was highly popular with the average Briton. "If he stays up late at a party . . . he rides out early in the morning and is first in the hunting field. If he happens to fall off his horse . . . he is quick to risk his neck again over the next fence. The Prince takes everything, throwing his heart over first." If, in the eyes of most people, he had a fault, it was that at the age of forty-one he was still a bachelor. What the British public did not know (a "voluntary" censorship was already at work in the Empire's press) was that he had already met the woman who might become the future Queen of England. Beautiful, popular in London society, an American, twice married, "clever and vital," with "vast allure for every shy man who came her way," her name was Wallis Warfield Simpson.

The girl who was to be called in 1936 "the most famous woman in the world today, the most romantic figure of all times," was born Bessie Wallis Warfield in Blue Ridge Summit, Pennsylvania, June 19, 1896, the only child of Teackle Wallis and Alice (Montague) Warfield. The annals of the Warfield family went back to Norman England. The descendants of Richard Warfield, who founded the American branch of the family in 1662, were wealthy Maryland landowners. Wallis' grandfather, Henry M. Warfield, imprisoned as a Southern sympathizer in the Civil War period, afterward became a director of the Baltimore and Ohio Railroad. Her uncle "Sol" Warfield was president of the Seaboard Air Line Railway. A rich man, devoted to his niece, he provided for her education and left her a sizable trust fund in his will.

Young Wallis went to the Oldfields private school in Cockeysville, Maryland, and spent some of her summers at Miss Noland's Camp for Girls, with "occasional exciting visits" to the home of Aunt Bessie Merryman in Washington. At the time the Prince of Wales was a young lieutenant in the Grenadier Guards in 1914, Wallis Warfield was making her debut in Baltimore. She had many admirers, but it was a United States Navy flier, Lieutenant Commander Earl Winfield Spencer, Jr., whom she married. They had met each other in Florida in 1915, and the marriage, which followed a romance begun in the excitement of war days, did not last; after an attempt at reconciliation in China, where Commander Spencer had been stationed, the couple were divorced.

Wallis Warfield lived quietly for a time in Warrenton, Virginia; then she accompanied her aunt, Mrs. Merryman, to Europe. In London the recently divorced Ernest Aldrich Simpson, American-born British subject, soon made it plain to Wallis Warfield how much he admired her. In 1928 they were married. The Simpsons' popularity increased: guests who dined at Mrs. Simpson's mirror-topped table were London's most distinguished personages, and in June 1931 Mrs. Simpson was presented at Court. On the evening of the presentation Mr. and Mrs. Simpson went to a party given by Lady Furness, at which the Prince of Wales was present. That night the Prince brought Mr. and Mrs. Simpson to their home in his car.

A brief visit to America in 1933 was the only interruption of Mrs. Simpson's fashionable London life. Guests at her exclusive parties usually included Lady Diana Duff Cooper, Lord and Lady Louis Mountbatten '42, Lady Mendl, sometimes Ambassador von Ribbentrop '41, often such well known Americans as John Gunther '41 and the late Alexander Woollcott '41. Wallis Simpson, as a hostess at this time, was said to have "the charm of a controlled, sophisticated woman, quick to sympathize and quick to understand the problems of others." That the Prince was increasingly attracted to Mrs. Simpson was soon noticed. The friendship that developed was based on mutual interests. "Both like country life and the races and dancing. Both prefer informal to formal social functions. Mrs. Simpson's devotion to flowers and his fondness for gardening are allied."

On January 20, 1936 George V died, and the Prince of Wales became King Edward VIII. Ears were pricked up when Edward asked Parliament, in considering his income, to make provision for his eventual marriage. The King's guests in May 1936, as reported in the Court Circular, included Mr. and Mrs. Ernest Simpson, and, when the King cruised on his private yacht in August, photographs in American newspapers showed Wallis Simpson beside the King. "The world wondered and England waited in a conspiracy of silence." Then, in October, Mrs. Simpson filed suit for divorce, which was granted by decree nisi the same month. (Such a decree is made absolute in not less than six months unless cause to the contrary is shown.) Growing rumors that the King intended to marry Mrs. Simpson could not be suppressed.

Conservative Britons became uneasy. The unorthodox romance was not the only thing about the new King which they viewed with alarm. Prime Minister Stanley Baldwin and others disliked the King's free mingling with rank and file Britishers. His remarks to East Coast miners that their living conditions were "a shame" and his promise to the Welsh jobless that "something would be done" also disturbed Government heads. Commentators have since agreed that certain pro-German tendencies Edward showed did not ease the political aspects of the situation. The clash between Baldwin and the King reached a climax in late November of 1936, and the storm broke when the self-imposed British press censorship released the news of the Bishop of Bradford's reproof to the King. The Bishop expressed the hope that the King was aware of his "need of God's grace," adding, "Some of us wish he gave more positive signs of such awareness." At this the London press released full details of the great romance and all England knew a constitutional crisis was at hand. The King expressed his willingness to contract a morganatic marriage, but Prime Minister Baldwin said he would resign rather than introduce such an act before Parliament. Conservative Winston Churchill '42 and Laborite Josiah Wedgewood '42 stood behind the King, as did the powerful publishers Lords Rothermere and Beaverbrook '40. Most of the working classes were for letting Edward "pick his own girl."

But with the clergy and the conservative influences in the Empire arrayed against him, Edward had no choice but abdication. On December 11 the Speaker of the House of Commons read to a hushed chamber: "I, Edward, do hereby declare my irrevocable determination to renounce the throne for myself and my descendants." The next day the world listened to Edward's final radio broadcast: "At long last I am able to say a few words of my own. I have never wanted to withhold anything but until now it has not been constitutionally possible for me to speak. . . . I have found it impossible to carry on the heavy burden of responsibility and to discharge the duties of King as I would wish to do without the help and support of the woman I love."

That night Edward, now the Duke of Windsor—the new title his brother King George VI '42 conferred on him—left for the Continent, proceeding to the estate of his friend Baron Eugene Daniel Rothschild in Austria. There he was later joined by Wallis Warfield after her divorce decree became final. They were married on June 3, 1937. For the next three years the famous couple lived under a cloud of rumor and conjecture. In England there was "an accumulating indifference" concerning Windsor; as for the Duchess, "there is no doubt whatever as to Albion's disapproval." The couple visited Germany "to study labor conditions under the Nazi regime . . . were escorted by protective Nazi officials, posed with Nazi leaders, including Hitler '42." In 1938 they went to live on the French Riviera in a luxurious villa staffed by twenty-two servants. Among their closest friends was Lady Mendl, of the Bonnet-Daladier '40 appeasement clique in France (*Friday*, August 9, 1940); another close friend was Charles Bedaux, who wanted to sponsor a trip to the United States for them, but whose unpopularity in labor and liberal circles raised an outcry loud enough to cause the trip to be canceled.

At the outbreak of the War the Duke hurried back to England to offer his services. He asked for a "real" war job, and was assigned as a liaison officer with British and French High Commands. He made a few trips to the Front during the winter, saw Lord Gort '40 a few times, but his headquarters remained at his house in Paris. In June 1940 it was reported that the Duke had relinquished his post and had gone with the Duchess to their residence near Cannes for an indefinite period. But when the German forces swept through France, the Windsors took refuge in Spain: their old friend, Sir Samuel Hoare '40, new British Ambassador in Madrid, made arrangements for

**WINDSOR, EDWARD, DUKE OF, and
WINDSOR, WALLIS, DUCHESS OF—**
Continued

their stay there. According to *Time* Magazine,
"the Spanish did not take Edward's military
career seriously enough to intern him as a
belligerent."

The ex-King had gone to Lisbon when an
official announcement was made in July 1940:
"His Majesty the King has been pleased to
appoint His Royal Highness, the Duke of
Windsor, to be Governor and Commander in
Chief of the Bahama Islands." The governorship of the small group of millionaire play-
ground islands off the coast of Florida, at a
salary of $12,000 a year, was (according to
critics of the Duke) probably the least important job given to a member of the British
Royal Family for many years. "Once sovereign
of 600,000,000 people and one-fourth of the
planet," wrote *PM*, the forty-six-year-old Duke
"would be head man of twenty-nine islands,
661 islets, 2,387 rocks [altogether, an area of
about 4,000 square miles], and a population of
68,000, mostly descendants of liberated Afri-
cans." Many Britons took a more kindly view
of Windsor's new status, however. One source
indicated that the appointment was the beginning of a $280,000,000 British colonial develop-
ment and welfare program; and others saw
Windsor in the role of good-will ambassador
to the New World. "The West Indies as a
whole," said the London *Times*, "may well receive the news as full of welcome significance
at a time when events in Europe and the
friendly interest of their great neighbor in the
north have demonstrated their high importance
in the international reckoning." The Duke himself was described by his secretary as "very
happy indeed" over the appointment.

On August 1, 1940 the famous couple sailed
on an American liner (the *Excalibur*) from
Lisbon to Bermuda. They were traveling light,
they said; there were three Cairn terriers,
three truckloads of baggage, a Buick automobile, a trailer which the Duke planned to
use as a baggage car, a sewing machine, golf
bags, a case each of champagne and gin, and
two cases of port. Meanwhile Bahamian society, having refurbished its uniforms and
checked its party wardrobes, awaited the arrival of the new Governor and his Duchess.

Accordingly, amid the most elaborate welcome
ever accorded a governor of the Bahamas, the
Duke, in August 1940, pledged his efforts to
help the colony meet its wartime problems. His
first concern was the leasing of air and naval
bases to the United States Government, which
he discussed with President Roosevelt '42 in December while the latter was cruising off the
Bahamas. The Duchess, for her part, supervised the renovation of the Government House
and became an active participant in Red Cross
and civic work.

In an interview in March 1941 with Fulton
Oursler '42, editor of *Liberty*, the Duke discussed international affairs. "When the War
is over," he said, "many strange things are
going to happen. There will be a new order
in Europe, whether it is imposed by Germany
or Great Britain. Labor is going to get a
more equitable distribution of the world's good
things in this new order." The new peace, he
said, "will have to be as just a settlement as
the human spirit can provide. . . . There will
have to be a world league with everybody in
it . . . but this time it will be buttressed with
police power. . . . When peace comes this
time there is going to be a new order of social
justice—don't make any mistake about that—
and when that time comes, what is your country going to do with its gold?"

Since their arrival in the Bahamas the Duke
and Duchess have made several trips to the
United States, for both business and pleasure.
The first one was late in 1941, when the Duke
came north to make a study of American CCC
camps, which he expected to use as the basis
for similar camps he hoped to establish in the
Islands for unskilled Negro workers. When
the Windsors again visited the United States
(in 1942) the Duke successfully promoted
trade for the Bahamas. When questioned on
the matter of rioting that had occurred among
native workers there, he said that "local rates
[of pay] must not be upset," but that an increase for the lowest paid workers was contemplated.

The War had played havoc with the Bahamas' tourist trade, greatly disturbing the Islands' economic life. In 1943, therefore, one
of the Duke's visits to the United States was
for the purpose of discussing the importation
of Bahamian laborers by that country as well
as the possibility of increased American use
of Bahamian exports. On that particular visit
to New York the Duchess appeared with the
Duke at various Service clubs and hospitals
and took the opportunity of making the rounds
of shops. The couple also visited Washington
and were there at the time of Winston
Churchill's visit. Questioned about his meeting with the President and Churchill, Windsor
said: "I did quite a lot of listening." Asked
if he regretted he was no longer King, his face
became grave: "I think that's old history now,
if you don't mind." He said he took pride in
the fact that wages and working conditions in
the Bahamas had been greatly improved since
he became Governor.

An indication of the progress he foresees
was his speech to the Bahama House of Assembly in December 1944. At this time he
declared that he was giving it another chance
to consider the secret ballot and labor and
social legislation that had been rejected at a
previous session: "After more than four years
of administration the Governor becomes very
conscious of the difficulty of avoiding repetition when addressing the Legislature. . . . My
insistence on the necessity of certain fundamental changes in your outlook is prompted
solely by my sincere interest in the colony's
welfare and by my desire that you shall not
find yourselves unprepared to face now the
conditions of a fast-changing world."

Since 1943 reports have circulated that the
Duke and Duchess are no longer happy in
their island post, reports promptly denied by
the Windsors themselves. In May 1944 Cornelius Vanderbilt wrote in the New York *Post*
that he had learned from an "unimpeachable
source" that the Duke of Windsor had tendered
his resignation as Governor and would attempt
to become an American citizen. The Duke
declared that the report was fantastic, and
from London came neither confirmation nor
denial of Vanderbilt's news story.

In the late summer of 1944 the Duke and Duchess of Windsor again came to the United States en route to their Canadian ranch. The former King said he planned to visit New York for a physical checkup and to go to Washington on official business, which included conferences with high British and American officials. If the Windsors had in mind any prospective change of residence, no hint at all of that was given to the public officials. (In August the Duchess entered a New York hospital for an appendectomy.) After a stay of four months, the Windsors returned to Nassau on November 8, the Duke "anxious to get back to work." In tribute to the former King, the London *Daily Express* said: "He has faithfully upheld the British cause in his lonely outpost . . . shown wisdom in his decisions and great dignity in his bearing."

The American press since 1940 has featured many stories on the home life of "Mr. and Mrs. Windsor." The Duchess, small but with a slenderness that seems to add to her height, has a face "distinctive for its high cheekbones, which artists invariably admire. Her brow is broad and well-proportioned. Her brown hair is parted in the center and drawn back in the softest of waves. . . . Her eyes are blue, her skin a creamy, pale tan. She has beautiful teeth of unusual whiteness, and generous lips." The Duchess, said one interviewer, is "completely well-gowned, completely gracious, completely composed. . . . At dinner she talks well and constantly. . . . Her most ardent admirers say she is so honest she will say first what she thinks, even if on second thought she has to regret it. . . . Her voice is two-toned—low and lower." The Duke, said another writer in 1941, is "still the restless princely personage who enjoys the mechanical setup of modern metropolitan life." He is said to be a trained listener, who rapidly grasps high spots and generalizations. He has a remarkable memory, and is a "youthfully energetic, fidgety man." He usually wears something that will match, or contrast pleasingly with, the costumes of the Duchess. The couple are fond of jigsaw puzzles; they also play a great deal of double solitaire, at which she usually wins. But Windsor's dominating passion, said one correspondent, is to have people "pay court to his Duchess." To any press photographer who might wish to photograph him alone he declares, "We are a team."

References

Friday 1:15+ Ag 9 '40 il pors
Ladies' H J 56:23+ Je '39 il pors
Liberty 18:12-17 Mr 22 '41 por
Life 10:118-22+ Je 9 '41 il pors
Lit Digest 122:13-14 N 28 '36
Newsweek 8:7-12 D 12 '36 il pors
Read Digest 29:40-3 N '36
Time 28:17-18 N 2 '36
Cook, T. R. comp. Essays in Modern Thought p89-97 1935
Eurich, A. C. and Wilson, E. C. In 1936 p605-11 1937
Wilson, E. H. Her Name Was Wallis Warfield 1936

WINDSOR, WALLIS (WARFIELD), DUCHESS OF *See* Windsor, E., Duke of, and Windsor, W. W., Duchess of

WINGATE, ORDE CHARLES 1903—Mar. 24, 1944 Major general in the British Army; leader of an Imperial air-borne Commando force in Burma at the time of his death in an airplane crash; one of the most colorful figures in modern warfare; his fabulous exploits had established him as the "Lawrence of Arabia" of the Second World War.

Obituary

N Y Times p1+ Ap 1 '44 por

WOOD, CHARLES ERSKINE SCOTT Feb. 20, 1852—Jan. 22, 1944 Poet; essayist; attorney; following graduation from West Point participated in several Indian campaigns and later wrote many myths of the North American Indians; as poet, called "a serious satirist"; works include *Heavenly Discourse* (1927); *Poet in the Desert* (1929); *Poems From the Range* (1929); *Earthly Discourse* (1937).

Obituary

N Y Times p17 Ja 24 '44

WOOD, SIR HENRY JOSEPH Mar. 3, 1869—Aug. 19, 1944 British conductor and composer; won international reputation as inaugurator and conductor of the Promenade Concert series at Queen's Hall (London) and of other special concert events; introduced much new music; was a favorite in America as well as England; declined offer in 1918 to become conductor of the Boston Symphony; composed under name of "Paul Klenovsky"; author of the *The Gentle Art of Singing* (1927-28), in four volumes, and *My Life of Music* (1938); died before he could see orchestra hall to which Britons were subscribing in his honor.

Obituary

N Y Times p23 Ag 20 '44 por

WOODSON, CARTER G(ODWIN) Dec. 19, 1875— Author; editor; publisher

Address: 1538 9th St., N.W., Washington, D.C.

The rich but long neglected field of Negro history has been opened to scholars chiefly through the efforts of one man, Carter Godwin Woodson. The son of former slaves, James and Anne Eliza (Riddle) Woodson, he was born December 19, 1875 at New Canton in Buckingham County, Virginia. As one of a large and poor family, young Woodson was brought up without "the ordinary comforts of life" and was not able to attend the district school during much of its five-month term because his parents needed him to work on the farm. He was able, however, "largely by self-instruction, to master the fundamentals of common school subjects by the time he was seventeen." Ambitious for more education, Carter and his brother Robert Henry moved to Huntington, West Virginia, where they hoped to attend the Douglass High School. But Carter was forced to earn his living as a miner in the Fayette County coal fields, and was able to devote only a few months annually to his schooling.

In 1895 Carter, who was then in his twentieth year, at last entered the Douglass High School, where he won his diploma in less than

CARTER G. WOODSON

two years. After an equal period of study at Berea College (Kentucky), then famous for its acceptance of both white and colored students (Kentucky law now forbids the teaching of Negroes within twenty-five miles of a school for white pupils) he began teaching at Winona, Fayette County. Four years after his graduation from the Douglass High School, Woodson returned as its principal. There he remained from 1900 to 1903; in the latter year, after completing his college studies in the summer vacations, Woodson received his Litt.B. degree from Berea College and took a position as supervisor of schools in the Philippines. During the four years in which Woodson held that position he learned to speak Spanish fluently. His summers were still devoted to college studies, now at the University of Chicago, from which he received his B.A. degree in 1907 and his M.A. a year later. Woodson also spent a year of study in Europe and Asia, including a semester at La Sorbonne (Paris), where he did graduate work in history and learned to speak fluent French.

After further study at Chicago, Woodson went to Harvard, where he specialized in history and political science. In 1909 he accepted a position as high school teacher in Washington, D.C., giving courses in French, Spanish, English, and history. This position enabled him to do research in the Library of Congress for a doctoral dissertation, *The Disruption of Virginia*. Presented at Harvard, it won him, in 1912, his Ph.D. degree.

Woodson continued to teach his high school classes and to do research on the history of the Negro. The year 1915, in which he founded the Association for the Study of Negro Life and History, saw the publication of his *The Education of the Negro Prior to 1861*; the following year marked the Association's first publication of a scientific quarterly, the *Journal of Negro History*. Woodson was its director-editor, and—since he was the

second Negro in the United States to become a trained historian—almost its entire active staff. Somehow he found time for teaching and for writing as well: in 1918 he was appointed principal of the Armstrong High School in Washington, D.C., and had another book, *A History of Negro Migration*, published.

One year later Woodson joined the faculty of Howard University (also in Washington) as Dean of the School of Liberal Arts, a position he held until 1920, when he went in the same capacity to West Virginia State College, at Institute, West Virginia. While active as Dean at West Virginia he organized and became president of the Associated Publishers, Inc., "to make possible the publication and circulation of valuable books on the Negro not acceptable to most publishers." (The Associated Publishers' list now includes a dozen books by Woodson, and half a dozen which he edited.) Woodson also found time during this period to write two books, both published in 1922: *The History of the Negro Church* and *The Negro in Our History*, the latter probably his most important work. Having completed the reorganization of his college department, he then retired from teaching to devote himself completely to research.

Woodson was convinced that if a race has no recorded history its achievements will be forgotten and finally claimed by other groups. The race thus "becomes a negligible factor in the thought of the world and stands the danger of being exterminated." Directly and indirectly, the contributions of the Negro race were, he found, overlooked, ignored, and even suppressed by the writers of history textbooks and the teachers who use them. Race prejudice, Woodson felt, grows naturally from the idea that the Negro race is inferior. "This is merely the logical result of tradition, the inevitable outcome of thorough instruction to the effect that the Negro has never contributed anything to the progress of mankind." But, in fact, "the achievements of the Negro properly set forth will crown him as a factor in early human progress and a maker of modern civilization."

"In his native country, moreover, the Negro produced in ancient times a civilization . . . [which] influenced the [Mediterranean] cultures," and "he taught the modern world trial by jury, music by stringed instruments, the domestication of the sheep, goat, and cow, and the use of iron by which science and invention have remade the universe. Must we let this generation continue ignorant of these eloquent facts?"

So well has Woodson succeeded as a historian that "in schools and colleges, and in the world at large, no term paper, no thesis, no monograph, and no book dealing with the Negro can well be written without consulting the volumes of the *Journal of Negro History*. . . . So indispensable is this publication that practically all of the larger college and university libraries of this country subscribe to it, and even some abroad." The *Journal* has subscribers in South America, Europe, Asia, and Africa.

"The establishment of Negro History Week in 1926," Woodson reports, by "dramatizing the achievements of the race, aroused Negroes and their co-workers throughout the United States—not to play up their grievances but to demonstrate what Negroes have actually achieved in spite of their handicaps. This celebration stimulated other efforts . . . for the improvement of Negroes. The hidden truths revealed at last to such large numbers exposed the bias in textbooks, bared the prejudice of teachers, and compelled here and there an enrichment of the curricula by treating the Negro in history as we do the Hebrew, the Greek, the Latin, and the Teuton. . . . The popularizing of Negro History Week made possible . . . the launching of the *Negro History Bulletin.* . . . The public desired a monthly publication nearer the level of the average reader than the *Journal of Negro History.* The staff, therefore, brought out in October 1937 the *Negro History Bulletin,* which appears nine times a year during the school months, beginning in October and closing with June."

"At present," Woodson sums up his activities, "the Association for the Study of Negro Life and History publishes two magazines, researches in Negro history, directs studies in clubs and schools which have done much to change the attitude of communities toward the Negro, promotes the home study of the Negro by mail, produces texts on the Negro for schools and colleges, collects and preserves the valuable documents of Negro history [thousands of which it has made accessible to the public in the Library of Congress], supplies libraries with special collections of rare books on the Negro, and educates promising and enterprising young students for service in historical research and for instruction in colleges and universities." This last service Woodson regards as "perhaps the outstanding achievement of the Association. In 1915 there were not half a dozen Negroes interested in or undertaking scientific historical research. Now the number runs into the hundreds. . . . The Association . . . has actually paid for training at the best graduate schools" for more than thirteen men and women. Even those Negro historians not officially connected with the Association "have been stimulated by the general effort and acknowledge their indebtedness to this undertaking."

The most remarkable feature of the Association is that it was pretty much of a "one-man job." Starting with nothing but his own abilities and enthusiasm, Woodson conceived the original plan, persuaded the first four members to join with him in organizing it, directed and financed the struggling Association. During its first three years he deprived himself of many necessities in order to make up the Association's deficits from his salary as a teacher in the Washington public schools. He edited the publications, directed the Association, and faced the problem of building a learned society from the ground up. Lacking trained Negro historians, Woodson was forced to create a staff of research specialists. Another and very difficult problem was that of finance. The Association has from the beginning had to depend mainly on what it could get from Negroes, a

relatively poor group, and from a few white people. Six years after the group had been organized Woodson succeeded in obtaining a grant of $25,000 from the Carnegie Corporation; later, two of $25,000 and $37,500 from the Laura Spelman Memorial; and, still later, a total of $32,500 from the Rockefeller Foundation, given on the condition that the sum be matched elsewhere. But research is an expensive undertaking and, as Woodson points out, "During the last twenty-five years the Association has not had at its disposal as much as some learned societies have had for one year. The funds on hand, then, have not counted so much as the sacrifices made by the staff and those who have cooperated with the Association in the prosecution of a long-neglected work." The financial situation became even more difficult when wealthy persons and foundations withdrew all assistance as the result of an attack made by certain individuals and agencies on the Association's policy of publishing whatever facts it found, "regardless of whom it affected." The Association was forced to present its case to the Negroes of the country and to appeal to them for assistance—in the very midst of the depression. Woodson considers that undoubtedly the greatest achievement of the Association is that it is now earning its own income and paying its way.

Acting as investigator as well as director-editor, Woodson has written a number of articles for the *Journal of Negro History.* In addition he has turned out a steady stream of scientific books, all dealing with the history of the Negro. Realizing that *The Negro in Our History* is too advanced for children's use, Woodson put the essential material into a textbook for junior high school pupils, *Negro Makers of History* (1928), following it with a high school text, *The Story of the Negro Retold* (1935). His other books include *Free Negro Owners of Slaves in the United States in 1830* (1925), *African Myths* (1928), *The Negro Wage-Earner* (1930, with Lorenzo Greene), *The Mis-Education of the Negro* (1933), and *African Heroes and Heroines* (1939). He has also directed several surveys and has edited their results.

Woodson has been honored with the Spingarn Medal, awarded him by the National Association for the Advancement of Colored People for outstanding achievement in the year 1926, and by an LL.D. from Virginia State College in 1941. Although nearing the biblical threescore and ten, he is still active as manager and director of the two enterprises he founded, and in 1944 is engaged in the preparation of a six-volume *Encyclopedia Africana.* Woodson has made one concession to the advancing years—on reaching fifty-five he gave up tennis in favor of walking. A collector of rare manuscripts, he is also "devoted to the theatre," and is particularly interested in the French drama. He has never married.

References

J Negro Hist 25:422-31 O '40
Bullock, R. W. In Spite of Handicaps 1927
Who's Who in America 1944-45

WOODWARD, SIR ARTHUR SMITH

May 23, 1864—Sept. 2, 1944 Geologist who co-operated with the late Charles Dawson in the discovery and interpretation of the Piltdown Man, found in 1912 in southern England, which provided anthropologists with invaluable evidence of past humanity nearly a million years ago; was head of the Geological Department of the British Museum from 1901 to 1924.

Obituary

N Y Times p19 S 4 '44

WRIGHT, HAROLD BELL

May 4, 1872 —May 24, 1944 Author and preacher; left the pulpit to become one of America's best-known and wealthiest fiction writers; although scorned by critics, his books were bought by millions; *Shepherd of the Hills* (1907) and *The Winning of Barbara Worth* (1911) were the two most widely read.

Obituary

N Y Times p21 My 25 '44 por

YAROSLAVSKY, EMELYAN

(yär-ō-släv'skē ē-mēl-yän') 1878 Dec. (?) 1943 Born Minei Izrailevich Gubelman, Yaroslavsky was a Soviet historian, publicist, and political spokes-man; one of the early Bolsheviks, he was president of the League of Militant Atheists, member of the Central Committee of the Russian Communist Party, and deputy of the Supreme Soviet.

Obituary

N Y Times p64 D 5 '43

YON, PIETRO A(LESSANDRO)

(yôn pē-ä'trō ales-sän'drō) Aug. 8, 1886—Nov. 22, 1943 Organist; musical director at St. Patrick's Cathedral in New York since 1926; composer of works for organ, orchestra and voice; honorary organist of the S.S. Basilica of St. Peter, in the Vatican.

Obituary

N Y Times p25 N 23 '43

YOUMANS, VINCENT

(yū'mənz) Sept. 27, 1898- Composer

Address: h. Carlton House, 22 E. 47th St., New York City

Vincent Youmans, one of America's most prolific, distinguished composers of musical comedy scores during the '20's, was forced to retire in 1933 because of ill health. For ten years there were no Youmans songs, but on his return to Broadway in 1943 he still held a significant place in the musical world—his songs "Tea for Two", "Sometimes I'm Happy", "I Want To Be Happy", "Flying Down to Rio", "Carioca," and others were still being sung. Because of their lasting appeal a cavalcade of Youmans' songs and the story of his life are to be perpetuated in celluloid. Arthur Schwartz has been assigned by Warner Brothers to produce the picture, which will be titled *Sometimes I'm Happy* and will co-star Ann Sheridan and Dennis Morgan.

Born in New York City, September 27, 1898, Vincent Youmans is the son of Vincent Miller and Lucy Gibson (Millie) Youmans. His parents were of English-Irish extraction. During the '90's and early 1900's his father was as famous as a hatter as Youmans is today as a composer. From their stores on lower and upper Broadway the firm of Daniel D. and Vincent M. Youmans dictated styles in men's silk hats and derbys and in "proper shapes in Ladies' Round Hats, Bonnetts, and Walking Hats." When Vincent reached the toddling age his parents moved from New York City to a Westchester suburb. His talent for music was discovered when at the age of four he began playing chords on the piano. Music lessons followed. His mother, he says, wanted him to learn to play for social occasions, but "drew the line at making music his profession." He was educated at private schools, at Trinity School in Mamaroneck, New York, and at the preparatory school, Heathcote Hall, in Rye, New York. Interested in machinery, young Youmans then decided to study engineering at the Sheffield Scientific School of Yale University.

Several months before he was to have entered Yale, however, Youmans decided against engineering for a career in Wall Street, where-upon he secured a clerk's position in a stock brokerage house in the summer of 1916. Upon the entrance of the United States into the First World War the next year, he enlisted in the United States Navy and was assigned to an entertainment unit at the Great Lakes Training Station. In producing and composing musical shows for the Navy young Youmans discovered his talent for creating popular music, and after the Armistice he secured a job in a New York music publishing house. His most valuable experience was gained while he worked for Victor Herbert, rehearsing the singers of the famous composer's musical productions. In speaking of this association, Youmans said, "There are no treatises or instruction books on how to write an operetta or musical comedy, so I was fortunate to work with a man like Herbert. I got something in less than a year that money could not buy."

When he was twenty Youmans composed the music of "Who's Who With You," a song interpolated into the score of *Piccadilly to Broadway*, a Ray Goetz production which failed to find favor on Broadway. His first big success came a year later in *Two Little Girls in Blue*, a musical comedy starring the late Jack Donahue and the Fairbanks twins. One of his hit numbers of this production was "Oh, Me! Oh, My! Oh, You!" The lyrics were written by Ira Gershwin.

The outstanding success of Youmans' career is his score for *No, No, Nanette*, a musical comedy, which made its debut in London on March 11, 1925. London reviewers gave it a sheaf of rave notices, and it made a record run of 665 performances during its first engagements and when it was brought back in 1936 remained there for 115 performances. When the New York company of the play opened on September 16, 1925 the New York *Herald Tribune* announced that *No, No Nanette* had "scored a hit that might be described as a triumph." The hit songs, "I Want To Be Happy" and "Tea for Two," literally achieved world-wide fame when seventeen companies of the musical encircled the globe, playing not only in Europe and South America but in China, New Zealand, the Philippine Islands, and Java. It earned over two million dollars for its producer and approximately a half million for its twenty-seven-year-old composer.

His next Broadway productions, *A Night Out* (1925) and *Oh, Please* (1926), proved to be less successful for Youmans, but in 1927 he again achieved a major success with *Hit the Deck*, whose score included the popular songs "Hallelujah" and "Sometimes I'm Happy." In this musical Youmans made his debut in the producing end of the theatre. In 1928 he wrote the score for *Rainbow*, but *Great Day* (1929) saw him again acting as composer and producer. "Without a Song" was its outstanding number. In 1930 Youmans' music was heard in *Smiles*, and in 1932 he wrote the score for the musical version of *Smilin' Through*. This was presented in New York under the title *Through the Years*, but failed to win the popularity the original play had. The composer contributed numbers to one more Broadway musical, *Take a Chance* (1932), before leaving the theatre world for Hollywood in 1933. His score for *Flying Down to Rio* (1933), the film which starred Fred Astaire and Ginger Rogers [41], was considered one of the most tuneful in film musicals; "Carioca" and "Orchids in the Moonlight" were the outstanding numbers. His music was also heard in *What a Widow* (1930), the movie which introduced Gloria Swanson as a singer.

The intensity with which Youmans had been working affected his health and at the insistence of his physicians he retired to Colorado Springs for a rest cure. As soon as he was physically able he turned to the study of serious music, which, he says, had been interrupted by his success in the popular musical field. He attended the Music School of Loyola University in New Orleans, where he studied harmony, instrumentation, and the history of liturgical music.

"Off and on for twelve years" Youmans says he has been working on an opera, for which he has written both libretto and score. On his return to Broadway in 1943 he told reporters: "It almost came off two years ago through the Spanish Franco's [42] Government. Then the War came along—so that was out. But if Spain joins the Allies, I'll do it." A symphony (which he has been working on for eight years) is a conventional four-movement score. Youmans says he must put in more work on it before it can be given a public hearing, but he hopes it may be heard next season in Mexico City with himself as conductor.

After six months of preparation and with the financial backing of Doris Duke Cromwell (the tobacco heiress), Youmans presented the first of his "comeback" productions under the title *Vincent Youmans' Ballet Revue* (previously known both as *The Cuban Revue* and *The Good Neighbors*) to Baltimore audiences on January 27, 1944. The production, billed as "a new form of entertainment," was an ambitious one, representing an outlay of $200,000 or more and having a cast of 150 players and some fifty musicians. The score for the

Ascap

VINCENT YOUMANS

revue was written by Ernesto Lecuona, the Cuban composer of "Siboney" and "Andalucía," with interpolations from the music of Maurice Ravel and Rimsky-Korsakoff. The revue also included two ballets by Léonide Massine [40] (in the classic style) and three others by Eugene Van Grona in his "typical modernistic groove." There was also a group of Frank Paris Puppeteers as interpreters of the fantasy plot. During the Baltimore engagement the entire show was drastically revamped and on February 10 during a Boston showing, although Youmans was much pleased with the press reviews, he announced the closing of the production for four weeks of further revision work. After that time he said he might take the revue to Mexico City, but its ultimate destination was Broadway.

Youmans, described by Lucius Beebe [40] as "smallish, dapper, and a facile talker," is popular in Broadway and in Park Avenue circles. He was married to Anne Varley, a specialty dancer in one of his productions, on February 7, 1927. Twins, Vincent and Cecily, were born in the first year of this marriage, which ended in divorce in 1933. On October 21, 1935 Youmans was married to Mildred Boots, a *Follies* girl.

References

Cue 12:12 My 8 '43 il por
N Y Herald Tribune VI p1 Ap 18 '43
N Y Post p11 Ap 24 '43
Baker's Biographical Dictionary of Musicians 1940
Who's Who in the Theatre 1939

YOUNG, ART(HUR HENRY) Jan. 14, 1866—Dec. 29, 1943 Cartoonist and author; veteran radical and crusader for better social conditions; contributed illustrations and cartoons to the old *Life*, the *Saturday Evening Post*, *Collier's*, the *Evening Mail*, the *Daily News*, *New Masses*; was author of *Trees at Night* (1927), *On My Way* (1928), *Art*

YOUNG, ART—*Continued*

Young's Inferno (1933), and *Art Young, His Life and Times* (1939); see sketch 1940 Yearbook.

Obituary

N Y Times p15 D 31 '43 por

YOUNG, KARL Nov. 2, 1879—Nov. 17, 1943 Professor of English at Yale University since 1923; student of the medieval drama and the writings of Geoffrey Chaucer; author of *The Origin and Development of the Story of Troilus and Criseyde* (1908), *The Drama of the Medieval Church* (1933), and other scholarly books and magazine articles.

Obituary

N Y Times p23 N 18 '43

ZANDONAI, RICCARDO (dzän"dō-nä'ē rēk-kär'dō) May 28, 1883—June (?), 1944 Italian operatic composer; best known for his operas *Francesca da Rimini* (1914) and *Guilietta e Romeo* (*Romeo and Juliet,* 1922); also wrote symphonic works and chamber music.

Obituary

N Y Times p13 Je 24 '44

ZOG I, KING OF THE ALBANIANS Oct. 8, 1895-

In 1944 Zog I, who has successively been Prime Minister, President, and King of the Albanians was still waiting in London, hoping for recognition of his "émigré Government" by the United Nations. It is recognition which most commentators believe very unlikely to come, although Zog has a number of followers among Albanian exiles in London and the United States, and even some British supporters. Churchill '42 and Cordell Hull '40 have both promised that Albania shall be free—and presumably most of the Albanian guerrillas, now fighting the Nazis in cooperation with Tito's '43 Partisans, are as eager for freedom from Zog as they were from the Italians. Albania itself has been accepted by the Allies as a co-belligerent, and in November 1944 Tirana, the capital, was liberated by Albanian partisans.

Ahmed Bey Zogu was born near Burgayeti in Albania, October 8, 1895, the son of the most powerful Moslem clan chieftain in North Albania, the head of the Mati tribe. ("Ahmed Zogu" means "Ahmed of the family of Zog" —and "Zog" itself means "Bird." "Zog I, Mbreti Shkuptarvet" therefore reads literally, "Bird the First, King of the Sons of the Eagle.") Ahmed Zogu was educated at Constantinople, first at the Lycée, or school for pages, then at the Officer's Academy, for at that time Albania was still under Turkish rule. In 1912 called back to Albania to take command of his tribe, he directed the campaign against the invading Serbs along with a cousin of his own age.

Albania is a half-mythical country of patriarchal clans, only 200 square miles larger than the state of Massachusetts, and with a population one-seventh that of Greater New York City. Long ago the Illyrians, from whom the Albanians claim descent, fought against the Romans; later they succumbed to the might of the Byzantine Empire and were "pressed back into their wild mountains by the Slav wave from the north." In 1389, after the war of Kossovo, they came under the sway of the Turks, but in the fifteenth century their hero, Skanderbeg, united them and won many battles against the Turks. After his death Albania again fell under Turkish domination, but for centuries the Albanians succeeded in retaining both their identity and their tribal customs. Always their highest patriotic duty was to resist government and evade taxes. Finally the Albanian League attempted to establish autonomy, and in 1912 Turkey granted autonomy to Albania after a general uprising. Although the Greeks, Serbs, Austro-Hungarians, and Italians all had designs on Albania, on November 28 of the same year, with the support of Vienna and Rome, Albania was declared an "independent" kingdom. This move was a result of Turkey's weakness in the Balkan wars. When the independence proclamation was made in the marketplace of Valona, Ahmed Zogu was among the eighty-odd notables present.

A German prince, Wilhelm von Wied, was then selected by the Great Powers as the ruler of the new mid-Adriatic buffer state, and in March 1914 he landed at Durazzo. Soon, however, there was an Italian-financed revolt against him, and in September he returned to Germany. Ahmed Zogu, who had been commander of the national forces in the Prince's Government and one of his most ardent supporters, hurriedly returned to his northern Mati district. From there he and his tribesmen joined the Austrians, who had penetrated Albania during the early stages of the First World War. The Austrians rewarded him with the title of "Imperial and Royal Colonel" and the Order of Franz Joseph; but later, suspecting him of intending to conspire with the Bulgars to re-establish Albanian independence, they invited him to the Habsburg Court in Vienna. He accepted the invitation, and found himself interned until the end of the War.

In 1915 the secret Treaty of London had promised Southern Albania to Italy in return for Italy's shift to the Allied side. Renewed rivalries among the Great Powers caused the rejection of the Italian claim, but after the Armistice the Italians occupied the south of the country without a declaration of war. In November 1918 Ahmed Zogu returned to Albania, and in February 1920 a temporary regency council of notables was set up at Lyusna (Lushniua) in order to organize resistance to the Italians and the French, who also were in Southern Albania. Ahmed Zogu was made Minister of the Interior and commander in chief of the Albanian armed forces. The French soon withdrew from Koritza, and on August 2, 1920 Italy recognized the independence of Albania, retaining only the island of Saseno, which commands the Bay of Valona.

Even before this the Serbs had invaded Albania and had reached the Mati valley, where they destroyed Ahmed Zogu's ancestral home. At that time Ahmed Zogu had been away in the south with the men of his tribe, fighting the Italians; but his mother, Sadije, had gathered the old men and boys of the valley and with this army had held the invaders at bay until her son could return in the fall. Upon his return Ahmed Zogu earned further glory for himself in the fighting against the Serbs, and later crushed numerous tribal insurrections and secured the recognition of Albania's independence by the Great Powers. After a tug-of-war between Italy and Yugoslavia and a bitter conflict with Greece (the Greek character of Southern Albania was generally recognized), the Council of Ambassadors drew Albania's boundary lines in November 1921, leaving to Italy the island of Saseno and control of Albania's foreign policy.

By 1923 young Ahmed Zogu was Prime Minister of Albania; he resisted the land reforms which were demanded by Albanians imbued with New World ideas. When his regime seemed to be favoring Yugoslavia in its foreign policy the Italians helped the rising of the progressive Fan Noli, a Harvard graduate and head of the Albanian Orthodox Church. Ahmed Zogu fled to Yugoslavia. He raised an army on Yugoslav territory, where he was supplied with men and material to fight his way back to Tirana. When he ousted Bishop Fan Noli on Christmas Day 1924 he was assisted by those landowners who feared that Fan Noli's idea of progress would rob them of their privileges, by his own clansmen, mercenaries, enemies of Noli's regime, a detachment of Wrangel's White Russians, and Yugoslav troops. Since Fan Noli's regime had established diplomatic relations with the Soviet Union, Ahmed Zogu did not have to fear the interference of the Great Powers in his revolt. Early in 1925 Albania was declared a republic, with Ahmed Zogu as president (elected by the National Assembly for a term of seven years). In 1928 the Mati chieftain had Albania proclaimed a kingdom again and himself proclaimed King, with the title of "Zog I." His spinster sisters were elevated to the rank of princesses and posed for pictures in gold-braided Hussars' uniforms. As for Zog himself, he had ordered a $5,000 wardrobe from Paris before the day of accession, and he "strutted on his palace balcony in rose-colored breeches, gold braid shining all over his august personage."

King Zog put Albania under Mussolini's '42 thumb long before the Italian occupation of 1939. In 1926 Il Duce was pressing for extended Ethiopian interests. According to *Time* Magazine, "To divert his attention British Foreign Secretary Sir Austen Chamberlain hinted that Albania was a more convenient outlet for Italian expansion and one, incidentally, less likely to interfere with British plans." When Mussolini sent a note to Albania insisting that he become the guarantor of Albania's "independence," the British Minister at Tirana informed Zog that "London expected Albania to reach an amicable agreement with Italy without undue delay." The Treaty of Tirana was signed on November 27, 1926 after a revolt in the north that had allegedly been stirred up by the Yugoslavs.

Within a year Italy had gained control of Albania's army and foreign policy, and was beginning to get an economic stranglehold on that undeveloped country—a country without even one yard of railroad track in use, and without a university of its own. Great tracts in Albania and virtual control of Albanian

ZOG I, KING OF THE ALBANIANS

petroleum deposits went to Italy, which forced "loans" on Zog whose amortization amounted to one-third of the receipts of the Italian budget. Albanian finance was "modernized," too: after the Italians gained control of the "Albanian National Bank" Albanian gold was shipped to Rome. Under Italian supervision, roads were built in districts where they were of military rather than industrial value (in any case, Albania never had as many as a thousand automobiles); and enough war supplies were pushed across the Adriatic to equip an army of nearly 350,000, although Albania's own Army was only 12,000 strong.

Nor did Zog's domestic policies make him particularly popular with his countrymen. He was responsible for a civil code modeled on that of France, a penal code based on the Italian example, the abolishment of polygamy, the prohibition of the wearing of veils by women, and agrarian reform (which was never really enforced). But his was no constitutional monarchy: he nominated his own Cabinet, and elections were not free. There was open corruption and graft in administration. Open criticism of the King was "treason," although Zog did grant amnesty to his former political opponents, Fan Noli's followers, and eventually made peace with the Bishop himself. And there were sporadic revolts, even though the Italians made it obvious that they were prepared to occupy Albanian territory again, if necessary, in order to keep Zog on his throne. Zog, as a result, became something of a hermit, seldom daring to leave home alone, rarely receiving visitors. In 1931, when he went to Vienna for medical treatment, he barely escaped assassination; and his mother had to watch over his kitchen to see that his food was not poisoned. Little wonder that the King once asked, sadly: "What have I to offer a bride?"

Not that he made no efforts to find a wife. Long before Zog became King of Albania he had signed a marriage contract with Shefquti Bey, a powerful chief, promising to take as his bride the Bey's daughter Fatima. When Zog came to the throne, however, he did not dare

ZOG I, KING OF THE ALBANIANS—
Continued

ally himself with the landowning class or arouse the jealousy of the other beys, and so he sought a bride elsewhere. Unable to win one of royal blood, in 1936 he reportedly offered a handsome fee to any marriage broker who could find him a comely bride with an income of a million a year. And then he fell in love with a photograph—the photograph of a twenty-two-year-old half-American girl, Countess Geraldine Apponyi of Hungary, who was both a Roman Catholic and penniless. (Seventy per cent of Zog's subjects are Moslems, 20 per cent Orthodox Christians, only about 10 per cent Catholic.) The couple were married in April 1938, the late Count Ciano '40 acting as Zog's witness. There were wedding presents from Hitler '42, Mussolini, Victor Emanuel '43, Metaxas' '40 Greek Government, and Franco '42—and the marriage ceremonies were described as something out of the Arabian Nights. On April 4 of the next year a son, Skander, was born.

But the Crown Prince did not come into the world under the happiest circumstances. In the spring of 1939 the Italians had begun accusing Zog of misusing Italian money, and on April 7 Italian warships began bombarding Albanian seaports, while Italian planes flew overhead, dropping leaflets announcing that "friendly" Italian troops were arriving to take over the country and "re-establish order, peace, and justice." Queen Geraldine immediately fled in an ambulance to Greece with her four-day-old son and two of Zog's sisters. The tiny Albanian Army was mobilized, but its resistance was overcome in a day. In two days the Italians occupied all the important points in Albania, and Count Ciano arrived to form a "provisional Albanian government." Once again the democracies remained relatively calm. After Il Duce merged the Albanian and Italian crowns and abolished Zog's foreign service, the United States State Department notified the Albanian Minister to the United States that his recognition was withdrawn. The next month the League of Nations delayed taking official notice of Zog's protest at Italy's seizure of Albania until it decided whether Zog was or was not still the rightful head of the Albanian State.

In the meanwhile Zog himself had lost no time in escaping from Albania: he reached Greece a day after his wife, with 115 court followers and ten heavy cases of valuables. (At the time of his escape he reportedly added the Albanian Treasury's gold reserve to his large personal fortune, previously deposited in Swiss and English banks.) Not long before France declared war on Germany he and his young wife appeared in Versailles, where they made their home in the Château de la Maye for a time. Then, after the fall of France, Zog was admitted to England as a "private citizen."

During Zog's absence his countrymen continued fighting the Axis. By November 1944, when the Germans finally yielded Tirana, the capital, to Albanian partisans, the major portion of the country had been liberated. At this time the Premier, Enver Hoxha, said in an interview that the partisans were entirely responsible for their own liberation. Relief assistance was badly needed in his devastated country, however, he revealed, but no Allied relief agency had ever offered to help. The next task facing his Government, he announced, was the election of a constitutional assembly to decide on a permanent form of government, for Albania was being rebuilt as a democracy. (There was some internal opposition to his regime from followers of Zog, he said, as well as open admiration of communism from other quarters.) To his interviewers Hoxha then outlined a program for universal suffrage and the guaranteeing of civil rights. He declared that he favored a "strong brotherhood" of the Balkan peoples, but did not wish to see a federation until boundary disputes had been settled.

Zog has been described as a "tall man of slight figure, blue-eyed and fair." He is a Moslem. In addition to Albanian he speaks German, French, Turkish, and Serbo-Croat. He plays tennis and poker with equal enthusiasm. "Fearless and a crack shot, he is as nimble as a mountain goat . . . and a master of court decorum, with great personal charm."

References

Commonweal 28:118-20 My 27 '38
Cur Hist 50:40-2 Mr '39; 31:341-4 N '29 il por map
Lit Digest 123:14 Ja 16 '37; 125-8 F 12 '38
Liv Age 354:516-19 Ag '38
N Y Post p23 D 16 '43
Newsweek 13:19-22 Ap 17 '39 il maps
Scholastic 34:18 Ap 22 '39
Time 31:20+ My 9 '38
International Who's Who 1942
Kovacs, F. W. L. The Untamed Balkans p41-52 1941
Roucek, J. C. The Politics of the Balkans p84-98 1939
Swire, J. King Zog's Albania 1937
Who's Who in Central and East Europe 1935-36

ZU REVENTLOW, ERNST GRAF *See*
Reventlow, E., Graf zu

BIOGRAPHICAL REFERENCES CONSULTED

The publication dates listed are those of volumes in CURRENT BIOGRAPHY's reference collection.

American Catholic Who's Who 1942-43

American Medical Directory 1942

American Men of Science 1938

American Women 1939-40

America's Young Men 1938-39

Baker's Biographical Dictionary of Musicians 1940

Baseball Register 1943

Blue Book of American Aviation 1940

Burke, J. B. Genealogical and Heraldic History of the Peerage and Baronetage, the Privy Council and Knightage 1936 (Burke's Peerage)

Catholic Who's Who 1941

Chemical Who's Who 1937

Chi è? 1936

China Handbook 1937-43

Congressional Directory 1945

Dictionary of the American Hierarchy 1940

Dictionnaire National des Contemporains 1936

Directory of Medical Specialists 1942

Ewen, D. ed. Composers of Today 1936

Ewen, D. Dictators of the Baton 1943

Ewen, D. ed. Living Musicians 1940

International Motion Picture Almanac 1943-44

International Press Who's Who; New Zealand 1938

International Who's Who 1942

Japan-Manchoukuo Year Book 1940

Kunitz, S. J., and Haycraft, H. eds. Junior Book of Authors 1934

Kunitz, S. J., and Haycraft, H. eds. Twentieth Century Authors 1942

Leaders in Education 1941

Mantle, B. Contemporary American Playwrights 1938

Millett, F. B. Contemporary American Authors 1940

National Cyclopaedia of American Biography, Current Volumes A-D 1930-34

New Standard Encyclopedia of Art 1939

New York City. Museum of Modern Art Twenty Centuries of Mexican Art 1940

Religious Leaders of America 1941-42

Sobel, B. ed. Theatre Handbook 1940

Streyckmans, F. B. Today's Young Men 1940

Texian Who's Who 1937

Thompson, O. ed. International Cyclopedia of Music and Musicians 1943

United States Government Manual 1944

Variety Radio Directory 1940-41

Vodarsky-Shiraeff, A. comp. Russian Composers and Musicians 1940

Webster's Biographical Dictionary 1943

Wer ist Wer 1937

Wer ist's? 1935

Who Is Who in Music 1941

Who's Who 1944

Who's Who Among North American Authors 1936-39

Who's Who Among Physicians and Surgeons 1938

Who's Who in America 1944-45

Who's Who in American Art 1940-41

Who's Who in American Education 1941-42

Who's Who in American Jewry 1938-39

Who's Who in Australia 1938

Who's Who in Aviation 1942-43

Who's Who in Canada 1936-37

Who's Who in Central and East-Europe 1935-36

Who's Who in China 1936

Who's Who in Colored America 1941-44

Who's Who in Commerce and Industry 1944

Who's Who in Engineering 1941

Who's Who in Japan 1937

Who's Who in Latin America 1940

Who's Who in Law 1937

Who's Who in Library Service 1933 & 1943

Who's Who in Major League Baseball 1937

Who's Who in New York 1938

Who's Who in New Zealand and the Western Pacific 1932

Who's Who in Polish America 1940

Who's Who in Railroading 1940

Who's Who in the Clergy 1935-36

Who's Who in the Major Leagues 1937

Who's Who in the Nation's Capital 1938-39

Who's Who in the Theatre 1939

Who's Who of the Allied Governments 1942-43

Women of Achievement 1940

PERIODICALS AND NEWSPAPERS CONSULTED

A. L. A. Bul—American Library Association Bulletin $3; free to members. American Library Assn, 520 N Michigan Ave, Chicago

Adult Ed J—Adult Education Journal $2. American Association for Adult Education, 525 W 120th St, New York
Formerly Journal of Adult Education

Adv & Selling—Advertising and Selling $3. Robbins Pub Co, Inc, 9 E 38th St, New York

Am Arch See Arch Rec

Am Artist—American Artist $3. Watson-Guptill Publications, Inc, 330 W 42nd St, New York
Formerly Art Instruction

Am Assn Univ Women J—Journal of the American Association of University Women $1. American Assn of University Women, 1634 I St, N W, Washington, D. C.

Am Federationist—American Federationist $2. American Federation of Labor, 901 Massachusetts Ave, Washington, D.C.

Am Hist R—American Historical Review $5; free to members of the American Historical Assn. Macmillan Co, 60 Fifth Ave, New York

Am Home—American Home $1.50. American Home Magazine Corp, 55 Fifth Ave, New York

Am Mag—American Magazine $2.50. Crowell-Collier Pub Co, Springfield, Ohio

Am Mag Art See Mag Art

Am Mercury—American Mercury $3. American Mercury, Inc, 570 Lexington Ave, New York

Am Photography—American Photography $2.50. American Photographic Pub Co, 353 Newbury St, Boston

Am Scand R—American Scandinavian Review $2; free to members. American Scandinavian Foundation, 116 E 64th St, New York

Am Scholar—American Scholar $2.50. United Chapters of the Phi Beta Kappa, 12 E 44th St, New York

Am Soc R—American Sociological Review $4 (to libraries $3; to students $2.50). American Sociological Society, F. S. Chapin, ed. U.S. Department of Agriculture, Washington, D.C.

Amerasia—Amerasia $2.50. Amerasia, 225 Fifth Ave, New York

Ann Am Acad—Annals of the American Academy of Political and Social Science $5; free to members. 3457 Walnut St, Philadelphia

Apollo—Apollo 35s. Field Press, Ltd, Field House, Bream's Bldgs, Chancery Lane, London, EC 4 ($7.50. 18 E 48th St, New York)
Temporary Address: Mundesley, nr Norwich, England

Apparel Arts—Apparel Arts $3. D. A. Smart 919 N Michigan Ave, Chicago

Arch Forum—Architectural Forum $4. Time, Inc, 330 E 22nd St, Chicago

Arch Rec—Architectural Record $3. F. W. Dodge Corp, 119 W 40th St, New York
American Architect and Architecture combined with Architectural Record March 1938.

Art Bul—Art Bulletin $10. College Art Assn, Inc, 625 Madison Ave, New York

Art Digest—Art Digest $3. Art Digest, Inc, 116 E 59th St, New York

Art N—Art News $5.50. Art Foundation, Inc, 136 E 57th St, New York

Arts & Dec—Arts and Decoration (discontinued)

Asia—Asia and the Americas $4. Asia Magazine, Inc, 40 E 49th St, New York

Asiatic R—Asiatic Review £1. East and West, Ltd, 3 Victoria St, London, SW 1

Atlan—Atlantic Monthly $5. Atlantic Monthly Co, 8 Arlington St, Boston

Bet Homes & Gard—Better Homes & Gardens $1.50. Meredith Pub Co, 1714 Locust St, Des Moines, Iowa

Book-of-the-Month Club N—Book-of-the-Month Club News Free to members. Book-of-the-Month Club, Inc, 385 Madison Ave, New York

Bookm (London) See Life & Letters To-day

Books (N Y Herald Tribune) See N Y Herald Tribune Books

Books (N Y Times) See N Y Times Book R

Bul Bibliog—Bulletin of Bibliography and Dramatic Index $3. F. W. Faxon Co, 83 Francis St, Boston, Mass.

Bul Museum Modern Art See New York City. Museum of Modern Art Bul

Bul Pan Am Union See Pan Am Union Bul

Business Week—Business Week $5. McGraw-Hill Pub Co, Inc, 330 W 42nd St, New York

Calif Arts & Arch—California Arts & Architecture $3.50. Western States Publishing Co, 3305 Wilshire Blvd, Los Angeles

Canad Forum—Canadian Forum $2. Canadian Forum, Ltd, 28 Wellington St, W, Toronto 1, Canada

Canad Hist R—Canadian Historical Review $2. University of Toronto Press, Toronto

Cath Lib World—Catholic Library World $5 or membership. Catholic Library Assn, University of Scranton, Scranton, Pa.

Cath School J—Catholic School Journal $2.50. Bruce Pub Co, 540 N Milwaukee St, Milwaukee, Wis.

Cath World—Catholic World $4. Missionary Society of St Paul the Apostle, 401 W 59th St, New York

Christian Cent—Christian Century $4. Christian Century Press, 407 S Dearborn St, Chicago

Christian Sci Mon—Christian Science Monitor (Atlantic edition) $12. Christian Science Pub Society, 1 Norway St, Boston

Christian Sci Mon Mag—Christian Science Monitor Weekly Magazine Section $2.60. Christian Science Pub Society, 1 Norway St, Boston

Col Engl—College English $3. University of Chicago Press, 5750 Ellis Ave, Chicago
Formerly English Journal (college edition)

Collier's—Collier's $3. Crowell-Collier Pub Co, Springfield, Ohio

Commonweal—Commonweal $5. Commonweal Pub Co, Inc, 386 Fourth Ave, New York

Cong Digest—Congressional Digest $5. Congressional Digest, 726 Jackson Pl, Washington, D. C.

Connoisseur—Connoisseur 43s. Connoisseur, Ltd, 28 & 30 Grosvenor Gardens, London, SW 1 ($7.50. Connoisseur and International Studio, 572 Madison Ave, New York)
Published quarterly after September 1941

Contemp—Contemporary Review $9.50. British Periodicals Ltd, 46-47 Chancery Lane, London, WC 2

Coronet—Coronet $3. D. A. Smart 919 N Michigan Ave, Chicago

Cue—Cue (Manhattan edition) $3. Cue Publishing Co, Inc, 6 E 39th St, New York

Cur Hist See Cur Hist ns

Cur Hist & Forum See Cur Hist ns

Cur Hist ns—Current History $2. Events Pub Co, Inc, 5528 W Oxford St, Philadelphia
Forum and Century combined with Current History May 23, 1940 as Current History and Forum.
Current History and Forum combined with Events July 21, 1941 and the name Current History restored.

Cur Opinion—Current Opinion (discontinued)

Delin—Delineator (discontinued)

Design—Design $3. Design Pub Co, 131 E State St, Columbus, Ohio

Dram Mir—Dramatic Mirror (discontinued)

Dublin R—Dublin Review 15s. Burns Oates & Washbourne, Ltd, 28 Ashley Pl, London, SW 1

Eccl R—Ecclesiastical Review $4. American Ecclesiastical Review, 1722 Archer St, Philadelphia

Educa—Education $4. Palmer Co, 370 Atlantic Ave, Boston

El Engl R—Elementary English Review $2.50. Elementary English Review, National Council of Teachers of English, 211 W 68th St, Chicago

Engl J—English Journal $3. University of Chicago Press, 5750 Ellis Ave, Chicago
Formerly English Journal (high school edition)

Engl J (Col edition) See Col Engl

Engl J (H S ed) See Engl J

Engl R See Nat R

Esquire—Esquire $5. Esquire, Inc, 919 N Michigan Ave, Chicago

Etude—Etude $2.50. Theodore Presser Co, 1712 Chestnut St, Philadelphia

Facts on File—Facts on File $25. Person's Index, Facts on File, Inc, 516 Fifth Ave, New York

Flying—Flying $4. Ziff-Davis Publishing Co, 540 N Michigan Ave, Chicago

Foreign Affairs—Foreign Affairs $5. Council on Foreign Relations, Inc, 45 E 65th St, New York

Foreign Policy Rep—Foreign Policy Reports $5. (to libraries subscription includes Foreign Policy Bulletins and 6 headline books); $3 to F. P. A. members. Foreign Policy Assn, Inc, 22 E 38th St, New York

Fortnightly—Fortnightly $8.50. Fortnightly Review, Ltd, 13 Buckingham St, London, WC 2

Fortune—Fortune $10. Time, Inc, 330 E 22nd St, Chicago

Forum See Cur Hist ns

Free France—Free France Free. French Press & Information Service, 501 Madison Ave, New York

Good H—Good Housekeeping $3.50. Hearst Magazines, Inc, 57th St & Eighth Ave, New York

Harper—Harper's Magazine $4. Harper & Bros, 49 E 33rd St, New York

Harper's Bazaar—Harper's Bazaar $5. Hearst Magazines, Inc, 572 Madison Ave, New York

Home & F See House B

Horn Book—Horn Book $2.50. Horn Book, Inc, 264 Boylston St, Boston

House & Gard—House and Garden $4. Condé Nast Publications, Inc, Graybar Bldg, 420 Lexington Ave, New York

House B—House Beautiful combined with Home and Field $4. Hearst Magazines, Inc, 572 Madison Ave, New York

Illus Lond N—Illustrated London News £4 9s 6d. 1 New Oxford St, London, WC 1 (American edition $16. British edition $18. International News Co, 131 Varick St, New York)

Ind Woman—Independent Woman $1.50. National Federation of Business and Professional Women's Clubs, Inc, 1819 Broadway, New York

Inland Printer—Inland Printer $4. Tradepress Pub Corp, 309 W Jackson Blvd, Chicago

J Adult Ed See Adult Ed J

J Home Econ—Journal of Home Economis $2.50. American Home Economics Assn, 620 Mills Bldg, Washington, D.C.

J Negro Hist—Journal of Negro History $4. Association for the Study of Negro Life and History, 1538 Ninth St, N W, Washington, D.C.

Ladies' H J—Ladies' Home Journal $2. Curtis Pub Co, Independence Sq, Philadelphia

Liberty—Liberty $3.50. Liberty Magazine, Inc, 205 E 42nd St, New York

Library J—Library Journal $5. R. R. Bowker Co, 62 W 45th St, New York

Life—Life $4.50. Time, Inc, 330 E 22nd St, Chicago

Life & Letters To-day—Life and Letters To-day 14s. 430 Strand, London, WC 2 ($3.50 International News Co, 131 Varick St, New York)
London Mercury absorbed Bookman January 1935
Life and Letters To-day absorbed London Mercury and Bookman May 1939

Lit Digest—Literary Digest (discontinued)

Liv Age—Living Age (discontinued)

London Mercury—London Mercury and Bookman See Life & Letters To-day

London Studio (Studio)—London Studio, American edition of the Studio $6. Studio Publications, Inc, 381 Fourth Ave, New York (28s; The Studio, Ltd, 66 Chandos Pl, London, WC 2)

Look—Look $2.50 Cowles Magazines, Inc, 511 Fifth Ave, New York

Mademoiselle—Mademoiselle $3. Street & Smith Publications, Inc, 122 E 42nd St, New York

Mag Art—Magazine of Art $5; free to members. American Federation of Arts, Barr Bldg, Farragut Sq, Washington, D. C.
Formerly American Magazine of Art

Mo Labor R—Monthly Labor Review $3.50. Superintendent of Documents, Washington, D. C.

Motion Pict Classic—Motion Picture Classic (discontinued)

Movie Classic—Movie Classic (discontinued)

Musical Am—Musical America $3. Musical America Corp, 113 W 57th St, New York

Musical Courier—Musical Courier $3. Music Periodicals Corp, 119 W 57th St, New York

Musical Q—Musical Quarterly $3. G. Schirmer, Inc. 3 E 43rd St, New York

Musician—Musician $3. AMF Artists Service, Inc, 139 E 47th St, New York

N Y Dram—New York Dramatic Mirror (discontinued)

N Y Herald Tribune—New York Herald Tribune $17, including Sunday edition. New York Tribune, Inc, 230 W 41st St, New York

N Y Herald Tribune Books—New York Herald Tribune Books $1. New York Tribune, Inc, 230 W 41st St. New York

N Y Post—New York Post $10, including Saturday edition. New York Post, Inc, 75 West St. New York

N Y Sun—New York Sun $12. New York Sun, Inc, 280 Broadway, New York

N Y Times—New York Times $17, including Sunday edition. The New York Times Co, 229 W 43rd St, New York

N Y Times Book R—New York Times Book Review $2. The New York Times Co, 229 W 43rd St, New York

N Y World-Telegram—New York World-Telegram $12. New York World-Telegram Corp, 125 Barclay St, New York

Nat Educ Assn J—Journal of the National Education Association $2; free to members. National Education Assn, 1201 16th St, N W, Washington, D. C.

Nat R—National Review 36s. Rolls House, 2 Bream's Bldgs, London, EC 4
Absorbed English Review August 1937

Nation—The Nation $5. The Nation, Inc, 20 Vesey St, New York

Nation's Bus—Nation's Business $3. Chamber of Commerce of the United States, 1615 H St, N W, Washington, D. C.

Natur Hist—Natural History $4. American Museum of Natural History, 79th St and Central Park West, New York

Nature—Nature Magazine $3. American Nature Assn, 1214 16th St, N W, Washington, D. C.

New England Q—New England Quarterly $4. New England Quarterly 200 Stevens Hall, Orono, Maine

New Repub—New Republic $5. Editorial Publications, Inc, 40 E 49th St, New York

New Statesman & Nation—New Statesman and Nation—Week-end Review 32s. 6d. 10 Great Turnstile, London, WC 1

New York City. Museum of Modern Art Bul—Bulletin of the Museum of Modern Art. 10c a copy; free to members. Museum of Modern Art, 11 W 53rd St, New York

New Yorker—New Yorker $6. F-R. Pub Corp, 25 W 43rd St, New York

Newsweek—Newsweek $5. Weekly Publications, Inc, Newsweek Bldg, 152 W 42nd St, New York

19th Cent—Nineteenth Century and After $8.75. Constable & Co, Ltd, 10 & 12 Orange St, London, WC 2

Opera N—Opera News $3; free to members. Metropolitan Opera Guild, Inc, 654 Madison Ave, New York

Pan Am Union Bul—Bulletin of the Pan American Union $1.50. Pan American Union, 17th St and Constitution Ave, N W, Washington, D. C.

Parnassus—Parnassus (discontinued)

Pencil P—Pencil Points $3. Reinhold Pub Corp, 330 W 42nd St, New York

Photoplay—Photoplay $1.80. Macfadden Publications, Inc, 205 E 42nd St, New York
  Combined with Movie Mirror

Pict R—Pictorial Review (discontinued)

PM—PM $15.50, including Sunday edition. Harry C. Holden, Subscription Manager, P.O. Box 81, Times Square Station, New York

Poetry—Poetry $3. 232 E Erie St, Chicago

Pol Sci Q—Political Science Quarterly $5; free to members. Academy of Political Science, Columbia University, New York

Pop Mech—Popular Mechanics Magazine $2.50. Popular Mechanics Co, 200 E Ontario St, Chicago

Pop Sci—Popular Science Monthly $2. Popular Science Pub Co, Inc, 353 Fourth Ave, New York

Progressive Educ—Progressive Education $3. American Education Fellowship 289 Fourth Ave, New York

Prométhée—Prométhée L'Amour de l'Art (discontinued)

Pub W—Publishers' Weekly $5. R. R. Bowker Co, 62 W 45th St, New York

Quar R—Quarterly Review 31s 4d. 50 Albermarle St, London, W 1. ($6.50 International News Co, 131 Varick St, New York)

Queen's Q—Queen's Quarterly $2. Queen's University, Kingston, Canada

R of Rs—Review of Reviews (discontinued)

Read Digest—Reader's Digest $3. Reader's Digest Assn, Inc, Pleasantville, N. Y.

Ref Shelf—Reference Shelf $6 per volume of ten bound numbers, published irregularly. The H. W. Wilson Co, 950-972 University Ave, New York

Rotarian—Rotarian $1.50. Rotary International, 35 E Wacker Drive, Chicago

Royal Inst Brit Arch J—Journal of the Royal Institute of British Architects £1 16s postpaid. The Institute, 66 Portland Pl, London, W 1
  Published monthly temporarily, November 1939.

Sat Eve Post—Saturday Evening Post $3. The Curtis Pub Co, Independence Sq, Philadelphia

Sat R Lit—Saturday Review of Literature $5. Saturday Review Associates, Inc, 25 W 45th St, New York

Sch & Soc—School and Society $5; free to members of the Society for the Advancement of Education. Science Press, N Queen St and McGovern Ave, Lancaster, Pa.

Sch Arts—School Arts $4. School Arts, Printers Bldg, Worcester, Mass.

Sch R—School Review $2.50. Department of Education, University of Chicago, 5835 Kimbark Ave, Chicago

Scholastic—Scholastic (high school teacher edition) $2. (combined, or teacher edition only); school group rate (two or more subscriptions to one address) $1 for special editions. $1.30 for combined edition. Scholastic Corp, 220 E 42nd St, New York

Sci Am—Scientific American $4. Munn & Co, Inc, 24 W 40th St, New York

Sci Mo—Scientific Monthly $5. American Assn for the Advancement of Science, Smithsonian Institution Bldg, Washington, D.C.

Sci N L—Science News Letter $5. Science Service, Inc, 1719 N St, N W, Washington, D. C.

Sci ns—Science (new series) $6. Science Press, N Queen St and McGovern Ave, Lancaster, Pa.

Scrib Com—Scribner's Commentator (discontinued)

Scrib Mag—Scribner's Magazine (discontinued)

So Atlan Q—South Atlantic Quarterly $3. Duke University Press, Durham, N. C.

Spec—Spectator 30s. 99 Gower St, London, WC 1

Studio (Am edition) See London Studio

Survey—Survey Mid-monthly $3. Survey Associates, Inc, 112 E 19th St, New York

Survey G—Survey Graphic $3. Survey Associates, Inc, 112 E 19th St, New York

Theatre Arts—Theatre Arts $3.50. Theatre Arts, Inc, 130 W 56th St, New York
  Formerly Theatre Arts Monthly

Time—Time $5. Time, Inc, 330 E 22nd St, Chicago

Travel—Travel $4. Robert M. McBride & Co, Inc, 116 E 16th St, New York

U S Bur Labor—Monthly Labor R See Mo Labor R

U S Bur Labor Bul—United States Bureau of Labor Statistics. Bulletins. Free to libraries. Bureau of Labor Statistics, Washington, D. C. Purchase orders, Superintendent of Documents, Washington, D. C.

U S News—United States News $4. United States News Bldg, 22nd and M Sts, N W, Washington, D. C.

U S Office Educ Bul—United States Office of Education. Bulletins. Free to libraries. Office of Education, Washington, D. C. Purchase orders, Superintendent of Documents, Washington, D. C.

Va Q R—Virginia Quarterly Review $3. University of Virginia, Charlottesville, Va.

Variety—Variety $10. Variety, Inc, 154 W 46th St, New York

Victor Record R—Victor Record Review 60c. Victor Record Review, Camden, N. J.

Vital Speeches—Vital Speeches of the Day $3. City News Pub Co, 33 W 42nd St, New York

Vogue—Vogue (Incorporating Vanity Fair) $6. Conde Nast Publications Inc, Greenwich, Connecticut

Wilson Lib Bul—Wilson Library Bulletin $1. The H. W. Wilson Co, 950-972 University Ave, New York
  Formerly Wilson Bulletin

Woman's H C—Woman's Home Companion $1.50. Crowell-Collier Pub Co, Springfield, Ohio

Writer—The Writer $3. The Writer, Inc, 8 Arlington St, Boston

Yale R ns—Yale Review $3. 143 Elm St, New Haven, Conn.

NECROLOGY—1944

This is an index to notices of deaths which occurred between November 16, 1943 and December 31, 1944. Deaths which occurred late in 1944 are recorded in early 1945 issues of CURRENT BIOGRAPHY; references to those issues are included in this index. See 1940-1943 Yearbooks for the necrologies for those years.

Ade, George
Alonso, José Ignacio Rivero y See Rivero (y Alonso), J. I.
Alvarez Quintero, Joaquín
Armstrong, Margaret (Neilson)

Bache, Jules S(emon)
Baekeland, Leo H(endrik)
Ballantine, Stuart
Banning, Kendall See Feb 1945
Barbour, Ralph Henry
Barbour, W. Warren
Barnes, Clifford W(ebster)
Barrère, Georges
Barton, William H(enry), Jr.
Bausch, Edward
Bausch, William
Beach, Amy Marcy See Beach, Mrs. H.H.A. Feb 1945
Beach, Mrs. H(enry) H(arris) A(ubrey) See Feb 1945
Beatrice Marie Victoria Feodora, Princess of England
Beck, Jozef
Bedaux, Charles E(ugene)
Bennett, Richard
Bestor, Arthur E(ugene)
Blair, David H.
Bogert, George H. See Feb 1945
Bogulawski, Moissaye
Bono, Emilio (Giuseppe Gaspare Giovanni) de
Bosworth, Hobart (Van Zandt)
Bowes-Lyon, Claud George, 14th Earl of Strathmore and Kinghorne See Strathmore and Kinghorne, C.G.B.-L.
Boyd, James
Brand, Max, pseud. See Faust, R.
Brentano, Arthur
Brinkley, Nell
Bristow, Joseph Little
Brookhart, Smith W(ildman) See Jan 1945
Bryan, George Sands
Burke, Charles H.
Busch, Carl

Caillaux, Joseph See Jan 1945
Cannon, James, Jr., Bishop
Carrel, Alexis (biog 1940)
Carter, John Ridgely
Castelnau, Edouard de Curieres de
Castillo, Ramón S. (biog 1941)
Cattell, J(ames) McKeen
Chaminade, Cécile (Louise Stéphanie)
Châtel, Yves (-Charles)
Chen, Eugene
Christie, John Walter

Ciano, Galeazzo, Conte (biog 1940)
Clapper, Raymond (biog 1940)
Cobb, Irvin S(hrewsbury)
Colijn, Hendricus See Jan 1945
Collier, William, Sr.
Cregar, Laird See Jan 1945
Cullen, Thomas H.

Dafoe, John Wesley
Dallin, Cyrus Edwin See Jan 1945
Dashwood, Mrs. Edmée Elizabeth Monica (de la Pasture) See Delafield, E. M.
Davenport, Charles B(enedict)
Davis, Norman H(ezekiah) (biog 1940)
Davis, Robert C(ourtney)
De Bono, Emilio (Giuseppe Gaspare Giovanni) See Bono, E. G. G. G. de
De Castelnau, Edouard de Curieres See Castelnau, E. de C. de
Delafield, E(dmée) M(onica)
Deloncle, Eugene
Des Portes, Fay Allen
Dewart, William T(hompson)
Dickerson, Roy E(rnest)
Dill, Sir John G(reer) (biog 1941)
Dinchart, Alan
Ditter, William J.
Dudley, Bide
Dudley, Walter Bronson See Dudley, B.

Eastman, Joseph B(artlett) (biog 1942)
Eboué, Felix Adolphe
Eicher, Edward C(layton) (biog 1941) See Jan 1945
Ertegun, Mehmet Munir See Jan 1945

Fall, Albert B(acon) See Jan 1945
Faust, Frederick
Ferguson, James Edward
Ferrero, Gina L(ombroso)
Flesch, Karl See Jan 1945
Flexner, Jennie M(aas) See Jan 1945
Floyd, William
Fulmer, Hampton Pitts

Gibson, Charles Dana See Feb 1945
Gifford, Sanford R(obinson)
Giraudoux, Jean
Goldthwaite, Anne
Gordon, Godfrey Jervis See Gordon, J.
Gordon, Jan

Gordon, Leon
Gubelman, Minei Izrailevich See Yaroslavsky, E.
Guedalla, Philip See Feb 1945
Guggenheim, Mrs. Daniel
Guggenheim, Florence (Shloss) See Guggenheim, Mrs. D.
Guiness, Walter Edward, 1st Baron Moyne See Moyne, W. E. G., 1st Baron
Gunn, Selskar Michael
Gwathmey, James T(ayloe)

Hackett, Walter
Hammond, Graeme M.
Hanna, Edward Joseph
Harding, Nelson See Feb 1945
Harsányi, Zsolt
Hart, Lorenz (biog 1940)
Haskin, Frederic J.
Hauck, Louise Platt
Henriot, Philippe
Hicks, Clarence J(ohn) See Feb 1945
Hitchcock, Thomas
Hodza, Milan
Hoover, Mrs. Herbert
Hoover, Lou Henry See Hoover, Mrs. H.
Horwood, Sir William T(homas) F(rancis)
Hull, John Adley
Hutchison, Miller Reese

Janson, Paul Emile
Jastrow, Joseph
Johnson, Douglas Wilson
Johnson, Paul B(urney)
Johnson, Philip G(ustav)
Jordana (y Souza), Francisco Gómez (biog 1944)

Kandinsky, Wassily See Feb 1945
Kelley, Edgar Stillman See Jan 1945
Kellogg, John Harvey
Kimball, James Henry
Knox, (William) Frank(lin) (biog 1940)
Koch, Frederick H(enry)
Koslowski, Leon

Landes, Bertha K(night)
Landis, Kenesaw Mountain (biog 1944) See Jan 1945
Langdon, Harry See Feb 1945
Leacock, Stephen (Butler)
Leary, John Joseph, Jr.

Lee, Blair See Feb 1945
Leigh-Mallory, Sir Trafford L(eigh) (biog 1944) See Mar 1945
Lewis, Lawrence
Lhevinne, Josef See Jan 1945
Lichtenberg, Bernard
Lincoln, Joseph C(rosby)
Linton, Frank B(enton) A(shley)
Lloyd, James T(ighlman)
Luhring, Oscar Raymond
Lutyens, Sir Edwin L(andseer) (biog 1942)
Lutz, Frank E(ugene)

MacCallum, William George
McGroarty, John Steven
Machado, Bernardino (Luiz)
McIntyre, Marvin H(unter)
McManamy, Frank
McMurtrie, Douglas C(rawford) (biog 1944)
McNair, Lesley J(ames) (biog 1942)
McNary, Charles L(inza) (biog 1940)
McPherson, Aimee Semple
Macrae, John
Maglione, Luigi, Cardinal
Maillol, Aristide (Joseph Bonaventure) (biog 1942)
Manson, John T(homas)
Mapes, Victor
Maria Theresa, Archduchess of Austria
Marquis, Albert Nelson
May, Charles H(enry)
Michael, Moina
Midgley, Thomas, Jr.
Miller, Benjamin Meek
Moffatt, James, Rev.
Molloy, Daniel M(urrah)
Mondriaan, Piet(er Cornelis)
Mordkin, Mikhail
Morris, Dave Hennen
Moses, George Higgins See Feb 1945
Moyne, Walter Edward Guinness, 1st Baron
Munch, Edvard (biog 1940)
Munk, Kaj

Norris, George W(illiam)

O'Connell, William (Henry), Cardinal (biog 1941)
O'Leary, James A.
Otero, Miguel Antonio

Paléologue (Georges) Maurice See Jan 1945
Palmer, John Leslie

Parker, Louis N(apoleon)
Peabody, Endicott, Rev. (biog 1940) See Jan 1945
Peroni, Carlo
Poiret, Paul
Potter, Beatrix
Poulton, Sir Edward Bagnall
Pucheu, Pierre

Quezon, Manuel L(uis) (biog 1941)
Quiller-Couch, Sir Arthur Thomas
Quintero, Joaquín (Alvarez) See Alvarez Quintero, J.

Ramm, Fredrik
Rand, James Henry, Sr.
Rank, Joseph
Ray, Charles
Reed, James A.
Renault, Louis
Reventlow, Ernst, Graf zu
Rivero (y Alonso), José Ignacio
Riza Shah Pahlavi
Roberts, Sir Charles G(eorge) D(ouglas)
Robinson, William Heath
Rolland, Romain See Feb 1945
Rommel, Erwin (biog 1942)
Roosevelt, Theodore, Jr.

Sachs, Bernard
Sanders, Jared Young
Schulthess, Edmund
Schulz, Leo
Sears, William Joseph, Sr.
Seitz, George B.
Selwyn, Edgar
Selznick, Myron
Sergius, Metropolitan
Seymour, Harriet Ayer
Simms, Ruth Hanna McCormick See Feb 1945
Singer, Israel J(oshua)
Smetona, Antanas
Smith, Alfred E(manuel) (biog 1944)
Smith, E(llison) Durant See Jan 1945
Smyth, Dame Ethel Mary
Steagall, Henry Bascom
Steele, Frederick Dorr
Stefan, Paul
Stephens, William D(ennison)
Stimson, Frederic Jesup
Stokes I(saac) N(ewton) Phelps See Feb 1945
Strathmore and Kinghorne, Claud George Bowes-Lyon, 14th Earl of
Straus, Percy Selden
Svinhufvud, Pehr Evind

Tarbell, Ida M(inerva)
Temple, William, Archbishop of Canterbury (biog 1942)
Tempski, Armine von
Thomason, John William, Jr.
Thompson, William Hale
Tietjens, Eunice
Treanor, Tom
Tyler, Alice S(arah)

Ullstein, Hermann
Underwood, Bert E(lias)

Vanderbilt, William K(issam)
Van Loon, Hendrik Willem
Van Nuys, Frederick
Vatutin, Nikolai F(edorovich) (biog 1944)
Velez, Lupe See Feb 1945
Vermilye, William Moorhead
Vienot, Pierre
Von Tempski, Armine See Tempski, Armine von

Waite, Henry Matson
Wakasugi, Kaname
Waller, Fats (biog 1942)
Waller, Thomas Wright See Waller, F.
Wang Ching-wei (biog 1940) See Jan 1945
Waterlow, Sir Sydney P(hilip) See Jan 1945
Weaver, Walter Reed
Werntz, Carl N.
Wheat, William Howard
White, Wilbert Webster, Rev.
White, William Allen (biog 1940)
Wiley, William Foust
Willkie, Wendell L(ewis) (biog 1940)
Wingate, Orde Charles
Wood, Charles Scott Erskine
Wood, Sir Henry Joseph
Woodward, Sir Arthur Smith
Wright, Harold Bell

Yaroslavsky, Emelyan
Yeats-Brown, Francis See Feb 1945
Yon, Pietro A(lessandro)
Young, Art(hur Henry) (biog 1940)
Young, Karl

Zandonai, Riccardo
Zu Reventlow, Ernst, Graf See Reventlow, E., Graf zu

CLASSIFICATION BY PROFESSION—1944

Architecture

Kiesler, Frederick J(ohn)
Lutyens, Sir Edwin L(andseer)
    obit (biog 1942)

Art

Albright, Ivan Le Lorraine
Armstrong, Margaret (Neilson)
    obit
Bache, Jules S(emon) obit
Baker, George
Beaton, Cecil (Walter Hardy)
Bonney, (Mabel) Thérèse
Brinkley, Nell obit
Caniff, Milton A(rthur)
Craven, Thomas
Evergood, Philip (Howard Francis Dixon)
Goldthwaite, Anne obit
Gordon, Jan obit
Gordon, Leon obit
Kiesler, Frederick J(ohn)
Kirby, Rollin
Linton, Frank B(enton) A(shley)
    obit
Losch, Tilly
McMurtrie, Douglas C(rawford)
    biog and obit
Maillol, Aristide (Joseph Bonaventure) obit (biog 1942)
Mondriaan, Piet(er Cornelis)
    obit
Munch, Edvard obit (biog 1940)
Peirce, Waldo
Potter, Beatrix obit
Robinson, William Heath obit
St. George, Thomas R(ichard)
Steele, Frederic Dorr obit
Steig, William
Thomason, John William, Jr.
    obit
Wellman, Frederick Creighton
Werntz, Carl N. obit
Young, Art(hur Henry) obit
    (biog 1940)

Aviation

Anderson, Frederick L(ewis)
Bates, H(erbert) E(rnest)
Candee, Robert C(hapin)
Coningham, Sir Arthur
Giles, Barney McKinney
Leigh-Mallory, Sir Trafford
    L(eigh)
Mitscher, Marc A(ndrew)
Weaver, Walter Reed obit

Business

Bache, Jules S(emon) obit
Bausch, Edward obit
Bausch, William obit

Brentano, Arthur obit
Bryan, George Sands obit
Cattell, J(ames) McKeen obit
Cooper, Kent
Engel, Carl obit
Farley, James A(loysius)
Griffis, Stanton
Gunn, Selskar Michael obit
Hannagan, Steve
Hickey, Margaret A.
Holmes, (Elias) Burton
Hopkins, Ernest Martin
Landon, Alf(red Mossman)
Lichtenberg, Bernard obit
McMurtrie, Douglas C(rawford)
    biog and obit
Macrae, John obit
Manson, John T(homas) obit
Marquis, Albert Nelson obit
Morris, Dave Hennen obit
Otero, Miguel Antonio obit
Paasikivi, Juho Kusti
Poiret, Paul obit
Rand, James Henry, Sr. obit
Roosevelt, Theodore, Jr. obit
Smart, David A.
Smith, Alfred E(manuel) biog
    and obit
Straus, Percy Selden obit
Underwood, Bert E(lias) obit
Wallace, DeWitt
Whalen, Grover A(loysius)

Dance

Draper, Paul
Graham, Martha
Losch, Tilly
Mordkin, Mikhail obit
Primus, Pearl

Diplomacy

Cadogan, Sir Alexander
    (George Montagu)
Carter, John Ridgely obit
Des Portes, Fay Allen obit
Hoppenot, Henri Etienne
Hurley, Patrick J(ay)
McGeachy, Mary (Agnes)
    Craig
Machado, Bernardino (Luiz)
    obit
Morris, Dave Hennen obit
Owen, Ruth Bryan
Palmer, John Leslie obit
Shang Chen
Stimson, Frederic Jesup obit
Wakasugi, Kaname obit

Education

Agar, Herbert (Sebastian)
Bestor, Arthur E(ugene) obit

Butler, Richard Austen
Cattell, J(ames) McKeen obit
Coffin, Henry Sloane
Croce, Benedetto
Dewey, John
Hastie, William H(enry)
Hopkins, Ernest Martin
Jastrow, Joseph obit
Kiesler, Frederick J(ohn)
Kingdon, Frank
Koch, Frederick H(enry) obit
Koslowski, Leon obit
Leacock, Stephen (Butler) obit
Lewis, C(live) S(taples)
Locke, Alain (Le Roy)
Lutz, Frank E(ugene) obit
Menthon, François de
Newcomer, Mabel
Odell, George C(linton) D(ensmore)
Ogden, C(harles) K(ay)
Petry, Lucile
Poulton, Sir Edward Bagnall
    obit
Quiller-Couch, Sir Arthur
    Thomas obit
Salter, Sir (James) Arthur
Shotwell, James T(homson)
Tyler, Alice S(arah) obit
Wecter, Dixon
Wellman, Frederick Creighton
Werntz, Carl N. obit
Wesley, Charles H(arris)
Woodson, Carter G(odwin)
Young, Karl obit

Finance

Carter, John Ridgely obit
Catto, Thomas Sivewright Catto,
    1st Baron
Griffis, Stanton
McKittrick, Thomas H(arrington)
Schacht, Hjalmar (Horace
    Greeley)

Government— International

Acland, Sir Richard (Thomas
    Dyke)
Beatrice Marie Victoria Feodora, Princess of England obit
Beck, Jozef obit
Björnsson, Sveinn
Bono, Emilio (Giuseppe Gaspare Giovanni) de obit
Bonomi, Ivanoe
Butler, Richard Austen
Cadogan, Sir Alexander
    (George Montagu)
Castelnau, Edouard de Curieres
    de obit

Castillo, Ramón S. obit (biog 1941)
Catto, Thomas Sivewright Catto, 1st Baron
Châtel, Yves (-Charles) obit
Chen, Eugene obit
Ciano, Galeazzo, Conte obit (biog 1940)
Davis, Norman H(ezekiah) obit
Dill, Sir John G(reer) obit (biog 1941)
Eboué, Felix Adolphe obit
Elizabeth, Princess of Great Britain
Grau San Martín, Ramón
Henriot, Philippe obit
Hodza, Milan obit
Horwood, Sir William T(homas) F(rancis) obit
Hume, Edgar Erskine
Janson, Paul Emile obit
Jordana (y Souza), Francisco Gómez biog and obit
Juliana, Crown Princess of the Netherlands
Koslowski, Leon obit
Law, Richard K(idston)
Leopold III, King of the Belgians
Lloyd George of Dwyfor, David Lloyd George, 1st Earl
Machado, Bernardino (Luiz) obit
Masaryk, Jan (Garrigue)
Michael V, King of Rumania
Mikolajczyk, Stanislaw
Moyne, Walter Edward Guinness, 1st Baron obit
Osmeña, Sergio
Paasikivi, Juho Kusti
Papandreou, George (Andreas)
Perón, Juan (Domingo)
Pucheu, Pierre obit
Quezon, Manuel L(uis) obit (biog 1941)
Riza Shah Pahlavi obit
Salter, Sir (James) Arthur
Schulthess, Edmund obit
Smetona, Antanas obit
Sun Fo
Svinhufvud, Pehr Evind obit
Vienot, Pierre obit
Vishinsky, Andrei Y(anuarievich)
Wakasugi, Kename obit
Windsor, Edward, Duke of
Yaroslavsky, Emelyan obit
Zog I, King of the Albanians

Government— United States

Austin, Warren R(obinson)
Barbour, W. Warren obit
Blair, David H. obit
Bristow, Joseph Little obit
Burke, Charles H. obit
Clayton, William L(ockhart)
Cullen, Thomas H. obit
Davis, Norman H(ezekiah) obit (biog 1940)
Des Portes, Fay Allen obit
Dewey, Thomas E(dmund) 1940, 1944

Dickerson, Roy E(rnest) obit
Ditter, J. William obit
Eastman, Joseph B(artlett) obit (biog 1942)
Fulmer, Hampton Pitts obit
Giegengack, A(ugustus) E(dward)
Griffis, Stanton
Guffey, Joseph F.
Hastie, William H(enry)
Hatch, Carl A(twood)
Hickey, Margaret A.
Hines, Frank T(homas)
Hurley, Patrick J(ay)
Johnson, Paul B(urney) obit
Knox, (William) Frank(lin) obit (biog 1940)
Krug, J(ulius) A(lbert)
La Follette, Robert M(arion, Jr.)
Landes, Bertha K(night) obit
Lewis, Lawrence obit
Lilienthal, David E(li)
Lloyd, James T(ighlman) obit
Luhring, Oscar Raymond obit
McGroarty, John Steven obit
McManamy, Frank obit
McNary, Charles L(inza) obit (biog 1940)
Maverick, Maury
Mead, James M(ichael)
Miller, Benjamin Meek obit
Norris, George W(illiam) obit
Norton, Mary T(eresa Hopkins)
O'Leary, James A. obit
Otera, Miguel Antonio obit
Petry, Lucile
Rankin, John E(lliott)
Reed, James A. obit
Roosevelt, Theodore, Jr. obit
Ross, Malcolm
Saltonstall, Leverett
Sanders, Jared Young obit
Sears, William Joseph, Sr. obit
Smith, Alfred E(manuel) biog and obit
Steagall, Henry Bascom obit
Stephens, William D(ennison) obit
Stimson, Frederic Jesup obit
Straus, Nathan
Thompson, William Hale obit
Van Nuys, Frederick obit
Vermilye, William Moorhead obit
Waite, Henry Matson obit
Warren, Earl
Wheat, William Howard obit
White, Harry D(exter)

Industry

Avery, Sewell (Lee)
Baekeland, Leo H(endrik) obit
Bedaux, Charles E(ugene) obit
Clayton, William L(ockhart)
Dow, Willard H(enry)
Firestone, Harvey S(amuel), Jr.
Ford, Henry
Gaylord, Robert (March)
Girdler, Tom M(ercer)
Jack, William S(aunders)

Johnson, Philip G(ustav) obit
Kellogg, John Harvey obit
Manson, John T(homas) obit
Noble, Edward J(ohn)
Pucheu, Pierre obit
Rank, Joseph obit
Renault, Louis obit
Straus, Nathan
Ullstein, Hermann obit
Vanderbilt, William K(issam) obit
Vermilye, William Moorhead obit

Journalism

Agar, Herbert (Sebastian)
Beatty, Bessie
Bonney, (Mabel) Thérèse
Chen, Eugene obit
Clapper, Raymond obit (biog 1940)
Close, Upton
Cobb, Irvin S(hrewsbury) obit
Cooper, Kent
Creel, George (Edward)
Dafoe, John Wesley obit
Daniell, (Francis) Raymond
Daniels, Josephus
Davenport, Marcia
Davenport, Russell W(heeler)
De Luce, Daniel
Dewart, William T(hompson) obit
Dudley, Bide obit
Fairfax, Beatrice
Faust, Frederick obit
Floyd, William obit
Fowler, Gene
Harsányi, Zsolt obit
Harsch, Joseph C(lose)
Haskin, Frederic J. obit
Heiden, Konrad
Hersey, John (Richard)
Kennedy, John B(right)
Kingdon, Frank
Knox, (William) Frank(lin) obit (biog 1940)
Kronenberger, Louis (Jr.)
Leary, John Joseph, Jr. obit
Lyons, Eugene
Mapes, Victor obit
Pacciardi, Randolfo
Pribichevich, Stoyan
Ramm, Fredrik obit
Reventlow, Ernst, Graf zu obit
Rivero (y Alonso), José Ignacio obit
Schultz, Sigrid (Lillian)
Sergio, Lisa
Sherrod, Robert (Lee)
Smedley, Agnes
Smith, Lillian (Eugenia)
Smyth, Dame Ethel Mary obit
Stefan, Paul obit
Stuart, Kenneth
Sulzberger, C(yrus) L(eo, 2d)
Swope, Herbert Bayard
Tarbell, Ida M(inerva) obit
Tobin, Richard L(ardner)
Treanor, Tom obit
Underwood, Bert E(lias) obit

Walker, Stanley
White, William Allen obit (biog 1940)
Wiley, William Foust obit
Woodson, Carter G(odwin)
Yaroslavsky, Emelyan obit

Labor

Acland, Sir Richard (Thomas Dyke)
Browder, Earl (Russell)
Deutsch, Julius
Hanna, Edward Joseph obit
Leary, John Joseph, Jr. obit
Norton, Mary T(eresa Hopkins)
Ross, Malcolm
Thomas, Norman (Mattoon)

Law

Austin, Warren R(obinson)
Dulles, John Foster
Hannegan, Robert E(mmet)
Hastie, William H(enry)
Hatch, Carl A(twood)
Hudson, Manley O(ttmer)
Hull, John Adley obit
Hurley, Patrick J(ay)
Landis, Kenesaw Mountain
Langner, Lawrence
Lilienthal, David E(li)
Luhring, Oscar Raymond obit
McGroarty, John Steven obit
Maverick, Maury
Menthon, François de
Miller, Benjamin Meek obit
Morris, Dave Hennen obit
O'Connor, Basil
Orlando, Vittorio Emanuele
Scheiberling, Edward N(icholas)
Schulthess, Edmund obit
Vishinsky, Andrei Y(anuarievich)
Warren, Earl
Willkie, Wendell L(ewis) obit
Wood, Charles Erskine Scott obit

Literature

Ade, George obit
Agar, Herbert (Sebastian)
Alvarez Quintero, Joaquín obit
Armstrong, Margaret (Neilson) obit
Barbour, Ralph Henry obit
Bates, H(erbert) E(rnest)
Beaton, Cecil (Walter Hardy)
Berlin, Ellin (Mackay)
Bowen, Catherine (Shober) Drinker
Boyd, James obit
Bromfield, Louis
Bryan, George Sands obit
Close, Upton
Cobb, Irvin S(hrewsbury) obit
Craven, Thomas
Croce, Benedetto
Dafoe, John Wesley obit

Davenport, Marcia
DeJong, David C(ornel)
Delafield, E(dmée) M(onica) obit
Dewey, John
Faust, Frederick obit
Ferrero, Gina L(ombroso) obit
Floyd, William obit
Forbes, Kathryn
Fowler, Gene
Gardner, Erle Stanley
Giraudoux, Jean obit
Gordon, Jan obit
Halsey, Margaret (Frances)
Harsányi, Zsolt obit
Hauck, Louise Platt obit
Hersey, John (Richard)
Hersholt, Jean
Holt, Rackham
Jackson, Charles (Reginald)
Janeway, Elizabeth (Hall)
Kimbrough, Emily
Kossak (-Szczucka), Zofia
Kronenberger, Louis (Jr.)
Leacock, Stephen (Butler) obit
Lewis, C(live) S(taples)
Lincoln, Joseph C(rosby) obit
Locke, Alain (Le Roy)
Mapes, Victor obit
Moffatt, James, Rev. obit
Munk, Kaj obit
Nin, Anaïs
Nock, Albert Jay
Ogden, C(harles) K(ay)
O'Hara, Mary
Owen, Ruth Bryan
Palmer, John Leslie obit
Peirce, Waldo
Pennell, Joseph Stanley
Potter, Beatrix obit
Quiller-Couch, Sir Arthur Thomas obit
Roberts, Sir Charles G(eorge) D(ouglas) obit
Roosevelt, Theodore, Jr. obit
Ross, Malcolm
Rosten, Norman
St. George, Thomas R(ichard)
Santayana, George
Shapiro, Karl (Jay)
Shaw, (George) Bernard
Singer, Israel J(oshua) obit
Smith, Lillian (Eugenia)
Smyth, Dame Ethel Mary obit
Stefan, Paul obit
Stimson, Frederic Jesup obit
Swarthout, Gladys
Tarbell, Ida M(inerva) obit
Tempski, Armine von obit
Thomason, John William, Jr. obit
Tietjens, Eunice obit
Van Druten, John (William)
Van Loon, Hendrik Willem obit
Walker, Stanley
Wasilewska, Wanda
Wellman, Frederick Creighton
White, William Allen obit (biog 1940)
Wood, Charles Erskine Scott obit
Wright, Harold Bell obit

Young, Art(hur Henry) obit (biog 1940)
Young, Karl obit

Medicine

Carrel, Alexis obit (biog 1940)
DeVoe, Ralph G(odwin)
Drew, Charles R(ichard)
Ferrero, Gina L(ombroso) obit
Fleming, Sir Alexander
Florey, Sir Howard W(alter)
Gifford, Sanford R(obinson) obit
Grau San Martín, Ramón
Gwathmey, James T(ayloe) obit
Hammond, Graeme M. obit
Horder, Thomas J(eeves), 1st Baron
Hume, Edgar Erskine
Kellogg, John Harvey obit
Kirk, Norman T(homas)
MacCallum, William George obit
May, Charles H(enry) obit
Sachs, Bernard obit
Schick, Béla
Wellman, Frederick Creighton

Military

Anderson, Frederick L(ewis)
Bagramian, Ivan C(hristoforovich)
Bates, H(erbert) E(rnest)
Bono, Emilio (Giuseppe Gaspare Giovanni) de obit
Candee, Robert C(hapin)
Castelnau, Edouard de Curieres de obit
Chernyakhovsky, Ivan D(anilovich)
Coningham, Sir Arthur
Craig, Malin
Crerar, H(enry) D(uncan) G(raham)
Dempsey, Miles Christopher
DeVoe, Ralph G(odwin)
Dill, Sir John G(reer) obit (biog 1941)
Giles, Barney McKinney
Hines, Frank T(homas)
Hitchcock, Thomas obit
Hull, John Adley obit
Hume, Edgar Erskine
Hurley, Patrick J(ay)
Jordana (y Souza), Francisco Gómez biog and obit
Kirk, Norman T(homas)
Koenig, Joseph-Pierre
Laycock, R(obert) E(dward)
Leclerc, Jacques-Philippe
Lee, John Clifford Hodges
Leese, Sir Oliver (William Hargreaves)
Leigh-Mallory, Sir Trafford L(eigh)
LeMay, Curtis E(merson)
Lentaigne, Walter D(avid) A(lexander)
McNair, Lesley J(ames) obit (biog 1942)

McNarney, Joseph T(aggart)
Malinovsky, Rodion Y(akovlevich)
Merrill, Frank (Dow)
Perón, Juan (Domingo)
Rokossovsky, Konstantin
Rommel, Erwin obit (biog 1942)
Roosevelt, Theodore, Jr. obit
St. George, Thomas R(ichard)
Shang Chen
Smith, Walter Bedell
Stuart, Kenneth
Urquhart, Sir Robert E(lliott)
Vatutin, Nikolai F(edorovich) biog and obit
Weaver, Walter Reed obit
Wingate, Orde Charles obit

Motion Pictures

Armstrong, Louis
Bennett, Richard obit
Bosworth, Hobart (Van Zandt) obit
Bracken, Eddie
Chodorov, Edward
Coburn, Charles
Collier, William, Sr. obit
De Havilland, Olivia
Dinehart, Alan obit
Douglas, Helen (Mary) Gahagan
D'Usseau, Arnaud
Faust, Frederick obit
Fontaine, Joan
Fowler, Gene
Gish, Dorothy
Gish, Lillian
Goldwyn, Samuel
Gow, James (Ellis)
Griffis, Stanton
Hammerstein, Oscar, 2d
Hannagan, Steve
Harrison, Joan (Mary)
Hersholt, Jean
Horne, Lena
Jones, Jennifer
Lee, Canada
Losch, Tilly
Martin, Mary
Moore, Grace
Muni, Paul
Nugent, Elliott
Ray, Charles obit
Seitz, George B. obit
Selwyn, Edgar obit
Selznick, Myron obit
Shaw, (George) Bernard
Smith, (Sir) C(harles) Aubrey
Sullavan, Margaret
Swarthout, Gladys
Van Druten, John (William)

Music

Adler, Larry
Antoine, Josephine
Armstrong, Louis
Baccaloni, Salvatore
Barber, Samuel
Barrère, Georges obit
Bernstein, Leonard

Boguslawski, Moissaye obit
Busch, Carl obit
Chaminade, Cécile (Louise Stéphanie) obit
Condon, Eddie
Damrosch, Walter (Johannes)
Davenport, Marcia
Douglas, Helen (Mary) Gahagan
Drake, Alfred
Dyer-Bennet, Richard
Engel, Carl obit
Hammerstein, Oscar, 2d
Hart, Lorenz obit (biog 1940)
Heifetz, Jascha
Hildegarde
Holm, Celeste
Horne, Lena
Kreisler, Fritz
Kurenko, Maria
Lecuona, Ernesto
Martin, Mary
Martinů, Bohuslav
Milanov, Zinka
Moore, Grace
Munn, Frank
O'Hara, Mary
Pelletier, Wilfred
Peroni, Carlo obit
Pons, Lily
Russell, Pee Wee
Sachs, Curt
Schultz, Leo obit
Smyth, Dame Ethel Mary obit
Spalding, Albert
Stefan, Paul obit
Straus, Oskar
Strauss, Richard
Swarthout, Gladys
Waller, Fats obit (biog 1942)
White, Josh
Wood, Sir Henry Joseph obit
Yon, Pietro A(lessandro) obit
Youmans, Vincent
Zandonai, Riccardo obit

Naval

Dauser, Sue S(ophia)
Gibbs, William Francis
Kinkaid, Thomas C(assin)
Kirk, Alan Goodrich
Knox, (William) Frank(lin) obit (biog 1940)
Mitscher, Marc A(ndrew)
Nelles, Percy Walker
Ramsay, Sir Bertram (Home)
Spruance, Raymond Ames
Thomason, John William, Jr. obit
Turner, R(ichmond) Kelly
Vian, Sir Philip (Louis)

Politics

Acland, Sir Richard (Thomas Dyke)
Beck, Jozef obit
Bedaux, Charles E(ugene) obit
Björnsson, Sveinn
Bono, Emilio (Giuseppe Gaspare Giovanni) de obit

Bonomi, Ivanoe
Bose, Subhas Chandra
Bristow, Joseph Little obit
Browder, Earl (Russell)
Brownell, Herbert, Jr.
Burke, Charles H. obit
Castelnau, Edouard de Curieres de obit
Castillo, Ramón S. obit (biog 1941)
Châtel, Yves (-Charles) obit
Chen, Eugene obit
Ciano, Galeazzo, Conte obit (biog 1940)
Cot, Pierre
Croce, Benedetto
Cullen, Thomas H. obit
Deloncle, Eugene obit
Deutsch, Julius
Dewey, Thomas E(dmund) 1940, 1944
Douglas, Helen (Mary) Gahagan
Farley, James A(loysius)
Ferguson, James Edward obit
Fulmer, Hampton Pitts obit
Grau San Martín, Ramón
Guffey, Joseph F.
Hannegan, Robert E(mmet)
Hatch, Carl A(twood)
Henriot, Philippe obit
Hodza, Milan obit
Janson, Paul Emile obit
Jordana (y Souza), Francisco Gómez biog and obit
Knox, (William) Frank(lin) obit (biog 1940)
Koslowski, Leon obit
La Follette, Robert M(arion, Jr.)
Landon, Alf(red Mossman)
Law, Richard K(idston)
Lloyd, James T(ighlman) obit
Lloyd George of Dwyfor, David Lloyd George, 1st Earl
Luhring, Oscar Raymond obit
McGroarty, John Steven obit
Machado, Bernardino (Luiz) obit
Masaryk, Jan (Garrigue)
Maverick, Maury
Mead, James M(ichael)
Menthon, François de
Mikolajczyk, Stanislaw
Moyne, Walter Edward Guinness, 1st Baron obit
Norris, George W(illiam) obit
Norton, Mary T(eresa Hopkins)
O'Leary, James A. obit
Orlando, Vittorio Emanuele
Osmeña, Sergio
Otero, Miguel Antonio obit
Paasikivi, Juho Kusti
Pacciardi, Randolfo
Papandreou, George (Andreas)
Perón, Juan (Domingo)
Pucheu, Pierre obit
Quezon, Manuel L(uis) obit (biog 1941)
Rankin, John E(lliott)
Reed, James A. obit
Riza Shah Pahlavi obit
Roosevelt, Theodore, Jr. obit

Salter, Sir (James) Arthur
Saltonstall, Leverett
Sanders, Jared Young   obit
Schacht, Hjalmar (Horace Greeley)
Schulthess, Edmund   obit
Sears, William Joseph, Sr.   obit
Smetona, Antanas   obit
Smith, Alfred E(manuel)   biog and obit
Sun Fo
Sun Yat-sen, Mme.
Svinhufvud, Pehr Evind   obit
Thomas, Norman (Mattoon)
Thompson, William Hale   obit
Van Nuys, Frederick   obit
Vienot, Pierre   obit
Vishinsky, Andrei Y(anuarievich)
Walker, Stanley
Wasilewska, Wanda
Willkie, Wendell L(ewis)   obit (biog 1940)
Yaroslavsky, Emelyan   obit

Radio

Antoine, Josephine
Beatty, Bessie
Carrington, Elaine Sterne
Close, Upton
Damrosch, Walter (Johannes)
Drake, Alfred
Dudley, Bide   obit
Dunninger, Joseph
Ferrer, José
Gardner, Erle Stanley
Harsch, Joseph C(lose)
Hersholt, Jean
Hildegarde
Jackson, Charles (Reginald)
Kennedy, John B(right)
Kingdon, Frank
Kurenko, Maria
Lee, Canada
Munn, Frank
Noble, Edward J(ohn)
Sergio, Lisa
Straus, Nathan
Swarthout, Gladys
Von Zell, Harry
White, Josh
Wilson, Don(ald Harlow)

Religion

Barnes, Clifford W(ebster)   obit
Cannon, James, Jr., Bishop   obit
Coffin, Henry Sloane
Hanna, Edward Joseph   obit
Kingdon, Frank
McPherson, Aimee Semple   obit
Maglione, Luigi, Cardinal   obit
Manson, John T(homas)   obit
Moffatt, James, Rev.   obit
Munk, Kaj   obit
O'Connell, William (Henry), Cardinal   obit (biog 1941)
Oxnam, G(arfield) Bromley, Bishop
Sergius, Metropolitan   obit

Temple, William, Archbishop of Canterbury   obit (biog 1942)
White, Wilbert Webster, Rev.   obit

Science

Baekeland, Leo H(endrik)   obit
Barton, William H(enry), Jr.   obit
Carrel, Alexis   obit (biog 1940)
Cattell, J(ames) McKeen   obit
Davenport, Charles B(enedict)   obit
Dickerson, Roy E(rnest)   obit
Dow, Willard H(enry)
Dunninger, Joseph
Fleming, Sir Alexander
Florey, Sir Howard W(alter)
Hutchison, Miller Reese   obit
Jastrow, Joseph   obit
Johnson, Douglas Wilson   obit
Kimball, James Henry   obit
Little, Clarence C(ook)
Lutz, Frank E(ugene)   obit
May, Charles H(enry)   obit
Midgley, Thomas, Jr.   obit
Molloy, Daniel M(urrah)   obit
Poulton, Sir Edward Bagnall   obit
Salter, Andrew
Wellman, Frederick Creighton
Woodward, Sir Arthur Smith   obit

Social Science

Agar, Herbert (Sebastian)
Croce, Benedetto
Dewey, John
Dulles, John Foster
Haskin, Frederic J.   obit
Heiden, Konrad
Hopkins, Ernest Martin
Kingdon, Frank
Leacock, Stephen (Butler)   obit
Moulton, Harold G(lenn)
Newcomer, Mabel
Oxnam, G(arfield) Bromley, Bishop
Salter, Sir (James) Arthur
Shotwell, James T(homson)
Straight, Michael (Whitney)
Wecter, Dixon
Wesley, Charles H(arris)
White, Harry D(exter)
Woodson, Carter G(odwin)

Social Service

Barnes, Clifford W(ebster)   obit
Belmont, Mrs. August
Bestor, Arthur E(ugene)   obit
Boardman, Mabel (Thorp)
Colvin, Mrs. D(avid) Leigh
Dauser, Sue S(ophia)
Davis, Norman H(ezekiah)   obit (biog 1940)
Davis, Robert C(ourtney)   obit
Ferrero, Gina L(ombroso)   obit
Gunn, Selskar Michael   obit
Hersholt, Jean
Horder, Thomas J(eeves), 1st Baron

Horwood, Sir William T(homas) F(rancis)   obit
Landes, Bertha K(night)   obit
McGeachy, Mary (Agnes) Craig
Molloy, Daniel M(urrah)   obit
O'Connor, Basil
Petry, Lucile
Sanger, Margaret (Higgins)
Seymour, Harriet Ayer   obit
Smith, Lillian (Eugenia)
Straus, Nathan

Sports

Hammond, Graeme M.   obit
Hitchcock, Thomas   obit
Landis, Kenesaw Mountain
Mack, Connie
Ruth, Babe
Sewell, Luke
Southworth, Billy
Stagg, (Amos) Alonzo
Swope, Herbert Bayard
Vanderbilt, William K(issam)   obit

Technology

Baekeland, Leo H(endrik)   obit
Ballantine, Stuart   obit
Bausch, Edward   obit
Bausch, William   obit
Christie, John Walker   obit
Dow, Willard H(enry)
Firestone, Harvey S(amuel), Jr.
Gibbs, William Francis
Hutchison, Miller Reese   obit
Johnson, Philip G(ustav)   obit
Midgley, Thomas, Jr.   obit
Waite, Henry Matson   obit

Theatre

Ade, George   obit
Alvarez Quintero, Joaquín   obit
Belmont, Mrs. August
Bennett, Richard   obit
Bosworth, Hobart (Van Zandt)   obit
Bracken, Eddie
Brown, Gilmor
Chodorov, Edward
Coburn, Charles
Collier, William, Sr.   obit
Dinehart, Alan   obit
Douglas, Helen (Mary) Gahagan
Drake, Alfred
Draper, Paul
Dudley, Bide   obit
D'Usseau, Arnaud
Ferguson, Elsie
Ferrer, José
Forbes, Kathryn
Giraudoux, Jean   obit
Gish, Dorothy
Gish, Lillian
Golden, John
Gow, James (Ellis)

Graham, Martha
Hackett, Walter obit
Hagen, Uta
Hammerstein, Oscar, 2d
Hart, Lorenz obit (biog 1940)
Helburn, Theresa
Holm, Celeste
Kiesler, Frederick J(ohn)
Koch, Frederick H(enry) obit
Kronenberger, Louis (Jr.)
Langner, Lawrence
Lecuona, Ernesto
Lee, Canada
McGroarty, John Steven obit
Mantle, (Robert) Burns
Mapes, Victor obit

Martin, Mary
Muni, Paul
Munk, Kaj obit
Nugent, Elliott
Odell, George C(linton) D(ensmore)
Palmer, John Leslie obit
Parker, Louis N(apoleon) obit
Pons, Lily
Rosten, Norman
Selwyn, Edgar obit
Shaw, (George) Bernard
Simms, Hilda
Singer, Israel J(oshua) obit
Smith, (Sir) C(harles) Aubrey
Sullavan, Margaret

Van Druten, John (William)
Youmans, Vincent

Other Classifications

Guggenheim, Mrs. Daniel obit
Hoover, Mrs. Herbert obit
McIntyre, Marvin H(unter) obit
Maria Theresa, Archduchess of Austria obit
Michael, Moina obit
Strathmore and Kinghorne, Claud George Bowes-Lyon, 14th Earl of obit
Windsor, Wallis (Warfield), Duchess of

BIOGRAPHIES OF WOMEN—1940 - 1944

Sanger, Margaret (Higgins) 1944
Sarojini Nayadu See Naidu, S. 1943
Savage, Augusta (Christine) 1941
Sayao, Bidu 1942
Schiaparelli, Elsa 1940
Schlauch, Margaret 1942
Schmitt, Gladys (Leonore) 1943
Schuller, Mary Craig McGeachy See McGeachy, M. A. C. 1944
Schultz, Sigrid (Lillian) 1944
Scott, Hazel (Dorothy) 1943
Seghers, Anna 1942
Seibert, Florence B(arbara) 1942
Sell, Hildegarde Loretta See Hildegarde 1944
Seredy, Kate 1940
Sergio, Lisa 1944
Seymour, Flora Warren 1942
Shiber, Etta 1943
Shore, Dinah 1942
Simkhovitch, Mary (Melinda) K(ingsbury) 1943
Simms, Hilda 1944
Skinner, Cornelia Otis 1942
Slye, Maud 1940
Smedley, Agnes 1944
Smith, Betty (Wehner) 1943
Smith, Ida B. Wise 1943
Smith, Kate 1940
Smith, Lillian (Eugenia) 1944
Soong Chingling See Sun Yat-sen, Mme. 1944
Spry, Constance 1940

Stanley, Winifred (C.) 1943
Steber, Eleanor 1943
Steen, Marguerite 1941
Stevens, Risë 1941
Stickney, Dorothy 1942
Stimson, Julia Catherine 1940
Stratton, Dorothy C(onstance) 1943
Streeter, Ruth Cheney 1943
Struther, Jan 1941
Sture-Vasa, Mary Alsop See O'Hara, M. 1944
Sues, (Ilona) Ralf 1944
Suesse, Dana 1940
Sullavan, Margaret 1944
Summerskill, Edith Clara 1943
Sun, Chingling (Soong) See Sun Yat-sen, Mme. 1944
Sun Yat-sen, Mme. 1944
Swarthout, Gladys 1944
Szold, Henrietta 1940

Tabouis, Geneviève 1940
Terrell, Mary Church 1942
Thompson, Dorothy 1940
Thorburg, Kerstin 1940
Tomasi, Mari 1941
Traubel, Helen 1940
Turner, Lana 1943

Undset, Sigrid 1940

Van Doren, Irita 1941
Varian, Dorothy 1943

Walker, Margaret (Abigail) 1943
Waln, Nora 1940
Warren, Althea (Hester) 1942
Wasilewska, Wanda 1944
Wason, Betty 1943
Waters, Ethel 1941
Webster, Margaret 1940
Welty, Eudora 1942
Wheaton, Elizabeth Lee 1942
Whipple, Maurine 1941
White, Margaret Bourke 1940
Whitney, Gertrude (Vanderbilt) biog 1941 obit 1942
Wicker, Ireene 1943
Wilbur, Bernice M(arion) 1943
Wilhelmina, Queen of the Netherlands 1940
Wilkinson, Ellen (Cicely) 1941
Windsor, Wallis (Warfield) Duchess of See Windsor, E., Duke of and Windsor, W. W., Duchess of 1944
Wolff, Maritta M. 1941
Wolff, Mary Evaline See Madeleva, Sister M. 1942
Wood, Peggy 1942
Woolley, Mary E(mma) 1942
Wright, Teresa 1943

Zorina, Vera 1941

CUMULATED INDEX—1940 - 1944

This is a cumulation of all names which appeared in CURRENT BIOGRAPHY from 1940 to 1944, inclusive. The year following each name in this index indicates the CURRENT BIOGRAPHY volume in which the biography or obituary notice appears.

Abbot, Anthony, pseud. See Oursler, F. 1942
Abbott, Berenice 1942
Abbott, Bud and Costello, Lou 1941
Abbott, Edith 1941
Abbott, Edwin Milton obit 1941
Abbott, George 1940
Abbott, Robert Sengstacke obit 1940
Abend, Hallett (Edward) 1942
Aberhart, William C. obit 1943
Abetz, Otto 1941
Abul Kalam Azad, Maulana 1942
Acheson, Albert R(obert) obit 1941
Acheson, Dean (Gooderham) 1941
Acland, Sir Richard (Thomas Dyke) 1944
Adamic, Louis 1940
Adamowski, Timothée obit 1943
Adams, Alva B(lanchard) obit 1942
Adams, Franklin P(ierce) 1941
Adams, James Truslow 1941
Adams, Joseph H(enry) obit 1941
Adams, Randolph G(reenfield) 1943
Adams, Thomas obit 1940
Addams, Clifford Isaac obit 1943
Addington, Sarah obit 1940
Addis Ababa, Pietro Badoglio, Duca d' 1940
Additon, Henrietta Silvis 1940
Ade, George obit 1944
Adkins, Charles obit 1941
Adler, Cyrus obit 1940
Adler, Guido obit 1941
Adler, Harry Clay obit 1940
Adler, Larry 1944
Adler, Mortimer Jerome 1940
Adrian, (Gilbert) 1941
Agar, Herbert (Sebastian) 1944
Aguirre Cerda, Pedro biog and obit 1941
Ahmed II, Sidi, Bey of Tunis obit 1942
Ainsworth, William Newman, Bishop obit 1942
Aitken, William Maxwell, 1st Baron Beaverbrook See Beaverbrook, W. M. A., 1st Baron 1940
Aked, Charles F(rederic), Rev. obit 1941
Alain, (Daniel A.) 1941
Alajálov, Constantin 1942
Albee, Fred H(oudlette) 1943
Albright, Ivan Le Lorraine 1944
Aldrich, Chester Holmes obit 1941
Aldrich, Richard S(teere) obit 1942
Aldrich, Winthrop Williams 1940

Aldridge, James 1943
Alegría, Ciro 1941
Alexander, Albert Victor 1940
Alexander, Franz 1942
Alexander, Sir Harold R(upert) L(eofric) G(eorge) 1942
Alexander, Harry Held obit 1941
Alexander, Ruth 1943
Alfonso XIII, Former King of Spain obit 1941
Allen, Edgar obit 1943
Allen, Florence (Ellinwood) 1941
Allen, Fred 1941
Allen, Gracie 1940
Allen, Jay (Cooke, Jr.) 1941
Allen, Joel Nott obit 1940
Allen, Larry 1942
Allen, Marion obit 1942
Allen, Robert Sharon See Pearson, D. A. R. and Allen, R. S. 1941
Allen, Terry (de la Mesa) 1943
Alley, Rewi 1943
Allyn, Lewis B. obit 1940
Almazán, Juan Andreu 1940
Alonso, José Ignacio Rivero y See Rivero (y Alonso), J. I. obit 1944
Alsberg, Carl Lucas obit 1940
Altenburg, Alexander obit 1940
Alter, George Elias obit 1940
Alvarez Quintero, Joaquín obit 1944
Alvear, Marcelo T. de See De Alvear, Marcelo T. de obit 1942
Amato, Pasquale obit 1942
Amedeo, Duke of Aosta obit 1942
Ameringer, Oscar obit 1943
Amery, L(eopold Charles Maurice) S(tennett) 1942
Ames, Joseph S(weetman) obit 1943
Amherst, Alicia-Margaret, Baroness Rockley See Rockley, A.-M. A. Baroness obit 1941
Amsden, Charles (Avery) obit 1941
Amsterdam, Birdie 1940
Amulree, William Warrender Mackenzie, 1st Baron of Strathbraan obit 1942
Andersen, Hendrik Christian obit 1941
Anderson, Abraham Archibald obit 1940
Anderson, Alexander E. obit 1943
Anderson, Frederick L(ewis) 1944
Anderson, George Everett obit 1940
Anderson, Sir John 1941
Anderson, John Crawford obit 1940
Anderson, John (Hargis) obit 1943

Anderson, Judith 1941
Anderson, Sir Kenneth A(rthur) N(oel) 1943
Anderson, Marian 1940
Anderson, Mary 1940
Anderson, Mary See Navarro, M. de obit 1940
Anderson, Maxwell 1942
Anderson, Sherwood obit 1941
Andino, Tiburcio Carías See Carías Andino, T. 1942
Andrews, C(harles) M(cLean) obit 1943
Andrews, Frank M(axwell) biog 1942 obit 1943
Andrews, John B(ertram) obit 1943
Andrews, Roy Chapman 1941
Angarita, Isaías Medina See Medina Angarita, I. 1942
Angell, James Rowland 1940
Anthony, John J. 1942
Antoine, Josephine 1944
Antonescu, Ion 1940
Appleton, Edward Dale obit 1942
Appleyard, Rollo obit 1943
Aranha, Oswaldo 1942
Aras, Tevfik Rüstü 1942
Archbishop of Canterbury See Lang, C. G., Archbishop of Canterbury 1941
Archbishop of Canterbury See Temple, W., Archbishop of Canterbury biog 1942 obit 1944
Arco, Georg Wilhelm Alexander Hans, Graf von obit 1940
Argentinita 1942
Argeseanu, George obit 1941
Arias, Arnulfo 1941
Armfield, Anne Constance See Smedley, C. obit 1941
Armour, Allison V(incent) obit 1941
Armstrong, Edwin Howard 1940
Armstrong, Louis 1944
Armstrong, Margaret (Neilson) obit 1944
Arno, Peter 1942
Arnold, Bion J(oseph) obit 1942
Arnold, George Stanleigh obit 1942
Arnold, Henry H(arley) 1942
Arnold, Thurman Wesley 1940
Arnold, William Richard, Mgr. 1942
Arnstein, Daniel (G.) 1942
Aronson, Louis V. obit 1940
Aronson, Naoum obit 1943
Arrau, Claudio 1942
Arroyo del Río, Carlos Alberto 1942
Arsonval, Jacques Arsène d' obit 1941
Arthur, J(oseph) C(harles) obit 1942